Peterson's College Money Handbook

2007

THOMSON
PETERSON'S

Australia • Canada • Mexico • Singapore • Spain • United Kingdom • United States

About Thomson Peterson's

Thomson Peterson's (www.petersons.com) is a leading provider of education information and advice, with books and online resources focusing on education search, test preparation, and financial aid. Its Web site offers searchable databases and interactive tools for contacting educational institutions, online practice tests and instruction, and planning tools for securing financial aid. Thomson Peterson's serves 110 million education consumers annually.

For more information, contact Thomson Peterson's, 2000 Lenox Drive, Lawrenceville, NJ 08648; 800-338-3282; or find us on the World Wide Web at www.petersons.com/about.

© 2006 Thomson Peterson's, a part of The Thomson Corporation
Thomson Learning™ is a trademark used herein under license.

Previous editions published as *Peterson's College Money Handbook* © 1983, 1984, 1985, 1986, 1987, 1988, 1989, 1990, 1991, 1996, 1997, 1998, 1999, 2000, 2001 2002, 2003, 2004, 2005 and as *Paying Less for College* © 1992, 1993, 1994, 1995

Peterson's makes every reasonable effort to obtain accurate, complete, and timely data from reliable sources. Nevertheless, Peterson's and the third-party data suppliers make no representation or warranty, either expressed or implied, as to the accuracy, timeliness, or completeness of the data or the results to be obtained from using the data, including, but not limited to, its quality, performance, merchantability, or fitness for a particular purpose, non-infringement or otherwise.

Neither Peterson's nor the third-party data suppliers warrant, guarantee, or make any representations that the results from using the data will be successful or will satisfy users' requirements. The entire risk to the results and performance is assumed by the user.

Editor: Linda Seghers; Production Editor: Susan W. Dilts; Copy Editor: Sally Ross; Research Project Manager: Dan Margolin; Research Associate: James Feichthaler; Programmer: Phyllis Johnson; Manufacturing Manager: Ray Golaszewski; Composition Manager: Linda M. Williams.

ALL RIGHTS RESERVED. No part of this work covered by the copyright herein may be reproduced or used in any form or by any means—graphic, electronic, or mechanical, including photocopying, recording, taping, Web distribution, or information storage and retrieval systems—without the prior written permission of the publisher.

For permission to use material from this text or product, submit a request online at www.thomsonrights.com

Any additional questions about permissions can be submitted by e-mail to thomsonrights@thomson.com

ISSN 1089-831X
ISBN-13: 978-0-7689-2324-7
ISBN-10: 0-7689-2324-7

Printed in the United States of America

10 9 8 7 6 5 4 3 2 1   08 07 06

Twenty-fourth Edition

Contents

A Note from the Peterson's Editors ... v

THE ABCs OF PAYING FOR COLLEGE
A Guide to Financing Your Child's College Education ... 2
Middle-Income Families: Making the Financial Aid Process Work ... 9
Common Questions Answered ... 11
Federal Financial Aid Programs ... 14
Analyzing Financial Aid Award Letters ... 18
Online Filing of FAFSA and CSS/PROFILE® Applications ... 25
Searching for Scholarships Online ... 27
How to Use This Guide ... 29

QUICK-REFERENCE CHART
College Costs At-a-Glance ... 37

PROFILES OF COLLEGE FINANCIAL AID PROGRAMS
Alphabetical Listings of College Financial Aid Programs ... 68

APPENDIX
State Scholarship and Grant Programs ... 618

INDEXES
Non-Need Scholarships for Undergraduates ... 680
Athletic Grants for Undergraduates ... 751
Co-op Programs ... 783
ROTC Programs ... 787
Tuition Waivers ... 795
Tuition Payment Alternatives ... 799

Other Recommended Titles

Peterson's Scholarships, Grants & Prizes
Peterson's Sports Scholarships & College Athletic Programs

A Note from the Peterson's Editors

The news media seem to constantly remind us that a college education is expensive. It certainly appears to be beyond the means of many Americans. The sticker price for four years at state-supported colleges can be more than $45,000, and private colleges and universities could cost more than $150,000. And these numbers continue to rise.

But there is good news. The system operates to provide the needed money so that most families and students are able to afford a college education while making only a reasonable financial sacrifice. However, because the college financial aid system is complex, finding the money is often easier said than done. That is why the process demands study, planning, calculation, flexibility, filling out forms, and meeting deadlines. Fortunately, for most people it can produce positive results. There are many ways to manage college costs and many channels through which you can receive help. Be sure to take full advantage of the opportunities that have been opened up to students and their families by the many organizations, foundations, and businesses that have organized to help you with the burden of college expenses.

For more than thirty-five years, Thomson Peterson's has given students and parents the most comprehensive, up-to-date information on how to get their fair share of the financial aid pie.

Peterson's College Money Handbook 2007 is both a quick reference and a comprehensive resource that puts valuable information about college costs and financial aid opportunities at your fingertips.

- **The ABCs of Paying for College** provides insight into federal financial aid programs that are available, offers an overview of the financial aid landscape, walks you through the process of filing for aid, and provides proven tips on how to successfully navigate the financial aid process to obtain the federal, state, and institutional aid you deserve.
- The **Quick-Reference Chart** offers a snapshot comparison of the financial aid programs available at more than 2,100 four-year institutions across the country.
- The **Profiles of College Financial Aid Programs** provide unbiased financial aid data for each of the more than 2,100 four-year institutions listed.
- The **Appendix** lists the state scholarship and grant programs offered by all fifty states and the District of Columbia.
- The six **Indexes** included in the back of the book allow you to search for specific award programs based on a variety of criteria, including merit-based awards, athletic grants, ROTC programs, and much more.

Thomson Peterson's publishes a full line of resources to help guide you and your family through the financial aid and college admission process. Peterson's publications can be found at your local bookstore, library, and high school guidance office, and you can access us online at www.petersons.com.

We welcome any comments or suggestions you may have about this publication and invite you to complete our online survey at www.petersons.com/booksurvey. Or you can fill out the survey at the back of this book, tear it out, and mail it to us at:

Publishing Department
Thomson Peterson's
2000 Lenox Drive
Lawrenceville, NJ 08648

Your feedback will help us to provide personalized solutions for your educational advancement.

The editors at Peterson's wish you the best of luck during the financial aid process!

The ABCs of Paying for College

A Guide to Financing Your Child's College Education

Don Betterton

Given the lifelong benefit of a college degree (college graduates are projected to earn in a lifetime $1 million more than those with only a high school diploma), higher education is a worthwhile investment. However, it is also an expensive one made even harder to manage by cost increases that have outpaced both inflation and gains in family income. This reality of higher education economics means that parental concern about how to pay for a child's college education is a dilemma that shows no sign of getting easier.

Because of the high cost involved (even the most inexpensive four-year education at a public institution costs about $10,000 a year), good information about college budgets and strategies for reducing the "sticker price" is essential. You have made a good start by taking the time to read *Peterson's College Money Handbook*. In the pages that follow, you will find valuable information about the four main sources of aid—federal, state, institutional, and private. Before you learn about the various programs, however, it will be helpful if you have an overview of how the college financial aid system operates and what long-range financing strategies are available.

Financial Aid

Financial aid refers to money that is awarded to a student, usually in a "package" that consists of gift aid (commonly called a scholarship or grant), a student loan, and a campus job.

College Costs

The starting point for organizing a plan to pay for your child's college education is to make a good estimate of the yearly cost of attendance. You can use the **College Cost Worksheet** on the next page to do this.

To estimate your college costs for 2007-08, refer to the tuition and fees and room and board figures shown in the **College Costs At-a-Glance** chart on page 39, and inflate 2005-06 costs by 10 percent. If 2004-05 costs are listed, inflate those numbers by 18 percent. If your child will commute from your home, use $2500 instead of the college's room and board charges and $900 for transportation. We have used $800 for books and $1300 for personal expenses. Finally, estimate the cost of two round trips if your home is more than a few hundred miles from the college. Add the items to calculate the total budget. You should now have a reasonably good estimate of college costs for 2007-08. (To determine the costs for later years, adding 5 percent per year will probably give you a fairly accurate estimate.)

Do You Qualify for Need-Based Aid?

The next step is to evaluate whether or not you are likely to qualify for financial aid based on need. This step is critical, since more than 90 percent of the yearly total of $128 billion in student aid is awarded only after a determination is made that the family lacks sufficient financial resources to pay the full cost of college on its own. To judge your chance of receiving need-based aid, it is necessary to estimate an Expected Family Contribution (EFC) according to a government formula known as the Federal Methodology (FM). You can do so by referring to the **Approximate Expected Family Contribution Chart** for 2007-08 on page 4.

Applying for Need-Based Aid

Because the federal government provides about 67 percent of all aid awarded, the application and need evaluation process is controlled by Congress and the U.S. Department of Education. The application is the Free Application for Federal Student Aid, or FAFSA. In addition, nearly every state that offers student assistance uses the federal government's system to award its own aid. Furthermore, in addition to arranging for the payment of federal and state aid, many colleges use the FAFSA to award their own funds to eligible students. (Note: In addition to the FAFSA, some colleges also ask the family to complete the CSS/PROFILE® application.)

The FAFSA is your "passport" to receiving your share of the billions of dollars awarded annually in need-based aid. Even if you're uncertain as to

A Guide to Financing Your Child's College Education

College Cost Worksheet

	College 1	College 2	College 3	Commuter College
Tuition and Fees	_____	_____	_____	_____
Room and Board	_____	_____	_____	$2,500
Books	$ 800	$ 800	$ 800	$ 750
Personal Expenses	$1,300	$1,300	$1,300	$1,300
Travel	_____	_____	_____	$ 900
Total Budget	_____	_____	_____	_____

whether or not you qualify for need-based aid, everyone who might need assistance in financing an education should pick up a FAFSA from the high school guidance office after mid-November 2006. This form will ask for 2006 financial data, and it should be filed after January 1, 2007, in time to meet the earliest college or state scholarship deadline. Within two to four weeks after you submit the form, you will receive a summary of the FAFSA information, called the Student Aid Report, or SAR. The SAR will give you the EFC and also allow you to make corrections to the data you submitted.

You can also apply for federal student aid via the Internet using FAFSA on the Web. FAFSA on the Web can be accessed at www.fafsa.ed.gov. Both the student and at least one parent should apply for a federal PIN number at www.pin.ed.gov. The PIN number serves as your electronic signature when applying for aid on the Web. (Note: Many colleges provide the option to apply for early decision or early action admission. If you apply for this before January 1, 2007, which is prior to when the FAFSA can be used, follow the college's instructions. Many colleges use either PROFILE or their own application form for early admission candidates.)

Awarding Aid

About the same time you receive the SAR, the colleges you list will receive your FAFSA information so they can calculate a financial aid award in a package that typically includes aid from at least one of the major sources—federal, state, college, or private. In addition, the award will probably consist of a combination of a scholarship or a grant, a loan, and a campus job. These last two pieces—loan and job—are called self-help aid because they require effort on your part (that is, the aid must be either earned through work or paid back later). Scholarships or grants are outright gifts that have no such obligation.

It is important that you understand each part of the package. You'll want to know, for example, how much is gift aid, the interest rate and repayment terms of the student loan, and how many hours per week the campus job requires. There should be an enclosure with the award letter that answers these questions. If not, make a list of your questions and call or visit the financial aid office.

Once you understand the terms of each item in the award letter, you should turn your attention to the "bottom line"—how much you will have to pay at each college where your child was accepted. In addition to understanding the aid award, this means having a good estimate of the college budget so you can accurately calculate how much you and your child will have to contribute. (Often, an aid package does not cover the entire need.) Colleges follow different practices in how much detail they include in their award notifications. Many colleges provide full information—types and amounts of aid, yearly costs, and the EFC divided into the parent and student shares. If these important items are missing or incomplete, you can do the work on your own. (See the

How Need Is Calculated and Aid Is Awarded

	College X	College Y
Total Cost of Attendance	$10,000	$ 24,000
− Expected Family Contribution	− 5,500	− 5,500
= Financial Need	$ 4,500	$ 18,500
− Grant Aid Awarded	− 675	−14,575
− Campus Job (Work-Study) Awarded	− 1,400	− 1,300
− Student Loan Awarded	− 2,425	− 2,625
= Unmet Need	0	0

Note: Sometimes an institution is unable to meet all need. The amount of unmet need is called "the gap."

A Guide to Financing Your Child's College Education

Approximate Expected Family Contribution Chart

Income Before Taxes

Assets / Family Size	$20,000	30,000	40,000	50,000	60,000	70,000	80,000	90,000	100,000
$20,000									
3	$ 0	900	2,500	4,400	7,000	10,400	13,800	16,700	19,900
4	0	50	1,700	3,400	5,600	8,700	12,100	15,100	18,300
5	0	0	850	2,500	4,400	7,000	10,400	13,600	16,800
6	0	0	50	1,700	3,300	5,500	8,500	11,900	15,100
$30,000									
3	$ 0	900	2,500	4,400	7,000	10,400	13,800	16,700	19,900
4	0	50	1,700	3,400	5,600	8,700	12,100	15,100	18,300
5	0	0	850	2,500	4,400	7,000	10,400	13,600	16,800
6	0	0	50	1,700	3,300	5,500	8,500	11,900	15,100
$40,000									
3	$ 0	900	2,500	4,400	7,000	10,400	13,800	16,700	19,900
4	0	50	1,700	3,400	5,600	8,700	12,100	15,100	18,300
5	0	0	850	2,500	4,400	7,000	10,400	13,600	16,800
6	0	0	50	1,700	3,300	5,500	8,500	11,900	15,100
$50,000									
3	$ 0	900	2,500	4,600	7,200	10,700	14,100	17,000	20,200
4	0	50	1,700	3,600	5,800	9,000	12,400	15,400	18,600
5	0	0	850	2,700	4,600	7,300	10,700	13,900	17,100
6	0	0	50	1,800	3,500	5,800	8,800	12,200	15,400
$60,000									
3	$ 0	900	2,500	5,000	7,600	11,100	14,500	17,500	20,800
4	0	50	1,700	4,000	6,200	9,400	12,800	15,900	19,200
5	0	0	850	3,100	5,000	7,700	11,100	14,400	17,700
6	0	0	50	2,200	3,900	6,200	9,200	12,700	16,000
$80,000									
3	$ 0	900	2,800	5,700	9,000	12,450	15,800	18,700	21,900
4	0	50	2,000	4,700	7,300	10,700	14,100	17,100	20,300
5	0	0	1,150	3,800	5,800	9,000	12,400	15,600	18,800
6	0	0	350	2,900	4,500	7,200	10,600	13,900	17,100
$100,000									
3	$ 0	900	3,100	6,800	10,200	13,600	16,900	19,850	23,100
4	0	50	2,300	5,400	8,400	11,800	15,200	18,250	21,500
5	0	0	1,450	4,250	6,800	10,150	13,500	16,700	20,000
6	0	0	650	3,200	5,300	8,300	11,700	15,000	18,250
$120,000									
3	$ 0	900	3,400	8,000	11,400	14,800	18,100	21,050	24,300
4	0	50	2,600	7,900	11,300	14,700	18,000	20,950	24,200
5	0	0	1,750	5,350	7,900	11,250	14,600	17,800	21,100
6	0	0	950	3,800	6,200	9,400	12,800	16,100	19,400
$140,000									
3	$ 0	900	3,700	9,200	12,600	16,000	19,300	22,250	25,500
4	0	50	2,900	9,100	12,500	15,900	19,200	22,150	25,400
5	0	0	2,050	6,450	9,000	12,350	15,700	18,900	22,200
6	0	0	1,250	4,500	7,100	10,500	13,900	17,300	20,500

This chart makes the following assumptions:

- Two parent family where age of older parent is 45
- Lower income families will file the 1040A or 1040EZ tax form
- Student income is less than $2300
- There are no student assets
- There is only one family member in college

All figures are estimates and may vary when the complete FAFSA or PROFILE application is submitted.

www.petersons.com Peterson's College Money Handbook 2007

A Guide to Financing Your Child's College Education

Comparing Financial Aid Awards and Family Contribution Worksheet

	College 1	College 2	College 3
Cost of Attendance	_____	_____	_____
Aid Awarded	_____	_____	_____
Grant/Scholarship	_____	_____	_____
Loan	_____	_____	_____
Job	_____	_____	_____
Total Aid	_____	_____	_____
Expected Family Contribution	_____	_____	_____
Student Contribution	_____	_____	_____
Parent Contribution	_____	_____	_____

Comparing Financial Aid Awards and Family Contribution Worksheet on this page.) For example, if only the college's direct charges for tuition, room, and board are shown on the award letter, make your own estimate of indirect costs like books, personal expenses, and travel. Then subtract the total aid awarded from the yearly cost to get the EFC. A portion of that amount may be your child's contribution (20 percent of his assets and 50 percent of his earnings over $3000) and the remainder is the parental share. If you can afford this amount at your child's first-choice college, the financial aid system has worked well for you, and your child's college enrollment plans can go forward.

But if you think your EFC is too high, you should contact the college's financial aid office and ask whether additional aid is available. Many colleges, private high-cost colleges in particular, are enrollment-oriented—they are willing to work with families to help make attendance at their institutions possible. Most colleges also allow applicants to appeal their financial aid awards, the budget used for you, or any of the elements used to determine the family contribution, especially if there are extenuating circumstances or if the information has changed since the application was submitted. Some colleges may also reconsider an award based on a "competitive appeal," the submission of a more favorable award letter from another college.

If your appeal is unsuccessful and there is still a gap between the expected family contribution and what you feel you can pay from income and savings, you are left with two choices. One option is for your child to attend a college where paying your share of the bill will not be a problem. (This assumes that an affordable option was included on your child's original list of colleges, a wise admission application strategy.) The second is to look into alternate methods of financing. At this stage, parental loans and tuition payment plans are the best financing options. A parental loan can bring the yearly cost down to a manageable level by spreading payments over a number of years. This is the type of financing that families use when purchasing a home or automobile. A tuition payment plan is essentially a short-term loan and allows you to pay the costs over ten to twelve months. It is an option for families who have the resources available but need help with managing their cash flow. See the "Financing Your Child's College Education" section for more information.

Non-Need-Based Aid

Regardless of whether you might qualify for a need-based award, it is always worthwhile to look into merit, or non-need, scholarships from sources such as foundations, agencies, religious groups, and service organizations. For a family that isn't eligible for need-based aid, merit scholarships are the only form of gift aid available. If you later qualify for a need-based award, a merit scholarship can be quite helpful in providing additional resources if the aid does not fully cover the costs. Even if the college meets 100 percent of need, a merit scholarship can benefit you by reducing the self-help (loan and job) portion of an award.

In searching for merit-based scholarships, keep in mind that there are relatively few awards (compared to those that are need-based), and most of them are highly competitive. Use the following checklist when investigating merit scholarships.

- Take advantage of any scholarships for which your child is automatically eligible based on parents' employer benefits, military service, association or church membership, other affiliations, or student or parent attributes (ethnic background, nationality, etc.). Company or union tuition remissions are the most common examples of these awards.

- Look for other awards for which your child might be eligible based on the characteristics and affiliations indicated above but where there is a selection process and an application is required. Free computerized searches are available on the Internet. (You should not pay a fee for a scholarship search.) Peterson's free scholarship search can be accessed by logging on to www.

A Guide to Financing Your Child's College Education

What Is CSS/PROFILE®?

There are many complexities in the financial aid process: knowing which aid is merit-based and which aid is need-based; understanding the difference between grants, loans, and work-study; and determining whether funds are from federal, state, institutional, or private sources.

In addition, the aid application process itself can be confusing. It can involve more than the Free Application for Federal Student Aid (FAFSA) and the Federal Methodology (FM). Among the approximately 2,100 four-year colleges, about 400 are private institutions with more than $2 billion of their own scholarship money. Many of these colleges feel that the federal aid system (FAFSA and FM) does not collect or evaluate information thoroughly enough for them to award their institutional funds. These colleges have made an arrangement with the College Scholarship Service, a branch of the College Board, to establish a separate application system.

The application is called the CSS/PROFILE®, and the need-analysis formula is referred to as the Institutional Methodology (IM). If you apply for financial aid at one of the colleges that uses PROFILE, the admission material will state that PROFILE is required in addition to the FAFSA. You should read the information carefully and file PROFILE to meet the earliest college deadline. Before you can receive PROFILE, however, you must register, either by phone or through the Web (http://www.collegeboard.org/finaid/fastud/html/proform.html), providing enough basic information so the PROFILE package can be designed specifically for you. The FAFSA is free, but there is a charge for PROFILE. As with the FAFSA, PROFILE can be submitted via the Internet.

In addition to the requirement by certain colleges that you submit both the FAFSA and PROFILE (when used, PROFILE is always in addition to the FAFSA; it does not replace it), you should understand that each system has its own method for analyzing a family's ability to pay for college. The main differences between PROFILE's Institutional Methodology and the FAFSA's Federal Methodology are:

- PROFILE includes equity in the family home as an asset; the FAFSA doesn't.

- PROFILE takes a broader look at assets not included on the FAFSA.

- PROFILE expects a minimum student contribution, usually in the form of summer earnings; the FAFSA has no such minimum.

- PROFILE may collect information on the noncustodial parent; the FAFSA does not.

- PROFILE allows for more professional judgment than the FAFSA. Medical expenses, private secondary school costs, and a variety of special circumstances are considered under PROFILE, subject to the discretion of the aid counselor on campus.

- PROFILE includes information on assets not reported on the FAFSA, including life insurance, annuities, retirement plans, etc.

To summarize: PROFILE's Institutional Methodology tends to be both more complete in its data collection and more rigorous in its analysis than the FAFSA's Federal Methodology. When IM results are compared to FM results for thousands of applicants, IM will usually come up with a somewhat higher expected parental contribution than FM.

---

petersons.com/finaid. Scholarship directories, such as *Peterson's Scholarships, Grants & Prizes*, which details more than 4,000 scholarship programs, are useful resources and can be found in bookstores, high school guidance offices, or public libraries.

- See if your state has a merit scholarship program.

- Look into national scholarship competitions. High school guidance counselors usually know about these scholarships. Examples of these awards are the National Merit

A Guide to Financing Your Child's College Education

Creditworthiness

If you will be borrowing to pay for your child's college education, making sure you qualify for a loan is critical. For the most part, that means your credit record must be free of default or delinquency. You can check your credit history with one or more of the following three major credit bureaus and clean up any adverse information that appears. The numbers below will offer specific information on what you need to provide to obtain a report. All of the credit bureaus accept credit report requests over their Web sites. You will usually be asked to provide your full name, phone number, social security number, birth date, and addresses for the last five years. You are entitled to a free report from each bureau.

Equifax
P.O. Box 740241
Atlanta, GA 30374
800-685-5000
http://www.equifax.com

Trans Union℠
P.O. Box 2000
Chester, PA 19022
800-888-4213
http://www.tuc.com

EXPERIAN National
Consumer
Assistance Center
475 Anton Boulevard
Costa Mesa, CA 92626
888-397-3742
800-972-0322
   (TTY/TDD)
http://www.experian.com

Scholarship, the Coca-Cola Scholarship, Aid Association for Lutherans, Gates Millennium Scholars, Intel Science Talent Search, and the U.S. Senate Youth Program.

- ROTC (Reserve Officers' Training Corps) scholarships are offered by the Army, Navy, Air Force, and Marine Corps. A full ROTC scholarship covers tuition, fees, textbook costs and, in some cases, a stipend. Acceptance of an ROTC scholarship entails a commitment to take military science courses and to serve for a specific number of years as an officer in the sponsoring branch of the service. Competition is heavy, and preference may be given to students in certain fields of study, such as engineering, languages, science, and health professions. Application procedures vary by service. Contact an armed services recruiter or high school guidance counselor for further information.

- Investigate community scholarships. High school guidance counselors usually have a list of these awards, and announcements are published in local newspapers. Most common are awards given by service organizations like the American Legion, Rotary International, and the local women's club.

If your child is strong academically (for example, a National Merit® Commended Student or better) or is very talented in fields such as athletics or performing/creative arts, you may want to consider colleges that offer their own merit awards to gifted students they wish to enroll. Refer to the *Non-Need Scholarships for Undergraduates* index.

In addition to merit scholarships, there are loan and job opportunities for students who do not qualify for need-based aid. Federal loan programs include the unsubsidized Federal Stafford and Direct Loans. See the "Federal Financial Aid Programs" article for more information. Some of the organizations that sponsor scholarships—for example, the Air Force Aid Society—also provide loans.

Note

A point of clarification about whether to put college savings in your name or your child's: If you are certain that your child will not be a candidate for need-based aid, there may be a tax advantage to accumulating money in his or her name name. However, when it comes to maximizing aid eligibility, it is important to understand that student assets are assessed at a 20 percent rate and parental assets at about 5 percent. Therefore, if your college savings are in your child's name, it may be wise to reestablish title to these funds before applying for financial aid. You should contact your financial planner or accountant before making any modifications to your asset structure.

A Guide to Financing Your Child's College Education

Work opportunities during the academic year are another type of assistance that is not restricted to aid recipients. Many colleges will, after assigning jobs to students on aid, open campus positions to all students looking for work. In addition, there are usually off-campus employment opportunities available to everyone.

Financing Your Child's College Education

In this section, "financing" means putting together resources to pay the balance due the college over and above payments from the primary sources of aid—grants, scholarships, student loans, and jobs. Financing strategies are important because the high cost of a college education today often requires a family, whether or not it receives aid, to think about stretching its college payment beyond the four-year period of enrollment. For high-cost colleges, it is not unreasonable to think about a 10-4-10 plan: ten years of saving; four years of paying college bills out of current income, savings, and borrowing; and ten years to repay a parental loan.

Savings

Although saving for college is always a good idea, many families are unclear about its advantages. Some families do not save because after normal living expenses have been covered, they do not have much money to set aside. An affordable but regular savings plan through a payroll deduction is usually the answer to the problem of spending your entire paycheck every month.

The second reason why saving for college is not a high priority is the belief that the financial aid system penalizes a family by lowering aid eligibility. The Federal Methodology of need determination is very kind to savers. In fact, savings are ignored completely for most families that earn less than $50,000. Savings in the form of home equity, retirement plans, and most annuities are excluded from the calculation. And even when savings are counted, a maximum of 5 percent of the total is expected each year. In other words, if a family has $40,000 in savings after an asset protection allowance is considered, the contribution is no greater than $2000. Given the impact of compound interest it is easy to see that a long-term savings plan can make paying for college much easier.

A sensible savings plan is important because of the financial advantage of saving compared to borrowing. The amount of money students borrow for college is now greater than the amount they receive in grants and scholarships. With loans becoming so widespread, savings should be carefully considered as an alternative to borrowing. Your incentive for saving is that a dollar saved is a dollar not borrowed.

Borrowing

Once you've calculated your "bottom-line" parental contribution and determined that the amount is not affordable out of your current income and assets, the most likely alternative is borrowing. First determine if you are eligible for a larger subsidized Federal Stafford or Direct Loan. Because no interest is due while your child attends college, these are the most favorable loans. If this is not possible, look into the unsubsidized Stafford or Direct Loan, which is not based on need but the interest accrues each year. The freshman year limit (either subsidized or unsubsidized) is $3500.

After you have taken out the maximum amount of student loans, the next step is to look into parental loans. The federal government's parent loan program is called PLUS and is the standard against which other loans should be judged. A local bank that participates in the PLUS program can give you a schedule of monthly repayments per $1000 borrowed. Use this repayment figure to compare other parental loans available from commercial lenders (including home equity loans), state programs, or colleges themselves. Choose the one that offers the best terms after all up-front costs, tax advantages, and the amount of monthly payments are considered. Be sure to check with your financial aid office before making a final decision. Often, the financial aid office will have reviewed the various programs that are available and can help direct you to the best choice.

Make Financial Aid Work for You

This overview is intended to provide you with a road map to help you think about financing strategies and navigate through the complexities of the financial aid process. Much of the information you will need to help you determine your plan to pay for your child's education can be found within the pages of this guide. First use the **Approximate Expected Family Contribution Chart** in conjunction with the **College Cost Worksheet** to estimate need eligibility. Complete the FAFSA (and PROFILE, if required). At the same time, look into merit scholarships. Once your child is accepted at a school, use the **Comparing Financial Aid Awards and Family Contribution Worksheet** to figure out your parental obligation. If you can't afford the payment, present your arguments to the institution's financial aid office before checking out the terms of PLUS and other parental loan options. And finally, if there are younger children at home, think about starting a college savings fund to get a head start on their future education costs.

If you are like millions of families that benefit from financial aid, it is likely that your child's college plans can go forward without undue worry about the costs involved. The key is to understand the financial aid system and to follow the best path for your family. The result of good information and good planning should be that you will receive your fair share of the billions of dollars available each year and that the cost of college will not prevent your child from attending.

Don Betterton is the Director of Undergraduate Financial Aid at Princeton University.

Middle-Income Families: Making the Financial Aid Process Work

Richard Woodland

The U.S. Department of Education's National Center for Education Statistics has researched how middle-income families finance a college education. Their 2001 report, *Middle Income Undergraduates: Where They Enroll and How They Pay for Their Education*, states that although 31 percent of middle-income families have the entire cost of college covered by financial aid, there is widespread angst among these families that, while they earn too much to qualify for grant assistance, they are too financially strapped to pay the spiraling cost of higher education.

First, we have to agree on what constitutes a "middle-income" family. For the purposes of the federal study, middle-income families are defined as those families with incomes between $35,000 and $70,000. The good news is that 52 percent of these families received grants, while the balance received loans. Other sources of aid, including work-study, also helped close the gap.

So how do these families do it? Is there a magic key that opens the door to significant amounts of grants and scholarships?

The report shows some interesting trends. One way middle-income families make college more affordable is by choosing a less expensive school. In fact, in the report, 29 percent of middle-income students chose to enroll in low- to moderate-cost schools, with a total cost of less than $8500 per year, including community colleges and lower-priced state colleges and universities. But almost half of these middle-income families chose higher-priced schools, with costs between $8500 and $16,000. The remaining 23 percent enrolled at the highest-priced schools, with costs above $16,000. Clearly cost is a factor, but middle-income families are not limiting their choices based on cost alone.

The report shows that families pay these higher costs through a combination of family assets, current income, and long-term borrowing. This is often referred to as the "past-present-future" model of financing. In fact, just by looking at the Expected Family Contributions, it is clear that there is a significant gap in what families need and what the financial aid process can provide. Families are closing this gap by making the necessary financial sacrifices to pay the current price of higher-cost schools, especially if they think their child is academically strong. The report concludes that parents are more likely to pay for a higher-priced education if their child scores above 2000 on the SAT.

Where to Start

The best place for middle-income families to start is their high school guidance office. Here they can find valuable information on financial aid and leads on local scholarships. Most guidance counselors report that there are far fewer applicants for these locally based scholarships than one would expect. So read the information they send home, and be sure to follow up during the application process. A few of those $500 to $1000 scholarships can really add up.

Second, be sure to attend a financial aid awareness program. If your school does not offer one, contact your local college financial aid office and see when and where one is available. These programs offer a lot of inside information on how the financial aid process works.

Next, be sure to file the correct applications for aid. Remember, each school can have a different set of requirements. For example, many higher-cost private colleges require the CSS/PROFILE® application, which should be filed in September or October of the senior year. Other schools may have their own institutional aid applications. All schools require the Free Application for Federal Student Aid (FAFSA). Watch the deadlines! It is important that you meet the school's published application deadline. Generally, schools are not very flexible about this, so be sure to double-check the due date of your application.

Finally, become a smart educational consumer. Thomson Peterson's has a wide range of resources available to help you understand the process. Be sure to check your local library, bookstore, and of course,

Middle-Income Families: Making the Financial Aid Process Work

the Internet. Two great Web sites to check out are www.petersons.com and www.finaid.org.

Closing the Gap

Once your child is accepted, you will receive an award notice outlining the aid you are eligible to receive. If you feel the offer is not sufficient, or if you have some unique financial problems, call the college or university's financial aid office to see if you can have your case reviewed. The financial aid office is the best source for putting the pieces together to help you finance your college education.

The financial aid office will help you determine what the "net price" is. This is the actual out-of-pocket cost that you will need to cover. Through a combination of student and parent loans, along with other forms of financial aid and family resources, most families are able to meet these expenses.

Furthermore, many students help close the gap by working throughout their college career. While this works for many students, research shows that too many hours spent away from studies can negatively affect academic success. Most experts feel that working 10 to 15 hours a week is optimal.

An overlooked source of aid is the recent tax credits given to middle-income families. Rather than extending eligibility for traditional sources of grant assistance to middle-income families, the federal tax system has built in a number of significant tax benefits for middle-income families, including the Hope Scholarship and Lifetime Learning Tax Credit. While it may take seven or eight months before you see the tax credit, families in this income group can safely count on this benefit, usually about $1500 to $2000 per student. This is real money in your pocket and you do not need to itemize your deductions to qualify for this tax credit. Another option for upper-middle-income families not qualifying for the Hope/Lifetime tax credit is a tuition and fee deduction of up to $4000 from their taxable income.

A tool to help you get a handle on the ever-rising costs of college is to assume you can pay a third of "net charges" from savings, another third from available (nonretirement) assets, and the rest from parent borrowing. If any one of these is not available, shift that amount to one of the other resources. But if it looks like you will be financing most or all of the costs from future income (borrowing), it may be wise to consider a lower-cost college.

Millions of middle-income families send their children to colleges and universities every year. Only 8 percent attend the lowest-priced schools. By using the concept of past-present-future financing, institutional assistance, federal and state aid, meaningful targeted tax relief, and student earnings, you can afford even the highest-priced schools.

Alternative Financing Options

For many families, traditional financial aid programs come up short in meeting the tuition bill each semester. Rather than exhausting their savings, many families are turning to private or alternative loans to help defray the cost. The world of private/alternative educational loans can be confusing. There are varying interest rates, loan fees, up-front costs, and capitalization dates. There is no single place to go and search for the best deal. But the private/alternative loan financing market is today's fastest-growing source of financial aid. Organizations such as *Sallie Mae* offer a number of money-saving options in alternative loan financing. Consult the micro-site content center at www.petersons.com/finaid for more information on the types of financing plans available.

The most common source of alternative funding is the federal Parent Loans for Undergraduate Students (PLUS). These are federally insured loans that offer creditworthy borrowers significant funding at reasonable interest rates. To qualify, you need to pass a credit check. It is a good idea to check your credit report annually. This can be done for free at FreeCreditReport.com. Contact the college financial aid office; some schools are in the Direct Loan program and will process the application from the financial aid office. Other schools will recommend a bank or other financial institution where you can begin the PLUS process. In general, you can borrow the full cost of tuition less any other aid received. This can run into the thousands of dollars.

Remember, though, that PLUS is not always the best deal. Many states have alternative loan programs that offer far better terms than PLUS. For example, New Jersey and Pennsylvania offer programs backed by state bond issues that generally are more attractive than the federal PLUS. Check with your state Higher Education Office or with a school in your area for more information. In most cases, these loans are portable, meaning they can be used at any school across the country. By doing some research you can save hundreds of dollars in interest charges.

Many schools have arranged special financing plans with private lenders. When you are working with the financial aid office to put your total aid package together, be sure to check for any special programs that may be available. There are many lenders available to help families finance higher education. You can trust the financial aid counselors. They do this work every day and can point you in the right direction.

Richard Woodland is Director of Financial Aid at Rutgers University–Camden.

Common Questions Answered

Q *Are a student's chances of being admitted to a college reduced if the student applies for financial aid?*

A Generally no. Nearly all colleges have a policy of "need-blind" admissions, which means that a student's financial need is not taken into account in the admission decision. There are a few selective colleges, however, that do consider ability to pay before deciding whether or not to admit a student. Some colleges will mention this in their literature; others may not. The best advice is to apply for financial aid if the student needs assistance to attend college.

Q *Are parents penalized for saving money for college?*

A No. As a matter of fact, families that have made a concerted effort to save money for college are in a much better position than those that have not. For example, a student from a family that has saved money may not have to borrow as much. Furthermore, the "taxing rate" on savings is quite low—only about 5 percent of the parents' assets are assessed and neither the home equity nor retirement savings are included. For example, a single 40-year-old parent who saved $40,000 for college expenses will have about $1900 counted as part of the parental contribution. Two parents, if the older one is 40 years old (a parent's age factors into the formulation), would have about $300 counted. (Note: The "taxing rate" for student assets is much higher—20 percent—compared to 5 percent for parents.)

Q *How does the financial aid system work in cases of divorce or separation? How are stepparents treated?*

A In cases of divorce or separation, the financial aid application(s) should be completed by the parent with whom the student lived for the longest period of time in the past twelve months (custodial parent). If the custodial parent has remarried, the stepparent is considered a family member and must complete the application along with the biological parent. If your family has any special circumstances, you should discuss these directly with the financial aid office. (Note: Colleges that award their own aid may ask the noncustodial biological parent to complete a separate aid application and a contribution will be calculated.)

Q *When are students considered independent of parental support in applying for financial aid?*

A The student must be at least 24 years of age in order to be considered independent. If younger than 24, the student must be married, be a graduate or professional student, have legal dependents other than a spouse, be an orphan or ward of the court, or be a veteran of the armed forces or on active military duty. However, in very unusual situations, students who can clearly document estrangement from their parents can appeal to the financial aid office for additional consideration.

Q *What can a family do if a job loss occurs?*

A Financial aid eligibility is based on the previous year's income. So the family's 2006 income would be reported to determine eligibility for the 2007-08 academic year. In that way, the family's income can be verified with an income tax return. But the previous year's income may not accurately reflect the current financial situation, particularly if a parent lost a job or retired. In these instances, the projected income for the coming year can be used instead. Families should discuss the situation directly with the financial aid office and be prepared to provide appropriate documentation.

Q *When my daughter first went to college, we applied for financial aid and were denied because our Expected Family Contribution was too high. Now, my son is a high school senior, and we will soon have two in college. Will we get the same results?*

A The results will definitely be different. Both your son and your daughter should apply. As we described earlier, need-based financial aid is based on your Expected Family Contribution, or EFC. When you have two children in college, this amount is divided in half for each child.

Common Questions Answered

Q: I've heard about the "middle-income squeeze" in regard to financial aid. What is it?

A: The so-called "middle-income squeeze" is the idea that low-income families qualify for aid, high-income families have adequate resources to pay for education, and those in the middle are not eligible for aid but do not have the ability to pay full college costs. There is no provision in the Federal Methodology that treats middle-income students differently than others (such as an income cutoff for eligibility). The Expected Family Contribution rises proportionately as income and assets increase. If a middle-income family does not qualify for aid, it is because the need analysis formula yields a contribution that exceeds college costs. But keep in mind that if a $65,000-income family does not qualify for grant aid at a public university with a $16,000 cost, the same family will likely be eligible for aid at a private college with a cost of $25,000 or more. Also, there are loan programs available to parents and students that are not based on need. Middle-income families should realize, however, that many of the grant programs funded by federal and state governments are directed at lower-income families. It is therefore likely that a larger share of an aid package for a middle-income student will consist of loans rather than grants.

Q: Given our financial condition, my daughter will be receiving financial aid. We will help out as much as we can, and, in fact, we ourselves will be borrowing. But I am concerned that she will have to take on a lot of loans in order to go to the college of her choice. Does she have any options?

A: She does. If offered a loan, she can decline all or part of it. One option is for her to ask in the financial aid office to have some of the loan changed to a work-study job. If this is not possible, she can find her own part-time work. Often there is an employment office on campus that can help her locate a job. In most cases, the more she works, the less she has to borrow. It is important to remember that the educational loans offered to students have very attractive terms and conditions, with flexible repayment options. Students should look upon these loans as a long-term investment that will reap significant rewards.

Q: Is it possible to change your financial aid package?

A: Yes. Most colleges have an appeal process. A request to change a need-based loan to a work-study job is usually approved if funds are available. A request to consider special financial circumstances may also be granted. At most colleges, a request for more grant money is rarely approved unless it is based on a change in the information reported. Applicants should speak with the financial aid office if they have concerns about their financial package. Some colleges may even respond to a competitive appeal, that is, a request to match another college's offer.

Q: My son was awarded a Federal Stafford Loan as part of his financial aid package. His award letter also indicated that we could take out a PLUS loan. How do we go about choosing our lender? Do we go to our local bank?

A: Read the material that came with the financial aid award letter. It is likely that the college has an "approved lender" list for Stafford and PLUS Loans. Although you can borrow from any bank, your loan application will be processed more quickly if you use a lender recommended by the college.

Q: The cost of attending college seems to be going up so much faster than the Consumer Price Index. Why is that, and how can I plan for my child's four years?

A: The cost of higher education cannot be compared to the Consumer Price Index (CPI). The CPI does not take into account most of the costs faced by colleges. For example, the dollars that universities spend on grants and scholarships have risen rapidly. Many universities have increased enrollment of students from less affluent families, further increasing the need for institutional financial aid. Colleges are expected to be on the cutting edge of technology, not only in research but also in the classroom and in the library. Many colleges have deferred needed maintenance and repairs that can now no longer be put off. In addition, there is market pressure to provide many expensive lifestyle amenities that were not expected ten years ago. In general, you can expect that college costs will rise at least 2 to 3 percent faster than inflation.

Q: I'm struggling with the idea that all students should apply to the college of their choice, regardless of cost, because financial aid will level the playing field. I feel I will be penalized because I have saved for college. My son has been required to save half of his allowance since age six for his college education. Will that count against him when he applies for financial aid? It's difficult to explain to him that his college choices may be limited because of the responsible choices and sacrifices we have made as a family. What can we do to make the most of our situation?

A: In general, it is always better to have planned ahead for college by saving. Families that have put away sufficient funds to pay for college will quickly realize that they have made the burden easier for themselves and their children. In today's college financing world, schools assume that paying for the cost of attendance is a 10-year commitment. So by saving when your child is young, you reap significant advantages from compound interest on the assets and reduce the need to borrow as much while in school. This should reduce the number of years after college that you will be burdened with student and parent loans. We advise families to spend the student's assets first, since the financial aid formulas count these more heavily than parental assets. Then, after the first year, you can explain to the college how you spent these

Common Questions Answered

assets, and why you might now need assistance. When looking at parental information, the income of the family is by far the most important component. Contrary to popular belief, parental assets play a minor role in the calculation of need. With this strategy, you have done the right thing, and in the long run, it should prove to be a wise financial plan.

Picking the right college also involves other factors. Students should select the colleges they are going to apply to in two ways. First and most important is to look at colleges that meet your son's academic and lifestyle interests. Most experts will tell him to pick a few "reach" schools (i.e., schools where he is not sure he has the grades and scores required) and at least one or two academically "safe" schools. He should also select one or two financially "safe" schools that you are sure you can afford with either moderate or little financial aid. Most students do not get into all of their first-choice schools, and not everyone can afford the schools they are admitted to. By working closely with the guidance office in high school and the admissions and financial aid offices at the college, you can maximize your options.

Q *My son was awarded a $2500 scholarship. This can be split and used for two years. When filling out the FAFSA, do we have to claim the full amount, or just the $1250 he plans to use the first year?*

A Congratulations to your son on the scholarship. Nowhere on the FAFSA should you report this scholarship. It is not considered income or an asset. However, once you choose a school to attend, you must notify the financial aid office for its advice on how to take the funds. But remember, do NOT report it on the FAFSA.

Q *I will be receiving a scholarship from my local high school. How will this scholarship be treated in my financial aid award?*

A Federal student aid regulations specify that all forms of aid must be included within the defined level of need. This means that additional aid, such as outside scholarships, must be combined with any need-based aid you receive; it may not be kept separate and used to reduce your family's contribution. If the college has not filled 100 percent of your need, it will usually allow outside scholarships to close the gap. Once your total need has been met, the college must reduce other aid and replace it with the outside award. Most colleges will allow you to use some, if not all, of an outside scholarship to replace self-help aid (loans and Federal Work-Study) rather than grant aid.

Q *I know we're supposed to apply for financial aid as soon as possible after January 1. What if I don't have my W-2s yet and my tax return isn't done?*

A The first financial aid application deadlines usually fall in early February. Most colleges use either March 1 or March 15 as their "priority filing date." Chances are you'll have your W-2 forms by then, but you won't have a completed tax return. If that is the case, complete the financial aid application using your best estimates. Then, when you receive the Student Aid Report (SAR), you can use your tax return to make corrections. Just be sure to check with each college for its deadline.

Q *Is there enough aid available to make it worthwhile for me to consider colleges that are more expensive than I can afford?*

A Definitely. More than $100 billion in aid is awarded to undergraduates every year. With more than half of all enrolled students qualifying for some type of assistance, this totals more than $5500 per student. You should view financial aid as a large, national system of tuition discounts, some given according to a student's ability and talent, others based on what a student's family can afford to pay. If you qualify for need-based financial aid, you will essentially pay only your calculated family contribution, regardless of the cost of the college. You will not pay the "sticker price" (the cost of attendance listed in the college catalog) but a lower rate that is reduced by the amount of aid you receive. No college should be ruled out until after financial aid is considered. In addition, when deciding which college to attend, consider that the short-term cost of a college education is only one criterion. If the college meets your educational needs and you are convinced it can launch you on an exciting career, a significant up-front investment may turn out to be a bargain over the long run.

Q *If I don't qualify for need-based aid, what options are available?*

A You should try to put together your own aid package to help reduce your parents' share. There are three sources to look into. First, search for merit scholarships. Second, seek employment, during both the summer and the academic year. The student employment office should be able to help you find a campus job. Third, look into borrowing. Even if you don't qualify for the need-based loan programs, the unsubsidized Federal Stafford and Direct Loans are available to all students. The terms and conditions are the same as the subsidized loan programs except that interest accrues while you are in college.

After you have contributed what you can through scholarships, employment, and loans, your parents will be faced with their share of the college bill. Many colleges have monthly payment plans that allow families to spread their payments over the academic year. If these monthly payments turn out to be more than your parents can afford, they can take out a parent loan. By borrowing from the college itself, from a commercial agency or lender, or through PLUS, your parents can extend their college payments over a ten-year period or longer. Borrowing reduces the monthly obligation to its lowest level, but the total amount paid will be the highest due to principal and interest payments. Before making a decision on where to borrow parental loan funds, be sure to first check with the financial aid office to determine what is the best source of alternative funds.

Federal Financial Aid Programs

There are a number of sources of financial aid available to students: federal and state governments, private agencies, and the colleges themselves. In addition, as discussed earlier, there are three different forms of aid: grants, earnings, and loans.

The federal government is the single largest source of financial aid for students. In the 2004–05 academic year, the U.S. Department of Education's student financial aid programs made $74 billion available in loans, grants, and other aid to nearly 10 million students, while 11 million families benefited from various education tax cuts and deductions. At the present time, there are four federal grant programs—Federal Pell Grant, Federal Supplemental Educational Opportunity Grant (FSEOG), Academic Competitiveness Grant, and National Smart Grant. There are three federal loan programs: Federal Perkins Loan, Direct Loan, and Stafford Loan. The federal government also has a job program, Federal Work-Study (FWS), which helps colleges provide employment for students. In addition to the student aid programs, there are also tuition tax credits and deductions. They are the HOPE Scholarship for freshmen and sophomores, the Lifetime Learning Tax Credit for undergraduate students after their second year, and the Tuition and Fees Tax Deduction.

The majority of federal higher education loans are made either in the Direct Loan program or the Stafford Loan program. The difference between these loans is the lending source, but, for the borrower, the terms and conditions are essentially the same. Both Direct and Stafford programs make available two kinds of loans: loans to students and PLUS loans to parents and graduate or professional students. These loans are either subsidized or unsubsidized. Subsidized loans are made on the basis of demonstrated student need and have the interest paid by the government during the time the student is in school. For the unsubsidized (non-need-based) loans and PLUS, interest begins to accrue as soon as the money is received.

To qualify for the Pell and FSEOG programs, Federal Work-Study, the Perkins Loan, and the subsidized Stafford Loan, you must demonstrate financial need.

Table Used to Estimate Federal Pell Grants for 2006–2007

Adjusted Gross Income	\$50,000	\$55,000	\$60,000	\$65,000	\$70,000	\$75,000	\$80,000	\$85,000
				Family Assets				
$ 5,000	$ 4,050	$ 4,050	$ 4,050	$ 4,050	$ 4,050	$ 4,050	$ 4,050	$ 4,050
$ 10,000	4,050	4,050	4,050	4,050	4,050	4,050	4,050	4,050
$ 15,000	4,050	4,050	4,050	4,050	4,050	4,050	4,050	4,050
$ 20,000	4,000	4,050	4,050	4,050	4,050	4,050	3,850	3,650
$ 25,000	3,850	3,650	3,450	3,350	2,850	2,650	2,450	2,250
$ 30,000	3,050	2,950	2,850	2,750	2,650	2,450	2,250	2,150
$ 35,000	2,050	1,950	1,850	1,750	1,650	1,550	1,450	1,350

Note: Based on family of four, one child enrolled in college, oldest parent age 41. This chart should only be used as an estimate since the formula to determine EFC takes into account a number of variables.

Federal Financial Aid Programs

Pell Grant

The Federal Pell Grant is the largest grant program; more than 5 million students receive Pell Grants annually. This grant is intended to be the starting point of assistance for lower-income families. Eligibility for a Federal Pell Grant depends on the Expected Family Contribution. The amount you receive will depend on your EFC and the cost of education at the college you will attend. The highest award depends on how much funding the program receives from the government. The maximum for 2006-07 is $4050.

To give you some idea of your possible eligibility for a Pell Grant, the table in this section may be helpful. The amounts shown are based on a family of four, with one student in college, no emergency expenses, no contribution from student income or assets, and college costs of at least $4050 per year. Pell Grants range from $400 to $4050.

Federal Supplemental Educational Opportunity Grant (FSEOG)

As its name implies, the Federal Supplemental Educational Opportunity Grant provides additional need-based federal grant money to supplement the Federal Pell Grant. Each participating college is given funds to award to especially needy students. The maximum award is $4000 per year, but the amount you receive depends on the college's policy, the availability of FSEOG funds, the total cost of education, and the amount of other aid awarded.

Academic Competitiveness Grants

New for the 2006–07 academic year, U.S citizens who are Pell Grant–eligible and who attended a "rigorous" high school program, as defined by the U.S. Secretary of Education, can receive up to $750 in their first year and $1300 in their second year if they have a minimum 3.0 GPA. More information about this program is available from your child's high school or college financial aid office.

National Smart Grants

Again a new program for 2006–07, third- and fourth-year undergraduates who are Pell Grant–eligible and major in math, science, technology, or certain foreign languages and have a minimum 3.0 in their major can qualify for a grant of up to $4000. More information about this program is available from your child's high school or college financial aid office.

Federal Work-Study (FWS)

This program provides jobs for students who demonstrate need. Salaries are paid by funds from the federal government as well as the college. You work on an hourly basis on or off campus and must be paid at least the federal minimum wage. You may earn only up to the amount awarded in the financial aid package.

Federal Perkins Loan

This is a low-interest (5 percent) loan for students with exceptional financial need. Federal Perkins Loans are made through the college's financial aid office with the college as the lender. You can borrow a maximum of $4000 per year for up to five years of undergraduate study. Borrowers may take up to ten years to repay the loan, beginning nine months after they graduate, leave school, or drop below half-time status. No interest accrues while they are in school, and, under certain conditions (e.g., they teach in low-income areas, work in law enforcement, are full-time nurses or medical technicians, serve as Peace Corps or VISTA volunteers, etc.), some or all of the loan can be cancelled. In addition, payments can be deferred under certain conditions such as unemployment.

Federal Stafford and Direct Loans

Stafford and Direct Loans generally have the same interest rates, loan maximums, deferments, and cancellation benefits. A Stafford Loan may be borrowed from a commercial lender, such as a bank or a credit union. A Direct Loan is borrowed directly from the U.S. Department of Education through the college's financial aid office.

The Direct and Stafford Loan programs carry a fixed interest rate of 6.8 percent. If a student qualifies for a need-based subsidized Stafford Loan, the interest is paid by the federal government while he is enrolled in college. There is also an unsubsidized Stafford Loan that is not based on need for which he is eligible.

The maximum amount dependent students may borrow in any one year is $3500 for freshmen, $4500 for sophomores, and $5500 for juniors and seniors, with a maximum of $23,000 for the total undergraduate program. The maximum amount independent students can borrow is $7500 for freshmen (of which no more than $3500 can be subsidized), $8500 for sophomores (of which no more than $4500 can be subsidized), and $10,500 for juniors and seniors (of which no more than $5500 can be subsidized). Borrowers may be charged a small origination fee (usually less than 3 percent), which is deducted from the loan proceeds. Some lenders offer reduced or no-fee loans.

To apply for a Stafford Loan, you must first complete a FAFSA to determine

Federal Financial Aid Programs

Federal Financial Aid Programs

Name of Program	Type of Program	Maximum Award Per Year
Federal Pell Grant	need-based grant	$4050
Federal Supplemental Educational Opportunity Grant (FSEOG)	need-based grant	$4000
Academic Competitiveness Grant	need/merit	freshman $750 sophomore $1300
National Smart Grant	need/merit/program	third and fourth-year undergraduates up to $4000
Federal Work-Study	need-based part-time job	no maximum
Federal Perkins Loan	need-based loan	$4000
Subsidized Stafford/Direct Loan	need-based student loan	$3500 (first year)
Unsubsidized Stafford/Direct Loan	non-need-based student loan	$3500 (first year, dependent student)

eligibility for a subsidized loan and then complete a separate loan application that is submitted to a lender. The financial aid office can help in selecting a lender. The lender will send a master promissory note through which you agree to repay the loan. The proceeds of the loan, less the origination fee, will be sent to the college to be either credited to your account or released to you directly. Direct Loans are processed by the financial aid office as part of your overall financial aid package.

Once the repayment period starts, borrowers of both subsidized and unsubsidized Stafford or Direct Loans have to pay a combination of interest and principal monthly for up to a ten-year period. There are a number of repayment options as well as opportunities to consolidate federal loans. There are also provisions for deferments and repayment forbearance, if needed.

Federal PLUS Loans

PLUS is for parents of dependent students to help families with cash-flow problems. There is no needs test to qualify. The loan has a fixed interest rate of 8.5 percent for Stafford Loans and 7.9 percent for Direct Loans (subject to change). There is no yearly limit; you can borrow up to the cost of your child's education, less other financial aid received. Repayment begins sixty days after the money is advanced. A small origination fee (usually about 3 percent or less) may be subtracted from the proceeds. Parent borrowers must generally have a good credit record to qualify. PLUS may be processed under either the Direct or Stafford Loan system, depending on the type of loan program for which the college has contracted.

Tuition Tax Credits

Tuition tax credits allow families to reduce their tax bill by the amount of out-of-pocket college tuition expense. Unlike a tax deduction, which is modified according to your tax bracket, a tax credit is a dollar-for-dollar reduction in taxes paid.

There are two programs: the HOPE Scholarship and the Lifetime Learning Tax Credit. As is true of many federal programs, there are numerous rules and restrictions that apply. You should check with your tax preparer or financial adviser for information about your own particular situation.

HOPE Scholarship

The HOPE Scholarship offsets some of the expense for the first two years of college or vocational school. Students or the parents of dependent students can claim an annual income tax credit of up to $1500—100 percent of the first $1000 of tuition and required fees and 50 percent of the second $1000. Grants, scholarships, and other tax-free educa-

Federal Financial Aid Programs

tional assistance must be deducted from the total tuition and fee payments.

This credit can be claimed for students who are in their first two years of college and who are enrolled on at least a half-time basis in a degree or certificate program for any portion of the year. This credit phases out for joint filers who have an income between $87,000 and $107,000 and for single filers who have between $43,000 and $53,000 of income. Parents may claim credits for more than one qualifying student. (The income figures are subject to change.)

Lifetime Learning Tax Credit

The Lifetime Learning Tax Credit is the counterpart of the HOPE Scholarship; it is for college juniors, seniors, graduate students, and part-time students pursuing lifelong learning to improve or upgrade their job skills. The qualifying taxpayer can claim an annual tax credit of up to $2000—20 percent of the first $10,000 of tuition. The credit is available for net tuition and fees, less grant aid. The total credit available is limited to $2000 per year per taxpayer (or joint-filing couple), and is phased out at the same income levels as the HOPE Scholarship. (The income figures are subject to change each year.)

Tuition and Fees Tax Deduction

The Tuition and Fees Tax Deduction could reduce taxable income by as much as $4000. This deduction is taken as an adjustment to income, which means you can claim this deduction even if you do not itemize deductions on Schedule A of Form 1040. This deduction may benefit taxpayers who do not qualify for either the Hope or Lifetime Learning Tax Credits.

Up to $4000 may be deducted for tuition and fees required for enrollment or attendance at an eligible postsecondary institution. Personal living and family expenses, including room and board, insurance, medical, and transportation, are not deductible expenses.

The exact amount of the Tuition and Fees Tax Deduction depends on the amount of qualified tuition and related expenses paid for one's self, spouse, or dependents, and your Adjusted Gross Income. Consult your tax preparer for more information.

AmeriCorps

AmeriCorps is a national umbrella group of service programs for students. Participants work in a public or private nonprofit agency and provide service to the community in one of four priority areas: education, human services, the environment, and public safety. In exchange, they earn a stipend (for living expenses) of between $7400 and $14,800 a year, health insurance coverage, and $4725 per year for up to two years to apply toward college expenses. Many student-loan lenders will postpone the repayment of student loans during service in AmeriCorps, and AmeriCorps will pay the interest that is accrued on qualified student loans for members who complete the service program. Participants can work before, during, or after college and can use the funds to either pay current educational expenses or repay federal student loans. For more information, visit www.americorps.org.

Analyzing Financial Award Letters

Richard Woodland

You have just received the financial aid award letters. Now what? This is the time to do a detailed analysis of each college's offer to help you pay for your child's education. Remember, accepting financial aid is a family matter. More often than not, parents need to borrow money to send their dependent children to college. You need to clearly understand the types of aid you and your child are being offered. How much is "free" money in the form of grants and/or scholarships that does not have to be repaid? If your financial aid award package includes loans, what are the terms and conditions for these loans? A good tool to have with you is the federal government's most recent issue of *The Student Guide*, available from the school's financial aid office or at http://studentaid.ed.gov/students/publications/student_guide/index.html. This publication is very helpful in explaining the federal grant and loan programs that are usually a part of the aid package.

Let's take a minute to explain what is meant by "financial aid award package." A college will offer an aid applicant a combination of aid types, "packaged" in the form of grants and scholarships, loans, and a work-study job, based on the information provided on the FAFSA and/or another application. Many schools use a priority filing date, which guarantees that all applications received by this date will be considered for the full range of institutional aid programs available. Late applicants (by even one day!) often are only awarded the basic aid programs from state and federal sources. *It is important to apply on time.*

Evaluate Each Letter

As each award letter comes in, read it through carefully. The following are some critical points to consider:

- **Does the Cost of Attendance (COA) include all projected costs?** Each award letter should state the school's academic year COA. Tuition, fees, room, board, books, transportation, and personal expenses are what normally make up the COA. Does the award letter itemize all these components? Or does it omit some? This is crucial because this is what you will need to budget for. If you need additional information, be sure to contact the financial aid office. They will be glad to provide you with information or answer any questions you may have about their costs.

- **What is your Expected Family Contribution (EFC)?** Is the school's—not just the federal government's—EFC listed on the award letter? Some schools may require a higher EFC than you expected. Be aware that the EFC may increase or decrease each year depending on the information you provide on the renewal FAFSA or other financial aid application.

- **Is there unmet need?** Does the aid package cover the difference between the COA and the EFC? Not every school can cover your full need. If the aid package does not cover your full need, does the information with the award letter provide you with alternative loan options? If not, contact the financial aid office for more information.

- **Is the scholarship renewable for four years?** If your child is awarded a scholarship based on scholastic achievement or talent, you need to ask these questions: Is there a minimum grade point average he has to maintain? Can he switch majors but keep the scholarship? Does he need to participate in an "honors college" program to maintain the scholarship? If he needs to change to part-time status, will the award amount be pro-rated, or does he need to maintain full-time status? If it is an athletic or "special talent" scholarship, will he continue to receive the award if for some reason he cannot continue with the specific program? Renewal of scholarship funds is often the biggest misunderstanding between families and colleges. Be sure you clearly understand the terms and conditions of all grants and scholarships.

- **What will the college do to your child's award if she receives outside, noninstitutional scholarships?** Will the award be used to cover unmet need or reduce her student loans? Will the college reduce her institutional grants or scholarships? Or will they reduce her work-study award? (This is a good time to compare each school's policy on this matter.) Remember, your overall aid

Analyzing Financial Award Letters

cannot total more than the COA, and many programs cannot exceed your financial need.

- **What are the interest rates of the loans that are offered?** Did another school offer you more than one loan and why? *Do not* sign the award letter until you understand your loan obligations. Again, *The Student Guide* can be very helpful with this part of the analysis.
- **Is the school likely to cover the same expenses every year?** In particular, ask if grant or scholarship funds are normally reduced or increased after the freshman year, even if family income and EFC remain the same. Some colleges will *increase* the self-help (loan, job) percentage every year but not necessarily the free money.
- **If work-study was awarded, how many hours a week will your child be expected to work?** If you feel working that many hours will have a negative impact on your child's academic performance, you may want to request that the awarded job funds be changed to a loan. You must ask immediately because funds are limited. Many schools are flexible with these funds early in the process.
- **What happens if (or more likely, when) tuition increases?** Check with the financial aid office to find out what its policy is for renewing an aid package. If, for example, tuition increases by 5 percent each of the next three years and your EFC remains the same, what will happen to your scholarships, grants, and loans?

You can always appeal your award letter if you feel that your needs are not being met, if your family situation has changed, or if you have received a better award from a competitive school. You have the right to ask for a reconsideration of your award. (Do not use the word *negotiate*.) When asking for reconsideration, be sure to provide the aid officer with all relevant information.

Compare Letters

After you have received and reviewed all the award letters from the schools your child is considering, the next step is to compare them and determine which schools are offering the best aid packages. Following are three sample award letters and a sample spreadsheet that shows you how to analyze and compare each school's awards.

Note: These award letters are simply for discussion purposes. They should not be considered to be representative award letters with an EFC of $9550.

Analyzing Financial Award Letters

UNIVERSITY A
FINANCIAL AID AWARD LETTER
2006–2007

Date: 4/21/06
ID#: 000000009

Dear Courtney Applicant,

We are pleased to inform you that you are eligible to receive the financial assistance indicated in the area labeled "Your Financial Aid." We estimated your budget based on the following assumptions:

In-state resident and living on campus.

	FALL	SPRING	TOTAL
Tuition and Fees	$3,849	$3,849	$ 7,698
Room & Board	3,769	3,770	7,539
Books	420	420	840
Transportation	973	974	1,947
Personal Expenses	369	369	738
Estimated Cost of Attendance	**$9,380**	**$9,382**	**$18,762**

Your Financial Aid

	FALL	SPRING	TOTAL
Federal Pell Grant	$1,950	$1,950	$ 3,900
Federal Direct Subsidized Loan	1,312	1,313	2,625
State Grant	432	432	864
Total Financial Aid	**$3,694**	**$3,695**	**$ 7,389**
Unmet Need	**$5,686**	**$5,687**	**$11,373**

What to Do Next:

- Verify that accurate assumptions have been used to determine your awards.
- Carefully review and follow the instructions on the Data Changes Form.
- To reduce or decline all or part of your loans, you must complete and return the Data Changes Form.
- We will assume you fully accept the awards above unless you submit changes to us immediately.
- Return corrections and required documents promptly.
- Retain this letter for your records.

Analyzing Financial Award Letters

UNIVERSITY B
FINANCIAL AID AWARD LETTER
2006–2007

Date: 4/21/06
ID#: 000000009

Dear Courtney Applicant,

We are pleased to inform you that you are eligible to receive the financial assistance indicated in the area labeled "Your Financial Aid." We estimated your budget based on the following assumptions:

Nonresident and living on campus.

	FALL	SPRING	TOTAL
Tuition and Fees	$ 9,085	$ 9,085	$18,170
Room & Board	2,835	2,835	5,670
Books	410	410	820
Transportation	875	875	1,750
Personal Expenses	378	377	755
Estimated Cost of Attendance	**$13,583**	**$13,582**	**$27,165**

Your Financial Aid

	FALL	SPRING	TOTAL
Federal Pell Grant	$ 1950	$ 1950	$ 3,900
Federal SEOG Grant	225	225	450
Academic Excellence Scholarship	500	500	1,000
Federal Work-Study Program	1,250	1,250	2,500
Federal Perkins Loan	1,250	1,250	2,500
Subsidized Stafford Loan	1,313	1,312	2,625
University Student Loan	2,000	2,000	4,000
Total Financial Aid	**$ 8,488**	**$ 8,487**	**$16,975**
Unmet Need	**$ 5,095**	**$ 5,095**	**$10,190**

What to Do Next:

- Verify that accurate assumptions have been used to determine your awards.
- Carefully review and follow the instructions on the Data Changes Form.
- To reduce or decline all or part of your loans, you must complete and return the Data Changes Form.
- We will assume you fully accept the awards above unless you submit changes to us immediately.
- Return corrections and required documents promptly.
- Retain this letter for your records.

Analyzing Financial Award Letters

UNIVERSITY C
FINANCIAL AID AWARD LETTER
2006–2007

Date: 4/21/06
ID#: 000000009

Dear Courtney Applicant,

We are pleased to inform you that you are eligible to receive the financial assistance indicated in the area labeled "Your Financial Aid." We estimated your budget based on the following assumptions:

Living on campus.

	FALL	SPRING	TOTAL
Tuition and Fees	$14,955	$14,955	$29,910
Room & Board	4,194	4,193	8,387
Books	450	450	900
Transportation	350	350	700
Personal Expenses	1,295	1,293	2,588
Estimated Cost of Attendance	**$21,244**	**$21,241**	**$42,485**

Your Financial Aid

	FALL	SPRING	TOTAL
Institutional Grant	$10,805	$10,805	$21,610
Federal Pell Grant	1,950	1,950	3,900
Federal SEOG Grant	2,000	2,000	4,000
Federal Work-Study Program	1,713	1,712	3,425
Total Financial Aid	**$16,468**	**$16,467**	**$32,935**
Unmet Need	**$ 4,776**	**$ 4,774**	**$ 9,550**

What to Do Next:

- Verify that accurate assumptions have been used to determine your awards.
- Carefully review and follow the instructions on the Data Changes Form.
- To reduce or decline all or part of your loans, you must complete and return the Data Changes Form.
- We will assume you fully accept the awards above unless you submit changes to us immediately.
- Return corrections and required documents promptly.
- Retain this letter for your records.

Analyzing Financial Award Letters

COMPARISON GRID

	University A (State University)	University B (Nonresident State University)	University C (Private College)
Cost of Attendance	**$18,762**	**$27,165**	**$42,485**
Tuition and Fees	7,698	18,170	29,910
Room and Board	7,539	5,670	8,367
Books	840	820	900
Transportation	1,947	1,750	700
Personal Expenses	738	755	2,558
Grants and Scholarships	4,764	5,350	29,510
Loans	2,625	5,525	0
Work-Study	0	2,500	3,425
Expected Family Contribution	9,550	9,550	9,550
Balance	$ 1,823	$ 640	$ 0

Some things to notice:

1. At all schools, the Federal Pell grant remains the same.
2. Even though University C (a private college) has the highest "sticker price," the net cost is less than the state schools.
3. University B is a state university, but you are classified as an out-of-state resident (or nonresident). Many students in this situation find that the higher out-of-state costs combined with lower grant aid make this a costly decision.
4. All schools assume that you will be residing in on-campus housing. But if you choose to commute to University A, you would save a substantial amount because you would not have the $7539 room and board cost.

Once you have entered all the information into a spreadsheet of your own and come up with the balances, here are some things to consider for each school:

- **How much is the balance?** Ideally, your balance should be $0, but look to see which school has the lowest balance amount.
- **What part of the aid package comes in the form of grants and scholarships?** It is important to note this because these awards (gift aid) do not have to be paid back.

- **Look at the loans.** Usually, the best financial deal contains more money in scholarships and less in loan dollars. Based on expected freshman-year borrowing, determine the debt burden at each school once your child graduates. You have to multiply the amount of your loan by four or five years, depending on how long it will take for your child to graduate. And remember that the loan amounts will probably increase each year. You also should take into consideration that you will have to borrow even more as the COA increases each year. To determine the best loan deal, consider:
  —What are the terms of the loans?
  —What are interest rates?
  —Do you pay the yearly interest rate during enrollment or is the interest subsidized or paid by the government?
  —Is any money due during enrollment or is it deferred until after graduation? Figuring out how much you will owe at each school at graduation will give you a clear picture of what your financial situation will be *after* graduation.

Analyzing Financial Award Letters

However, unless cost is your only concern, you shouldn't simply choose the school offering the lowest loan amounts. Many other factors need to be considered, such as academic and social environment. And you should never reject a school based solely on insufficient financial aid. Consult with an aid administrator to discuss possible alternatives.

Finally, if the college that costs the most is still the one your child wants to attend, there are a number of ways to find money to cover the gap between the aid package and your actual cost, including paying more than the EFC figure, increasing student borrowing, working more hours, and taking out a PLUS loan.

———————

Richard Woodland is Director of Financial Aid at Rutgers University–Camden.

Online Filing of FAFSA and CSS/PROFILE® Applications

Richard Woodland

Over the past few years, there have been major advancements in the way students apply both for admission to college and for financial aid. The two primary financial aid applications, the Free Application for Federal Student Aid (FAFSA) and the CSS/PROFILE® application from the College Scholarship Service now offer direct, online applications. FAFSA on the Web and PROFILE are available in both English and Spanish.

Why File Online?

There are two reasons why it is a good idea to file online. First, the online environment prevents you from making many mistakes. For example, if there is a question that is required of all applicants, you cannot inadvertently skip it. If the application software thinks your answer may not be accurate, it will prompt you to check it before proceeding. The financial aid process can be complicated, and applying online greatly reduces the chance for error. The second reason is turnaround time. The online applications are processed in a matter of days, not weeks. Since time is an important factor when applying for financial aid, it is prudent to have your application processed as quickly as possible.

Some Common Concerns About Online Filing

Both the FASFA and PROFILE online applications have become much more user-friendly. You do not have to be a computer expert to use these programs. Both applications allow you to save your completed data and return later if you are interrupted or need to gather additional information. Both systems use secure encryption technology to protect your privacy. FASFA information is shared with other federal agencies as required as part of the application process, online or paper. FAFSA information is also sent to your state of legal residence for state aid purposes and to any college or program your child lists on the application. The information on the application is highly personal, and every precaution is taken to safeguard your privacy.

Now, let's discuss some specific issues related to each application.

The FAFSA

The FAFSA is the universal application for all federal financial aid programs. It is the primary application used for most state and college financial aid programs. Before using the FAFSA online application, you need to secure an electronic signature, or Personal Identification Number (PIN). This is similar to the access codes used at ATM machines, online banking, etc. It is easy to obtain a PIN number. Simply go to www.pin.ed.gov and apply online. You will receive a reply via e-mail in about 48 hours. If your child is under 24 years of age, he or she and one parent will need a PIN number. If there is more than one child in college, a parent only needs one PIN number. However, each college applicant will need to have his or her own PIN.

The FASFA online application is not presented in the same format as the paper FAFSA. Although all of the questions are exactly the same, the order of some of the items on the online application has been rearranged to make it easier to complete and allow for some built-in skip-logic. You can easily obtain a copy of the electronic FAFSA by logging on to www.fafsa.ed.gov. Just click on "FAFSA on the Web Worksheet." Completing this first will make the online entry that much easier. There are a number of other worksheets available that can also make the process easier. You should print them out and decide which are applicable to your situation. Everyone should review Worksheets A, B, and C. If you have not completed your federal tax return, the "Income Estimator" worksheets are easy to use and can reduce much of the guesswork.

After completing the online FASFA, be sure to print a copy of the pages at the end of the process so that you have a copy of your answers and the confirmation number. Although lost applications are extremely rare, having this information will give you peace of mind. You can go online as often as you wish to check the status of your application.

The CSS/PROFILE®

The CSS/PROFILE® is a more comprehensive financial aid application that is used primarily at private, higher-cost

25

Online Filing of FAFSA and CSS/PROFILE® Applications

colleges and universities to award nonfederal student aid funds. Many private scholarship programs also use the PROFILE. A complete list of colleges and programs that use the PROFILE can be found at https://profileonline.collegeboard.com/index.jsp.

The PROFILE application has a $5 registration fee and an additional $18 for each school or program you select to receive your information. You must have a credit card, debit card, or checking account to use this service.

Note: A limited number of fee waivers are available for families with incomes below the poverty line. See your high school guidance officer for more information on the fee waiver program.

Complete information on the online PROFILE application is available at www.collegeboard.com/profile. Although the customized PROFILE application is processed in about one week, you should allow for enough processing time (usually 2 to 3 weeks) to meet the earliest deadline established by the school or program.

What Happens Next?

Both the FAFSA and CSS/PROFILE® processors want more applicants to use the online environment. Not only is the process easier for them, but it is faster and more accurate. Once you decide to apply online, the processors will only respond to you electronically. You will not receive any paper acknowledgments—all confirmations will be sent via e-mail. When it is time to reapply for aid in subsequent years (usually quite easy as most of the data are carried over from the previous application), all reminders will be sent to the e-mail address that is on file, so it is important to report any changes in your e-mail address.

It is easy to update the FAFSA following your initial application. For example, if you used estimated income information and now you have your federal tax return completed, you can simply return to www.fafsa.ed.gov and change your income figures. But be sure to go through the entire process and print out the updated confirmation page. In general, the PROFILE is a one-time application, filed well before tax season. Any updates are usually done directly through the schools.

Both processors offer helpful information, both in print and online. Check with your high school guidance office or local college financial aid office for additional assistance. If you need to call the FAFSA processor, the phone number is 800-4-FED-AID (toll-free). You can contact PROFILE customer service via e-mail at help@cssprofile.org or by phone at 305-829-9793.

Richard Woodland is Director of Financial Aid at Rutgers University–Camden.

Searching for Scholarships Online

Today's students need all the help they can get when looking for ways to pay for their college education. Skyrocketing tuition costs, state budget cuts, and diminished personal savings have combined to make financing a college education perhaps the number one concern for parents. College sticker shock is driving many families away from college. No wonder. The "purchasing power" of all aid programs from federal, state, and institutional sources has declined over the past two decades. State education budgets have been slashed. In 2005–06, as compared to 2004–05, tuition at public institutions increased 7.1 percent; private tuition increased by 5.9 percent. And it's not only lower-income families who are affected. Some families fear they make *too much* money to qualify for financial aid. Regardless of their situation, most families struggle to make sense of the college financial aid process and to decide which aid package is the right one for them.

Despite the confusion, students and parents can and should continue to research as many sources as possible to find the money they need. The Internet can be a great source of information. There are many worthwhile sites that are ready to help you search and apply for your fair share of awards, including Thomson Peterson's comprehensive financial aid site at www.petersons.com/finaid.

Thomson Peterson's "Pay For School"

Expert Advice

By logging on to www.petersons.com/finaid you gain access to comprehensive articles that describe the ins and outs of federal and state funding; tips for filing the FAFSA and the CSS/PROFILE®; step-by-step advice on what your child should be doing junior and senior years of high school; and an audio clip of an interview with a financial aid expert. Links to state programs and agencies connect you directly to those resources. The "Advice Center" lets you access articles on specific topics, such as 529 Plans, loans and payment plans, scholarship scams, and the military. There is also a section called "Financial Aid This Month," where the latest-breaking news on government aid programs and other college funding topics is posted.

Scholarship Search

Thomson Peterson's free Scholarship Search connects you to more than 1.8 million scholarships, grants, and prizes totaling nearly $8 billion and lets you do an individualized search for awards that match your financial and educational needs. In just three easy steps, your child can register; complete a customized profile indicating his or her scholastic and personal background, intended major, work experi-

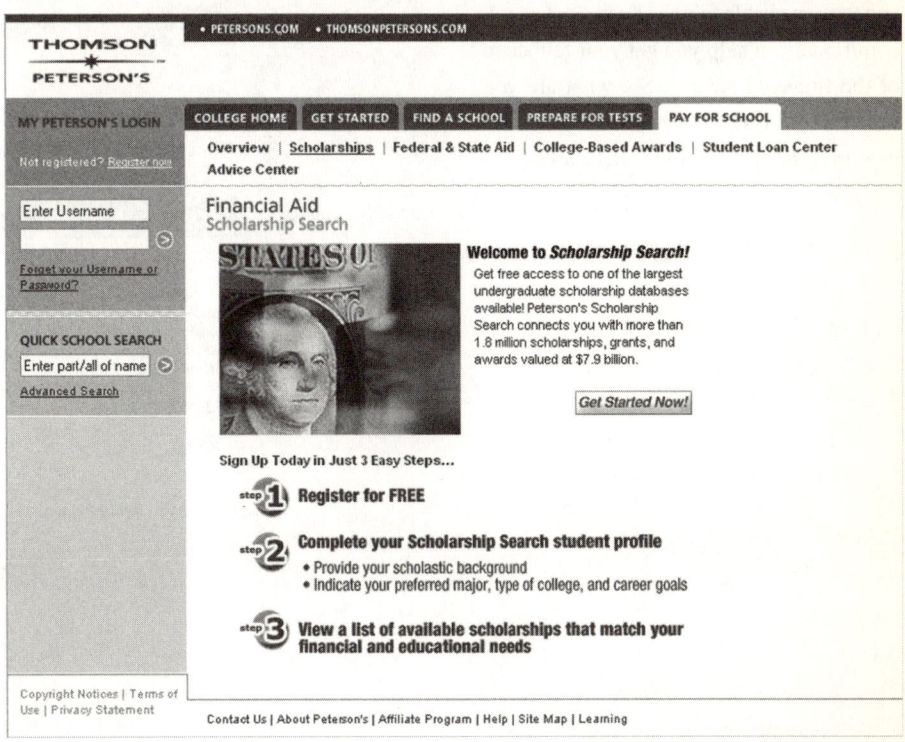

Searching for Scholarships Online

ence, and a host of other criteria; and access a list of scholarships that match your family's needs. Each scholarship is described in detail, including eligibility and application requirements and contact information, with links to its e-mail address and Web site. Finding money for college couldn't be easier!

Interactive Tools

When it's time to get to the nuts and bolts of your college financial planning, Peterson's has the tools to help. You can access a calculator to find your Estimated Family Contribution (EFC) as well as a College Financial Planning calculator that lets your student figure out his or her own personal savings plan. After receiving award letters from the colleges, you and your child can use the Award Analyzer, which helps you compare award letters and determine which school is prepared to give you the most aid. You simply enter the information from each award letter you received, press the Calculate button, and discover which school has offered your child the best package.

Searching and applying for financial aid is a complicated process. The resources and tools available to you at www.petersons.com/finaid can help you get your fair share of the financial aid pie. So, what are you waiting for? Log on! Free money for college may be just a mouse click away.

How to Use This Guide

Quick-Reference Chart

The amount of aid available at colleges can vary greatly. "College Costs At-a-Glance" lists the percent of freshmen who applied for and received need-based gift aid and the percent of those whose need was fully met. Also listed are the average freshman financial aid package, the average cost after aid, and the average graduate indebtedness.

Profiles of College Financial Aid Programs

After the federal government, colleges provide the largest amount of financial aid to students. In addition, they control most of the money channeled to students from the federal government. The amount and makeup of your financial aid package will depend on the institution's particular circumstances and its decisions concerning your application. The main section of this book shows you the pattern and extent of each college's current awards. The profiles present detailed factual and statistical data for each school in a uniform format to enable easy, quick references and comparisons. Items that could not be collected in time for publication are designated as *N/A*. Items for which the specific figures could not be gathered in time are given as *available*. Colleges that supplied no data are listed by name and address only so that you do not overlook them in your search for colleges.

There is much anecdotal evidence that students and their families fail to apply for financial aid under the misconception that student aid goes only to poor families. Financial need in the context of college expenses is not the same as being needy in the broad social context. Middle-class families typically qualify for need-based financial aid; at expensive schools, even upper-middle-income families can qualify for need-based financial aid. Thomson Peterson's encourages you to apply for financial aid whether or not you think that you will qualify.

To help you understand the definition and significance of each item, the following outline of the profile format explains what is covered in each section. The term college or colleges is frequently used below to refer to any institution of higher education, regardless of its official definition.

The College

The name of the college is the official name as it appears on the institution's charter. The city and state listed are the official location of the school. The subhead line shows tuition and required fees, as they were charged to the majority of full-time undergraduate students in the 2005–06 academic year. Any exceptions to the 2005–06 academic year are so noted. For a public institution, the tuition and fees shown are for state residents, and this is noted. If a college's annual expenses are expressed as a comprehensive fee (including full-time tuition, mandatory fees, and college room and board), this is noted, as are any unusual definitions, such as tuition only. The average undergraduate aid package is the average total package of grant, loan, and work-study aid that was awarded to meet the officially defined financial need of full-time undergraduates enrolled in fall 2005 (or fall 2004) who applied for financial aid, were determined to have need, and then actually received financial aid. This information appears in more detail in each profile.

About the Institution

This paragraph gives the reader a brief introduction to a college. It contains the following elements:

Institutional Control

Private institutions are designated as *independent* (nonprofit), *independent/religious* (sponsored by or affiliated with a religious group or having a nondenominational or interdenominational religious orientation), or *proprietary* (profit-making). Public institutions are designated by their primary source of support, such as *federal*, *state*, *commonwealth* (Puerto Rico), *territory* (U.S. territories), *county*, *district* (an administrative unit of public education, often having boundaries different from those of units of local government), *state- and locally-supported* ("locally" refers to county, district, or city), *state-supported* (funded by the state), or *state-related* (funded primarily by the state but administered autonomously).

Type of Student Body

The categories are *men* (100 percent of student body), *coed-primarily men*, *women* (100 percent of student body), *coed-primarily women*, and *coed*. A few schools are designated as *undergraduate: women only, graduate: coed* or *undergraduate: men only, graduate: coed*.

Degrees Awarded

Associate, *bachelor's* (baccalaureate), *master's*, *doctoral* (doctorate), and *first pro-*

How to Use This Guide

fessional (in such fields as law and medicine). There are no institutions in this book that award the associate degree only. Many award the bachelor's as their highest degree. Your student will need to discuss this with you and his or her guidance counselor to decide whether a college that concentrates on undergraduate education or an institution with professional schools and research activities better meets his or her needs.

Number of Undergraduate Majors

This shows the number of academic fields in which the institution offers associate and/or bachelor's degrees. The purpose of this is to give you an indication of the range of subjects available.

Enrollment

These figures are based on the actual number of full-time and part-time students enrolled in degree programs as of fall 2005. In most instances, they are designated as *total enrollment* (for the specific college or university) and *freshmen*. If the institution is a university and its total enrollment figure includes graduate students, a separate figure for *undergraduates* may be provided. If the profiled institution is a subunit of a university, the figures may be designated *total university enrollment* for the entire university and *total unit enrollment* for the specific subunit.

Methodology Used for Determining Need

Private colleges usually have larger financial aid programs, but public colleges usually have lower sticker prices, especially for in-state or local students. At a public college, your financial need will be less, and you will receive a smaller financial aid package. The note on whether a college uses federal (FAFSA) or institutional methodology (usually PROFILE) will let you know whether you will have to complete one or two kinds of financial aid application forms. Federal Methodology is the needs-analysis formula used by the U.S. Department of Education to determine the Expected Family Contribution (EFC), which, when subtracted from the cost of attendance at an institution, determines the financial need of a student. There is no relative advantage or disadvantage to using one methodology over the other.

Undergraduate Expenses

If provided by the institution, the one-time application fee is listed. Costs are given for the 2006–07 academic year (or estimated for the 2006–07 academic year) or for the 2005–06 academic year if 2006–07 figures were not yet available. Annual expenses may be expressed as a comprehensive fee (including full-time tuition, mandatory fees, and college room and board) or may be given as separate figures for full-time tuition, fees, room and board, or room only. For public institutions where tuition differs according to state residence, separate figures are given for area or state residents and for nonresidents. Part-time tuition is expressed in terms of a per-unit rate (per credit, per semester hour, etc.), as specified by the institution.

The tuition structure at some institutions is complex. Freshmen and sophomores may be charged a different rate from that charged juniors and seniors, a professional or vocational division may have a different fee structure from the liberal arts division of the same institution, or part-time tuition may be prorated on a sliding scale according to the number of credit hours taken. Tuition and fees may vary according to academic program, campus/location, class time (day, evening, weekend), course/credit load, course level, degree level, reciprocity agreements, and student level. If tuition and fees differ for international students, the rate charged is listed.

Room and board charges are reported as an average for one academic year and may vary according to board plan selected, campus/location, gender, type of housing facility, or student level. If no college-owned or -operated housing facilities are offered, the phrase *college housing not available* will appear.

If a college offers a *guaranteed tuition* plan, it promises that the tuition rate of an entering student will not increase for the entire term of enrollment, from entrance to graduation. Other payment plans might include *tuition prepayment*, which allows an entering student to lock in the current tuition rate for the entire term of enrollment by paying the full amount in advance rather than year by year, and *installment* and *deferred payment* plans, which allow students to delay the payment of the full tuition.

Guaranteed tuition and tuition prepayment help you to plan the total cost of your child's education and can save you from the financial distress sometimes caused by tuition hikes. Colleges that offer such plans may also help you to arrange financing, which in the long run can cost less than the total of four years of increasing tuition rates. Deferred payment or installment payments may better fit your personal financial situation, especially if you do not qualify for financial aid and, due to other financial commitments, find that obtaining the entire amount due is burdensome. Carefully investigate these plans, however, to see what premium you may pay at the end to allow you to defer immediate payment.

Freshman Financial Aid

Usually, these are actual figures for the 2005–06 term, beginning in fall 2005; figures may also be estimated for that term, or they could be 2004–05 figures. The particular term for which these data apply is indicated. The figures are for degree-seeking full-time freshman students. The first figure is the number of freshmen who applied for any kind of financial aid. The next figure is the percentage of those freshmen financial aid applicants who were determined to have financial need—that is, through the formal needs-assessment process, had a calculated expected family contribution that was less than the total college cost. The next figure is the percentage of this group of eligible freshmen who received any financial aid. The next figure is the percentage of this preceding group of eligible aid recipients whose need was fully met by financial aid. The *Average percent of need met* is the average percentage of financial need met for freshmen who received any need-based aid. The *Average financial aid package* is the average dollar amount awarded (need-based or non-need-based) to freshmen who applied for aid, were deemed eligible, and received any aid; awards used to reduce the expected family contribution are excluded from this average. The final line in most profiles is the percentage of freshmen who had no financial need but who received non-need-based aid other than athletic scholarships or special-group tuition benefits.

What do these data mean to you? If financial aid is important in your comparison of colleges, the relative percentage of students who received any aid, whose need was fully met, and the average percentage of need met have the most weight. These figures reflect the relative abundance of student aid available to the average eligible applicant. The average dollar amount of the aid package has real meaning, but only in relation to the college's expense; you will be especially interested in the difference between this figure and the costs figure, which is what the average student (in any given statistical group, there actually may be no average individual) will have to pay. Of course, if the financial aid package is largely loans rather than grants, you will have to pay this amount eventually. Relative differences in the figures of the number of students who apply for aid and who are deemed eligible can hinge on any number of factors: the relative sticker price of the college, the relative level of wealth of the students' families, the proportion of only children in college and students with siblings in college (families with two or more children in college are more likely to apply for aid and be considered eligible), or the relative sophistication in financial aid matters (or quality of college counseling they may have received) of the students and their families. While these may be interesting, they will not mean too much to most students and families. If you are among the unlucky (or, perhaps, lucky) families who do not qualify for need-based financial aid, the final sentence of this paragraph in the profile will be of interest because it reveals the relative policies that the college has in distributing merit-based aid to students who cannot demonstrate need.

Undergraduate Financial Aid

This is the parallel paragraph to the Freshman Financial Aid paragraph (see above). The same definitions apply, except that the group being considered is degree-seeking full-time undergraduate students (including freshmen).

There are cases of students who chose a particular college because they received a really generous financial aid package in their freshman year and then had to scramble to pay the tuition bill in their later years. If a financial aid package is a key factor in your child's decision to attend a particular college, you want to be certain that the package offered to all undergraduates is not too far from that offered to freshmen. The key figures are those for the percentage of students who received any aid, the percentage of financial aid recipients whose need was fully met, the average percentage of need met, and the dollar figure of the average financial aid package. Generally, colleges assume that after the freshman year, students develop study habits and time-management skills that will allow them to take on part-time and summer employment without hurting their academic performance. So, the proportion of self-help aid (work-study and student loans) in the financial aid package tends to increase after the freshman year. This pattern, which is true of most colleges, can be verified below, in the freshman-undergraduate figures in the paragraph on Gift Aid (Need-Based).

Gift Aid (Need-Based)

Total amount is the total dollar figure in 2005–06 (actual or estimated) or 2004–05 (actual) of need-based scholarships and grant (gift) aid awarded to degree-seeking full-time and part-time students that was used to meet financial need. The percentages of this aid from federal, state, institutional (college or university), and external (e.g., foundations, civic organizations, etc.) sources are shown. *Receiving aid* shows the percentages (and number, in parentheses) of freshmen and of all undergraduates who applied for aid, were considered eligible, and received any need-based gift aid. *Scholarships, grants, and awards by category* cites major categories of need-based gift aid provided by the college; these include Federal Pell Grants, Federal Supplemental Educational Opportunity Grants (FSEOG), state scholarships, private scholarships, college/university gift aid from institutional funds, United Negro College Fund aid, Federal Nursing Scholarships, and others.

Scholarships and grants are gifts awarded to students that do not need to be repaid. These are preferable to loans, which have to be repaid, or work-study wages, which may take time away from studies and personal pursuits. The total amount of need-based gift aid has to be placed into the context of the total number of undergraduate students (shown above, in the About the Institution paragraph) and the relative expense of the institution. Filing the FAFSA automatically puts you in line to receive any available federal grants for which you may qualify. However, if the college that your child is considering has a higher

How to Use This Guide

than usual proportion of gift aid coming from state, institutional, or external sources, be sure to check with the financial aid office to find out what these sources may be and how to apply for them. For almost all colleges, the percentage of freshmen receiving need-based gift aid will be higher than the percentage of all undergraduates receiving need-based gift aid. However, if your family is dependent on need-based gift aid and the particular college your child is considering shows a sharper drop from the freshman to undergraduate years than other colleges of a similar type, you might want to think about how this change will affect your ability to pay for later years at this college.

Gift Aid (Non-Need-Based)

Total amount is the total dollar figure in 2005–06 (actual or estimated) or 2004–05 (actual) of non-need-based scholarships and grant (gift) aid awarded to degree-seeking full-time and part-time students. Non-need-based aid that was used to meet financial need is not included in this total. The percentages of this aid from federal, state, institutional (college or university), and external (e.g., National Merit Scholarships, civic, religious, fraternal organizations, etc.) sources are shown. *Receiving aid* shows the percentages (and number, in parentheses) of freshmen and of all undergraduates who did not receive need-based aid but who received non-need-based gift aid. *Average award* is the average dollar amount of awards to the students in this immediately preceding group. *Scholarships, grants, and awards by category* cites the major categories in which non-need-based awards are available and the number of awards made in that category (in parentheses, the total dollar value of these awards). The categories listed are *Academic Interests/Achievement*, *Creative Arts/Performance*, *Special Achievements/Activities*, and *Special Characteristics*. *Tuition waivers* indicate special categories of students (minority students, children of alumni, college employees or children of employees, adult students, and senior citizens) who may qualify for a full or partial waiver of tuition. *ROTC* indicates Army, Naval, and Air Force ROTC programs that are offered on campus; a program offered by arrangement on another campus is indicated by the word *cooperative*.

This section covers college-administered scholarships awarded to undergraduates on the basis of merit or personal attributes without regard to need. If you do not qualify for financial aid but nevertheless lack the resources to pay for college, non-need-based awards will be of special interest to you. Some personal characteristics are completely beyond an individual's control, and talents and achievements take a number of years to develop or attain. However, certain criteria for these awards, such as religious involvement, community service, and special academic interests can be attained in a relatively brief period of time. ROTC programs offer such benefits as tuition, the cost of textbooks, and living allowances. In return, you must fulfill a service obligation after graduating from college. Because they can be a significant help in paying for college, these programs have become quite competitive. Certain subject areas, such as nursing, health care, or the technical fields, are in stronger demand than others. Among the obligations to consider about ROTC are that you must spend a regular portion of your available time in military training programs and that ROTC entails a multiyear commitment after your graduation to serve as an officer in the armed services branch sponsoring the program.

Loans

The figures here represent loans that are part of the financial aid award package. These are typically offered at rates lower than can be found in the normal loan marketplace. *Student loans* represents the total dollar amount of loans from all sources to full-time and part-time degree-seeking undergraduates or their parents. The percentage of these loans that goes to meet financial need and the percentage that goes to pay the non-need portion (the expected family contribution) are indicated. The percentage of a past graduating class who borrowed through any loan program (except parent loans) while enrolled at the college is shown, as is the average dollar figure per-borrower of cumulative undergraduate indebtedness (this does not include loans from other institutions). *Parent loans* shows the total amount borrowed through parent loan programs as well as the percentages that were applied to the need-based and non-need-based portions of financial need. *Programs* indicates the major loan programs available to undergraduates. These include Direct and Stafford Loans (subsidized and unsubsidized and PLUS), Perkins Loans, Federal Nursing Loans, state loans, college/university loans, and other types.

Loans are forms of aid that must be repaid with interest. Most people will borrow money to pay college costs. The loans available through financial aid programs are offered at very favorable interest rates. Student loans are preferable to parent loans because the payoff is deferred. In comparing colleges, the dollar amount of total indebtedness of the last class is a factor to be considered. Typically, this amount would increase proportionate to the tuition. However, if it does not, this could mean that the college provides relatively generous grant or work-study aid rather than loans in its financial aid package.

Work-Study

The total dollar amounts, number, and average dollar amount of *Federal Work-Study* (FWS) jobs appear first. The total dollar figure of *State or other work-study/employment*, if available, is shown, as is the percentage of those dollars that go to meet financial need. The number of part-time jobs available on campus to undergraduates, other than work-study, is shown last.

FWS is a federally funded program that enables students with demonstrated need to earn money by working on or off campus, usually in a nonprofit organization. FWS jobs are a special category of jobs that are open to students only through the financial aid office. Other kinds of part-time jobs are routinely available at most colleges and may vary widely. In comparing colleges, you may find characteristic differences in how the "self-help" amounts (loans and work-study) are apportioned.

Athletic Awards
The total dollar amount of athletic scholarships given by the college to undergraduate students, including percentages that are need-based and non-need-based, is indicated.

If your child is a serious student-athlete candidate, this may provide a broad context, but actual awards will depend upon her specific talents and the college's athletic needs at the particular time. If she is a good athlete but not of starter caliber in a marquee sport, she might be able to secure a partial scholarship, depending on talent and the college's needs. In this case, the number of students receiving athletic awards in relation to the number of total undergraduates may be important.

Applying for Financial Aid
Required financial aid forms include the FAFSA (Free Application for Federal Student Aid), the institution's own form, CSS/PROFILE®, a state aid form, a noncustodial (divorced/separated) parent's statement, a business/farm supplement, and others. The college's financial aid application deadline is noted as the *Financial aid deadline* and is shown in one of three ways: as a specific date if it is an absolute deadline; noted as *Continuous*, which means processing goes on without a deadline or until all available aid has been awarded; or as a date with the note *(priority)*, meaning that you are encouraged to apply before that date in order to have the best chance of obtaining aid. *Notification date* is listed as either a specific date or *Continuous*. The date by which your child must reply to the college with her decision to accept or decline its financial aid package is listed as either a specific date or as a number of weeks from the date of notification.

Be prepared to check early with the colleges your child is interested in as to exactly which forms will be required from you. All colleges require the FAFSA for students applying for federal aid. In most cases, colleges have a limited amount of funds set aside to use as financial aid. It is possible that the first eligible students will get a larger share of what is available.

Contact
The name, title, address, telephone and fax numbers, and e-mail address of the person to contact for further information (student financial aid contact, chief financial aid officer, or office of financial aid) are given at the end of the profile. You should feel free to write or call for any materials you need or if you have questions.

Appendix
This section lists more than 400 state-specific grants and loans. Eligibility requirements, award amounts, and contact information are given for all programs.

Indexes
Six indexes in the back of the book allow you to search for particular award programs based on the following criteria:

Non-Need Scholarships for Undergraduates
This index lists the colleges that report that they offer scholarships based on academic interests, abilities, achievements, or personal characteristics other than financial need. Specific categories appear in alphabetical order under the following broad groups:

- Academic Interests/Achievements
- Creative Arts/Performance
- Special Achievements/Activities
- Special Characteristics

See the index for specific categories in each group.

Athletic Grants for Undergraduates
This index lists the colleges that report offering scholarships on the basis of athletic abilities.

Co-op Programs
This index lists colleges that report offering cooperative education programs. These are formal arrangements with off-campus employers that are designed to allow students to combine study and work, often in a position related to the student's field of study. Salaries typically are set at regular marketplace levels, and academic credit is often given.

ROTC Programs
This index lists colleges that offer Reserve Officers' Training Corps programs. The index is arranged by the branch of service that sponsors the program.

Tuition Waivers
This index lists colleges that report offering full or partial tuition waivers for certain categories of students. A majority of colleges offer tuition waivers to employees or children of employees. Because this benefit is so common and the affected employees usually are aware of it, no separate index of schools

How to Use This Guide

offering this option is provided. However, this information is included in the individual college profiles.

Tuition Payment Alternatives

This index lists colleges that report offering tuition payment alternatives. These payment alternatives include deferred payment plans, guaranteed tuition plans, installment payment plans, and prepayment plans.

Data Collection Procedures

The data contained in the college chart, profiles, and indexes were collected in fall and winter 2005 and spring 2006 through *Thomson Peterson's Annual Survey of Undergraduate Financial Aid* and the *Thomson Peterson's Annual Survey of Undergraduate Institutions*. Questionnaires were sent to the more than 2,100 institutions of higher education that are accredited in the U.S. and U.S. territories and offer full four- or five-year baccalaureate degrees via full-time on-campus programs of study. Officials at the colleges—usually financial aid or admission officers but sometimes registrars or institutional research staff members—completed and returned the forms. Thomson Peterson's has every reason to believe that the data presented in this book are accurate. However, students should always confirm costs and other facts with a specific school at the time of application, since colleges can and do change policies and fees whenever necessary.

The state aid data presented in *Peterson's College Money Handbook* was submitted by state officials (usually the director of the state scholarship commission) to Thomson Peterson's in spring 2006. Because regulations for any government-sponsored program may be changed at any time, you should request written descriptive materials from the office administering a program in which you are interested.

Criteria for Inclusion in This Book

Peterson's College Money Handbook 2007 covers accredited baccalaureate-degree-granting institutions in the United States and U.S. territories. Institutions have full accreditation or candidate-for-accreditation (preaccreditation) status granted by an institutional or specialized accrediting body recognized by the U.S. Department of Education or Council for Higher Education Accreditation. Recognized institutional accrediting bodies, which consider each institution as a whole, are the six regional associations of schools and colleges (Middle States, New England, North Central, Northwest, Southern, and Western), each of which is responsible for a specified portion of the United States and its territories; the Association for Biblical Higher Education (ABHE); the Accrediting Council for Independent Colleges and Schools (ACICS); the Accrediting Commission of Career Schools and Colleges of Technology (ACCSCT); the Distance Education and Training Council (DETC); the American Academy for Liberal Education; the Council on Occupational Education; and the Transnational Association of Christian Colleges and Schools (TRACS). Program registration by the New York State Board of Regents is considered to be the equivalent of institutional accreditation, since the Board requires that all programs offered by an institution meet its standards before recognition is granted. There are recognized specialized accrediting bodies in more than forty different fields, each of which is authorized to accredit specific programs in its particular field. This can serve as the equivalent of institutional accreditation for specialized institutions that offer programs in one field only (schools of art, music, optometry, theology, etc.).

Quick-Reference Chart

College Costs At-a-Glance

Michael Steidel

To help shed some light on the typical patterns of financial aid offered by colleges, we have prepared the following chart. This chart can help you to better understand financial aid practices in general, form realistic expectations about the amounts of aid that might be provided by specific colleges or universities, and prepare for meaningful discussions with the financial aid officers at colleges you are considering. The data appearing in the chart have been supplied by the schools themselves and are also shown in the individual college profiles.

Tuition and fees are based on the total of full-time tuition and mandatory fees for the 2006–07 academic year (or estimated 2006–07) or for the 2005–06 academic year if 2006–07 figures are not available. More information about these costs, as well as the costs of room and board and the year for which they are current, can be found in the individual college profiles. For institutions that have two or more tuition rates for different categories of students or types of programs, the lowest rate is used in figuring the cost.

The colleges are listed alphabetically by state. An "NR" in any individual column indicates that the applicable data element was "Not Reported."

The chart is divided into seven columns of information for each college:

A. Institutional Control
Whether the school is independent (ind.), including independent, independent–religious, and proprietary, or public, including federal, state, commonwealth, territory, county, district, city, state, local, and state-related.

B. Tuition and Fees
Based on the total of full-time tuition and mandatory fees. An asterisk indicates that the school includes room and board in their mandatory fees.

C. Room and Board
If a school has room and board costs that vary according to the type of accommodation and meal plan, either the lowest figures are represented or the figures are for the most common room arrangement and a full meal plan. If a school has only housing arrangements, a dagger appears to the right of the number. An "NA" will appear in this column if no college-owned or -operated housing facilities are offered.

D. Percent of Eligible Freshmen Receiving Need-Based Gift Awards
Calculated by dividing the number of freshman students determined to have need who received need-based gift aid by the number of full-time freshmen.

E. Percent of Freshmen Whose Need Was Fully Met
Calculated by dividing the number of freshman students whose financial need was fully met by the number of freshmen with need.

F. Average Financial Aid Package for Freshmen
The average dollar amount from all sources, including *gift aid* (scholarships and grants) and *self-help* (jobs and loans), awarded to aided freshmen. Note that this aid package may exceed tuition and fees if the average aid package included coverage of room and board expenses.

G. Average Net Cost After Aid
Average aid package subtracted from published costs (tuition, fees, room, and board) to produce what the average student will have to pay.

H. Graduate's Average Indebtedness
Average per-student indebtedness of graduating seniors.

Because personal situations vary widely, it is very important to note that an individual's aid package can be quite different from the averages. Moreover, the data shown for each school can fluctuate widely from year to year, depending on the number of applicants, the amount of need to be met, and the financial resources and policies of the college. Our intent in presenting this chart is to provide you with useful facts and figures that can serve as general guidelines in your pursuit of financial aid. We caution you to use the data only as a jumping-off point for further investigation and analysis, not as a means to rank or select colleges.

After you have narrowed down the colleges in which you are interested based on academic and personal criteria, we recommend that you carefully study this chart. From it, you can develop a list of questions for financial aid officers at the colleges you are seriously considering attending. Here are just a few questions you might want to ask:

- What are the specific types and sources of aid provided to freshmen at this school?
- What factors does this college consider in determining whether a

College Costs At-a-Glance

financial aid applicant is qualified for its need-based aid programs?

- How does the college determine the combination of types of aid that make up an individual's package?
- How are non-need-based awards treated: as a part of the aid package or as a part of the parental/family contribution?
- Does this school "guarantee" financial aid and, if so, how is its policy implemented? Guaranteed aid means that, by policy, 100 percent of need is met for all students judged to have need. Implementation determines *how* need is met and varies widely from school to school. For example, grade point average may determine the apportioning of scholarship, loan, and work-study aid. Rules for freshmen may be different from those for upperclass students.
- To what degree is the admission process "need-blind"? Need-blind means that admission decisions are made without regard to the student's need for financial aid.
- What are the norms and practices for upperclass students? Our chart presents information on *freshman* financial aid only; however, the financial aid office should be able and willing to provide you with comparable figures for upperclass students. A college might offer a wonderful package for the freshman year, then leave you mostly on your own to fund the remaining three years. Or the school may provide a higher proportion of scholarship money for freshmen, then rebalance its aid packages to contain more self-help aid (loans and work-study) in upperclass years. There is an assumption that, all other factors being equal, students who have settled into the pattern of college time management can handle more work-study hours than freshmen. Grade point average, tuition increases, changes in parental financial circumstances, and other factors may also affect the redistribution.

Michael Steidel is Director of Admissions at Carnegie Mellon University.

College Costs At-a-Glance

	Institutional Control ind.=independent; pub.=public	Tuition and Fees	Room and Board	Percent of Eligible Freshmen Receiving Need-Based Gift Awards	Percent of Freshmen Whose Need Was Fully Met	Average Financial Aid Package for Freshmen	Average Net Cost After Aid	Graduate's Average Indebtedness
Alabama								
Alabama Agricultural and Mechanical University	pub.	$ 4940	NR	96%	1%	$ 3,680	$ 1,260	$17,125
Athens State University	pub.	$ 3870	$ 900†	NR	NR	NR	NR	$12,510
Auburn University	pub.	$ 5516	$7232	73%	17%	$ 7,286	$ 5,462	$19,423
Auburn University Montgomery	pub.	$ 4640	$4890	75%	21%	$ 5,733	$ 3,797	$15,000
Faulkner University	ind.	$11,425	$5400	69%	12%	$ 6,000	$10,825	$18,700
Heritage Christian University	ind.	$ 8264	$1650†	NR	NR	$ 1,058	$ 8,856	$23,236
Jacksonville State University	pub.	$ 4040	$3258	8%	50%	$ 3,800	$ 3,498	$17,125
Judson College	ind.	$ 9900	$7190	100%	15%	$11,477	$ 5,613	$15,690
Samford University	ind.	$14,642	$5616	94%	27%	$12,976	$ 7,282	$17,532
South University	ind.	$11,475	NA	100%	NR	$ 5,768	$ 5,707	$ 9600
Spring Hill College	ind.	$20,948	$7730	100%	23%	$20,217	$ 8,461	$14,074
Tuskegee University	ind.	$12,700	$7887	85%	70%	$13,824	$ 6,763	$30,000
The University of Alabama	pub.	$ 4864	$5024	54%	34%	$ 7,887	$ 2,001	$18,545
The University of Alabama at Birmingham	pub.	$ 4792	$3390†	62%	13%	$10,410	—	$17,594
The University of Alabama in Huntsville	pub.	$ 4688	$5320	51%	16%	$ 5,324	$ 4,684	$17,272
University of North Alabama	pub.	$ 4366	$4170	62%	28%	$ 3,722	$ 4,814	NR
The University of West Alabama	pub.	$ 4326	$3285	NR	NR	NR	NR	$16,043
Alaska								
Alaska Bible College	ind.	$ 5950	$4750	100%	NR	NR	NR	$ 8500
Alaska Pacific University	ind.	$19,610	$6800	82%	36%	NR	NR	$39,463
University of Alaska Fairbanks	pub.	$ 4518	$5580	71%	28%	$ 7,830	$ 2,268	$13,432
University of Alaska Southeast	pub.	$ 3856	$6714	60%	19%	$ 6,134	$ 4,436	$19,979
Arizona								
Arizona State University	pub.	$ 4406	$6768	91%	20%	$ 7,790	$ 3,384	$17,016
Arizona State University at the Polytechnic Campus	pub.	$ 4346	$5155	NR	NR	NR	NR	NR
Arizona State University West	pub.	$ 4346	$5836†	96%	11%	$ 6,807	$ 3,375	$16,438
The Art Institute of Phoenix	ind.	$18,144	$5217†	NR	NR	NR	NR	NR
Collins College: A School of Design and Technology	ind.	$13,875	$2970†	72%	3%	$10,000	$ 6,845	$18,000
Embry-Riddle Aeronautical University	ind.	$23,490	$6516	100%	NR	$11,544	$18,462	$49,532
Midwestern University, Glendale Campus	ind.	$15,556	$8785	NR	NR	NR	NR	$51,174
Northern Arizona University	pub.	$ 4393	$5960	59%	19%	$ 6,938	$ 3,415	$16,473
Prescott College	ind.	$19,511	NA	30%	NR	$ 7,974	$11,537	$18,235
University of Phoenix Online Campus	ind.	$13,880	NA	96%	NR	$ 4,697	$ 9,183	NR
University of Phoenix–Phoenix Campus	ind.	$10,325	NA	86%	NR	$ 4,030	$ 6,295	NR
University of Phoenix–Southern Arizona Campus	ind.	$10,235	NA	100%	NR	$ 4,839	$ 5,396	NR
Arkansas								
Arkansas State University	pub.	$ 5440	$4190	96%	23%	$ 6,100	$ 3,530	$18,500
Arkansas Tech University	pub.	$ 4700	$4290	78%	28%	$ 3,393	$ 5,597	$17,064
Harding University	ind.	$11,200	$5312	93%	25%	$ 8,594	$ 7,918	$18,301
Hendrix College	ind.	$21,636	$6310	99%	33%	$16,492	$11,454	$15,271
John Brown University	ind.	$15,280	$5630	91%	16%	$10,413	$10,497	$19,262
Lyon College	ind.	$14,860	$6270	100%	42%	$13,235	$ 7,895	$15,956

NA = not applicable; NR = not reported; * = includes room and board; † = room only.

College Costs At-a-Glance

	Institutional Control ind.=independent; pub.=public	Tuition and Fees	Room and Board	Percent of Eligible Freshmen Receiving Need-Based Gift Awards	Percent of Freshmen Whose Need Was Fully Met	Average Financial Aid Package for Freshmen	Average Net Cost After Aid	Graduate's Average Indebtedness
Arkansas—*continued*								
Ouachita Baptist University	ind.	$16,990	$ 5000	86%	39%	$12,995	$ 8,995	$14,016
Southern Arkansas University–Magnolia	pub.	$ 4290	$ 3790	93%	82%	$ 1,511	$ 6,569	$14,162
University of Arkansas	pub.	$ 5494	$ 6365	59%	28%	$ 9,405	$ 2,454	$19,862
University of Phoenix–Little Rock Campus	ind.	$10,100	NA	100%	NR	$ 1,666	$ 8,434	NR
University of the Ozarks	ind.	$14,950	$ 5260	100%	16%	$16,008	$ 4,202	$12,866
California								
Academy of Art University	ind.	$14,480	$12,000	46%	NR	$ 5,500	$20,980	$32,000
Alliant International University	ind.	$14,370	$ 7800	100%	29%	$21,250	$ 920	$17,125
Art Center College of Design	ind.	$28,000	NA	70%	NR	$12,836	$15,164	$70,000
Azusa Pacific University	ind.	$22,160	$ 6366	97%	16%	$14,070	$14,456	$19,487
Biola University	ind.	$23,882	$ 7116	79%	12%	$14,019	$16,979	$28,007
California Baptist University	ind.	$17,470	$ 6310	97%	22%	$ 9,860	$13,920	$21,700
California Institute of Technology	ind.	$27,309	$ 8814	100%	100%	$27,702	$ 8,421	$ 5395
California Institute of the Arts	ind.	$27,725	$ 7697	97%	12%	$23,990	$11,432	$34,602
California Lutheran University	ind.	$23,370	$ 8320	100%	52%	$19,776	$11,914	$21,140
California Polytechnic State University, San Luis Obispo	pub.	$ 4245	$ 8145	78%	5%	$ 6,588	$ 5,802	$13,788
California State University, Bakersfield	pub.	$ 2959	$ 5946	88%	7%	$ 6,820	$ 2,085	$ 4144
California State University, Chico	pub.	$ 3370	$ 7993	63%	10%	$ 6,032	$ 5,331	NR
California State University, Dominguez Hills	pub.	$ 3618	$ 5850†	98%	5%	$ 7,488	$ 1,980	$15,232
California State University, East Bay	pub.	$ 2916	$ 6759†	87%	11%	$ 7,141	$ 2,534	$12,312
California State University, Fresno	pub.	$ 3037	$ 7344	77%	32%	$ 4,384	$ 5,997	$10,958
California State University, Fullerton	pub.	$ 2990	$ 4504†	88%	2%	$ 6,561	$ 933	$14,071
California State University, Sacramento	pub.	$16,866	$ 7458	87%	5%	$ 8,626	$15,698	$10,868
California State University, San Marcos	pub.	$ 3062	$ 7470†	99%	NR	$ 5,851	$ 4,681	$13,112
California State University, Stanislaus	pub.	$ 3030	$ 8253	85%	2%	$ 6,800	$ 4,483	$16,200
Chapman University	ind.	$30,748	$10,500	100%	100%	$22,516	$18,732	$19,237
Claremont McKenna College	ind.	$32,650	$10,270	100%	100%	$25,976	$16,944	$10,518
Concordia University	ind.	$21,130	$ 7060	95%	23%	$19,857	$ 8,333	$19,200
Dominican University of California	ind.	$28,070	$11,300	99%	10%	$20,825	$18,545	$49,337
Fresno Pacific University	ind.	$20,790	$ 5990	100%	22%	$18,241	$ 8,539	$13,334
Harvey Mudd College	ind.	$31,940	$10,412	97%	100%	$27,245	$15,107	$16,055
Holy Names University	ind.	$22,710	NR	97%	19%	$16,560	$ 6,150	$ 7229
La Sierra University	ind.	$20,634	$ 5873	100%	15%	$14,997	$11,510	$24,680
The Master's College and Seminary	ind.	$19,230	$ 6620	98%	16%	$14,368	$11,482	$15,383
Menlo College	ind.	$24,450	$ 9600	100%	12%	$21,171	$12,879	$21,905
Mount St. Mary's College	ind.	$24,150	$ 8747	84%	12%	$17,925	$14,972	NR
National University	ind.	$ 8352	NA	67%	NR	$ 3,145	$ 5,207	$23,432
Occidental College	ind.	$33,644	$ 9042	98%	100%	$26,747	$15,939	$20,640
Otis College of Art and Design	ind.	$27,546	NR	100%	1%	$12,993	$14,553	$29,717
Pacific Oaks College	ind.	$16,380	NA	NR	NR	NR	NR	NR
Pacific Union College	ind.	$19,125	$ 5430	100%	41%	$14,600	$ 9,955	$14,000
Pepperdine University (Malibu)	ind.	$32,740	$ 9500	95%	52%	$30,500	$11,740	$31,848

NA = not applicable; NR = not reported; * = includes room and board; † = room only; — = not available.

College Costs At-a-Glance

	Institutional Control ind.=independent; pub.=public	Tuition and Fees	Room and Board	Percent of Eligible Freshmen Receiving Need-Based Gift Awards	Percent of Freshmen Whose Need Was Fully Met	Average Financial Aid Package for Freshmen	Average Net Cost After Aid	Graduate's Average Indebtedness
California—*continued*								
Pitzer College	ind.	$33,012	$ 8632	100%	100%	$28,858	$12,786	$20,900
Pomona College	ind.	$29,923	$10,851	100%	100%	$30,474	$10,300	$11,250
Saint Mary's College of California	ind.	$27,280	$10,010	92%	8%	$20,109	$17,181	$21,892
Samuel Merritt College	ind.	$29,576	$ 5903†	100%	NR	$21,833	$13,646	$36,250
San Diego Christian College	ind.	$17,342	$ 7180	71%	70%	$12,705	$11,817	$16,000
San Diego State University	pub.	$ 3155	$ 9849	68%	11%	$ 6,100	$ 6,904	$14,500
San Francisco State University	pub.	$ 3370	$ 9124	71%	8%	$ 7,532	$ 4,962	$15,376
San Jose State University	pub.	$13,462	$ 8718	88%	8%	$ 6,329	$15,851	$ 5733
Santa Clara University	ind.	$28,899	$10,032	88%	67%	$17,578	$21,353	$17,620
Scripps College	ind.	$31,500	$ 9500	100%	100%	$26,229	$14,771	$12,907
Shasta Bible College	ind.	$ 6750	$ 1650†	100%	NR	$ 4,275	$ 4,125	NR
Simpson University	ind.	$17,800	$ 6200	90%	7%	$ 8,459	$15,541	$17,600
Sonoma State University	pub.	$ 3616	$ 8890	77%	80%	$ 6,400	$ 6,106	$ 5030
Stanford University	ind.	$31,200	$ 9932	98%	89%	$28,122	$13,010	$15,172
Thomas Aquinas College	ind.	$19,300	$ 6000	88%	100%	$15,806	$ 9,494	$14,000
University of California, Berkeley	pub.	$ 6558	$13,074	92%	51%	$16,460	$ 3,172	$13,171
University of California, Davis	pub.	$ 7593	$11,239	95%	16%	$12,281	$ 6,551	$12,701
University of California, Irvine	pub.	$ 6141	$ 9875	83%	52%	$12,377	$ 3,639	$13,587
University of California, Los Angeles	pub.	$ 6504	$11,928	97%	36%	$14,748	$ 3,684	$14,431
University of California, Riverside	pub.	$ 7250	$10,200	88%	56%	$14,746	$ 2,704	$14,814
University of California, San Diego	pub.	$ 6681	$ 9421	94%	28%	$13,479	$ 2,623	$14,689
University of California, Santa Barbara	pub.	$ 6993	$10,577	86%	50%	$13,502	$ 4,068	NR
University of California, Santa Cruz	pub.	$ 7603	$11,571	88%	49%	$14,307	$ 4,867	$13,374
University of Judaism	ind.	$19,330	$13,046	94%	100%	$19,860	$12,516	$17,000
University of Phoenix–Bay Area Campus	ind.	$13,550	NA	NR	NR	NR	NR	NR
University of Phoenix–Central Valley Campus	ind.	$12,335	NA	NR	NR	NR	NR	NR
University of Phoenix–Sacramento Valley Campus	ind.	$12,785	NA	NR	NR	NR	NR	NR
University of Phoenix–San Diego Campus	ind.	$12,500	NA	100%	NR	$ 8,245	$ 4,255	NR
University of Phoenix–Southern California Campus	ind.	$13,685	NA	100%	NR	$ 4,250	$ 9,435	NR
University of Redlands	ind.	$27,164	$ 9000	98%	54%	$25,155	$11,009	$15,024
University of San Diego	ind.	$30,704	$10,960	95%	37%	$16,603	$25,061	$27,722
University of Southern California	ind.	$32,008	$ 9610	88%	95%	$28,371	$13,247	$19,131
University of the Pacific	ind.	$26,088	$ 8478	99%	29%	$21,946	$12,620	NR
Vanguard University of Southern California	ind.	$20,315	$ 6756	80%	14%	$15,502	$11,569	$16,979
Westmont College	ind.	$27,806	$ 8866	97%	11%	$16,502	$20,170	$16,999
Whittier College	ind.	$26,138	$ 7928	90%	31%	$22,027	$12,039	$27,335
Woodbury University	ind.	$23,474	$ 8198	100%	5%	$17,279	$14,393	$20,134
Colorado								
The Colorado College	ind.	$30,048	$ 7620	100%	89%	$28,058	$ 9,610	NR
Colorado School of Mines	pub.	$ 8143	$ 6750	86%	79%	$13,800	$ 1,093	$17,700
Colorado State University	pub.	$ 4562	$ 6316	74%	43%	$ 6,758	$ 4,120	$16,887
Fort Lewis College	pub.	$ 5692	$ 6160	59%	16%	$ 5,192	$ 6,660	$16,966

NA = not applicable; NR = not reported; * = includes room and board; † = room only; — = not available.

College Costs At-a-Glance

	Institutional Control ind.=independent; pub.=public	Tuition and Fees	Room and Board	Percent of Eligible Freshmen Receiving Need-Based Gift Awards	Percent of Freshmen Whose Need Was Fully Met	Average Financial Aid Package for Freshmen	Average Net Cost After Aid	Graduate's Average Indebtedness
Colorado—*continued*								
Johnson & Wales University	ind.	$ 20,826	$ 8500	76%	3%	$14,382	$14,944	$14,798
Mesa State College	pub.	$ 3442	NR	75%	22%	$ 4,014	—	$17,634
Metropolitan State College of Denver	pub.	$ 2859	NA	75%	1%	$ 4,226	—	$10,902
Rocky Mountain College of Art & Design	ind.	$ 17,880	$ 3840†	36%	25%	$ 6,507	$15,213	$18,000
University of Colorado at Boulder	pub.	$ 5372	$ 7980	91%	74%	$ 7,964	$ 5,388	$17,225
University of Colorado at Colorado Springs	pub.	$ 4888	$ 6418	78%	12%	$ 5,756	$ 5,550	$12,438
University of Colorado at Denver and Health Sciences Center—Downtown Denver Campus	pub.	$ 5021	NA	81%	9%	$ 5,362	—	$16,933
University of Denver	ind.	$ 28,410	$ 8749	98%	15%	$21,710	$15,449	$22,633
University of Northern Colorado	pub.	$ 3837	$ 6412	50%	46%	$ 7,928	$ 2,321	NR
University of Phoenix–Denver Campus	ind.	$ 10,040	NA	100%	NR	$ 2,471	$ 7,569	NR
University of Phoenix–Southern Colorado Campus	ind.	$ 10,049	NA	NR	NR	NR	NR	NR
Western State College of Colorado	pub.	$ 3207	$ 6976	50%	15%	$ 6,625	$ 3,558	$16,000
Connecticut								
Albertus Magnus College	ind.	$ 17,310	$ 7550	89%	14%	$ 8,760	$16,100	$12,625
Central Connecticut State University	pub.	$ 6164	$ 7456	74%	12%	$ 5,943	$ 7,677	$10,500
Connecticut College	ind.	$41,975*	NR	87%	100%	$25,156	$16,819	$22,542
Fairfield University	ind.	$ 30,255	$ 9600	91%	30%	$17,929	$21,926	$25,081
Lyme Academy College of Fine Arts	ind.	$ 16,916	NA	80%	NR	$10,950	$ 5,966	NR
Quinnipiac University	ind.	$ 26,280	$10,700	98%	12%	$14,369	$22,611	$25,794
Sacred Heart University	ind.	$ 23,750	$ 9654	98%	29%	$13,922	$19,482	$19,926
Southern Connecticut State University	pub.	$ 6442	$ 8031	71%	39%	$ 6,368	$ 8,105	NR
Trinity College	ind.	$ 33,630	$ 8590	96%	100%	$27,916	$14,304	$18,122
University of Connecticut	pub.	$ 8362	$ 8266	79%	15%	$ 9,035	$ 7,593	$19,410
University of Hartford	ind.	$ 25,766	$ 9922	97%	10%	$14,471	$21,217	$25,553
University of New Haven	ind.	$ 22,982	$ 9550	97%	17%	$15,093	$17,439	$30,399
Wesleyan University	ind.	$ 35,230	$ 9540	96%	100%	$28,280	$16,490	$22,395
Yale University	ind.	$ 31,460	$ 9540	99%	100%	$30,125	$10,875	$14,306
Delaware								
University of Delaware	pub.	$ 7318	$ 6824	78%	48%	$10,400	$ 3,742	$15,200
District of Columbia								
American University	ind.	$ 29,701	$11,342	76%	49%	$24,350	$16,693	$19,766
The Catholic University of America	ind.	$ 26,000	$ 9838	99%	52%	$17,465	$18,373	NR
Corcoran College of Art and Design	ind.	$ 22,800	$10,050	87%	NR	$ 6,139	$26,711	$34,153
Gallaudet University	ind.	$ 10,250	$ 8500	99%	38%	$14,806	$ 3,944	$14,071
Georgetown University	ind.	$ 32,024	$11,159	98%	100%	$27,000	$16,183	$23,700
Howard University	ind.	$ 12,295	$ 6186	49%	23%	$16,313	$ 2,168	$16,566
University of the District of Columbia	pub.	$ 2070	NA	44%	27%	$ 4,930	—	$16,270
Florida								
The Baptist College of Florida	ind.	$ 7250	$ 3570	95%	9%	$ 4,932	$ 5,888	$13,257
Clearwater Christian College	ind.	$ 12,500	$ 5330	59%	3%	$ 7,875	$ 9,955	$16,300
Eckerd College	ind.	$ 27,618	$ 7868	100%	27%	$19,716	$15,770	$ 9448

NA = not applicable; NR = not reported; * = includes room and board; † = room only; — = not available.

College Costs At-a-Glance

	Institutional Control ind.=independent; pub.=public	Tuition and Fees	Room and Board	Percent of Eligible Freshmen Receiving Need-Based Gift Awards	Percent of Freshmen Whose Need Was Fully Met	Average Financial Aid Package for Freshmen	Average Net Cost After Aid	Graduate's Average Indebtedness
Florida—*continued*								
Embry-Riddle Aeronautical University	ind.	$23,500	$6936	100%	NR	$11,738	$18,698	$52,276
Embry-Riddle Aeronautical University, Extended Campus	ind.	$ 4224	NR	69%	NR	$ 4,934	—	$11,565
Flagler College	ind.	$ 8600	$5190	39%	31%	$10,182	$ 3,608	$15,037
Florida Agricultural and Mechanical University	pub.	$ 3318	$5766	68%	10%	$ 7,303	$ 1,781	$30,454
Florida Atlantic University	pub.	$ 3259	$7962	90%	16%	$ 6,631	$ 4,590	NR
Florida Christian College	ind.	$ 9720	$2200†	52%	2%	$ 4,585	$ 7,335	$15,353
Florida College	ind.	$10,730	$5200	70%	6%	$ 9,116	$ 6,814	$ 2111
Florida Gulf Coast University	pub.	$ 3420	$7460	62%	20%	$ 6,058	$ 4,822	$13,245
Florida Institute of Technology	ind.	$25,150	$6800	82%	33%	$21,186	$10,764	$24,535
Florida Metropolitan University–Tampa Campus	ind.	$ 9900	NA	75%	58%	$ 6,625	$ 3,275	$12,000
Florida Southern College	ind.	$19,165	$6800	95%	42%	$18,403	$ 7,562	$16,072
Florida State University	pub.	$ 3208	$6778	68%	73%	$ 8,430	$ 1,556	$16,597
International College	ind.	$ 9500	NA	76%	6%	$ 6,925	$ 2,575	$18,400
Jacksonville University	ind.	$19,970	$6460	66%	20%	$17,510	$ 8,920	$21,483
Johnson & Wales University	ind.	$20,826	$9300	93%	1%	$16,741	$13,385	$18,633
Lynn University	ind.	$27,350	$9650	98%	10%	$14,320	$22,680	$15,154
New College of Florida	pub.	$ 3797	$6750	100%	72%	$12,085	—	$12,252
Northwood University, Florida Campus	ind.	$15,801	$7515	85%	16%	$12,669	$10,647	$15,704
Nova Southeastern University	ind.	$17,800	$6520	56%	10%	$13,826	$10,494	$28,785
Palm Beach Atlantic University	ind.	$17,350	$6680	55%	48%	$ 2,540	$21,490	$24,393
Ringling School of Art and Design	ind.	$21,400	$9165	84%	5%	$ 8,319	$22,246	$30,558
Rollins College	ind.	$29,224	$9142	98%	29%	$27,618	$10,748	$15,438
Saint Leo University	ind.	$14,680	$7460	100%	35%	$15,223	$ 6,917	$15,300
St. Thomas University	ind.	$17,860	$5630	80%	40%	NR	NR	$12,000
Southeastern University	ind.	$11,500	$5678	97%	12%	$ 7,007	$10,171	$21,650
Stetson University	ind.	$25,450	$7275	100%	43%	$22,588	$10,137	$21,500
University of Florida	pub.	$ 3094	$6260	55%	36%	$ 9,763	—	$14,835
University of Miami	ind.	$29,020	$8906	97%	34%	$23,188	$14,738	$19,140
University of North Florida	pub.	$ 3269	$6640	52%	39%	$ 1,441	$ 8,468	$16,707
University of Phoenix–Central Florida Campus	ind.	$10,520	NA	NR	NR	NR	NR	NR
University of Phoenix–North Florida Campus	ind.	$10,520	NA	100%	NR	$ 2,525	$ 7,995	NR
University of Phoenix–South Florida Campus	ind.	$10,520	NA	100%	NR	$ 500	$10,020	NR
University of Phoenix–West Florida Campus	ind.	$10,520	NA	100%	NR	$ 500	$10,020	NR
University of South Florida	pub.	$ 3384	$6900	50%	5%	$ 7,824	$ 2,460	$17,434
The University of Tampa	ind.	$18,848	$6936	97%	22%	$14,268	$11,516	$23,051
Webber International University	ind.	$14,390	$4700	100%	24%	$12,470	$ 6,620	$16,329
Georgia								
Agnes Scott College	ind.	$23,570	$8500	100%	70%	$23,295	$ 8,775	$22,018
Armstrong Atlantic State University	pub.	$ 3350	$4980†	48%	85%	$ 5,818	$ 2,512	$11,000
Augusta State University	pub.	$ 2920	$4920†	80%	2%	$10,919	—	$16,092
Berry College	ind.	$18,950	$7164	100%	33%	$13,669	$12,445	$12,028
Brenau University	ind.	$16,440	$8550	100%	36%	$17,587	$ 7,403	$17,953

NA = not applicable; NR = not reported; * = includes room and board; † = room only; — = not available.

College Costs At-a-Glance

	Institutional Control ind.=independent; pub.=public	Tuition and Fees	Room and Board	Percent of Eligible Freshmen Receiving Need-Based Gift Awards	Percent of Freshmen Whose Need Was Fully Met	Average Financial Aid Package for Freshmen	Average Net Cost After Aid	Graduate's Average Indebtedness
Georgia—*continued*								
Brewton-Parker College	ind.	$12,684	$ 4820	100%	10%	$ 9,409	$ 8,095	$23,445
Clark Atlanta University	ind.	$14,522	$ 6816	68%	47%	$14,103	$ 7,235	$17,751
Columbus State University	pub.	$ 2944	$ 5720	93%	66%	$ 3,474	$ 5,190	NR
Dalton State College	pub.	$ 1592	NA	55%	9%	$ 1,526	$ 66	$ 4049
Emory University	ind.	$30,794	$ 9752	90%	100%	$26,335	$14,211	$22,175
Georgia College & State University	pub.	$ 4142	$ 6878	38%	3%	$ 4,995	$ 6,025	$15,128
Georgia Institute of Technology	pub.	$ 4648	$ 6802	54%	44%	$ 8,644	$ 2,806	$17,001
Georgia Southern University	pub.	$ 3462	$ 6300	95%	20%	$ 6,148	$ 3,614	$17,913
Georgia Southwestern State University	pub.	$ 3034	$ 4810	64%	15%	$ 6,169	$ 1,675	$15,346
Kennesaw State University	pub.	$ 3044	$ 5880†	41%	15%	$ 7,975	$ 949	$15,346
LaGrange College	ind.	$16,200	$ 6674	100%	43%	$15,488	$ 7,386	$17,074
Life University	ind.	$ 7065	$10,980	62%	40%	$ 6,100	$11,945	$13,000
Macon State College	pub.	$ 1730	NA	80%	10%	$ 5,334	—	NR
Medical College of Georgia	pub.	$ 4056	$ 2334†	NR	NR	NR	NR	$19,694
Mercer University	ind.	$23,460	$ 7413	100%	58%	$23,519	$ 7,354	$11,075
North Georgia College & State University	pub.	$ 3068	$ 4596	52%	53%	$ 6,122	$ 1,542	NR
Oglethorpe University	ind.	$22,300	$ 8000	100%	66%	$23,190	$ 7,110	$16,273
Savannah College of Art and Design	ind.	$23,450	$ 9595	27%	46%	$10,400	$22,645	$24,700
Shorter College	ind.	$13,500	$ 6200	100%	22%	$11,495	$ 8,205	$16,193
Southern Polytechnic State University	pub.	$ 3174	$ 5490	33%	55%	$ 2,284	$ 6,380	$12,706
Toccoa Falls College	ind.	$12,050	$ 4600	100%	13%	$ 9,336	$ 7,314	$17,273
University of Georgia	pub.	$ 4628	$ 6376	97%	39%	$ 7,290	$ 3,714	$13,422
University of Phoenix–Atlanta Campus	ind.	$11,150	NA	NR	NR	NR	NR	NR
University of Phoenix–Columbus Georgia Campus	ind.	$10,880	NA	100%	NR	$ 1,137	$ 9,743	NR
University of West Georgia	pub.	$ 3270	$ 5568	97%	19%	$ 6,478	$ 2,360	$14,555
Valdosta State University	pub.	$ 3278	$ 5524	93%	83%	$ 8,244	$ 558	$16,220
Wesleyan College	ind.	$12,110	$ 7450	100%	27%	$11,641	$ 7,919	$20,988
Hawaii								
Brigham Young University–Hawaii	ind.	$ 2760	$ 4980	78%	65%	$ 5,700	$ 2,040	$ 9794
Chaminade University of Honolulu	ind.	$14,960	$ 9380	99%	13%	$11,862	$12,478	$22,263
Hawai'i Pacific University	ind.	$11,630	$ 9450	48%	14%	$10,239	$10,841	$17,125
University of Hawaii at Hilo	pub.	$ 2604	$ 5374	87%	22%	$ 5,008	$ 2,970	$14,145
University of Hawaii at Manoa	pub.	$ 4513	$ 6690	79%	24%	$ 5,334	$ 5,869	$12,459
University of Phoenix–Hawaii Campus	ind.	$12,110	NA	NR	NR	NR	NR	NR
Idaho								
Albertson College of Idaho	ind.	$16,000	$ 6191	62%	21%	$13,320	$ 8,871	$25,343
Idaho State University	pub.	$11,700	$ 5030	69%	10%	$ 4,505	$12,225	$19,299
Lewis-Clark State College	pub.	$ 3714	$ 4500	70%	7%	$ 3,950	$ 4,264	NR
Northwest Nazarene University	ind.	$18,770	$ 5010	75%	19%	$12,522	$11,258	$24,405
University of Idaho	pub.	$ 3968	$ 5342	58%	31%	$ 8,151	$ 1,159	$20,002
University of Phoenix–Idaho Campus	ind.	$10,460	NA	NR	NR	NR	NR	NR

NA = not applicable; NR = not reported; * = includes room and board; † = room only; — = not available.

College Costs At-a-Glance

	Institutional Control ind.=independent; pub.=public	Tuition and Fees	Room and Board	Percent of Eligible Freshmen Receiving Need-Based Gift Awards	Percent of Freshmen Whose Need Was Fully Met	Average Financial Aid Package for Freshmen	Average Net Cost After Aid	Graduate's Average Indebtedness
Illinois								
Aurora University	ind.	$16,180	$ 6590	67%	40%	$18,062	$ 4,708	$18,374
Benedictine University	ind.	$19,210	$ 6600	58%	38%	$13,630	$12,180	NR
Blessing-Rieman College of Nursing	ind.	$14,250	$ 5775	NR	NR	NR	NR	$11,000
Bradley University	ind.	$18,830	$ 6450	99%	51%	$13,984	$11,296	$15,079
DePaul University	ind.	$21,040	$ 8865	76%	14%	$16,928	$12,977	$21,061
Dominican University	ind.	$20,050	$ 6320	100%	29%	$16,146	$10,224	$14,923
Eastern Illinois University	pub.	$ 6373	$ 6196	45%	72%	$ 9,412	$ 3,157	$15,538
Elmhurst College	ind.	$21,600	$ 6906	92%	39%	$15,492	$13,014	$16,080
Eureka College	ind.	$13,400	$ 5880	65%	55%	$15,741	$ 3,539	$15,352
Greenville College	ind.	$17,242	$ 5904	100%	15%	$15,099	$ 8,047	$19,820
Illinois College	ind.	$17,100	$ 6500	78%	37%	$13,253	$10,347	$11,105
Illinois State University	pub.	$ 7091	$ 5748	62%	43%	$ 7,848	$ 4,991	$15,616
Illinois Wesleyan University	ind.	$29,076	$ 6714	100%	57%	$19,424	$16,366	$21,846
Knox College	ind.	$26,100	$ 6285	100%	47%	$21,171	$11,214	$19,642
Lake Forest College	ind.	$27,334	$ 6526	100%	100%	$21,385	$12,475	$18,306
Lexington College	ind.	$17,040	NA	16%	6%	$13,500	$ 3,540	$ 5000
Lincoln Christian College	ind.	$10,200	$ 4900	NR	NR	$ 7,500	$ 7,600	$15,555
Loyola University Chicago	ind.	$26,906	$ 9614	96%	12%	$20,066	$16,454	$24,299
MacMurray College	ind.	$15,750	$ 5998	100%	13%	$12,703	$ 9,045	$16,920
McKendree College	ind.	$18,900	$ 7380	99%	24%	$17,047	$ 9,233	$16,322
Northeastern Illinois University	pub.	$ 5646	NA	94%	6%	$ 6,141	—	$12,284
Northern Illinois University	pub.	$ 6439	$ 5950	59%	22%	$ 8,880	$ 3,509	$17,773
Northwestern University	ind.	$33,559	$10,266	96%	100%	$24,912	$18,913	$18,362
Olivet Nazarene University	ind.	$16,490	$ 6100	99%	31%	$12,610	$ 9,980	$20,062
Principia College	ind.	$21,450	$ 7896	88%	66%	$19,672	$ 9,674	$12,740
Quincy University	ind.	$19,010	$ 6960	100%	30%	$15,162	$10,808	$16,837
Robert Morris College	ind.	$15,900	NR	98%	4%	$10,187	$ 5,713	$18,479
Roosevelt University	ind.	$14,430	$ 7990	65%	16%	$13,142	$ 9,278	NR
Saint Francis Medical Center College of Nursing	ind.	$10,650	$ 1880†	NR	NR	NR	NR	$ 8171
Saint Xavier University	ind.	$18,520	$ 7078	100%	20%	$17,222	$ 8,376	$20,470
Southern Illinois University Carbondale	pub.	$ 6831	$ 5560	82%	82%	$ 8,397	$ 3,994	$14,708
Southern Illinois University Edwardsville	pub.	$ 5179	$ 5819	75%	23%	$ 8,055	$ 2,943	$18,145
Trinity International University	ind.	$19,366	$ 6320	60%	5%	$14,902	$10,784	$17,129
University of Illinois at Springfield	pub.	$ 5335	$ 7110	56%	62%	$ 7,946	$ 4,499	$11,069
University of Illinois at Urbana–Champaign	pub.	$ 8624	$ 7176	59%	51%	$ 9,050	$ 6,750	$15,526
University of Phoenix–Chicago Campus	ind.	$11,705	NA	100%	NR	$ 1,274	$10,431	NR
University of St. Francis	ind.	$19,150	$ 7280	56%	92%	$16,007	$10,423	$15,662
VanderCook College of Music	ind.	$17,890	$ 8050	NR	NR	NR	NR	NR
Western Illinois University	pub.	$ 6899	$ 6143	67%	33%	$ 6,643	$ 6,399	$14,850
Wheaton College	ind.	$21,100	$ 6600	82%	29%	$18,867	$ 8,833	$18,717
Indiana								
Ball State University	pub.	$ 6458	$ 6680	71%	30%	$ 7,426	$ 5,712	$17,418

NA = not applicable; NR = not reported; * = includes room and board; † = room only; — = not available.

College Costs At-a-Glance

College Costs At-a-Glance	Institutional Control ind.=independent; pub.=public	Tuition and Fees	Room and Board	Percent of Eligible Freshmen Receiving Need-Based Gift Awards	Percent of Freshmen Whose Need Was Fully Met	Average Financial Aid Package for Freshmen	Average Net Cost After Aid	Graduate's Average Indebtedness
Indiana—*continued*								
Butler University	ind.	$23,774	$8170	99%	25%	$17,725	$14,219	NR
Calumet College of Saint Joseph	ind.	$ 9900	NA	100%	NR	NR	NR	$15,968
DePauw University	ind.	$27,780	$7800	76%	70%	$25,384	$10,196	$15,635
Goshen College	ind.	$20,300	$6700	100%	34%	$16,599	$10,401	$18,680
Grace College	ind.	$16,020	$6150	100%	32%	$11,587	$10,583	$25,588
Hanover College	ind.	$21,650	$6500	100%	35%	$15,581	$12,569	$16,658
Huntington University	ind.	$18,860	$6530	95%	21%	$13,942	$11,448	$18,290
Indiana State University	pub.	$ 5864	$5938	60%	14%	$ 6,528	$ 5,274	$11,331
Indiana University Bloomington	pub.	$ 7112	$6240	35%	4%	$ 6,859	$ 6,493	$21,251
Indiana University East	pub.	$ 4806	NA	69%	4%	$ 4,835	—	$24,729
Indiana University Kokomo	pub.	$ 4835	NA	58%	19%	$ 4,969	—	$15,195
Indiana University Northwest	pub.	$ 4902	NA	67%	10%	$ 6,371	—	$18,394
Indiana University–Purdue University Fort Wayne	pub.	$ 5067	$4750†	62%	6%	$ 5,176	$ 4,641	$16,880
Indiana University–Purdue University Indianapolis	pub.	$ 6219	$4740	57%	3%	$ 5,941	$ 5,018	$23,041
Indiana University South Bend	pub.	$ 4989	NA	61%	6%	$ 4,935	$ 54	$20,199
Indiana University Southeast	pub.	$ 4880	NA	52%	3%	$ 5,122	—	$18,570
Manchester College	ind.	$20,500	$4500†	100%	45%	$18,533	$ 6,467	$18,254
Marian College	ind.	$19,060	$6300	61%	51%	$17,749	$ 7,611	$14,815
Purdue University	pub.	$ 7096	NR	33%	33%	$11,673	—	$18,978
Purdue University Calumet	pub.	$ 4714	$3990†	76%	NR	$ 3,420	$ 5,284	$19,941
Rose-Hulman Institute of Technology	ind.	$27,138	$7419	99%	9%	$23,161	$11,396	$33,105
Saint Joseph's College	ind.	$19,760	$6480	99%	36%	$17,773	$ 8,467	$23,417
Saint Mary's College	ind.	$25,580	$8425	82%	26%	$18,878	$15,127	$24,617
Taylor University	ind.	$20,746	$5630	93%	26%	$13,886	$12,490	$17,910
Taylor University Fort Wayne	ind.	$17,714	$4960	100%	42%	$15,850	$ 6,824	$15,650
Tri-State University	ind.	$21,210	$6240	69%	100%	$15,043	$12,407	$15,400
University of Evansville	ind.	$21,660	$6660	100%	81%	$20,635	$ 7,685	$21,142
University of Phoenix–Indianapolis Campus	ind.	$10,340	NA	100%	NR	$ 2,025	$ 8,315	NR
University of Saint Francis	ind.	$18,478	$5834	100%	30%	$12,237	$12,075	$22,709
University of Southern Indiana	pub.	$ 4304	$6368	74%	14%	$ 4,985	$ 5,687	$15,724
Valparaiso University	ind.	$22,750	$6220	100%	27%	$18,070	$10,900	$23,853
Wabash College	ind.	$23,388	$6728	99%	100%	$22,859	$ 7,257	$17,328
Iowa								
Allen College	ind.	$13,472	$5712	92%	NR	$ 1,850	$17,334	$21,383
Buena Vista University	ind.	$21,688	$6054	99%	14%	$20,629	$ 7,113	$29,059
Central College	ind.	$20,972	$7224	100%	23%	$16,944	$11,252	$23,490
Clarke College	ind.	$18,945	$6445	100%	26%	$18,461	$ 6,929	$19,492
Coe College	ind.	$25,120	$6550	99%	27%	$21,766	$ 9,904	$20,237
Cornell College	ind.	$23,680	$6430	100%	52%	$21,795	$ 8,315	$23,185
Dordt College	ind.	$17,640	$4900	100%	15%	$15,941	$ 6,599	$16,600
Drake University	ind.	$21,462	$6170	98%	33%	$17,549	$10,083	$25,691
Emmaus Bible College	ind.	$ 8210	$4162	100%	NR	$ 4,760	$ 7,612	$15,890

NA = not applicable; NR = not reported; * = includes room and board; † = room only; — = not available.

College Costs At-a-Glance

	Institutional Control ind.=independent; pub.=public	Tuition and Fees	Room and Board	Percent of Eligible Freshmen Receiving Need-Based Gift Awards	Percent of Freshmen Whose Need Was Fully Met	Average Financial Aid Package for Freshmen	Average Net Cost After Aid	Graduate's Average Indebtedness
Iowa—*continued*								
Faith Baptist Bible College and Theological Seminary	ind.	$11,204	$4316	86%	5%	$ 7,043	$ 8,477	$15,006
Graceland University	ind.	$16,150	$5400	100%	35%	$16,607	$ 4,943	$23,198
Grand View College	ind.	$16,110	$5664	99%	16%	$13,777	$ 7,997	$18,463
Iowa Wesleyan College	ind.	$17,800	$5530	100%	53%	$16,275	$ 7,055	$20,794
Loras College	ind.	$21,098	$6095	84%	32%	$18,336	$ 8,857	$24,320
Luther College	ind.	$26,380	$4290	100%	40%	$19,627	$11,043	$18,504
Maharishi University of Management	ind.	$24,430	$6000	100%	26%	$29,630	$ 800	$19,545
Morningside College	ind.	$18,080	$5624	80%	64%	$16,962	$ 6,742	$26,816
Mount Mercy College	ind.	$18,030	$5680	100%	47%	$15,850	$ 7,860	$22,530
Simpson College	ind.	$20,911	$5922	100%	22%	$19,099	$ 7,734	$24,403
The University of Iowa	pub.	$ 5935	$6912	61%	100%	$ 7,213	$ 5,634	$19,886
University of Northern Iowa	pub.	$ 5602	$5531	71%	23%	$ 6,011	$ 5,122	$20,239
Waldorf College	ind.	$15,520	$4620	100%	32%	$12,494	$ 7,646	$14,782
Wartburg College	ind.	$21,130	$5765	100%	36%	$17,853	$ 9,042	$22,122
William Penn University	ind.	$15,945	$4982	100%	31%	$17,782	$ 3,145	$22,169
Kansas								
Benedictine College	ind.	$15,760	$7208	99%	46%	$12,379	$10,589	$22,333
Bethany College	ind.	$16,210	$5270	77%	45%	$16,682	$ 4,798	$16,925
Bethel College	ind.	$15,550	$6100	74%	38%	$15,486	$ 6,164	$19,122
Emporia State University	pub.	$ 3306	$4787	63%	30%	$ 4,480	$ 3,613	$16,197
Fort Hays State University	pub.	$ 2442	$6190	95%	22%	$ 5,345	$ 3,287	$15,077
Kansas State University	pub.	$ 5124	$5772	65%	12%	$ 6,003	$ 4,893	$19,000
Manhattan Christian College	ind.	$ 9638	$5590	61%	16%	$ 8,268	$ 6,960	$12,046
MidAmerica Nazarene University	ind.	$15,968	$5830	99%	2%	$10,620	$11,178	$19,222
Newman University	ind.	$17,308	$5372	82%	12%	$11,470	$11,210	$19,049
Pittsburg State University	pub.	$ 3562	$4550	87%	14%	$ 6,120	$ 1,992	$10,742
Tabor College	ind.	$15,934	$5670	86%	25%	$16,198	$ 5,406	$20,181
University of Kansas	pub.	$ 5413	$5502	84%	23%	$ 5,933	$ 4,982	$17,243
University of Phoenix–Wichita Campus	ind.	$11,000	NR	NR	NR	NR	NR	NR
Wichita State University	pub.	$ 4231	$5070	47%	12%	$ 2,514	$ 6,787	$18,840
Kentucky								
Alice Lloyd College	ind.	$ 1150	$3750	100%	40%	$ 9,143	—	$ 3495
Asbury College	ind.	$18,956	$4806	99%	29%	$13,654	$10,108	$22,016
Berea College	ind.	$ 516	$4980	100%	27%	$25,921	—	$ 7299
Campbellsville University	ind.	$16,340	$5932	99%	29%	$12,230	$10,042	$18,437
Centre College	ind.	$23,110	$7700	99%	42%	$18,893	$11,917	$13,700
Clear Creek Baptist Bible College	ind.	$ 4520	$3310	100%	NR	$ 4,910	$ 2,920	NR
Georgetown College	ind.	$20,700	$6070	100%	59%	$18,350	$ 8,420	$15,018
Kentucky State University	pub.	$ 4468	$5620	NR	NR	NR	NR	NR
Kentucky Wesleyan College	ind.	$13,600	$5750	100%	24%	$12,560	$ 6,790	$11,191
Lindsey Wilson College	ind.	$14,438	$6163	97%	29%	$10,932	$ 9,669	$ 9389
Midway College	ind.	$13,950	$6200	97%	21%	$12,678	$ 7,472	$15,407

NA = not applicable; NR = not reported; * = includes room and board; † = room only; — = not available.

College Costs At-a-Glance

College Costs At-a-Glance	Institutional Control ind.=independent; pub.=public	Tuition and Fees	Room and Board	Percent of Eligible Freshmen Receiving Need-Based Gift Awards	Percent of Freshmen Whose Need Was Fully Met	Average Financial Aid Package for Freshmen	Average Net Cost After Aid	Graduate's Average Indebtedness
Kentucky—*continued*								
Morehead State University	pub.	$ 4320	$4830	71%	36%	$ 7,449	$ 1,701	$16,995
Murray State University	pub.	$ 4428	$4472	75%	94%	$ 4,593	$ 4,307	$17,617
Pikeville College	ind.	$ 11,500	$5000	100%	65%	$11,903	$ 4,597	$15,208
Thomas More College	ind.	$ 18,320	$6150	94%	100%	$17,950	$ 6,520	$25,779
Transylvania University	ind.	$ 19,650	$6590	100%	31%	$15,892	$10,348	$15,673
Union College	ind.	$ 15,290	$4600	100%	18%	$12,928	$ 6,962	$14,626
University of Kentucky	pub.	$ 5812	$5129	51%	45%	$ 7,252	$ 3,689	$17,692
University of Louisville	pub.	$ 5532	$6036	94%	17%	$ 8,229	$ 3,339	$15,128
University of the Cumberlands	ind.	$ 13,658	$6326	69%	59%	$14,014	$ 5,970	$16,083
Western Kentucky University	pub.	$ 5316	$4876	61%	28%	$ 7,012	$ 3,180	$12,946
Louisiana								
Centenary College of Louisiana	ind.	$ 18,900	$6780	100%	42%	$12,811	$12,869	$17,300
Grambling State University	pub.	$ 3506	$4034	85%	5%	$ 5,950	$ 1,590	$30,000
Louisiana State University and Agricultural and Mechanical College	pub.	$ 4419	$6330	95%	22%	$ 7,293	$ 3,456	$19,258
Louisiana Tech University	pub.	$ 4375	$4035	93%	19%	$ 5,257	$ 3,153	$15,861
Loyola University New Orleans	ind.	$ 25,246	$8312	100%	43%	$19,284	$14,274	$18,543
Nicholls State University	pub.	$ 3389	$3720	89%	65%	$ 5,027	$ 2,082	$12,738
Northwestern State University of Louisiana	pub.	$ 3393	$3626	84%	NR	$ 4,482	$ 2,537	$17,442
Southeastern Louisiana University	pub.	$ 3341	$5180	55%	NR	$ 4,005	$ 4,516	$12,527
Southern University and Agricultural and Mechanical College	pub.	$ 3592	$4646	65%	12%	$ 8,455	—	$23,000
University of Louisiana at Lafayette	pub.	$ 3324	$3478	93%	13%	$ 4,800	$ 2,002	NR
University of New Orleans	pub.	$ 3810	$4590†	66%	11%	$ 5,331	$ 3,069	$22,272
University of Phoenix–Louisiana Campus	ind.	$ 9680	NA	100%	NR	$ 8,954	$ 726	NR
Xavier University of Louisiana	ind.	$ 13,100	$7100	NR	1%	$ 3,921	$16,279	$20,083
Maine								
Bates College	ind.	$42,100*	NR	98%	97%	$27,545	$14,555	$13,636
Bowdoin College	ind.	$ 32,990	$8670	97%	100%	$26,643	$15,017	$15,300
Colby College	ind.	$41,770*	NR	94%	100%	$28,493	$13,277	$18,479
College of the Atlantic	ind.	$ 28,075	$7600	99%	97%	$23,369	$12,306	$16,705
Husson College	ind.	$ 11,380	$6030	97%	29%	$ 7,328	$10,082	$16,940
Maine Maritime Academy	pub.	$ 7620	$6720	77%	12%	$11,475	$ 2,865	$27,000
New England School of Communications	ind.	$ 9590	$6030	59%	69%	$ 5,615	$10,005	$30,000
Saint Joseph's College of Maine	ind.	$ 20,605	$8580	100%	43%	$16,037	$13,148	$28,195
Thomas College	ind.	$ 17,730	$7430	100%	19%	$16,464	$ 8,696	$19,125
Unity College	ind.	$ 17,680	$6630	100%	33%	$13,934	$10,376	NR
University of Maine	pub.	$ 6910	$6732	85%	26%	$ 9,170	$ 4,472	$20,700
University of Maine at Farmington	pub.	$ 5631	$5984	84%	15%	$ 8,398	$ 3,217	$16,289
University of Maine at Presque Isle	pub.	$ 4820	$5246	90%	41%	$ 6,790	$ 3,276	$11,181
University of New England	ind.	$ 22,275	$8730	100%	21%	$18,574	$12,431	$37,507
University of Southern Maine	pub.	$ 5906	$6755	81%	20%	$ 7,333	$ 5,328	$21,800
Maryland								
Capitol College	ind.	$ 17,688	$3869†	92%	18%	$ 8,550	$13,007	$23,772

NA = not applicable; NR = not reported; * = includes room and board; † = room only; — = not available.

College Costs At-a-Glance

College Costs At-a-Glance	Institutional Control ind.=independent; pub.=public	Tuition and Fees	Room and Board	Percent of Eligible Freshmen Receiving Need-Based Gift Awards	Percent of Freshmen Whose Need Was Fully Met	Average Financial Aid Package for Freshmen	Average Net Cost After Aid	Graduate's Average Indebtedness
Maryland—continued								
College of Notre Dame of Maryland	ind.	$ 21,600	$ 8000	87%	53%	$21,109	$ 8,491	$19,211
Coppin State University	pub.	$ 4879	$ 6239	80%	12%	$ 6,218	$ 4,900	$17,843
Frostburg State University	pub.	$ 6616	$ 6442	80%	22%	$ 6,637	$ 6,421	$15,678
Goucher College	ind.	$ 27,525	$ 9475	95%	38%	$19,849	$17,151	$16,062
The Johns Hopkins University	ind.	$ 34,400	$10,622	87%	100%	$29,472	$15,550	$14,000
Loyola College in Maryland	ind.	$ 29,683	$ 9215	78%	98%	$21,375	$17,523	$15,680
McDaniel College	ind.	$ 27,280	$ 5900	99%	30%	$19,667	$13,513	$21,416
Mount St. Mary's University	ind.	$ 24,030	$ 8690	100%	28%	$15,918	$16,802	$15,964
Salisbury University	pub.	$ 6376	$ 6932	72%	18%	$ 5,140	$ 8,168	$15,831
Sojourner-Douglass College	ind.	$ 6748	NA	74%	NR	$ 8,290	—	NR
Towson University	pub.	$ 7096	$ 6828	60%	23%	$ 5,816	$ 8,108	$14,808
University of Baltimore	pub.	$ 6793	NA	NR	NR	NR	NR	$18,050
University of Maryland, Baltimore County	pub.	$ 8520	$ 8090	67%	27%	$ 9,335	$ 7,275	$19,018
University of Maryland, College Park	pub.	$ 7821	$ 8075	64%	31%	$11,800	$ 4,096	$14,076
University of Phoenix–Maryland Campus	ind.	$ 12,510	NA	NR	NR	NR	NR	NR
Villa Julie College	ind.	$ 15,674	$ 9548	95%	25%	$10,876	$14,346	$15,580
Washington College	ind.	$ 28,790	$ 6200	97%	70%	$15,528	$19,462	$20,483
Massachusetts								
American International College	ind.	$ 20,990	$ 9270	95%	17%	$21,668	$ 8,592	$29,700
Amherst College	ind.	$ 33,005	$ 8585	97%	100%	$32,333	$ 9,257	$12,109
Anna Maria College	ind.	$ 21,880	$ 7935	97%	23%	$16,855	$12,960	$23,513
Assumption College	ind.	$ 26,310	$ 5775	99%	18%	$14,854	$17,231	$21,773
Atlantic Union College	ind.	$17,600*	NR	98%	19%	$ 9,609	$ 7,991	$20,023
Babson College	ind.	$ 32,256	$11,222	91%	88%	$26,171	$17,307	$24,900
Becker College	ind.	$ 18,425	$ 8000	99%	9%	$ 9,984	$16,441	$33,046
Bentley College	ind.	$ 28,614	$10,170	87%	24%	$22,288	$16,496	$27,132
Boston College	ind.	$ 31,438	$10,845	94%	100%	$26,614	$15,669	$15,723
The Boston Conservatory	ind.	$ 27,835	$14,320	29%	5%	$15,580	$26,575	$15,000
Boston University	ind.	$ 31,966	$10,080	87%	55%	$27,009	$15,037	$21,196
Brandeis University	ind.	$ 32,501	$ 9050	95%	30%	$22,176	$19,375	$21,437
Bridgewater State College	pub.	$ 5506	$ 6614	93%	NR	$ 5,375	$ 6,745	$15,065
Clark University	ind.	$ 31,465	$ 5900	100%	68%	$21,898	$15,467	$18,990
College of the Holy Cross	ind.	$ 31,444	$ 9220	76%	100%	$22,216	$18,448	$19,390
Curry College	ind.	$ 24,300	$ 9640	98%	4%	$15,060	$18,880	$25,051
Elms College	ind.	$ 21,520	$ 8400	100%	31%	$13,697	$16,223	$23,226
Emerson College	ind.	$ 24,622	$10,420	83%	76%	$13,843	$21,199	$16,222
Emmanuel College	ind.	$ 22,300	$ 9700	84%	31%	$16,047	$15,953	$15,523
Endicott College	ind.	$ 20,390	$ 9766	72%	11%	$11,704	$18,452	$18,000
Fitchburg State College	pub.	$ 5002	$ 6274	81%	93%	NR	NR	$10,660
Gordon College	ind.	$ 22,924	$ 6270	98%	20%	$13,799	$15,395	$11,193
Hampshire College	ind.	$ 32,519	$ 8519	99%	59%	$24,510	$16,528	$17,825
Harvard University	ind.	$ 33,709	$ 9946	99%	100%	$31,868	$11,787	$ 8769

NA = not applicable; NR = not reported; * = includes room and board; † = room only; — = not available.

College Costs At-a-Glance

	Institutional Control ind.=independent; pub.=public	Tuition and Fees	Room and Board	Percent of Eligible Freshmen Receiving Need-Based Gift Awards	Percent of Freshmen Whose Need Was Fully Met	Average Financial Aid Package for Freshmen	Average Net Cost After Aid	Graduate's Average Indebtedness
Massachusetts—*continued*								
Lasell College	ind.	$20,900	$ 9200	99%	9%	$15,100	$15,000	$20,800
Lesley University	ind.	$24,450	$10,500	100%	10%	$16,791	$18,159	$14,000
Massachusetts College of Art	pub.	$ 6850	$ 9800	59%	NR	$ 5,626	$11,024	NR
Massachusetts College of Pharmacy and Health Sciences	ind.	$21,050	$11,220	89%	8%	$12,024	$20,246	$47,248
Massachusetts Institute of Technology	ind.	$32,300	$ 9500	97%	100%	$28,383	$13,417	$19,748
Massachusetts Maritime Academy	pub.	$ 5107	$ 6464	45%	51%	$ 5,925	$ 5,646	$12,972
Merrimack College	ind.	$24,650	$ 9730	100%	84%	$17,500	$16,880	$17,125
Montserrat College of Art	ind.	$20,679	$ 5300†	100%	NR	$10,457	$15,522	NR
Mount Holyoke College	ind.	$32,598	$ 9550	97%	100%	$27,525	$14,623	$19,877
Northeastern University	ind.	$28,792	$10,550	97%	17%	$16,939	$22,403	NR
Regis College	ind.	$21,525	$ 9825	94%	9%	$20,803	$10,547	$24,094
School of the Museum of Fine Arts, Boston	ind.	$24,760	$10,795†	99%	NR	$14,981	$20,574	$23,898
Simmons College	ind.	$25,440	$10,200	88%	6%	$17,312	$18,328	$26,300
Smith College	ind.	$30,754	$10,720	100%	100%	$29,183	$12,291	$25,023
Stonehill College	ind.	$25,540	$10,564	97%	28%	$17,917	$18,187	$19,712
Suffolk University	ind.	$21,220	$11,940	83%	15%	$12,025	$21,135	$19,012
Tufts University	ind.	$32,621	$ 9397	93%	100%	$25,199	$16,819	$14,400
University of Massachusetts Amherst	pub.	$ 9595	NR	71%	13%	$ 9,590	$ 5	$14,672
University of Massachusetts Dartmouth	pub.	$ 8036	$ 7634	82%	68%	$10,700	$ 4,970	$16,214
University of Massachusetts Lowell	pub.	$ 8166	$ 6311	92%	74%	$ 8,192	$ 6,285	$15,167
University of Phoenix–Boston Campus	ind.	$13,580	NA	NR	NR	NR	NR	NR
University of Phoenix–Central Massachusetts Campus	ind.	$13,580	NA	NR	NR	NR	NR	NR
Wellesley College	ind.	$31,348	$ 9682	96%	100%	$27,999	$13,031	$11,821
Wentworth Institute of Technology	ind.	$18,500	$ 9000	34%	4%	$ 8,443	$19,057	$20,928
Western New England College	ind.	$23,164	$ 8890	100%	9%	$14,994	$17,060	NR
Westfield State College	pub.	$ 5657	$ 6470	47%	23%	$ 5,548	$ 6,579	NR
Wheaton College	ind.	$32,350	$ 7830	95%	41%	$22,540	$17,640	$22,380
Worcester Polytechnic Institute	ind.	$33,270	$ 9840	98%	42%	$20,979	$22,131	$27,384
Worcester State College	pub.	$ 5079	$ 7420	85%	45%	$ 5,494	$ 7,005	$11,843
Michigan								
Adrian College	ind.	$18,630	$ 6270	100%	85%	$17,672	$ 7,228	$20,849
Albion College	ind.	$24,296	$ 6928	100%	61%	$20,774	$10,450	$23,010
Alma College	ind.	$21,134	$ 7410	100%	27%	$18,620	$ 9,924	$18,947
Andrews University	ind.	$16,506	$ 5280	70%	40%	$18,990	$ 2,796	$23,195
Calvin College	ind.	$19,150	$ 6585	100%	26%	$13,700	$12,035	$19,400
Central Michigan University	pub.	$ 5868	$ 6376	92%	79%	$ 9,620	$ 2,624	$16,537
College for Creative Studies	ind.	$24,635	$ 3900†	NR	NR	NR	NR	$30,000
Concordia University	ind.	$18,205	$ 6948	100%	26%	$16,979	$ 8,174	$28,280
Cornerstone University	ind.	$14,700	$ 5800	100%	24%	$13,534	$ 6,966	$23,710
Davenport University (Dearborn)	ind.	$ 8880	NR	88%	NR	NR	NR	$ 8459
Davenport University (Traverse City)	ind.	$ 8880	$ 4200†	93%	7%	$ 8,034	$ 5,046	$ 8459
Eastern Michigan University	pub.	$ 6541	$ 6356	58%	5%	$ 6,404	$ 6,493	$21,397

NA = not applicable; NR = not reported; * = includes room and board; † = room only; — = not available.

College Costs At-a-Glance

College Costs At-a-Glance	Institutional Control ind.=independent; pub.=public	Tuition and Fees	Room and Board	Percent of Eligible Freshmen Receiving Need-Based Gift Awards	Percent of Freshmen Whose Need Was Fully Met	Average Financial Aid Package for Freshmen	Average Net Cost After Aid	Graduate's Average Indebtedness
Michigan—*continued*								
Ferris State University	pub.	$ 6882	$6816	60%	10%	$ 7,000	$ 6,698	$15,000
Finlandia University	ind.	$15,533	$5314	78%	3%	$14,000	$ 6,847	$17,500
Grace Bible College	ind.	$10,950	$6860	100%	2%	$ 6,130	$11,680	$17,286
Grand Valley State University	pub.	$ 6220	$6360	85%	100%	$ 7,117	$ 5,463	$16,606
Hillsdale College	ind.	$17,410	$6750	100%	50%	$12,750	$11,410	$17,000
Hope College	ind.	$21,540	$6668	77%	38%	$18,557	$ 9,651	$20,507
Kettering University	ind.	$23,748	$5440	90%	15%	$15,416	$13,772	$40,617
Kuyper College	ind.	$12,208	$5700	100%	22%	$ 7,670	$10,238	$12,900
Lake Superior State University	pub.	$ 6306	$6536	61%	NR	$ 8,262	$ 4,580	$17,458
Lawrence Technological University	ind.	$19,443	$7266	95%	7%	$11,119	$15,590	$24,250
Michigan State University	pub.	$ 7587	$5744	55%	32%	$ 8,892	$ 4,439	$21,037
Michigan Technological University	pub.	$ 8194	$6375	89%	36%	$ 9,010	$ 5,559	$17,000
Northern Michigan University	pub.	$ 5958	$6013	66%	28%	$ 6,480	$ 5,491	$16,829
Northwood University	ind.	$15,533	$6942	90%	28%	$14,645	$ 7,830	$18,389
Spring Arbor University	ind.	$16,666	$5810	99%	48%	$16,177	$ 6,299	$11,989
University of Michigan	pub.	$ 9400	$7374	54%	90%	$ 8,079	$ 8,695	$22,312
University of Michigan–Dearborn	pub.	$ 6841	NA	63%	14%	$ 4,011	$ 2,830	$20,509
University of Michigan–Flint	pub.	$ 6398	NA	58%	3%	$ 5,621	$ 777	$21,888
University of Phoenix–Metro Detroit Campus	ind.	$11,900	NA	100%	NR	$ 1,341	$10,559	NR
University of Phoenix–West Michigan Campus	ind.	$11,660	NA	NR	NR	NR	NR	NR
Walsh College of Accountancy and Business Administration	ind.	$ 9230	NA	NR	NR	NR	NR	$10,306
Wayne State University	pub.	$ 6439	$5350	72%	7%	$ 6,233	$ 5,556	$19,329
Minnesota								
Augsburg College	ind.	$23,422	$6604	98%	20%	$15,487	$14,539	$25,750
Bemidji State University	pub.	$ 6014	$5014	71%	24%	$ 6,806	$ 4,222	$18,247
Bethany Lutheran College	ind.	$16,508	$5278	100%	33%	$12,830	$ 8,956	$18,654
Bethel University	ind.	$22,700	$7140	100%	23%	$15,451	$14,389	$25,325
Carleton College	ind.	$34,272	$8592	95%	100%	$25,462	$17,402	$17,842
College of Saint Benedict	ind.	$23,454	$6637	95%	58%	$20,417	$ 9,674	$24,764
College of St. Catherine	ind.	$21,385	$6120	75%	18%	$24,647	$ 2,858	$27,519
The College of St. Scholastica	ind.	$22,240	$6216	89%	80%	$17,321	$11,135	$29,942
College of Visual Arts	ind.	$18,040	NA	79%	3%	$ 6,269	$11,771	$43,860
Concordia University, St. Paul	ind.	$22,378	$6596	100%	25%	$16,187	$12,787	$20,715
Crown College	ind.	$17,054	$7016	69%	9%	$10,007	$14,063	$22,672
Gustavus Adolphus College	ind.	$24,865	$6065	99%	NR	$18,202	$12,728	$19,500
Hamline University	ind.	$23,157	$6910	79%	52%	$23,872	$ 6,195	$22,265
Macalester College	ind.	$31,038	$7982	100%	100%	$24,854	$14,166	$14,889
Minnesota State University Mankato	pub.	$ 5846	$5083	58%	45%	$ 6,365	$ 4,564	$16,500
Northwestern College	ind.	$19,100	$6120	100%	9%	$14,091	$11,129	$21,778
St. Cloud State University	pub.	$ 5322	$4688	79%	71%	$10,137	—	$20,431
Saint Mary's University of Minnesota	ind.	$20,739	$5900	100%	61%	$13,925	$12,714	$26,633
University of Minnesota, Duluth	pub.	$ 8928	$5546	81%	56%	$ 7,122	$ 7,352	$20,205

NA = not applicable; NR = not reported; * = includes room and board; † = room only; — = not available.

College Costs At-a-Glance

	Institutional Control ind.=independent; pub.=public	Tuition and Fees	Room and Board	Percent of Eligible Freshmen Receiving Need-Based Gift Awards	Percent of Freshmen Whose Need Was Fully Met	Average Financial Aid Package for Freshmen	Average Net Cost After Aid	Graduate's Average Indebtedness
Minnesota—*continued*								
University of Minnesota, Morris	pub.	$ 9721	$ 5750	90%	44%	$12,676	$ 2,795	$15,490
University of Minnesota, Twin Cities Campus	pub.	$ 8622	$ 6722	76%	51%	$11,075	$ 4,269	NR
University of St. Thomas	ind.	$30,380*	NR	100%	49%	$17,103	$13,277	$26,621
Winona State University	pub.	$ 7727	$ 5000	47%	13%	$ 4,657	$ 8,070	$16,588
Mississippi								
Belhaven College	ind.	$ 14,774	$ 5704	86%	25%	$10,562	$ 9,916	$18,126
Blue Mountain College	ind.	$ 7320	$ 3766	50%	82%	$ 8,738	$ 2,348	$11,484
Millsaps College	ind.	$ 20,690	$ 7566	100%	32%	$18,185	$10,071	$22,285
Mississippi State University	pub.	$ 4312	$ 5859	93%	29%	$ 7,405	$ 2,766	$18,230
University of Southern Mississippi	pub.	$ 4342	$ 5800	67%	20%	$ 6,156	$ 3,986	$15,776
Wesley College	ind.	$ 7600	$ 3380	21%	NR	$ 5,400	$ 5,580	$15,000
William Carey College	ind.	$ 8415	$ 3465	NR	NR	NR	NR	$16,000
Missouri								
Avila University	ind.	$ 16,700	$ 5400	98%	27%	$10,776	$11,324	$16,398
Calvary Bible College and Theological Seminary	ind.	$ 7296	$ 3700	83%	6%	$ 6,356	$ 4,640	$17,098
Central Missouri State University	pub.	$ 5835	$ 5109	53%	17%	$ 3,897	$ 7,047	$ 9632
College of the Ozarks	ind.	$ 280	$ 4100	100%	31%	$15,098	—	$ 4648
Culver-Stockton College	ind.	$ 15,250	$ 6546	100%	21%	$12,226	$ 9,570	$18,429
Evangel University	ind.	$ 12,750	$ 4620	90%	10%	$ 8,121	$ 9,249	$22,105
Hannibal-LaGrange College	ind.	$ 11,780	$ 4610	54%	NR	NR	NR	$16,689
Harris-Stowe State University	pub.	$ 4800	$ 5400†	100%	50%	$ 6,625	$ 3,575	$16,000
Kansas City Art Institute	ind.	$ 22,392	$ 7150	100%	13%	$15,912	$13,630	$30,000
Lincoln University	pub.	$ 4602	$ 3790	65%	16%	$ 6,000	$ 2,392	$20,974
Lindenwood University	ind.	$ 12,240	$ 6000	NR	NR	NR	NR	NR
Maryville University of Saint Louis	ind.	$ 17,320	$ 7350	100%	16%	$14,794	$ 9,876	$26,310
Messenger College	ind.	$ 5410	$ 3500	100%	NR	$ 4,700	$ 4,210	$27,790
Missouri State University	pub.	$ 5454	$ 5294	79%	24%	$ 5,748	$ 5,000	$12,997
Rockhurst University	ind.	$ 19,210	$ 5900	63%	28%	$19,921	$ 5,189	$17,890
St. Louis Christian College	ind.	$ 8450	$ 5000	100%	20%	$11,150	$ 2,300	$14,585
St. Louis College of Pharmacy	ind.	$ 19,180	$ 7510	100%	20%	$11,023	$15,667	$80,000
Saint Louis University	ind.	$ 26,448	$ 8230	97%	18%	$19,543	$15,135	$24,552
Southeast Missouri State University	pub.	$ 5145	$ 5351	83%	19%	$ 5,952	$ 4,544	$16,006
Southwest Baptist University	ind.	$ 14,100	$ 4200	49%	25%	$11,247	$ 7,053	$11,268
Stephens College	ind.	$ 20,500	$ 7975	82%	28%	$17,252	$11,223	$19,396
Truman State University	pub.	$ 5812	$ 5380	51%	65%	$ 6,682	$ 4,510	$16,656
University of Missouri–Columbia	pub.	$ 7745	$ 6245	89%	25%	$11,955	$ 2,035	$17,907
University of Missouri–Kansas City	pub.	$ 6819	NR	69%	60%	$11,089	—	$16,387
University of Missouri–St. Louis	pub.	$ 7618	$ 6428	78%	15%	$ 8,802	$ 5,244	$19,435
University of Phoenix–Kansas City Campus	ind.	$ 11,705	NA	NR	NR	NR	NR	NR
University of Phoenix–St. Louis Campus	ind.	$ 12,110	NA	100%	NR	$ 1,274	$10,836	NR
University of Phoenix–Springfield Campus	ind.	$ 10,010	NA	NR	NR	NR	NR	NR
Washington University in St. Louis	ind.	$ 33,788	$10,452	97%	100%	$25,347	$18,893	NR

NA = not applicable; NR = not reported; * = includes room and board; † = room only; — = not available.

College Costs At-a-Glance

	Institutional Control ind.=independent; pub.=public	Tuition and Fees	Room and Board	Percent of Eligible Freshmen Receiving Need-Based Gift Awards	Percent of Freshmen Whose Need Was Fully Met	Average Financial Aid Package for Freshmen	Average Net Cost After Aid	Graduate's Average Indebtedness
Missouri—continued								
Webster University	ind.	$17,210	$6737	86%	NR	$17,548	$ 6,399	$18,690
Westminster College	ind.	$15,030	$6140	100%	36%	$15,325	$ 5,845	$17,534
William Jewell College	ind.	$20,150	$5510	100%	NR	$16,295	$ 9,365	$17,133
William Woods University	ind.	$15,120	$5900	100%	30%	$12,541	$ 8,479	$13,865
Montana								
Carroll College	ind.	$17,078	$6406	89%	18%	$14,916	$ 8,568	$25,659
Montana State University	pub.	$ 5221	$6150	80%	12%	$ 6,869	$ 4,502	$18,081
Montana State University–Billings	pub.	$ 4856	$4050	78%	14%	$ 6,459	$ 2,447	$15,719
Montana Tech of The University of Montana	pub.	$ 4816	$5106	71%	50%	$ 5,000	$ 4,922	$19,000
University of Great Falls	ind.	$15,220	$5500	57%	5%	$10,541	$10,179	$26,450
Nebraska								
College of Saint Mary	ind.	$18,110	$5900	98%	12%	$10,891	$13,119	$18,047
Concordia University	ind.	$17,724	$4710	79%	70%	$15,389	$ 7,045	$15,522
Creighton University	ind.	$22,378	$7540	100%	48%	$21,204	$ 8,714	$26,013
Doane College	ind.	$17,536	$4922	97%	54%	$14,636	$ 7,822	$14,915
Midland Lutheran College	ind.	$19,510	$4950	100%	32%	$15,059	$ 9,401	$19,698
Nebraska Wesleyan University	ind.	$18,410	$5015	99%	15%	$13,361	$10,064	$17,100
University of Nebraska at Kearney	pub.	$ 4493	$5326	89%	56%	$ 6,994	$ 2,825	$16,808
University of Nebraska at Omaha	pub.	$ 4825	$6140	61%	NR	NR	NR	$16,900
University of Nebraska–Lincoln	pub.	$ 5540	$6008	88%	28%	$ 8,606	$ 2,942	$16,909
University of Nebraska Medical Center	pub.	$ 7418	NA	NR	NR	NR	NR	$24,192
Wayne State College	pub.	$ 3803	$4300	67%	26%	$ 3,209	$ 4,894	NR
Nevada								
University of Nevada, Las Vegas	pub.	$ 3818	$8326	40%	50%	$ 5,801	$ 6,343	$17,394
University of Nevada, Reno	pub.	$ 3270	$7785	87%	14%	$ 4,802	$ 6,253	$15,696
New Hampshire								
Chester College of New England	ind.	$14,965	$7600	29%	NR	$ 5,805	$16,760	$40,695
Daniel Webster College	ind.	$22,955	$8450	92%	NR	$15,361	$16,044	$37,945
Dartmouth College	ind.	$32,046	$9390	97%	100%	$29,921	$11,515	$19,305
Franklin Pierce College	ind.	$25,300	$8200	99%	11%	$15,089	$18,411	$28,036
Keene State College	pub.	$ 7818	$7027	70%	19%	$ 7,385	$ 7,460	$20,065
Magdalen College	ind.	$10,750	$6500	100%	100%	$12,859	$ 4,391	$15,350
New England College	ind.	$23,010	$8456	99%	61%	$20,820	$10,646	$31,753
New Hampshire Institute of Art	ind.	$12,080	$5700†	NR	NR	NR	NR	NR
Plymouth State University	pub.	$ 7028	$6780	62%	4%	$ 6,411	$ 7,397	$23,088
Southern New Hampshire University	ind.	$21,714	$8480	96%	11%	$14,016	$16,178	$21,138
Thomas More College of Liberal Arts	ind.	$10,650	$8000	100%	NR	$11,229	$ 7,421	$17,878
University of New Hampshire	pub.	$10,401	$7584	70%	25%	$15,275	$ 2,710	$21,459
University of New Hampshire at Manchester	pub.	$ 7163	NA	47%	11%	$ 6,262	$ 901	$16,437
New Jersey								
Bloomfield College	ind.	$15,100	$7400	96%	56%	$15,837	$ 6,663	NR
Centenary College	ind.	$20,870	$7900	95%	16%	$15,397	$13,373	$20,407

NA = not applicable; NR = not reported; * = includes room and board; † = room only; — = not available.

College Costs At-a-Glance

College Costs At-a-Glance	Institutional Control ind.=independent; pub.=public	Tuition and Fees	Room and Board	Percent of Eligible Freshmen Receiving Need-Based Gift Awards	Percent of Freshmen Whose Need Was Fully Met	Average Financial Aid Package for Freshmen	Average Net Cost After Aid	Graduate's Average Indebtedness
New Jersey—*continued*								
The College of New Jersey	pub.	$ 9707	$ 8458	51%	12%	$12,202	$ 5,963	$17,673
Drew University	ind.	$31,286	$ 8412	99%	37%	$21,339	$18,359	$17,586
Felician College	ind.	$18,200	$ 7950	100%	20%	$13,600	$12,550	$19,500
Kean University	pub.	$ 7507	$ 8374	99%	9%	$ 7,427	$ 8,454	$13,128
Monmouth University	ind.	$20,686	$ 8270	37%	12%	$13,575	$15,381	$27,600
Montclair State University	pub.	$ 7709	$ 8618	50%	29%	$ 6,376	$ 9,951	$16,654
New Jersey City University	pub.	$ 7040	$ 7306	76%	11%	$ 7,661	$ 6,685	NR
Princeton University	ind.	$33,000	$ 9200	100%	100%	$29,692	$12,508	$ 4370
Ramapo College of New Jersey	pub.	$ 8792	$ 9464	50%	16%	$10,615	$ 7,641	$15,937
The Richard Stockton College of New Jersey	pub.	$ 8394	$ 7902	54%	59%	$12,104	$ 4,192	$15,875
Rider University	ind.	$23,470	$ 8840	96%	20%	$17,925	$14,385	$28,636
Rowan University	pub.	$ 8607	$ 8242	64%	35%	$ 5,716	$11,133	$ 9575
Rutgers, The State University of New Jersey, Camden	pub.	$ 9028	$ 8088	71%	37%	$10,174	$ 6,942	$17,378
Rutgers, The State University of New Jersey, Newark	pub.	$ 8812	$ 8984	78%	26%	$10,615	$ 7,181	$16,553
Rutgers, The State University of New Jersey, New Brunswick/Piscataway	pub.	$ 9221	$ 8838	62%	41%	$11,555	$ 6,504	$15,362
Stevens Institute of Technology	ind.	$31,835	$ 9500	80%	27%	$25,792	$15,543	$14,113
William Paterson University of New Jersey	pub.	$ 8740	$ 9070	57%	28%	$ 9,845	$ 7,965	$11,483
New Mexico								
College of Santa Fe	ind.	$22,276	$ 6702	87%	20%	$18,101	$10,877	$17,540
College of the Southwest	ind.	$ 9300	$ 5000	77%	42%	$10,163	$ 4,137	$17,420
New Mexico State University	pub.	$ 3918	$ 5332	95%	15%	$ 7,745	$ 1,505	NR
University of Phoenix–New Mexico Campus	ind.	$ 9950	NA	100%	NR	$ 3,788	$ 6,162	NR
New York								
Adelphi University	ind.	$19,720	$ 9190	91%	NR	$14,100	$14,810	$22,000
Alfred University	ind.	$20,960	$ 9746	100%	85%	$19,396	$11,310	$19,125
Bard College	ind.	$34,080	$ 9850	95%	58%	$25,265	$18,665	$18,345
Barnard College	ind.	$30,676	$11,126	96%	100%	$27,708	$14,094	$19,121
Bernard M. Baruch College of the City University of New York	pub.	$ 4320	NA	83%	26%	$ 5,406	—	$11,700
Cazenovia College	ind.	$18,940	$ 7510	98%	18%	$13,000	$13,450	$27,321
City College of the City University of New York	pub.	$ 4080	NA	90%	75%	$ 5,214	—	$16,500
Clarkson University	ind.	$25,585	$ 9345	80%	NR	$20,516	$14,414	$19,942
Colgate University	ind.	$33,105	$ 8065	100%	100%	$31,901	$ 9,269	$13,452
College of Mount Saint Vincent	ind.	$21,550	$ 8500	100%	NR	$15,296	$14,754	$17,000
The College of Saint Rose	ind.	$17,954	$ 7816	92%	4%	$ 7,885	$17,885	$19,459
College of Staten Island of the City University of New York	pub.	$ 4328	NA	98%	9%	$ 5,773	—	NR
Columbia University, School of General Studies	ind.	$32,176	$ 8540	NR	NR	NR	NR	NR
Cooper Union for the Advancement of Science and Art	ind.	$ 1500	$13,360	100%	82%	$27,500	—	$11,617
Cornell University	ind.	$31,467	$10,250	95%	100%	$26,900	$14,817	$23,450
The Culinary Institute of America	ind.	$20,160	$ 6820	NR	NR	NR	NR	$18,000
Daemen College	ind.	$16,800	$ 7780	92%	27%	$15,506	$ 9,074	$13,323
Dowling College	ind.	$13,800	$ 5748†	100%	5%	$12,945	$ 6,603	$18,920
Elmira College	ind.	$30,050	$ 9100	100%	16%	$21,877	$17,273	$25,347

NA = not applicable; NR = not reported; * = includes room and board; † = room only; — = not available.

College Costs At-a-Glance

	Institutional Control ind.=independent; pub.=public	Tuition and Fees	Room and Board	Percent of Eligible Freshmen Receiving Need-Based Gift Awards	Percent of Freshmen Whose Need Was Fully Met	Average Financial Aid Package for Freshmen	Average Net Cost After Aid	Graduate's Average Indebtedness
New York—*continued*								
Fashion Institute of Technology	pub.	$ 4770	$ 8409	73%	27%	$ 6,815	$ 6,364	$12,869
Five Towns College	ind.	$14,100	$10,250	78%	15%	$ 4,860	$19,490	$15,100
Fordham University	ind.	$27,725	$10,895	95%	20%	$21,197	$17,423	$16,590
Hilbert College	ind.	$14,900	$ 5580	100%	18%	$11,258	$ 9,222	$21,948
Hobart and William Smith Colleges	ind.	$32,737	$ 8386	100%	75%	$24,525	$16,598	$21,454
Hofstra University	ind.	$21,530	$ 9300	89%	19%	$12,950	$17,880	$20,500
Houghton College	ind.	$19,420	$ 6560	100%	27%	$15,114	$10,866	$16,028
Iona College	ind.	$20,980	$ 9898	33%	20%	$13,309	$17,569	$21,495
Ithaca College	ind.	$25,194	$ 9950	87%	52%	$22,583	$12,561	NR
John Jay College of Criminal Justice of the City University of New York	pub.	$ 4259	NA	NR	NR	$ 6,800	—	$13,240
Lehman College of the City University of New York	pub.	$ 4288	NA	92%	2%	$ 3,524	$ 764	$10,500
Le Moyne College	ind.	$21,280	$ 8290	100%	31%	$18,335	$11,235	$19,137
Long Island University, Brooklyn Campus	ind.	$24,328	$ 7810	98%	49%	$12,778	$19,360	$32,200
Manhattan College	ind.	$20,350	$ 9325	97%	13%	$12,941	$16,734	$15,715
Manhattan School of Music	ind.	$29,960	$12,800	64%	7%	$15,312	$27,448	$17,658
Mannes College The New School for Music	ind.	$26,130	$11,750	NR	25%	$11,396	$26,484	$18,025
Marist College	ind.	$21,202	$ 9364	100%	24%	$14,765	$15,801	$20,419
Marymount Manhattan College	ind.	$19,638	$12,090	100%	41%	$11,573	$20,155	$29,706
Medgar Evers College of the City University of New York	pub.	$ 4230	NA	96%	NR	NR	NR	NR
Molloy College	ind.	$16,460	NA	98%	29%	$ 9,905	$ 6,555	$23,000
Monroe College (Bronx)	ind.	$ 9760	$ 6900	100%	36%	$ 9,905	$ 6,755	$ 5307
Nazareth College of Rochester	ind.	$19,874	$ 8360	100%	NR	$16,383	$11,851	$19,785
New York Institute of Technology	ind.	$19,236	$10,804	95%	14%	$13,224	$16,816	$17,125
New York School of Interior Design	ind.	$18,820	NA	75%	NR	$ 6,500	$12,320	$13,250
New York University	ind.	$31,690	$11,480	93%	NR	$20,047	$23,123	$29,480
Niagara University	ind.	$19,800	$ 8450	100%	61%	$17,285	$10,965	$17,163
Nyack College	ind.	$15,400	$ 7600	99%	14%	$12,972	$10,028	$17,271
Paul Smith's College of Arts and Sciences	ind.	$18,170	$ 7420	99%	16%	$14,752	$10,838	$ 6625
Rensselaer Polytechnic Institute	ind.	$31,857	$ 9431	100%	57%	$28,075	$13,213	$27,235
Roberts Wesleyan College	ind.	$20,286	$ 7448	100%	18%	$16,898	$10,836	NR
Rochester Institute of Technology	ind.	$23,619	$ 8451	95%	83%	$17,600	$14,470	$22,000
Russell Sage College	ind.	$23,520	$ 7540	65%	3%	NR	NR	$21,000
Sage College of Albany	ind.	$16,870	$ 7540	64%	NR	NR	NR	$ 9200
St. Bonaventure University	ind.	$22,515	$ 7760	100%	34%	$18,581	$11,694	$16,900
St. Francis College	ind.	$12,710	$ 8000	81%	18%	$ 3,936	$16,774	NR
St. John Fisher College	ind.	$19,560	$ 8300	100%	12%	$16,570	$11,290	$25,833
St. John's University	ind.	$24,970	$11,470	92%	12%	$17,328	$19,112	$21,122
St. Joseph's College, New York	ind.	$12,236	NA	100%	58%	$11,000	$ 1,236	$16,805
St. Joseph's College, Suffolk Campus	ind.	$12,766	NA	100%	74%	$ 7,638	$ 5,128	$15,014
St. Lawrence University	ind.	$32,150	$ 8180	99%	55%	$31,869	$ 8,461	$26,274
Sarah Lawrence College	ind.	$34,042	$11,464	96%	90%	$25,580	$19,926	$13,607
Skidmore College	ind.	$32,659	$ 9120	100%	84%	$26,224	$15,555	$16,078

NA = not applicable; NR = not reported; * = includes room and board; † = room only; — = not available.

College Costs At-a-Glance

	Institutional Control ind.=independent; pub.=public	Tuition and Fees	Room and Board	Percent of Eligible Freshmen Receiving Need-Based Gift Awards	Percent of Freshmen Whose Need Was Fully Met	Average Financial Aid Package for Freshmen	Average Net Cost After Aid	Graduate's Average Indebtedness
New York—*continued*								
State University of New York at Binghamton	pub.	$ 5838	$ 8150	90%	90%	$11,069	$ 2,919	$14,734
State University of New York at Buffalo	pub.	$ 6068	$ 7626	62%	48%	$ 5,902	$ 7,792	$16,700
State University of New York at New Paltz	pub.	$ 5360	$ 7230	90%	22%	$ 2,092	$10,498	$18,900
State University of New York at Oswego	pub.	$ 5322	$ 8340	95%	27%	$ 7,771	$ 5,891	$18,917
State University of New York at Plattsburgh	pub.	$ 5296	$ 7066	96%	28%	$ 8,628	$ 3,734	$17,596
State University of New York College at Cortland	pub.	$ 4350	$ 7850	89%	15%	$ 9,113	$ 3,087	NR
State University of New York College at Geneseo	pub.	$ 5520	$ 7390	81%	75%	$ 8,635	$ 4,275	$16,000
State University of New York College at Old Westbury	pub.	$ 5072	$ 8083	NR	NR	$ 6,661	$ 6,494	$14,532
State University of New York College at Oneonta	pub.	$ 5367	$ 7538	90%	15%	$ 7,955	$ 4,950	$ 8308
State University of New York College at Potsdam	pub.	$ 5289	$ 7670	95%	80%	$12,295	$ 664	$16,117
State University of New York College of Agriculture and Technology at Cobleskill	pub.	$ 5345	$ 7270	90%	4%	$ 6,675	$ 5,940	$ 6300
State University of New York College of Environmental Science and Forestry	pub.	$ 5032	$10,180	57%	100%	$10,850	$ 4,362	$19,000
State University of New York, Fredonia	pub.	$ 5441	$ 6940	95%	22%	$ 6,751	$ 5,630	$12,500
State University of New York Institute of Technology	pub.	$ 5285	$ 7290	93%	28%	$ 8,354	$ 4,221	$16,318
State University of New York Upstate Medical University	pub.	$ 9166	$ 3585†	NR	NR	NR	NR	$ 9970
Stony Brook University, State University of New York	pub.	$ 5575	$ 8050	94%	10%	$ 8,066	$ 5,559	$14,437
Syracuse University	ind.	$ 28,285	$10,370	90%	65%	$21,135	$17,520	$19,200
Union College	ind.	$41,595*	NR	100%	100%	$26,636	$14,959	$16,705
University at Albany, State University of New York	pub.	$ 5887	$ 8050	95%	13%	$ 8,071	$ 5,866	$14,392
University of Rochester	ind.	$ 31,297	$10,188	100%	100%	$25,741	$15,744	$26,100
Utica College	ind.	$ 22,340	$ 9056	100%	9%	$19,483	$11,913	$25,565
Vassar College	ind.	$ 33,800	$ 7900	100%	100%	$27,803	$13,897	$19,038
Vaughn College of Aeronautics and Technology	ind.	$ 13,680	NA	100%	12%	$ 5,600	$ 8,080	$17,125
Webb Institute	ind.	$ 0	$ 8340	17%	33%	$ 2,626	$ 5,714	$11,612
Wells College	ind.	$ 16,680	$ 7500	100%	29%	$16,897	$ 7,283	$17,125
York College of the City University of New York	pub.	$ 4000	NA	99%	NR	$ 3,313	$ 687	NR
North Carolina								
Appalachian State University	pub.	$ 3918	$ 4960	86%	35%	$ 5,820	$ 3,058	$15,433
Barton College	ind.	$ 16,670	$ 5800	65%	17%	$15,226	$ 7,244	$17,272
Belmont Abbey College	ind.	$ 16,724	$ 8586	100%	20%	$13,526	$11,784	$16,025
Bennett College For Women	ind.	$ 13,239	$ 5850	84%	5%	$ 8,449	$10,640	$15,531
Brevard College	ind.	$ 15,990	$ 5980	100%	25%	$14,075	$ 7,895	$19,293
Cabarrus College of Health Sciences	ind.	$ 7300	NA	NR	NR	NR	NR	NR
Campbell University	ind.	$ 17,027	$ 5808	68%	27%	$15,748	$ 7,087	$14,200
Catawba College	ind.	$ 18,750	$ 6250	66%	33%	$15,811	$ 9,189	$18,731
Chowan University	ind.	$ 14,750	$ 6600	98%	11%	$12,525	$ 8,825	$23,370
Davidson College	ind.	$ 28,667	$ 8158	92%	100%	$17,844	$18,981	$22,954
Duke University	ind.	$ 33,963	$ 9152	97%	100%	$27,347	$15,768	$24,391
East Carolina University	pub.	$ 3627	$ 6840	67%	97%	$ 7,978	$ 2,489	$19,614
Elon University	ind.	$ 18,949	$ 6422	87%	NR	$11,753	$13,618	$21,687
Guilford College	ind.	$ 23,020	$ 6690	100%	27%	$17,950	$11,760	$20,150

NA = not applicable; NR = not reported; * = includes room and board; † = room only; — = not available.

College Costs At-a-Glance

	Institutional Control ind.=independent; pub.=public	Tuition and Fees	Room and Board	Percent of Eligible Freshmen Receiving Need-Based Gift Awards	Percent of Freshmen Whose Need Was Fully Met	Average Financial Aid Package for Freshmen	Average Net Cost After Aid	Graduate's Average Indebtedness
North Carolina—*continued*								
Johnson & Wales University	ind.	$20,826	$8300	92%	1%	$15,217	$13,909	NR
Meredith College	ind.	$21,200	$5940	100%	16%	$13,726	$13,414	$21,266
Methodist College	ind.	$17,850	$6770	99%	62%	$13,990	$10,630	$19,989
Montreat College	ind.	$15,560	$5008	99%	12%	$11,143	$ 9,425	$19,166
Mount Olive College	ind.	$12,620	$4952	99%	20%	$ 7,075	$10,497	$ 8901
North Carolina Agricultural and Technical State University	pub.	$ 3124	$5254	78%	4%	$ 5,720	$ 2,658	$20,052
North Carolina State University	pub.	$ 4784	$7040	98%	37%	$ 8,162	$ 3,662	$14,505
Peace College	ind.	$19,250	$6918	100%	12%	$14,649	$11,519	NR
St. Andrews Presbyterian College	ind.	$18,062	$6694	100%	28%	$10,212	$14,544	$10,591
The University of North Carolina at Asheville	pub.	$ 3525	$5712	94%	29%	$ 5,984	$ 3,253	$15,309
The University of North Carolina at Chapel Hill	pub.	$ 4613	$6516	100%	82%	$ 9,801	$ 1,328	$13,801
The University of North Carolina at Greensboro	pub.	$ 3813	$5706	45%	23%	$ 6,113	$ 3,406	$13,661
The University of North Carolina at Pembroke	pub.	$ 2980	$4890	90%	10%	$ 5,943	$ 1,927	$14,766
The University of North Carolina Wilmington	pub.	$ 3695	$6412	80%	70%	$ 5,611	$ 4,496	$15,620
University of Phoenix–Charlotte Campus	ind.	$10,730	NA	NR	NR	NR	NR	NR
University of Phoenix–Raleigh Campus	ind.	$10,730	NA	100%	NR	$ 867	$ 9,863	NR
Wake Forest University	ind.	$32,140	$8800	98%	39%	$22,513	$18,427	$22,831
Warren Wilson College	ind.	$20,126	$6000	86%	15%	$10,382	$15,744	$16,211
Wingate University	ind.	$16,850	$6450	89%	24%	$11,582	$11,718	$21,971
Winston-Salem State University	pub.	$ 2805	$5298	91%	NR	$ 3,606	$ 4,497	$10,200
North Dakota								
Dickinson State University	pub.	$ 4979	$3694	NR	NR	NR	NR	NR
Jamestown College	ind.	$10,550	$4340	100%	18%	$ 8,516	$ 6,374	$21,131
Mayville State University	pub.	$ 4943	$3724	53%	41%	$ 6,028	$ 2,639	$18,190
Medcenter One College of Nursing	ind.	$ 9151	$1800†	NR	NR	NR	NR	$ 9910
University of Mary	ind.	$11,324	$4050	100%	19%	NR	NR	NR
University of North Dakota	pub.	$ 5327	$4787	39%	39%	$ 9,175	$ 939	$26,225
Valley City State University	pub.	$ 5160	$4694	96%	27%	$ 5,194	$ 4,660	$18,394
Ohio								
Antioch College	ind.	$27,214	$7000	97%	100%	$17,521	$16,693	$17,125
Antioch University McGregor	ind.	$12,513	NA	NR	NR	NR	NR	$28,500
Ashland University	ind.	$21,430	$7790	100%	NR	NR	NR	$18,250
Baldwin-Wallace College	ind.	$21,236	$6974	100%	55%	$16,231	$11,979	$16,250
Bluffton University	ind.	$20,570	$7082	100%	70%	$18,587	$ 9,065	$27,441
Bowling Green State University	pub.	$ 8560	$6434	43%	15%	$ 7,277	$ 7,717	$21,594
Case Western Reserve University	ind.	$31,688	$9280	100%	82%	$29,351	$11,617	$20,597
Cedarville University	ind.	$17,120	$5010	40%	57%	$15,800	$ 6,330	$19,258
Cincinnati Christian University	ind.	$ 9690	$5390	95%	15%	$ 6,848	$ 8,232	$13,891
The Cleveland Institute of Art	ind.	$27,177	$9136	100%	5%	$16,331	$19,982	$37,543
Cleveland Institute of Music	ind.	$26,870	$8726	100%	36%	$15,770	$19,826	$24,819
Cleveland State University	pub.	$ 6792	$6809	82%	5%	$ 6,510	$ 7,091	NR
College of Mount St. Joseph	ind.	$18,790	$6070	98%	63%	$16,596	$ 8,264	$13,400

NA = not applicable; NR = not reported; * = includes room and board; † = room only; — = not available.

College Costs At-a-Glance

College Costs At-a-Glance	Institutional Control ind.=independent; pub.=public	Tuition and Fees	Room and Board	Percent of Eligible Freshmen Receiving Need-Based Gift Awards	Percent of Freshmen Whose Need Was Fully Met	Average Financial Aid Package for Freshmen	Average Net Cost After Aid	Graduate's Average Indebtedness
Ohio—*continued*								
The College of Wooster	ind.	$28,230	$7060	100%	91%	$23,486	$11,804	$19,989
Columbus College of Art & Design	ind.	$20,278	$6450	100%	21%	$14,576	$12,152	$27,693
David N. Myers University	ind.	$ 9840	NA	96%	19%	$ 9,981	—	$19,300
Defiance College	ind.	$19,740	$6170	51%	NR	$14,053	$11,857	$17,359
Denison University	ind.	$28,920	$8120	100%	40%	$24,545	$12,495	$14,657
Heidelberg College	ind.	$16,134	$7108	100%	11%	$14,403	$ 8,839	$26,125
Kent State University	pub.	$ 7954	$6640	77%	12%	$ 6,958	$ 7,636	$21,066
Kenyon College	ind.	$33,930	$5570	96%	59%	$23,874	$15,626	$19,190
Laura and Alvin Siegal College of Judaic Studies	ind.	$15,025	NA	100%	NR	$ 1,000	$14,025	NR
Malone College	ind.	$17,790	$6400	100%	16%	$13,038	$11,152	$18,482
Miami University	pub.	$21,487	$7610	59%	36%	$16,255	$12,842	$21,522
Mount Union College	ind.	$19,850	$5990	100%	24%	$16,776	$ 9,064	$21,268
Mount Vernon Nazarene University	ind.	$16,726	$5090	100%	17%	$12,095	$ 9,721	$20,293
Ohio Northern University	ind.	$28,260	$7080	70%	38%	$23,865	$11,475	$38,203
The Ohio State University	pub.	$ 8082	$7275	95%	30%	$ 9,588	$ 5,769	$17,821
Ohio University	pub.	$ 8235	$7686	43%	17%	$ 6,318	$ 9,603	$18,101
Ohio University–Zanesville	pub.	$ 4596	NA	61%	27%	$ 5,594	—	$18,101
Ohio Wesleyan University	ind.	$28,280	$7550	100%	30%	$21,893	$13,937	$22,619
Tiffin University	ind.	$15,870	$6775	44%	19%	$14,383	$ 8,262	$19,994
The University of Akron	pub.	$ 7958	$7208	52%	5%	$ 6,168	$ 8,998	$15,036
University of Cincinnati	pub.	$ 8883	$7890	48%	6%	$ 7,618	$ 9,155	$16,794
University of Dayton	ind.	$22,846	$6780	98%	50%	$13,473	$16,153	$20,151
The University of Findlay	ind.	$21,746	$7492	100%	20%	$16,059	$13,179	$17,000
University of Phoenix–Cincinnati Campus	ind.	$12,110	NA	NR	NR	NR	NR	NR
University of Phoenix–Cleveland Campus	ind.	$12,110	NA	100%	NR	$ 7,055	$ 5,055	NR
University of Phoenix–Columbus Ohio Campus	ind.	$12,110	NA	NR	NR	NR	NR	NR
The University of Toledo	pub.	$ 7494	$8312	83%	10%	$ 6,364	$ 9,442	$21,531
Urbana University	ind.	$16,254	$6612	51%	66%	$10,412	$12,454	$20,462
Wittenberg University	ind.	$29,280	$7498	100%	46%	$23,495	$13,283	$21,615
Xavier University	ind.	$22,430	$8640	97%	29%	$15,226	$15,844	$19,300
Youngstown State University	pub.	$ 6333	$6280	NR	NR	NR	NR	NR
Oklahoma								
East Central University	pub.	$ 3566	$3000	75%	36%	$ 7,395	—	$16,169
Northwestern Oklahoma State University	pub.	$ 3270	$2980	87%	43%	$ 5,235	$ 1,015	$ 9476
Oklahoma Baptist University	ind.	$13,846	$4140	94%	62%	$12,983	$ 5,003	$16,614
Oklahoma Panhandle State University	pub.	$ 3392	$4270	NR	NR	NR	NR	NR
Oklahoma State University	pub.	$ 4365	$5848	74%	19%	$ 8,669	$ 1,544	$17,844
Oral Roberts University	ind.	$15,880	$6770	96%	53%	$13,969	$ 8,681	$27,956
Southeastern Oklahoma State University	pub.	$ 3372	$3910	59%	44%	$ 1,059	$ 6,223	$ 6124
Southwestern Christian University	ind.	$ 8250	$4000	89%	53%	$ 7,925	$ 4,325	$17,000
University of Central Oklahoma	pub.	$ 3618	$4476	96%	42%	$ 3,762	$ 4,332	$14,142
University of Oklahoma	pub.	$ 4408	$6361	21%	47%	$ 8,492	$ 2,277	$18,494

NA = not applicable; NR = not reported; * = includes room and board; † = room only; — = not available.

College Costs At-a-Glance

	Institutional Control ind.=independent; pub.=public	Tuition and Fees	Room and Board	Percent of Eligible Freshmen Receiving Need-Based Gift Awards	Percent of Freshmen Whose Need Was Fully Met	Average Financial Aid Package for Freshmen	Average Net Cost After Aid	Graduate's Average Indebtedness
Oklahoma—*continued*								
University of Phoenix–Oklahoma City Campus	ind.	$ 9920	NA	100%	NR	$ 1,857	$ 8,063	NR
University of Phoenix–Tulsa Campus	ind.	$ 9920	NA	100%	NR	$ 1,265	$ 8,655	NR
University of Science and Arts of Oklahoma	pub.	$ 3480	$ 4170	95%	22%	$ 6,034	$ 1,616	$11,378
University of Tulsa	ind.	$20,738	$ 7052	43%	56%	$16,030	$11,760	$23,824
Oregon								
Cascade College	ind.	$12,800	$ 6120	20%	NR	$12,213	$ 6,707	$24,988
Corban College	ind.	$19,294	$ 7084	100%	9%	$12,195	$14,183	$23,400
Eugene Bible College	ind.	$ 8300	$ 4575	53%	NR	$ 5,800	$ 7,075	$10,550
Lewis & Clark College	ind.	$27,710	$ 7648	100%	31%	$23,877	$11,481	$19,124
Linfield College	ind.	$23,022	$ 6610	80%	39%	$18,671	$10,961	$24,594
Northwest Christian College	ind.	$19,890	$ 6424	100%	19%	$15,076	$11,238	$17,585
Oregon Health & Science University	pub.	$ 9113	NR	NR	NR	NR	NR	$27,425
Pacific University	ind.	$22,534	$ 6468	97%	39%	$18,266	$10,736	$25,581
Portland State University	pub.	$ 4961	$ 8445	53%	10%	$ 5,526	$ 7,880	$18,085
Reed College	ind.	$32,590	$ 8516	93%	96%	$28,205	$12,901	$17,175
Southern Oregon University	pub.	$ 4986	$ 6468	89%	20%	$ 6,899	$ 4,555	$22,944
University of Oregon	pub.	$ 5613	$ 7496	47%	18%	$ 7,138	$ 5,971	$18,029
University of Phoenix–Oregon Campus	ind.	$10,970	NA	NR	NR	NR	NR	NR
University of Portland	ind.	$24,900	$ 7400	100%	25%	$20,356	$11,944	$22,253
Western Oregon University	pub.	$ 4332	$ 6276	81%	11%	$ 5,929	$ 4,679	$19,422
Willamette University	ind.	$28,416	$ 7000	100%	39%	$23,382	$12,034	$18,756
Pennsylvania								
Albright College	ind.	$26,032	$ 7888	100%	18%	$20,149	$13,771	$24,671
Allegheny College	ind.	$28,300	$ 7000	100%	52%	$21,575	$13,725	$24,825
Alvernia College	ind.	$19,089	$ 7299	100%	36%	$13,986	$12,402	$ 6985
Bloomsburg University of Pennsylvania	pub.	$ 6226	$ 5376	51%	90%	$ 9,362	$ 2,240	$16,442
Bryn Mawr College	ind.	$32,230	$10,550	95%	98%	$28,226	$14,554	$17,018
Bucknell University	ind.	$36,002	$ 7366	100%	100%	$23,100	$20,268	$17,400
Cabrini College	ind.	$24,000	$ 9340	72%	18%	$20,113	$13,227	$17,400
Carnegie Mellon University	ind.	$34,578	$ 9280	96%	36%	$21,613	$22,245	$26,500
Cedar Crest College	ind.	$23,012	$ 7953	100%	17%	$17,103	$13,862	$22,820
Chestnut Hill College	ind.	$22,750	$ 7950	100%	1%	$ 8,000	$22,700	$26,250
College Misericordia	ind.	$19,700	$ 8250	99%	18%	$13,168	$14,782	$18,013
Delaware Valley College	ind.	$21,814	$ 8130	92%	77%	$16,050	$13,894	$17,482
Dickinson College	ind.	$32,120	$ 8050	97%	83%	$27,977	$12,193	$20,982
Drexel University	ind.	$24,280	$10,515	39%	14%	$15,921	$18,874	$25,347
Duquesne University	ind.	$21,480	$ 8054	87%	58%	$16,697	$12,837	$21,493
East Stroudsburg University of Pennsylvania	pub.	$ 6462	$ 4794	56%	61%	$ 3,832	$ 7,424	$21,900
Edinboro University of Pennsylvania	pub.	$ 6290	$ 5518	99%	6%	$ 5,639	$ 6,169	$17,034
Elizabethtown College	ind.	$26,950	$ 7300	100%	32%	$16,500	$17,750	$29,233
Franklin and Marshall College	ind.	$32,530	$ 8060	98%	100%	$25,565	$15,025	$19,391
Gannon University	ind.	$18,690	$ 7410	98%	19%	$15,454	$10,646	$24,148

NA = not applicable; NR = not reported; * = includes room and board; † = room only; — = not available.

College Costs At-a-Glance

	Institutional Control ind.=independent; pub.=public	Tuition and Fees	Room and Board	Percent of Eligible Freshmen Receiving Need-Based Gift Awards	Percent of Freshmen Whose Need Was Fully Met	Average Financial Aid Package for Freshmen	Average Net Cost After Aid	Graduate's Average Indebtedness
Pennsylvania—*continued*								
Geneva College	ind.	$17,475	$6770	99%	19%	$13,822	$10,423	$23,425
Gettysburg College	ind.	$32,070	$7794	100%	100%	$24,487	$15,377	$21,810
Grove City College	ind.	$10,640	$5344	100%	15%	$ 5,393	$10,591	$23,409
Gwynedd-Mercy College	ind.	$19,220	$8300	100%	75%	$14,446	$13,074	$18,708
Haverford College	ind.	$31,760	$9840	98%	100%	$27,787	$13,813	$16,330
Indiana University of Pennsylvania	pub.	$ 6085	$4866	72%	12%	$ 7,772	$ 3,179	$18,105
Juniata College	ind.	$27,540	$7680	98%	18%	$18,763	$16,457	$22,131
King's College	ind.	$21,220	$8590	78%	18%	$16,135	$13,675	$17,263
Lancaster Bible College	ind.	$12,360	$5700	78%	14%	$ 8,303	$ 9,757	$15,807
Lebanon Valley College	ind.	$24,860	$6840	100%	38%	$18,041	$13,659	$24,236
Lehigh University	ind.	$31,420	$8560	90%	43%	$24,245	$15,735	$23,418
Lincoln University	pub.	$ 7618	$6792	78%	7%	$ 8,434	$ 5,976	$21,000
Lock Haven University of Pennsylvania	pub.	$ 6258	$5840	62%	55%	$ 6,111	$ 5,987	$19,500
Lycoming College	ind.	$24,080	$6542	100%	17%	$18,277	$12,345	$23,343
Mansfield University of Pennsylvania	pub.	$ 6408	$5868	73%	43%	$10,082	$ 2,194	$22,821
Marywood University	ind.	$21,640	$9100	100%	16%	$14,467	$16,273	$31,073
Mercyhurst College	ind.	$19,113	$7074	100%	79%	$16,288	$ 9,899	$21,000
Messiah College	ind.	$22,110	$6800	88%	26%	$12,349	$16,561	$27,322
Millersville University of Pennsylvania	pub.	$ 6235	$5878	83%	12%	$ 6,581	$ 5,532	$16,103
Moore College of Art & Design	ind.	$23,602	$8654	100%	6%	$13,311	$18,945	$22,652
Moravian College	ind.	$25,263	$7530	99%	18%	$16,827	$15,966	NR
Mount Aloysius College	ind.	$14,650	$6190	100%	NR	$11,000	$ 9,840	$20,970
Neumann College	ind.	$17,920	$8076	85%	60%	$17,000	$ 8,996	$20,000
Pennsylvania College of Technology	pub.	$10,080	$6900	NR	NR	NR	NR	NR
The Pennsylvania State University Abington College	pub.	$10,190	NA	80%	5%	$ 9,598	$ 592	$22,400
The Pennsylvania State University Altoona College	pub.	$10,626	$6530	71%	6%	$11,540	$ 5,616	$22,400
The Pennsylvania State University at Erie, The Behrend College	pub.	$10,626	$6530	71%	8%	$12,337	$ 4,819	$22,400
The Pennsylvania State University Berks Campus of the Berks–Lehigh Valley College	pub.	$10,626	$7140	66%	3%	$10,997	$ 6,769	$22,400
The Pennsylvania State University Harrisburg Campus	pub.	$10,616	$8030	68%	14%	$12,828	$ 5,818	$22,400
The Pennsylvania State University University Park Campus	pub.	$11,508	$6530	55%	11%	$13,937	$ 4,101	$22,400
Philadelphia Biblical University	ind.	$15,875	$6550	100%	33%	$12,597	$ 9,828	$15,000
Philadelphia University	ind.	$22,140	$7936	100%	15%	$16,642	$13,434	$22,917
Robert Morris University	ind.	$15,152	$7670	98%	29%	$13,207	$ 9,615	NR
Rosemont College	ind.	$20,550	$8800	100%	24%	$19,792	$ 9,558	$23,091
Saint Francis University	ind.	$21,410	$7568	100%	38%	$17,141	$11,837	$14,100
Saint Joseph's University	ind.	$27,455	$9973	76%	23%	$12,854	$24,574	$16,120
Saint Vincent College	ind.	$21,679	$6874	100%	25%	$15,568	$12,985	NR
Seton Hill University	ind.	$21,990	$7030	100%	14%	$17,458	$11,562	$26,281
Shippensburg University of Pennsylvania	pub.	$ 6175	$5710	81%	13%	$ 5,780	$ 6,105	$17,976
Slippery Rock University of Pennsylvania	pub.	$ 6275	$4796	80%	63%	$ 6,548	$ 4,523	$20,054
Swarthmore College	ind.	$31,516	$9764	100%	100%	$29,935	$11,345	$12,413
Temple University	pub.	$ 9640	$7794	100%	31%	$13,429	$ 4,005	$25,493

NA = not applicable; NR = not reported; * = includes room and board; † = room only; — = not available.

College Costs At-a-Glance

College Costs At-a-Glance	Institutional Control ind.=independent; pub.=public	Tuition and Fees	Room and Board	Percent of Eligible Freshmen Receiving Need-Based Gift Awards	Percent of Freshmen Whose Need Was Fully Met	Average Financial Aid Package for Freshmen	Average Net Cost After Aid	Graduate's Average Indebtedness
Pennsylvania—*continued*								
Thiel College	ind.	$17,590	$ 6990	100%	20%	$14,960	$ 9,620	$20,000
Thomas Jefferson University	ind.	$21,975	NR	67%	4%	NR	NR	$25,975
University of Pennsylvania	ind.	$32,364	$ 9402	93%	100%	$26,978	$14,788	$21,133
University of Phoenix–Philadelphia Campus	ind.	$13,610	NA	100%	NR	$ 2,008	$11,602	NR
University of Phoenix–Pittsburgh Campus	ind.	$13,610	NA	NR	NR	NR	NR	NR
University of Pittsburgh	pub.	$11,436	$ 7430	67%	44%	$12,085	$ 6,781	$17,051
University of Pittsburgh at Bradford	pub.	$10,538	$ 6470	73%	18%	$11,400	$ 5,608	$19,313
University of Pittsburgh at Greensburg	pub.	$10,562	$ 7210	70%	41%	$ 6,840	$10,932	$17,125
University of Pittsburgh at Johnstown	pub.	$10,500	$ 6100	92%	10%	$ 8,013	$ 8,587	$18,962
Ursinus College	ind.	$31,600	$ 7350	100%	75%	$24,927	$14,023	$18,000
Valley Forge Christian College	ind.	$11,700	$ 5850	89%	5%	$ 6,455	$11,095	$27,186
Villanova University	ind.	$29,435	$ 9362	91%	23%	$22,149	$16,648	$28,549
Washington & Jefferson College	ind.	$26,330	$ 7160	98%	22%	$19,380	$14,110	$17,000
Waynesburg College	ind.	$14,810	$ 6080	100%	26%	$12,338	$ 8,552	$20,000
Westminster College	ind.	$24,325	$ 7070	100%	28%	$17,951	$13,444	$20,386
Widener University	ind.	$24,970	$ 8520	94%	19%	$21,490	$12,000	$26,348
Wilkes University	ind.	$21,646	$ 9240	100%	18%	$17,438	$13,448	$25,164
Wilson College	ind.	$20,050	$ 7610	100%	21%	$15,252	$12,408	$25,534
York College of Pennsylvania	ind.	$10,050	$ 6500	74%	20%	$ 6,708	$ 9,842	$18,198
Puerto Rico								
Pontifical Catholic University of Puerto Rico	ind.	$ 4938	$ 3140	98%	3%	$ 6,930	$ 1,148	$ 3500
University of Phoenix–Puerto Rico Campus	ind.	$ 6200	NA	NR	NR	NR	NR	NR
Rhode Island								
Bryant University	ind.	$24,762	$ 9568	90%	13%	$15,587	$18,743	$29,222
Johnson & Wales University	ind.	$20,826	$ 7300	91%	2%	$14,058	$14,068	$17,704
Roger Williams University	ind.	$24,066	$10,693	70%	53%	$15,111	$19,648	$28,147
Salve Regina University	ind.	$23,950	$ 9500	96%	12%	$15,523	$17,927	$27,332
University of Rhode Island	pub.	$ 7284	$ 8114	93%	83%	$12,009	$ 3,389	$16,200
South Carolina								
Anderson University	ind.	$16,550	$ 6400	99%	30%	$16,985	$ 5,965	$15,125
The Citadel, The Military College of South Carolina	pub.	$ 7520	$ 4840	70%	7%	$ 8,364	$ 3,996	$16,127
Clemson University	pub.	$ 9016	$ 5780	36%	38%	$10,712	$ 4,084	$15,730
Coastal Carolina University	pub.	$ 6860	$ 6280	36%	34%	$ 6,868	$ 6,272	$20,923
College of Charleston	pub.	$ 6668	$ 6948	67%	30%	$ 8,192	$ 5,424	$16,143
Columbia College	ind.	$19,214	$ 5818	98%	71%	$21,723	$ 3,309	$25,333
Converse College	ind.	$22,234	$ 6848	100%	40%	$18,438	$10,644	$16,641
Erskine College	ind.	$19,042	$ 6426	97%	32%	$17,200	$ 8,268	$17,500
Francis Marion University	pub.	$ 5984	$ 5350	78%	NR	NR	NR	$19,968
Furman University	ind.	$26,352	$ 6912	100%	45%	$24,047	$ 9,217	$21,860
Limestone College	ind.	$15,000	$ 6000	97%	21%	$10,023	$10,977	$16,175
Newberry College	ind.	$19,631	$ 6880	100%	32%	$13,857	$12,654	$13,477
North Greenville College	ind.	$10,350	$ 5950	NR	NR	NR	NR	$10,000

NA = not applicable; NR = not reported; * = includes room and board; † = room only; — = not available.

College Costs At-a-Glance

College Costs At-a-Glance	Institutional Control ind.=independent; pub.=public	Tuition and Fees	Room and Board	Percent of Eligible Freshmen Receiving Need-Based Gift Awards	Percent of Freshmen Whose Need Was Fully Met	Average Financial Aid Package for Freshmen	Average Net Cost After Aid	Graduate's Average Indebtedness
South Carolina—*continued*								
South Carolina State University	pub.	$ 6665	$6028	NR	NR	NR	NR	$23,580
Southern Methodist College	ind.	$ 5200	$4200	100%	NR	$ 2,025	$ 7,375	$12,600
University of South Carolina	pub.	$ 6914	$6080	48%	30%	$ 9,067	$ 3,927	$18,699
University of South Carolina Upstate	pub.	$ 6762	$5160	62%	21%	$ 7,846	$ 4,076	$17,238
Winthrop University	pub.	$ 8756	$5352	99%	24%	$ 9,675	$ 4,433	$18,793
Wofford College	ind.	$24,130	$6805	100%	54%	$21,456	$ 9,479	$10,242
South Dakota								
Augustana College	ind.	$19,986	$5472	100%	14%	$16,422	$ 9,036	$18,956
Black Hills State University	pub.	$ 5072	$3663	NR	NR	NR	NR	$23,435
Dakota State University	pub.	$ 4831	$3727	61%	21%	$ 6,405	$ 2,153	$19,492
Mount Marty College	ind.	$15,730	$4860	99%	17%	$14,336	$ 6,254	$26,304
Northern State University	pub.	$ 4699	$3980	85%	100%	$ 5,861	$ 2,818	$19,864
Presentation College	ind.	$12,300	$4775	72%	18%	$ 7,357	$ 9,718	$21,152
South Dakota School of Mines and Technology	pub.	$ 4757	$2867	64%	44%	$ 6,631	$ 993	$ 1623
South Dakota State University	pub.	$ 4732	$4769	51%	69%	$ 6,312	$ 3,189	$19,520
The University of South Dakota	pub.	$ 4829	$4240	50%	85%	$ 4,339	$ 4,730	$19,535
Tennessee								
American Baptist College of American Baptist Theological Seminary	ind.	$ 4172	$1600†	100%	NR	$ 2,025	$ 3,747	NR
Austin Peay State University	pub.	$ 4635	$4800	55%	NR	$ 6,351	$ 3,084	NR
Belmont University	ind.	$17,260	$8650	74%	31%	$ 5,464	$20,446	$18,007
Bryan College	ind.	$14,800	$4470	56%	NR	$12,804	$ 6,466	$17,660
Carson-Newman College	ind.	$16,060	$5200	99%	30%	$13,763	$ 7,497	$16,512
Christian Brothers University	ind.	$19,150	$5500	49%	35%	$17,630	$ 7,020	$24,463
East Tennessee State University	pub.	$ 4487	$4822	85%	30%	$ 6,103	$ 3,206	$17,988
Freed-Hardeman University	ind.	$13,092	$3700†	97%	26%	$11,621	$ 5,171	$22,792
Free Will Baptist Bible College	ind.	$11,166	$4708	NR	NR	NR	NR	$14,509
Johnson Bible College	ind.	$ 6490	$4090	98%	NR	$ 2,586	$ 7,994	$16,809
King College	ind.	$18,345	$6200	100%	27%	$14,907	$ 9,638	$16,635
Lee University	ind.	$ 9610	$5170	88%	26%	$ 8,116	$ 6,664	$26,482
LeMoyne-Owen College	ind.	$14,658	$4620	96%	7%	$ 7,992	$11,286	$15,528
Lipscomb University	ind.	$14,557	$6410	78%	100%	$12,038	$ 8,929	NR
Maryville College	ind.	$22,224	$7000	100%	34%	$23,787	$ 5,437	$18,473
Memphis College of Art	ind.	$17,460	NR	67%	69%	$ 6,500	$10,960	$20,000
Middle Tennessee State University	pub.	$ 4600	$5626	55%	58%	$ 7,311	$ 2,915	$20,438
Milligan College	ind.	$17,240	$4750	61%	38%	$11,803	$10,187	$18,769
Sewanee: The University of the South	ind.	$27,095	$7550	100%	78%	$21,576	$13,069	$14,926
Southern Adventist University	ind.	$14,784	$4604	55%	1%	$12,000	$ 7,388	$10,935
Tennessee State University	pub.	$ 4639	$4270	72%	8%	$ 6,075	$ 2,834	$22,517
Tennessee Technological University	pub.	$ 4660	$6650	57%	28%	$ 6,849	$ 4,461	$14,164
Trevecca Nazarene University	ind.	$14,774	$6470	96%	26%	$10,502	$10,742	$24,000
Tusculum College	ind.	$16,215	$6500	72%	4%	$10,336	$12,379	$20,928
Union University	ind.	$16,450	$5470	95%	NR	$12,200	$ 9,720	$17,645

NA = not applicable; NR = not reported; * = includes room and board; † = room only; — = not available.

College Costs At-a-Glance

	Institutional Control ind.=independent; pub.=public	Tuition and Fees	Room and Board	Percent of Eligible Freshmen Receiving Need-Based Gift Awards	Percent of Freshmen Whose Need Was Fully Met	Average Financial Aid Package for Freshmen	Average Net Cost After Aid	Graduate's Average Indebtedness
Tennessee—*continued*								
University of Memphis	pub.	$ 5084	$ 6069	91%	12%	$ 6,073	$ 5,080	$21,908
University of Phoenix–Nashville Campus	ind.	$10,730	NR	NR	NR	NR	NR	NR
The University of Tennessee at Martin	pub.	$ 4493	$ 4220	62%	39%	$ 8,275	$ 438	$16,749
Vanderbilt University	ind.	$31,700	$10,286	89%	99%	$32,265	$ 9,721	$19,585
Watkins College of Art and Design	ind.	$12,720	$ 5600†	48%	NR	$ 7,500	$10,820	$18,000
Texas								
Abilene Christian University	ind.	$15,160	$ 5670	100%	25%	$10,806	$10,024	$26,413
Arlington Baptist College	ind.	$ 5450	$ 3800	NR	100%	$ 5,379	$ 3,871	$ 7800
The Art Institute of Dallas	ind.	$17,542	$ 4896†	78%	NR	$ 6,528	$15,910	$23,125
Austin College	ind.	$23,540	$ 7741	100%	99%	$21,571	$ 9,710	$26,164
Baylor University	ind.	$22,814	$ 7125	100%	16%	$16,482	$13,457	NR
Concordia University at Austin	ind.	$16,850	$ 6900	90%	31%	$14,130	$ 9,620	$20,202
Dallas Baptist University	ind.	$12,270	$ 4770	76%	57%	$ 5,024	$12,016	$18,763
East Texas Baptist University	ind.	$12,840	$ 3873	77%	25%	$10,258	$ 6,455	$16,777
Hardin-Simmons University	ind.	$15,626	$ 4580	73%	27%	$13,492	$ 6,714	$26,144
Houston Baptist University	ind.	$16,500	$ 4500	99%	29%	$ 9,672	$11,328	$17,256
Lamar University	pub.	$ 2880	$ 5254	NR	19%	$ 1,300	$ 6,834	$ 7100
LeTourneau University	ind.	$15,890	$ 6286	100%	16%	$12,747	$ 9,429	$28,426
Lubbock Christian University	ind.	$12,560	$ 4250	100%	16%	$10,102	$ 6,708	$22,192
Midwestern State University	pub.	$ 4566	$ 5220	90%	20%	$ 6,215	$ 3,571	$16,041
Northwood University, Texas Campus	ind.	$15,801	$ 6636	85%	17%	$14,938	$ 7,499	$16,346
Rice University	ind.	$23,746	$ 8980	100%	100%	$22,949	$ 9,777	$14,166
St. Edward's University	ind.	$18,800	$ 6900	96%	48%	$15,124	$10,576	$24,280
Schreiner University	ind.	$15,142	$ 7332	99%	11%	$10,366	$12,108	$21,455
Southwestern University	ind.	$21,900	$ 6547	100%	64%	$20,426	$ 8,021	$18,446
Stephen F. Austin State University	pub.	$ 4718	$ 5459	76%	27%	$ 4,394	$ 5,783	$17,243
Texas A&M University	pub.	$ 6399	$ 6952	92%	66%	$11,418	$ 1,933	$16,027
Texas A&M University at Galveston	pub.	$ 5118	$ 4870	55%	27%	$10,122	—	$11,156
Texas A&M University–Commerce	pub.	$ 3834	$ 5740	92%	15%	$ 6,769	$ 2,805	$18,182
Texas Christian University	ind.	$21,320	$ 6980	90%	47%	$14,193	$14,107	NR
Texas Lutheran University	ind.	$18,840	$ 5600	94%	25%	$12,748	$11,692	$28,300
Texas Southern University	pub.	$ 3772	$ 6056	85%	29%	$14,065	—	$25,310
Texas State University-San Marcos	pub.	$ 5252	$ 5610	74%	13%	$ 9,827	$ 1,035	$16,863
Texas Tech University	pub.	$ 6152	$ 6875	57%	6%	$ 5,824	$ 7,203	$19,972
Texas Woman's University	pub.	$ 5010	$ 5598	71%	87%	$ 9,312	$ 1,296	$18,125
University of Dallas	ind.	$21,805	$ 7332	99%	21%	$13,959	$15,178	$21,700
University of Mary Hardin-Baylor	ind.	$15,710	$ 4200	88%	24%	$10,113	$ 9,797	$15,819
University of Phoenix–Dallas Campus	ind.	$11,345	NA	100%	NR	$ 999	$10,346	NR
University of Phoenix–Houston Campus	ind.	$11,345	NA	100%	NR	$ 3,606	$ 7,739	NR
University of St. Thomas	ind.	$17,110	$ 6700	98%	12%	$12,985	$10,825	$21,626
The University of Texas at Arlington	pub.	$ 5563	$ 5345	69%	16%	$ 7,898	$ 3,010	$16,780
The University of Texas at Austin	pub.	$ 6972	$ 7638	87%	91%	$ 9,175	$ 5,435	$16,000

NA = not applicable; NR = not reported; * = includes room and board; † = room only; — = not available.

College Costs At-a-Glance

College Costs At-a-Glance	Institutional Control ind.=independent; pub.=public	Tuition and Fees	Room and Board	Percent of Eligible Freshmen Receiving Need-Based Gift Awards	Percent of Freshmen Whose Need Was Fully Met	Average Financial Aid Package for Freshmen	Average Net Cost After Aid	Graduate's Average Indebtedness
Texas—*continued*								
The University of Texas at Dallas	pub.	$ 6831	$6244	70%	45%	$11,115	$ 1,960	NR
The University of Texas at El Paso	pub.	$ 5064	$4095†	91%	14%	$ 7,823	$ 1,336	$ 6538
The University of Texas at San Antonio	pub.	$ 5858	$7190	77%	10%	$ 5,624	$ 7,424	$16,054
The University of Texas at Tyler	pub.	$ 4250	$7010	89%	26%	$ 7,054	$ 4,206	$14,581
The University of Texas Health Science Center at Houston	pub.	$ 5602	NR	63%	NR	$16,950	—	$19,235
The University of Texas Medical Branch	pub.	$ 2690	$2322†	NR	NR	NR	NR	NR
The University of Texas–Pan American	pub.	$ 4160	$4333	95%	3%	$ 7,271	$ 1,222	$11,499
Wayland Baptist University	ind.	$ 9900	$3584	97%	21%	$ 9,200	$ 4,284	$13,972
West Texas A&M University	pub.	$ 3756	$4916	71%	100%	$ 5,958	$ 2,714	$13,136
Utah								
University of Phoenix–Utah Campus	ind.	$ 10,580	NA	100%	NR	$ 1,801	$ 8,779	NR
University of Utah	pub.	$ 4342	$5422	75%	16%	$ 7,506	$ 2,258	$12,806
Utah State University	pub.	$ 3672	$4330	62%	13%	$ 3,400	$ 4,602	$12,430
Vermont								
Bennington College	ind.	$ 33,570	$8320	99%	4%	$24,069	$17,821	$20,340
Burlington College	ind.	$ 15,600	$4500†	80%	NR	$ 7,259	$12,841	$21,577
Champlain College	ind.	$ 14,910	$9695	77%	19%	$ 8,795	$15,810	NR
College of St. Joseph	ind.	$ 14,900	$7150	100%	33%	$15,053	$ 6,997	$21,967
Goddard College	ind.	$ 10,706	NA	57%	NR	$ 5,263	$ 5,443	$21,591
Green Mountain College	ind.	$ 22,204	$7690	100%	29%	$19,403	$10,491	$23,894
Marlboro College	ind.	$ 27,790	$8190	100%	NR	NR	NR	$18,404
Middlebury College	ind.	$42,120*	NR	100%	100%	$26,032	$16,088	NR
Southern Vermont College	ind.	$ 14,373	$6944	96%	27%	$11,944	$ 9,373	$17,606
Sterling College	ind.	$ 16,950	$6336	100%	NR	$13,979	$ 9,307	$28,251
University of Vermont	pub.	$ 10,748	$7332	88%	98%	$17,342	$ 738	$20,142
Vermont Technical College	pub.	$ 7926	$6674	81%	13%	$ 8,400	$ 6,200	$12,600
Virgin Islands								
University of the Virgin Islands	pub.	$ 3726	$7550	94%	3%	$ 4,026	$ 7,250	$ 3380
Virginia								
Averett University	ind.	$ 19,040	$6560	100%	14%	$13,795	$11,805	$16,398
Bridgewater College	ind.	$ 20,190	$9060	100%	32%	$17,535	$11,715	$25,780
Christendom College	ind.	$ 16,740	$6066	98%	100%	$11,622	$11,184	$11,080
Christopher Newport University	pub.	$ 5826	$7500	75%	25%	$ 5,677	$ 7,649	$11,936
The College of William and Mary	pub.	$ 7778	$6417	73%	43%	$10,237	$ 3,958	$14,524
Emory & Henry College	ind.	$ 19,530	$7040	100%	29%	$14,955	$11,615	$15,465
Ferrum College	ind.	$ 18,020	$6300	100%	13%	$16,184	$ 8,136	$16,300
George Mason University	pub.	$ 5880	$6480	76%	10%	$ 7,518	$ 4,842	$13,607
Hampden-Sydney College	ind.	$ 26,170	$8125	100%	41%	$18,482	$15,813	$16,244
Hampton University	ind.	$ 14,182	$6746	46%	83%	$ 2,893	$18,035	$ 3645
Hollins University	ind.	$ 22,945	$8160	100%	25%	$18,826	$12,279	$16,853
James Madison University	pub.	$ 5886	$6372	49%	94%	$ 7,769	$ 4,489	$12,591
Lynchburg College	ind.	$ 24,245	$6400	100%	30%	$18,519	$12,126	$18,517

NA = not applicable; NR = not reported; * = includes room and board; † = room only; — = not available.

College Costs At-a-Glance

	Institutional Control ind.=independent; pub.=public	Tuition and Fees	Room and Board	Percent of Eligible Freshmen Receiving Need-Based Gift Awards	Percent of Freshmen Whose Need Was Fully Met	Average Financial Aid Package for Freshmen	Average Net Cost After Aid	Graduate's Average Indebtedness
Virginia—*continued*								
Mary Baldwin College	ind.	$20,605	$5860	99%	48%	$21,886	$ 4,579	$21,000
Marymount University	ind.	$18,114	$7820	78%	22%	$13,777	$12,157	$24,950
Radford University	pub.	$ 5130	$6120	65%	70%	$ 6,554	$ 4,696	$17,265
Randolph-Macon College	ind.	$23,945	$7305	100%	25%	$19,042	$12,208	$15,130
Randolph-Macon Woman's College	ind.	$22,930	$8610	100%	51%	$21,686	$ 9,854	$25,500
Roanoke College	ind.	$23,453	$7295	76%	23%	$19,176	$11,572	$18,543
Shenandoah University	ind.	$20,050	$7550	52%	19%	$14,411	$13,189	$19,518
Southern Virginia University	ind.	$15,826	$4300	98%	18%	$ 8,395	$11,731	$15,444
Sweet Briar College	ind.	$23,340	$9480	68%	95%	$14,480	$18,340	$17,808
University of Mary Washington	pub.	$ 5634	$6002	90%	9%	$ 4,450	$ 7,186	$12,665
University of Phoenix–Northern Virginia Campus	ind.	$12,365	NA	100%	NR	$ 9,733	$ 2,632	NR
University of Phoenix–Richmond Campus	ind.	$11,930	NR	NR	NR	NR	NR	NR
University of Richmond	ind.	$36,550	$6060	98%	97%	$27,202	$15,408	$18,500
University of Virginia	pub.	$ 7370	$6389	90%	100%	$15,251	—	$15,176
Virginia Commonwealth University	pub.	$ 5385	$7042	78%	5%	$ 6,845	$ 5,582	$20,069
Virginia Intermont College	ind.	$16,450	$5750	97%	7%	$12,445	$ 9,755	$18,700
Virginia Military Institute	pub.	$ 6988	$5666	97%	37%	$11,017	$ 1,637	$14,367
Virginia Polytechnic Institute and State University	pub.	$ 6378	$4400	69%	3%	$ 7,999	$ 2,779	$18,385
Virginia Union University	ind.	$12,770	$5662	59%	32%	$12,207	$ 6,225	$17,568
Virginia Wesleyan College	ind.	$23,136	$6850	37%	5%	$14,326	$15,660	$20,386
Washington and Lee University	ind.	$28,635	$7225	86%	87%	$25,256	$10,604	$17,105
Washington								
Bastyr University	ind.	$15,381	$2460†	NR	NR	NR	NR	$21,000
Central Washington University	pub.	$ 4806	$6924	73%	26%	$ 7,022	$ 4,708	$27,025
Eastern Washington University	pub.	$ 4281	$5733	79%	17%	$ 9,521	$ 493	$18,097
The Evergreen State College	pub.	$ 4337	$6924	53%	46%	$10,271	$ 990	$13,818
Gonzaga University	ind.	$23,578	$6700	100%	20%	$13,857	$16,421	$23,113
Northwest University	ind.	$18,144	$6450	99%	27%	$12,163	$12,431	$19,171
Pacific Lutheran University	ind.	$22,040	$6765	79%	44%	$19,012	$ 9,793	$22,372
Saint Martin's University	ind.	$20,965	$6400	100%	47%	$19,549	$ 7,816	$27,846
Seattle Pacific University	ind.	$21,783	$7572	98%	22%	$18,573	$10,782	$22,569
Seattle University	ind.	$22,905	$7158	96%	44%	$21,431	$ 8,632	$25,311
Trinity Lutheran College	ind.	$21,582	$8725	NR	NR	NR	NR	NR
University of Phoenix–Spokane Campus	ind.	$10,310	NA	NR	NR	NR	NR	NR
University of Phoenix–Washington Campus	ind.	$11,615	NA	NR	NR	NR	NR	NR
University of Puget Sound	ind.	$28,460	$7140	98%	27%	$20,591	$15,009	$25,842
Walla Walla College	ind.	$19,917	$4572	82%	24%	$16,018	$ 8,471	$23,668
Washington State University	pub.	$ 5432	NR	57%	31%	$ 8,846	—	$21,201
Western Washington University	pub.	$ 4738	$6524	82%	24%	$ 8,542	$ 2,720	$15,784
Whitman College	ind.	$28,640	$7470	100%	78%	$21,400	$14,710	$16,200
Whitworth College	ind.	$24,154	$7030	99%	23%	$16,733	$14,451	$18,246

NA = not applicable; NR = not reported; * = includes room and board; † = room only; — = not available.

Peterson's College Money Handbook 2007

College Costs At-a-Glance

	Institutional Control ind.=independent; pub.=public	Tuition and Fees	Room and Board	Percent of Eligible Freshmen Receiving Need-Based Gift Awards	Percent of Freshmen Whose Need Was Fully Met	Average Financial Aid Package for Freshmen	Average Net Cost After Aid	Graduate's Average Indebtedness
West Virginia								
Alderson-Broaddus College	ind.	$18,136	$5870	96%	3%	$16,600	$ 7,406	$26,313
Bluefield State College	pub.	$ 3410	NA	100%	36%	$ 5,600	—	$14,300
Davis & Elkins College	ind.	$16,832	$6104	45%	46%	$14,744	$ 8,192	$18,015
Fairmont State University	pub.	$ 4412	$5674	76%	8%	$ 5,000	$ 5,086	$17,500
Glenville State College	pub.	$ 3628	$5150	75%	25%	$ 8,173	$ 605	$16,079
Marshall University	pub.	$ 3932	$6272	66%	35%	$ 7,158	$ 3,046	$16,639
Mountain State University	ind.	$ 7350	$5526	81%	NR	$ 4,875	$ 8,001	$23,570
Shepherd University	pub.	$ 4046	$6020	47%	NR	$ 7,677	$ 2,389	$14,887
West Virginia University	pub.	$ 4164	$6342	50%	45%	$ 6,379	$ 4,127	$13,798
West Virginia Wesleyan College	ind.	$21,250	$5550	100%	35%	$21,577	$ 5,223	$19,750
Wheeling Jesuit University	ind.	$21,350	$6450	87%	45%	$19,113	$ 8,687	$16,309
Wisconsin								
Alverno College	ind.	$15,418	$6210	NR	NR	NR	NR	NR
Bellin College of Nursing	ind.	$14,768	NA	NR	NR	NR	NR	$25,305
Beloit College	ind.	$26,884	$5924	98%	100%	$18,593	$14,215	$14,781
Carroll College	ind.	$19,910	$6070	100%	56%	$15,260	$10,720	$18,404
Carthage College	ind.	$23,650	$6800	100%	28%	$14,452	$15,998	NR
Concordia University Wisconsin	ind.	$17,280	$6540	96%	37%	$18,229	$ 5,591	$17,270
Lakeland College	ind.	$16,796	$5420	99%	19%	$13,145	$ 9,071	$15,552
Lawrence University	ind.	$29,598	$6381	100%	100%	$22,900	$13,079	$19,294
Maranatha Baptist Bible College	ind.	$ 8510	$5000	56%	1%	$ 6,161	$ 7,349	$14,431
Marian College of Fond du Lac	ind.	$16,705	$5070	100%	43%	$15,399	$ 6,376	$20,000
Marquette University	ind.	$25,074	$8160	88%	34%	$17,835	$15,399	$26,345
Milwaukee School of Engineering	ind.	$24,960	$6189	100%	14%	$16,517	$14,632	$31,808
Mount Mary College	ind.	$17,105	$5790	100%	18%	$12,026	$10,869	$19,040
Northland College	ind.	$20,789	$5891	98%	17%	$15,600	$11,080	$18,983
Ripon College	ind.	$22,437	$6060	100%	43%	$18,083	$10,414	$16,492
St. Norbert College	ind.	$22,509	$6068	100%	36%	$16,937	$11,640	$24,808
Silver Lake College	ind.	$17,108	$4400†	100%	11%	$16,405	$ 5,103	$18,934
University of Phoenix–Wisconsin Campus	ind.	$11,345	NA	NR	NR	NR	NR	NR
University of Wisconsin–Eau Claire	pub.	$ 5178	$4737	59%	69%	$ 6,570	$ 3,345	$16,953
University of Wisconsin–Green Bay	pub.	$ 5425	$4698	65%	34%	$ 7,360	$ 2,763	$12,222
University of Wisconsin–La Crosse	pub.	$ 5225	$4820	47%	87%	$ 4,874	$ 5,171	$13,948
University of Wisconsin–Madison	pub.	$ 6617	$6500	60%	41%	$11,240	$ 1,877	$18,630
University of Wisconsin–Parkside	pub.	$ 5001	$5500	96%	91%	$ 4,780	$ 5,721	$17,158
University of Wisconsin–Stevens Point	pub.	$ 5062	$4322	47%	65%	$ 5,301	$ 4,083	$14,975
University of Wisconsin–Stout	pub.	$ 6592	$4572	50%	45%	$ 6,893	$ 4,271	$18,496
University of Wisconsin–Whitewater	pub.	$ 5080	$4210	43%	44%	$ 5,866	$ 3,424	$17,394
Wyoming								
University of Wyoming	pub.	$ 3426	$6240	47%	22%	$ 6,512	$ 3,154	$16,741

NA = not applicable; NR = not reported; * = includes room and board; † = room only; — = not available.

Profiles of College Financial Aid Programs

ABILENE CHRISTIAN UNIVERSITY
Abilene, TX

Tuition & fees: $15,160 **Average undergraduate aid package:** $10,777

ABOUT THE INSTITUTION Independent religious, coed. Awards: associate, bachelor's, master's, doctoral, and first professional degrees and post-bachelor's and post-master's certificates. 78 undergraduate majors. Total enrollment: 4,685. Undergraduates: 4,120. Freshmen: 1,031. Federal methodology is used as a basis for awarding need-based institutional aid.

UNDERGRADUATE EXPENSES for 2005–06 *Application fee:* $25. *Comprehensive fee:* $20,830 includes full-time tuition ($14,610), mandatory fees ($550), and room and board ($5670). *College room only:* $2750. Full-time tuition and fees vary according to course load. Room and board charges vary according to board plan and housing facility. *Part-time tuition:* $487 per semester hour. *Part-time fees:* $26.50 per semester hour; $10 per term. Part-time tuition and fees vary according to course load. *Payment plans:* Tuition prepayment, installment.

FRESHMAN FINANCIAL AID (Fall 2004) 993 applied for aid; of those 65% were deemed to have need. 100% of freshmen with need received aid; of those 25% had need fully met. *Average percent of need met:* 72% (excluding resources awarded to replace EFC). *Average financial aid package:* $10,806 (excluding resources awarded to replace EFC). 30% of all full-time freshmen had no need and received non-need-based gift aid.

UNDERGRADUATE FINANCIAL AID (Fall 2004) 3,902 applied for aid; of those 63% were deemed to have need. 100% of undergraduates with need received aid; of those 27% had need fully met. *Average percent of need met:* 71% (excluding resources awarded to replace EFC). *Average financial aid package:* $10,777 (excluding resources awarded to replace EFC). 26% of all full-time undergraduates had no need and received non-need-based gift aid.

GIFT AID (NEED-BASED) *Total amount:* $17,426,216 (18% federal, 29% state, 46% institutional, 7% external sources). *Receiving aid:* Freshmen: 64% (650); All full-time undergraduates: 60% (2,403). *Average award:* Freshmen: $8521; Undergraduates: $7510. *Scholarships, grants, and awards:* Federal Pell, FSEOG, state, private, college/university gift aid from institutional funds, United Negro College Fund.

GIFT AID (NON-NEED-BASED) *Total amount:* $5,929,884 (80% institutional, 20% external sources). *Receiving aid:* Freshmen: 59% (605); Undergraduates: 46% (1,862). *Average Award:* Freshmen: $6726; Undergraduates: $5551. *Scholarships, grants, and awards by category: Academic Interests/Achievement:* agriculture, biological sciences, business, communication, education, English, foreign languages, general academic interests/achievements, mathematics, physical sciences, religion/biblical studies, social sciences. *Creative Arts/Performance:* art/fine arts, debating, journalism/publications, music, theater/drama. *Special Achievements/Activities:* cheerleading/drum major, leadership. *Special Characteristics:* 873 awards ($2,762,377 total): children of faculty/staff, ethnic background, first-generation college students, local/state students, members of minority groups, out-of-state students, previous college experience, relatives of clergy, religious affiliation. *Tuition waivers:* Full or partial for employees or children of employees.

LOANS *Student loans:* $21,716,386 (39% need-based, 61% non-need-based). 71% of past graduating class borrowed through all loan programs. *Average indebtedness per student:* $26,413. *Average need-based loan:* Freshmen: $2795; Undergraduates: $4031. *Parent loans:* $5,413,402 (100% non-need-based). *Programs:* FFEL (Subsidized and Unsubsidized Stafford, PLUS), Perkins, state, college/university.

WORK-STUDY *Federal work-study:* Total amount: $413,663; 440 jobs averaging $1454. *State or other work-study/employment:* Total amount: $1,342,049 (9% need-based, 91% non-need-based). Part-time jobs available.

ATHLETIC AWARDS *Total amount:* $2,221,762 (52% need-based, 48% non-need-based).

APPLYING FOR FINANCIAL AID *Required financial aid forms:* FAFSA, institution's own form. *Financial aid deadline (priority):* 3/1. *Notification date:* Continuous beginning 4/1. Students must reply within 3 weeks of notification.

CONTACT Director of Student Financial Services, Abilene Christian University, ACU Box 29007, Abilene, TX 79699-9007, 325-674-2643 or toll-free 800-460-6228.

ACADEMY OF ART UNIVERSITY
San Francisco, CA

Tuition & fees: $14,480 **Average undergraduate aid package:** $6821

ABOUT THE INSTITUTION Proprietary, coed. Awards: associate, bachelor's, and master's degrees. 26 undergraduate majors. Total enrollment: 8,270. Undergraduates: 6,686. Freshmen: 1,775. Federal methodology is used as a basis for awarding need-based institutional aid.

UNDERGRADUATE EXPENSES for 2006–07 *Application fee:* $100. *Comprehensive fee:* $26,480 includes full-time tuition ($14,400), mandatory fees ($80), and room and board ($12,000). *College room only:* $8400.

FRESHMAN FINANCIAL AID (Fall 2004) 328 applied for aid; of those 85% were deemed to have need. 86% of freshmen with need received aid. *Average percent of need met:* 25% (excluding resources awarded to replace EFC). *Average financial aid package:* $5500 (excluding resources awarded to replace EFC).

UNDERGRADUATE FINANCIAL AID (Fall 2004) 2,255 applied for aid; of those 89% were deemed to have need. 77% of undergraduates with need received aid. *Average percent of need met:* 38% (excluding resources awarded to replace EFC). *Average financial aid package:* $6821 (excluding resources awarded to replace EFC).

GIFT AID (NEED-BASED) *Total amount:* $6,767,078 (75% federal, 25% state). *Receiving aid:* Freshmen: 14% (110); All full-time undergraduates: 19% (784). *Average award:* Freshmen: $4144; Undergraduates: $4831. *Scholarships, grants, and awards:* Federal Pell, FSEOG, state, private.

GIFT AID (NON-NEED-BASED) *Total amount:* $1,012,129 (100% institutional). *Receiving aid:* Freshmen: 1% (11); Undergraduates: 1% (59).

LOANS *Student loans:* $31,848,533 (52% need-based, 48% non-need-based). 51% of past graduating class borrowed through all loan programs. *Average indebtedness per student:* $32,000. *Average need-based loan:* Freshmen: $2555; Undergraduates: $3523. *Parent loans:* $16,905,025 (100% non-need-based). *Programs:* Federal Direct (Subsidized and Unsubsidized Stafford, PLUS), alternative loans.

WORK-STUDY *Federal work-study:* Total amount: $131,412; 64 jobs averaging $2053.

APPLYING FOR FINANCIAL AID *Required financial aid forms:* FAFSA, institution's own form. *Financial aid deadline (priority):* 3/2. *Notification date:* Continuous beginning 7/1. Students must reply within 3 weeks of notification.

CONTACT Mr. Joe Vollaro, Executive Vice President of Financial Aid and Compliance, Academy of Art University, 79 New Montgomery Street, San Francisco, CA 94105-3410, 415-274-8688 or toll-free 800-544-ARTS. *Fax:* 415-296-2098. *E-mail:* jvollaro@academyart.edu.

ADAMS STATE COLLEGE
Alamosa, CO

CONTACT Phil Schroeder, Student Financial Aid Director, Adams State College, 208 Edgemont Boulevard, Alamosa, CO 81102, 719-587-7306 or toll-free 800-824-6494. *Fax:* 719-587-7366.

ADELPHI UNIVERSITY
Garden City, NY

Tuition & fees: $19,720 **Average undergraduate aid package:** $14,100

ABOUT THE INSTITUTION Independent, coed. Awards: associate, bachelor's, master's, and doctoral degrees and post-bachelor's and post-master's certificates. 41 undergraduate majors. Total enrollment: 7,898. Undergraduates: 4,758. Freshmen: 770. Federal methodology is used as a basis for awarding need-based institutional aid.

UNDERGRADUATE EXPENSES for 2005–06 *Application fee:* $35. *Comprehensive fee:* $28,910 includes full-time tuition ($18,620), mandatory fees ($1100), and room and board ($9190). *College room only:* $5990. Full-time tuition and fees vary according to course level, location, and program. Room and board charges vary according to board plan and housing facility. *Part-time tuition:* $600 per credit. *Part-time fees:* $550 per year. Part-time tuition and fees vary according to course level, location, and program. *Payment plans:* Tuition prepayment, installment, deferred payment.

FRESHMAN FINANCIAL AID (Fall 2004) 693 applied for aid; of those 85% were deemed to have need. 100% of freshmen with need received aid. *Average percent of need met:* 29% (excluding resources awarded to replace EFC). *Average financial aid package:* $14,100 (excluding resources awarded to replace EFC). 24% of all full-time freshmen had no need and received non-need-based gift aid.
UNDERGRADUATE FINANCIAL AID (Fall 2004) 2,854 applied for aid; of those 87% were deemed to have need. 100% of undergraduates with need received aid; of those 1% had need fully met. *Average percent of need met:* 31% (excluding resources awarded to replace EFC). *Average financial aid package:* $14,100 (excluding resources awarded to replace EFC). 20% of all full-time undergraduates had no need and received non-need-based gift aid.
GIFT AID (NEED-BASED) *Total amount:* $19,837,573 (16% federal, 25% state, 59% institutional). *Receiving aid:* Freshmen: 70% (535); All full-time undergraduates: 59% (2,213). *Average award:* Freshmen: $4958; Undergraduates: $4825. *Scholarships, grants, and awards:* Federal Pell, FSEOG, state, private, college/university gift aid from institutional funds, United Negro College Fund, endowed-donor scholarships.
GIFT AID (NON-NEED-BASED) *Total amount:* $6,067,751 (80% institutional, 20% external sources). *Receiving aid:* Freshmen: 52% (402); Undergraduates: 41% (1,529). *Average Award:* Freshmen: $8901; Undergraduates: $7823. *Scholarships, grants, and awards by category:* Academic Interests/Achievement: 2,341 awards ($16,329,651 total): communication, foreign languages, general academic interests/achievements. Creative Arts/Performance: 344 awards ($2,614,824 total): art/fine arts, dance, music, performing arts, theater/drama. Special Achievements/Activities: 244 awards ($217,350 total): community service, general special achievements/activities, memberships. Special Characteristics: 220 awards ($1,083,705 total): children and siblings of alumni, children of faculty/staff. *Tuition waivers:* Full or partial for employees or children of employees. *ROTC:* Army cooperative, Air Force cooperative.
LOANS *Student loans:* $23,863,946 (73% need-based, 27% non-need-based). 81% of past graduating class borrowed through all loan programs. *Average indebtedness per student:* $22,000. *Average need-based loan:* Freshmen: $3240; Undergraduates: $4094. *Parent loans:* $29,265,524 (76% need-based, 24% non-need-based). *Programs:* FFEL (Subsidized and Unsubsidized Stafford, PLUS), Perkins, Federal Nursing, alternative loans.
WORK-STUDY *Federal work-study:* Total amount: $1,063,285; 693 jobs averaging $1746. *State or other work-study/employment:* Total amount: $1,091,233 (100% non-need-based). 652 part-time jobs averaging $1674.
ATHLETIC AWARDS *Total amount:* $1,631,884 (58% need-based, 42% non-need-based).
APPLYING FOR FINANCIAL AID *Required financial aid forms:* FAFSA, state aid form. *Financial aid deadline (priority):* 3/1. *Notification date:* Continuous beginning 3/1.
CONTACT Ms. Sheryl Mihopulos, Director of Student Financial Services, Adelphi University, 1 South Avenue, PO Box 701, Garden City, NY 11530, 516-877-3080 or toll-free 800-ADELPHI. *Fax:* 516-877-3380.

ADRIAN COLLEGE
Adrian, MI

Tuition & fees: $18,630	Average undergraduate aid package: $17,074

ABOUT THE INSTITUTION Independent religious, coed. Awards: associate and bachelor's degrees. 44 undergraduate majors. Total enrollment: 1,013. Undergraduates: 1,013. Freshmen: 293. Both federal and institutional methodology are used as a basis for awarding need-based institutional aid.
UNDERGRADUATE EXPENSES for 2005–06 *Application fee:* $20. *Comprehensive fee:* $24,900 includes full-time tuition ($18,530), mandatory fees ($100), and room and board ($6270). *College room only:* $2880. Room and board charges vary according to board plan. *Payment plan:* Installment.
FRESHMAN FINANCIAL AID (Fall 2005, est.) 267 applied for aid; of those 82% were deemed to have need. 100% of freshmen with need received aid; of those 85% had need fully met. *Average percent of need met:* 100% (excluding resources awarded to replace EFC). *Average financial aid package:* $17,672 (excluding resources awarded to replace EFC). 16% of all full-time freshmen had no need and received non-need-based gift aid.
UNDERGRADUATE FINANCIAL AID (Fall 2005, est.) 923 applied for aid; of those 79% were deemed to have need. 100% of undergraduates with need received aid; of those 69% had need fully met. *Average percent of need met:* 98% (excluding resources awarded to replace EFC). *Average financial aid package:* $17,074 (excluding resources awarded to replace EFC). 20% of all full-time undergraduates had no need and received non-need-based gift aid.
GIFT AID (NEED-BASED) *Total amount:* $7,170,144 (12% federal, 13% state, 73% institutional, 2% external sources). *Receiving aid:* Freshmen: 82% (220); All full-time undergraduates: 78% (729). *Average award:* Freshmen: $11,481; Undergraduates: $10,282. *Scholarships, grants, and awards:* Federal Pell, FSEOG, state, private, college/university gift aid from institutional funds.
GIFT AID (NON-NEED-BASED) *Total amount:* $431,489 (31% state, 58% institutional, 11% external sources). *Receiving aid:* Freshmen: 34% (92); Undergraduates: 35% (327). *Average Award:* Freshmen: $8281; Undergraduates: $8059. *Scholarships, grants, and awards by category:* Academic Interests/Achievement: 852 awards ($4,618,195 total): business, general academic interests/achievements. Creative Arts/Performance: 241 awards ($424,500 total): art/fine arts, music, theater/drama. Special Achievements/Activities: 40 awards ($40,000 total): religious involvement. Special Characteristics: 66 awards ($221,102 total): children and siblings of alumni, children of faculty/staff, children of union members/company employees, international students, religious affiliation. *Tuition waivers:* Full or partial for children of alumni, employees or children of employees.
LOANS *Student loans:* $4,455,757 (63% need-based, 37% non-need-based). 79% of past graduating class borrowed through all loan programs. *Average indebtedness per student:* $20,849. *Average need-based loan:* Freshmen: $3505; Undergraduates: $4235. *Parent loans:* $6,798,706 (4% need-based, 96% non-need-based). *Programs:* FFEL (Subsidized and Unsubsidized Stafford, PLUS), Perkins.
WORK-STUDY *Federal work-study:* Total amount: $183,211; 102 jobs averaging $1800. *State or other work-study/employment:* Total amount: $723,466 (98% need-based, 2% non-need-based). 414 part-time jobs averaging $1747.
APPLYING FOR FINANCIAL AID *Required financial aid form:* FAFSA. *Financial aid deadline (priority):* 3/1. *Notification date:* Continuous beginning 3/15. Students must reply by 5/1 or within 2 weeks of notification.
CONTACT Mr. Michael Hague, Associate Vice President for Student Financial Services, Adrian College, 110 South Madison Street, Adrian, MI 49221-2575, 517-265-5161 Ext. 4523 or toll-free 800-877-2246. *E-mail:* mhague@adrian.edu.

AGNES SCOTT COLLEGE
Decatur, GA

Tuition & fees: $23,570	Average undergraduate aid package: $24,314

ABOUT THE INSTITUTION Independent religious, undergraduate: women only; graduate: coed. Awards: bachelor's and master's degrees and post-bachelor's certificates. 27 undergraduate majors. Total enrollment: 1,016. Undergraduates: 1,003. Freshmen: 229. Both federal and institutional methodology are used as a basis for awarding need-based institutional aid.
UNDERGRADUATE EXPENSES for 2005–06 *Application fee:* $35. *Comprehensive fee:* $32,070 includes full-time tuition ($23,260), mandatory fees ($310), and room and board ($8500). *College room only:* $4250. Room and board charges vary according to board plan and housing facility. *Part-time tuition:* $970 per credit hour. *Part-time fees:* $310 per year. Part-time tuition and fees vary according to course load. *Payment plan:* Installment.
FRESHMAN FINANCIAL AID (Fall 2005, est.) 193 applied for aid; of those 78% were deemed to have need. 100% of freshmen with need received aid; of those 70% had need fully met. *Average percent of need met:* 96% (excluding resources awarded to replace EFC). *Average financial aid package:* $23,295 (excluding resources awarded to replace EFC). 33% of all full-time freshmen had no need and received non-need-based gift aid.
UNDERGRADUATE FINANCIAL AID (Fall 2005, est.) 631 applied for aid; of those 85% were deemed to have need. 100% of undergraduates with need received aid; of those 70% had need fully met. *Average percent of need met:* 97% (excluding resources awarded to replace EFC). *Average financial aid package:* $24,314 (excluding resources awarded to replace EFC). 33% of all full-time undergraduates had no need and received non-need-based gift aid.
GIFT AID (NEED-BASED) *Total amount:* $9,573,535 (9% federal, 7% state, 83% institutional, 1% external sources). *Receiving aid:* Freshmen: 66% (151); All full-time undergraduates: 63% (533). *Average award:* Freshmen: $17,390; Undergraduates: $17,866. *Scholarships, grants, and awards:* Federal Pell, FSEOG, state, private, college/university gift aid from institutional funds.

Agnes Scott College

GIFT AID (NON-NEED-BASED) *Total amount:* $4,373,621 (14% state, 84% institutional, 2% external sources). *Receiving aid:* Freshmen: 31% (72); Undergraduates: 21% (177). *Average Award:* Freshmen: $13,438; Undergraduates: $12,976. *Scholarships, grants, and awards by category:* Academic Interests/Achievement: 669 awards ($6,587,000 total): general academic interests/achievements. *Creative Arts/Performance:* 24 awards ($56,375 total): music. *Special Achievements/Activities:* 11 awards ($64,000 total): community service, leadership. *Special Characteristics:* adult students, children of educators, children of faculty/staff, international students, local/state students, religious affiliation. *Tuition waivers:* Full or partial for employees or children of employees. *ROTC:* Air Force cooperative.
LOANS *Student loans:* $3,071,310 (61% need-based, 39% non-need-based). 71% of past graduating class borrowed through all loan programs. *Average indebtedness per student:* $22,018. *Average need-based loan:* Freshmen: $2606; Undergraduates: $3923. *Parent loans:* $1,982,303 (5% need-based, 95% non-need-based). *Programs:* FFEL (Subsidized and Unsubsidized Stafford, PLUS), college/university.
WORK-STUDY *Federal work-study:* Total amount: $849,523; 429 jobs averaging $1980. *State or other work-study/employment:* Total amount: $241,200 (38% need-based, 62% non-need-based). 125 part-time jobs averaging $1930.
APPLYING FOR FINANCIAL AID *Required financial aid forms:* FAFSA, previous year's tax returns. *Financial aid deadline:* 5/1 (priority: 2/15). *Notification date:* Continuous beginning 3/1. Students must reply by 5/1 or within 2 weeks of notification.
CONTACT Karen Smith, Director of Financial Aid, Agnes Scott College, 141 East College Avenue, Decatur, GA 30030-3797, 404-471-6395 or toll-free 800-868-8602. *Fax:* 404-471-6159. *E-mail:* finaid@agnesscott.edu.

ALABAMA AGRICULTURAL AND MECHANICAL UNIVERSITY
Huntsville, AL

Tuition & fees (AL res): $4940 **Average undergraduate aid package: $5705**

ABOUT THE INSTITUTION State-supported, coed. Awards: bachelor's, master's, and doctoral degrees. 36 undergraduate majors. Total enrollment: 6,323. Undergraduates: 5,091. Freshmen: 1,208. Federal methodology is used as a basis for awarding need-based institutional aid.
UNDERGRADUATE EXPENSES for 2005–06 *Application fee:* $10. *Tuition, state resident:* full-time $4420.
FRESHMAN FINANCIAL AID (Fall 2005, est.) 2786 applied for aid; of those 89% were deemed to have need. 33% of freshmen with need received aid; of those 1% had need fully met. *Average percent of need met:* 9% (excluding resources awarded to replace EFC). *Average financial aid package:* $3680 (excluding resources awarded to replace EFC). 2% of all full-time freshmen had no need and received non-need-based gift aid.
UNDERGRADUATE FINANCIAL AID (Fall 2005, est.) 7,840 applied for aid; of those 89% were deemed to have need. 59% of undergraduates with need received aid; of those 8% had need fully met. *Average percent of need met:* 26% (excluding resources awarded to replace EFC). *Average financial aid package:* $5705 (excluding resources awarded to replace EFC). 8% of all full-time undergraduates had no need and received non-need-based gift aid.
GIFT AID (NEED-BASED) *Total amount:* $20,427,500 (70% federal, 28% institutional, 2% external sources). *Receiving aid:* Freshmen: 27% (784); All full-time undergraduates: 42% (3,575). *Average award:* Freshmen: $3526; Undergraduates: $4333. *Scholarships, grants, and awards:* Federal Pell, FSEOG, state, private, college/university gift aid from institutional funds, United Negro College Fund.
GIFT AID (NON-NEED-BASED) *Total amount:* $4,776,835 (2% federal, 93% institutional, 5% external sources). *Receiving aid:* Freshmen: 1; Undergraduates: 2% (180). *Average Award:* Freshmen: $4247; Undergraduates: $8700. *Scholarships, grants, and awards by category:* Academic Interests/Achievement: general academic interests/achievements. *Creative Arts/Performance:* music, theater/drama. *Special Characteristics:* children of faculty/staff, parents of current students. *ROTC:* Army.
LOANS *Student loans:* $25,755,218 (85% need-based, 15% non-need-based). 66% of past graduating class borrowed through all loan programs. *Average indebtedness per student:* $17,125. *Average need-based loan:* Freshmen: $2769; Andergraduates: $3006. *Parent loans:* $5,644,997 (55% need-based, 45% non-need-based). *Programs:* Federal Direct (Subsidized and Unsubsidized Stafford, PLUS), FFEL (Subsidized and Unsubsidized Stafford, PLUS), Perkins, state.
WORK-STUDY *Federal work-study:* Total amount: $478,174; jobs available. *State or other work-study/employment:* Part-time jobs available.
APPLYING FOR FINANCIAL AID *Required financial aid forms:* FAFSA, institution's own form. *Financial aid deadline (priority):* 3/1. *Notification date:* Continuous beginning 5/1. Students must reply within 2 weeks of notification.
CONTACT Dr. Carlos Clark, Financial Aid Officer, Alabama Agricultural and Mechanical University, 4900 Meridian Street, Normal, AL 35762, 256-851-5400 or toll-free 800-553-0816. *Fax:* 256-851-5407.

ALABAMA STATE UNIVERSITY
Montgomery, AL

CONTACT Mrs. Dorenda A. Adams, Director of Financial Aid, Alabama State University, PO Box 271, Montgomery, AL 36101-0271, 334-229-4323 or toll-free 800-253-5037. *Fax:* 334-299-4924. *E-mail:* dadams@asunet.alasu.edu.

ALASKA BIBLE COLLEGE
Glennallen, AK

Tuition & fees: $5950 **Average undergraduate aid package: N/A**

ABOUT THE INSTITUTION Independent nondenominational, coed. Awards: associate and bachelor's degrees. 1 undergraduate major. Total enrollment: 48. Undergraduates: 48. Freshmen: 4. Institutional methodology is used as a basis for awarding need-based institutional aid.
UNDERGRADUATE EXPENSES for 2006–07 *Application fee:* $35. *Comprehensive fee:* $10,700 includes full-time tuition ($5950) and room and board ($4750). *Part-time tuition:* $260 per credit hour.
FRESHMAN FINANCIAL AID (Fall 2004) 9 applied for aid; of those 89% were deemed to have need. 100% of freshmen with need received aid.
UNDERGRADUATE FINANCIAL AID (Fall 2004) 35 applied for aid; of those 94% were deemed to have need. 100% of undergraduates with need received aid.
GIFT AID (NEED-BASED) *Total amount:* $59,316 (41% institutional, 59% external sources). *Receiving aid:* Freshmen: 89% (8); All full-time undergraduates: 87% (33). *Scholarships, grants, and awards:* private, college/university gift aid from institutional funds.
GIFT AID (NON-NEED-BASED) *Total amount:* $27,796 (100% institutional). *Receiving aid:* Freshmen: 44% (4); Undergraduates: 11% (4). *Scholarships, grants, and awards by category:* Academic Interests/Achievement: 4 awards ($4000 total): general academic interests/achievements, religion/biblical studies. *Creative Arts/Performance:* 1 award ($250 total): music. *Special Achievements/Activities:* 1 award ($250 total): religious involvement. *Special Characteristics:* 3 awards: children of faculty/staff, local/state students, religious affiliation, spouses of current students.
LOANS *Student loans:* $161,711 (100% need-based). 32% of past graduating class borrowed through all loan programs. *Average indebtedness per student:* $8500. *Programs:* state.
WORK-STUDY *State or other work-study/employment:* Total amount: $35,092 (100% need-based). 27 part-time jobs averaging $1800.
APPLYING FOR FINANCIAL AID *Required financial aid form:* institution's own form. *Financial aid deadline:* 7/1 (priority: 7/1). *Notification date:* 8/1. Students must reply within 2 weeks of notification.
CONTACT Kevin Newman, Financial Aid Officer, Alaska Bible College, PO Box 289, Glennallen, AK 99588-0289, 907-822-3201 Ext. 253 or toll-free 800-478-7884. *Fax:* 907-822-5027. *E-mail:* knewman@akbible.edu.

ALASKA PACIFIC UNIVERSITY
Anchorage, AK

Tuition & fees: $19,610 **Average undergraduate aid package: N/A**

ABOUT THE INSTITUTION Independent, coed. Awards: associate, bachelor's, and master's degrees. 12 undergraduate majors. Total enrollment: 800. Undergraduates: 580. Freshmen: 51. Both federal and institutional methodology are used as a basis for awarding need-based institutional aid.

UNDERGRADUATE EXPENSES for 2006–07 *Application fee:* $25. *Comprehensive fee:* $26,410 includes full-time tuition ($19,500), mandatory fees ($110), and room and board ($6800). *Part-time tuition:* $812 per semester hour. *Part-time fees:* $55 per term.
FRESHMAN FINANCIAL AID (Fall 2004) 36 applied for aid; of those 92% were deemed to have need. 100% of freshmen with need received aid; of those 36% had need fully met. *Average percent of need met:* 86% (excluding resources awarded to replace EFC). 8% of all full-time freshmen had no need and received non-need-based gift aid.
UNDERGRADUATE FINANCIAL AID (Fall 2004) 239 applied for aid; of those 90% were deemed to have need. 100% of undergraduates with need received aid; of those 35% had need fully met. *Average percent of need met:* 81% (excluding resources awarded to replace EFC). 26% of all full-time undergraduates had no need and received non-need-based gift aid.
GIFT AID (NEED-BASED) *Total amount:* $765,894 (53% federal, 3% state, 44% institutional). *Receiving aid:* Freshmen: 69% (27); All full-time undergraduates: 63% (189). *Average award:* Freshmen: $2945; Undergraduates: $2863. *Scholarships, grants, and awards:* Federal Pell, FSEOG, state, private, college/university gift aid from institutional funds, Bureau of Indian Affairs Grants.
GIFT AID (NON-NEED-BASED) *Total amount:* $1,421,715 (77% institutional, 23% external sources). *Receiving aid:* Freshmen: 74% (29); Undergraduates: 65% (194). *Average Award:* Freshmen: $6665; Undergraduates: $1736. *Scholarships, grants, and awards by category: Academic Interests/Achievement:* 152 awards ($572,035 total): biological sciences, business, education, general academic interests/achievements, humanities, physical sciences, social sciences. *Special Achievements/Activities:* 88 awards ($167,402 total): community service, general special achievements/activities, leadership, religious involvement. *Special Characteristics:* 136 awards ($317,487 total): children and siblings of alumni, children of faculty/staff, ethnic background, general special characteristics, international students, local/state students, members of minority groups, out-of-state students, religious affiliation.
LOANS *Student loans:* $2,898,448 (29% need-based, 71% non-need-based). 66% of past graduating class borrowed through all loan programs. *Average indebtedness per student:* $39,463. *Average need-based loan:* Freshmen: $2625; Undergraduates: $3813. *Parent loans:* $214,078 (100% non-need-based). *Programs:* FFEL (Subsidized and Unsubsidized Stafford, PLUS), state.
WORK-STUDY *Federal work-study:* Total amount: $56,901; 31 jobs averaging $1836. *State or other work-study/employment:* Part-time jobs available.
APPLYING FOR FINANCIAL AID *Required financial aid form:* FAFSA. *Financial aid deadline (priority):* 4/15. *Notification date:* Continuous beginning 2/1. Students must reply within 4 weeks of notification.
CONTACT Peter Miller, Director of Financial Aid, Alaska Pacific University, 4101 University Drive, Grant Hall, Room 115, Anchorage, AK 99508-4672, 907-564-8341 or toll-free 800-252-7528. *Fax:* 907-564-8372. *E-mail:* sfs@alaskapacific.edu.

ALBANY COLLEGE OF PHARMACY OF UNION UNIVERSITY
Albany, NY

CONTACT Tiffany M. Gutierrez, Director of Financial Aid, Albany College of Pharmacy of Union University, 106 New Scotland Avenue, Albany, NY 12208-3425, 518-445-7256 or toll-free 888-203-8010. *Fax:* 518-445-7322. *E-mail:* gutierrt@mail.acp.edu.

ALBANY STATE UNIVERSITY
Albany, GA

CONTACT Ms. Kathleen J. Caldwell, Director of Financial Aid, Albany State University, 504 College Drive, Albany, GA 31705-2717, 912-430-4650 or toll-free 800-822-RAMS (in-state). *Fax:* 912-430-3936. *E-mail:* finaid@asurams.edu.

ALBERTSON COLLEGE OF IDAHO
Caldwell, ID

Tuition & fees: $16,000	Average undergraduate aid package: $13,993

ABOUT THE INSTITUTION Independent, coed. Awards: bachelor's and master's degrees. 26 undergraduate majors. Total enrollment: 818. Undergraduates: 800. Freshmen: 196. Federal methodology is used as a basis for awarding need-based institutional aid.
UNDERGRADUATE EXPENSES for 2006–07 *Application fee:* $50. *Comprehensive fee:* $22,191 includes full-time tuition ($16,000) and room and board ($6191). *College room only:* $2700. *Part-time tuition:* $670 per credit.
FRESHMAN FINANCIAL AID (Fall 2005, est.) 157 applied for aid; of those 89% were deemed to have need. 100% of freshmen with need received aid; of those 21% had need fully met. *Average percent of need met:* 89% (excluding resources awarded to replace EFC). *Average financial aid package:* $13,320 (excluding resources awarded to replace EFC). 29% of all full-time freshmen had no need and received non-need-based gift aid.
UNDERGRADUATE FINANCIAL AID (Fall 2005, est.) 572 applied for aid; of those 85% were deemed to have need. 99% of undergraduates with need received aid; of those 15% had need fully met. *Average percent of need met:* 83% (excluding resources awarded to replace EFC). *Average financial aid package:* $13,993 (excluding resources awarded to replace EFC). 32% of all full-time undergraduates had no need and received non-need-based gift aid.
GIFT AID (NEED-BASED) *Total amount:* $1,947,446 (39% federal, 1% state, 37% institutional, 23% external sources). *Receiving aid:* Freshmen: 45% (86); All full-time undergraduates: 39% (297). *Average award:* Freshmen: $3737; Undergraduates: $4060. *Scholarships, grants, and awards:* Federal Pell, FSEOG, state, private, college/university gift aid from institutional funds.
GIFT AID (NON-NEED-BASED) *Total amount:* $3,941,448 (4% state, 96% institutional). *Receiving aid:* Freshmen: 70% (134); Undergraduates: 60% (455). *Average Award:* Freshmen: $8667; Undergraduates: $7791. *Scholarships, grants, and awards by category: Academic Interests/Achievement:* $3,321,666 total: biological sciences, education, general academic interests/achievements. *Creative Arts/Performance:* $281,686 total: art/fine arts, debating, music, theater/drama. *Special Achievements/Activities:* $1500 total: junior miss. *Special Characteristics:* $764,601 total: children and siblings of alumni, children of faculty/staff, ethnic background, handicapped students, international students, local/state students, members of minority groups, religious affiliation, siblings of current students. *ROTC:* Army cooperative.
LOANS *Student loans:* $13,423,052 (12% need-based, 88% non-need-based). 94% of past graduating class borrowed through all loan programs. *Average indebtedness per student:* $25,343. *Average need-based loan:* Freshmen: $3515; Undergraduates: $4444. *Parent loans:* $1,047,696 (100% non-need-based). *Programs:* Federal Direct (Subsidized and Unsubsidized Stafford, PLUS), Perkins, alternative loans.
WORK-STUDY *Federal work-study:* Total amount: $171,089; 179 jobs averaging $977. *State or other work-study/employment:* Total amount: $81,773 (29% need-based, 71% non-need-based). 89 part-time jobs averaging $919.
ATHLETIC AWARDS *Total amount:* $847,399 (100% non-need-based).
APPLYING FOR FINANCIAL AID *Required financial aid forms:* FAFSA, institution's own form. *Financial aid deadline (priority):* 2/15. *Notification date:* Continuous beginning 12/1. Students must reply within 3 weeks of notification.
CONTACT Juanitta M. Pearson, Director, Office of Student Financial Services, Albertson College of Idaho, 2112 Cleveland Boulevard, Campus Box 39, Caldwell, ID 83605-4432, 208-459-5307 or toll-free 800-244-3246. *Fax:* 208-459-5844. *E-mail:* jpearson@albertson.edu.

ALBERTUS MAGNUS COLLEGE
New Haven, CT

Tuition & fees: $17,310	Average undergraduate aid package: $9050

ABOUT THE INSTITUTION Independent Roman Catholic, coed. Awards: associate, bachelor's, and master's degrees. 56 undergraduate majors. Total enrollment: 2,230. Undergraduates: 1,782. Freshmen: 193. Federal methodology is used as a basis for awarding need-based institutional aid.
UNDERGRADUATE EXPENSES for 2005–06 *Application fee:* $35. *Comprehensive fee:* $24,860 includes full-time tuition ($16,600), mandatory fees ($710), and room and board ($7550). Full-time tuition and fees vary according to class time and program. *Part-time tuition:* $1726 per course. Part-time tuition and fees vary according to class time and program. *Payment plan:* Installment.
FRESHMAN FINANCIAL AID (Fall 2004) 72 applied for aid; of those 97% were deemed to have need. 100% of freshmen with need received aid; of those 14% had need fully met. *Average percent of need met:* 46% (excluding resources

Albertus Magnus College

awarded to replace EFC). *Average financial aid package:* $8760 (excluding resources awarded to replace EFC). 8% of all full-time freshmen had no need and received non-need-based gift aid.
UNDERGRADUATE FINANCIAL AID (Fall 2004) 366 applied for aid; of those 90% were deemed to have need. 100% of undergraduates with need received aid; of those 23% had need fully met. *Average percent of need met:* 52% (excluding resources awarded to replace EFC). *Average financial aid package:* $9050 (excluding resources awarded to replace EFC). 19% of all full-time undergraduates had no need and received non-need-based gift aid.
GIFT AID (NEED-BASED) *Total amount:* $2,254,461 (25% federal, 62% state, 13% institutional). *Receiving aid:* Freshmen: 52% (62); All full-time undergraduates: 83% (308). *Average award:* Freshmen: $6720; Undergraduates: $6950. *Scholarships, grants, and awards:* Federal Pell, FSEOG, state, college/university gift aid from institutional funds.
GIFT AID (NON-NEED-BASED) *Total amount:* $1,170,990 (5% state, 86% institutional, 9% external sources). *Receiving aid:* Freshmen: 35% (42); Undergraduates: 58% (214). *Average Award:* Freshmen: $4300; Undergraduates: $6570. *Scholarships, grants, and awards by category: Academic Interests/Achievement:* 130 awards ($552,630 total): biological sciences, business, communication, computer science, education, English, foreign languages, general academic interests/achievements, humanities, international studies, mathematics, physical sciences, premedicine, religion/biblical studies, social sciences. *Creative Arts/Performance:* art/fine arts, performing arts, theater/drama. *Special Achievements/Activities:* community service, leadership. *Special Characteristics:* 8 awards ($40,000 total): religious affiliation. *Tuition waivers:* Full or partial for employees or children of employees, senior citizens.
LOANS *Student loans:* $2,435,014 (47% need-based, 53% non-need-based). 85% of past graduating class borrowed through all loan programs. *Average indebtedness per student:* $12,625. *Average need-based loan:* Freshmen: $3550; Undergraduates: $3600. *Parent loans:* $536,755 (100% non-need-based). *Programs:* FFEL (Subsidized and Unsubsidized Stafford, PLUS), Perkins.
WORK-STUDY *Federal work-study:* Total amount: $89,448; 74 jobs averaging $1208. *State or other work-study/employment:* Total amount: $94,000 (100% need-based). 33 part-time jobs averaging $2849.
APPLYING FOR FINANCIAL AID *Required financial aid forms:* FAFSA, institution's own form. *Financial aid deadline (priority):* 3/15. *Notification date:* 4/15. Students must reply within 2 weeks of notification.
CONTACT Andrew Foster, Director of Financial Aid, Albertus Magnus College, 700 Prospect Street, New Haven, CT 06511-1189, 203-773-8508 or toll-free 800-578-9160. *Fax:* 203-773-8972. *E-mail:* financial_aid@albertus.edu.

ALBION COLLEGE
Albion, MI

Tuition & fees: $24,296	Average undergraduate aid package: $20,101

ABOUT THE INSTITUTION Independent Methodist, coed. Awards: bachelor's degrees. 37 undergraduate majors. Total enrollment: 1,979. Undergraduates: 1,979. Freshmen: 574. Federal methodology is used as a basis for awarding need-based institutional aid.
UNDERGRADUATE EXPENSES for 2005–06 *Application fee:* $20. *Comprehensive fee:* $31,224 includes full-time tuition ($24,012), mandatory fees ($284), and room and board ($6928). *College room only:* $3388. Room and board charges vary according to housing facility. *Part-time tuition:* $1020 per semester hour. *Payment plans:* Tuition prepayment, installment, deferred payment.
FRESHMAN FINANCIAL AID (Fall 2005, est.) 421 applied for aid; of those 81% were deemed to have need. 100% of freshmen with need received aid; of those 61% had need fully met. *Average percent of need met:* 95% (excluding resources awarded to replace EFC). *Average financial aid package:* $20,774 (excluding resources awarded to replace EFC). 37% of all full-time freshmen had no need and received non-need-based gift aid.
UNDERGRADUATE FINANCIAL AID (Fall 2005, est.) 1,388 applied for aid; of those 85% were deemed to have need. 100% of undergraduates with need received aid; of those 59% had need fully met. *Average percent of need met:* 94% (excluding resources awarded to replace EFC). *Average financial aid package:* $20,101 (excluding resources awarded to replace EFC). 37% of all full-time undergraduates had no need and received non-need-based gift aid.
GIFT AID (NEED-BASED) *Total amount:* $19,704,640 (5% federal, 12% state, 80% institutional, 3% external sources). *Receiving aid:* Freshmen: 60% (342); All full-time undergraduates: 60% (1,178). *Average award:* Freshmen: $17,560;

Undergraduates: $15,969. *Scholarships, grants, and awards:* Federal Pell, FSEOG, state, private, college/university gift aid from institutional funds.
GIFT AID (NON-NEED-BASED) *Total amount:* $8,691,296 (5% state, 93% institutional, 2% external sources). *Receiving aid:* Freshmen: 58% (329); Undergraduates: 57% (1,108). *Average Award:* Freshmen: $12,346; Undergraduates: $11,250. *Scholarships, grants, and awards by category: Academic Interests/Achievement:* 1,724 awards ($18,667,577 total): business, communication, education, general academic interests/achievements, mathematics, premedicine. *Creative Arts/Performance:* 203 awards ($250,100 total): art/fine arts, music, performing arts, theater/drama. *Special Characteristics:* 276 awards ($414,606 total): children and siblings of alumni, relatives of clergy. *Tuition waivers:* Full or partial for children of alumni, employees or children of employees.
LOANS *Student loans:* $8,683,481 (45% need-based, 55% non-need-based). 63% of past graduating class borrowed through all loan programs. *Average indebtedness per student:* $23,010. *Average need-based loan:* Freshmen: $3373; Undergraduates: $4444. *Parent loans:* $1,826,829 (100% non-need-based). *Programs:* FFEL (Subsidized and Unsubsidized Stafford, PLUS), Perkins, state.
WORK-STUDY *Federal work-study:* Total amount: $726,501; 569 jobs averaging $1277.
APPLYING FOR FINANCIAL AID *Required financial aid form:* FAFSA. *Financial aid deadline (priority):* 3/1. *Notification date:* Continuous beginning 3/15.
CONTACT Doug Kellar, Associate Vice President for Enrollment, Albion College, Kellogg Center Box 4670, Albion, MI 49224-1831, 517-629-0440 or toll-free 800-858-6770. *Fax:* 517-629-0581. *E-mail:* dkellar@albion.edu.

ALBRIGHT COLLEGE
Reading, PA

Tuition & fees: $26,032	Average undergraduate aid package: $17,140

ABOUT THE INSTITUTION Independent religious, coed. Awards: bachelor's and master's degrees. 45 undergraduate majors. Total enrollment: 2,180. Undergraduates: 2,112. Freshmen: 451. Federal methodology is used as a basis for awarding need-based institutional aid.
UNDERGRADUATE EXPENSES for 2005–06 *Application fee:* $25. *Comprehensive fee:* $33,920 includes full-time tuition ($25,232), mandatory fees ($800), and room and board ($7888). *College room only:* $4490. Full-time tuition and fees vary according to program. Room and board charges vary according to board plan and housing facility. *Part-time tuition:* $3154 per course. Part-time tuition and fees vary according to class time. *Payment plan:* Installment.
FRESHMAN FINANCIAL AID (Fall 2005, est.) 406 applied for aid; of those 90% were deemed to have need. 100% of freshmen with need received aid; of those 18% had need fully met. *Average percent of need met:* 78% (excluding resources awarded to replace EFC). *Average financial aid package:* $20,149 (excluding resources awarded to replace EFC). 15% of all full-time freshmen had no need and received non-need-based gift aid.
UNDERGRADUATE FINANCIAL AID (Fall 2005, est.) 1,759 applied for aid; of those 88% were deemed to have need. 99% of undergraduates with need received aid; of those 20% had need fully met. *Average percent of need met:* 75% (excluding resources awarded to replace EFC). *Average financial aid package:* $17,140 (excluding resources awarded to replace EFC). 15% of all full-time undergraduates had no need and received non-need-based gift aid.
GIFT AID (NEED-BASED) *Total amount:* $20,112,958 (10% federal, 10% state, 73% institutional, 7% external sources). *Receiving aid:* Freshmen: 81% (364); All full-time undergraduates: 68% (1,483). *Average award:* Freshmen: $16,255; Undergraduates: $13,532. *Scholarships, grants, and awards:* Federal Pell, FSEOG, state, private, college/university gift aid from institutional funds.
GIFT AID (NON-NEED-BASED) *Total amount:* $3,790,952 (1% state, 77% institutional, 22% external sources). *Receiving aid:* Freshmen: 11% (50); Undergraduates: 9% (202). *Average Award:* Freshmen: $14,327; Undergraduates: $1230. *Scholarships, grants, and awards by category: Academic Interests/Achievement:* 53 awards ($46,750 total): general academic interests/achievements, religion/biblical studies. *Creative Arts/Performance:* 60 awards ($70,000 total): art/fine arts, music, theater/drama. *Special Achievements/Activities:* 44 awards ($26,250 total): junior miss, memberships. *Special Characteristics:* 205 awards ($424,800 total): children and siblings of alumni, international students, members of minority groups, siblings of current students. *Tuition waivers:* Full or partial for children of alumni, employees or children of employees, senior citizens.
LOANS *Student loans:* $12,923,413 (68% need-based, 32% non-need-based). 88% of past graduating class borrowed through all loan programs. *Average

indebtedness per student: $24,671. ***Average need-based loan:*** Freshmen: $3948; Undergraduates: $4248. ***Parent loans:*** $4,273,164 (35% need-based, 65% non-need-based). ***Programs:*** FFEL (Subsidized and Unsubsidized Stafford, PLUS), Perkins, private educational loans.

WORK-STUDY *Federal work-study:* Total amount: $665,346. ***State or other work-study/employment:*** Total amount: $577,521 (5% need-based, 95% non-need-based).

APPLYING FOR FINANCIAL AID *Required financial aid form:* FAFSA. ***Financial aid deadline (priority):*** 3/1. ***Notification date:*** Continuous beginning 2/14. Students must reply within 2 weeks of notification.

CONTACT Mary Ellen Duffy, Director of Financial Aid, Albright College, PO Box 15234, Reading, PA 19612-5234, 610-921-7515 or toll-free 800-252-1856. *Fax:* 610-921-7729. *E-mail:* meduffy@alb.edu.

ALCORN STATE UNIVERSITY
Alcorn State, MS

ABOUT THE INSTITUTION State-supported, coed. Awards: associate, bachelor's, and master's degrees and post-master's certificates. 37 undergraduate majors. Total enrollment: 3,544. Undergraduates: 2,962. Freshmen: 497.

GIFT AID (NEED-BASED) *Scholarships, grants, and awards:* Federal Pell, FSEOG, state, private, college/university gift aid from institutional funds.

GIFT AID (NON-NEED-BASED) *Scholarships, grants, and awards by category: Academic Interests/Achievement:* general academic interests/achievements. *Creative Arts/Performance:* music. *Special Characteristics:* children of faculty/staff, local/state students, members of minority groups.

LOANS *Programs:* Federal Direct (Subsidized and Unsubsidized Stafford, PLUS).

APPLYING FOR FINANCIAL AID *Required financial aid forms:* FAFSA, institution's own form.

CONTACT Juanita M. Russell, Director of Financial Aid, Alcorn State University, 1000 ASU Drive #28, Alcorn State, MS 39096-7500, 601-877-6190 or toll-free 800-222-6790. *Fax:* 601-877-6110. *E-mail:* juanita@lorman.alcorn.edu.

ALDERSON-BROADDUS COLLEGE
Philippi, WV

Tuition & fees: $18,136   **Average undergraduate aid package: $20,020**

ABOUT THE INSTITUTION Independent religious, coed. Awards: associate, bachelor's, and master's degrees. 43 undergraduate majors. Total enrollment: 779. Undergraduates: 648. Freshmen: 125. Federal methodology is used as a basis for awarding need-based institutional aid.

UNDERGRADUATE EXPENSES for 2005–06 *Application fee:* $10. ***Comprehensive fee:*** $24,006 includes full-time tuition ($17,970), mandatory fees ($166), and room and board ($5870). ***College room only:*** $2860. Full-time tuition and fees vary according to degree level. Room and board charges vary according to housing facility. ***Part-time tuition:*** $598 per credit hour. ***Part-time fees:*** $41.50 per term. Part-time tuition and fees vary according to degree level. ***Payment plan:*** Installment.

FRESHMAN FINANCIAL AID (Fall 2004) 150 applied for aid; of those 97% were deemed to have need. 100% of freshmen with need received aid; of those 3% had need fully met. *Average percent of need met:* 79% (excluding resources awarded to replace EFC). *Average financial aid package:* $16,600 (excluding resources awarded to replace EFC). 1% of all full-time freshmen had no need and received non-need-based gift aid.

UNDERGRADUATE FINANCIAL AID (Fall 2004) 602 applied for aid; of those 91% were deemed to have need. 100% of undergraduates with need received aid; of those 5% had need fully met. *Average percent of need met:* 91% (excluding resources awarded to replace EFC). *Average financial aid package:* $20,020 (excluding resources awarded to replace EFC). 5% of all full-time undergraduates had no need and received non-need-based gift aid.

GIFT AID (NEED-BASED) *Total amount:* $5,627,922 (20% federal, 9% state, 65% institutional, 6% external sources). ***Receiving aid:*** Freshmen: 93% (139); All full-time undergraduates: 83% (503). ***Average award:*** Freshmen: $9160; Undergraduates: $10,404. ***Scholarships, grants, and awards:*** Federal Pell, FSEOG, state, private, college/university gift aid from institutional funds, Federal Nursing, National Health Service Corp.

GIFT AID (NON-NEED-BASED) *Total amount:* $651,742 (10% federal, 48% state, 38% institutional, 4% external sources). ***Receiving aid:*** Freshmen: 12% (18); Undergraduates: 13% (78). ***Average Award:*** Freshmen: $6750; Undergraduates: $9266. ***Scholarships, grants, and awards by category:*** *Academic Interests/Achievement:* 572 awards ($2,696,741 total): biological sciences, business, communication, computer science, education, general academic interests/achievements, health fields, humanities, mathematics, physical sciences, premedicine, religion/biblical studies, social sciences. *Creative Arts/Performance:* 71 awards ($491,415 total): art/fine arts, creative writing, debating, journalism, publications, music, performing arts, theater/drama. *Special Achievements/Activities:* general special achievements/activities, leadership. *Special Characteristics:* 45 awards ($412,729 total): children of faculty/staff, ethnic background, general special characteristics, international students, religious affiliation. ***Tuition waivers:*** Full or partial for employees or children of employees.

LOANS *Student loans:* $4,360,947 (58% need-based, 42% non-need-based). 86% of past graduating class borrowed through all loan programs. *Average indebtedness per student:* $26,313. ***Average need-based loan:*** Freshmen: $3319; Undergraduates: $4547. ***Parent loans:*** $535,553 (100% non-need-based). ***Programs:*** FFEL (Subsidized and Unsubsidized Stafford, PLUS), Perkins, Federal Nursing.

WORK-STUDY *Federal work-study:* Total amount: $286,480; 240 jobs averaging $1400. ***State or other work-study/employment:*** Total amount: $217,681 (100% non-need-based). 122 part-time jobs averaging $1400.

ATHLETIC AWARDS *Total amount:* $775,896 (100% non-need-based).

APPLYING FOR FINANCIAL AID *Required financial aid form:* FAFSA. ***Financial aid deadline (priority):*** 3/1. ***Notification date:*** Continuous beginning 2/15. Students must reply within 2 weeks of notification.

CONTACT Brian Weingart, Director of Financial Aid, Alderson-Broaddus College, College Hill Road, Philippi, WV 26416, 304-457-6354 or toll-free 800-263-1549. *Fax:* 304-457-6239.

ALFRED UNIVERSITY
Alfred, NY

Tuition & fees: $20,960   **Average undergraduate aid package: $19,364**

ABOUT THE INSTITUTION Independent, coed. Awards: bachelor's, master's, and doctoral degrees and post-master's certificates. 41 undergraduate majors. Total enrollment: 2,235. Undergraduates: 1,961. Freshmen: 429. Both federal and institutional methodology are used as a basis for awarding need-based institutional aid.

UNDERGRADUATE EXPENSES for 2005–06 *Application fee:* $40. ***Comprehensive fee:*** $30,706 includes full-time tuition ($20,150), mandatory fees ($810), and room and board ($9746). ***College room only:*** $5076. Full-time tuition and fees vary according to student level. Room and board charges vary according to board plan and housing facility. ***Part-time tuition:*** $658 per credit hour. Part-time tuition and fees vary according to course load. ***Payment plans:*** Tuition prepayment, installment, deferred payment.

FRESHMAN FINANCIAL AID (Fall 2004) 452 applied for aid; of those 90% were deemed to have need. 100% of freshmen with need received aid; of those 85% had need fully met. *Average percent of need met:* 94% (excluding resources awarded to replace EFC). *Average financial aid package:* $19,396 (excluding resources awarded to replace EFC).

UNDERGRADUATE FINANCIAL AID (Fall 2004) 1,731 applied for aid; of those 92% were deemed to have need. 100% of undergraduates with need received aid; of those 75% had need fully met. *Average percent of need met:* 90% (excluding resources awarded to replace EFC). *Average financial aid package:* $19,364 (excluding resources awarded to replace EFC). 13% of all full-time undergraduates had no need and received non-need-based gift aid.

GIFT AID (NEED-BASED) *Total amount:* $20,829,000 (12% federal, 13% state, 75% institutional). ***Receiving aid:*** Freshmen: 405; All full-time undergraduates: 80% (1,559). ***Average award:*** Freshmen: $14,574; Undergraduates: $14,364. ***Scholarships, grants, and awards:*** Federal Pell, FSEOG, state, private, college/university gift aid from institutional funds.

GIFT AID (NON-NEED-BASED) *Total amount:* $2,876,000 (3% federal, 2% state, 78% institutional, 17% external sources). ***Receiving aid:*** Freshmen: 235; Undergraduates: 41% (801). ***Average Award:*** Freshmen: $7136; Undergraduates: $6680. ***Scholarships, grants, and awards by category:*** *Academic Interests/Achievement:* biological sciences, business, communication, computer science, education, engineering/technologies, English, foreign languages, general academic interests/achievements, humanities, international studies, mathematics, military science, physical sciences, premedicine, social sciences. *Creative Arts/Performance:* art/fine arts, general creative arts/performance, performing arts. *Special Achievements/Activities:* leadership. *Special Characteristics:* children of

Alfred University

educators, children of faculty/staff, international students. *Tuition waivers:* Full or partial for employees or children of employees. *ROTC:* Army cooperative.
LOANS *Student loans:* $10,063,000 (65% need-based, 35% non-need-based). 89% of past graduating class borrowed through all loan programs. *Average indebtedness per student:* $19,125. *Average need-based loan:* Freshmen: $4146; Undergraduates: $4904. *Parent loans:* $2,633,000 (100% non-need-based). *Programs:* FFEL (Subsidized and Unsubsidized Stafford, PLUS), Perkins, college/university, alternative loans.
WORK-STUDY *Federal work-study:* Total amount: $1,447,000; 1,064 jobs averaging $1328. *State or other work-study/employment:* Total amount: $20,000 (100% non-need-based). Part-time jobs available.
APPLYING FOR FINANCIAL AID *Required financial aid forms:* FAFSA, institution's own form, state aid form, noncustodial (divorced/separated) parent's statement, business/farm supplement. *Financial aid deadline:* Continuous. *Notification date:* Continuous beginning 2/15. Students must reply by 5/1 or within 2 weeks of notification.
CONTACT Mr. Earl Pierce, Director of Financial Aid, Alfred University, Alumni Hall, One Saxon Drive, Alfred, NY 14802-1205, 607-871-2159 or toll-free 800-541-9229. *Fax:* 607-871-2252. *E-mail:* pierce@alfred.edu.

ALICE LLOYD COLLEGE
Pippa Passes, KY

Tuition & fees: $1150   Average undergraduate aid package: $8678

ABOUT THE INSTITUTION Independent, coed. Awards: bachelor's degrees. 14 undergraduate majors. Total enrollment: 593. Undergraduates: 593. Freshmen: 175. Federal methodology is used as a basis for awarding need-based institutional aid.
UNDERGRADUATE EXPENSES for 2005–06 includes mandatory fees ($1150) and room and board ($3750). *College room only:* $1730. *Part-time tuition:* $212 per credit hour. Full-time students in the 108-county service area are granted guaranteed tuition. *Payment plan:* Deferred payment.
FRESHMAN FINANCIAL AID (Fall 2005, est.) 188 applied for aid; of those 54% were deemed to have need. 100% of freshmen with need received aid; of those 40% had need fully met. *Average percent of need met:* 65% (excluding resources awarded to replace EFC). *Average financial aid package:* $9143 (excluding resources awarded to replace EFC). 46% of all full-time freshmen had no need and received non-need-based gift aid.
UNDERGRADUATE FINANCIAL AID (Fall 2005, est.) 589 applied for aid; of those 54% were deemed to have need. 100% of undergraduates with need received aid; of those 31% had need fully met. *Average percent of need met:* 60% (excluding resources awarded to replace EFC). *Average financial aid package:* $8678 (excluding resources awarded to replace EFC). 41% of all full-time undergraduates had no need and received non-need-based gift aid.
GIFT AID (NEED-BASED) *Total amount:* $2,484,170 (40% federal, 44% state, 16% institutional). *Receiving aid:* Freshmen: 54% (101); All full-time undergraduates: 54% (318). *Average award:* Freshmen: $7543; Undergraduates: $7087. *Scholarships, grants, and awards:* Federal Pell, FSEOG, state, private, college/university gift aid from institutional funds.
GIFT AID (NON-NEED-BASED) *Total amount:* $1,516,120 (39% state, 60% institutional, 1% external sources). *Receiving aid:* Undergraduates: 54% (318). *Average Award:* Freshmen: $4712; Undergraduates: $4970. *Scholarships, grants, and awards by category:* Special Achievements/Activities: 31 awards ($226,850 total): general special achievements/activities. Special Characteristics: 15 awards ($57,765 total): members of minority groups. *Tuition waivers:* Full or partial for minority students, employees or children of employees.
LOANS *Student loans:* $277,000 (51% need-based, 49% non-need-based). 56% of past graduating class borrowed through all loan programs. *Average indebtedness per student:* $3495. *Average need-based loan:* Freshmen: $308; Undergraduates: $501. *Parent loans:* $54,000 (100% non-need-based). *Programs:* FFEL (Subsidized and Unsubsidized Stafford, PLUS), college/university, Bagby Loans (for freshmen).
WORK-STUDY *Federal work-study:* Total amount: $710,000; 402 jobs averaging $1600. *State or other work-study/employment:* Total amount: $400,000 (100% non-need-based). 241 part-time jobs averaging $1591.
ATHLETIC AWARDS Total amount: $226,000 (100% non-need-based).
APPLYING FOR FINANCIAL AID *Required financial aid form:* FAFSA. *Financial aid deadline (priority):* 3/15. *Notification date:* Continuous beginning 4/15.
CONTACT Ms. Nancy M. Melton, Director of Financial Aid, Alice Lloyd College, 100 Purpose Road, Pippa Passes, KY 41844, 606-368-6059. *E-mail:* nancymelton@alc.edu.

ALLEGHENY COLLEGE
Meadville, PA

Tuition & fees: $28,300   Average undergraduate aid package: $21,250

ABOUT THE INSTITUTION Independent, coed. Awards: bachelor's degrees. 47 undergraduate majors. Total enrollment: 2,053. Undergraduates: 2,053. Freshmen: 564. Federal methodology is used as a basis for awarding need-based institutional aid.
UNDERGRADUATE EXPENSES for 2006–07 *Application fee:* $35. *Comprehensive fee:* $35,300 includes full-time tuition ($28,000), mandatory fees ($300), and room and board ($7000). *College room only:* $3600. *Part-time tuition:* $1167 per credit hour. *Part-time fees:* $150 per term.
FRESHMAN FINANCIAL AID (Fall 2005, est.) 478 applied for aid; of those 83% were deemed to have need. 100% of freshmen with need received aid; of those 52% had need fully met. *Average percent of need met:* 94% (excluding resources awarded to replace EFC). *Average financial aid package:* $21,575 (excluding resources awarded to replace EFC). 28% of all full-time freshmen had no need and received non-need-based gift aid.
UNDERGRADUATE FINANCIAL AID (Fall 2005, est.) 1,584 applied for aid; of those 86% were deemed to have need. 100% of undergraduates with need received aid; of those 45% had need fully met. *Average percent of need met:* 92% (excluding resources awarded to replace EFC). *Average financial aid package:* $21,250 (excluding resources awarded to replace EFC). 28% of all full-time undergraduates had no need and received non-need-based gift aid.
GIFT AID (NEED-BASED) *Total amount:* $19,880,835 (5% federal, 11% state, 80% institutional, 4% external sources). *Receiving aid:* Freshmen: 70% (395); All full-time undergraduates: 68% (1,361). *Average award:* Freshmen: $15,625; Undergraduates: $14,950. *Scholarships, grants, and awards:* Federal Pell, FSEOG, state, private, college/university gift aid from institutional funds.
GIFT AID (NON-NEED-BASED) *Total amount:* $7,624,254 (94% institutional, 6% external sources). *Receiving aid:* Freshmen: 18% (99); Undergraduates: 13% (267). *Average Award:* Freshmen: $10,835; Undergraduates: $10,635. *Scholarships, grants, and awards by category:* Academic Interests/Achievement: 1,593 awards ($18,043,842 total): general academic interests/achievements. Special Characteristics: 72 awards ($1,297,575 total): adult students, children of educators, children of faculty/staff, international students.
LOANS *Student loans:* $11,787,419 (43% need-based, 57% non-need-based). 78% of past graduating class borrowed through all loan programs. *Average indebtedness per student:* $24,825. *Average need-based loan:* Freshmen: $4360; Undergraduates: $4720. *Parent loans:* $3,212,296 (100% non-need-based). *Programs:* FFEL (Subsidized and Unsubsidized Stafford, PLUS), Perkins, private loans from commercial lenders.
WORK-STUDY *Federal work-study:* Total amount: $1,654,620; 1,041 jobs averaging $1590. *State or other work-study/employment:* Total amount: $645,582 (100% non-need-based). 384 part-time jobs averaging $1680.
APPLYING FOR FINANCIAL AID *Required financial aid form:* FAFSA. *Financial aid deadline (priority):* 2/15. *Notification date:* Continuous beginning 3/1. Students must reply by 5/1 or within 4 weeks of notification.
CONTACT Ms. Sheryle Proper, Director of Financial Aid, Allegheny College, 520 North Main Street, Meadville, PA 16335, 814-332-2701 or toll-free 800-521-5293. *Fax:* 814-337-0431. *E-mail:* fao@allegheny.edu.

ALLEGHENY WESLEYAN COLLEGE
Salem, OH

CONTACT Financial Aid Office, Allegheny Wesleyan College, 2161 Woodsdale Road, Salem, OH 44460, 330-337-6403 or toll-free 800-292-3153.

ALLEN COLLEGE
Waterloo, IA

Tuition & fees: $13,472   Average undergraduate aid package: $7580

ABOUT THE INSTITUTION Independent, coed, primarily women. Awards: associate, bachelor's, and master's degrees (liberal arts and general education courses

offered at either University of North Iowa or Wartburg College). 2 undergraduate majors. Total enrollment: 404. Undergraduates: 374. Freshmen: 18. Federal methodology is used as a basis for awarding need-based institutional aid.
UNDERGRADUATE EXPENSES for 2006–07 *Application fee:* $50. *Comprehensive fee:* $19,184 includes full-time tuition ($11,958), mandatory fees ($1514), and room and board ($5712). *College room only:* $2666. *Part-time tuition:* $415 per credit hour. *Part-time fees:* $37 per credit hour; $170 per term.
GIFT AID (NEED-BASED) *Total amount:* $757,372 (33% federal, 57% state, 10% institutional). *Receiving aid:* Freshmen: 67% (22); All full-time undergraduates: 57% (157). *Average award:* Freshmen: $3113; Undergraduates: $4528. *Scholarships, grants, and awards:* Federal Pell, FSEOG, state, private, college/university gift aid from institutional funds, Federal Nursing, Federal Scholarships for Disadvantaged Students.
GIFT AID (NON-NEED-BASED) *Total amount:* $17,877 (52% institutional, 48% external sources). *Average Award:* Freshmen: $397; Undergraduates: $1153. *Scholarships, grants, and awards by category: Academic Interests/Achievement:* 20 awards ($12,101 total): health fields. *Special Achievements/Activities:* community service, general special achievements/activities, leadership. *Special Characteristics:* local/state students, members of minority groups, out-of-state students. *ROTC:* Army cooperative.
LOANS *Student loans:* $1,766,240 (57% need-based, 43% non-need-based). 86% of past graduating class borrowed through all loan programs. *Average indebtedness per student:* $21,383. *Average need-based loan:* Freshmen: $1849; Undergraduates: $3491. *Parent loans:* $455,835 (29% need-based, 71% non-need-based). *Programs:* Federal Direct (Subsidized and Unsubsidized Stafford, PLUS), Perkins, Federal Nursing, state, college/university.
APPLYING FOR FINANCIAL AID *Required financial aid forms:* FAFSA, institution's own form. *Financial aid deadline:* Continuous. *Notification date:* Continuous beginning 4/1.
CONTACT Kathie S. Walters, Financial Aid Director, Allen College, Barrett Forum, 1825 Logan Avenue, Waterloo, IA 50703, 319-226-2003. *Fax:* 319-226-2051. *E-mail:* walterks@ihs.org.

ALLEN UNIVERSITY
Columbia, SC

CONTACT Ms. Donna Foster, Director of Financial Aid, Allen University, 1530 Harden Street, Columbia, SC 29204-1085, 803-376-5736 or toll-free 877-625-5368 (in-state). *E-mail:* donnaf@allenuniversity.edu.

ALLIANT INTERNATIONAL UNIVERSITY
San Diego, CA

Tuition & fees: $14,370 **Average undergraduate aid package: $21,250**

ABOUT THE INSTITUTION Independent, coed. Awards: bachelor's, master's, and doctoral degrees and post-bachelor's certificates. 10 undergraduate majors. Total enrollment: 3,487. Undergraduates: 254. Freshmen: 21. Federal methodology is used as a basis for awarding need-based institutional aid.
UNDERGRADUATE EXPENSES for 2006–07 *Application fee:* $45. *Comprehensive fee:* $22,170 includes full-time tuition ($14,000), mandatory fees ($370), and room and board ($7800). *Part-time tuition:* $515 per unit.
FRESHMAN FINANCIAL AID (Fall 2005, est.) 67 applied for aid; of those 82% were deemed to have need. 100% of freshmen with need received aid; of those 29% had need fully met. *Average percent of need met:* 80% (excluding resources awarded to replace EFC). *Average financial aid package:* $21,250 (excluding resources awarded to replace EFC). 21% of all full-time freshmen had no need and received non-need-based gift aid.
UNDERGRADUATE FINANCIAL AID (Fall 2005, est.) 266 applied for aid; of those 67% were deemed to have need. 100% of undergraduates with need received aid; of those 27% had need fully met. *Average percent of need met:* 80% (excluding resources awarded to replace EFC). *Average financial aid package:* $21,250 (excluding resources awarded to replace EFC). 18% of all full-time undergraduates had no need and received non-need-based gift aid.
GIFT AID (NEED-BASED) *Total amount:* $797,597 (53% federal, 47% state). *Receiving aid:* Freshmen: 79% (55); All full-time undergraduates: 62% (179). *Average award:* Freshmen: $6000; Undergraduates: $6000. *Scholarships, grants, and awards:* Federal Pell, FSEOG, state, private, college/university gift aid from institutional funds.

GIFT AID (NON-NEED-BASED) *Total amount:* $1,102,875 (98% institutional, 2% external sources). *Receiving aid:* Freshmen: 79% (55); Undergraduates: 62% (179). *Average Award:* Freshmen: $3500; Undergraduates: $3000. *Scholarships, grants, and awards by category: Academic Interests/Achievement:* business, communication, computer science, education, English, foreign languages, general academic interests/achievements, humanities, international studies, social sciences. *Special Achievements/Activities:* community service, general special achievements/activities, leadership. *Special Characteristics:* children and siblings of alumni, children of current students, children of faculty/staff, ethnic background, international students, local/state students, members of minority groups. *ROTC:* Army cooperative.
LOANS *Student loans:* $809,961 (63% need-based, 37% non-need-based). 67% of past graduating class borrowed through all loan programs. *Average indebtedness per student:* $17,125. *Average need-based loan:* Freshmen: $2625; Undergraduates: $3500. *Parent loans:* $275,444 (100% non-need-based). *Programs:* FFEL (Subsidized and Unsubsidized Stafford, PLUS), Perkins, alternative loans.
WORK-STUDY *Federal work-study:* Total amount: $108,562; 55 jobs averaging $4100. *State or other work-study/employment:* Total amount: $45,255 (100% need-based). 30 part-time jobs averaging $4207.
ATHLETIC AWARDS *Total amount:* $317,520 (100% non-need-based).
APPLYING FOR FINANCIAL AID *Required financial aid form:* FAFSA. *Financial aid deadline (priority):* 3/2. *Notification date:* Continuous beginning 4/1. Students must reply within 3 weeks of notification.
CONTACT Deborah Spindler, Director of Financial Aid, Alliant International University, 10455 Pomerado Road, San Diego, CA 92131-1799, 858-635-4559 Ext. 4700 or toll-free 866-825-5426. *Fax:* 858-635-4848.

ALMA COLLEGE
Alma, MI

Tuition & fees: $21,134 **Average undergraduate aid package: $17,812**

ABOUT THE INSTITUTION Independent Presbyterian, coed. Awards: bachelor's degrees. 69 undergraduate majors. Total enrollment: 1,284. Undergraduates: 1,284. Freshmen: 336. Federal methodology is used as a basis for awarding need-based institutional aid.
UNDERGRADUATE EXPENSES for 2005–06 *Application fee:* $25. *Comprehensive fee:* $28,544 includes full-time tuition ($20,934), mandatory fees ($200), and room and board ($7410). *College room only:* $3650. Room and board charges vary according to board plan and housing facility. *Part-time tuition:* $810 per credit. Part-time tuition and fees vary according to course load. *Payment plans:* Installment, deferred payment.
FRESHMAN FINANCIAL AID (Fall 2005, est.) 336 applied for aid; of those 76% were deemed to have need. 100% of freshmen with need received aid; of those 27% had need fully met. *Average percent of need met:* 85% (excluding resources awarded to replace EFC). *Average financial aid package:* $18,620 (excluding resources awarded to replace EFC). 22% of all full-time freshmen had no need and received non-need-based gift aid.
UNDERGRADUATE FINANCIAL AID (Fall 2005, est.) 1,238 applied for aid; of those 76% were deemed to have need. 100% of undergraduates with need received aid; of those 27% had need fully met. *Average percent of need met:* 84% (excluding resources awarded to replace EFC). *Average financial aid package:* $17,812 (excluding resources awarded to replace EFC). 23% of all full-time undergraduates had no need and received non-need-based gift aid.
GIFT AID (NEED-BASED) *Total amount:* $12,285,516 (7% federal, 15% state, 75% institutional, 3% external sources). *Receiving aid:* Freshmen: 76% (257); All full-time undergraduates: 75% (933). *Average award:* Freshmen: $14,978; Undergraduates: $13,480. *Scholarships, grants, and awards:* Federal Pell, FSEOG, state, private, college/university gift aid from institutional funds.
GIFT AID (NON-NEED-BASED) *Total amount:* $3,201,195 (7% state, 84% institutional, 9% external sources). *Receiving aid:* Freshmen: 11% (38); Undergraduates: 9% (116). *Average Award:* Freshmen: $16,029; Undergraduates: $12,840. *Scholarships, grants, and awards by category: Academic Interests/Achievement:* 254 awards ($2,189,639 total): general academic interests/achievements. *Creative Arts/Performance:* 334 awards ($638,420 total): art/fine arts, dance, music, theater/drama. *Special Achievements/Activities:* 3 awards ($6250 total): leadership. *Special Characteristics:* 268 awards ($872,871 total): children and siblings of alumni, children of faculty/staff, previous college experience. *Tuition waivers:* Full or partial for employees or children of employees. *ROTC:* Army cooperative.

Alma College

LOANS *Student loans:* $6,419,932 (67% need-based, 33% non-need-based). 87% of past graduating class borrowed through all loan programs. *Average indebtedness per student:* $18,947. *Average need-based loan:* Freshmen: $4562; Undergraduates: $5228. *Parent loans:* $2,554,434 (32% need-based, 68% non-need-based). *Programs:* Federal Direct (Subsidized and Unsubsidized Stafford, PLUS), Perkins, state, college/university, alternative loans.
WORK-STUDY *Federal work-study:* Total amount: $173,000; 140 jobs averaging $950. *State or other work-study/employment:* Total amount: $22,000 (100% need-based). 30 part-time jobs averaging $700.
APPLYING FOR FINANCIAL AID *Required financial aid form:* FAFSA. *Financial aid deadline (priority):* 3/1. *Notification date:* Continuous beginning 3/1. Students must reply within 3 weeks of notification.
CONTACT Mr. Christopher A. Brown, Director of Student Financial Assistance, Alma College, 614 West Superior Street, Alma, MI 48801-1599, 989-463-7347 or toll-free 800-321-ALMA. *Fax:* 989-463-7993. *E-mail:* cabrown@alma.edu.

ALVERNIA COLLEGE
Reading, PA

Tuition & fees: $19,089   **Average undergraduate aid package: $12,225**

ABOUT THE INSTITUTION Independent Roman Catholic, coed. Awards: associate, bachelor's, and master's degrees and post-bachelor's and post-master's certificates. 40 undergraduate majors. Total enrollment: 2,735. Undergraduates: 1,996. Freshmen: 277. Federal methodology is used as a basis for awarding need-based institutional aid.
UNDERGRADUATE EXPENSES for 2005–06 *Application fee:* $25. *Comprehensive fee:* $26,388 includes full-time tuition ($18,900), mandatory fees ($189), and room and board ($7299). *College room only:* $3477. Full-time tuition and fees vary according to class time and reciprocity agreements. Room and board charges vary according to board plan and housing facility. *Part-time tuition:* $555 per credit. Part-time tuition and fees vary according to class time and course load. *Payment plan:* Installment.
FRESHMAN FINANCIAL AID (Fall 2005, est.) 269 applied for aid; of those 89% were deemed to have need. 100% of freshmen with need received aid; of those 36% had need fully met. *Average percent of need met:* 84% (excluding resources awarded to replace EFC). *Average financial aid package:* $13,986 (excluding resources awarded to replace EFC). 10% of all full-time freshmen had no need and received non-need-based gift aid.
UNDERGRADUATE FINANCIAL AID (Fall 2005, est.) 1,178 applied for aid; of those 98% were deemed to have need. 100% of undergraduates with need received aid; of those 9% had need fully met. *Average percent of need met:* 79% (excluding resources awarded to replace EFC). *Average financial aid package:* $12,225 (excluding resources awarded to replace EFC). 2% of all full-time undergraduates had no need and received non-need-based gift aid.
GIFT AID (NEED-BASED) *Total amount:* $10,844,818 (16% federal, 14% state, 69% institutional, 1% external sources). *Receiving aid:* Freshmen: 84% (240); All full-time undergraduates: 94% (1,151). *Average award:* Freshmen: $6784; Undergraduates: $6521. *Scholarships, grants, and awards:* Federal Pell, FSEOG, state, private, college/university gift aid from institutional funds.
GIFT AID (NON-NEED-BASED) *Total amount:* $915,357 (2% state, 98% institutional). *Receiving aid:* Freshmen: 1% (2); Undergraduates: 11% (136). *Average Award:* Freshmen: $7800; Undergraduates: $6500. *Scholarships, grants, and awards by category: Academic Interests/Achievement:* 20 awards ($120,000 total): general academic interests/achievements. *Special Achievements/Activities:* 20 awards ($60,000 total): community service, junior miss, leadership, religious involvement. *Special Characteristics:* children and siblings of alumni, children of faculty/staff, international students, local/state students, out-of-state students, previous college experience, religious affiliation, siblings of current students. *Tuition waivers:* Full or partial for employees or children of employees, senior citizens. *ROTC:* Army cooperative.
LOANS *Student loans:* $9,218,608 (80% need-based, 20% non-need-based). 91% of past graduating class borrowed through all loan programs. *Average indebtedness per student:* $6985. *Average need-based loan:* Freshmen: $3496; Undergraduates: $5482. *Parent loans:* $1,261,445 (100% need-based). *Programs:* FFEL (Subsidized and Unsubsidized Stafford, PLUS), Perkins, college/university, Health Professions Loans.
WORK-STUDY *Federal work-study:* Total amount: $682,044; 620 jobs averaging $1950. *State or other work-study/employment:* Total amount: $89,780 (5% need-based, 95% non-need-based). Part-time jobs available.
APPLYING FOR FINANCIAL AID *Required financial aid forms:* FAFSA, state aid form, noncustodial (divorced/separated) parent's statement. *Financial aid deadline:* Continuous. *Notification date:* Continuous beginning 2/10. Students must reply within 2 weeks of notification.
CONTACT Lora Myers, Director of Financial Aid, Alvernia College, 400 St. Bernardine Street, Reading, PA 19607-1799, 610-796-8200 Ext. 1473 or toll-free 888-ALVERNIA (in-state). *Fax:* 610-796-8336. *E-mail:* bra.myers@alvernia.edu.

ALVERNO COLLEGE
Milwaukee, WI

Tuition & fees: $15,418   **Average undergraduate aid package: N/A**

ABOUT THE INSTITUTION Independent Roman Catholic, undergraduate: women only; graduate: coed. Awards: associate, bachelor's, and master's degrees and post-bachelor's certificates (also offers weekend program with significant enrollment not reflected in profile). 42 undergraduate majors. Total enrollment: 2,372. Undergraduates: 2,176. Freshmen: 280. Federal methodology is used as a basis for awarding need-based institutional aid.
UNDERGRADUATE EXPENSES for 2005–06 *Application fee:* $20. *Comprehensive fee:* $21,628 includes full-time tuition ($15,168), mandatory fees ($250), and room and board ($6210). *College room only:* $2100. Full-time tuition and fees vary according to class time and program. Room and board charges vary according to board plan and housing facility. *Part-time tuition:* $632 per credit. *Part-time fees:* $125 per term. Part-time tuition and fees vary according to class time and program. *Payment plans:* Installment, deferred payment.
GIFT AID (NEED-BASED) *Total amount:* $10,836,574 (30% federal, 24% state, 46% institutional). *Scholarships, grants, and awards:* Federal Pell, FSEOG, state, private, college/university gift aid from institutional funds, transfer student scholarships.
GIFT AID (NON-NEED-BASED) *Total amount:* $308,638 (100% external sources). *Scholarships, grants, and awards by category: Academic Interests/Achievement:* general academic interests/achievements. *Creative Arts/Performance:* art/fine arts, music. *Special Achievements/Activities:* community service. *Special Characteristics:* children and siblings of alumni. *Tuition waivers:* Full or partial for employees or children of employees. *ROTC:* Army cooperative, Air Force cooperative.
LOANS *Student loans:* $12,417,942 (52% need-based, 48% non-need-based). *Parent loans:* $519,836 (100% non-need-based). *Programs:* FFEL (Subsidized and Unsubsidized Stafford, PLUS), Perkins, Federal Nursing.
WORK-STUDY *Federal work-study:* Total amount: $211,495; 148 jobs averaging $1429.
APPLYING FOR FINANCIAL AID *Required financial aid forms:* FAFSA, institution's own form, business/farm supplement, income tax forms. *Financial aid deadline (priority):* 4/1. *Notification date:* Continuous beginning 4/15. Students must reply within 2 weeks of notification.
CONTACT Mark Levine, Director of Financial Aid, Alverno College, 3400 South 43rd Street, PO Box 343922, Milwaukee, WI 53234-3922, 414-382-6046 or toll-free 800-933-3401. *Fax:* 414-382-6354. *E-mail:* mark.levine@alverno.edu.

AMERICAN ACADEMY OF ART
Chicago, IL

CONTACT Ms. Ione Fitzgerald, Director of Financial Aid, American Academy of Art, 332 South Michigan Avenue, Suite 300, Chicago, IL 60604, 312-461-0600. *Fax:* 312-294-9570.

AMERICAN BAPTIST COLLEGE OF AMERICAN BAPTIST THEOLOGICAL SEMINARY
Nashville, TN

Tuition & fees: $4172   **Average undergraduate aid package: $2025**

ABOUT THE INSTITUTION Independent Baptist, coed. Awards: associate and bachelor's degrees. 2 undergraduate majors. Total enrollment: 112. Undergraduates: 112. Freshmen: 10. Federal methodology is used as a basis for awarding need-based institutional aid.

UNDERGRADUATE EXPENSES for 2005–06 *Application fee:* $20. *Tuition:* full-time $4032; part-time $168 per credit hour. *Required fees:* full-time $140; $140 per term part-time. Full-time tuition and fees vary according to course load. Part-time tuition and fees vary according to course load. Room and board charges vary according to housing facility. *Payment plan:* Deferred payment.
FRESHMAN FINANCIAL AID (Fall 2005, est.) 5 applied for aid; of those 100% were deemed to have need. 100% of freshmen with need received aid. *Average percent of need met:* 80% (excluding resources awarded to replace EFC). *Average financial aid package:* $2025 (excluding resources awarded to replace EFC).
UNDERGRADUATE FINANCIAL AID (Fall 2005, est.) 52 applied for aid; of those 100% were deemed to have need. 92% of undergraduates with need received aid. *Average percent of need met:* 80% (excluding resources awarded to replace EFC). *Average financial aid package:* $2025 (excluding resources awarded to replace EFC).
GIFT AID (NEED-BASED) *Total amount:* $255,377 (62% federal, 13% state, 25% external sources). *Receiving aid:* Freshmen: 71% (5); All full-time undergraduates: 20% (13). *Average award:* Freshmen: $1161; Undergraduates: $1161. *Scholarships, grants, and awards:* Federal Pell, FSEOG, state.
GIFT AID (NON-NEED-BASED) *Receiving aid:* Freshmen: 14% (1); Undergraduates: 3% (2). *Scholarships, grants, and awards by category: Special Characteristics:* religious affiliation.
WORK-STUDY *Federal work-study:* Total amount: $7391; 2 jobs averaging $3695.
APPLYING FOR FINANCIAL AID *Required financial aid form:* FAFSA. *Financial aid deadline:* 7/23 (priority: 1/1). *Notification date:* Continuous beginning 7/30. Students must reply by 8/1 or within 2 weeks of notification.
CONTACT Marcella Lockhart, Executive Assistant for Administrator, American Baptist College of American Baptist Theological Seminary, 1800 Baptist World Center Drive, Nashville, TN 37207, 615-256-1463 Ext. 2227. *Fax:* 615-226-7855. *E-mail:* mlockhart@abcnash.edu.

AMERICAN INDIAN COLLEGE OF THE ASSEMBLIES OF GOD, INC.
Phoenix, AZ

CONTACT Office of Student Financial Aid, American Indian College of the Assemblies of God, Inc., 10020 North Fifteenth Avenue, Phoenix, AZ 85021-2199, 800-933-3828.

AMERICAN INTERCONTINENTAL UNIVERSITY
Los Angeles, CA

CONTACT Mr. Joe Johnson, Director of Financial Aid, American InterContinental University, 12655 West Jefferson Boulevard, Los Angeles, CA 90066, 310-302-2000 Ext. 2447 or toll-free 800-333-2652 (out-of-state). *Fax:* 310-302-2002.

AMERICAN INTERCONTINENTAL UNIVERSITY
Weston, FL

CONTACT Financial Aid Office, American InterContinental University, 2250 North Commerce Parkway, Suite 100, Weston, FL 33326, 954-446-6100 or toll-free 866-248-4723 (out-of-state).

AMERICAN INTERCONTINENTAL UNIVERSITY
Atlanta, GA

CONTACT Sherry Rizzi, Financial Aid Director, American InterContinental University, 3330 Peachtree Road NE, Atlanta, GA 30326, 404-965-5796 or toll-free 888-999-4248 (out-of-state). *Fax:* 404-965-5704.

AMERICAN INTERCONTINENTAL UNIVERSITY
Atlanta, GA

CONTACT Financial Aid Office, American InterContinental University, 6600 Peachtree-Dunwoody Road, 500 Embassy Row, Atlanta, GA 30328, 404-965-6500 or toll-free 800-255-6839.

AMERICAN INTERCONTINENTAL UNIVERSITY
Houston, TX

CONTACT Financial Aid Office, American InterContinental University, 9999 Richmond Avenue, Houston, TX 77042, 832-242-5788.

AMERICAN INTERCONTINENTAL UNIVERSITY ONLINE
Hoffman Estates, IL

CONTACT Financial Aid Office, American InterContinental University Online, 5550 Prairie Stone Parkway, Suite 400, Hoffman Estates, IL 60192, 847-851-5000 or toll-free 877-701-3800.

AMERICAN INTERNATIONAL COLLEGE
Springfield, MA

Tuition & fees: $20,990   Average undergraduate aid package: $20,200

ABOUT THE INSTITUTION Independent, coed. Awards: associate, bachelor's, master's, and doctoral degrees and post-bachelor's and post-master's certificates. 45 undergraduate majors. Total enrollment: 1,815. Undergraduates: 1,398. Freshmen: 331. Federal methodology is used as a basis for awarding need-based institutional aid.
UNDERGRADUATE EXPENSES for 2006–07 *Application fee:* $20. *Comprehensive fee:* $30,260 includes full-time tuition ($20,990) and room and board ($9270). *Part-time tuition:* $470 per credit.
FRESHMAN FINANCIAL AID (Fall 2005, est.) 331 applied for aid; of those 99% were deemed to have need. 100% of freshmen with need received aid; of those 17% had need fully met. *Average percent of need met:* 85% (excluding resources awarded to replace EFC). *Average financial aid package:* $21,668 (excluding resources awarded to replace EFC). 13% of all full-time freshmen had no need and received non-need-based gift aid.
UNDERGRADUATE FINANCIAL AID (Fall 2005, est.) 1,214 applied for aid; of those 92% were deemed to have need. 98% of undergraduates with need received aid; of those 22% had need fully met. *Average percent of need met:* 82% (excluding resources awarded to replace EFC). *Average financial aid package:* $20,200 (excluding resources awarded to replace EFC). 15% of all full-time undergraduates had no need and received non-need-based gift aid.
GIFT AID (NEED-BASED) *Total amount:* $9,571,124 (17% federal, 5% state, 76% institutional, 2% external sources). *Receiving aid:* Freshmen: 94% (311); All full-time undergraduates: 72% (872). *Average award:* Freshmen: $12,821; Undergraduates: $10,813. *Scholarships, grants, and awards:* Federal Pell, FSEOG, state, private, college/university gift aid from institutional funds.
GIFT AID (NON-NEED-BASED) *Receiving aid:* Freshmen: 85% (281); Undergraduates: 78% (945). *Average Award:* Freshmen: $7499; Undergraduates: $6741. *Scholarships, grants, and awards by category: Academic Interests/Achievement:* 501 awards ($7,296,569 total): general academic interests/achievements. *Special Achievements/Activities:* 10 awards ($66,000 total): general special achievements/activities. *ROTC:* Army cooperative, Air Force cooperative.
LOANS *Student loans:* $9,460,270 (53% need-based, 47% non-need-based). 85% of past graduating class borrowed through all loan programs. *Average indebtedness per student:* $29,700. *Average need-based loan:* Freshmen: $3758; Undergraduates: $4653. *Parent loans:* $1,546,190 (100% need-based). *Programs:* FFEL (Subsidized and Unsubsidized Stafford, PLUS), Perkins, state, college/university, alternative loans.
WORK-STUDY *Federal work-study:* Total amount: $666,400; 277 jobs averaging $2400. *State or other work-study/employment:* Total amount: $295,000 (100% non-need-based). 123 part-time jobs averaging $2400.

American International College

ATHLETIC AWARDS *Total amount:* $2,136,501 (100% need-based).

APPLYING FOR FINANCIAL AID *Required financial aid form:* FAFSA. *Financial aid deadline (priority):* 5/1. *Notification date:* Continuous beginning 3/15. Students must reply within 2 weeks of notification.

CONTACT Ms. Irene D. Martin, Director of Financial Aid, American International College, 1000 State Street, Springfield, MA 01109-3189, 413-205-3259. *Fax:* 413-205-3912. *E-mail:* finaid@aic.edu.

AMERICAN UNIVERSITY
Washington, DC

Tuition & fees: $29,701   Average undergraduate aid package: $26,453

ABOUT THE INSTITUTION Independent Methodist, coed. Awards: associate, bachelor's, master's, doctoral, and first professional degrees and post-bachelor's certificates. 53 undergraduate majors. Total enrollment: 11,279. Undergraduates: 5,921. Freshmen: 1,223. Both federal and institutional methodology are used as a basis for awarding need-based institutional aid.

UNDERGRADUATE EXPENSES for 2006–07 *Application fee:* $45. *Comprehensive fee:* $41,043 includes full-time tuition ($29,205), mandatory fees ($496), and room and board ($11,342). *College room only:* $7197. *Part-time tuition:* $973 per semester hour. *Part-time fees:* $159 per year.

FRESHMAN FINANCIAL AID (Fall 2005, est.) 911 applied for aid; of those 69% were deemed to have need. 100% of freshmen with need received aid; of those 49% had need fully met. *Average percent of need met:* 68% (excluding resources awarded to replace EFC). *Average financial aid package:* $24,350 (excluding resources awarded to replace EFC). 22% of all full-time freshmen had no need and received non-need-based gift aid.

UNDERGRADUATE FINANCIAL AID (Fall 2005, est.) 3,460 applied for aid; of those 82% were deemed to have need. 97% of undergraduates with need received aid; of those 51% had need fully met. *Average percent of need met:* 75% (excluding resources awarded to replace EFC). *Average financial aid package:* $26,453 (excluding resources awarded to replace EFC). 13% of all full-time undergraduates had no need and received non-need-based gift aid.

GIFT AID (NEED-BASED) *Total amount:* $31,944,276 (11% federal, 84% institutional, 5% external sources). *Receiving aid:* Freshmen: 39% (481); All full-time undergraduates: 37% (2,212). *Average award:* Freshmen: $13,745; Undergraduates: $13,534. *Scholarships, grants, and awards:* Federal Pell, FSEOG, state, private, college/university gift aid from institutional funds.

GIFT AID (NON-NEED-BASED) *Total amount:* $20,664,791 (100% institutional). *Receiving aid:* Freshmen: 14% (170); Undergraduates: 10% (610). *Average Award:* Freshmen: $16,046; Undergraduates: $15,708. *Scholarships, grants, and awards by category: Academic Interests/Achievement:* general academic interests/achievements. *Creative Arts/Performance:* general creative arts/performance. *Special Achievements/Activities:* general special achievements/activities, leadership, memberships. *Special Characteristics:* adult students, children and siblings of alumni, children of faculty/staff, ethnic background, first-generation college students, local/state students, members of minority groups, previous college experience, relatives of clergy, spouses of current students. *ROTC:* Army cooperative, Air Force cooperative.

LOANS *Student loans:* $36,623,971 (59% need-based, 41% non-need-based). 50% of past graduating class borrowed through all loan programs. *Average indebtedness per student:* $19,766. *Average need-based loan:* Freshmen: $5784; Undergraduates: $8191. *Parent loans:* $11,694,688 (100% non-need-based). *Programs:* Federal Direct (Subsidized and Unsubsidized Stafford, PLUS), FFEL (PLUS), Perkins, college/university.

WORK-STUDY *Federal work-study:* Total amount: $4,080,467; 2,169 jobs averaging $2016.

ATHLETIC AWARDS *Total amount:* $2,975,566 (100% non-need-based).

APPLYING FOR FINANCIAL AID *Required financial aid forms:* FAFSA, institution's own form. *Financial aid deadline:* 2/15. *Notification date:* 4/1. Students must reply by 5/1 or within 4 weeks of notification.

CONTACT Brian Lee Sang, Office of Enrollment, American University, 4400 Massachusetts Avenue, NW, Washington, DC 20016-8001, 202-885-6100. *Fax:* 202-885-1025. *E-mail:* financialaid@american.edu.

AMERICAN UNIVERSITY OF PUERTO RICO
Bayamón, PR

ABOUT THE INSTITUTION Independent, coed. Awards: associate and bachelor's degrees. 9 undergraduate majors. Total enrollment: 3,691. Undergraduates: 3,691.

GIFT AID (NEED-BASED) *Scholarships, grants, and awards:* Federal Pell, FSEOG, state, college/university gift aid from institutional funds.

LOANS *Programs:* Federal Direct (Subsidized and Unsubsidized Stafford, PLUS).

WORK-STUDY *Federal work-study:* Total amount: $352,896; jobs available.

APPLYING FOR FINANCIAL AID *Required financial aid forms:* FAFSA, institution's own form.

CONTACT Mr. Yahaira Melendez, Financial Aid Director, American University of Puerto Rico, PO Box 2037, Bayamón, PR 00960-2037, 787-620-2040 Ext. 2031. *Fax:* 787-785-7377. *E-mail:* melendezy@aupr.edu.

AMHERST COLLEGE
Amherst, MA

Tuition & fees: $33,005   Average undergraduate aid package: $31,048

ABOUT THE INSTITUTION Independent, coed. Awards: bachelor's degrees. 36 undergraduate majors. Total enrollment: 1,623. Undergraduates: 1,623. Freshmen: 431. Institutional methodology is used as a basis for awarding need-based institutional aid.

UNDERGRADUATE EXPENSES for 2005–06 *Application fee:* $55. *Comprehensive fee:* $41,590 includes full-time tuition ($32,395), mandatory fees ($610), and room and board ($8585). *College room only:* $4600. *Payment plans:* Installment, deferred payment.

FRESHMAN FINANCIAL AID (Fall 2005, est.) 247 applied for aid; of those 81% were deemed to have need. 100% of freshmen with need received aid; of those 100% had need fully met. *Average percent of need met:* 100% (excluding resources awarded to replace EFC). *Average financial aid package:* $32,333 (excluding resources awarded to replace EFC).

UNDERGRADUATE FINANCIAL AID (Fall 2005, est.) 947 applied for aid; of those 81% were deemed to have need. 100% of undergraduates with need received aid; of those 100% had need fully met. *Average percent of need met:* 100% (excluding resources awarded to replace EFC). *Average financial aid package:* $31,048 (excluding resources awarded to replace EFC).

GIFT AID (NEED-BASED) *Total amount:* $22,141,112 (4% federal, 93% institutional, 3% external sources). *Receiving aid:* Freshmen: 46% (193); All full-time undergraduates: 46% (743). *Average award:* Freshmen: $29,373; Undergraduates: $28,713. *Scholarships, grants, and awards:* Federal Pell, FSEOG, state, private, college/university gift aid from institutional funds, United Negro College Fund.

GIFT AID (NON-NEED-BASED) *Total amount:* $1,503,704 (4% federal, 2% state, 94% external sources). *Receiving aid:* Freshmen: 20% (85); Undergraduates: 11% (175).

LOANS *Student loans:* $2,360,216 (67% need-based, 33% non-need-based). 47% of past graduating class borrowed through all loan programs. *Average indebtedness per student:* $12,109. *Average need-based loan:* Freshmen: $1620; Undergraduates: $2935. *Parent loans:* $2,599,712 (100% non-need-based). *Programs:* Federal Direct (Subsidized and Unsubsidized Stafford, PLUS, Perkins, college/university.

WORK-STUDY *Federal work-study:* Total amount: $811,954; jobs available. *State or other work-study/employment:* Total amount: $234,024 (100% need-based). Part-time jobs available.

APPLYING FOR FINANCIAL AID *Required financial aid forms:* FAFSA, CSS Financial Aid PROFILE, noncustodial (divorced/separated) parent's statement, income tax form(s), W-2 forms. *Financial aid deadline (priority):* 2/15. *Notification date:* 4/1. Students must reply by 5/1.

CONTACT Joe Paul Case, Dean/Director of Financial Aid, Amherst College, 202 Converse Hall, PO Box 5000, Amherst, MA 01002-5000, 413-542-2296. *Fax:* 413-542-2628. *E-mail:* finaid@amherst.edu.

ANDERSON UNIVERSITY
Anderson, IN

ABOUT THE INSTITUTION Independent religious, coed. Awards: associate, bachelor's, master's, doctoral, and first professional degrees. 58 undergraduate majors. Total enrollment: 2,811. Undergraduates: 2,337. Freshmen: 582.
GIFT AID (NEED-BASED) *Scholarships, grants, and awards:* Federal Pell, FSEOG, state, private, college/university gift aid from institutional funds.
GIFT AID (NON-NEED-BASED) *Scholarships, grants, and awards by category: Academic Interests/Achievement:* general academic interests/achievements. *Creative Arts/Performance:* art/fine arts, music. *Special Achievements/Activities:* leadership. *Special Characteristics:* adult students, children of faculty/staff, international students, relatives of clergy.
LOANS *Programs:* FFEL (Subsidized and Unsubsidized Stafford, PLUS), Perkins, GATE Loans.
WORK-STUDY *Federal work-study:* Total amount: $2,314,444; 1,048 jobs averaging $2208. *State or other work-study/employment:* Part-time jobs available.
APPLYING FOR FINANCIAL AID *Required financial aid form:* FAFSA.
CONTACT Mr. Kenneth Nieman, Director of Student Financial Services, Anderson University, 1100 East Fifth Street, Anderson, IN 46012-3495, 765-641-4180 or toll-free 800-421-3014 (in-state), 800-428-6414 (out-of-state). *Fax:* 765-641-3831. *E-mail:* kfnieman@anderson.edu.

ANDERSON UNIVERSITY
Anderson, SC

Tuition & fees: $16,550	Average undergraduate aid package: $15,834

ABOUT THE INSTITUTION Independent Baptist, coed. Awards: bachelor's and master's degrees. 46 undergraduate majors. Total enrollment: 1,644. Undergraduates: 1,644. Freshmen: 371. Federal methodology is used as a basis for awarding need-based institutional aid.
UNDERGRADUATE EXPENSES for 2006–07 *Application fee:* $25. *Comprehensive fee:* $22,950 includes full-time tuition ($15,400), mandatory fees ($1150), and room and board ($6400). *College room only:* $3250. *Part-time tuition:* $410 per credit hour.
FRESHMAN FINANCIAL AID (Fall 2005, est.) 362 applied for aid; of those 89% were deemed to have need. 100% of freshmen with need received aid; of those 30% had need fully met. *Average percent of need met:* 64% (excluding resources awarded to replace EFC). *Average financial aid package:* $16,985 (excluding resources awarded to replace EFC). 10% of all full-time freshmen had no need and received non-need-based gift aid.
UNDERGRADUATE FINANCIAL AID (Fall 2005, est.) 1,228 applied for aid; of those 90% were deemed to have need. 99% of undergraduates with need received aid; of those 29% had need fully met. *Average percent of need met:* 66% (excluding resources awarded to replace EFC). *Average financial aid package:* $15,834 (excluding resources awarded to replace EFC). 8% of all full-time undergraduates had no need and received non-need-based gift aid.
GIFT AID (NEED-BASED) *Total amount:* $8,423,467 (17% federal, 22% state, 61% institutional). *Receiving aid:* Freshmen: 87% (319); All full-time undergraduates: 83% (1,056). *Average award:* Freshmen: $8098; Undergraduates: $7160. *Scholarships, grants, and awards:* Federal Pell, FSEOG, state, college/university gift aid from institutional funds.
GIFT AID (NON-NEED-BASED) *Total amount:* $3,090,365 (100% state). *Receiving aid:* Freshmen: 78% (288); Undergraduates: 56% (719). *Average Award:* Freshmen: $5772; Undergraduates: $5652. *ROTC:* Army cooperative, Air Force cooperative.
LOANS *Student loans:* $3,382,574 (89% need-based, 11% non-need-based). 76% of past graduating class borrowed through all loan programs. *Average indebtedness per student:* $15,125. *Average need-based loan:* Freshmen: $3608; Undergraduates: $4596. *Parent loans:* $3,284,030 (100% need-based). *Programs:* FFEL (Subsidized and Unsubsidized Stafford, PLUS), Perkins.
WORK-STUDY *Federal work-study:* Total amount: $234,672; 127 jobs averaging $1662. *State or other work-study/employment:* Part-time jobs available.
ATHLETIC AWARDS Total amount: $888,509 (100% non-need-based).
APPLYING FOR FINANCIAL AID *Required financial aid form:* FAFSA. *Financial aid deadline:* 7/30 (priority: 3/1). *Notification date:* Continuous beginning 3/15. Students must reply within 2 weeks of notification.

CONTACT Jeff Holliday, Director of Financial Aid, Anderson University, 316 Boulevard, Anderson, SC 29621-4035, 864-231-2070 or toll-free 800-542-3594. *Fax:* 864-231-2008. *E-mail:* jholliday@ac.edu.

ANDREWS UNIVERSITY
Berrien Springs, MI

Tuition & fees: $16,506	Average undergraduate aid package: $21,103

ABOUT THE INSTITUTION Independent Seventh-day Adventist, coed. Awards: associate, bachelor's, master's, doctoral, and first professional degrees and post-master's certificates. 82 undergraduate majors. Total enrollment: 3,087. Undergraduates: 1,726. Freshmen: 305. Federal methodology is used as a basis for awarding need-based institutional aid.
UNDERGRADUATE EXPENSES for 2005–06 *Application fee:* $30. *Comprehensive fee:* $21,786 includes full-time tuition ($16,030), mandatory fees ($476), and room and board ($5280). *College room only:* $2850. Full-time tuition and fees vary according to course load. Room and board charges vary according to board plan. *Part-time tuition:* $670 per credit hour. Part-time tuition and fees vary according to course load. *Payment plan:* Installment.
FRESHMAN FINANCIAL AID (Fall 2005, est.) 305 applied for aid; of those 66% were deemed to have need. 100% of freshmen with need received aid; of those 40% had need fully met. *Average percent of need met:* 100% (excluding resources awarded to replace EFC). *Average financial aid package:* $18,990 (excluding resources awarded to replace EFC). 33% of all full-time freshmen had no need and received non-need-based gift aid.
UNDERGRADUATE FINANCIAL AID (Fall 2005, est.) 1,542 applied for aid; of those 65% were deemed to have need. 100% of undergraduates with need received aid; of those 47% had need fully met. *Average percent of need met:* 98% (excluding resources awarded to replace EFC). *Average financial aid package:* $21,103 (excluding resources awarded to replace EFC). 33% of all full-time undergraduates had no need and received non-need-based gift aid.
GIFT AID (NEED-BASED) *Total amount:* $5,445,899 (37% federal, 6% state, 57% institutional). *Receiving aid:* Freshmen: 46% (141); All full-time undergraduates: 48% (751). *Average award:* Freshmen: $6060; Undergraduates: $7105. *Scholarships, grants, and awards:* Federal Pell, FSEOG, state, private, college/university gift aid from institutional funds.
GIFT AID (NON-NEED-BASED) *Total amount:* $8,194,830 (3% state, 69% institutional, 28% external sources). *Receiving aid:* Freshmen: 65% (199); Undergraduates: 60% (925). *Average Award:* Freshmen: $6121; Undergraduates: $5472. *Scholarships, grants, and awards by category: Academic Interests/Achievement:* 1,521 awards ($4,974,087 total): general academic interests/achievements. *Creative Arts/Performance:* 65 awards ($56,294 total): music. *Special Achievements/Activities:* 202 awards ($214,804 total): leadership, religious involvement. *Special Characteristics:* 112 awards ($977,630 total): children of faculty/staff, general special characteristics, international students. *Tuition waivers:* Full or partial for employees or children of employees, senior citizens.
LOANS *Student loans:* $12,002,659 (30% need-based, 70% non-need-based). 66% of past graduating class borrowed through all loan programs. *Average indebtedness per student:* $23,195. *Average need-based loan:* Freshmen: $5960; Undergraduates: $7477. *Parent loans:* $2,467,064 (100% non-need-based). *Programs:* Federal Direct (Subsidized and Unsubsidized Stafford, PLUS), Perkins.
WORK-STUDY *Federal work-study:* Total amount: $652,930; 600 jobs averaging $1306. *State or other work-study/employment:* Total amount: $302,460 (100% need-based). 252 part-time jobs averaging $1200.
APPLYING FOR FINANCIAL AID *Required financial aid forms:* FAFSA, institution's own form. *Financial aid deadline:* Continuous. *Notification date:* Continuous beginning 3/1.
CONTACT Cynthia Schulz, Assistant Director of Student Financial Services, Andrews University, Student Financial Services Administration Building, Berrien Springs, MI 49104, 269-471-3221 or toll-free 800-253-2874. *Fax:* 269-471-3228.

ANGELO STATE UNIVERSITY
San Angelo, TX

ABOUT THE INSTITUTION State-supported, coed. Awards: associate, bachelor's, and master's degrees. 40 undergraduate majors. Total enrollment: 6,156. Undergraduates: 5,709. Freshmen: 1,304.

Angelo State University

GIFT AID (NEED-BASED) *Scholarships, grants, and awards:* Federal Pell, FSEOG, state, private, college/university gift aid from institutional funds.
GIFT AID (NON-NEED-BASED) *Scholarships, grants, and awards by category: Academic Interests/Achievement:* agriculture, biological sciences, business, communication, computer science, education, English, foreign languages, general academic interests/achievements, international studies, mathematics, military science, physical sciences, premedicine, social sciences. *Creative Arts/Performance:* art/fine arts, dance, journalism/publications, music, performing arts, theater/drama. *Special Achievements/Activities:* cheerleading/drum major, general special achievements/activities, hobbies/interests, leadership, memberships, rodeo.
LOANS *Programs:* FFEL (Subsidized and Unsubsidized Stafford, PLUS), Perkins, state, college/university, alternative loans.
APPLYING FOR FINANCIAL AID *Required financial aid forms:* FAFSA, institution's own form.
CONTACT Ms. Lyn Wheeler, Director of Financial Aid, Angelo State University, ASU Station #11015, San Angelo, TX 76909-1015, 325-942-2246 or toll-free 800-946-8627 (in-state). *Fax:* 325-942-2082. *E-mail:* lyn.wheeler@angelo.edu.

ANNA MARIA COLLEGE
Paxton, MA

Tuition & fees: $21,880 **Average undergraduate aid package: $15,242**

ABOUT THE INSTITUTION Independent Roman Catholic, coed. Awards: associate, bachelor's, and master's degrees and post-bachelor's and post-master's certificates. 28 undergraduate majors. Total enrollment: 1,042. Undergraduates: 745. Freshmen: 163. Federal methodology is used as a basis for awarding need-based institutional aid.
UNDERGRADUATE EXPENSES for 2005–06 *Application fee:* $40. *Comprehensive fee:* $29,815 includes full-time tuition ($19,900), mandatory fees ($1980), and room and board ($7935). *Part-time tuition:* $663.33 per credit hour.
FRESHMAN FINANCIAL AID (Fall 2005, est.) 142 applied for aid; of those 91% were deemed to have need. 100% of freshmen with need received aid; of those 23% had need fully met. *Average percent of need met:* 78% (excluding resources awarded to replace EFC). *Average financial aid package:* $16,855 (excluding resources awarded to replace EFC). 11% of all full-time freshmen had no need and received non-need-based gift aid.
UNDERGRADUATE FINANCIAL AID (Fall 2005, est.) 482 applied for aid; of those 91% were deemed to have need. 99% of undergraduates with need received aid; of those 27% had need fully met. *Average percent of need met:* 75% (excluding resources awarded to replace EFC). *Average financial aid package:* $15,242 (excluding resources awarded to replace EFC). 14% of all full-time undergraduates had no need and received non-need-based gift aid.
GIFT AID (NEED-BASED) *Total amount:* $4,650,743 (10% federal, 7% state, 82% institutional, 1% external sources). *Receiving aid:* Freshmen: 78% (125); All full-time undergraduates: 78% (419). *Average award:* Freshmen: $11,071; Undergraduates: $10,958. *Scholarships, grants, and awards:* Federal Pell, FSEOG, state, private, college/university gift aid from institutional funds, United Negro College Fund, Federal Nursing.
GIFT AID (NON-NEED-BASED) *Total amount:* $843,807 (99% institutional, 1% external sources). *Receiving aid:* Freshmen: 75% (121); Undergraduates: 66% (355). *Average Award:* Freshmen: $8226; Undergraduates: $6913. *Scholarships, grants, and awards by category: Academic Interests/Achievement:* 330 awards ($1,944,500 total): general academic interests/achievements. *Creative Arts/Performance:* 8 awards ($23,500 total): music. *Special Achievements/Activities:* 91 awards ($114,750 total): religious involvement. *Special Characteristics:* 178 awards ($629,036 total): children and siblings of alumni, children of faculty/staff, children with a deceased or disabled parent, general special characteristics, local/state students, previous college experience, siblings of current students. *ROTC:* Air Force cooperative.
LOANS *Student loans:* $5,832,167 (84% need-based, 16% non-need-based). 86% of past graduating class borrowed through all loan programs. *Average indebtedness per student:* $23,513. *Average need-based loan:* Freshmen: $2843; Undergraduates: $4178. *Parent loans:* $1,009,571 (28% need-based, 72% non-need-based). *Programs:* FFEL (Subsidized and Unsubsidized Stafford, PLUS), Perkins, state, college/university.
WORK-STUDY *Federal work-study:* Total amount: $90,500; 82 jobs averaging $1103.
APPLYING FOR FINANCIAL AID *Required financial aid form:* FAFSA. *Financial aid deadline:* Continuous. *Notification date:* Continuous beginning 3/15. Students must reply within 4 weeks of notification.
CONTACT Nicole Brennan, Director of Financial Aid and Admission, Anna Maria College, 50 Sunset Lane, Paxton, MA 01612-1198, 508-849-3367 or toll-free 800-344-4586 Ext. 360. *Fax:* 508-849-3362. *E-mail:* nbrennan@annamaria.edu.

ANTIOCH COLLEGE
Yellow Springs, OH

Tuition & fees: $27,214 **Average undergraduate aid package: $22,853**

ABOUT THE INSTITUTION Independent, coed. Awards: bachelor's degrees. 56 undergraduate majors. Total enrollment: 470. Undergraduates: 464. Freshmen: 46.
UNDERGRADUATE EXPENSES for 2006–07 *Comprehensive fee:* $34,214 includes full-time tuition ($26,492), mandatory fees ($722), and room and board ($7000). *College room only:* $3426. *Part-time tuition:* $435 per credit hour.
FRESHMAN FINANCIAL AID (Fall 2005, est.) 46 applied for aid; of those 85% were deemed to have need. 100% of freshmen with need received aid; of those 100% had need fully met. *Average percent of need met:* 100% (excluding resources awarded to replace EFC). *Average financial aid package:* $17,521 (excluding resources awarded to replace EFC). 13% of all full-time freshmen had no need and received non-need-based gift aid.
UNDERGRADUATE FINANCIAL AID (Fall 2005, est.) 299 applied for aid; of those 95% were deemed to have need. 100% of undergraduates with need received aid; of those 100% had need fully met. *Average percent of need met:* 100% (excluding resources awarded to replace EFC). *Average financial aid package:* $22,853 (excluding resources awarded to replace EFC). 4% of all full-time undergraduates had no need and received non-need-based gift aid.
GIFT AID (NEED-BASED) *Total amount:* $3,539,487 (25% federal, 4% state, 71% institutional). *Receiving aid:* Freshmen: 72% (38); All full-time undergraduates: 70% (258). *Average award:* Freshmen: $11,898; Undergraduates: $13,719. *Scholarships, grants, and awards:* Federal Pell, FSEOG, state, private, college/university gift aid from institutional funds.
GIFT AID (NON-NEED-BASED) *Total amount:* $2,545,376 (4% state, 93% institutional, 3% external sources). *Receiving aid:* Freshmen: 74% (39); Undergraduates: 75% (275). *Average Award:* Freshmen: $15,929; Undergraduates: $9571. *Scholarships, grants, and awards by category: Academic Interests/Achievement:* 23 awards ($156,214 total): biological sciences, education, general academic interests/achievements, humanities, international studies, mathematics, physical sciences, social sciences. *Special Characteristics:* 150 awards ($367,875 total): local/state students.
LOANS *Student loans:* $1,604,464 (82% need-based, 18% non-need-based). 97% of past graduating class borrowed through all loan programs. *Average indebtedness per student:* $17,125. *Average need-based loan:* Freshmen: $2852; Undergraduates: $4910. *Parent loans:* $1,568,404 (100% non-need-based). *Programs:* FFEL (Subsidized and Unsubsidized Stafford, PLUS), Perkins.
WORK-STUDY *Federal work-study:* Total amount: $528,000; 263 jobs averaging $2500. *State or other work-study/employment:* Total amount: $74,500 (100% non-need-based). Part-time jobs available (averaging $1000).
APPLYING FOR FINANCIAL AID *Required financial aid forms:* FAFSA, institution's own form. *Financial aid deadline (priority):* 2/1. *Notification date:* 3/1. Students must reply by 4/16.
CONTACT Jennifer Rhyner, Associate Director of Admissions and Financial Aid, Antioch College, 795 Livermore Street, Yellow Springs, OH 45387, 937-769-1120 or toll-free 800-543-9436. *Fax:* 937-769-1133. *E-mail:* jrhyner@antioch-college.edu.

ANTIOCH UNIVERSITY MCGREGOR
Yellow Springs, OH

Tuition & fees: $12,513 **Average undergraduate aid package: $5000**

ABOUT THE INSTITUTION Independent, coed. Awards: bachelor's and master's degrees and post-master's certificates. 6 undergraduate majors. Total enrollment: 695. Undergraduates: 152. Both federal and institutional methodology are used as a basis for awarding need-based institutional aid.

UNDERGRADUATE EXPENSES for 2006–07 *Application fee:* $45. *Tuition:* full-time $12,288; part-time $256 per credit hour. *Required fees:* full-time $225; $75 per term part-time.
UNDERGRADUATE FINANCIAL AID (Fall 2004) 193 applied for aid; of those 97% were deemed to have need. 100% of undergraduates with need received aid. *Average percent of need met:* 45% (excluding resources awarded to replace EFC). *Average financial aid package:* $5000 (excluding resources awarded to replace EFC). 2% of all full-time undergraduates had no need and received non-need-based gift aid.
GIFT AID (NEED-BASED) *Total amount:* $218,835 (75% federal, 25% state). *Receiving aid:* All full-time undergraduates: 16% (70). *Average award:* Undergraduates: $2735. *Scholarships, grants, and awards:* Federal Pell, FSEOG, state.
GIFT AID (NON-NEED-BASED) *Total amount:* $36,072 (100% state). *Receiving aid:* Undergraduates: 15% (66).
LOANS *Student loans:* $1,934,600 (50% need-based, 50% non-need-based). 60% of past graduating class borrowed through all loan programs. *Average indebtedness per student:* $28,500. *Average need-based loan:* Undergraduates: $1170. *Programs:* FFEL (Subsidized and Unsubsidized Stafford, PLUS), Perkins.
WORK-STUDY *Federal work-study:* Total amount: $2503; 2 jobs averaging $1100.
APPLYING FOR FINANCIAL AID *Required financial aid forms:* FAFSA, institution's own form. *Financial aid deadline:* Continuous. *Notification date:* Continuous beginning 3/1.
CONTACT Kathy John, Director of Financial Aid, Antioch University McGregor, 800 Livermore Street, Yellow Springs, OH 45387-1609, 937-769-1840 or toll-free 937-769-1818. *Fax:* 937-769-1804. *E-mail:* kjohn@mcgregor.edu.

ANTIOCH UNIVERSITY SANTA BARBARA
Santa Barbara, CA

CONTACT Cecilia Schneider, Financial Aid Director, Antioch University Santa Barbara, 801 Garden Street, Santa Barbara, CA 93101-1580, 805-962-8179 Ext. 108. *Fax:* 805-962-4786.

ANTIOCH UNIVERSITY SEATTLE
Seattle, WA

Tuition & fees: N/R **Average undergraduate aid package:** $6681

ABOUT THE INSTITUTION Independent, coed. Awards: bachelor's, master's, and doctoral degrees. 1 undergraduate major. Total enrollment: 950. Undergraduates: 209. Federal methodology is used as a basis for awarding need-based institutional aid.
UNDERGRADUATE FINANCIAL AID (Fall 2004) 300 applied for aid; of those 83% were deemed to have need. 100% of undergraduates with need received aid; of those 60% had need fully met. *Average percent of need met:* 75% (excluding resources awarded to replace EFC). *Average financial aid package:* $6681 (excluding resources awarded to replace EFC).
GIFT AID (NEED-BASED) *Total amount:* $1,088,886 (26% federal, 31% state, 10% institutional, 33% external sources). *Receiving aid:* All full-time undergraduates: 43% (150). *Average award:* Undergraduates: $4000. *Scholarships, grants, and awards:* Federal Pell, FSEOG, state, private, college/university gift aid from institutional funds, United Negro College Fund.
GIFT AID (NON-NEED-BASED) *Receiving aid:* Undergraduates: 4% (15). *Tuition waivers:* Full or partial for employees or children of employees.
LOANS *Student loans:* $1,706,553 (53% need-based, 47% non-need-based). 85% of past graduating class borrowed through all loan programs. *Average indebtedness per student:* $15,999. *Average need-based loan:* Undergraduates: $5500. *Parent loans:* $8125 (100% non-need-based). *Programs:* FFEL (Subsidized and Unsubsidized Stafford, PLUS), Perkins.
WORK-STUDY *Federal work-study:* Total amount: $105,000; 18 jobs averaging $6000. *State or other work-study/employment:* Total amount: $10,000 (100% need-based). 2 part-time jobs averaging $5000.
APPLYING FOR FINANCIAL AID *Required financial aid form:* FAFSA. *Financial aid deadline (priority):* 4/15. *Notification date:* Continuous beginning 3/15. Students must reply within 2 weeks of notification.

CONTACT Katy Gilroy, Director of Financial Aid, Antioch University Seattle, 2326 Sixth Avenue, Seattle, WA 98121-1814, 206-268-4004. *Fax:* 206-268-4242. *E-mail:* kgilroy@antiochseattle.edu.

APEX SCHOOL OF THEOLOGY
Durham, NC

CONTACT Financial Aid Office, Apex School of Theology, 5104 Revere Road, Durham, NC 27713, 919-572-1625.

APPALACHIAN BIBLE COLLEGE
Bradley, WV

ABOUT THE INSTITUTION Independent nondenominational, coed. Awards: associate and bachelor's degrees. 2 undergraduate majors. Total enrollment: 304. Undergraduates: 304. Freshmen: 54.
GIFT AID (NEED-BASED) *Scholarships, grants, and awards:* Federal Pell, FSEOG, state, private, college/university gift aid from institutional funds.
GIFT AID (NON-NEED-BASED) *Scholarships, grants, and awards by category: Academic Interests/Achievement:* general academic interests/achievements, religion/biblical studies. *Special Achievements/Activities:* general special achievements/activities, religious involvement. *Special Characteristics:* children and siblings of alumni, children of educators, children of faculty/staff, general special characteristics, international students, married students, relatives of clergy, religious affiliation, spouses of current students, veterans.
LOANS *Programs:* FFEL (Subsidized and Unsubsidized Stafford, PLUS).
APPLYING FOR FINANCIAL AID *Required financial aid forms:* FAFSA, institution's own form.
CONTACT Mrs. Shirley Carfrey, Director of Financial Aid, Appalachian Bible College, PO Box ABC, Sandbranch Road, Bradley, WV 25818, 304-877-6428 Ext. 3244 or toll-free 800-678-9ABC Ext. 3213. *Fax:* 304-877-5082. *E-mail:* scarfrey@abc.edu.

APPALACHIAN STATE UNIVERSITY
Boone, NC

Tuition & fees (NC res): $3918 **Average undergraduate aid package:** $6383

ABOUT THE INSTITUTION State-supported, coed. Awards: bachelor's, master's, and doctoral degrees and post-master's certificates. 84 undergraduate majors. Total enrollment: 14,653. Undergraduates: 12,986. Freshmen: 2,543. Federal methodology is used as a basis for awarding need-based institutional aid.
UNDERGRADUATE EXPENSES for 2006–07 *Application fee:* $45. *Tuition, state resident:* full-time $2221; part-time $80 per credit hour. *Tuition, nonresident:* full-time $11,963; part-time $425 per credit hour. *College room and board:* $4960; *room only:* $3100.
FRESHMAN FINANCIAL AID (Fall 2005, est.) 1666 applied for aid; of those 49% were deemed to have need. 95% of freshmen with need received aid; of those 35% had need fully met. *Average percent of need met:* 74% (excluding resources awarded to replace EFC). *Average financial aid package:* $5820 (excluding resources awarded to replace EFC). 10% of all full-time freshmen had no need and received non-need-based gift aid.
UNDERGRADUATE FINANCIAL AID (Fall 2005, est.) 7,337 applied for aid; of those 57% were deemed to have need. 96% of undergraduates with need received aid; of those 40% had need fully met. *Average percent of need met:* 77% (excluding resources awarded to replace EFC). *Average financial aid package:* $6383 (excluding resources awarded to replace EFC). 6% of all full-time undergraduates had no need and received non-need-based gift aid.
GIFT AID (NEED-BASED) *Total amount:* $13,945,410 (47% federal, 36% state, 10% institutional, 7% external sources). *Receiving aid:* Freshmen: 27% (675); All full-time undergraduates: 27% (3,321). *Average award:* Freshmen: $4450; Undergraduates: $4286. *Scholarships, grants, and awards:* Federal Pell, FSEOG, state, private, college/university gift aid from institutional funds.
GIFT AID (NON-NEED-BASED) *Total amount:* $3,662,772 (13% federal, 32% state, 28% institutional, 27% external sources). *Receiving aid:* Freshmen: 11% (269); Undergraduates: 7% (843). *Average Award:* Freshmen: $2015; Undergraduates: $2875. *Scholarships, grants, and awards by category: Academic Interests/Achievement:* 4,025 awards ($2,418,364 total): general academic interests/achievements. *Creative Arts/Performance:* general creative arts/performance. *Special Achievements/Activities:* general special achievements/activities. *Special*

Appalachian State University

Characteristics: 462 awards ($1,683,235 total): first-generation college students, general special characteristics, handicapped students, members of minority groups, out-of-state students, veterans, veterans' children. *ROTC:* Army.
LOANS *Student loans:* $24,832,139 (69% need-based, 31% non-need-based). 50% of past graduating class borrowed through all loan programs. *Average indebtedness per student:* $15,433. *Average need-based loan:* Freshmen: $2526; Undergraduates: $3399. *Parent loans:* $15,680,997 (48% need-based, 52% non-need-based). *Programs:* FFEL (Subsidized and Unsubsidized Stafford, PLUS), Perkins, college/university.
WORK-STUDY *Federal work-study:* Total amount: $552,571; 344 jobs averaging $1800. *State or other work-study/employment:* Total amount: $4,561,812 (100% non-need-based). 1,687 part-time jobs averaging $673.
ATHLETIC AWARDS *Total amount:* $2,316,023 (39% need-based, 61% non-need-based).
APPLYING FOR FINANCIAL AID *Required financial aid form:* FAFSA. *Financial aid deadline (priority):* 3/15. *Notification date:* Continuous beginning 4/1. Students must reply within 3 weeks of notification.
CONTACT Kay Stroud, Associate Director of Student Financial Aid, Appalachian State University, Office of Student Financial Aid, ASU Box 32059, Boone, NC 28608-2059, 828-262-8687. *Fax:* 828-262-2585. *E-mail:* stroudkn@appstate.edu.

AQUINAS COLLEGE
Grand Rapids, MI

CONTACT David J. Steffee, Director Financial Aid, Aquinas College, 1607 Robinson Road, Grand Rapids, MI 49506-1799, 616-459-8281 Ext. 5127 or toll-free 800-678-9593. *Fax:* 616-732-4547. *E-mail:* steffdav@aquinas.edu.

AQUINAS COLLEGE
Nashville, TN

ABOUT THE INSTITUTION Independent Roman Catholic, coed. Awards: associate and bachelor's degrees and post-bachelor's certificates. 6 undergraduate majors. Total enrollment: 902. Undergraduates: 902.
GIFT AID (NEED-BASED) *Scholarships, grants, and awards:* Federal Pell, FSEOG, state, private, college/university gift aid from institutional funds.
GIFT AID (NON-NEED-BASED) *Scholarships, grants, and awards by category:* Academic Interests/Achievement: business, education, general academic interests/achievements, health fields. *Special Achievements/Activities:* leadership. *Special Characteristics:* general special characteristics.
LOANS *Programs:* FFEL (Subsidized and Unsubsidized Stafford, PLUS), alternative loans.
APPLYING FOR FINANCIAL AID *Required financial aid form:* institution's own form.
CONTACT Zelena O'Sullivan, Director of Financial Aid, Aquinas College, 4210 Harding Road, Nashville, TN 37205-2005, 615-297-7545 Ext. 431 or toll-free 800-649-9956. *Fax:* 615-279-3891. *E-mail:* osullivanz@aquinas-tn.edu.

ARCADIA UNIVERSITY
Glenside, PA

ABOUT THE INSTITUTION Independent religious, coed. Awards: bachelor's, master's, and doctoral degrees. 52 undergraduate majors. Total enrollment: 3,403. Undergraduates: 1,955. Freshmen: 441.
GIFT AID (NEED-BASED) *Scholarships, grants, and awards:* Federal Pell, FSEOG, state, private, college/university gift aid from institutional funds.
GIFT AID (NON-NEED-BASED) *Scholarships, grants, and awards by category:* Academic Interests/Achievement: general academic interests/achievements. *Creative Arts/Performance:* applied art and design, art/fine arts, theater/drama. *Special Achievements/Activities:* community service, general special achievements/activities, leadership, memberships. *Special Characteristics:* children and siblings of alumni, relatives of clergy, religious affiliation.
LOANS *Programs:* FFEL (Subsidized and Unsubsidized Stafford, PLUS), Perkins, college/university.
WORK-STUDY *Federal work-study:* Total amount: $1,193,635; 914 jobs averaging $1294. *State or other work-study/employment:* Total amount: $220,110 (100% non-need-based). 224 part-time jobs averaging $870.

APPLYING FOR FINANCIAL AID *Required financial aid forms:* FAFSA, institution's own form.
CONTACT Elizabeth Rihl Lewinsky, Director of Financial Aid, Arcadia University, 450 South Easton Road, Glenside, PA 19038, 215-572-2980 or toll-free 877-ARCADIA. *Fax:* 215-572-4049. *E-mail:* finaid@arcadia.edu.

ARGOSY UNIVERSITY/ATLANTA
Atlanta, GA

CONTACT Ashley Manker, Financial Aid Office, Argosy University/Atlanta, One Lakeside Commons, Building One, 990 Hammond Drive, 11th Floor, Atlanta, GA 30328, 770-671-1200 Ext. 1036 or toll-free 888-671-4777. *Fax:* 770-407-1110. *E-mail:* amanker@argosyu.edu.

ARGOSY UNIVERSITY/CHICAGO
Chicago, IL

CONTACT Ardie Elgersma, Financial Aid Office, Argosy University/Chicago, Two First National Plaza, 20 South Clark Street, Third Floor, Chicago, IL 60603, 312-201-0200 Ext. 3909 or toll-free 800-626-4123 (in-state). *Fax:* 312-201-1907. *E-mail:* aelgersma@argosyu.edu.

ARGOSY UNIVERSITY/DALLAS
Dallas, TX

CONTACT Beth Kirkman, Financial Aid Office, Argosy University/Dallas, One North Park, Suite 315, 8950 North Central Expressway, Dallas, TX 75231, 214-459-2204 or toll-free 866-954-9900. *Fax:* 214-696-3900. *E-mail:* bkirkman@argosyu.edu.

ARGOSY UNIVERSITY/HAWAI'I
Honolulu, HI

CONTACT Mary Vee Cheung, Financial Aid Office, Argosy University/Hawai'i, 400 Pacific Tower, 1001 Bishop Street, Honolulu, HI 96813, 808-536-5555 Ext. 204 or toll-free 888-323-2777 (in-state). *Fax:* 808-536-5505. *E-mail:* mvee@argosyu.edu.

ARGOSY UNIVERSITY/NASHVILLE
Franklin, TN

CONTACT Financial Aid Office, Argosy University/Nashville, 341 Cool Springs Boulevard, Suite 210, Franklin, TN 37067-7226, 615-369-0616.

ARGOSY UNIVERSITY/PHOENIX
Phoenix, AZ

CONTACT Amy Vincent, Financial Aid Office, Argosy University/Phoenix, 2301 West Dunlap, Suite 211, Phoenix, AZ 85021, 602-216-2600 or toll-free 866-216-2777. *Fax:* 602-216-2601. *E-mail:* avincent@argosyu.edu.

ARGOSY UNIVERSITY/SAN FRANCISCO BAY AREA
Point Richmond, CA

CONTACT Adrian Ramos, Financial Aid Office, Argosy University/San Francisco Bay Area, 999 Canal Boulevard, Point Richmond, CA 94804, 510-215-0277 Ext. 217 or toll-free 866-215-2777 Ext. 205 (in-state), 866-215-2777 (out-of-state). *Fax:* 510-215-0299. *E-mail:* aramos@argosyu.edu.

ARGOSY UNIVERSITY/SARASOTA
Sarasota, FL

CONTACT Deborah Kerris, Financial Aid Office, Argosy University/Sarasota, 5250 17th Street, Sarasota, FL 34235, 800-331-5995 Ext. 244 or toll-free 800-331-5995. *Fax:* 941-371-8910. *E-mail:* dkerris@argosyu.edu.

ARGOSY UNIVERSITY/SCHAUMBURG
Schaumburg, IL

CONTACT Virginia Carlin, Financial Aid Office, Argosy University/Schaumburg, One Continental Towers, 1701 Golf Road, Suite 101, Rolling Meadows, IL 60008, 847-290-7400 or toll-free 866-290-2777. *Fax:* 847-290-8432. *E-mail:* vcarlin@argosyu.edu.

ARGOSY UNIVERSITY/SEATTLE
Seattle, WA

CONTACT Eun-Ju Lee, Assistant Director of Student Services, Argosy University/Seattle, 1019 Eighth Avenue North, Seattle, WA 98109, 206-283-4500 Ext. 235 or toll-free 866-283-2777 (out-of-state). *Fax:* 206-283-5777. *E-mail:* elee@argosyu.edu.

ARGOSY UNIVERSITY/TAMPA
Tampa, FL

CONTACT Donna Page, Financial Aid Office, Argosy University/Tampa, 4401 North Hines Avenue, Tampa, FL 33614, 813-393-5290 or toll-free 800-850-6488 Ext. 5260 (in-state), 800-850-6488 (out-of-state). *Fax:* 813-874-1989. *E-mail:* dpage@edmc.edu.

ARGOSY UNIVERSITY/WASHINGTON D.C.
Arlington, VA

CONTACT Financial Aid Office, Argosy University/Washington D.C., 1550 Wilson Boulevard, Suite 600, Arlington, VA 22209, 703-526-5800 or toll-free 866-703-2777 Ext. 5833.

ARIZONA STATE UNIVERSITY
Tempe, AZ

Tuition & fees (AZ res): $4406   **Average undergraduate aid package: $8300**

ABOUT THE INSTITUTION State-supported, coed. Awards: bachelor's, master's, doctoral, and first professional degrees and post-bachelor's and post-master's certificates. 86 undergraduate majors. Total enrollment: 51,612. Undergraduates: 41,256. Freshmen: 7,706. Federal methodology is used as a basis for awarding need-based institutional aid.
UNDERGRADUATE EXPENSES for 2005–06 *Application fee:* $25; $50 for nonresidents. *Tuition, state resident:* full-time $4311; part-time $225 per credit. *Tuition, nonresident:* full-time $15,000; part-time $625 per credit. *Required fees:* full-time $95; $24 per term part-time. Full-time tuition and fees vary according to program. Part-time tuition and fees vary according to program. *College room and board:* $6768; *room only:* $4275. Room and board charges vary according to board plan and housing facility. *Payment plan:* Installment.
FRESHMAN FINANCIAL AID (Fall 2004) 3851 applied for aid; of those 68% were deemed to have need. 100% of freshmen with need received aid; of those 20% had need fully met. *Average percent of need met:* 64% (excluding resources awarded to replace EFC). *Average financial aid package:* $7790 (excluding resources awarded to replace EFC). 22% of all full-time freshmen had no need and received non-need-based gift aid.
UNDERGRADUATE FINANCIAL AID (Fall 2004) 17,079 applied for aid; of those 77% were deemed to have need. 100% of undergraduates with need received aid; of those 17% had need fully met. *Average percent of need met:* 63% (excluding resources awarded to replace EFC). *Average financial aid package:* $8300 (excluding resources awarded to replace EFC). 13% of all full-time undergraduates had no need and received non-need-based gift aid.
GIFT AID (NEED-BASED) *Total amount:* $64,158,475 (40% federal, 1% state, 49% institutional, 10% external sources). *Receiving aid:* Freshmen: 35% (2,397); All full-time undergraduates: 34% (10,827). *Average award:* Freshmen: $5946; Undergraduates: $5423. *Scholarships, grants, and awards:* Federal Pell, FSEOG, state, private, college/university gift aid from institutional funds, Federal Nursing.
GIFT AID (NON-NEED-BASED) *Total amount:* $29,430,943 (1% state, 81% institutional, 18% external sources). *Receiving aid:* Freshmen: 5% (329); Undergraduates: 3% (797). *Average Award:* Freshmen: $5463; Undergraduates: $5426. *Scholarships, grants, and awards by category:* Academic Interests/Achievement: architecture, area/ethnic studies, biological sciences, business, communication, computer science, education, engineering/technologies, English, foreign languages, general academic interests/achievements, health fields, home economics, humanities, mathematics, military science, physical sciences, premedicine, social sciences. *Creative Arts/Performance:* applied art and design, art/fine arts, cinema/film/broadcasting, creative writing, dance, debating, general creative arts/performance, journalism/publications, music, performing arts, theater/drama. *Special Achievements/Activities:* general special achievements/activities. *Tuition waivers:* Full or partial for employees or children of employees. *ROTC:* Army, Air Force.
LOANS *Student loans:* $91,304,035 (75% need-based, 25% non-need-based). 51% of past graduating class borrowed through all loan programs. *Average indebtedness per student:* $17,016. *Average need-based loan:* Freshmen: $2729; Undergraduates: $4173. *Parent loans:* $28,614,033 (29% need-based, 71% non-need-based). *Programs:* Federal Direct (Subsidized and Unsubsidized Stafford, PLUS), FFEL (PLUS), Perkins.
WORK-STUDY *Federal work-study:* Total amount: $1,344,175; 615 jobs averaging $2228. *State or other work-study/employment:* Total amount: $12,354,453 (24% need-based, 76% non-need-based). 4,493 part-time jobs averaging $2892.
ATHLETIC AWARDS *Total amount:* $5,642,850 (23% need-based, 77% non-need-based).
APPLYING FOR FINANCIAL AID *Required financial aid form:* FAFSA. *Financial aid deadline (priority):* 3/1.
CONTACT Craig Fennell, Director of Student Financial Assistance, Arizona State University, Box 870412, Tempe, AZ 85287-0412, 480-965-3355. *Fax:* 480-965-9484. *E-mail:* financialaid@asu.edu.

ARIZONA STATE UNIVERSITY AT THE POLYTECHNIC CAMPUS
Mesa, AZ

Tuition & fees (AZ res): $4346   **Average undergraduate aid package: $8301**

ABOUT THE INSTITUTION State-supported, coed. Awards: bachelor's and master's degrees. 25 undergraduate majors. Total enrollment: 4,865. Undergraduates: 4,083. Freshmen: 227. Federal methodology is used as a basis for awarding need-based institutional aid.
UNDERGRADUATE EXPENSES for 2005–06 *Application fee:* $50. *Tuition, state resident:* full-time $4301; part-time $221 per credit hour. *Tuition, nonresident:* full-time $13,918; part-time $580 per credit hour. Full-time tuition and fees vary according to degree level, location, and program. Part-time tuition and fees vary according to course load, degree level, location, and program. *College room and board:* $5155; *room only:* $2655. Room and board charges vary according to board plan, housing facility, and student level. *Payment plan:* Installment.
FRESHMAN FINANCIAL AID (Fall 2004) 2 applied for aid; of those 50% were deemed to have need. 100% of freshmen with need received aid. 50% of all full-time freshmen had no need and received non-need-based gift aid.
UNDERGRADUATE FINANCIAL AID (Fall 2004) 793 applied for aid; of those 78% were deemed to have need. 100% of undergraduates with need received aid; of those 13% had need fully met. *Average percent of need met:* 60% (excluding resources awarded to replace EFC). *Average financial aid package:* $8301 (excluding resources awarded to replace EFC). 15% of all full-time undergraduates had no need and received non-need-based gift aid.
GIFT AID (NEED-BASED) *Total amount:* $4,243,931 (45% federal, 46% institutional, 9% external sources). *Receiving aid:* All full-time undergraduates: 42% (496). *Average award:* Undergraduates: $4815. *Scholarships, grants, and awards:* Federal Pell, FSEOG, state, private, college/university gift aid from institutional funds.
GIFT AID (NON-NEED-BASED) *Total amount:* $461,245 (63% institutional, 37% external sources). *Receiving aid:* Undergraduates: 1. *Average Award:* Freshmen: $8025; Undergraduates: $6703. *Scholarships, grants, and awards by category:* Academic Interests/Achievement: general academic interests/achievements. *Creative Arts/Performance:* general creative arts/performance. *Special Achievements/Activities:* general special achievements/activities. *Special Characteristics:* general special characteristics. *Tuition waivers:* Full or partial for employees or children of employees. *ROTC:* Army cooperative, Air Force cooperative.
LOANS *Student loans:* $8,853,015 (77% need-based, 23% non-need-based). *Average need-based loan:* Undergraduates: $5071. *Parent loans:* $1,444,167

Arizona State University at the Polytechnic Campus

(34% need-based, 66% non-need-based). *Programs:* Federal Direct (Subsidized and Unsubsidized Stafford, PLUS), FFEL (PLUS), Perkins.
WORK-STUDY *Federal work-study:* Total amount: $55,741; 26 jobs averaging $2144. *State or other work-study/employment:* Total amount: $3,985,398 (5% need-based, 95% non-need-based). 185 part-time jobs averaging $3056.
ATHLETIC AWARDS *Total amount:* $49,258 (100% non-need-based).
APPLYING FOR FINANCIAL AID *Required financial aid form:* FAFSA. *Financial aid deadline (priority):* 3/1. *Notification date:* Continuous beginning 4/15. Students must reply within 4 weeks of notification.
CONTACT Heather Klotz, Financial Aid Counselor, Arizona State University at the Polytechnic Campus, 7001 East Williams Field Road, Building 370, Mesa, AZ 85212, 480-727-1042. *Fax:* 480-727-1008. *E-mail:* heather.klotz@asu.edu.

ARIZONA STATE UNIVERSITY EAST
Mesa, AZ

See Arizona State University at the Polytechnic Campus.

ARIZONA STATE UNIVERSITY WEST
Phoenix, AZ

Tuition & fees (AZ res): $4346   **Average undergraduate aid package: $7926**

ABOUT THE INSTITUTION State-supported, coed. Awards: bachelor's and master's degrees and post-bachelor's certificates. 23 undergraduate majors. Total enrollment: 7,734. Undergraduates: 6,620. Freshmen: 487. Federal methodology is used as a basis for awarding need-based institutional aid.
UNDERGRADUATE EXPENSES for 2005–06 *Application fee:* $50. *Tuition, state resident:* full-time $4251; part-time $221 per credit hour. *Tuition, nonresident:* full-time $15,000; part-time $625 per credit hour. Part-time tuition and fees vary according to course load. *College room and board: room only:* $5836. *Payment plan:* Installment.
FRESHMAN FINANCIAL AID (Fall 2004) 239 applied for aid; of those 77% were deemed to have need. 100% of freshmen with need received aid; of those 11% had need fully met. *Average percent of need met:* 63% (excluding resources awarded to replace EFC). *Average financial aid package:* $6807 (excluding resources awarded to replace EFC). 17% of all full-time freshmen had no need and received non-need-based gift aid.
UNDERGRADUATE FINANCIAL AID (Fall 2004) 2,265 applied for aid; of those 85% were deemed to have need. 100% of undergraduates with need received aid; of those 14% had need fully met. *Average percent of need met:* 61% (excluding resources awarded to replace EFC). *Average financial aid package:* $7926 (excluding resources awarded to replace EFC). 7% of all full-time undergraduates had no need and received non-need-based gift aid.
GIFT AID (NEED-BASED) *Total amount:* $9,815,010 (48% federal, 44% institutional, 8% external sources). *Receiving aid:* Freshmen: 47% (176); All full-time undergraduates: 45% (1,567). *Average award:* Freshmen: $5776; Undergraduates: $5160. *Scholarships, grants, and awards:* Federal Pell, FSEOG, state, private, college/university gift aid from institutional funds.
GIFT AID (NON-NEED-BASED) *Total amount:* $1,312,786 (80% institutional, 20% external sources). *Receiving aid:* Freshmen: 3% (10); Undergraduates: 1% (52). *Average Award:* Freshmen: $3842; Undergraduates: $3613. *Scholarships, grants, and awards by category: Academic Interests/Achievement:* general academic interests/achievements. *Tuition waivers:* Full or partial for employees or children of employees.
LOANS *Student loans:* $17,428,814 (82% need-based, 18% non-need-based). 56% of past graduating class borrowed through all loan programs. *Average indebtedness per student:* $16,438. *Average need-based loan:* Freshmen: $2447; Undergraduates: $4619. *Parent loans:* $859,508 (30% need-based, 70% non-need-based). *Programs:* Federal Direct (Subsidized and Unsubsidized Stafford), FFEL (PLUS), Perkins, college/university.
WORK-STUDY *Federal work-study:* Total amount: $262,513; 94 jobs averaging $2793. *State or other work-study/employment:* Total amount: $546,659 (32% need-based, 68% non-need-based). 201 part-time jobs averaging $2720.
APPLYING FOR FINANCIAL AID *Required financial aid form:* FAFSA. *Financial aid deadline:* 3/1 (priority: 2/15). *Notification date:* Continuous beginning 3/15. Students must reply within 4 weeks of notification.
CONTACT Leah Samudio, Financial Aid Manager, Arizona State University West, 4701 West Thunderbird Road, PO Box 37100, Phoenix, AZ 85069-7100, 602-543-8178. *E-mail:* leah.samudio@asu.edu.

ARKANSAS BAPTIST COLLEGE
Little Rock, AR

CONTACT Director of Financial Aid, Arkansas Baptist College, 1600 Bishop Street, Little Rock, AR 72202-6067, 501-374-7856.

ARKANSAS STATE UNIVERSITY
Jonesboro, AR

Tuition & fees (AR res): $5440   **Average undergraduate aid package: $6000**

ABOUT THE INSTITUTION State-supported, coed. Awards: associate, bachelor's, master's, and doctoral degrees and post-bachelor's and post-master's certificates (specialist). 80 undergraduate majors. Total enrollment: 10,414. Undergraduates: 9,138. Freshmen: 1,584. Federal methodology is used as a basis for awarding need-based institutional aid.
UNDERGRADUATE EXPENSES for 2005–06 *Application fee:* $15. *Tuition, state resident:* full-time $4260; part-time $142 per credit hour. *Tuition, nonresident:* full-time $10,965; part-time $365.50 per credit hour. *Required fees:* full-time $1180; $37 per credit hour or $25 per term part-time. Full-time tuition and fees vary according to course load, location, and program. Part-time tuition and fees vary according to course load, location, and program. *College room and board:* $4190. Room and board charges vary according to board plan and housing facility. *Payment plan:* Installment.
FRESHMAN FINANCIAL AID (Fall 2005, est.) 1339 applied for aid; of those 95% were deemed to have need. 97% of freshmen with need received aid; of those 23% had need fully met. *Average percent of need met:* 67% (excluding resources awarded to replace EFC). *Average financial aid package:* $6100 (excluding resources awarded to replace EFC). 19% of all full-time freshmen had no need and received non-need-based gift aid.
UNDERGRADUATE FINANCIAL AID (Fall 2005, est.) 6,395 applied for aid; of those 88% were deemed to have need. 95% of undergraduates with need received aid; of those 28% had need fully met. *Average percent of need met:* 55% (excluding resources awarded to replace EFC). *Average financial aid package:* $6000 (excluding resources awarded to replace EFC). 11% of all full-time undergraduates had no need and received non-need-based gift aid.
GIFT AID (NEED-BASED) *Total amount:* $25,847,599 (42% federal, 13% state, 37% institutional, 8% external sources). *Receiving aid:* Freshmen: 79% (1,184); All full-time undergraduates: 66% (4,734). *Average award:* Freshmen: $5900; Undergraduates: $5400. *Scholarships, grants, and awards:* Federal Pell, FSEOG, state, private, college/university gift aid from institutional funds.
GIFT AID (NON-NEED-BASED) *Receiving aid:* Freshmen: 34% (513); Undergraduates: 39% (2,798). *Average Award:* Freshmen: $5000; Undergraduates: $5000. *Scholarships, grants, and awards by category: Academic Interests/Achievement:* 3,010 awards ($8,265,431 total): agriculture, biological sciences, business, communication, computer science, education, engineering/technologies, English, general academic interests/achievements, health fields, humanities, library science, mathematics, military science, physical sciences, premedicine, social sciences. *Creative Arts/Performance:* 284 awards ($721,775 total): art/fine arts, cinema/film/broadcasting, debating, journalism/publications, music, performing arts, theater/drama. *Special Achievements/Activities:* 310 awards ($399,231 total): cheerleading/drum major, community service, general special achievements/activities. *Special Characteristics:* 155 awards ($370,929 total): adult students, children and siblings of alumni, children of faculty/staff, ethnic background, first-generation college students, general special characteristics, handicapped students, local/state students, members of minority groups, out-of-state students, veterans, veterans' children. *Tuition waivers:* Full or partial for children of alumni, employees or children of employees, senior citizens. *ROTC:* Army.
LOANS *Student loans:* $25,450,242 (69% need-based, 31% non-need-based). 68% of past graduating class borrowed through all loan programs. *Average indebtedness per student:* $18,500. *Average need-based loan:* Freshmen: $3100; Undergraduates: $4100. *Programs:* FFEL (Subsidized and Unsubsidized Stafford, PLUS), Perkins.
WORK-STUDY *Federal work-study:* Total amount: $879,959; 280 jobs averaging $2900. *State or other work-study/employment:* Total amount: $2,000,000 (100% non-need-based). Part-time jobs available.
ATHLETIC AWARDS *Total amount:* $1,899,311 (100% non-need-based).
APPLYING FOR FINANCIAL AID *Required financial aid forms:* FAFSA, institution's own form. *Financial aid deadline:* 7/1 (priority: 2/15). *Notification date:* Continuous beginning 6/1. Students must reply within 2 weeks of notification.

CONTACT Mr. Gregory Thornburg, Director of Financial Aid/Dean of Enrollment Services, Arkansas State University, PO Box 1620, State University, AR 72467, 870-972-2310 or toll-free 800-382-3030 (in-state). *Fax:* 870-972-2794. *E-mail:* gthorn@astate.edu.

ARKANSAS TECH UNIVERSITY
Russellville, AR

Tuition & fees (AR res): $4700   **Average undergraduate aid package: $4381**

ABOUT THE INSTITUTION State-supported, coed. Awards: associate, bachelor's, and master's degrees (Educational Specialist's). 53 undergraduate majors. Total enrollment: 6,842. Undergraduates: 6,328. Freshmen: 1,529. Federal methodology is used as a basis for awarding need-based institutional aid.

UNDERGRADUATE EXPENSES for 2005–06 *Tuition, state resident:* full-time $4290; part-time $143 per credit hour. *Tuition, nonresident:* full-time $8580; part-time $286 per credit hour. *Required fees:* full-time $410; $4 per credit hour or $145 per term part-time. Full-time tuition and fees vary according to course load and location. Part-time tuition and fees vary according to course load and location. *College room and board:* $4290; *room only:* $2290. Room and board charges vary according to board plan and housing facility. *Payment plans:* Installment, deferred payment.

FRESHMAN FINANCIAL AID (Fall 2004) 1075 applied for aid; of those 84% were deemed to have need. 99% of freshmen with need received aid; of those 28% had need fully met. *Average percent of need met:* 37% (excluding resources awarded to replace EFC). *Average financial aid package:* $3393 (excluding resources awarded to replace EFC). 25% of all full-time freshmen had no need and received non-need-based gift aid.

UNDERGRADUATE FINANCIAL AID (Fall 2004) 3,760 applied for aid; of those 88% were deemed to have need. 99% of undergraduates with need received aid; of those 26% had need fully met. *Average percent of need met:* 41% (excluding resources awarded to replace EFC). *Average financial aid package:* $4381 (excluding resources awarded to replace EFC). 18% of all full-time undergraduates had no need and received non-need-based gift aid.

GIFT AID (NEED-BASED) *Total amount:* $9,092,558 (81% federal, 19% state). *Receiving aid:* Freshmen: 49% (693); All full-time undergraduates: 47% (2,463). *Average award:* Freshmen: $2516; Undergraduates: $2478. *Scholarships, grants, and awards:* Federal Pell, FSEOG, state, private, college/university gift aid from institutional funds.

GIFT AID (NON-NEED-BASED) *Total amount:* $9,486,549 (2% federal, 7% state, 82% institutional, 9% external sources). *Receiving aid:* Freshmen: 36% (501); Undergraduates: 23% (1,203). *Average Award:* Freshmen: $5655; Undergraduates: $5643. *Scholarships, grants, and awards by category: Academic Interests/Achievement:* 1,350 awards ($5,865,868 total): agriculture, engineering/technologies, general academic interests/achievements. *Creative Arts/Performance:* 279 awards ($528,390 total): creative writing, general creative arts/performance, music. *Special Achievements/Activities:* 65 awards ($46,966 total): general special achievements/activities, leadership. *Special Characteristics:* 536 awards ($864,173 total): adult students, children of faculty/staff, ethnic background, general special characteristics, international students, out-of-state students, public servants. *Tuition waivers:* Full or partial for employees or children of employees, senior citizens. *ROTC:* Army cooperative.

LOANS *Student loans:* $16,950,388 (55% need-based, 45% non-need-based). 53% of past graduating class borrowed through all loan programs. *Average indebtedness per student:* $17,064. *Average need-based loan:* Freshmen: $843; Undergraduates: $1826. *Parent loans:* $824,385 (100% non-need-based). *Programs:* FFEL (Subsidized and Unsubsidized Stafford, PLUS), Perkins.

WORK-STUDY *Federal work-study:* Total amount: $272,895; 250 jobs averaging $1109. *State or other work-study/employment:* Total amount: $494,181 (100% non-need-based). 435 part-time jobs averaging $1077.

ATHLETIC AWARDS *Total amount:* $685,232 (100% non-need-based).

APPLYING FOR FINANCIAL AID *Required financial aid form:* FAFSA. *Financial aid deadline (priority):* 4/15. *Notification date:* Continuous beginning 5/1. Students must reply within 2 weeks of notification.

CONTACT Niki Harrison, Financial Aid Officer, Arkansas Tech University, Bryan Student Services Building, Room 117, Russellville, AR 72801-2222, 479-968-0399 or toll-free 800-582-6953. *Fax:* 479-964-0857. *E-mail:* niki.harrison@atu.edu.

ARLINGTON BAPTIST COLLEGE
Arlington, TX

Tuition & fees: $5450   **Average undergraduate aid package: $5379**

ABOUT THE INSTITUTION Independent Baptist, coed. Awards: bachelor's degrees. 10 undergraduate majors. Total enrollment: 181. Undergraduates: 181. Freshmen: 35. Federal methodology is used as a basis for awarding need-based institutional aid.

UNDERGRADUATE EXPENSES for 2006–07 *Application fee:* $15. *Comprehensive fee:* $9250 includes full-time tuition ($4950), mandatory fees ($500), and room and board ($3800). *Part-time tuition:* $165 per hour.

FRESHMAN FINANCIAL AID (Fall 2004) 38 applied for aid; of those 84% were deemed to have need. 100% of freshmen with need received aid; of those 100% had need fully met. *Average financial aid package:* $5379 (excluding resources awarded to replace EFC).

UNDERGRADUATE FINANCIAL AID (Fall 2004) 163 applied for aid; of those 93% were deemed to have need. 100% of undergraduates with need received aid; of those 100% had need fully met. *Average financial aid package:* $5379 (excluding resources awarded to replace EFC).

GIFT AID (NEED-BASED) *Total amount:* $361,409 (55% federal, 45% institutional). *Scholarships, grants, and awards:* Federal Pell, private, college/university gift aid from institutional funds.

GIFT AID (NON-NEED-BASED) *Scholarships, grants, and awards by category: Special Characteristics:* children of faculty/staff, spouses of current students.

LOANS *Student loans:* $577,610 (100% need-based). 65% of past graduating class borrowed through all loan programs. *Average indebtedness per student:* $7800. *Programs:* FFEL (Subsidized and Unsubsidized Stafford, PLUS).

WORK-STUDY Federal work-study jobs available.

APPLYING FOR FINANCIAL AID *Required financial aid form:* FAFSA. *Financial aid deadline (priority):* 8/1. *Notification date:* Continuous beginning 9/1.

CONTACT Mr. David B. Clogston Jr., Business Manager, Arlington Baptist College, 3001 West Division Street, Arlington, TX 76012-3425, 817-461-8741 Ext. 110. *Fax:* 817-274-1138.

ARMSTRONG ATLANTIC STATE UNIVERSITY
Savannah, GA

Tuition & fees (GA res): $3350   **Average undergraduate aid package: $6848**

ABOUT THE INSTITUTION State-supported, coed. Awards: associate, bachelor's, and master's degrees. 34 undergraduate majors. Total enrollment: 6,710. Undergraduates: 5,915. Freshmen: 794. Federal methodology is used as a basis for awarding need-based institutional aid.

UNDERGRADUATE EXPENSES for 2005–06 *Application fee:* $20. *Tuition, state resident:* full-time $2894; part-time $102 per hour. *Tuition, nonresident:* full-time $10,210; part-time $407 per hour. *Required fees:* full-time $456; $213 per term part-time. Full-time tuition and fees vary according to program. Part-time tuition and fees vary according to course load and program. *College room and board: room only:* $4980. Room and board charges vary according to housing facility.

FRESHMAN FINANCIAL AID (Fall 2004) 659 applied for aid; of those 62% were deemed to have need. 100% of freshmen with need received aid; of those 85% had need fully met. *Average percent of need met:* 85% (excluding resources awarded to replace EFC). *Average financial aid package:* $5818 (excluding resources awarded to replace EFC). 34% of all full-time freshmen had no need and received non-need-based gift aid.

UNDERGRADUATE FINANCIAL AID (Fall 2004) 3,058 applied for aid; of those 65% were deemed to have need. 100% of undergraduates with need received aid; of those 85% had need fully met. *Average percent of need met:* 85% (excluding resources awarded to replace EFC). *Average financial aid package:* $6848 (excluding resources awarded to replace EFC). 19% of all full-time undergraduates had no need and received non-need-based gift aid.

GIFT AID (NEED-BASED) *Total amount:* $4,786,812 (98% federal, 1% state, 1% external sources). *Receiving aid:* Freshmen: 26% (199); All full-time undergraduates: 34% (1,214). *Average award:* Freshmen: $2706; Undergraduates: $2796. *Scholarships, grants, and awards:* Federal Pell, FSEOG, state, private, college/university gift aid from institutional funds, Federal Nursing.

Armstrong Atlantic State University

GIFT AID (NON-NEED-BASED) *Total amount:* $4,965,272 (92% state, 2% institutional, 6% external sources). *Receiving aid:* Freshmen: 40% (310); Undergraduates: 24% (849). *Average Award: Freshmen:* $2989; *Undergraduates:* $2779. *Scholarships, grants, and awards by category: Academic Interests/Achievement:* 361 awards ($433,748 total): biological sciences, computer science, education, engineering/technologies, English, foreign languages, general academic interests/achievements, health fields, humanities, international studies, mathematics, military science, physical sciences. *Creative Arts/Performance:* 87 awards ($52,011 total): art/fine arts, music. *Special Achievements/Activities:* community service. *Special Characteristics:* 15 awards ($37,614 total): international students, religious affiliation. *Tuition waivers:* Full or partial for senior citizens. *ROTC:* Army, Naval cooperative.
LOANS *Student loans:* $12,773,421 (58% need-based, 42% non-need-based). 55% of past graduating class borrowed through all loan programs. *Average indebtedness per student:* $11,000. *Average need-based loan:* Freshmen: $2368; Undergraduates: $3418. *Parent loans:* $381,391 (100% non-need-based). *Programs:* FFEL (Subsidized and Unsubsidized Stafford, PLUS), state, college/university, alternative loans.
WORK-STUDY *Federal work-study:* Total amount: $349,362; 100 jobs averaging $3500. *State or other work-study/employment:* Part-time jobs available.
ATHLETIC AWARDS *Total amount:* $620,861 (100% non-need-based).
APPLYING FOR FINANCIAL AID *Required financial aid form:* FAFSA. *Financial aid deadline (priority):* 3/15. *Notification date:* Continuous beginning 4/1. Students must reply within 2 weeks of notification.
CONTACT Lee Ann Kirkland, Director of Financial Aid, Armstrong Atlantic State University, 11935 Abercorn Street, Savannah, GA 31419-1997, 912-921-5990 or toll-free 800-633-2349. *Fax:* 912-921-7357. *E-mail:* finaid@mail.armstrong.edu.

ART ACADEMY OF CINCINNATI
Cincinnati, OH

ABOUT THE INSTITUTION Independent, coed. Awards: associate, bachelor's, and master's degrees. 11 undergraduate majors. Total enrollment: 164. Undergraduates: 163. Freshmen: 52.
GIFT AID (NEED-BASED) *Scholarships, grants, and awards:* Federal Pell, FSEOG, state, private, college/university gift aid from institutional funds.
GIFT AID (NON-NEED-BASED) *Scholarships, grants, and awards by category: Creative Arts/Performance:* applied art and design, art/fine arts.
LOANS *Programs:* FFEL (Subsidized and Unsubsidized Stafford, PLUS), college/university, alternative loans.
APPLYING FOR FINANCIAL AID *Required financial aid form:* FAFSA.
CONTACT Ms. Karen Geiger, Director of Financial Aid, Art Academy of Cincinnati, 1125 Saint Gregory Street, Cincinnati, OH 45202-1700, 513-562-8773 or toll-free 800-323-5692 (in-state). *Fax:* 513-562-8778. *E-mail:* financialaid@artacademy.edu.

ART CENTER COLLEGE OF DESIGN
Pasadena, CA

Tuition & fees: $28,000	Average undergraduate aid package: $13,708

ABOUT THE INSTITUTION Independent, coed. Awards: bachelor's and master's degrees. 19 undergraduate majors. Total enrollment: 1,642. Undergraduates: 1,512. Freshmen: 90. Federal methodology is used as a basis for awarding need-based institutional aid.
UNDERGRADUATE EXPENSES for 2005–06 *Application fee:* $45. *Tuition:* full-time $27,800. *Payment plan:* Installment.
FRESHMAN FINANCIAL AID (Fall 2005, est.) 195 applied for aid. *Average percent of need met:* 58% (excluding resources awarded to replace EFC). *Average financial aid package:* $12,836 (excluding resources awarded to replace EFC).
UNDERGRADUATE FINANCIAL AID (Fall 2005, est.) 1,090 applied for aid. *Average percent of need met:* 60% (excluding resources awarded to replace EFC). *Average financial aid package:* $13,708 (excluding resources awarded to replace EFC).
GIFT AID (NEED-BASED) *Total amount:* $6,884,285 (28% federal, 22% state, 49% institutional, 1% external sources). *Receiving aid:* Freshmen: 42% (136); All full-time undergraduates: 65% (834). *Average award:* Freshmen: $8588; Undergraduates: $8227. *Scholarships, grants, and awards:* Federal Pell, FSEOG, state, private, college/university gift aid from institutional funds.
GIFT AID (NON-NEED-BASED) *Scholarships, grants, and awards by category: Creative Arts/Performance:* art/fine arts. *Tuition waivers:* Full or partial for employees or children of employees.
LOANS *Student loans:* $6,330,081 (82% need-based, 18% non-need-based). 70% of past graduating class borrowed through all loan programs. *Average indebtedness per student:* $70,000. *Average need-based loan:* Freshmen: $4026; Undergraduates: $5283. *Parent loans:* $1,938,819 (100% non-need-based). *Programs:* FFEL (Subsidized and Unsubsidized Stafford, PLUS), college/university, alternative loans.
WORK-STUDY *Federal work-study:* Total amount: $300,000; 150 jobs averaging $2000.
APPLYING FOR FINANCIAL AID *Required financial aid form:* FAFSA. *Financial aid deadline (priority):* 3/1. *Notification date:* Continuous beginning 5/1. Students must reply within 4 weeks of notification.
CONTACT Clema McKenzie, Director of Financial Aid, Art Center College of Design, 1700 Lida Street, Pasadena, CA 91103-1999, 626-396-2215. *Fax:* 626-683-8684.

THE ART CENTER DESIGN COLLEGE
Tucson, AZ

CONTACT Ms. Margarita Carey, Education Finance Director, The Art Center Design College, 2525 North Country Club Road, Tucson, AZ 85716-2505, 520-325-0123 or toll-free 800-825-8753. *Fax:* 520-325-5535.

THE ART INSTITUTE OF ATLANTA
Atlanta, GA

CONTACT Rena Marroquin, Financial Aid Office, The Art Institute of Atlanta, 6600 Peachtree Dunwoody Road, 100 Embassy Road, Atlanta, GA 30326, 770-394-8300 or toll-free 800-275-4242.

THE ART INSTITUTE OF BOSTON AT LESLEY UNIVERSITY
Boston, MA

CONTACT Financial Aid Officer, The Art Institute of Boston at Lesley University, 700 Beacon Street, Boston, MA 02215-2598, 617-349-8714 or toll-free 800-773-0494 (in-state). *Fax:* 617-437-1226.

THE ART INSTITUTE OF CALIFORNIA–INLAND EMPIRE
San Bernardino, CA

CONTACT Financial Aid Office, The Art Institute of California–Inland Empire, 630 East Brier Drive, San Bernardino, CA 92408, 909-915-2100 or toll-free 800-353-0812 (out-of-state).

THE ART INSTITUTE OF CALIFORNIA–LOS ANGELES
Santa Monica, CA

CONTACT Financial Aid Office, The Art Institute of California–Los Angeles, 2900 31st Street, Santa Monica, CA 90405-3035, 310-752-4700 or toll-free 888-646-4610.

THE ART INSTITUTE OF CALIFORNIA–ORANGE COUNTY
Santa Ana, CA

CONTACT Financial Aid Office, The Art Institute of California–Orange County, 3601 West Sunflower Avenue, Santa Ana, CA 92704-9888, 714-830-0200 or toll-free 888-549-3055.

THE ART INSTITUTE OF CALIFORNIA–SAN DIEGO
San Diego, CA

CONTACT Monica McCormick, Financial Aid Administrator, The Art Institute of California–San Diego, 10025 Mesa Rim Road, San Diego, CA 92121, 619-546-0602 or toll-free 800-591-2422 Ext. 3117 (in-state).

THE ART INSTITUTE OF CALIFORNIA–SAN FRANCISCO
San Francisco, CA

CONTACT Director of Student Financial Services, The Art Institute of California–San Francisco, 1170 Market Street, San Francisco, CA 94102-4908, 415-865-0198 or toll-free 888-493-3261. *Fax:* 415-863-5831.

THE ART INSTITUTE OF COLORADO
Denver, CO

ABOUT THE INSTITUTION Proprietary, coed. Awards: associate and bachelor's degrees. 10 undergraduate majors. Total enrollment: 2,886. Undergraduates: 2,886. Freshmen: 670.
GIFT AID (NEED-BASED) *Scholarships, grants, and awards:* Federal Pell, FSEOG, state, private, college/university gift aid from institutional funds.
GIFT AID (NON-NEED-BASED) *Scholarships, grants, and awards by category: Academic Interests/Achievement:* general academic interests/achievements. *Creative Arts/Performance:* applied art and design, art/fine arts, cinema/film/broadcasting, general creative arts/performance. *Special Achievements/Activities:* general special achievements/activities, junior miss.
LOANS *Programs:* FFEL (Subsidized and Unsubsidized Stafford, PLUS), Perkins, state.
WORK-STUDY *Federal work-study:* Total amount: $88,142; jobs available. *State or other work-study/employment:* Total amount: $208,110 (100% need-based). 34 part-time jobs available.
APPLYING FOR FINANCIAL AID *Required financial aid forms:* FAFSA, institution's own form.
CONTACT Shannon May, Director of Student Financial Services, The Art Institute of Colorado, 1200 Lincoln Street, Denver, CO 80203-2903, 303-837-0825 Ext. 4747 or toll-free 800-275-2420. *Fax:* 303-860-8520. *E-mail:* mays@aii.edu.

THE ART INSTITUTE OF DALLAS
Dallas, TX

Tuition & fees: $17,542	Average undergraduate aid package: $6528

ABOUT THE INSTITUTION Proprietary, coed. Awards: associate and bachelor's degrees. 10 undergraduate majors. Total enrollment: 1,304. Undergraduates: 1,304. Freshmen: 260. Federal methodology is used as a basis for awarding need-based institutional aid.
UNDERGRADUATE EXPENSES for 2006–07 *Application fee:* $50. *Tuition:* full-time $17,542; part-time $390 per credit hour.
FRESHMAN FINANCIAL AID (Fall 2004) 185 applied for aid; of those 92% were deemed to have need. 100% of freshmen with need received aid. *Average percent of need met:* 45% (excluding resources awarded to replace EFC). *Average financial aid package:* $6528 (excluding resources awarded to replace EFC). 7% of all full-time freshmen had no need and received non-need-based gift aid.
UNDERGRADUATE FINANCIAL AID (Fall 2004) 799 applied for aid; of those 97% were deemed to have need. 100% of undergraduates with need received aid. *Average percent of need met:* 45% (excluding resources awarded to replace EFC). *Average financial aid package:* $6528 (excluding resources awarded to replace EFC). 2% of all full-time undergraduates had no need and received non-need-based gift aid.
GIFT AID (NEED-BASED) *Total amount:* $527,121 (89% institutional, 11% external sources). *Receiving aid:* Freshmen: 57% (133); All full-time undergraduates: 59% (587). *Average award:* Freshmen: $838; Undergraduates: $838. *Scholarships, grants, and awards:* Federal Pell, FSEOG, private, college/university gift aid from institutional funds.

GIFT AID (NON-NEED-BASED) *Receiving aid:* Freshmen: 7% (16); Undergraduates: 3% (31). *Average Award:* Freshmen: $1066; Undergraduates: $2100.
LOANS *Student loans:* $6,792,600 (100% need-based). 83% of past graduating class borrowed through all loan programs. *Average indebtedness per student:* $23,125. *Average need-based loan:* Freshmen: $3028; Undergraduates: $3028. *Parent loans:* $6,792,600 (100% need-based). *Programs:* FFEL (Subsidized and Unsubsidized Stafford, PLUS), Perkins.
WORK-STUDY *Federal work-study:* Total amount: $91,765; 33 jobs averaging $2000. *State or other work-study/employment:* 49 part-time jobs averaging $3748.
APPLYING FOR FINANCIAL AID *Required financial aid forms:* FAFSA, institution's own form. *Financial aid deadline (priority):* 4/15. *Notification date:* Continuous beginning 7/1.
CONTACT Lisa McGaha, Director of Student Financial Services, The Art Institute of Dallas, 8080 Park Lane, Dallas, TX 75231, 214-692-8080 Ext. 1258 or toll-free 800-275-4243. *Fax:* 214-692-6541. *E-mail:* lmcgaha@aii.edu.

THE ART INSTITUTE OF FORT LAUDERDALE
Fort Lauderdale, FL

CONTACT Office of Student Financial Services, The Art Institute of Fort Lauderdale, 1799 Southeast 17th Street Causeway, Fort Lauderdale, FL 33316-3000, 954-527-1799 or toll-free 800-275-7603.

THE ART INSTITUTE OF HOUSTON
Houston, TX

CONTACT Sara Benson, Director of Accounting and Financial Services, The Art Institute of Houston, 1900 Yorktown, Houston, TX 77056, 713-623-2040 Ext. 780 or toll-free 800-275-4244. *Fax:* 713-966-2700. *E-mail:* bensons@aii.edu.

THE ART INSTITUTE OF INDIANAPOLIS
Indianapolis, IN

CONTACT Financial Aid Office, The Art Institute of Indianapolis, 3500 Depauw Boulevard, Indianapolis, IN 46268, 866-441-9031.

THE ART INSTITUTE OF LAS VEGAS
Henderson, NV

CONTACT Financial Aid Office, The Art Institute of Las Vegas, 2350 Corporate Circle Drive, Henderson, NV 89074, 702-369-9944.

THE ART INSTITUTE OF PHOENIX
Phoenix, AZ

Tuition & fees: $18,144	Average undergraduate aid package: N/A

ABOUT THE INSTITUTION Proprietary, coed. Awards: associate and bachelor's degrees. 7 undergraduate majors. Total enrollment: 1,114. Undergraduates: 1,114. Freshmen: 439. Federal methodology is used as a basis for awarding need-based institutional aid.
UNDERGRADUATE EXPENSES for 2005–06 *Application fee:* $50. *One-time required fee:* $100. *Tuition:* full-time $18,144; part-time $378 per credit hour. Full-time tuition and fees vary according to course load. Part-time tuition and fees vary according to course load. *Payment plans:* Guaranteed tuition, installment.
GIFT AID (NEED-BASED) *Total amount:* $1,777,300 (91% federal, 9% institutional). *Scholarships, grants, and awards:* Federal Pell, FSEOG, state, private, college/university gift aid from institutional funds.
GIFT AID (NON-NEED-BASED) *Total amount:* $564,397 (81% institutional, 19% external sources). *Tuition waivers:* Full or partial for employees or children of employees.
LOANS *Student loans:* $11,670,486 (41% need-based, 59% non-need-based). *Parent loans:* $5,050,113 (100% non-need-based). *Programs:* FFEL (Subsidized and Unsubsidized Stafford, PLUS), Perkins, private alternative loans.

The Art Institute of Phoenix

WORK-STUDY *Federal work-study:* Total amount: $42,632; 22 jobs averaging $2087.
APPLYING FOR FINANCIAL AID *Required financial aid form:* FAFSA. *Financial aid deadline:* Continuous. *Notification date:* Continuous beginning 3/1. Students must reply within 2 weeks of notification.
CONTACT Dorena Spitler, Director of Student Financial Services, The Art Institute of Phoenix, 2233 West Dunlap Avenue, Phoenix, AZ 85021, 602-331-7500 Ext. 7510 or toll-free 800-474-2479. *Fax:* 602-331-5302. *E-mail:* aspitler@aii.edu.

THE ART INSTITUTE OF PITTSBURGH
Pittsburgh, PA

CONTACT Ms. Gayle J. Knight, Student Financial Services Director, The Art Institute of Pittsburgh, 526 Penn Avenue, Pittsburgh, PA 15222-3269, 412-263-6600 or toll-free 800-275-2470.

THE ART INSTITUTE OF PORTLAND
Portland, OR

ABOUT THE INSTITUTION Proprietary, coed. Awards: associate and bachelor's degrees. 7 undergraduate majors. Total enrollment: 1,583. Undergraduates: 1,583. Freshmen: 232.
GIFT AID (NEED-BASED) *Scholarships, grants, and awards:* Federal Pell, FSEOG, private, college/university gift aid from institutional funds, Bureau of Indian Affairs Grants.
GIFT AID (NON-NEED-BASED) *Scholarships, grants, and awards by category: Creative Arts/Performance:* applied art and design, general creative arts/performance. *Special Characteristics:* children of faculty/staff.
LOANS *Programs:* FFEL (Subsidized and Unsubsidized Stafford, PLUS), state, alternative loans.
WORK-STUDY *Federal work-study:* Total amount: $73,701; 30 jobs averaging $2457.
APPLYING FOR FINANCIAL AID *Required financial aid forms:* FAFSA, financial aid transcript (for transfers).
CONTACT Mr. Mickey Jacobson, Director of Student Financial Services, The Art Institute of Portland, 1122 Northwest Davis Street, Portland, OR 97209-2911, 503-228-6528 Ext. 4728 or toll-free 888-228-6528. *Fax:* 503-228-4227. *E-mail:* mjacobson@aii.edu.

THE ART INSTITUTE OF SEATTLE
Seattle, WA

CONTACT Shelly DuBois, Vice President/Director of Administrative and Financial Services, The Art Institute of Seattle, 2323 Elliott Avenue, Seattle, WA 98121, 206-448-0900 or toll-free 800-275-2471. *Fax:* 206-448-2501.

THE ART INSTITUTE OF TAMPA
Tampa, FL

CONTACT Financial Aid Office, The Art Institute of Tampa, 4401 North Himes Avenue, Suite 150, Tampa, FL 33614, 866-703-3277.

THE ART INSTITUTE OF WASHINGTON
Arlington, VA

CONTACT Director of Student Financial Services, The Art Institute of Washington, 1820 North Fort Myer Drive, Arlington, VA 22209, 703-247-6849 or toll-free 877-303-3771. *Fax:* 703-247-6829.

THE ART INSTITUTES INTERNATIONAL MINNESOTA
Minneapolis, MN

CONTACT Tiffany Robb, Student Financial Planner, The Art Institutes International Minnesota, 825 2nd Avenue South, Minneapolis, MN 55402, 612-332-3361 Ext. 110 or toll-free 800-777-3643. *Fax:* 612-332-3934. *E-mail:* robbt@aii.edu.

ASBURY COLLEGE
Wilmore, KY

Tuition & fees: $18,956 **Average undergraduate aid package:** $13,506

ABOUT THE INSTITUTION Independent nondenominational, coed. Awards: bachelor's and master's degrees. 37 undergraduate majors. Total enrollment: 1,293. Undergraduates: 1,229. Freshmen: 277. Federal methodology is used as a basis for awarding need-based institutional aid.
UNDERGRADUATE EXPENSES for 2005–06 *Application fee:* $30. *Comprehensive fee:* $23,762 includes full-time tuition ($18,808), mandatory fees ($148), and room and board ($4806). *College room only:* $2810. Full-time tuition and fees vary according to course load. Room and board charges vary according to board plan, housing facility, and location. *Part-time tuition:* $723 per semester hour. Part-time tuition and fees vary according to course load. *Payment plans:* Installment, deferred payment.
FRESHMAN FINANCIAL AID (Fall 2005, est.) 253 applied for aid; of those 85% were deemed to have need. 100% of freshmen with need received aid; of those 29% had need fully met. *Average percent of need met:* 81% (excluding resources awarded to replace EFC). *Average financial aid package:* $13,654 (excluding resources awarded to replace EFC). 13% of all full-time freshmen had no need and received non-need-based gift aid.
UNDERGRADUATE FINANCIAL AID (Fall 2005, est.) 913 applied for aid; of those 87% were deemed to have need. 100% of undergraduates with need received aid; of those 24% had need fully met. *Average percent of need met:* 78% (excluding resources awarded to replace EFC). *Average financial aid package:* $13,506 (excluding resources awarded to replace EFC). 9% of all full-time undergraduates had no need and received non-need-based gift aid.
GIFT AID (NEED-BASED) *Total amount:* $5,458,729 (16% federal, 16% state, 59% institutional, 9% external sources). *Receiving aid:* Freshmen: 76% (210); All full-time undergraduates: 69% (774). *Average award:* Freshmen: $8273; Undergraduates: $8075. *Scholarships, grants, and awards:* Federal Pell, FSEOG, state, private, college/university gift aid from institutional funds.
GIFT AID (NON-NEED-BASED) *Total amount:* $2,674,295 (5% state, 90% institutional, 5% external sources). *Receiving aid:* Freshmen: 34% (95); Undergraduates: 22% (249). *Average Award:* Freshmen: $10,951; Undergraduates:* $10,356. *Scholarships, grants, and awards by category: Academic Interests/Achievement:* general academic interests/achievements. *Creative Arts/Performance:* music. *Special Achievements/Activities:* leadership. *Special Characteristics:* children and siblings of alumni, children of faculty/staff, ethnic background, international students, siblings of current students. *Tuition waivers:* Full or partial for employees or children of employees, senior citizens. *ROTC:* Army cooperative, Air Force cooperative.
LOANS *Student loans:* $4,937,528 (92% need-based, 8% non-need-based). 70% of past graduating class borrowed through all loan programs. *Average indebtedness per student:* $22,016. *Average need-based loan:* Freshmen: $2696; Undergraduates: $3737. *Parent loans:* $1,482,275 (92% need-based, 8% non-need-based). *Programs:* FFEL (Subsidized and Unsubsidized Stafford, PLUS), Perkins, state, college/university, private alternative loans.
WORK-STUDY *Federal work-study:* Total amount: $484,896; jobs available. *State or other work-study/employment:* Total amount: $560,184 (100% need-based). Part-time jobs available.
ATHLETIC AWARDS *Total amount:* $80,552 (82% need-based, 18% non-need-based).
APPLYING FOR FINANCIAL AID *Required financial aid forms:* FAFSA, institution's own form. *Financial aid deadline (priority):* 3/1. *Notification date:* Continuous beginning 2/15. Students must reply within 4 weeks of notification.
CONTACT Ronald Anderson, Director of Financial Aid, Asbury College, One Macklem Drive, Wilmore, KY 40390, 859-858-2508 Ext. 2195 or toll-free 800-888-1818. *Fax:* 859-858-3921. *E-mail:* ron.anderson@asbury.edu.

ASHFORD UNIVERSITY
Clinton, IA

Tuition & fees: N/R **Average undergraduate aid package:** $10,201

ABOUT THE INSTITUTION Proprietary, coed. Awards: bachelor's and master's degrees. 32 undergraduate majors. Total enrollment: 459. Undergraduates: 391. Freshmen: 52. Federal methodology is used as a basis for awarding need-based institutional aid.

FRESHMAN FINANCIAL AID (Fall 2005, est.) 64 applied for aid; of those 83% were deemed to have need. 100% of freshmen with need received aid; of those 8% had need fully met. *Average percent of need met:* 72% (excluding resources awarded to replace EFC). *Average financial aid package:* $10,241 (excluding resources awarded to replace EFC). 20% of all full-time freshmen had no need and received non-need-based gift aid.
UNDERGRADUATE FINANCIAL AID (Fall 2005, est.) 350 applied for aid; of those 89% were deemed to have need. 100% of undergraduates with need received aid; of those 15% had need fully met. *Average percent of need met:* 73% (excluding resources awarded to replace EFC). *Average financial aid package:* $10,201 (excluding resources awarded to replace EFC). 13% of all full-time undergraduates had no need and received non-need-based gift aid.
GIFT AID (NEED-BASED) *Total amount:* $1,827,723 (26% federal, 20% state, 54% institutional). *Receiving aid:* Freshmen: 79% (52); All full-time undergraduates: 83% (298). *Average award:* Freshmen: $7683; Undergraduates: $7122. *Scholarships, grants, and awards:* Federal Pell, FSEOG, state, private, college/university gift aid from institutional funds.
GIFT AID (NON-NEED-BASED) *Total amount:* $203,473 (1% state, 92% institutional, 7% external sources). *Receiving aid:* Freshmen: 5% (3); Undergraduates: 8% (30). *Average Award: Freshmen:* $11,660; *Undergraduates:* $10,099. *Scholarships, grants, and awards by category: Academic Interests/Achievement:* general academic interests/achievements. *Special Characteristics:* children of faculty/staff, international students. *Tuition waivers:* Full or partial for children of alumni, employees or children of employees, senior citizens.
LOANS *Student loans:* $2,184,341 (74% need-based, 26% non-need-based). 99% of past graduating class borrowed through all loan programs. *Average indebtedness per student:* $20,468. *Average need-based loan:* Freshmen: $2178; Undergraduates: $3492. *Parent loans:* $548,927 (32% need-based, 68% non-need-based). *Programs:* FFEL (Subsidized and Unsubsidized Stafford, PLUS), Perkins, state.
WORK-STUDY *Federal work-study:* Total amount: $91,430; 55 jobs averaging $1650. *State or other work-study/employment:* Total amount: $42,289 (5% need-based, 95% non-need-based). 25 part-time jobs averaging $1650.
ATHLETIC AWARDS *Total amount:* $458,560 (68% need-based, 32% non-need-based).
APPLYING FOR FINANCIAL AID *Required financial aid forms:* FAFSA, institution's own form. *Financial aid deadline:* 8/1 (priority: 3/1). *Notification date:* Continuous beginning 3/1. Students must reply within 2 weeks of notification.
CONTACT Lisa Kramer, Director of Financial Aid, Ashford University, 400 North Bluff Boulevard, PO Box 2967, Clinton, IA 52733-2967, 563-242-4023 Ext. 1243 or toll-free 800-242-4153. Fax: 563-242-8684.

ASHLAND UNIVERSITY
Ashland, OH

Tuition & fees: $21,430	Average undergraduate aid package: N/A

ABOUT THE INSTITUTION Independent religious, coed. Awards: associate, bachelor's, master's, doctoral, and first professional degrees. 70 undergraduate majors. Total enrollment: 6,472. Undergraduates: 2,791. Freshmen: 550. Federal methodology is used as a basis for awarding need-based institutional aid.
UNDERGRADUATE EXPENSES for 2006–07 *Application fee:* $25. *Comprehensive fee:* $29,220 includes full-time tuition ($20,666), mandatory fees ($764), and room and board ($7790). *College room only:* $4184. *Part-time tuition:* $635 per credit hour.
FRESHMAN FINANCIAL AID (Fall 2005, est.) 534 applied for aid; of those 81% were deemed to have need. 100% of freshmen with need received aid. *Average percent of need met:* 90% (excluding resources awarded to replace EFC). 17% of all full-time freshmen had no need and received non-need-based gift aid.
UNDERGRADUATE FINANCIAL AID (Fall 2005, est.) 2,252 applied for aid; of those 78% were deemed to have need. 100% of undergraduates with need received aid. *Average percent of need met:* 90% (excluding resources awarded to replace EFC). 16% of all full-time undergraduates had no need and received non-need-based gift aid.
GIFT AID (NEED-BASED) *Total amount:* $16,033,480 (11% federal, 17% state, 69% institutional, 3% external sources). *Receiving aid:* Freshmen: 79% (430); All full-time undergraduates: 78% (1,758). *Average award:* Freshmen: $11,729; Undergraduates: $11,409. *Scholarships, grants, and awards:* Federal Pell, FSEOG, state, private.
GIFT AID (NON-NEED-BASED) *Total amount:* $2,521,555 (15% state, 77% institutional, 8% external sources). *Average Award: Freshmen:* $7170; *Undergraduates:* $6206. *Scholarships, grants, and awards by category: Academic Interests/Achievement:* 1,197 awards ($6,481,790 total): general academic interests/achievements, mathematics, physical sciences, social sciences. *Creative Arts/Performance:* 174 awards ($341,375 total): art/fine arts, music, theater/drama. *Special Characteristics:* 351 awards ($2,141,841 total): children and siblings of alumni, children of faculty/staff, international students, relatives of clergy, religious affiliation.
LOANS *Student loans:* $10,602,033 (92% need-based, 8% non-need-based). 75% of past graduating class borrowed through all loan programs. *Average indebtedness per student:* $18,250. *Average need-based loan:* Freshmen: $3192; Undergraduates: $4183. *Parent loans:* $4,007,748 (78% need-based, 22% non-need-based). *Programs:* Federal Direct (Subsidized and Unsubsidized Stafford, PLUS), Perkins, college/university.
WORK-STUDY *Federal work-study:* Total amount: $2,127,225; 1,155 jobs averaging $1841. *State or other work-study/employment:* Total amount: $651,443 (42% need-based, 58% non-need-based).
ATHLETIC AWARDS *Total amount:* $3,511,188 (71% need-based, 29% non-need-based).
APPLYING FOR FINANCIAL AID *Required financial aid forms:* FAFSA, institution's own form. *Financial aid deadline:* Continuous. *Notification date:* Continuous beginning 3/15. Students must reply within 3 weeks of notification.
CONTACT Mr. Stephen C. Howell, Director of Financial Aid, Ashland University, 401 College Avenue, Room 310, Ashland, OH 44805-3702, 419-289-5944 or toll-free 800-882-1548. Fax: 419-289-5976. E-mail: showell@ashland.edu.

ASPEN UNIVERSITY
Denver, CO

CONTACT Financial Aid Office, Aspen University, 501 South Cherry Street, Suite 350, Denver, CO 80246, 303-333-4224 or toll-free 800-441-4746 Ext. 177 (in-state).

ASSUMPTION COLLEGE
Worcester, MA

Tuition & fees: $26,310	Average undergraduate aid package: $15,462

ABOUT THE INSTITUTION Independent Roman Catholic, coed. Awards: bachelor's and master's degrees and post-master's certificates. 31 undergraduate majors. Total enrollment: 2,451. Undergraduates: 2,124. Freshmen: 565. Federal methodology is used as a basis for awarding need-based institutional aid.
UNDERGRADUATE EXPENSES for 2006–07 *Application fee:* $50. *Comprehensive fee:* $32,085 includes full-time tuition ($25,895), mandatory fees ($415), and room and board ($5775). *College room only:* $3395.
FRESHMAN FINANCIAL AID (Fall 2005, est.) 483 applied for aid; of those 82% were deemed to have need. 100% of freshmen with need received aid; of those 18% had need fully met. *Average percent of need met:* 70% (excluding resources awarded to replace EFC). *Average financial aid package:* $14,854 (excluding resources awarded to replace EFC). 23% of all full-time freshmen had no need and received non-need-based gift aid.
UNDERGRADUATE FINANCIAL AID (Fall 2005, est.) 1,717 applied for aid; of those 86% were deemed to have need. 99% of undergraduates with need received aid; of those 20% had need fully met. *Average percent of need met:* 72% (excluding resources awarded to replace EFC). *Average financial aid package:* $15,462 (excluding resources awarded to replace EFC). 23% of all full-time undergraduates had no need and received non-need-based gift aid.
GIFT AID (NEED-BASED) *Total amount:* $15,897,127 (5% federal, 5% state, 87% institutional, 3% external sources). *Receiving aid:* Freshmen: 69% (392); All full-time undergraduates: 69% (1,441). *Average award:* Freshmen: $12,018; Undergraduates: $11,400. *Scholarships, grants, and awards:* Federal Pell, FSEOG, state, private, college/university gift aid from institutional funds.
GIFT AID (NON-NEED-BASED) *Total amount:* $3,897,207 (94% institutional, 6% external sources). *Receiving aid:* Freshmen: 10% (55); Undergraduates: 7% (151). *Average Award: Freshmen:* $15,059; *Undergraduates:* $13,992. *Scholarships, grants, and awards by category: Academic Interests/Achievement:* 1,149 awards ($10,265,663 total): general academic interests/achievements. *ROTC:* Army cooperative, Air Force cooperative.

Assumption College

LOANS *Student loans:* $12,050,499 (65% need-based, 35% non-need-based). 76% of past graduating class borrowed through all loan programs. *Average indebtedness per student:* $21,773. *Average need-based loan:* Freshmen: $3000; Undergraduates: $4451. *Parent loans:* $7,293,707 (28% need-based, 72% non-need-based). *Programs:* FFEL (Subsidized and Unsubsidized Stafford, PLUS), Perkins, state, college/university.
WORK-STUDY *Federal work-study:* Total amount: $649,090; 436 jobs averaging $1488.
ATHLETIC AWARDS Total amount: $736,266 (21% need-based, 79% non-need-based).
APPLYING FOR FINANCIAL AID *Required financial aid form:* FAFSA. *Financial aid deadline:* 2/1. *Notification date:* Continuous beginning 2/16. Students must reply by 5/1.
CONTACT Karen Puntillo, Director of Financial Aid, Assumption College, 500 Salisbury Street, Worcester, MA 01609-1296, 508-767-7157 or toll-free 888-882-7786. *Fax:* 508-767-7376. *E-mail:* fa@assumption.edu.

ATHENS STATE UNIVERSITY
Athens, AL

Tuition & fees (AL res): $3870   **Average undergraduate aid package:** N/A

ABOUT THE INSTITUTION State-supported, coed. Awards: bachelor's degrees. 29 undergraduate majors. Total enrollment: 2,643. Undergraduates: 2,643. Federal methodology is used as a basis for awarding need-based institutional aid.
UNDERGRADUATE EXPENSES for 2005–06 *Application fee:* $30. *Tuition, state resident:* full-time $3330; part-time $111 per semester hour. *Tuition, nonresident:* full-time $6660; part-time $222 per semester hour. *Required fees:* full-time $540; $18 per semester hour. *College room and board: room only:* $900.
UNDERGRADUATE FINANCIAL AID (Fall 2004) 2,827 applied for aid; of those 60% were deemed to have need. 94% of undergraduates with need received aid.
GIFT AID (NEED-BASED) *Total amount:* $2,424,738 (100% federal). *Receiving aid:* All full-time undergraduates: 30% (1,067). *Scholarships, grants, and awards:* Federal Pell, FSEOG, state, private, college/university gift aid from institutional funds.
GIFT AID (NON-NEED-BASED) *Total amount:* $2,760,481 (16% federal, 29% state, 27% institutional, 28% external sources). *Scholarships, grants, and awards by category: Academic Interests/Achievement:* 89 awards ($731,643 total): biological sciences, business, computer science, education, English, general academic interests/achievements, humanities, international studies, mathematics, physical sciences, religion/biblical studies, social sciences. *Creative Arts/Performance:* art/fine arts, journalism/publications. *Special Achievements/Activities:* cheerleading/drum major, general special achievements/activities, leadership. *Special Characteristics:* children and siblings of alumni, children of faculty/staff. *Tuition waivers:* Full or partial for employees or children of employees, senior citizens.
LOANS *Student loans:* $8,651,242 (55% need-based, 45% non-need-based). 54% of past graduating class borrowed through all loan programs. *Average indebtedness per student:* $12,510. *Programs:* Federal Direct (Subsidized and Unsubsidized Stafford).
WORK-STUDY *Federal work-study:* Total amount: $60,313; 16 jobs averaging $3769. *State or other work-study/employment:* Total amount: $125,000 (100% non-need-based). 25 part-time jobs averaging $5000.
APPLYING FOR FINANCIAL AID *Required financial aid form:* FAFSA. *Financial aid deadline:* Continuous. *Notification date:* Continuous beginning 5/1. Students must reply within 2 weeks of notification.
CONTACT Renee Stanford, Financial Aid Officer, Athens State University, 300 North Beaty Street, Athens, AL 35611, 256-233-8122 or toll-free 800-522-0272. *Fax:* 256-233-8178. *E-mail:* renee.stanford@athens.edu.

ATLANTA CHRISTIAN COLLEGE
East Point, GA

CONTACT Blair Walker, Director of Financial Aid, Atlanta Christian College, 2605 Ben Hill Road, East Point, GA 30344, 404-761-8861 or toll-free 800-776-1ACC. *Fax:* 404-669-2024. *E-mail:* blairw@acc.edu.

ATLANTIC COLLEGE
Guaynabo, PR

ABOUT THE INSTITUTION Independent. Awards: associate and bachelor's degrees. Total enrollment: 656.
GIFT AID (NEED-BASED) *Scholarships, grants, and awards:* Federal Pell, FSEOG, state.
LOANS *Programs:* FFEL (Subsidized and Unsubsidized Stafford, PLUS).
APPLYING FOR FINANCIAL AID *Required financial aid forms:* FAFSA, institution's own form, commonwealth aid form.
CONTACT Mrs. Velma Aponte, Financial Aid Coordinator, Atlantic College, Calle Colton #9, Guaynabo, PR 00970, 787-720-1092. *E-mail:* atlaneco@coqui.net.

ATLANTIC UNION COLLEGE
South Lancaster, MA

Comprehensive fee: $17,600   **Average undergraduate aid package:** $10,766

ABOUT THE INSTITUTION Independent Seventh-day Adventist, coed. Awards: associate, bachelor's, and master's degrees. 45 undergraduate majors. Total enrollment: 473. Undergraduates: 398. Federal methodology is used as a basis for awarding need-based institutional aid.
UNDERGRADUATE EXPENSES for 2005–06 *Application fee:* $25. *Comprehensive fee:* $17,600. Full-time tuition and fees vary according to program. Room and board charges vary according to board plan and housing facility. *Part-time tuition:* $525 per credit hour. Part-time tuition and fees vary according to class time and program. *Payment plan:* Guaranteed tuition.
FRESHMAN FINANCIAL AID (Fall 2005, est.) 66 applied for aid; of those 86% were deemed to have need. 100% of freshmen with need received aid; of those 19% had need fully met. *Average percent of need met:* 71% (excluding resources awarded to replace EFC). *Average financial aid package:* $9609 (excluding resources awarded to replace EFC). 44% of all full-time freshmen had no need and received non-need-based gift aid.
UNDERGRADUATE FINANCIAL AID (Fall 2005, est.) 304 applied for aid; of those 90% were deemed to have need. 100% of undergraduates with need received aid; of those 16% had need fully met. *Average percent of need met:* 74% (excluding resources awarded to replace EFC). *Average financial aid package:* $10,766 (excluding resources awarded to replace EFC). 31% of all full-time undergraduates had no need and received non-need-based gift aid.
GIFT AID (NEED-BASED) *Total amount:* $1,908,202 (44% federal, 5% state, 42% institutional, 9% external sources). *Receiving aid:* Freshmen: 52% (56); All full-time undergraduates: 65% (260). *Average award:* Freshmen: $6899; Undergraduates: $6649. *Scholarships, grants, and awards:* Federal Pell, FSEOG, state, private, college/university gift aid from institutional funds.
GIFT AID (NON-NEED-BASED) *Total amount:* $647,387 (70% institutional, 30% external sources). *Receiving aid:* Freshmen: 6% (6); Undergraduates: 4% (17). *Average Award:* Freshmen: $4838; Undergraduates: $7199. *Scholarships, grants, and awards by category: Academic Interests/Achievement:* 21 awards ($5150 total): business, computer science, education, English, general academic interests/achievements, health fields, mathematics, premedicine, religion/biblical studies. *Creative Arts/Performance:* 66 awards ($293,500 total): music. *Special Achievements/Activities:* 42 awards ($60,150 total): leadership. *Special Characteristics:* 53 awards ($168,829 total): adult students, children of current students, children of faculty/staff, international students, out-of-state students, siblings of current students. *Tuition waivers:* Full or partial for employees or children of employees, senior citizens.
LOANS *Student loans:* $2,776,469 (72% need-based, 28% non-need-based). 100% of past graduating class borrowed through all loan programs. *Average indebtedness per student:* $20,023. *Average need-based loan:* Freshmen: $2929; Undergraduates: $4279. *Parent loans:* $199,730 (53% need-based, 47% non-need-based). *Programs:* FFEL (Subsidized and Unsubsidized Stafford, PLUS), Perkins, Federal Nursing, state, college/university, TERI Loans, Signature Loans, Campus Door.
WORK-STUDY *Federal work-study:* Total amount: $114,648; 92 jobs averaging $1247. *State or other work-study/employment:* Total amount: $165,724 (29% need-based, 71% non-need-based). 45 part-time jobs averaging $576.
APPLYING FOR FINANCIAL AID *Required financial aid form:* FAFSA. *Financial aid deadline (priority):* 4/15. *Notification date:* Continuous beginning 4/16. Students must reply within 2 weeks of notification.

CONTACT Sandra Boucher, Director of Financial Aid, Atlantic Union College, PO Box 1000, South Lancaster, MA 01561-1000, 978-368-2284 or toll-free 800-282-2030. *Fax:* 978-368-2283. *E-mail:* sboucher@atlanticuc.edu.

AUBURN UNIVERSITY
Auburn University, AL

Tuition & fees (AL res): $5516   **Average undergraduate aid package:** $7607

ABOUT THE INSTITUTION State-supported, coed. Awards: bachelor's, master's, doctoral, and first professional degrees and post-master's certificates. 138 undergraduate majors. Total enrollment: 23,333. Undergraduates: 19,254. Freshmen: 4,197. Federal methodology is used as a basis for awarding need-based institutional aid.

UNDERGRADUATE EXPENSES for 2006–07 *Application fee:* $25. *Tuition, state resident:* full-time $5278. *Tuition, nonresident:* full-time $14,878. *College room and board:* $7232; *room only:* $3060.

FRESHMAN FINANCIAL AID (Fall 2004) 1757 applied for aid; of those 69% were deemed to have need. 93% of freshmen with need received aid; of those 17% had need fully met. *Average percent of need met:* 46% (excluding resources awarded to replace EFC). *Average financial aid package:* $7286 (excluding resources awarded to replace EFC). 8% of all full-time freshmen had no need and received non-need-based gift aid.

UNDERGRADUATE FINANCIAL AID (Fall 2004) 7,959 applied for aid; of those 79% were deemed to have need. 96% of undergraduates with need received aid; of those 12% had need fully met. *Average percent of need met:* 47% (excluding resources awarded to replace EFC). *Average financial aid package:* $7607 (excluding resources awarded to replace EFC). 5% of all full-time undergraduates had no need and received non-need-based gift aid.

GIFT AID (NEED-BASED) *Total amount:* $17,218,718 (50% federal, 7% state, 24% institutional, 19% external sources). *Receiving aid:* Freshmen: 23% (816); All full-time undergraduates: 22% (3,835). *Average award:* Freshmen: $4417; Undergraduates: $4228. *Scholarships, grants, and awards:* Federal Pell, FSEOG, state, private, college/university gift aid from institutional funds.

GIFT AID (NON-NEED-BASED) *Total amount:* $4,946,291 (8% state, 2% institutional, 90% external sources). *Receiving aid:* Freshmen: 3% (100); Undergraduates: 2% (294). *Average Award:* Freshmen: $3047; Undergraduates: $3616. *Scholarships, grants, and awards by category: Academic Interests/Achievement:* agriculture, architecture, biological sciences, business, communication, computer science, education, engineering/technologies, English, foreign languages, general academic interests/achievements, health fields, home economics, humanities, international studies, mathematics, physical sciences, premedicine, social sciences. *Creative Arts/Performance:* applied art and design, art/fine arts, cinema/film/broadcasting, creative writing, journalism/publications, music, performing arts, theater/drama. *Special Achievements/Activities:* cheerleading/drum major, leadership, memberships. *Special Characteristics:* children and siblings of alumni, children of faculty/staff, children of union members/company employees, ethnic background, local/state students, married students, out-of-state students. *ROTC:* Army, Naval, Air Force.

LOANS *Student loans:* $43,322,532 (73% need-based, 27% non-need-based). 65% of past graduating class borrowed through all loan programs. *Average indebtedness per student:* $19,423. *Average need-based loan:* Freshmen: $2935; Undergraduates: $3985. *Parent loans:* $17,258,939 (33% need-based, 67% non-need-based). *Programs:* FFEL (Subsidized and Unsubsidized Stafford, PLUS), Perkins, college/university.

WORK-STUDY *Federal work-study:* Total amount: $1,486,158; 496 jobs averaging $2996.

ATHLETIC AWARDS *Total amount:* $6,945,263 (31% need-based, 69% non-need-based).

APPLYING FOR FINANCIAL AID *Required financial aid forms:* FAFSA, institution's own form. *Financial aid deadline (priority):* 3/1. *Notification date:* Continuous. Students must reply within 2 weeks of notification.

CONTACT Mr. Mike Reynolds, Director of Student Financial Services, Auburn University, 203 Mary Martin Hall, Auburn University, AL 36849, 334-844-4634 or toll-free 800-AUBURN9 (in-state). *Fax:* 334-844-6085. *E-mail:* finaid7@auburn.edu.

AUBURN UNIVERSITY MONTGOMERY
Montgomery, AL

Tuition & fees (AL res): $4640   **Average undergraduate aid package:** $7516

ABOUT THE INSTITUTION State-supported, coed. Awards: bachelor's, master's, and doctoral degrees and post-master's certificates. 24 undergraduate majors. Total enrollment: 5,128. Undergraduates: 4,300. Freshmen: 758. Federal methodology is used as a basis for awarding need-based institutional aid.

UNDERGRADUATE EXPENSES for 2005–06 *Application fee:* $25. *Tuition, state resident:* full-time $4410; part-time $147 per semester hour. *Tuition, nonresident:* full-time $13,230; part-time $441 per semester hour. *Required fees:* full-time $230; $5 per semester hour or $40 per term part-time. Full-time tuition and fees vary according to course load. *College room and board:* $4890; *room only:* $2400. Room and board charges vary according to housing facility. *Payment plan:* Deferred payment.

FRESHMAN FINANCIAL AID (Fall 2004) 382 applied for aid; of those 98% were deemed to have need. 78% of freshmen with need received aid; of those 21% had need fully met. *Average financial aid package:* $5733 (excluding resources awarded to replace EFC).

UNDERGRADUATE FINANCIAL AID (Fall 2004) 1,948 applied for aid; of those 93% were deemed to have need. 78% of undergraduates with need received aid; of those 20% had need fully met. *Average financial aid package:* $7516 (excluding resources awarded to replace EFC).

GIFT AID (NEED-BASED) *Total amount:* $6,114,599 (76% federal, 20% institutional, 4% external sources). *Receiving aid:* Freshmen: 36% (219); All full-time undergraduates: 4% (105). *Average award:* Freshmen: $3450; Undergraduates: $3275. *Scholarships, grants, and awards:* Federal Pell, FSEOG, state, college/university gift aid from institutional funds.

GIFT AID (NON-NEED-BASED) *Scholarships, grants, and awards by category: Academic Interests/Achievement:* 392 awards ($1,100,000 total): general academic interests/achievements. *Tuition waivers:* Full or partial for employees or children of employees. *ROTC:* Army, Air Force cooperative.

LOANS *Student loans:* $16,859,798 (100% need-based). 45% of past graduating class borrowed through all loan programs. *Average indebtedness per student:* $15,000. *Average need-based loan:* Freshmen: $2327; Undergraduates: $3525. *Parent loans:* $412,590 (100% need-based). *Programs:* FFEL (Subsidized and Unsubsidized Stafford, PLUS), Perkins.

WORK-STUDY *Federal work-study:* Total amount: $226,425; 73 jobs averaging $3385.

APPLYING FOR FINANCIAL AID *Required financial aid form:* FAFSA. *Financial aid deadline (priority):* 3/1. *Notification date:* 5/15. Students must reply within 3 weeks of notification.

CONTACT Dan Miller, Director of Financial Aid, Auburn University Montgomery, PO Box 244023, Montgomery, AL 36124-4023, 334-244-3570 or toll-free 800-227-2649 (in-state). *Fax:* 334-244-3913. *E-mail:* dmiller7@mail.aum.edu.

AUGSBURG COLLEGE
Minneapolis, MN

Tuition & fees: $23,422   **Average undergraduate aid package:** $12,700

ABOUT THE INSTITUTION Independent Lutheran, coed. Awards: bachelor's and master's degrees and post-bachelor's and post-master's certificates. 64 undergraduate majors. Total enrollment: 3,508. Undergraduates: 2,835. Freshmen: 335. Federal methodology is used as a basis for awarding need-based institutional aid.

UNDERGRADUATE EXPENSES for 2006–07 *Application fee:* $25. *Comprehensive fee:* $30,026 includes full-time tuition ($22,900), mandatory fees ($522), and room and board ($6604). *College room only:* $3396. *Part-time tuition:* $2866 per course. *Part-time fees:* $86 per course.

FRESHMAN FINANCIAL AID (Fall 2004) 248 applied for aid; of those 81% were deemed to have need. 99% of freshmen with need received aid; of those 20% had need fully met. *Average percent of need met:* 74% (excluding resources awarded to replace EFC). *Average financial aid package:* $15,487 (excluding resources awarded to replace EFC). 21% of all full-time freshmen had no need and received non-need-based gift aid.

UNDERGRADUATE FINANCIAL AID (Fall 2004) 1,683 applied for aid; of those 87% were deemed to have need. 100% of undergraduates with need received aid; of those 13% had need fully met. *Average percent of need met:* 61%

Augsburg College

(excluding resources awarded to replace EFC). *Average financial aid package:* $12,700 (excluding resources awarded to replace EFC). 16% of all full-time undergraduates had no need and received non-need-based gift aid.
GIFT AID (NEED-BASED) *Total amount:* $14,165,196 (17% federal, 15% state, 60% institutional, 8% external sources). *Receiving aid:* Freshmen: 50% (196); All full-time undergraduates: 60% (1,250). *Average award:* Freshmen: $11,877; Undergraduates: $9709. *Scholarships, grants, and awards:* Federal Pell, FSEOG, state, private, college/university gift aid from institutional funds, Federal Nursing.
GIFT AID (NON-NEED-BASED) *Total amount:* $2,528,421 (1% state, 69% institutional, 30% external sources). *Receiving aid:* Freshmen: 7% (26); Undergraduates: 5% (114). *Average Award:* Freshmen: $17,302; Undergraduates: $18,724. *Scholarships, grants, and awards by category: Academic Interests/Achievement:* biological sciences, business, communication, computer science, education, English, foreign languages, general academic interests/achievements, health fields, international studies, mathematics, physical sciences, religion/biblical studies, social sciences. *Creative Arts/Performance:* music, performing arts, theater/drama. *Special Achievements/Activities:* community service, general special achievements/activities, junior miss, leadership, religious involvement. *Special Characteristics:* children and siblings of alumni, international students, members of minority groups, relatives of clergy, siblings of current students. *ROTC:* Army cooperative, Naval cooperative, Air Force cooperative.
LOANS *Student loans:* $21,298,534 (99% need-based, 1% non-need-based). 74% of past graduating class borrowed through all loan programs. *Average indebtedness per student:* $25,750. *Average need-based loan:* Freshmen: $3212; Undergraduates: $4200. *Parent loans:* $1,620,733 (13% need-based, 87% non-need-based). *Programs:* FFEL (Subsidized and Unsubsidized Stafford, PLUS), Perkins, Federal Nursing, state.
WORK-STUDY *Federal work-study:* Total amount: $358,778; 174 jobs averaging $2062. *State or other work-study/employment:* Total amount: $1,163,576 (100% need-based). 494 part-time jobs averaging $2355.
APPLYING FOR FINANCIAL AID *Required financial aid forms:* FAFSA, institution's own form. *Financial aid deadline:* 4/15. *Notification date:* Continuous. Students must reply within 3 weeks of notification.
CONTACT Mr. Paul L. Terrio, Director of Financial Aid, Augsburg College, 2211 Riverside Avenue, Minneapolis, MN 55454-1351, 612-330-1049 or toll-free 800-788-5678. *Fax:* 612-330-1308. *E-mail:* terriop@augsburg.edu.

AUGUSTANA COLLEGE
Rock Island, IL

CONTACT Sue Standley, Director of Financial Aid, Augustana College, 639 38th Street, Rock Island, IL 61201-2296, 309-794-7207 or toll-free 800-798-8100. *Fax:* 309-794-7174. *E-mail:* afass@augustana.edu.

AUGUSTANA COLLEGE
Sioux Falls, SD

Tuition & fees: $19,986   **Average undergraduate aid package:** $15,183

ABOUT THE INSTITUTION Independent religious, coed. Awards: bachelor's and master's degrees. 52 undergraduate majors. Total enrollment: 1,745. Undergraduates: 1,714. Freshmen: 391. Federal methodology is used as a basis for awarding need-based institutional aid.
UNDERGRADUATE EXPENSES for 2006–07 *Comprehensive fee:* $25,458 includes full-time tuition ($19,750), mandatory fees ($236), and room and board ($5472). *College room only:* $2700.
FRESHMAN FINANCIAL AID (Fall 2005, est.) 338 applied for aid; of those 87% were deemed to have need. 100% of freshmen with need received aid; of those 14% had need fully met. *Average percent of need met:* 93% (excluding resources awarded to replace EFC). *Average financial aid package:* $16,422 (excluding resources awarded to replace EFC). 23% of all full-time freshmen had no need and received non-need-based gift aid.
UNDERGRADUATE FINANCIAL AID (Fall 2005, est.) 1,301 applied for aid; of those 85% were deemed to have need. 100% of undergraduates with need received aid; of those 16% had need fully met. *Average percent of need met:* 89% (excluding resources awarded to replace EFC). *Average financial aid package:* $15,183 (excluding resources awarded to replace EFC). 30% of all full-time undergraduates had no need and received non-need-based gift aid.
GIFT AID (NEED-BASED) *Total amount:* $9,715,587 (15% federal, 79% institutional, 6% external sources). *Receiving aid:* Freshmen: 76% (295); All full-time undergraduates: 68% (1,104). *Average award:* Freshmen: $11,798; Undergraduates: $10,674. *Scholarships, grants, and awards:* Federal Pell, FSEOG, state, private, college/university gift aid from institutional funds, need-linked special talent scholarships and minority scholarships.
GIFT AID (NON-NEED-BASED) *Total amount:* $4,095,964 (3% state, 86% institutional, 11% external sources). *Receiving aid:* Freshmen: 75% (293); Undergraduates: 67% (1,083). *Average Award:* Freshmen: $8407; Undergraduates: $7223. *Scholarships, grants, and awards by category: Academic Interests/Achievement:* biological sciences, business, communication, computer science, education, English, foreign languages, general academic interests/achievements, health fields, humanities, international studies, mathematics, physical sciences, premedicine, religion/biblical studies, social sciences. *Creative Arts/Performance:* art/fine arts, music, performing arts, theater/drama. *Special Achievements/Activities:* general special achievements/activities, leadership. *Special Characteristics:* children and siblings of alumni, children of current students, children of faculty/staff, ethnic background, international students, local/state students, members of minority groups, religious affiliation, siblings of current students, spouses of current students, veterans.
LOANS *Student loans:* $8,741,080 (62% need-based, 38% non-need-based). 79% of past graduating class borrowed through all loan programs. *Average indebtedness per student:* $18,956. *Average need-based loan:* Freshmen: $4869; Undergraduates: $5007. *Parent loans:* $1,456,633 (18% need-based, 82% non-need-based). *Programs:* FFEL (Subsidized and Unsubsidized Stafford, PLUS), Perkins, Federal Nursing, college/university, Minnesota SELF Loans, alternative loans.
WORK-STUDY *Federal work-study:* Total amount: $636,971; 444 jobs averaging $1315. *State or other work-study/employment:* Total amount: $75,437 (8% need-based, 92% non-need-based). 105 part-time jobs averaging $720.
ATHLETIC AWARDS *Total amount:* $1,813,748 (46% need-based, 54% non-need-based).
APPLYING FOR FINANCIAL AID *Required financial aid form:* FAFSA. *Financial aid deadline (priority):* 3/1. *Notification date:* Continuous beginning 4/1. Students must reply by 5/1 or within 3 weeks of notification.
CONTACT Ms. Brenda L. Murtha, Director of Financial Aid, Augustana College, 2001 South Summit Avenue, Sioux Falls, SD 57197, 605-274-5216 or toll-free 800-727-2844 Ext. 5516 (in-state), 800-727-2844 (out-of-state). *Fax:* 605-274-5295. *E-mail:* brenda.murtha@augie.edu.

AUGUSTA STATE UNIVERSITY
Augusta, GA

Tuition & fees (GA res): $2920   **Average undergraduate aid package:** $12,389

ABOUT THE INSTITUTION State-supported, coed. Awards: associate, bachelor's, and master's degrees and post-master's certificates. 33 undergraduate majors. Total enrollment: 6,312. Undergraduates: 5,461. Freshmen: 1,034. Federal methodology is used as a basis for awarding need-based institutional aid.
UNDERGRADUATE EXPENSES for 2005–06 *Application fee:* $20. *Tuition, state resident:* full-time $2438; part-time $102 per hour. *Tuition, nonresident:* full-time $9754; part-time $407 per hour. *Required fees:* full-time $482; $241 per term part-time. *College room and board: room only:* $4920.
FRESHMAN FINANCIAL AID (Fall 2004) 727 applied for aid; of those 75% were deemed to have need. 97% of freshmen with need received aid; of those 2% had need fully met. *Average percent of need met:* 70% (excluding resources awarded to replace EFC). *Average financial aid package:* $10,919 (excluding resources awarded to replace EFC). 28% of all full-time freshmen had no need and received non-need-based gift aid.
UNDERGRADUATE FINANCIAL AID (Fall 2004) 2,604 applied for aid; of those 74% were deemed to have need. 95% of undergraduates with need received aid; of those 4% had need fully met. *Average percent of need met:* 70% (excluding resources awarded to replace EFC). *Average financial aid package:* $12,389 (excluding resources awarded to replace EFC). 19% of all full-time undergraduates had no need and received non-need-based gift aid.
GIFT AID (NEED-BASED) *Total amount:* $8,809,855 (100% federal). *Receiving aid:* Freshmen: 53% (418); All full-time undergraduates: 38% (1,392). *Average award:* Freshmen: $6691; Undergraduates: $7454. *Scholarships, grants, and awards:* Federal Pell, FSEOG, state, private, college/university gift aid from institutional funds.

GIFT AID (NON-NEED-BASED) *Total amount:* $7,014,312 (91% state, 5% institutional, 4% external sources). *Receiving aid:* Freshmen: 33% (260); Undergraduates: 18% (657). *Average Award:* Freshmen: $502; Undergraduates: $506. *Scholarships, grants, and awards by category:* Academic Interests/Achievement: 35 awards ($49,033 total): biological sciences, business, communication, computer science, education, English, general academic interests/achievements, health fields, mathematics, military science, physical sciences, social sciences. *Creative Arts/Performance:* 50 awards ($29,407 total): art/fine arts, creative writing, general creative arts/performance, music, performing arts, theater/drama. *Special Achievements/Activities:* 21 awards ($21,010 total): community service, general special achievements/activities, hobbies/interests, leadership. *Special Characteristics:* 1,926 awards ($4,846,872 total): general special characteristics, handicapped students, local/state students. *Tuition waivers:* Full or partial for employees or children of employees, senior citizens. *ROTC:* Army.
LOANS *Student loans:* $13,397,188 (59% need-based, 41% non-need-based). 64% of past graduating class borrowed through all loan programs. *Average indebtedness per student:* $16,092. *Average need-based loan:* Freshmen: $5353; Undergraduates: $7395. *Parent loans:* $113,621 (100% non-need-based). *Programs:* FFEL (Subsidized and Unsubsidized Stafford, PLUS), Perkins, state, college/university, alternative loans.
WORK-STUDY *Federal work-study:* Total amount: $219,140; 77 jobs averaging $2830. *State or other work-study/employment:* 204 part-time jobs averaging $1734.
ATHLETIC AWARDS *Total amount:* $557,998 (100% non-need-based).
APPLYING FOR FINANCIAL AID *Required financial aid form:* FAFSA. *Financial aid deadline:* 5/1 (priority: 4/15). *Notification date:* Continuous.
CONTACT Ms. Roxanne Padgett, Assistant Director of Financial Aid, Augusta State University, 2500 Walton Way, Augusta, GA 30904-2200, 706-737-1431 or toll-free 800-341-4373. *Fax:* 706-737-1777. *E-mail:* bpadgett@aug.edu.

AURORA UNIVERSITY
Aurora, IL

Tuition & fees: $16,180 — **Average undergraduate aid package: $17,348**

ABOUT THE INSTITUTION Independent, coed. Awards: bachelor's, master's, and doctoral degrees and post-bachelor's and post-master's certificates. 32 undergraduate majors. Total enrollment: 3,556. Undergraduates: 1,907. Freshmen: 385. Federal methodology is used as a basis for awarding need-based institutional aid.
UNDERGRADUATE EXPENSES for 2006–07 *Application fee:* $25. *Comprehensive fee:* $22,770 includes full-time tuition ($16,080), mandatory fees ($100), and room and board ($6590). *College room only:* $2994. *Part-time tuition:* $495 per semester hour.
FRESHMAN FINANCIAL AID (Fall 2005, est.) 383 applied for aid; of those 83% were deemed to have need. 100% of freshmen with need received aid; of those 40% had need fully met. *Average percent of need met:* 90% (excluding resources awarded to replace EFC). *Average financial aid package:* $18,062 (excluding resources awarded to replace EFC). 16% of all full-time freshmen had no need and received non-need-based gift aid.
UNDERGRADUATE FINANCIAL AID (Fall 2005, est.) 1,663 applied for aid; of those 77% were deemed to have need. 100% of undergraduates with need received aid; of those 41% had need fully met. *Average percent of need met:* 89% (excluding resources awarded to replace EFC). *Average financial aid package:* $17,348 (excluding resources awarded to replace EFC). 21% of all full-time undergraduates had no need and received non-need-based gift aid.
GIFT AID (NEED-BASED) *Total amount:* $5,406,428 (34% federal, 58% state, 8% institutional). *Receiving aid:* Freshmen: 56% (213); All full-time undergraduates: 53% (897). *Average award:* Freshmen: $6095; Undergraduates: $5855. *Scholarships, grants, and awards:* Federal Pell, FSEOG, state, private, college/university gift aid from institutional funds.
GIFT AID (NON-NEED-BASED) *Total amount:* $10,243,502 (97% institutional, 3% external sources). *Receiving aid:* Freshmen: 82% (313); Undergraduates: 73% (1,227). *Average Award:* Freshmen: $9959; Undergraduates: $8703. *Scholarships, grants, and awards by category:* Academic Interests/Achievement: 1,914 awards ($9,772,464 total): education, general academic interests/achievements, mathematics. *Special Achievements/Activities:* 133 awards ($301,357 total): general special achievements/activities. *Special Characteristics:* 231 awards ($398,597 total): children and siblings of alumni, children of educators, children of faculty/staff, out-of-state students, parents of current students, siblings of current students, spouses of current students.
LOANS *Student loans:* $8,315,403 (47% need-based, 53% non-need-based). 74% of past graduating class borrowed through all loan programs. *Average indebtedness per student:* $18,374. *Average need-based loan:* Freshmen: $2455; Undergraduates: $3811. *Parent loans:* $1,259,526 (100% non-need-based). *Programs:* FFEL (Subsidized and Unsubsidized Stafford, PLUS), Perkins, college/university.
WORK-STUDY *Federal work-study:* Total amount: $942,187; 608 jobs averaging $1550.
APPLYING FOR FINANCIAL AID *Required financial aid form:* FAFSA. *Financial aid deadline (priority):* 4/15. *Notification date:* Continuous beginning 3/1. Students must reply by 5/1 or within 3 weeks of notification.
CONTACT Heather Gutierrez, Dean of Student Financial Services, Aurora University, 347 South Gladstone Avenue, Aurora, IL 60506-4892, 630-844-5533 or toll-free 800-742-5281. *Fax:* 630-844-5535. *E-mail:* finaid@aurora.edu.

AUSTIN COLLEGE
Sherman, TX

Tuition & fees: $23,540 — **Average undergraduate aid package: $20,989**

ABOUT THE INSTITUTION Independent Presbyterian, coed. Awards: bachelor's and master's degrees. 31 undergraduate majors. Total enrollment: 1,327. Undergraduates: 1,298. Freshmen: 348. Federal methodology is used as a basis for awarding need-based institutional aid.
UNDERGRADUATE EXPENSES for 2006–07 *Application fee:* $35. *Comprehensive fee:* $31,281 includes full-time tuition ($23,355), mandatory fees ($185), and room and board ($7741). *College room only:* $3554. *Part-time tuition:* $3385 per course.
FRESHMAN FINANCIAL AID (Fall 2005, est.) 273 applied for aid; of those 71% were deemed to have need. 100% of freshmen with need received aid; of those 99% had need fully met. *Average percent of need met:* 100% (excluding resources awarded to replace EFC). *Average financial aid package:* $21,571 (excluding resources awarded to replace EFC). 40% of all full-time freshmen had no need and received non-need-based gift aid.
UNDERGRADUATE FINANCIAL AID (Fall 2005, est.) 913 applied for aid; of those 78% were deemed to have need. 100% of undergraduates with need received aid; of those 96% had need fully met. *Average percent of need met:* 99% (excluding resources awarded to replace EFC). *Average financial aid package:* $20,989 (excluding resources awarded to replace EFC). 38% of all full-time undergraduates had no need and received non-need-based gift aid.
GIFT AID (NEED-BASED) *Total amount:* $9,356,821 (10% federal, 19% state, 69% institutional, 2% external sources). *Receiving aid:* Freshmen: 56% (194); All full-time undergraduates: 54% (715). *Average award:* Freshmen: $14,574; Undergraduates: $13,446. *Scholarships, grants, and awards:* Federal Pell, FSEOG, state, private, college/university gift aid from institutional funds.
GIFT AID (NON-NEED-BASED) *Total amount:* $5,497,408 (95% institutional, 5% external sources). *Receiving aid:* Freshmen: 20% (69); Undergraduates: 16% (219). *Average Award:* Freshmen: $9328; Undergraduates: $9199. *Scholarships, grants, and awards by category:* Academic Interests/Achievement: biological sciences, business, communication, education, engineering/technologies, English, foreign languages, general academic interests/achievements, health fields, humanities, international studies, physical sciences, premedicine, religion/biblical studies, social sciences. *Creative Arts/Performance:* art/fine arts, music, theater/drama. *Special Achievements/Activities:* general special achievements/activities, leadership, religious involvement. *Special Characteristics:* children of faculty/staff, ethnic background, first-generation college students, handicapped students, international students, local/state students, relatives of clergy.
LOANS *Student loans:* $7,037,051 (53% need-based, 47% non-need-based). 82% of past graduating class borrowed through all loan programs. *Average indebtedness per student:* $26,164. *Average need-based loan:* Freshmen: $5724; Undergraduates: $5857. *Parent loans:* $6,725,890 (4% need-based, 96% non-need-based). *Programs:* FFEL (Subsidized and Unsubsidized Stafford, PLUS), Perkins, state, college/university, alternative loans through various sources.
WORK-STUDY *Federal work-study:* Total amount: $493,541; 321 jobs averaging $1538. *State or other work-study/employment:* Total amount: $273,018 (9% need-based, 91% non-need-based). 192 part-time jobs averaging $1422.

Austin College

APPLYING FOR FINANCIAL AID *Required financial aid forms:* FAFSA, institution's own form. *Financial aid deadline (priority):* 4/1. *Notification date:* Continuous beginning 3/1. Students must reply by 5/1.
CONTACT Mrs. Laurie Coulter, Director of Financial Aid, Austin College, 900 North Grand Avenue, Sherman, TX 75090, 903-813-2900 or toll-free 800-442-5363. *E-mail:* finaid@austincollege.edu.

AUSTIN GRADUATE SCHOOL OF THEOLOGY
Austin, TX

ABOUT THE INSTITUTION Independent religious, coed. Awards: bachelor's and master's degrees. 1 undergraduate major. Total enrollment: 61. Undergraduates: 27.
GIFT AID (NEED-BASED) *Scholarships, grants, and awards:* Federal Pell, FSEOG, college/university gift aid from institutional funds.
GIFT AID (NON-NEED-BASED) *Scholarships, grants, and awards by category: Academic Interests/Achievement:* religion/biblical studies.
LOANS *Programs:* FFEL (Subsidized and Unsubsidized Stafford, PLUS), college/university.
APPLYING FOR FINANCIAL AID *Required financial aid forms:* FAFSA, institution's own form.
CONTACT David Arthur, Financial Aid Officer, Austin Graduate School of Theology, 1909 University Avenue, Austin, TX 78705-5610, 512-476-2772 Ext. 204 or toll-free 866-AUS-GRAD. *Fax:* 512-476-3919. *E-mail:* darthur@austingrad.edu.

AUSTIN PEAY STATE UNIVERSITY
Clarksville, TN

Tuition & fees (TN res): $4635 **Average undergraduate aid package: $6269**

ABOUT THE INSTITUTION State-supported, coed. Awards: associate, bachelor's, and master's degrees and post-bachelor's and post-master's certificates. 34 undergraduate majors. Total enrollment: 8,813. Undergraduates: 8,216. Freshmen: 1,408. Federal methodology is used as a basis for awarding need-based institutional aid.
UNDERGRADUATE EXPENSES for 2005–06 *Application fee:* $15. *Tuition, state resident:* full-time $3678; part-time $161 per credit hour. *Tuition, nonresident:* full-time $12,990; part-time $565 per credit hour. *Required fees:* full-time $957; $41 per credit hour or $4 per term part-time. Part-time tuition and fees vary according to location. *College room and board:* $4800; *room only:* $2900. Room and board charges vary according to board plan and housing facility. *Payment plans:* Installment, deferred payment.
FRESHMAN FINANCIAL AID (Fall 2004) 1087 applied for aid; of those 82% were deemed to have need. 99% of freshmen with need received aid. *Average financial aid package:* $6351 (excluding resources awarded to replace EFC). 15% of all full-time freshmen had no need and received non-need-based gift aid.
UNDERGRADUATE FINANCIAL AID (Fall 2004) 4,580 applied for aid; of those 89% were deemed to have need. 98% of undergraduates with need received aid. *Average financial aid package:* $6269 (excluding resources awarded to replace EFC). 6% of all full-time undergraduates had no need and received non-need-based gift aid.
GIFT AID (NEED-BASED) *Total amount:* $11,755,509 (84% federal, 16% state). *Receiving aid:* Freshmen: 40% (479); All full-time undergraduates: 45% (2,577). *Average award:* Freshmen: $3921; Undergraduates: $3698. *Scholarships, grants, and awards:* Federal Pell, FSEOG, state, private, college/university gift aid from institutional funds, corporate.
GIFT AID (NON-NEED-BASED) *Total amount:* $8,741,210 (36% state, 22% institutional, 42% external sources). *Receiving aid:* Freshmen: 59% (707); Undergraduates: 29% (1,689). *Average Award:* Freshmen: $3782; Undergraduates: $3856. *Scholarships, grants, and awards by category: Academic Interests/Achievement:* 194 awards ($327,302 total): biological sciences, business, education, general academic interests/achievements, humanities, mathematics, military science, social sciences. *Creative Arts/Performance:* 276 awards ($318,922 total): art/fine arts, creative writing, debating, journalism/publications, music, theater/drama. *Special Achievements/Activities:* 563 awards ($745,589 total): general special achievements/activities, leadership. *Special Characteristics:* 61 awards ($78,472 total): children of educators, children of faculty/staff, general special characteristics, members of minority groups, veterans. *Tuition waivers:* Full or partial for employees or children of employees, senior citizens. *ROTC:* Army.
LOANS *Student loans:* $20,866,425 (57% need-based, 43% non-need-based). *Parent loans:* $1,310,495 (100% non-need-based). *Programs:* FFEL (Subsidized and Unsubsidized Stafford, PLUS), Perkins.
WORK-STUDY *Federal work-study:* Total amount: $307,618; 155 jobs averaging $2000. *State or other work-study/employment:* Total amount: $571,500 (100% non-need-based). 410 part-time jobs averaging $1394.
ATHLETIC AWARDS *Total amount:* $1,069,202 (100% non-need-based).
APPLYING FOR FINANCIAL AID *Required financial aid form:* FAFSA. *Financial aid deadline (priority):* 4/1. *Notification date:* Continuous beginning 5/1. Students must reply within 2 weeks of notification.
CONTACT Greg Ross, Associate Director of Student Financial Aid, Austin Peay State University, PO Box 4546, Clarksville, TN 37044-0001, 931-221-7907 or toll-free 800-844-2778 (out-of-state). *Fax:* 931-221-6329. *E-mail:* rossg@apsu.edu.

AVE MARIA COLLEGE
Ypsilanti, MI

CONTACT Mr. Bob Hickey, Director of Financial Aid, Ave Maria College, 300 West Forest Avenue, Ypsilanti, MI 48197, 734-337-4504 or toll-free 866-866-3030. *Fax:* 734-337-4140. *E-mail:* bhickey@avemaria.edu.

AVE MARIA UNIVERSITY
Naples, FL

CONTACT Financial Aid Office, Ave Maria University, 1025 Commons Circle, Naples, FL 34119, 239-280-2554 or toll-free 877-AVE-UNIV.

AVERETT UNIVERSITY
Danville, VA

Tuition & fees: $19,040 **Average undergraduate aid package: $14,298**

ABOUT THE INSTITUTION Independent religious, coed. Awards: associate, bachelor's, and master's degrees. 64 undergraduate majors. Total enrollment: 1,487. Undergraduates: 241. Freshmen: 231. Federal methodology is used as a basis for awarding need-based institutional aid.
UNDERGRADUATE EXPENSES for 2005–06 *Comprehensive fee:* $25,600 includes full-time tuition ($18,040), mandatory fees ($1000), and room and board ($6560). *College room only:* $4800. Room and board charges vary according to board plan and housing facility. *Part-time tuition:* $305 per credit. *Part-time fees:* $250 per term. Part-time tuition and fees vary according to course load, location, and program. *Payment plan:* Installment.
FRESHMAN FINANCIAL AID (Fall 2005, est.) 219 applied for aid; of those 86% were deemed to have need. 100% of freshmen with need received aid; of those 14% had need fully met. *Average percent of need met:* 70% (excluding resources awarded to replace EFC). *Average financial aid package:* $13,795 (excluding resources awarded to replace EFC). 22% of all full-time freshmen had no need and received non-need-based gift aid.
UNDERGRADUATE FINANCIAL AID (Fall 2005, est.) 743 applied for aid; of those 90% were deemed to have need. 100% of undergraduates with need received aid; of those 19% had need fully met. *Average percent of need met:* 74% (excluding resources awarded to replace EFC). *Average financial aid package:* $14,298 (excluding resources awarded to replace EFC). 19% of all full-time undergraduates had no need and received non-need-based gift aid.
GIFT AID (NEED-BASED) *Total amount:* $7,032,538 (15% federal, 16% state, 61% institutional, 8% external sources). *Receiving aid:* Freshmen: 78% (188); All full-time undergraduates: 81% (667). *Average award:* Freshmen: $10,296; Undergraduates: $10,456. *Scholarships, grants, and awards:* Federal Pell, FSEOG, state, private, college/university gift aid from institutional funds.
GIFT AID (NON-NEED-BASED) *Total amount:* $1,812,717 (20% state, 69% institutional, 11% external sources). *Receiving aid:* Freshmen: 9% (21); Undergraduates: 19% (156). *Average Award:* Freshmen: $13,240; Undergraduates: $12,692. *Scholarships, grants, and awards by category: Academic Interests/Achievement:* 96 awards ($185,156 total): biological sciences, business, education, engineering/technologies, English, foreign languages, general

academic interests/achievements, health fields, home economics, humanities, mathematics, physical sciences, premedicine, religion/biblical studies. *Creative Arts/Performance:* 20 awards ($12,162 total): art/fine arts, journalism/publications, music, theater/drama. *Special Achievements/Activities:* 9 awards ($9501 total): general special achievements/activities, leadership, memberships, religious involvement. *Special Characteristics:* 219 awards ($190,123 total): adult students, children and siblings of alumni, children of union members/company employees, first-generation college students, general special characteristics, international students, local/state students, out-of-state students, relatives of clergy, religious affiliation. *Tuition waivers:* Full or partial for employees or children of employees, senior citizens.
LOANS *Student loans:* $5,299,567 (73% need-based, 27% non-need-based). 70% of past graduating class borrowed through all loan programs. *Average indebtedness per student:* $16,398. *Average need-based loan:* Freshmen: $3568; Undergraduates: $4255. *Parent loans:* $1,501,218 (29% need-based, 71% non-need-based). *Programs:* FFEL (Subsidized and Unsubsidized Stafford, PLUS), Perkins, alternative loans.
WORK-STUDY *Federal work-study:* Total amount: $172,027; 173 jobs averaging $994.
APPLYING FOR FINANCIAL AID *Required financial aid forms:* FAFSA, state aid form. *Financial aid deadline (priority):* 4/1. *Notification date:* Continuous beginning 2/15. Students must reply within 2 weeks of notification.
CONTACT Carl Bradsher, Dean of Financial Assistance, Averett University, 420 West Main Street, Danville, VA 24541-3692, 434-791-5646 or toll-free 800-AVERETT. *Fax:* 434-791-5647. *E-mail:* carl.bradsher@averett.edu.

AVILA UNIVERSITY
Kansas City, MO

Tuition & fees: $16,700	Average undergraduate aid package: $11,751

ABOUT THE INSTITUTION Independent Roman Catholic, coed. Awards: bachelor's and master's degrees. 32 undergraduate majors. Total enrollment: 1,697. Undergraduates: 1,214. Freshmen: 154. Federal methodology is used as a basis for awarding need-based institutional aid.
UNDERGRADUATE EXPENSES for 2005–06 *Comprehensive fee:* $22,100 includes full-time tuition ($16,300), mandatory fees ($400), and room and board ($5400). Full-time tuition and fees vary according to course load. Room and board charges vary according to board plan and housing facility. *Part-time tuition:* $365 per credit hour. *Part-time fees:* $13 per credit hour. Part-time tuition and fees vary according to course load. *Payment plans:* Guaranteed tuition, installment, deferred payment.
FRESHMAN FINANCIAL AID (Fall 2005, est.) 613 applied for aid; of those 86% were deemed to have need. 24% of freshmen with need received aid; of those 27% had need fully met. *Average percent of need met:* 13% (excluding resources awarded to replace EFC). *Average financial aid package:* $10,776 (excluding resources awarded to replace EFC). 17% of all full-time freshmen had no need and received non-need-based gift aid.
UNDERGRADUATE FINANCIAL AID (Fall 2005, est.) 1,912 applied for aid; of those 88% were deemed to have need. 43% of undergraduates with need received aid; of those 23% had need fully met. *Average percent of need met:* 25% (excluding resources awarded to replace EFC). *Average financial aid package:* $11,751 (excluding resources awarded to replace EFC). 13% of all full-time undergraduates had no need and received non-need-based gift aid.
GIFT AID (NEED-BASED) *Total amount:* $5,264,337 (20% federal, 5% state, 70% institutional, 5% external sources). *Receiving aid:* Freshmen: 16% (122); All full-time undergraduates: 31% (683). *Average award:* Freshmen: $8020; Undergraduates: $7465. *Scholarships, grants, and awards:* Federal Pell, FSEOG, state, private, college/university gift aid from institutional funds.
GIFT AID (NON-NEED-BASED) *Total amount:* $1,922,018 (2% state, 93% institutional, 5% external sources). *Receiving aid:* Freshmen: 3% (25); Undergraduates: 4% (89). *Average Award:* Freshmen: $6608; Undergraduates: $8933. *Scholarships, grants, and awards by category: Academic Interests/Achievement:* biological sciences, communication, general academic interests/achievements, humanities, premedicine. *Creative Arts/Performance:* art/fine arts, music, performing arts, theater/drama. *Special Characteristics:* children and siblings of alumni, children of current students, children of faculty/staff, religious affiliation, siblings of current students, spouses of current students. *Tuition waivers:* Full or partial for children of alumni, employees or children of employees, senior citizens. *ROTC:* Army cooperative.

LOANS *Student loans:* $6,826,666 (75% need-based, 25% non-need-based). 100% of past graduating class borrowed through all loan programs. *Average indebtedness per student:* $16,398. *Average need-based loan:* Freshmen: $3424; Undergraduates: $5221. *Parent loans:* $1,439,432 (33% need-based, 67% non-need-based). *Programs:* FFEL (Subsidized and Unsubsidized Stafford, PLUS), Perkins.
WORK-STUDY *Federal work-study:* Total amount: $211,104; jobs available. *State or other work-study/employment:* Total amount: $96,239 (16% need-based, 84% non-need-based). Part-time jobs available.
ATHLETIC AWARDS *Total amount:* $120,705 (64% need-based, 36% non-need-based).
APPLYING FOR FINANCIAL AID *Required financial aid form:* FAFSA. *Financial aid deadline:* Continuous. *Notification date:* Continuous beginning 2/1. Students must reply by 7/1 or within 3 weeks of notification.
CONTACT Kimberly Warren, Director of Financial Aid, Avila University, 11901 Wornall Road, Kansas City, MO 64145, 816-501-3782 or toll-free 800-GO-AVILA. *Fax:* 816-501-2462. *E-mail:* kimberly.warren@avila.edu.

AZUSA PACIFIC UNIVERSITY
Azusa, CA

Tuition & fees: $22,160	Average undergraduate aid package: $15,983

ABOUT THE INSTITUTION Independent nondenominational, coed. Awards: bachelor's, master's, doctoral, and first professional degrees. 37 undergraduate majors. Total enrollment: 8,162. Undergraduates: 4,441. Freshmen: 903. Federal methodology is used as a basis for awarding need-based institutional aid.
UNDERGRADUATE EXPENSES for 2005–06 *Application fee:* $45. *Comprehensive fee:* $28,526 includes full-time tuition ($21,500), mandatory fees ($660), and room and board ($6366). *College room only:* $3510. Full-time tuition and fees vary according to course load. Room and board charges vary according to board plan, housing facility, and student level. *Part-time tuition:* $900 per unit. Part-time tuition and fees vary according to course load. *Payment plan:* Installment.
FRESHMAN FINANCIAL AID (Fall 2004) 897 applied for aid; of those 63% were deemed to have need. 100% of freshmen with need received aid; of those 16% had need fully met. *Average percent of need met:* 70% (excluding resources awarded to replace EFC). *Average financial aid package:* $14,070 (excluding resources awarded to replace EFC). 30% of all full-time freshmen had no need and received non-need-based gift aid.
UNDERGRADUATE FINANCIAL AID (Fall 2004) 3,770 applied for aid; of those 64% were deemed to have need. 100% of undergraduates with need received aid; of those 17% had need fully met. *Average percent of need met:* 76% (excluding resources awarded to replace EFC). *Average financial aid package:* $15,983 (excluding resources awarded to replace EFC). 23% of all full-time undergraduates had no need and received non-need-based gift aid.
GIFT AID (NEED-BASED) *Total amount:* $22,620,674 (23% federal, 33% state, 39% institutional, 5% external sources). *Receiving aid:* Freshmen: 62% (552); All full-time undergraduates: 58% (2,179). *Average award:* Freshmen: $9499; Undergraduates: $9790. *Scholarships, grants, and awards:* Federal Pell, FSEOG, state, private, college/university gift aid from institutional funds, Federal Nursing.
GIFT AID (NON-NEED-BASED) *Total amount:* $5,760,114 (20% federal, 2% state, 67% institutional, 11% external sources). *Receiving aid:* Freshmen: 31% (281); Undergraduates: 27% (1,006). *Average Award:* Freshmen: $3794; Undergraduates: $3839. *Scholarships, grants, and awards by category: Academic Interests/Achievement:* 6,938 awards ($8,950,326 total): biological sciences, computer science, general academic interests/achievements, health fields, religion/biblical studies. *Creative Arts/Performance:* 1,283 awards ($1,288,343 total): debating, music, theater/drama. *Special Achievements/Activities:* 859 awards ($376,076 total): cheerleading/drum major, leadership, religious involvement. *Special Characteristics:* 975 awards ($2,032,927 total): children of faculty/staff, ethnic background, international students, relatives of clergy, religious affiliation, siblings of current students. *Tuition waivers:* Full or partial for employees or children of employees. *ROTC:* Army cooperative.
LOANS *Student loans:* $17,951,603 (77% need-based, 23% non-need-based). 49% of past graduating class borrowed through all loan programs. *Average indebtedness per student:* $19,487. *Average need-based loan:* Freshmen: $3706; Undergraduates: $5564. *Parent loans:* $9,356,587 (50% need-based, 50% non-need-based). *Programs:* FFEL (Subsidized and Unsubsidized Stafford, PLUS), Perkins, Federal Nursing.

Azusa Pacific University

WORK-STUDY *Federal work-study:* Total amount: $2,519,173; 463 jobs averaging $1430.
ATHLETIC AWARDS *Total amount:* $2,470,262 (14% need-based, 86% non-need-based).
APPLYING FOR FINANCIAL AID *Required financial aid forms:* FAFSA, institution's own form. *Financial aid deadline:* 7/1 (priority: 3/2). *Notification date:* Continuous beginning 3/1. Students must reply within 3 weeks of notification.
CONTACT Todd Ross, Interim Director, Student Financial Services, Azusa Pacific University, 901 East Alosta Avenue, PO Box 7000, Azusa, CA 91702-7000, 626-812-3009 or toll-free 800-TALK-APU. *E-mail:* tross@apu.edu.

BABSON COLLEGE
Wellesley, MA

Tuition & fees: $32,256   Average undergraduate aid package: $26,018

ABOUT THE INSTITUTION Independent, coed. Awards: bachelor's and master's degrees and post-master's certificates. 24 undergraduate majors. Total enrollment: 3,210. Undergraduates: 1,725. Freshmen: 420. Both federal and institutional methodology are used as a basis for awarding need-based institutional aid.
UNDERGRADUATE EXPENSES for 2006–07 *Application fee:* $60. *Comprehensive fee:* $43,478 includes full-time tuition ($32,256) and room and board ($11,222). *College room only:* $7242.
FRESHMAN FINANCIAL AID (Fall 2005, est.) 232 applied for aid; of those 75% were deemed to have need. 100% of freshmen with need received aid; of those 88% had need fully met. *Average percent of need met:* 97% (excluding resources awarded to replace EFC). *Average financial aid package:* $26,171 (excluding resources awarded to replace EFC). 9% of all full-time freshmen had no need and received non-need-based gift aid.
UNDERGRADUATE FINANCIAL AID (Fall 2005, est.) 779 applied for aid; of those 92% were deemed to have need. 100% of undergraduates with need received aid; of those 88% had need fully met. *Average percent of need met:* 97% (excluding resources awarded to replace EFC). *Average financial aid package:* $26,018 (excluding resources awarded to replace EFC). 8% of all full-time undergraduates had no need and received non-need-based gift aid.
GIFT AID (NEED-BASED) *Total amount:* $15,442,000 (6% federal, 2% state, 92% institutional). *Receiving aid:* Freshmen: 38% (159); All full-time undergraduates: 39% (667). *Average award:* Freshmen: $21,633; Undergraduates: $20,807. *Scholarships, grants, and awards:* Federal Pell, FSEOG, state, college/university gift aid from institutional funds.
GIFT AID (NON-NEED-BASED) *Total amount:* $1,477,000 (81% institutional, 19% external sources). *Receiving aid:* Freshmen: 7% (28); Undergraduates: 7% (122). *Average Award:* Freshmen: $14,445; Undergraduates: $9153. *Scholarships, grants, and awards by category:* Academic Interests/Achievement: 138 awards ($1,800,000 total): general academic interests/achievements. *Special Achievements/Activities:* 155 awards ($2,150,000 total): leadership. *ROTC:* Army cooperative, Naval cooperative, Air Force cooperative.
LOANS *Student loans:* $6,271,000 (45% need-based, 55% non-need-based). 48% of past graduating class borrowed through all loan programs. *Average indebtedness per student:* $24,900. *Average need-based loan:* Freshmen: $3123; Undergraduates: $3932. *Parent loans:* $3,669,000 (100% non-need-based). *Programs:* FFEL (Subsidized and Unsubsidized Stafford, PLUS), Perkins, state.
WORK-STUDY *Federal work-study:* Total amount: $415,000; 284 jobs averaging $1460. *State or other work-study/employment:* Total amount: $1,020,000 (100% non-need-based). 424 part-time jobs averaging $2400.
APPLYING FOR FINANCIAL AID *Required financial aid forms:* FAFSA, CSS Financial Aid PROFILE, noncustodial (divorced/separated) parent's statement, business/farm supplement, federal income tax form(s), W-2 forms, verification worksheet. *Financial aid deadline:* 2/15 (priority: 2/15). *Notification date:* 4/1. Students must reply by 5/1.
CONTACT Ms. Melissa Shaak, Director of Financial Aid, Babson College, Hollister Hall, 3rd Floor, Babson Park, MA 02457-0310, 781-239-4219 or toll-free 800-488-3696. *Fax:* 781-239-5510. *E-mail:* shaak@babson.edu.

BACONE COLLEGE
Muskogee, OK

CONTACT Office of Financial Aid, Bacone College, 2299 Old Bacone Road, Muskogee, OK 74403-1597, 918-683-4581 Ext. 7298 or toll-free 888-682-5514 Ext. 7340. *Fax:* 918-682-5514. *E-mail:* financialaid@bacone.edu.

BAKER UNIVERSITY
Baldwin City, KS

ABOUT THE INSTITUTION Independent United Methodist, coed. Awards: bachelor's degrees. 37 undergraduate majors. Total enrollment: 916. Undergraduates: 916. Freshmen: 239.
GIFT AID (NEED-BASED) *Scholarships, grants, and awards:* Federal Pell, FSEOG, state, private, college/university gift aid from institutional funds.
GIFT AID (NON-NEED-BASED) *Scholarships, grants, and awards by category:* Academic Interests/Achievement: general academic interests/achievements. *Creative Arts/Performance:* art/fine arts, cinema/film/broadcasting, dance, debating, journalism/publications, music, theater/drama. *Special Achievements/Activities:* cheerleading/drum major, leadership, religious involvement. *Special Characteristics:* children and siblings of alumni, children of faculty/staff, ethnic background, international students, members of minority groups, out-of-state students, relatives of clergy.
LOANS *Programs:* FFEL (Subsidized and Unsubsidized Stafford, PLUS), Perkins, college/university, alternative loans.
WORK-STUDY *Federal work-study:* Total amount: $252,828; jobs available. *State or other work-study/employment:* Total amount: $182,055 (100% non-need-based). Part-time jobs available.
APPLYING FOR FINANCIAL AID *Required financial aid forms:* FAFSA, institution's own form.
CONTACT Mrs. Jeanne Mott, Financial Aid Director, Baker University, Box 65, Baldwin City, KS 66006-0065, 785-594-4595 or toll-free 800-873-4282. *Fax:* 785-594-8358.

BALDWIN-WALLACE COLLEGE
Berea, OH

Tuition & fees: $21,236   Average undergraduate aid package: $13,355

ABOUT THE INSTITUTION Independent Methodist, coed. Awards: bachelor's and master's degrees. 62 undergraduate majors. Total enrollment: 4,469. Undergraduates: 3,681. Freshmen: 599. Federal methodology is used as a basis for awarding need-based institutional aid.
UNDERGRADUATE EXPENSES for 2006–07 *Application fee:* $25. *Comprehensive fee:* $28,210 includes full-time tuition ($21,236) and room and board ($6974). *College room only:* $3406. *Part-time tuition:* $674.
FRESHMAN FINANCIAL AID (Fall 2005, est.) 576 applied for aid; of those 82% were deemed to have need. 100% of freshmen with need received aid; of those 55% had need fully met. *Average percent of need met:* 88% (excluding resources awarded to replace EFC). *Average financial aid package:* $16,231 (excluding resources awarded to replace EFC). 18% of all full-time freshmen had no need and received non-need-based gift aid.
UNDERGRADUATE FINANCIAL AID (Fall 2005, est.) 2,701 applied for aid; of those 85% were deemed to have need. 100% of undergraduates with need received aid; of those 64% had need fully met. *Average percent of need met:* 87% (excluding resources awarded to replace EFC). *Average financial aid package:* $13,355 (excluding resources awarded to replace EFC). 23% of all full-time undergraduates had no need and received non-need-based gift aid.
GIFT AID (NEED-BASED) *Total amount:* $23,350,135 (11% federal, 14% state, 73% institutional, 2% external sources). *Receiving aid:* Freshmen: 79% (473); All full-time undergraduates: 77% (2,289). *Average award:* Freshmen: $11,837; Undergraduates: $9956. *Scholarships, grants, and awards:* Federal Pell, FSEOG, state, private, college/university gift aid from institutional funds.
GIFT AID (NON-NEED-BASED) *Total amount:* $7,399,373 (8% state, 82% institutional, 10% external sources). *Receiving aid:* Freshmen: 41% (243); Undergraduates: 14% (410). *Average Award:* Freshmen: $7860; Undergraduates: $7975. *Scholarships, grants, and awards by category:* Academic Interests/Achievement: 2,356 awards ($14,055,720 total): general academic interests/achievements. *Creative Arts/Performance:* 90 awards ($213,000 total): music. *Special Achievements/Activities:* 142 awards ($406,250 total): leadership. *Special Characteristics:* 554 awards ($1,130,650 total): children and siblings of alumni, members of minority groups, religious affiliation, siblings of current students. *ROTC:* Air Force cooperative.
LOANS *Student loans:* $17,048,000 (58% need-based, 42% non-need-based). 95% of past graduating class borrowed through all loan programs. *Average indebtedness per student:* $16,250. *Average need-based loan:* Freshmen: $2875;

Undergraduates: $3440. *Parent loans:* $5,796,103 (40% need-based, 60% non-need-based). *Programs:* FFEL (Subsidized and Unsubsidized Stafford, PLUS), Perkins.
WORK-STUDY *Federal work-study:* Total amount: $466,000; 741 jobs averaging $629. *State or other work-study/employment:* Total amount: $993,000 (42% need-based, 58% non-need-based). 741 part-time jobs averaging $1312.
APPLYING FOR FINANCIAL AID *Required financial aid form:* FAFSA. *Financial aid deadline:* 9/1 (priority: 5/1). *Notification date:* Continuous beginning 2/14.
CONTACT Dr. George L. Rolleston, Director of Financial Aid, Baldwin-Wallace College, 275 Eastland Road, Berea, OH 44017-2088, 440-826-2108 or toll-free 877-BWAPPLY (in-state). *E-mail:* grollest@bw.edu.

BALL STATE UNIVERSITY
Muncie, IN

Tuition & fees (IN res): $6458   Average undergraduate aid package: $7663

ABOUT THE INSTITUTION State-supported, coed. Awards: associate, bachelor's, master's, and doctoral degrees and post-bachelor's and post-master's certificates. 124 undergraduate majors. Total enrollment: 20,351. Undergraduates: 17,426. Freshmen: 3,692. Federal methodology is used as a basis for awarding need-based institutional aid.
UNDERGRADUATE EXPENSES for 2005–06 *Application fee:* $25. *Tuition, state resident:* full-time $6030; part-time $221 per credit hour. *Tuition, nonresident:* full-time $15,790; part-time $569 per credit hour. *College room and board:* $6680.
FRESHMAN FINANCIAL AID (Fall 2005, est.) 3113 applied for aid; of those 69% were deemed to have need. 99% of freshmen with need received aid; of those 30% had need fully met. *Average percent of need met:* 61% (excluding resources awarded to replace EFC). *Average financial aid package:* $7426 (excluding resources awarded to replace EFC). 20% of all full-time freshmen had no need and received non-need-based gift aid.
UNDERGRADUATE FINANCIAL AID (Fall 2005, est.) 12,168 applied for aid; of those 73% were deemed to have need. 99% of undergraduates with need received aid; of those 35% had need fully met. *Average percent of need met:* 68% (excluding resources awarded to replace EFC). *Average financial aid package:* $7663 (excluding resources awarded to replace EFC). 9% of all full-time undergraduates had no need and received non-need-based gift aid.
GIFT AID (NEED-BASED) *Total amount:* $29,709,305 (34% federal, 57% state, 9% institutional). *Receiving aid:* Freshmen: 41% (1,511); All full-time undergraduates: 36% (5,748). *Average award:* Freshmen: $4522; Undergraduates: $4672. *Scholarships, grants, and awards:* Federal Pell, FSEOG, state, private, college/university gift aid from institutional funds.
GIFT AID (NON-NEED-BASED) *Total amount:* $19,855,142 (7% federal, 19% state, 54% institutional, 20% external sources). *Receiving aid:* Freshmen: 29% (1,066); Undergraduates: 19% (3,007). *Average Award:* Freshmen: $3256; Undergraduates: $3804. *Scholarships, grants, and awards by category:* Academic Interests/Achievement: 1,876 awards ($7,081,385 total): architecture, biological sciences, business, communication, education, English, foreign languages, general academic interests/achievements, health fields, mathematics, social sciences. Creative Arts/Performance: 231 awards ($217,345 total): art/fine arts, dance, general creative arts/performance, journalism/publications, music, theater/drama. Special Achievements/Activities: 36 awards ($99,612 total): leadership. Special Characteristics: 301 awards ($977,893 total): children and siblings of alumni, children of faculty/staff. *ROTC:* Army.
LOANS *Student loans:* $56,981,770 (48% need-based, 52% non-need-based). 62% of past graduating class borrowed through all loan programs. *Average indebtedness per student:* $17,418. *Average need-based loan:* Freshmen: $2794; Undergraduates: $3620. *Parent loans:* $77,681,022 (100% non-need-based). *Programs:* Federal Direct (Subsidized and Unsubsidized Stafford, PLUS), Perkins.
WORK-STUDY *Federal work-study:* Total amount: $2,596,590; 1,105 jobs averaging $2350. *State or other work-study/employment:* Total amount: $6,645,991 (11% need-based, 89% non-need-based). 4,763 part-time jobs averaging $1395.
ATHLETIC AWARDS *Total amount:* $4,194,399 (100% non-need-based).
APPLYING FOR FINANCIAL AID *Required financial aid form:* FAFSA. *Financial aid deadline (priority):* 3/1. *Notification date:* Continuous beginning 4/1.
CONTACT Robert Zellers, Director of Scholarships and Financial Aid, Ball State University, Lucina Hall, Room 202, Muncie, IN 47306-1099, 765-285-8898 or toll-free 800-482-4BSU. *Fax:* 765-285-2173. *E-mail:* finaid@bsu.edu.

BALTIMORE HEBREW UNIVERSITY
Baltimore, MD

CONTACT Ms. Yelena Feldman, Financial Aid Counselor, Baltimore Hebrew University, 5800 Park Heights Avenue, Baltimore, MD 21215-3996, 410-578-6913 or toll-free 888-248-7420 (out-of-state). *Fax:* 410-578-6940.

BAPTIST BIBLE COLLEGE
Springfield, MO

CONTACT Ms. Shirley Cutburth, Director of Financial Aid, Baptist Bible College, 628 East Kearney, Springfield, MO 65803-3498, 417-268-6034. *Fax:* 417-268-6694.

BAPTIST BIBLE COLLEGE OF PENNSYLVANIA
Clarks Summit, PA

CONTACT Mr. Thomas Pollock, Director of Student Financial Services, Baptist Bible College of Pennsylvania, 538 Venard Road, Clarks Summit, PA 18411, 570-586-2400 Ext. 9205 or toll-free 800-451-7664. *Fax:* 570-586-1753. *E-mail:* tpollock@bbc.edu.

THE BAPTIST COLLEGE OF FLORIDA
Graceville, FL

Tuition & fees: $7250   Average undergraduate aid package: $6118

ABOUT THE INSTITUTION Independent Southern Baptist, coed. Awards: associate and bachelor's degrees. 9 undergraduate majors. Total enrollment: 623. Undergraduates: 623. Freshmen: 48. Federal methodology is used as a basis for awarding need-based institutional aid.
UNDERGRADUATE EXPENSES for 2005–06 *Application fee:* $20. *Comprehensive fee:* $10,820 includes full-time tuition ($6900), mandatory fees ($350), and room and board ($3570). Full-time tuition and fees vary according to course load. Room and board charges vary according to board plan and housing facility. *Part-time tuition:* $230 per semester hour. *Part-time fees:* $175 per term. Part-time tuition and fees vary according to course load. *Payment plan:* Installment.
FRESHMAN FINANCIAL AID (Fall 2004) 50 applied for aid; of those 86% were deemed to have need. 100% of freshmen with need received aid; of those 9% had need fully met. *Average percent of need met:* 55% (excluding resources awarded to replace EFC). *Average financial aid package:* $4932 (excluding resources awarded to replace EFC). 26% of all full-time freshmen had no need and received non-need-based gift aid.
UNDERGRADUATE FINANCIAL AID (Fall 2004) 366 applied for aid; of those 91% were deemed to have need. 100% of undergraduates with need received aid; of those 9% had need fully met. *Average percent of need met:* 59% (excluding resources awarded to replace EFC). *Average financial aid package:* $6118 (excluding resources awarded to replace EFC). 16% of all full-time undergraduates had no need and received non-need-based gift aid.
GIFT AID (NEED-BASED) *Total amount:* $1,534,425 (54% federal, 20% state, 26% external sources). *Receiving aid:* Freshmen: 71% (41); All full-time undergraduates: 80% (317). *Average award:* Freshmen: $3833; Undergraduates: $4070. *Scholarships, grants, and awards:* Federal Pell, FSEOG, state, private, college/university gift aid from institutional funds.
GIFT AID (NON-NEED-BASED) *Total amount:* $212,067 (42% state, 58% external sources). *Receiving aid:* Freshmen: 7% (4); Undergraduates: 6% (24). *Average Award:* Freshmen: $3490; Undergraduates: $3367. *Scholarships, grants, and awards by category:* Academic Interests/Achievement: 302 awards ($321,540 total): education, religion/biblical studies. Creative Arts/Performance: 10 awards ($31,739 total): music. Special Characteristics: 304 awards ($322,162 total): children with a deceased or disabled parent, religious affiliation, spouses of current students. *Tuition waivers:* Full or partial for employees or children of employees.
LOANS *Student loans:* $1,290,793 (88% need-based, 12% non-need-based). 53% of past graduating class borrowed through all loan programs. *Average indebtedness per student:* $13,257. *Average need-based loan:* Freshmen: $1947;

The Baptist College of Florida

Undergraduates: $3056. *Parent loans:* $50,769 (33% need-based, 67% non-need-based). *Programs:* FFEL (Subsidized and Unsubsidized Stafford, PLUS), college/university.

WORK-STUDY *Federal work-study:* Total amount: $43,864; 38 jobs averaging $1154.

APPLYING FOR FINANCIAL AID *Required financial aid forms:* FAFSA, institution's own form, state aid form, business/farm supplement. *Financial aid deadline:* 5/15 (priority: 3/1). *Notification date:* Continuous beginning 6/15. Students must reply within 4 weeks of notification.

CONTACT Angela Rathel, Director of Financial Aid, The Baptist College of Florida, 5400 College Drive, Graceville, FL 32440-3306, 850-263-3261 Ext. 461 or toll-free 800-328-2660 Ext. 460. *Fax:* 850-263-2141. *E-mail:* finaid@baptistcollege.edu.

BAPTIST COLLEGE OF HEALTH SCIENCES
Memphis, TN

CONTACT Ms. Janet Bonney-Baker, Financial Aid Officer, Baptist College of Health Sciences, 1003 Monroe Avenue, Memphis, TN 38104, 901-227-6805 or toll-free 866-575-2247. *Fax:* 901-227-4311. *E-mail:* janet.bonney@bchs.edu.

BAPTIST MISSIONARY ASSOCIATION THEOLOGICAL SEMINARY
Jacksonville, TX

CONTACT Dr. Philip Attebery, Dean/Registrar, Baptist Missionary Association Theological Seminary, 1530 East Pine Street, Jacksonville, TX 75766-5407, 903-586-2501. *Fax:* 903-586-0378. *E-mail:* bmatsem@bmats.edu.

BAPTIST UNIVERSITY OF THE AMERICAS
San Antonio, TX

CONTACT Financial Aid Office, Baptist University of the Americas, 8019 South Pan Am Expressway, San Antonio, TX 78224-2701, 210-924-4338 or toll-free 800-721-1396.

BARBER-SCOTIA COLLEGE
Concord, NC

CONTACT Financial Aid Counselor, Barber-Scotia College, 145 Cabarrus Avenue, Concord, NC 28025-5187, 704-789-2908 or toll-free 800-610-0778. *Fax:* 704-789-2911.

BARCLAY COLLEGE
Haviland, KS

CONTACT Christina Foster, Financial Aid Coordinator, Barclay College, 607 North Kingman, Haviland, KS 67059, 800-862-0226. *Fax:* 620-862-5403. *E-mail:* financialaid@barclaycollege.edu.

BARD COLLEGE
Annandale-on-Hudson, NY

Tuition & fees: $34,080 — **Average undergraduate aid package: $25,107**

ABOUT THE INSTITUTION Independent, coed. Awards: associate, bachelor's, master's, and doctoral degrees. 88 undergraduate majors. Total enrollment: 1,858. Undergraduates: 1,585. Freshmen: 515. Both federal and institutional methodology are used as a basis for awarding need-based institutional aid.

UNDERGRADUATE EXPENSES for 2006–07 *Application fee:* $50. *Comprehensive fee:* $43,930 includes full-time tuition ($34,080) and room and board ($9850). *College room only:* $4950. *Part-time tuition:* $1066 per credit. *Part-time fees:* $351 per term.

FRESHMAN FINANCIAL AID (Fall 2005, est.) 359 applied for aid; of those 81% were deemed to have need. 100% of freshmen with need received aid; of those 58% had need fully met. *Average percent of need met:* 87% (excluding resources awarded to replace EFC). *Average financial aid package:* $25,265 (excluding resources awarded to replace EFC). 6% of all full-time freshmen had no need and received non-need-based gift aid.

UNDERGRADUATE FINANCIAL AID (Fall 2005, est.) 1,047 applied for aid; of those 85% were deemed to have need. 100% of undergraduates with need received aid; of those 54% had need fully met. *Average percent of need met:* 89% (excluding resources awarded to replace EFC). *Average financial aid package:* $25,107 (excluding resources awarded to replace EFC). 4% of all full-time undergraduates had no need and received non-need-based gift aid.

GIFT AID (NEED-BASED) *Total amount:* $17,387,612 (6% federal, 4% state, 88% institutional, 2% external sources). *Receiving aid:* Freshmen: 53% (274); All full-time undergraduates: 52% (784). *Average award:* Freshmen: $24,046; Undergraduates: $23,892. *Scholarships, grants, and awards:* Federal Pell, FSEOG, state, private, college/university gift aid from institutional funds.

GIFT AID (NON-NEED-BASED) *Total amount:* $804,961 (2% state, 92% institutional, 6% external sources). *Average Award:* Freshmen: $9708; Undergraduates: $10,750. *Scholarships, grants, and awards by category: Academic Interests/Achievement:* 30 awards ($214,250 total): biological sciences, mathematics, physical sciences. *Special Achievements/Activities:* leadership. *Special Characteristics:* 19 awards ($451,000 total): children of educators, children of faculty/staff.

LOANS *Student loans:* $4,767,513 (90% need-based, 10% non-need-based). 71% of past graduating class borrowed through all loan programs. *Average indebtedness per student:* $18,345. *Average need-based loan:* Freshmen: $1614; Undergraduates: $3700. *Parent loans:* $4,036,924 (57% need-based, 43% non-need-based). *Programs:* FFEL (Subsidized and Unsubsidized Stafford, PLUS), Perkins, college/university loans from institutional funds (for international students only).

WORK-STUDY *Federal work-study:* Total amount: $868,810; 557 jobs averaging $1560. *State or other work-study/employment:* Total amount: $226,915 (100% need-based). 137 part-time jobs averaging $1650.

APPLYING FOR FINANCIAL AID *Required financial aid forms:* FAFSA, CSS Financial Aid PROFILE, state aid form, noncustodial (divorced/separated) parent's statement, business/farm supplement. *Financial aid deadline:* 2/15 (priority: 2/1). *Notification date:* 4/1. Students must reply by 5/1 or within 2 weeks of notification.

CONTACT Denise Ann Ackerman, Director of Financial Aid, Bard College, Annandale Road, Annandale-on-Hudson, NY 12504, 845-758-7525. *Fax:* 845-758-7336. *E-mail:* ackerman@bard.edu.

BARNARD COLLEGE
New York, NY

Tuition & fees: $30,676 — **Average undergraduate aid package: $28,402**

ABOUT THE INSTITUTION Independent, women only. Awards: bachelor's degrees. 66 undergraduate majors. Total enrollment: 2,356. Undergraduates: 2,356. Freshmen: 571. Both federal and institutional methodology are used as a basis for awarding need-based institutional aid.

UNDERGRADUATE EXPENSES for 2005–06 *Application fee:* $45. *Comprehensive fee:* $41,802 includes full-time tuition ($29,364), mandatory fees ($1312), and room and board ($11,126). *College room only:* $6764. Room and board charges vary according to board plan and housing facility. *Part-time tuition:* $980 per credit. *Payment plans:* Installment, deferred payment.

FRESHMAN FINANCIAL AID (Fall 2005, est.) 328 applied for aid; of those 73% were deemed to have need. 100% of freshmen with need received aid; of those 100% had need fully met. *Average percent of need met:* 100% (excluding resources awarded to replace EFC). *Average financial aid package:* $27,708 (excluding resources awarded to replace EFC).

UNDERGRADUATE FINANCIAL AID (Fall 2005, est.) 1,116 applied for aid; of those 86% were deemed to have need. 100% of undergraduates with need received aid; of those 100% had need fully met. *Average percent of need met:* 100% (excluding resources awarded to replace EFC). *Average financial aid package:* $28,402 (excluding resources awarded to replace EFC).

GIFT AID (NEED-BASED) *Total amount:* $22,457,619 (7% federal, 7% state, 84% institutional, 2% external sources). *Receiving aid:* Freshmen: 40% (230); All full-time undergraduates: 41% (922). *Average award:* Freshmen: $25,453; Undergraduates: $24,244. *Scholarships, grants, and awards:* Federal Pell, FSEOG, state, private, college/university gift aid from institutional funds.

GIFT AID (NON-NEED-BASED) *Total amount:* $471,491 (12% state, 88% external sources). *Tuition waivers:* Full or partial for employees or children of employees.
LOANS *Student loans:* $5,126,439 (71% need-based, 29% non-need-based). 46% of past graduating class borrowed through all loan programs. *Average indebtedness per student:* $19,121. *Average need-based loan:* Freshmen: $2625; Undergraduates: $4006. *Parent loans:* $6,377,860 (100% non-need-based). *Programs:* FFEL (Subsidized and Unsubsidized Stafford, PLUS), Perkins, state, college/university, alternative loans.
WORK-STUDY *Federal work-study:* Total amount: $583,621; 372 jobs averaging $1568. *State or other work-study/employment:* Total amount: $1,126,681 (65% need-based, 35% non-need-based). 620 part-time jobs averaging $1817.
APPLYING FOR FINANCIAL AID *Required financial aid forms:* FAFSA, institution's own form, CSS Financial Aid PROFILE, state aid form, noncustodial (divorced/separated) parent's statement, business/farm supplement, federal income tax form(s). *Financial aid deadline:* 2/1. *Notification date:* 4/1. Students must reply by 5/1.
CONTACT Dr. Alison Rabil, Director of Financial Aid, Barnard College, 3009 Broadway, New York, NY 10027-6598, 212-854-2154. *Fax:* 212-531-1058. *E-mail:* finaid@barnard.edu.

BARNES-JEWISH COLLEGE OF NURSING AND ALLIED HEALTH
St. Louis, MO

CONTACT Regina Blackshear, Chief Financial Aid Officer, Barnes-Jewish College of Nursing and Allied Health, 306 South Kingshighway, St. Louis, MO 63110-1091, 314-454-7770 or toll-free 800-832-9009 (in-state).

BARRY UNIVERSITY
Miami Shores, FL

ABOUT THE INSTITUTION Independent Roman Catholic, coed. Awards: bachelor's, master's, doctoral, and first professional degrees and post-bachelor's certificates. 58 undergraduate majors. Total enrollment: 9,207. Undergraduates: 5,942. Freshmen: 553.
GIFT AID (NEED-BASED) *Scholarships, grants, and awards:* Federal Pell, FSEOG, state, private, college/university gift aid from institutional funds, Federal Nursing.
GIFT AID (NON-NEED-BASED) *Scholarships, grants, and awards by category: Academic Interests/Achievement:* general academic interests/achievements. *Creative Arts/Performance:* applied art and design, art/fine arts, theater/drama. *Special Achievements/Activities:* community service, general special achievements/activities, leadership, memberships, religious involvement.
LOANS *Programs:* FFEL (Subsidized and Unsubsidized Stafford, PLUS), Perkins, Federal Nursing, college/university, alternative loans.
WORK-STUDY *Federal work-study:* Total amount: $977,516; 598 jobs averaging $2432. *State or other work-study/employment:* Total amount: $226,595 (100% non-need-based). Part-time jobs available.
APPLYING FOR FINANCIAL AID *Required financial aid form:* FAFSA.
CONTACT Mr. Dart Humeston, Assistant Dean of Enrollment Services/Director of Financial Aid, Barry University, 11300 Northeast Second Avenue, Miami Shores, FL 33161-6695, 305-899-3673 or toll-free 800-695-2279. *E-mail:* finaid@mail.barry.edu.

BARTON COLLEGE
Wilson, NC

Tuition & fees: $16,670   **Average undergraduate aid package: $14,952**

ABOUT THE INSTITUTION Independent religious, coed. Awards: bachelor's degrees and post-bachelor's certificates. 32 undergraduate majors. Total enrollment: 1,189. Undergraduates: 1,189. Freshmen: 247. Federal methodology is used as a basis for awarding need-based institutional aid.
UNDERGRADUATE EXPENSES for 2005–06 *Application fee:* $25. *Comprehensive fee:* $22,470 includes full-time tuition ($15,390), mandatory fees ($1280), and room and board ($5800). *College room only:* $2774. Full-time tuition and fees vary according to course load and program. Room and board charges vary according to housing facility. *Part-time tuition:* $654 per credit hour. Part-time tuition and fees vary according to course load and program. *Payment plan:* Installment.
FRESHMAN FINANCIAL AID (Fall 2005, est.) 215 applied for aid; of those 89% were deemed to have need. 100% of freshmen with need received aid; of those 17% had need fully met. *Average percent of need met:* 75% (excluding resources awarded to replace EFC). *Average financial aid package:* $15,226 (excluding resources awarded to replace EFC). 15% of all full-time freshmen had no need and received non-need-based gift aid.
UNDERGRADUATE FINANCIAL AID (Fall 2005, est.) 709 applied for aid; of those 92% were deemed to have need. 100% of undergraduates with need received aid; of those 15% had need fully met. *Average percent of need met:* 72% (excluding resources awarded to replace EFC). *Average financial aid package:* $14,952 (excluding resources awarded to replace EFC). 20% of all full-time undergraduates had no need and received non-need-based gift aid.
GIFT AID (NEED-BASED) *Total amount:* $2,281,515 (53% federal, 43% state, 1% institutional, 3% external sources). *Receiving aid:* Freshmen: 51% (125); All full-time undergraduates: 49% (450). *Average award:* Freshmen: $4790; Undergraduates: $4645. *Scholarships, grants, and awards:* Federal Pell, FSEOG, state, private, college/university gift aid from institutional funds, Federal Nursing.
GIFT AID (NON-NEED-BASED) *Total amount:* $2,791,019 (48% state, 45% institutional, 7% external sources). *Receiving aid:* Freshmen: 72% (177); Undergraduates: 65% (596). *Average Award:* Freshmen: $2289; Undergraduates: $2590. *Scholarships, grants, and awards by category: Academic Interests/Achievement:* 1,224 awards ($2,443,183 total): biological sciences, business, communication, computer science, education, English, general academic interests/achievements, health fields, humanities, mathematics, physical sciences, religion/biblical studies, social sciences. *Creative Arts/Performance:* 12 awards ($7200 total): art/fine arts, music, theater/drama. *Special Achievements/Activities:* 23 awards ($38,500 total): general special achievements/activities, leadership, religious involvement. *Special Characteristics:* 145 awards ($478,000 total): adult students, children and siblings of alumni, children of faculty/staff, international students, local/state students, relatives of clergy, religious affiliation, siblings of current students, veterans. *Tuition waivers:* Full or partial for children of alumni, employees or children of employees, adult students, senior citizens.
LOANS *Student loans:* $5,226,946 (49% need-based, 51% non-need-based). 71% of past graduating class borrowed through all loan programs. *Average indebtedness per student:* $17,272. *Average need-based loan:* Freshmen: $2858; Undergraduates: $4309. *Parent loans:* $1,226,331 (100% non-need-based). *Programs:* FFEL (Subsidized and Unsubsidized Stafford, PLUS), Perkins, alternative loans.
WORK-STUDY *Federal work-study:* Total amount: $517,540; 460 jobs averaging $1107.
ATHLETIC AWARDS *Total amount:* $796,935 (100% non-need-based).
APPLYING FOR FINANCIAL AID *Required financial aid form:* FAFSA. *Financial aid deadline (priority):* 4/1. *Notification date:* Continuous beginning 2/1. Students must reply by 5/1 or within 2 weeks of notification.
CONTACT Ms. Bettie Westbrook, Director of Financial Aid, Barton College, Box 5000, Wilson, NC 27893, 252-399-6316 or toll-free 800-345-4973. *Fax:* 252-399-6572. *E-mail:* aid@barton.edu.

BASTYR UNIVERSITY
Kenmore, WA

Tuition & fees: $15,381   **Average undergraduate aid package: $16,050**

ABOUT THE INSTITUTION Independent, coed. Awards: bachelor's, master's, and first professional degrees and post-bachelor's, post-master's, and first professional certificates. 6 undergraduate majors. Total enrollment: 1,098. Undergraduates: 264. Entering class: . Federal methodology is used as a basis for awarding need-based institutional aid.
UNDERGRADUATE EXPENSES for 2005–06 *Application fee:* $60. *Tuition:* full-time $13,770; part-time $306 per credit. Full-time tuition and fees vary according to course load and program. Part-time tuition and fees vary according to course load and program. Room and board charges vary according to board plan and housing facility.
UNDERGRADUATE FINANCIAL AID (Fall 2004) 200 applied for aid; of those 100% were deemed to have need. 95% of undergraduates with need received

Bastyr University

aid. *Average percent of need met:* 50% (excluding resources awarded to replace EFC). *Average financial aid package:* $16,050 (excluding resources awarded to replace EFC).
GIFT AID (NEED-BASED) *Total amount:* $811,164 (51% federal, 31% state, 15% institutional, 3% external sources). *Receiving aid:* All full-time undergraduates: 78% (190). *Average award:* Undergraduates: $8005. *Scholarships, grants, and awards:* Federal Pell, FSEOG, state, private, college/university gift aid from institutional funds.
GIFT AID (NON-NEED-BASED) *Scholarships, grants, and awards by category: Academic Interests/Achievement:* health fields. *Tuition waivers:* Full or partial for employees or children of employees.
LOANS *Student loans:* $2,705,000 (100% need-based). 80% of past graduating class borrowed through all loan programs. *Average indebtedness per student:* $21,000. *Average need-based loan:* Undergraduates: $5500. *Parent loans:* $25,700 (100% need-based). *Programs:* FFEL (Subsidized and Unsubsidized Stafford, PLUS), Perkins.
WORK-STUDY *Federal work-study:* Total amount: $64,693; 40 jobs averaging $3000. *State or other work-study/employment:* Total amount: $32,704 (100% need-based). 31 part-time jobs averaging $3000.
APPLYING FOR FINANCIAL AID *Required financial aid forms:* FAFSA, institution's own form. *Financial aid deadline (priority):* 5/1. *Notification date:* Continuous beginning 5/15. Students must reply within 3 weeks of notification.
CONTACT Maria Rebecchi, Assistant Director of Financial Aid, Bastyr University, 14500 Juanita Drive NE, Kenmore, WA 98028-4966, 425-602-3081. *Fax:* 425-602-3090. *E-mail:* finaid@bastyr.edu.

BATES COLLEGE
Lewiston, ME

Comprehensive fee: $42,100   **Average undergraduate aid package: $27,428**

ABOUT THE INSTITUTION Independent, coed. Awards: bachelor's degrees. 36 undergraduate majors. Total enrollment: 1,730. Undergraduates: 1,730. Freshmen: 490. Both federal and institutional methodology are used as a basis for awarding need-based institutional aid.
UNDERGRADUATE EXPENSES for 2005–06 *Application fee:* $60. *Comprehensive fee:* $42,100. *Payment plans:* Tuition prepayment, installment.
FRESHMAN FINANCIAL AID (Fall 2005, est.) 239 applied for aid; of those 87% were deemed to have need. 88% of freshmen with need received aid; of those 97% had need fully met. *Average percent of need met:* 100% (excluding resources awarded to replace EFC). *Average financial aid package:* $27,545 (excluding resources awarded to replace EFC).
UNDERGRADUATE FINANCIAL AID (Fall 2005, est.) 819 applied for aid; of those 91% were deemed to have need. 90% of undergraduates with need received aid; of those 96% had need fully met. *Average percent of need met:* 100% (excluding resources awarded to replace EFC). *Average financial aid package:* $27,428 (excluding resources awarded to replace EFC).
GIFT AID (NEED-BASED) *Total amount:* $15,600,317 (4% federal, 96% institutional). *Receiving aid:* Freshmen: 36% (178); All full-time undergraduates: 39% (650). *Average award:* Freshmen: $24,369; Undergraduates: $24,000. *Scholarships, grants, and awards:* Federal Pell, FSEOG, state, private, college/university gift aid from institutional funds.
GIFT AID (NON-NEED-BASED) *Tuition waivers:* Full or partial for employees or children of employees.
LOANS *Student loans:* $3,174,068 (58% need-based, 42% non-need-based). 46% of past graduating class borrowed through all loan programs. *Average indebtedness per student:* $13,636. *Average need-based loan:* Freshmen: $3282; Undergraduates: $3877. *Parent loans:* $3,030,025 (100% non-need-based). *Programs:* FFEL (Subsidized and Unsubsidized Stafford, PLUS), Perkins, state.
WORK-STUDY *Federal work-study:* Total amount: $924,892; 573 jobs averaging $1614. *State or other work-study/employment:* Total amount: $116,000 (100% need-based). 71 part-time jobs averaging $1633.
APPLYING FOR FINANCIAL AID *Required financial aid forms:* FAFSA, CSS Financial Aid PROFILE, noncustodial (divorced/separated) parent's statement, business/farm supplement. *Financial aid deadline:* 2/1. *Notification date:* 4/1. Students must reply by 5/1.
CONTACT Catherine D. Ganung, Director of Student Financial Services, Bates College, 44 Mountain Avenue, Lewiston, ME 04240, 207-786-6096. *Fax:* 207-786-8350. *E-mail:* cganung@bates.edu.

BAYAMÓN CENTRAL UNIVERSITY
Bayamón, PR

CONTACT Financial Aid Director, Bayamón Central University, PO Box 1725, Bayamón, PR 00960-1725, 787-786-3030 Ext. 2115. *Fax:* 787-785-4365.

BAYLOR UNIVERSITY
Waco, TX

Tuition & fees: $22,814   **Average undergraduate aid package: $15,392**

ABOUT THE INSTITUTION Independent Baptist, coed. Awards: bachelor's, master's, doctoral, and first professional degrees and post-master's certificates. 132 undergraduate majors. Total enrollment: 13,975. Undergraduates: 11,825. Freshmen: 3,168. Federal methodology is used as a basis for awarding need-based institutional aid.
UNDERGRADUATE EXPENSES for 2006–07 *Application fee:* $50. *Comprehensive fee:* $29,939 includes full-time tuition ($20,574), mandatory fees ($2240), and room and board ($7125). *College room only:* $3600. *Part-time tuition:* $857 per semester hour. *Part-time fees:* $82 per semester hour.
FRESHMAN FINANCIAL AID (Fall 2005, est.) 2282 applied for aid; of those 76% were deemed to have need. 100% of freshmen with need received aid; of those 16% had need fully met. *Average percent of need met:* 70% (excluding resources awarded to replace EFC). *Average financial aid package:* $16,482 (excluding resources awarded to replace EFC). 35% of all full-time freshmen had no need and received non-need-based gift aid.
UNDERGRADUATE FINANCIAL AID (Fall 2005, est.) 7,223 applied for aid; of those 81% were deemed to have need. 99% of undergraduates with need received aid; of those 19% had need fully met. *Average percent of need met:* 67% (excluding resources awarded to replace EFC). *Average financial aid package:* $15,392 (excluding resources awarded to replace EFC). 31% of all full-time undergraduates had no need and received non-need-based gift aid.
GIFT AID (NEED-BASED) *Total amount:* $58,271,065 (11% federal, 20% state, 63% institutional, 6% external sources). *Receiving aid:* Freshmen: 55% (1,737); All full-time undergraduates: 48% (5,453). *Average award:* Freshmen: $12,114; Undergraduates: $10,925. *Scholarships, grants, and awards:* Federal Pell, FSEOG, state, private, college/university gift aid from institutional funds.
GIFT AID (NON-NEED-BASED) *Total amount:* $26,472,953 (87% institutional, 13% external sources). *Receiving aid:* Freshmen: 54% (1,703); Undergraduates: 38% (4,394). *Average Award:* Freshmen: $6880; Undergraduates: $6981. *Scholarships, grants, and awards by category: Academic Interests/Achievement:* 8,845 awards ($40,645,523 total): business, communication, computer science, education, engineering/technologies, English, foreign languages, general academic interests/achievements, health fields, home economics, humanities, international studies, mathematics, military science, physical sciences, premedicine, religion/biblical studies, social sciences. *Creative Arts/Performance:* 533 awards ($1,759,604 total): art/fine arts, cinema/film/broadcasting, debating, journalism/publications, music, theater/drama. *Special Achievements/Activities:* 452 awards ($1,070,488 total): community service, leadership, religious involvement. *Special Characteristics:* 288 awards ($4,154,933 total): children of faculty/staff. *ROTC:* Air Force.
LOANS *Student loans:* $57,764,211 (68% need-based, 32% non-need-based). *Average need-based loan:* Freshmen: $2015; Undergraduates: $2394. *Parent loans:* $20,542,554 (25% need-based, 75% non-need-based). *Programs:* FFEL (Subsidized and Unsubsidized Stafford, PLUS), Perkins, Federal Nursing, state, college/university.
WORK-STUDY *Federal work-study:* Total amount: $8,851,155; 3,384 jobs averaging $2616. *State or other work-study/employment:* Part-time jobs available.
ATHLETIC AWARDS Total amount: $5,983,793 (28% need-based, 72% non-need-based).
APPLYING FOR FINANCIAL AID *Required financial aid form:* FAFSA. *Financial aid deadline (priority):* 3/1. *Notification date:* Continuous beginning 3/1. Students must reply by 5/1 or within 2 weeks of notification.
CONTACT Office of Admission Services, Baylor University, PO Box 97056, Waco, TX 76798-7056, 254-710-3435 or toll-free 800-BAYLOR U. *Fax:* 254-710-3436. *E-mail:* admissions@baylor.edu.

BAY PATH COLLEGE
Longmeadow, MA

ABOUT THE INSTITUTION Independent, undergraduate: women only; graduate: coed. Awards: associate, bachelor's, and master's degrees and post-bachelor's certificates. 13 undergraduate majors. Total enrollment: 1,456. Undergraduates: 1,343. Freshmen: 182.

GIFT AID (NEED-BASED) *Scholarships, grants, and awards:* Federal Pell, FSEOG, state, private, college/university gift aid from institutional funds.

GIFT AID (NON-NEED-BASED) *Scholarships, grants, and awards by category: Academic Interests/Achievement:* general academic interests/achievements. *Creative Arts/Performance:* dance, performing arts, theater/drama. *Special Achievements/Activities:* general special achievements/activities, memberships. *Special Characteristics:* adult students, children of faculty/staff, children of public servants, children with a deceased or disabled parent, general special characteristics, international students, out-of-state students, siblings of current students, twins.

LOANS *Programs:* Federal Direct (Subsidized and Unsubsidized Stafford, PLUS), FFEL (Subsidized and Unsubsidized Stafford, PLUS), Perkins, state.

WORK-STUDY *Federal work-study:* Total amount: $161,481; 146 jobs averaging $2000.

APPLYING FOR FINANCIAL AID *Required financial aid forms:* FAFSA, institution's own form.

CONTACT Phyllis Brand, Financial Aid Assistant, Bay Path College, 588 Longmeadow Street, Longmeadow, MA 01106-2292, 413-565-1261 or toll-free 800-782-7284 Ext. 331. *Fax:* 413-565-1101. *E-mail:* pbrand@baypath.edu.

BEACON COLLEGE
Leesburg, FL

CONTACT Financial Aid Office, Beacon College, 105 East Main Street, Leesburg, FL 34748, 352-787-7660.

BEACON UNIVERSITY
Columbus, GA

Tuition & fees: N/R	Average undergraduate aid package: $3636

ABOUT THE INSTITUTION Independent religious, coed. Awards: associate, bachelor's, master's, and doctoral degrees. 3 undergraduate majors. Total enrollment: 141. Undergraduates: 107. Federal methodology is used as a basis for awarding need-based institutional aid.

FRESHMAN FINANCIAL AID (Fall 2004) 11 applied for aid; of those 100% were deemed to have need. 100% of freshmen with need received aid; of those 100% had need fully met. *Average percent of need met:* 100% (excluding resources awarded to replace EFC). *Average financial aid package:* $3709 (excluding resources awarded to replace EFC).

UNDERGRADUATE FINANCIAL AID (Fall 2004) 53 applied for aid; of those 100% were deemed to have need. 100% of undergraduates with need received aid; of those 100% had need fully met. *Average percent of need met:* 100% (excluding resources awarded to replace EFC). *Average financial aid package:* $3636 (excluding resources awarded to replace EFC).

GIFT AID (NEED-BASED) *Total amount:* $195,589 (96% federal, 4% external sources). *Receiving aid:* Freshmen: 82% (9); All full-time undergraduates: 74% (39). *Average award:* Freshmen: $2681; Undergraduates: $3040. *Scholarships, grants, and awards:* Federal Pell.

GIFT AID (NON-NEED-BASED) *Receiving aid:* Freshmen: 64% (7); Undergraduates: 68% (36). *Scholarships, grants, and awards by category: Academic Interests/Achievement:* business, religion/biblical studies, social sciences. *Tuition waivers:* Full or partial for employees or children of employees.

LOANS *Student loans:* $548,715 (52% need-based, 48% non-need-based). 68% of past graduating class borrowed through all loan programs. *Average indebtedness per student:* $19,659. *Average need-based loan:* Freshmen: $3607; Undergraduates: $3195. *Programs:* FFEL (Subsidized and Unsubsidized Stafford, PLUS).

APPLYING FOR FINANCIAL AID *Required financial aid forms:* FAFSA, institution's own form. *Financial aid deadline:* Continuous. *Notification date:* Continuous beginning 7/15. Students must reply within 2 weeks of notification.

CONTACT Mrs. Rita Roberts, Director of Student Financial Affairs, Beacon University, 6003 Veterans Parkway, Columbus, GA 31909-4663, 706-323-5364 Ext. 254. *Fax:* 706-323-5891. *E-mail:* rita.roberts@beacon.edu.

BECKER COLLEGE
Worcester, MA

Tuition & fees: $18,425	Average undergraduate aid package: $9490

ABOUT THE INSTITUTION Independent, coed. Awards: associate and bachelor's degrees (also includes Leicester, MA small town campus). 30 undergraduate majors. Total enrollment: 1,660. Undergraduates: 1,660. Freshmen: 496. Federal methodology is used as a basis for awarding need-based institutional aid.

UNDERGRADUATE EXPENSES for 2005–06 *Application fee:* $30. *Comprehensive fee:* $26,425 includes full-time tuition ($18,000), mandatory fees ($425), and room and board ($8000). *Part-time tuition:* $750 per credit hour. Part-time tuition and fees vary according to program. *Payment plan:* Installment.

FRESHMAN FINANCIAL AID (Fall 2005, est.) 432 applied for aid; of those 92% were deemed to have need. 99% of freshmen with need received aid; of those 9% had need fully met. *Average percent of need met:* 48% (excluding resources awarded to replace EFC). *Average financial aid package:* $9984 (excluding resources awarded to replace EFC). 17% of all full-time freshmen had no need and received non-need-based gift aid.

UNDERGRADUATE FINANCIAL AID (Fall 2005, est.) 1,077 applied for aid; of those 91% were deemed to have need. 99% of undergraduates with need received aid; of those 8% had need fully met. *Average percent of need met:* 47% (excluding resources awarded to replace EFC). *Average financial aid package:* $9490 (excluding resources awarded to replace EFC). 13% of all full-time undergraduates had no need and received non-need-based gift aid.

GIFT AID (NEED-BASED) *Total amount:* $6,462,299 (25% federal, 7% state, 64% institutional, 4% external sources). *Receiving aid:* Freshmen: 81% (389); All full-time undergraduates: 81% (920). *Average award:* Freshmen: $7445; Undergraduates: $6735. *Scholarships, grants, and awards:* Federal Pell, FSEOG, state, private, college/university gift aid from institutional funds.

GIFT AID (NON-NEED-BASED) *Total amount:* $338,985 (2% federal, 2% state, 93% institutional, 3% external sources). *Receiving aid:* Freshmen: 3% (15); Undergraduates: 2% (23). *Average Award:* Freshmen: $11,281; Undergraduates:* $12,241. *Scholarships, grants, and awards by category: Academic Interests/Achievement:* 21 awards ($35,000 total): general academic interests/achievements. *Special Achievements/Activities:* general special achievements/activities, leadership. *Special Characteristics:* 42 awards ($267,180 total): children of faculty/staff, siblings of current students, twins. *Tuition waivers:* Full or partial for employees or children of employees, senior citizens. *ROTC:* Army cooperative, Naval cooperative, Air Force cooperative.

LOANS *Student loans:* $12,608,439 (72% need-based, 28% non-need-based). 100% of past graduating class borrowed through all loan programs. *Average indebtedness per student:* $33,046. *Average need-based loan:* Freshmen: $2361; Undergraduates: $2988. *Parent loans:* $3,112,906 (49% need-based, 51% non-need-based). *Programs:* FFEL (Subsidized and Unsubsidized Stafford, PLUS), state, alternative loans.

WORK-STUDY *Federal work-study:* Total amount: $300,175; 450 jobs averaging $879.

APPLYING FOR FINANCIAL AID *Required financial aid form:* FAFSA. *Financial aid deadline (priority):* 3/1. *Notification date:* Continuous. Students must reply within 2 weeks of notification.

CONTACT Denise Lawrie, Director of Financial Aid, Becker College, 61 Sever Street, PO Box 15071, Worcester, MA 01615-0071, 508-791-9241 Ext. 242 or toll-free 877-5BECKER Ext. 245. *Fax:* 508-890-1511. *E-mail:* lawrie@beckercollege.edu.

BEIS MEDRASH HEICHAL DOVID
Far Rockaway, NY

CONTACT Financial Aid Office, Beis Medrash Heichal Dovid, 257 Beach 17th Street, Far Rockaway, NY 11691, 718-868-2300.

Belhaven College

BELHAVEN COLLEGE
Jackson, MS

Tuition & fees: $14,774   **Average undergraduate aid package: $9795**

ABOUT THE INSTITUTION Independent Presbyterian, coed. Awards: associate, bachelor's, and master's degrees. 26 undergraduate majors. Total enrollment: 2,580. Undergraduates: 2,238. Freshmen: 202. Federal methodology is used as a basis for awarding need-based institutional aid.

UNDERGRADUATE EXPENSES for 2006–07 *Application fee:* $25. *Comprehensive fee:* $20,478 includes full-time tuition ($14,124), mandatory fees ($650), and room and board ($5704). *Part-time tuition:* $350 per semester hour.

FRESHMAN FINANCIAL AID (Fall 2005, est.) 166 applied for aid; of those 72% were deemed to have need. 100% of freshmen with need received aid; of those 25% had need fully met. *Average percent of need met:* 56% (excluding resources awarded to replace EFC). *Average financial aid package:* $10,562 (excluding resources awarded to replace EFC). 30% of all full-time freshmen had no need and received non-need-based gift aid.

UNDERGRADUATE FINANCIAL AID (Fall 2005, est.) 1,996 applied for aid; of those 94% were deemed to have need. 100% of undergraduates with need received aid; of those 4% had need fully met. *Average percent of need met:* 53% (excluding resources awarded to replace EFC). *Average financial aid package:* $9795 (excluding resources awarded to replace EFC). 8% of all full-time undergraduates had no need and received non-need-based gift aid.

GIFT AID (NEED-BASED) *Total amount:* $3,103,145 (97% federal, 3% state). *Receiving aid:* Freshmen: 50% (102); All full-time undergraduates: 79% (1,720). *Average award:* Freshmen: $7973; Undergraduates: $7090. *Scholarships, grants, and awards:* Federal Pell, FSEOG, state, private, college/university gift aid from institutional funds.

GIFT AID (NON-NEED-BASED) *Total amount:* $3,954,764 (8% state, 87% institutional, 5% external sources). *Receiving aid:* Freshmen: 44% (88); Undergraduates: 69% (1,503). *Average Award:* Freshmen: $8056; Undergraduates: $7041. *Scholarships, grants, and awards by category: Academic Interests/Achievement:* 732 awards ($2,135,171 total): biological sciences, business, communication, computer science, education, English, foreign languages, general academic interests/achievements, humanities, mathematics, premedicine, religion/biblical studies, social sciences. *Creative Arts/Performance:* 166 awards ($275,667 total): applied art and design, art/fine arts, creative writing, dance, journalism/publications, music, performing arts, theater/drama. *Special Achievements/Activities:* 441 awards ($183,225 total): cheerleading/drum major, general special achievements/activities, junior miss, leadership. *Special Characteristics:* 176 awards ($231,800 total): children of faculty/staff, general special characteristics, international students, local/state students, relatives of clergy, religious affiliation.

LOANS *Student loans:* $12,446,916 (52% need-based, 48% non-need-based). 87% of past graduating class borrowed through all loan programs. *Average indebtedness per student:* $18,126. *Average need-based loan:* Freshmen: $3000; Undergraduates: $4310. *Parent loans:* $909,730 (100% non-need-based). *Programs:* FFEL (Subsidized and Unsubsidized Stafford, PLUS), Perkins.

WORK-STUDY *Federal work-study:* Total amount: $179,789; 123 jobs averaging $1600.

ATHLETIC AWARDS *Total amount:* $1,447,522 (100% non-need-based).

APPLYING FOR FINANCIAL AID *Required financial aid forms:* FAFSA, state aid form. *Financial aid deadline (priority):* 3/1. *Notification date:* Continuous beginning 3/1. Students must reply within 4 weeks of notification.

CONTACT Ms. Linda Phillips, Assistant Vice President for Institutional Advancement, Belhaven College, 1500 Peachtree Street, Box 159, Jackson, MS 39202-1789, 601-968-5934 or toll-free 800-960-5940. *Fax:* 601-353-0701. *E-mail:* lphillips@belhaven.edu.

BELLARMINE UNIVERSITY
Louisville, KY

CONTACT Associate Director of Financial Aid, Bellarmine University, 2001 Newburg Road, Louisville, KY 40205-0671, 502-452-8124 or toll-free 800-274-4723 Ext. 8131. *Fax:* 502-452-8002.

BELLEVUE UNIVERSITY
Bellevue, NE

ABOUT THE INSTITUTION Independent, coed. Awards: bachelor's and master's degrees. 14 undergraduate majors. Total enrollment: 5,929. Undergraduates: 4,447. Freshmen: 84.

GIFT AID (NEED-BASED) *Scholarships, grants, and awards:* Federal Pell, FSEOG, state.

GIFT AID (NON-NEED-BASED) *Scholarships, grants, and awards by category: Academic Interests/Achievement:* business, general academic interests/achievements, humanities, mathematics, social sciences.

LOANS *Programs:* FFEL (Subsidized and Unsubsidized Stafford, PLUS).

APPLYING FOR FINANCIAL AID *Required financial aid forms:* FAFSA, institution's own form.

CONTACT Mr. Jon Dotterer, Director of Financial Aid, Bellevue University, 1000 Galvin Road South, Bellevue, NE 68005, 402-293-3762 or toll-free 800-756-7920. *Fax:* 402-293-2062.

BELLIN COLLEGE OF NURSING
Green Bay, WI

Tuition & fees: $14,768   **Average undergraduate aid package: $12,285**

ABOUT THE INSTITUTION Independent, coed, primarily women. Awards: bachelor's and master's degrees. 1 undergraduate major. Total enrollment: 239. Undergraduates: 216. Freshmen: 32. Federal methodology is used as a basis for awarding need-based institutional aid.

UNDERGRADUATE EXPENSES for 2005–06 *Application fee:* $30. *Tuition:* full-time $14,500; part-time $684 per credit. Full-time tuition and fees vary according to course level. Part-time tuition and fees vary according to course load. *Payment plan:* Installment.

UNDERGRADUATE FINANCIAL AID (Fall 2004) 109 applied for aid; of those 90% were deemed to have need. 100% of undergraduates with need received aid; of those 11% had need fully met. *Average percent of need met:* 87% (excluding resources awarded to replace EFC). *Average financial aid package:* $12,285 (excluding resources awarded to replace EFC). 2% of all full-time undergraduates had no need and received non-need-based gift aid.

GIFT AID (NEED-BASED) *Total amount:* $564,306 (14% federal, 16% state, 49% institutional, 21% external sources). *Receiving aid:* All full-time undergraduates: 54% (97). *Average award:* Undergraduates: $5588. *Scholarships, grants, and awards:* Federal Pell, FSEOG, state, private, college/university gift aid from institutional funds.

GIFT AID (NON-NEED-BASED) *Total amount:* $14,130 (35% institutional, 65% external sources). *Receiving aid:* Undergraduates: 1% (1). *Average Award:* Undergraduates: $1225. *Scholarships, grants, and awards by category: Academic Interests/Achievement:* 53 awards ($58,267 total): general academic interests/achievements. *ROTC:* Army cooperative.

LOANS *Student loans:* $1,026,111 (74% need-based, 26% non-need-based). 93% of past graduating class borrowed through all loan programs. *Average indebtedness per student:* $25,305. *Average need-based loan:* Undergraduates: $5224. *Parent loans:* $175,864 (41% need-based, 59% non-need-based). *Programs:* FFEL (Subsidized and Unsubsidized Stafford, PLUS), state.

WORK-STUDY *Federal work-study:* Total amount: $7100; 6 jobs averaging $1183.

APPLYING FOR FINANCIAL AID *Required financial aid form:* FAFSA. *Financial aid deadline (priority):* 3/1. *Notification date:* 4/1. Students must reply within 2 weeks of notification.

CONTACT Ms. Lena C. Goodman, Director of Financial Aid, Bellin College of Nursing, 725 South Webster Avenue, PO Box 23400, Green Bay, WI 54305-3400, 920-433-5801 or toll-free 800-236-8707. *Fax:* 920-433-7416. *E-mail:* lena.goodman@bcon.edu.

BELMONT ABBEY COLLEGE
Belmont, NC

Tuition & fees: $16,724   **Average undergraduate aid package: $12,082**

ABOUT THE INSTITUTION Independent Roman Catholic, coed. Awards: bachelor's degrees. 23 undergraduate majors. Total enrollment: 800. Undergraduates: 800. Freshmen: 174. Federal methodology is used as a basis for awarding need-based institutional aid.

UNDERGRADUATE EXPENSES for 2005–06 *Application fee:* $35. *One-time required fee:* $672. *Comprehensive fee:* $25,310 includes full-time tuition ($15,910), mandatory fees ($814), and room and board ($8586). *College room only:* $4829. Full-time tuition and fees vary according to class time, course level, course load, location, program, reciprocity agreements, and student level. Room and board charges vary according to board plan, housing facility, location, and student level. *Part-time tuition:* $499 per credit. *Part-time fees:* $201 per hour. Part-time tuition and fees vary according to class time, course level, course load, location, reciprocity agreements, and student level. *Payment plans:* Installment, deferred payment.

FRESHMAN FINANCIAL AID (Fall 2005, est.) 206 applied for aid; of those 82% were deemed to have need. 99% of freshmen with need received aid; of those 20% had need fully met. *Average percent of need met:* 63% (excluding resources awarded to replace EFC). *Average financial aid package:* $13,526 (excluding resources awarded to replace EFC). 31% of all full-time freshmen had no need and received non-need-based gift aid.

UNDERGRADUATE FINANCIAL AID (Fall 2005, est.) 679 applied for aid; of those 89% were deemed to have need. 98% of undergraduates with need received aid; of those 16% had need fully met. *Average percent of need met:* 57% (excluding resources awarded to replace EFC). *Average financial aid package:* $12,082 (excluding resources awarded to replace EFC). 26% of all full-time undergraduates had no need and received non-need-based gift aid.

GIFT AID (NEED-BASED) *Total amount:* $4,886,484 (15% federal, 21% state, 56% institutional, 8% external sources). *Receiving aid:* Freshmen: 62% (168); All full-time undergraduates: 64% (587). *Average award:* Freshmen: $11,491; Undergraduates: $8984. *Scholarships, grants, and awards:* Federal Pell, FSEOG, state, private, college/university gift aid from institutional funds.

GIFT AID (NON-NEED-BASED) *Total amount:* $1,904,658 (9% state, 82% institutional, 9% external sources). *Receiving aid:* Freshmen: 11% (29); Undergraduates: 7% (66). *Average Award:* Freshmen: $15,006; Undergraduates:* $11,769. *Scholarships, grants, and awards by category: Academic Interests/Achievement:* 535 awards ($2,986,633 total): general academic interests/achievements. *Creative Arts/Performance:* 16 awards ($26,885 total): theater/drama. *Special Achievements/Activities:* 34 awards ($61,031 total): religious involvement. *Special Characteristics:* 22 awards ($135,163 total): children of faculty/staff. *Tuition waivers:* Full or partial for employees or children of employees, senior citizens. *ROTC:* Army cooperative, Air Force cooperative.

LOANS *Student loans:* $3,332,215 (61% need-based, 39% non-need-based). 70% of past graduating class borrowed through all loan programs. *Average indebtedness per student:* $16,025. *Average need-based loan:* Freshmen: $2116; Undergraduates: $3383. *Parent loans:* $4,246,452 (38% need-based, 62% non-need-based). *Programs:* Federal Direct (Subsidized and Unsubsidized Stafford, PLUS), Perkins.

WORK-STUDY *Federal work-study:* Total amount: $151,727; 164 jobs averaging $925.

ATHLETIC AWARDS *Total amount:* $919,070 (49% need-based, 51% non-need-based).

APPLYING FOR FINANCIAL AID *Required financial aid form:* FAFSA. *Financial aid deadline (priority):* 4/1. *Notification date:* Continuous beginning 3/1. Students must reply within 2 weeks of notification.

CONTACT Ms. Julie Hodge, Associate Director of Financial Aid, Belmont Abbey College, 100 Belmont Mt. Holly Road, Belmont, NC 28012-1802, 704-825-6718 or toll-free 888-BAC-0110. Fax: 704-825-6882. E-mail: juliehodge@bac.edu.

BELMONT UNIVERSITY
Nashville, TN

Tuition & fees: $17,260	Average undergraduate aid package: $6524

ABOUT THE INSTITUTION Independent Baptist, coed. Awards: bachelor's, master's, and doctoral degrees and post-master's certificates. 67 undergraduate majors. Total enrollment: 4,319. Undergraduates: 3,645. Freshmen: 797. Federal methodology is used as a basis for awarding need-based institutional aid.

UNDERGRADUATE EXPENSES for 2005–06 *Application fee:* $35. *Comprehensive fee:* $25,910 includes full-time tuition ($16,360), mandatory fees ($900), and room and board ($8650). *College room only:* $5300. Full-time tuition and fees vary according to class time and course load. Room and board charges vary according to board plan, housing facility, and location. *Part-time tuition:* $625 per credit hour. *Part-time fees:* $300 per term. Part-time tuition and fees vary according to course load. *Payment plans:* Installment, deferred payment.

FRESHMAN FINANCIAL AID (Fall 2004) 657 applied for aid; of those 58% were deemed to have need. 96% of freshmen with need received aid; of those 31% had need fully met. *Average percent of need met:* 45% (excluding resources awarded to replace EFC). *Average financial aid package:* $5464 (excluding resources awarded to replace EFC). 22% of all full-time freshmen had no need and received non-need-based gift aid.

UNDERGRADUATE FINANCIAL AID (Fall 2004) 2,441 applied for aid; of those 63% were deemed to have need. 98% of undergraduates with need received aid; of those 21% had need fully met. *Average percent of need met:* 41% (excluding resources awarded to replace EFC). *Average financial aid package:* $6524 (excluding resources awarded to replace EFC). 16% of all full-time undergraduates had no need and received non-need-based gift aid.

GIFT AID (NEED-BASED) *Total amount:* $6,475,826 (22% federal, 25% state, 42% institutional, 11% external sources). *Receiving aid:* Freshmen: 37% (272); All full-time undergraduates: 37% (1,086). *Average award:* Freshmen: $4797; Undergraduates: $4512. *Scholarships, grants, and awards:* Federal Pell, FSEOG, state, private, college/university gift aid from institutional funds.

GIFT AID (NON-NEED-BASED) *Total amount:* $5,204,382 (100% institutional). *Receiving aid:* Freshmen: 31% (226); Undergraduates: 22% (636). *Average Award:* Freshmen: $4344; Undergraduates: $4269. *Scholarships, grants, and awards by category: Academic Interests/Achievement:* 714 awards ($2,954,483 total): general academic interests/achievements, religion/biblical studies. *Creative Arts/Performance:* 191 awards ($217,250 total): music. *Special Characteristics:* 45 awards ($539,133 total): children of faculty/staff. *Tuition waivers:* Full or partial for employees or children of employees, senior citizens. *ROTC:* Army cooperative, Naval cooperative.

LOANS *Student loans:* $11,240,968 (100% need-based). 56% of past graduating class borrowed through all loan programs. *Average indebtedness per student:* $18,007. *Average need-based loan:* Freshmen: $2586; Undergraduates: $4207. *Parent loans:* $8,827,379 (100% non-need-based). *Programs:* FFEL (Subsidized and Unsubsidized Stafford, PLUS), Perkins, college/university.

WORK-STUDY *Federal work-study:* Total amount: $311,236; 221 jobs averaging $1412.

ATHLETIC AWARDS *Total amount:* $2,366,536 (100% non-need-based).

APPLYING FOR FINANCIAL AID *Required financial aid form:* FAFSA. *Financial aid deadline (priority):* 3/1. *Notification date:* Continuous beginning 3/15. Students must reply by 5/1 or within 2 weeks of notification.

CONTACT Mrs. Paula A. Gill, Director, Student Financial Services, Belmont University, 1900 Belmont Boulevard, Nashville, TN 37212-3757, 615-460-6403 or toll-free 800-56E-NROL. E-mail: gillp@mail.belmont.edu.

BELOIT COLLEGE
Beloit, WI

Tuition & fees: $26,884	Average undergraduate aid package: $19,108

ABOUT THE INSTITUTION Independent, coed. Awards: bachelor's degrees. 56 undergraduate majors. Total enrollment: 1,385. Undergraduates: 1,385. Freshmen: 326. Both federal and institutional methodology are used as a basis for awarding need-based institutional aid.

UNDERGRADUATE EXPENSES for 2005–06 *Application fee:* $35. *Comprehensive fee:* $32,808 includes full-time tuition ($26,664), mandatory fees ($220), and room and board ($5924). *College room only:* $2890. Room and board charges vary according to board plan. *Part-time tuition:* $3334 per course. *Payment plan:* Installment.

FRESHMAN FINANCIAL AID (Fall 2005, est.) 309 applied for aid; of those 85% were deemed to have need. 100% of freshmen with need received aid; of those 100% had need fully met. *Average percent of need met:* 100% (excluding resources awarded to replace EFC). *Average financial aid package:* $18,593 (excluding resources awarded to replace EFC). 10% of all full-time freshmen had no need and received non-need-based gift aid.

UNDERGRADUATE FINANCIAL AID (Fall 2005, est.) 1,209 applied for aid; of those 82% were deemed to have need. 100% of undergraduates with need received aid; of those 100% had need fully met. *Average percent of need met:* 100% (excluding resources awarded to replace EFC). *Average financial aid*

Beloit College

package: $19,108 (excluding resources awarded to replace EFC). 13% of all full-time undergraduates had no need and received non-need-based gift aid. **GIFT AID (NEED-BASED)** *Total amount:* $14,523,635 (5% federal, 3% state, 90% institutional, 2% external sources). *Receiving aid:* Freshmen: 79% (257); All full-time undergraduates: 76% (983). *Average award:* Freshmen: $15,676; Undergraduates: $14,736. *Scholarships, grants, and awards:* Federal Pell, FSEOG, state, private, college/university gift aid from institutional funds. **GIFT AID (NON-NEED-BASED)** *Total amount:* $2,522,767 (95% institutional, 5% external sources). *Receiving aid:* Freshmen: 52% (169); Undergraduates: 42% (548). *Average Award:* Freshmen: $12,990; Undergraduates: $11,791. *Scholarships, grants, and awards by category:* Academic Interests/Achievement: 188 awards ($2,115,034 total): general academic interests/achievements. *Creative Arts/Performance:* 22 awards ($86,000 total): music. *Special Achievements/Activities:* 35 awards ($119,000 total): community service, general special achievements/activities. *Special Characteristics:* 36 awards ($181,400 total): members of minority groups, siblings of current students. *Tuition waivers:* Full or partial for employees or children of employees. **LOANS** *Student loans:* $5,581,019 (59% need-based, 41% non-need-based). 62% of past graduating class borrowed through all loan programs. *Average indebtedness per student:* $14,781. *Average need-based loan:* Freshmen: $4420; Undergraduates: $5872. *Parent loans:* $2,563,550 (100% non-need-based). *Programs:* FFEL (Subsidized and Unsubsidized Stafford, PLUS), Perkins, college/university. **WORK-STUDY** *Federal work-study:* Total amount: $750,610; 526 jobs averaging $1427. *State or other work-study/employment:* Total amount: $566,377 (83% need-based, 17% non-need-based). 517 part-time jobs averaging $1096. **APPLYING FOR FINANCIAL AID** *Required financial aid forms:* FAFSA, institution's own form, state aid form. *Financial aid deadline (priority):* 3/1. *Notification date:* Continuous beginning 4/1. Students must reply by 5/1 or within 2 weeks of notification. **CONTACT** Mr. Jon Urish, Senior Associate Director of Admissions and Financial Aid, Beloit College, 700 College Street, Beloit, WI 53511-5596, 800-356-0751 or toll-free 800-9-BELOIT. *Fax:* 608-363-2075. *E-mail:* urishj@beloit.edu.

BEMIDJI STATE UNIVERSITY
Bemidji, MN

Tuition & fees (MN res): $6014   **Average undergraduate aid package:** $7579

ABOUT THE INSTITUTION State-supported, coed. Awards: associate, bachelor's, and master's degrees. 72 undergraduate majors. Total enrollment: 4,893. Undergraduates: 4,456. Freshmen: 633. Federal methodology is used as a basis for awarding need-based institutional aid.
UNDERGRADUATE EXPENSES for 2005–06 *Application fee:* $20. *Tuition, state resident:* full-time $5246; part-time $190.50 per credit. *Required fees:* full-time $768; $83.89 per credit. Part-time tuition and fees vary according to course load. *College room and board:* $5014; *room only:* $3214. Room and board charges vary according to board plan and housing facility. *Payment plan:* Installment.
FRESHMAN FINANCIAL AID (Fall 2005, est.) 433 applied for aid; of those 68% were deemed to have need. 99% of freshmen with need received aid; of those 24% had need fully met. *Average percent of need met:* 71% (excluding resources awarded to replace EFC). *Average financial aid package:* $6806 (excluding resources awarded to replace EFC). 24% of all full-time freshmen had no need and received non-need-based gift aid.
UNDERGRADUATE FINANCIAL AID (Fall 2005, est.) 2,528 applied for aid; of those 76% were deemed to have need. 99% of undergraduates with need received aid; of those 31% had need fully met. *Average percent of need met:* 77% (excluding resources awarded to replace EFC). *Average financial aid package:* $7579 (excluding resources awarded to replace EFC). 17% of all full-time undergraduates had no need and received non-need-based gift aid.
GIFT AID (NEED-BASED) *Total amount:* $6,722,311 (55% federal, 36% state, 1% institutional, 8% external sources). *Receiving aid:* Freshmen: 38% (208); All full-time undergraduates: 41% (1,377). *Average award:* Freshmen: $4185; Undergraduates: $4115. *Scholarships, grants, and awards:* Federal Pell, FSEOG, state, private, college/university gift aid from institutional funds.
GIFT AID (NON-NEED-BASED) *Total amount:* $4,431,018 (17% federal, 26% state, 41% institutional, 16% external sources). *Receiving aid:* Freshmen: 29% (159); Undergraduates: 35% (1,189). *Average Award:* Freshmen: $5733; Undergraduates: $6607. *Scholarships, grants, and awards by category:*

Academic Interests/Achievement: 493 awards ($595,955 total): general academic interests/achievements. *Creative Arts/Performance:* 38 awards ($79,152 total). *Special Characteristics:* 130 awards ($253,685 total): children and siblings of alumni, children of faculty/staff, international students, out-of-state students. *Tuition waivers:* Full or partial for employees or children of employees, senior citizens.
LOANS *Student loans:* $15,987,192 (42% need-based, 58% non-need-based). 77% of past graduating class borrowed through all loan programs. *Average indebtedness per student:* $18,247. *Average need-based loan:* Freshmen: $2663; Undergraduates: $3392. *Parent loans:* $465,859 (100% non-need-based). *Programs:* Federal Direct (Subsidized and Unsubsidized Stafford, PLUS), Perkins, state, Alaska Loans, Canada Student Loans, Norwest Collegiate Loans, CitiAssist Loans and other alternative loans.
WORK-STUDY *Federal work-study:* Total amount: $415,837; 217 jobs averaging $1916. *State or other work-study/employment:* Total amount: $1,972,648 (28% need-based, 72% non-need-based). 279 part-time jobs averaging $1962.
ATHLETIC AWARDS Total amount: $691,736 (100% non-need-based).
APPLYING FOR FINANCIAL AID *Required financial aid forms:* FAFSA, institution's own form. *Financial aid deadline (priority):* 5/15. *Notification date:* Continuous beginning 5/15.
CONTACT Marjorie Gilderalaws, Financial Aid Office, Bemidji State University, 1500 Birchmont Drive, NE, Bemidji, MN 56601-2699, 218-755-2034 or toll-free 800-475-2001 (in-state), 800-652-9747 (out-of-state). *Fax:* 218-755-4361. *E-mail:* mgilderslecve@bcmidjistate.edu.

BENEDICT COLLEGE
Columbia, SC

CONTACT Assistant Director of Financial Aid, Benedict College, 1600 Harden Street, Columbia, SC 29204, 803-253-5105 or toll-free 800-868-6598 (in-state).

BENEDICTINE COLLEGE
Atchison, KS

Tuition & fees: $15,760   **Average undergraduate aid package:** $13,973

ABOUT THE INSTITUTION Independent Roman Catholic, coed. Awards: associate, bachelor's, and master's degrees. 34 undergraduate majors. Total enrollment: 1,508. Undergraduates: 1,456. Freshmen: 304. Federal methodology is used as a basis for awarding need-based institutional aid.
UNDERGRADUATE EXPENSES for 2005–06 *Application fee:* $25. *Comprehensive fee:* $22,968 includes full-time tuition ($15,110), mandatory fees ($650), and room and board ($7208). *College room only:* $2730. Full-time tuition and fees vary according to course load and degree level. Room and board charges vary according to board plan and housing facility. *Part-time tuition:* $450 per credit hour. Part-time tuition and fees vary according to course load and degree level. *Payment plan:* Installment.
FRESHMAN FINANCIAL AID (Fall 2005, est.) 303 applied for aid; of those 76% were deemed to have need. 100% of freshmen with need received aid; of those 46% had need fully met. *Average percent of need met:* 59% (excluding resources awarded to replace EFC). *Average financial aid package:* $12,379 (excluding resources awarded to replace EFC). 17% of all full-time freshmen had no need and received non-need-based gift aid.
UNDERGRADUATE FINANCIAL AID (Fall 2005, est.) 1,162 applied for aid; of those 78% were deemed to have need. 100% of undergraduates with need received aid; of those 44% had need fully met. *Average percent of need met:* 67% (excluding resources awarded to replace EFC). *Average financial aid package:* $13,973 (excluding resources awarded to replace EFC). 17% of all full-time undergraduates had no need and received non-need-based gift aid.
GIFT AID (NEED-BASED) *Total amount:* $6,584,606 (18% federal, 10% state, 67% institutional, 5% external sources). *Receiving aid:* Freshmen: 76% (229); All full-time undergraduates: 74% (875). *Average award:* Freshmen: $8647; Undergraduates: $11,150. *Scholarships, grants, and awards:* Federal Pell, FSEOG, state, private, college/university gift aid from institutional funds.
GIFT AID (NON-NEED-BASED) *Total amount:* $347,934 (100% institutional). *Average Award:* Freshmen: $6037; Undergraduates: $4680. *Scholarships, grants, and awards by category:* Academic Interests/Achievement: 812 awards ($4,735,624 total): general academic interests/achievements. *Creative Arts/Performance:* 100 awards ($104,026 total): music, theater/drama. *Special Achievements/Activities:* 165 awards ($293,902 total): general special achievements/

activities. *Special Characteristics:* 93 awards ($252,629 total): children of educators, ethnic background, general special characteristics, international students, local/state students, members of minority groups, out-of-state students, religious affiliation, veterans' children. *Tuition waivers:* Full or partial for employees or children of employees, senior citizens. *ROTC:* Army.
LOANS *Student loans:* $6,148,512 (59% need-based, 41% non-need-based). 62% of past graduating class borrowed through all loan programs. *Average indebtedness per student:* $22,333. *Average need-based loan:* Freshmen: $3142; Undergraduates: $6418. *Parent loans:* $1,479,969 (100% non-need-based). *Programs:* FFEL (Subsidized and Unsubsidized Stafford, PLUS), Perkins, alternative loans.
WORK-STUDY *Federal work-study:* Total amount: $305,701; 372 jobs averaging $822. *State or other work-study/employment:* Total amount: $39,966 (100% non-need-based). 73 part-time jobs averaging $547.
ATHLETIC AWARDS *Total amount:* $2,924,942 (100% need-based).
APPLYING FOR FINANCIAL AID *Required financial aid form:* FAFSA. *Financial aid deadline (priority):* 3/15. *Notification date:* Continuous beginning 2/1. Students must reply within 2 weeks of notification.
CONTACT Mr. Keith Jaloma, Assistant Dean of Enrollment Management/Director of Financial Aid, Benedictine College, 1020 North Second Street, Atchison, KS 66002-1499, 913-360-7484 or toll-free 800-467-5340. *Fax:* 913-367-5462. *E-mail:* kjaloma@benedictine.edu.

BENEDICTINE UNIVERSITY
Lisle, IL

Tuition & fees: $19,210   **Average undergraduate aid package: $11,980**

ABOUT THE INSTITUTION Independent Roman Catholic, coed. Awards: associate, bachelor's, master's, and doctoral degrees and post-bachelor's certificates. 51 undergraduate majors. Total enrollment: 3,400. Undergraduates: 2,320. Freshmen: 311. Federal methodology is used as a basis for awarding need-based institutional aid.
UNDERGRADUATE EXPENSES for 2005–06 *Application fee:* $40. *Comprehensive fee:* $25,810 includes full-time tuition ($18,700), mandatory fees ($510), and room and board ($6600). Full-time tuition and fees vary according to class time, degree level, and location. Room and board charges vary according to board plan and housing facility. *Part-time tuition:* $630 per credit hour. *Part-time fees:* $15 per credit hour. Part-time tuition and fees vary according to class time and degree level. *Payment plan:* Installment.
FRESHMAN FINANCIAL AID (Fall 2005, est.) 252 applied for aid; of those 100% were deemed to have need. 99% of freshmen with need received aid; of those 38% had need fully met. *Average percent of need met:* 87% (excluding resources awarded to replace EFC). *Average financial aid package:* $13,630 (excluding resources awarded to replace EFC). 17% of all full-time freshmen had no need and received non-need-based gift aid.
UNDERGRADUATE FINANCIAL AID (Fall 2005, est.) 1,135 applied for aid; of those 100% were deemed to have need. 98% of undergraduates with need received aid; of those 40% had need fully met. *Average percent of need met:* 85% (excluding resources awarded to replace EFC). *Average financial aid package:* $11,980 (excluding resources awarded to replace EFC). 18% of all full-time undergraduates had no need and received non-need-based gift aid.
GIFT AID (NEED-BASED) *Total amount:* $4,819,198 (36% federal, 57% state, 7% institutional). *Receiving aid:* Freshmen: 47% (144); All full-time undergraduates: 42% (640). *Average award:* Freshmen: $6897; Undergraduates: $6350. *Scholarships, grants, and awards:* Federal Pell, FSEOG, state, private, college/university gift aid from institutional funds.
GIFT AID (NON-NEED-BASED) *Total amount:* $7,991,778 (98% institutional, 2% external sources). *Receiving aid:* Freshmen: 80% (245); Undergraduates: 58% (886). *Average Award:* Freshmen: $6305; Undergraduates: $6720. *Scholarships, grants, and awards by category: Academic Interests/Achievement:* general academic interests/achievements. *Creative Arts/Performance:* music. *Special Characteristics:* children and siblings of alumni, out-of-state students, previous college experience, siblings of current students. *Tuition waivers:* Full or partial for employees or children of employees. *ROTC:* Army cooperative.
LOANS *Student loans:* $10,415,179 (45% need-based, 55% non-need-based). *Average need-based loan:* Freshmen: $3383; Undergraduates: $4170. *Parent loans:* $8,699,214 (100% non-need-based). *Programs:* FFEL (Subsidized and Unsubsidized Stafford, PLUS), Perkins, alternative loans.
WORK-STUDY *Federal work-study:* Total amount: $193,161; jobs available.

APPLYING FOR FINANCIAL AID *Required financial aid forms:* FAFSA, institution's own form. *Financial aid deadline:* Continuous. *Notification date:* Continuous beginning 2/1. Students must reply within 2 weeks of notification.
CONTACT Diane Battistella, Director, Benedictine Central, Benedictine University, 5700 College Road, Lisle, IL 60532, 630-829-6415 or toll-free 888-829-6363 (out-of-state). *Fax:* 630-829-6456. *E-mail:* dbattistella@ben.edu.

BENNETT COLLEGE FOR WOMEN
Greensboro, NC

Tuition & fees: $13,239   **Average undergraduate aid package: $9393**

ABOUT THE INSTITUTION Independent United Methodist, women only. Awards: bachelor's degrees. 23 undergraduate majors. Total enrollment: 572. Undergraduates: 572. Freshmen: 205. Federal methodology is used as a basis for awarding need-based institutional aid.
UNDERGRADUATE EXPENSES for 2005–06 *Application fee:* $30. *Comprehensive fee:* $19,089 includes full-time tuition ($11,509), mandatory fees ($1730), and room and board ($5850). *College room only:* $2937. *Part-time tuition:* $479 per credit hour. *Part-time fees:* $718 per term. *Payment plan:* Deferred payment.
FRESHMAN FINANCIAL AID (Fall 2005, est.) 169 applied for aid; of those 90% were deemed to have need. 99% of freshmen with need received aid; of those 5% had need fully met. *Average percent of need met:* 42% (excluding resources awarded to replace EFC). *Average financial aid package:* $8449 (excluding resources awarded to replace EFC). 11% of all full-time freshmen had no need and received non-need-based gift aid.
UNDERGRADUATE FINANCIAL AID (Fall 2005, est.) 526 applied for aid; of those 94% were deemed to have need. 98% of undergraduates with need received aid; of those 5% had need fully met. *Average percent of need met:* 45% (excluding resources awarded to replace EFC). *Average financial aid package:* $9393 (excluding resources awarded to replace EFC). 8% of all full-time undergraduates had no need and received non-need-based gift aid.
GIFT AID (NEED-BASED) *Total amount:* $3,086,487 (38% federal, 17% state, 32% institutional, 13% external sources). *Receiving aid:* Freshmen: 61% (126); All full-time undergraduates: 75% (427). *Average award:* Freshmen: $7191; Undergraduates: $7196. *Scholarships, grants, and awards:* Federal Pell, FSEOG, state, private, college/university gift aid from institutional funds, United Negro College Fund, United Methodist Church Scholarships.
GIFT AID (NON-NEED-BASED) *Total amount:* $270,222 (10% state, 73% institutional, 17% external sources). *Receiving aid:* Freshmen: 2% (5); Undergraduates: 2% (14). *Average Award:* Freshmen: $15,347; Undergraduates: $16,857. *Scholarships, grants, and awards by category: Academic Interests/Achievement:* 227 awards ($1,234,702 total): business, general academic interests/achievements, mathematics. *Special Achievements/Activities:* general special achievements/activities. *Special Characteristics:* children of faculty/staff, relatives of clergy, religious affiliation. *Tuition waivers:* Full or partial for employees or children of employees. *ROTC:* Army cooperative, Air Force cooperative.
LOANS *Student loans:* $4,507,300 (84% need-based, 16% non-need-based). 100% of past graduating class borrowed through all loan programs. *Average indebtedness per student:* $15,531. *Average need-based loan:* Freshmen: $2282; Undergraduates: $3043. *Parent loans:* $1,570,546 (100% non-need-based). *Programs:* FFEL (Subsidized and Unsubsidized Stafford, PLUS), Perkins.
WORK-STUDY *Federal work-study:* Total amount: $118,213; 82 jobs averaging $1800.
APPLYING FOR FINANCIAL AID *Required financial aid forms:* FAFSA, institution's own form, state aid form. *Financial aid deadline:* 3/15. *Notification date:* Continuous beginning 2/20. Students must reply within 2 weeks of notification.
CONTACT Monty K. Hickman, Financial Aid Director, Bennett College For Women, 900 East Washington Street, Greensboro, NC 27401, 336-370-8677. *Fax:* 336-517-2204. *E-mail:* mhickman@bennett.edu.

BENNINGTON COLLEGE
Bennington, VT

Tuition & fees: $33,570   **Average undergraduate aid package: $25,712**

ABOUT THE INSTITUTION Independent, coed. Awards: bachelor's and master's degrees and post-bachelor's certificates. 86 undergraduate majors. Total enroll-

Bennington College

ment: 725. Undergraduates: 571. Freshmen: 137. Both federal and institutional methodology are used as a basis for awarding need-based institutional aid.
UNDERGRADUATE EXPENSES for 2005–06 *Application fee:* $60. *Comprehensive fee:* $41,890 includes full-time tuition ($32,700), mandatory fees ($870), and room and board ($8320). *College room only:* $4460. *Part-time tuition:* $1050 per credit. *Payment plan:* Installment.
FRESHMAN FINANCIAL AID (Fall 2005, est.) 98 applied for aid; of those 93% were deemed to have need. 100% of freshmen with need received aid; of those 4% had need fully met. *Average percent of need met:* 75% (excluding resources awarded to replace EFC). *Average financial aid package:* $24,069 (excluding resources awarded to replace EFC). 2% of all full-time freshmen had no need and received non-need-based gift aid.
UNDERGRADUATE FINANCIAL AID (Fall 2005, est.) 409 applied for aid; of those 95% were deemed to have need. 100% of undergraduates with need received aid; of those 3% had need fully met. *Average percent of need met:* 74% (excluding resources awarded to replace EFC). *Average financial aid package:* $25,712 (excluding resources awarded to replace EFC). 5% of all full-time undergraduates had no need and received non-need-based gift aid.
GIFT AID (NEED-BASED) *Total amount:* $8,149,346 (8% federal, 89% institutional, 3% external sources). *Receiving aid:* Freshmen: 66% (90); All full-time undergraduates: 67% (380). *Average award:* Freshmen: $21,211; Undergraduates: $21,449. *Scholarships, grants, and awards:* Federal Pell, FSEOG, state, private, college/university gift aid from institutional funds.
GIFT AID (NON-NEED-BASED) *Total amount:* $225,943 (73% institutional, 27% external sources). *Receiving aid:* Freshmen: 2% (3); Undergraduates: 1% (5). *Average Award:* Freshmen: $7325; Undergraduates: $7498. *Scholarships, grants, and awards by category:* Academic Interests/Achievement: general academic interests/achievements. Creative Arts/Performance: general creative arts/performance. Special Achievements/Activities: general special achievements/activities. Special Characteristics: children of educators, children of faculty/staff, general special characteristics. *Tuition waivers:* Full or partial for employees or children of employees.
LOANS *Student loans:* $2,453,224 (82% need-based, 18% non-need-based). 72% of past graduating class borrowed through all loan programs. *Average indebtedness per student:* $20,340. *Average need-based loan:* Freshmen: $2281; Undergraduates: $3798. *Parent loans:* $2,327,451 (46% need-based, 54% non-need-based). *Programs:* FFEL (Subsidized and Unsubsidized Stafford, PLUS), college/university.
WORK-STUDY *Federal work-study:* Total amount: $367,174; jobs available (averaging $1700). *State or other work-study/employment:* Total amount: $33,800 (91% need-based, 9% non-need-based). Part-time jobs available (averaging $1700).
APPLYING FOR FINANCIAL AID *Required financial aid forms:* FAFSA, institution's own form, CSS Financial Aid PROFILE, noncustodial (divorced/separated) parent's statement, student and parent federal tax returns. *Financial aid deadline (priority):* 3/1. *Notification date:* 3/30. Students must reply by 5/1 or within 2 weeks of notification.
CONTACT Meg Woolmington, Financial Aid Director, Bennington College, One College Drive, Bennington, VT 05201, 802-440-4325 or toll-free 800-833-6845. *Fax:* 802-440-4350. *E-mail:* finaid@bennington.edu.

BENTLEY COLLEGE
Waltham, MA

Tuition & fees: $28,614	Average undergraduate aid package: $21,726

ABOUT THE INSTITUTION Independent, coed. Awards: associate, bachelor's, and master's degrees and post-bachelor's and post-master's certificates. 14 undergraduate majors. Total enrollment: 5,565. Undergraduates: 4,294. Freshmen: 937. Both federal and institutional methodology are used as a basis for awarding need-based institutional aid.
UNDERGRADUATE EXPENSES for 2005–06 *Application fee:* $50. *Comprehensive fee:* $38,784 includes full-time tuition ($28,390), mandatory fees ($224), and room and board ($10,170). *College room only:* $6060. Full-time tuition and fees vary according to student level. Room and board charges vary according to board plan and housing facility. *Part-time tuition:* $1368 per course. *Part-time fees:* $10 per term. Part-time tuition and fees vary according to class time and student level. *Payment plan:* Installment.
FRESHMAN FINANCIAL AID (Fall 2004) 737 applied for aid; of those 69% were deemed to have need. 100% of freshmen with need received aid; of those 24% had need fully met. *Average percent of need met:* 91% (excluding resources awarded to replace EFC). *Average financial aid package:* $22,288 (excluding resources awarded to replace EFC). 10% of all full-time freshmen had no need and received non-need-based gift aid.
UNDERGRADUATE FINANCIAL AID (Fall 2004) 2,862 applied for aid; of those 72% were deemed to have need. 99% of undergraduates with need received aid; of those 25% had need fully met. *Average percent of need met:* 89% (excluding resources awarded to replace EFC). *Average financial aid package:* $21,726 (excluding resources awarded to replace EFC). 9% of all full-time undergraduates had no need and received non-need-based gift aid.
GIFT AID (NEED-BASED) *Total amount:* $25,473,818 (9% federal, 5% state, 86% institutional). *Receiving aid:* Freshmen: 48% (444); All full-time undergraduates: 42% (1,691). *Average award:* Freshmen: $16,755; Undergraduates: $16,755. *Scholarships, grants, and awards:* Federal Pell, FSEOG, state, private, college/university gift aid from institutional funds.
GIFT AID (NON-NEED-BASED) *Total amount:* $11,002,294 (91% institutional, 9% external sources). *Receiving aid:* Freshmen: 13% (121); Undergraduates: 13% (536). *Average Award:* Freshmen: $11,409; Undergraduates: $11,276. *Scholarships, grants, and awards by category:* Academic Interests/Achievement: 830 awards ($9,628,295 total): general academic interests/achievements. *Special Achievements/Activities:* 16 awards ($107,500 total): community service. *Special Characteristics:* 33 awards ($710,217 total): members of minority groups. *Tuition waivers:* Full or partial for employees or children of employees. *ROTC:* Army cooperative.
LOANS *Student loans:* $19,457,977 (49% need-based, 51% non-need-based). 65% of past graduating class borrowed through all loan programs. *Average indebtedness per student:* $27,132. *Average need-based loan:* Freshmen: $3940; Undergraduates: $4958. *Parent loans:* $9,298,586 (100% non-need-based). *Programs:* FFEL (Subsidized and Unsubsidized Stafford, PLUS), Perkins, state, college/university, Veterans Education Benefits.
WORK-STUDY *Federal work-study:* Total amount: $2,407,283; 1,386 jobs averaging $1588. *State or other work-study/employment:* Total amount: $797,047 (100% non-need-based). 499 part-time jobs averaging $2014.
ATHLETIC AWARDS *Total amount:* $1,755,344 (42% need-based, 58% non-need-based).
APPLYING FOR FINANCIAL AID *Required financial aid forms:* FAFSA, CSS Financial Aid PROFILE, noncustodial (divorced/separated) parent's statement, business/farm supplement. *Financial aid deadline:* 2/1. *Notification date:* Continuous beginning 3/25.
CONTACT Ms. Donna Kendall, Director of Financial Assistance, Bentley College, 175 Forest Street, Waltham, MA 02452-4705, 781-891-3441 or toll-free 800-523-2354. *Fax:* 781-891-2448. *E-mail:* finaid@bentley.edu.

BEREA COLLEGE
Berea, KY

Tuition & fees: $516	Average undergraduate aid package: $26,299

ABOUT THE INSTITUTION Independent, coed. Awards: bachelor's degrees. 52 undergraduate majors. Total enrollment: 1,595. Undergraduates: 1,595. Freshmen: 378. Federal methodology is used as a basis for awarding need-based institutional aid.
UNDERGRADUATE EXPENSES for 2005–06 includes mandatory fees ($516) and room and board ($4980). Financial aid is provided to all students for tuition costs.
FRESHMAN FINANCIAL AID (Fall 2005, est.) 378 applied for aid; of those 100% were deemed to have need. 100% of freshmen with need received aid; of those 27% had need fully met. *Average percent of need met:* 90% (excluding resources awarded to replace EFC). *Average financial aid package:* $25,921 (excluding resources awarded to replace EFC).
UNDERGRADUATE FINANCIAL AID (Fall 2005, est.) 1,520 applied for aid; of those 100% were deemed to have need. 100% of undergraduates with need received aid; of those 23% had need fully met. *Average percent of need met:* 92% (excluding resources awarded to replace EFC). *Average financial aid package:* $26,299 (excluding resources awarded to replace EFC).
GIFT AID (NEED-BASED) *Total amount:* $37,558,655 (11% federal, 7% state, 82% institutional). *Receiving aid:* Freshmen: 100% (378); All full-time undergraduates: 100% (1,520). *Average award:* Freshmen: $24,545; Undergraduates: $24,062. *Scholarships, grants, and awards:* Federal Pell, FSEOG, state, private, college/university gift aid from institutional funds.

LOANS *Student loans:* $1,805,707 (52% need-based, 48% non-need-based). 79% of past graduating class borrowed through all loan programs. *Average indebtedness per student:* $7299. *Average need-based loan:* Freshmen: $696; Undergraduates: $1190. *Parent loans:* $20,429 (100% need-based). *Programs:* FFEL (Subsidized and Unsubsidized Stafford, PLUS), Perkins, college/university.
WORK-STUDY *Federal work-study:* Total amount: $1,963,593; 1,201 jobs averaging $1585. *State or other work-study/employment:* Total amount: $495,170 (100% need-based). 319 part-time jobs averaging $1529.
APPLYING FOR FINANCIAL AID *Required financial aid form:* FAFSA. *Financial aid deadline:* 8/1 (priority: 4/15). *Notification date:* Continuous beginning 4/19.
CONTACT Bryan Erslan, Student Financial Aid Services, Berea College, CPO 2172, Berea, KY 40404, 859-985-3310 or toll-free 800-326-5948. *Fax:* 859-985-3914. *E-mail:* bryan_erslan@berea.edu.

BERKLEE COLLEGE OF MUSIC
Boston, MA

ABOUT THE INSTITUTION Independent, coed. Awards: bachelor's degrees. 12 undergraduate majors. Total enrollment: 4,037. Undergraduates: 4,037.
GIFT AID (NEED-BASED) *Scholarships, grants, and awards:* Federal Pell, FSEOG, state, private, college/university gift aid from institutional funds.
GIFT AID (NON-NEED-BASED) *Scholarships, grants, and awards by category: Creative Arts/Performance:* music.
LOANS *Programs:* Federal Direct (Subsidized and Unsubsidized Stafford, PLUS), Perkins, state.
WORK-STUDY *Federal work-study:* Total amount: $285,925; 269 jobs averaging $1063. *State or other work-study/employment:* Total amount: $277,301 (100% non-need-based). Part-time jobs available.
APPLYING FOR FINANCIAL AID *Required financial aid form:* FAFSA.
CONTACT Julie Poorman, Director of Financial Aid, Berklee College of Music, 1140 Boylston Street, Boston, MA 02215-3693, 617-747-2274 or toll-free 800-BERKLEE. *Fax:* 617-747-2073. *E-mail:* jpoorman@berklee.edu.

BERNARD M. BARUCH COLLEGE OF THE CITY UNIVERSITY OF NEW YORK
New York, NY

Tuition & fees (NY res): $4320   **Average undergraduate aid package:** $4800

ABOUT THE INSTITUTION State and locally supported, coed. Awards: bachelor's, master's, and doctoral degrees and post-master's certificates. 33 undergraduate majors. Total enrollment: 15,756. Undergraduates: 12,844. Freshmen: 1,641. Federal methodology is used as a basis for awarding need-based institutional aid.
UNDERGRADUATE EXPENSES for 2006–07 *Application fee:* $65. *Tuition, state resident:* full-time $4000; part-time $170 per credit. *Tuition, nonresident:* full-time $8640; part-time $360 per credit. *Required fees:* full-time $320; $80 per term part-time.
FRESHMAN FINANCIAL AID (Fall 2005, est.) 1471 applied for aid; of those 84% were deemed to have need. 98% of freshmen with need received aid; of those 26% had need fully met. *Average percent of need met:* 67% (excluding resources awarded to replace EFC). *Average financial aid package:* $5406 (excluding resources awarded to replace EFC). 6% of all full-time freshmen had no need and received non-need-based gift aid.
UNDERGRADUATE FINANCIAL AID (Fall 2005, est.) 8,198 applied for aid; of those 98% were deemed to have need. 100% of undergraduates with need received aid; of those 8% had need fully met. *Average percent of need met:* 63% (excluding resources awarded to replace EFC). *Average financial aid package:* $4800 (excluding resources awarded to replace EFC). 7% of all full-time undergraduates had no need and received non-need-based gift aid.
GIFT AID (NEED-BASED) *Total amount:* $34,360,000 (47% federal, 53% state). *Receiving aid:* Freshmen: 62% (1,001); All full-time undergraduates: 70% (6,807). *Average award:* Freshmen: $4800; Undergraduates: $3725. *Scholarships, grants, and awards:* Federal Pell, FSEOG, state, college/university gift aid from institutional funds.
GIFT AID (NON-NEED-BASED) *Total amount:* $6,100,000 (41% state, 18% institutional, 41% external sources). *Receiving aid:* Freshmen: 12% (190); Undergraduates: 13% (1,300). *Average Award:* Freshmen: $1600; Undergraduates:* $1800. *Scholarships, grants, and awards by category: Academic Interests/Achievement:* general academic interests/achievements.
LOANS *Student loans:* $13,000,000 (62% need-based, 38% non-need-based). 22% of past graduating class borrowed through all loan programs. *Average indebtedness per student:* $11,700. *Average need-based loan:* Freshmen: $2300; Undergraduates: $2900. *Parent loans:* $180,000 (100% non-need-based). *Programs:* Federal Direct (Subsidized and Unsubsidized Stafford, PLUS), Perkins.
WORK-STUDY *Federal work-study:* Total amount: $300,000; 520 jobs available. *State or other work-study/employment:* Total amount: $500,000 (100% non-need-based). Part-time jobs available.
APPLYING FOR FINANCIAL AID *Required financial aid forms:* FAFSA, state aid form. *Financial aid deadline:* 4/30 (priority: 3/15). *Notification date:* Continuous. Students must reply by 6/1 or within 6 weeks of notification.
CONTACT Financial Aid Office, Bernard M. Baruch College of the City University of New York, 151 East 25th Street, Room 720, New York, NY 10010-5585, 646-312-1360. *Fax:* 646-312-1363. *E-mail:* financial_aid@baruch.cuny.edu.

BERRY COLLEGE
Mount Berry, GA

Tuition & fees: $18,950   **Average undergraduate aid package:** $14,794

ABOUT THE INSTITUTION Independent interdenominational, coed. Awards: bachelor's and master's degrees and post-master's certificates. 39 undergraduate majors. Total enrollment: 1,970. Undergraduates: 1,863. Freshmen: 513. Federal methodology is used as a basis for awarding need-based institutional aid.
UNDERGRADUATE EXPENSES for 2006–07 *Application fee:* $50. *Comprehensive fee:* $26,114 includes full-time tuition ($18,950) and room and board ($7164). *College room only:* $4024.
FRESHMAN FINANCIAL AID (Fall 2005, est.) 401 applied for aid; of those 74% were deemed to have need. 100% of freshmen with need received aid; of those 33% had need fully met. *Average percent of need met:* 81% (excluding resources awarded to replace EFC). *Average financial aid package:* $13,669 (excluding resources awarded to replace EFC). 41% of all full-time freshmen had no need and received non-need-based gift aid.
UNDERGRADUATE FINANCIAL AID (Fall 2005, est.) 1,327 applied for aid; of those 78% were deemed to have need. 99% of undergraduates with need received aid; of those 23% had need fully met. *Average percent of need met:* 82% (excluding resources awarded to replace EFC). *Average financial aid package:* $14,794 (excluding resources awarded to replace EFC). 42% of all full-time undergraduates had no need and received non-need-based gift aid.
GIFT AID (NEED-BASED) *Total amount:* $11,352,521 (9% federal, 20% state, 67% institutional, 4% external sources). *Receiving aid:* Freshmen: 59% (295); All full-time undergraduates: 57% (1,021). *Average award:* Freshmen: $11,487; Undergraduates: $11,398. *Scholarships, grants, and awards:* Federal Pell, FSEOG, state, private, college/university gift aid from institutional funds.
GIFT AID (NON-NEED-BASED) *Total amount:* $6,877,596 (35% state, 58% institutional, 7% external sources). *Receiving aid:* Freshmen: 16% (79); Undergraduates: 10% (187). *Average Award:* Freshmen: $11,889; Undergraduates:* $12,112. *Scholarships, grants, and awards by category: Academic Interests/Achievement:* 860 awards ($4,850,000 total): agriculture, communication, education, English, general academic interests/achievements, humanities, religion/biblical studies. *Creative Arts/Performance:* 125 awards ($275,000 total): art/fine arts, debating, journalism/publications, music, theater/drama. *Special Achievements/Activities:* 73 awards ($135,000 total): community service, religious involvement. *Special Characteristics:* 200 awards ($788,500 total): adult students, children of faculty/staff, ethnic background, local/state students, members of minority groups.
LOANS *Student loans:* $3,770,973 (72% need-based, 28% non-need-based). 50% of past graduating class borrowed through all loan programs. *Average indebtedness per student:* $12,028. *Average need-based loan:* Freshmen: $2395; Undergraduates: $2826. *Parent loans:* $3,997,892 (21% need-based, 79% non-need-based). *Programs:* FFEL (Subsidized and Unsubsidized Stafford, PLUS), Perkins, college/university.
WORK-STUDY *Federal work-study:* Total amount: $872,522; 416 jobs averaging $2723. *State or other work-study/employment:* Total amount: $2,864,939 (18% need-based, 82% non-need-based). 1,028 part-time jobs averaging $2991.

Berry College

ATHLETIC AWARDS *Total amount:* $1,568,156 (26% need-based, 74% non-need-based).
APPLYING FOR FINANCIAL AID *Required financial aid forms:* FAFSA, institution's own form, state aid form. *Financial aid deadline (priority):* 4/1. *Notification date:* Continuous beginning 3/1. Students must reply by 5/1.
CONTACT Timothy H. Tarpley, Director of Financial Aid, Berry College, 2277 Martha Berry Highway, NW, Mount Berry, GA 30149-5007, 706-236-2276 or toll-free 800-237-7942. Fax: 706-290-2160. E-mail: wfron@berry.edu.

BETHANY COLLEGE
Lindsborg, KS

Tuition & fees: $16,210 | **Average undergraduate aid package: $16,612**

ABOUT THE INSTITUTION Independent Lutheran, coed. Awards: bachelor's degrees. 41 undergraduate majors. Total enrollment: 588. Undergraduates: 588. Freshmen: 148. Federal methodology is used as a basis for awarding need-based institutional aid.
UNDERGRADUATE EXPENSES for 2006–07 *Application fee:* $20. *Comprehensive fee:* $21,480 includes full-time tuition ($16,000), mandatory fees ($210), and room and board ($5270). *College room only:* $2850. *Part-time tuition:* $300 per credit hour.
FRESHMAN FINANCIAL AID (Fall 2005, est.) 143 applied for aid; of those 81% were deemed to have need. 100% of freshmen with need received aid; of those 45% had need fully met. *Average percent of need met:* 97% (excluding resources awarded to replace EFC). *Average financial aid package:* $16,682 (excluding resources awarded to replace EFC). 7% of all full-time freshmen had no need and received non-need-based gift aid.
UNDERGRADUATE FINANCIAL AID (Fall 2005, est.) 531 applied for aid; of those 85% were deemed to have need. 100% of undergraduates with need received aid; of those 46% had need fully met. *Average percent of need met:* 96% (excluding resources awarded to replace EFC). *Average financial aid package:* $16,612 (excluding resources awarded to replace EFC). 5% of all full-time undergraduates had no need and received non-need-based gift aid.
GIFT AID (NEED-BASED) *Total amount:* $1,935,046 (36% federal, 25% state, 39% institutional). *Receiving aid:* Freshmen: 60% (89); All full-time undergraduates: 67% (368). *Average award:* Freshmen: $4942; Undergraduates: $5404. *Scholarships, grants, and awards:* Federal Pell, FSEOG, state, private, college/university gift aid from institutional funds.
GIFT AID (NON-NEED-BASED) *Total amount:* $538,492 (74% institutional, 26% external sources). *Receiving aid:* Freshmen: 22% (33); Undergraduates: 24% (130). *Average Award:* Freshmen: $4750; Undergraduates: $6189. *Scholarships, grants, and awards by category:* Academic Interests/Achievement: 361 awards ($1,395,245 total): general academic interests/achievements. Creative Arts/Performance: 113 awards ($318,300 total): art/fine arts, music, theater/drama. Special Achievements/Activities: 8 awards ($6000 total): cheerleading/drum major. Special Characteristics: 18 awards ($119,030 total): international students, relatives of clergy.
LOANS *Student loans:* $2,844,099 (63% need-based, 37% non-need-based). 82% of past graduating class borrowed through all loan programs. *Average indebtedness per student:* $16,925. *Average need-based loan:* Freshmen: $4430; Undergraduates: $4822. *Parent loans:* $400,634 (100% non-need-based). *Programs:* FFEL (Subsidized and Unsubsidized Stafford, PLUS), Perkins, college/university.
WORK-STUDY *Federal work-study:* Total amount: $173,000; 115 jobs averaging $1500. *State or other work-study/employment:* Total amount: $150,000 (100% non-need-based). 100 part-time jobs averaging $1500.
ATHLETIC AWARDS *Total amount:* $1,088,589 (82% need-based, 18% non-need-based).
APPLYING FOR FINANCIAL AID *Required financial aid form:* FAFSA. *Financial aid deadline:* Continuous. *Notification date:* Continuous beginning 2/1. Students must reply within 3 weeks of notification.
CONTACT Ms. Brenda Meagher, Director of Financial Aid, Bethany College, 421 North First Street, Lindsborg, KS 67456-1897, 785-227-3311 Ext. 8248 or toll-free 800-826-2281. Fax: 785-227-2004. E-mail: meagherb@bethanylb.edu.

BETHANY COLLEGE
Bethany, WV

ABOUT THE INSTITUTION Independent religious, coed. Awards: bachelor's degrees. 33 undergraduate majors. Total enrollment: 902. Undergraduates: 902. Freshmen: 226.
GIFT AID (NEED-BASED) *Scholarships, grants, and awards:* Federal Pell, FSEOG, state, private, college/university gift aid from institutional funds.
GIFT AID (NON-NEED-BASED) *Scholarships, grants, and awards by category:* Academic Interests/Achievement: general academic interests/achievements. Creative Arts/Performance: music. Special Achievements/Activities: leadership, religious involvement. Special Characteristics: children and siblings of alumni, children of faculty/staff, ethnic background, international students, local/state students, relatives of clergy, religious affiliation.
LOANS *Programs:* Federal Direct (Subsidized and Unsubsidized Stafford, PLUS), Perkins, alternative loans.
WORK-STUDY *Federal work-study:* Total amount: $650,000; 423 jobs averaging $1100. *State or other work-study/employment:* Total amount: $115,000 (100% non-need-based). 310 part-time jobs averaging $290.
APPLYING FOR FINANCIAL AID *Required financial aid forms:* FAFSA, institution's own form.
CONTACT Financial Aid Office, Bethany College, Main Street, Bethany, WV 26032, 304-829-7141 or toll-free 800-922-7611 (out-of-state).

BETHANY LUTHERAN COLLEGE
Mankato, MN

Tuition & fees: $16,508 | **Average undergraduate aid package: $13,187**

ABOUT THE INSTITUTION Independent Lutheran, coed. Awards: associate and bachelor's degrees. 16 undergraduate majors. Total enrollment: 566. Undergraduates: 566. Freshmen: 152. Federal methodology is used as a basis for awarding need-based institutional aid.
UNDERGRADUATE EXPENSES for 2006–07 *One-time required fee:* $130. *Comprehensive fee:* $21,786 includes full-time tuition ($16,248), mandatory fees ($260), and room and board ($5278). *College room only:* $1988. *Part-time tuition:* $690 per credit. *Part-time fees:* $130 per term.
FRESHMAN FINANCIAL AID (Fall 2004) 148 applied for aid; of those 91% were deemed to have need. 100% of freshmen with need received aid; of those 33% had need fully met. *Average percent of need met:* 86% (excluding resources awarded to replace EFC). *Average financial aid package:* $12,830 (excluding resources awarded to replace EFC). 14% of all full-time freshmen had no need and received non-need-based gift aid.
UNDERGRADUATE FINANCIAL AID (Fall 2004) 487 applied for aid; of those 92% were deemed to have need. 100% of undergraduates with need received aid; of those 30% had need fully met. *Average percent of need met:* 87% (excluding resources awarded to replace EFC). *Average financial aid package:* $13,187 (excluding resources awarded to replace EFC). 15% of all full-time undergraduates had no need and received non-need-based gift aid.
GIFT AID (NEED-BASED) *Total amount:* $3,749,594 (16% federal, 19% state, 61% institutional, 4% external sources). *Receiving aid:* Freshmen: 82% (135); All full-time undergraduates: 82% (448). *Average award:* Freshmen: $9512; Undergraduates: $9398. *Scholarships, grants, and awards:* Federal Pell, FSEOG, state, private, college/university gift aid from institutional funds.
GIFT AID (NON-NEED-BASED) *Total amount:* $321,628 (1% state, 88% institutional, 11% external sources). *Receiving aid:* Freshmen: 8% (14); Undergraduates: 8% (44). *Average Award:* Freshmen: $7219; Undergraduates: $7076. *Scholarships, grants, and awards by category:* Creative Arts/Performance: 103 awards ($171,000 total): art/fine arts, debating, journalism/publications, music, theater/drama. Special Characteristics: 33 awards ($372,659 total): children of faculty/staff. *ROTC:* Army cooperative.
LOANS *Student loans:* $2,716,006 (65% need-based, 35% non-need-based). 75% of past graduating class borrowed through all loan programs. *Average indebtedness per student:* $18,654. *Average need-based loan:* Freshmen: $3384; Undergraduates: $4044. *Parent loans:* $303,358 (33% need-based, 67% non-need-based). *Programs:* FFEL (Subsidized and Unsubsidized Stafford, PLUS), Perkins, state, alternative loans.
WORK-STUDY *Federal work-study:* Total amount: $36,807; 37 jobs averaging $995. *State or other work-study/employment:* Total amount: $199,881 (44% need-based, 56% non-need-based). 251 part-time jobs averaging $803.

ATHLETIC AWARDS *Total amount:* $44,000 (82% need-based, 18% non-need-based).
APPLYING FOR FINANCIAL AID *Required financial aid forms:* FAFSA, institution's own form, business/farm supplement, federal income tax form(s), W-2 forms. *Financial aid deadline (priority):* 4/15. *Notification date:* Continuous. Students must reply within 3 weeks of notification.
CONTACT Financial Aid Office, Bethany Lutheran College, 700 Luther Drive, Mankato, MN 56001-6163, 507-344-7328 or toll-free 800-944-3066 Ext. 331. *Fax:* 507-344-7376.

BETHANY UNIVERSITY
Scotts Valley, CA

CONTACT Deborah Snow, Financial Aid Director, Bethany University, 800 Bethany Drive, Scotts Valley, CA 95066-2820, 831-438-3800 Ext. 1477 or toll-free 800-843-9410. *Fax:* 831-461-1533.

BETH BENJAMIN ACADEMY OF CONNECTICUT
Stamford, CT

CONTACT Financial Aid Office, Beth Benjamin Academy of Connecticut, 132 Prospect Street, Stamford, CT 06901-1202, 203-325-4351.

BETHEL COLLEGE
Mishawaka, IN

CONTACT Mr. Guy A. Fisher, Director of Financial Aid, Bethel College, 1001 West McKinley Avenue, Mishawaka, IN 46545-5591, 574-257-3316 or toll-free 800-422-4101. *Fax:* 574-257-3326. *E-mail:* fisherg@bethelcollege.edu.

BETHEL COLLEGE
North Newton, KS

Tuition & fees: $15,550 | **Average undergraduate aid package:** $15,829

ABOUT THE INSTITUTION Independent religious, coed. Awards: bachelor's degrees. 27 undergraduate majors. Total enrollment: 514. Undergraduates: 514. Freshmen: 96. Federal methodology is used as a basis for awarding need-based institutional aid.
UNDERGRADUATE EXPENSES for 2005–06 *Application fee:* $20. *Comprehensive fee:* $21,650 includes full-time tuition ($15,550) and room and board ($6100). *College room only:* $3200. Full-time tuition and fees vary according to course load. Room and board charges vary according to board plan and housing facility. *Part-time tuition:* $550 per credit hour. Part-time tuition and fees vary according to course load. *Payment plans:* Installment, deferred payment.
FRESHMAN FINANCIAL AID (Fall 2004) 106 applied for aid; of those 94% were deemed to have need. 100% of freshmen with need received aid; of those 38% had need fully met. *Average percent of need met:* 90% (excluding resources awarded to replace EFC). *Average financial aid package:* $15,486 (excluding resources awarded to replace EFC). 12% of all full-time freshmen had no need and received non-need-based gift aid.
UNDERGRADUATE FINANCIAL AID (Fall 2004) 421 applied for aid; of those 97% were deemed to have need. 100% of undergraduates with need received aid; of those 31% had need fully met. *Average percent of need met:* 88% (excluding resources awarded to replace EFC). *Average financial aid package:* $15,829 (excluding resources awarded to replace EFC). 12% of all full-time undergraduates had no need and received non-need-based gift aid.
GIFT AID (NEED-BASED) *Total amount:* $1,261,677 (50% federal, 32% state, 18% institutional). *Receiving aid:* Freshmen: 64% (74); All full-time undergraduates: 65% (311). *Average award:* Freshmen: $4464; Undergraduates: $4739. *Scholarships, grants, and awards:* Federal Pell, FSEOG, state, college/university gift aid from institutional funds.
GIFT AID (NON-NEED-BASED) *Total amount:* $2,162,525 (87% institutional, 13% external sources). *Receiving aid:* Freshmen: 86% (100); Undergraduates: 72% (346). *Average Award:* Freshmen: $7797; Undergraduates: $6384. *Scholarships, grants, and awards by category: Academic Interests/Achievement:* 313 awards ($1,154,056 total): general academic interests/achievements. *Creative Arts/Performance:* 111 awards ($165,990 total): art/fine arts, debating, music,

theater/drama. *Special Characteristics:* 335 awards ($407,040 total): children and siblings of alumni, children of faculty/staff, international students, previous college experience, relatives of clergy, religious affiliation. *Tuition waivers:* Full or partial for children of alumni, employees or children of employees, senior citizens.
LOANS *Student loans:* $2,582,884 (70% need-based, 30% non-need-based). 84% of past graduating class borrowed through all loan programs. *Average indebtedness per student:* $19,122. *Average need-based loan:* Freshmen: $3817; Undergraduates: $5209. *Parent loans:* $704,826 (100% non-need-based). *Programs:* FFEL (Subsidized and Unsubsidized Stafford, PLUS), Perkins.
WORK-STUDY *Federal work-study:* Total amount: $384,501; 271 jobs averaging $1419. *State or other work-study/employment:* Total amount: $144,331 (100% need-based). 207 part-time jobs averaging $694.
ATHLETIC AWARDS *Total amount:* $413,255 (100% non-need-based).
APPLYING FOR FINANCIAL AID *Required financial aid form:* FAFSA. *Financial aid deadline (priority):* 3/15. *Notification date:* Continuous. Students must reply by 5/1 or within 2 weeks of notification.
CONTACT Mr. Tony Graber, Financial Aid Director, Bethel College, 300 East 27th Street, North Newton, KS 67117, 316-284-5232 or toll-free 800-522-1887 Ext. 230. *Fax:* 316-284-5845. *E-mail:* tgraber@bethelks.edu.

BETHEL COLLEGE
McKenzie, TN

ABOUT THE INSTITUTION Independent Cumberland Presbyterian, coed. Awards: bachelor's, master's, and first professional degrees. 24 undergraduate majors. Total enrollment: 1,297. Undergraduates: 1,134. Freshmen: 260.
GIFT AID (NEED-BASED) *Scholarships, grants, and awards:* college/university gift aid from institutional funds.
GIFT AID (NON-NEED-BASED) *Scholarships, grants, and awards by category: Academic Interests/Achievement:* general academic interests/achievements, religion/biblical studies. *Creative Arts/Performance:* music. *Special Characteristics:* children of faculty/staff, local/state students, religious affiliation.
LOANS *Programs:* FFEL (Subsidized and Unsubsidized Stafford, PLUS), Perkins, alternative loans.
APPLYING FOR FINANCIAL AID *Required financial aid forms:* FAFSA, institution's own form.
CONTACT Laura Bateman, Office of Financial Aid, Bethel College, 325 Cherry Avenue, McKenzie, TN 38201, 901-352-4007. *Fax:* 901-352-4069.

BETHEL UNIVERSITY
St. Paul, MN

Tuition & fees: $22,700 | **Average undergraduate aid package:** $14,918

ABOUT THE INSTITUTION Independent religious, coed. Awards: associate, bachelor's, and master's degrees and post-bachelor's and post-master's certificates. 55 undergraduate majors. Total enrollment: 3,857. Undergraduates: 3,197. Freshmen: 726. Federal methodology is used as a basis for awarding need-based institutional aid.
UNDERGRADUATE EXPENSES for 2006–07 *Application fee:* $25. *Comprehensive fee:* $29,840 includes full-time tuition ($22,590), mandatory fees ($110), and room and board ($7140). *College room only:* $4260. *Part-time tuition:* $865 per credit.
FRESHMAN FINANCIAL AID (Fall 2005, est.) 568 applied for aid; of those 81% were deemed to have need. 100% of freshmen with need received aid; of those 23% had need fully met. *Average percent of need met:* 79% (excluding resources awarded to replace EFC). *Average financial aid package:* $15,451 (excluding resources awarded to replace EFC). 25% of all full-time freshmen had no need and received non-need-based gift aid.
UNDERGRADUATE FINANCIAL AID (Fall 2005, est.) 2,136 applied for aid; of those 84% were deemed to have need. 100% of undergraduates with need received aid; of those 24% had need fully met. *Average percent of need met:* 78% (excluding resources awarded to replace EFC). *Average financial aid package:* $14,918 (excluding resources awarded to replace EFC). 25% of all full-time undergraduates had no need and received non-need-based gift aid.
GIFT AID (NEED-BASED) *Total amount:* $15,870,000 (10% federal, 15% state, 69% institutional, 6% external sources). *Receiving aid:* Freshmen: 64% (461); All full-time undergraduates: 66% (1,783). *Average award:* Freshmen: $9817;

Bethel University

Undergraduates: $8846. *Scholarships, grants, and awards:* Federal Pell, FSEOG, state, private, college/university gift aid from institutional funds.
GIFT AID (NON-NEED-BASED) *Total amount:* $2,990,000 (89% institutional, 11% external sources). *Receiving aid:* Freshmen: 5% (39); Undergraduates: 5% (142). *Average Award:* Freshmen: $4580; *Undergraduates:* $3545. *Scholarships, grants, and awards by category: Academic Interests/Achievement:* 1,490 awards ($4,620,000 total): general academic interests/achievements. *Creative Arts/Performance:* 106 awards ($160,000 total): art/fine arts, debating, music, theater/drama. *Special Achievements/Activities:* 2,010 awards ($2,250,000 total): community service, junior miss, leadership, religious involvement. *Special Characteristics:* 1,260 awards ($3,485,000 total): children and siblings of alumni, children of faculty/staff, ethnic background, international students, members of minority groups, out-of-state students, relatives of clergy, religious affiliation. *ROTC:* Army cooperative, Air Force cooperative.
LOANS *Student loans:* $7,260,000 (100% need-based). 75% of past graduating class borrowed through all loan programs. *Average indebtedness per student:* $25,325. *Average need-based loan:* Freshmen: $3979; Undergraduates: $4368. *Programs:* FFEL (Subsidized and Unsubsidized Stafford, PLUS), Perkins, state, alternative loans.
WORK-STUDY *Federal work-study:* Total amount: $860,000; 450 jobs averaging $1570. *State or other work-study/employment:* Total amount: $4,100,000 (85% need-based, 15% non-need-based). 1,300 part-time jobs averaging $1600.
APPLYING FOR FINANCIAL AID *Required financial aid forms:* FAFSA, institution's own form. *Financial aid deadline (priority):* 4/15. *Notification date:* Continuous beginning 3/1. Students must reply by 5/1 or within 3 weeks of notification.
CONTACT Mr. Jeffrey D. Olson, Director of Financial Aid, Bethel University, 3900 Bethel Drive, St. Paul, MN 55112-6999, 651-638-6241 or toll-free 800-255-8706 Ext. 6242. *Fax:* 651-635-1491. *E-mail:* jeff-olson@bethel.edu.

BETHESDA CHRISTIAN UNIVERSITY
Anaheim, CA

CONTACT Myongha Prince, Financial Aid Administrator, Bethesda Christian University, 730 North Euclid Street, Anaheim, CA 92801, 714-517-1945 Ext. 130. *Fax:* 714-517-1948. *E-mail:* financialaid@bcu.edu.

BETH HAMEDRASH SHAAREI YOSHER INSTITUTE
Brooklyn, NY

CONTACT Financial Aid Office, Beth HaMedrash Shaarei Yosher Institute, 4102-10 16th Avenue, Brooklyn, NY 11204, 718-854-2290.

BETH HATALMUD RABBINICAL COLLEGE
Brooklyn, NY

CONTACT Financial Aid Office, Beth Hatalmud Rabbinical College, 2127 82nd Street, Brooklyn, NY 11204, 718-259-2525.

BETH MEDRASH GOVOHA
Lakewood, NJ

CONTACT Financial Aid Office, Beth Medrash Govoha, 617 Sixth Street, Lakewood, NJ 08701-2797, 732-367-1060.

BETHUNE-COOKMAN COLLEGE
Daytona Beach, FL

ABOUT THE INSTITUTION Independent Methodist, coed. Awards: bachelor's degrees. 37 undergraduate majors. Total enrollment: 3,090. Undergraduates: 3,090. Freshmen: 949.
GIFT AID (NEED-BASED) *Scholarships, grants, and awards:* Federal Pell, FSEOG, state, private, college/university gift aid from institutional funds, United Negro College Fund, Federal Nursing.
GIFT AID (NON-NEED-BASED) *Scholarships, grants, and awards by category: Academic Interests/Achievement:* general academic interests/achievements.
LOANS *Programs:* Federal Direct (Subsidized and Unsubsidized Stafford, PLUS), FFEL (PLUS).
WORK-STUDY *Federal work-study:* Total amount: $569,068; 300 jobs averaging $1660. *State or other work-study/employment:* Total amount: $203,008 (100% non-need-based). 125 part-time jobs averaging $1660.
APPLYING FOR FINANCIAL AID *Required financial aid form:* FAFSA.
CONTACT Mr. Joseph Coleman, Director of Financial Aid, Bethune-Cookman College, 640 Mary McLeod Bethune Boulevard, Daytona Beach, FL 32114-3099, 386-481-2626 or toll-free 800-448-0228. *Fax:* 386-481-2621. *E-mail:* colemanj@cookman.edu.

BEULAH HEIGHTS BIBLE COLLEGE
Atlanta, GA

Tuition & fees: N/R	Average undergraduate aid package: $8591

ABOUT THE INSTITUTION Independent Pentecostal, coed. Awards: associate and bachelor's degrees. 2 undergraduate majors. Total enrollment: 620. Undergraduates: 620. Freshmen: 155. Federal methodology is used as a basis for awarding need-based institutional aid.
FRESHMAN FINANCIAL AID (Fall 2005, est.) 13 applied for aid; of those 100% were deemed to have need. 100% of freshmen with need received aid. *Average percent of need met:* 80% (excluding resources awarded to replace EFC). *Average financial aid package:* $6223 (excluding resources awarded to replace EFC).
UNDERGRADUATE FINANCIAL AID (Fall 2005, est.) 140 applied for aid; of those 100% were deemed to have need. 100% of undergraduates with need received aid. *Average percent of need met:* 80% (excluding resources awarded to replace EFC). *Average financial aid package:* $8591 (excluding resources awarded to replace EFC).
GIFT AID (NEED-BASED) *Total amount:* $830,502 (87% federal, 13% institutional). *Receiving aid:* Freshmen: 32% (8); All full-time undergraduates: 43% (100). *Average award:* Freshmen: $3330; Undergraduates: $3441. *Scholarships, grants, and awards:* Federal Pell, FSEOG, private, college/university gift aid from institutional funds.
GIFT AID (NON-NEED-BASED) *Scholarships, grants, and awards by category: Special Characteristics:* 36 awards ($107,173 total): children of faculty/staff, general special characteristics, international students, married students, religious affiliation, spouses of current students. *Tuition waivers:* Full or partial for employees or children of employees.
LOANS *Student loans:* $2,346,625 (56% need-based, 44% non-need-based). 59% of past graduating class borrowed through all loan programs. *Average indebtedness per student:* $29,712. *Average need-based loan:* Freshmen: $2094; Undergraduates: $3781. *Parent loans:* $8000 (100% need-based). *Programs:* FFEL (Subsidized and Unsubsidized Stafford, PLUS).
WORK-STUDY *Federal work-study:* Total amount: $45,724; 13 jobs averaging $3402.
APPLYING FOR FINANCIAL AID *Required financial aid forms:* FAFSA, institution's own form. *Financial aid deadline (priority):* 5/15. *Notification date:* 7/30. Students must reply within 2 weeks of notification.
CONTACT Ms. Patricia Banks, Financial Aid Director, Beulah Heights Bible College, 892 Berne Street, SE, Atlanta, GA 30316, 404-627-2681 or toll-free 888-777-BHBC. *Fax:* 404-627-0702. *E-mail:* pat.banks@beulah.org.

BIOLA UNIVERSITY
La Mirada, CA

Tuition & fees: $23,882	Average undergraduate aid package: $15,200

ABOUT THE INSTITUTION Independent interdenominational, coed. Awards: bachelor's, master's, doctoral, and first professional degrees. 39 undergraduate majors. Total enrollment: 5,455. Undergraduates: 3,246. Freshmen: 781. Federal methodology is used as a basis for awarding need-based institutional aid.
UNDERGRADUATE EXPENSES for 2006–07 *Application fee:* $45. *Comprehensive fee:* $30,998 includes full-time tuition ($23,782), mandatory fees ($100), and room and board ($7116). *College room only:* $3756. *Part-time tuition:* $942 per unit.
FRESHMAN FINANCIAL AID (Fall 2004) 565 applied for aid; of those 83% were deemed to have need. 100% of freshmen with need received aid; of those 12% had need fully met. *Average percent of need met:* 67% (excluding resources

awarded to replace EFC). *Average financial aid package:* $14,019 (excluding resources awarded to replace EFC). 16% of all full-time freshmen had no need and received non-need-based gift aid.
UNDERGRADUATE FINANCIAL AID (Fall 2004) 2,216 applied for aid; of those 87% were deemed to have need. 100% of undergraduates with need received aid; of those 13% had need fully met. *Average percent of need met:* 70% (excluding resources awarded to replace EFC). *Average financial aid package:* $15,200 (excluding resources awarded to replace EFC). 11% of all full-time undergraduates had no need and received non-need-based gift aid.
GIFT AID (NEED-BASED) *Total amount:* $19,786,499 (13% federal, 32% state, 50% institutional, 5% external sources). *Receiving aid:* Freshmen: 54% (370); All full-time undergraduates: 52% (1,550). *Average award:* Freshmen: $9134; Undergraduates: $9514. *Scholarships, grants, and awards:* Federal Pell, FSEOG, state, private, college/university gift aid from institutional funds.
GIFT AID (NON-NEED-BASED) *Total amount:* $1,271,170 (79% institutional, 21% external sources). *Receiving aid:* Freshmen: 55% (381); Undergraduates: 49% (1,437). *Average Award:* Freshmen: $10,381; Undergraduates: $11,205. *Scholarships, grants, and awards by category: Academic Interests/Achievement:* 1,253 awards ($4,952,931 total): communication, general academic interests/achievements, health fields. *Creative Arts/Performance:* 184 awards ($494,560 total): art/fine arts, debating, journalism/publications, music, performing arts, theater/drama. *Special Achievements/Activities:* 205 awards ($517,928 total): community service. *Special Characteristics:* 751 awards ($1,040,870 total): adult students, children of faculty/staff, ethnic background, international students, relatives of clergy. *ROTC:* Army cooperative, Air Force cooperative.
LOANS *Student loans:* $14,783,642 (81% need-based, 19% non-need-based). 74% of past graduating class borrowed through all loan programs. *Average indebtedness per student:* $28,007. *Average need-based loan:* Freshmen: $2479; Undergraduates: $2969. *Parent loans:* $4,484,913 (100% need-based). *Programs:* FFEL (Subsidized and Unsubsidized Stafford, PLUS), Perkins, Federal Nursing, college/university, alternative loans.
WORK-STUDY *Federal work-study:* Total amount: $289,561; 85 jobs averaging $3011.
ATHLETIC AWARDS *Total amount:* $1,121,945 (100% need-based).
APPLYING FOR FINANCIAL AID *Required financial aid forms:* FAFSA, state aid form. *Financial aid deadline:* Continuous. *Notification date:* Continuous beginning 5/1.
CONTACT Financial Aid Office, Biola University, 13800 Biola Avenue, La Mirada, CA 90639-0001, 562-903-4742 or toll-free 800-652-4652. *Fax:* 562-906-4541. *E-mail:* finaid@biola.edu.

BIRMINGHAM-SOUTHERN COLLEGE
Birmingham, AL

CONTACT Financial Aid Office, Birmingham-Southern College, 900 Arkadelphia Road, Box 549016, Birmingham, AL 35254, 205-226-4688 or toll-free 800-523-5793. *Fax:* 205-226-3082. *E-mail:* finaid@bsc.edu.

BIRTHINGWAY COLLEGE OF MIDWIFERY
Portland, OR

CONTACT Financial Aid Office, Birthingway College of Midwifery, 12113 SE Foster Road, Portland, OR 97299, 503-760-3131.

BLACKBURN COLLEGE
Carlinville, IL

CONTACT Mrs. Jane Kelsey, Financial Aid Administrator, Blackburn College, 700 College Avenue, Carlinville, IL 62626-1498, 217-854-3231 Ext. 4227 or toll-free 800-233-3550. *Fax:* 217-854-3731.

BLACK HILLS STATE UNIVERSITY
Spearfish, SD

Tuition & fees (SD res): $5072	Average undergraduate aid package: $4361

ABOUT THE INSTITUTION State-supported, coed. Awards: associate, bachelor's, and master's degrees and post-bachelor's and post-master's certificates. 47 undergraduate majors. Total enrollment: 3,846. Undergraduates: 3,653. Freshmen: 657. Federal methodology is used as a basis for awarding need-based institutional aid.
UNDERGRADUATE EXPENSES for 2005–06 *Application fee:* $20. *Tuition, state resident:* full-time $2444; part-time $76.35 per credit. *Tuition, nonresident:* full-time $7764; part-time $242.60 per credit. *Required fees:* full-time $2628; $82.10 per credit. Full-time tuition and fees vary according to course load and reciprocity agreements. Part-time tuition and fees vary according to course load and reciprocity agreements. *College room and board:* $3663; *room only:* $2078. Room and board charges vary according to board plan and housing facility. *Payment plans:* Installment, deferred payment.
UNDERGRADUATE FINANCIAL AID (Fall 2004) *Average financial aid package:* $4361 (excluding resources awarded to replace EFC).
GIFT AID (NEED-BASED) *Total amount:* $3,705,267 (94% federal, 6% external sources). *Scholarships, grants, and awards:* Federal Pell, FSEOG, state, private, college/university gift aid from institutional funds.
GIFT AID (NON-NEED-BASED) *Total amount:* $849,051 (1% federal, 3% state, 42% institutional, 54% external sources). *Scholarships, grants, and awards by category: Academic Interests/Achievement:* biological sciences, business, communication, computer science, education, English, foreign languages, general academic interests/achievements, health fields, humanities, mathematics, military science, physical sciences, social sciences. *Creative Arts/Performance:* art/fine arts, music, theater/drama. *Tuition waivers:* Full or partial for employees or children of employees, senior citizens. *ROTC:* Army.
LOANS *Student loans:* $13,250,171 (52% need-based, 48% non-need-based). 85% of past graduating class borrowed through all loan programs. *Average indebtedness per student:* $23,435. *Parent loans:* $433,335 (100% non-need-based). *Programs:* FFEL (Subsidized and Unsubsidized Stafford, PLUS), Perkins.
WORK-STUDY *Federal work-study:* Total amount: $277,366; 221 jobs averaging $1255. *State or other work-study/employment:* Total amount: $661,104 (100% non-need-based). 588 part-time jobs averaging $1124.
ATHLETIC AWARDS *Total amount:* $306,386 (100% non-need-based).
APPLYING FOR FINANCIAL AID *Required financial aid form:* FAFSA. *Financial aid deadline (priority):* 3/1. *Notification date:* Continuous beginning 5/1. Students must reply within 3 weeks of notification.
CONTACT Ms. Deb Henriksen, Director of Financial Aid, Black Hills State University, 1200 University Street, Box 9670, Spearfish, SD 57799-9670, 605-642-6581 or toll-free 800-255-2478. *Fax:* 605-642-6254. *E-mail:* debhenriksen@bhsu.edu.

BLESSING-RIEMAN COLLEGE OF NURSING
Quincy, IL

Tuition & fees: $14,250	Average undergraduate aid package: N/A

ABOUT THE INSTITUTION Independent, coed, primarily women. Awards: bachelor's degrees. 1 undergraduate major. Total enrollment: 211. Undergraduates: 211. Freshmen: 29. Federal methodology is used as a basis for awarding need-based institutional aid.
UNDERGRADUATE EXPENSES for 2005–06 *Comprehensive fee:* $20,025 includes full-time tuition ($13,900), mandatory fees ($350), and room and board ($5775). Full-time tuition and fees vary according to course load, location, and student level. Room and board charges vary according to location. Part-time tuition and fees vary according to course load, location, and student level. *Payment plan:* Installment.
UNDERGRADUATE FINANCIAL AID (Fall 2004) 118 applied for aid; of those 100% were deemed to have need. 100% of undergraduates with need received aid. *Average percent of need met:* 75% (excluding resources awarded to replace EFC).
GIFT AID (NEED-BASED) *Total amount:* $550,801 (27% federal, 18% state, 47% institutional, 8% external sources). *Receiving aid:* All full-time undergraduates: 100% (118). *Scholarships, grants, and awards:* Federal Pell, state, private, college/university gift aid from institutional funds.
GIFT AID (NON-NEED-BASED) *Tuition waivers:* Full or partial for employees or children of employees.
LOANS *Student loans:* $429,803 (100% need-based). 70% of past graduating class borrowed through all loan programs. *Average indebtedness per student:* $11,000. *Parent loans:* $47,907 (100% need-based). *Programs:* FFEL (Subsidized and Unsubsidized Stafford, PLUS), Federal Nursing, college/university.
APPLYING FOR FINANCIAL AID *Required financial aid form:* FAFSA. *Financial aid deadline:* Continuous.

Blessing-Rieman College of Nursing

CONTACT Ms. Sara Brehm, Financial Aid Officer, Blessing-Rieman College of Nursing, Broadway at 11th Street, Quincy, IL 62301, 217-223-8400 Ext. 6993 or toll-free 800-877-9140 Ext. 6964. *Fax:* 217-223-1781. *E-mail:* sbrehm@blessinghospital.org.

BLOOMFIELD COLLEGE
Bloomfield, NJ

Tuition & fees: $15,100   **Average undergraduate aid package:** $15,061

ABOUT THE INSTITUTION Independent religious, coed. Awards: bachelor's degrees. 56 undergraduate majors. Total enrollment: 2,212. Undergraduates: 2,212. Freshmen: 413. Federal methodology is used as a basis for awarding need-based institutional aid.

UNDERGRADUATE EXPENSES for 2005–06 *Application fee:* $35. *Comprehensive fee:* $22,500 includes full-time tuition ($14,850), mandatory fees ($250), and room and board ($7400). *College room only:* $3700. *Part-time tuition:* $1495 per course. *Part-time fees:* $30 per term. Part-time tuition and fees vary according to course load. *Payment plans:* Installment, deferred payment.

FRESHMAN FINANCIAL AID (Fall 2005, est.) 398 applied for aid; of those 90% were deemed to have need. 99% of freshmen with need received aid; of those 56% had need fully met. *Average percent of need met:* 70% (excluding resources awarded to replace EFC). *Average financial aid package:* $15,837 (excluding resources awarded to replace EFC). 5% of all full-time freshmen had no need and received non-need-based gift aid.

UNDERGRADUATE FINANCIAL AID (Fall 2005, est.) 1,571 applied for aid; of those 90% were deemed to have need. 100% of undergraduates with need received aid; of those 46% had need fully met. *Average percent of need met:* 64% (excluding resources awarded to replace EFC). *Average financial aid package:* $15,061 (excluding resources awarded to replace EFC). 3% of all full-time undergraduates had no need and received non-need-based gift aid.

GIFT AID (NEED-BASED) *Total amount:* $14,371,849 (26% federal, 51% state, 23% institutional). *Receiving aid:* Freshmen: 84% (338); All full-time undergraduates: 80% (1,314). *Average award:* Freshmen: $12,071; Undergraduates: $10,205. *Scholarships, grants, and awards:* Federal Pell, FSEOG, state, private, college/university gift aid from institutional funds.

GIFT AID (NON-NEED-BASED) *Total amount:* $1,442,054 (1% state, 76% institutional, 23% external sources). *Receiving aid:* Freshmen: 24% (97); Undergraduates: 21% (340). *Average Award:* Freshmen: $5523; Undergraduates: $5265. *Scholarships, grants, and awards by category:* Academic Interests/Achievement: 126 awards ($600,152 total): biological sciences, business, computer science, education, English, general academic interests/achievements, health fields, humanities, physical sciences, social sciences. *Creative Arts/Performance:* art/fine arts. *Special Achievements/Activities:* 218 awards ($1,246,433 total): community service, general special achievements/activities. *Special Characteristics:* 79 awards ($123,179 total): adult students, children and siblings of alumni, general special characteristics, previous college experience. *Tuition waivers:* Full or partial for employees or children of employees, senior citizens. *ROTC:* Army cooperative.

LOANS *Student loans:* $6,771,467 (99% need-based, 1% non-need-based). *Average need-based loan:* Freshmen: $2838; Undergraduates: $4441. *Parent loans:* $835,775 (100% need-based). *Programs:* FFEL (Subsidized and Unsubsidized Stafford, PLUS).

WORK-STUDY *Federal work-study:* Total amount: $539,831; 347 jobs averaging $1434. *State or other work-study/employment:* 22 part-time jobs averaging $5584.

ATHLETIC AWARDS *Total amount:* $848,395 (100% non-need-based).

APPLYING FOR FINANCIAL AID *Required financial aid form:* FAFSA. *Financial aid deadline:* 10/1 (priority: 3/15). *Notification date:* Continuous beginning 3/15. Students must reply by 3/15 or within 2 weeks of notification.

CONTACT Mr. Luis Gonzalez, Director of Financial Aid, Bloomfield College, Bloomfield College, 467 Franklin Street, Bloomfield, NJ 07003-9981, 973-748-9000 Ext. 212 or toll-free 800-848-4555 Ext. 230. *Fax:* 973-748-9735. *E-mail:* l_gonzalez@bloomfield.edu.

BLOOMSBURG UNIVERSITY OF PENNSYLVANIA
Bloomsburg, PA

Tuition & fees (PA res): $6226   **Average undergraduate aid package:** $9356

ABOUT THE INSTITUTION State-supported, coed. Awards: associate, bachelor's, master's, and doctoral degrees and post-bachelor's certificates. 51 undergraduate majors. Total enrollment: 8,570. Undergraduates: 7,783. Freshmen: 1,697. Federal methodology is used as a basis for awarding need-based institutional aid.

UNDERGRADUATE EXPENSES for 2005–06 *Application fee:* $30. *Tuition, state resident:* full-time $4906; part-time $204 per credit. *Tuition, nonresident:* full-time $12,266; part-time $511 per credit. *Required fees:* full-time $1320; $39 per credit or $61. Full-time tuition and fees vary according to course load. Part-time tuition and fees vary according to course load. *College room and board:* $5376; *room only:* $3126. Room and board charges vary according to board plan and housing facility. *Payment plan:* Installment.

FRESHMAN FINANCIAL AID (Fall 2005, est.) 1490 applied for aid; of those 95% were deemed to have need. 97% of freshmen with need received aid; of those 90% had need fully met. *Average percent of need met:* 65% (excluding resources awarded to replace EFC). *Average financial aid package:* $9362 (excluding resources awarded to replace EFC). 2% of all full-time freshmen had no need and received non-need-based gift aid.

UNDERGRADUATE FINANCIAL AID (Fall 2005, est.) 6,347 applied for aid; of those 95% were deemed to have need. 94% of undergraduates with need received aid; of those 90% had need fully met. *Average percent of need met:* 65% (excluding resources awarded to replace EFC). *Average financial aid package:* $9356 (excluding resources awarded to replace EFC). 1% of all full-time undergraduates had no need and received non-need-based gift aid.

GIFT AID (NEED-BASED) *Total amount:* $11,959,764 (41% federal, 53% state, 2% institutional, 4% external sources). *Receiving aid:* Freshmen: 41% (699); All full-time undergraduates: 39% (2,829). *Average award:* Freshmen: $4491; Undergraduates: $4105. *Scholarships, grants, and awards:* Federal Pell, FSEOG, state, private, college/university gift aid from institutional funds.

GIFT AID (NON-NEED-BASED) *Total amount:* $3,118,177 (26% federal, 11% state, 22% institutional, 41% external sources). *Receiving aid:* Freshmen: 21% (363); Undergraduates: 15% (1,109). *Average Award:* Freshmen: $1476; Undergraduates: $1642. *Scholarships, grants, and awards by category:* Academic Interests/Achievement: 372 awards ($346,215 total): biological sciences, business, communication, computer science, education, English, foreign languages, general academic interests/achievements, health fields, humanities, international studies, mathematics, physical sciences, religion/biblical studies, social sciences. *Special Characteristics:* 230 awards ($769,496 total): children of faculty/staff, international students. *Tuition waivers:* Full or partial for minority students, employees or children of employees, senior citizens. *ROTC:* Army, Air Force cooperative.

LOANS *Student loans:* $24,702,089 (49% need-based, 51% non-need-based). 68% of past graduating class borrowed through all loan programs. *Average indebtedness per student:* $16,442. *Average need-based loan:* Freshmen: $2479; Undergraduates: $3540. *Parent loans:* $6,530,384 (100% non-need-based). *Programs:* FFEL (Subsidized and Unsubsidized Stafford, PLUS), Perkins, state, alternative loans.

WORK-STUDY *Federal work-study:* Total amount: $2,626,492; 1,031 jobs averaging $2548. *State or other work-study/employment:* Total amount: $3,295,256 (100% non-need-based). 1,133 part-time jobs averaging $2908.

ATHLETIC AWARDS *Total amount:* $451,150 (100% non-need-based).

APPLYING FOR FINANCIAL AID *Required financial aid form:* FAFSA. *Financial aid deadline (priority):* 3/15. *Notification date:* Continuous beginning 4/1.

CONTACT Mr. Thomas M. Lyons, Director of Financial Aid, Bloomsburg University of Pennsylvania, 119 Warren Student Services Center, 400 East 2nd Street, Bloomsburg, PA 17815-1301, 570-389-4279. *Fax:* 570-389-4795. *E-mail:* tlyons@bloomu.edu.

BLUEFIELD COLLEGE
Bluefield, VA

CONTACT Mrs. Debbie Checchio, Director of Financial Aid, Bluefield College, 3000 College Drive, Bluefield, VA 24605, 276-326-4215 or toll-free 800-872-0175. *Fax:* 276-326-4356. *E-mail:* dchecchio@bluefield.edu.

BLUEFIELD STATE COLLEGE
Bluefield, WV

Tuition & fees (WV res): $3410   **Average undergraduate aid package: $5600**

ABOUT THE INSTITUTION State-supported, coed. Awards: associate and bachelor's degrees. 28 undergraduate majors. Total enrollment: 1,708. Undergraduates: 1,708. Freshmen: 251. Federal methodology is used as a basis for awarding need-based institutional aid.

UNDERGRADUATE EXPENSES for 2005–06 *Tuition, state resident:* full-time $3410; part-time $142 per credit. *Tuition, nonresident:* full-time $7014; part-time $292 per credit. Full-time tuition and fees vary according to degree level, program, and reciprocity agreements. Part-time tuition and fees vary according to course load, program, and reciprocity agreements. *Payment plans:* Installment, deferred payment.

FRESHMAN FINANCIAL AID (Fall 2005, est.) 200 applied for aid; of those 90% were deemed to have need. 100% of freshmen with need received aid; of those 36% had need fully met. *Average percent of need met:* 68% (excluding resources awarded to replace EFC). *Average financial aid package:* $5600 (excluding resources awarded to replace EFC). 19% of all full-time freshmen had no need and received non-need-based gift aid.

UNDERGRADUATE FINANCIAL AID (Fall 2005, est.) 980 applied for aid; of those 92% were deemed to have need. 100% of undergraduates with need received aid; of those 13% had need fully met. *Average percent of need met:* 68% (excluding resources awarded to replace EFC). *Average financial aid package:* $5600 (excluding resources awarded to replace EFC). 27% of all full-time undergraduates had no need and received non-need-based gift aid.

GIFT AID (NEED-BASED) *Total amount:* $4,318,000 (81% federal, 19% state). *Receiving aid:* Freshmen: 73% (180); All full-time undergraduates: 64% (900). *Average award:* Freshmen: $3000; Undergraduates: $3100. *Scholarships, grants, and awards:* Federal Pell, FSEOG, state, private, college/university gift aid from institutional funds.

GIFT AID (NON-NEED-BASED) *Total amount:* $1,560,000 (15% state, 14% institutional, 71% external sources). *Receiving aid:* Freshmen: 14% (35); Undergraduates: 7% (95). *Average Award:* Freshmen: $1400; Undergraduates: $1400. *Scholarships, grants, and awards by category: Academic Interests/Achievement:* 400 awards ($200,000 total): engineering/technologies, general academic interests/achievements. *Special Achievements/Activities:* 10 awards ($5000 total): cheerleading/drum major, general special achievements/activities, junior miss, leadership. *Special Characteristics:* 1 award ($500 total): general special characteristics. *Tuition waivers:* Full or partial for senior citizens.

LOANS *Student loans:* $4,700,000 (57% need-based, 43% non-need-based). 52% of past graduating class borrowed through all loan programs. *Average indebtedness per student:* $14,300. *Average need-based loan:* Freshmen: $3200; Undergraduates: $3200. *Parent loans:* $160,000 (100% non-need-based). *Programs:* Federal Direct (Subsidized and Unsubsidized Stafford, PLUS), Perkins.

WORK-STUDY *Federal work-study:* Total amount: $180,000; 115 jobs averaging $1650. *State or other work-study/employment:* Total amount: $230,000 (100% non-need-based). 160 part-time jobs averaging $1800.

ATHLETIC AWARDS *Total amount:* $91,000 (100% non-need-based).

APPLYING FOR FINANCIAL AID *Required financial aid forms:* FAFSA, institution's own form. *Financial aid deadline (priority):* 3/1. *Notification date:* 6/1.

CONTACT Mr. Tom Ilse, Director of Financial Aid, Bluefield State College, 219 Rock Street, Bluefield, WV 24701-2198, 304-327-4020 or toll-free 800-344-8892 Ext. 4065 (in-state), 800-654-7798 Ext. 4065 (out-of-state). *Fax:* 304-325-7747. *E-mail:* tilse@bluefieldstate.edu.

BLUE MOUNTAIN COLLEGE
Blue Mountain, MS

Tuition & fees: $7320   **Average undergraduate aid package: $7942**

ABOUT THE INSTITUTION Independent Southern Baptist, coed. Awards: bachelor's degrees. 28 undergraduate majors. Total enrollment: 365. Undergraduates: 365. Freshmen: 45. Federal methodology is used as a basis for awarding need-based institutional aid.

UNDERGRADUATE EXPENSES for 2005–06 *Application fee:* $10. *Comprehensive fee:* $11,086 includes full-time tuition ($6780), mandatory fees ($540), and room and board ($3766). *College room only:* $1400. Full-time tuition and fees vary according to course load. Room and board charges vary according to board plan and gender. *Part-time tuition:* $230 per hour. *Part-time fees:* $80 per term. Part-time tuition and fees vary according to course load. *Payment plan:* Installment.

FRESHMAN FINANCIAL AID (Fall 2005, est.) 36 applied for aid; of those 78% were deemed to have need. 100% of freshmen with need received aid; of those 82% had need fully met. *Average percent of need met:* 82% (excluding resources awarded to replace EFC). *Average financial aid package:* $8738 (excluding resources awarded to replace EFC). 17% of all full-time freshmen had no need and received non-need-based gift aid.

UNDERGRADUATE FINANCIAL AID (Fall 2005, est.) 231 applied for aid; of those 87% were deemed to have need. 100% of undergraduates with need received aid; of those 54% had need fully met. *Average percent of need met:* 46% (excluding resources awarded to replace EFC). *Average financial aid package:* $7942 (excluding resources awarded to replace EFC). 11% of all full-time undergraduates had no need and received non-need-based gift aid.

GIFT AID (NEED-BASED) *Total amount:* $487,397 (99% federal, 1% state). *Receiving aid:* Freshmen: 33% (14); All full-time undergraduates: 49% (136). *Average award:* Freshmen: $2225; Undergraduates: $2830. *Scholarships, grants, and awards:* Federal Pell, FSEOG, state, private, college/university gift aid from institutional funds.

GIFT AID (NON-NEED-BASED) *Total amount:* $692,930 (38% state, 57% institutional, 5% external sources). *Receiving aid:* Freshmen: 62% (26); Undergraduates: 72% (200). *Average Award:* Freshmen: $3525; Undergraduates: $4041. *Scholarships, grants, and awards by category: Academic Interests/Achievement:* biological sciences, business, education, English, general academic interests/achievements, mathematics, premedicine, religion/biblical studies, social sciences. *Creative Arts/Performance:* music, theater/drama. *Special Achievements/Activities:* leadership, memberships, religious involvement. *Special Characteristics:* children and siblings of alumni, children of current students, children of faculty/staff, children of workers in trades, general special characteristics, married students, parents of current students, relatives of clergy, religious affiliation, siblings of current students, spouses of current students. *Tuition waivers:* Full or partial for employees or children of employees.

LOANS *Student loans:* $1,171,838 (80% need-based, 20% non-need-based). 83% of past graduating class borrowed through all loan programs. *Average indebtedness per student:* $11,484. *Average need-based loan:* Freshmen: $2673; Undergraduates: $3592. *Parent loans:* $23,568 (100% non-need-based). *Programs:* FFEL (Subsidized and Unsubsidized Stafford, PLUS), Perkins.

WORK-STUDY *Federal work-study:* Total amount: $79,572; 52 jobs averaging $1400. *State or other work-study/employment:* Total amount: $68,720 (100% non-need-based). 46 part-time jobs averaging $1400.

ATHLETIC AWARDS *Total amount:* $184,339 (100% non-need-based).

APPLYING FOR FINANCIAL AID *Required financial aid forms:* FAFSA, institution's own form. *Financial aid deadline (priority):* 3/1. *Notification date:* Continuous. Students must reply within 2 weeks of notification.

CONTACT Angie Gossett, Director of Financial Aid, Blue Mountain College, PO Box 160, Blue Mountain, MS 38610-0160, 662-685-4771 Ext. 141 or toll-free 800-235-0136. *Fax:* 662-685-4776. *E-mail:* agossett@bmc.edu.

BLUFFTON UNIVERSITY
Bluffton, OH

Tuition & fees: $20,570   **Average undergraduate aid package: $18,106**

ABOUT THE INSTITUTION Independent Mennonite, coed. Awards: bachelor's and master's degrees. 39 undergraduate majors. Total enrollment: 1,211. Undergraduates: 1,079. Freshmen: 230. Both federal and institutional methodology are used as a basis for awarding need-based institutional aid.

UNDERGRADUATE EXPENSES for 2006–07 *Application fee:* $20. *Comprehensive fee:* $27,652 includes full-time tuition ($20,170), mandatory fees ($400), and room and board ($7082). *College room only:* $3260. *Part-time tuition:* $840 per credit hour.

FRESHMAN FINANCIAL AID (Fall 2005, est.) 220 applied for aid; of those 94% were deemed to have need. 100% of freshmen with need received aid; of those 70% had need fully met. *Average percent of need met:* 96% (excluding resources awarded to replace EFC). *Average financial aid package:* $18,587 (excluding resources awarded to replace EFC). 10% of all full-time freshmen had no need and received non-need-based gift aid.

UNDERGRADUATE FINANCIAL AID (Fall 2005, est.) 785 applied for aid; of those 94% were deemed to have need. 100% of undergraduates with need

Bluffton University

received aid; of those 48% had need fully met. *Average percent of need met:* 91% (excluding resources awarded to replace EFC). *Average financial aid package:* $18,106 (excluding resources awarded to replace EFC). 10% of all full-time undergraduates had no need and received non-need-based gift aid.
GIFT AID (NEED-BASED) *Total amount:* $8,777,645 (11% federal, 14% state, 67% institutional, 8% external sources). *Receiving aid:* Freshmen: 90% (207); All full-time undergraduates: 74% (740). *Average award:* Freshmen: $13,712; Undergraduates: $12,147. *Scholarships, grants, and awards:* Federal Pell, FSEOG, state, private, college/university gift aid from institutional funds.
GIFT AID (NON-NEED-BASED) *Total amount:* $1,631,787 (6% state, 70% institutional, 24% external sources). *Receiving aid:* Freshmen: 7% (17); Undergraduates: 6% (62). *Average Award:* Freshmen: $8110; Undergraduates: $8087. *Scholarships, grants, and awards by category: Academic Interests/Achievement:* 502 awards ($3,626,005 total): general academic interests/achievements. *Creative Arts/Performance:* 23 awards ($21,800 total): art/fine arts, music. *Special Achievements/Activities:* 66 awards ($196,693 total): leadership. *Special Characteristics:* 430 awards ($1,155,267 total): children of faculty/staff, international students, members of minority groups, out-of-state students, relatives of clergy, religious affiliation.
LOANS *Student loans:* $6,725,796 (95% need-based, 5% non-need-based). 77% of past graduating class borrowed through all loan programs. *Average indebtedness per student:* $27,441. *Average need-based loan:* Freshmen: $3820; Undergraduates: $4759. *Parent loans:* $2,048,012 (71% need-based, 29% non-need-based). *Programs:* FFEL (Subsidized and Unsubsidized Stafford, PLUS), Perkins, college/university, alternative loans.
WORK-STUDY *Federal work-study:* Total amount: $932,943; 617 jobs averaging $1528. *State or other work-study/employment:* Total amount: $467,015 (57% need-based, 43% non-need-based). 301 part-time jobs averaging $1566.
APPLYING FOR FINANCIAL AID *Required financial aid form:* FAFSA. *Financial aid deadline:* 10/1 (priority: 5/1). *Notification date:* Continuous beginning 3/1. Students must reply within 3 weeks of notification.
CONTACT Lawrence Matthews, Director of Financial Aid, Bluffton University, 1 University Drive, Bluffton, OH 45817-2104, 419-358-3266 or toll-free 800-488-3257. *Fax:* 419-358-3073. *E-mail:* matthewsl@bluffton.edu.

BOB JONES UNIVERSITY
Greenville, SC

CONTACT Mr. Chris Baker, Director of Financial Aid, Bob Jones University, 1700 Wade Hampton Boulevard, Greenville, SC 29614, 803-242-5100 Ext. 3037 or toll-free 800-BJANDME.

BOISE BIBLE COLLEGE
Boise, ID

CONTACT Beth Turner, Financial Aid Counselor, Boise Bible College, 8695 West Marigold Street, Boise, ID 83714-1220, 208-376-7731 Ext. 12 or toll-free 800-893-7755. *Fax:* 208-376-7743. *E-mail:* betht@boisebible.edu.

BOISE STATE UNIVERSITY
Boise, ID

ABOUT THE INSTITUTION State-supported, coed. Awards: associate, bachelor's, master's, and doctoral degrees. 97 undergraduate majors. Total enrollment: 18,586. Undergraduates: 16,925. Freshmen: 2,501.
GIFT AID (NEED-BASED) *Scholarships, grants, and awards:* Federal Pell, FSEOG, state, private, college/university gift aid from institutional funds, Leveraged Educational Assistance Program (LEAP).
GIFT AID (NON-NEED-BASED) *Scholarships, grants, and awards by category: Academic Interests/Achievement:* biological sciences, business, communication, computer science, education, engineering/technologies, English, foreign languages, general academic interests/achievements, health fields, humanities, international studies, mathematics, military science, physical sciences, premedicine, social sciences. *Creative Arts/Performance:* art/fine arts, dance, debating, general creative arts/performance, journalism/publications, music, performing arts, theater/drama. *Special Achievements/Activities:* cheerleading/drum major, community service, leadership, rodeo. *Special Characteristics:* ethnic background, first-generation college students, general special characteristics, handicapped students, international students, local/state students, members of minority groups, out-of-state students, previous college experience, spouses of current students, veterans, veterans' children.
LOANS *Programs:* Federal Direct (Subsidized and Unsubsidized Stafford, PLUS), Perkins, state, college/university, Alaska Loans.
WORK-STUDY *Federal work-study:* Total amount: $700,000; jobs available (averaging $4000). *State or other work-study/employment:* Total amount: $560,000 (96% need-based, 4% non-need-based). Part-time jobs available (averaging $4000).
APPLYING FOR FINANCIAL AID *Required financial aid form:* FAFSA.
CONTACT Office of Financial Aid and Scholarships, Boise State University, Administration Building, Room 123, 1910 University Drive, Boise, ID 83725-1315, 208-426-1664 or toll-free 800-632-6586 (in-state), 800-824-7017 (out-of-state). *Fax:* 208-426-1305. *E-mail:* faquest@boisestate.edu.

BORICUA COLLEGE
New York, NY

CONTACT Ms. Rosalia Cruz, Financial Aid Administrator, Boricua College, 3755 Broadway, New York, NY 10032-1560, 212-694-1000 Ext. 611.

BOSTON ARCHITECTURAL COLLEGE
Boston, MA

ABOUT THE INSTITUTION Independent, coed. Awards: bachelor's and master's degrees. 2 undergraduate majors. Total enrollment: 910. Undergraduates: 507. Freshmen: 72.
GIFT AID (NEED-BASED) *Scholarships, grants, and awards:* Federal Pell, state, college/university gift aid from institutional funds.
GIFT AID (NON-NEED-BASED) *Scholarships, grants, and awards by category: Academic Interests/Achievement:* architecture.
LOANS *Programs:* FFEL (Subsidized and Unsubsidized Stafford, PLUS).
APPLYING FOR FINANCIAL AID *Required financial aid form:* FAFSA.
CONTACT Maureen Samways, Director of Financial Aid, Boston Architectural College, 320 Newbury Street, Boston, MA 02115, 617-585-0125 or toll-free 877-585-0100. *Fax:* 617-585-0131. *E-mail:* maureen.samways@the-bac.edu.

BOSTON BAPTIST COLLEGE
Boston, MA

CONTACT Curt A. Wiedenroth, Financial Aid Director, Boston Baptist College, 950 Metropolitan Avenue, Boston, MA 02136, 617-364-3510 or toll-free 888-235-2014 (out-of-state). *Fax:* 617-364-0723. *E-mail:* cw9083@aol.com.

BOSTON COLLEGE
Chestnut Hill, MA

Tuition & fees: $31,438   **Average undergraduate aid package:** $27,292

ABOUT THE INSTITUTION Independent Roman Catholic (Jesuit), coed. Awards: bachelor's, master's, doctoral, and first professional degrees and post-master's certificates (also offers continuing education program with significant enrollment not reflected in profile). 45 undergraduate majors. Total enrollment: 13,755. Undergraduates: 9,019. Freshmen: 2,174. Institutional methodology is used as a basis for awarding need-based institutional aid.
UNDERGRADUATE EXPENSES for 2005-06 *Application fee:* $70. *One-time required fee:* $355. *Comprehensive fee:* $42,283 includes full-time tuition ($30,950), mandatory fees ($488), and room and board ($10,845). *College room only:* $6945. Room and board charges vary according to housing facility. *Payment plans:* Tuition prepayment, installment.
FRESHMAN FINANCIAL AID (Fall 2004) 1441 applied for aid; of those 67% were deemed to have need. 100% of freshmen with need received aid; of those 100% had need fully met. *Average percent of need met:* 100% (excluding resources awarded to replace EFC). *Average financial aid package:* $26,614 (excluding resources awarded to replace EFC). 1% of all full-time freshmen had no need and received non-need-based gift aid.
UNDERGRADUATE FINANCIAL AID (Fall 2004) 4,785 applied for aid; of those 76% were deemed to have need. 100% of undergraduates with need received aid; of those 100% had need fully met. *Average percent of need met:* 100%

Bowdoin College

(excluding resources awarded to replace EFC). *Average financial aid package:* $27,292 (excluding resources awarded to replace EFC). 1% of all full-time undergraduates had no need and received non-need-based gift aid.
GIFT AID (NEED-BASED) *Total amount:* $61,720,079 (7% federal, 2% state, 87% institutional, 4% external sources). *Receiving aid:* Freshmen: 39% (905); All full-time undergraduates: 36% (3,305). *Average award:* Freshmen: $19,072; Undergraduates: $18,342. *Scholarships, grants, and awards:* Federal Pell, FSEOG, state, private, college/university gift aid from institutional funds.
GIFT AID (NON-NEED-BASED) *Total amount:* $2,317,798 (99% institutional, 1% external sources). *Receiving aid:* Freshmen: 2% (35); Undergraduates: 3% (252). *Average Award:* Freshmen: $10,085; Undergraduates: $8051. *Scholarships, grants, and awards by category:* Academic Interests/Achievement: 87 awards ($2,317,798 total): general academic interests/achievements, military science. *Tuition waivers:* Full or partial for employees or children of employees. *ROTC:* Army cooperative, Air Force cooperative.
LOANS *Student loans:* $19,757,296 (85% need-based, 15% non-need-based). 48% of past graduating class borrowed through all loan programs. *Average indebtedness per student:* $15,723. *Average need-based loan:* Freshmen: $3707; Undergraduates: $4721. *Parent loans:* $30,345,826 (100% non-need-based). *Programs:* FFEL (Subsidized and Unsubsidized Stafford, PLUS), Perkins, Federal Nursing, state.
WORK-STUDY *Federal work-study:* Total amount: $7,028,725; 2,764 jobs averaging $1775.
ATHLETIC AWARDS *Total amount:* $9,300,726 (100% non-need-based).
APPLYING FOR FINANCIAL AID *Required financial aid forms:* FAFSA, CSS Financial Aid PROFILE, noncustodial (divorced/separated) parent's statement, business/farm supplement, federal income tax form(s), W-2 forms. *Financial aid deadline (priority):* 2/1. *Notification date:* 4/1. Students must reply by 5/1.
CONTACT Office of Financial Services, Boston College, Lyons Hall, Chestnut Hill, MA 02467, 800-294-0294 or toll-free 800-360-2522. *Fax:* 617-552-4889. *E-mail:* studentservices@bc.edu.

THE BOSTON CONSERVATORY
Boston, MA

Tuition & fees: $27,835 — Average undergraduate aid package: $15,931

ABOUT THE INSTITUTION Independent, coed. Awards: bachelor's and master's degrees and post-bachelor's and post-master's certificates. 9 undergraduate majors. Total enrollment: 537. Undergraduates: 407. Freshmen: 122. Institutional methodology is used as a basis for awarding need-based institutional aid.
UNDERGRADUATE EXPENSES for 2006–07 *Application fee:* $105. *Comprehensive fee:* $42,155 includes full-time tuition ($26,400), mandatory fees ($1435), and room and board ($14,320).
FRESHMAN FINANCIAL AID (Fall 2005, est.) 120 applied for aid; of those 62% were deemed to have need. 74% of freshmen with need received aid; of those 5% had need fully met. *Average percent of need met:* 50% (excluding resources awarded to replace EFC). *Average financial aid package:* $15,580 (excluding resources awarded to replace EFC). 10% of all full-time freshmen had no need and received non-need-based gift aid.
UNDERGRADUATE FINANCIAL AID (Fall 2005, est.) 396 applied for aid; of those 59% were deemed to have need. 95% of undergraduates with need received aid; of those 22% had need fully met. *Average percent of need met:* 50% (excluding resources awarded to replace EFC). *Average financial aid package:* $15,931 (excluding resources awarded to replace EFC). 13% of all full-time undergraduates had no need and received non-need-based gift aid.
GIFT AID (NEED-BASED) *Total amount:* $231,107 (95% federal, 5% state). *Receiving aid:* Freshmen: 13% (16); All full-time undergraduates: 13% (53). *Average award:* Freshmen: $3841; Undergraduates: $4163. *Scholarships, grants, and awards:* Federal Pell, FSEOG, state, private, college/university gift aid from institutional funds.
GIFT AID (NON-NEED-BASED) *Total amount:* $1,933,892 (94% institutional, 6% external sources). *Receiving aid:* Freshmen: 26% (32); Undergraduates: 42% (169). *Average Award:* Freshmen: $12,708; Undergraduates: $11,031. *Scholarships, grants, and awards by category:* Creative Arts/Performance: 262 awards ($2,499,923 total): dance, music, theater/drama.
LOANS *Student loans:* $805,597 (100% need-based). 68% of past graduating class borrowed through all loan programs. *Average indebtedness per student:* $15,000. *Average need-based loan:* Freshmen: $2629; Undergraduates: $4331.

Parent loans: $4,228,309 (100% non-need-based). *Programs:* FFEL (Subsidized and Unsubsidized Stafford, PLUS), college/university, alternative loans.
WORK-STUDY *Federal work-study:* Total amount: $127,000; 90 jobs averaging $1025. *State or other work-study/employment:* Total amount: $40,000 (100% need-based). 30 part-time jobs averaging $1335.
APPLYING FOR FINANCIAL AID *Required financial aid forms:* FAFSA, institution's own form. *Financial aid deadline:* 2/1. *Notification date:* 4/1. Students must reply by 5/1.
CONTACT Jessica Raine, Financial Aid Assistant, The Boston Conservatory, 8 The Fenway, Boston, MA 02215, 617-912-9147. *Fax:* 617-536-1496. *E-mail:* jraine@bostonconservatory.edu.

BOSTON UNIVERSITY
Boston, MA

Tuition & fees: $31,966 — Average undergraduate aid package: $27,633

ABOUT THE INSTITUTION Independent, coed. Awards: bachelor's, master's, doctoral, and first professional degrees and post-bachelor's, post-master's, and first professional certificates. 121 undergraduate majors. Total enrollment: 30,957. Undergraduates: 18,694. Freshmen: 4,212. Both federal and institutional methodology are used as a basis for awarding need-based institutional aid.
UNDERGRADUATE EXPENSES for 2005–06 *Application fee:* $70. *Comprehensive fee:* $42,046 includes full-time tuition ($31,530), mandatory fees ($436), and room and board ($10,080). *College room only:* $6450. Full-time tuition and fees vary according to class time and degree level. Room and board charges vary according to board plan and housing facility. *Part-time tuition:* $985 per credit. *Part-time fees:* $40. Part-time tuition and fees vary according to class time, course load, and degree level. *Payment plans:* Tuition prepayment, installment.
GIFT AID (NEED-BASED) *Total amount:* $149,397,023 (7% federal, 2% state, 87% institutional, 4% external sources). *Receiving aid:* Freshmen: 44% (1,868); All full-time undergraduates: 38% (6,897). *Average award:* Freshmen: $19,149; Undergraduates: $18,831. *Scholarships, grants, and awards:* Federal Pell, FSEOG, state, private, college/university gift aid from institutional funds.
GIFT AID (NON-NEED-BASED) *Total amount:* $30,120,602 (10% federal, 77% institutional, 13% external sources). *Receiving aid:* Freshmen: 23% (948); Undergraduates: 11% (2,091). *Average Award:* Freshmen: $15,849; Undergraduates: $16,606. *Scholarships, grants, and awards by category:* Academic Interests/Achievement: 2,442 awards ($33,889,142 total): education, engineering/technologies, foreign languages, general academic interests/achievements. Creative Arts/Performance: 196 awards ($1,312,640 total): art/fine arts, music, theater/drama. Special Achievements/Activities: 89 awards ($179,880 total): general special achievements/activities, leadership, memberships. Special Characteristics: 709 awards ($8,292,465 total): children and siblings of alumni, local/state students, relatives of clergy, religious affiliation. *Tuition waivers:* Full or partial for employees or children of employees, senior citizens. *ROTC:* Army, Naval, Air Force.
LOANS *Student loans:* $59,709,347 (66% need-based, 34% non-need-based). 57% of past graduating class borrowed through all loan programs. *Average indebtedness per student:* $21,196. *Average need-based loan:* Freshmen: $3593; Undergraduates: $4835. *Parent loans:* $48,089,445 (28% need-based, 72% non-need-based). *Programs:* Federal Direct (Subsidized and Unsubsidized Stafford, PLUS), Perkins, state, alternative loans.
ATHLETIC AWARDS *Total amount:* $8,755,602 (16% need-based, 84% non-need-based).
APPLYING FOR FINANCIAL AID *Required financial aid forms:* FAFSA, CSS Financial Aid PROFILE. *Financial aid deadline (priority):* 2/15. *Notification date:* Continuous beginning 2/15. Students must reply by 5/1 or within 2 weeks of notification.
CONTACT Christine McGuire, Director of Financial Assistance, Boston University, 881 Commonwealth Avenue, 5th Floor, Boston, MA 02215, 617-353-4176. *Fax:* 617-353-8200. *E-mail:* finaid@bu.edu.

BOWDOIN COLLEGE
Brunswick, ME

Tuition & fees: $32,990 — Average undergraduate aid package: $25,250

Bowdoin College

ABOUT THE INSTITUTION Independent, coed. Awards: bachelor's degrees. 43 undergraduate majors. Total enrollment: 1,666. Undergraduates: 1,666. Freshmen: 477. Institutional methodology is used as a basis for awarding need-based institutional aid.

UNDERGRADUATE EXPENSES for 2005–06 *Application fee:* $60. *Comprehensive fee:* $41,660 includes full-time tuition ($32,650), mandatory fees ($340), and room and board ($8670). *College room only:* $3900. Room and board charges vary according to board plan. *Payment plans:* Installment, deferred payment.

FRESHMAN FINANCIAL AID (Fall 2004) 258 applied for aid; of those 79% were deemed to have need. 100% of freshmen with need received aid; of those 100% had need fully met. *Average percent of need met:* 100% (excluding resources awarded to replace EFC). *Average financial aid package:* $26,643 (excluding resources awarded to replace EFC). 3% of all full-time freshmen had no need and received non-need-based gift aid.

UNDERGRADUATE FINANCIAL AID (Fall 2004) 912 applied for aid; of those 90% were deemed to have need. 100% of undergraduates with need received aid; of those 100% had need fully met. *Average percent of need met:* 100% (excluding resources awarded to replace EFC). *Average financial aid package:* $25,250 (excluding resources awarded to replace EFC). 3% of all full-time undergraduates had no need and received non-need-based gift aid.

GIFT AID (NEED-BASED) *Total amount:* $17,117,857 (6% federal, 1% state, 89% institutional, 4% external sources). *Receiving aid:* Freshmen: 42% (196); All full-time undergraduates: 46% (762). *Average award:* Freshmen: $23,702; Undergraduates: $22,520. *Scholarships, grants, and awards:* Federal Pell, FSEOG, state, private, college/university gift aid from institutional funds.

GIFT AID (NON-NEED-BASED) *Total amount:* $577,172 (29% institutional, 71% external sources). *Receiving aid:* Freshmen: 1% (3); Undergraduates: 1% (11). *Average Award:* Freshmen: $1000; Undergraduates: $1000. *Scholarships, grants, and awards by category: Academic Interests/Achievement:* 51 awards ($51,000 total): general academic interests/achievements. *Special Achievements/Activities:* leadership. *Special Characteristics:* children of faculty/staff. *Tuition waivers:* Full or partial for employees or children of employees.

LOANS *Student loans:* $2,977,073 (71% need-based, 29% non-need-based). 54% of past graduating class borrowed through all loan programs. *Average indebtedness per student:* $15,300. *Average need-based loan:* Freshmen: $3268; Undergraduates: $3851. *Parent loans:* $3,412,858 (100% non-need-based). *Programs:* FFEL (Subsidized and Unsubsidized Stafford, PLUS), Perkins, state, college/university.

WORK-STUDY *Federal work-study:* Total amount: $400,000; 267 jobs averaging $1500. *State or other work-study/employment:* Total amount: $626,550 (95% need-based, 5% non-need-based). 398 part-time jobs averaging $1500.

APPLYING FOR FINANCIAL AID *Required financial aid forms:* FAFSA, institution's own form, CSS Financial Aid PROFILE, noncustodial (divorced/separated) parent's statement, business/farm supplement. *Financial aid deadline:* 2/15. *Notification date:* 4/5. Students must reply by 5/1 or within 1 week of notification.

CONTACT Mr. Stephen H. Joyce, Director of Student Aid, Bowdoin College, 5300 College Station, Brunswick, ME 04011-8444, 207-725-3273. *Fax:* 207-725-3864. *E-mail:* sjoyce@bowdoin.edu.

BOWIE STATE UNIVERSITY
Bowie, MD

ABOUT THE INSTITUTION State-supported, coed. Awards: bachelor's, master's, and doctoral degrees and post-bachelor's certificates. 29 undergraduate majors. Total enrollment: 5,415. Undergraduates: 4,027. Freshmen: 649.

GIFT AID (NEED-BASED) *Scholarships, grants, and awards:* Federal Pell, FSEOG, state, private, college/university gift aid from institutional funds.

GIFT AID (NON-NEED-BASED) *Scholarships, grants, and awards by category: Academic Interests/Achievement:* biological sciences, business, communication, computer science, engineering/technologies, mathematics, military science. *Creative Arts/Performance:* applied art and design, art/fine arts, general creative arts/performance, music. *Special Characteristics:* first-generation college students.

LOANS *Programs:* Federal Direct (Subsidized and Unsubsidized Stafford, PLUS), Perkins.

APPLYING FOR FINANCIAL AID *Required financial aid form:* FAFSA.

CONTACT Veronica Pickett, Financial Aid Director, Bowie State University, 14000 Jericho Park Road, Bowie, MD 20715, 301-860-3543 or toll-free 877-772-6943. *Fax:* 301-860-3549. *E-mail:* vpickett@bowiestate.edu.

BOWLING GREEN STATE UNIVERSITY
Bowling Green, OH

Tuition & fees (OH res): $8560   **Average undergraduate aid package: $7798**

ABOUT THE INSTITUTION State-supported, coed. Awards: bachelor's, master's, and doctoral degrees and post-master's certificates. 131 undergraduate majors. Total enrollment: 19,016. Undergraduates: 16,079. Freshmen: 3,603. Federal methodology is used as a basis for awarding need-based institutional aid.

UNDERGRADUATE EXPENSES for 2005–06 *Application fee:* $35. *Tuition, state resident:* full-time $7314; part-time $357 per credit hour. *Tuition, nonresident:* full-time $14,622; part-time $706 per credit hour. *Required fees:* full-time $1246; $62 per credit hour. Part-time tuition and fees vary according to course load. *College room and board:* $6434; *room only:* $3934. Room and board charges vary according to board plan and housing facility. *Payment plan:* Installment.

FRESHMAN FINANCIAL AID (Fall 2004) 3145 applied for aid; of those 78% were deemed to have need. 100% of freshmen with need received aid; of those 15% had need fully met. *Average percent of need met:* 50% (excluding resources awarded to replace EFC). *Average financial aid package:* $7277 (excluding resources awarded to replace EFC). 9% of all full-time freshmen had no need and received non-need-based gift aid.

UNDERGRADUATE FINANCIAL AID (Fall 2004) 11,140 applied for aid; of those 82% were deemed to have need. 99% of undergraduates with need received aid; of those 14% had need fully met. *Average percent of need met:* 52% (excluding resources awarded to replace EFC). *Average financial aid package:* $7798 (excluding resources awarded to replace EFC). 9% of all full-time undergraduates had no need and received non-need-based gift aid.

GIFT AID (NEED-BASED) *Total amount:* $15,595,163 (72% federal, 20% state, 8% institutional). *Receiving aid:* Freshmen: 27% (1,053); All full-time undergraduates: 26% (4,195). *Average award:* Freshmen: $3571; Undergraduates: $3510. *Scholarships, grants, and awards:* Federal Pell, FSEOG, state, private, college/university gift aid from institutional funds.

GIFT AID (NON-NEED-BASED) *Total amount:* $27,636,975 (3% federal, 16% state, 69% institutional, 12% external sources). *Receiving aid:* Freshmen: 34% (1,312); Undergraduates: 22% (3,503). *Average Award:* Freshmen: $5077; Undergraduates: $4577. *Scholarships, grants, and awards by category: Academic Interests/Achievement:* biological sciences, business, communication, computer science, education, engineering/technologies, English, foreign languages, general academic interests/achievements, health fields, home economics, humanities, international studies, mathematics, military science, physical sciences, social sciences. *Creative Arts/Performance:* art/fine arts, cinema/film/broadcasting, creative writing, dance, debating, journalism/publications, music, performing arts, theater/drama. *Special Achievements/Activities:* general special achievements/activities, leadership. *Special Characteristics:* children and siblings of alumni, children of faculty/staff, general special characteristics, international students, members of minority groups. *Tuition waivers:* Full or partial for employees or children of employees, senior citizens. *ROTC:* Army, Air Force.

LOANS *Student loans:* $72,624,764 (42% need-based, 58% non-need-based). 72% of past graduating class borrowed through all loan programs. *Average indebtedness per student:* $21,594. *Average need-based loan:* Freshmen: $2751; Undergraduates: $3795. *Parent loans:* $15,517,166 (100% non-need-based). *Programs:* Federal Direct (Subsidized and Unsubsidized Stafford, PLUS), Perkins, Federal Nursing, state, college/university, Alternative Loans.

WORK-STUDY *Federal work-study:* Total amount: $801,699; 959 jobs averaging $836.

ATHLETIC AWARDS *Total amount:* $4,247,522 (100% non-need-based).

APPLYING FOR FINANCIAL AID *Required financial aid form:* FAFSA. *Financial aid deadline:* Continuous. *Notification date:* Continuous beginning 4/15. Students must reply within 3 weeks of notification.

CONTACT Tina Coulter, Assistant Director, Office of Student Financial Aid, Bowling Green State University, 231 Administration Building, Bowling Green, OH 43403, 419-372-2651. *Fax:* 419-372-0404.

BRADLEY UNIVERSITY
Peoria, IL

Tuition & fees: $18,830   **Average undergraduate aid package: $13,037**

ABOUT THE INSTITUTION Independent, coed. Awards: bachelor's, master's, and first professional degrees. 74 undergraduate majors. Total enrollment: 6,154. Undergraduates: 5,369. Freshmen: 1,136. Federal methodology is used as a basis for awarding need-based institutional aid.
UNDERGRADUATE EXPENSES for 2005–06 *Application fee:* $35. *Comprehensive fee:* $25,280 includes full-time tuition ($18,700), mandatory fees ($130), and room and board ($6450). *College room only:* $3700. Full-time tuition and fees vary according to program. Room and board charges vary according to board plan. *Part-time tuition:* $510 per credit. Part-time tuition and fees vary according to course load. *Payment plans:* Installment, deferred payment.
FRESHMAN FINANCIAL AID (Fall 2004) 931 applied for aid; of those 73% were deemed to have need. 100% of freshmen with need received aid; of those 51% had need fully met. *Average percent of need met:* 82% (excluding resources awarded to replace EFC). *Average financial aid package:* $13,984 (excluding resources awarded to replace EFC). 23% of all full-time freshmen had no need and received non-need-based gift aid.
UNDERGRADUATE FINANCIAL AID (Fall 2004) 4,220 applied for aid; of those 85% were deemed to have need. 100% of undergraduates with need received aid; of those 36% had need fully met. *Average percent of need met:* 80% (excluding resources awarded to replace EFC). *Average financial aid package:* $13,037 (excluding resources awarded to replace EFC). 20% of all full-time undergraduates had no need and received non-need-based gift aid.
GIFT AID (NEED-BASED) *Total amount:* $32,777,961 (9% federal, 20% state, 68% institutional, 3% external sources). *Receiving aid:* Freshmen: 65% (674); All full-time undergraduates: 68% (3,415). *Average award:* Freshmen: $10,648; Undergraduates: $8715. *Scholarships, grants, and awards:* Federal Pell, FSEOG, state, private, college/university gift aid from institutional funds.
GIFT AID (NON-NEED-BASED) *Total amount:* $7,047,345 (1% state, 93% institutional, 6% external sources). *Receiving aid:* Freshmen: 9% (95); Undergraduates: 7% (369). *Average Award:* Freshmen: $9581; Undergraduates: $9556. *Scholarships, grants, and awards by category:* Academic Interests/Achievement: 3,009 awards ($19,766,240 total): general academic interests/achievements. Creative Arts/Performance: 206 awards ($241,990 total): art/fine arts, music, theater/drama. Special Achievements/Activities: 51 awards ($52,447 total): community service, leadership. Special Characteristics: 917 awards ($3,661,442 total): children and siblings of alumni, children of faculty/staff, members of minority groups. *Tuition waivers:* Full or partial for employees or children of employees, senior citizens. *ROTC:* Army.
LOANS *Student loans:* $24,232,594 (70% need-based, 30% non-need-based). 74% of past graduating class borrowed through all loan programs. *Average indebtedness per student:* $15,079. *Average need-based loan:* Freshmen: $3699; Undergraduates: $5718. *Parent loans:* $6,820,255 (29% need-based, 71% non-need-based). *Programs:* Federal Direct (Subsidized and Unsubsidized Stafford, PLUS), FFEL (PLUS), Perkins, Federal Nursing.
WORK-STUDY *Federal work-study:* Total amount: $1,805,290; 637 jobs averaging $1600.
ATHLETIC AWARDS *Total amount:* $1,989,552 (45% need-based, 55% non-need-based).
APPLYING FOR FINANCIAL AID *Required financial aid form:* FAFSA. *Financial aid deadline (priority):* 3/1. *Notification date:* Continuous. Students must reply within 3 weeks of notification.
CONTACT Mr. David L. Pardieck, Director of Financial Assistance, Bradley University, 1501 West Bradley Avenue, Peoria, IL 61625-0002, 309-677-3089 or toll-free 800-447-6460. *E-mail:* dlp@bradley.edu.

BRANDEIS UNIVERSITY
Waltham, MA

Tuition & fees: $32,501	Average undergraduate aid package: $23,816

ABOUT THE INSTITUTION Independent, coed. Awards: bachelor's, master's, and doctoral degrees and post-bachelor's certificates. 46 undergraduate majors. Total enrollment: 5,189. Undergraduates: 3,267. Freshmen: 739. Institutional methodology is used as a basis for awarding need-based institutional aid.
UNDERGRADUATE EXPENSES for 2005–06 *Application fee:* $55. *Comprehensive fee:* $41,551 includes full-time tuition ($31,532), mandatory fees ($969), and room and board ($9050). *College room only:* $5083. Room and board charges vary according to board plan and housing facility. *Part-time tuition:* $986 per credit. Part-time tuition and fees vary according to course load. *Payment plan:* Installment.
FRESHMAN FINANCIAL AID (Fall 2005, est.) 581 applied for aid; of those 69% were deemed to have need. 100% of freshmen with need received aid; of those 30% had need fully met. *Average percent of need met:* 83% (excluding resources awarded to replace EFC). *Average financial aid package:* $22,176 (excluding resources awarded to replace EFC). 79% of all full-time freshmen had no need and received non-need-based gift aid.
UNDERGRADUATE FINANCIAL AID (Fall 2005, est.) 1,904 applied for aid; of those 80% were deemed to have need. 100% of undergraduates with need received aid; of those 29% had need fully met. *Average percent of need met:* 83% (excluding resources awarded to replace EFC). *Average financial aid package:* $23,816 (excluding resources awarded to replace EFC). 24% of all full-time undergraduates had no need and received non-need-based gift aid.
GIFT AID (NEED-BASED) *Total amount:* $27,056,302 (7% federal, 2% state, 89% institutional, 2% external sources). *Receiving aid:* Freshmen: 52% (381); All full-time undergraduates: 45% (1,453). *Average award:* Freshmen: $19,252; Undergraduates: $18,620. *Scholarships, grants, and awards:* Federal Pell, FSEOG, state, private, college/university gift aid from institutional funds.
GIFT AID (NON-NEED-BASED) *Total amount:* $11,430,075 (90% institutional, 10% external sources). *Receiving aid:* Freshmen: 8% (56); Undergraduates: 4% (142). *Average Award:* Freshmen: $18,159; Undergraduates: $18,144. *Scholarships, grants, and awards by category:* Academic Interests/Achievement: 765 awards: general academic interests/achievements. *Tuition waivers:* Full or partial for employees or children of employees. *ROTC:* Army cooperative, Air Force cooperative.
LOANS *Student loans:* $11,429,132 (66% need-based, 34% non-need-based). 61% of past graduating class borrowed through all loan programs. *Average indebtedness per student:* $21,437. *Average need-based loan:* Freshmen: $3826; Undergraduates: $5744. *Parent loans:* $6,566,315 (30% need-based, 70% non-need-based). *Programs:* Federal Direct (Subsidized and Unsubsidized Stafford, PLUS), FFEL (Subsidized and Unsubsidized Stafford, PLUS), Perkins, state, college/university.
WORK-STUDY *Federal work-study:* Total amount: $1,325,539; jobs available. *State or other work-study/employment:* Total amount: $542,115 (22% need-based, 78% non-need-based). Part-time jobs available.
APPLYING FOR FINANCIAL AID *Required financial aid forms:* FAFSA, institution's own form, CSS Financial Aid PROFILE, noncustodial (divorced/separated) parent's statement, business/farm supplement. *Financial aid deadline:* 4/1 (priority: 1/15). *Notification date:* 4/1. Students must reply by 5/1.
CONTACT Peter Giumette, Director of Financial Aid, Brandeis University, 415 South Street, Kutz Hall 121, MS 027, Waltham, MA 02454-9110, 781-736-3700 or toll-free 800-622-0622 (out-of-state). *Fax:* 781-736-3719. *E-mail:* sfs@brandeis.edu.

BRENAU UNIVERSITY
Gainesville, GA

Tuition & fees: $16,440	Average undergraduate aid package: $14,861

ABOUT THE INSTITUTION Independent, undergraduate: women only; graduate: coed. Awards: bachelor's and master's degrees and post-master's certificates (also offers coed evening and weekend programs with significant enrollment not reflected in profile). 35 undergraduate majors. Total enrollment: 743. Undergraduates: 711. Freshmen: 174. Federal methodology is used as a basis for awarding need-based institutional aid.
UNDERGRADUATE EXPENSES for 2005–06 *Application fee:* $35. *Comprehensive fee:* $24,990 includes full-time tuition ($16,440) and room and board ($8550). Full-time tuition and fees vary according to class time, location, and program. Room and board charges vary according to housing facility. *Part-time tuition:* $548 per semester hour. *Part-time fees:* $75 per term. Part-time tuition and fees vary according to class time, location, and program. *Payment plan:* Installment.
FRESHMAN FINANCIAL AID (Fall 2005, est.) 138 applied for aid; of those 88% were deemed to have need. 100% of freshmen with need received aid; of those 36% had need fully met. *Average percent of need met:* 87% (excluding resources awarded to replace EFC). *Average financial aid package:* $17,587 (excluding resources awarded to replace EFC). 22% of all full-time freshmen had no need and received non-need-based gift aid.
UNDERGRADUATE FINANCIAL AID (Fall 2005, est.) 543 applied for aid; of those 90% were deemed to have need. 100% of undergraduates with need received aid; of those 33% had need fully met. *Average percent of need met:* 80% (excluding resources awarded to replace EFC). *Average financial aid*

Brenau University

package: $14,861 (excluding resources awarded to replace EFC). 18% of all full-time undergraduates had no need and received non-need-based gift aid. **GIFT AID (NEED-BASED)** *Total amount:* $6,254,529 (13% federal, 19% state, 67% institutional, 1% external sources). *Receiving aid:* Freshmen: 71% (122); All full-time undergraduates: 73% (486). *Average award:* Freshmen: $14,175; Undergraduates: $12,411. *Scholarships, grants, and awards:* Federal Pell, FSEOG, state, private, college/university gift aid from institutional funds. **GIFT AID (NON-NEED-BASED)** *Total amount:* $1,505,097 (24% state, 75% institutional, 1% external sources). *Receiving aid:* Freshmen: 17% (29); Undergraduates: 12% (82). *Average Award:* Freshmen: $7960; Undergraduates: $7643. *Scholarships, grants, and awards by category: Academic Interests/Achievement:* 417 awards ($2,367,645 total): biological sciences, business, communication, education, general academic interests/achievements, health fields, humanities. *Creative Arts/Performance:* 110 awards ($258,225 total): applied art and design, art/fine arts, cinema/film/broadcasting, creative writing, dance, journalism/publications, music, theater/drama. *Special Achievements/Activities:* 65 awards ($390,989 total): general special achievements/activities, leadership. *Special Characteristics:* 12 awards ($112,855 total): children of faculty/staff, first-generation college students, general special characteristics, international students. *Tuition waivers:* Full or partial for employees or children of employees.
LOANS *Student loans:* $2,145,687 (50% need-based, 50% non-need-based). 65% of past graduating class borrowed through all loan programs. *Average indebtedness per student:* $17,953. *Average need-based loan:* Freshmen: $2406; Undergraduates: $3439. *Parent loans:* $316,756 (100% non-need-based). *Programs:* FFEL (Subsidized and Unsubsidized Stafford, PLUS), Perkins, state.
WORK-STUDY *Federal work-study:* Total amount: $217,672; 127 jobs averaging $1714. *State or other work-study/employment:* Total amount: $10,850 (100% non-need-based). 6 part-time jobs averaging $1808.
ATHLETIC AWARDS *Total amount:* $303,100 (53% need-based, 47% non-need-based).
APPLYING FOR FINANCIAL AID *Required financial aid forms:* FAFSA, state aid form. *Financial aid deadline (priority):* 4/1. *Notification date:* Continuous beginning 3/1.
CONTACT Pam Barrett, Director of Financial Aid, Brenau University, 500 Washington Street, SE, Gainesville, GA 30501-3697, 770-534-6152 or toll-free 800-252-5119. *Fax:* 770-538-4306. *E-mail:* pbarrett@brenau.edu.

BRESCIA UNIVERSITY
Owensboro, KY

CONTACT Martie Ruxer-Boyken, Director of Financial Aid, Brescia University, 717 Frederica Street, Owensboro, KY 42301-3023, 270-686-4290 or toll-free 877-273-7242. *Fax:* 270-686-4266. *E-mail:* martieb@brescia.edu.

BREVARD COLLEGE
Brevard, NC

Tuition & fees: $15,990 | **Average undergraduate aid package: $15,245**

ABOUT THE INSTITUTION Independent United Methodist, coed. Awards: bachelor's degrees. 22 undergraduate majors. Total enrollment: 597. Undergraduates: 597. Freshmen: 148. Federal methodology is used as a basis for awarding need-based institutional aid.
UNDERGRADUATE EXPENSES for 2005–06 *Application fee:* $30. *Comprehensive fee:* $21,970 includes full-time tuition ($15,620), mandatory fees ($370), and room and board ($5980). Full-time tuition and fees vary according to course load. Room and board charges vary according to board plan and housing facility. *Part-time tuition:* $620 per credit hour. *Part-time fees:* $20 per term. Part-time tuition and fees vary according to course load. *Payment plan:* Installment.
FRESHMAN FINANCIAL AID (Fall 2005, est.) 113 applied for aid; of those 88% were deemed to have need. 100% of freshmen with need received aid; of those 25% had need fully met. *Average percent of need met:* 78% (excluding resources awarded to replace EFC). *Average financial aid package:* $14,075 (excluding resources awarded to replace EFC). 24% of all full-time freshmen had no need and received non-need-based gift aid.
UNDERGRADUATE FINANCIAL AID (Fall 2005, est.) 413 applied for aid; of those 86% were deemed to have need. 99% of undergraduates with need received aid; of those 30% had need fully met. *Average percent of need met:* 82% (excluding resources awarded to replace EFC). *Average financial aid package:* $15,245 (excluding resources awarded to replace EFC). 16% of all full-time undergraduates had no need and received non-need-based gift aid.
GIFT AID (NEED-BASED) *Total amount:* $2,796,750 (22% federal, 11% state, 64% institutional, 3% external sources). *Receiving aid:* Freshmen: 67% (99); All full-time undergraduates: 62% (352). *Average award:* Freshmen: $10,264; Undergraduates: $10,172. *Scholarships, grants, and awards:* Federal Pell, FSEOG, state, private, college/university gift aid from institutional funds.
GIFT AID (NON-NEED-BASED) *Total amount:* $1,085,350 (40% state, 52% institutional, 8% external sources). *Receiving aid:* Freshmen: 3% (5); Undergraduates: 4% (25). *Average Award:* Freshmen: $7215; Undergraduates: $6015. *Scholarships, grants, and awards by category: Academic Interests/Achievement:* 265 awards ($690,000 total): biological sciences, business, English, general academic interests/achievements, health fields, mathematics, physical sciences, premedicine, social sciences. *Creative Arts/Performance:* 90 awards ($141,100 total): art/fine arts, journalism/publications, music, theater/drama. *Special Achievements/Activities:* 110 awards ($134,900 total): cheerleading/drum major, community service, general special achievements/activities, hobbies/interests, leadership. *Special Characteristics:* 400 awards ($720,850 total): children of faculty/staff, local/state students, previous college experience, relatives of clergy, religious affiliation, veterans' children. *Tuition waivers:* Full or partial for employees or children of employees, senior citizens.
LOANS *Student loans:* $2,027,600 (55% need-based, 45% non-need-based). 63% of past graduating class borrowed through all loan programs. *Average indebtedness per student:* $19,293. *Average need-based loan:* Freshmen: $2984; Undergraduates: $3829. *Parent loans:* $835,450 (38% need-based, 62% non-need-based). *Programs:* FFEL (Subsidized and Unsubsidized Stafford, PLUS), Perkins.
WORK-STUDY *Federal work-study:* Total amount: $48,000; 95 jobs averaging $1150. *State or other work-study/employment:* Total amount: $50,000 (100% non-need-based). 55 part-time jobs averaging $1280.
ATHLETIC AWARDS *Total amount:* $602,800 (56% need-based, 44% non-need-based).
APPLYING FOR FINANCIAL AID *Required financial aid forms:* FAFSA, state aid form. *Financial aid deadline (priority):* 4/15. *Notification date:* Continuous beginning 2/1. Students must reply within 4 weeks of notification.
CONTACT Ms. Lisanne J. Masterson, Director of Financial Aid, Brevard College, 400 North Broad Street, Brevard, NC 28712, 828-884-8287 or toll-free 800-527-9090. *Fax:* 828-884-3790. *E-mail:* finaid@brevard.edu.

BREWTON-PARKER COLLEGE
Mt. Vernon, GA

Tuition & fees: $12,684 | **Average undergraduate aid package: $10,062**

ABOUT THE INSTITUTION Independent Southern Baptist, coed. Awards: associate and bachelor's degrees. 31 undergraduate majors. Total enrollment: 1,094. Undergraduates: 1,094. Freshmen: 273. Federal methodology is used as a basis for awarding need-based institutional aid.
UNDERGRADUATE EXPENSES for 2005–06 *Application fee:* $25. *Comprehensive fee:* $17,504 includes full-time tuition ($11,584), mandatory fees ($1100), and room and board ($4820). *College room only:* $2150. Room and board charges vary according to board plan and housing facility. *Part-time tuition:* $362 per credit hour. *Part-time fees:* $275 per term. *Payment plan:* Installment.
FRESHMAN FINANCIAL AID (Fall 2004) 201 applied for aid; of those 92% were deemed to have need. 99% of freshmen with need received aid; of those 10% had need fully met. *Average percent of need met:* 62% (excluding resources awarded to replace EFC). *Average financial aid package:* $9409 (excluding resources awarded to replace EFC). 10% of all full-time freshmen had no need and received non-need-based gift aid.
UNDERGRADUATE FINANCIAL AID (Fall 2004) 791 applied for aid; of those 93% were deemed to have need. 99% of undergraduates with need received aid; of those 11% had need fully met. *Average percent of need met:* 59% (excluding resources awarded to replace EFC). *Average financial aid package:* $10,062 (excluding resources awarded to replace EFC). 9% of all full-time undergraduates had no need and received non-need-based gift aid.
GIFT AID (NEED-BASED) *Total amount:* $6,484,000 (28% federal, 25% state, 40% institutional, 7% external sources). *Receiving aid:* Freshmen: 89% (184); All full-time undergraduates: 90% (728). *Average award:* Freshmen: $7405;

Undergraduates: $7206. *Scholarships, grants, and awards:* Federal Pell, FSEOG, state, private, college/university gift aid from institutional funds, Georgia Baptist Funds; Ministerial Grants.
GIFT AID (NON-NEED-BASED) *Total amount:* $663,221 (35% state, 51% institutional, 14% external sources). *Receiving aid:* Freshmen: 8% (16); Undergraduates: 7% (57). *Average Award:* Freshmen: $7135; Undergraduates: $6773. *Scholarships, grants, and awards by category: Academic Interests/Achievement:* 987 awards ($1,065,750 total): biological sciences, business, communication, education, general academic interests/achievements, mathematics, religion/biblical studies. *Creative Arts/Performance:* 48 awards ($96,229 total): art/fine arts, journalism/publications, music, theater/drama. *Special Achievements/Activities:* 304 awards ($222,880 total): cheerleading/drum major, general special achievements/activities, leadership. *Special Characteristics:* 1,185 awards ($1,963,859 total): children of faculty/staff, first-generation college students, general special characteristics, international students, local/state students, out-of-state students, relatives of clergy, religious affiliation. *Tuition waivers:* Full or partial for employees or children of employees, senior citizens.
LOANS *Student loans:* $5,744,456 (91% need-based, 9% non-need-based). 89% of past graduating class borrowed through all loan programs. *Average indebtedness per student:* $23,445. *Average need-based loan:* Freshmen: $2249; Undergraduates: $3245. *Parent loans:* $584,669 (49% need-based, 51% non-need-based). *Programs:* FFEL (Subsidized and Unsubsidized Stafford, PLUS), Perkins.
WORK-STUDY *Federal work-study:* Total amount: $163,547; 237 jobs averaging $856. *State or other work-study/employment:* Total amount: $59,950 (18% need-based, 82% non-need-based). 57 part-time jobs averaging $1067.
ATHLETIC AWARDS Total amount: $702,850 (67% need-based, 33% non-need-based).
APPLYING FOR FINANCIAL AID *Required financial aid forms:* FAFSA, state aid form. *Financial aid deadline (priority):* 4/1. *Notification date:* Continuous beginning 2/27.
CONTACT Ms. Rachel Jones, Assistant Director of Financial Aid, Brewton-Parker College, Financial Aid #2018, PO Box 197, Mt. Vernon, GA 30445-0197, 800-342-1087 Ext. 215 or toll-free 800-342-1087. *Fax:* 912-583-3598. *E-mail:* finaid@bpc.edu.

BRIARCLIFFE COLLEGE
Bethpage, NY

CONTACT Johanna Kelly, Financial Aid Director, Briarcliffe College, 1055 Stewart Avenue, Bethpage, NY 11714, 516-918-3600 or toll-free 888-333-1150 (in-state).

BRIAR CLIFF UNIVERSITY
Sioux City, IA

CONTACT Financial Aid Office, Briar Cliff University, 3303 Rebecca Street, PO Box 2100, Sioux City, IA 51104-2100, 712-279-5200 or toll-free 800-662-3303 Ext. 5200. *Fax:* 712-279-5410.

BRIDGEWATER COLLEGE
Bridgewater, VA

Tuition & fees: $20,190 | **Average undergraduate aid package:** $17,309

ABOUT THE INSTITUTION Independent religious, coed. Awards: bachelor's degrees. 34 undergraduate majors. Total enrollment: 1,506. Undergraduates: 1,506. Freshmen: 394. Federal methodology is used as a basis for awarding need-based institutional aid.
UNDERGRADUATE EXPENSES for 2006–07 *Application fee:* $30. *Comprehensive fee:* $29,250 includes full-time tuition ($20,190) and room and board ($9060). *College room only:* $4595. *Part-time tuition:* $650 per credit hour. *Part-time fees:* $30.
FRESHMAN FINANCIAL AID (Fall 2005, est.) 348 applied for aid; of those 79% were deemed to have need. 100% of freshmen with need received aid; of those 32% had need fully met. *Average percent of need met:* 85% (excluding resources awarded to replace EFC). *Average financial aid package:* $17,535 (excluding resources awarded to replace EFC). 29% of all full-time freshmen had no need and received non-need-based gift aid.

UNDERGRADUATE FINANCIAL AID (Fall 2005, est.) 1,216 applied for aid; of those 83% were deemed to have need. 100% of undergraduates with need received aid; of those 31% had need fully met. *Average percent of need met:* 84% (excluding resources awarded to replace EFC). *Average financial aid package:* $17,309 (excluding resources awarded to replace EFC). 30% of all full-time undergraduates had no need and received non-need-based gift aid.
GIFT AID (NEED-BASED) *Total amount:* $13,300,606 (8% federal, 15% state, 74% institutional, 3% external sources). *Receiving aid:* Freshmen: 70% (275); All full-time undergraduates: 68% (1,012). *Average award:* Freshmen: $14,547; Undergraduates: $13,371. *Scholarships, grants, and awards:* Federal Pell, FSEOG, state, private, college/university gift aid from institutional funds.
GIFT AID (NON-NEED-BASED) *Total amount:* $4,391,421 (19% state, 80% institutional, 1% external sources). *Receiving aid:* Freshmen: 70% (274); Undergraduates: 68% (1,006). *Average Award:* Freshmen: $9016; Undergraduates: $7895. *Scholarships, grants, and awards by category: Academic Interests/Achievement:* 980 awards ($8,065,388 total): general academic interests/achievements. *Creative Arts/Performance:* 33 awards ($26,000 total): music. *Special Characteristics:* 517 awards ($1,345,390 total): ethnic background, international students, out-of-state students, religious affiliation, siblings of current students.
LOANS *Student loans:* $7,746,525 (71% need-based, 29% non-need-based). 69% of past graduating class borrowed through all loan programs. *Average indebtedness per student:* $25,780. *Average need-based loan:* Freshmen: $2570; Undergraduates: $3537. *Parent loans:* $2,806,751 (75% need-based, 25% non-need-based). *Programs:* FFEL (Subsidized and Unsubsidized Stafford, PLUS), Perkins, GATE Loans.
WORK-STUDY *Federal work-study:* Total amount: $405,617; 347 jobs averaging $1169. *State or other work-study/employment:* Total amount: $98,865 (37% need-based, 63% non-need-based). 39 part-time jobs averaging $930.
APPLYING FOR FINANCIAL AID *Required financial aid forms:* FAFSA, state aid form. *Financial aid deadline (priority):* 3/1. *Notification date:* Continuous beginning 3/15. Students must reply within 2 weeks of notification.
CONTACT Mr. J. Vern Fairchilds, Director of Financial Aid, Bridgewater College, College Box 27, Bridgewater, VA 22812-1599, 540-828-5376 or toll-free 800-759-8328. *Fax:* 540-828-5671. *E-mail:* vfairchi@bridgewater.edu.

BRIDGEWATER STATE COLLEGE
Bridgewater, MA

Tuition & fees (MA res): $5506 | **Average undergraduate aid package:** $6635

ABOUT THE INSTITUTION State-supported, coed. Awards: bachelor's and master's degrees and post-bachelor's and post-master's certificates. 75 undergraduate majors. Total enrollment: 9,649. Undergraduates: 7,851. Federal methodology is used as a basis for awarding need-based institutional aid.
UNDERGRADUATE EXPENSES for 2005–06 *Application fee:* $25. *Tuition, state resident:* full-time $910; part-time $38 per credit hour. *Tuition, nonresident:* full-time $7050; part-time $294 per credit hour. *Required fees:* full-time $4596; $188 per credit hour. *College room and board:* $6614; *room only:* $4114. Room and board charges vary according to board plan and housing facility. *Payment plan:* Installment.
FRESHMAN FINANCIAL AID (Fall 2004) 1012 applied for aid; of those 70% were deemed to have need. 100% of freshmen with need received aid. *Average percent of need met:* 51% (excluding resources awarded to replace EFC). *Average financial aid package:* $5375 (excluding resources awarded to replace EFC). 2% of all full-time freshmen had no need and received non-need-based gift aid.
UNDERGRADUATE FINANCIAL AID (Fall 2004) 4,512 applied for aid; of those 73% were deemed to have need. 99% of undergraduates with need received aid. *Average percent of need met:* 67% (excluding resources awarded to replace EFC). *Average financial aid package:* $6635 (excluding resources awarded to replace EFC). 2% of all full-time undergraduates had no need and received non-need-based gift aid.
GIFT AID (NEED-BASED) *Total amount:* $7,425,386 (50% federal, 39% state, 11% institutional). *Receiving aid:* Freshmen: 52% (654); All full-time undergraduates: 46% (2,899). *Average award:* Freshmen: $2356; Undergraduates: $3048. *Scholarships, grants, and awards:* Federal Pell, FSEOG, state, private, college/university gift aid from institutional funds.
GIFT AID (NON-NEED-BASED) *Total amount:* $868,880 (15% state, 41% institutional, 44% external sources). *Receiving aid:* Freshmen: 1% (15);

Bridgewater State College

Undergraduates: 1% (40). **Average Award:** Freshmen: $3069; Undergraduates: $2540. **Scholarships, grants, and awards by category:** Academic Interests/Achievement: general academic interests/achievements. **Tuition waivers:** Full or partial for employees or children of employees. **ROTC:** Army cooperative, Air Force cooperative.

LOANS **Student loans:** $21,741,323 (47% need-based, 53% non-need-based). 31% of past graduating class borrowed through all loan programs. *Average indebtedness per student:* $15,065. **Average need-based loan:** Freshmen: $2688; Undergraduates: $3608. **Parent loans:** $2,650,323 (100% non-need-based). **Programs:** Federal Direct (Subsidized and Unsubsidized Stafford, PLUS), Perkins, state.

WORK-STUDY **Federal work-study:** Total amount: $574,075; 450 jobs averaging $1275.

APPLYING FOR FINANCIAL AID *Required financial aid form:* FAFSA. **Financial aid deadline (priority):** 3/1. **Notification date:** 3/15.

CONTACT Catherine M. Kedski, Office of Financial Aid, Bridgewater State College, Tillinghast Hall, Bridgewater, MA 02325-0001, 508-531-1341. *Fax:* 508-531-1728. *E-mail:* ckedski@bridgew.edu.

BRIGHAM YOUNG UNIVERSITY
Provo, UT

ABOUT THE INSTITUTION Independent religious, coed. Awards: bachelor's, master's, doctoral, and first professional degrees. 210 undergraduate majors. Total enrollment: 34,067. Undergraduates: 30,798. Freshmen: 4,533.

GIFT AID (NEED-BASED) *Scholarships, grants, and awards:* Federal Pell, state, private, college/university gift aid from institutional funds.

GIFT AID (NON-NEED-BASED) *Scholarships, grants, and awards by category: Academic Interests/Achievement:* agriculture, area/ethnic studies, biological sciences, business, communication, computer science, education, engineering/technologies, English, foreign languages, general academic interests/achievements, health fields, home economics, humanities, international studies, mathematics, military science, physical sciences, premedicine, religion/biblical studies, social sciences. *Creative Arts/Performance:* applied art and design, art/fine arts, cinema/film/broadcasting, creative writing, dance, journalism/publications, music, performing arts, theater/drama. *Special Achievements/Activities:* cheerleading/drum major, community service, general special achievements/activities, leadership, memberships. *Special Characteristics:* adult students, ethnic background, general special characteristics, handicapped students, international students, local/state students, members of minority groups, out-of-state students, religious affiliation.

LOANS *Programs:* FFEL (Subsidized and Unsubsidized Stafford, PLUS), college/university.

APPLYING FOR FINANCIAL AID *Required financial aid form:* FAFSA.

CONTACT Paul R. Conrad, Director of Financial Aid, Brigham Young University, A-41 Abraham Smoot Building, Provo, UT 84602-1009, 801-378-4104. *Fax:* 801-422-0234. *E-mail:* financial_aid@byu.edu.

BRIGHAM YOUNG UNIVERSITY–HAWAII
Laie, HI

| Tuition & fees: $2760 | Average undergraduate aid package: $7900 |

ABOUT THE INSTITUTION Independent Latter-day Saints, coed. Awards: associate and bachelor's degrees and post-bachelor's certificates. 51 undergraduate majors. Total enrollment: 2,486. Undergraduates: 2,486. Freshmen: 206. Institutional methodology is used as a basis for awarding need-based institutional aid.

UNDERGRADUATE EXPENSES for 2005–06 *Application fee:* $30. *Comprehensive fee:* $7740 includes full-time tuition ($2760) and room and board ($4980). Full-time tuition and fees vary according to course load. Room and board charges vary according to board plan and housing facility. *Part-time tuition:* $187 per credit. *Payment plan:* Installment.

FRESHMAN FINANCIAL AID (Fall 2005, est.) 180 applied for aid; of those 92% were deemed to have need. 93% of freshmen with need received aid; of those 65% had need fully met. *Average percent of need met:* 80% (excluding resources awarded to replace EFC). *Average financial aid package:* $5700 (excluding resources awarded to replace EFC). 12% of all full-time freshmen had no need and received non-need-based gift aid.

UNDERGRADUATE FINANCIAL AID (Fall 2005, est.) 1,900 applied for aid; of those 89% were deemed to have need. 94% of undergraduates with need received aid; of those 75% had need fully met. *Average percent of need met:* 80% (excluding resources awarded to replace EFC). *Average financial aid package:* $7900 (excluding resources awarded to replace EFC). 5% of all full-time undergraduates had no need and received non-need-based gift aid.

GIFT AID (NEED-BASED) *Total amount:* $3,285,117 (53% federal, 35% institutional, 12% external sources). *Receiving aid:* Freshmen: 58% (120); All full-time undergraduates: 67% (1,500). **Average award:** Freshmen: $3200; Undergraduates: $4000. **Scholarships, grants, and awards:** Federal Pell, state, private, college/university gift aid from institutional funds.

GIFT AID (NON-NEED-BASED) *Total amount:* $1,737,713 (99% institutional, 1% external sources). *Receiving aid:* Freshmen: 15% (30); Undergraduates: 36% (800). **Average Award:** Freshmen: $1400; Undergraduates: $1400. **Scholarships, grants, and awards by category:** Academic Interests/Achievement: area/ethnic studies, biological sciences, business, communication, computer science, education, English, foreign languages, general academic interests/achievements, humanities, international studies, mathematics, physical sciences, religion/biblical studies, social sciences. *Creative Arts/Performance:* art/fine arts, creative writing, journalism/publications, music, theater/drama. *Special Achievements/Activities:* cheerleading/drum major, community service, general special achievements/activities, junior miss, leadership, religious involvement. *Special Characteristics:* children and siblings of alumni, children of educators, children of faculty/staff, ethnic background, international students, local/state students, married students, members of minority groups, religious affiliation, veterans. **Tuition waivers:** Full or partial for employees or children of employees. **ROTC:** Army cooperative, Naval cooperative, Air Force cooperative.

LOANS *Student loans:* $2,153,695 (72% need-based, 28% non-need-based). 25% of past graduating class borrowed through all loan programs. *Average indebtedness per student:* $9794. **Average need-based loan:** Freshmen: $2000; Undergraduates: $2000. **Parent loans:** $26,428 (100% non-need-based). **Programs:** FFEL (Subsidized and Unsubsidized Stafford, PLUS), college/university.

WORK-STUDY *State or other work-study/employment:* Total amount: $9,250,593 (53% need-based, 47% non-need-based). Part-time jobs available.

ATHLETIC AWARDS *Total amount:* $356,095 (80% need-based, 20% non-need-based).

APPLYING FOR FINANCIAL AID *Required financial aid form:* FAFSA. **Financial aid deadline:** 3/31 (priority: 3/1). **Notification date:** Continuous beginning 6/30.

CONTACT Mr. Wes Duke, Director of Financial Aid, Brigham Young University–Hawaii, BYUH #1980, 55-220 Kulanui Street, Laie, HI 96762, 808-293-3530. *Fax:* 808-293-3349. *E-mail:* duekw@byuh.edu.

BROOKLYN COLLEGE OF THE CITY UNIVERSITY OF NEW YORK
Brooklyn, NY

CONTACT Sherwood Johnson, Director of Financial Aid, Brooklyn College of the City University of New York, 2900 Bedford Avenue, Brooklyn, NY 11210-2889, 718-951-5045. *Fax:* 718-951-4778. *E-mail:* sjohnson@brooklyn.cuny.edu.

BROOKS INSTITUTE OF PHOTOGRAPHY
Santa Barbara, CA

CONTACT Debra Johnson, Financial Aid Officer, Brooks Institute of Photography, 801 Alston Road, Santa Barbara, CA 93108, 805-966-3888 Ext. 3032 or toll-free 888-304-3456 (out-of-state). *Fax:* 805-966-2909.

BROWN UNIVERSITY
Providence, RI

CONTACT Michael Bartini, Director of Financial Aid, Brown University, Box 1827, Providence, RI 02912, 401-863-2721. *Fax:* 401-863-7575. *E-mail:* financial_aid@brown.edu.

BRYAN COLLEGE
Dayton, TN

Tuition & fees: $14,800 **Average undergraduate aid package:** $10,039

ABOUT THE INSTITUTION Independent interdenominational, coed. Awards: associate and bachelor's degrees. 39 undergraduate majors. Total enrollment: 775. Undergraduates: 775. Freshmen: 184. Both federal and institutional methodology are used as a basis for awarding need-based institutional aid.

UNDERGRADUATE EXPENSES for 2005–06 *Application fee:* $30. *Comprehensive fee:* $19,270 includes full-time tuition ($14,800) and room and board ($4470). *Part-time tuition:* $625 per credit hour. *Payment plan:* Installment.

FRESHMAN FINANCIAL AID (Fall 2004) 130 applied for aid; of those 92% were deemed to have need. 100% of freshmen with need received aid. *Average percent of need met:* 73% (excluding resources awarded to replace EFC). *Average financial aid package:* $12,804 (excluding resources awarded to replace EFC). 32% of all full-time freshmen had no need and received non-need-based gift aid.

UNDERGRADUATE FINANCIAL AID (Fall 2004) 561 applied for aid; of those 84% were deemed to have need. 100% of undergraduates with need received aid. *Average percent of need met:* 71% (excluding resources awarded to replace EFC). *Average financial aid package:* $10,039 (excluding resources awarded to replace EFC). 23% of all full-time undergraduates had no need and received non-need-based gift aid.

GIFT AID (NEED-BASED) *Total amount:* $1,046,442 (57% federal, 27% state, 16% institutional). *Receiving aid:* Freshmen: 50% (67); All full-time undergraduates: 44% (276). *Average award:* Freshmen: $3507; Undergraduates: $4409. *Scholarships, grants, and awards:* Federal Pell, FSEOG, state, private, college/university gift aid from institutional funds.

GIFT AID (NON-NEED-BASED) *Total amount:* $1,782,009 (10% state, 80% institutional, 10% external sources). *Receiving aid:* Freshmen: 90% (120); Undergraduates: 75% (472). *Average Award:* Freshmen: $4766; Undergraduates:* $4417. *Scholarships, grants, and awards by category:* Academic Interests/Achievement: 332 awards ($926,750 total): biological sciences, business, communication, computer science, education, English, foreign languages, general academic interests/achievements, humanities, mathematics, physical sciences, premedicine, religion/biblical studies, social sciences. *Creative Arts/Performance:* 41 awards ($37,950 total): art/fine arts, journalism/publications, music, performing arts, theater/drama. *Special Achievements/Activities:* 63 awards ($51,551 total): cheerleading/drum major, community service, general special achievements/activities, leadership, religious involvement. *Special Characteristics:* 144 awards ($797,789 total): children and siblings of alumni, children of current students, children of educators, children of faculty/staff, general special characteristics, handicapped students, international students, local/state students, relatives of clergy, religious affiliation, spouses of current students. *Tuition waivers:* Full or partial for children of alumni, employees or children of employees.

LOANS *Student loans:* $2,430,719 (70% need-based, 30% non-need-based). 66% of past graduating class borrowed through all loan programs. *Average indebtedness per student:* $17,660. *Average need-based loan:* Freshmen: $3945; Undergraduates: $4140. *Parent loans:* $897,137 (100% non-need-based). *Programs:* FFEL (Subsidized and Unsubsidized Stafford, PLUS), Perkins, state, college/university.

WORK-STUDY *Federal work-study:* Total amount: $208,000; 183 jobs averaging $1500.

ATHLETIC AWARDS *Total amount:* $505,765 (100% non-need-based).

APPLYING FOR FINANCIAL AID *Required financial aid forms:* FAFSA, institution's own form. *Financial aid deadline (priority):* 3/1. *Notification date:* Continuous beginning 1/1. Students must reply within 2 weeks of notification.

CONTACT Michael Sapienza, Director of Financial Aid, Bryan College, PO Box 7000, Dayton, TN 37321-7000, 423-775-7339 or toll-free 800-277-9522. *Fax:* 423-775-7300. *E-mail:* finaid@bryan.edu.

BRYANT AND STRATTON COLLEGE
Cleveland, OH

CONTACT Bill Davenport, Financial Aid Supervisor, Bryant and Stratton College, 1700 East 13th Street, Cleveland, OH 44114-3203, 216-771-1700. *Fax:* 216-771-7787.

BRYANT AND STRATTON COLLEGE, WAUWATOSA CAMPUS
Wauwatosa, WI

CONTACT Financial Aid Office, Bryant and Stratton College, Wauwatosa Campus, 10950 W. Potter Road, Wauwatosa, WI 53226, 414-302-7000.

BRYANT UNIVERSITY
Smithfield, RI

Tuition & fees: $24,762 **Average undergraduate aid package:** $15,270

ABOUT THE INSTITUTION Independent, coed. Awards: bachelor's and master's degrees and post-master's certificates. 16 undergraduate majors. Total enrollment: 3,642. Undergraduates: 3,203. Freshmen: 822. Federal methodology is used as a basis for awarding need-based institutional aid.

UNDERGRADUATE EXPENSES for 2005–06 *Application fee:* $50. *Comprehensive fee:* $34,330 includes full-time tuition ($24,762) and room and board ($9568). *College room only:* $5550. Full-time tuition and fees vary according to course load. Room and board charges vary according to board plan and housing facility. *Part-time tuition:* $891 per course. Part-time tuition and fees vary according to course load. Full-time tuition includes cost of personal laptop computer. *Payment plan:* Installment.

FRESHMAN FINANCIAL AID (Fall 2005, est.) 668 applied for aid; of those 84% were deemed to have need. 100% of freshmen with need received aid; of those 13% had need fully met. *Average percent of need met:* 76% (excluding resources awarded to replace EFC). *Average financial aid package:* $15,587 (excluding resources awarded to replace EFC). 10% of all full-time freshmen had no need and received non-need-based gift aid.

UNDERGRADUATE FINANCIAL AID (Fall 2005, est.) 2,256 applied for aid; of those 86% were deemed to have need. 100% of undergraduates with need received aid; of those 11% had need fully met. *Average percent of need met:* 74% (excluding resources awarded to replace EFC). *Average financial aid package:* $15,270 (excluding resources awarded to replace EFC). 15% of all full-time undergraduates had no need and received non-need-based gift aid.

GIFT AID (NEED-BASED) *Total amount:* $17,903,626 (6% federal, 3% state, 81% institutional, 10% external sources). *Receiving aid:* Freshmen: 61% (503); All full-time undergraduates: 51% (1,539). *Average award:* Freshmen: $8739; Undergraduates: $8615. *Scholarships, grants, and awards:* Federal Pell, FSEOG, state, private, college/university gift aid from institutional funds.

GIFT AID (NON-NEED-BASED) *Total amount:* $7,760,809 (80% institutional, 20% external sources). *Receiving aid:* Freshmen: 32% (260); Undergraduates: 32% (970). *Average Award:* Freshmen: $9336; Undergraduates: $7721. *Scholarships, grants, and awards by category:* Academic Interests/Achievement: 731 awards ($6,277,098 total): engineering/technologies, general academic interests/achievements. *Special Characteristics:* 136 awards ($866,775 total): children and siblings of alumni, local/state students, members of minority groups, siblings of current students. *Tuition waivers:* Full or partial for employees or children of employees. *ROTC:* Army.

LOANS *Student loans:* $19,637,164 (45% need-based, 55% non-need-based). 60% of past graduating class borrowed through all loan programs. *Average indebtedness per student:* $29,222. *Average need-based loan:* Freshmen: $4165; Undergraduates: $4899. *Parent loans:* $7,708,152 (11% need-based, 89% non-need-based). *Programs:* Federal Direct (Subsidized and Unsubsidized Stafford), FFEL (PLUS), Perkins, alternative loans.

WORK-STUDY *Federal work-study:* Total amount: $385,811; 425 jobs averaging $1572. *State or other work-study/employment:* Total amount: $1,889,019 (100% need-based). 979 part-time jobs averaging $1385.

ATHLETIC AWARDS *Total amount:* $1,639,468 (56% need-based, 44% non-need-based).

APPLYING FOR FINANCIAL AID *Required financial aid form:* FAFSA. *Financial aid deadline (priority):* 2/15. *Notification date:* 3/24. Students must reply by 5/1.

CONTACT Mr. John B. Canning, Director of Financial Aid, Bryant University, Office of Financial Aid, 1150 Douglas Pike, Smithfield, RI 02917-1284, 401-232-6020 or toll-free 800-622-7001. *Fax:* 401-232-6293. *E-mail:* jcanning@bryant.edu.

Bryn Athyn College of the New Church

BRYN ATHYN COLLEGE OF THE NEW CHURCH
Bryn Athyn, PA

CONTACT Les Alden, Business Manager, Bryn Athyn College of the New Church, Box 711, Bryn Athyn, PA 19009, 215-938-2635. *Fax:* 215-938-2616. *E-mail:* wlalden@newchurch.edu.

BRYN MAWR COLLEGE
Bryn Mawr, PA

Tuition & fees: $32,230   Average undergraduate aid package: $27,582

ABOUT THE INSTITUTION Independent, undergraduate: women only; graduate: coed. Awards: bachelor's, master's, and doctoral degrees and post-bachelor's certificates. 33 undergraduate majors. Total enrollment: 1,799. Undergraduates: 1,346. Freshmen: 354. Both federal and institutional methodology are used as a basis for awarding need-based institutional aid.
UNDERGRADUATE EXPENSES for 2006–07 *Application fee:* $50. *Comprehensive fee:* $42,780 includes full-time tuition ($32,230) and room and board ($10,550). *College room only:* $6030. *Part-time tuition:* $3990 per course.
FRESHMAN FINANCIAL AID (Fall 2005, est.) 252 applied for aid; of those 80% were deemed to have need. 100% of freshmen with need received aid; of those 98% had need fully met. *Average percent of need met:* 98% (excluding resources awarded to replace EFC). *Average financial aid package:* $28,226 (excluding resources awarded to replace EFC). 3% of all full-time freshmen had no need and received non-need-based gift aid.
UNDERGRADUATE FINANCIAL AID (Fall 2005, est.) 810 applied for aid; of those 88% were deemed to have need. 100% of undergraduates with need received aid; of those 98% had need fully met. *Average percent of need met:* 98% (excluding resources awarded to replace EFC). *Average financial aid package:* $27,582 (excluding resources awarded to replace EFC). 2% of all full-time undergraduates had no need and received non-need-based gift aid.
GIFT AID (NEED-BASED) *Total amount:* $14,928,437 (4% federal, 2% state, 92% institutional, 2% external sources). *Receiving aid:* Freshmen: 54% (192); All full-time undergraduates: 52% (679). *Average award:* Freshmen: $24,396; Undergraduates: $22,888. *Scholarships, grants, and awards:* Federal Pell, FSEOG, state, college/university gift aid from institutional funds.
GIFT AID (NON-NEED-BASED) *Total amount:* $472,865 (2% federal, 74% institutional, 24% external sources). *Receiving aid:* Freshmen: 3% (10); Undergraduates: 2% (28). *Average Award:* Freshmen: $10,397; Undergraduates: $11,082. *ROTC:* Air Force cooperative.
LOANS *Student loans:* $3,487,817 (72% need-based, 28% non-need-based). 57% of past graduating class borrowed through all loan programs. *Average indebtedness per student:* $17,018. *Average need-based loan:* Freshmen: $3525; Undergraduates: $4479. *Parent loans:* $3,377,760 (100% non-need-based). *Programs:* FFEL (Subsidized and Unsubsidized Stafford, PLUS), Perkins.
WORK-STUDY *Federal work-study:* Total amount: $923,300; 555 jobs averaging $1776. *State or other work-study/employment:* Total amount: $164,976 (100% need-based). 67 part-time jobs averaging $1904.
APPLYING FOR FINANCIAL AID *Required financial aid forms:* FAFSA, CSS Financial Aid PROFILE, business/farm supplement, income tax form(s) student and parent tax returns. *Financial aid deadline:* 2/4. *Notification date:* 3/23. Students must reply by 5/1.
CONTACT Ethel M. Desmarais, Director of Financial Aid, Bryn Mawr College, 101 North Merion Avenue, Bryn Mawr, PA 19010-2899, 610-526-7922 or toll-free 800-BMC-1885 (out-of-state). *Fax:* 610-526-5249. *E-mail:* edesmara@brynmawr.edu.

BUCKNELL UNIVERSITY
Lewisburg, PA

Tuition & fees: $36,002   Average undergraduate aid package: $21,000

ABOUT THE INSTITUTION Independent, coed. Awards: bachelor's and master's degrees. 54 undergraduate majors. Total enrollment: 3,648. Undergraduates: 3,505. Freshmen: 920. Both federal and institutional methodology are used as a basis for awarding need-based institutional aid.
UNDERGRADUATE EXPENSES for 2006–07 *Application fee:* $60. *Comprehensive fee:* $43,368 includes full-time tuition ($35,802), mandatory fees ($200), and room and board ($7366). *College room only:* $3972. *Part-time tuition:* $3930 per course.
FRESHMAN FINANCIAL AID (Fall 2005, est.) 541 applied for aid; of those 77% were deemed to have need. 100% of freshmen with need received aid; of those 100% had need fully met. *Average percent of need met:* 100% (excluding resources awarded to replace EFC). *Average financial aid package:* $23,100 (excluding resources awarded to replace EFC). 2% of all full-time freshmen had no need and received non-need-based gift aid.
UNDERGRADUATE FINANCIAL AID (Fall 2005, est.) 2,023 applied for aid; of those 82% were deemed to have need. 100% of undergraduates with need received aid; of those 100% had need fully met. *Average percent of need met:* 100% (excluding resources awarded to replace EFC). *Average financial aid package:* $21,000 (excluding resources awarded to replace EFC). 1% of all full-time undergraduates had no need and received non-need-based gift aid.
GIFT AID (NEED-BASED) *Total amount:* $30,734,050 (5% federal, 4% state, 88% institutional, 3% external sources). *Receiving aid:* Freshmen: 45% (418); All full-time undergraduates: 45% (1,534). *Average award:* Freshmen: $18,400; Undergraduates: $17,300. *Scholarships, grants, and awards:* Federal Pell, FSEOG, state, private, college/university gift aid from institutional funds.
GIFT AID (NON-NEED-BASED) *Total amount:* $400,000 (100% institutional). *Receiving aid:* Freshmen: 2% (16); Undergraduates: 1% (28). *Average Award:* Freshmen: $14,540; Undergraduates: $12,356. *Scholarships, grants, and awards by category:* Academic Interests/Achievement: 10 awards ($150,900 total): business, engineering/technologies, general academic interests/achievements, physical sciences. Creative Arts/Performance: 21 awards ($139,000 total): art/fine arts, music, performing arts. Special Achievements/Activities: 10 awards ($326,080 total): general special achievements/activities. *ROTC:* Army.
LOANS *Student loans:* $12,000,000 (100% need-based). 62% of past graduating class borrowed through all loan programs. *Average indebtedness per student:* $17,400. *Average need-based loan:* Freshmen: $4000; Undergraduates: $5200. *Parent loans:* $7,194,810 (100% non-need-based). *Programs:* FFEL (Subsidized and Unsubsidized Stafford, PLUS), Perkins.
WORK-STUDY *Federal work-study:* Total amount: $1,500,000; 1,000 jobs averaging $1500. *State or other work-study/employment:* Total amount: $90,000 (100% need-based). 60 part-time jobs averaging $1500.
ATHLETIC AWARDS *Total amount:* $180,000 (100% non-need-based).
APPLYING FOR FINANCIAL AID *Required financial aid forms:* FAFSA, CSS Financial Aid PROFILE, noncustodial (divorced/separated) parent's statement. *Financial aid deadline:* 1/1. *Notification date:* 4/1. Students must reply by 5/1.
CONTACT Andrea Leithner, Director of Financial Aid, Bucknell University, Office of Financial Aid, Lewisburg, PA 17837, 570-577-1331. *Fax:* 570-577-1481.

BUENA VISTA UNIVERSITY
Storm Lake, IA

Tuition & fees: $21,688   Average undergraduate aid package: $19,994

ABOUT THE INSTITUTION Independent religious, coed. Awards: bachelor's and master's degrees. 58 undergraduate majors. Total enrollment: 1,283. Undergraduates: 1,214. Freshmen: 287. Federal methodology is used as a basis for awarding need-based institutional aid.
UNDERGRADUATE EXPENSES for 2005–06 *Application fee:* $25. *Comprehensive fee:* $27,742 includes full-time tuition ($21,688) and room and board ($6054). *Part-time tuition:* $729 per semester hour.
FRESHMAN FINANCIAL AID (Fall 2005, est.) 282 applied for aid; of those 94% were deemed to have need. 100% of freshmen with need received aid; of those 14% had need fully met. *Average percent of need met:* 90% (excluding resources awarded to replace EFC). *Average financial aid package:* $20,629 (excluding resources awarded to replace EFC). 6% of all full-time freshmen had no need and received non-need-based gift aid.
UNDERGRADUATE FINANCIAL AID (Fall 2005, est.) 1,162 applied for aid; of those 95% were deemed to have need. 100% of undergraduates with need received aid; of those 28% had need fully met. *Average percent of need met:* 91% (excluding resources awarded to replace EFC). *Average financial aid package:* $19,994 (excluding resources awarded to replace EFC). 5% of all full-time undergraduates had no need and received non-need-based gift aid.
GIFT AID (NEED-BASED) *Total amount:* $10,957,230 (13% federal, 23% state, 64% institutional). *Receiving aid:* Freshmen: 92% (263); All full-time undergradu-

ates: 90% (1,082). **Average award:** Freshmen: $7463; Undergraduates: $9608. **Scholarships, grants, and awards:** Federal Pell, FSEOG, state, private, college/university gift aid from institutional funds.
GIFT AID (NON-NEED-BASED) Total amount: $5,588,300 (94% institutional, 6% external sources). **Receiving aid:** Freshmen: 85% (245); Undergraduates: 68% (814). **Average Award:** *Freshmen:* $8842; *Undergraduates:* $6550. **Scholarships, grants, and awards by category:** *Academic Interests/Achievement:* 902 awards ($6,550,957 total): biological sciences, business, computer science, education, general academic interests/achievements, humanities, international studies, mathematics. *Creative Arts/Performance:* 98 awards ($130,157 total): art/fine arts, music, theater/drama. *Special Achievements/Activities:* 219 awards ($1,305,016 total): general special achievements/activities, leadership. *Special Characteristics:* 299 awards ($846,312 total): children of faculty/staff, ethnic background, international students, out-of-state students, religious affiliation, siblings of current students. **Tuition waivers:** Full or partial for employees or children of employees.
LOANS Student loans: $5,579,928 (82% need-based, 18% non-need-based). 92% of past graduating class borrowed through all loan programs. *Average indebtedness per student:* $29,059. **Average need-based loan:** Freshmen: $4149; Undergraduates: $4689. **Programs:** FFEL (Subsidized and Unsubsidized Stafford, PLUS), Perkins, college/university.
WORK-STUDY Federal work-study: Total amount: $654,619; 595 jobs averaging $1060. **State or other work-study/employment:** Total amount: $153,131 (100% non-need-based). 154 part-time jobs averaging $1001.
APPLYING FOR FINANCIAL AID Required financial aid form: FAFSA. **Financial aid deadline (priority):** 6/1. **Notification date:** Continuous beginning 3/5. Students must reply by 5/1 or within 2 weeks of notification.
CONTACT Mrs. Leanne Valentine, Director of Financial Assistance, Buena Vista University, 610 West Fourth Street, Storm Lake, IA 50588, 712-749-2164 or toll-free 800-383-9600. *Fax:* 712-749-1451. *E-mail:* valentinel@bvu.edu.

BUFFALO STATE COLLEGE, STATE UNIVERSITY OF NEW YORK
Buffalo, NY

CONTACT Mr. Kent McGowan, Director of Financial Aid, Buffalo State College, State University of New York, 1300 Elmwood Avenue, Buffalo, NY 14222-1095, 716-878-4902. *Fax:* 716-878-4903.

BURLINGTON COLLEGE
Burlington, VT

Tuition & fees: $15,600   **Average undergraduate aid package: $10,170**

ABOUT THE INSTITUTION Independent, coed. Awards: associate and bachelor's degrees. 20 undergraduate majors. Total enrollment: 241. Undergraduates: 241. Freshmen: 17. Federal methodology is used as a basis for awarding need-based institutional aid.
UNDERGRADUATE EXPENSES for 2006–07 Application fee: $35. **Tuition:** full-time $15,600; part-time $515 per credit hour.
FRESHMAN FINANCIAL AID (Fall 2005, est.) 5 applied for aid; of those 100% were deemed to have need. 100% of freshmen with need received aid. *Average percent of need met:* 50% (excluding resources awarded to replace EFC). *Average financial aid package:* $7259 (excluding resources awarded to replace EFC).
UNDERGRADUATE FINANCIAL AID (Fall 2005, est.) 70 applied for aid; of those 96% were deemed to have need. 99% of undergraduates with need received aid; of those 3% had need fully met. *Average percent of need met:* 58% (excluding resources awarded to replace EFC). *Average financial aid package:* $10,170 (excluding resources awarded to replace EFC).
GIFT AID (NEED-BASED) Total amount: $387,974 (54% federal, 40% state, 2% institutional, 4% external sources). **Receiving aid:** Freshmen: 57% (4); All full-time undergraduates: 45% (46). **Average award:** Freshmen: $2268; Undergraduates: $4927. **Scholarships, grants, and awards:** Federal Pell, FSEOG, state, private, college/university gift aid from institutional funds.
GIFT AID (NON-NEED-BASED) Scholarships, grants, and awards by category: *Special Achievements/Activities:* general special achievements/activities.
LOANS Student loans: $1,127,077 (90% need-based, 10% non-need-based). 85% of past graduating class borrowed through all loan programs. *Average indebtedness per student:* $21,577. **Average need-based loan:** Freshmen: $4994; Undergraduates: $6495. **Parent loans:** $133,166 (50% need-based, 50% non-need-based). **Programs:** FFEL (Subsidized and Unsubsidized Stafford, PLUS), Perkins.
WORK-STUDY Federal work-study: Total amount: $62,341; 50 jobs averaging $1247.
APPLYING FOR FINANCIAL AID Required financial aid form: FAFSA. **Financial aid deadline:** Continuous. **Notification date:** Continuous beginning 4/1. Students must reply within 4 weeks of notification.
CONTACT Ms. Yvonne Whitaker, Assistant Director of Financial Aid Services, Burlington College, PO Box 2000, Winooski, VT 05404, 877-685-7787 or toll-free 800-862-9616. *Fax:* 802-654-3765. *E-mail:* bc@vsac.org.

BUTLER UNIVERSITY
Indianapolis, IN

Tuition & fees: $23,774   **Average undergraduate aid package: $17,568**

ABOUT THE INSTITUTION Independent, coed. Awards: bachelor's, master's, and first professional degrees. 52 undergraduate majors. Total enrollment: 4,384. Undergraduates: 3,651. Freshmen: 867. Federal methodology is used as a basis for awarding need-based institutional aid.
UNDERGRADUATE EXPENSES for 2005–06 Application fee: $35. **Comprehensive fee:** $31,944 includes full-time tuition ($23,530), mandatory fees ($244), and room and board ($8170). **College room only:** $3980. Full-time tuition and fees vary according to program. Room and board charges vary according to housing facility. **Part-time tuition:** $980 per credit. Part-time tuition and fees vary according to program. **Payment plan:** Installment.
FRESHMAN FINANCIAL AID (Fall 2005, est.) 801 applied for aid; of those 68% were deemed to have need. 100% of freshmen with need received aid; of those 25% had need fully met. *Average financial aid package:* $17,725 (excluding resources awarded to replace EFC). 26% of all full-time freshmen had no need and received non-need-based gift aid.
UNDERGRADUATE FINANCIAL AID (Fall 2005, est.) 3,439 applied for aid; of those 67% were deemed to have need. 100% of undergraduates with need received aid; of those 21% had need fully met. *Average financial aid package:* $17,568 (excluding resources awarded to replace EFC). 26% of all full-time undergraduates had no need and received non-need-based gift aid.
GIFT AID (NEED-BASED) Total amount: $27,172,350 (5% federal, 12% state, 74% institutional, 9% external sources). **Receiving aid:** Freshmen: 62% (533); All full-time undergraduates: 57% (2,173). **Average award:** Freshmen: $13,818; Undergraduates: $12,850. **Scholarships, grants, and awards:** Federal Pell, FSEOG, state, private, college/university gift aid from institutional funds.
GIFT AID (NON-NEED-BASED) Total amount: $11,033,995 (78% institutional, 22% external sources). **Receiving aid:** Freshmen: 13% (115); Undergraduates: 9% (356). **Average Award:** *Freshmen:* $8525; *Undergraduates:* $9445. **Scholarships, grants, and awards by category:** *Academic Interests/Achievement:* biological sciences, business, communication, computer science, education, engineering/technologies, English, foreign languages, general academic interests/achievements, humanities, international studies, mathematics, physical sciences, social sciences. *Creative Arts/Performance:* art/fine arts, cinema/film/broadcasting, dance, music, theater/drama. **Tuition waivers:** Full or partial for employees or children of employees. **ROTC:** Army, Air Force cooperative.
LOANS Student loans: $22,500,190 (64% need-based, 36% non-need-based). 62% of past graduating class borrowed through all loan programs. **Average need-based loan:** Freshmen: $3590; Undergraduates: $5245. **Parent loans:** $4,573,050 (20% need-based, 80% non-need-based). **Programs:** FFEL (Subsidized and Unsubsidized Stafford, PLUS), Perkins.
WORK-STUDY Federal work-study: Total amount: $221,500; jobs available. **State or other work-study/employment:** Part-time jobs available.
ATHLETIC AWARDS Total amount: $3,194,376 (23% need-based, 77% non-need-based).
APPLYING FOR FINANCIAL AID Required financial aid form: FAFSA. **Financial aid deadline (priority):** 3/1. **Notification date:** 3/15. Students must reply within 3 weeks of notification.
CONTACT Ms. Kristine Butz, Associate Director of Financial Aid, Butler University, 4600 Sunset Avenue, Indianapolis, IN 46208-3485, 317-940-8200 or toll-free 888-940-8100. *Fax:* 317-940-8250. *E-mail:* kbutz@butler.edu.

Cabarrus College of Health Sciences

CABARRUS COLLEGE OF HEALTH SCIENCES
Concord, NC

Tuition & fees: $7300   **Average undergraduate aid package:** N/A

ABOUT THE INSTITUTION Independent, coed, primarily women. Awards: associate and bachelor's degrees. 6 undergraduate majors. Total enrollment: 308. Undergraduates: 308. Freshmen: 21. Federal methodology is used as a basis for awarding need-based institutional aid.
UNDERGRADUATE EXPENSES for 2006–07 *Application fee:* $35. *Tuition:* full-time $7300; part-time $230 per hour.
GIFT AID (NEED-BASED) *Total amount:* $539,747 (36% federal, 42% state, 4% institutional, 18% external sources). *Scholarships, grants, and awards:* Federal Pell, FSEOG, state, private, college/university gift aid from institutional funds.
GIFT AID (NON-NEED-BASED) *Total amount:* $278,725 (99% state, 1% institutional). *Scholarships, grants, and awards by category:* Special Characteristics: ethnic background, first-generation college students.
LOANS *Student loans:* $1,227,117 (40% need-based, 60% non-need-based). *Parent loans:* $36,153 (100% need-based). *Programs:* FFEL (Subsidized and Unsubsidized Stafford, PLUS), state.
WORK-STUDY *Federal work-study:* Total amount: $15,000; 20 jobs available. *State or other work-study/employment:* Total amount: $43,405 (100% need-based).
APPLYING FOR FINANCIAL AID *Required financial aid form:* FAFSA. *Financial aid deadline (priority):* 4/15. *Notification date:* Continuous beginning 7/1. Students must reply within 2 weeks of notification.
CONTACT Joanne Yurchison, Business Officer, Cabarrus College of Health Sciences, 431 Copperfield Boulevard NE, Concord, NC 28025, 704-783-1754. *Fax:* 704-783-1764. *E-mail:* jyurch@northeastmedical.org.

CABRINI COLLEGE
Radnor, PA

Tuition & fees: $24,000   **Average undergraduate aid package:** $19,399

ABOUT THE INSTITUTION Independent Roman Catholic, coed. Awards: bachelor's and master's degrees and post-bachelor's certificates. 38 undergraduate majors. Total enrollment: 2,318. Undergraduates: 1,739. Freshmen: 534. Federal methodology is used as a basis for awarding need-based institutional aid.
UNDERGRADUATE EXPENSES for 2005–06 *Application fee:* $35. *Comprehensive fee:* $33,340 includes full-time tuition ($23,200), mandatory fees ($800), and room and board ($9340). Full-time tuition and fees vary according to location. Room and board charges vary according to board plan and housing facility. *Part-time tuition:* $395 per credit hour. *Part-time fees:* $45 per term. Part-time tuition and fees vary according to course load. *Payment plan:* Installment.
FRESHMAN FINANCIAL AID (Fall 2005, est.) 482 applied for aid; of those 86% were deemed to have need. 100% of freshmen with need received aid; of those 18% had need fully met. *Average percent of need met:* 88% (excluding resources awarded to replace EFC). *Average financial aid package:* $20,113 (excluding resources awarded to replace EFC). 13% of all full-time freshmen had no need and received non-need-based gift aid.
UNDERGRADUATE FINANCIAL AID (Fall 2005, est.) 1,279 applied for aid; of those 88% were deemed to have need. 100% of undergraduates with need received aid; of those 16% had need fully met. *Average percent of need met:* 84% (excluding resources awarded to replace EFC). *Average financial aid package:* $19,399 (excluding resources awarded to replace EFC). 9% of all full-time undergraduates had no need and received non-need-based gift aid.
GIFT AID (NEED-BASED) *Total amount:* $5,049,997 (20% federal, 28% state, 52% institutional). *Receiving aid:* Freshmen: 57% (298); All full-time undergraduates: 56% (868). *Average award:* Freshmen: $5065; Undergraduates: $5659. *Scholarships, grants, and awards:* Federal Pell, FSEOG, state, private, college/university gift aid from institutional funds.
GIFT AID (NON-NEED-BASED) *Total amount:* $10,500,191 (98% institutional, 2% external sources). *Receiving aid:* Freshmen: 75% (396); Undergraduates: 69% (1,067). *Average Award:* Freshmen: $8670; Undergraduates: $7154. *Scholarships, grants, and awards by category:* Academic Interests/Achievement: general academic interests/achievements. Special Characteristics: children and siblings of alumni, children of faculty/staff, ethnic background, siblings of current students. *Tuition waivers:* Full or partial for children of alumni, employees or children of employees, senior citizens. *ROTC:* Army cooperative.
LOANS *Student loans:* $9,109,751 (40% need-based, 60% non-need-based). 84% of past graduating class borrowed through all loan programs. *Average indebtedness per student:* $17,400. *Average need-based loan:* Freshmen: $2932; Undergraduates: $3919. *Parent loans:* $5,756,951 (71% need-based, 29% non-need-based). *Programs:* FFEL (Subsidized and Unsubsidized Stafford, PLUS), Perkins, alternative loans.
WORK-STUDY *Federal work-study:* Total amount: $166,080; 203 jobs averaging $765.
APPLYING FOR FINANCIAL AID *Required financial aid form:* FAFSA. *Financial aid deadline:* Continuous. *Notification date:* Continuous beginning 2/15.
CONTACT Mike Colahan, Director of Financial Aid, Cabrini College, 610 King of Prussia Road, Grace Hall, Radnor, PA 19087-3698, 610-902-8420 or toll-free 800-848-1003. *Fax:* 610-902-8426.

CALDWELL COLLEGE
Caldwell, NJ

ABOUT THE INSTITUTION Independent Roman Catholic, coed. Awards: bachelor's and master's degrees and post-bachelor's and post-master's certificates. 26 undergraduate majors. Total enrollment: 2,229. Undergraduates: 1,671. Freshmen: 298.
GIFT AID (NEED-BASED) *Scholarships, grants, and awards:* Federal Pell, FSEOG, state, private, college/university gift aid from institutional funds.
GIFT AID (NON-NEED-BASED) *Scholarships, grants, and awards by category:* Academic Interests/Achievement: general academic interests/achievements.
LOANS *Programs:* Federal Direct (Subsidized and Unsubsidized Stafford, PLUS), FFEL (Subsidized and Unsubsidized Stafford, PLUS), college/university.
WORK-STUDY *Federal work-study:* Total amount: $38,000; 159 jobs averaging $1500. *State or other work-study/employment:* Total amount: $10,000 (100% need-based).
APPLYING FOR FINANCIAL AID *Required financial aid forms:* FAFSA, state aid form.
CONTACT Ms. Lissa B. Anderson, Executive Director of Financial Aid, Caldwell College, Caldwell College, 9 Ryerson Avenue, Caldwell, NJ 07006, 973-618-3221 or toll-free 888-864-9516 (out-of-state). *E-mail:* landerson@caldwell.edu.

CALIFORNIA BAPTIST UNIVERSITY
Riverside, CA

Tuition & fees: $17,470   **Average undergraduate aid package:** $11,670

ABOUT THE INSTITUTION Independent Southern Baptist, coed. Awards: bachelor's and master's degrees. 32 undergraduate majors. Total enrollment: 3,105. Undergraduates: 2,415. Freshmen: 321. Federal methodology is used as a basis for awarding need-based institutional aid.
UNDERGRADUATE EXPENSES for 2005–06 *Application fee:* $45. *Comprehensive fee:* $23,780 includes full-time tuition ($16,250), mandatory fees ($1220), and room and board ($6310). *College room only:* $2640. Full-time tuition and fees vary according to class time and program. Room and board charges vary according to board plan and housing facility. *Part-time tuition:* $625 per semester hour. Part-time tuition and fees vary according to class time and program. *Payment plan:* Installment.
FRESHMAN FINANCIAL AID (Fall 2005, est.) 311 applied for aid; of those 96% were deemed to have need. 100% of freshmen with need received aid; of those 22% had need fully met. *Average percent of need met:* 70% (excluding resources awarded to replace EFC). *Average financial aid package:* $9860 (excluding resources awarded to replace EFC). 4% of all full-time freshmen had no need and received non-need-based gift aid.
UNDERGRADUATE FINANCIAL AID (Fall 2005, est.) 1,958 applied for aid; of those 97% were deemed to have need. 100% of undergraduates with need received aid; of those 20% had need fully met. *Average percent of need met:* 67% (excluding resources awarded to replace EFC). *Average financial aid package:* $11,670 (excluding resources awarded to replace EFC). 2% of all full-time undergraduates had no need and received non-need-based gift aid.
GIFT AID (NEED-BASED) *Total amount:* $10,906,218 (22% federal, 46% state, 29% institutional, 3% external sources). *Receiving aid:* Freshmen: 91% (289); All full-time undergraduates: 95% (1,887). *Average award:* Freshmen: $7700;

Undergraduates: $8920. *Scholarships, grants, and awards:* Federal Pell, FSEOG, state, private, college/university gift aid from institutional funds.
GIFT AID (NON-NEED-BASED) *Total amount:* $2,232,984 (77% institutional, 23% external sources). *Receiving aid:* Freshmen: 89% (281); Undergraduates: 94% (1,862). *Average Award:* Freshmen: $5150; Undergraduates: $5900. *Scholarships, grants, and awards by category:* Academic Interests/Achievement: 376 awards ($876,873 total): general academic interests/achievements, religion/biblical studies. *Creative Arts/Performance:* 291 awards ($874,748 total): art/fine arts, music, theater/drama. *Special Characteristics:* 643 awards ($1,406,140 total): adult students, children and siblings of alumni, children of faculty/staff, relatives of clergy, siblings of current students. *Tuition waivers:* Full or partial for employees or children of employees. *ROTC:* Army cooperative, Air Force cooperative.
LOANS *Student loans:* $20,867,468 (75% need-based, 25% non-need-based). 87% of past graduating class borrowed through all loan programs. *Average indebtedness per student:* $21,700. *Average need-based loan:* Freshmen: $2430; Undergraduates: $4360. *Parent loans:* $2,433,114 (40% need-based, 60% non-need-based). *Programs:* FFEL (Subsidized and Unsubsidized Stafford, PLUS), Perkins, alternative loans.
WORK-STUDY *Federal work-study:* Total amount: $126,435; 149 jobs averaging $849.
ATHLETIC AWARDS *Total amount:* $1,856,313 (40% need-based, 60% non-need-based).
APPLYING FOR FINANCIAL AID *Required financial aid forms:* FAFSA, state aid form. *Financial aid deadline (priority):* 3/2. *Notification date:* Continuous beginning 3/1. Students must reply by 4/1 or within 3 weeks of notification.
CONTACT Ms. Bekah Reed, Senior Financial Aid Counselor, California Baptist University, 8432 Magnolia Avenue, Riverside, CA 92504-3297, 951-343-4236 or toll-free 877-228-8866. *Fax:* 951-343-4518. *E-mail:* eterry@calbaptist.edu.

CALIFORNIA CHRISTIAN COLLEGE
Fresno, CA
CONTACT Mindy Scroggins, Financial Aid Coordinator, California Christian College, 4881 East University, Fresno, CA 93703, 559-455-5580. *Fax:* 559-251-4231. *E-mail:* cccfadir@aol.com.

CALIFORNIA COAST UNIVERSITY
Santa Ana, CA
CONTACT Financial Aid Office, California Coast University, 700 North Main Street, Santa Ana, CA 92701, 714-547-9625 or toll-free 888-CCU-UNIV (out-of-state).

CALIFORNIA COLLEGE FOR HEALTH SCIENCES
Salt Lake City, UT
CONTACT Financial Aid Director, California College for Health Sciences, 2423 Hoover Avenue, National City, CA 91950-6605, 619-477-4800 or toll-free 800-791-7353. *Fax:* 619-477-5202.

CALIFORNIA COLLEGE OF THE ARTS
San Francisco, CA
ABOUT THE INSTITUTION Independent, coed. Awards: bachelor's and master's degrees. 17 undergraduate majors. Total enrollment: 1,616. Undergraduates: 1,312. Freshmen: 181.
GIFT AID (NEED-BASED) *Scholarships, grants, and awards:* Federal Pell, FSEOG, state, private, college/university gift aid from institutional funds.
GIFT AID (NON-NEED-BASED) *Scholarships, grants, and awards by category:* Academic Interests/Achievement: architecture, general academic interests/achievements. *Creative Arts/Performance:* applied art and design, art/fine arts, creative writing, general creative arts/performance.
LOANS *Programs:* FFEL (Subsidized and Unsubsidized Stafford, PLUS), Perkins, private education loans.
WORK-STUDY *Federal work-study:* Total amount: $366,784; 321 jobs averaging $1534. *State or other work-study/employment:* Total amount: $157,029 (100% non-need-based). 81 part-time jobs averaging $1938.

APPLYING FOR FINANCIAL AID *Required financial aid form:* FAFSA.
CONTACT Financial Aid Office, California College of the Arts, 1111 Eighth Street, San Francisco, CA 94107, 415-703-9528 or toll-free 800-447-1ART. *Fax:* 415-551-9261. *E-mail:* finaid@ccac.edu.

CALIFORNIA DESIGN COLLEGE
Los Angeles, CA
CONTACT Mr. Jason F. Li, Director of Financial Aid, California Design College, 3440 Wilshire Boulevard, Seventh Floor, Los Angeles, CA 90010, 213-251-3636 Ext. 209 or toll-free 213-251-3636 (in-state), 877-468-6232 (out-of-state). *Fax:* 213-385-3545. *E-mail:* jason@cdc.edu.

CALIFORNIA INSTITUTE OF INTEGRAL STUDIES
San Francisco, CA
CONTACT Financial Aid Office, California Institute of Integral Studies, 1453 Mission Street, San Francisco, CA 94103, 415-575-6122. *Fax:* 415-575-1268. *E-mail:* finaid@ciis.edu.

CALIFORNIA INSTITUTE OF TECHNOLOGY
Pasadena, CA

Tuition & fees: $27,309   **Average undergraduate aid package: $28,508**

ABOUT THE INSTITUTION Independent, coed. Awards: bachelor's, master's, and doctoral degrees. 32 undergraduate majors. Total enrollment: 2,172. Undergraduates: 891. Freshmen: 191. Both federal and institutional methodology are used as a basis for awarding need-based institutional aid.
UNDERGRADUATE EXPENSES for 2005–06 *Application fee:* $50. *Comprehensive fee:* $36,123 includes full-time tuition ($27,309) and room and board ($8814). *Payment plans:* Installment, deferred payment.
FRESHMAN FINANCIAL AID (Fall 2005, est.) 179 applied for aid; of those 69% were deemed to have need. 100% of freshmen with need received aid; of those 100% had need fully met. *Average percent of need met:* 100% (excluding resources awarded to replace EFC). *Average financial aid package:* $27,702 (excluding resources awarded to replace EFC). 6% of all full-time freshmen had no need and received non-need-based gift aid.
UNDERGRADUATE FINANCIAL AID (Fall 2005, est.) 635 applied for aid; of those 78% were deemed to have need. 100% of undergraduates with need received aid; of those 100% had need fully met. *Average percent of need met:* 100% (excluding resources awarded to replace EFC). *Average financial aid package:* $28,508 (excluding resources awarded to replace EFC). 9% of all full-time undergraduates had no need and received non-need-based gift aid.
GIFT AID (NEED-BASED) *Total amount:* $13,317,147 (5% federal, 6% state, 86% institutional, 3% external sources). *Receiving aid:* Freshmen: 53% (124); All full-time undergraduates: 53% (488). *Average award:* Freshmen: $26,303; Undergraduates: $27,325. *Scholarships, grants, and awards:* Federal Pell, FSEOG, state, private, college/university gift aid from institutional funds.
GIFT AID (NON-NEED-BASED) *Total amount:* $3,280,154 (4% state, 73% institutional, 23% external sources). *Receiving aid:* Freshmen: 5% (12); Undergraduates: 3% (24). *Average Award:* Freshmen: $29,399; Undergraduates: $29,818. *Scholarships, grants, and awards by category:* Academic Interests/Achievement: 78 awards ($2,325,000 total): general academic interests/achievements. *Tuition waivers:* Full or partial for employees or children of employees. *ROTC:* Army cooperative, Air Force cooperative.
LOANS *Student loans:* $618,076 (50% need-based, 50% non-need-based). 45% of past graduating class borrowed through all loan programs. *Average indebtedness per student:* $5395. *Average need-based loan:* Freshmen: $1503; Undergraduates: $1491. *Parent loans:* $767,420 (100% non-need-based). *Programs:* Federal Direct (Subsidized and Unsubsidized Stafford, PLUS), Perkins, college/university.
WORK-STUDY *Federal work-study:* Total amount: $411,411; 271 jobs averaging $1517. *State or other work-study/employment:* Total amount: $63,114 (100% need-based). 36 part-time jobs averaging $1753.
APPLYING FOR FINANCIAL AID *Required financial aid forms:* FAFSA, CSS Financial Aid PROFILE, state aid form, noncustodial (divorced/separated) parent's

California Institute of Technology

statement, business/farm supplement. *Financial aid deadline (priority):* 1/15. *Notification date:* 4/15. Students must reply by 5/1 or within 4 weeks of notification.
CONTACT David Levy, Director of Financial Aid, California Institute of Technology, Financial Aid Office, MC 110-87, Pasadena, CA 91125-0001, 626-395-6280. *Fax:* 626-564-8136. *E-mail:* davidlevy@finaid.caltech.edu.

CALIFORNIA INSTITUTE OF THE ARTS
Valencia, CA

Tuition & fees: $27,725	Average undergraduate aid package: $26,206

ABOUT THE INSTITUTION Independent, coed. Awards: bachelor's and master's degrees and post-bachelor's certificates. 23 undergraduate majors. Total enrollment: 1,327. Undergraduates: 821. Freshmen: 138. Federal methodology is used as a basis for awarding need-based institutional aid.
UNDERGRADUATE EXPENSES for 2005–06 *Application fee:* $65. *Comprehensive fee:* $35,422 includes full-time tuition ($27,260), mandatory fees ($465), and room and board ($7697). *College room only:* $4095. Full-time tuition and fees vary according to course load. Room and board charges vary according to board plan, housing facility, and location. *Payment plan:* Deferred payment.
FRESHMAN FINANCIAL AID (Fall 2005, est.) 108 applied for aid; of those 72% were deemed to have need. 99% of freshmen with need received aid; of those 12% had need fully met. *Average percent of need met:* 86% (excluding resources awarded to replace EFC). *Average financial aid package:* $23,990 (excluding resources awarded to replace EFC). 14% of all full-time freshmen had no need and received non-need-based gift aid.
UNDERGRADUATE FINANCIAL AID (Fall 2005, est.) 640 applied for aid; of those 82% were deemed to have need. 99% of undergraduates with need received aid; of those 9% had need fully met. *Average percent of need met:* 85% (excluding resources awarded to replace EFC). *Average financial aid package:* $26,206 (excluding resources awarded to replace EFC). 11% of all full-time undergraduates had no need and received non-need-based gift aid.
GIFT AID (NEED-BASED) *Total amount:* $6,096,820 (18% federal, 14% state, 66% institutional, 2% external sources). *Receiving aid:* Freshmen: 54% (75); All full-time undergraduates: 66% (516). *Average award:* Freshmen: $9746; Undergraduates: $11,781. *Scholarships, grants, and awards:* Federal Pell, FSEOG, state, private, college/university gift aid from institutional funds.
GIFT AID (NON-NEED-BASED) *Total amount:* $462,460 (98% institutional, 2% external sources). *Average Award:* Freshmen: $2978; Undergraduates: $5032. *Scholarships, grants, and awards by category:* Creative Arts/Performance: 90 awards ($452,910 total): applied art and design, art/fine arts, cinema/film/broadcasting, creative writing, dance, music, performing arts, theater/drama. *Tuition waivers:* Full or partial for employees or children of employees.
LOANS *Student loans:* $6,512,066 (91% need-based, 9% non-need-based). 76% of past graduating class borrowed through all loan programs. *Average indebtedness per student:* $34,602. *Average need-based loan:* Freshmen: $3586; Undergraduates: $5431. *Parent loans:* $1,921,732 (71% need-based, 29% non-need-based). *Programs:* FFEL (Subsidized and Unsubsidized Stafford, PLUS), Perkins, college/university.
WORK-STUDY *Federal work-study:* Total amount: $355,537; 192 jobs averaging $1852. *State or other work-study/employment:* Total amount: $18,700 (100% need-based). 11 part-time jobs averaging $1700.
APPLYING FOR FINANCIAL AID *Required financial aid form:* FAFSA. *Financial aid deadline (priority):* 3/2. *Notification date:* Continuous beginning 4/1. Students must reply by 5/1 or within 3 weeks of notification.
CONTACT Ms. Bobbi Heuer, Director of Financial Aid, California Institute of the Arts, 24700 McBean Parkway, Valencia, CA 91355-2340, 661-253-7869 or toll-free 800-545-2787. *Fax:* 661-287-3816.

CALIFORNIA LUTHERAN UNIVERSITY
Thousand Oaks, CA

Tuition & fees: $23,370	Average undergraduate aid package: $17,890

ABOUT THE INSTITUTION Independent Lutheran, coed. Awards: bachelor's, master's, and doctoral degrees and post-bachelor's and post-master's certificates. 51 undergraduate majors. Total enrollment: 3,212. Undergraduates: 2,095. Freshmen: 385. Federal methodology is used as a basis for awarding need-based institutional aid.
UNDERGRADUATE EXPENSES for 2005–06 *Application fee:* $45. *Comprehensive fee:* $31,690 includes full-time tuition ($23,170), mandatory fees ($200), and room and board ($8320). *College room only:* $4330. Room and board charges vary according to board plan. *Part-time tuition:* $750 per unit. *Part-time fees:* $200 per year. *Payment plan:* Installment.
FRESHMAN FINANCIAL AID (Fall 2004) 350 applied for aid; of those 81% were deemed to have need. 100% of freshmen with need received aid; of those 52% had need fully met. *Average percent of need met:* 86% (excluding resources awarded to replace EFC). *Average financial aid package:* $19,776 (excluding resources awarded to replace EFC). 29% of all full-time freshmen had no need and received non-need-based gift aid.
UNDERGRADUATE FINANCIAL AID (Fall 2004) 1,330 applied for aid; of those 85% were deemed to have need. 100% of undergraduates with need received aid; of those 45% had need fully met. *Average percent of need met:* 87% (excluding resources awarded to replace EFC). *Average financial aid package:* $17,890 (excluding resources awarded to replace EFC). 23% of all full-time undergraduates had no need and received non-need-based gift aid.
GIFT AID (NEED-BASED) *Total amount:* $16,268,720 (6% federal, 18% state, 73% institutional, 3% external sources). *Receiving aid:* Freshmen: 71% (284); All full-time undergraduates: 64% (1,134). *Average award:* Freshmen: $16,616; Undergraduates: $13,751. *Scholarships, grants, and awards:* Federal Pell, FSEOG, state, private, college/university gift aid from institutional funds.
GIFT AID (NON-NEED-BASED) *Total amount:* $3,609,034 (96% institutional, 4% external sources). *Receiving aid:* Freshmen: 36% (144); Undergraduates: 28% (495). *Average Award:* Freshmen: $8484; Undergraduates: $8130. *Scholarships, grants, and awards by category:* Academic Interests/Achievement: 476 awards ($3,332,000 total): biological sciences, business, communication, computer science, education, English, foreign languages, general academic interests/achievements, humanities, international studies, mathematics, physical sciences, religion/biblical studies, social sciences. Creative Arts/Performance: 75 awards ($136,179 total): art/fine arts, creative writing, journalism/publications, music, performing arts, theater/drama. Special Achievements/Activities: 18 awards ($22,000 total): community service, general special achievements/activities, leadership, religious involvement. Special Characteristics: 127 awards ($190,500 total): adult students, children and siblings of alumni, children of faculty/staff, ethnic background, first-generation college students, international students, relatives of clergy, religious affiliation. *Tuition waivers:* Full or partial for employees or children of employees. *ROTC:* Army cooperative, Air Force cooperative.
LOANS *Student loans:* $8,463,194 (88% need-based, 12% non-need-based). 86% of past graduating class borrowed through all loan programs. *Average indebtedness per student:* $21,140. *Average need-based loan:* Freshmen: $2099; Undergraduates: $3593. *Parent loans:* $9,973,881 (29% need-based, 71% non-need-based). *Programs:* FFEL (Subsidized and Unsubsidized Stafford, PLUS), Perkins.
WORK-STUDY *Federal work-study:* Total amount: $758,319; 527 jobs averaging $2000. *State or other work-study/employment:* Total amount: $324,318 (100% non-need-based). 200 part-time jobs averaging $2000.
APPLYING FOR FINANCIAL AID *Required financial aid forms:* FAFSA, loan application. *Financial aid deadline (priority):* 3/2. *Notification date:* Continuous beginning 2/25. Students must reply by 5/1 or within 2 weeks of notification.
CONTACT Matthew Ward, Dean, Undergraduate Enrollment, California Lutheran University, 60 West Olsen Road, Thousand Oaks, CA 91360-2787, 805-493-3115 or toll-free 877-258-3678. *Fax:* 805-493-3114.

CALIFORNIA MARITIME ACADEMY
Vallejo, CA

CONTACT Financial Aid Manager, California Maritime Academy, 200 Maritime Academy Drive, Vallejo, CA 94590-0644, 707-654-1275 or toll-free 800-561-1945. *Fax:* 707-654-1007.

CALIFORNIA POLYTECHNIC STATE UNIVERSITY, SAN LUIS OBISPO
San Luis Obispo, CA

Tuition & fees (CA res): $4245	Average undergraduate aid package: $7516

ABOUT THE INSTITUTION State-supported, coed. Awards: bachelor's and master's degrees. 60 undergraduate majors. Total enrollment: 18,475. Undergraduates: 17,488. Freshmen: 3,372. Federal methodology is used as a basis for awarding need-based institutional aid.
UNDERGRADUATE EXPENSES for 2005–06 *Application fee:* $55. *Tuition, state resident:* full-time $0. *Tuition, nonresident:* full-time $10,170; part-time $226 per unit. *Required fees:* full-time $4245; $2853 per year part-time. Full-time tuition and fees vary according to course load and program. Part-time tuition and fees vary according to course load and program. *College room and board:* $8145; *room only:* $4583. Room and board charges vary according to board plan and housing facility. *Payment plan:* Installment.
FRESHMAN FINANCIAL AID (Fall 2004) 1942 applied for aid; of those 51% were deemed to have need. 91% of freshmen with need received aid; of those 5% had need fully met. *Average percent of need met:* 64% (excluding resources awarded to replace EFC). *Average financial aid package:* $6588 (excluding resources awarded to replace EFC).
UNDERGRADUATE FINANCIAL AID (Fall 2004) 8,167 applied for aid; of those 70% were deemed to have need. 95% of undergraduates with need received aid; of those 5% had need fully met. *Average percent of need met:* 67% (excluding resources awarded to replace EFC). *Average financial aid package:* $7516 (excluding resources awarded to replace EFC).
GIFT AID (NEED-BASED) *Total amount:* $28,547,998 (33% federal, 42% state, 15% institutional, 10% external sources). *Receiving aid:* Freshmen: 25% (715); All full-time undergraduates: 25% (3,939). *Average award:* Freshmen: $1459; Undergraduates: $1711. *Scholarships, grants, and awards:* Federal Pell, FSEOG, state, private, college/university gift aid from institutional funds.
GIFT AID (NON-NEED-BASED) *Receiving aid:* Freshmen: 9% (266); Undergraduates: 4% (650). *Scholarships, grants, and awards by category: Academic Interests/Achievement:* agriculture, architecture, biological sciences, business, communication, computer science, education, engineering/technologies, English, foreign languages, general academic interests/achievements, health fields, home economics, humanities, international studies, library science, mathematics, military science, physical sciences, social sciences. *Creative Arts/Performance:* applied art and design, art/fine arts, cinema/film/broadcasting, creative writing, dance, debating, general creative arts/performance, journalism/publications, music, performing arts, theater/drama. *Special Achievements/Activities:* community service, leadership, rodeo. *Special Characteristics:* general special characteristics. *Tuition waivers:* Full or partial for employees or children of employees. *ROTC:* Army.
LOANS *Student loans:* $49,329,377 (40% need-based, 60% non-need-based). 35% of past graduating class borrowed through all loan programs. *Average indebtedness per student:* $13,788. *Average need-based loan:* Freshmen: $2466; Undergraduates: $3901. *Parent loans:* $15,956,024 (100% non-need-based). *Programs:* FFEL (Subsidized and Unsubsidized Stafford, PLUS), Perkins, college/university, alternative loans.
WORK-STUDY *Federal work-study:* Total amount: $686,519; jobs available.
ATHLETIC AWARDS *Total amount:* $2,972,658 (100% need-based).
APPLYING FOR FINANCIAL AID *Required financial aid forms:* FAFSA, institution's own form. *Financial aid deadline:* 6/30 (priority: 3/1). *Notification date:* Continuous beginning 4/15. Students must reply within 8 weeks of notification.
CONTACT Lois Kelly, Director, Financial Aid, California Polytechnic State University, San Luis Obispo, Cal Poly State University, San Luis Obispo, CA 93407, 805-756-5993. *Fax:* 805-756-7243. *E-mail:* lkelly@calpoly.edu.

CALIFORNIA STATE POLYTECHNIC UNIVERSITY, POMONA
Pomona, CA

CONTACT Diana Minor, Associate Director of Financial Aid, California State Polytechnic University, Pomona, 3801 West Temple Avenue, Pomona, CA 91768-2557, 909-869-3704. *Fax:* 909-869-4757. *E-mail:* dyminor@csupomona.edu.

CALIFORNIA STATE UNIVERSITY, BAKERSFIELD
Bakersfield, CA

Tuition & fees (CA res): $2959   **Average undergraduate aid package:** $7007

California State University, Chico

ABOUT THE INSTITUTION State-supported, coed. Awards: bachelor's and master's degrees. 30 undergraduate majors. Total enrollment: 7,549. Undergraduates: 5,960. Freshmen: 782. Federal methodology is used as a basis for awarding need-based institutional aid.
UNDERGRADUATE EXPENSES for 2005–06 *Application fee:* $55. *Tuition, state resident:* full-time $0. *Tuition, nonresident:* full-time $6780; part-time $226 per unit. *Required fees:* full-time $2959; $579 per term part-time. *College room and board:* $5946.
FRESHMAN FINANCIAL AID (Fall 2004) 616 applied for aid; of those 82% were deemed to have need. 95% of freshmen with need received aid; of those 7% had need fully met. *Average percent of need met:* 79% (excluding resources awarded to replace EFC). *Average financial aid package:* $6820 (excluding resources awarded to replace EFC). 8% of all full-time freshmen had no need and received non-need-based gift aid.
UNDERGRADUATE FINANCIAL AID (Fall 2004) 4,080 applied for aid; of those 88% were deemed to have need. 95% of undergraduates with need received aid; of those 10% had need fully met. *Average percent of need met:* 81% (excluding resources awarded to replace EFC). *Average financial aid package:* $7007 (excluding resources awarded to replace EFC). 4% of all full-time undergraduates had no need and received non-need-based gift aid.
GIFT AID (NEED-BASED) *Total amount:* $15,647,972 (49% federal, 51% state). *Receiving aid:* Freshmen: 54% (421); All full-time undergraduates: 50% (2,835). *Average award:* Freshmen: $6124; Undergraduates: $5336. *Scholarships, grants, and awards:* Federal Pell, FSEOG, state, private, college/university gift aid from institutional funds, Federal Nursing.
GIFT AID (NON-NEED-BASED) *Total amount:* $1,181,040 (55% institutional, 45% external sources). *Receiving aid:* Freshmen: 17% (134); Undergraduates: 7% (418). *Average Award:* Freshmen: $1514; Undergraduates: $1702. *Scholarships, grants, and awards by category: Academic Interests/Achievement:* 605 awards ($915,835 total): architecture, biological sciences, business, communication, education, general academic interests/achievements, health fields, mathematics, physical sciences, social sciences. *Creative Arts/Performance:* 75 awards ($46,168 total): art/fine arts, dance, music, theater/drama. *Special Achievements/Activities:* 21 awards ($29,350 total): community service, general special achievements/activities. *Special Characteristics:* 165 awards ($199,687 total): adult students, children of faculty/staff, children of union members/company employees, first-generation college students, general special characteristics, handicapped students.
LOANS *Student loans:* $9,330,450 (79% need-based, 21% non-need-based). 12% of past graduating class borrowed through all loan programs. *Average indebtedness per student:* $4144. *Average need-based loan:* Freshmen: $2293; Undergraduates: $3726. *Parent loans:* $196,100 (100% non-need-based). *Programs:* Federal Direct (Subsidized and Unsubsidized Stafford, PLUS), Perkins, Federal Nursing, college/university.
WORK-STUDY *Federal work-study:* Total amount: $323,940; 177 jobs averaging $1942.
ATHLETIC AWARDS *Total amount:* $568,920 (100% non-need-based).
APPLYING FOR FINANCIAL AID *Required financial aid form:* FAFSA. *Financial aid deadline (priority):* 3/2. *Notification date:* 4/1. Students must reply within 3 weeks of notification.
CONTACT Mr. John Casdorph, Associate Director of Financial Aid, California State University, Bakersfield, 9001 Stockdale Highway, Bakersfield, CA 93311-1099, 661-664-3265 or toll-free 800-788-2782 (in-state). *Fax:* 661-665-6800. *E-mail:* jcasdorph@csub.edu.

CALIFORNIA STATE UNIVERSITY CHANNEL ISLANDS
Camarillo, CA

CONTACT Financial Aid Office, California State University Channel Islands, One University Drive, Camarillo, CA 93012, 805-437-8979.

CALIFORNIA STATE UNIVERSITY, CHICO
Chico, CA

Tuition & fees (CA res): $3370   **Average undergraduate aid package:** $7875

ABOUT THE INSTITUTION State-supported, coed. Awards: bachelor's and master's degrees and post-bachelor's and post-master's certificates. 120 undergraduate

California State University, Chico

majors. Total enrollment: 15,919. Undergraduates: 14,526. Freshmen: 2,335. Federal methodology is used as a basis for awarding need-based institutional aid.
UNDERGRADUATE EXPENSES for 2005–06 *Application fee:* $55. *Tuition, state resident:* full-time $0. *Tuition, nonresident:* full-time $12,690; part-time $339 per unit. *Required fees:* full-time $3370; $425 per term part-time. Part-time tuition and fees vary according to course load. *College room and board:* $7993; *room only:* $5550. Room and board charges vary according to board plan and housing facility. *Payment plans:* Installment, deferred payment.
FRESHMAN FINANCIAL AID (Fall 2005, est.) 1337 applied for aid; of those 95% were deemed to have need. 83% of freshmen with need received aid; of those 10% had need fully met. *Average percent of need met:* 65% (excluding resources awarded to replace EFC). *Average financial aid package:* $6032 (excluding resources awarded to replace EFC). 1% of all full-time freshmen had no need and received non-need-based gift aid.
UNDERGRADUATE FINANCIAL AID (Fall 2005, est.) 7,361 applied for aid; of those 97% were deemed to have need. 93% of undergraduates with need received aid; of those 13% had need fully met. *Average percent of need met:* 78% (excluding resources awarded to replace EFC). *Average financial aid package:* $7875 (excluding resources awarded to replace EFC). 1% of all full-time undergraduates had no need and received non-need-based gift aid.
GIFT AID (NEED-BASED) *Total amount:* $29,684,709 (47% federal, 53% state). *Receiving aid:* Freshmen: 30% (665); All full-time undergraduates: 35% (4,476). *Average award:* Freshmen: $5345; Undergraduates: $5400. *Scholarships, grants, and awards:* Federal Pell, FSEOG, state, private, college/university gift aid from institutional funds, United Negro College Fund.
GIFT AID (NON-NEED-BASED) *Total amount:* $2,261,842 (1% federal, 1% state, 42% institutional, 56% external sources). *Receiving aid:* Freshmen: 12% (256); Undergraduates: 19% (2,480). *Average Award:* Freshmen: $148; Undergraduates: $1245. *Scholarships, grants, and awards by category:* Academic Interests/Achievement: agriculture, area/ethnic studies, biological sciences, business, communication, computer science, education, engineering/technologies, English, foreign languages, general academic interests/achievements, health fields, humanities, international studies, mathematics, physical sciences, social sciences. Creative Arts/Performance: applied art and design, art/fine arts, cinema/film/broadcasting, creative writing, dance, debating, general creative arts/performance, journalism/publications, music, performing arts, theater/drama. Special Achievements/Activities: community service, general special achievements/activities, hobbies/interests, leadership, memberships. Special Characteristics: adult students, children of faculty/staff, ethnic background, first-generation college students, handicapped students, international students, local/state students, married students, members of minority groups, out-of-state students. *Tuition waivers:* Full or partial for employees or children of employees, senior citizens.
LOANS *Student loans:* $51,706,920 (53% need-based, 47% non-need-based). *Average need-based loan:* Freshmen: $2796; Undergraduates: $4155. *Parent loans:* $3,199,393 (100% non-need-based). *Programs:* Federal Direct (Subsidized and Unsubsidized Stafford, PLUS), Perkins, college/university.
WORK-STUDY *Federal work-study:* Total amount: $5,016,345; 750 jobs averaging $2500.
ATHLETIC AWARDS Total amount: $362,362 (70% need-based, 30% non-need-based).
APPLYING FOR FINANCIAL AID *Required financial aid forms:* FAFSA, scholarship application form. *Financial aid deadline:* Continuous. *Notification date:* Continuous beginning 2/15.
CONTACT Yvonne Lydon, Administrative Support Coordinator, California State University, Chico, Financial Aid Office, Chico, CA 95929-0705, 530-898-6451 or toll-free 800-542-4426. Fax: 530-898-6883. E-mail: ylydon@csuchico.edu.

CALIFORNIA STATE UNIVERSITY, DOMINGUEZ HILLS
Carson, CA

Tuition & fees (CA res): $3618   **Average undergraduate aid package: $8239**

ABOUT THE INSTITUTION State-supported, coed. Awards: bachelor's and master's degrees. 70 undergraduate majors. Total enrollment: 12,357. Undergraduates: 8,943. Freshmen: 786. Federal methodology is used as a basis for awarding need-based institutional aid.
UNDERGRADUATE EXPENSES for 2006–07 *Application fee:* $55. *Tuition, state resident:* full-time $0. *Tuition, nonresident:* part-time $339 per unit. *College room and board: room only:* $5850.
FRESHMAN FINANCIAL AID (Fall 2005, est.) 542 applied for aid; of those 94% were deemed to have need. 100% of freshmen with need received aid; of those 5% had need fully met. *Average percent of need met:* 71% (excluding resources awarded to replace EFC). *Average financial aid package:* $7488 (excluding resources awarded to replace EFC). 2% of all full-time freshmen had no need and received non-need-based gift aid.
UNDERGRADUATE FINANCIAL AID (Fall 2005, est.) 4,730 applied for aid; of those 94% were deemed to have need. 98% of undergraduates with need received aid; of those 5% had need fully met. *Average percent of need met:* 67% (excluding resources awarded to replace EFC). *Average financial aid package:* $8239 (excluding resources awarded to replace EFC). 1% of all full-time undergraduates had no need and received non-need-based gift aid.
GIFT AID (NEED-BASED) *Total amount:* $22,652,459 (48% federal, 50% state, 2% external sources). *Receiving aid:* Freshmen: 71% (500); All full-time undergraduates: 82% (4,355). *Average award:* Freshmen: $5637; Undergraduates: $4975. *Scholarships, grants, and awards:* Federal Pell, FSEOG, state, private, college/university gift aid from institutional funds.
GIFT AID (NON-NEED-BASED) *Total amount:* $674,996 (46% federal, 46% state, 4% institutional, 4% external sources). *Receiving aid:* Freshmen: 11% (79); Undergraduates: 6% (336). *Average Award:* Freshmen: $3403; Undergraduates: $2669. *Scholarships, grants, and awards by category:* Academic Interests/Achievement: 505 awards ($873,420 total): general academic interests/achievements. Special Characteristics: 66 awards ($106,588 total): ethnic background, members of minority groups. *ROTC:* Army cooperative, Air Force cooperative.
LOANS *Student loans:* $13,416,256 (90% need-based, 10% non-need-based). 32% of past graduating class borrowed through all loan programs. *Average indebtedness per student:* $15,232. *Average need-based loan:* Freshmen: $2465; Undergraduates: $4258. *Parent loans:* $43,450 (70% need-based, 30% non-need-based). *Programs:* Federal Direct (Subsidized and Unsubsidized Stafford), FFEL (PLUS), Perkins.
WORK-STUDY *Federal work-study:* Total amount: $314,746; 240 jobs averaging $1312.
ATHLETIC AWARDS Total amount: $230,604 (78% need-based, 22% non-need-based).
APPLYING FOR FINANCIAL AID *Required financial aid forms:* FAFSA, institution's own form, state aid form. *Financial aid deadline:* 4/15 (priority: 3/2). *Notification date:* Continuous. Students must reply within 4 weeks of notification.
CONTACT Mrs. Delores S. Lee, Director of Financial Aid, California State University, Dominguez Hills, 1000 East Victoria Street, Carson, CA 90747-0001, 310-243-3691. E-mail: dslee@csudh.edu.

CALIFORNIA STATE UNIVERSITY, EAST BAY
Hayward, CA

Tuition & fees (CA res): $2916   **Average undergraduate aid package: $7952**

ABOUT THE INSTITUTION State-supported, coed. Awards: bachelor's and master's degrees and post-bachelor's certificates. 91 undergraduate majors. Total enrollment: 12,535. Undergraduates: 9,129. Freshmen: 696. Federal methodology is used as a basis for awarding need-based institutional aid.
UNDERGRADUATE EXPENSES for 2005–06 *Application fee:* $55. *Tuition, state resident:* full-time $0. *Tuition, nonresident:* full-time $10,170. *College room and board: room only:* $6759.
FRESHMAN FINANCIAL AID (Fall 2005, est.) 275 applied for aid; of those 90% were deemed to have need. 97% of freshmen with need received aid; of those 11% had need fully met. *Average percent of need met:* 68% (excluding resources awarded to replace EFC). *Average financial aid package:* $7141 (excluding resources awarded to replace EFC).
UNDERGRADUATE FINANCIAL AID (Fall 2005, est.) 3,277 applied for aid; of those 99% were deemed to have need. 99% of undergraduates with need received aid; of those 9% had need fully met. *Average percent of need met:* 64% (excluding resources awarded to replace EFC). *Average financial aid package:* $7952 (excluding resources awarded to replace EFC).
GIFT AID (NEED-BASED) *Total amount:* $17,658,320 (48% federal, 52% state). *Receiving aid:* Freshmen: 30% (209); All full-time undergraduates: 36% (2,622).

California State University, Fullerton

Average award: Freshmen: $7128; Undergraduates: $6301. *Scholarships, grants, and awards:* Federal Pell, FSEOG, state, private, college/university gift aid from institutional funds.
GIFT AID (NON-NEED-BASED) *Scholarships, grants, and awards by category: Academic Interests/Achievement:* general academic interests/achievements. *Creative Arts/Performance:* 5 awards ($4100 total): music.
LOANS *Student loans:* $14,554,207 (81% need-based, 19% non-need-based). 37% of past graduating class borrowed through all loan programs. *Average indebtedness per student:* $12,312. *Average need-based loan:* Freshmen: $2668; Undergraduates: $5900. *Parent loans:* $897,275 (20% need-based, 80% non-need-based). *Programs:* FFEL (Subsidized and Unsubsidized Stafford, PLUS), Perkins, college/university.
WORK-STUDY *Federal work-study:* Total amount: $573,803; jobs available.
APPLYING FOR FINANCIAL AID *Required financial aid form:* FAFSA. *Financial aid deadline (priority):* 3/2. *Notification date:* Continuous beginning 5/31. Students must reply within 3 weeks of notification.
CONTACT Office of Financial Aid, California State University, East Bay, 25800 Carlos Bee Boulevard, Hayward, CA 94542-3028, 510-885-2784. *Fax:* 510-885-2161. *E-mail:* oskes@csueastbay.edu.

CALIFORNIA STATE UNIVERSITY, FRESNO
Fresno, CA

Tuition & fees (CA res): $3037   **Average undergraduate aid package:** $5077

ABOUT THE INSTITUTION State-supported, coed. Awards: bachelor's, master's, and doctoral degrees. 87 undergraduate majors. Total enrollment: 20,371. Undergraduates: 17,428. Freshmen: 2,438. Federal methodology is used as a basis for awarding need-based institutional aid.
UNDERGRADUATE EXPENSES for 2006–07 *Application fee:* $55. *Tuition, state resident:* full-time $0. *Tuition, nonresident:* full-time $13,207; part-time $339 per unit. *Required fees:* full-time $3037; $990 per term part-time. *College room and board:* $7344.
FRESHMAN FINANCIAL AID (Fall 2005, est.) 1330 applied for aid; of those 84% were deemed to have need. 95% of freshmen with need received aid; of those 32% had need fully met. *Average percent of need met:* 25% (excluding resources awarded to replace EFC). *Average financial aid package:* $4384 (excluding resources awarded to replace EFC). 2% of all full-time freshmen had no need and received non-need-based gift aid.
UNDERGRADUATE FINANCIAL AID (Fall 2005, est.) 10,626 applied for aid; of those 91% were deemed to have need. 94% of undergraduates with need received aid; of those 42% had need fully met. *Average percent of need met:* 39% (excluding resources awarded to replace EFC). *Average financial aid package:* $5077 (excluding resources awarded to replace EFC). 1% of all full-time undergraduates had no need and received non-need-based gift aid.
GIFT AID (NEED-BASED) *Total amount:* $46,559,210 (48% federal, 52% state). *Receiving aid:* Freshmen: 35% (810); All full-time undergraduates: 47% (7,023). *Average award:* Freshmen: $4387; Undergraduates: $4631. *Scholarships, grants, and awards:* Federal Pell, FSEOG, state, private, college/university gift aid from institutional funds.
GIFT AID (NON-NEED-BASED) *Total amount:* $4,479,956 (51% institutional, 49% external sources). *Receiving aid:* Freshmen: 11% (256); Undergraduates: 11% (1,582). *Average Award:* Freshmen: $1513; Undergraduates: $2101. *Scholarships, grants, and awards by category: Academic Interests/Achievement:* 1,255 awards ($2,169,367 total): agriculture, area/ethnic studies, biological sciences, business, communication, education, engineering/technologies, English, foreign languages, general academic interests/achievements, health fields, humanities, mathematics, social sciences. *Creative Arts/Performance:* 233 awards ($181,463 total): art/fine arts, journalism/publications, music, theater/drama. *Special Achievements/Activities:* 59 awards ($75,000 total): community service. *Special Characteristics:* 7 awards ($7650 total): handicapped students, local/state students. *ROTC:* Army, Air Force.
LOANS *Student loans:* $24,176,607 (66% need-based, 34% non-need-based). 43% of past graduating class borrowed through all loan programs. *Average indebtedness per student:* $10,958. *Average need-based loan:* Freshmen: $2205; Undergraduates: $3473. *Parent loans:* $1,482,589 (100% non-need-based). *Programs:* FFEL (Subsidized and Unsubsidized Stafford, PLUS), Perkins, Federal Nursing, college/university.
WORK-STUDY *Federal work-study:* Total amount: $988,050; 312 jobs averaging $3140.
ATHLETIC AWARDS *Total amount:* $2,943,110 (100% non-need-based).
APPLYING FOR FINANCIAL AID *Required financial aid form:* FAFSA. *Financial aid deadline (priority):* 3/1. *Notification date:* Continuous beginning 4/1. Students must reply within 3 weeks of notification.
CONTACT Financial Aid Office, California State University, Fresno, 5150 North Maple Avenue, Mail Stop JA 64, Fresno, CA 93740, 559-278-2182. *Fax:* 559-278-4833.

CALIFORNIA STATE UNIVERSITY, FULLERTON
Fullerton, CA

Tuition & fees (CA res): $2990   **Average undergraduate aid package:** $6897

ABOUT THE INSTITUTION State-supported, coed. Awards: bachelor's and master's degrees. 88 undergraduate majors. Total enrollment: 35,040. Undergraduates: 29,462. Freshmen: 3,943. Federal methodology is used as a basis for awarding need-based institutional aid.
UNDERGRADUATE EXPENSES for 2005–06 *Application fee:* $55. *Tuition, state resident:* full-time $0. *Tuition, nonresident:* full-time $10,170; part-time $339 per unit. *Required fees:* full-time $2990; $967 per term part-time. Full-time tuition and fees vary according to course load. Part-time tuition and fees vary according to course load. *College room and board: room only:* $4504. *Payment plans:* Installment, deferred payment.
FRESHMAN FINANCIAL AID (Fall 2005, est.) 1767 applied for aid; of those 75% were deemed to have need. 75% of freshmen with need received aid; of those 2% had need fully met. *Average percent of need met:* 60% (excluding resources awarded to replace EFC). *Average financial aid package:* $6561 (excluding resources awarded to replace EFC). 7% of all full-time freshmen had no need and received non-need-based gift aid.
UNDERGRADUATE FINANCIAL AID (Fall 2005, est.) 8,275 applied for aid; of those 82% were deemed to have need. 76% of undergraduates with need received aid; of those 2% had need fully met. *Average percent of need met:* 61% (excluding resources awarded to replace EFC). *Average financial aid package:* $6897 (excluding resources awarded to replace EFC). 5% of all full-time undergraduates had no need and received non-need-based gift aid.
GIFT AID (NEED-BASED) *Total amount:* $48,541,849 (44% federal, 53% state, 1% institutional, 2% external sources). *Receiving aid:* Freshmen: 25% (883); All full-time undergraduates: 21% (4,129). *Average award:* Freshmen: $6144; Undergraduates: $5727. *Scholarships, grants, and awards:* Federal Pell, FSEOG, state, private, college/university gift aid from institutional funds.
GIFT AID (NON-NEED-BASED) *Total amount:* $835,338 (21% institutional, 79% external sources). *Average Award:* Freshmen: $3757; Undergraduates: $4525. *Scholarships, grants, and awards by category: Academic Interests/Achievement:* 1,558 awards ($2,796,149 total): business, communication, engineering/technologies, general academic interests/achievements, humanities, mathematics, military science, social sciences. *Creative Arts/Performance:* 83 awards ($41,500 total): art/fine arts, music. *Special Achievements/Activities:* 57 awards ($59,000 total): general special achievements/activities, leadership. *Special Characteristics:* 41 awards ($208,674 total): general special characteristics. *Tuition waivers:* Full or partial for employees or children of employees, senior citizens. *ROTC:* Army.
LOANS *Student loans:* $39,111,571 (62% need-based, 38% non-need-based). 37% of past graduating class borrowed through all loan programs. *Average indebtedness per student:* $14,071. *Average need-based loan:* Freshmen: $2756; Undergraduates: $4099. *Parent loans:* $2,416,848 (100% non-need-based). *Programs:* FFEL (Subsidized and Unsubsidized Stafford, PLUS), Perkins, college/university.
WORK-STUDY *Federal work-study:* Total amount: $1,258,409; 1,552 jobs averaging $3062.
ATHLETIC AWARDS *Total amount:* $1,883,373 (10% need-based, 90% non-need-based).
APPLYING FOR FINANCIAL AID *Required financial aid form:* FAFSA. *Financial aid deadline (priority):* 3/2. *Notification date:* Continuous beginning 4/2. Students must reply within 3 weeks of notification.
CONTACT Ms. Deborah S. McCracken, Director of Financial Aid, California State University, Fullerton, 800 North State College Boulevard, Fullerton, CA 92831-3599, 714-278-3128. *Fax:* 714-278-1328. *E-mail:* dmccracken@fullerton.edu.

California State University, Hayward

CALIFORNIA STATE UNIVERSITY, HAYWARD
Hayward, CA

See California State University, East Bay.

CALIFORNIA STATE UNIVERSITY, LONG BEACH
Long Beach, CA

CONTACT Office of Financial Aid, California State University, Long Beach, 1250 Bellflower Boulevard, Long Beach, CA 90840, 562-985-8403.

CALIFORNIA STATE UNIVERSITY, LOS ANGELES
Los Angeles, CA

CONTACT Lindy W. Fong, Director, Center for Student Financial Aid, California State University, Los Angeles, 5151 State University Drive, Los Angeles, CA 90032, 323-343-3247. *Fax:* 323-343-3166. *E-mail:* lfong@cslanet.calstatela.edu.

CALIFORNIA STATE UNIVERSITY, MONTEREY BAY
Seaside, CA

CONTACT Campus Service Center, California State University, Monterey Bay, 100 Campus Center, Seaside, CA 93955-8001, 831-582-4074. *Fax:* 831-582-3782.

CALIFORNIA STATE UNIVERSITY, NORTHRIDGE
Northridge, CA

CONTACT Kathryn J. Anderson, Director of Financial Aid and Scholarships, California State University, Northridge, 18111 Nordhoff Street, Northridge, CA 91330-8307, 818-677-3827. *Fax:* 818-677-6787. *E-mail:* kathryn.anderson@csun.edu.

CALIFORNIA STATE UNIVERSITY, SACRAMENTO
Sacramento, CA

Tuition & fees: N/R   Average undergraduate aid package: $6753

ABOUT THE INSTITUTION State-supported, coed. Awards: bachelor's, master's, and doctoral degrees. 84 undergraduate majors. Total enrollment: 27,932. Undergraduates: 23,028. Freshmen: 2,518. Federal methodology is used as a basis for awarding need-based institutional aid.
UNDERGRADUATE EXPENSES for 2006–07 *Application fee:* $55. *Tuition, nonresident:* full-time $13,242; part-time $339 per unit. *Required fees:* full-time $3624; $276 per term part-time. *College room and board:* $7458.
FRESHMAN FINANCIAL AID (Fall 2005, est.) 1507 applied for aid; of those 76% were deemed to have need. 91% of freshmen with need received aid; of those 5% had need fully met. *Average percent of need met:* 67% (excluding resources awarded to replace EFC). *Average financial aid package:* $8626 (excluding resources awarded to replace EFC). 5% of all full-time freshmen had no need and received non-need-based gift aid.
UNDERGRADUATE FINANCIAL AID (Fall 2005, est.) 10,629 applied for aid; of those 85% were deemed to have need. 93% of undergraduates with need received aid; of those 9% had need fully met. *Average percent of need met:* 67% (excluding resources awarded to replace EFC). *Average financial aid package:* $6753 (excluding resources awarded to replace EFC). 5% of all full-time undergraduates had no need and received non-need-based gift aid.
GIFT AID (NEED-BASED) *Total amount:* $45,116,481 (45% federal, 51% state, 1% institutional, 3% external sources). *Receiving aid:* Freshmen: 44% (905); All full-time undergraduates: 38% (6,674). *Average award:* Freshmen: $2326; Undergraduates: $2216. *Scholarships, grants, and awards:* Federal Pell, FSEOG, state, private, college/university gift aid from institutional funds, Federal Nursing.
GIFT AID (NON-NEED-BASED) *Total amount:* $21,537 (100% institutional). *Receiving aid:* Undergraduates: 10. *Average Award:* Freshmen: $5675; Undergraduates: $5960. *Scholarships, grants, and awards by category: Academic Interests/Achievement:* general academic interests/achievements. *Creative Arts/Performance:* general creative arts/performance. *Special Achievements/Activities:* general special achievements/activities. *Special Characteristics:* general special characteristics. *ROTC:* Army cooperative, Air Force.
LOANS *Student loans:* $40,313,362 (61% need-based, 39% non-need-based). 40% of past graduating class borrowed through all loan programs. *Average indebtedness per student:* $10,868. *Average need-based loan:* Freshmen: $2461; Undergraduates: $4018. *Parent loans:* $8,535,607 (100% non-need-based). *Programs:* Federal Direct (Subsidized and Unsubsidized Stafford), FFEL (PLUS), Perkins, Federal Nursing, state, college/university.
WORK-STUDY *Federal work-study:* Total amount: $1,039,658; 431 jobs averaging $2412.
ATHLETIC AWARDS Total amount: $2,304,503 (100% need-based).
APPLYING FOR FINANCIAL AID *Required financial aid form:* FAFSA. *Financial aid deadline (priority):* 3/2. *Notification date:* 4/1. Students must reply within 2 weeks of notification.
CONTACT Linda Joy Clemons, Financial Aid Director, California State University, Sacramento, 6000 J Street, Sacramento, CA 95819-6044, 916-278-6554. *Fax:* 916-278-6082. *E-mail:* ljclemons@csus.edu.

CALIFORNIA STATE UNIVERSITY, SAN BERNARDINO
San Bernardino, CA

ABOUT THE INSTITUTION State-supported, coed. Awards: bachelor's and master's degrees. 51 undergraduate majors. Total enrollment: 16,431. Undergraduates: 12,464. Freshmen: 1,692.
GIFT AID (NEED-BASED) *Scholarships, grants, and awards:* Federal Pell, FSEOG, state, college/university gift aid from institutional funds.
GIFT AID (NON-NEED-BASED) *Scholarships, grants, and awards by category: Academic Interests/Achievement:* biological sciences, business, computer science, education, foreign languages, general academic interests/achievements, health fields. *Creative Arts/Performance:* art/fine arts, music, theater/drama. *Special Achievements/Activities:* community service, general special achievements/activities, hobbies/interests. *Special Characteristics:* children of public servants, children with a deceased or disabled parent, ethnic background, first-generation college students, handicapped students.
LOANS *Programs:* Federal Direct (Subsidized and Unsubsidized Stafford), FFEL (PLUS), Perkins.
APPLYING FOR FINANCIAL AID *Required financial aid forms:* FAFSA, state aid form.
CONTACT Lois E. Madsen, Director of Financial Aid, California State University, San Bernardino, 5500 University Parkway, San Bernardino, CA 92407-2397, 909-880-5223. *Fax:* 909-880-7024. *E-mail:* lemadsen@csusb.edu.

CALIFORNIA STATE UNIVERSITY, SAN MARCOS
San Marcos, CA

Tuition & fees (CA res): $3062   Average undergraduate aid package: $6946

ABOUT THE INSTITUTION State-supported, coed. Awards: bachelor's and master's degrees. 23 undergraduate majors. Total enrollment: 6,956. Undergraduates: 6,327. Freshmen: 804. Federal methodology is used as a basis for awarding need-based institutional aid.
UNDERGRADUATE EXPENSES for 2005–06 *Application fee:* $55. *Tuition, state resident:* full-time $0. *Tuition, nonresident:* full-time $8136; part-time $339 per credit hour. Part-time tuition and fees vary according to course load. *College room and board: room only:* $7470. Room and board charges vary according to housing facility.
FRESHMAN FINANCIAL AID (Fall 2004) 306 applied for aid; of those 71% were deemed to have need. 84% of freshmen with need received aid. *Average financial aid package:* $5851 (excluding resources awarded to replace EFC).

UNDERGRADUATE FINANCIAL AID (Fall 2004) 2,081 applied for aid; of those 83% were deemed to have need. 91% of undergraduates with need received aid. *Average financial aid package:* $6946 (excluding resources awarded to replace EFC).
GIFT AID (NEED-BASED) *Total amount:* $9,407,763 (43% federal, 50% state, 6% institutional, 1% external sources). *Receiving aid:* Freshmen: 33% (179); All full-time undergraduates: 40% (1,575). *Average award:* Undergraduates: $3831. *Scholarships, grants, and awards:* Federal Pell, FSEOG, state, private, college/university gift aid from institutional funds.
GIFT AID (NON-NEED-BASED) *Receiving aid:* Freshmen: 2; Undergraduates: 10. *Scholarships, grants, and awards by category:* Academic Interests/Achievement: general academic interests/achievements, mathematics. *Tuition waivers:* Full or partial for employees or children of employees, senior citizens. *ROTC:* Army cooperative, Naval cooperative, Air Force cooperative.
LOANS *Student loans:* $10,203,967 (57% need-based, 43% non-need-based). 40% of past graduating class borrowed through all loan programs. *Average indebtedness per student:* $13,112. *Average need-based loan:* Undergraduates: $4099. *Parent loans:* $317,996 (100% non-need-based). *Programs:* Federal Direct (Subsidized and Unsubsidized Stafford, PLUS), Perkins, college/university.
WORK-STUDY *Federal work-study:* Total amount: $286,372; 193 jobs averaging $2035. *State or other work-study/employment:* 18 part-time jobs averaging $821.
ATHLETIC AWARDS *Total amount:* $121,239 (100% non-need-based).
APPLYING FOR FINANCIAL AID *Required financial aid form:* FAFSA. *Financial aid deadline (priority):* 3/2. *Notification date:* 4/15.
CONTACT Addalou Davis, Director of Financial Aid, California State University, San Marcos, 333 South Twin Oaks Valley Road, San Marcos, CA 92096-0001, 760-750-4852. *Fax:* 760-750-3047. *E-mail:* finaid@csusm.edu.

CALIFORNIA STATE UNIVERSITY, STANISLAUS
Turlock, CA

Tuition & fees (CA res): $3030   Average undergraduate aid package: $6897

ABOUT THE INSTITUTION State-supported, coed. Awards: bachelor's and master's degrees. 35 undergraduate majors. Total enrollment: 8,137. Undergraduates: 6,483. Freshmen: 870. Federal methodology is used as a basis for awarding need-based institutional aid.
UNDERGRADUATE EXPENSES for 2005–06 *Application fee:* $55. *Tuition, state resident:* full-time $0. *Tuition, nonresident:* full-time $10,170; part-time $339 per unit. *Required fees:* full-time $3030; $855.50 per term part-time. *College room and board:* $8253; *room only:* $5612. Room and board charges vary according to board plan and housing facility. *Payment plans:* Installment, deferred payment.
FRESHMAN FINANCIAL AID (Fall 2005, est.) 678 applied for aid; of those 71% were deemed to have need. 96% of freshmen with need received aid; of those 2% had need fully met. *Average percent of need met:* 67% (excluding resources awarded to replace EFC). *Average financial aid package:* $6800 (excluding resources awarded to replace EFC). 4% of all full-time freshmen had no need and received non-need-based gift aid.
UNDERGRADUATE FINANCIAL AID (Fall 2005, est.) 3,926 applied for aid; of those 63% were deemed to have need. 97% of undergraduates with need received aid; of those 2% had need fully met. *Average percent of need met:* 63% (excluding resources awarded to replace EFC). *Average financial aid package:* $6897 (excluding resources awarded to replace EFC). 1% of all full-time undergraduates had no need and received non-need-based gift aid.
GIFT AID (NEED-BASED) *Total amount:* $16,747,146 (49% federal, 50% state, 1% institutional). *Receiving aid:* Freshmen: 54% (392); All full-time undergraduates: 44% (1,988). *Average award:* Freshmen: $4303; Undergraduates: $4346. *Scholarships, grants, and awards:* Federal Pell, FSEOG, state, private, college/university gift aid from institutional funds.
GIFT AID (NON-NEED-BASED) *Total amount:* $920,846 (33% institutional, 67% external sources). *Receiving aid:* Freshmen: 3% (24); Undergraduates: 2% (99). *Average Award:* Freshmen: $1237; Undergraduates: $1429. *Scholarships, grants, and awards by category:* Academic Interests/Achievement: 86 awards ($137,980 total): agriculture, area/ethnic studies, biological sciences, business, communication, computer science, education, English, foreign languages, general academic interests/achievements, health fields, humanities, mathematics, physical sciences, premedicine, social sciences. *Creative Arts/Performance:* 31 awards ($828,250 total): art/fine arts, music. *Special Achievements/Activities:* 132 awards ($196,416 total): community service, general special achievements/activities, leadership, memberships. *Special Characteristics:* 58 awards ($171,056 total): children of faculty/staff, ethnic background, first-generation college students, general special characteristics, local/state students, members of minority groups. *Tuition waivers:* Full or partial for employees or children of employees, adult students, senior citizens.
LOANS *Student loans:* $13,029,986 (100% need-based). 23% of past graduating class borrowed through all loan programs. *Average indebtedness per student:* $16,200. *Average need-based loan:* Freshmen: $2754; Undergraduates: $3139. *Parent loans:* $945,059 (100% non-need-based). *Programs:* FFEL (Subsidized and Unsubsidized Stafford, PLUS), Perkins, college/university.
WORK-STUDY *Federal work-study:* Total amount: $443,385; 172 jobs averaging $2848. *State or other work-study/employment:* Part-time jobs available.
ATHLETIC AWARDS *Total amount:* $280,950 (100% non-need-based).
APPLYING FOR FINANCIAL AID *Required financial aid forms:* FAFSA, state aid form. *Financial aid deadline (priority):* 3/2. *Notification date:* Continuous beginning 3/15. Students must reply within 3 weeks of notification.
CONTACT Mr. David Gomes, Interim Director of Financial Aid, California State University, Stanislaus, 801 West Monte Vista Avenue, Turlock, CA 95382, 209-667-3336 or toll-free 800-300-7420 (in-state). *Fax:* 209-664-7064. *E-mail:* dgomes@stan.csustan.edu.

CALIFORNIA UNIVERSITY OF PENNSYLVANIA
California, PA

CONTACT Financial Aid Office, California University of Pennsylvania, 250 University Avenue, California, PA 15419-1394, 724-938-4415.

CALUMET COLLEGE OF SAINT JOSEPH
Whiting, IN

Tuition & fees: $9900   Average undergraduate aid package: N/A

ABOUT THE INSTITUTION Independent Roman Catholic, coed. Awards: associate, bachelor's, and master's degrees and post-bachelor's certificates. 28 undergraduate majors. Total enrollment: 1,265. Undergraduates: 1,182. Freshmen: 60. Both federal and institutional methodology are used as a basis for awarding need-based institutional aid.
UNDERGRADUATE EXPENSES for 2005–06 *Tuition:* full-time $9900; part-time $330 per credit hour. *Payment plan:* Installment.
FRESHMAN FINANCIAL AID (Fall 2004) 104 applied for aid; of those 88% were deemed to have need. 62% of freshmen with need received aid.
UNDERGRADUATE FINANCIAL AID (Fall 2004) 436 applied for aid; of those 86% were deemed to have need. 72% of undergraduates with need received aid.
GIFT AID (NEED-BASED) *Total amount:* $3,117,639 (47% federal, 36% state, 7% institutional, 10% external sources). *Receiving aid:* Freshmen: 52% (56); All full-time undergraduates: 55% (245). *Scholarships, grants, and awards:* Federal Pell, FSEOG, state, private, college/university gift aid from institutional funds, United Negro College Fund.
GIFT AID (NON-NEED-BASED) *Total amount:* $708,931 (100% institutional). *Tuition waivers:* Full or partial for children of alumni, employees or children of employees, senior citizens.
LOANS *Student loans:* $5,444,294 (47% need-based, 53% non-need-based). 65% of past graduating class borrowed through all loan programs. *Average indebtedness per student:* $15,968. *Parent loans:* $67,282 (100% need-based). *Programs:* FFEL (Subsidized and Unsubsidized Stafford, PLUS).
WORK-STUDY *Federal work-study:* Total amount: $109,968; 47 jobs averaging $1771. *State or other work-study/employment:* Part-time jobs available.
ATHLETIC AWARDS *Total amount:* $422,414 (100% non-need-based).
APPLYING FOR FINANCIAL AID *Required financial aid form:* FAFSA. *Financial aid deadline (priority):* 3/1. *Notification date:* Continuous.
CONTACT Chuck Walz, Director of Admissions and Financial Aid, Calumet College of Saint Joseph, 2400 New York Avenue, Whiting, IN 46394, 219-473-4379 or toll-free 877-700-9100. *E-mail:* cwalz@ccsj.edu.

Calvary Bible College and Theological Seminary

CALVARY BIBLE COLLEGE AND THEOLOGICAL SEMINARY
Kansas City, MO

Tuition & fees: $7296   **Average undergraduate aid package:** $5054

ABOUT THE INSTITUTION Independent nondenominational, coed. Awards: associate, bachelor's, master's, and first professional degrees. 17 undergraduate majors. Total enrollment: 348. Undergraduates: 288. Freshmen: 40. Federal methodology is used as a basis for awarding need-based institutional aid.
UNDERGRADUATE EXPENSES for 2005–06 *Application fee:* $25. *Comprehensive fee:* $10,996 includes full-time tuition ($6720), mandatory fees ($576), and room and board ($3700). *College room only:* $1750. *Part-time tuition:* $240 per credit hour. *Part-time fees:* $19 per credit.
FRESHMAN FINANCIAL AID (Fall 2004) 20 applied for aid; of those 90% were deemed to have need. 100% of freshmen with need received aid; of those 6% had need fully met. *Average percent of need met:* 6% (excluding resources awarded to replace EFC). *Average financial aid package:* $6356 (excluding resources awarded to replace EFC).
UNDERGRADUATE FINANCIAL AID (Fall 2004) 168 applied for aid; of those 86% were deemed to have need. 100% of undergraduates with need received aid; of those 21% had need fully met. *Average percent of need met:* 5% (excluding resources awarded to replace EFC). *Average financial aid package:* $5054 (excluding resources awarded to replace EFC).
GIFT AID (NEED-BASED) *Total amount:* $367,605 (76% federal, 24% institutional). *Receiving aid:* Freshmen: 54% (15); All full-time undergraduates: 56% (105). *Average award:* Freshmen: $2278; Undergraduates: $2622. *Scholarships, grants, and awards:* Federal Pell, FSEOG, private, college/university gift aid from institutional funds.
GIFT AID (NON-NEED-BASED) *Total amount:* $64,256 (100% external sources). *Receiving aid:* Freshmen: 29% (8); Undergraduates: 17% (32). *Scholarships, grants, and awards by category: Academic Interests/Achievement:* general academic interests/achievements. *Special Achievements/Activities:* general special achievements/activities, religious involvement. *Special Characteristics:* children and siblings of alumni, children of educators, children of faculty/staff, relatives of clergy, siblings of current students, spouses of current students.
LOANS *Student loans:* $634,817 (75% need-based, 25% non-need-based). 64% of past graduating class borrowed through all loan programs. *Average indebtedness per student:* $17,098. *Average need-based loan:* Freshmen: $849; Undergraduates: $2280. *Parent loans:* $50,941 (100% need-based). *Programs:* FFEL (Subsidized and Unsubsidized Stafford, PLUS), alternative loans.
WORK-STUDY *Federal work-study:* Total amount: $13,686; 10 jobs averaging $1368.
APPLYING FOR FINANCIAL AID *Required financial aid forms:* FAFSA, institution's own form. *Financial aid deadline:* 4/1 (priority: 3/1). *Notification date:* Continuous beginning 5/15.
CONTACT Rachael Russiaky, Financial Aid Administrator, Calvary Bible College and Theological Seminary, 15800 Calvary Road, Kansas City, MO 64147-1341, 816-322-5152 Ext. 1323 or toll-free 800-326-3960. *Fax:* 816-331-4474. *E-mail:* finaid@calvary.edu.

CALVIN COLLEGE
Grand Rapids, MI

Tuition & fees: $19,150   **Average undergraduate aid package:** $13,000

ABOUT THE INSTITUTION Independent religious, coed. Awards: bachelor's and master's degrees and post-bachelor's certificates. 83 undergraduate majors. Total enrollment: 4,177. Undergraduates: 4,125. Freshmen: 1,007. Both federal and institutional methodology are used as a basis for awarding need-based institutional aid.
UNDERGRADUATE EXPENSES for 2005–06 *Application fee:* $35. *Comprehensive fee:* $25,735 includes full-time tuition ($18,925), mandatory fees ($225), and room and board ($6585). *College room only:* $3580. Full-time tuition and fees vary according to program. Room and board charges vary according to board plan. *Part-time tuition:* $460 per credit hour. Part-time tuition and fees vary according to course load. *Payment plans:* Tuition prepayment, installment.
FRESHMAN FINANCIAL AID (Fall 2005, est.) 831 applied for aid; of those 76% were deemed to have need. 100% of freshmen with need received aid; of those 26% had need fully met. *Average percent of need met:* 83% (excluding resources awarded to replace EFC). *Average financial aid package:* $13,700 (excluding resources awarded to replace EFC). 32% of all full-time freshmen had no need and received non-need-based gift aid.
UNDERGRADUATE FINANCIAL AID (Fall 2005, est.) 2,963 applied for aid; of those 82% were deemed to have need. 100% of undergraduates with need received aid; of those 22% had need fully met. *Average percent of need met:* 80% (excluding resources awarded to replace EFC). *Average financial aid package:* $13,000 (excluding resources awarded to replace EFC). 29% of all full-time undergraduates had no need and received non-need-based gift aid.
GIFT AID (NEED-BASED) *Total amount:* $21,100,000 (11% federal, 13% state, 73% institutional, 3% external sources). *Receiving aid:* Freshmen: 62% (626); All full-time undergraduates: 61% (2,408). *Average award:* Freshmen: $9200; Undergraduates: $8300. *Scholarships, grants, and awards:* Federal Pell, FSEOG, state, private, college/university gift aid from institutional funds.
GIFT AID (NON-NEED-BASED) *Total amount:* $5,700,000 (1% federal, 7% state, 88% institutional, 4% external sources). *Receiving aid:* Freshmen: 15% (156); Undergraduates: 12% (471). *Average Award:* Freshmen: $4200; Undergraduates: $3800. *Scholarships, grants, and awards by category: Academic Interests/Achievement:* 3,490 awards ($9,600,000 total): biological sciences, business, communication, computer science, education, engineering/technologies, English, foreign languages, general academic interests/achievements, health fields, humanities, international studies, mathematics, physical sciences, premedicine, religion/biblical studies, social sciences. *Creative Arts/Performance:* 75 awards ($85,000 total): art/fine arts, music, performing arts, theater/drama. *Special Achievements/Activities:* 105 awards ($70,000 total): community service, religious involvement. *Special Characteristics:* 2,950 awards ($4,150,000 total): children and siblings of alumni, children of faculty/staff, children of union members/company employees, ethnic background, handicapped students, international students, members of minority groups, religious affiliation. *Tuition waivers:* Full or partial for employees or children of employees. *ROTC:* Army cooperative.
LOANS *Student loans:* $17,300,000 (70% need-based, 30% non-need-based). 67% of past graduating class borrowed through all loan programs. *Average indebtedness per student:* $19,400. *Average need-based loan:* Freshmen: $4000; Undergraduates: $6100. *Parent loans:* $1,400,000 (21% need-based, 79% non-need-based). *Programs:* Federal Direct (Subsidized and Unsubsidized Stafford, PLUS), Perkins, state, college/university, alternative loans.
WORK-STUDY *Federal work-study:* Total amount: $900,000; 710 jobs averaging $1140. *State or other work-study/employment:* Total amount: $1,312,000 (5% need-based, 95% non-need-based). 1,100 part-time jobs averaging $1200.
APPLYING FOR FINANCIAL AID *Required financial aid forms:* FAFSA, institution's own form. *Financial aid deadline (priority):* 2/15. *Notification date:* Continuous beginning 3/15.
CONTACT Mr. Dave Brummel, Financial Aid Counselor, Calvin College, Spoelhof Center 356, 3201 Burton Street, SE, Grand Rapids, MI 49546-4388, 616-526-6134 or toll-free 800-688-0122. *Fax:* 616-526-6883. *E-mail:* dlbrum@calvin.edu.

CAMBRIDGE COLLEGE
Cambridge, MA

CONTACT Dr. Gerri Major, Director of Financial Aid, Cambridge College, 1000 Massachusetts Avenue, Cambridge, MA 02138, 617-868-1000 Ext. 137 or toll-free 800-877-4723. *Fax:* 617-349-3561. *E-mail:* gmajor@idea.cambridge.edu.

CAMERON UNIVERSITY
Lawton, OK

ABOUT THE INSTITUTION State-supported, coed. Awards: bachelor's and master's degrees. 39 undergraduate majors. Total enrollment: 5,873. Undergraduates: 5,439. Freshmen: 943.
GIFT AID (NEED-BASED) *Scholarships, grants, and awards:* Federal Pell, FSEOG, state, private, college/university gift aid from institutional funds.
GIFT AID (NON-NEED-BASED) *Scholarships, grants, and awards by category: Academic Interests/Achievement:* agriculture, biological sciences, business, communication, computer science, education, engineering/technologies, English, foreign languages, general academic interests/achievements, mathematics, military science, social sciences. *Creative Arts/Performance:* art/fine arts, creative writ-

ing, debating, journalism/publications, music, theater/drama. *Special Achievements/Activities:* leadership. *Special Characteristics:* members of minority groups.
LOANS *Programs:* FFEL (Subsidized and Unsubsidized Stafford, PLUS).
APPLYING FOR FINANCIAL AID *Required financial aid form:* FAFSA.
CONTACT Caryn Pacheco, Financial Aid Director, Cameron University, 2800 West Gore Boulevard, Lawton, OK 73505-6377, 580-581-2293 or toll-free 888-454-7600. *Fax:* 580-581-2556.

CAMPBELLSVILLE UNIVERSITY
Campbellsville, KY

Tuition & fees: $16,340	Average undergraduate aid package: $11,897

ABOUT THE INSTITUTION Independent religious, coed. Awards: associate, bachelor's, and master's degrees and post-bachelor's certificates. 54 undergraduate majors. Total enrollment: 2,286. Undergraduates: 1,836. Freshmen: 356. Federal methodology is used as a basis for awarding need-based institutional aid.
UNDERGRADUATE EXPENSES for 2006–07 *Application fee:* $20. *Comprehensive fee:* $22,272 includes full-time tuition ($15,960), mandatory fees ($380), and room and board ($5932).
FRESHMAN FINANCIAL AID (Fall 2004) 387 applied for aid; of those 89% were deemed to have need. 99% of freshmen with need received aid; of those 29% had need fully met. *Average percent of need met:* 75% (excluding resources awarded to replace EFC). *Average financial aid package:* $12,230 (excluding resources awarded to replace EFC). 22% of all full-time freshmen had no need and received non-need-based gift aid.
UNDERGRADUATE FINANCIAL AID (Fall 2004) 1,142 applied for aid; of those 91% were deemed to have need. 99% of undergraduates with need received aid; of those 25% had need fully met. *Average percent of need met:* 72% (excluding resources awarded to replace EFC). *Average financial aid package:* $11,897 (excluding resources awarded to replace EFC). 16% of all full-time undergraduates had no need and received non-need-based gift aid.
GIFT AID (NEED-BASED) *Total amount:* $9,618,018 (19% federal, 34% state, 42% institutional, 5% external sources). *Receiving aid:* Freshmen: 86% (340); All full-time undergraduates: 76% (1,010). *Average award:* Freshmen: $9632; Undergraduates: $8953. *Scholarships, grants, and awards:* Federal Pell, FSEOG, state, college/university gift aid from institutional funds.
GIFT AID (NON-NEED-BASED) *Total amount:* $1,785,256 (19% state, 73% institutional, 8% external sources). *Receiving aid:* Freshmen: 11% (42); Undergraduates: 8% (110). *Average Award:* Freshmen: $6583; Undergraduates: $7860. *Scholarships, grants, and awards by category: Academic Interests/Achievement:* 393 awards ($1,775,178 total): biological sciences, business, communication, computer science, education, English, general academic interests/achievements, humanities, mathematics, physical sciences, premedicine, religion/biblical studies, social sciences. *Creative Arts/Performance:* 157 awards ($383,099 total): art/fine arts, journalism/publications, music, theater/drama. *Special Achievements/Activities:* 205 awards ($552,062 total): cheerleading/drum major, junior miss, leadership, religious involvement. *Special Characteristics:* 100 awards ($502,596 total): adult students, children of educators, international students, relatives of clergy, religious affiliation.
LOANS *Student loans:* $4,956,315 (76% need-based, 24% non-need-based). 80% of past graduating class borrowed through all loan programs. *Average indebtedness per student:* $18,437. *Average need-based loan:* Freshmen: $2779; Undergraduates: $3447. *Parent loans:* $796,963 (56% need-based, 44% non-need-based). *Programs:* FFEL (Subsidized and Unsubsidized Stafford, PLUS), Perkins, college/university.
WORK-STUDY *Federal work-study:* Total amount: $433,580; 330 jobs averaging $1314. *State or other work-study/employment:* Total amount: $154,308 (6% need-based, 94% non-need-based). 80 part-time jobs averaging $1929.
ATHLETIC AWARDS *Total amount:* $1,385,502 (60% need-based, 40% non-need-based).
APPLYING FOR FINANCIAL AID *Required financial aid form:* FAFSA. *Financial aid deadline (priority):* 3/1. *Notification date:* Continuous beginning 3/15. Students must reply within 3 weeks of notification.
CONTACT Mr. Aaron Gabehart, Financial Aid Counselor, Campbellsville University, 1 University Drive, Campbellsville, KY 42718, 270-789-5305 or toll-free 800-264-6014. *Fax:* 270-789-5050. *E-mail:* finaid@campbellsville.edu.

CAMPBELL UNIVERSITY
Buies Creek, NC

Tuition & fees: $17,027	Average undergraduate aid package: $12,204

ABOUT THE INSTITUTION Independent religious, coed. Awards: associate, bachelor's, master's, doctoral, and first professional degrees. 98 undergraduate majors. Total enrollment: 3,645. Undergraduates: 2,692. Freshmen: 730. Federal methodology is used as a basis for awarding need-based institutional aid.
UNDERGRADUATE EXPENSES for 2006–07 *Application fee:* $35. *Comprehensive fee:* $22,835 includes full-time tuition ($17,027) and room and board ($5808).
FRESHMAN FINANCIAL AID (Fall 2005, est.) 653 applied for aid; of those 82% were deemed to have need. 100% of freshmen with need received aid; of those 27% had need fully met. *Average percent of need met:* 100% (excluding resources awarded to replace EFC). *Average financial aid package:* $15,748 (excluding resources awarded to replace EFC). 19% of all full-time freshmen had no need and received non-need-based gift aid.
UNDERGRADUATE FINANCIAL AID (Fall 2005, est.) 1,856 applied for aid; of those 86% were deemed to have need. 100% of undergraduates with need received aid; of those 20% had need fully met. *Average percent of need met:* 100% (excluding resources awarded to replace EFC). *Average financial aid package:* $12,204 (excluding resources awarded to replace EFC). 14% of all full-time undergraduates had no need and received non-need-based gift aid.
GIFT AID (NEED-BASED) *Total amount:* $14,157,249 (25% federal, 30% state, 42% institutional, 3% external sources). *Receiving aid:* Freshmen: 51% (365); All full-time undergraduates: 39% (1,091). *Average award:* Freshmen: $3851; Undergraduates: $4083. *Scholarships, grants, and awards:* Federal Pell, FSEOG, state, private, college/university gift aid from institutional funds.
GIFT AID (NON-NEED-BASED) *Total amount:* $8,674,817 (5% federal, 32% state, 58% institutional, 5% external sources). *Receiving aid:* Freshmen: 72% (517); Undergraduates: 53% (1,475). *Average Award:* Freshmen: $7452; Undergraduates: $6134. *Scholarships, grants, and awards by category: Academic Interests/Achievement:* 1,567 awards ($8,614,373 total): general academic interests/achievements. *Creative Arts/Performance:* 79 awards ($72,470 total): art/fine arts, creative writing, journalism/publications, music, theater/drama. *Special Achievements/Activities:* 86 awards ($80,500 total): cheerleading/drum major, junior miss, religious involvement. *Special Characteristics:* 105 awards ($645,354 total): children of faculty/staff. *ROTC:* Army.
LOANS *Student loans:* $15,934,317 (87% need-based, 13% non-need-based). 65% of past graduating class borrowed through all loan programs. *Average indebtedness per student:* $14,200. *Average need-based loan:* Freshmen: $2809; Undergraduates: $4382. *Parent loans:* $10,836,131 (80% need-based, 20% non-need-based). *Programs:* FFEL (Subsidized and Unsubsidized Stafford, PLUS), Perkins, state.
WORK-STUDY *Federal work-study:* Total amount: $1,108,805; 933 jobs averaging $1188. *State or other work-study/employment:* Total amount: $430,000 (100% non-need-based). 565 part-time jobs averaging $761.
ATHLETIC AWARDS *Total amount:* $2,261,787 (70% need-based, 30% non-need-based).
APPLYING FOR FINANCIAL AID *Required financial aid form:* FAFSA. *Financial aid deadline (priority):* 3/15. *Notification date:* Continuous beginning 3/1. Students must reply within 2 weeks of notification.
CONTACT Office of Financial Aid, Campbell University, PO Box 36, Buies Creek, NC 27506, 910-893-1310 or toll-free 800-334-4111.

CANISIUS COLLEGE
Buffalo, NY

ABOUT THE INSTITUTION Independent Roman Catholic (Jesuit), coed. Awards: bachelor's and master's degrees and post-master's certificates. 54 undergraduate majors. Total enrollment: 4,979. Undergraduates: 3,591. Freshmen: 775.
GIFT AID (NEED-BASED) *Scholarships, grants, and awards:* Federal Pell, FSEOG, state, private, college/university gift aid from institutional funds.
GIFT AID (NON-NEED-BASED) *Scholarships, grants, and awards by category: Academic Interests/Achievement:* general academic interests/achievements. *Creative Arts/Performance:* art/fine arts, music. *Special Achievements/Activities:* community service, leadership, religious involvement. *Special Characteristics:* children and siblings of alumni, children of educators, children of faculty/staff, international students, religious affiliation, siblings of current students, spouses of current students.

Canisius College

LOANS *Programs:* FFEL (Subsidized and Unsubsidized Stafford, PLUS), Perkins, college/university.
WORK-STUDY *Federal work-study:* Total amount: $815,713; 584 jobs averaging $1396. *State or other work-study/employment:* Total amount: $87,239 (39% need-based, 61% non-need-based). Part-time jobs available.
APPLYING FOR FINANCIAL AID *Required financial aid forms:* FAFSA, institution's own form, state aid form.
CONTACT Mr. Curtis Gaume, Director of Student Financial Aid, Canisius College, 2001 Main Street, Buffalo, NY 14208-1098, 716-888-2300 or toll-free 800-843-1517. *Fax:* 716-888-2377. *E-mail:* gaume@canisius.edu.

CAPELLA UNIVERSITY
Minneapolis, MN

CONTACT University Services, Capella University, 222 South Ninth Street, Minneapolis, MN 55402, 888-227-3552 or toll-free 888-CAPELLA.

CAPITAL UNIVERSITY
Columbus, OH

CONTACT Office of Financial Aid, Capital University, 2199 East Main Street, Columbus, OH 43209-2394, 614-236-6511 or toll-free 800-289-6289. *Fax:* 614-236-6926. *E-mail:* finaid@capital.edu.

CAPITOL COLLEGE
Laurel, MD

Tuition & fees: $17,688 | **Average undergraduate aid package: $9155**

ABOUT THE INSTITUTION Independent, coed. Awards: associate, bachelor's, and master's degrees and post-bachelor's certificates. 7 undergraduate majors. Total enrollment: 801. Undergraduates: 630. Freshmen: 61. Federal methodology is used as a basis for awarding need-based institutional aid.
UNDERGRADUATE EXPENSES for 2005–06 *Application fee:* $25. *Tuition:* full-time $17,688. Room and board charges vary according to housing facility. *Payment plans:* Installment, deferred payment.
FRESHMAN FINANCIAL AID (Fall 2005, est.) 64 applied for aid; of those 94% were deemed to have need. 100% of freshmen with need received aid; of those 18% had need fully met. *Average percent of need met:* 40% (excluding resources awarded to replace EFC). *Average financial aid package:* $8550 (excluding resources awarded to replace EFC).
UNDERGRADUATE FINANCIAL AID (Fall 2005, est.) 186 applied for aid; of those 93% were deemed to have need. 99% of undergraduates with need received aid; of those 14% had need fully met. *Average percent of need met:* 45% (excluding resources awarded to replace EFC). *Average financial aid package:* $9155 (excluding resources awarded to replace EFC). 3% of all full-time undergraduates had no need and received non-need-based gift aid.
GIFT AID (NEED-BASED) *Total amount:* $1,576,947 (23% federal, 18% state, 40% institutional, 19% external sources). *Receiving aid:* Freshmen: 83% (55); All full-time undergraduates: 67% (150). *Average award:* Freshmen: $6908; Undergraduates: $6797. *Scholarships, grants, and awards:* Federal Pell, FSEOG, state, private, college/university gift aid from institutional funds.
GIFT AID (NON-NEED-BASED) *Total amount:* $281,841 (9% state, 69% institutional, 22% external sources). *Receiving aid:* Freshmen: 21% (14); Undergraduates: 16% (36). *Average Award:* Undergraduates: $6083. *Tuition waivers:* Full or partial for employees or children of employees. *ROTC:* Army cooperative.
LOANS *Student loans:* $1,823,775 (76% need-based, 24% non-need-based). 63% of past graduating class borrowed through all loan programs. *Average indebtedness per student:* $23,772. *Average need-based loan:* Freshmen: $3457; Undergraduates: $4027. *Parent loans:* $956,743 (62% need-based, 38% non-need-based). *Programs:* FFEL (Subsidized and Unsubsidized Stafford, PLUS), Perkins.
WORK-STUDY *Federal work-study:* Total amount: $68,528; 40 jobs averaging $2000. *State or other work-study/employment:* 30 part-time jobs averaging $3800.
APPLYING FOR FINANCIAL AID *Required financial aid forms:* FAFSA, institution's own form. *Financial aid deadline:* Continuous. *Notification date:* Continuous. Students must reply within 3 weeks of notification.

CONTACT Suzanne Thompson, Director of Financial Aid, Capitol College, 11301 Springfield Road, Laurel, MD 20708-9759, 301-369-2800 Ext. 3037 or toll-free 800-950-1992. *Fax:* 301-369-2328. *E-mail:* sthompson@capitol-college.edu.

CARDINAL STRITCH UNIVERSITY
Milwaukee, WI

CONTACT Financial Aid Director, Cardinal Stritch University, 6801 North Yates Road, Milwaukee, WI 53217-3985, 414-410-4000 or toll-free 800-347-8822 Ext. 4040.

CARIBBEAN UNIVERSITY
Bayamón, PR

CONTACT Financial Aid Office, Caribbean University, Box 493, Bayamón, PR 00960-0493, 787-780-0070.

CARLETON COLLEGE
Northfield, MN

Tuition & fees: $34,272 | **Average undergraduate aid package: $26,649**

ABOUT THE INSTITUTION Independent, coed. Awards: bachelor's degrees. 35 undergraduate majors. Total enrollment: 1,959. Undergraduates: 1,959. Freshmen: 541. Both federal and institutional methodology are used as a basis for awarding need-based institutional aid.
UNDERGRADUATE EXPENSES for 2006–07 *Application fee:* $30. *Comprehensive fee:* $42,864 includes full-time tuition ($34,083), mandatory fees ($189), and room and board ($8592). *College room only:* $4299.
FRESHMAN FINANCIAL AID (Fall 2004) 414 applied for aid; of those 89% were deemed to have need. 100% of freshmen with need received aid; of those 100% had need fully met. *Average percent of need met:* 100% (excluding resources awarded to replace EFC). *Average financial aid package:* $25,462 (excluding resources awarded to replace EFC). 6% of all full-time freshmen had no need and received non-need-based gift aid.
UNDERGRADUATE FINANCIAL AID (Fall 2004) 1,708 applied for aid; of those 68% were deemed to have need. 100% of undergraduates with need received aid; of those 100% had need fully met. *Average percent of need met:* 100% (excluding resources awarded to replace EFC). *Average financial aid package:* $26,649 (excluding resources awarded to replace EFC). 8% of all full-time undergraduates had no need and received non-need-based gift aid.
GIFT AID (NEED-BASED) *Total amount:* $20,696,590 (3% federal, 2% state, 92% institutional, 3% external sources). *Receiving aid:* Freshmen: 65% (350); All full-time undergraduates: 58% (1,131). *Average award:* Freshmen: $21,611; Undergraduates: $20,842. *Scholarships, grants, and awards:* Federal Pell, FSEOG, state, private, college/university gift aid from institutional funds.
GIFT AID (NON-NEED-BASED) *Total amount:* $1,045,017 (2% federal, 50% institutional, 48% external sources). *Receiving aid:* Freshmen: 14% (75); Undergraduates: 10% (196). *Average Award:* Freshmen: $3803; Undergraduates: $4876. *Scholarships, grants, and awards by category:* Academic Interests/Achievement: 257 awards ($521,530 total): general academic interests/achievements. Creative Arts/Performance: 5 awards ($4400 total): music.
LOANS *Student loans:* $5,500,406 (91% need-based, 9% non-need-based). 60% of past graduating class borrowed through all loan programs. *Average indebtedness per student:* $17,842. *Average need-based loan:* Freshmen: $2730; Undergraduates: $3691. *Parent loans:* $2,267,601 (100% non-need-based). *Programs:* FFEL (Subsidized and Unsubsidized Stafford, PLUS), Perkins, state, college/university.
WORK-STUDY *Federal work-study:* Total amount: $840,472; 343 jobs averaging $2445. *State or other work-study/employment:* Total amount: $2,766,197 (65% need-based, 35% non-need-based). 1,257 part-time jobs averaging $2283.
APPLYING FOR FINANCIAL AID *Required financial aid forms:* FAFSA, CSS Financial Aid PROFILE, noncustodial (divorced/separated) parent's statement, business/farm supplement. *Financial aid deadline:* 2/15 (priority: 2/15). *Notification date:* 4/1. Students must reply by 5/1 or within 2 weeks of notification.
CONTACT Mr. Rodney M. Oto, Director of Student Financial Services, Carleton College, One North College Street, Northfield, MN 55057-4001, 507-646-4138 or toll-free 800-995-2275. *Fax:* 507-646-4269.

CARLOS ALBIZU UNIVERSITY
San Juan, PR

CONTACT Financial Aid Office, Carlos Albizu University, 151 Tanca Street, San Juan, PR 00901, 787-725-6500.

CARLOS ALBIZU UNIVERSITY, MIAMI CAMPUS
Miami, FL

CONTACT Maria V. Chavez, Senior Financial Aid Officer, Carlos Albizu University, Miami Campus, 2173 Northwest 99th Avenue, Miami, FL 33172, 305-593-1223 Ext. 153 or toll-free 800-672-3246. *Fax:* 305-593-8902. *E-mail:* mchavez@albizu.edu.

CARLOW UNIVERSITY
Pittsburgh, PA

CONTACT Ms. Natalie Wilson, Director of Financial Aid, Carlow University, 3333 Fifth Avenue, Pittsburgh, PA 15213-3165, 412-578-6171 or toll-free 800-333-CARLOW.

CARNEGIE MELLON UNIVERSITY
Pittsburgh, PA

Tuition & fees: $34,578 **Average undergraduate aid package: $22,143**

ABOUT THE INSTITUTION Independent, coed. Awards: bachelor's, master's, and doctoral degrees and post-master's certificates. 71 undergraduate majors. Total enrollment: 10,017. Undergraduates: 5,623. Freshmen: 1,409. Federal methodology is used as a basis for awarding need-based institutional aid.

UNDERGRADUATE EXPENSES for 2006–07 *Application fee:* $60. *Comprehensive fee:* $43,858 includes full-time tuition ($34,180), mandatory fees ($398), and room and board ($9280). *College room only:* $5440. *Part-time tuition:* $475 per unit. *Part-time fees:* $199 per term.

FRESHMAN FINANCIAL AID (Fall 2005, est.) 969 applied for aid; of those 78% were deemed to have need. 100% of freshmen with need received aid; of those 36% had need fully met. *Average percent of need met:* 80% (excluding resources awarded to replace EFC). *Average financial aid package:* $21,613 (excluding resources awarded to replace EFC). 8% of all full-time freshmen had no need and received non-need-based gift aid.

UNDERGRADUATE FINANCIAL AID (Fall 2005, est.) 3,200 applied for aid; of those 86% were deemed to have need. 99% of undergraduates with need received aid; of those 37% had need fully met. *Average percent of need met:* 81% (excluding resources awarded to replace EFC). *Average financial aid package:* $22,143 (excluding resources awarded to replace EFC). 9% of all full-time undergraduates had no need and received non-need-based gift aid.

GIFT AID (NEED-BASED) *Total amount:* $43,209,875 (8% federal, 3% state, 85% institutional, 4% external sources). *Receiving aid:* Freshmen: 51% (724); All full-time undergraduates: 48% (2,579). *Average award:* Freshmen: $17,288; Undergraduates: $16,636. *Scholarships, grants, and awards:* Federal Pell, FSEOG, state, private, college/university gift aid from institutional funds.

GIFT AID (NON-NEED-BASED) *Total amount:* $13,285,302 (87% institutional, 13% external sources). *Receiving aid:* Freshmen: 23% (329); Undergraduates: 24% (1,273). *Average Award:* Freshmen: $11,533; Undergraduates: $12,318. *Scholarships, grants, and awards by category:* Academic Interests/Achievement: 1,195 awards ($9,564,498 total): general academic interests/achievements. Creative Arts/Performance: art/fine arts, music, theater/drama. *ROTC:* Army, Naval, Air Force.

LOANS *Student loans:* $19,137,036 (91% need-based, 9% non-need-based). 48% of past graduating class borrowed through all loan programs. *Average indebtedness per student:* $26,500. *Average need-based loan:* Freshmen: $3470; Undergraduates: $4853. *Parent loans:* $9,428,016 (14% need-based, 86% non-need-based). *Programs:* FFEL (Subsidized and Unsubsidized Stafford, PLUS), Perkins, GATE Loans.

WORK-STUDY *Federal work-study:* Total amount: $4,737,736; 2,012 jobs averaging $2355. *State or other work-study/employment:* 19 part-time jobs averaging $2247.

APPLYING FOR FINANCIAL AID *Required financial aid forms:* FAFSA, institution's own form, parent and student federal income tax returns, parents' W-2 forms. *Financial aid deadline:* 5/1 (priority: 2/15). *Notification date:* 3/15.

CONTACT Linda M. Anderson, Director, Enrollment Services, Carnegie Mellon University, 5000 Forbes Avenue, Pittsburgh, PA 15213-3890, 412-268-8186. *Fax:* 412-268-8084. *E-mail:* thehub@andrew.cmu.edu.

CARROLL COLLEGE
Helena, MT

Tuition & fees: $17,078 **Average undergraduate aid package: $15,113**

ABOUT THE INSTITUTION Independent Roman Catholic, coed. Awards: associate and bachelor's degrees. 56 undergraduate majors. Total enrollment: 1,452. Undergraduates: 1,452. Freshmen: 304. Federal methodology is used as a basis for awarding need-based institutional aid.

UNDERGRADUATE EXPENSES for 2005–06 *Application fee:* $35. *Comprehensive fee:* $23,484 includes full-time tuition ($16,778), mandatory fees ($300), and room and board ($6406). *College room only:* $3046. Full-time tuition and fees vary according to course load. Room and board charges vary according to board plan and housing facility. *Part-time tuition:* $558 per credit hour. Part-time tuition and fees vary according to course load. *Payment plan:* Installment.

FRESHMAN FINANCIAL AID (Fall 2005, est.) 300 applied for aid; of those 68% were deemed to have need. 100% of freshmen with need received aid; of those 18% had need fully met. *Average percent of need met:* 81% (excluding resources awarded to replace EFC). *Average financial aid package:* $14,916 (excluding resources awarded to replace EFC). 33% of all full-time freshmen had no need and received non-need-based gift aid.

UNDERGRADUATE FINANCIAL AID (Fall 2005, est.) 1,224 applied for aid; of those 67% were deemed to have need. 100% of undergraduates with need received aid; of those 13% had need fully met. *Average percent of need met:* 80% (excluding resources awarded to replace EFC). *Average financial aid package:* $15,113 (excluding resources awarded to replace EFC). 30% of all full-time undergraduates had no need and received non-need-based gift aid.

GIFT AID (NEED-BASED) *Total amount:* $7,197,362 (16% federal, 1% state, 78% institutional, 5% external sources). *Receiving aid:* Freshmen: 60% (181); All full-time undergraduates: 62% (763). *Average award:* Freshmen: $9394; Undergraduates: $9053. *Scholarships, grants, and awards:* Federal Pell, FSEOG, state, private, college/university gift aid from institutional funds.

GIFT AID (NON-NEED-BASED) *Total amount:* $2,932,759 (2% federal, 91% institutional, 7% external sources). *Receiving aid:* Freshmen: 9% (26); Undergraduates: 5% (67). *Average Award:* Freshmen: $6575; Undergraduates: $6123. *Scholarships, grants, and awards by category:* Academic Interests/Achievement: 1,162 awards ($10,772,453 total): general academic interests/achievements. Creative Arts/Performance: 27 awards ($36,250 total): debating, theater/drama. Special Achievements/Activities: 175 awards ($1,243,540 total): general special achievements/activities, religious involvement. Special Characteristics: 143 awards ($813,799 total): children of faculty/staff, children of union members/company employees, international students, siblings of current students, spouses of current students, veterans. *Tuition waivers:* Full or partial for employees or children of employees, senior citizens. *ROTC:* Army.

LOANS *Student loans:* $6,508,808 (49% need-based, 51% non-need-based). 75% of past graduating class borrowed through all loan programs. *Average indebtedness per student:* $25,659. *Average need-based loan:* Freshmen: $4617; Undergraduates: $4831. *Parent loans:* $911,154 (7% need-based, 93% non-need-based). *Programs:* FFEL (Subsidized and Unsubsidized Stafford, PLUS), Perkins.

WORK-STUDY *Federal work-study:* Total amount: $1,015,746; 457 jobs averaging $2207. *State or other work-study/employment:* Total amount: $3856 (75% need-based, 25% non-need-based). 9 part-time jobs averaging $2411.

ATHLETIC AWARDS *Total amount:* $1,249,516 (45% need-based, 55% non-need-based).

APPLYING FOR FINANCIAL AID *Required financial aid form:* FAFSA. *Financial aid deadline:* Continuous. *Notification date:* Continuous beginning 3/1. Students must reply within 4 weeks of notification.

CONTACT Ms. Janet Riis, Director of Financial Aid, Carroll College, 1601 North Benton Avenue, Helena, MT 59625-0002, 406-447-5423 or toll-free 800-992-3648. *Fax:* 406-447-4533. *E-mail:* jriis@carroll.edu.

Carroll College

CARROLL COLLEGE
Waukesha, WI

Tuition & fees: $19,910 **Average undergraduate aid package:** $15,075

ABOUT THE INSTITUTION Independent Presbyterian, coed. Awards: bachelor's and master's degrees. 76 undergraduate majors. Total enrollment: 3,123. Undergraduates: 2,882. Freshmen: 610. Both federal and institutional methodology are used as a basis for awarding need-based institutional aid.
UNDERGRADUATE EXPENSES for 2006–07 *Comprehensive fee:* $25,980 includes full-time tuition ($19,500), mandatory fees ($410), and room and board ($6070). *College room only:* $3300. *Part-time tuition:* $235 per credit.
FRESHMAN FINANCIAL AID (Fall 2005, est.) 557 applied for aid; of those 81% were deemed to have need. 100% of freshmen with need received aid; of those 56% had need fully met. *Average percent of need met:* 94% (excluding resources awarded to replace EFC). *Average financial aid package:* $15,260 (excluding resources awarded to replace EFC). 24% of all full-time freshmen had no need and received non-need-based gift aid.
UNDERGRADUATE FINANCIAL AID (Fall 2005, est.) 2,005 applied for aid; of those 86% were deemed to have need. 100% of undergraduates with need received aid; of those 70% had need fully met. *Average percent of need met:* 96% (excluding resources awarded to replace EFC). *Average financial aid package:* $15,075 (excluding resources awarded to replace EFC). 22% of all full-time undergraduates had no need and received non-need-based gift aid.
GIFT AID (NEED-BASED) *Total amount:* $18,152,710 (9% federal, 12% state, 76% institutional, 3% external sources). *Receiving aid:* Freshmen: 75% (451); All full-time undergraduates: 75% (1,730). *Average award:* Freshmen: $10,512; Undergraduates: $9401. *Scholarships, grants, and awards:* Federal Pell, FSEOG, state, private, college/university gift aid from institutional funds.
GIFT AID (NON-NEED-BASED) *Total amount:* $4,891,852 (1% federal, 1% state, 94% institutional, 4% external sources). *Receiving aid:* Freshmen: 63% (374); Undergraduates: 65% (1,496). *Average Award:* Freshmen: $7902; Undergraduates: $7258. *Scholarships, grants, and awards by category: Academic Interests/Achievement:* 2,079 awards ($10,986,077 total): biological sciences, business, computer science, education, general academic interests/achievements, health fields, humanities, international studies, mathematics, physical sciences, premedicine, social sciences. *Creative Arts/Performance:* 118 awards ($193,000 total): art/fine arts, journalism/publications, music, performing arts, theater/drama. *Special Achievements/Activities:* 114 awards ($102,600 total): general special achievements/activities, junior miss, leadership, memberships, religious involvement. *Special Characteristics:* 1,061 awards ($1,261,502 total): adult students, children and siblings of alumni, children of current students, children of faculty/staff, general special characteristics, international students, siblings of current students, spouses of current students. *ROTC:* Air Force cooperative.
LOANS *Student loans:* $12,537,059 (51% need-based, 49% non-need-based). 57% of past graduating class borrowed through all loan programs. *Average indebtedness per student:* $18,404. *Average need-based loan:* Freshmen: $2531; Undergraduates: $4013. *Parent loans:* $2,540,014 (75% need-based, 25% non-need-based). *Programs:* FFEL (Subsidized and Unsubsidized Stafford, PLUS), Perkins, state, college/university.
WORK-STUDY *Federal work-study:* Total amount: $445,680; 595 jobs averaging $1677. *State or other work-study/employment:* Total amount: $615,465 (100% non-need-based). 659 part-time jobs averaging $1564.
APPLYING FOR FINANCIAL AID *Required financial aid form:* FAFSA. *Financial aid deadline:* Continuous. *Notification date:* Continuous beginning 2/15. Students must reply by 5/1 or within 2 weeks of notification.
CONTACT Dawn Scott, Director of Financial Aid, Carroll College, 100 North East Avenue, Waukesha, WI 53186-5593, 262-524-7297 or toll-free 800-CARROLL. *Fax:* 262-951-3037. *E-mail:* dthomas@cc.edu.

CARSON-NEWMAN COLLEGE
Jefferson City, TN

Tuition & fees: $16,060 **Average undergraduate aid package:** $12,839

ABOUT THE INSTITUTION Independent Southern Baptist, coed. Awards: associate, bachelor's, and master's degrees. 68 undergraduate majors. Total enrollment: 1,993. Undergraduates: 1,851. Freshmen: 449. Federal methodology is used as a basis for awarding need-based institutional aid.
UNDERGRADUATE EXPENSES for 2006–07 *Application fee:* $25. *Comprehensive fee:* $21,260 includes full-time tuition ($15,300), mandatory fees ($760), and room and board ($5200). *College room only:* $2250. *Part-time tuition:* $635 per semester hour.
FRESHMAN FINANCIAL AID (Fall 2005, est.) 422 applied for aid; of those 80% were deemed to have need. 100% of freshmen with need received aid; of those 30% had need fully met. *Average percent of need met:* 83% (excluding resources awarded to replace EFC). *Average financial aid package:* $13,763 (excluding resources awarded to replace EFC). 22% of all full-time freshmen had no need and received non-need-based gift aid.
UNDERGRADUATE FINANCIAL AID (Fall 2005, est.) 1,570 applied for aid; of those 81% were deemed to have need. 100% of undergraduates with need received aid; of those 37% had need fully met. *Average percent of need met:* 82% (excluding resources awarded to replace EFC). *Average financial aid package:* $12,839 (excluding resources awarded to replace EFC). 26% of all full-time undergraduates had no need and received non-need-based gift aid.
GIFT AID (NEED-BASED) *Total amount:* $11,904,348 (20% federal, 18% state, 59% institutional, 3% external sources). *Receiving aid:* Freshmen: 75% (335); All full-time undergraduates: 69% (1,213). *Average award:* Freshmen: $10,414; Undergraduates: $8983. *Scholarships, grants, and awards:* Federal Pell, FSEOG, state, private, college/university gift aid from institutional funds.
GIFT AID (NON-NEED-BASED) *Total amount:* $2,134,959 (6% federal, 21% state, 69% institutional, 4% external sources). *Receiving aid:* Freshmen: 22% (101); Undergraduates: 25% (445). *Average Award:* Freshmen: $9649; Undergraduates: $9120. *Scholarships, grants, and awards by category: Academic Interests/Achievement:* biological sciences, business, education, general academic interests/achievements, home economics, mathematics, military science, religion/biblical studies. *Creative Arts/Performance:* art/fine arts, debating, journalism/publications, music. *Special Achievements/Activities:* leadership, memberships. *Special Characteristics:* children and siblings of alumni, members of minority groups, relatives of clergy, siblings of current students. *ROTC:* Army, Air Force cooperative.
LOANS *Student loans:* $5,847,335 (90% need-based, 10% non-need-based). 71% of past graduating class borrowed through all loan programs. *Average indebtedness per student:* $16,512. *Average need-based loan:* Freshmen: $2714; Undergraduates: $3790. *Parent loans:* $1,622,734 (80% need-based, 20% non-need-based). *Programs:* FFEL (Subsidized and Unsubsidized Stafford, PLUS), Perkins, state, college/university, alternative loans.
WORK-STUDY *Federal work-study:* Total amount: $437,565; jobs available. *State or other work-study/employment:* Total amount: $319,830 (76% need-based, 24% non-need-based). Part-time jobs available.
ATHLETIC AWARDS Total amount: $1,468,545 (90% need-based, 10% non-need-based).
APPLYING FOR FINANCIAL AID *Required financial aid forms:* FAFSA, institution's own form. *Financial aid deadline (priority):* 4/1. *Notification date:* Continuous. Students must reply within 2 weeks of notification.
CONTACT Danette Seale, Director of Financial Aid, Carson-Newman College, c/o Financial Aid, Jefferson City, TN 37760, 865-471-3247 or toll-free 800-678-9061. *Fax:* 865-471-3502. *E-mail:* dseale@cn.edu.

CARTHAGE COLLEGE
Kenosha, WI

Tuition & fees: $23,650 **Average undergraduate aid package:** $15,314

ABOUT THE INSTITUTION Independent religious, coed. Awards: bachelor's and master's degrees. 48 undergraduate majors. Total enrollment: 2,699. Undergraduates: 2,594. Freshmen: 598. Both federal and institutional methodology are used as a basis for awarding need-based institutional aid.
UNDERGRADUATE EXPENSES for 2006–07 *Application fee:* $25. *Comprehensive fee:* $30,450 includes full-time tuition ($23,650) and room and board ($6800). *Part-time tuition:* $345 per credit hour.
FRESHMAN FINANCIAL AID (Fall 2005, est.) 519 applied for aid; of those 82% were deemed to have need. 100% of freshmen with need received aid; of those 28% had need fully met. *Average percent of need met:* 69% (excluding resources awarded to replace EFC). *Average financial aid package:* $14,452 (excluding resources awarded to replace EFC). 24% of all full-time freshmen had no need and received non-need-based gift aid.
UNDERGRADUATE FINANCIAL AID (Fall 2005, est.) 1,850 applied for aid; of those 85% were deemed to have need. 100% of undergraduates with need

received aid; of those 32% had need fully met. *Average percent of need met:* 72% (excluding resources awarded to replace EFC). *Average financial aid package:* $15,314 (excluding resources awarded to replace EFC). 25% of all full-time undergraduates had no need and received non-need-based gift aid.
GIFT AID (NEED-BASED) *Total amount:* $16,998,746 (8% federal, 6% state, 83% institutional, 3% external sources). *Receiving aid:* Freshmen: 74% (427); All full-time undergraduates: 72% (1,557). *Average award:* Freshmen: $10,520; Undergraduates: $10,634. *Scholarships, grants, and awards:* Federal Pell, FSEOG, state, private, college/university gift aid from institutional funds.
GIFT AID (NON-NEED-BASED) *Total amount:* $5,781,622 (94% institutional, 6% external sources). *Receiving aid:* Freshmen: 12% (68); Undergraduates: 10% (216). *Average Award:* Freshmen: $11,011; Undergraduates: $11,579. *Scholarships, grants, and awards by category:* Academic Interests/Achievement: biological sciences, computer science, engineering/technologies, foreign languages, general academic interests/achievements, health fields, mathematics, physical sciences, premedicine. *Creative Arts/Performance:* applied art and design, art/fine arts, music, theater/drama. *Special Achievements/Activities:* general special achievements/activities, leadership, religious involvement. *Special Characteristics:* children and siblings of alumni, children of educators, children of faculty/staff, children of public servants, local/state students, members of minority groups, previous college experience, relatives of clergy, religious affiliation, siblings of current students. *ROTC:* Army cooperative, Air Force cooperative.
LOANS *Student loans:* $12,972,905 (71% need-based, 29% non-need-based). *Average need-based loan:* Freshmen: $4554; Undergraduates: $5663. *Parent loans:* $4,566,180 (40% need-based, 60% non-need-based). *Programs:* FFEL (Subsidized and Unsubsidized Stafford, PLUS), Perkins, Federal Nursing, state, college/university.
WORK-STUDY *Federal work-study:* Total amount: $143,756; jobs available (averaging $1200). *State or other work-study/employment:* Total amount: $195,325 (43% need-based, 57% non-need-based). Part-time jobs available.
APPLYING FOR FINANCIAL AID *Required financial aid form:* FAFSA. *Financial aid deadline (priority):* 2/15. *Notification date:* Continuous.
CONTACT William Henderson, Director of Student Financial Planning, Carthage College, 2001 Alford Park Drive, Kenosha, WI 53140, 262-551-6001 or toll-free 800-351-4058. *Fax:* 262-551-5762. *E-mail:* whenderson@carthage.edu.

CASCADE COLLEGE
Portland, OR

Tuition & fees: $12,800	Average undergraduate aid package: $11,825

ABOUT THE INSTITUTION Independent religious, coed. Awards: bachelor's degrees. 9 undergraduate majors. Total enrollment: 292. Undergraduates: 292. Freshmen: 93. Federal methodology is used as a basis for awarding need-based institutional aid.
UNDERGRADUATE EXPENSES for 2006–07 *Application fee:* $25. *Comprehensive fee:* $18,920 includes full-time tuition ($12,200), mandatory fees ($600), and room and board ($6120). *Part-time tuition:* $510 per semester hour.
FRESHMAN FINANCIAL AID (Fall 2005, est.) 86 applied for aid; of those 87% were deemed to have need. 100% of freshmen with need received aid. *Average percent of need met:* 51% (excluding resources awarded to replace EFC). *Average financial aid package:* $12,213 (excluding resources awarded to replace EFC). 15% of all full-time freshmen had no need and received non-need-based gift aid.
UNDERGRADUATE FINANCIAL AID (Fall 2005, est.) 246 applied for aid; of those 88% were deemed to have need. 100% of undergraduates with need received aid; of those .5% had need fully met. *Average percent of need met:* 50% (excluding resources awarded to replace EFC). *Average financial aid package:* $11,825 (excluding resources awarded to replace EFC). 17% of all full-time undergraduates had no need and received non-need-based gift aid.
GIFT AID (NEED-BASED) *Total amount:* $620,017 (65% federal, 1% state, 27% institutional, 7% external sources). *Receiving aid:* Freshmen: 16% (15); All full-time undergraduates: 79% (216). *Average award:* Freshmen: $1541; Undergraduates: $1559. *Scholarships, grants, and awards:* Federal Pell, FSEOG, private, college/university gift aid from institutional funds.
GIFT AID (NON-NEED-BASED) *Total amount:* $882,797 (93% institutional, 7% external sources). *Receiving aid:* Freshmen: 77% (73); Undergraduates: 70% (191). *Average Award:* Freshmen: $5452; Undergraduates: $3850. *Scholarships, grants, and awards by category:* Academic Interests/Achievement: 162 awards ($509,684 total): biological sciences, business, communication, education, English, general academic interests/achievements, international studies, religion/biblical studies. *Creative Arts/Performance:* 65 awards ($103,840 total): journalism/publications, music, theater/drama. *Special Achievements/Activities:* 25 awards ($24,000 total): general special achievements/activities, leadership, memberships. *Special Characteristics:* 133 awards ($177,600 total): children and siblings of alumni, children of current students, children of faculty/staff, general special characteristics, international students, out-of-state students, parents of current students, siblings of current students, spouses of current students. *ROTC:* Army cooperative, Air Force cooperative.
LOANS *Student loans:* $1,536,407 (42% need-based, 58% non-need-based). 87% of past graduating class borrowed through all loan programs. *Average indebtedness per student:* $24,988. *Average need-based loan:* Freshmen: $2597; Undergraduates: $3638. *Parent loans:* $316,276 (100% non-need-based). *Programs:* FFEL (Subsidized and Unsubsidized Stafford, PLUS), alternative loans.
WORK-STUDY *Federal work-study:* Total amount: $173,771; 87 jobs averaging $1997. *State or other work-study/employment:* Total amount: $20,000 (100% non-need-based). 11 part-time jobs averaging $1818.
ATHLETIC AWARDS Total amount: $347,794 (100% non-need-based).
APPLYING FOR FINANCIAL AID *Required financial aid forms:* FAFSA, institution's own form. *Financial aid deadline:* 8/15 (priority: 5/15). *Notification date:* Continuous.
CONTACT Jim Murphy, Director of Financial Services, Cascade College, 9101 East Burnside Street, Portland, OR 97216-1515, 503-257-1218 or toll-free 800-550-7678. *Fax:* 503-257-1222. *E-mail:* jmurphy@cascade.edu.

CASE WESTERN RESERVE UNIVERSITY
Cleveland, OH

Tuition & fees: $31,688	Average undergraduate aid package: $28,931

ABOUT THE INSTITUTION Independent, coed. Awards: bachelor's, master's, doctoral, and first professional degrees. 63 undergraduate majors. Total enrollment: 9,615. Undergraduates: 3,949. Freshmen: 1,162. Both federal and institutional methodology are used as a basis for awarding need-based institutional aid.
UNDERGRADUATE EXPENSES for 2006–07 *Application fee:* $35. *Comprehensive fee:* $40,968 includes full-time tuition ($31,090), mandatory fees ($598), and room and board ($9280). *College room only:* $5440. *Part-time tuition:* $1296 per credit hour.
FRESHMAN FINANCIAL AID (Fall 2005, est.) 991 applied for aid; of those 82% were deemed to have need. 100% of freshmen with need received aid; of those 82% had need fully met. *Average percent of need met:* 96% (excluding resources awarded to replace EFC). *Average financial aid package:* $29,351 (excluding resources awarded to replace EFC). 24% of all full-time freshmen had no need and received non-need-based gift aid.
UNDERGRADUATE FINANCIAL AID (Fall 2005, est.) 2,549 applied for aid; of those 88% were deemed to have need. 100% of undergraduates with need received aid; of those 88% had need fully met. *Average percent of need met:* 92% (excluding resources awarded to replace EFC). *Average financial aid package:* $28,931 (excluding resources awarded to replace EFC). 29% of all full-time undergraduates had no need and received non-need-based gift aid.
GIFT AID (NEED-BASED) *Total amount:* $43,645,426 (7% federal, 6% state, 83% institutional, 4% external sources). *Receiving aid:* Freshmen: 70% (809); All full-time undergraduates: 59% (2,231). *Average award:* Freshmen: $20,713; Undergraduates: $18,391. *Scholarships, grants, and awards:* Federal Pell, FSEOG, state, private, college/university gift aid from institutional funds.
GIFT AID (NON-NEED-BASED) *Total amount:* $14,579,769 (1% federal, 5% state, 90% institutional, 4% external sources). *Receiving aid:* Freshmen: 60% (696); Undergraduates: 50% (1,884). *Average Award:* Freshmen: $15,206; Undergraduates: $11,852. *Scholarships, grants, and awards by category:* Academic Interests/Achievement: 1,431 awards ($20,168,504 total): biological sciences, business, communication, computer science, engineering/technologies, English, general academic interests/achievements, health fields, humanities, international studies, mathematics, physical sciences, premedicine, religion/biblical studies, social sciences. *Creative Arts/Performance:* 26 awards ($143,700 total): art/fine arts, creative writing, dance, general creative arts/performance, music, theater/drama. *Special Achievements/Activities:* 84 awards ($247,516 total): leadership. *Special Characteristics:* 198 awards ($5,141,111 total): children of faculty/staff. *ROTC:* Army cooperative, Air Force cooperative.

Case Western Reserve University

LOANS *Student loans:* $23,040,868 (52% need-based, 48% non-need-based). 67% of past graduating class borrowed through all loan programs. *Average indebtedness per student:* $20,597. *Average need-based loan:* Freshmen: $4836; Undergraduates: $5349. *Parent loans:* $3,036,254 (89% need-based, 11% non-need-based). *Programs:* FFEL (Subsidized and Unsubsidized Stafford, PLUS), Perkins, Federal Nursing, state, college/university, alternative loans-Custom Signature.
WORK-STUDY *Federal work-study:* Total amount: $3,073,447; 2,113 jobs averaging $2576.
APPLYING FOR FINANCIAL AID *Required financial aid forms:* FAFSA, noncustodial (divorced/separated) parent's statement, business/farm supplement, income tax form(s), W-2 forms. *Financial aid deadline (priority):* 2/15. *Notification date:* Continuous beginning 3/15. Students must reply by 5/1 or within 2 weeks of notification.
CONTACT Ms. Nancy Issa, Associate Director of University Financial Aid, Case Western Reserve University, 10900 Euclid Avenue, Cleveland, OH 44106-7049, 216-368-4530. *Fax:* 216-368-5054. *E-mail:* nxi@po.cwru.edu.

CASTLETON STATE COLLEGE
Castleton, VT

ABOUT THE INSTITUTION State-supported, coed. Awards: associate, bachelor's, and master's degrees and post-master's certificates. 42 undergraduate majors. Total enrollment: 2,392. Undergraduates: 1,891. Freshmen: 462.
GIFT AID (NEED-BASED) *Scholarships, grants, and awards:* Federal Pell, FSEOG, state, private, college/university gift aid from institutional funds.
GIFT AID (NON-NEED-BASED) *Scholarships, grants, and awards by category: Academic Interests/Achievement:* foreign languages, general academic interests/achievements. *Creative Arts/Performance:* applied art and design, art/fine arts, music.
LOANS *Programs:* FFEL (Subsidized and Unsubsidized Stafford, PLUS), Perkins, Federal Nursing, state.
APPLYING FOR FINANCIAL AID *Required financial aid forms:* FAFSA, state aid form.
CONTACT Audrey Reed, Director of Financial Aid, Castleton State College, Castleton, VT 05735, 802-468-1286 or toll-free 800-639-8521. *Fax:* 802-468-6470. *E-mail:* audrey.reed@castleton.edu.

CATAWBA COLLEGE
Salisbury, NC

Tuition & fees: $18,750 **Average undergraduate aid package: $13,193**

ABOUT THE INSTITUTION Independent religious, coed. Awards: bachelor's and master's degrees. 42 undergraduate majors. Total enrollment: 1,288. Undergraduates: 1,256. Freshmen: 223. Federal methodology is used as a basis for awarding need-based institutional aid.
UNDERGRADUATE EXPENSES for 2005–06 *Application fee:* $25. *Comprehensive fee:* $25,000 includes full-time tuition ($18,750) and room and board ($6250). Full-time tuition and fees vary according to class time. *Part-time tuition:* $500 per semester hour. Part-time tuition and fees vary according to class time, course load, and degree level. *Payment plan:* Installment.
FRESHMAN FINANCIAL AID (Fall 2004) 234 applied for aid; of those 81% were deemed to have need. 100% of freshmen with need received aid; of those 33% had need fully met. *Average percent of need met:* 80% (excluding resources awarded to replace EFC). *Average financial aid package:* $15,811 (excluding resources awarded to replace EFC). 15% of all full-time freshmen had no need and received non-need-based gift aid.
UNDERGRADUATE FINANCIAL AID (Fall 2004) 1,085 applied for aid; of those 86% were deemed to have need. 98% of undergraduates with need received aid; of those 30% had need fully met. *Average percent of need met:* 84% (excluding resources awarded to replace EFC). *Average financial aid package:* $13,193 (excluding resources awarded to replace EFC). 9% of all full-time undergraduates had no need and received non-need-based gift aid.
GIFT AID (NEED-BASED) *Total amount:* $2,358,435 (56% federal, 44% state). *Receiving aid:* Freshmen: 48% (126); All full-time undergraduates: 44% (601). *Average award:* Freshmen: $3958; Undergraduates: $4032. *Scholarships, grants, and awards:* Federal Pell, FSEOG, state, private, college/university gift aid from institutional funds.
GIFT AID (NON-NEED-BASED) *Total amount:* $6,619,209 (23% state, 74% institutional, 3% external sources). *Receiving aid:* Freshmen: 73% (190); Undergraduates: 66% (910). *Average Award:* Freshmen: $4921; Undergraduates: $7047. *Scholarships, grants, and awards by category: Academic Interests/Achievement:* 900 awards ($4,724,524 total): education, general academic interests/achievements. *Creative Arts/Performance:* 87 awards ($138,875 total): music, theater/drama. *Special Characteristics:* 12 awards ($107,925 total): children of faculty/staff. *Tuition waivers:* Full or partial for employees or children of employees. *ROTC:* Army cooperative.
LOANS *Student loans:* $5,363,758 (40% need-based, 60% non-need-based). 78% of past graduating class borrowed through all loan programs. *Average indebtedness per student:* $18,731. *Average need-based loan:* Freshmen: $4239; Undergraduates: $4153. *Parent loans:* $1,826,267 (100% non-need-based). *Programs:* FFEL (Subsidized and Unsubsidized Stafford, PLUS), Perkins, college/university, TERI Loans, Nellie Mae Loans, Advantage Loans, alternative loans, Citiassist Loans, "Extra" loans.
WORK-STUDY *Federal work-study:* Total amount: $271,878; 226 jobs averaging $1203. *State or other work-study/employment:* Total amount: $214,578 (100% non-need-based). 182 part-time jobs averaging $1179.
ATHLETIC AWARDS *Total amount:* $1,718,022 (100% non-need-based).
APPLYING FOR FINANCIAL AID *Required financial aid forms:* FAFSA, state aid form. *Financial aid deadline (priority):* 3/15. *Notification date:* Continuous. Students must reply within 2 weeks of notification.
CONTACT Melanie McCulloh, Director of Scholarships and Financial Aid, Catawba College, 2300 West Innes Street, Salisbury, NC 28144-2488, 704-637-4416 or toll-free 800-CATAWBA. *Fax:* 704-637-4252. *E-mail:* mcmccull@catawba.edu.

THE CATHOLIC UNIVERSITY OF AMERICA
Washington, DC

Tuition & fees: $26,000 **Average undergraduate aid package: $16,279**

ABOUT THE INSTITUTION Independent religious, coed. Awards: bachelor's, master's, doctoral, and first professional degrees and post-master's certificates. 77 undergraduate majors. Total enrollment: 6,130. Undergraduates: 3,053. Freshmen: 792. Federal methodology is used as a basis for awarding need-based institutional aid.
UNDERGRADUATE EXPENSES for 2005–06 *Application fee:* $55. *One-time required fee:* $365. *Comprehensive fee:* $35,838 includes full-time tuition ($24,800), mandatory fees ($1200), and room and board ($9838). *College room only:* $5646. Full-time tuition and fees vary according to program. Room and board charges vary according to board plan and housing facility. *Part-time tuition:* $940 per credit. *Part-time fees:* $605 per year. Part-time tuition and fees vary according to course load. *Payment plans:* Tuition prepayment, installment.
FRESHMAN FINANCIAL AID (Fall 2005, est.) 587 applied for aid; of those 76% were deemed to have need. 100% of freshmen with need received aid; of those 52% had need fully met. *Average percent of need met:* 84% (excluding resources awarded to replace EFC). *Average financial aid package:* $17,465 (excluding resources awarded to replace EFC). 41% of all full-time freshmen had no need and received non-need-based gift aid.
UNDERGRADUATE FINANCIAL AID (Fall 2005, est.) 1,799 applied for aid; of those 81% were deemed to have need. 99% of undergraduates with need received aid; of those 53% had need fully met. *Average percent of need met:* 83% (excluding resources awarded to replace EFC). *Average financial aid package:* $16,279 (excluding resources awarded to replace EFC). 40% of all full-time undergraduates had no need and received non-need-based gift aid.
GIFT AID (NEED-BASED) *Total amount:* $17,218,779 (5% federal, 1% state, 91% institutional, 3% external sources). *Receiving aid:* Freshmen: 56% (443); All full-time undergraduates: 50% (1,377). *Average award:* Freshmen: $13,234; Undergraduates: $12,339. *Scholarships, grants, and awards:* Federal Pell, FSEOG, state, private, college/university gift aid from institutional funds, Federal Nursing.
GIFT AID (NON-NEED-BASED) *Total amount:* $9,923,705 (98% institutional, 2% external sources). *Average Award:* Freshmen: $8224; Undergraduates: $8962. *Scholarships, grants, and awards by category: Academic Interests/Achievement:* general academic interests/achievements. *Creative Arts/Performance:* music, theater/drama. *Special Achievements/Activities:* general special achievements/activities. *Special Characteristics:* adult students, children of faculty/staff, ethnic background, first-generation college students, handicapped students, local/state students, religious affiliation, siblings of current students,

twins. *Tuition waivers:* Full or partial for employees or children of employees. *ROTC:* Army cooperative, Naval cooperative, Air Force cooperative.
LOANS *Student loans:* $12,996,207 (83% need-based, 17% non-need-based). *Average need-based loan:* Freshmen: $3730; Undergraduates: $4793. *Parent loans:* $8,551,451 (70% need-based, 30% non-need-based). *Programs:* FFEL (Subsidized and Unsubsidized Stafford, PLUS), Perkins, Federal Nursing, college/university, Commercial Loans.
WORK-STUDY *Federal work-study:* Total amount: $1,176,727; jobs available.
APPLYING FOR FINANCIAL AID *Required financial aid form:* FAFSA. *Financial aid deadline:* 4/15 (priority: 2/1). *Notification date:* Continuous beginning 4/1. Students must reply by 5/1 or within 2 weeks of notification.
CONTACT Ms. Doris Torosian, Director of Financial Aid, The Catholic University of America, 620 Michigan Avenue, NE, 6 McMahon Hall, Washington, DC 20064, 202-319-5307 or toll-free 202-319-5305 (in-state), 800-673-2772 (out-of-state). *Fax:* 202-319-5573. *E-mail:* torosian@cua.edu.

CAZENOVIA COLLEGE
Cazenovia, NY

Tuition & fees: $18,940   **Average undergraduate aid package:** $13,500

ABOUT THE INSTITUTION Independent, coed. Awards: associate and bachelor's degrees. 21 undergraduate majors. Total enrollment: 1,124. Undergraduates: 1,124. Freshmen: 285. Federal methodology is used as a basis for awarding need-based institutional aid.
UNDERGRADUATE EXPENSES for 2005–06 *Application fee:* $30. *Comprehensive fee:* $26,450 includes full-time tuition ($18,940) and room and board ($7510). *College room only:* $4200. Full-time tuition and fees vary according to course load. Room and board charges vary according to board plan. *Part-time tuition:* $400 per credit. *Part-time fees:* $100. Part-time tuition and fees vary according to class time and course load. *Payment plan:* Installment.
FRESHMAN FINANCIAL AID (Fall 2005, est.) 265 applied for aid; of those 88% were deemed to have need. 100% of freshmen with need received aid; of those 18% had need fully met. *Average percent of need met:* 70% (excluding resources awarded to replace EFC). *Average financial aid package:* $13,000 (excluding resources awarded to replace EFC). 9% of all full-time freshmen had no need and received non-need-based gift aid.
UNDERGRADUATE FINANCIAL AID (Fall 2005, est.) 725 applied for aid; of those 91% were deemed to have need. 100% of undergraduates with need received aid; of those 18% had need fully met. *Average percent of need met:* 70% (excluding resources awarded to replace EFC). *Average financial aid package:* $13,500 (excluding resources awarded to replace EFC). 7% of all full-time undergraduates had no need and received non-need-based gift aid.
GIFT AID (NEED-BASED) *Total amount:* $7,940,101 (13% federal, 17% state, 67% institutional, 3% external sources). *Receiving aid:* Freshmen: 80% (229); All full-time undergraduates: 60% (484). *Average award:* Freshmen: $8500; Undergraduates: $8000. *Scholarships, grants, and awards:* Federal Pell, FSEOG, state, private, college/university gift aid from institutional funds.
GIFT AID (NON-NEED-BASED) *Total amount:* $932,918 (3% state, 92% institutional, 5% external sources). *Receiving aid:* Freshmen: 9% (25); Undergraduates: 9% (70). *Average Award:* Freshmen: $5788; Undergraduates: $5000. *Scholarships, grants, and awards by category: Academic Interests/Achievement:* general academic interests/achievements. *Tuition waivers:* Full or partial for employees or children of employees. *ROTC:* Army cooperative, Air Force cooperative.
LOANS *Student loans:* $4,943,560 (83% need-based, 17% non-need-based). 85% of past graduating class borrowed through all loan programs. *Average indebtedness per student:* $27,321. *Average need-based loan:* Freshmen: $2626; Undergraduates: $3063. *Parent loans:* $1,767,000 (70% need-based, 30% non-need-based). *Programs:* Federal Direct (Subsidized and Unsubsidized Stafford, PLUS).
WORK-STUDY *Federal work-study:* Total amount: $224,294; 242 jobs averaging $927.
APPLYING FOR FINANCIAL AID *Required financial aid forms:* FAFSA, state aid form. *Financial aid deadline (priority):* 3/15. *Notification date:* Continuous beginning 11/1. Students must reply by 5/1 or within 2 weeks of notification.
CONTACT Christine L. Mandel, Director of Financial Aid, Cazenovia College, 3 Sullivan Street, Cazenovia, NY 13035, 315-655-7887 or toll-free 800-654-3210. *Fax:* 315-655-7219. *E-mail:* finaid@cazenovia.edu.

CEDAR CREST COLLEGE
Allentown, PA

Tuition & fees: $23,012   **Average undergraduate aid package:** $15,960

ABOUT THE INSTITUTION Independent religious, women only. Awards: associate, bachelor's, and master's degrees and post-bachelor's certificates. 53 undergraduate majors. Total enrollment: 1,856. Undergraduates: 1,784. Freshmen: 320. Federal methodology is used as a basis for awarding need-based institutional aid.
UNDERGRADUATE EXPENSES for 2005–06 *Application fee:* $30. *Comprehensive fee:* $30,965 includes full-time tuition ($22,712), mandatory fees ($300), and room and board ($7953). Full-time tuition and fees vary according to course load. Room and board charges vary according to board plan. Part-time tuition and fees vary according to class time. *Payment plan:* Installment.
FRESHMAN FINANCIAL AID (Fall 2005, est.) 197 applied for aid; of those 87% were deemed to have need. 100% of freshmen with need received aid; of those 17% had need fully met. *Average percent of need met:* 76% (excluding resources awarded to replace EFC). *Average financial aid package:* $17,103 (excluding resources awarded to replace EFC). 13% of all full-time freshmen had no need and received non-need-based gift aid.
UNDERGRADUATE FINANCIAL AID (Fall 2005, est.) 883 applied for aid; of those 91% were deemed to have need. 100% of undergraduates with need received aid; of those 16% had need fully met. *Average percent of need met:* 74% (excluding resources awarded to replace EFC). *Average financial aid package:* $15,960 (excluding resources awarded to replace EFC). 11% of all full-time undergraduates had no need and received non-need-based gift aid.
GIFT AID (NEED-BASED) *Total amount:* $10,135,864 (13% federal, 16% state, 66% institutional, 5% external sources). *Receiving aid:* Freshmen: 85% (171); All full-time undergraduates: 85% (772). *Average award:* Freshmen: $13,349; Undergraduates: $12,194. *Scholarships, grants, and awards:* Federal Pell, FSEOG, state, private, college/university gift aid from institutional funds.
GIFT AID (NON-NEED-BASED) *Total amount:* $1,318,704 (2% state, 76% institutional, 22% external sources). *Receiving aid:* Freshmen: 10% (21); Undergraduates: 9% (80). *Average Award:* Freshmen: $10,132; Undergraduates: $13,887. *Scholarships, grants, and awards by category: Academic Interests/Achievement:* 344 awards ($2,698,543 total): general academic interests/achievements. *Creative Arts/Performance:* 119 awards ($173,250 total): art/fine arts, dance, performing arts, theater/drama. *Special Achievements/Activities:* 62 awards ($72,059 total): community service, general special achievements/activities, junior miss, leadership, memberships, religious involvement. *Special Characteristics:* 84 awards ($288,092 total): adult students, children and siblings of alumni, general special characteristics, previous college experience, relatives of clergy, religious affiliation, siblings of current students. *Tuition waivers:* Full or partial for children of alumni, employees or children of employees. *ROTC:* Army cooperative.
LOANS *Student loans:* $9,557,156 (74% need-based, 26% non-need-based). 97% of past graduating class borrowed through all loan programs. *Average indebtedness per student:* $22,820. *Average need-based loan:* Freshmen: $3391; Undergraduates: $4110. *Parent loans:* $1,906,802 (38% need-based, 62% non-need-based). *Programs:* FFEL (Subsidized and Unsubsidized Stafford, PLUS), Perkins, Federal Nursing, college/university.
WORK-STUDY *Federal work-study:* Total amount: $130,085; 87 jobs averaging $1500. *State or other work-study/employment:* Total amount: $581,365 (67% need-based, 33% non-need-based). 341 part-time jobs averaging $1700.
APPLYING FOR FINANCIAL AID *Required financial aid forms:* FAFSA, institution's own form. *Financial aid deadline (priority):* 5/1. *Notification date:* Continuous. Students must reply by 5/1.
CONTACT Ms. Lori Williams, Director of Financial Aid, Cedar Crest College, 100 College Drive, Allentown, PA 18104-6196, 610-740-3785 or toll-free 800-360-1222. *Fax:* 610-606-4653. *E-mail:* finaid@cedarcrest.edu.

CEDARVILLE UNIVERSITY
Cedarville, OH

Tuition & fees: $17,120   **Average undergraduate aid package:** $15,778

Cedarville University

ABOUT THE INSTITUTION Independent Baptist, coed. Awards: bachelor's and master's degrees. 78 undergraduate majors. Total enrollment: 3,113. Undergraduates: 3,090. Freshmen: 763. Federal methodology is used as a basis for awarding need-based institutional aid.

UNDERGRADUATE EXPENSES for 2006–07 *Application fee:* $30. *Comprehensive fee:* $22,130 includes full-time tuition ($17,120) and room and board ($5010). *College room only:* $2684. *Part-time tuition:* $535 per credit hour.

FRESHMAN FINANCIAL AID (Fall 2004) 730 applied for aid; of those 80% were deemed to have need. 99% of freshmen with need received aid; of those 57% had need fully met. *Average percent of need met:* 24% (excluding resources awarded to replace EFC). *Average financial aid package:* $15,800 (excluding resources awarded to replace EFC). 25% of all full-time freshmen had no need and received non-need-based gift aid.

UNDERGRADUATE FINANCIAL AID (Fall 2004) 2,073 applied for aid; of those 85% were deemed to have need. 99% of undergraduates with need received aid; of those 53% had need fully met. *Average percent of need met:* 38% (excluding resources awarded to replace EFC). *Average financial aid package:* $15,778 (excluding resources awarded to replace EFC). 19% of all full-time undergraduates had no need and received non-need-based gift aid.

GIFT AID (NEED-BASED) *Total amount:* $3,548,840 (43% federal, 11% state, 42% institutional, 4% external sources). *Receiving aid:* Freshmen: 26% (232); All full-time undergraduates: 32% (928). *Average award:* Freshmen: $1422; Undergraduates: $1879. *Scholarships, grants, and awards:* Federal Pell, FSEOG, state, private, college/university gift aid from institutional funds.

GIFT AID (NON-NEED-BASED) *Total amount:* $9,370,281 (13% state, 60% institutional, 27% external sources). *Receiving aid:* Freshmen: 56% (499); Undergraduates: 42% (1,205). *Average Award:* Freshmen: $8620; Undergraduates: $9457. *Scholarships, grants, and awards by category:* Academic Interests/Achievement: 763 awards ($1,455,327 total): general academic interests/achievements. Creative Arts/Performance: 66 awards ($86,275 total): debating, music. Special Achievements/Activities: 454 awards ($672,637 total): leadership. Special Characteristics: 231 awards ($2,199,858 total): children and siblings of alumni, children of faculty/staff, ethnic background, general special characteristics, religious affiliation, veterans. *ROTC:* Army cooperative, Air Force cooperative.

LOANS *Student loans:* $10,051,880 (62% need-based, 38% non-need-based). 67% of past graduating class borrowed through all loan programs. *Average indebtedness per student:* $19,258. *Average need-based loan:* Freshmen: $2723; Undergraduates: $4129. *Parent loans:* $13,171,233 (100% non-need-based). *Programs:* FFEL (Subsidized and Unsubsidized Stafford, PLUS), Perkins, Federal Nursing, college/university.

WORK-STUDY *Federal work-study:* Total amount: $316,442; 403 jobs averaging $785. *State or other work-study/employment:* Total amount: $1,300,982 (100% non-need-based). 1,417 part-time jobs averaging $918.

ATHLETIC AWARDS *Total amount:* $563,974 (100% non-need-based).

APPLYING FOR FINANCIAL AID *Required financial aid form:* FAFSA. *Financial aid deadline (priority):* 3/1. *Notification date:* Continuous beginning 3/1. Students must reply within 4 weeks of notification.

CONTACT Mr. Fred Merritt, Director of Financial Aid, Cedarville University, 251 North Main Street, Cedarville, OH 45314-0601, 937-766-7866 or toll-free 800-CEDARVILLE. *E-mail:* merrittf@cedarville.edu.

CENTENARY COLLEGE
Hackettstown, NJ

Tuition & fees: $20,870	Average undergraduate aid package: $13,229

ABOUT THE INSTITUTION Independent religious, coed. Awards: associate, bachelor's, and master's degrees and post-bachelor's certificates. 24 undergraduate majors. Total enrollment: 2,472. Undergraduates: 1,887. Freshmen: 248. Federal methodology is used as a basis for awarding need-based institutional aid.

UNDERGRADUATE EXPENSES for 2005–06 *Application fee:* $30. *Comprehensive fee:* $28,770 includes full-time tuition ($19,840), mandatory fees ($1030), and room and board ($7900). Full-time tuition and fees vary according to location and program. *Part-time tuition:* $395 per credit. *Part-time fees:* $10 per term. Part-time tuition and fees vary according to location and program. *Payment plan:* Installment.

FRESHMAN FINANCIAL AID (Fall 2005, est.) 252 applied for aid; of those 86% were deemed to have need. 100% of freshmen with need received aid; of those 16% had need fully met. *Average percent of need met:* 69% (excluding resources awarded to replace EFC). *Average financial aid package:* $15,397 (excluding resources awarded to replace EFC). 14% of all full-time freshmen had no need and received non-need-based gift aid.

UNDERGRADUATE FINANCIAL AID (Fall 2005, est.) 1,094 applied for aid; of those 84% were deemed to have need. 100% of undergraduates with need received aid; of those 16% had need fully met. *Average percent of need met:* 65% (excluding resources awarded to replace EFC). *Average financial aid package:* $13,229 (excluding resources awarded to replace EFC). 13% of all full-time undergraduates had no need and received non-need-based gift aid.

GIFT AID (NEED-BASED) *Total amount:* $8,782,838 (12% federal, 26% state, 53% institutional, 9% external sources). *Receiving aid:* Freshmen: 81% (205); All full-time undergraduates: 77% (837). *Average award:* Freshmen: $12,832; Undergraduates: $10,244. *Scholarships, grants, and awards:* Federal Pell, FSEOG, state, private, college/university gift aid from institutional funds.

GIFT AID (NON-NEED-BASED) *Total amount:* $851,380 (78% institutional, 22% external sources). *Receiving aid:* Freshmen: 7% (18); Undergraduates: 7% (75). *Average Award:* Freshmen: $15,272; Undergraduates: $12,699. *Scholarships, grants, and awards by category:* Academic Interests/Achievement: 402 awards ($2,312,425 total): general academic interests/achievements. Special Achievements/Activities: 89 awards ($379,875 total): leadership. Special Characteristics: 574 awards ($1,590,388 total): children and siblings of alumni, children of faculty/staff, ethnic background, general special characteristics, local/state students, out-of-state students, previous college experience, religious affiliation, siblings of current students. *Tuition waivers:* Full or partial for children of alumni, employees or children of employees, senior citizens.

LOANS *Student loans:* $7,758,538 (73% need-based, 27% non-need-based). 92% of past graduating class borrowed through all loan programs. *Average indebtedness per student:* $20,407. *Average need-based loan:* Freshmen: $3436; Undergraduates: $4223. *Parent loans:* $2,829,115 (38% need-based, 62% non-need-based). *Programs:* FFEL (Subsidized and Unsubsidized Stafford, PLUS), Perkins, state, NJ Class Loans.

WORK-STUDY *Federal work-study:* Total amount: $69,606; 110 jobs averaging $990. *State or other work-study/employment:* Total amount: $161,679 (44% need-based, 56% non-need-based). 206 part-time jobs averaging $860.

APPLYING FOR FINANCIAL AID *Required financial aid form:* FAFSA. *Financial aid deadline (priority):* 4/15. *Notification date:* Continuous. Students must reply within 2 weeks of notification.

CONTACT Michael Corso, Director of Financial Aid, Centenary College, 400 Jefferson Street, Hackettstown, NJ 07840-2100, 908-852-1400 Ext. 2207 or toll-free 800-236-8679. *Fax:* 908-813-2632.

CENTENARY COLLEGE OF LOUISIANA
Shreveport, LA

Tuition & fees: $18,900	Average undergraduate aid package: $13,618

ABOUT THE INSTITUTION Independent United Methodist, coed. Awards: bachelor's and master's degrees. 66 undergraduate majors. Total enrollment: 1,044. Undergraduates: 904. Freshmen: 232. Federal methodology is used as a basis for awarding need-based institutional aid.

UNDERGRADUATE EXPENSES for 2006–07 *Application fee:* $30. *Comprehensive fee:* $25,680 includes full-time tuition ($18,900) and room and board ($6780). *College room only:* $3310. *Part-time tuition:* $630 per semester hour. *Part-time fees:* $50 per term.

FRESHMAN FINANCIAL AID (Fall 2004) 205 applied for aid; of those 73% were deemed to have need. 100% of freshmen with need received aid; of those 42% had need fully met. *Average percent of need met:* 71% (excluding resources awarded to replace EFC). *Average financial aid package:* $12,811 (excluding resources awarded to replace EFC). 25% of all full-time freshmen had no need and received non-need-based gift aid.

UNDERGRADUATE FINANCIAL AID (Fall 2004) 732 applied for aid; of those 75% were deemed to have need. 96% of undergraduates with need received aid; of those 40% had need fully met. *Average percent of need met:* 75% (excluding resources awarded to replace EFC). *Average financial aid package:* $13,618 (excluding resources awarded to replace EFC). 28% of all full-time undergraduates had no need and received non-need-based gift aid.

GIFT AID (NEED-BASED) *Total amount:* $6,035,121 (10% federal, 15% state, 73% institutional, 2% external sources). *Receiving aid:* Freshmen: 64% (149); All full-time undergraduates: 60% (529). *Average award:* Freshmen: $11,168;

Undergraduates: $11,289. *Scholarships, grants, and awards:* Federal Pell, FSEOG, state, private, college/university gift aid from institutional funds.

GIFT AID (NON-NEED-BASED) *Total amount:* $4,139,264 (12% state, 86% institutional, 2% external sources). *Receiving aid:* Freshmen: 19% (44); Undergraduates: 18% (160). *Average Award:* Freshmen: $9639; Undergraduates: $10,270. *Scholarships, grants, and awards by category: Academic Interests/Achievement:* 652 awards ($5,497,850 total): biological sciences, business, communication, education, engineering/technologies, English, foreign languages, general academic interests/achievements, health fields, humanities, mathematics, physical sciences, premedicine, religion/biblical studies, social sciences. *Creative Arts/Performance:* 213 awards ($682,961 total): art/fine arts, dance, general creative arts/performance, music, performing arts, theater/drama. *Special Achievements/Activities:* 177 awards ($366,913 total): community service, general special achievements/activities, leadership, religious involvement. *Special Characteristics:* 129 awards ($506,711 total): children of educators, children of faculty/staff, ethnic background, general special characteristics, international students, local/state students, members of minority groups, out-of-state students, relatives of clergy, religious affiliation.

LOANS *Student loans:* $2,005,088 (51% need-based, 49% non-need-based). 53% of past graduating class borrowed through all loan programs. *Average indebtedness per student:* $17,300. *Average need-based loan:* Freshmen: $2702; Undergraduates: $3631. *Parent loans:* $1,649,996 (100% non-need-based). *Programs:* FFEL (Subsidized and Unsubsidized Stafford, PLUS), Perkins.

WORK-STUDY *Federal work-study:* Total amount: $238,636; 162 jobs averaging $1457. *State or other work-study/employment:* Total amount: $68,100 (100% non-need-based). 63 part-time jobs averaging $1111.

ATHLETIC AWARDS *Total amount:* $2,211,724 (41% need-based, 59% non-need-based).

APPLYING FOR FINANCIAL AID *Required financial aid forms:* FAFSA, institution's own form. *Financial aid deadline (priority):* 2/15. *Notification date:* 3/15. Students must reply by 5/1.

CONTACT Ms. Mary Sue Rix, Director of Financial Aid, Centenary College of Louisiana, PO Box 41188, Shreveport, LA 71134-1188, 318-869-5137 or toll-free 800-234-4448. *Fax:* 318-841-7266. *E-mail:* msrix@centenary.edu.

CENTRAL BAPTIST COLLEGE
Conway, AR

CONTACT Christi Bell, Financial Aid Director, Central Baptist College, 1501 College Avenue, Conway, AR 72032-6470, 800-205-6872 Ext. 185 or toll-free 800-205-6872. *Fax:* 501-329-2941. *E-mail:* financialaid@cbc.edu.

CENTRAL BIBLE COLLEGE
Springfield, MO

ABOUT THE INSTITUTION Independent Assemblies of God, coed. Awards: associate and bachelor's degrees. 7 undergraduate majors. Total enrollment: 817. Undergraduates: 817. Freshmen: 189.

GIFT AID (NEED-BASED) *Scholarships, grants, and awards:* Federal Pell, FSEOG, college/university gift aid from institutional funds.

GIFT AID (NON-NEED-BASED) *Scholarships, grants, and awards by category: Academic Interests/Achievement:* general academic interests/achievements. *Creative Arts/Performance:* art/fine arts, music, theater/drama. *Special Achievements/Activities:* community service, religious involvement. *Special Characteristics:* children of faculty/staff, ethnic background, relatives of clergy, religious affiliation, siblings of current students, spouses of current students.

LOANS *Programs:* FFEL (Subsidized and Unsubsidized Stafford, PLUS), Perkins, college/university.

WORK-STUDY *Federal work-study:* Total amount: $164,635; 125 jobs averaging $1317.

APPLYING FOR FINANCIAL AID *Required financial aid form:* FAFSA.

CONTACT Rick Woolverton, Director of Financial Aid, Central Bible College, 3000 North Grant, Springfield, MO 65803-1096, 417-833-2551 or toll-free 800-831-4222 Ext. 1184. *Fax:* 417-833-2168.

CENTRAL CHRISTIAN COLLEGE OF KANSAS
McPherson, KS

ABOUT THE INSTITUTION Independent Free Methodist, coed. Awards: associate and bachelor's degrees. 84 undergraduate majors. Total enrollment: 336. Undergraduates: 336. Freshmen: 97.

GIFT AID (NEED-BASED) *Scholarships, grants, and awards:* Federal Pell, FSEOG, state, private.

GIFT AID (NON-NEED-BASED) *Scholarships, grants, and awards by category: Academic Interests/Achievement:* general academic interests/achievements, religion/biblical studies. *Creative Arts/Performance:* music, theater/drama. *Special Achievements/Activities:* cheerleading/drum major, general special achievements/activities, leadership, religious involvement. *Special Characteristics:* children of faculty/staff, relatives of clergy.

LOANS *Programs:* FFEL (Subsidized and Unsubsidized Stafford, PLUS), Perkins.

WORK-STUDY *Federal work-study:* Total amount: $58,725; 58 jobs averaging $1000.

APPLYING FOR FINANCIAL AID *Required financial aid form:* FAFSA.

CONTACT Mike Reimer, Financial Aid Director, Central Christian College of Kansas, 1200 South Main, PO Box 1403, McPherson, KS 67460, 620-241-0723 Ext. 333 or toll-free 800-835-0078 Ext. 337. *Fax:* 620-241-6032. *E-mail:* miker@centralchristian.edu.

CENTRAL CHRISTIAN COLLEGE OF THE BIBLE
Moberly, MO

Tuition & fees: N/R   **Average undergraduate aid package:** $12,879

ABOUT THE INSTITUTION Independent religious, coed. Awards: associate and bachelor's degrees. 7 undergraduate majors. Total enrollment: 531. Undergraduates: 531. Freshmen: 163. Both federal and institutional methodology are used as a basis for awarding need-based institutional aid.

UNDERGRADUATE EXPENSES for 2005–06 *Application fee:* $25. Every full-time student receives a full tuition scholarship.

FRESHMAN FINANCIAL AID (Fall 2004) 200 applied for aid; of those 90% were deemed to have need. 100% of freshmen with need received aid; of those 44% had need fully met. *Average percent of need met:* 81% (excluding resources awarded to replace EFC). *Average financial aid package:* $14,903 (excluding resources awarded to replace EFC). 27% of all full-time freshmen had no need and received non-need-based gift aid.

UNDERGRADUATE FINANCIAL AID (Fall 2004) 561 applied for aid; of those 74% were deemed to have need. 100% of undergraduates with need received aid; of those 25% had need fully met. *Average percent of need met:* 81% (excluding resources awarded to replace EFC). *Average financial aid package:* $12,879 (excluding resources awarded to replace EFC). 26% of all full-time undergraduates had no need and received non-need-based gift aid.

GIFT AID (NEED-BASED) *Total amount:* $909,962 (100% federal). *Receiving aid:* Freshmen: 59% (146); All full-time undergraduates: 44% (248). *Average award:* Freshmen: $2335; Undergraduates: $2718. *Scholarships, grants, and awards:* Federal Pell, FSEOG, private, college/university gift aid from institutional funds.

GIFT AID (NON-NEED-BASED) *Total amount:* $2,817,392 (98% institutional, 2% external sources). *Receiving aid:* Freshmen: 30% (75); Undergraduates: 26% (146). *Average Award:* Freshmen: $6300; Undergraduates: $6300. *Scholarships, grants, and awards by category: Academic Interests/Achievement:* 547 awards ($2,756,335 total): religion/biblical studies.

LOANS *Student loans:* $1,163,727 (60% need-based, 40% non-need-based). 66% of past graduating class borrowed through all loan programs. *Average indebtedness per student:* $10,762. *Average need-based loan:* Freshmen: $2366; Undergraduates: $2692. *Parent loans:* $135,635 (100% need-based). *Programs:* FFEL (Subsidized and Unsubsidized Stafford, PLUS), alternative loans.

WORK-STUDY *Federal work-study:* Total amount: $13,000; 10 jobs averaging $1100.

APPLYING FOR FINANCIAL AID *Financial aid deadline:* Continuous. *Notification date:* Continuous beginning 4/1. Students must reply by 6/15 or within 2 weeks of notification.

Central Christian College of the Bible

CONTACT Rhonda J. Dunham, Financial Aid Director, Central Christian College of the Bible, 911 East Urbandale Drive, Moberly, MO 65270-1997, 660-263-3900 Ext. 121 or toll-free 888-263-3900 (in-state). *Fax:* 660-263-3936. *E-mail:* rdunham@cccb.edu.

CENTRAL COLLEGE
Pella, IA

Tuition & fees: $20,972 | **Average undergraduate aid package: $16,987**

ABOUT THE INSTITUTION Independent religious, coed. Awards: bachelor's degrees. 35 undergraduate majors. Total enrollment: 1,635. Undergraduates: 1,635. Freshmen: 366. Federal methodology is used as a basis for awarding need-based institutional aid.
UNDERGRADUATE EXPENSES for 2006–07 *Application fee:* $25. *Comprehensive fee:* $28,196 includes full-time tuition ($20,972) and room and board ($7224). *College room only:* $3542. *Part-time tuition:* $728 per semester hour.
FRESHMAN FINANCIAL AID (Fall 2005, est.) 351 applied for aid; of those 86% were deemed to have need. 100% of freshmen with need received aid; of those 23% had need fully met. *Average percent of need met:* 82% (excluding resources awarded to replace EFC). *Average financial aid package:* $16,944 (excluding resources awarded to replace EFC). 17% of all full-time freshmen had no need and received non-need-based gift aid.
UNDERGRADUATE FINANCIAL AID (Fall 2005, est.) 1,341 applied for aid; of those 91% were deemed to have need. 100% of undergraduates with need received aid; of those 16% had need fully met. *Average percent of need met:* 81% (excluding resources awarded to replace EFC). *Average financial aid package:* $16,987 (excluding resources awarded to replace EFC). 19% of all full-time undergraduates had no need and received non-need-based gift aid.
GIFT AID (NEED-BASED) *Total amount:* $14,012,272 (7% federal, 18% state, 72% institutional, 3% external sources). *Receiving aid:* Freshmen: 83% (302); All full-time undergraduates: 80% (1,207). *Average award:* Freshmen: $12,500; Undergraduates: $11,542. *Scholarships, grants, and awards:* Federal Pell, FSEOG, state, private, college/university gift aid from institutional funds.
GIFT AID (NON-NEED-BASED) *Total amount:* $2,880,452 (1% state, 94% institutional, 5% external sources). *Receiving aid:* Freshmen: 13% (48); Undergraduates: 9% (140). *Average Award:* Freshmen: $8486; Undergraduates:* $8000. *Scholarships, grants, and awards by category: Academic Interests/Achievement:* biological sciences, business, communication, computer science, education, foreign languages, general academic interests/achievements, health fields, humanities, international studies, mathematics, physical sciences, religion/biblical studies. *Creative Arts/Performance:* art/fine arts, music, theater/drama. *Special Achievements/Activities:* religious involvement. *Special Characteristics:* children and siblings of alumni, children of current students, children of faculty/staff, general special characteristics, handicapped students, international students, members of minority groups, out-of-state students, previous college experience, religious affiliation, siblings of current students.
LOANS *Student loans:* $9,395,936 (67% need-based, 33% non-need-based). 85% of past graduating class borrowed through all loan programs. *Average indebtedness per student:* $23,490. *Average need-based loan:* Freshmen: $3139; Undergraduates: $4208. *Parent loans:* $1,606,532 (24% need-based, 76% non-need-based). *Programs:* Federal Direct (Subsidized and Unsubsidized Stafford, PLUS), Perkins, college/university, alternative loans.
WORK-STUDY *Federal work-study:* Total amount: $873,488; 761 jobs averaging $1148. *State or other work-study/employment:* Total amount: $583,272 (26% need-based, 74% non-need-based). 511 part-time jobs averaging $1141.
APPLYING FOR FINANCIAL AID *Required financial aid form:* FAFSA. *Financial aid deadline (priority):* 3/15. *Notification date:* Continuous beginning 3/15. Students must reply by 5/1 or within 2 weeks of notification.
CONTACT Ms. Jean Vander Wert, Director of Financial Aid, Central College, 812 University Street, Box 5800, Pella, IA 50219-1999, 641-628-5336 or toll-free 877-462-3687 (in-state), 877-462-3689 (out-of-state). *Fax:* 641-628-7199. *E-mail:* vanderwertj@central.edu.

CENTRAL CONNECTICUT STATE UNIVERSITY
New Britain, CT

Tuition & fees (CT res): $6164 | **Average undergraduate aid package: $6522**

ABOUT THE INSTITUTION State-supported, coed. Awards: bachelor's, master's, and doctoral degrees and post-bachelor's and post-master's certificates. 53 undergraduate majors. Total enrollment: 12,315. Undergraduates: 9,678. Freshmen: 1,356. Federal methodology is used as a basis for awarding need-based institutional aid.
UNDERGRADUATE EXPENSES for 2005–06 *Application fee:* $50. *Tuition, state resident:* full-time $3034; part-time $290 per credit. *Tuition, nonresident:* full-time $9820; part-time $290 per credit. *Required fees:* full-time $3130; $55 per term part-time. Full-time tuition and fees vary according to course level, course load, and reciprocity agreements. Part-time tuition and fees vary according to course level and course load. *College room and board:* $7456; *room only:* $4250. Room and board charges vary according to board plan. *Payment plan:* Installment.
FRESHMAN FINANCIAL AID (Fall 2005, est.) 966 applied for aid; of those 65% were deemed to have need. 97% of freshmen with need received aid; of those 12% had need fully met. *Average percent of need met:* 68% (excluding resources awarded to replace EFC). *Average financial aid package:* $5943 (excluding resources awarded to replace EFC). 9% of all full-time freshmen had no need and received non-need-based gift aid.
UNDERGRADUATE FINANCIAL AID (Fall 2005, est.) 5,196 applied for aid; of those 77% were deemed to have need. 98% of undergraduates with need received aid; of those 10% had need fully met. *Average percent of need met:* 75% (excluding resources awarded to replace EFC). *Average financial aid package:* $6522 (excluding resources awarded to replace EFC). 5% of all full-time undergraduates had no need and received non-need-based gift aid.
GIFT AID (NEED-BASED) *Total amount:* $10,619,702 (43% federal, 24% state, 33% institutional). *Receiving aid:* Freshmen: 38% (450); All full-time undergraduates: 41% (2,806). *Average award:* Freshmen: $4352; Undergraduates: $4931. *Scholarships, grants, and awards:* Federal Pell, FSEOG, state, private, college/university gift aid from institutional funds.
GIFT AID (NON-NEED-BASED) *Total amount:* $12,606,511 (94% institutional, 6% external sources). *Receiving aid:* Freshmen: 5% (64); Undergraduates: 5% (353). *Average Award:* Freshmen: $2602; Undergraduates: $2624. *Scholarships, grants, and awards by category: Academic Interests/Achievement:* general academic interests/achievements. *Special Characteristics:* members of minority groups. *Tuition waivers:* Full or partial for employees or children of employees, senior citizens. *ROTC:* Army cooperative, Air Force cooperative.
LOANS *Student loans:* $27,433,784 (58% need-based, 42% non-need-based). 38% of past graduating class borrowed through all loan programs. *Average indebtedness per student:* $10,500. *Average need-based loan:* Freshmen: $2950; Undergraduates: $3950. *Parent loans:* $3,360,290 (100% non-need-based). *Programs:* Federal Direct (Subsidized and Unsubsidized Stafford, PLUS, FFEL (Subsidized and Unsubsidized Stafford, PLUS), Perkins.
WORK-STUDY *Federal work-study:* Total amount: $325,000; 289 jobs averaging $1990. *State or other work-study/employment:* 110 part-time jobs averaging $544.
ATHLETIC AWARDS *Total amount:* $1,725,699 (100% non-need-based).
APPLYING FOR FINANCIAL AID *Required financial aid forms:* FAFSA, institution's own form. *Financial aid deadline (priority):* 3/1. *Notification date:* Continuous. Students must reply within 3 weeks of notification.
CONTACT Ms. Keri Lupachino, Assistant Director of Financial Aid, Central Connecticut State University, Memorial Hall, Room 103, 1615 Stanley Street, New Britain, CT 06050-4010, 860-832-2200 or toll-free 800-755-2278 (in-state). *Fax:* 860-832-1105. *E-mail:* lupachinok@ccsu.edu.

CENTRAL METHODIST UNIVERSITY
Fayette, MO

ABOUT THE INSTITUTION Independent Methodist, coed. Awards: associate, bachelor's, and master's degrees. 47 undergraduate majors. Total enrollment: 781. Undergraduates: 781. Freshmen: 193.
GIFT AID (NEED-BASED) *Scholarships, grants, and awards:* Federal Pell, FSEOG, state, private, college/university gift aid from institutional funds.
GIFT AID (NON-NEED-BASED) *Scholarships, grants, and awards by category: Academic Interests/Achievement:* biological sciences, business, communication, computer science, education, English, foreign languages, general academic interests/achievements, health fields, humanities, mathematics, physical sciences, premedicine, religion/biblical studies, social sciences. *Creative Arts/Performance:* music, theater/drama. *Special Achievements/Activities:* cheerleading/drum major, leadership, religious involvement. *Special Characteristics:* children

and siblings of alumni, children of faculty/staff, general special characteristics, international students, relatives of clergy, religious affiliation, siblings of current students, spouses of current students.
LOANS *Programs:* FFEL (Subsidized and Unsubsidized Stafford, PLUS), college/university.
APPLYING FOR FINANCIAL AID *Required financial aid form:* FAFSA.
CONTACT Linda Mackey, Director of Financial Assistance, Central Methodist University, 411 CMC Square, Fayette, MO 65248-1198, 660-248-6244 or toll-free 888-CMU-1854 (in-state). *Fax:* 660-248-6288. *E-mail:* lmackey@cmc.edu.

CENTRAL MICHIGAN UNIVERSITY
Mount Pleasant, MI

Tuition & fees (MI res): $5868   Average undergraduate aid package: $9632

ABOUT THE INSTITUTION State-supported, coed. Awards: bachelor's, master's, and doctoral degrees and post-bachelor's and post-master's certificates. 117 undergraduate majors. Total enrollment: 27,221. Undergraduates: 19,997. Freshmen: 3,737. Federal methodology is used as a basis for awarding need-based institutional aid.
UNDERGRADUATE EXPENSES for 2005–06 *Application fee:* $35. *Tuition, state resident:* full-time $5868; part-time $195.60 per credit. *Tuition, nonresident:* full-time $13,632; part-time $454.40 per credit. Full-time tuition and fees vary according to student level. Part-time tuition and fees vary according to student level. *College room and board:* $6376; *room only:* $3188. Room and board charges vary according to board plan, housing facility, and location. *Payment plans:* Guaranteed tuition, installment.
FRESHMAN FINANCIAL AID (Fall 2005, est.) 2900 applied for aid; of those 68% were deemed to have need. 99% of freshmen with need received aid; of those 79% had need fully met. *Average percent of need met:* 99% (excluding resources awarded to replace EFC). *Average financial aid package:* $9620 (excluding resources awarded to replace EFC). 16% of all full-time freshmen had no need and received non-need-based gift aid.
UNDERGRADUATE FINANCIAL AID (Fall 2005, est.) 12,235 applied for aid; of those 75% were deemed to have need. 99% of undergraduates with need received aid; of those 72% had need fully met. *Average percent of need met:* 94% (excluding resources awarded to replace EFC). *Average financial aid package:* $9632 (excluding resources awarded to replace EFC). 10% of all full-time undergraduates had no need and received non-need-based gift aid.
GIFT AID (NEED-BASED) *Total amount:* $27,720,711 (49% federal, 20% state, 27% institutional, 4% external sources). *Receiving aid:* Freshmen: 48% (1,784); All full-time undergraduates: 40% (7,082). *Average award:* Freshmen: $4784; Undergraduates: $3929. *Scholarships, grants, and awards:* Federal Pell, FSEOG, state, private, college/university gift aid from institutional funds.
GIFT AID (NON-NEED-BASED) *Total amount:* $12,146,505 (7% federal, 29% state, 51% institutional, 13% external sources). *Receiving aid:* Freshmen: 9% (320); Undergraduates: 4% (628). *Average Award:* Freshmen: $3357; Undergraduates:* $3096. *Scholarships, grants, and awards by category: Academic Interests/Achievement:* 8,777 awards ($13,498,496 total): biological sciences, business, communication, computer science, education, engineering/technologies, English, foreign languages, general academic interests/achievements, health fields, humanities, mathematics, military science, physical sciences, social sciences. *Creative Arts/Performance:* 209 awards ($223,593 total): applied art and design, art/fine arts, cinema/film/broadcasting, creative writing, dance, journalism/publications, music, performing arts, theater/drama. *Special Achievements/Activities:* 404 awards ($1,293,345 total): leadership. *Special Characteristics:* 1,012 awards ($2,962,660 total): children and siblings of alumni, children of faculty/staff, children of union members/company employees, first-generation college students, international students, local/state students, members of minority groups, out-of-state students, veterans, veterans' children. *Tuition waivers:* Full or partial for children of alumni, employees or children of employees, senior citizens. *ROTC:* Army.
LOANS *Student loans:* $62,711,614 (73% need-based, 27% non-need-based). 64% of past graduating class borrowed through all loan programs. *Average indebtedness per student:* $16,537. *Average need-based loan:* Freshmen: $3605; Undergraduates: $5129. *Parent loans:* $24,492,798 (39% need-based, 61% non-need-based). *Programs:* Federal Direct (Subsidized and Unsubsidized Stafford, PLUS), Perkins, state, alternative loans.
WORK-STUDY *Federal work-study:* Total amount: $1,599,194; 796 jobs averaging $1841. *State or other work-study/employment:* Total amount: $6,782,713 (34% need-based, 66% non-need-based). 3,664 part-time jobs averaging $1851.

ATHLETIC AWARDS *Total amount:* $3,147,909 (31% need-based, 69% non-need-based).
APPLYING FOR FINANCIAL AID *Required financial aid form:* FAFSA. *Financial aid deadline (priority):* 3/1. *Notification date:* Continuous beginning 4/1.
CONTACT Mr. Michael Owens, Director of Scholarships and Financial Aid, Central Michigan University, WA 202, Mount Pleasant, MI 48859, 989-774-7428 or toll-free 888-292-5366. *Fax:* 989-774-3634. *E-mail:* owens1ma@cmich.edu.

CENTRAL MISSOURI STATE UNIVERSITY
Warrensburg, MO

Tuition & fees (MO res): $5835   Average undergraduate aid package: $4160

ABOUT THE INSTITUTION State-supported, coed. Awards: associate, bachelor's, and master's degrees and post-bachelor's and post-master's certificates. 72 undergraduate majors. Total enrollment: 10,604. Undergraduates: 8,817. Freshmen: 1,575. Federal methodology is used as a basis for awarding need-based institutional aid.
UNDERGRADUATE EXPENSES for 2006–07 *Application fee:* $30. *Tuition, state resident:* full-time $5835. *Tuition, nonresident:* full-time $11,250. *College room and board:* $5109; *room only:* $3406.
FRESHMAN FINANCIAL AID (Fall 2004) 1172 applied for aid; of those 69% were deemed to have need. 97% of freshmen with need received aid; of those 17% had need fully met. *Average percent of need met:* 77% (excluding resources awarded to replace EFC). *Average financial aid package:* $3897 (excluding resources awarded to replace EFC). 39% of all full-time freshmen had no need and received non-need-based gift aid.
UNDERGRADUATE FINANCIAL AID (Fall 2004) 5,965 applied for aid; of those 77% were deemed to have need. 98% of undergraduates with need received aid; of those 21% had need fully met. *Average percent of need met:* 98% (excluding resources awarded to replace EFC). *Average financial aid package:* $4160 (excluding resources awarded to replace EFC). 31% of all full-time undergraduates had no need and received non-need-based gift aid.
GIFT AID (NEED-BASED) *Total amount:* $4,593,830 (96% federal, 4% state). *Receiving aid:* Freshmen: 29% (420); All full-time undergraduates: 38% (2,676). *Average award:* Freshmen: $1631; Undergraduates: $1735. *Scholarships, grants, and awards:* Federal Pell, FSEOG, state, private, college/university gift aid from institutional funds.
GIFT AID (NON-NEED-BASED) *Total amount:* $7,760,220 (3% federal, 6% state, 70% institutional, 21% external sources). *Receiving aid:* Freshmen: 40% (572); Undergraduates: 33% (2,331). *Average Award:* Freshmen: $2690; Undergraduates: $2139. *Scholarships, grants, and awards by category: Academic Interests/Achievement:* 455 awards ($185,000 total): agriculture, area/ethnic studies, biological sciences, business, communication, computer science, education, engineering/technologies, English, foreign languages, general academic interests/achievements, health fields, home economics, humanities, library science, mathematics, military science, physical sciences, premedicine, religion/biblical studies, social sciences. *Creative Arts/Performance:* 705 awards ($230,000 total): applied art and design, art/fine arts, cinema/film/broadcasting, creative writing, debating, journalism/publications, music, performing arts, theater/drama. *Special Achievements/Activities:* 60 awards ($40,000 total): cheerleading/drum major, leadership. *Special Characteristics:* 546 awards ($536,450 total): adult students, children and siblings of alumni, children of faculty/staff, ethnic background, members of minority groups, out-of-state students, previous college experience. *ROTC:* Army, Air Force cooperative.
LOANS *Student loans:* $12,387,463 (58% need-based, 42% non-need-based). 63% of past graduating class borrowed through all loan programs. *Average indebtedness per student:* $9632. *Average need-based loan:* Freshmen: $1258; Undergraduates: $2146. *Parent loans:* $3,791,267 (100% non-need-based). *Programs:* Federal Direct (Subsidized and Unsubsidized Stafford, PLUS), Perkins, state.
WORK-STUDY *Federal work-study:* Total amount: $176,910; 309 jobs averaging $1192. *State or other work-study/employment:* Total amount: $799,672 (100% non-need-based). 1,286 part-time jobs averaging $787.
ATHLETIC AWARDS *Total amount:* $1,625,530 (100% non-need-based).
APPLYING FOR FINANCIAL AID *Required financial aid form:* FAFSA. *Financial aid deadline (priority):* 4/1. *Notification date:* Continuous beginning 3/1. Students must reply within 3 weeks of notification.

Central Missouri State University

CONTACT Mr. Phil Shreves, Director of Student Financial Assistance, Central Missouri State University, Office of Financial Aid, Administration Building 104, Warrensburg, MO 64093, 660-543-4040 or toll-free 800-729-2678 (in-state). *Fax:* 660-543-8080. *E-mail:* fedaid@cmsuvmb.cmsu.edu.

CENTRAL PENNSYLVANIA COLLEGE
Summerdale, PA

ABOUT THE INSTITUTION Proprietary, coed. Awards: associate and bachelor's degrees. 22 undergraduate majors. Total enrollment: 981. Undergraduates: 981. Freshmen: 213.

GIFT AID (NEED-BASED) *Scholarships, grants, and awards:* Federal Pell, FSEOG, state, private, college/university gift aid from institutional funds.

GIFT AID (NON-NEED-BASED) *Scholarships, grants, and awards by category: Academic Interests/Achievement:* general academic interests/achievements. *Special Achievements/Activities:* leadership, memberships. *Special Characteristics:* general special characteristics, out-of-state students.

LOANS *Programs:* FFEL (Subsidized and Unsubsidized Stafford, PLUS).

APPLYING FOR FINANCIAL AID *Required financial aid forms:* FAFSA, institution's own form, state aid form, Federal Stafford Loan.

CONTACT Kathy Shepard, Financial Aid Director, Central Pennsylvania College, College Hill Road, Summerdale, PA 17093, 717-728-2261 or toll-free 800-759-2727 Ext. 2201. *Fax:* 717-728-2300. *E-mail:* financial-aid@centralpenn.edu.

CENTRAL STATE UNIVERSITY
Wilberforce, OH

CONTACT Veronica J. Leech, Director of Student Financial Aid, Central State University, PO Box 1004, Wilberforce, OH 45384, 937-376-6579 or toll-free 800-388-CSU1 (in-state).

CENTRAL WASHINGTON UNIVERSITY
Ellensburg, WA

Tuition & fees (WA res): $4806   **Average undergraduate aid package:** $7996

ABOUT THE INSTITUTION State-supported, coed. Awards: bachelor's and master's degrees and post-bachelor's certificates. 72 undergraduate majors. Total enrollment: 10,190. Undergraduates: 9,617. Freshmen: 1,437. Federal methodology is used as a basis for awarding need-based institutional aid.

UNDERGRADUATE EXPENSES for 2006–07 *Application fee:* $50. *Tuition, state resident:* full-time $4182. *Tuition, nonresident:* full-time $12,477. *College room and board:* $6924.

FRESHMAN FINANCIAL AID (Fall 2004) 1010 applied for aid; of those 66% were deemed to have need. 93% of freshmen with need received aid; of those 26% had need fully met. *Average percent of need met:* 70% (excluding resources awarded to replace EFC). *Average financial aid package:* $7022 (excluding resources awarded to replace EFC). 1% of all full-time freshmen had no need and received non-need-based gift aid.

UNDERGRADUATE FINANCIAL AID (Fall 2004) 5,773 applied for aid; of those 76% were deemed to have need. 95% of undergraduates with need received aid; of those 26% had need fully met. *Average percent of need met:* 73% (excluding resources awarded to replace EFC). *Average financial aid package:* $7996 (excluding resources awarded to replace EFC). 1% of all full-time undergraduates had no need and received non-need-based gift aid.

GIFT AID (NEED-BASED) *Total amount:* $15,679,890 (40% federal, 43% state, 8% institutional, 9% external sources). *Receiving aid:* Freshmen: 33% (455); All full-time undergraduates: 36% (2,971). *Average award:* Freshmen: $1931; Undergraduates: $2309. *Scholarships, grants, and awards:* Federal Pell, FSEOG, state, private, college/university gift aid from institutional funds, Title III grants, McNair scholarships, WA Regional Achievers Awards.

GIFT AID (NON-NEED-BASED) *Total amount:* $305,012 (20% state, 1% institutional, 79% external sources). *Receiving aid:* Freshmen: 1; Undergraduates: 3. *Average Award:* Freshmen: $513; Undergraduates: $731. *Scholarships, grants, and awards by category: Academic Interests/Achievement:* 963 awards ($2,930,702 total): business, communication, computer science, education, engineering/technologies, English, foreign languages, general academic interests/achievements, health fields, international studies, mathematics, military science, physical sciences, premedicine. *Creative Arts/Performance:* 90 awards ($260,000 total): applied art and design, art/fine arts, journalism/publications, music, performing arts, theater/drama. *Special Achievements/Activities:* 30 awards ($80,000 total): community service, general special achievements/activities, hobbies/interests, leadership, memberships. *Special Characteristics:* adult students, children and siblings of alumni, general special characteristics, handicapped students, local/state students, previous college experience. *ROTC:* Army, Air Force.

LOANS *Student loans:* $27,139,346 (74% need-based, 26% non-need-based). 63% of past graduating class borrowed through all loan programs. *Average indebtedness per student:* $27,025. *Average need-based loan:* Freshmen: $2350; Undergraduates: $3387. *Parent loans:* $13,507,814 (44% need-based, 56% non-need-based). *Programs:* Federal Direct (Subsidized and Unsubsidized Stafford, PLUS), FFEL (Subsidized and Unsubsidized Stafford, PLUS), Perkins, state, college/university.

WORK-STUDY *Federal work-study:* Total amount: $539,182; 205 jobs averaging $2630. *State or other work-study/employment:* Total amount: $535,202 (100% need-based). 197 part-time jobs averaging $2793.

ATHLETIC AWARDS *Total amount:* $321,665 (77% need-based, 23% non-need-based).

APPLYING FOR FINANCIAL AID *Required financial aid form:* FAFSA. *Financial aid deadline (priority):* 3/1. *Notification date:* Continuous beginning 4/15. Students must reply within 4 weeks of notification.

CONTACT Ms. Agnes Canedo, Director of Financial Aid, Central Washington University, 400 East University Way, Ellensburg, WA 98926-7495, 509-963-3049 or toll-free 866-298-4968. *Fax:* 509-963-1788. *E-mail:* canedoa@cwu.edu.

CENTRAL YESHIVA TOMCHEI TMIMIM-LUBAVITCH
Brooklyn, NY

CONTACT Rabbi Moshe M. Gluckowsky, Director of Financial Aid, Central Yeshiva Tomchei Tmimim-Lubavitch, 841-853 Ocean Parkway, Brooklyn, NY 11230, 718-859-2277.

CENTRE COLLEGE
Danville, KY

Tuition & fees: $23,110   **Average undergraduate aid package:** $18,526

ABOUT THE INSTITUTION Independent religious, coed. Awards: bachelor's degrees. 28 undergraduate majors. Total enrollment: 1,130. Undergraduates: 1,130. Freshmen: 316. Both federal and institutional methodology are used as a basis for awarding need-based institutional aid.

UNDERGRADUATE EXPENSES for 2005–06 *Application fee:* $40. *Comprehensive fee:* $30,810 includes full-time tuition ($23,110) and room and board ($7700). *College room only:* $3900. Room and board charges vary according to board plan. *Part-time tuition:* $830 per credit hour. Part-time tuition and fees vary according to course load. *Payment plan:* Installment.

FRESHMAN FINANCIAL AID (Fall 2005, est.) 252 applied for aid; of those 72% were deemed to have need. 100% of freshmen with need received aid; of those 42% had need fully met. *Average percent of need met:* 90% (excluding resources awarded to replace EFC). *Average financial aid package:* $18,893 (excluding resources awarded to replace EFC). 39% of all full-time freshmen had no need and received non-need-based gift aid.

UNDERGRADUATE FINANCIAL AID (Fall 2005, est.) 828 applied for aid; of those 82% were deemed to have need. 100% of undergraduates with need received aid; of those 38% had need fully met. *Average percent of need met:* 88% (excluding resources awarded to replace EFC). *Average financial aid package:* $18,526 (excluding resources awarded to replace EFC). 34% of all full-time undergraduates had no need and received non-need-based gift aid.

GIFT AID (NEED-BASED) *Total amount:* $10,684,807 (5% federal, 20% state, 72% institutional, 3% external sources). *Receiving aid:* Freshmen: 57% (180); All full-time undergraduates: 60% (675). *Average award:* Freshmen: $17,281; Undergraduates: $15,809. *Scholarships, grants, and awards:* Federal Pell, FSEOG, state, private, college/university gift aid from institutional funds.

GIFT AID (NON-NEED-BASED) *Total amount:* $4,079,784 (13% state, 85% institutional, 2% external sources). *Average Award:* Freshmen: $11,224; Undergraduates: $10,381. *Scholarships, grants, and awards by category: Academic Interests/Achievement:* 744 awards ($5,978,610 total): general academic interests/achievements. *Creative Arts/Performance:* 78 awards ($272,500 total): music, theater/drama. *Special Characteristics:* 148 awards ($948,621 total):

children and siblings of alumni, children of faculty/staff, ethnic background, first-generation college students. *Tuition waivers:* Full or partial for children of alumni, employees or children of employees. *ROTC:* Army cooperative, Air Force cooperative.
LOANS *Student loans:* $2,709,963 (67% need-based, 33% non-need-based). 58% of past graduating class borrowed through all loan programs. *Average indebtedness per student:* $13,700. *Average need-based loan:* Freshmen: $2716; Undergraduates: $4110. *Parent loans:* $1,736,999 (100% non-need-based). *Programs:* FFEL (Subsidized and Unsubsidized Stafford, PLUS), Perkins, college/university.
WORK-STUDY *Federal work-study:* Total amount: $371,785; 274 jobs averaging $1374. *State or other work-study/employment:* Total amount: $58,050 (24% need-based, 76% non-need-based). 30 part-time jobs averaging $1860.
APPLYING FOR FINANCIAL AID *Required financial aid forms:* FAFSA, institution's own form. *Financial aid deadline:* 3/1. *Notification date:* 4/1. Students must reply by 5/1.
CONTACT Ms. Elaine Larson, Director of Student Financial Planning, Centre College, 600 West Walnut Street, Danville, KY 40422-1394, 859-238-5365 or toll-free 800-423-6236. *Fax:* 859-238-5373. *E-mail:* finaid@centre.edu.

CHADRON STATE COLLEGE
Chadron, NE

ABOUT THE INSTITUTION State-supported, coed. Awards: bachelor's and master's degrees. 46 undergraduate majors. Total enrollment: 2,636. Undergraduates: 2,316. Freshmen: 326.
GIFT AID (NEED-BASED) *Scholarships, grants, and awards:* Federal Pell, FSEOG, state, college/university gift aid from institutional funds.
LOANS *Programs:* Federal Direct (Subsidized and Unsubsidized Stafford, PLUS), FFEL (Subsidized and Unsubsidized Stafford, PLUS), Perkins.
WORK-STUDY *Federal work-study:* Total amount: $440,904; jobs available.
APPLYING FOR FINANCIAL AID *Required financial aid forms:* FAFSA, institution's own form.
CONTACT Ms. Sherry Douglas, Director of Financial Aid, Chadron State College, 1000 Main Street, Chadron, NE 69337, 308-432-6230 or toll-free 800-242-3766 (in-state). *Fax:* 308-432-6229. *E-mail:* finaid@csc.edu.

CHAMINADE UNIVERSITY OF HONOLULU
Honolulu, HI

Tuition & fees: $14,960   **Average undergraduate aid package: $12,846**

ABOUT THE INSTITUTION Independent Roman Catholic, coed. Awards: associate, bachelor's, and master's degrees and post-bachelor's certificates. 22 undergraduate majors. Total enrollment: 1,810. Undergraduates: 1,106. Freshmen: 261. Federal methodology is used as a basis for awarding need-based institutional aid.
UNDERGRADUATE EXPENSES for 2006-07 *Application fee:* $50. *Comprehensive fee:* $24,340 includes full-time tuition ($14,820), mandatory fees ($140), and room and board ($9380). *College room only:* $4980. *Part-time tuition:* $494 per credit.
FRESHMAN FINANCIAL AID (Fall 2004) 202 applied for aid; of those 83% were deemed to have need. 100% of freshmen with need received aid; of those 13% had need fully met. *Average percent of need met:* 65% (excluding resources awarded to replace EFC). *Average financial aid package:* $11,862 (excluding resources awarded to replace EFC). 14% of all full-time freshmen had no need and received non-need-based gift aid.
UNDERGRADUATE FINANCIAL AID (Fall 2004) 852 applied for aid; of those 89% were deemed to have need. 100% of undergraduates with need received aid; of those 14% had need fully met. *Average percent of need met:* 65% (excluding resources awarded to replace EFC). *Average financial aid package:* $12,846 (excluding resources awarded to replace EFC). 17% of all full-time undergraduates had no need and received non-need-based gift aid.
GIFT AID (NEED-BASED) *Total amount:* $6,682,275 (25% federal, 60% institutional, 15% external sources). *Receiving aid:* Freshmen: 67% (166); All full-time undergraduates: 73% (757). *Average award:* Freshmen: $8258; Undergraduates: $8257. *Scholarships, grants, and awards:* Federal Pell, FSEOG, state, private, college/university gift aid from institutional funds.
GIFT AID (NON-NEED-BASED) *Total amount:* $1,087,935 (86% institutional, 14% external sources). *Receiving aid:* Freshmen: 7% (18); Undergraduates: 7% (77). *Average Award:* Freshmen: $4994; Undergraduates: $4565. *Scholarships, grants, and awards by category:* Academic Interests/Achievement: 992 awards ($4,434,024 total): general academic interests/achievements. *ROTC:* Army cooperative, Air Force cooperative.
LOANS *Student loans:* $5,614,698 (77% need-based, 23% non-need-based). 56% of past graduating class borrowed through all loan programs. *Average indebtedness per student:* $22,263. *Average need-based loan:* Freshmen: $2879; Undergraduates: $4156. *Parent loans:* $3,640,772 (38% need-based, 62% non-need-based). *Programs:* FFEL (Subsidized and Unsubsidized Stafford, PLUS), Perkins, alternative loans.
WORK-STUDY *Federal work-study:* Total amount: $175,000; 120 jobs averaging $1500.
ATHLETIC AWARDS *Total amount:* $491,358 (72% need-based, 28% non-need-based).
APPLYING FOR FINANCIAL AID *Required financial aid form:* FAFSA. *Financial aid deadline (priority):* 3/1. *Notification date:* Continuous. Students must reply within 4 weeks of notification.
CONTACT Mr. Eric Nemoto, Associate Dean of Enrollment Management, Chaminade University of Honolulu, 3140 Waialae Avenue, Honolulu, HI 96816-1578, 808-735-4780 or toll-free 800-735-3733 (out-of-state). *Fax:* 808-739-8362. *E-mail:* enemoto@chaminade.edu.

CHAMPLAIN COLLEGE
Burlington, VT

Tuition & fees: $14,910   **Average undergraduate aid package: $9185**

ABOUT THE INSTITUTION Independent, coed. Awards: associate, bachelor's, and master's degrees. 57 undergraduate majors. Total enrollment: 2,529. Undergraduates: 2,472. Freshmen: 461. Both federal and institutional methodology are used as a basis for awarding need-based institutional aid.
UNDERGRADUATE EXPENSES for 2005-06 *Application fee:* $40. *Comprehensive fee:* $24,605 includes full-time tuition ($14,660), mandatory fees ($250), and room and board ($9695). *College room only:* $5855. Full-time tuition and fees vary according to course load. Room and board charges vary according to board plan and housing facility. *Part-time tuition:* $420 per credit hour. Part-time tuition and fees vary according to course load. *Payment plan:* Installment.
FRESHMAN FINANCIAL AID (Fall 2004) 361 applied for aid; of those 74% were deemed to have need. 96% of freshmen with need received aid; of those 19% had need fully met. *Average percent of need met:* 58% (excluding resources awarded to replace EFC). *Average financial aid package:* $8795 (excluding resources awarded to replace EFC). 7% of all full-time freshmen had no need and received non-need-based gift aid.
UNDERGRADUATE FINANCIAL AID (Fall 2004) 1,701 applied for aid; of those 60% were deemed to have need. 96% of undergraduates with need received aid; of those 21% had need fully met. *Average percent of need met:* 63% (excluding resources awarded to replace EFC). *Average financial aid package:* $9185 (excluding resources awarded to replace EFC). 1% of all full-time undergraduates had no need and received non-need-based gift aid.
GIFT AID (NEED-BASED) *Total amount:* $4,541,247 (34% federal, 36% state, 21% institutional, 9% external sources). *Receiving aid:* Freshmen: 50% (199); All full-time undergraduates: 43% (749). *Average award:* Freshmen: $4869; Undergraduates: $5134. *Scholarships, grants, and awards:* Federal Pell, FSEOG, state, private, college/university gift aid from institutional funds.
GIFT AID (NON-NEED-BASED) *Total amount:* $197,479 (71% institutional, 29% external sources). *Receiving aid:* Freshmen: 1% (5); Undergraduates: 1% (19). *Average Award:* Freshmen: $4538; Undergraduates: $3453. *Scholarships, grants, and awards by category:* Academic Interests/Achievement: 9 awards ($9800 total): business, communication, health fields. *Tuition waivers:* Full or partial for employees or children of employees, senior citizens. *ROTC:* Army cooperative.
LOANS *Student loans:* $11,032,946 (67% need-based, 33% non-need-based). *Average need-based loan:* Freshmen: $4886; Undergraduates: $5218. *Parent loans:* $5,742,999 (36% need-based, 64% non-need-based). *Programs:* FFEL (Subsidized and Unsubsidized Stafford, PLUS), Perkins, state.
WORK-STUDY *Federal work-study:* Total amount: $311,053; 231 jobs averaging $1437.
APPLYING FOR FINANCIAL AID *Required financial aid forms:* FAFSA, institution's own form, state aid form, noncustodial (divorced/separated) parent's statement. *Financial aid deadline (priority):* 5/1. *Notification date:* Continuous beginning 3/1. Students must reply within 2 weeks of notification.

Champlain College

CONTACT David B. Myette, Director of Financial Aid, Champlain College, 163 South Willard Street, Burlington, VT 05401, 802-860-2730 or toll-free 800-570-5858. *Fax:* 802-860-2775. *E-mail:* myette@champlain.edu.

CHAPMAN UNIVERSITY
Orange, CA

Tuition & fees: $30,748 | Average undergraduate aid package: $20,774

ABOUT THE INSTITUTION Independent religious, coed. Awards: bachelor's, master's, and first professional degrees and post-bachelor's certificates. 54 undergraduate majors. Total enrollment: 5,732. Undergraduates: 3,864. Freshmen: 853. Both federal and institutional methodology are used as a basis for awarding need-based institutional aid.
UNDERGRADUATE EXPENSES for 2006–07 *Application fee:* $55. *Comprehensive fee:* $41,248 includes full-time tuition ($29,900), mandatory fees ($848), and room and board ($10,500). *Part-time tuition:* $920 per credit.
FRESHMAN FINANCIAL AID (Fall 2004) 661 applied for aid; of those 72% were deemed to have need. 100% of freshmen with need received aid; of those 100% had need fully met. *Average percent of need met:* 100% (excluding resources awarded to replace EFC). *Average financial aid package:* $22,516 (excluding resources awarded to replace EFC). 13% of all full-time freshmen had no need and received non-need-based gift aid.
UNDERGRADUATE FINANCIAL AID (Fall 2004) 3,142 applied for aid; of those 71% were deemed to have need. 100% of undergraduates with need received aid; of those 100% had need fully met. *Average percent of need met:* 100% (excluding resources awarded to replace EFC). *Average financial aid package:* $20,774 (excluding resources awarded to replace EFC). 14% of all full-time undergraduates had no need and received non-need-based gift aid.
GIFT AID (NEED-BASED) *Total amount:* $34,599,261 (9% federal, 13% state, 75% institutional, 3% external sources). *Receiving aid:* Freshmen: 63% (472); All full-time undergraduates: 61% (2,204). *Average award:* Freshmen: $19,640; Undergraduates: $17,219. *Scholarships, grants, and awards:* Federal Pell, FSEOG, state, private, college/university gift aid from institutional funds.
GIFT AID (NON-NEED-BASED) *Total amount:* $7,928,421 (98% institutional, 2% external sources). *Average Award:* Freshmen: $16,440; Undergraduates: $14,755. *Scholarships, grants, and awards by category:* Academic Interests/Achievement: 69 awards ($134,500 total): biological sciences, physical sciences. Creative Arts/Performance: 253 awards ($1,334,697 total): art/fine arts, cinema/film/broadcasting, creative writing, dance, music, performing arts, theater/drama. Special Characteristics: 38 awards ($38,000 total): children and siblings of alumni. *ROTC:* Army cooperative, Air Force cooperative.
LOANS *Student loans:* $12,575,233 (92% need-based, 8% non-need-based). 64% of past graduating class borrowed through all loan programs. *Average indebtedness per student:* $19,237. *Average need-based loan:* Freshmen: $3557; Undergraduates: $4429. *Parent loans:* $8,676,708 (76% need-based, 24% non-need-based). *Programs:* FFEL (Subsidized and Unsubsidized Stafford, PLUS), Perkins, college/university.
WORK-STUDY *Federal work-study:* Total amount: $1,188,446; 697 jobs averaging $1705.
APPLYING FOR FINANCIAL AID *Required financial aid forms:* FAFSA, state aid form. *Financial aid deadline (priority):* 3/2. *Notification date:* Continuous beginning 3/15. Students must reply within 3 weeks of notification.
CONTACT Gregory L. Ball, Director of Financial Aid, Chapman University, One University Drive, Orange, CA 92866, 714-997-6741 or toll-free 888-CUAPPLY. *Fax:* 714-997-6743. *E-mail:* gball@chapman.edu.

CHARLES R. DREW UNIVERSITY OF MEDICINE AND SCIENCE
Los Angeles, CA

CONTACT Financial Aid Office, Charles R. Drew University of Medicine and Science, 1731 East 120th Street, Los Angeles, CA 90059, 323-563-4824. *Fax:* 323-569-0597.

CHARLESTON SOUTHERN UNIVERSITY
Charleston, SC

CONTACT Director of Financial Aid, Charleston Southern University, PO Box 118087, 9200 University Boulevard, Charleston, SC 29423-8087, 843-863-7050 or toll-free 800-947-7474. *Fax:* 843-863-7070.

CHARTER OAK STATE COLLEGE
New Britain, CT

ABOUT THE INSTITUTION State-supported, coed. Awards: associate and bachelor's degrees (offers only external degree programs). 1 undergraduate major. Total enrollment: 1,902. Undergraduates: 1,902.
GIFT AID (NEED-BASED) *Scholarships, grants, and awards:* Federal Pell, state, college/university gift aid from institutional funds, foundation grants.
GIFT AID (NON-NEED-BASED) *Scholarships, grants, and awards by category:* Academic Interests/Achievement: general academic interests/achievements.
LOANS *Programs:* FFEL (Subsidized and Unsubsidized Stafford, PLUS), alternative loans.
APPLYING FOR FINANCIAL AID *Required financial aid forms:* FAFSA, institution's own form.
CONTACT Velma Walters, Director, Financial Aid, Charter Oak State College, 55 Paul J. Manafort Drive, New Britain, CT 06053-2142, 860-832-3872. *Fax:* 860-832-3999. *E-mail:* sfa@charteroak.edu.

CHATHAM COLLEGE
Pittsburgh, PA

ABOUT THE INSTITUTION Independent, undergraduate: women only; graduate: coed. Awards: bachelor's, master's, and doctoral degrees and post-bachelor's and post-master's certificates. 46 undergraduate majors. Total enrollment: 1,440. Undergraduates: 794. Freshmen: 119.
GIFT AID (NEED-BASED) *Scholarships, grants, and awards:* Federal Pell, FSEOG, state, private, college/university gift aid from institutional funds.
GIFT AID (NON-NEED-BASED) *Scholarships, grants, and awards by category:* Academic Interests/Achievement: biological sciences, business, communication, education, English, general academic interests/achievements, international studies, mathematics, physical sciences, premedicine, social sciences. Creative Arts/Performance: theater/drama. Special Characteristics: children and siblings of alumni, children of faculty/staff, siblings of current students.
LOANS *Programs:* FFEL (Subsidized and Unsubsidized Stafford, PLUS), Perkins, alternative loans.
WORK-STUDY *Federal work-study:* Total amount: $370,151; 180 jobs averaging $2200. *State or other work-study/employment:* Total amount: $34,700 (100% non-need-based). 25 part-time jobs averaging $1500.
APPLYING FOR FINANCIAL AID *Required financial aid form:* FAFSA.
CONTACT Jennifer Burns, Director of Financial Aid, Chatham College, Woodland Road, Pittsburgh, PA 15232-2826, 800-837-1610 or toll-free 800-837-1290. *Fax:* 412-365-1643. *E-mail:* jburns@chatham.edu.

CHESTER COLLEGE OF NEW ENGLAND
Chester, NH

Tuition & fees: $14,965 | Average undergraduate aid package: $7442

ABOUT THE INSTITUTION Independent, coed. Awards: bachelor's degrees. 6 undergraduate majors. Total enrollment: 217. Undergraduates: 217. Federal methodology is used as a basis for awarding need-based institutional aid.
UNDERGRADUATE EXPENSES for 2006–07 *Application fee:* $35. *Comprehensive fee:* $22,565 includes full-time tuition ($14,700), mandatory fees ($265), and room and board ($7600). *Part-time tuition:* $465 per credit. *Part-time fees:* $500 per year.
FRESHMAN FINANCIAL AID (Fall 2005, est.) 58 applied for aid; of those 100% were deemed to have need. 100% of freshmen with need received aid. *Average percent of need met:* 38% (excluding resources awarded to replace EFC). *Average financial aid package:* $5805 (excluding resources awarded to replace EFC). 7% of all full-time freshmen had no need and received non-need-based gift aid.

UNDERGRADUATE FINANCIAL AID (Fall 2005, est.) 186 applied for aid; of those 100% were deemed to have need. 94% of undergraduates with need received aid. *Average percent of need met:* 38% (excluding resources awarded to replace EFC). *Average financial aid package:* $7442 (excluding resources awarded to replace EFC). 6% of all full-time undergraduates had no need and received non-need-based gift aid.
GIFT AID (NEED-BASED) *Total amount:* $200,682 (84% federal, 16% state). *Receiving aid:* Freshmen: 20% (17); All full-time undergraduates: 25% (57). *Average award:* Freshmen: $2535; Undergraduates: $3520. *Scholarships, grants, and awards:* Federal Pell, FSEOG, state, private, college/university gift aid from institutional funds.
GIFT AID (NON-NEED-BASED) *Total amount:* $502,825 (91% institutional, 9% external sources). *Receiving aid:* Freshmen: 41% (36); Undergraduates: 47% (106). *Average Award:* Freshmen: $5816; Undergraduates: $4367. *Scholarships, grants, and awards by category: Academic Interests/Achievement:* 128 awards ($456,275 total): general academic interests/achievements. *Creative Arts/Performance:* 117 awards ($428,150 total): applied art and design, art/fine arts, creative writing.
LOANS *Student loans:* $1,838,163 (30% need-based, 70% non-need-based). 81% of past graduating class borrowed through all loan programs. *Average indebtedness per student:* $40,695. *Average need-based loan:* Freshmen: $2485; Undergraduates: $3529. *Parent loans:* $445,191 (100% non-need-based). *Programs:* FFEL (Subsidized and Unsubsidized Stafford, PLUS), alternative loans.
WORK-STUDY *Federal work-study:* Total amount: $10,476; 44 jobs averaging $536.
APPLYING FOR FINANCIAL AID *Required financial aid form:* FAFSA. *Financial aid deadline (priority):* 3/15. *Notification date:* Continuous beginning 4/1. Students must reply within 2 weeks of notification.
CONTACT Jason Graves, Director of Financial Aid, Chester College of New England, 40 Chester Street, Chester, NH 03036-4331, 603-887-4401 Ext. 7404 or toll-free 800-974-6372. *Fax:* 603-887-1777. *E-mail:* financialaid@chestercollege.edu.

CHESTNUT HILL COLLEGE
Philadelphia, PA

Tuition & fees: $22,750	Average undergraduate aid package: $8500

ABOUT THE INSTITUTION Independent Roman Catholic, coed, primarily women. Awards: associate, bachelor's, master's, and doctoral degrees and post-bachelor's and post-master's certificates (profile includes figures from both traditional and accelerated (part-time) programs). 37 undergraduate majors. Total enrollment: 1,719. Undergraduates: 1,039. Freshmen: 216. Federal methodology is used as a basis for awarding need-based institutional aid.
UNDERGRADUATE EXPENSES for 2006–07 *Application fee:* $35. *Comprehensive fee:* $30,700 includes full-time tuition ($22,750) and room and board ($7950). *Part-time tuition:* $500 per credit.
FRESHMAN FINANCIAL AID (Fall 2004) 208 applied for aid; of those 80% were deemed to have need. 100% of freshmen with need received aid; of those 1% had need fully met. *Average percent of need met:* 48% (excluding resources awarded to replace EFC). *Average financial aid package:* $8000 (excluding resources awarded to replace EFC). 7% of all full-time freshmen had no need and received non-need-based gift aid.
UNDERGRADUATE FINANCIAL AID (Fall 2004) 750 applied for aid; of those 85% were deemed to have need. 100% of undergraduates with need received aid; of those 1% had need fully met. *Average percent of need met:* 56% (excluding resources awarded to replace EFC). *Average financial aid package:* $8500 (excluding resources awarded to replace EFC). 11% of all full-time undergraduates had no need and received non-need-based gift aid.
GIFT AID (NEED-BASED) *Total amount:* $3,145,799 (32% federal, 32% state, 32% institutional, 4% external sources). *Receiving aid:* Freshmen: 77% (167); All full-time undergraduates: 79% (634). *Average award:* Freshmen: $6000; Undergraduates: $6500. *Scholarships, grants, and awards:* Federal Pell, FSEOG, state, private, college/university gift aid from institutional funds.
GIFT AID (NON-NEED-BASED) *Total amount:* $3,359,304 (100% institutional). *Receiving aid:* Freshmen: 69% (148); Undergraduates: 73% (583). *Average Award:* Freshmen: $5000; Undergraduates: $6000. *Scholarships, grants, and awards by category: Special Achievements/Activities:* 1 award ($500 total): leadership. *Special Characteristics:* 36 awards ($120,770 total): children and siblings of alumni, international students, religious affiliation.
LOANS *Student loans:* $4,811,571 (49% need-based, 51% non-need-based). 67% of past graduating class borrowed through all loan programs. *Average indebtedness per student:* $26,250. *Average need-based loan:* Freshmen: $2625; Undergraduates: $4281. *Parent loans:* $2,040,828 (59% need-based, 41% non-need-based). *Programs:* FFEL (Subsidized and Unsubsidized Stafford, PLUS), Perkins.
WORK-STUDY *Federal work-study:* Total amount: $168,444; 306 jobs averaging $1000.
APPLYING FOR FINANCIAL AID *Required financial aid form:* FAFSA. *Financial aid deadline:* 4/15. *Notification date:* Continuous beginning 1/31. Students must reply by 5/1 or within 2 weeks of notification.
CONTACT Crystal Filer-Ogden, Director of Financial Aid, Chestnut Hill College, Chestnut Hill College, 9601 Germantown Avenue, Philadelphia, PA 19118-2693, 215-248-7182 or toll-free 800-248-0052 (out-of-state). *Fax:* 215-242-7217. *E-mail:* finaid@chc.edu.

CHEYNEY UNIVERSITY OF PENNSYLVANIA
Cheyney, PA

CONTACT Mr. James Brown, Director of Financial Aid, Cheyney University of Pennsylvania, 1837 University Circle, Cheyney, PA 19319, 610-399-2302 or toll-free 800-CHEYNEY. *Fax:* 610-399-2411. *E-mail:* jbrown@cheyney.edu.

CHICAGO STATE UNIVERSITY
Chicago, IL

CONTACT Director of Student Financial Aid, Chicago State University, 9501 South Martin Luther King Drive, Chicago, IL 60628, 773-995-2304.

CHOWAN UNIVERSITY
Murfreesboro, NC

Tuition & fees: $14,750	Average undergraduate aid package: $12,504

ABOUT THE INSTITUTION Independent Baptist, coed. Awards: associate and bachelor's degrees. 37 undergraduate majors. Total enrollment: 800. Undergraduates: 800. Freshmen: 315. Federal methodology is used as a basis for awarding need-based institutional aid.
UNDERGRADUATE EXPENSES for 2005–06 *Application fee:* $20. *Comprehensive fee:* $21,350 includes full-time tuition ($14,600), mandatory fees ($150), and room and board ($6600). *College room only:* $3100. Room and board charges vary according to board plan. *Part-time tuition:* $230 per hour. Part-time tuition and fees vary according to course load. *Payment plans:* Installment, deferred payment.
FRESHMAN FINANCIAL AID (Fall 2005, est.) 255 applied for aid; of those 93% were deemed to have need. 100% of freshmen with need received aid; of those 11% had need fully met. *Average percent of need met:* 69% (excluding resources awarded to replace EFC). *Average financial aid package:* $12,525 (excluding resources awarded to replace EFC). 10% of all full-time freshmen had no need and received non-need-based gift aid.
UNDERGRADUATE FINANCIAL AID (Fall 2005, est.) 630 applied for aid; of those 92% were deemed to have need. 100% of undergraduates with need received aid; of those 13% had need fully met. *Average percent of need met:* 69% (excluding resources awarded to replace EFC). *Average financial aid package:* $12,504 (excluding resources awarded to replace EFC). 12% of all full-time undergraduates had no need and received non-need-based gift aid.
GIFT AID (NEED-BASED) *Total amount:* $5,520,408 (25% federal, 9% state, 55% institutional, 11% external sources). *Receiving aid:* Freshmen: 87% (232); All full-time undergraduates: 85% (567). *Average award:* Freshmen: $10,033; Undergraduates: $9259. *Scholarships, grants, and awards:* Federal Pell, FSEOG, state, private, college/university gift aid from institutional funds.
GIFT AID (NON-NEED-BASED) *Total amount:* $632,052 (13% state, 72% institutional, 15% external sources). *Receiving aid:* Freshmen: 7% (18); Undergraduates: 6% (41). *Average Award:* Freshmen: $8897; Undergraduates: $11,297. *Scholarships, grants, and awards by category: Academic Interests/Achievement:* 461 awards ($1,697,493 total): general academic interests/achievements. *Creative Arts/Performance:* 24 awards ($52,400 total): music. *Special Achievements/Activities:* 77 awards ($285,354 total): leadership. *Special*

Chowan University

Characteristics: 320 awards ($475,008 total): children of faculty/staff, first-generation college students, international students, local/state students, relatives of clergy, religious affiliation. *Tuition waivers:* Full or partial for employees or children of employees, senior citizens.

LOANS *Student loans:* $4,456,822 (83% need-based, 17% non-need-based). 80% of past graduating class borrowed through all loan programs. *Average indebtedness per student:* $23,370. *Average need-based loan:* Freshmen: $2807; Undergraduates: $3560. *Parent loans:* $1,605,960 (35% need-based, 65% non-need-based). *Programs:* FFEL (Subsidized and Unsubsidized Stafford, PLUS), Perkins, state, alternative loans.

WORK-STUDY *Federal work-study:* Total amount: $176,055; 274 jobs averaging $642. *State or other work-study/employment:* 86 part-time jobs averaging $1550.

ATHLETIC AWARDS Total amount: $189,354 (74% need-based, 26% non-need-based).

APPLYING FOR FINANCIAL AID *Required financial aid form:* FAFSA. *Financial aid deadline (priority):* 5/1. *Notification date:* Continuous beginning 3/1. Students must reply within 2 weeks of notification.

CONTACT Mrs. Stephanie W. Harrell, Director of Financial Aid, Chowan University, 200 Jones Drive, Murfreesboro, NC 27855, 252-398-1229 or toll-free 800-488-4101. Fax: 252-398-6513. E-mail: harres@chowan.edu.

CHRISTENDOM COLLEGE
Front Royal, VA

Tuition & fees: $16,740   **Average undergraduate aid package:** $10,782

ABOUT THE INSTITUTION Independent Roman Catholic, coed. Awards: associate, bachelor's, and master's degrees. 8 undergraduate majors. Total enrollment: 435. Undergraduates: 379. Freshmen: 105. Institutional methodology is used as a basis for awarding need-based institutional aid.

UNDERGRADUATE EXPENSES for 2006–07 *Application fee:* $25. *Comprehensive fee:* $22,806 includes full-time tuition ($16,290), mandatory fees ($450), and room and board ($6066).

FRESHMAN FINANCIAL AID (Fall 2005, est.) 76 applied for aid; of those 67% were deemed to have need. 100% of freshmen with need received aid; of those 100% had need fully met. *Average percent of need met:* 90% (excluding resources awarded to replace EFC). *Average financial aid package:* $11,622 (excluding resources awarded to replace EFC). 31% of all full-time freshmen had no need and received non-need-based gift aid.

UNDERGRADUATE FINANCIAL AID (Fall 2005, est.) 236 applied for aid; of those 76% were deemed to have need. 100% of undergraduates with need received aid; of those 100% had need fully met. *Average percent of need met:* 90% (excluding resources awarded to replace EFC). *Average financial aid package:* $10,782 (excluding resources awarded to replace EFC). 22% of all full-time undergraduates had no need and received non-need-based gift aid.

GIFT AID (NEED-BASED) *Total amount:* $1,118,000 (100% institutional). *Receiving aid:* Freshmen: 48% (50); All full-time undergraduates: 48% (179). *Average award:* Freshmen: $8500; Undergraduates: $8975. *Scholarships, grants, and awards:* private, college/university gift aid from institutional funds.

GIFT AID (NON-NEED-BASED) *Total amount:* $457,651 (92% institutional, 8% external sources). *Average Award:* Freshmen: $6480; Undergraduates: $5114. *Scholarships, grants, and awards by category:* Academic Interests/Achievement: 136 awards ($630,590 total): general academic interests/achievements.

LOANS *Student loans:* $989,229 (100% need-based). 55% of past graduating class borrowed through all loan programs. *Average indebtedness per student:* $11,080. *Average need-based loan:* Freshmen: $4705; Undergraduates: $4380. *Programs:* college/university.

WORK-STUDY *State or other work-study/employment:* Total amount: $240,500 (100% need-based). 130 part-time jobs averaging $1850.

APPLYING FOR FINANCIAL AID *Required financial aid form:* institution's own form. *Financial aid deadline (priority):* 4/1. *Notification date:* Continuous beginning 2/1. Students must reply within 4 weeks of notification.

CONTACT Mrs. Alisa Polk, Financial Aid Officer, Christendom College, 134 Christendom Drive, Front Royal, VA 22630-5103, 800-877-5456 Ext. 214 or toll-free 800-877-5456 Ext. 290. Fax: 540-636-1655. E-mail: finaid@christendom.edu.

CHRISTIAN BROTHERS UNIVERSITY
Memphis, TN

Tuition & fees: $19,150   **Average undergraduate aid package:** $14,897

ABOUT THE INSTITUTION Independent Roman Catholic, coed. Awards: bachelor's and master's degrees. 27 undergraduate majors. Total enrollment: 1,778. Undergraduates: 1,493. Freshmen: 258. Both federal and institutional methodology are used as a basis for awarding need-based institutional aid.

UNDERGRADUATE EXPENSES for 2005–06 *Application fee:* $25. *Comprehensive fee:* $24,650 includes full-time tuition ($18,630), mandatory fees ($520), and room and board ($5500). *College room only:* $2480. Full-time tuition and fees vary according to class time. Room and board charges vary according to board plan and housing facility. *Part-time tuition:* $585 per credit hour. Part-time tuition and fees vary according to class time. *Payment plans:* Installment, deferred payment.

FRESHMAN FINANCIAL AID (Fall 2005, est.) 225 applied for aid; of those 77% were deemed to have need. 100% of freshmen with need received aid; of those 35% had need fully met. *Average percent of need met:* 93% (excluding resources awarded to replace EFC). *Average financial aid package:* $17,630 (excluding resources awarded to replace EFC). 23% of all full-time freshmen had no need and received non-need-based gift aid.

UNDERGRADUATE FINANCIAL AID (Fall 2005, est.) 969 applied for aid; of those 81% were deemed to have need. 100% of undergraduates with need received aid; of those 22% had need fully met. *Average percent of need met:* 79% (excluding resources awarded to replace EFC). *Average financial aid package:* $14,897 (excluding resources awarded to replace EFC). 25% of all full-time undergraduates had no need and received non-need-based gift aid.

GIFT AID (NEED-BASED) *Total amount:* $2,911,920 (57% federal, 43% state). *Receiving aid:* Freshmen: 35% (85); All full-time undergraduates: 36% (417). *Average award:* Freshmen: $5386; Undergraduates: $6028. *Scholarships, grants, and awards:* Federal Pell, FSEOG, state, private, college/university gift aid from institutional funds.

GIFT AID (NON-NEED-BASED) *Total amount:* $8,634,527 (12% state, 84% institutional, 4% external sources). *Receiving aid:* Freshmen: 69% (167); Undergraduates: 55% (635). *Average Award:* Freshmen: $7951; Undergraduates: $9419. *Scholarships, grants, and awards by category:* Academic Interests/Achievement: 750 awards ($5,264,285 total): engineering/technologies, general academic interests/achievements. Creative Arts/Performance: 1 award ($2000 total): general creative arts/performance. Special Achievements/Activities: 83 awards ($328,817 total): general special achievements/activities, leadership. Special Characteristics: 587 awards ($1,624,072 total): children and siblings of alumni, children of faculty/staff, general special characteristics, religious affiliation. *Tuition waivers:* Full or partial for children of alumni, employees or children of employees. *ROTC:* Army cooperative, Naval cooperative, Air Force cooperative.

LOANS *Student loans:* $6,538,781 (44% need-based, 56% non-need-based). 63% of past graduating class borrowed through all loan programs. *Average indebtedness per student:* $24,463. *Average need-based loan:* Freshmen: $3105; Undergraduates: $4054. *Parent loans:* $705,334 (100% non-need-based). *Programs:* FFEL (Subsidized and Unsubsidized Stafford, PLUS), Perkins, college/university, alternative loans.

WORK-STUDY *Federal work-study:* Total amount: $207,400; 201 jobs averaging $1032. *State or other work-study/employment:* Total amount: $192,600 (100% non-need-based). 192 part-time jobs averaging $1003.

ATHLETIC AWARDS Total amount: $948,357 (100% non-need-based).

APPLYING FOR FINANCIAL AID *Required financial aid form:* FAFSA. *Financial aid deadline (priority):* 2/15. *Notification date:* Continuous beginning 2/28. Students must reply by 5/1 or within 2 weeks of notification.

CONTACT Mr. Jim Shannon, Student Financial Resources Director, Christian Brothers University, 650 East Parkway South, Memphis, TN 38104, 901-321-3305 or toll-free 800-288-7576. E-mail: jshannon@cbu.edu.

CHRISTIAN HERITAGE COLLEGE
El Cajon, CA

See San Diego Christian College.

CHRISTIAN LIFE COLLEGE
Mount Prospect, IL

CONTACT Jeanna Wilson, Office of Financial Aid, Christian Life College, 400 East Gregory Street, Mt. Prospect, IL 60056, 847-259-1840. *Fax:* 847-259-3888.

CHRISTOPHER NEWPORT UNIVERSITY
Newport News, VA

Tuition & fees (VA res): $5826   **Average undergraduate aid package: $6245**

ABOUT THE INSTITUTION State-supported, coed. Awards: bachelor's and master's degrees. 38 undergraduate majors. Total enrollment: 4,699. Undergraduates: 4,536. Freshmen: 1,250. Federal methodology is used as a basis for awarding need-based institutional aid.
UNDERGRADUATE EXPENSES for 2005–06 *Application fee:* $35. *Tuition, state resident:* full-time $3442; part-time $143 per credit hour. *Tuition, nonresident:* full-time $10,464; part-time $436 per credit hour. *Required fees:* full-time $2384; $99. Full-time tuition and fees vary according to course load. Part-time tuition and fees vary according to course load. *College room and board:* $7500. Room and board charges vary according to housing facility. *Payment plan:* Installment.
FRESHMAN FINANCIAL AID (Fall 2004) 1083 applied for aid; of those 61% were deemed to have need. 68% of freshmen with need received aid; of those 25% had need fully met. *Average percent of need met:* 76% (excluding resources awarded to replace EFC). *Average financial aid package:* $5677 (excluding resources awarded to replace EFC). 10% of all full-time freshmen had no need and received non-need-based gift aid.
UNDERGRADUATE FINANCIAL AID (Fall 2004) 2,904 applied for aid; of those 68% were deemed to have need. 81% of undergraduates with need received aid; of those 25% had need fully met. *Average percent of need met:* 77% (excluding resources awarded to replace EFC). *Average financial aid package:* $6245 (excluding resources awarded to replace EFC). 9% of all full-time undergraduates had no need and received non-need-based gift aid.
GIFT AID (NEED-BASED) *Total amount:* $4,748,329 (37% federal, 61% state, 2% institutional). *Receiving aid:* Freshmen: 28% (333); All full-time undergraduates: 28% (1,151). *Average award:* Freshmen: $3964; Undergraduates: $3965. *Scholarships, grants, and awards:* Federal Pell, FSEOG, state, private, college/university gift aid from institutional funds.
GIFT AID (NON-NEED-BASED) *Total amount:* $1,037,860 (38% institutional, 62% external sources). *Receiving aid:* Freshmen: 13% (157); Undergraduates: 8% (332). *Average Award:* Freshmen: $1578; Undergraduates: $1443. *Scholarships, grants, and awards by category:* Academic Interests/Achievement: 52 awards ($88,674 total): business, communication, computer science, education, English, foreign languages, general academic interests/achievements, humanities, mathematics, military science, religion/biblical studies. *Creative Arts/Performance:* 31 awards ($30,200 total): art/fine arts, music, theater/drama. *Special Achievements/Activities:* 238 awards ($278,706 total): general special achievements/activities, leadership. *Tuition waivers:* Full or partial for employees or children of employees, senior citizens. *ROTC:* Army.
LOANS *Student loans:* $9,839,788 (46% need-based, 54% non-need-based). 51% of past graduating class borrowed through all loan programs. *Average indebtedness per student:* $11,936. *Average need-based loan:* Freshmen: $2147; Undergraduates: $3191. *Parent loans:* $3,568,539 (100% non-need-based). *Programs:* FFEL (Subsidized and Unsubsidized Stafford, PLUS), state, college/university, alternative loans.
WORK-STUDY *Federal work-study:* Total amount: $157,541; 199 jobs averaging $792. *State or other work-study/employment:* Total amount: $1,583,860 (100% non-need-based). 797 part-time jobs averaging $1987.
APPLYING FOR FINANCIAL AID *Required financial aid form:* FAFSA. *Financial aid deadline (priority):* 3/1. *Notification date:* Continuous beginning 2/1. Students must reply within 3 weeks of notification.
CONTACT Mary L. Wigginton, Director of Financial Aid, Christopher Newport University, 1 University Place, Newport News, VA 23606, 757-594-7278 or toll-free 800-333-4268. *Fax:* 757-594-7113.

CINCINNATI CHRISTIAN UNIVERSITY
Cincinnati, OH

Tuition & fees: $9690   **Average undergraduate aid package: $7707**

ABOUT THE INSTITUTION Independent religious, coed. Awards: associate, bachelor's, master's, and first professional degrees. 12 undergraduate majors. Total enrollment: 922. Undergraduates: 626. Freshmen: 135. Federal methodology is used as a basis for awarding need-based institutional aid.
UNDERGRADUATE EXPENSES for 2005–06 *Application fee:* $35. *Comprehensive fee:* $15,080 includes full-time tuition ($9120), mandatory fees ($570), and room and board ($5390). *Part-time tuition:* $285 per credit hour. *Part-time fees:* $75 per term.
FRESHMAN FINANCIAL AID (Fall 2004) 113 applied for aid; of those 87% were deemed to have need. 100% of freshmen with need received aid; of those 15% had need fully met. *Average percent of need met:* 55% (excluding resources awarded to replace EFC). *Average financial aid package:* $6848 (excluding resources awarded to replace EFC). 13% of all full-time freshmen had no need and received non-need-based gift aid.
UNDERGRADUATE FINANCIAL AID (Fall 2004) 529 applied for aid; of those 87% were deemed to have need. 100% of undergraduates with need received aid; of those 14% had need fully met. *Average percent of need met:* 56% (excluding resources awarded to replace EFC). *Average financial aid package:* $7707 (excluding resources awarded to replace EFC). 13% of all full-time undergraduates had no need and received non-need-based gift aid.
GIFT AID (NEED-BASED) *Total amount:* $2,082,115 (31% federal, 26% state, 23% institutional, 20% external sources). *Receiving aid:* Freshmen: 82% (93); All full-time undergraduates: 82% (433). *Average award:* Freshmen: $4443; Undergraduates: $4484. *Scholarships, grants, and awards:* Federal Pell, FSEOG, state, college/university gift aid from institutional funds.
GIFT AID (NON-NEED-BASED) *Total amount:* $323,559 (18% state, 40% institutional, 42% external sources). *Receiving aid:* Freshmen: 8% (9); Undergraduates: 7% (37). *Average Award:* Freshmen: $13,225; Undergraduates: $10,808. *Scholarships, grants, and awards by category:* Creative Arts/Performance: 8 awards ($4900 total): music. *Special Characteristics:* 112 awards ($344,021 total): children of current students, children of faculty/staff, international students, married students, parents of current students, siblings of current students, spouses of current students, twins.
LOANS *Student loans:* $3,036,045 (81% need-based, 19% non-need-based). 100% of past graduating class borrowed through all loan programs. *Average indebtedness per student:* $13,891. *Parent loans:* $1,059,311 (38% need-based, 62% non-need-based). *Programs:* FFEL (Subsidized and Unsubsidized Stafford, PLUS), alternative loans.
WORK-STUDY *Federal work-study:* Total amount: $76,489; 197 jobs averaging $429.
APPLYING FOR FINANCIAL AID *Required financial aid forms:* FAFSA, institution's own form, state aid form. *Financial aid deadline (priority):* 3/15. *Notification date:* Continuous beginning 4/1. Students must reply within 2 weeks of notification.
CONTACT Robbin D. Moore, Financial Aid Coordinator, Cincinnati Christian University, 2700 Glenway Avenue, Cincinnati, OH 45204-1799, 513-244-8450 or toll-free 800-949-4CBC. *Fax:* 513-244-8140. *E-mail:* financialaid@ccuniversity.edu.

CIRCLEVILLE BIBLE COLLEGE
Circleville, OH

CONTACT Financial Aid Officer, Circleville Bible College, 1476 Lancaster Pike, PO Box 458, Circleville, OH 43113-9487, 740-477-7774 or toll-free 800-701-0222. *Fax:* 740-477-7755.

THE CITADEL, THE MILITARY COLLEGE OF SOUTH CAROLINA
Charleston, SC

Tuition & fees (SC res): $7520   **Average undergraduate aid package: $8846**

ABOUT THE INSTITUTION State-supported, coed, primarily men. Awards: bachelor's and master's degrees and post-master's certificates. 23 undergradu-

The Citadel, The Military College of South Carolina

ate majors. Total enrollment: 3,386. Undergraduates: 2,238. Freshmen: 585. Federal methodology is used as a basis for awarding need-based institutional aid.
UNDERGRADUATE EXPENSES for 2005–06 *Application fee:* $40. *Tuition, state resident:* full-time $6522; part-time $198 per credit hour. *Tuition, nonresident:* full-time $15,918; part-time $397 per credit hour. *Required fees:* full-time $998; $15 per term part-time. *College room and board:* $4840.
FRESHMAN FINANCIAL AID (Fall 2005, est.) 458 applied for aid; of those 70% were deemed to have need. 96% of freshmen with need received aid; of those 7% had need fully met. *Average percent of need met:* 47% (excluding resources awarded to replace EFC). *Average financial aid package:* $8364 (excluding resources awarded to replace EFC). 11% of all full-time freshmen had no need and received non-need-based gift aid.
UNDERGRADUATE FINANCIAL AID (Fall 2005, est.) 1,442 applied for aid; of those 74% were deemed to have need. 97% of undergraduates with need received aid; of those 13% had need fully met. *Average percent of need met:* 58% (excluding resources awarded to replace EFC). *Average financial aid package:* $8846 (excluding resources awarded to replace EFC). 12% of all full-time undergraduates had no need and received non-need-based gift aid.
GIFT AID (NEED-BASED) *Total amount:* $4,088,894 (26% federal, 25% state, 49% institutional). *Receiving aid:* Freshmen: 37% (216); All full-time undergraduates: 32% (684). *Average award:* Freshmen: $9233; Undergraduates: $9498. *Scholarships, grants, and awards:* Federal Pell, FSEOG, state, private, college/university gift aid from institutional funds.
GIFT AID (NON-NEED-BASED) *Total amount:* $6,698,633 (13% state, 34% institutional, 53% external sources). *Receiving aid:* Freshmen: 30% (175); Undergraduates: 25% (532). *Average Award:* Freshmen: $8777; Undergraduates: $6578. *Scholarships, grants, and awards by category: Academic Interests/Achievement:* 600 awards ($1,800,000 total): biological sciences, business, engineering/technologies, general academic interests/achievements, humanities, military science, religion/biblical studies. *Creative Arts/Performance:* 6 awards ($30,000 total): journalism/publications, music. *Special Achievements/Activities:* 10 awards ($35,000 total): community service, leadership, religious involvement. *Special Characteristics:* 60 awards ($140,000 total): children and siblings of alumni, children with a deceased or disabled parent, local/state students, out-of-state students. *Tuition waivers:* Full or partial for senior citizens. *ROTC:* Army, Naval, Air Force.
LOANS *Student loans:* $4,479,910 (81% need-based, 19% non-need-based). 59% of past graduating class borrowed through all loan programs. *Average indebtedness per student:* $16,127. *Average need-based loan:* Freshmen: $2852; Undergraduates: $4142. *Parent loans:* $8,356,966 (72% need-based, 28% non-need-based). *Programs:* Federal Direct (Subsidized and Unsubsidized Stafford, PLUS), Perkins, state, college/university.
WORK-STUDY *Federal work-study:* Total amount: $20,840; 21 jobs averaging $1121.
ATHLETIC AWARDS *Total amount:* $3,295,562 (48% need-based, 52% non-need-based).
APPLYING FOR FINANCIAL AID *Required financial aid form:* FAFSA. *Financial aid deadline (priority):* 2/28. *Notification date:* 3/15. Students must reply within 2 weeks of notification.
CONTACT Lt. Col. Hank M. Fuller, Director of Financial Aid and Scholarships, The Citadel, The Military College of South Carolina, 171 Moultrie Street, Charleston, SC 29409, 843-953-5187 or toll-free 800-868-1842. *Fax:* 843-953-6759. *E-mail:* fullerh@citadel.edu.

CITY COLLEGE OF THE CITY UNIVERSITY OF NEW YORK
New York, NY

Tuition & fees (NY res): $4080	Average undergraduate aid package: $7100

ABOUT THE INSTITUTION State and locally supported, coed. Awards: bachelor's, master's, and first professional degrees and post-master's certificates. 66 undergraduate majors. Total enrollment: 12,440. Undergraduates: 9,494. Freshmen: 1,326. Federal methodology is used as a basis for awarding need-based institutional aid.
UNDERGRADUATE EXPENSES for 2005–06 *Application fee:* $65. *Tuition, state resident:* full-time $4080; part-time $170 per credit. *Tuition, nonresident:* full-time $8640; part-time $360 per credit. Full-time tuition and fees vary according to class time and program. Part-time tuition and fees vary according to class time, course load, and program. *Payment plan:* Deferred payment.
FRESHMAN FINANCIAL AID (Fall 2005, est.) 833 applied for aid; of those 85% were deemed to have need. 90% of freshmen with need received aid; of those 75% had need fully met. *Average percent of need met:* 74% (excluding resources awarded to replace EFC). *Average financial aid package:* $5214 (excluding resources awarded to replace EFC). 32% of all full-time freshmen had no need and received non-need-based gift aid.
UNDERGRADUATE FINANCIAL AID (Fall 2005, est.) 5,687 applied for aid; of those 95% were deemed to have need. 95% of undergraduates with need received aid; of those 55% had need fully met. *Average percent of need met:* 70% (excluding resources awarded to replace EFC). *Average financial aid package:* $7100 (excluding resources awarded to replace EFC). 14% of all full-time undergraduates had no need and received non-need-based gift aid.
GIFT AID (NEED-BASED) *Total amount:* $26,599,500 (52% federal, 46% state, 2% institutional). *Receiving aid:* Freshmen: 58% (573); All full-time undergraduates: 73% (4,875). *Average award:* Freshmen: $5106; Undergraduates: $5271. *Scholarships, grants, and awards:* Federal Pell, FSEOG, state, private, college/university gift aid from institutional funds.
GIFT AID (NON-NEED-BASED) *Total amount:* $2,601,900 (11% state, 83% institutional, 6% external sources). *Receiving aid:* Freshmen: 36% (350); Undergraduates: 9% (590). *Average Award:* Freshmen: $1759; Undergraduates:* $2200. *Scholarships, grants, and awards by category: Academic Interests/Achievement:* architecture, area/ethnic studies, biological sciences, communication, computer science, education, engineering/technologies, English, foreign languages, general academic interests/achievements, humanities, international studies, mathematics, premedicine, social sciences. *Creative Arts/Performance:* applied art and design, art/fine arts, cinema/film/broadcasting, creative writing, general creative arts/performance, music, performing arts. *Special Achievements/Activities:* community service, general special achievements/activities, leadership. *Tuition waivers:* Full or partial for senior citizens. *ROTC:* Army cooperative, Air Force cooperative.
LOANS *Student loans:* $13,820,000 (95% need-based, 5% non-need-based). 35% of past graduating class borrowed through all loan programs. *Average indebtedness per student:* $16,500. *Average need-based loan:* Freshmen: $1500; Undergraduates: $3200. *Parent loans:* $166,000 (100% non-need-based). *Programs:* Federal Direct (Subsidized and Unsubsidized Stafford, PLUS, Perkins.
WORK-STUDY *Federal work-study:* Total amount: $2,277,000; 2,009 jobs averaging $1444.
APPLYING FOR FINANCIAL AID *Required financial aid forms:* FAFSA, state aid form. *Financial aid deadline (priority):* 4/1. *Notification date:* Continuous beginning 3/31.
CONTACT Thelma Mason, Director of Financial Aid, City College of the City University of New York, 160 Convent Avenue, Administration Building, Room 104, New York, NY 10031, 212-650-5819. *Fax:* 212-650-5829. *E-mail:* thelma@finance.ccny.cuny.edu.

CITY UNIVERSITY
Bellevue, WA

ABOUT THE INSTITUTION Independent, coed. Awards: associate, bachelor's, and master's degrees and post-bachelor's certificates. 10 undergraduate majors. Total enrollment: 4,020. Undergraduates: 1,794. Freshmen: 16.
GIFT AID (NEED-BASED) *Scholarships, grants, and awards:* Federal Pell, FSEOG, private, college/university gift aid from institutional funds.
GIFT AID (NON-NEED-BASED) *Scholarships, grants, and awards by category: Academic Interests/Achievement:* general academic interests/achievements.
LOANS *Programs:* FFEL (Subsidized and Unsubsidized Stafford, PLUS).
APPLYING FOR FINANCIAL AID *Required financial aid forms:* FAFSA, institution's own form.
CONTACT Ms. Jean L. Roberts, Director of Student Financial Services, City University, 11900 Northeast 1st Street, Bellevue, WA 98005, 425-709-5251 or toll-free 888-42-CITYU. *Fax:* 425-709-5263. *E-mail:* jroberts@cityu.edu.

CLAFLIN UNIVERSITY
Orangeburg, SC

CONTACT Director of Student Financial Aid, Claflin University, Tingly Hall, Suite 12, 400 Magnolia Street, Orangeburg, SC 29115, 803-535-5720 or toll-free 800-922-1276 (in-state).

CLAREMONT MCKENNA COLLEGE
Claremont, CA

Tuition & fees: $32,650   **Average undergraduate aid package:** $25,674

ABOUT THE INSTITUTION Independent, coed. Awards: bachelor's degrees. 83 undergraduate majors. Total enrollment: 1,139. Undergraduates: 1,139. Freshmen: 271. Both federal and institutional methodology are used as a basis for awarding need-based institutional aid.
UNDERGRADUATE EXPENSES for 2005–06 *Application fee:* $60. *Comprehensive fee:* $42,920 includes full-time tuition ($30,800), mandatory fees ($1850), and room and board ($10,270). *College room only:* $5160. Full-time tuition and fees vary according to reciprocity agreements. Room and board charges vary according to board plan and housing facility. *Part-time tuition:* $5100 per course. *Payment plans:* Tuition prepayment, installment.
FRESHMAN FINANCIAL AID (Fall 2005, est.) 164 applied for aid; of those 77% were deemed to have need. 100% of freshmen with need received aid; of those 100% had need fully met. *Average percent of need met:* 100% (excluding resources awarded to replace EFC). *Average financial aid package:* $25,976 (excluding resources awarded to replace EFC). 4% of all full-time freshmen had no need and received non-need-based gift aid.
UNDERGRADUATE FINANCIAL AID (Fall 2005, est.) 660 applied for aid; of those 86% were deemed to have need. 100% of undergraduates with need received aid; of those 100% had need fully met. *Average percent of need met:* 100% (excluding resources awarded to replace EFC). *Average financial aid package:* $25,674 (excluding resources awarded to replace EFC). 6% of all full-time undergraduates had no need and received non-need-based gift aid.
GIFT AID (NEED-BASED) *Total amount:* $12,916,263 (4% federal, 7% state, 86% institutional, 3% external sources). *Receiving aid:* Freshmen: 47% (127); All full-time undergraduates: 50% (565). *Average award:* Freshmen: $23,460; Undergraduates: $22,823. *Scholarships, grants, and awards:* Federal Pell, FSEOG, state, private, college/university gift aid from institutional funds.
GIFT AID (NON-NEED-BASED) *Total amount:* $683,083 (64% institutional, 36% external sources). *Receiving aid:* Freshmen: 24% (65); Undergraduates: 19% (221). *Average Award:* Freshmen: $4800; Undergraduates: $6116. *Scholarships, grants, and awards by category: Academic Interests/Achievement:* 143 awards ($546,500 total): general academic interests/achievements. *Special Characteristics:* 33 awards ($162,500 total): ethnic background. *Tuition waivers:* Full or partial for employees or children of employees. *ROTC:* Army, Air Force cooperative.
LOANS *Student loans:* $3,224,456 (31% need-based, 69% non-need-based). 51% of past graduating class borrowed through all loan programs. *Average indebtedness per student:* $10,518. *Average need-based loan:* Freshmen: $2991; Undergraduates: $3406. *Parent loans:* $1,486,815 (100% need-based). *Programs:* FFEL (Subsidized and Unsubsidized Stafford, PLUS), Perkins, college/university, alternative loans.
WORK-STUDY *Federal work-study:* Total amount: $250,000; 372 jobs averaging $1476. *State or other work-study/employment:* Total amount: $950,000 (11% need-based, 89% non-need-based). 57 part-time jobs averaging $951.
APPLYING FOR FINANCIAL AID *Required financial aid forms:* FAFSA, CSS Financial Aid PROFILE. *Financial aid deadline:* 2/1. *Notification date:* 4/1. Students must reply by 5/1.
CONTACT Ms. Georgette R. DeVeres, Director of Financial Aid/Associate Dean of Admission, Claremont McKenna College, 890 Columbia Avenue, Claremont, CA 91711, 909-621-8356. *Fax:* 909-621-8516. *E-mail:* gdeveres@claremontmckenna.edu.

CLARION UNIVERSITY OF PENNSYLVANIA
Clarion, PA

ABOUT THE INSTITUTION State-supported, coed. Awards: associate, bachelor's, and master's degrees and post-master's certificates. 55 undergraduate majors. Total enrollment: 6,338. Undergraduates: 5,744. Freshmen: 1,241.
GIFT AID (NEED-BASED) *Scholarships, grants, and awards:* Federal Pell, FSEOG, state, private, college/university gift aid from institutional funds, United Negro College Fund.
GIFT AID (NON-NEED-BASED) *Scholarships, grants, and awards by category: Academic Interests/Achievement:* biological sciences, business, communication, computer science, education, English, foreign languages, general academic interests/achievements, humanities, international studies, library science, mathematics, physical sciences, premedicine, social sciences. *Creative Arts/Performance:* art/fine arts, performing arts, theater/drama. *Special Achievements/Activities:* leadership. *Special Characteristics:* children of faculty/staff, ethnic background, local/state students, members of minority groups, veterans.
LOANS *Programs:* FFEL (Subsidized and Unsubsidized Stafford, PLUS), Perkins.
APPLYING FOR FINANCIAL AID *Required financial aid form:* FAFSA.
CONTACT Ms. Mary Jo Phillips, Freshman Financial Aid Adviser, Clarion University of Pennsylvania, 890 Wood Street, Clarion, PA 16214, 814-393-2315 or toll-free 800-672-7171. *E-mail:* maphillips@clarion.edu.

CLARK ATLANTA UNIVERSITY
Atlanta, GA

Tuition & fees: $14,522   **Average undergraduate aid package:** $10,935

ABOUT THE INSTITUTION Independent United Methodist, coed. Awards: bachelor's, master's, and doctoral degrees and post-bachelor's and post-master's certificates. 47 undergraduate majors. Total enrollment: 4,598. Undergraduates: 3,701. Freshmen: 813. Federal methodology is used as a basis for awarding need-based institutional aid.
UNDERGRADUATE EXPENSES for 2005–06 *Application fee:* $35. *Comprehensive fee:* $21,338 includes full-time tuition ($14,522) and room and board ($6816). Room and board charges vary according to board plan and housing facility. *Payment plan:* Deferred payment.
FRESHMAN FINANCIAL AID (Fall 2005, est.) 965 applied for aid; of those 94% were deemed to have need. 99% of freshmen with need received aid; of those 47% had need fully met. *Average percent of need met:* 6% (excluding resources awarded to replace EFC). *Average financial aid package:* $14,103 (excluding resources awarded to replace EFC).
UNDERGRADUATE FINANCIAL AID (Fall 2005, est.) 3,883 applied for aid; of those 96% were deemed to have need. 99% of undergraduates with need received aid; of those 43% had need fully met. *Average percent of need met:* 8% (excluding resources awarded to replace EFC). *Average financial aid package:* $10,935 (excluding resources awarded to replace EFC).
GIFT AID (NEED-BASED) *Total amount:* $13,166,452 (52% federal, 48% institutional). *Receiving aid:* Freshmen: 62% (613); All full-time undergraduates: 64% (2,586). *Average award:* Freshmen: $5651; Undergraduates: $3818. *Scholarships, grants, and awards:* Federal Pell, FSEOG, state, private, college/university gift aid from institutional funds, United Negro College Fund.
GIFT AID (NON-NEED-BASED) *Total amount:* $5,945,941 (38% state, 62% external sources). *Receiving aid:* Freshmen: 28% (274); Undergraduates: 27% (1,112). *Scholarships, grants, and awards by category: Academic Interests/Achievement:* general academic interests/achievements. *Creative Arts/Performance:* music. *Special Achievements/Activities:* general special achievements/activities, leadership. *Special Characteristics:* general special characteristics. *Tuition waivers:* Full or partial for employees or children of employees. *ROTC:* Army, Air Force.
LOANS *Student loans:* $25,574,979 (55% need-based, 45% non-need-based). 10% of past graduating class borrowed through all loan programs. *Average indebtedness per student:* $17,751. *Average need-based loan:* Freshmen: $3534; Undergraduates: $4526. *Parent loans:* $14,867,493 (100% non-need-based). *Programs:* FFEL (Subsidized and Unsubsidized Stafford, PLUS), Perkins.
WORK-STUDY *Federal work-study:* Total amount: $842,633; 229 jobs averaging $1335.
ATHLETIC AWARDS *Total amount:* $1,220,002 (100% non-need-based).
APPLYING FOR FINANCIAL AID *Required financial aid form:* FAFSA. *Financial aid deadline (priority):* 4/1. *Notification date:* Continuous beginning 2/15. Students must reply within 2 weeks of notification.
CONTACT Office of Financial Aid, Clark Atlanta University, 223 James P. Brawley Drive, Atlanta, GA 30314, 404-880-8992 or toll-free 800-688-3228. *Fax:* 404-880-8070. *E-mail:* studentfinancialaid@cau.edu.

CLARKE COLLEGE
Dubuque, IA

Tuition & fees: $18,945   **Average undergraduate aid package:** $16,631

Clarke College

ABOUT THE INSTITUTION Independent Roman Catholic, coed. Awards: associate, bachelor's, and master's degrees. 42 undergraduate majors. Total enrollment: 1,246. Undergraduates: 1,021. Freshmen: 158. Federal methodology is used as a basis for awarding need-based institutional aid.
UNDERGRADUATE EXPENSES for 2005–06 *Application fee:* $25. *Comprehensive fee:* $25,390 includes full-time tuition ($18,360), mandatory fees ($585), and room and board ($6445). *College room only:* $3135. Full-time tuition and fees vary according to class time. Room and board charges vary according to board plan and housing facility. *Part-time tuition:* $465 per credit hour. Part-time tuition and fees vary according to class time. *Payment plans:* Installment, deferred payment.
FRESHMAN FINANCIAL AID (Fall 2005, est.) 151 applied for aid; of those 96% were deemed to have need. 100% of freshmen with need received aid; of those 26% had need fully met. *Average percent of need met:* 100% (excluding resources awarded to replace EFC). *Average financial aid package:* $18,461 (excluding resources awarded to replace EFC). 6% of all full-time freshmen had no need and received non-need-based gift aid.
UNDERGRADUATE FINANCIAL AID (Fall 2005, est.) 767 applied for aid; of those 91% were deemed to have need. 100% of undergraduates with need received aid; of those 27% had need fully met. *Average percent of need met:* 100% (excluding resources awarded to replace EFC). *Average financial aid package:* $16,631 (excluding resources awarded to replace EFC). 11% of all full-time undergraduates had no need and received non-need-based gift aid.
GIFT AID (NEED-BASED) *Total amount:* $8,210,801 (12% federal, 17% state, 70% institutional, 1% external sources). *Receiving aid:* Freshmen: 94% (145); All full-time undergraduates: 85% (691). *Average award:* Freshmen: $15,777; Undergraduates: $12,897. *Scholarships, grants, and awards:* Federal Pell, FSEOG, state, private, college/university gift aid from institutional funds.
GIFT AID (NON-NEED-BASED) *Total amount:* $546,766 (96% institutional, 4% external sources). *Receiving aid:* Freshmen: 88% (137); Undergraduates: 76% (622). *Average Award:* Freshmen: $13,125; Undergraduates: $12,108. *Scholarships, grants, and awards by category:* Academic Interests/Achievement: 567 awards ($2,775,721 total): computer science, foreign languages, general academic interests/achievements. Creative Arts/Performance: 74 awards ($158,000 total): art/fine arts, music, theater/drama. Special Achievements/Activities: 17 awards ($15,700 total): leadership. Special Characteristics: 813 awards ($1,311,995 total): children and siblings of alumni, children of faculty/staff, children with a deceased or disabled parent, general special characteristics, international students, local/state students, members of minority groups, relatives of clergy, religious affiliation, siblings of current students. *Tuition waivers:* Full or partial for children of alumni, employees or children of employees, adult students, senior citizens.
LOANS *Student loans:* $5,590,298 (53% need-based, 47% non-need-based). 72% of past graduating class borrowed through all loan programs. *Average indebtedness per student:* $19,492. *Average need-based loan:* Freshmen: $2618; Undergraduates: $4237. *Parent loans:* $615,974 (80% need-based, 20% non-need-based). *Programs:* FFEL (Subsidized and Unsubsidized Stafford, PLUS), Perkins, Federal Nursing, state, college/university, alternative loans.
WORK-STUDY *Federal work-study:* Total amount: $285,771; 240 jobs averaging $1191. *State or other work-study/employment:* Part-time jobs available.
APPLYING FOR FINANCIAL AID *Required financial aid form:* FAFSA. *Financial aid deadline (priority):* 4/15. *Notification date:* Continuous beginning 3/15. Students must reply by 5/1 or within 2 weeks of notification.
CONTACT Ann Heisler, Director of Financial Aid, Clarke College, 1550 Clarke Drive, Dubuque, IA 52001-3198, 563-588-6327 or toll-free 800-383-2345. *Fax:* 563-584-8666. *E-mail:* ann.heisler@clarke.edu.

CLARKSON COLLEGE
Omaha, NE

CONTACT Pam Shelton, Director of Financial Aid, Clarkson College, 101 South 42nd Street, Omaha, NE 68131-2739, 402-552-2749 or toll-free 800-647-5500. *Fax:* 402-552-6165. *E-mail:* shelton@clarksoncollege.edu.

CLARKSON UNIVERSITY
Potsdam, NY

Tuition & fees: $25,585   **Average undergraduate aid package: $18,723**

ABOUT THE INSTITUTION Independent, coed. Awards: bachelor's, master's, and doctoral degrees. 60 undergraduate majors. Total enrollment: 3,045. Undergraduates: 2,648. Freshmen: 630. Federal methodology is used as a basis for awarding need-based institutional aid.
UNDERGRADUATE EXPENSES for 2005–06 *Application fee:* $50. *Comprehensive fee:* $34,930 includes full-time tuition ($25,185), mandatory fees ($400), and room and board ($9345). *College room only:* $4896. Full-time tuition and fees vary according to course load. Room and board charges vary according to housing facility. *Part-time tuition:* $840 per credit. Part-time tuition and fees vary according to course load. *Payment plans:* Tuition prepayment, installment.
FRESHMAN FINANCIAL AID (Fall 2005, est.) 560 applied for aid; of those 88% were deemed to have need. 100% of freshmen with need received aid. *Average percent of need met:* 87% (excluding resources awarded to replace EFC). *Average financial aid package:* $20,516 (excluding resources awarded to replace EFC). 7% of all full-time freshmen had no need and received non-need-based gift aid.
UNDERGRADUATE FINANCIAL AID (Fall 2005, est.) 2,337 applied for aid; of those 90% were deemed to have need. 93% of undergraduates with need received aid. *Average percent of need met:* 87% (excluding resources awarded to replace EFC). *Average financial aid package:* $18,723 (excluding resources awarded to replace EFC). 8% of all full-time undergraduates had no need and received non-need-based gift aid.
GIFT AID (NEED-BASED) *Total amount:* $36,815,845 (6% federal, 9% state, 81% institutional, 4% external sources). *Receiving aid:* Freshmen: 63% (396); All full-time undergraduates: 65% (1,711). *Average award:* Freshmen: $13,506; Undergraduates: $11,200. *Scholarships, grants, and awards:* Federal Pell, FSEOG, state, private, college/university gift aid from institutional funds.
GIFT AID (NON-NEED-BASED) *Total amount:* $1,903,944 (3% state, 93% institutional, 4% external sources). *Receiving aid:* Freshmen: 17% (110); Undergraduates: 9% (250). *Average Award:* Freshmen: $7628; Undergraduates: $7873. *Scholarships, grants, and awards by category:* Academic Interests/Achievement: 1,138 awards ($4,110,225 total): biological sciences, business, computer science, engineering/technologies, general academic interests/achievements, humanities, mathematics, military science, physical sciences. Special Achievements/Activities: 672 awards ($5,167,600 total): general special achievements/activities, leadership. Special Characteristics: 360 awards ($2,620,096 total): children of faculty/staff, general special characteristics, international students, local/state students, members of minority groups. *Tuition waivers:* Full or partial for employees or children of employees. *ROTC:* Army, Air Force.
LOANS *Student loans:* $20,320,889 (94% need-based, 6% non-need-based). 81% of past graduating class borrowed through all loan programs. *Average indebtedness per student:* $19,942. *Average need-based loan:* Freshmen: $2926; Undergraduates: $4294. *Parent loans:* $4,504,094 (87% need-based, 13% non-need-based). *Programs:* Federal Direct (Subsidized and Unsubsidized Stafford, PLUS), Perkins, college/university, GATE Loans.
WORK-STUDY *Federal work-study:* Total amount: $651,995; 711 jobs averaging $917. *State or other work-study/employment:* Total amount: $313,433 (59% need-based, 41% non-need-based). 110 state part-time jobs averaging $946.
ATHLETIC AWARDS *Total amount:* $1,149,582 (100% non-need-based).
APPLYING FOR FINANCIAL AID *Required financial aid forms:* FAFSA, institution's own form, state aid form. *Financial aid deadline (priority):* 3/1. *Notification date:* 3/23. Students must reply by 5/1 or within 2 weeks of notification.
CONTACT April L. Grant, Associate Director of Financial Aid, Clarkson University, Box 5615, Cubley-Reynolds, Potsdam, NY 13699-5615, 315-268-6413 or toll-free 800-527-6577. *E-mail:* agrant@clarkson.edu.

CLARK UNIVERSITY
Worcester, MA

Tuition & fees: $31,465   **Average undergraduate aid package: $21,898**

ABOUT THE INSTITUTION Independent, coed. Awards: bachelor's, master's, and doctoral degrees and post-bachelor's and post-master's certificates. 49 undergraduate majors. Total enrollment: 3,118. Undergraduates: 2,255. Freshmen: 560. Institutional methodology is used as a basis for awarding need-based institutional aid.
UNDERGRADUATE EXPENSES for 2005–06 *Application fee:* $50. *Comprehensive fee:* $37,365 includes full-time tuition ($31,200), mandatory fees ($265), and room and board ($5900). *College room only:* $3550. Room and board charges

vary according to board plan and housing facility. *Part-time tuition:* $915.63 per credit hour. *Payment plans:* Tuition prepayment, installment.
FRESHMAN FINANCIAL AID (Fall 2005, est.) 408 applied for aid; of those 76% were deemed to have need. 98% of freshmen with need received aid; of those 68% had need fully met. *Average percent of need met:* 93% (excluding resources awarded to replace EFC). *Average financial aid package:* $21,898 (excluding resources awarded to replace EFC). 26% of all full-time freshmen had no need and received non-need-based gift aid.
UNDERGRADUATE FINANCIAL AID (Fall 2005, est.) 1,525 applied for aid; of those 76% were deemed to have need. 98% of undergraduates with need received aid; of those 68% had need fully met. *Average percent of need met:* 93% (excluding resources awarded to replace EFC). *Average financial aid package:* $21,898 (excluding resources awarded to replace EFC). 26% of all full-time undergraduates had no need and received non-need-based gift aid.
GIFT AID (NEED-BASED) *Total amount:* $17,930,100 (10% federal, 3% state, 85% institutional, 2% external sources). *Receiving aid:* Freshmen: 54% (301); All full-time undergraduates: 54% (1,125). *Average award:* Freshmen: $17,645; Undergraduates: $17,645. *Scholarships, grants, and awards:* Federal Pell, FSEOG, state, college/university gift aid from institutional funds.
GIFT AID (NON-NEED-BASED) *Total amount:* $6,721,295 (100% institutional). *Receiving aid:* Freshmen: 29% (161); Undergraduates: 29% (602). *Average Award:* Freshmen: $11,591; Undergraduates: $11,591. *Scholarships, grants, and awards by category: Academic Interests/Achievement:* general academic interests/achievements. *Special Achievements/Activities:* community service, general special achievements/activities. *Tuition waivers:* Full or partial for employees or children of employees. *ROTC:* Army cooperative, Naval cooperative, Air Force cooperative.
LOANS *Student loans:* $8,200,109 (64% need-based, 36% non-need-based). 88% of past graduating class borrowed through all loan programs. *Average indebtedness per student:* $18,990. *Average need-based loan:* Freshmen: $3208; Undergraduates: $3208. *Parent loans:* $4,219,949 (2% need-based, 98% non-need-based). *Programs:* FFEL (Subsidized and Unsubsidized Stafford, PLUS), Perkins, state, college/university.
WORK-STUDY *Federal work-study:* Total amount: $1,358,165; jobs available.
APPLYING FOR FINANCIAL AID *Required financial aid forms:* FAFSA, CSS Financial Aid PROFILE. *Financial aid deadline (priority):* 2/1. *Notification date:* 3/31. Students must reply by 5/1.
CONTACT Dr. Jeffrey J. Himmelberger, Coordinator, Clark University, 950 Main Street, Worcester, MA 01610-1477, 508-793-7374 or toll-free 800-GO-CLARK. *Fax:* 508-421-3764. *E-mail:* jhimmelberger@clarku.edu.

CLAYTON STATE UNIVERSITY
Morrow, GA

ABOUT THE INSTITUTION State-supported, coed. Awards: associate and bachelor's degrees. 93 undergraduate majors. Total enrollment: 6,152. Undergraduates: 6,152. Freshmen: 631.
GIFT AID (NEED-BASED) *Scholarships, grants, and awards:* Federal Pell, FSEOG, state, college/university gift aid from institutional funds, Federal Nursing.
GIFT AID (NON-NEED-BASED) *Scholarships, grants, and awards by category: Special Characteristics:* general special characteristics.
LOANS *Programs:* FFEL (Subsidized and Unsubsidized Stafford, PLUS), Federal Nursing, state.
WORK-STUDY *Federal work-study:* Total amount: $67,988; jobs available.
APPLYING FOR FINANCIAL AID *Required financial aid forms:* FAFSA, institution's own form, state aid form.
CONTACT Melody Hodge, Director of Financial Aid, Clayton State University, 5900 North Lee Street, Morrow, GA 30260, 770-961-3511. *Fax:* 770-960-4258. *E-mail:* financialaid@mail.clayton.edu.

CLEAR CREEK BAPTIST BIBLE COLLEGE
Pineville, KY

Tuition & fees: $4520	Average undergraduate aid package: $4872

ABOUT THE INSTITUTION Independent Southern Baptist, coed, primarily men. Awards: bachelor's degrees. 2 undergraduate majors. Total enrollment: 212. Undergraduates: 212. Both federal and institutional methodology are used as a basis for awarding need-based institutional aid.
UNDERGRADUATE EXPENSES for 2005–06 *Application fee:* $40. *Comprehensive fee:* $7830 includes full-time tuition ($4520) and room and board ($3310). *College room only:* $1870. *Part-time tuition:* $205 per semester hour.
FRESHMAN FINANCIAL AID (Fall 2005, est.) 22 applied for aid; of those 100% were deemed to have need. 100% of freshmen with need received aid. *Average percent of need met:* 41% (excluding resources awarded to replace EFC). *Average financial aid package:* $4910 (excluding resources awarded to replace EFC). 19% of all full-time freshmen had no need and received non-need-based gift aid.
UNDERGRADUATE FINANCIAL AID (Fall 2005, est.) 146 applied for aid; of those 77% were deemed to have need. 100% of undergraduates with need received aid. *Average percent of need met:* 40% (excluding resources awarded to replace EFC). *Average financial aid package:* $4872 (excluding resources awarded to replace EFC). 20% of all full-time undergraduates had no need and received non-need-based gift aid.
GIFT AID (NEED-BASED) *Total amount:* $725,542 (61% federal, 5% state, 26% institutional, 8% external sources). *Receiving aid:* Freshmen: 85% (22); All full-time undergraduates: 67% (112). *Scholarships, grants, and awards:* Federal Pell, FSEOG, state, private, college/university gift aid from institutional funds.
GIFT AID (NON-NEED-BASED) *Total amount:* $171,843 (50% federal, 50% institutional). *Receiving aid:* Freshmen: 65% (17); Undergraduates: 37% (62). *Average Award:* Freshmen: $680; Undergraduates: $887. *Scholarships, grants, and awards by category: Academic Interests/Achievement:* 8 awards ($1350 total): general academic interests/achievements. *Creative Arts/Performance:* 7 awards ($1400 total): music. *Special Characteristics:* 2 awards ($1132 total): handicapped students, international students.
WORK-STUDY *Federal work-study:* Total amount: $28,562; 24 jobs averaging $1190. *State or other work-study/employment:* Total amount: $9521 (100% need-based). 24 part-time jobs averaging $396.
APPLYING FOR FINANCIAL AID *Required financial aid forms:* FAFSA, institution's own form. *Financial aid deadline (priority):* 6/30. *Notification date:* 7/1.
CONTACT Mr. Sam Risner, Director of Financial Aid, Clear Creek Baptist Bible College, 300 Clear Creek Road, Pineville, KY 40977-9754, 606-337-3196 Ext. 142. *Fax:* 606-337-2372. *E-mail:* srisner@ccbbc.edu.

CLEARWATER CHRISTIAN COLLEGE
Clearwater, FL

Tuition & fees: $12,500	Average undergraduate aid package: $8245

ABOUT THE INSTITUTION Independent nondenominational, coed. Awards: associate and bachelor's degrees. 25 undergraduate majors. Total enrollment: 582. Undergraduates: 582. Freshmen: 149. Federal methodology is used as a basis for awarding need-based institutional aid.
UNDERGRADUATE EXPENSES for 2006–07 *Application fee:* $35. *Comprehensive fee:* $17,830 includes full-time tuition ($11,860), mandatory fees ($640), and room and board ($5330). *Part-time tuition:* $460 per hour.
FRESHMAN FINANCIAL AID (Fall 2005, est.) 150 applied for aid; of those 100% were deemed to have need. 96% of freshmen with need received aid; of those 3% had need fully met. *Average percent of need met:* 31% (excluding resources awarded to replace EFC). *Average financial aid package:* $7875 (excluding resources awarded to replace EFC).
UNDERGRADUATE FINANCIAL AID (Fall 2005, est.) 581 applied for aid; of those 100% were deemed to have need. 95% of undergraduates with need received aid; of those 3% had need fully met. *Average percent of need met:* 47% (excluding resources awarded to replace EFC). *Average financial aid package:* $8245 (excluding resources awarded to replace EFC).
GIFT AID (NEED-BASED) *Total amount:* $759,931 (74% federal, 21% state, 5% institutional). *Receiving aid:* Freshmen: 57% (85); All full-time undergraduates: 40% (233). *Average award:* Freshmen: $4110; Undergraduates: $4002. *Scholarships, grants, and awards:* Federal Pell, FSEOG, state, private, college/university gift aid from institutional funds.
GIFT AID (NON-NEED-BASED) *Total amount:* $1,938,480 (47% state, 44% institutional, 9% external sources). *Receiving aid:* Freshmen: 84% (126); Undergraduates: 55% (319). *Scholarships, grants, and awards by category: Academic Interests/Achievement:* 119 awards ($272,350 total): business, education, general academic interests/achievements, premedicine, religion/biblical studies. *Creative Arts/Performance:* 31 awards ($61,750 total): music. *Special Achievements/Activities:* 11 awards ($53,655 total): leadership. *Special*

Clearwater Christian College

Characteristics: 66 awards ($49,500 total): children and siblings of alumni, ethnic background, religious affiliation, siblings of current students. *ROTC:* Army cooperative, Air Force cooperative.
LOANS *Student loans:* $1,565,959 (51% need-based, 49% non-need-based). 64% of past graduating class borrowed through all loan programs. *Average indebtedness per student:* $16,300. *Average need-based loan:* Freshmen: $2373; Undergraduates: $3923. *Parent loans:* $692,666 (100% non-need-based). *Programs:* FFEL (Subsidized and Unsubsidized Stafford, PLUS), state, alternative loans.
WORK-STUDY *Federal work-study:* Total amount: $33,547; 50 jobs averaging $670. *State or other work-study/employment:* Total amount: $12,239 (100% need-based). 20 part-time jobs averaging $612.
APPLYING FOR FINANCIAL AID *Required financial aid forms:* FAFSA, institution's own form, state aid form. *Financial aid deadline (priority):* 3/15. *Notification date:* Continuous beginning 1/1. Students must reply within 2 weeks of notification.
CONTACT Mrs. Ruth Strum, Director of Financial Aid, Clearwater Christian College, 3400 Gulf-to-Bay Boulevard, Clearwater, FL 33759-4595, 727-726-1153 Ext. 214 or toll-free 800-348-4463. *Fax:* 727-791-1347. *E-mail:* ruthstrum@clearwater.edu.

CLEARY UNIVERSITY
Ann Arbor, MI

ABOUT THE INSTITUTION Independent, coed. Awards: associate, bachelor's, and master's degrees. 10 undergraduate majors. Total enrollment: 597. Undergraduates: 563.
GIFT AID (NEED-BASED) *Scholarships, grants, and awards:* Federal Pell, FSEOG, state, private, college/university gift aid from institutional funds.
GIFT AID (NON-NEED-BASED) *Scholarships, grants, and awards by category: Academic Interests/Achievement:* business, general academic interests/achievements. *Special Achievements/Activities:* community service, general special achievements/activities. *Special Characteristics:* adult students, children of faculty/staff.
LOANS *Programs:* FFEL (Subsidized and Unsubsidized Stafford, PLUS).
WORK-STUDY *Federal work-study:* Total amount: $41,600; 13 jobs averaging $3124. *State or other work-study/employment:* Part-time jobs available.
APPLYING FOR FINANCIAL AID *Required financial aid forms:* FAFSA, institution's own form.
CONTACT Vesta Smith-Campbell, Director of Financial Aid, Cleary University, 3750 Cleary Drive, Howell, MI 48843, 800-589-1979 Ext. 2234 or toll-free 888-5-CLEARY Ext. 2249. *Fax:* 517-552-8022. *E-mail:* vscampbell@cleary.edu.

CLEMSON UNIVERSITY
Clemson, SC

Tuition & fees (SC res): $9016   **Average undergraduate aid package:** $9154

ABOUT THE INSTITUTION State-supported, coed. Awards: bachelor's, master's, and doctoral degrees. 77 undergraduate majors. Total enrollment: 17,165. Undergraduates: 14,096. Freshmen: 2,882. Federal methodology is used as a basis for awarding need-based institutional aid.
UNDERGRADUATE EXPENSES for 2005–06 *Application fee:* $50. *Tuition, state resident:* full-time $9016; part-time $364 per hour. *Tuition, nonresident:* full-time $18,640; part-time $760 per hour. Full-time tuition and fees vary according to course load and program. Part-time tuition and fees vary according to course load and program. *College room and board:* $5780; *room only:* $3470. Room and board charges vary according to board plan and housing facility. *Payment plan:* Installment.
FRESHMAN FINANCIAL AID (Fall 2005, est.) 1898 applied for aid; of those 66% were deemed to have need. 98% of freshmen with need received aid; of those 38% had need fully met. *Average percent of need met:* 30% (excluding resources awarded to replace EFC). *Average financial aid package:* $10,712 (excluding resources awarded to replace EFC). 25% of all full-time freshmen had no need and received non-need-based gift aid.
UNDERGRADUATE FINANCIAL AID (Fall 2005, est.) 7,325 applied for aid; of those 74% were deemed to have need. 96% of undergraduates with need received aid; of those 26% had need fully met. *Average percent of need met:* 39% (excluding resources awarded to replace EFC). *Average financial aid package:* $9154 (excluding resources awarded to replace EFC). 18% of all full-time undergraduates had no need and received non-need-based gift aid.
GIFT AID (NEED-BASED) *Total amount:* $9,900,771 (54% federal, 21% state, 10% institutional, 15% external sources). *Receiving aid:* Freshmen: 15% (444); All full-time undergraduates: 18% (2,468). *Average award:* Freshmen: $3508; Undergraduates: $3337. *Scholarships, grants, and awards:* Federal Pell, FSEOG, state, private, college/university gift aid from institutional funds, Federal Nursing.
GIFT AID (NON-NEED-BASED) *Total amount:* $40,189,476 (72% state, 17% institutional, 11% external sources). *Receiving aid:* Freshmen: 38% (1,100); Undergraduates: 22% (3,029). *Average Award:* Freshmen: $4542; Undergraduates: $3671. *Scholarships, grants, and awards by category: Academic Interests/Achievement:* agriculture, architecture, biological sciences, business, communication, computer science, education, engineering/technologies, English, foreign languages, general academic interests/achievements, health fields, humanities, international studies, mathematics, military science, physical sciences, premedicine, social sciences. *Creative Arts/Performance:* applied art and design, art/fine arts, performing arts, theater/drama. *Special Achievements/Activities:* community service, general special achievements/activities, leadership. *Special Characteristics:* children of faculty/staff, ethnic background, local/state students, members of minority groups. *Tuition waivers:* Full or partial for senior citizens. *ROTC:* Army, Air Force.
LOANS *Student loans:* $40,838,266 (41% need-based, 59% non-need-based). 44% of past graduating class borrowed through all loan programs. *Average indebtedness per student:* $15,730. *Average need-based loan:* Freshmen: $3017; Undergraduates: $4192. *Parent loans:* $11,476,545 (100% non-need-based). *Programs:* FFEL (Subsidized and Unsubsidized Stafford, PLUS), Perkins, state, college/university, private loans.
WORK-STUDY *Federal work-study:* Total amount: $1,322,615; 629 jobs averaging $2101. *State or other work-study/employment:* Total amount: $8,242,000 (100% non-need-based). 3,300 part-time jobs averaging $2496.
ATHLETIC AWARDS Total amount: $4,051,059 (100% non-need-based).
APPLYING FOR FINANCIAL AID *Required financial aid form:* FAFSA. *Financial aid deadline (priority):* 4/1. *Notification date:* Continuous beginning 4/15. Students must reply within 3 weeks of notification.
CONTACT Mr. Marvin G. Carmichael, Director of Financial Aid, Clemson University, G01 Sikes Hall, Clemson, SC 29634-5123, 864-656-2280. *Fax:* 864-656-1831. *E-mail:* finaid@clemson.edu.

THE CLEVELAND INSTITUTE OF ART
Cleveland, OH

Tuition & fees: $27,177   **Average undergraduate aid package:** $16,015

ABOUT THE INSTITUTION Independent, coed. Awards: bachelor's and master's degrees. 17 undergraduate majors. Total enrollment: 610. Undergraduates: 604. Freshmen: 123. Federal methodology is used as a basis for awarding need-based institutional aid.
UNDERGRADUATE EXPENSES for 2005–06 *Application fee:* $30. *Comprehensive fee:* $36,313 includes full-time tuition ($24,917), mandatory fees ($2260), and room and board ($9136). *College room only:* $5480. Room and board charges vary according to board plan and housing facility. *Part-time tuition:* $1045 per credit. *Part-time fees:* $90 per credit. Part-time tuition and fees vary according to course load. *Payment plan:* Deferred payment.
FRESHMAN FINANCIAL AID (Fall 2005, est.) 82 applied for aid; of those 96% were deemed to have need. 100% of freshmen with need received aid; of those 5% had need fully met. *Average percent of need met:* 55% (excluding resources awarded to replace EFC). *Average financial aid package:* $16,331 (excluding resources awarded to replace EFC). 22% of all full-time freshmen had no need and received non-need-based gift aid.
UNDERGRADUATE FINANCIAL AID (Fall 2005, est.) 445 applied for aid; of those 93% were deemed to have need. 100% of undergraduates with need received aid; of those 6% had need fully met. *Average percent of need met:* 53% (excluding resources awarded to replace EFC). *Average financial aid package:* $16,015 (excluding resources awarded to replace EFC). 17% of all full-time undergraduates had no need and received non-need-based gift aid.
GIFT AID (NEED-BASED) *Total amount:* $4,403,441 (13% federal, 14% state, 68% institutional, 5% external sources). *Receiving aid:* Freshmen: 86% (79); All full-time undergraduates: 81% (411). *Average award:* Freshmen: $11,766; Undergraduates: $10,431. *Scholarships, grants, and awards:* Federal Pell, FSEOG, state, private, college/university gift aid from institutional funds.

Cleveland State University

GIFT AID (NON-NEED-BASED) *Total amount:* $856,098 (7% state, 92% institutional, 1% external sources). *Receiving aid:* Freshmen: 3% (3); Undergraduates: 4% (21). *Average Award: Freshmen:* $9654; *Undergraduates:* $12,369. *Scholarships, grants, and awards by category: Academic Interests/Achievement:* 33 awards ($66,760 total): general academic interests/achievements. *Creative Arts/Performance:* 464 awards ($3,069,228 total): art/fine arts. *Tuition waivers:* Full or partial for employees or children of employees.

LOANS *Student loans:* $5,183,309 (83% need-based, 17% non-need-based). 89% of past graduating class borrowed through all loan programs. *Average indebtedness per student:* $37,543. *Average need-based loan: Freshmen:* $3694; Undergraduates: $4622. *Parent loans:* $1,139,874 (67% need-based, 33% non-need-based). *Programs:* FFEL (Subsidized and Unsubsidized Stafford, PLUS), Perkins.

WORK-STUDY *Federal work-study:* Total amount: $230,138; 225 jobs averaging $1023.

APPLYING FOR FINANCIAL AID *Required financial aid forms:* FAFSA, institution's own form. *Financial aid deadline (priority):* 3/15. *Notification date:* Continuous beginning 3/16. Students must reply within 4 weeks of notification.

CONTACT Delores Hall, Assistant Director of Financial Aid, The Cleveland Institute of Art, 11141 East Boulevard, Cleveland, OH 44106-1700, 216-421-7425 or toll-free 800-223-4700. *Fax:* 216-754-3634. *E-mail:* financialaid@cia.edu.

CLEVELAND INSTITUTE OF MUSIC
Cleveland, OH

Tuition & fees: $26,870 **Average undergraduate aid package:** $17,544

ABOUT THE INSTITUTION Independent, coed. Awards: bachelor's, master's, and doctoral degrees and post-bachelor's certificates. 6 undergraduate majors. Total enrollment: 409. Undergraduates: 244. Freshmen: 71. Federal methodology is used as a basis for awarding need-based institutional aid.

UNDERGRADUATE EXPENSES for 2005–06 *Application fee:* $100. *Comprehensive fee:* $35,596 includes full-time tuition ($25,870), mandatory fees ($1000), and room and board ($8726). *College room only:* $5120. Room and board charges vary according to board plan. *Part-time tuition:* $1078 per credit hour. *Payment plan:* Installment.

FRESHMAN FINANCIAL AID (Fall 2005, est.) 54 applied for aid; of those 72% were deemed to have need. 100% of freshmen with need received aid; of those 36% had need fully met. *Average percent of need met:* 74% (excluding resources awarded to replace EFC). *Average financial aid package:* $15,770 (excluding resources awarded to replace EFC). 33% of all full-time freshmen had no need and received non-need-based gift aid.

UNDERGRADUATE FINANCIAL AID (Fall 2005, est.) 207 applied for aid; of those 74% were deemed to have need. 100% of undergraduates with need received aid; of those 27% had need fully met. *Average percent of need met:* 72% (excluding resources awarded to replace EFC). *Average financial aid package:* $17,544 (excluding resources awarded to replace EFC). 37% of all full-time undergraduates had no need and received non-need-based gift aid.

GIFT AID (NEED-BASED) *Total amount:* $1,852,098 (7% federal, 3% state, 86% institutional, 4% external sources). *Receiving aid: Freshmen:* 65% (39); All full-time undergraduates: 62% (153). *Average award: Freshmen:* $12,626; Undergraduates: $12,051. *Scholarships, grants, and awards:* Federal Pell, FSEOG, state, private, college/university gift aid from institutional funds.

GIFT AID (NON-NEED-BASED) *Total amount:* $968,881 (2% state, 86% institutional, 12% external sources). *Receiving aid: Freshmen:* 20% (12); Undergraduates: 10% (24). *Average Award: Freshmen:* $13,614; Undergraduates: $12,724. *Scholarships, grants, and awards by category: Creative Arts/Performance:* music. *Tuition waivers:* Full or partial for employees or children of employees. *ROTC:* Army cooperative, Air Force cooperative.

LOANS *Student loans:* $1,241,022 (72% need-based, 28% non-need-based). 71% of past graduating class borrowed through all loan programs. *Average indebtedness per student:* $24,819. *Average need-based loan: Freshmen:* $3868; Undergraduates: $5528. *Parent loans:* $724,056 (33% need-based, 67% non-need-based). *Programs:* Federal Direct (Subsidized and Unsubsidized Stafford, PLUS), Perkins, college/university, private/alternative loans.

WORK-STUDY *Federal work-study:* Total amount: $143,894; 95 jobs averaging $1515. *State or other work-study/employment:* Total amount: $56,638 (100% non-need-based). 43 part-time jobs averaging $1294.

APPLYING FOR FINANCIAL AID *Required financial aid forms:* FAFSA, institution's own form. *Financial aid deadline:* 2/15 (priority: 2/15). *Notification date:* 4/1. Students must reply by 5/1.

CONTACT Ms. Kristie Gripp, Director of Financial Aid, Cleveland Institute of Music, 11021 East Boulevard, Cleveland, OH 44106-1776, 216-791-5000 Ext. 262. *Fax:* 216-795-3141. *E-mail:* kxg26@cwru.edu.

CLEVELAND STATE UNIVERSITY
Cleveland, OH

Tuition & fees (OH res): $6792 **Average undergraduate aid package:** $7247

ABOUT THE INSTITUTION State-supported, coed. Awards: bachelor's, master's, doctoral, and first professional degrees and post-bachelor's and post-master's certificates. 83 undergraduate majors. Total enrollment: 15,722. Undergraduates: 9,953. Freshmen: 1,079. Federal methodology is used as a basis for awarding need-based institutional aid.

UNDERGRADUATE EXPENSES for 2005–06 *Application fee:* $30. *Tuition, state resident:* full-time $6792; part-time $283 per semester hour. *Tuition, nonresident:* full-time $9216; part-time $384 per semester hour. Full-time tuition and fees vary according to program and student level. Part-time tuition and fees vary according to program and student level. *College room and board:* $6809; *room only:* $4091. Room and board charges vary according to board plan and housing facility. *Payment plan:* Installment.

FRESHMAN FINANCIAL AID (Fall 2005, est.) 829 applied for aid; of those 89% were deemed to have need. 97% of freshmen with need received aid; of those 5% had need fully met. *Average percent of need met:* 43% (excluding resources awarded to replace EFC). *Average financial aid package:* $6510 (excluding resources awarded to replace EFC). 11% of all full-time freshmen had no need and received non-need-based gift aid.

UNDERGRADUATE FINANCIAL AID (Fall 2005, est.) 5,284 applied for aid; of those 90% were deemed to have need. 98% of undergraduates with need received aid; of those 8% had need fully met. *Average percent of need met:* 48% (excluding resources awarded to replace EFC). *Average financial aid package:* $7247 (excluding resources awarded to replace EFC). 11% of all full-time undergraduates had no need and received non-need-based gift aid.

GIFT AID (NEED-BASED) *Total amount:* $18,093,197 (60% federal, 19% state, 14% institutional, 7% external sources). *Receiving aid: Freshmen:* 57% (587); All full-time undergraduates: 52% (3,455). *Average award: Freshmen:* $5200; Undergraduates: $4979. *Scholarships, grants, and awards:* Federal Pell, FSEOG, state, private, college/university gift aid from institutional funds.

GIFT AID (NON-NEED-BASED) *Total amount:* $1,613,551 (7% state, 75% institutional, 18% external sources). *Receiving aid: Freshmen:* 1% (15); Undergraduates: 1% (68). *Average Award: Freshmen:* $8887; *Undergraduates:* $8133. *Scholarships, grants, and awards by category: Academic Interests/Achievement:* engineering/technologies, general academic interests/achievements. *Creative Arts/Performance:* art/fine arts, creative writing, dance, music, theater/drama. *Special Characteristics:* general special characteristics. *Tuition waivers:* Full or partial for employees or children of employees, senior citizens. *ROTC:* Army cooperative, Naval cooperative, Air Force cooperative.

LOANS *Student loans:* $37,243,580 (85% need-based, 15% non-need-based). *Average need-based loan: Freshmen:* $2699; Undergraduates: $3901. *Parent loans:* $6,927,560 (36% need-based, 64% non-need-based). *Programs:* FFEL (Subsidized and Unsubsidized Stafford, PLUS), Perkins, state, alternative loans.

WORK-STUDY *Federal work-study:* Total amount: $749,189; jobs available. *State or other work-study/employment:* Total amount: $3763 (100% need-based). Part-time jobs available.

ATHLETIC AWARDS *Total amount:* $1,965,892 (34% need-based, 66% non-need-based).

APPLYING FOR FINANCIAL AID *Required financial aid forms:* FAFSA, income tax form(s), if selected for verification by Department of Education or the Institution, verification documents. *Financial aid deadline (priority):* 2/15. *Notification date:* Continuous beginning 3/15. Students must reply within 4 weeks of notification.

CONTACT Director of Financial Aid, Cleveland State University, 2121 Euclid Avenue, University Center, Room 560, Cleveland, OH 44115, 216-687-3764 or toll-free 888-CSU-OHIO.

Coastal Carolina University

COASTAL CAROLINA UNIVERSITY
Conway, SC

Tuition & fees (SC res): $6860 **Average undergraduate aid package:** $7717

ABOUT THE INSTITUTION State-supported, coed. Awards: bachelor's and master's degrees and post-bachelor's certificates. 31 undergraduate majors. Total enrollment: 7,613. Undergraduates: 6,397. Freshmen: 1,498. Federal methodology is used as a basis for awarding need-based institutional aid.

UNDERGRADUATE EXPENSES for 2005–06 *Application fee:* $45. *Tuition, state resident:* full-time $6780; part-time $290 per credit hour. *Tuition, nonresident:* full-time $15,020; part-time $630 per credit hour. Full-time tuition and fees vary according to course load. Part-time tuition and fees vary according to course load. *College room and board:* $6280; *room only:* $4020. Room and board charges vary according to board plan and housing facility. *Payment plans:* Installment, deferred payment.

FRESHMAN FINANCIAL AID (Fall 2004) 1021 applied for aid; of those 82% were deemed to have need. 100% of freshmen with need received aid; of those 34% had need fully met. *Average percent of need met:* 58% (excluding resources awarded to replace EFC). *Average financial aid package:* $6868 (excluding resources awarded to replace EFC). 25% of all full-time freshmen had no need and received non-need-based gift aid.

UNDERGRADUATE FINANCIAL AID (Fall 2004) 4,061 applied for aid; of those 86% were deemed to have need. 100% of undergraduates with need received aid; of those 32% had need fully met. *Average percent of need met:* 57% (excluding resources awarded to replace EFC). *Average financial aid package:* $7717 (excluding resources awarded to replace EFC). 21% of all full-time undergraduates had no need and received non-need-based gift aid.

GIFT AID (NEED-BASED) *Total amount:* $5,016,870 (89% federal, 11% state). *Receiving aid:* Freshmen: 23% (300); All full-time undergraduates: 26% (1,364). *Average award:* Freshmen: $3347; Undergraduates: $3387. *Scholarships, grants, and awards:* Federal Pell, FSEOG, state, private, college/university gift aid from institutional funds.

GIFT AID (NON-NEED-BASED) *Total amount:* $7,821,302 (66% state, 12% institutional, 22% external sources). *Receiving aid:* Freshmen: 33% (441); Undergraduates: 19% (1,001). *Average Award:* Freshmen: $7125; Undergraduates:* $7128. *Scholarships, grants, and awards by category: Academic Interests/Achievement:* 1,034 awards ($2,881,578 total): biological sciences, business, education, general academic interests/achievements, humanities, mathematics. *Creative Arts/Performance:* 36 awards ($29,850 total): art/fine arts, music, theater/drama. *Special Characteristics:* 600 awards ($3,087,166 total): general special characteristics, international students, local/state students, out-of-state students, veterans' children. *Tuition waivers:* Full or partial for employees or children of employees, senior citizens.

LOANS *Student loans:* $22,528,396 (43% need-based, 57% non-need-based). 62% of past graduating class borrowed through all loan programs. *Average indebtedness per student:* $20,923. *Average need-based loan:* Freshmen: $6088; Undergraduates: $7287. *Parent loans:* $7,982,866 (100% non-need-based). *Programs:* FFEL (Subsidized and Unsubsidized Stafford, PLUS), Perkins, state.

WORK-STUDY *Federal work-study:* Total amount: $322,939; 210 jobs averaging $1407. *State or other work-study/employment:* Total amount: $826,350 (3% need-based, 97% non-need-based). 598 part-time jobs averaging $2354.

ATHLETIC AWARDS Total amount: $1,735,019 (100% non-need-based).

APPLYING FOR FINANCIAL AID *Required financial aid form:* FAFSA. *Financial aid deadline (priority):* 4/1. *Notification date:* Continuous beginning 3/1.

CONTACT Dawn Hitchcock, Interim Director of Financial Aid, Coastal Carolina University, PO Box 261954, Conway, SC 29528-6054, 843-349-2325 or toll-free 800-277-7000. *Fax:* 843-349-2347. *E-mail:* dawn@coastal.edu.

COE COLLEGE
Cedar Rapids, IA

Tuition & fees: $25,120 **Average undergraduate aid package:** $20,370

ABOUT THE INSTITUTION Independent religious, coed. Awards: bachelor's and master's degrees. 64 undergraduate majors. Total enrollment: 1,355. Undergraduates: 1,331. Freshmen: 316. Both federal and institutional methodology are used as a basis for awarding need-based institutional aid.

UNDERGRADUATE EXPENSES for 2006–07 *Application fee:* $30. *Comprehensive fee:* $31,670 includes full-time tuition ($24,830), mandatory fees ($290), and room and board ($6550). *College room only:* $2990. *Part-time tuition:* $3200 per course.

FRESHMAN FINANCIAL AID (Fall 2005, est.) 283 applied for aid; of those 89% were deemed to have need. 100% of freshmen with need received aid; of those 27% had need fully met. *Average percent of need met:* 96% (excluding resources awarded to replace EFC). *Average financial aid package:* $21,766 (excluding resources awarded to replace EFC). 21% of all full-time freshmen had no need and received non-need-based gift aid.

UNDERGRADUATE FINANCIAL AID (Fall 2005, est.) 1,058 applied for aid; of those 91% were deemed to have need. 100% of undergraduates with need received aid; of those 20% had need fully met. *Average percent of need met:* 90% (excluding resources awarded to replace EFC). *Average financial aid package:* $20,370 (excluding resources awarded to replace EFC). 20% of all full-time undergraduates had no need and received non-need-based gift aid.

GIFT AID (NEED-BASED) *Total amount:* $13,418,755 (7% federal, 14% state, 77% institutional, 2% external sources). *Receiving aid:* Freshmen: 79% (251); All full-time undergraduates: 75% (939). *Average award:* Freshmen: $16,012; Undergraduates: $14,228. *Scholarships, grants, and awards:* Federal Pell, FSEOG, state, private, college/university gift aid from institutional funds, ROTC.

GIFT AID (NON-NEED-BASED) *Total amount:* $3,442,246 (97% institutional, 3% external sources). *Receiving aid:* Freshmen: 18% (57); Undergraduates: 11% (136). *Average Award:* Freshmen: $13,496; Undergraduates: $11,287. *Scholarships, grants, and awards by category: Academic Interests/Achievement:* 1,224 awards ($8,642,528 total): biological sciences, business, foreign languages, general academic interests/achievements, physical sciences, premedicine. *Creative Arts/Performance:* 362 awards ($997,037 total): art/fine arts, creative writing, music, performing arts, theater/drama. *Special Achievements/Activities:* 322 awards ($1,009,737 total). *Special Characteristics:* 322 awards ($1,009,737 total): adult students, children and siblings of alumni, children of faculty/staff, international students, siblings of current students. *ROTC:* Army cooperative, Air Force cooperative.

LOANS *Student loans:* $7,221,456 (72% need-based, 28% non-need-based). 76% of past graduating class borrowed through all loan programs. *Average indebtedness per student:* $20,237. *Average need-based loan:* Freshmen: $4727; Undergraduates: $6229. *Parent loans:* $1,970,974 (25% need-based, 75% non-need-based). *Programs:* Federal Direct (Subsidized and Unsubsidized Stafford, PLUS), Perkins, college/university.

WORK-STUDY *Federal work-study:* Total amount: $517,800; jobs available (averaging $1200). *State or other work-study/employment:* Total amount: $151,350 (5% need-based, 95% non-need-based). Part-time jobs available (averaging $1200).

APPLYING FOR FINANCIAL AID *Required financial aid form:* FAFSA. *Financial aid deadline (priority):* 3/1. *Notification date:* Continuous beginning 3/15. Students must reply by 5/1 or within 2 weeks of notification.

CONTACT Ms. Barbara Hoffman, Director of Financial Aid, Coe College, 1220 1st Avenue, NE, Cedar Rapids, IA 52402-5070, 319-399-8540 or toll-free 877-225-5263. *Fax:* 319-399-8886.

COGSWELL POLYTECHNICAL COLLEGE
Sunnyvale, CA

CONTACT Guillermo S. Gaeta, Financial Aid Director, Cogswell Polytechnical College, 1175 Bordeaux Drive, Sunnyvale, CA 94089, 408-541-0100 Ext. 107 or toll-free 800-264-7955. *Fax:* 408-747-0766. *E-mail:* ggaeta@cogswell.edu.

COKER COLLEGE
Hartsville, SC

CONTACT Betty Williams, Director of Financial Aid, Coker College, 300 East College Avenue, Hartsville, SC 29550, 843-383-8055 or toll-free 800-950-1908. *Fax:* 843-383-8056. *E-mail:* bwilliams@coker.edu.

THE COLBURN SCHOOL CONSERVATORY OF MUSIC
Los Angeles, CA

CONTACT Financial Aid Office, The Colburn School Conservatory of Music, 200 South Grand Avenue, Los Angeles, CA 90012, 213-621-2200.

COLBY COLLEGE
Waterville, ME

Comprehensive fee: $41,770 **Average undergraduate aid package:** $27,177

ABOUT THE INSTITUTION Independent, coed. Awards: bachelor's degrees. 41 undergraduate majors. Total enrollment: 1,871. Undergraduates: 1,871. Freshmen: 511. Both federal and institutional methodology are used as a basis for awarding need-based institutional aid.

UNDERGRADUATE EXPENSES for 2005–06 *Comprehensive fee:* $41,770.

FRESHMAN FINANCIAL AID (Fall 2005, est.) 267 applied for aid; of those 80% were deemed to have need. 100% of freshmen with need received aid; of those 100% had need fully met. *Average percent of need met:* 100% (excluding resources awarded to replace EFC). *Average financial aid package:* $28,493 (excluding resources awarded to replace EFC).

UNDERGRADUATE FINANCIAL AID (Fall 2005, est.) 830 applied for aid; of those 87% were deemed to have need. 100% of undergraduates with need received aid; of those 100% had need fully met. *Average percent of need met:* 100% (excluding resources awarded to replace EFC). *Average financial aid package:* $27,177 (excluding resources awarded to replace EFC).

GIFT AID (NEED-BASED) *Total amount:* $17,214,337 (5% federal, 92% institutional, 3% external sources). *Receiving aid:* Freshmen: 39% (201); All full-time undergraduates: 36% (679). *Average award:* Freshmen: $27,190; Undergraduates: $25,352. *Scholarships, grants, and awards:* Federal Pell, FSEOG, state, private, college/university gift aid from institutional funds.

GIFT AID (NON-NEED-BASED) *ROTC:* Army cooperative.

LOANS *Student loans:* $3,485,119 (43% need-based, 57% non-need-based). 43% of past graduating class borrowed through all loan programs. *Average indebtedness per student:* $18,479. *Average need-based loan:* Freshmen: $3043; Undergraduates: $3306. *Parent loans:* $2,554,472 (100% non-need-based). *Programs:* Federal Direct (Subsidized and Unsubsidized Stafford, PLUS), FFEL (Subsidized and Unsubsidized Stafford, PLUS), Perkins, state, college/university, alternative loans.

WORK-STUDY *Federal work-study:* Total amount: $649,339; 444 jobs averaging $1463. *State or other work-study/employment:* Total amount: $148,555 (100% need-based). 91 part-time jobs averaging $1635.

APPLYING FOR FINANCIAL AID *Required financial aid forms:* FAFSA, either institution's own financial aid form or CSS/Financial Aid PROFILE and institutional supplement. *Financial aid deadline:* 2/1. *Notification date:* 4/1. Students must reply by 5/1.

CONTACT Ms. Lucia Whittelsey, Director of Financial Aid, Colby College, 4850 Mayflower Hill, Waterville, ME 04901-8848, 207-859-4832 or toll-free 800-723-3032. *Fax:* 207-859-4828. *E-mail:* finaid@colby.edu.

COLBY-SAWYER COLLEGE
New London, NH

ABOUT THE INSTITUTION Independent, coed. Awards: associate and bachelor's degrees. 20 undergraduate majors. Total enrollment: 971. Undergraduates: 971. Freshmen: 282.

GIFT AID (NEED-BASED) *Scholarships, grants, and awards:* Federal Pell, FSEOG, state, private, college/university gift aid from institutional funds.

GIFT AID (NON-NEED-BASED) *Scholarships, grants, and awards by category: Academic Interests/Achievement:* general academic interests/achievements. *Creative Arts/Performance:* art/fine arts, creative writing, music. *Special Achievements/Activities:* community service, leadership. *Special Characteristics:* children of faculty/staff.

LOANS *Programs:* FFEL (Subsidized and Unsubsidized Stafford, PLUS), Perkins, state, college/university.

APPLYING FOR FINANCIAL AID *Required financial aid forms:* FAFSA, institution's own form.

CONTACT Office of Financial Aid, Colby-Sawyer College, 541 Main Street, New London, NH 03257-7835, 603-526-3717 or toll-free 800-272-1015. *Fax:* 603-526-3452. *E-mail:* cscfinaid@colby-sawyer.edu.

COLEGIO BIBLICO PENTECOSTAL
St. Just, PR

CONTACT Mr. Eric Ayala, Director of Financial Aid, Colegio Biblico Pentecostal, PO Box 901, St. Just, PR 00978-0901, 787-761-0640.

COLEGIO PENTECOSTAL MIZPA
Río Piedras, PR

CONTACT Financial Aid Office, Colegio Pentecostal Mizpa, Bo Caimito Road 199, Apartado 20966, Río Piedras, PR 00928-0966, 787-720-4476.

COLEMAN COLLEGE
La Mesa, CA

CONTACT Financial Aid Office, Coleman College, 7380 Parkway Drive, La Mesa, CA 91942, 619-465-3990. *Fax:* 619-465-0162. *E-mail:* faoffice@coleman.edu.

COLGATE UNIVERSITY
Hamilton, NY

Tuition & fees: $33,105 **Average undergraduate aid package:** $27,795

ABOUT THE INSTITUTION Independent, coed. Awards: bachelor's and master's degrees. 52 undergraduate majors. Total enrollment: 2,779. Undergraduates: 2,771. Freshmen: 729. Both federal and institutional methodology are used as a basis for awarding need-based institutional aid.

UNDERGRADUATE EXPENSES for 2005–06 *Application fee:* $55. *Comprehensive fee:* $41,170 includes full-time tuition ($32,885), mandatory fees ($220), and room and board ($8065). *College room only:* $3895. Full-time tuition and fees vary according to course load. Room and board charges vary according to board plan and housing facility. *Part-time tuition:* $4111 per course. Part-time tuition and fees vary according to course load. *Payment plans:* Tuition prepayment, installment, deferred payment.

FRESHMAN FINANCIAL AID (Fall 2005, est.) 272 applied for aid; of those 81% were deemed to have need. 100% of freshmen with need received aid; of those 100% had need fully met. *Average percent of need met:* 100% (excluding resources awarded to replace EFC). *Average financial aid package:* $31,901 (excluding resources awarded to replace EFC).

UNDERGRADUATE FINANCIAL AID (Fall 2005, est.) 1,265 applied for aid; of those 94% were deemed to have need. 100% of undergraduates with need received aid; of those 100% had need fully met. *Average percent of need met:* 100% (excluding resources awarded to replace EFC). *Average financial aid package:* $27,795 (excluding resources awarded to replace EFC).

GIFT AID (NEED-BASED) *Total amount:* $28,262,569 (3% federal, 3% state, 91% institutional, 3% external sources). *Receiving aid:* Freshmen: 30% (219); All full-time undergraduates: 39% (1,073). *Average award:* Freshmen: $27,326; Undergraduates: $25,396. *Scholarships, grants, and awards:* Federal Pell, FSEOG, state, college/university gift aid from institutional funds.

GIFT AID (NON-NEED-BASED) *Receiving aid:* Freshmen: 5% (37); Undergraduates: 3% (70). *Tuition waivers:* Full or partial for employees or children of employees. *ROTC:* Army cooperative.

LOANS *Student loans:* $3,926,957 (72% need-based, 28% non-need-based). 38% of past graduating class borrowed through all loan programs. *Average indebtedness per student:* $13,452. *Average need-based loan:* Freshmen: $2571; Undergraduates: $4350. *Parent loans:* $4,002,648 (100% non-need-based). *Programs:* FFEL (Subsidized and Unsubsidized Stafford, PLUS), Perkins.

WORK-STUDY *Federal work-study:* Total amount: $1,136,365; 601 jobs averaging $1890. *State or other work-study/employment:* Total amount: $533,707 (100% need-based). 297 part-time jobs averaging $1797.

ATHLETIC AWARDS *Total amount:* $2,171,068 (100% non-need-based).

APPLYING FOR FINANCIAL AID *Required financial aid forms:* FAFSA, CSS Financial Aid PROFILE, noncustodial (divorced/separated) parent's statement, business/farm supplement. *Financial aid deadline:* 1/15. *Notification date:* 4/1. Students must reply by 5/1 or within 2 weeks of notification.

CONTACT Financial Aid Office, Colgate University, 13 Oak Drive, Hamilton, NY 13346, 315-228-7431. *Fax:* 315-228-7050. *E-mail:* financialaid@colgate.edu.

College for Creative Studies

COLLEGE FOR CREATIVE STUDIES
Detroit, MI

Tuition & fees: $24,635 — Average undergraduate aid package: N/A

ABOUT THE INSTITUTION Independent, coed. Awards: bachelor's degrees. Total enrollment: 1,291. Undergraduates: 1,291. Freshmen: 207. Federal methodology is used as a basis for awarding need-based institutional aid.

UNDERGRADUATE EXPENSES for 2006–07 *Application fee:* $35. *Tuition:* full-time $23,490; part-time $788 per credit hour. *Required fees:* full-time $1145; $563 per term part-time.

GIFT AID (NEED-BASED) *Total amount:* $3,688,394 (29% federal, 20% state, 51% institutional). *Scholarships, grants, and awards:* Federal Pell, FSEOG, state, private, college/university gift aid from institutional funds.

GIFT AID (NON-NEED-BASED) *Total amount:* $3,983,523 (8% state, 79% institutional, 13% external sources). *Scholarships, grants, and awards by category: Creative Arts/Performance:* applied art and design, art/fine arts.

LOANS *Student loans:* $10,251,889 (100% need-based). 70% of past graduating class borrowed through all loan programs. *Average indebtedness per student:* $30,000. *Parent loans:* $2,500,496 (100% need-based). *Programs:* FFEL (Subsidized and Unsubsidized Stafford, PLUS), state, alternative loans.

WORK-STUDY *Federal work-study:* Total amount: $100,000; jobs available (averaging $1000). *State or other work-study/employment:* Total amount: $25,145 (100% need-based). Part-time jobs available (averaging $1000).

APPLYING FOR FINANCIAL AID *Required financial aid form:* FAFSA. *Financial aid deadline (priority):* 7/1. *Notification date:* Continuous beginning 3/15. Students must reply within 3 weeks of notification.

CONTACT Financial Aid Office, College for Creative Studies, 201 East Kirby, Detroit, MI 48202-4034, 313-664-7495 or toll-free 800-952-ARTS. *Fax:* 313-872-1521. *E-mail:* finaid@ccscad.edu.

COLLEGE MISERICORDIA
Dallas, PA

Tuition & fees: $19,700 — Average undergraduate aid package: $13,722

ABOUT THE INSTITUTION Independent Roman Catholic, coed. Awards: bachelor's, master's, and doctoral degrees and post-bachelor's and post-master's certificates. 26 undergraduate majors. Total enrollment: 2,343. Undergraduates: 2,072. Freshmen: 335. Federal methodology is used as a basis for awarding need-based institutional aid.

UNDERGRADUATE EXPENSES for 2005–06 *Application fee:* $25. *Comprehensive fee:* $27,950 includes full-time tuition ($18,700), mandatory fees ($1000), and room and board ($8250). *College room only:* $4730. Room and board charges vary according to board plan and housing facility. *Part-time tuition:* $425 per credit. Part-time tuition and fees vary according to location. *Payment plans:* Installment, deferred payment.

FRESHMAN FINANCIAL AID (Fall 2005, est.) 302 applied for aid; of those 86% were deemed to have need. 100% of freshmen with need received aid; of those 18% had need fully met. *Average percent of need met:* 72% (excluding resources awarded to replace EFC). *Average financial aid package:* $13,168 (excluding resources awarded to replace EFC). 13% of all full-time freshmen had no need and received non-need-based gift aid.

UNDERGRADUATE FINANCIAL AID (Fall 2005, est.) 1,305 applied for aid; of those 89% were deemed to have need. 100% of undergraduates with need received aid; of those 23% had need fully met. *Average percent of need met:* 75% (excluding resources awarded to replace EFC). *Average financial aid package:* $13,722 (excluding resources awarded to replace EFC). 10% of all full-time undergraduates had no need and received non-need-based gift aid.

GIFT AID (NEED-BASED) *Total amount:* $11,344,462 (11% federal, 18% state, 70% institutional, 1% external sources). *Receiving aid:* Freshmen: 80% (258); All full-time undergraduates: 80% (1,146). *Average award:* Freshmen: $9934; Undergraduates: $9527. *Scholarships, grants, and awards:* Federal Pell, FSEOG, state, private, college/university gift aid from institutional funds, Federal Nursing.

GIFT AID (NON-NEED-BASED) *Total amount:* $1,914,782 (95% institutional, 5% external sources). *Receiving aid:* Freshmen: 14% (45); Undergraduates: 17% (238). *Average Award:* Freshmen: $6835; Undergraduates: $6008. *Scholarships, grants, and awards by category: Academic Interests/Achievement:* 1,002 awards ($4,022,050 total): business, computer science, education, general academic interests/achievements, health fields, social sciences. *Special Achievements/Activities:* 929 awards ($2,262,150 total): community service, general special achievements/activities, leadership. *Special Characteristics:* 578 awards ($1,243,904 total): children and siblings of alumni, children of current students, children of faculty/staff, general special characteristics, out-of-state students, previous college experience, relatives of clergy, religious affiliation, siblings of current students. *Tuition waivers:* Full or partial for employees or children of employees. *ROTC:* Army cooperative, Air Force cooperative.

LOANS *Student loans:* $10,545,869 (70% need-based, 30% non-need-based). 87% of past graduating class borrowed through all loan programs. *Average indebtedness per student:* $18,013. *Average need-based loan:* Freshmen: $5176; Undergraduates: $6224. *Parent loans:* $3,057,438 (31% need-based, 69% non-need-based). *Programs:* FFEL (Subsidized and Unsubsidized Stafford, PLUS), Perkins, Federal Nursing, state.

WORK-STUDY *Federal work-study:* Total amount: $239,270; 200 jobs averaging $1200.

APPLYING FOR FINANCIAL AID *Required financial aid forms:* FAFSA, institution's own form. *Financial aid deadline (priority):* 3/1. *Notification date:* 3/15. Students must reply within 2 weeks of notification.

CONTACT Margaret R. Charnick, Director of Financial Aid, College Misericordia, 301 Lake Street, Dallas, PA 18612-1098, 570-674-6280 or toll-free 866-262-6363 (in-state), 866-2626363 (out-of-state). *Fax:* 570-675-2441. *E-mail:* pcharnic@misericordia.edu.

COLLEGE OF BIBLICAL STUDIES–HOUSTON
Houston, TX

CONTACT Financial Aid Office, College of Biblical Studies–Houston, 6000 Dale Carnegie Drive, Houston, TX 77036, 713-785-5995.

COLLEGE OF CHARLESTON
Charleston, SC

Tuition & fees (SC res): $6668 — Average undergraduate aid package: $8971

ABOUT THE INSTITUTION State-supported, coed. Awards: bachelor's and master's degrees (also offers graduate degree programs through University of Charleston, South Carolina). 43 undergraduate majors. Total enrollment: 11,332. Undergraduates: 9,878. Freshmen: 1,993. Federal methodology is used as a basis for awarding need-based institutional aid.

UNDERGRADUATE EXPENSES for 2005–06 *Application fee:* $45. *Tuition, state resident:* full-time $6668; part-time $278 per semester hour. *Tuition, nonresident:* full-time $15,342; part-time $639 per semester hour. Part-time tuition and fees vary according to course load. *College room and board:* $6948; *room only:* $4768. Room and board charges vary according to board plan and housing facility. *Payment plan:* Installment.

FRESHMAN FINANCIAL AID (Fall 2005, est.) 1234 applied for aid; of those 65% were deemed to have need. 96% of freshmen with need received aid; of those 30% had need fully met. *Average percent of need met:* 61% (excluding resources awarded to replace EFC). *Average financial aid package:* $8192 (excluding resources awarded to replace EFC). 13% of all full-time freshmen had no need and received non-need-based gift aid.

UNDERGRADUATE FINANCIAL AID (Fall 2005, est.) 4,720 applied for aid; of those 73% were deemed to have need. 96% of undergraduates with need received aid; of those 25% had need fully met. *Average percent of need met:* 62% (excluding resources awarded to replace EFC). *Average financial aid package:* $8971 (excluding resources awarded to replace EFC). 10% of all full-time undergraduates had no need and received non-need-based gift aid.

GIFT AID (NEED-BASED) *Total amount:* $11,900,002 (35% federal, 46% state, 14% institutional, 5% external sources). *Receiving aid:* Freshmen: 26% (518); All full-time undergraduates: 23% (2,092). *Average award:* Freshmen: $3204; Undergraduates: $2997. *Scholarships, grants, and awards:* Federal Pell, FSEOG, state, private, college/university gift aid from institutional funds.

GIFT AID (NON-NEED-BASED) *Total amount:* $16,660,475 (64% state, 32% institutional, 4% external sources). *Receiving aid:* Freshmen: 29% (580); Undergraduates: 16% (1,404). *Average Award:* Freshmen: $8897; Undergraduates: $10,293. *Scholarships, grants, and awards by category: Academic Interests/Achievement:* biological sciences, business, communication, computer science, education, engineering/technologies, English, foreign languages, general academic interests/achievements, health fields, humanities, mathematics, physical sciences, premedicine, social sciences. *Creative Arts/Performance:* art/fine

arts, music, performing arts, theater/drama. *Special Characteristics:* general special characteristics. *Tuition waivers:* Full or partial for senior citizens. *ROTC:* Air Force cooperative.
LOANS *Student loans:* $22,826,099 (58% need-based, 42% non-need-based). 46% of past graduating class borrowed through all loan programs. *Average indebtedness per student:* $16,143. *Average need-based loan:* Freshmen: $2333; Undergraduates: $3563. *Parent loans:* $18,828,610 (48% need-based, 52% non-need-based). *Programs:* Federal Direct (Subsidized and Unsubsidized Stafford, PLUS), Perkins.
WORK-STUDY *Federal work-study:* Total amount: $454,440; jobs available. *State or other work-study/employment:* Total amount: $1,951,584 (100% non-need-based). Part-time jobs available.
ATHLETIC AWARDS *Total amount:* $2,189,540 (18% need-based, 82% non-need-based).
APPLYING FOR FINANCIAL AID *Required financial aid form:* FAFSA. *Financial aid deadline (priority):* 3/15. *Notification date:* Continuous beginning 4/10.
CONTACT Mr. Don Griggs, Financial Aid Director, College of Charleston, 66 George Street, Charleston, SC 29424, 843-953-5540 or toll-free 843-953-5670 (in-state). *Fax:* 843-953-7192.

COLLEGE OF MOUNT ST. JOSEPH
Cincinnati, OH

Tuition & fees: $18,790	Average undergraduate aid package: $15,832

ABOUT THE INSTITUTION Independent Roman Catholic, coed. Awards: associate, bachelor's, and master's degrees and post-bachelor's certificates. 39 undergraduate majors. Total enrollment: 2,233. Undergraduates: 1,935. Freshmen: 315. Federal methodology is used as a basis for awarding need-based institutional aid.
UNDERGRADUATE EXPENSES for 2005–06 *Application fee:* $25. *Comprehensive fee:* $24,860 includes full-time tuition ($18,400), mandatory fees ($390), and room and board ($6070). *College room only:* $3000. Full-time tuition and fees vary according to course load, program, and reciprocity agreements. Room and board charges vary according to board plan and housing facility. *Part-time tuition:* $430 per semester hour. *Part-time fees:* $65 per term. Part-time tuition and fees vary according to course load, location, program, and reciprocity agreements. *Payment plans:* Installment, deferred payment.
FRESHMAN FINANCIAL AID (Fall 2005, est.) 274 applied for aid; of those 91% were deemed to have need. 100% of freshmen with need received aid; of those 63% had need fully met. *Average percent of need met:* 90% (excluding resources awarded to replace EFC). *Average financial aid package:* $16,596 (excluding resources awarded to replace EFC). 11% of all full-time freshmen had no need and received non-need-based gift aid.
UNDERGRADUATE FINANCIAL AID (Fall 2005, est.) 1,278 applied for aid; of those 71% were deemed to have need. 100% of undergraduates with need received aid; of those 53% had need fully met. *Average percent of need met:* 90% (excluding resources awarded to replace EFC). *Average financial aid package:* $15,832 (excluding resources awarded to replace EFC). 12% of all full-time undergraduates had no need and received non-need-based gift aid.
GIFT AID (NEED-BASED) *Total amount:* $10,723,848 (14% federal, 17% state, 66% institutional, 3% external sources). *Receiving aid:* Freshmen: 80% (245); All full-time undergraduates: 57% (757). *Average award:* Freshmen: $8787; Undergraduates: $6998. *Scholarships, grants, and awards:* Federal Pell, FSEOG, state, private, college/university gift aid from institutional funds.
GIFT AID (NON-NEED-BASED) *Total amount:* $524,430 (20% state, 78% institutional, 2% external sources). *Receiving aid:* Freshmen: 56% (171); Undergraduates: 32% (422). *Average Award:* Freshmen: $7264; Undergraduates: $6990. *Scholarships, grants, and awards by category: Academic Interests/Achievement:* 607 awards ($3,301,356 total): general academic interests/achievements. *Creative Arts/Performance:* 79 awards ($81,875 total): art/fine arts, music. *Special Achievements/Activities:* 49 awards ($71,875 total): community service, leadership. *Special Characteristics:* 33 awards ($433,432 total): adult students, children and siblings of alumni, children of faculty/staff. *Tuition waivers:* Full or partial for employees or children of employees, senior citizens. *ROTC:* Army cooperative, Air Force cooperative.
LOANS *Student loans:* $12,069,579 (94% need-based, 6% non-need-based). 80% of past graduating class borrowed through all loan programs. *Average indebtedness per student:* $13,400. *Average need-based loan:* Freshmen: $3730; Undergraduates: $4737. *Parent loans:* $1,651,919 (86% need-based, 14% non-need-based). *Programs:* FFEL (Subsidized and Unsubsidized Stafford, PLUS), Perkins, Federal Nursing, state.
WORK-STUDY *Federal work-study:* Total amount: $174,000; 188 jobs averaging $1431. *State or other work-study/employment:* Total amount: $183,111 (100% need-based). 71 part-time jobs averaging $1397.
APPLYING FOR FINANCIAL AID *Required financial aid form:* FAFSA. *Financial aid deadline (priority):* 3/1. *Notification date:* Continuous beginning 2/15. Students must reply by 5/1 or within 4 weeks of notification.
CONTACT Ms. Kathryn Kelly, Director of Student Administrative Services, College of Mount St. Joseph, 5701 Delhi Road, Cincinnati, OH 45233-1670, 513-244-4418 or toll-free 800-654-9314. *Fax:* 513-244-4201. *E-mail:* kathy_kelly@mail.msj.edu.

COLLEGE OF MOUNT SAINT VINCENT
Riverdale, NY

Tuition & fees: $21,550	Average undergraduate aid package: $17,000

ABOUT THE INSTITUTION Independent, coed. Awards: associate, bachelor's, and master's degrees and post-master's certificates. 31 undergraduate majors. Total enrollment: 1,855. Undergraduates: 1,527. Freshmen: 345. Federal methodology is used as a basis for awarding need-based institutional aid.
UNDERGRADUATE EXPENSES for 2006–07 *Application fee:* $35. *Comprehensive fee:* $30,050 includes full-time tuition ($21,000), mandatory fees ($550), and room and board ($8500). *Part-time tuition:* $685 per credit. *Part-time fees:* $75 per term.
FRESHMAN FINANCIAL AID (Fall 2004) 333 applied for aid; of those 86% were deemed to have need. 100% of freshmen with need received aid. *Average percent of need met:* 74% (excluding resources awarded to replace EFC). *Average financial aid package:* $15,296 (excluding resources awarded to replace EFC).
UNDERGRADUATE FINANCIAL AID (Fall 2004) 1,019 applied for aid; of those 86% were deemed to have need. 100% of undergraduates with need received aid. *Average percent of need met:* 74% (excluding resources awarded to replace EFC). *Average financial aid package:* $17,000 (excluding resources awarded to replace EFC).
GIFT AID (NEED-BASED) *Total amount:* $14,210,000 (13% federal, 16% state, 70% institutional, 1% external sources). *Receiving aid:* Freshmen: 82% (288); All full-time undergraduates: 71% (881). *Average award:* Freshmen: $8553; Undergraduates: $7500. *Scholarships, grants, and awards:* Federal Pell, FSEOG, state, private, college/university gift aid from institutional funds.
GIFT AID (NON-NEED-BASED) *Scholarships, grants, and awards by category: Academic Interests/Achievement:* general academic interests/achievements. *Special Achievements/Activities:* leadership. *Special Characteristics:* children and siblings of alumni, children of faculty/staff, siblings of current students. *ROTC:* Army cooperative, Air Force cooperative.
LOANS *Student loans:* $7,480,000 (100% need-based). 80% of past graduating class borrowed through all loan programs. *Average indebtedness per student:* $17,000. *Average need-based loan:* Freshmen: $2500; Undergraduates: $4100. *Parent loans:* $3,000,000 (100% need-based). *Programs:* FFEL (Subsidized and Unsubsidized Stafford, PLUS), Perkins.
WORK-STUDY *Federal work-study:* Total amount: $123,000; jobs available.
APPLYING FOR FINANCIAL AID *Required financial aid forms:* FAFSA, state aid form. *Financial aid deadline:* Continuous. *Notification date:* Continuous beginning 3/1. Students must reply by 5/1 or within 2 weeks of notification.
CONTACT Ms. Monica Simotas, Director of Financial Aid, College of Mount Saint Vincent, 6301 Riverdale Avenue, Riverdale, NY 10471, 718-405-3290 or toll-free 800-665-CMSV. *Fax:* 718-405-3490. *E-mail:* msimotas@mountsaintvincent.edu.

THE COLLEGE OF NEW JERSEY
Ewing, NJ

Tuition & fees (NJ res): $9707	Average undergraduate aid package: $11,010

ABOUT THE INSTITUTION State-supported, coed. Awards: bachelor's and master's degrees and post-bachelor's and post-master's certificates. 53 undergraduate majors. Total enrollment: 6,768. Undergraduates: 5,895. Freshmen: 1,236. Federal methodology is used as a basis for awarding need-based institutional aid.

The College of New Jersey

UNDERGRADUATE EXPENSES for 2005–06 *Application fee:* $50. *Tuition, state resident:* full-time $7051; part-time $249.75 per credit. *Tuition, nonresident:* full-time $12,314; part-time $436 per credit. *Required fees:* full-time $2656; $93.10 per credit. Part-time tuition and fees vary according to course load. *College room and board:* $8458; *room only:* $6090. Room and board charges vary according to board plan. *Payment plan:* Installment.
FRESHMAN FINANCIAL AID (Fall 2005, est.) 428 applied for aid; of those 100% were deemed to have need. 94% of freshmen with need received aid; of those 12% had need fully met. *Average percent of need met:* 51% (excluding resources awarded to replace EFC). *Average financial aid package:* $12,202 (excluding resources awarded to replace EFC). 47% of all full-time freshmen had no need and received non-need-based gift aid.
UNDERGRADUATE FINANCIAL AID (Fall 2005, est.) 1,945 applied for aid; of those 100% were deemed to have need. 96% of undergraduates with need received aid; of those 15% had need fully met. *Average percent of need met:* 55% (excluding resources awarded to replace EFC). *Average financial aid package:* $11,010 (excluding resources awarded to replace EFC). 37% of all full-time undergraduates had no need and received non-need-based gift aid.
GIFT AID (NEED-BASED) *Total amount:* $7,988,754 (29% federal, 51% state, 20% institutional). *Receiving aid:* Freshmen: 17% (205); All full-time undergraduates: 15% (877). *Average award:* Freshmen: $12,033; Undergraduates: $9003. *Scholarships, grants, and awards:* Federal Pell, FSEOG, state, private, college/university gift aid from institutional funds, Federal Nursing.
GIFT AID (NON-NEED-BASED) *Total amount:* $16,240,737 (36% state, 57% institutional, 7% external sources). *Receiving aid:* Freshmen: 21% (262); Undergraduates: 20% (1,128). *Average Award:* Freshmen: $3684; Undergraduates:* $4079. *Scholarships, grants, and awards by category:* Academic Interests/Achievement: engineering/technologies, general academic interests/achievements, physical sciences. Creative Arts/Performance: art/fine arts, music. Special Characteristics: children with a deceased or disabled parent, members of minority groups. *Tuition waivers:* Full or partial for employees or children of employees, senior citizens. *ROTC:* Army cooperative, Air Force cooperative.
LOANS *Student loans:* $19,564,137 (41% need-based, 59% non-need-based). 51% of past graduating class borrowed through all loan programs. *Average indebtedness per student:* $17,673. *Average need-based loan:* Freshmen: $5337; Undergraduates: $6876. *Parent loans:* $5,051,080 (100% non-need-based). *Programs:* FFEL (Subsidized and Unsubsidized Stafford, PLUS), Perkins, Federal Nursing, state.
WORK-STUDY *Federal work-study:* Total amount: $318,950; 287 jobs averaging $1215. *State or other work-study/employment:* Part-time jobs available.
APPLYING FOR FINANCIAL AID *Required financial aid form:* FAFSA. *Financial aid deadline:* 10/1 (priority: 3/1). *Notification date:* Continuous beginning 7/15. Students must reply within 2 weeks of notification.
CONTACT Jamie Hightower, Director of Financial Aid and Student Accounts, The College of New Jersey, PO Box 7718, Ewing, NJ 08628, 609-771-2211 or toll-free 800-624-0967. *Fax:* 609-637-5154. *E-mail:* hightowe@tcnj.edu.

THE COLLEGE OF NEW ROCHELLE
New Rochelle, NY

ABOUT THE INSTITUTION Independent, coed, primarily women. Awards: bachelor's and master's degrees and post-bachelor's and post-master's certificates (also offers a non-traditional adult program with significant enrollment not reflected in profile). 36 undergraduate majors. Total enrollment: 2,306. Undergraduates: 1,106. Freshmen: 180.
GIFT AID (NEED-BASED) *Scholarships, grants, and awards:* Federal Pell, FSEOG, state, private, college/university gift aid from institutional funds.
GIFT AID (NON-NEED-BASED) *Scholarships, grants, and awards by category:* Academic Interests/Achievement: area/ethnic studies, biological sciences, business, communication, education, English, foreign languages, general academic interests/achievements, health fields, humanities, mathematics, physical sciences, premedicine, religion/biblical studies, social sciences. Creative Arts/Performance: applied art and design, art/fine arts, cinema/film/broadcasting, creative writing, dance, debating, general creative arts/performance, journalism/publications, music, performing arts, theater/drama. Special Achievements/Activities: community service, general special achievements/activities, hobbies/interests, junior miss, leadership, memberships, religious involvement. Special Characteristics: children of current students, children of faculty/staff, general special characteristics, out-of-state students, parents of current students, previous college experience, siblings of current students, spouses of current students.

LOANS *Programs:* Federal Direct (Subsidized and Unsubsidized Stafford), FFEL (PLUS), Perkins, Federal Nursing.
APPLYING FOR FINANCIAL AID *Required financial aid forms:* FAFSA, institution's own form, federal income tax form(s).
CONTACT Anne Pelak, Director of Financial Aid, The College of New Rochelle, 29 Castle Place, New Rochelle, NY 10805-2339, 914-654-5551 or toll-free 800-933-5923. *Fax:* 914-654-5420. *E-mail:* apelak@cnr.edu.

COLLEGE OF NOTRE DAME OF MARYLAND
Baltimore, MD

Tuition & fees: $21,600 **Average undergraduate aid package: $18,061**

ABOUT THE INSTITUTION Independent Roman Catholic, undergraduate: women only; graduate: coed. Awards: bachelor's, master's, and doctoral degrees and post-bachelor's certificates. 33 undergraduate majors. Total enrollment: 3,307. Undergraduates: 1,686. Freshmen: 201. Federal methodology is used as a basis for awarding need-based institutional aid.
UNDERGRADUATE EXPENSES for 2005–06 *Application fee:* $25. *Comprehensive fee:* $29,600 includes full-time tuition ($21,100), mandatory fees ($500), and room and board ($8000). *Part-time tuition:* $345 per credit. *Part-time fees:* $60 per term. *Payment plan:* Installment.
FRESHMAN FINANCIAL AID (Fall 2005, est.) 138 applied for aid; of those 85% were deemed to have need. 98% of freshmen with need received aid; of those 53% had need fully met. *Average percent of need met:* 92% (excluding resources awarded to replace EFC). *Average financial aid package:* $21,109 (excluding resources awarded to replace EFC). 13% of all full-time freshmen had no need and received non-need-based gift aid.
UNDERGRADUATE FINANCIAL AID (Fall 2005, est.) 503 applied for aid; of those 89% were deemed to have need. 99% of undergraduates with need received aid; of those 26% had need fully met. *Average percent of need met:* 75% (excluding resources awarded to replace EFC). *Average financial aid package:* $18,061 (excluding resources awarded to replace EFC). 8% of all full-time undergraduates had no need and received non-need-based gift aid.
GIFT AID (NEED-BASED) *Total amount:* $6,463,162 (13% federal, 16% state, 68% institutional, 3% external sources). *Receiving aid:* Freshmen: 68% (100); All full-time undergraduates: 65% (385). *Average award:* Freshmen: $8419; Undergraduates: $8635. *Scholarships, grants, and awards:* Federal Pell, FSEOG, state, private, college/university gift aid from institutional funds.
GIFT AID (NON-NEED-BASED) *Total amount:* $1,316,982 (5% state, 92% institutional, 3% external sources). *Receiving aid:* Freshmen: 55% (81); Undergraduates: 59% (350). *Average Award:* Freshmen: $10,225; Undergraduates:* $9055. *Scholarships, grants, and awards by category:* Academic Interests/Achievement: 182 awards ($1,865,993 total): general academic interests/achievements. Creative Arts/Performance: 58 awards ($256,500 total): art/fine arts, general creative arts/performance. Special Achievements/Activities: 276 awards ($1,165,706 total): community service, general special achievements/activities, leadership, memberships, religious involvement. Special Characteristics: 9 awards ($52,755 total): international students. *Tuition waivers:* Full or partial for employees or children of employees. *ROTC:* Army cooperative.
LOANS *Student loans:* $5,097,767 (87% need-based, 13% non-need-based). 71% of past graduating class borrowed through all loan programs. *Average indebtedness per student:* $19,211. *Average need-based loan:* Freshmen: $3368; Undergraduates: $4221. *Parent loans:* $962,656 (83% need-based, 17% non-need-based). *Programs:* FFEL (Subsidized and Unsubsidized Stafford, PLUS), Perkins.
WORK-STUDY *Federal work-study:* Total amount: $79,885; 66 jobs averaging $1210.
APPLYING FOR FINANCIAL AID *Required financial aid form:* FAFSA. *Financial aid deadline (priority):* 2/15. *Notification date:* Continuous beginning 3/1. Students must reply by 5/1.
CONTACT Zhanna Goltser, Director of Financial Aid, College of Notre Dame of Maryland, 4701 North Charles Street, Baltimore, MD 21210-2404, 410-532-5369 or toll-free 800-435-0200 (in-state), 800-435-0300 (out-of-state). *Fax:* 410-532-6287. *E-mail:* finaid@ndm.edu.

COLLEGE OF SAINT BENEDICT
Saint Joseph, MN

Tuition & fees: $23,454   **Average undergraduate aid package:** $19,044

ABOUT THE INSTITUTION Independent Roman Catholic, coed, primarily women. Awards: bachelor's degrees (coordinate with Saint John's University for men). 49 undergraduate majors. Total enrollment: 2,045. Undergraduates: 2,045. Freshmen: 576. Federal methodology is used as a basis for awarding need-based institutional aid.

UNDERGRADUATE EXPENSES for 2005–06 *Comprehensive fee:* $30,091 includes full-time tuition ($23,064), mandatory fees ($390), and room and board ($6637). *College room only:* $3419. Room and board charges vary according to board plan and housing facility. *Part-time tuition:* $961 per credit. *Part-time fees:* $195 per term. Part-time tuition and fees vary according to course load. *Payment plans:* Tuition prepayment, installment.

FRESHMAN FINANCIAL AID (Fall 2005, est.) 474 applied for aid; of those 83% were deemed to have need. 100% of freshmen with need received aid; of those 58% had need fully met. *Average percent of need met:* 94% (excluding resources awarded to replace EFC). *Average financial aid package:* $20,417 (excluding resources awarded to replace EFC). 28% of all full-time freshmen had no need and received non-need-based gift aid.

UNDERGRADUATE FINANCIAL AID (Fall 2005, est.) 1,517 applied for aid; of those 86% were deemed to have need. 100% of undergraduates with need received aid; of those 43% had need fully met. *Average percent of need met:* 91% (excluding resources awarded to replace EFC). *Average financial aid package:* $19,044 (excluding resources awarded to replace EFC). 29% of all full-time undergraduates had no need and received non-need-based gift aid.

GIFT AID (NEED-BASED) *Total amount:* $15,884,124 (7% federal, 12% state, 77% institutional, 4% external sources). *Receiving aid:* Freshmen: 65% (375); All full-time undergraduates: 61% (1,215). *Average award:* Freshmen: $14,435; Undergraduates: $12,290. *Scholarships, grants, and awards:* Federal Pell, FSEOG, state, private, college/university gift aid from institutional funds.

GIFT AID (NON-NEED-BASED) *Total amount:* $5,759,780 (96% institutional, 4% external sources). *Receiving aid:* Freshmen: 65% (375); Undergraduates: 61% (1,215). *Average Award:* Freshmen: $9605; Undergraduates: $8210. *Scholarships, grants, and awards by category: Academic Interests/Achievement:* general academic interests/achievements, military science. *Creative Arts/Performance:* art/fine arts, music, theater/drama. *Special Achievements/Activities:* junior miss, memberships. *Special Characteristics:* ethnic background, international students. *Tuition waivers:* Full or partial for employees or children of employees. *ROTC:* Army cooperative.

LOANS *Student loans:* $10,753,879 (90% need-based, 10% non-need-based). 72% of past graduating class borrowed through all loan programs. *Average indebtedness per student:* $24,764. *Average need-based loan:* Freshmen: $5107; Undergraduates: $6030. *Parent loans:* $3,077,151 (73% need-based, 27% non-need-based). *Programs:* FFEL (Subsidized and Unsubsidized Stafford, PLUS), Perkins, state, alternative loans.

WORK-STUDY *Federal work-study:* Total amount: $1,172,173; 600 jobs averaging $2000. *State or other work-study/employment:* Total amount: $1,500,529 (68% need-based, 32% non-need-based). 300 part-time jobs averaging $2000.

APPLYING FOR FINANCIAL AID *Required financial aid forms:* FAFSA, institution's own form. *Financial aid deadline (priority):* 3/15. *Notification date:* Continuous beginning 3/1. Students must reply by 5/1.

CONTACT Ms. Jane Haugen, Executive Director of Financial Aid, College of Saint Benedict, 37 South College Avenue, Saint Joseph, MN 56374-2099, 320-363-5388 or toll-free 800-544-1489. *Fax:* 320-363-6099. *E-mail:* jhaugen@csbsju.edu.

COLLEGE OF ST. CATHERINE
St. Paul, MN

Tuition & fees: $21,385   **Average undergraduate aid package:** $22,474

ABOUT THE INSTITUTION Independent Roman Catholic, undergraduate: women only; graduate: coed. Awards: associate, bachelor's, master's, and doctoral degrees and post-bachelor's certificates. 76 undergraduate majors. Total enrollment: 4,907. Undergraduates: 3,605. Freshmen: 413. Federal methodology is used as a basis for awarding need-based institutional aid.

UNDERGRADUATE EXPENSES for 2005–06 *Comprehensive fee:* $27,505 includes full-time tuition ($21,060), mandatory fees ($325), and room and board ($6120). *College room only:* $3420. Full-time tuition and fees vary according to class time. Room and board charges vary according to board plan and housing facility. *Part-time tuition:* $702 per credit. Part-time tuition and fees vary according to class time.

FRESHMAN FINANCIAL AID (Fall 2005, est.) 306 applied for aid; of those 85% were deemed to have need. 97% of freshmen with need received aid; of those 18% had need fully met. *Average percent of need met:* 78% (excluding resources awarded to replace EFC). *Average financial aid package:* $24,647 (excluding resources awarded to replace EFC). 19% of all full-time freshmen had no need and received non-need-based gift aid.

UNDERGRADUATE FINANCIAL AID (Fall 2005, est.) 1,426 applied for aid; of those 86% were deemed to have need. 97% of undergraduates with need received aid; of those 16% had need fully met. *Average percent of need met:* 76% (excluding resources awarded to replace EFC). *Average financial aid package:* $22,474 (excluding resources awarded to replace EFC). 16% of all full-time undergraduates had no need and received non-need-based gift aid.

GIFT AID (NEED-BASED) *Total amount:* $11,063,914 (26% federal, 25% state, 47% institutional, 2% external sources). *Receiving aid:* Freshmen: 54% (189); All full-time undergraduates: 58% (1,006). *Average award:* Freshmen: $7991; Undergraduates: $7248. *Scholarships, grants, and awards:* Federal Pell, FSEOG, state, private, college/university gift aid from institutional funds, Federal Nursing.

GIFT AID (NON-NEED-BASED) *Total amount:* $8,122,792 (84% institutional, 16% external sources). *Receiving aid:* Freshmen: 60% (210); Undergraduates: 48% (819). *Average Award:* Freshmen: $17,660; Undergraduates: $12,876. *Scholarships, grants, and awards by category: Academic Interests/Achievement:* business, education, English, foreign languages, general academic interests/achievements, health fields, home economics, humanities, mathematics, physical sciences, premedicine, social sciences. *Creative Arts/Performance:* art/fine arts, music. *Special Achievements/Activities:* community service, general special achievements/activities, leadership, memberships. *Special Characteristics:* adult students, children and siblings of alumni, children of educators, children of faculty/staff, ethnic background, general special characteristics, international students, local/state students, out-of-state students, religious affiliation, siblings of current students. *Tuition waivers:* Full or partial for employees or children of employees, senior citizens. *ROTC:* Air Force cooperative.

LOANS *Student loans:* $23,766,998 (41% need-based, 59% non-need-based). 78% of past graduating class borrowed through all loan programs. *Average indebtedness per student:* $27,519. *Average need-based loan:* Freshmen: $3710; Undergraduates: $4887. *Parent loans:* $3,285,081 (100% non-need-based). *Programs:* FFEL (Subsidized and Unsubsidized Stafford, PLUS), Perkins, Federal Nursing, state, alternative loans.

WORK-STUDY *Federal work-study:* Total amount: $684,029; 500 jobs available. *State or other work-study/employment:* Total amount: $646,488 (74% need-based, 26% non-need-based). Part-time jobs available.

APPLYING FOR FINANCIAL AID *Required financial aid forms:* FAFSA, institution's own form. *Financial aid deadline (priority):* 4/15. *Notification date:* Continuous. Students must reply within 2 weeks of notification.

CONTACT Sandy Sundstrom, Director of Financial Aid, College of St. Catherine, Mail #F-11, 2004 Randolph Avenue, St. Paul, MN 55105-1789, 651-690-6540 or toll-free 800-656-5283 (in-state). *Fax:* 651-690-6558.

COLLEGE OF ST. CATHERINE–MINNEAPOLIS
Minneapolis, MN

CONTACT Mr. Cal Mosley, Associate Dean/Director of Financial Aid, College of St. Catherine–Minneapolis, 601 25th Avenue South, Minneapolis, MN 55454, 651-690-8600 or toll-free 800-945-4599 Ext. 7800. *Fax:* 651-690-8119. *E-mail:* pajohnson@stkate.edu.

COLLEGE OF SAINT ELIZABETH
Morristown, NJ

CONTACT Vincent Tunstall, Director of Financial Aid, College of Saint Elizabeth, 2 Convent Road, Morristown, NJ 07960-6989, 973-290-4445 or toll-free 800-210-7900. *Fax:* 973-290-4421.

COLLEGE OF ST. JOSEPH
Rutland, VT

Tuition & fees: $14,900   **Average undergraduate aid package:** $12,874

ABOUT THE INSTITUTION Independent Roman Catholic, coed. Awards: associate, bachelor's, and master's degrees and post-bachelor's certificates. 20 undergraduate majors. Total enrollment: 450. Undergraduates: 271. Federal methodology is used as a basis for awarding need-based institutional aid.

UNDERGRADUATE EXPENSES for 2006–07 *Application fee:* $25. *Comprehensive fee:* $22,050 includes full-time tuition ($14,650), mandatory fees ($250), and room and board ($7150). *Part-time tuition:* $245 per credit. *Part-time fees:* $45 per term.

FRESHMAN FINANCIAL AID (Fall 2005, est.) 43 applied for aid; of those 84% were deemed to have need. 100% of freshmen with need received aid; of those 33% had need fully met. *Average percent of need met:* 84% (excluding resources awarded to replace EFC). *Average financial aid package:* $15,053 (excluding resources awarded to replace EFC). 16% of all full-time freshmen had no need and received non-need-based gift aid.

UNDERGRADUATE FINANCIAL AID (Fall 2005, est.) 162 applied for aid; of those 91% were deemed to have need. 99% of undergraduates with need received aid; of those 28% had need fully met. *Average percent of need met:* 76% (excluding resources awarded to replace EFC). *Average financial aid package:* $12,874 (excluding resources awarded to replace EFC). 9% of all full-time undergraduates had no need and received non-need-based gift aid.

GIFT AID (NEED-BASED) *Total amount:* $1,187,841 (28% federal, 20% state, 47% institutional, 5% external sources). *Receiving aid:* Freshmen: 84% (36); All full-time undergraduates: 90% (146). *Average award:* Freshmen: $10,156; Undergraduates: $7430. *Scholarships, grants, and awards:* Federal Pell, FSEOG, state, private, college/university gift aid from institutional funds.

GIFT AID (NON-NEED-BASED) *Total amount:* $67,711 (93% institutional, 7% external sources). *Receiving aid:* Undergraduates: 2% (4). *Average Award:* Freshmen: $12,273; Undergraduates: $11,020. *Scholarships, grants and awards by category:* Academic Interests/Achievement: 45 awards ($182,575 total): general academic interests/achievements. Special Achievements/Activities: 3 awards ($4000 total): community service, leadership. Special Characteristics: 51 awards ($98,830 total): general special characteristics, local/state students, previous college experience, religious affiliation.

LOANS *Student loans:* $1,393,907 (74% need-based, 26% non-need-based). 69% of past graduating class borrowed through all loan programs. *Average indebtedness per student:* $21,967. *Average need-based loan:* Freshmen: $2625; Undergraduates: $5046. *Parent loans:* $193,147 (25% need-based, 75% non-need-based). *Programs:* FFEL (Subsidized and Unsubsidized Stafford, PLUS), Perkins.

WORK-STUDY *Federal work-study:* Total amount: $37,400; 38 jobs averaging $980. *State or other work-study/employment:* Total amount: $72,900 (92% need-based, 8% non-need-based). 77 part-time jobs averaging $945.

APPLYING FOR FINANCIAL AID *Required financial aid forms:* FAFSA, institution's own form. *Financial aid deadline:* Continuous. *Notification date:* Continuous beginning 3/15. Students must reply within 2 weeks of notification.

CONTACT Yvonne Payrits, Financial Aid Coordinator, College of St. Joseph, 71 Clement Road, Rutland, VT 05701-3899, 802-773-5900 Ext. 3218 or toll-free 877-270-9998 (in-state). *Fax:* 802-773-5900. *E-mail:* finaid@csj.edu.

COLLEGE OF SAINT MARY
Omaha, NE

Tuition & fees: $18,110   **Average undergraduate aid package:** $10,520

ABOUT THE INSTITUTION Independent Roman Catholic, women only. Awards: associate, bachelor's, and master's degrees. 27 undergraduate majors. Total enrollment: 1,015. Undergraduates: 999. Freshmen: 107. Federal methodology is used as a basis for awarding need-based institutional aid.

UNDERGRADUATE EXPENSES for 2005–06 *Application fee:* $30. *Comprehensive fee:* $24,010 includes full-time tuition ($17,750), mandatory fees ($360), and room and board ($5900). Room and board charges vary according to housing facility. *Part-time tuition:* $550 per credit hour. *Part-time fees:* $12 per credit hour. Part-time tuition and fees vary according to class time. *Payment plans:* Installment, deferred payment.

FRESHMAN FINANCIAL AID (Fall 2005, est.) 211 applied for aid; of those 87% were deemed to have need. 89% of freshmen with need received aid; of those 12% had need fully met. *Average percent of need met:* 52% (excluding resources awarded to replace EFC). *Average financial aid package:* $10,891 (excluding resources awarded to replace EFC). 34% of all full-time freshmen had no need and received non-need-based gift aid.

UNDERGRADUATE FINANCIAL AID (Fall 2005, est.) 968 applied for aid; of those 91% were deemed to have need. 89% of undergraduates with need received aid; of those 13% had need fully met. *Average percent of need met:* 52% (excluding resources awarded to replace EFC). *Average financial aid package:* $10,520 (excluding resources awarded to replace EFC). 16% of all full-time undergraduates had no need and received non-need-based gift aid.

GIFT AID (NEED-BASED) *Total amount:* $5,438,196 (32% federal, 4% state, 58% institutional, 6% external sources). *Receiving aid:* Freshmen: 45% (161); All full-time undergraduates: 60% (721). *Average award:* Freshmen: $8316; Undergraduates: $7268. *Scholarships, grants, and awards:* Federal Pell, FSEOG, state, college/university gift aid from institutional funds.

GIFT AID (NON-NEED-BASED) *Total amount:* $1,149,462 (89% institutional, 11% external sources). *Receiving aid:* Freshmen: 3% (12); Undergraduates: 3% (38). *Average Award:* Freshmen: $6757; Undergraduates: $8042. *Scholarships, grants, and awards by category:* Academic Interests/Achievement: general academic interests/achievements. Creative Arts/Performance: music. Special Achievements/Activities: community service, leadership. *Tuition waivers:* Full or partial for employees or children of employees, senior citizens. *ROTC:* Army cooperative, Air Force cooperative.

LOANS *Student loans:* $7,173,664 (79% need-based, 21% non-need-based). 90% of past graduating class borrowed through all loan programs. *Average indebtedness per student:* $18,047. *Average need-based loan:* Freshmen: $3252; Undergraduates: $4259. *Parent loans:* $1,684,313 (52% need-based, 48% non-need-based). *Programs:* FFEL (Subsidized and Unsubsidized Stafford, PLUS), Perkins, Federal Nursing.

WORK-STUDY *Federal work-study:* Total amount: $146,044; 116 jobs averaging $1259. *State or other work-study/employment:* Total amount: $52,200 (44% need-based, 56% non-need-based). Part-time jobs available.

ATHLETIC AWARDS *Total amount:* $297,884 (64% need-based, 36% non-need-based).

APPLYING FOR FINANCIAL AID *Required financial aid form:* FAFSA. *Financial aid deadline (priority):* 3/1. *Notification date:* Continuous beginning 3/1. Students must reply within 2 weeks of notification.

CONTACT Caprice E. Calamaio, Director/Express Center, College of Saint Mary, 7000 Mercy Road, Omaha, NE 68106, 402-399-2415 or toll-free 800-926-5534. *Fax:* 402-399-2480. *E-mail:* ccalamaio@csm.edu.

THE COLLEGE OF SAINT ROSE
Albany, NY

Tuition & fees: $17,954   **Average undergraduate aid package:** $7278

ABOUT THE INSTITUTION Independent, coed. Awards: bachelor's and master's degrees and post-bachelor's and post-master's certificates. 42 undergraduate majors. Total enrollment: 5,149. Undergraduates: 3,078. Freshmen: 598. Federal methodology is used as a basis for awarding need-based institutional aid.

UNDERGRADUATE EXPENSES for 2005–06 *Application fee:* $35. *Comprehensive fee:* $25,770 includes full-time tuition ($17,368), mandatory fees ($586), and room and board ($7816). *College room only:* $3684. Full-time tuition and fees vary according to course load and program. Room and board charges vary according to board plan. *Part-time tuition:* $578 per credit hour. Part-time tuition and fees vary according to class time. *Payment plan:* Deferred payment.

FRESHMAN FINANCIAL AID (Fall 2004) 506 applied for aid; of those 83% were deemed to have need. 100% of freshmen with need received aid; of those 4% had need fully met. *Average percent of need met:* 36% (excluding resources awarded to replace EFC). *Average financial aid package:* $7885 (excluding resources awarded to replace EFC). 12% of all full-time freshmen had no need and received non-need-based gift aid.

UNDERGRADUATE FINANCIAL AID (Fall 2004) 2,511 applied for aid; of those 86% were deemed to have need. 99% of undergraduates with need received aid; of those 3% had need fully met. *Average percent of need met:* 36% (excluding resources awarded to replace EFC). *Average financial aid package:* $7278 (excluding resources awarded to replace EFC). 8% of all full-time undergraduates had no need and received non-need-based gift aid.

GIFT AID (NEED-BASED) *Total amount:* $17,002,617 (14% federal, 19% state, 44% institutional, 23% external sources). *Receiving aid:* Freshmen: 65% (384); All full-time undergraduates: 73% (2,041). *Average award:* Freshmen: $3673; Undergraduates: $3339. *Scholarships, grants, and awards:* Federal Pell, FSEOG, state, private, college/university gift aid from institutional funds.
GIFT AID (NON-NEED-BASED) *Total amount:* $1,599,632 (5% state, 63% institutional, 32% external sources). *Average Award:* Freshmen: $2353; Undergraduates: $1808. *Scholarships, grants, and awards by category: Academic Interests/Achievement:* 684 awards ($2,593,711 total): business, education, engineering/technologies, English, foreign languages, general academic interests/achievements, mathematics, premedicine, social sciences. *Creative Arts/Performance:* art/fine arts, music. *Special Achievements/Activities:* community service. *Special Characteristics:* adult students, children and siblings of alumni, children of union members/company employees, ethnic background, general special characteristics, members of minority groups, siblings of current students, twins. *Tuition waivers:* Full or partial for employees or children of employees.
LOANS *Student loans:* $9,088,199 (67% need-based, 33% non-need-based). 82% of past graduating class borrowed through all loan programs. *Average indebtedness per student:* $19,459. *Average need-based loan:* Freshmen: $1261; Undergraduates: $1177. *Parent loans:* $4,210,586 (87% need-based, 13% non-need-based). *Programs:* FFEL (Subsidized and Unsubsidized Stafford, PLUS).
WORK-STUDY *Federal work-study:* Total amount: $483,874; 406 jobs averaging $815. *State or other work-study/employment:* Total amount: $293,936 (76% need-based, 24% non-need-based). 83 part-time jobs averaging $892.
ATHLETIC AWARDS *Total amount:* $1,382,886 (75% need-based, 25% non-need-based).
APPLYING FOR FINANCIAL AID *Required financial aid form:* FAFSA. *Financial aid deadline:* 3/1 (priority: 3/1). *Notification date:* Continuous beginning 3/15. Students must reply by 5/1 or within 2 weeks of notification.
CONTACT Steven Dwire, Director of Financial Aid, The College of Saint Rose, 432 Western Avenue, Albertus Hall, Room 206, Albany, NY 12203-1419, 518-458-4915 or toll-free 800-637-8556. *Fax:* 518-454-2802. *E-mail:* finaid@strose.edu.

THE COLLEGE OF ST. SCHOLASTICA
Duluth, MN

Tuition & fees: $22,240	Average undergraduate aid package: $17,059

ABOUT THE INSTITUTION Independent religious, coed. Awards: bachelor's, master's, and first professional degrees and post-bachelor's and post-master's certificates. 33 undergraduate majors. Total enrollment: 3,238. Undergraduates: 2,613. Freshmen: 508. Federal methodology is used as a basis for awarding need-based institutional aid.
UNDERGRADUATE EXPENSES for 2005–06 *Application fee:* $25. *Comprehensive fee:* $28,456 includes full-time tuition ($22,110), mandatory fees ($130), and room and board ($6216). *College room only:* $3556. Full-time tuition and fees vary according to class time. Room and board charges vary according to board plan and housing facility. *Part-time tuition:* $688 per credit hour. Part-time tuition and fees vary according to class time and course load. *Payment plan:* Installment.
FRESHMAN FINANCIAL AID (Fall 2005, est.) 429 applied for aid; of those 88% were deemed to have need. 99% of freshmen with need received aid; of those 80% had need fully met. *Average percent of need met:* 80% (excluding resources awarded to replace EFC). *Average financial aid package:* $17,321 (excluding resources awarded to replace EFC). 18% of all full-time freshmen had no need and received non-need-based gift aid.
UNDERGRADUATE FINANCIAL AID (Fall 2005, est.) 1,627 applied for aid; of those 90% were deemed to have need. 99% of undergraduates with need received aid; of those 85% had need fully met. *Average percent of need met:* 84% (excluding resources awarded to replace EFC). *Average financial aid package:* $17,059 (excluding resources awarded to replace EFC). 17% of all full-time undergraduates had no need and received non-need-based gift aid.
GIFT AID (NEED-BASED) *Total amount:* $8,180,702 (19% federal, 27% state, 54% institutional). *Receiving aid:* Freshmen: 68% (332); All full-time undergraduates: 70% (1,325). *Average award:* Freshmen: $4877; Undergraduates: $5618. *Scholarships, grants, and awards:* Federal Pell, FSEOG, state, private, college/university gift aid from institutional funds.

GIFT AID (NON-NEED-BASED) *Total amount:* $13,821,082 (3% federal, 91% institutional, 6% external sources). *Receiving aid:* Freshmen: 74% (362); Undergraduates: 69% (1,309). *Average Award:* Freshmen: $9381; Undergraduates: $8003. *Scholarships, grants, and awards by category: Academic Interests/Achievement:* 1,610 awards ($12,214,381 total): general academic interests/achievements. *Creative Arts/Performance:* 11 awards ($4845 total): music. *Special Characteristics:* 903 awards ($2,898,739 total): children and siblings of alumni, children of faculty/staff, international students, members of minority groups, previous college experience, religious affiliation, siblings of current students. *Tuition waivers:* Full or partial for children of alumni, employees or children of employees, senior citizens. *ROTC:* Air Force cooperative.
LOANS *Student loans:* $12,881,270 (38% need-based, 62% non-need-based). 84% of past graduating class borrowed through all loan programs. *Average indebtedness per student:* $29,942. *Average need-based loan:* Freshmen: $3368; Undergraduates: $4571. *Parent loans:* $1,556,385 (100% non-need-based). *Programs:* FFEL (Subsidized and Unsubsidized Stafford, PLUS), Perkins, Federal Nursing, state, private supplemental loans.
WORK-STUDY *Federal work-study:* Total amount: $463,656; 231 jobs averaging $2016. *State or other work-study/employment:* Total amount: $714,532 (45% need-based, 55% non-need-based). 138 part-time jobs averaging $2347.
APPLYING FOR FINANCIAL AID *Required financial aid forms:* FAFSA, institution's own form. *Financial aid deadline (priority):* 3/15. *Notification date:* Continuous beginning 3/1. Students must reply by 5/1 or within 2 weeks of notification.
CONTACT Mr. Jon P. Erickson, Director of Financial Aid, The College of St. Scholastica, 1200 Kenwood Avenue, Duluth, MN 55811-4199, 218-723-6725 or toll-free 800-249-6412. *Fax:* 218-733-2229. *E-mail:* jerickso@css.edu.

THE COLLEGE OF SAINT THOMAS MORE
Fort Worth, TX

CONTACT Mrs. Sharon Kirk, Financial Aid Officer, The College of Saint Thomas More, 3013 Lubbock Avenue, Fort Worth, TX 76109-2323, 817-923-8459 or toll-free 800-583-6489 (out-of-state). *Fax:* 817-924-3206. *E-mail:* more-info@cstm.edu.

COLLEGE OF SANTA FE
Santa Fe, NM

Tuition & fees: $22,276	Average undergraduate aid package: $18,934

ABOUT THE INSTITUTION Independent, coed. Awards: associate, bachelor's, and master's degrees. 43 undergraduate majors. Total enrollment: 1,661. Undergraduates: 1,342. Freshmen: 141. Federal methodology is used as a basis for awarding need-based institutional aid.
UNDERGRADUATE EXPENSES for 2005–06 *Application fee:* $35. *Comprehensive fee:* $28,978 includes full-time tuition ($21,530), mandatory fees ($746), and room and board ($6702). *College room only:* $3204. Room and board charges vary according to board plan and housing facility. *Part-time tuition:* $720 per credit hour. *Part-time fees:* $16 per credit hour. *Payment plan:* Installment.
FRESHMAN FINANCIAL AID (Fall 2005, est.) 97 applied for aid; of those 86% were deemed to have need. 99% of freshmen with need received aid; of those 20% had need fully met. *Average percent of need met:* 77% (excluding resources awarded to replace EFC). *Average financial aid package:* $18,101 (excluding resources awarded to replace EFC). 12% of all full-time freshmen had no need and received non-need-based gift aid.
UNDERGRADUATE FINANCIAL AID (Fall 2005, est.) 469 applied for aid; of those 89% were deemed to have need. 100% of undergraduates with need received aid; of those 12% had need fully met. *Average percent of need met:* 77% (excluding resources awarded to replace EFC). *Average financial aid package:* $18,934 (excluding resources awarded to replace EFC). 15% of all full-time undergraduates had no need and received non-need-based gift aid.
GIFT AID (NEED-BASED) *Total amount:* $4,476,282 (28% federal, 19% state, 53% institutional). *Receiving aid:* Freshmen: 55% (71); All full-time undergraduates: 60% (373). *Average award:* Freshmen: $7782; Undergraduates: $10,083. *Scholarships, grants, and awards:* Federal Pell, FSEOG, state, private, college/university gift aid from institutional funds.
GIFT AID (NON-NEED-BASED) *Total amount:* $1,315,378 (1% federal, 93% institutional, 6% external sources). *Receiving aid:* Freshmen: 61% (79); Undergraduates: 33% (205). *Average Award:* Freshmen: $6133; Undergraduates: $4011. *Scholarships, grants, and awards by category: Academic Interests/*

College of Santa Fe

Achievement: general academic interests/achievements. *Creative Arts/Performance:* applied art and design, art/fine arts, cinema/film/broadcasting, creative writing, dance, general creative arts/performance, journalism/publications, music, performing arts, theater/drama. *Special Achievements/Activities:* general special achievements/activities. *Special Characteristics:* children and siblings of alumni, general special characteristics. *Tuition waivers:* Full or partial for employees or children of employees, senior citizens. *ROTC:* Air Force cooperative.
LOANS *Student loans:* $5,011,372 (55% need-based, 45% non-need-based). 63% of past graduating class borrowed through all loan programs. *Average indebtedness per student:* $17,540. *Average need-based loan:* Freshmen: $3661; Undergraduates: $4700. *Parent loans:* $1,690,326 (100% non-need-based). *Programs:* FFEL (Subsidized and Unsubsidized Stafford, PLUS), Perkins, state, college/university.
WORK-STUDY *Federal work-study:* Total amount: $222,711; jobs available. *State or other work-study/employment:* Total amount: $189,257 (52% need-based, 48% non-need-based). Part-time jobs available.
ATHLETIC AWARDS Total amount: $69,842 (100% non-need-based).
APPLYING FOR FINANCIAL AID *Required financial aid form:* FAFSA. *Financial aid deadline (priority):* 3/15. *Notification date:* Continuous beginning 3/1. Students must reply by 5/1 or within 2 weeks of notification.
CONTACT Ms. Jill Robertson, Director, Student Financial Services, College of Santa Fe, 1600 St. Michael's Drive, Santa Fe, NM 87505-7634, 505-473-6454 or toll-free 800-456-2673. *Fax:* 505-473-6464.

COLLEGE OF STATEN ISLAND OF THE CITY UNIVERSITY OF NEW YORK
Staten Island, NY

Tuition & fees (NY res): $4328 — **Average undergraduate aid package: $6101**

ABOUT THE INSTITUTION State and locally supported, coed. Awards: associate, bachelor's, and master's degrees and post-master's certificates. 40 undergraduate majors. Total enrollment: 12,083. Undergraduates: 10,920. Freshmen: 2,197. Federal methodology is used as a basis for awarding need-based institutional aid.
UNDERGRADUATE EXPENSES for 2005–06 *Application fee:* $65. *Tuition, state resident:* full-time $4000; part-time $250 per credit. *Tuition, nonresident:* full-time $8640; part-time $530 per credit. *Required fees:* full-time $328; $90.35 per term part-time. Full-time tuition and fees vary according to course load. Part-time tuition and fees vary according to course load. *Payment plan:* Installment.
FRESHMAN FINANCIAL AID (Fall 2005, est.) 1490 applied for aid; of those 71% were deemed to have need. 97% of freshmen with need received aid; of those 9% had need fully met. *Average percent of need met:* 59% (excluding resources awarded to replace EFC). *Average financial aid package:* $5773 (excluding resources awarded to replace EFC). 9% of all full-time freshmen had no need and received non-need-based gift aid.
UNDERGRADUATE FINANCIAL AID (Fall 2005, est.) 5,202 applied for aid; of those 76% were deemed to have need. 96% of undergraduates with need received aid; of those 7% had need fully met. *Average percent of need met:* 58% (excluding resources awarded to replace EFC). *Average financial aid package:* $6101 (excluding resources awarded to replace EFC). 5% of all full-time undergraduates had no need and received non-need-based gift aid.
GIFT AID (NEED-BASED) *Total amount:* $21,477,401 (49% federal, 47% state, 4% external sources). *Receiving aid:* Freshmen: 53% (996); All full-time undergraduates: 50% (3,644). *Average award:* Freshmen: $5087; Undergraduates: $4991. *Scholarships, grants, and awards:* Federal Pell, FSEOG, state, private, college/university gift aid from institutional funds, Federal Nursing.
GIFT AID (NON-NEED-BASED) *Total amount:* $1,736,727 (1% federal, 45% state, 54% external sources). *Receiving aid:* Freshmen: 12% (231); Undergraduates: 6% (419). *Average Award:* Freshmen: $1929; Undergraduates: $2682. *Scholarships, grants, and awards by category:* Academic Interests/Achievement: 162 awards ($252,206 total): biological sciences, business, computer science, education, engineering/technologies, general academic interests/achievements, health fields, international studies, mathematics, physical sciences, premedicine. *Creative Arts/Performance:* 4 awards ($4050 total): art/fine arts, music, theater/drama. *Special Achievements/Activities:* 5 awards ($5500 total): general special achievements/activities. *Special Characteristics:* 7 awards ($8500 total): children of public servants, children with a deceased or disabled parent, general special characteristics, handicapped students, international students, members of minority groups, public servants, spouses of deceased or disabled public servants, veterans' children. *Tuition waivers:* Full or partial for employees or children of employees, senior citizens.
LOANS *Student loans:* $6,996,510 (100% need-based). *Average need-based loan:* Freshmen: $2526; Undergraduates: $3366. *Programs:* Federal Direct (Subsidized and Unsubsidized Stafford, PLUS), Perkins.
WORK-STUDY *Federal work-study:* Total amount: $1,329,600; 341 jobs averaging $1372.
APPLYING FOR FINANCIAL AID *Required financial aid forms:* FAFSA, state aid form. *Financial aid deadline (priority):* 3/31. *Notification date:* Continuous beginning 6/30.
CONTACT Sherman Whipkey, Director of Financial Aid, College of Staten Island of the City University of New York, 2800 Victory Boulevard, 2A-401A, Staten Island, NY 10314-6600, 718-982-2030. *Fax:* 718-982-2037. *E-mail:* whipkey@mail.csi.cuny.edu.

COLLEGE OF THE ATLANTIC
Bar Harbor, ME

Tuition & fees: $28,075 — **Average undergraduate aid package: $24,478**

ABOUT THE INSTITUTION Independent, coed. Awards: bachelor's and master's degrees. 37 undergraduate majors. Total enrollment: 318. Undergraduates: 310. Freshmen: 82. Both federal and institutional methodology are used as a basis for awarding need-based institutional aid.
UNDERGRADUATE EXPENSES for 2006–07 *Application fee:* $45. *Comprehensive fee:* $35,675 includes full-time tuition ($27,700), mandatory fees ($375), and room and board ($7600). *College room only:* $4700. *Part-time tuition:* $9234 per term. *Part-time fees:* $125 per term.
FRESHMAN FINANCIAL AID (Fall 2004) 78 applied for aid; of those 99% were deemed to have need. 100% of freshmen with need received aid; of those 97% had need fully met. *Average percent of need met:* 97% (excluding resources awarded to replace EFC). *Average financial aid package:* $23,369 (excluding resources awarded to replace EFC). 15% of all full-time freshmen had no need and received non-need-based gift aid.
UNDERGRADUATE FINANCIAL AID (Fall 2004) 280 applied for aid; of those 98% were deemed to have need. 100% of undergraduates with need received aid; of those 95% had need fully met. *Average percent of need met:* 95% (excluding resources awarded to replace EFC). *Average financial aid package:* $24,478 (excluding resources awarded to replace EFC). 6% of all full-time undergraduates had no need and received non-need-based gift aid.
GIFT AID (NEED-BASED) *Total amount:* $5,334,103 (6% federal, 1% state, 54% institutional, 39% external sources). *Receiving aid:* Freshmen: 94% (76); All full-time undergraduates: 85% (253). *Average award:* Freshmen: $20,016; Undergraduates: $20,849. *Scholarships, grants, and awards:* Federal Pell, FSEOG, state, private, college/university gift aid from institutional funds.
GIFT AID (NON-NEED-BASED) *Total amount:* $50,000 (100% institutional). *Receiving aid:* Freshmen: 15% (12); Undergraduates: 16% (46). *Average Award:* Freshmen: $5500; Undergraduates: $4200. *Scholarships, grants, and awards by category:* Academic Interests/Achievement: 68 awards ($306,000 total): general academic interests/achievements. *Special Achievements/Activities:* 68 awards ($306,000 total): community service, general special achievements/activities, leadership.
LOANS *Student loans:* $1,102,206 (69% need-based, 31% non-need-based). 57% of past graduating class borrowed through all loan programs. *Average indebtedness per student:* $16,705. *Average need-based loan:* Freshmen: $3026; Undergraduates: $3990. *Parent loans:* $369,309 (100% non-need-based). *Programs:* FFEL (Subsidized and Unsubsidized Stafford, PLUS), Perkins.
WORK-STUDY *Federal work-study:* Total amount: $339,623; 173 jobs averaging $1963. *State or other work-study/employment:* Total amount: $68,698 (100% need-based). 53 part-time jobs averaging $1296.
APPLYING FOR FINANCIAL AID *Required financial aid forms:* FAFSA, institution's own form, noncustodial (divorced/separated) parent's statement, financial aid transcript (for transfers). *Financial aid deadline (priority):* 2/15. *Notification date:* 4/1. Students must reply by 5/1 or within 2 weeks of notification.
CONTACT Bruce Hazam, Director of Financial Aid, College of the Atlantic, 105 Eden Street, Bar Harbor, ME 04609-1198, 207-288-5015 Ext. 232 or toll-free 800-528-0025. *Fax:* 207-288-4126. *E-mail:* bhazam@ecology.coa.edu.

COLLEGE OF THE HOLY CROSS
Worcester, MA

Tuition & fees: $31,444 **Average undergraduate aid package:** $21,254

ABOUT THE INSTITUTION Independent Roman Catholic (Jesuit), coed. Awards: bachelor's degrees. 33 undergraduate majors. Total enrollment: 2,816. Undergraduates: 2,816. Freshmen: 721. Both federal and institutional methodology are used as a basis for awarding need-based institutional aid.

UNDERGRADUATE EXPENSES for 2005–06 *Application fee:* $50. *Comprehensive fee:* $40,664 includes full-time tuition ($30,960), mandatory fees ($484), and room and board ($9220). *College room only:* $4610. Room and board charges vary according to board plan and housing facility. *Payment plan:* Installment.

FRESHMAN FINANCIAL AID (Fall 2005, est.) 522 applied for aid; of those 84% were deemed to have need. 96% of freshmen with need received aid; of those 100% had need fully met. *Average percent of need met:* 100% (excluding resources awarded to replace EFC). *Average financial aid package:* $22,216 (excluding resources awarded to replace EFC). 6% of all full-time freshmen had no need and received non-need-based gift aid.

UNDERGRADUATE FINANCIAL AID (Fall 2005, est.) 1,688 applied for aid; of those 89% were deemed to have need. 99% of undergraduates with need received aid; of those 100% had need fully met. *Average percent of need met:* 100% (excluding resources awarded to replace EFC). *Average financial aid package:* $21,254 (excluding resources awarded to replace EFC). 3% of all full-time undergraduates had no need and received non-need-based gift aid.

GIFT AID (NEED-BASED) *Total amount:* $20,276,946 (7% federal, 3% state, 83% institutional, 7% external sources). *Receiving aid:* Freshmen: 44% (319); All full-time undergraduates: 44% (1,219). *Average award:* Freshmen: $20,573; Undergraduates: $18,110. *Scholarships, grants, and awards:* Federal Pell, FSEOG, state, private, college/university gift aid from institutional funds.

GIFT AID (NON-NEED-BASED) *Total amount:* $2,933,812 (100% institutional). *Receiving aid:* Freshmen: 7% (53); Undergraduates: 4% (98). *Average Award:* Freshmen: $1790; Undergraduates: $15,517. *Scholarships, grants, and awards by category:* Academic Interests/Achievement: 153 awards ($2,047,675 total): general academic interests/achievements, humanities, military science. Creative Arts/Performance: 5 awards ($154,800 total): music. Special Characteristics: 21 awards ($650,160 total): children of faculty/staff. *Tuition waivers:* Full or partial for employees or children of employees. *ROTC:* Army cooperative, Naval, Air Force cooperative.

LOANS *Student loans:* $8,233,893 (76% need-based, 24% non-need-based). 52% of past graduating class borrowed through all loan programs. *Average indebtedness per student:* $19,390. *Average need-based loan:* Freshmen: $3513; Undergraduates: $4198. *Parent loans:* $9,540,200 (100% non-need-based). *Programs:* FFEL (Subsidized and Unsubsidized Stafford, PLUS), Perkins, MEFA Loans.

WORK-STUDY *Federal work-study:* Total amount: $1,329,309; 886 jobs averaging $1500.

ATHLETIC AWARDS *Total amount:* $4,637,471 (81% need-based, 19% non-need-based).

APPLYING FOR FINANCIAL AID *Required financial aid forms:* FAFSA, CSS Financial Aid PROFILE, noncustodial (divorced/separated) parent's statement, business/farm supplement, federal income tax form(s). *Financial aid deadline:* 2/1. *Notification date:* 4/2. Students must reply by 5/1.

CONTACT Lynne Myers, Director of Financial Aid, College of the Holy Cross, One College Street, Worcester, MA 01610-2395, 508-793-2265 or toll-free 800-442-2421. *Fax:* 508-793-2527.

COLLEGE OF THE HUMANITIES AND SCIENCES, HARRISON MIDDLETON UNIVERSITY
Tempe, AZ

CONTACT Financial Aid Office, College of the Humanities and Sciences, Harrison Middleton University, 1105 East Broadway, Tempe, AZ 85282, 480-317-5955 or toll-free 877-248-6724.

COLLEGE OF THE OZARKS
Point Lookout, MO

Tuition & fees: $280 **Average undergraduate aid package:** $14,849

ABOUT THE INSTITUTION Independent Presbyterian, coed. Awards: bachelor's degrees. 95 undergraduate majors. Total enrollment: 1,333. Undergraduates: 1,333. Freshmen: 240. Federal methodology is used as a basis for awarding need-based institutional aid.

UNDERGRADUATE EXPENSES for 2006–07 includes mandatory fees ($280) and room and board ($4100). *College room only:* $2000. *Part-time tuition:* $295 per credit hour. *Part-time fees:* $140 per term.

FRESHMAN FINANCIAL AID (Fall 2005, est.) 243 applied for aid; of those 94% were deemed to have need. 100% of freshmen with need received aid; of those 31% had need fully met. *Average percent of need met:* 84% (excluding resources awarded to replace EFC). *Average financial aid package:* $15,098 (excluding resources awarded to replace EFC). 12% of all full-time freshmen had no need and received non-need-based gift aid.

UNDERGRADUATE FINANCIAL AID (Fall 2005, est.) 1,283 applied for aid; of those 93% were deemed to have need. 100% of undergraduates with need received aid; of those 41% had need fully met. *Average percent of need met:* 86% (excluding resources awarded to replace EFC). *Average financial aid package:* $14,849 (excluding resources awarded to replace EFC). 9% of all full-time undergraduates had no need and received non-need-based gift aid.

GIFT AID (NEED-BASED) *Total amount:* $15,310,478 (12% federal, 6% state, 82% institutional). *Receiving aid:* Freshmen: 86% (229); All full-time undergraduates: 90% (1,194). *Average award:* Freshmen: $12,527; Undergraduates: $12,519. *Scholarships, grants, and awards:* Federal Pell, FSEOG, state, private, college/university gift aid from institutional funds.

GIFT AID (NON-NEED-BASED) *Total amount:* $3,009,497 (93% institutional, 7% external sources). *Receiving aid:* Freshmen: 13% (35); Undergraduates: 22% (287). *Average Award:* Freshmen: $13,267; Undergraduates: $15,220. *Scholarships, grants, and awards by category:* Academic Interests/Achievement: general academic interests/achievements. *ROTC:* Army.

LOANS *Student loans:* $400,000 (100% non-need-based). 5% of past graduating class borrowed through all loan programs. *Average indebtedness per student:* $4648. *Programs:* alternative loans.

WORK-STUDY *Federal work-study:* Total amount: $2,585,000; 778 jobs averaging $2884. *State or other work-study/employment:* Total amount: $1,829,162 (19% need-based, 81% non-need-based). 700 part-time jobs averaging $2884.

ATHLETIC AWARDS *Total amount:* $160,710 (34% need-based, 66% non-need-based).

APPLYING FOR FINANCIAL AID *Required financial aid forms:* FAFSA, federal income tax form(s). *Financial aid deadline (priority):* 2/15. *Notification date:* 7/1.

CONTACT Kyla R. McCarty, Director of Financial Aid, College of the Ozarks, PO Box 17, Point Lookout, MO 65726, 417-334-6411 Ext. 4290 or toll-free 800-222-0525. *Fax:* 417-334-6737.

COLLEGE OF THE SOUTHWEST
Hobbs, NM

Tuition & fees: $9300 **Average undergraduate aid package:** $8437

ABOUT THE INSTITUTION Independent, coed. Awards: bachelor's and master's degrees. 22 undergraduate majors. Total enrollment: 741. Undergraduates: 608. Freshmen: 90. Federal methodology is used as a basis for awarding need-based institutional aid.

UNDERGRADUATE EXPENSES for 2005–06 *Application fee:* $25. *Comprehensive fee:* $14,300 includes full-time tuition ($9300) and room and board ($5000). Full-time tuition and fees vary according to course load. Room and board charges vary according to housing facility. *Part-time tuition:* $310 per semester hour. Part-time tuition and fees vary according to course load. *Payment plan:* Deferred payment.

FRESHMAN FINANCIAL AID (Fall 2005, est.) 72 applied for aid; of those 83% were deemed to have need. 100% of freshmen with need received aid; of those 42% had need fully met. *Average percent of need met:* 76% (excluding resources awarded to replace EFC). *Average financial aid package:* $10,163 (excluding resources awarded to replace EFC). 14% of all full-time freshmen had no need and received non-need-based gift aid.

College of the Southwest

UNDERGRADUATE FINANCIAL AID (Fall 2005, est.) 484 applied for aid; of those 84% were deemed to have need. 99% of undergraduates with need received aid; of those 39% had need fully met. *Average percent of need met:* 62% (excluding resources awarded to replace EFC). *Average financial aid package:* $8437 (excluding resources awarded to replace EFC). 16% of all full-time undergraduates had no need and received non-need-based gift aid.
GIFT AID (NEED-BASED) *Total amount:* $1,308,969 (64% federal, 36% state). *Receiving aid:* Freshmen: 62% (46); All full-time undergraduates: 60% (294). *Average award:* Freshmen: $5166; Undergraduates: $4104. *Scholarships, grants, and awards:* Federal Pell, FSEOG, state, private, college/university gift aid from institutional funds.
GIFT AID (NON-NEED-BASED) *Total amount:* $656,542 (82% institutional, 18% external sources). *Receiving aid:* Freshmen: 54% (40); Undergraduates: 52% (259). *Average Award:* Freshmen: $4698; Undergraduates: $3402. *Scholarships, grants, and awards by category:* Academic Interests/Achievement: 69 awards ($81,393 total): business, education, English, general academic interests/achievements, mathematics, social sciences. Creative Arts/Performance: 12 awards ($7100 total): music, theater/drama. Special Achievements/Activities: 14 awards ($11,909 total): general special achievements/activities. Special Characteristics: 18 awards ($78,095 total): children of faculty/staff, first-generation college students, relatives of clergy. *Tuition waivers:* Full or partial for employees or children of employees.
LOANS *Student loans:* $2,505,375 (60% need-based, 40% non-need-based). 66% of past graduating class borrowed through all loan programs. *Average indebtedness per student:* $17,420. *Average need-based loan:* Freshmen: $2465; Undergraduates: $3768. *Parent loans:* $135,855 (100% non-need-based). *Programs:* FFEL (Subsidized and Unsubsidized Stafford, PLUS), state.
WORK-STUDY *Federal work-study:* Total amount: $59,300; 43 jobs averaging $1395. *State or other work-study/employment:* Total amount: $64,550 (100% need-based). 50 part-time jobs averaging $1236.
ATHLETIC AWARDS Total amount: $432,117 (100% non-need-based).
APPLYING FOR FINANCIAL AID *Required financial aid forms:* FAFSA, institution's own form. *Financial aid deadline:* 8/1 (priority: 4/1). *Notification date:* Continuous beginning 3/15. Students must reply within 2 weeks of notification.
CONTACT Kerrie Mitchell, Senior Financial Aid Officer, College of the Southwest, 6610 Lovington Highway, Hobbs, NM 88240-9129, 505-392-6561 Ext. 1048 or toll-free 800-530-4400. *Fax:* 505-392-6006. *E-mail:* kmitchell@csw.edu.

COLLEGE OF VISUAL ARTS
St. Paul, MN

Tuition & fees: $18,040 **Average undergraduate aid package:** $8429

ABOUT THE INSTITUTION Independent, coed. Awards: bachelor's degrees. 7 undergraduate majors. Total enrollment: 202. Undergraduates: 202. Freshmen: 49. Federal methodology is used as a basis for awarding need-based institutional aid.
UNDERGRADUATE EXPENSES for 2005–06 *Application fee:* $40. *Tuition:* full-time $17,510; part-time $875 per credit. *Required fees:* full-time $530; $53 per course. Full-time tuition and fees vary according to course load. Part-time tuition and fees vary according to course load. *Payment plan:* Installment.
FRESHMAN FINANCIAL AID (Fall 2005, est.) 49 applied for aid; of those 84% were deemed to have need. 95% of freshmen with need received aid; of those 3% had need fully met. *Average percent of need met:* 36% (excluding resources awarded to replace EFC). *Average financial aid package:* $6269 (excluding resources awarded to replace EFC). 7% of all full-time freshmen had no need and received non-need-based gift aid.
UNDERGRADUATE FINANCIAL AID (Fall 2005, est.) 96 applied for aid; of those 92% were deemed to have need. 100% of undergraduates with need received aid; of those 3% had need fully met. *Average percent of need met:* 42% (excluding resources awarded to replace EFC). *Average financial aid package:* $8429 (excluding resources awarded to replace EFC). 9% of all full-time undergraduates had no need and received non-need-based gift aid.
GIFT AID (NEED-BASED) *Total amount:* $428,923 (34% federal, 38% state, 28% institutional). *Receiving aid:* Freshmen: 57% (31); All full-time undergraduates: 62% (72). *Average award:* Freshmen: $2117; Undergraduates: $1939. *Scholarships, grants, and awards:* Federal Pell, FSEOG, state, private, college/university gift aid from institutional funds.
GIFT AID (NON-NEED-BASED) *Total amount:* $34,763 (84% institutional, 16% external sources). *Receiving aid:* Freshmen: 26% (14); Undergraduates: 21% (25). *Average Award:* Freshmen: $2300; Undergraduates: $1991. *Scholarships, grants, and awards by category:* Academic Interests/Achievement: 39 awards ($59,688 total): general academic interests/achievements. Creative Arts/Performance: 28 awards ($52,375 total): art/fine arts. Special Characteristics: 1 award ($18,040 total): children of faculty/staff. *Tuition waivers:* Full or partial for employees or children of employees.
LOANS *Student loans:* $1,250,280 (81% need-based, 19% non-need-based). 76% of past graduating class borrowed through all loan programs. *Average indebtedness per student:* $43,860. *Average need-based loan:* Freshmen: $2494; Undergraduates: $4336. *Parent loans:* $97,593 (48% need-based, 52% non-need-based). *Programs:* FFEL (Subsidized and Unsubsidized Stafford, PLUS), state, alternative loans.
WORK-STUDY *Federal work-study:* Total amount: $35,496; 19 jobs averaging $1932. *State or other work-study/employment:* Total amount: $65,179 (32% need-based, 68% non-need-based). 25 part-time jobs averaging $2048.
APPLYING FOR FINANCIAL AID *Required financial aid forms:* FAFSA, institution's own form. *Financial aid deadline:* 6/1 (priority: 4/1). *Notification date:* Continuous beginning 1/1. Students must reply within 2 weeks of notification.
CONTACT Mrs. Bonnie Burgoyne, Director of Financial Aid, College of Visual Arts, 344 Summit Avenue, St. Paul, MN 55102-2124, 651-224-3416 or toll-free 800-224-1536. *Fax:* 651-224-8854. *E-mail:* bburgoyne@cva.edu.

THE COLLEGE OF WILLIAM AND MARY
Williamsburg, VA

Tuition & fees (VA res): $7778 **Average undergraduate aid package:** $10,682

ABOUT THE INSTITUTION State-supported, coed. Awards: bachelor's, master's, doctoral, and first professional degrees and post-master's certificates. 44 undergraduate majors. Total enrollment: 7,544. Undergraduates: 5,594. Freshmen: 1,344. Federal methodology is used as a basis for awarding need-based institutional aid.
UNDERGRADUATE EXPENSES for 2005–06 *Application fee:* $60. *Tuition, state resident:* full-time $4730; part-time $180 per credit hour. *Tuition, nonresident:* full-time $20,000; part-time $710 per credit hour. Full-time tuition and fees vary according to program. Part-time tuition and fees vary according to program. *College room and board:* $6417; *room only:* $3856. Room and board charges vary according to board plan and housing facility. *Payment plan:* Installment.
FRESHMAN FINANCIAL AID (Fall 2005, est.) 798 applied for aid; of those 43% were deemed to have need. 100% of freshmen with need received aid; of those 43% had need fully met. *Average percent of need met:* 88% (excluding resources awarded to replace EFC). *Average financial aid package:* $10,237 (excluding resources awarded to replace EFC). 2% of all full-time freshmen had no need and received non-need-based gift aid.
UNDERGRADUATE FINANCIAL AID (Fall 2005, est.) 2,575 applied for aid; of those 58% were deemed to have need. 100% of undergraduates with need received aid; of those 46% had need fully met. *Average percent of need met:* 87% (excluding resources awarded to replace EFC). *Average financial aid package:* $10,682 (excluding resources awarded to replace EFC). 5% of all full-time undergraduates had no need and received non-need-based gift aid.
GIFT AID (NEED-BASED) *Total amount:* $10,262,176 (13% federal, 21% state, 57% institutional, 9% external sources). *Receiving aid:* Freshmen: 19% (252); All full-time undergraduates: 22% (1,209). *Average award:* Freshmen: $10,303; Undergraduates: $10,445. *Scholarships, grants, and awards:* Federal Pell, FSEOG, state, private, college/university gift aid from institutional funds.
GIFT AID (NON-NEED-BASED) *Total amount:* $5,123,410 (2% federal, 28% institutional, 70% external sources). *Receiving aid:* Freshmen: 13% (177); Undergraduates: 10% (528). *Average Award:* Freshmen: $7167; Undergraduates: $5237. *Scholarships, grants, and awards by category:* Academic Interests/Achievement: 186 awards ($1,400,000 total): general academic interests/achievements. Creative Arts/Performance: 12 awards ($4035 total): art/fine arts, music. *Tuition waivers:* Full or partial for employees or children of employees, senior citizens. *ROTC:* Army.
LOANS *Student loans:* $8,961,779 (65% need-based, 35% non-need-based). 34% of past graduating class borrowed through all loan programs. *Average indebtedness per student:* $14,524. *Average need-based loan:* Freshmen: $2129; Undergraduates: $2648. *Parent loans:* $6,869,064 (48% need-based, 52% non-need-based). *Programs:* FFEL (Subsidized and Unsubsidized Stafford, PLUS), Perkins.

WORK-STUDY *Federal work-study:* Total amount: $140,044; 80 jobs averaging $760.
ATHLETIC AWARDS Total amount: $4,262,058 (18% need-based, 82% non-need-based).
APPLYING FOR FINANCIAL AID *Required financial aid form:* FAFSA. *Financial aid deadline (priority):* 2/15. *Notification date:* Continuous beginning 3/15. Students must reply by 5/1 or within 2 weeks of notification.
CONTACT Mr. Edward P. Irish, Director of Financial Aid, The College of William and Mary, PO Box 8795, Williamsburg, VA 23187-8795, 757-221-2425. *Fax:* 757-221-2515. *E-mail:* epiris@wm.edu.

THE COLLEGE OF WOOSTER
Wooster, OH

Tuition & fees: $28,230   Average undergraduate aid package: $23,837

ABOUT THE INSTITUTION Independent religious, coed. Awards: bachelor's degrees. 45 undergraduate majors. Total enrollment: 1,846. Undergraduates: 1,846. Freshmen: 535. Both federal and institutional methodology are used as a basis for awarding need-based institutional aid.
UNDERGRADUATE EXPENSES for 2005–06 *Application fee:* $40. *Comprehensive fee:* $35,290 includes full-time tuition ($28,230) and room and board ($7060). *College room only:* $3210. Full-time tuition and fees vary according to course load and reciprocity agreements. Part-time tuition and fees vary according to course load. *Payment plan:* Installment.
FRESHMAN FINANCIAL AID (Fall 2005, est.) 406 applied for aid; of those 77% were deemed to have need. 100% of freshmen with need received aid; of those 91% had need fully met. *Average percent of need met:* 92% (excluding resources awarded to replace EFC). *Average financial aid package:* $23,486 (excluding resources awarded to replace EFC). 37% of all full-time freshmen had no need and received non-need-based gift aid.
UNDERGRADUATE FINANCIAL AID (Fall 2005, est.) 1,212 applied for aid; of those 86% were deemed to have need. 100% of undergraduates with need received aid; of those 91% had need fully met. *Average percent of need met:* 93% (excluding resources awarded to replace EFC). *Average financial aid package:* $23,837 (excluding resources awarded to replace EFC). 27% of all full-time undergraduates had no need and received non-need-based gift aid.
GIFT AID (NEED-BASED) *Total amount:* $19,433,870 (5% federal, 4% state, 89% institutional, 2% external sources). *Receiving aid:* Freshmen: 59% (313); All full-time undergraduates: 57% (1,036). *Average award:* Freshmen: $17,281; Undergraduates: $17,286. *Scholarships, grants, and awards:* Federal Pell, FSEOG, state, private, college/university gift aid from institutional funds.
GIFT AID (NON-NEED-BASED) *Total amount:* $9,101,733 (4% state, 94% institutional, 2% external sources). *Receiving aid:* Freshmen: 14% (73); Undergraduates: 9% (159). *Average Award:* Freshmen: $12,591; Undergraduates: $11,350. *Scholarships, grants, and awards by category:* Academic Interests/Achievement: 1,241 awards ($13,585,000 total): biological sciences, general academic interests/achievements, mathematics, physical sciences, social sciences. Creative Arts/Performance: 55 awards ($220,000 total): dance, music, theater/drama. Special Achievements/Activities: 212 awards ($1,150,000 total): community service, leadership, religious involvement. Special Characteristics: 262 awards ($3,100,000 total): children of faculty/staff, international students, local/state students, members of minority groups. *Tuition waivers:* Full or partial for employees or children of employees.
LOANS *Student loans:* $7,392,419 (64% need-based, 36% non-need-based). 55% of past graduating class borrowed through all loan programs. *Average indebtedness per student:* $19,989. *Average need-based loan:* Freshmen: $5564; Undergraduates: $6333. *Parent loans:* $3,201,756 (13% need-based, 87% non-need-based). *Programs:* Federal Direct (Subsidized and Unsubsidized Stafford, PLUS), Perkins.
WORK-STUDY *Federal work-study:* Total amount: $968,799; 690 jobs averaging $1342. *State or other work-study/employment:* Total amount: $173,450 (87% need-based, 13% non-need-based). 118 part-time jobs averaging $1931.
APPLYING FOR FINANCIAL AID *Required financial aid forms:* FAFSA, institution's own form, CSS Financial Aid PROFILE. *Financial aid deadline:* 9/1 (priority): 2/15). *Notification date:* 3/15. Students must reply by 5/1 or within 4 weeks of notification.
CONTACT Office of Financial Aid, The College of Wooster, 1189 Beall Avenue, Wooster, OH 44691, 330-263-2317 or toll-free 800-877-9905. *Fax:* 330-263-2634. *E-mail:* financialaid@wooster.edu.

COLLINS COLLEGE: A SCHOOL OF DESIGN AND TECHNOLOGY
Tempe, AZ

Tuition & fees: $13,875   Average undergraduate aid package: $11,500

ABOUT THE INSTITUTION Proprietary, coed. Awards: associate and bachelor's degrees. 6 undergraduate majors. Total enrollment: 1,828. Undergraduates: 1,828. Federal methodology is used as a basis for awarding need-based institutional aid.
UNDERGRADUATE EXPENSES for 2005–06 *Application fee:* $50. *Tuition:* full-time $13,875. Full-time tuition and fees vary according to class time, course level, course load, degree level, location, program, reciprocity agreements, and student level. Part-time tuition and fees vary according to class time, course level, course load, degree level, reciprocity agreements, and student level. *Payment plan:* Guaranteed tuition.
FRESHMAN FINANCIAL AID (Fall 2005, est.) 2150 applied for aid; of those 97% were deemed to have need. 99% of freshmen with need received aid; of those 3% had need fully met. *Average percent of need met:* 59% (excluding resources awarded to replace EFC). *Average financial aid package:* $10,000 (excluding resources awarded to replace EFC). 1% of all full-time freshmen had no need and received non-need-based gift aid.
UNDERGRADUATE FINANCIAL AID (Fall 2005, est.) 2,736 applied for aid; of those 94% were deemed to have need. 99% of undergraduates with need received aid; of those 3% had need fully met. *Average percent of need met:* 65% (excluding resources awarded to replace EFC). *Average financial aid package:* $11,500 (excluding resources awarded to replace EFC). 1% of all full-time undergraduates had no need and received non-need-based gift aid.
GIFT AID (NEED-BASED) *Total amount:* $3,242,661 (89% federal, 11% external sources). *Receiving aid:* Freshmen: 62% (1,472); All full-time undergraduates: 46% (1,682). *Average award:* Freshmen: $4000; Undergraduates: $4000. *Scholarships, grants, and awards:* Federal Pell, FSEOG, state, private, college/university gift aid from institutional funds.
GIFT AID (NON-NEED-BASED) *Total amount:* $244,824 (65% institutional, 35% external sources). *Receiving aid:* Freshmen: 2% (58); Undergraduates: 2% (61). *Average Award:* Freshmen: $8000; Undergraduates: $11,500. *Scholarships, grants, and awards by category:* Creative Arts/Performance: applied art and design. *Tuition waivers:* Full or partial for employees or children of employees.
LOANS *Student loans:* $13,492,886 (28% need-based, 72% non-need-based). 74% of past graduating class borrowed through all loan programs. *Average indebtedness per student:* $18,000. *Average need-based loan:* Freshmen: $3370; Undergraduates: $4880. *Parent loans:* $6,132,748 (100% non-need-based). *Programs:* FFEL (Subsidized and Unsubsidized Stafford, PLUS), college/university.
WORK-STUDY *Federal work-study:* Total amount: $212,862; 65 jobs averaging $3000. *State or other work-study/employment:* Total amount: $24,093 (100% need-based).
APPLYING FOR FINANCIAL AID *Required financial aid forms:* FAFSA, institution's own form. *Financial aid deadline:* Continuous. *Notification date:* Continuous beginning 3/1. Students must reply within 2 weeks of notification.
CONTACT Carol Clapp, Director of Financial Aid, Collins College: A School of Design and Technology, 1140 South Priest Drive, Tempe, AZ 85281, 480-966-3000 Ext. 127 or toll-free 800-876-7070 (out-of-state). *Fax:* 480-446-1172. *E-mail:* cclapp@collinscollege.edu.

COLORADO CHRISTIAN UNIVERSITY
Lakewood, CO

ABOUT THE INSTITUTION Independent interdenominational, coed. Awards: associate, bachelor's, and master's degrees. 26 undergraduate majors. Total enrollment: 2,142. Undergraduates: 1,826. Freshmen: 207.
GIFT AID (NEED-BASED) *Scholarships, grants, and awards:* Federal Pell, FSEOG, private, college/university gift aid from institutional funds.
GIFT AID (NON-NEED-BASED) *Scholarships, grants, and awards by category:* Academic Interests/Achievement: general academic interests/achievements. Creative Arts/Performance: music, theater/drama. Special Achievements/Activities: community service, leadership, religious involvement. Special Characteristics: children of faculty/staff, first-generation college students.

Colorado Christian University

LOANS *Programs:* FFEL (Subsidized and Unsubsidized Stafford, PLUS), Perkins.

WORK-STUDY *Federal work-study:* Total amount: $19,327; 16 jobs averaging $2000. *State or other work-study/employment:* Total amount: $74,175 (12% need-based, 88% non-need-based). Part-time jobs available.

APPLYING FOR FINANCIAL AID *Required financial aid form:* FAFSA.

CONTACT Steve Woodburn, Director of Financial Aid, Colorado Christian University, 180 South Garrison Street, Lakewood, CO 80226-7499, 303-963-3230 or toll-free 800-44-FAITH. *Fax:* 303-963-3231. *E-mail:* sfs@ccu.edu.

THE COLORADO COLLEGE
Colorado Springs, CO

Tuition & fees: $30,048   Average undergraduate aid package: $27,522

ABOUT THE INSTITUTION Independent, coed. Awards: bachelor's and master's degrees (master's degree in education only). 46 undergraduate majors. Total enrollment: 2,016. Undergraduates: 1,977. Freshmen: 469. Both federal and institutional methodology are used as a basis for awarding need-based institutional aid.

UNDERGRADUATE EXPENSES for 2005–06 *Application fee:* $50. *Comprehensive fee:* $37,668 includes full-time tuition ($30,048) and room and board ($7620). *College room only:* $4116. Room and board charges vary according to board plan. *Part-time tuition:* $948.38 per credit hour. *Payment plan:* Installment.

FRESHMAN FINANCIAL AID (Fall 2005, est.) 239 applied for aid; of those 87% were deemed to have need. 100% of freshmen with need received aid; of those 89% had need fully met. *Average percent of need met:* 98% (excluding resources awarded to replace EFC). *Average financial aid package:* $28,058 (excluding resources awarded to replace EFC). 12% of all full-time freshmen had no need and received non-need-based gift aid.

UNDERGRADUATE FINANCIAL AID (Fall 2005, est.) 963 applied for aid; of those 91% were deemed to have need. 100% of undergraduates with need received aid; of those 67% had need fully met. *Average percent of need met:* 91% (excluding resources awarded to replace EFC). *Average financial aid package:* $27,522 (excluding resources awarded to replace EFC). 11% of all full-time undergraduates had no need and received non-need-based gift aid.

GIFT AID (NEED-BASED) *Total amount:* $18,451,568 (5% federal, 2% state, 90% institutional, 3% external sources). *Receiving aid:* Freshmen: 44% (208); All full-time undergraduates: 41% (790). *Average award:* Freshmen: $24,621; Undergraduates: $23,717. *Scholarships, grants, and awards:* Federal Pell, FSEOG, state, private, college/university gift aid from institutional funds.

GIFT AID (NON-NEED-BASED) *Total amount:* $3,885,423 (1% state, 78% institutional, 21% external sources). *Receiving aid:* Freshmen: 7% (34); Undergraduates: 5% (103). *Average Award:* Freshmen: $9053; Undergraduates: $15,144. *Scholarships, grants, and awards by category:* Academic Interests/Achievement: 160 awards ($1,700,000 total): biological sciences, general academic interests/achievements, mathematics, physical sciences. *Special Characteristics:* 29 awards ($857,878 total): international students. *Tuition waivers:* Full or partial for employees or children of employees. *ROTC:* Army cooperative.

LOANS *Student loans:* $3,636,660 (66% need-based, 34% non-need-based). *Average need-based loan:* Freshmen: $3521; Undergraduates: $4835. *Parent loans:* $3,214,428 (19% need-based, 81% non-need-based). *Programs:* FFEL (Subsidized and Unsubsidized Stafford, PLUS), Perkins.

WORK-STUDY *Federal work-study:* Total amount: $479,655; 310 jobs averaging $1550. *State or other work-study/employment:* Total amount: $375,334 (73% need-based, 27% non-need-based). 232 part-time jobs averaging $1618.

ATHLETIC AWARDS *Total amount:* $1,085,364 (100% non-need-based).

APPLYING FOR FINANCIAL AID *Required financial aid forms:* FAFSA, CSS Financial Aid PROFILE, noncustodial (divorced/separated) parent's statement, federal income tax form(s) for parents and student. *Financial aid deadline:* 2/15 (priority: 2/15). *Notification date:* 3/20. Students must reply by 5/1.

CONTACT Mr. James M. Swanson, Director of Financial Aid, The Colorado College, 14 East Cache La Poudre Street, Colorado Springs, CO 80903-3294, 719-389-6651 or toll-free 800-542-7214. *Fax:* 719-389-6173. *E-mail:* FinancialAid@ColoradoCollege.edu.

COLORADO SCHOOL OF MINES
Golden, CO

Tuition & fees (CO res): $8143   Average undergraduate aid package: $13,800

ABOUT THE INSTITUTION State-supported, coed. Awards: bachelor's, master's, doctoral, and first professional degrees. 16 undergraduate majors. Total enrollment: 3,921. Undergraduates: 3,098. Freshmen: 824. Federal methodology is used as a basis for awarding need-based institutional aid.

UNDERGRADUATE EXPENSES for 2005–06 *Application fee:* $45. *Tuition, state resident:* full-time $7248; part-time $382 per semester hour. *Tuition, nonresident:* full-time $19,830; part-time $661 per semester hour. *Required fees:* full-time $895; $60 per semester hour. Part-time tuition and fees vary according to course load. *College room and board:* $6750; *room only:* $3550. Room and board charges vary according to board plan and housing facility. *Payment plan:* Installment.

FRESHMAN FINANCIAL AID (Fall 2005, est.) 632 applied for aid; of those 91% were deemed to have need. 100% of freshmen with need received aid; of those 79% had need fully met. *Average percent of need met:* 93% (excluding resources awarded to replace EFC). *Average financial aid package:* $13,800 (excluding resources awarded to replace EFC). 10% of all full-time freshmen had no need and received non-need-based gift aid.

UNDERGRADUATE FINANCIAL AID (Fall 2005, est.) 2,072 applied for aid; of those 91% were deemed to have need. 100% of undergraduates with need received aid; of those 82% had need fully met. *Average percent of need met:* 93% (excluding resources awarded to replace EFC). *Average financial aid package:* $13,800 (excluding resources awarded to replace EFC). 10% of all full-time undergraduates had no need and received non-need-based gift aid.

GIFT AID (NEED-BASED) *Total amount:* $7,772,000 (19% federal, 12% state, 57% institutional, 12% external sources). *Receiving aid:* Freshmen: 61% (496); All full-time undergraduates: 60% (1,660). *Average award:* Freshmen: $7100; Undergraduates: $7100. *Scholarships, grants, and awards:* Federal Pell, FSEOG, state, private, college/university gift aid from institutional funds.

GIFT AID (NON-NEED-BASED) *Total amount:* $3,052,000 (2% state, 69% institutional, 29% external sources). *Receiving aid:* Freshmen: 24% (195); Undergraduates: 23% (630). *Average Award:* Freshmen: $5100; Undergraduates: $5100. *Scholarships, grants, and awards by category:* Academic Interests/Achievement: 350 awards ($1,100,000 total): business, computer science, engineering/technologies, general academic interests/achievements, mathematics, military science, physical sciences. *Special Characteristics:* 10 awards ($10,000 total): children and siblings of alumni. *ROTC:* Army.

LOANS *Student loans:* $8,150,000 (63% need-based, 37% non-need-based). 69% of past graduating class borrowed through all loan programs. *Average indebtedness per student:* $17,700. *Average need-based loan:* Freshmen: $4200; Undergraduates: $4200. *Parent loans:* $2,900,000 (100% non-need-based). *Programs:* FFEL (Subsidized and Unsubsidized Stafford, PLUS), Perkins, college/university.

WORK-STUDY *Federal work-study:* Total amount: $198,000; 164 jobs averaging $1200. *State or other work-study/employment:* Total amount: $668,000 (55% need-based, 45% non-need-based). 560 part-time jobs averaging $1200.

ATHLETIC AWARDS *Total amount:* $1,050,000 (66% need-based, 34% non-need-based).

APPLYING FOR FINANCIAL AID *Required financial aid form:* FAFSA. *Financial aid deadline (priority):* 3/1. *Notification date:* 4/1. Students must reply by 5/1 or within 2 weeks of notification.

CONTACT Mr. Roger A. Koester, Director of Financial Aid, Colorado School of Mines, 1500 Illinois Street, Golden, CO 80401-1887, 303-273-3220 or toll-free 800-446-9488 Ext. 3220 (out-of-state). *Fax:* 303-384-2252. *E-mail:* rkoester@mines.edu.

COLORADO STATE UNIVERSITY
Fort Collins, CO

Tuition & fees (CO res): $4562   Average undergraduate aid package: $8188

ABOUT THE INSTITUTION State-supported, coed. Awards: bachelor's, master's, doctoral, and first professional degrees. 118 undergraduate majors. Total enrollment: 27,133. Undergraduates: 21,506. Freshmen: 3,893. Federal methodology is used as a basis for awarding need-based institutional aid.

UNDERGRADUATE EXPENSES for 2005–06 *Application fee:* $50. *Tuition, state resident:* full-time $3381; part-time $188 per credit. *Tuition, nonresident:* full-time $14,343; part-time $797 per credit. Part-time tuition and fees vary according to course load. *College room and board:* $6316; *room only:* $2852. Room and board charges vary according to board plan and housing facility. *Payment plan:* Installment.

FRESHMAN FINANCIAL AID (Fall 2004) 2328 applied for aid; of those 62% were deemed to have need. 100% of freshmen with need received aid; of those 43% had need fully met. *Average percent of need met:* 87% (excluding resources awarded to replace EFC). *Average financial aid package:* $6758 (excluding resources awarded to replace EFC). 7% of all full-time freshmen had no need and received non-need-based gift aid.

UNDERGRADUATE FINANCIAL AID (Fall 2004) 10,741 applied for aid; of those 70% were deemed to have need. 100% of undergraduates with need received aid; of those 50% had need fully met. *Average percent of need met:* 82% (excluding resources awarded to replace EFC). *Average financial aid package:* $8188 (excluding resources awarded to replace EFC). 5% of all full-time undergraduates had no need and received non-need-based gift aid.

GIFT AID (NEED-BASED) *Total amount:* $24,899,074 (50% federal, 19% state, 21% institutional, 10% external sources). *Receiving aid:* Freshmen: 27% (1,074); All full-time undergraduates: 27% (5,197). *Average award:* Freshmen: $5707; Undergraduates: $4914. *Scholarships, grants, and awards:* Federal Pell, FSEOG, state, private, college/university gift aid from institutional funds.

GIFT AID (NON-NEED-BASED) *Total amount:* $5,648,741 (20% federal, 9% state, 41% institutional, 30% external sources). *Average Award:* Freshmen: $2599; *Undergraduates:* $2275. *Scholarships, grants, and awards by category: Academic Interests/Achievement:* 4,029 awards ($7,443,337 total): general academic interests/achievements. *Creative Arts/Performance:* 153 awards ($150,000 total): art/fine arts, creative writing, dance, music, theater/drama. *Special Achievements/Activities:* 252 awards ($628,763 total): general special achievements/activities. *Special Characteristics:* 495 awards ($942,985 total): children of faculty/staff, first-generation college students. *Tuition waivers:* Full or partial for employees or children of employees. *ROTC:* Army, Air Force.

LOANS *Student loans:* $50,886,884 (74% need-based, 26% non-need-based). 52% of past graduating class borrowed through all loan programs. *Average indebtedness per student:* $16,887. *Average need-based loan:* Freshmen: $3318; Undergraduates: $5355. *Parent loans:* $25,444,467 (55% need-based, 45% non-need-based). *Programs:* Federal Direct (Subsidized and Unsubsidized Stafford, PLUS), Perkins, college/university, alternative loans.

WORK-STUDY *Federal work-study:* Total amount: $847,258; 492 jobs averaging $1893. *State or other work-study/employment:* Total amount: $1,947,069 (75% need-based, 25% non-need-based). 1,120 part-time jobs averaging $1790.

ATHLETIC AWARDS *Total amount:* $3,720,827 (28% need-based, 72% non-need-based).

APPLYING FOR FINANCIAL AID *Required financial aid form:* FAFSA. *Financial aid deadline (priority):* 3/1. *Notification date:* Continuous beginning 3/1.

CONTACT Office of Student Financial Services, Colorado State University, Room 103, Administration Annex Building, Fort Collins, CO 80523-8024, 970-491-6321. *E-mail:* sfs@colostate.edu.

COLORADO STATE UNIVERSITY-PUEBLO
Pueblo, CO

ABOUT THE INSTITUTION State-supported, coed. Awards: bachelor's and master's degrees. 65 undergraduate majors. Total enrollment: 5,835. Undergraduates: 5,417. Freshmen: 709.

GIFT AID (NEED-BASED) *Scholarships, grants, and awards:* Federal Pell, FSEOG, state, private, college/university gift aid from institutional funds.

GIFT AID (NON-NEED-BASED) *Scholarships, grants, and awards by category: Academic Interests/Achievement:* biological sciences, business, computer science, engineering/technologies, general academic interests/achievements, international studies, mathematics, premedicine, social sciences. *Creative Arts/Performance:* applied art and design, art/fine arts, cinema/film/broadcasting, journalism/publications, music, performing arts, theater/drama. *Special Achievements/Activities:* community service, general special achievements/activities, leadership. *Special Characteristics:* first-generation college students, general special characteristics.

LOANS *Programs:* FFEL (Subsidized and Unsubsidized Stafford, PLUS), Perkins.

APPLYING FOR FINANCIAL AID *Required financial aid form:* FAFSA.

CONTACT Director of Student Financial Services, Colorado State University-Pueblo, 2200 Bonforte Boulevard, Pueblo, CO 81001-4901, 719-549-2913. *Fax:* 719-549-2088.

COLORADO TECHNICAL UNIVERSITY
Colorado Springs, CO

CONTACT Anne Marie Alba, Financial Aid Coordinator, Colorado Technical University, 4435 North Chestnut Street, Colorado Springs, CO 80907-3896, 719-598-0200. *Fax:* 719-598-3740.

COLORADO TECHNICAL UNIVERSITY DENVER CAMPUS
Greenwood Village, CO

CONTACT Ms. Natalie Dietsch, Financial Aid Manager, Colorado Technical University Denver Campus, 5775 Denver Tech Center Boulevard, Suite 100, Greenwood Village, CO 80111, 303-694-6600. *Fax:* 303-694-6673.

COLORADO TECHNICAL UNIVERSITY SIOUX FALLS CAMPUS
Sioux Falls, SD

CONTACT Vikki Van Hull, Financial Aid Officer, Colorado Technical University Sioux Falls Campus, 3901 West 59th Street, Sioux Falls, SD 57108, 605-361-0200 Ext. 140. *Fax:* 605-361-5954. *E-mail:* vvanhull@sf.coloradotech.edu.

COLUMBIA COLLEGE
Columbia, MO

ABOUT THE INSTITUTION Independent religious, coed. Awards: associate, bachelor's, and master's degrees (offers continuing education program with significant enrollment not reflected in profile). 37 undergraduate majors. Total enrollment: 1,149. Undergraduates: 1,009. Freshmen: 163.

GIFT AID (NEED-BASED) *Scholarships, grants, and awards:* Federal Pell, FSEOG, state, private, college/university gift aid from institutional funds, VA, vocational rehabilitation.

GIFT AID (NON-NEED-BASED) *Scholarships, grants, and awards by category: Academic Interests/Achievement:* biological sciences, business, education, English, general academic interests/achievements, humanities, physical sciences, religion/biblical studies, social sciences. *Creative Arts/Performance:* applied art and design, art/fine arts, music. *Special Achievements/Activities:* leadership, memberships, religious involvement. *Special Characteristics:* children and siblings of alumni, children of current students, children of educators, children of faculty/staff, children of union members/company employees, children with a deceased or disabled parent, international students, local/state students, parents of current students, previous college experience, religious affiliation, siblings of current students, spouses of current students, veterans.

LOANS *Programs:* Federal Direct (Subsidized and Unsubsidized Stafford, PLUS), Perkins.

WORK-STUDY *Federal work-study:* Total amount: $51,063; 92 jobs averaging $555.

APPLYING FOR FINANCIAL AID *Required financial aid forms:* FAFSA, institution's own form.

CONTACT Sharon Abernathy, Director of Financial Aid, Columbia College, 1001 Rogers Street, Columbia, MO 65216-0002, 573-875-7360 or toll-free 800-231-2391 Ext. 7366. *E-mail:* saabernathy@ccis.edu.

COLUMBIA COLLEGE
New York, NY

ABOUT THE INSTITUTION Independent, coed. Awards: bachelor's degrees. 64 undergraduate majors. Total enrollment: 4,225. Undergraduates: 4,225. Freshmen: 1,024.

GIFT AID (NEED-BASED) *Scholarships, grants, and awards:* Federal Pell, FSEOG, state, private, college/university gift aid from institutional funds.

LOANS *Programs:* FFEL (Subsidized and Unsubsidized Stafford, PLUS), Perkins, alternative loans.

Columbia College

WORK-STUDY *Federal work-study:* Total amount: $3,166,203; 1,347 jobs averaging $2350. *State or other work-study/employment:* Total amount: $347,910 (100% need-based). 130 part-time jobs averaging $2676.
APPLYING FOR FINANCIAL AID *Required financial aid forms:* FAFSA, institution's own form, CSS Financial Aid PROFILE, noncustodial (divorced/separated) parent's statement, parent and student income tax form(s).
CONTACT Office of Financial Aid and Educational Financing, Columbia College, 407 Lerner Hall MC 2802, 1130 Amsterdam Avenue, New York, NY 10027, 212-854-3711. *Fax:* 212-854-8223. *E-mail:* ugrad-finaid@columbia.edu.

COLUMBIA COLLEGE
Caguas, PR

CONTACT Financial Aid Officer, Columbia College, Carr 183, Km 1.7, PO Box 8517, Caguas, PR 00726, 787-743-4041 Ext. 244 or toll-free 800-981-4877 Ext. 239 (in-state).

COLUMBIA COLLEGE
Columbia, SC

Tuition & fees: $19,214 **Average undergraduate aid package: $20,052**

ABOUT THE INSTITUTION Independent United Methodist, undergraduate: women only; graduate: coed. Awards: bachelor's and master's degrees. 39 undergraduate majors. Total enrollment: 1,493. Undergraduates: 1,108. Freshmen: 211. Federal methodology is used as a basis for awarding need-based institutional aid.
UNDERGRADUATE EXPENSES for 2005–06 *Application fee:* $25. *Comprehensive fee:* $25,032 includes full-time tuition ($18,864), mandatory fees ($350), and room and board ($5818). *College room only:* $3034. Full-time tuition and fees vary according to class time. Room and board charges vary according to board plan and housing facility. *Part-time tuition:* $506 per credit hour. Part-time tuition and fees vary according to course load. *Payment plans:* Tuition prepayment, installment.
FRESHMAN FINANCIAL AID (Fall 2005, est.) 240 applied for aid; of those 83% were deemed to have need. 100% of freshmen with need received aid; of those 71% had need fully met. *Average percent of need met:* 82% (excluding resources awarded to replace EFC). *Average financial aid package:* $21,723 (excluding resources awarded to replace EFC). 20% of all full-time freshmen had no need and received non-need-based gift aid.
UNDERGRADUATE FINANCIAL AID (Fall 2005, est.) 794 applied for aid; of those 88% were deemed to have need. 100% of undergraduates with need received aid; of those 45% had need fully met. *Average percent of need met:* 70% (excluding resources awarded to replace EFC). *Average financial aid package:* $20,052 (excluding resources awarded to replace EFC). 17% of all full-time undergraduates had no need and received non-need-based gift aid.
GIFT AID (NEED-BASED) *Total amount:* $4,717,208 (34% federal, 32% state, 33% institutional, 1% external sources). *Receiving aid:* Freshmen: 75% (195); All full-time undergraduates: 75% (669). *Average award:* Freshmen: $8309; Undergraduates: $8495. *Scholarships, grants, and awards:* Federal Pell, FSEOG, state, private, college/university gift aid from institutional funds.
GIFT AID (NON-NEED-BASED) *Total amount:* $6,735,519 (29% state, 64% institutional, 7% external sources). *Receiving aid:* Freshmen: 50% (131); Undergraduates: 29% (262). *Average Award:* Freshmen: $9656; Undergraduates: $7775. *Scholarships, grants, and awards by category:* Academic Interests/Achievement: 736 awards ($1,480,587 total): biological sciences, business, communication, education, English, foreign languages, general academic interests/achievements, humanities, mathematics, religion/biblical studies. Creative Arts/Performance: 108 awards ($257,500 total): applied art and design, art/fine arts, dance, music. Special Achievements/Activities: 199 awards ($469,719 total): leadership. Special Characteristics: 22 awards ($116,584 total): children of faculty/staff, relatives of clergy. *Tuition waivers:* Full or partial for employees or children of employees. *ROTC:* Army cooperative, Naval cooperative, Air Force cooperative.
LOANS *Student loans:* $9,809,010 (48% need-based, 52% non-need-based). 87% of past graduating class borrowed through all loan programs. *Average indebtedness per student:* $25,333. *Average need-based loan:* Freshmen: $3444; Undergraduates: $3810. *Parent loans:* $550,111 (100% non-need-based). *Programs:* FFEL (Subsidized and Unsubsidized Stafford, PLUS), Perkins, state, South Carolina Teacher Loans, United Methodist Student Loans.

WORK-STUDY *Federal work-study:* Total amount: $285,246; 200 jobs averaging $1000. *State or other work-study/employment:* Total amount: $70,757 (100% need-based). Part-time jobs available.
ATHLETIC AWARDS *Total amount:* $119,750 (100% non-need-based).
APPLYING FOR FINANCIAL AID *Required financial aid form:* FAFSA. *Financial aid deadline (priority):* 3/15. *Notification date:* Continuous beginning 4/1. Students must reply within 2 weeks of notification.
CONTACT Anita Kaminer Elliott, Director of Financial Aid, Columbia College, 1301 Columbia College Drive, Columbia, SC 29203-5998, 803-786-3612 or toll-free 800-277-1301. *Fax:* 803-786-3560.

COLUMBIA COLLEGE CHICAGO
Chicago, IL

ABOUT THE INSTITUTION Independent, coed. Awards: bachelor's and master's degrees and post-bachelor's certificates. 42 undergraduate majors. Total enrollment: 10,842. Undergraduates: 10,144. Freshmen: 1,829.
GIFT AID (NEED-BASED) *Scholarships, grants, and awards:* Federal Pell, FSEOG, state, private, college/university gift aid from institutional funds.
GIFT AID (NON-NEED-BASED) *Scholarships, grants, and awards by category:* Academic Interests/Achievement: business, communication, education, general academic interests/achievements. Creative Arts/Performance: applied art and design, art/fine arts, cinema/film/broadcasting, creative writing, dance, journalism/publications, music, performing arts, theater/drama. Special Achievements/Activities: leadership. Special Characteristics: children of faculty/staff, first-generation college students, handicapped students.
LOANS *Programs:* Federal Direct (Subsidized and Unsubsidized Stafford, PLUS).
APPLYING FOR FINANCIAL AID *Required financial aid forms:* FAFSA, institution's own form.
CONTACT Mr. Timothy Bauhs, Executive Director of Student Financial Services, Columbia College Chicago, 600 South Michigan Avenue, Chicago, IL 60605-1996, 312-663-1600 Ext. 7054 or toll-free 312-663-1600 Ext. 7130 (in-state). *Fax:* 312-986-1091. *E-mail:* tbauhs@colum.edu.

COLUMBIA COLLEGE HOLLYWOOD
Tarzana, CA

ABOUT THE INSTITUTION Independent, coed. Awards: associate and bachelor's degrees. 5 undergraduate majors. Total enrollment: 177. Undergraduates: 177.
GIFT AID (NEED-BASED) *Scholarships, grants, and awards:* Federal Pell, FSEOG, state, private.
LOANS *Programs:* FFEL (Subsidized and Unsubsidized Stafford, PLUS).
APPLYING FOR FINANCIAL AID *Required financial aid forms:* FAFSA, institution's own form.
CONTACT Mr. Chris Freeman, Financial Aid Administrator, Columbia College Hollywood, 18618 Oxnard Street, Tarzana, CA 91356, 818-345-8414 Ext. 110 or toll-free 800-785-0585 (in-state). *Fax:* 818-345-9053. *E-mail:* finaid@columbiacollege.edu.

COLUMBIA INTERNATIONAL UNIVERSITY
Columbia, SC

ABOUT THE INSTITUTION Independent nondenominational, coed. Awards: associate, bachelor's, master's, doctoral, and first professional degrees and post-bachelor's certificates. 15 undergraduate majors. Total enrollment: 1,013. Undergraduates: 550. Freshmen: 93.
GIFT AID (NEED-BASED) *Scholarships, grants, and awards:* Federal Pell, FSEOG, state, private, college/university gift aid from institutional funds.
GIFT AID (NON-NEED-BASED) *Scholarships, grants, and awards by category:* Academic Interests/Achievement: general academic interests/achievements, international studies, religion/biblical studies. Creative Arts/Performance: music, performing arts. Special Achievements/Activities: general special achievements/activities, leadership, religious involvement. Special Characteristics: children and siblings of alumni, ethnic background, first-generation college students, international students, married students, relatives of clergy, religious affiliation, spouses of current students, veterans, veterans' children.
LOANS *Programs:* FFEL (Subsidized and Unsubsidized Stafford, PLUS).
APPLYING FOR FINANCIAL AID *Required financial aid forms:* FAFSA, institution's own form.

CONTACT Mr. Robert Patton, Financial Aid Counselor, Columbia International University, PO Box 3122, Columbia, SC 29230-3122, 803-754-4100 Ext. 3036 or toll-free 800-777-2227 Ext. 3024. *Fax:* 803-691-0739. *E-mail:* yesciu@ciu.edu.

COLUMBIA UNION COLLEGE
Takoma Park, MD

CONTACT Elaine Oliver, Director, Financial Aid, Columbia Union College, 7600 Flower Avenue, Takoma Park, MD 20912, 301-891-4005 or toll-free 800-835-4212.

COLUMBIA UNIVERSITY, SCHOOL OF GENERAL STUDIES
New York, NY

Tuition & fees: $32,176	Average undergraduate aid package: N/A

ABOUT THE INSTITUTION Independent, coed. Awards: bachelor's degrees and post-bachelor's certificates. 45 undergraduate majors. Total enrollment: 1,579. Undergraduates: 1,146. Freshmen: 63. Both federal and institutional methodology are used as a basis for awarding need-based institutional aid.
UNDERGRADUATE EXPENSES for 2005–06 *Application fee:* $65. *Comprehensive fee:* $40,716 includes full-time tuition ($30,900), mandatory fees ($1276), and room and board ($8540). *College room only:* $5450. Full-time tuition and fees vary according to course load. Room and board charges vary according to housing facility. *Part-time tuition:* $1030 per credit. Part-time tuition and fees vary according to course load. *Payment plans:* Tuition prepayment, deferred payment.
GIFT AID (NEED-BASED) *Total amount:* $5,788,695 (30% federal, 10% state, 59% institutional, 1% external sources). *Scholarships, grants, and awards:* Federal Pell, FSEOG, state, private, college/university gift aid from institutional funds.
GIFT AID (NON-NEED-BASED) *Total amount:* $1,533,077 (48% federal, 47% institutional, 5% external sources). *Scholarships, grants, and awards by category:* Academic Interests/Achievement: general academic interests/achievements. *Tuition waivers:* Full or partial for employees or children of employees.
LOANS *Student loans:* $9,432,013 (57% need-based, 43% non-need-based). *Parent loans:* $2,229,394 (100% non-need-based). *Programs:* FFEL (Subsidized and Unsubsidized Stafford, PLUS), Perkins, college/university.
WORK-STUDY *Federal work-study:* Total amount: $561,532; 243 jobs averaging $2313.
APPLYING FOR FINANCIAL AID *Required financial aid forms:* FAFSA, institution's own form. *Financial aid deadline (priority):* 6/1. *Notification date:* Continuous. Students must reply within 2 weeks of notification.
CONTACT Student Financial Planning, Columbia University, School of General Studies, 208 Kent Hall, New York, NY 10027, 212-854-7040 or toll-free 800-895-1169 (out-of-state).

COLUMBIA UNIVERSITY, THE FU FOUNDATION SCHOOL OF ENGINEERING AND APPLIED SCIENCE
New York, NY

ABOUT THE INSTITUTION Independent, coed. Awards: bachelor's, master's, and doctoral degrees. 15 undergraduate majors. Total enrollment: 1,436. Undergraduates: 1,436. Freshmen: 315.
GIFT AID (NEED-BASED) *Scholarships, grants, and awards:* Federal Pell, FSEOG, state, private, college/university gift aid from institutional funds.
LOANS *Programs:* FFEL (Subsidized and Unsubsidized Stafford, PLUS), Perkins, alternative loans.
WORK-STUDY *Federal work-study:* Total amount: $1,368,051; 594 jobs averaging $2300. *State or other work-study/employment:* Total amount: $221,490 (100% need-based). 64 part-time jobs averaging $3460.
APPLYING FOR FINANCIAL AID *Required financial aid forms:* FAFSA, institution's own form, CSS Financial Aid PROFILE, noncustodial (divorced/separated) parent's statement, student and parent income tax form(s).

CONTACT Office of Financial Aid and Educational Financing, Columbia University, The Fu Foundation School of Engineering and Applied Science, 407 Lerner Hall, 1130 Amsterdam Avenue, New York, NY 10027, 212-854-3711. *Fax:* 212-854-8223. *E-mail:* ugrad-finaid@columbia.edu.

COLUMBUS COLLEGE OF ART & DESIGN
Columbus, OH

Tuition & fees: $20,278	Average undergraduate aid package: $14,477

ABOUT THE INSTITUTION Independent, coed. Awards: bachelor's degrees. 7 undergraduate majors. Total enrollment: 1,455. Undergraduates: 1,455. Freshmen: 207. Federal methodology is used as a basis for awarding need-based institutional aid.
UNDERGRADUATE EXPENSES for 2005–06 *Application fee:* $25. *Comprehensive fee:* $26,728 includes full-time tuition ($19,728), mandatory fees ($550), and room and board ($6450). Room and board charges vary according to housing facility and student level. *Part-time tuition:* $822 per credit. *Part-time fees:* $275 per term. Part-time tuition and fees vary according to course load. *Payment plans:* Installment, deferred payment.
FRESHMAN FINANCIAL AID (Fall 2005, est.) 309 applied for aid; of those 83% were deemed to have need. 100% of freshmen with need received aid; of those 21% had need fully met. *Average percent of need met:* 67% (excluding resources awarded to replace EFC). *Average financial aid package:* $14,576 (excluding resources awarded to replace EFC). 25% of all full-time freshmen had no need and received non-need-based gift aid.
UNDERGRADUATE FINANCIAL AID (Fall 2005, est.) 1,178 applied for aid; of those 87% were deemed to have need. 100% of undergraduates with need received aid; of those 20% had need fully met. *Average percent of need met:* 67% (excluding resources awarded to replace EFC). *Average financial aid package:* $14,477 (excluding resources awarded to replace EFC). 20% of all full-time undergraduates had no need and received non-need-based gift aid.
GIFT AID (NEED-BASED) *Total amount:* $9,972,505 (13% federal, 15% state, 69% institutional, 3% external sources). *Receiving aid:* Freshmen: 74% (257); All full-time undergraduates: 78% (1,013). *Average award:* Freshmen: $10,600; Undergraduates: $9614. *Scholarships, grants, and awards:* Federal Pell, FSEOG, state, private, college/university gift aid from institutional funds.
GIFT AID (NON-NEED-BASED) *Total amount:* $2,218,255 (7% state, 90% institutional, 3% external sources). *Receiving aid:* Freshmen: 5% (16); Undergraduates: 5% (70). *Average Award:* Freshmen: $11,569; Undergraduates: $11,225. *Scholarships, grants, and awards by category:* Creative Arts/Performance: 1,211 awards ($8,884,637 total): art/fine arts. *Special Characteristics:* 10 awards ($171,288 total): children of educators, children of faculty/staff, local/state students. *Tuition waivers:* Full or partial for employees or children of employees.
LOANS *Student loans:* $8,580,034 (71% need-based, 29% non-need-based). 99% of past graduating class borrowed through all loan programs. *Average indebtedness per student:* $27,693. *Average need-based loan:* Freshmen: $4652; Undergraduates: $5447. *Parent loans:* $4,623,982 (56% need-based, 44% non-need-based). *Programs:* FFEL (Subsidized and Unsubsidized Stafford, PLUS), Perkins, state.
WORK-STUDY *Federal work-study:* Total amount: $135,677; 136 jobs averaging $3250. *State or other work-study/employment:* 227 part-time jobs averaging $3000.
APPLYING FOR FINANCIAL AID *Required financial aid forms:* FAFSA, institution's own form, income tax forms, verification statement. *Financial aid deadline (priority):* 3/3. *Notification date:* 3/15. Students must reply within 2 weeks of notification.
CONTACT Mrs. Anna Schofield, Director of Financial Aid, Columbus College of Art & Design, 107 North Ninth Street, Columbus, OH 43215-1758, 614-224-9101 Ext. 3274 or toll-free 877-997-2223. *Fax:* 614-222-4034. *E-mail:* aschofield@ccad.edu.

COLUMBUS STATE UNIVERSITY
Columbus, GA

Tuition & fees (GA res): $2944	Average undergraduate aid package: $3988

ABOUT THE INSTITUTION State-supported, coed. Awards: associate, bachelor's, and master's degrees and post-bachelor's and post-master's certificates. 68

Columbus State University

undergraduate majors. Total enrollment: 7,475. Undergraduates: 6,624. Freshmen: 1,184. Federal methodology is used as a basis for awarding need-based institutional aid.
UNDERGRADUATE EXPENSES for 2005–06 *Application fee:* $25. *Tuition, state resident:* full-time $2438; part-time $102 per semester hour. *Tuition, nonresident:* full-time $9754; part-time $407 per semester hour. *College room and board:* $5720; *room only:* $3510. Room and board charges vary according to board plan and location.
FRESHMAN FINANCIAL AID (Fall 2005, est.) 680 applied for aid; of those 73% were deemed to have need. 87% of freshmen with need received aid; of those 66% had need fully met. *Average percent of need met:* 58% (excluding resources awarded to replace EFC). *Average financial aid package:* $3474 (excluding resources awarded to replace EFC). 34% of all full-time freshmen had no need and received non-need-based gift aid.
UNDERGRADUATE FINANCIAL AID (Fall 2005, est.) 2,666 applied for aid; of those 83% were deemed to have need. 94% of undergraduates with need received aid; of those 67% had need fully met. *Average percent of need met:* 69% (excluding resources awarded to replace EFC). *Average financial aid package:* $3988 (excluding resources awarded to replace EFC). 27% of all full-time undergraduates had no need and received non-need-based gift aid.
GIFT AID (NEED-BASED) *Total amount:* $2,922,680 (96% federal, 1% state, 2% institutional, 1% external sources). *Receiving aid:* Freshmen: 39% (398); All full-time undergraduates: 47% (2,079). *Average award:* Freshmen: $2491; Undergraduates: $3214. *Scholarships, grants, and awards:* Federal Pell, FSEOG, state, private, college/university gift aid from institutional funds.
GIFT AID (NON-NEED-BASED) *Total amount:* $3,638,607 (75% state, 16% institutional, 9% external sources). *Receiving aid:* Freshmen: 30% (305); Undergraduates: 32% (1,409). *Average Award:* Freshmen: $1638; Undergraduates:* $1672. *Scholarships, grants, and awards by category: Academic Interests/Achievement:* biological sciences, business, communication, computer science, education, English, general academic interests/achievements, health fields, humanities, international studies, military science, physical sciences. *Creative Arts/Performance:* art/fine arts, music, performing arts, theater/drama. *Special Achievements/Activities:* cheerleading/drum major, community service, general special achievements/activities, leadership. *Tuition waivers:* Full or partial for employees or children of employees, senior citizens. *ROTC:* Army.
LOANS *Student loans:* $19,523,663 (54% need-based, 46% non-need-based). 71% of past graduating class borrowed through all loan programs. *Average need-based loan:* Freshmen: $2620; Undergraduates: $3456. *Parent loans:* $653,534 (100% need-based). *Programs:* Federal Direct (Subsidized and Unsubsidized Stafford, PLUS), Perkins, state, college/university.
WORK-STUDY *Federal work-study:* Total amount: $140,000; 46 jobs averaging $3000.
ATHLETIC AWARDS *Total amount:* $344,100 (100% non-need-based).
APPLYING FOR FINANCIAL AID *Required financial aid form:* FAFSA. *Financial aid deadline (priority):* 5/1. *Notification date:* Continuous beginning 6/1.
CONTACT Ms. Janis Bowles, Director of Financial Aid, Columbus State University, 4225 University Avenue, Columbus, GA 31907-5645, 706-568-2036 or toll-free 866-264-2035. *Fax:* 706-568-2230. *E-mail:* bowles_janis@colstate.edu.

CONCEPTION SEMINARY COLLEGE
Conception, MO

CONTACT Br. Justin Hernandez, OSB, Director of Financial Aid, Conception Seminary College, PO Box 502, Conception, MO 64433-0502, 660-944-2851. *Fax:* 660-944-2829. *E-mail:* justin@conception.edu.

CONCORDIA COLLEGE
Selma, AL

CONTACT Financial Aid Office, Concordia College, 1804 Green Street, Selma, AL 36701, 334-874-5700. *Fax:* 334-874-3728.

CONCORDIA COLLEGE
Moorhead, MN

ABOUT THE INSTITUTION Independent religious, coed. Awards: bachelor's and master's degrees. 81 undergraduate majors. Total enrollment: 2,764. Undergraduates: 2,759. Freshmen: 773.

GIFT AID (NEED-BASED) *Scholarships, grants, and awards:* Federal Pell, FSEOG, state, private, college/university gift aid from institutional funds.
GIFT AID (NON-NEED-BASED) *Scholarships, grants, and awards by category: Academic Interests/Achievement:* general academic interests/achievements. *Creative Arts/Performance:* debating, music, theater/drama. *Special Characteristics:* international students, members of minority groups.
LOANS *Programs:* FFEL (Subsidized and Unsubsidized Stafford, PLUS), Perkins, state, college/university, alternative loans.
APPLYING FOR FINANCIAL AID *Required financial aid forms:* FAFSA, institution's own form.
CONTACT Mr. Dale E. Thornton, Financial Aid Director, Concordia College, 901 South 8th Street, Moorhead, MN 56562, 218-299-3010 or toll-free 800-699-9897. *Fax:* 218-299-3025. *E-mail:* thornton@cord.edu.

CONCORDIA COLLEGE
Bronxville, NY

CONTACT Mr. Ken Fick, Director of Financial Aid, Concordia College, 171 White Plains Road, Bronxville, NY 10708, 914-337-9300 Ext. 2146 or toll-free 800-YES-COLLEGE. *Fax:* 914-395-4500. *E-mail:* financialaid@concordia-ny.edu.

CONCORDIA UNIVERSITY
Irvine, CA

Tuition & fees: $21,130	Average undergraduate aid package: $19,204

ABOUT THE INSTITUTION Independent religious, coed. Awards: bachelor's and master's degrees and post-bachelor's certificates (associate's degree for international students only). 23 undergraduate majors. Total enrollment: 2,092. Undergraduates: 1,445. Freshmen: 265. Federal methodology is used as a basis for awarding need-based institutional aid.
UNDERGRADUATE EXPENSES for 2006–07 *Application fee:* $50. *Comprehensive fee:* $28,190 includes full-time tuition ($21,130) and room and board ($7060). *College room only:* $4380. *Part-time tuition:* $600 per unit.
FRESHMAN FINANCIAL AID (Fall 2005, est.) 273 applied for aid; of those 73% were deemed to have need. 100% of freshmen with need received aid; of those 23% had need fully met. *Average percent of need met:* 70% (excluding resources awarded to replace EFC). *Average financial aid package:* $19,857 (excluding resources awarded to replace EFC). 18% of all full-time freshmen had no need and received non-need-based gift aid.
UNDERGRADUATE FINANCIAL AID (Fall 2005, est.) 1,242 applied for aid; of those 71% were deemed to have need. 99% of undergraduates with need received aid; of those 25% had need fully met. *Average percent of need met:* 70% (excluding resources awarded to replace EFC). *Average financial aid package:* $19,204 (excluding resources awarded to replace EFC). 20% of all full-time undergraduates had no need and received non-need-based gift aid.
GIFT AID (NEED-BASED) *Total amount:* $8,374,685 (12% federal, 25% state, 62% institutional, 1% external sources). *Receiving aid:* Freshmen: 69% (190); All full-time undergraduates: 60% (794). *Average award:* Freshmen: $10,652; Undergraduates: $10,480. *Scholarships, grants, and awards:* Federal Pell, FSEOG, state, private, college/university gift aid from institutional funds.
GIFT AID (NON-NEED-BASED) *Total amount:* $2,177,905 (100% institutional). *Receiving aid:* Freshmen: 10% (29); Undergraduates: 8% (112). *Average Award:* Freshmen: $6333; Undergraduates: $6151. *Scholarships, grants, and awards by category: Academic Interests/Achievement:* 944 awards ($3,157,594 total): general academic interests/achievements, religion/biblical studies. *Creative Arts/Performance:* 186 awards ($297,700 total): applied art and design, debating, music, theater/drama. *Special Achievements/Activities:* general special achievements/activities. *Special Characteristics:* 455 awards: children of faculty/staff, ethnic background, religious affiliation, siblings of current students.
LOANS *Student loans:* $5,982,217 (43% need-based, 57% non-need-based). 74% of past graduating class borrowed through all loan programs. *Average indebtedness per student:* $19,200. *Average need-based loan:* Freshmen: $2583; Undergraduates: $4030. *Parent loans:* $2,020,847 (100% non-need-based). *Programs:* FFEL (Subsidized and Unsubsidized Stafford, PLUS), alternative loan.
WORK-STUDY *Federal work-study:* Total amount: $77,624; 42 jobs averaging $1765. *State or other work-study/employment:* Total amount: $304,838 (100% need-based). 179 part-time jobs averaging $1690.

ATHLETIC AWARDS *Total amount:* $1,379,817 (52% need-based, 48% non-need-based).

APPLYING FOR FINANCIAL AID *Required financial aid forms:* FAFSA, institution's own form. *Financial aid deadline:* 4/1 (priority: 3/2). *Notification date:* Continuous. Students must reply within 4 weeks of notification.

CONTACT Lori McDonald, Director of Financial Aid, Concordia University, 1530 Concordia West, Irvine, CA 92612-3299, 949-854-8002 Ext. 1170 or toll-free 800-229-1200. *Fax:* 949-854-6709. *E-mail:* lori.mcdonald@cui.edu.

CONCORDIA UNIVERSITY
River Forest, IL

CONTACT Assistant Director of Student Financial Planning, Concordia University, 7400 Augusta Street, River Forest, IL 60305-1499, 708-209-3113 or toll-free 800-285-2668.

CONCORDIA UNIVERSITY
Ann Arbor, MI

Tuition & fees: $18,205   **Average undergraduate aid package: $16,827**

ABOUT THE INSTITUTION Independent religious, coed. Awards: associate, bachelor's, and master's degrees. 45 undergraduate majors. Total enrollment: 600. Undergraduates: 559. Freshmen: 115. Federal methodology is used as a basis for awarding need-based institutional aid.

UNDERGRADUATE EXPENSES for 2005–06 *Application fee:* $25. *One-time required fee:* $100. *Comprehensive fee:* $25,153 includes full-time tuition ($18,035), mandatory fees ($170), and room and board ($6948). *College room only:* $5042. Full-time tuition and fees vary according to course load, degree level, and program. *Part-time tuition:* $590 per credit hour. Part-time tuition and fees vary according to course load, degree level, and program. *Payment plan:* Installment.

FRESHMAN FINANCIAL AID (Fall 2005, est.) 110 applied for aid; of those 85% were deemed to have need. 100% of freshmen with need received aid; of those 26% had need fully met. *Average percent of need met:* 83% (excluding resources awarded to replace EFC). *Average financial aid package:* $16,979 (excluding resources awarded to replace EFC). 16% of all full-time freshmen had no need and received non-need-based gift aid.

UNDERGRADUATE FINANCIAL AID (Fall 2005, est.) 472 applied for aid; of those 87% were deemed to have need. 100% of undergraduates with need received aid; of those 35% had need fully met. *Average percent of need met:* 84% (excluding resources awarded to replace EFC). *Average financial aid package:* $16,827 (excluding resources awarded to replace EFC). 14% of all full-time undergraduates had no need and received non-need-based gift aid.

GIFT AID (NEED-BASED) *Total amount:* $3,451,504 (14% federal, 17% state, 60% institutional, 9% external sources). *Receiving aid:* Freshmen: 80% (94); All full-time undergraduates: 78% (398). *Average award:* Freshmen: $11,610; Undergraduates: $10,016. *Scholarships, grants, and awards:* Federal Pell, FSEOG, state, private, college/university gift aid from institutional funds.

GIFT AID (NON-NEED-BASED) *Total amount:* $477,655 (16% state, 54% institutional, 30% external sources). *Receiving aid:* Freshmen: 13% (15); Undergraduates: 13% (68). *Average Award:* Freshmen: $3830; Undergraduates: $6352. *Scholarships, grants, and awards by category: Academic Interests/Achievement:* general academic interests/achievements, religion/biblical studies. *Creative Arts/Performance:* art/fine arts, music, performing arts, theater/drama. *Special Achievements/Activities:* general special achievements/activities. *Special Characteristics:* children and siblings of alumni, children of faculty/staff, ethnic background, relatives of clergy, religious affiliation, siblings of current students. *Tuition waivers:* Full or partial for employees or children of employees. *ROTC:* Army cooperative, Air Force cooperative.

LOANS *Student loans:* $3,139,973 (66% need-based, 34% non-need-based). 83% of past graduating class borrowed through all loan programs. *Average indebtedness per student:* $28,280. *Average need-based loan:* Freshmen: $4328; Undergraduates: $5004. *Parent loans:* $395,745 (25% need-based, 75% non-need-based). *Programs:* FFEL (Subsidized and Unsubsidized Stafford, PLUS), Perkins.

WORK-STUDY *Federal work-study:* Total amount: $55,438; jobs available. *State or other work-study/employment:* Total amount: $17,903 (69% need-based, 31% non-need-based). Part-time jobs available.

ATHLETIC AWARDS *Total amount:* $897,391 (64% need-based, 36% non-need-based).

APPLYING FOR FINANCIAL AID *Required financial aid forms:* FAFSA, institution's own form, Tax returns tw-25. *Financial aid deadline (priority):* 3/1. *Notification date:* Continuous. Students must reply by 5/1 or within 4 weeks of notification.

CONTACT Sandy Tarbox, Financial Aid Office, Concordia University, 4090 Geddes Road, Ann Arbor, MI 48105-2797, 734-995-4622 or toll-free 800-253-0680. *Fax:* 734-995-4610. *E-mail:* sandy.tarbox@cuaa.edu.

CONCORDIA UNIVERSITY
Seward, NE

Tuition & fees: $17,724   **Average undergraduate aid package: $15,019**

ABOUT THE INSTITUTION Independent religious, coed. Awards: bachelor's and master's degrees. 73 undergraduate majors. Total enrollment: 1,317. Undergraduates: 1,202. Freshmen: 222. Federal methodology is used as a basis for awarding need-based institutional aid.

UNDERGRADUATE EXPENSES for 2005–06 *Application fee:* $25. *Comprehensive fee:* $22,434 includes full-time tuition ($17,724) and room and board ($4710). Room and board charges vary according to board plan. Part-time tuition and fees vary according to course load. *Payment plan:* Installment.

FRESHMAN FINANCIAL AID (Fall 2005, est.) 242 applied for aid; of those 87% were deemed to have need. 100% of freshmen with need received aid; of those 70% had need fully met. *Average percent of need met:* 90% (excluding resources awarded to replace EFC). *Average financial aid package:* $15,389 (excluding resources awarded to replace EFC). 18% of all full-time freshmen had no need and received non-need-based gift aid.

UNDERGRADUATE FINANCIAL AID (Fall 2005, est.) 982 applied for aid; of those 87% were deemed to have need. 100% of undergraduates with need received aid; of those 75% had need fully met. *Average percent of need met:* 91% (excluding resources awarded to replace EFC). *Average financial aid package:* $15,019 (excluding resources awarded to replace EFC). 20% of all full-time undergraduates had no need and received non-need-based gift aid.

GIFT AID (NEED-BASED) *Total amount:* $2,346,197 (36% federal, 4% state, 44% institutional, 16% external sources). *Receiving aid:* Freshmen: 57% (165); All full-time undergraduates: 64% (683). *Average award:* Freshmen: $3842; Undergraduates: $4741. *Scholarships, grants, and awards:* Federal Pell, FSEOG, state, private, college/university gift aid from institutional funds.

GIFT AID (NON-NEED-BASED) *Total amount:* $6,027,065 (81% institutional, 19% external sources). *Receiving aid:* Freshmen: 73% (210); Undergraduates: 78% (837). *Average Award:* Freshmen: $6140; Undergraduates: $5896. *Scholarships, grants, and awards by category: Academic Interests/Achievement:* 1,382 awards ($3,909,984 total): biological sciences, business, communication, computer science, education, English, general academic interests/achievements, health fields, humanities, mathematics, physical sciences, premedicine, religion/biblical studies, social sciences. *Creative Arts/Performance:* 148 awards ($288,000 total): art/fine arts, music, theater/drama. *Special Achievements/Activities:* 557 awards ($571,125 total): memberships, religious involvement. *Special Characteristics:* 232 awards ($363,111 total): children and siblings of alumni, children of educators, children of faculty/staff, international students, local/state students, members of minority groups. *Tuition waivers:* Full or partial for employees or children of employees. *ROTC:* Army cooperative, Air Force cooperative.

LOANS *Student loans:* $3,805,489 (64% need-based, 36% non-need-based). 86% of past graduating class borrowed through all loan programs. *Average indebtedness per student:* $15,522. *Average need-based loan:* Freshmen: $2431; Undergraduates: $3572. *Parent loans:* $2,666,653 (100% non-need-based). *Programs:* FFEL (Subsidized and Unsubsidized Stafford, PLUS), Perkins.

WORK-STUDY *Federal work-study:* Total amount: $103,408; 161 jobs averaging $693. *State or other work-study/employment:* Part-time jobs available.

ATHLETIC AWARDS *Total amount:* $1,484,954 (100% non-need-based).

APPLYING FOR FINANCIAL AID *Required financial aid forms:* FAFSA, institution's own form. *Financial aid deadline (priority):* 3/1. *Notification date:* Continuous beginning 3/31. Students must reply within 4 weeks of notification.

CONTACT Mrs. Gloria F. Hennig, Director of Student Financial Services, Concordia University, 800 North Columbia Avenue, Seward, NE 68434-1599, 402-643-7270 or toll-free 800-535-5494. *Fax:* 402-643-3519. *E-mail:* gloria.hennig@cune.edu.

Concordia University

CONCORDIA UNIVERSITY
Portland, OR

ABOUT THE INSTITUTION Independent religious, coed. Awards: associate, bachelor's, and master's degrees and post-bachelor's certificates. 32 undergraduate majors. Total enrollment: 1,506. Undergraduates: 1,006. Freshmen: 171.
GIFT AID (NEED-BASED) *Scholarships, grants, and awards:* Federal Pell, FSEOG, state, private, college/university gift aid from institutional funds.
GIFT AID (NON-NEED-BASED) *Scholarships, grants, and awards by category: Academic Interests/Achievement:* general academic interests/achievements, religion/biblical studies. *Creative Arts/Performance:* music. *Special Achievements/Activities:* leadership, religious involvement. *Special Characteristics:* children of faculty/staff, relatives of clergy, religious affiliation.
LOANS *Programs:* FFEL (Subsidized and Unsubsidized Stafford, PLUS), Perkins, alternative loans.
APPLYING FOR FINANCIAL AID *Required financial aid form:* FAFSA.
CONTACT Mr. James W. Cullen, Director of Financial Aid, Concordia University, 2811 Northeast Holman Street, Portland, OR 97211-6099, 503-493-6508 or toll-free 800-321-9371. *Fax:* 503-280-8661. *E-mail:* jcullen@cu-portland.edu.

CONCORDIA UNIVERSITY AT AUSTIN
Austin, TX

Tuition & fees: $16,850   **Average undergraduate aid package: $15,222**

ABOUT THE INSTITUTION Independent religious, coed. Awards: associate, bachelor's, and master's degrees and post-bachelor's certificates. 21 undergraduate majors. Total enrollment: 1,219. Undergraduates: 1,129. Freshmen: 206. Federal methodology is used as a basis for awarding need-based institutional aid.
UNDERGRADUATE EXPENSES for 2005–06 *Application fee:* $25. *Comprehensive fee:* $23,750 includes full-time tuition ($16,850) and room and board ($6900). Full-time tuition and fees vary according to course load and location. Room and board charges vary according to board plan. Part-time tuition and fees vary according to location.
FRESHMAN FINANCIAL AID (Fall 2005, est.) 183 applied for aid; of those 74% were deemed to have need. 100% of freshmen with need received aid; of those 31% had need fully met. *Average percent of need met:* 73% (excluding resources awarded to replace EFC). *Average financial aid package:* $14,130 (excluding resources awarded to replace EFC). 27% of all full-time freshmen had no need and received non-need-based gift aid.
UNDERGRADUATE FINANCIAL AID (Fall 2005, est.) 635 applied for aid; of those 77% were deemed to have need. 100% of undergraduates with need received aid; of those 45% had need fully met. *Average percent of need met:* 81% (excluding resources awarded to replace EFC). *Average financial aid package:* $15,222 (excluding resources awarded to replace EFC). 18% of all full-time undergraduates had no need and received non-need-based gift aid.
GIFT AID (NEED-BASED) *Total amount:* $3,688,914 (22% federal, 25% state, 53% institutional). *Receiving aid:* Freshmen: 62% (121); All full-time undergraduates: 54% (399). *Average award:* Freshmen: $8638; Undergraduates: $8735. *Scholarships, grants, and awards:* Federal Pell, FSEOG, state, college/university gift aid from institutional funds.
GIFT AID (NON-NEED-BASED) *Total amount:* $1,909,903 (2% federal, 9% state, 89% institutional). *Receiving aid:* Freshmen: 29% (57); Undergraduates: 28% (208). *Average Award:* Freshmen: $7347; Undergraduates: $6844. *Scholarships, grants, and awards by category: Academic Interests/Achievement:* 279 awards ($1,606,220 total): general academic interests/achievements. *Creative Arts/Performance:* 8 awards ($24,225 total): music. *Special Achievements/Activities:* 124 awards ($751,742 total): religious involvement. *Special Characteristics:* children and siblings of alumni. *Tuition waivers:* Full or partial for employees or children of employees. **ROTC:** Army cooperative, Air Force cooperative.
LOANS *Student loans:* $4,677,902 (100% need-based). 68% of past graduating class borrowed through all loan programs. *Average indebtedness per student:* $20,202. *Average need-based loan:* Freshmen: $4389; Undergraduates: $6411. *Parent loans:* $705,276 (100% need-based). *Programs:* FFEL (Subsidized and Unsubsidized Stafford, PLUS), state.
WORK-STUDY *Federal work-study:* Total amount: $121,560; 82 jobs averaging $1579. *State or other work-study/employment:* Total amount: $9712 (100% need-based). 6 part-time jobs averaging $1619.
APPLYING FOR FINANCIAL AID *Required financial aid forms:* FAFSA, institution's own form. *Financial aid deadline (priority):* 5/1. *Notification date:* Continuous beginning 2/15. Students must reply by 5/1 or within 2 weeks of notification.
CONTACT Cathy L. Schryer, Director of Student Financial Services, Concordia University at Austin, 3400 Interstate 35 North, Austin, TX 78705-2799, 512-486-1283 or toll-free 800-285-4252.

CONCORDIA UNIVERSITY, ST. PAUL
St. Paul, MN

Tuition & fees: $22,378   **Average undergraduate aid package: $11,874**

ABOUT THE INSTITUTION Independent religious, coed. Awards: associate, bachelor's, and master's degrees and post-bachelor's certificates. 43 undergraduate majors. Total enrollment: 2,069. Undergraduates: 1,736. Freshmen: 165. Federal methodology is used as a basis for awarding need-based institutional aid.
UNDERGRADUATE EXPENSES for 2006–07 *Application fee:* $30. *Comprehensive fee:* $28,974 includes full-time tuition ($22,378) and room and board ($6596). *Part-time tuition:* $466 per credit.
FRESHMAN FINANCIAL AID (Fall 2005, est.) 163 applied for aid; of those 86% were deemed to have need. 100% of freshmen with need received aid; of those 25% had need fully met. *Average percent of need met:* 78% (excluding resources awarded to replace EFC). *Average financial aid package:* $16,187 (excluding resources awarded to replace EFC). 12% of all full-time freshmen had no need and received non-need-based gift aid.
UNDERGRADUATE FINANCIAL AID (Fall 2005, est.) 1,127 applied for aid; of those 85% were deemed to have need. 100% of undergraduates with need received aid; of those 17% had need fully met. *Average percent of need met:* 65% (excluding resources awarded to replace EFC). *Average financial aid package:* $11,874 (excluding resources awarded to replace EFC). 6% of all full-time undergraduates had no need and received non-need-based gift aid.
GIFT AID (NEED-BASED) *Total amount:* $7,389,696 (15% federal, 15% state, 60% institutional, 10% external sources). *Receiving aid:* Freshmen: 85% (140); All full-time undergraduates: 53% (759). *Average award:* Freshmen: $13,391; Undergraduates: $9760. *Scholarships, grants, and awards:* Federal Pell, FSEOG, state, private, college/university gift aid from institutional funds.
GIFT AID (NON-NEED-BASED) *Total amount:* $716,279 (4% state, 75% institutional, 21% external sources). *Average Award:* Freshmen: $6035; Undergraduates: $6202. *Scholarships, grants, and awards by category: Academic Interests/Achievement:* 727 awards ($2,548,031 total): biological sciences, business, communication, English, general academic interests/achievements, mathematics, physical sciences, religion/biblical studies, social sciences. *Creative Arts/Performance:* 125 awards ($152,650 total): art/fine arts, journalism/publications, music, theater/drama. *Special Characteristics:* 200 awards ($352,101 total): children of faculty/staff, religious affiliation. **ROTC:** Army cooperative, Naval cooperative, Air Force cooperative.
LOANS *Student loans:* $7,911,901 (90% need-based, 10% non-need-based). 68% of past graduating class borrowed through all loan programs. *Average indebtedness per student:* $20,715. *Average need-based loan:* Freshmen: $2748; Undergraduates: $4154. *Parent loans:* $1,139,486 (81% need-based, 19% non-need-based). *Programs:* FFEL (Subsidized and Unsubsidized Stafford, PLUS), Perkins, state.
WORK-STUDY *Federal work-study:* Total amount: $225,715; 139 jobs averaging $1624. *State or other work-study/employment:* Total amount: $482,468 (100% need-based). 297 part-time jobs averaging $1624.
ATHLETIC AWARDS *Total amount:* $1,075,642 (81% need-based, 19% non-need-based).
APPLYING FOR FINANCIAL AID *Required financial aid forms:* FAFSA, institution's own form. *Financial aid deadline (priority):* 5/1. *Notification date:* Continuous. Students must reply within 3 weeks of notification.
CONTACT Brian Heinemann, Financial Aid Director, Concordia University, St. Paul, 275 North Syndicate Street, St. Paul, MN 55104-5494, 651-603-6300 or toll-free 800-333-4705. *Fax:* 651-641-8889. *E-mail:* heinemann@csp.edu.

CONCORDIA UNIVERSITY WISCONSIN
Mequon, WI

Tuition & fees: $17,280   **Average undergraduate aid package: $17,213**

ABOUT THE INSTITUTION Independent religious, coed. Awards: associate, bachelor's, master's, and doctoral degrees and post-bachelor's certificates. 62 undergraduate majors. Total enrollment: 5,418. Undergraduates: 3,982. Freshmen: 387. Federal methodology is used as a basis for awarding need-based institutional aid.
UNDERGRADUATE EXPENSES for 2005–06 *Application fee:* $35. *Comprehensive fee:* $23,820 includes full-time tuition ($17,190), mandatory fees ($90), and room and board ($6540). Full-time tuition and fees vary according to program. Room and board charges vary according to board plan. *Part-time tuition:* $716 per credit hour. Part-time tuition and fees vary according to class time and program. *Payment plans:* Guaranteed tuition, installment, deferred payment.
FRESHMAN FINANCIAL AID (Fall 2005, est.) 373 applied for aid; of those 80% were deemed to have need. 100% of freshmen with need received aid; of those 37% had need fully met. *Average percent of need met:* 78% (excluding resources awarded to replace EFC). *Average financial aid package:* $18,229 (excluding resources awarded to replace EFC). 20% of all full-time freshmen had no need and received non-need-based gift aid.
UNDERGRADUATE FINANCIAL AID (Fall 2005, est.) 1,579 applied for aid; of those 83% were deemed to have need. 100% of undergraduates with need received aid; of those 35% had need fully met. *Average percent of need met:* 78% (excluding resources awarded to replace EFC). *Average financial aid package:* $17,213 (excluding resources awarded to replace EFC). 15% of all full-time undergraduates had no need and received non-need-based gift aid.
GIFT AID (NEED-BASED) *Total amount:* $5,217,228 (37% federal, 34% state, 15% institutional, 14% external sources). *Receiving aid:* Freshmen: 75% (287); All full-time undergraduates: 72% (1,230). *Average award:* Freshmen: $10,099; Undergraduates: $9146. *Scholarships, grants, and awards:* Federal Pell, FSEOG, state, private, college/university gift aid from institutional funds.
GIFT AID (NON-NEED-BASED) *Total amount:* $3,309,251 (1% state, 99% institutional). *Receiving aid:* Freshmen: 27% (102); Undergraduates: 24% (402). *Average Award:* Freshmen: $7529; Undergraduates: $7182. *Scholarships, grants, and awards by category:* Academic Interests/Achievement: 652 awards ($2,891,434 total): general academic interests/achievements. Creative Arts/Performance: 34 awards ($25,000 total): music, performing arts. Special Achievements/Activities: 86 awards ($153,164 total): leadership. Special Characteristics: 635 awards ($2,025,534 total): children of faculty/staff, out-of-state students, religious affiliation. *Tuition waivers:* Full or partial for employees or children of employees.
LOANS *Student loans:* $12,010,595 (62% need-based, 38% non-need-based). 68% of past graduating class borrowed through all loan programs. *Average indebtedness per student:* $17,270. *Average need-based loan:* Freshmen: $4860; Undergraduates: $5570. *Parent loans:* $2,304,203 (100% non-need-based). *Programs:* Federal Direct (Subsidized and Unsubsidized Stafford, PLUS), FFEL (Subsidized and Unsubsidized Stafford, PLUS), Perkins, state.
WORK-STUDY *Federal work-study:* Total amount: $7500; 80 jobs averaging $1600. *State or other work-study/employment:* 80 part-time jobs averaging $400.
APPLYING FOR FINANCIAL AID *Required financial aid forms:* FAFSA, institution's own form. *Financial aid deadline (priority):* 5/1. *Notification date:* Continuous beginning 1/15. Students must reply within 3 weeks of notification.
CONTACT Mr. Steven P. Taylor, Director of Financial Aid, Concordia University Wisconsin, 12800 North Lake Shore Drive, Mequon, WI 53097-2402, 262-243-4392 or toll-free 888-628-9472. *Fax:* 262-243-2636. *E-mail:* steve.taylor@cuw.edu.

CONCORD UNIVERSITY
Athens, WV

CONTACT Patricia Harmon, Financial Aid Director, Concord University, PO Box 1000, Athens, WV 24712-1000, 304-384-6069 or toll-free 888-384-5249. *Fax:* 304-384-9044.

CONNECTICUT COLLEGE
New London, CT

Comprehensive fee: $41,975	Average undergraduate aid package: $26,012

ABOUT THE INSTITUTION Independent, coed. Awards: bachelor's and master's degrees. 56 undergraduate majors. Total enrollment: 1,898. Undergraduates: 1,887. Freshmen: 492. Both federal and institutional methodology are used as a basis for awarding need-based institutional aid.
UNDERGRADUATE EXPENSES for 2005–06 *Application fee:* $60. *Comprehensive fee:* $41,975. Full-time tuition and fees vary according to program. *Part-time tuition:* $975 per credit hour. Part-time tuition and fees vary according to program. *Payment plan:* Installment.
FRESHMAN FINANCIAL AID (Fall 2005, est.) 246 applied for aid; of those 82% were deemed to have need. 100% of freshmen with need received aid; of those 100% had need fully met. *Average percent of need met:* 100% (excluding resources awarded to replace EFC). *Average financial aid package:* $25,156 (excluding resources awarded to replace EFC).
UNDERGRADUATE FINANCIAL AID (Fall 2005, est.) 908 applied for aid; of those 88% were deemed to have need. 100% of undergraduates with need received aid; of those 100% had need fully met. *Average percent of need met:* 100% (excluding resources awarded to replace EFC). *Average financial aid package:* $26,012 (excluding resources awarded to replace EFC).
GIFT AID (NEED-BASED) *Total amount:* $17,291,203 (4% federal, 3% state, 90% institutional, 3% external sources). *Receiving aid:* Freshmen: 35% (175); All full-time undergraduates: 37% (706). *Average award:* Freshmen: $24,277; Undergraduates: $23,755. *Scholarships, grants, and awards:* Federal Pell, FSEOG, state, college/university gift aid from institutional funds.
GIFT AID (NON-NEED-BASED) *Total amount:* $407,019 (100% external sources). *Tuition waivers:* Full or partial for employees or children of employees, senior citizens.
LOANS *Student loans:* $3,811,544 (66% need-based, 34% non-need-based). 44% of past graduating class borrowed through all loan programs. *Average indebtedness per student:* $22,542. *Average need-based loan:* Freshmen: $2826; Undergraduates: $4079. *Parent loans:* $6,080,072 (100% non-need-based). *Programs:* FFEL (Subsidized and Unsubsidized Stafford, PLUS), Perkins, college/university.
WORK-STUDY *Federal work-study:* Total amount: $832,313; 686 jobs averaging $1214. *State or other work-study/employment:* Total amount: $14,210 (100% need-based). 18 part-time jobs averaging $789.
APPLYING FOR FINANCIAL AID *Required financial aid forms:* FAFSA, CSS Financial Aid PROFILE, noncustodial (divorced/separated) parent's statement, business/farm supplement. *Financial aid deadline:* 2/1. *Notification date:* 4/1. Students must reply by 5/1 or within 2 weeks of notification.
CONTACT Ms. Elaine Solinga, Director of Financial Aid Services, Connecticut College, 270 Mohegan Avenue, New London, CT 06320-4196, 860-439-2058. *Fax:* 860-439-5357. *E-mail:* finaid@conncoll.edu.

CONSERVATORY OF MUSIC OF PUERTO RICO
San Juan, PR

CONTACT Mr. Jorge Medina, Director of Financial Aid, Conservatory of Music of Puerto Rico, 350 Rafael Lamar Street at FDR Avenue, San Juan, PR 00918, 787-751-0160 Ext. 230. *Fax:* 787-758-8268. *E-mail:* jmedina@cmpr.gobierno.pr.

CONVERSE COLLEGE
Spartanburg, SC

Tuition & fees: $22,234	Average undergraduate aid package: $18,431

ABOUT THE INSTITUTION Independent, undergraduate: women only; graduate: coed. Awards: bachelor's and master's degrees and post-master's certificates. 40 undergraduate majors. Total enrollment: 2,176. Undergraduates: 776. Freshmen: 213. Federal methodology is used as a basis for awarding need-based institutional aid.
UNDERGRADUATE EXPENSES for 2006–07 *Application fee:* $40. *Comprehensive fee:* $29,082 includes full-time tuition ($22,234) and room and board ($6848). *Part-time tuition:* $720 per credit hour. *Part-time fees:* $20 per term.
FRESHMAN FINANCIAL AID (Fall 2005, est.) 139 applied for aid; of those 85% were deemed to have need. 100% of freshmen with need received aid; of those 40% had need fully met. *Average percent of need met:* 89% (excluding resources

Converse College

awarded to replace EFC). *Average financial aid package:* $18,438 (excluding resources awarded to replace EFC). 32% of all full-time freshmen had no need and received non-need-based gift aid.

UNDERGRADUATE FINANCIAL AID (Fall 2005, est.) 443 applied for aid; of those 91% were deemed to have need. 100% of undergraduates with need received aid; of those 36% had need fully met. *Average percent of need met:* 87% (excluding resources awarded to replace EFC). *Average financial aid package:* $18,431 (excluding resources awarded to replace EFC). 29% of all full-time undergraduates had no need and received non-need-based gift aid.

GIFT AID (NEED-BASED) *Total amount:* $6,253,314 (11% federal, 20% state, 67% institutional, 2% external sources). *Receiving aid:* Freshmen: 62% (118); All full-time undergraduates: 70% (402). *Average award:* Freshmen: $16,115; Undergraduates: $15,292. *Scholarships, grants, and awards:* Federal Pell, FSEOG, state, private, college/university gift aid from institutional funds.

GIFT AID (NON-NEED-BASED) *Total amount:* $3,348,105 (23% state, 74% institutional, 3% external sources). *Receiving aid:* Freshmen: 23% (44); Undergraduates: 21% (120). *Average Award: Freshmen:* $15,966; *Undergraduates:* $16,637. *Scholarships, grants, and awards by category: Academic Interests/Achievement:* 342 awards ($3,946,696 total): general academic interests/achievements. *Creative Arts/Performance:* 134 awards ($1,129,792 total): applied art and design, music, theater/drama. *Special Achievements/Activities:* 89 awards ($640,300 total): leadership. *Special Characteristics:* 56 awards ($1,106,605 total): children and siblings of alumni, children of faculty/staff. *ROTC:* Army cooperative.

LOANS *Student loans:* $2,648,133 (81% need-based, 19% non-need-based). 58% of past graduating class borrowed through all loan programs. *Average indebtedness per student:* $16,641. *Average need-based loan:* Freshmen: $3440; Undergraduates: $4426. *Parent loans:* $850,177 (16% need-based, 84% non-need-based). *Programs:* FFEL (Subsidized and Unsubsidized Stafford, PLUS), Perkins, state.

WORK-STUDY *Federal work-study:* Total amount: $219,200; 149 jobs averaging $1425. *State or other work-study/employment:* 76 part-time jobs averaging $1000.

ATHLETIC AWARDS *Total amount:* $288,096 (44% need-based, 56% non-need-based).

APPLYING FOR FINANCIAL AID *Required financial aid form:* FAFSA. *Financial aid deadline (priority):* 3/1. *Notification date:* Continuous beginning 3/15. Students must reply by 5/1 or within 2 weeks of notification.

CONTACT Ms. Margaret P. Collins, Director of Financial Assistance, Converse College, 580 East Main Street, Spartanburg, SC 29302-0006, 864-596-9019 or toll-free 800-766-1125. *Fax:* 864-596-9749. *E-mail:* peggy.collins@converse.edu.

COOPER UNION FOR THE ADVANCEMENT OF SCIENCE AND ART
New York, NY

Tuition & fees: $1500 **Average undergraduate aid package:** $27,500

ABOUT THE INSTITUTION Independent, coed. Awards: bachelor's degrees (also offers master's program primarily made up of currently-enrolled students). 8 undergraduate majors. Total enrollment: 1,003. Undergraduates: 949. Freshmen: 216. Both federal and institutional methodology are used as a basis for awarding need-based institutional aid.

UNDERGRADUATE EXPENSES for 2006–07 *Application fee:* $50. *One-time required fee:* $150. includes mandatory fees ($1500) and room and board ($13,360). *College room only:* $9360.

FRESHMAN FINANCIAL AID (Fall 2004) 209 applied for aid; of those 37% were deemed to have need. 100% of freshmen with need received aid; of those 82% had need fully met. *Average percent of need met:* 90% (excluding resources awarded to replace EFC). *Average financial aid package:* $27,500 (excluding resources awarded to replace EFC). 100% of all full-time freshmen had no need and received non-need-based gift aid.

UNDERGRADUATE FINANCIAL AID (Fall 2004) 395 applied for aid; of those 77% were deemed to have need. 100% of undergraduates with need received aid; of those 86% had need fully met. *Average percent of need met:* 92% (excluding resources awarded to replace EFC). *Average financial aid package:* $27,500 (excluding resources awarded to replace EFC). 100% of all full-time undergraduates had no need and received non-need-based gift aid.

GIFT AID (NEED-BASED) *Total amount:* $1,790,311 (30% federal, 24% state, 32% institutional, 14% external sources). *Receiving aid:* Freshmen: 35% (78); All full-time undergraduates: 33% (305). *Average award:* Freshmen: $3325; Undergraduates: $3586. *Scholarships, grants, and awards:* Federal Pell, FSEOG, state, private, college/university gift aid from institutional funds.

GIFT AID (NON-NEED-BASED) *Total amount:* $25,145,000 (100% institutional). *Receiving aid:* Freshmen: 35% (78); Undergraduates: 33% (305). *Average Award:* Freshmen: $27,500; Undergraduates: $27,500. *Scholarships, grants, and awards by category: Academic Interests/Achievement:* architecture, engineering/technologies. *Creative Arts/Performance:* art/fine arts.

LOANS *Student loans:* $948,368 (90% need-based, 10% non-need-based). 32% of past graduating class borrowed through all loan programs. *Average indebtedness per student:* $11,617. *Average need-based loan:* Freshmen: $1848; Undergraduates: $3319. *Parent loans:* $232,194 (60% need-based, 40% non-need-based). *Programs:* FFEL (Subsidized and Unsubsidized Stafford, PLUS), Perkins, college/university.

WORK-STUDY *Federal work-study:* Total amount: $40,222; 59 jobs averaging $682. *State or other work-study/employment:* Total amount: $506,868 (33% need-based, 67% non-need-based). 455 part-time jobs averaging $1114.

APPLYING FOR FINANCIAL AID *Required financial aid forms:* FAFSA, CSS Financial Aid PROFILE. *Financial aid deadline:* 6/1 (priority: 4/15). *Notification date:* 6/1. Students must reply by 6/30 or within 2 weeks of notification.

CONTACT Ms. Mary Ruokonen, Director of Financial Aid, Cooper Union for the Advancement of Science and Art, 30 Cooper Square, New York, NY 10003-7120, 212-353-4130. *Fax:* 212-353-4343. *E-mail:* ruokon@cooper.edu.

COPPIN STATE UNIVERSITY
Baltimore, MD

Tuition & fees (MD res): $4879 **Average undergraduate aid package:** $6966

ABOUT THE INSTITUTION State-supported, coed. Awards: bachelor's and master's degrees. 26 undergraduate majors. Total enrollment: 4,003. Undergraduates: 3,092. Federal methodology is used as a basis for awarding need-based institutional aid.

UNDERGRADUATE EXPENSES for 2005–06 *Application fee:* $35. *Tuition, state resident:* full-time $3527; part-time $151 per credit hour. *Tuition, nonresident:* full-time $10,048; part-time $347 per credit hour. *Required fees:* full-time $1352; $22 per credit hour or $150 per term part-time. *College room and board:* $6239; *room only:* $3881.

FRESHMAN FINANCIAL AID (Fall 2005, est.) 571 applied for aid; of those 100% were deemed to have need. 91% of freshmen with need received aid; of those 12% had need fully met. *Average percent of need met:* 56% (excluding resources awarded to replace EFC). *Average financial aid package:* $6218 (excluding resources awarded to replace EFC). 1% of all full-time freshmen had no need and received non-need-based gift aid.

UNDERGRADUATE FINANCIAL AID (Fall 2005, est.) 2,311 applied for aid; of those 100% were deemed to have need. 90% of undergraduates with need received aid; of those 12% had need fully met. *Average percent of need met:* 63% (excluding resources awarded to replace EFC). *Average financial aid package:* $6966 (excluding resources awarded to replace EFC). 1% of all full-time undergraduates had no need and received non-need-based gift aid.

GIFT AID (NEED-BASED) *Total amount:* $8,806,193 (71% federal, 27% state, 2% institutional). *Receiving aid:* Freshmen: 64% (415); All full-time undergraduates: 63% (1,689). *Average award:* Freshmen: $4827; Undergraduates: $4521. *Scholarships, grants, and awards:* Federal Pell, FSEOG, state, private, college/university gift aid from institutional funds, Federal Nursing.

GIFT AID (NON-NEED-BASED) *Total amount:* $828,907 (4% federal, 19% state, 57% institutional, 20% external sources). *Receiving aid:* Freshmen: 12% (81); Undergraduates: 9% (244). *Average Award:* Freshmen: $2904; *Undergraduates:* $2521. *Scholarships, grants, and awards by category: Academic Interests/Achievement:* general academic interests/achievements. *ROTC:* Army.

LOANS *Student loans:* $12,854,194 (74% need-based, 26% non-need-based). 90% of past graduating class borrowed through all loan programs. *Average indebtedness per student:* $17,843. *Average need-based loan:* Freshmen: $3245; Undergraduates: $4154. *Parent loans:* $756,601 (100% non-need-based). *Programs:* Federal Direct (Subsidized and Unsubsidized Stafford), FFEL (PLUS), Perkins, alternative loans from lenders.

WORK-STUDY *Federal work-study:* Total amount: $426,138; 165 jobs averaging $2044.

ATHLETIC AWARDS *Total amount:* $1,033,660 (100% non-need-based).
APPLYING FOR FINANCIAL AID *Required financial aid form:* FAFSA. *Financial aid deadline (priority):* 3/1. *Notification date:* 4/15. Students must reply within 4 weeks of notification.
CONTACT Fay Tayree, Associate Director of Financial Aid, Coppin State University, 2500 West North Avenue, Baltimore, MD 21216-3698, 410-951-3636 or toll-free 800-635-3674. Fax: 410-951-3637. E-mail: ftayree@coppin.edu.

CORBAN COLLEGE
Salem, OR

Tuition & fees: $19,294   Average undergraduate aid package: $12,117

ABOUT THE INSTITUTION Independent religious, coed. Awards: associate, bachelor's, and master's degrees. 46 undergraduate majors. Total enrollment: 851. Undergraduates: 804. Freshmen: 205. Federal methodology is used as a basis for awarding need-based institutional aid.
UNDERGRADUATE EXPENSES for 2006–07 *Application fee:* $40. *Comprehensive fee:* $26,378 includes full-time tuition ($19,084), mandatory fees ($210), and room and board ($7084). *Part-time tuition:* $795 per credit.
FRESHMAN FINANCIAL AID (Fall 2005, est.) 186 applied for aid; of those 90% were deemed to have need. 100% of freshmen with need received aid; of those 9% had need fully met. *Average percent of need met:* 62% (excluding resources awarded to replace EFC). *Average financial aid package:* $12,195 (excluding resources awarded to replace EFC). 13% of all full-time freshmen had no need and received non-need-based gift aid.
UNDERGRADUATE FINANCIAL AID (Fall 2005, est.) 606 applied for aid; of those 92% were deemed to have need. 100% of undergraduates with need received aid; of those 13% had need fully met. *Average percent of need met:* 61% (excluding resources awarded to replace EFC). *Average financial aid package:* $12,117 (excluding resources awarded to replace EFC). 13% of all full-time undergraduates had no need and received non-need-based gift aid.
GIFT AID (NEED-BASED) *Total amount:* $4,340,183 (13% federal, 5% state, 72% institutional, 10% external sources). *Receiving aid:* Freshmen: 86% (168); All full-time undergraduates: 86% (558). *Average award:* Freshmen: $9593; Undergraduates: $8955. *Scholarships, grants, and awards:* Federal Pell, FSEOG, state, private, college/university gift aid from institutional funds.
GIFT AID (NON-NEED-BASED) *Total amount:* $473,397 (83% institutional, 17% external sources). *Receiving aid:* Freshmen: 3% (6); Undergraduates: 6% (42). *Average Award:* Freshmen: $10,006; Undergraduates: $7847. *Scholarships, grants, and awards by category:* Academic Interests/Achievement: 451 awards ($1,556,000 total): general academic interests/achievements. Creative Arts/Performance: 18 awards ($31,750 total): music, performing arts. Special Achievements/Activities: 120 awards ($78,800 total): general special achievements/activities, hobbies/interests, leadership, memberships, religious involvement. Special Characteristics: 162 awards ($191,000 total): children and siblings of alumni, children of faculty/staff, international students, relatives of clergy, siblings of current students. *ROTC:* Army cooperative, Air Force cooperative.
LOANS *Student loans:* $4,145,883 (76% need-based, 24% non-need-based). 70% of past graduating class borrowed through all loan programs. *Average indebtedness per student:* $23,400. *Average need-based loan:* Freshmen: $3036; Undergraduates: $3846. *Parent loans:* $804,287 (55% need-based, 45% non-need-based). *Programs:* Federal Direct (Subsidized and Unsubsidized Stafford, PLUS), Perkins, state, alternative loans.
WORK-STUDY *Federal work-study:* Total amount: $68,141; 110 jobs averaging $619.
ATHLETIC AWARDS *Total amount:* $651,418 (79% need-based, 21% non-need-based).
APPLYING FOR FINANCIAL AID *Required financial aid form:* FAFSA. *Financial aid deadline (priority):* 2/15. *Notification date:* Continuous beginning 3/1. Students must reply within 4 weeks of notification.
CONTACT Nathan Warthan, Director of Financial Aid, Corban College, 5000 Deer Park Drive, SE, Salem, OR 97301-9392, 503-375-7006 or toll-free 800-845-3005 (out-of-state). Fax: 503-585-4316. E-mail: nwarthan@corban.edu.

CORCORAN COLLEGE OF ART AND DESIGN
Washington, DC

Tuition & fees: $22,800   Average undergraduate aid package: $9437

ABOUT THE INSTITUTION Independent, coed. Awards: associate, bachelor's, and master's degrees. 10 undergraduate majors. Total enrollment: 590. Undergraduates: 520. Freshmen: 52. Federal methodology is used as a basis for awarding need-based institutional aid.
UNDERGRADUATE EXPENSES for 2005–06 *Application fee:* $40. *Comprehensive fee:* $32,850 includes full-time tuition ($22,700), mandatory fees ($100), and room and board ($10,050). *College room only:* $8150. Full-time tuition and fees vary according to degree level. *Part-time tuition:* $630 per credit. *Part-time fees:* $100. Part-time tuition and fees vary according to degree level. *Payment plan:* Installment.
FRESHMAN FINANCIAL AID (Fall 2004) 67 applied for aid; of those 100% were deemed to have need. 100% of freshmen with need received aid. *Average percent of need met:* 42% (excluding resources awarded to replace EFC). *Average financial aid package:* $6139 (excluding resources awarded to replace EFC). 12% of all full-time freshmen had no need and received non-need-based gift aid.
UNDERGRADUATE FINANCIAL AID (Fall 2004) 235 applied for aid; of those 100% were deemed to have need. 100% of undergraduates with need received aid. *Average percent of need met:* 26% (excluding resources awarded to replace EFC). *Average financial aid package:* $9437 (excluding resources awarded to replace EFC). 20% of all full-time undergraduates had no need and received non-need-based gift aid.
GIFT AID (NEED-BASED) *Total amount:* $1,106,414 (48% federal, 2% state, 50% external sources). *Receiving aid:* Freshmen: 75% (58); All full-time undergraduates: 61% (186). *Average award:* Freshmen: $4640; Undergraduates: $5948. *Scholarships, grants, and awards:* Federal Pell, FSEOG, state, college/university gift aid from institutional funds.
GIFT AID (NON-NEED-BASED) *Total amount:* $754,810 (1% state, 49% institutional, 50% external sources). *Receiving aid:* Freshmen: 52% (40); Undergraduates: 66% (203). *Average Award:* Freshmen: $9390; Undergraduates: $4257. *Scholarships, grants, and awards by category:* Academic Interests/Achievement: 282 awards ($605,325 total): general academic interests/achievements. Creative Arts/Performance: 53 awards ($365,455 total): applied art and design. *Tuition waivers:* Full or partial for employees or children of employees.
LOANS *Student loans:* $2,406,139 (43% need-based, 57% non-need-based). 73% of past graduating class borrowed through all loan programs. *Average indebtedness per student:* $34,153. *Average need-based loan:* Freshmen: $3506; Undergraduates: $4749. *Parent loans:* $1,308,027 (100% non-need-based). *Programs:* FFEL (Subsidized and Unsubsidized Stafford, PLUS), Perkins.
WORK-STUDY *Federal work-study:* Total amount: $81,925; 88 jobs averaging $942.
APPLYING FOR FINANCIAL AID *Required financial aid forms:* FAFSA, institution's own form. *Financial aid deadline (priority):* 4/15. *Notification date:* Continuous. Students must reply within 2 weeks of notification.
CONTACT Diane Morris, Financial Aid Director, Corcoran College of Art and Design, 500 17th Street, NW, Washington, DC 20006-4804, 202-639-1816 or toll-free 888-CORCORAN (out-of-state). Fax: 202-737-6921. E-mail: dmorris@corcoran.org.

CORNELL COLLEGE
Mount Vernon, IA

Tuition & fees: $23,680   Average undergraduate aid package: $18,510

ABOUT THE INSTITUTION Independent Methodist, coed. Awards: bachelor's degrees. 46 undergraduate majors. Total enrollment: 1,179. Undergraduates: 1,179. Freshmen: 319. Both federal and institutional methodology are used as a basis for awarding need-based institutional aid.
UNDERGRADUATE EXPENSES for 2005–06 *Application fee:* $30. *Comprehensive fee:* $30,110 includes full-time tuition ($23,500), mandatory fees ($180), and room and board ($6430). *College room only:* $3010. Full-time tuition and fees vary according to reciprocity agreements. Room and board charges vary according to board plan. *Part-time tuition:* $734 per credit. *Part-time fees:* $180 per year. Part-time tuition and fees vary according to course load. *Payment plan:* Installment.
FRESHMAN FINANCIAL AID (Fall 2005, est.) 268 applied for aid; of those 83% were deemed to have need. 100% of freshmen with need received aid; of those 52% had need fully met. *Average percent of need met:* 100% (excluding

Cornell College

resources awarded to replace EFC). *Average financial aid package:* $21,795 (excluding resources awarded to replace EFC). 27% of all full-time freshmen had no need and received non-need-based gift aid.

UNDERGRADUATE FINANCIAL AID (Fall 2005, est.) 1,051 applied for aid; of those 89% were deemed to have need. 100% of undergraduates with need received aid; of those 50% had need fully met. *Average percent of need met:* 91% (excluding resources awarded to replace EFC). *Average financial aid package:* $18,510 (excluding resources awarded to replace EFC). 25% of all full-time undergraduates had no need and received non-need-based gift aid.

GIFT AID (NEED-BASED) *Total amount:* $14,107,129 (6% federal, 5% state, 86% institutional, 3% external sources). *Receiving aid:* Freshmen: 70% (222); All full-time undergraduates: 80% (940). *Average award:* Freshmen: $17,905; Undergraduates: $15,005. *Scholarships, grants, and awards:* Federal Pell, FSEOG, state, private, college/university gift aid from institutional funds.

GIFT AID (NON-NEED-BASED) *Total amount:* $3,453,414 (99% institutional, 1% external sources). *Receiving aid:* Freshmen: 65% (207); Undergraduates: 66% (773). *Average Award:* Freshmen: $10,950; Undergraduates: $11,705. *Scholarships, grants, and awards by category: Academic Interests/Achievement:* 390 awards ($5,130,830 total): general academic interests/achievements. *Creative Arts/Performance:* 156 awards ($1,182,397 total): art/fine arts, music, theater/drama. *Special Achievements/Activities:* 453 awards ($3,674,268 total): community service, religious involvement. *Special Characteristics:* 142 awards ($1,703,265 total): children of educators, children of faculty/staff, ethnic background, international students, local/state students. *Tuition waivers:* Full or partial for employees or children of employees, adult students, senior citizens.

LOANS *Student loans:* $4,273,285 (65% need-based, 35% non-need-based). 78% of past graduating class borrowed through all loan programs. *Average indebtedness per student:* $23,185. *Average need-based loan:* Freshmen: $3155; Undergraduates: $4370. *Parent loans:* $784,515 (100% non-need-based). *Programs:* FFEL (Subsidized and Unsubsidized Stafford, PLUS), Perkins, state, college/university.

WORK-STUDY *Federal work-study:* Total amount: $534,345; 515 jobs averaging $1038. *State or other work-study/employment:* Total amount: $184,936 (100% non-need-based). 193 part-time jobs averaging $960.

APPLYING FOR FINANCIAL AID *Required financial aid forms:* FAFSA, institution's own form, noncustodial (divorced/separated) parent's statement. *Financial aid deadline:* 3/1. *Notification date:* Continuous beginning 12/15. Students must reply by 5/1 or within 2 weeks of notification.

CONTACT Ms. Cindi P. Reints, Director of Financial Assistance, Cornell College, Wade House, 600 1st Street West, Mount Vernon, IA 52314-1098, 319-895-4216 or toll-free 800-747-1112. Fax: 319-895-4106. E-mail: creints@cornellcollege.edu.

CORNELL UNIVERSITY
Ithaca, NY

Tuition & fees: $31,467 **Average undergraduate aid package: $27,100**

ABOUT THE INSTITUTION Independent, coed. Awards: bachelor's, master's, doctoral, and first professional degrees. 156 undergraduate majors. Total enrollment: 19,447. Undergraduates: 13,515. Freshmen: 3,076. Institutional methodology is used as a basis for awarding need-based institutional aid.

UNDERGRADUATE EXPENSES for 2005-06 *Application fee:* $65. *Comprehensive fee:* $41,717 includes full-time tuition ($31,300), mandatory fees ($167), and room and board ($10,250). *College room only:* $6080. Room and board charges vary according to board plan and housing facility. *Payment plan:* Installment.

FRESHMAN FINANCIAL AID (Fall 2005, est.) 1967 applied for aid; of those 76% were deemed to have need. 100% of freshmen with need received aid; of those 100% had need fully met. *Average percent of need met:* 100% (excluding resources awarded to replace EFC). *Average financial aid package:* $26,900 (excluding resources awarded to replace EFC).

UNDERGRADUATE FINANCIAL AID (Fall 2005, est.) 7,235 applied for aid; of those 88% were deemed to have need. 100% of undergraduates with need received aid; of those 100% had need fully met. *Average percent of need met:* 100% (excluding resources awarded to replace EFC). *Average financial aid package:* $27,100 (excluding resources awarded to replace EFC).

GIFT AID (NEED-BASED) *Total amount:* $123,538,000 (8% federal, 5% state, 82% institutional, 5% external sources). *Receiving aid:* Freshmen: 46% (1,421); All full-time undergraduates: 44% (5,997). *Average award:* Freshmen: $21,000; Undergraduates: $20,600. *Scholarships, grants, and awards:* Federal Pell, FSEOG, state, private, college/university gift aid from institutional funds.

GIFT AID (NON-NEED-BASED) *Tuition waivers:* Full or partial for employees or children of employees. *ROTC:* Army, Air Force.

LOANS *Student loans:* $45,404,000 (100% need-based). 54% of past graduating class borrowed through all loan programs. *Average indebtedness per student:* $23,450. *Average need-based loan:* Freshmen: $6300; Undergraduates: $7600. *Parent loans:* $10,772,000 (100% need-based). *Programs:* Federal Direct (Subsidized and Unsubsidized Stafford, PLUS), FFEL (Subsidized and Unsubsidized Stafford, PLUS), Perkins, college/university, Key Bank Alternative Loans.

WORK-STUDY *Federal work-study:* Total amount: $8,423,000; 5,262 jobs averaging $1881.

APPLYING FOR FINANCIAL AID *Required financial aid forms:* FAFSA, institution's own form, CSS Financial Aid PROFILE, noncustodial (divorced/separated) parent's statement, business/farm supplement, Prior year tax. *Financial aid deadline:* 2/11. *Notification date:* 4/1. Students must reply by 5/1 or within 2 weeks of notification.

CONTACT Mr. Thomas Keane, Director of Financial Aid and Student Employment, Cornell University, 410 Thurston Avenue, Ithaca, NY 14853-2488, 607-255-5147.

CORNERSTONE UNIVERSITY
Grand Rapids, MI

Tuition & fees: $14,700 **Average undergraduate aid package: $13,320**

ABOUT THE INSTITUTION Independent nondenominational, coed. Awards: associate, bachelor's, master's, and first professional degrees. 52 undergraduate majors. Total enrollment: 2,515. Undergraduates: 2,172. Freshmen: 384. Federal methodology is used as a basis for awarding need-based institutional aid.

UNDERGRADUATE EXPENSES for 2005-06 *Application fee:* $25. *Comprehensive fee:* $20,500 includes full-time tuition ($14,700) and room and board ($5800). *College room only:* $2650. Room and board charges vary according to board plan. *Part-time tuition:* $595 per hour. Part-time tuition and fees vary according to course load. *Payment plan:* Installment.

FRESHMAN FINANCIAL AID (Fall 2004) 269 applied for aid; of those 83% were deemed to have need. 100% of freshmen with need received aid; of those 24% had need fully met. *Average percent of need met:* 88% (excluding resources awarded to replace EFC). *Average financial aid package:* $13,534 (excluding resources awarded to replace EFC). 16% of all full-time freshmen had no need and received non-need-based gift aid.

UNDERGRADUATE FINANCIAL AID (Fall 2004) 1,108 applied for aid; of those 79% were deemed to have need. 100% of undergraduates with need received aid; of those 20% had need fully met. *Average percent of need met:* 85% (excluding resources awarded to replace EFC). *Average financial aid package:* $13,320 (excluding resources awarded to replace EFC). 16% of all full-time undergraduates had no need and received non-need-based gift aid.

GIFT AID (NEED-BASED) *Total amount:* $5,782,631 (21% federal, 22% state, 53% institutional, 4% external sources). *Receiving aid:* Freshmen: 82% (222); All full-time undergraduates: 76% (865). *Average award:* Freshmen: $7852; Undergraduates: $6656. *Scholarships, grants, and awards:* Federal Pell, FSEOG, state, private, college/university gift aid from institutional funds.

GIFT AID (NON-NEED-BASED) *Total amount:* $1,044,386 (27% state, 65% institutional, 8% external sources). *Receiving aid:* Freshmen: 79% (214); Undergraduates: 71% (806). *Average Award:* Freshmen: $4756; Undergraduates: $3472. *Scholarships, grants, and awards by category: Academic Interests/Achievement:* 987 awards ($1,937,925 total): business, education, general academic interests/achievements, religion/biblical studies. *Creative Arts/Performance:* 76 awards ($214,472 total): music. *Special Achievements/Activities:* 73 awards ($101,442 total): leadership, religious involvement. *Special Characteristics:* 256 awards ($194,572 total): children and siblings of alumni, children of faculty/staff, children of union members/company employees, ethnic background, general special characteristics, international students, members of minority groups, out-of-state students. *Tuition waivers:* Full or partial for employees or children of employees. *ROTC:* Army cooperative.

LOANS *Student loans:* $7,657,504 (75% need-based, 25% non-need-based). 79% of past graduating class borrowed through all loan programs. *Average indebtedness per student:* $23,710. *Average need-based loan:* Freshmen: $3160;

Undergraduates: $4077. *Parent loans:* $605,312 (44% need-based, 56% non-need-based). *Programs:* FFEL (Subsidized and Unsubsidized Stafford, PLUS), Perkins, state, college/university.
WORK-STUDY *Federal work-study:* Total amount: $214,083; 148 jobs averaging $1447. *State or other work-study/employment:* Total amount: $50,750 (100% need-based). 32 part-time jobs averaging $1586.
ATHLETIC AWARDS *Total amount:* $723,150 (58% need-based, 42% non-need-based).
APPLYING FOR FINANCIAL AID *Required financial aid form:* FAFSA. *Financial aid deadline:* 3/1. *Notification date:* Continuous beginning 3/1. Students must reply within 2 weeks of notification.
CONTACT Mr. Geoff Marsh, Director of Student Financial Services, Cornerstone University, 1001 East Beltline Avenue, NE, Grand Rapids, MI 49525-5897, 616-222-1424 or toll-free 800-787-9778. *Fax:* 616-222-1400. *E-mail:* geoff_a_marsh@cornerstone.edu.

CORNISH COLLEGE OF THE ARTS
Seattle, WA

ABOUT THE INSTITUTION Independent, coed. Awards: bachelor's degrees. 16 undergraduate majors. Total enrollment: 768. Undergraduates: 768. Freshmen: 164.
GIFT AID (NEED-BASED) *Scholarships, grants, and awards:* Federal Pell, FSEOG, state, private, college/university gift aid from institutional funds.
GIFT AID (NON-NEED-BASED) *Scholarships, grants, and awards by category:* Academic Interests/Achievement: general academic interests/achievements. Creative Arts/Performance: art/fine arts, dance, music, theater/drama.
LOANS *Programs:* FFEL (Subsidized and Unsubsidized Stafford, PLUS), Perkins, college/university.
APPLYING FOR FINANCIAL AID *Required financial aid forms:* FAFSA, institution's own form.
CONTACT Sharron Starling, Office of Admissions, Cornish College of the Arts, 1000 Lenora Street, Seattle, WA 98121, 206-726-5017 or toll-free 800-726-ARTS. *Fax:* 206-720-1011. *E-mail:* admissions@cornish.edu.

COVENANT COLLEGE
Lookout Mountain, GA

CONTACT Mrs. Carolyn Hays, Assistant Director of Student Financial Planning, Covenant College, 14049 Scenic Highway, Lookout Mountain, GA 30750, 706-820-1560 Ext. 1150 or toll-free 888-451-2683. *Fax:* 706-820-2820. *E-mail:* hays@covenant.edu.

COX COLLEGE OF NURSING AND HEALTH SCIENCES
Springfield, MO

CONTACT Brenda Smith, Financial Aid Coordinator, Cox College of Nursing and Health Sciences, 1423 North Jefferson Avenue, Springfield, MO 65802, 417-269-3401 or toll-free 866-898-5355 (in-state). *Fax:* 417-269-3586. *E-mail:* bjsmit1@coxcollege.edu.

CREIGHTON UNIVERSITY
Omaha, NE

Tuition & fees: $22,378	Average undergraduate aid package: $20,201

ABOUT THE INSTITUTION Independent Roman Catholic (Jesuit), coed. Awards: associate, bachelor's, master's, doctoral, and first professional degrees. 46 undergraduate majors. Total enrollment: 6,791. Undergraduates: 3,988. Freshmen: 971. Federal methodology is used as a basis for awarding need-based institutional aid.
UNDERGRADUATE EXPENSES for 2005–06 *Application fee:* $40. *Comprehensive fee:* $29,918 includes full-time tuition ($21,576), mandatory fees ($802), and room and board ($7540). *College room only:* $4250. Room and board charges vary according to board plan and housing facility. *Part-time tuition:* $675 per semester hour. *Part-time fees:* $134 per semester hour. *Payment plan:* Installment.
FRESHMAN FINANCIAL AID (Fall 2005, est.) 766 applied for aid; of those 78% were deemed to have need. 97% of freshmen with need received aid; of those 48% had need fully met. *Average percent of need met:* 91% (excluding resources awarded to replace EFC). *Average financial aid package:* $21,204 (excluding resources awarded to replace EFC). 36% of all full-time freshmen had no need and received non-need-based gift aid.
UNDERGRADUATE FINANCIAL AID (Fall 2005, est.) 2,570 applied for aid; of those 83% were deemed to have need. 100% of undergraduates with need received aid; of those 48% had need fully met. *Average percent of need met:* 86% (excluding resources awarded to replace EFC). *Average financial aid package:* $20,201 (excluding resources awarded to replace EFC). 34% of all full-time undergraduates had no need and received non-need-based gift aid.
GIFT AID (NEED-BASED) *Total amount:* $22,230,605 (10% federal, 1% state, 82% institutional, 7% external sources). *Receiving aid:* Freshmen: 59% (577); All full-time undergraduates: 53% (1,986). *Average award:* Freshmen: $15,096; Undergraduates: $12,003. *Scholarships, grants, and awards:* Federal Pell, FSEOG, state, private, college/university gift aid from institutional funds, Federal Nursing.
GIFT AID (NON-NEED-BASED) *Total amount:* $9,020,945 (97% institutional, 3% external sources). *Receiving aid:* Freshmen: 48% (463); Undergraduates: 37% (1,378). *Average Award:* Freshmen: $8752; Undergraduates: $8627. *Scholarships, grants, and awards by category:* Academic Interests/Achievement: business, education, general academic interests/achievements, military science. Creative Arts/Performance: art/fine arts, creative writing, debating. Special Characteristics: children of faculty/staff, first-generation college students, handicapped students, local/state students, members of minority groups, religious affiliation, siblings of current students. *Tuition waivers:* Full or partial for employees or children of employees, adult students. *ROTC:* Army, Air Force cooperative.
LOANS *Student loans:* $13,484,288 (76% need-based, 24% non-need-based). 74% of past graduating class borrowed through all loan programs. *Average indebtedness per student:* $26,013. *Average need-based loan:* Freshmen: $5188; Undergraduates: $6575. *Parent loans:* $5,216,803 (100% non-need-based). *Programs:* FFEL (Subsidized and Unsubsidized Stafford, PLUS), Perkins, Federal Nursing, college/university.
WORK-STUDY *Federal work-study:* Total amount: $1,533,785; 846 jobs averaging $1724.
ATHLETIC AWARDS *Total amount:* $2,073,186 (9% need-based, 91% non-need-based).
APPLYING FOR FINANCIAL AID *Required financial aid forms:* FAFSA, institution's own form. *Financial aid deadline (priority):* 5/15. *Notification date:* Continuous. Students must reply within 4 weeks of notification.
CONTACT Sarah Sell, Assistant Director of Financial Aid, Creighton University, 2500 California Plaza, Omaha, NE 68178, 402-280-2731 or toll-free 800-282-5835. *Fax:* 402-280-2895. *E-mail:* sarahsell@creighton.edu.

CRICHTON COLLEGE
Memphis, TN

CONTACT Mrs. Dede Pirtle, Financial Aid Director, Crichton College, 255 North Highland, Memphis, TN 38111, 901-320-9700 Ext. 1030 or toll-free 800-960-9777. *Fax:* 901-320-9709. *E-mail:* dede@crichton.edu.

THE CRISWELL COLLEGE
Dallas, TX

CONTACT Kirk Spencer, Financial Aid Director, The Criswell College, 4010 Gaston Avenue, Dallas, TX 75246, 800-899-0012. *Fax:* 214-818-1310. *E-mail:* kspencer@criswell.edu.

CROSSROADS BIBLE COLLEGE
Indianapolis, IN

CONTACT Mrs. Phyllis Dodson, Director of Financial Aid, Crossroads Bible College, 601 North Shortridge Road, Indianapolis, IN 46219, 317-352-8736 Ext. 28 or toll-free 800-273-2224 Ext. 230. *Fax:* 317-352-9145.

Crossroads College

CROSSROADS COLLEGE
Rochester, MN

CONTACT Polly Kellogg-Bradley, Director of Financial Aid, Crossroads College, 920 Mayowood Road SW, Rochester, MN 55902-2275, 507-535-3308 or toll-free 800-456-7651. *Fax:* 507-288-9046. *E-mail:* pkellogbradley@crossroadscollege.edu.

CROWN COLLEGE
St. Bonifacius, MN

Tuition & fees: $17,054   **Average undergraduate aid package: $11,529**

ABOUT THE INSTITUTION Independent religious, coed. Awards: associate, bachelor's, and master's degrees. 30 undergraduate majors. Total enrollment: 1,304. Undergraduates: 1,188. Freshmen: 171. Both federal and institutional methodology are used as a basis for awarding need-based institutional aid.
UNDERGRADUATE EXPENSES for 2006–07 *Application fee:* $35. *Comprehensive fee:* $24,070 includes full-time tuition ($17,054) and room and board ($7016). *College room only:* $3652. *Part-time tuition:* $713 per credit.
FRESHMAN FINANCIAL AID (Fall 2004) 151 applied for aid; of those 91% were deemed to have need. 100% of freshmen with need received aid; of those 9% had need fully met. *Average percent of need met:* 57% (excluding resources awarded to replace EFC). *Average financial aid package:* $10,007 (excluding resources awarded to replace EFC). 8% of all full-time freshmen had no need and received non-need-based gift aid.
UNDERGRADUATE FINANCIAL AID (Fall 2004) 577 applied for aid; of those 87% were deemed to have need. 100% of undergraduates with need received aid; of those 8% had need fully met. *Average percent of need met:* 61% (excluding resources awarded to replace EFC). *Average financial aid package:* $11,529 (excluding resources awarded to replace EFC). 8% of all full-time undergraduates had no need and received non-need-based gift aid.
GIFT AID (NEED-BASED) *Total amount:* $1,771,131 (46% federal, 34% state, 20% institutional). *Receiving aid:* Freshmen: 56% (94); All full-time undergraduates: 47% (371). *Average award:* Freshmen: $4036; Undergraduates: $4675. *Scholarships, grants, and awards:* Federal Pell, FSEOG, state, private, college/university gift aid from institutional funds.
GIFT AID (NON-NEED-BASED) *Total amount:* $1,991,126 (92% institutional, 8% external sources). *Receiving aid:* Freshmen: 76% (128); Undergraduates: 58% (462). *Average Award:* Freshmen: $2500; Undergraduates: $2606. *Scholarships, grants, and awards by category:* Academic Interests/Achievement: 444 awards ($644,690 total): general academic interests/achievements. *Creative Arts/Performance:* 24 awards ($28,225 total): music. *Special Achievements/Activities:* 72 awards ($342,338 total): leadership. *Special Characteristics:* 142 awards ($402,245 total): children of faculty/staff, international students, members of minority groups, relatives of clergy, siblings of current students.
LOANS *Student loans:* $4,293,773 (43% need-based, 57% non-need-based). 85% of past graduating class borrowed through all loan programs. *Average indebtedness per student:* $22,672. *Average need-based loan:* Freshmen: $3193; Undergraduates: $4075. *Parent loans:* $748,019 (100% non-need-based). *Programs:* FFEL (Subsidized and Unsubsidized Stafford, PLUS), Perkins, state, SELF Loans, CitiAssist Loans, Signature Loans, Bremer Education Loans, U.S. Bank No Fee Educational Loans.
WORK-STUDY *Federal work-study:* Total amount: $348,368; 182 jobs averaging $2132. *State or other work-study/employment:* Total amount: $8796 (100% need-based). 5 part-time jobs averaging $3160.
APPLYING FOR FINANCIAL AID *Required financial aid forms:* FAFSA, institution's own form. *Financial aid deadline (priority):* 4/1. *Notification date:* Continuous beginning 4/2. Students must reply within 4 weeks of notification.
CONTACT Cheryl Fernandez, Director of Financial Aid, Crown College, 8700 College View Drive, St. Bonifacius, MN 55375-9001, 952-446-4177 or toll-free 800-68-CROWN. *Fax:* 952-446-4178. *E-mail:* finlaid@crown.edu.

THE CULINARY INSTITUTE OF AMERICA
Hyde Park, NY

Tuition & fees: $20,160   **Average undergraduate aid package: $11,229**

ABOUT THE INSTITUTION Independent, coed. Awards: bachelor's degrees. 2 undergraduate majors. Total enrollment: 2,713. Undergraduates: 2,713. Federal methodology is used as a basis for awarding need-based institutional aid.
UNDERGRADUATE EXPENSES for 2005–06 *Application fee:* $30. *Comprehensive fee:* $26,980 includes full-time tuition ($19,180), mandatory fees ($980), and room and board ($6820). Full-time tuition and fees vary according to degree level. Room and board charges vary according to housing facility. *Payment plan:* Installment.
UNDERGRADUATE FINANCIAL AID (Fall 2004) 2,415 applied for aid; of those 91% were deemed to have need. 97% of undergraduates with need received aid; of those 4% had need fully met. *Average percent of need met:* 43% (excluding resources awarded to replace EFC). *Average financial aid package:* $11,229 (excluding resources awarded to replace EFC). 8% of all full-time undergraduates had no need and received non-need-based gift aid.
GIFT AID (NEED-BASED) *Total amount:* $11,121,321 (23% federal, 7% state, 65% institutional, 5% external sources). *Receiving aid:* All full-time undergraduates: 77% (1,960). *Average award:* Undergraduates: $3000. *Scholarships, grants, and awards:* Federal Pell, FSEOG, state, private, college/university gift aid from institutional funds.
GIFT AID (NON-NEED-BASED) *Total amount:* $2,190,657 (7% federal, 2% state, 91% institutional). *Receiving aid:* Undergraduates: 39% (1,000). *Average Award:* Undergraduates: $3000. *Scholarships, grants, and awards by category:* Academic Interests/Achievement: 513 awards ($1,000,000 total): general academic interests/achievements. *Creative Arts/Performance:* 11 awards ($75,000 total): general creative arts/performance. *Special Achievements/Activities:* 10 awards ($50,000 total): general special achievements/activities. *Special Characteristics:* adult students, children and siblings of alumni, children of faculty/staff, general special characteristics, handicapped students, international students, members of minority groups, veterans. *Tuition waivers:* Full or partial for employees or children of employees.
LOANS *Student loans:* $25,844,275 (78% need-based, 22% non-need-based). 92% of past graduating class borrowed through all loan programs. *Average indebtedness per student:* $18,000. *Average need-based loan:* Undergraduates: $3252. *Parent loans:* $5,771,131 (100% non-need-based). *Programs:* FFEL (Subsidized and Unsubsidized Stafford, PLUS), Perkins, alternative loans.
WORK-STUDY *Federal work-study:* Total amount: $525,729; 928 jobs averaging $567.
APPLYING FOR FINANCIAL AID *Required financial aid form:* FAFSA. *Financial aid deadline:* 2/15. *Notification date:* Continuous beginning 4/15. Students must reply within 2 weeks of notification.
CONTACT Patricia A. Arcuri, Director of Financial Aid, The Culinary Institute of America, 1946 Campus Drive, Hyde Park, NY 12538-1499, 845-451-1243 or toll-free 800-CULINARY. *Fax:* 845-905-4030. *E-mail:* p_arcuri@culinary.edu.

CULVER-STOCKTON COLLEGE
Canton, MO

Tuition & fees: $15,250   **Average undergraduate aid package: $11,986**

ABOUT THE INSTITUTION Independent religious, coed. Awards: bachelor's degrees. 29 undergraduate majors. Total enrollment: 840. Undergraduates: 840. Freshmen: 155. Federal methodology is used as a basis for awarding need-based institutional aid.
UNDERGRADUATE EXPENSES for 2006–07 *Application fee:* $25. *Comprehensive fee:* $21,796 includes full-time tuition ($15,250) and room and board ($6546). *College room only:* $3030. *Part-time tuition:* $400 per credit hour. *Part-time fees:* $10 per credit hour.
FRESHMAN FINANCIAL AID (Fall 2005, est.) 153 applied for aid; of those 92% were deemed to have need. 100% of freshmen with need received aid; of those 21% had need fully met. *Average percent of need met:* 74% (excluding resources awarded to replace EFC). *Average financial aid package:* $12,226 (excluding resources awarded to replace EFC). 8% of all full-time freshmen had no need and received non-need-based gift aid.
UNDERGRADUATE FINANCIAL AID (Fall 2005, est.) 722 applied for aid; of those 89% were deemed to have need. 100% of undergraduates with need received aid; of those 26% had need fully met. *Average percent of need met:* 75% (excluding resources awarded to replace EFC). *Average financial aid package:* $11,986 (excluding resources awarded to replace EFC). 10% of all full-time undergraduates had no need and received non-need-based gift aid.

GIFT AID (NEED-BASED) *Total amount:* $4,587,878 (18% federal, 7% state, 73% institutional, 2% external sources). *Receiving aid:* Freshmen: 92% (141); All full-time undergraduates: 89% (643). *Average award:* Freshmen: $9537; Undergraduates: $8650. *Scholarships, grants, and awards:* Federal Pell, FSEOG, state, private, college/university gift aid from institutional funds.
GIFT AID (NON-NEED-BASED) *Total amount:* $700,254 (2% state, 86% institutional, 12% external sources). *Receiving aid:* Freshmen: 17% (26); Undergraduates: 15% (108). *Average Award:* Freshmen: $14,200; Undergraduates: $12,103. *Scholarships, grants, and awards by category:* Academic Interests/Achievement: 422 awards ($2,101,721 total): general academic interests/achievements, international studies. *Creative Arts/Performance:* 184 awards ($373,600 total): art/fine arts, debating, music, theater/drama. *Special Achievements/Activities:* 22 awards ($9750 total): cheerleading/drum major, leadership. *Special Characteristics:* 134 awards ($341,146 total): children and siblings of alumni, children of faculty/staff, international students, local/state students, religious affiliation.
LOANS *Student loans:* $4,626,112 (67% need-based, 33% non-need-based). 89% of past graduating class borrowed through all loan programs. *Average indebtedness per student:* $18,429. *Average need-based loan:* Freshmen: $2899; Undergraduates: $3680. *Parent loans:* $1,526,939 (36% need-based, 64% non-need-based). *Programs:* Federal Direct (Subsidized and Unsubsidized Stafford, PLUS), Perkins, Federal Nursing, state, college/university.
WORK-STUDY *Federal work-study:* Total amount: $73,717; 60 jobs averaging $1229. *State or other work-study/employment:* Total amount: $188,701 (47% need-based, 53% non-need-based). 161 part-time jobs averaging $1419.
ATHLETIC AWARDS *Total amount:* $1,037,413 (77% need-based, 23% non-need-based).
APPLYING FOR FINANCIAL AID *Required financial aid form:* FAFSA. *Financial aid deadline:* 6/15 (priority: 4/1). *Notification date:* Continuous beginning 2/15. Students must reply within 2 weeks of notification.
CONTACT Ms. Tina M. Wiseman, Director of Financial Aid, Culver-Stockton College, One College Hill, Canton, MO 63435, 573-288-6306 Ext. 6307 or toll-free 800-537-1883. *Fax:* 573-288-6308. *E-mail:* twiseman@culver.edu.

CUMBERLAND COLLEGE
Williamsburg, KY

See University of the Cumberlands.

CUMBERLAND UNIVERSITY
Lebanon, TN

CONTACT Mr. Larry Vaughan, Director of Financial Aid, Cumberland University, One Cumberland Square, Lebanon, TN 37087-3554, 615-444-2562 Ext. 1222 or toll-free 800-467-0562. *Fax:* 615-443-8424. *E-mail:* lvaughan@cumberland.edu.

CURRY COLLEGE
Milton, MA

Tuition & fees: $24,300	Average undergraduate aid package: $14,733

ABOUT THE INSTITUTION Independent, coed. Awards: bachelor's and master's degrees. 28 undergraduate majors. Total enrollment: 3,202. Undergraduates: 2,955. Freshmen: 593. Federal methodology is used as a basis for awarding need-based institutional aid.
UNDERGRADUATE EXPENSES for 2006–07 *Application fee:* $40. *Comprehensive fee:* $33,940 includes full-time tuition ($23,400), mandatory fees ($900), and room and board ($9640). *College room only:* $5640.
FRESHMAN FINANCIAL AID (Fall 2005, est.) 429 applied for aid; of those 100% were deemed to have need. 99% of freshmen with need received aid; of those 4% had need fully met. *Average percent of need met:* 67% (excluding resources awarded to replace EFC). *Average financial aid package:* $15,060 (excluding resources awarded to replace EFC).
UNDERGRADUATE FINANCIAL AID (Fall 2005, est.) 1,332 applied for aid; of those 98% were deemed to have need. 99% of undergraduates with need received aid; of those 6% had need fully met. *Average percent of need met:* 68% (excluding resources awarded to replace EFC). *Average financial aid package:* $14,733 (excluding resources awarded to replace EFC). 1% of all full-time undergraduates had no need and received non-need-based gift aid.

GIFT AID (NEED-BASED) *Total amount:* $12,871,492 (11% federal, 6% state, 79% institutional, 4% external sources). *Receiving aid:* Freshmen: 70% (414); All full-time undergraduates: 60% (1,184). *Average award:* Freshmen: $10,531; Undergraduates: $9925. *Scholarships, grants, and awards:* Federal Pell, FSEOG, state, private, college/university gift aid from institutional funds.
GIFT AID (NON-NEED-BASED) *Total amount:* $681,247 (27% institutional, 73% external sources). *Receiving aid:* Undergraduates: 1% (10). *Average Award:* Undergraduates: $4379. *Scholarships, grants, and awards by category:* Academic Interests/Achievement: 152 awards ($610,250 total): general academic interests/achievements. *ROTC:* Army cooperative.
LOANS *Student loans:* $13,926,683 (37% need-based, 63% non-need-based). 55% of past graduating class borrowed through all loan programs. *Average indebtedness per student:* $25,051. *Average need-based loan:* Freshmen: $2618; Undergraduates: $3764. *Parent loans:* $7,180,762 (100% non-need-based). *Programs:* FFEL (Subsidized and Unsubsidized Stafford, PLUS), Perkins, state.
WORK-STUDY *Federal work-study:* Total amount: $834,846; 728 jobs averaging $1147. *State or other work-study/employment:* Total amount: $2500 (100% non-need-based). 3 part-time jobs averaging $833.
APPLYING FOR FINANCIAL AID *Required financial aid form:* FAFSA. *Financial aid deadline (priority):* 3/1. *Notification date:* Continuous beginning 3/1. Students must reply by 5/1.
CONTACT Stephanny Elias, Director of Student Financial Services, Curry College, 1071 Blue Hill Avenue, Milton, MA 02186-2395, 617-333-2146 or toll-free 800-669-0686. *Fax:* 617-333-2915.

THE CURTIS INSTITUTE OF MUSIC
Philadelphia, PA

Tuition & fees: N/R	Average undergraduate aid package: $10,778

ABOUT THE INSTITUTION Independent, coed. Awards: bachelor's and master's degrees. 5 undergraduate majors. Total enrollment: 160. Undergraduates: 144. Both federal and institutional methodology are used as a basis for awarding need-based institutional aid.
FRESHMAN FINANCIAL AID (Fall 2005, est.) 11 applied for aid; of those 100% were deemed to have need. 100% of freshmen with need received aid; of those 27% had need fully met. *Average percent of need met:* 79% (excluding resources awarded to replace EFC). *Average financial aid package:* $7549 (excluding resources awarded to replace EFC).
UNDERGRADUATE FINANCIAL AID (Fall 2005, est.) 68 applied for aid; of those 100% were deemed to have need. 100% of undergraduates with need received aid; of those 40% had need fully met. *Average percent of need met:* 92% (excluding resources awarded to replace EFC). *Average financial aid package:* $10,778 (excluding resources awarded to replace EFC).
GIFT AID (NEED-BASED) *Total amount:* $330,126 (11% federal, 84% institutional, 5% external sources). *Receiving aid:* Freshmen: 29% (5); All full-time undergraduates: 65% (49). *Average award:* Freshmen: $5100; Undergraduates: $6430. *Scholarships, grants, and awards:* Federal Pell, college/university gift aid from institutional funds.
GIFT AID (NON-NEED-BASED) *Scholarships, grants, and awards by category:* Creative Arts/Performance: music.
LOANS *Student loans:* $269,050 (100% need-based). 45% of past graduating class borrowed through all loan programs. *Average indebtedness per student:* $16,161. *Average need-based loan:* Freshmen: $2743; Undergraduates: $3957. *Parent loans:* $5578 (100% need-based). *Programs:* FFEL (Subsidized and Unsubsidized Stafford, PLUS), TERI Loans.
WORK-STUDY *State or other work-study/employment:* Total amount: $133,720 (100% need-based). 66 part-time jobs averaging $2026.
APPLYING FOR FINANCIAL AID *Required financial aid forms:* FAFSA, institution's own form, CSS Financial Aid PROFILE, noncustodial (divorced/separated) parent's statement, bank statements, tax returns. *Financial aid deadline:* 3/1. *Notification date:* 4/1. Students must reply by 5/1.
CONTACT Janice Miller, Director of Student Financial Assistance, The Curtis Institute of Music, 1726 Locust Street, Philadelphia, PA 19103-6107, 215-893-5252. *E-mail:* janice.miller@curtis.edu.

Daemen College

DAEMEN COLLEGE
Amherst, NY

Tuition & fees: $16,800 | **Average undergraduate aid package:** $14,419

ABOUT THE INSTITUTION Independent, coed. Awards: bachelor's, master's, and first professional degrees and post-bachelor's and post-master's certificates. 32 undergraduate majors. Total enrollment: 2,315. Undergraduates: 1,603. Freshmen: 366. Federal methodology is used as a basis for awarding need-based institutional aid.
UNDERGRADUATE EXPENSES for 2005–06 *Application fee:* $25. *Comprehensive fee:* $24,580 includes full-time tuition ($16,350), mandatory fees ($450), and room and board ($7780). Room and board charges vary according to board plan and housing facility. *Part-time tuition:* $545 per credit. *Part-time fees:* $4 per credit; $68 per term. Part-time tuition and fees vary according to course load. *Payment plans:* Installment, deferred payment.
FRESHMAN FINANCIAL AID (Fall 2005, est.) 319 applied for aid; of those 100% were deemed to have need. 100% of freshmen with need received aid; of those 27% had need fully met. *Average percent of need met:* 84% (excluding resources awarded to replace EFC). *Average financial aid package:* $15,506 (excluding resources awarded to replace EFC). 10% of all full-time freshmen had no need and received non-need-based gift aid.
UNDERGRADUATE FINANCIAL AID (Fall 2005, est.) 1,088 applied for aid; of those 100% were deemed to have need. 100% of undergraduates with need received aid; of those 30% had need fully met. *Average percent of need met:* 87% (excluding resources awarded to replace EFC). *Average financial aid package:* $14,419 (excluding resources awarded to replace EFC). 16% of all full-time undergraduates had no need and received non-need-based gift aid.
GIFT AID (NEED-BASED) *Total amount:* $7,683,604 (21% federal, 32% state, 47% institutional). *Receiving aid:* Freshmen: 80% (292); All full-time undergraduates: 78% (987). *Average award:* Freshmen: $7938; Undergraduates: $6951. *Scholarships, grants, and awards:* Federal Pell, FSEOG, state, private, college/university gift aid from institutional funds.
GIFT AID (NON-NEED-BASED) *Total amount:* $5,844,659 (1% state, 99% institutional). *Receiving aid:* Freshmen: 69% (253); Undergraduates: 69% (879). *Average Award:* Freshmen: $6132; Undergraduates: $5369. *Scholarships, grants, and awards by category:* Academic Interests/Achievement: 914 awards ($4,102,012 total): general academic interests/achievements. Creative Arts/Performance: 7 awards ($3500 total): art/fine arts. Special Characteristics: 38 awards ($491,808 total): children and siblings of alumni, children of faculty/staff, general special characteristics, siblings of current students. *Tuition waivers:* Full or partial for employees or children of employees, senior citizens. **ROTC:** Army cooperative.
LOANS *Student loans:* $8,385,027 (86% need-based, 14% non-need-based). 78% of past graduating class borrowed through all loan programs. *Average indebtedness per student:* $13,323. *Average need-based loan:* Freshmen: $3228; Undergraduates: $4054. *Parent loans:* $1,257,098 (77% need-based, 23% non-need-based). *Programs:* FFEL (Subsidized and Unsubsidized Stafford, PLUS), Perkins, college/university, alternative loans.
WORK-STUDY *Federal work-study:* Total amount: $855,695; 290 jobs averaging $1067. *State or other work-study/employment:* Total amount: $73,400 (69% need-based, 31% non-need-based). 30 part-time jobs averaging $1163.
ATHLETIC AWARDS *Total amount:* $494,227 (67% need-based, 33% non-need-based).
APPLYING FOR FINANCIAL AID *Required financial aid forms:* FAFSA, state aid form. *Financial aid deadline (priority):* 2/15. *Notification date:* Continuous. Students must reply within 2 weeks of notification.
CONTACT Jeffrey Pagano, Director of Financial Aid, Daemen College, 4380 Main Street, Amherst, NY 14226-3592, 716-839-8254 or toll-free 800-462-7652. *Fax:* 716-839-8378. *E-mail:* jpagano@daemen.edu.

DAKOTA STATE UNIVERSITY
Madison, SD

Tuition & fees (SD res): $4831 | **Average undergraduate aid package:** $6449

ABOUT THE INSTITUTION State-supported, coed. Awards: associate, bachelor's, and master's degrees. 30 undergraduate majors. Total enrollment: 2,319. Undergraduates: 2,081. Freshmen: 311. Federal methodology is used as a basis for awarding need-based institutional aid.
UNDERGRADUATE EXPENSES for 2005–06 *Application fee:* $20. *Tuition, state resident:* full-time $2290; part-time $161 per credit hour. *Tuition, nonresident:* full-time $7278; part-time $327 per credit hour. Full-time tuition and fees vary according to location and reciprocity agreements. Part-time tuition and fees vary according to location and reciprocity agreements. *College room and board:* $3727; *room only:* $1815. Room and board charges vary according to board plan and housing facility. *Payment plans:* Installment, deferred payment.
FRESHMAN FINANCIAL AID (Fall 2004) 226 applied for aid; of those 76% were deemed to have need. 99% of freshmen with need received aid; of those 21% had need fully met. *Average percent of need met:* 87% (excluding resources awarded to replace EFC). *Average financial aid package:* $6405 (excluding resources awarded to replace EFC). 20% of all full-time freshmen had no need and received non-need-based gift aid.
UNDERGRADUATE FINANCIAL AID (Fall 2004) 1,020 applied for aid; of those 81% were deemed to have need. 100% of undergraduates with need received aid; of those 24% had need fully met. *Average percent of need met:* 86% (excluding resources awarded to replace EFC). *Average financial aid package:* $6449 (excluding resources awarded to replace EFC). 15% of all full-time undergraduates had no need and received non-need-based gift aid.
GIFT AID (NEED-BASED) *Total amount:* $2,083,881 (77% federal, 12% institutional, 11% external sources). *Receiving aid:* Freshmen: 41% (104); All full-time undergraduates: 39% (460). *Average award:* Freshmen: $2820; Undergraduates: $2836. *Scholarships, grants, and awards:* Federal Pell, FSEOG, state, private, college/university gift aid from institutional funds.
GIFT AID (NON-NEED-BASED) *Total amount:* $215,984 (10% state, 46% institutional, 44% external sources). *Receiving aid:* Freshmen: 37% (92); Undergraduates: 25% (297). *Average Award:* Freshmen: $5249; Undergraduates: $5680. *Scholarships, grants, and awards by category:* Academic Interests/Achievement: business, communication, computer science, education, English, general academic interests/achievements, mathematics. Creative Arts/Performance: music. Special Achievements/Activities: general special achievements/activities. Special Characteristics: children and siblings of alumni, ethnic background, local/state students, members of minority groups. *Tuition waivers:* Full or partial for employees or children of employees, senior citizens. **ROTC:** Air Force cooperative.
LOANS *Student loans:* $6,380,075 (71% need-based, 29% non-need-based). 90% of past graduating class borrowed through all loan programs. *Average indebtedness per student:* $19,492. *Average need-based loan:* Freshmen: $3488; Undergraduates: $4814. *Parent loans:* $504,541 (71% need-based, 29% non-need-based). *Programs:* FFEL (Subsidized and Unsubsidized Stafford, PLUS), Perkins, alternative loans.
WORK-STUDY *Federal work-study:* Total amount: $345,549; 165 jobs averaging $2094. *State or other work-study/employment:* Total amount: $307,460 (100% need-based). 196 part-time jobs averaging $1569.
ATHLETIC AWARDS *Total amount:* $159,251 (71% need-based, 29% non-need-based).
APPLYING FOR FINANCIAL AID *Required financial aid form:* FAFSA. *Financial aid deadline (priority):* 3/1. *Notification date:* Continuous beginning 4/10. Students must reply within 2 weeks of notification.
CONTACT Denise Grayson, Financial Aid Director, Dakota State University, 103 Heston Hall, 820 North Washington Avenue, Madison, SD 57042-1799, 605-256-5158 or toll-free 888-DSU-9988. *Fax:* 605-256-5316. *E-mail:* dsuinfo@pluto.dsu.edu.

DAKOTA WESLEYAN UNIVERSITY
Mitchell, SD

CONTACT Marci Farmer, Administrative Assistant for Academic Affairs, Dakota Wesleyan University, 1200 West University Avenue, Mitchell, SD 57301-4398, 605-995-2645 or toll-free 800-333-8506. *Fax:* 605-995-2643. *E-mail:* mafarmer@dwu.edu.

DALLAS BAPTIST UNIVERSITY
Dallas, TX

Tuition & fees: $12,270 | **Average undergraduate aid package:** $10,262

ABOUT THE INSTITUTION Independent religious, coed. Awards: associate, bachelor's, and master's degrees and post-bachelor's certificates. 45 undergraduate majors. Total enrollment: 4,988. Undergraduates: 3,567. Freshmen: 362. Federal methodology is used as a basis for awarding need-based institutional aid.

UNDERGRADUATE EXPENSES for 2005–06 *Application fee:* $25. *Comprehensive fee:* $17,040 includes full-time tuition ($12,270) and room and board ($4770). *College room only:* $1900. Room and board charges vary according to board plan and housing facility. *Part-time tuition:* $409 per credit hour. *Payment plan:* Installment.

FRESHMAN FINANCIAL AID (Fall 2005, est.) 330 applied for aid; of those 61% were deemed to have need. 98% of freshmen with need received aid; of those 57% had need fully met. *Average percent of need met:* 70% (excluding resources awarded to replace EFC). *Average financial aid package:* $5024 (excluding resources awarded to replace EFC). 20% of all full-time freshmen had no need and received non-need-based gift aid.

UNDERGRADUATE FINANCIAL AID (Fall 2005, est.) 1,756 applied for aid; of those 68% were deemed to have need. 98% of undergraduates with need received aid; of those 42% had need fully met. *Average percent of need met:* 79% (excluding resources awarded to replace EFC). *Average financial aid package:* $10,262 (excluding resources awarded to replace EFC). 21% of all full-time undergraduates had no need and received non-need-based gift aid.

GIFT AID (NEED-BASED) *Total amount:* $4,386,362 (46% federal, 54% state). *Receiving aid:* Freshmen: 42% (150); All full-time undergraduates: 41% (864). *Average award:* Freshmen: $2742; Undergraduates: $2767. *Scholarships, grants, and awards:* Federal Pell, FSEOG, state, private, college/university gift aid from institutional funds.

GIFT AID (NON-NEED-BASED) *Total amount:* $8,178,630 (69% institutional, 31% external sources). *Receiving aid:* Freshmen: 48% (173); Undergraduates: 42% (877). *Average Award:* Freshmen: $9403; Undergraduates: $9093. *Scholarships, grants, and awards by category:* Academic Interests/Achievement: 1,322 awards ($2,690,686 total): business, communication, computer science, education, general academic interests/achievements, humanities, mathematics, premedicine, religion/biblical studies. *Creative Arts/Performance:* 57 awards ($145,200 total): music. *Special Achievements/Activities:* 1,126 awards ($2,680,132 total): community service, general special achievements/activities, leadership, memberships, religious involvement. *Special Characteristics:* 238 awards ($600,870 total): children of faculty/staff, general special characteristics, relatives of clergy, religious affiliation. *Tuition waivers:* Full or partial for employees or children of employees. *ROTC:* Army cooperative, Air Force cooperative.

LOANS *Student loans:* $13,271,686 (41% need-based, 59% non-need-based). 51% of past graduating class borrowed through all loan programs. *Average indebtedness per student:* $18,763. *Average need-based loan:* Freshmen: $2438; Undergraduates: $3398. *Parent loans:* $1,735,700 (100% non-need-based). *Programs:* FFEL (Subsidized and Unsubsidized Stafford, PLUS), Perkins, state, college/university.

WORK-STUDY *Federal work-study:* Total amount: $327,506; 146 jobs averaging $2133. *State or other work-study/employment:* Total amount: $31,577 (100% need-based). 46 part-time jobs averaging $752.

ATHLETIC AWARDS *Total amount:* $628,658 (100% non-need-based).

APPLYING FOR FINANCIAL AID *Required financial aid forms:* FAFSA, institution's own form. *Financial aid deadline:* Continuous. *Notification date:* Continuous.

CONTACT Mr. Donald Zackary, Director of Financial Aid, Dallas Baptist University, 3000 Mountain Creek Parkway, Dallas, TX 75211-9299, 214-333-5363 or toll-free 800-460-1328. *Fax:* 214-333-5586. *E-mail:* donz@dbu.edu.

DALLAS CHRISTIAN COLLEGE
Dallas, TX

Tuition & fees: N/R **Average undergraduate aid package:** $3940

ABOUT THE INSTITUTION Independent religious, coed. Awards: bachelor's degrees and post-bachelor's certificates. 3 undergraduate majors. Total enrollment: 366. Undergraduates: 366. Freshmen: 52. Federal methodology is used as a basis for awarding need-based institutional aid.

FRESHMAN FINANCIAL AID (Fall 2005, est.) 38 applied for aid; of those 74% were deemed to have need. *Average percent of need met:* 52% (excluding resources awarded to replace EFC). *Average financial aid package:* $5700 (excluding resources awarded to replace EFC). 9% of all full-time freshmen had no need and received non-need-based gift aid.

UNDERGRADUATE FINANCIAL AID (Fall 2005, est.) 189 applied for aid; of those 70% were deemed to have need. *Average percent of need met:* 43% (excluding resources awarded to replace EFC). *Average financial aid package:* $3940 (excluding resources awarded to replace EFC). 11% of all full-time undergraduates had no need and received non-need-based gift aid.

GIFT AID (NEED-BASED) *Total amount:* $502,684 (60% federal, 28% state, 10% institutional, 2% external sources). *Receiving aid:* Freshmen: 36% (16); All full-time undergraduates: 17% (40). *Average award:* Freshmen: $1080; Undergraduates: $1282. *Scholarships, grants, and awards:* Federal Pell, FSEOG, private, college/university gift aid from institutional funds.

GIFT AID (NON-NEED-BASED) *Total amount:* $427,790 (68% institutional, 32% external sources). *Receiving aid:* Freshmen: 27% (12); Undergraduates: 12% (28). *Average Award:* Freshmen: $1904; Undergraduates: $3664. *Scholarships, grants, and awards by category:* Academic Interests/Achievement: 66 awards ($273,693 total): education, general academic interests/achievements, religion/biblical studies. *Creative Arts/Performance:* 20 awards ($8000 total): music. *Special Achievements/Activities:* 45 awards ($43,850 total): general special achievements/activities, leadership. *Special Characteristics:* 31 awards ($62,270 total): children of faculty/staff, general special characteristics, religious affiliation. *Tuition waivers:* Full or partial for employees or children of employees.

LOANS *Student loans:* $1,159,448 (53% need-based, 47% non-need-based). 74% of past graduating class borrowed through all loan programs. *Average indebtedness per student:* $15,000. *Average need-based loan:* Freshmen: $2624; Undergraduates: $3589. *Parent loans:* $126,800 (100% non-need-based). *Programs:* FFEL (Subsidized and Unsubsidized Stafford, PLUS).

WORK-STUDY *Federal work-study:* Total amount: $25,258; 36 jobs averaging $1404.

APPLYING FOR FINANCIAL AID *Required financial aid forms:* FAFSA, institution's own form. *Financial aid deadline:* Continuous. *Notification date:* Continuous beginning 5/10. Students must reply within 2 weeks of notification.

CONTACT Robin L. Walker, Director of Student Financial Aid, Dallas Christian College, 2700 Christian Parkway, Dallas, TX 75234-7299, 972-241-3371 Ext. 105. *Fax:* 972-241-8021. *E-mail:* finaid@dallas.edu.

DALTON STATE COLLEGE
Dalton, GA

Tuition & fees (GA res): $1592 **Average undergraduate aid package:** $1470

ABOUT THE INSTITUTION State-supported, coed. Awards: associate and bachelor's degrees. 64 undergraduate majors. Total enrollment: 4,267. Undergraduates: 4,267. Federal methodology is used as a basis for awarding need-based institutional aid.

UNDERGRADUATE EXPENSES for 2005–06 *Application fee:* $25. *Tuition, area resident:* part-time $66.75 per credit hour. *Tuition, state resident:* full-time $1592. *Tuition, nonresident:* full-time $5996.

FRESHMAN FINANCIAL AID (Fall 2005, est.) 346 applied for aid; of those 69% were deemed to have need. 97% of freshmen with need received aid; of those 9% had need fully met. *Average percent of need met:* 74% (excluding resources awarded to replace EFC). *Average financial aid package:* $1526 (excluding resources awarded to replace EFC). 5% of all full-time freshmen had no need and received non-need-based gift aid.

UNDERGRADUATE FINANCIAL AID (Fall 2005, est.) 1,055 applied for aid; of those 74% were deemed to have need. 92% of undergraduates with need received aid; of those 12% had need fully met. *Average percent of need met:* 70% (excluding resources awarded to replace EFC). *Average financial aid package:* $1470 (excluding resources awarded to replace EFC). 6% of all full-time undergraduates had no need and received non-need-based gift aid.

GIFT AID (NEED-BASED) *Total amount:* $3,418,974 (56% federal, 38% state, 1% institutional, 5% external sources). *Receiving aid:* Freshmen: 30% (127); All full-time undergraduates: 42% (494). *Average award:* Freshmen: $1539; Undergraduates: $1492. *Scholarships, grants, and awards:* Federal Pell, FSEOG, state, private, college/university gift aid from institutional funds.

GIFT AID (NON-NEED-BASED) *Total amount:* $3,817,441 (47% federal, 46% state, 1% institutional, 6% external sources). *Receiving aid:* Freshmen: 44% (187); Undergraduates: 36% (425). *Average Award:* Freshmen: $1061; Undergraduates: $446. *Scholarships, grants, and awards by category:* Academic Interests/Achievement: 14 awards ($17,225 total): business, education, engineering/technologies, health fields, humanities. *Special Achievements/*

Dalton State College

Activities: 5 awards ($1900 total): hobbies/interests, memberships. *Special Characteristics:* 7 awards ($4400 total): adult students, children and siblings of alumni, children of faculty/staff.
LOANS *Student loans:* $1,532,952 (57% need-based, 43% non-need-based). 1% of past graduating class borrowed through all loan programs. *Average indebtedness per student:* $4049. *Average need-based loan:* Freshmen: $1221; Undergraduates: $1167. *Programs:* FFEL (Subsidized and Unsubsidized Stafford, PLUS), state.
WORK-STUDY *Federal work-study:* Total amount: $82,639; 91 jobs averaging $1433. *State or other work-study/employment:* Total amount: $566,979 (41% need-based, 59% non-need-based). 98 part-time jobs averaging $3665.
APPLYING FOR FINANCIAL AID *Required financial aid form:* FAFSA. *Financial aid deadline (priority):* 6/1. *Notification date:* Continuous beginning 4/1.
CONTACT Dianne Cox, Director of Student Financial Aid, Dalton State College, 650 College Drive, Dalton, GA 30720, 706-272-4545 or toll-free 800-829-4436. *Fax:* 706-272-2458. *E-mail:* dcox@daltonstate.edu.

DANA COLLEGE
Blair, NE

CONTACT Kris Weigelt, Assistant Director, Financial Aid, Dana College, 2848 College Drive, Blair, NE 68008-1099, 402-426-7245 or toll-free 800-444-3262. *Fax:* 402-426-7225. *E-mail:* kweigelt@fs1.dana.edu.

DANIEL WEBSTER COLLEGE
Nashua, NH

Tuition & fees: $22,955 — **Average undergraduate aid package: $15,584**

ABOUT THE INSTITUTION Independent, coed. Awards: associate and bachelor's degrees. 16 undergraduate majors. Total enrollment: 1,109. Undergraduates: 1,050. Freshmen: 141. Federal methodology is used as a basis for awarding need-based institutional aid.
UNDERGRADUATE EXPENSES for 2005–06 *Application fee:* $35. *Comprehensive fee:* $31,405 includes full-time tuition ($22,130), mandatory fees ($825), and room and board ($8450). *Payment plan:* Installment.
FRESHMAN FINANCIAL AID (Fall 2005, est.) 185 applied for aid; of those 92% were deemed to have need. 100% of freshmen with need received aid. *Average percent of need met:* 75% (excluding resources awarded to replace EFC). *Average financial aid package:* $15,361 (excluding resources awarded to replace EFC). 14% of all full-time freshmen had no need and received non-need-based gift aid.
UNDERGRADUATE FINANCIAL AID (Fall 2005, est.) 567 applied for aid; of those 98% were deemed to have need. 100% of undergraduates with need received aid. *Average percent of need met:* 72% (excluding resources awarded to replace EFC). *Average financial aid package:* $15,584 (excluding resources awarded to replace EFC). 8% of all full-time undergraduates had no need and received non-need-based gift aid.
GIFT AID (NEED-BASED) *Total amount:* $2,835,259 (16% federal, 3% state, 78% institutional, 3% external sources). *Receiving aid:* Freshmen: 81% (157); All full-time undergraduates: 84% (490). *Scholarships, grants, and awards:* Federal Pell, FSEOG, state, private, college/university gift aid from institutional funds.
GIFT AID (NON-NEED-BASED) *Total amount:* $2,760,678 (100% institutional). *Receiving aid:* Freshmen: 87% (168); Undergraduates: 72% (419). *Average Award:* Freshmen: $5500; Undergraduates: $6755. *Scholarships, grants, and awards by category:* Academic Interests/Achievement: $2,649,158 total: business, computer science, engineering/technologies, general academic interests/achievements, social sciences. *Special Achievements/Activities:* 12 awards ($111,520 total): general special achievements/activities, leadership. *Tuition waivers:* Full or partial for employees or children of employees. *ROTC:* Army cooperative, Air Force cooperative.
LOANS *Student loans:* $2,134,845 (83% need-based, 17% non-need-based). 95% of past graduating class borrowed through all loan programs. *Average indebtedness per student:* $37,945. *Average need-based loan:* Freshmen: $4273; Undergraduates: $3588. *Parent loans:* $3,968,549 (100% non-need-based). *Programs:* Federal Direct (Subsidized and Unsubsidized Stafford, PLUS), Perkins, Signature Loans.
WORK-STUDY *Federal work-study:* Total amount: $663,994; 372 jobs averaging $2000. *State or other work-study/employment:* Part-time jobs available.

APPLYING FOR FINANCIAL AID *Required financial aid forms:* FAFSA, institution's own form. *Financial aid deadline (priority):* 3/1. *Notification date:* Continuous beginning 4/1. Students must reply within 3 weeks of notification.
CONTACT Anne-Marie Caruso, Director of Financial Assistance, Daniel Webster College, 20 University Drive, Nashua, NH 03063-1300, 603-577-6590 or toll-free 800-325-6876. *Fax:* 603-577-6593. *E-mail:* caruso@dwc.edu.

DARKEI NOAM RABBINICAL COLLEGE
Brooklyn, NY

CONTACT Ms. Rivi Horowitz, Director of Financial Aid, Darkei Noam Rabbinical College, 2822 Avenue J, Brooklyn, NY 11219, 718-338-6464.

DARTMOUTH COLLEGE
Hanover, NH

Tuition & fees: $32,046 — **Average undergraduate aid package: $27,934**

ABOUT THE INSTITUTION Independent, coed. Awards: bachelor's, master's, doctoral, and first professional degrees. 60 undergraduate majors. Total enrollment: 5,780. Undergraduates: 4,110. Freshmen: 1,075. Both federal and institutional methodology are used as a basis for awarding need-based institutional aid.
UNDERGRADUATE EXPENSES for 2005–06 *Application fee:* $70. *Comprehensive fee:* $41,436 includes full-time tuition ($31,770), mandatory fees ($276), and room and board ($9390). *College room only:* $5640. Room and board charges vary according to board plan. *Payment plan:* Tuition prepayment.
FRESHMAN FINANCIAL AID (Fall 2004) 656 applied for aid; of those 79% were deemed to have need. 100% of freshmen with need received aid; of those 100% had need fully met. *Average percent of need met:* 100% (excluding resources awarded to replace EFC). *Average financial aid package:* $29,921 (excluding resources awarded to replace EFC). 1% of all full-time freshmen had no need and received non-need-based gift aid.
UNDERGRADUATE FINANCIAL AID (Fall 2004) 2,481 applied for aid; of those 83% were deemed to have need. 100% of undergraduates with need received aid; of those 100% had need fully met. *Average percent of need met:* 100% (excluding resources awarded to replace EFC). *Average financial aid package:* $27,934 (excluding resources awarded to replace EFC). 1% of all full-time undergraduates had no need and received non-need-based gift aid.
GIFT AID (NEED-BASED) *Total amount:* $46,576,444 (8% federal, 88% institutional, 4% external sources). *Receiving aid:* Freshmen: 47% (506); All full-time undergraduates: 48% (1,932). *Average award:* Freshmen: $26,838; Undergraduates: $24,114. *Scholarships, grants, and awards:* Federal Pell, FSEOG, state, college/university gift aid from institutional funds.
GIFT AID (NON-NEED-BASED) *Total amount:* $753,859 (23% federal, 1% institutional, 76% external sources). *Average Award:* Freshmen: $450; Undergraduates: $420. *ROTC:* Army cooperative.
LOANS *Student loans:* $11,089,888 (67% need-based, 33% non-need-based). 48% of past graduating class borrowed through all loan programs. *Average indebtedness per student:* $19,305. *Average need-based loan:* Freshmen: $3138; Undergraduates: $4349. *Parent loans:* $7,114,237 (100% non-need-based). *Programs:* FFEL (Subsidized and Unsubsidized Stafford, PLUS), Perkins, college/university.
WORK-STUDY *Federal work-study:* Total amount: $3,010,167; 1,616 jobs averaging $1862. *State or other work-study/employment:* Total amount: $462,140 (100% need-based). 270 part-time jobs averaging $1711.
APPLYING FOR FINANCIAL AID *Required financial aid forms:* FAFSA, CSS Financial Aid PROFILE, noncustodial (divorced/separated) parent's statement, business/farm supplement, W-2 forms, federal income tax form(s). *Financial aid deadline:* 2/1. *Notification date:* 4/2. Students must reply by 5/1.
CONTACT Ms. Virginia S. Hazen, Director of Financial Aid, Dartmouth College, 6024 McNutt Hall, Hanover, NH 03755, 603-646-2451 or toll-free 603-646-2875 (in-state). *Fax:* 603-646-1414. *E-mail:* virginia.s.hazen@dartmouth.edu.

DAVENPORT UNIVERSITY
Dearborn, MI

Tuition & fees: $8880 — **Average undergraduate aid package: N/A**

ABOUT THE INSTITUTION Independent, coed. Awards: associate, bachelor's, and master's degrees and post-bachelor's certificates. 26 undergraduate majors. Total enrollment: 12,822. Undergraduates: 12,066. Freshmen: 1,231.
UNDERGRADUATE EXPENSES for 2005–06 *Application fee:* $25. *Tuition:* full-time $8760; part-time $365 per credit hour.
FRESHMAN FINANCIAL AID (Fall 2004) 37 applied for aid; of those 97% were deemed to have need. 94% of freshmen with need received aid. *Average percent of need met:* 16% (excluding resources awarded to replace EFC). 2% of all full-time freshmen had no need and received non-need-based gift aid.
UNDERGRADUATE FINANCIAL AID (Fall 2004) 724 applied for aid; of those 96% were deemed to have need. 98% of undergraduates with need received aid; of those 2% had need fully met. *Average percent of need met:* 75% (excluding resources awarded to replace EFC). 4% of all full-time undergraduates had no need and received non-need-based gift aid.
GIFT AID (NEED-BASED) *Total amount:* $30,968,057 (63% federal, 32% state, 5% institutional). *Receiving aid:* Freshmen: 73% (30); All full-time undergraduates: 66% (551). *Average award:* Freshmen: $1680; Undergraduates: $3818. *Scholarships, grants, and awards:* Federal Pell, FSEOG, state, private, college/university gift aid from institutional funds.
GIFT AID (NON-NEED-BASED) *Total amount:* $10,570,465 (3% state, 96% institutional, 1% external sources). *Receiving aid:* Freshmen: 2% (1); Undergraduates: 20% (164). *Average Award:* Freshmen $4598; Undergraduates: $8607. *Scholarships, grants, and awards by category: Special Characteristics:* 114 awards ($3348 total): children of faculty/staff.
LOANS *Student loans:* $55,483,797 (59% need-based, 41% non-need-based). 74% of past graduating class borrowed through all loan programs. *Average indebtedness per student:* $8459. *Average need-based loan:* Freshmen: $2315; Undergraduates: $5186. *Parent loans:* $819,176 (100% non-need-based). *Programs:* FFEL (Subsidized and Unsubsidized Stafford, PLUS), alternative loans.
WORK-STUDY *Federal work-study:* Total amount: $1,063,093; 333 jobs averaging $3192. *State or other work-study/employment:* Total amount: $502,594 (100% need-based). 149 part-time jobs averaging $3373.
ATHLETIC AWARDS *Total amount:* $133,936 (100% non-need-based).
APPLYING FOR FINANCIAL AID *Required financial aid forms:* FAFSA, scholarship app., if applicable. *Financial aid deadline (priority):* 3/1. *Notification date:* Continuous beginning 3/1.
CONTACT Mrs. Susan Crkovski, Executive Director of Financial Aid, Davenport University, 4801 Oakman Boulevard, Dearborn, MI 48126-3799, 313-581-4400 Ext. 217 or toll-free 800-632-9569. *Fax:* 313-581-1955. *E-mail:* susan.crkovski@davenport.edu.

DAVENPORT UNIVERSITY
Flint, MI

CONTACT Ms. Rita Miller, Director of Financial Aid, Davenport University, 3488 North Jennings Road, Flint, MI 48504-1700, 810-789-2200 or toll-free 800-727-1443. *Fax:* 810-789-2266. *E-mail:* flrmiller@dcb.edu.

DAVENPORT UNIVERSITY
Gaylord, MI

CONTACT Office of Financial Aid, Davenport University, 80 Livingston Boulevard, Gaylord, MI 49735, 989-705-3720 or toll-free 800-632-9569. *Fax:* 989-705-3727.

DAVENPORT UNIVERSITY
Grand Rapids, MI

CONTACT Mary Kay Bethune, Vice President for Financial Aid, Davenport University, 415 East Fulton Street, Grand Rapids, MI 49503, 616-451-3511 or toll-free 800-632-9569. *E-mail:* marykay.bethune@davenport.edu.

DAVENPORT UNIVERSITY
Holland, MI

CONTACT Office of Financial Aid, Davenport University, 643 South Waverly Road, Holland, MI 49423, 616-395-4600 or toll-free 800-632-9569. *Fax:* 616-395-4698.

DAVENPORT UNIVERSITY
Kalamazoo, MI

CONTACT Ms. Linda Reischer, Director of Financial Aid, Davenport University, 4123 West Main Street, Kalamazoo, MI 49006-2791, 269-552-3320 or toll-free 800-632-9569. *Fax:* 269-552-3305. *E-mail:* linda.reischer@davenport.edu.

DAVENPORT UNIVERSITY
Lansing, MI

CONTACT Libby Jean, Acting Director of Financial Aid, Davenport University, 220 East Kalamazoo Street, Lansing, MI 48933-2197, 517-484-2600 Ext. 8226 or toll-free 800-632-9569. *Fax:* 517-484-1132. *E-mail:* libby.jean@davenport.edu.

DAVENPORT UNIVERSITY
Lapeer, MI

CONTACT Office of Financial Aid, Davenport University, 550 Lake Drive, Suite B, Lapeer, MI 48446, 810-664-9655 or toll-free 800-632-9569. *Fax:* 810-664-1912.

DAVENPORT UNIVERSITY
Traverse City, MI

Tuition & fees: $8880   **Average undergraduate aid package:** $9728

ABOUT THE INSTITUTION Independent, coed. Awards: associate, bachelor's, and master's degrees and post-bachelor's certificates. Total enrollment: 12,822. Undergraduates: 12,066. Freshmen: 1,231. Federal methodology is used as a basis for awarding need-based institutional aid.
UNDERGRADUATE EXPENSES for 2005–06 *Application fee:* $25. *Tuition:* full-time $8760; part-time $365 per credit hour.
GIFT AID (NEED-BASED) *Total amount:* $32,702,935 (57% federal, 30% state, 13% institutional). *Receiving aid:* Freshmen: 77% (540); All full-time undergraduates: 77% (2,940). *Average award:* Freshmen: $4037; Undergraduates: $4271. *Scholarships, grants, and awards:* Federal Pell, FSEOG, state, private, college/university gift aid from institutional funds, State of MI Nursing Scholarships.
GIFT AID (NON-NEED-BASED) *Total amount:* $330,876 (72% state, 28% external sources). *Receiving aid:* Freshmen: 45% (316); Undergraduates: 23% (887). *Average Award:* Freshmen: $3475; Undergraduates: $5685.
LOANS *Student loans:* $51,228,538 (99% need-based, 1% non-need-based). 77% of past graduating class borrowed through all loan programs. *Average indebtedness per student:* $8459. *Average need-based loan:* Freshmen: $2400; Undergraduates: $3397. *Parent loans:* $729,826 (100% need-based). *Programs:* FFEL (Subsidized and Unsubsidized Stafford, PLUS), state.
ATHLETIC AWARDS *Total amount:* $62,737 (100% non-need-based).
APPLYING FOR FINANCIAL AID *Required financial aid form:* FAFSA. *Financial aid deadline (priority):* 3/1. *Notification date:* Continuous beginning 3/1.
CONTACT Office of Financial Aid, Davenport University, 2200 Dendrinos Drive, Suite 110, Traverse City, MI 49684, 231-995-1740 or toll-free 866-925-3884 (out-of-state). *Fax:* 231-995-1743.

DAVENPORT UNIVERSITY
Warren, MI

CONTACT Ms. Carol Agee, Director of Financial Aid, Davenport University, 27500 Dequindre Road, Warren, MI 48092-5209, 586-558-8700 Ext. 230 or toll-free 800-632-9569. *Fax:* 586-558-7528. *E-mail:* carol.agee@davenport.edu.

DAVID N. MYERS UNIVERSITY
Cleveland, OH

Tuition & fees: $9840   **Average undergraduate aid package:** $8731

David N. Myers University

ABOUT THE INSTITUTION Independent, coed. Awards: associate, bachelor's, and master's degrees. 14 undergraduate majors. Total enrollment: 1,177. Undergraduates: 1,096. Freshmen: 115. Federal methodology is used as a basis for awarding need-based institutional aid.

UNDERGRADUATE EXPENSES for 2005–06 *Application fee:* $25. *Tuition:* full-time $9840.

FRESHMAN FINANCIAL AID (Fall 2004) 112 applied for aid; of those 92% were deemed to have need. 100% of freshmen with need received aid; of those 19% had need fully met. *Average percent of need met:* 74% (excluding resources awarded to replace EFC). *Average financial aid package:* $9981 (excluding resources awarded to replace EFC).

UNDERGRADUATE FINANCIAL AID (Fall 2004) 743 applied for aid; of those 95% were deemed to have need. 89% of undergraduates with need received aid; of those 4% had need fully met. *Average percent of need met:* 55% (excluding resources awarded to replace EFC). *Average financial aid package:* $8731 (excluding resources awarded to replace EFC). 3% of all full-time undergraduates had no need and received non-need-based gift aid.

GIFT AID (NEED-BASED) *Total amount:* $3,551,851 (46% federal, 35% state, 18% institutional, 1% external sources). *Receiving aid:* Freshmen: 74% (99); All full-time undergraduates: 62% (578). *Average award:* Freshmen: $5424; Undergraduates: $5464. *Scholarships, grants, and awards:* Federal Pell, FSEOG, state, private, college/university gift aid from institutional funds, United Negro College Fund.

GIFT AID (NON-NEED-BASED) *Total amount:* $59,929 (24% state, 76% institutional). *Receiving aid:* Freshmen: 2% (2); Undergraduates: 1% (7). *Average Award:* Undergraduates: $8675. *Scholarships, grants, and awards by category:* Academic Interests/Achievement: 39 awards ($45,369 total): business, general academic interests/achievements. *Special Achievements/Activities:* 35 awards ($31,500 total): leadership.

LOANS *Student loans:* $6,412,348 (90% need-based, 10% non-need-based). 68% of past graduating class borrowed through all loan programs. *Average indebtedness per student:* $19,300. *Average need-based loan:* Freshmen: $4329; Undergraduates: $3851. *Parent loans:* $92,953 (34% need-based, 66% non-need-based). *Programs:* FFEL (Subsidized and Unsubsidized Stafford, PLUS), Perkins.

WORK-STUDY *Federal work-study:* Total amount: $114,452; 105 jobs averaging $1080.

ATHLETIC AWARDS *Total amount:* $130,164 (100% need-based).

APPLYING FOR FINANCIAL AID *Required financial aid forms:* FAFSA, institution's own form. *Financial aid deadline (priority):* 3/15. *Notification date:* Continuous beginning 4/1. Students must reply within 3 weeks of notification.

CONTACT Miria Batig, Director of Financial Aid, David N. Myers University, 3921 Chester Avenue, Cleveland, OH 44114, 216-361-2739 or toll-free 800-424-3953. *Fax:* 216-361-9096. *E-mail:* mbatig@myers.edu.

DAVIDSON COLLEGE
Davidson, NC

Tuition & fees: $28,667	Average undergraduate aid package: $18,024

ABOUT THE INSTITUTION Independent Presbyterian, coed. Awards: bachelor's degrees. 21 undergraduate majors. Total enrollment: 1,683. Undergraduates: 1,683. Freshmen: 460. Both federal and institutional methodology are used as a basis for awarding need-based institutional aid.

UNDERGRADUATE EXPENSES for 2005–06 *Application fee:* $50. *Comprehensive fee:* $36,825 includes full-time tuition ($28,667) and room and board ($8158). *College room only:* $4308.

FRESHMAN FINANCIAL AID (Fall 2004) 262 applied for aid; of those 61% were deemed to have need. 100% of freshmen with need received aid; of those 100% had need fully met. *Average percent of need met:* 100% (excluding resources awarded to replace EFC). *Average financial aid package:* $17,844 (excluding resources awarded to replace EFC). 21% of all full-time freshmen had no need and received non-need-based gift aid.

UNDERGRADUATE FINANCIAL AID (Fall 2004) 728 applied for aid; of those 81% were deemed to have need. 100% of undergraduates with need received aid; of those 100% had need fully met. *Average percent of need met:* 100% (excluding resources awarded to replace EFC). *Average financial aid package:* $18,024 (excluding resources awarded to replace EFC). 22% of all full-time undergraduates had no need and received non-need-based gift aid.

GIFT AID (NEED-BASED) *Total amount:* $10,758,229 (5% federal, 5% state, 90% institutional). *Receiving aid:* Freshmen: 32% (147); All full-time undergraduates: 32% (553). *Average award:* Freshmen: $16,871; Undergraduates: $15,766. *Scholarships, grants, and awards:* Federal Pell, FSEOG, state, private, college/university gift aid from institutional funds, need-linked special talent scholarships.

GIFT AID (NON-NEED-BASED) *Total amount:* $4,915,031 (10% federal, 8% state, 66% institutional, 16% external sources). *Receiving aid:* Freshmen: 6% (30); Undergraduates: 5% (83). *Average Award:* Freshmen: $10,115; Undergraduates: $8824. *Scholarships, grants, and awards by category:* Academic Interests/Achievement: 250 awards ($2,719,585 total): biological sciences, education, foreign languages, general academic interests/achievements, mathematics, physical sciences, premedicine. *Creative Arts/Performance:* 33 awards ($200,250 total): art/fine arts, creative writing, music, theater/drama. *Special Achievements/Activities:* 46 awards ($632,015 total): community service, general special achievements/activities, leadership, religious involvement. *Special Characteristics:* 86 awards ($1,135,750 total): children of faculty/staff, general special characteristics, relatives of clergy. *ROTC:* Army, Air Force cooperative.

LOANS *Student loans:* $3,955,667 (67% need-based, 33% non-need-based). 34% of past graduating class borrowed through all loan programs. *Average indebtedness per student:* $22,954. *Average need-based loan:* Freshmen: $3063; Undergraduates: $3926. *Parent loans:* $2,713,442 (100% non-need-based). *Programs:* FFEL (Subsidized and Unsubsidized Stafford, PLUS), Perkins, alternative loans.

WORK-STUDY *Federal work-study:* Total amount: $402,868; 265 jobs averaging $1595. *State or other work-study/employment:* Total amount: $290,954 (80% need-based, 20% non-need-based). 142 part-time jobs averaging $1445.

ATHLETIC AWARDS *Total amount:* $2,231,457 (100% non-need-based).

APPLYING FOR FINANCIAL AID *Required financial aid forms:* FAFSA, CSS Financial Aid PROFILE, noncustodial (divorced/separated) parent's statement, business/farm supplement, parent and student tax returns and W-2 forms; coporate tax returns, if applicable. *Financial aid deadline (priority):* 2/15. *Notification date:* 4/1. Students must reply by 5/1.

CONTACT Kathleen Stevenson, Senior Associate Dean of Admission and Financial Aid, Davidson College, 413 North Main Street, Box 7157, Davidson, NC 28035-7157, 704-894-2232 or toll-free 800-768-0380. *Fax:* 704-894-2845. *E-mail:* kastevenson@davidson.edu.

DAVIS & ELKINS COLLEGE
Elkins, WV

Tuition & fees: $16,832	Average undergraduate aid package: $15,367

ABOUT THE INSTITUTION Independent Presbyterian, coed. Awards: associate and bachelor's degrees. 48 undergraduate majors. Total enrollment: 624. Undergraduates: 624. Freshmen: 104. Federal methodology is used as a basis for awarding need-based institutional aid.

UNDERGRADUATE EXPENSES for 2005–06 *Application fee:* $35. *Comprehensive fee:* $22,936 includes full-time tuition ($16,312), mandatory fees ($520), and room and board ($6104). Full-time tuition and fees vary according to course load. Room and board charges vary according to board plan. *Part-time tuition:* $525 per credit hour. Part-time tuition and fees vary according to course load. *Payment plan:* Installment.

FRESHMAN FINANCIAL AID (Fall 2004) 124 applied for aid; of those 72% were deemed to have need. 100% of freshmen with need received aid; of those 46% had need fully met. *Average percent of need met:* 86% (excluding resources awarded to replace EFC). *Average financial aid package:* $14,744 (excluding resources awarded to replace EFC). 28% of all full-time freshmen had no need and received non-need-based gift aid.

UNDERGRADUATE FINANCIAL AID (Fall 2004) 567 applied for aid; of those 79% were deemed to have need. 100% of undergraduates with need received aid; of those 33% had need fully met. *Average percent of need met:* 81% (excluding resources awarded to replace EFC). *Average financial aid package:* $15,367 (excluding resources awarded to replace EFC). 17% of all full-time undergraduates had no need and received non-need-based gift aid.

GIFT AID (NEED-BASED) *Total amount:* $1,381,947 (74% federal, 26% state). *Receiving aid:* Freshmen: 32% (40); All full-time undergraduates: 48% (277). *Average award:* Freshmen: $2115; Undergraduates: $2297. *Scholarships, grants, and awards:* Federal Pell, FSEOG, state, private, college/university gift aid from institutional funds.

GIFT AID (NON-NEED-BASED) *Total amount:* $3,011,155 (1% federal, 8% state, 81% institutional, 10% external sources). *Receiving aid:* Freshmen: 72% (89); Undergraduates: 79% (450). *Average Award: Freshmen:* $1760; *Undergraduates:* $1621. *Scholarships, grants, and awards by category: Academic Interests/Achievement:* 808 awards ($1,743,722 total): biological sciences, business, computer science, education, engineering/technologies, general academic interests/achievements, health fields, physical sciences, religion/biblical studies. *Creative Arts/Performance:* 60 awards ($109,100 total): art/fine arts, music, performing arts, theater/drama. *Special Achievements/Activities:* 64 awards ($62,500 total): leadership, religious involvement. *Special Characteristics:* 337 awards ($520,482 total): children of faculty/staff, first-generation college students, local/state students, religious affiliation. *Tuition waivers:* Full or partial for employees or children of employees.
LOANS *Student loans:* $3,762,875 (37% need-based, 63% non-need-based). 78% of past graduating class borrowed through all loan programs. *Average indebtedness per student:* $18,015. *Average need-based loan:* Freshmen: $2219; Undergraduates: $3188. *Parent loans:* $328,255 (100% non-need-based). *Programs:* FFEL (Subsidized and Unsubsidized Stafford, PLUS), Perkins, college/university.
WORK-STUDY *Federal work-study:* Total amount: $238,983; 172 jobs averaging $1007. *State or other work-study/employment:* Total amount: $73,673 (100% non-need-based). 26 part-time jobs averaging $1090.
ATHLETIC AWARDS Total amount: $640,427 (100% non-need-based).
APPLYING FOR FINANCIAL AID *Required financial aid form:* FAFSA. *Financial aid deadline:* Continuous. *Notification date:* Continuous. Students must reply within 2 weeks of notification.
CONTACT Susan M. George, Director of Financial Planning, Davis & Elkins College, 100 Campus Drive, Elkins, WV 26241-3996, 304-637-1373 or toll-free 800-624-3157 Ext. 1230. *Fax:* 304-637-1986. *E-mail:* ssw@davisandelkins.edu.

DAVIS COLLEGE
Johnson City, NY

CONTACT Mr. James P. Devine, Financial Aid Director, Davis College, PO Box 601, Bible School Park, NY 13737-0601, 607-729-1581 Ext. 401 or toll-free 800-331-4137 Ext. 406. *Fax:* 607-770-6886. *E-mail:* financialaid@practical.edu.

DEACONESS COLLEGE OF NURSING
St. Louis, MO

CONTACT Financial Aid Counselor, Deaconess College of Nursing, 6150 Oakland Avenue, St. Louis, MO 63139-3215, 314-768-5604 or toll-free 800-942-4310.

DEFIANCE COLLEGE
Defiance, OH

Tuition & fees: $19,740	Average undergraduate aid package: $14,129

ABOUT THE INSTITUTION Independent religious, coed. Awards: associate, bachelor's, and master's degrees. 38 undergraduate majors. Total enrollment: 930. Undergraduates: 827. Freshmen: 244. Federal methodology is used as a basis for awarding need-based institutional aid.
UNDERGRADUATE EXPENSES for 2006–07 *Application fee:* $25. *Comprehensive fee:* $25,910 includes full-time tuition ($19,260), mandatory fees ($480), and room and board ($6170). *College room only:* $3150. *Part-time tuition:* $325 per credit hour. *Part-time fees:* $65 per term.
FRESHMAN FINANCIAL AID (Fall 2005, est.) 153 applied for aid; of those 90% were deemed to have need. 100% of freshmen with need received aid. *Average percent of need met:* 81% (excluding resources awarded to replace EFC). *Average financial aid package:* $14,053 (excluding resources awarded to replace EFC). 4% of all full-time freshmen had no need and received non-need-based gift aid.
UNDERGRADUATE FINANCIAL AID (Fall 2005, est.) 644 applied for aid; of those 89% were deemed to have need. 100% of undergraduates with need received aid. *Average percent of need met:* 83% (excluding resources awarded to replace EFC). *Average financial aid package:* $14,129 (excluding resources awarded to replace EFC). 8% of all full-time undergraduates had no need and received non-need-based gift aid.
GIFT AID (NEED-BASED) *Total amount:* $1,346,244 (54% federal, 38% state, 8% institutional). *Receiving aid:* Freshmen: 44% (70); All full-time undergraduates: 46% (321). *Average award:* Freshmen: $2341; Undergraduates: $1821. *Scholarships, grants, and awards:* Federal Pell, FSEOG, state, private, college/university gift aid from institutional funds.
GIFT AID (NON-NEED-BASED) *Total amount:* $5,654,343 (9% state, 86% institutional, 5% external sources). *Receiving aid:* Freshmen: 86% (138); Undergraduates: 83% (576). *Average Award:* Freshmen: $12,417; Undergraduates: $7863. *Scholarships, grants, and awards by category: Academic Interests/Achievement:* biological sciences, business, communication, computer science, education, general academic interests/achievements, humanities, mathematics, physical sciences, premedicine, religion/biblical studies, social sciences. *Special Achievements/Activities:* community service, general special achievements/activities, leadership, religious involvement. *Special Characteristics:* children of faculty/staff, children with a deceased or disabled parent, first-generation college students, general special characteristics, international students, local/state students, members of minority groups, out-of-state students, previous college experience, relatives of clergy, religious affiliation.
LOANS *Student loans:* $5,413,610 (45% need-based, 55% non-need-based). 76% of past graduating class borrowed through all loan programs. *Average indebtedness per student:* $17,359. *Average need-based loan:* Freshmen: $3276; Undergraduates: $3401. *Parent loans:* $1,009,569 (100% non-need-based). *Programs:* FFEL (Subsidized and Unsubsidized Stafford, PLUS), Perkins, alternative loans.
WORK-STUDY *Federal work-study:* Total amount: $88,429; 138 jobs averaging $640. *State or other work-study/employment:* Total amount: $123,311 (100% non-need-based). 154 part-time jobs averaging $800.
APPLYING FOR FINANCIAL AID *Required financial aid form:* FAFSA. *Financial aid deadline (priority):* 3/1. *Notification date:* Continuous. Students must reply within 3 weeks of notification.
CONTACT Ms. Amy Francis, Director of Financial Aid, Defiance College, 701 North Clinton Street, Defiance, OH 43512-1610, 419-784-4010 Ext. 376 or toll-free 800-520-4632 Ext. 2359.

DELAWARE STATE UNIVERSITY
Dover, DE

ABOUT THE INSTITUTION State-supported, coed. Awards: bachelor's, master's, and doctoral degrees. 85 undergraduate majors. Total enrollment: 3,722. Undergraduates: 3,440. Freshmen: 940.
GIFT AID (NEED-BASED) *Scholarships, grants, and awards:* Federal Pell, FSEOG, state, Federal Nursing.
GIFT AID (NON-NEED-BASED) *Scholarships, grants, and awards by category: Academic Interests/Achievement:* general academic interests/achievements. *Creative Arts/Performance:* music. *Special Achievements/Activities:* general special achievements/activities. *Special Characteristics:* out-of-state students.
LOANS *Programs:* FFEL (Subsidized and Unsubsidized Stafford, PLUS), Perkins, Federal Nursing.
WORK-STUDY *Federal work-study:* Total amount: $234,423; jobs available. *State or other work-study/employment:* Total amount: $146,816 (100% non-need-based). Part-time jobs available.
APPLYING FOR FINANCIAL AID *Required financial aid form:* FAFSA.
CONTACT Associate Director of Financial Aid, Delaware State University, 1200 North DuPont Highway, Dover, DE 19901-2277, 302-857-6250 or toll-free 800-845-2544.

DELAWARE VALLEY COLLEGE
Doylestown, PA

Tuition & fees: $21,814	Average undergraduate aid package: $17,760

ABOUT THE INSTITUTION Independent, coed. Awards: associate, bachelor's, and master's degrees and post-bachelor's certificates. 28 undergraduate majors. Total enrollment: 2,070. Undergraduates: 1,999. Freshmen: 451. Federal methodology is used as a basis for awarding need-based institutional aid.
UNDERGRADUATE EXPENSES for 2005–06 *Application fee:* $35. *Comprehensive fee:* $29,944 includes full-time tuition ($20,664), mandatory fees ($1150), and room and board ($8130). *College room only:* $3686. Full-time tuition and fees vary according to program. Room and board charges vary according to board plan. *Part-time tuition:* $560 per credit.
FRESHMAN FINANCIAL AID (Fall 2005, est.) 392 applied for aid; of those 90% were deemed to have need. 92% of freshmen with need received aid; of those

Delaware Valley College

77% had need fully met. *Average percent of need met:* 79% (excluding resources awarded to replace EFC). *Average financial aid package:* $16,050 (excluding resources awarded to replace EFC). 20% of all full-time freshmen had no need and received non-need-based gift aid.
UNDERGRADUATE FINANCIAL AID (Fall 2005, est.) 1,310 applied for aid; of those 98% were deemed to have need. 98% of undergraduates with need received aid; of those 69% had need fully met. *Average percent of need met:* 85% (excluding resources awarded to replace EFC). *Average financial aid package:* $17,760 (excluding resources awarded to replace EFC). 22% of all full-time undergraduates had no need and received non-need-based gift aid.
GIFT AID (NEED-BASED) *Total amount:* $13,480,292 (10% federal, 12% state, 77% institutional, 1% external sources). *Receiving aid:* Freshmen: 66% (297); All full-time undergraduates: 64% (1,031). *Average award:* Freshmen: $13,410; Undergraduates: $13,075. *Scholarships, grants, and awards:* Federal Pell, FSEOG, state, private, college/university gift aid from institutional funds.
GIFT AID (NON-NEED-BASED) *Total amount:* $3,274,304 (3% state, 95% institutional, 2% external sources). *Receiving aid:* Freshmen: 12% (56); Undergraduates: 13% (203). *Average Award:* Freshmen: $9754; Undergraduates: $8302. *Scholarships, grants, and awards by category:* Academic Interests/Achievement: 352 awards ($3,274,304 total): general academic interests/achievements. Creative Arts/Performance: 36 awards ($17,200 total): music. Special Achievements/Activities: 1 award ($1000 total): memberships. Special Characteristics: 2 awards ($1000 total): handicapped students. *Tuition waivers:* Full or partial for employees or children of employees.
LOANS *Student loans:* $6,909,690 (58% need-based, 42% non-need-based). 68% of past graduating class borrowed through all loan programs. *Average indebtedness per student:* $17,482. *Average need-based loan:* Freshmen: $2275; Undergraduates: $3709. *Parent loans:* $5,847,668 (27% need-based, 73% non-need-based). *Programs:* FFEL (Subsidized and Unsubsidized Stafford, PLUS), Perkins, state, alternative loans.
WORK-STUDY *Federal work-study:* Total amount: $160,000; 117 jobs averaging $1624. *State or other work-study/employment:* Total amount: $400,000 (75% need-based, 25% non-need-based).
APPLYING FOR FINANCIAL AID *Required financial aid form:* FAFSA. *Financial aid deadline (priority):* 4/1. *Notification date:* Continuous. Students must reply by 5/1.
CONTACT Mr. Robert Sauer, Director of Student Financial Aid, Delaware Valley College, 700 East Butler Avenue, Doylestown, PA 18901-2697, 215-489-2297 or toll-free 800-2DELVAL (in-state). *E-mail:* finaid@devalcol.edu.

DELTA STATE UNIVERSITY
Cleveland, MS

CONTACT Ms. Ann Margaret Mullins, Director of Student Financial Assistance, Delta State University, PO Box 3154, Cleveland, MS 38733-0001, 662-846-4670 or toll-free 800-468-6378. *E-mail:* amullins@deltastate.edu.

DENISON UNIVERSITY
Granville, OH

Tuition & fees: $28,920	Average undergraduate aid package: $25,367

ABOUT THE INSTITUTION Independent, coed. Awards: bachelor's degrees. 39 undergraduate majors. Total enrollment: 2,329. Undergraduates: 2,329. Freshmen: 622. Federal methodology is used as a basis for awarding need-based institutional aid.
UNDERGRADUATE EXPENSES for 2005–06 *Application fee:* $40. *Comprehensive fee:* $37,040 includes full-time tuition ($28,170), mandatory fees ($750), and room and board ($8120). *College room only:* $4470. Room and board charges vary according to housing facility. *Part-time tuition:* $880 per semester hour. Part-time tuition and fees vary according to course load. *Payment plan:* Installment.
FRESHMAN FINANCIAL AID (Fall 2005, est.) 374 applied for aid; of those 76% were deemed to have need. 100% of freshmen with need received aid; of those 40% had need fully met. *Average percent of need met:* 93% (excluding resources awarded to replace EFC). *Average financial aid package:* $24,545 (excluding resources awarded to replace EFC). 46% of all full-time freshmen had no need and received non-need-based gift aid.
UNDERGRADUATE FINANCIAL AID (Fall 2005, est.) 1,229 applied for aid; of those 82% were deemed to have need. 100% of undergraduates with need received aid; of those 40% had need fully met. *Average percent of need met:* 93% (excluding resources awarded to replace EFC). *Average financial aid package:* $25,367 (excluding resources awarded to replace EFC). 51% of all full-time undergraduates had no need and received non-need-based gift aid.
GIFT AID (NEED-BASED) *Total amount:* $18,090,122 (4% federal, 2% state, 94% institutional). *Receiving aid:* Freshmen: 46% (285); All full-time undergraduates: 44% (1,003). *Average award:* Freshmen: $24,545; Undergraduates: $25,367. *Scholarships, grants, and awards:* Federal Pell, FSEOG, state, private, college/university gift aid from institutional funds.
GIFT AID (NON-NEED-BASED) *Total amount:* $17,407,180 (1% federal, 5% state, 90% institutional, 4% external sources). *Receiving aid:* Freshmen: 40% (251); Undergraduates: 40% (924). *Average Award:* Freshmen: $12,213; Undergraduates: $12,464. *Scholarships, grants, and awards by category:* Academic Interests/Achievement: 1,867 awards ($22,818,701 total): biological sciences, communication, English, foreign languages, general academic interests/achievements, humanities, physical sciences. Creative Arts/Performance: 147 awards ($284,454 total): art/fine arts, dance, music, theater/drama. Special Achievements/Activities: 14 awards ($16,160 total): leadership. Special Characteristics: 120 awards ($2,168,536 total): members of minority groups. *Tuition waivers:* Full or partial for employees or children of employees. *ROTC:* Army cooperative.
LOANS *Student loans:* $5,254,589 (92% need-based, 8% non-need-based). 49% of past graduating class borrowed through all loan programs. *Average indebtedness per student:* $14,657. *Average need-based loan:* Freshmen: $4182; Undergraduates: $5013. *Parent loans:* $2,762,373 (100% non-need-based). *Programs:* Federal Direct (Subsidized and Unsubsidized Stafford, PLUS), Perkins, college/university.
WORK-STUDY *Federal work-study:* Total amount: $985,473; 537 jobs averaging $1762. *State or other work-study/employment:* Total amount: $2,253,712 (100% non-need-based). 1,255 part-time jobs averaging $2071.
APPLYING FOR FINANCIAL AID *Required financial aid form:* FAFSA. *Financial aid deadline (priority):* 2/15. *Notification date:* 3/30. Students must reply by 5/1 or within 2 weeks of notification.
CONTACT Ms. Nancy Hoover, Director of Financial Aid, Denison University, PO Box M, Granville, OH 43023-0613, 740-587-6279 or toll-free 800-DENISON. *Fax:* 740-587-5706. *E-mail:* hoover@denison.edu.

DePAUL UNIVERSITY
Chicago, IL

Tuition & fees: $21,040	Average undergraduate aid package: $16,309

ABOUT THE INSTITUTION Independent Roman Catholic, coed. Awards: bachelor's, master's, doctoral, and first professional degrees and post-bachelor's and post-master's certificates. 100 undergraduate majors. Total enrollment: 23,148. Undergraduates: 14,740. Freshmen: 2,400. Federal methodology is used as a basis for awarding need-based institutional aid.
UNDERGRADUATE EXPENSES for 2005–06 *Application fee:* $40. *Comprehensive fee:* $29,905 includes full-time tuition ($20,900), mandatory fees ($140), and room and board ($8865). *College room only:* $6507. Full-time tuition and fees vary according to program. Room and board charges vary according to board plan, housing facility, and location. *Part-time tuition:* $384 per quarter hour. Part-time tuition and fees vary according to program. *Payment plans:* Installment, deferred payment.
FRESHMAN FINANCIAL AID (Fall 2005, est.) 1826 applied for aid; of those 83% were deemed to have need. 96% of freshmen with need received aid; of those 14% had need fully met. *Average percent of need met:* 70% (excluding resources awarded to replace EFC). *Average financial aid package:* $16,928 (excluding resources awarded to replace EFC). 11% of all full-time freshmen had no need and received non-need-based gift aid.
UNDERGRADUATE FINANCIAL AID (Fall 2005, est.) 8,121 applied for aid; of those 87% were deemed to have need. 96% of undergraduates with need received aid; of those 14% had need fully met. *Average percent of need met:* 68% (excluding resources awarded to replace EFC). *Average financial aid package:* $16,309 (excluding resources awarded to replace EFC). 7% of all full-time undergraduates had no need and received non-need-based gift aid.
GIFT AID (NEED-BASED) *Total amount:* $59,200,000 (21% federal, 22% state, 56% institutional, 1% external sources). *Receiving aid:* Freshmen: 46% (1,093); All full-time undergraduates: 49% (5,524). *Average award:* Freshmen: $11,853;

Undergraduates: $10,461. *Scholarships, grants, and awards:* Federal Pell, FSEOG, state, private, college/university gift aid from institutional funds, United Negro College Fund.
GIFT AID (NON-NEED-BASED) *Total amount:* $19,170,000 (1% state, 91% institutional, 8% external sources). *Receiving aid:* Freshmen: 27% (652); Undergraduates: 17% (1,967). *Average Award:* Freshmen: $8900; Undergraduates: $8144. *Scholarships, grants, and awards by category:* Academic Interests/Achievement: 1,650 awards ($8,500,000 total): biological sciences, business, computer science, education, general academic interests/achievements. *Creative Arts/Performance:* 375 awards ($2,600,000 total): art/fine arts, debating, music, performing arts, theater/drama. *Special Achievements/Activities:* 70 awards ($250,000 total): community service. *Special Characteristics:* children of faculty/staff. *Tuition waivers:* Full or partial for employees or children of employees. *ROTC:* Army cooperative.
LOANS *Student loans:* $84,000,000 (64% need-based, 36% non-need-based). 65% of past graduating class borrowed through all loan programs. *Average indebtedness per student:* $21,061. *Average need-based loan:* Freshmen: $3312; Undergraduates: $4581. *Parent loans:* $28,500,000 (100% non-need-based). *Programs:* Federal Direct (Subsidized and Unsubsidized Stafford, PLUS), Perkins.
WORK-STUDY *Federal work-study:* Total amount: $2,200,000; 890 jobs averaging $2472. *State or other work-study/employment:* Total amount: $4,140,000 (31% need-based, 69% non-need-based). Part-time jobs available.
ATHLETIC AWARDS *Total amount:* $3,500,000 (100% non-need-based).
APPLYING FOR FINANCIAL AID *Required financial aid form:* FAFSA. *Financial aid deadline:* 4/1 (priority: 3/1). *Notification date:* Continuous. Students must reply by 5/1 or within 4 weeks of notification.
CONTACT Christopher Rone, Associate Director of Financial Aid, DePaul University, 1 East Jackson Boulevard, Suite 9000, Chicago, IL 60604-2287, 773-325-7815. *Fax:* 773-325-7746.

DePAUW UNIVERSITY
Greencastle, IN

Tuition & fees: $27,780	Average undergraduate aid package: $24,873

ABOUT THE INSTITUTION Independent religious, coed. Awards: bachelor's degrees. 45 undergraduate majors. Total enrollment: 2,397. Undergraduates: 2,397. Freshmen: 586. Both federal and institutional methodology are used as a basis for awarding need-based institutional aid.
UNDERGRADUATE EXPENSES for 2006–07 *Application fee:* $40. *Comprehensive fee:* $35,580 includes full-time tuition ($27,400), mandatory fees ($380), and room and board ($7800). *College room only:* $4100. *Part-time tuition:* $856.25 per semester hour.
FRESHMAN FINANCIAL AID (Fall 2005, est.) 407 applied for aid; of those 75% were deemed to have need. 100% of freshmen with need received aid; of those 70% had need fully met. *Average percent of need met:* 97% (excluding resources awarded to replace EFC). *Average financial aid package:* $25,384 (excluding resources awarded to replace EFC). 46% of all full-time freshmen had no need and received non-need-based gift aid.
UNDERGRADUATE FINANCIAL AID (Fall 2005, est.) 1,342 applied for aid; of those 81% were deemed to have need. 100% of undergraduates with need received aid; of those 91% had need fully met. *Average percent of need met:* 98% (excluding resources awarded to replace EFC). *Average financial aid package:* $24,873 (excluding resources awarded to replace EFC). 49% of all full-time undergraduates had no need and received non-need-based gift aid.
GIFT AID (NEED-BASED) *Total amount:* $16,814,102 (5% federal, 8% state, 83% institutional, 4% external sources). *Receiving aid:* Freshmen: 40% (232); All full-time undergraduates: 36% (840). *Average award:* Freshmen: $14,841; Undergraduates: $14,486. *Scholarships, grants, and awards:* Federal Pell, FSEOG, state, private, college/university gift aid from institutional funds.
GIFT AID (NON-NEED-BASED) *Total amount:* $20,234,760 (89% institutional, 11% external sources). *Receiving aid:* Freshmen: 38% (221); Undergraduates: 32% (755). *Average Award:* Freshmen: $11,203; Undergraduates: $12,345. *Scholarships, grants, and awards by category:* Academic Interests/Achievement: biological sciences, business, communication, computer science, foreign languages, general academic interests/achievements, humanities, international studies, mathematics, physical sciences. *Creative Arts/Performance:* art/fine arts, cinema/film/broadcasting, journalism/publications, music. *Special Achievements/Activities:* community service, leadership. *Special Characteristics:* children and siblings of alumni, children of faculty/staff, ethnic background, international students, members of minority groups, relatives of clergy, religious affiliation. *ROTC:* Army cooperative, Air Force cooperative.
LOANS *Student loans:* $6,764,102 (72% need-based, 28% non-need-based). 55% of past graduating class borrowed through all loan programs. *Average indebtedness per student:* $15,635. *Average need-based loan:* Freshmen: $3745; Undergraduates: $4637. *Parent loans:* $4,558,039 (46% need-based, 54% non-need-based). *Programs:* FFEL (Subsidized and Unsubsidized Stafford, PLUS), Perkins, college/university, alternative loans.
WORK-STUDY *Federal work-study:* Total amount: $986,013; 698 jobs averaging $1412. *State or other work-study/employment:* Total amount: $20,800 (45% need-based, 55% non-need-based). 17 part-time jobs averaging $1224.
APPLYING FOR FINANCIAL AID *Required financial aid forms:* FAFSA, institution's own form. *Financial aid deadline:* 2/15. *Notification date:* 3/31. Students must reply by 5/1.
CONTACT Joanne L. Haymaker, Associate Director of Financial Aid, DePauw University, 313 South Locust Street, Greencastle, IN 46135-0037, 765-658-4030 or toll-free 800-447-2495. *Fax:* 765-658-4177. *E-mail:* jhaymaker@depauw.edu.

DeSALES UNIVERSITY
Center Valley, PA

ABOUT THE INSTITUTION Independent Roman Catholic, coed. Awards: bachelor's and master's degrees and post-bachelor's and post-master's certificates. 38 undergraduate majors. Total enrollment: 3,282. Undergraduates: 2,489. Freshmen: 434.
GIFT AID (NEED-BASED) *Scholarships, grants, and awards:* Federal Pell, FSEOG, state, private, college/university gift aid from institutional funds.
GIFT AID (NON-NEED-BASED) *Scholarships, grants, and awards by category:* Academic Interests/Achievement: biological sciences, business, communication, computer science, education, English, foreign languages, general academic interests/achievements, health fields, humanities, mathematics, military science, physical sciences, premedicine, religion/biblical studies, social sciences. *Creative Arts/Performance:* cinema/film/broadcasting, creative writing, dance, general creative arts/performance, music, performing arts, theater/drama. *Special Achievements/Activities:* general special achievements/activities, leadership. *Special Characteristics:* children of educators, children of faculty/staff, relatives of clergy, religious affiliation, siblings of current students.
LOANS *Programs:* FFEL (Subsidized and Unsubsidized Stafford, PLUS), Perkins, Federal Nursing, alternative loans.
WORK-STUDY *Federal work-study:* Total amount: $567,399; 324 jobs averaging $631. *State or other work-study/employment:* Total amount: $251,800 (47% need-based, 53% non-need-based). 234 part-time jobs averaging $631.
APPLYING FOR FINANCIAL AID *Required financial aid forms:* FAFSA, institution's own form, state aid form.
CONTACT Mr. Peter Rautzhan, Director of Admissions and Financial Aid, DeSales University, 2755 Station Avenue, Center Valley, PA 18034-9568, 610-282-1100 Ext. 1332 or toll-free 877-4DESALES (in-state), 800-228-5114 (out-of-state). *Fax:* 610-282-0131. *E-mail:* peter.rautzhan@desales.edu.

DESIGN INSTITUTE OF SAN DIEGO
San Diego, CA

CONTACT Financial Aid Office, Design Institute of San Diego, 8555 Commerce Avenue, San Diego, CA 92121, 858-566-1200 or toll-free 800-619-4337.

DeVRY INSTITUTE OF TECHNOLOGY
Long Island City, NY

CONTACT Elvira Senese, Dean of Student Finance, DeVry Institute of Technology, 30-20 Thomson Avenue, Long Island City, NY 11101, 718-472-2728 or toll-free 866-338-7934. *Fax:* 718-269-4284.

DeVRY UNIVERSITY
Mesa, AZ

CONTACT Financial Aid Office, DeVry University, 1201 South Alma School Road, Mesa, AZ 85210-2011, 480-827-1511.

DeVRY UNIVERSITY
Phoenix, AZ
CONTACT Kathy Wyse, Dean of Student Finance, DeVry University, 2149 West Dunlap Avenue, Phoenix, AZ 85021-2995, 602-870-9222 or toll-free 866-338-7934. *Fax:* 602-870-1209.

DeVRY UNIVERSITY
Elk Grove, CA
CONTACT Financial Aid Office, DeVry University, Sacramento Center, 2218 Kausen Drive, Elk Grove, CA 95758, 916-478-2847 or toll-free 866-573-3879.

DeVRY UNIVERSITY
Fremont, CA
CONTACT Kim Kane, Director of Student Finance, DeVry University, 6600 Dumbarton Circle, Fremont, CA 94555, 510-574-1100 or toll-free 888-393-3879. *Fax:* 510-742-0868.

DeVRY UNIVERSITY
Irvine, CA
CONTACT Financial Aid Office, DeVry University, 3333 Michelson Drive, Suite 420, Irvine, CA 92612-1682, 949-752-5631.

DeVRY UNIVERSITY
Long Beach, CA
CONTACT Kathy Odom, Director of Financial Aid, DeVry University, 3880 Kilroy Airport Way, Long Beach, CA 90806, 562-427-0861 or toll-free 800-597-0444. *Fax:* 562-989-1578.

DeVRY UNIVERSITY
Pomona, CA
CONTACT Kathy Odom, Director of Financial Aid, DeVry University, 901 Corporate Center Drive, Pomona, CA 91768-2642, 909-622-8866 or toll-free 866-338-7934. *Fax:* 909-623-5666.

DeVRY UNIVERSITY
San Diego, CA
CONTACT Financial Aid Office, DeVry University, 2655 Camino Del Rio North, Suite 201, San Diego, CA 92108-1633, 619-683-2446.

DeVRY UNIVERSITY
San Francisco, CA
CONTACT Financial Aid Office, DeVry University, 455 Market Street, Suite 1650, San Francisco, CA 94105-2472, 415-243-8787.

DeVRY UNIVERSITY
West Hills, CA
CONTACT Ann Logan, Dean of Student Finance, DeVry University, 22801 Roscoe Boulevard, West Hills, CA 91304, 818-932-3001 or toll-free 888-610-0800. *Fax:* 818-932-3131.

DeVRY UNIVERSITY
Broomfield, CO
CONTACT Terry Bargas, Director of Financial Aid, DeVry University, 925 South Niagara Street, Denver, CO 80224, 303-329-3340. *Fax:* 303-321-3412.

DeVRY UNIVERSITY
Colorado Springs, CO
CONTACT Carol Oppman, Director of Financial Aid, DeVry University, 225 South Union Boulevard, Colorado Springs, CO 80910, 719-632-3000 or toll-free 866-338-7934. *Fax:* 719-632-1909.

DeVRY UNIVERSITY
Westminster, CO
CONTACT Office of Financial Aid, DeVry University, 1870 West 122nd Avenue, Westminster, CO 80234-2010, 303-280-7400 or toll-free 866-338-7934.

DeVRY UNIVERSITY
Miami, FL
CONTACT Financial Aid Office, DeVry University, 200 South Biscayne Boulevard, Suite 500, Miami, FL 33131-5351, 786-425-1113.

DeVRY UNIVERSITY
Miramar, FL
CONTACT Office of Financial Aid, DeVry University, 2300 Southwest 145th Avenue, Miramar, FL 33027, 954-499-9700 or toll-free 866-338-7934.

DeVRY UNIVERSITY
Orlando, FL
CONTACT Estrella Velazquez-Domenech, Director of Student Finance, DeVry University, 4000 Millenia Boulevard, Orlando, FL 32839, 407-345-2816 or toll-free 866-338-7934. *Fax:* 407-355-4855.

DeVRY UNIVERSITY
Tampa, FL
CONTACT Financial Aid Office, DeVry University, 3030 North Rocky Point Drive West, Suite 100, Tampa, FL 33607-5901, 813-288-8994.

DeVRY UNIVERSITY
Alpharetta, GA
CONTACT David Pickett, Assistant Director of Financial Aid, DeVry University, 2555 Northwinds Parkway, Alpharetta, GA 30004, 770-521-4900 or toll-free 866-338-7934. *Fax:* 770-664-8024.

DeVRY UNIVERSITY
Atlanta, GA
CONTACT Financial Aid Office, DeVry University, Fifteen Piedmont Center, Plaza Level 100, Atlanta, GA 30305-1543, 404-296-7400.

DeVRY UNIVERSITY
Decatur, GA
CONTACT Robin Winston, Director of Financial Aid, DeVry University, 250 North Arcadia Avenue, Decatur, GA 30030-2198, 404-292-7900 or toll-free 866-338-7934. *Fax:* 404-292-2321.

DeVRY UNIVERSITY
Duluth, GA
CONTACT Financial Aid Office, DeVry University, 3505 Koger Boulevard, Suite 170, Duluth, GA 30096-7671, 678-380-9780.

DeVRY UNIVERSITY
Addison, IL
CONTACT Sejal Amin, Director of Student Finance, DeVry University, 1221 North Swift Road, Addison, IL 60101-6106, 630-953-1300 or toll-free 800-346-5420.

DeVRY UNIVERSITY
Chicago, IL
CONTACT Milena Dobrina, Director of Financial Aid, DeVry University, 3300 North Campbell Avenue, Chicago, IL 60618-5994, 773-929-8500 or toll-free 800-383-3879. *Fax:* 773-348-1780.

DeVRY UNIVERSITY
Elgin, IL
CONTACT Financial Aid Office, DeVry University, 385 Airport Road, Elgin, IL 60123-9341, 847-622-1135.

DeVRY UNIVERSITY
Gurnee, IL
CONTACT Financial Aid Office, DeVry University, 1075 Tri-State Parkway, Suite 800, Gurnee, IL 60031-9126, 847-855-2649 or toll-free 866-563-3879.

DeVRY UNIVERSITY
Naperville, IL
CONTACT Financial Aid Office, DeVry University, 2056 Westings Avenue, Suite 40, Naperville, IL 60563-2361, 630-428-9086.

DeVRY UNIVERSITY
Oakbrook Terrace, IL
CONTACT Financial Aid Office, DeVry University, One Tower Lane, Oakbrook Terrace, IL 60181, 630-574-1960.

DeVRY UNIVERSITY
Tinley Park, IL
CONTACT Director of Student Finance, DeVry University, 18624 West Creek Drive, Tinley Park, IL 60477, 708-342-3300 or toll-free 866-338-7934. *Fax:* 708-342-3120.

DeVRY UNIVERSITY
Indianapolis, IN
CONTACT Financial Aid Office, DeVry University, 9100 Keystone Crossing, Suite 350, Indianapolis, IN 46240-2158, 317-581-8854 or toll-free 866-513-3879.

DeVRY UNIVERSITY
Merrillville, IN
CONTACT Financial Aid Office, DeVry University, Twin Towers, 1000 East 80th Place, Suite 222 Mall, Merrillville, IN 46410-5673, 219-736-7440.

DeVRY UNIVERSITY
Bethesda, MD
CONTACT Financial Aid Office, DeVry University, 4550 Montgomery Avenue. Suite 100 North, Bethesda, MD 20814-3304, 301-652-8477 or toll-free 866-338-7934.

DeVRY UNIVERSITY
Edina, MN
CONTACT Financial Aid Office, DeVry University, 7700 France Avenue South, Suite 575, Edina, MN 55435, 952-838-1860 or toll-free 866-338-7934 (in-state).

DeVRY UNIVERSITY
Kansas City, MO
CONTACT Maureen Kelly, Senior Associate Director of Financial Aid, DeVry University, 11224 Holmes Street, Kansas City, MO 64131-3698, 816-941-0430 or toll-free 800-821-3766.

DeVRY UNIVERSITY
Kansas City, MO
CONTACT Financial Aid Office, DeVry University, City Center Square, 1100 Main Street, Suite 118, Kansas City, MO 64105-2112, 816-221-1300.

DeVRY UNIVERSITY
St. Louis, MO
CONTACT Financial Aid Office, DeVry University, 1801 Park 270 Drive, Suite 260, St. Louis, MO 63146-4020, 314-542-4222.

DeVRY UNIVERSITY
Henderson, NV
CONTACT Financial Aid Office, DeVry University, 2490 Paseo Verde Parkway, Suite 150, Henderson, NV 89074-7120, 702-933-9700 or toll-free 866-783-3879.

DeVRY UNIVERSITY
North Brunswick, NJ
CONTACT Albert Cama, Director of Financial Aid, DeVry University, 630 US Highway 1, North Brunswick, NJ 08902, 732-435-4880 or toll-free 866-338-7934. *Fax:* 732-435-4867.

DeVRY UNIVERSITY
Charlotte, NC
CONTACT Financial Aid Office, DeVry University, 4521 Sharon Road, Suite 145, Charlotte, NC 28211-3627, 704-362-2345 or toll-free 866-923-3879.

DeVRY UNIVERSITY
Cleveland, OH
CONTACT Financial Aid Office, DeVry University, 200 Public Square, Suite 150, Cleveland, OH 44114-2301, 216-781-8000.

DeVRY UNIVERSITY
Columbus, OH
CONTACT Cynthia Price, Director of Financial Aid, DeVry University, 1350 Alum Creek Drive, Columbus, OH 43209-2705, 614-253-7291 or toll-free 800-426-2206. *Fax:* 614-252-4108.

DeVRY UNIVERSITY
Seven Hills, OH
CONTACT Financial Aid Office, DeVry University, The Genesis Building, 6000 Lombardo Center, Seven Hills, OH 44131-6907, 216-328-8754 or toll-free 866-453-3879.

DeVry University

DeVRY UNIVERSITY
Portland, OR
CONTACT Financial Aid Office, DeVry University, Peterkort Center II, 9755 SW Barnes Road, Suite 150, Portland, OR 97225-6651, 503-296-7468 or toll-free 866-338-7934.

DeVRY UNIVERSITY
Chesterbrook, PA
CONTACT Financial Aid Office, DeVry University, 701 Lee Road, Suite 103, Chesterbrook, PA 19087-5612, 610-889-9980.

DeVRY UNIVERSITY
Fort Washington, PA
CONTACT Financial Aid Office, DeVry University, 1140 Virginia Drive, Fort Washington, PA 19034, 215-591-5700 or toll-free 866-338-7934.

DeVRY UNIVERSITY
Pittsburgh, PA
CONTACT Financial Aid Office, DeVry University, FreeMarkets Center, 210 Sixth Avenue, Suite 200, Pittsburgh, PA 15222-9123, 412-642-9072 or toll-free 866-77DEVRY.

DeVRY UNIVERSITY
Houston, TX
CONTACT Financial Aid Office, DeVry University, 11125 Equity Drive, Houston, TX 77041, 713-850-0888 or toll-free 866-338-7934.

DeVRY UNIVERSITY
Irving, TX
CONTACT Tommy Sims, Financial Aid Officer, DeVry University, 4800 Regent Boulevard, Irving, TX 75063-2440, 972-929-6777 or toll-free 866-338-7934.

DeVRY UNIVERSITY
Plano, TX
CONTACT Financial Aid Office, DeVry University, Plano Corporate Center II, 2301 West Plano Parkway, Suite 101, Plano, TX 75075-8435, 972-943-8041.

DeVRY UNIVERSITY
Arlington, VA
CONTACT Roberta McDevitt, Director of Student Finance, DeVry University, 2341 Jefferson Davis Highway, Arlington, VA 22202, 866-338-7932 or toll-free 866-563-3900. Fax: 703-414-4040.

DeVRY UNIVERSITY
McLean, VA
CONTACT Financial Aid Office, DeVry University, 1751 Pinnacle Drive, Suite 250, McLean, VA 22102-3832, 703-556-9669.

DeVRY UNIVERSITY
Bellevue, WA
CONTACT Financial Aid Office, DeVry University, 500 108th Avenue NE, Suite 320, Bellevue, WA 98004-5519, 425-455-2242.

DeVRY UNIVERSITY
Federal Way, WA
CONTACT Diane Rooney, Assistant Director of Student Finance, DeVry University, 3600 South 344th Way, Federal Way, WA 98001, 253-943-2800 or toll-free 866-338-7934. Fax: 253-943-5503.

DeVRY UNIVERSITY
Milwaukee, WI
CONTACT Financial Aid Office, DeVry University, 100 East Wisconsin Avenue, Suite 2550, Milwaukee, WI 53202-4107, 414-278-7677 or toll-free 866-683-3879.

DeVRY UNIVERSITY
Waukesha, WI
CONTACT Financial Aid Office, DeVry University, 20935 Swenson Drive, Suite 450, Waukesha, WI 53186-4047, 262-798-9889.

DeVRY UNIVERSITY ONLINE
Oakbrook Terrace, IL
CONTACT Financial Aid Office, DeVry University Online, One Tower Lane, Suite 1000, Oakbrook Terrace, IL 60181, 630-574-1960 or toll-free 866-338-7934.

DICKINSON COLLEGE
Carlisle, PA

Tuition & fees: $32,120   Average undergraduate aid package: $27,496

ABOUT THE INSTITUTION Independent, coed. Awards: bachelor's degrees. 46 undergraduate majors. Total enrollment: 2,352. Undergraduates: 2,352. Freshmen: 648. Both federal and institutional methodology are used as a basis for awarding need-based institutional aid.

UNDERGRADUATE EXPENSES for 2005–06 *Application fee:* $60. *One-time required fee:* $25. *Comprehensive fee:* $40,170 includes full-time tuition ($31,800), mandatory fees ($320), and room and board ($8050). *College room only:* $4150. Room and board charges vary according to housing facility. *Part-time tuition:* $3975 per course. *Part-time fees:* $40 per credit. *Payment plan:* Installment.

FRESHMAN FINANCIAL AID (Fall 2005, est.) 422 applied for aid; of those 78% were deemed to have need. 98% of freshmen with need received aid; of those 83% had need fully met. *Average percent of need met:* 99% (excluding resources awarded to replace EFC). *Average financial aid package:* $27,977 (excluding resources awarded to replace EFC). 10% of all full-time freshmen had no need and received non-need-based gift aid.

UNDERGRADUATE FINANCIAL AID (Fall 2005, est.) 1,340 applied for aid; of those 85% were deemed to have need. 99% of undergraduates with need received aid; of those 72% had need fully met. *Average percent of need met:* 96% (excluding resources awarded to replace EFC). *Average financial aid package:* $27,496 (excluding resources awarded to replace EFC). 12% of all full-time undergraduates had no need and received non-need-based gift aid.

GIFT AID (NEED-BASED) *Total amount:* $22,275,477 (5% federal, 3% state, 89% institutional, 3% external sources). *Receiving aid:* Freshmen: 48% (313); All full-time undergraduates: 47% (1,070). *Average award:* Freshmen: $22,575; Undergraduates: $20,818. *Scholarships, grants, and awards:* Federal Pell, FSEOG, state, private, college/university gift aid from institutional funds.

GIFT AID (NON-NEED-BASED) *Total amount:* $4,578,577 (8% federal, 82% institutional, 10% external sources). *Receiving aid:* Freshmen: 7% (45); Undergraduates: 6% (135). *Average Award:* Freshmen: $10,973; Undergraduates: $12,318. *Scholarships, grants, and awards by category:* Academic Interests/Achievement: general academic interests/achievements, military science. Special Achievements/Activities: general special achievements/activities, leadership. Special Characteristics: children and siblings of alumni, children of faculty/staff, international students. *Tuition waivers:* Full or partial for employees or children of employees. *ROTC:* Army.

LOANS *Student loans:* $7,222,547 (74% need-based, 26% non-need-based). 62% of past graduating class borrowed through all loan programs. *Average*

indebtedness per student: $20,982. ***Average need-based loan:*** Freshmen: $3628; Undergraduates: $5224. ***Parent loans:*** $5,192,879 (35% need-based, 65% non-need-based). ***Programs:*** FFEL (Subsidized and Unsubsidized Stafford, PLUS), Perkins, college/university.
WORK-STUDY *Federal work-study:* Total amount: $1,411,694; 754 jobs averaging $1872. ***State or other work-study/employment:*** Total amount: $451,640 (69% need-based, 31% non-need-based). 149 part-time jobs averaging $3031.
APPLYING FOR FINANCIAL AID *Required financial aid forms:* FAFSA, CSS Financial Aid PROFILE, state aid form, noncustodial (divorced/separated) parent's statement, business/farm supplement. ***Financial aid deadline:*** 2/1 (priority: 11/15). ***Notification date:*** 3/20. Students must reply by 5/1 or within 2 weeks of notification.
CONTACT Judith B. Carter, Director of Financial Aid, Dickinson College, PO Box 1773, Carlisle, PA 17013-2896, 717-245-1308 or toll-free 800-644-1773. *Fax:* 717-245-1972. *E-mail:* finaid@dickinson.edu.

DICKINSON STATE UNIVERSITY
Dickinson, ND

Tuition & fees (ND res): $4979 | **Average undergraduate aid package:** N/A

ABOUT THE INSTITUTION State-supported, coed. Awards: associate and bachelor's degrees. 43 undergraduate majors. Total enrollment: 2,516. Undergraduates: 2,516. Freshmen: 351. Federal methodology is used as a basis for awarding need-based institutional aid.
UNDERGRADUATE EXPENSES for 2005–06 *Application fee:* $35. ***Tuition, state resident:*** full-time $4154. ***Tuition, nonresident:*** full-time $9712. Full-time tuition and fees vary according to location, program, and reciprocity agreements. Part-time tuition and fees vary according to course load, location, program, and reciprocity agreements. ***College room and board:*** $3694. Room and board charges vary according to board plan.
GIFT AID (NEED-BASED) *Total amount:* $2,457,768 (96% federal, 4% state). ***Scholarships, grants, and awards:*** Federal Pell, FSEOG, state, college/university gift aid from institutional funds, National Guard tuition waivers, staff waivers.
GIFT AID (NON-NEED-BASED) *Scholarships, grants, and awards by category: Academic Interests/Achievement:* 537 awards ($436,665 total): agriculture, biological sciences, business, communication, computer science, education, English, foreign languages, general academic interests/achievements, health fields, humanities, mathematics, physical sciences, premedicine, social sciences. *Creative Arts/Performance:* 111 awards ($60,090 total): art/fine arts, creative writing, journalism/publications, music, theater/drama. *Special Achievements/Activities:* 32 awards ($43,570 total): cheerleading/drum major, leadership, rodeo. *Special Characteristics:* 399 awards ($1,206,770 total): children of faculty/staff, children with a deceased or disabled parent, ethnic background, general special characteristics, international students, members of minority groups, veterans, veterans' children. ***Tuition waivers:*** Full or partial for minority students, employees or children of employees, senior citizens.
LOANS *Student loans:* $7,314,104 (57% need-based, 43% non-need-based). ***Parent loans:*** $197,877 (100% non-need-based). ***Programs:*** FFEL (Subsidized and Unsubsidized Stafford, PLUS), Perkins, Federal Nursing, state, college/university, Alaska Loans, alternative loans.
WORK-STUDY *Federal work-study:* Total amount: $199,095; jobs available. ***State or other work-study/employment:*** Part-time jobs available.
APPLYING FOR FINANCIAL AID *Required financial aid form:* FAFSA. ***Financial aid deadline (priority):*** 3/15. ***Notification date:*** 6/5. Students must reply within 2 weeks of notification.
CONTACT Ms. Sandy Klein, Director of Financial Aid, Dickinson State University, 291 Campus Drive, Dickinson, ND 58601-4896, 701-483-2371 or toll-free 800-279-4295. *Fax:* 701-483-2720. *E-mail:* sandy.klein@dsu.nodak.edu.

DILLARD UNIVERSITY
New Orleans, LA

ABOUT THE INSTITUTION Independent interdenominational, coed. Awards: bachelor's degrees. 51 undergraduate majors. Total enrollment: 2,155. Undergraduates: 2,155. Freshmen: 501.
GIFT AID (NEED-BASED) *Scholarships, grants, and awards:* Federal Pell, FSEOG, state, private, college/university gift aid from institutional funds, United Negro College Fund.

GIFT AID (NON-NEED-BASED) *Scholarships, grants, and awards by category: Academic Interests/Achievement:* general academic interests/achievements. *Creative Arts/Performance:* art/fine arts, music, theater/drama. *Special Characteristics:* children of faculty/staff, religious affiliation.
LOANS *Programs:* FFEL (Subsidized and Unsubsidized Stafford, PLUS), Perkins, alternative loans.
APPLYING FOR FINANCIAL AID *Required financial aid forms:* FAFSA, institution's own form.
CONTACT Mrs. Cynthia Thornton, Director of Financial Aid, Dillard University, 2601 Gentilly Boulevard, New Orleans, LA 70122-3097, 504-816-4677 or toll-free 800-216-6637 (out-of-state). *Fax:* 504-816-4353. *E-mail:* cthornton@dillard.edu.

DOANE COLLEGE
Crete, NE

Tuition & fees: $17,536 | **Average undergraduate aid package:** $14,009

ABOUT THE INSTITUTION Independent religious, coed. Awards: bachelor's and master's degrees (non-traditional undergraduate programs and graduate programs offered at Lincoln campus). 40 undergraduate majors. Total enrollment: 2,394. Undergraduates: 1,596. Freshmen: 265. Federal methodology is used as a basis for awarding need-based institutional aid.
UNDERGRADUATE EXPENSES for 2005–06 *Application fee:* $15. ***Comprehensive fee:*** $22,458 includes full-time tuition ($17,186), mandatory fees ($350), and room and board ($4922). ***College room only:*** $1850. Full-time tuition and fees vary according to location. Room and board charges vary according to board plan, housing facility, and location. ***Part-time tuition:*** $573 per credit hour. ***Part-time fees:*** $120 per year. Part-time tuition and fees vary according to degree level and location. ***Payment plan:*** Installment.
FRESHMAN FINANCIAL AID (Fall 2005, est.) 258 applied for aid; of those 88% were deemed to have need. 100% of freshmen with need received aid; of those 54% had need fully met. *Average percent of need met:* 97% (excluding resources awarded to replace EFC). *Average financial aid package:* $14,636 (excluding resources awarded to replace EFC). 6% of all full-time freshmen had no need and received non-need-based gift aid.
UNDERGRADUATE FINANCIAL AID (Fall 2005, est.) 872 applied for aid; of those 86% were deemed to have need. 100% of undergraduates with need received aid; of those 52% had need fully met. *Average percent of need met:* 93% (excluding resources awarded to replace EFC). *Average financial aid package:* $14,009 (excluding resources awarded to replace EFC). 9% of all full-time undergraduates had no need and received non-need-based gift aid.
GIFT AID (NEED-BASED) *Total amount:* $3,744,804 (25% federal, 7% state, 52% institutional, 16% external sources). ***Receiving aid:*** Freshmen: 84% (219); All full-time undergraduates: 75% (727). ***Average award:*** Freshmen: $11,039; Undergraduates: $10,138. ***Scholarships, grants, and awards:*** Federal Pell, FSEOG, state, private, college/university gift aid from institutional funds.
GIFT AID (NON-NEED-BASED) *Total amount:* $3,233,277 (100% institutional). ***Receiving aid:*** Freshmen: 3% (7); Undergraduates: 3% (25). ***Average Award:*** Freshmen: $9056; Undergraduates: $9358. ***Scholarships, grants, and awards by category: Creative Arts/Performance:*** art/fine arts, debating, music, theater/drama. *Special Characteristics:* religious affiliation, siblings of current students. ***Tuition waivers:*** Full or partial for employees or children of employees, senior citizens. ***ROTC:*** Army cooperative, Air Force cooperative.
LOANS *Student loans:* $3,534,671 (71% need-based, 29% non-need-based). 79% of past graduating class borrowed through all loan programs. *Average indebtedness per student:* $14,915. ***Average need-based loan:*** Freshmen: $3371; Undergraduates: $4212. ***Parent loans:*** $3,120,367 (100% non-need-based). ***Programs:*** FFEL (Subsidized and Unsubsidized Stafford, PLUS), Perkins.
WORK-STUDY *Federal work-study:* Total amount: $336,305; jobs available. ***State or other work-study/employment:*** Total amount: $128,505 (100% non-need-based). Part-time jobs available.
ATHLETIC AWARDS *Total amount:* $1,469,398 (57% need-based, 43% non-need-based).
APPLYING FOR FINANCIAL AID *Required financial aid form:* FAFSA. ***Financial aid deadline (priority):*** 3/1. ***Notification date:*** Continuous beginning 3/1. Students must reply within 2 weeks of notification.
CONTACT Ms. Janet Dodson, Director of Financial Aid, Doane College, 1014 Boswell Avenue, Crete, NE 68333-2430, 402-826-8260 or toll-free 800-333-6263. *Fax:* 402-826-8600. *E-mail:* janet.dodson@doane.edu.

Dominican College

DOMINICAN COLLEGE
Orangeburg, NY

ABOUT THE INSTITUTION Independent, coed. Awards: associate, bachelor's, master's, and doctoral degrees. 35 undergraduate majors. Total enrollment: 1,530. Undergraduates: 1,409. Freshmen: 290.

GIFT AID (NEED-BASED) *Scholarships, grants, and awards:* Federal Pell, FSEOG, state, private, college/university gift aid from institutional funds.

GIFT AID (NON-NEED-BASED) *Scholarships, grants, and awards by category: Academic Interests/Achievement:* general academic interests/achievements. *Special Achievements/Activities:* community service, leadership, memberships. *Special Characteristics:* children of faculty/staff, general special characteristics, relatives of clergy.

LOANS *Programs:* FFEL (Subsidized and Unsubsidized Stafford, PLUS), Perkins, Federal Nursing.

WORK-STUDY *Federal work-study:* Total amount: $254,817; 138 jobs averaging $1806. *State or other work-study/employment:* Total amount: $53,173 (73% need-based, 27% non-need-based). 25 part-time jobs averaging $2102.

APPLYING FOR FINANCIAL AID *Required financial aid forms:* FAFSA, state aid form.

CONTACT Ms. Eileen Felske, Director of Financial Aid, Dominican College, 470 Western Highway, Orangeburg, NY 10962-1210, 845-359-7800 Ext. 225 or toll-free 866-432-4636. *Fax:* 845-359-2313. *E-mail:* eileen.felske@dc.edu.

DOMINICAN UNIVERSITY
River Forest, IL

Tuition & fees: $20,050 **Average undergraduate aid package: $15,046**

ABOUT THE INSTITUTION Independent Roman Catholic, coed. Awards: bachelor's and master's degrees and post-master's certificates. 46 undergraduate majors. Total enrollment: 3,250. Undergraduates: 1,337. Freshmen: 269. Federal methodology is used as a basis for awarding need-based institutional aid.

UNDERGRADUATE EXPENSES for 2005–06 *Application fee:* $25. *Comprehensive fee:* $26,370 includes full-time tuition ($19,950), mandatory fees ($100), and room and board ($6320). Full-time tuition and fees vary according to program. Room and board charges vary according to board plan and housing facility. *Part-time tuition:* $665 per semester hour. *Part-time fees:* $10 per course. Part-time tuition and fees vary according to location and program. *Payment plan:* Installment.

FRESHMAN FINANCIAL AID (Fall 2005, est.) 228 applied for aid; of those 91% were deemed to have need. 100% of freshmen with need received aid; of those 29% had need fully met. *Average percent of need met:* 87% (excluding resources awarded to replace EFC). *Average financial aid package:* $16,146 (excluding resources awarded to replace EFC). 19% of all full-time freshmen had no need and received non-need-based gift aid.

UNDERGRADUATE FINANCIAL AID (Fall 2005, est.) 945 applied for aid; of those 89% were deemed to have need. 100% of undergraduates with need received aid; of those 27% had need fully met. *Average percent of need met:* 80% (excluding resources awarded to replace EFC). *Average financial aid package:* $15,046 (excluding resources awarded to replace EFC). 18% of all full-time undergraduates had no need and received non-need-based gift aid.

GIFT AID (NEED-BASED) *Total amount:* $9,371,011 (12% federal, 24% state, 62% institutional, 2% external sources). *Receiving aid:* Freshmen: 77% (207); All full-time undergraduates: 80% (824). *Average award:* Freshmen: $12,860; Undergraduates: $11,237. *Scholarships, grants, and awards:* Federal Pell, FSEOG, state, private, college/university gift aid from institutional funds.

GIFT AID (NON-NEED-BASED) *Total amount:* $1,541,388 (1% state, 96% institutional, 3% external sources). *Receiving aid:* Freshmen: 20% (54); Undergraduates: 14% (149). *Average Award:* Freshmen: $11,056; Undergraduates: $11,282. *Scholarships, grants, and awards by category: Academic Interests/Achievement:* 646 awards ($3,799,754 total): general academic interests/achievements, physical sciences. *Special Achievements/Activities:* 13 awards ($36,500 total): leadership. *Special Characteristics:* 94 awards ($230,005 total): children and siblings of alumni, children of faculty/staff, international students, siblings of current students, twins. *Tuition waivers:* Full or partial for children of alumni, employees or children of employees.

LOANS *Student loans:* $5,376,930 (72% need-based, 28% non-need-based). 60% of past graduating class borrowed through all loan programs. *Average indebtedness per student:* $14,923. *Average need-based loan:* Freshmen: $2485; Undergraduates: $3763. *Parent loans:* $1,335,828 (100% non-need-based). *Programs:* FFEL (Subsidized and Unsubsidized Stafford, PLUS), Perkins.

WORK-STUDY *Federal work-study:* Total amount: $617,516; 326 jobs averaging $1865. *State or other work-study/employment:* Total amount: $359,918 (8% need-based, 92% non-need-based). 181 part-time jobs averaging $1975.

APPLYING FOR FINANCIAL AID *Required financial aid form:* FAFSA. *Financial aid deadline (priority):* 6/1. *Notification date:* Continuous beginning 3/1. Students must reply within 2 weeks of notification.

CONTACT Michael Shields, Director of Financial Aid, Dominican University, 7900 West Division Street, River Forest, IL 60305-1099, 708-524-6807 or toll-free 800-828-8475. *Fax:* 708-366-6478. *E-mail:* mshields@dom.edu.

DOMINICAN UNIVERSITY OF CALIFORNIA
San Rafael, CA

Tuition & fees: $28,070 **Average undergraduate aid package: $20,605**

ABOUT THE INSTITUTION Independent religious, coed. Awards: bachelor's and master's degrees and post-bachelor's certificates. 28 undergraduate majors. Total enrollment: 1,631. Undergraduates: 1,177. Freshmen: 227. Federal methodology is used as a basis for awarding need-based institutional aid.

UNDERGRADUATE EXPENSES for 2006–07 *Application fee:* $40. *Comprehensive fee:* $39,370 includes full-time tuition ($27,770), mandatory fees ($300), and room and board ($11,300). *College room only:* $6580. *Part-time tuition:* $1160 per unit. *Part-time fees:* $150 per term.

FRESHMAN FINANCIAL AID (Fall 2005, est.) 195 applied for aid; of those 84% were deemed to have need. 100% of freshmen with need received aid; of those 10% had need fully met. *Average percent of need met:* 14% (excluding resources awarded to replace EFC). *Average financial aid package:* $20,825 (excluding resources awarded to replace EFC). 11% of all full-time freshmen had no need and received non-need-based gift aid.

UNDERGRADUATE FINANCIAL AID (Fall 2005, est.) 946 applied for aid; of those 93% were deemed to have need. 100% of undergraduates with need received aid; of those 8% had need fully met. *Average percent of need met:* 15% (excluding resources awarded to replace EFC). *Average financial aid package:* $20,605 (excluding resources awarded to replace EFC). 13% of all full-time undergraduates had no need and received non-need-based gift aid.

GIFT AID (NEED-BASED) *Total amount:* $12,365,129 (10% federal, 17% state, 68% institutional, 5% external sources). *Receiving aid:* Freshmen: 71% (162); All full-time undergraduates: 73% (840). *Average award:* Freshmen: $6023; Undergraduates: $5682. *Scholarships, grants, and awards:* Federal Pell, FSEOG, state, private, college/university gift aid from institutional funds, Federal Nursing.

GIFT AID (NON-NEED-BASED) *Total amount:* $1,342,190 (99% institutional, 1% external sources). *Receiving aid:* Undergraduates: 3. *Average Award:* Freshmen: $8990; Undergraduates: $7474. *Scholarships, grants, and awards by category: Academic Interests/Achievement:* 929 awards ($6,908,184 total): general academic interests/achievements. *Creative Arts/Performance:* 9 awards ($17,000 total): music. *Special Achievements/Activities:* 2 awards ($12,000 total): community service, general special achievements/activities. *Special Characteristics:* 498 awards ($2,428,932 total): adult students, children and siblings of alumni, children of faculty/staff, ethnic background, first-generation college students, international students, local/state students, members of minority groups, out-of-state students.

LOANS *Student loans:* $8,665,536 (98% need-based, 2% non-need-based). 70% of past graduating class borrowed through all loan programs. *Average indebtedness per student:* $49,337. *Average need-based loan:* Freshmen: $3378; Undergraduates: $4778. *Parent loans:* $9,732,336 (99% need-based, 1% non-need-based). *Programs:* FFEL (Subsidized and Unsubsidized Stafford, PLUS), Perkins, Private loans.

WORK-STUDY *Federal work-study:* Total amount: $693,184; 284 jobs averaging $2431. *State or other work-study/employment:* Total amount: $206,998 (71% need-based, 29% non-need-based). 24 part-time jobs averaging $7751.

ATHLETIC AWARDS Total amount: $252,355 (77% need-based, 23% non-need-based).

APPLYING FOR FINANCIAL AID *Required financial aid forms:* FAFSA, institution's own form, state aid form. *Financial aid deadline (priority):* 3/2. *Notification date:* Continuous beginning 3/15. Students must reply within 2 weeks of notification.

CONTACT Audrey Tanne, Assistant Vice President for Financial Aid and Student Services, Dominican University of California, 50 Acacia Avenue, San Rafael, CA 94901-2298, 415-257-1321 or toll-free 888-323-6763. *Fax:* 415-485-3294. *E-mail:* atanner@dominican.edu.

DORDT COLLEGE
Sioux Center, IA

Tuition & fees: $17,640 | Average undergraduate aid package: $15,719

ABOUT THE INSTITUTION Independent Christian Reformed, coed. Awards: associate, bachelor's, and master's degrees. 86 undergraduate majors. Total enrollment: 1,327. Undergraduates: 1,254. Freshmen: 344. Federal methodology is used as a basis for awarding need-based institutional aid.

UNDERGRADUATE EXPENSES for 2005–06 *Application fee:* $25. *Comprehensive fee:* $22,540 includes full-time tuition ($17,400), mandatory fees ($240), and room and board ($4900). *College room only:* $2580. Room and board charges vary according to board plan and housing facility. *Part-time tuition:* $690 per credit hour. *Part-time fees:* $120 per term. *Payment plan:* Installment.

FRESHMAN FINANCIAL AID (Fall 2005, est.) 320 applied for aid; of those 87% were deemed to have need. 100% of freshmen with need received aid; of those 15% had need fully met. *Average percent of need met:* 85% (excluding resources awarded to replace EFC). *Average financial aid package:* $15,941 (excluding resources awarded to replace EFC). 21% of all full-time freshmen had no need and received non-need-based gift aid.

UNDERGRADUATE FINANCIAL AID (Fall 2005, est.) 1,021 applied for aid; of those 89% were deemed to have need. 100% of undergraduates with need received aid; of those 13% had need fully met. *Average percent of need met:* 86% (excluding resources awarded to replace EFC). *Average financial aid package:* $15,719 (excluding resources awarded to replace EFC). 20% of all full-time undergraduates had no need and received non-need-based gift aid.

GIFT AID (NEED-BASED) *Total amount:* $8,460,647 (12% federal, 13% state, 68% institutional, 7% external sources). *Receiving aid:* Freshmen: 78% (278); All full-time undergraduates: 76% (905). *Average award:* Freshmen: $9623; Undergraduates: $8731. *Scholarships, grants, and awards:* Federal Pell, FSEOG, state, private, college/university gift aid from institutional funds.

GIFT AID (NON-NEED-BASED) *Total amount:* $1,296,186 (91% institutional, 9% external sources). *Average Award:* Freshmen: $8277; Undergraduates: $8179. *Scholarships, grants, and awards by category: Academic Interests/Achievement:* agriculture, biological sciences, business, communication, computer science, education, engineering/technologies, English, foreign languages, general academic interests/achievements, humanities, mathematics, physical sciences, premedicine, religion/biblical studies, social sciences. *Creative Arts/Performance:* 223 awards ($389,045 total): journalism/publications, music, theater/drama. *Special Achievements/Activities:* general special achievements/activities, leadership. *Special Characteristics:* children and siblings of alumni, children of faculty/staff, general special characteristics, handicapped students, international students, local/state students, members of minority groups, out-of-state students, religious affiliation. *Tuition waivers:* Full or partial for employees or children of employees, senior citizens.

LOANS *Student loans:* $6,025,242 (92% need-based, 8% non-need-based). 79% of past graduating class borrowed through all loan programs. *Average indebtedness per student:* $16,600. *Average need-based loan:* Freshmen: $4173; Undergraduates: $4487. *Parent loans:* $1,907,567 (88% need-based, 12% non-need-based). *Programs:* FFEL (Subsidized and Unsubsidized Stafford, PLUS), Perkins, state, college/university, alternative loans.

WORK-STUDY *Federal work-study:* Total amount: $690,100; 578 jobs averaging $1300. *State or other work-study/employment:* Total amount: $758,470 (71% need-based, 29% non-need-based). 472 part-time jobs averaging $1300.

ATHLETIC AWARDS *Total amount:* $503,400 (73% need-based, 27% non-need-based).

APPLYING FOR FINANCIAL AID *Required financial aid forms:* FAFSA, institution's own form. *Financial aid deadline (priority):* 4/1. *Notification date:* Continuous beginning 3/5. Students must reply within 3 weeks of notification.

CONTACT Michael Epema, Director of Financial Aid, Dordt College, 498 4th Avenue NE, Sioux Center, IA 51250-1697, 712-722-6087 Ext. 6082 or toll-free 800-343-6738. *Fax:* 712-722-1967.

DOWLING COLLEGE
Oakdale, NY

Tuition & fees: $13,800 | Average undergraduate aid package: $13,385

ABOUT THE INSTITUTION Independent, coed. Awards: bachelor's, master's, and doctoral degrees and post-bachelor's and post-master's certificates. 52 undergraduate majors. Total enrollment: 6,379. Undergraduates: 3,627. Freshmen: 465. Federal methodology is used as a basis for awarding need-based institutional aid.

UNDERGRADUATE EXPENSES for 2005–06 *Application fee:* $25. *Tuition:* full-time $12,960; part-time $540 per credit hour. *Required fees:* full-time $840; $137.50 per term part-time. Part-time tuition and fees vary according to course load and degree level. Room and board charges vary according to housing facility and location. *Payment plans:* Installment, deferred payment.

FRESHMAN FINANCIAL AID (Fall 2005, est.) 373 applied for aid; of those 83% were deemed to have need. 99% of freshmen with need received aid; of those 5% had need fully met. *Average percent of need met:* 87% (excluding resources awarded to replace EFC). *Average financial aid package:* $12,945 (excluding resources awarded to replace EFC). 24% of all full-time freshmen had no need and received non-need-based gift aid.

UNDERGRADUATE FINANCIAL AID (Fall 2005, est.) 1,782 applied for aid; of those 86% were deemed to have need. 98% of undergraduates with need received aid; of those 9% had need fully met. *Average percent of need met:* 87% (excluding resources awarded to replace EFC). *Average financial aid package:* $13,385 (excluding resources awarded to replace EFC). 14% of all full-time undergraduates had no need and received non-need-based gift aid.

GIFT AID (NEED-BASED) *Total amount:* $10,704,889 (25% federal, 31% state, 43% institutional, 1% external sources). *Receiving aid:* Freshmen: 69% (306); All full-time undergraduates: 65% (1,500). *Average award:* Freshmen: $2742; Undergraduates: $2804. *Scholarships, grants, and awards:* Federal Pell, FSEOG, state, private, college/university gift aid from institutional funds.

GIFT AID (NON-NEED-BASED) *Total amount:* $2,074,636 (2% federal, 4% state, 94% institutional). *Average Award:* Freshmen: $4111; Undergraduates: $3690. *Scholarships, grants, and awards by category: Academic Interests/Achievement:* business, education, general academic interests/achievements. *Special Achievements/Activities:* general special achievements/activities. *Special Characteristics:* children and siblings of alumni, children of educators, children of faculty/staff, children of public servants, children of union members/company employees, children of workers in trades, first-generation college students, general special characteristics, local/state students, public servants. *Tuition waivers:* Full or partial for minority students, children of alumni, employees or children of employees, adult students, senior citizens. *ROTC:* Air Force cooperative.

LOANS *Student loans:* $15,397,802 (72% need-based, 28% non-need-based). 81% of past graduating class borrowed through all loan programs. *Average indebtedness per student:* $18,920. *Average need-based loan:* Freshmen: $2469; Undergraduates: $3691. *Parent loans:* $1,893,351 (69% need-based, 31% non-need-based). *Programs:* Federal Direct (Subsidized and Unsubsidized Stafford, PLUS), FFEL (PLUS), Perkins, alternative loans.

WORK-STUDY Federal work-study jobs available. *State or other work-study/employment:* Part-time jobs available.

ATHLETIC AWARDS *Total amount:* $1,786,236 (45% need-based, 55% non-need-based).

APPLYING FOR FINANCIAL AID *Required financial aid forms:* FAFSA, institution's own form, state aid form. *Financial aid deadline (priority):* 4/1. *Notification date:* Continuous beginning 2/1.

CONTACT Diane Beltrani, Director of Enrollment Services/Financial Aid, Dowling College, Idle Hour Boulevard, Oakdale, NY 11769-1999, 631-244-3385 or toll-free 800-DOWLING. *Fax:* 631-563-3827. *E-mail:* beltranb@dowling.edu.

DRAKE UNIVERSITY
Des Moines, IA

Tuition & fees: $21,462 | Average undergraduate aid package: $17,453

ABOUT THE INSTITUTION Independent, coed. Awards: bachelor's, master's, doctoral, and first professional degrees and post-master's certificates. 66

Drake University

undergraduate majors. Total enrollment: 5,277. Undergraduates: 3,141. Freshmen: 809. Federal methodology is used as a basis for awarding need-based institutional aid.

UNDERGRADUATE EXPENSES for 2005–06 *Application fee:* $25. *Comprehensive fee:* $27,632 includes full-time tuition ($21,100), mandatory fees ($362), and room and board ($6170). *College room only:* $3000. Full-time tuition and fees vary according to class time, course load, and student level. Room and board charges vary according to board plan. *Part-time tuition:* $430 per hour. *Part-time fees:* $8 per hour. Part-time tuition and fees vary according to class time. *Payment plan:* Installment.

FRESHMAN FINANCIAL AID (Fall 2005, est.) 691 applied for aid; of those 77% were deemed to have need. 100% of freshmen with need received aid; of those 33% had need fully met. *Average percent of need met:* 87% (excluding resources awarded to replace EFC). *Average financial aid package:* $17,549 (excluding resources awarded to replace EFC). 30% of all full-time freshmen had no need and received non-need-based gift aid.

UNDERGRADUATE FINANCIAL AID (Fall 2005, est.) 2,147 applied for aid; of those 83% were deemed to have need. 100% of undergraduates with need received aid; of those 34% had need fully met. *Average percent of need met:* 84% (excluding resources awarded to replace EFC). *Average financial aid package:* $17,453 (excluding resources awarded to replace EFC). 31% of all full-time undergraduates had no need and received non-need-based gift aid.

GIFT AID (NEED-BASED) *Total amount:* $18,887,970 (9% federal, 10% state, 78% institutional, 3% external sources). *Receiving aid:* Freshmen: 65% (524); All full-time undergraduates: 61% (1,744). *Average award:* Freshmen: $11,627; Undergraduates: $10,719. *Scholarships, grants, and awards:* Federal Pell, FSEOG, state, private, college/university gift aid from institutional funds.

GIFT AID (NON-NEED-BASED) *Total amount:* $10,296,210 (2% federal, 93% institutional, 5% external sources). *Receiving aid:* Freshmen: 15% (122); Undergraduates: 13% (374). *Average Award:* Freshmen: $9486; Undergraduates:* $9026. *Scholarships, grants, and awards by category:* Academic Interests/Achievement: 2,207 awards ($17,315,376 total): general academic interests/achievements. Creative Arts/Performance: 262 awards ($751,480 total): art/fine arts, music, theater/drama. Special Characteristics: 283 awards ($706,513 total): children and siblings of alumni, ethnic background, members of minority groups. *Tuition waivers:* Full or partial for children of alumni, employees or children of employees, senior citizens. *ROTC:* Army, Air Force cooperative.

LOANS *Student loans:* $23,692,370 (47% need-based, 53% non-need-based). 70% of past graduating class borrowed through all loan programs. *Average indebtedness per student:* $25,691. *Average need-based loan:* Freshmen: $4643; Undergraduates: $5472. *Parent loans:* $20,330,935 (10% need-based, 90% non-need-based). *Programs:* FFEL (Subsidized and Unsubsidized Stafford, PLUS), Perkins, college/university.

WORK-STUDY *Federal work-study:* Total amount: $1,853,249; 1,220 jobs averaging $1519. *State or other work-study/employment:* Total amount: $302,800 (43% need-based, 57% non-need-based). 44 part-time jobs averaging $6882.

ATHLETIC AWARDS *Total amount:* $2,564,094 (28% need-based, 72% non-need-based).

APPLYING FOR FINANCIAL AID *Required financial aid form:* FAFSA. *Financial aid deadline (priority):* 3/1. *Notification date:* Continuous beginning 3/1. Students must reply by 5/1 or within 3 weeks of notification.

CONTACT Office of Student Financial Planning, Drake University, 2507 University Avenue, Des Moines, IA 50311-4516, 800-44-DRAKE Ext. 2905 or toll-free 800-44DRAKE Ext. 3181. *Fax:* 515-271-4042.

DREW UNIVERSITY
Madison, NJ

Tuition & fees: $31,286	Average undergraduate aid package: $22,093

ABOUT THE INSTITUTION Independent religious, coed. Awards: bachelor's, master's, doctoral, and first professional degrees and post-bachelor's certificates. 30 undergraduate majors. Total enrollment: 2,627. Undergraduates: 1,613. Freshmen: 391. Institutional methodology is used as a basis for awarding need-based institutional aid.

UNDERGRADUATE EXPENSES for 2005–06 *Application fee:* $50. *Comprehensive fee:* $39,698 includes full-time tuition ($30,740), mandatory fees ($546), and room and board ($8412). *College room only:* $5438. Full-time tuition and fees vary according to course load. Room and board charges vary according to board plan and housing facility. *Part-time tuition:* $1280 per credit. *Part-time fees:* $22.75 per credit; $273. Part-time tuition and fees vary according to course load. *Payment plans:* Tuition prepayment, installment, deferred payment.

FRESHMAN FINANCIAL AID (Fall 2004) 302 applied for aid; of those 75% were deemed to have need. 99% of freshmen with need received aid; of those 37% had need fully met. *Average percent of need met:* 83% (excluding resources awarded to replace EFC). *Average financial aid package:* $21,339 (excluding resources awarded to replace EFC). 31% of all full-time freshmen had no need and received non-need-based gift aid.

UNDERGRADUATE FINANCIAL AID (Fall 2004) 980 applied for aid; of those 79% were deemed to have need. 99% of undergraduates with need received aid; of those 33% had need fully met. *Average percent of need met:* 82% (excluding resources awarded to replace EFC). *Average financial aid package:* $22,093 (excluding resources awarded to replace EFC). 28% of all full-time undergraduates had no need and received non-need-based gift aid.

GIFT AID (NEED-BASED) *Total amount:* $12,451,633 (8% federal, 12% state, 77% institutional, 3% external sources). *Receiving aid:* Freshmen: 53% (221); All full-time undergraduates: 49% (756). *Average award:* Freshmen: $17,027; Undergraduates: $16,470. *Scholarships, grants, and awards:* Federal Pell, FSEOG, state, private, college/university gift aid from institutional funds.

GIFT AID (NON-NEED-BASED) *Total amount:* $6,161,291 (5% state, 92% institutional, 3% external sources). *Receiving aid:* Freshmen: 13% (53); Undergraduates: 8% (117). *Average Award:* Freshmen: $12,259; Undergraduates:* $11,802. *Scholarships, grants, and awards by category:* Academic Interests/Achievement: 1,084 awards ($10,552,794 total): general academic interests/achievements. Creative Arts/Performance: 20 awards ($195,000 total): general creative arts/performance. Special Characteristics: 41 awards ($267,978 total): general special characteristics. *Tuition waivers:* Full or partial for employees or children of employees, senior citizens. *ROTC:* Army cooperative, Air Force cooperative.

LOANS *Student loans:* $4,073,767 (76% need-based, 24% non-need-based). 60% of past graduating class borrowed through all loan programs. *Average indebtedness per student:* $17,586. *Average need-based loan:* Freshmen: $3536; Undergraduates: $4978. *Parent loans:* $6,961,172 (25% need-based, 75% non-need-based). *Programs:* FFEL (Subsidized and Unsubsidized Stafford, PLUS), Perkins, state.

WORK-STUDY *Federal work-study:* Total amount: $414,290; 339 jobs averaging $1222. *State or other work-study/employment:* Total amount: $244,200 (58% need-based, 42% non-need-based). 30 part-time jobs averaging $8140.

APPLYING FOR FINANCIAL AID *Required financial aid forms:* FAFSA, CSS Financial Aid PROFILE. *Financial aid deadline:* 2/15. *Notification date:* 3/30. Students must reply by 5/1.

CONTACT Suzanne Tang, Acting Director of Financial Assistance, Drew University, 36 Madison Avenue, Madison, NJ 07940-1493, 973-408-3112. *Fax:* 973-408-3188.

DREXEL UNIVERSITY
Philadelphia, PA

Tuition & fees: $24,280	Average undergraduate aid package: $15,076

ABOUT THE INSTITUTION Independent, coed. Awards: associate, bachelor's, master's, doctoral, and first professional degrees and post-bachelor's, post-master's, and first professional certificates. 55 undergraduate majors. Total enrollment: 18,466. Undergraduates: 12,357. Freshmen: 2,503. Federal methodology is used as a basis for awarding need-based institutional aid.

UNDERGRADUATE EXPENSES for 2005–06 *Application fee:* $50. *Comprehensive fee:* $34,795 includes full-time tuition ($22,700), mandatory fees ($1580), and room and board ($10,515). *College room only:* $6255. Full-time tuition and fees vary according to course load, program, and student level. Room and board charges vary according to board plan and housing facility. *Part-time tuition:* $500 per credit. *Part-time fees:* $100 per term. Part-time tuition and fees vary according to course load and program. *Payment plan:* Installment.

FRESHMAN FINANCIAL AID (Fall 2005, est.) 2257 applied for aid; of those 74% were deemed to have need. 100% of freshmen with need received aid; of those 14% had need fully met. *Average percent of need met:* 64% (excluding resources awarded to replace EFC). *Average financial aid package:* $15,921 (excluding resources awarded to replace EFC). 22% of all full-time freshmen had no need and received non-need-based gift aid.

UNDERGRADUATE FINANCIAL AID (Fall 2005, est.) 8,758 applied for aid; of those 74% were deemed to have need. 99% of undergraduates with need

received aid; of those 11% had need fully met. *Average percent of need met:* 59% (excluding resources awarded to replace EFC). *Average financial aid package:* $15,076 (excluding resources awarded to replace EFC). 19% of all full-time undergraduates had no need and received non-need-based gift aid.
GIFT AID (NEED-BASED) *Total amount:* $13,390,217 (50% federal, 47% state, 1% institutional, 2% external sources). *Receiving aid:* Freshmen: 26% (647); All full-time undergraduates: 26% (2,619). *Average award:* Freshmen: $4388; Undergraduates: $4672. *Scholarships, grants, and awards:* Federal Pell, FSEOG, state, private, college/university gift aid from institutional funds, United Negro College Fund.
GIFT AID (NON-NEED-BASED) *Total amount:* $76,093,360 (99% institutional, 1% external sources). *Receiving aid:* Freshmen: 67% (1,638); Undergraduates: 57% (5,754). *Average Award:* Freshmen: $9890; Undergraduates: $9206. *Scholarships, grants, and awards by category:* Academic Interests/Achievement: 4,102 awards ($43,584,115 total): general academic interests/achievements. Creative Arts/Performance: 117 awards ($163,900 total): dance, music, performing arts, theater/drama. Special Achievements/Activities: 25 awards ($36,700 total): cheerleading/drum major. Special Characteristics: 868 awards ($1,208,852 total): children and siblings of alumni, siblings of current students, twins. *Tuition waivers:* Full or partial for employees or children of employees. *ROTC:* Army, Air Force cooperative.
LOANS *Student loans:* $72,773,804 (57% need-based, 43% non-need-based). 85% of past graduating class borrowed through all loan programs. *Average indebtedness per student:* $25,347. *Average need-based loan:* Freshmen: $3002; Undergraduates: $4299. *Parent loans:* $22,556,092 (100% non-need-based). *Programs:* FFEL (Subsidized and Unsubsidized Stafford, PLUS), Perkins, college/university.
WORK-STUDY *Federal work-study:* Total amount: $4,998,860; jobs available.
ATHLETIC AWARDS *Total amount:* $4,086,314 (100% non-need-based).
APPLYING FOR FINANCIAL AID *Required financial aid form:* FAFSA. *Financial aid deadline:* 3/15. *Notification date:* Continuous beginning 3/15.
CONTACT Melissa Englund, Director of Financial Aid, Drexel University, 3141 Chestnut Street, Main Building, Room 106, Philadelphia, PA 19104-2875, 215-895-2537 or toll-free 800-2-DREXEL. *Fax:* 215-895-6903.

DRURY UNIVERSITY
Springfield, MO

CONTACT Ms. Annette Avery, Director of Financial Aid, Drury University, 900 North Benton Avenue, Springfield, MO 65802-3791, 417-873-7312 or toll-free 800-922-2274. *Fax:* 417-873-6906. *E-mail:* aavery@lib.drury.edu.

DUKE UNIVERSITY
Durham, NC

Tuition & fees: $33,963 | **Average undergraduate aid package: $27,842**

ABOUT THE INSTITUTION Independent religious, coed. Awards: bachelor's, master's, doctoral, and first professional degrees and post-bachelor's and post-master's certificates. 45 undergraduate majors. Total enrollment: 14,075. Undergraduates: 6,534. Freshmen: 1,724. Both federal and institutional methodology are used as a basis for awarding need-based institutional aid.
UNDERGRADUATE EXPENSES for 2006–07 *Application fee:* $70. *Comprehensive fee:* $43,115 includes full-time tuition ($32,845), mandatory fees ($1118), and room and board ($9152). *College room only:* $4950.
FRESHMAN FINANCIAL AID (Fall 2005, est.) 900 applied for aid; of those 86% were deemed to have need. 100% of freshmen with need received aid; of those 100% had need fully met. *Average percent of need met:* 100% (excluding resources awarded to replace EFC). *Average financial aid package:* $27,347 (excluding resources awarded to replace EFC). 1% of all full-time freshmen had no need and received non-need-based gift aid.
UNDERGRADUATE FINANCIAL AID (Fall 2005, est.) 2,851 applied for aid; of those 91% were deemed to have need. 100% of undergraduates with need received aid; of those 100% had need fully met. *Average percent of need met:* 100% (excluding resources awarded to replace EFC). *Average financial aid package:* $27,842 (excluding resources awarded to replace EFC). 4% of all full-time undergraduates had no need and received non-need-based gift aid.
GIFT AID (NEED-BASED) *Total amount:* $55,891,388 (5% federal, 3% state, 85% institutional, 7% external sources). *Receiving aid:* Freshmen: 44% (750); All full-time undergraduates: 38% (2,454). *Average award:* Freshmen: $24,354; Undergraduates: $23,928. *Scholarships, grants, and awards:* Federal Pell, FSEOG, state, private, college/university gift aid from institutional funds.
GIFT AID (NON-NEED-BASED) *Total amount:* $8,745,443 (9% state, 63% institutional, 28% external sources). *Receiving aid:* Freshmen: 5% (78); Undergraduates: 3% (213). *Average Award:* Freshmen: $31,264; Undergraduates: $24,016. *Scholarships, grants, and awards by category:* Academic Interests/Achievement: 113 awards ($3,706,600 total): general academic interests/achievements, mathematics. Creative Arts/Performance: creative writing. Special Achievements/Activities: 72 awards ($2,452,878 total): general special achievements/activities, leadership. Special Characteristics: 40 awards ($1,368,607 total): children and siblings of alumni, ethnic background, local/state students. *ROTC:* Army, Air Force.
LOANS *Student loans:* $15,248,678 (85% need-based, 15% non-need-based). 46% of past graduating class borrowed through all loan programs. *Average indebtedness per student:* $24,391. *Average need-based loan:* Freshmen: $3035; Undergraduates: $4270. *Parent loans:* $12,888,215 (57% need-based, 43% non-need-based). *Programs:* FFEL (Subsidized and Unsubsidized Stafford, PLUS), Perkins, college/university, alternative loans.
WORK-STUDY *Federal work-study:* Total amount: $3,251,210; 1,805 jobs averaging $1866. *State or other work-study/employment:* Total amount: $950,378 (58% need-based, 42% non-need-based). 617 part-time jobs averaging $1515.
ATHLETIC AWARDS *Total amount:* $10,044,468 (21% need-based, 79% non-need-based).
APPLYING FOR FINANCIAL AID *Required financial aid forms:* FAFSA, CSS Financial Aid PROFILE, noncustodial (divorced/separated) parent's statement, business/farm supplement, income tax form(s). *Financial aid deadline:* 2/1. *Notification date:* 4/1. Students must reply by 5/1.
CONTACT Kelly Kay, Assistant Director, Undergraduate Financial Aid, Duke University, 2122 Campus Drive, Durham, NC 27708-0397, 919-684-6225. *Fax:* 919-660-9811. *E-mail:* finaid@duke.edu.

DUQUESNE UNIVERSITY
Pittsburgh, PA

Tuition & fees: $21,480 | **Average undergraduate aid package: $15,919**

ABOUT THE INSTITUTION Independent Roman Catholic, coed. Awards: bachelor's, master's, doctoral, and first professional degrees and post-bachelor's and post-master's certificates. 74 undergraduate majors. Total enrollment: 9,916. Undergraduates: 5,650. Freshmen: 1,328. Federal methodology is used as a basis for awarding need-based institutional aid.
UNDERGRADUATE EXPENSES for 2005–06 *Application fee:* $50. *Comprehensive fee:* $29,534 includes full-time tuition ($19,721), mandatory fees ($1759), and room and board ($8054). *College room only:* $4394. Full-time tuition and fees vary according to program. Room and board charges vary according to board plan and housing facility. *Part-time tuition:* $641 per credit. *Part-time fees:* $69 per credit. Part-time tuition and fees vary according to program. *Payment plans:* Installment, deferred payment.
FRESHMAN FINANCIAL AID (Fall 2005, est.) 1162 applied for aid; of those 84% were deemed to have need. 100% of freshmen with need received aid; of those 58% had need fully met. *Average percent of need met:* 90% (excluding resources awarded to replace EFC). *Average financial aid package:* $16,697 (excluding resources awarded to replace EFC). 23% of all full-time freshmen had no need and received non-need-based gift aid.
UNDERGRADUATE FINANCIAL AID (Fall 2005, est.) 4,111 applied for aid; of those 86% were deemed to have need. 100% of undergraduates with need received aid; of those 58% had need fully met. *Average percent of need met:* 87% (excluding resources awarded to replace EFC). *Average financial aid package:* $15,919 (excluding resources awarded to replace EFC). 21% of all full-time undergraduates had no need and received non-need-based gift aid.
GIFT AID (NEED-BASED) *Total amount:* $34,069,318 (9% federal, 18% state, 64% institutional, 9% external sources). *Receiving aid:* Freshmen: 65% (856); All full-time undergraduates: 56% (3,007). *Average award:* Freshmen: $7108; Undergraduates: $6350. *Scholarships, grants, and awards:* Federal Pell, FSEOG, state, private, college/university gift aid from institutional funds, United Negro College Fund.
GIFT AID (NON-NEED-BASED) *Total amount:* $9,458,733 (1% state, 92% institutional, 7% external sources). *Receiving aid:* Freshmen: 58% (765); Undergraduates: 42% (2,227). *Average Award:* Freshmen: $6851; Undergraduates: $8077. *Scholarships, grants, and awards by category:* Academic Interests/

Duquesne University

Achievement: 4,067 awards ($17,993,289 total): general academic interests/achievements. *Creative Arts/Performance:* 219 awards ($1,516,353 total): dance, music. *Special Characteristics:* 806 awards ($9,651,524 total): children and siblings of alumni, children of faculty/staff, general special characteristics, international students, members of minority groups, relatives of clergy, religious affiliation. *Tuition waivers:* Full or partial for employees or children of employees, senior citizens. *ROTC:* Army, Naval cooperative, Air Force cooperative.
LOANS *Student loans:* $31,869,711 (89% need-based, 11% non-need-based). 78% of past graduating class borrowed through all loan programs. *Average indebtedness per student:* $21,493. *Average need-based loan:* Freshmen: $3267; Undergraduates: $4257. *Parent loans:* $11,038,191 (82% need-based, 18% non-need-based). *Programs:* FFEL (Subsidized and Unsubsidized Stafford, PLUS), Perkins, Federal Nursing, Private Alternative Loans.
WORK-STUDY *Federal work-study:* Total amount: $5,817,786; 1,650 jobs averaging $2979.
ATHLETIC AWARDS Total amount: $21,031,847 (8% need-based, 92% non-need-based).
APPLYING FOR FINANCIAL AID *Required financial aid forms:* FAFSA, institution's own form. *Financial aid deadline:* 5/1. *Notification date:* Continuous beginning 3/1. Students must reply by 5/1 or within 3 weeks of notification.
CONTACT Mr. Richard C. Esposito, Director of Financial Aid, Duquesne University, 600 Forbes Avenue, Pittsburgh, PA 15282-0299, 412-396-6607 or toll-free 800-456-0590. *Fax:* 412-396-5284. *E-mail:* esposito@duq.edu.

D'YOUVILLE COLLEGE
Buffalo, NY

ABOUT THE INSTITUTION Independent, coed. Awards: bachelor's, master's, doctoral, and first professional degrees and post-bachelor's and post-master's certificates. 33 undergraduate majors. Total enrollment: 2,906. Undergraduates: 1,482. Freshmen: 145.
GIFT AID (NEED-BASED) *Scholarships, grants, and awards:* Federal Pell, FSEOG, state, private, college/university gift aid from institutional funds.
GIFT AID (NON-NEED-BASED) *Scholarships, grants, and awards by category: Academic Interests/Achievement:* biological sciences, business, education, English, general academic interests/achievements, health fields, humanities, international studies, premedicine, social sciences. *Special Characteristics:* children and siblings of alumni, children of faculty/staff.
LOANS *Programs:* FFEL (Subsidized and Unsubsidized Stafford, PLUS), Perkins, Federal Nursing, college/university.
APPLYING FOR FINANCIAL AID *Required financial aid form:* FAFSA.
CONTACT Ms. Lorraine A. Metz, Director of Financial Aid, D'Youville College, 320 Porter Avenue, Buffalo, NY 14201-1084, 716-829-7500 or toll-free 800-777-3921. *Fax:* 716-829-7779. *E-mail:* metzla@dyc.edu.

EARLHAM COLLEGE
Richmond, IN

CONTACT Mr. Robert W. Arnold, Director of Financial Aid, Earlham College, National Road West, Richmond, IN 47374-4095, 765-983-1217 or toll-free 800-327-5426. *Fax:* 765-983-1299.

EAST CAROLINA UNIVERSITY
Greenville, NC

Tuition & fees (NC res): $3627	Average undergraduate aid package: $8502

ABOUT THE INSTITUTION State-supported, coed. Awards: bachelor's, master's, doctoral, and first professional degrees and post-master's certificates. 91 undergraduate majors. Total enrollment: 23,164. Undergraduates: 17,728. Freshmen: 3,273. Federal methodology is used as a basis for awarding need-based institutional aid.
UNDERGRADUATE EXPENSES for 2005–06 *Application fee:* $50. *Tuition, state resident:* full-time $2135. *Tuition, nonresident:* full-time $12,649. Part-time tuition and fees vary according to course load. *College room and board:* $6840; *room only:* $3790. Room and board charges vary according to board plan and housing facility. *Payment plans:* Installment, deferred payment.
FRESHMAN FINANCIAL AID (Fall 2005, est.) 2485 applied for aid; of those 56% were deemed to have need. 100% of freshmen with need received aid; of those 97% had need fully met. *Average percent of need met:* 23% (excluding resources awarded to replace EFC). *Average financial aid package:* $7978 (excluding resources awarded to replace EFC). 4% of all full-time freshmen had no need and received non-need-based gift aid.
UNDERGRADUATE FINANCIAL AID (Fall 2005, est.) 9,365 applied for aid; of those 48% were deemed to have need. 100% of undergraduates with need received aid; of those 98% had need fully met. *Average percent of need met:* 27% (excluding resources awarded to replace EFC). *Average financial aid package:* $8502 (excluding resources awarded to replace EFC). 6% of all full-time undergraduates had no need and received non-need-based gift aid.
GIFT AID (NEED-BASED) *Total amount:* $25,373,834 (63% federal, 27% state, 10% institutional). *Receiving aid:* Freshmen: 29% (933); All full-time undergraduates: 18% (2,827). *Average award:* Freshmen: $8843; Undergraduates: $9372. *Scholarships, grants, and awards:* Federal Pell, FSEOG, state, private, college/university gift aid from institutional funds.
GIFT AID (NON-NEED-BASED) *Total amount:* $6,867,975 (37% state, 31% institutional, 32% external sources). *Receiving aid:* Freshmen: 8% (258); Undergraduates: 5% (859). *Average Award:* Freshmen: $7582; Undergraduates: $9562. *Scholarships, grants, and awards by category: Academic Interests/Achievement:* biological sciences, business, education, general academic interests/achievements, health fields, home economics, humanities, military science. *Creative Arts/Performance:* applied art and design, art/fine arts, music. *Special Achievements/Activities:* leadership. *Special Characteristics:* adult students, children of faculty/staff, ethnic background, handicapped students, local/state students. *Tuition waivers:* Full or partial for employees or children of employees, senior citizens. *ROTC:* Army, Air Force.
LOANS *Student loans:* $55,944,593 (50% need-based, 50% non-need-based). 79% of past graduating class borrowed through all loan programs. *Average indebtedness per student:* $19,614. *Average need-based loan:* Freshmen: $5391; Undergraduates: $6664. *Parent loans:* $13,987,933 (100% non-need-based). *Programs:* FFEL (Subsidized and Unsubsidized Stafford, PLUS), Perkins, Federal Nursing.
WORK-STUDY *Federal work-study:* Total amount: $623,581; 382 jobs averaging $1584. *State or other work-study/employment:* Total amount: $940,697 (100% need-based). 127 part-time jobs averaging $7344.
ATHLETIC AWARDS Total amount: $3,824,696 (100% non-need-based).
APPLYING FOR FINANCIAL AID *Required financial aid form:* FAFSA. *Financial aid deadline (priority):* 4/15. *Notification date:* 3/15. Students must reply within 2 weeks of notification.
CONTACT Rose Mary Stelma, Director, Student Financial Aid, East Carolina University, Office of Financial Aid, East 5th Street, Greenville, NC 27858-4353, 252-328-6610. *Fax:* 252-328-4347. *E-mail:* pattersonba@ecu.edu.

EAST CENTRAL UNIVERSITY
Ada, OK

Tuition & fees (OK res): $3566	Average undergraduate aid package: $8211

ABOUT THE INSTITUTION State-supported, coed. Awards: bachelor's and master's degrees. 82 undergraduate majors. Total enrollment: 4,571. Undergraduates: 3,803. Freshmen: 572. Federal methodology is used as a basis for awarding need-based institutional aid.
UNDERGRADUATE EXPENSES for 2005–06 *Application fee:* $20. *Tuition, state resident:* full-time $2,722; part-time $75.11 per semester hour. *Tuition, nonresident:* full-time $5,739; part-time $229.55 per semester hour. *Required fees:* full-time $844; $31.80 per semester hour or $23.50 per term part-time. Full-time tuition and fees vary according to course load. Part-time tuition and fees vary according to course load. *College room and board:* $3000; *room only:* $1070. Room and board charges vary according to board plan and housing facility.
FRESHMAN FINANCIAL AID (Fall 2005, est.) 396 applied for aid; of those 85% were deemed to have need. 98% of freshmen with need received aid; of those 36% had need fully met. *Average percent of need met:* 60% (excluding resources awarded to replace EFC). *Average financial aid package:* $7395 (excluding resources awarded to replace EFC). 9% of all full-time freshmen had no need and received non-need-based gift aid.
UNDERGRADUATE FINANCIAL AID (Fall 2005, est.) 1,967 applied for aid; of those 89% were deemed to have need. 98% of undergraduates with need received aid; of those 37% had need fully met. *Average percent of need met:* 66% (excluding resources awarded to replace EFC). *Average financial aid*

package: $8211 (excluding resources awarded to replace EFC). 8% of all full-time undergraduates had no need and received non-need-based gift aid.
GIFT AID (NEED-BASED) *Total amount:* $8,299,878 (71% federal, 29% state). *Receiving aid:* Freshmen: 35% (248); All full-time undergraduates: 39% (1,265). *Average award:* Freshmen: $4979; Undergraduates: $3452. *Scholarships, grants, and awards:* Federal Pell, FSEOG, state, private, college/university gift aid from institutional funds.
GIFT AID (NON-NEED-BASED) *Total amount:* $2,775,619 (29% institutional, 71% external sources). *Receiving aid:* Freshmen: 22% (156); Undergraduates: 23% (728). *Average Award:* Freshmen: $1878; Undergraduates: $3234. *Scholarships, grants, and awards by category: Academic Interests/Achievement:* 680 awards ($487,806 total): communication, general academic interests/achievements. *Creative Arts/Performance:* 114 awards ($180,016 total): music, theater/drama. *Special Achievements/Activities:* 8 awards ($3650 total): cheerleading/drum major. *Special Characteristics:* 375 awards ($851,772 total): children of faculty/staff, general special characteristics, members of minority groups, out-of-state students, previous college experience, veterans, veterans' children. *Tuition waivers:* Full or partial for employees or children of employees, senior citizens.
LOANS *Student loans:* $12,529,335 (62% need-based, 38% non-need-based). 64% of past graduating class borrowed through all loan programs. *Average indebtedness per student:* $16,169. *Average need-based loan:* Freshmen: $1693; Undergraduates: $3273. *Parent loans:* $203,635 (100% non-need-based). *Programs:* FFEL (Subsidized and Unsubsidized Stafford, PLUS), Perkins, college/university.
WORK-STUDY *Federal work-study:* Total amount: $411,210; 196 jobs averaging $2098. *State or other work-study/employment:* Total amount: $880,299 (100% non-need-based). 427 part-time jobs averaging $2062.
ATHLETIC AWARDS *Total amount:* $825,302 (100% non-need-based).
APPLYING FOR FINANCIAL AID *Required financial aid form:* FAFSA. *Financial aid deadline (priority):* 3/1. *Notification date:* Continuous beginning 4/15. Students must reply within 2 weeks of notification.
CONTACT Marcia Carter, Director of Financial Aid, East Central University, 1100 East 14th, Ada, OK 74820-6899, 580-332-8000 Ext. 242. *Fax:* 580-436-5612.

EASTERN CONNECTICUT STATE UNIVERSITY
Willimantic, CT

CONTACT Assistant to the Director of Financial Aid, Eastern Connecticut State University, 83 Windham Street, Willimantic, CT 06226-2295, 860-465-4428 or toll-free 877-353-3278. *Fax:* 860-465-4440.

EASTERN ILLINOIS UNIVERSITY
Charleston, IL

Tuition & fees (IL res): $6373	Average undergraduate aid package: $9783

ABOUT THE INSTITUTION State-supported, coed. Awards: bachelor's and master's degrees and post-bachelor's and post-master's certificates. 42 undergraduate majors. Total enrollment: 12,129. Undergraduates: 10,375. Freshmen: 1,668. Federal methodology is used as a basis for awarding need-based institutional aid.
UNDERGRADUATE EXPENSES for 2005–06 *Application fee:* $30. *Tuition, state resident:* full-time $4629; part-time $154 per credit hour. *Tuition, nonresident:* full-time $13,887; part-time $463 per credit hour. *Required fees:* full-time $1744; $63 per credit hour. Full-time tuition and fees vary according to course load. Part-time tuition and fees vary according to course load. *College room and board:* $6196. Room and board charges vary according to board plan and housing facility. *Payment plan:* Installment.
FRESHMAN FINANCIAL AID (Fall 2005, est.) 1306 applied for aid; of those 72% were deemed to have need. 89% of freshmen with need received aid; of those 72% had need fully met. *Average percent of need met:* 17% (excluding resources awarded to replace EFC). *Average financial aid package:* $9412 (excluding resources awarded to replace EFC). 5% of all full-time freshmen had no need and received non-need-based gift aid.
UNDERGRADUATE FINANCIAL AID (Fall 2005, est.) 6,350 applied for aid; of those 77% were deemed to have need. 89% of undergraduates with need received aid; of those 72% had need fully met. *Average percent of need met:* 19% (excluding resources awarded to replace EFC). *Average financial aid package:* $9783 (excluding resources awarded to replace EFC). 3% of all full-time undergraduates had no need and received non-need-based gift aid.
GIFT AID (NEED-BASED) *Total amount:* $14,997,966 (33% federal, 52% state, 10% institutional, 5% external sources). *Receiving aid:* Freshmen: 22% (380); All full-time undergraduates: 22% (2,072). *Average award:* Freshmen: $2750; Undergraduates: $2886. *Scholarships, grants, and awards:* Federal Pell, FSEOG, state, college/university gift aid from institutional funds.
GIFT AID (NON-NEED-BASED) *Total amount:* $3,813,029 (2% federal, 25% state, 54% institutional, 19% external sources). *Receiving aid:* Freshmen: 25% (426); Undergraduates: 22% (1,999). *Average Award:* Freshmen: $5967; Undergraduates: $7140. *Tuition waivers:* Full or partial for employees or children of employees. *ROTC:* Army.
LOANS *Student loans:* $25,408,239 (76% need-based, 24% non-need-based). 63% of past graduating class borrowed through all loan programs. *Average indebtedness per student:* $15,538. *Average need-based loan:* Freshmen: $2436; Undergraduates: $3461. *Parent loans:* $3,570,899 (55% need-based, 45% non-need-based). *Programs:* Federal Direct (Subsidized and Unsubsidized Stafford, PLUS), Perkins.
WORK-STUDY *Federal work-study:* Total amount: $608,744; 458 jobs averaging $1329. *State or other work-study/employment:* Total amount: $1500 (100% need-based). Part-time jobs available.
ATHLETIC AWARDS *Total amount:* $2,399,410 (26% need-based, 74% non-need-based).
APPLYING FOR FINANCIAL AID *Required financial aid form:* FAFSA. *Financial aid deadline (priority):* 3/1. *Notification date:* Continuous beginning 3/1. Students must reply within 2 weeks of notification.
CONTACT Tracy L. Hall, Assistant Director of Financial Aid, Eastern Illinois University, 600 Lincoln Avenue, Charleston, IL 61920-3099, 217-581-7511 or toll-free 800-252-5711. *Fax:* 217-581-6422. *E-mail:* cstlh@eiu.edu.

EASTERN KENTUCKY UNIVERSITY
Richmond, KY

CONTACT Ms. Shelley Park, Director of Student Financial Assistance, Eastern Kentucky University, 521 Lancaster Avenue, Student Services Building, CPO 59, Richmond, KY 40475-3102, 859-622-2361 or toll-free 800-465-9191 (in-state). *E-mail:* shelley.park@eku.edu.

EASTERN MENNONITE UNIVERSITY
Harrisonburg, VA

ABOUT THE INSTITUTION Independent Mennonite, coed. Awards: associate, bachelor's, master's, and first professional degrees and post-bachelor's certificates. 58 undergraduate majors. Total enrollment: 1,301. Undergraduates: 1,012. Freshmen: 202.
GIFT AID (NEED-BASED) *Scholarships, grants, and awards:* Federal Pell, FSEOG, state, private, college/university gift aid from institutional funds.
GIFT AID (NON-NEED-BASED) *Scholarships, grants, and awards by category: Academic Interests/Achievement:* biological sciences, business, education, English, foreign languages, general academic interests/achievements, humanities, mathematics, physical sciences, premedicine, religion/biblical studies, social sciences. *Creative Arts/Performance:* art/fine arts, music. *Special Achievements/Activities:* general special achievements/activities, religious involvement. *Special Characteristics:* children and siblings of alumni, children of faculty/staff, ethnic background, general special characteristics, international students, religious affiliation.
LOANS *Programs:* FFEL (Subsidized and Unsubsidized Stafford, PLUS), Perkins, Federal Nursing.
APPLYING FOR FINANCIAL AID *Required financial aid forms:* FAFSA, state aid form.
CONTACT Ms. Renee Leap, Assistant Director of Financial Assistance, Eastern Mennonite University, 1200 Park Road, Harrisonburg, VA 22802-2462, 540-432-4138 or toll-free 800-368-2665. *Fax:* 540-432-4081. *E-mail:* leapr@emu.edu.

EASTERN MICHIGAN UNIVERSITY
Ypsilanti, MI

Tuition & fees (MI res): $6541	Average undergraduate aid package: $6472

Eastern Michigan University

ABOUT THE INSTITUTION State-supported, coed. Awards: bachelor's, master's, and doctoral degrees and post-bachelor's and post-master's certificates. 132 undergraduate majors. Total enrollment: 23,240. Undergraduates: 18,578. Freshmen: 2,386. Federal methodology is used as a basis for awarding need-based institutional aid.

UNDERGRADUATE EXPENSES for 2005–06 *Application fee:* $30. *Tuition, state resident:* full-time $5463; part-time $182.10 per credit hour. *Tuition, nonresident:* full-time $16,818; part-time $560.60 per credit hour. *Required fees:* full-time $1078; $33.25 per credit hour or $40 per term part-time. *College room and board:* $6356.

FRESHMAN FINANCIAL AID (Fall 2004) 1791 applied for aid; of those 73% were deemed to have need. 96% of freshmen with need received aid; of those 5% had need fully met. *Average percent of need met:* 62% (excluding resources awarded to replace EFC). *Average financial aid package:* $6404 (excluding resources awarded to replace EFC). 14% of all full-time freshmen had no need and received non-need-based gift aid.

UNDERGRADUATE FINANCIAL AID (Fall 2004) 8,433 applied for aid; of those 81% were deemed to have need. 97% of undergraduates with need received aid; of those 2% had need fully met. *Average percent of need met:* 60% (excluding resources awarded to replace EFC). *Average financial aid package:* $6472 (excluding resources awarded to replace EFC). 8% of all full-time undergraduates had no need and received non-need-based gift aid.

GIFT AID (NEED-BASED) *Total amount:* $13,882,570 (87% federal, 8% state, 5% institutional). *Receiving aid:* Freshmen: 32% (733); All full-time undergraduates: 29% (3,781). *Average award:* Freshmen: $3471; Undergraduates: $3146. *Scholarships, grants, and awards:* Federal Pell, FSEOG, state, private, college/university gift aid from institutional funds.

GIFT AID (NON-NEED-BASED) *Total amount:* $14,606,167 (19% state, 40% institutional, 41% external sources). *Receiving aid:* Freshmen: 30% (690); Undergraduates: 16% (2,059). *Average Award:* Freshmen: $2041; Undergraduates: $2516. *Scholarships, grants, and awards by category:* Academic Interests/Achievement: 3,950 awards ($8,756,311 total): agriculture, architecture, biological sciences, business, communication, computer science, education, engineering/technologies, English, foreign languages, general academic interests/achievements, health fields, home economics, humanities, mathematics, physical sciences, religion/biblical studies, social sciences. *Creative Arts/Performance:* 145 awards ($103,444 total): applied art and design, art/fine arts, cinema/film/broadcasting, creative writing, dance, debating, general creative arts/performance, music, performing arts, theater/drama. *Special Achievements/Activities:* 211 awards ($160,302 total): general special achievements/activities, leadership, memberships, religious involvement. *Special Characteristics:* 179 awards ($1,074,781 total): children and siblings of alumni, ethnic background, international students, members of minority groups, out-of-state students, previous college experience, religious affiliation. *ROTC:* Army, Naval cooperative, Air Force cooperative.

LOANS *Student loans:* $62,755,187 (46% need-based, 54% non-need-based). 58% of past graduating class borrowed through all loan programs. *Average indebtedness per student:* $21,397. *Average need-based loan:* Freshmen: $3088; Undergraduates: $4044. *Parent loans:* $8,352,186 (100% non-need-based). *Programs:* FFEL (Subsidized and Unsubsidized Stafford, PLUS), Perkins, college/university, Alternative (private) loans.

WORK-STUDY *Federal work-study:* Total amount: $868,634; 529 jobs averaging $1642. *State or other work-study/employment:* Total amount: $366,740 (100% need-based). 253 part-time jobs averaging $1450.

ATHLETIC AWARDS *Total amount:* $4,167,011 (100% non-need-based).

APPLYING FOR FINANCIAL AID *Required financial aid form:* FAFSA. *Financial aid deadline (priority):* 3/15. *Notification date:* Continuous beginning 3/15.

CONTACT Ms. Bernice A. Lindke, Associate Vice President, Enrollment Services, Eastern Michigan University, 403 Pierce Hall, Ypsilanti, MI 48197, 734-487-1048 or toll-free 800-GO TO EMU. *Fax:* 734-487-4281. *E-mail:* bernice.lindke@emich.edu.

EASTERN NAZARENE COLLEGE
Quincy, MA

CONTACT Financial Aid Department, Eastern Nazarene College, 23 East Elm Avenue, Quincy, MA 02170, 617-745-3712 or toll-free 800-88-ENC88. *Fax:* 617-745-3929. *E-mail:* finaid@enc.edu.

EASTERN NEW MEXICO UNIVERSITY
Portales, NM

CONTACT Ms. Patricia Willis, Financial Aid Specialist, Eastern New Mexico University, Station 54, Portales, NM 88130, 505-562-2194 or toll-free 800-367-3668. *Fax:* 505-562-2198. *E-mail:* pat.willis@enmu.edu.

EASTERN OREGON UNIVERSITY
La Grande, OR

ABOUT THE INSTITUTION State-supported, coed. Awards: bachelor's and master's degrees. 32 undergraduate majors. Total enrollment: 3,533. Undergraduates: 3,197. Freshmen: 383.

GIFT AID (NEED-BASED) *Scholarships, grants, and awards:* Federal Pell, FSEOG, state, private, college/university gift aid from institutional funds.

GIFT AID (NON-NEED-BASED) *Scholarships, grants, and awards by category:* Academic Interests/Achievement: agriculture, biological sciences, business, education, general academic interests/achievements, mathematics, physical sciences. *Creative Arts/Performance:* art/fine arts, music, theater/drama. *Special Achievements/Activities:* community service, leadership, rodeo. *Special Characteristics:* adult students, general special characteristics, international students, members of minority groups, out-of-state students.

LOANS *Programs:* Federal Direct (Subsidized and Unsubsidized Stafford, PLUS), FFEL (Subsidized and Unsubsidized Stafford, PLUS), Perkins.

WORK-STUDY *Federal work-study:* Total amount: $336,861; 245 jobs averaging $1553.

APPLYING FOR FINANCIAL AID *Required financial aid form:* FAFSA.

CONTACT Mr. Eric Bucks, Director of Financial Aid, Eastern Oregon University, One University Boulevard, La Grande, OR 97850-2899, 541-962-3550 or toll-free 800-452-8639 (in-state), 800-452-3393 (out-of-state). *Fax:* 541-962-3661. *E-mail:* eric.bucks@eou.edu.

EASTERN UNIVERSITY
St. Davids, PA

CONTACT Financial Aid Office, Eastern University, 1300 Eagle Road, St. Davids, PA 19087-3696, 610-341-5842 or toll-free 800-452-0996. *Fax:* 610-341-1492. *E-mail:* finaid@eastern.edu.

EASTERN WASHINGTON UNIVERSITY
Cheney, WA

Tuition & fees (WA res): $4281 | **Average undergraduate aid package: $10,381**

ABOUT THE INSTITUTION State-supported, coed. Awards: bachelor's, master's, and doctoral degrees. 109 undergraduate majors. Total enrollment: 10,908. Undergraduates: 9,603. Freshmen: 1,637. Federal methodology is used as a basis for awarding need-based institutional aid.

UNDERGRADUATE EXPENSES for 2005–06 *Application fee:* $50. *Tuition, state resident:* full-time $4044; part-time $135 per credit. *Tuition, nonresident:* full-time $17,756; part-time $444 per credit. *Required fees:* full-time $237; $79 per term part-time. Full-time tuition and fees vary according to course load. Part-time tuition and fees vary according to course load. *College room and board:* $5733. Room and board charges vary according to board plan and housing facility. *Payment plan:* Installment.

FRESHMAN FINANCIAL AID (Fall 2004) 1451 applied for aid; of those 76% were deemed to have need. 97% of freshmen with need received aid; of those 17% had need fully met. *Average percent of need met:* 35% (excluding resources awarded to replace EFC). *Average financial aid package:* $9521 (excluding resources awarded to replace EFC). 3% of all full-time freshmen had no need and received non-need-based gift aid.

UNDERGRADUATE FINANCIAL AID (Fall 2004) 5,725 applied for aid; of those 83% were deemed to have need. 97% of undergraduates with need received aid; of those 15% had need fully met. *Average percent of need met:* 38% (excluding resources awarded to replace EFC). *Average financial aid package:* $10,381 (excluding resources awarded to replace EFC). 2% of all full-time undergraduates had no need and received non-need-based gift aid.

GIFT AID (NEED-BASED) *Total amount:* $20,657,740 (46% federal, 36% state, 9% institutional, 9% external sources). *Receiving aid:* Freshmen: 45% (847);

All full-time undergraduates: 46% (3,466). *Average award:* Freshmen: $4286; Undergraduates: $4627. *Scholarships, grants, and awards:* Federal Pell, FSEOG, state, private, college/university gift aid from institutional funds.
GIFT AID (NON-NEED-BASED) *Total amount:* $258,916 (18% institutional, 82% external sources). *Receiving aid:* Freshmen: 17% (323); Undergraduates: 10% (769). *Average Award:* Freshmen: $3704; Undergraduates: $3136. *Scholarships, grants, and awards by category:* Academic Interests/Achievement: 488 awards ($547,000 total): biological sciences, business, computer science, education, engineering/technologies, English, foreign languages, general academic interests/achievements, health fields, mathematics, physical sciences, social sciences. *Creative Arts/Performance:* 57 awards ($61,000 total): art/fine arts, cinema/film/broadcasting, creative writing, journalism/publications, music, theater/drama. *Special Characteristics:* 250 awards ($450,000 total): children and siblings of alumni, children of union members/company employees, ethnic background, handicapped students, local/state students. *Tuition waivers:* Full or partial for employees or children of employees. *ROTC:* Army.
LOANS *Student loans:* $42,272,290 (90% need-based, 10% non-need-based). 70% of past graduating class borrowed through all loan programs. *Average indebtedness per student:* $18,097. *Average need-based loan:* Freshmen: $2351; Undergraduates: $3684. *Parent loans:* $6,483,966 (62% need-based, 38% non-need-based). *Programs:* FFEL (Subsidized and Unsubsidized Stafford, PLUS), Perkins.
WORK-STUDY *Federal work-study:* Total amount: $474,378; 261 jobs averaging $1817. *State or other work-study/employment:* Total amount: $820,791 (100% need-based). 503 part-time jobs averaging $2061.
ATHLETIC AWARDS *Total amount:* $1,166,952 (44% need-based, 56% non-need-based).
APPLYING FOR FINANCIAL AID *Required financial aid form:* FAFSA. *Financial aid deadline (priority):* 2/15. *Notification date:* Continuous beginning 4/1. Students must reply within 4 weeks of notification.
CONTACT Bruce DeFrates, Financial Aid Director, Eastern Washington University, 102 Sutton Hall, Cheney, WA 99004-2447, 509-359-2314. *Fax:* 509-359-4330. *E-mail:* finaid@mail.ewu.edu.

EAST STROUDSBURG UNIVERSITY OF PENNSYLVANIA
East Stroudsburg, PA

Tuition & fees (PA res): $6462   **Average undergraduate aid package: $5224**

ABOUT THE INSTITUTION State-supported, coed. Awards: associate, bachelor's, and master's degrees. 50 undergraduate majors. Total enrollment: 6,793. Undergraduates: 5,596. Freshmen: 1,101. Federal methodology is used as a basis for awarding need-based institutional aid.
UNDERGRADUATE EXPENSES for 2005–06 *Application fee:* $35. *Tuition, area resident:* part-time $204 per credit. *Tuition, state resident:* full-time $4906; part-time $204 per credit. *Tuition, nonresident:* full-time $12,266; part-time $511 per credit. *Required fees:* full-time $1556; $55 per credit. Part-time tuition and fees vary according to course load. *College room and board:* $4794; *room only:* $3098. Room and board charges vary according to board plan and housing facility. *Payment plan:* Installment.
FRESHMAN FINANCIAL AID (Fall 2004) 959 applied for aid; of those 69% were deemed to have need. 94% of freshmen with need received aid; of those 61% had need fully met. *Average percent of need met:* 76% (excluding resources awarded to replace EFC). *Average financial aid package:* $3832 (excluding resources awarded to replace EFC). 24% of all full-time freshmen had no need and received non-need-based gift aid.
UNDERGRADUATE FINANCIAL AID (Fall 2004) 3,902 applied for aid; of those 74% were deemed to have need. 99% of undergraduates with need received aid; of those 74% had need fully met. *Average percent of need met:* 86% (excluding resources awarded to replace EFC). *Average financial aid package:* $5224 (excluding resources awarded to replace EFC). 20% of all full-time undergraduates had no need and received non-need-based gift aid.
GIFT AID (NEED-BASED) *Total amount:* $7,500,119 (44% federal, 41% state, 10% institutional, 5% external sources). *Receiving aid:* Freshmen: 34% (343); All full-time undergraduates: 37% (1,673). *Average award:* Freshmen: $3269; Undergraduates: $3489. *Scholarships, grants, and awards:* Federal Pell, FSEOG, state, private, college/university gift aid from institutional funds.
GIFT AID (NON-NEED-BASED) *Receiving aid:* Freshmen: 3% (34); Undergraduates: 3% (149). *Average Award:* Freshmen: $6761; Undergraduates: $7415.

Scholarships, grants, and awards by category: Academic Interests/Achievement: 386 awards ($320,390 total): biological sciences, business, communication, computer science, education, English, foreign languages, general academic interests/achievements, health fields, mathematics, physical sciences, social sciences. *Creative Arts/Performance:* 13 awards ($7850 total): applied art and design, music, theater/drama. *Special Achievements/Activities:* 46 awards ($7950 total): general special achievements/activities. *Special Characteristics:* 56 awards ($214,394 total): adult students, handicapped students, international students, members of minority groups. *Tuition waivers:* Full or partial for employees or children of employees, senior citizens. *ROTC:* Army cooperative, Air Force cooperative.
LOANS *Student loans:* $19,525,357 (56% need-based, 44% non-need-based). 69% of past graduating class borrowed through all loan programs. *Average indebtedness per student:* $21,900. *Average need-based loan:* Freshmen: $2506; Undergraduates: $3780. *Parent loans:* $4,333,745 (100% non-need-based). *Programs:* FFEL (Subsidized and Unsubsidized Stafford, PLUS), Perkins, alternative loans.
WORK-STUDY *Federal work-study:* Total amount: $375,356; 346 jobs averaging $1085. *State or other work-study/employment:* Total amount: $966,093 (100% non-need-based). 752 part-time jobs averaging $1285.
ATHLETIC AWARDS *Total amount:* $382,449 (100% need-based).
APPLYING FOR FINANCIAL AID *Required financial aid form:* FAFSA. *Financial aid deadline:* 3/1. *Notification date:* 4/1. Students must reply by 5/1.
CONTACT Georgia K. Prell, Director of Enrollment Services, East Stroudsburg University of Pennsylvania, 200 Prospect Street, East Stroudsburg, PA 18301-2999, 570-422-2820 or toll-free 877-230-5547. *Fax:* 570-422-2849.

EAST TENNESSEE STATE UNIVERSITY
Johnson City, TN

Tuition & fees (TN res): $4487   **Average undergraduate aid package: $4762**

ABOUT THE INSTITUTION State-supported, coed. Awards: associate, bachelor's, master's, doctoral, and first professional degrees and post-bachelor's and post-master's certificates. 38 undergraduate majors. Total enrollment: 11,894. Undergraduates: 9,770. Freshmen: 1,595. Federal methodology is used as a basis for awarding need-based institutional aid.
UNDERGRADUATE EXPENSES for 2005–06 *Application fee:* $15. *Tuition, state resident:* full-time $3678; part-time $161 per hour. *Tuition, nonresident:* full-time $12,990; part-time $565 per hour. Full-time tuition and fees vary according to course load and program. *College room and board:* $4822; *room only:* $2512. Room and board charges vary according to board plan and housing facility. *Payment plans:* Installment, deferred payment.
FRESHMAN FINANCIAL AID (Fall 2005, est.) 969 applied for aid; of those 74% were deemed to have need. 98% of freshmen with need received aid; of those 30% had need fully met. *Average percent of need met:* 82% (excluding resources awarded to replace EFC). *Average financial aid package:* $6103 (excluding resources awarded to replace EFC). 6% of all full-time freshmen had no need and received non-need-based gift aid.
UNDERGRADUATE FINANCIAL AID (Fall 2005, est.) 6,671 applied for aid; of those 70% were deemed to have need. 97% of undergraduates with need received aid; of those 45% had need fully met. *Average percent of need met:* 82% (excluding resources awarded to replace EFC). *Average financial aid package:* $4762 (excluding resources awarded to replace EFC). 14% of all full-time undergraduates had no need and received non-need-based gift aid.
GIFT AID (NEED-BASED) *Total amount:* $20,536,007 (45% federal, 55% state). *Receiving aid:* Freshmen: 38% (600); All full-time undergraduates: 41% (3,345). *Average award:* Freshmen: $3851; Undergraduates: $3009. *Scholarships, grants, and awards:* Federal Pell, FSEOG, state, private, college/university gift aid from institutional funds, Federal Nursing.
GIFT AID (NON-NEED-BASED) *Total amount:* $6,921,581 (6% federal, 15% state, 60% institutional, 19% external sources). *Receiving aid:* Freshmen: 11% (173); Undergraduates: 15% (1,232). *Average Award:* Freshmen: $3686; Undergraduates: $3054. *Scholarships, grants, and awards by category:* Academic Interests/Achievement: biological sciences, business, computer science, education, engineering/technologies, English, general academic interests/achievements, health fields, mathematics, military science, social sciences. *Creative Arts/Performance:* art/fine arts, journalism/publications, music, theater/drama. *Special Achievements/Activities:* leadership, memberships. Special

East Tennessee State University

Characteristics: children of union members/company employees, members of minority groups. *Tuition waivers:* Full or partial for employees or children of employees, senior citizens. *ROTC:* Army.

LOANS *Student loans:* $30,249,190 (64% need-based, 36% non-need-based). 58% of past graduating class borrowed through all loan programs. *Average indebtedness per student:* $17,988. *Average need-based loan:* Freshmen: $845; Undergraduates: $3216. *Parent loans:* $3,106,487 (100% non-need-based). *Programs:* FFEL (Subsidized and Unsubsidized Stafford, PLUS), Perkins, Federal Nursing, college/university.

WORK-STUDY *Federal work-study:* Total amount: $2,154,601; 1,674 jobs averaging $1272. *State or other work-study/employment:* Total amount: $489,940 (100% non-need-based). 412 part-time jobs averaging $1189.

ATHLETIC AWARDS *Total amount:* $1,940,658 (100% non-need-based).

APPLYING FOR FINANCIAL AID *Required financial aid form:* FAFSA. *Financial aid deadline (priority):* 4/15. *Notification date:* Continuous beginning 5/1. Students must reply within 3 weeks of notification.

CONTACT Cindy A. Johnson, Assistant Director of Financial Aid, East Tennessee State University, PO Box 70722, Johnson City, TN 37614, 423-439-4300 or toll-free 800-462-3878.

EAST TEXAS BAPTIST UNIVERSITY
Marshall, TX

Tuition & fees: $12,840 | **Average undergraduate aid package: $11,930**

ABOUT THE INSTITUTION Independent Baptist, coed. Awards: associate and bachelor's degrees. 44 undergraduate majors. Total enrollment: 1,326. Undergraduates: 1,326. Freshmen: 303. Federal methodology is used as a basis for awarding need-based institutional aid.

UNDERGRADUATE EXPENSES for 2005–06 *Application fee:* $25. *Comprehensive fee:* $16,713 includes full-time tuition ($12,840) and room and board ($3873). Room and board charges vary according to board plan and housing facility. *Part-time tuition:* $400 per semester hour. *Payment plans:* Guaranteed tuition, installment.

FRESHMAN FINANCIAL AID (Fall 2005, est.) 294 applied for aid; of those 82% were deemed to have need. 100% of freshmen with need received aid; of those 25% had need fully met. *Average percent of need met:* 89% (excluding resources awarded to replace EFC). *Average financial aid package:* $10,258 (excluding resources awarded to replace EFC). 17% of all full-time freshmen had no need and received non-need-based gift aid.

UNDERGRADUATE FINANCIAL AID (Fall 2005, est.) 1,082 applied for aid; of those 83% were deemed to have need. 100% of undergraduates with need received aid; of those 26% had need fully met. *Average percent of need met:* 85% (excluding resources awarded to replace EFC). *Average financial aid package:* $11,930 (excluding resources awarded to replace EFC). 16% of all full-time undergraduates had no need and received non-need-based gift aid.

GIFT AID (NEED-BASED) *Total amount:* $3,664,934 (43% federal, 57% state). *Receiving aid:* Freshmen: 62% (186); All full-time undergraduates: 61% (720). *Average award:* Freshmen: $5284; Undergraduates: $7492. *Scholarships, grants, and awards:* Federal Pell, FSEOG, state, private, college/university gift aid from institutional funds.

GIFT AID (NON-NEED-BASED) *Total amount:* $4,699,379 (85% institutional, 15% external sources). *Receiving aid:* Freshmen: 79% (238); Undergraduates: 71% (832). *Average Award:* Freshmen: $4858; Undergraduates: $5768. *Scholarships, grants, and awards by category: Academic Interests/Achievement:* biological sciences, business, communication, computer science, education, English, foreign languages, general academic interests/achievements, health fields, mathematics, physical sciences, religion/biblical studies. *Creative Arts/Performance:* music, theater/drama. *Special Achievements/Activities:* cheerleading/drum major, general special achievements/activities, leadership, religious involvement. *Special Characteristics:* children and siblings of alumni, children of educators, children of faculty/staff, general special characteristics, international students, local/state students, previous college experience, religious affiliation, siblings of current students, twins. *Tuition waivers:* Full or partial for employees or children of employees.

LOANS *Student loans:* $5,591,930 (47% need-based, 53% non-need-based). 81% of past graduating class borrowed through all loan programs. *Average indebtedness per student:* $16,777. *Average need-based loan:* Freshmen: $2605;

Undergraduates: $3743. *Parent loans:* $1,111,886 (100% non-need-based). *Programs:* FFEL (Subsidized and Unsubsidized Stafford, PLUS), Perkins, state, college/university.

WORK-STUDY *Federal work-study:* Total amount: $141,456; 144 jobs averaging $1108. *State or other work-study/employment:* Total amount: $391,658 (7% need-based, 93% non-need-based). 303 part-time jobs averaging $1099.

APPLYING FOR FINANCIAL AID *Required financial aid forms:* FAFSA, institution's own form. *Financial aid deadline (priority):* 6/1. *Notification date:* Continuous. Students must reply within 3 weeks of notification.

CONTACT Katherine Evans, Director of Financial Aid, East Texas Baptist University, 1209 North Grove Street, Marshall, TX 75670-1498, 903-923-2137 or toll-free 800-804-ETBU. *Fax:* 903-934-8120.

EAST-WEST UNIVERSITY
Chicago, IL

CONTACT Financial Aid Office, East-West University, 816 South Michigan Avenue, Chicago, IL 60605-2103, 312-939-0111 Ext. 1809.

ECKERD COLLEGE
St. Petersburg, FL

Tuition & fees: $27,618 | **Average undergraduate aid package: $18,961**

ABOUT THE INSTITUTION Independent Presbyterian, coed. Awards: bachelor's degrees. 36 undergraduate majors. Total enrollment: 1,779. Undergraduates: 1,779. Federal methodology is used as a basis for awarding need-based institutional aid.

UNDERGRADUATE EXPENSES for 2006–07 *Application fee:* $35. *Comprehensive fee:* $35,486 includes full-time tuition ($27,352), mandatory fees ($266), and room and board ($7868). *College room only:* $4072. *Part-time tuition:* $3300 per course.

FRESHMAN FINANCIAL AID (Fall 2005, est.) 347 applied for aid; of those 79% were deemed to have need. 100% of freshmen with need received aid; of those 27% had need fully met. *Average percent of need met:* 87% (excluding resources awarded to replace EFC). *Average financial aid package:* $19,716 (excluding resources awarded to replace EFC). 20% of all full-time freshmen had no need and received non-need-based gift aid.

UNDERGRADUATE FINANCIAL AID (Fall 2005, est.) 1,103 applied for aid; of those 84% were deemed to have need. 100% of undergraduates with need received aid; of those 17% had need fully met. *Average percent of need met:* 79% (excluding resources awarded to replace EFC). *Average financial aid package:* $18,961 (excluding resources awarded to replace EFC). 35% of all full-time undergraduates had no need and received non-need-based gift aid.

GIFT AID (NEED-BASED) *Total amount:* $12,722,947 (8% federal, 9% state, 80% institutional, 3% external sources). *Receiving aid:* Freshmen: 58% (272); All full-time undergraduates: 56% (923). *Average award:* Freshmen: $17,956; Undergraduates: $14,307. *Scholarships, grants, and awards:* Federal Pell, FSEOG, state, private, college/university gift aid from institutional funds.

GIFT AID (NON-NEED-BASED) *Total amount:* $6,229,692 (11% state, 85% institutional, 4% external sources). *Average Award:* Freshmen: $9250; Undergraduates: $8617. *Scholarships, grants, and awards by category: Academic Interests/Achievement:* 500 awards ($4,000,000 total): general academic interests/achievements. *Creative Arts/Performance:* 40 awards ($200,000 total): art/fine arts, creative writing, music, theater/drama. *Special Achievements/Activities:* 100 awards ($500,000 total): community service, leadership. *Special Characteristics:* 233 awards ($1,116,402 total): children of faculty/staff, international students, local/state students, religious affiliation. *ROTC:* Army cooperative, Air Force cooperative.

LOANS *Student loans:* $6,717,582 (63% need-based, 37% non-need-based). 59% of past graduating class borrowed through all loan programs. *Average indebtedness per student:* $9448. *Average need-based loan:* Freshmen: $2204; Undergraduates: $4383. *Parent loans:* $2,572,336 (34% need-based, 66% non-need-based). *Programs:* FFEL (Subsidized and Unsubsidized Stafford, PLUS), Perkins, college/university.

WORK-STUDY *Federal work-study:* Total amount: $1,370,018; 661 jobs averaging $2000. *State or other work-study/employment:* Total amount: $141,755 (100% non-need-based). 75 part-time jobs averaging $1500.

ATHLETIC AWARDS *Total amount:* $452,438 (36% need-based, 64% non-need-based).

APPLYING FOR FINANCIAL AID *Required financial aid form:* FAFSA. *Financial aid deadline (priority):* 4/1. *Notification date:* Continuous. Students must reply by 5/1.
CONTACT Dr. Pat Garrett Watkins, Director of Financial Aid, Eckerd College, 4200 54th Avenue, South, St. Petersburg, FL 33711, 727-864-8334 or toll-free 800-456-9009. *Fax:* 727-866-2304. *E-mail:* watkinpe@eckerd.edu.

EDGEWOOD COLLEGE
Madison, WI

ABOUT THE INSTITUTION Independent Roman Catholic, coed. Awards: associate, bachelor's, master's, and doctoral degrees. 41 undergraduate majors. Total enrollment: 2,646. Undergraduates: 2,023. Freshmen: 287.
GIFT AID (NEED-BASED) *Scholarships, grants, and awards:* Federal Pell, FSEOG, state, private, college/university gift aid from institutional funds.
GIFT AID (NON-NEED-BASED) *Scholarships, grants, and awards by category: Academic Interests/Achievement:* foreign languages, general academic interests/achievements. *Creative Arts/Performance:* art/fine arts, creative writing, music, performing arts, theater/drama. *Special Achievements/Activities:* community service, hobbies/interests, leadership. *Special Characteristics:* first-generation college students, handicapped students, local/state students, members of minority groups, religious affiliation.
LOANS *Programs:* FFEL (Subsidized and Unsubsidized Stafford, PLUS), Perkins, state, college/university.
APPLYING FOR FINANCIAL AID *Required financial aid forms:* FAFSA, institution's own form.
CONTACT Kari Gribble, Director for Financial Aid, Edgewood College, 1000 Edgewood College Drive, Madison, WI 53711-1997, 608-663-2206 or toll-free 800-444-4861 Ext. 2294.

EDINBORO UNIVERSITY OF PENNSYLVANIA
Edinboro, PA

Tuition & fees (PA res): $6290	Average undergraduate aid package: $6402

ABOUT THE INSTITUTION State-supported, coed. Awards: associate, bachelor's, and master's degrees and post-bachelor's and post-master's certificates. 55 undergraduate majors. Total enrollment: 7,691. Undergraduates: 6,523. Freshmen: 1,326. Federal methodology is used as a basis for awarding need-based institutional aid.
UNDERGRADUATE EXPENSES for 2005–06 *Application fee:* $30. *Tuition, state resident:* full-time $4906; part-time $204 per credit. *Tuition, nonresident:* full-time $9814; part-time $409 per credit. *Required fees:* full-time $1384; $52.32 per credit. Part-time tuition and fees vary according to course load. *College room and board:* $5518; *room only:* $3400. Room and board charges vary according to board plan. *Payment plan:* Installment.
FRESHMAN FINANCIAL AID (Fall 2004) 1195 applied for aid; of those 86% were deemed to have need. 97% of freshmen with need received aid; of those 6% had need fully met. *Average percent of need met:* 78% (excluding resources awarded to replace EFC). *Average financial aid package:* $5639 (excluding resources awarded to replace EFC). 8% of all full-time freshmen had no need and received non-need-based gift aid.
UNDERGRADUATE FINANCIAL AID (Fall 2004) 5,462 applied for aid; of those 87% were deemed to have need. 98% of undergraduates with need received aid; of those 7% had need fully met. *Average percent of need met:* 81% (excluding resources awarded to replace EFC). *Average financial aid package:* $6402 (excluding resources awarded to replace EFC). 11% of all full-time undergraduates had no need and received non-need-based gift aid.
GIFT AID (NEED-BASED) *Total amount:* $13,186,398 (56% federal, 44% state). *Receiving aid:* Freshmen: 80% (992); All full-time undergraduates: 77% (4,640). *Average award:* Freshmen: $2832; Undergraduates: $1825. *Scholarships, grants, and awards:* Federal Pell, FSEOG, state, private, college/university gift aid from institutional funds.
GIFT AID (NON-NEED-BASED) *Total amount:* $2,009,981 (20% state, 47% institutional, 33% external sources). *Receiving aid:* Freshmen: 28% (350); Undergraduates: 16% (948). *Average Award:* Freshmen: $2444; Undergraduates: $1900. *Scholarships, grants, and awards by category: Academic Interests/Achievement:* 260 awards ($286,000 total): biological sciences, business, communication, computer science, education, engineering/technologies, English, foreign languages, general academic interests/achievements, health fields, humanities, mathematics, military science, physical sciences, premedicine, religion/biblical studies, social sciences. *Creative Arts/Performance:* 31 awards ($14,500 total): art/fine arts, cinema/film/broadcasting, journalism/publications, music. *Special Achievements/Activities:* 5 awards ($3500 total): general special achievements/activities. *Special Characteristics:* 856 awards ($2,422,311 total): adult students, children and siblings of alumni, children of faculty/staff, children of union members/company employees, children with a deceased or disabled parent, first-generation college students, general special characteristics, handicapped students, international students, local/state students, members of minority groups, out-of-state students, religious affiliation, veterans, veterans' children. *Tuition waivers:* Full or partial for minority students, employees or children of employees. *ROTC:* Army.
LOANS *Student loans:* $35,255,825 (52% need-based, 48% non-need-based). 67% of past graduating class borrowed through all loan programs. *Average indebtedness per student:* $17,034. *Average need-based loan:* Freshmen: $2107; Undergraduates: $3227. *Parent loans:* $4,527,765 (100% non-need-based). *Programs:* FFEL (Subsidized and Unsubsidized Stafford, PLUS), Perkins, Federal Nursing, college/university.
WORK-STUDY *Federal work-study:* Total amount: $731,407; 571 jobs averaging $1281. *State or other work-study/employment:* Total amount: $903,412 (100% non-need-based). 801 part-time jobs averaging $1128.
ATHLETIC AWARDS *Total amount:* $728,877 (1% need-based, 99% non-need-based).
APPLYING FOR FINANCIAL AID *Required financial aid form:* FAFSA. *Financial aid deadline (priority):* 3/15. *Notification date:* 3/31. Students must reply within 2 weeks of notification.
CONTACT Ms. Dorothy Body, Assistant Vice President for Student Financial Support and Services, Edinboro University of Pennsylvania, Hamilton Hall, Edinboro, PA 16444, 814-732-5555 Ext. 266 or toll-free 888-846-2676 (in-state), 800-626-2203 (out-of-state). *Fax:* 814-732-2129. *E-mail:* dbody@edinboro.edu.

EDWARD WATERS COLLEGE
Jacksonville, FL

CONTACT Gabriel Mbomeh, Director of Financial Aid, Edward Waters College, 1658 Kings Road, Jacksonville, FL 32209-6199, 904-366-2528 or toll-free 888-898-3191.

ELECTRONIC DATA PROCESSING COLLEGE OF PUERTO RICO
Hato Rey, PR

CONTACT Dean of Financial Aid, Electronic Data Processing College of Puerto Rico, PO Box 192303, San Juan, PR 00919-2303, 787-765-3560 Ext. 4713. *Fax:* 787-765-2650.

ELECTRONIC DATA PROCESSING COLLEGE OF PUERTO RICO–SAN SEBASTIAN
San Sebastian, PR

CONTACT Financial Aid Office, Electronic Data Processing College of Puerto Rico–San Sebastian, Avenue Betances #49, San Sebastian, PR 00685, 787-896-2137.

ELIZABETH CITY STATE UNIVERSITY
Elizabeth City, NC

CONTACT Assistant Director of Financial Aid, Elizabeth City State University, 1704 Weeksville Road, Campus Box 914, Elizabeth City, NC 27909-7806, 252-335-3285 or toll-free 800-347-3278. *Fax:* 252-335-3716.

ELIZABETHTOWN COLLEGE
Elizabethtown, PA

Tuition & fees: $26,950	Average undergraduate aid package: $16,420

Elizabethtown College

ABOUT THE INSTITUTION Independent religious, coed. Awards: associate, bachelor's, and master's degrees and post-bachelor's certificates. 50 undergraduate majors. Total enrollment: 2,248. Undergraduates: 1,895. Freshmen: 508. Both federal and institutional methodology are used as a basis for awarding need-based institutional aid.

UNDERGRADUATE EXPENSES for 2006–07 *Application fee:* $30. *Comprehensive fee:* $34,250 includes full-time tuition ($26,950) and room and board ($7300). *College room only:* $3650. *Part-time tuition:* $660 per credit hour.

FRESHMAN FINANCIAL AID (Fall 2005, est.) 451 applied for aid; of those 81% were deemed to have need. 100% of freshmen with need received aid; of those 32% had need fully met. *Average percent of need met:* 83% (excluding resources awarded to replace EFC). *Average financial aid package:* $16,500 (excluding resources awarded to replace EFC). 14% of all full-time freshmen had no need and received non-need-based gift aid.

UNDERGRADUATE FINANCIAL AID (Fall 2005, est.) 1,555 applied for aid; of those 87% were deemed to have need. 100% of undergraduates with need received aid; of those 28% had need fully met. *Average percent of need met:* 79% (excluding resources awarded to replace EFC). *Average financial aid package:* $16,420 (excluding resources awarded to replace EFC). 9% of all full-time undergraduates had no need and received non-need-based gift aid.

GIFT AID (NEED-BASED) *Total amount:* $21,659,417 (5% federal, 10% state, 77% institutional, 8% external sources). *Receiving aid:* Freshmen: 72% (366); All full-time undergraduates: 70% (1,344). *Average award:* Freshmen: $15,210; Undergraduates: $14,244. *Scholarships, grants, and awards:* Federal Pell, FSEOG, state, private, college/university gift aid from institutional funds.

GIFT AID (NON-NEED-BASED) *Total amount:* $2,551,975 (1% state, 80% institutional, 19% external sources). *Receiving aid:* Freshmen: 15% (77); Undergraduates: 11% (209). *Average Award:* Freshmen: $14,816; Undergraduates: $15,442. *Scholarships, grants, and awards by category:* Academic Interests/Achievement: biological sciences, business, communication, computer science, education, engineering/technologies, English, foreign languages, general academic interests/achievements, health fields, humanities, international studies, mathematics, physical sciences, premedicine, religion/biblical studies, social sciences. Creative Arts/Performance: art/fine arts, music, performing arts, theater/drama. Special Achievements/Activities: religious involvement. Special Characteristics: children of faculty/staff, international students, local/state students, members of minority groups, religious affiliation, siblings of current students.

LOANS *Student loans:* $10,555,567 (58% need-based, 42% non-need-based). 77% of past graduating class borrowed through all loan programs. *Average indebtedness per student:* $29,233. *Average need-based loan:* Freshmen: $2927; Undergraduates: $3914. *Parent loans:* $4,648,246 (19% need-based, 81% non-need-based). *Programs:* FFEL (Subsidized and Unsubsidized Stafford, PLUS), Perkins, state, college/university.

WORK-STUDY *Federal work-study:* Total amount: $1,129,682; 881 jobs averaging $1282.

APPLYING FOR FINANCIAL AID *Required financial aid forms:* FAFSA, institution's own form, state aid form, federal income tax form(s), W-2 forms. *Financial aid deadline (priority):* 3/15. *Notification date:* Continuous beginning 3/15. Students must reply by 5/1 or within 2 weeks of notification.

CONTACT Elizabeth K. McCloud, Director of Financial Aid, Elizabethtown College, 1 Alpha Drive, Elizabethtown, PA 17022-2298, 717-361-1404. *Fax:* 717-361-1514. *E-mail:* mcclouek@etown.edu.

ELMHURST COLLEGE
Elmhurst, IL

Tuition & fees: $21,600	Average undergraduate aid package: $15,512

ABOUT THE INSTITUTION Independent religious, coed. Awards: bachelor's and master's degrees. 67 undergraduate majors. Total enrollment: 2,670. Undergraduates: 2,484. Freshmen: 415. Federal methodology is used as a basis for awarding need-based institutional aid.

UNDERGRADUATE EXPENSES for 2005–06 *Application fee:* $25. *Comprehensive fee:* $28,506 includes full-time tuition ($21,600) and room and board ($6906). *College room only:* $3816. Room and board charges vary according to board plan and housing facility. *Part-time tuition:* $614 per semester hour. *Payment plan:* Installment.

FRESHMAN FINANCIAL AID (Fall 2005, est.) 395 applied for aid; of those 82% were deemed to have need. 100% of freshmen with need received aid; of those 39% had need fully met. *Average percent of need met:* 93% (excluding resources awarded to replace EFC). *Average financial aid package:* $15,492 (excluding resources awarded to replace EFC). 20% of all full-time freshmen had no need and received non-need-based gift aid.

UNDERGRADUATE FINANCIAL AID (Fall 2005, est.) 1,915 applied for aid; of those 86% were deemed to have need. 100% of undergraduates with need received aid; of those 29% had need fully met. *Average percent of need met:* 91% (excluding resources awarded to replace EFC). *Average financial aid package:* $15,512 (excluding resources awarded to replace EFC). 20% of all full-time undergraduates had no need and received non-need-based gift aid.

GIFT AID (NEED-BASED) *Total amount:* $18,341,567 (10% federal, 19% state, 70% institutional, 1% external sources). *Receiving aid:* Freshmen: 64% (300); All full-time undergraduates: 70% (1,648). *Average award:* Freshmen: $14,284; Undergraduates: $11,156. *Scholarships, grants, and awards:* Federal Pell, FSEOG, state, private, college/university gift aid from institutional funds.

GIFT AID (NON-NEED-BASED) *Total amount:* $4,725,782 (2% state, 97% institutional, 1% external sources). *Receiving aid:* Freshmen: 16% (74); Undergraduates: 8% (196). *Average Award:* Freshmen: $9976; Undergraduates: $8374. *Scholarships, grants, and awards by category:* Academic Interests/Achievement: 1,021 awards ($8,709,182 total): biological sciences, business, communication, computer science, education, English, foreign languages, general academic interests/achievements, health fields, humanities, mathematics, physical sciences, premedicine, religion/biblical studies. Creative Arts/Performance: 163 awards ($205,570 total): art/fine arts, music, theater/drama. Special Achievements/Activities: 2 awards ($2000 total): community service. Special Characteristics: 232 awards ($1,220,638 total): children and siblings of alumni, children of current students, ethnic background, members of minority groups, religious affiliation, siblings of current students, spouses of current students. *Tuition waivers:* Full or partial for employees or children of employees, senior citizens. *ROTC:* Army cooperative, Air Force cooperative.

LOANS *Student loans:* $12,313,327 (49% need-based, 51% non-need-based). 75% of past graduating class borrowed through all loan programs. *Average indebtedness per student:* $16,080. *Average need-based loan:* Freshmen: $3500; Undergraduates: $3745. *Parent loans:* $4,114,853 (33% need-based, 67% non-need-based). *Programs:* Federal Direct (Subsidized and Unsubsidized Stafford, PLUS), Perkins, alternative loans.

WORK-STUDY *Federal work-study:* Total amount: $255,690; 293 jobs averaging $873. *State or other work-study/employment:* Total amount: $474,853 (100% non-need-based). 240 part-time jobs averaging $1978.

APPLYING FOR FINANCIAL AID *Required financial aid form:* FAFSA. *Financial aid deadline (priority):* 4/15. *Notification date:* Continuous beginning 3/1. Students must reply within 3 weeks of notification.

CONTACT Ruth A. Pusich, Director of Financial Aid, Elmhurst College, Goebel Hall 106A, 190 Prospect Avenue, Elmhurst, IL 60126-3296, 630-617-3080 or toll-free 800-697-1871 (out-of-state). *Fax:* 630-617-5188. *E-mail:* ruthp@elmhurst.edu.

ELMIRA COLLEGE
Elmira, NY

Tuition & fees: $30,050	Average undergraduate aid package: $21,435

ABOUT THE INSTITUTION Independent, coed. Awards: bachelor's and master's degrees. 67 undergraduate majors. Total enrollment: 1,853. Undergraduates: 1,484. Freshmen: 323. Federal methodology is used as a basis for awarding need-based institutional aid.

UNDERGRADUATE EXPENSES for 2006–07 *Application fee:* $50. *Comprehensive fee:* $39,150 includes full-time tuition ($29,000), mandatory fees ($1050), and room and board ($9100). *Part-time tuition:* $270 per credit.

FRESHMAN FINANCIAL AID (Fall 2005, est.) 272 applied for aid; of those 92% were deemed to have need. 100% of freshmen with need received aid; of those 16% had need fully met. *Average percent of need met:* 80% (excluding resources awarded to replace EFC). *Average financial aid package:* $21,877 (excluding resources awarded to replace EFC). 17% of all full-time freshmen had no need and received non-need-based gift aid.

UNDERGRADUATE FINANCIAL AID (Fall 2005, est.) 1,001 applied for aid; of those 92% were deemed to have need. 100% of undergraduates with need received aid; of those 16% had need fully met. *Average percent of need met:* 80% (excluding resources awarded to replace EFC). *Average financial aid package:* $21,435 (excluding resources awarded to replace EFC). 18% of all full-time undergraduates had no need and received non-need-based gift aid.

GIFT AID (NEED-BASED) *Total amount:* $14,711,333 (6% federal, 7% state, 85% institutional, 2% external sources). *Receiving aid:* Freshmen: 82% (249); All full-time undergraduates: 78% (914). *Average award:* Freshmen: $17,500; Undergraduates: $16,130. *Scholarships, grants, and awards:* Federal Pell, FSEOG, state, private, college/university gift aid from institutional funds.
GIFT AID (NON-NEED-BASED) *Total amount:* $3,092,348 (2% state, 94% institutional, 4% external sources). *Receiving aid:* Freshmen: 10% (31); Undergraduates: 9% (108). *Average Award:* Freshmen: $15,861; Undergraduates: $15,717. *Scholarships, grants, and awards by category: Academic Interests/Achievement:* 745 awards ($8,858,524 total): general academic interests/achievements. *Special Achievements/Activities:* 97 awards ($397,200 total): leadership. *Special Characteristics:* 108 awards ($1,309,472 total): children of faculty/staff, international students, local/state students, previous college experience, siblings of current students. *ROTC:* Army, Air Force cooperative.
LOANS *Student loans:* $9,220,290 (69% need-based, 31% non-need-based). 69% of past graduating class borrowed through all loan programs. *Average indebtedness per student:* $25,347. *Average need-based loan:* Freshmen: $4631; Undergraduates: $5795. *Parent loans:* $2,347,746 (33% need-based, 67% non-need-based). *Programs:* FFEL (Subsidized and Unsubsidized Stafford, PLUS), Perkins, college/university, GATE Loans, alternative loans.
WORK-STUDY *Federal work-study:* Total amount: $363,744; 364 jobs averaging $1000. *State or other work-study/employment:* Total amount: $240,775 (51% need-based, 49% non-need-based). 195 part-time jobs averaging $1200.
APPLYING FOR FINANCIAL AID *Required financial aid forms:* FAFSA, state aid form. *Financial aid deadline (priority):* 2/1. *Notification date:* Continuous beginning 2/15. Students must reply by 5/1 or within 3 weeks of notification.
CONTACT Kathleen L. Cohen, Dean of Financial Aid, Elmira College, Hamilton Hall, One Park Place, Elmira, NY 14901-2099, 607-735-1728 or toll-free 800-935-6472. *Fax:* 607-735-1718. *E-mail:* kcohen@elmira.edu.

ELMS COLLEGE
Chicopee, MA

Tuition & fees: $21,520 **Average undergraduate aid package: $14,959**

ABOUT THE INSTITUTION Independent Roman Catholic, coed, primarily women. Awards: associate, bachelor's, and master's degrees and post-bachelor's certificates. 42 undergraduate majors. Total enrollment: 1,234. Undergraduates: 1,066. Freshmen: 145. Both federal and institutional methodology are used as a basis for awarding need-based institutional aid.
UNDERGRADUATE EXPENSES for 2006–07 *Application fee:* $30. *Comprehensive fee:* $29,920 includes full-time tuition ($21,520) and room and board ($8400). *Part-time tuition:* $440 per credit. *Part-time fees:* $20 per term.
FRESHMAN FINANCIAL AID (Fall 2004) 116 applied for aid; of those 90% were deemed to have need. 100% of freshmen with need received aid; of those 31% had need fully met. *Average percent of need met:* 80% (excluding resources awarded to replace EFC). *Average financial aid package:* $13,697 (excluding resources awarded to replace EFC). 19% of all full-time freshmen had no need and received non-need-based gift aid.
UNDERGRADUATE FINANCIAL AID (Fall 2004) 526 applied for aid; of those 92% were deemed to have need. 100% of undergraduates with need received aid; of those 31% had need fully met. *Average percent of need met:* 80% (excluding resources awarded to replace EFC). *Average financial aid package:* $14,959 (excluding resources awarded to replace EFC). 15% of all full-time undergraduates had no need and received non-need-based gift aid.
GIFT AID (NEED-BASED) *Total amount:* $4,913,424 (14% federal, 9% state, 75% institutional, 2% external sources). *Receiving aid:* Freshmen: 80% (104); All full-time undergraduates: 82% (473). *Average award:* Freshmen: $9969; Undergraduates: $9496. *Scholarships, grants, and awards:* Federal Pell, FSEOG, state, private, college/university gift aid from institutional funds.
GIFT AID (NON-NEED-BASED) *Total amount:* $732,519 (98% institutional, 2% external sources). *Receiving aid:* Freshmen: 11% (14); Undergraduates: 6% (36). *Average Award:* Freshmen: $11,304; Undergraduates: $11,183. *Scholarships, grants, and awards by category: Academic Interests/Achievement:* 148 awards ($588,525 total): general academic interests/achievements. *Special Characteristics:* 87 awards ($316,600 total): children of faculty/staff, general special characteristics, religious affiliation. *ROTC:* Army cooperative, Air Force cooperative.
LOANS *Student loans:* $4,950,293 (70% need-based, 30% non-need-based). 96% of past graduating class borrowed through all loan programs. *Average indebtedness per student:* $23,226. *Average need-based loan:* Freshmen: $3700; Undergraduates: $5553. *Parent loans:* $1,044,524 (40% need-based, 60% non-need-based). *Programs:* FFEL (Subsidized and Unsubsidized Stafford, PLUS), Perkins, state, alternative loans, MEFA Loans, Signature Loans.
WORK-STUDY *Federal work-study:* Total amount: $254,652; 164 jobs averaging $1328. *State or other work-study/employment:* Total amount: $56,000 (12% need-based, 88% non-need-based).
APPLYING FOR FINANCIAL AID *Required financial aid forms:* FAFSA, institution's own form. *Financial aid deadline (priority):* 3/1. *Notification date:* Continuous beginning 3/15. Students must reply by 5/1.
CONTACT Ms. April Arcouette, Assistant Director of Student Financial Aid Services, Elms College, 291 Springfield Street, Chicopee, MA 01013-2839, 413-265-2249 or toll-free 800-255-ELMS. *Fax:* 413-265-2671. *E-mail:* arcouettea@elms.edu.

ELON UNIVERSITY
Elon, NC

Tuition & fees: $18,949 **Average undergraduate aid package: $12,161**

ABOUT THE INSTITUTION Independent religious, coed. Awards: bachelor's, master's, doctoral, and first professional degrees. 51 undergraduate majors. Total enrollment: 4,956. Undergraduates: 4,702. Freshmen: 1,237. Institutional methodology is used as a basis for awarding need-based institutional aid.
UNDERGRADUATE EXPENSES for 2005–06 *Application fee:* $40. *Comprehensive fee:* $25,371 includes full-time tuition ($18,699), mandatory fees ($250), and room and board ($6422). Room and board charges vary according to board plan and housing facility. *Part-time tuition:* $588 per hour. *Part-time fees:* $125 per term. Part-time tuition and fees vary according to course load. *Payment plan:* Installment.
FRESHMAN FINANCIAL AID (Fall 2005, est.) 734 applied for aid; of those 60% were deemed to have need. 99% of freshmen with need received aid. *Average percent of need met:* 68% (excluding resources awarded to replace EFC). *Average financial aid package:* $11,753 (excluding resources awarded to replace EFC). 22% of all full-time freshmen had no need and received non-need-based gift aid.
UNDERGRADUATE FINANCIAL AID (Fall 2005, est.) 2,182 applied for aid; of those 71% were deemed to have need. 99% of undergraduates with need received aid. *Average percent of need met:* 67% (excluding resources awarded to replace EFC). *Average financial aid package:* $12,161 (excluding resources awarded to replace EFC). 21% of all full-time undergraduates had no need and received non-need-based gift aid.
GIFT AID (NEED-BASED) *Total amount:* $10,680,258 (11% federal, 28% state, 58% institutional, 3% external sources). *Receiving aid:* Freshmen: 31% (383); All full-time undergraduates: 30% (1,389). *Average award:* Freshmen: $7332; Undergraduates: $6799. *Scholarships, grants, and awards:* Federal Pell, FSEOG, state, private, college/university gift aid from institutional funds.
GIFT AID (NON-NEED-BASED) *Total amount:* $5,335,488 (26% state, 69% institutional, 5% external sources). *Receiving aid:* Freshmen: 5% (63); Undergraduates: 4% (170). *Average Award:* Freshmen: $4544; Undergraduates:* $4119. *Scholarships, grants, and awards by category: Academic Interests/Achievement:* 1,702 awards ($5,646,768 total): biological sciences, business, communication, computer science, education, engineering/technologies, general academic interests/achievements, mathematics, military science, physical sciences, premedicine, religion/biblical studies, social sciences. *Creative Arts/Performance:* 55 awards ($116,180 total): art/fine arts, journalism/publications, music, performing arts, theater/drama. *Special Achievements/Activities:* 142 awards ($59,775 total): community service, general special achievements/activities, leadership, religious involvement. *Special Characteristics:* 63 awards ($645,735 total): children of faculty/staff, first-generation college students, relatives of clergy. *Tuition waivers:* Full or partial for employees or children of employees. *ROTC:* Army, Air Force cooperative.
LOANS *Student loans:* $12,535,897 (42% need-based, 58% non-need-based). 45% of past graduating class borrowed through all loan programs. *Average indebtedness per student:* $21,687. *Average need-based loan:* Freshmen: $2768; Undergraduates: $3771. *Parent loans:* $8,992,165 (35% need-based, 65% non-need-based). *Programs:* FFEL (Subsidized and Unsubsidized Stafford, PLUS), Perkins, state, college/university, alternative loans.
WORK-STUDY *Federal work-study:* Total amount: $2,023,429; 864 jobs averaging $2283.

Elon University

ATHLETIC AWARDS *Total amount:* $3,711,635 (45% need-based, 55% non-need-based).
APPLYING FOR FINANCIAL AID *Required financial aid forms:* FAFSA, institution's own form, CSS Financial Aid PROFILE. *Financial aid deadline (priority):* 2/15. *Notification date:* Continuous beginning 3/30.
CONTACT Pat Murphy, Director of Financial Planning, Elon University, 2700 Campus Box, Elon, NC 27244, 336-278-7640 or toll-free 800-334-8448. *E-mail:* murphyp@elon.edu.

EMBRY-RIDDLE AERONAUTICAL UNIVERSITY
Prescott, AZ

Tuition & fees: $23,490 **Average undergraduate aid package: $13,896**

ABOUT THE INSTITUTION Independent, coed. Awards: bachelor's and master's degrees. 11 undergraduate majors. Total enrollment: 1,685. Undergraduates: 1,653. Freshmen: 359. Federal methodology is used as a basis for awarding need-based institutional aid.
UNDERGRADUATE EXPENSES for 2005–06 *Application fee:* $50. *Comprehensive fee:* $30,006 includes full-time tuition ($22,820), mandatory fees ($670), and room and board ($6516). *College room only:* $3580. *Part-time tuition:* $955 per credit hour.
FRESHMAN FINANCIAL AID (Fall 2004) 319 applied for aid; of those 79% were deemed to have need. 100% of freshmen with need received aid. *Average financial aid package:* $11,544 (excluding resources awarded to replace EFC).
UNDERGRADUATE FINANCIAL AID (Fall 2004) 1,078 applied for aid; of those 86% were deemed to have need. 100% of undergraduates with need received aid. *Average financial aid package:* $13,896 (excluding resources awarded to replace EFC).
GIFT AID (NEED-BASED) *Total amount:* $12,554,383 (10% federal, 60% institutional, 30% external sources). *Receiving aid:* Freshmen: 70% (251); All full-time undergraduates: 60% (881). *Average award:* Freshmen: $7464; Undergraduates: $7834. *Scholarships, grants, and awards:* Federal Pell, FSEOG, state, private, college/university gift aid from institutional funds.
GIFT AID (NON-NEED-BASED) *Scholarships, grants, and awards by category: Academic Interests/Achievement:* 523 awards ($3,106,834 total): general academic interests/achievements. *Special Achievements/Activities:* 16 awards ($75,250 total): leadership. *Special Characteristics:* 54 awards ($595,243 total): children and siblings of alumni, children of faculty/staff. *ROTC:* Army, Air Force.
LOANS *Student loans:* $13,300,671 (100% need-based). 73% of past graduating class borrowed through all loan programs. *Average indebtedness per student:* $49,532. *Average need-based loan:* Freshmen: $3470; Undergraduates: $4683. *Parent loans:* $6,568,754 (100% need-based). *Programs:* FFEL (Subsidized and Unsubsidized Stafford, PLUS), Perkins.
WORK-STUDY *Federal work-study:* Total amount: $67,089; 78 jobs averaging $860. *State or other work-study/employment:* Total amount: $902,713 (100% need-based). 462 part-time jobs averaging $1953.
ATHLETIC AWARDS *Total amount:* $603,716 (100% need-based).
APPLYING FOR FINANCIAL AID *Required financial aid form:* FAFSA. *Financial aid deadline:* Continuous. *Notification date:* Continuous beginning 3/1. Students must reply within 4 weeks of notification.
CONTACT Mr. Dan Lupin, Director of Financial Aid, Embry-Riddle Aeronautical University, 3700 Willow Creek Road, Prescott, AZ 86301-3720, 928-777-3765 or toll-free 800-888-3728. *E-mail:* lupind@erau.edu.

EMBRY-RIDDLE AERONAUTICAL UNIVERSITY
Daytona Beach, FL

Tuition & fees: $23,500 **Average undergraduate aid package: $13,221**

ABOUT THE INSTITUTION Independent, coed. Awards: bachelor's and master's degrees. 19 undergraduate majors. Total enrollment: 4,776. Undergraduates: 4,382. Freshmen: 977. Federal methodology is used as a basis for awarding need-based institutional aid.
UNDERGRADUATE EXPENSES for 2005–06 *Application fee:* $50. *Comprehensive fee:* $30,436 includes full-time tuition ($22,820), mandatory fees ($680), and room and board ($6936). *College room only:* $2800. *Part-time tuition:* $855 per credit hour.
FRESHMAN FINANCIAL AID (Fall 2005, est.) 806 applied for aid; of those 83% were deemed to have need. 100% of freshmen with need received aid. *Average financial aid package:* $11,738 (excluding resources awarded to replace EFC).
UNDERGRADUATE FINANCIAL AID (Fall 2005, est.) 2,830 applied for aid; of those 87% were deemed to have need. 100% of undergraduates with need received aid. *Average financial aid package:* $13,221 (excluding resources awarded to replace EFC).
GIFT AID (NEED-BASED) *Total amount:* $27,705,054 (10% federal, 14% state, 50% institutional, 26% external sources). *Receiving aid:* Freshmen: 68% (667); All full-time undergraduates: 55% (2,249). *Average award:* Freshmen: $7380; Undergraduates: $7070. *Scholarships, grants, and awards:* Federal Pell, FSEOG, state, private, college/university gift aid from institutional funds.
GIFT AID (NON-NEED-BASED) *Scholarships, grants, and awards by category: Academic Interests/Achievement:* 1,952 awards ($8,431,948 total): general academic interests/achievements. *Special Achievements/Activities:* 60 awards ($160,883 total): leadership. *Special Characteristics:* 140 awards ($1,401,324 total): children and siblings of alumni, children of faculty/staff, siblings of current students. *ROTC:* Army, Naval, Air Force.
LOANS *Student loans:* $36,256,559 (100% need-based). 68% of past graduating class borrowed through all loan programs. *Average indebtedness per student:* $52,276. *Average need-based loan:* Freshmen: $3169; Undergraduates: $4510. *Parent loans:* $18,667,083 (100% need-based). *Programs:* FFEL (Subsidized and Unsubsidized Stafford, PLUS), Perkins.
WORK-STUDY *Federal work-study:* Total amount: $268,787; 229 jobs averaging $1173. *State or other work-study/employment:* Total amount: $3,180,364 (100% need-based). 1,309 part-time jobs averaging $2429.
ATHLETIC AWARDS *Total amount:* $1,365,474 (100% need-based).
APPLYING FOR FINANCIAL AID *Required financial aid form:* FAFSA. *Financial aid deadline:* Continuous. *Notification date:* Continuous beginning 3/1. Students must reply within 4 weeks of notification.
CONTACT Maria A. Shaulis, Director of Financial Aid, Embry-Riddle Aeronautical University, 600 South Clyde Morris Boulevard, Daytona Beach, FL 32114-3900, 800-943-6279 or toll-free 800-862-2416. *Fax:* 386-226-6307. *E-mail:* maria.shaulis@erau.edu.

EMBRY-RIDDLE AERONAUTICAL UNIVERSITY, EXTENDED CAMPUS
Daytona Beach, FL

Tuition & fees: $4224 **Average undergraduate aid package: $5128**

ABOUT THE INSTITUTION Independent, coed. Awards: associate, bachelor's, and master's degrees (programs offered at 100 military bases worldwide). 4 undergraduate majors. Total enrollment: 16,255. Undergraduates: 12,560. Freshmen: 506. Federal methodology is used as a basis for awarding need-based institutional aid.
UNDERGRADUATE EXPENSES for 2005–06 *Application fee:* $50. *Tuition:* full-time $4224.
FRESHMAN FINANCIAL AID (Fall 2005, est.) 18 applied for aid; of those 89% were deemed to have need. 100% of freshmen with need received aid. *Average financial aid package:* $4934 (excluding resources awarded to replace EFC).
UNDERGRADUATE FINANCIAL AID (Fall 2005, est.) 587 applied for aid; of those 85% were deemed to have need. 98% of undergraduates with need received aid. *Average financial aid package:* $5128 (excluding resources awarded to replace EFC).
GIFT AID (NEED-BASED) *Total amount:* $3,215,856 (68% federal, 31% state, 1% external sources). *Receiving aid:* Freshmen: 16% (11); All full-time undergraduates: 14% (307). *Average award:* Freshmen: $3623; Undergraduates: $3036. *Scholarships, grants, and awards:* Federal Pell, state, private, college/university gift aid from institutional funds.
GIFT AID (NON-NEED-BASED) *Scholarships, grants, and awards by category: Academic Interests/Achievement:* 24 awards ($1750 total): general academic interests/achievements. *Special Achievements/Activities:* 102 awards ($16,762 total): leadership. *Special Characteristics:* 11 awards ($30,465 total): children of faculty/staff.

LOANS *Student loans:* $12,675,794 (100% need-based). 18% of past graduating class borrowed through all loan programs. *Average indebtedness per student:* $11,565. *Average need-based loan:* Freshmen: $2606; Undergraduates: $3696. *Parent loans:* $95,074 (100% need-based). *Programs:* Federal Direct (Subsidized and Unsubsidized Stafford, PLUS).

APPLYING FOR FINANCIAL AID *Required financial aid form:* FAFSA. *Financial aid deadline:* Continuous. *Notification date:* Continuous beginning 3/1. Students must reply within 4 weeks of notification.

CONTACT Maria A. Shaulis, Director of Financial Aid, Embry-Riddle Aeronautical University, Extended Campus, 600 South Clyde Morris Boulevard, Daytona Beach, FL 32114-3900, 800-943-6279 or toll-free 800-522-6787. *Fax:* 386-226-6307. *E-mail:* maria.shaulis@erau.edu.

EMERSON COLLEGE
Boston, MA

Tuition & fees: $24,622   Average undergraduate aid package: $14,230

ABOUT THE INSTITUTION Independent, coed. Awards: bachelor's, master's, and doctoral degrees. 29 undergraduate majors. Total enrollment: 4,326. Undergraduates: 3,373. Freshmen: 721. Both federal and institutional methodology are used as a basis for awarding need-based institutional aid.

UNDERGRADUATE EXPENSES for 2005–06 *Application fee:* $60. *Comprehensive fee:* $35,042 includes full-time tuition ($24,064), mandatory fees ($558), and room and board ($10,420). *College room only:* $6200. *Part-time tuition:* $752 per credit hour. *Payment plan:* Installment.

FRESHMAN FINANCIAL AID (Fall 2004) 539 applied for aid; of those 74% were deemed to have need. 100% of freshmen with need received aid; of those 76% had need fully met. *Average percent of need met:* 76% (excluding resources awarded to replace EFC). *Average financial aid package:* $13,843 (excluding resources awarded to replace EFC). 21% of all full-time freshmen had no need and received non-need-based gift aid.

UNDERGRADUATE FINANCIAL AID (Fall 2004) 1,915 applied for aid; of those 84% were deemed to have need. 100% of undergraduates with need received aid; of those 67% had need fully met. *Average percent of need met:* 67% (excluding resources awarded to replace EFC). *Average financial aid package:* $14,230 (excluding resources awarded to replace EFC). 13% of all full-time undergraduates had no need and received non-need-based gift aid.

GIFT AID (NEED-BASED) *Total amount:* $14,609,738 (10% federal, 3% state, 82% institutional, 5% external sources). *Receiving aid:* Freshmen: 46% (330); All full-time undergraduates: 41% (1,266). *Average award:* Freshmen: $11,814; Undergraduates: $10,846. *Scholarships, grants, and awards:* Federal Pell, FSEOG, state, private, college/university gift aid from institutional funds.

GIFT AID (NON-NEED-BASED) *Total amount:* $965,749 (81% institutional, 19% external sources). *Receiving aid:* Freshmen: 12% (84); Undergraduates: 10% (297). *Average Award:* Freshmen: $9590; Undergraduates: $12,763. *Scholarships, grants, and awards by category:* Academic Interests/Achievement: 348 awards ($2,774,335 total): general academic interests/achievements. Creative Arts/Performance: 32 awards ($133,600 total): performing arts. *Tuition waivers:* Full or partial for employees or children of employees.

LOANS *Student loans:* $20,223,200 (65% need-based, 35% non-need-based). 55% of past graduating class borrowed through all loan programs. *Average indebtedness per student:* $16,222. *Average need-based loan:* Freshmen: $3545; Undergraduates: $4285. *Parent loans:* $7,162,081 (42% need-based, 58% non-need-based). *Programs:* FFEL (Subsidized and Unsubsidized Stafford, PLUS), Perkins, state.

WORK-STUDY *Federal work-study:* Total amount: $571,268; 445 jobs averaging $2000. *State or other work-study/employment:* Total amount: $766,690 (77% need-based, 23% non-need-based). 41 part-time jobs averaging $10,648.

APPLYING FOR FINANCIAL AID *Required financial aid forms:* FAFSA, CSS Financial Aid PROFILE, noncustodial (divorced/separated) parent's statement, business/farm supplement, Income Tax Returns. *Financial aid deadline (priority):* 3/1. *Notification date:* 4/1. Students must reply by 5/1 or within 3 weeks of notification.

CONTACT Michelle Smith, Director, Office of Student Financial Services, Emerson College, 120 Boylston Street, Boston, MA 02116-4624, 617-824-8655. *Fax:* 617-824-8619. *E-mail:* finaid@emerson.edu.

EMMANUEL COLLEGE
Franklin Springs, GA

CONTACT Mary Beadles, Director of Financial Aid, Emmanuel College, PO Box 129, Franklin Springs, GA 30639-0129, 706-245-2844 or toll-free 800-860-8800 (in-state). *Fax:* 706-245-4424. *E-mail:* mbeadles@emmanuel-college.edu.

EMMANUEL COLLEGE
Boston, MA

Tuition & fees: $22,300   Average undergraduate aid package: $16,201

ABOUT THE INSTITUTION Independent Roman Catholic, coed. Awards: bachelor's and master's degrees and post-master's certificates. 35 undergraduate majors. Total enrollment: 2,296. Undergraduates: 2,096. Freshmen: 438. Federal methodology is used as a basis for awarding need-based institutional aid.

UNDERGRADUATE EXPENSES for 2005–06 *Application fee:* $40. *Comprehensive fee:* $32,000 includes full-time tuition ($21,900), mandatory fees ($400), and room and board ($9700). Full-time tuition and fees vary according to course load, degree level, and program. Room and board charges vary according to housing facility. *Part-time tuition:* $684 per credit. Part-time tuition and fees vary according to program. *Payment plan:* Installment.

FRESHMAN FINANCIAL AID (Fall 2005, est.) 387 applied for aid; of those 86% were deemed to have need. 100% of freshmen with need received aid; of those 31% had need fully met. *Average percent of need met:* 68% (excluding resources awarded to replace EFC). *Average financial aid package:* $16,047 (excluding resources awarded to replace EFC). 11% of all full-time freshmen had no need and received non-need-based gift aid.

UNDERGRADUATE FINANCIAL AID (Fall 2005, est.) 1,372 applied for aid; of those 85% were deemed to have need. 100% of undergraduates with need received aid; of those 18% had need fully met. *Average percent of need met:* 70% (excluding resources awarded to replace EFC). *Average financial aid package:* $16,201 (excluding resources awarded to replace EFC). 14% of all full-time undergraduates had no need and received non-need-based gift aid.

GIFT AID (NEED-BASED) *Total amount:* $13,449,179 (9% federal, 7% state, 80% institutional, 4% external sources). *Receiving aid:* Freshmen: 65% (280); All full-time undergraduates: 61% (905). *Average award:* Freshmen: $10,057; Undergraduates: $8209. *Scholarships, grants, and awards:* Federal Pell, FSEOG, state, private, college/university gift aid from institutional funds.

GIFT AID (NON-NEED-BASED) *Total amount:* $2,091,471 (95% institutional, 5% external sources). *Receiving aid:* Freshmen: 28% (122); Undergraduates: 37% (549). *Average Award:* Freshmen: $11,641; Undergraduates: $9202. *Scholarships, grants, and awards by category:* Academic Interests/Achievement: 555 awards ($5,936,152 total): biological sciences, education, engineering/technologies, foreign languages, general academic interests/achievements, health fields, humanities, mathematics, physical sciences, religion/biblical studies, social sciences. Creative Arts/Performance: 1 award ($3375 total): general creative arts/performance. Special Achievements/Activities: 31 awards ($77,500 total): community service. Special Characteristics: 176 awards ($627,531 total): children and siblings of alumni, children of educators, children of faculty/staff, children of union members/company employees, ethnic background, general special characteristics, handicapped students, international students, local/state students, religious affiliation, siblings of current students. *Tuition waivers:* Full or partial for employees or children of employees. *ROTC:* Army cooperative.

LOANS *Student loans:* $11,327,936 (37% need-based, 63% non-need-based). 71% of past graduating class borrowed through all loan programs. *Average indebtedness per student:* $15,523. *Average need-based loan:* Freshmen: $3449; Undergraduates: $4368. *Parent loans:* $4,210,373 (100% need-based). *Programs:* FFEL (Subsidized and Unsubsidized Stafford, PLUS), Perkins, state, alternative loans.

WORK-STUDY *Federal work-study:* Total amount: $420,000; 454 jobs averaging $925. *State or other work-study/employment:* Total amount: $300,000 (100% non-need-based). 282 part-time jobs averaging $1063.

APPLYING FOR FINANCIAL AID *Required financial aid forms:* FAFSA, institution's own form. *Financial aid deadline (priority):* 4/1. *Notification date:* Continuous. Students must reply within 2 weeks of notification.

CONTACT Jennifer Porter, Director of Student Financial Services, Emmanuel College, 400 The Fenway, Boston, MA 02115, 617-735-9938. *Fax:* 617-735-9939. *E-mail:* porterj@emmanuel.edu.

Emmaus Bible College

EMMAUS BIBLE COLLEGE
Dubuque, IA

Tuition & fees: $8210 **Average undergraduate aid package:** $5195

ABOUT THE INSTITUTION Independent nondenominational, coed. Awards: associate and bachelor's degrees. 5 undergraduate majors. Total enrollment: 296. Undergraduates: 296. Freshmen: 59. Federal methodology is used as a basis for awarding need-based institutional aid.
UNDERGRADUATE EXPENSES for 2005–06 *Application fee:* $25. *Comprehensive fee:* $12,372 includes full-time tuition ($7700), mandatory fees ($510), and room and board ($4162). Full-time tuition and fees vary according to course load. *Part-time tuition:* $342 per credit hour. Part-time tuition and fees vary according to course load. *Payment plan:* Installment.
FRESHMAN FINANCIAL AID (Fall 2005, est.) 99 applied for aid; of those 62% were deemed to have need. 84% of freshmen with need received aid. *Average percent of need met:* 56% (excluding resources awarded to replace EFC). *Average financial aid package:* $4760 (excluding resources awarded to replace EFC).
UNDERGRADUATE FINANCIAL AID (Fall 2005, est.) 212 applied for aid; of those 68% were deemed to have need. 86% of undergraduates with need received aid. *Average percent of need met:* 74% (excluding resources awarded to replace EFC). *Average financial aid package:* $5195 (excluding resources awarded to replace EFC).
GIFT AID (NEED-BASED) *Total amount:* $705,538 (49% federal, 32% institutional, 19% external sources). *Receiving aid:* Freshmen: 42% (51); All full-time undergraduates: 43% (115). *Average award:* Freshmen: $2677; Undergraduates: $2841. *Scholarships, grants, and awards:* Federal Pell, FSEOG, private, college/university gift aid from institutional funds.
GIFT AID (NON-NEED-BASED) *Receiving aid:* Freshmen: 24% (29); Undergraduates: 34% (91). *Scholarships, grants, and awards by category: Academic Interests/Achievement:* 93 awards ($60,850 total): general academic interests/achievements. *Creative Arts/Performance:* 4 awards ($800 total): music. *Special Achievements/Activities:* 29 awards ($32,889 total): leadership, religious involvement. *Special Characteristics:* 11 awards ($70,265 total): children of faculty/staff. *Tuition waivers:* Full or partial for employees or children of employees.
LOANS *Student loans:* $903,170 (49% need-based, 51% non-need-based). 79% of past graduating class borrowed through all loan programs. *Average indebtedness per student:* $15,890. *Average need-based loan:* Freshmen: $3108; Undergraduates: $3638. *Parent loans:* $56,990 (100% need-based). *Programs:* FFEL (Subsidized and Unsubsidized Stafford, PLUS), alternative loans.
APPLYING FOR FINANCIAL AID *Required financial aid forms:* FAFSA, institution's own form. *Financial aid deadline:* 6/10. *Notification date:* Continuous.
CONTACT Joel Laos, Financial Aid Director, Emmaus Bible College, 2570 Asbury Road, Dubuque, IA 52001-3097, 563-588-8000 Ext. 1309 or toll-free 800-397-2425. *Fax:* 563-557-0573. *E-mail:* financialaid@emmaus.edu.

EMORY & HENRY COLLEGE
Emory, VA

Tuition & fees: $19,530 **Average undergraduate aid package:** $14,362

ABOUT THE INSTITUTION Independent United Methodist, coed. Awards: bachelor's and master's degrees. 37 undergraduate majors. Total enrollment: 1,101. Undergraduates: 1,027. Freshmen: 338. Federal methodology is used as a basis for awarding need-based institutional aid.
UNDERGRADUATE EXPENSES for 2005–06 *Application fee:* $30. *Comprehensive fee:* $26,570 includes full-time tuition ($19,530) and room and board ($7040). *College room only:* $3500. Full-time tuition and fees vary according to course load. Room and board charges vary according to board plan. *Part-time tuition:* $815 per hour. Part-time tuition and fees vary according to course load. *Payment plan:* Installment.
FRESHMAN FINANCIAL AID (Fall 2005, est.) 317 applied for aid; of those 87% were deemed to have need. 100% of freshmen with need received aid; of those 29% had need fully met. *Average percent of need met:* 74% (excluding resources awarded to replace EFC). *Average financial aid package:* $14,955 (excluding resources awarded to replace EFC). 18% of all full-time freshmen had no need and received non-need-based gift aid.
UNDERGRADUATE FINANCIAL AID (Fall 2005, est.) 878 applied for aid; of those 90% were deemed to have need. 100% of undergraduates with need received aid; of those 25% had need fully met. *Average percent of need met:* 72% (excluding resources awarded to replace EFC). *Average financial aid package:* $14,362 (excluding resources awarded to replace EFC). 20% of all full-time undergraduates had no need and received non-need-based gift aid.
GIFT AID (NEED-BASED) *Total amount:* $10,094,457 (10% federal, 14% state, 71% institutional, 5% external sources). *Receiving aid:* Freshmen: 82% (276); All full-time undergraduates: 79% (794). *Average award:* Freshmen: $11,711; Undergraduates: $10,834. *Scholarships, grants, and awards:* Federal Pell, FSEOG, state, private, college/university gift aid from institutional funds.
GIFT AID (NON-NEED-BASED) *Total amount:* $1,881,650 (17% state, 83% institutional). *Receiving aid:* Freshmen: 18% (62); Undergraduates: 21% (213). *Average Award:* Freshmen: $14,046; Undergraduates: $10,072. *Scholarships, grants, and awards by category: Academic Interests/Achievement:* 98 awards ($200,692 total): international studies, premedicine, religion/biblical studies. *Special Characteristics:* 23 awards ($215,202 total): children of educators, children of faculty/staff, ethnic background, out-of-state students, previous college experience, relatives of clergy, religious affiliation. *Tuition waivers:* Full or partial for employees or children of employees.
LOANS *Student loans:* $2,635,677 (88% need-based, 12% non-need-based). 76% of past graduating class borrowed through all loan programs. *Average indebtedness per student:* $15,465. *Average need-based loan:* Freshmen: $2543; Undergraduates: $3197. *Parent loans:* $3,764,100 (80% need-based, 20% non-need-based). *Programs:* FFEL (Subsidized and Unsubsidized Stafford, PLUS), Perkins, college/university.
WORK-STUDY *Federal work-study:* Total amount: $554,744; 271 jobs averaging $1863.
APPLYING FOR FINANCIAL AID *Required financial aid forms:* FAFSA, state aid form. *Financial aid deadline (priority):* 4/1. *Notification date:* Continuous beginning 2/1. Students must reply within 2 weeks of notification.
CONTACT Scarlett Cortner, Coordinator of Financial Aid, Emory & Henry College, PO Box 10, Emory, VA 24327-0010, 276-944-6115 or toll-free 800-848-5493. *Fax:* 276-944-6935. *E-mail:* scortner@ehc.edu.

EMORY UNIVERSITY
Atlanta, GA

Tuition & fees: $30,794 **Average undergraduate aid package:** $27,599

ABOUT THE INSTITUTION Independent Methodist, coed. Awards: associate, bachelor's, master's, doctoral, and first professional degrees (enrollment figures include Emory University, Oxford College; application data for main campus only). 57 undergraduate majors. Total enrollment: 12,134. Undergraduates: 6,510. Freshmen: 1,637. Both federal and institutional methodology are used as a basis for awarding need-based institutional aid.
UNDERGRADUATE EXPENSES for 2005–06 *Application fee:* $50. *Comprehensive fee:* $40,546 includes full-time tuition ($30,400), mandatory fees ($394), and room and board ($9752). *College room only:* $6112. Room and board charges vary according to board plan, housing facility, and student level. *Part-time tuition:* $1267 per credit. *Payment plans:* Tuition prepayment, installment.
FRESHMAN FINANCIAL AID (Fall 2005, est.) 832 applied for aid; of those 76% were deemed to have need. 100% of freshmen with need received aid; of those 100% had need fully met. *Average percent of need met:* 100% (excluding resources awarded to replace EFC). *Average financial aid package:* $26,335 (excluding resources awarded to replace EFC). 5% of all full-time freshmen had no need and received non-need-based gift aid.
UNDERGRADUATE FINANCIAL AID (Fall 2005, est.) 2,888 applied for aid; of those 83% were deemed to have need. 100% of undergraduates with need received aid; of those 100% had need fully met. *Average percent of need met:* 100% (excluding resources awarded to replace EFC). *Average financial aid package:* $27,599 (excluding resources awarded to replace EFC). 6% of all full-time undergraduates had no need and received non-need-based gift aid.
GIFT AID (NEED-BASED) *Total amount:* $44,030,729 (7% federal, 4% state, 86% institutional, 3% external sources). *Receiving aid:* Freshmen: 35% (566); All full-time undergraduates: 35% (2,247). *Average award:* Freshmen: $21,616; Undergraduates: $21,236. *Scholarships, grants, and awards:* Federal Pell, FSEOG, state, private, college/university gift aid from institutional funds.
GIFT AID (NON-NEED-BASED) *Total amount:* $11,951,967 (18% state, 71% institutional, 11% external sources). *Receiving aid:* Freshmen: 16% (262);

Undergraduates: 16% (1,009). *Average Award: Freshmen:* $16,047; *Undergraduates:* $17,985. *Scholarships, grants, and awards by category:* Academic Interests/Achievement: 720 awards ($11,255,968 total): general academic interests/achievements. *Creative Arts/Performance:* 5 awards ($147,380 total): debating, music, performing arts. *Special Achievements/Activities:* 3 awards ($2590 total): memberships. *Special Characteristics:* 1,592 awards ($16,258,202 total): children of faculty/staff, local/state students, relatives of clergy, religious affiliation, veterans. *Tuition waivers:* Full or partial for employees or children of employees. *ROTC:* Air Force cooperative.
LOANS *Student loans:* $15,660,254 (55% need-based, 45% non-need-based). 40% of past graduating class borrowed through all loan programs. *Average indebtedness per student:* $22,175. *Average need-based loan: Freshmen:* $3529; Undergraduates: $5355. *Parent loans:* $12,139,109 (100% non-need-based). *Programs:* FFEL (Subsidized and Unsubsidized Stafford, PLUS), Perkins, Federal Nursing, state, college/university.
WORK-STUDY *Federal work-study:* Total amount: $3,050,141; 1,757 jobs averaging $1735. *State or other work-study/employment:* Total amount: $747,742 (50% need-based, 50% non-need-based). 106 part-time jobs averaging $7403.
APPLYING FOR FINANCIAL AID *Required financial aid forms:* FAFSA, CSS Financial Aid PROFILE. *Financial aid deadline:* 4/1 (priority: 2/15). *Notification date:* 4/15. Students must reply within 4 weeks of notification.
CONTACT Julia Padgett, Director of Financial Aid, Emory University, 200 Dowman Drive, Boisfeuillet Jones Center, Suite 300, Atlanta, GA 30322-1100, 404-727-6039 or toll-free 800-727-6036. *Fax:* 404-727-6709. *E-mail:* finaid@emory.edu.

EMPORIA STATE UNIVERSITY
Emporia, KS

| Tuition & fees (KS res): $3306 | Average undergraduate aid package: $5730 |

ABOUT THE INSTITUTION State-supported, coed. Awards: bachelor's, master's, and doctoral degrees and post-bachelor's and post-master's certificates. 33 undergraduate majors. Total enrollment: 6,288. Undergraduates: 4,351. Freshmen: 739. Federal methodology is used as a basis for awarding need-based institutional aid.
UNDERGRADUATE EXPENSES for 2005–06 *Application fee:* $30. *Tuition, state resident:* full-time $2638; part-time $88 per credit hour. *Tuition, nonresident:* full-time $9990; part-time $333 per credit hour. *Required fees:* full-time $668; $41 per credit hour. Full-time tuition and fees vary according to degree level. Part-time tuition and fees vary according to degree level. *College room and board:* $4787; *room only:* $2363. Room and board charges vary according to board plan and housing facility. *Payment plans:* Installment, deferred payment.
FRESHMAN FINANCIAL AID (Fall 2004) 665 applied for aid; of those 64% were deemed to have need. 100% of freshmen with need received aid; of those 30% had need fully met. *Average percent of need met:* 63% (excluding resources awarded to replace EFC). *Average financial aid package:* $4480 (excluding resources awarded to replace EFC). 15% of all full-time freshmen had no need and received non-need-based gift aid.
UNDERGRADUATE FINANCIAL AID (Fall 2004) 3,288 applied for aid; of those 68% were deemed to have need. 100% of undergraduates with need received aid; of those 29% had need fully met. *Average percent of need met:* 68% (excluding resources awarded to replace EFC). *Average financial aid package:* $5730 (excluding resources awarded to replace EFC). 8% of all full-time undergraduates had no need and received non-need-based gift aid.
GIFT AID (NEED-BASED) *Total amount:* $6,186,724 (70% federal, 7% state, 13% institutional, 10% external sources). *Receiving aid: Freshmen:* 37% (267); All full-time undergraduates: 38% (1,431). *Average award: Freshmen:* $1474; Undergraduates: $1740. *Scholarships, grants, and awards:* Federal Pell, FSEOG, state, private, college/university gift aid from institutional funds, Jones Foundation Grants.
GIFT AID (NON-NEED-BASED) *Total amount:* $1,126,793 (1% federal, 5% state, 63% institutional, 31% external sources). *Receiving aid: Freshmen:* 42% (304); Undergraduates: 27% (1,037). *Average Award: Freshmen:* $799; Undergraduates: $944. *Scholarships, grants, and awards by category:* Academic Interests/Achievement: 2,077 awards ($1,044,988 total): biological sciences, business, communication, computer science, education, engineering/technologies, English, foreign languages, general academic interests/achievements, health fields, humanities, library science, mathematics, physical sciences, premedicine, social sciences. *Creative Arts/Performance:* 212 awards ($167,555 total): art/fine arts, creative writing, debating, music, theater/drama. *Special Achievements/Activities:* 13 awards ($5616 total): memberships. *Special Characteristics:* 33 awards ($19,767 total): children and siblings of alumni, children of faculty/staff, children of union members/company employees, handicapped students, international students, members of minority groups, religious affiliation, veterans, veterans' children. *Tuition waivers:* Full or partial for employees or children of employees, senior citizens.
LOANS *Student loans:* $14,312,735 (67% need-based, 33% non-need-based). 72% of past graduating class borrowed through all loan programs. *Average indebtedness per student:* $16,197. *Average need-based loan: Freshmen:* $2135; Undergraduates: $3088. *Parent loans:* $615,302 (12% need-based, 88% non-need-based). *Programs:* FFEL (Subsidized and Unsubsidized Stafford, PLUS), Perkins, Alaska Loans, alternative loans.
WORK-STUDY *Federal work-study:* Total amount: $409,921; 288 jobs averaging $1423. *State or other work-study/employment:* Total amount: $38,969 (53% need-based, 47% non-need-based). 23 part-time jobs averaging $1694.
ATHLETIC AWARDS *Total amount:* $907,508 (43% need-based, 57% non-need-based).
APPLYING FOR FINANCIAL AID *Required financial aid forms:* FAFSA, state aid form. *Financial aid deadline (priority):* 3/15. *Notification date:* Continuous. Students must reply within 2 weeks of notification.
CONTACT Elaine Henrie, Director of Financial Aid, Emporia State University, 1200 Commercial Street, Campus Box 4038, Emporia, KS 66801-5087, 620-341-5457 or toll-free 877-GOTOESU (in-state), 877-468-6378 (out-of-state). *Fax:* 620-341-6088. *E-mail:* henrieel@emporia.edu.

ENDICOTT COLLEGE
Beverly, MA

| Tuition & fees: $20,390 | Average undergraduate aid package: $12,361 |

ABOUT THE INSTITUTION Independent, coed. Awards: associate, bachelor's, and master's degrees. 22 undergraduate majors. Total enrollment: 3,326. Undergraduates: 2,038. Freshmen: 501. Federal methodology is used as a basis for awarding need-based institutional aid.
UNDERGRADUATE EXPENSES for 2005–06 *Application fee:* $40. *Comprehensive fee:* $30,156 includes full-time tuition ($19,690), mandatory fees ($700), and room and board ($9766). *College room only:* $6846. Full-time tuition and fees vary according to student level. Room and board charges vary according to board plan and housing facility. *Part-time tuition:* $615 per credit. *Part-time fees:* $200 per term. Part-time tuition and fees vary according to student level. *Payment plan:* Installment.
FRESHMAN FINANCIAL AID (Fall 2005, est.) 359 applied for aid; of those 76% were deemed to have need. 100% of freshmen with need received aid; of those 11% had need fully met. *Average percent of need met:* 55% (excluding resources awarded to replace EFC). *Average financial aid package:* $11,704 (excluding resources awarded to replace EFC). 12% of all full-time freshmen had no need and received non-need-based gift aid.
UNDERGRADUATE FINANCIAL AID (Fall 2005, est.) 1,441 applied for aid; of those 74% were deemed to have need. 99% of undergraduates with need received aid; of those 14% had need fully met. *Average percent of need met:* 58% (excluding resources awarded to replace EFC). *Average financial aid package:* $12,361 (excluding resources awarded to replace EFC). 15% of all full-time undergraduates had no need and received non-need-based gift aid.
GIFT AID (NEED-BASED) *Total amount:* $7,072,021 (9% federal, 4% state, 87% institutional). *Receiving aid: Freshmen:* 39% (196); All full-time undergraduates: 46% (782). *Average award: Freshmen:* $6359; Undergraduates: $5725. *Scholarships, grants, and awards:* Federal Pell, FSEOG, state, private, college/university gift aid from institutional funds.
GIFT AID (NON-NEED-BASED) *Total amount:* $2,188,699 (86% institutional, 14% external sources). *Receiving aid: Freshmen:* 32% (159); Undergraduates: 32% (553). *Average Award: Freshmen:* $4469; Undergraduates: $6763. *Scholarships, grants, and awards by category:* Academic Interests/Achievement: 717 awards ($3,692,895 total): business, education, general academic interests/achievements, health fields. *Creative Arts/Performance:* 4 awards ($2000 total): art/fine arts. *Special Achievements/Activities:* 10 awards ($13,800 total): community service, general special achievements/activities, leadership, religious involvement. *Special Characteristics:* 130 awards ($670,982 total): children and siblings of alumni, children of educators, general special characteristics, international students, local/state students, religious affiliation. *Tuition waivers:* Full or partial for employees or children of employees. *ROTC:* Army cooperative.

Endicott College

LOANS *Student loans:* $5,583,958 (71% need-based, 29% non-need-based). 62% of past graduating class borrowed through all loan programs. *Average indebtedness per student:* $18,000. *Average need-based loan:* Freshmen: $2851; Undergraduates: $4066. *Parent loans:* $9,887,421 (100% non-need-based). *Programs:* FFEL (Subsidized and Unsubsidized Stafford, PLUS), Perkins, state, college/university.

WORK-STUDY *Federal work-study:* Total amount: $250,000; 325 jobs averaging $1500.

APPLYING FOR FINANCIAL AID *Required financial aid forms:* FAFSA, institution's own form. *Financial aid deadline (priority):* 3/15. *Notification date:* Continuous beginning 3/15. Students must reply within 2 weeks of notification.

CONTACT Ms. Marcia Toomey, Director of Financial Aid, Endicott College, 376 Hale Street, Beverly, MA 01915-2096, 978-232-2060 or toll-free 800-325-1114 (out-of-state). *Fax:* 978-232-2085. *E-mail:* mtoomey@endicott.edu.

ERSKINE COLLEGE
Due West, SC

Tuition & fees: $19,042	Average undergraduate aid package: $17,200

ABOUT THE INSTITUTION Independent religious, coed. Awards: bachelor's, master's, doctoral, and first professional degrees. 30 undergraduate majors. Total enrollment: 890. Undergraduates: 594. Freshmen: 181. Both federal and institutional methodology are used as a basis for awarding need-based institutional aid.

UNDERGRADUATE EXPENSES for 2005–06 *Application fee:* $25. *Comprehensive fee:* $25,468 includes full-time tuition ($17,700), mandatory fees ($1342), and room and board ($6426). Room and board charges vary according to board plan and housing facility. *Payment plan:* Installment.

FRESHMAN FINANCIAL AID (Fall 2004) 173 applied for aid; of those 85% were deemed to have need. 100% of freshmen with need received aid; of those 32% had need fully met. *Average percent of need met:* 85% (excluding resources awarded to replace EFC). *Average financial aid package:* $17,200 (excluding resources awarded to replace EFC). 25% of all full-time freshmen had no need and received non-need-based gift aid.

UNDERGRADUATE FINANCIAL AID (Fall 2004) 592 applied for aid; of those 84% were deemed to have need. 100% of undergraduates with need received aid; of those 32% had need fully met. *Average percent of need met:* 84% (excluding resources awarded to replace EFC). *Average financial aid package:* $17,200 (excluding resources awarded to replace EFC). 18% of all full-time undergraduates had no need and received non-need-based gift aid.

GIFT AID (NEED-BASED) *Total amount:* $2,617,671 (19% federal, 34% state, 47% institutional). *Receiving aid:* Freshmen: 78% (142); All full-time undergraduates: 79% (487). *Average award:* Freshmen: $9800; Undergraduates: $9800. *Scholarships, grants, and awards:* Federal Pell, FSEOG, state, private, college/university gift aid from institutional funds.

GIFT AID (NON-NEED-BASED) *Total amount:* $6,543,603 (20% state, 75% institutional, 5% external sources). *Receiving aid:* Freshmen: 74% (134); Undergraduates: 74% (457). *Average Award:* Freshmen: $9075; Undergraduates: $8672. *Scholarships, grants, and awards by category: Academic Interests/Achievement:* biological sciences, business, education, English, foreign languages, general academic interests/achievements, mathematics, premedicine, religion/biblical studies, social sciences. *Creative Arts/Performance:* music, theater/drama. *Special Achievements/Activities:* general special achievements/activities, leadership, memberships. *Special Characteristics:* children and siblings of alumni, children of faculty/staff, children with a deceased or disabled parent, ethnic background, first-generation college students, members of minority groups, out-of-state students, relatives of clergy, religious affiliation, siblings of current students. *Tuition waivers:* Full or partial for children of alumni, employees or children of employees.

LOANS *Student loans:* $1,950,059 (57% need-based, 43% non-need-based). 71% of past graduating class borrowed through all loan programs. *Average indebtedness per student:* $17,500. *Average need-based loan:* Freshmen: $2500; Undergraduates: $3450. *Parent loans:* $251,986 (100% non-need-based). *Programs:* FFEL (Subsidized and Unsubsidized Stafford, PLUS), Perkins, college/university, teacher loans.

WORK-STUDY *Federal work-study:* Total amount: $108,869; jobs available. *State or other work-study/employment:* Total amount: $39,148 (100% non-need-based). Part-time jobs available.

ATHLETIC AWARDS *Total amount:* $690,648 (100% non-need-based).

APPLYING FOR FINANCIAL AID *Required financial aid forms:* FAFSA, institution's own form. *Financial aid deadline (priority):* 4/1. *Notification date:* Continuous beginning 12/15. Students must reply within 2 weeks of notification.

CONTACT Rebecca Pressley, Director of Financial Aid, Erskine College, PO Box 337, Due West, SC 29639, 864-379-8832 or toll-free 800-241-8721. *Fax:* 864-379-2172. *E-mail:* pressley@erskine.edu.

ESCUELA DE ARTES PLASTICAS DE PUERTO RICO
San Juan, PR

CONTACT Ms. Marion E. Muñoz, Financial Aid Administrator, Escuela de Artes Plasticas de Puerto Rico, PO Box 9021112, San Juan, PR 00902-1112, 787-725-8120 Ext. 231. *Fax:* 787-725-8111. *E-mail:* mmunoz@coqui.net.

EUGENE BIBLE COLLEGE
Eugene, OR

Tuition & fees: $8300	Average undergraduate aid package: $6500

ABOUT THE INSTITUTION Independent religious, coed. Awards: bachelor's degrees. 7 undergraduate majors. Total enrollment: 203. Undergraduates: 203. Freshmen: 64. Both federal and institutional methodology are used as a basis for awarding need-based institutional aid.

UNDERGRADUATE EXPENSES for 2005–06 *Application fee:* $30. *Comprehensive fee:* $12,875 includes full-time tuition ($7500), mandatory fees ($800), and room and board ($4575). *Part-time tuition:* $220 per credit hour.

FRESHMAN FINANCIAL AID (Fall 2004) 33 applied for aid; of those 45% were deemed to have need. 100% of freshmen with need received aid. *Average percent of need met:* 31% (excluding resources awarded to replace EFC). *Average financial aid package:* $5800 (excluding resources awarded to replace EFC). 3% of all full-time freshmen had no need and received non-need-based gift aid.

UNDERGRADUATE FINANCIAL AID (Fall 2004) 149 applied for aid; of those 87% were deemed to have need. 100% of undergraduates with need received aid; of those 1% had need fully met. *Average percent of need met:* 42% (excluding resources awarded to replace EFC). *Average financial aid package:* $6500 (excluding resources awarded to replace EFC). 1% of all full-time undergraduates had no need and received non-need-based gift aid.

GIFT AID (NEED-BASED) *Total amount:* $251,705 (97% federal, 3% institutional). *Receiving aid:* Freshmen: 24% (8); All full-time undergraduates: 51% (89). *Average award:* Freshmen: $3200; Undergraduates: $3000. *Scholarships, grants, and awards:* Federal Pell, FSEOG, private, college/university gift aid from institutional funds.

GIFT AID (NON-NEED-BASED) *Total amount:* $52,890 (52% institutional, 48% external sources). *Receiving aid:* Freshmen: 42% (14); Undergraduates: 34% (59). *Average Award:* Freshmen: $100; Undergraduates: $100. *Scholarships, grants, and awards by category: Academic Interests/Achievement:* general academic interests/achievements, religion/biblical studies. *Creative Arts/Performance:* music. *Special Achievements/Activities:* 2 awards ($5500 total): community service, general special achievements/activities, hobbies/interests, leadership, religious involvement. *Special Characteristics:* 56 awards ($35,400 total): general special characteristics, international students, married students, out-of-state students, relatives of clergy, spouses of current students, veterans, veterans' children.

LOANS *Student loans:* $1,154,062 (80% need-based, 20% non-need-based). 82% of past graduating class borrowed through all loan programs. *Average indebtedness per student:* $10,550. *Average need-based loan:* Freshmen: $2625; Undergraduates: $3850. *Parent loans:* $282,517 (100% non-need-based). *Programs:* FFEL (Subsidized and Unsubsidized Stafford, PLUS), college/university, Key Alternative Loans.

WORK-STUDY *Federal work-study:* Total amount: $12,740; 6 jobs averaging $2123. *State or other work-study/employment:* Total amount: $50,025 (100% non-need-based). 23 part-time jobs averaging $2175.

ATHLETIC AWARDS *Total amount:* $3000 (100% non-need-based).

APPLYING FOR FINANCIAL AID *Required financial aid forms:* FAFSA, institution's own form, CSS Financial Aid PROFILE. *Financial aid deadline:* 9/1 (priority: 3/1). *Notification date:* Continuous beginning 4/1. Students must reply by 9/1.

CONTACT Mrs. Rulena Mellor, Financial Aid Director, Eugene Bible College, 2155 Bailey Hill Road, Eugene, OR 97405-1194, 541-485-1780 Ext. 125 or toll-free 800-322-2638. *Fax:* 541-343-5801. *E-mail:* finaid@ebc.edu.

EUGENE LANG COLLEGE THE NEW SCHOOL FOR LIBERAL ARTS
New York, NY

CONTACT Financial Aid Counselor, Eugene Lang College The New School for Liberal Arts, 65 West 11th Street, New York, NY 10011, 212-229-5665 or toll-free 877-528-3321.

EUREKA COLLEGE
Eureka, IL

Tuition & fees: $13,400   Average undergraduate aid package: $15,467

ABOUT THE INSTITUTION Independent religious, coed. Awards: bachelor's degrees. 42 undergraduate majors. Total enrollment: 516. Undergraduates: 516. Freshmen: 138. Federal methodology is used as a basis for awarding need-based institutional aid.
UNDERGRADUATE EXPENSES for 2005–06 *Comprehensive fee:* $19,280 includes full-time tuition ($13,000), mandatory fees ($400), and room and board ($5880). *College room only:* $2820. Full-time tuition and fees vary according to course load and program. Room and board charges vary according to board plan and housing facility. *Part-time tuition:* $375 per semester hour. Part-time tuition and fees vary according to course load and program. *Payment plan:* Installment.
FRESHMAN FINANCIAL AID (Fall 2005, est.) 130 applied for aid; of those 85% were deemed to have need. 100% of freshmen with need received aid; of those 55% had need fully met. *Average percent of need met:* 80% (excluding resources awarded to replace EFC). *Average financial aid package:* $15,741 (excluding resources awarded to replace EFC). 2% of all full-time freshmen had no need and received non-need-based gift aid.
UNDERGRADUATE FINANCIAL AID (Fall 2005, est.) 448 applied for aid; of those 88% were deemed to have need. 100% of undergraduates with need received aid; of those 79% had need fully met. *Average percent of need met:* 81% (excluding resources awarded to replace EFC). *Average financial aid package:* $15,467 (excluding resources awarded to replace EFC). 2% of all full-time undergraduates had no need and received non-need-based gift aid.
GIFT AID (NEED-BASED) *Total amount:* $3,935,960 (14% federal, 28% state, 56% institutional, 2% external sources). *Receiving aid:* Freshmen: 49% (71); All full-time undergraduates: 73% (369). *Average award:* Freshmen: $11,896; Undergraduates: $10,666. *Scholarships, grants, and awards:* Federal Pell, FSEOG, state, private, college/university gift aid from institutional funds.
GIFT AID (NON-NEED-BASED) *Total amount:* $391,093 (1% state, 99% institutional). *Receiving aid:* Freshmen: 23% (34); Undergraduates: 20% (102). *Average Award:* Freshmen: $2333; Undergraduates: $4125. *Scholarships, grants, and awards by category:* Academic Interests/Achievement: 394 awards ($2,162,619 total): general academic interests/achievements. Creative Arts/Performance: 59 awards ($79,793 total): art/fine arts, performing arts. Special Achievements/Activities: 20 awards ($291,395 total): leadership. Special Characteristics: 49 awards ($177,645 total): children of faculty/staff, religious affiliation. *Tuition waivers:* Full or partial for children of alumni, employees or children of employees, senior citizens.
LOANS *Student loans:* $2,078,104 (60% need-based, 40% non-need-based). 89% of past graduating class borrowed through all loan programs. *Average indebtedness per student:* $15,352. *Average need-based loan:* Freshmen: $1906; Undergraduates: $3798. *Parent loans:* $605,855 (100% non-need-based). *Programs:* FFEL (Subsidized and Unsubsidized Stafford, PLUS), Perkins, college/university, alternative loans.
WORK-STUDY *Federal work-study:* Total amount: $90,952; 88 jobs averaging $1034. *State or other work-study/employment:* Total amount: $131,228 (100% non-need-based). 70 part-time jobs averaging $1875.
APPLYING FOR FINANCIAL AID *Required financial aid form:* FAFSA. *Financial aid deadline (priority):* 4/15. *Notification date:* 5/1. Students must reply within 2 weeks of notification.
CONTACT Ms. Ellen Rigsby, Assistant Dean and Director of Financial Aid, Eureka College, 300 East College Avenue, Eureka, IL 61530, 309-467-6311 or toll-free 888-4-EUREKA. *Fax:* 309-467-6897. *E-mail:* eraid@eureka.edu.

EVANGEL UNIVERSITY
Springfield, MO

Tuition & fees: $12,750   Average undergraduate aid package: $8620

ABOUT THE INSTITUTION Independent religious, coed. Awards: associate, bachelor's, and master's degrees. 56 undergraduate majors. Total enrollment: 1,801. Undergraduates: 1,721. Freshmen: 423. Federal methodology is used as a basis for awarding need-based institutional aid.
UNDERGRADUATE EXPENSES for 2005–06 *Application fee:* $25. *Comprehensive fee:* $17,370 includes full-time tuition ($12,040), mandatory fees ($710), and room and board ($4620). *College room only:* $2270. Full-time tuition and fees vary according to course load. Room and board charges vary according to board plan. *Part-time tuition:* $469 per credit hour. *Part-time fees:* $235 per term. *Payment plan:* Installment.
FRESHMAN FINANCIAL AID (Fall 2004) 307 applied for aid; of those 85% were deemed to have need. 98% of freshmen with need received aid; of those 10% had need fully met. *Average percent of need met:* 45% (excluding resources awarded to replace EFC). *Average financial aid package:* $8121 (excluding resources awarded to replace EFC). 22% of all full-time freshmen had no need and received non-need-based gift aid.
UNDERGRADUATE FINANCIAL AID (Fall 2004) 1,328 applied for aid; of those 88% were deemed to have need. 98% of undergraduates with need received aid; of those 8% had need fully met. *Average percent of need met:* 41% (excluding resources awarded to replace EFC). *Average financial aid package:* $8620 (excluding resources awarded to replace EFC). 18% of all full-time undergraduates had no need and received non-need-based gift aid.
GIFT AID (NEED-BASED) *Total amount:* $4,067,622 (44% federal, 2% state, 37% institutional, 17% external sources). *Receiving aid:* Freshmen: 58% (232); All full-time undergraduates: 61% (965). *Average award:* Freshmen: $5596; Undergraduates: $5158. *Scholarships, grants, and awards:* Federal Pell, FSEOG, state, college/university gift aid from institutional funds.
GIFT AID (NON-NEED-BASED) *Total amount:* $731,156 (64% institutional, 36% external sources). *Receiving aid:* Freshmen: 5% (18); Undergraduates: 4% (59). *Average Award:* Freshmen: $6000; Undergraduates: $7686. *Scholarships, grants, and awards by category:* Academic Interests/Achievement: 900 awards ($1,664,865 total): business, communication, computer science, education, engineering/technologies, English, foreign languages, general academic interests/achievements, humanities, mathematics, physical sciences, premedicine, religion/biblical studies, social sciences. Creative Arts/Performance: 154 awards ($223,095 total): art/fine arts, debating, music. Special Achievements/Activities: 387 awards ($1,530,738 total): cheerleading/drum major, general special achievements/activities, leadership, religious involvement. Special Characteristics: 307 awards ($1,442,641 total): children of faculty/staff, general special characteristics, religious affiliation. *Tuition waivers:* Full or partial for employees or children of employees. *ROTC:* Army.
LOANS *Student loans:* $10,367,726 (79% need-based, 21% non-need-based). 86% of past graduating class borrowed through all loan programs. *Average indebtedness per student:* $22,105. *Average need-based loan:* Freshmen: $3249; Undergraduates: $4469. *Parent loans:* $2,423,584 (41% need-based, 59% non-need-based). *Programs:* FFEL (Subsidized and Unsubsidized Stafford, PLUS), Perkins, college/university.
WORK-STUDY *Federal work-study:* Total amount: $521,309; 413 jobs averaging $963. *State or other work-study/employment:* Total amount: $119,768 (66% need-based, 34% non-need-based). 115 part-time jobs averaging $1075.
ATHLETIC AWARDS *Total amount:* $1,190,028 (65% need-based, 35% non-need-based).
APPLYING FOR FINANCIAL AID *Required financial aid form:* FAFSA. *Financial aid deadline (priority):* 3/1. *Notification date:* Continuous beginning 4/1. Students must reply within 4 weeks of notification.
CONTACT Mrs. Kathy White, Director of Financial Aid, Evangel University, 1111 North Glenstone Avenue, Springfield, MO 65802-2191, 417-865-2811 Ext. 7264 or toll-free 800-382-6435 (in-state). *E-mail:* whitek@evangel.edu.

EVERGLADES UNIVERSITY
Boca Raton, FL

CONTACT Fred Pfeffer, Financial Aid Office, Everglades University, 1500 Northwest 49th Street, Fort Lauderdale, FL 33309, 888-772-6077. *Fax:* 954-772-2695. *E-mail:* fredp@evergladesuniversity.edu.

Everglades University

EVERGLADES UNIVERSITY
Sarasota, FL

CONTACT Financial Aid Office, Everglades University, 6151 Lake Osprey Drive, Sarasota, FL 34240, 941-907-2262 or toll-free 866-907-2262.

THE EVERGREEN STATE COLLEGE
Olympia, WA

Tuition & fees (WA res): $4337   **Average undergraduate aid package: $11,066**

ABOUT THE INSTITUTION State-supported, coed. Awards: bachelor's and master's degrees. 23 undergraduate majors. Total enrollment: 4,470. Undergraduates: 4,171. Freshmen: 605. Federal methodology is used as a basis for awarding need-based institutional aid.

UNDERGRADUATE EXPENSES for 2005–06 *Application fee:* $50. *Tuition, state resident:* full-time $4128; part-time $137.60 per quarter hour. *Tuition, nonresident:* full-time $14,538; part-time $484.60 per quarter hour. *Required fees:* full-time $209; $2.05 per quarter hour or $41 per term part-time. Full-time tuition and fees vary according to course load and degree level. Part-time tuition and fees vary according to course load and degree level. *College room and board:* $6924; *room only:* $4482. Room and board charges vary according to board plan, housing facility, and student level. *Payment plan:* Installment.

FRESHMAN FINANCIAL AID (Fall 2004) 415 applied for aid; of those 55% were deemed to have need. 95% of freshmen with need received aid; of those 46% had need fully met. *Average percent of need met:* 77% (excluding resources awarded to replace EFC). *Average financial aid package:* $10,271 (excluding resources awarded to replace EFC). 2% of all full-time freshmen had no need and received non-need-based gift aid.

UNDERGRADUATE FINANCIAL AID (Fall 2004) 2,906 applied for aid; of those 75% were deemed to have need. 96% of undergraduates with need received aid; of those 42% had need fully met. *Average percent of need met:* 81% (excluding resources awarded to replace EFC). *Average financial aid package:* $11,066 (excluding resources awarded to replace EFC). 1% of all full-time undergraduates had no need and received non-need-based gift aid.

GIFT AID (NEED-BASED) *Total amount:* $8,593,307 (51% federal, 39% state, 8% institutional, 2% external sources). *Receiving aid:* Freshmen: 24% (116); All full-time undergraduates: 44% (1,580). *Average award:* Freshmen: $4815; Undergraduates: $5672. *Scholarships, grants, and awards:* Federal Pell, FSEOG, state, private, college/university gift aid from institutional funds.

GIFT AID (NON-NEED-BASED) *Total amount:* $1,240,148 (16% state, 13% institutional, 71% external sources). *Receiving aid:* Freshmen: 28% (132); Undergraduates: 9% (309). *Average Award:* Freshmen: $3900; Undergraduates: $3793. *Scholarships, grants, and awards by category: Academic Interests/Achievement:* 383 awards ($398,692 total): general academic interests/achievements. *Creative Arts/Performance:* 24 awards ($58,129 total): applied art and design, art/fine arts, creative writing. *Special Achievements/Activities:* 15 awards ($32,524 total): community service, general special achievements/activities. *Special Characteristics:* 50 awards ($157,252 total): adult students, first-generation college students, members of minority groups. *Tuition waivers:* Full or partial for employees or children of employees.

LOANS *Student loans:* $11,581,868 (62% need-based, 38% non-need-based). 59% of past graduating class borrowed through all loan programs. *Average indebtedness per student:* $13,818. *Average need-based loan:* Freshmen: $2862; Undergraduates: $4871. *Parent loans:* $3,388,760 (50% need-based, 50% non-need-based). *Programs:* FFEL (Subsidized and Unsubsidized Stafford, PLUS), Perkins, college/university.

WORK-STUDY *Federal work-study:* Total amount: $389,698; 196 jobs averaging $1988. *State or other work-study/employment:* Total amount: $346,961 (100% need-based). 154 part-time jobs averaging $2253.

ATHLETIC AWARDS *Total amount:* $66,986 (100% need-based).

APPLYING FOR FINANCIAL AID *Required financial aid forms:* FAFSA, institution's own form. *Financial aid deadline (priority):* 3/15. *Notification date:* Continuous beginning 4/15. Students must reply within 4 weeks of notification.

CONTACT Financial Aid Office, The Evergreen State College, 2700 Evergreen Parkway NW, Olympia, WA 98505, 360-867-6205. *Fax:* 360-866-6576.

EXCELSIOR COLLEGE
Albany, NY

Tuition & fees: N/R   **Average undergraduate aid package: N/A**

ABOUT THE INSTITUTION Independent, coed. Awards: associate, bachelor's, and master's degrees and post-bachelor's certificates (offers only external degree programs). 42 undergraduate majors. Total enrollment: 28,464. Undergraduates: 27,844. Both federal and institutional methodology are used as a basis for awarding need-based institutional aid.

UNDERGRADUATE EXPENSES for 2006–07 *Application fee:* $65. *Tuition:* part-time $250 per credit hour. *Required fees:* $515 per year part-time.

GIFT AID (NEED-BASED) *Total amount:* $254,209 (51% state, 46% institutional, 3% external sources). *Scholarships, grants, and awards:* state, private, college/university gift aid from institutional funds.

GIFT AID (NON-NEED-BASED) *Total amount:* $146,335 (100% external sources). *Scholarships, grants, and awards by category: Academic Interests/Achievement:* general academic interests/achievements. *Special Characteristics:* veterans, veterans' children.

LOANS *Student loans:* $1,828,773 (100% non-need-based). 1% of past graduating class borrowed through all loan programs. *Average indebtedness per student:* $5410. *Programs:* alternative loans, PLATO Loans, Excel, Citi Assist, Key.

APPLYING FOR FINANCIAL AID *Required financial aid form:* institution's own form. *Financial aid deadline (priority):* 7/1. *Notification date:* Continuous.

CONTACT Donna L. Cooper, Director of Financial Aid, Excelsior College, 7 Columbia Circle, Albany, NY 12203-5159, 518-464-8500 or toll-free 888-647-2388. *Fax:* 518-464-8777.

FAIRFIELD UNIVERSITY
Fairfield, CT

Tuition & fees: $30,255   **Average undergraduate aid package: $17,079**

ABOUT THE INSTITUTION Independent Roman Catholic (Jesuit), coed. Awards: bachelor's and master's degrees and post-master's certificates. 35 undergraduate majors. Total enrollment: 5,173. Undergraduates: 4,073. Freshmen: 940. Federal methodology is used as a basis for awarding need-based institutional aid.

UNDERGRADUATE EXPENSES for 2005–06 *Application fee:* $55. *Comprehensive fee:* $39,855 includes full-time tuition ($29,750), mandatory fees ($505), and room and board ($9600). *College room only:* $5560. Full-time tuition and fees vary according to student level. Room and board charges vary according to board plan and housing facility. *Part-time tuition:* $395 per credit. *Part-time fees:* $60 per term. Part-time tuition and fees vary according to course load and program. *Payment plan:* Installment.

FRESHMAN FINANCIAL AID (Fall 2005, est.) 673 applied for aid; of those 74% were deemed to have need. 99% of freshmen with need received aid; of those 30% had need fully met. *Average percent of need met:* 69% (excluding resources awarded to replace EFC). *Average financial aid package:* $17,929 (excluding resources awarded to replace EFC). 6% of all full-time freshmen had no need and received non-need-based gift aid.

UNDERGRADUATE FINANCIAL AID (Fall 2005, est.) 2,056 applied for aid; of those 81% were deemed to have need. 99% of undergraduates with need received aid; of those 26% had need fully met. *Average percent of need met:* 65% (excluding resources awarded to replace EFC). *Average financial aid package:* $17,079 (excluding resources awarded to replace EFC). 7% of all full-time undergraduates had no need and received non-need-based gift aid.

GIFT AID (NEED-BASED) *Total amount:* $18,699,956 (10% federal, 1% state, 89% institutional). *Receiving aid:* Freshmen: 48% (452); All full-time undergraduates: 42% (1,472). *Average award:* Freshmen: $13,151; Undergraduates: $11,906. *Scholarships, grants, and awards:* Federal Pell, FSEOG, state, private, college/university gift aid from institutional funds, United Negro College Fund.

GIFT AID (NON-NEED-BASED) *Total amount:* $5,968,504 (92% institutional, 8% external sources). *Receiving aid:* Freshmen: 15% (139); Undergraduates: 12% (419). *Average Award:* Freshmen: $11,803; Undergraduates: $10,723. *Scholarships, grants, and awards by category: Academic Interests/Achievement:* 580 awards ($6,223,940 total): biological sciences, business, education, engineering/technologies, foreign languages, general academic interests/achievements, physical sciences. *Creative Arts/Performance:* 26 awards ($24,630 total): art/fine arts, music, performing arts. *Special Achievements/Activities:* 27

awards ($79,000 total): religious involvement. *Special Characteristics:* 12 awards ($69,250 total): children and siblings of alumni, ethnic background, first-generation college students, members of minority groups, religious affiliation. *Tuition waivers:* Full or partial for employees or children of employees. **ROTC:** Army cooperative.

LOANS *Student loans:* $17,828,514 (38% need-based, 62% non-need-based). 63% of past graduating class borrowed through all loan programs. *Average indebtedness per student:* $25,081. *Average need-based loan:* Freshmen: $3484; Undergraduates: $4111. *Parent loans:* $6,546,426 (100% non-need-based). *Programs:* FFEL (Subsidized and Unsubsidized Stafford, PLUS), Perkins, Federal Nursing, alternative loans.

WORK-STUDY *Federal work-study:* Total amount: $802,686; 445 jobs averaging $1440.

ATHLETIC AWARDS *Total amount:* $3,092,356 (100% non-need-based).

APPLYING FOR FINANCIAL AID *Required financial aid forms:* FAFSA, CSS Financial Aid PROFILE, business/farm supplement. *Financial aid deadline:* 2/15 (priority: 2/15). *Notification date:* 4/1. Students must reply by 5/1 or within 2 weeks of notification.

CONTACT Mr. Erin Chiaro, Director of Financial Aid, Fairfield University, 1073 North Benson Road, Fairfield, CT 06824-5195, 203-254-4125. *Fax:* 203-254-4008. *E-mail:* echiaro@mail.fairfield.edu.

FAIRLEIGH DICKINSON UNIVERSITY, COLLEGE AT FLORHAM
Madison, NJ

ABOUT THE INSTITUTION Independent, coed. Awards: associate, bachelor's, and master's degrees and post-bachelor's and post-master's certificates. 30 undergraduate majors. Total enrollment: 3,481. Undergraduates: 2,595. Freshmen: 613.

GIFT AID (NEED-BASED) *Scholarships, grants, and awards:* Federal Pell, FSEOG, state, private, college/university gift aid from institutional funds, United Negro College Fund, Federal Nursing.

LOANS *Programs:* FFEL (Subsidized and Unsubsidized Stafford, PLUS), Perkins, Federal Nursing, state.

APPLYING FOR FINANCIAL AID *Required financial aid form:* FAFSA.

CONTACT Financial Aid Office, Fairleigh Dickinson University, College at Florham, 285 Madison Avenue, Madison, NJ 07940-1099, 973-443-8700 or toll-free 800-338-8803.

FAIRLEIGH DICKINSON UNIVERSITY, METROPOLITAN CAMPUS
Teaneck, NJ

ABOUT THE INSTITUTION Independent, coed. Awards: associate, bachelor's, master's, and doctoral degrees and post-bachelor's and post-master's certificates. 43 undergraduate majors. Total enrollment: 7,937. Undergraduates: 5,444. Freshmen: 497.

GIFT AID (NEED-BASED) *Scholarships, grants, and awards:* Federal Pell, FSEOG, state, private, college/university gift aid from institutional funds, United Negro College Fund, Federal Nursing.

LOANS *Programs:* FFEL (Subsidized and Unsubsidized Stafford, PLUS), Perkins, Federal Nursing, state.

APPLYING FOR FINANCIAL AID *Required financial aid form:* FAFSA.

CONTACT Financial Aid Office, Fairleigh Dickinson University, Metropolitan Campus, 100 River Road, Teaneck, NJ 07666-1914, 201-692-2363 or toll-free 800-338-8803.

FAIRMONT STATE UNIVERSITY
Fairmont, WV

Tuition & fees (WV res): $4412   **Average undergraduate aid package: $5676**

ABOUT THE INSTITUTION State-supported, coed. Awards: associate, bachelor's, and master's degrees. 60 undergraduate majors. Total enrollment: 7,759. Undergraduates: 7,520. Freshmen: 1,291. Federal methodology is used as a basis for awarding need-based institutional aid.

UNDERGRADUATE EXPENSES for 2005–06 *Tuition, state resident:* full-time $4218; part-time $155 per hour. *Tuition, nonresident:* full-time $8808; part-time $331 per hour. *Required fees:* full-time $194; $177 per credit hour. *College room and board:* $5674; *room only:* $2814.

FRESHMAN FINANCIAL AID (Fall 2004) 1234 applied for aid; of those 85% were deemed to have need. 97% of freshmen with need received aid; of those 8% had need fully met. *Average percent of need met:* 63% (excluding resources awarded to replace EFC). *Average financial aid package:* $5000 (excluding resources awarded to replace EFC). 8% of all full-time freshmen had no need and received non-need-based gift aid.

UNDERGRADUATE FINANCIAL AID (Fall 2004) 4,868 applied for aid; of those 87% were deemed to have need. 97% of undergraduates with need received aid; of those 7% had need fully met. *Average percent of need met:* 67% (excluding resources awarded to replace EFC). *Average financial aid package:* $5676 (excluding resources awarded to replace EFC). 8% of all full-time undergraduates had no need and received non-need-based gift aid.

GIFT AID (NEED-BASED) *Total amount:* $10,263,092 (80% federal, 14% state, 3% institutional, 3% external sources). *Receiving aid:* Freshmen: 58% (769); All full-time undergraduates: 52% (3,032). *Average award:* Freshmen: $6949; Undergraduates: $8077. *Scholarships, grants, and awards:* Federal Pell, FSEOG, state, private, college/university gift aid from institutional funds.

GIFT AID (NON-NEED-BASED) *Total amount:* $949,845 (71% state, 15% institutional, 14% external sources). *Receiving aid:* Freshmen: 11% (142); Undergraduates: 6% (381). *Average Award:* Freshmen: $687; Undergraduates: $946. *Scholarships, grants, and awards by category:* Academic Interests/Achievement: 420 awards ($400,000 total): architecture, business, communication, computer science, education, engineering/technologies, English, foreign languages, general academic interests/achievements, health fields, home economics, humanities, mathematics, physical sciences, social sciences. *Creative Arts/Performance:* 75 awards ($75,000 total): art/fine arts, debating, music, theater/drama. *Special Achievements/Activities:* 10 awards ($10,000 total): cheerleading/drum major. *Special Characteristics:* 50 awards ($75,000 total): children and siblings of alumni, general special characteristics, international students, local/state students, members of minority groups, out-of-state students. **ROTC:** Army.

LOANS *Student loans:* $15,912,711 (59% need-based, 41% non-need-based). 94% of past graduating class borrowed through all loan programs. *Average indebtedness per student:* $17,500. *Average need-based loan:* Freshmen: $2328; Undergraduates: $2997. *Parent loans:* $1,268,208 (82% need-based, 18% non-need-based). *Programs:* Federal Direct (Subsidized and Unsubsidized Stafford, PLUS), Perkins.

WORK-STUDY *Federal work-study:* Total amount: $319,901; 292 jobs averaging $1164. *State or other work-study/employment:* Total amount: $410,844 (100% non-need-based). 396 part-time jobs averaging $1037.

ATHLETIC AWARDS *Total amount:* $574,440 (59% need-based, 41% non-need-based).

APPLYING FOR FINANCIAL AID *Required financial aid forms:* FAFSA, state aid form. *Financial aid deadline:* 2/1 (priority: 3/1). *Notification date:* Continuous beginning 4/15. Students must reply within 2 weeks of notification.

CONTACT Sandra K. Oerly-Bennett, Director of Financial Aid and Scholarships, Fairmont State University, 1201 Locust Avenue, Fairmont, WV 26554, 304-367-4213 or toll-free 800-641-5678. *Fax:* 304-367-4584. *E-mail:* financialaid@fairmontstate.edu.

FAITH BAPTIST BIBLE COLLEGE AND THEOLOGICAL SEMINARY
Ankeny, IA

Tuition & fees: $11,204   **Average undergraduate aid package: $7124**

ABOUT THE INSTITUTION Independent religious, coed. Awards: associate, bachelor's, master's, and first professional degrees. 10 undergraduate majors. Total enrollment: 479. Undergraduates: 328. Freshmen: 86. Federal methodology is used as a basis for awarding need-based institutional aid.

UNDERGRADUATE EXPENSES for 2005–06 *Application fee:* $25. *Comprehensive fee:* $15,520 includes full-time tuition ($10,804), mandatory fees ($400), and room and board ($4316). *College room only:* $2010. Full-time tuition and fees vary according to course load. Room and board charges vary according to board plan. *Part-time tuition:* $395 per semester hour. *Part-time fees:* $95 per term.

Faith Baptist Bible College and Theological Seminary

FRESHMAN FINANCIAL AID (Fall 2004) 104 applied for aid; of those 90% were deemed to have need. 100% of freshmen with need received aid; of those 5% had need fully met. *Average percent of need met:* 46% (excluding resources awarded to replace EFC). *Average financial aid package:* $7043 (excluding resources awarded to replace EFC). 9% of all full-time freshmen had no need and received non-need-based gift aid.
UNDERGRADUATE FINANCIAL AID (Fall 2004) 311 applied for aid; of those 93% were deemed to have need. 100% of undergraduates with need received aid; of those 2% had need fully met. *Average percent of need met:* 48% (excluding resources awarded to replace EFC). *Average financial aid package:* $7124 (excluding resources awarded to replace EFC). 7% of all full-time undergraduates had no need and received non-need-based gift aid.
GIFT AID (NEED-BASED) *Total amount:* $1,136,762 (30% federal, 39% state, 31% institutional). *Receiving aid:* Freshmen: 71% (81); All full-time undergraduates: 73% (232). *Average award:* Freshmen: $5250; Undergraduates: $6299. *Scholarships, grants, and awards:* Federal Pell, state, private, college/university gift aid from institutional funds.
GIFT AID (NON-NEED-BASED) *Total amount:* $337,670 (57% institutional, 43% external sources). *Receiving aid:* Freshmen: 80% (91); Undergraduates: 43% (135). *Average Award:* Freshmen: $255; Undergraduates: $2465. *Scholarships, grants, and awards by category:* Academic Interests/Achievement: 131 awards ($87,988 total): general academic interests/achievements. Creative Arts/Performance: 23 awards ($32,450 total): music. Special Achievements/Activities: 1 award ($200 total): leadership. Special Characteristics: 93 awards ($160,470 total): children of faculty/staff, relatives of clergy. *Tuition waivers:* Full or partial for employees or children of employees.
LOANS *Student loans:* $1,348,003 (51% need-based, 49% non-need-based). 89% of past graduating class borrowed through all loan programs. *Average indebtedness per student:* $15,006. *Average need-based loan:* Freshmen: $2163; Undergraduates: $3142. *Parent loans:* $75,904 (100% non-need-based). *Programs:* FFEL (Subsidized and Unsubsidized Stafford, PLUS).
APPLYING FOR FINANCIAL AID *Required financial aid form:* FAFSA. *Financial aid deadline (priority):* 3/1. *Notification date:* Continuous. Students must reply within 4 weeks of notification.
CONTACT Mr. Breck Appell, Director of Financial Assistance, Faith Baptist Bible College and Theological Seminary, 1900 Northwest 4th Street, Ankeny, IA 50021-2152, 515-964-0601 or toll-free 888-FAITH 4U. *Fax:* 515-964-1638.

FARMINGDALE STATE UNIVERSITY OF NEW YORK
Farmingdale, NY

CONTACT Dionne Walker-Belgrave, Assistant Director of Financial Aid, Farmingdale State University of New York, 2350 Broadhollow Road, Route 110, Farmingdale, NY 11735, 631-420-2328 or toll-free 877-4-FARMINGDALE. *Fax:* 631-420-3662.

FASHION INSTITUTE OF TECHNOLOGY
New York, NY

Tuition & fees (NY res): $4770 | **Average undergraduate aid package:** $7555

ABOUT THE INSTITUTION State and locally supported, coed, primarily women. Awards: associate, bachelor's, and master's degrees. 21 undergraduate majors. Total enrollment: 10,381. Undergraduates: 10,199. Freshmen: 1,028. Federal methodology is used as a basis for awarding need-based institutional aid.
UNDERGRADUATE EXPENSES for 2006–07 *Application fee:* $40. *Tuition, state resident:* full-time $4350; part-time $181 per credit. *Tuition, nonresident:* full-time $10,610; part-time $442 per credit. *Required fees:* full-time $420; $30 per term part-time. *College room and board:* $8409; *room only:* $7519.
FRESHMAN FINANCIAL AID (Fall 2005, est.) 739 applied for aid; of those 47% were deemed to have need. 98% of freshmen with need received aid; of those 27% had need fully met. *Average percent of need met:* 73% (excluding resources awarded to replace EFC). *Average financial aid package:* $6815 (excluding resources awarded to replace EFC). 3% of all full-time freshmen had no need and received non-need-based gift aid.
UNDERGRADUATE FINANCIAL AID (Fall 2005, est.) 4,317 applied for aid; of those 45% were deemed to have need. 98% of undergraduates with need received aid; of those 22% had need fully met. *Average percent of need met:* 71% (excluding resources awarded to replace EFC). *Average financial aid package:* $7555 (excluding resources awarded to replace EFC). 1% of all full-time undergraduates had no need and received non-need-based gift aid.
GIFT AID (NEED-BASED) *Total amount:* $9,729,806 (53% federal, 41% state, 6% institutional). *Receiving aid:* Freshmen: 23% (247); All full-time undergraduates: 20% (1,393). *Average award:* Freshmen: $3984; Undergraduates: $4138. *Scholarships, grants, and awards:* Federal Pell, FSEOG, state, private, college/university gift aid from institutional funds.
GIFT AID (NON-NEED-BASED) *Total amount:* $612,886 (13% institutional, 87% external sources). *Receiving aid:* Freshmen: 5% (59); Undergraduates: 2% (137). *Average Award:* Freshmen: $2045; Undergraduates: $2208. *Scholarships, grants, and awards by category:* Creative Arts/Performance: 162 awards ($79,250 total): applied art and design.
LOANS *Student loans:* $18,464,885 (40% need-based, 60% non-need-based). 39% of past graduating class borrowed through all loan programs. *Average indebtedness per student:* $12,869. *Average need-based loan:* Freshmen: $2548; Undergraduates: $3664. *Parent loans:* $3,771,612 (100% non-need-based). *Programs:* FFEL (Subsidized and Unsubsidized Stafford, PLUS, Perkins, alternative loans.
WORK-STUDY *Federal work-study:* Total amount: $999,062; 458 jobs averaging $2048.
APPLYING FOR FINANCIAL AID *Required financial aid forms:* FAFSA, state aid form. *Financial aid deadline (priority):* 2/15. *Notification date:* Continuous beginning 4/15. Students must reply within 2 weeks of notification.
CONTACT Financial Aid Office, Fashion Institute of Technology, Seventh Avenue at 27th Street, New York, NY 10001-5992, 212-217-7439 or toll-free 800-GOTOFIT (out-of-state).

FAULKNER UNIVERSITY
Montgomery, AL

Tuition & fees: $11,425 | **Average undergraduate aid package:** $7300

ABOUT THE INSTITUTION Independent religious, coed. Awards: associate, bachelor's, master's, and first professional degrees. 48 undergraduate majors. Total enrollment: 2,583. Undergraduates: 2,225. Freshmen: 238. Federal methodology is used as a basis for awarding need-based institutional aid.
UNDERGRADUATE EXPENSES for 2006–07 *Application fee:* $10. *Comprehensive fee:* $16,825 includes full-time tuition ($11,400), mandatory fees ($25), and room and board ($5400). *College room only:* $2500. *Part-time tuition:* $395 per semester hour.
FRESHMAN FINANCIAL AID (Fall 2005, est.) 169 applied for aid; of those 79% were deemed to have need. 100% of freshmen with need received aid; of those 12% had need fully met. *Average percent of need met:* 60% (excluding resources awarded to replace EFC). *Average financial aid package:* $6000 (excluding resources awarded to replace EFC). 6% of all full-time freshmen had no need and received non-need-based gift aid.
UNDERGRADUATE FINANCIAL AID (Fall 2005, est.) 1,413 applied for aid; of those 80% were deemed to have need. 100% of undergraduates with need received aid; of those 10% had need fully met. *Average percent of need met:* 60% (excluding resources awarded to replace EFC). *Average financial aid package:* $7300 (excluding resources awarded to replace EFC). 3% of all full-time undergraduates had no need and received non-need-based gift aid.
GIFT AID (NEED-BASED) *Total amount:* $4,600,000 (100% federal). *Receiving aid:* Freshmen: 49% (93); All full-time undergraduates: 50% (790). *Average award:* Freshmen: $3600; Undergraduates: $3800. *Scholarships, grants, and awards:* Federal Pell, FSEOG, state, private, college/university gift aid from institutional funds.
GIFT AID (NON-NEED-BASED) *Total amount:* $2,846,030 (16% state, 77% institutional, 7% external sources). *Receiving aid:* Freshmen: 43% (80); Undergraduates: 43% (677). *Average Award:* Freshmen: $2200; Undergraduates: $2500. *Scholarships, grants, and awards by category:* Academic Interests/Achievement: 386 awards ($990,900 total): general academic interests/achievements, religion/biblical studies. Creative Arts/Performance: 26 awards ($15,100 total): journalism/publications, music, theater/drama. Special Achievements/Activities: 321 awards ($261,000 total): cheerleading/drum major, leadership, religious involvement. Special Characteristics: 113 awards ($86,730 total): adult students, children and siblings of alumni, children of faculty/staff, relatives of clergy, siblings of current students. *ROTC:* Army cooperative, Air Force cooperative.

LOANS *Student loans:* $17,800,000 (51% need-based, 49% non-need-based). 80% of past graduating class borrowed through all loan programs. *Average indebtedness per student:* $18,700. *Average need-based loan:* Freshmen: $2625; Undergraduates: $5300. *Parent loans:* $570,000 (100% non-need-based). *Programs:* FFEL (Subsidized and Unsubsidized Stafford, PLUS), Perkins.
WORK-STUDY *Federal work-study:* Total amount: $208,222; 128 jobs averaging $1500. *State or other work-study/employment:* Total amount: $2291 (100% non-need-based). 4 part-time jobs averaging $746.
ATHLETIC AWARDS *Total amount* $769,687 (100% non-need-based).
APPLYING FOR FINANCIAL AID *Required financial aid forms:* FAFSA, institution's own form, state aid form. *Financial aid deadline (priority):* 5/1.
CONTACT William G. Jackson II, Director of Financial Aid, Faulkner University, 5345 Atlanta Highway, Montgomery, AL 36109-3398, 334-386-7195 or toll-free 800-879-9816. *Fax:* 334-386-7201.

FAYETTEVILLE STATE UNIVERSITY
Fayetteville, NC

CONTACT Lois L. McKoy, Director of Financial Aid, Fayetteville State University, 1200 Murchison Road, Fayetteville, NC 28301-4298, 910-672-1325 or toll-free 800-222-2594. *Fax:* 910-672-1423. *E-mail:* lmckoy@uncfsu.edu.

FELICIAN COLLEGE
Lodi, NJ

Tuition & fees: $18,200	Average undergraduate aid package: $13,161

ABOUT THE INSTITUTION Independent Roman Catholic, coed. Awards: associate, bachelor's, and master's degrees. 40 undergraduate majors. Total enrollment: 1,806. Undergraduates: 1,550. Freshmen: 261. Federal methodology is used as a basis for awarding need-based institutional aid.
UNDERGRADUATE EXPENSES for 2006–07 *Application fee:* $30. *Comprehensive fee:* $26,150 includes full-time tuition ($17,300), mandatory fees ($900), and room and board ($7950). *Part-time tuition:* $575 per credit.
FRESHMAN FINANCIAL AID (Fall 2004) 213 applied for aid; of those 56% were deemed to have need. 100% of freshmen with need received aid; of those 20% had need fully met. *Average percent of need met:* 85% (excluding resources awarded to replace EFC). *Average financial aid package:* $13,600 (excluding resources awarded to replace EFC). 13% of all full-time freshmen had no need and received non-need-based gift aid.
UNDERGRADUATE FINANCIAL AID (Fall 2004) 1,231 applied for aid; of those 90% were deemed to have need. 100% of undergraduates with need received aid; of those 13% had need fully met. *Average percent of need met:* 85% (excluding resources awarded to replace EFC). *Average financial aid package:* $13,161 (excluding resources awarded to replace EFC). 8% of all full-time undergraduates had no need and received non-need-based gift aid.
GIFT AID (NEED-BASED) *Total amount:* $3,767,047 (34% federal, 65% state, 1% institutional). *Receiving aid:* Freshmen: 49% (119); All full-time undergraduates: 50% (725). *Average award:* Freshmen: $6000; Undergraduates: $6000. *Scholarships, grants, and awards:* Federal Pell, FSEOG, state, private, college/university gift aid from institutional funds.
GIFT AID (NON-NEED-BASED) *Total amount:* $1,440,371 (99% institutional, 1% external sources). *Receiving aid:* Freshmen: 15% (36); Undergraduates: 15% (217). *Average Award:* Freshmen: $9962; Undergraduates: $9962. *Scholarships, grants, and awards by category: Academic Interests/Achievement:* 124 awards ($224,000 total): area/ethnic studies, biological sciences, business, computer science, education, English, general academic interests/achievements, health fields, mathematics, premedicine, religion/biblical studies, social sciences.
LOANS *Student loans:* $6,734,444 (39% need-based, 61% non-need-based). 85% of past graduating class borrowed through all loan programs. *Average indebtedness per student:* $19,500. *Average need-based loan:* Freshmen: $3500; Undergraduates: $4300. *Parent loans:* $1,185,758 (100% non-need-based). *Programs:* FFEL (Subsidized and Unsubsidized Stafford, PLUS), state, Alternative Loans.
WORK-STUDY *Federal work-study:* Total amount: $84,728; 108 jobs averaging $1300. *State or other work-study/employment:* Total amount: $140,147 (100% non-need-based).
ATHLETIC AWARDS *Total amount:* $1,185,565 (100% non-need-based).
APPLYING FOR FINANCIAL AID *Required financial aid form:* FAFSA. *Financial aid deadline:* Continuous. *Notification date:* Continuous beginning 4/1.

CONTACT Norma Betz, Financial Aid Director, Felician College, 262 South Main Street, Lodi, NJ 07644, 201-559-6040. *Fax:* 201-559-6188. *E-mail:* betzn@inet.felician.edu.

FERRIS STATE UNIVERSITY
Big Rapids, MI

Tuition & fees (MI res): $6882	Average undergraduate aid package: $8000

ABOUT THE INSTITUTION State-supported, coed. Awards: associate, bachelor's, master's, and first professional degrees (Associate). 93 undergraduate majors. Total enrollment: 12,547. Undergraduates: 11,437. Freshmen: 2,240. Federal methodology is used as a basis for awarding need-based institutional aid.
UNDERGRADUATE EXPENSES for 2005–06 *Application fee:* $30. *Tuition, state resident:* full-time $6740; part-time $265 per credit hour. *Tuition, nonresident:* full-time $13,480; part-time $530 per credit hour. Full-time tuition and fees vary according to reciprocity agreements. *College room and board:* $6816; *room only:* $3462. Room and board charges vary according to board plan and housing facility. *Payment plans:* Installment, deferred payment.
FRESHMAN FINANCIAL AID (Fall 2005, est.) 2030 applied for aid; of those 86% were deemed to have need. 77% of freshmen with need received aid; of those 10% had need fully met. *Average percent of need met:* 70% (excluding resources awarded to replace EFC). *Average financial aid package:* $7000 (excluding resources awarded to replace EFC). 7% of all full-time freshmen had no need and received non-need-based gift aid.
UNDERGRADUATE FINANCIAL AID (Fall 2005, est.) 8,417 applied for aid; of those 86% were deemed to have need. 81% of undergraduates with need received aid; of those 10% had need fully met. *Average percent of need met:* 75% (excluding resources awarded to replace EFC). *Average financial aid package:* $8000 (excluding resources awarded to replace EFC). 4% of all full-time undergraduates had no need and received non-need-based gift aid.
GIFT AID (NEED-BASED) *Total amount:* $13,977,296 (69% federal, 21% state, 10% institutional). *Receiving aid:* Freshmen: 36% (798); All full-time undergraduates: 40% (3,510). *Average award:* Freshmen: $3000; Undergraduates: $3500. *Scholarships, grants, and awards:* Federal Pell, FSEOG, state, private, college/university gift aid from institutional funds.
GIFT AID (NON-NEED-BASED) *Total amount:* $8,906,381 (32% state, 51% institutional, 17% external sources). *Receiving aid:* Freshmen: 14% (308); Undergraduates: 8% (734). *Average Award:* Freshmen: $2000; Undergraduates: $2000. *Scholarships, grants, and awards by category: Academic Interests/Achievement:* 1,350 awards ($2,000,000 total): general academic interests/achievements. *Creative Arts/Performance:* 175 awards ($87,500 total): debating, general creative arts/performance, journalism/publications, music, theater/drama. *Special Characteristics:* 450 awards ($1,195,000 total): children of faculty/staff, general special characteristics. *Tuition waivers:* Full or partial for employees or children of employees. *ROTC:* Army cooperative.
LOANS *Student loans:* $45,931,776 (60% need-based, 40% non-need-based). 85% of past graduating class borrowed through all loan programs. *Average indebtedness per student:* $15,000. *Average need-based loan:* Freshmen: $2000; Undergraduates: $3500. *Parent loans:* $4,537,839 (100% non-need-based). *Programs:* Federal Direct (Subsidized and Unsubsidized Stafford, PLUS), Perkins, Federal Nursing, college/university, alternative loans.
WORK-STUDY *Federal work-study:* Total amount: $650,000; 566 jobs averaging $1030. *State or other work-study/employment:* Total amount: $236,000 (100% need-based). 120 part-time jobs averaging $1820.
ATHLETIC AWARDS *Total amount:* $1,374,793 (100% non-need-based).
APPLYING FOR FINANCIAL AID *Required financial aid form:* FAFSA. *Financial aid deadline (priority):* 3/1. *Notification date:* Continuous beginning 4/1. Students must reply within 2 weeks of notification.
CONTACT Carla Erlewine, Associate Director of Financial Aid, Ferris State University, 1201 South State Street, CSS 101, Big Rapids, MI 49307-2020, 231-591-2110 or toll-free 800-433-7747. *Fax:* 231-591-2950. *E-mail:* erlewinc@ferris.edu.

FERRUM COLLEGE
Ferrum, VA

Tuition & fees: $18,020	Average undergraduate aid package: $14,639

Ferrum College

ABOUT THE INSTITUTION Independent United Methodist, coed. Awards: bachelor's degrees. 33 undergraduate majors. Total enrollment: 991. Undergraduates: 991. Freshmen: 346. Federal methodology is used as a basis for awarding need-based institutional aid.

UNDERGRADUATE EXPENSES for 2005–06 *Application fee:* $25. *Comprehensive fee:* $24,320 includes full-time tuition ($17,990), mandatory fees ($30), and room and board ($6300). Room and board charges vary according to housing facility. *Part-time tuition:* $360 per hour. Part-time tuition and fees vary according to course load. *Payment plan:* Installment.

FRESHMAN FINANCIAL AID (Fall 2004) 328 applied for aid; of those 75% were deemed to have need. 100% of freshmen with need received aid; of those 13% had need fully met. *Average percent of need met:* 74% (excluding resources awarded to replace EFC). *Average financial aid package:* $16,184 (excluding resources awarded to replace EFC). 24% of all full-time freshmen had no need and received non-need-based gift aid.

UNDERGRADUATE FINANCIAL AID (Fall 2004) 958 applied for aid; of those 76% were deemed to have need. 100% of undergraduates with need received aid; of those 11% had need fully met. *Average percent of need met:* 85% (excluding resources awarded to replace EFC). *Average financial aid package:* $14,639 (excluding resources awarded to replace EFC). 18% of all full-time undergraduates had no need and received non-need-based gift aid.

GIFT AID (NEED-BASED) *Total amount:* $7,842,902 (16% federal, 18% state, 63% institutional, 3% external sources). *Receiving aid:* Freshmen: 73% (245); All full-time undergraduates: 76% (732). *Average award:* Freshmen: $9725; Undergraduates: $10,075. *Scholarships, grants, and awards:* Federal Pell, FSEOG, state, private, college/university gift aid from institutional funds.

GIFT AID (NON-NEED-BASED) *Total amount:* $1,263,579 (29% state, 68% institutional, 3% external sources). *Receiving aid:* Freshmen: 19% (62); Undergraduates: 19% (183). *Average Award:* Freshmen: $6249; Undergraduates: $6487. *Scholarships, grants, and awards by category: Academic Interests/Achievement:* 537 awards ($1,968,020 total): general academic interests/achievements. *Creative Arts/Performance:* 40 awards ($45,250 total): art/fine arts, performing arts, theater/drama. *Special Achievements/Activities:* 171 awards ($285,337 total): community service, general special achievements/activities, leadership, religious involvement. *Special Characteristics:* 319 awards ($1,004,109 total): adult students, children and siblings of alumni, children of educators, children of faculty/staff, international students, local/state students, out-of-state students, relatives of clergy, religious affiliation, siblings of current students. *Tuition waivers:* Full or partial for employees or children of employees, senior citizens.

LOANS *Student loans:* $4,252,803 (91% need-based, 9% non-need-based). 74% of past graduating class borrowed through all loan programs. *Average indebtedness per student:* $16,300. *Average need-based loan:* Freshmen: $2406; Undergraduates: $3829. *Parent loans:* $2,645,057 (78% need-based, 22% non-need-based). *Programs:* FFEL (Subsidized and Unsubsidized Stafford, PLUS), Perkins, alternative loans.

WORK-STUDY *Federal work-study:* Total amount: $240,304; 294 jobs averaging $845. *State or other work-study/employment:* Total amount: $35,349 (89% need-based, 11% non-need-based). 46 part-time jobs averaging $768.

APPLYING FOR FINANCIAL AID *Required financial aid forms:* FAFSA, state aid form. *Financial aid deadline (priority):* 3/1. *Notification date:* Continuous beginning 3/15.

CONTACT Heather Hollandsworth, Associate Director of Financial Aid, Ferrum College, PO Box 1000, Spilman-Daniel House, Ferrum, VA 24088-9001, 540-365-4282 or toll-free 800-868-9797. *Fax:* 540-365-4266.

FINLANDIA UNIVERSITY
Hancock, MI

Tuition & fees: $15,533	Average undergraduate aid package: $13,000

ABOUT THE INSTITUTION Independent religious, coed. Awards: associate and bachelor's degrees. 15 undergraduate majors. Total enrollment: 548. Undergraduates: 548. Freshmen: 107. Federal methodology is used as a basis for awarding need-based institutional aid.

UNDERGRADUATE EXPENSES for 2005–06 *Application fee:* $30. *Comprehensive fee:* $20,847 includes full-time tuition ($15,434), mandatory fees ($99), and room and board ($5314). Full-time tuition and fees vary according to program. Room and board charges vary according to housing facility. *Part-time tuition:* $520 per credit. *Part-time fees:* $99 per year. Part-time tuition and fees vary according to course load, degree level, and program. *Payment plan:* Installment.

FRESHMAN FINANCIAL AID (Fall 2004) 108 applied for aid; of those 87% were deemed to have need. 100% of freshmen with need received aid; of those 3% had need fully met. *Average percent of need met:* 80% (excluding resources awarded to replace EFC). *Average financial aid package:* $14,000 (excluding resources awarded to replace EFC). 17% of all full-time freshmen had no need and received non-need-based gift aid.

UNDERGRADUATE FINANCIAL AID (Fall 2004) 435 applied for aid; of those 99% were deemed to have need. 100% of undergraduates with need received aid; of those 1% had need fully met. *Average percent of need met:* 90% (excluding resources awarded to replace EFC). *Average financial aid package:* $13,000 (excluding resources awarded to replace EFC). 4% of all full-time undergraduates had no need and received non-need-based gift aid.

GIFT AID (NEED-BASED) *Total amount:* $4,090,840 (35% federal, 18% state, 45% institutional, 2% external sources). *Receiving aid:* Freshmen: 67% (73); All full-time undergraduates: 93% (417). *Average award:* Freshmen: $5000; Undergraduates: $5000. *Scholarships, grants, and awards:* Federal Pell, FSEOG, state, private, college/university gift aid from institutional funds.

GIFT AID (NON-NEED-BASED) *Total amount:* $4,058,627 (36% federal, 17% state, 46% institutional, 1% external sources). *Receiving aid:* Freshmen: 81% (88); Undergraduates: 96% (429). *Average Award:* Freshmen: $4000; Undergraduates: $4000. *Scholarships, grants, and awards by category: Academic Interests/Achievement:* 157 awards ($211,076 total). *Creative Arts/Performance:* art/fine arts, general creative arts/performance. *Special Achievements/Activities:* community service, general special achievements/activities, leadership, religious involvement. *Special Characteristics:* 141 awards ($169,275 total): children of current students, children of faculty/staff, first-generation college students, international students, religious affiliation, siblings of current students, spouses of current students, twins. *Tuition waivers:* Full or partial for employees or children of employees. *ROTC:* Army cooperative, Air Force cooperative.

LOANS *Student loans:* $5,677,007 (49% need-based, 51% non-need-based). 90% of past graduating class borrowed through all loan programs. *Average indebtedness per student:* $17,500. *Average need-based loan:* Freshmen: $2625; Undergraduates: $3500. *Parent loans:* $175,182 (49% need-based, 51% non-need-based). *Programs:* FFEL (Subsidized and Unsubsidized Stafford, PLUS), state, Private Loan Program.

WORK-STUDY *Federal work-study:* Total amount: $236,250; 154 jobs averaging $1600. *State or other work-study/employment:* Total amount: $63,030 (50% need-based, 50% non-need-based). 25 part-time jobs averaging $1200.

APPLYING FOR FINANCIAL AID *Required financial aid forms:* FAFSA, institution's own form. *Financial aid deadline (priority):* 3/1. *Notification date:* 3/1. Students must reply within 3 weeks of notification.

CONTACT Sandy Turnquist, Director of Financial Aid, Finlandia University, 601 Quincy Street, Hancock, MI 49930, 906-487-7240 or toll-free 877-202-5491. *Fax:* 906-487-7509. *E-mail:* sandy.turnquist@finlandia.edu.

FISK UNIVERSITY
Nashville, TN

CONTACT Director of Financial Aid, Fisk University, 1000 17th Avenue North, Nashville, TN 37208-3051, 615-329-8585 or toll-free 800-443-FISK. *Fax:* 615-329-8774.

FITCHBURG STATE COLLEGE
Fitchburg, MA

Tuition & fees (MA res): $5002	Average undergraduate aid package: N/A

ABOUT THE INSTITUTION State-supported, coed. Awards: bachelor's and master's degrees and post-bachelor's and post-master's certificates. 59 undergraduate majors. Total enrollment: 5,340. Undergraduates: 3,653. Freshmen: 607. Federal methodology is used as a basis for awarding need-based institutional aid.

UNDERGRADUATE EXPENSES for 2006–07 *Application fee:* $10. *Tuition, state resident:* full-time $970; part-time $40.42 per credit. *Tuition, nonresident:* full-time $7050; part-time $293.75 per credit. *Required fees:* full-time $4032; $168 per credit. *College room and board:* $6274.

FRESHMAN FINANCIAL AID (Fall 2004) 669 applied for aid; of those 58% were deemed to have need. 96% of freshmen with need received aid; of those 93% had need fully met. *Average percent of need met:* 93% (excluding resources awarded to replace EFC). 6% of all full-time freshmen had no need and received non-need-based gift aid.

UNDERGRADUATE FINANCIAL AID (Fall 2004) 2,380 applied for aid; of those 60% were deemed to have need. 97% of undergraduates with need received aid; of those 93% had need fully met. *Average percent of need met:* 93% (excluding resources awarded to replace EFC). 2% of all full-time undergraduates had no need and received non-need-based gift aid.
GIFT AID (NEED-BASED) *Total amount:* $4,631,218 (44% federal, 39% state, 17% institutional). *Receiving aid:* Freshmen: 41% (301); All full-time undergraduates: 37% (1,056). *Scholarships, grants, and awards:* Federal Pell, FSEOG, state, private, college/university gift aid from institutional funds.
GIFT AID (NON-NEED-BASED) *Total amount:* $917,688 (6% state, 64% institutional, 30% external sources). *Receiving aid:* Freshmen: 15% (106); Undergraduates: 10% (287). *Average Award:* Freshmen: $2347; Undergraduates: $2384. *Scholarships, grants, and awards by category: Academic Interests/Achievement:* 350 awards ($585,750 total): biological sciences, business, communication, computer science, education, English, general academic interests/achievements, health fields, mathematics, social sciences. *Special Achievements/Activities:* 85 awards ($332,400 total): general special achievements/activities, leadership. *Special Characteristics:* 16 awards ($16,500 total): adult students, children and siblings of alumni. *ROTC:* Air Force cooperative.
LOANS *Student loans:* $6,456,538 (56% need-based, 44% non-need-based). 55% of past graduating class borrowed through all loan programs. *Average indebtedness per student:* $10,660. *Parent loans:* $896,578 (100% non-need-based). *Programs:* Federal Direct (Subsidized and Unsubsidized Stafford, PLUS), Perkins, Federal Nursing, state.
WORK-STUDY *Federal work-study:* Total amount: $259,393; 240 jobs averaging $1080.
APPLYING FOR FINANCIAL AID *Required financial aid form:* FAFSA. *Financial aid deadline (priority):* 3/1. *Notification date:* Continuous beginning 3/15. Students must reply within 2 weeks of notification.
CONTACT Pamela McCafferty, Director of Financial Aid, Fitchburg State College, 160 Pearl Street, Fitchburg, MA 01420-2697, 978-665-3156 or toll-free 800-705-9692. *Fax:* 978-665-3559. *E-mail:* finaid@fsc.edu.

FIVE TOWNS COLLEGE
Dix Hills, NY

Tuition & fees: $14,100   **Average undergraduate aid package: $6000**

ABOUT THE INSTITUTION Independent, coed. Awards: associate, bachelor's, master's, and doctoral degrees. 19 undergraduate majors. Total enrollment: 1,162. Undergraduates: 1,088. Freshmen: 267. Federal methodology is used as a basis for awarding need-based institutional aid.
UNDERGRADUATE EXPENSES for 2005–06 *Application fee:* $35. *Comprehensive fee:* $24,350 includes full-time tuition ($14,100) and room and board ($10,250). Room and board charges vary according to board plan and location. *Part-time tuition:* $585 per credit. *Payment plan:* Installment.
FRESHMAN FINANCIAL AID (Fall 2005, est.) 207 applied for aid; of those 80% were deemed to have need. 100% of freshmen with need received aid; of those 15% had need fully met. *Average percent of need met:* 45% (excluding resources awarded to replace EFC). *Average financial aid package:* $4860 (excluding resources awarded to replace EFC). 8% of all full-time freshmen had no need and received non-need-based gift aid.
UNDERGRADUATE FINANCIAL AID (Fall 2005, est.) 784 applied for aid; of those 80% were deemed to have need. 100% of undergraduates with need received aid; of those 13% had need fully met. *Average percent of need met:* 45% (excluding resources awarded to replace EFC). *Average financial aid package:* $6000 (excluding resources awarded to replace EFC). 4% of all full-time undergraduates had no need and received non-need-based gift aid.
GIFT AID (NEED-BASED) *Total amount:* $2,872,300 (36% federal, 55% state, 5% institutional, 4% external sources). *Receiving aid:* Freshmen: 49% (130); All full-time undergraduates: 45% (490). *Average award:* Freshmen: $5700; Undergraduates: $5000. *Scholarships, grants, and awards:* Federal Pell, FSEOG, state, private, college/university gift aid from institutional funds.
GIFT AID (NON-NEED-BASED) *Total amount:* $1,120,000 (100% institutional). *Receiving aid:* Freshmen: 26% (70); Undergraduates: 25% (270). *Average Award:* Freshmen: $3400; Undergraduates: $3400. *Scholarships, grants, and awards by category: Academic Interests/Achievement:* 300 awards ($960,000 total): business, education, general academic interests/achievements. *Creative Arts/Performance:* 118 awards ($290,000 total): cinema/film/broadcasting, music, theater/drama. *Tuition waivers:* Full or partial for employees or children of employees.
LOANS *Student loans:* $6,024,000 (39% need-based, 61% non-need-based). 77% of past graduating class borrowed through all loan programs. *Average indebtedness per student:* $15,100. *Average need-based loan:* Freshmen: $2625; Undergraduates: $3200. *Parent loans:* $3,079,110 (100% non-need-based). *Programs:* Federal Direct (Subsidized and Unsubsidized Stafford, PLUS).
WORK-STUDY *Federal work-study:* Total amount: $120,000; 150 jobs averaging $900.
APPLYING FOR FINANCIAL AID *Required financial aid forms:* FAFSA, institution's own form, state aid form. *Financial aid deadline (priority):* 3/31. *Notification date:* Continuous beginning 5/1. Students must reply within 4 weeks of notification.
CONTACT Ms. Mary Venezia, Financial Aid/Director, Five Towns College, 305 North Service Road, Dix Hills, NY 11746-6055, 631-656-2113. *Fax:* 631-656-2191. *E-mail:* mvenezia@ftc.edu.

FLAGLER COLLEGE
St. Augustine, FL

Tuition & fees: $8600   **Average undergraduate aid package: $10,752**

ABOUT THE INSTITUTION Independent, coed. Awards: bachelor's degrees. 23 undergraduate majors. Total enrollment: 2,157. Undergraduates: 2,157. Freshmen: 461. Federal methodology is used as a basis for awarding need-based institutional aid.
UNDERGRADUATE EXPENSES for 2005–06 *Application fee:* $30. *Comprehensive fee:* $13,790 includes full-time tuition ($8600) and room and board ($5190). *College room only:* $2130. *Part-time tuition:* $295 per credit hour.
FRESHMAN FINANCIAL AID (Fall 2005, est.) 333 applied for aid; of those 63% were deemed to have need. 99% of freshmen with need received aid; of those 31% had need fully met. *Average percent of need met:* 75% (excluding resources awarded to replace EFC). *Average financial aid package:* $10,182 (excluding resources awarded to replace EFC). 2% of all full-time freshmen had no need and received non-need-based gift aid.
UNDERGRADUATE FINANCIAL AID (Fall 2005, est.) 1,344 applied for aid; of those 71% were deemed to have need. 100% of undergraduates with need received aid; of those 33% had need fully met. *Average percent of need met:* 79% (excluding resources awarded to replace EFC). *Average financial aid package:* $10,752 (excluding resources awarded to replace EFC). 3% of all full-time undergraduates had no need and received non-need-based gift aid.
GIFT AID (NEED-BASED) *Total amount:* $3,714,218 (24% federal, 68% state, 5% institutional, 3% external sources). *Receiving aid:* Freshmen: 17% (80); All full-time undergraduates: 21% (445). *Average award:* Freshmen: $3152; Undergraduates: $3060. *Scholarships, grants, and awards:* Federal Pell, FSEOG, state, private, college/university gift aid from institutional funds.
GIFT AID (NON-NEED-BASED) *Total amount:* $4,114,999 (90% state, 6% institutional, 4% external sources). *Receiving aid:* Freshmen: 36% (165); Undergraduates: 34% (709). *Average Award:* Freshmen: $7869; Undergraduates: $2293. *Scholarships, grants, and awards by category: Academic Interests/Achievement:* 34 awards ($20,545 total): business, communication, education, English, foreign languages, general academic interests/achievements, humanities, religion/biblical studies, social sciences. *Creative Arts/Performance:* 4 awards ($6850 total): applied art and design, art/fine arts, cinema/film/broadcasting, performing arts, theater/drama. *Special Achievements/Activities:* 81 awards ($279,872 total): general special achievements/activities, leadership, memberships, religious involvement. *Special Characteristics:* 67 awards ($196,870 total): children of faculty/staff, ethnic background, first-generation college students, general special characteristics, local/state students, members of minority groups, out-of-state students. *Tuition waivers:* Full or partial for employees or children of employees.
LOANS *Student loans:* $5,172,510 (67% need-based, 33% non-need-based). 55% of past graduating class borrowed through all loan programs. *Average indebtedness per student:* $15,037. *Average need-based loan:* Freshmen: $2721; Undergraduates: $3787. *Parent loans:* $1,248,020 (50% need-based, 50% non-need-based). *Programs:* Federal Direct (Subsidized and Unsubsidized Stafford, PLUS), Perkins.

Flagler College

WORK-STUDY *Federal work-study:* Total amount: $141,760; 167 jobs averaging $849. *State or other work-study/employment:* Total amount: $59,211 (37% need-based, 63% non-need-based). 72 part-time jobs averaging $922.
ATHLETIC AWARDS Total amount: $410,932 (37% need-based, 63% non-need-based).
APPLYING FOR FINANCIAL AID *Required financial aid forms:* FAFSA, institution's own form. *Financial aid deadline (priority):* 4/1. *Notification date:* Continuous beginning 3/1. Students must reply within 2 weeks of notification.
CONTACT Ms. Sheia Pleasant, Assistant Director of Financial Aid, Flagler College, PO Box 1027, St. Augustine, FL 32085-1027, 904-819-6225 or toll-free 800-304-4208. *Fax:* 904-819-6453. *E-mail:* spleasant@flagler.edu.

FLORIDA AGRICULTURAL AND MECHANICAL UNIVERSITY
Tallahassee, FL

Tuition & fees (FL res): $3318	Average undergraduate aid package: $8353

ABOUT THE INSTITUTION State-supported, coed. Awards: associate, bachelor's, master's, doctoral, and first professional degrees. 84 undergraduate majors. Total enrollment: 13,064. Undergraduates: 10,576. Freshmen: 2,001. Federal methodology is used as a basis for awarding need-based institutional aid.
UNDERGRADUATE EXPENSES for 2005–06 *Application fee:* $20. *Tuition, state resident:* full-time $3318; part-time $110.60 per credit hour. *Tuition, nonresident:* full-time $16,662; part-time $555.40 per credit hour. Full-time tuition and fees vary according to course load. Part-time tuition and fees vary according to course load. *College room and board:* $5766; *room only:* $3476. Room and board charges vary according to board plan and housing facility. *Payment plans:* Tuition prepayment, deferred payment.
FRESHMAN FINANCIAL AID (Fall 2004) 1868 applied for aid; of those 87% were deemed to have need. 98% of freshmen with need received aid; of those 10% had need fully met. *Average percent of need met:* 63% (excluding resources awarded to replace EFC). *Average financial aid package:* $7303 (excluding resources awarded to replace EFC). 7% of all full-time freshmen had no need and received non-need-based gift aid.
UNDERGRADUATE FINANCIAL AID (Fall 2004) 9,383 applied for aid; of those 91% were deemed to have need. 97% of undergraduates with need received aid; of those 10% had need fully met. *Average percent of need met:* 69% (excluding resources awarded to replace EFC). *Average financial aid package:* $8353 (excluding resources awarded to replace EFC). 4% of all full-time undergraduates had no need and received non-need-based gift aid.
GIFT AID (NEED-BASED) *Total amount:* $26,507,838 (78% federal, 15% state, 7% external sources). *Receiving aid:* Freshmen: 53% (1,076); All full-time undergraduates: 54% (5,802). *Average award:* Freshmen: $4295; Undergraduates: $4297. *Scholarships, grants, and awards:* Federal Pell, FSEOG, state, private, college/university gift aid from institutional funds, United Negro College Fund, Federal Nursing.
GIFT AID (NON-NEED-BASED) *Total amount:* $14,433,132 (20% state, 58% institutional, 22% external sources). *Receiving aid:* Freshmen: 34% (686); Undergraduates: 22% (2,386). *Average Award:* Freshmen: $6283; Undergraduates: $6584. *Scholarships, grants, and awards by category:* Academic Interests/Achievement: agriculture, business, engineering/technologies, general academic interests/achievements, health fields. *Tuition waivers:* Full or partial for employees or children of employees, senior citizens. *ROTC:* Army, Naval, Air Force cooperative.
LOANS *Student loans:* $52,234,982 (60% need-based, 40% non-need-based). 82% of past graduating class borrowed through all loan programs. *Average indebtedness per student:* $30,454. *Average need-based loan:* Freshmen: $2725; Undergraduates: $4108. *Parent loans:* $10,333,875 (100% non-need-based). *Programs:* Federal Direct (Subsidized and Unsubsidized Stafford, PLUS), Perkins.
WORK-STUDY *Federal work-study:* Total amount: $835,116; 524 jobs averaging $1227.
ATHLETIC AWARDS *Total amount:* $2,867,782 (100% non-need-based).
APPLYING FOR FINANCIAL AID *Required financial aid form:* FAFSA. *Financial aid deadline:* 6/30 (priority: 3/1). *Notification date:* Continuous. Students must reply within 2 weeks of notification.
CONTACT Dr. Joel V. Harrell, Director of Student Financial Aid, Florida Agricultural and Mechanical University, 101 Foote-Hilyer Administration Center, Tallahassee, FL 32307, 850-599-3730. *E-mail:* joel.harrell@famu.edu.

FLORIDA ATLANTIC UNIVERSITY
Boca Raton, FL

Tuition & fees (FL res): $3259	Average undergraduate aid package: $7012

ABOUT THE INSTITUTION State-supported, coed. Awards: associate, bachelor's, master's, and doctoral degrees and post-master's certificates. 62 undergraduate majors. Total enrollment: 25,704. Undergraduates: 21,505. Freshmen: 2,478. Federal methodology is used as a basis for awarding need-based institutional aid.
UNDERGRADUATE EXPENSES for 2005–06 *Application fee:* $30. *Tuition, state resident:* full-time $2147; part-time $108.64 per credit hour. *Tuition, nonresident:* full-time $14,653; part-time $546.36 per credit hour. Full-time tuition and fees vary according to course load. Part-time tuition and fees vary according to course load. *College room and board:* $7962. Room and board charges vary according to board plan and housing facility. *Payment plans:* Tuition prepayment, installment, deferred payment.
FRESHMAN FINANCIAL AID (Fall 2005, est.) 1666 applied for aid; of those 52% were deemed to have need. 96% of freshmen with need received aid; of those 16% had need fully met. *Average percent of need met:* 87% (excluding resources awarded to replace EFC). *Average financial aid package:* $6631 (excluding resources awarded to replace EFC). 5% of all full-time freshmen had no need and received non-need-based gift aid.
UNDERGRADUATE FINANCIAL AID (Fall 2005, est.) 8,537 applied for aid; of those 65% were deemed to have need. 96% of undergraduates with need received aid; of those 14% had need fully met. *Average percent of need met:* 74% (excluding resources awarded to replace EFC). *Average financial aid package:* $7012 (excluding resources awarded to replace EFC). 4% of all full-time undergraduates had no need and received non-need-based gift aid.
GIFT AID (NEED-BASED) *Total amount:* $28,755,120 (44% federal, 44% state, 4% institutional, 8% external sources). *Receiving aid:* Freshmen: 37% (753); All full-time undergraduates: 39% (4,515). *Average award:* Freshmen: $5854; Undergraduates: $5796. *Scholarships, grants, and awards:* Federal Pell, FSEOG, state, private, college/university gift aid from institutional funds, Federal Nursing.
GIFT AID (NON-NEED-BASED) *Average Award:* Freshmen: $2236; Undergraduates: $2315. *Scholarships, grants, and awards by category:* Academic Interests/Achievement: business, engineering/technologies, general academic interests/achievements, physical sciences, social sciences. Creative Arts/Performance: music, performing arts. *Tuition waivers:* Full or partial for employees or children of employees, senior citizens. *ROTC:* Army cooperative, Air Force cooperative.
LOANS *Student loans:* $43,133,918 (51% need-based, 49% non-need-based). *Average need-based loan:* Freshmen: $2372; Undergraduates: $3741. *Parent loans:* $2,755,403 (100% non-need-based). *Programs:* FFEL (Subsidized and Unsubsidized Stafford, PLUS), Perkins, college/university.
WORK-STUDY *Federal work-study:* Total amount: $529,933; 134 jobs averaging $3201. *State or other work-study/employment:* Total amount: $10,576 (100% need-based). Part-time jobs available.
ATHLETIC AWARDS *Total amount:* $2,589,741 (100% need-based).
APPLYING FOR FINANCIAL AID *Required financial aid form:* FAFSA. *Financial aid deadline (priority):* 3/1. *Notification date:* Continuous beginning 5/1. Students must reply within 3 weeks of notification.
CONTACT Carole Pfeilsticker, Director of Student Financial Aid, Florida Atlantic University, 777 Glades Road, Student Services Building, Room 227, Boca Raton, FL 33431-0991, 561-297-3528 or toll-free 800-299-4FAU. *E-mail:* pfeilsti@fau.edu.

FLORIDA ATLANTIC UNIVERSITY, JUPITER CAMPUS
Jupiter, FL

CONTACT Financial Aid Office, Florida Atlantic University, Jupiter Campus, 5353 Parkside Drive, Jupiter, FL 33458, 561-799-8500 or toll-free 561-799-8502 (in-state).

FLORIDA CHRISTIAN COLLEGE
Kissimmee, FL

Tuition & fees: $9720	Average undergraduate aid package: $5947

ABOUT THE INSTITUTION Independent religious, coed. Awards: associate and bachelor's degrees. 3 undergraduate majors. Total enrollment: 259. Undergraduates: 259. Federal methodology is used as a basis for awarding need-based institutional aid.
UNDERGRADUATE EXPENSES for 2005–06 *Application fee:* $25. *Tuition:* full-time $9280; part-time $290 per credit. Full-time tuition and fees vary according to course load. Part-time tuition and fees vary according to course load. *Payment plan:* Guaranteed tuition.
FRESHMAN FINANCIAL AID (Fall 2005, est.) 46 applied for aid; of those 100% were deemed to have need. 100% of freshmen with need received aid; of those 2% had need fully met. *Average percent of need met:* 35% (excluding resources awarded to replace EFC). *Average financial aid package:* $4585 (excluding resources awarded to replace EFC). 10% of all full-time freshmen had no need and received non-need-based gift aid.
UNDERGRADUATE FINANCIAL AID (Fall 2005, est.) 186 applied for aid; of those 100% were deemed to have need. 100% of undergraduates with need received aid; of those 3% had need fully met. *Average percent of need met:* 46% (excluding resources awarded to replace EFC). *Average financial aid package:* $5947 (excluding resources awarded to replace EFC). 5% of all full-time undergraduates had no need and received non-need-based gift aid.
GIFT AID (NEED-BASED) *Total amount:* $347,124 (75% federal, 17% state, 8% institutional). *Receiving aid:* Freshmen: 49% (24); All full-time undergraduates: 63% (117). *Average award:* Freshmen: $2278; Undergraduates: $2788. *Scholarships, grants, and awards:* Federal Pell, FSEOG, state, private, college/university gift aid from institutional funds.
GIFT AID (NON-NEED-BASED) *Total amount:* $433,381 (24% state, 30% institutional, 46% external sources). *Receiving aid:* Freshmen: 73% (36); Undergraduates: 76% (142). *Average Award:* Freshmen: $2500; Undergraduates:* $2000. *Scholarships, grants, and awards by category: Academic Interests/Achievement:* 47 awards ($45,558 total): education, religion/biblical studies. *Creative Arts/Performance:* 17 awards ($32,120 total): music. *Special Characteristics:* 150 awards ($73,270 total): children and siblings of alumni, children of faculty/staff, relatives of clergy, religious affiliation, spouses of current students.
LOANS *Student loans:* $552,226 (64% need-based, 36% non-need-based). 77% of past graduating class borrowed through all loan programs. *Average indebtedness per student:* $15,353. *Average need-based loan:* Freshmen: $2123; Undergraduates: $3418. *Parent loans:* $104,516 (100% non-need-based). *Programs:* FFEL (Subsidized and Unsubsidized Stafford, PLUS), alternative loans, Sallie Mae Loans.
WORK-STUDY *Federal work-study:* Total amount: $41,917; 38 jobs averaging $1103.
APPLYING FOR FINANCIAL AID *Required financial aid forms:* FAFSA, institution's own form. *Financial aid deadline:* 7/15 (priority: 5/1). *Notification date:* Continuous.
CONTACT Ms. Sandra Peppard, Director of Student Financial Aid, Florida Christian College, 1011 Bill Beck Boulevard, Kissimmee, FL 34744-5301, 407-847-8966 Ext. 365 or toll-free 888-GO-TO-FCC (in-state). *Fax:* 407-847-3925. *E-mail:* sandi.peppard@fcc.edu.

FLORIDA COLLEGE
Temple Terrace, FL

Tuition & fees: $10,730	Average undergraduate aid package: $9356

ABOUT THE INSTITUTION Independent, coed. Awards: associate and bachelor's degrees. 3 undergraduate majors. Total enrollment: 456. Undergraduates: 456. Freshmen: 209. Both federal and institutional methodology are used as a basis for awarding need-based institutional aid.
UNDERGRADUATE EXPENSES for 2005–06 *Application fee:* $25. *Comprehensive fee:* $15,930 includes full-time tuition ($10,180), mandatory fees ($550), and room and board ($5200). Room and board charges vary according to board plan and housing facility. *Part-time tuition:* $410 per semester hour. *Part-time fees:* $200 per term. *Payment plan:* Installment.
FRESHMAN FINANCIAL AID (Fall 2004) 102 applied for aid; of those 100% were deemed to have need. 100% of freshmen with need received aid; of those 6% had need fully met. *Average percent of need met:* 36% (excluding resources awarded to replace EFC). *Average financial aid package:* $9116 (excluding resources awarded to replace EFC). 35% of all full-time freshmen had no need and received non-need-based gift aid.

UNDERGRADUATE FINANCIAL AID (Fall 2004) 227 applied for aid; of those 100% were deemed to have need. 100% of undergraduates with need received aid; of those 10% had need fully met. *Average percent of need met:* 37% (excluding resources awarded to replace EFC). *Average financial aid package:* $9356 (excluding resources awarded to replace EFC). 32% of all full-time undergraduates had no need and received non-need-based gift aid.
GIFT AID (NEED-BASED) *Total amount:* $1,150,483 (28% federal, 2% state, 12% institutional, 58% external sources). *Receiving aid:* Freshmen: 34% (71); All full-time undergraduates: 36% (164). *Average award:* Freshmen: $2605; Undergraduates: $2616. *Scholarships, grants, and awards:* Federal Pell, FSEOG, state, private, college/university gift aid from institutional funds.
GIFT AID (NON-NEED-BASED) *Total amount:* $1,025,873 (43% state, 31% institutional, 26% external sources). *Receiving aid:* Freshmen: 34% (71); Undergraduates: 36% (164). *Average Award:* Freshmen: $777; Undergraduates:* $774. *Scholarships, grants, and awards by category: Academic Interests/Achievement:* general academic interests/achievements. *Creative Arts/Performance:* debating, journalism/publications, music, theater/drama. *Special Characteristics:* children of educators, children of faculty/staff. *Tuition waivers:* Full or partial for employees or children of employees. *ROTC:* Army cooperative, Air Force cooperative.
LOANS *Student loans:* $1,260,910 (59% need-based, 41% non-need-based). 62% of past graduating class borrowed through all loan programs. *Average indebtedness per student:* $2111. *Average need-based loan:* Freshmen: $1646; Undergraduates: $1915. *Parent loans:* $1,163,498 (100% non-need-based). *Programs:* FFEL (Subsidized and Unsubsidized Stafford, PLUS), Perkins.
WORK-STUDY *Federal work-study:* Total amount: $19,399; jobs available. *State or other work-study/employment:* Total amount: $197,582 (100% non-need-based). Part-time jobs available.
ATHLETIC AWARDS Total amount: $255,025 (100% non-need-based).
APPLYING FOR FINANCIAL AID *Required financial aid form:* FAFSA. *Financial aid deadline:* 8/1 (priority: 4/1). *Notification date:* Continuous. Students must reply within 2 weeks of notification.
CONTACT Lisa McClister, Financial Aid Officer, Florida College, 119 North Glen Arven Avenue, Temple Terrace, FL 33617, 813-849-6720 or toll-free 800-326-7655. *Fax:* 813-899-6772. *E-mail:* mcclisterl@floridacollege.edu.

FLORIDA GULF COAST UNIVERSITY
Fort Myers, FL

Tuition & fees (FL res): $3420	Average undergraduate aid package: $7210

ABOUT THE INSTITUTION State-supported, coed. Awards: associate, bachelor's, and master's degrees. 26 undergraduate majors. Total enrollment: 7,249. Undergraduates: 6,138. Freshmen: 1,343. Federal methodology is used as a basis for awarding need-based institutional aid.
UNDERGRADUATE EXPENSES for 2005–06 *Application fee:* $30. *Tuition, state resident:* full-time $3260; part-time $108.67 per credit. *Tuition, nonresident:* full-time $15,249; part-time $508.31 per credit. *Required fees:* full-time $160; $2 per credit or $100 per year part-time. Full-time tuition and fees vary according to course load. Part-time tuition and fees vary according to course load. *College room and board:* $7460; *room only:* $3620. Room and board charges vary according to board plan.
FRESHMAN FINANCIAL AID (Fall 2004) 760 applied for aid; of those 45% were deemed to have need. 100% of freshmen with need received aid; of those 20% had need fully met. *Average percent of need met:* 66% (excluding resources awarded to replace EFC). *Average financial aid package:* $6058 (excluding resources awarded to replace EFC). 42% of all full-time freshmen had no need and received non-need-based gift aid.
UNDERGRADUATE FINANCIAL AID (Fall 2004) 2,802 applied for aid; of those 54% were deemed to have need. 100% of undergraduates with need received aid; of those 22% had need fully met. *Average percent of need met:* 69% (excluding resources awarded to replace EFC). *Average financial aid package:* $7210 (excluding resources awarded to replace EFC). 29% of all full-time undergraduates had no need and received non-need-based gift aid.
GIFT AID (NEED-BASED) *Total amount:* $4,332,992 (63% federal, 13% state, 22% institutional, 2% external sources). *Receiving aid:* Freshmen: 23% (209); All full-time undergraduates: 28% (1,043). *Average award:* Freshmen: $3044; Undergraduates: $3432. *Scholarships, grants, and awards:* Federal Pell, FSEOG, state, private, college/university gift aid from institutional funds.

Florida Gulf Coast University

GIFT AID (NON-NEED-BASED) *Total amount:* $5,141,561 (77% state, 11% institutional, 12% external sources). *Receiving aid:* Freshmen: 29% (270); Undergraduates: 21% (786). *Average Award:* Freshmen: $1550; Undergraduates: $1992. *Scholarships, grants, and awards by category: Academic Interests/Achievement:* biological sciences, business, education, engineering/technologies, general academic interests/achievements, health fields, humanities, mathematics, physical sciences, religion/biblical studies, social sciences. *Creative Arts/Performance:* art/fine arts, music. *Special Achievements/Activities:* community service, leadership. *Special Characteristics:* adult students, ethnic background, handicapped students, international students, local/state students, members of minority groups, out-of-state students. *Tuition waivers:* Full or partial for employees or children of employees, senior citizens.
LOANS *Student loans:* $13,588,184 (61% need-based, 39% non-need-based). 47% of past graduating class borrowed through all loan programs. *Average indebtedness per student:* $13,245. *Average need-based loan:* Freshmen: $2351; Undergraduates: $4545. *Programs:* FFEL (Subsidized and Unsubsidized Stafford, PLUS), state.
WORK-STUDY *Federal work-study:* Total amount: $114,600; 65 jobs averaging $1763. *State or other work-study/employment:* Total amount: $2,480,371 (100% need-based). 580 part-time jobs averaging $4277.
ATHLETIC AWARDS *Total amount:* $456,617 (100% non-need-based).
APPLYING FOR FINANCIAL AID *Required financial aid forms:* FAFSA, institution's own form. *Financial aid deadline:* 3/15 (priority: 2/1). *Notification date:* Continuous beginning 2/15. Students must reply within 4 weeks of notification.
CONTACT Kevin McGowan, Director of Student Financial Aid and Scholarships, Florida Gulf Coast University, 10501 FGCU Boulevard South, Fort Myers, FL 33965, 239-590-7920 or toll-free 888-889-1095. *Fax:* 239-590-7923. *E-mail:* faso@fgcu.edu.

FLORIDA INSTITUTE OF TECHNOLOGY
Melbourne, FL

Tuition & fees: $25,150   **Average undergraduate aid package: $21,102**

ABOUT THE INSTITUTION Independent, coed. Awards: bachelor's, master's, and doctoral degrees and post-master's certificates. 47 undergraduate majors. Total enrollment: 4,745. Undergraduates: 2,358. Freshmen: 604. Federal methodology is used as a basis for awarding need-based institutional aid.
UNDERGRADUATE EXPENSES for 2005-06 *Application fee:* $50. *Comprehensive fee:* $31,950 includes full-time tuition ($25,150) and room and board ($6800). *College room only:* $4000. Full-time tuition and fees vary according to course load and program. Room and board charges vary according to board plan and housing facility. *Part-time tuition:* $765 per credit hour. Part-time tuition and fees vary according to course load and program. *Payment plan:* Installment.
FRESHMAN FINANCIAL AID (Fall 2005, est.) 525 applied for aid; of those 83% were deemed to have need. 100% of freshmen with need received aid; of those 33% had need fully met. *Average percent of need met:* 86% (excluding resources awarded to replace EFC). *Average financial aid package:* $21,186 (excluding resources awarded to replace EFC). 26% of all full-time freshmen had no need and received non-need-based gift aid.
UNDERGRADUATE FINANCIAL AID (Fall 2005, est.) 1,611 applied for aid; of those 89% were deemed to have need. 100% of undergraduates with need received aid; of those 31% had need fully met. *Average percent of need met:* 84% (excluding resources awarded to replace EFC). *Average financial aid package:* $21,102 (excluding resources awarded to replace EFC). 26% of all full-time undergraduates had no need and received non-need-based gift aid.
GIFT AID (NEED-BASED) *Total amount:* $18,429,643 (12% federal, 15% state, 71% institutional, 2% external sources). *Receiving aid:* Freshmen: 59% (358); All full-time undergraduates: 55% (1,238). *Average award:* Freshmen: $15,031; Undergraduates: $14,095. *Scholarships, grants, and awards:* Federal Pell, FSEOG, state, private, college/university gift aid from institutional funds.
GIFT AID (NON-NEED-BASED) *Total amount:* $5,912,168 (11% federal, 12% state, 75% institutional, 2% external sources). *Receiving aid:* Freshmen: 71% (431); Undergraduates: 51% (1,161). *Average Award:* Freshmen: $8473; Undergraduates: $7526. *Scholarships, grants, and awards by category: Academic Interests/Achievement:* 1,642 awards ($11,346,772 total): general academic interests/achievements, military science. *Special Characteristics:* 242 awards ($1,284,849 total): children and siblings of alumni, children of faculty/staff, general special characteristics, previous college experience. *Tuition waivers:* Full or partial for employees or children of employees, senior citizens.
ROTC: Army.
LOANS *Student loans:* $15,738,134 (88% need-based, 12% non-need-based). 54% of past graduating class borrowed through all loan programs. *Average indebtedness per student:* $24,535. *Average need-based loan:* Freshmen: $3927; Undergraduates: $4724. *Parent loans:* $3,060,687 (90% need-based, 10% non-need-based). *Programs:* FFEL (Subsidized and Unsubsidized Stafford, PLUS), Perkins, college/university, alternative loans.
WORK-STUDY *Federal work-study:* Total amount: $894,391; 610 jobs averaging $1466. *State or other work-study/employment:* Total amount: $31,235 (100% need-based). 14 part-time jobs averaging $2402.
ATHLETIC AWARDS *Total amount:* $1,782,075 (63% need-based, 37% non-need-based).
APPLYING FOR FINANCIAL AID *Required financial aid forms:* FAFSA, state aid form. *Financial aid deadline (priority):* 3/15. *Notification date:* Continuous beginning 2/15. Students must reply by 5/1 or within 4 weeks of notification.
CONTACT Ann Munroe, Financial Aid Administrative Clerk, Florida Institute of Technology, 150 West University Boulevard, Melbourne, FL 32901-6975, 321-674-8070 or toll-free 800-888-4348. *Fax:* 321-724-2778. *E-mail:* dtouma@fit.edu.

FLORIDA INTERNATIONAL UNIVERSITY
Miami, FL

CONTACT Maria A. Tolon, Associate Director, Financial Aid, Florida International University, University Park PC 125, Miami, FL 33199, 305-348-2340. *Fax:* 305-348-2346. *E-mail:* tolonm@fiu.edu.

FLORIDA MEMORIAL COLLEGE
Miami-Dade, FL

CONTACT Brian Phillip, Director of Financial Aid, Florida Memorial College, 15800 Northwest 42nd Avenue, Miami, FL 33054, 305-626-3745 or toll-free 800-822-1362. *Fax:* 305-626-3106.

FLORIDA METROPOLITAN UNIVERSITY–BRANDON CAMPUS
Tampa, FL

CONTACT Ms. Ginger Waymire, Director of Financial Aid, Florida Metropolitan University–Brandon Campus, 3924 Coconut Palm Drive, Tampa, FL 33619, 813-621-0041 Ext. 118 or toll-free 877-338-0068. *Fax:* 813-621-6283. *E-mail:* gwaymire@cci.edu.

FLORIDA METROPOLITAN UNIVERSITY–JACKSONVILLE CAMPUS
Jacksonville, FL

CONTACT Financial Aid Office, Florida Metropolitan University–Jacksonville Campus, 8226 Phillips Highway, Jacksonville, FL 32256, 904-731-4949 or toll-free 888-741-4271.

FLORIDA METROPOLITAN UNIVERSITY–LAKELAND CAMPUS
Lakeland, FL

CONTACT Brian Jones, Senior Finance Officer, Florida Metropolitan University–Lakeland Campus, Office of Financial Aid, 995 East Memorial Boulevard, Lakeland, FL 33801, 863-686-1444 Ext. 118 or toll-free 877-225-0014 (in-state). *Fax:* 863-682-1077.

FLORIDA METROPOLITAN UNIVERSITY–MELBOURNE CAMPUS
Melbourne, FL

CONTACT Ronda Nabb-Landolfi, Director of Student Financial Aid, Florida Metropolitan University–Melbourne Campus, 2401 North Harbor City Boulevard, Melbourne, FL 32935-6657, 321-253-2929 Ext. 19.

Florida Southern College

FLORIDA METROPOLITAN UNIVERSITY–NORTH ORLANDO CAMPUS
Orlando, FL

CONTACT Ms. Linda Kaisrlik, Director of Student Finance, Florida Metropolitan University–North Orlando Campus, 5421 Diplomat Circle, Orlando, FL 32810-5674, 407-628-5870 Ext. 118 or toll-free 800-628-5870.

FLORIDA METROPOLITAN UNIVERSITY–PINELLAS CAMPUS
Clearwater, FL

Tuition & fees: N/R   **Average undergraduate aid package:** $7500

ABOUT THE INSTITUTION Proprietary, coed. Awards: associate, bachelor's, and master's degrees. 6 undergraduate majors. Total enrollment: 1,201. Undergraduates: 1,057. Federal methodology is used as a basis for awarding need-based institutional aid.
FRESHMAN FINANCIAL AID (Fall 2005, est.) 403 applied for aid; of those 50% were deemed to have need. 100% of freshmen with need received aid. *Average percent of need met:* 85% (excluding resources awarded to replace EFC). *Average financial aid package:* $6625 (excluding resources awarded to replace EFC).
UNDERGRADUATE FINANCIAL AID (Fall 2005, est.) 651 applied for aid; of those 84% were deemed to have need. 100% of undergraduates with need received aid. *Average percent of need met:* 90% (excluding resources awarded to replace EFC). *Average financial aid package:* $7500 (excluding resources awarded to replace EFC).
GIFT AID (NEED-BASED) *Total amount:* $12,350 (33% federal, 6% state, 61% institutional). *Receiving aid:* Freshmen: 50% (201). *Average award:* Freshmen: $2700; Undergraduates: $2700. *Scholarships, grants, and awards:* Federal Pell, FSEOG, state, private, college/university gift aid from institutional funds.
GIFT AID (NON-NEED-BASED) *Total amount:* $7500 (100% institutional). *Receiving aid:* Freshmen: 50% (201); Undergraduates: 69% (550). *Scholarships, grants, and awards by category: Academic Interests/Achievement:* business, computer science, general academic interests/achievements, health fields.
LOANS *Student loans:* $11,369,000 (43% need-based, 57% non-need-based). 80% of past graduating class borrowed through all loan programs. *Average indebtedness per student:* $30,000. *Parent loans:* $35,000 (100% non-need-based). *Programs:* FFEL (Subsidized and Unsubsidized Stafford, PLUS), Signature Loans; career training; NLSC.
WORK-STUDY *Federal work-study:* Total amount: $80,000; 6 jobs averaging $9000.
APPLYING FOR FINANCIAL AID *Required financial aid form:* FAFSA. *Financial aid deadline:* Continuous. *Notification date:* Continuous.
CONTACT Ms. Rebeca Handsaker, Director of Student Finance, Florida Metropolitan University–Pinellas Campus, 2471 North McMullen Booth Road, Clearwater, FL 33759, 727-725-2688 Ext. 166 or toll-free 800-353-FMUS. *Fax:* 727-796-3406.

FLORIDA METROPOLITAN UNIVERSITY–POMPANO BEACH CAMPUS
Pompano Beach, FL

CONTACT Sharon Scheible, Director of Student Financial Aid, Florida Metropolitan University–Pompano Beach Campus, 1040 Bayview Drive, Fort Lauderdale, FL 33304-2522, 954-568-1600 Ext. 52 or toll-free 800-468-0168. *Fax:* 954-564-5283. *E-mail:* scheible@cci.edu.

FLORIDA METROPOLITAN UNIVERSITY–SOUTH ORLANDO CAMPUS
Orlando, FL

CONTACT Sherri Williams, Director of Financial Aid, Florida Metropolitan University–South Orlando Campus, 2411 Sand Lake Road, Orlando, FL 32809, 407-851-2525 or toll-free 888-471-4270 (out-of-state).

FLORIDA METROPOLITAN UNIVERSITY–TAMPA CAMPUS
Tampa, FL

Tuition & fees: $9900   **Average undergraduate aid package:** $6625

ABOUT THE INSTITUTION Proprietary, coed. Awards: associate, bachelor's, and master's degrees. 10 undergraduate majors. Total enrollment: 1,390. Undergraduates: 1,281. Freshmen: 167. Federal methodology is used as a basis for awarding need-based institutional aid.
UNDERGRADUATE EXPENSES for 2005–06 *Application fee:* $25. *Tuition:* full-time $9720; part-time $270 per quarter hour. *Required fees:* full-time $180; $60 per term part-time. Full-time tuition and fees vary according to program. Part-time tuition and fees vary according to program. *Payment plan:* Installment.
FRESHMAN FINANCIAL AID (Fall 2005, est.) 385 applied for aid; of those 100% were deemed to have need. 100% of freshmen with need received aid; of those 58% had need fully met. *Average percent of need met:* 83% (excluding resources awarded to replace EFC). *Average financial aid package:* $6625 (excluding resources awarded to replace EFC).
UNDERGRADUATE FINANCIAL AID (Fall 2005, est.) 1,054 applied for aid; of those 100% were deemed to have need. 100% of undergraduates with need received aid; of those 81% had need fully met. *Average percent of need met:* 83% (excluding resources awarded to replace EFC). *Average financial aid package:* $6625 (excluding resources awarded to replace EFC).
GIFT AID (NEED-BASED) *Total amount:* $3,695,233 (97% federal, 3% state). *Receiving aid:* Freshmen: 64% (288); All full-time undergraduates: 81% (1,001). *Average award:* Freshmen: $1350; Undergraduates: $1350. *Scholarships, grants, and awards:* Federal Pell, FSEOG, state, private, college/university gift aid from institutional funds.
GIFT AID (NON-NEED-BASED) *Receiving aid:* Freshmen: 54% (243); Undergraduates: 75% (930). *Tuition waivers:* Full or partial for employees or children of employees.
LOANS *Student loans:* $10,121,333 (56% need-based, 44% non-need-based). 81% of past graduating class borrowed through all loan programs. *Average indebtedness per student:* $12,000. *Average need-based loan:* Freshmen: $2625; Undergraduates: $2625. *Parent loans:* $429,000 (100% non-need-based). *Programs:* FFEL (Subsidized and Unsubsidized Stafford, PLUS).
WORK-STUDY *Federal work-study:* Total amount: $101,000; 25 jobs averaging $4000.
APPLYING FOR FINANCIAL AID *Required financial aid form:* FAFSA. *Financial aid deadline:* Continuous. *Notification date:* Continuous.
CONTACT Mr. Rod Kirkwood, Financial Aid Director, Florida Metropolitan University–Tampa Campus, 3319 West Hillsborough Avenue, Tampa, FL 33614, 813-879-6000 Ext. 145. *Fax:* 813-871-2483. *E-mail:* rkirkwoo@cci.edu.

FLORIDA SOUTHERN COLLEGE
Lakeland, FL

Tuition & fees: $19,165   **Average undergraduate aid package:** $16,993

ABOUT THE INSTITUTION Independent religious, coed. Awards: bachelor's and master's degrees. 57 undergraduate majors. Total enrollment: 1,921. Undergraduates: 1,816. Freshmen: 483. Federal methodology is used as a basis for awarding need-based institutional aid.
UNDERGRADUATE EXPENSES for 2005–06 *Application fee:* $30. *Comprehensive fee:* $25,965 includes full-time tuition ($18,765), mandatory fees ($400), and room and board ($6800). *College room only:* $3750. Full-time tuition and fees vary according to student level. Room and board charges vary according to board plan and housing facility. *Part-time tuition:* $500 per credit hour. *Part-time fees:* $400 per year. *Payment plan:* Installment.
FRESHMAN FINANCIAL AID (Fall 2005, est.) 395 applied for aid; of those 78% were deemed to have need. 100% of freshmen with need received aid; of those 42% had need fully met. *Average percent of need met:* 72% (excluding resources awarded to replace EFC). *Average financial aid package:* $18,403 (excluding resources awarded to replace EFC). 18% of all full-time freshmen had no need and received non-need-based gift aid.
UNDERGRADUATE FINANCIAL AID (Fall 2005, est.) 1,507 applied for aid; of those 84% were deemed to have need. 99% of undergraduates with need received aid; of those 34% had need fully met. *Average percent of need met:*

Florida Southern College

64% (excluding resources awarded to replace EFC). *Average financial aid package:* $16,993 (excluding resources awarded to replace EFC). 13% of all full-time undergraduates had no need and received non-need-based gift aid.
GIFT AID (NEED-BASED) *Total amount:* $16,006,562 (9% federal, 33% state, 53% institutional, 5% external sources). *Receiving aid:* Freshmen: 64% (295); All full-time undergraduates: 68% (1,192). *Average award:* Freshmen: $14,611; Undergraduates: $13,078. *Scholarships, grants, and awards:* Federal Pell, FSEOG, state, private, college/university gift aid from institutional funds.
GIFT AID (NON-NEED-BASED) *Total amount:* $1,078,103 (10% state, 88% institutional, 2% external sources). *Receiving aid:* Freshmen: 45% (210); Undergraduates: 36% (641). *Average Award:* Freshmen: $13,388; Undergraduates:* $13,443. *Scholarships, grants, and awards by category: Academic Interests/Achievement:* 1,261 awards ($5,675,649 total): agriculture, biological sciences, business, communication, education, general academic interests/achievements, physical sciences, religion/biblical studies, social sciences. *Creative Arts/Performance:* 341 awards ($603,781 total): art/fine arts, music, theater/drama. *Special Achievements/Activities:* 758 awards ($1,818,374 total): community service, general special achievements/activities, leadership. *Special Characteristics:* 1,050 awards ($3,248,832 total): children and siblings of alumni, children of faculty/staff, general special characteristics, local/state students, out-of-state students, relatives of clergy, siblings of current students. *Tuition waivers:* Full or partial for children of alumni, employees or children of employees. *ROTC:* Army, Air Force cooperative.
LOANS *Student loans:* $4,723,704 (94% need-based, 6% non-need-based). 67% of past graduating class borrowed through all loan programs. *Average indebtedness per student:* $16,072. *Average need-based loan:* Freshmen: $4331; Undergraduates: $5199. *Programs:* FFEL (Subsidized and Unsubsidized Stafford, PLUS), Perkins.
WORK-STUDY *Federal work-study:* Total amount: $436,601; 356 jobs averaging $1226. *State or other work-study/employment:* Total amount: $169,162 (81% need-based, 19% non-need-based). 73 part-time jobs averaging $1871.
ATHLETIC AWARDS *Total amount:* $1,430,996 (95% need-based, 5% non-need-based).
APPLYING FOR FINANCIAL AID *Required financial aid forms:* FAFSA, institution's own form. *Financial aid deadline:* 8/1 (priority: 4/1). *Notification date:* Continuous beginning 3/15.
CONTACT David M. Bodwell, Financial Aid Director, Florida Southern College, 111 Lake Hollingsworth Drive, Lakeland, FL 33801-5698, 863-680-4140 or toll-free 800-274-4131. *Fax:* 863-680-4567. *E-mail:* dbodwell@flsouthern.edu.

FLORIDA STATE UNIVERSITY
Tallahassee, FL

Tuition & fees (FL res): $3208   **Average undergraduate aid package:** $8752

ABOUT THE INSTITUTION State-supported, coed. Awards: associate, bachelor's, master's, doctoral, and first professional degrees and post-bachelor's and post-master's certificates. 157 undergraduate majors. Total enrollment: 39,146. Undergraduates: 30,785. Freshmen: 6,063. Federal methodology is used as a basis for awarding need-based institutional aid.
UNDERGRADUATE EXPENSES for 2005–06 *Application fee:* $30. *Tuition, state resident:* full-time $3208; part-time $106.93 per credit hour. *Tuition, nonresident:* full-time $16,340; part-time $544.67 per credit hour. Full-time tuition and fees vary according to location. Part-time tuition and fees vary according to location. *College room and board:* $6778; *room only:* $3600. Room and board charges vary according to board plan and housing facility. *Payment plans:* Tuition prepayment, installment.
FRESHMAN FINANCIAL AID (Fall 2005, est.) 3835 applied for aid; of those 53% were deemed to have need. 100% of freshmen with need received aid; of those 73% had need fully met. *Average percent of need met:* 65% (excluding resources awarded to replace EFC). *Average financial aid package:* $8430 (excluding resources awarded to replace EFC). 7% of all full-time freshmen had no need and received non-need-based gift aid.
UNDERGRADUATE FINANCIAL AID (Fall 2005, est.) 15,351 applied for aid; of those 57% were deemed to have need. 100% of undergraduates with need received aid; of those 76% had need fully met. *Average percent of need met:* 70% (excluding resources awarded to replace EFC). *Average financial aid package:* $8752 (excluding resources awarded to replace EFC). 4% of all full-time undergraduates had no need and received non-need-based gift aid.
GIFT AID (NEED-BASED) *Total amount:* $51,186,729 (38% federal, 33% state, 26% institutional, 3% external sources). *Receiving aid:* Freshmen: 23% (1,376); All full-time undergraduates: 21% (5,721). *Average award:* Freshmen: $2817; Undergraduates: $3003. *Scholarships, grants, and awards:* Federal Pell, FSEOG, state, private, college/university gift aid from institutional funds.
GIFT AID (NON-NEED-BASED) *Total amount:* $41,372,226 (78% state, 17% institutional, 5% external sources). *Receiving aid:* Freshmen: 31% (1,847); Undergraduates: 22% (5,850). *Average Award:* Freshmen: $1946; Undergraduates:* $1797. *Scholarships, grants, and awards by category: Academic Interests/Achievement:* general academic interests/achievements. *Creative Arts/Performance:* music. *Special Characteristics:* local/state students. *Tuition waivers:* Full or partial for employees or children of employees, senior citizens. *ROTC:* Army, Naval cooperative, Air Force.
LOANS *Student loans:* $54,556,620 (59% need-based, 41% non-need-based). 52% of past graduating class borrowed through all loan programs. *Average indebtedness per student:* $16,597. *Average need-based loan:* Freshmen: $2160; Undergraduates: $3122. *Parent loans:* $9,647,471 (22% need-based, 78% non-need-based). *Programs:* FFEL (Subsidized and Unsubsidized Stafford, PLUS), Perkins, college/university.
WORK-STUDY *Federal work-study:* Total amount: $1,356,838; 719 jobs averaging $1459. *State or other work-study/employment:* Part-time jobs available.
ATHLETIC AWARDS *Total amount:* $1,951,342 (7% need-based, 93% non-need-based).
APPLYING FOR FINANCIAL AID *Required financial aid form:* FAFSA. *Financial aid deadline (priority):* 2/15. *Notification date:* Continuous beginning 3/15. Students must reply within 2 weeks of notification.
CONTACT Darryl Marshall, Director of Financial Aid, Florida State University, University Center A4400, Tallahassee, FL 32306-2430, 850-644-5716. *Fax:* 850-644-6404. *E-mail:* ofacs@admin.fsu.edu.

FONTBONNE UNIVERSITY
St. Louis, MO

CONTACT Financial Aid Office, Fontbonne University, 6800 Wydown Boulevard, St. Louis, MO 63105-3098, 314-889-1414. *Fax:* 314-889-1451.

FORDHAM UNIVERSITY
New York, NY

Tuition & fees: $27,725   **Average undergraduate aid package:** $19,953

ABOUT THE INSTITUTION Independent Roman Catholic (Jesuit), coed. Awards: bachelor's, master's, doctoral, and first professional degrees and post-master's certificates (branch locations at Rose Hill and Lincoln Center). 94 undergraduate majors. Total enrollment: 14,664. Undergraduates: 7,528. Freshmen: 1,755. Both federal and institutional methodology are used as a basis for awarding need-based institutional aid.
UNDERGRADUATE EXPENSES for 2006–07 *Application fee:* $50. *Comprehensive fee:* $38,620 includes full-time tuition ($27,725) and room and board ($10,895). *College room only:* $7260.
FRESHMAN FINANCIAL AID (Fall 2004) 1332 applied for aid; of those 87% were deemed to have need. 99% of freshmen with need received aid; of those 20% had need fully met. *Average percent of need met:* 82% (excluding resources awarded to replace EFC). *Average financial aid package:* $21,197 (excluding resources awarded to replace EFC). 8% of all full-time freshmen had no need and received non-need-based gift aid.
UNDERGRADUATE FINANCIAL AID (Fall 2004) 4,936 applied for aid; of those 89% were deemed to have need. 99% of undergraduates with need received aid; of those 21% had need fully met. *Average percent of need met:* 77% (excluding resources awarded to replace EFC). *Average financial aid package:* $19,953 (excluding resources awarded to replace EFC). 9% of all full-time undergraduates had no need and received non-need-based gift aid.
GIFT AID (NEED-BASED) *Total amount:* $59,146,006 (10% federal, 11% state, 76% institutional, 3% external sources). *Receiving aid:* Freshmen: 65% (1,094); All full-time undergraduates: 62% (4,136). *Average award:* Freshmen: $17,493; Undergraduates: $15,096. *Scholarships, grants, and awards:* Federal Pell, FSEOG, state, private, college/university gift aid from institutional funds.
GIFT AID (NON-NEED-BASED) *Total amount:* $6,058,555 (1% federal, 2% state, 80% institutional, 17% external sources). *Receiving aid:* Freshmen: 4% (66); Undergraduates: 4% (259). *Average Award:* Freshmen: $7444; Undergradu-

ates: $8005. *Scholarships, grants, and awards by category: Academic Interests/Achievement:* communication, foreign languages, general academic interests/achievements. *Creative Arts/Performance:* music. *Special Achievements/Activities:* general special achievements/activities. *Special Characteristics:* children and siblings of alumni, children of faculty/staff, children of union members/company employees, children with a deceased or disabled parent, handicapped students, veterans, veterans' children. *ROTC:* Army, Naval cooperative, Air Force cooperative.
LOANS *Student loans:* $31,155,532 (68% need-based, 32% non-need-based). 66% of past graduating class borrowed through all loan programs. *Average indebtedness per student:* $16,590. *Average need-based loan:* Freshmen: $3267; Undergraduates: $4396. *Parent loans:* $16,071,789 (33% need-based, 67% non-need-based). *Programs:* FFEL (Subsidized and Unsubsidized Stafford, PLUS), Perkins.
WORK-STUDY *Federal work-study:* Total amount: $3,465,293; 1,295 jobs averaging $2676. *State or other work-study/employment:* Total amount: $923,430 (51% need-based, 49% non-need-based). 99 part-time jobs averaging $9328.
ATHLETIC AWARDS Total amount: $5,876,016 (67% need-based, 33% non-need-based).
APPLYING FOR FINANCIAL AID *Required financial aid forms:* FAFSA, CSS Financial Aid PROFILE, noncustodial (divorced/separated) parent's statement, business/farm supplement. *Financial aid deadline:* 2/1 (priority: 2/1). *Notification date:* Continuous beginning 4/1. Students must reply by 5/1 or within 2 weeks of notification.
CONTACT Calvin Brian Ghanoo, Senior Associate Director of Student Financial Services, Fordham University, 441 East Fordham Road, Thebaud Hall, New York, NY 10458, 718-817-3800 or toll-free 800-FORDHAM. *E-mail:* ghanoo@fordham.edu.

FORT HAYS STATE UNIVERSITY
Hays, KS

Tuition & fees (KS res): $2442	Average undergraduate aid package: $5749

ABOUT THE INSTITUTION State-supported, coed. Awards: associate, bachelor's, and master's degrees and post-master's certificates. 55 undergraduate majors. Total enrollment: 7,373. Undergraduates: 5,920. Freshmen: 904. Federal methodology is used as a basis for awarding need-based institutional aid.
UNDERGRADUATE EXPENSES for 2005–06 *Application fee:* $30. *Tuition, state resident:* full-time $1886; part-time $101.75 per credit hour. *Tuition, nonresident:* full-time $7104; part-time $319.17 per credit hour. Full-time tuition and fees vary according to course load, location, and reciprocity agreements. Part-time tuition and fees vary according to course load and location. *College room and board:* $6190; *room only:* $3577. Room and board charges vary according to board plan, housing facility, and student level. *Payment plan:* Installment.
FRESHMAN FINANCIAL AID (Fall 2004) 597 applied for aid; of those 79% were deemed to have need. 98% of freshmen with need received aid; of those 22% had need fully met. *Average percent of need met:* 64% (excluding resources awarded to replace EFC). *Average financial aid package:* $5345 (excluding resources awarded to replace EFC). 38% of all full-time freshmen had no need and received non-need-based gift aid.
UNDERGRADUATE FINANCIAL AID (Fall 2004) 3,295 applied for aid; of those 82% were deemed to have need. 98% of undergraduates with need received aid; of those 21% had need fully met. *Average percent of need met:* 64% (excluding resources awarded to replace EFC). *Average financial aid package:* $5749 (excluding resources awarded to replace EFC). 29% of all full-time undergraduates had no need and received non-need-based gift aid.
GIFT AID (NEED-BASED) *Total amount:* $7,298,222 (70% federal, 7% state, 7% institutional, 16% external sources). *Receiving aid:* Freshmen: 56% (438); All full-time undergraduates: 53% (2,102). *Average award:* Freshmen: $3401; Undergraduates: $3174. *Scholarships, grants, and awards:* Federal Pell, FSEOG, state, private, college/university gift aid from institutional funds, athletic.
GIFT AID (NON-NEED-BASED) *Total amount:* $1,171,758 (1% federal, 29% institutional, 70% external sources). *Receiving aid:* Freshmen: 5% (39); Undergraduates: 3% (119). *Average Award:* Freshmen: $2030; Undergraduates: $2995. *Scholarships, grants, and awards by category: Academic Interests/Achievement:* agriculture, biological sciences, business, communication, computer science, education, engineering/technologies, English, foreign languages, general academic interests/achievements, health fields, humanities, international studies, library science, mathematics, physical sciences, premedicine, social sciences. *Creative Arts/Performance:* applied art and design, art/fine arts, cinema/film/broadcasting, creative writing, debating, journalism/publications, music, performing arts, theater/drama. *Special Achievements/Activities:* cheerleading/drum major, rodeo. *Special Characteristics:* adult students, members of minority groups. *Tuition waivers:* Full or partial for senior citizens.
LOANS *Student loans:* $17,413,446 (75% need-based, 25% non-need-based). 43% of past graduating class borrowed through all loan programs. *Average indebtedness per student:* $15,077. *Average need-based loan:* Freshmen: $2394; Undergraduates: $3427. *Parent loans:* $388,446 (19% need-based, 81% non-need-based). *Programs:* FFEL (Subsidized and Unsubsidized Stafford, PLUS), Perkins, college/university.
WORK-STUDY *Federal work-study:* Total amount: $663,820; 400 jobs available. *State or other work-study/employment:* Total amount: $128,106 (36% need-based, 64% non-need-based). Part-time jobs available.
ATHLETIC AWARDS Total amount: $933,889 (56% need-based, 44% non-need-based).
APPLYING FOR FINANCIAL AID *Required financial aid forms:* FAFSA, state aid form. *Financial aid deadline (priority):* 3/15. *Notification date:* Continuous beginning 3/15. Students must reply within 3 weeks of notification.
CONTACT Craig Karlin, Director of Financial Assistance, Fort Hays State University, Custer Hall, Room 306, 600 Park Street, Hays, KS 67601, 785-628-4408 or toll-free 800-628-FHSU. *Fax:* 785-628-4014. *E-mail:* finaid@fhsu.edu.

FORT LEWIS COLLEGE
Durango, CO

Tuition & fees (CO res): $5692	Average undergraduate aid package: $6456

ABOUT THE INSTITUTION State-supported, coed. Awards: bachelor's degrees. 56 undergraduate majors. Total enrollment: 3,946. Undergraduates: 3,946. Freshmen: 910. Federal methodology is used as a basis for awarding need-based institutional aid.
UNDERGRADUATE EXPENSES for 2005–06 *Application fee:* $30. *Tuition, state resident:* full-time $4862; part-time $121 per credit hour. *Tuition, nonresident:* full-time $12,870; part-time $643 per credit hour. *Required fees:* full-time $830; $45.75 per credit hour. Full-time tuition and fees vary according to reciprocity agreements. Part-time tuition and fees vary according to course load and reciprocity agreements. *College room and board:* $6160; *room only:* $3258. Room and board charges vary according to board plan and housing facility.
FRESHMAN FINANCIAL AID (Fall 2004) 599 applied for aid; of those 69% were deemed to have need. 98% of freshmen with need received aid; of those 16% had need fully met. *Average percent of need met:* 64% (excluding resources awarded to replace EFC). *Average financial aid package:* $5192 (excluding resources awarded to replace EFC). 8% of all full-time freshmen had no need and received non-need-based gift aid.
UNDERGRADUATE FINANCIAL AID (Fall 2004) 2,346 applied for aid; of those 79% were deemed to have need. 97% of undergraduates with need received aid; of those 16% had need fully met. *Average percent of need met:* 69% (excluding resources awarded to replace EFC). *Average financial aid package:* $6456 (excluding resources awarded to replace EFC). 6% of all full-time undergraduates had no need and received non-need-based gift aid.
GIFT AID (NEED-BASED) *Total amount:* $6,534,480 (65% federal, 13% state, 16% institutional, 6% external sources). *Receiving aid:* Freshmen: 25% (240); All full-time undergraduates: 31% (1,145). *Average award:* Freshmen: $3192; Undergraduates: $3616. *Scholarships, grants, and awards:* Federal Pell, FSEOG, state, private, college/university gift aid from institutional funds.
GIFT AID (NON-NEED-BASED) *Total amount:* $1,164,957 (2% federal, 6% state, 56% institutional, 36% external sources). *Receiving aid:* Freshmen: 19% (181); Undergraduates: 18% (656). *Average Award:* Freshmen: $1547; Undergraduates: $1504. *Scholarships, grants, and awards by category: Academic Interests/Achievement:* 418 awards ($530,747 total): agriculture, area/ethnic studies, biological sciences, business, communication, computer science, education, English, general academic interests/achievements, humanities, mathematics, physical sciences, social sciences. *Creative Arts/Performance:* 53 awards ($27,418 total): art/fine arts, music, performing arts, theater/drama. *Special Achievements/Activities:* 62 awards ($92,493 total): general special achievements/activities, leadership. *Special Characteristics:* 126 awards ($115,171 total): children of faculty/staff, ethnic background, first-generation college students, general special characteristics, handicapped students, international students, local/state students, out-of-state students, veterans' children. *Tuition waivers:* Full or partial for minority students, employees or children of employees.

Fort Lewis College

LOANS *Student loans:* $8,593,653 (77% need-based, 23% non-need-based). 60% of past graduating class borrowed through all loan programs. *Average indebtedness per student:* $16,966. *Average need-based loan:* Freshmen: $2140; Undergraduates: $3180. *Parent loans:* $1,650,121 (68% need-based, 32% non-need-based). *Programs:* FFEL (Subsidized and Unsubsidized Stafford, PLUS), Perkins, college/university.
WORK-STUDY *Federal work-study:* Total amount: $261,817; 177 jobs averaging $2500. *State or other work-study/employment:* Total amount: $780,114 (69% need-based, 31% non-need-based). 179 part-time jobs averaging $2400.
ATHLETIC AWARDS Total amount: $420,576 (40% need-based, 60% non-need-based).
APPLYING FOR FINANCIAL AID *Required financial aid form:* FAFSA. *Financial aid deadline:* Continuous. *Notification date:* Continuous beginning 4/1. Students must reply within 2 weeks of notification.
CONTACT Ms. Elaine Redwine, Director of Financial Aid, Fort Lewis College, 1000 Rim Drive, Durango, CO 81301-3999, 970-247-7464. *Fax:* 970-247-7108. *E-mail:* redwine_e@fortlewis.edu.

FORT VALLEY STATE UNIVERSITY
Fort Valley, GA

CONTACT Financial Aid Director, Fort Valley State University, PO Box 4129, Fort Valley, GA 31030-3298, 478-825-6182 or toll-free 800-248-7343. *Fax:* 478-825-6976.

FRAMINGHAM STATE COLLEGE
Framingham, MA

ABOUT THE INSTITUTION State-supported, coed. Awards: bachelor's and master's degrees and post-bachelor's certificates. 89 undergraduate majors. Total enrollment: 5,874. Undergraduates: 3,772. Freshmen: 670.
GIFT AID (NEED-BASED) *Scholarships, grants, and awards:* Federal Pell, FSEOG, state, college/university gift aid from institutional funds, Federal Nursing.
GIFT AID (NON-NEED-BASED) *Scholarships, grants, and awards by category:* Academic Interests/Achievement: biological sciences, education, general academic interests/achievements, home economics, physical sciences. *Special Characteristics:* children of faculty/staff, children of public servants, children of union members/company employees, local/state students, veterans.
LOANS *Programs:* Federal Direct (Subsidized and Unsubsidized Stafford, PLUS), FFEL (Subsidized and Unsubsidized Stafford, PLUS), Perkins, Federal Nursing, state, college/university.
WORK-STUDY *Federal work-study:* Total amount: $340,000; jobs available.
APPLYING FOR FINANCIAL AID *Required financial aid form:* FAFSA.
CONTACT Financial Aid Office, Framingham State College, 100 State Street, PO Box 9101, Framingham, MA 01701-9101, 508-626-4534. *Fax:* 508-626-4598.

FRANCISCAN UNIVERSITY OF STEUBENVILLE
Steubenville, OH

CONTACT John Herrmann, Director of Student Financial Services, Franciscan University of Steubenville, 1235 University Boulevard, Steubenville, OH 43952-1763, 740-283-6211 or toll-free 800-783-6220. *Fax:* 740-284-5469. *E-mail:* jherrmann@franciscan.edu.

FRANCIS MARION UNIVERSITY
Florence, SC

Tuition & fees (SC res): $5984   **Average undergraduate aid package:** N/A

ABOUT THE INSTITUTION State-supported, coed. Awards: bachelor's and master's degrees. 30 undergraduate majors. Total enrollment: 4,008. Undergraduates: 3,500. Freshmen: 803. Federal methodology is used as a basis for awarding need-based institutional aid.
UNDERGRADUATE EXPENSES for 2005–06 *Application fee:* $30. *Tuition, state resident:* full-time $5849; part-time $292.45 per credit hour. *Tuition, nonresident:* full-time $11,698; part-time $584.90 per credit hour. *Required fees:* full-time $135; $2 per credit hour. Part-time tuition and fees vary according to course load. *College room and board:* $5350; *room only:* $2880. Room and board charges vary according to board plan and housing facility. *Payment plan:* Installment.
FRESHMAN FINANCIAL AID (Fall 2004) 398 applied for aid; of those 83% were deemed to have need. 96% of freshmen with need received aid.
UNDERGRADUATE FINANCIAL AID (Fall 2004) 1,970 applied for aid; of those 78% were deemed to have need. 87% of undergraduates with need received aid.
GIFT AID (NEED-BASED) Total amount: $4,715,936 (87% federal, 13% state). *Receiving aid:* Freshmen: 33% (248); All full-time undergraduates: 34% (1,002). *Scholarships, grants, and awards:* Federal Pell, FSEOG, state, private.
GIFT AID (NON-NEED-BASED) Total amount: $5,782,978 (78% state, 14% institutional, 8% external sources). *Scholarships, grants, and awards by category:* Academic Interests/Achievement: biological sciences, business, education, English, general academic interests/achievements, health fields, humanities, mathematics, premedicine, social sciences. *Creative Arts/Performance:* art/fine arts, music, theater/drama. *Special Achievements/Activities:* cheerleading/drum major. *Special Characteristics:* adult students, children and siblings of alumni, children of faculty/staff, handicapped students, international students, out-of-state students, spouses of deceased or disabled public servants, veterans, veterans' children. *Tuition waivers:* Full or partial for employees or children of employees, senior citizens.
LOANS *Student loans:* $13,905,479 (50% need-based, 50% non-need-based). *Average indebtedness per student:* $19,968. *Parent loans:* $623,998 (100% non-need-based). *Programs:* FFEL (Subsidized and Unsubsidized Stafford, PLUS), Perkins, state.
WORK-STUDY *Federal work-study:* Total amount: $177,672; 132 jobs averaging $1346. *State or other work-study/employment:* Total amount: $496,089 (100% non-need-based). Part-time jobs available.
ATHLETIC AWARDS Total amount: $443,427 (100% non-need-based).
APPLYING FOR FINANCIAL AID *Required financial aid forms:* FAFSA, institution's own form. *Financial aid deadline (priority):* 3/1. *Notification date:* 4/1.
CONTACT Kim Ellisor, Director of Financial Assistance, Francis Marion University, PO Box 100547, Florence, SC 29501-0547, 843-661-1190 or toll-free 800-368-7551.

FRANKLIN AND MARSHALL COLLEGE
Lancaster, PA

Tuition & fees: $32,530   **Average undergraduate aid package:** $24,283

ABOUT THE INSTITUTION Independent, coed. Awards: bachelor's degrees. 38 undergraduate majors. Total enrollment: 2,025. Undergraduates: 2,025. Freshmen: 582. Both federal and institutional methodology are used as a basis for awarding need-based institutional aid.
UNDERGRADUATE EXPENSES for 2005–06 *Application fee:* $50. *Comprehensive fee:* $40,590 includes full-time tuition ($32,480), mandatory fees ($50), and room and board ($8060). *College room only:* $5250. Full-time tuition and fees vary according to reciprocity agreements. Room and board charges vary according to board plan and housing facility. *Part-time tuition:* $4060 per course. Part-time tuition and fees vary according to course load. *Payment plans:* Installment, deferred payment.
FRESHMAN FINANCIAL AID (Fall 2005, est.) 475 applied for aid; of those 77% were deemed to have need. 99% of freshmen with need received aid; of those 100% had need fully met. *Average percent of need met:* 100% (excluding resources awarded to replace EFC). *Average financial aid package:* $25,565 (excluding resources awarded to replace EFC). 24% of all full-time freshmen had no need and received non-need-based gift aid.
UNDERGRADUATE FINANCIAL AID (Fall 2005, est.) 1,446 applied for aid; of those 65% were deemed to have need. 100% of undergraduates with need received aid; of those 99% had need fully met. *Average percent of need met:* 100% (excluding resources awarded to replace EFC). *Average financial aid package:* $24,283 (excluding resources awarded to replace EFC). 24% of all full-time undergraduates had no need and received non-need-based gift aid.
GIFT AID (NEED-BASED) Total amount: $16,233,909 (4% federal, 4% state, 92% institutional). *Receiving aid:* Freshmen: 61% (356); All full-time undergraduates: 45% (891). *Average award:* Freshmen: $20,967; Undergraduates: $19,856. *Scholarships, grants, and awards:* Federal Pell, FSEOG, state, private, college/university gift aid from institutional funds.

GIFT AID (NON-NEED-BASED) *Total amount:* $3,967,002 (92% institutional, 8% external sources). *Receiving aid:* Freshmen: 23% (133); Undergraduates: 22% (433). *Average Award:* Freshmen: $8209; Undergraduates: $8826. *Scholarships, grants, and awards by category: Academic Interests/Achievement:* 670 awards ($5,482,000 total): general academic interests/achievements. *Creative Arts/Performance:* 35 awards ($87,500 total): music. *Special Characteristics:* 56 awards: children of faculty/staff, members of minority groups. *Tuition waivers:* Full or partial for employees or children of employees.
LOANS *Student loans:* $7,075,772 (61% need-based, 39% non-need-based). 61% of past graduating class borrowed through all loan programs. *Average indebtedness per student:* $19,391. *Average need-based loan:* Freshmen: $3507; Undergraduates: $5040. *Parent loans:* $5,152,970 (100% non-need-based). *Programs:* FFEL (Subsidized and Unsubsidized Stafford, PLUS), Perkins, college/university.
WORK-STUDY *Federal work-study:* Total amount: $935,150; jobs available (averaging $1400). *State or other work-study/employment:* Total amount: $800,000 (100% non-need-based). Part-time jobs available.
APPLYING FOR FINANCIAL AID *Required financial aid forms:* FAFSA, institution's own form, CSS Financial Aid PROFILE, noncustodial (divorced/separated) parent's statement, business/farm supplement, federal income tax form(s), W-2 forms. *Financial aid deadline:* 3/1 (priority: 2/1). *Notification date:* 4/1. Students must reply by 5/1.
CONTACT Mr. Christopher K. Hanlon, Director of Student Aid, Franklin and Marshall College, PO Box 3003, Lancaster, PA 17604-3003, 717-291-3991. *Fax:* 717-291-4389. *E-mail:* c_hanlon@admin.fandm.edu.

FRANKLIN COLLEGE
Franklin, IN

ABOUT THE INSTITUTION Independent religious, coed. Awards: bachelor's degrees. 32 undergraduate majors. Total enrollment: 1,003. Undergraduates: 1,003. Freshmen: 273.
GIFT AID (NEED-BASED) *Scholarships, grants, and awards:* Federal Pell, FSEOG, state, private, college/university gift aid from institutional funds.
GIFT AID (NON-NEED-BASED) *Scholarships, grants, and awards by category: Academic Interests/Achievement:* general academic interests/achievements, mathematics. *Creative Arts/Performance:* journalism/publications, music, performing arts, theater/drama. *Special Characteristics:* children and siblings of alumni, children of faculty/staff, ethnic background, local/state students, religious affiliation.
LOANS *Programs:* FFEL (Subsidized and Unsubsidized Stafford, PLUS), Perkins, college/university.
APPLYING FOR FINANCIAL AID *Required financial aid forms:* FAFSA, institution's own form.
CONTACT Richard A. Nash, Director of Financial Aid, Franklin College, 101 Branigin Boulevard, Franklin, IN 46131-2598, 317-738-8075 or toll-free 800-852-0232. *Fax:* 317-738-8072. *E-mail:* rnash@franklincollege.edu.

FRANKLIN PIERCE COLLEGE
Rindge, NH

Tuition & fees: $25,300	Average undergraduate aid package: $16,346

ABOUT THE INSTITUTION Independent, coed. Awards: bachelor's degrees (profile does not reflect significant enrollment at 6 continuing education sites; master's degree is only offered at these sites). 50 undergraduate majors. Total enrollment: 1,635. Undergraduates: 1,635. Freshmen: 507. Federal methodology is used as a basis for awarding need-based institutional aid.
UNDERGRADUATE EXPENSES for 2006–07 *Comprehensive fee:* $33,500 includes full-time tuition ($24,300), mandatory fees ($1000), and room and board ($8200). *College room only:* $4600. *Part-time tuition:* $810 per credit.
FRESHMAN FINANCIAL AID (Fall 2005, est.) 398 applied for aid; of those 87% were deemed to have need. 100% of freshmen with need received aid; of those 11% had need fully met. *Average percent of need met:* 64% (excluding resources awarded to replace EFC). *Average financial aid package:* $15,089 (excluding resources awarded to replace EFC). 19% of all full-time freshmen had no need and received non-need-based gift aid.
UNDERGRADUATE FINANCIAL AID (Fall 2005, est.) 1,306 applied for aid; of those 91% were deemed to have need. 100% of undergraduates with need received aid; of those 11% had need fully met. *Average percent of need met:* 67% (excluding resources awarded to replace EFC). *Average financial aid package:* $16,346 (excluding resources awarded to replace EFC). 19% of all full-time undergraduates had no need and received non-need-based gift aid.
GIFT AID (NEED-BASED) *Total amount:* $12,986,099 (9% federal, 1% state, 89% institutional, 1% external sources). *Receiving aid:* Freshmen: 67% (340); All full-time undergraduates: 73% (1,160). *Average award:* Freshmen: $12,044; Undergraduates: $11,888. *Scholarships, grants, and awards:* Federal Pell, FSEOG, state, private, college/university gift aid from institutional funds, United Negro College Fund.
GIFT AID (NON-NEED-BASED) *Total amount:* $2,665,231 (99% institutional, 1% external sources). *Receiving aid:* Freshmen: 6% (29); Undergraduates: 6% (92). *Average Award:* Freshmen: $10,786; Undergraduates: $11,589. *Scholarships, grants, and awards by category: Academic Interests/Achievement:* 1,330 awards ($9,605,692 total): communication, general academic interests/achievements. *Creative Arts/Performance:* 19 awards ($37,000 total): performing arts, theater/drama. *Special Characteristics:* 218 awards ($1,405,711 total): adult students, children and siblings of alumni, children of current students, children of educators, children of faculty/staff, general special characteristics, international students, local/state students, married students, parents of current students, siblings of current students, spouses of current students. *ROTC:* Army cooperative, Air Force cooperative.
LOANS *Student loans:* $13,444,424 (69% need-based, 31% non-need-based). 80% of past graduating class borrowed through all loan programs. *Average indebtedness per student:* $28,036. *Average need-based loan:* Freshmen: $2875; Undergraduates: $4486. *Parent loans:* $3,888,309 (46% need-based, 54% non-need-based). *Programs:* FFEL (Subsidized and Unsubsidized Stafford, PLUS), Perkins, state.
WORK-STUDY *Federal work-study:* Total amount: $635,492; 758 jobs averaging $1467. *State or other work-study/employment:* Total amount: $300,690 (34% need-based, 66% non-need-based). 183 part-time jobs averaging $2128.
ATHLETIC AWARDS *Total amount:* $1,100,978 (39% need-based, 61% non-need-based).
APPLYING FOR FINANCIAL AID *Required financial aid form:* FAFSA. *Financial aid deadline (priority):* 3/1. *Notification date:* Continuous beginning 4/1. Students must reply within 4 weeks of notification.
CONTACT Kenneth Ferreira, Director of Financial Aid, Franklin Pierce College, College Road, PO Box 60, Rindge, NH 03461-0060, 603-899-4180 or toll-free 800-437-0048. *Fax:* 603-899-4372. *E-mail:* ferreirak@fpc.edu.

FRANKLIN UNIVERSITY
Columbus, OH

CONTACT Ms. Marlowe Collier, Financial Aid Assistant, Franklin University, 201 South Grant Avenue, Columbus, OH 43215-5399, 614-797-4700 or toll-free 877-341-6300. *Fax:* 614-220-8931. *E-mail:* finaid@franklin.edu.

FREED-HARDEMAN UNIVERSITY
Henderson, TN

Tuition & fees: $13,092	Average undergraduate aid package: $10,706

ABOUT THE INSTITUTION Independent religious, coed. Awards: bachelor's and master's degrees and post-master's certificates. 53 undergraduate majors. Total enrollment: 2,030. Undergraduates: 1,500. Freshmen: 374. Federal methodology is used as a basis for awarding need-based institutional aid.
UNDERGRADUATE EXPENSES for 2006–07 *Tuition:* full-time $11,000.
FRESHMAN FINANCIAL AID (Fall 2004) 327 applied for aid; of those 86% were deemed to have need. 99% of freshmen with need received aid; of those 26% had need fully met. *Average percent of need met:* 71% (excluding resources awarded to replace EFC). *Average financial aid package:* $11,621 (excluding resources awarded to replace EFC). 22% of all full-time freshmen had no need and received non-need-based gift aid.
UNDERGRADUATE FINANCIAL AID (Fall 2004) 1,031 applied for aid; of those 85% were deemed to have need. 98% of undergraduates with need received aid; of those 19% had need fully met. *Average percent of need met:* 62% (excluding resources awarded to replace EFC). *Average financial aid package:* $10,706 (excluding resources awarded to replace EFC). 20% of all full-time undergraduates had no need and received non-need-based gift aid.
GIFT AID (NEED-BASED) *Total amount:* $7,730,233 (19% federal, 19% state, 59% institutional, 3% external sources). *Receiving aid:* Freshmen: 71% (269);

Freed-Hardeman University

All full-time undergraduates: 69% (785). *Average award:* Freshmen: $9114; Undergraduates: $7795. *Scholarships, grants, and awards:* Federal Pell, FSEOG, state, private, college/university gift aid from institutional funds.
GIFT AID (NON-NEED-BASED) *Total amount:* $3,090,638 (15% state, 80% institutional, 5% external sources). *Receiving aid:* Freshmen: 16% (59); Undergraduates: 12% (135). *Average Award: Freshmen:* $12,566; *Undergraduates:* $12,850. *Scholarships, grants, and awards by category:* Academic Interests/Achievement: biological sciences, business, computer science, education, engineering/technologies, English, general academic interests/achievements, humanities, mathematics, physical sciences, premedicine, religion/biblical studies. Creative Arts/Performance: art/fine arts, cinema/film/broadcasting, journalism/publications, music, performing arts, theater/drama. Special Achievements/Activities: leadership. Special Characteristics: adult students, children of faculty/staff.
LOANS *Student loans:* $9,774,849 (74% need-based, 26% non-need-based). 81% of past graduating class borrowed through all loan programs. *Average indebtedness per student:* $22,792. *Average need-based loan:* Freshmen: $3270; Undergraduates: $3875. *Parent loans:* $3,278,648 (34% need-based, 66% non-need-based). *Programs:* FFEL (Subsidized and Unsubsidized Stafford, PLUS), Perkins, alternative loans.
WORK-STUDY *Federal work-study:* Total amount: $501,307; jobs available. *State or other work-study/employment:* Part-time jobs available.
APPLYING FOR FINANCIAL AID *Required financial aid form:* FAFSA. *Financial aid deadline (priority):* 3/1. *Notification date:* Continuous beginning 3/1. Students must reply within 4 weeks of notification.
CONTACT Larry Cyr, Director of Financial Aid, Freed-Hardeman University, 158 East Main Street, Henderson, TN 38340-2399, 731-989-6662 or toll-free 800-630-3480. *Fax:* 731-989-6775. *E-mail:* lcyr@fhu.edu.

FREE WILL BAPTIST BIBLE COLLEGE
Nashville, TN

Tuition & fees: $11,166 | **Average undergraduate aid package:** N/A

ABOUT THE INSTITUTION Independent Free Will Baptist, coed. Awards: associate and bachelor's degrees. 12 undergraduate majors. Total enrollment: 377. Undergraduates: 377. Federal methodology is used as a basis for awarding need-based institutional aid.
UNDERGRADUATE EXPENSES for 2006–07 *Application fee:* $35. *Comprehensive fee:* $15,874 includes full-time tuition ($10,470), mandatory fees ($696), and room and board ($4708). *Part-time tuition:* $349 per semester hour.
GIFT AID (NEED-BASED) *Total amount:* $843,141 (39% federal, 4% state, 43% institutional, 14% external sources). *Scholarships, grants, and awards:* Federal Pell, FSEOG, state, private, college/university gift aid from institutional funds.
GIFT AID (NON-NEED-BASED) *Total amount:* $77,425 (100% state). *Scholarships, grants, and awards by category:* Special Characteristics: 46 awards ($100,781 total): children of faculty/staff, international students, married students, relatives of clergy, veterans, veterans' children. *ROTC:* Army cooperative, Air Force cooperative.
LOANS *Student loans:* $1,155,791 (71% need-based, 29% non-need-based). 70% of past graduating class borrowed through all loan programs. *Average indebtedness per student:* $14,509. *Parent loans:* $395,715 (100% non-need-based). *Programs:* FFEL (Subsidized and Unsubsidized Stafford, PLUS), alternative loans.
WORK-STUDY *Federal work-study:* Total amount: $22,359; 16 jobs averaging $1397. *State or other work-study/employment:* Total amount: $130,188 (100% non-need-based). 90 part-time jobs averaging $1447.
APPLYING FOR FINANCIAL AID *Required financial aid forms:* FAFSA, institution's own form. *Financial aid deadline (priority):* 4/15. *Notification date:* Continuous beginning 7/1.
CONTACT Jeff Caudill, Director of Enrollment Services, Free Will Baptist Bible College, 3606 West End Avenue, Nashville, TN 37205, 615-844-5000 or toll-free 800-763-9222. *Fax:* 615-269-6028. *E-mail:* jcaudill@fwbbc.edu.

FRESNO PACIFIC UNIVERSITY
Fresno, CA

Tuition & fees: $20,790 | **Average undergraduate aid package:** $16,919

ABOUT THE INSTITUTION Independent religious, coed. Awards: associate, bachelor's, and master's degrees. 42 undergraduate majors. Total enrollment: 2,371. Undergraduates: 1,492. Freshmen: 212. Federal methodology is used as a basis for awarding need-based institutional aid.
UNDERGRADUATE EXPENSES for 2006–07 *Application fee:* $40. *Comprehensive fee:* $26,780 includes full-time tuition ($20,550), mandatory fees ($240), and room and board ($5990). *Part-time tuition:* $735 per unit.
FRESHMAN FINANCIAL AID (Fall 2004) 178 applied for aid; of those 90% were deemed to have need. 100% of freshmen with need received aid; of those 22% had need fully met. *Average percent of need met:* 82% (excluding resources awarded to replace EFC). *Average financial aid package:* $18,241 (excluding resources awarded to replace EFC). 3% of all full-time freshmen had no need and received non-need-based gift aid.
UNDERGRADUATE FINANCIAL AID (Fall 2004) 1,009 applied for aid; of those 87% were deemed to have need. 100% of undergraduates with need received aid; of those 65% had need fully met. *Average percent of need met:* 85% (excluding resources awarded to replace EFC). *Average financial aid package:* $16,919 (excluding resources awarded to replace EFC). 4% of all full-time undergraduates had no need and received non-need-based gift aid.
GIFT AID (NEED-BASED) *Total amount:* $11,436,835 (16% federal, 40% state, 44% institutional). *Receiving aid:* Freshmen: 90% (161); All full-time undergraduates: 75% (817). *Average award:* Freshmen: $11,812; Undergraduates: $11,488. *Scholarships, grants, and awards:* Federal Pell, FSEOG, state, private, college/university gift aid from institutional funds.
GIFT AID (NON-NEED-BASED) *Total amount:* $955,731 (61% institutional, 39% external sources). *Receiving aid:* Freshmen: 39% (70); Undergraduates: 33% (363). *Average Award: Freshmen:* $917; *Undergraduates:* $789. *Scholarships, grants, and awards by category:* Academic Interests/Achievement: 505 awards ($1,513,656 total): general academic interests/achievements, humanities, religion/biblical studies, social sciences. Creative Arts/Performance: 106 awards ($172,225 total): art/fine arts, journalism/publications, music, theater/drama. Special Achievements/Activities: general special achievements/activities, leadership, memberships, religious involvement. Special Characteristics: children of faculty/staff, ethnic background, international students, members of minority groups, religious affiliation.
LOANS *Student loans:* $20,891,469 (100% need-based). 50% of past graduating class borrowed through all loan programs. *Average indebtedness per student:* $13,334. *Average need-based loan:* Freshmen: $5088; Undergraduates: $4244. *Parent loans:* $685,791 (100% need-based). *Programs:* FFEL (Subsidized and Unsubsidized Stafford, PLUS), Perkins, alternative loans.
WORK-STUDY *Federal work-study:* Total amount: $1,304,651; 463 jobs averaging $2718. *State or other work-study/employment:* Part-time jobs available.
ATHLETIC AWARDS Total amount: $935,866 (100% need-based).
APPLYING FOR FINANCIAL AID *Required financial aid forms:* FAFSA, institution's own form. *Financial aid deadline (priority):* 3/2. *Notification date:* Continuous beginning 2/21. Students must reply by 7/30 or within 3 weeks of notification.
CONTACT Amber Blodgett, Associate Director of Financial Aid, Fresno Pacific University, 1717 South Chestnut Avenue, #2004, Fresno, CA 93702, 559-453-7137 or toll-free 800-660-6089 (in-state). *Fax:* 559-453-5595. *E-mail:* finaid@fresno.edu.

FRIENDS UNIVERSITY
Wichita, KS

Tuition & fees: N/R | **Average undergraduate aid package:** $9673

ABOUT THE INSTITUTION Independent, coed. Awards: associate, bachelor's, and master's degrees. 59 undergraduate majors. Total enrollment: 3,190. Undergraduates: 2,629. Federal methodology is used as a basis for awarding need-based institutional aid.
FRESHMAN FINANCIAL AID (Fall 2005, est.) 286 applied for aid; of those 90% were deemed to have need. 99% of freshmen with need received aid; of those 44% had need fully met. *Average percent of need met:* 66% (excluding resources awarded to replace EFC). *Average financial aid package:* $9501 (excluding resources awarded to replace EFC). 11% of all full-time freshmen had no need and received non-need-based gift aid.
UNDERGRADUATE FINANCIAL AID (Fall 2005, est.) 1,653 applied for aid; of those 92% were deemed to have need. 99% of undergraduates with need received aid; of those 38% had need fully met. *Average percent of need met:* 45% (excluding resources awarded to replace EFC). *Average financial aid*

package: $9673 (excluding resources awarded to replace EFC). 12% of all full-time undergraduates had no need and received non-need-based gift aid.
GIFT AID (NEED-BASED) *Total amount:* $8,342,258 (32% federal, 9% state, 45% institutional, 14% external sources). *Receiving aid:* Freshmen: 54% (204); All full-time undergraduates: 49% (861). *Average award:* Freshmen: $2592; Undergraduates: $2735. *Scholarships, grants, and awards:* Federal Pell, FSEOG, state, private, college/university gift aid from institutional funds.
GIFT AID (NON-NEED-BASED) *Total amount:* $689,561 (53% institutional, 47% external sources). *Receiving aid:* Freshmen: 45% (168); Undergraduates: 54% (943). *Average Award:* Freshmen: $1628; Undergraduates: $1427. *Scholarships, grants, and awards by category:* Academic Interests/Achievement: 785 awards ($2,693,825 total): biological sciences, business, communication, computer science, education, English, foreign languages, general academic interests/achievements, health fields, humanities, mathematics, physical sciences, premedicine, religion/biblical studies, social sciences. *Creative Arts/Performance:* 237 awards ($450,299 total): applied art and design, art/fine arts, dance, music, performing arts, theater/drama. *Special Achievements/Activities:* 114 awards ($54,500 total): leadership. *Special Characteristics:* 102 awards ($35,250 total): children and siblings of alumni, international students, relatives of clergy, religious affiliation.
LOANS *Student loans:* $13,881,920 (51% need-based, 49% non-need-based). 100% of past graduating class borrowed through all loan programs. *Average indebtedness per student:* $17,750. *Average need-based loan:* Freshmen: $2235; Undergraduates: $3480. *Parent loans:* $910,773 (100% non-need-based). *Programs:* FFEL (Subsidized and Unsubsidized Stafford, PLUS), Perkins, college/university.
WORK-STUDY *Federal work-study:* Total amount: $267,548; 239 jobs averaging $1221. *State or other work-study/employment:* Total amount: $453,373 (100% non-need-based). 185 part-time jobs averaging $1608.
ATHLETIC AWARDS *Total amount:* $893,303 (100% non-need-based).
APPLYING FOR FINANCIAL AID *Required financial aid forms:* FAFSA, institution's own form. *Financial aid deadline (priority):* 3/15. *Notification date:* Continuous beginning 3/1. Students must reply within 3 weeks of notification.
CONTACT Brandon Pierce, Director of Financial Aid, Friends University, 2100 University Street, Wichita, KS 67213, 316-295-5658 or toll-free 800-577-2233. *Fax:* 316-295-5703. *E-mail:* piercb@friends.edu.

FROSTBURG STATE UNIVERSITY
Frostburg, MD

Tuition & fees (MD res): $6616 **Average undergraduate aid package: $6906**

ABOUT THE INSTITUTION State-supported, coed. Awards: bachelor's and master's degrees and post-bachelor's and post-master's certificates. 46 undergraduate majors. Total enrollment: 5,041. Undergraduates: 4,321. Freshmen: 929. Both federal and institutional methodology are used as a basis for awarding need-based institutional aid.
UNDERGRADUATE EXPENSES for 2006–07 *Application fee:* $30. *Tuition, state resident:* full-time $5224; part-time $216 per credit hour. *Tuition, nonresident:* full-time $14,050; part-time $396 per credit hour. *Required fees:* full-time $1392; $67 per credit hour or $9 per term part-time. *College room and board:* $6442; *room only:* $3132.
FRESHMAN FINANCIAL AID (Fall 2005, est.) 742 applied for aid; of those 68% were deemed to have need. 100% of freshmen with need received aid; of those 22% had need fully met. *Average percent of need met:* 66% (excluding resources awarded to replace EFC). *Average financial aid package:* $6637 (excluding resources awarded to replace EFC). 15% of all full-time freshmen had no need and received non-need-based gift aid.
UNDERGRADUATE FINANCIAL AID (Fall 2005, est.) 2,969 applied for aid; of those 68% were deemed to have need. 100% of undergraduates with need received aid; of those 26% had need fully met. *Average percent of need met:* 71% (excluding resources awarded to replace EFC). *Average financial aid package:* $6906 (excluding resources awarded to replace EFC). 10% of all full-time undergraduates had no need and received non-need-based gift aid.
GIFT AID (NEED-BASED) *Total amount:* $6,944,245 (42% federal, 40% state, 12% institutional, 6% external sources). *Receiving aid:* Freshmen: 42% (407); All full-time undergraduates: 36% (1,514). *Average award:* Freshmen: $4439; Undergraduates: $4075. *Scholarships, grants, and awards:* Federal Pell, FSEOG, state, private, college/university gift aid from institutional funds.

GIFT AID (NON-NEED-BASED) *Total amount:* $3,717,132 (19% state, 47% institutional, 34% external sources). *Receiving aid:* Freshmen: 20% (190); Undergraduates: 13% (548). *Average Award:* Freshmen: $2142; Undergraduates: $2452. *Scholarships, grants, and awards by category:* Academic Interests/Achievement: 543 awards ($1,087,500 total): biological sciences, business, communication, computer science, education, engineering/technologies, English, foreign languages, general academic interests/achievements, health fields, humanities, international studies, mathematics, physical sciences, premedicine, social sciences. *Creative Arts/Performance:* 79 awards ($83,000 total): art/fine arts, creative writing, dance, journalism/publications, music, performing arts, theater/drama. *Special Achievements/Activities:* 59 awards ($23,350 total): community service, leadership. *Special Characteristics:* 243 awards ($154,427 total): adult students, children and siblings of alumni, children of union members/company employees, international students, local/state students, out-of-state students, veterans, veterans' children.
LOANS *Student loans:* $12,297,533 (45% need-based, 55% non-need-based). 61% of past graduating class borrowed through all loan programs. *Average indebtedness per student:* $15,678. *Average need-based loan:* Freshmen: $2237; Undergraduates: $3320. *Parent loans:* $4,217,375 (100% non-need-based). *Programs:* FFEL (Subsidized and Unsubsidized Stafford, PLUS), Perkins.
WORK-STUDY *Federal work-study:* Total amount: $69,153; 179 jobs averaging $386. *State or other work-study/employment:* Total amount: $268,981 (100% non-need-based). 518 part-time jobs averaging $519.
APPLYING FOR FINANCIAL AID *Required financial aid form:* FAFSA. *Financial aid deadline (priority):* 3/1. *Notification date:* Continuous beginning 3/15. Students must reply within 3 weeks of notification.
CONTACT Mrs. Angela Hovatter, Director of Financial Aid, Frostburg State University, 101 Braddock Road, Frostburg, MD 21532-1099, 301-687-4301. *Fax:* 301-687-7074.

FURMAN UNIVERSITY
Greenville, SC

Tuition & fees: $26,352 **Average undergraduate aid package: $22,162**

ABOUT THE INSTITUTION Independent, coed. Awards: bachelor's and master's degrees and post-bachelor's certificates. 48 undergraduate majors. Total enrollment: 3,221. Undergraduates: 2,804. Freshmen: 689. Both federal and institutional methodology are used as a basis for awarding need-based institutional aid.
UNDERGRADUATE EXPENSES for 2005–06 *Application fee:* $40. *Comprehensive fee:* $33,264 includes full-time tuition ($25,888), mandatory fees ($464), and room and board ($6912). *College room only:* $3712. Room and board charges vary according to board plan and housing facility. *Part-time tuition:* $809 per credit hour. Part-time tuition and fees vary according to course load. *Payment plan:* Installment.
FRESHMAN FINANCIAL AID (Fall 2005, est.) 406 applied for aid; of those 71% were deemed to have need. 100% of freshmen with need received aid; of those 45% had need fully met. *Average percent of need met:* 91% (excluding resources awarded to replace EFC). *Average financial aid package:* $24,047 (excluding resources awarded to replace EFC). 33% of all full-time freshmen had no need and received non-need-based gift aid.
UNDERGRADUATE FINANCIAL AID (Fall 2005, est.) 1,473 applied for aid; of those 80% were deemed to have need. 100% of undergraduates with need received aid; of those 43% had need fully met. *Average percent of need met:* 86% (excluding resources awarded to replace EFC). *Average financial aid package:* $22,162 (excluding resources awarded to replace EFC). 28% of all full-time undergraduates had no need and received non-need-based gift aid.
GIFT AID (NEED-BASED) *Total amount:* $15,722,925 (8% federal, 8% state, 79% institutional, 5% external sources). *Receiving aid:* Freshmen: 42% (289); All full-time undergraduates: 44% (1,179). *Average award:* Freshmen: $21,735; Undergraduates: $18,486. *Scholarships, grants, and awards:* Federal Pell, FSEOG, state, private, college/university gift aid from institutional funds.
GIFT AID (NON-NEED-BASED) *Total amount:* $14,263,517 (26% state, 66% institutional, 8% external sources). *Receiving aid:* Freshmen: 35% (241); Undergraduates: 37% (1,000). *Average Award:* Freshmen: $10,830; Undergraduates: $10,198. *Scholarships, grants, and awards by category:* Academic Interests/Achievement: 1,241 awards ($13,232,902 total): area/ethnic studies, biological sciences, business, communication, computer science, education, engineering/technologies, English, foreign languages, general academic interests/achievements, health fields, humanities, international studies, mathematics, military science, physical sciences, premedicine, religion/biblical studies, social

Furman University

sciences. *Creative Arts/Performance:* 193 awards ($1,088,704 total): art/fine arts, creative writing, music, theater/drama. *Special Achievements/Activities:* 24 awards ($114,646 total): community service, leadership, religious involvement. *Special Characteristics:* 1,034 awards ($6,833,955 total): children of faculty/staff, ethnic background, international students, local/state students, relatives of clergy, religious affiliation, veterans. *Tuition waivers:* Full or partial for employees or children of employees. *ROTC:* Army.

LOANS *Student loans:* $7,914,489 (83% need-based, 17% non-need-based). 38% of past graduating class borrowed through all loan programs. *Average indebtedness per student:* $21,860. *Average need-based loan:* Freshmen: $1705; Undergraduates: $3096. *Parent loans:* $3,184,727 (58% need-based, 42% non-need-based). *Programs:* FFEL (Subsidized and Unsubsidized Stafford, PLUS), Perkins, state, alternative loans.

WORK-STUDY *Federal work-study:* Total amount: $685,285; 442 jobs averaging $1550.

ATHLETIC AWARDS *Total amount:* $5,303,820 (40% need-based, 60% non-need-based).

APPLYING FOR FINANCIAL AID *Required financial aid forms:* FAFSA, institution's own form, state aid form, South Carolina residents must complete required SC forms. *Financial aid deadline:* 1/15. *Notification date:* 3/15. Students must reply by 5/1.

CONTACT Martin Carney, Director of Financial Aid, Furman University, 3300 Poinsett Highway, Greenville, SC 29613, 864-294-2204. *Fax:* 864-294-3127. *E-mail:* martin.carney@furman.edu.

GALLAUDET UNIVERSITY
Washington, DC

Tuition & fees: $10,250 | **Average undergraduate aid package: $14,284**

ABOUT THE INSTITUTION Independent, coed. Awards: bachelor's, master's, and doctoral degrees and post-bachelor's certificates (undergraduate programs are open primarily to the hearing-impaired). 52 undergraduate majors. Total enrollment: 1,834. Undergraduates: 1,207. Freshmen: 227. Federal methodology is used as a basis for awarding need-based institutional aid.

UNDERGRADUATE EXPENSES for 2005–06 *Application fee:* $50. *Comprehensive fee:* $18,750 includes full-time tuition ($9920), mandatory fees ($330), and room and board ($8500). *College room only:* $4850. Room and board charges vary according to board plan. *Part-time tuition:* $481.50 per credit. *Payment plan:* Installment.

FRESHMAN FINANCIAL AID (Fall 2005, est.) 202 applied for aid; of those 86% were deemed to have need. 98% of freshmen with need received aid; of those 38% had need fully met. *Average percent of need met:* 83% (excluding resources awarded to replace EFC). *Average financial aid package:* $14,806 (excluding resources awarded to replace EFC). 5% of all full-time freshmen had no need and received non-need-based gift aid.

UNDERGRADUATE FINANCIAL AID (Fall 2005, est.) 1,033 applied for aid; of those 90% were deemed to have need. 94% of undergraduates with need received aid; of those 34% had need fully met. *Average percent of need met:* 75% (excluding resources awarded to replace EFC). *Average financial aid package:* $14,284 (excluding resources awarded to replace EFC). 1% of all full-time undergraduates had no need and received non-need-based gift aid.

GIFT AID (NEED-BASED) *Total amount:* $10,301,502 (14% federal, 63% state, 21% institutional, 2% external sources). *Receiving aid:* Freshmen: 70% (169); All full-time undergraduates: 65% (852). *Average award:* Freshmen: $13,874; Undergraduates: $12,969. *Scholarships, grants, and awards:* Federal Pell, FSEOG, state, private, college/university gift aid from institutional funds.

GIFT AID (NON-NEED-BASED) *Total amount:* $1,703,763 (82% state, 16% institutional, 2% external sources). *Receiving aid:* Freshmen: 24% (58); Undergraduates: 20% (265). *Average Award:* Freshmen: $3785; Undergraduates: $4323. *Scholarships, grants, and awards by category:* Academic Interests/Achievement: general academic interests/achievements. *Special Characteristics:* children of educators, children of faculty/staff, handicapped students, international students. *Tuition waivers:* Full or partial for employees or children of employees.

LOANS *Student loans:* $2,032,096 (92% need-based, 8% non-need-based). 59% of past graduating class borrowed through all loan programs. *Average indebtedness per student:* $14,071. *Average need-based loan:* Freshmen: $2156; Undergraduates: $2926. *Parent loans:* $468,754 (76% need-based, 24% non-need-based). *Programs:* FFEL (Subsidized and Unsubsidized Stafford, PLUS), Perkins.

WORK-STUDY *Federal work-study:* Total amount: $42,199; 46 jobs averaging $1229.

APPLYING FOR FINANCIAL AID *Required financial aid forms:* FAFSA, institution's own form. *Financial aid deadline (priority):* 7/1. *Notification date:* Continuous beginning 4/1. Students must reply within 4 weeks of notification.

CONTACT Mrs. Nancy C. Goodman, Director of Financial Aid, Gallaudet University, 800 Florida Avenue, NE, Washington, DC 20002-3695, 202-651-5290 or toll-free 800-995-0550 (out-of-state). *Fax:* 202-651-5740.

GANNON UNIVERSITY
Erie, PA

Tuition & fees: $18,690 | **Average undergraduate aid package: $15,226**

ABOUT THE INSTITUTION Independent Roman Catholic, coed. Awards: bachelor's, master's, and doctoral degrees and post-bachelor's and post-master's certificates (associate). 65 undergraduate majors. Total enrollment: 3,590. Undergraduates: 2,574. Freshmen: 632. Federal methodology is used as a basis for awarding need-based institutional aid.

UNDERGRADUATE EXPENSES for 2005–06 *Application fee:* $25. *Comprehensive fee:* $26,100 includes full-time tuition ($18,220), mandatory fees ($470), and room and board ($7410). *College room only:* $4020. Full-time tuition and fees vary according to class time and program. Room and board charges vary according to board plan and housing facility. *Part-time tuition:* $565 per credit hour. *Part-time fees:* $15 per credit hour. Part-time tuition and fees vary according to class time and program. *Payment plans:* Installment, deferred payment.

FRESHMAN FINANCIAL AID (Fall 2005, est.) 597 applied for aid; of those 90% were deemed to have need. 100% of freshmen with need received aid; of those 19% had need fully met. *Average percent of need met:* 75% (excluding resources awarded to replace EFC). *Average financial aid package:* $15,454 (excluding resources awarded to replace EFC). 10% of all full-time freshmen had no need and received non-need-based gift aid.

UNDERGRADUATE FINANCIAL AID (Fall 2005, est.) 2,053 applied for aid; of those 91% were deemed to have need. 99% of undergraduates with need received aid; of those 18% had need fully met. *Average percent of need met:* 72% (excluding resources awarded to replace EFC). *Average financial aid package:* $15,226 (excluding resources awarded to replace EFC). 10% of all full-time undergraduates had no need and received non-need-based gift aid.

GIFT AID (NEED-BASED) *Total amount:* $23,676,898 (11% federal, 30% state, 55% institutional, 4% external sources). *Receiving aid:* Freshmen: 85% (527); All full-time undergraduates: 83% (1,821). *Average award:* Freshmen: $12,687; Undergraduates: $11,609. *Scholarships, grants, and awards:* Federal Pell, FSEOG, state, private, college/university gift aid from institutional funds, Federal Nursing.

GIFT AID (NON-NEED-BASED) *Total amount:* $1,782,419 (94% institutional, 6% external sources). *Receiving aid:* Freshmen: 10% (63); Undergraduates: 9% (200). *Average Award:* Freshmen: $6764; Undergraduates: $6260. *Scholarships, grants, and awards by category:* Academic Interests/Achievement: 1,579 awards ($5,885,842 total): biological sciences, business, education, engineering/technologies, English, foreign languages, general academic interests/achievements, international studies, mathematics, premedicine, religion/biblical studies. *Creative Arts/Performance:* 71 awards ($117,250 total): music, theater/drama. *Special Achievements/Activities:* 1,434 awards ($2,063,861 total): community service, leadership. *Special Characteristics:* 572 awards ($627,240 total): adult students, ethnic background, international students, members of minority groups, religious affiliation. *Tuition waivers:* Full or partial for employees or children of employees, senior citizens. *ROTC:* Army.

LOANS *Student loans:* $10,150,323 (65% need-based, 35% non-need-based). 75% of past graduating class borrowed through all loan programs. *Average indebtedness per student:* $24,148. *Average need-based loan:* Freshmen: $2182; Undergraduates: $3728. *Parent loans:* $2,862,018 (100% non-need-based). *Programs:* Federal Direct (Subsidized and Unsubsidized Stafford, PLUS), FFEL (Subsidized and Unsubsidized Stafford, PLUS), Perkins, Federal Nursing.

WORK-STUDY *Federal work-study:* Total amount: $651,695; 549 jobs averaging $1187. *State or other work-study/employment:* Total amount: $276,885 (100% non-need-based). 254 part-time jobs averaging $1090.

ATHLETIC AWARDS *Total amount:* $2,518,812 (73% need-based, 27% non-need-based).
APPLYING FOR FINANCIAL AID *Required financial aid forms:* FAFSA, institution's own form. *Financial aid deadline (priority):* 3/15. *Notification date:* Continuous beginning 11/1. Students must reply within 4 weeks of notification.
CONTACT Ms. Sharon Krahe, Director of Financial Aid, Gannon University, 109 University Square, Erie, PA 16541, 814-871-7670 or toll-free 800-GANNONU. *Fax:* 814-871-5826. *E-mail:* krahe001@gannon.edu.

GARDNER-WEBB UNIVERSITY
Boiling Springs, NC

CONTACT Ms. Cindy Wallace, Assistant Director of Financial Planning, Gardner-Webb University, PO Box 955, Boiling Springs, NC 28017, 704-406-4243 or toll-free 800-253-6472. *Fax:* 704-406-4102. *E-mail:* cwallace@gardner-webb.edu.

GENEVA COLLEGE
Beaver Falls, PA

Tuition & fees: $17,475   **Average undergraduate aid package:** $13,360

ABOUT THE INSTITUTION Independent religious, coed. Awards: associate, bachelor's, and master's degrees. 38 undergraduate majors. Total enrollment: 2,141. Undergraduates: 1,809. Both federal and institutional methodology are used as a basis for awarding need-based institutional aid.
UNDERGRADUATE EXPENSES for 2005–06 *Application fee:* $25. *Comprehensive fee:* $24,245 includes full-time tuition ($16,910), mandatory fees ($565), and room and board ($6770). *College room only:* $3530. Full-time tuition and fees vary according to course load. Room and board charges vary according to board plan and housing facility. *Part-time tuition:* $565 per credit. Part-time tuition and fees vary according to course load. *Payment plan:* Installment.
FRESHMAN FINANCIAL AID (Fall 2005, est.) 319 applied for aid; of those 87% were deemed to have need. 100% of freshmen with need received aid; of those 19% had need fully met. *Average percent of need met:* 76% (excluding resources awarded to replace EFC). *Average financial aid package:* $13,822 (excluding resources awarded to replace EFC). 13% of all full-time freshmen had no need and received non-need-based gift aid.
UNDERGRADUATE FINANCIAL AID (Fall 2005, est.) 1,210 applied for aid; of those 91% were deemed to have need. 100% of undergraduates with need received aid; of those 23% had need fully met. *Average percent of need met:* 77% (excluding resources awarded to replace EFC). *Average financial aid package:* $13,360 (excluding resources awarded to replace EFC). 15% of all full-time undergraduates had no need and received non-need-based gift aid.
GIFT AID (NEED-BASED) *Total amount:* $9,713,059 (14% federal, 21% state, 60% institutional, 5% external sources). *Receiving aid:* Freshmen: 86% (275); All full-time undergraduates: 82% (1,082). *Average award:* Freshmen: $10,284; Undergraduates: $9647. *Scholarships, grants, and awards:* Federal Pell, FSEOG, state, private, college/university gift aid from institutional funds.
GIFT AID (NON-NEED-BASED) *Total amount:* $1,268,758 (7% state, 86% institutional, 7% external sources). *Receiving aid:* Freshmen: 8% (25); Undergraduates: 9% (122). *Average Award:* Freshmen: $9354; Undergraduates: $8558. *Scholarships, grants, and awards by category:* Academic Interests/Achievement: engineering/technologies, general academic interests/achievements, religion/biblical studies. Creative Arts/Performance: music. Special Characteristics: children of faculty/staff, relatives of clergy, religious affiliation. *Tuition waivers:* Full or partial for minority students, employees or children of employees. *ROTC:* Army cooperative.
LOANS *Student loans:* $8,417,507 (67% need-based, 33% non-need-based). 91% of past graduating class borrowed through all loan programs. *Average indebtedness per student:* $23,425. *Average need-based loan:* Freshmen: $3106; Undergraduates: $3634. *Parent loans:* $1,575,020 (41% need-based, 59% non-need-based). *Programs:* FFEL (Subsidized and Unsubsidized Stafford, PLUS), Perkins.
WORK-STUDY *Federal work-study:* Total amount: $720,608; jobs available (averaging $2000).
ATHLETIC AWARDS *Total amount:* $787,483 (76% need-based, 24% non-need-based).

APPLYING FOR FINANCIAL AID *Required financial aid form:* FAFSA. *Financial aid deadline (priority):* 3/15. *Notification date:* Continuous. Students must reply within 4 weeks of notification.
CONTACT Mr. Steve Bell, Director of Financial Aid, Geneva College, 3200 College Avenue, Beaver Falls, PA 15010-3599, 800-847-8255. *Fax:* 724-847-6776. *E-mail:* financialaid@geneva.edu.

GEORGE FOX UNIVERSITY
Newberg, OR

CONTACT Associate Director of Financial Aid, George Fox University, 414 North Meridian, Newberg, OR 97132-2697, 503-554-2235 or toll-free 800-765-4369. *Fax:* 503-554-3880.

GEORGE MASON UNIVERSITY
Fairfax, VA

Tuition & fees (VA res): $5880   **Average undergraduate aid package:** $7878

ABOUT THE INSTITUTION State-supported, coed. Awards: bachelor's, master's, doctoral, and first professional degrees and post-bachelor's certificates. 47 undergraduate majors. Total enrollment: 29,728. Undergraduates: 18,091. Freshmen: 2,529. Federal methodology is used as a basis for awarding need-based institutional aid.
UNDERGRADUATE EXPENSES for 2005–06 *Application fee:* $60. *Tuition, state resident:* full-time $4356; part-time $181.50 per credit. *Tuition, nonresident:* full-time $15,636; part-time $651.50 per credit. *Required fees:* full-time $1524; $63.50 per credit. Full-time tuition and fees vary according to course load. Part-time tuition and fees vary according to course load. *College room and board:* $6480; *room only:* $3700. Room and board charges vary according to board plan and housing facility. *Payment plans:* Installment, deferred payment.
FRESHMAN FINANCIAL AID (Fall 2004) 1380 applied for aid; of those 67% were deemed to have need. 94% of freshmen with need received aid; of those 10% had need fully met. *Average percent of need met:* 64% (excluding resources awarded to replace EFC). *Average financial aid package:* $7518 (excluding resources awarded to replace EFC). 9% of all full-time freshmen had no need and received non-need-based gift aid.
UNDERGRADUATE FINANCIAL AID (Fall 2004) 6,833 applied for aid; of those 75% were deemed to have need. 96% of undergraduates with need received aid; of those 14% had need fully met. *Average percent of need met:* 70% (excluding resources awarded to replace EFC). *Average financial aid package:* $7878 (excluding resources awarded to replace EFC). 5% of all full-time undergraduates had no need and received non-need-based gift aid.
GIFT AID (NEED-BASED) *Total amount:* $17,434,524 (49% federal, 45% state, 6% institutional). *Receiving aid:* Freshmen: 30% (656); All full-time undergraduates: 28% (3,649). *Average award:* Freshmen: $4708; Undergraduates: $4363. *Scholarships, grants, and awards:* Federal Pell, FSEOG, state, private, college/university gift aid from institutional funds.
GIFT AID (NON-NEED-BASED) *Total amount:* $4,385,464 (40% institutional, 60% external sources). *Receiving aid:* Freshmen: 12% (256); Undergraduates: 5% (677). *Average Award:* Freshmen: $3964; Undergraduates: $4084. *Scholarships, grants, and awards by category:* Academic Interests/Achievement: 595 awards ($1,759,661 total): general academic interests/achievements. Creative Arts/Performance: general creative arts/performance. Special Characteristics: general special characteristics. *Tuition waivers:* Full or partial for employees or children of employees, senior citizens. *ROTC:* Army, Air Force cooperative.
LOANS *Student loans:* $34,738,436 (66% need-based, 34% non-need-based). 47% of past graduating class borrowed through all loan programs. *Average indebtedness per student:* $13,607. *Average need-based loan:* Freshmen: $2787; Undergraduates: $3956. *Parent loans:* $7,260,697 (28% need-based, 72% non-need-based). *Programs:* FFEL (Subsidized and Unsubsidized Stafford, PLUS), Perkins, Federal Nursing.
WORK-STUDY *Federal work-study:* Total amount: $901,183; 377 jobs averaging $2387.
ATHLETIC AWARDS *Total amount:* $2,568,917 (100% non-need-based).
APPLYING FOR FINANCIAL AID *Required financial aid form:* FAFSA. *Financial aid deadline (priority):* 3/1. *Notification date:* Continuous beginning 4/1. Students must reply within 3 weeks of notification.

George Mason University

CONTACT Office of Student Financial Aid, George Mason University, Mail Stop 3B5, Fairfax, VA 22030-4444, 703-993-2353. *Fax:* 703-993-2350. *E-mail:* finaid@gmu.edu.

GEORGE MEANY CENTER FOR LABOR STUDIES-THE NATIONAL LABOR COLLEGE
Silver Spring, MD

CONTACT Financial Aid Office, George Meany Center for Labor Studies-The National Labor College, 10000 New Hampshire Avenue, Silver Spring, MD 20903, 301-431-6400 or toll-free 800-GMC-4CDP.

GEORGETOWN COLLEGE
Georgetown, KY

Tuition & fees: $20,700 — **Average undergraduate aid package: $17,844**

ABOUT THE INSTITUTION Independent religious, coed. Awards: bachelor's and master's degrees and post-master's certificates. 32 undergraduate majors. Total enrollment: 1,904. Undergraduates: 1,365. Freshmen: 416. Federal methodology is used as a basis for awarding need-based institutional aid.
UNDERGRADUATE EXPENSES for 2006–07 *Application fee:* $30. *Comprehensive fee:* $26,770 includes full-time tuition ($20,700) and room and board ($6070). *College room only:* $2940. *Part-time tuition:* $860 per hour.
FRESHMAN FINANCIAL AID (Fall 2005, est.) 353 applied for aid; of those 76% were deemed to have need. 100% of freshmen with need received aid; of those 59% had need fully met. *Average percent of need met:* 91% (excluding resources awarded to replace EFC). *Average financial aid package:* $18,350 (excluding resources awarded to replace EFC). 35% of all full-time freshmen had no need and received non-need-based gift aid.
UNDERGRADUATE FINANCIAL AID (Fall 2005, est.) 1,043 applied for aid; of those 83% were deemed to have need. 100% of undergraduates with need received aid; of those 59% had need fully met. *Average percent of need met:* 92% (excluding resources awarded to replace EFC). *Average financial aid package:* $17,844 (excluding resources awarded to replace EFC). 32% of all full-time undergraduates had no need and received non-need-based gift aid.
GIFT AID (NEED-BASED) *Total amount:* $10,221,970 (9% federal, 19% state, 68% institutional, 4% external sources). *Receiving aid:* Freshmen: 64% (268); All full-time undergraduates: 66% (862). *Average award:* Freshmen: $14,359; Undergraduates: $13,703. *Scholarships, grants, and awards:* Federal Pell, FSEOG, state, private, college/university gift aid from institutional funds.
GIFT AID (NON-NEED-BASED) *Total amount:* $5,597,682 (32% state, 65% institutional, 3% external sources). *Receiving aid:* Freshmen: 20% (83); Undergraduates: 16% (206). *Average Award:* Freshmen: $9139; Undergraduates: $8581. *Scholarships, grants, and awards by category:* Academic Interests/Achievement: 726 awards ($5,256,349 total): general academic interests/achievements. Creative Arts/Performance: 153 awards ($184,844 total): art/fine arts, music, performing arts, theater/drama. Special Achievements/Activities: 260 awards ($393,771 total): junior miss, leadership, religious involvement. Special Characteristics: 297 awards ($512,343 total): children of faculty/staff, local/state students, relatives of clergy, religious affiliation. *ROTC:* Army cooperative, Air Force cooperative.
LOANS *Student loans:* $4,418,856 (48% need-based, 52% non-need-based). 69% of past graduating class borrowed through all loan programs. *Average indebtedness per student:* $15,018. *Average need-based loan:* Freshmen: $3284; Undergraduates: $4145. *Parent loans:* $1,615,754 (100% non-need-based). *Programs:* FFEL (Subsidized and Unsubsidized Stafford, PLUS), Perkins, college/university.
WORK-STUDY *Federal work-study:* Total amount: $549,730; 505 jobs averaging $1074. *State or other work-study/employment:* Part-time jobs available.
ATHLETIC AWARDS *Total amount:* $1,123,886 (51% need-based, 49% non-need-based).
APPLYING FOR FINANCIAL AID *Required financial aid form:* FAFSA. *Financial aid deadline (priority):* 2/15. *Notification date:* Continuous beginning 3/15. Students must reply by 5/1.
CONTACT Rhyan Conyers, Director of Financial Planning, Georgetown College, 400 East College Street, Georgetown, KY 40324-1696, 502-863-8027 or toll-free 800-788-9985. *E-mail:* financialaid@georgetowncollege.edu.

GEORGETOWN UNIVERSITY
Washington, DC

Tuition & fees: $32,024 — **Average undergraduate aid package: $25,600**

ABOUT THE INSTITUTION Independent Roman Catholic (Jesuit), coed. Awards: bachelor's, master's, doctoral, and first professional degrees. 46 undergraduate majors. Total enrollment: 13,652. Undergraduates: 6,719. Freshmen: 1,551. Both federal and institutional methodology are used as a basis for awarding need-based institutional aid.
UNDERGRADUATE EXPENSES for 2005–06 *Application fee:* $60. *Comprehensive fee:* $43,183 includes full-time tuition ($31,656), mandatory fees ($368), and room and board ($11,159). *College room only:* $7410. Room and board charges vary according to board plan and housing facility. *Part-time tuition:* $1319 per credit hour. Part-time tuition and fees vary according to course level. *Payment plans:* Installment, deferred payment.
FRESHMAN FINANCIAL AID (Fall 2005, est.) 862 applied for aid; of those 75% were deemed to have need. 99% of freshmen with need received aid; of those 100% had need fully met. *Average percent of need met:* 100% (excluding resources awarded to replace EFC). *Average financial aid package:* $27,000 (excluding resources awarded to replace EFC).
UNDERGRADUATE FINANCIAL AID (Fall 2005, est.) 3,043 applied for aid; of those 86% were deemed to have need. 99% of undergraduates with need received aid; of those 100% had need fully met. *Average percent of need met:* 100% (excluding resources awarded to replace EFC). *Average financial aid package:* $25,600 (excluding resources awarded to replace EFC). 1% of all full-time undergraduates had no need and received non-need-based gift aid.
GIFT AID (NEED-BASED) *Total amount:* $53,680,000 (7% federal, 88% institutional, 5% external sources). *Receiving aid:* Freshmen: 41% (627); All full-time undergraduates: 37% (2,319). *Average award:* Freshmen: $23,000; Undergraduates: $19,300. *Scholarships, grants, and awards:* Federal Pell, FSEOG, state, private, college/university gift aid from institutional funds.
GIFT AID (NON-NEED-BASED) *Total amount:* $2,400,000 (50% federal, 50% external sources). *Receiving aid:* Freshmen: 7; Undergraduates: 21. *Average Award:* Undergraduates: $30,730. *Scholarships, grants, and awards by category:* Special Characteristics: children of faculty/staff. *Tuition waivers:* Full or partial for employees or children of employees. *ROTC:* Army, Naval cooperative, Air Force cooperative.
LOANS *Student loans:* $19,500,000 (55% need-based, 45% non-need-based). 45% of past graduating class borrowed through all loan programs. *Average indebtedness per student:* $23,700. *Average need-based loan:* Freshmen: $1800; Undergraduates: $3600. *Parent loans:* $16,300,000 (100% non-need-based). *Programs:* FFEL (Subsidized and Unsubsidized Stafford, PLUS), Perkins, Federal Nursing.
WORK-STUDY *Federal work-study:* Total amount: $5,500,000; 1,835 jobs averaging $3000.
ATHLETIC AWARDS *Total amount:* $4,100,000 (27% need-based, 73% non-need-based).
APPLYING FOR FINANCIAL AID *Required financial aid forms:* FAFSA, CSS Financial Aid PROFILE, noncustodial (divorced/separated) parent's statement, business/farm supplement. *Financial aid deadline:* 2/1. *Notification date:* 4/1. Students must reply by 5/1 or within 2 weeks of notification.
CONTACT Ms. Patricia A. McWade, Dean of Student Financial Services, Georgetown University, 37th and O Street, NW, Box 1252, Washington, DC 20057, 202-687-4547. *Fax:* 202-687-6542. *E-mail:* mcwadep@georgetown.edu.

THE GEORGE WASHINGTON UNIVERSITY
Washington, DC

ABOUT THE INSTITUTION Independent, coed. Awards: associate, bachelor's, master's, doctoral, and first professional degrees and post-bachelor's and post-master's certificates. 79 undergraduate majors. Total enrollment: 24,099. Undergraduates: 10,761. Freshmen: 2,413.
GIFT AID (NEED-BASED) *Scholarships, grants, and awards:* Federal Pell, FSEOG, state, college/university gift aid from institutional funds.
GIFT AID (NON-NEED-BASED) *Scholarships, grants, and awards by category:* Academic Interests/Achievement: engineering/technologies, general academic interests/achievements, mathematics. Creative Arts/Performance: debating, music, performing arts, theater/drama.
LOANS *Programs:* FFEL (Subsidized and Unsubsidized Stafford, PLUS), Perkins.

APPLYING FOR FINANCIAL AID *Required financial aid forms:* FAFSA, CSS Financial Aid PROFILE.
CONTACT Dan Small, Director of Student Financial Assistance, The George Washington University, 2121 Eye Street, NW, Rice Hall, 3rd Floor, Washington, DC 20052, 202-994-6620 or toll-free 800-447-3765. *Fax:* 202-994-0906. *E-mail:* finaid@gwu.edu.

GEORGIA COLLEGE & STATE UNIVERSITY
Milledgeville, GA

Tuition & fees (GA res): $4142   **Average undergraduate aid package:** $5167

ABOUT THE INSTITUTION State-supported, coed. Awards: bachelor's and master's degrees and post-master's certificates. 34 undergraduate majors. Total enrollment: 5,659. Undergraduates: 4,798. Freshmen: 1,036. Federal methodology is used as a basis for awarding need-based institutional aid.
UNDERGRADUATE EXPENSES for 2005–06 *Application fee:* $25. *Tuition, state resident:* full-time $3404; part-time $142 per semester hour. *Tuition, nonresident:* full-time $13,616; part-time $568 per semester hour. *Required fees:* full-time $738; $369 per term part-time. Full-time tuition and fees vary according to location. Part-time tuition and fees vary according to course load and location. *College room and board:* $6878; *room only:* $3690. Room and board charges vary according to board plan and housing facility.
FRESHMAN FINANCIAL AID (Fall 2004) 885 applied for aid; of those 35% were deemed to have need. 99% of freshmen with need received aid; of those 3% had need fully met. *Average percent of need met:* 71% (excluding resources awarded to replace EFC). *Average financial aid package:* $4995 (excluding resources awarded to replace EFC). 3% of all full-time freshmen had no need and received non-need-based gift aid.
UNDERGRADUATE FINANCIAL AID (Fall 2004) 3,609 applied for aid; of those 46% were deemed to have need. 96% of undergraduates with need received aid; of those 1% had need fully met. *Average percent of need met:* 70% (excluding resources awarded to replace EFC). *Average financial aid package:* $5167 (excluding resources awarded to replace EFC). 2% of all full-time undergraduates had no need and received non-need-based gift aid.
GIFT AID (NEED-BASED) *Total amount:* $2,610,251 (99% federal, 1% state). *Receiving aid:* Freshmen: 13% (116); All full-time undergraduates: 19% (774). *Average award:* Freshmen: $2620; Undergraduates: $2616. *Scholarships, grants, and awards:* Federal Pell, FSEOG, state, college/university gift aid from institutional funds.
GIFT AID (NON-NEED-BASED) *Total amount:* $10,313,987 (92% state, 4% institutional, 4% external sources). *Receiving aid:* Freshmen: 33% (304); Undergraduates: 39% (1,543). *Average Award:* Freshmen: $1365; Undergraduates: $1362. *Scholarships, grants, and awards by category:* Academic Interests/Achievement: business, computer science, education, English, foreign languages, general academic interests/achievements, health fields, humanities, international studies, mathematics, physical sciences, social sciences. Creative Arts/Performance: applied art and design, art/fine arts, creative writing, debating, journalism/publications, music, performing arts, theater/drama. Special Achievements/Activities: community service, general special achievements/activities, leadership. Special Characteristics: children of faculty/staff, children with a deceased or disabled parent, handicapped students, international students, local/state students, members of minority groups, out-of-state students, religious affiliation. *Tuition waivers:* Full or partial for employees or children of employees, senior citizens.
ROTC: Army cooperative.
LOANS *Student loans:* $10,607,871 (59% need-based, 41% non-need-based). 57% of past graduating class borrowed through all loan programs. *Average indebtedness per student:* $15,128. *Average need-based loan:* Freshmen: $2630; Undergraduates: $2560. *Parent loans:* $905,917 (100% non-need-based). *Programs:* Federal Direct (PLUS), FFEL (Subsidized and Unsubsidized Stafford, PLUS), Perkins, state, college/university.
WORK-STUDY *Federal work-study:* Total amount: $145,980; 181 jobs averaging $1190.
ATHLETIC AWARDS *Total amount:* $511,270 (100% non-need-based).
APPLYING FOR FINANCIAL AID *Required financial aid form:* FAFSA. *Financial aid deadline:* Continuous. *Notification date:* Continuous beginning 3/1. Students must reply within 2 weeks of notification.
CONTACT Mrs. Cathy Crawley, Associate Director of Financial Aid, Georgia College & State University, Campus Box 30, Milledgeville, GA 31061, 478-445-5149 or toll-free 800-342-0471 (in-state). *Fax:* 478-445-0729. *E-mail:* cathy.crawley@gcsu.edu.

GEORGIA INSTITUTE OF TECHNOLOGY
Atlanta, GA

Tuition & fees (GA res): $4648   **Average undergraduate aid package:** $8222

ABOUT THE INSTITUTION State-supported, coed. Awards: bachelor's, master's, and doctoral degrees. 34 undergraduate majors. Total enrollment: 17,135. Undergraduates: 11,841. Freshmen: 2,425. Federal methodology is used as a basis for awarding need-based institutional aid.
UNDERGRADUATE EXPENSES for 2005–06 *Application fee:* $50. *Tuition, state resident:* full-time $3638; part-time $152 per hour. *Tuition, nonresident:* full-time $17,980; part-time $750 per hour. *Required fees:* full-time $1010; $505 per term part-time. Part-time tuition and fees vary according to course load. *College room and board:* $6802; *room only:* $3992. Room and board charges vary according to board plan and housing facility.
FRESHMAN FINANCIAL AID (Fall 2005, est.) 1855 applied for aid; of those 40% were deemed to have need. 98% of freshmen with need received aid; of those 44% had need fully met. *Average percent of need met:* 76% (excluding resources awarded to replace EFC). *Average financial aid package:* $8644 (excluding resources awarded to replace EFC). 9% of all full-time freshmen had no need and received non-need-based gift aid.
UNDERGRADUATE FINANCIAL AID (Fall 2005, est.) 6,440 applied for aid; of those 53% were deemed to have need. 97% of undergraduates with need received aid; of those 43% had need fully met. *Average percent of need met:* 72% (excluding resources awarded to replace EFC). *Average financial aid package:* $8222 (excluding resources awarded to replace EFC). 7% of all full-time undergraduates had no need and received non-need-based gift aid.
GIFT AID (NEED-BASED) *Total amount:* $17,747,784 (25% federal, 32% state, 34% institutional, 9% external sources). *Receiving aid:* Freshmen: 16% (397); All full-time undergraduates: 18% (1,934). *Average award:* Freshmen: $5224; Undergraduates: $4390. *Scholarships, grants, and awards:* Federal Pell, FSEOG, state, private, college/university gift aid from institutional funds.
GIFT AID (NON-NEED-BASED) *Total amount:* $19,499,161 (1% federal, 74% state, 10% institutional, 15% external sources). *Receiving aid:* Freshmen: 21% (505); Undergraduates: 16% (1,734). *Average Award:* Freshmen: $2511; Undergraduates: $3041. *Scholarships, grants, and awards by category:* Academic Interests/Achievement: 1,782 awards ($5,114,409 total): architecture, biological sciences, computer science, engineering/technologies, general academic interests/achievements, physical sciences. Special Achievements/Activities: 226 awards ($2,034,716 total): leadership. Special Characteristics: 162 awards ($490,966 total): children of faculty/staff, children of union members/company employees, ethnic background, general special characteristics, handicapped students, local/state students, members of minority groups, out-of-state students.
ROTC: Army, Naval, Air Force.
LOANS *Student loans:* $22,810,667 (64% need-based, 36% non-need-based). 49% of past graduating class borrowed through all loan programs. *Average indebtedness per student:* $17,001. *Average need-based loan:* Freshmen: $3504; Undergraduates: $3770. *Parent loans:* $16,253,220 (51% need-based, 49% non-need-based). *Programs:* FFEL (Subsidized and Unsubsidized Stafford, PLUS), Perkins, college/university.
WORK-STUDY *Federal work-study:* Total amount: $1,332,403; 219 jobs averaging $2100.
ATHLETIC AWARDS *Total amount:* $4,499,360 (32% need-based, 68% non-need-based).
APPLYING FOR FINANCIAL AID *Required financial aid forms:* FAFSA, institution's own form. *Financial aid deadline:* 3/1 (priority: 3/1). *Notification date:* Continuous beginning 4/1. Students must reply by 5/1.
CONTACT Ms. Marie Mons, Director of Student Financial Planning and Services, Georgia Institute of Technology, 225 North Avenue, NW, Atlanta, GA 30332-0460, 404-894-4160. *Fax:* 404-894-7412. *E-mail:* marie.mons@finaid.gatech.edu.

GEORGIAN COURT UNIVERSITY
Lakewood, NJ

ABOUT THE INSTITUTION Independent Roman Catholic, undergraduate: women only; graduate: coed. Awards: bachelor's and master's degrees and post-bachelor's and post-master's certificates. 26 undergraduate majors. Total enrollment: 3,153. Undergraduates: 1,999. Freshmen: 188.

Georgian Court University

GIFT AID (NEED-BASED) *Scholarships, grants, and awards:* Federal Pell, FSEOG, state, private, college/university gift aid from institutional funds.
GIFT AID (NON-NEED-BASED) *Scholarships, grants, and awards by category: Academic Interests/Achievement:* biological sciences, business, English, foreign languages, general academic interests/achievements, mathematics, physical sciences. *Creative Arts/Performance:* art/fine arts, creative writing, music. *Special Achievements/Activities:* general special achievements/activities. *Special Characteristics:* children of faculty/staff, religious affiliation, spouses of current students, veterans.
LOANS *Programs:* Federal Direct (Subsidized and Unsubsidized Stafford, PLUS), FFEL (Subsidized and Unsubsidized Stafford, PLUS), Perkins, state.
APPLYING FOR FINANCIAL AID *Required financial aid forms:* FAFSA, institution's own form.
CONTACT Carol Straus, Director of Financial Aid, Georgian Court University, 900 Lakewood Avenue, Lakewood, NJ 08701-2697, 732-364-2200 Ext. 2258 or toll-free 800-458-8422. *Fax:* 732-987-2012. *E-mail:* financialaid@georgian.edu.

GEORGIA SOUTHERN UNIVERSITY
Statesboro, GA

Tuition & fees (GA res): $3462 **Average undergraduate aid package: $6652**

ABOUT THE INSTITUTION State-supported, coed. Awards: bachelor's, master's, and doctoral degrees and post-master's certificates. 79 undergraduate majors. Total enrollment: 16,646. Undergraduates: 14,650. Freshmen: 3,145. Federal methodology is used as a basis for awarding need-based institutional aid.
UNDERGRADUATE EXPENSES for 2005–06 *Application fee:* $50. *Tuition, state resident:* full-time $2438; part-time $102 per semester hour. *Tuition, nonresident:* full-time $9754; part-time $407 per semester hour. *Required fees:* full-time $1024; $512 per term part-time. Full-time tuition and fees vary according to degree level and location. Part-time tuition and fees vary according to course load, degree level, and location. *College room and board:* $6300; *room only:* $3968. Room and board charges vary according to board plan and housing facility.
FRESHMAN FINANCIAL AID (Fall 2004) 2812 applied for aid; of those 52% were deemed to have need. 98% of freshmen with need received aid; of those 20% had need fully met. *Average percent of need met:* 66% (excluding resources awarded to replace EFC). *Average financial aid package:* $6148 (excluding resources awarded to replace EFC). 3% of all full-time freshmen had no need and received non-need-based gift aid.
UNDERGRADUATE FINANCIAL AID (Fall 2004) 10,981 applied for aid; of those 61% were deemed to have need. 97% of undergraduates with need received aid; of those 17% had need fully met. *Average percent of need met:* 65% (excluding resources awarded to replace EFC). *Average financial aid package:* $6652 (excluding resources awarded to replace EFC). 2% of all full-time undergraduates had no need and received non-need-based gift aid.
GIFT AID (NEED-BASED) *Total amount:* $23,386,925 (51% federal, 46% state, 1% institutional, 2% external sources). *Receiving aid:* Freshmen: 46% (1,363); All full-time undergraduates: 43% (5,418). *Average award:* Freshmen: $4871; Undergraduates: $4306. *Scholarships, grants, and awards:* Federal Pell, FSEOG, state, private, college/university gift aid from institutional funds, Georgia HOPE Scholarships, Federal work study.
GIFT AID (NON-NEED-BASED) *Total amount:* $10,833,080 (92% state, 5% institutional, 3% external sources). *Receiving aid:* Freshmen: 5% (162); Undergraduates: 3% (438). *Average Award:* Freshmen: $1348; Undergraduates: $1343. *Scholarships, grants, and awards by category: Academic Interests/Achievement:* 525 awards ($686,788 total): biological sciences, business, communication, education, engineering/technologies, English, foreign languages, general academic interests/achievements, health fields, humanities, international studies, mathematics, military science, social sciences. *Creative Arts/Performance:* 68 awards ($67,200 total): art/fine arts, cinema/film/broadcasting, general creative arts/performance, music, theater/drama. *Special Achievements/Activities:* 272 awards ($133,750 total): community service, junior miss, leadership, memberships. *Special Characteristics:* 15 awards ($48,753 total): children and siblings of alumni, children of public servants, first-generation college students, handicapped students, married students, members of minority groups. *Tuition waivers:* Full or partial for employees or children of employees, senior citizens. *ROTC:* Army.
LOANS *Student loans:* $36,294,195 (71% need-based, 29% non-need-based). 70% of past graduating class borrowed through all loan programs. *Average indebtedness per student:* $17,913. *Average need-based loan:* Freshmen: $2414; Undergraduates: $3828. *Parent loans:* $5,493,303 (56% need-based, 44% non-need-based). *Programs:* Federal Direct (Subsidized and Unsubsidized Stafford, PLUS), Perkins, Service-Cancelable State Direct Student Loans, external alternative loans.
WORK-STUDY *Federal work-study:* Total amount: $390,597; 316 jobs averaging $1236.
ATHLETIC AWARDS Total amount: $1,728,110 (51% need-based, 49% non-need-based).
APPLYING FOR FINANCIAL AID *Required financial aid form:* FAFSA. *Financial aid deadline (priority):* 3/31. *Notification date:* Continuous beginning 4/15.
CONTACT Ms. Elise Boyett, Associate Director of Financial Aid, Georgia Southern University, Box 8065, Statesboro, GA 30460-8065, 912-681-5413. *Fax:* 912-681-0573. *E-mail:* eboyett@georgiasouthern.edu.

GEORGIA SOUTHWESTERN STATE UNIVERSITY
Americus, GA

Tuition & fees (GA res): $3034 **Average undergraduate aid package: $6219**

ABOUT THE INSTITUTION State-supported, coed. Awards: associate, bachelor's, and master's degrees and post-master's certificates. 64 undergraduate majors. Total enrollment: 2,427. Undergraduates: 2,238. Freshmen: 385. Federal methodology is used as a basis for awarding need-based institutional aid.
UNDERGRADUATE EXPENSES for 2005–06 *Application fee:* $25. *Tuition, state resident:* full-time $2438; part-time $102 per semester hour. *Tuition, nonresident:* full-time $9754; part-time $407 per semester hour. *Required fees:* full-time $596; $289 per term part-time. Part-time tuition and fees vary according to course load. *College room and board:* $4810; *room only:* $2620. Room and board charges vary according to board plan and housing facility.
FRESHMAN FINANCIAL AID (Fall 2005, est.) 299 applied for aid; of those 77% were deemed to have need. 99% of freshmen with need received aid; of those 15% had need fully met. *Average percent of need met:* 59% (excluding resources awarded to replace EFC). *Average financial aid package:* $6169 (excluding resources awarded to replace EFC). 11% of all full-time freshmen had no need and received non-need-based gift aid.
UNDERGRADUATE FINANCIAL AID (Fall 2005, est.) 1,299 applied for aid; of those 82% were deemed to have need. 99% of undergraduates with need received aid; of those 9% had need fully met. *Average percent of need met:* 55% (excluding resources awarded to replace EFC). *Average financial aid package:* $6219 (excluding resources awarded to replace EFC). 8% of all full-time undergraduates had no need and received non-need-based gift aid.
GIFT AID (NEED-BASED) *Total amount:* $2,646,048 (96% federal, 4% state). *Receiving aid:* Freshmen: 41% (146); All full-time undergraduates: 43% (736). *Average award:* Freshmen: $3086; Undergraduates: $3018. *Scholarships, grants, and awards:* Federal Pell, FSEOG, state, private, college/university gift aid from institutional funds.
GIFT AID (NON-NEED-BASED) *Total amount:* $2,796,207 (80% state, 15% institutional, 5% external sources). *Receiving aid:* Freshmen: 48% (173); Undergraduates: 30% (505). *Average Award:* Freshmen: $1846; Undergraduates: $2961. *Scholarships, grants, and awards by category: Academic Interests/Achievement:* general academic interests/achievements. *Creative Arts/Performance:* art/fine arts, music. *Special Achievements/Activities:* leadership. *Tuition waivers:* Full or partial for senior citizens.
LOANS *Student loans:* $5,175,698 (58% need-based, 42% non-need-based). 68% of past graduating class borrowed through all loan programs. *Average indebtedness per student:* $15,346. *Average need-based loan:* Freshmen: $2313; Undergraduates: $3249. *Parent loans:* $108,004 (100% non-need-based). *Programs:* FFEL (Subsidized and Unsubsidized Stafford, PLUS), Perkins, state, college/university.
WORK-STUDY *Federal work-study:* Total amount: $114,458; 82 jobs averaging $1396. *State or other work-study/employment:* Part-time jobs available.
ATHLETIC AWARDS Total amount: $322,808 (100% non-need-based).
APPLYING FOR FINANCIAL AID *Required financial aid forms:* FAFSA, institution's own form. *Financial aid deadline (priority):* 4/1. *Notification date:* Continuous beginning 5/1. Students must reply within 8 weeks of notification.
CONTACT Ms. Freida Jones, Director of Financial Aid, Georgia Southwestern State University, 800 Georgia Southwestern State University Drive, Americus, GA 31709-4693, 229-928-1378 or toll-free 800-338-0082. *Fax:* 229-931-2061.

GEORGIA STATE UNIVERSITY
Atlanta, GA

ABOUT THE INSTITUTION State-supported, coed. Awards: bachelor's, master's, doctoral, and first professional degrees and post-bachelor's, post-master's, and first professional certificates. 48 undergraduate majors. Total enrollment: 25,945. Undergraduates: 18,960. Freshmen: 2,291.
GIFT AID (NEED-BASED) *Scholarships, grants, and awards:* Federal Pell, FSEOG, state, private, college/university gift aid from institutional funds.
GIFT AID (NON-NEED-BASED) *Scholarships, grants, and awards by category: Academic Interests/Achievement:* general academic interests/achievements. *Creative Arts/Performance:* applied art and design, art/fine arts, journalism/publications, music, performing arts, theater/drama. *Special Achievements/Activities:* community service, leadership, memberships.
LOANS *Programs:* Federal Direct (Subsidized and Unsubsidized Stafford, PLUS), Perkins, state, college/university.
APPLYING FOR FINANCIAL AID *Required financial aid forms:* FAFSA, Hope Alternate Application (for Hope Scholarships only).
CONTACT Financial Aid Office, Georgia State University, 102 Sparks Hall, Atlanta, GA 30303, 404-651-2227.

GETTYSBURG COLLEGE
Gettysburg, PA

Tuition & fees: $32,070 — **Average undergraduate aid package: $25,089**

ABOUT THE INSTITUTION Independent religious, coed. Awards: bachelor's degrees. 83 undergraduate majors. Total enrollment: 2,463. Undergraduates: 2,463. Freshmen: 697. Both federal and institutional methodology are used as a basis for awarding need-based institutional aid.
UNDERGRADUATE EXPENSES for 2005–06 *Application fee:* $45. *Comprehensive fee:* $39,864 includes full-time tuition ($31,790), mandatory fees ($280), and room and board ($7794). *College room only:* $4134. Room and board charges vary according to board plan and housing facility. *Part-time tuition:* $3450 per course. *Payment plans:* Tuition prepayment, installment.
FRESHMAN FINANCIAL AID (Fall 2005, est.) 479 applied for aid; of those 80% were deemed to have need. 100% of freshmen with need received aid; of those 100% had need fully met. *Average percent of need met:* 100% (excluding resources awarded to replace EFC). *Average financial aid package:* $24,487 (excluding resources awarded to replace EFC). 14% of all full-time freshmen had no need and received non-need-based gift aid.
UNDERGRADUATE FINANCIAL AID (Fall 2005, est.) 1,696 applied for aid; of those 87% were deemed to have need. 100% of undergraduates with need received aid; of those 100% had need fully met. *Average percent of need met:* 100% (excluding resources awarded to replace EFC). *Average financial aid package:* $25,089 (excluding resources awarded to replace EFC). 12% of all full-time undergraduates had no need and received non-need-based gift aid.
GIFT AID (NEED-BASED) *Total amount:* $28,960,420 (4% federal, 3% state, 91% institutional, 2% external sources). *Receiving aid:* Freshmen: 55% (384); All full-time undergraduates: 56% (1,452). *Average award:* Freshmen: $20,095; Undergraduates: $19,711. *Scholarships, grants, and awards:* Federal Pell, FSEOG, state, private, college/university gift aid from institutional funds.
GIFT AID (NON-NEED-BASED) *Total amount:* $3,470,388 (1% state, 84% institutional, 15% external sources). *Receiving aid:* Freshmen: 30% (212); Undergraduates: 22% (561). *Average Award:* Freshmen: $9060; Undergraduates: $9571. *Scholarships, grants, and awards by category: Academic Interests/Achievement:* 810 awards ($8,095,500 total): general academic interests/achievements. *Creative Arts/Performance:* 20 awards ($100,000 total): music. *Tuition waivers:* Full or partial for employees or children of employees. *ROTC:* Army cooperative.
LOANS *Student loans:* $10,020,110 (56% need-based, 44% non-need-based). 59% of past graduating class borrowed through all loan programs. *Average indebtedness per student:* $21,810. *Average need-based loan:* Freshmen: $3466; Undergraduates: $4495. *Parent loans:* $7,157,303 (100% non-need-based). *Programs:* FFEL (Subsidized and Unsubsidized Stafford, PLUS), Perkins, college/university.
WORK-STUDY *Federal work-study:* Total amount: $509,230; 546 jobs averaging $933. *State or other work-study/employment:* Total amount: $644,862 (14% need-based, 86% non-need-based). 732 part-time jobs averaging $838.
APPLYING FOR FINANCIAL AID *Required financial aid forms:* FAFSA, CSS Financial Aid PROFILE, business/farm supplement, income tax form(s) and verification worksheet. *Financial aid deadline:* 2/15. *Notification date:* 3/27. Students must reply by 5/1.
CONTACT Timothy A. Opgenorth, Director of Financial Aid, Gettysburg College, 300 North Washington Street, Box 438, Gettysburg, PA 17325, 717-337-6611 or toll-free 800-431-0803. *Fax:* 717-337-8555. *E-mail:* finaid@gettysburg.edu.

GLENVILLE STATE COLLEGE
Glenville, WV

Tuition & fees (WV res): $3628 — **Average undergraduate aid package: $8736**

ABOUT THE INSTITUTION State-supported, coed. Awards: associate and bachelor's degrees. 31 undergraduate majors. Total enrollment: 1,392. Undergraduates: 1,392. Federal methodology is used as a basis for awarding need-based institutional aid.
UNDERGRADUATE EXPENSES for 2005–06 *Tuition, state resident:* full-time $3628; part-time $151.17 per credit hour. *Tuition, nonresident:* full-time $8640; part-time $360 per credit hour. *College room and board:* $5150; *room only:* $2500. Room and board charges vary according to housing facility. *Payment plan:* Installment.
FRESHMAN FINANCIAL AID (Fall 2005, est.) 282 applied for aid; of those 86% were deemed to have need. 95% of freshmen with need received aid; of those 25% had need fully met. *Average percent of need met:* 79% (excluding resources awarded to replace EFC). *Average financial aid package:* $8173 (excluding resources awarded to replace EFC). 9% of all full-time freshmen had no need and received non-need-based gift aid.
UNDERGRADUATE FINANCIAL AID (Fall 2005, est.) 1,045 applied for aid; of those 86% were deemed to have need. 97% of undergraduates with need received aid; of those 30% had need fully met. *Average percent of need met:* 82% (excluding resources awarded to replace EFC). *Average financial aid package:* $8736 (excluding resources awarded to replace EFC). 8% of all full-time undergraduates had no need and received non-need-based gift aid.
GIFT AID (NEED-BASED) *Total amount:* $6,222,120 (37% federal, 13% state, 50% external sources). *Receiving aid:* Freshmen: 57% (173); All full-time undergraduates: 55% (659). *Average award:* Freshmen: $4484; Undergraduates: $4455. *Scholarships, grants, and awards:* Federal Pell, FSEOG, state, private, college/university gift aid from institutional funds.
GIFT AID (NON-NEED-BASED) *Total amount:* $1,128,726 (56% state, 21% institutional, 23% external sources). *Receiving aid:* Freshmen: 40% (120); Undergraduates: 32% (386). *Average Award:* Freshmen: $2359; Undergraduates: $2387. *Scholarships, grants, and awards by category: Academic Interests/Achievement:* 175 awards ($236,756 total): biological sciences, education, English, general academic interests/achievements, mathematics. *Creative Arts/Performance:* 18 awards ($31,519 total): music. *Special Characteristics:* 2 awards ($2000 total): first-generation college students, veterans' children. *Tuition waivers:* Full or partial for senior citizens.
LOANS *Student loans:* $3,967,063 (62% need-based, 38% non-need-based). 75% of past graduating class borrowed through all loan programs. *Average indebtedness per student:* $16,079. *Average need-based loan:* Freshmen: $3029; Undergraduates: $4087. *Parent loans:* $441,236 (100% non-need-based). *Programs:* Federal Direct (Subsidized and Unsubsidized Stafford, PLUS).
WORK-STUDY *Federal work-study:* Total amount: $137,056; 116 jobs averaging $1181. *State or other work-study/employment:* Total amount: $242,419 (100% non-need-based). 255 part-time jobs averaging $950.
ATHLETIC AWARDS Total amount: $384,699 (100% non-need-based).
APPLYING FOR FINANCIAL AID *Required financial aid form:* FAFSA. *Financial aid deadline (priority):* 3/1. *Notification date:* Continuous beginning 4/1. Students must reply within 3 weeks of notification.
CONTACT Ms. Karen Lay, Director of Financial Aid, Glenville State College, 200 High Street, Glenville, WV 26351-1200, 304-462-4103 Ext. 5 or toll-free 800-924-2010 (in-state). *Fax:* 304-462-4407. *E-mail:* karen.lay@glenville.edu.

GLOBE INSTITUTE OF TECHNOLOGY
New York, NY

CONTACT Office of Admissions, Globe Institute of Technology, 291 Broadway, 2nd Floor, New York, NY 10007, 212-349-4330 or toll-free 877-394-5623. *Fax:* 212-227-5920. *E-mail:* admission@globe.edu.

Goddard College

GODDARD COLLEGE
Plainfield, VT

Tuition & fees: $10,706 | **Average undergraduate aid package:** $6426

ABOUT THE INSTITUTION Independent, coed. Awards: bachelor's and master's degrees. 5 undergraduate majors. Total enrollment: 560. Undergraduates: 165. Freshmen: 7. Federal methodology is used as a basis for awarding need-based institutional aid.

UNDERGRADUATE EXPENSES for 2005–06 *Application fee:* $40. *Tuition:* full-time $9806. *Payment plan:* Installment.

FRESHMAN FINANCIAL AID (Fall 2005, est.) 7 applied for aid; of those 100% were deemed to have need. 100% of freshmen with need received aid. *Average percent of need met:* 37% (excluding resources awarded to replace EFC). *Average financial aid package:* $5263 (excluding resources awarded to replace EFC).

UNDERGRADUATE FINANCIAL AID (Fall 2005, est.) 149 applied for aid; of those 96% were deemed to have need. 98% of undergraduates with need received aid; of those 2% had need fully met. *Average percent of need met:* 43% (excluding resources awarded to replace EFC). *Average financial aid package:* $6426 (excluding resources awarded to replace EFC). 2% of all full-time undergraduates had no need and received non-need-based gift aid.

GIFT AID (NEED-BASED) *Total amount:* $362,002 (70% federal, 8% state, 22% external sources). *Receiving aid:* Freshmen: 36% (4); All full-time undergraduates: 47% (94). *Average award:* Freshmen: $5400; Undergraduates: $3819. *Scholarships, grants, and awards:* Federal Pell, FSEOG, state, private, college/university gift aid from institutional funds.

GIFT AID (NON-NEED-BASED) *Total amount:* $30,983 (100% external sources). *Receiving aid:* Undergraduates: 1% (1). *Average Award:* Undergraduates: $8820. *Tuition waivers:* Full or partial for employees or children of employees.

LOANS *Student loans:* $1,088,576 (91% need-based, 9% non-need-based). 84% of past graduating class borrowed through all loan programs. *Average indebtedness per student:* $21,591. *Average need-based loan:* Freshmen: $2177; Undergraduates: $4223. *Parent loans:* $71,904 (71% need-based, 29% non-need-based). *Programs:* FFEL (Subsidized and Unsubsidized Stafford, PLUS), Perkins, college/university.

APPLYING FOR FINANCIAL AID *Required financial aid form:* FAFSA. *Financial aid deadline (priority):* 3/1. *Notification date:* Continuous. Students must reply within 2 weeks of notification.

CONTACT Beverly Jene, Director of Financial Aid, Goddard College, 123 Pitkin Road, Plainfield, VT 05667, 802-454-8311 Ext. 324 or toll-free 800-906-8312 Ext. 243. *Fax:* 802-454-1029. *E-mail:* jeneb@goddard.edu.

GOD'S BIBLE SCHOOL AND COLLEGE
Cincinnati, OH

CONTACT Mrs. Lori Waggoner, Financial Aid Director, God's Bible School and College, 1810 Young Street, Cincinnati, OH 45202-6899, 513-721-7944 Ext. 205 or toll-free 800-486-4637. *Fax:* 513-721-1357. *E-mail:* lwaggoner@gbs.edu.

GOLDEN GATE UNIVERSITY
San Francisco, CA

CONTACT Ken Walsh, Associate Director of Financial Services, Golden Gate University, 536 Mission Street, San Francisco, CA 94105-2968, 415-442-7262 or toll-free 800-448-4968. *Fax:* 415-442-7819. *E-mail:* kwalsh@ggu.edu.

GOLDEY-BEACOM COLLEGE
Wilmington, DE

ABOUT THE INSTITUTION Independent, coed. Awards: associate, bachelor's, and master's degrees. 7 undergraduate majors. Total enrollment: 1,324. Undergraduates: 1,049.

GIFT AID (NEED-BASED) *Scholarships, grants, and awards:* Federal Pell, FSEOG, state, private, college/university gift aid from institutional funds.

GIFT AID (NON-NEED-BASED) *Scholarships, grants, and awards by category: Academic Interests/Achievement:* business.

LOANS *Programs:* FFEL (Subsidized and Unsubsidized Stafford, PLUS), Perkins.

APPLYING FOR FINANCIAL AID *Required financial aid form:* FAFSA.

CONTACT Jane H. Lysle, Dean of Enrollment Management, Goldey-Beacom College, 4701 Limestone Road, Wilmington, DE 19808-1999, 302-225-6274 or toll-free 800-833-4877. *Fax:* 302-998-8631. *E-mail:* lyslej@goldey.gbc.edu.

GONZAGA UNIVERSITY
Spokane, WA

Tuition & fees: $23,578 | **Average undergraduate aid package:** $13,724

ABOUT THE INSTITUTION Independent Roman Catholic, coed. Awards: bachelor's, master's, doctoral, and first professional degrees and post-master's certificates. 51 undergraduate majors. Total enrollment: 6,377. Undergraduates: 4,152. Freshmen: 986. Federal methodology is used as a basis for awarding need-based institutional aid.

UNDERGRADUATE EXPENSES for 2005–06 *Application fee:* $45. *Comprehensive fee:* $30,278 includes full-time tuition ($23,140), mandatory fees ($438), and room and board ($6700). *College room only:* $3400. Room and board charges vary according to board plan and housing facility. *Part-time tuition:* $670 per credit. *Part-time fees:* $45 per term. *Payment plans:* Installment, deferred payment.

FRESHMAN FINANCIAL AID (Fall 2004) 824 applied for aid; of those 74% were deemed to have need. 100% of freshmen with need received aid; of those 20% had need fully met. *Average percent of need met:* 83% (excluding resources awarded to replace EFC). *Average financial aid package:* $13,857 (excluding resources awarded to replace EFC). 32% of all full-time freshmen had no need and received non-need-based gift aid.

UNDERGRADUATE FINANCIAL AID (Fall 2004) 3,019 applied for aid; of those 82% were deemed to have need. 98% of undergraduates with need received aid; of those 28% had need fully met. *Average percent of need met:* 84% (excluding resources awarded to replace EFC). *Average financial aid package:* $13,724 (excluding resources awarded to replace EFC). 31% of all full-time undergraduates had no need and received non-need-based gift aid.

GIFT AID (NEED-BASED) *Total amount:* $24,962,576 (10% federal, 8% state, 77% institutional, 5% external sources). *Receiving aid:* Freshmen: 63% (608); All full-time undergraduates: 62% (2,421). *Average award:* Freshmen: $12,554; Undergraduates: $11,832. *Scholarships, grants, and awards:* Federal Pell, FSEOG, state, private, college/university gift aid from institutional funds, United Negro College Fund, Federal Nursing.

GIFT AID (NON-NEED-BASED) *Total amount:* $10,548,709 (87% institutional, 13% external sources). *Receiving aid:* Freshmen: 25% (239); Undergraduates: 25% (962). *Average Award:* Freshmen: $5638; Undergraduates: $6523. *Scholarships, grants, and awards by category: Academic Interests/Achievement:* 55 awards ($97,800 total): business, engineering/technologies. *Creative Arts/Performance:* 85 awards ($158,917 total): debating, music. *Special Achievements/Activities:* 120 awards ($528,000 total): leadership. *Special Characteristics:* 369 awards ($2,234,543 total): children and siblings of alumni, children of faculty/staff, members of minority groups, siblings of current students. *Tuition waivers:* Full or partial for employees or children of employees. *ROTC:* Army.

LOANS *Student loans:* $16,997,652 (72% need-based, 28% non-need-based). 68% of past graduating class borrowed through all loan programs. *Average indebtedness per student:* $23,113. *Average need-based loan:* Freshmen: $4097; Undergraduates: $5013. *Parent loans:* $6,090,205 (78% need-based, 22% non-need-based). *Programs:* FFEL (Subsidized and Unsubsidized Stafford, PLUS), Perkins, Federal Nursing, state, college/university.

WORK-STUDY *Federal work-study:* Total amount: $1,384,580; 463 jobs averaging $2990. *State or other work-study/employment:* Total amount: $1,261,286 (100% need-based). 306 part-time jobs averaging $4124.

ATHLETIC AWARDS *Total amount:* $2,261,647 (21% need-based, 79% non-need-based).

APPLYING FOR FINANCIAL AID *Required financial aid form:* FAFSA. *Financial aid deadline (priority):* 2/1. *Notification date:* Continuous beginning 3/1. Students must reply by 5/1 or within 3 weeks of notification.

CONTACT Darlene Hendrickson, Director of Operations for Financial Aid, Gonzaga University, 502 East Boone Avenue, Spokane, WA 99258-0072, 509-323-6568 or toll-free 800-322-2584 Ext. 6572. *Fax:* 509-323-5816. *E-mail:* hendrickson@gonzaga.edu.

GORDON COLLEGE
Wenham, MA

Tuition & fees: $22,924   **Average undergraduate aid package:** $14,540

ABOUT THE INSTITUTION Independent nondenominational, coed. Awards: bachelor's and master's degrees. 32 undergraduate majors. Total enrollment: 1,650. Undergraduates: 1,589. Freshmen: 414. Both federal and institutional methodology are used as a basis for awarding need-based institutional aid.

UNDERGRADUATE EXPENSES for 2005–06 *Application fee:* $50. *Comprehensive fee:* $29,194 includes full-time tuition ($21,930), mandatory fees ($994), and room and board ($6270). *College room only:* $4200. Room and board charges vary according to board plan and housing facility. *Part-time fees:* $1550 per credit; $248.50 per term. Part-time tuition and fees vary according to course load. *Payment plan:* Installment.

FRESHMAN FINANCIAL AID (Fall 2005, est.) 329 applied for aid; of those 81% were deemed to have need. 100% of freshmen with need received aid; of those 20% had need fully met. *Average percent of need met:* 71% (excluding resources awarded to replace EFC). *Average financial aid package:* $13,799 (excluding resources awarded to replace EFC). 43% of all full-time freshmen had no need and received non-need-based gift aid.

UNDERGRADUATE FINANCIAL AID (Fall 2005, est.) 1,189 applied for aid; of those 86% were deemed to have need. 100% of undergraduates with need received aid; of those 18% had need fully met. *Average percent of need met:* 70% (excluding resources awarded to replace EFC). *Average financial aid package:* $14,540 (excluding resources awarded to replace EFC). 30% of all full-time undergraduates had no need and received non-need-based gift aid.

GIFT AID (NEED-BASED) *Total amount:* $10,222,348 (8% federal, 4% state, 78% institutional, 10% external sources). *Receiving aid:* Freshmen: 51% (260); All full-time undergraduates: 65% (989). *Average award:* Freshmen: $10,626; Undergraduates: $10,093. *Scholarships, grants, and awards:* Federal Pell, FSEOG, state, private, college/university gift aid from institutional funds.

GIFT AID (NON-NEED-BASED) *Total amount:* $4,761,982 (79% institutional, 21% external sources). *Receiving aid:* Freshmen: 7% (36); Undergraduates: 7% (101). *Average Award:* Freshmen: $11,444; Undergraduates: $2383. *Scholarships, grants, and awards by category:* Academic Interests/Achievement: 940 awards ($5,727,560 total): general academic interests/achievements. Creative Arts/Performance: 46 awards ($140,250 total): music. Special Achievements/Activities: 84 awards ($922,500 total): leadership. Special Characteristics: 107 awards ($49,000 total): children and siblings of alumni, relatives of clergy. *Tuition waivers:* Full or partial for employees or children of employees. *ROTC:* Army cooperative, Air Force cooperative.

LOANS *Student loans:* $10,332,013 (65% need-based, 35% non-need-based). 47% of past graduating class borrowed through all loan programs. *Average indebtedness per student:* $11,193. *Average need-based loan:* Freshmen: $2964; Undergraduates: $4473. *Parent loans:* $2,898,636 (40% need-based, 60% non-need-based). *Programs:* FFEL (Subsidized and Unsubsidized Stafford, PLUS), Perkins, state, college/university.

WORK-STUDY *Federal work-study:* Total amount: $856,414; 151 jobs averaging $1503.

APPLYING FOR FINANCIAL AID *Required financial aid forms:* FAFSA, CSS Financial Aid PROFILE, state aid form. *Financial aid deadline (priority):* 3/1. *Notification date:* 4/15. Students must reply by 5/1 or within 2 weeks of notification.

CONTACT Barbara Ruth Layne, Associate Vice President and Student Services, Gordon College, 255 Grapevine Road, Wenham, MA 01984-1899, 978-867-4246 or toll-free 866-464-6736. *Fax:* 978-867-4657. *E-mail:* blayne@hope.gordon.edu.

GOSHEN COLLEGE
Goshen, IN

Tuition & fees: $20,300   **Average undergraduate aid package:** $16,555

ABOUT THE INSTITUTION Independent Mennonite, coed. Awards: bachelor's degrees. 48 undergraduate majors. Total enrollment: 922. Undergraduates: 922. Freshmen: 198. Federal methodology is used as a basis for awarding need-based institutional aid.

UNDERGRADUATE EXPENSES for 2006–07 *Application fee:* $25. *Comprehensive fee:* $27,000 includes full-time tuition ($20,300) and room and board ($6700). *College room only:* $3600. *Part-time tuition:* $800 per credit hour.

FRESHMAN FINANCIAL AID (Fall 2005, est.) 195 applied for aid; of those 76% were deemed to have need. 99% of freshmen with need received aid; of those 34% had need fully met. *Average percent of need met:* 88% (excluding resources awarded to replace EFC). *Average financial aid package:* $16,599 (excluding resources awarded to replace EFC). 13% of all full-time freshmen had no need and received non-need-based gift aid.

UNDERGRADUATE FINANCIAL AID (Fall 2005, est.) 786 applied for aid; of those 78% were deemed to have need. 100% of undergraduates with need received aid; of those 30% had need fully met. *Average percent of need met:* 87% (excluding resources awarded to replace EFC). *Average financial aid package:* $16,555 (excluding resources awarded to replace EFC). 7% of all full-time undergraduates had no need and received non-need-based gift aid.

GIFT AID (NEED-BASED) *Total amount:* $6,915,183 (9% federal, 14% state, 66% institutional, 11% external sources). *Receiving aid:* Freshmen: 76% (148); All full-time undergraduates: 78% (613). *Average award:* Freshmen: $12,385; Undergraduates: $11,680. *Scholarships, grants, and awards:* Federal Pell, FSEOG, state, private, college/university gift aid from institutional funds.

GIFT AID (NON-NEED-BASED) *Total amount:* $1,365,762 (3% federal, 73% institutional, 24% external sources). *Receiving aid:* Freshmen: 70% (137); Undergraduates: 70% (549). *Average Award:* Freshmen: $8208; Undergraduates: $8031. *Scholarships, grants, and awards by category:* Academic Interests/Achievement: 536 awards ($2,669,344 total): business, communication, education, general academic interests/achievements. Creative Arts/Performance: 66 awards ($90,250 total): music. Special Characteristics: 57 awards ($669,953 total): international students.

LOANS *Student loans:* $3,257,218 (63% need-based, 37% non-need-based). 69% of past graduating class borrowed through all loan programs. *Average indebtedness per student:* $18,680. *Average need-based loan:* Freshmen: $3401; Undergraduates: $4887. *Parent loans:* $946,073 (100% non-need-based). *Programs:* Federal Direct (Subsidized and Unsubsidized Stafford, PLUS), Perkins, Federal Nursing, college/university.

WORK-STUDY *Federal work-study:* Total amount: $475,593; 614 jobs averaging $775. *State or other work-study/employment:* Total amount: $22,354 (95% need-based, 5% non-need-based). 16 part-time jobs averaging $1320.

ATHLETIC AWARDS *Total amount:* $469,184 (89% need-based, 11% non-need-based).

APPLYING FOR FINANCIAL AID *Required financial aid forms:* FAFSA, institution's own form. *Financial aid deadline (priority):* 2/15. *Notification date:* Continuous beginning 3/1. Students must reply by 5/1 or within 2 weeks of notification.

CONTACT Mr. Galen Graber, Director of Enrollment, Goshen College, 1700 South Main Street, Goshen, IN 46526-4794, 574-535-7525 or toll-free 800-348-7422. *Fax:* 574-535-7654.

GOUCHER COLLEGE
Baltimore, MD

Tuition & fees: $27,525   **Average undergraduate aid package:** $19,481

ABOUT THE INSTITUTION Independent, coed. Awards: bachelor's and master's degrees and post-bachelor's certificates. 31 undergraduate majors. Total enrollment: 2,233. Undergraduates: 1,346. Freshmen: 340. Both federal and institutional methodology are used as a basis for awarding need-based institutional aid.

UNDERGRADUATE EXPENSES for 2005–06 *Application fee:* $40. *Comprehensive fee:* $37,000 includes full-time tuition ($27,100), mandatory fees ($425), and room and board ($9475). *College room only:* $5625. Room and board charges vary according to board plan and housing facility. *Part-time tuition:* $950 per credit hour. *Payment plans:* Tuition prepayment, installment.

FRESHMAN FINANCIAL AID (Fall 2004) 293 applied for aid; of those 78% were deemed to have need. 100% of freshmen with need received aid; of those 38% had need fully met. *Average percent of need met:* 81% (excluding resources awarded to replace EFC). *Average financial aid package:* $19,849 (excluding resources awarded to replace EFC). 20% of all full-time freshmen had no need and received non-need-based gift aid.

UNDERGRADUATE FINANCIAL AID (Fall 2004) 878 applied for aid; of those 90% were deemed to have need. 100% of undergraduates with need received aid; of those 21% had need fully met. *Average percent of need met:* 68% (excluding resources awarded to replace EFC). *Average financial aid package:*

Goucher College

$19,481 (excluding resources awarded to replace EFC). 26% of all full-time undergraduates had no need and received non-need-based gift aid.
GIFT AID (NEED-BASED) Total amount: $10,812,747 (7% federal, 5% state, 86% institutional, 2% external sources). *Receiving aid:* Freshmen: 54% (218); All full-time undergraduates: 56% (746). *Average award:* Freshmen: $13,722; Undergraduates: $13,556. *Scholarships, grants, and awards:* Federal Pell, FSEOG, state, private, college/university gift aid from institutional funds.
GIFT AID (NON-NEED-BASED) Total amount: $3,802,851 (1% state, 97% institutional, 2% external sources). *Receiving aid:* Freshmen: 23% (92); Undergraduates: 12% (162). *Average Award:* Freshmen: $9420; *Undergraduates:* $8825. *Scholarships, grants, and awards by category:* Creative Arts/Performance: 11 awards ($55,000 total): art/fine arts, dance, music, performing arts, theater/drama. *Tuition waivers:* Full or partial for employees or children of employees, adult students, senior citizens. *ROTC:* Army cooperative.
LOANS Student loans: $3,577,507 (94% need-based, 6% non-need-based). 68% of past graduating class borrowed through all loan programs. *Average indebtedness per student:* $16,062. *Average need-based loan:* Freshmen: $3607; Undergraduates: $3755. *Parent loans:* $3,252,907 (63% need-based, 37% non-need-based). *Programs:* FFEL (Subsidized and Unsubsidized Stafford, PLUS), Perkins, college/university.
WORK-STUDY Federal work-study: Total amount: $364,133; 286 jobs averaging $1273. *State or other work-study/employment:* Total amount: $143,841 (100% non-need-based). 502 part-time jobs averaging $287.
APPLYING FOR FINANCIAL AID *Required financial aid forms:* FAFSA, CSS Financial Aid PROFILE. *Financial aid deadline (priority):* 2/15. *Notification date:* 4/1. Students must reply by 5/1 or within 2 weeks of notification.
CONTACT Sharon Hassan, Director of Student Financial Aid, Goucher College, 1021 Dulaney Valley Road, Baltimore, MD 21204-2794, 410-337-6141 or toll-free 800-468-2437. *Fax:* 410-337-6504.

GOVERNORS STATE UNIVERSITY
University Park, IL

CONTACT Financial Aid Office, Governors State University, One University Parkway, University Park, IL 60466-0975, 708-534-4480.

GRACE BIBLE COLLEGE
Grand Rapids, MI

Tuition & fees: $10,950   **Average undergraduate aid package: $7578**

ABOUT THE INSTITUTION Independent religious, coed. Awards: associate and bachelor's degrees. 21 undergraduate majors. Total enrollment: 161. Undergraduates: 161. Freshmen: 33. Federal methodology is used as a basis for awarding need-based institutional aid.
UNDERGRADUATE EXPENSES for 2005–06 *Comprehensive fee:* $17,810 includes full-time tuition ($10,450), mandatory fees ($500), and room and board ($6860). Room and board charges vary according to housing facility. *Part-time tuition:* $450 per semester hour. Part-time tuition and fees vary according to course load. *Payment plan:* Installment.
FRESHMAN FINANCIAL AID (Fall 2004) 42 applied for aid; of those 95% were deemed to have need. 100% of freshmen with need received aid; of those 2% had need fully met. *Average percent of need met:* 47% (excluding resources awarded to replace EFC). *Average financial aid package:* $6130 (excluding resources awarded to replace EFC). 7% of all full-time freshmen had no need and received non-need-based gift aid.
UNDERGRADUATE FINANCIAL AID (Fall 2004) 141 applied for aid; of those 95% were deemed to have need. 100% of undergraduates with need received aid; of those 4% had need fully met. *Average percent of need met:* 59% (excluding resources awarded to replace EFC). *Average financial aid package:* $7578 (excluding resources awarded to replace EFC). 5% of all full-time undergraduates had no need and received non-need-based gift aid.
GIFT AID (NEED-BASED) Total amount: $531,211 (31% federal, 37% state, 26% institutional, 6% external sources). *Receiving aid:* Freshmen: 91% (40); All full-time undergraduates: 85% (134). *Average award:* Freshmen: $4383; Undergraduates: $5066. *Scholarships, grants, and awards:* Federal Pell, FSEOG, state, private, college/university gift aid from institutional funds.
GIFT AID (NON-NEED-BASED) Total amount: $33,841 (13% state, 65% institutional, 22% external sources). *Receiving aid:* Freshmen: 5% (2); Undergraduates: 4% (7). *Average Award:* Freshmen: $1013; Undergraduates: $1138. *Scholarships, grants, and awards by category:* Academic Interests/Achievement: 76 awards ($47,959 total): general academic interests/achievements. Creative Arts/Performance: 12 awards ($12,250 total): music. Special Characteristics: 20 awards ($78,063 total): children of faculty/staff, general special characteristics, relatives of clergy. *Tuition waivers:* Full or partial for employees or children of employees. *ROTC:* Army cooperative.
LOANS Student loans: $906,103 (65% need-based, 35% non-need-based). 78% of past graduating class borrowed through all loan programs. *Average indebtedness per student:* $17,286. *Average need-based loan:* Freshmen: $2401; Undergraduates: $3497. *Parent loans:* $149,618 (53% need-based, 47% non-need-based). *Programs:* FFEL (Subsidized and Unsubsidized Stafford, PLUS).
WORK-STUDY Federal work-study: Total amount: $29,833; 38 jobs averaging $785. *State or other work-study/employment:* Total amount: $6813 (100% need-based). 15 part-time jobs averaging $454.
APPLYING FOR FINANCIAL AID *Required financial aid form:* FAFSA. *Financial aid deadline (priority):* 2/28. *Notification date:* Continuous beginning 5/15.
CONTACT Ms. Marlene DeVries, Director of Financial Aid, Grace Bible College, 1011 Aldon Street, SW, PO Box 910, Grand Rapids, MI 49509-1921, 616-538-2330 or toll-free 800-968-1887. *Fax:* 616-538-0599.

GRACE COLLEGE
Winona Lake, IN

Tuition & fees: $16,020   **Average undergraduate aid package: $12,899**

ABOUT THE INSTITUTION Independent religious, coed. Awards: associate, bachelor's, master's, doctoral, and first professional degrees. 39 undergraduate majors. Total enrollment: 1,275. Undergraduates: 1,128. Freshmen: 217. Federal methodology is used as a basis for awarding need-based institutional aid.
UNDERGRADUATE EXPENSES for 2005–06 *Application fee:* $20. *Comprehensive fee:* $22,170 includes full-time tuition ($15,620), mandatory fees ($400), and room and board ($6150). *College room only:* $3070. Room and board charges vary according to board plan and housing facility. *Part-time tuition:* $295 per credit. *Part-time fees:* $280 per year. Part-time tuition and fees vary according to course load. *Payment plan:* Installment.
FRESHMAN FINANCIAL AID (Fall 2005, est.) 197 applied for aid; of those 85% were deemed to have need. 100% of freshmen with need received aid; of those 32% had need fully met. *Average percent of need met:* 80% (excluding resources awarded to replace EFC). *Average financial aid package:* $11,587 (excluding resources awarded to replace EFC). 17% of all full-time freshmen had no need and received non-need-based gift aid.
UNDERGRADUATE FINANCIAL AID (Fall 2005, est.) 670 applied for aid; of those 87% were deemed to have need. 100% of undergraduates with need received aid; of those 32% had need fully met. *Average percent of need met:* 83% (excluding resources awarded to replace EFC). *Average financial aid package:* $12,899 (excluding resources awarded to replace EFC). 20% of all full-time undergraduates had no need and received non-need-based gift aid.
GIFT AID (NEED-BASED) Total amount: $4,210,816 (16% federal, 30% state, 39% institutional, 15% external sources). *Receiving aid:* Freshmen: 64% (167); All full-time undergraduates: 74% (568). *Average award:* Freshmen: $7876; Undergraduates: $8034. *Scholarships, grants, and awards:* Federal Pell, FSEOG, state, college/university gift aid from institutional funds.
GIFT AID (NON-NEED-BASED) Total amount: $1,051,857 (60% institutional, 40% external sources). *Receiving aid:* Freshmen: 12% (31); Undergraduates: 8% (64). *Average Award:* Freshmen: $14,709; Undergraduates: $12,154. *Scholarships, grants, and awards by category:* Academic Interests/Achievement: 590 awards ($1,547,673 total): general academic interests/achievements. Creative Arts/Performance: 44 awards ($44,125 total): art/fine arts, music, theater/drama. Special Characteristics: 155 awards ($541,135 total): children of faculty/staff, relatives of clergy. *Tuition waivers:* Full or partial for employees or children of employees.
LOANS Student loans: $4,533,992 (72% need-based, 28% non-need-based). 94% of past graduating class borrowed through all loan programs. *Average indebtedness per student:* $25,588. *Average need-based loan:* Freshmen: $4284; Undergraduates: $5503. *Parent loans:* $3,594,760 (24% need-based, 76% non-need-based). *Programs:* FFEL (Subsidized and Unsubsidized Stafford, PLUS), Perkins.
WORK-STUDY Federal work-study: Total amount: $164,165; 302 jobs averaging $1300.

ATHLETIC AWARDS *Total amount:* $763,516 (60% need-based, 40% non-need-based).
APPLYING FOR FINANCIAL AID *Required financial aid form:* FAFSA. *Financial aid deadline (priority):* 3/10. *Notification date:* Continuous beginning 3/15. Students must reply by 5/1.
CONTACT Office of Student Financial Aid Services, Grace College, 200 Seminary Drive, Winona Lake, IN 46590-1294, 800-544-7223 Ext. 6162 or toll-free 800-54-GRACE Ext. 6412 (in-state), 800-54 GRACE Ext. 6412 (out-of-state). *Fax:* 574-372-5144. *E-mail:* financialaid@grace.edu.

GRACELAND UNIVERSITY
Lamoni, IA

Tuition & fees: $16,150	Average undergraduate aid package: $14,364

ABOUT THE INSTITUTION Independent Community of Christ, coed. Awards: bachelor's and master's degrees and post-master's certificates. 54 undergraduate majors. Total enrollment: 2,351. Undergraduates: 1,945. Freshmen: 307. Federal methodology is used as a basis for awarding need-based institutional aid.
UNDERGRADUATE EXPENSES for 2005–06 *Application fee:* $50. *Comprehensive fee:* $21,550 includes full-time tuition ($16,000), mandatory fees ($150), and room and board ($5400). Full-time tuition and fees vary according to course load and location. Room and board charges vary according to board plan, housing facility, and location. *Part-time tuition:* $500 per semester hour. Part-time tuition and fees vary according to location. *Payment plan:* Installment.
FRESHMAN FINANCIAL AID (Fall 2005, est.) 214 applied for aid; of those 85% were deemed to have need. 99% of freshmen with need received aid; of those 35% had need fully met. *Average percent of need met:* 88% (excluding resources awarded to replace EFC). *Average financial aid package:* $16,607 (excluding resources awarded to replace EFC). 20% of all full-time freshmen had no need and received non-need-based gift aid.
UNDERGRADUATE FINANCIAL AID (Fall 2005, est.) 1,148 applied for aid; of those 84% were deemed to have need. 97% of undergraduates with need received aid; of those 25% had need fully met. *Average percent of need met:* 80% (excluding resources awarded to replace EFC). *Average financial aid package:* $14,364 (excluding resources awarded to replace EFC). 20% of all full-time undergraduates had no need and received non-need-based gift aid.
GIFT AID (NEED-BASED) *Total amount:* $7,697,458 (21% federal, 9% state, 64% institutional, 6% external sources). *Receiving aid:* Freshmen: 68% (179); All full-time undergraduates: 57% (873). *Average award:* Freshmen: $12,468; Undergraduates: $10,308. *Scholarships, grants, and awards:* Federal Pell, FSEOG, state, private, college/university gift aid from institutional funds.
GIFT AID (NON-NEED-BASED) *Total amount:* $3,489,162 (3% federal, 83% institutional, 14% external sources). *Receiving aid:* Freshmen: 39% (103); Undergraduates: 27% (413). *Average Award:* Freshmen: $8574; Undergraduates: $9894. *Scholarships, grants, and awards by category: Academic Interests/Achievement:* 988 awards ($3,804,674 total): computer science, engineering/technologies, English, general academic interests/achievements, physical sciences. *Creative Arts/Performance:* 296 awards ($550,210 total): applied art and design, creative writing, music, theater/drama. *Special Achievements/Activities:* 292 awards ($282,701 total): cheerleading/drum major, general special achievements/activities, leadership, religious involvement. *Special Characteristics:* 1,514 awards ($4,099,388 total): children and siblings of alumni, children of faculty/staff, children of public servants, first-generation college students, general special characteristics, international students, local/state students, members of minority groups, religious affiliation. *Tuition waivers:* Full or partial for employees or children of employees, senior citizens.
LOANS *Student loans:* $8,299,641 (71% need-based, 29% non-need-based). 77% of past graduating class borrowed through all loan programs. *Average indebtedness per student:* $23,198. *Average need-based loan:* Freshmen: $4489; Undergraduates: $5078. *Parent loans:* $808,280 (26% need-based, 74% non-need-based). *Programs:* Federal Direct (Subsidized and Unsubsidized Stafford, PLUS), Perkins, state, college/university.
WORK-STUDY *Federal work-study:* Total amount: $552,611; 335 jobs averaging $1650. *State or other work-study/employment:* Total amount: $431,389 (11% need-based, 89% non-need-based). 363 part-time jobs averaging $1188.
ATHLETIC AWARDS *Total amount:* $1,561,885 (64% need-based, 36% non-need-based).

APPLYING FOR FINANCIAL AID *Required financial aid form:* FAFSA. *Financial aid deadline:* Continuous. *Notification date:* Continuous beginning 2/1. Students must reply within 2 weeks of notification.
CONTACT Mrs. Sherry Mesle-Morain, Director of Financial Aid, Graceland University, 1 University Place, Lamoni, IA 50140, 641-784-5140 or toll-free 866-GRACELAND. *Fax:* 641-784-5488. *E-mail:* smorain@graceland.edu.

GRACE UNIVERSITY
Omaha, NE

ABOUT THE INSTITUTION Independent interdenominational, coed. Awards: associate, bachelor's, and master's degrees. 39 undergraduate majors. Total enrollment: 513. Undergraduates: 427. Freshmen: 122.
GIFT AID (NEED-BASED) *Scholarships, grants, and awards:* Federal Pell, FSEOG, state, college/university gift aid from institutional funds.
GIFT AID (NON-NEED-BASED) *Scholarships, grants, and awards by category: Academic Interests/Achievement:* business, education, general academic interests/achievements, health fields, international studies, religion/biblical studies. *Creative Arts/Performance:* cinema/film/broadcasting, music. *Special Achievements/Activities:* general special achievements/activities, leadership, religious involvement. *Special Characteristics:* adult students, children and siblings of alumni, children of faculty/staff, general special characteristics, international students, married students, members of minority groups, out-of-state students, relatives of clergy, religious affiliation, siblings of current students, spouses of current students.
LOANS *Programs:* FFEL (Subsidized and Unsubsidized Stafford, PLUS).
APPLYING FOR FINANCIAL AID *Required financial aid form:* FAFSA.
CONTACT Office of Financial Aid, Grace University, 1311 South Ninth Street, Omaha, NE 68108-3629, 402-449-2810 or toll-free 800-383-1422. *Fax:* 402-341-9587. *E-mail:* gufinaid@graceu.edu.

GRAMBLING STATE UNIVERSITY
Grambling, LA

Tuition & fees (LA res): $3506	Average undergraduate aid package: $6800

ABOUT THE INSTITUTION State-supported, coed. Awards: associate, bachelor's, master's, and doctoral degrees. 51 undergraduate majors. Total enrollment: 5,039. Undergraduates: 4,440. Freshmen: 1,156. Federal methodology is used as a basis for awarding need-based institutional aid.
UNDERGRADUATE EXPENSES for 2005–06 *Application fee:* $20. *Tuition, state resident:* full-time $2232; part-time $558 per term. *Tuition, nonresident:* full-time $7582; part-time $558 per term. Part-time tuition and fees vary according to course load. *College room and board:* $4034; *room only:* $2138. Room and board charges vary according to housing facility. *Payment plan:* Deferred payment.
FRESHMAN FINANCIAL AID (Fall 2005, est.) 1086 applied for aid; of those 90% were deemed to have need. 99% of freshmen with need received aid; of those 5% had need fully met. *Average percent of need met:* 78% (excluding resources awarded to replace EFC). *Average financial aid package:* $5950 (excluding resources awarded to replace EFC). 3% of all full-time freshmen had no need and received non-need-based gift aid.
UNDERGRADUATE FINANCIAL AID (Fall 2005, est.) 3,856 applied for aid; of those 91% were deemed to have need. 99% of undergraduates with need received aid; of those 10% had need fully met. *Average percent of need met:* 80% (excluding resources awarded to replace EFC). *Average financial aid package:* $6800 (excluding resources awarded to replace EFC). 4% of all full-time undergraduates had no need and received non-need-based gift aid.
GIFT AID (NEED-BASED) *Total amount:* $10,322,896 (100% federal). *Receiving aid:* Freshmen: 73% (828); All full-time undergraduates: 69% (2,874). *Average award:* Freshmen: $4000; Undergraduates: $4000. *Scholarships, grants, and awards:* Federal Pell, FSEOG, state.
GIFT AID (NON-NEED-BASED) *Total amount:* $2,027,044 (24% state, 58% institutional, 18% external sources). *Receiving aid:* Freshmen: 20% (225); Undergraduates: 22% (929). *Average Award:* Freshmen: $2800; Undergraduates: $2800. *Scholarships, grants, and awards by category: Academic Interests/Achievement:* 658 awards ($818,844 total): biological sciences, business, communication, computer science, education, engineering/technologies, English, foreign languages, general academic interests/achievements, health fields, home economics, humanities, mathematics, military science, physical sciences, premedicine, social sciences. *Creative Arts/Performance:* 198 awards ($119,434

Grambling State University

total): dance, general creative arts/performance, music, performing arts, theater/drama. *Special Achievements/Activities:* 5 awards ($8081 total): cheerleading/drum major, junior miss, leadership. *Special Characteristics:* 1,051 awards ($3,750,350 total): children and siblings of alumni, children of faculty/staff, children of public servants, ethnic background, international students, local/state students, members of minority groups, out-of-state students, public servants, veterans, veterans' children. *Tuition waivers:* Full or partial for children of alumni, employees or children of employees, senior citizens. *ROTC:* Army, Air Force.

LOANS *Student loans:* $22,480,779 (53% need-based, 47% non-need-based). 85% of past graduating class borrowed through all loan programs. *Average indebtedness per student:* $30,000. *Average need-based loan:* Freshmen: $2625; Undergraduates: $3875. *Parent loans:* $774,011 (100% non-need-based). *Programs:* FFEL (Subsidized and Unsubsidized Stafford, PLUS), alternative loans.

WORK-STUDY *Federal work-study:* Total amount: $753,810; 788 jobs averaging $957. *State or other work-study/employment:* Total amount: $75,000 (100% non-need-based). 72 part-time jobs averaging $1030.

ATHLETIC AWARDS *Total amount:* $1,058,305 (100% non-need-based).

APPLYING FOR FINANCIAL AID *Required financial aid form:* FAFSA. *Financial aid deadline:* 4/1. *Notification date:* Continuous beginning 3/1. Students must reply within 2 weeks of notification.

CONTACT Mrs. Anne Rugege, Assistant Director of Student Financial Aid and Scholarships, Grambling State University, PO Box 629, Grambling, LA 71245, 318-274-6415. *Fax:* 318-274-3358.

GRAND CANYON UNIVERSITY
Phoenix, AZ

ABOUT THE INSTITUTION Independent Southern Baptist, coed. Awards: bachelor's and master's degrees. 55 undergraduate majors. Total enrollment: 4,113. Undergraduates: 1,609. Freshmen: 371.

GIFT AID (NEED-BASED) *Scholarships, grants, and awards:* Federal Pell, FSEOG, state, private, college/university gift aid from institutional funds, Bureau of Indian Affairs Grants.

GIFT AID (NON-NEED-BASED) *Scholarships, grants, and awards by category: Academic Interests/Achievement:* biological sciences, business, communication, education, English, general academic interests/achievements, health fields, humanities, mathematics, military science, physical sciences, premedicine, religion/biblical studies, social sciences. *Creative Arts/Performance:* applied art and design, art/fine arts, music, performing arts, theater/drama. *Special Achievements/Activities:* leadership, memberships. *Special Characteristics:* children and siblings of alumni, children of faculty/staff, ethnic background, members of minority groups, out-of-state students, relatives of clergy, religious affiliation.

LOANS *Programs:* FFEL (Subsidized and Unsubsidized Stafford, PLUS), Perkins, state, alternative loans.

APPLYING FOR FINANCIAL AID *Required financial aid forms:* FAFSA, Different forms of aid.

CONTACT Director of Financial Aid, Grand Canyon University, 3300 West Camelback Road, PO Box 11097, Phoenix, AZ 85017-3030, 800-800-9776 Ext. 2885 or toll-free 800-800-9776 (in-state). *Fax:* 602-589-2044.

GRAND VALLEY STATE UNIVERSITY
Allendale, MI

Tuition & fees (MI res): $6220	Average undergraduate aid package: $7049

ABOUT THE INSTITUTION State-supported, coed. Awards: bachelor's and master's degrees and post-bachelor's and post-master's certificates. 122 undergraduate majors. Total enrollment: 22,565. Undergraduates: 18,903. Freshmen: 3,412. Federal methodology is used as a basis for awarding need-based institutional aid.

UNDERGRADUATE EXPENSES for 2005–06 *Application fee:* $30. *Tuition, state resident:* full-time $6220; part-time $271 per credit hour. *Tuition, nonresident:* full-time $12,510; part-time $532 per credit hour. Full-time tuition and fees vary according to course level, program, and student level. Part-time tuition and fees vary according to course level, course load, program, and student level. *College room and board:* $6360. Room and board charges vary according to board plan, housing facility, and location. *Payment plans:* Installment, deferred payment.

FRESHMAN FINANCIAL AID (Fall 2005, est.) 3092 applied for aid; of those 65% were deemed to have need. 100% of freshmen with need received aid; of those 100% had need fully met. *Average percent of need met:* 100% (excluding resources awarded to replace EFC). *Average financial aid package:* $7117 (excluding resources awarded to replace EFC). 37% of all full-time freshmen had no need and received non-need-based gift aid.

UNDERGRADUATE FINANCIAL AID (Fall 2005, est.) 12,999 applied for aid; of those 70% were deemed to have need. 100% of undergraduates with need received aid; of those 85% had need fully met. *Average percent of need met:* 85% (excluding resources awarded to replace EFC). *Average financial aid package:* $7049 (excluding resources awarded to replace EFC). 14% of all full-time undergraduates had no need and received non-need-based gift aid.

GIFT AID (NEED-BASED) *Total amount:* $26,306,047 (46% federal, 29% state, 25% institutional). *Receiving aid:* Freshmen: 50% (1,708); All full-time undergraduates: 34% (5,608). *Average award:* Freshmen: $4190; Undergraduates: $3081. *Scholarships, grants, and awards:* Federal Pell, FSEOG, state, private, college/university gift aid from institutional funds, Federal Nursing.

GIFT AID (NON-NEED-BASED) *Total amount:* $14,778,255 (25% state, 55% institutional, 20% external sources). *Receiving aid:* Freshmen: 57% (1,932); Undergraduates: 12% (1,980). *Average Award:* Freshmen: $2340; Undergraduates:* $2078. *Scholarships, grants, and awards by category: Academic Interests/Achievement:* 800 awards ($2,505,000 total): general academic interests/achievements. *Creative Arts/Performance:* 190 awards ($210,000 total): art/fine arts, music, theater/drama. *Special Characteristics:* 1,150 awards ($4,300,000 total): children of faculty/staff, children of union members/company employees, handicapped students, local/state students, members of minority groups, out-of-state students. *Tuition waivers:* Full or partial for employees or children of employees.

LOANS *Student loans:* $78,160,800 (66% need-based, 34% non-need-based). 73% of past graduating class borrowed through all loan programs. *Average indebtedness per student:* $16,606. *Average need-based loan:* Freshmen: $2638; Undergraduates: $3419. *Parent loans:* $5,200,000 (100% non-need-based). *Programs:* Federal Direct (Subsidized and Unsubsidized Stafford, PLUS), Perkins, Federal Nursing, state.

WORK-STUDY *Federal work-study:* Total amount: $1,051,897; 865 jobs averaging $1200. *State or other work-study/employment:* Total amount: $6,564,240 (6% need-based, 94% non-need-based). 261 part-time jobs averaging $1340.

ATHLETIC AWARDS *Total amount:* $2,180,928 (100% non-need-based).

APPLYING FOR FINANCIAL AID *Required financial aid form:* FAFSA. *Financial aid deadline (priority):* 2/15. *Notification date:* 4/1. Students must reply within 3 weeks of notification.

CONTACT Mr. Ken Fridsma, Director of Financial Aid, Grand Valley State University, 100 Student Services Building, Allendale, MI 49401-9403, 616-331-3234 or toll-free 800-748-0246. *Fax:* 616-331-3180. *E-mail:* fridsmak@gvsu.edu.

GRAND VIEW COLLEGE
Des Moines, IA

Tuition & fees: $16,110	Average undergraduate aid package: $12,144

ABOUT THE INSTITUTION Independent religious, coed. Awards: associate and bachelor's degrees and post-bachelor's certificates. 29 undergraduate majors. Total enrollment: 1,761. Undergraduates: 1,761. Freshmen: 221. Federal methodology is used as a basis for awarding need-based institutional aid.

UNDERGRADUATE EXPENSES for 2005–06 *Application fee:* $35. *Comprehensive fee:* $21,774 includes full-time tuition ($15,750), mandatory fees ($360), and room and board ($5664). Full-time tuition and fees vary according to class time. Room and board charges vary according to board plan and housing facility. *Part-time tuition:* $425 per hour. Part-time tuition and fees vary according to class time. *Payment plan:* Installment.

FRESHMAN FINANCIAL AID (Fall 2005, est.) 202 applied for aid; of those 82% were deemed to have need. 99% of freshmen with need received aid; of those 16% had need fully met. *Average percent of need met:* 80% (excluding resources awarded to replace EFC). *Average financial aid package:* $13,777 (excluding resources awarded to replace EFC). 24% of all full-time freshmen had no need and received non-need-based gift aid.

UNDERGRADUATE FINANCIAL AID (Fall 2005, est.) 1,300 applied for aid; of those 86% were deemed to have need. 99% of undergraduates with need received aid; of those 17% had need fully met. *Average percent of need met:* 74% (excluding resources awarded to replace EFC). *Average financial aid package:* $12,144 (excluding resources awarded to replace EFC). 18% of all full-time undergraduates had no need and received non-need-based gift aid.
GIFT AID (NEED-BASED) *Total amount:* $9,363,076 (17% federal, 32% state, 46% institutional, 5% external sources). *Receiving aid:* Freshmen: 73% (162); All full-time undergraduates: 80% (1,104). *Average award:* Freshmen: $10,895; Undergraduates: $8448. *Scholarships, grants, and awards:* Federal Pell, FSEOG, state, private, college/university gift aid from institutional funds.
GIFT AID (NON-NEED-BASED) *Total amount:* $1,397,489 (3% federal, 6% state, 82% institutional, 9% external sources). *Receiving aid:* Freshmen: 8% (18); Undergraduates: 7% (92). *Average Award:* Freshmen: $12,735; Undergraduates: $11,108. *Scholarships, grants, and awards by category: Academic Interests/Achievement:* 777 awards ($3,075,480 total): general academic interests/achievements. *Creative Arts/Performance:* 57 awards ($64,150 total): art/fine arts, music, theater/drama. *Special Achievements/Activities:* 1 award ($500 total): junior miss. *Special Characteristics:* 118 awards ($444,526 total): children and siblings of alumni, children of educators, children of faculty/staff. *Tuition waivers:* Full or partial for employees or children of employees, senior citizens. **ROTC:** Army cooperative, Air Force cooperative.
LOANS *Student loans:* $12,089,278 (61% need-based, 39% non-need-based). 94% of past graduating class borrowed through all loan programs. *Average indebtedness per student:* $18,463. *Average need-based loan:* Freshmen: $3000; Undergraduates: $3867. *Parent loans:* $456,687 (20% need-based, 80% non-need-based). *Programs:* FFEL (Subsidized and Unsubsidized Stafford, PLUS), Perkins, Federal Nursing.
WORK-STUDY *Federal work-study:* Total amount: $322,402; 230 jobs averaging $1500. *State or other work-study/employment:* Total amount: $905 (100% need-based). 1 part-time job averaging $905.
ATHLETIC AWARDS *Total amount:* $553,770 (55% need-based, 45% non-need-based).
APPLYING FOR FINANCIAL AID *Required financial aid form:* FAFSA. *Financial aid deadline (priority):* 3/1. *Notification date:* Continuous beginning 3/15. Students must reply by 5/1 or within 4 weeks of notification.
CONTACT Michele Dunne, Director of Financial Aid, Grand View College, 1200 Grandview Avenue, Des Moines, IA 50316-1599, 515-263-2820 or toll-free 800-444-6083 Ext. 2810. *Fax:* 515-263-6191. *E-mail:* mdunne@gvc.edu.

GRATZ COLLEGE
Melrose Park, PA

CONTACT Karen West, Student Financial Services Adviser, Gratz College, 7605 Old York Road, Melrose Park, PA 19027, 215-635-7300 Ext. 163 or toll-free 800-475-4635 Ext. 140 (out-of-state). *Fax:* 215-635-7320.

GREAT LAKES CHRISTIAN COLLEGE
Lansing, MI

CONTACT Financial Aid Officer, Great Lakes Christian College, 6211 West Willow Highway, Lansing, MI 48917-1299, 517-321-0242 or toll-free 800-YES-GLCC.

GREEN MOUNTAIN COLLEGE
Poultney, VT

Tuition & fees: $22,204   **Average undergraduate aid package:** $19,049

ABOUT THE INSTITUTION Independent religious, coed. Awards: bachelor's and master's degrees. 24 undergraduate majors. Total enrollment: 696. Undergraduates: 696. Freshmen: 254. Federal methodology is used as a basis for awarding need-based institutional aid.
UNDERGRADUATE EXPENSES for 2005–06 *Application fee:* $30. *Comprehensive fee:* $29,894 includes full-time tuition ($21,604), mandatory fees ($600), and room and board ($7690). *College room only:* $4700. Full-time tuition and fees vary according to course load. Room and board charges vary according to housing facility. *Part-time tuition:* $720 per credit hour. Part-time tuition and fees vary according to course load. *Payment plan:* Installment.
FRESHMAN FINANCIAL AID (Fall 2005, est.) 224 applied for aid; of those 90% were deemed to have need. 100% of freshmen with need received aid; of those 29% had need fully met. *Average percent of need met:* 80% (excluding resources awarded to replace EFC). *Average financial aid package:* $19,403 (excluding resources awarded to replace EFC). 19% of all full-time freshmen had no need and received non-need-based gift aid.
UNDERGRADUATE FINANCIAL AID (Fall 2005, est.) 573 applied for aid; of those 88% were deemed to have need. 99% of undergraduates with need received aid; of those 29% had need fully met. *Average percent of need met:* 78% (excluding resources awarded to replace EFC). *Average financial aid package:* $19,049 (excluding resources awarded to replace EFC). 14% of all full-time undergraduates had no need and received non-need-based gift aid.
GIFT AID (NEED-BASED) *Total amount:* $6,014,347 (19% federal, 4% state, 76% institutional, 1% external sources). *Receiving aid:* Freshmen: 74% (200); All full-time undergraduates: 77% (477). *Average award:* Freshmen: $14,444; Undergraduates: $12,939. *Scholarships, grants, and awards:* Federal Pell, FSEOG, state, private, college/university gift aid from institutional funds.
GIFT AID (NON-NEED-BASED) *Total amount:* $388,977 (94% institutional, 6% external sources). *Receiving aid:* Freshmen: 7% (18); Undergraduates: 4% (27). *Average Award:* Freshmen: $14,489; Undergraduates: $15,767. *Scholarships, grants, and awards by category: Creative Arts/Performance:* 14 awards ($23,200 total): art/fine arts, music, performing arts, theater/drama. *Special Achievements/Activities:* 72 awards ($132,783 total): community service, leadership, religious involvement. *Special Characteristics:* 49 awards ($181,418 total): children and siblings of alumni, children of current students, international students, local/state students, parents of current students, relatives of clergy, siblings of current students. *Tuition waivers:* Full or partial for employees or children of employees.
LOANS *Student loans:* $4,846,301 (68% need-based, 32% non-need-based). 95% of past graduating class borrowed through all loan programs. *Average indebtedness per student:* $23,894. *Average need-based loan:* Freshmen: $4492; Undergraduates: $6251. *Parent loans:* $1,591,645 (41% need-based, 59% non-need-based). *Programs:* FFEL (Subsidized and Unsubsidized Stafford, PLUS).
WORK-STUDY *Federal work-study:* Total amount: $186,802; 159 jobs averaging $1500. *State or other work-study/employment:* Total amount: $365,320 (100% need-based). 271 part-time jobs averaging $1500.
APPLYING FOR FINANCIAL AID *Required financial aid forms:* FAFSA, CSS Financial Aid PROFILE. *Financial aid deadline (priority):* 3/1. *Notification date:* Continuous beginning 1/1. Students must reply by 5/1 or within 4 weeks of notification.
CONTACT Wendy J. Ellis, Director of Financial Aid, Green Mountain College, One College Circle, Poultney, VT 05764-1199, 800-776-6675 Ext. 8210 or toll-free 800-776-6675 (out-of-state). *Fax:* 802-287-8099. *E-mail:* ellisw@greenmtn.edu.

GREENSBORO COLLEGE
Greensboro, NC

CONTACT Mr. Ron Elmore, Director of Financial Aid, Greensboro College, 815 West Market Street, Greensboro, NC 27401-1875, 336-272-7102 Ext. 339 or toll-free 800-346-8226. *Fax:* 336-271-6634. *E-mail:* relmore@gborocollege.edu.

GREENVILLE COLLEGE
Greenville, IL

Tuition & fees: $17,242   **Average undergraduate aid package:** $14,307

ABOUT THE INSTITUTION Independent Free Methodist, coed. Awards: bachelor's and master's degrees. 51 undergraduate majors. Total enrollment: 1,350. Undergraduates: 1,215. Freshmen: 252. Federal methodology is used as a basis for awarding need-based institutional aid.
UNDERGRADUATE EXPENSES for 2005–06 *Application fee:* $25. *Comprehensive fee:* $23,146 includes full-time tuition ($17,142), mandatory fees ($100), and room and board ($5904). *College room only:* $2794. Room and board charges vary according to housing facility. *Part-time tuition:* $361 per credit hour. Part-time tuition and fees vary according to course load.
FRESHMAN FINANCIAL AID (Fall 2005, est.) 233 applied for aid; of those 91% were deemed to have need. 100% of freshmen with need received aid; of those 15% had need fully met. *Average percent of need met:* 79% (excluding resources awarded to replace EFC). *Average financial aid package:* $15,099 (excluding resources awarded to replace EFC). 18% of all full-time freshmen had no need and received non-need-based gift aid.

Greenville College

UNDERGRADUATE FINANCIAL AID (Fall 2005, est.) 829 applied for aid; of those 92% were deemed to have need. 100% of undergraduates with need received aid; of those 15% had need fully met. *Average percent of need met:* 78% (excluding resources awarded to replace EFC). *Average financial aid package:* $14,307 (excluding resources awarded to replace EFC). 15% of all full-time undergraduates had no need and received non-need-based gift aid.
GIFT AID (NEED-BASED) *Total amount:* $7,609,197 (13% federal, 18% state, 66% institutional, 3% external sources). *Receiving aid:* Freshmen: 82% (211); All full-time undergraduates: 85% (760). *Average award:* Freshmen: $11,207; Undergraduates: $9913. *Scholarships, grants, and awards:* Federal Pell, FSEOG, state, private, college/university gift aid from institutional funds.
GIFT AID (NON-NEED-BASED) *Total amount:* $896,050 (1% state, 91% institutional, 8% external sources). *Receiving aid:* Freshmen: 7% (17); Undergraduates: 6% (52). *Average Award:* Freshmen: $6065; Undergraduates: $8104. *Scholarships, grants, and awards by category: Academic Interests/Achievement:* 486 awards ($2,062,522 total): biological sciences, business, education, engineering/technologies, general academic interests/achievements, mathematics, physical sciences, religion/biblical studies. *Creative Arts/Performance:* 131 awards ($141,000 total): applied art and design, art/fine arts, music, performing arts. *Special Achievements/Activities:* 540 awards ($992,590 total): leadership, memberships, religious involvement. *Special Characteristics:* 594 awards ($1,349,800 total): children and siblings of alumni, children of faculty/staff, international students, local/state students, out-of-state students, relatives of clergy, religious affiliation, siblings of current students. *Tuition waivers:* Full or partial for employees or children of employees, senior citizens.
LOANS *Student loans:* $4,632,846 (79% need-based, 21% non-need-based). 85% of past graduating class borrowed through all loan programs. *Average indebtedness per student:* $19,820. *Average need-based loan:* Freshmen: $3322; Undergraduates: $4000. *Parent loans:* $1,770,949 (38% need-based, 62% non-need-based). *Programs:* FFEL (Subsidized and Unsubsidized Stafford, PLUS), Perkins, college/university.
WORK-STUDY *Federal work-study:* Total amount: $289,000; 212 jobs averaging $1390. *State or other work-study/employment:* Total amount: $23,000 (100% non-need-based). 26 part-time jobs averaging $827.
APPLYING FOR FINANCIAL AID *Required financial aid form:* FAFSA. *Financial aid deadline:* Continuous. *Notification date:* Continuous beginning 3/15. Students must reply within 3 weeks of notification.
CONTACT Mr. Karl Somerville, Director of Financial Aid, Greenville College, 315 East College Avenue, Greenville, IL 62246-0159, 618-664-7110 or toll-free 800-345-4440. *Fax:* 618-664-9841. *E-mail:* karl.somerville@greenville.edu.

GRINNELL COLLEGE
Grinnell, IA

ABOUT THE INSTITUTION Independent, coed. Awards: bachelor's degrees. 24 undergraduate majors. Total enrollment: 1,577. Undergraduates: 1,577. Freshmen: 387.
GIFT AID (NEED-BASED) *Scholarships, grants, and awards:* Federal Pell, FSEOG, state, private, college/university gift aid from institutional funds.
GIFT AID (NON-NEED-BASED) *Scholarships, grants, and awards by category: Academic Interests/Achievement:* general academic interests/achievements.
LOANS *Programs:* FFEL (Subsidized and Unsubsidized Stafford, PLUS), Perkins, college/university.
WORK-STUDY *Federal work-study:* Total amount: $758,772; 469 jobs averaging $1618. *State or other work-study/employment:* Total amount: $458,111 (54% need-based, 46% non-need-based). 257 part-time jobs averaging $1783.
APPLYING FOR FINANCIAL AID *Required financial aid forms:* FAFSA, institution's own form, noncustodial (divorced/separated) parent's statement.
CONTACT Mr. Arnold Woods, Director of Student Financial Aid, Grinnell College, 1121 Park Street, Grinnell, IA 50112-1690, 641-269-3250 or toll-free 800-247-0113. *Fax:* 641-269-4937. *E-mail:* woods@grinnell.edu.

GROVE CITY COLLEGE
Grove City, PA

Tuition & fees: $10,640	Average undergraduate aid package: $5175

ABOUT THE INSTITUTION Independent Presbyterian, coed. Awards: bachelor's degrees. 45 undergraduate majors. Total enrollment: 2,341. Undergraduates: 2,341. Freshmen: 580. Institutional methodology is used as a basis for awarding need-based institutional aid.
UNDERGRADUATE EXPENSES for 2005–06 *Application fee:* $50. *Comprehensive fee:* $15,984 includes full-time tuition ($10,440), mandatory fees ($200), and room and board ($5344). Full-time tuition and fees vary according to course load. *Part-time tuition:* $334 per credit. *Payment plan:* Installment.
FRESHMAN FINANCIAL AID (Fall 2005, est.) 352 applied for aid; of those 68% were deemed to have need. 100% of freshmen with need received aid; of those 15% had need fully met. *Average percent of need met:* 56% (excluding resources awarded to replace EFC). *Average financial aid package:* $5393 (excluding resources awarded to replace EFC). 31% of all full-time freshmen had no need and received non-need-based gift aid.
UNDERGRADUATE FINANCIAL AID (Fall 2005, est.) 1,006 applied for aid; of those 83% were deemed to have need. 98% of undergraduates with need received aid; of those 10% had need fully met. *Average percent of need met:* 49% (excluding resources awarded to replace EFC). *Average financial aid package:* $5175 (excluding resources awarded to replace EFC). 34% of all full-time undergraduates had no need and received non-need-based gift aid.
GIFT AID (NEED-BASED) *Total amount:* $3,802,629 (23% state, 63% institutional, 14% external sources). *Receiving aid:* Freshmen: 41% (240); All full-time undergraduates: 33% (764). *Average award:* Freshmen: $5104; Undergraduates: $4971. *Scholarships, grants, and awards:* state, private, college/university gift aid from institutional funds.
GIFT AID (NON-NEED-BASED) *Total amount:* $1,527,191 (5% state, 50% institutional, 45% external sources). *Receiving aid:* Freshmen: 6% (36); Undergraduates: 3% (77). *Average Award:* Freshmen: $4919; Undergraduates: $6260. *Scholarships, grants, and awards by category: Academic Interests/Achievement:* 541 awards ($922,261 total): biological sciences, business, communication, education, engineering/technologies, English, foreign languages, general academic interests/achievements, physical sciences, religion/biblical studies, social sciences. *Creative Arts/Performance:* 5 awards ($6000 total): creative writing, music. *Special Achievements/Activities:* 19 awards ($43,250 total): general special achievements/activities, leadership, memberships, religious involvement. *Special Characteristics:* 7 awards ($32,200 total): ethnic background, general special characteristics, members of minority groups. *Tuition waivers:* Full or partial for employees or children of employees. *ROTC:* Army cooperative.
LOANS *Student loans:* $7,729,915 (100% non-need-based). 53% of past graduating class borrowed through all loan programs. *Average indebtedness per student:* $23,409. *Programs:* alternative loans.
WORK-STUDY *State or other work-study/employment:* Total amount: $10,825 (100% non-need-based). 18 part-time jobs averaging $600.
APPLYING FOR FINANCIAL AID *Required financial aid forms:* institution's own form, state aid form. *Financial aid deadline:* 4/15. *Notification date:* Continuous beginning 3/15.
CONTACT Patty Peterson, Director of Financial Aid, Grove City College, 100 Campus Drive, Grove City, PA 16127-2104, 724-458-3300. *Fax:* 724-450-4040. *E-mail:* financialaid@gcc.edu.

GUILFORD COLLEGE
Greensboro, NC

Tuition & fees: $23,020	Average undergraduate aid package: $11,661

ABOUT THE INSTITUTION Independent religious, coed. Awards: bachelor's degrees. 37 undergraduate majors. Total enrollment: 2,682. Undergraduates: 2,682. Freshmen: 460. Federal methodology is used as a basis for awarding need-based institutional aid.
UNDERGRADUATE EXPENSES for 2006–07 *Application fee:* $25. *Comprehensive fee:* $29,710 includes full-time tuition ($22,690), mandatory fees ($330), and room and board ($6690). *Part-time tuition:* $700 per credit hour. *Part-time fees:* $330 per year.
FRESHMAN FINANCIAL AID (Fall 2005, est.) 315 applied for aid; of those 74% were deemed to have need. 100% of freshmen with need received aid; of those 27% had need fully met. *Average percent of need met:* 87% (excluding resources awarded to replace EFC). *Average financial aid package:* $17,950 (excluding resources awarded to replace EFC). 19% of all full-time freshmen had no need and received non-need-based gift aid.

UNDERGRADUATE FINANCIAL AID (Fall 2005, est.) 1,201 applied for aid; of those 87% were deemed to have need. 99% of undergraduates with need received aid; of those 18% had need fully met. *Average percent of need met:* 67% (excluding resources awarded to replace EFC). *Average financial aid package:* $11,661 (excluding resources awarded to replace EFC). 26% of all full-time undergraduates had no need and received non-need-based gift aid.
GIFT AID (NEED-BASED) *Total amount:* $8,360,532 (21% federal, 23% state, 53% institutional, 3% external sources). *Receiving aid:* Freshmen: 57% (233); All full-time undergraduates: 65% (999). *Average award:* Freshmen: $13,772; Undergraduates: $8325. *Scholarships, grants, and awards:* Federal Pell, FSEOG, state, private, college/university gift aid from institutional funds.
GIFT AID (NON-NEED-BASED) *Total amount:* $2,527,839 (10% state, 80% institutional, 10% external sources). *Receiving aid:* Freshmen: 29% (119); Undergraduates: 49% (758). *Average Award:* Freshmen: $8116; Undergraduates: $7006. *Scholarships, grants, and awards by category: Academic Interests/Achievement:* 1,215 awards ($4,750,175 total): biological sciences, general academic interests/achievements. *Creative Arts/Performance:* 36 awards ($42,780 total): music, theater/drama. *Special Achievements/Activities:* 25 awards ($75,525 total): religious involvement. *Special Characteristics:* 310 awards ($554,173 total): children of faculty/staff, first-generation college students, local/state students.
LOANS *Student loans:* $6,222,943 (90% need-based, 10% non-need-based). 61% of past graduating class borrowed through all loan programs. *Average indebtedness per student:* $20,150. *Average need-based loan:* Freshmen: $4695; Undergraduates: $4145. *Parent loans:* $1,104,871 (77% need-based, 23% non-need-based). *Programs:* FFEL (Subsidized and Unsubsidized Stafford, PLUS), Perkins, college/university.
WORK-STUDY *Federal work-study:* Total amount: $155,643; 184 jobs averaging $1225. *State or other work-study/employment:* Total amount: $88,295 (67% need-based, 33% non-need-based). 128 part-time jobs averaging $1200.
APPLYING FOR FINANCIAL AID *Required financial aid forms:* FAFSA, noncustodial (divorced/separated) parent's statement, business/farm supplement. *Financial aid deadline (priority):* 3/1. *Notification date:* Continuous beginning 2/1. Students must reply within 2 weeks of notification.
CONTACT Mr. Anthony E. Gurley, Associate Dean of Enrollment, Guilford College, 5800 West Friendly Avenue, Greensboro, NC 27410, 336-316-2142 or toll-free 800-992-7759. *Fax:* 336-316-2952. *E-mail:* agurley@guilford.edu.

GUSTAVUS ADOLPHUS COLLEGE
St. Peter, MN

Tuition & fees: $24,865   Average undergraduate aid package: $16,526

ABOUT THE INSTITUTION Independent religious, coed. Awards: bachelor's degrees. 64 undergraduate majors. Total enrollment: 2,603. Undergraduates: 2,603. Freshmen: 705. Both federal and institutional methodology are used as a basis for awarding need-based institutional aid.
UNDERGRADUATE EXPENSES for 2005–06 *Comprehensive fee:* $30,930 includes full-time tuition ($24,500), mandatory fees ($365), and room and board ($6065). *College room only:* $3665. Full-time tuition and fees vary according to student level. Room and board charges vary according to board plan, housing facility, and student level. *Part-time tuition:* $3000 per course. *Payment plans:* Guaranteed tuition, tuition prepayment, installment.
FRESHMAN FINANCIAL AID (Fall 2004) 525 applied for aid; of those 82% were deemed to have need. 100% of freshmen with need received aid. *Average percent of need met:* 91% (excluding resources awarded to replace EFC). *Average financial aid package:* $18,202 (excluding resources awarded to replace EFC). 29% of all full-time freshmen had no need and received non-need-based gift aid.
UNDERGRADUATE FINANCIAL AID (Fall 2004) 1,970 applied for aid; of those 83% were deemed to have need. 100% of undergraduates with need received aid. *Average percent of need met:* 87% (excluding resources awarded to replace EFC). *Average financial aid package:* $16,526 (excluding resources awarded to replace EFC). 27% of all full-time undergraduates had no need and received non-need-based gift aid.
GIFT AID (NEED-BASED) *Total amount:* $19,542,780 (8% federal, 11% state, 77% institutional, 4% external sources). *Receiving aid:* Freshmen: 64% (424); All full-time undergraduates: 63% (1,619). *Average award:* Freshmen: $14,145; Undergraduates: $12,271. *Scholarships, grants, and awards:* Federal Pell, FSEOG, state, private, college/university gift aid from institutional funds.

GIFT AID (NON-NEED-BASED) *Total amount:* $4,901,736 (1% federal, 89% institutional, 10% external sources). *Receiving aid:* Freshmen: 8% (54); Undergraduates: 7% (177). *Average Award:* Freshmen: $5914; Undergraduates: $5532. *Scholarships, grants, and awards by category: Academic Interests/Achievement:* 493 awards ($2,371,812 total): general academic interests/achievements. *Creative Arts/Performance:* 60 awards ($168,037 total): music, theater/drama. *Special Achievements/Activities:* 212 awards ($156,250 total): community service. *Special Characteristics:* 70 awards ($105,000 total): children and siblings of alumni. *Tuition waivers:* Full or partial for employees or children of employees. *ROTC:* Army cooperative.
LOANS *Student loans:* $12,683,322 (54% need-based, 46% non-need-based). 68% of past graduating class borrowed through all loan programs. *Average indebtedness per student:* $19,500. *Average need-based loan:* Freshmen: $3668; Undergraduates: $4277. *Parent loans:* $2,053,268 (14% need-based, 86% non-need-based). *Programs:* Federal Direct (Subsidized and Unsubsidized Stafford, PLUS), Perkins, state, private/alternative education loans from banks.
WORK-STUDY *Federal work-study:* Total amount: $995,730; 672 jobs averaging $1482. *State or other work-study/employment:* Total amount: $1,119,111 (68% need-based, 32% non-need-based). 784 part-time jobs averaging $1427.
APPLYING FOR FINANCIAL AID *Required financial aid forms:* FAFSA, institution's own form. *Financial aid deadline (priority):* 2/15. *Notification date:* Continuous beginning 3/1. Students must reply by 5/1 or within 2 weeks of notification.
CONTACT Mr. Kirk Carlson, Associate Director of Student Financial Assistance, Gustavus Adolphus College, 800 West College Avenue, St. Peter, MN 56082-1498, 507-933-7527 or toll-free 800-GUSTAVU(S). *Fax:* 507-933-7727. *E-mail:* kcarlson@gustavus.edu.

GUTENBERG COLLEGE
Eugene, OR

CONTACT Financial Aid Office, Gutenberg College, 1883 University Street, Eugene, OR 97403, 541-683-5141.

GWYNEDD-MERCY COLLEGE
Gwynedd Valley, PA

Tuition & fees: $19,220   Average undergraduate aid package: $13,485

ABOUT THE INSTITUTION Independent Roman Catholic, coed. Awards: associate, bachelor's, and master's degrees and post-bachelor's and post-master's certificates. 36 undergraduate majors. Total enrollment: 2,723. Undergraduates: 2,180. Freshmen: 315. Federal methodology is used as a basis for awarding need-based institutional aid.
UNDERGRADUATE EXPENSES for 2006–07 *Application fee:* $25. *Comprehensive fee:* $27,520 includes full-time tuition ($18,720), mandatory fees ($500), and room and board ($8300). *Part-time tuition:* $415 per credit. *Part-time fees:* $10 per credit.
FRESHMAN FINANCIAL AID (Fall 2004) 251 applied for aid; of those 85% were deemed to have need. 100% of freshmen with need received aid; of those 75% had need fully met. *Average percent of need met:* 85% (excluding resources awarded to replace EFC). *Average financial aid package:* $14,446 (excluding resources awarded to replace EFC). 28% of all full-time freshmen had no need and received non-need-based gift aid.
UNDERGRADUATE FINANCIAL AID (Fall 2004) 1,135 applied for aid; of those 79% were deemed to have need. 100% of undergraduates with need received aid; of those 35% had need fully met. *Average percent of need met:* 82% (excluding resources awarded to replace EFC). *Average financial aid package:* $13,485 (excluding resources awarded to replace EFC). 18% of all full-time undergraduates had no need and received non-need-based gift aid.
GIFT AID (NEED-BASED) *Total amount:* $9,400,889 (12% federal, 21% state, 65% institutional, 2% external sources). *Receiving aid:* Freshmen: 76% (213); All full-time undergraduates: 65% (820). *Average award:* Freshmen: $10,686; Undergraduates: $9867. *Scholarships, grants, and awards:* Federal Pell, FSEOG, state, private, college/university gift aid from institutional funds.
GIFT AID (NON-NEED-BASED) *Total amount:* $1,588,184 (97% institutional, 3% external sources). *Receiving aid:* Freshmen: 61% (170); Undergraduates: 57% (720). *Average Award:* Freshmen: $9712; Undergraduates: $9321. *Scholarships, grants, and awards by category: Academic Interests/Achievement:* 560 awards ($3,524,590 total): general academic interests/achievements. *Special*

Gwynedd-Mercy College

Achievements/Activities: 158 awards ($540,500 total): general special achievements/activities. *Special Characteristics:* 6 awards ($9000 total): children and siblings of alumni, siblings of current students.
LOANS *Student loans:* $6,865,342 (56% need-based, 44% non-need-based). 85% of past graduating class borrowed through all loan programs. *Average indebtedness per student:* $18,708. *Average need-based loan:* Freshmen: $3082; Undergraduates: $5560. *Parent loans:* $1,399,280 (10% need-based, 90% non-need-based). *Programs:* FFEL (Subsidized and Unsubsidized Stafford, PLUS), Perkins, Federal Nursing, alternative loans.
WORK-STUDY *Federal work-study:* Total amount: $290,234; 192 jobs averaging $1090. *State or other work-study/employment:* Total amount: $17,036 (100% need-based). 17 part-time jobs averaging $1002.
APPLYING FOR FINANCIAL AID *Required financial aid forms:* FAFSA, institution's own form. *Financial aid deadline (priority):* 3/1. *Notification date:* Continuous beginning 3/1. Students must reply by 5/1.
CONTACT Sr. Barbara A. Kaufmann, Director of Student Financial Aid, Gwynedd-Mercy College, PO Box 901, Gwynedd Valley, PA 19437-0901, 215-641-5570 or toll-free 800-DIAL-GMC (in-state). *Fax:* 215-641-5556.

HAMILTON COLLEGE
Clinton, NY

ABOUT THE INSTITUTION Independent, coed. Awards: bachelor's degrees. 46 undergraduate majors. Total enrollment: 1,812. Undergraduates: 1,812. Freshmen: 498.
GIFT AID (NEED-BASED) *Scholarships, grants, and awards:* Federal Pell, FSEOG, state, private, college/university gift aid from institutional funds.
GIFT AID (NON-NEED-BASED) *Scholarships, grants, and awards by category: Academic Interests/Achievement:* general academic interests/achievements. *Creative Arts/Performance:* general creative arts/performance. *Special Achievements/Activities:* general special achievements/activities. *Special Characteristics:* general special characteristics.
LOANS *Programs:* FFEL (Subsidized and Unsubsidized Stafford, PLUS), Perkins, college/university.
WORK-STUDY *Federal work-study:* Total amount: $570,166; jobs available (averaging $1600).
APPLYING FOR FINANCIAL AID *Required financial aid forms:* FAFSA, institution's own form, CSS Financial Aid PROFILE, state aid form, noncustodial (divorced/separated) parent's statement, business/farm supplement.
CONTACT Mr. Kevin Michaelsen, Associate Director of Financial Aid, Hamilton College, 198 College Hill Road, Clinton, NY 13323, 315-859-4395 or toll-free 800-843-2655. *Fax:* 315-859-4457. *E-mail:* kmichael@hamilton.edu.

HAMILTON TECHNICAL COLLEGE
Davenport, IA

CONTACT Ms. Lisa Boyd, Executive Vice President/Director of Financial Aid, Hamilton Technical College, 1011 East 53rd Street, Davenport, IA 52807-2653, 563-386-3570 Ext. 33. *Fax:* 563-386-6756.

HAMLINE UNIVERSITY
St. Paul, MN

Tuition & fees: $23,157	Average undergraduate aid package: $23,824

ABOUT THE INSTITUTION Independent religious, coed. Awards: bachelor's, master's, doctoral, and first professional degrees and post-bachelor's certificates. 61 undergraduate majors. Total enrollment: 4,550. Undergraduates: 2,046. Freshmen: 461. Federal methodology is used as a basis for awarding need-based institutional aid.
UNDERGRADUATE EXPENSES for 2005–06 *Comprehensive fee:* $30,067 includes full-time tuition ($22,758), mandatory fees ($399), and room and board ($6910). *College room only:* $3484. Full-time tuition and fees vary according to student level. Room and board charges vary according to board plan and housing facility. *Part-time tuition:* $700 per credit. Part-time tuition and fees vary according to course load and student level. *Payment plan:* Installment.
FRESHMAN FINANCIAL AID (Fall 2005, est.) 443 applied for aid; of those 80% were deemed to have need. 100% of freshmen with need received aid; of those 52% had need fully met. *Average percent of need met:* 87% (excluding resources awarded to replace EFC). *Average financial aid package:* $23,872 (excluding resources awarded to replace EFC). 19% of all full-time freshmen had no need and received non-need-based gift aid.
UNDERGRADUATE FINANCIAL AID (Fall 2005, est.) 1,807 applied for aid; of those 79% were deemed to have need. 100% of undergraduates with need received aid; of those 48% had need fully met. *Average percent of need met:* 85% (excluding resources awarded to replace EFC). *Average financial aid package:* $23,824 (excluding resources awarded to replace EFC). 19% of all full-time undergraduates had no need and received non-need-based gift aid.
GIFT AID (NEED-BASED) *Total amount:* $10,362,017 (16% federal, 23% state, 59% institutional, 2% external sources). *Receiving aid:* Freshmen: 61% (279); All full-time undergraduates: 66% (1,245). *Average award:* Freshmen: $7169; Undergraduates: $7011. *Scholarships, grants, and awards:* Federal Pell, FSEOG, state, private, college/university gift aid from institutional funds.
GIFT AID (NON-NEED-BASED) *Total amount:* $10,425,057 (86% institutional, 14% external sources). *Receiving aid:* Freshmen: 52% (239); Undergraduates: 51% (974). *Average Award:* Freshmen: $17,543; Undergraduates: $14,611. *Scholarships, grants, and awards by category: Academic Interests/Achievement:* 1,077 awards ($6,981,072 total): area/ethnic studies, biological sciences, communication, English, foreign languages, general academic interests/achievements, health fields, physical sciences, premedicine. *Creative Arts/Performance:* 3 awards ($9000 total): art/fine arts, creative writing, music, theater/drama. *Special Achievements/Activities:* junior miss. *Special Characteristics:* 91 awards ($726,475 total): children with a deceased or disabled parent, ethnic background, general special characteristics, international students, local/state students, members of minority groups. *Tuition waivers:* Full or partial for employees or children of employees. *ROTC:* Air Force cooperative.
LOANS *Student loans:* $15,560,112 (34% need-based, 66% non-need-based). 81% of past graduating class borrowed through all loan programs. *Average indebtedness per student:* $22,265. *Average need-based loan:* Freshmen: $2893; Undergraduates: $3631. *Parent loans:* $2,490,049 (100% non-need-based). *Programs:* FFEL (Subsidized and Unsubsidized Stafford, PLUS), Perkins.
WORK-STUDY *Federal work-study:* Total amount: $1,307,164; 491 jobs averaging $2614. *State or other work-study/employment:* Total amount: $2,534,280 (53% need-based, 47% non-need-based). 982 part-time jobs averaging $2521.
APPLYING FOR FINANCIAL AID *Required financial aid form:* FAFSA. *Financial aid deadline (priority):* 3/1. *Notification date:* Continuous. Students must reply within 2 weeks of notification.
CONTACT Ms. Cheryl Anderson-Dooley, Associate Director, Financial Aid, Hamline University, 1536 Hewitt Avenue, MS C1915, St. Paul, MN 55104, 651-523-2280 or toll-free 800-753-9753. *Fax:* 651-523-2585. *E-mail:* cdooley@gw.hamline.edu.

HAMPDEN-SYDNEY COLLEGE
Hampden-Sydney, VA

Tuition & fees: $26,170	Average undergraduate aid package: $17,891

ABOUT THE INSTITUTION Independent religious, men only. Awards: bachelor's degrees. 28 undergraduate majors. Total enrollment: 1,060. Undergraduates: 1,060. Freshmen: 322. Both federal and institutional methodology are used as a basis for awarding need-based institutional aid.
UNDERGRADUATE EXPENSES for 2006–07 *Application fee:* $30. *Comprehensive fee:* $34,295 includes full-time tuition ($25,166), mandatory fees ($1004), and room and board ($8125). *College room only:* $3436. *Part-time tuition:* $748 per credit hour.
FRESHMAN FINANCIAL AID (Fall 2005, est.) 240 applied for aid; of those 66% were deemed to have need. 100% of freshmen with need received aid; of those 41% had need fully met. *Average percent of need met:* 88% (excluding resources awarded to replace EFC). *Average financial aid package:* $18,482 (excluding resources awarded to replace EFC). 50% of all full-time freshmen had no need and received non-need-based gift aid.
UNDERGRADUATE FINANCIAL AID (Fall 2005, est.) 662 applied for aid; of those 75% were deemed to have need. 100% of undergraduates with need received aid; of those 37% had need fully met. *Average percent of need met:* 84% (excluding resources awarded to replace EFC). *Average financial aid package:* $17,891 (excluding resources awarded to replace EFC). 50% of all full-time undergraduates had no need and received non-need-based gift aid.

GIFT AID (NEED-BASED) *Total amount:* $6,905,568 (5% federal, 11% state, 80% institutional, 4% external sources). *Receiving aid:* Freshmen: 49% (159); All full-time undergraduates: 47% (494). *Average award:* Freshmen: $15,444; Undergraduates: $14,035. *Scholarships, grants, and awards:* Federal Pell, FSEOG, state, private, college/university gift aid from institutional funds.
GIFT AID (NON-NEED-BASED) *Total amount:* $5,087,569 (19% state, 73% institutional, 8% external sources). *Receiving aid:* Freshmen: 14% (46); Undergraduates: 11% (119). *Average Award:* Freshmen: $21,697; Undergraduates:* $16,595. *Scholarships, grants, and awards by category:* Academic Interests/Achievement: 376 awards ($4,202,034 total): biological sciences, education, general academic interests/achievements, health fields, premedicine, religion/biblical studies. *Creative Arts/Performance:* 1 award ($5000 total): music. *Special Achievements/Activities:* 277 awards ($755,250 total): general special achievements/activities, leadership. *Special Characteristics:* 22 awards ($310,012 total): children of educators, children of faculty/staff, out-of-state students, religious affiliation. *ROTC:* Army cooperative.
LOANS *Student loans:* $4,245,197 (42% need-based, 58% non-need-based). 54% of past graduating class borrowed through all loan programs. *Average indebtedness per student:* $16,244. *Average need-based loan:* Freshmen: $2974; Undergraduates: $4134. *Parent loans:* $7,951,342 (14% need-based, 86% non-need-based). *Programs:* FFEL (Subsidized and Unsubsidized Stafford, PLUS), Perkins, college/university.
WORK-STUDY *Federal work-study:* Total amount: $394,793; 257 jobs averaging $1536.
APPLYING FOR FINANCIAL AID *Required financial aid forms:* FAFSA, CSS Financial Aid PROFILE. *Financial aid deadline (priority):* 3/1. *Notification date:* Continuous. Students must reply by 5/1 or within 2 weeks of notification.
CONTACT Mrs. Lynn Clements, Assistant Director of Financial Aid, Hampden-Sydney College, PO Box 726, Hampden-Sydney, VA 23943-0667, 434-223-6119 or toll-free 800-755-0733. *Fax:* 434-223-6075. *E-mail:* lclements@hsc.edu.

HAMPSHIRE COLLEGE
Amherst, MA

Tuition & fees: $32,519 — **Average undergraduate aid package: $25,660**

ABOUT THE INSTITUTION Independent, coed. Awards: bachelor's degrees. 46 undergraduate majors. Total enrollment: 1,376. Undergraduates: 1,376. Freshmen: 392. Institutional methodology is used as a basis for awarding need-based institutional aid.
UNDERGRADUATE EXPENSES for 2005–06 *Application fee:* $55. *Comprehensive fee:* $41,038 includes full-time tuition ($31,939), mandatory fees ($580), and room and board ($8519). *College room only:* $5433. Room and board charges vary according to board plan. *Payment plan:* Installment.
FRESHMAN FINANCIAL AID (Fall 2005, est.) 240 applied for aid; of those 90% were deemed to have need. 100% of freshmen with need received aid; of those 59% had need fully met. *Average percent of need met:* 96% (excluding resources awarded to replace EFC). *Average financial aid package:* $24,510 (excluding resources awarded to replace EFC). 11% of all full-time freshmen had no need and received non-need-based gift aid.
UNDERGRADUATE FINANCIAL AID (Fall 2005, est.) 822 applied for aid; of those 91% were deemed to have need. 100% of undergraduates with need received aid; of those 83% had need fully met. *Average percent of need met:* 96% (excluding resources awarded to replace EFC). *Average financial aid package:* $25,660 (excluding resources awarded to replace EFC). 5% of all full-time undergraduates had no need and received non-need-based gift aid.
GIFT AID (NEED-BASED) *Total amount:* $15,765,255 (6% federal, 1% state, 91% institutional, 2% external sources). *Receiving aid:* Freshmen: 64% (214); All full-time undergraduates: 56% (750). *Average award:* Freshmen: $19,785; Undergraduates: $19,180. *Scholarships, grants, and awards:* Federal Pell, FSEOG, state, private, college/university gift aid from institutional funds.
GIFT AID (NON-NEED-BASED) *Total amount:* $1,082,180 (4% state, 58% institutional, 38% external sources). *Receiving aid:* Freshmen: 22% (74); Undergraduates: 13% (181). *Average Award:* Freshmen: $3700; Undergraduates: $3865. *Scholarships, grants, and awards by category:* Academic Interests/Achievement: 412 awards ($912,000 total): general academic interests/achievements, international studies, physical sciences, social sciences. *Creative Arts/Performance:* 1 award ($3500 total): creative writing. *Special Achievements/Activities:* 26 awards ($233,200 total): community service, leadership. *Special Characteristics:* 11 awards ($150,000 total): children of faculty/staff. *Tuition waivers:* Full or partial for employees or children of employees. *ROTC:* Army cooperative.
LOANS *Student loans:* $2,744,455 (91% need-based, 9% non-need-based). 52% of past graduating class borrowed through all loan programs. *Average indebtedness per student:* $17,825. *Average need-based loan:* Freshmen: $2625; Undergraduates: $4155. *Parent loans:* $5,136,495 (73% need-based, 27% non-need-based). *Programs:* Federal Direct (Subsidized and Unsubsidized Stafford), FFEL (PLUS), Perkins.
WORK-STUDY *Federal work-study:* Total amount: $1,163,945; 587 jobs averaging $2300. *State or other work-study/employment:* Total amount: $594,645 (68% need-based, 32% non-need-based). 250 part-time jobs averaging $2300.
APPLYING FOR FINANCIAL AID *Required financial aid forms:* FAFSA, institution's own form, CSS Financial Aid PROFILE, noncustodial (divorced/separated) parent's statement. *Financial aid deadline (priority):* 2/1. *Notification date:* 4/1. Students must reply by 5/1 or within 2 weeks of notification.
CONTACT Ms. Kathleen Methot, Director of Financial Aid, Hampshire College, 893 West Street, Amherst, MA 01002, 413-559-5484 or toll-free 877-937-4267 (out-of-state). *Fax:* 413-559-5585. *E-mail:* sfs@hampshire.edu.

HAMPTON UNIVERSITY
Hampton, VA

Tuition & fees: $14,182 — **Average undergraduate aid package: $3220**

ABOUT THE INSTITUTION Independent, coed. Awards: associate, bachelor's, master's, doctoral, and first professional degrees. 83 undergraduate majors. Total enrollment: 6,209. Undergraduates: 5,325. Freshmen: 1,201. Federal methodology is used as a basis for awarding need-based institutional aid.
UNDERGRADUATE EXPENSES for 2005–06 *Application fee:* $25. *Comprehensive fee:* $20,928 includes full-time tuition ($12,722), mandatory fees ($1460), and room and board ($6746). *College room only:* $3580. Full-time tuition and fees vary according to degree level. Room and board charges vary according to board plan and housing facility. *Part-time tuition:* $320 per credit. *Payment plan:* Deferred payment.
FRESHMAN FINANCIAL AID (Fall 2005, est.) 1087 applied for aid; of those 83% were deemed to have need. 90% of freshmen with need received aid; of those 83% had need fully met. *Average percent of need met:* 46% (excluding resources awarded to replace EFC). *Average financial aid package:* $2893 (excluding resources awarded to replace EFC). 9% of all full-time freshmen had no need and received non-need-based gift aid.
UNDERGRADUATE FINANCIAL AID (Fall 2005, est.) 4,053 applied for aid; of those 93% were deemed to have need. 88% of undergraduates with need received aid; of those 88% had need fully met. *Average percent of need met:* 46% (excluding resources awarded to replace EFC). *Average financial aid package:* $3220 (excluding resources awarded to replace EFC). 6% of all full-time undergraduates had no need and received non-need-based gift aid.
GIFT AID (NEED-BASED) *Total amount:* $9,055,934 (39% federal, 13% state, 32% institutional, 16% external sources). *Receiving aid:* Freshmen: 32% (372); All full-time undergraduates: 31% (1,535). *Average award:* Freshmen: $1800; Undergraduates: $2058. *Scholarships, grants, and awards:* Federal Pell, FSEOG, state, private, college/university gift aid from institutional funds, Federal Nursing.
GIFT AID (NON-NEED-BASED) *Total amount:* $1,388,348 (10% state, 84% institutional, 6% external sources). *Receiving aid:* Freshmen: 24% (277); Undergraduates: 27% (1,341). *Average Award:* Freshmen: $6152; Undergraduates: $7474. *Scholarships, grants, and awards by category:* Academic Interests/Achievement: general academic interests/achievements. *Creative Arts/Performance:* music. *Special Characteristics:* international students, members of minority groups. *Tuition waivers:* Full or partial for employees or children of employees. *ROTC:* Army, Naval.
LOANS *Student loans:* $11,522,991 (91% need-based, 9% non-need-based). 28% of past graduating class borrowed through all loan programs. *Average indebtedness per student:* $3645. *Average need-based loan:* Freshmen: $2066; Undergraduates: $2892. *Parent loans:* $11,341,776 (79% need-based, 21% non-need-based). *Programs:* FFEL (Subsidized and Unsubsidized Stafford, PLUS), Perkins, Federal Nursing, college/university.
WORK-STUDY *Federal work-study:* Total amount: $319,803; 378 jobs averaging $1800.
ATHLETIC AWARDS *Total amount:* $1,335,143 (93% need-based, 7% non-need-based).

Hampton University

APPLYING FOR FINANCIAL AID *Required financial aid form:* FAFSA. *Financial aid deadline:* 3/1. *Notification date:* Continuous beginning 4/15. Students must reply within 2 weeks of notification.
CONTACT Marcia Boyd, Director, Financial Aid, Hampton University, Hampton University, Office of Financial Aid and Scholarships, Hampton, VA 23668, 757-727-5332 or toll-free 800-624-3328. *Fax:* 757-728-6567. *E-mail:* marcia.boyd@hamptonu.edu.

HANNIBAL-LAGRANGE COLLEGE
Hannibal, MO

| Tuition & fees: $11,780 | Average undergraduate aid package: N/A |

ABOUT THE INSTITUTION Independent Southern Baptist, coed. Awards: associate and bachelor's degrees. 43 undergraduate majors. Total enrollment: 1,057. Undergraduates: 1,057. Freshmen: 119. Federal methodology is used as a basis for awarding need-based institutional aid.
UNDERGRADUATE EXPENSES for 2005–06 *Application fee:* $25. *Comprehensive fee:* $16,390 includes full-time tuition ($11,420), mandatory fees ($360), and room and board ($4610). Full-time tuition and fees vary according to course load. Room and board charges vary according to board plan and housing facility. *Part-time tuition:* $380 per hour. *Part-time fees:* $90 per term. Part-time tuition and fees vary according to course load. *Payment plan:* Installment.
FRESHMAN FINANCIAL AID (Fall 2005, est.) 100% of freshmen with need received aid.
UNDERGRADUATE FINANCIAL AID (Fall 2005, est.) 100% of undergraduates with need received aid.
GIFT AID (NEED-BASED) *Total amount:* $845,441 (84% federal, 16% state). *Receiving aid:* Freshmen: 32% (43); All full-time undergraduates: 72% (462). *Average award:* Freshmen: $1244; Undergraduates: $3206. *Scholarships, grants, and awards:* Federal Pell, FSEOG, state, private.
GIFT AID (NON-NEED-BASED) *Total amount:* $861,983 (4% state, 72% institutional, 24% external sources). *Receiving aid:* Freshmen: 55% (75); Undergraduates: 52% (335). *Scholarships, grants, and awards by category:* Academic Interests/Achievement: general academic interests/achievements, religion/biblical studies. Creative Arts/Performance: art/fine arts, journalism/publications, music, performing arts, theater/drama. Special Characteristics: children of faculty/staff, public servants, relatives of clergy, religious affiliation. *Tuition waivers:* Full or partial for employees or children of employees.
LOANS *Student loans:* $3,281,454 (53% need-based, 47% non-need-based). *Average indebtedness per student:* $16,689. *Average need-based loan:* Freshmen: $2287; Undergraduates: $6359. *Programs:* FFEL (Subsidized and Unsubsidized Stafford, PLUS), Perkins.
WORK-STUDY *Federal work-study:* 85 jobs averaging $550. *State or other work-study/employment:* Total amount: $28,875 (100% non-need-based).
ATHLETIC AWARDS *Total amount:* $644,566 (100% non-need-based).
APPLYING FOR FINANCIAL AID *Required financial aid forms:* FAFSA, institution's own form. *Financial aid deadline:* Continuous.
CONTACT Amy Blackwell, Director of Financial Aid, Hannibal-LaGrange College, 2800 Palmyra Road, Hannibal, MO 63401-1940, 573-221-3675 Ext. 279 or toll-free 800-HLG-1119. *Fax:* 573-221-6594.

HANOVER COLLEGE
Hanover, IN

| Tuition & fees: $21,650 | Average undergraduate aid package: $16,673 |

ABOUT THE INSTITUTION Independent Presbyterian, coed. Awards: bachelor's degrees. 29 undergraduate majors. Total enrollment: 1,008. Undergraduates: 1,008. Freshmen: 265. Federal methodology is used as a basis for awarding need-based institutional aid.
UNDERGRADUATE EXPENSES for 2005–06 *Application fee:* $35. *Comprehensive fee:* $28,150 includes full-time tuition ($21,150), mandatory fees ($500), and room and board ($6500). *College room only:* $3100. Full-time tuition and fees vary according to reciprocity agreements. Room and board charges vary according to housing facility and location. *Part-time tuition:* $2350 per unit. Part-time tuition and fees vary according to course load and reciprocity agreements. *Payment plan:* Installment.
FRESHMAN FINANCIAL AID (Fall 2004) 367 applied for aid; of those 84% were deemed to have need. 100% of freshmen with need received aid; of those 35% had need fully met. *Average percent of need met:* 75% (excluding resources awarded to replace EFC). *Average financial aid package:* $15,581 (excluding resources awarded to replace EFC). 18% of all full-time freshmen had no need and received non-need-based gift aid.
UNDERGRADUATE FINANCIAL AID (Fall 2004) 890 applied for aid; of those 86% were deemed to have need. 100% of undergraduates with need received aid; of those 38% had need fully met. *Average percent of need met:* 81% (excluding resources awarded to replace EFC). *Average financial aid package:* $16,673 (excluding resources awarded to replace EFC). 27% of all full-time undergraduates had no need and received non-need-based gift aid.
GIFT AID (NEED-BASED) *Total amount:* $10,552,499 (6% federal, 12% state, 73% institutional, 9% external sources). *Receiving aid:* Freshmen: 81% (309); All full-time undergraduates: 73% (768). *Average award:* Freshmen: $13,462; Undergraduates: $13,382. *Scholarships, grants, and awards:* Federal Pell, state, private, college/university gift aid from institutional funds.
GIFT AID (NON-NEED-BASED) *Total amount:* $3,436,567 (1% federal, 89% institutional, 10% external sources). *Receiving aid:* Freshmen: 19% (71); Undergraduates: 13% (139). *Average Award:* Freshmen: $13,763; Undergraduates: $12,643. *Scholarships, grants, and awards by category:* Academic Interests/Achievement: general academic interests/achievements. Creative Arts/Performance: 44 awards ($98,500 total): music, theater/drama. Special Characteristics: children and siblings of alumni, children of faculty/staff, international students, members of minority groups, out-of-state students, religious affiliation, siblings of current students. *Tuition waivers:* Full or partial for employees or children of employees, senior citizens.
LOANS *Student loans:* $3,092,872 (62% need-based, 38% non-need-based). 63% of past graduating class borrowed through all loan programs. *Average indebtedness per student:* $16,658. *Average need-based loan:* Freshmen: $2788; Undergraduates: $3076. *Parent loans:* $1,597,846 (25% need-based, 75% non-need-based). *Programs:* FFEL (Subsidized and Unsubsidized Stafford, PLUS), college/university.
APPLYING FOR FINANCIAL AID *Required financial aid form:* FAFSA. *Financial aid deadline (priority):* 3/10. *Notification date:* Continuous beginning 3/1. Students must reply by 5/1.
CONTACT Jon Riester, Director of Financial Aid, Hanover College, PO Box 108, Hanover, IN 47243-0108, 800-213-2178. *Fax:* 812-866-7098. *E-mail:* finaid@hanover.edu.

HARDING UNIVERSITY
Searcy, AR

| Tuition & fees: $11,200 | Average undergraduate aid package: $8581 |

ABOUT THE INSTITUTION Independent religious, coed. Awards: bachelor's and master's degrees. 96 undergraduate majors. Total enrollment: 5,744. Undergraduates: 4,092. Freshmen: 960. Federal methodology is used as a basis for awarding need-based institutional aid.
UNDERGRADUATE EXPENSES for 2005–06 *Application fee:* $35. *Comprehensive fee:* $16,512 includes full-time tuition ($10,800), mandatory fees ($400), and room and board ($5312). *College room only:* $2636. Full-time tuition and fees vary according to course load. Room and board charges vary according to board plan and housing facility. *Part-time tuition:* $360 per semester hour. *Part-time fees:* $20 per semester hour. Part-time tuition and fees vary according to course load. *Payment plan:* Installment.
FRESHMAN FINANCIAL AID (Fall 2005, est.) 733 applied for aid; of those 70% were deemed to have need. 99% of freshmen with need received aid; of those 25% had need fully met. *Average percent of need met:* 71% (excluding resources awarded to replace EFC). *Average financial aid package:* $8594 (excluding resources awarded to replace EFC). 20% of all full-time freshmen had no need and received non-need-based gift aid.
UNDERGRADUATE FINANCIAL AID (Fall 2005, est.) 2,945 applied for aid; of those 74% were deemed to have need. 99% of undergraduates with need received aid; of those 22% had need fully met. *Average percent of need met:* 68% (excluding resources awarded to replace EFC). *Average financial aid package:* $8581 (excluding resources awarded to replace EFC). 13% of all full-time undergraduates had no need and received non-need-based gift aid.
GIFT AID (NEED-BASED) *Total amount:* $8,420,153 (39% federal, 6% state, 51% institutional, 4% external sources). *Receiving aid:* Freshmen: 49% (470); All full-time undergraduates: 47% (1,841). *Average award:* Freshmen: $5605; Undergraduates: $4990. *Scholarships, grants, and awards:* Federal Pell, FSEOG, state, private, college/university gift aid from institutional funds.

GIFT AID (NON-NEED-BASED) *Total amount:* $2,577,017 (10% state, 78% institutional, 12% external sources). *Receiving aid:* Freshmen: 7% (71); Undergraduates: 6% (251). *Average Award:* Freshmen: $3298; Undergraduates: $3261. *Scholarships, grants, and awards by category: Academic Interests/Achievement:* 2,123 awards ($4,650,100 total): general academic interests/achievements. *Creative Arts/Performance:* 125 awards ($1,452,229 total): music. *Special Achievements/Activities:* 159 awards ($259,600 total): cheerleading/drum major, religious involvement. *Special Characteristics:* 97 awards ($253,900 total): children with a deceased or disabled parent, international students, siblings of current students. *Tuition waivers:* Full or partial for employees or children of employees, senior citizens. *ROTC:* Army cooperative.
LOANS *Student loans:* $20,625,880 (64% need-based, 36% non-need-based). 66% of past graduating class borrowed through all loan programs. *Average indebtedness per student:* $18,301. *Average need-based loan:* Freshmen: $3374; Undergraduates: $4583. *Parent loans:* $5,207,855 (22% need-based, 78% non-need-based). *Programs:* FFEL (Subsidized and Unsubsidized Stafford, PLUS), Perkins, Federal Nursing, state, college/university.
WORK-STUDY *Federal work-study:* Total amount: $423,711; 570 jobs averaging $743. *State or other work-study/employment:* Total amount: $742,464 (26% need-based, 74% non-need-based). 1,005 part-time jobs averaging $738.
ATHLETIC AWARDS *Total amount:* $885,931 (46% need-based, 54% non-need-based).
APPLYING FOR FINANCIAL AID *Required financial aid form:* FAFSA. *Financial aid deadline:* Continuous. *Notification date:* Continuous beginning 2/15. Students must reply within 2 weeks of notification.
CONTACT Dr. Jonathan C. Roberts, Director of Student Financial Services, Harding University, Box 12282, Searcy, AR 72149-0001, 501-279-4257 or toll-free 800-477-4407. *Fax:* 501-279-4129. *E-mail:* jroberts@harding.edu.

HARDIN-SIMMONS UNIVERSITY
Abilene, TX

Tuition & fees: $15,626   Average undergraduate aid package: $13,530

ABOUT THE INSTITUTION Independent Baptist, coed. Awards: bachelor's, master's, doctoral, and first professional degrees and post-bachelor's certificates. 73 undergraduate majors. Total enrollment: 2,435. Undergraduates: 1,991. Freshmen: 436. Federal methodology is used as a basis for awarding need-based institutional aid.
UNDERGRADUATE EXPENSES for 2006–07 *Application fee:* $50. *Comprehensive fee:* $20,206 includes full-time tuition ($14,850), mandatory fees ($776), and room and board ($4580). *College room only:* $2365. *Part-time tuition:* $495 per semester hour. *Part-time fees:* $96 per term.
FRESHMAN FINANCIAL AID (Fall 2005, est.) 434 applied for aid; of those 71% were deemed to have need. 100% of freshmen with need received aid; of those 27% had need fully met. *Average percent of need met:* 67% (excluding resources awarded to replace EFC). *Average financial aid package:* $13,492 (excluding resources awarded to replace EFC). 18% of all full-time freshmen had no need and received non-need-based gift aid.
UNDERGRADUATE FINANCIAL AID (Fall 2005, est.) 1,690 applied for aid; of those 73% were deemed to have need. 100% of undergraduates with need received aid; of those 20% had need fully met. *Average percent of need met:* 70% (excluding resources awarded to replace EFC). *Average financial aid package:* $13,530 (excluding resources awarded to replace EFC). 13% of all full-time undergraduates had no need and received non-need-based gift aid.
GIFT AID (NEED-BASED) *Total amount:* $11,263,390 (18% federal, 26% state, 51% institutional, 5% external sources). *Receiving aid:* Freshmen: 51% (222); All full-time undergraduates: 52% (932). *Average award:* Freshmen: $4431; Undergraduates: $4812. *Scholarships, grants, and awards:* Federal Pell, FSEOG, state, private, college/university gift aid from institutional funds.
GIFT AID (NON-NEED-BASED) *Receiving aid:* Freshmen: 66% (289); Undergraduates: 58% (1,032). *Average Award:* Freshmen: $4548; Undergraduates: $3751. *Scholarships, grants, and awards by category: Academic Interests/Achievement:* 1,278 awards ($4,831,862 total): biological sciences, business, communication, education, English, foreign languages, general academic interests/achievements, health fields, humanities, mathematics, physical sciences, premedicine, religion/biblical studies, social sciences. *Creative Arts/Performance:* 120 awards ($627,535 total): art/fine arts, creative writing, journalism/publications, music, theater/drama. *Special Achievements/Activities:* 43 awards ($113,925 total): general special achievements/activities, junior miss, leadership. *Special Characteristics:* 236 awards ($808,954 total): children of faculty/staff, ethnic background, general special characteristics, local/state students, out-of-state students, public servants, relatives of clergy, religious affiliation, siblings of current students.
LOANS *Student loans:* $13,931,632 (42% need-based, 58% non-need-based). 72% of past graduating class borrowed through all loan programs. *Average indebtedness per student:* $26,144. *Average need-based loan:* Freshmen: $2394; Undergraduates: $3803. *Parent loans:* $1,204,981 (100% non-need-based). *Programs:* FFEL (Subsidized and Unsubsidized Stafford, PLUS), Perkins, state, college/university.
WORK-STUDY *Federal work-study:* Total amount: $148,753; 136 jobs averaging $1554. *State or other work-study/employment:* Total amount: $237,035 (6% need-based, 94% non-need-based). 204 part-time jobs averaging $1199.
APPLYING FOR FINANCIAL AID *Required financial aid form:* FAFSA. *Financial aid deadline (priority):* 3/15. *Notification date:* Continuous beginning 1/1.
CONTACT Jim Jones, Director of Financial Aid, Hardin-Simmons University, PO Box 16050, Abilene, TX 79698-6050, 325-670-5891 or toll-free 877-464-7889. *Fax:* 325-670-5822. *E-mail:* jjones@hsutx.edu.

HARRINGTON COLLEGE OF DESIGN
Chicago, IL

CONTACT Ms. Renee Darosky, Director of Financial Aid, Harrington College of Design, 410 South Michigan Avenue, Chicago, IL 60605-1496, 312-939-4975 or toll-free 877-939-4975. *Fax:* 312-697-8058. *E-mail:* financialaid@interiordesign.edu.

HARRIS-STOWE STATE UNIVERSITY
St. Louis, MO

Tuition & fees (MO res): $4800   Average undergraduate aid package: $7350

ABOUT THE INSTITUTION State-supported, coed. Awards: bachelor's degrees and post-bachelor's certificates. 17 undergraduate majors. Total enrollment: 1,662. Undergraduates: 1,662. Freshmen: 293. Federal methodology is used as a basis for awarding need-based institutional aid.
UNDERGRADUATE EXPENSES for 2006–07 *Application fee:* $15. *Tuition, state resident:* full-time $4650; part-time $145 per hour. *Tuition, nonresident:* full-time $8570; part-time $285.65 per hour. *Required fees:* full-time $150; $150 per term part-time. *College room and board:* room only: $5400.
GIFT AID (NEED-BASED) *Total amount:* $6,070,000 (99% federal, 1% state). *Receiving aid:* Freshmen: 72% (120); All full-time undergraduates: 88% (780). *Average award:* Freshmen: $3074; Undergraduates: $4000. *Scholarships, grants, and awards:* Federal Pell, FSEOG, state, private, college/university gift aid from institutional funds.
GIFT AID (NON-NEED-BASED) *Total amount:* $571,152 (66% institutional, 34% external sources). *Receiving aid:* Freshmen: 42% (70); Undergraduates: 19% (165). *Average Award:* Freshmen: $1500; Undergraduates: $2000. *Scholarships, grants, and awards by category: Academic Interests/Achievement:* general academic interests/achievements. *Creative Arts/Performance:* 34 awards ($57,300 total): music, theater/drama. *ROTC:* Air Force cooperative.
LOANS *Student loans:* $26,000,000 (96% need-based, 4% non-need-based). 85% of past graduating class borrowed through all loan programs. *Average indebtedness per student:* $16,000. *Average need-based loan:* Freshmen: $2512; Undergraduates: $4000. *Programs:* FFEL (Subsidized and Unsubsidized Stafford, PLUS), college/university.
ATHLETIC AWARDS *Total amount:* $315,000 (100% non-need-based).
APPLYING FOR FINANCIAL AID *Required financial aid forms:* FAFSA, institution's own form. *Financial aid deadline (priority):* 4/1. *Notification date:* Continuous. Students must reply within 3 weeks of notification.
CONTACT Regina Blackshear, Director of Financial Aid, Harris-Stowe State University, 3026 Laclede Avenue, St. Louis, MO 63103-2136, 314-340-3502. *Fax:* 314-340-3503.

HARTWICK COLLEGE
Oneonta, NY

CONTACT Kathleen Ryan-O'Neill, Director, Financial Aid Department, Hartwick College, One Hartwick Drive, Oneonta, NY 13820, 607-431-4158 or toll-free 888-HARTWICK (out-of-state). *Fax:* 607-431-4006. *E-mail:* oneillk@hartwick.edu.

Harvard University

HARVARD UNIVERSITY
Cambridge, MA

Tuition & fees: $33,709 **Average undergraduate aid package:** $30,780

ABOUT THE INSTITUTION Independent, coed. Awards: bachelor's, master's, doctoral, and first professional degrees. 141 undergraduate majors. Total enrollment: 19,376. Undergraduates: 6,649. Freshmen: 1,648. Both federal and institutional methodology are used as a basis for awarding need-based institutional aid.

UNDERGRADUATE EXPENSES for 2006–07 *Application fee:* $65. *Comprehensive fee:* $43,655 includes full-time tuition ($30,275), mandatory fees ($3434), and room and board ($9946). *College room only:* $5328.

FRESHMAN FINANCIAL AID (Fall 2005, est.) 1036 applied for aid; of those 82% were deemed to have need. 100% of freshmen with need received aid; of those 100% had need fully met. *Average percent of need met:* 100% (excluding resources awarded to replace EFC). *Average financial aid package:* $31,868 (excluding resources awarded to replace EFC).

UNDERGRADUATE FINANCIAL AID (Fall 2005, est.) 3,655 applied for aid; of those 90% were deemed to have need. 100% of undergraduates with need received aid; of those 100% had need fully met. *Average percent of need met:* 100% (excluding resources awarded to replace EFC). *Average financial aid package:* $30,780 (excluding resources awarded to replace EFC).

GIFT AID (NEED-BASED) *Total amount:* $93,037,400 (5% federal, 1% state, 89% institutional, 5% external sources). *Receiving aid:* Freshmen: 52% (848); All full-time undergraduates: 49% (3,260). *Average award:* Freshmen: $29,956; Undergraduates: $28,317. *Scholarships, grants, and awards:* Federal Pell, FSEOG, state, private, college/university gift aid from institutional funds.

GIFT AID (NON-NEED-BASED) *Total amount:* $6,372,112 (25% federal, 75% external sources). *ROTC:* Army cooperative, Air Force cooperative.

LOANS *Student loans:* $6,133,345 (63% need-based, 37% non-need-based). 49% of past graduating class borrowed through all loan programs. *Average indebtedness per student:* $8769. *Average need-based loan:* Freshmen: $2967; Undergraduates: $3228. *Parent loans:* $14,269,333 (100% non-need-based). *Programs:* Federal Direct (Subsidized and Unsubsidized Stafford, PLUS), Perkins, state, college/university.

WORK-STUDY *Federal work-study:* Total amount: $2,959,437; 1,233 jobs averaging $2400. *State or other work-study/employment:* Total amount: $2,831,858 (80% need-based, 20% non-need-based). 1,231 part-time jobs averaging $2300.

APPLYING FOR FINANCIAL AID *Required financial aid forms:* FAFSA, CSS Financial Aid PROFILE, noncustodial (divorced/separated) parent's statement, business/farm supplement, income tax form(s). *Financial aid deadline (priority):* 2/1. *Notification date:* 4/1. Students must reply by 5/1 or within 2 weeks of notification.

CONTACT Financial Aid Office, Harvard University, 312 Byerly Hall, 8 Garden Street, Cambridge, MA 02138, 617-495-1581. *Fax:* 617-496-0256.

HARVEY MUDD COLLEGE
Claremont, CA

Tuition & fees: $31,940 **Average undergraduate aid package:** $25,315

ABOUT THE INSTITUTION Independent, coed. Awards: bachelor's and master's degrees. 6 undergraduate majors. Total enrollment: 743. Undergraduates: 743. Both federal and institutional methodology are used as a basis for awarding need-based institutional aid.

UNDERGRADUATE EXPENSES for 2005–06 *Application fee:* $50. *Comprehensive fee:* $42,352 includes full-time tuition ($31,738), mandatory fees ($202), and room and board ($10,412). *College room only:* $5282. Room and board charges vary according to board plan. *Payment plan:* Installment.

FRESHMAN FINANCIAL AID (Fall 2005, est.) 151 applied for aid; of those 74% were deemed to have need. 100% of freshmen with need received aid; of those 100% had need fully met. *Average percent of need met:* 100% (excluding resources awarded to replace EFC). *Average financial aid package:* $27,245 (excluding resources awarded to replace EFC). 22% of all full-time freshmen had no need and received non-need-based gift aid.

UNDERGRADUATE FINANCIAL AID (Fall 2005, est.) 474 applied for aid; of those 85% were deemed to have need. 100% of undergraduates with need received aid; of those 100% had need fully met. *Average percent of need met:* 100% (excluding resources awarded to replace EFC). *Average financial aid package:* $25,315 (excluding resources awarded to replace EFC). 21% of all full-time undergraduates had no need and received non-need-based gift aid.

GIFT AID (NEED-BASED) *Total amount:* $8,280,122 (5% federal, 9% state, 86% institutional). *Receiving aid:* Freshmen: 56% (109); All full-time undergraduates: 51% (387). *Average award:* Freshmen: $25,595; Undergraduates: $22,062. *Scholarships, grants, and awards:* Federal Pell, FSEOG, state, private, college/university gift aid from institutional funds.

GIFT AID (NON-NEED-BASED) *Total amount:* $1,722,164 (1% state, 47% institutional, 52% external sources). *Receiving aid:* Freshmen: 22% (43); Undergraduates: 21% (156). *Average Award:* Freshmen: $6574; Undergraduates: $5157. *Scholarships, grants, and awards by category:* Academic Interests/Achievement: 271 awards ($1,801,633 total): general academic interests/achievements. *Tuition waivers:* Full or partial for employees or children of employees. *ROTC:* Army cooperative, Air Force.

LOANS *Student loans:* $1,911,340 (60% need-based, 40% non-need-based). 60% of past graduating class borrowed through all loan programs. *Average indebtedness per student:* $16,055. *Average need-based loan:* Freshmen: $3597; Undergraduates: $4246. *Parent loans:* $2,463,054 (100% non-need-based). *Programs:* FFEL (Subsidized and Unsubsidized Stafford, PLUS), Perkins, college/university, alternative loans.

WORK-STUDY *Federal work-study:* Total amount: $421,601; 222 jobs averaging $1899. *State or other work-study/employment:* Total amount: $22,264 (100% need-based). 11 part-time jobs averaging $2024.

APPLYING FOR FINANCIAL AID *Required financial aid forms:* FAFSA, CSS Financial Aid PROFILE, state aid form, noncustodial (divorced/separated) parent's statement, business/farm supplement. *Financial aid deadline:* 2/1. *Notification date:* 4/1. Students must reply by 5/1 or within 2 weeks of notification.

CONTACT Gilma Lopez, Office of Financial Aid, Harvey Mudd College, 301 Platt Boulevard, Claremont, CA 91711-5994, 909-621-8055. *Fax:* 909-607-7046. *E-mail:* financial_aid@hmc.edu.

HASKELL INDIAN NATIONS UNIVERSITY
Lawrence, KS

CONTACT Reta Beaver, Director of Financial Aid, Haskell Indian Nations University, 155 Indian Avenue, Box 5027, Lawrence, KS 66046-4800, 785-749-8468. *Fax:* 785-832-6617.

HASTINGS COLLEGE
Hastings, NE

ABOUT THE INSTITUTION Independent Presbyterian, coed. Awards: bachelor's and master's degrees. 81 undergraduate majors. Total enrollment: 1,189. Undergraduates: 1,144. Freshmen: 318.

GIFT AID (NEED-BASED) *Scholarships, grants, and awards:* Federal Pell, FSEOG, state, private, college/university gift aid from institutional funds.

GIFT AID (NON-NEED-BASED) *Scholarships, grants, and awards by category:* Academic Interests/Achievement: communication, general academic interests/achievements, religion/biblical studies. *Creative Arts/Performance:* art/fine arts, debating, music, performing arts, theater/drama. *Special Characteristics:* adult students, children of educators, children of faculty/staff, relatives of clergy, religious affiliation, siblings of current students.

LOANS *Programs:* FFEL (Subsidized and Unsubsidized Stafford, PLUS), Perkins, college/university.

WORK-STUDY *Federal work-study:* Total amount: $68,355; jobs available (averaging $600). *State or other work-study/employment:* Total amount: $116,277 (36% need-based, 64% non-need-based). Part-time jobs available.

APPLYING FOR FINANCIAL AID *Required financial aid forms:* FAFSA, institution's own form.

CONTACT Mr. Ian Roberts, Associate Vice President-Administration, Hastings College, 7th and Turner, Hastings, NE 68901, 402-461-7455 or toll-free 800-532-7642. *Fax:* 402-461-7714. *E-mail:* iroberts@hastings.edu.

HAVERFORD COLLEGE
Haverford, PA

Tuition & fees: $31,760 **Average undergraduate aid package:** $26,990

ABOUT THE INSTITUTION Independent, coed. Awards: bachelor's degrees. 44 undergraduate majors. Total enrollment: 1,168. Undergraduates: 1,168. Freshmen: 316. Institutional methodology is used as a basis for awarding need-based institutional aid.
UNDERGRADUATE EXPENSES for 2005–06 *Application fee:* $60. *Comprehensive fee:* $41,600 includes full-time tuition ($31,466), mandatory fees ($294), and room and board ($9840). *College room only:* $5540. *Payment plan:* Installment.
FRESHMAN FINANCIAL AID (Fall 2005, est.) 180 applied for aid; of those 73% were deemed to have need. 100% of freshmen with need received aid; of those 100% had need fully met. *Average percent of need met:* 100% (excluding resources awarded to replace EFC). *Average financial aid package:* $27,787 (excluding resources awarded to replace EFC).
UNDERGRADUATE FINANCIAL AID (Fall 2005, est.) 585 applied for aid; of those 86% were deemed to have need. 100% of undergraduates with need received aid; of those 100% had need fully met. *Average percent of need met:* 100% (excluding resources awarded to replace EFC). *Average financial aid package:* $26,990 (excluding resources awarded to replace EFC).
GIFT AID (NEED-BASED) *Total amount:* $11,532,229 (4% federal, 2% state, 91% institutional, 3% external sources). *Receiving aid:* Freshmen: 41% (130); All full-time undergraduates: 41% (479). *Average award:* Freshmen: $25,462; Undergraduates: $24,073. *Scholarships, grants, and awards:* Federal Pell, FSEOG, state, private, college/university gift aid from institutional funds.
GIFT AID (NON-NEED-BASED) *Tuition waivers:* Full or partial for employees or children of employees.
LOANS *Student loans:* $1,543,085 (78% need-based, 22% non-need-based). 36% of past graduating class borrowed through all loan programs. *Average indebtedness per student:* $16,330. *Average need-based loan:* Freshmen: $2727; Undergraduates: $3884. *Parent loans:* $2,954,545 (100% non-need-based). *Programs:* FFEL (Subsidized and Unsubsidized Stafford, PLUS), Perkins.
WORK-STUDY *Federal work-study:* Total amount: $314,045; jobs available. *State or other work-study/employment:* Total amount: $462,031 (48% need-based, 52% non-need-based). Part-time jobs available.
APPLYING FOR FINANCIAL AID *Required financial aid forms:* FAFSA, CSS Financial Aid PROFILE, state aid form, noncustodial (divorced/separated) parent's statement, business/farm supplement. *Financial aid deadline:* 1/31. *Notification date:* 4/15. Students must reply by 5/1.
CONTACT Mr. David J. Hoy, Director of Financial Aid Office, Haverford College, 370 Lancaster Avenue, Haverford, PA 19041-1392, 610-896-1350. *Fax:* 610-896-1338. *E-mail:* finaid@haverford.edu.

HAWAI'I PACIFIC UNIVERSITY
Honolulu, HI

Tuition & fees: $11,630 | Average undergraduate aid package: $10,465

ABOUT THE INSTITUTION Independent, coed. Awards: associate, bachelor's, and master's degrees and post-bachelor's and post-master's certificates. 55 undergraduate majors. Total enrollment: 8,046. Undergraduates: 6,911. Freshmen: 647. Federal methodology is used as a basis for awarding need-based institutional aid.
UNDERGRADUATE EXPENSES for 2005–06 *Application fee:* $50. *Comprehensive fee:* $21,080 includes full-time tuition ($11,550), mandatory fees ($80), and room and board ($9450). Full-time tuition and fees vary according to course load, program, and student level. Room and board charges vary according to housing facility. *Part-time tuition:* $225 per credit. Part-time tuition and fees vary according to course load. *Payment plan:* Installment.
FRESHMAN FINANCIAL AID (Fall 2005, est.) 513 applied for aid; of those 52% were deemed to have need. 94% of freshmen with need received aid; of those 14% had need fully met. *Average percent of need met:* 75% (excluding resources awarded to replace EFC). *Average financial aid package:* $10,239 (excluding resources awarded to replace EFC). 42% of all full-time freshmen had no need and received non-need-based gift aid.
UNDERGRADUATE FINANCIAL AID (Fall 2005, est.) 2,686 applied for aid; of those 57% were deemed to have need. 97% of undergraduates with need received aid; of those 20% had need fully met. *Average percent of need met:* 71% (excluding resources awarded to replace EFC). *Average financial aid package:* $10,465 (excluding resources awarded to replace EFC). 24% of all full-time undergraduates had no need and received non-need-based gift aid.
GIFT AID (NEED-BASED) *Total amount:* $3,498,718 (100% federal). *Receiving aid:* Freshmen: 19% (119); All full-time undergraduates: 19% (766). *Average award:* Freshmen: $4066; Undergraduates: $3915. *Scholarships, grants, and awards:* Federal Pell, FSEOG, state, private, college/university gift aid from institutional funds.
GIFT AID (NON-NEED-BASED) *Total amount:* $8,112,176 (78% institutional, 22% external sources). *Receiving aid:* Freshmen: 17% (106); Undergraduates: 12% (494). *Average Award:* Freshmen: $6115; Undergraduates: $6543. *Scholarships, grants, and awards by category:* Academic Interests/Achievement: 334 awards ($2,389,812 total): biological sciences, business, communication, general academic interests/achievements, health fields, social sciences. *Creative Arts/Performance:* 108 awards ($935,567 total): dance, journalism/publications, music. *Special Achievements/Activities:* 402 awards ($2,774,010 total): cheerleading/drum major, hobbies/interests, leadership, memberships, religious involvement. *Special Characteristics:* 214 awards ($568,254 total): ethnic background, international students, local/state students, out-of-state students, previous college experience, relatives of clergy, religious affiliation. *Tuition waivers:* Full or partial for employees or children of employees. *ROTC:* Army cooperative, Air Force cooperative.
LOANS *Student loans:* $14,210,353 (100% need-based). 36% of past graduating class borrowed through all loan programs. *Average indebtedness per student:* $17,125. *Average need-based loan:* Freshmen: $2806; Undergraduates: $4145. *Parent loans:* $8,311,978 (100% need-based). *Programs:* FFEL (Subsidized and Unsubsidized Stafford, PLUS), Perkins, Federal Nursing.
WORK-STUDY *Federal work-study:* Total amount: $858,126; 382 jobs averaging $2250.
ATHLETIC AWARDS *Total amount:* $1,240,525 (100% non-need-based).
APPLYING FOR FINANCIAL AID *Required financial aid form:* FAFSA. *Financial aid deadline (priority):* 3/1. *Notification date:* Continuous beginning 4/1. Students must reply within 3 weeks of notification.
CONTACT Adam Hatch, Director of Financial Aid, Hawai'i Pacific University, 1164 Bishop Street, Honolulu, HI 96813-2785, 808-544-0253 or toll-free 866-225-5478 (out-of-state). *Fax:* 808-544-0884. *E-mail:* financialaid@hpu.edu.

HAWAI'I THEOLOGICAL SEMINARY
Honolulu, HI

CONTACT Mr. Jon Rawlings, Executive Vice President, Hawai'i Theological Seminary, 20 Dowsett Avenue, Honolulu, HI 96817, 808-595-4247. *Fax:* 808-595-4779. *E-mail:* icgs@hawaii.rr.com.

HEBREW COLLEGE
Newton Centre, MA

CONTACT Ms. Norma Frankel, Registrar, Hebrew College, 160 Herrick Road, Newton Centre, MA 02459, 617-559-8612 or toll-free 800-866-4814 Ext. 8619. *Fax:* 617-559-8601.

HEBREW THEOLOGICAL COLLEGE
Skokie, IL

CONTACT Ms. Rhoda Morris, Financial Aid Administrator, Hebrew Theological College, 7135 Carpenter Road, Skokie, IL 60077-3263, 847-982-2500. *Fax:* 847-674-6381.

HEIDELBERG COLLEGE
Tiffin, OH

Tuition & fees: $16,134 | Average undergraduate aid package: $14,130

ABOUT THE INSTITUTION Independent religious, coed. Awards: bachelor's and master's degrees. 46 undergraduate majors. Total enrollment: 1,435. Undergraduates: 1,230. Freshmen: 328. Federal methodology is used as a basis for awarding need-based institutional aid.
UNDERGRADUATE EXPENSES for 2005–06 *Application fee:* $25. *Comprehensive fee:* $23,242 includes full-time tuition ($15,740), mandatory fees ($394), and room and board ($7108). *College room only:* $3296. Full-time tuition and fees vary according to course load, degree level, and location. Room and board charges vary according to board plan and housing facility. *Part-time tuition:* $504 per semester hour. Part-time tuition and fees vary according to degree level and location. *Payment plans:* Installment, deferred payment.

Heidelberg College

FRESHMAN FINANCIAL AID (Fall 2005, est.) 290 applied for aid; of those 92% were deemed to have need. 100% of freshmen with need received aid; of those 11% had need fully met. *Average percent of need met:* 83% (excluding resources awarded to replace EFC). *Average financial aid package:* $14,403 (excluding resources awarded to replace EFC). 8% of all full-time freshmen had no need and received non-need-based gift aid.
UNDERGRADUATE FINANCIAL AID (Fall 2005, est.) 955 applied for aid; of those 92% were deemed to have need. 100% of undergraduates with need received aid; of those 17% had need fully met. *Average percent of need met:* 86% (excluding resources awarded to replace EFC). *Average financial aid package:* $14,130 (excluding resources awarded to replace EFC). 7% of all full-time undergraduates had no need and received non-need-based gift aid.
GIFT AID (NEED-BASED) *Total amount:* $9,175,650 (13% federal, 16% state, 69% institutional, 2% external sources). *Receiving aid:* Freshmen: 82% (266); All full-time undergraduates: 81% (879). *Average award:* Freshmen: $10,739; Undergraduates: $9894. *Scholarships, grants, and awards:* Federal Pell, FSEOG, state, private, college/university gift aid from institutional funds.
GIFT AID (NON-NEED-BASED) *Total amount:* $1,196,137 (12% state, 83% institutional, 5% external sources). *Receiving aid:* Freshmen: 74% (241); Undergraduates: 79% (866). *Average Award:* Freshmen: $7696; Undergraduates:* $6518. *Scholarships, grants, and awards by category:* Academic Interests/Achievement: 611 awards ($2,492,415 total): general academic interests/achievements, mathematics, physical sciences. Creative Arts/Performance: 77 awards ($118,000 total): music. Special Achievements/Activities: religious involvement. Special Characteristics: 135 awards ($513,275 total): children of faculty/staff, local/state students, out-of-state students, relatives of clergy, religious affiliation. *Tuition waivers:* Full or partial for employees or children of employees. *ROTC:* Army cooperative, Air Force cooperative.
LOANS *Student loans:* $4,714,938 (94% need-based, 6% non-need-based). 87% of past graduating class borrowed through all loan programs. *Average indebtedness per student:* $26,125. *Average need-based loan:* Freshmen: $3564; Undergraduates: $4349. *Parent loans:* $1,100,285 (88% need-based, 12% non-need-based). *Programs:* FFEL (Subsidized and Unsubsidized Stafford, PLUS), Perkins.
WORK-STUDY *Federal work-study:* Total amount: $549,215; 574 jobs averaging $979. *State or other work-study/employment:* Total amount: $48,460 (93% need-based, 7% non-need-based). 15 part-time jobs averaging $3230.
APPLYING FOR FINANCIAL AID *Required financial aid form:* FAFSA. *Financial aid deadline (priority):* 3/1. *Notification date:* Continuous beginning 3/15. Students must reply within 2 weeks of notification.
CONTACT Ms. Juli L. Weininger, Director of Financial Aid, Heidelberg College, 310 East Market Street, Tiffin, OH 44883-2462, 419-448-2293 or toll-free 800-434-3352. *Fax:* 419-448-2296.

HELLENIC COLLEGE
Brookline, MA

CONTACT George A. Georgenes, Director of Financial Aid, Hellenic College, 50 Goddard Avenue, Brookline, MA 02146-7496, 617-731-3500 or toll-free 866-424-2338. *Fax:* 617-850-1465 Ext. 1297. *E-mail:* ggeorgenes@hchc.edu.

HENDERSON STATE UNIVERSITY
Arkadelphia, AR

CONTACT Ms. Jo Holland, Director of Financial Aid, Henderson State University, Box 7812, 1100 Henderson Street, Arkadelphia, AR 71999-0001, 870-230-5094 or toll-free 800-228-7333. *Fax:* 870-230-5144. *E-mail:* hollanj@hsu.edu.

HENDRIX COLLEGE
Conway, AR

Tuition & fees: $21,636	Average undergraduate aid package: $15,279

ABOUT THE INSTITUTION Independent United Methodist, coed. Awards: bachelor's and master's degrees. 26 undergraduate majors. Total enrollment: 1,031. Undergraduates: 1,022. Freshmen: 280. Federal methodology is used as a basis for awarding need-based institutional aid.
UNDERGRADUATE EXPENSES for 2005–06 *Application fee:* $40. *Comprehensive fee:* $27,946 includes full-time tuition ($21,336), mandatory fees ($300), and room and board ($6310). *College room only:* $2760. Full-time tuition and fees vary according to course load. Room and board charges vary according to board plan and housing facility. *Part-time tuition:* $2248 per course. *Part-time fees:* $40 per year. Part-time tuition and fees vary according to course load. *Payment plan:* Installment.
FRESHMAN FINANCIAL AID (Fall 2005, est.) 234 applied for aid; of those 69% were deemed to have need. 100% of freshmen with need received aid; of those 33% had need fully met. *Average percent of need met:* 82% (excluding resources awarded to replace EFC). *Average financial aid package:* $16,492 (excluding resources awarded to replace EFC). 42% of all full-time freshmen had no need and received non-need-based gift aid.
UNDERGRADUATE FINANCIAL AID (Fall 2005, est.) 719 applied for aid; of those 78% were deemed to have need. 100% of undergraduates with need received aid; of those 34% had need fully met. *Average percent of need met:* 82% (excluding resources awarded to replace EFC). *Average financial aid package:* $15,279 (excluding resources awarded to replace EFC). 42% of all full-time undergraduates had no need and received non-need-based gift aid.
GIFT AID (NEED-BASED) *Total amount:* $5,904,771 (11% federal, 7% state, 78% institutional, 4% external sources). *Receiving aid:* Freshmen: 54% (160); All full-time undergraduates: 55% (555). *Average award:* Freshmen: $12,844; Undergraduates: $10,978. *Scholarships, grants, and awards:* Federal Pell, FSEOG, state, private, college/university gift aid from institutional funds.
GIFT AID (NON-NEED-BASED) *Total amount:* $4,753,804 (12% state, 84% institutional, 4% external sources). *Receiving aid:* Freshmen: 14% (41); Undergraduates: 11% (110). *Average Award:* Freshmen: $18,202; Undergraduates:* $15,588. *Scholarships, grants, and awards by category:* Academic Interests/Achievement: 779 awards ($5,104,962 total): general academic interests/achievements. Creative Arts/Performance: 115 awards ($140,500 total): art/fine arts, dance, music, theater/drama. Special Achievements/Activities: 112 awards ($241,114 total): leadership, religious involvement. Special Characteristics: 46 awards ($528,491 total): children of faculty/staff, international students, previous college experience, relatives of clergy. *Tuition waivers:* Full or partial for employees or children of employees. *ROTC:* Army cooperative.
LOANS *Student loans:* $3,664,289 (64% need-based, 36% non-need-based). 78% of past graduating class borrowed through all loan programs. *Average indebtedness per student:* $15,271. *Average need-based loan:* Freshmen: $3733; Undergraduates: $4425. *Parent loans:* $3,903,684 (17% need-based, 83% non-need-based). *Programs:* FFEL (Subsidized and Unsubsidized Stafford, PLUS), Perkins, United Methodist Loan.
WORK-STUDY *Federal work-study:* Total amount: $435,076; 310 jobs averaging $1403. *State or other work-study/employment:* Total amount: $186,190 (13% need-based, 87% non-need-based). 187 part-time jobs averaging $996.
APPLYING FOR FINANCIAL AID *Required financial aid forms:* FAFSA, institution's own form, state aid form. *Financial aid deadline (priority):* 2/15. *Notification date:* Continuous beginning 2/16. Students must reply by 5/1 or within 2 weeks of notification.
CONTACT Mark Bandré, Director of Financial Aid, Hendrix College, 1600 Washington Avenue, Conway, AR 72032, 501-450-1368 or toll-free 800-277-9017. *Fax:* 501-450-3871. *E-mail:* student_aid@hendrix.edu.

HENRY COGSWELL COLLEGE
Everett, WA

CONTACT Financial Aid Director, Henry Cogswell College, 3002 Colby Avenue, Everett, WA 98201, 425-258-3351 Ext. 117 or toll-free 866-411-4221. *Fax:* 425-257-0405. *E-mail:* financialaid@henrycogswell.edu.

HERITAGE BIBLE COLLEGE
Dunn, NC

CONTACT Mrs. Vickie Williford, Director of Financial Aid, Heritage Bible College, Box 1628, Dunn, NC 28335, 800-297-6351 or toll-free 800-297-6351 Ext. 230. *Fax:* 910-892-1809. *E-mail:* vwilliford@heritagebiblecollege.org.

HERITAGE CHRISTIAN UNIVERSITY
Florence, AL

Tuition & fees: $8264	Average undergraduate aid package: $2165

ABOUT THE INSTITUTION Independent religious, coed, primarily men. Awards: associate, bachelor's, and master's degrees. 1 undergraduate major. Total enrollment: 123. Undergraduates: 109. Freshmen: 4. Federal methodology is used as a basis for awarding need-based institutional aid.
UNDERGRADUATE EXPENSES for 2005–06 *Application fee:* $25. *Tuition:* full-time $7784; part-time $278 per hour. *Required fees:* full-time $480; $20 per hour. *Payment plans:* Installment, deferred payment.
FRESHMAN FINANCIAL AID (Fall 2004) 3 applied for aid; of those 67% were deemed to have need. 100% of freshmen with need received aid. *Average percent of need met:* 43% (excluding resources awarded to replace EFC). *Average financial aid package:* $1058 (excluding resources awarded to replace EFC). 33% of all full-time freshmen had no need and received non-need-based gift aid.
UNDERGRADUATE FINANCIAL AID (Fall 2004) 29 applied for aid; of those 97% were deemed to have need. 100% of undergraduates with need received aid. *Average percent of need met:* 29% (excluding resources awarded to replace EFC). *Average financial aid package:* $2165 (excluding resources awarded to replace EFC). 24% of all full-time undergraduates had no need and received non-need-based gift aid.
GIFT AID (NEED-BASED) *Total amount:* $152,188 (100% federal). *Scholarships, grants, and awards:* Federal Pell, FSEOG, college/university gift aid from institutional funds.
GIFT AID (NON-NEED-BASED) *Total amount:* $98,492 (100% institutional). *Receiving aid:* Freshmen: 100% (3); Undergraduates: 44% (20). *Average Award:* Freshmen: $500; Undergraduates: $5589. *Scholarships, grants, and awards by category: Academic Interests/Achievement:* general academic interests/achievements. *Special Characteristics:* 6 awards ($11,744 total): children and siblings of alumni, children of educators, children of faculty/staff, spouses of current students. *Tuition waivers:* Full or partial for employees or children of employees.
LOANS *Student loans:* $362,856 (54% need-based, 46% non-need-based). 69% of past graduating class borrowed through all loan programs. *Average indebtedness per student:* $23,236. *Parent loans:* $11,640 (100% need-based). *Programs:* FFEL (Subsidized and Unsubsidized Stafford, PLUS).
WORK-STUDY *Federal work-study:* Total amount: $8066; 10 jobs averaging $1234.
APPLYING FOR FINANCIAL AID *Required financial aid forms:* FAFSA, federal income tax form(s). *Financial aid deadline (priority):* 6/1. *Notification date:* Continuous beginning 7/15. Students must reply within 2 weeks of notification.
CONTACT Angie Horton, Financial Aid Counselor, Heritage Christian University, PO Box HCU, Florence, AL 35630, 800-367-3565 Ext. 24 or toll-free 800-367-3565. *Fax:* 256-766-9289. *E-mail:* ahorton@hcu.edu.

HERITAGE UNIVERSITY
Toppenish, WA

ABOUT THE INSTITUTION Independent, coed. Awards: associate, bachelor's, and master's degrees and post-bachelor's certificates. 25 undergraduate majors. Total enrollment: 1,311. Undergraduates: 806. Freshmen: 89.
GIFT AID (NEED-BASED) *Scholarships, grants, and awards:* Federal Pell, FSEOG, state, private, college/university gift aid from institutional funds.
GIFT AID (NON-NEED-BASED) *Scholarships, grants, and awards by category: Academic Interests/Achievement:* biological sciences, business, communication, computer science, education, general academic interests/achievements, physical sciences, social sciences.
LOANS *Programs:* FFEL (Subsidized and Unsubsidized Stafford, PLUS), Perkins.
APPLYING FOR FINANCIAL AID *Required financial aid forms:* FAFSA, institution's own form.
CONTACT Mr. Norberto Espindola, Director of Enrollment Management Services, Heritage University, 3240 Fort Road, Toppenish, WA 98948-9599, 509-865-8500 or toll-free 888-272-6190 (in-state). *Fax:* 509-865-8659. *E-mail:* financial_aid@heritage.edu.

HIGH POINT UNIVERSITY
High Point, NC

CONTACT Dana D. Kelly, Director of Financial Aid, High Point University, Box 3232, University Station, 833 Montlieu Avenue, High Point, NC 27262, 336-841-9128 or toll-free 800-345-6993. *Fax:* 336-884-0221. *E-mail:* dkelly@highpoint.edu.

HILBERT COLLEGE
Hamburg, NY

Tuition & fees: $14,900   **Average undergraduate aid package:** $10,157

ABOUT THE INSTITUTION Independent, coed. Awards: associate and bachelor's degrees. 13 undergraduate majors. Total enrollment: 1,109. Undergraduates: 1,109. Freshmen: 147. Federal methodology is used as a basis for awarding need-based institutional aid.
UNDERGRADUATE EXPENSES for 2005–06 *Application fee:* $20. *Comprehensive fee:* $20,480 includes full-time tuition ($14,300), mandatory fees ($600), and room and board ($5580). *College room only:* $2400. Full-time tuition and fees vary according to course load. Room and board charges vary according to board plan and housing facility. *Part-time tuition:* $332 per credit hour. *Part-time fees:* $13 per credit hour; $55 per term. Part-time tuition and fees vary according to course load. *Payment plans:* Installment, deferred payment.
FRESHMAN FINANCIAL AID (Fall 2005, est.) 170 applied for aid; of those 91% were deemed to have need. 99% of freshmen with need received aid; of those 18% had need fully met. *Average percent of need met:* 74% (excluding resources awarded to replace EFC). *Average financial aid package:* $11,258 (excluding resources awarded to replace EFC). 11% of all full-time freshmen had no need and received non-need-based gift aid.
UNDERGRADUATE FINANCIAL AID (Fall 2005, est.) 823 applied for aid; of those 89% were deemed to have need. 99% of undergraduates with need received aid; of those 29% had need fully met. *Average percent of need met:* 77% (excluding resources awarded to replace EFC). *Average financial aid package:* $10,157 (excluding resources awarded to replace EFC). 11% of all full-time undergraduates had no need and received non-need-based gift aid.
GIFT AID (NEED-BASED) *Total amount:* $4,669,455 (23% federal, 30% state, 38% institutional, 9% external sources). *Receiving aid:* Freshmen: 86% (153); All full-time undergraduates: 85% (710). *Average award:* Freshmen: $7802; Undergraduates: $6287. *Scholarships, grants, and awards:* Federal Pell, FSEOG, state, private, college/university gift aid from institutional funds.
GIFT AID (NON-NEED-BASED) *Total amount:* $360,318 (16% state, 50% institutional, 34% external sources). *Receiving aid:* Freshmen: 3% (6); Undergraduates: 6% (51). *Average Award:* Freshmen: $8980; Undergraduates: $9608. *Scholarships, grants, and awards by category: Academic Interests/Achievement:* 84 awards ($162,000 total): general academic interests/achievements. *Special Achievements/Activities:* 44 awards ($61,500 total): leadership. *Special Characteristics:* 51 awards ($52,000 total): children and siblings of alumni, members of minority groups, siblings of current students. *Tuition waivers:* Full or partial for children of alumni, employees or children of employees, senior citizens.
LOANS *Student loans:* $6,448,703 (65% need-based, 35% non-need-based). 91% of past graduating class borrowed through all loan programs. *Average indebtedness per student:* $21,948. *Average need-based loan:* Freshmen: $3476; Undergraduates: $4324. *Parent loans:* $747,361 (29% need-based, 71% non-need-based). *Programs:* FFEL (Subsidized and Unsubsidized Stafford, PLUS), Perkins, alternative loans.
WORK-STUDY *Federal work-study:* Total amount: $96,907; 68 jobs averaging $1425.
APPLYING FOR FINANCIAL AID *Required financial aid form:* FAFSA. *Financial aid deadline:* 5/1 (priority: 3/1). *Notification date:* Continuous beginning 3/15. Students must reply within 2 weeks of notification.
CONTACT Beverly Chudy, Director of Financial Aid, Hilbert College, 5200 South Park Avenue, Hamburg, NY 14075-1597, 716-649-7900 Ext. 207. *Fax:* 716-649-1152. *E-mail:* bchudy@hilbert.edu.

HILLSDALE COLLEGE
Hillsdale, MI

Tuition & fees: $17,410   **Average undergraduate aid package:** $13,000

ABOUT THE INSTITUTION Independent, coed. Awards: bachelor's degrees. 43 undergraduate majors. Total enrollment: 1,304. Undergraduates: 1,304. Freshmen: 340. Both federal and institutional methodology are used as a basis for awarding need-based institutional aid.
UNDERGRADUATE EXPENSES for 2005–06 *Application fee:* $35. *Comprehensive fee:* $24,160 includes full-time tuition ($17,000), mandatory fees ($410), and room and board ($6750). *College room only:* $3350. Room and board charges

Hillsdale College

vary according to board plan. *Part-time tuition:* $670 per semester hour. *Payment plans:* Tuition prepayment, installment, deferred payment.
FRESHMAN FINANCIAL AID (Fall 2005, est.) 155 applied for aid; of those 77% were deemed to have need. 100% of freshmen with need received aid; of those 50% had need fully met. *Average percent of need met:* 75% (excluding resources awarded to replace EFC). *Average financial aid package:* $12,750 (excluding resources awarded to replace EFC). 26% of all full-time freshmen had no need and received non-need-based gift aid.
UNDERGRADUATE FINANCIAL AID (Fall 2005, est.) 473 applied for aid; of those 85% were deemed to have need. 100% of undergraduates with need received aid; of those 62% had need fully met. *Average percent of need met:* 80% (excluding resources awarded to replace EFC). *Average financial aid package:* $13,000 (excluding resources awarded to replace EFC). 26% of all full-time undergraduates had no need and received non-need-based gift aid.
GIFT AID (NEED-BASED) *Total amount:* $6,865,000 (5% state, 95% institutional). *Receiving aid:* Freshmen: 37% (120); All full-time undergraduates: 32% (400). *Average award:* Freshmen: $6800; Undergraduates: $6000. *Scholarships, grants, and awards:* state, private, college/university gift aid from institutional funds.
GIFT AID (NON-NEED-BASED) *Total amount:* $2,138,000 (14% state, 72% institutional, 14% external sources). *Receiving aid:* Freshmen: 25% (80); Undergraduates: 25% (320). *Average Award:* Freshmen: $5700; Undergraduates: $6750. *Scholarships, grants, and awards by category: Academic Interests/Achievement:* 675 awards ($2,200,000 total): biological sciences, business, education, English, foreign languages, general academic interests/achievements, health fields, humanities, international studies, mathematics, physical sciences, premedicine, religion/biblical studies. *Creative Arts/Performance:* 60 awards ($120,000 total): art/fine arts, debating, journalism/publications, music, theater/drama. *Special Achievements/Activities:* 245 awards ($1,000,000 total): community service, general special achievements/activities, leadership. *Special Characteristics:* 40 awards ($330,000 total): children of faculty/staff, international students. *Tuition waivers:* Full or partial for children of alumni, employees or children of employees.
LOANS *Student loans:* $4,586,000 (41% need-based, 59% non-need-based). 65% of past graduating class borrowed through all loan programs. *Average indebtedness per student:* $17,000. *Average need-based loan:* Freshmen: $2500; Undergraduates: $5000. *Programs:* college/university, alternative loans.
ATHLETIC AWARDS *Total amount:* $1,857,000 (100% non-need-based).
APPLYING FOR FINANCIAL AID *Required financial aid forms:* institution's own form, noncustodial (divorced/separated) parent's statement, business/farm supplement, FAFSA (for state aid only). *Financial aid deadline:* 4/1 (priority: 2/15). *Notification date:* Continuous beginning 2/15. Students must reply by 5/1 or within 3 weeks of notification.
CONTACT Mr. Rich Moeggengberg, Director of Student Financial Aid, Hillsdale College, 33 East College Street, Hillsdale, MI 49242-1298, 517-607-2550. *Fax:* 517-607-2298. *E-mail:* rich.moeggenbeng@hillsdale.edu.

HILLSDALE FREE WILL BAPTIST COLLEGE
Moore, OK

CONTACT Ms. Pamela Thompson, Director of Admissions and Financial Aid, Hillsdale Free Will Baptist College, PO Box 7208, Moore, OK 73153-1208, 405-912-9006. *Fax:* 405-912-9050. *E-mail:* pamthompson@hc.edu.

HIRAM COLLEGE
Hiram, OH

CONTACT Ann Marie Gruber, Associate Director of Financial Aid, Hiram College, Box 67, Hiram, OH 44234-0067, 330-569-5107 or toll-free 800-362-5280. *Fax:* 330-569-5499.

HOBART AND WILLIAM SMITH COLLEGES
Geneva, NY

Tuition & fees: $32,737	Average undergraduate aid package: $24,316

ABOUT THE INSTITUTION Independent, coed. Awards: bachelor's degrees. 54 undergraduate majors. Total enrollment: 1,883. Undergraduates: 1,868. Freshmen: 545. Both federal and institutional methodology are used as a basis for awarding need-based institutional aid.

UNDERGRADUATE EXPENSES for 2005–06 *Application fee:* $45. *Comprehensive fee:* $41,123 includes full-time tuition ($31,850), mandatory fees ($887), and room and board ($8386). Room and board charges vary according to board plan. *Payment plans:* Tuition prepayment, installment.
FRESHMAN FINANCIAL AID (Fall 2005, est.) 394 applied for aid; of those 80% were deemed to have need. 100% of freshmen with need received aid; of those 75% had need fully met. *Average percent of need met:* 92% (excluding resources awarded to replace EFC). *Average financial aid package:* $24,525 (excluding resources awarded to replace EFC). 23% of all full-time freshmen had no need and received non-need-based gift aid.
UNDERGRADUATE FINANCIAL AID (Fall 2005, est.) 1,332 applied for aid; of those 85% were deemed to have need. 100% of undergraduates with need received aid; of those 76% had need fully met. *Average percent of need met:* 89% (excluding resources awarded to replace EFC). *Average financial aid package:* $24,316 (excluding resources awarded to replace EFC). 20% of all full-time undergraduates had no need and received non-need-based gift aid.
GIFT AID (NEED-BASED) *Total amount:* $22,838,667 (7% federal, 7% state, 83% institutional, 3% external sources). *Receiving aid:* Freshmen: 58% (316); All full-time undergraduates: 60% (1,115). *Average award:* Freshmen: $21,967; Undergraduates: $20,483. *Scholarships, grants, and awards:* Federal Pell, FSEOG, state, private, college/university gift aid from institutional funds.
GIFT AID (NON-NEED-BASED) *Total amount:* $4,291,124 (1% state, 88% institutional, 11% external sources). *Receiving aid:* Freshmen: 9% (50); Undergraduates: 7% (133). *Average Award:* Freshmen: $10,301; Undergraduates: $8971. *Scholarships, grants, and awards by category: Academic Interests/Achievement:* 79 awards ($1,002,429 total): general academic interests/achievements. *Creative Arts/Performance:* 13 awards ($117,000 total): art/fine arts, creative writing, dance, music, performing arts. *Special Achievements/Activities:* 25 awards ($212,500 total): leadership. *Tuition waivers:* Full or partial for employees or children of employees.
LOANS *Student loans:* $8,111,198 (65% need-based, 35% non-need-based). 65% of past graduating class borrowed through all loan programs. *Average indebtedness per student:* $21,454. *Average need-based loan:* Freshmen: $2325; Undergraduates: $3638. *Parent loans:* $5,503,605 (26% need-based, 74% non-need-based). *Programs:* FFEL (Subsidized and Unsubsidized Stafford, PLUS), Perkins.
WORK-STUDY *Federal work-study:* Total amount: $1,487,212; 938 jobs averaging $1586. *State or other work-study/employment:* Total amount: $635,656 (14% need-based, 86% non-need-based). 366 part-time jobs averaging $1736.
APPLYING FOR FINANCIAL AID *Required financial aid forms:* FAFSA, CSS Financial Aid PROFILE, state aid form, noncustodial (divorced/separated) parent's statement, income tax form(s). *Financial aid deadline:* 3/15 (priority: 2/15). *Notification date:* 4/1. Students must reply by 5/1 or within 3 weeks of notification.
CONTACT Samantha Veeder, Director of Financial Aid, Hobart and William Smith Colleges, Geneva, NY 14456-3397, 315-781-3315 or toll-free 800-245-0100. *Fax:* 315-781-3655. *E-mail:* finaid@hws.edu.

HOBE SOUND BIBLE COLLEGE
Hobe Sound, FL

CONTACT Director of Financial Aid, Hobe Sound Bible College, PO Box 1065, Hobe Sound, FL 33475-1065, 561-546-5534 or toll-free 800-881-5534. *Fax:* 561-545-1422.

HOFSTRA UNIVERSITY
Hempstead, NY

Tuition & fees: $21,530	Average undergraduate aid package: $12,750

ABOUT THE INSTITUTION Independent, coed. Awards: bachelor's, master's, doctoral, and first professional degrees and post-bachelor's and post-master's certificates. 128 undergraduate majors. Total enrollment: 12,890. Undergraduates: 8,884. Freshmen: 1,774. Federal methodology is used as a basis for awarding need-based institutional aid.

UNDERGRADUATE EXPENSES for 2005–06 *Application fee:* $50. *Comprehensive fee:* $30,830 includes full-time tuition ($20,500), mandatory fees ($1030), and room and board ($9300). *College room only:* $6200. Full-time tuition and fees vary according to course load and program. Room and board charges vary according to board plan and housing facility. *Part-time tuition:* $670 per

semester hour. *Part-time fees:* $155 per term. Part-time tuition and fees vary according to course load and program. *Payment plans:* Installment, deferred payment.
FRESHMAN FINANCIAL AID (Fall 2005, est.) 1400 applied for aid; of those 79% were deemed to have need. 98% of freshmen with need received aid; of those 19% had need fully met. *Average percent of need met:* 55% (excluding resources awarded to replace EFC). *Average financial aid package:* $12,950 (excluding resources awarded to replace EFC). 20% of all full-time freshmen had no need and received non-need-based gift aid.
UNDERGRADUATE FINANCIAL AID (Fall 2005, est.) 5,760 applied for aid; of those 82% were deemed to have need. 99% of undergraduates with need received aid; of those 16% had need fully met. *Average percent of need met:* 52% (excluding resources awarded to replace EFC). *Average financial aid package:* $12,750 (excluding resources awarded to replace EFC). 14% of all full-time undergraduates had no need and received non-need-based gift aid.
GIFT AID (NEED-BASED) *Total amount:* $32,245,000 (20% federal, 21% state, 55% institutional, 4% external sources). *Receiving aid:* Freshmen: 55% (965); All full-time undergraduates: 52% (4,070). *Average award:* Freshmen: $10,100; Undergraduates: $8475. *Scholarships, grants, and awards:* Federal Pell, FSEOG, state, private, college/university gift aid from institutional funds.
GIFT AID (NON-NEED-BASED) *Total amount:* $12,390,000 (2% federal, 5% state, 86% institutional, 7% external sources). *Receiving aid:* Freshmen: 9% (155); Undergraduates: 6% (455). *Average Award:* Freshmen: $9800; Undergraduates: $8050. *Scholarships, grants, and awards by category: Academic Interests/Achievement:* 3,313 awards ($22,370,676 total): communication, general academic interests/achievements. *Creative Arts/Performance:* 156 awards ($301,619 total): art/fine arts, dance, music, theater/drama. *Special Achievements/Activities:* 112 awards ($245,138 total): general special achievements/activities, leadership. *Special Characteristics:* 116 awards ($269,796 total): general special characteristics. *Tuition waivers:* Full or partial for employees or children of employees, senior citizens. *ROTC:* Army.
LOANS *Student loans:* $47,000,000 (72% need-based, 28% non-need-based). 61% of past graduating class borrowed through all loan programs. *Average indebtedness per student:* $20,500. *Average need-based loan:* Freshmen: $3025; Undergraduates: $4400. *Parent loans:* $37,385,000 (41% need-based, 59% non-need-based). *Programs:* FFEL (Subsidized and Unsubsidized Stafford, PLUS).
WORK-STUDY *Federal work-study:* Total amount: $1,200,000; 550 jobs averaging $2200. *State or other work-study/employment:* Total amount: $5,110,000 (26% need-based, 74% non-need-based). 2,200 part-time jobs averaging $2300.
ATHLETIC AWARDS *Total amount:* $7,000,000 (44% need-based, 56% non-need-based).
APPLYING FOR FINANCIAL AID *Required financial aid forms:* FAFSA, state aid form. *Financial aid deadline (priority):* 2/15. *Notification date:* Continuous beginning 3/15. Students must reply within 2 weeks of notification.
CONTACT Sandra Filby, Assistant Director of Financial Aid, Hofstra University, 126 Hofstra University, Hempstead, NY 11549, 516-463-4335 or toll-free 800-HOFSTRA. *Fax:* 516-463-4936. *E-mail:* sandra.a.filbry@hofstra.edu.

HOLLINS UNIVERSITY
Roanoke, VA

Tuition & fees: $22,945   **Average undergraduate aid package: $17,913**

ABOUT THE INSTITUTION Independent, undergraduate: women only; graduate: coed. Awards: bachelor's and master's degrees and post-master's certificates. 30 undergraduate majors. Total enrollment: 1,123. Undergraduates: 848. Freshmen: 184. Federal methodology is used as a basis for awarding need-based institutional aid.
UNDERGRADUATE EXPENSES for 2005–06 *Application fee:* $35. *Comprehensive fee:* $31,105 includes full-time tuition ($22,470), mandatory fees ($475), and room and board ($8160). *College room only:* $4880. *Part-time tuition:* $702 per credit. *Payment plan:* Installment.
FRESHMAN FINANCIAL AID (Fall 2005, est.) 165 applied for aid; of those 79% were deemed to have need. 100% of freshmen with need received aid; of those 25% had need fully met. *Average percent of need met:* 81% (excluding resources awarded to replace EFC). *Average financial aid package:* $18,826 (excluding resources awarded to replace EFC). 29% of all full-time freshmen had no need and received non-need-based gift aid.
UNDERGRADUATE FINANCIAL AID (Fall 2005, est.) 744 applied for aid; of those 64% were deemed to have need. 100% of undergraduates with need received aid; of those 21% had need fully met. *Average percent of need met:* 75% (excluding resources awarded to replace EFC). *Average financial aid package:* $17,913 (excluding resources awarded to replace EFC). 25% of all full-time undergraduates had no need and received non-need-based gift aid.
GIFT AID (NEED-BASED) *Total amount:* $7,347,711 (11% federal, 11% state, 77% institutional, 1% external sources). *Receiving aid:* Freshmen: 71% (130); All full-time undergraduates: 61% (474). *Average award:* Freshmen: $13,042; Undergraduates: $14,983. *Scholarships, grants, and awards:* Federal Pell, FSEOG, state, private, college/university gift aid from institutional funds.
GIFT AID (NON-NEED-BASED) *Total amount:* $2,417,396 (7% state, 91% institutional, 2% external sources). *Receiving aid:* Freshmen: 33% (61); Undergraduates: 36% (277). *Average Award:* Freshmen: $8414; Undergraduates: $9830. *Scholarships, grants, and awards by category: Academic Interests/Achievement:* 411 awards ($3,787,315 total): general academic interests/achievements. *Creative Arts/Performance:* 114 awards ($472,811 total): art/fine arts, creative writing, dance, music. *Special Achievements/Activities:* 47 awards ($237,500 total): community service, leadership. *Special Characteristics:* 276 awards ($424,151 total): children and siblings of alumni, international students, local/state students, out-of-state students, veterans. *Tuition waivers:* Full or partial for employees or children of employees.
LOANS *Student loans:* $3,492,767 (63% need-based, 37% non-need-based). 64% of past graduating class borrowed through all loan programs. *Average indebtedness per student:* $16,853. *Average need-based loan:* Freshmen: $3287; Undergraduates: $4761. *Parent loans:* $1,782,518 (86% need-based, 14% non-need-based). *Programs:* Federal Direct (Subsidized and Unsubsidized Stafford, PLUS), Perkins, college/university, Key Alternative Loans, PLATO Loans, CitiAssist Loans, GATE Loans, Sallie Mae Loans, OneChoice loans.
WORK-STUDY *Federal work-study:* Total amount: $586,965; 278 jobs averaging $2111. *State or other work-study/employment:* Total amount: $167,600 (100% non-need-based). 86 part-time jobs averaging $1948.
APPLYING FOR FINANCIAL AID *Required financial aid forms:* FAFSA, state aid form. *Financial aid deadline:* 2/15 (priority: 2/1). *Notification date:* Continuous beginning 3/15. Students must reply by 5/1.
CONTACT Mrs. Amy J. Moore, Director of Scholarships and Financial Assistance, Hollins University, PO Box 9718, Roanoke, VA 24020-1688, 540-362-6332 or toll-free 800-456-9595. *Fax:* 540-362-6093. *E-mail:* amoore@hollins.edu.

HOLY FAMILY UNIVERSITY
Philadelphia, PA

CONTACT Financial Aid Office, Holy Family University, Grant and Frankford Avenues, Philadelphia, PA 19114-2094, 215-637-5538 or toll-free 800-637-1191. *Fax:* 215-599-1694. *E-mail:* hfcfinaid@holyfamily.edu.

HOLY NAMES UNIVERSITY
Oakland, CA

Tuition & fees: $22,710   **Average undergraduate aid package: $16,215**

ABOUT THE INSTITUTION Independent Roman Catholic, coed, primarily women. Awards: bachelor's and master's degrees and post-bachelor's certificates. 26 undergraduate majors. Total enrollment: 1,093. Undergraduates: 686. Freshmen: 90. Federal methodology is used as a basis for awarding need-based institutional aid.
UNDERGRADUATE EXPENSES for 2006–07 *Application fee:* $50. *Tuition:* full-time $22,470.
FRESHMAN FINANCIAL AID (Fall 2005, est.) 89 applied for aid; of those 93% were deemed to have need. 94% of freshmen with need received aid; of those 19% had need fully met. *Average percent of need met:* 67% (excluding resources awarded to replace EFC). *Average financial aid package:* $16,560 (excluding resources awarded to replace EFC). 13% of all full-time freshmen had no need and received non-need-based gift aid.
UNDERGRADUATE FINANCIAL AID (Fall 2005, est.) 442 applied for aid; of those 85% were deemed to have need. 97% of undergraduates with need received aid; of those 8% had need fully met. *Average percent of need met:* 84% (excluding resources awarded to replace EFC). *Average financial aid package:* $16,215 (excluding resources awarded to replace EFC). 2% of all full-time undergraduates had no need and received non-need-based gift aid.
GIFT AID (NEED-BASED) *Total amount:* $4,463,858 (15% federal, 18% state, 60% institutional, 7% external sources). *Receiving aid:* Freshmen: 85% (76);

Holy Names University

All full-time undergraduates: 79% (351). *Average award:* Freshmen: $8558; Undergraduates: $13,570. *Scholarships, grants, and awards:* Federal Pell, FSEOG, state, private, college/university gift aid from institutional funds.
GIFT AID (NON-NEED-BASED) *Total amount:* $342,304 (2% state, 92% institutional, 6% external sources). *Receiving aid:* Freshmen: 15% (13); Undergraduates: 69% (307). *Average Award:* Freshmen: $18,958; *Undergraduates:* $18,286. *Scholarships, grants, and awards by category: Academic Interests/Achievement:* 72 awards ($503,100 total): general academic interests/achievements. *Creative Arts/Performance:* 8 awards ($26,879 total): music. *Special Achievements/Activities:* 10 awards ($8500 total): community service. *Special Characteristics:* 31 awards ($132,904 total): children and siblings of alumni, ethnic background, international students, religious affiliation. *ROTC:* Army cooperative, Air Force cooperative.
LOANS *Student loans:* $2,163,330 (82% need-based, 18% non-need-based). 94% of past graduating class borrowed through all loan programs. *Average indebtedness per student:* $7229. *Average need-based loan:* Freshmen: $2842; Undergraduates: $3458. *Parent loans:* $1,633,371 (41% need-based, 59% non-need-based). *Programs:* FFEL (Subsidized and Unsubsidized Stafford, PLUS), Perkins, alternative loans.
WORK-STUDY *Federal work-study:* Total amount: $84,760; 50 jobs averaging $1699.
ATHLETIC AWARDS *Total amount:* $535,363 (79% need-based, 21% non-need-based).
APPLYING FOR FINANCIAL AID *Required financial aid forms:* FAFSA, state aid form. *Financial aid deadline (priority):* 3/2. *Notification date:* Continuous beginning 3/1. Students must reply by 5/1 or within 2 weeks of notification.
CONTACT Christina Miller, Director of Financial Aid, Holy Names University, 3500 Mountain Boulevard, Oakland, CA 94619-1699, 510-436-1327 or toll-free 800-430-1321. *Fax:* 510-436-1199. *E-mail:* miller@hnu.edu.

HOOD COLLEGE
Frederick, MD

CONTACT Director of Financial Aid, Hood College, 401 Rosemont Avenue, Frederick, MD 21701-8575, 301-696-3411 or toll-free 800-922-1599. *E-mail:* finaid@hood.edu.

HOPE COLLEGE
Holland, MI

Tuition & fees: $21,540 **Average undergraduate aid package: $18,174**

ABOUT THE INSTITUTION Independent religious, coed. Awards: bachelor's degrees. 84 undergraduate majors. Total enrollment: 3,141. Undergraduates: 3,141. Freshmen: 775. Federal methodology is used as a basis for awarding need-based institutional aid.
UNDERGRADUATE EXPENSES for 2005–06 *Application fee:* $35. *Comprehensive fee:* $28,208 includes full-time tuition ($21,420), mandatory fees ($120), and room and board ($6668). *College room only:* $3040. Full-time tuition and fees vary according to course load. Room and board charges vary according to board plan. *Payment plan:* Installment.
FRESHMAN FINANCIAL AID (Fall 2005, est.) 601 applied for aid; of those 75% were deemed to have need. 100% of freshmen with need received aid; of those 38% had need fully met. *Average percent of need met:* 87% (excluding resources awarded to replace EFC). *Average financial aid package:* $18,557 (excluding resources awarded to replace EFC). 33% of all full-time freshmen had no need and received non-need-based gift aid.
UNDERGRADUATE FINANCIAL AID (Fall 2005, est.) 2,027 applied for aid; of those 81% were deemed to have need. 100% of undergraduates with need received aid; of those 32% had need fully met. *Average percent of need met:* 86% (excluding resources awarded to replace EFC). *Average financial aid package:* $18,174 (excluding resources awarded to replace EFC). 29% of all full-time undergraduates had no need and received non-need-based gift aid.
GIFT AID (NEED-BASED) *Total amount:* $16,415,405 (7% federal, 12% state, 79% institutional, 2% external sources). *Receiving aid:* Freshmen: 46% (345); All full-time undergraduates: 50% (1,379). *Average award:* Freshmen: $14,394; Undergraduates: $12,739. *Scholarships, grants, and awards:* Federal Pell, FSEOG, state, private, college/university gift aid from institutional funds.
GIFT AID (NON-NEED-BASED) *Total amount:* $8,769,549 (1% federal, 13% state, 75% institutional, 11% external sources). *Receiving aid:* Freshmen: 56% (418); Undergraduates: 44% (1,231). *Average Award:* Freshmen: $7164; Undergraduates: $6863. *Scholarships, grants, and awards by category: Academic Interests/Achievement:* 1,992 awards ($12,070,162 total): general academic interests/achievements. *Creative Arts/Performance:* 140 awards ($350,538 total): art/fine arts, creative writing, dance, music, theater/drama. *ROTC:* Army cooperative.
LOANS *Student loans:* $11,959,149 (49% need-based, 51% non-need-based). 62% of past graduating class borrowed through all loan programs. *Average indebtedness per student:* $20,507. *Average need-based loan:* Freshmen: $3373; Undergraduates: $4696. *Parent loans:* $3,630,810 (100% non-need-based). *Programs:* Federal Direct (Subsidized and Unsubsidized Stafford, PLUS), Perkins, state, college/university.
WORK-STUDY *Federal work-study:* Total amount: $322,715; 249 jobs averaging $1296. *State or other work-study/employment:* Total amount: $1,610,727 (63% need-based, 37% non-need-based). 560 part-time jobs averaging $1804.
APPLYING FOR FINANCIAL AID *Required financial aid forms:* FAFSA, institution's own form. *Financial aid deadline (priority):* 3/1. *Notification date:* Continuous beginning 3/15. Students must reply by 5/1 or within 2 weeks of notification.
CONTACT Ms. Phyllis Hooyman, Director of Financial Aid, Hope College, 141 East 12th Street, PO Box 9000, Holland, MI 49422-9000, 616-395-7765 or toll-free 800-968-7850. *Fax:* 616-395-7160. *E-mail:* hooyman@hope.edu.

HOPE INTERNATIONAL UNIVERSITY
Fullerton, CA

CONTACT Mr. Mai Bui, Director of Financial Aid, Hope International University, 2500 East Nutwood Avenue, Fullerton, CA 92831, 714-879-3901 or toll-free 800-762-1294. *Fax:* 714-526-0231. *E-mail:* mbui@hiu.edu.

HOUGHTON COLLEGE
Houghton, NY

Tuition & fees: $19,420 **Average undergraduate aid package: $14,861**

ABOUT THE INSTITUTION Independent Wesleyan, coed. Awards: associate, bachelor's, and master's degrees. 52 undergraduate majors. Total enrollment: 1,411. Undergraduates: 1,398. Freshmen: 321. Both federal and institutional methodology are used as a basis for awarding need-based institutional aid.
UNDERGRADUATE EXPENSES for 2005–06 *Application fee:* $40. *Comprehensive fee:* $25,980 includes full-time tuition ($19,420) and room and board ($6560). Full-time tuition and fees vary according to class time, program, and reciprocity agreements. Room and board charges vary according to board plan and housing facility. *Part-time tuition:* $812 per hour. *Payment plan:* Installment.
FRESHMAN FINANCIAL AID (Fall 2005, est.) 289 applied for aid; of those 91% were deemed to have need. 99% of freshmen with need received aid; of those 27% had need fully met. *Average percent of need met:* 72% (excluding resources awarded to replace EFC). *Average financial aid package:* $15,114 (excluding resources awarded to replace EFC). 13% of all full-time freshmen had no need and received non-need-based gift aid.
UNDERGRADUATE FINANCIAL AID (Fall 2005, est.) 1,118 applied for aid; of those 91% were deemed to have need. 100% of undergraduates with need received aid; of those 29% had need fully met. *Average percent of need met:* 72% (excluding resources awarded to replace EFC). *Average financial aid package:* $14,861 (excluding resources awarded to replace EFC). 5% of all full-time undergraduates had no need and received non-need-based gift aid.
GIFT AID (NEED-BASED) *Total amount:* $8,489,909 (13% federal, 17% state, 61% institutional, 9% external sources). *Receiving aid:* Freshmen: 72% (260); All full-time undergraduates: 66% (883). *Average award:* Freshmen: $11,024; Undergraduates: $9422. *Scholarships, grants, and awards:* Federal Pell, FSEOG, state, private, college/university gift aid from institutional funds, United Negro College Fund.
GIFT AID (NON-NEED-BASED) *Total amount:* $1,233,696 (2% state, 86% institutional, 12% external sources). *Receiving aid:* Freshmen: 20% (71); Undergraduates: 22% (297). *Average Award:* Freshmen: $4629; Undergraduates: $10,810. *Scholarships, grants, and awards by category: Academic Interests/Achievement:* 603 awards ($2,098,008 total): general academic interests/achievements. *Creative Arts/Performance:* 73 awards ($127,084 total): art/fine arts, music. *Special Achievements/Activities:* 153 awards ($333,395 total): religious involvement. *Special Characteristics:* 304 awards ($391,270 total):

children and siblings of alumni, relatives of clergy, religious affiliation, siblings of current students. *Tuition waivers:* Full or partial for employees or children of employees, senior citizens. *ROTC:* Army cooperative.
LOANS *Student loans:* $4,179,838 (95% need-based, 5% non-need-based). 71% of past graduating class borrowed through all loan programs. *Average indebtedness per student:* $16,028. *Average need-based loan:* Freshmen: $3051; Undergraduates: $3697. *Parent loans:* $2,277,293 (93% need-based, 7% non-need-based). *Programs:* FFEL (Subsidized and Unsubsidized Stafford, PLUS), Perkins, college/university, alternative loans.
WORK-STUDY *Federal work-study:* Total amount: $1,279,500; 788 jobs averaging $1500. *State or other work-study/employment:* 43 part-time jobs averaging $1500.
ATHLETIC AWARDS *Total amount:* $487,965 (78% need-based, 22% non-need-based).
APPLYING FOR FINANCIAL AID *Required financial aid forms:* FAFSA, state aid form. *Financial aid deadline (priority):* 3/1. *Notification date:* Continuous beginning 3/15. Students must reply within 4 weeks of notification.
CONTACT Mr. Troy Martin, Director of Financial Aid, Houghton College, One Willard Avenue, Houghton, NY 14744, 716-567-9328 or toll-free 800-777-2556. *Fax:* 716-567-9610. *E-mail:* troy.martin@houghton.edu.

HOUSTON BAPTIST UNIVERSITY
Houston, TX

Tuition & fees: $16,500	Average undergraduate aid package: $11,149

ABOUT THE INSTITUTION Independent Baptist, coed. Awards: associate, bachelor's, and master's degrees and post-bachelor's and post-master's certificates. 65 undergraduate majors. Total enrollment: 2,294. Undergraduates: 1,932. Freshmen: 313. Federal methodology is used as a basis for awarding need-based institutional aid.
UNDERGRADUATE EXPENSES for 2006–07 *Application fee:* $25. *Comprehensive fee:* $21,000 includes full-time tuition ($16,500) and room and board ($4500). *College room only:* $2355. *Part-time tuition:* $550 per semester hour.
FRESHMAN FINANCIAL AID (Fall 2005, est.) 141 applied for aid; of those 77% were deemed to have need. 100% of freshmen with need received aid; of those 29% had need fully met. *Average percent of need met:* 63% (excluding resources awarded to replace EFC). *Average financial aid package:* $9672 (excluding resources awarded to replace EFC). 23% of all full-time freshmen had no need and received non-need-based gift aid.
UNDERGRADUATE FINANCIAL AID (Fall 2005, est.) 642 applied for aid; of those 84% were deemed to have need. 100% of undergraduates with need received aid; of those 19% had need fully met. *Average percent of need met:* 65% (excluding resources awarded to replace EFC). *Average financial aid package:* $11,149 (excluding resources awarded to replace EFC). 16% of all full-time undergraduates had no need and received non-need-based gift aid.
GIFT AID (NEED-BASED) *Total amount:* $6,989,730 (31% federal, 35% state, 26% institutional, 8% external sources). *Receiving aid:* Freshmen: 77% (108); All full-time undergraduates: 81% (523). *Average award:* Freshmen: $7635; Undergraduates: $7987. *Scholarships, grants, and awards:* Federal Pell, FSEOG, state, private, college/university gift aid from institutional funds.
GIFT AID (NON-NEED-BASED) *Total amount:* $871,667 (1% federal, 3% state, 77% institutional, 19% external sources). *Receiving aid:* Freshmen: 14% (20); Undergraduates: 8% (54). *Average Award:* Freshmen: $15,620; Undergraduates: $14,701. *Scholarships, grants, and awards by category: Academic Interests/Achievement:* 625 awards ($2,554,700 total): general academic interests/achievements, health fields, religion/biblical studies. *Creative Arts/Performance:* 135 awards ($302,000 total): art/fine arts, music. *Special Achievements/Activities:* 13 awards ($13,200 total): cheerleading/drum major, general special achievements/activities. *Special Characteristics:* 56 awards ($331,600 total): children of faculty/staff, general special characteristics, relatives of clergy. *ROTC:* Army cooperative.
LOANS *Student loans:* $7,443,691 (81% need-based, 19% non-need-based). 83% of past graduating class borrowed through all loan programs. *Average indebtedness per student:* $17,256. *Average need-based loan:* Freshmen: $2001; Undergraduates: $3355. *Parent loans:* $2,673,851 (27% need-based, 73% non-need-based). *Programs:* FFEL (Subsidized and Unsubsidized Stafford, PLUS), state, alternative loans.
WORK-STUDY *Federal work-study:* Total amount: $897,540; jobs available. *State or other work-study/employment:* Part-time jobs available.

ATHLETIC AWARDS *Total amount:* $652,021 (86% need-based, 14% non-need-based).
APPLYING FOR FINANCIAL AID *Required financial aid form:* FAFSA. *Financial aid deadline:* 4/15 (priority: 3/1). *Notification date:* Continuous beginning 3/1.
CONTACT Sherry Byrd, Director of Student Aid Programs, Houston Baptist University, 109 Administration Building, 7502 Fondren Road, Houston, TX 77074-3298, 281-649-3471 or toll-free 800-696-3210. *Fax:* 281-649-3298.

HOWARD PAYNE UNIVERSITY
Brownwood, TX

ABOUT THE INSTITUTION Independent religious, coed. Awards: associate and bachelor's degrees. 77 undergraduate majors. Total enrollment: 1,319. Undergraduates: 1,319. Freshmen: 302.
GIFT AID (NEED-BASED) *Scholarships, grants, and awards:* Federal Pell, FSEOG, state, private, college/university gift aid from institutional funds.
GIFT AID (NON-NEED-BASED) *Scholarships, grants, and awards by category: Academic Interests/Achievement:* biological sciences, business, communication, education, English, general academic interests/achievements, mathematics, physical sciences, premedicine, religion/biblical studies, social sciences. *Creative Arts/Performance:* art/fine arts, music, theater/drama. *Special Achievements/Activities:* community service, leadership, religious involvement. *Special Characteristics:* children and siblings of alumni, children of faculty/staff, local/state students, relatives of clergy, religious affiliation.
LOANS *Programs:* FFEL (Subsidized and Unsubsidized Stafford, PLUS), Perkins, state.
WORK-STUDY *Federal work-study:* Total amount: $80,474; 118 jobs averaging $2000. *State or other work-study/employment:* Total amount: $15,000 (100% need-based). 9 part-time jobs averaging $2000.
APPLYING FOR FINANCIAL AID *Required financial aid forms:* FAFSA, institution's own form.
CONTACT Glenda Huff, Director of Financial Aid, Howard Payne University, 1000 Fisk Avenue, Brownwood, TX 76801, 325-649-8014 or toll-free 800-880-4478. *Fax:* 325-649-8901. *E-mail:* ghuff@hputx.edu.

HOWARD UNIVERSITY
Washington, DC

Tuition & fees: $12,295	Average undergraduate aid package: $17,077

ABOUT THE INSTITUTION Independent, coed. Awards: bachelor's, master's, doctoral, and first professional degrees and post-master's and first professional certificates. 64 undergraduate majors. Total enrollment: 10,623. Undergraduates: 7,112. Freshmen: 1,451. Federal methodology is used as a basis for awarding need-based institutional aid.
UNDERGRADUATE EXPENSES for 2005–06 *Application fee:* $45. *Comprehensive fee:* $18,481 includes full-time tuition ($11,490), mandatory fees ($805), and room and board ($6186). *College room only:* $3736. Room and board charges vary according to board plan and housing facility. *Part-time tuition:* $479 per credit hour. *Payment plan:* Deferred payment.
FRESHMAN FINANCIAL AID (Fall 2004) 1182 applied for aid; of those 88% were deemed to have need. 95% of freshmen with need received aid; of those 23% had need fully met. *Average percent of need met:* 71% (excluding resources awarded to replace EFC). *Average financial aid package:* $16,313 (excluding resources awarded to replace EFC). 12% of all full-time freshmen had no need and received non-need-based gift aid.
UNDERGRADUATE FINANCIAL AID (Fall 2004) 4,571 applied for aid; of those 96% were deemed to have need. 97% of undergraduates with need received aid; of those 21% had need fully met. *Average percent of need met:* 75% (excluding resources awarded to replace EFC). *Average financial aid package:* $17,077 (excluding resources awarded to replace EFC). 13% of all full-time undergraduates had no need and received non-need-based gift aid.
GIFT AID (NEED-BASED) *Total amount:* $46,760,589 (19% federal, 72% institutional, 9% external sources). *Receiving aid:* Freshmen: 34% (482); All full-time undergraduates: 36% (2,445). *Average award:* Freshmen: $4134; Undergraduates: $4559. *Scholarships, grants, and awards:* Federal Pell, FSEOG, state, private, college/university gift aid from institutional funds, Federal Nursing.
GIFT AID (NON-NEED-BASED) *Receiving aid:* Freshmen: 64% (905); Undergraduates: 25% (1,706). *Average Award:* Freshmen: $12,989; Undergraduates: $10,147. *Scholarships, grants, and awards by category: Creative Arts/

Howard University

Performance: art/fine arts, dance, music. *Tuition waivers:* Full or partial for employees or children of employees. *ROTC:* Army, Air Force.
LOANS *Student loans:* $82,431,644 (100% need-based). 90% of past graduating class borrowed through all loan programs. *Average indebtedness per student:* $16,566. *Average need-based loan:* Freshmen: $3603; Undergraduates: $3636. *Parent loans:* $26,532,569 (100% need-based). *Programs:* Federal Direct (Subsidized and Unsubsidized Stafford, PLUS), FFEL (Subsidized and Unsubsidized Stafford, PLUS), Perkins, Federal Nursing, district, college/university.
WORK-STUDY *Federal work-study:* Total amount: $1,511,173; 431 jobs averaging $3667. *State or other work-study/employment:* Total amount: $799,504 (100% need-based). 223 part-time jobs averaging $3590.
ATHLETIC AWARDS *Total amount:* $4,515,723 (100% need-based).
APPLYING FOR FINANCIAL AID *Required financial aid form:* FAFSA. *Financial aid deadline:* 8/15 (priority: 2/15). *Notification date:* Continuous beginning 4/1. Students must reply by 6/1 or within 2 weeks of notification.
CONTACT Mr. Steven G. Johnson, Director of Financial Aid and Scholarships, Howard University, 2400 Sixth Street, NW, Washington, DC 20059-0002, 202-806-2762 or toll-free 800-HOWARD-U. *Fax:* 202-806-2818.

HUMBOLDT STATE UNIVERSITY
Arcata, CA

Tuition & fees: N/R **Average undergraduate aid package:** $8257

ABOUT THE INSTITUTION State-supported, coed. Awards: bachelor's and master's degrees. 78 undergraduate majors. Total enrollment: 7,550. Undergraduates: 6,529. Freshmen: 760. Federal methodology is used as a basis for awarding need-based institutional aid.
FRESHMAN FINANCIAL AID (Fall 2004) 533 applied for aid; of those 71% were deemed to have need. 93% of freshmen with need received aid; of those 15% had need fully met. *Average percent of need met:* 81% (excluding resources awarded to replace EFC). *Average financial aid package:* $8471 (excluding resources awarded to replace EFC).
UNDERGRADUATE FINANCIAL AID (Fall 2004) 3,789 applied for aid; of those 85% were deemed to have need. 96% of undergraduates with need received aid; of those 10% had need fully met. *Average percent of need met:* 77% (excluding resources awarded to replace EFC). *Average financial aid package:* $8257 (excluding resources awarded to replace EFC).
GIFT AID (NEED-BASED) *Total amount:* $17,866,654 (50% federal, 41% state, 4% institutional, 5% external sources). *Receiving aid:* Freshmen: 35% (279); All full-time undergraduates: 46% (2,670). *Average award:* Freshmen: $2022; Undergraduates: $2619. *Scholarships, grants, and awards:* Federal Pell, FSEOG, state, private, college/university gift aid from institutional funds.
GIFT AID (NON-NEED-BASED) *Scholarships, grants, and awards by category: Academic Interests/Achievement:* general academic interests/achievements. *Tuition waivers:* Full or partial for employees or children of employees, senior citizens.
LOANS *Student loans:* $17,167,205 (100% need-based). 35% of past graduating class borrowed through all loan programs. *Average indebtedness per student:* $12,730. *Average need-based loan:* Freshmen: $2269; Undergraduates: $2851. *Parent loans:* $2,517,268 (100% need-based). *Programs:* Federal Direct (Subsidized and Unsubsidized Stafford, PLUS), Perkins.
WORK-STUDY *Federal work-study:* Total amount: $467,347; 300 jobs averaging $2000.
ATHLETIC AWARDS *Total amount:* $350,989 (100% need-based).
APPLYING FOR FINANCIAL AID *Required financial aid form:* FAFSA. *Financial aid deadline (priority):* 3/2. *Notification date:* Continuous beginning 3/7.
CONTACT Kim Coughlin-Lamphear, Director of Financial Aid, Humboldt State University, 1 Harpst Street, Arcata, CA 95521-8299, 707-826-4321. *E-mail:* coughlin@humboldt.edu.

HUMPHREYS COLLEGE
Stockton, CA

ABOUT THE INSTITUTION Independent, coed. Awards: associate, bachelor's, and first professional degrees. 13 undergraduate majors. Total enrollment: 721. Undergraduates: 597.
GIFT AID (NEED-BASED) *Scholarships, grants, and awards:* Federal Pell, FSEOG, state.
GIFT AID (NON-NEED-BASED) *Scholarships, grants, and awards by category: Academic Interests/Achievement:* business, computer science, general academic interests/achievements. *Special Achievements/Activities:* community service. *Special Characteristics:* ethnic background, members of minority groups.
LOANS *Programs:* FFEL (Subsidized and Unsubsidized Stafford, PLUS).
APPLYING FOR FINANCIAL AID *Required financial aid form:* FAFSA.
CONTACT Judi LaFeber, Director of Financial Aid, Humphreys College, 6650 Inglewood Avenue, Stockton, CA 95207-3896, 209-478-0800. *Fax:* 209-478-8721.

HUNTER COLLEGE OF THE CITY UNIVERSITY OF NEW YORK
New York, NY

CONTACT Kevin McGowan, Director of Financial Aid, Hunter College of the City University of New York, 695 Park Avenue, New York, NY 10021-5085, 212-772-4820.

HUNTINGDON COLLEGE
Montgomery, AL

CONTACT Belinda Goris, Student Financial Aid Director, Huntingdon College, 1500 East Fairview Avenue, Montgomery, AL 36106-2148, 334-833-4519 or toll-free 800-763-0313. *E-mail:* bgoris@huntingdon.edu.

HUNTINGTON UNIVERSITY
Huntington, IN

Tuition & fees: $18,860 **Average undergraduate aid package:** $12,751

ABOUT THE INSTITUTION Independent religious, coed. Awards: associate, bachelor's, and master's degrees. 58 undergraduate majors. Total enrollment: 1,019. Undergraduates: 949. Freshmen: 229. Federal methodology is used as a basis for awarding need-based institutional aid.
UNDERGRADUATE EXPENSES for 2006–07 *Application fee:* $20. *Comprehensive fee:* $25,390 includes full-time tuition ($18,420), mandatory fees ($440), and room and board ($6530). *Part-time tuition:* $530 per semester hour.
FRESHMAN FINANCIAL AID (Fall 2005, est.) 203 applied for aid; of those 85% were deemed to have need. 100% of freshmen with need received aid; of those 21% had need fully met. *Average percent of need met:* 77% (excluding resources awarded to replace EFC). *Average financial aid package:* $13,942 (excluding resources awarded to replace EFC). 20% of all full-time freshmen had no need and received non-need-based gift aid.
UNDERGRADUATE FINANCIAL AID (Fall 2005, est.) 692 applied for aid; of those 87% were deemed to have need. 100% of undergraduates with need received aid; of those 17% had need fully met. *Average percent of need met:* 72% (excluding resources awarded to replace EFC). *Average financial aid package:* $12,751 (excluding resources awarded to replace EFC). 13% of all full-time undergraduates had no need and received non-need-based gift aid.
GIFT AID (NEED-BASED) *Total amount:* $5,274,419 (12% federal, 26% state, 55% institutional, 7% external sources). *Receiving aid:* Freshmen: 74% (165); All full-time undergraduates: 66% (546). *Average award:* Freshmen: $11,883; Undergraduates: $10,409. *Scholarships, grants, and awards:* Federal Pell, FSEOG, state, private, college/university gift aid from institutional funds.
GIFT AID (NON-NEED-BASED) *Total amount:* $861,904 (81% institutional, 19% external sources). *Receiving aid:* Freshmen: 26% (59); Undergraduates: 18% (149). *Average Award:* Freshmen: $7171; Undergraduates: $6328. *Scholarships, grants, and awards by category: Academic Interests/Achievement:* 444 awards ($1,501,830 total): general academic interests/achievements. *Creative Arts/Performance:* 74 awards ($89,650 total): art/fine arts, journalism/publications, music, theater/drama. *Special Achievements/Activities:* 6 awards ($3593 total): cheerleading/drum major. *Special Characteristics:* 554 awards ($1,612,307 total): children and siblings of alumni, children of current students, children of faculty/staff, international students, parents of current students, relatives of clergy, religious affiliation, siblings of current students, spouses of current students.
LOANS *Student loans:* $4,033,100 (68% need-based, 32% non-need-based). 62% of past graduating class borrowed through all loan programs. *Average indebtedness per student:* $18,290. *Average need-based loan:* Freshmen: $3067;

Undergraduates: $4118. *Parent loans:* $1,276,285 (34% need-based, 66% non-need-based). *Programs:* FFEL (Subsidized and Unsubsidized Stafford, PLUS), Perkins.
WORK-STUDY *Federal work-study:* Total amount: $302,356; 202 jobs averaging $1837.
ATHLETIC AWARDS *Total amount:* $703,518 (63% need-based, 37% non-need-based).
APPLYING FOR FINANCIAL AID *Required financial aid form:* FAFSA. *Financial aid deadline (priority):* 3/1. *Notification date:* Continuous beginning 3/1. Students must reply by 5/1 or within 2 weeks of notification.
CONTACT Mrs. Cindy Kreps, Financial Aid Secretary, Huntington University, 2303 College Avenue, Huntington, IN 46750, 260-359-4015 or toll-free 800-642-6493. *Fax:* 260-358-3699. *E-mail:* ckreps@huntington.edu.

HUSSIAN SCHOOL OF ART
Philadelphia, PA

CONTACT Ms. Susan Cohen, Financial Aid and Placement Director, Hussian School of Art, 1118 Market Street, Philadelphia, PA 19107-3679, 215-981-0900.

HUSSON COLLEGE
Bangor, ME

| Tuition & fees: $11,380 | Average undergraduate aid package: $7835 |

ABOUT THE INSTITUTION Independent, coed. Awards: associate, bachelor's, and master's degrees and post-bachelor's and post-master's certificates. 28 undergraduate majors. Total enrollment: 2,245. Undergraduates: 1,977. Freshmen: 334. Federal methodology is used as a basis for awarding need-based institutional aid.
UNDERGRADUATE EXPENSES for 2005-06 *Application fee:* $25. *Comprehensive fee:* $17,410 includes full-time tuition ($11,130), mandatory fees ($250), and room and board ($6030). Full-time tuition and fees vary according to class time. *Part-time tuition:* $371 per credit hour. Part-time tuition and fees vary according to class time and course load. *Payment plans:* Tuition prepayment, installment.
FRESHMAN FINANCIAL AID (Fall 2005, est.) 816 applied for aid; of those 67% were deemed to have need. 96% of freshmen with need received aid; of those 29% had need fully met. *Average percent of need met:* 76% (excluding resources awarded to replace EFC). *Average financial aid package:* $7328 (excluding resources awarded to replace EFC). 22% of all full-time freshmen had no need and received non-need-based gift aid.
UNDERGRADUATE FINANCIAL AID (Fall 2005, est.) 2,008 applied for aid; of those 73% were deemed to have need. 95% of undergraduates with need received aid; of those 19% had need fully met. *Average percent of need met:* 72% (excluding resources awarded to replace EFC). *Average financial aid package:* $7835 (excluding resources awarded to replace EFC). 15% of all full-time undergraduates had no need and received non-need-based gift aid.
GIFT AID (NEED-BASED) *Total amount:* $7,384,844 (39% federal, 10% state, 44% institutional, 7% external sources). *Receiving aid:* Freshmen: 55% (505); All full-time undergraduates: 61% (1,293). *Average award:* Freshmen: $5746; Undergraduates: $5363. *Scholarships, grants, and awards:* Federal Pell, FSEOG, state, private, college/university gift aid from institutional funds.
GIFT AID (NON-NEED-BASED) *Total amount:* $895,586 (17% federal, 1% state, 74% institutional, 8% external sources). *Receiving aid:* Freshmen: 12% (110); Undergraduates: 7% (157). *Average Award:* Freshmen: $4614; Undergraduates: $6286. *Scholarships, grants, and awards by category:* Academic Interests/Achievement: 152 awards ($15,897 total): business, computer science, education, general academic interests/achievements, health fields. *Special Achievements/Activities:* general special achievements/activities, leadership. *Special Characteristics:* children of union members/company employees. *Tuition waivers:* Full or partial for employees or children of employees, senior citizens. *ROTC:* Army cooperative, Naval cooperative.
LOANS *Student loans:* $9,296,210 (65% need-based, 35% non-need-based). 100% of past graduating class borrowed through all loan programs. *Average indebtedness per student:* $16,940. *Average need-based loan:* Freshmen: $2176; Undergraduates: $3252. *Parent loans:* $1,564,120 (35% need-based, 65% non-need-based). *Programs:* FFEL (Subsidized and Unsubsidized Stafford, PLUS), Perkins, alternative loans.

WORK-STUDY *Federal work-study:* Total amount: $566,311; 450 jobs averaging $1300.
APPLYING FOR FINANCIAL AID *Required financial aid forms:* FAFSA, state aid form. *Financial aid deadline (priority):* 4/15. *Notification date:* Continuous beginning 2/15. Students must reply by 5/1 or within 2 weeks of notification.
CONTACT Linda B. Conant, Director of Financial Aid, Husson College, One College Circle, Bangor, ME 04401, 207-941-7156 or toll-free 800-4-HUSSON. *Fax:* 207-973-1038. *E-mail:* conantl@husson.edu.

HUSTON-TILLOTSON UNIVERSITY
Austin, TX

CONTACT Anthony P. Barrientez, Director of Financial Aid, Huston-Tillotson University, 900 Chicon Street, Austin, TX 78702, 512-505-3031.

IDAHO STATE UNIVERSITY
Pocatello, ID

| Tuition & fees: N/R | Average undergraduate aid package: $11,201 |

ABOUT THE INSTITUTION State-supported, coed. Awards: bachelor's, master's, doctoral, and first professional degrees and post-bachelor's, post-master's, and first professional certificates. 100 undergraduate majors. Total enrollment: 13,977. Undergraduates: 11,652. Freshmen: 1,653. Federal methodology is used as a basis for awarding need-based institutional aid.
UNDERGRADUATE EXPENSES for 2006-07 *Application fee:* $40. *One-time required fee:* $330. *Tuition, nonresident:* full-time $7700. *College room and board:* $5030; *room only:* $2100.
FRESHMAN FINANCIAL AID (Fall 2005, est.) 781 applied for aid; of those 75% were deemed to have need. 97% of freshmen with need received aid; of those 10% had need fully met. *Average percent of need met:* 57% (excluding resources awarded to replace EFC). *Average financial aid package:* $4505 (excluding resources awarded to replace EFC). 35% of all full-time freshmen had no need and received non-need-based gift aid.
UNDERGRADUATE FINANCIAL AID (Fall 2005, est.) 6,012 applied for aid; of those 89% were deemed to have need. 98% of undergraduates with need received aid; of those 46% had need fully met. *Average percent of need met:* 77% (excluding resources awarded to replace EFC). *Average financial aid package:* $11,201 (excluding resources awarded to replace EFC). 17% of all full-time undergraduates had no need and received non-need-based gift aid.
GIFT AID (NEED-BASED) *Total amount:* $16,727,661 (99% federal, 1% state). *Receiving aid:* Freshmen: 38% (393); All full-time undergraduates: 57% (4,262). *Average award:* Freshmen: $2532; Undergraduates: $5530. *Scholarships, grants, and awards:* Federal Pell, FSEOG, state, private.
GIFT AID (NON-NEED-BASED) *Total amount:* $7,907,760 (3% federal, 12% state, 42% institutional, 43% external sources). *Receiving aid:* Freshmen: 41% (422); Undergraduates: 35% (2,583). *Average Award:* Freshmen: $4879; Undergraduates: $9889. *Scholarships, grants, and awards by category:* Academic Interests/Achievement: 2,687 awards ($2,884,386 total): biological sciences, business, communication, computer science, education, engineering/technologies, English, foreign languages, general academic interests/achievements, health fields, home economics, humanities, international studies, mathematics, military science, physical sciences, premedicine, religion/biblical studies, social sciences. *Creative Arts/Performance:* 288 awards ($165,765 total): art/fine arts, debating, music, performing arts, theater/drama. *Special Achievements/Activities:* 120 awards ($66,410 total): general special achievements/activities, junior miss, leadership, memberships, rodeo. *Special Characteristics:* 1,682 awards ($916,735 total): children and siblings of alumni, children of faculty/staff, first-generation college students, handicapped students, local/state students, members of minority groups, out-of-state students. *ROTC:* Army cooperative.
LOANS *Student loans:* $39,343,793 (56% need-based, 44% non-need-based). 69% of past graduating class borrowed through all loan programs. *Average indebtedness per student:* $19,299. *Average need-based loan:* Freshmen: $2259; Undergraduates: $6839. *Parent loans:* $397,174 (100% non-need-based). *Programs:* Federal Direct (Subsidized and Unsubsidized Stafford, PLUS), Perkins.
WORK-STUDY *Federal work-study:* Total amount: $1,020,800; 950 jobs averaging $1074. *State or other work-study/employment:* Total amount: $456,728 (100% need-based). 707 part-time jobs averaging $646.
ATHLETIC AWARDS *Total amount:* $2,428,831 (100% non-need-based).

Idaho State University

APPLYING FOR FINANCIAL AID *Required financial aid form:* FAFSA. *Financial aid deadline:* Continuous. *Notification date:* Continuous beginning 5/1.

CONTACT Mr. Doug Severs, Director of Financial Aid, Idaho State University, Campus Box 8077, Pocatello, ID 83209, 208-282-2981. *Fax:* 208-282-4755. *E-mail:* sevedoug@isu.edu.

ILLINOIS COLLEGE
Jacksonville, IL

Tuition & fees: $17,100 | Average undergraduate aid package: $13,570

ABOUT THE INSTITUTION Independent interdenominational, coed. Awards: bachelor's degrees. 44 undergraduate majors. Total enrollment: 1,030. Undergraduates: 1,030. Freshmen: 257. Federal methodology is used as a basis for awarding need-based institutional aid.

UNDERGRADUATE EXPENSES for 2006–07 *Application fee:* $25. *Comprehensive fee:* $23,600 includes full-time tuition ($17,100) and room and board ($6500). *Part-time tuition:* $712 per credit hour.

FRESHMAN FINANCIAL AID (Fall 2005, est.) 241 applied for aid; of those 82% were deemed to have need. 100% of freshmen with need received aid; of those 37% had need fully met. *Average percent of need met:* 82% (excluding resources awarded to replace EFC). *Average financial aid package:* $13,253 (excluding resources awarded to replace EFC). 19% of all full-time freshmen had no need and received non-need-based gift aid.

UNDERGRADUATE FINANCIAL AID (Fall 2005, est.) 902 applied for aid; of those 85% were deemed to have need. 100% of undergraduates with need received aid; of those 35% had need fully met. *Average percent of need met:* 85% (excluding resources awarded to replace EFC). *Average financial aid package:* $13,570 (excluding resources awarded to replace EFC). 18% of all full-time undergraduates had no need and received non-need-based gift aid.

GIFT AID (NEED-BASED) *Total amount:* $6,584,498 (10% federal, 29% state, 59% institutional, 2% external sources). *Receiving aid:* Freshmen: 60% (154); All full-time undergraduates: 62% (635). *Average award:* Freshmen: $6176; Undergraduates: $6292. *Scholarships, grants, and awards:* Federal Pell, FSEOG, state, private, college/university gift aid from institutional funds.

GIFT AID (NON-NEED-BASED) *Total amount:* $1,662,098 (92% institutional, 8% external sources). *Receiving aid:* Freshmen: 69% (177); Undergraduates: 60% (617). *Average Award:* Freshmen: $6489; Undergraduates: $5587. *Scholarships, grants, and awards by category:* Academic Interests/Achievement: 634 awards ($3,564,423 total): general academic interests/achievements. Creative Arts/Performance: 58 awards ($47,085 total): art/fine arts, music, theater/drama. Special Characteristics: 188 awards ($683,899 total): children of faculty/staff, ethnic background, international students, members of minority groups, out-of-state students, previous college experience, religious affiliation.

LOANS *Student loans:* $4,676,640 (59% need-based, 41% non-need-based). 95% of past graduating class borrowed through all loan programs. *Average indebtedness per student:* $11,105. *Average need-based loan:* Freshmen: $3556; Undergraduates: $4307. *Parent loans:* $1,266,532 (100% non-need-based). *Programs:* FFEL (Subsidized and Unsubsidized Stafford, PLUS), Perkins.

WORK-STUDY *Federal work-study:* Total amount: $805,183; 526 jobs averaging $1530. *State or other work-study/employment:* Total amount: $319,161 (100% non-need-based). 375 part-time jobs averaging $851.

APPLYING FOR FINANCIAL AID *Required financial aid form:* FAFSA. *Financial aid deadline (priority):* 3/1. *Notification date:* Continuous. Students must reply within 2 weeks of notification.

CONTACT Kate Taylor, Director of Financial Aid, Illinois College, 1101 West College Avenue, Jacksonville, IL 62650-2299, 217-245-3035 or toll-free 866-464-5265. *Fax:* 217-245-3274. *E-mail:* finaid@hilltop.ic.edu.

THE ILLINOIS INSTITUTE OF ART–CHICAGO
Chicago, IL

CONTACT Director of Student Financial Services, The Illinois Institute of Art–Chicago, 350 North Orleans Street, Suite 136, Chicago, IL 60654-1593, 800-351-3450.

THE ILLINOIS INSTITUTE OF ART–SCHAUMBURG
Schaumburg, IL

CONTACT Financial Aid Office, The Illinois Institute of Art–Schaumburg, 1000 North Plaza Drive, Schaumburg, IL 60173, 800-314-3450.

ILLINOIS INSTITUTE OF TECHNOLOGY
Chicago, IL

CONTACT Virginia Foster, Director of Student Finances, Illinois Institute of Technology, 3300 South Federal Street, Chicago, IL 60616, 312-567-5725 or toll-free 800-448-2329 (out-of-state). *Fax:* 312-567-3982. *E-mail:* foster@iit.edu.

ILLINOIS STATE UNIVERSITY
Normal, IL

Tuition & fees (IL res): $7091 | Average undergraduate aid package: $9056

ABOUT THE INSTITUTION State-supported, coed. Awards: bachelor's, master's, and doctoral degrees and post-bachelor's and post-master's certificates. 61 undergraduate majors. Total enrollment: 20,653. Undergraduates: 17,858. Freshmen: 3,179. Federal methodology is used as a basis for awarding need-based institutional aid.

UNDERGRADUATE EXPENSES for 2005–06 *Application fee:* $30. *Tuition, state resident:* full-time $5400; part-time $180 per credit hour. *Tuition, nonresident:* full-time $11,280; part-time $376 per credit hour. *Required fees:* full-time $1691; $46.70 per credit hour or $700.50 per term part-time. Full-time tuition and fees vary according to course load. Part-time tuition and fees vary according to course load. *College room and board:* $5748; *room only:* $3010. Room and board charges vary according to board plan. *Payment plans:* Guaranteed tuition, installment.

FRESHMAN FINANCIAL AID (Fall 2005, est.) 2421 applied for aid; of those 57% were deemed to have need. 97% of freshmen with need received aid; of those 43% had need fully met. *Average percent of need met:* 79% (excluding resources awarded to replace EFC). *Average financial aid package:* $7848 (excluding resources awarded to replace EFC). 1% of all full-time freshmen had no need and received non-need-based gift aid.

UNDERGRADUATE FINANCIAL AID (Fall 2005, est.) 10,999 applied for aid; of those 69% were deemed to have need. 98% of undergraduates with need received aid; of those 47% had need fully met. *Average percent of need met:* 83% (excluding resources awarded to replace EFC). *Average financial aid package:* $9056 (excluding resources awarded to replace EFC). 2% of all full-time undergraduates had no need and received non-need-based gift aid.

GIFT AID (NEED-BASED) *Total amount:* $33,806,942 (33% federal, 53% state, 11% institutional, 3% external sources). *Receiving aid:* Freshmen: 26% (833); All full-time undergraduates: 11% (1,795). *Average award:* Freshmen: $6496; Undergraduates: $6844. *Scholarships, grants, and awards:* Federal Pell, FSEOG, state, private, college/university gift aid from institutional funds, Federal Nursing.

GIFT AID (NON-NEED-BASED) *Total amount:* $6,529,661 (10% federal, 49% state, 28% institutional, 13% external sources). *Receiving aid:* Freshmen: 12% (391); Undergraduates: 10% (1,611). *Average Award:* Freshmen: $3318; Undergraduates: $4230. *Scholarships, grants, and awards by category:* Academic Interests/Achievement: 401 awards ($1,479,480 total): agriculture, biological sciences, business, communication, computer science, education, engineering/technologies, English, foreign languages, general academic interests/achievements, health fields, home economics, humanities, international studies, library science, mathematics, military science, physical sciences, premedicine, social sciences. Creative Arts/Performance: 174 awards ($191,139 total): applied art and design, art/fine arts, cinema/film/broadcasting, creative writing, debating, general creative arts/performance, music, performing arts, theater/drama. Special Achievements/Activities: 1 award ($1000 total): community service, leadership. Special Characteristics: 381 awards ($1,318,687 total): children of faculty/staff, children of union members/company employees, children with a deceased or disabled parent, first-generation college students, general special characteristics, members of minority groups, previous college experience. *Tuition waivers:* Full or partial for minority students, employees or children of employees, senior citizens. *ROTC:* Army.

LOANS *Student loans:* $53,402,569 (58% need-based, 42% non-need-based). 59% of past graduating class borrowed through all loan programs. *Average indebtedness per student:* $15,616. *Average need-based loan:* Freshmen: $3988; Undergraduates: $4921. *Parent loans:* $13,521,992 (19% need-based, 81% non-need-based). *Programs:* Federal Direct (Subsidized and Unsubsidized Stafford, PLUS), Perkins, Federal Nursing, alternative loans.

WORK-STUDY *Federal work-study:* Total amount: $1,274,235; 658 jobs averaging $1937. *State or other work-study/employment:* Total amount: $98,869 (50% need-based, 50% non-need-based). 43 part-time jobs averaging $2299.

ATHLETIC AWARDS *Total amount:* $2,770,794 (18% need-based, 82% non-need-based).

APPLYING FOR FINANCIAL AID *Required financial aid form:* FAFSA. *Financial aid deadline (priority):* 3/1. *Notification date:* Continuous beginning 4/1.

CONTACT Mr. David Krueger, Assistant Director of Financial Aid, Illinois State University, Campus Box 2320, Normal, IL 61790-2320, 309-438-2231 or toll-free 800-366-2478 (in-state). *E-mail:* askfao@ilstu.edu.

ILLINOIS WESLEYAN UNIVERSITY
Bloomington, IL

Tuition & fees: $29,076   **Average undergraduate aid package:** $18,285

ABOUT THE INSTITUTION Independent, coed. Awards: bachelor's degrees. 52 undergraduate majors. Total enrollment: 2,146. Undergraduates: 2,146. Freshmen: 565. Both federal and institutional methodology are used as a basis for awarding need-based institutional aid.

UNDERGRADUATE EXPENSES for 2006–07 *Comprehensive fee:* $35,790 includes full-time tuition ($28,926), mandatory fees ($150), and room and board ($6714). *College room only:* $4104. *Part-time tuition:* $3619 per course.

FRESHMAN FINANCIAL AID (Fall 2005, est.) 429 applied for aid; of those 79% were deemed to have need. 100% of freshmen with need received aid; of those 57% had need fully met. *Average percent of need met:* 91% (excluding resources awarded to replace EFC). *Average financial aid package:* $19,424 (excluding resources awarded to replace EFC). 28% of all full-time freshmen had no need and received non-need-based gift aid.

UNDERGRADUATE FINANCIAL AID (Fall 2005, est.) 1,302 applied for aid; of those 89% were deemed to have need. 100% of undergraduates with need received aid; of those 49% had need fully met. *Average percent of need met:* 93% (excluding resources awarded to replace EFC). *Average financial aid package:* $18,285 (excluding resources awarded to replace EFC). 31% of all full-time undergraduates had no need and received non-need-based gift aid.

GIFT AID (NEED-BASED) *Total amount:* $15,221,511 (5% federal, 11% state, 82% institutional, 2% external sources). *Receiving aid:* Freshmen: 59% (335); All full-time undergraduates: 54% (1,160). *Average award:* Freshmen: $14,897; Undergraduates: $13,565. *Scholarships, grants, and awards:* Federal Pell, FSEOG, state, private, college/university gift aid from institutional funds.

GIFT AID (NON-NEED-BASED) *Total amount:* $6,221,472 (1% federal, 98% institutional, 1% external sources). *Receiving aid:* Freshmen: 8% (48); Undergraduates: 4% (81). *Average Award:* Freshmen: $8062; Undergraduates: $8691. *Scholarships, grants, and awards by category: Academic Interests/Achievement:* 574 awards ($4,404,450 total): general academic interests/achievements. *Creative Arts/Performance:* 157 awards ($1,324,710 total): art/fine arts, music, theater/drama. *Special Achievements/Activities:* community service, general special achievements/activities, hobbies/interests, leadership. *Special Characteristics:* 42 awards ($709,349 total): children of faculty/staff, international students. *ROTC:* Army cooperative.

LOANS *Student loans:* $6,356,406 (74% need-based, 26% non-need-based). 67% of past graduating class borrowed through all loan programs. *Average indebtedness per student:* $21,846. *Average need-based loan:* Freshmen: $4197; Undergraduates: $4935. *Parent loans:* $3,031,906 (100% non-need-based). *Programs:* FFEL (Subsidized and Unsubsidized Stafford, PLUS), Perkins, Federal Nursing, college/university.

WORK-STUDY *Federal work-study:* Total amount: $690,915; 326 jobs averaging $2119. *State or other work-study/employment:* Total amount: $1,482,212 (79% need-based, 21% non-need-based). 577 part-time jobs averaging $1985.

APPLYING FOR FINANCIAL AID *Required financial aid forms:* FAFSA, institution's own form, business/farm supplement. *Financial aid deadline:* 3/1 (priority: 3/1). *Notification date:* Continuous beginning 2/1. Students must reply by 5/1.

CONTACT Mr. Lynn Nichelson, Director of Financial Aid, Illinois Wesleyan University, 1312 North Park Street, PO Box 2900, Bloomington, IL 61702-2900, 309-556-3096 or toll-free 800-332-2498. *Fax:* 309-556-3833. *E-mail:* lnichels@titan.iwu.edu.

IMMACULATA UNIVERSITY
Immaculata, PA

CONTACT Mr. Peter Lysionek, Director of Student Financial Aid, Immaculata University, 1145 King Road, Box 500, Immaculata, PA 19345, 610-647-4400 Ext. 3026 or toll-free 877-428-6328. *Fax:* 610-640-0836. *E-mail:* plysionek@immaculata.edu.

INDIANA STATE UNIVERSITY
Terre Haute, IN

Tuition & fees (IN res): $5864   **Average undergraduate aid package:** $7125

ABOUT THE INSTITUTION State-supported, coed. Awards: associate, bachelor's, master's, and doctoral degrees and post-bachelor's and post-master's certificates. 76 undergraduate majors. Total enrollment: 10,679. Undergraduates: 8,670. Freshmen: 1,642. Federal methodology is used as a basis for awarding need-based institutional aid.

UNDERGRADUATE EXPENSES for 2005–06 *Application fee:* $25. *Tuition, state resident:* full-time $5756; part-time $208 per credit hour. *Tuition, nonresident:* full-time $12,752; part-time $450 per credit hour. *Required fees:* full-time $108; $54 per term part-time. Full-time tuition and fees vary according to course load. *College room and board:* $5938; *room only:* $3150. Room and board charges vary according to board plan, housing facility, and student level. *Payment plan:* Installment.

FRESHMAN FINANCIAL AID (Fall 2004) 1575 applied for aid; of those 79% were deemed to have need. 93% of freshmen with need received aid; of those 14% had need fully met. *Average percent of need met:* 72% (excluding resources awarded to replace EFC). *Average financial aid package:* $6528 (excluding resources awarded to replace EFC). 10% of all full-time freshmen had no need and received non-need-based gift aid.

UNDERGRADUATE FINANCIAL AID (Fall 2004) 6,350 applied for aid; of those 81% were deemed to have need. 95% of undergraduates with need received aid; of those 19% had need fully met. *Average percent of need met:* 78% (excluding resources awarded to replace EFC). *Average financial aid package:* $7125 (excluding resources awarded to replace EFC). 8% of all full-time undergraduates had no need and received non-need-based gift aid.

GIFT AID (NEED-BASED) *Total amount:* $14,212,215 (52% federal, 43% state, 3% institutional, 2% external sources). *Receiving aid:* Freshmen: 38% (695); All full-time undergraduates: 37% (3,017). *Average award:* Freshmen: $4790; Undergraduates: $4532. *Scholarships, grants, and awards:* Federal Pell, FSEOG, state, private, college/university gift aid from institutional funds.

GIFT AID (NON-NEED-BASED) *Total amount:* $8,674,853 (31% state, 51% institutional, 18% external sources). *Receiving aid:* Freshmen: 31% (565); Undergraduates: 22% (1,761). *Average Award:* Freshmen: $3735; Undergraduates: $3200. *Scholarships, grants, and awards by category: Academic Interests/Achievement:* 713 awards ($1,765,968 total): general academic interests/achievements. *Creative Arts/Performance:* 100 awards ($124,200 total): art/fine arts, performing arts. *Special Characteristics:* 205 awards ($473,077 total): children and siblings of alumni, children of faculty/staff, children with a deceased or disabled parent, members of minority groups, veterans' children. *Tuition waivers:* Full or partial for employees or children of employees. *ROTC:* Army, Air Force.

LOANS *Student loans:* $28,356,563 (52% need-based, 48% non-need-based). 61% of past graduating class borrowed through all loan programs. *Average indebtedness per student:* $11,331. *Average need-based loan:* Freshmen: $2615; Undergraduates: $3776. *Parent loans:* $5,792,065 (100% non-need-based). *Programs:* FFEL (Subsidized and Unsubsidized Stafford, PLUS), Perkins.

WORK-STUDY *Federal work-study:* Total amount: $457,008; 419 jobs averaging $1093. *State or other work-study/employment:* Part-time jobs available.

ATHLETIC AWARDS *Total amount:* $2,422,546 (100% non-need-based).

APPLYING FOR FINANCIAL AID *Required financial aid form:* FAFSA. *Financial aid deadline:* 3/1 (priority: 3/1). *Notification date:* Continuous beginning 4/15.

Indiana State University

CONTACT Brenda Hall, Senior Associate Director, Indiana State University, Tirey Hall, Room 150, Terre Haute, IN 47809-1401, 812-237-2215 or toll-free 800-742-0891. *Fax:* 812-237-4330. *E-mail:* finaid@indstate.edu.

INDIANA TECH
Fort Wayne, IN

CONTACT Financial Aid Office, Indiana Tech, 1600 East Washington Boulevard, Fort Wayne, IN 46803-1297, 800-937-2448 or toll-free 888-666-TECH (out-of-state). *Fax:* 219-422-1578.

INDIANA UNIVERSITY BLOOMINGTON
Bloomington, IN

Tuition & fees (IN res): $7112   **Average undergraduate aid package: $6840**

ABOUT THE INSTITUTION State-supported, coed. Awards: associate, bachelor's, master's, doctoral, and first professional degrees and post-bachelor's and post-master's certificates. 140 undergraduate majors. Total enrollment: 37,958. Undergraduates: 29,562. Freshmen: 6,949. Federal methodology is used as a basis for awarding need-based institutional aid.

UNDERGRADUATE EXPENSES for 2005–06 *Application fee:* $50. *Tuition, state resident:* full-time $6291; part-time $196.40 per credit hour. *Tuition, nonresident:* full-time $18,687; part-time $584.05 per credit hour. Full-time tuition and fees vary according to location, program, and student level. Part-time tuition and fees vary according to course load, location, program, and student level. *College room and board:* $6240; *room only:* $3760. Room and board charges vary according to board plan and housing facility. *Payment plan:* Deferred payment.

FRESHMAN FINANCIAL AID (Fall 2005, est.) 5756 applied for aid; of those 68% were deemed to have need. 99% of freshmen with need received aid; of those 4% had need fully met. *Average percent of need met:* 51% (excluding resources awarded to replace EFC). *Average financial aid package:* $6859 (excluding resources awarded to replace EFC). 12% of all full-time freshmen had no need and received non-need-based gift aid.

UNDERGRADUATE FINANCIAL AID (Fall 2005, est.) 20,406 applied for aid; of those 75% were deemed to have need. 98% of undergraduates with need received aid; of those 7% had need fully met. *Average percent of need met:* 59% (excluding resources awarded to replace EFC). *Average financial aid package:* $6840 (excluding resources awarded to replace EFC). 6% of all full-time undergraduates had no need and received non-need-based gift aid.

GIFT AID (NEED-BASED) *Total amount:* $30,816,994 (42% federal, 48% state, 10% institutional). *Receiving aid:* Freshmen: 19% (1,346); All full-time undergraduates: 19% (5,418). *Average award:* Freshmen: $6813; Undergraduates: $5546. *Scholarships, grants, and awards:* Federal Pell, FSEOG, state, private, college/university gift aid from institutional funds.

GIFT AID (NON-NEED-BASED) *Total amount:* $41,860,588 (7% federal, 6% state, 71% institutional, 16% external sources). *Receiving aid:* Freshmen: 34% (2,357); Undergraduates: 28% (7,905). *Average Award:* Freshmen: $4254; Undergraduates: $4333. *Scholarships, grants, and awards by category: Academic Interests/Achievement:* general academic interests/achievements. *Creative Arts/Performance:* general creative arts/performance. *Special Achievements/Activities:* general special achievements/activities. *Special Characteristics:* general special characteristics. *Tuition waivers:* Full or partial for employees or children of employees. *ROTC:* Army, Air Force.

LOANS *Student loans:* $60,876,752 (60% need-based, 40% non-need-based). 44% of past graduating class borrowed through all loan programs. *Average indebtedness per student:* $21,251. *Average need-based loan:* Freshmen: $3284; Undergraduates: $4161. *Parent loans:* $36,237,090 (100% non-need-based). *Programs:* Federal Direct (Subsidized and Unsubsidized Stafford, PLUS), Perkins, Federal Nursing, college/university.

WORK-STUDY *Federal work-study:* Total amount: $1,479,174; 1,016 jobs averaging $1456.

ATHLETIC AWARDS Total amount: $6,372,997 (100% non-need-based).

APPLYING FOR FINANCIAL AID *Required financial aid form:* FAFSA. *Financial aid deadline:* Continuous. *Notification date:* Continuous beginning 4/1.

CONTACT Automated Client Inquiry System, Indiana University Bloomington, Franklin Hall, Room 208, Bloomington, IN 47405, 812-855-RSVP. *Fax:* 812-856-RSVP. *E-mail:* rsvposfa@indiana.edu.

INDIANA UNIVERSITY EAST
Richmond, IN

Tuition & fees (IN res): $4806   **Average undergraduate aid package: $5918**

ABOUT THE INSTITUTION State-supported, coed. Awards: associate and bachelor's degrees and post-bachelor's certificates. 21 undergraduate majors. Total enrollment: 2,459. Undergraduates: 2,392. Freshmen: 372. Federal methodology is used as a basis for awarding need-based institutional aid.

UNDERGRADUATE EXPENSES for 2005–06 *Application fee:* $25. *Tuition, state resident:* full-time $4475; part-time $149.15 per credit hour. *Tuition, nonresident:* full-time $11,153; part-time $371.75 per credit hour. Full-time tuition and fees vary according to course load and reciprocity agreements. Part-time tuition and fees vary according to course load and reciprocity agreements. *Payment plan:* Deferred payment.

FRESHMAN FINANCIAL AID (Fall 2005, est.) 259 applied for aid; of those 76% were deemed to have need. 98% of freshmen with need received aid; of those 4% had need fully met. *Average percent of need met:* 53% (excluding resources awarded to replace EFC). *Average financial aid package:* $4835 (excluding resources awarded to replace EFC). 6% of all full-time freshmen had no need and received non-need-based gift aid.

UNDERGRADUATE FINANCIAL AID (Fall 2005, est.) 1,133 applied for aid; of those 80% were deemed to have need. 98% of undergraduates with need received aid; of those 8% had need fully met. *Average percent of need met:* 59% (excluding resources awarded to replace EFC). *Average financial aid package:* $5918 (excluding resources awarded to replace EFC). 4% of all full-time undergraduates had no need and received non-need-based gift aid.

GIFT AID (NEED-BASED) *Total amount:* $3,450,925 (69% federal, 31% state). *Receiving aid:* Freshmen: 48% (135); All full-time undergraduates: 52% (658). *Average award:* Freshmen: $4489; Undergraduates: $4272. *Scholarships, grants, and awards:* Federal Pell, FSEOG, state, private, college/university gift aid from institutional funds.

GIFT AID (NON-NEED-BASED) *Total amount:* $631,316 (42% federal, 20% state, 19% institutional, 19% external sources). *Receiving aid:* Freshmen: 27% (76); Undergraduates: 15% (189). *Average Award:* Freshmen: $1764; Undergraduates: $1737. *Scholarships, grants, and awards by category: Academic Interests/Achievement:* general academic interests/achievements. *Creative Arts/Performance:* general creative arts/performance. *Special Achievements/Activities:* general special achievements/activities. *Special Characteristics:* general special characteristics. *Tuition waivers:* Full or partial for employees or children of employees.

LOANS *Student loans:* $6,159,512 (51% need-based, 49% non-need-based). 59% of past graduating class borrowed through all loan programs. *Average indebtedness per student:* $24,729. *Average need-based loan:* Freshmen: $2333; Undergraduates: $3240. *Parent loans:* $79,164 (100% non-need-based). *Programs:* FFEL (Subsidized and Unsubsidized Stafford, PLUS), Perkins, Federal Nursing, college/university.

WORK-STUDY *Federal work-study:* Total amount: $133,057; 42 jobs averaging $3168.

APPLYING FOR FINANCIAL AID *Required financial aid forms:* FAFSA, institution's own form. *Financial aid deadline (priority):* 3/1. *Notification date:* Continuous beginning 5/1. Students must reply within 2 weeks of notification.

CONTACT James Bland, Financial Aid Director, Indiana University East, 2325 Chester Boulevard, Whitewater Hall, Richmond, IN 47374-1289, 765-973-8276 or toll-free 800-959-EAST. *Fax:* 765-973-8388. *E-mail:* jabland@indiana.edu.

INDIANA UNIVERSITY KOKOMO
Kokomo, IN

Tuition & fees (IN res): $4835   **Average undergraduate aid package: $6081**

ABOUT THE INSTITUTION State-supported, coed. Awards: associate, bachelor's, and master's degrees and post-bachelor's certificates. 17 undergraduate majors. Total enrollment: 2,895. Undergraduates: 2,737. Freshmen: 476. Federal methodology is used as a basis for awarding need-based institutional aid.

UNDERGRADUATE EXPENSES for 2005–06 *Application fee:* $30. *Tuition, state resident:* full-time $4475; part-time $149.15 per credit hour. *Tuition, nonresident:* full-time $11,153; part-time $371.75 per credit hour. Full-time tuition and fees vary according to course load. Part-time tuition and fees vary according to course load. *Payment plan:* Deferred payment.

FRESHMAN FINANCIAL AID (Fall 2005, est.) 309 applied for aid; of those 63% were deemed to have need. 97% of freshmen with need received aid; of those 19% had need fully met. *Average percent of need met:* 70% (excluding resources awarded to replace EFC). *Average financial aid package:* $4969 (excluding resources awarded to replace EFC). 8% of all full-time freshmen had no need and received non-need-based gift aid.
UNDERGRADUATE FINANCIAL AID (Fall 2005, est.) 1,077 applied for aid; of those 69% were deemed to have need. 98% of undergraduates with need received aid; of those 19% had need fully met. *Average percent of need met:* 73% (excluding resources awarded to replace EFC). *Average financial aid package:* $6081 (excluding resources awarded to replace EFC). 6% of all full-time undergraduates had no need and received non-need-based gift aid.
GIFT AID (NEED-BASED) *Total amount:* $2,661,453 (65% federal, 32% state, 3% institutional). *Receiving aid:* Freshmen: 29% (111); All full-time undergraduates: 34% (479). *Average award:* Freshmen: $4466; Undergraduates: $4288. *Scholarships, grants, and awards:* Federal Pell, FSEOG, state, private, college/university gift aid from institutional funds.
GIFT AID (NON-NEED-BASED) *Total amount:* $990,453 (39% federal, 27% state, 17% institutional, 17% external sources). *Receiving aid:* Freshmen: 16% (60); Undergraduates: 15% (209). *Average Award:* Freshmen: $1801; Undergraduates: $2022. *Scholarships, grants, and awards by category:* Academic Interests/Achievement: general academic interests/achievements. Special Characteristics: general special characteristics. *Tuition waivers:* Full or partial for employees or children of employees. *ROTC:* Army cooperative.
LOANS *Student loans:* $6,935,177 (43% need-based, 57% non-need-based). 38% of past graduating class borrowed through all loan programs. *Average indebtedness per student:* $15,195. *Average need-based loan:* Freshmen: $2077; Undergraduates: $3043. *Parent loans:* $149,495 (100% non-need-based). *Programs:* FFEL (Subsidized and Unsubsidized Stafford, PLUS), Perkins, Federal Nursing, college/university.
WORK-STUDY *Federal work-study:* Total amount: $116,600; 78 jobs averaging $1495.
APPLYING FOR FINANCIAL AID *Required financial aid forms:* FAFSA, institution's own form. *Financial aid deadline (priority):* 3/1. *Notification date:* Continuous beginning 5/1.
CONTACT Jackie Kennedy-Fletcher, Director of Financial Aid, Indiana University Kokomo, 2300 South Washington Street, PO Box 9003, Kelley Student Center, Room 201H, Kokomo, IN 46904-9003, 765-455-9431 or toll-free 888-875-4485. *E-mail:* jacfletc@iuk.edu.

INDIANA UNIVERSITY NORTHWEST
Gary, IN

Tuition & fees (IN res): $4902   **Average undergraduate aid package:** $7363

ABOUT THE INSTITUTION State-supported, coed. Awards: associate, bachelor's, and master's degrees and post-bachelor's certificates. 44 undergraduate majors. Total enrollment: 4,987. Undergraduates: 4,387. Freshmen: 604. Federal methodology is used as a basis for awarding need-based institutional aid.
UNDERGRADUATE EXPENSES for 2005–06 *Application fee:* $35. *Tuition, state resident:* full-time $4475; part-time $149.15 per credit hour. *Tuition, nonresident:* full-time $11,153; part-time $371.75 per credit hour. Full-time tuition and fees vary according to course load. Part-time tuition and fees vary according to course load. *Payment plans:* Installment, deferred payment.
FRESHMAN FINANCIAL AID (Fall 2005, est.) 379 applied for aid; of those 73% were deemed to have need. 98% of freshmen with need received aid; of those 10% had need fully met. *Average percent of need met:* 60% (excluding resources awarded to replace EFC). *Average financial aid package:* $6371 (excluding resources awarded to replace EFC). 3% of all full-time freshmen had no need and received non-need-based gift aid.
UNDERGRADUATE FINANCIAL AID (Fall 2005, est.) 1,908 applied for aid; of those 79% were deemed to have need. 99% of undergraduates with need received aid; of those 10% had need fully met. *Average percent of need met:* 64% (excluding resources awarded to replace EFC). *Average financial aid package:* $7363 (excluding resources awarded to replace EFC). 2% of all full-time undergraduates had no need and received non-need-based gift aid.
GIFT AID (NEED-BASED) *Total amount:* $6,519,457 (63% federal, 37% state). *Receiving aid:* Freshmen: 39% (182); All full-time undergraduates: 43% (1,037).
Average award: Freshmen: $4845; Undergraduates: $4944. *Scholarships, grants, and awards:* Federal Pell, FSEOG, state, private, college/university gift aid from institutional funds, Federal Nursing.
GIFT AID (NON-NEED-BASED) *Total amount:* $1,050,719 (14% federal, 12% state, 56% institutional, 18% external sources). *Receiving aid:* Freshmen: 12% (55); Undergraduates: 11% (257). *Average Award:* Freshmen: $4037; Undergraduates: $2983. *Scholarships, grants, and awards by category:* Academic Interests/Achievement: general academic interests/achievements. Creative Arts/Performance: general creative arts/performance. Special Achievements/Activities: general special achievements/activities. Special Characteristics: general special characteristics. *Tuition waivers:* Full or partial for employees or children of employees, senior citizens. *ROTC:* Army.
LOANS *Student loans:* $13,683,186 (46% need-based, 54% non-need-based). 45% of past graduating class borrowed through all loan programs. *Average indebtedness per student:* $18,394. *Average need-based loan:* Freshmen: $2233; Undergraduates: $3264. *Parent loans:* $216,380 (100% non-need-based). *Programs:* FFEL (Subsidized and Unsubsidized Stafford, PLUS), Perkins, college/university.
WORK-STUDY *Federal work-study:* Total amount: $1,320,688; 491 jobs averaging $2690.
ATHLETIC AWARDS *Total amount:* $12,600 (100% non-need-based).
APPLYING FOR FINANCIAL AID *Required financial aid forms:* FAFSA, institution's own form. *Financial aid deadline (priority):* 3/1. *Notification date:* Continuous beginning 5/1. Students must reply within 2 weeks of notification.
CONTACT Dianne Mickey, Director of Scholarships and Financial Aid, Indiana University Northwest, 3400 Broadway, Hawthorn Hall, Room 101, Gary, IN 46408-1197, 219-980-6767 or toll-free 800-968-7486. *Fax:* 219-981-4219.

INDIANA UNIVERSITY OF PENNSYLVANIA
Indiana, PA

Tuition & fees (PA res): $6085   **Average undergraduate aid package:** $7498

ABOUT THE INSTITUTION State-supported, coed. Awards: associate, bachelor's, master's, and doctoral degrees and post-bachelor's and post-master's certificates. 74 undergraduate majors. Total enrollment: 14,081. Undergraduates: 12,047. Freshmen: 2,509. Federal methodology is used as a basis for awarding need-based institutional aid.
UNDERGRADUATE EXPENSES for 2005–06 *Application fee:* $30. *Tuition, state resident:* full-time $4810; part-time $204 per credit hour. *Tuition, nonresident:* full-time $12,026; part-time $511 per credit hour. *Required fees:* full-time $1275; $20.40 per credit hour or $167 per term part-time. Full-time tuition and fees vary according to course load, location, and reciprocity agreements. Part-time tuition and fees vary according to course load, location, and reciprocity agreements. *College room and board:* $4866; *room only:* $2740. Room and board charges vary according to board plan, housing facility, and location. *Payment plans:* Installment, deferred payment.
FRESHMAN FINANCIAL AID (Fall 2004) 2313 applied for aid; of those 76% were deemed to have need. 100% of freshmen with need received aid; of those 12% had need fully met. *Average percent of need met:* 79% (excluding resources awarded to replace EFC). *Average financial aid package:* $7772 (excluding resources awarded to replace EFC). 6% of all full-time freshmen had no need and received non-need-based gift aid.
UNDERGRADUATE FINANCIAL AID (Fall 2004) 9,186 applied for aid; of those 80% were deemed to have need. 99% of undergraduates with need received aid; of those 11% had need fully met. *Average percent of need met:* 76% (excluding resources awarded to replace EFC). *Average financial aid package:* $7498 (excluding resources awarded to replace EFC). 3% of all full-time undergraduates had no need and received non-need-based gift aid.
GIFT AID (NEED-BASED) *Total amount:* $21,467,540 (53% federal, 47% state). *Receiving aid:* Freshmen: 48% (1,262); All full-time undergraduates: 48% (5,316). *Average award:* Freshmen: $4052; Undergraduates: $3876. *Scholarships, grants, and awards:* Federal Pell, FSEOG, state, private, college/university gift aid from institutional funds.
GIFT AID (NON-NEED-BASED) *Total amount:* $5,415,533 (1% state, 45% institutional, 54% external sources). *Receiving aid:* Freshmen: 23% (612); Undergraduates: 14% (1,540). *Average Award:* Freshmen: $1368; Undergraduates: $2250. *Scholarships, grants, and awards by category:* Academic Interests/Achievement: 1,129 awards ($1,873,229 total): area/ethnic studies, biological sciences, business, communication, computer science, education, engineering/

Indiana University of Pennsylvania

technologies, English, foreign languages, general academic interests/achievements, health fields, home economics, humanities, international studies, mathematics, physical sciences, premedicine, social sciences. *Creative Arts/Performance:* applied art and design, art/fine arts, dance, general creative arts/performance, journalism/publications, music, performing arts, theater/drama. *Special Achievements/Activities:* community service, general special achievements/activities, hobbies/interests, leadership. *Special Characteristics:* 813 awards ($3,417,151 total): adult students, children of faculty/staff, ethnic background, international students. *Tuition waivers:* Full or partial for minority students, employees or children of employees. *ROTC:* Army.
LOANS *Student loans:* $46,369,781 (54% need-based, 46% non-need-based). 80% of past graduating class borrowed through all loan programs. *Average indebtedness per student:* $18,105. *Average need-based loan:* Freshmen: $3037; Undergraduates: $3698. *Parent loans:* $7,480,092 (100% non-need-based). *Programs:* FFEL (Subsidized and Unsubsidized Stafford, PLUS), Perkins, alternative loans.
WORK-STUDY *Federal work-study:* Total amount: $5,245,229; 1,358 jobs averaging $1315. *State or other work-study/employment:* Total amount: $1,115,776 (100% non-need-based). 1,367 part-time jobs averaging $1197.
ATHLETIC AWARDS *Total amount:* $740,064 (100% non-need-based).
APPLYING FOR FINANCIAL AID *Required financial aid forms:* FAFSA, state aid form. *Financial aid deadline:* 4/15. *Notification date:* Continuous beginning 3/15.
CONTACT Mrs. Patricia C. McCarthy, Interim Director of Financial Aid, Indiana University of Pennsylvania, 213 Clark Hall, Indiana, PA 15705, 724-357-2218 or toll-free 800-442-6830. Fax: 724-357-2094. E-mail: mccarthy@iup.edu.

INDIANA UNIVERSITY–PURDUE UNIVERSITY FORT WAYNE
Fort Wayne, IN

Tuition & fees (IN res): $5067   **Average undergraduate aid package: $5976**

ABOUT THE INSTITUTION State-supported, coed. Awards: associate, bachelor's, and master's degrees and post-bachelor's certificates. 97 undergraduate majors. Total enrollment: 11,795. Undergraduates: 11,028. Freshmen: 1,788. Federal methodology is used as a basis for awarding need-based institutional aid.
UNDERGRADUATE EXPENSES for 2005–06 *Application fee:* $30. *Tuition, state resident:* full-time $4523; part-time $168 per semester hour. *Tuition, nonresident:* full-time $11,142; part-time $413 per semester hour. *Required fees:* full-time $544; $20 per semester hour. Full-time tuition and fees vary according to course load, location, and student level. Part-time tuition and fees vary according to course load, location, and student level. *College room and board: room only:* $4750. Room and board charges vary according to housing facility. *Payment plans:* Installment, deferred payment.
FRESHMAN FINANCIAL AID (Fall 2004) 1296 applied for aid; of those 76% were deemed to have need. 93% of freshmen with need received aid; of those 6% had need fully met. *Average percent of need met:* 69% (excluding resources awarded to replace EFC). *Average financial aid package:* $5176 (excluding resources awarded to replace EFC). 26% of all full-time freshmen had no need and received non-need-based gift aid.
UNDERGRADUATE FINANCIAL AID (Fall 2004) 5,029 applied for aid; of those 80% were deemed to have need. 96% of undergraduates with need received aid; of those 9% had need fully met. *Average percent of need met:* 78% (excluding resources awarded to replace EFC). *Average financial aid package:* $5976 (excluding resources awarded to replace EFC). 18% of all full-time undergraduates had no need and received non-need-based gift aid.
GIFT AID (NEED-BASED) *Total amount:* $13,938,567 (57% federal, 38% state, 5% institutional). *Receiving aid:* Freshmen: 35% (565); All full-time undergraduates: 38% (2,497). *Average award:* Freshmen: $3786; Undergraduates: $4049. *Scholarships, grants, and awards:* Federal Pell, FSEOG, state, private, college/university gift aid from institutional funds.
GIFT AID (NON-NEED-BASED) *Total amount:* $3,638,058 (12% federal, 24% state, 18% institutional, 46% external sources). *Receiving aid:* Freshmen: 11% (184); Undergraduates: 9% (604). *Average Award:* Freshmen: $1618; Undergraduates: $1806. *Scholarships, grants, and awards by category:* Academic Interests/Achievement: 224 awards ($198,759 total): biological sciences, business, communication, computer science, education, engineering/technologies, English, foreign languages, general academic interests/achievements, health fields, humanities, mathematics, physical sciences, premedicine, social sciences. Creative Arts/Performance: 49 awards ($31,800 total): art/fine arts, music, theater/drama. *Special Characteristics:* 976 awards ($1,549,197 total): children and siblings of alumni, children of faculty/staff, children with a deceased or disabled parent, handicapped students, local/state students, spouses of deceased or disabled public servants. *Tuition waivers:* Full or partial for employees or children of employees, senior citizens.
LOANS *Student loans:* $31,139,844 (54% need-based, 46% non-need-based). 60% of past graduating class borrowed through all loan programs. *Average indebtedness per student:* $16,880. *Average need-based loan:* Freshmen: $2333; Undergraduates: $3028. *Parent loans:* $1,095,290 (100% non-need-based). *Programs:* FFEL (Subsidized and Unsubsidized Stafford, PLUS), Perkins.
WORK-STUDY *Federal work-study:* Total amount: $270,921; 171 jobs averaging $1584.
ATHLETIC AWARDS *Total amount:* $1,068,929 (100% non-need-based).
APPLYING FOR FINANCIAL AID *Required financial aid form:* FAFSA. *Financial aid deadline (priority):* 3/10. *Notification date:* 4/30. Students must reply within 4 weeks of notification.
CONTACT Mr. Joel Wenger, Director of Financial Aid, Indiana University–Purdue University Fort Wayne, 2101 East Coliseum Boulevard, Fort Wayne, IN 46805-1499, 260-481-6130 or toll-free 800-324-4739 (in-state). E-mail: wengerj@ipfw.edu.

INDIANA UNIVERSITY–PURDUE UNIVERSITY INDIANAPOLIS
Indianapolis, IN

Tuition & fees (IN res): $6219   **Average undergraduate aid package: $6929**

ABOUT THE INSTITUTION State-supported, coed. Awards: associate, bachelor's, master's, doctoral, and first professional degrees and post-bachelor's certificates. 77 undergraduate majors. Total enrollment: 29,933. Undergraduates: 21,438. Freshmen: 2,746. Federal methodology is used as a basis for awarding need-based institutional aid.
UNDERGRADUATE EXPENSES for 2005–06 *Application fee:* $50. *Tuition, state resident:* full-time $5625; part-time $188 per credit hour. *Tuition, nonresident:* full-time $15,953; part-time $532 per credit hour. Full-time tuition and fees vary according to course load and program. Part-time tuition and fees vary according to course load and program. *College room and board:* $4740; room only: $2340. Room and board charges vary according to board plan and housing facility. *Payment plans:* Installment, deferred payment.
FRESHMAN FINANCIAL AID (Fall 2005, est.) 2069 applied for aid; of those 71% were deemed to have need. 96% of freshmen with need received aid; of those 3% had need fully met. *Average percent of need met:* 50% (excluding resources awarded to replace EFC). *Average financial aid package:* $5941 (excluding resources awarded to replace EFC). 9% of all full-time freshmen had no need and received non-need-based gift aid.
UNDERGRADUATE FINANCIAL AID (Fall 2005, est.) 10,679 applied for aid; of those 79% were deemed to have need. 97% of undergraduates with need received aid; of those 4% had need fully met. *Average percent of need met:* 51% (excluding resources awarded to replace EFC). *Average financial aid package:* $6929 (excluding resources awarded to replace EFC). 4% of all full-time undergraduates had no need and received non-need-based gift aid.
GIFT AID (NEED-BASED) *Total amount:* $25,561,953 (55% federal, 44% state, 1% institutional). *Receiving aid:* Freshmen: 34% (818); All full-time undergraduates: 34% (4,635). *Average award:* Freshmen: $5135; Undergraduates: $4829. *Scholarships, grants, and awards:* Federal Pell, FSEOG, state, private, college/university gift aid from institutional funds.
GIFT AID (NON-NEED-BASED) *Total amount:* $14,071,564 (44% federal, 15% state, 28% institutional, 13% external sources). *Receiving aid:* Freshmen: 24% (583); Undergraduates: 17% (2,351). *Average Award:* Freshmen: $2659; Undergraduates: $3061. *Scholarships, grants, and awards by category:* Academic Interests/Achievement: general academic interests/achievements. Creative Arts/Performance: general creative arts/performance. Special Achievements/Activities: general special achievements/activities. *Special Characteristics:* general special characteristics. *Tuition waivers:* Full or partial for employees or children of employees. *ROTC:* Army, Naval cooperative, Air Force cooperative.
LOANS *Student loans:* $57,004,108 (54% need-based, 46% non-need-based). 52% of past graduating class borrowed through all loan programs. *Average indebtedness per student:* $23,041. *Average need-based loan:* Freshmen: $2344;

Undergraduates: $3704. **Parent loans:** $3,015,355 (100% non-need-based). **Programs:** FFEL (Subsidized and Unsubsidized Stafford, PLUS), Perkins, Federal Nursing, college/university.
WORK-STUDY *Federal work-study:* Total amount: $2,723,632; 813 jobs averaging $3350.
ATHLETIC AWARDS *Total amount:* $1,250,945 (100% non-need-based).
APPLYING FOR FINANCIAL AID *Required financial aid form:* FAFSA. *Financial aid deadline (priority):* 3/1. *Notification date:* Continuous beginning 4/1.
CONTACT Kathy Purris, Director of Financial Aid Services, Indiana University–Purdue University Indianapolis, 425 North University Boulevard, Cavanaugh Hall, Room 103, Indianapolis, IN 46202-5145, 317-278-FAST. *Fax:* 317-274-5930.

INDIANA UNIVERSITY SOUTH BEND
South Bend, IN

Tuition & fees (IN res): $4989 **Average undergraduate aid package: $6050**

ABOUT THE INSTITUTION State-supported, coed. Awards: associate, bachelor's, and master's degrees and post-bachelor's certificates. 53 undergraduate majors. Total enrollment: 7,459. Undergraduates: 6,324. Freshmen: 1,006. Federal methodology is used as a basis for awarding need-based institutional aid.
UNDERGRADUATE EXPENSES for 2005–06 *Application fee:* $43. *Tuition, state resident:* full-time $4583; part-time $152.75 per credit hour. *Tuition, nonresident:* full-time $12,002; part-time $400.05 per credit hour. Full-time tuition and fees vary according to course load. Part-time tuition and fees vary according to course load. *Payment plan:* Deferred payment.
FRESHMAN FINANCIAL AID (Fall 2005, est.) 695 applied for aid; of those 68% were deemed to have need. 100% of freshmen with need received aid; of those 6% had need fully met. *Average percent of need met:* 55% (excluding resources awarded to replace EFC). *Average financial aid package:* $4935 (excluding resources awarded to replace EFC). 10% of all full-time freshmen had no need and received non-need-based gift aid.
UNDERGRADUATE FINANCIAL AID (Fall 2005, est.) 2,890 applied for aid; of those 74% were deemed to have need. 99% of undergraduates with need received aid; of those 7% had need fully met. *Average percent of need met:* 58% (excluding resources awarded to replace EFC). *Average financial aid package:* $6050 (excluding resources awarded to replace EFC). 4% of all full-time undergraduates had no need and received non-need-based gift aid.
GIFT AID (NEED-BASED) *Total amount:* $7,245,519 (62% federal, 38% state). *Receiving aid:* Freshmen: 36% (287); All full-time undergraduates: 39% (1,393). *Average award:* Freshmen: $4072; Undergraduates: $4153. **Scholarships, grants, and awards:** Federal Pell, FSEOG, state, private, college/university gift aid from institutional funds.
GIFT AID (NON-NEED-BASED) *Total amount:* $2,307,626 (40% federal, 14% state, 26% institutional, 20% external sources). *Receiving aid:* Freshmen: 22% (181); Undergraduates: 13% (457). *Average Award:* Freshmen: $1357; Undergraduates: $1966. **Scholarships, grants, and awards by category:** *Academic Interests/Achievement:* general academic interests/achievements. *Creative Arts/Performance:* general creative arts/performance. *Special Achievements/Activities:* general special achievements/activities. *Special Characteristics:* general special characteristics. *Tuition waivers:* Full or partial for employees or children of employees. *ROTC:* Army cooperative, Naval cooperative, Air Force cooperative.
LOANS *Student loans:* $14,045,383 (52% need-based, 48% non-need-based). 53% of past graduating class borrowed through all loan programs. *Average indebtedness per student:* $20,199. *Average need-based loan:* Freshmen: $2194; Undergraduates: $3277. *Parent loans:* $706,616 (100% non-need-based). **Programs:** Federal Direct (Subsidized and Unsubsidized Stafford, PLUS), Perkins, Federal Nursing, college/university.
WORK-STUDY *Federal work-study:* Total amount: $409,230; 178 jobs averaging $2299.
ATHLETIC AWARDS *Total amount:* $76,393 (100% non-need-based).
APPLYING FOR FINANCIAL AID *Required financial aid forms:* FAFSA, institution's own form. *Financial aid deadline (priority):* 3/1. *Notification date:* Continuous beginning 5/1. Students must reply within 2 weeks of notification.
CONTACT Bev Cooper, Financial Aid Director, Indiana University South Bend, 1700 Mishawaka Avenue, PO Box 7111, South Bend, IN 46634-7111, 219-237-4357 or toll-free 877-GO-2-IUSB. *E-mail:* beacoope@iusb.edu.

INDIANA UNIVERSITY SOUTHEAST
New Albany, IN

Tuition & fees (IN res): $4880 **Average undergraduate aid package: $6127**

ABOUT THE INSTITUTION State-supported, coed. Awards: associate, bachelor's, and master's degrees and post-bachelor's certificates. 37 undergraduate majors. Total enrollment: 6,164. Undergraduates: 5,300. Freshmen: 753. Federal methodology is used as a basis for awarding need-based institutional aid.
UNDERGRADUATE EXPENSES for 2005–06 *Application fee:* $30. *Tuition, state resident:* full-time $4475; part-time $149.15 per credit hour. *Tuition, nonresident:* full-time $11,153; part-time $371.75 per credit hour. Full-time tuition and fees vary according to course load and reciprocity agreements. Part-time tuition and fees vary according to course load and reciprocity agreements. *Payment plan:* Deferred payment.
FRESHMAN FINANCIAL AID (Fall 2005, est.) 544 applied for aid; of those 76% were deemed to have need. 99% of freshmen with need received aid; of those 3% had need fully met. *Average percent of need met:* 47% (excluding resources awarded to replace EFC). *Average financial aid package:* $5122 (excluding resources awarded to replace EFC). 8% of all full-time freshmen had no need and received non-need-based gift aid.
UNDERGRADUATE FINANCIAL AID (Fall 2005, est.) 2,355 applied for aid; of those 80% were deemed to have need. 98% of undergraduates with need received aid; of those 5% had need fully met. *Average percent of need met:* 52% (excluding resources awarded to replace EFC). *Average financial aid package:* $6127 (excluding resources awarded to replace EFC). 3% of all full-time undergraduates had no need and received non-need-based gift aid.
GIFT AID (NEED-BASED) *Total amount:* $5,758,969 (60% federal, 35% state, 5% institutional). *Receiving aid:* Freshmen: 32% (212); All full-time undergraduates: 33% (1,061). *Average award:* Freshmen: $4898; Undergraduates: $4560. **Scholarships, grants, and awards:** Federal Pell, FSEOG, state, private, college/university gift aid from institutional funds.
GIFT AID (NON-NEED-BASED) *Total amount:* $1,383,729 (6% federal, 19% state, 39% institutional, 36% external sources). *Receiving aid:* Freshmen: 23% (156); Undergraduates: 15% (478). *Average Award:* Freshmen: $2647; Undergraduates: $2376. **Scholarships, grants, and awards by category:** *Academic Interests/Achievement:* general academic interests/achievements. *Creative Arts/Performance:* general creative arts/performance. *Special Achievements/Activities:* general special achievements/activities. *Special Characteristics:* general special characteristics. *Tuition waivers:* Full or partial for employees or children of employees. *ROTC:* Army cooperative, Air Force cooperative.
LOANS *Student loans:* $13,423,572 (53% need-based, 47% non-need-based). 42% of past graduating class borrowed through all loan programs. *Average indebtedness per student:* $18,570. *Average need-based loan:* Freshmen: $2475; Undergraduates: $3772. *Parent loans:* $168,550 (100% non-need-based). **Programs:** FFEL (Subsidized and Unsubsidized Stafford, PLUS), Perkins, Federal Nursing, college/university.
WORK-STUDY *Federal work-study:* Total amount: $470,640; 230 jobs averaging $2046.
ATHLETIC AWARDS *Total amount:* $66,050 (100% non-need-based).
APPLYING FOR FINANCIAL AID *Required financial aid forms:* FAFSA, institution's own form. *Financial aid deadline (priority):* 3/1. *Notification date:* Continuous beginning 5/1.
CONTACT Brittany Hubbard, Director of Financial Aid, Indiana University Southeast, LB-002, New Albany, IN 47150, 812-941-2246 or toll-free 800-852-8835 (in-state). *E-mail:* mibarlow@ius.edu.

INDIANA WESLEYAN UNIVERSITY
Marion, IN

CONTACT Director of Financial Aid, Indiana Wesleyan University, 4201 South Washington Street, Marion, IN 46953-4999, 765-677-2116 or toll-free 800-332-6901. *Fax:* 765-677-2809.

INSTITUTE OF COMPUTER TECHNOLOGY
Los Angeles, CA

CONTACT Office of Financial Aid, Institute of Computer Technology, 3200 Wilshire Boulevard, Los Angeles, CA 90010, 213-381-3333 or toll-free 800-57 GO ICT (in-state). *Fax:* 213-383-9369.

Inter American University of Puerto Rico, Aguadilla Campus

INTER AMERICAN UNIVERSITY OF PUERTO RICO, AGUADILLA CAMPUS
Aguadilla, PR

CONTACT Mr. Juan Gonzalez, Director of Financial Aid, Inter American University of Puerto Rico, Aguadilla Campus, PO Box 20000, Aguadilla, PR 00605, 787-891-0925 Ext. 2108. *Fax:* 787-882-3020.

INTER AMERICAN UNIVERSITY OF PUERTO RICO, ARECIBO CAMPUS
Arecibo, PR

CONTACT Ramón O. de Jesús, Financial Aid Director, Inter American University of Puerto Rico, Arecibo Campus, PO Box 4050, Arecibo, PR 00614-4050, 787-878-5475 Ext. 2275. *Fax:* 787-880-1624.

INTER AMERICAN UNIVERSITY OF PUERTO RICO, BARRANQUITAS CAMPUS
Barranquitas, PR

CONTACT Mr. Eduardo Fontánez Colón, Financial Aid Officer, Inter American University of Puerto Rico, Barranquitas Campus, Box 517, Barranquitas, PR 00794, 787-857-3600 Ext. 2049. *Fax:* 787-857-2244.

INTER AMERICAN UNIVERSITY OF PUERTO RICO, BAYAMÓN CAMPUS
Bayamón, PR

CONTACT Financial Aid Office, Inter American University of Puerto Rico, Bayamón Campus, 500 Road 830, Bayamon, PR 00957, 787-279-1912 Ext. 2025.

INTER AMERICAN UNIVERSITY OF PUERTO RICO, FAJARDO CAMPUS
Fajardo, PR

CONTACT Financial Aid Director, Inter American University of Puerto Rico, Fajardo Campus, Call Box 700003, Fajardo, PR 00738-7003, 787-863-2390 Ext. 2208.

INTER AMERICAN UNIVERSITY OF PUERTO RICO, GUAYAMA CAMPUS
Guayama, PR

Tuition & fees: N/R	Average undergraduate aid package: $1551

ABOUT THE INSTITUTION Independent, coed. Awards: associate, bachelor's, and master's degrees. 15 undergraduate majors. Total enrollment: 2,273. Federal methodology is used as a basis for awarding need-based institutional aid.
FRESHMAN FINANCIAL AID (Fall 2004) 287 applied for aid; of those 94% were deemed to have need. 79% of freshmen with need received aid; of those .5% had need fully met. *Average percent of need met:* 2% (excluding resources awarded to replace EFC). *Average financial aid package:* $224 (excluding resources awarded to replace EFC).
UNDERGRADUATE FINANCIAL AID (Fall 2004) 1,180 applied for aid; of those 95% were deemed to have need. 82% of undergraduates with need received aid; of those 1% had need fully met. *Average percent of need met:* 16% (excluding resources awarded to replace EFC). *Average financial aid package:* $1551 (excluding resources awarded to replace EFC).
GIFT AID (NEED-BASED) *Total amount:* $7,605,119 (93% federal, 3% state, 4% institutional). *Receiving aid:* Freshmen: 38% (168); All full-time undergraduates: 37% (662). *Average award:* Freshmen: $113; Undergraduates: $480. *Scholarships, grants, and awards:* Federal Pell, FSEOG, state, college/university gift aid from institutional funds, Federal Nursing.
GIFT AID (NON-NEED-BASED) *Receiving aid:* Freshmen: 1; Undergraduates: 1.
ROTC: Army cooperative.
LOANS *Student loans:* $3,467,125 (100% need-based). 80% of past graduating class borrowed through all loan programs. *Average need-based loan:* Freshmen: $236; Undergraduates: $2000. *Programs:* Federal Direct (Subsidized and Unsubsidized Stafford, PLUS), Perkins, Federal Nursing.
WORK-STUDY *Federal work-study:* Total amount: $116,143; 116 jobs averaging $1000. *State or other work-study/employment:* Part-time jobs available.
ATHLETIC AWARDS *Total amount:* $13,964 (100% need-based).
APPLYING FOR FINANCIAL AID *Required financial aid form:* FAFSA. *Financial aid deadline:* Continuous. *Notification date:* Continuous beginning 7/1. Students must reply within 5 weeks of notification.
CONTACT Sr. Jose A. Vechini, Director of Financial Aid Office, Inter American University of Puerto Rico, Guayama Campus, Call Box 10004, Guyama, PR 00785, 787-864-2222 Ext. 2206 or toll-free 787-864-2222 Ext. 2243 (in-state). *Fax:* 787-864-8232. *E-mail:* javechi@inter.edu.

INTER AMERICAN UNIVERSITY OF PUERTO RICO, METROPOLITAN CAMPUS
San Juan, PR

CONTACT Mrs. Luz M. Medina, Acting Director of Financial Aid, Inter American University of Puerto Rico, Metropolitan Campus, PO Box 191293, San Juan, PR 00919-1293, 787-758-2891. *Fax:* 787-250-0782.

INTER AMERICAN UNIVERSITY OF PUERTO RICO, PONCE CAMPUS
Mercedita, PR

CONTACT Financial Aid Officer, Inter American University of Puerto Rico, Ponce Campus, Street #1, Km 123.2, Mercedita, PR 00715-2201, 787-284-1912 Ext. 2015.

INTER AMERICAN UNIVERSITY OF PUERTO RICO, SAN GERMÁN CAMPUS
San Germán, PR

ABOUT THE INSTITUTION Independent, coed. Awards: associate, bachelor's, master's, and doctoral degrees and post-bachelor's certificates. 57 undergraduate majors. Total enrollment: 5,764. Undergraduates: 4,872. Freshmen: 861.
GIFT AID (NEED-BASED) *Scholarships, grants, and awards:* Federal Pell, FSEOG, state, college/university gift aid from institutional funds.
GIFT AID (NON-NEED-BASED) *Scholarships, grants, and awards by category: Academic Interests/Achievement:* general academic interests/achievements.
LOANS *Programs:* Federal Direct (Subsidized and Unsubsidized Stafford, PLUS), Perkins.
APPLYING FOR FINANCIAL AID *Required financial aid forms:* FAFSA, institution's own form.
CONTACT Ms. María I. Lugo, Financial Aid Director, Inter American University of Puerto Rico, San Germán Campus, PO Box 5100, San Germán, PR 00683-5008, 787-264-1912 Ext. 7252. *Fax:* 787-892-6350.

INTERIOR DESIGNERS INSTITUTE
Newport Beach, CA

CONTACT Office of Financial Aid, Interior Designers Institute, 1061 Camelback Road, Newport Beach, CA 92660, 949-675-4451.

INTERNATIONAL ACADEMY OF DESIGN & TECHNOLOGY
Tampa, FL

CONTACT Financial Aid Office, International Academy of Design & Technology, 5225 Memorial Highway, Tampa, FL 33634-7350, 813-881-0007 or toll-free 800-ACADEMY. *Fax:* 813-881-3440.

INTERNATIONAL ACADEMY OF DESIGN & TECHNOLOGY
Chicago, IL

CONTACT Barbara Williams, Financial Aid Director, International Academy of Design & Technology, 1 North State Street, Suite 400, Chicago, IL 60602, 312-980-9200 or toll-free 877-ACADEMY (out-of-state). *Fax:* 312-541-3929.

INTERNATIONAL BAPTIST COLLEGE
Tempe, AZ

CONTACT Financial Aid Office, International Baptist College, 2150 East Southern Avenue, Tempe, AZ 85282, 480-838-7070 or toll-free 800-422-4858. *Fax:* 480-838-5432.

INTERNATIONAL COLLEGE
Naples, FL

Tuition & fees: $9500   **Average undergraduate aid package: $7830**

ABOUT THE INSTITUTION Independent, coed. Awards: associate, bachelor's, and master's degrees. 13 undergraduate majors. Total enrollment: 1,544. Undergraduates: 1,342. Freshmen: 138. Federal methodology is used as a basis for awarding need-based institutional aid.
UNDERGRADUATE EXPENSES for 2005–06 *Application fee:* $20. *Tuition:* full-time $9120; part-time $380 per credit. *Required fees:* full-time $380; $190 per term. *Payment plan:* Installment.
FRESHMAN FINANCIAL AID (Fall 2005, est.) 160 applied for aid; of those 90% were deemed to have need. 100% of freshmen with need received aid; of those 6% had need fully met. *Average percent of need met:* 1% (excluding resources awarded to replace EFC). *Average financial aid package:* $6925 (excluding resources awarded to replace EFC).
UNDERGRADUATE FINANCIAL AID (Fall 2005, est.) 1,001 applied for aid; of those 90% were deemed to have need. 100% of undergraduates with need received aid; of those 6% had need fully met. *Average percent of need met:* 1% (excluding resources awarded to replace EFC). *Average financial aid package:* $7830 (excluding resources awarded to replace EFC).
GIFT AID (NEED-BASED) *Total amount:* $2,840,615 (94% federal, 5% state, 1% external sources). *Receiving aid:* Freshmen: 64% (109); All full-time undergraduates: 65% (685). *Average award:* Freshmen: $3600; Undergraduates: $3750. *Scholarships, grants, and awards:* Federal Pell, FSEOG, state, private, college/university gift aid from institutional funds.
GIFT AID (NON-NEED-BASED) *Total amount:* $3,083,961 (88% state, 10% institutional, 2% external sources). *Receiving aid:* Freshmen: 80% (135); Undergraduates: 80% (842). *Scholarships, grants, and awards by category:* Special Achievements/Activities: 245 awards ($303,230 total): general special achievements/activities. *Tuition waivers:* Full or partial for employees or children of employees.
LOANS *Student loans:* $12,325,788 (49% need-based, 51% non-need-based). 76% of past graduating class borrowed through all loan programs. *Average indebtedness per student:* $18,400. *Average need-based loan:* Freshmen: $1313; Undergraduates: $3300. *Parent loans:* $197,894 (100% non-need-based). *Programs:* FFEL (Subsidized and Unsubsidized Stafford, PLUS).
WORK-STUDY *Federal work-study:* Total amount: $108,924; 48 jobs averaging $2269.
APPLYING FOR FINANCIAL AID *Required financial aid form:* FAFSA. *Financial aid deadline:* Continuous. *Notification date:* Continuous.
CONTACT Mr. Joe Gilchrist, Vice President of Student Financial Assistance, International College, 2655 Northbrooke Drive, Naples, FL 34119, 239-513-1122 Ext. 116 or toll-free 800-466-8017. *Fax:* 239-513-9579. *E-mail:* jgilchrist@internationalcollege.edu.

INTERNATIONAL COLLEGE AND GRADUATE SCHOOL
Honolulu, HI

See Hawai'i Theological Seminary.

INTERNATIONAL IMPORT-EXPORT INSTITUTE
Phoenix, AZ

CONTACT Financial Aid Office, International Import-Export Institute, 2432 West Peoria Avenue, Suite 1026, Phoenix, AZ 85029, 602-648-5750 or toll-free 800-474-8013.

IONA COLLEGE
New Rochelle, NY

Tuition & fees: $20,980   **Average undergraduate aid package: $13,384**

ABOUT THE INSTITUTION Independent religious, coed. Awards: bachelor's and master's degrees and post-bachelor's and post-master's certificates. 58 undergraduate majors. Total enrollment: 4,184. Undergraduates: 3,365. Freshmen: 779. Federal methodology is used as a basis for awarding need-based institutional aid.
UNDERGRADUATE EXPENSES for 2005–06 *Application fee:* $50. *Comprehensive fee:* $30,878 includes full-time tuition ($20,110), mandatory fees ($870), and room and board ($9898). Full-time tuition and fees vary according to class time. Room and board charges vary according to housing facility. *Part-time tuition:* $667 per credit. *Part-time fees:* $370 per term. Part-time tuition and fees vary according to class time and course load. *Payment plan:* Installment.
FRESHMAN FINANCIAL AID (Fall 2005, est.) 763 applied for aid; of those 80% were deemed to have need. 99% of freshmen with need received aid; of those 20% had need fully met. *Average percent of need met:* 19% (excluding resources awarded to replace EFC). *Average financial aid package:* $13,309 (excluding resources awarded to replace EFC). 18% of all full-time freshmen had no need and received non-need-based gift aid.
UNDERGRADUATE FINANCIAL AID (Fall 2005, est.) 2,966 applied for aid; of those 79% were deemed to have need. 99% of undergraduates with need received aid; of those 21% had need fully met. *Average percent of need met:* 23% (excluding resources awarded to replace EFC). *Average financial aid package:* $13,384 (excluding resources awarded to replace EFC). 18% of all full-time undergraduates had no need and received non-need-based gift aid.
GIFT AID (NEED-BASED) *Total amount:* $6,529,279 (37% federal, 58% state, 1% institutional, 4% external sources). *Receiving aid:* Freshmen: 26% (200); All full-time undergraduates: 27% (830). *Average award:* Freshmen: $3788; Undergraduates: $3258. *Scholarships, grants, and awards:* Federal Pell, FSEOG, state, private, college/university gift aid from institutional funds.
GIFT AID (NON-NEED-BASED) *Total amount:* $20,384,879 (99% institutional, 1% external sources). *Receiving aid:* Freshmen: 77% (603); Undergraduates: 71% (2,223). *Average Award:* Freshmen: $9635; Undergraduates: $9753. *Scholarships, grants, and awards by category:* Academic Interests/Achievement: 2,822 awards ($19,086,976 total): general academic interests/achievements. *Creative Arts/Performance:* 32 awards ($88,550 total): music. *Special Characteristics:* 166 awards ($599,265 total): children and siblings of alumni, children of faculty/staff, religious affiliation, siblings of current students. *Tuition waivers:* Full or partial for employees or children of employees, senior citizens. *ROTC:* Army cooperative.
LOANS *Student loans:* $14,071,207 (40% need-based, 60% non-need-based). 70% of past graduating class borrowed through all loan programs. *Average indebtedness per student:* $21,495. *Average need-based loan:* Freshmen: $2367; Undergraduates: $2794. *Parent loans:* $6,804,713 (100% non-need-based). *Programs:* FFEL (Subsidized and Unsubsidized Stafford, PLUS), Perkins, alternative loans.
WORK-STUDY *Federal work-study:* Total amount: $576,682; 513 jobs averaging $1099. *State or other work-study/employment:* Total amount: $380,000 (100% non-need-based). 188 part-time jobs averaging $1513.
ATHLETIC AWARDS *Total amount:* $1,975,711 (100% non-need-based).
APPLYING FOR FINANCIAL AID *Required financial aid forms:* FAFSA, institution's own form, state aid form. *Financial aid deadline (priority):* 4/15. *Notification date:* Continuous beginning 12/20. Students must reply by 5/1 or within 2 weeks of notification.
CONTACT Mary Grant, Director of Financial Aid, Iona College, 715 North Avenue, New Rochelle, NY 10801-1890, 914-633-2676 or toll-free 800-231-IONA (in-state). *Fax:* 914-633-2486.

IOWA STATE UNIVERSITY OF SCIENCE AND TECHNOLOGY
Ames, IA

ABOUT THE INSTITUTION State-supported, coed. Awards: bachelor's, master's, doctoral, and first professional degrees and post-master's certificates. 116 undergraduate majors. Total enrollment: 25,741. Undergraduates: 20,732. Freshmen: 3,769.

GIFT AID (NEED-BASED) *Scholarships, grants, and awards:* Federal Pell, FSEOG, state, college/university gift aid from institutional funds.

GIFT AID (NON-NEED-BASED) *Scholarships, grants, and awards by category: Academic Interests/Achievement:* agriculture, architecture, area/ethnic studies, biological sciences, business, communication, computer science, education, engineering/technologies, English, foreign languages, general academic interests/achievements, health fields, home economics, humanities, international studies, library science, mathematics, military science, physical sciences, premedicine, social sciences. *Creative Arts/Performance:* applied art and design, art/fine arts, journalism/publications, music, theater/drama. *Special Achievements/Activities:* community service, general special achievements/activities, leadership, rodeo. *Special Characteristics:* adult students, children and siblings of alumni, ethnic background, first-generation college students, general special characteristics, international students, local/state students, members of minority groups, out-of-state students, religious affiliation.

LOANS *Programs:* Federal Direct (Subsidized and Unsubsidized Stafford, PLUS), Perkins, state, college/university, private alternative loans.

WORK-STUDY *Federal work-study:* Total amount: $1,062,405; 779 jobs averaging $2168. *State or other work-study/employment:* 9,458 part-time jobs averaging $1779.

APPLYING FOR FINANCIAL AID *Required financial aid form:* FAFSA.

CONTACT Roberta Johnson, Director of Financial Aid, Iowa State University of Science and Technology, 0210 Beardshear Hall, Ames, IA 50011, 515-294-2223 or toll-free 800-262-3810. *Fax:* 515-294-3622. *E-mail:* rljohns@iastate.edu.

IOWA WESLEYAN COLLEGE
Mount Pleasant, IA

Tuition & fees: $17,800 | **Average undergraduate aid package: $14,852**

ABOUT THE INSTITUTION Independent United Methodist, coed. Awards: bachelor's degrees. 40 undergraduate majors. Total enrollment: 849. Undergraduates: 849. Federal methodology is used as a basis for awarding need-based institutional aid.

UNDERGRADUATE EXPENSES for 2006–07 *Comprehensive fee:* $23,330 includes full-time tuition ($17,800) and room and board ($5530). *College room only:* $2280. *Part-time tuition:* $439 per credit hour.

FRESHMAN FINANCIAL AID (Fall 2005, est.) 119 applied for aid; of those 73% were deemed to have need. 100% of freshmen with need received aid; of those 53% had need fully met. *Average percent of need met:* 93% (excluding resources awarded to replace EFC). *Average financial aid package:* $16,275 (excluding resources awarded to replace EFC). 12% of all full-time freshmen had no need and received non-need-based gift aid.

UNDERGRADUATE FINANCIAL AID (Fall 2005, est.) 615 applied for aid; of those 96% were deemed to have need. 100% of undergraduates with need received aid; of those 46% had need fully met. *Average percent of need met:* 89% (excluding resources awarded to replace EFC). *Average financial aid package:* $14,852 (excluding resources awarded to replace EFC). 5% of all full-time undergraduates had no need and received non-need-based gift aid.

GIFT AID (NEED-BASED) *Total amount:* $4,122,269 (25% federal, 19% state, 53% institutional, 3% external sources). *Receiving aid:* Freshmen: 64% (87); All full-time undergraduates: 92% (593). *Average award:* Freshmen: $10,278; Undergraduates: $7833. *Scholarships, grants, and awards:* Federal Pell, FSEOG, state, private, college/university gift aid from institutional funds.

GIFT AID (NON-NEED-BASED) *Total amount:* $1,433,743 (10% state, 89% institutional, 1% external sources). *Receiving aid:* Freshmen: 64% (87); Undergraduates: 92% (593). *Average Award:* Freshmen: $10,525; Undergraduates: $7564. *Scholarships, grants, and awards by category: Academic Interests/Achievement:* 200 awards ($788,435 total): general academic interests/achievements. *Creative Arts/Performance:* 35 awards ($79,301 total): art/fine arts, music. *Special Achievements/Activities:* 115 awards ($336,635 total): cheerleading/drum major, community service, leadership, religious involvement. *Special Characteristics:* 335 awards ($1,379,369 total): children and siblings of alumni, children of faculty/staff, international students, out-of-state students, relatives of clergy, religious affiliation.

LOANS *Student loans:* $4,667,009 (54% need-based, 46% non-need-based). 90% of past graduating class borrowed through all loan programs. *Average indebtedness per student:* $20,794. *Average need-based loan:* Freshmen: $2600; Undergraduates: $5000. *Parent loans:* $338,031 (29% need-based, 71% non-need-based). *Programs:* FFEL (Subsidized and Unsubsidized Stafford, PLUS), Perkins, state, alternative loans.

WORK-STUDY *Federal work-study:* Total amount: $139,438; 119 jobs averaging $1200. *State or other work-study/employment:* Total amount: $84,675 (59% need-based, 41% non-need-based). 47 part-time jobs averaging $1000.

ATHLETIC AWARDS *Total amount:* $1,485,045 (75% need-based, 25% non-need-based).

APPLYING FOR FINANCIAL AID *Required financial aid form:* FAFSA. *Financial aid deadline (priority):* 4/1. *Notification date:* Continuous beginning 3/1. Students must reply within 3 weeks of notification.

CONTACT Melissa Kilbride, Director of Financial Aid, Iowa Wesleyan College, 601 North Main Street, Mount Pleasant, IA 52641-1398, 319-385-6242 or toll-free 800-582-2383 Ext. 6231. *Fax:* 319-385-6219. *E-mail:* mkilbride@iwc.edu.

ITHACA COLLEGE
Ithaca, NY

Tuition & fees: $25,194 | **Average undergraduate aid package: $21,810**

ABOUT THE INSTITUTION Independent, coed. Awards: bachelor's, master's, and doctoral degrees. 105 undergraduate majors. Total enrollment: 6,412. Undergraduates: 6,098. Freshmen: 1,680. Institutional methodology is used as a basis for awarding need-based institutional aid.

UNDERGRADUATE EXPENSES for 2005–06 *Application fee:* $55. *Comprehensive fee:* $35,144 includes full-time tuition ($25,194) and room and board ($9950). *College room only:* $5120. *Part-time tuition:* $840 per credit hour.

FRESHMAN FINANCIAL AID (Fall 2005, est.) 1358 applied for aid; of those 92% were deemed to have need. 100% of freshmen with need received aid; of those 52% had need fully met. *Average percent of need met:* 89% (excluding resources awarded to replace EFC). *Average financial aid package:* $22,583 (excluding resources awarded to replace EFC). 8% of all full-time freshmen had no need and received non-need-based gift aid.

UNDERGRADUATE FINANCIAL AID (Fall 2005, est.) 4,553 applied for aid; of those 92% were deemed to have need. 100% of undergraduates with need received aid; of those 46% had need fully met. *Average percent of need met:* 87% (excluding resources awarded to replace EFC). *Average financial aid package:* $21,810 (excluding resources awarded to replace EFC). 10% of all full-time undergraduates had no need and received non-need-based gift aid.

GIFT AID (NEED-BASED) *Total amount:* $54,426,246 (7% federal, 7% state, 84% institutional, 2% external sources). *Receiving aid:* Freshmen: 65% (1,090); All full-time undergraduates: 65% (3,881). *Average award:* Freshmen: $14,710; Undergraduates: $13,967. *Scholarships, grants, and awards:* Federal Pell, FSEOG, state, private, college/university gift aid from institutional funds.

GIFT AID (NON-NEED-BASED) *Total amount:* $9,391,085 (1% federal, 1% state, 92% institutional, 6% external sources). *Receiving aid:* Freshmen: 18% (304); Undergraduates: 14% (826). *Average Award:* Freshmen: $8411; Undergraduates: $9582. *Scholarships, grants, and awards by category: Academic Interests/Achievement:* 2,014 awards ($16,687,116 total): communication, general academic interests/achievements. *Creative Arts/Performance:* 24 awards ($290,388 total): dance, journalism/publications, music, performing arts, theater/drama. *Special Achievements/Activities:* 108 awards ($642,000 total): leadership. *Special Characteristics:* 300 awards ($301,000 total): children and siblings of alumni, siblings of current students. *ROTC:* Army cooperative, Air Force cooperative.

LOANS *Student loans:* $25,631,514 (88% need-based, 12% non-need-based). *Average need-based loan:* Freshmen: $6768; Undergraduates: $6091. *Parent loans:* $11,708,021 (22% need-based, 78% non-need-based). *Programs:* FFEL (Subsidized and Unsubsidized Stafford, PLUS), Perkins, college/university.

WORK-STUDY *Federal work-study:* Total amount: $1,350,000; jobs available. *State or other work-study/employment:* Total amount: $8,039,434 (56% need-based, 44% non-need-based). Part-time jobs available.

APPLYING FOR FINANCIAL AID *Required financial aid forms:* FAFSA, CSS Profile required of early decision applicants; deadline Nov. 1. *Financial aid deadline (priority):* 2/1. *Notification date:* Continuous beginning 2/15.
CONTACT Mr. Larry Chambers, Director of Financial Aid, Ithaca College, 350 Egbert Hall, Ithaca, NY 14850, 800-429-4275 or toll-free 800-429-4274. *Fax:* 607-274-1895. *E-mail:* finaid@ithaca.edu.

ITT TECHNICAL INSTITUTE
Tempe, AZ

CONTACT Financial Aid Office, ITT Technical Institute, 5005 S. Wendler Drive, Tempe, AZ 85282, 602-437-7500 or toll-free 800-879-4881.

ITT TECHNICAL INSTITUTE
Lexington, KY

CONTACT Financial Aid Office, ITT Technical Institute, 2473 Fortune Drive, Suite 180, Lexington, KY 40509, 859-246-3300.

JACKSON STATE UNIVERSITY
Jackson, MS

CONTACT Director of Financial Aid, Jackson State University, 1400 J.R. Lynch Street, PO Box 17065, Jackson, MS 39217, 601-968-2227 or toll-free 800-682-5390 (in-state), 800-848-6817 (out-of-state).

JACKSONVILLE STATE UNIVERSITY
Jacksonville, AL

Tuition & fees (AL res): $4040 **Average undergraduate aid package: $6200**

ABOUT THE INSTITUTION State-supported, coed. Awards: bachelor's and master's degrees and post-master's certificates. 58 undergraduate majors. Total enrollment: 9,110. Undergraduates: 7,285. Freshmen: 1,151. Federal methodology is used as a basis for awarding need-based institutional aid.
UNDERGRADUATE EXPENSES for 2005–06 *Application fee:* $20. *Tuition, state resident:* full-time $4040; part-time $169 per credit hour. *Tuition, nonresident:* full-time $8080; part-time $338 per credit hour. *College room and board:* $3258; *room only:* $1680. Room and board charges vary according to board plan and housing facility.
FRESHMAN FINANCIAL AID (Fall 2004) 908 applied for aid; of those 94% were deemed to have need. 100% of freshmen with need received aid; of those 50% had need fully met. *Average percent of need met:* 70% (excluding resources awarded to replace EFC). *Average financial aid package:* $3800 (excluding resources awarded to replace EFC). 15% of all full-time freshmen had no need and received non-need-based gift aid.
UNDERGRADUATE FINANCIAL AID (Fall 2004) 4,785 applied for aid; of those 94% were deemed to have need. 100% of undergraduates with need received aid; of those 50% had need fully met. *Average percent of need met:* 80% (excluding resources awarded to replace EFC). *Average financial aid package:* $6200 (excluding resources awarded to replace EFC). 14% of all full-time undergraduates had no need and received non-need-based gift aid.
GIFT AID (NEED-BASED) *Total amount:* $19,092,856 (52% federal, 1% state, 24% institutional, 23% external sources). *Receiving aid:* Freshmen: 6% (68); All full-time undergraduates: 6% (357). *Average award:* Freshmen: $2100; Undergraduates: $3500. *Scholarships, grants, and awards:* Federal Pell, FSEOG, state, private, college/university gift aid from institutional funds, Federal Nursing.
GIFT AID (NON-NEED-BASED) *Total amount:* $35,350 (100% external sources). *Receiving aid:* Freshmen: 35% (401); Undergraduates: 36% (2,116). *Average Award:* Freshmen: $1000; Undergraduates: $1000. *Scholarships, grants, and awards by category:* Academic Interests/Achievement: biological sciences, business, communication, computer science, education, English, health fields, home economics, humanities, mathematics, military science, physical sciences, social sciences. Creative Arts/Performance: art/fine arts, journalism/publications, music, theater/drama. Special Achievements/Activities: general special achievements/activities. *Tuition waivers:* Full or partial for employees or children of employees. *ROTC:* Army.
LOANS *Student loans:* $38,000,000 (65% need-based, 35% non-need-based). 46% of past graduating class borrowed through all loan programs. *Average indebtedness per student:* $17,125. *Average need-based loan:* Undergraduates: $5250. *Parent loans:* $1,200,000 (100% non-need-based). *Programs:* FFEL (Subsidized and Unsubsidized Stafford, PLUS), college/university.
WORK-STUDY *Federal work-study:* Total amount: $442,490; 380 jobs averaging $1164. *State or other work-study/employment:* Total amount: $1,302,222 (100% non-need-based). 517 part-time jobs averaging $2518.
ATHLETIC AWARDS *Total amount:* $1,828,533 (100% non-need-based).
APPLYING FOR FINANCIAL AID *Required financial aid forms:* FAFSA, institution's own form. *Financial aid deadline (priority):* 3/15. *Notification date:* Continuous beginning 5/15. Students must reply within 2 weeks of notification.
CONTACT Mrs. Vicki Adams, Director of Financial Aid, Jacksonville State University, 700 Pelham Road North, Jacksonville, AL 36265-9982, 256-782-5006 Ext. 8399 or toll-free 800-231-5291. *Fax:* 256-782-5476. *E-mail:* finaid@jsu.edu.

JACKSONVILLE UNIVERSITY
Jacksonville, FL

Tuition & fees: $19,970 **Average undergraduate aid package: $16,571**

ABOUT THE INSTITUTION Independent, coed. Awards: bachelor's and master's degrees and first professional certificates. 58 undergraduate majors. Total enrollment: 2,948. Undergraduates: 2,561. Freshmen: 466. Federal methodology is used as a basis for awarding need-based institutional aid.
UNDERGRADUATE EXPENSES for 2005–06 *Application fee:* $30. *Comprehensive fee:* $26,430 includes full-time tuition ($19,970) and room and board ($6460). *College room only:* $3030. *Part-time tuition:* $666 per credit hour.
FRESHMAN FINANCIAL AID (Fall 2005, est.) 439 applied for aid; of those 87% were deemed to have need. 100% of freshmen with need received aid; of those 20% had need fully met. *Average percent of need met:* 81% (excluding resources awarded to replace EFC). *Average financial aid package:* $17,510 (excluding resources awarded to replace EFC). 13% of all full-time freshmen had no need and received non-need-based gift aid.
UNDERGRADUATE FINANCIAL AID (Fall 2005, est.) 1,511 applied for aid; of those 82% were deemed to have need. 100% of undergraduates with need received aid; of those 27% had need fully met. *Average percent of need met:* 82% (excluding resources awarded to replace EFC). *Average financial aid package:* $16,571 (excluding resources awarded to replace EFC). 16% of all full-time undergraduates had no need and received non-need-based gift aid.
GIFT AID (NEED-BASED) *Total amount:* $14,305,501 (21% federal, 19% state, 58% institutional, 2% external sources). *Receiving aid:* Freshmen: 48% (253); All full-time undergraduates: 48% (836). *Average award:* Freshmen: $7103; Undergraduates: $5331. *Scholarships, grants, and awards:* Federal Pell, FSEOG, state, private, college/university gift aid from institutional funds.
GIFT AID (NON-NEED-BASED) *Total amount:* $2,585,186 (16% federal, 25% state, 56% institutional, 3% external sources). *Receiving aid:* Freshmen: 69% (365); Undergraduates: 66% (1,159). *Average Award:* Freshmen: $5355; Undergraduates: $5066. *Scholarships, grants, and awards by category:* Academic Interests/Achievement: 1,109 awards ($5,825,566 total): business, general academic interests/achievements. Creative Arts/Performance: 93 awards ($313,550 total): general creative arts/performance. Special Achievements/Activities: community service, general special achievements/activities, leadership. Special Characteristics: 283 awards ($1,712,892 total): children and siblings of alumni, children of current students, children of faculty/staff, international students, siblings of current students, spouses of current students. *ROTC:* Naval.
LOANS *Student loans:* $9,191,380 (89% need-based, 11% non-need-based). 53% of past graduating class borrowed through all loan programs. *Average indebtedness per student:* $21,483. *Average need-based loan:* Freshmen: $4291; Undergraduates: $3963. *Parent loans:* $2,609,176 (79% need-based, 21% non-need-based). *Programs:* FFEL (Subsidized and Unsubsidized Stafford, PLUS), Perkins, college/university, Navy ROTC.
WORK-STUDY *Federal work-study:* Total amount: $535,315; 200 jobs averaging $2000.
ATHLETIC AWARDS *Total amount:* $1,465,934 (81% need-based, 19% non-need-based).
APPLYING FOR FINANCIAL AID *Required financial aid form:* FAFSA. *Financial aid deadline:* 3/15 (priority: 2/1). *Notification date:* Continuous beginning 2/1. Students must reply by 5/1 or within 3 weeks of notification.

Jacksonville University

CONTACT Mrs. Catherine Huntress, Director of Student Financial Assistance, Jacksonville University, 2800 University Boulevard North, Jacksonville, FL 32211, 904-256-7060 or toll-free 800-225-2027. *Fax:* 904-256-7148. *E-mail:* chuntres@ju.edu.

JAMES MADISON UNIVERSITY
Harrisonburg, VA

Tuition & fees (VA res): $5886 | **Average undergraduate aid package: $6822**

ABOUT THE INSTITUTION State-supported, coed. Awards: bachelor's, master's, and doctoral degrees (also offers specialist in education degree). 46 undergraduate majors. Total enrollment: 16,938. Undergraduates: 15,618. Freshmen: 3,798. Federal methodology is used as a basis for awarding need-based institutional aid.

UNDERGRADUATE EXPENSES for 2005–06 *Application fee:* $40. *Tuition, state resident:* full-time $5886. *Tuition, nonresident:* full-time $15,322. Part-time tuition and fees vary according to course load. *College room and board:* $6372; *room only:* $3278. Room and board charges vary according to board plan and housing facility. *Payment plan:* Installment.

FRESHMAN FINANCIAL AID (Fall 2005, est.) 2769 applied for aid; of those 51% were deemed to have need. 86% of freshmen with need received aid; of those 94% had need fully met. *Average percent of need met:* 62% (excluding resources awarded to replace EFC). *Average financial aid package:* $7769 (excluding resources awarded to replace EFC). 3% of all full-time freshmen had no need and received non-need-based gift aid.

UNDERGRADUATE FINANCIAL AID (Fall 2005, est.) 12,082 applied for aid; of those 60% were deemed to have need. 62% of undergraduates with need received aid; of those 69% had need fully met. *Average percent of need met:* 50% (excluding resources awarded to replace EFC). *Average financial aid package:* $6822 (excluding resources awarded to replace EFC). 1% of all full-time undergraduates had no need and received non-need-based gift aid.

GIFT AID (NEED-BASED) *Total amount:* $11,127,434 (31% federal, 37% state, 16% institutional, 16% external sources). *Receiving aid:* Freshmen: 16% (593); All full-time undergraduates: 12% (1,777). *Average award:* Freshmen: $5827; Undergraduates: $5332. *Scholarships, grants, and awards:* Federal Pell, FSEOG, state, private, college/university gift aid from institutional funds.

GIFT AID (NON-NEED-BASED) *Total amount:* $2,360,618 (5% state, 80% institutional, 15% external sources). *Receiving aid:* Freshmen: 13% (488); Undergraduates: 7% (975). *Average Award:* Freshmen: $2246; Undergraduates: $2049. *Scholarships, grants, and awards by category:* Academic Interests/Achievement: 691 awards ($931,636 total): architecture, biological sciences, business, computer science, education, engineering/technologies, English, general academic interests/achievements, health fields, humanities, international studies, mathematics, military science, physical sciences, premedicine, religion/biblical studies, social sciences. *Creative Arts/Performance:* 156 awards ($153,055 total): art/fine arts, cinema/film/broadcasting, dance, journalism/publications, music, theater/drama. *Special Achievements/Activities:* 105 awards ($67,520 total): cheerleading/drum major, general special achievements/activities, leadership. *Special Characteristics:* 42 awards ($61,930 total): children and siblings of alumni, children of faculty/staff, handicapped students, international students, out-of-state students, siblings of current students. *Tuition waivers:* Full or partial for employees or children of employees, senior citizens. *ROTC:* Army, Air Force cooperative.

LOANS *Student loans:* $39,400,076 (43% need-based, 57% non-need-based). 53% of past graduating class borrowed through all loan programs. *Average indebtedness per student:* $12,591. *Average need-based loan:* Freshmen: $2904; Undergraduates: $3640. *Parent loans:* $28,312,209 (100% non-need-based). *Programs:* FFEL (Subsidized and Unsubsidized Stafford, PLUS), Perkins.

WORK-STUDY *Federal work-study:* Total amount: $2,844,063; 1,640 jobs averaging $1734. *State or other work-study/employment:* Total amount: $4,504,000 (100% non-need-based). 2,460 part-time jobs averaging $1831.

ATHLETIC AWARDS *Total amount:* $3,619,846 (100% non-need-based).

APPLYING FOR FINANCIAL AID *Required financial aid form:* FAFSA. *Financial aid deadline (priority):* 3/1. *Notification date:* Continuous beginning 4/1. Students must reply within 4 weeks of notification.

CONTACT Lisa L. Turner, Director of Financial Aid and Scholarships, James Madison University, Warren Hall B504, MSC 3519, Harrisonburg, VA 22807, 540-568-7820.

JAMESTOWN COLLEGE
Jamestown, ND

Tuition & fees: $10,550 | **Average undergraduate aid package: $8094**

ABOUT THE INSTITUTION Independent Presbyterian, coed. Awards: bachelor's degrees. 43 undergraduate majors. Total enrollment: 1,026. Undergraduates: 1,026. Freshmen: 286. Both federal and institutional methodology are used as a basis for awarding need-based institutional aid.

UNDERGRADUATE EXPENSES for 2006–07 *Application fee:* $20. *Comprehensive fee:* $14,890 includes full-time tuition ($10,550) and room and board ($4340). *College room only:* $1850. *Part-time tuition:* $295 per credit.

FRESHMAN FINANCIAL AID (Fall 2005, est.) 272 applied for aid; of those 78% were deemed to have need. 100% of freshmen with need received aid; of those 18% had need fully met. *Average percent of need met:* 67% (excluding resources awarded to replace EFC). *Average financial aid package:* $8516 (excluding resources awarded to replace EFC). 22% of all full-time freshmen had no need and received non-need-based gift aid.

UNDERGRADUATE FINANCIAL AID (Fall 2005, est.) 958 applied for aid; of those 81% were deemed to have need. 100% of undergraduates with need received aid; of those 20% had need fully met. *Average percent of need met:* 65% (excluding resources awarded to replace EFC). *Average financial aid package:* $8094 (excluding resources awarded to replace EFC). 19% of all full-time undergraduates had no need and received non-need-based gift aid.

GIFT AID (NEED-BASED) *Total amount:* $3,292,942 (29% federal, 4% state, 58% institutional, 9% external sources). *Receiving aid:* Freshmen: 78% (213); All full-time undergraduates: 81% (777). *Average award:* Freshmen: $6087; Undergraduates: $4844. *Scholarships, grants, and awards:* Federal Pell, FSEOG, state, private, college/university gift aid from institutional funds, Federal Nursing.

GIFT AID (NON-NEED-BASED) *Total amount:* $697,347 (84% institutional, 16% external sources). *Receiving aid:* Freshmen: 10% (27); Undergraduates: 8% (75). *Average Award:* Freshmen: $7050; Undergraduates: $7821. *Scholarships, grants, and awards by category:* Academic Interests/Achievement: 336 awards ($953,184 total): general academic interests/achievements, physical sciences. *Creative Arts/Performance:* 12 awards ($9250 total): art/fine arts. *Special Achievements/Activities:* 32 awards ($19,093 total): leadership. *Special Characteristics:* 63 awards ($253,185 total): children of faculty/staff, general special characteristics, international students, relatives of clergy, religious affiliation, spouses of current students.

LOANS *Student loans:* $5,119,453 (65% need-based, 35% non-need-based). 95% of past graduating class borrowed through all loan programs. *Average indebtedness per student:* $21,131. *Average need-based loan:* Freshmen: $3073; Undergraduates: $3848. *Parent loans:* $341,270 (25% need-based, 75% non-need-based). *Programs:* FFEL (Subsidized and Unsubsidized Stafford, PLUS), Perkins, college/university, alternative loans.

WORK-STUDY *Federal work-study:* Total amount: $228,625; 293 jobs averaging $780. *State or other work-study/employment:* Total amount: $43,202 (100% non-need-based). 52 part-time jobs averaging $881.

ATHLETIC AWARDS *Total amount:* $637,290 (73% need-based, 27% non-need-based).

APPLYING FOR FINANCIAL AID *Required financial aid form:* FAFSA. *Financial aid deadline (priority):* 3/15. *Notification date:* Continuous beginning 4/1. Students must reply within 6 weeks of notification.

CONTACT Margery Michael, Director of Financial Aid, Jamestown College, 6085 College Lane, Jamestown, ND 58405, 701-252-3467 Ext. 2556 or toll-free 800-336-2554. *Fax:* 701-253-4318. *E-mail:* mmichael@jc.edu.

JARVIS CHRISTIAN COLLEGE
Hawkins, TX

CONTACT Assistant Director of Financial Aid, Jarvis Christian College, PO Box 1470, Hawkins, TX 75765, 903-769-5743. *Fax:* 903-769-4842.

JEFFERSON COLLEGE OF HEALTH SCIENCES
Roanoke, VA

Tuition & fees: N/R | **Average undergraduate aid package: $10,391**

ABOUT THE INSTITUTION Independent, coed. Awards: associate and bachelor's degrees. 13 undergraduate majors. Total enrollment: 697. Undergraduates: 697. Freshmen: 77. Federal methodology is used as a basis for awarding need-based institutional aid.

FRESHMAN FINANCIAL AID (Fall 2005, est.) 228 applied for aid; of those 47% were deemed to have need. 70% of freshmen with need received aid; of those 7% had need fully met. *Average percent of need met:* 46% (excluding resources awarded to replace EFC). *Average financial aid package:* $9999 (excluding resources awarded to replace EFC). 2% of all full-time freshmen had no need and received non-need-based gift aid.

UNDERGRADUATE FINANCIAL AID (Fall 2005, est.) 894 applied for aid; of those 58% were deemed to have need. 79% of undergraduates with need received aid; of those 9% had need fully met. *Average percent of need met:* 47% (excluding resources awarded to replace EFC). *Average financial aid package:* $10,391 (excluding resources awarded to replace EFC). 4% of all full-time undergraduates had no need and received non-need-based gift aid.

GIFT AID (NEED-BASED) *Total amount:* $3,324,506 (20% federal, 23% state, 32% institutional, 25% external sources). *Receiving aid:* Freshmen: 6% (75); All full-time undergraduates: 18% (392). *Average award:* Freshmen: $6685; Undergraduates: $6270. *Scholarships, grants, and awards:* Federal Pell, FSEOG, state, private, college/university gift aid from institutional funds.

GIFT AID (NON-NEED-BASED) *Total amount:* $1,003,519 (19% state, 22% institutional, 59% external sources). *Receiving aid:* Freshmen: 4; Undergraduates: 1% (21). *Average Award:* Freshmen: $6932; Undergraduates: $9164. *Scholarships, grants, and awards by category:* Academic Interests/Achievement: 471 awards ($1,134,130 total): biological sciences, health fields. *Special Characteristics:* 461 awards ($969,069 total): local/state students. *Tuition waivers:* Full or partial for employees or children of employees.

LOANS *Student loans:* $4,684,407 (86% need-based, 14% non-need-based). 71% of past graduating class borrowed through all loan programs. *Average indebtedness per student:* $20,780. *Average need-based loan:* Freshmen: $2658; Undergraduates: $4409. *Parent loans:* $726,817 (49% need-based, 51% non-need-based). *Programs:* FFEL (Subsidized and Unsubsidized Stafford, PLUS), alternative loans.

WORK-STUDY *Federal work-study:* Total amount: $261,453; 185 jobs averaging $1414. *State or other work-study/employment:* Total amount: $5581 (69% need-based, 31% non-need-based).

APPLYING FOR FINANCIAL AID *Required financial aid forms:* FAFSA, state aid form. *Financial aid deadline (priority):* 3/1. *Notification date:* Continuous beginning 5/1.

CONTACT Debra A. Johnson, Director of Financial Aid, Jefferson College of Health Sciences, 920 South Jefferson Street, PO Box 13186, Roanoke, VA 24031-3186, 540-985-8492 or toll-free 888-985-8483. *Fax:* 540-224-6916. *E-mail:* djohnson@jchs.edu.

JEWISH HOSPITAL COLLEGE OF NURSING AND ALLIED HEALTH
St. Louis, MO

See Barnes-Jewish College of Nursing and Allied Health.

THE JEWISH THEOLOGICAL SEMINARY
New York, NY

CONTACT Linda Levine, Registrar/Director of Financial Aid, The Jewish Theological Seminary, 3080 Broadway, New York, NY 10027-4649, 212-678-8007. *Fax:* 212-678-8947. *E-mail:* financialaid@jtsa.edu.

JOHN BROWN UNIVERSITY
Siloam Springs, AR

Tuition & fees: $15,280   **Average undergraduate aid package: $8195**

ABOUT THE INSTITUTION Independent interdenominational, coed. Awards: bachelor's and master's degrees. 59 undergraduate majors. Total enrollment: 1,904. Undergraduates: 1,659. Freshmen: 262. Federal methodology is used as a basis for awarding need-based institutional aid.

UNDERGRADUATE EXPENSES for 2005–06 *Application fee:* $25. *Comprehensive fee:* $20,910 includes full-time tuition ($14,544), mandatory fees ($736), and room and board ($5630). Full-time tuition and fees vary according to program. Room and board charges vary according to board plan and housing facility. *Part-time tuition:* $600 per semester hour. Part-time tuition and fees vary according to course load and program. *Payment plan:* Installment.

FRESHMAN FINANCIAL AID (Fall 2005, est.) 221 applied for aid; of those 82% were deemed to have need. 100% of freshmen with need received aid; of those 16% had need fully met. *Average percent of need met:* 50% (excluding resources awarded to replace EFC). *Average financial aid package:* $10,413 (excluding resources awarded to replace EFC). 24% of all full-time freshmen had no need and received non-need-based gift aid.

UNDERGRADUATE FINANCIAL AID (Fall 2005, est.) 1,163 applied for aid; of those 85% were deemed to have need. 100% of undergraduates with need received aid; of those 6% had need fully met. *Average percent of need met:* 50% (excluding resources awarded to replace EFC). *Average financial aid package:* $8195 (excluding resources awarded to replace EFC). 16% of all full-time undergraduates had no need and received non-need-based gift aid.

GIFT AID (NEED-BASED) *Total amount:* $6,247,244 (20% federal, 4% state, 76% institutional). *Receiving aid:* Freshmen: 63% (166); All full-time undergraduates: 48% (751). *Average award:* Freshmen: $5030; Undergraduates: $7121. *Scholarships, grants, and awards:* Federal Pell, FSEOG, state, private, college/university gift aid from institutional funds.

GIFT AID (NON-NEED-BASED) *Total amount:* $2,337,914 (5% state, 95% institutional). *Receiving aid:* Freshmen: 61% (161); Undergraduates: 33% (519). *Average Award:* Freshmen: $3868; Undergraduates: $4121. *Scholarships, grants, and awards by category:* Academic Interests/Achievement: 745 awards ($2,201,916 total): general academic interests/achievements. *Creative Arts/Performance:* 69 awards ($104,725 total): journalism/publications, music. *Special Achievements/Activities:* 217 awards ($206,500 total): cheerleading/drum major, leadership. *Special Characteristics:* 367 awards ($879,095 total): children and siblings of alumni, children of educators, children of faculty/staff, ethnic background, international students, members of minority groups, relatives of clergy, siblings of current students. *Tuition waivers:* Full or partial for minority students, children of alumni, employees or children of employees, adult students, senior citizens. *ROTC:* Army cooperative, Air Force cooperative.

LOANS *Student loans:* $3,871,579 (100% need-based). 60% of past graduating class borrowed through all loan programs. *Average indebtedness per student:* $19,262. *Average need-based loan:* Freshmen: $3573; Undergraduates: $4496. *Parent loans:* $1,467,486 (99% need-based, 1% non-need-based). *Programs:* FFEL (Subsidized and Unsubsidized Stafford, PLUS), Perkins, state.

WORK-STUDY *Federal work-study:* Total amount: $428,930; 297 jobs averaging $1362. *State or other work-study/employment:* Total amount: $329,330 (71% need-based, 29% non-need-based). 255 part-time jobs averaging $1318.

ATHLETIC AWARDS *Total amount:* $1,027,714 (43% need-based, 57% non-need-based).

APPLYING FOR FINANCIAL AID *Required financial aid forms:* FAFSA, institution's own form. *Financial aid deadline (priority):* 3/1. *Notification date:* Continuous beginning 3/1. Students must reply by 6/1 or within 4 weeks of notification.

CONTACT Mrs. Emily Nichols, Assistant Director of Student Financial Aid, John Brown University, 2000 West University Street, Siloam Springs, AR 72761-2121, 479-524-7115 or toll-free 877-JBU-INFO. *Fax:* 479-524-7405. *E-mail:* emnichols@jbu.edu.

JOHN CARROLL UNIVERSITY
University Heights, OH

CONTACT Financial Aid Counselor, John Carroll University, 20700 North Park Boulevard, University Heights, OH 44118-4581, 216-397-4248. *Fax:* 216-397-3098. *E-mail:* jcuofa@jcu.edu.

JOHN F. KENNEDY UNIVERSITY
Pleasant Hill, CA

Tuition & fees: N/R   **Average undergraduate aid package: $7000**

ABOUT THE INSTITUTION Independent, coed. Awards: bachelor's, master's, doctoral, and first professional degrees and post-bachelor's certificates. 6 undergraduate majors. Total enrollment: 1,653. Undergraduates: 197. Federal methodology is used as a basis for awarding need-based institutional aid.

UNDERGRADUATE FINANCIAL AID (Fall 2005, est.) 11 applied for aid; of those 100% were deemed to have need. 100% of undergraduates with need received

John F. Kennedy University

aid; of those 100% had need fully met. *Average percent of need met:* 60% (excluding resources awarded to replace EFC). *Average financial aid package:* $7000 (excluding resources awarded to replace EFC).
GIFT AID (NEED-BASED) *Total amount:* $148,751 (82% federal, 8% state, 10% institutional). *Receiving aid:* All full-time undergraduates: 16% (4). *Average award:* Undergraduates: $1000. *Scholarships, grants, and awards:* Federal Pell, FSEOG, state, private, college/university gift aid from institutional funds.
GIFT AID (NON-NEED-BASED) *Tuition waivers:* Full or partial for employees or children of employees.
LOANS *Student loans:* $4,300,000 (7% need-based, 93% non-need-based). 51% of past graduating class borrowed through all loan programs. *Average indebtedness per student:* $23,000. *Average need-based loan:* Undergraduates: $6000. *Parent loans:* $68,981 (72% need-based, 28% non-need-based). *Programs:* FFEL (Subsidized and Unsubsidized Stafford, PLUS), Perkins, college/university.
APPLYING FOR FINANCIAL AID *Required financial aid forms:* FAFSA, institution's own form. *Financial aid deadline (priority):* 3/2. *Notification date:* Continuous.
CONTACT Mindy Bergeron, Director of Financial Aid, John F. Kennedy University, 100 Ellinwood Way, Pleasant Hill, CA 94523, 925-969-3385 or toll-free 800-696-JFKU. *Fax:* 925-969-3390. *E-mail:* bergeron@jfku.edu.

JOHN JAY COLLEGE OF CRIMINAL JUSTICE OF THE CITY UNIVERSITY OF NEW YORK
New York, NY

Tuition & fees (NY res): $4259 **Average undergraduate aid package: $6800**

ABOUT THE INSTITUTION State and locally supported, coed. Awards: associate, bachelor's, master's, and doctoral degrees and post-bachelor's certificates. 16 undergraduate majors. Total enrollment: 12,984. Undergraduates: 11,515. Federal methodology is used as a basis for awarding need-based institutional aid.
UNDERGRADUATE EXPENSES for 2005–06 *Application fee:* $50. *Tuition, state resident:* full-time $4000; part-time $170 per credit. *Tuition, nonresident:* full-time $8640; part-time $360 per credit. *Required fees:* full-time $259; $82.35 per term part-time. Full-time tuition and fees vary according to course level and course load. Part-time tuition and fees vary according to course level and course load. *Payment plan:* Installment.
FRESHMAN FINANCIAL AID (Fall 2004) 2400 applied for aid; of those 100% were deemed to have need. *Average percent of need met:* 85% (excluding resources awarded to replace EFC). *Average financial aid package:* $6800 (excluding resources awarded to replace EFC).
UNDERGRADUATE FINANCIAL AID (Fall 2004) 7,228 applied for aid; of those 100% were deemed to have need. *Average percent of need met:* 85% (excluding resources awarded to replace EFC). *Average financial aid package:* $6800 (excluding resources awarded to replace EFC).
GIFT AID (NEED-BASED) *Total amount:* $38,126,694 (51% federal, 48% state, 1% institutional). *Receiving aid:* Freshmen: 76% (2,018); All full-time undergraduates: 80% (7,228). *Average award:* Freshmen: $2770; Undergraduates: $3544. *Scholarships, grants, and awards:* Federal Pell, FSEOG, state, college/university gift aid from institutional funds.
GIFT AID (NON-NEED-BASED) *Total amount:* $545,500 (100% external sources). *Receiving aid:* Undergraduates: 8% (718). *Scholarships, grants, and awards by category: Academic Interests/Achievement:* general academic interests/achievements. *ROTC:* Air Force cooperative.
LOANS *Student loans:* $18,053,186 (93% need-based, 7% non-need-based). 45% of past graduating class borrowed through all loan programs. *Average indebtedness per student:* $13,240. *Average need-based loan:* Undergraduates: $1751. *Parent loans:* $698,736 (100% need-based). *Programs:* Federal Direct (Subsidized and Unsubsidized Stafford, PLUS), Perkins, alternative loans.
WORK-STUDY *Federal work-study:* Total amount: $2,734,323; 442 jobs averaging $1064. *State or other work-study/employment:* Part-time jobs available.
APPLYING FOR FINANCIAL AID *Required financial aid form:* FAFSA. *Financial aid deadline (priority):* 6/1. *Notification date:* Continuous. Students must reply within 2 weeks of notification.
CONTACT Mr. Arnold Osansky, Associate Director of Financial Aid, John Jay College of Criminal Justice of the City University of New York, 445 West 59th Street, New York, NY 10019-1093, 212-237-8158 or toll-free 877-JOHNJAY. *Fax:* 212-237-8936. *E-mail:* aosansky@jjay.cuny.edu.

THE JOHNS HOPKINS UNIVERSITY
Baltimore, MD

Tuition & fees: $34,400 **Average undergraduate aid package: $26,553**

ABOUT THE INSTITUTION Independent, coed. Awards: bachelor's, master's, doctoral, and first professional degrees and post-bachelor's and post-master's certificates. 59 undergraduate majors. Total enrollment: 6,025. Undergraduates: 4,417. Freshmen: 1,154. Both federal and institutional methodology are used as a basis for awarding need-based institutional aid.
UNDERGRADUATE EXPENSES for 2006–07 *Application fee:* $60. *Comprehensive fee:* $45,022 includes full-time tuition ($33,900), mandatory fees ($500), and room and board ($10,622). *College room only:* $6096. *Part-time tuition:* $1130 per credit.
FRESHMAN FINANCIAL AID (Fall 2005, est.) 746 applied for aid; of those 77% were deemed to have need. 98% of freshmen with need received aid; of those 100% had need fully met. *Average percent of need met:* 100% (excluding resources awarded to replace EFC). *Average financial aid package:* $29,472 (excluding resources awarded to replace EFC). 1% of all full-time freshmen had no need and received non-need-based gift aid.
UNDERGRADUATE FINANCIAL AID (Fall 2005, est.) 2,591 applied for aid; of those 82% were deemed to have need. 98% of undergraduates with need received aid; of those 100% had need fully met. *Average percent of need met:* 96% (excluding resources awarded to replace EFC). *Average financial aid package:* $26,553 (excluding resources awarded to replace EFC). 4% of all full-time undergraduates had no need and received non-need-based gift aid.
GIFT AID (NEED-BASED) *Total amount:* $41,196,284 (5% federal, 3% state, 88% institutional, 4% external sources). *Receiving aid:* Freshmen: 42% (483); All full-time undergraduates: 41% (1,754). *Average award:* Freshmen: $23,713; Undergraduates: $17,776. *Scholarships, grants, and awards:* Federal Pell, FSEOG, state, private, college/university gift aid from institutional funds.
GIFT AID (NON-NEED-BASED) *Total amount:* $1,472,836 (22% federal, 16% state, 49% institutional, 13% external sources). *Receiving aid:* Freshmen: 5% (54); Undergraduates: 9% (373). *Average Award:* Freshmen: $24,579; Undergraduates: $12,609. *Scholarships, grants, and awards by category: Academic Interests/Achievement:* 76 awards ($1,640,754 total): engineering/technologies, general academic interests/achievements. *Special Characteristics:* 50 awards ($916,980 total): children of faculty/staff. *ROTC:* Army, Air Force cooperative.
LOANS *Student loans:* $11,322,304 (86% need-based, 14% non-need-based). 52% of past graduating class borrowed through all loan programs. *Average indebtedness per student:* $14,000. *Average need-based loan:* Freshmen: $2715; Undergraduates: $4087. *Parent loans:* $10,934,641 (73% need-based, 27% non-need-based). *Programs:* Federal Direct (Subsidized and Unsubsidized Stafford), FFEL (PLUS), Perkins, college/university.
WORK-STUDY *Federal work-study:* Total amount: $3,567,730; 1,516 jobs averaging $2413. *State or other work-study/employment:* Part-time jobs available.
ATHLETIC AWARDS *Total amount:* $1,050,704 (41% need-based, 59% non-need-based).
APPLYING FOR FINANCIAL AID *Required financial aid forms:* FAFSA, CSS Financial Aid PROFILE, noncustodial (divorced/separated) parent's statement, business/farm supplement, prior and current year federal income tax form(s). *Financial aid deadline:* 2/15 (priority: 2/1). *Notification date:* 4/1. Students must reply by 5/1 or within 2 weeks of notification.
CONTACT Dr. Ellen Frishberg, University Director of Student Financial Services, The Johns Hopkins University, 146 Garland Hall, Baltimore, MD 21218, 410-516-8028. *Fax:* 410-516-6015. *E-mail:* efrish@jhu.edu.

JOHNSON & WALES UNIVERSITY
Denver, CO

Tuition & fees: $20,826 **Average undergraduate aid package: $12,710**

ABOUT THE INSTITUTION Independent, coed. Awards: associate and bachelor's degrees. 18 undergraduate majors. Total enrollment: 1,544. Undergraduates: 1,544. Freshmen: 386. Federal methodology is used as a basis for awarding need-based institutional aid.
UNDERGRADUATE EXPENSES for 2006–07 *Comprehensive fee:* $29,326 includes full-time tuition ($19,875), mandatory fees ($951), and room and board ($8500). *Part-time tuition:* $368 per quarter hour.

Johnson & Wales University

FRESHMAN FINANCIAL AID (Fall 2005, est.) 343 applied for aid; of those 87% were deemed to have need. 100% of freshmen with need received aid; of those 3% had need fully met. *Average percent of need met:* 65% (excluding resources awarded to replace EFC). *Average financial aid package:* $14,382 (excluding resources awarded to replace EFC). 15% of all full-time freshmen had no need and received non-need-based gift aid.
UNDERGRADUATE FINANCIAL AID (Fall 2005, est.) 1,276 applied for aid; of those 88% were deemed to have need. 99% of undergraduates with need received aid; of those 5% had need fully met. *Average percent of need met:* 65% (excluding resources awarded to replace EFC). *Average financial aid package:* $12,710 (excluding resources awarded to replace EFC). 17% of all full-time undergraduates had no need and received non-need-based gift aid.
GIFT AID (NEED-BASED) *Total amount:* $3,449,649 (42% federal, 58% institutional). *Receiving aid:* Freshmen: 59% (226); All full-time undergraduates: 51% (778). *Average award:* Freshmen: $5180; Undergraduates: $5184. *Scholarships, grants, and awards:* Federal Pell, FSEOG, state, private, college/university gift aid from institutional funds.
GIFT AID (NON-NEED-BASED) *Total amount:* $5,833,933 (90% institutional, 10% external sources). *Receiving aid:* Freshmen: 57% (218); Undergraduates: 52% (796). *Average Award:* Freshmen: $5014; Undergraduates: $5084. *Scholarships, grants, and awards by category: Academic Interests/Achievement:* general academic interests/achievements. *Special Achievements/Activities:* memberships. *Special Characteristics:* children of faculty/staff.
LOANS *Student loans:* $11,241,048 (65% need-based, 35% non-need-based). 74% of past graduating class borrowed through all loan programs. *Average indebtedness per student:* $14,798. *Average need-based loan:* Freshmen: $6255; Undergraduates: $5736. *Parent loans:* $3,144,480 (100% non-need-based). *Programs:* FFEL (Subsidized and Unsubsidized Stafford, PLUS), Perkins, state, college/university.
WORK-STUDY *Federal work-study:* Total amount: $612,560; jobs available.
APPLYING FOR FINANCIAL AID *Required financial aid forms:* FAFSA, CSS Financial Aid PROFILE. *Financial aid deadline:* Continuous. *Notification date:* Continuous beginning 3/1. Students must reply within 2 weeks of notification.
CONTACT Ms. Lynn Robinson, Director of Financial Aid, Johnson & Wales University, 8 Abbott Park Place, Providence, RI 02903, 401-598-4648 or toll-free 877-598-3368. *Fax:* 401-598-1040. *E-mail:* fp@jwu.edu.

JOHNSON & WALES UNIVERSITY
North Miami, FL

Tuition & fees: $20,826 | **Average undergraduate aid package: $14,240**

ABOUT THE INSTITUTION Independent, coed. Awards: associate and bachelor's degrees. 16 undergraduate majors. Total enrollment: 2,452. Undergraduates: 2,452. Freshmen: 716. Federal methodology is used as a basis for awarding need-based institutional aid.
UNDERGRADUATE EXPENSES for 2006–07 *Comprehensive fee:* $30,126 includes full-time tuition ($19,875), mandatory fees ($951), and room and board ($9300). *Part-time tuition:* $368 per quarter hour.
FRESHMAN FINANCIAL AID (Fall 2005, est.) 622 applied for aid; of those 95% were deemed to have need. 98% of freshmen with need received aid; of those 1% had need fully met. *Average percent of need met:* 65% (excluding resources awarded to replace EFC). *Average financial aid package:* $16,741 (excluding resources awarded to replace EFC). 9% of all full-time freshmen had no need and received non-need-based gift aid.
UNDERGRADUATE FINANCIAL AID (Fall 2005, est.) 1,990 applied for aid; of those 95% were deemed to have need. 99% of undergraduates with need received aid; of those 2% had need fully met. *Average percent of need met:* 65% (excluding resources awarded to replace EFC). *Average financial aid package:* $14,240 (excluding resources awarded to replace EFC). 10% of all full-time undergraduates had no need and received non-need-based gift aid.
GIFT AID (NON-NEED-BASED) *Total amount:* $5,861,282 (5% state, 82% institutional, 13% external sources). *Receiving aid:* Freshmen: 51% (360); Undergraduates: 46% (1,063). *Average Award:* Freshmen: $4670; Undergraduates: $5098. *Scholarships, grants, and awards by category: Academic Interests/Achievement:* general academic interests/achievements. *Special Achievements/Activities:* memberships. *Special Characteristics:* children of faculty/staff.
LOANS *Student loans:* $20,050,945 (76% need-based, 24% non-need-based). 75% of past graduating class borrowed through all loan programs. *Average indebtedness per student:* $18,633. *Average need-based loan:* Freshmen: $6856; Undergraduates: $6249. *Parent loans:* $4,300,478 (100% non-need-based). *Programs:* FFEL (Subsidized and Unsubsidized Stafford, PLUS), Perkins, state, college/university.
WORK-STUDY *Federal work-study:* Total amount: $1,575,542; jobs available. *State or other work-study/employment:* Total amount: $8150 (100% need-based). Part-time jobs available.
APPLYING FOR FINANCIAL AID *Required financial aid forms:* FAFSA, CSS Financial Aid PROFILE. *Financial aid deadline:* Continuous. *Notification date:* Continuous beginning 3/1. Students must reply within 2 weeks of notification.
CONTACT Ms. Lynn Robinson, Director of Financial Aid, Johnson & Wales University, 8 Abbott Park Place, Providence, RI 02903, 401-598-4648 or toll-free 800-232-2433. *Fax:* 401-598-1040. *E-mail:* fp@jwu.edu.

JOHNSON & WALES UNIVERSITY
Charlotte, NC

Tuition & fees: $20,826 | **Average undergraduate aid package: $13,109**

ABOUT THE INSTITUTION Independent, coed. Awards: associate and bachelor's degrees. 13 undergraduate majors. Total enrollment: 2,156. Undergraduates: 2,156. Freshmen: 791. Federal methodology is used as a basis for awarding need-based institutional aid.
UNDERGRADUATE EXPENSES for 2006–07 *Comprehensive fee:* $29,126 includes full-time tuition ($19,875), mandatory fees ($951), and room and board ($8300). *Part-time tuition:* $368 per quarter hour.
FRESHMAN FINANCIAL AID (Fall 2005, est.) 726 applied for aid; of those 90% were deemed to have need. 100% of freshmen with need received aid; of those 1% had need fully met. *Average percent of need met:* 63% (excluding resources awarded to replace EFC). *Average financial aid package:* $15,217 (excluding resources awarded to replace EFC). 12% of all full-time freshmen had no need and received non-need-based gift aid.
UNDERGRADUATE FINANCIAL AID (Fall 2005, est.) 1,960 applied for aid; of those 90% were deemed to have need. 99% of undergraduates with need received aid; of those 3% had need fully met. *Average percent of need met:* 64% (excluding resources awarded to replace EFC). *Average financial aid package:* $13,109 (excluding resources awarded to replace EFC). 12% of all full-time undergraduates had no need and received non-need-based gift aid.
GIFT AID (NEED-BASED) *Total amount:* $6,739,762 (38% federal, 8% state, 54% institutional). *Receiving aid:* Freshmen: 76% (599); All full-time undergraduates: 68% (1,452). *Average award:* Freshmen: $5512; Undergraduates: $5178. *Scholarships, grants, and awards:* Federal Pell, FSEOG, state, private, college/university gift aid from institutional funds.
GIFT AID (NON-NEED-BASED) *Total amount:* $6,972,321 (15% state, 77% institutional, 8% external sources). *Receiving aid:* Freshmen: 66% (518); Undergraduates: 64% (1,368). *Average Award:* Freshmen: $4428; Undergraduates: $4348. *Scholarships, grants, and awards by category: Academic Interests/Achievement:* general academic interests/achievements. *Special Achievements/Activities:* memberships. *Special Characteristics:* children of faculty/staff.
LOANS *Student loans:* $17,125,423 (70% need-based, 30% non-need-based). *Average need-based loan:* Freshmen: $6361; Undergraduates: $5857. *Parent loans:* $4,609,668 (100% non-need-based). *Programs:* FFEL (Subsidized and Unsubsidized Stafford, PLUS), Perkins, state, college/university.
WORK-STUDY *Federal work-study:* Total amount: $1,159,980; jobs available.
APPLYING FOR FINANCIAL AID *Required financial aid forms:* FAFSA, CSS Financial Aid PROFILE. *Financial aid deadline:* Continuous. *Notification date:* Continuous beginning 3/1.
CONTACT Ms. Lynn Robinson, Director of Financial Aid, Johnson & Wales University, 8 Abbott Park Place, Providence, RI 02903, 401-598-1648 or toll-free 866-598-2427. *Fax:* 401-598-4751. *E-mail:* fp@jwu.edu.

JOHNSON & WALES UNIVERSITY
Providence, RI

Tuition & fees: $20,826 | **Average undergraduate aid package: $12,009**

ABOUT THE INSTITUTION Independent, coed. Awards: associate, bachelor's, master's, and doctoral degrees (branch locations in Charleston, SC; Denver, CO; North Miami, FL; Norfolk, VA; Gothenberg, Sweden). 38 undergraduate majors. Total enrollment: 10,171. Undergraduates: 9,337. Freshmen: 2,493. Federal methodology is used as a basis for awarding need-based institutional aid.

Johnson & Wales University

UNDERGRADUATE EXPENSES for 2006–07 *Comprehensive fee:* $28,126 includes full-time tuition ($19,875), mandatory fees ($951), and room and board ($7300). *Part-time tuition:* $368 per quarter hour.

FRESHMAN FINANCIAL AID (Fall 2005, est.) 2069 applied for aid; of those 87% were deemed to have need. 99% of freshmen with need received aid; of those 2% had need fully met. *Average percent of need met:* 63% (excluding resources awarded to replace EFC). *Average financial aid package:* $14,058 (excluding resources awarded to replace EFC). 12% of all full-time freshmen had no need and received non-need-based gift aid.

UNDERGRADUATE FINANCIAL AID (Fall 2005, est.) 6,924 applied for aid; of those 88% were deemed to have need. 99% of undergraduates with need received aid; of those 5% had need fully met. *Average percent of need met:* 64% (excluding resources awarded to replace EFC). *Average financial aid package:* $12,009 (excluding resources awarded to replace EFC). 13% of all full-time undergraduates had no need and received non-need-based gift aid.

GIFT AID (NEED-BASED) *Total amount:* $21,356,380 (38% federal, 4% state, 58% institutional). *Receiving aid:* Freshmen: 67% (1,622); All full-time undergraduates: 57% (4,762). *Average award:* Freshmen: $5175; Undergraduates: $4900. *Scholarships, grants, and awards:* Federal Pell, FSEOG, state, private, college/university gift aid from institutional funds.

GIFT AID (NON-NEED-BASED) *Total amount:* $21,188,838 (86% institutional, 14% external sources). *Receiving aid:* Freshmen: 41% (1,005); Undergraduates: 41% (3,479). *Average Award:* Freshmen: $4090; Undergraduates: $4455. *Scholarships, grants, and awards by category:* Academic Interests/Achievement: general academic interests/achievements. Special Achievements/Activities: memberships. Special Characteristics: children of faculty/staff.

LOANS *Student loans:* $64,288,717 (65% need-based, 35% non-need-based). 68% of past graduating class borrowed through all loan programs. *Average indebtedness per student:* $17,704. *Average need-based loan:* Freshmen: $6203; Undergraduates: $5788. *Parent loans:* $17,908,180 (100% non-need-based). *Programs:* FFEL (Subsidized and Unsubsidized Stafford, PLUS), Perkins, state, college/university.

WORK-STUDY *Federal work-study:* Total amount: $3,966,982; jobs available.

APPLYING FOR FINANCIAL AID *Required financial aid forms:* FAFSA, CSS Financial Aid PROFILE. *Financial aid deadline:* Continuous. *Notification date:* Continuous beginning 3/1. Students must reply within 2 weeks of notification.

CONTACT Ms. Lynn Robinson, Director of Financial Aid, Johnson & Wales University, 8 Abbott Park Place, Providence, RI 02903, 401-598-4648 or toll-free 800-598-1000 (in-state), 800-342-5598 (out-of-state). *Fax:* 401-598-1040.

JOHNSON BIBLE COLLEGE
Knoxville, TN

Tuition & fees: $6490	Average undergraduate aid package: $2757

ABOUT THE INSTITUTION Independent religious, coed. Awards: associate, bachelor's, and master's degrees. 6 undergraduate majors. Total enrollment: 889. Undergraduates: 756. Freshmen: 147. Federal methodology is used as a basis for awarding need-based institutional aid.

UNDERGRADUATE EXPENSES for 2005–06 *Application fee:* $35. *Comprehensive fee:* $10,580 includes full-time tuition ($5800), mandatory fees ($690), and room and board ($4090). *College room only:* $2595. Room and board charges vary according to board plan and housing facility. *Part-time tuition:* $242 per semester hour. *Part-time fees:* $20.42 per semester hour. Part-time tuition and fees vary according to course load. *Payment plan:* Installment.

FRESHMAN FINANCIAL AID (Fall 2005, est.) 241 applied for aid; of those 80% were deemed to have need. 100% of freshmen with need received aid. *Average percent of need met:* 49% (excluding resources awarded to replace EFC). *Average financial aid package:* $2586 (excluding resources awarded to replace EFC).

UNDERGRADUATE FINANCIAL AID (Fall 2005, est.) 733 applied for aid; of those 87% were deemed to have need. 100% of undergraduates with need received aid. *Average percent of need met:* 34% (excluding resources awarded to replace EFC). *Average financial aid package:* $2757 (excluding resources awarded to replace EFC).

GIFT AID (NEED-BASED) *Total amount:* $2,506,253 (12% federal, 4% state, 84% institutional). *Receiving aid:* Freshmen: 79% (191); All full-time undergraduates: 84% (615). *Average award:* Freshmen: $1200; Undergraduates: $1396. *Scholarships, grants, and awards:* Federal Pell, FSEOG, state, private, college/university gift aid from institutional funds.

GIFT AID (NON-NEED-BASED) *Total amount:* $311,241 (100% external sources). *Receiving aid:* Freshmen: 34% (81); Undergraduates: 34% (252). *Scholarships, grants, and awards by category:* Academic Interests/Achievement: 563 awards ($493,103 total): communication, education, general academic interests/achievements, religion/biblical studies. Creative Arts/Performance: 8 awards ($3625 total): art/fine arts, general creative arts/performance, music. Special Achievements/Activities: 183 awards ($33,950 total): community service, general special achievements/activities, leadership, religious involvement. Special Characteristics: 216 awards ($136,086 total): children of current students, children of educators, children of faculty/staff, ethnic background, general special characteristics, international students, married students, members of minority groups, parents of current students, relatives of clergy, religious affiliation, siblings of current students, spouses of current students. *Tuition waivers:* Full or partial for employees or children of employees.

LOANS *Student loans:* $775,553 (55% need-based, 45% non-need-based). 72% of past graduating class borrowed through all loan programs. *Average indebtedness per student:* $16,809. *Average need-based loan:* Freshmen: $1078; Undergraduates: $1459. *Parent loans:* $199,301 (100% non-need-based). *Programs:* FFEL (Subsidized and Unsubsidized Stafford, PLUS), college/university, alternative loans.

WORK-STUDY *Federal work-study:* Total amount: $71,695; 103 jobs averaging $696.

APPLYING FOR FINANCIAL AID *Required financial aid forms:* FAFSA, institution's own form. *Financial aid deadline (priority):* 5/1. *Notification date:* Continuous beginning 5/15. Students must reply within 2 weeks of notification.

CONTACT Mrs. Janette Overton, Financial Aid Director, Johnson Bible College, 7900 Johnson Drive, Knoxville, TN 37998, 865-251-2303 Ext. 2292 or toll-free 800-827-2122. *Fax:* 865-251-2337. *E-mail:* joverton@jbc.edu.

JOHNSON C. SMITH UNIVERSITY
Charlotte, NC

ABOUT THE INSTITUTION Independent, coed. Awards: bachelor's degrees. 37 undergraduate majors. Total enrollment: 1,404. Undergraduates: 1,404. Freshmen: 444.

GIFT AID (NEED-BASED) *Scholarships, grants, and awards:* Federal Pell, FSEOG, state, private, college/university gift aid from institutional funds, United Negro College Fund.

GIFT AID (NON-NEED-BASED) *Scholarships, grants, and awards by category:* Academic Interests/Achievement: computer science, general academic interests/achievements, mathematics. Creative Arts/Performance: music. Special Achievements/Activities: community service, general special achievements/activities, leadership. Special Characteristics: children of faculty/staff, ethnic background, siblings of current students.

LOANS *Programs:* Federal Direct (Subsidized and Unsubsidized Stafford, PLUS), FFEL (PLUS), Perkins, alternative loans.

APPLYING FOR FINANCIAL AID *Required financial aid form:* FAFSA.

CONTACT Ms. Cynthia Anderson, Director of Financial Aid, Johnson C. Smith University, 100 Beatties Ford Road, Charlotte, NC 28216, 704-378-1035 or toll-free 800-782-7303. *Fax:* 704-378-1292.

JOHNSON STATE COLLEGE
Johnson, VT

CONTACT Ms. Kimberly Goodell, Financial Aid Officer, Johnson State College, 337 College Hill, Johnson, VT 05656-9405, 802-635-2356 or toll-free 800-635-2356. *Fax:* 802-635-1463. *E-mail:* goodellk@badger.jsc.vsc.edu.

JOHN WESLEY COLLEGE
High Point, NC

ABOUT THE INSTITUTION Independent interdenominational, coed. Awards: associate and bachelor's degrees. 10 undergraduate majors. Total enrollment: 130. Undergraduates: 130. Freshmen: 9.

GIFT AID (NEED-BASED) *Scholarships, grants, and awards:* Federal Pell, FSEOG, private, college/university gift aid from institutional funds.

GIFT AID (NON-NEED-BASED) *Scholarships, grants, and awards by category:* Academic Interests/Achievement: education, general academic interests/achievements, religion/biblical studies. Special Achievements/Activities: religious

involvement. *Special Characteristics:* children of faculty/staff, general special characteristics, married students, spouses of current students.
LOANS *Programs:* FFEL (Subsidized and Unsubsidized Stafford, PLUS).
APPLYING FOR FINANCIAL AID *Required financial aid forms:* FAFSA, institution's own form.
CONTACT Mrs. Shirley Carter, Director of Financial Aid, John Wesley College, 2314 North Centennial Street, High Point, NC 27265-3197, 336-889-2262. *Fax:* 336-889-2261. *E-mail:* scarter@johnwesley.edu.

JONES COLLEGE
Jacksonville, FL

CONTACT Mrs. Becky Davis, Director of Financial Assistance, Jones College, 5353 Arlington Expressway, Jacksonville, FL 32211-5540, 904-743-1122. *Fax:* 904-743-4446.

JONES COLLEGE
Miami, FL

CONTACT Financial Aid Office, Jones College, 11430 North Kendall Drive, Suite 200, Miami, FL 33176, 305-275-9996.

JONES INTERNATIONAL UNIVERSITY
Centennial, CO

ABOUT THE INSTITUTION Proprietary, coed. Awards: bachelor's and master's degrees (offers only online degree programs). 5 undergraduate majors. Total enrollment: 1,411. Undergraduates: 255.
GIFT AID (NEED-BASED) *Scholarships, grants, and awards:* Federal Pell, private, Sallie Mae CASHE Scholarships.
LOANS *Programs:* Federal Direct (Subsidized and Unsubsidized Stafford, PLUS), Sallie Mae Loans, PLATO Loans, alternative loans.
APPLYING FOR FINANCIAL AID *Required financial aid forms:* FAFSA, noncustodial (divorced/separated) parent's statement, Master Promissory Note.
CONTACT Steve Bidwell, Director of Financial And Accounting, Jones International University, 9697 East Mineral Avenue, Englewood, CO 80112, 303-784-8284 or toll-free 800-811-5663. *Fax:* 303-784-8524. *E-mail:* marketing@jonesknowledge.com.

JUDSON COLLEGE
Marion, AL

Tuition & fees: $9900	Average undergraduate aid package: $10,963

ABOUT THE INSTITUTION Independent Baptist, women only. Awards: bachelor's degrees. 23 undergraduate majors. Total enrollment: 331. Undergraduates: 331. Freshmen: 79. Both federal and institutional methodology are used as a basis for awarding need-based institutional aid.
UNDERGRADUATE EXPENSES for 2006–07 *Application fee:* $30. *Comprehensive fee:* $17,090 includes full-time tuition ($9900) and room and board ($7190). *Part-time tuition:* $322 per semester hour.
FRESHMAN FINANCIAL AID (Fall 2005, est.) 79 applied for aid; of those 84% were deemed to have need. 100% of freshmen with need received aid; of those 15% had need fully met. *Average percent of need met:* 77% (excluding resources awarded to replace EFC). *Average financial aid package:* $11,477 (excluding resources awarded to replace EFC). 16% of all full-time freshmen had no need and received non-need-based gift aid.
UNDERGRADUATE FINANCIAL AID (Fall 2005, est.) 191 applied for aid; of those 97% were deemed to have need. 100% of undergraduates with need received aid; of those 22% had need fully met. *Average percent of need met:* 81% (excluding resources awarded to replace EFC). *Average financial aid package:* $10,963 (excluding resources awarded to replace EFC). 14% of all full-time undergraduates had no need and received non-need-based gift aid.
GIFT AID (NEED-BASED) *Total amount:* $1,173,422 (26% federal, 5% state, 63% institutional, 6% external sources). *Receiving aid:* Freshmen: 84% (66); All full-time undergraduates: 77% (184). *Average award:* Freshmen: $7376; Undergraduates: $6668. *Scholarships, grants, and awards:* Federal Pell, FSEOG, state, private, college/university gift aid from institutional funds.

GIFT AID (NON-NEED-BASED) *Total amount:* $224,720 (3% state, 89% institutional, 8% external sources). *Receiving aid:* Freshmen: 8% (6); Undergraduates: 5% (13). *Average Award:* Freshmen: $5903; Undergraduates: $4971. *Scholarships, grants, and awards by category:* Academic Interests/Achievement: 14 awards ($52,000 total): general academic interests/achievements. Creative Arts/Performance: 22 awards ($18,150 total): art/fine arts, music. Special Achievements/Activities: 6 awards ($3500 total): general special achievements/activities, junior miss. *Special Characteristics:* 5 awards ($50,000 total): children of educators, children of faculty/staff, relatives of clergy, religious affiliation. *ROTC:* Army cooperative.
LOANS *Student loans:* $822,464 (67% need-based, 33% non-need-based). 77% of past graduating class borrowed through all loan programs. *Average indebtedness per student:* $15,690. *Average need-based loan:* Freshmen: $2611; Undergraduates: $3582. *Parent loans:* $198,876 (94% need-based, 6% non-need-based). *Programs:* FFEL (Subsidized and Unsubsidized Stafford, PLUS), Perkins, college/university.
WORK-STUDY *Federal work-study:* Total amount: $60,191; 50 jobs averaging $1204. *State or other work-study/employment:* Total amount: $104,798 (94% need-based, 6% non-need-based). 79 part-time jobs averaging $1124.
ATHLETIC AWARDS *Total amount:* $112,000 (97% need-based, 3% non-need-based).
APPLYING FOR FINANCIAL AID *Required financial aid forms:* FAFSA, institution's own form, state aid form. *Financial aid deadline (priority):* 3/1. *Notification date:* Continuous beginning 3/15. Students must reply within 2 weeks of notification.
CONTACT Mrs. Doris A. Wilson, Director of Financial Aid, Judson College, PO Box 120, Marion, AL 36756, 334-683-5157 or toll-free 800-447-9472. *Fax:* 334-683-5282. *E-mail:* dwilson@judson.edu.

JUDSON COLLEGE
Elgin, IL

CONTACT Amy Wemken, Financial Aid Counselor, Judson College, 1151 North State Street, Elgin, IL 60123-1498, 847-695-2534 or toll-free 800-879-5376. *E-mail:* awemken@judsoncollege.edu.

THE JUILLIARD SCHOOL
New York, NY

CONTACT Mary K. Gray, Associate Dean for Admissions, The Juilliard School, 60 Lincoln Center Plaza, New York, NY 10023, 212-799-5000 Ext. 223. *Fax:* 212-769-6420.

JUNIATA COLLEGE
Huntingdon, PA

Tuition & fees: $27,540	Average undergraduate aid package: $18,539

ABOUT THE INSTITUTION Independent religious, coed. Awards: bachelor's degrees. 87 undergraduate majors. Total enrollment: 1,449. Undergraduates: 1,449. Freshmen: 390. Federal methodology is used as a basis for awarding need-based institutional aid.
UNDERGRADUATE EXPENSES for 2006–07 *Application fee:* $30. *Comprehensive fee:* $35,220 includes full-time tuition ($26,900), mandatory fees ($640), and room and board ($7680). *College room only:* $4030.
FRESHMAN FINANCIAL AID (Fall 2005, est.) 347 applied for aid; of those 89% were deemed to have need. 100% of freshmen with need received aid; of those 18% had need fully met. *Average percent of need met:* 79% (excluding resources awarded to replace EFC). *Average financial aid package:* $18,763 (excluding resources awarded to replace EFC). 19% of all full-time freshmen had no need and received non-need-based gift aid.
UNDERGRADUATE FINANCIAL AID (Fall 2005, est.) 1,219 applied for aid; of those 90% were deemed to have need. 100% of undergraduates with need received aid; of those 34% had need fully met. *Average percent of need met:* 77% (excluding resources awarded to replace EFC). *Average financial aid package:* $18,539 (excluding resources awarded to replace EFC). 23% of all full-time undergraduates had no need and received non-need-based gift aid.
GIFT AID (NEED-BASED) *Total amount:* $5,094,328 (5% federal, 10% state, 81% institutional, 4% external sources). *Receiving aid:* Freshmen: 78% (304); All full-time undergraduates: 72% (1,049). *Average award:* Freshmen: $15,668;

Juniata College

Undergraduates: $14,789. **Scholarships, grants, and awards:** Federal Pell, FSEOG, state, private, college/university gift aid from institutional funds.
GIFT AID (NON-NEED-BASED) Total amount: $907,239 (99% institutional, 1% external sources). **Receiving aid:** Freshmen: 72% (278); Undergraduates: 66% (962). **Average Award:** Freshmen: $12,358; Undergraduates: $12,311. **Scholarships, grants, and awards by category:** Academic Interests/Achievement: business, general academic interests/achievements, premedicine. Creative Arts/Performance: general creative arts/performance. Special Achievements/Activities: community service, leadership. Special Characteristics: adult students, children and siblings of alumni, children of faculty/staff, ethnic background, international students, religious affiliation.
LOANS Student loans: $1,724,693 (90% need-based, 10% non-need-based). 77% of past graduating class borrowed through all loan programs. *Average indebtedness per student:* $22,131. **Average need-based loan:** Freshmen: $3448; Undergraduates: $3981. **Parent loans:** $1,117,675 (96% need-based, 4% non-need-based). **Programs:** FFEL (Subsidized and Unsubsidized Stafford, PLUS), Perkins.
WORK-STUDY *Federal work-study:* Total amount: $250,825; 752 jobs averaging $629. **State or other work-study/employment:** Total amount: $172,200 (100% non-need-based). Part-time jobs available.
APPLYING FOR FINANCIAL AID *Required financial aid form:* FAFSA. **Financial aid deadline:** 3/1 (priority: 3/1). **Notification date:** Continuous beginning 2/1. Students must reply by 5/1 or within 2 weeks of notification.
CONTACT Mr. Randall S. Rennell, Director of Student Financial Planning, Juniata College, 1700 Moore Street, Huntingdon, PA 16652-2119, 814-641-3142 or toll-free 877-JUNIATA. *Fax:* 814-641-5311. *E-mail:* rennelr@juniata.edu.

KALAMAZOO COLLEGE
Kalamazoo, MI

ABOUT THE INSTITUTION Independent religious, coed. Awards: bachelor's degrees. 24 undergraduate majors. Total enrollment: 1,263. Undergraduates: 1,263. Freshmen: 367.
GIFT AID (NEED-BASED) Scholarships, grants, and awards: Federal Pell, FSEOG, state, private, college/university gift aid from institutional funds.
GIFT AID (NON-NEED-BASED) Scholarships, grants, and awards by category: Academic Interests/Achievement: biological sciences, English, foreign languages, general academic interests/achievements, mathematics, physical sciences, social sciences. Creative Arts/Performance: art/fine arts, cinema/film/broadcasting, music, theater/drama. Special Achievements/Activities: general special achievements/activities. Special Characteristics: children of faculty/staff.
LOANS Programs: Federal Direct (Subsidized and Unsubsidized Stafford, PLUS), Perkins, state.
WORK-STUDY *Federal work-study:* Total amount: $332,000; 440 jobs averaging $1500. **State or other work-study/employment:** Total amount: $10,000 (100% need-based). 12 part-time jobs averaging $834.
APPLYING FOR FINANCIAL AID *Required financial aid forms:* FAFSA, institution's own form.
CONTACT Judy Clark, Assistant Director of Financial Aid, Kalamazoo College, 1200 Academy Street, Kalamazoo, MI 49006-3295, 269-337-7192 or toll-free 800-253-3602. *Fax:* 269-337-7390.

KANSAS CITY ART INSTITUTE
Kansas City, MO

Tuition & fees: $22,392	Average undergraduate aid package: $15,004

ABOUT THE INSTITUTION Independent, coed. Awards: bachelor's degrees. 12 undergraduate majors. Total enrollment: 588. Undergraduates: 588. Freshmen: 86. Federal methodology is used as a basis for awarding need-based institutional aid.
UNDERGRADUATE EXPENSES for 2005–06 *Application fee:* $35. **Comprehensive fee:** $29,542 includes full-time tuition ($21,446), mandatory fees ($946), and room and board ($7150). Full-time tuition and fees vary according to program. Room and board charges vary according to board plan and housing facility. **Part-time tuition:** $850 per credit hour. **Part-time fees:** $46 per credit hour. Part-time tuition and fees vary according to program.
FRESHMAN FINANCIAL AID (Fall 2005, est.) 104 applied for aid; of those 88% were deemed to have need. 99% of freshmen with need received aid; of those 13% had need fully met. *Average percent of need met:* 65% (excluding resources awarded to replace EFC). *Average financial aid package:* $15,912 (excluding resources awarded to replace EFC). 22% of all full-time freshmen had no need and received non-need-based gift aid.
UNDERGRADUATE FINANCIAL AID (Fall 2005, est.) 539 applied for aid; of those 90% were deemed to have need. 100% of undergraduates with need received aid; of those 10% had need fully met. *Average percent of need met:* 59% (excluding resources awarded to replace EFC). *Average financial aid package:* $15,004 (excluding resources awarded to replace EFC). 20% of all full-time undergraduates had no need and received non-need-based gift aid.
GIFT AID (NEED-BASED) Total amount: $5,020,055 (14% federal, 4% state, 77% institutional, 5% external sources). **Receiving aid:** Freshmen: 77% (90); All full-time undergraduates: 79% (481). **Average award:** Freshmen: $12,244; Undergraduates: $10,366. **Scholarships, grants, and awards:** Federal Pell, FSEOG, state, private, college/university gift aid from institutional funds.
GIFT AID (NON-NEED-BASED) Total amount: $1,098,517 (1% state, 86% institutional, 13% external sources). **Receiving aid:** Freshmen: 9% (11); Undergraduates: 6% (36). **Average Award:** Freshmen: $10,860; Undergraduates: $11,786. **Scholarships, grants, and awards by category:** Creative Arts/Performance: 443 awards ($3,254,128 total): art/fine arts. **Tuition waivers:** Full or partial for employees or children of employees.
LOANS Student loans: $4,722,105 (86% need-based, 14% non-need-based). 86% of past graduating class borrowed through all loan programs. *Average indebtedness per student:* $30,000. **Average need-based loan:** Freshmen: $4011; Undergraduates: $4830. **Parent loans:** $2,201,666 (52% need-based, 48% non-need-based). **Programs:** FFEL (Subsidized and Unsubsidized Stafford, PLUS), Perkins, alternative loans.
WORK-STUDY *Federal work-study:* Total amount: $123,614; 124 jobs averaging $997. **State or other work-study/employment:** Total amount: $30,000 (3% need-based, 97% non-need-based). 30 part-time jobs averaging $1000.
APPLYING FOR FINANCIAL AID *Required financial aid form:* FAFSA. **Financial aid deadline (priority):** 3/1. **Notification date:** Continuous beginning 3/15. Students must reply within 2 weeks of notification.
CONTACT Ms. Christal D. Williams, Director of Financial Aid, Kansas City Art Institute, 4415 Warwick Boulevard, Kansas City, MO 64111-1874, 816-802-3448 or toll-free 800-522-5224. *Fax:* 816-802-3453. *E-mail:* cdwilliams@kcai.edu.

KANSAS CITY COLLEGE
Kansas City, MO

Tuition & fees: N/R	Average undergraduate aid package: $10,000

ABOUT THE INSTITUTION Proprietary, coed. Awards: associate and bachelor's degrees. 2 undergraduate majors. Total enrollment: 123. Undergraduates: 123. Both federal and institutional methodology are used as a basis for awarding need-based institutional aid.
FRESHMAN FINANCIAL AID (Fall 2005, est.) 65 applied for aid; of those 89% were deemed to have need. 100% of freshmen with need received aid. *Average percent of need met:* 98% (excluding resources awarded to replace EFC). *Average financial aid package:* $10,000 (excluding resources awarded to replace EFC).
UNDERGRADUATE FINANCIAL AID (Fall 2005, est.) 131 applied for aid; of those 89% were deemed to have need. 88% of undergraduates with need received aid. *Average percent of need met:* 98% (excluding resources awarded to replace EFC). *Average financial aid package:* $10,000 (excluding resources awarded to replace EFC).
GIFT AID (NEED-BASED) Total amount: $179,676 (100% federal). **Receiving aid:** Freshmen: 89% (58); All full-time undergraduates: 79% (103). **Average award:** Freshmen: $3000; Undergraduates: $3000. **Scholarships, grants, and awards:** Federal Pell.
GIFT AID (NON-NEED-BASED) Receiving aid: Undergraduates: 2% (3).
LOANS Student loans: $541,263 (100% need-based). 30% of past graduating class borrowed through all loan programs. *Average indebtedness per student:* $20,000. **Average need-based loan:** Freshmen: $3200; Undergraduates: $3200. **Parent loans:** $20,618 (100% need-based). **Programs:** FFEL (Subsidized and Unsubsidized Stafford, PLUS).
APPLYING FOR FINANCIAL AID *Required financial aid forms:* FAFSA, institution's own form, federal income tax form(s). **Financial aid deadline:** Continuous. **Notification date:** Continuous.

CONTACT Cori Deaton, Financial Aid Office, Kansas City College, 800 East 101st Terrace, Suite 100, Kansas City, MO 64131, 816-444-2232 or toll-free 877-582-3963 (out-of-state).

KANSAS STATE UNIVERSITY
Manhattan, KS

Tuition & fees (KS res): $5124   **Average undergraduate aid package: $6341**

ABOUT THE INSTITUTION State-supported, coed. Awards: associate, bachelor's, master's, doctoral, and first professional degrees. 78 undergraduate majors. Total enrollment: 23,182. Undergraduates: 18,838. Freshmen: 3,309. Federal methodology is used as a basis for awarding need-based institutional aid.

UNDERGRADUATE EXPENSES for 2005–06 *Application fee:* $30. *Tuition, state resident:* full-time $4560; part-time $152 per credit hour. *Tuition, nonresident:* full-time $13,890; part-time $463 per credit hour. *College room and board:* $5772. Room and board charges vary according to board plan. *Payment plans:* Installment, deferred payment.

FRESHMAN FINANCIAL AID (Fall 2004) 2404 applied for aid; of those 70% were deemed to have need. 99% of freshmen with need received aid; of those 12% had need fully met. *Average percent of need met:* 63% (excluding resources awarded to replace EFC). *Average financial aid package:* $6003 (excluding resources awarded to replace EFC). 12% of all full-time freshmen had no need and received non-need-based gift aid.

UNDERGRADUATE FINANCIAL AID (Fall 2004) 11,908 applied for aid; of those 78% were deemed to have need. 99% of undergraduates with need received aid; of those 13% had need fully met. *Average percent of need met:* 65% (excluding resources awarded to replace EFC). *Average financial aid package:* $6341 (excluding resources awarded to replace EFC). 7% of all full-time undergraduates had no need and received non-need-based gift aid.

GIFT AID (NEED-BASED) *Total amount:* $26,775,284 (48% federal, 2% state, 40% institutional, 10% external sources). *Receiving aid:* Freshmen: 33% (1,075); All full-time undergraduates: 34% (5,717). *Average award:* Freshmen: $3034; Undergraduates: $3092. *Scholarships, grants, and awards:* Federal Pell, FSEOG, state, private, college/university gift aid from institutional funds.

GIFT AID (NON-NEED-BASED) *Total amount:* $3,047,219 (1% state, 68% institutional, 31% external sources). *Receiving aid:* Freshmen: 30% (981); Undergraduates: 18% (3,063). *Average Award:* Freshmen: $2297; Undergraduates: $1786. *Scholarships, grants, and awards by category:* Academic Interests/Achievement: agriculture, architecture, biological sciences, business, communication, computer science, education, engineering/technologies, English, foreign languages, general academic interests/achievements, health fields, home economics, humanities, mathematics, military science, physical sciences, premedicine, social sciences. *Creative Arts/Performance:* art/fine arts, debating, music, theater/drama. *Special Achievements/Activities:* general special achievements/activities, leadership. *Special Characteristics:* adult students, children and siblings of alumni, general special characteristics. *Tuition waivers:* Full or partial for employees or children of employees. *ROTC:* Army, Air Force.

LOANS *Student loans:* $61,429,176 (74% need-based, 26% non-need-based). 55% of past graduating class borrowed through all loan programs. *Average indebtedness per student:* $19,000. *Average need-based loan:* Freshmen: $2862; Undergraduates: $4015. *Parent loans:* $24,494,465 (72% need-based, 28% non-need-based). *Programs:* FFEL (Subsidized and Unsubsidized Stafford, PLUS), Perkins, college/university, Alternative student loans.

WORK-STUDY *Federal work-study:* Total amount: $898,742; 663 jobs averaging $1700. *State or other work-study/employment:* Total amount: $180,347 (65% need-based, 35% non-need-based).

ATHLETIC AWARDS *Total amount:* $4,000,622 (84% need-based, 16% non-need-based).

APPLYING FOR FINANCIAL AID *Required financial aid form:* FAFSA. *Financial aid deadline (priority):* 3/1. *Notification date:* Continuous beginning 3/15. Students must reply within 2 weeks of notification.

CONTACT Mr. Larry Moeder, Director of Admissions and Student Financial Assistance, Kansas State University, 104 Fairchild Hall, Manhattan, KS 66506, 785-532-6420 or toll-free 800-432-8270 (in-state). *E-mail:* larrym@ksu.edu.

KANSAS WESLEYAN UNIVERSITY
Salina, KS

CONTACT Mrs. Glenna Alexander, Director of Financial Assistance, Kansas Wesleyan University, 100 East Claflin, Salina, KS 67401-6196, 785-827-5541 Ext. 1130 or toll-free 800-874-1154 Ext. 1285. *Fax:* 785-827-0927. *E-mail:* kglennaa@acck.edu.

KEAN UNIVERSITY
Union, NJ

Tuition & fees (NJ res): $7507   **Average undergraduate aid package: $7929**

ABOUT THE INSTITUTION State-supported, coed. Awards: bachelor's and master's degrees and post-bachelor's and post-master's certificates. 48 undergraduate majors. Total enrollment: 12,958. Undergraduates: 10,035. Freshmen: 1,432. Federal methodology is used as a basis for awarding need-based institutional aid.

UNDERGRADUATE EXPENSES for 2005–06 *Application fee:* $50. *Tuition, state resident:* full-time $4898; part-time $163.25 per credit. *Tuition, nonresident:* full-time $7530; part-time $251 per credit. *Required fees:* full-time $2609; $87.70 per credit. Part-time tuition and fees vary according to course load. *College room and board:* $8374; *room only:* $5892. Room and board charges vary according to board plan and housing facility. *Payment plans:* Installment, deferred payment.

FRESHMAN FINANCIAL AID (Fall 2005, est.) 1167 applied for aid; of those 72% were deemed to have need. 96% of freshmen with need received aid; of those 9% had need fully met. *Average percent of need met:* 54% (excluding resources awarded to replace EFC). *Average financial aid package:* $7427 (excluding resources awarded to replace EFC). 4% of all full-time freshmen had no need and received non-need-based gift aid.

UNDERGRADUATE FINANCIAL AID (Fall 2005, est.) 5,817 applied for aid; of those 72% were deemed to have need. 94% of undergraduates with need received aid; of those 17% had need fully met. *Average percent of need met:* 54% (excluding resources awarded to replace EFC). *Average financial aid package:* $7929 (excluding resources awarded to replace EFC). 2% of all full-time undergraduates had no need and received non-need-based gift aid.

GIFT AID (NEED-BASED) *Total amount:* $16,959,112 (48% federal, 45% state, 7% institutional). *Receiving aid:* Freshmen: 57% (795); All full-time undergraduates: 52% (3,891). *Average award:* Freshmen: $6091; Undergraduates: $5705. *Scholarships, grants, and awards:* Federal Pell, FSEOG, state, private, college/university gift aid from institutional funds.

GIFT AID (NON-NEED-BASED) *Total amount:* $42,000 (100% state). *Average Award:* Freshmen: $2564; Undergraduates: $2184. *Scholarships, grants, and awards by category:* Academic Interests/Achievement: 507 awards ($959,358 total): business, education, general academic interests/achievements, health fields, humanities. *Creative Arts/Performance:* 13 awards ($35,785 total): applied art and design, art/fine arts, music, theater/drama. *Special Achievements/Activities:* community service, leadership. *Special Characteristics:* 143 awards ($257,548 total): general special characteristics. *Tuition waivers:* Full or partial for employees or children of employees, senior citizens. *ROTC:* Army cooperative, Air Force cooperative.

LOANS *Student loans:* $30,150,015 (50% need-based, 50% non-need-based). 40% of past graduating class borrowed through all loan programs. *Average indebtedness per student:* $13,128. *Average need-based loan:* Freshmen: $2688; Undergraduates: $3848. *Parent loans:* $3,424,936 (100% non-need-based). *Programs:* Federal Direct (Subsidized and Unsubsidized Stafford, PLUS), Perkins.

WORK-STUDY *Federal work-study:* Total amount: $9600; 459 jobs averaging $1198.

APPLYING FOR FINANCIAL AID *Required financial aid form:* FAFSA. *Financial aid deadline (priority):* 3/15. *Notification date:* Continuous beginning 3/15. Students must reply by 5/1.

CONTACT Sandra Bembry, Director of Financial Aid, Kean University, 1000 Morris Avenue, Union, NJ 07083, 908-737-3190. *Fax:* 908-737-3200.

KEENE STATE COLLEGE
Keene, NH

Tuition & fees (NH res): $7818   **Average undergraduate aid package: $7382**

Keene State College

ABOUT THE INSTITUTION State-supported, coed. Awards: bachelor's and master's degrees and post-bachelor's and post-master's certificates. 87 undergraduate majors. Total enrollment: 4,846. Undergraduates: 4,729. Freshmen: 1,008. Federal methodology is used as a basis for awarding need-based institutional aid.

UNDERGRADUATE EXPENSES for 2005–06 *Application fee:* $35. *Tuition, state resident:* full-time $5780; part-time $241 per credit. *Tuition, nonresident:* full-time $13,050; part-time $544 per credit. *Required fees:* full-time $2038; $77 per credit. Part-time tuition and fees vary according to course load and degree level. *College room and board:* $7027; *room only:* $4700. Room and board charges vary according to board plan and housing facility. *Payment plan:* Installment.

FRESHMAN FINANCIAL AID (Fall 2004) 906 applied for aid; of those 71% were deemed to have need. 97% of freshmen with need received aid; of those 19% had need fully met. *Average percent of need met:* 70% (excluding resources awarded to replace EFC). *Average financial aid package:* $7385 (excluding resources awarded to replace EFC). 8% of all full-time freshmen had no need and received non-need-based gift aid.

UNDERGRADUATE FINANCIAL AID (Fall 2004) 3,207 applied for aid; of those 74% were deemed to have need. 98% of undergraduates with need received aid; of those 25% had need fully met. *Average percent of need met:* 73% (excluding resources awarded to replace EFC). *Average financial aid package:* $7382 (excluding resources awarded to replace EFC). 8% of all full-time undergraduates had no need and received non-need-based gift aid.

GIFT AID (NEED-BASED) *Total amount:* $6,301,519 (39% federal, 7% state, 44% institutional, 10% external sources). *Receiving aid:* Freshmen: 40% (436); All full-time undergraduates: 35% (1,537). *Average award:* Freshmen: $4458; Undergraduates: $4003. *Scholarships, grants, and awards:* Federal Pell, FSEOG, state, private, college/university gift aid from institutional funds.

GIFT AID (NON-NEED-BASED) *Total amount:* $2,551,997 (79% institutional, 21% external sources). *Receiving aid:* Freshmen: 14% (154); Undergraduates: 12% (533). *Average Award:* Freshmen: $2187; Undergraduates: $2471. *Scholarships, grants, and awards by category: Academic Interests/Achievement:* 543 awards ($1,117,001 total): general academic interests/achievements. *Creative Arts/Performance:* 22 awards ($64,000 total): applied art and design, art/fine arts, cinema/film/broadcasting, dance, general creative arts/performance, music, theater/drama. *Special Achievements/Activities:* 13 awards ($37,600 total): general special achievements/activities. *Tuition waivers:* Full or partial for employees or children of employees. *ROTC:* Air Force cooperative.

LOANS *Student loans:* $18,238,782 (44% need-based, 56% non-need-based). 74% of past graduating class borrowed through all loan programs. *Average indebtedness per student:* $20,065. *Average need-based loan:* Freshmen: $2934; Undergraduates: $3638. *Parent loans:* $5,791,973 (100% non-need-based). *Programs:* FFEL (Subsidized and Unsubsidized Stafford, PLUS), Perkins, college/university.

WORK-STUDY *Federal work-study:* Total amount: $1,846,645; 612 jobs averaging $816. *State or other work-study/employment:* Total amount: $510,905 (100% non-need-based). 552 part-time jobs averaging $9216.

APPLYING FOR FINANCIAL AID *Required financial aid form:* FAFSA. *Financial aid deadline:* 3/1. *Notification date:* Continuous. Students must reply within 4 weeks of notification.

CONTACT Ms. Patricia Blodgett, Director of Student Financial Management, Keene State College, 229 Main Street, Keene, NH 03435-2606, 603-358-2280 or toll-free 800-572-1909. *Fax:* 603-358-2794. *E-mail:* pblodget@keene.edu.

KEHILATH YAKOV RABBINICAL SEMINARY
Brooklyn, NY

CONTACT Financial Aid Office, Kehilath Yakov Rabbinical Seminary, 206 Wilson Street, Brooklyn, NY 11211-7207, 718-963-1212.

KENDALL COLLEGE
Chicago, IL

CONTACT Cynthia Sabo, Director of Financial Aid, Kendall College, 2408 Orrington Avenue, Evanston, IL 60201, 847-448-2349 or toll-free 866-667-3344 (in-state), 877-588-8860 (out-of-state). *Fax:* 847-448-2403.

KENNESAW STATE UNIVERSITY
Kennesaw, GA

Tuition & fees (GA res): $3044   **Average undergraduate aid package:** $9524

ABOUT THE INSTITUTION State-supported, coed. Awards: bachelor's and master's degrees. 44 undergraduate majors. Total enrollment: 18,556. Undergraduates: 16,739. Freshmen: 2,114. Federal methodology is used as a basis for awarding need-based institutional aid.

UNDERGRADUATE EXPENSES for 2005–06 *Application fee:* $40. *Tuition, state resident:* full-time $2438; part-time $102 per credit hour. *Tuition, nonresident:* full-time $9754; part-time $407 per credit hour. *Required fees:* full-time $606; $303 per term part-time. Part-time tuition and fees vary according to course load. *College room and board: room only:* $5880. Room and board charges vary according to housing facility. *Payment plan:* Deferred payment.

FRESHMAN FINANCIAL AID (Fall 2005, est.) 1836 applied for aid; of those 39% were deemed to have need. 100% of freshmen with need received aid; of those 15% had need fully met. *Average percent of need met:* 19% (excluding resources awarded to replace EFC). *Average financial aid package:* $7975 (excluding resources awarded to replace EFC). 51% of all full-time freshmen had no need and received non-need-based gift aid.

UNDERGRADUATE FINANCIAL AID (Fall 2005, est.) 8,568 applied for aid; of those 48% were deemed to have need. 100% of undergraduates with need received aid; of those 16% had need fully met. *Average percent of need met:* 22% (excluding resources awarded to replace EFC). *Average financial aid package:* $9524 (excluding resources awarded to replace EFC). 30% of all full-time undergraduates had no need and received non-need-based gift aid.

GIFT AID (NEED-BASED) *Total amount:* $10,744,792 (99% federal, 1% institutional). *Receiving aid:* Freshmen: 14% (294); All full-time undergraduates: 19% (2,045). *Average award:* Freshmen: $2698; Undergraduates: $2690. *Scholarships, grants, and awards:* Federal Pell, FSEOG, state, private, college/university gift aid from institutional funds.

GIFT AID (NON-NEED-BASED) *Total amount:* $22,922,919 (98% state, 1% institutional, 1% external sources). *Receiving aid:* Freshmen: 30% (631); Undergraduates: 16% (1,705). *Average Award:* Freshmen: $1636; Undergraduates:* $1672. *Scholarships, grants, and awards by category: Academic Interests/Achievement:* 110 awards ($217,483 total): biological sciences, business, communication, computer science, education, English, foreign languages, general academic interests/achievements, health fields, humanities, international studies, mathematics, physical sciences, premedicine, social sciences. *Creative Arts/Performance:* 23 awards ($18,000 total): music, performing arts, theater/drama. *Special Achievements/Activities:* 5 awards ($6001 total): community service, leadership, memberships. *Special Characteristics:* 16 awards ($31,000 total): children and siblings of alumni, children of union members/company employees, children of workers in trades, ethnic background, general special characteristics, handicapped students, international students, local/state students, members of minority groups, religious affiliation, veterans' children. *Tuition waivers:* Full or partial for senior citizens. *ROTC:* Army, Air Force.

LOANS *Student loans:* $23,873,929 (93% need-based, 7% non-need-based). 45% of past graduating class borrowed through all loan programs. *Average indebtedness per student:* $15,346. *Average need-based loan:* Freshmen: $2366; Undergraduates: $3402. *Parent loans:* $604,327 (100% non-need-based). *Programs:* FFEL (Subsidized and Unsubsidized Stafford, PLUS), Perkins, Federal Nursing, state.

WORK-STUDY *Federal work-study:* Total amount: $378,558; 325 jobs averaging $1112.

ATHLETIC AWARDS *Total amount:* $1,384,652 (100% non-need-based).

APPLYING FOR FINANCIAL AID *Required financial aid forms:* FAFSA, state aid form. *Financial aid deadline (priority):* 4/1. *Notification date:* Continuous beginning 5/15.

CONTACT Mr. Michael C. Roberts, Director of Student Financial Aid, Kennesaw State University, 1000 Chastain Road, Kennesaw, GA 30144-5591, 770-499-3240. *Fax:* 770-423-6708. *E-mail:* finaid@kennesaw.edu.

KENT STATE UNIVERSITY
Kent, OH

Tuition & fees (OH res): $7954   **Average undergraduate aid package:** $7040

ABOUT THE INSTITUTION State-supported, coed. Awards: associate, bachelor's, master's, and doctoral degrees and post-bachelor's and post-master's certificates. 125 undergraduate majors. Total enrollment: 23,622. Undergraduates: 18,745. Freshmen: 3,814. Federal methodology is used as a basis for awarding need-based institutional aid.
UNDERGRADUATE EXPENSES for 2005–06 *Application fee:* $30. **Tuition, state resident:** full-time $7954; part-time $363 per credit hour. **Tuition, nonresident:** full-time $15,386; part-time $701 per credit hour. Full-time tuition and fees vary according to course level, course load, degree level, location, program, reciprocity agreements, and student level. Part-time tuition and fees vary according to course level, course load, degree level, location, program, reciprocity agreements, and student level. *College room and board:* $6640; *room only:* $4040. Room and board charges vary according to board plan and housing facility. *Payment plans:* Tuition prepayment, installment, deferred payment.
FRESHMAN FINANCIAL AID (Fall 2005, est.) 3002 applied for aid; of those 79% were deemed to have need. 100% of freshmen with need received aid; of those 12% had need fully met. *Average percent of need met:* 55% (excluding resources awarded to replace EFC). *Average financial aid package:* $6958 (excluding resources awarded to replace EFC). 9% of all full-time freshmen had no need and received non-need-based gift aid.
UNDERGRADUATE FINANCIAL AID (Fall 2005, est.) 11,107 applied for aid; of those 84% were deemed to have need. 100% of undergraduates with need received aid; of those 13% had need fully met. *Average percent of need met:* 56% (excluding resources awarded to replace EFC). *Average financial aid package:* $7040 (excluding resources awarded to replace EFC). 7% of all full-time undergraduates had no need and received non-need-based gift aid.
GIFT AID (NEED-BASED) *Total amount:* $31,753,364 (46% federal, 17% state, 32% institutional, 5% external sources). *Receiving aid:* Freshmen: 48% (1,815); All full-time undergraduates: 35% (6,390). *Average award:* Freshmen: $4868; Undergraduates: $4670. *Scholarships, grants, and awards:* Federal Pell, FSEOG, state, private, college/university gift aid from institutional funds.
GIFT AID (NON-NEED-BASED) *Total amount:* $7,192,648 (2% federal, 15% state, 72% institutional, 11% external sources). *Receiving aid:* Freshmen: 7% (282); Undergraduates: 3% (618). *Average Award:* Freshmen: $4178; Undergraduates: $3761. *Scholarships, grants, and awards by category:* Academic Interests/Achievement: architecture, area/ethnic studies, biological sciences, business, communication, computer science, education, English, general academic interests/achievements, health fields, international studies, library science, mathematics, military science, physical sciences, social sciences. Creative Arts/Performance: art/fine arts, journalism/publications, music, theater/drama. Special Achievements/Activities: community service, general special achievements/activities, leadership. Special Characteristics: adult students, children and siblings of alumni, children of faculty/staff, children of union members/company employees, children with a deceased or disabled parent, ethnic background, handicapped students, international students, members of minority groups, out-of-state students. *Tuition waivers:* Full or partial for employees or children of employees. *ROTC:* Army, Air Force.
LOANS *Student loans:* $68,821,165 (84% need-based, 16% non-need-based). 69% of past graduating class borrowed through all loan programs. *Average indebtedness per student:* $21,066. *Average need-based loan:* Freshmen: $3233; Undergraduates: $3820. *Parent loans:* $52,211,695 (28% need-based, 72% non-need-based). *Programs:* Federal Direct (Subsidized and Unsubsidized Stafford, PLUS), Perkins, Federal Nursing, state, college/university, alternative loans.
WORK-STUDY *Federal work-study:* Total amount: $559,830; 1,042 jobs averaging $2316.
ATHLETIC AWARDS Total amount: $4,062,778 (53% need-based, 47% non-need-based).
APPLYING FOR FINANCIAL AID *Required financial aid forms:* FAFSA, University Scholarship Application. *Financial aid deadline (priority):* 3/1. *Notification date:* 3/15. Students must reply within 2 weeks of notification.
CONTACT Constance Dubick, Associate Director of Student Financial Aid, Kent State University, 103 Michael Schwartz Center, PO Box 5190, Kent, OH 44242-0001, 330-672-2972 or toll-free 800-988-KENT. Fax: 330-672-4014. E-mail: cdubick@kent.edu.

KENTUCKY CHRISTIAN UNIVERSITY
Grayson, KY

Tuition & fees: N/R	Average undergraduate aid package: $11,728

ABOUT THE INSTITUTION Independent religious, coed. Awards: associate, bachelor's, and master's degrees. 13 undergraduate majors. Total enrollment: 559. Undergraduates: 544. Freshmen: 127. Federal methodology is used as a basis for awarding need-based institutional aid.
FRESHMAN FINANCIAL AID (Fall 2005, est.) 125 applied for aid; of those 86% were deemed to have need. 100% of freshmen with need received aid; of those 13% had need fully met. *Average percent of need met:* 74% (excluding resources awarded to replace EFC). *Average financial aid package:* $11,098 (excluding resources awarded to replace EFC). 16% of all full-time freshmen had no need and received non-need-based gift aid.
UNDERGRADUATE FINANCIAL AID (Fall 2005, est.) 515 applied for aid; of those 88% were deemed to have need. 100% of undergraduates with need received aid; of those 21% had need fully met. *Average percent of need met:* 74% (excluding resources awarded to replace EFC). *Average financial aid package:* $11,728 (excluding resources awarded to replace EFC). 13% of all full-time undergraduates had no need and received non-need-based gift aid.
GIFT AID (NEED-BASED) *Total amount:* $1,645,876 (44% federal, 32% state, 24% institutional). *Receiving aid:* Freshmen: 67% (91); All full-time undergraduates: 62% (347). *Average award:* Freshmen: $5032; Undergraduates: $4743. *Scholarships, grants, and awards:* Federal Pell, FSEOG, state, private, college/university gift aid from institutional funds.
GIFT AID (NON-NEED-BASED) *Total amount:* $2,274,892 (8% state, 71% institutional, 21% external sources). *Receiving aid:* Freshmen: 79% (107); Undergraduates: 78% (434). *Average Award:* Freshmen: $2333; Undergraduates: $2919. *Scholarships, grants, and awards by category:* Academic Interests/Achievement: 529 awards ($1,197,174 total): business, education, general academic interests/achievements, religion/biblical studies. Creative Arts/Performance: 43 awards ($126,418 total): debating, music, performing arts, theater/drama. Special Achievements/Activities: 45 awards ($58,674 total): community service, general special achievements/activities, leadership, religious involvement. Special Characteristics: 55 awards ($241,558 total): children and siblings of alumni, children of faculty/staff, general special characteristics, international students, members of minority groups, religious affiliation. *Tuition waivers:* Full or partial for minority students, employees or children of employees.
LOANS *Student loans:* $2,634,797 (54% need-based, 46% non-need-based). 84% of past graduating class borrowed through all loan programs. *Average indebtedness per student:* $25,731. *Average need-based loan:* Freshmen: $2905; Undergraduates: $3656. *Parent loans:* $606,640 (100% non-need-based). *Programs:* FFEL (Subsidized and Unsubsidized Stafford, PLUS), Perkins.
WORK-STUDY *Federal work-study:* Total amount: $405,092; 227 jobs averaging $1785. *State or other work-study/employment:* Total amount: $92,542 (100% non-need-based). 52 part-time jobs averaging $1780.
APPLYING FOR FINANCIAL AID *Required financial aid form:* FAFSA. *Financial aid deadline (priority):* 4/1. *Notification date:* Continuous beginning 3/15. Students must reply within 2 weeks of notification.
CONTACT Mrs. Jennie M. Bender, Director of Financial Aid, Kentucky Christian University, 100 Academic Parkway, Grayson, KY 41143-2205, 606-474-3226 or toll-free 800-522-3181. Fax: 606-474-3155. E-mail: jbender@kcu.edu.

KENTUCKY MOUNTAIN BIBLE COLLEGE
Vancleve, KY

ABOUT THE INSTITUTION Independent interdenominational, coed. Awards: associate and bachelor's degrees. 5 undergraduate majors. Total enrollment: 79. Undergraduates: 79.
GIFT AID (NEED-BASED) *Scholarships, grants, and awards:* Federal Pell, FSEOG, state, private, college/university gift aid from institutional funds.
GIFT AID (NON-NEED-BASED) *Scholarships, grants, and awards by category:* Academic Interests/Achievement: general academic interests/achievements. Creative Arts/Performance: music, theater/drama. Special Characteristics: children of faculty/staff.
LOANS *Programs:* FFEL (Subsidized and Unsubsidized Stafford, PLUS), college/university.
APPLYING FOR FINANCIAL AID *Required financial aid form:* FAFSA.
CONTACT Ms. Sara Klopping, Director of Financial Aid, Kentucky Mountain Bible College, PO Box 10, Vancleve, KY 41385-0010, 800-879-KMBC Ext. 142 or toll-free 800-879-KMBC Ext. 130 (in-state), 800-879-KMBC Ext. 136 (out-of-state). Fax: 606-693-0495.

Kentucky State University

KENTUCKY STATE UNIVERSITY
Frankfort, KY

Tuition & fees (KY res): $4468 **Average undergraduate aid package:** N/A

ABOUT THE INSTITUTION State-related, coed. Awards: associate, bachelor's, and master's degrees. 31 undergraduate majors. Total enrollment: 2,386. Undergraduates: 2,228. Freshmen: 420. Federal methodology is used as a basis for awarding need-based institutional aid.

UNDERGRADUATE EXPENSES for 2005–06 *Application fee:* $22. *Tuition, state resident:* full-time $3550; part-time $148 per credit. *Tuition, nonresident:* full-time $9992; part-time $419 per credit. *Required fees:* full-time $918; $20 per credit or $49 per term part-time. Full-time tuition and fees vary according to class time, course level, course load, location, program, reciprocity agreements, and student level. Part-time tuition and fees vary according to class time, course level, course load, location, program, reciprocity agreements, and student level. *College room and board:* $5620; *room only:* $2592. Room and board charges vary according to board plan, housing facility, location, and student level. *Payment plans:* Installment, deferred payment.

FRESHMAN FINANCIAL AID (Fall 2005, est.) 277 applied for aid; of those 99% were deemed to have need. 100% of freshmen with need received aid. 39% of all full-time freshmen had no need and received non-need-based gift aid.

UNDERGRADUATE FINANCIAL AID (Fall 2005, est.) 1,470 applied for aid; of those 52% were deemed to have need. 100% of undergraduates with need received aid. 23% of all full-time undergraduates had no need and received non-need-based gift aid.

GIFT AID (NEED-BASED) *Total amount:* $4,470,783 (77% federal, 19% state, 4% institutional). *Scholarships, grants, and awards:* Federal Pell, FSEOG, state, private, college/university gift aid from institutional funds, Federal Nursing.

GIFT AID (NON-NEED-BASED) *Total amount:* $2,502,394 (78% institutional, 22% external sources). *Average Award: Freshmen:* $2673; *Undergraduates:* $3869. *Scholarships, grants, and awards by category: Academic Interests/Achievement:* 29 awards ($30,000 total): general academic interests/achievements, mathematics. *Creative Arts/Performance:* 150 awards ($529,700 total): art/fine arts, music. *Special Characteristics:* adult students, children with a deceased or disabled parent, handicapped students. *Tuition waivers:* Full or partial for employees or children of employees, senior citizens. *ROTC:* Air Force cooperative.

LOANS *Student loans:* $9,087,506 (52% need-based, 48% non-need-based). 60% of past graduating class borrowed through all loan programs. *Parent loans:* $2,302,125 (100% non-need-based). *Programs:* Federal Direct (Subsidized and Unsubsidized Stafford, PLUS), Perkins.

WORK-STUDY *Federal work-study:* Total amount: $715,502; 500 jobs available.

ATHLETIC AWARDS *Total amount:* $727,288 (100% non-need-based).

APPLYING FOR FINANCIAL AID *Required financial aid form:* FAFSA. *Financial aid deadline:* 5/31 (priority: 4/15). *Notification date:* Continuous. Students must reply within 2 weeks of notification.

CONTACT Myrna C. Bryant, Assistant Director of Financial Aid, Kentucky State University, 400 East Main Street, Frankfort, KY 40601, 502-597-6025 or toll-free 800-633-9415 (in-state), 800-325-1716 (out-of-state). *E-mail:* myrna.bryant@kysu.edu.

KENTUCKY WESLEYAN COLLEGE
Owensboro, KY

Tuition & fees: $13,600 **Average undergraduate aid package:** $12,214

ABOUT THE INSTITUTION Independent Methodist, coed. Awards: bachelor's degrees. 41 undergraduate majors. Total enrollment: 755. Undergraduates: 755. Freshmen: 209. Federal methodology is used as a basis for awarding need-based institutional aid.

UNDERGRADUATE EXPENSES for 2006–07 *Comprehensive fee:* $19,350 includes full-time tuition ($13,200), mandatory fees ($400), and room and board ($5750). *College room only:* $2600. *Part-time tuition:* $400 per credit hour.

FRESHMAN FINANCIAL AID (Fall 2005, est.) 210 applied for aid; of those 90% were deemed to have need. 100% of freshmen with need received aid; of those 24% had need fully met. *Average percent of need met:* 76% (excluding resources awarded to replace EFC). *Average financial aid package:* $12,560 (excluding resources awarded to replace EFC). 16% of all full-time freshmen had no need and received non-need-based gift aid.

UNDERGRADUATE FINANCIAL AID (Fall 2005, est.) 698 applied for aid; of those 88% were deemed to have need. 100% of undergraduates with need received aid; of those 23% had need fully met. *Average percent of need met:* 75% (excluding resources awarded to replace EFC). *Average financial aid package:* $12,214 (excluding resources awarded to replace EFC). 16% of all full-time undergraduates had no need and received non-need-based gift aid.

GIFT AID (NEED-BASED) *Total amount:* $6,009,405 (14% federal, 27% state, 54% institutional, 5% external sources). *Receiving aid: Freshmen:* 84% (190); *All full-time undergraduates:* 84% (615). *Average award: Freshmen:* $10,724; *Undergraduates:* $9766. *Scholarships, grants, and awards:* Federal Pell, FSEOG, state, private, college/university gift aid from institutional funds.

GIFT AID (NON-NEED-BASED) *Total amount:* $1,431,885 (15% state, 77% institutional, 8% external sources). *Receiving aid: Freshmen:* 15% (34); *Undergraduates:* 14% (103). *Average Award: Freshmen:* $10,397; *Undergraduates:* $10,887. *Scholarships, grants, and awards by category: Academic Interests/Achievement:* 480 awards ($2,303,143 total): general academic interests/achievements. *Creative Arts/Performance:* 38 awards ($58,485 total): art/fine arts, music, theater/drama. *Special Achievements/Activities:* 108 awards ($228,017 total): junior miss, leadership. *Special Characteristics:* 185 awards ($321,463 total): children and siblings of alumni, children of faculty/staff, children of union members/company employees, general special characteristics, out-of-state students, relatives of clergy, religious affiliation, siblings of current students.

LOANS *Student loans:* $2,244,685 (72% need-based, 28% non-need-based). 69% of past graduating class borrowed through all loan programs. *Average indebtedness per student:* $11,191. *Average need-based loan: Freshmen:* $1993; *Undergraduates:* $2902. *Parent loans:* $761,680 (47% need-based, 53% non-need-based). *Programs:* FFEL (Subsidized and Unsubsidized Stafford, PLUS), Perkins, alternative loans.

WORK-STUDY *Federal work-study:* Total amount: $193,403; 190 jobs averaging $1000.

APPLYING FOR FINANCIAL AID *Required financial aid form:* FAFSA. *Financial aid deadline (priority):* 3/15. *Notification date:* Continuous beginning 2/15. Students must reply by 5/1 or within 2 weeks of notification.

CONTACT Mr. Kurt Osborne, Director of Financial Aid, Kentucky Wesleyan College, 3000 Frederica Street, Owensboro, KY 42302, 270-852-3130 or toll-free 800-999-0592 (in-state), 800-990-0592 (out-of-state). *Fax:* 270-926-3196. *E-mail:* kosborne@kwc.edu.

KENYON COLLEGE
Gambier, OH

Tuition & fees: $33,930 **Average undergraduate aid package:** $24,982

ABOUT THE INSTITUTION Independent, coed. Awards: bachelor's degrees. 54 undergraduate majors. Total enrollment: 1,661. Undergraduates: 1,661. Freshmen: 440. Both federal and institutional methodology are used as a basis for awarding need-based institutional aid.

UNDERGRADUATE EXPENSES for 2005–06 *Application fee:* $50. *Comprehensive fee:* $39,500 includes full-time tuition ($32,980), mandatory fees ($950), and room and board ($5570). *College room only:* $2620. Room and board charges vary according to housing facility. *Part-time tuition:* $825 per credit hour. *Payment plan:* Installment.

FRESHMAN FINANCIAL AID (Fall 2005, est.) 227 applied for aid; of those 90% were deemed to have need. 100% of freshmen with need received aid; of those 59% had need fully met. *Average percent of need met:* 98% (excluding resources awarded to replace EFC). *Average financial aid package:* $23,874 (excluding resources awarded to replace EFC). 25% of all full-time freshmen had no need and received non-need-based gift aid.

UNDERGRADUATE FINANCIAL AID (Fall 2005, est.) 897 applied for aid; of those 83% were deemed to have need. 99% of undergraduates with need received aid; of those 54% had need fully met. *Average percent of need met:* 98% (excluding resources awarded to replace EFC). *Average financial aid package:* $24,982 (excluding resources awarded to replace EFC). 23% of all full-time undergraduates had no need and received non-need-based gift aid.

GIFT AID (NEED-BASED) *Total amount:* $15,591,196 (4% federal, 2% state, 81% institutional, 13% external sources). *Receiving aid: Freshmen:* 45% (196); *All full-time undergraduates:* 41% (712). *Average award: Freshmen:* $22,525; *Undergraduates:* $21,897. *Scholarships, grants, and awards:* Federal Pell, FSEOG, state, private, college/university gift aid from institutional funds.

GIFT AID (NON-NEED-BASED) *Total amount:* $3,781,110 (6% state, 81% institutional, 13% external sources). *Receiving aid:* Freshmen: 23% (100); Undergraduates: 17% (296). *Average Award:* Freshmen: $13,085; Undergraduates: $12,072. *Scholarships, grants, and awards by category:* Academic Interests/Achievement: 356 awards ($3,074,026 total): general academic interests/achievements. *Special Characteristics:* 44 awards ($630,276 total): ethnic background. *Tuition waivers:* Full or partial for employees or children of employees.
LOANS *Student loans:* $5,221,088 (51% need-based, 49% non-need-based). 60% of past graduating class borrowed through all loan programs. *Average indebtedness per student:* $19,190. *Average need-based loan:* Freshmen: $2140; Undergraduates: $3810. *Parent loans:* $3,597,889 (8% need-based, 92% non-need-based). *Programs:* FFEL (Subsidized and Unsubsidized Stafford, PLUS), Perkins, college/university.
WORK-STUDY *Federal work-study:* Total amount: $128,120; 282 jobs averaging $570. *State or other work-study/employment:* Total amount: $368,140 (62% need-based, 38% non-need-based). 231 part-time jobs averaging $555.
APPLYING FOR FINANCIAL AID *Required financial aid forms:* FAFSA, CSS Financial Aid PROFILE, noncustodial (divorced/separated) parent's statement, income tax form(s). *Financial aid deadline (priority):* 2/15. *Notification date:* 4/1. Students must reply by 5/1.
CONTACT Mr. Craig Daugherty, Director of Financial Aid, Kenyon College, Stephens Hall, Gambier, OH 43022-9623, 740-427-5430 or toll-free 800-848-2468. *Fax:* 740-427-5240. *E-mail:* daugherty@kenyon.edu.

KETTERING UNIVERSITY
Flint, MI

Tuition & fees: $23,748 | **Average undergraduate aid package: $13,833**

ABOUT THE INSTITUTION Independent, coed. Awards: bachelor's and master's degrees. 22 undergraduate majors. Total enrollment: 2,935. Undergraduates: 2,411. Freshmen: 495. Federal methodology is used as a basis for awarding need-based institutional aid.
UNDERGRADUATE EXPENSES for 2005–06 *Application fee:* $35. *Comprehensive fee:* $29,188 includes full-time tuition ($23,360), mandatory fees ($388), and room and board ($5440). *College room only:* $3432. Room and board charges vary according to student level. *Part-time tuition:* $730 per credit. *Payment plan:* Installment.
FRESHMAN FINANCIAL AID (Fall 2005, est.) 445 applied for aid; of those 89% were deemed to have need. 100% of freshmen with need received aid; of those 15% had need fully met. *Average percent of need met:* 29% (excluding resources awarded to replace EFC). *Average financial aid package:* $15,416 (excluding resources awarded to replace EFC). 16% of all full-time freshmen had no need and received non-need-based gift aid.
UNDERGRADUATE FINANCIAL AID (Fall 2005, est.) 1,778 applied for aid; of those 92% were deemed to have need. 100% of undergraduates with need received aid; of those 11% had need fully met. *Average percent of need met:* 46% (excluding resources awarded to replace EFC). *Average financial aid package:* $13,833 (excluding resources awarded to replace EFC). 19% of all full-time undergraduates had no need and received non-need-based gift aid.
GIFT AID (NEED-BASED) *Total amount:* $13,526,667 (11% federal, 14% state, 71% institutional, 4% external sources). *Receiving aid:* Freshmen: 72% (358); All full-time undergraduates: 61% (1,465). *Average award:* Freshmen: $11,999; Undergraduates: $9237. *Scholarships, grants, and awards:* Federal Pell, FSEOG, state, private, college/university gift aid from institutional funds.
GIFT AID (NON-NEED-BASED) *Total amount:* $4,555,257 (5% state, 86% institutional, 9% external sources). *Receiving aid:* Freshmen: 77% (382); Undergraduates: 56% (1,361). *Average Award:* Freshmen: $9039; Undergraduates: $6945. *Scholarships, grants, and awards by category:* Academic Interests/Achievement: 1,640 awards ($10,591,918 total): business, computer science, engineering/technologies, general academic interests/achievements, mathematics, physical sciences. *Special Achievements/Activities:* 42 awards ($182,000 total): general special achievements/activities, memberships. *Special Characteristics:* 219 awards ($908,086 total): children and siblings of alumni, children of faculty/staff, members of minority groups, siblings of current students. *Tuition waivers:* Full or partial for employees or children of employees.
LOANS *Student loans:* $22,816,129 (83% need-based, 17% non-need-based). 59% of past graduating class borrowed through all loan programs. *Average indebtedness per student:* $40,617. *Average need-based loan:* Freshmen: $2556;

Undergraduates: $3974. *Parent loans:* $1,431,004 (85% need-based, 15% non-need-based). *Programs:* FFEL (Subsidized and Unsubsidized Stafford, PLUS), state, alternative loans.
WORK-STUDY *Federal work-study:* Total amount: $337,625; 224 jobs averaging $637. *State or other work-study/employment:* Total amount: $19,956 (100% need-based). 65 part-time jobs averaging $236.
APPLYING FOR FINANCIAL AID *Required financial aid form:* FAFSA. *Financial aid deadline (priority):* 2/14. *Notification date:* Continuous beginning 2/15. Students must reply within 2 weeks of notification.
CONTACT Diane Bice, Director of Financial Aid, Kettering University, 1700 West Third Avenue, Flint, MI 48504-4898, 800-955-4464 Ext. 7859 or toll-free 800-955-4464 Ext. 7865 (in-state), 800-955-4464 (out-of-state). *Fax:* 810-762-9807. *E-mail:* finaid@kettering.edu.

KEUKA COLLEGE
Keuka Park, NY

ABOUT THE INSTITUTION Independent religious, coed. Awards: bachelor's and master's degrees. 34 undergraduate majors. Total enrollment: 1,368. Undergraduates: 1,268. Freshmen: 287.
GIFT AID (NEED-BASED) *Scholarships, grants, and awards:* Federal Pell, FSEOG, state, private, college/university gift aid from institutional funds.
GIFT AID (NON-NEED-BASED) *Scholarships, grants, and awards by category:* Academic Interests/Achievement: general academic interests/achievements, international studies. *Special Achievements/Activities:* community service, general special achievements/activities, leadership. *Special Characteristics:* children and siblings of alumni, children of faculty/staff, international students, siblings of current students.
LOANS *Programs:* FFEL (Subsidized and Unsubsidized Stafford, PLUS), Perkins.
APPLYING FOR FINANCIAL AID *Required financial aid form:* FAFSA.
CONTACT Jennifer Bates, Director of Financial Aid, Keuka College, Financial Aid Office, Keuka Park, NY 14478-0098, 315-279-5232 or toll-free 800-33-KEUKA. *Fax:* 315-536-5327. *E-mail:* jbates@mail.keuka.edu.

KING COLLEGE
Bristol, TN

Tuition & fees: $18,345 | **Average undergraduate aid package: $15,045**

ABOUT THE INSTITUTION Independent religious, coed. Awards: bachelor's and master's degrees. 49 undergraduate majors. Total enrollment: 970. Undergraduates: 873. Freshmen: 209. Federal methodology is used as a basis for awarding need-based institutional aid.
UNDERGRADUATE EXPENSES for 2006–07 *Application fee:* $20. *Comprehensive fee:* $24,545 includes full-time tuition ($17,291), mandatory fees ($1054), and room and board ($6200). *College room only:* $3100. *Part-time tuition:* $575 per credit hour.
FRESHMAN FINANCIAL AID (Fall 2005, est.) 197 applied for aid; of those 81% were deemed to have need. 100% of freshmen with need received aid; of those 27% had need fully met. *Average percent of need met:* 77% (excluding resources awarded to replace EFC). *Average financial aid package:* $14,907 (excluding resources awarded to replace EFC). 17% of all full-time freshmen had no need and received non-need-based gift aid.
UNDERGRADUATE FINANCIAL AID (Fall 2005, est.) 709 applied for aid; of those 86% were deemed to have need. 100% of undergraduates with need received aid; of those 24% had need fully met. *Average percent of need met:* 77% (excluding resources awarded to replace EFC). *Average financial aid package:* $15,045 (excluding resources awarded to replace EFC). 16% of all full-time undergraduates had no need and received non-need-based gift aid.
GIFT AID (NEED-BASED) *Total amount:* $6,000,487 (14% federal, 12% state, 63% institutional, 11% external sources). *Receiving aid:* Freshmen: 77% (160); All full-time undergraduates: 74% (591). *Average award:* Freshmen: $13,391; Undergraduates: $12,080. *Scholarships, grants, and awards:* Federal Pell, FSEOG, state, private, college/university gift aid from institutional funds.
GIFT AID (NON-NEED-BASED) *Total amount:* $1,578,435 (19% state, 58% institutional, 23% external sources). *Receiving aid:* Freshmen: 19% (39); Undergraduates: 15% (118). *Average Award:* Freshmen: $12,027; Undergraduates: $9793. *Scholarships, grants, and awards by category:* Academic Interests/Achievement: 407 awards ($3,101,788 total): general academic interests/achievements. *Creative Arts/Performance:* 26 awards ($25,000 total): music,

King College

performing arts, theater/drama. *Special Achievements/Activities:* 287 awards ($1,840,091 total): community service, general special achievements/activities. *Special Characteristics:* 23 awards ($222,757 total): children of faculty/staff, members of minority groups, relatives of clergy.

LOANS *Student loans:* $3,407,275 (76% need-based, 24% non-need-based). 99% of past graduating class borrowed through all loan programs. *Average indebtedness per student:* $16,635. *Average need-based loan:* Freshmen: $2618; Undergraduates: $4335. *Parent loans:* $808,162 (41% need-based, 59% non-need-based). *Programs:* FFEL (Subsidized and Unsubsidized Stafford, PLUS), Perkins, college/university.

WORK-STUDY *Federal work-study:* Total amount: $65,622; 96 jobs averaging $684. *State or other work-study/employment:* Part-time jobs available.

ATHLETIC AWARDS *Total amount:* $1,908,460 (64% need-based, 36% non-need-based).

APPLYING FOR FINANCIAL AID *Required financial aid form:* FAFSA. *Financial aid deadline (priority):* 3/1. *Notification date:* Continuous beginning 3/1. Students must reply within 2 weeks of notification.

CONTACT Brenda L. Clark, Director of Financial Aid, King College, 1350 King College Road, Bristol, TN 37620-2699, 423-652-4728 or toll-free 800-362-0014. Fax: 423-652-6039. E-mail: blclark@king.edu.

THE KING'S COLLEGE
New York, NY

CONTACT Financial Aid Office, The King's College, 350 Fifth Avenue, 15th Floor Empire State Building, New York, NY 10118, 212-659-7200 or toll-free 888-969-7200 Ext. 3610.

KING'S COLLEGE
Wilkes-Barre, PA

Tuition & fees: $21,220   **Average undergraduate aid package:** $15,220

ABOUT THE INSTITUTION Independent Roman Catholic, coed. Awards: associate, bachelor's, and master's degrees and post-bachelor's certificates. 40 undergraduate majors. Total enrollment: 2,323. Undergraduates: 2,110. Freshmen: 480. Federal methodology is used as a basis for awarding need-based institutional aid.

UNDERGRADUATE EXPENSES for 2005–06 *Application fee:* $30. *Comprehensive fee:* $29,810 includes full-time tuition ($20,320), mandatory fees ($900), and room and board ($8590). *College room only:* $3980. Room and board charges vary according to board plan and housing facility. *Part-time tuition:* $495 per credit hour. *Payment plans:* Installment, deferred payment.

FRESHMAN FINANCIAL AID (Fall 2005, est.) 449 applied for aid; of those 89% were deemed to have need. 100% of freshmen with need received aid; of those 18% had need fully met. *Average percent of need met:* 76% (excluding resources awarded to replace EFC). *Average financial aid package:* $16,135 (excluding resources awarded to replace EFC). 16% of all full-time freshmen had no need and received non-need-based gift aid.

UNDERGRADUATE FINANCIAL AID (Fall 2005, est.) 1,689 applied for aid; of those 89% were deemed to have need. 100% of undergraduates with need received aid; of those 20% had need fully met. *Average percent of need met:* 71% (excluding resources awarded to replace EFC). *Average financial aid package:* $15,220 (excluding resources awarded to replace EFC). 17% of all full-time undergraduates had no need and received non-need-based gift aid.

GIFT AID (NEED-BASED) *Total amount:* $17,107,698 (9% federal, 16% state, 74% institutional, 1% external sources). *Receiving aid:* Freshmen: 65% (310); All full-time undergraduates: 64% (1,182). *Average award:* Freshmen: $5699; Undergraduates: $6373. *Scholarships, grants, and awards:* Federal Pell, FSEOG, state, private, college/university gift aid from institutional funds.

GIFT AID (NON-NEED-BASED) *Total amount:* $2,876,313 (4% federal, 91% institutional, 5% external sources). *Receiving aid:* Freshmen: 81% (390); Undergraduates: 61% (1,123). *Average Award:* Freshmen: $7964; Undergraduates: $8242. *Scholarships, grants, and awards by category: Academic Interests/Achievement:* 1,068 awards ($9,360,174 total): biological sciences, business, communication, computer science, education, English, foreign languages, general academic interests/achievements, health fields, humanities, mathematics, physical sciences, premedicine, religion/biblical studies, social sciences. *Creative Arts/Performance:* debating, journalism/publications. *Special Achievements/Activities:* 378 awards ($1,790,965 total): community service, general special achievements/activities, leadership. *Special Characteristics:* 235 awards ($1,325,290 total): children of educators, children of faculty/staff, international students, members of minority groups, relatives of clergy, siblings of current students. *Tuition waivers:* Full or partial for employees or children of employees, senior citizens. *ROTC:* Army, Air Force.

LOANS *Student loans:* $8,404,166 (86% need-based, 14% non-need-based). 88% of past graduating class borrowed through all loan programs. *Average indebtedness per student:* $17,263. *Average need-based loan:* Freshmen: $3674; Undergraduates: $4369. *Parent loans:* $3,989,084 (85% need-based, 15% non-need-based). *Programs:* FFEL (Subsidized and Unsubsidized Stafford, PLUS), Perkins, alternative loans.

WORK-STUDY *Federal work-study:* Total amount: $280,000; 350 jobs averaging $800. *State or other work-study/employment:* Total amount: $175,874 (78% need-based, 22% non-need-based). 175 part-time jobs averaging $1000.

APPLYING FOR FINANCIAL AID *Required financial aid forms:* FAFSA, institution's own form. *Financial aid deadline (priority):* 2/15. *Notification date:* Continuous beginning 3/1. Students must reply by 5/1 or within 2 weeks of notification.

CONTACT Ellen E. McGuire, Director of Financial Aid, King's College, 133 North River Street, Wilkes-Barre, PA 18711-0801, 570-208-5868 or toll-free 888-KINGSPA. Fax: 570-208-6015. E-mail: finaid@kings.edu.

THE KING'S COLLEGE AND SEMINARY
Van Nuys, CA

CONTACT Financial Aid Office, The King's College and Seminary, 14800 Sherman Way, Van Nuys, CA 91405-8040, 818-779-8040 or toll-free 888-779-8040 (in-state).

KNOX COLLEGE
Galesburg, IL

Tuition & fees: $26,100   **Average undergraduate aid package:** $21,317

ABOUT THE INSTITUTION Independent, coed. Awards: bachelor's degrees. 33 undergraduate majors. Total enrollment: 1,245. Undergraduates: 1,245. Freshmen: 325. Both federal and institutional methodology are used as a basis for awarding need-based institutional aid.

UNDERGRADUATE EXPENSES for 2005–06 *Application fee:* $40. *Comprehensive fee:* $32,385 includes full-time tuition ($25,815), mandatory fees ($285), and room and board ($6285). *College room only:* $2784. Room and board charges vary according to board plan. *Part-time tuition:* $870 per credit. Part-time tuition and fees vary according to course load. *Payment plan:* Installment.

FRESHMAN FINANCIAL AID (Fall 2005, est.) 271 applied for aid; of those 80% were deemed to have need. 100% of freshmen with need received aid; of those 47% had need fully met. *Average percent of need met:* 95% (excluding resources awarded to replace EFC). *Average financial aid package:* $21,171 (excluding resources awarded to replace EFC). 30% of all full-time freshmen had no need and received non-need-based gift aid.

UNDERGRADUATE FINANCIAL AID (Fall 2005, est.) 956 applied for aid; of those 84% were deemed to have need. 100% of undergraduates with need received aid; of those 47% had need fully met. *Average percent of need met:* 95% (excluding resources awarded to replace EFC). *Average financial aid package:* $21,317 (excluding resources awarded to replace EFC). 29% of all full-time undergraduates had no need and received non-need-based gift aid.

GIFT AID (NEED-BASED) *Total amount:* $13,019,923 (7% federal, 8% state, 82% institutional, 3% external sources). *Receiving aid:* Freshmen: 66% (216); All full-time undergraduates: 67% (805). *Average award:* Freshmen: $16,474; Undergraduates: $16,117. *Scholarships, grants, and awards:* Federal Pell, FSEOG, state, private, college/university gift aid from institutional funds.

GIFT AID (NON-NEED-BASED) *Total amount:* $3,504,029 (98% institutional, 2% external sources). *Receiving aid:* Freshmen: 10% (31); Undergraduates: 9% (112). *Average Award:* Freshmen: $9869; Undergraduates: $10,011. *Scholarships, grants, and awards by category: Academic Interests/Achievement:* general academic interests/achievements, mathematics. *Creative Arts/Performance:* art/fine arts, creative writing, dance, music, theater/drama. *Special Achievements/Activities:* community service. *Tuition waivers:* Full or partial for employees or children of employees.

LOANS *Student loans:* $4,870,748 (63% need-based, 37% non-need-based). 68% of past graduating class borrowed through all loan programs. *Average indebtedness per student:* $19,642. *Average need-based loan:* Freshmen: $4424;

Undergraduates: $5138. **Parent loans:** $2,390,962 (100% non-need-based). **Programs:** Federal Direct (Subsidized and Unsubsidized Stafford, PLUS), Perkins, college/university.
WORK-STUDY *Federal work-study:* Total amount: $1,031,191; 589 jobs averaging $1749. *State or other work-study/employment:* Total amount: $148,936 (83% need-based, 17% non-need-based). 94 part-time jobs averaging $1590.
APPLYING FOR FINANCIAL AID *Required financial aid forms:* FAFSA, institution's own form, income tax form(s). *Financial aid deadline (priority):* 2/15. *Notification date:* 4/15. Students must reply by 5/1 or within 2 weeks of notification.
CONTACT Ms. Teresa K. Jackson, Director of Financial Aid, Knox College, 2 East South Street, Galesburg, IL 61401, 309-341-7130 or toll-free 800-678-KNOX. *Fax:* 309-341-7070. *E-mail:* tjackson@knox.edu.

KOL YAAKOV TORAH CENTER
Monsey, NY

CONTACT Office of Financial Aid, Kol Yaakov Torah Center, 29 West Maple Avenue, Monsey, NY 10952-2954, 914-425-3863.

KUTZTOWN UNIVERSITY OF PENNSYLVANIA
Kutztown, PA

ABOUT THE INSTITUTION State-supported, coed. Awards: bachelor's and master's degrees and post-bachelor's certificates. 62 undergraduate majors. Total enrollment: 9,864. Undergraduates: 8,806. Freshmen: 1,912.
GIFT AID (NEED-BASED) *Scholarships, grants, and awards:* Federal Pell, FSEOG, state, private, college/university gift aid from institutional funds.
GIFT AID (NON-NEED-BASED) *Scholarships, grants, and awards by category: Academic Interests/Achievement:* business, communication, computer science, education, English, foreign languages, general academic interests/achievements, humanities, library science, mathematics, physical sciences. *Creative Arts/Performance:* applied art and design, art/fine arts, dance, music, theater/drama. *Special Achievements/Activities:* general special achievements/activities, leadership, religious involvement. *Special Characteristics:* children of faculty/staff, children of union members/company employees, handicapped students.
LOANS *Programs:* FFEL (Subsidized and Unsubsidized Stafford, PLUS), Perkins.
APPLYING FOR FINANCIAL AID *Required financial aid form:* FAFSA.
CONTACT Ms. Anita Faust, Director of Financial Aid, Kutztown University of Pennsylvania, 209A Stratton Administration Center, Kutztown, PA 19530-0730, 610-683-4077 or toll-free 877-628-1915. *Fax:* 610-683-1380. *E-mail:* faust@kutztown.edu.

KUYPER COLLEGE
Grand Rapids, MI

Tuition & fees: $12,208	Average undergraduate aid package: $6773

ABOUT THE INSTITUTION Independent religious, coed. Awards: associate and bachelor's degrees and post-bachelor's certificates. 21 undergraduate majors. Total enrollment: 274. Undergraduates: 270. Freshmen: 49. Federal methodology is used as a basis for awarding need-based institutional aid.
UNDERGRADUATE EXPENSES for 2005–06 *Application fee:* $25. *Comprehensive fee:* $17,908 includes full-time tuition ($11,700), mandatory fees ($508), and room and board ($5700). *College room only:* $2300. Full-time tuition and fees vary according to course load and student level. Room and board charges vary according to board plan, housing facility, and student level. *Part-time tuition:* $525 per credit hour. Part-time tuition and fees vary according to course load. *Payment plan:* Installment.
FRESHMAN FINANCIAL AID (Fall 2005, est.) 42 applied for aid; of those 90% were deemed to have need. 97% of freshmen with need received aid; of those 22% had need fully met. *Average percent of need met:* 64% (excluding resources awarded to replace EFC). *Average financial aid package:* $7670 (excluding resources awarded to replace EFC). 13% of all full-time freshmen had no need and received non-need-based gift aid.
UNDERGRADUATE FINANCIAL AID (Fall 2005, est.) 200 applied for aid; of those 84% were deemed to have need. 99% of undergraduates with need received aid; of those 19% had need fully met. *Average percent of need met:* 67% (excluding resources awarded to replace EFC). *Average financial aid package:* $6773 (excluding resources awarded to replace EFC). 12% of all full-time undergraduates had no need and received non-need-based gift aid.
GIFT AID (NEED-BASED) *Total amount:* $862,252 (29% federal, 35% state, 34% institutional, 2% external sources). *Receiving aid:* Freshmen: 80% (37); All full-time undergraduates: 75% (165). *Average award:* Freshmen: $5921; Undergraduates: $2394. *Scholarships, grants, and awards:* Federal Pell, FSEOG, state, private, college/university gift aid from institutional funds.
GIFT AID (NON-NEED-BASED) *Total amount:* $85,182 (15% state, 84% institutional, 1% external sources). *Receiving aid:* Freshmen: 11% (5); Undergraduates: 5% (10). *Average Award:* Freshmen: $1850; Undergraduates: $2055. *Scholarships, grants, and awards by category: Academic Interests/Achievement:* 86 awards ($46,341 total): general academic interests/achievements. *Special Achievements/Activities:* 18 awards ($41,250 total): leadership, religious involvement. *Special Characteristics:* 31 awards ($189,548 total): children of faculty/staff, international students, members of minority groups. *Tuition waivers:* Full or partial for employees or children of employees.
LOANS *Student loans:* $992,289 (60% need-based, 40% non-need-based). 48% of past graduating class borrowed through all loan programs. *Average indebtedness per student:* $12,900. *Average need-based loan:* Freshmen: $2588; Undergraduates: $3629. *Parent loans:* $9140 (78% need-based, 22% non-need-based). *Programs:* FFEL (Subsidized and Unsubsidized Stafford, PLUS), alternative loans.
WORK-STUDY *Federal work-study:* Total amount: $33,082; 33 jobs averaging $1000. *State or other work-study/employment:* Total amount: $266,918 (2% need-based, 98% non-need-based). 58 part-time jobs averaging $3000.
APPLYING FOR FINANCIAL AID *Required financial aid forms:* FAFSA, institution's own form. *Financial aid deadline (priority):* 3/1. *Notification date:* Continuous beginning 3/20. Students must reply within 2 weeks of notification.
CONTACT Ms. Agnes Russell, Director of Financial Aid, Kuyper College, 3333 East Beltline NE, Grand Rapids, MI 49525-9749, 616-222-3000 Ext. 656 or toll-free 800-511-3749. *Fax:* 616-222-3045. *E-mail:* arussell@kuyper.edu.

LABORATORY INSTITUTE OF MERCHANDISING
New York, NY

ABOUT THE INSTITUTION Proprietary, coed, primarily women. Awards: associate and bachelor's degrees. 2 undergraduate majors. Total enrollment: 792. Undergraduates: 792. Freshmen: 197.
GIFT AID (NEED-BASED) *Scholarships, grants, and awards:* Federal Pell, FSEOG, state, college/university gift aid from institutional funds.
GIFT AID (NON-NEED-BASED) *Scholarships, grants, and awards by category: Academic Interests/Achievement:* general academic interests/achievements. *Special Achievements/Activities:* memberships. *Special Characteristics:* local/state students.
LOANS *Programs:* Federal Direct (Subsidized and Unsubsidized Stafford, PLUS).
APPLYING FOR FINANCIAL AID *Required financial aid forms:* FAFSA, institution's own form.
CONTACT Mr. Christopher Barto, Director of Financial Aid, Laboratory Institute of Merchandising, 12 East 53rd Street, New York, NY 10022-5268, 212-752-1530 or toll-free 800-677-1323. *Fax:* 212-317-8602. *E-mail:* cbarto@limcollege.edu.

LAFAYETTE COLLEGE
Easton, PA

ABOUT THE INSTITUTION Independent religious, coed. Awards: bachelor's degrees. 34 undergraduate majors. Total enrollment: 2,346. Undergraduates: 2,346. Freshmen: 597.
GIFT AID (NEED-BASED) *Scholarships, grants, and awards:* Federal Pell, FSEOG, state, private, college/university gift aid from institutional funds.
GIFT AID (NON-NEED-BASED) *Scholarships, grants, and awards by category: Academic Interests/Achievement:* general academic interests/achievements.
LOANS *Programs:* FFEL (Subsidized and Unsubsidized Stafford, PLUS), Perkins, state, college/university.
APPLYING FOR FINANCIAL AID *Required financial aid forms:* FAFSA, CSS Financial Aid PROFILE, business/farm supplement, CSS/Financial Aid non-custodial profile.

Lafayette College

CONTACT Arlinda DeNardo, Director Financial Aid, Lafayette College, 107 Markle Hall, Easton, PA 18042-1777, 610-330-5055. *Fax:* 610-330-5758. *E-mail:* denardoa@lafayette.edu.

LAGRANGE COLLEGE
LaGrange, GA

| Tuition & fees: $16,200 | Average undergraduate aid package: $14,700 |

ABOUT THE INSTITUTION Independent United Methodist, coed. Awards: associate, bachelor's, and master's degrees. 33 undergraduate majors. Total enrollment: 1,046. Undergraduates: 986. Freshmen: 205. Federal methodology is used as a basis for awarding need-based institutional aid.

UNDERGRADUATE EXPENSES for 2005–06 *Application fee:* $20. *Comprehensive fee:* $22,874 includes full-time tuition ($16,200) and room and board ($6674). Full-time tuition and fees vary according to class time, degree level, location, and program. Room and board charges vary according to housing facility. *Part-time tuition:* $668 per hour. Part-time tuition and fees vary according to class time, degree level, location, and program. *Payment plan:* Installment.

FRESHMAN FINANCIAL AID (Fall 2004) 194 applied for aid; of those 85% were deemed to have need. 100% of freshmen with need received aid; of those 43% had need fully met. *Average percent of need met:* 86% (excluding resources awarded to replace EFC). *Average financial aid package:* $15,488 (excluding resources awarded to replace EFC). 21% of all full-time freshmen had no need and received non-need-based gift aid.

UNDERGRADUATE FINANCIAL AID (Fall 2004) 723 applied for aid; of those 83% were deemed to have need. 100% of undergraduates with need received aid; of those 39% had need fully met. *Average percent of need met:* 80% (excluding resources awarded to replace EFC). *Average financial aid package:* $14,700 (excluding resources awarded to replace EFC). 20% of all full-time undergraduates had no need and received non-need-based gift aid.

GIFT AID (NEED-BASED) *Total amount:* $6,043,918 (16% federal, 24% state, 56% institutional, 4% external sources). *Receiving aid:* Freshmen: 74% (164); All full-time undergraduates: 73% (600). *Average award:* Freshmen: $12,796; Undergraduates: $10,526. *Scholarships, grants, and awards:* Federal Pell, FSEOG, state, private, college/university gift aid from institutional funds.

GIFT AID (NON-NEED-BASED) *Total amount:* $2,288,684 (22% state, 66% institutional, 12% external sources). *Receiving aid:* Freshmen: 22% (48); Undergraduates: 15% (124). *Average Award:* Freshmen: $6735; Undergraduates: $6368. *Scholarships, grants, and awards by category: Academic Interests/Achievement:* 624 awards ($2,175,690 total): biological sciences, business, computer science, education, English, general academic interests/achievements, health fields, physical sciences, religion/biblical studies, social sciences. *Creative Arts/Performance:* 57 awards ($112,397 total): applied art and design, art/fine arts, music, theater/drama. *Special Achievements/Activities:* 16 awards ($48,500 total): community service, leadership. *Special Characteristics:* 131 awards ($637,381 total): children of faculty/staff, ethnic background, first-generation college students, relatives of clergy, religious affiliation. *Tuition waivers:* Full or partial for employees or children of employees.

LOANS *Student loans:* $3,631,997 (76% need-based, 24% non-need-based). 79% of past graduating class borrowed through all loan programs. *Average indebtedness per student:* $17,074. *Average need-based loan:* Freshmen: $2717; Undergraduates: $5676. *Parent loans:* $981,849 (12% need-based, 88% non-need-based). *Programs:* FFEL (Subsidized and Unsubsidized Stafford, PLUS), Perkins.

WORK-STUDY *Federal work-study:* Total amount: $71,717; 94 jobs averaging $763. *State or other work-study/employment:* Total amount: $319,446 (33% need-based, 67% non-need-based). 347 part-time jobs averaging $921.

APPLYING FOR FINANCIAL AID *Required financial aid forms:* FAFSA, institution's own form, state aid form. *Financial aid deadline:* 3/1. *Notification date:* Continuous beginning 3/1. Students must reply by 8/15 or within 2 weeks of notification.

CONTACT Sylvia Smith, Director of Financial Aid, LaGrange College, 601 Broad Street, LaGrange, GA 30240-2999, 706-880-8229 or toll-free 800-593-2885. *E-mail:* ssmith@lagrange.edu.

LAGUNA COLLEGE OF ART & DESIGN
Laguna Beach, CA

ABOUT THE INSTITUTION Independent, coed. Awards: bachelor's degrees. 12 undergraduate majors. Total enrollment: 310. Undergraduates: 310. Freshmen: 70.

GIFT AID (NEED-BASED) *Scholarships, grants, and awards:* Federal Pell, FSEOG, state, private, college/university gift aid from institutional funds.

GIFT AID (NON-NEED-BASED) *Scholarships, grants, and awards by category: Academic Interests/Achievement:* general academic interests/achievements. *Creative Arts/Performance:* applied art and design, art/fine arts.

LOANS *Programs:* FFEL (Subsidized and Unsubsidized Stafford, PLUS).

APPLYING FOR FINANCIAL AID *Required financial aid form:* FAFSA.

CONTACT Christopher Brown, Director of Student Services, Laguna College of Art & Design, 2222 Laguna Canyon Road, Laguna Beach, CA 92651-1136, 949-376-6000 or toll-free 800-255-0762. *Fax:* 949-497-5220. *E-mail:* cbrown@lagunacollege.edu.

LAKE ERIE COLLEGE
Painesville, OH

ABOUT THE INSTITUTION Independent, coed. Awards: bachelor's and master's degrees. 29 undergraduate majors. Total enrollment: 952. Undergraduates: 682. Freshmen: 118.

GIFT AID (NEED-BASED) *Scholarships, grants, and awards:* Federal Pell, FSEOG, state, private, college/university gift aid from institutional funds.

GIFT AID (NON-NEED-BASED) *Scholarships, grants, and awards by category: Academic Interests/Achievement:* biological sciences, business, foreign languages, general academic interests/achievements, mathematics, physical sciences, social sciences. *Creative Arts/Performance:* art/fine arts, dance, general creative arts/performance, music, performing arts, theater/drama. *Special Achievements/Activities:* community service, general special achievements/activities, hobbies/interests. *Special Characteristics:* children of faculty/staff, twins.

LOANS *Programs:* FFEL (Subsidized and Unsubsidized Stafford, PLUS), Perkins, college/university.

APPLYING FOR FINANCIAL AID *Required financial aid form:* FAFSA.

CONTACT Patricia Canfield, Director of Financial Aid, Lake Erie College, 391 West Washington Street, Painesville, OH 44077-3389, 440-375-7100 or toll-free 800-916-0904. *Fax:* 440-375-7005.

LAKE FOREST COLLEGE
Lake Forest, IL

| Tuition & fees: $27,334 | Average undergraduate aid package: $21,562 |

ABOUT THE INSTITUTION Independent, coed. Awards: bachelor's and master's degrees. 32 undergraduate majors. Total enrollment: 1,435. Undergraduates: 1,418. Freshmen: 358. Both federal and institutional methodology are used as a basis for awarding need-based institutional aid.

UNDERGRADUATE EXPENSES for 2005–06 *Application fee:* $40. *Comprehensive fee:* $33,860 includes full-time tuition ($27,000), mandatory fees ($334), and room and board ($6526). *College room only:* $3456. Room and board charges vary according to housing facility. *Part-time tuition:* $3375 per course. *Payment plan:* Installment.

FRESHMAN FINANCIAL AID (Fall 2005, est.) 329 applied for aid; of those 89% were deemed to have need. 100% of freshmen with need received aid; of those 100% had need fully met. *Average percent of need met:* 100% (excluding resources awarded to replace EFC). *Average financial aid package:* $21,385 (excluding resources awarded to replace EFC). 9% of all full-time freshmen had no need and received non-need-based gift aid.

UNDERGRADUATE FINANCIAL AID (Fall 2005, est.) 1,277 applied for aid; of those 84% were deemed to have need. 100% of undergraduates with need received aid; of those 100% had need fully met. *Average percent of need met:* 100% (excluding resources awarded to replace EFC). *Average financial aid package:* $21,562 (excluding resources awarded to replace EFC). 15% of all full-time undergraduates had no need and received non-need-based gift aid.

GIFT AID (NEED-BASED) *Total amount:* $19,015,199 (8% federal, 7% state, 83% institutional, 2% external sources). *Receiving aid:* Freshmen: 82% (292); All full-time undergraduates: 78% (1,070). *Average award:* Freshmen: $18,006;

Undergraduates: $17,771. **Scholarships, grants, and awards:** Federal Pell, FSEOG, state, private, college/university gift aid from institutional funds.
GIFT AID (NON-NEED-BASED) Total amount: $2,297,400 (97% institutional, 3% external sources). **Average Award:** Freshmen: $9544; Undergraduates: $10,967. **Scholarships, grants, and awards by category:** *Academic Interests/Achievement:* 813 awards ($7,383,842 total): biological sciences, foreign languages, general academic interests/achievements, physical sciences. *Creative Arts/Performance:* 216 awards ($746,100 total): art/fine arts, creative writing, music, theater/drama. *Special Achievements/Activities:* 169 awards ($573,000 total): leadership. *Special Characteristics:* 50 awards ($564,700 total): children and siblings of alumni, general special characteristics, previous college experience. **Tuition waivers:** Full or partial for employees or children of employees.
LOANS Student loans: $4,198,386 (100% need-based). 53% of past graduating class borrowed through all loan programs. *Average indebtedness per student:* $18,306. **Average need-based loan:** Freshmen: $4159; Undergraduates: $4821. **Parent loans:** $2,107,842 (98% need-based, 2% non-need-based). **Programs:** FFEL (Subsidized and Unsubsidized Stafford, PLUS), Perkins, college/university, Alternative loans.
WORK-STUDY Federal work-study: Total amount: $930,585; 528 jobs averaging $1765.
APPLYING FOR FINANCIAL AID Required financial aid forms: FAFSA, federal income tax form(s). **Financial aid deadline (priority):** 3/1. **Notification date:** 3/15. Students must reply by 5/1.
CONTACT Mr. Jerry Cebrzynski, Director of Financial Aid, Lake Forest College, 555 North Sheridan Road, Lake Forest, IL 60045-2399, 847-735-5104 or toll-free 800-828-4751. *Fax:* 847-735-6271. *E-mail:* cebrzynski@lakeforest.edu.

LAKELAND COLLEGE
Sheboygan, WI

Tuition & fees: $16,796	Average undergraduate aid package: $11,271

ABOUT THE INSTITUTION Independent religious, coed. Awards: bachelor's and master's degrees. 29 undergraduate majors. Total enrollment: 4,021. Undergraduates: 3,373. Freshmen: 243. Federal methodology is used as a basis for awarding need-based institutional aid.
UNDERGRADUATE EXPENSES for 2006-07 Application fee: $20. **Comprehensive fee:** $22,216 includes full-time tuition ($16,080), mandatory fees ($716), and room and board ($5420). **College room only:** $3882. **Part-time tuition:** $1608 per course.
FRESHMAN FINANCIAL AID (Fall 2005, est.) 223 applied for aid; of those 87% were deemed to have need. 96% of freshmen with need received aid; of those 19% had need fully met. *Average percent of need met:* 74% (excluding resources awarded to replace EFC). *Average financial aid package:* $13,145 (excluding resources awarded to replace EFC). 30% of all full-time freshmen had no need and received non-need-based gift aid.
UNDERGRADUATE FINANCIAL AID (Fall 2005, est.) 1,080 applied for aid; of those 85% were deemed to have need. 99% of undergraduates with need received aid; of those 25% had need fully met. *Average percent of need met:* 73% (excluding resources awarded to replace EFC). *Average financial aid package:* $11,271 (excluding resources awarded to replace EFC). 22% of all full-time undergraduates had no need and received non-need-based gift aid.
GIFT AID (NEED-BASED) Total amount: $7,225,756 (21% federal, 13% state, 60% institutional, 6% external sources). **Receiving aid:** Freshmen: 60% (184); All full-time undergraduates: 64% (814). **Average award:** Freshmen: $9755; Undergraduates: $8110. **Scholarships, grants, and awards:** Federal Pell, FSEOG, state, private, college/university gift aid from institutional funds.
GIFT AID (NON-NEED-BASED) Total amount: $1,749,488 (1% state, 93% institutional, 6% external sources). **Receiving aid:** Freshmen: 5% (16); Undergraduates: 6% (70). **Average Award:** Freshmen: $6795; Undergraduates: $8273. **Scholarships, grants, and awards by category:** *Academic Interests/Achievement:* 455 awards ($2,680,000 total): business, engineering/technologies, English, general academic interests/achievements, religion/biblical studies. *Creative Arts/Performance:* 15 awards ($30,500 total): art/fine arts, creative writing, journalism/publications, music, performing arts. *Special Achievements/Activities:* 48 awards ($65,200 total): community service, leadership, religious involvement. *Special Characteristics:* 138 awards ($488,371 total): children of faculty/staff, religious affiliation, siblings of current students.
LOANS Student loans: $11,206,958 (73% need-based, 27% non-need-based). 86% of past graduating class borrowed through all loan programs. *Average indebtedness per student:* $15,552. **Average need-based loan:** Freshmen: $3095; Undergraduates: $4108. **Parent loans:** $625,960 (32% need-based, 68% non-need-based). **Programs:** FFEL (Subsidized and Unsubsidized Stafford, PLUS), Perkins, alternative loans.
WORK-STUDY Federal work-study: Total amount: $329,806; 200 jobs averaging $1650. **State or other work-study/employment:** Total amount: $268,349 (13% need-based, 87% non-need-based). 160 part-time jobs averaging $1650.
APPLYING FOR FINANCIAL AID Required financial aid forms: FAFSA, institution's own form. **Financial aid deadline:** 7/1 (priority: 5/1). **Notification date:** Continuous beginning 3/1. Students must reply within 2 weeks of notification.
CONTACT Ms. Patty Taylor, Interim Director of Financial Aid, Lakeland College, PO Box 359, Sheboygan, WI 53082-0359, 920-565-1214 or toll-free 800-242-3347 (in-state). *Fax:* 920-565-1470.

LAKE SUPERIOR STATE UNIVERSITY
Sault Sainte Marie, MI

Tuition & fees (MI res): $6306	Average undergraduate aid package: $8594

ABOUT THE INSTITUTION State-supported, coed. Awards: associate, bachelor's, and master's degrees. 63 undergraduate majors. Total enrollment: 2,888. Undergraduates: 2,888. Freshmen: 554. Both federal and institutional methodology are used as a basis for awarding need-based institutional aid.
UNDERGRADUATE EXPENSES for 2005-06 Application fee: $20. **Tuition, state resident:** full-time $5988; part-time $249.50 per credit hour. **Tuition, nonresident:** full-time $11,976; part-time $499 per credit hour. **Required fees:** full-time $318; $7 per credit hour or $75 per term part-time. Full-time tuition and fees vary according to reciprocity agreements. Part-time tuition and fees vary according to course load and reciprocity agreements. **College room and board:** $6536. Room and board charges vary according to board plan and housing facility. **Payment plans:** Installment, deferred payment.
FRESHMAN FINANCIAL AID (Fall 2004) 537 applied for aid; of those 77% were deemed to have need. 100% of freshmen with need received aid. *Average percent of need met:* 78% (excluding resources awarded to replace EFC). *Average financial aid package:* $8262 (excluding resources awarded to replace EFC). 11% of all full-time freshmen had no need and received non-need-based gift aid.
UNDERGRADUATE FINANCIAL AID (Fall 2004) 2,149 applied for aid; of those 74% were deemed to have need. 100% of undergraduates with need received aid. *Average percent of need met:* 81% (excluding resources awarded to replace EFC). *Average financial aid package:* $8594 (excluding resources awarded to replace EFC). 7% of all full-time undergraduates had no need and received non-need-based gift aid.
GIFT AID (NEED-BASED) Total amount: $3,375,962 (76% federal, 19% state, 5% institutional). **Receiving aid:** Freshmen: 44% (249); All full-time undergraduates: 39% (976). **Average award:** Freshmen: $3338; Undergraduates: $3160. **Scholarships, grants, and awards:** Federal Pell, FSEOG, state, private, college/university gift aid from institutional funds, Federal Nursing, third party payments.
GIFT AID (NON-NEED-BASED) Total amount: $3,305,628 (34% state, 48% institutional, 18% external sources). **Receiving aid:** Freshmen: 72% (407); Undergraduates: 50% (1,257). **Average Award:** Freshmen: $2359; Undergraduates: $2475. **Scholarships, grants, and awards by category:** *Academic Interests/Achievement:* general academic interests/achievements. *Creative Arts/Performance:* general creative arts/performance. *Special Achievements/Activities:* general special achievements/activities. *Special Characteristics:* general special characteristics. **Tuition waivers:** Full or partial for minority students, children of alumni, employees or children of employees, senior citizens.
LOANS Student loans: $9,234,267 (100% need-based). 63% of past graduating class borrowed through all loan programs. *Average indebtedness per student:* $17,458. **Average need-based loan:** Freshmen: $3164; Undergraduates: $4528. **Parent loans:** $1,459,156 (100% need-based). **Programs:** Federal Direct (Subsidized and Unsubsidized Stafford, PLUS), Perkins, Federal Nursing, state.
WORK-STUDY Federal work-study: Total amount: $463,303; jobs available. **State or other work-study/employment:** Total amount: $279,195 (100% need-based). Part-time jobs available.
ATHLETIC AWARDS Total amount: $773,985 (100% non-need-based).
APPLYING FOR FINANCIAL AID Required financial aid form: FAFSA. **Financial aid deadline (priority):** 2/21. **Notification date:** Continuous. Students must reply within 3 weeks of notification.

Lake Superior State University

CONTACT Mr. Dan Arnold, Financial Aid Officer, Lake Superior State University, 650 West Easterday Avenue, Sault Sainte Marie, MI 49783, 906-635-2678 or toll-free 888-800-LSSU Ext. 2231. *E-mail:* finaaid@lssu.edu.

LAKEVIEW COLLEGE OF NURSING
Danville, IL

CONTACT Director of Financial Aid, Lakeview College of Nursing, 903 North Logan Avenue, Danville, IL 61832, 217-443-5238 or toll-free 217-443-5238 Ext. 5454 (in-state).

LAMAR UNIVERSITY
Beaumont, TX

Tuition & fees (TX res): $2880	Average undergraduate aid package: $1237

ABOUT THE INSTITUTION State-supported, coed. Awards: associate, bachelor's, master's, and doctoral degrees. 102 undergraduate majors. Total enrollment: 10,595. Undergraduates: 9,684. Freshmen: 1,683. Federal methodology is used as a basis for awarding need-based institutional aid.

UNDERGRADUATE EXPENSES for 2005–06 *Tuition, area resident:* part-time $1262 per term. *Tuition, state resident:* full-time $2880. *Tuition, nonresident:* full-time $9504; part-time $4813 per term. *Required fees:* $512 per term part-time. Part-time tuition and fees vary according to course load. *College room and board:* $5254; *room only:* $3600. Room and board charges vary according to board plan and housing facility. *Payment plan:* Installment.

FRESHMAN FINANCIAL AID (Fall 2005, est.) 1109 applied for aid; of those 64% were deemed to have need. 84% of freshmen with need received aid; of those 19% had need fully met. *Average percent of need met:* 65% (excluding resources awarded to replace EFC). *Average financial aid package:* $1300 (excluding resources awarded to replace EFC). 38% of all full-time freshmen had no need and received non-need-based gift aid.

UNDERGRADUATE FINANCIAL AID (Fall 2005, est.) 4,696 applied for aid; of those 67% were deemed to have need. 84% of undergraduates with need received aid; of those 8% had need fully met. *Average percent of need met:* 30% (excluding resources awarded to replace EFC). *Average financial aid package:* $1237 (excluding resources awarded to replace EFC). 17% of all full-time undergraduates had no need and received non-need-based gift aid.

GIFT AID (NEED-BASED) *Total amount:* $13,512,921 (69% federal, 30% state, 1% institutional). *Scholarships, grants, and awards:* Federal Pell, FSEOG, state, college/university gift aid from institutional funds.

GIFT AID (NON-NEED-BASED) *Total amount:* $4,655,787 (73% institutional, 27% external sources). *Receiving aid:* Freshmen: 30% (475); Undergraduates: 13% (878). *Average Award:* Freshmen: $900; Undergraduates: $900. *Scholarships, grants, and awards by category: Academic Interests/Achievement:* general academic interests/achievements. *Creative Arts/Performance:* general creative arts/performance. *Special Achievements/Activities:* general special achievements/activities.

LOANS *Student loans:* $21,998,875 (51% need-based, 49% non-need-based). 20% of past graduating class borrowed through all loan programs. *Average indebtedness per student:* $7100. *Parent loans:* $1,090,295 (100% need-based). *Programs:* FFEL (Subsidized and Unsubsidized Stafford, PLUS), Perkins, state, college/university.

WORK-STUDY *Federal work-study:* Total amount: $164,476; 94 jobs averaging $3000. *State or other work-study/employment:* Total amount: $46,904 (100% need-based). 21 part-time jobs averaging $3000.

ATHLETIC AWARDS *Total amount:* $148,996 (100% non-need-based).

APPLYING FOR FINANCIAL AID *Required financial aid forms:* FAFSA, institution's own form. *Financial aid deadline (priority):* 4/1. *Notification date:* Continuous beginning 5/1. Students must reply within 2 weeks of notification.

CONTACT Financial Aid Department, Lamar University, PO Box 10042, Beaumont, TX 77710, 409-880-8450. *Fax:* 409-880-8934. *E-mail:* finaid@hal.lamar.edu.

LAMBUTH UNIVERSITY
Jackson, TN

ABOUT THE INSTITUTION Independent United Methodist, coed. Awards: bachelor's degrees. 70 undergraduate majors. Total enrollment: 805. Undergraduates: 805. Freshmen: 234.

GIFT AID (NEED-BASED) *Scholarships, grants, and awards:* Federal Pell, FSEOG, state, private, college/university gift aid from institutional funds.

GIFT AID (NON-NEED-BASED) *Scholarships, grants, and awards by category: Academic Interests/Achievement:* biological sciences, business, communication, computer science, education, English, foreign languages, general academic interests/achievements, home economics, humanities, international studies, mathematics, physical sciences, premedicine, religion/biblical studies, social sciences. *Creative Arts/Performance:* dance, music, theater/drama. *Special Achievements/Activities:* cheerleading/drum major. *Special Characteristics:* children and siblings of alumni, children of faculty/staff, relatives of clergy, religious affiliation.

LOANS *Programs:* FFEL (Subsidized and Unsubsidized Stafford, PLUS), Perkins, United Methodist Student Loans.

WORK-STUDY *Federal work-study:* Total amount: $184,580; 188 jobs averaging $982. *State or other work-study/employment:* Total amount: $48,999 (100% non-need-based). 42 part-time jobs averaging $1167.

APPLYING FOR FINANCIAL AID *Required financial aid forms:* FAFSA, institution's own form.

CONTACT Ms. Lisa A. Warmath, Director of Scholarships and Financial Aid, Lambuth University, 705 Lambuth Boulevard, Jackson, TN 38301, 731-425-3331 or toll-free 800-526-2884. *Fax:* 731-425-3496. *E-mail:* warmath@lambuth.edu.

LANCASTER BIBLE COLLEGE
Lancaster, PA

Tuition & fees: $12,360	Average undergraduate aid package: $8871

ABOUT THE INSTITUTION Independent nondenominational, coed. Awards: associate, bachelor's, and master's degrees and post-bachelor's certificates. 17 undergraduate majors. Total enrollment: 1,001. Undergraduates: 829. Freshmen: 121. Federal methodology is used as a basis for awarding need-based institutional aid.

UNDERGRADUATE EXPENSES for 2005–06 *Application fee:* $25. *Comprehensive fee:* $18,060 includes full-time tuition ($11,850), mandatory fees ($510), and room and board ($5700). *College room only:* $2500. *Part-time tuition:* $417 per credit. *Part-time fees:* $19 per credit.

FRESHMAN FINANCIAL AID (Fall 2005, est.) 105 applied for aid; of those 83% were deemed to have need. 99% of freshmen with need received aid; of those 14% had need fully met. *Average percent of need met:* 60% (excluding resources awarded to replace EFC). *Average financial aid package:* $8303 (excluding resources awarded to replace EFC). 17% of all full-time freshmen had no need and received non-need-based gift aid.

UNDERGRADUATE FINANCIAL AID (Fall 2005, est.) 510 applied for aid; of those 89% were deemed to have need. 100% of undergraduates with need received aid; of those 14% had need fully met. *Average percent of need met:* 74% (excluding resources awarded to replace EFC). *Average financial aid package:* $8871 (excluding resources awarded to replace EFC). 15% of all full-time undergraduates had no need and received non-need-based gift aid.

GIFT AID (NEED-BASED) *Total amount:* $2,561,893 (20% federal, 24% state, 52% institutional, 4% external sources). *Receiving aid:* Freshmen: 57% (67); All full-time undergraduates: 63% (344). *Average award:* Freshmen: $4980; Undergraduates: $4790. *Scholarships, grants, and awards:* Federal Pell, FSEOG, state, private, college/university gift aid from institutional funds, Office of Vocational Rehabilitation, Blindness and Visual Services Awards.

GIFT AID (NON-NEED-BASED) *Total amount:* $393,181 (90% institutional, 10% external sources). *Receiving aid:* Freshmen: 52% (61); Undergraduates: 53% (290). *Average Award:* Freshmen: $4551; Undergraduates: $4826. *Scholarships, grants, and awards by category: Academic Interests/Achievement:* 211 awards ($404,944 total): general academic interests/achievements. *Creative Arts/Performance:* 20 awards ($42,156 total): general creative arts/performance, music. *Special Achievements/Activities:* 95 awards ($79,100 total): general special achievements/activities, leadership, religious involvement. *Special Characteristics:* 395 awards ($1,215,752 total): adult students, children and siblings of alumni, children of current students, children of faculty/staff, international students, married students, previous college experience, relatives of clergy, religious affiliation, siblings of current students, spouses of current students.

LOANS *Student loans:* $2,336,361 (78% need-based, 22% non-need-based). 48% of past graduating class borrowed through all loan programs. *Average

indebtedness per student: $15,807. ***Average need-based loan:*** Freshmen: $2447; Undergraduates: $3568. ***Parent loans:*** $837,950 (39% need-based, 61% non-need-based). ***Programs:*** FFEL (Subsidized and Unsubsidized Stafford, PLUS), Perkins, state, alternative loans.
WORK-STUDY *Federal work-study:* Total amount: $104,312; 99 jobs averaging $1500.
APPLYING FOR FINANCIAL AID *Required financial aid forms:* FAFSA, state aid form. ***Financial aid deadline (priority):*** 5/1. ***Notification date:*** Continuous beginning 3/15. Students must reply within 3 weeks of notification.
CONTACT Karen Fox, Director of Financial Aid, Lancaster Bible College, PO Box 83403, Lancaster, PA 17608-3403, 717-560-8254 Ext. 5352 or toll-free 866-LBC4YOU. *Fax:* 717-560-8216. *E-mail:* kfox@lbc.edu.

LANDER UNIVERSITY
Greenwood, SC

CONTACT Director of Financial Aid, Lander University, 320 Stanley Avenue, Greenwood, SC 29649, 864-388-8340 or toll-free 888-452-6337. *Fax:* 864-388-8811. *E-mail:* fhardin@lander.edu.

LANE COLLEGE
Jackson, TN

CONTACT Ms. Ursula Singleton, Director of Financial Aid, Lane College, 545 Lane Avenue, Jackson, TN 38301, 731-426-7536 or toll-free 800-960-7533. *Fax:* 731-426-7652. *E-mail:* fao@lanecollege.edu.

LANGSTON UNIVERSITY
Langston, OK

ABOUT THE INSTITUTION State-supported, coed. Awards: associate, bachelor's, and master's degrees. 56 undergraduate majors. Total enrollment: 3,008. Undergraduates: 2,896. Freshmen: 481.
GIFT AID (NEED-BASED) *Scholarships, grants, and awards:* Federal Pell, FSEOG, state.
GIFT AID (NON-NEED-BASED) *Scholarships, grants, and awards by category: Academic Interests/Achievement:* agriculture, business, education, engineering/technologies, general academic interests/achievements, health fields. *Creative Arts/Performance:* music. *Special Achievements/Activities:* cheerleading/drum major, leadership. *Special Characteristics:* ethnic background.
LOANS *Programs:* Federal Direct (Subsidized and Unsubsidized Stafford, PLUS), FFEL (Subsidized and Unsubsidized Stafford, PLUS).
APPLYING FOR FINANCIAL AID *Required financial aid forms:* FAFSA, institution's own form.
CONTACT Yvonne Maxwell, Director of Financial Aid, Langston University, Page Hall, Room 311, Langston, OK 73050, 405-466-3282 or toll-free 405-466-3428 (in-state). *Fax:* 405-466-2986. *E-mail:* ymaxwell@lunet.edu.

LA ROCHE COLLEGE
Pittsburgh, PA

ABOUT THE INSTITUTION Independent religious, coed. Awards: associate, bachelor's, and master's degrees. 34 undergraduate majors. Total enrollment: 1,707. Undergraduates: 1,500. Freshmen: 305.
GIFT AID (NEED-BASED) *Scholarships, grants, and awards:* Federal Pell, FSEOG, state, private, college/university gift aid from institutional funds.
GIFT AID (NON-NEED-BASED) *Scholarships, grants, and awards by category: Creative Arts/Performance:* applied art and design.
LOANS *Programs:* FFEL (Subsidized and Unsubsidized Stafford, PLUS), Perkins, state.
WORK-STUDY *Federal work-study:* Total amount: $815,367; jobs available (averaging $2000).
APPLYING FOR FINANCIAL AID *Required financial aid forms:* FAFSA, institution's own form, state aid form.
CONTACT Mr. John F. Matsko, Director of Financial Aid, La Roche College, 9000 Babcock Boulevard, Pittsburgh, PA 15237-5898, 412-536-1120 or toll-free 800-838-4LRC. *Fax:* 412-536-1072. *E-mail:* matskoj1@laroche.edu.

LA SALLE UNIVERSITY
Philadelphia, PA

ABOUT THE INSTITUTION Independent Roman Catholic, coed. Awards: associate, bachelor's, master's, and doctoral degrees and post-bachelor's and post-master's certificates. 61 undergraduate majors. Total enrollment: 6,138. Undergraduates: 4,339. Freshmen: 822.
GIFT AID (NEED-BASED) *Scholarships, grants, and awards:* Federal Pell, FSEOG, state, private, college/university gift aid from institutional funds.
GIFT AID (NON-NEED-BASED) *Scholarships, grants, and awards by category: Academic Interests/Achievement:* general academic interests/achievements. *Special Achievements/Activities:* community service. *Special Characteristics:* children of faculty/staff.
LOANS *Programs:* FFEL (Subsidized and Unsubsidized Stafford, PLUS), Perkins.
APPLYING FOR FINANCIAL AID *Required financial aid form:* FAFSA.
CONTACT Robert G. Voss, Dean of Admission and Financial Aid, La Salle University, 1900 West Olney Avenue, Philadelphia, PA 19141-1199, 215-951-1500 or toll-free 800-328-1910.

LASELL COLLEGE
Newton, MA

Tuition & fees: $20,900	Average undergraduate aid package: $14,900

ABOUT THE INSTITUTION Independent, coed. Awards: bachelor's and master's degrees. 28 undergraduate majors. Total enrollment: 1,253. Undergraduates: 1,216. Freshmen: 374. Both federal and institutional methodology are used as a basis for awarding need-based institutional aid.
UNDERGRADUATE EXPENSES for 2006–07 *Application fee:* $40. ***Comprehensive fee:*** $30,100 includes full-time tuition ($19,900), mandatory fees ($1000), and room and board ($9200). ***Part-time tuition:*** $660 per credit hour. ***Part-time fees:*** $250.
FRESHMAN FINANCIAL AID (Fall 2005, est.) 337 applied for aid; of those 88% were deemed to have need. 100% of freshmen with need received aid; of those 9% had need fully met. *Average percent of need met:* 68% (excluding resources awarded to replace EFC). *Average financial aid package:* $15,100 (excluding resources awarded to replace EFC). 12% of all full-time freshmen had no need and received non-need-based gift aid.
UNDERGRADUATE FINANCIAL AID (Fall 2005, est.) 1,198 applied for aid; of those 90% were deemed to have need. 94% of undergraduates with need received aid; of those 13% had need fully met. *Average percent of need met:* 67% (excluding resources awarded to replace EFC). *Average financial aid package:* $14,900 (excluding resources awarded to replace EFC). 13% of all full-time undergraduates had no need and received non-need-based gift aid.
GIFT AID (NEED-BASED) *Total amount:* $11,556,257 (11% federal, 5% state, 82% institutional, 2% external sources). *Receiving aid:* Freshmen: 78% (292); All full-time undergraduates: 84% (1,012). *Average award:* Freshmen: $12,200; Undergraduates: $12,200. *Scholarships, grants, and awards:* Federal Pell, FSEOG, state, private, college/university gift aid from institutional funds.
GIFT AID (NON-NEED-BASED) *Total amount:* $1,095,246 (1% state, 94% institutional, 5% external sources). *Receiving aid:* Freshmen: 5% (19); Undergraduates: 5% (65). *Average Award:* Freshmen: $14,800; Undergraduates: $14,700. *Scholarships, grants, and awards by category: Academic Interests/Achievement:* 135 awards ($565,000 total): general academic interests/achievements. *Special Achievements/Activities:* 41 awards ($117,000 total): community service, general special achievements/activities. *Special Characteristics:* 21 awards ($30,635 total): children and siblings of alumni, children of faculty/staff, siblings of current students, twins.
LOANS *Student loans:* $7,992,279 (65% need-based, 35% non-need-based). 93% of past graduating class borrowed through all loan programs. *Average indebtedness per student:* $20,800. ***Average need-based loan:*** Freshmen: $2500; Undergraduates: $3500. ***Parent loans:*** $3,524,266 (40% need-based, 60% non-need-based). ***Programs:*** FFEL (Subsidized and Unsubsidized Stafford, PLUS), Perkins, state, alternative loans.
WORK-STUDY *Federal work-study:* Total amount: $290,500; 632 jobs averaging $2000.
APPLYING FOR FINANCIAL AID *Required financial aid forms:* FAFSA, institution's own form. ***Financial aid deadline (priority):*** 3/1. ***Notification date:*** Continuous. Students must reply within 4 weeks of notification.

Lasell College

CONTACT Michele R. Kosboth, Director of Student Financial Planning, Lasell College, 1844 Commonwealth Avenue, Newton, MA 02466-2709, 617-243-2227 or toll-free 888-LASELL-4. *Fax:* 617-243-2326. *E-mail:* finaid@lasell.edu.

LA SIERRA UNIVERSITY
Riverside, CA

Tuition & fees: $20,634	Average undergraduate aid package: $15,090

ABOUT THE INSTITUTION Independent Seventh-day Adventist, coed. Awards: bachelor's, master's, and doctoral degrees and post-bachelor's and post-master's certificates. 33 undergraduate majors. Total enrollment: 1,941. Undergraduates: 1,638. Freshmen: 388. Federal methodology is used as a basis for awarding need-based institutional aid.

UNDERGRADUATE EXPENSES for 2006–07 *Application fee:* $30. *Comprehensive fee:* $26,507 includes full-time tuition ($19,908), mandatory fees ($726), and room and board ($5873). *Part-time tuition:* $553 per unit.

FRESHMAN FINANCIAL AID (Fall 2004) 296 applied for aid; of those 89% were deemed to have need. 99% of freshmen with need received aid; of those 15% had need fully met. *Average percent of need met:* 71% (excluding resources awarded to replace EFC). *Average financial aid package:* $14,997 (excluding resources awarded to replace EFC). 25% of all full-time freshmen had no need and received non-need-based gift aid.

UNDERGRADUATE FINANCIAL AID (Fall 2004) 1,079 applied for aid; of those 91% were deemed to have need. 100% of undergraduates with need received aid; of those 12% had need fully met. *Average percent of need met:* 67% (excluding resources awarded to replace EFC). *Average financial aid package:* $15,090 (excluding resources awarded to replace EFC). 26% of all full-time undergraduates had no need and received non-need-based gift aid.

GIFT AID (NEED-BASED) *Total amount:* $11,636,450 (19% federal, 28% state, 42% institutional, 11% external sources). *Receiving aid:* Freshmen: 75% (262); All full-time undergraduates: 71% (968). *Average award:* Freshmen: $12,940; Undergraduates: $11,444. *Scholarships, grants, and awards:* Federal Pell, FSEOG, state, private, college/university gift aid from institutional funds.

GIFT AID (NON-NEED-BASED) *Total amount:* $2,503,007 (1% state, 81% institutional, 18% external sources). *Average Award:* Freshmen: $6776; Undergraduates: $5156. *Scholarships, grants, and awards by category:* Academic Interests/Achievement: general academic interests/achievements. Creative Arts/Performance: music, theater/drama. Special Achievements/Activities: leadership. Special Characteristics: adult students, children of faculty/staff, relatives of clergy, religious affiliation, siblings of current students.

LOANS *Student loans:* $7,718,721 (92% need-based, 8% non-need-based). 70% of past graduating class borrowed through all loan programs. *Average indebtedness per student:* $24,680. *Average need-based loan:* Freshmen: $2995; Undergraduates: $4814. *Parent loans:* $1,865,955 (78% need-based, 22% non-need-based). *Programs:* FFEL (Subsidized and Unsubsidized Stafford, PLUS), Perkins.

WORK-STUDY *Federal work-study:* Total amount: $661,954; 309 jobs averaging $2142.

APPLYING FOR FINANCIAL AID *Required financial aid forms:* FAFSA, state aid form. *Financial aid deadline (priority):* 3/2. *Notification date:* Continuous beginning 4/15. Students must reply by 9/1.

CONTACT Financial Aid Office, La Sierra University, 4500 Riverwalk Parkway, Riverside, CA 92515, 951-785-2175 or toll-free 800-874-5587. *Fax:* 951-785-2942. *E-mail:* sfs@lasierra.edu.

LAURA AND ALVIN SIEGAL COLLEGE OF JUDAIC STUDIES
Beachwood, OH

Tuition & fees: $15,025	Average undergraduate aid package: $1000

ABOUT THE INSTITUTION Independent, coed. Awards: bachelor's and master's degrees. 7 undergraduate majors. Total enrollment: 146. Undergraduates: 11. Freshmen: 1. Institutional methodology is used as a basis for awarding need-based institutional aid.

UNDERGRADUATE EXPENSES for 2005–06 *Application fee:* $50. *Tuition:* full-time $15,000; part-time $500 per credit. Full-time tuition and fees vary according to course load. Part-time tuition and fees vary according to course load. *Payment plan:* Installment.

FRESHMAN FINANCIAL AID (Fall 2005, est.) 1 applied for aid; of those 100% were deemed to have need. 100% of freshmen with need received aid. *Average percent of need met:* 40% (excluding resources awarded to replace EFC). *Average financial aid package:* $1000 (excluding resources awarded to replace EFC).

UNDERGRADUATE FINANCIAL AID (Fall 2005, est.) 1 applied for aid; of those 100% were deemed to have need. 100% of undergraduates with need received aid. *Average percent of need met:* 40% (excluding resources awarded to replace EFC). *Average financial aid package:* $1000 (excluding resources awarded to replace EFC).

GIFT AID (NEED-BASED) *Total amount:* $77,997 (100% institutional). *Receiving aid:* Freshmen: 100% (1); All full-time undergraduates: 100% (1). *Average award:* Freshmen: $1000; Undergraduates: $1000. *Scholarships, grants, and awards:* college/university gift aid from institutional funds.

GIFT AID (NON-NEED-BASED) *Scholarships, grants, and awards by category:* Academic Interests/Achievement: education, religion/biblical studies. *Tuition waivers:* Full or partial for employees or children of employees.

APPLYING FOR FINANCIAL AID *Required financial aid form:* institution's own form. *Financial aid deadline:* Continuous. *Notification date:* Continuous. Students must reply within 2 weeks of notification.

CONTACT Ruth Kronick, Director of Student Services, Laura and Alvin Siegal College of Judaic Studies, 26500 Shaker Boulevard, Cleveland, OH 44122, 216-464-4050 Ext. 101 or toll-free 888-336-2257. *Fax:* 216-464-5278. *E-mail:* rkronick@siegalcollege.edu.

LAWRENCE TECHNOLOGICAL UNIVERSITY
Southfield, MI

Tuition & fees: $19,443	Average undergraduate aid package: $10,157

ABOUT THE INSTITUTION Independent, coed. Awards: associate, bachelor's, master's, and doctoral degrees. 34 undergraduate majors. Total enrollment: 4,122. Undergraduates: 2,868. Freshmen: 332. Federal methodology is used as a basis for awarding need-based institutional aid.

UNDERGRADUATE EXPENSES for 2006–07 *Application fee:* $30. *Comprehensive fee:* $26,709 includes full-time tuition ($19,073), mandatory fees ($370), and room and board ($7266). *College room only:* $5286. *Part-time tuition:* $635 per credit hour. *Part-time fees:* $185 per term.

FRESHMAN FINANCIAL AID (Fall 2004) 269 applied for aid; of those 70% were deemed to have need. 100% of freshmen with need received aid; of those 7% had need fully met. *Average percent of need met:* 78% (excluding resources awarded to replace EFC). *Average financial aid package:* $11,119 (excluding resources awarded to replace EFC). 18% of all full-time freshmen had no need and received non-need-based gift aid.

UNDERGRADUATE FINANCIAL AID (Fall 2004) 1,166 applied for aid; of those 78% were deemed to have need. 100% of undergraduates with need received aid; of those 6% had need fully met. *Average percent of need met:* 80% (excluding resources awarded to replace EFC). *Average financial aid package:* $10,157 (excluding resources awarded to replace EFC). 18% of all full-time undergraduates had no need and received non-need-based gift aid.

GIFT AID (NEED-BASED) *Total amount:* $6,758,137 (18% federal, 31% state, 49% institutional, 2% external sources). *Receiving aid:* Freshmen: 58% (179); All full-time undergraduates: 52% (831). *Average award:* Freshmen: $7317; Undergraduates: $6783. *Scholarships, grants, and awards:* Federal Pell, FSEOG, state, private, college/university gift aid from institutional funds, Michigan National Guard and ROTC.

GIFT AID (NON-NEED-BASED) *Total amount:* $3,052,408 (13% federal, 14% state, 70% institutional, 3% external sources). *Receiving aid:* Freshmen: 49% (152); Undergraduates: 36% (569). *Average Award:* Freshmen: $5359; Undergraduates: $5816. *Scholarships, grants, and awards by category:* Academic Interests/Achievement: 1,243 awards ($5,624,876 total): architecture, business, computer science, education, engineering/technologies, general academic interests/achievements, humanities, international studies, mathematics, military science, physical sciences. *Special Achievements/Activities:* general

special achievements/activities. *Special Characteristics:* 74 awards ($583,243 total): children of faculty/staff, members of minority groups. *ROTC:* Army cooperative, Air Force cooperative.
LOANS *Student loans:* $8,218,020 (82% need-based, 18% non-need-based). 50% of past graduating class borrowed through all loan programs. *Average indebtedness per student:* $24,250. *Average need-based loan:* Freshmen: $2696; Undergraduates: $4126. *Parent loans:* $3,607,035 (74% need-based, 26% non-need-based). *Programs:* FFEL (Subsidized and Unsubsidized Stafford, PLUS), Perkins, state, college/university, alternative loans.
WORK-STUDY *Federal work-study:* Total amount: $1,224,087; 140 jobs averaging $4000. *State or other work-study/employment:* Total amount: $44,000 (100% need-based). 18 part-time jobs averaging $2000.
APPLYING FOR FINANCIAL AID *Required financial aid form:* FAFSA. *Financial aid deadline (priority):* 4/1. *Notification date:* Continuous beginning 4/1. Students must reply within 2 weeks of notification.
CONTACT Mr. Mark Martin, Director of Financial Aid, Lawrence Technological University, 21000 West Ten Mile Road, Southfield, MI 48075-1058, 248-204-2126 or toll-free 800-225-5588. *Fax:* 248-204-2124. *E-mail:* m_martin@ltu.edu.

LAWRENCE UNIVERSITY
Appleton, WI

Tuition & fees: $29,598   Average undergraduate aid package: $22,900

ABOUT THE INSTITUTION Independent, coed. Awards: bachelor's degrees. 58 undergraduate majors. Total enrollment: 1,450. Undergraduates: 1,450. Freshmen: 401. Institutional methodology is used as a basis for awarding need-based institutional aid.
UNDERGRADUATE EXPENSES for 2006–07 *Application fee:* $40. *Comprehensive fee:* $35,979 includes full-time tuition ($29,376), mandatory fees ($222), and room and board ($6381). *College room only:* $2934.
FRESHMAN FINANCIAL AID (Fall 2005, est.) 318 applied for aid; of those 79% were deemed to have need. 100% of freshmen with need received aid; of those 100% had need fully met. *Average percent of need met:* 100% (excluding resources awarded to replace EFC). *Average financial aid package:* $22,900 (excluding resources awarded to replace EFC). 31% of all full-time freshmen had no need and received non-need-based gift aid.
UNDERGRADUATE FINANCIAL AID (Fall 2005, est.) 1,061 applied for aid; of those 81% were deemed to have need. 100% of undergraduates with need received aid; of those 100% had need fully met. *Average percent of need met:* 100% (excluding resources awarded to replace EFC). *Average financial aid package:* $22,900 (excluding resources awarded to replace EFC). 31% of all full-time undergraduates had no need and received non-need-based gift aid.
GIFT AID (NEED-BASED) *Total amount:* $13,808,915 (6% federal, 6% state, 85% institutional, 3% external sources). *Receiving aid:* Freshmen: 62% (250); All full-time undergraduates: 61% (856). *Average award:* Freshmen: $17,080; Undergraduates: $16,061. *Scholarships, grants, and awards:* Federal Pell, FSEOG, state, private, college/university gift aid from institutional funds.
GIFT AID (NON-NEED-BASED) *Total amount:* $4,195,875 (96% institutional, 4% external sources). *Average Award:* Freshmen: $9251; Undergraduates: $9270. *Scholarships, grants, and awards by category:* Academic Interests/Achievement: 709 awards ($5,788,430 total): general academic interests/achievements. Creative Arts/Performance: 197 awards ($1,413,462 total): music. *Special Characteristics:* 96 awards ($472,072 total): children and siblings of alumni, members of minority groups.
LOANS *Student loans:* $5,129,859 (82% need-based, 18% non-need-based). 66% of past graduating class borrowed through all loan programs. *Average indebtedness per student:* $19,294. *Average need-based loan:* Freshmen: $4510; Undergraduates: $5660. *Parent loans:* $2,886,898 (100% non-need-based). *Programs:* Federal Direct (Subsidized and Unsubsidized Stafford, PLUS), FFEL (PLUS), Perkins, college/university, alternative loans.
WORK-STUDY *Federal work-study:* Total amount: $1,292,849; 626 jobs averaging $2065. *State or other work-study/employment:* Total amount: $854,132 (100% non-need-based). 417 part-time jobs averaging $2048.
APPLYING FOR FINANCIAL AID *Required financial aid forms:* FAFSA, institution's own form, signed copies of 2005 federal tax returns and W-2 for parents and students. *Financial aid deadline (priority):* 3/15. *Notification date:* Continuous beginning 3/15. Students must reply by 5/1.

CONTACT Mrs. Sara Beth Holman, Director of Financial Aid, Lawrence University, PO Box 599, Appleton, WI 54912-0599, 920-832-6583 or toll-free 800-227-0982. *Fax:* 920-832-6582. *E-mail:* sara.b.holman@lawrence.edu.

LEBANON VALLEY COLLEGE
Annville, PA

Tuition & fees: $24,860   Average undergraduate aid package: $17,982

ABOUT THE INSTITUTION Independent United Methodist, coed. Awards: associate, bachelor's, master's, and first professional degrees and post-bachelor's certificates. 53 undergraduate majors. Total enrollment: 1,915. Undergraduates: 1,774. Freshmen: 454. Federal methodology is used as a basis for awarding need-based institutional aid.
UNDERGRADUATE EXPENSES for 2005–06 *Application fee:* $30. *Comprehensive fee:* $31,700 includes full-time tuition ($24,210), mandatory fees ($650), and room and board ($6840). *College room only:* $3340. Room and board charges vary according to board plan and housing facility. *Part-time tuition:* $440 per credit. Part-time tuition and fees vary according to class time and degree level. *Payment plan:* Installment.
FRESHMAN FINANCIAL AID (Fall 2005, est.) 426 applied for aid; of those 86% were deemed to have need. 100% of freshmen with need received aid; of those 38% had need fully met. *Average percent of need met:* 88% (excluding resources awarded to replace EFC). *Average financial aid package:* $18,041 (excluding resources awarded to replace EFC). 17% of all full-time freshmen had no need and received non-need-based gift aid.
UNDERGRADUATE FINANCIAL AID (Fall 2005, est.) 1,430 applied for aid; of those 87% were deemed to have need. 100% of undergraduates with need received aid; of those 38% had need fully met. *Average percent of need met:* 88% (excluding resources awarded to replace EFC). *Average financial aid package:* $17,982 (excluding resources awarded to replace EFC). 18% of all full-time undergraduates had no need and received non-need-based gift aid.
GIFT AID (NEED-BASED) *Total amount:* $15,537,505 (5% federal, 13% state, 82% institutional). *Receiving aid:* Freshmen: 80% (364); All full-time undergraduates: 77% (1,232). *Average award:* Freshmen: $15,235; Undergraduates: $14,836. *Scholarships, grants, and awards:* Federal Pell, FSEOG, state, private, college/university gift aid from institutional funds.
GIFT AID (NON-NEED-BASED) *Total amount:* $4,580,021 (2% state, 83% institutional, 15% external sources). *Receiving aid:* Freshmen: 13% (59); Undergraduates: 11% (171). *Average Award:* Freshmen: $10,125; Undergraduates: $10,104. *Scholarships, grants, and awards by category:* Academic Interests/Achievement: $12,744,043 total: biological sciences, general academic interests/achievements. Creative Arts/Performance: 32 awards ($32,000 total): music. Special Achievements/Activities: 105 awards ($52,500 total): general special achievements/activities, junior miss. *Special Characteristics:* 183 awards ($917,951 total): children and siblings of alumni, children of faculty/staff, ethnic background, international students. *Tuition waivers:* Full or partial for employees or children of employees, senior citizens. *ROTC:* Army cooperative.
LOANS *Student loans:* $10,951,273 (39% need-based, 61% non-need-based). 73% of past graduating class borrowed through all loan programs. *Average indebtedness per student:* $24,236. *Average need-based loan:* Freshmen: $3622; Undergraduates: $4222. *Parent loans:* $5,124,912 (100% non-need-based). *Programs:* FFEL (Subsidized and Unsubsidized Stafford, PLUS), Perkins.
WORK-STUDY *Federal work-study:* Total amount: $1,019,144; 790 jobs averaging $1266.
APPLYING FOR FINANCIAL AID *Required financial aid forms:* FAFSA, institution's own form. *Financial aid deadline (priority):* 3/1. *Notification date:* Continuous beginning 3/1. Students must reply by 5/1 or within 2 weeks of notification.
CONTACT Kendra M. Feigert, Director of Financial Aid, Lebanon Valley College, 101 North College Avenue, Annville, PA 17003, 866-582-4236 or toll-free 866-LVC-4ADM. *Fax:* 717-867-6027. *E-mail:* feigert@lvc.edu.

LEES-MCRAE COLLEGE
Banner Elk, NC

CONTACT Lester McKenzie, Assistant Dean of Students for Financial Aid, Lees-McRae College, PO Box 128, Banner Elk, NC 28604-0128, 828-898-8793 or toll-free 800-280-4562. *Fax:* 828-898-8814. *E-mail:* mckenzie@lmc.edu.

Lee University

LEE UNIVERSITY
Cleveland, TN

Tuition & fees: $9610 **Average undergraduate aid package:** $7911

ABOUT THE INSTITUTION Independent religious, coed. Awards: bachelor's and master's degrees. 33 undergraduate majors. Total enrollment: 3,930. Undergraduates: 3,648. Freshmen: 761. Federal methodology is used as a basis for awarding need-based institutional aid.
UNDERGRADUATE EXPENSES for 2005–06 *Application fee:* $25. *Comprehensive fee:* $14,780 includes full-time tuition ($9400), mandatory fees ($210), and room and board ($5170). *College room only:* $2680. Full-time tuition and fees vary according to program. Room and board charges vary according to board plan and housing facility. *Part-time tuition:* $392 per credit hour. *Part-time fees:* $30 per term. Part-time tuition and fees vary according to program. *Payment plan:* Deferred payment.
FRESHMAN FINANCIAL AID (Fall 2005, est.) 583 applied for aid; of those 79% were deemed to have need. 99% of freshmen with need received aid; of those 26% had need fully met. *Average percent of need met:* 62% (excluding resources awarded to replace EFC). *Average financial aid package:* $8116 (excluding resources awarded to replace EFC). 46% of all full-time freshmen had no need and received non-need-based gift aid.
UNDERGRADUATE FINANCIAL AID (Fall 2005, est.) 2,481 applied for aid; of those 82% were deemed to have need. 98% of undergraduates with need received aid; of those 17% had need fully met. *Average percent of need met:* 54% (excluding resources awarded to replace EFC). *Average financial aid package:* $7911 (excluding resources awarded to replace EFC). 26% of all full-time undergraduates had no need and received non-need-based gift aid.
GIFT AID (NEED-BASED) *Total amount:* $8,652,892 (37% federal, 18% state, 41% institutional, 4% external sources). *Receiving aid:* Freshmen: 53% (402); All full-time undergraduates: 48% (1,585). *Average award:* Freshmen: $7000; Undergraduates: $5752. *Scholarships, grants, and awards:* Federal Pell, FSEOG, state, private, college/university gift aid from institutional funds.
GIFT AID (NON-NEED-BASED) *Total amount:* $4,276,348 (17% state, 76% institutional, 7% external sources). *Receiving aid:* Freshmen: 11% (86); Undergraduates: 6% (200). *Average Award:* Freshmen: $6772; Undergraduates:* $7114. *Scholarships, grants, and awards by category: Academic Interests/Achievement:* 1,062 awards ($5,014,811 total): biological sciences, business, communication, education, general academic interests/achievements, religion/biblical studies. *Creative Arts/Performance:* 197 awards ($172,685 total): music, theater/drama. *Special Achievements/Activities:* 36 awards ($64,600 total): cheerleading/drum major, leadership, religious involvement. *Special Characteristics:* 178 awards ($751,401 total): children of faculty/staff, local/state students, siblings of current students, spouses of current students. *Tuition waivers:* Full or partial for employees or children of employees.
LOANS *Student loans:* $13,917,063 (75% need-based, 25% non-need-based). 71% of past graduating class borrowed through all loan programs. *Average indebtedness per student:* $26,482. *Average need-based loan:* Freshmen: $2819; Undergraduates: $4041. *Parent loans:* $2,853,912 (37% need-based, 63% non-need-based). *Programs:* FFEL (Subsidized and Unsubsidized Stafford, PLUS), Perkins, college/university.
WORK-STUDY *Federal work-study:* Total amount: $296,032; 180 jobs averaging $1648. *State or other work-study/employment:* Total amount: $420,000 (100% non-need-based). 300 part-time jobs averaging $1400.
ATHLETIC AWARDS *Total amount:* $1,142,587 (26% need-based, 74% non-need-based).
APPLYING FOR FINANCIAL AID *Required financial aid forms:* FAFSA, institution's own form. *Financial aid deadline (priority):* 3/15. *Notification date:* Continuous beginning 2/1. Students must reply within 3 weeks of notification.
CONTACT Mr. Michael Ellis, Director of Student Financial Aid, Lee University, 1120 North Ocoee Street, Cleveland, TN 37320-3450, 423-614-8300 or toll-free 800-533-9930. *Fax:* 423-614-8308. *E-mail:* finaid@leeuniversity.edu.

LEHIGH UNIVERSITY
Bethlehem, PA

Tuition & fees: $31,420 **Average undergraduate aid package:** $25,403

ABOUT THE INSTITUTION Independent, coed. Awards: bachelor's, master's, and doctoral degrees and post-bachelor's and post-master's certificates. 77 undergraduate majors. Total enrollment: 6,748. Undergraduates: 4,679. Freshmen: 1,223. Institutional methodology is used as a basis for awarding need-based institutional aid.
UNDERGRADUATE EXPENSES for 2005–06 *Application fee:* $60. *Comprehensive fee:* $39,980 includes full-time tuition ($31,180), mandatory fees ($240), and room and board ($8560). *College room only:* $4890. Room and board charges vary according to board plan and student level. *Part-time tuition:* $1300 per credit. *Payment plans:* Tuition prepayment, installment.
FRESHMAN FINANCIAL AID (Fall 2005, est.) 754 applied for aid; of those 76% were deemed to have need. 99% of freshmen with need received aid; of those 43% had need fully met. *Average percent of need met:* 97% (excluding resources awarded to replace EFC). *Average financial aid package:* $24,245 (excluding resources awarded to replace EFC). 8% of all full-time freshmen had no need and received non-need-based gift aid.
UNDERGRADUATE FINANCIAL AID (Fall 2005, est.) 2,514 applied for aid; of those 85% were deemed to have need. 99% of undergraduates with need received aid; of those 53% had need fully met. *Average percent of need met:* 98% (excluding resources awarded to replace EFC). *Average financial aid package:* $25,403 (excluding resources awarded to replace EFC). 6% of all full-time undergraduates had no need and received non-need-based gift aid.
GIFT AID (NEED-BASED) *Total amount:* $38,144,460 (4% federal, 4% state, 92% institutional). *Receiving aid:* Freshmen: 42% (513); All full-time undergraduates: 42% (1,925). *Average award:* Freshmen: $19,990; Undergraduates: $20,441. *Scholarships, grants, and awards:* Federal Pell, FSEOG, state, private, college/university gift aid from institutional funds, United Negro College Fund.
GIFT AID (NON-NEED-BASED) *Total amount:* $6,332,993 (1% federal, 76% institutional, 23% external sources). *Receiving aid:* Freshmen: 7% (83); Undergraduates: 6% (255). *Average Award:* Freshmen: $10,759; Undergraduates:* $9808. *Scholarships, grants, and awards by category: Academic Interests/Achievement:* 430 awards ($4,464,340 total): communication, general academic interests/achievements, military science. *Creative Arts/Performance:* 28 awards ($47,700 total): general creative arts/performance, music, performing arts, theater/drama. *Special Achievements/Activities:* general special achievements/activities. *Tuition waivers:* Full or partial for employees or children of employees, senior citizens. *ROTC:* Army.
LOANS *Student loans:* $18,558,593 (47% need-based, 53% non-need-based). 52% of past graduating class borrowed through all loan programs. *Average indebtedness per student:* $23,418. *Average need-based loan:* Freshmen: $3215; Undergraduates: $4325. *Parent loans:* $8,051,922 (100% non-need-based). *Programs:* FFEL (Subsidized and Unsubsidized Stafford, PLUS), Perkins, college/university, alternative loans.
WORK-STUDY *Federal work-study:* Total amount: $2,042,945; 1,302 jobs averaging $1569. *State or other work-study/employment:* Total amount: $757,193 (7% need-based, 93% non-need-based). 224 part-time jobs averaging $3380.
ATHLETIC AWARDS *Total amount:* $2,490,340 (56% need-based, 44% non-need-based).
APPLYING FOR FINANCIAL AID *Required financial aid forms:* FAFSA, CSS Financial Aid PROFILE, noncustodial (divorced/separated) parent's statement, business/farm supplement. *Financial aid deadline:* 2/1. *Notification date:* 3/30. Students must reply by 5/1 or within 3 weeks of notification.
CONTACT Linda F. Bell, Director of Financial Aid, Lehigh University, 218 West Packer Avenue, Bethlehem, PA 18015-3094, 610-758-3181. *Fax:* 610-758-6211. *E-mail:* lfn0@lehigh.edu.

LEHMAN COLLEGE OF THE CITY UNIVERSITY OF NEW YORK
Bronx, NY

Tuition & fees (NY res): $4288 **Average undergraduate aid package:** $3537

ABOUT THE INSTITUTION State and locally supported, coed. Awards: bachelor's and master's degrees and post-master's certificates. 53 undergraduate majors. Total enrollment: 10,615. Undergraduates: 8,442. Freshmen: 804. Federal methodology is used as a basis for awarding need-based institutional aid.
UNDERGRADUATE EXPENSES for 2006–07 *Application fee:* $50. *Tuition, state resident:* full-time $4000; part-time $170 per credit. *Tuition, nonresident:* full-time $10,800; part-time $360 per credit.
FRESHMAN FINANCIAL AID (Fall 2005, est.) 697 applied for aid; of those 100% were deemed to have need. 100% of freshmen with need received aid; of those 2% had need fully met. *Average percent of need met:* 72% (excluding

resources awarded to replace EFC). *Average financial aid package:* $3524 (excluding resources awarded to replace EFC). 7% of all full-time freshmen had no need and received non-need-based gift aid.
UNDERGRADUATE FINANCIAL AID (Fall 2005, est.) 4,275 applied for aid; of those 99% were deemed to have need. 100% of undergraduates with need received aid; of those 2% had need fully met. *Average percent of need met:* 68% (excluding resources awarded to replace EFC). *Average financial aid package:* $3537 (excluding resources awarded to replace EFC). 2% of all full-time undergraduates had no need and received non-need-based gift aid.
GIFT AID (NEED-BASED) *Total amount:* $25,565,576 (56% federal, 43% state, 1% institutional). *Receiving aid:* Freshmen: 80% (634); All full-time undergraduates: 77% (3,927). *Average award:* Freshmen: $1531; Undergraduates: $1361. *Scholarships, grants, and awards:* Federal Pell, FSEOG, state, college/university gift aid from institutional funds.
GIFT AID (NON-NEED-BASED) *Total amount:* $591,966 (13% state, 24% institutional, 63% external sources). *Receiving aid:* Freshmen: 36% (285); Undergraduates: 11% (585). *Average Award:* Freshmen: $1219; Undergraduates: $1400. *ROTC:* Army cooperative.
LOANS *Student loans:* $5,500,365 (100% need-based). 35% of past graduating class borrowed through all loan programs. *Average indebtedness per student:* $10,500. *Average need-based loan:* Freshmen: $1440; Undergraduates: $1559. *Parent loans:* $40,210 (100% non-need-based). *Programs:* Federal Direct (Subsidized and Unsubsidized Stafford, PLUS), Perkins.
WORK-STUDY *Federal work-study:* Total amount: $1,683,322; 510 jobs averaging $950.
APPLYING FOR FINANCIAL AID *Required financial aid forms:* FAFSA, state aid form. *Financial aid deadline:* Continuous. *Notification date:* Continuous beginning 3/1.
CONTACT David Martinez, Director of Financial Aid, Lehman College of the City University of New York, 250 Bedford Park Boulevard West, Bronx, NY 10468-1589, 718-960-8545 or toll-free 877-Lehman1 (out-of-state). *Fax:* 718-960-8328. *E-mail:* idmlc@cunyvm.cuny.edu.

LE MOYNE COLLEGE
Syracuse, NY

Tuition & fees: $21,280   **Average undergraduate aid package:** $17,168

ABOUT THE INSTITUTION Independent Roman Catholic (Jesuit), coed. Awards: bachelor's and master's degrees and post-bachelor's and post-master's certificates. 54 undergraduate majors. Total enrollment: 3,580. Undergraduates: 2,789. Freshmen: 520. Both federal and institutional methodology are used as a basis for awarding need-based institutional aid.
UNDERGRADUATE EXPENSES for 2005–06 *Application fee:* $35. *Comprehensive fee:* $29,570 includes full-time tuition ($20,770), mandatory fees ($510), and room and board ($8290). *College room only:* $5240. Room and board charges vary according to board plan and housing facility. *Part-time tuition:* $441 per credit hour. Part-time tuition and fees vary according to class time. *Payment plans:* Installment, deferred payment.
FRESHMAN FINANCIAL AID (Fall 2004) 389 applied for aid; of those 100% were deemed to have need. 100% of freshmen with need received aid; of those 31% had need fully met. *Average percent of need met:* 88% (excluding resources awarded to replace EFC). *Average financial aid package:* $18,335 (excluding resources awarded to replace EFC). 10% of all full-time freshmen had no need and received non-need-based gift aid.
UNDERGRADUATE FINANCIAL AID (Fall 2004) 2,090 applied for aid; of those 91% were deemed to have need. 100% of undergraduates with need received aid; of those 31% had need fully met. *Average percent of need met:* 82% (excluding resources awarded to replace EFC). *Average financial aid package:* $17,168 (excluding resources awarded to replace EFC). 9% of all full-time undergraduates had no need and received non-need-based gift aid.
GIFT AID (NEED-BASED) *Total amount:* $22,156,841 (11% federal, 17% state, 70% institutional, 2% external sources). *Receiving aid:* Freshmen: 82% (389); All full-time undergraduates: 81% (1,857). *Average award:* Freshmen: $14,765; Undergraduates: $12,977. *Scholarships, grants, and awards:* Federal Pell, FSEOG, state, private, college/university gift aid from institutional funds.
GIFT AID (NON-NEED-BASED) *Total amount:* $2,117,960 (4% state, 94% institutional, 2% external sources). *Receiving aid:* Freshmen: 48% (228); Undergraduates: 43% (975). *Average Award:* Freshmen: $9133; Undergraduates: $8704. *Scholarships, grants, and awards by category:* Academic Interests/Achievement: 325 awards ($3,884,450 total): general academic interests/achievements. *Special Achievements/Activities:* 500 awards ($2,880,200 total): leadership. *Special Characteristics:* 84 awards ($275,000 total): children and siblings of alumni, members of minority groups. *Tuition waivers:* Full or partial for employees or children of employees. *ROTC:* Army cooperative, Air Force cooperative.
LOANS *Student loans:* $10,983,484 (95% need-based, 5% non-need-based). 87% of past graduating class borrowed through all loan programs. *Average indebtedness per student:* $19,137. *Average need-based loan:* Freshmen: $3286; Undergraduates: $4599. *Parent loans:* $3,314,652 (86% need-based, 14% non-need-based). *Programs:* FFEL (Subsidized and Unsubsidized Stafford, PLUS), Perkins.
WORK-STUDY *Federal work-study:* Total amount: $290,600; 380 jobs averaging $900.
ATHLETIC AWARDS *Total amount:* $1,170,069 (77% need-based, 23% non-need-based).
APPLYING FOR FINANCIAL AID *Required financial aid forms:* FAFSA, institution's own form, state aid form. *Financial aid deadline (priority):* 2/1. *Notification date:* 3/15. Students must reply by 5/1 or within 2 weeks of notification.
CONTACT Mr. William Cheetham, Director of Financial Aid, Le Moyne College, Financial Aid Office, Syracuse, NY 13214-1301, 315-445-4400 or toll-free 800-333-4733. *Fax:* 315-445-4182. *E-mail:* cheethwc@lemoyne.edu.

LEMOYNE-OWEN COLLEGE
Memphis, TN

Tuition & fees: $14,658   **Average undergraduate aid package:** $8915

ABOUT THE INSTITUTION Independent religious, coed. Awards: bachelor's degrees and post-bachelor's certificates. 20 undergraduate majors. Total enrollment: 809. Undergraduates: 809. Freshmen: 112. Federal methodology is used as a basis for awarding need-based institutional aid.
UNDERGRADUATE EXPENSES for 2005–06 *Application fee:* $25. *Comprehensive fee:* $19,278 includes full-time tuition ($14,458), mandatory fees ($200), and room and board ($4620). *College room only:* $2420. Room and board charges vary according to board plan. *Payment plan:* Installment.
FRESHMAN FINANCIAL AID (Fall 2004) 110 applied for aid; of those 95% were deemed to have need. 98% of freshmen with need received aid; of those 7% had need fully met. *Average percent of need met:* 56% (excluding resources awarded to replace EFC). *Average financial aid package:* $7992 (excluding resources awarded to replace EFC). 10% of all full-time freshmen had no need and received non-need-based gift aid.
UNDERGRADUATE FINANCIAL AID (Fall 2004) 493 applied for aid; of those 96% were deemed to have need. 98% of undergraduates with need received aid; of those 7% had need fully met. *Average percent of need met:* 58% (excluding resources awarded to replace EFC). *Average financial aid package:* $8915 (excluding resources awarded to replace EFC). 5% of all full-time undergraduates had no need and received non-need-based gift aid.
GIFT AID (NEED-BASED) *Total amount:* $4,665,486 (52% federal, 23% state, 16% institutional, 9% external sources). *Receiving aid:* Freshmen: 84% (98); All full-time undergraduates: 85% (428). *Average award:* Freshmen: $6024; Undergraduates: $6304. *Scholarships, grants, and awards:* Federal Pell, FSEOG, state, private, college/university gift aid from institutional funds, United Negro College Fund.
GIFT AID (NON-NEED-BASED) *Total amount:* $355,748 (2% state, 78% institutional, 20% external sources). *Receiving aid:* Freshmen: 4% (5); Undergraduates: 4% (19). *Average Award:* Freshmen: $8117; Undergraduates: $8072. *Scholarships, grants, and awards by category:* Academic Interests/Achievement: 86 awards ($413,661 total): general academic interests/achievements. *Creative Arts/Performance:* 25 awards ($172,948 total): journalism/publications, music. *Special Characteristics:* 12 awards ($72,157 total): children of faculty/staff. *Tuition waivers:* Full or partial for employees or children of employees. *ROTC:* Army cooperative, Air Force cooperative.
LOANS *Student loans:* $3,995,662 (95% need-based, 5% non-need-based). 94% of past graduating class borrowed through all loan programs. *Average indebtedness per student:* $15,528. *Average need-based loan:* Freshmen: $2262; Undergraduates: $3121. *Parent loans:* $433,088 (74% need-based, 26% non-need-based). *Programs:* Federal Direct (Subsidized and Unsubsidized Stafford, PLUS).

LeMoyne-Owen College

WORK-STUDY *Federal work-study:* Total amount: $242,386; 317 jobs averaging $731.
ATHLETIC AWARDS Total amount: $527,385 (77% need-based, 23% non-need-based).
APPLYING FOR FINANCIAL AID *Required financial aid forms:* FAFSA, institution's own form. *Financial aid deadline (priority):* 4/1. *Notification date:* Continuous beginning 5/1. Students must reply within 2 weeks of notification.
CONTACT Phyllis Wilson, Director of Student Financial Services, LeMoyne-Owen College, 807 Walker Avenue, Memphis, TN 38126-6595, 901-435-1550. *Fax:* 901-435-1574. *E-mail:* phyllis_wilson@loc.edu.

LENOIR-RHYNE COLLEGE
Hickory, NC

ABOUT THE INSTITUTION Independent Lutheran, coed. Awards: bachelor's and master's degrees. 54 undergraduate majors. Total enrollment: 1,579. Undergraduates: 1,407. Freshmen: 322.
GIFT AID (NEED-BASED) *Scholarships, grants, and awards:* Federal Pell, FSEOG, state, private, college/university gift aid from institutional funds, Federal Nursing.
GIFT AID (NON-NEED-BASED) *Scholarships, grants, and awards by category: Academic Interests/Achievement:* general academic interests/achievements. *Creative Arts/Performance:* music. *Special Achievements/Activities:* cheerleading/drum major, community service, leadership. *Special Characteristics:* children and siblings of alumni, children of faculty/staff, local/state students, relatives of clergy, religious affiliation, siblings of current students.
LOANS *Programs:* FFEL (Subsidized and Unsubsidized Stafford, PLUS), Perkins, Federal Nursing, state.
WORK-STUDY *Federal work-study:* Total amount: $129,592; 168 jobs averaging $771. *State or other work-study/employment:* Total amount: $121,547 (100% need-based). 137 part-time jobs averaging $887.
APPLYING FOR FINANCIAL AID *Required financial aid forms:* FAFSA, institution's own form.
CONTACT Mrs. Rachel Nichols, Dean of Admissions and Financial Aid, Lenoir-Rhyne College, PO Box 7227, Hickory, NC 28603, 828-328-7300 or toll-free 800-277-5721. *Fax:* 828-328-7039. *E-mail:* admission@lrc.edu.

LESLEY UNIVERSITY
Cambridge, MA

Tuition & fees: $24,450	Average undergraduate aid package: $15,843

ABOUT THE INSTITUTION Independent, coed. Awards: associate, bachelor's, master's, and doctoral degrees and post-bachelor's and post-master's certificates. 22 undergraduate majors. Total enrollment: 7,298. Undergraduates: 1,265. Freshmen: 267. Both federal and institutional methodology are used as a basis for awarding need-based institutional aid.
UNDERGRADUATE EXPENSES for 2005–06 *Application fee:* $40. *One-time required fee:* $950. *Comprehensive fee:* $34,950 includes full-time tuition ($24,200), mandatory fees ($250), and room and board ($10,500). *College room only:* $6400. Full-time tuition and fees vary according to program. Room and board charges vary according to housing facility. *Part-time tuition:* $1020 per credit. *Payment plan:* Installment.
FRESHMAN FINANCIAL AID (Fall 2005, est.) 234 applied for aid; of those 81% were deemed to have need. 100% of freshmen with need received aid; of those 10% had need fully met. *Average percent of need met:* 70% (excluding resources awarded to replace EFC). *Average financial aid package:* $16,791 (excluding resources awarded to replace EFC). 16% of all full-time freshmen had no need and received non-need-based gift aid.
UNDERGRADUATE FINANCIAL AID (Fall 2005, est.) 874 applied for aid; of those 81% were deemed to have need. 100% of undergraduates with need received aid; of those 26% had need fully met. *Average percent of need met:* 70% (excluding resources awarded to replace EFC). *Average financial aid package:* $15,843 (excluding resources awarded to replace EFC). 10% of all full-time undergraduates had no need and received non-need-based gift aid.
GIFT AID (NEED-BASED) *Total amount:* $6,090,503 (17% federal, 7% state, 70% institutional, 6% external sources). *Receiving aid:* Freshmen: 76% (189); All full-time undergraduates: 67% (666). *Average award:* Freshmen: $12,741; Undergraduates: $11,142. *Scholarships, grants, and awards:* Federal Pell, FSEOG, state, private, college/university gift aid from institutional funds.
GIFT AID (NON-NEED-BASED) *Total amount:* $2,973,704 (100% institutional). *Receiving aid:* Freshmen: 49% (121); Undergraduates: 19% (185). *Average Award:* Freshmen: $5938; Undergraduates: $6056. *Scholarships, grants, and awards by category: Academic Interests/Achievement:* 4 awards ($80,410 total): general academic interests/achievements. *Creative Arts/Performance:* 9 awards ($10,500 total): art/fine arts. *Special Achievements/Activities:* 205 awards ($966,586 total): general special achievements/activities. *Special Characteristics:* 59 awards ($653,774 total): ethnic background, local/state students, members of minority groups. *Tuition waivers:* Full or partial for employees or children of employees.
LOANS *Student loans:* $3,779,573 (74% need-based, 26% non-need-based). 90% of past graduating class borrowed through all loan programs. *Average indebtedness per student:* $14,000. *Average need-based loan:* Freshmen: $3507; Undergraduates: $4183. *Parent loans:* $1,919,242 (100% non-need-based). *Programs:* FFEL (Subsidized and Unsubsidized Stafford, PLUS), Perkins, state.
WORK-STUDY *Federal work-study:* Total amount: $301,000; 232 jobs averaging $1270. *State or other work-study/employment:* 135 part-time jobs averaging $2016.
APPLYING FOR FINANCIAL AID *Required financial aid forms:* FAFSA, institution's own form. *Financial aid deadline (priority):* 3/15. *Notification date:* 4/1.
CONTACT Financial Aid Office, Lesley University, 29 Everett Street, Cambridge, MA 02138-2790, 617-349-8581 or toll-free 800-999-1959 Ext. 8800. *Fax:* 617-349-8667. *E-mail:* finaid@lesley.edu.

LETOURNEAU UNIVERSITY
Longview, TX

Tuition & fees: $15,890	Average undergraduate aid package: $12,703

ABOUT THE INSTITUTION Independent nondenominational, coed. Awards: associate, bachelor's, and master's degrees. 41 undergraduate majors. Total enrollment: 3,980. Undergraduates: 3,606. Freshmen: 352. Federal methodology is used as a basis for awarding need-based institutional aid.
UNDERGRADUATE EXPENSES for 2005–06 *Application fee:* $25. *Comprehensive fee:* $22,176 includes full-time tuition ($15,710), mandatory fees ($180), and room and board ($6286). Room and board charges vary according to board plan. *Part-time tuition:* $280 per hour. Part-time tuition and fees vary according to course load. *Payment plan:* Installment.
FRESHMAN FINANCIAL AID (Fall 2004) 286 applied for aid; of those 81% were deemed to have need. 100% of freshmen with need received aid; of those 16% had need fully met. *Average percent of need met:* 73% (excluding resources awarded to replace EFC). *Average financial aid package:* $12,747 (excluding resources awarded to replace EFC). 21% of all full-time freshmen had no need and received non-need-based gift aid.
UNDERGRADUATE FINANCIAL AID (Fall 2004) 949 applied for aid; of those 85% were deemed to have need. 100% of undergraduates with need received aid; of those 18% had need fully met. *Average percent of need met:* 73% (excluding resources awarded to replace EFC). *Average financial aid package:* $12,703 (excluding resources awarded to replace EFC). 16% of all full-time undergraduates had no need and received non-need-based gift aid.
GIFT AID (NEED-BASED) *Total amount:* $6,439,175 (44% federal, 18% state, 38% institutional). *Receiving aid:* Freshmen: 71% (232); All full-time undergraduates: 25% (301). *Average award:* Freshmen: $9049; Undergraduates: $8145. *Scholarships, grants, and awards:* Federal Pell, FSEOG, state, private, college/university gift aid from institutional funds.
GIFT AID (NON-NEED-BASED) *Total amount:* $2,870,173 (1% federal, 85% institutional, 14% external sources). *Receiving aid:* Freshmen: 54% (178); Undergraduates: 36% (438). *Average Award:* Freshmen: $1650; Undergraduates: $4083. *Scholarships, grants, and awards by category: Academic Interests/Achievement:* general academic interests/achievements. *Special Achievements/Activities:* general special achievements/activities. *Special Characteristics:* children of faculty/staff, international students, local/state students, relatives of clergy, spouses of current students. *Tuition waivers:* Full or partial for employees or children of employees.
LOANS *Student loans:* $24,438,625 (42% need-based, 58% non-need-based). 87% of past graduating class borrowed through all loan programs. *Average indebtedness per student:* $28,426. *Average need-based loan:* Freshmen: $2819; Undergraduates: $3944. *Parent loans:* $2,248,150 (100% non-need-based). *Programs:* FFEL (Subsidized and Unsubsidized Stafford, PLUS), Perkins.

WORK-STUDY *Federal work-study:* Total amount: $187,218; jobs available. *State or other work-study/employment:* Total amount: $26,779 (100% need-based). Part-time jobs available.

APPLYING FOR FINANCIAL AID *Required financial aid form:* FAFSA. *Financial aid deadline (priority):* 2/15. *Notification date:* Continuous beginning 3/1. Students must reply within 3 weeks of notification.

CONTACT Ms. Delinda Hall, Director of Financial Aid, LeTourneau University, 2100 South Mobberly Avenue, PO Box 7001, Longview, TX 75607, 903-233-3430 or toll-free 800-759-8811. *Fax:* 903-233-3411. *E-mail:* finaid@letu.edu.

LEWIS & CLARK COLLEGE
Portland, OR

| Tuition & fees: $27,710 | Average undergraduate aid package: $24,380 |

ABOUT THE INSTITUTION Independent, coed. Awards: bachelor's, master's, doctoral, and first professional degrees and post-master's certificates. 29 undergraduate majors. Total enrollment: 3,433. Undergraduates: 1,964. Freshmen: 490. Federal methodology is used as a basis for awarding need-based institutional aid.

UNDERGRADUATE EXPENSES for 2005–06 *Application fee:* $50. *Comprehensive fee:* $35,358 includes full-time tuition ($27,494), mandatory fees ($216), and room and board ($7648). *College room only:* $3974. Room and board charges vary according to board plan and housing facility. *Part-time tuition:* $1386 per credit hour. *Payment plan:* Installment.

FRESHMAN FINANCIAL AID (Fall 2005, est.) 415 applied for aid; of those 84% were deemed to have need. 100% of freshmen with need received aid; of those 31% had need fully met. *Average percent of need met:* 89% (excluding resources awarded to replace EFC). *Average financial aid package:* $23,877 (excluding resources awarded to replace EFC). 15% of all full-time freshmen had no need and received non-need-based gift aid.

UNDERGRADUATE FINANCIAL AID (Fall 2005, est.) 1,283 applied for aid; of those 89% were deemed to have need. 97% of undergraduates with need received aid; of those 34% had need fully met. *Average percent of need met:* 88% (excluding resources awarded to replace EFC). *Average financial aid package:* $24,380 (excluding resources awarded to replace EFC). 13% of all full-time undergraduates had no need and received non-need-based gift aid.

GIFT AID (NEED-BASED) *Total amount:* $18,030,861 (7% federal, 1% state, 89% institutional, 3% external sources). *Receiving aid:* Freshmen: 65% (347); All full-time undergraduates: 60% (1,099). *Average award:* Freshmen: $20,037; Undergraduates: $19,352. *Scholarships, grants, and awards:* Federal Pell, FSEOG, state, private, college/university gift aid from institutional funds.

GIFT AID (NON-NEED-BASED) *Total amount:* $1,978,197 (96% institutional, 4% external sources). *Receiving aid:* Freshmen: 3% (14); Undergraduates: 3% (46). *Average Award:* Freshmen: $7965; Undergraduates: $7876. *Scholarships, grants, and awards by category: Academic Interests/Achievement:* 672 awards ($5,319,792 total): general academic interests/achievements. *Creative Arts/Performance:* 39 awards ($143,878 total): debating, music. *Special Achievements/Activities:* 97 awards ($483,000 total): community service. *Tuition waivers:* Full or partial for employees or children of employees.

LOANS *Student loans:* $5,840,812 (93% need-based, 7% non-need-based). 58% of past graduating class borrowed through all loan programs. *Average indebtedness per student:* $19,124. *Average need-based loan:* Freshmen: $4319; Undergraduates: $5262. *Parent loans:* $2,163,842 (82% need-based, 18% non-need-based). *Programs:* FFEL (Subsidized and Unsubsidized Stafford, PLUS), Perkins.

WORK-STUDY *Federal work-study:* Total amount: $1,398,908; 674 jobs averaging $2034.

APPLYING FOR FINANCIAL AID *Required financial aid form:* FAFSA. *Financial aid deadline (priority):* 3/1. *Notification date:* Continuous beginning 3/1. Students must reply by 5/1.

CONTACT Glendi Gaddis, Director of Student Financial Services, Lewis & Clark College, Templeton Student Center, MS 56, Portland, OR 97219-7899, 503-768-7096 or toll-free 800-444-4111. *Fax:* 503-768-7074. *E-mail:* sfs@lclark.edu.

LEWIS-CLARK STATE COLLEGE
Lewiston, ID

| Tuition & fees (ID res): $3714 | Average undergraduate aid package: $5452 |

ABOUT THE INSTITUTION State-supported, coed. Awards: associate and bachelor's degrees. 50 undergraduate majors. Total enrollment: 3,451. Undergraduates: 3,451. Freshmen: 469. Federal methodology is used as a basis for awarding need-based institutional aid.

UNDERGRADUATE EXPENSES for 2005–06 *Application fee:* $35. *Tuition, area resident:* part-time $185 per credit. *Tuition, state resident:* full-time $3714; part-time $185 per credit. *Tuition, nonresident:* full-time $10,266. *Required fees:* $11 per credit. Full-time tuition and fees vary according to course load and reciprocity agreements. *College room and board:* $4500; *room only:* $1900. Room and board charges vary according to board plan and housing facility. *Payment plan:* Deferred payment.

FRESHMAN FINANCIAL AID (Fall 2004) 393 applied for aid; of those 86% were deemed to have need. 98% of freshmen with need received aid; of those 7% had need fully met. *Average percent of need met:* 7% (excluding resources awarded to replace EFC). *Average financial aid package:* $3950 (excluding resources awarded to replace EFC). 13% of all full-time freshmen had no need and received non-need-based gift aid.

UNDERGRADUATE FINANCIAL AID (Fall 2004) 1,862 applied for aid; of those 90% were deemed to have need. 98% of undergraduates with need received aid; of those 11% had need fully met. *Average percent of need met:* 11% (excluding resources awarded to replace EFC). *Average financial aid package:* $5452 (excluding resources awarded to replace EFC). 7% of all full-time undergraduates had no need and received non-need-based gift aid.

GIFT AID (NEED-BASED) *Total amount:* $5,432,855 (80% federal, 1% state, 9% institutional, 10% external sources). *Receiving aid:* Freshmen: 51% (231); All full-time undergraduates: 53% (1,225). *Average award:* Freshmen: $3018; Undergraduates: $3125. *Scholarships, grants, and awards:* Federal Pell, FSEOG, state, private, college/university gift aid from institutional funds.

GIFT AID (NON-NEED-BASED) *Total amount:* $560,021 (71% institutional, 29% external sources). *Receiving aid:* Freshmen: 30% (139); Undergraduates: 14% (329). *Average Award:* Freshmen: $2221; Undergraduates: $2478. *Scholarships, grants, and awards by category: Academic Interests/Achievement:* 169 awards ($176,909 total): business, education, English, general academic interests/achievements, health fields, humanities, mathematics, social sciences. *Creative Arts/Performance:* 22 awards ($53,610 total): art/fine arts, creative writing, music, theater/drama. *Special Achievements/Activities:* 32 awards ($7500 total): junior miss, leadership, rodeo. *Special Characteristics:* 208 awards ($559,850 total): ethnic background, first-generation college students, local/state students, members of minority groups, out-of-state students. *Tuition waivers:* Full or partial for employees or children of employees, senior citizens. *ROTC:* Army, Air Force cooperative.

LOANS *Student loans:* $9,237,147 (71% need-based, 29% non-need-based). 61% of past graduating class borrowed through all loan programs. *Average need-based loan:* Freshmen: $2203; Undergraduates: $3552. *Parent loans:* $349,149 (100% non-need-based). *Programs:* FFEL (Subsidized and Unsubsidized Stafford, PLUS), Perkins, Federal Nursing.

WORK-STUDY *Federal work-study:* Total amount: $125,888; 96 jobs averaging $1311. *State or other work-study/employment:* Total amount: $97,991 (84% need-based, 16% non-need-based). 77 part-time jobs averaging $1272.

ATHLETIC AWARDS *Total amount:* $818,830 (100% non-need-based).

APPLYING FOR FINANCIAL AID *Required financial aid form:* FAFSA. *Financial aid deadline (priority):* 3/1. *Notification date:* Continuous beginning 4/15. Students must reply within 2 weeks of notification.

CONTACT Ms. Laura Hughes, Director of Financial Aid, Lewis-Clark State College, 500 8th Avenue, Lewiston, ID 83501-2698, 208-792-2224 or toll-free 800-933-LCSC Ext. 2210. *Fax:* 208-792-2063. *E-mail:* lhughes@lcsc.edu.

LEWIS UNIVERSITY
Romeoville, IL

CONTACT Ms. Janeen Decharinte, Director of Financial Aid, Lewis University, One University Parkway, Romeoville, IL 60446, 815-836-5262 or toll-free 800-897-9000. *Fax:* 815-836-5135. *E-mail:* decharja@lewisu.edu.

LEXINGTON COLLEGE
Chicago, IL

| Tuition & fees: $17,040 | Average undergraduate aid package: $8700 |

Lexington College

ABOUT THE INSTITUTION Independent, women only. Awards: associate and bachelor's degrees. 12 undergraduate majors. Total enrollment: 56. Undergraduates: 56. Freshmen: 15. Federal methodology is used as a basis for awarding need-based institutional aid.
UNDERGRADUATE EXPENSES for 2005–06 *Application fee:* $30. *Tuition:* full-time $16,100; part-time $530 per credit hour. *Required fees:* full-time $940; $200 per term part-time. *Payment plan:* Installment.
FRESHMAN FINANCIAL AID (Fall 2005, est.) 31 applied for aid; of those 100% were deemed to have need. 100% of freshmen with need received aid; of those 6% had need fully met. *Average percent of need met:* 89% (excluding resources awarded to replace EFC). *Average financial aid package:* $13,500 (excluding resources awarded to replace EFC).
UNDERGRADUATE FINANCIAL AID (Fall 2005, est.) 51 applied for aid; of those 100% were deemed to have need. 100% of undergraduates with need received aid; of those 12% had need fully met. *Average percent of need met:* 93% (excluding resources awarded to replace EFC). *Average financial aid package:* $8700 (excluding resources awarded to replace EFC).
GIFT AID (NEED-BASED) *Total amount:* $501,007 (24% federal, 26% state, 33% institutional, 17% external sources). *Receiving aid:* Freshmen: 16% (5); All full-time undergraduates: 100% (51). *Average award:* Freshmen: $11,500; Undergraduates: $7900. *Scholarships, grants, and awards:* Federal Pell, FSEOG, state, private, college/university gift aid from institutional funds.
GIFT AID (NON-NEED-BASED) *Tuition waivers:* Full or partial for employees or children of employees.
LOANS *Student loans:* $188,560 (95% need-based, 5% non-need-based). 50% of past graduating class borrowed through all loan programs. *Average indebtedness per student:* $5000. *Average need-based loan:* Undergraduates: $3500. *Parent loans:* $16,340 (100% need-based). *Programs:* FFEL (Subsidized and Unsubsidized Stafford, PLUS), Sallie Mae Signature Student Loans, alternative loans.
WORK-STUDY *Federal work-study:* Total amount: $5000; 5 jobs averaging $5000.
APPLYING FOR FINANCIAL AID *Required financial aid form:* FAFSA. *Financial aid deadline:* 10/1 (priority: 5/15). *Notification date:* Continuous.
CONTACT Maria Lebron-Cardona, Director of Financial Aid, Lexington College, 310 South Peoria Street, Suite 512, Chicago, IL 60607, 312-226-6294 Ext. 227. *Fax:* 312-226-6405. *E-mail:* finaid@lexingtoncollege.edu.

LIBERTY UNIVERSITY
Lynchburg, VA

ABOUT THE INSTITUTION Independent nondenominational, coed. Awards: associate, bachelor's, master's, doctoral, and first professional degrees and post-master's certificates (also offers external degree program with significant enrollment not reflected in profile). 51 undergraduate majors. Total enrollment: 12,458. Undergraduates: 9,975. Freshmen: 1,985.
GIFT AID (NEED-BASED) *Scholarships, grants, and awards:* Federal Pell, FSEOG, state, private, college/university gift aid from institutional funds.
GIFT AID (NON-NEED-BASED) *Scholarships, grants, and awards by category: Academic Interests/Achievement:* general academic interests/achievements. *Creative Arts/Performance:* art/fine arts, debating, journalism/publications, music, performing arts. *Special Achievements/Activities:* cheerleading/drum major, general special achievements/activities, leadership, religious involvement. *Special Characteristics:* international students, religious affiliation.
LOANS *Programs:* FFEL (Subsidized and Unsubsidized Stafford, PLUS).
WORK-STUDY *Federal work-study:* Total amount: $3,171,874; 2,712 jobs averaging $1170.
APPLYING FOR FINANCIAL AID *Required financial aid form:* FAFSA.
CONTACT Rhonda Allbeck, Director, Financial Aid Office, Liberty University, 1971 University Boulevard, Lynchburg, VA 24502, 434-582-2288 or toll-free 800-543-5317. *Fax:* 434-582-2053. *E-mail:* rfallbeck@liberty.edu.

LIFE PACIFIC COLLEGE
San Dimas, CA

ABOUT THE INSTITUTION Independent religious, coed. Awards: associate and bachelor's degrees. 3 undergraduate majors. Total enrollment: 528. Undergraduates: 534. Freshmen: 79.
GIFT AID (NEED-BASED) *Scholarships, grants, and awards:* Federal Pell, FSEOG, state, private, college/university gift aid from institutional funds.
GIFT AID (NON-NEED-BASED) *Scholarships, grants, and awards by category: Academic Interests/Achievement:* general academic interests/achievements. *Special Characteristics:* children of faculty/staff, relatives of clergy.
LOANS *Programs:* FFEL (Subsidized and Unsubsidized Stafford, PLUS).
APPLYING FOR FINANCIAL AID *Required financial aid forms:* FAFSA, state aid form.
CONTACT Mrs. Becky Huyck, Director of Financial Aid, Life Pacific College, 1100 Covina Boulevard, San Dimas, CA 91773-3298, 909-599-5433 Ext. 319 or toll-free 877-886-5433 Ext. 314. *Fax:* 909-599-6690. *E-mail:* bhuyck@lifepacific.edu.

LIFE UNIVERSITY
Marietta, GA

Tuition & fees: $7065 | **Average undergraduate aid package: $6100**

ABOUT THE INSTITUTION Independent, coed. Awards: associate, bachelor's, master's, and first professional degrees. 5 undergraduate majors. Total enrollment: 1,473. Undergraduates: 476. Federal methodology is used as a basis for awarding need-based institutional aid.
UNDERGRADUATE EXPENSES for 2005–06 *Application fee:* $50. *Comprehensive fee:* $18,045 includes full-time tuition ($6750), mandatory fees ($315), and room and board ($10,980). Full-time tuition and fees vary according to course load. *Part-time tuition:* $148 per hour. *Part-time fees:* $105 per term. Part-time tuition and fees vary according to course load.
FRESHMAN FINANCIAL AID (Fall 2005, est.) 78 applied for aid; of those 91% were deemed to have need. 96% of freshmen with need received aid; of those 40% had need fully met. *Average percent of need met:* 38% (excluding resources awarded to replace EFC). *Average financial aid package:* $6100 (excluding resources awarded to replace EFC). 2% of all full-time freshmen had no need and received non-need-based gift aid.
UNDERGRADUATE FINANCIAL AID (Fall 2005, est.) 373 applied for aid; of those 93% were deemed to have need. 98% of undergraduates with need received aid; of those 16% had need fully met. *Average percent of need met:* 15% (excluding resources awarded to replace EFC). *Average financial aid package:* $6100 (excluding resources awarded to replace EFC). 1% of all full-time undergraduates had no need and received non-need-based gift aid.
GIFT AID (NEED-BASED) *Total amount:* $600,500 (100% federal). *Receiving aid:* Freshmen: 35% (42); All full-time undergraduates: 30% (148). *Average award:* Freshmen: $4200; Undergraduates: $3700. *Scholarships, grants, and awards:* Federal Pell, FSEOG, state, private, college/university gift aid from institutional funds.
GIFT AID (NON-NEED-BASED) *Total amount:* $398,000 (41% state, 50% institutional, 9% external sources). *Receiving aid:* Freshmen: 28% (33); Undergraduates: 23% (114). *Average Award:* Freshmen: $3460; Undergraduates: $3680. *Scholarships, grants, and awards by category: Academic Interests/Achievement:* 19 awards ($73,000 total): general academic interests/achievements. *Tuition waivers:* Full or partial for employees or children of employees.
LOANS *Student loans:* $3,100,000 (52% need-based, 48% non-need-based). 69% of past graduating class borrowed through all loan programs. *Average indebtedness per student:* $13,000. *Average need-based loan:* Freshmen: $3100; Undergraduates: $3200. *Parent loans:* $95,000 (100% non-need-based). *Programs:* FFEL (Subsidized and Unsubsidized Stafford, PLUS), Perkins, college/university, alternative loans.
WORK-STUDY *Federal work-study:* Total amount: $135,000; 156 jobs averaging $900.
ATHLETIC AWARDS *Total amount:* $100,500 (100% non-need-based).
APPLYING FOR FINANCIAL AID *Required financial aid forms:* FAFSA, institution's own form. *Financial aid deadline (priority):* 3/1. *Notification date:* Continuous beginning 5/1.
CONTACT Diane Clark, Director of Financial Aid, Life University, 1269 Barclay Circle, Marietta, GA 30060, 770-426-2901 or toll-free 800-543-3202 (in-state). *Fax:* 770-426-2926. *E-mail:* finaid@life.edu.

LIMESTONE COLLEGE
Gaffney, SC

Tuition & fees: $15,000 | **Average undergraduate aid package: $10,129**

ABOUT THE INSTITUTION Independent, coed. Awards: associate and bachelor's degrees. 45 undergraduate majors. Total enrollment: 676. Undergraduates: 676. Freshmen: 172. Federal methodology is used as a basis for awarding need-based institutional aid.
UNDERGRADUATE EXPENSES for 2006–07 *Application fee:* $25. *Comprehensive fee:* $21,000 includes full-time tuition ($15,000) and room and board ($6000). *Part-time tuition:* $625 per credit hour.
FRESHMAN FINANCIAL AID (Fall 2004) 180 applied for aid; of those 84% were deemed to have need. 100% of freshmen with need received aid; of those 21% had need fully met. *Average percent of need met:* 66% (excluding resources awarded to replace EFC). *Average financial aid package:* $10,023 (excluding resources awarded to replace EFC). 18% of all full-time freshmen had no need and received non-need-based gift aid.
UNDERGRADUATE FINANCIAL AID (Fall 2004) 578 applied for aid; of those 90% were deemed to have need. 100% of undergraduates with need received aid; of those 19% had need fully met. *Average percent of need met:* 63% (excluding resources awarded to replace EFC). *Average financial aid package:* $10,129 (excluding resources awarded to replace EFC). 16% of all full-time undergraduates had no need and received non-need-based gift aid.
GIFT AID (NEED-BASED) *Total amount:* $2,992,864 (30% federal, 25% state, 40% institutional, 5% external sources). *Receiving aid:* Freshmen: 59% (147); All full-time undergraduates: 74% (496). *Average award:* Freshmen: $7644; Undergraduates: $7227. *Scholarships, grants, and awards:* Federal Pell, FSEOG, state, private, college/university gift aid from institutional funds.
GIFT AID (NON-NEED-BASED) *Total amount:* $769,167 (25% state, 61% institutional, 14% external sources). *Receiving aid:* Freshmen: 12% (31); Undergraduates: 15% (98). *Average Award:* Freshmen: $7565; Undergraduates: $6921. *Scholarships, grants, and awards by category: Academic Interests/Achievement:* 115 awards ($329,325 total): biological sciences, business, communication, computer science, education, English, general academic interests/achievements, humanities, mathematics, physical sciences, religion/biblical studies, social sciences. *Creative Arts/Performance:* 34 awards ($81,313 total): art/fine arts, music, performing arts, theater/drama. *Special Achievements/Activities:* 293 awards ($426,120 total): cheerleading/drum major, leadership, religious involvement. *Special Characteristics:* 423 awards ($615,540 total): children and siblings of alumni, children of faculty/staff, first-generation college students, local/state students, out-of-state students, siblings of current students. *ROTC:* Army cooperative.
LOANS *Student loans:* $3,160,722 (83% need-based, 17% non-need-based). 66% of past graduating class borrowed through all loan programs. *Average indebtedness per student:* $16,175. *Average need-based loan:* Freshmen: $2372; Undergraduates: $3345. *Parent loans:* $744,249 (48% need-based, 52% non-need-based). *Programs:* FFEL (Subsidized and Unsubsidized Stafford, PLUS), Perkins.
WORK-STUDY *Federal work-study:* Total amount: $162,059; 82 jobs averaging $1861. *State or other work-study/employment:* Total amount: $85,635 (38% need-based, 62% non-need-based). 89 part-time jobs averaging $833.
ATHLETIC AWARDS *Total amount:* $927,960 (58% need-based, 42% non-need-based).
APPLYING FOR FINANCIAL AID *Required financial aid form:* FAFSA. *Financial aid deadline (priority):* 2/1. *Notification date:* Continuous beginning 1/15. Students must reply within 3 weeks of notification.
CONTACT Mrs. Lauren Mack, Director of Financial Aid, Limestone College, 1115 College Drive, Gaffney, SC 29340-3799, 864-488-4567 or toll-free 800-795-7151 Ext. 554. *Fax:* 864-487-8706. *E-mail:* lmack@limestone.edu.

LINCOLN CHRISTIAN COLLEGE
Lincoln, IL

Tuition & fees: $10,200   **Average undergraduate aid package:** $8000

ABOUT THE INSTITUTION Independent religious, coed. Awards: associate and bachelor's degrees. 13 undergraduate majors. Total enrollment: 708. Undergraduates: 708. Freshmen: 182. Federal methodology is used as a basis for awarding need-based institutional aid.
UNDERGRADUATE EXPENSES for 2006–07 *Application fee:* $20. *Comprehensive fee:* $15,100 includes full-time tuition ($10,200) and room and board ($4900). *Part-time tuition:* $340 per semester hour.
FRESHMAN FINANCIAL AID (Fall 2005, est.) 160 applied for aid; of those 80% were deemed to have need. 100% of freshmen with need received aid. *Average percent of need met:* 80% (excluding resources awarded to replace EFC). *Average financial aid package:* $7500 (excluding resources awarded to replace EFC). 22% of all full-time freshmen had no need and received non-need-based gift aid.
UNDERGRADUATE FINANCIAL AID (Fall 2005, est.) 632 applied for aid; of those 80% were deemed to have need. 100% of undergraduates with need received aid. *Average percent of need met:* 80% (excluding resources awarded to replace EFC). *Average financial aid package:* $8000 (excluding resources awarded to replace EFC). 9% of all full-time undergraduates had no need and received non-need-based gift aid.
GIFT AID (NEED-BASED) *Total amount:* $2,122,525 (33% federal, 48% state, 19% institutional). *Scholarships, grants, and awards:* Federal Pell, FSEOG, state.
GIFT AID (NON-NEED-BASED) *Total amount:* $777,521 (2% state, 45% institutional, 53% external sources). *Scholarships, grants, and awards by category: Academic Interests/Achievement:* 45 awards ($148,450 total): general academic interests/achievements. *Special Achievements/Activities:* 28 awards ($48,600 total): community service, leadership. *Special Characteristics:* 22 awards ($150,341 total): children of faculty/staff.
LOANS *Student loans:* $2,271,461 (64% need-based, 36% non-need-based). 74% of past graduating class borrowed through all loan programs. *Average indebtedness per student:* $15,555. *Parent loans:* $365,273 (100% non-need-based). *Programs:* FFEL (Subsidized and Unsubsidized Stafford, PLUS), Perkins, college/university.
WORK-STUDY *Federal work-study:* Total amount: $87,753; 100 jobs averaging $780. *State or other work-study/employment:* Total amount: $130,000 (23% need-based, 77% non-need-based). 109 part-time jobs averaging $1224.
APPLYING FOR FINANCIAL AID *Required financial aid form:* FAFSA. *Financial aid deadline:* Continuous. *Notification date:* Continuous beginning 3/1. Students must reply within 2 weeks of notification.
CONTACT Nancy Siddens, Co-Director of Financial Aid, Lincoln Christian College, 100 Campus View Drive, Lincoln, IL 62656, 217-732-3168 Ext. 2250 or toll-free 888-522-5228. *Fax:* 217-732-4199. *E-mail:* finaid@lccs.edu.

LINCOLN MEMORIAL UNIVERSITY
Harrogate, TN

ABOUT THE INSTITUTION Independent, coed. Awards: associate, bachelor's, and master's degrees and post-master's certificates. 43 undergraduate majors. Total enrollment: 2,802. Undergraduates: 1,316. Freshmen: 184.
GIFT AID (NEED-BASED) *Scholarships, grants, and awards:* Federal Pell, FSEOG, state, private, college/university gift aid from institutional funds.
GIFT AID (NON-NEED-BASED) *Scholarships, grants, and awards by category: Academic Interests/Achievement:* general academic interests/achievements. *Creative Arts/Performance:* music. *Special Achievements/Activities:* cheerleading/drum major. *Special Characteristics:* children of faculty/staff.
LOANS *Programs:* FFEL (Subsidized and Unsubsidized Stafford, PLUS), Perkins.
APPLYING FOR FINANCIAL AID *Required financial aid form:* FAFSA.
CONTACT Celena Rader-Lombdin, Director of Financial Aid, Lincoln Memorial University, Cumberland Gap Parkway, Harrogate, TN 37752-1901, 423-869-6465 or toll-free 800-325-0900. *Fax:* 423-869-6347. *E-mail:* clambdin@lmunet.edu.

LINCOLN UNIVERSITY
Jefferson City, MO

Tuition & fees (MO res): $4602   **Average undergraduate aid package:** $8000

ABOUT THE INSTITUTION State-supported, coed. Awards: associate, bachelor's, and master's degrees and post-master's certificates. 41 undergraduate majors. Total enrollment: 3,180. Undergraduates: 2,953. Freshmen: 632. Federal methodology is used as a basis for awarding need-based institutional aid.
UNDERGRADUATE EXPENSES for 2006–07 *Application fee:* $17. *Tuition, state resident:* full-time $4412; part-time $147.08 per credit hour. *Tuition, nonresident:* full-time $8059; part-time $268.62 per credit hour. *Required fees:* full-time $190; $5 per credit hour or $20 per term part-time. *College room and board:* $3790; *room only:* $1850.
FRESHMAN FINANCIAL AID (Fall 2005, est.) 528 applied for aid; of those 91% were deemed to have need. 90% of freshmen with need received aid; of those 16% had need fully met. *Average percent of need met:* 30% (excluding resources

Lincoln University

awarded to replace EFC). *Average financial aid package:* $6000 (excluding resources awarded to replace EFC). 8% of all full-time freshmen had no need and received non-need-based gift aid.

UNDERGRADUATE FINANCIAL AID (Fall 2005, est.) 1,608 applied for aid; of those 94% were deemed to have need. 93% of undergraduates with need received aid; of those 15% had need fully met. *Average percent of need met:* 35% (excluding resources awarded to replace EFC). *Average financial aid package:* $8000 (excluding resources awarded to replace EFC). 11% of all full-time undergraduates had no need and received non-need-based gift aid.

GIFT AID (NEED-BASED) *Total amount:* $4,755,755 (77% federal, 2% state, 17% institutional, 4% external sources). *Receiving aid:* Freshmen: 46% (278); All full-time undergraduates: 40% (808). *Average award:* Freshmen: $3000; Undergraduates: $3000. *Scholarships, grants, and awards:* Federal Pell, FSEOG, state, private, college/university gift aid from institutional funds, Federal Nursing.

GIFT AID (NON-NEED-BASED) *Total amount:* $635,265 (10% federal, 1% state, 88% institutional, 1% external sources). *Receiving aid:* Freshmen: 16% (98); Undergraduates: 30% (608). *Average Award:* Freshmen: $2000; Undergraduates: $3000. *Scholarships, grants, and awards by category:* Academic Interests/Achievement: 80 awards ($440,506 total): agriculture, education, general academic interests/achievements, military science. *Creative Arts/Performance:* 82 awards ($179,759 total): art/fine arts, journalism/publications, music. *ROTC:* Army.

LOANS *Student loans:* $5,217,741 (99% need-based, 1% non-need-based). 58% of past graduating class borrowed through all loan programs. *Average indebtedness per student:* $20,974. *Average need-based loan:* Freshmen: $1000; Undergraduates: $2000. *Parent loans:* $1,035,468 (100% non-need-based). *Programs:* FFEL (Subsidized and Unsubsidized Stafford, PLUS).

WORK-STUDY *Federal work-study:* Total amount: $192,396; 241 jobs averaging $1200. *State or other work-study/employment:* Total amount: $151,000 (100% non-need-based). 40 part-time jobs averaging $1000.

ATHLETIC AWARDS *Total amount:* $721,978 (100% non-need-based).

APPLYING FOR FINANCIAL AID *Required financial aid forms:* FAFSA, institution's own form. *Financial aid deadline (priority):* 3/1. *Notification date:* Continuous beginning 3/20. Students must reply within 2 weeks of notification.

CONTACT Mr. Alfred Robinson, Director of Financial Aid, Lincoln University, 820 Chestnut Street, Jefferson City, MO 65102-0029, 573-681-6156 or toll-free 800-521-5052. *Fax:* 573-681-5871.

LINCOLN UNIVERSITY
Lincoln University, PA

Tuition & fees (PA res): $7618   **Average undergraduate aid package:** $9118

ABOUT THE INSTITUTION State-related, coed. Awards: bachelor's and master's degrees. 46 undergraduate majors. Total enrollment: 2,278. Undergraduates: 1,714. Freshmen: 636.

UNDERGRADUATE EXPENSES for 2005–06 *Application fee:* $20. *Tuition, state resident:* full-time $5236; part-time $284 per credit hour. *Tuition, nonresident:* full-time $8912; part-time $459 per credit hour. Part-time tuition and fees vary according to course load. *College room and board:* $6792; room only: $3692. Room and board charges vary according to board plan. *Payment plans:* Installment, deferred payment.

FRESHMAN FINANCIAL AID (Fall 2005, est.) 599 applied for aid; of those 92% were deemed to have need. 99% of freshmen with need received aid; of those 7% had need fully met. *Average percent of need met:* 45% (excluding resources awarded to replace EFC). *Average financial aid package:* $8434 (excluding resources awarded to replace EFC). 3% of all full-time freshmen had no need and received non-need-based gift aid.

UNDERGRADUATE FINANCIAL AID (Fall 2005, est.) 1,494 applied for aid; of those 92% were deemed to have need. 99% of undergraduates with need received aid; of those 8% had need fully met. *Average percent of need met:* 49% (excluding resources awarded to replace EFC). *Average financial aid package:* $9118 (excluding resources awarded to replace EFC). 6% of all full-time undergraduates had no need and received non-need-based gift aid.

GIFT AID (NEED-BASED) *Total amount:* $5,463,810 (66% federal, 27% state, 1% institutional, 6% external sources). *Receiving aid:* Freshmen: 68% (426); All full-time undergraduates: 64% (1,058). *Average award:* Freshmen: $5142; Undergraduates: $4889. *Scholarships, grants, and awards:* Federal Pell, FSEOG, state, private, college/university gift aid from institutional funds, United Negro College Fund.

GIFT AID (NON-NEED-BASED) *Total amount:* $3,022,649 (89% institutional, 11% external sources). *Receiving aid:* Freshmen: 33% (210); Undergraduates: 30% (502). *Average Award:* Freshmen: $8096; Undergraduates: $8509. *Scholarships, grants, and awards by category:* Academic Interests/Achievement: 56 awards ($189,457 total): biological sciences, business, communication, computer science, education, general academic interests/achievements, humanities, mathematics, physical sciences, social sciences. *Creative Arts/Performance:* 49 awards ($38,050 total): music. *Special Achievements/Activities:* 2 awards ($6000 total): community service. *Special Characteristics:* 199 awards ($598,126 total): children and siblings of alumni, children of faculty/staff, international students. *Tuition waivers:* Full or partial for employees or children of employees. *ROTC:* Army cooperative, Air Force cooperative.

LOANS *Student loans:* $10,149,329 (82% need-based, 18% non-need-based). 78% of past graduating class borrowed through all loan programs. *Average indebtedness per student:* $21,000. *Average need-based loan:* Freshmen: $2673; Undergraduates: $3490. *Parent loans:* $3,055,203 (100% non-need-based). *Programs:* FFEL (Subsidized and Unsubsidized Stafford, PLUS), Perkins.

WORK-STUDY *Federal work-study:* Total amount: $370,938; 329 jobs averaging $791. *State or other work-study/employment:* Total amount: $99,784 (100% need-based). 25 part-time jobs averaging $863.

APPLYING FOR FINANCIAL AID *Required financial aid form:* FAFSA. *Financial aid deadline:* 5/1 (priority: 5/1). *Notification date:* Continuous beginning 5/1. Students must reply within 2 weeks of notification.

CONTACT Thelma Ross, Director of Financial Aid, Lincoln University, PO Box 179, 1570 Baltimore Pike, Lincoln University, PA 19352, 610-932-8300 Ext. 3564 or toll-free 800-790-0191. *Fax:* 610-932-1298. *E-mail:* tross@lincoln.edu.

LINDENWOOD UNIVERSITY
St. Charles, MO

Tuition & fees: $12,240   **Average undergraduate aid package:** N/A

ABOUT THE INSTITUTION Independent Presbyterian, coed. Awards: bachelor's and master's degrees and post-master's certificates (education specialist). 88 undergraduate majors. Total enrollment: 9,076. Undergraduates: 5,738. Freshmen: 821. Federal methodology is used as a basis for awarding need-based institutional aid.

UNDERGRADUATE EXPENSES for 2006–07 *Application fee:* $30. *Comprehensive fee:* $18,240 includes full-time tuition ($12,000), mandatory fees ($240), and room and board ($6000). *College room only:* $3000. *Part-time tuition:* $330 per credit hour.

GIFT AID (NEED-BASED) *Total amount:* $21,887,236 (19% federal, 8% state, 73% institutional). *Scholarships, grants, and awards:* Federal Pell, FSEOG, state, private, college/university gift aid from institutional funds.

GIFT AID (NON-NEED-BASED) *Total amount:* $9,179,954 (2% state, 96% institutional, 2% external sources). *Scholarships, grants, and awards by category:* Academic Interests/Achievement: biological sciences, business, communication, computer science, education, engineering/technologies, English, foreign languages, general academic interests/achievements, health fields, humanities, international studies, library science, mathematics, military science, physical sciences, premedicine, social sciences. *Creative Arts/Performance:* applied art and design, art/fine arts, cinema/film/broadcasting, dance, general creative arts/performance, music, performing arts, theater/drama. *Special Achievements/Activities:* cheerleading/drum major, community service, general special achievements/activities, junior miss, leadership. *ROTC:* Army, Air Force cooperative.

LOANS *Student loans:* $19,778,324 (59% need-based, 41% non-need-based). *Parent loans:* $2,589,047 (100% non-need-based). *Programs:* FFEL (Subsidized and Unsubsidized Stafford, PLUS), Perkins.

WORK-STUDY *Federal work-study:* Total amount: $406,345; jobs available (averaging $1800). *State or other work-study/employment:* Total amount: $3,710,616 (61% need-based, 39% non-need-based). Part-time jobs available.

APPLYING FOR FINANCIAL AID *Required financial aid form:* FAFSA. *Financial aid deadline (priority):* 3/15. *Notification date:* Continuous. Students must reply within 1 week of notification.

CONTACT Lori Bode, Director of Financial Aid, Lindenwood University, 209 South Kingshighway, St. Charles, MO 63301-1695, 636-949-4925. *Fax:* 636-949-4924.

LINDSEY WILSON COLLEGE
Columbia, KY

Tuition & fees: $14,438   **Average undergraduate aid package:** $9963

ABOUT THE INSTITUTION Independent United Methodist, coed. Awards: associate, bachelor's, and master's degrees. 37 undergraduate majors. Total enrollment: 1,902. Undergraduates: 1,622. Freshmen: 422. Federal methodology is used as a basis for awarding need-based institutional aid.
UNDERGRADUATE EXPENSES for 2006–07 Comprehensive fee: $20,601 includes full-time tuition ($14,208), mandatory fees ($230), and room and board ($6163). *Part-time tuition:* $592 per credit hour.
FRESHMAN FINANCIAL AID (Fall 2004) 395 applied for aid; of those 92% were deemed to have need. 100% of freshmen with need received aid; of those 29% had need fully met. *Average financial aid package:* $10,932 (excluding resources awarded to replace EFC).
UNDERGRADUATE FINANCIAL AID (Fall 2004) 1,516 applied for aid; of those 91% were deemed to have need. 100% of undergraduates with need received aid; of those 23% had need fully met. *Average financial aid package:* $9963 (excluding resources awarded to replace EFC).
GIFT AID (NEED-BASED) *Total amount:* $12,462,472 (24% federal, 32% state, 39% institutional, 5% external sources). *Receiving aid:* Freshmen: 89% (352); All full-time undergraduates: 89% (1,353). *Average award:* Freshmen: $10,987; Undergraduates: $10,386. *Scholarships, grants, and awards:* Federal Pell, FSEOG, state, private, college/university gift aid from institutional funds.
GIFT AID (NON-NEED-BASED) *Total amount:* $560,571 (1% state, 90% institutional, 9% external sources). *Scholarships, grants, and awards by category: Academic Interests/Achievement:* general academic interests/achievements. *Creative Arts/Performance:* $218,560 total: debating, theater/drama. *Special Achievements/Activities:* junior miss, leadership, religious involvement. *Special Characteristics:* 239 awards ($2,623,035 total): children of faculty/staff, members of minority groups. **ROTC:** Army cooperative.
LOANS *Student loans:* $8,909,270 (100% need-based). 99% of past graduating class borrowed through all loan programs. *Average indebtedness per student:* $9389. *Average need-based loan:* Freshmen: $4003; Undergraduates: $3398. *Parent loans:* $111,954 (100% need-based). *Programs:* FFEL (Subsidized and Unsubsidized Stafford, PLUS), Perkins, college/university.
WORK-STUDY *Federal work-study:* Total amount: $283,052; 464 jobs averaging $1200. *State or other work-study/employment:* Total amount: $22,535 (29% need-based, 71% non-need-based). Part-time jobs available.
ATHLETIC AWARDS Total amount: $2,184,402 (36% need-based, 64% non-need-based).
APPLYING FOR FINANCIAL AID *Required financial aid forms:* FAFSA, institution's own form. *Financial aid deadline (priority):* 4/1. *Notification date:* Continuous beginning 4/15. Students must reply within 2 weeks of notification.
CONTACT Ms. Marilyn D. Radford, Assistant Director of Student Financial Services, Lindsey Wilson College, 210 Lindsey Wilson Street, Columbia, KY 42728-1298, 270-384-8022 or toll-free 800-264-0138. *Fax:* 270-384-8591. *E-mail:* radfordm@lindsey.edu.

LINFIELD COLLEGE
McMinnville, OR

Tuition & fees: $23,022   **Average undergraduate aid package:** $17,653

ABOUT THE INSTITUTION Independent American Baptist Churches in the USA, coed. Awards: bachelor's degrees. 34 undergraduate majors. Total enrollment: 1,750. Undergraduates: 1,750. Freshmen: 488. Federal methodology is used as a basis for awarding need-based institutional aid.
UNDERGRADUATE EXPENSES for 2005–06 *Application fee:* $40. **Comprehensive fee:** $29,632 includes full-time tuition ($22,790), mandatory fees ($232), and room and board ($6610). *College room only:* $3540. Room and board charges vary according to board plan and housing facility. *Part-time tuition:* $710 per credit. *Part-time fees:* $68 per term. Part-time tuition and fees vary according to course load. *Payment plan:* Installment.
FRESHMAN FINANCIAL AID (Fall 2005, est.) 317 applied for aid; of those 100% were deemed to have need. 100% of freshmen with need received aid; of those 39% had need fully met. *Average percent of need met:* 85% (excluding resources awarded to replace EFC). *Average financial aid package:* $18,671 (excluding resources awarded to replace EFC). 25% of all full-time freshmen had no need and received non-need-based gift aid.
UNDERGRADUATE FINANCIAL AID (Fall 2005, est.) 1,112 applied for aid; of those 100% were deemed to have need. 100% of undergraduates with need received aid; of those 39% had need fully met. *Average percent of need met:* 85% (excluding resources awarded to replace EFC). *Average financial aid package:* $17,653 (excluding resources awarded to replace EFC). 22% of all full-time undergraduates had no need and received non-need-based gift aid.
GIFT AID (NEED-BASED) *Total amount:* $13,649,707 (8% federal, 3% state, 81% institutional, 8% external sources). *Receiving aid:* Freshmen: 52% (254); All full-time undergraduates: 52% (863). *Average award:* Freshmen: $7730; Undergraduates: $6672. *Scholarships, grants, and awards:* Federal Pell, FSEOG, state, private, college/university gift aid from institutional funds.
GIFT AID (NON-NEED-BASED) *Total amount:* $3,742,257 (94% institutional, 6% external sources). *Receiving aid:* Freshmen: 43% (211); Undergraduates: 42% (700). *Average Award:* Freshmen: $9390; Undergraduates: $8946. *Scholarships, grants, and awards by category: Academic Interests/Achievement:* 148 awards ($482,800 total): general academic interests/achievements. *Creative Arts/Performance:* 40 awards ($72,000 total): debating, music. *Special Achievements/Activities:* 37 awards ($73,000 total): leadership. *Special Characteristics:* 31 awards ($680,995 total): children of faculty/staff. *Tuition waivers:* Full or partial for employees or children of employees, senior citizens. **ROTC:** Air Force cooperative.
LOANS *Student loans:* $8,280,847 (90% need-based, 10% non-need-based). 75% of past graduating class borrowed through all loan programs. *Average indebtedness per student:* $24,594. *Average need-based loan:* Freshmen: $3304; Undergraduates: $4457. *Parent loans:* $656,904 (100% non-need-based). *Programs:* FFEL (Subsidized and Unsubsidized Stafford, PLUS), Perkins, college/university, alternative loans.
WORK-STUDY *Federal work-study:* Total amount: $1,301,773; 755 jobs averaging $1724. *State or other work-study/employment:* Total amount: $622,942 (100% non-need-based). 610 part-time jobs averaging $1021.
APPLYING FOR FINANCIAL AID *Required financial aid form:* FAFSA. *Financial aid deadline (priority):* 2/1. *Notification date:* 4/1. Students must reply by 5/1.
CONTACT Crisanne Werner, Associate Director of Financial Aid, Linfield College, 900 Southeast Baker Street, McMinnville, OR 97128-6894, 503-883-2225 or toll-free 800-640-2287. *Fax:* 503-883-2486. *E-mail:* finaid@linfield.edu.

LIPSCOMB UNIVERSITY
Nashville, TN

Tuition & fees: $14,557   **Average undergraduate aid package:** $10,316

ABOUT THE INSTITUTION Independent religious, coed. Awards: bachelor's, master's, and first professional degrees. 58 undergraduate majors. Total enrollment: 2,518. Undergraduates: 2,297. Freshmen: 526. Federal methodology is used as a basis for awarding need-based institutional aid.
UNDERGRADUATE EXPENSES for 2005–06 *Application fee:* $50. **Comprehensive fee:** $20,967 includes full-time tuition ($13,928), mandatory fees ($629), and room and board ($6410). Full-time tuition and fees vary according to class time and degree level. Room and board charges vary according to board plan and housing facility. *Part-time tuition:* $525 per hour. *Part-time fees:* $629 per year. Part-time tuition and fees vary according to class time and degree level. *Payment plans:* Installment, deferred payment.
FRESHMAN FINANCIAL AID (Fall 2005, est.) 470 applied for aid; of those 66% were deemed to have need. 86% of freshmen with need received aid; of those 100% had need fully met. *Average percent of need met:* 77% (excluding resources awarded to replace EFC). *Average financial aid package:* $12,038 (excluding resources awarded to replace EFC). 35% of all full-time freshmen had no need and received non-need-based gift aid.
UNDERGRADUATE FINANCIAL AID (Fall 2005, est.) 1,583 applied for aid; of those 81% were deemed to have need. 86% of undergraduates with need received aid; of those 99% had need fully met. *Average percent of need met:* 79% (excluding resources awarded to replace EFC). *Average financial aid package:* $10,316 (excluding resources awarded to replace EFC). 46% of all full-time undergraduates had no need and received non-need-based gift aid.
GIFT AID (NEED-BASED) *Total amount:* $4,242,272 (26% federal, 8% state, 43% institutional, 23% external sources). *Receiving aid:* Freshmen: 40% (207); All full-time undergraduates: 42% (892). *Average award:* Freshmen: $2731;

Lipscomb University

Undergraduates: $2916. *Scholarships, grants, and awards:* Federal Pell, FSEOG, state, private, college/university gift aid from institutional funds.
GIFT AID (NON-NEED-BASED) *Total amount:* $9,658,019 (22% state, 78% institutional). *Receiving aid:* Freshmen: 42% (221); Undergraduates: 38% (792). *Average Award:* Freshmen: $3685; Undergraduates: $5495. *Scholarships, grants, and awards by category:* Academic Interests/Achievement: general academic interests/achievements, religion/biblical studies. *Creative Arts/Performance:* art/fine arts, music, theater/drama. *Special Achievements/Activities:* cheerleading/drum major, leadership, religious involvement. *Special Characteristics:* adult students, children of educators, children of faculty/staff, children with a deceased or disabled parent, international students, members of minority groups, relatives of clergy. *Tuition waivers:* Full or partial for minority students, employees or children of employees. *ROTC:* Army cooperative, Air Force cooperative.
LOANS *Student loans:* $6,374,317 (100% need-based). *Average need-based loan:* Freshmen: $3351; Undergraduates: $4004. *Parent loans:* $2,966,504 (100% non-need-based). *Programs:* FFEL (Subsidized and Unsubsidized Stafford, PLUS), Perkins.
WORK-STUDY *Federal work-study:* Total amount: $62,410; jobs available.
ATHLETIC AWARDS Total amount: $4,999,539 (100% non-need-based).
APPLYING FOR FINANCIAL AID *Required financial aid form:* FAFSA. *Financial aid deadline (priority):* 3/1. *Notification date:* Continuous beginning 3/15.
CONTACT Mrs. Karita McCaleb Waters, Director of Financial Aid, Lipscomb University, 3901 Granny White Pike, Nashville, TN 37204-3951, 615-269-1791 or toll-free 877-582-4766. *Fax:* 615-386-7640. *E-mail:* karita.waters@lipscomb.edu.

LIVINGSTONE COLLEGE
Salisbury, NC

CONTACT Mrs. Terry Jefferies, Financial Aid Director, Livingstone College, 701 West Monroe Street, Price Building, Salisbury, NC 28144-5298, 704-216-6069 or toll-free 800-835-3435. *Fax:* 704-216-6319. *E-mail:* tjefferies@livingstone.edu.

LOCK HAVEN UNIVERSITY OF PENNSYLVANIA
Lock Haven, PA

Tuition & fees (PA res): $6258	Average undergraduate aid package: $6562

ABOUT THE INSTITUTION State-supported, coed. Awards: associate, bachelor's, and master's degrees. 56 undergraduate majors. Total enrollment: 5,283. Undergraduates: 4,977. Freshmen: 1,247. Federal methodology is used as a basis for awarding need-based institutional aid.
UNDERGRADUATE EXPENSES for 2005–06 *Application fee:* $25. *Tuition, state resident:* full-time $4906; part-time $204 per credit. *Tuition, nonresident:* full-time $10,266; part-time $428 per credit. *Required fees:* full-time $1352; $38 per credit or $98 per term part-time. Full-time tuition and fees vary according to course load and location. Part-time tuition and fees vary according to course load and location. *College room and board:* $5840; *room only:* $3204. Room and board charges vary according to board plan and housing facility. *Payment plans:* Installment, deferred payment.
FRESHMAN FINANCIAL AID (Fall 2005, est.) 1109 applied for aid; of those 78% were deemed to have need. 100% of freshmen with need received aid; of those 55% had need fully met. *Average percent of need met:* 73% (excluding resources awarded to replace EFC). *Average financial aid package:* $6111 (excluding resources awarded to replace EFC). 3% of all full-time freshmen had no need and received non-need-based gift aid.
UNDERGRADUATE FINANCIAL AID (Fall 2005, est.) 4,457 applied for aid; of those 76% were deemed to have need. 100% of undergraduates with need received aid; of those 61% had need fully met. *Average percent of need met:* 77% (excluding resources awarded to replace EFC). *Average financial aid package:* $6562 (excluding resources awarded to replace EFC). 4% of all full-time undergraduates had no need and received non-need-based gift aid.
GIFT AID (NEED-BASED) *Total amount:* $8,973,560 (50% federal, 49% state, 1% institutional). *Receiving aid:* Freshmen: 46% (533); All full-time undergraduates: 53% (2,492). *Average award:* Freshmen: $4283; Undergraduates: $4922. *Scholarships, grants, and awards:* Federal Pell, FSEOG, state, private, college/university gift aid from institutional funds.
GIFT AID (NON-NEED-BASED) *Total amount:* $851,695 (2% state, 8% institutional, 90% external sources). *Receiving aid:* Freshmen: 7% (79); Undergraduates: 6% (289). *Average Award:* Freshmen: $1200; Undergraduates: $1575. *Scholarships, grants, and awards by category:* Academic Interests/Achievement: 195 awards ($164,183 total): biological sciences, communication, education, English, foreign languages, general academic interests/achievements, international studies, library science, mathematics, physical sciences, social sciences. *Creative Arts/Performance:* 7 awards ($10,410 total): art/fine arts, journalism/publications, music. *Special Achievements/Activities:* 12 awards ($12,500 total): leadership, memberships. *Special Characteristics:* 94 awards ($398,200 total): handicapped students, local/state students, members of minority groups, previous college experience. *Tuition waivers:* Full or partial for minority students, employees or children of employees, senior citizens. *ROTC:* Army.
LOANS *Student loans:* $22,373,799 (100% need-based). 75% of past graduating class borrowed through all loan programs. *Average indebtedness per student:* $19,500. *Average need-based loan:* Freshmen: $2500; Undergraduates: $3797. *Parent loans:* $3,947,106 (100% non-need-based). *Programs:* FFEL (Subsidized and Unsubsidized Stafford, PLUS), Perkins.
WORK-STUDY *Federal work-study:* Total amount: $335,173; 253 jobs averaging $1174. *State or other work-study/employment:* Total amount: $748,028 (29% need-based, 71% non-need-based). 951 part-time jobs averaging $711.
ATHLETIC AWARDS Total amount: $575,953 (40% need-based, 60% non-need-based).
APPLYING FOR FINANCIAL AID *Required financial aid forms:* FAFSA, institution's own form. *Financial aid deadline (priority):* 3/15. *Notification date:* Continuous. Students must reply by 5/1 or within 2 weeks of notification.
CONTACT James Theeuwes, Director, Financial Services, Lock Haven University of Pennsylvania, Russell Hall 118, Lock Haven, PA 17745-2390, 570-893-2344 or toll-free 800-332-8900 (in-state), 800-233-8978 (out-of-state). *Fax:* 570-893-2918. *E-mail:* jtheeuwe@lhup.edu.

LOGAN UNIVERSITY-COLLEGE OF CHIROPRACTIC
Chesterfield, MO

CONTACT Linda K. Haman, Director of Financial Aid, Logan University-College of Chiropractic, 1851 Schoettler Road, PO Box 1065, Chesterfield, MO 63006-1065, 636-227-2100 Ext. 141 or toll-free 800-533-9210.

LOMA LINDA UNIVERSITY
Loma Linda, CA

CONTACT Verdell Schaefer, Director of Financial Aid, Loma Linda University, 11139 Anderson Street, Loma Linda, CA 92350, 909-558-4509. *Fax:* 909-558-4879. *E-mail:* finaid@univ.llu.edu.

LONG ISLAND UNIVERSITY, BROOKLYN CAMPUS
Brooklyn, NY

Tuition & fees: $24,328	Average undergraduate aid package: $12,399

ABOUT THE INSTITUTION Independent, coed. Awards: associate, bachelor's, master's, doctoral, and first professional degrees and post-bachelor's, post-master's, and first professional certificates. 64 undergraduate majors. Total enrollment: 8,144. Undergraduates: 5,331. Freshmen: 1,086. Both federal and institutional methodology are used as a basis for awarding need-based institutional aid.
UNDERGRADUATE EXPENSES for 2005–06 *Application fee:* $30. *Comprehensive fee:* $32,138 includes full-time tuition ($23,188), mandatory fees ($1140), and room and board ($7810). *College room only:* $4640. Full-time tuition and fees vary according to program. Room and board charges vary according to board plan and housing facility. *Part-time tuition:* $689 per credit. *Part-time fees:* $590 per year. Part-time tuition and fees vary according to course load and program. *Payment plan:* Deferred payment.
FRESHMAN FINANCIAL AID (Fall 2005, est.) 929 applied for aid; of those 81% were deemed to have need. 98% of freshmen with need received aid; of those 49% had need fully met. *Average percent of need met:* 52% (excluding resources

awarded to replace EFC). *Average financial aid package:* $12,778 (excluding resources awarded to replace EFC). 10% of all full-time freshmen had no need and received non-need-based gift aid.
UNDERGRADUATE FINANCIAL AID (Fall 2005, est.) 4,059 applied for aid; of those 94% were deemed to have need. 97% of undergraduates with need received aid; of those 46% had need fully met. *Average percent of need met:* 45% (excluding resources awarded to replace EFC). *Average financial aid package:* $12,399 (excluding resources awarded to replace EFC). 4% of all full-time undergraduates had no need and received non-need-based gift aid.
GIFT AID (NEED-BASED) *Total amount:* $35,355,075 (33% federal, 31% state, 33% institutional, 3% external sources). *Receiving aid:* Freshmen: 74% (725); All full-time undergraduates: 81% (3,553). *Average award:* Freshmen: $10,018; Undergraduates: $8744. *Scholarships, grants, and awards:* Federal Pell, FSEOG, state, private, college/university gift aid from institutional funds, Scholarships for Disadvantaged Students (Nursing and Pharmacy).
GIFT AID (NON-NEED-BASED) *Total amount:* $1,777,064 (95% institutional, 5% external sources). *Receiving aid:* Freshmen: 2% (22); Undergraduates: 3% (111). *Average Award:* Freshmen: $16,860; Undergraduates: $19,604. *Scholarships, grants, and awards by category: Academic Interests/Achievement:* communication, education, general academic interests/achievements, health fields. *Creative Arts/Performance:* art/fine arts, cinema/film/broadcasting, dance, music. *Special Achievements/Activities:* cheerleading/drum major, general special achievements/activities, leadership. *Special Characteristics:* $4,943,242 total: children and siblings of alumni, children of faculty/staff, ethnic background, first-generation college students, general special characteristics, international students. *Tuition waivers:* Full or partial for employees or children of employees.
LOANS *Student loans:* $34,038,377 (85% need-based, 15% non-need-based). 97% of past graduating class borrowed through all loan programs. *Average indebtedness per student:* $32,200. *Average need-based loan:* Freshmen: $2945; Undergraduates: $4300. *Parent loans:* $21,881,145 (100% non-need-based). *Programs:* Federal Direct (Subsidized and Unsubsidized Stafford, PLUS), Perkins, Federal Health Professions Student Loans, alternative loans.
WORK-STUDY *Federal work-study:* Total amount: $1,707,332; jobs available. *State or other work-study/employment:* Part-time jobs available.
ATHLETIC AWARDS Total amount: $4,060,806 (92% need-based, 8% non-need-based).
APPLYING FOR FINANCIAL AID *Required financial aid form:* FAFSA. *Financial aid deadline:* Continuous. *Notification date:* Continuous beginning 4/1. Students must reply within 4 weeks of notification.
CONTACT Ms. Rose Iannicelli, Dean of Financial Services, Long Island University, Brooklyn Campus, 1 University Plaza, Brooklyn, NY 11201-8423, 718-488-1037 or toll-free 800-LIU-PLAN. *Fax:* 718-488-3343.

LONG ISLAND UNIVERSITY, C.W. POST CAMPUS
Brookville, NY

CONTACT Office of Financial Assistance, Long Island University, C.W. Post Campus, 720 Northern Boulevard, Brookville, NY 11548-1300, 516-299-2338 or toll-free 800-LIU-PLAN. *Fax:* 516-299-3833. *E-mail:* finaid@cwpost.liu.edu.

LONGWOOD UNIVERSITY
Farmville, VA

ABOUT THE INSTITUTION State-supported, coed. Awards: bachelor's and master's degrees. 74 undergraduate majors. Total enrollment: 4,289. Undergraduates: 3,739. Freshmen: 980.
GIFT AID (NEED-BASED) *Scholarships, grants, and awards:* Federal Pell, FSEOG, state, private, college/university gift aid from institutional funds.
GIFT AID (NON-NEED-BASED) *Scholarships, grants, and awards by category: Academic Interests/Achievement:* biological sciences, business, computer science, education, English, general academic interests/achievements, humanities, mathematics, social sciences. *Creative Arts/Performance:* art/fine arts, general creative arts/performance, music, theater/drama. *Special Achievements/Activities:* memberships. *Special Characteristics:* children and siblings of alumni, general special characteristics, local/state students.
LOANS *Programs:* FFEL (Subsidized and Unsubsidized Stafford, PLUS), Perkins, college/university.
APPLYING FOR FINANCIAL AID *Required financial aid form:* FAFSA.

CONTACT Michael Barree, Financial Aid Director, Longwood University, 201 High Street, Farmville, VA 23909, 434-395-2077 or toll-free 800-281-4677. *Fax:* 434-395-2829. *E-mail:* barreemw@longwood.edu.

LORAS COLLEGE
Dubuque, IA

Tuition & fees: $21,098   **Average undergraduate aid package:** $18,374

ABOUT THE INSTITUTION Independent Roman Catholic, coed. Awards: associate, bachelor's, and master's degrees. 54 undergraduate majors. Total enrollment: 1,683. Undergraduates: 1,594. Freshmen: 370. Federal methodology is used as a basis for awarding need-based institutional aid.
UNDERGRADUATE EXPENSES for 2005–06 *Application fee:* $25. *Comprehensive fee:* $27,193 includes full-time tuition ($19,990), mandatory fees ($1108), and room and board ($6095). *College room only:* $3100. Full-time tuition and fees vary according to course load and degree level. Room and board charges vary according to board plan and housing facility. *Part-time tuition:* $400 per credit. *Payment plan:* Installment.
FRESHMAN FINANCIAL AID (Fall 2005, est.) 342 applied for aid; of those 96% were deemed to have need. 100% of freshmen with need received aid; of those 32% had need fully met. *Average percent of need met:* 85% (excluding resources awarded to replace EFC). *Average financial aid package:* $18,336 (excluding resources awarded to replace EFC). 10% of all full-time freshmen had no need and received non-need-based gift aid.
UNDERGRADUATE FINANCIAL AID (Fall 2005, est.) 1,285 applied for aid; of those 90% were deemed to have need. 100% of undergraduates with need received aid; of those 33% had need fully met. *Average percent of need met:* 88% (excluding resources awarded to replace EFC). *Average financial aid package:* $18,374 (excluding resources awarded to replace EFC). 32% of all full-time undergraduates had no need and received non-need-based gift aid.
GIFT AID (NEED-BASED) *Total amount:* $11,002,391 (9% federal, 15% state, 76% institutional). *Receiving aid:* Freshmen: 76% (276); All full-time undergraduates: 68% (1,025). *Average award:* Freshmen: $8192; Undergraduates: $8170. *Scholarships, grants, and awards:* Federal Pell, FSEOG, state, college/university gift aid from institutional funds.
GIFT AID (NON-NEED-BASED) *Total amount:* $4,586,524 (96% institutional, 4% external sources). *Receiving aid:* Freshmen: 88% (321); Undergraduates: 66% (1,000). *Average Award:* Freshmen: $6467; Undergraduates: $8289. *Scholarships, grants, and awards by category: Academic Interests/Achievement:* 1,325 awards ($7,575,000 total): engineering/technologies, general academic interests/achievements, physical sciences. *Creative Arts/Performance:* 43 awards ($39,938 total): music. *Special Achievements/Activities:* memberships, religious involvement. *Special Characteristics:* 456 awards ($426,288 total): children and siblings of alumni, siblings of current students. *Tuition waivers:* Full or partial for employees or children of employees, senior citizens.
LOANS *Student loans:* $9,291,698 (47% need-based, 53% non-need-based). 94% of past graduating class borrowed through all loan programs. *Average indebtedness per student:* $24,320. *Average need-based loan:* Freshmen: $4242; Undergraduates: $4230. *Parent loans:* $800,835 (100% non-need-based). *Programs:* FFEL (Subsidized and Unsubsidized Stafford, PLUS), Perkins, college/university.
WORK-STUDY *Federal work-study:* Total amount: $242,652; 280 jobs averaging $942. *State or other work-study/employment:* Total amount: $533,869 (100% non-need-based). 254 part-time jobs averaging $2581.
APPLYING FOR FINANCIAL AID *Required financial aid form:* FAFSA. *Financial aid deadline (priority):* 4/15. *Notification date:* Continuous beginning 3/6. Students must reply within 3 weeks of notification.
CONTACT Ms. Julie A. Dunn, Director of Financial Planning, Loras College, 1450 Alta Vista Street, Dubuque, IA 52004-0178, 563-588-7136 or toll-free 800-245-6727. *Fax:* 563-588-7119. *E-mail:* Julie.Dunn@loras.edu.

LOUISIANA COLLEGE
Pineville, LA

CONTACT Shelley Jinks, Financial Aid Director, Louisiana College, 1140 College Drive, Pineville, LA 71359-0001, 318-487-7386 or toll-free 800-487-1906. *Fax:* 318-487-7449. *E-mail:* jinks@lacollege.edu.

Louisiana State University and Agricultural and Mechanical College

LOUISIANA STATE UNIVERSITY AND AGRICULTURAL AND MECHANICAL COLLEGE
Baton Rouge, LA

Tuition & fees (LA res): $4419 **Average undergraduate aid package:** $8006

ABOUT THE INSTITUTION State-supported, coed. Awards: bachelor's, master's, doctoral, and first professional degrees and post-master's certificates. 69 undergraduate majors. Total enrollment: 31,264. Undergraduates: 25,705. Freshmen: 4,970. Federal methodology is used as a basis for awarding need-based institutional aid.

UNDERGRADUATE EXPENSES for 2005–06 *Application fee:* $40. *Tuition, state resident:* full-time $2981. *Tuition, nonresident:* full-time $11,281. Part-time tuition and fees vary according to course load. *College room and board:* $6330; *room only:* $3930. Room and board charges vary according to board plan and housing facility. *Payment plan:* Deferred payment.

FRESHMAN FINANCIAL AID (Fall 2004) 3055 applied for aid; of those 63% were deemed to have need. 97% of freshmen with need received aid; of those 22% had need fully met. *Average percent of need met:* 68% (excluding resources awarded to replace EFC). *Average financial aid package:* $7293 (excluding resources awarded to replace EFC). 14% of all full-time freshmen had no need and received non-need-based gift aid.

UNDERGRADUATE FINANCIAL AID (Fall 2004) 12,775 applied for aid; of those 70% were deemed to have need. 96% of undergraduates with need received aid; of those 20% had need fully met. *Average percent of need met:* 65% (excluding resources awarded to replace EFC). *Average financial aid package:* $8006 (excluding resources awarded to replace EFC). 10% of all full-time undergraduates had no need and received non-need-based gift aid.

GIFT AID (NEED-BASED) *Total amount:* $33,245,154 (40% federal, 42% state, 16% institutional, 2% external sources). *Receiving aid:* Freshmen: 31% (1,784); All full-time undergraduates: 30% (7,264). *Average award:* Freshmen: $5311; Undergraduates: $5132. *Scholarships, grants, and awards:* Federal Pell, FSEOG, state, private, college/university gift aid from institutional funds.

GIFT AID (NON-NEED-BASED) *Total amount:* $44,399,595 (1% federal, 73% state, 21% institutional, 5% external sources). *Receiving aid:* Freshmen: 1% (80); Undergraduates: 1% (190). *Average Award:* Freshmen: $2941; Undergraduates: $3607. *Scholarships, grants, and awards by category: Academic Interests/Achievement:* 621 awards ($946,174 total): agriculture, architecture, biological sciences, business, communication, computer science, education, engineering/technologies, English, foreign languages, general academic interests/achievements, home economics, humanities, mathematics, military science, physical sciences, premedicine. *Creative Arts/Performance:* 157 awards ($916,017 total): applied art and design, art/fine arts, journalism/publications, music, performing arts, theater/drama. *Special Achievements/Activities:* leadership. *Special Characteristics:* 320 awards ($1,369,653 total): children and siblings of alumni, children with a deceased or disabled parent, general special characteristics. *Tuition waivers:* Full or partial for children of alumni, employees or children of employees. *ROTC:* Army, Naval cooperative, Air Force.

LOANS *Student loans:* $47,745,168 (70% need-based, 30% non-need-based). 49% of past graduating class borrowed through all loan programs. *Average indebtedness per student:* $19,258. *Average need-based loan:* Freshmen: $2392; Undergraduates: $3864. *Parent loans:* $10,929,582 (27% need-based, 73% non-need-based). *Programs:* FFEL (Subsidized and Unsubsidized Stafford, PLUS).

WORK-STUDY *Federal work-study:* Total amount: $1,592,266; 927 jobs averaging $1316. *State or other work-study/employment:* Total amount: $14,320,473 (21% need-based, 79% non-need-based). 6,743 part-time jobs averaging $2087.

ATHLETIC AWARDS *Total amount:* $4,403,867 (33% need-based, 67% non-need-based).

APPLYING FOR FINANCIAL AID *Required financial aid forms:* FAFSA, institution's own form. *Financial aid deadline (priority):* 3/1. *Notification date:* 3/1. Students must reply within 2 weeks of notification.

CONTACT Mary G. Parker, Director of Student Aid and Scholarships, Louisiana State University and Agricultural and Mechanical College, LSU 208 Coates Hall, Baton Rouge, LA 70803-3103, 225-578-3113. *Fax:* 225-578-9460. *E-mail:* financialaid@lsu.edu.

LOUISIANA STATE UNIVERSITY HEALTH SCIENCES CENTER
New Orleans, LA

CONTACT Mr. Patrick Gorman, Director of Financial Aid, Louisiana State University Health Sciences Center, 433 Bolivar Street, New Orleans, LA 70112, 504-568-4821. *Fax:* 504-599-1390.

LOUISIANA STATE UNIVERSITY IN SHREVEPORT
Shreveport, LA

CONTACT Office of Student Financial Aid, Louisiana State University in Shreveport, One University Place, Shreveport, LA 71115-2399, 318-797-5363 or toll-free 800-229-5957 (in-state). *Fax:* 318-797-5366.

LOUISIANA TECH UNIVERSITY
Ruston, LA

Tuition & fees (LA res): $4375 **Average undergraduate aid package:** $5909

ABOUT THE INSTITUTION State-supported, coed. Awards: associate, bachelor's, master's, and doctoral degrees and first professional certificates. 79 undergraduate majors. Total enrollment: 11,691. Undergraduates: 9,318. Freshmen: 1,914. Both federal and institutional methodology are used as a basis for awarding need-based institutional aid.

UNDERGRADUATE EXPENSES for 2005–06 *Application fee:* $20. *Tuition, state resident:* full-time $3914. *Tuition, nonresident:* full-time $8819. *College room and board:* $4035; *room only:* $2130. *Payment plans:* Installment, deferred payment.

FRESHMAN FINANCIAL AID (Fall 2005, est.) 1545 applied for aid; of those 82% were deemed to have need. 92% of freshmen with need received aid; of those 19% had need fully met. *Average percent of need met:* 53% (excluding resources awarded to replace EFC). *Average financial aid package:* $5257 (excluding resources awarded to replace EFC). 45% of all full-time freshmen had no need and received non-need-based gift aid.

UNDERGRADUATE FINANCIAL AID (Fall 2005, est.) 7,331 applied for aid; of those 63% were deemed to have need. 89% of undergraduates with need received aid; of those 14% had need fully met. *Average percent of need met:* 48% (excluding resources awarded to replace EFC). *Average financial aid package:* $5909 (excluding resources awarded to replace EFC). 27% of all full-time undergraduates had no need and received non-need-based gift aid.

GIFT AID (NEED-BASED) *Total amount:* $16,045,037 (54% federal, 30% state, 13% institutional, 3% external sources). *Receiving aid:* Freshmen: 65% (1,079); All full-time undergraduates: 47% (3,568). *Average award:* Freshmen: $4271; Undergraduates: $4435. *Scholarships, grants, and awards:* Federal Pell, FSEOG, state, private, college/university gift aid from institutional funds.

GIFT AID (NON-NEED-BASED) *Total amount:* $8,609,087 (1% federal, 67% state, 25% institutional, 7% external sources). *Receiving aid:* Freshmen: 12% (200); Undergraduates: 7% (510). *Average Award:* Freshmen: $5222; Undergraduates: $5757. *Scholarships, grants, and awards by category: Academic Interests/Achievement:* 6,205 awards ($23,800,000 total): agriculture, architecture, biological sciences, business, computer science, education, engineering/technologies, English, foreign languages, general academic interests/achievements, health fields, home economics, humanities, library science, mathematics, military science, physical sciences, social sciences. *Creative Arts/Performance:* 424 awards ($497,259 total): debating, journalism/publications, music, performing arts, theater/drama. *Special Achievements/Activities:* 56 awards ($91,795 total): cheerleading/drum major. *Special Characteristics:* 389 awards ($1,774,998 total): children of faculty/staff, children with a deceased or disabled parent, out-of-state students, public servants, spouses of deceased or disabled public servants. *Tuition waivers:* Full or partial for children of alumni, employees or children of employees, senior citizens. *ROTC:* Army cooperative, Naval.

LOANS *Student loans:* $23,125,850 (66% need-based, 34% non-need-based). 82% of past graduating class borrowed through all loan programs. *Average indebtedness per student:* $15,861. *Average need-based loan:* Freshmen: $2048; Undergraduates: $3027. *Parent loans:* $2,626,356 (20% need-based, 80% non-need-based). *Programs:* FFEL (Subsidized and Unsubsidized Stafford, PLUS), Perkins, state.

WORK-STUDY *Federal work-study:* Total amount: $805,531; 304 jobs averaging $2756. *State or other work-study/employment:* Total amount: $527,211 (100% need-based). 1,150 part-time jobs averaging $1770.
ATHLETIC AWARDS *Total amount:* $1,139,454 (82% need-based, 18% non-need-based).
APPLYING FOR FINANCIAL AID *Required financial aid forms:* FAFSA, institution's own form. *Financial aid deadline:* Continuous. *Notification date:* Continuous beginning 4/1. Students must reply within 4 weeks of notification.
CONTACT Financial Aid Office, Louisiana Tech University, PO Box 7925, Ruston, LA 71272, 318-257-2641 or toll-free 800-528-3241. *Fax:* 318-257-2628. *E-mail:* techaid@ltfa.latech.edu.

LOURDES COLLEGE
Sylvania, OH

ABOUT THE INSTITUTION Independent Roman Catholic, coed. Awards: associate, bachelor's, and master's degrees. 21 undergraduate majors. Total enrollment: 1,460. Undergraduates: 1,390. Freshmen: 105.
GIFT AID (NEED-BASED) *Scholarships, grants, and awards:* Federal Pell, FSEOG, state, private, college/university gift aid from institutional funds.
GIFT AID (NON-NEED-BASED) *Scholarships, grants, and awards by category: Academic Interests/Achievement:* general academic interests/achievements. *Creative Arts/Performance:* art/fine arts, music. *Special Achievements/Activities:* general special achievements/activities. *Special Characteristics:* children of faculty/staff, international students, local/state students, members of minority groups.
LOANS *Programs:* FFEL (Subsidized and Unsubsidized Stafford, PLUS), Perkins, state, college/university, alternative loans.
APPLYING FOR FINANCIAL AID *Required financial aid form:* FAFSA.
CONTACT Greg Guzman, Director of Financial Aid, Lourdes College, 6832 Convent Boulevard, Sylvania, OH 43560-2898, 419-824-3732 or toll-free 800-878-3210 Ext. 1299. *Fax:* 419-882-3987. *E-mail:* finaid@lourdes.edu.

LOYOLA COLLEGE IN MARYLAND
Baltimore, MD

Tuition & fees: $29,683 **Average undergraduate aid package: $20,465**

ABOUT THE INSTITUTION Independent Roman Catholic (Jesuit), coed. Awards: bachelor's, master's, and doctoral degrees and post-master's certificates. 32 undergraduate majors. Total enrollment: 6,187. Undergraduates: 3,556. Freshmen: 898. Institutional methodology is used as a basis for awarding need-based institutional aid.
UNDERGRADUATE EXPENSES for 2005–06 *Application fee:* $50. *Comprehensive fee:* $38,898 includes full-time tuition ($28,683), mandatory fees ($1000), and room and board ($9215). *College room only:* $7215. Full-time tuition and fees vary according to student level. Room and board charges vary according to board plan. *Part-time tuition:* $486 per credit. *Part-time fees:* $25 per term.
FRESHMAN FINANCIAL AID (Fall 2005, est.) 635 applied for aid; of those 70% were deemed to have need. 100% of freshmen with need received aid; of those 98% had need fully met. *Average percent of need met:* 97% (excluding resources awarded to replace EFC). *Average financial aid package:* $21,375 (excluding resources awarded to replace EFC). 9% of all full-time freshmen had no need and received non-need-based gift aid.
UNDERGRADUATE FINANCIAL AID (Fall 2005, est.) 1,985 applied for aid; of those 77% were deemed to have need. 100% of undergraduates with need received aid; of those 96% had need fully met. *Average percent of need met:* 98% (excluding resources awarded to replace EFC). *Average financial aid package:* $20,465 (excluding resources awarded to replace EFC). 11% of all full-time undergraduates had no need and received non-need-based gift aid.
GIFT AID (NEED-BASED) *Total amount:* $21,832,315 (6% federal, 3% state, 88% institutional, 3% external sources). *Receiving aid:* Freshmen: 39% (346); All full-time undergraduates: 33% (1,138). *Average award:* Freshmen: $13,545; Undergraduates: $12,785. *Scholarships, grants, and awards:* Federal Pell, FSEOG, state, private, college/university gift aid from institutional funds.
GIFT AID (NON-NEED-BASED) *Total amount:* $5,316,696 (7% federal, 1% state, 81% institutional, 11% external sources). *Receiving aid:* Freshmen: 21% (192); Undergraduates: 17% (603). *Average Award:* Freshmen: $10,076; Undergraduates: $11,176. *Scholarships, grants, and awards by category: Academic Interests/Achievement:* 685 awards ($6,646,720 total): general academic interests/achievements. *Special Characteristics:* 99 awards ($1,306,050 total):

members of minority groups. *Tuition waivers:* Full or partial for employees or children of employees. *ROTC:* Army, Air Force cooperative.
LOANS *Student loans:* $12,499,797 (53% need-based, 47% non-need-based). 74% of past graduating class borrowed through all loan programs. *Average indebtedness per student:* $15,680. *Average need-based loan:* Freshmen: $5880; Undergraduates: $5730. *Parent loans:* $12,126,828 (100% non-need-based). *Programs:* Federal Direct (Subsidized and Unsubsidized Stafford), FFEL (PLUS), Perkins, college/university.
WORK-STUDY *Federal work-study:* Total amount: $826,307; 436 jobs averaging $1615. *State or other work-study/employment:* Total amount: $654,593 (61% need-based, 39% non-need-based). 83 part-time jobs averaging $9285.
ATHLETIC AWARDS *Total amount:* $3,926,894 (29% need-based, 71% non-need-based).
APPLYING FOR FINANCIAL AID *Required financial aid forms:* FAFSA, CSS Financial Aid PROFILE, noncustodial (divorced/separated) parent's statement, business/farm supplement. *Financial aid deadline:* 2/15. *Notification date:* 4/1. Students must reply by 5/1.
CONTACT Ms. Tricia Selby, Director of Financial Aid, Loyola College in Maryland, 4501 North Charles Street, Baltimore, MD 21210-2699, 410-617-2680 or toll-free 800-221-9107 Ext. 2252 (in-state). *Fax:* 410-617-5413. *E-mail:* tdselby@loyola.edu.

LOYOLA MARYMOUNT UNIVERSITY
Los Angeles, CA

ABOUT THE INSTITUTION Independent Roman Catholic, coed. Awards: bachelor's, master's, doctoral, and first professional degrees and post-bachelor's certificates. 48 undergraduate majors. Total enrollment: 8,855. Undergraduates: 5,721. Freshmen: 1,391.
GIFT AID (NEED-BASED) *Scholarships, grants, and awards:* Federal Pell, FSEOG, state, private, college/university gift aid from institutional funds.
GIFT AID (NON-NEED-BASED) *Scholarships, grants, and awards by category: Academic Interests/Achievement:* general academic interests/achievements. *Creative Arts/Performance:* art/fine arts, debating, music. *Special Achievements/Activities:* community service, religious involvement.
LOANS *Programs:* FFEL (Subsidized and Unsubsidized Stafford, PLUS), Perkins, college/university.
WORK-STUDY *Federal work-study:* Total amount: $5,938,654; 1,600 jobs averaging $2000. *State or other work-study/employment:* Total amount: $900,885 (100% non-need-based). 579 part-time jobs averaging $2800.
APPLYING FOR FINANCIAL AID *Required financial aid forms:* FAFSA, CSS Financial Aid PROFILE, state aid form.
CONTACT Financial Aid Office, Loyola Marymount University, One LMU Drive, Los Angeles, CA 90045-8350, 310-338-2753 or toll-free 800-LMU-INFO. *E-mail:* finaid@lmu.edu.

LOYOLA UNIVERSITY CHICAGO
Chicago, IL

Tuition & fees: $26,906 **Average undergraduate aid package: $20,367**

ABOUT THE INSTITUTION Independent Roman Catholic (Jesuit), coed. Awards: bachelor's, master's, doctoral, and first professional degrees and post-bachelor's and post-master's certificates (also offers adult part-time program with significant enrollment not reflected in profile). 51 undergraduate majors. Total enrollment: 14,764. Undergraduates: 9,240. Freshmen: 2,080. Federal methodology is used as a basis for awarding need-based institutional aid.
UNDERGRADUATE EXPENSES for 2006–07 *Application fee:* $25. *Comprehensive fee:* $36,520 includes full-time tuition ($26,150), mandatory fees ($756), and room and board ($9614). *College room only:* $6490. *Part-time tuition:* $530 per semester hour. *Part-time fees:* $75.
FRESHMAN FINANCIAL AID (Fall 2005, est.) 1807 applied for aid; of those 85% were deemed to have need. 100% of freshmen with need received aid; of those 12% had need fully met. *Average percent of need met:* 80% (excluding resources awarded to replace EFC). *Average financial aid package:* $20,066 (excluding resources awarded to replace EFC). 10% of all full-time freshmen had no need and received non-need-based gift aid.
UNDERGRADUATE FINANCIAL AID (Fall 2005, est.) 6,408 applied for aid; of those 88% were deemed to have need. 100% of undergraduates with need received aid; of those 13% had need fully met. *Average percent of need met:*

Loyola University Chicago

79% (excluding resources awarded to replace EFC). *Average financial aid package:* $20,367 (excluding resources awarded to replace EFC). 7% of all full-time undergraduates had no need and received non-need-based gift aid.
GIFT AID (NEED-BASED) *Total amount:* $74,626,048 (10% federal, 12% state, 76% institutional, 2% external sources). *Receiving aid:* Freshmen: 71% (1,461); All full-time undergraduates: 67% (5,291). *Average award:* Freshmen: $12,434; Undergraduates: $11,760. *Scholarships, grants, and awards:* Federal Pell, FSEOG, state, private, college/university gift aid from institutional funds.
GIFT AID (NON-NEED-BASED) *Total amount:* $6,296,015 (93% institutional, 7% external sources). *Receiving aid:* Freshmen: 5% (111); Undergraduates: 5% (383). *Average Award:* Freshmen: $6553; Undergraduates: $7205. *Scholarships, grants, and awards by category: Academic Interests/Achievement:* 3,829 awards ($28,774,667 total): general academic interests/achievements. *Creative Arts/Performance:* 46 awards ($113,400 total): art/fine arts, debating, journalism/publications, music, theater/drama. *Special Achievements/Activities:* 129 awards ($572,278 total): community service, general special achievements/activities, leadership, memberships. *Special Characteristics:* 1,618 awards ($3,810,611 total): adult students, general special characteristics, religious affiliation. *ROTC:* Army cooperative, Naval cooperative.
LOANS *Student loans:* $42,217,729 (72% need-based, 28% non-need-based). 68% of past graduating class borrowed through all loan programs. *Average indebtedness per student:* $24,299. *Average need-based loan:* Freshmen: $2739; Undergraduates: $3971. *Parent loans:* $12,153,042 (40% need-based, 60% non-need-based). *Programs:* FFEL (Subsidized and Unsubsidized Stafford, PLUS), Perkins, Federal Nursing.
WORK-STUDY *Federal work-study:* Total amount: $7,788,016; 3,742 jobs averaging $2081.
ATHLETIC AWARDS *Total amount:* $2,690,638 (45% need-based, 55% non-need-based).
APPLYING FOR FINANCIAL AID *Required financial aid form:* FAFSA. *Financial aid deadline (priority):* 3/1. *Notification date:* Continuous beginning 2/15. Students must reply within 3 weeks of notification.
CONTACT Mr. Eric Weems, Director of Financial Aid, Loyola University Chicago, 6525 North Sheridan Road, Sullivan Center, Chicago, IL 60626, 773-508-3155 or toll-free 800-262-2373. *Fax:* 773-508-3177. *E-mail:* lufinaid@luc.edu.

LOYOLA UNIVERSITY NEW ORLEANS
New Orleans, LA

Tuition & fees: $25,246 — **Average undergraduate aid package: $18,013**

ABOUT THE INSTITUTION Independent Roman Catholic (Jesuit), coed. Awards: bachelor's, master's, and first professional degrees and post-bachelor's and post-master's certificates. 49 undergraduate majors. Total enrollment: 5,423. Undergraduates: 3,688. Freshmen: 815. Federal methodology is used as a basis for awarding need-based institutional aid.
UNDERGRADUATE EXPENSES for 2005–06 *Application fee:* $20. *Comprehensive fee:* $33,558 includes full-time tuition ($24,410), mandatory fees ($836), and room and board ($8312). *College room only:* $5166. Room and board charges vary according to board plan and housing facility. *Part-time tuition:* $696 per credit hour. *Payment plan:* Installment.
FRESHMAN FINANCIAL AID (Fall 2004) 612 applied for aid; of those 79% were deemed to have need. 100% of freshmen with need received aid; of those 43% had need fully met. *Average percent of need met:* 86% (excluding resources awarded to replace EFC). *Average financial aid package:* $19,284 (excluding resources awarded to replace EFC). 25% of all full-time freshmen had no need and received non-need-based gift aid.
UNDERGRADUATE FINANCIAL AID (Fall 2004) 2,067 applied for aid; of those 80% were deemed to have need. 100% of undergraduates with need received aid; of those 41% had need fully met. *Average percent of need met:* 85% (excluding resources awarded to replace EFC). *Average financial aid package:* $18,013 (excluding resources awarded to replace EFC). 35% of all full-time undergraduates had no need and received non-need-based gift aid.
GIFT AID (NEED-BASED) *Total amount:* $20,907,608 (10% federal, 7% state, 81% institutional, 2% external sources). *Receiving aid:* Freshmen: 59% (481); All full-time undergraduates: 52% (1,629). *Average award:* Freshmen: $14,770; Undergraduates: $12,927. *Scholarships, grants, and awards:* Federal Pell, FSEOG, private, college/university gift aid from institutional funds.
GIFT AID (NON-NEED-BASED) *Total amount:* $14,064,121 (8% state, 89% institutional, 3% external sources). *Receiving aid:* Freshmen: 10% (81); Undergraduates: 9% (285). *Average Award:* Freshmen: $10,642; Undergraduates: $9669. *Scholarships, grants, and awards by category: Academic Interests/Achievement:* 766 awards ($6,926,625 total): general academic interests/achievements. *Creative Arts/Performance:* general creative arts/performance. *Special Characteristics:* 49 awards ($805,156 total): children of faculty/staff. *Tuition waivers:* Full or partial for employees or children of employees, senior citizens. *ROTC:* Army cooperative, Naval cooperative, Air Force cooperative.
LOANS *Student loans:* $10,287,252 (67% need-based, 33% non-need-based). 61% of past graduating class borrowed through all loan programs. *Average indebtedness per student:* $18,543. *Average need-based loan:* Freshmen: $4730; Undergraduates: $5831. *Parent loans:* $4,202,961 (24% need-based, 76% non-need-based). *Programs:* FFEL (Subsidized and Unsubsidized Stafford, PLUS), Perkins.
WORK-STUDY *Federal work-study:* Total amount: $1,397,985; 764 jobs averaging $1858.
APPLYING FOR FINANCIAL AID *Required financial aid form:* FAFSA. *Financial aid deadline (priority):* 2/15. *Notification date:* Continuous beginning 3/1. Students must reply by 5/1 or within 2 weeks of notification.
CONTACT Catherine Simoneaux, Director of Scholarships and Financial Aid, Loyola University New Orleans, 6363 St. Charles Avenue, Box 206, New Orleans, LA 70118-6195, 504-865-3231 or toll-free 800-4-LOYOLA. *Fax:* 504-865-3233. *E-mail:* finaid@loyno.edu.

LUBBOCK CHRISTIAN UNIVERSITY
Lubbock, TX

Tuition & fees: $12,560 — **Average undergraduate aid package: $11,165**

ABOUT THE INSTITUTION Independent religious, coed. Awards: bachelor's, master's, and first professional degrees. 44 undergraduate majors. Total enrollment: 2,076. Undergraduates: 1,832. Freshmen: 320. Federal methodology is used as a basis for awarding need-based institutional aid.
UNDERGRADUATE EXPENSES for 2005–06 *Application fee:* $25. *Comprehensive fee:* $16,810 includes full-time tuition ($11,644), mandatory fees ($916), and room and board ($4250). Full-time tuition and fees vary according to program. Room and board charges vary according to board plan and housing facility. *Part-time tuition:* $375 per semester hour. *Part-time fees:* $402 per term. Part-time tuition and fees vary according to course load and program. *Payment plan:* Installment.
FRESHMAN FINANCIAL AID (Fall 2005, est.) 224 applied for aid; of those 83% were deemed to have need. 100% of freshmen with need received aid; of those 16% had need fully met. *Average percent of need met:* 76% (excluding resources awarded to replace EFC). *Average financial aid package:* $10,102 (excluding resources awarded to replace EFC). 25% of all full-time freshmen had no need and received non-need-based gift aid.
UNDERGRADUATE FINANCIAL AID (Fall 2005, est.) 981 applied for aid; of those 86% were deemed to have need. 100% of undergraduates with need received aid; of those 10% had need fully met. *Average percent of need met:* 73% (excluding resources awarded to replace EFC). *Average financial aid package:* $11,165 (excluding resources awarded to replace EFC). 18% of all full-time undergraduates had no need and received non-need-based gift aid.
GIFT AID (NEED-BASED) *Total amount:* $6,655,179 (30% federal, 35% state, 29% institutional, 6% external sources). *Receiving aid:* Freshmen: 73% (186); All full-time undergraduates: 75% (822). *Average award:* Freshmen: $6893; Undergraduates: $7405. *Scholarships, grants, and awards:* Federal Pell, FSEOG, state, college/university gift aid from institutional funds.
GIFT AID (NON-NEED-BASED) *Total amount:* $944,330 (1% state, 85% institutional, 14% external sources). *Receiving aid:* Freshmen: 10% (25); Undergraduates: 6% (66). *Average Award:* Freshmen: $9527; Undergraduates: $10,630. *Scholarships, grants, and awards by category: Academic Interests/Achievement:* agriculture, business, communication, computer science, education, English, foreign languages, general academic interests/achievements, humanities, physical sciences, religion/biblical studies, social sciences. *Creative Arts/Performance:* art/fine arts, journalism/publications, music, performing arts, theater/drama. *Special Achievements/Activities:* 37 awards ($42,161 total): cheerleading/drum major, leadership. *Special Characteristics:* 52 awards ($337,644 total): children of faculty/staff, general special characteristics. *Tuition waivers:* Full or partial for employees or children of employees. *ROTC:* Army cooperative, Air Force cooperative.
LOANS *Student loans:* $11,671,176 (76% need-based, 24% non-need-based). 81% of past graduating class borrowed through all loan programs. *Average*

indebtedness per student: $22,192. **Average need-based loan:** Freshmen: $2975; Undergraduates: $3661. **Parent loans:** $2,392,693 (26% need-based, 74% non-need-based). **Programs:** FFEL (Subsidized and Unsubsidized Stafford, PLUS), Perkins, state.
WORK-STUDY *Federal work-study:* Total amount: $817,553; 848 jobs averaging $2000. **State or other work-study/employment:** Total amount: $25,849 (41% need-based, 59% non-need-based). 116 part-time jobs averaging $223.
ATHLETIC AWARDS *Total amount:* $801,727 (44% need-based, 56% non-need-based).
APPLYING FOR FINANCIAL AID *Required financial aid forms:* FAFSA, institution's own form. *Financial aid deadline (priority):* 6/1. *Notification date:* Continuous beginning 3/1.
CONTACT Amy Hardesty, Financial Aid Director, Lubbock Christian University, 5601 19th Street, Lubbock, TX 79407, 806-720-7176 or toll-free 800-933-7601. *Fax:* 806-720-7185. *E-mail:* amy.hardesty@lcu.edu.

LUTHER COLLEGE
Decorah, IA

Tuition & fees: $26,380 | Average undergraduate aid package: $19,374

ABOUT THE INSTITUTION Independent religious, coed. Awards: bachelor's degrees. 41 undergraduate majors. Total enrollment: 2,545. Undergraduates: 2,545. Freshmen: 631. Federal methodology is used as a basis for awarding need-based institutional aid.
UNDERGRADUATE EXPENSES for 2006–07 *Application fee:* $25. *Comprehensive fee:* $30,670 includes full-time tuition ($26,380) and room and board ($4290). *College room only:* $2100. *Part-time tuition:* $924 per semester hour.
FRESHMAN FINANCIAL AID (Fall 2005, est.) 564 applied for aid; of those 81% were deemed to have need. 100% of freshmen with need received aid; of those 40% had need fully met. *Average percent of need met:* 90% (excluding resources awarded to replace EFC). *Average financial aid package:* $19,627 (excluding resources awarded to replace EFC). 23% of all full-time freshmen had no need and received non-need-based gift aid.
UNDERGRADUATE FINANCIAL AID (Fall 2005, est.) 2,082 applied for aid; of those 84% were deemed to have need. 100% of undergraduates with need received aid; of those 36% had need fully met. *Average percent of need met:* 88% (excluding resources awarded to replace EFC). *Average financial aid package:* $19,374 (excluding resources awarded to replace EFC). 29% of all full-time undergraduates had no need and received non-need-based gift aid.
GIFT AID (NEED-BASED) *Total amount:* $20,604,160 (8% federal, 7% state, 81% institutional, 4% external sources). *Receiving aid:* Freshmen: 73% (458); All full-time undergraduates: 71% (1,729). *Average award:* Freshmen: $18,463; Undergraduates: $12,386. *Scholarships, grants, and awards:* Federal Pell, FSEOG, state, private, college/university gift aid from institutional funds.
GIFT AID (NON-NEED-BASED) *Total amount:* $4,612,658 (90% institutional, 10% external sources). *Receiving aid:* Freshmen: 5% (34); Undergraduates: 4% (89). *Average Award:* Freshmen: $8563; Undergraduates: $6301. *Scholarships, grants, and awards by category:* Academic Interests/Achievement: 1,639 awards ($10,382,227 total): general academic interests/achievements. Creative Arts/Performance: 815 awards ($1,722,435 total): music. Special Characteristics: 654 awards ($843,939 total): children and siblings of alumni, members of minority groups, religious affiliation.
LOANS *Student loans:* $9,419,972 (80% need-based, 20% non-need-based). 76% of past graduating class borrowed through all loan programs. *Average indebtedness per student:* $18,504. *Average need-based loan:* Freshmen: $4640; Undergraduates: $5150. *Parent loans:* $5,124,628 (46% need-based, 54% non-need-based). *Programs:* Federal Direct (Subsidized and Unsubsidized Stafford, PLUS), Perkins, college/university.
WORK-STUDY *Federal work-study:* Total amount: $1,575,829; 943 jobs averaging $1671. *State or other work-study/employment:* Total amount: $1,887,586 (14% need-based, 86% non-need-based). 1,052 part-time jobs averaging $1794.
APPLYING FOR FINANCIAL AID *Required financial aid forms:* FAFSA, institution's own form. *Financial aid deadline (priority):* 3/1. *Notification date:* Continuous beginning 3/15. Students must reply by 5/1.
CONTACT Ms. Janice Cordell, Director of Student Financial Planning, Luther College, 700 College Drive, Decorah, IA 52101-1045, 563-387-1018 or toll-free 800-458-8437. *E-mail:* cordellj@luther.edu.

LUTHER RICE UNIVERSITY
Lithonia, GA

ABOUT THE INSTITUTION Independent Baptist, coed. Awards: bachelor's, master's, and doctoral degrees. 2 undergraduate majors. Total enrollment: 1,600. Undergraduates: 655. Freshmen: 33.
GIFT AID (NEED-BASED) *Scholarships, grants, and awards:* Federal Pell, FSEOG, college/university gift aid from institutional funds.
LOANS *Programs:* FFEL (Subsidized and Unsubsidized Stafford, PLUS).
APPLYING FOR FINANCIAL AID *Required financial aid forms:* FAFSA, institution's own form.
CONTACT Gary W. Cooke, Director of Financial Aid, Luther Rice University, 3038 Evans Mill Road, Lithonia, GA 30038-2418, 770-484-1204 Ext. 241 or toll-free 800-442-1577. *Fax:* 678-990-5388. *E-mail:* gcooke@lrs.edu.

LYCOMING COLLEGE
Williamsport, PA

Tuition & fees: $24,080 | Average undergraduate aid package: $17,826

ABOUT THE INSTITUTION Independent United Methodist, coed. Awards: bachelor's degrees. 49 undergraduate majors. Total enrollment: 1,467. Undergraduates: 1,467. Freshmen: 357. Federal methodology is used as a basis for awarding need-based institutional aid.
UNDERGRADUATE EXPENSES for 2005–06 *Application fee:* $35. *Comprehensive fee:* $30,622 includes full-time tuition ($23,680), mandatory fees ($400), and room and board ($6542). *College room only:* $3356. Full-time tuition and fees vary according to course load. Room and board charges vary according to housing facility. *Part-time tuition:* $740 per credit hour. *Payment plan:* Installment.
FRESHMAN FINANCIAL AID (Fall 2005, est.) 330 applied for aid; of those 89% were deemed to have need. 100% of freshmen with need received aid; of those 17% had need fully met. *Average percent of need met:* 76% (excluding resources awarded to replace EFC). *Average financial aid package:* $18,277 (excluding resources awarded to replace EFC). 13% of all full-time freshmen had no need and received non-need-based gift aid.
UNDERGRADUATE FINANCIAL AID (Fall 2005, est.) 1,315 applied for aid; of those 91% were deemed to have need. 100% of undergraduates with need received aid; of those 23% had need fully met. *Average percent of need met:* 77% (excluding resources awarded to replace EFC). *Average financial aid package:* $17,826 (excluding resources awarded to replace EFC). 13% of all full-time undergraduates had no need and received non-need-based gift aid.
GIFT AID (NEED-BASED) *Total amount:* $15,626,769 (7% federal, 12% state, 77% institutional, 4% external sources). *Receiving aid:* Freshmen: 82% (293); All full-time undergraduates: 82% (1,191). *Average award:* Freshmen: $14,694; Undergraduates: $13,513. *Scholarships, grants, and awards:* Federal Pell, FSEOG, state, private, college/university gift aid from institutional funds.
GIFT AID (NON-NEED-BASED) *Total amount:* $2,348,538 (3% state, 87% institutional, 10% external sources). *Receiving aid:* Freshmen: 10% (34); Undergraduates: 7% (103). *Average Award:* Freshmen: $9504; Undergraduates: $8949. *Scholarships, grants, and awards by category:* Academic Interests/Achievement: 772 awards ($6,323,955 total): biological sciences, business, communication, computer science, education, English, foreign languages, general academic interests/achievements, health fields, humanities, international studies, mathematics, physical sciences, premedicine, religion/biblical studies, social sciences. Creative Arts/Performance: 175 awards ($327,550 total): art/fine arts, creative writing, music, theater/drama. Special Achievements/Activities: 55 awards ($95,375 total): general special achievements/activities, leadership. Special Characteristics: 50 awards ($1,057,587 total): children of educators, children of faculty/staff, relatives of clergy. *Tuition waivers:* Full or partial for employees or children of employees. *ROTC:* Army cooperative.
LOANS *Student loans:* $9,221,845 (67% need-based, 33% non-need-based). 87% of past graduating class borrowed through all loan programs. *Average indebtedness per student:* $23,343. *Average need-based loan:* Freshmen: $3489; Undergraduates: $4261. *Parent loans:* $4,712,354 (36% need-based, 64% non-need-based). *Programs:* FFEL (Subsidized and Unsubsidized Stafford, PLUS), Perkins, college/university.
WORK-STUDY *Federal work-study:* Total amount: $557,826; 491 jobs averaging $1136. *State or other work-study/employment:* Part-time jobs available.

Lycoming College

APPLYING FOR FINANCIAL AID *Required financial aid forms:* FAFSA, institution's own form, state aid form. *Financial aid deadline (priority):* 3/1. *Notification date:* Continuous beginning 3/1. Students must reply by 5/1.
CONTACT Mrs. Jamie Lowthert, Director of Financial Aid, Lycoming College, 700 College Place, Long Hall, Williamsport, PA 17701-5192, 570-321-4040 or toll-free 800-345-3920 Ext. 4026. *Fax:* 570-321-4993. *E-mail:* lowthert@lycoming.edu.

LYME ACADEMY COLLEGE OF FINE ARTS
Old Lyme, CT

Tuition & fees: $16,916   **Average undergraduate aid package:** $10,573

ABOUT THE INSTITUTION Independent, coed. Awards: bachelor's degrees. 3 undergraduate majors. Total enrollment: 160. Undergraduates: 160. Freshmen: 14. Both federal and institutional methodology are used as a basis for awarding need-based institutional aid.
UNDERGRADUATE EXPENSES for 2005–06 *Application fee:* $35. *Tuition:* full-time $16,416.
FRESHMAN FINANCIAL AID (Fall 2005, est.) 100% of freshmen with need received aid. *Average financial aid package:* $10,950 (excluding resources awarded to replace EFC). 20% of all full-time freshmen had no need and received non-need-based gift aid.
UNDERGRADUATE FINANCIAL AID (Fall 2005, est.) *Average financial aid package:* $10,573 (excluding resources awarded to replace EFC). 14% of all full-time undergraduates had no need and received non-need-based gift aid.
GIFT AID (NEED-BASED) *Total amount:* $203,957 (40% federal, 34% state, 26% external sources). *Receiving aid:* Freshmen: 80% (8). *Scholarships, grants, and awards:* Federal Pell, FSEOG, state, private, college/university gift aid from institutional funds.
GIFT AID (NON-NEED-BASED) *Total amount:* $260,600 (100% institutional). *Scholarships, grants, and awards by category:* Creative Arts/Performance: art/fine arts.
LOANS *Student loans:* $430,934 (56% need-based, 44% non-need-based). 50% of past graduating class borrowed through all loan programs. *Average need-based loan:* Freshmen: $2625. *Parent loans:* $150,482 (100% non-need-based). *Programs:* FFEL (Subsidized and Unsubsidized Stafford, PLUS), Nellie Mae Loans, EXCEL Loans, TERI Loans, Connecticut Student Loan Foundation FFELP loans, alternative loans.
WORK-STUDY *Federal work-study:* Total amount: $5666; 7 jobs averaging $809. *State or other work-study/employment:* Total amount: $3442 (100% need-based). 3 part-time jobs averaging $1306.
APPLYING FOR FINANCIAL AID *Required financial aid forms:* FAFSA, institution's own form, CSS Financial Aid PROFILE, business/farm supplement. *Financial aid deadline (priority):* 2/15. *Notification date:* Continuous beginning 2/15. Students must reply by 5/1 or within 2 weeks of notification.
CONTACT Mr. Jim Falconer, Director of Financial Aid, Lyme Academy College of Fine Arts, 84 Lyme Street, Old Lyme, CT 06371, 860-434-5232 Ext. 114. *Fax:* 860-434-8725. *E-mail:* jfalconer@lymeacademy.edu.

LYNCHBURG COLLEGE
Lynchburg, VA

Tuition & fees: $24,245   **Average undergraduate aid package:** $18,221

ABOUT THE INSTITUTION Independent religious, coed. Awards: bachelor's and master's degrees. 47 undergraduate majors. Total enrollment: 2,428. Undergraduates: 2,049. Freshmen: 557. Both federal and institutional methodology are used as a basis for awarding need-based institutional aid.
UNDERGRADUATE EXPENSES for 2006–07 *Application fee:* $30. *Comprehensive fee:* $30,645 includes full-time tuition ($23,700), mandatory fees ($545), and room and board ($6400). *College room only:* $3200. *Part-time tuition:* $335 per credit hour.
FRESHMAN FINANCIAL AID (Fall 2005, est.) 457 applied for aid; of those 77% were deemed to have need. 100% of freshmen with need received aid; of those 30% had need fully met. *Average percent of need met:* 90% (excluding resources awarded to replace EFC). *Average financial aid package:* $18,519 (excluding resources awarded to replace EFC). 36% of all full-time freshmen had no need and received non-need-based gift aid.
UNDERGRADUATE FINANCIAL AID (Fall 2005, est.) 1,491 applied for aid; of those 82% were deemed to have need. 100% of undergraduates with need received aid; of those 34% had need fully met. *Average percent of need met:* 87% (excluding resources awarded to replace EFC). *Average financial aid package:* $18,221 (excluding resources awarded to replace EFC). 36% of all full-time undergraduates had no need and received non-need-based gift aid.
GIFT AID (NEED-BASED) *Total amount:* $19,655,571 (6% federal, 10% state, 80% institutional, 4% external sources). *Receiving aid:* Freshmen: 63% (351); All full-time undergraduates: 63% (1,214). *Average award:* Freshmen: $15,060; Undergraduates: $13,610. *Scholarships, grants, and awards:* Federal Pell, FSEOG, state, college/university gift aid from institutional funds.
GIFT AID (NON-NEED-BASED) *Total amount:* $3,304,825 (33% state, 59% institutional, 8% external sources). *Receiving aid:* Freshmen: 35% (196); Undergraduates: 40% (778). *Average Award:* Freshmen: $8379; Undergraduates: $8196. *Scholarships, grants, and awards by category:* Academic Interests/Achievement: general academic interests/achievements. Creative Arts/Performance: music. Special Achievements/Activities: community service, leadership. Special Characteristics: children of faculty/staff.
LOANS *Student loans:* $9,288,268 (70% need-based, 30% non-need-based). 65% of past graduating class borrowed through all loan programs. *Average indebtedness per student:* $18,517. *Average need-based loan:* Freshmen: $3076; Undergraduates: $4000. *Parent loans:* $5,102,596 (70% need-based, 30% non-need-based). *Programs:* FFEL (Subsidized and Unsubsidized Stafford, PLUS), Perkins.
WORK-STUDY *Federal work-study:* Total amount: $200,000; 352 jobs averaging $1088. *State or other work-study/employment:* Total amount: $635,913 (25% need-based, 75% non-need-based). 465 part-time jobs averaging $1373.
APPLYING FOR FINANCIAL AID *Required financial aid forms:* FAFSA, state aid form. *Financial aid deadline (priority):* 3/1. *Notification date:* Continuous beginning 3/10. Students must reply by 5/1 or within 2 weeks of notification.
CONTACT Mrs. Michelle Davis, Director of Financial Aid, Lynchburg College, 1501 Lakeside Drive, Lynchburg, VA 24501-3199, 434-544-8228 or toll-free 800-426-8101. *Fax:* 434-544-8653.

LYNDON STATE COLLEGE
Lyndonville, VT

CONTACT Ms. Terry Van Zile, Assistant Director of Financial Aid, Lyndon State College, PO Box 919, Lyndonville, VT 05851, 802-626-6217 or toll-free 800-225-1998. *E-mail:* theresa.vanzile@lsc.vsc.edu.

LYNN UNIVERSITY
Boca Raton, FL

Tuition & fees: $27,350   **Average undergraduate aid package:** $16,051

ABOUT THE INSTITUTION Independent, coed. Awards: bachelor's, master's, and doctoral degrees and post-bachelor's and post-master's certificates. 39 undergraduate majors. Total enrollment: 2,747. Undergraduates: 2,283. Freshmen: 651. Federal methodology is used as a basis for awarding need-based institutional aid.
UNDERGRADUATE EXPENSES for 2006–07 *Application fee:* $35. *Comprehensive fee:* $37,000 includes full-time tuition ($26,200), mandatory fees ($1150), and room and board ($9650). *Part-time tuition:* $760 per credit hour.
FRESHMAN FINANCIAL AID (Fall 2004) 273 applied for aid; of those 78% were deemed to have need. 99% of freshmen with need received aid; of those 10% had need fully met. *Average percent of need met:* 51% (excluding resources awarded to replace EFC). *Average financial aid package:* $14,320 (excluding resources awarded to replace EFC). 32% of all full-time freshmen had no need and received non-need-based gift aid.
UNDERGRADUATE FINANCIAL AID (Fall 2004) 734 applied for aid; of those 84% were deemed to have need. 99% of undergraduates with need received aid; of those 12% had need fully met. *Average percent of need met:* 55% (excluding resources awarded to replace EFC). *Average financial aid package:* $16,051 (excluding resources awarded to replace EFC). 29% of all full-time undergraduates had no need and received non-need-based gift aid.
GIFT AID (NEED-BASED) *Total amount:* $6,586,776 (17% federal, 10% state, 66% institutional, 7% external sources). *Receiving aid:* Freshmen: 28% (205); All full-time undergraduates: 36% (594). *Average award:* Freshmen: $11,591;

Undergraduates: $12,320. **Scholarships, grants, and awards:** Federal Pell, FSEOG, state, private, college/university gift aid from institutional funds.
GIFT AID (NON-NEED-BASED) Total amount: $3,940,285 (15% state, 63% institutional, 22% external sources). **Receiving aid:** Freshmen: 1% (10); Undergraduates: 2% (35). **Average Award:** Freshmen: $12,376; Undergraduates: $12,527. **Scholarships, grants, and awards by category:** Academic Interests/Achievement: 530 awards ($3,339,431 total): business, communication, general academic interests/achievements. Creative Arts/Performance: 28 awards ($639,304 total): music. Special Achievements/Activities: 2 awards ($44,462 total): leadership, religious involvement. Special Characteristics: 44 awards ($390,960 total): children of faculty/staff, siblings of current students. **ROTC:** Air Force cooperative.
LOANS Student loans: $5,905,658 (74% need-based, 26% non-need-based). 68% of past graduating class borrowed through all loan programs. *Average indebtedness per student:* $15,154. **Average need-based loan:** Freshmen: $3084; Undergraduates: $4304. **Parent loans:** $5,080,892 (44% need-based, 56% non-need-based). **Programs:** FFEL (Subsidized and Unsubsidized Stafford, PLUS), Perkins, state, college/university.
WORK-STUDY Federal work-study: Total amount: $154,016; 175 jobs averaging $1119. **State or other work-study/employment:** Total amount: $248,180 (27% need-based, 73% non-need-based). 39 part-time jobs averaging $5432.
ATHLETIC AWARDS Total amount: $2,276,524 (33% need-based, 67% non-need-based).
APPLYING FOR FINANCIAL AID *Required financial aid forms:* FAFSA, institution's own form. *Financial aid deadline (priority):* 3/1. *Notification date:* Continuous beginning 2/1. Students must reply within 2 weeks of notification.
CONTACT William Healy, Director of Student Financial Services, Lynn University, 3601 North Military Trail, Boca Raton, FL 33431-5598, 561-237-7814 or toll-free 800-888-5966. *Fax:* 561-237-7189. *E-mail:* whealy@lynn.edu.

LYON COLLEGE
Batesville, AR

Tuition & fees: $14,860   **Average undergraduate aid package:** $13,749

ABOUT THE INSTITUTION Independent Presbyterian, coed. Awards: bachelor's degrees. 18 undergraduate majors. Total enrollment: 488. Undergraduates: 488. Freshmen: 112. Federal methodology is used as a basis for awarding need-based institutional aid.
UNDERGRADUATE EXPENSES for 2006–07 Application fee: $25. **Comprehensive fee:** $21,130 includes full-time tuition ($14,420), mandatory fees ($440), and room and board ($6270). **College room only:** $2580. **Part-time tuition:** $600 per credit hour.
FRESHMAN FINANCIAL AID (Fall 2005, est.) 87 applied for aid; of those 75% were deemed to have need. 100% of freshmen with need received aid; of those 42% had need fully met. *Average percent of need met:* 85% (excluding resources awarded to replace EFC). *Average financial aid package:* $13,235 (excluding resources awarded to replace EFC). 33% of all full-time freshmen had no need and received non-need-based gift aid.
UNDERGRADUATE FINANCIAL AID (Fall 2005, est.) 373 applied for aid; of those 86% were deemed to have need. 100% of undergraduates with need received aid; of those 29% had need fully met. *Average percent of need met:* 77% (excluding resources awarded to replace EFC). *Average financial aid package:* $13,749 (excluding resources awarded to replace EFC). 27% of all full-time undergraduates had no need and received non-need-based gift aid.
GIFT AID (NEED-BASED) Total amount: $2,849,276 (22% federal, 10% state, 64% institutional, 4% external sources). **Receiving aid:** Freshmen: 59% (65); All full-time undergraduates: 70% (319). **Average award:** Freshmen: $10,531; Undergraduates: $9953. **Scholarships, grants, and awards:** Federal Pell, FSEOG, state, private, college/university gift aid from institutional funds.
GIFT AID (NON-NEED-BASED) Total amount: $1,293,087 (20% state, 76% institutional, 4% external sources). **Receiving aid:** Freshmen: 17% (19); Undergraduates: 12% (57). **Average Award:** Freshmen: $11,096; Undergraduates: $10,421. **Scholarships, grants, and awards by category:** Academic Interests/Achievement: 453 awards ($1,813,656 total): general academic interests/achievements. Creative Arts/Performance: 24 awards ($56,915 total): art/fine arts, music, theater/drama. Special Achievements/Activities: 26 awards ($91,000 total): leadership. Special Characteristics: 31 awards ($100,616 total): children of faculty/staff, ethnic background, local/state students, members of minority groups, religious affiliation.

LOANS Student loans: $1,785,500 (78% need-based, 22% non-need-based). 92% of past graduating class borrowed through all loan programs. *Average indebtedness per student:* $15,956. **Average need-based loan:** Freshmen: $3464; Undergraduates: $4616. **Parent loans:** $470,680 (30% need-based, 70% non-need-based). **Programs:** FFEL (Subsidized and Unsubsidized Stafford, PLUS), Perkins.
WORK-STUDY Federal work-study: Total amount: $139,783; 121 jobs averaging $1152. **State or other work-study/employment:** Total amount: $10,000 (100% non-need-based). 10 part-time jobs averaging $1000.
ATHLETIC AWARDS Total amount: $783,175 (39% need-based, 61% non-need-based).
APPLYING FOR FINANCIAL AID *Required financial aid form:* FAFSA. *Financial aid deadline (priority):* 3/15. *Notification date:* Continuous beginning 3/1. Students must reply by 8/15.
CONTACT Ms. Louise Strauser, Assistant Director of Student Financial Assistance, Lyon College, 2300 Highland Road, Batesville, AR 72501, 870-698-4257 or toll-free 800-423-2542. *Fax:* 870-793-1791. *E-mail:* financialaid@lyon.edu.

MACALESTER COLLEGE
St. Paul, MN

Tuition & fees: $31,038   **Average undergraduate aid package:** $25,238

ABOUT THE INSTITUTION Independent Presbyterian, coed. Awards: bachelor's degrees. 38 undergraduate majors. Total enrollment: 1,869. Undergraduates: 1,869. Freshmen: 491. Institutional methodology is used as a basis for awarding need-based institutional aid.
UNDERGRADUATE EXPENSES for 2006–07 Application fee: $40. **Comprehensive fee:** $39,020 includes full-time tuition ($30,870), mandatory fees ($168), and room and board ($7982). **College room only:** $4208. **Part-time tuition:** $965 per semester hour.
FRESHMAN FINANCIAL AID (Fall 2005, est.) 377 applied for aid; of those 92% were deemed to have need. 100% of freshmen with need received aid; of those 100% had need fully met. *Average percent of need met:* 100% (excluding resources awarded to replace EFC). *Average financial aid package:* $24,854 (excluding resources awarded to replace EFC). 6% of all full-time freshmen had no need and received non-need-based gift aid.
UNDERGRADUATE FINANCIAL AID (Fall 2005, est.) 1,311 applied for aid; of those 96% were deemed to have need. 100% of undergraduates with need received aid; of those 100% had need fully met. *Average percent of need met:* 100% (excluding resources awarded to replace EFC). *Average financial aid package:* $25,238 (excluding resources awarded to replace EFC). 6% of all full-time undergraduates had no need and received non-need-based gift aid.
GIFT AID (NEED-BASED) Total amount: $25,054,999 (3% federal, 2% state, 90% institutional, 5% external sources). **Receiving aid:** Freshmen: 71% (347); All full-time undergraduates: 69% (1,258). **Average award:** Freshmen: $20,455; Undergraduates: $19,806. **Scholarships, grants, and awards:** Federal Pell, FSEOG, state, private, college/university gift aid from institutional funds.
GIFT AID (NON-NEED-BASED) Total amount: $575,037 (2% federal, 89% institutional, 9% external sources). **Average Award:** Freshmen: $3806; Undergraduates: $4686. **Scholarships, grants, and awards by category:** Academic Interests/Achievement: 397 awards ($1,110,150 total): general academic interests/achievements. Special Characteristics: 165 awards ($532,750 total): ethnic background. **ROTC:** Naval cooperative, Air Force cooperative.
LOANS Student loans: $5,920,435 (96% need-based, 4% non-need-based). 75% of past graduating class borrowed through all loan programs. *Average indebtedness per student:* $14,889. **Average need-based loan:** Freshmen: $2896; Undergraduates: $3627. **Parent loans:** $2,102,904 (100% non-need-based). **Programs:** FFEL (Subsidized and Unsubsidized Stafford, PLUS), Perkins, state.
WORK-STUDY Federal work-study: Total amount: $500,972; 315 jobs averaging $1591. **State or other work-study/employment:** Total amount: $1,896,965 (98% need-based, 2% non-need-based). 936 part-time jobs averaging $2026.
APPLYING FOR FINANCIAL AID *Required financial aid forms:* FAFSA, CSS Financial Aid PROFILE, noncustodial (divorced/separated) parent's statement. *Financial aid deadline (priority):* 2/8. *Notification date:* 4/1. Students must reply by 5/1.
CONTACT Financial Aid Office, Macalester College, 1600 Grand Avenue, St. Paul, MN 55105, 651-696-6214 or toll-free 800-231-7974. *Fax:* 651-696-6866. *E-mail:* finaid@macalester.edu.

MACHZIKEI HADATH RABBINICAL COLLEGE
Brooklyn, NY

CONTACT Rabbi Baruch Rozmarin, Director of Financial Aid, Machzikei Hadath Rabbinical College, 5407 16th Avenue, Brooklyn, NY 11204-1805, 718-854-8777.

MACMURRAY COLLEGE
Jacksonville, IL

Tuition & fees: $15,750   **Average undergraduate aid package:** $13,591

ABOUT THE INSTITUTION Independent United Methodist, coed. Awards: associate and bachelor's degrees. 39 undergraduate majors. Total enrollment: 703. Undergraduates: 703. Freshmen: 164. Federal methodology is used as a basis for awarding need-based institutional aid.

UNDERGRADUATE EXPENSES for 2006–07 *Comprehensive fee:* $21,748 includes full-time tuition ($15,500), mandatory fees ($250), and room and board ($5998). *College room only:* $2732. *Part-time tuition:* $250 per credit hour. *Part-time fees:* $35 per term.

FRESHMAN FINANCIAL AID (Fall 2005, est.) 167 applied for aid; of those 90% were deemed to have need. 100% of freshmen with need received aid; of those 13% had need fully met. *Average percent of need met:* 72% (excluding resources awarded to replace EFC). *Average financial aid package:* $12,703 (excluding resources awarded to replace EFC). 10% of all full-time freshmen had no need and received non-need-based gift aid.

UNDERGRADUATE FINANCIAL AID (Fall 2005, est.) 638 applied for aid; of those 90% were deemed to have need. 100% of undergraduates with need received aid; of those 15% had need fully met. *Average percent of need met:* 75% (excluding resources awarded to replace EFC). *Average financial aid package:* $13,591 (excluding resources awarded to replace EFC). 9% of all full-time undergraduates had no need and received non-need-based gift aid.

GIFT AID (NEED-BASED) *Total amount:* $5,752,935 (18% federal, 27% state, 53% institutional, 2% external sources). *Receiving aid:* Freshmen: 90% (150); All full-time undergraduates: 89% (571). *Average award:* Freshmen: $10,204; Undergraduates: $9942. *Scholarships, grants, and awards:* Federal Pell, FSEOG, state, private, college/university gift aid from institutional funds.

GIFT AID (NON-NEED-BASED) *Total amount:* $581,848 (1% federal, 94% institutional, 5% external sources). *Receiving aid:* Freshmen: 9% (15); Undergraduates: 7% (45). *Average Award:* Freshmen: $15,033; Undergraduates: $12,548. *Scholarships, grants, and awards by category:* Academic Interests/Achievement: 293 awards ($660,397 total): biological sciences, education, English, foreign languages, general academic interests/achievements, health fields, physical sciences, religion/biblical studies, social sciences. *Creative Arts/Performance:* 26 awards ($51,750 total): art/fine arts, music, theater/drama. *Special Achievements/Activities:* 20 awards ($40,400 total): leadership, religious involvement. *Special Characteristics:* 102 awards ($302,318 total): children and siblings of alumni, children of faculty/staff, international students, out-of-state students, previous college experience, religious affiliation, siblings of current students.

LOANS *Student loans:* $4,124,613 (78% need-based, 22% non-need-based). 91% of past graduating class borrowed through all loan programs. *Average indebtedness per student:* $16,920. *Average need-based loan:* Freshmen: $3111; Undergraduates: $4184. *Parent loans:* $563,343 (43% need-based, 57% non-need-based). *Programs:* FFEL (Subsidized and Unsubsidized Stafford, PLUS), Perkins.

WORK-STUDY *Federal work-study:* Total amount: $61,170; 66 jobs averaging $920. *State or other work-study/employment:* Total amount: $82,000 (100% non-need-based). 86 part-time jobs averaging $1139.

APPLYING FOR FINANCIAL AID *Required financial aid form:* FAFSA. *Financial aid deadline (priority):* 5/31. *Notification date:* Continuous. Students must reply within 2 weeks of notification.

CONTACT Dena Dobson, Director of Financial Aid, MacMurray College, 447 East College Avenue, Jacksonville, IL 62650, 217-479-7041 or toll-free 800-252-7485 (in-state). *Fax:* 217-291-0702. *E-mail:* dena.dobson@mac.edu.

MACON STATE COLLEGE
Macon, GA

Tuition & fees (GA res): $1730   **Average undergraduate aid package:** $5984

ABOUT THE INSTITUTION State-supported, coed. Awards: associate and bachelor's degrees. 58 undergraduate majors. Total enrollment: 6,150. Undergraduates: 6,150. Federal methodology is used as a basis for awarding need-based institutional aid.

UNDERGRADUATE EXPENSES for 2005–06 *Application fee:* $20. *One-time required fee:* $25. *Tuition, state resident:* full-time $1542; part-time $65 per credit hour. *Tuition, nonresident:* full-time $6166; part-time $257 per credit hour. *Required fees:* full-time $188; $94 per term part-time.

FRESHMAN FINANCIAL AID (Fall 2004) 100% of freshmen with need received aid; of those 10% had need fully met. *Average financial aid package:* $5334 (excluding resources awarded to replace EFC). 30% of all full-time freshmen had no need and received non-need-based gift aid.

UNDERGRADUATE FINANCIAL AID (Fall 2004) 100% of undergraduates with need received aid; of those 3% had need fully met. *Average percent of need met:* 46% (excluding resources awarded to replace EFC). *Average financial aid package:* $5984 (excluding resources awarded to replace EFC). 21% of all full-time undergraduates had no need and received non-need-based gift aid.

GIFT AID (NEED-BASED) *Total amount:* $5,416,682 (99% federal, 1% state). *Receiving aid:* Freshmen: 45% (322); All full-time undergraduates: 44% (1,095). *Average award:* Freshmen: $3152; Undergraduates: $3031. *Scholarships, grants, and awards:* Federal Pell, FSEOG, state, college/university gift aid from institutional funds, Georgia HOPE Scholarships.

GIFT AID (NON-NEED-BASED) *Total amount:* $2,930,386 (99% state, 1% external sources). *Receiving aid:* Freshmen: 33% (235); Undergraduates: 22% (543). *Average Award:* Freshmen: $1871; Undergraduates: $1826. *Tuition waivers:* Full or partial for senior citizens.

LOANS *Student loans:* $8,434,786 (51% need-based, 49% non-need-based). *Average need-based loan:* Freshmen: $2158; Undergraduates: $2749. *Parent loans:* $74,213 (100% non-need-based). *Programs:* FFEL (Subsidized and Unsubsidized Stafford, PLUS), state.

WORK-STUDY *Federal work-study:* Total amount: $167,541; 106 jobs available. *State or other work-study/employment:* Part-time jobs available.

APPLYING FOR FINANCIAL AID *Required financial aid forms:* FAFSA, state aid form. *Financial aid deadline (priority):* 4/1. *Notification date:* Continuous beginning 4/15.

CONTACT Office of Financial Aid, Macon State College, 100 College Station Drive, Macon, GA 31206, 478-471-2717 or toll-free 800-272-7619 Ext. 2800. *Fax:* 478-471-2790. *E-mail:* fainfo@mail.maconstate.edu.

MADONNA UNIVERSITY
Livonia, MI

CONTACT Financial Aid Secretary, Madonna University, 36600 Schoolcraft Road, Livonia, MI 48150-1173, 734-432-5663 or toll-free 800-852-4951.

MAGDALEN COLLEGE
Warner, NH

Tuition & fees: $10,750   **Average undergraduate aid package:** $12,642

ABOUT THE INSTITUTION Independent Roman Catholic, coed. Awards: associate and bachelor's degrees. 1 undergraduate major. Total enrollment: 73. Undergraduates: 73. Freshmen: 28. Institutional methodology is used as a basis for awarding need-based institutional aid.

UNDERGRADUATE EXPENSES for 2005–06 *Application fee:* $35. *Comprehensive fee:* $17,250 includes full-time tuition ($10,750) and room and board ($6500).

FRESHMAN FINANCIAL AID (Fall 2005, est.) 16 applied for aid; of those 100% were deemed to have need. 100% of freshmen with need received aid; of those 100% had need fully met. *Average percent of need met:* 100% (excluding resources awarded to replace EFC). *Average financial aid package:* $12,859 (excluding resources awarded to replace EFC).

UNDERGRADUATE FINANCIAL AID (Fall 2005, est.) 41 applied for aid; of those 100% were deemed to have need. 100% of undergraduates with need received

aid; of those 100% had need fully met. *Average percent of need met:* 100% (excluding resources awarded to replace EFC). *Average financial aid package:* $12,642 (excluding resources awarded to replace EFC).
GIFT AID (NEED-BASED) *Total amount:* $114,600 (98% institutional, 2% external sources). *Receiving aid:* Freshmen: 59% (16); All full-time undergraduates: 59% (41). *Average award:* Freshmen: $2719; Undergraduates: $2502. *Scholarships, grants, and awards:* private, college/university gift aid from institutional funds.
GIFT AID (NON-NEED-BASED) *Tuition waivers:* Full or partial for employees or children of employees.
LOANS *Student loans:* $243,350 (100% need-based). 65% of past graduating class borrowed through all loan programs. *Average indebtedness per student:* $15,350. *Programs:* college/university, alternative loans.
WORK-STUDY *State or other work-study/employment:* Total amount: $15,000 (100% need-based). 15 part-time jobs averaging $1000.
APPLYING FOR FINANCIAL AID *Required financial aid form:* institution's own form. *Financial aid deadline:* Continuous. *Notification date:* 7/1. Students must reply within 4 weeks of notification.
CONTACT Gail Crowdes, Assistant to Executive Vice President, Magdalen College, 511 Kearsarge Mountain Road, Warner, NH 03278, 603-456-2656 or toll-free 877-498-1723 (out-of-state). *Fax:* 603-456-2660. *E-mail:* gcrowdes@magdalen.edu.

MAGNOLIA BIBLE COLLEGE
Kosciusko, MS

ABOUT THE INSTITUTION Independent religious, coed, primarily men. Awards: bachelor's degrees. 1 undergraduate major. Total enrollment: 41. Undergraduates: 41. Freshmen: 1.
GIFT AID (NEED-BASED) *Scholarships, grants, and awards:* Federal Pell, FSEOG, state, college/university gift aid from institutional funds.
GIFT AID (NON-NEED-BASED) *Scholarships, grants, and awards by category: Academic Interests/Achievement:* general academic interests/achievements, religion/biblical studies. *Special Characteristics:* children of faculty/staff, general special characteristics, spouses of current students.
LOANS *Programs:* FFEL (Subsidized and Unsubsidized Stafford, PLUS).
APPLYING FOR FINANCIAL AID *Required financial aid form:* FAFSA.
CONTACT Allen Coker, Financial Aid Director, Magnolia Bible College, PO Box 1109, Kosciusko, MS 39090-1109, 662-289-2896 or toll-free 800-748-8655 (in-state). *Fax:* 662-289-1850. *E-mail:* acoker@magnolia.edu.

MAHARISHI UNIVERSITY OF MANAGEMENT
Fairfield, IA

Tuition & fees: $24,430   **Average undergraduate aid package: $29,630**

ABOUT THE INSTITUTION Independent, coed. Awards: bachelor's, master's, and doctoral degrees and post-bachelor's certificates. 10 undergraduate majors. Total enrollment: 741. Undergraduates: 218. Freshmen: 31. Federal methodology is used as a basis for awarding need-based institutional aid.
UNDERGRADUATE EXPENSES for 2006–07 *Application fee:* $15. *Comprehensive fee:* $30,430 includes full-time tuition ($24,000), mandatory fees ($430), and room and board ($6000).
FRESHMAN FINANCIAL AID (Fall 2005, est.) 29 applied for aid; of those 93% were deemed to have need. 100% of freshmen with need received aid; of those 26% had need fully met. *Average percent of need met:* 87% (excluding resources awarded to replace EFC). *Average financial aid package:* $29,630 (excluding resources awarded to replace EFC). 3% of all full-time freshmen had no need and received non-need-based gift aid.
UNDERGRADUATE FINANCIAL AID (Fall 2005, est.) 193 applied for aid; of those 98% were deemed to have need. 100% of undergraduates with need received aid; of those 69% had need fully met. *Average percent of need met:* 87% (excluding resources awarded to replace EFC). *Average financial aid package:* $29,630 (excluding resources awarded to replace EFC). 2% of all full-time undergraduates had no need and received non-need-based gift aid.
GIFT AID (NEED-BASED) *Total amount:* $2,064,188 (21% federal, 10% state, 69% institutional). *Receiving aid:* Freshmen: 87% (27); All full-time undergradu-

ates: 92% (190). *Average award:* Freshmen: $21,405; Undergraduates: $19,717. *Scholarships, grants, and awards:* Federal Pell, FSEOG, state, private, college/university gift aid from institutional funds.
GIFT AID (NON-NEED-BASED) *Total amount:* $163,950 (100% institutional). *Average Award:* Freshmen: $10,000; Undergraduates: $5900. *Scholarships, grants, and awards by category: Academic Interests/Achievement:* 7 awards ($90,450 total): general academic interests/achievements. *Creative Arts/Performance:* 5 awards ($3500 total): creative writing, music. *Special Characteristics:* 411 awards ($411,218 total): children of faculty/staff, ethnic background, veterans, veterans' children.
LOANS *Student loans:* $1,373,571 (68% need-based, 32% non-need-based). 94% of past graduating class borrowed through all loan programs. *Average indebtedness per student:* $19,545. *Average need-based loan:* Freshmen: $6625; Undergraduates: $8281. *Parent loans:* $24,448 (100% non-need-based). *Programs:* FFEL (Subsidized and Unsubsidized Stafford, PLUS), Perkins, college/university, alternative loans.
WORK-STUDY *Federal work-study:* Total amount: $142,631; 102 jobs averaging $1398. *State or other work-study/employment:* Total amount: $27,900 (100% need-based). 25 part-time jobs averaging $1116.
APPLYING FOR FINANCIAL AID *Required financial aid form:* FAFSA. *Financial aid deadline (priority):* 4/15. *Notification date:* Continuous. Students must reply by 5/30 or within 4 weeks of notification.
CONTACT Mr. Bill Christensen, Associate Director of Financial Aid, Maharishi University of Management, 1000 North 4th Street, DB 1127, Fairfield, IA 52557-1127, 641-472-1156 or toll-free 800-369-6480. *Fax:* 641-472-1133. *E-mail:* bchrist@mum.edu.

MAINE COLLEGE OF ART
Portland, ME

ABOUT THE INSTITUTION Independent, coed. Awards: bachelor's and master's degrees. 9 undergraduate majors. Total enrollment: 490. Undergraduates: 458. Freshmen: 125.
GIFT AID (NEED-BASED) *Scholarships, grants, and awards:* Federal Pell, FSEOG, state, private, college/university gift aid from institutional funds.
GIFT AID (NON-NEED-BASED) *Scholarships, grants, and awards by category: Creative Arts/Performance:* art/fine arts. *Special Characteristics:* children of faculty/staff.
LOANS *Programs:* FFEL (Subsidized and Unsubsidized Stafford, PLUS), Perkins, alternative loans.
WORK-STUDY *Federal work-study:* Total amount: $155,174; 69 jobs averaging $2249.
APPLYING FOR FINANCIAL AID *Required financial aid form:* FAFSA.
CONTACT Michelle A. Leclerc, Director of Financial Aid, Maine College of Art, 97 Spring Street, Portland, ME 04101-3987, 207-775-3052 or toll-free 800-639-4808. *Fax:* 207-772-5069. *E-mail:* mleclerc@meca.edu.

MAINE MARITIME ACADEMY
Castine, ME

Tuition & fees (ME res): $7620   **Average undergraduate aid package: $10,667**

ABOUT THE INSTITUTION State-supported, coed, primarily men. Awards: associate, bachelor's, and master's degrees. 11 undergraduate majors. Total enrollment: 861. Undergraduates: 846. Freshmen: 241. Federal methodology is used as a basis for awarding need-based institutional aid.
UNDERGRADUATE EXPENSES for 2005–06 *Application fee:* $15. *Tuition, state resident:* full-time $6380; part-time $230 per credit hour. *Tuition, nonresident:* full-time $9570; part-time $410 per credit hour. Full-time tuition and fees vary according to program. Part-time tuition and fees vary according to program. *College room and board:* $6720; *room only:* $2420. Room and board charges vary according to board plan. *Payment plan:* Installment.
FRESHMAN FINANCIAL AID (Fall 2004) 169 applied for aid; of those 81% were deemed to have need. 100% of freshmen with need received aid; of those 12% had need fully met. *Average percent of need met:* 65% (excluding resources awarded to replace EFC). *Average financial aid package:* $11,475 (excluding resources awarded to replace EFC). 6% of all full-time freshmen had no need and received non-need-based gift aid.
UNDERGRADUATE FINANCIAL AID (Fall 2004) 660 applied for aid; of those 83% were deemed to have need. 100% of undergraduates with need received

Maine Maritime Academy

aid; of those 13% had need fully met. *Average percent of need met:* 60% (excluding resources awarded to replace EFC). *Average financial aid package:* $10,667 (excluding resources awarded to replace EFC). 4% of all full-time undergraduates had no need and received non-need-based gift aid.

GIFT AID (NEED-BASED) *Total amount:* $1,577,810 (56% federal, 12% state, 20% institutional, 12% external sources). *Receiving aid:* Freshmen: 48% (105); All full-time undergraduates: 50% (395). *Average award:* Freshmen: $3701; Undergraduates: $4417. *Scholarships, grants, and awards:* Federal Pell, FSEOG, state, private, college/university gift aid from institutional funds.

GIFT AID (NON-NEED-BASED) *Total amount:* $552,222 (30% federal, 7% state, 61% institutional, 2% external sources). *Receiving aid:* Freshmen: 14% (31); Undergraduates: 12% (95). *Average Award:* Freshmen: $2500; Undergraduates: $2500. *Scholarships, grants, and awards by category: Academic Interests/Achievement:* 139 awards ($339,425 total): biological sciences, business, engineering/technologies, general academic interests/achievements. *Special Characteristics:* 12 awards ($68,540 total): children of faculty/staff. *ROTC:* Army, Naval.

LOANS *Student loans:* $4,837,698 (46% need-based, 54% non-need-based). 90% of past graduating class borrowed through all loan programs. *Average indebtedness per student:* $27,000. *Average need-based loan:* Freshmen: $4095; Undergraduates: $4698. *Parent loans:* $933,848 (32% need-based, 68% non-need-based). *Programs:* FFEL (Subsidized and Unsubsidized Stafford, PLUS), Perkins, college/university, alternative loans.

WORK-STUDY *Federal work-study:* Total amount: $99,418; 174 jobs averaging $571.

APPLYING FOR FINANCIAL AID *Required financial aid form:* FAFSA. *Financial aid deadline (priority):* 4/15. *Notification date:* Continuous. Students must reply within 3 weeks of notification.

CONTACT Ms. Holly Bayle, Assistant Director of Financial Aid, Maine Maritime Academy, Pleasant Street, Castine, ME 04420, 207-326-2205 or toll-free 800-464-6565 (in-state), 800-227-8465 (out-of-state). *Fax:* 207-326-2515. *E-mail:* bbayle@mma.edu.

MALONE COLLEGE
Canton, OH

| Tuition & fees: $17,790 | Average undergraduate aid package: $12,194 |

ABOUT THE INSTITUTION Independent religious, coed. Awards: bachelor's and master's degrees and post-bachelor's certificates. 43 undergraduate majors. Total enrollment: 2,277. Undergraduates: 1,920. Freshmen: 361. Federal methodology is used as a basis for awarding need-based institutional aid.

UNDERGRADUATE EXPENSES for 2006–07 *Application fee:* $20. *Comprehensive fee:* $24,190 includes full-time tuition ($17,520), mandatory fees ($270), and room and board ($6400). *College room only:* $3300. *Part-time tuition:* $330 per semester hour. *Part-time fees:* $67.50 per term.

FRESHMAN FINANCIAL AID (Fall 2005, est.) 334 applied for aid; of those 88% were deemed to have need. 100% of freshmen with need received aid; of those 16% had need fully met. *Average percent of need met:* 70% (excluding resources awarded to replace EFC). *Average financial aid package:* $13,038 (excluding resources awarded to replace EFC). 12% of all full-time freshmen had no need and received non-need-based gift aid.

UNDERGRADUATE FINANCIAL AID (Fall 2005, est.) 1,416 applied for aid; of those 88% were deemed to have need. 100% of undergraduates with need received aid; of those 18% had need fully met. *Average percent of need met:* 71% (excluding resources awarded to replace EFC). *Average financial aid package:* $12,194 (excluding resources awarded to replace EFC). 11% of all full-time undergraduates had no need and received non-need-based gift aid.

GIFT AID (NEED-BASED) *Total amount:* $9,008,123 (19% federal, 22% state, 52% institutional, 7% external sources). *Receiving aid:* Freshmen: 82% (293); All full-time undergraduates: 74% (1,238). *Average award:* Freshmen: $9703; Undergraduates: $8344. *Scholarships, grants, and awards:* Federal Pell, FSEOG, state, private, college/university gift aid from institutional funds.

GIFT AID (NON-NEED-BASED) *Total amount:* $1,489,769 (19% state, 67% institutional, 14% external sources). *Receiving aid:* Freshmen: 81% (288); Undergraduates: 72% (1,208). *Average Award:* Freshmen: $4726; Undergraduates: $4524. *Scholarships, grants, and awards by category: Academic Interests/Achievement:* 1,219 awards ($3,295,314 total): biological sciences, business, communication, computer science, education, English, foreign languages, general academic interests/achievements, health fields, humanities, international studies, mathematics, physical sciences, premedicine, religion/biblical studies, social sciences. *Creative Arts/Performance:* 77 awards ($92,450 total): debating, journalism/publications, music, theater/drama. *Special Achievements/Activities:* 169 awards ($255,568 total): community service, junior miss, leadership, religious involvement. *Special Characteristics:* 272 awards ($860,570 total): children and siblings of alumni, children of faculty/staff, international students, parents of current students, relatives of clergy, religious affiliation, siblings of current students, spouses of current students. *ROTC:* Army cooperative, Air Force cooperative.

LOANS *Student loans:* $8,437,166 (90% need-based, 10% non-need-based). 72% of past graduating class borrowed through all loan programs. *Average indebtedness per student:* $18,482. *Average need-based loan:* Freshmen: $3167; Undergraduates: $4074. *Parent loans:* $2,135,471 (90% need-based, 10% non-need-based). *Programs:* FFEL (Subsidized and Unsubsidized Stafford, PLUS), Perkins, state, college/university, alternative loans.

WORK-STUDY *Federal work-study:* Total amount: $572,500; 292 jobs averaging $1961. *State or other work-study/employment:* Total amount: $158,318 (66% need-based, 34% non-need-based). 64 part-time jobs averaging $2474.

ATHLETIC AWARDS *Total amount:* $1,646,721 (74% need-based, 26% non-need-based).

APPLYING FOR FINANCIAL AID *Required financial aid forms:* FAFSA, Verification documents if chosen for verification. *Financial aid deadline:* 7/31 (priority: 3/1). *Notification date:* Continuous beginning 3/1. Students must reply within 2 weeks of notification.

CONTACT Mr. Michael Bole, Director of Financial Aid, Malone College, 515 25th Street, NW, Canton, OH 44709-3897, 330-471-8162 or toll-free 800-521-1146. *Fax:* 330-471-8478. *E-mail:* mbole@malone.edu.

MANCHESTER COLLEGE
North Manchester, IN

| Tuition & fees: $20,500 | Average undergraduate aid package: $17,375 |

ABOUT THE INSTITUTION Independent religious, coed. Awards: associate, bachelor's, and master's degrees. 59 undergraduate majors. Total enrollment: 1,104. Undergraduates: 1,094. Freshmen: 330. Federal methodology is used as a basis for awarding need-based institutional aid.

UNDERGRADUATE EXPENSES for 2006–07 *Application fee:* $25. *Tuition:* full-time $19,800; part-time $670 per credit hour.

FRESHMAN FINANCIAL AID (Fall 2005, est.) 318 applied for aid; of those 89% were deemed to have need. 100% of freshmen with need received aid; of those 45% had need fully met. *Average percent of need met:* 93% (excluding resources awarded to replace EFC). *Average financial aid package:* $18,533 (excluding resources awarded to replace EFC). 9% of all full-time freshmen had no need and received non-need-based gift aid.

UNDERGRADUATE FINANCIAL AID (Fall 2005, est.) 980 applied for aid; of those 92% were deemed to have need. 99% of undergraduates with need received aid; of those 43% had need fully met. *Average percent of need met:* 88% (excluding resources awarded to replace EFC). *Average financial aid package:* $17,375 (excluding resources awarded to replace EFC). 6% of all full-time undergraduates had no need and received non-need-based gift aid.

GIFT AID (NEED-BASED) *Total amount:* $12,251,073 (8% federal, 24% state, 66% institutional, 2% external sources). *Receiving aid:* Freshmen: 86% (283); All full-time undergraduates: 85% (889). *Average award:* Freshmen: $15,334; Undergraduates: $13,794. *Scholarships, grants, and awards:* Federal Pell, FSEOG, state, private, college/university gift aid from institutional funds.

GIFT AID (NON-NEED-BASED) *Total amount:* $1,471,830 (97% institutional, 3% external sources). *Receiving aid:* Freshmen: 66% (217); Undergraduates: 62% (645). *Average Award:* Freshmen: $8667; Undergraduates: $8648. *Scholarships, grants, and awards by category: Academic Interests/Achievement:* business, English, foreign languages, general academic interests/achievements, humanities. *Special Characteristics:* children and siblings of alumni, ethnic background, international students, members of minority groups, previous college experience, religious affiliation.

LOANS *Student loans:* $2,762,670 (94% need-based, 6% non-need-based). 70% of past graduating class borrowed through all loan programs. *Average indebtedness per student:* $18,254. *Average need-based loan:* Freshmen: $2213; Undergraduates: $3202. *Parent loans:* $1,528,676 (90% need-based, 10% non-need-based). *Programs:* FFEL (Subsidized and Unsubsidized Stafford, PLUS), Perkins.

WORK-STUDY *Federal work-study:* Total amount: $800,913; jobs available (averaging $1500). *State or other work-study/employment:* Total amount: $671,750 (69% need-based, 31% non-need-based). Part-time jobs available.
APPLYING FOR FINANCIAL AID *Required financial aid form:* FAFSA. *Financial aid deadline (priority):* 3/1. *Notification date:* Continuous beginning 3/1. Students must reply within 2 weeks of notification.
CONTACT Ms. Gina Voelz, Director of Financial Aid, Manchester College, 604 East College Avenue, North Manchester, IN 46962-1225, 260-982-5066 or toll-free 800-852-3648. *Fax:* 260-982-6868. *E-mail:* glvoelz@manchester.edu.

MANHATTAN CHRISTIAN COLLEGE
Manhattan, KS

Tuition & fees: $9638	Average undergraduate aid package: $8938

ABOUT THE INSTITUTION Independent religious, coed. Awards: associate and bachelor's degrees. 9 undergraduate majors. Total enrollment: 331. Undergraduates: 331. Freshmen: 83. Federal methodology is used as a basis for awarding need-based institutional aid.
UNDERGRADUATE EXPENSES for 2005–06 *Application fee:* $25. *Comprehensive fee:* $15,228 includes full-time tuition ($9444), mandatory fees ($194), and room and board ($5590). Room and board charges vary according to board plan. *Part-time tuition:* $389 per hour. Part-time tuition and fees vary according to course load. *Payment plan:* Deferred payment.
FRESHMAN FINANCIAL AID (Fall 2004) 80 applied for aid; of those 76% were deemed to have need. 100% of freshmen with need received aid; of those 16% had need fully met. *Average percent of need met:* 74% (excluding resources awarded to replace EFC). *Average financial aid package:* $8268 (excluding resources awarded to replace EFC). 22% of all full-time freshmen had no need and received non-need-based gift aid.
UNDERGRADUATE FINANCIAL AID (Fall 2004) 334 applied for aid; of those 79% were deemed to have need. 100% of undergraduates with need received aid; of those 8% had need fully met. *Average percent of need met:* 72% (excluding resources awarded to replace EFC). *Average financial aid package:* $8938 (excluding resources awarded to replace EFC). 18% of all full-time undergraduates had no need and received non-need-based gift aid.
GIFT AID (NEED-BASED) *Total amount:* $502,062 (68% federal, 28% state, 4% institutional). *Receiving aid:* Freshmen: 45% (37); All full-time undergraduates: 40% (160). *Average award:* Freshmen: $3126; Undergraduates: $3024. *Scholarships, grants, and awards:* Federal Pell, FSEOG, state, private, college/university gift aid from institutional funds.
GIFT AID (NON-NEED-BASED) *Total amount:* $967,745 (1% state, 67% institutional, 32% external sources). *Receiving aid:* Freshmen: 73% (61); Undergraduates: 49% (197). *Average Award:* Freshmen: $3319; Undergraduates: $3432. *Scholarships, grants, and awards by category: Academic Interests/Achievement:* 186 awards ($439,063 total): general academic interests/achievements, religion/biblical studies. *Creative Arts/Performance:* 8 awards ($4250 total): music. *Special Achievements/Activities:* 13 awards ($69,889 total): leadership. *Special Characteristics:* 8 awards ($30,068 total): children of faculty/staff. *Tuition waivers:* Full or partial for employees or children of employees, senior citizens. *ROTC:* Army cooperative, Air Force cooperative.
LOANS *Student loans:* $1,176,945 (64% need-based, 36% non-need-based). 75% of past graduating class borrowed through all loan programs. *Average indebtedness per student:* $12,046. *Average need-based loan:* Freshmen: $2725; Undergraduates: $3569. *Parent loans:* $273,641 (100% non-need-based). *Programs:* FFEL (Subsidized and Unsubsidized Stafford, PLUS), Perkins.
WORK-STUDY *Federal work-study:* Total amount: $74,825; 74 jobs averaging $1011.
APPLYING FOR FINANCIAL AID *Required financial aid forms:* FAFSA, state aid form. *Notification date:* Continuous beginning 3/5. Students must reply within 2 weeks of notification.
CONTACT Mrs. Margaret Carlisle, Director of Financial Aid, Manhattan Christian College, 1415 Anderson Avenue, Manhattan, KS 66502-4081, 785-539-3571 or toll-free 877-246-4622. *E-mail:* carlisle@mccks.edu.

MANHATTAN COLLEGE
Riverdale, NY

Tuition & fees: $20,350	Average undergraduate aid package: $13,606

ABOUT THE INSTITUTION Independent religious, coed. Awards: bachelor's and master's degrees and post-master's certificates. 41 undergraduate majors. Total enrollment: 3,425. Undergraduates: 3,026. Freshmen: 721. Federal methodology is used as a basis for awarding need-based institutional aid.
UNDERGRADUATE EXPENSES for 2006–07 *Application fee:* $50. *Comprehensive fee:* $29,675 includes full-time tuition ($20,350) and room and board ($9325).
FRESHMAN FINANCIAL AID (Fall 2005, est.) 581 applied for aid; of those 75% were deemed to have need. 97% of freshmen with need received aid; of those 13% had need fully met. *Average percent of need met:* 62% (excluding resources awarded to replace EFC). *Average financial aid package:* $12,941 (excluding resources awarded to replace EFC). 17% of all full-time freshmen had no need and received non-need-based gift aid.
UNDERGRADUATE FINANCIAL AID (Fall 2005, est.) 2,261 applied for aid; of those 81% were deemed to have need. 97% of undergraduates with need received aid; of those 15% had need fully met. *Average percent of need met:* 64% (excluding resources awarded to replace EFC). *Average financial aid package:* $13,606 (excluding resources awarded to replace EFC). 16% of all full-time undergraduates had no need and received non-need-based gift aid.
GIFT AID (NEED-BASED) *Total amount:* $18,643,004 (11% federal, 13% state, 75% institutional, 1% external sources). *Receiving aid:* Freshmen: 60% (410); All full-time undergraduates: 59% (1,707). *Average award:* Freshmen: $11,262; Undergraduates: $10,791. *Scholarships, grants, and awards:* Federal Pell, FSEOG, state, private, college/university gift aid from institutional funds.
GIFT AID (NON-NEED-BASED) *Total amount:* $5,130,283 (3% state, 96% institutional, 1% external sources). *Receiving aid:* Freshmen: 8% (54); Undergraduates: 9% (257). *Average Award:* Freshmen: $8340; Undergraduates: $7052. *Scholarships, grants, and awards by category: Academic Interests/Achievement:* 600 awards ($1,600,000 total): biological sciences, business, computer science, foreign languages, general academic interests/achievements, mathematics, military science. *Creative Arts/Performance:* 30 awards ($25,000 total): music. *Special Achievements/Activities:* 300 awards ($1,200,000 total): community service, leadership. *Special Characteristics:* 90 awards ($530,848 total): children of faculty/staff. *ROTC:* Army cooperative, Air Force.
LOANS *Student loans:* $13,804,175 (38% need-based, 62% non-need-based). 79% of past graduating class borrowed through all loan programs. *Average indebtedness per student:* $15,715. *Average need-based loan:* Freshmen: $2634; Undergraduates: $3984. *Parent loans:* $5,939,671 (73% need-based, 27% non-need-based). *Programs:* Federal Direct (Subsidized and Unsubsidized Stafford, PLUS), FFEL (Subsidized and Unsubsidized Stafford, PLUS), Perkins.
WORK-STUDY *Federal work-study:* Total amount: $449,107; 504 jobs averaging $891. *State or other work-study/employment:* Total amount: $300,000 (100% non-need-based). 211 part-time jobs averaging $1421.
ATHLETIC AWARDS *Total amount:* $2,573,365 (44% need-based, 56% non-need-based).
APPLYING FOR FINANCIAL AID *Required financial aid forms:* FAFSA, institution's own form, state aid form. *Financial aid deadline (priority):* 3/1. *Notification date:* 4/1. Students must reply by 5/1.
CONTACT Mr. Edward Keough, Director of Student Financial Services, Manhattan College, 4513 Manhattan College Parkway, Riverdale, NY 10471, 718-862-7100 or toll-free 800-622-9235 (in-state). *Fax:* 718-862-8027. *E-mail:* finaid@manhattan.edu.

MANHATTAN SCHOOL OF MUSIC
New York, NY

Tuition & fees: $29,960	Average undergraduate aid package: $12,080

ABOUT THE INSTITUTION Independent, coed. Awards: bachelor's, master's, and doctoral degrees and post-bachelor's and post-master's certificates. 6 undergraduate majors. Total enrollment: 891. Undergraduates: 416. Freshmen: 98. Both federal and institutional methodology are used as a basis for awarding need-based institutional aid.
UNDERGRADUATE EXPENSES for 2006–07 *Application fee:* $100. *Comprehensive fee:* $42,760 includes full-time tuition ($27,400), mandatory fees ($2560), and room and board ($12,800). *College room only:* $8400. *Part-time tuition:* $1200 per credit.
FRESHMAN FINANCIAL AID (Fall 2004) 76 applied for aid; of those 100% were deemed to have need. 100% of freshmen with need received aid; of those 7% had need fully met. *Average percent of need met:* 39% (excluding resources

Manhattan School of Music

awarded to replace EFC). *Average financial aid package:* $15,312 (excluding resources awarded to replace EFC). 15% of all full-time freshmen had no need and received non-need-based gift aid.
UNDERGRADUATE FINANCIAL AID (Fall 2004) 291 applied for aid; of those 100% were deemed to have need. 100% of undergraduates with need received aid; of those 4% had need fully met. *Average percent of need met:* 32% (excluding resources awarded to replace EFC). *Average financial aid package:* $12,080 (excluding resources awarded to replace EFC). 5% of all full-time undergraduates had no need and received non-need-based gift aid.
GIFT AID (NEED-BASED) *Total amount:* $2,403,447 (18% federal, 5% state, 71% institutional, 6% external sources). *Receiving aid:* Freshmen: 47% (49); All full-time undergraduates: 54% (226). *Average award:* Freshmen: $13,286; Undergraduates: $10,576. *Scholarships, grants, and awards:* Federal Pell, FSEOG, state, private, college/university gift aid from institutional funds.
GIFT AID (NON-NEED-BASED) *Total amount:* $131,500 (100% institutional). *Receiving aid:* Freshmen: 4% (4); Undergraduates: 6% (25). *Average Award:* Freshmen: $8917; Undergraduates: $8583. *Scholarships, grants, and awards by category:* Creative Arts/Performance: 43 awards ($131,500 total): music.
LOANS *Student loans:* $1,973,049 (96% need-based, 4% non-need-based). 45% of past graduating class borrowed through all loan programs. *Average indebtedness per student:* $17,658. *Average need-based loan:* Freshmen: $3508; Undergraduates: $4080. *Parent loans:* $2,654,492 (91% need-based, 9% non-need-based). *Programs:* FFEL (Subsidized and Unsubsidized Stafford, PLUS), Perkins.
WORK-STUDY *Federal work-study:* Total amount: $106,835; 82 jobs averaging $1303.
APPLYING FOR FINANCIAL AID *Required financial aid forms:* FAFSA, institution's own form, CSS Financial Aid PROFILE, verification worksheet. *Financial aid deadline (priority):* 3/1. *Notification date:* 4/1. Students must reply by 5/1 or within 2 weeks of notification.
CONTACT Ms. Amy Anderson, Assistant Dean of Admission and Financial Aid, Manhattan School of Music, 120 Claremont Avenue, New York, NY 10027-4698, 212-749-2802 Ext. 4501. *Fax:* 212-749-3025. *E-mail:* aanderson@msmnyc.edu.

MANHATTANVILLE COLLEGE
Purchase, NY

ABOUT THE INSTITUTION Independent, coed. Awards: bachelor's and master's degrees. 42 undergraduate majors. Total enrollment: 2,806. Undergraduates: 1,781. Freshmen: 504.
GIFT AID (NEED-BASED) *Scholarships, grants, and awards:* Federal Pell, FSEOG, state, private, college/university gift aid from institutional funds.
GIFT AID (NON-NEED-BASED) *Scholarships, grants, and awards by category:* Academic Interests/Achievement: general academic interests/achievements. Creative Arts/Performance: art/fine arts. Special Achievements/Activities: community service.
LOANS *Programs:* FFEL (Subsidized and Unsubsidized Stafford, PLUS), Perkins.
APPLYING FOR FINANCIAL AID *Required financial aid forms:* FAFSA, state aid form.
CONTACT Maria A. Barlaam, Director of Financial Aid, Manhattanville College, 2900 Purchase Street, Purchase, NY 10577-2132, 914-323-5357 or toll-free 800-328-4553. *Fax:* 914-323-5382. *E-mail:* barlaamm@mville.edu.

MANNES COLLEGE THE NEW SCHOOL FOR MUSIC
New York, NY

Tuition & fees: $26,130   **Average undergraduate aid package:** $12,162

ABOUT THE INSTITUTION Independent, coed. Awards: bachelor's and master's degrees and post-bachelor's certificates. 7 undergraduate majors. Total enrollment: 366. Undergraduates: 208. Freshmen: 38. Federal methodology is used as a basis for awarding need-based institutional aid.
UNDERGRADUATE EXPENSES for 2005–06 *Application fee:* $100. *Comprehensive fee:* $37,880 includes full-time tuition ($25,560), mandatory fees ($570), and room and board ($11,750). *College room only:* $8750. Full-time tuition and fees vary according to degree level and program. Room and board charges vary according to board plan. *Part-time tuition:* $842 per credit.
FRESHMAN FINANCIAL AID (Fall 2005, est.) 21 applied for aid; of those 38% were deemed to have need. 100% of freshmen with need received aid; of those 25% had need fully met. *Average percent of need met:* 57% (excluding resources awarded to replace EFC). *Average financial aid package:* $11,396 (excluding resources awarded to replace EFC). 29% of all full-time freshmen had no need and received non-need-based gift aid.
UNDERGRADUATE FINANCIAL AID (Fall 2005, est.) 116 applied for aid; of those 43% were deemed to have need. 92% of undergraduates with need received aid; of those 35% had need fully met. *Average percent of need met:* 34% (excluding resources awarded to replace EFC). *Average financial aid package:* $12,162 (excluding resources awarded to replace EFC). 30% of all full-time undergraduates had no need and received non-need-based gift aid.
GIFT AID (NEED-BASED) *Total amount:* $211,906 (34% federal, 19% state, 47% institutional). *Average award:* Freshmen: $3116; Undergraduates: $4335. *Scholarships, grants, and awards:* Federal Pell, FSEOG, private, college/university gift aid from institutional funds.
GIFT AID (NON-NEED-BASED) *Total amount:* $1,066,122 (100% institutional). *Receiving aid:* Freshmen: 29% (7); Undergraduates: 30% (39). *Average Award:* Freshmen: $11,993; Undergraduates: $9876. *Scholarships, grants, and awards by category:* Academic Interests/Achievement: general academic interests/achievements. Creative Arts/Performance: music. Special Achievements/Activities: general special achievements/activities.
LOANS *Student loans:* $539,523 (37% need-based, 63% non-need-based). 60% of past graduating class borrowed through all loan programs. *Average indebtedness per student:* $18,025. *Average need-based loan:* Freshmen: $2625; Undergraduates: $3884. *Parent loans:* $260,547 (100% non-need-based). *Programs:* FFEL (Subsidized and Unsubsidized Stafford, PLUS), Perkins.
WORK-STUDY *Federal work-study:* Total amount: $23,500; jobs available.
APPLYING FOR FINANCIAL AID *Required financial aid forms:* FAFSA, state aid form. *Financial aid deadline (priority):* 3/1. *Notification date:* 3/1. Students must reply within 4 weeks of notification.
CONTACT Financial Aid Counselor, Mannes College The New School for Music, 150 West 85th Street, New York, NY 10024-4402, 212-580-0210 or toll-free 800-292-3040. *Fax:* 212-580-1738.

MANSFIELD UNIVERSITY OF PENNSYLVANIA
Mansfield, PA

Tuition & fees (PA res): $6408   **Average undergraduate aid package:** $10,934

ABOUT THE INSTITUTION State-supported, coed. Awards: associate, bachelor's, and master's degrees. 82 undergraduate majors. Total enrollment: 3,390. Undergraduates: 2,986. Freshmen: 680. Federal methodology is used as a basis for awarding need-based institutional aid.
UNDERGRADUATE EXPENSES for 2005–06 *Application fee:* $25. *Tuition, state resident:* full-time $4906; part-time $204 per credit. *Tuition, nonresident:* full-time $12,266; part-time $511 per credit. *Required fees:* full-time $1502; $78 per credit. Part-time tuition and fees vary according to course load. *College room and board:* $5868. Room and board charges vary according to board plan. *Payment plans:* Installment, deferred payment.
FRESHMAN FINANCIAL AID (Fall 2004) 656 applied for aid; of those 80% were deemed to have need. 100% of freshmen with need received aid; of those 43% had need fully met. *Average percent of need met:* 52% (excluding resources awarded to replace EFC). *Average financial aid package:* $10,082 (excluding resources awarded to replace EFC). 5% of all full-time freshmen had no need and received non-need-based gift aid.
UNDERGRADUATE FINANCIAL AID (Fall 2004) 2,649 applied for aid; of those 82% were deemed to have need. 100% of undergraduates with need received aid; of those 44% had need fully met. *Average percent of need met:* 56% (excluding resources awarded to replace EFC). *Average financial aid package:* $10,934 (excluding resources awarded to replace EFC). 3% of all full-time undergraduates had no need and received non-need-based gift aid.
GIFT AID (NEED-BASED) *Total amount:* $9,475,480 (38% federal, 61% state, 1% external sources). *Receiving aid:* Freshmen: 55% (388); All full-time undergraduates: 55% (1,618). *Average award:* Freshmen: $4051; Undergraduates: $3924. *Scholarships, grants, and awards:* Federal Pell, FSEOG, state, private, college/university gift aid from institutional funds, United Negro College Fund, Federal Nursing.

GIFT AID (NON-NEED-BASED) *Total amount:* $1,454,812 (13% state, 45% institutional, 42% external sources). *Receiving aid:* Freshmen: 16% (113); Undergraduates: 12% (343). *Average Award: Freshmen:* $1534; *Undergraduates:* $1830. *Scholarships, grants, and awards by category:* Academic Interests/Achievement: biological sciences, communication, education, general academic interests/achievements, health fields, mathematics, physical sciences. *Creative Arts/Performance:* art/fine arts, journalism/publications, music. *Special Characteristics:* local/state students, members of minority groups. *Tuition waivers:* Full or partial for employees or children of employees, senior citizens.
LOANS *Student loans:* $17,377,086 (48% need-based, 52% non-need-based). 77% of past graduating class borrowed through all loan programs. *Average indebtedness per student:* $22,821. *Average need-based loan: Freshmen:* $2600; Undergraduates: $3636. *Parent loans:* $1,280,869 (100% non-need-based). *Programs:* FFEL (Subsidized and Unsubsidized Stafford, PLUS), Perkins, Federal Nursing, state, alternative loans.
WORK-STUDY *Federal work-study:* Total amount: $411,937; jobs available. *State or other work-study/employment:* Total amount: $560,885 (100% non-need-based). Part-time jobs available.
ATHLETIC AWARDS *Total amount:* $387,384 (100% non-need-based).
APPLYING FOR FINANCIAL AID *Required financial aid forms:* FAFSA, institution's own form. *Financial aid deadline (priority):* 3/15. *Notification date:* Continuous beginning 3/15. Students must reply within 2 weeks of notification.
CONTACT Ms. Darcie Stephens, Director of Financial Aid, Mansfield University of Pennsylvania, 109 South Hall, Mansfield, PA 16933, 570-662-4854 or toll-free 800-577-6826. *Fax:* 570-662-4136.

MAPLE SPRINGS BAPTIST BIBLE COLLEGE AND SEMINARY
Capitol Heights, MD

CONTACT Ms. Fannie G. Thompson, Director of Business Affairs, Maple Springs Baptist Bible College and Seminary, 4130 Belt Road, Capitol Heights, MD 20743, 301-736-3631. *Fax:* 301-735-6507.

MARANATHA BAPTIST BIBLE COLLEGE
Watertown, WI

Tuition & fees: $8510	Average undergraduate aid package: $6574

ABOUT THE INSTITUTION Independent Baptist, coed. Awards: associate, bachelor's, and master's degrees. 19 undergraduate majors. Total enrollment: 904. Undergraduates: 850. Freshmen: 246. Federal methodology is used as a basis for awarding need-based institutional aid.
UNDERGRADUATE EXPENSES for 2005–06 *Application fee:* $40. *Comprehensive fee:* $13,510 includes full-time tuition ($7680), mandatory fees ($830), and room and board ($5000). Full-time tuition and fees vary according to course level. *Part-time tuition:* $240 per semester hour. Part-time tuition and fees vary according to course level.
FRESHMAN FINANCIAL AID (Fall 2004) 184 applied for aid; of those 91% were deemed to have need. 100% of freshmen with need received aid; of those 1% had need fully met. *Average percent of need met:* 55% (excluding resources awarded to replace EFC). *Average financial aid package:* $6161 (excluding resources awarded to replace EFC). 4% of all full-time freshmen had no need and received non-need-based gift aid.
UNDERGRADUATE FINANCIAL AID (Fall 2004) 685 applied for aid; of those 93% were deemed to have need. 100% of undergraduates with need received aid; of those 1% had need fully met. *Average percent of need met:* 58% (excluding resources awarded to replace EFC). *Average financial aid package:* $6574 (excluding resources awarded to replace EFC). 2% of all full-time undergraduates had no need and received non-need-based gift aid.
GIFT AID (NEED-BASED) *Total amount:* $1,408,213 (67% federal, 14% state, 12% institutional, 7% external sources). *Receiving aid:* Freshmen: 48% (94); All full-time undergraduates: 46% (358). *Average award: Freshmen:* $2724; Undergraduates: $2609. *Scholarships, grants, and awards:* Federal Pell, FSEOG, state, private, college/university gift aid from institutional funds.
GIFT AID (NON-NEED-BASED) *Total amount:* $96,344 (14% state, 42% institutional, 44% external sources). *Receiving aid:* Freshmen: 3% (5); Undergraduates: 2% (18). *Average Award: Freshmen:* $482; Undergraduates: $715. *Scholarships, grants, and awards by category:* Academic Interests/Achievement: 64 awards ($46,325 total): business, general academic interests/achievements, religion/biblical studies. *Special Characteristics:* 193 awards ($395,065 total): children and siblings of alumni, children of educators, children of faculty/staff, relatives of clergy, spouses of current students. *Tuition waivers:* Full or partial for employees or children of employees. *ROTC:* Air Force.
LOANS *Student loans:* $1,960,692 (94% need-based, 6% non-need-based). 47% of past graduating class borrowed through all loan programs. *Average indebtedness per student:* $14,431. *Average need-based loan: Freshmen:* $2401; Undergraduates: $3443. *Parent loans:* $441,847 (85% need-based, 15% non-need-based). *Programs:* FFEL (Subsidized and Unsubsidized Stafford, PLUS), state, alternative loans.
WORK-STUDY *State or other work-study/employment:* Total amount: $1,656,007 (100% need-based). 323 part-time jobs averaging $3112.
APPLYING FOR FINANCIAL AID *Required financial aid form:* FAFSA. *Financial aid deadline (priority):* 3/1. *Notification date:* Continuous. Students must reply within 2 weeks of notification.
CONTACT Mr. Bruce Roth, Associate Director of Financial Aid, Maranatha Baptist Bible College, 745 West Main Street, Watertown, WI 53094, 920-206-2318 or toll-free 800-622-2947. *Fax:* 920-261-9109. *E-mail:* financialaid@mbbc.edu.

MARIAN COLLEGE
Indianapolis, IN

Tuition & fees: $19,060	Average undergraduate aid package: $15,345

ABOUT THE INSTITUTION Independent Roman Catholic, coed. Awards: associate, bachelor's, and master's degrees. 36 undergraduate majors. Total enrollment: 1,685. Undergraduates: 1,666. Freshmen: 269. Federal methodology is used as a basis for awarding need-based institutional aid.
UNDERGRADUATE EXPENSES for 2005–06 *Application fee:* $20. *Comprehensive fee:* $25,360 includes full-time tuition ($18,400), mandatory fees ($660), and room and board ($6300). Full-time tuition and fees vary according to class time and course load. Room and board charges vary according to board plan and housing facility. *Part-time tuition:* $780 per credit hour. Part-time tuition and fees vary according to class time and course load. *Payment plans:* Installment, deferred payment.
FRESHMAN FINANCIAL AID (Fall 2005, est.) 175 applied for aid; of those 89% were deemed to have need. 100% of freshmen with need received aid; of those 51% had need fully met. *Average percent of need met:* 95% (excluding resources awarded to replace EFC). *Average financial aid package:* $17,749 (excluding resources awarded to replace EFC). 16% of all full-time freshmen had no need and received non-need-based gift aid.
UNDERGRADUATE FINANCIAL AID (Fall 2005, est.) 959 applied for aid; of those 90% were deemed to have need. 100% of undergraduates with need received aid; of those 33% had need fully met. *Average percent of need met:* 72% (excluding resources awarded to replace EFC). *Average financial aid package:* $15,345 (excluding resources awarded to replace EFC). 12% of all full-time undergraduates had no need and received non-need-based gift aid.
GIFT AID (NEED-BASED) *Total amount:* $8,468,838 (20% federal, 36% state, 44% institutional). *Receiving aid:* Freshmen: 52% (95); All full-time undergraduates: 49% (534). *Average award: Freshmen:* $5396; Undergraduates: $5044. *Scholarships, grants, and awards:* Federal Pell, FSEOG, state, private, college/university gift aid from institutional funds.
GIFT AID (NON-NEED-BASED) *Total amount:* $2,706,040 (81% institutional, 19% external sources). *Receiving aid:* Freshmen: 84% (154); Undergraduates: 42% (457). *Average Award: Freshmen:* $8994; Undergraduates: $6901. *Scholarships, grants, and awards by category:* Academic Interests/Achievement: 316 awards ($1,659,000 total): area/ethnic studies, general academic interests/achievements, religion/biblical studies. *Creative Arts/Performance:* 22 awards ($80,000 total): applied art and design, art/fine arts, music, performing arts, theater/drama. *Special Achievements/Activities:* 150 awards ($275,000 total): community service, religious involvement. *Special Characteristics:* 270 awards ($760,000 total): adult students, children and siblings of alumni, children of faculty/staff, international students, members of minority groups, religious affiliation, siblings of current students, spouses of current students. *Tuition waivers:* Full or partial for children of alumni, employees or children of employees, senior citizens. *ROTC:* Army cooperative.
LOANS *Student loans:* $8,913,482 (57% need-based, 43% non-need-based). 80% of past graduating class borrowed through all loan programs. *Average indebtedness per student:* $14,815. *Average need-based loan: Freshmen:* $2433;

Marian College

Undergraduates: $3302. **Parent loans:** $1,616,935 (100% non-need-based). **Programs:** FFEL (Subsidized and Unsubsidized Stafford, PLUS), Perkins, college/university.

WORK-STUDY *Federal work-study:* Total amount: $213,826; 200 jobs averaging $1500. *State or other work-study/employment:* Total amount: $69,960 (100% non-need-based). Part-time jobs available.

ATHLETIC AWARDS Total amount: $10,601,709 (89% need-based, 11% non-need-based).

APPLYING FOR FINANCIAL AID *Required financial aid forms:* FAFSA, institution's own form. *Financial aid deadline (priority):* 3/1. *Notification date:* Continuous beginning 3/15. Students must reply within 4 weeks of notification.

CONTACT Mr. John E. Shelton, Dean of Financial Aid, Marian College, 3200 Cold Spring Road, Indianapolis, IN 46222-1997, 317-955-6040 or toll-free 800-772-7264 (in-state). *Fax:* 317-955-6424. *E-mail:* jshelton@marian.edu.

MARIAN COLLEGE OF FOND DU LAC
Fond du Lac, WI

| Tuition & fees: $16,705 | Average undergraduate aid package: $16,359 |

ABOUT THE INSTITUTION Independent Roman Catholic, coed. Awards: bachelor's, master's, and doctoral degrees. 50 undergraduate majors. Total enrollment: 2,975. Undergraduates: 2,077. Freshmen: 261. Federal methodology is used as a basis for awarding need-based institutional aid.

UNDERGRADUATE EXPENSES for 2005–06 *Application fee:* $20. *Comprehensive fee:* $21,775 includes full-time tuition ($16,380), mandatory fees ($325), and room and board ($5070). *College room only:* $3350. Full-time tuition and fees vary according to class time and program. Room and board charges vary according to board plan and housing facility. *Part-time tuition:* $280 per credit. *Part-time fees:* $80 per term. Part-time tuition and fees vary according to class time, course load, and program. *Payment plan:* Installment.

FRESHMAN FINANCIAL AID (Fall 2005, est.) 261 applied for aid; of those 85% were deemed to have need. 100% of freshmen with need received aid; of those 43% had need fully met. *Average percent of need met:* 90% (excluding resources awarded to replace EFC). *Average financial aid package:* $15,399 (excluding resources awarded to replace EFC). 14% of all full-time freshmen had no need and received non-need-based gift aid.

UNDERGRADUATE FINANCIAL AID (Fall 2005, est.) 1,269 applied for aid; of those 84% were deemed to have need. 100% of undergraduates with need received aid; of those 40% had need fully met. *Average percent of need met:* 92% (excluding resources awarded to replace EFC). *Average financial aid package:* $16,359 (excluding resources awarded to replace EFC). 14% of all full-time undergraduates had no need and received non-need-based gift aid.

GIFT AID (NEED-BASED) *Total amount:* $9,288,855 (16% federal, 21% state, 61% institutional, 2% external sources). *Receiving aid:* Freshmen: 84% (220); All full-time undergraduates: 75% (999). *Average award:* Freshmen: $9521; Undergraduates: $8986. *Scholarships, grants, and awards:* Federal Pell, FSEOG, state, private, college/university gift aid from institutional funds, endowed scholarships.

GIFT AID (NON-NEED-BASED) *Total amount:* $1,099,168 (7% state, 89% institutional, 4% external sources). *Receiving aid:* Freshmen: 78% (204); Undergraduates: 65% (876). *Average Award:* Freshmen: $4964; Undergraduates: $4484. *Scholarships, grants, and awards by category:* Academic Interests/Achievement: 1,184 awards ($5,020,765 total): general academic interests/achievements. *Creative Arts/Performance:* 39 awards ($56,800 total): music. *Special Characteristics:* 78 awards ($273,171 total): children of faculty/staff, children with a deceased or disabled parent, siblings of current students. *Tuition waivers:* Full or partial for employees or children of employees, senior citizens. *ROTC:* Army.

LOANS *Student loans:* $10,381,847 (69% need-based, 31% non-need-based). 90% of past graduating class borrowed through all loan programs. *Average indebtedness per student:* $20,000. *Average need-based loan:* Freshmen: $3488; Undergraduates: $5309. *Parent loans:* $1,168,562 (68% need-based, 32% non-need-based). *Programs:* FFEL (Subsidized and Unsubsidized Stafford, PLUS), Perkins, Federal Nursing.

WORK-STUDY *Federal work-study:* Total amount: $1,062,241; 568 jobs averaging $1870. *State or other work-study/employment:* Total amount: $286,412 (100% non-need-based). 335 part-time jobs averaging $1000.

APPLYING FOR FINANCIAL AID *Required financial aid forms:* FAFSA, institution's own form. *Financial aid deadline (priority):* 3/1. *Notification date:* Continuous. Students must reply within 4 weeks of notification.

CONTACT Ms. Debra E. McKinney, Director of Financial Aid, Marian College of Fond du Lac, 45 South National Avenue, Fond du Lac, WI 54935-4699, 920-923-7614 or toll-free 800-2-MARIAN Ext. 7652 (in-state). *Fax:* 920-923-8767. *E-mail:* dmckinney@mariancollege.edu.

MARIETTA COLLEGE
Marietta, OH

ABOUT THE INSTITUTION Independent, coed. Awards: associate, bachelor's, and master's degrees. 40 undergraduate majors. Total enrollment: 1,461. Undergraduates: 1,344. Freshmen: 387.

GIFT AID (NEED-BASED) *Scholarships, grants, and awards:* Federal Pell, FSEOG, state, private, college/university gift aid from institutional funds.

GIFT AID (NON-NEED-BASED) *Scholarships, grants, and awards by category:* Academic Interests/Achievement: general academic interests/achievements. Creative Arts/Performance: art/fine arts. Special Achievements/Activities: general special achievements/activities. Special Characteristics: children and siblings of alumni, members of minority groups, siblings of current students.

LOANS *Programs:* Federal Direct (Subsidized and Unsubsidized Stafford, PLUS).

APPLYING FOR FINANCIAL AID *Required financial aid form:* FAFSA.

CONTACT Mr. Gary Craig, Dean of Enrollment, Marietta College, 215 Fifth Street, Marietta, OH 45750-4000, 740-376-4712 or toll-free 800-331-7896. *Fax:* 740-376-4990. *E-mail:* finaid@marietta.edu.

MARIST COLLEGE
Poughkeepsie, NY

| Tuition & fees: $21,202 | Average undergraduate aid package: $13,439 |

ABOUT THE INSTITUTION Independent, coed. Awards: bachelor's and master's degrees. 50 undergraduate majors. Total enrollment: 5,744. Undergraduates: 4,896. Freshmen: 1,017. Federal methodology is used as a basis for awarding need-based institutional aid.

UNDERGRADUATE EXPENSES for 2006–07 *Application fee:* $40. *Comprehensive fee:* $30,566 includes full-time tuition ($20,712), mandatory fees ($490), and room and board ($9364). *College room only:* $5964. *Part-time tuition:* $475 per credit. *Part-time fees:* $65 per term.

FRESHMAN FINANCIAL AID (Fall 2005, est.) 858 applied for aid; of those 73% were deemed to have need. 100% of freshmen with need received aid; of those 24% had need fully met. *Average percent of need met:* 78% (excluding resources awarded to replace EFC). *Average financial aid package:* $14,765 (excluding resources awarded to replace EFC). 27% of all full-time freshmen had no need and received non-need-based gift aid.

UNDERGRADUATE FINANCIAL AID (Fall 2005, est.) 3,449 applied for aid; of those 79% were deemed to have need. 100% of undergraduates with need received aid; of those 18% had need fully met. *Average percent of need met:* 68% (excluding resources awarded to replace EFC). *Average financial aid package:* $13,439 (excluding resources awarded to replace EFC). 18% of all full-time undergraduates had no need and received non-need-based gift aid.

GIFT AID (NEED-BASED) *Total amount:* $15,529,537 (14% federal, 19% state, 63% institutional, 4% external sources). *Receiving aid:* Freshmen: 61% (621); All full-time undergraduates: 58% (2,581). *Average award:* Freshmen: $10,971; Undergraduates: $9099. *Scholarships, grants, and awards:* Federal Pell, FSEOG, state, private, college/university gift aid from institutional funds.

GIFT AID (NON-NEED-BASED) *Total amount:* $12,670,318 (97% institutional, 3% external sources). *Receiving aid:* Freshmen: 40% (408); Undergraduates: 30% (1,335). *Average Award:* Freshmen: $6314; Undergraduates: $5837. *Scholarships, grants, and awards by category:* Academic Interests/Achievement: general academic interests/achievements. Creative Arts/Performance: debating, music. Special Achievements/Activities: general special achievements/activities. *ROTC:* Army.

LOANS *Student loans:* $24,560,381 (43% need-based, 57% non-need-based). 54% of past graduating class borrowed through all loan programs. *Average indebtedness per student:* $20,419. *Average need-based loan:* Freshmen: $3565; Undergraduates: $4741. *Parent loans:* $8,772,770 (100% non-need-based).

Programs: FFEL (Subsidized and Unsubsidized Stafford, PLUS), Perkins, alternative loans, Key Alternative Loans, CitiAssist Loans, TERI Loans, Signature Loans, EXCEL Loans.

WORK-STUDY *Federal work-study:* Total amount: $1,850,227; 611 jobs averaging $1226. *State or other work-study/employment:* Total amount: $669,395 (100% non-need-based). 502 part-time jobs averaging $1055.

ATHLETIC AWARDS Total amount: $2,408,634 (100% non-need-based).

APPLYING FOR FINANCIAL AID *Required financial aid forms:* FAFSA, institution's own form. *Financial aid deadline:* 5/1 (priority: 2/15). *Notification date:* Continuous beginning 3/15. Students must reply by 5/1 or within 2 weeks of notification.

CONTACT Joseph R. Weglarz, Director of Financial Aid, Marist College, 3399 North Road, Poughkeepsie, NY 12601, 845-575-3230 or toll-free 800-436-5483. *Fax:* 845-575-3099. *E-mail:* joseph.weglarz@marist.edu.

MARLBORO COLLEGE
Marlboro, VT

Tuition & fees: $27,790 | **Average undergraduate aid package: N/A**

ABOUT THE INSTITUTION Independent, coed. Awards: bachelor's, master's, and first professional degrees. 77 undergraduate majors. Total enrollment: 387. Undergraduates: 340. Freshmen: 79. Federal methodology is used as a basis for awarding need-based institutional aid.

UNDERGRADUATE EXPENSES for 2005–06 *Application fee:* $50. *Comprehensive fee:* $35,980 includes full-time tuition ($26,940), mandatory fees ($850), and room and board ($8190). *College room only:* $4540. *Part-time tuition:* $890 per credit. *Payment plan:* Installment.

FRESHMAN FINANCIAL AID (Fall 2005, est.) 63 applied for aid; of those 79% were deemed to have need. 100% of freshmen with need received aid. *Average percent of need met:* 80% (excluding resources awarded to replace EFC). 6% of all full-time freshmen had no need and received non-need-based gift aid.

UNDERGRADUATE FINANCIAL AID (Fall 2005, est.) 263 applied for aid; of those 93% were deemed to have need. 100% of undergraduates with need received aid. *Average percent of need met:* 80% (excluding resources awarded to replace EFC). 8% of all full-time undergraduates had no need and received non-need-based gift aid.

GIFT AID (NEED-BASED) *Total amount:* $3,957,951 (9% federal, 2% state, 84% institutional, 5% external sources). *Receiving aid:* Freshmen: 63% (50); All full-time undergraduates: 68% (223). *Average award:* Freshmen: $10,000; Undergraduates: $7621. *Scholarships, grants, and awards:* Federal Pell, FSEOG, state, private, college/university gift aid from institutional funds.

GIFT AID (NON-NEED-BASED) *Total amount:* $3,816,964 (3% state, 83% institutional, 14% external sources). *Receiving aid:* Freshmen: 22% (17); Undergraduates: 14% (45). *Average Award:* Freshmen: $10,000; *Undergraduates:* $7621. *Scholarships, grants, and awards by category:* Academic Interests/Achievement: 62 awards ($580,000 total): general academic interests/achievements. *Special Achievements/Activities:* 5 awards ($50,000 total): community service. *Tuition waivers:* Full or partial for employees or children of employees, senior citizens.

LOANS *Student loans:* $2,592,568 (59% need-based, 41% non-need-based). 80% of past graduating class borrowed through all loan programs. *Average indebtedness per student:* $18,404. *Average need-based loan:* Freshmen: $2465; Undergraduates: $3728. *Parent loans:* $2,881,347 (44% need-based, 56% non-need-based). *Programs:* FFEL (Subsidized and Unsubsidized Stafford, PLUS), state.

WORK-STUDY *Federal work-study:* Total amount: $329,924; 244 jobs averaging $2050. *State or other work-study/employment:* Total amount: $60,150 (100% non-need-based). 2 part-time jobs averaging $2000.

APPLYING FOR FINANCIAL AID *Required financial aid form:* FAFSA. *Financial aid deadline:* 3/1. *Notification date:* 4/1. Students must reply by 5/1 or within 2 weeks of notification.

CONTACT Alan E. Young, Dean of Enrollment Management, Marlboro College, South Road, PO Box A, Marlboro, VT 05344-0300, 802-258-9261 or toll-free 800-343-0049. *Fax:* 802-258-9300. *E-mail:* finaid@marlboro.edu.

MARQUETTE UNIVERSITY
Milwaukee, WI

Tuition & fees: $25,074 | **Average undergraduate aid package: $16,770**

ABOUT THE INSTITUTION Independent Roman Catholic (Jesuit), coed. Awards: associate, bachelor's, master's, doctoral, and first professional degrees and post-master's certificates. 85 undergraduate majors. Total enrollment: 11,594. Undergraduates: 8,010. Freshmen: 1,784. Federal methodology is used as a basis for awarding need-based institutional aid.

UNDERGRADUATE EXPENSES for 2006–07 *Application fee:* $30. *Comprehensive fee:* $33,234 includes full-time tuition ($24,670), mandatory fees ($404), and room and board ($8160). *College room only:* $5304. *Part-time tuition:* $725 per credit. *Part-time fees:* $465 per credit.

FRESHMAN FINANCIAL AID (Fall 2005, est.) 1421 applied for aid; of those 77% were deemed to have need. 100% of freshmen with need received aid; of those 34% had need fully met. *Average percent of need met:* 78% (excluding resources awarded to replace EFC). *Average financial aid package:* $17,835 (excluding resources awarded to replace EFC). 11% of all full-time freshmen had no need and received non-need-based gift aid.

UNDERGRADUATE FINANCIAL AID (Fall 2005, est.) 5,468 applied for aid; of those 84% were deemed to have need. 96% of undergraduates with need received aid; of those 32% had need fully met. *Average percent of need met:* 74% (excluding resources awarded to replace EFC). *Average financial aid package:* $16,770 (excluding resources awarded to replace EFC). 7% of all full-time undergraduates had no need and received non-need-based gift aid.

GIFT AID (NEED-BASED) *Total amount:* $45,001,929 (10% federal, 8% state, 77% institutional, 5% external sources). *Receiving aid:* Freshmen: 54% (965); All full-time undergraduates: 52% (3,902). *Average award:* Freshmen: $14,044; Undergraduates: $11,445. *Scholarships, grants, and awards:* Federal Pell, FSEOG, state, private, college/university gift aid from institutional funds.

GIFT AID (NON-NEED-BASED) *Total amount:* $21,944,929 (1% federal, 75% institutional, 24% external sources). *Receiving aid:* Freshmen: 7% (131); Undergraduates: 6% (417). *Average Award:* Freshmen: $8828; *Undergraduates:* $7953. *Scholarships, grants, and awards by category:* Academic Interests/Achievement: biological sciences, business, communication, engineering/technologies, foreign languages, general academic interests/achievements, health fields, mathematics. *Special Characteristics:* 155 awards ($3,426,601 total): children of faculty/staff. *ROTC:* Army, Naval, Air Force.

LOANS *Student loans:* $33,426,567 (86% need-based, 14% non-need-based). 53% of past graduating class borrowed through all loan programs. *Average indebtedness per student:* $26,345. *Average need-based loan:* Freshmen: $3696; Undergraduates: $4991. *Parent loans:* $20,703,144 (68% need-based, 32% non-need-based). *Programs:* Federal Direct (Subsidized and Unsubsidized Stafford, PLUS), Perkins, Federal Nursing, state, college/university, alternative loans.

WORK-STUDY *Federal work-study:* Total amount: $1,823,746; 894 jobs averaging $2500. *State or other work-study/employment:* Total amount: $2,097,283 (100% non-need-based). Part-time jobs available.

ATHLETIC AWARDS Total amount: $2,628,353 (14% need-based, 86% non-need-based).

APPLYING FOR FINANCIAL AID *Required financial aid form:* FAFSA. *Financial aid deadline:* Continuous. *Notification date:* 3/21. Students must reply by 5/1 or within 3 weeks of notification.

CONTACT Daniel L. Goyette, Director of Financial Aid, Marquette University, Office of Student Financial Aid, 1212 Building, Room 415, Milwaukee, WI 53201-1881, 414-288-7390 or toll-free 800-222-6544. *Fax:* 414-288-1718. *E-mail:* financialaid@marquette.edu.

MARSHALL UNIVERSITY
Huntington, WV

Tuition & fees (WV res): $3932 | **Average undergraduate aid package: $7022**

ABOUT THE INSTITUTION State-supported, coed. Awards: associate, bachelor's, master's, doctoral, and first professional degrees and post-master's certificates. 46 undergraduate majors. Total enrollment: 13,988. Undergraduates: 9,841. Freshmen: 1,715. Federal methodology is used as a basis for awarding need-based institutional aid.

Marshall University

UNDERGRADUATE EXPENSES for 2005–06 *Application fee:* $25. *Tuition, state resident:* full-time $3932; part-time $155.75 per credit hour. *Tuition, nonresident:* full-time $10,634; part-time $423.25 per credit hour. Full-time tuition and fees vary according to degree level, location, program, and reciprocity agreements. Part-time tuition and fees vary according to course load, degree level, location, program, and reciprocity agreements. *College room and board:* $6272; *room only:* $3496. Room and board charges vary according to board plan and housing facility. *Payment plan:* Installment.
FRESHMAN FINANCIAL AID (Fall 2005, est.) 1273 applied for aid; of those 71% were deemed to have need. 98% of freshmen with need received aid; of those 35% had need fully met. *Average percent of need met:* 53% (excluding resources awarded to replace EFC). *Average financial aid package:* $7158 (excluding resources awarded to replace EFC). 22% of all full-time freshmen had no need and received non-need-based gift aid.
UNDERGRADUATE FINANCIAL AID (Fall 2005, est.) 6,383 applied for aid; of those 73% were deemed to have need. 99% of undergraduates with need received aid; of those 40% had need fully met. *Average percent of need met:* 58% (excluding resources awarded to replace EFC). *Average financial aid package:* $7022 (excluding resources awarded to replace EFC). 20% of all full-time undergraduates had no need and received non-need-based gift aid.
GIFT AID (NEED-BASED) *Total amount:* $14,964,380 (71% federal, 29% state). *Receiving aid:* Freshmen: 41% (587); All full-time undergraduates: 36% (3,068). *Average award:* Freshmen: $3940; Undergraduates: $3924. *Scholarships, grants, and awards:* Federal Pell, FSEOG, state, private, college/university gift aid from institutional funds.
GIFT AID (NON-NEED-BASED) *Total amount:* $13,262,135 (57% state, 27% institutional, 16% external sources). *Receiving aid:* Freshmen: 35% (500); Undergraduates: 20% (1,692). *Average Award:* Freshmen: $5238; Undergraduates: $5038. *Scholarships, grants, and awards by category:* Academic Interests/Achievement: 2,254 awards ($3,579,902 total): general academic interests/achievements. Creative Arts/Performance: applied art and design, art/fine arts, cinema/film/broadcasting, creative writing, dance, debating, general creative arts/performance, journalism/publications, music, performing arts, theater/drama. Special Characteristics: 38 awards ($23,887 total): children of faculty/staff. *Tuition waivers:* Full or partial for senior citizens. *ROTC:* Army.
LOANS *Student loans:* $28,643,559 (91% need-based, 9% non-need-based). 58% of past graduating class borrowed through all loan programs. *Average indebtedness per student:* $16,639. *Average need-based loan:* Freshmen: $3696; Undergraduates: $4814. *Parent loans:* $3,828,559 (100% non-need-based). *Programs:* Federal Direct (Subsidized and Unsubsidized Stafford, PLUS), Perkins, state, college/university, alternative loans through outside sources.
WORK-STUDY *Federal work-study:* Total amount: $632,497; 359 jobs averaging $1761. *State or other work-study/employment:* Total amount: $349,745 (100% non-need-based). 58 part-time jobs averaging $6030.
ATHLETIC AWARDS Total amount: $3,657,092 (100% non-need-based).
APPLYING FOR FINANCIAL AID *Required financial aid form:* FAFSA. *Financial aid deadline (priority):* 3/1. *Notification date:* 4/15. Students must reply within 2 weeks of notification.
CONTACT Ms. Nadine A. Hamrick, Associate Director of Student Financial Aid, Marshall University, One John Marshall Drive, Huntington, WV 25755, 304-696-2277 or toll-free 800-642-3499 (in-state). *Fax:* 304-696-3242. *E-mail:* hamrick@marshall.edu.

MARS HILL COLLEGE
Mars Hill, NC

ABOUT THE INSTITUTION Independent Baptist, coed. Awards: bachelor's degrees. 63 undergraduate majors. Total enrollment: 1,378. Undergraduates: 1,378. Freshmen: 348.
GIFT AID (NEED-BASED) *Scholarships, grants, and awards:* Federal Pell, FSEOG, state, private, college/university gift aid from institutional funds.
GIFT AID (NON-NEED-BASED) *Scholarships, grants, and awards by category:* Academic Interests/Achievement: general academic interests/achievements. Creative Arts/Performance: dance, music, theater/drama. Special Achievements/Activities: cheerleading/drum major. Special Characteristics: children of faculty/staff.
LOANS *Programs:* FFEL (Subsidized and Unsubsidized Stafford, PLUS), Perkins.
APPLYING FOR FINANCIAL AID *Required financial aid forms:* FAFSA, state aid form.
CONTACT Myrtle Martin, Director of Financial Aid, Mars Hill College, PO Box 370, Mars Hill, NC 28754, 828-689-1123 or toll-free 866-MHC-4-YOU. *Fax:* 828-689-1300.

MARTIN LUTHER COLLEGE
New Ulm, MN

CONTACT Mr. Gene Slettedahl, Director of Financial Aid, Martin Luther College, 1995 Luther Court, New Ulm, MN 56073, 507-354-8221 Ext. 225. *Fax:* 507-354-8225. *E-mail:* slettega@mlc-wels.edu.

MARTIN METHODIST COLLEGE
Pulaski, TN

ABOUT THE INSTITUTION Independent United Methodist, coed. Awards: bachelor's degrees. 64 undergraduate majors. Total enrollment: 714. Undergraduates: 714. Freshmen: 209.
GIFT AID (NEED-BASED) *Scholarships, grants, and awards:* Federal Pell, FSEOG, state, private, college/university gift aid from institutional funds.
GIFT AID (NON-NEED-BASED) *Scholarships, grants, and awards by category:* Academic Interests/Achievement: biological sciences, business, education, general academic interests/achievements, religion/biblical studies. Creative Arts/Performance: art/fine arts, music, theater/drama. Special Achievements/Activities: cheerleading/drum major. Special Characteristics: children of faculty/staff, local/state students, religious affiliation.
LOANS *Programs:* FFEL (Subsidized and Unsubsidized Stafford, PLUS), United Methodist Student Loans.
WORK-STUDY *Federal work-study:* Total amount: $50,499; 50 jobs averaging $1010. *State or other work-study/employment:* Total amount: $81,000 (59% need-based, 41% non-need-based). 61 part-time jobs averaging $1311.
APPLYING FOR FINANCIAL AID *Required financial aid forms:* FAFSA, institution's own form.
CONTACT Ms. Anita Beecham, Financial Aid Assistant, Martin Methodist College, 433 West Madison Street, Pulaski, TN 38478-2716, 931-363-9808 or toll-free 800-467-1273. *Fax:* 931-363-9818. *E-mail:* abeecham@martinmethodist.edu.

MARTIN UNIVERSITY
Indianapolis, IN

ABOUT THE INSTITUTION Independent, coed. Awards: bachelor's and master's degrees. 28 undergraduate majors. Total enrollment: 571. Undergraduates: 465. Freshmen: 49.
GIFT AID (NEED-BASED) *Scholarships, grants, and awards:* Federal Pell, FSEOG, state, private, college/university gift aid from institutional funds.
LOANS *Programs:* FFEL (Subsidized and Unsubsidized Stafford, PLUS), Charles E. Schell Foundation Loans.
WORK-STUDY *Federal work-study:* Total amount: $23,000; 9 jobs averaging $2445.
APPLYING FOR FINANCIAL AID *Required financial aid form:* FAFSA.
CONTACT Mason M. Moton, Director of Financial Aid, Martin University, 2171 Avondale Place, PO Box 18567, Indianapolis, IN 46218-3867, 317-543-3670. *Fax:* 317-543-4790. *E-mail:* mmoton@martin.edu.

MARY BALDWIN COLLEGE
Staunton, VA

Tuition & fees: $20,605   **Average undergraduate aid package:** $19,942

ABOUT THE INSTITUTION Independent, coed, primarily women. Awards: bachelor's and master's degrees. 30 undergraduate majors. Total enrollment: 1,740. Undergraduates: 1,535. Freshmen: 267. Federal methodology is used as a basis for awarding need-based institutional aid.
UNDERGRADUATE EXPENSES for 2005–06 *Application fee:* $35. *Comprehensive fee:* $26,465 includes full-time tuition ($20,405), mandatory fees ($200), and room and board ($5860). *College room only:* $3738. Full-time tuition and fees vary according to degree level. Room and board charges vary according to housing facility. *Part-time tuition:* $345 per credit hour. Part-time tuition and fees vary according to degree level. *Payment plan:* Installment.

FRESHMAN FINANCIAL AID (Fall 2005, est.) 213 applied for aid; of those 86% were deemed to have need. 99% of freshmen with need received aid; of those 48% had need fully met. *Average percent of need met:* 88% (excluding resources awarded to replace EFC). *Average financial aid package:* $21,886 (excluding resources awarded to replace EFC). 21% of all full-time freshmen had no need and received non-need-based gift aid.

UNDERGRADUATE FINANCIAL AID (Fall 2005, est.) 900 applied for aid; of those 87% were deemed to have need. 100% of undergraduates with need received aid; of those 45% had need fully met. *Average percent of need met:* 88% (excluding resources awarded to replace EFC). *Average financial aid package:* $19,942 (excluding resources awarded to replace EFC). 20% of all full-time undergraduates had no need and received non-need-based gift aid.

GIFT AID (NEED-BASED) *Total amount:* $8,522,333 (15% federal, 18% state, 63% institutional, 4% external sources). *Receiving aid:* Freshmen: 76% (182); All full-time undergraduates: 74% (768). *Average award:* Freshmen: $11,910; Undergraduates: $9827. *Scholarships, grants, and awards:* Federal Pell, FSEOG, state, private, college/university gift aid from institutional funds.

GIFT AID (NON-NEED-BASED) *Total amount:* $1,336,026 (15% state, 76% institutional, 9% external sources). *Receiving aid:* Freshmen: 75% (180); Undergraduates: 75% (775). *Average Award:* Freshmen: $11,322; Undergraduates: $12,260. *Scholarships, grants, and awards by category:* Academic Interests/Achievement: 755 awards ($4,147,754 total): general academic interests/achievements. Special Achievements/Activities: 31 awards ($62,000 total): leadership. Special Characteristics: 12 awards ($190,199 total): children of educators, children of faculty/staff. *Tuition waivers:* Full or partial for employees or children of employees. *ROTC:* Army, Naval cooperative, Air Force cooperative.

LOANS *Student loans:* $5,712,692 (98% need-based, 2% non-need-based). 87% of past graduating class borrowed through all loan programs. *Average indebtedness per student:* $21,000. *Average need-based loan:* Freshmen: $1840; Undergraduates: $3266. *Parent loans:* $2,727,395 (90% need-based, 10% non-need-based). *Programs:* FFEL (Subsidized and Unsubsidized Stafford, PLUS), Perkins, alternative loans.

WORK-STUDY *Federal work-study:* Total amount: $481,450; 349 jobs averaging $1379. *State or other work-study/employment:* Total amount: $117,123 (80% need-based, 20% non-need-based). 103 part-time jobs averaging $1137.

APPLYING FOR FINANCIAL AID *Required financial aid forms:* FAFSA, state aid form (for VA residents only). *Financial aid deadline:* 5/15. *Notification date:* Continuous. Students must reply within 3 weeks of notification.

CONTACT Lisa Branson, Executive Director of Admissions and Financial Aid, Mary Baldwin College, Office of Financial Aid and Student Campus Employment, Staunton, VA 24401, 540-887-7022 or toll-free 800-468-2262. *Fax:* 540-887-7229. *E-mail:* lbranson@mbc.edu.

MARYGROVE COLLEGE
Detroit, MI

CONTACT Mr. Donald Hurt, Director of Financial Aid, Marygrove College, 8425 West McNichols Road, Detroit, MI 48221-2599, 313-862-8000 Ext. 436 or toll-free 866-313-1297.

MARYLAND INSTITUTE COLLEGE OF ART
Baltimore, MD

CONTACT Ms. Diane Prengaman, Associate Vice President for Financial Aid, Maryland Institute College of Art, 1300 Mount Royal Avenue, Baltimore, MD 21217, 410-225-2285. *Fax:* 410-225-2337. *E-mail:* dprengam@mica.edu.

MARYLHURST UNIVERSITY
Marylhurst, OR

ABOUT THE INSTITUTION Independent Roman Catholic, coed. Awards: bachelor's and master's degrees and post-bachelor's certificates. 22 undergraduate majors. Total enrollment: 1,268. Undergraduates: 879. Freshmen: 10.

GIFT AID (NEED-BASED) *Scholarships, grants, and awards:* Federal Pell, FSEOG, state, private, college/university gift aid from institutional funds, United Negro College Fund.

LOANS *Programs:* FFEL (Subsidized and Unsubsidized Stafford, PLUS), Perkins.

APPLYING FOR FINANCIAL AID *Required financial aid form:* FAFSA.

CONTACT Marlena McKee-Flores, Office of Financial Aid, Marylhurst University, 17600 Pacific Highway, PO Box 261, Marylhurst, OR 97036, 503-699-6253 or toll-free 800-634-9982. *Fax:* 503-635-6585. *E-mail:* finaid@marylhurst.edu.

MARYMOUNT MANHATTAN COLLEGE
New York, NY

Tuition & fees: $19,638   **Average undergraduate aid package: $11,386**

ABOUT THE INSTITUTION Independent, coed. Awards: bachelor's degrees. 20 undergraduate majors. Total enrollment: 2,007. Undergraduates: 2,007. Freshmen: 447. Both federal and institutional methodology are used as a basis for awarding need-based institutional aid.

UNDERGRADUATE EXPENSES for 2006–07 *Application fee:* $60. *Comprehensive fee:* $31,728 includes full-time tuition ($18,748), mandatory fees ($890), and room and board ($12,090). *College room only:* $10,090. *Part-time tuition:* $590 per credit. *Part-time fees:* $393 per term.

FRESHMAN FINANCIAL AID (Fall 2005, est.) 100% of freshmen with need received aid; of those 41% had need fully met. *Average percent of need met:* 46% (excluding resources awarded to replace EFC). *Average financial aid package:* $11,573 (excluding resources awarded to replace EFC). 34% of all full-time freshmen had no need and received non-need-based gift aid.

UNDERGRADUATE FINANCIAL AID (Fall 2005, est.) 100% of undergraduates with need received aid; of those 13% had need fully met. *Average percent of need met:* 46% (excluding resources awarded to replace EFC). *Average financial aid package:* $11,386 (excluding resources awarded to replace EFC). 12% of all full-time undergraduates had no need and received non-need-based gift aid.

GIFT AID (NEED-BASED) *Total amount:* $4,365,954 (24% federal, 25% state, 51% institutional). *Receiving aid:* Freshmen: 70% (302); All full-time undergraduates: 63% (1,002). *Average award:* Freshmen: $3469; Undergraduates: $4222. *Scholarships, grants, and awards:* Federal Pell, FSEOG, state, private, college/university gift aid from institutional funds.

GIFT AID (NON-NEED-BASED) *Total amount:* $2,861,895 (92% institutional, 8% external sources). *Receiving aid:* Freshmen: 70% (302); Undergraduates: 32% (513). *Average Award:* Freshmen: $4243; Undergraduates: $4122. *Scholarships, grants, and awards by category:* Academic Interests/Achievement: biological sciences, business, communication, education, English, general academic interests/achievements, humanities, international studies, premedicine, social sciences. Creative Arts/Performance: dance, theater/drama. Special Achievements/Activities: leadership.

LOANS *Student loans:* $7,655,912 (58% need-based, 42% non-need-based). 57% of past graduating class borrowed through all loan programs. *Average indebtedness per student:* $29,706. *Average need-based loan:* Freshmen: $2594; Undergraduates: $3711. *Parent loans:* $14,279,142 (39% need-based, 61% non-need-based). *Programs:* FFEL (Subsidized and Unsubsidized Stafford, PLUS).

WORK-STUDY *Federal work-study:* Total amount: $288,812; jobs available. *State or other work-study/employment:* Part-time jobs available.

APPLYING FOR FINANCIAL AID *Required financial aid form:* FAFSA. *Financial aid deadline (priority):* 3/15. *Notification date:* Continuous. Students must reply within 4 weeks of notification.

CONTACT Maria DeInnocentiis, Director of Financial Aid, Marymount Manhattan College, 221 East 71st Street, New York, NY 10021-4597, 212-517-0480 or toll-free 800-MARYMOUNT (out-of-state). *Fax:* 212-517-0491.

MARYMOUNT UNIVERSITY
Arlington, VA

Tuition & fees: $18,114   **Average undergraduate aid package: $12,511**

ABOUT THE INSTITUTION Independent religious, coed. Awards: bachelor's, master's, and doctoral degrees and post-bachelor's and post-master's certificates (Associate). 37 undergraduate majors. Total enrollment: 3,684. Undergraduates: 2,327. Freshmen: 426. Both federal and institutional methodology are used as a basis for awarding need-based institutional aid.

UNDERGRADUATE EXPENSES for 2005–06 *Application fee:* $35. *Comprehensive fee:* $25,934 includes full-time tuition ($17,970), mandatory fees ($144), and room and board ($7820). *Part-time tuition:* $582 per credit hour. *Part-time fees:* $6 per credit hour. *Payment plan:* Installment.

FRESHMAN FINANCIAL AID (Fall 2005, est.) 325 applied for aid; of those 76% were deemed to have need. 98% of freshmen with need received aid; of those

Marymount University

22% had need fully met. *Average percent of need met:* 78% (excluding resources awarded to replace EFC). *Average financial aid package:* $13,777 (excluding resources awarded to replace EFC). 23% of all full-time freshmen had no need and received non-need-based gift aid.
UNDERGRADUATE FINANCIAL AID (Fall 2005, est.) 1,332 applied for aid; of those 80% were deemed to have need. 98% of undergraduates with need received aid; of those 16% had need fully met. *Average percent of need met:* 70% (excluding resources awarded to replace EFC). *Average financial aid package:* $12,511 (excluding resources awarded to replace EFC). 17% of all full-time undergraduates had no need and received non-need-based gift aid.
GIFT AID (NEED-BASED) *Total amount:* $5,468,375 (26% federal, 1% state, 73% institutional). *Receiving aid:* Freshmen: 44% (187); All full-time undergraduates: 41% (758). *Average award:* Freshmen: $7253; Undergraduates: $6834. *Scholarships, grants, and awards:* Federal Pell, FSEOG, state, private, college/university gift aid from institutional funds.
GIFT AID (NON-NEED-BASED) *Total amount:* $7,577,689 (1% federal, 21% state, 77% institutional, 1% external sources). *Receiving aid:* Freshmen: 43% (181); Undergraduates: 38% (708). *Average Award:* Freshmen: $8147; Undergraduates: $8343. *Scholarships, grants, and awards by category: Academic Interests/Achievement:* 560 awards ($4,517,800 total): general academic interests/achievements. *Special Achievements/Activities:* 74 awards ($102,932 total): community service, leadership, memberships. *Special Characteristics:* 32 awards ($217,083 total): children and siblings of alumni, children of current students, children of faculty/staff, parents of current students, siblings of current students. *Tuition waivers:* Full or partial for children of alumni, employees or children of employees, senior citizens. *ROTC:* Army cooperative.
LOANS *Student loans:* $9,225,994 (39% need-based, 61% non-need-based). 71% of past graduating class borrowed through all loan programs. *Average indebtedness per student:* $24,950. *Average need-based loan:* Freshmen: $2629; Undergraduates: $3805. *Parent loans:* $4,486,062 (100% non-need-based). *Programs:* Federal Direct (Subsidized and Unsubsidized Stafford), FFEL (PLUS), Perkins.
WORK-STUDY *Federal work-study:* Total amount: $459,915; 274 jobs averaging $1850.
APPLYING FOR FINANCIAL AID *Required financial aid forms:* FAFSA, state aid form. *Financial aid deadline (priority):* 3/1. *Notification date:* Continuous beginning 3/15.
CONTACT Ms. Debbie A. Raines, Director of Financial Aid, Marymount University, 2807 North Glebe Road, Arlington, VA 22207-4299, 703-284-1530 or toll-free 800-548-7638. Fax: 703-516-4771. E-mail: admissions@marymount.edu.

MARYVILLE COLLEGE
Maryville, TN

Tuition & fees: $22,224 | **Average undergraduate aid package: $20,380**

ABOUT THE INSTITUTION Independent Presbyterian, coed. Awards: bachelor's degrees. 50 undergraduate majors. Total enrollment: 1,146. Undergraduates: 1,146. Freshmen: 333. Federal methodology is used as a basis for awarding need-based institutional aid.
UNDERGRADUATE EXPENSES for 2005–06 *Application fee:* $25. *Comprehensive fee:* $29,224 includes full-time tuition ($21,624), mandatory fees ($600), and room and board ($7000). *College room only:* $3500. Full-time tuition and fees vary according to course load. Room and board charges vary according to board plan, housing facility, and location. *Part-time tuition:* $901 per hour. *Part-time fees:* $13.50 per hour. Part-time tuition and fees vary according to course load. *Payment plan:* Installment.
FRESHMAN FINANCIAL AID (Fall 2005, est.) 333 applied for aid; of those 81% were deemed to have need. 100% of freshmen with need received aid; of those 34% had need fully met. *Average percent of need met:* 91% (excluding resources awarded to replace EFC). *Average financial aid package:* $23,787 (excluding resources awarded to replace EFC). 19% of all full-time freshmen had no need and received non-need-based gift aid.
UNDERGRADUATE FINANCIAL AID (Fall 2005, est.) 1,120 applied for aid; of those 77% were deemed to have need. 100% of undergraduates with need received aid; of those 56% had need fully met. *Average percent of need met:* 92% (excluding resources awarded to replace EFC). *Average financial aid package:* $20,380 (excluding resources awarded to replace EFC). 22% of all full-time undergraduates had no need and received non-need-based gift aid.

GIFT AID (NEED-BASED) *Total amount:* $15,949,039 (7% federal, 4% state, 79% institutional, 10% external sources). *Receiving aid:* Freshmen: 81% (270); All full-time undergraduates: 74% (824). *Average award:* Freshmen: $13,991; Undergraduates: $13,670. *Scholarships, grants, and awards:* Federal Pell, FSEOG, state, private, college/university gift aid from institutional funds.
GIFT AID (NON-NEED-BASED) *Total amount:* $827,524 (46% institutional, 54% external sources). *Receiving aid:* Freshmen: 80% (266); Undergraduates: 53% (591). *Average Award:* Freshmen: $2285; Undergraduates: $1535. *Scholarships, grants, and awards by category: Academic Interests/Achievement:* 1,011 awards ($9,905,204 total): general academic interests/achievements. *Creative Arts/Performance:* 96 awards ($241,200 total): art/fine arts, music, theater/drama. *Special Achievements/Activities:* 148 awards ($581,650 total): community service, leadership. *Special Characteristics:* 146 awards ($673,423 total): children and siblings of alumni, children of faculty/staff, local/state students, members of minority groups, religious affiliation. *Tuition waivers:* Full or partial for employees or children of employees.
LOANS *Student loans:* $3,520,555 (61% need-based, 39% non-need-based). 87% of past graduating class borrowed through all loan programs. *Average indebtedness per student:* $18,473. *Average need-based loan:* Freshmen: $2890; Undergraduates: $5086. *Parent loans:* $1,174,658 (100% non-need-based). *Programs:* FFEL (Subsidized and Unsubsidized Stafford, PLUS), Perkins, state, college/university.
WORK-STUDY *Federal work-study:* Total amount: $645,567; 441 jobs averaging $1464. *State or other work-study/employment:* Total amount: $286,443 (83% need-based, 17% non-need-based). 162 part-time jobs averaging $1768.
APPLYING FOR FINANCIAL AID *Required financial aid form:* FAFSA. *Financial aid deadline (priority):* 3/1. *Notification date:* Continuous beginning 3/15. Students must reply within 4 weeks of notification.
CONTACT Mr. Richard Brand, Director of Financial Aid, Maryville College, 502 East Lamar Alexander Parkway, Maryville, TN 37804-5907, 865-981-8100 or toll-free 800-597-2687. E-mail: richard.brand@maryvillecollege.edu.

MARYVILLE UNIVERSITY OF SAINT LOUIS
St. Louis, MO

Tuition & fees: $17,320 | **Average undergraduate aid package: $14,272**

ABOUT THE INSTITUTION Independent, coed. Awards: bachelor's, master's, and doctoral degrees. 48 undergraduate majors. Total enrollment: 3,223. Undergraduates: 2,659. Freshmen: 335. Both federal and institutional methodology are used as a basis for awarding need-based institutional aid.
UNDERGRADUATE EXPENSES for 2005–06 *Application fee:* $25. *Comprehensive fee:* $24,670 includes full-time tuition ($17,000), mandatory fees ($320), and room and board ($7350). *College room only:* $6425. Full-time tuition and fees vary according to course load. Room and board charges vary according to housing facility. *Part-time tuition:* $510 per credit hour. *Part-time fees:* $80 per term. Part-time tuition and fees vary according to class time. *Payment plans:* Installment, deferred payment.
FRESHMAN FINANCIAL AID (Fall 2005, est.) 295 applied for aid; of those 82% were deemed to have need. 100% of freshmen with need received aid; of those 16% had need fully met. *Average percent of need met:* 78% (excluding resources awarded to replace EFC). *Average financial aid package:* $14,794 (excluding resources awarded to replace EFC). 21% of all full-time freshmen had no need and received non-need-based gift aid.
UNDERGRADUATE FINANCIAL AID (Fall 2005, est.) 1,357 applied for aid; of those 86% were deemed to have need. 99% of undergraduates with need received aid; of those 13% had need fully met. *Average percent of need met:* 75% (excluding resources awarded to replace EFC). *Average financial aid package:* $14,272 (excluding resources awarded to replace EFC). 18% of all full-time undergraduates had no need and received non-need-based gift aid.
GIFT AID (NEED-BASED) *Total amount:* $8,896,293 (14% federal, 7% state, 77% institutional, 2% external sources). *Receiving aid:* Freshmen: 75% (240); All full-time undergraduates: 70% (1,131). *Average award:* Freshmen: $9108; Undergraduates: $7795. *Scholarships, grants, and awards:* Federal Pell, FSEOG, state, private, college/university gift aid from institutional funds.
GIFT AID (NON-NEED-BASED) *Total amount:* $1,894,922 (5% state, 87% institutional, 8% external sources). *Receiving aid:* Freshmen: 7% (24); Undergraduates: 5% (77). *Average Award:* Freshmen: $4769; Undergraduates: $4639. *Scholarships, grants, and awards by category: Academic Interests/Achievement:* 1,816 awards ($5,375,710 total): education, general academic interests/achievements, health fields. *Creative Arts/Performance:* 25 awards

($47,050 total): art/fine arts. *Special Achievements/Activities:* 325 awards ($218,863 total): community service, general special achievements/activities, leadership. *Special Characteristics:* 47 awards ($54,967 total): children of current students, members of minority groups, parents of current students, religious affiliation, siblings of current students, spouses of current students, twins. *Tuition waivers:* Full or partial for employees or children of employees, senior citizens. *ROTC:* Army cooperative.
LOANS *Student loans:* $9,839,598 (60% need-based, 40% non-need-based). 60% of past graduating class borrowed through all loan programs. *Average indebtedness per student:* $26,310. *Average need-based loan:* Freshmen: $2657; Undergraduates: $3833. *Parent loans:* $3,350,972 (40% need-based, 60% non-need-based). *Programs:* Federal Direct (Subsidized and Unsubsidized Stafford, PLUS), Perkins, Sallie Mae Signature Loans, Keybank Loans, TERI Loans, CitiAssist Loans, MOHELA ED Cash Loans, Wells Fargo Loans, Nelnet.
WORK-STUDY *Federal work-study:* Total amount: $269,531; 224 jobs averaging $1203. *State or other work-study/employment:* Total amount: $224,886 (88% need-based, 12% non-need-based). 102 part-time jobs averaging $2205.
APPLYING FOR FINANCIAL AID *Required financial aid forms:* FAFSA, institution's own form. *Financial aid deadline (priority):* 3/1. *Notification date:* Continuous beginning 3/15. Students must reply by 5/1 or within 2 weeks of notification.
CONTACT Ms. Martha Harbaugh, Director of Financial Aid, Maryville University of Saint Louis, 13550 Conway Road, St. Louis, MO 63141-7299, 800-627-9855 Ext. 9360 or toll-free 800-627-9855. *Fax:* 314-529-9199. *E-mail:* fin_aid@maryville.edu.

MARYWOOD UNIVERSITY
Scranton, PA

Tuition & fees: $21,640   **Average undergraduate aid package: $14,499**

ABOUT THE INSTITUTION Independent Roman Catholic, coed. Awards: associate, bachelor's, master's, and doctoral degrees and post-bachelor's and post-master's certificates. 86 undergraduate majors. Total enrollment: 3,127. Undergraduates: 1,811. Freshmen: 342. Federal methodology is used as a basis for awarding need-based institutional aid.
UNDERGRADUATE EXPENSES for 2005–06 *Application fee:* $30. *Comprehensive fee:* $30,740 includes full-time tuition ($20,700), mandatory fees ($940), and room and board ($9100). *College room only:* $5152. Room and board charges vary according to board plan and housing facility. *Part-time tuition:* $643 per credit. *Part-time fees:* $190 per term. Part-time tuition and fees vary according to course load. *Payment plans:* Installment, deferred payment.
GIFT AID (NEED-BASED) *Total amount:* $11,190,930 (18% federal, 21% state, 59% institutional, 2% external sources). *Receiving aid:* Freshmen: 85% (237); All full-time undergraduates: 83% (1,270). *Average award:* Freshmen: $11,073; Undergraduates: $10,319. *Scholarships, grants, and awards:* Federal Pell, FSEOG, state, private, college/university gift aid from institutional funds.
GIFT AID (NON-NEED-BASED) *Total amount:* $2,070,088 (96% institutional, 4% external sources). *Receiving aid:* Freshmen: 9% (24); Undergraduates: 7% (111). *Average Award:* Freshmen: $8110; Undergraduates: $6929. *Scholarships, grants, and awards by category: Academic Interests/Achievement:* 121 awards ($830,614 total): business, communication, education, foreign languages, general academic interests/achievements, health fields, mathematics, religion/biblical studies. *Creative Arts/Performance:* 33 awards ($36,100 total): art/fine arts, cinema/film/broadcasting, journalism/publications, music, performing arts, theater/drama. *Special Achievements/Activities:* 158 awards ($723,389 total): community service, general special achievements/activities, leadership. *Special Characteristics:* 59 awards: adult students, children and siblings of alumni, children of current students, children of faculty/staff, children of workers in trades, ethnic background, general special characteristics, international students, local/state students, religious affiliation, siblings of current students, spouses of current students. *Tuition waivers:* Full or partial for employees or children of employees, senior citizens. *ROTC:* Army cooperative, Air Force cooperative.
LOANS *Student loans:* $10,354,884 (75% need-based, 25% non-need-based). 89% of past graduating class borrowed through all loan programs. *Average indebtedness per student:* $31,073. *Average need-based loan:* Freshmen: $2765; Undergraduates: $4185. *Parent loans:* $1,934,478 (36% need-based, 64% non-need-based). *Programs:* FFEL (Subsidized and Unsubsidized Stafford, PLUS), Perkins, state, alternative loans.
APPLYING FOR FINANCIAL AID *Required financial aid forms:* FAFSA, institution's own form. *Financial aid deadline:* Continuous. *Notification date:* Continuous beginning 3/1. Students must reply by 5/1 or within 3 weeks of notification.

CONTACT Mr. Stanley F. Skrutski, Director of Financial Aid, Marywood University, 2300 Adams Avenue, Scranton, PA 18509-1598, 570-348-6225 or toll-free 800-346-5014. *Fax:* 570-961-4739. *E-mail:* skrutski@ac.marywood.edu.

MASSACHUSETTS COLLEGE OF ART
Boston, MA

Tuition & fees (MA res): $6850   **Average undergraduate aid package: $7239**

ABOUT THE INSTITUTION State-supported, coed. Awards: bachelor's and master's degrees and post-bachelor's certificates. 17 undergraduate majors. Total enrollment: 2,130. Undergraduates: 1,994. Freshmen: 265. Federal methodology is used as a basis for awarding need-based institutional aid.
UNDERGRADUATE EXPENSES for 2005–06 *Application fee:* $30. *Tuition, state resident:* full-time $6850. *Tuition, nonresident:* full-time $19,200. *College room and board:* $9800.
FRESHMAN FINANCIAL AID (Fall 2005, est.) 216 applied for aid; of those 75% were deemed to have need. 100% of freshmen with need received aid. *Average financial aid package:* $5626 (excluding resources awarded to replace EFC).
UNDERGRADUATE FINANCIAL AID (Fall 2005, est.) 996 applied for aid; of those 78% were deemed to have need. 100% of undergraduates with need received aid. *Average financial aid package:* $7239 (excluding resources awarded to replace EFC).
GIFT AID (NEED-BASED) *Total amount:* $2,739,848 (43% federal, 34% state, 23% institutional). *Receiving aid:* Freshmen: 36% (95); All full-time undergraduates: 37% (507). *Average award:* Freshmen: $5189; Undergraduates: $5101. *Scholarships, grants, and awards:* Federal Pell, FSEOG, state, private, college/university gift aid from institutional funds.
GIFT AID (NON-NEED-BASED) *Total amount:* $429,680 (100% external sources). *Receiving aid:* Freshmen: 19% (50); Undergraduates: 12% (165). *Scholarships, grants, and awards by category: Special Characteristics:* children of faculty/staff, children of union members/company employees, veterans.
LOANS *Student loans:* $5,973,685 (51% need-based, 49% non-need-based). *Average need-based loan:* Freshmen: $2654; Undergraduates: $3988. *Parent loans:* $3,890,608 (100% non-need-based). *Programs:* Federal Direct (Subsidized and Unsubsidized Stafford, PLUS), FFEL (Subsidized and Unsubsidized Stafford, PLUS), Perkins, state, college/university, alternative loans.
WORK-STUDY *Federal work-study:* Total amount: $281,810; 167 jobs averaging $1519.
APPLYING FOR FINANCIAL AID *Required financial aid form:* FAFSA. *Financial aid deadline (priority):* 3/15. *Notification date:* Continuous. Students must reply within 3 weeks of notification.
CONTACT Ken Berryhill, Director of Financial Aid, Massachusetts College of Art, 621 Huntington Avenue, Boston, MA 02115-5882, 617-879-7846. *Fax:* 617-879-7880. *E-mail:* kberryhill@massart.edu.

MASSACHUSETTS COLLEGE OF LIBERAL ARTS
North Adams, MA

CONTACT Elizabeth M. Petri, Director of Financial Aid, Massachusetts College of Liberal Arts, 375 Church Street, Eldridge Hall, Room 112, North Adams, MA 01247, 413-662-5219 or toll-free 800-292-6632 (in-state). *E-mail:* epetri@mcla.edu.

MASSACHUSETTS COLLEGE OF PHARMACY AND HEALTH SCIENCES
Boston, MA

Tuition & fees: $21,050   **Average undergraduate aid package: $10,043**

ABOUT THE INSTITUTION Independent, coed. Awards: bachelor's, master's, doctoral, and first professional degrees and post-bachelor's certificates. 10 undergraduate majors. Total enrollment: 2,896. Undergraduates: 1,886. Freshmen: 406. Federal methodology is used as a basis for awarding need-based institutional aid.

Massachusetts College of Pharmacy and Health Sciences

UNDERGRADUATE EXPENSES for 2005–06 *Application fee:* $70. *Comprehensive fee:* $32,270 includes full-time tuition ($20,400), mandatory fees ($650), and room and board ($11,220). *College room only:* $7900. *Part-time tuition:* $750 per credit. *Part-time fees:* $160 per term.

FRESHMAN FINANCIAL AID (Fall 2005, est.) 377 applied for aid; of those 89% were deemed to have need. 99% of freshmen with need received aid; of those 8% had need fully met. *Average percent of need met:* 48% (excluding resources awarded to replace EFC). *Average financial aid package:* $12,024 (excluding resources awarded to replace EFC). 14% of all full-time freshmen had no need and received non-need-based gift aid.

UNDERGRADUATE FINANCIAL AID (Fall 2005, est.) 1,625 applied for aid; of those 93% were deemed to have need. 98% of undergraduates with need received aid; of those 5% had need fully met. *Average percent of need met:* 34% (excluding resources awarded to replace EFC). *Average financial aid package:* $10,043 (excluding resources awarded to replace EFC). 9% of all full-time undergraduates had no need and received non-need-based gift aid.

GIFT AID (NEED-BASED) *Total amount:* $7,763,547 (21% federal, 8% state, 64% institutional, 7% external sources). *Receiving aid:* Freshmen: 75% (296); All full-time undergraduates: 67% (1,159). *Average award:* Freshmen: $8227; Undergraduates: $6507. *Scholarships, grants, and awards:* Federal Pell, FSEOG, state, private, college/university gift aid from institutional funds.

GIFT AID (NON-NEED-BASED) *Total amount:* $621,314 (86% institutional, 14% external sources). *Receiving aid:* Freshmen: 4% (17); Undergraduates: 1% (23). *Average Award:* Freshmen: $10,288; Undergraduates: $15,600. *Scholarships, grants, and awards by category: Academic Interests/Achievement:* general academic interests/achievements. *Special Characteristics:* children of faculty/staff. *ROTC:* Army cooperative, Air Force cooperative.

LOANS *Student loans:* $30,561,727 (79% need-based, 21% non-need-based). 75% of past graduating class borrowed through all loan programs. *Average indebtedness per student:* $47,248. *Average need-based loan:* Freshmen: $4666; Undergraduates: $4826. *Parent loans:* $2,019,834 (57% need-based, 43% non-need-based). *Programs:* FFEL (Subsidized and Unsubsidized Stafford, PLUS), Perkins, state.

WORK-STUDY *Federal work-study:* Total amount: $384,936; jobs available.

APPLYING FOR FINANCIAL AID *Required financial aid form:* FAFSA. *Financial aid deadline (priority):* 3/15. *Notification date:* Continuous beginning 2/20. Students must reply by 5/1 or within 2 weeks of notification.

CONTACT Ms. Carrie Glass, Director of Student Financial Services, Massachusetts College of Pharmacy and Health Sciences, 179 Longwood Avenue, Boston, MA 02115-5896, 617-732-2199 or toll-free 617-732-2850 (in-state), 800-225-5506 (out-of-state). Fax: 617-732-2082. E-mail: carrie.glass@mcphs.edu.

MASSACHUSETTS INSTITUTE OF TECHNOLOGY
Cambridge, MA

Tuition & fees: $32,300   **Average undergraduate aid package:** $27,800

ABOUT THE INSTITUTION Independent, coed. Awards: bachelor's, master's, and doctoral degrees. 33 undergraduate majors. Total enrollment: 10,206. Undergraduates: 4,066. Freshmen: 996. Institutional methodology is used as a basis for awarding need-based institutional aid.

UNDERGRADUATE EXPENSES for 2005–06 *Application fee:* $65. *Comprehensive fee:* $41,800 includes full-time tuition ($32,100), mandatory fees ($200), and room and board ($9500). *College room only:* $5250. Room and board charges vary according to board plan and housing facility. *Part-time tuition:* $505 per unit. Part-time tuition and fees vary according to course load. *Payment plan:* Installment.

GIFT AID (NEED-BASED) *Total amount:* $63,584,572 (10% federal, 79% institutional, 11% external sources). *Receiving aid:* Freshmen: 64% (693); All full-time undergraduates: 61% (2,486). *Average award:* Freshmen: $25,666; Undergraduates: $24,244. *Scholarships, grants, and awards:* Federal Pell, FSEOG, state, private, college/university gift aid from institutional funds.

GIFT AID (NON-NEED-BASED) *Total amount:* $695,311 (23% federal, 77% external sources). *Tuition waivers:* Full or partial for employees or children of employees. *ROTC:* Army, Naval, Air Force.

LOANS *Student loans:* $10,357,130 (87% need-based, 13% non-need-based). 50% of past graduating class borrowed through all loan programs. *Average indebtedness per student:* $19,748. *Average need-based loan:* Freshmen: $3321; Undergraduates: $3897. *Parent loans:* $7,614,516 (100% non-need-based). *Programs:* Federal Direct (Subsidized and Unsubsidized Stafford, PLUS), Perkins, college/university.

APPLYING FOR FINANCIAL AID *Required financial aid forms:* FAFSA, CSS Financial Aid PROFILE, noncustodial (divorced/separated) parent's statement, business/farm supplement, parents' complete federal income returns from prior year. *Financial aid deadline:* 2/1 (priority: 2/1). *Notification date:* 4/1. Students must reply by 5/1.

CONTACT Student Financial Services, Massachusetts Institute of Technology, 77 Massachusetts Avenue, Room 11-320, Cambridge, MA 02139-4307, 617-253-4971. Fax: 617-253-9859. E-mail: finaid@mit.edu.

MASSACHUSETTS MARITIME ACADEMY
Buzzards Bay, MA

Tuition & fees (area res): $5107   **Average undergraduate aid package:** $5125

ABOUT THE INSTITUTION State-supported, coed, primarily men. Awards: bachelor's and master's degrees and first professional certificates. 8 undergraduate majors. Total enrollment: 1,008. Undergraduates: 969. Freshmen: 266. Federal methodology is used as a basis for awarding need-based institutional aid.

UNDERGRADUATE EXPENSES for 2005–06 *Application fee:* $50. *Tuition, area resident:* full-time $1062. *Tuition, state resident:* full-time $1591. *Tuition, nonresident:* full-time $11,591. *College room and board:* $6464; *room only:* $3286. *Payment plan:* Installment.

FRESHMAN FINANCIAL AID (Fall 2005, est.) 246 applied for aid; of those 65% were deemed to have need. 100% of freshmen with need received aid; of those 51% had need fully met. *Average percent of need met:* 45% (excluding resources awarded to replace EFC). *Average financial aid package:* $5925 (excluding resources awarded to replace EFC). 28% of all full-time freshmen had no need and received non-need-based gift aid.

UNDERGRADUATE FINANCIAL AID (Fall 2005, est.) 654 applied for aid; of those 65% were deemed to have need. 100% of undergraduates with need received aid; of those 57% had need fully met. *Average percent of need met:* 57% (excluding resources awarded to replace EFC). *Average financial aid package:* $5125 (excluding resources awarded to replace EFC). 14% of all full-time undergraduates had no need and received non-need-based gift aid.

GIFT AID (NEED-BASED) *Total amount:* $879,233 (52% federal, 36% state, 12% external sources). *Receiving aid:* Freshmen: 27% (72); All full-time undergraduates: 26% (246). *Average award:* Freshmen: $1030; Undergraduates: $1707. *Scholarships, grants, and awards:* Federal Pell, FSEOG, state, private, college/university gift aid from institutional funds.

GIFT AID (NON-NEED-BASED) *Total amount:* $497,403 (91% institutional, 9% external sources). *Receiving aid:* Freshmen: 34% (92); Undergraduates: 26% (249). *Average Award:* Freshmen: $1030; Undergraduates: $1707. *Scholarships, grants, and awards by category: Academic Interests/Achievement:* 135 awards ($219,732 total): general academic interests/achievements. *Creative Arts/Performance:* 3 awards ($3090 total): theater/drama. *Special Achievements/Activities:* 52 awards ($53,560 total): leadership. *Special Characteristics:* 45 awards ($108,813 total): children and siblings of alumni, children of faculty/staff, international students, veterans. *Tuition waivers:* Full or partial for employees or children of employees. *ROTC:* Army cooperative, Naval.

LOANS *Student loans:* $3,467,353 (36% need-based, 64% non-need-based). 82% of past graduating class borrowed through all loan programs. *Average indebtedness per student:* $12,972. *Average need-based loan:* Freshmen: $2625; Undergraduates: $3643. *Parent loans:* $897,352 (100% non-need-based). *Programs:* Federal Direct (Subsidized and Unsubsidized Stafford, PLUS).

WORK-STUDY *Federal work-study:* Total amount: $89,583; 147 jobs averaging $1233.

APPLYING FOR FINANCIAL AID *Required financial aid forms:* FAFSA, institution's own form. *Financial aid deadline (priority):* 4/30. *Notification date:* Continuous beginning 4/1.

CONTACT Mrs. Elizabeth Benway, Director of Financial Aid, Massachusetts Maritime Academy, 101 Academy Drive, Buzzards Bay, MA 02532, 508-830-5086 or toll-free 800-544-3411. Fax: 508-830-5077. E-mail: ebenway@maritime.edu.

THE MASTER'S COLLEGE AND SEMINARY
Santa Clarita, CA

Tuition & fees: $19,230 **Average undergraduate aid package:** $15,054

ABOUT THE INSTITUTION Independent nondenominational, coed. Awards: bachelor's, master's, doctoral, and first professional degrees and first professional certificates. 47 undergraduate majors. Total enrollment: 1,537. Undergraduates: 1,139. Freshmen: 187. Federal methodology is used as a basis for awarding need-based institutional aid.

UNDERGRADUATE EXPENSES for 2005–06 *Application fee:* $55. *Comprehensive fee:* $25,850 includes full-time tuition ($19,230) and room and board ($6620). *College room only:* $3660. Full-time tuition and fees vary according to course load, degree level, and program. Room and board charges vary according to board plan. *Part-time tuition:* $805 per credit hour. Part-time tuition and fees vary according to course load, degree level, and program. *Payment plan:* Installment.

FRESHMAN FINANCIAL AID (Fall 2005, est.) 168 applied for aid; of those 84% were deemed to have need. 99% of freshmen with need received aid; of those 16% had need fully met. *Average percent of need met:* 69% (excluding resources awarded to replace EFC). *Average financial aid package:* $14,368 (excluding resources awarded to replace EFC). 20% of all full-time freshmen had no need and received non-need-based gift aid.

UNDERGRADUATE FINANCIAL AID (Fall 2005, est.) 838 applied for aid; of those 88% were deemed to have need. 99% of undergraduates with need received aid; of those 23% had need fully met. *Average percent of need met:* 69% (excluding resources awarded to replace EFC). *Average financial aid package:* $15,054 (excluding resources awarded to replace EFC). 19% of all full-time undergraduates had no need and received non-need-based gift aid.

GIFT AID (NEED-BASED) *Total amount:* $6,698,429 (11% federal, 27% state, 46% institutional, 16% external sources). *Receiving aid:* Freshmen: 53% (137); All full-time undergraduates: 66% (679). *Average award:* Freshmen: $10,540; Undergraduates: $10,405. *Scholarships, grants, and awards:* Federal Pell, FSEOG, state, private, college/university gift aid from institutional funds.

GIFT AID (NON-NEED-BASED) *Total amount:* $1,484,119 (72% institutional, 28% external sources). *Receiving aid:* Freshmen: 6% (15); Undergraduates: 5% (49). *Average Award:* Freshmen: $9392; Undergraduates: $9833. *Scholarships, grants, and awards by category: Academic Interests/Achievement:* 467 awards ($2,317,885 total): biological sciences, business, education, general academic interests/achievements, mathematics, physical sciences, religion/biblical studies, social sciences. *Creative Arts/Performance:* 74 awards ($198,450 total): music. *Special Achievements/Activities:* 53 awards ($115,000 total): leadership. *Special Characteristics:* 225 awards ($1,023,922 total): children and siblings of alumni, children of faculty/staff, general special characteristics, international students, relatives of clergy. *Tuition waivers:* Full or partial for employees or children of employees.

LOANS *Student loans:* $4,463,447 (78% need-based, 22% non-need-based). 54% of past graduating class borrowed through all loan programs. *Average indebtedness per student:* $15,383. *Average need-based loan:* Freshmen: $2995; Undergraduates: $4634. *Parent loans:* $2,267,796 (51% need-based, 49% non-need-based). *Programs:* FFEL (Subsidized and Unsubsidized Stafford, PLUS), Perkins, alternative loans.

WORK-STUDY *Federal work-study:* Total amount: $108,000; 45 jobs averaging $2666. *State or other work-study/employment:* Total amount: $1,045,019 (74% need-based, 26% non-need-based). Part-time jobs available.

ATHLETIC AWARDS *Total amount:* $908,398 (56% need-based, 44% non-need-based).

APPLYING FOR FINANCIAL AID *Required financial aid forms:* FAFSA, institution's own form, state aid form. *Financial aid deadline (priority):* 3/2. *Notification date:* Continuous. Students must reply by 5/1 or within 2 weeks of notification.

CONTACT Gary Edwards, Director of Financial Aid, The Master's College and Seminary, 21726 Placerita Canyon Road, Santa Clarita, CA 91321-1200, 661-259-3540 Ext. 3391 or toll-free 800-568-6248. Fax: 661-362-2693. E-mail: gedwards@masters.edu.

MAYVILLE STATE UNIVERSITY
Mayville, ND

Tuition & fees (ND res): $4943 **Average undergraduate aid package:** $6854

ABOUT THE INSTITUTION State-supported, coed. Awards: associate and bachelor's degrees. 37 undergraduate majors. Total enrollment: 912. Undergraduates: 912. Freshmen: 145. Federal methodology is used as a basis for awarding need-based institutional aid.

UNDERGRADUATE EXPENSES for 2005–06 *Application fee:* $35. *Tuition, state resident:* full-time $3300; part-time $137.50 per credit hour. *Tuition, nonresident:* full-time $8811; part-time $367.14 per hour. *Required fees:* full-time $1643; $68.45 per credit hour. Full-time tuition and fees vary according to course load and reciprocity agreements. Part-time tuition and fees vary according to course load and reciprocity agreements. *College room and board:* $3724; room only: $1524. Room and board charges vary according to board plan and housing facility. *Payment plan:* Installment.

FRESHMAN FINANCIAL AID (Fall 2004) 126 applied for aid; of those 78% were deemed to have need. 95% of freshmen with need received aid; of those 41% had need fully met. *Average percent of need met:* 76% (excluding resources awarded to replace EFC). *Average financial aid package:* $6028 (excluding resources awarded to replace EFC). 6% of all full-time freshmen had no need and received non-need-based gift aid.

UNDERGRADUATE FINANCIAL AID (Fall 2004) 532 applied for aid; of those 82% were deemed to have need. 99% of undergraduates with need received aid; of those 54% had need fully met. *Average percent of need met:* 84% (excluding resources awarded to replace EFC). *Average financial aid package:* $6854 (excluding resources awarded to replace EFC). 2% of all full-time undergraduates had no need and received non-need-based gift aid.

GIFT AID (NEED-BASED) *Total amount:* $774,734 (89% federal, 2% state, 4% institutional, 5% external sources). *Receiving aid:* Freshmen: 30% (49); All full-time undergraduates: 35% (236). *Average award:* Freshmen: $2752; Undergraduates: $3343. *Scholarships, grants, and awards:* Federal Pell, FSEOG, state.

GIFT AID (NON-NEED-BASED) *Total amount:* $83,129 (3% state, 51% institutional, 46% external sources). *Receiving aid:* Freshmen: 30% (49); Undergraduates: 18% (120). *Average Award:* Freshmen: $849; Undergraduates: $929. *Scholarships, grants, and awards by category: Academic Interests/Achievement:* 131 awards ($50,201 total): biological sciences, business, education, English, general academic interests/achievements, library science, mathematics, physical sciences. *Creative Arts/Performance:* 8 awards ($3000 total): music. *Special Achievements/Activities:* 20 awards ($12,600 total): leadership. *Special Characteristics:* 150 awards ($454,447 total): children of faculty/staff, international students, local/state students, members of minority groups, out-of-state students. *Tuition waivers:* Full or partial for minority students, employees or children of employees, senior citizens. *ROTC:* Army cooperative, Air Force.

LOANS *Student loans:* $2,428,923 (92% need-based, 8% non-need-based). 77% of past graduating class borrowed through all loan programs. *Average indebtedness per student:* $18,190. *Average need-based loan:* Freshmen: $2848; Undergraduates: $4356. *Parent loans:* $151,892 (30% need-based, 70% non-need-based). *Programs:* FFEL (Subsidized and Unsubsidized Stafford, PLUS), Perkins, college/university.

WORK-STUDY *Federal work-study:* Total amount: $83,625; 83 jobs averaging $1007.

ATHLETIC AWARDS *Total amount:* $103,836 (53% need-based, 47% non-need-based).

APPLYING FOR FINANCIAL AID *Required financial aid form:* FAFSA. *Financial aid deadline (priority):* 3/15. *Notification date:* Continuous. Students must reply within 2 weeks of notification.

CONTACT Ms. Shirley Hanson, Director of Student Financial Aid, Mayville State University, 330 3rd Street NE, Mayville, ND 58257-1299, 701-788-4767 or toll-free 800-437-4104. E-mail: s.hanson@mayvillestate.edu.

McDANIEL COLLEGE
Westminster, MD

Tuition & fees: $27,280 **Average undergraduate aid package:** $20,398

ABOUT THE INSTITUTION Independent, coed. Awards: bachelor's and master's degrees. 28 undergraduate majors. Total enrollment: 3,524. Undergraduates: 1,695. Freshmen: 448. Both federal and institutional methodology are used as a basis for awarding need-based institutional aid.

McDaniel College

UNDERGRADUATE EXPENSES for 2006–07 *Application fee:* $50. *Comprehensive fee:* $33,180 includes full-time tuition ($26,980), mandatory fees ($300), and room and board ($5900). *College room only:* $3200. *Part-time tuition:* $843 per credit. *Part-time fees:* $150 per term.

FRESHMAN FINANCIAL AID (Fall 2005, est.) 369 applied for aid; of those 77% were deemed to have need. 100% of freshmen with need received aid; of those 30% had need fully met. *Average percent of need met:* 95% (excluding resources awarded to replace EFC). *Average financial aid package:* $19,667 (excluding resources awarded to replace EFC). 63% of all full-time freshmen had no need and received non-need-based gift aid.

UNDERGRADUATE FINANCIAL AID (Fall 2005, est.) 1,210 applied for aid; of those 85% were deemed to have need. 98% of undergraduates with need received aid; of those 30% had need fully met. *Average percent of need met:* 94% (excluding resources awarded to replace EFC). *Average financial aid package:* $20,398 (excluding resources awarded to replace EFC). 33% of all full-time undergraduates had no need and received non-need-based gift aid.

GIFT AID (NEED-BASED) *Total amount:* $14,460,772 (6% federal, 10% state, 84% institutional). *Receiving aid:* Freshmen: 62% (279); All full-time undergraduates: 61% (983). *Average award:* Freshmen: $9330; Undergraduates: $9091. *Scholarships, grants, and awards:* Federal Pell, FSEOG, state, private, college/university gift aid from institutional funds.

GIFT AID (NON-NEED-BASED) *Total amount:* $6,710,249 (7% state, 85% institutional, 8% external sources). *Average Award:* Freshmen: $10,562; Undergraduates: $10,326. *Scholarships, grants, and awards by category: Academic Interests/Achievement:* 1,140 awards ($10,417,355 total): general academic interests/achievements. *Special Achievements/Activities:* 4 awards ($8000 total): junior miss, leadership. *Special Characteristics:* 308 awards ($445,296 total): local/state students, previous college experience, siblings of current students. *ROTC:* Army.

LOANS *Student loans:* $6,857,079 (48% need-based, 52% non-need-based). 60% of past graduating class borrowed through all loan programs. *Average indebtedness per student:* $21,416. *Average need-based loan:* Freshmen: $3892; Undergraduates: $4505. *Parent loans:* $2,629,824 (100% non-need-based). *Programs:* FFEL (Subsidized and Unsubsidized Stafford, PLUS), Perkins, college/university.

WORK-STUDY *Federal work-study:* Total amount: $162,036; 196 jobs averaging $1000. *State or other work-study/employment:* Total amount: $154,505 (100% non-need-based). 112 part-time jobs averaging $1379.

APPLYING FOR FINANCIAL AID *Required financial aid forms:* FAFSA, institution's own form, federal income tax form(s). *Financial aid deadline (priority):* 3/1. *Notification date:* Continuous beginning 3/1. Students must reply by 5/1 or within 2 weeks of notification.

CONTACT Financial Aid Office, McDaniel College, 2 College Hill, Westminster, MD 21157-4390, 410-857-2233 or toll-free 800-638-5005. *Fax:* 410-857-2729. *E-mail:* finaid@mcdaniel.edu.

McKENDREE COLLEGE
Lebanon, IL

Tuition & fees: $18,900   Average undergraduate aid package: $15,473

ABOUT THE INSTITUTION Independent religious, coed. Awards: bachelor's and master's degrees. 50 undergraduate majors. Total enrollment: 2,585. Undergraduates: 2,257. Freshmen: 274. Federal methodology is used as a basis for awarding need-based institutional aid.

UNDERGRADUATE EXPENSES for 2006–07 *Application fee:* $40. *Comprehensive fee:* $26,280 includes full-time tuition ($18,300), mandatory fees ($600), and room and board ($7380). *College room only:* $3900. *Part-time tuition:* $615 per hour.

FRESHMAN FINANCIAL AID (Fall 2005, est.) 238 applied for aid; of those 87% were deemed to have need. 100% of freshmen with need received aid; of those 24% had need fully met. *Average percent of need met:* 86% (excluding resources awarded to replace EFC). *Average financial aid package:* $17,047 (excluding resources awarded to replace EFC). 20% of all full-time freshmen had no need and received non-need-based gift aid.

UNDERGRADUATE FINANCIAL AID (Fall 2005, est.) 1,095 applied for aid; of those 89% were deemed to have need. 100% of undergraduates with need received aid; of those 24% had need fully met. *Average percent of need met:* 81% (excluding resources awarded to replace EFC). *Average financial aid package:* $15,473 (excluding resources awarded to replace EFC). 21% of all full-time undergraduates had no need and received non-need-based gift aid.

GIFT AID (NEED-BASED) *Total amount:* $10,470,278 (13% federal, 21% state, 64% institutional, 2% external sources). *Receiving aid:* Freshmen: 79% (205); All full-time undergraduates: 77% (971). *Average award:* Freshmen: $14,846; Undergraduates: $12,144. *Scholarships, grants, and awards:* Federal Pell, FSEOG, state, private, college/university gift aid from institutional funds.

GIFT AID (NON-NEED-BASED) *Total amount:* $2,406,697 (1% state, 92% institutional, 7% external sources). *Receiving aid:* Freshmen: 15% (39); Undergraduates: 12% (156). *Average Award:* Freshmen: $13,940; Undergraduates: $11,327. *Scholarships, grants, and awards by category: Academic Interests/Achievement:* 651 awards ($3,681,609 total): biological sciences, business, general academic interests/achievements, religion/biblical studies. *Creative Arts/Performance:* 134 awards ($356,966 total): music. *Special Achievements/Activities:* 44 awards ($105,830 total): cheerleading/drum major, community service, leadership. *Special Characteristics:* 169 awards ($382,595 total): children of faculty/staff, general special characteristics, out-of-state students, religious affiliation. *ROTC:* Army cooperative, Air Force cooperative.

LOANS *Student loans:* $5,262,219 (73% need-based, 27% non-need-based). 57% of past graduating class borrowed through all loan programs. *Average indebtedness per student:* $16,322. *Average need-based loan:* Freshmen: $2323; Undergraduates: $3627. *Parent loans:* $2,836,516 (25% need-based, 75% non-need-based). *Programs:* FFEL (Subsidized and Unsubsidized Stafford, PLUS), Perkins.

WORK-STUDY *Federal work-study:* Total amount: $577,198; 409 jobs averaging $1874. *State or other work-study/employment:* Total amount: $246,299 (2% need-based, 98% non-need-based). 218 part-time jobs averaging $1239.

ATHLETIC AWARDS Total amount: $2,376,652 (55% need-based, 45% non-need-based).

APPLYING FOR FINANCIAL AID *Required financial aid forms:* FAFSA, institution's own form. *Financial aid deadline (priority):* 5/31. *Notification date:* Continuous beginning 3/1.

CONTACT Cynthia Kiefer, Director of Financial Aid, McKendree College, 701 College Road, Lebanon, IL 62254-1299, 618-537-6827 or toll-free 800-232-7228 Ext. 6831. *Fax:* 618-537-6530. *E-mail:* cjkiefer@mckendree.edu.

McMURRY UNIVERSITY
Abilene, TX

ABOUT THE INSTITUTION Independent United Methodist, coed. Awards: bachelor's degrees. 46 undergraduate majors. Total enrollment: 1,430. Undergraduates: 1,430. Freshmen: 292.

GIFT AID (NEED-BASED) *Scholarships, grants, and awards:* Federal Pell, FSEOG, state, private, college/university gift aid from institutional funds.

GIFT AID (NON-NEED-BASED) *Scholarships, grants, and awards by category: Academic Interests/Achievement:* general academic interests/achievements, religion/biblical studies. *Creative Arts/Performance:* art/fine arts, music. *Special Achievements/Activities:* general special achievements/activities, junior miss. *Special Characteristics:* children of faculty/staff, international students, local/state students, out-of-state students, previous college experience, relatives of clergy, religious affiliation, veterans.

LOANS *Programs:* FFEL (Subsidized and Unsubsidized Stafford, PLUS), Perkins, state, Alternative Loan.

APPLYING FOR FINANCIAL AID *Required financial aid forms:* FAFSA, institution's own form.

CONTACT Ms. Kathyrn Martin, Director of Financial Aid, McMurry University, Box 908, McMurry Station, Abilene, TX 79697, 325-793-4713 or toll-free 800-477-0077. *Fax:* 325-793-4718. *E-mail:* martink@mcmurryadm.mcm.edu.

McNEESE STATE UNIVERSITY
Lake Charles, LA

CONTACT Ms. Taina J. Savoit, Director of Financial Aid, McNeese State University, PO Box 93260, Lake Charles, LA 70609-3260, 337-475-5065 or toll-free 800-622-3352. *Fax:* 337-475-5068. *E-mail:* tsavoit@mail.mcneese.edu.

McPHERSON COLLEGE
McPherson, KS

ABOUT THE INSTITUTION Independent religious, coed. Awards: associate and bachelor's degrees. 44 undergraduate majors. Total enrollment: 464. Undergraduates: 464. Freshmen: 115.
GIFT AID (NEED-BASED) *Scholarships, grants, and awards:* Federal Pell, FSEOG, state, private, college/university gift aid from institutional funds.
GIFT AID (NON-NEED-BASED) *Scholarships, grants, and awards by category: Academic Interests/Achievement:* general academic interests/achievements. *Special Characteristics:* local/state students, religious affiliation.
LOANS *Programs:* FFEL (Subsidized and Unsubsidized Stafford, PLUS), Perkins.
APPLYING FOR FINANCIAL AID *Required financial aid forms:* FAFSA, state aid form.
CONTACT Ms. Carol L. Williams, Director of Admissions and Financial Aid, McPherson College, PO Box 1402, McPherson, KS 67460-1402, 316-241-0731 Ext. 1270 or toll-free 800-365-7402. *Fax:* 316-241-8443. *E-mail:* williamc@mcpherson.edu.

MEDAILLE COLLEGE
Buffalo, NY

CONTACT Ms. Jacqueline Matheny, Director of Enrollment Management and Admissions, Medaille College, 18 Agassiz Circle, Buffalo, NY 14214-2695, 716-884-3411 Ext. 203 or toll-free 800-292-1582 (in-state). *Fax:* 716-884-0291.

MEDCENTER ONE COLLEGE OF NURSING
Bismarck, ND

Tuition & fees: $9151 **Average undergraduate aid package:** $12,680

ABOUT THE INSTITUTION Independent, coed, primarily women. Awards: bachelor's degrees. 1 undergraduate major. Total enrollment: 88. Undergraduates: 88. Both federal and institutional methodology are used as a basis for awarding need-based institutional aid.
UNDERGRADUATE EXPENSES for 2005–06 *Application fee:* $40. *Tuition:* full-time $8400; part-time $350 per credit. *Required fees:* full-time $751; $5.25 per credit or $499 per term part-time. Part-time tuition and fees vary according to course load.
UNDERGRADUATE FINANCIAL AID (Fall 2005, est.) 88 applied for aid; of those 73% were deemed to have need. 100% of undergraduates with need received aid; of those 80% had need fully met. *Average percent of need met:* 95% (excluding resources awarded to replace EFC). *Average financial aid package:* $12,680 (excluding resources awarded to replace EFC). 8% of all full-time undergraduates had no need and received non-need-based gift aid.
GIFT AID (NEED-BASED) *Total amount:* $132,560 (82% federal, 10% state, 8% institutional). *Receiving aid:* All full-time undergraduates: 33% (29). *Average award:* Undergraduates: $3402. *Scholarships, grants, and awards:* Federal Pell, FSEOG, state, private, college/university gift aid from institutional funds.
GIFT AID (NON-NEED-BASED) *Total amount:* $19,910 (25% institutional, 75% external sources). *Receiving aid:* Undergraduates: 9% (8). *Average Award:* Undergraduates: $779. *Scholarships, grants, and awards by category: Academic Interests/Achievement:* 8 awards ($5022 total): general academic interests/achievements, health fields. *Special Achievements/Activities:* 15 awards ($1500 total): memberships. *Special Characteristics:* 4 awards ($2450 total): children and siblings of alumni, local/state students.
LOANS *Student loans:* $1,122,866 (17% need-based, 83% non-need-based). 95% of past graduating class borrowed through all loan programs. *Average indebtedness per student:* $9910. *Average need-based loan:* Undergraduates: $3719. *Parent loans:* $6000 (100% non-need-based). *Programs:* FFEL (Subsidized and Unsubsidized Stafford, PLUS), Perkins, Federal Nursing, college/university.
WORK-STUDY *Federal work-study:* Total amount: $7450; 7 jobs averaging $1100.
APPLYING FOR FINANCIAL AID *Required financial aid forms:* FAFSA, institution's own form, institutional scholarship application form. *Financial aid deadline (priority):* 3/15. *Notification date:* 6/15. Students must reply within 2 weeks of notification.

CONTACT Ms. Janell Thomas, Financial Aid Director, Medcenter One College of Nursing, 512 North 7th Street, Bismarck, ND 58501-4494, 701-323-6270. *Fax:* 701-323-6967. *E-mail:* jthomas@mohs.org.

MEDCENTRAL COLLEGE OF NURSING
Mansfield, OH

CONTACT Financial Aid Office, MedCentral College of Nursing, 335 Glessner Avenue, Mansfield, OH 44903, 419-520-2600 or toll-free 877-656-4360.

MEDGAR EVERS COLLEGE OF THE CITY UNIVERSITY OF NEW YORK
Brooklyn, NY

Tuition & fees (NY res): $4230 **Average undergraduate aid package:** N/A

ABOUT THE INSTITUTION State and locally supported, coed. Awards: associate and bachelor's degrees. 19 undergraduate majors. Total enrollment: 5,212. Undergraduates: 5,212. Freshmen: 787. Federal methodology is used as a basis for awarding need-based institutional aid.
UNDERGRADUATE EXPENSES for 2005–06 *Application fee:* $60. *Tuition, state resident:* full-time $4000; part-time $170 per credit. *Tuition, nonresident:* full-time $8640; part-time $360 per credit. *Required fees:* full-time $230; $78.35 per term part-time. *Payment plans:* Installment, deferred payment.
GIFT AID (NEED-BASED) *Total amount:* $15,688,748 (55% federal, 44% state, 1% institutional). *Receiving aid:* Freshmen: 73% (507); All full-time undergraduates: 71% (2,228). *Scholarships, grants, and awards:* Federal Pell, FSEOG, state, private, college/university gift aid from institutional funds.
GIFT AID (NON-NEED-BASED) *Total amount:* $20,500 (100% external sources). *Receiving aid:* Freshmen: 2; Undergraduates: 1% (17). *Scholarships, grants, and awards by category: Academic Interests/Achievement:* 17 awards ($10,128 total): general academic interests/achievements.
LOANS *Student loans:* $935,394 (91% need-based, 9% non-need-based). *Programs:* Federal Direct (Subsidized and Unsubsidized Stafford, PLUS), FFEL (Subsidized and Unsubsidized Stafford, PLUS), Perkins.
WORK-STUDY *Federal work-study:* Total amount: $1,121,836; 218 jobs averaging $1144.
APPLYING FOR FINANCIAL AID *Required financial aid forms:* FAFSA, state aid form, University Financial Aid Information Supplemental Request (FASIR). *Financial aid deadline (priority):* 4/1. *Notification date:* Continuous beginning 9/1.
CONTACT Conley James, Director of Financial Aid (Acting), Medgar Evers College of the City University of New York, 1650 Bedford Avenue, Brooklyn, NY 11225, 718-270-6038. *Fax:* 718-270-6194. *E-mail:* conley@mec.cuny.edu.

MEDICAL COLLEGE OF GEORGIA
Augusta, GA

Tuition & fees (GA res): $4056 **Average undergraduate aid package:** $8646

ABOUT THE INSTITUTION State-supported, coed. Awards: bachelor's, master's, doctoral, and first professional degrees and post-bachelor's certificates. 10 undergraduate majors. Total enrollment: 2,115. Undergraduates: 725. Federal methodology is used as a basis for awarding need-based institutional aid.
UNDERGRADUATE EXPENSES for 2005–06 *Tuition, state resident:* full-time $3638; part-time $152 per hour. *Tuition, nonresident:* full-time $14,552; part-time $607 per hour. *Required fees:* full-time $418; $209 per term part-time. Full-time tuition and fees vary according to location. Part-time tuition and fees vary according to course load and location. *College room and board: room only:* $2334. Room and board charges vary according to housing facility.
UNDERGRADUATE FINANCIAL AID (Fall 2004) 404 applied for aid; of those 90% were deemed to have need. 98% of undergraduates with need received aid; of those 10% had need fully met. *Average percent of need met:* 50% (excluding resources awarded to replace EFC). *Average financial aid package:* $8646 (excluding resources awarded to replace EFC). 20% of all full-time undergraduates had no need and received non-need-based gift aid.
GIFT AID (NEED-BASED) *Total amount:* $1,339,302 (35% federal, 52% state, 9% institutional, 4% external sources). *Receiving aid:* All full-time undergradu-

Medical College of Georgia

ates: 55% (262). *Average award:* Undergraduates: $4232. *Scholarships, grants, and awards:* Federal Pell, FSEOG, state, private, college/university gift aid from institutional funds, Federal Nursing.
GIFT AID (NON-NEED-BASED) *Total amount:* $533,630 (97% state, 3% external sources). *Receiving aid:* Undergraduates: 4% (17). *Average Award:* Undergraduates: $7622. *Scholarships, grants, and awards by category:* Academic Interests/Achievement: 452 awards ($3,835,863 total): health fields. *Special Characteristics:* 170 awards ($139,994 total): religious affiliation.
LOANS *Student loans:* $4,061,996 (77% need-based, 23% non-need-based). 90% of past graduating class borrowed through all loan programs. *Average indebtedness per student:* $19,694. *Average need-based loan:* Undergraduates: $6349. *Parent loans:* $55,902 (53% need-based, 47% non-need-based). *Programs:* FFEL (Subsidized and Unsubsidized Stafford, PLUS), Perkins, Federal Nursing, state, college/university.
WORK-STUDY *Federal work-study:* Total amount: $40,182; 98 jobs averaging $1892.
APPLYING FOR FINANCIAL AID *Required financial aid forms:* FAFSA, institution's own form. *Financial aid deadline (priority):* 3/31. *Notification date:* Continuous beginning 4/30. Students must reply within 2 weeks of notification.
CONTACT Cynthia Parks, Interim Director of Student Financial Aid, Medical College of Georgia, 2013 Administration Building, 1120 Fifteenth Street, Augusta, GA 30912-7320, 706-721-4901 or toll-free 800-519-3388 (in-state). *Fax:* 706-721-9407. *E-mail:* osfa@mail.mcg.edu.

MEDICAL UNIVERSITY OF SOUTH CAROLINA
Charleston, SC

ABOUT THE INSTITUTION State-supported, coed. Awards: bachelor's, master's, doctoral, and first professional degrees and post-bachelor's certificates. 3 undergraduate majors. Total enrollment: 2,428. Undergraduates: 332.
GIFT AID (NEED-BASED) *Scholarships, grants, and awards:* Federal Pell, FSEOG, state, private, college/university gift aid from institutional funds, Federal Nursing, Scholarships for Disadvantaged Students (SDS).
GIFT AID (NON-NEED-BASED) *Scholarships, grants, and awards by category:* Academic Interests/Achievement: general academic interests/achievements, health fields. *Special Characteristics:* ethnic background, general special characteristics, local/state students, members of minority groups.
LOANS *Programs:* FFEL (Subsidized and Unsubsidized Stafford, PLUS), Perkins, Federal Nursing, state, Health Professions Loans, Loans for Disadvantaged Students program, Primary Care Loans, alternative loans, TERI Loans.
APPLYING FOR FINANCIAL AID *Required financial aid forms:* FAFSA, institution's own form, income tax forms.
CONTACT William H. Vandiver, Associate Director for Financial Aid Services, Medical University of South Carolina, 45 Courtenay Drive, PO Box 250176, Charleston, SC 29425, 843-792-2536. *Fax:* 843-792-2060. *E-mail:* vandivew@musc.edu.

MEMPHIS COLLEGE OF ART
Memphis, TN

Tuition & fees: $17,460 **Average undergraduate aid package:** $7000

ABOUT THE INSTITUTION Independent, coed. Awards: bachelor's and master's degrees. 20 undergraduate majors. Total enrollment: 326. Undergraduates: 314. Freshmen: 60. Both federal and institutional methodology are used as a basis for awarding need-based institutional aid.
UNDERGRADUATE EXPENSES for 2005–06 *Application fee:* $25. *Tuition:* full-time $17,400; part-time $2225 per course.
FRESHMAN FINANCIAL AID (Fall 2005, est.) 55 applied for aid; of those 89% were deemed to have need. 100% of freshmen with need received aid; of those 69% had need fully met. *Average percent of need met:* 90% (excluding resources awarded to replace EFC). *Average financial aid package:* $6500 (excluding resources awarded to replace EFC). 13% of all full-time freshmen had no need and received non-need-based gift aid.
UNDERGRADUATE FINANCIAL AID (Fall 2005, est.) 231 applied for aid; of those 90% were deemed to have need. 100% of undergraduates with need received aid; of those 54% had need fully met. *Average percent of need met:* 95% (excluding resources awarded to replace EFC). *Average financial aid package:* $7000 (excluding resources awarded to replace EFC). 23% of all full-time undergraduates had no need and received non-need-based gift aid.
GIFT AID (NEED-BASED) *Total amount:* $751,879 (61% federal, 29% state, 10% institutional). *Receiving aid:* Freshmen: 59% (33); All full-time undergraduates: 48% (129). *Average Award:* Freshmen: $3000; Undergraduates: $3000. *Scholarships, grants, and awards:* Federal Pell, FSEOG, state, private, college/university gift aid from institutional funds.
GIFT AID (NON-NEED-BASED) *Total amount:* $1,148,650 (7% state, 89% institutional, 4% external sources). *Receiving aid:* Freshmen: 73% (41); Undergraduates: 77% (208). *Average Award:* Freshmen: $3500; Undergraduates: $5500. *Scholarships, grants, and awards by category:* Academic Interests/Achievement: 263 awards ($934,627 total): general academic interests/achievements. Creative Arts/Performance: 42 awards ($77,950 total): applied art and design, art/fine arts. *Special Characteristics:* 14 awards ($10,500 total): previous college experience.
LOANS *Student loans:* $2,310,901 (37% need-based, 63% non-need-based). 90% of past graduating class borrowed through all loan programs. *Average indebtedness per student:* $20,000. *Average need-based loan:* Freshmen: $3500; Undergraduates: $5500. *Parent loans:* $1,055,316 (100% non-need-based). *Programs:* Federal Direct (Subsidized and Unsubsidized Stafford, PLUS), FFEL (Subsidized and Unsubsidized Stafford, PLUS), Perkins, college/university.
WORK-STUDY *Federal work-study:* Total amount: $67,000; 67 jobs averaging $1000. *State or other work-study/employment:* Total amount: $55,000 (100% non-need-based). 55 part-time jobs averaging $1000.
APPLYING FOR FINANCIAL AID *Required financial aid form:* FAFSA. *Financial aid deadline (priority):* 3/1. *Notification date:* Continuous beginning 4/1. Students must reply within 3 weeks of notification.
CONTACT Kara Ziegemeier, Director of Financial Aid, Memphis College of Art, 1930 Poplar Avenue, Memphis, TN 38104-2764, 901-272-5136 or toll-free 800-727-1088. *Fax:* 901-272-5134. *E-mail:* kziegemeier@mca.edu.

MENLO COLLEGE
Atherton, CA

Tuition & fees: $24,450 **Average undergraduate aid package:** $20,559

ABOUT THE INSTITUTION Independent, coed. Awards: bachelor's degrees. 3 undergraduate majors. Total enrollment: 769. Undergraduates: 769. Freshmen: 183. Federal methodology is used as a basis for awarding need-based institutional aid.
UNDERGRADUATE EXPENSES for 2005–06 *Application fee:* $40. *Comprehensive fee:* $34,050 includes full-time tuition ($24,300), mandatory fees ($150), and room and board ($9600). Full-time tuition and fees vary according to program. Room and board charges vary according to housing facility. *Part-time tuition:* $1000 per unit. *Part-time fees:* $75. Part-time tuition and fees vary according to course load and program. *Payment plan:* Installment.
FRESHMAN FINANCIAL AID (Fall 2005, est.) 127 applied for aid; of those 90% were deemed to have need. 100% of freshmen with need received aid; of those 12% had need fully met. *Average percent of need met:* 75% (excluding resources awarded to replace EFC). *Average financial aid package:* $21,171 (excluding resources awarded to replace EFC). 28% of all full-time freshmen had no need and received non-need-based gift aid.
UNDERGRADUATE FINANCIAL AID (Fall 2005, est.) 458 applied for aid; of those 92% were deemed to have need. 100% of undergraduates with need received aid; of those 12% had need fully met. *Average percent of need met:* 73% (excluding resources awarded to replace EFC). *Average financial aid package:* $20,559 (excluding resources awarded to replace EFC). 27% of all full-time undergraduates had no need and received non-need-based gift aid.
GIFT AID (NEED-BASED) *Total amount:* $6,753,994 (10% federal, 12% state, 75% institutional, 3% external sources). *Receiving aid:* Freshmen: 62% (114); All full-time undergraduates: 62% (418). *Average award:* Freshmen: $17,676; Undergraduates: $16,123. *Scholarships, grants, and awards:* Federal Pell, FSEOG, state, college/university gift aid from institutional funds.
GIFT AID (NON-NEED-BASED) *Total amount:* $1,672,976 (1% state, 95% institutional, 4% external sources). *Receiving aid:* Freshmen: 5% (9); Undergraduates: 4% (26). *Average Award:* Freshmen: $10,664; Undergraduates: $11,479. *Scholarships, grants, and awards by category:* Academic Interests/Achievement: 535 awards ($4,156,050 total): general academic interests/

achievements. *Special Achievements/Activities:* 456 awards ($3,883,225 total): community service. *Tuition waivers:* Full or partial for employees or children of employees. *ROTC:* Army cooperative.
LOANS *Student loans:* $2,986,794 (77% need-based, 23% non-need-based). 67% of past graduating class borrowed through all loan programs. *Average indebtedness per student:* $21,905. *Average need-based loan:* Freshmen: $3414; Undergraduates: $4756. *Parent loans:* $1,887,789 (46% need-based, 54% non-need-based). *Programs:* FFEL (Subsidized and Unsubsidized Stafford, PLUS).
WORK-STUDY *Federal work-study:* Total amount: $200,791; 290 jobs averaging $1000.
APPLYING FOR FINANCIAL AID *Required financial aid forms:* FAFSA, state aid form. *Financial aid deadline (priority):* 3/2. *Notification date:* Continuous beginning 3/15.
CONTACT Elinore Burkhardt, Director of Financial Aid, Menlo College, 1000 El Camino Real, Atherton, CA 94027-4301, 650-543-3880 or toll-free 800-556-3656. *Fax:* 650-543-4103.

MERCER UNIVERSITY
Macon, GA

| Tuition & fees: $23,460 | Average undergraduate aid package: $23,102 |

ABOUT THE INSTITUTION Independent Baptist, coed. Awards: bachelor's, master's, doctoral, and first professional degrees and post-bachelor's, post-master's, and first professional certificates. 49 undergraduate majors. Total enrollment: 7,154. Undergraduates: 4,498. Freshmen: 685. Federal methodology is used as a basis for awarding need-based institutional aid.
UNDERGRADUATE EXPENSES for 2005–06 *Application fee:* $50. *Comprehensive fee:* $30,873 includes full-time tuition ($23,460) and room and board ($7413). *College room only:* $3570. Full-time tuition and fees vary according to class time, course load, and location. Room and board charges vary according to board plan, housing facility, and location. *Part-time tuition:* $782 per credit hour. Part-time tuition and fees vary according to class time, course load, and location. *Payment plan:* Installment.
FRESHMAN FINANCIAL AID (Fall 2005, est.) 537 applied for aid; of those 78% were deemed to have need. 100% of freshmen with need received aid; of those 58% had need fully met. *Average percent of need met:* 93% (excluding resources awarded to replace EFC). *Average financial aid package:* $23,519 (excluding resources awarded to replace EFC). 31% of all full-time freshmen had no need and received non-need-based gift aid.
UNDERGRADUATE FINANCIAL AID (Fall 2005, est.) 1,812 applied for aid; of those 82% were deemed to have need. 100% of undergraduates with need received aid; of those 51% had need fully met. *Average percent of need met:* 91% (excluding resources awarded to replace EFC). *Average financial aid package:* $23,102 (excluding resources awarded to replace EFC). 33% of all full-time undergraduates had no need and received non-need-based gift aid.
GIFT AID (NEED-BASED) *Total amount:* $20,200,743 (10% federal, 12% state, 74% institutional, 4% external sources). *Receiving aid:* Freshmen: 68% (417); All full-time undergraduates: 64% (1,476). *Average award:* Freshmen: $15,670; Undergraduates: $14,556. *Scholarships, grants, and awards:* Federal Pell, FSEOG, state, college/university gift aid from institutional funds, Federal Nursing.
GIFT AID (NON-NEED-BASED) *Total amount:* $13,173,119 (18% state, 77% institutional, 5% external sources). *Receiving aid:* Freshmen: 25% (155); Undergraduates: 19% (438). *Average Award:* Freshmen: $17,027; Undergraduates: $15,854. *Scholarships, grants, and awards by category: Academic Interests/Achievement:* 2,283 awards ($18,193,705 total): biological sciences, business, education, engineering/technologies, English, foreign languages, general academic interests/achievements, international studies, military science, religion/biblical studies. *Creative Arts/Performance:* 132 awards ($431,220 total): art/fine arts, debating, music, theater/drama. *Special Achievements/Activities:* 16 awards ($148,339 total): community service, general special achievements/activities, junior miss, memberships. *Special Characteristics:* 2,344 awards ($7,265,544 total): adult students, children of faculty/staff, children of public servants, children of union members/company employees, general special characteristics, international students, local/state students, members of minority groups, relatives of clergy, religious affiliation, siblings of current students. *Tuition waivers:* Full or partial for employees or children of employees. *ROTC:* Army.
LOANS *Student loans:* $9,693,320 (63% need-based, 37% non-need-based). 63% of past graduating class borrowed through all loan programs. *Average indebtedness per student:* $11,075. *Average need-based loan:* Freshmen: $5006; Undergraduates: $6668. *Parent loans:* $2,803,514 (29% need-based, 71% non-need-based). *Programs:* Federal Direct (Subsidized and Unsubsidized Stafford, PLUS), Perkins, Federal Nursing, college/university.
WORK-STUDY *Federal work-study:* Total amount: $919,829; jobs available.
ATHLETIC AWARDS Total amount: $2,960,517 (31% need-based, 69% non-need-based).
APPLYING FOR FINANCIAL AID *Required financial aid forms:* FAFSA, institution's own form, state aid form (for GA residents only). *Financial aid deadline (priority):* 4/1. *Notification date:* Continuous beginning 3/15. Students must reply within 2 weeks of notification.
CONTACT Ms. Carol Williams, Associate Vice President, Financial Planning, Mercer University, 1400 Coleman Avenue, Macon, GA 31207-0003, 478-301-2670 or toll-free 800-840-8577. *Fax:* 478-301-2671. *E-mail:* williams_ck@mercer.edu.

MERCY COLLEGE
Dobbs Ferry, NY

ABOUT THE INSTITUTION Independent, coed. Awards: associate, bachelor's, and master's degrees. 40 undergraduate majors. Total enrollment: 9,539. Undergraduates: 5,636. Freshmen: 605.
GIFT AID (NEED-BASED) *Scholarships, grants, and awards:* Federal Pell, FSEOG, state, private, college/university gift aid from institutional funds.
GIFT AID (NON-NEED-BASED) *Scholarships, grants, and awards by category: Academic Interests/Achievement:* general academic interests/achievements.
LOANS *Programs:* FFEL (Subsidized and Unsubsidized Stafford, PLUS), Federal Nursing.
WORK-STUDY *Federal work-study:* Total amount: $734,000; jobs available.
APPLYING FOR FINANCIAL AID *Required financial aid forms:* FAFSA, state aid form.
CONTACT Director of Financial Aid, Mercy College, 28 Wells Avenue, 5th Floor, Yonkers, NY 00701, 800-MERCY-NY. *Fax:* 914-375-8582. *E-mail:* @mercy.edu.

MERCY COLLEGE OF HEALTH SCIENCES
Des Moines, IA

ABOUT THE INSTITUTION Independent religious, coed, primarily women. Awards: associate and bachelor's degrees. 6 undergraduate majors. Total enrollment: 660. Undergraduates: 660. Freshmen: 69.
GIFT AID (NEED-BASED) *Scholarships, grants, and awards:* Federal Pell, FSEOG, state, private, college/university gift aid from institutional funds.
GIFT AID (NON-NEED-BASED) *Scholarships, grants, and awards by category: Academic Interests/Achievement:* general academic interests/achievements, health fields. *Special Achievements/Activities:* community service. *Special Characteristics:* children of union members/company employees, ethnic background, previous college experience.
LOANS *Programs:* FFEL (Subsidized and Unsubsidized Stafford, PLUS).
APPLYING FOR FINANCIAL AID *Required financial aid form:* FAFSA.
CONTACT Lisa Croat, Financial Aid Assistant Coordinator, Mercy College of Health Sciences, 928 Sixth Avenue, Des Moines, IA 50309, 515-643-6720 or toll-free 800-637-2994. *Fax:* 515-643-6702. *E-mail:* lcroat@mercydesmoines.org.

MERCYHURST COLLEGE
Erie, PA

| Tuition & fees: $19,113 | Average undergraduate aid package: $10,261 |

ABOUT THE INSTITUTION Independent Roman Catholic, coed. Awards: associate, bachelor's, and master's degrees and post-bachelor's certificates. 107 undergraduate majors. Total enrollment: 4,120. Undergraduates: 3,840. Freshmen: 696. Federal methodology is used as a basis for awarding need-based institutional aid.
UNDERGRADUATE EXPENSES for 2005–06 *Application fee:* $30. *Comprehensive fee:* $26,187 includes full-time tuition ($17,760), mandatory fees ($1353), and room and board ($7074). *College room only:* $3576. Room and board charges vary according to board plan and housing facility. *Part-time tuition:* $592 per credit. Part-time tuition and fees vary according to course load and location. *Payment plan:* Installment.

Mercyhurst College

FRESHMAN FINANCIAL AID (Fall 2005, est.) 691 applied for aid; of those 74% were deemed to have need. 100% of freshmen with need received aid; of those 79% had need fully met. *Average percent of need met:* 87% (excluding resources awarded to replace EFC). *Average financial aid package:* $16,288 (excluding resources awarded to replace EFC). 21% of all full-time freshmen had no need and received non-need-based gift aid.
UNDERGRADUATE FINANCIAL AID (Fall 2005, est.) 3,079 applied for aid; of those 84% were deemed to have need. 100% of undergraduates with need received aid; of those 81% had need fully met. *Average percent of need met:* 89% (excluding resources awarded to replace EFC). *Average financial aid package:* $10,261 (excluding resources awarded to replace EFC).
GIFT AID (NEED-BASED) Total amount: $18,433,556 (10% federal, 13% state, 75% institutional, 2% external sources). *Receiving aid:* Freshmen: 73% (506); All full-time undergraduates: 76% (2,562). *Average award:* Freshmen: $9322; Undergraduates: $5433. *Scholarships, grants, and awards:* Federal Pell, FSEOG, state, private, college/university gift aid from institutional funds.
GIFT AID (NON-NEED-BASED) Total amount: $3,697,781 (4% state, 95% institutional, 1% external sources). *Receiving aid:* Freshmen: 29% (203); Undergraduates: 22% (739). *Average Award:* Freshmen: $8673. *Scholarships, grants, and awards by category:* Academic Interests/Achievement: 634 awards ($3,469,568 total): general academic interests/achievements, physical sciences, premedicine, social sciences. *Creative Arts/Performance:* 141 awards ($697,334 total): applied art and design, art/fine arts, dance, music. *Special Achievements/Activities:* 310 awards ($1,339,139 total): community service, general special achievements/activities, leadership, religious involvement. *Special Characteristics:* 41 awards ($158,004 total): adult students, children and siblings of alumni, children of faculty/staff, local/state students. *Tuition waivers:* Full or partial for employees or children of employees, adult students. *ROTC:* Army cooperative, Air Force cooperative.
LOANS Student loans: $13,542,829 (90% need-based, 10% non-need-based). 93% of past graduating class borrowed through all loan programs. *Average indebtedness per student:* $21,000. *Average need-based loan:* Freshmen: $2515; Undergraduates: $3224. *Parent loans:* $3,889,154 (79% need-based, 21% non-need-based). *Programs:* FFEL (Subsidized and Unsubsidized Stafford, PLUS), Perkins, college/university.
WORK-STUDY *Federal work-study:* Total amount: $362,626; 248 jobs averaging $1400. *State or other work-study/employment:* Total amount: $1,676,056 (79% need-based, 21% non-need-based). 1,404 part-time jobs averaging $1202.
ATHLETIC AWARDS *Total amount:* $4,378,170 (57% need-based, 43% non-need-based).
APPLYING FOR FINANCIAL AID *Required financial aid forms:* FAFSA, institution's own form. *Financial aid deadline:* 5/1 (priority: 3/1). *Notification date:* Continuous beginning 2/1.
CONTACT Dan Shumate, Interim Director, Financial Aid, Mercyhurst College, 501 East 38th Street, Erie, PA 16546, 814-824-2288 or toll-free 800-825-1926 Ext. 2202. *Fax:* 814-824-2438. *E-mail:* dshumate@mercyhurst.edu.

MEREDITH COLLEGE
Raleigh, NC

Tuition & fees: $21,200   **Average undergraduate aid package: $14,059**

ABOUT THE INSTITUTION Independent, undergraduate: women only; graduate: coed. Awards: bachelor's and master's degrees and post-bachelor's certificates. 57 undergraduate majors. Total enrollment: 2,168. Undergraduates: 2,015. Freshmen: 459. Federal methodology is used as a basis for awarding need-based institutional aid.
UNDERGRADUATE EXPENSES for 2006–07 *Application fee:* $40. *Comprehensive fee:* $27,140 includes full-time tuition ($21,150), mandatory fees ($50), and room and board ($5940). *Part-time tuition:* $555 per credit hour.
FRESHMAN FINANCIAL AID (Fall 2005, est.) 376 applied for aid; of those 82% were deemed to have need. 100% of freshmen with need received aid; of those 16% had need fully met. *Average percent of need met:* 70% (excluding resources awarded to replace EFC). *Average financial aid package:* $13,726 (excluding resources awarded to replace EFC). 20% of all full-time freshmen had no need and received non-need-based gift aid.
UNDERGRADUATE FINANCIAL AID (Fall 2005, est.) 1,274 applied for aid; of those 86% were deemed to have need. 100% of undergraduates with need received aid; of those 12% had need fully met. *Average percent of need met:* 70% (excluding resources awarded to replace EFC). *Average financial aid package:* $14,059 (excluding resources awarded to replace EFC). 12% of all full-time undergraduates had no need and received non-need-based gift aid.
GIFT AID (NEED-BASED) Total amount: $11,451,299 (12% federal, 32% state, 49% institutional, 7% external sources). *Receiving aid:* Freshmen: 69% (310); All full-time undergraduates: 67% (1,082). *Average award:* Freshmen: $11,719; Undergraduates: $10,948. *Scholarships, grants, and awards:* Federal Pell, FSEOG, state, private, college/university gift aid from institutional funds.
GIFT AID (NON-NEED-BASED) Total amount: $2,666,056 (37% state, 44% institutional, 19% external sources). *Receiving aid:* Freshmen: 8% (37); Undergraduates: 6% (89). *Average Award:* Freshmen: $5189; Undergraduates: $5089. *Scholarships, grants, and awards by category:* Academic Interests/Achievement: 564 awards ($2,455,300 total): biological sciences, computer science, education, general academic interests/achievements, mathematics, physical sciences, religion/biblical studies. *Creative Arts/Performance:* 51 awards ($101,180 total): applied art and design, art/fine arts, creative writing, music. *Special Achievements/Activities:* 20 awards ($58,750 total): community service, leadership. *Special Characteristics:* 60 awards ($123,525 total): adult students, children of faculty/staff, ethnic background, first-generation college students, international students, members of minority groups, out-of-state students, previous college experience, religious affiliation. *ROTC:* Army cooperative, Air Force cooperative.
LOANS Student loans: $9,281,053 (70% need-based, 30% non-need-based). 79% of past graduating class borrowed through all loan programs. *Average indebtedness per student:* $21,266. *Average need-based loan:* Freshmen: $2773; Undergraduates: $3858. *Parent loans:* $2,209,878 (15% need-based, 85% non-need-based). *Programs:* FFEL (Subsidized and Unsubsidized Stafford, PLUS), Perkins, college/university.
WORK-STUDY *Federal work-study:* Total amount: $134,010; 110 jobs averaging $1218. *State or other work-study/employment:* Total amount: $439,015 (99% need-based, 1% non-need-based). 362 part-time jobs averaging $1213.
APPLYING FOR FINANCIAL AID *Required financial aid form:* FAFSA. *Financial aid deadline (priority):* 2/15. *Notification date:* Continuous beginning 3/15. Students must reply by 5/1 or within 2 weeks of notification.
CONTACT Mr. Kevin Michaelsen, Director of Financial Assistance, Meredith College, 3800 Hillsborough Street, Raleigh, NC 27607-5298, 919-760-8565 or toll-free 800-MEREDITH. *Fax:* 919-760-2375. *E-mail:* michaelsen@meredith.edu.

MERRIMACK COLLEGE
North Andover, MA

Tuition & fees: $24,650   **Average undergraduate aid package: $18,000**

ABOUT THE INSTITUTION Independent Roman Catholic, coed. Awards: associate, bachelor's, and master's degrees. 41 undergraduate majors. Total enrollment: 2,188. Undergraduates: 2,154. Freshmen: 556. Federal methodology is used as a basis for awarding need-based institutional aid.
UNDERGRADUATE EXPENSES for 2005–06 *Application fee:* $50. *Comprehensive fee:* $34,380 includes full-time tuition ($24,200), mandatory fees ($450), and room and board ($9730). *College room only:* $5500. Full-time tuition and fees vary according to program and student level. Room and board charges vary according to board plan and housing facility. *Part-time tuition:* $900 per credit. *Part-time fees:* $55 per term. Part-time tuition and fees vary according to class time, course level, course load, and degree level. *Payment plan:* Installment.
FRESHMAN FINANCIAL AID (Fall 2005, est.) 440 applied for aid; of those 92% were deemed to have need. 100% of freshmen with need received aid; of those 84% had need fully met. *Average percent of need met:* 70% (excluding resources awarded to replace EFC). *Average financial aid package:* $17,500 (excluding resources awarded to replace EFC). 7% of all full-time freshmen had no need and received non-need-based gift aid.
UNDERGRADUATE FINANCIAL AID (Fall 2005, est.) 1,496 applied for aid; of those 79% were deemed to have need. 100% of undergraduates with need received aid; of those 85% had need fully met. *Average percent of need met:* 65% (excluding resources awarded to replace EFC). *Average financial aid package:* $18,000 (excluding resources awarded to replace EFC). 8% of all full-time undergraduates had no need and received non-need-based gift aid.
GIFT AID (NEED-BASED) Total amount: $12,082,406 (5% federal, 5% state, 90% institutional). *Receiving aid:* Freshmen: 74% (405); All full-time undergraduates: 61% (1,186). *Average award:* Freshmen: $13,000; Undergraduates: $12,000. *Scholarships, grants, and awards:* Federal Pell, FSEOG, state, private, college/university gift aid from institutional funds.

GIFT AID (NON-NEED-BASED) *Total amount:* $1,058,000 (81% institutional, 19% external sources). *Receiving aid:* Freshmen: 8% (45); Undergraduates: 14% (274). *Average Award:* Freshmen: $10,000; Undergraduates: $10,000. *Scholarships, grants, and awards by category: Academic Interests/Achievement:* 60 awards ($600,000 total): general academic interests/achievements. *Creative Arts/Performance:* 2 awards ($20,625 total): theater/drama. *Special Achievements/Activities:* 20 awards ($200,000 total): leadership. *Special Characteristics:* 75 awards ($1,180,538 total): children and siblings of alumni, children of faculty/staff, relatives of clergy, siblings of current students. *Tuition waivers:* Full or partial for employees or children of employees, senior citizens. *ROTC:* Air Force cooperative.

LOANS *Student loans:* $9,625,654 (40% need-based, 60% non-need-based). 70% of past graduating class borrowed through all loan programs. *Average indebtedness per student:* $17,125. *Average need-based loan:* Freshmen: $3625; Undergraduates: $5500. *Parent loans:* $4,575,564 (100% non-need-based). *Programs:* FFEL (Subsidized and Unsubsidized Stafford, PLUS), Perkins, state, college/university, MEFA Loans, alternative loans.

WORK-STUDY *Federal work-study:* Total amount: $165,245; 138 jobs averaging $1200. *State or other work-study/employment:* Total amount: $821,249 (100% non-need-based). 410 part-time jobs averaging $2000.

ATHLETIC AWARDS *Total amount:* $2,795,224 (18% need-based, 82% non-need-based).

APPLYING FOR FINANCIAL AID *Required financial aid forms:* FAFSA, noncustodial (divorced/separated) parent's statement, business/farm supplement, Sibling. *Financial aid deadline:* 2/1. *Notification date:* Continuous beginning 3/1. Students must reply by 5/1.

CONTACT Christine A. Mordach, Director of Student Financial Aid and Scholarships, Merrimack College, 315 Turnpike Street, North Andover, MA 01845, 978-837-5186. *Fax:* 978-837-5067. *E-mail:* christine.mordach@merrimack.edu.

MESA STATE COLLEGE
Grand Junction, CO

Tuition & fees (CO res): $3442	Average undergraduate aid package: $5206

ABOUT THE INSTITUTION State-supported, coed. Awards: associate, bachelor's, and master's degrees. 67 undergraduate majors. Total enrollment: 6,062. Undergraduates: 6,034. Freshmen: 1,288. Federal methodology is used as a basis for awarding need-based institutional aid.

UNDERGRADUATE EXPENSES for 2006–07 *Application fee:* $30. *Tuition, state resident:* full-time $3442; part-time $132.40 per hour. *Tuition, nonresident:* full-time $10,660; part-time $410 per hour.

FRESHMAN FINANCIAL AID (Fall 2005, est.) 828 applied for aid; of those 74% were deemed to have need. 100% of freshmen with need received aid; of those 22% had need fully met. *Average percent of need met:* 57% (excluding resources awarded to replace EFC). *Average financial aid package:* $4014 (excluding resources awarded to replace EFC). 5% of all full-time freshmen had no need and received non-need-based gift aid.

UNDERGRADUATE FINANCIAL AID (Fall 2005, est.) 3,261 applied for aid; of those 83% were deemed to have need. 97% of undergraduates with need received aid; of those 16% had need fully met. *Average percent of need met:* 60% (excluding resources awarded to replace EFC). *Average financial aid package:* $5206 (excluding resources awarded to replace EFC). 4% of all full-time undergraduates had no need and received non-need-based gift aid.

GIFT AID (NEED-BASED) *Total amount:* $7,387,143 (76% federal, 24% state). *Receiving aid:* Freshmen: 40% (457); All full-time undergraduates: 43% (1,943). *Average award:* Freshmen: $3126; Undergraduates: $3546. *Scholarships, grants, and awards:* Federal Pell, FSEOG, state, private, college/university gift aid from institutional funds.

GIFT AID (NON-NEED-BASED) *Total amount:* $2,430,775 (7% state, 31% institutional, 62% external sources). *Receiving aid:* Freshmen: 50% (574); Undergraduates: 7% (310). *Average Award:* Freshmen: $1887; Undergraduates: $1893. *Scholarships, grants, and awards by category: Academic Interests/Achievement:* 698 awards ($828,986 total): biological sciences, business, communication, computer science, education, engineering/technologies, English, general academic interests/achievements, health fields, humanities, mathematics, physical sciences, social sciences. *Creative Arts/Performance:* 47 awards ($19,873 total): art/fine arts, creative writing, journalism/publications, music, theater/drama. *Special Achievements/Activities:* general special achievements/activities, hobbies/interests. *Special Characteristics:* 112 awards ($137,866 total): first-generation college students, international students, local/state students, members of minority groups, out-of-state students.

LOANS *Student loans:* $13,080,525 (55% need-based, 45% non-need-based). 53% of past graduating class borrowed through all loan programs. *Average indebtedness per student:* $17,634. *Average need-based loan:* Freshmen: $2288; Undergraduates: $3188. *Parent loans:* $1,718,146 (100% non-need-based). *Programs:* FFEL (Subsidized and Unsubsidized Stafford, PLUS), Perkins.

WORK-STUDY *Federal work-study:* Total amount: $267,337; 189 jobs averaging $1428. *State or other work-study/employment:* Total amount: $629,511 (77% need-based, 23% non-need-based). 394 part-time jobs averaging $1669.

ATHLETIC AWARDS *Total amount:* $470,557 (100% non-need-based).

APPLYING FOR FINANCIAL AID *Required financial aid form:* FAFSA. *Financial aid deadline (priority):* 3/1. *Notification date:* Continuous beginning 4/1.

CONTACT Mr. Curt Martin, Director of Financial Aid, Mesa State College, 1100 North Avenue, Grand Junction, CO 81501-3122, 970-248-1396 or toll-free 800-982-MESA. *Fax:* 970-248-1191. *E-mail:* cmartin@mesastate.edu.

MESIVTA OF EASTERN PARKWAY RABBINICAL SEMINARY
Brooklyn, NY

CONTACT Rabbi Joseph Halberstadt, Dean, Mesivta of Eastern Parkway Rabbinical Seminary, 510 Dahill Road, Brooklyn, NY 11218-5559, 718-438-1002.

MESIVTA TIFERETH JERUSALEM OF AMERICA
New York, NY

CONTACT Rabbi Dickstein, Director of Financial Aid, Mesivta Tifereth Jerusalem of America, 141 East Broadway, New York, NY 10002-6301, 212-964-2830.

MESIVTA TORAH VODAATH RABBINICAL SEMINARY
Brooklyn, NY

CONTACT Mrs. Kayla Goldring, Director of Financial Aid, Mesivta Torah Vodaath Rabbinical Seminary, 425 East Ninth Street, Brooklyn, NY 11218-5209, 718-941-8000.

MESSENGER COLLEGE
Joplin, MO

Tuition & fees: $5410	Average undergraduate aid package: $5800

ABOUT THE INSTITUTION Independent Pentecostal, coed. Awards: associate and bachelor's degrees. 13 undergraduate majors. Total enrollment: 100. Undergraduates: 100. Freshmen: 31. Federal methodology is used as a basis for awarding need-based institutional aid.

UNDERGRADUATE EXPENSES for 2005–06 *Application fee:* $35. *Comprehensive fee:* $8910 includes full-time tuition ($4950), mandatory fees ($460), and room and board ($3500). Room and board charges vary according to housing facility. *Part-time tuition:* $165 per credit hour. *Payment plan:* Installment.

FRESHMAN FINANCIAL AID (Fall 2005, est.) 23 applied for aid; of those 96% were deemed to have need. 100% of freshmen with need received aid. *Average percent of need met:* 52% (excluding resources awarded to replace EFC). *Average financial aid package:* $4700 (excluding resources awarded to replace EFC).

UNDERGRADUATE FINANCIAL AID (Fall 2005, est.) 99 applied for aid; of those 96% were deemed to have need. 100% of undergraduates with need received aid. *Average percent of need met:* 55% (excluding resources awarded to replace EFC). *Average financial aid package:* $5800 (excluding resources awarded to replace EFC).

GIFT AID (NEED-BASED) *Total amount:* $197,695 (93% federal, 3% institutional, 4% external sources). *Receiving aid:* Freshmen: 88% (22); All full-time undergraduates: 91% (95). *Average award:* Freshmen: $3500; Undergraduates: $3600. *Scholarships, grants, and awards:* Federal Pell, FSEOG, private.

Messenger College

GIFT AID (NON-NEED-BASED) *Scholarships, grants, and awards by category: Academic Interests/Achievement:* education, general academic interests/achievements, religion/biblical studies. *Special Achievements/Activities:* religious involvement. *Special Characteristics:* religious affiliation. *Tuition waivers:* Full or partial for employees or children of employees.

LOANS *Student loans:* $304,792 (100% need-based). 100% of past graduating class borrowed through all loan programs. *Average indebtedness per student:* $27,790. *Average need-based loan:* Freshmen: $2625; Undergraduates: $3875. *Parent loans:* $17,000 (100% need-based). *Programs:* FFEL (Subsidized and Unsubsidized Stafford, PLUS).

WORK-STUDY *Federal work-study:* Total amount: $10,875; 14 jobs averaging $777.

APPLYING FOR FINANCIAL AID *Required financial aid form:* FAFSA. *Financial aid deadline:* Continuous. *Notification date:* Continuous.

CONTACT Sharon Shackelford, Financial Aid Director, Messenger College, 300 East 50th Street, Joplin, MO 64804, 417-624-7070 Ext. 308 or toll-free 800-385-8940 (in-state). *Fax:* 417-624-5070.

MESSIAH COLLEGE
Grantham, PA

| Tuition & fees: $22,110 | Average undergraduate aid package: $11,017 |

ABOUT THE INSTITUTION Independent interdenominational, coed. Awards: bachelor's degrees. 64 undergraduate majors. Total enrollment: 2,916. Undergraduates: 2,916. Freshmen: 707. Federal methodology is used as a basis for awarding need-based institutional aid.

UNDERGRADUATE EXPENSES for 2005–06 *Application fee:* $30. *Comprehensive fee:* $28,910 includes full-time tuition ($21,420), mandatory fees ($690), and room and board ($6800). *College room only:* $3540. Room and board charges vary according to board plan, housing facility, and location. *Part-time tuition:* $890 per credit. *Part-time fees:* $28 per credit. *Payment plan:* Installment.

FRESHMAN FINANCIAL AID (Fall 2005, est.) 605 applied for aid; of those 80% were deemed to have need. 100% of freshmen with need received aid; of those 26% had need fully met. *Average percent of need met:* 63% (excluding resources awarded to replace EFC). *Average financial aid package:* $12,349 (excluding resources awarded to replace EFC). 18% of all full-time freshmen had no need and received non-need-based gift aid.

UNDERGRADUATE FINANCIAL AID (Fall 2005, est.) 2,279 applied for aid; of those 86% were deemed to have need. 100% of undergraduates with need received aid; of those 27% had need fully met. *Average percent of need met:* 61% (excluding resources awarded to replace EFC). *Average financial aid package:* $11,017 (excluding resources awarded to replace EFC). 19% of all full-time undergraduates had no need and received non-need-based gift aid.

GIFT AID (NEED-BASED) *Total amount:* $17,899,135 (8% federal, 12% state, 76% institutional, 4% external sources). *Receiving aid:* Freshmen: 60% (424); All full-time undergraduates: 63% (1,807). *Average award:* Freshmen: $4742; Undergraduates: $3910. *Scholarships, grants, and awards:* Federal Pell, FSEOG, state, private, college/university gift aid from institutional funds.

GIFT AID (NON-NEED-BASED) *Total amount:* $6,225,625 (94% institutional, 6% external sources). *Receiving aid:* Freshmen: 64% (454); Undergraduates: 60% (1,708). *Average Award:* Freshmen: $8095; Undergraduates: $7726. *Scholarships, grants, and awards by category: Academic Interests/Achievement:* general academic interests/achievements. *Creative Arts/Performance:* art/fine arts, music, theater/drama. *Special Achievements/Activities:* leadership. *Special Characteristics:* adult students, children and siblings of alumni, children of faculty/staff, relatives of clergy, religious affiliation, siblings of current students, spouses of current students. *Tuition waivers:* Full or partial for minority students, children of alumni, employees or children of employees, adult students, senior citizens.

LOANS *Student loans:* $14,097,072 (68% need-based, 32% non-need-based). 70% of past graduating class borrowed through all loan programs. *Average indebtedness per student:* $27,322. *Average need-based loan:* Freshmen: $2069; Undergraduates: $3010. *Parent loans:* $4,093,912 (40% need-based, 60% non-need-based). *Programs:* Federal Direct (Subsidized and Unsubsidized Stafford, PLUS), Perkins, Federal Nursing.

WORK-STUDY *Federal work-study:* Total amount: $1,435,213; 723 jobs averaging $1973. *State or other work-study/employment:* Total amount: $1,793,083 (40% need-based, 60% non-need-based). 761 part-time jobs averaging $2356.

APPLYING FOR FINANCIAL AID *Required financial aid form:* FAFSA. *Financial aid deadline (priority):* 4/1. *Notification date:* Continuous beginning 3/15. Students must reply by 5/1 or within 4 weeks of notification.

CONTACT Mr. Michael Strite, Assistant Director of Financial Aid, Messiah College, PO Box 3006, One College Avenue, Grantham, PA 17027, 717-691-6007 or toll-free 800-233-4220. *Fax:* 717-796-4791. *E-mail:* mstrite@messiah.edu.

METHODIST COLLEGE
Fayetteville, NC

| Tuition & fees: $17,850 | Average undergraduate aid package: $15,822 |

ABOUT THE INSTITUTION Independent United Methodist, coed. Awards: associate, bachelor's, and master's degrees. 56 undergraduate majors. Total enrollment: 2,257. Undergraduates: 2,195. Freshmen: 518. Federal methodology is used as a basis for awarding need-based institutional aid.

UNDERGRADUATE EXPENSES for 2005–06 *Application fee:* $25. *Comprehensive fee:* $24,620 includes full-time tuition ($17,580), mandatory fees ($270), and room and board ($6770). Full-time tuition and fees vary according to class time. Room and board charges vary according to board plan and housing facility. *Part-time tuition:* $570 per semester hour. Part-time tuition and fees vary according to class time. *Payment plans:* Installment, deferred payment.

FRESHMAN FINANCIAL AID (Fall 2004) 410 applied for aid; of those 82% were deemed to have need. 100% of freshmen with need received aid; of those 62% had need fully met. *Average percent of need met:* 74% (excluding resources awarded to replace EFC). *Average financial aid package:* $13,990 (excluding resources awarded to replace EFC). 11% of all full-time freshmen had no need and received non-need-based gift aid.

UNDERGRADUATE FINANCIAL AID (Fall 2004) 1,441 applied for aid; of those 88% were deemed to have need. 100% of undergraduates with need received aid; of those 59% had need fully met. *Average percent of need met:* 73% (excluding resources awarded to replace EFC). *Average financial aid package:* $15,822 (excluding resources awarded to replace EFC). 9% of all full-time undergraduates had no need and received non-need-based gift aid.

GIFT AID (NEED-BASED) *Total amount:* $8,843,374 (21% federal, 14% state, 64% institutional, 1% external sources). *Receiving aid:* Freshmen: 77% (336); All full-time undergraduates: 73% (1,260). *Average award:* Freshmen: $7850; Undergraduates: $6679. *Scholarships, grants, and awards:* Federal Pell, FSEOG, state, private, college/university gift aid from institutional funds.

GIFT AID (NON-NEED-BASED) *Total amount:* $6,286,843 (33% federal, 26% state, 33% institutional, 8% external sources). *Receiving aid:* Freshmen: 57% (250); Undergraduates: 58% (1,001). *Average Award:* Freshmen: $3201; Undergraduates: $5929. *Scholarships, grants, and awards by category: Academic Interests/Achievement:* 556 awards ($2,782,303 total): English, general academic interests/achievements. *Creative Arts/Performance:* 125 awards ($88,600 total): debating, music, theater/drama. *Special Achievements/Activities:* 34 awards ($11,750 total): cheerleading/drum major, leadership. *Special Characteristics:* 328 awards ($556,089 total): children and siblings of alumni, children of faculty/staff, relatives of clergy, religious affiliation. *Tuition waivers:* Full or partial for employees or children of employees, senior citizens. *ROTC:* Army, Air Force cooperative.

LOANS *Student loans:* $8,626,679 (50% need-based, 50% non-need-based). 75% of past graduating class borrowed through all loan programs. *Average indebtedness per student:* $19,989. *Average need-based loan:* Freshmen: $2429; Undergraduates: $3505. *Parent loans:* $2,943,779 (100% non-need-based). *Programs:* FFEL (Subsidized and Unsubsidized Stafford, PLUS), Perkins.

WORK-STUDY *Federal work-study:* Total amount: $217,514; 504 jobs averaging $476. *State or other work-study/employment:* Total amount: $43,037 (100% non-need-based). 54 part-time jobs averaging $797.

APPLYING FOR FINANCIAL AID *Required financial aid form:* FAFSA. *Financial aid deadline:* Continuous. *Notification date:* Continuous beginning 3/6. Students must reply within 2 weeks of notification.

CONTACT Financial Aid Office, Methodist College, 5400 Ramsey Street, Fayetteville, NC 28311-1420, 910-630-7307 or toll-free 800-488-7110 Ext. 7027. *Fax:* 910-630-7285.

METROPOLITAN COLLEGE
Oklahoma City, OK

CONTACT Office of Financial Aid, Metropolitan College, 1900 Northwest Expressway, Suite R302, Oklahoma City, OK 73118, 405-843-1000. *Fax:* 405-843-2325.

METROPOLITAN COLLEGE
Tulsa, OK

CONTACT Office of Financial Aid, Metropolitan College, 10820 East 45th Street, Suite 101B, Tulsa, OK 74136, 918-627-9429. *Fax:* 918-627-2122.

METROPOLITAN COLLEGE OF COURT REPORTING
Phoenix, AZ

CONTACT Financial Aid Director, Metropolitan College of Court Reporting, 4640 East Elwood Street, #12, Phoenix, AZ 85040, 480-955-5900. *Fax:* 480-894-8999.

METROPOLITAN COLLEGE OF COURT REPORTING
Albuquerque, NM

CONTACT Director of Financial Aid, Metropolitan College of Court Reporting, 1717 Louisiana Boulevard NE, Suite 207, Albuquerque, NM 87110-7027, 505-888-3400. *Fax:* 505-254-3738.

METROPOLITAN COLLEGE OF NEW YORK
New York, NY

CONTACT Rosibel Gomez, Financial Aid Director, Metropolitan College of New York, 75 Varick Street, New York, NY 10013-1919, 212-343-1234 Ext. 5004 or toll-free 800-33-THINK Ext. 5001 (in-state). *Fax:* 212-343-7399.

METROPOLITAN STATE COLLEGE OF DENVER
Denver, CO

Tuition & fees (CO res): $2859 | **Average undergraduate aid package: $6234**

ABOUT THE INSTITUTION State-supported, coed. Awards: bachelor's degrees. 49 undergraduate majors. Total enrollment: 20,761. Undergraduates: 20,761. Freshmen: 2,490. Federal methodology is used as a basis for awarding need-based institutional aid.
UNDERGRADUATE EXPENSES for 2005–06 *Application fee:* $25. *Tuition, state resident:* full-time $2283. *Tuition, nonresident:* full-time $9366. Full-time tuition and fees vary according to course load and location. Part-time tuition and fees vary according to course load and location. *Payment plans:* Installment, deferred payment.
FRESHMAN FINANCIAL AID (Fall 2004) 924 applied for aid; of those 83% were deemed to have need. 100% of freshmen with need received aid; of those 1% had need fully met. *Average percent of need met:* 25% (excluding resources awarded to replace EFC). *Average financial aid package:* $4226 (excluding resources awarded to replace EFC). 1% of all full-time freshmen had no need and received non-need-based gift aid.
UNDERGRADUATE FINANCIAL AID (Fall 2004) 6,412 applied for aid; of those 84% were deemed to have need. 100% of undergraduates with need received aid; of those 4% had need fully met. *Average percent of need met:* 24% (excluding resources awarded to replace EFC). *Average financial aid package:* $6234 (excluding resources awarded to replace EFC). 1% of all full-time undergraduates had no need and received non-need-based gift aid.
GIFT AID (NEED-BASED) *Total amount:* $21,228,811 (67% federal, 21% state, 10% institutional, 2% external sources). *Receiving aid:* Freshmen: 29% (577); All full-time undergraduates: 31% (3,731). *Average award:* Freshmen: $3271; Undergraduates: $3814. *Scholarships, grants, and awards:* Federal Pell, FSEOG, state, private, college/university gift aid from institutional funds.
GIFT AID (NON-NEED-BASED) *Total amount:* $1,005,244 (5% federal, 29% state, 45% institutional, 21% external sources). *Receiving aid:* Freshmen: 1% (29); Undergraduates: 3% (322). *Average Award:* Freshmen: $1942; Undergraduates: $2368. *Scholarships, grants, and awards by category:* Academic Interests/Achievement: 1,317 awards ($1,632,596 total): biological sciences, business, communication, computer science, education, engineering/technologies, English, foreign languages, general academic interests/achievements, health fields, humanities, mathematics, physical sciences, social sciences. Creative Arts/Performance: 62 awards ($45,859 total): art/fine arts, music, theater/drama. Special Achievements/Activities: 52 awards ($100,690 total): general special achievements/activities. *Tuition waivers:* Full or partial for senior citizens. *ROTC:* Army cooperative, Air Force cooperative.
LOANS *Student loans:* $44,504,863 (87% need-based, 13% non-need-based). 56% of past graduating class borrowed through all loan programs. *Average indebtedness per student:* $10,902. *Average need-based loan:* Freshmen: $3536; Undergraduates: $6139. *Parent loans:* $821,296 (59% need-based, 41% non-need-based). *Programs:* FFEL (Subsidized and Unsubsidized Stafford, PLUS), Perkins.
WORK-STUDY *Federal work-study:* Total amount: $659,603; 157 jobs averaging $2866. *State or other work-study/employment:* Total amount: $396,730 (35% need-based, 65% non-need-based). 312 part-time jobs averaging $4045.
ATHLETIC AWARDS *Total amount:* $867,550 (29% need-based, 71% non-need-based).
APPLYING FOR FINANCIAL AID *Required financial aid form:* FAFSA. *Financial aid deadline:* Continuous. *Notification date:* Continuous beginning 4/1.
CONTACT Office of Financial Aid, Metropolitan State College of Denver, PO Box 173362, Denver, CO 80217-3362, 303-556-8593. *Fax:* 303-556-4927.

METROPOLITAN STATE UNIVERSITY
St. Paul, MN

CONTACT Mr. Michael Uran, Director of Financial Aid, Metropolitan State University, Founder's Hall, Room 105, 700 East 7th Street, St. Paul, MN 55106-5000, 651-793-1414. *E-mail:* finaid@metrostate.edu.

MIAMI INTERNATIONAL UNIVERSITY OF ART & DESIGN
Miami, FL

CONTACT Mitzie Forrest, Financial Aid Director, Miami International University of Art & Design, 1737 Bayshore Drive, Miami, FL 33132, 800-225-9023 Ext. 125 or toll-free 800-225-9023. *Fax:* 305-374-7946.

MIAMI UNIVERSITY
Oxford, OH

Tuition & fees (OH res): $21,487 | **Average undergraduate aid package: $15,665**

ABOUT THE INSTITUTION State-related, coed. Awards: associate, bachelor's, master's, and doctoral degrees and post-master's certificates. 112 undergraduate majors. Total enrollment: 16,338. Undergraduates: 14,643. Freshmen: 3,162. Federal methodology is used as a basis for awarding need-based institutional aid.
UNDERGRADUATE EXPENSES for 2005–06 *Application fee:* $45. *Tuition, state resident:* full-time $19,877. *Tuition, nonresident:* full-time $19,877. *College room and board:* $7610; *room only:* $3860. Room and board charges vary according to board plan and housing facility. Ohio residents receive a minimum of $10,000 in resident scholarships. *Payment plan:* Installment.
FRESHMAN FINANCIAL AID (Fall 2005, est.) 2178 applied for aid; of those 67% were deemed to have need. 99% of freshmen with need received aid; of those 36% had need fully met. *Average percent of need met:* 78% (excluding resources awarded to replace EFC). *Average financial aid package:* $16,255 (excluding resources awarded to replace EFC). 36% of all full-time freshmen had no need and received non-need-based gift aid.
UNDERGRADUATE FINANCIAL AID (Fall 2005, est.) 7,335 applied for aid; of those 79% were deemed to have need. 100% of undergraduates with need received aid; of those 29% had need fully met. *Average percent of need met:*

Miami University

75% (excluding resources awarded to replace EFC). *Average financial aid package:* $15,665 (excluding resources awarded to replace EFC). 40% of all full-time undergraduates had no need and received non-need-based gift aid.

GIFT AID (NEED-BASED) *Total amount:* $11,025,174 (40% federal, 9% state, 51% institutional). *Receiving aid:* Freshmen: 27% (854); All full-time undergraduates: 17% (2,497). *Average award:* Freshmen: $3056; Undergraduates: $4005. *Scholarships, grants, and awards:* Federal Pell, FSEOG, state, private, college/university gift aid from institutional funds.

GIFT AID (NON-NEED-BASED) *Total amount:* $140,235,005 (96% institutional, 4% external sources). *Receiving aid:* Freshmen: 43% (1,347); Undergraduates: 37% (5,293). *Average Award:* Freshmen: $10,901; Undergraduates: $11,606. *Scholarships, grants, and awards by category: Academic Interests/Achievement:* architecture, education, engineering/technologies, general academic interests/achievements. *Creative Arts/Performance:* art/fine arts, music, theater/drama. *Special Achievements/Activities:* general special achievements/activities, leadership. *Special Characteristics:* children of faculty/staff, local/state students, members of minority groups, out-of-state students. *Tuition waivers:* Full or partial for employees or children of employees. *ROTC:* Army cooperative, Naval, Air Force.

LOANS *Student loans:* $49,122,004 (34% need-based, 66% non-need-based). 48% of past graduating class borrowed through all loan programs. *Average indebtedness per student:* $21,522. *Average need-based loan:* Freshmen: $2790; Undergraduates: $3947. *Parent loans:* $16,989,543 (100% non-need-based). *Programs:* Federal Direct (Subsidized and Unsubsidized Stafford, PLUS), Perkins, Federal Nursing, college/university, bank alternative loans.

WORK-STUDY *Federal work-study:* Total amount: $1,485,964; 951 jobs averaging $1650.

ATHLETIC AWARDS Total amount: $5,931,951 (100% non-need-based).

APPLYING FOR FINANCIAL AID *Required financial aid form:* FAFSA. *Financial aid deadline (priority):* 2/15. *Notification date:* Continuous beginning 3/31. Students must reply by 5/1 or within 3 weeks of notification.

CONTACT Chuck Knepfle, Office of Student Financial Aid, Miami University, Campus Avenue Building, Oxford, OH 45056-3427, 513-529-8734. *Fax:* 513-529-8713. *E-mail:* financialaid@muohio.edu.

MICHIGAN JEWISH INSTITUTE
Oak Park, MI

CONTACT Financial Aid Office, Michigan Jewish Institute, 25401 Coolidge Highway, Oak Park, MI 48237-1304, 248-414-6900.

MICHIGAN STATE UNIVERSITY
East Lansing, MI

Tuition & fees (MI res): $7587 **Average undergraduate aid package:** $8468

ABOUT THE INSTITUTION State-supported, coed. Awards: bachelor's, master's, doctoral, and first professional degrees and post-master's certificates. 130 undergraduate majors. Total enrollment: 45,166. Undergraduates: 35,678. Freshmen: 7,485. Federal methodology is used as a basis for awarding need-based institutional aid.

UNDERGRADUATE EXPENSES for 2005–06 *Application fee:* $35. *Tuition, state resident:* full-time $6705; part-time $223.50 per credit. *Tuition, nonresident:* full-time $18,458; part-time $615.25 per credit. *Required fees:* full-time $882; $882 per year part-time. Full-time tuition and fees vary according to course load, degree level, program, and student level. Part-time tuition and fees vary according to course load, degree level, program, and student level. *College room and board:* $5744; *room only:* $2488. Room and board charges vary according to board plan and housing facility. *Payment plan:* Deferred payment.

FRESHMAN FINANCIAL AID (Fall 2005, est.) 4934 applied for aid; of those 63% were deemed to have need. 100% of freshmen with need received aid; of those 32% had need fully met. *Average percent of need met:* 78% (excluding resources awarded to replace EFC). *Average financial aid package:* $8892 (excluding resources awarded to replace EFC). 8% of all full-time freshmen had no need and received non-need-based gift aid.

UNDERGRADUATE FINANCIAL AID (Fall 2005, est.) 18,563 applied for aid; of those 69% were deemed to have need. 99% of undergraduates with need received aid; of those 27% had need fully met. *Average percent of need met:* 72% (excluding resources awarded to replace EFC). *Average financial aid package:* $8468 (excluding resources awarded to replace EFC). 7% of all full-time undergraduates had no need and received non-need-based gift aid.

GIFT AID (NEED-BASED) *Total amount:* $36,468,444 (52% federal, 48% institutional). *Receiving aid:* Freshmen: 23% (1,710); All full-time undergraduates: 25% (7,912). *Average award:* Freshmen: $4322; Undergraduates: $4167. *Scholarships, grants, and awards:* Federal Pell, FSEOG, state, private, college/university gift aid from institutional funds, United Negro College Fund, Federal Nursing.

GIFT AID (NON-NEED-BASED) *Total amount:* $71,424,186 (3% federal, 52% state, 29% institutional, 16% external sources). *Receiving aid:* Freshmen: 42% (3,062); Undergraduates: 30% (9,694). *Average Award:* Freshmen: $3779; Undergraduates: $3824. *Scholarships, grants, and awards by category: Academic Interests/Achievement:* agriculture, architecture, biological sciences, business, communication, computer science, education, engineering/technologies, English, foreign languages, general academic interests/achievements, health fields, international studies, mathematics, military science, physical sciences, social sciences. *Creative Arts/Performance:* creative writing, debating, journalism/publications, music, performing arts, theater/drama. *Special Achievements/Activities:* community service, hobbies/interests, junior miss, leadership, memberships, rodeo. *Special Characteristics:* children and siblings of alumni, children of faculty/staff, children of union members/company employees, ethnic background, first-generation college students, handicapped students, international students, local/state students, members of minority groups, out-of-state students, public servants, religious affiliation, spouses of deceased or disabled public servants, veterans, veterans' children. *Tuition waivers:* Full or partial for employees or children of employees. *ROTC:* Army, Air Force.

LOANS *Student loans:* $97,046,256 (47% need-based, 53% non-need-based). *Average indebtedness per student:* $21,037. *Average need-based loan:* Freshmen: $2748; Undergraduates: $3861. *Parent loans:* $46,126,985 (100% non-need-based). *Programs:* FFEL (Subsidized and Unsubsidized Stafford, PLUS), Perkins, Federal Nursing, state, college/university.

WORK-STUDY *Federal work-study:* Total amount: $2,823,617; 1,700 jobs averaging $1500. *State or other work-study/employment:* Total amount: $412,090 (100% need-based). 320 part-time jobs averaging $900.

ATHLETIC AWARDS Total amount: $6,805,197 (33% need-based, 67% non-need-based).

APPLYING FOR FINANCIAL AID *Required financial aid form:* FAFSA. *Financial aid deadline:* 6/30 (priority: 3/1). *Notification date:* Continuous beginning 3/15. Students must reply within 4 weeks of notification.

CONTACT Mr. Keith Williams, Associate Director, Michigan State University, 252 Student Services Building, East Lansing, MI 48824-1113, 517-353-5940. *Fax:* 517-432-1155. *E-mail:* willi398@msu.edu.

MICHIGAN TECHNOLOGICAL UNIVERSITY
Houghton, MI

Tuition & fees (MI res): $8194 **Average undergraduate aid package:** $9061

ABOUT THE INSTITUTION State-supported, coed. Awards: associate, bachelor's, master's, and doctoral degrees and post-bachelor's certificates. 88 undergraduate majors. Total enrollment: 6,510. Undergraduates: 5,614. Freshmen: 1,327. Federal methodology is used as a basis for awarding need-based institutional aid.

UNDERGRADUATE EXPENSES for 2005–06 *Application fee:* $40. *Tuition, state resident:* full-time $7560; part-time $252 per credit hour. *Tuition, nonresident:* full-time $18,750; part-time $625 per credit hour. *Required fees:* full-time $634; $316.86 per term part-time. Full-time tuition and fees vary according to course load, location, and program. Part-time tuition and fees vary according to course load, location, and program. *College room and board:* $6375; *room only:* $3120. Room and board charges vary according to board plan and housing facility. *Payment plans:* Installment, deferred payment.

FRESHMAN FINANCIAL AID (Fall 2004) 1022 applied for aid; of those 65% were deemed to have need. 99% of freshmen with need received aid; of those 36% had need fully met. *Average percent of need met:* 79% (excluding resources awarded to replace EFC). *Average financial aid package:* $9010 (excluding resources awarded to replace EFC). 41% of all full-time freshmen had no need and received non-need-based gift aid.

UNDERGRADUATE FINANCIAL AID (Fall 2004) 3,809 applied for aid; of those 76% were deemed to have need. 96% of undergraduates with need received aid; of those 39% had need fully met. *Average percent of need met:* 75% (excluding resources awarded to replace EFC). *Average financial aid package:* $9061 (excluding resources awarded to replace EFC). 35% of all full-time undergraduates had no need and received non-need-based gift aid.

GIFT AID (NEED-BASED) *Total amount:* $13,588,921 (24% federal, 17% state, 47% institutional, 12% external sources). *Receiving aid:* Freshmen: 48% (582); All full-time undergraduates: 43% (2,453). *Average award:* Freshmen: $5439; Undergraduates: $4847. *Scholarships, grants, and awards:* Federal Pell, FSEOG, state, private, college/university gift aid from institutional funds.
GIFT AID (NON-NEED-BASED) *Total amount:* $7,239,074 (10% state, 50% institutional, 40% external sources). *Receiving aid:* Freshmen: 41% (504); Undergraduates: 28% (1,573). *Average Award:* Freshmen: $2372; Undergraduates: $2179. *Scholarships, grants, and awards by category: Academic Interests/Achievement:* 1,069 awards ($1,441,922 total): biological sciences, business, communication, computer science, education, engineering/technologies, general academic interests/achievements, humanities, mathematics, physical sciences, premedicine, social sciences. *Special Achievements/Activities:* 25 awards ($10,000 total): leadership. *Special Characteristics:* 2,357 awards ($7,381,737 total): children and siblings of alumni, children of faculty/staff, ethnic background, general special characteristics, international students, local/state students, members of minority groups, out-of-state students, previous college experience. *Tuition waivers:* Full or partial for children of alumni, employees or children of employees, senior citizens. *ROTC:* Army, Air Force.
LOANS *Student loans:* $18,491,909 (79% need-based, 21% non-need-based). 59% of past graduating class borrowed through all loan programs. *Average indebtedness per student:* $17,000. *Average need-based loan:* Freshmen: $3369; Undergraduates: $4374. *Parent loans:* $2,869,630 (58% need-based, 42% non-need-based). *Programs:* Federal Direct (Subsidized and Unsubsidized Stafford, PLUS), Perkins, state, college/university, external private loans.
WORK-STUDY *Federal work-study:* Total amount: $306,788; 231 jobs averaging $1407. *State or other work-study/employment:* Total amount: $3,857,165 (2% need-based, 98% non-need-based). 2,491 part-time jobs averaging $1550.
ATHLETIC AWARDS *Total amount:* $1,597,860 (26% need-based, 74% non-need-based).
APPLYING FOR FINANCIAL AID *Required financial aid form:* FAFSA. *Financial aid deadline (priority):* 2/18. *Notification date:* Continuous beginning 3/1. Students must reply within 4 weeks of notification.
CONTACT Adrene Remali, Manager of Information Systems, Michigan Technological University, 1400 Townsend Drive, Houghton, MI 49931-1295, 906-487-3222 or toll-free 888-MTU-1885. *Fax:* 906-487-3042. *E-mail:* adrene@mtu.edu.

MID-AMERICA CHRISTIAN UNIVERSITY
Oklahoma City, OK

CONTACT Mr. Todd Martin, Director of Financial Aid, Mid-America Christian University, 3500 Southwest 119th Street, Oklahoma City, OK 73170-4504, 405-691-3800. *Fax:* 405-692-3165. *E-mail:* tmartin@mabc.edu.

MIDAMERICA NAZARENE UNIVERSITY
Olathe, KS

Tuition & fees: $15,968	Average undergraduate aid package: $10,028

ABOUT THE INSTITUTION Independent religious, coed. Awards: associate, bachelor's, and master's degrees. 40 undergraduate majors. Total enrollment: 1,779. Undergraduates: 1,357. Freshmen: 216. Federal methodology is used as a basis for awarding need-based institutional aid.
UNDERGRADUATE EXPENSES for 2006-07 *Application fee:* $25. *Comprehensive fee:* $21,798 includes full-time tuition ($14,968), mandatory fees ($1000), and room and board ($5830). *Part-time tuition:* $500 per semester hour. *Part-time fees:* $500 per term.
FRESHMAN FINANCIAL AID (Fall 2005, est.) 196 applied for aid; of those 85% were deemed to have need. 100% of freshmen with need received aid; of those 2% had need fully met. *Average percent of need met:* 62% (excluding resources awarded to replace EFC). *Average financial aid package:* $10,620 (excluding resources awarded to replace EFC). 19% of all full-time freshmen had no need and received non-need-based gift aid.
UNDERGRADUATE FINANCIAL AID (Fall 2005, est.) 978 applied for aid; of those 86% were deemed to have need. 100% of undergraduates with need received aid; of those 1% had need fully met. *Average percent of need met:* 60% (excluding resources awarded to replace EFC). *Average financial aid package:* $10,028 (excluding resources awarded to replace EFC). 15% of all full-time undergraduates had no need and received non-need-based gift aid.

GIFT AID (NEED-BASED) *Total amount:* $3,712,079 (28% federal, 15% state, 51% institutional, 6% external sources). *Receiving aid:* Freshmen: 77% (165); All full-time undergraduates: 61% (732). *Average award:* Freshmen: $7247; Undergraduates: $6260. *Scholarships, grants, and awards:* Federal Pell, FSEOG, state, private, college/university gift aid from institutional funds.
GIFT AID (NON-NEED-BASED) *Total amount:* $664,395 (89% institutional, 11% external sources). *Receiving aid:* Freshmen: 7% (16); Undergraduates: 4% (49). *Average Award:* Freshmen: $2695; Undergraduates: $2921. *Scholarships, grants, and awards by category: Academic Interests/Achievement:* agriculture, general academic interests/achievements, health fields. *Creative Arts/Performance:* cinema/film/broadcasting, music. *Special Achievements/Activities:* cheerleading/drum major, leadership. *Special Characteristics:* children of faculty/staff, general special characteristics, relatives of clergy, religious affiliation. *ROTC:* Army cooperative, Air Force cooperative.
LOANS *Student loans:* $7,826,319 (49% need-based, 51% non-need-based). 80% of past graduating class borrowed through all loan programs. *Average indebtedness per student:* $19,222. *Average need-based loan:* Freshmen: $4149; Undergraduates: $5861. *Parent loans:* $865,362 (30% need-based, 70% non-need-based). *Programs:* FFEL (Subsidized and Unsubsidized Stafford, PLUS), Perkins, Federal Nursing.
WORK-STUDY *Federal work-study:* Total amount: $19,650; jobs available.
ATHLETIC AWARDS *Total amount:* $1,513,044 (47% need-based, 53% non-need-based).
APPLYING FOR FINANCIAL AID *Required financial aid forms:* FAFSA, institution's own form. *Financial aid deadline (priority):* 3/1. *Notification date:* Continuous. Students must reply within 2 weeks of notification.
CONTACT Rhonda L. Cole, Director of Student Financial Services, MidAmerica Nazarene University, 2030 East College Way, Olathe, KS 66062-1899, 913-791-3298 or toll-free 800-800-8887. *Fax:* 913-791-3482. *E-mail:* rcole@mnu.edu.

MID-CONTINENT UNIVERSITY
Mayfield, KY

ABOUT THE INSTITUTION Independent Southern Baptist, coed. Awards: associate and bachelor's degrees. 13 undergraduate majors. Total enrollment: 649. Undergraduates: 649. Freshmen: 164.
GIFT AID (NEED-BASED) *Scholarships, grants, and awards:* Federal Pell, FSEOG, state, private, college/university gift aid from institutional funds.
GIFT AID (NON-NEED-BASED) *Scholarships, grants, and awards by category: Academic Interests/Achievement:* education, English, general academic interests/achievements, humanities, religion/biblical studies, social sciences. *Special Characteristics:* children and siblings of alumni, children of faculty/staff, children of union members/company employees, married students, relatives of clergy.
LOANS *Programs:* Federal Direct (Subsidized and Unsubsidized Stafford, PLUS), FFEL (Subsidized and Unsubsidized Stafford, PLUS).
WORK-STUDY *Federal work-study:* Total amount: $53,445; 40 jobs averaging $1650. *State or other work-study/employment:* Part-time jobs available.
APPLYING FOR FINANCIAL AID *Required financial aid forms:* FAFSA, institution's own form.
CONTACT Kent Youngblood, Director of Financial Aid, Mid-Continent University, 99 Powell Road East, Mayfield, KY 42066, 270-251-9400 Ext. 260. *Fax:* 270-251-9475. *E-mail:* kyoungblood@midcontinent.edu.

MIDDLEBURY COLLEGE
Middlebury, VT

Comprehensive fee: $42,120	Average undergraduate aid package: $27,354

ABOUT THE INSTITUTION Independent, coed. Awards: bachelor's, master's, and doctoral degrees. 44 undergraduate majors. Total enrollment: 2,455. Undergraduates: 2,455. Freshmen: 553. Both federal and institutional methodology are used as a basis for awarding need-based institutional aid.
UNDERGRADUATE EXPENSES for 2005-06 *Application fee:* $55. *Comprehensive fee:* $42,120. *Payment plan:* Tuition prepayment.
FRESHMAN FINANCIAL AID (Fall 2004) 318 applied for aid; of those 81% were deemed to have need. 100% of freshmen with need received aid; of those 100% had need fully met. *Average percent of need met:* 100% (excluding resources awarded to replace EFC). *Average financial aid package:* $26,032 (excluding resources awarded to replace EFC).

Middlebury College

UNDERGRADUATE FINANCIAL AID (Fall 2004) 1,144 applied for aid; of those 88% were deemed to have need. 100% of undergraduates with need received aid; of those 100% had need fully met. *Average percent of need met:* 100% (excluding resources awarded to replace EFC). *Average financial aid package:* $27,354 (excluding resources awarded to replace EFC).
GIFT AID (NEED-BASED) *Total amount:* $28,384,522 (4% federal, 1% state, 91% institutional, 4% external sources). *Receiving aid:* Freshmen: 45% (257); All full-time undergraduates: 43% (1,011). *Average award:* Freshmen: $24,002; Undergraduates: $24,468. *Scholarships, grants, and awards:* Federal Pell, FSEOG, state, private, college/university gift aid from institutional funds.
GIFT AID (NON-NEED-BASED) *Tuition waivers:* Full or partial for employees or children of employees. *ROTC:* Army cooperative.
LOANS *Student loans:* $5,297,188 (70% need-based, 30% non-need-based). *Average need-based loan:* Freshmen: $3411; Undergraduates: $4011. *Parent loans:* $6,786,902 (100% non-need-based). *Programs:* Federal Direct (Subsidized and Unsubsidized Stafford, PLUS), Perkins, college/university.
WORK-STUDY *Federal work-study:* Total amount: $304,265; jobs available. *State or other work-study/employment:* Total amount: $1,032,168 (100% need-based). Part-time jobs available.
APPLYING FOR FINANCIAL AID *Required financial aid forms:* FAFSA, CSS Financial Aid PROFILE, noncustodial (divorced/separated) parent's statement, business/farm supplement, federal income tax return. *Financial aid deadline (priority):* 12/31. *Notification date:* 4/1. Students must reply by 5/1.
CONTACT Marguerite Corbin, Financial Aid Assistant, Middlebury College, Emma Willard House, Middlebury, VT 05753, 802-443-5158. *E-mail:* financialaid@middlebury.edu.

MIDDLE TENNESSEE STATE UNIVERSITY
Murfreesboro, TN

Tuition & fees (TN res): $4600   **Average undergraduate aid package:** $5593

ABOUT THE INSTITUTION State-supported, coed. Awards: bachelor's, master's, and doctoral degrees and post-bachelor's and post-master's certificates. 61 undergraduate majors. Total enrollment: 22,554. Undergraduates: 20,389. Freshmen: 3,208. Federal methodology is used as a basis for awarding need-based institutional aid.
UNDERGRADUATE EXPENSES for 2005–06 *Application fee:* $25. *Tuition, state resident:* full-time $3678; part-time $161 per semester hour. *Tuition, nonresident:* full-time $12,990; part-time $565 per semester hour. Part-time tuition and fees vary according to course load. *College room and board:* $5626; *room only:* $3478. Room and board charges vary according to board plan and housing facility. *Payment plan:* Deferred payment.
FRESHMAN FINANCIAL AID (Fall 2005, est.) 3130 applied for aid; of those 60% were deemed to have need. 98% of freshmen with need received aid; of those 58% had need fully met. *Average percent of need met:* 81% (excluding resources awarded to replace EFC). *Average financial aid package:* $7311 (excluding resources awarded to replace EFC). 35% of all full-time freshmen had no need and received non-need-based gift aid.
UNDERGRADUATE FINANCIAL AID (Fall 2005, est.) 13,686 applied for aid; of those 62% were deemed to have need. 97% of undergraduates with need received aid; of those 68% had need fully met. *Average percent of need met:* 77% (excluding resources awarded to replace EFC). *Average financial aid package:* $5593 (excluding resources awarded to replace EFC). 21% of all full-time undergraduates had no need and received non-need-based gift aid.
GIFT AID (NEED-BASED) *Total amount:* $21,417,121 (74% federal, 19% state, 7% external sources). *Receiving aid:* Freshmen: 31% (1,009); All full-time undergraduates: 27% (4,598). *Average award:* Freshmen: $2647; Undergraduates: $1905. *Scholarships, grants, and awards:* Federal Pell, FSEOG, state, private, college/university gift aid from institutional funds, Federal Nursing.
GIFT AID (NON-NEED-BASED) *Total amount:* $24,920,690 (64% state, 21% institutional, 15% external sources). *Receiving aid:* Freshmen: 43% (1,394); Undergraduates: 20% (3,537). *Average Award:* Freshmen: $4816; Undergraduates: $2948. *Scholarships, grants, and awards by category:* Academic Interests/Achievement: 1,924 awards ($5,153,519 total): agriculture, biological sciences, business, communication, computer science, education, engineering/technologies, English, foreign languages, general academic interests/achievements, health fields, home economics, humanities, international studies, mathematics, military science, physical sciences, premedicine, social sciences. *Creative Arts/Performance:* 538 awards ($354,804 total): dance, debating, journalism/publications, music, theater/drama. *Special Achievements/Activities:* 88 awards ($227,108 total): cheerleading/drum major, general special achievements/activities, leadership. *Special Characteristics:* 710 awards ($1,429,335 total): adult students, local/state students, members of minority groups. *Tuition waivers:* Full or partial for employees or children of employees, senior citizens. *ROTC:* Army, Air Force cooperative.
LOANS *Student loans:* $54,480,997 (100% need-based). 7% of past graduating class borrowed through all loan programs. *Average indebtedness per student:* $20,438. *Average need-based loan:* Freshmen: $1815; Undergraduates: $5396. *Parent loans:* $8,174,855 (100% non-need-based). *Programs:* FFEL (Subsidized and Unsubsidized Stafford, PLUS), Perkins, college/university.
WORK-STUDY *Federal work-study:* Total amount: $699,683; 283 jobs averaging $2472.
ATHLETIC AWARDS *Total amount:* $4,338,128 (100% non-need-based).
APPLYING FOR FINANCIAL AID *Required financial aid form:* FAFSA. *Financial aid deadline (priority):* 5/15. *Notification date:* Continuous beginning 4/15. Students must reply within 2 weeks of notification.
CONTACT David Hutton, Financial Aid Director, Middle Tennessee State University, 218 Cope Administration Building, Murfreesboro, TN 37132, 615-898-2830 or toll-free 800-331-MTSU (in-state), 800-433-MTSU (out-of-state). *Fax:* 615-898-5167.

MIDLAND LUTHERAN COLLEGE
Fremont, NE

Tuition & fees: $19,510   **Average undergraduate aid package:** $15,639

ABOUT THE INSTITUTION Independent Lutheran, coed. Awards: associate and bachelor's degrees. 57 undergraduate majors. Total enrollment: 909. Undergraduates: 909. Freshmen: 249. Both federal and institutional methodology are used as a basis for awarding need-based institutional aid.
UNDERGRADUATE EXPENSES for 2006–07 *Application fee:* $30. *Comprehensive fee:* $24,460 includes full-time tuition ($19,510) and room and board ($4950). *College room only:* $2190.
FRESHMAN FINANCIAL AID (Fall 2004) 246 applied for aid; of those 90% were deemed to have need. 100% of freshmen with need received aid; of those 32% had need fully met. *Average percent of need met:* 89% (excluding resources awarded to replace EFC). *Average financial aid package:* $15,059 (excluding resources awarded to replace EFC). 4% of all full-time freshmen had no need and received non-need-based gift aid.
UNDERGRADUATE FINANCIAL AID (Fall 2004) 856 applied for aid; of those 91% were deemed to have need. 100% of undergraduates with need received aid; of those 47% had need fully met. *Average percent of need met:* 95% (excluding resources awarded to replace EFC). *Average financial aid package:* $15,639 (excluding resources awarded to replace EFC). 6% of all full-time undergraduates had no need and received non-need-based gift aid.
GIFT AID (NEED-BASED) *Total amount:* $2,136,095 (56% federal, 10% state, 34% institutional). *Receiving aid:* Freshmen: 87% (222); All full-time undergraduates: 84% (775). *Average award:* Freshmen: $9746; Undergraduates: $9311. *Scholarships, grants, and awards:* Federal Pell, FSEOG, state, private, college/university gift aid from institutional funds.
GIFT AID (NON-NEED-BASED) *Total amount:* $486,517 (29% institutional, 71% external sources). *Average Award:* Freshmen: $8550; Undergraduates: $8083. *Scholarships, grants, and awards by category:* Academic Interests/Achievement: general academic interests/achievements. *Creative Arts/Performance:* art/fine arts, debating, journalism/publications, music, theater/drama. *Special Achievements/Activities:* community service, general special achievements/activities, leadership, religious involvement. *Special Characteristics:* children and siblings of alumni, handicapped students, international students, members of minority groups, religious affiliation, siblings of current students.
LOANS *Student loans:* $4,685,760 (87% need-based, 13% non-need-based). 87% of past graduating class borrowed through all loan programs. *Average indebtedness per student:* $19,698. *Average need-based loan:* Freshmen: $4991; Undergraduates: $6038. *Parent loans:* $1,335,113 (100% non-need-based). *Programs:* FFEL (Subsidized and Unsubsidized Stafford, PLUS), Perkins, college/university.
WORK-STUDY *Federal work-study:* Total amount: $178,741; 196 jobs averaging $904. *State or other work-study/employment:* Total amount: $206,437 (100% non-need-based). 139 part-time jobs averaging $1480.

ATHLETIC AWARDS *Total amount:* $1,938,336 (78% need-based, 22% non-need-based).
APPLYING FOR FINANCIAL AID *Required financial aid form:* FAFSA. *Financial aid deadline:* Continuous. *Notification date:* Continuous beginning 3/1. Students must reply within 2 weeks of notification.
CONTACT Mr. Doug G. Watson, Associate Vice President, Midland Lutheran College, 900 North Clarkson Street, Fremont, NE 68025-4200, 402-721-5480 Ext. 6521 or toll-free 800-642-8382 Ext. 6501. *Fax:* 402-721-6513. *E-mail:* watson@mlc.edu.

MIDSTATE COLLEGE
Peoria, IL

CONTACT Janet Ozuna, Director of Financial Aid/Business Manager, Midstate College, 411 West Northmoor Road, Peoria, IL 61614, 309-692-4092. *Fax:* 309-692-3893.

MIDWAY COLLEGE
Midway, KY

Tuition & fees: $13,950 **Average undergraduate aid package: $12,196**

ABOUT THE INSTITUTION Independent religious, women only. Awards: associate and bachelor's degrees. 20 undergraduate majors. Total enrollment: 1,279. Undergraduates: 1,279. Freshmen: 159. Federal methodology is used as a basis for awarding need-based institutional aid.
UNDERGRADUATE EXPENSES for 2005–06 *Application fee:* $25. *Comprehensive fee:* $20,150 includes full-time tuition ($13,800), mandatory fees ($150), and room and board ($6200). *College room only:* $3000. Full-time tuition and fees vary according to class time, location, and program. Room and board charges vary according to board plan and housing facility. *Part-time tuition:* $460 per semester hour. Part-time tuition and fees vary according to class time, location, and program. *Payment plan:* Deferred payment.
FRESHMAN FINANCIAL AID (Fall 2004) 116 applied for aid; of those 91% were deemed to have need. 100% of freshmen with need received aid; of those 21% had need fully met. *Average percent of need met:* 57% (excluding resources awarded to replace EFC). *Average financial aid package:* $12,678 (excluding resources awarded to replace EFC). 2% of all full-time freshmen had no need and received non-need-based gift aid.
UNDERGRADUATE FINANCIAL AID (Fall 2004) 771 applied for aid; of those 91% were deemed to have need. 100% of undergraduates with need received aid; of those 26% had need fully met. *Average percent of need met:* 59% (excluding resources awarded to replace EFC). *Average financial aid package:* $12,196 (excluding resources awarded to replace EFC). 1% of all full-time undergraduates had no need and received non-need-based gift aid.
GIFT AID (NEED-BASED) *Total amount:* $4,689,803 (31% federal, 43% state, 14% institutional, 12% external sources). *Receiving aid:* Freshmen: 79% (102); All full-time undergraduates: 75% (658). *Average award:* Freshmen: $6530; Undergraduates: $5792. *Scholarships, grants, and awards:* Federal Pell, FSEOG, state, private, college/university gift aid from institutional funds.
GIFT AID (NON-NEED-BASED) *Total amount:* $335,271 (28% institutional, 72% external sources). *Receiving aid:* Freshmen: 6% (8); Undergraduates: 7% (60). *Average Award:* Freshmen: $2417; Undergraduates: $3756. *Scholarships, grants, and awards by category:* Academic Interests/Achievement: agriculture, business, general academic interests/achievements, health fields, premedicine. Creative Arts/Performance: art/fine arts, music. Special Achievements/Activities: general special achievements/activities, junior miss, leadership, religious involvement. Special Characteristics: children and siblings of alumni, children of faculty/staff, members of minority groups, relatives of clergy, religious affiliation, veterans. *Tuition waivers:* Full or partial for employees or children of employees, senior citizens. *ROTC:* Army cooperative.
LOANS *Student loans:* $5,162,351 (91% need-based, 9% non-need-based). 80% of past graduating class borrowed through all loan programs. *Average indebtedness per student:* $15,407. *Average need-based loan:* Freshmen: $2475; Undergraduates: $3658. *Parent loans:* $838,581 (87% need-based, 13% non-need-based). *Programs:* FFEL (Subsidized and Unsubsidized Stafford, PLUS), Perkins, college/university.
WORK-STUDY *Federal work-study:* Total amount: $158,491; 113 jobs averaging $1372. *State or other work-study/employment:* Part-time jobs available.

ATHLETIC AWARDS *Total amount:* $286,923 (97% need-based, 3% non-need-based).
APPLYING FOR FINANCIAL AID *Required financial aid forms:* FAFSA, institution's own form. *Financial aid deadline (priority):* 3/15. *Notification date:* Continuous. Students must reply within 4 weeks of notification.
CONTACT Katie Valentine, Director of Financial Aid, Midway College, 512 East Stephens Street, Midway, KY 40347-1120, 859-846-5410 or toll-free 800-755-0031. *Fax:* 859-846-5751. *E-mail:* kvalentine@midway.edu.

MIDWESTERN STATE UNIVERSITY
Wichita Falls, TX

Tuition & fees (TX res): $4566 **Average undergraduate aid package: $6459**

ABOUT THE INSTITUTION State-supported, coed. Awards: associate, bachelor's, and master's degrees and post-bachelor's certificates. 58 undergraduate majors. Total enrollment: 6,279. Undergraduates: 5,544. Freshmen: 875. Federal methodology is used as a basis for awarding need-based institutional aid.
UNDERGRADUATE EXPENSES for 2006–07 *Application fee:* $25. *Tuition, state resident:* full-time $1500; part-time $50 per credit hour. *Tuition, nonresident:* full-time $9750; part-time $325 per credit hour. *College room and board:* $5220; *room only:* $2660.
FRESHMAN FINANCIAL AID (Fall 2005, est.) 100% of freshmen with need received aid; of those 20% had need fully met. *Average percent of need met:* 70% (excluding resources awarded to replace EFC). *Average financial aid package:* $6215 (excluding resources awarded to replace EFC). 24% of all full-time freshmen had no need and received non-need-based gift aid.
UNDERGRADUATE FINANCIAL AID (Fall 2005, est.) 99% of undergraduates with need received aid; of those 20% had need fully met. *Average percent of need met:* 70% (excluding resources awarded to replace EFC). *Average financial aid package:* $6459 (excluding resources awarded to replace EFC). 21% of all full-time undergraduates had no need and received non-need-based gift aid.
GIFT AID (NEED-BASED) *Total amount:* $7,267,279 (60% federal, 29% state, 7% institutional, 4% external sources). *Receiving aid:* Freshmen: 41% (348); All full-time undergraduates: 40% (1,611). *Average award:* Freshmen: $4414; Undergraduates: $4038. *Scholarships, grants, and awards:* Federal Pell, FSEOG, state, private, college/university gift aid from institutional funds.
GIFT AID (NON-NEED-BASED) *Total amount:* $1,110,738 (21% federal, 3% state, 73% institutional, 3% external sources). *Receiving aid:* Freshmen: 1% (7); Undergraduates: 1% (27). *Average Award:* Freshmen: $1489; Undergraduates: $1472. *Scholarships, grants, and awards by category:* Academic Interests/Achievement: business, computer science, education, English, general academic interests/achievements, health fields, mathematics, social sciences. Creative Arts/Performance: art/fine arts, general creative arts/performance, music, theater/drama. Special Achievements/Activities: cheerleading/drum major, general special achievements/activities, leadership, memberships. Special Characteristics: children of faculty/staff, general special characteristics, handicapped students, international students, out-of-state students, veterans. *ROTC:* Air Force cooperative.
LOANS *Student loans:* $12,576,460 (70% need-based, 30% non-need-based). 46% of past graduating class borrowed through all loan programs. *Average indebtedness per student:* $16,041. *Average need-based loan:* Freshmen: $2526; Undergraduates: $3304. *Parent loans:* $2,912,860 (33% need-based, 67% non-need-based). *Programs:* Federal Direct (Subsidized and Unsubsidized Stafford, PLUS), FFEL (Subsidized and Unsubsidized Stafford, PLUS), Perkins, state, college/university.
WORK-STUDY *Federal work-study:* Total amount: $130,110; 47 jobs averaging $2768. *State or other work-study/employment:* Total amount: $45,955 (100% need-based). 20 part-time jobs averaging $2298.
ATHLETIC AWARDS *Total amount:* $419,106 (31% need-based, 69% non-need-based).
APPLYING FOR FINANCIAL AID *Required financial aid forms:* FAFSA, institution's own form. *Financial aid deadline (priority):* 5/1. *Notification date:* Continuous.
CONTACT Ms. Kathy Pennartz, Director of Financial Aid, Midwestern State University, 3410 Taft Boulevard, Wichita Falls, TX 76308-2099, 940-397-4214 or toll-free 800-842-1922. *Fax:* 940-397-4852. *E-mail:* financial-aid@mwsu.edu.

Midwestern University, Glendale Campus

MIDWESTERN UNIVERSITY, GLENDALE CAMPUS
Glendale, AZ

| Tuition & fees: $15,556 | Average undergraduate aid package: $9257 |

ABOUT THE INSTITUTION Independent, coed. Awards: bachelor's, master's, and doctoral degrees and post-bachelor's certificates. 1 undergraduate major. Total enrollment: 1,117. Undergraduates: 20. Federal methodology is used as a basis for awarding need-based institutional aid.
UNDERGRADUATE EXPENSES for 2005–06 *Comprehensive fee:* $24,341 includes full-time tuition ($15,306), mandatory fees ($250), and room and board ($8785). *College room only:* $5670.
UNDERGRADUATE FINANCIAL AID (Fall 2005, est.) 114 applied for aid; of those 95% were deemed to have need. 100% of undergraduates with need received aid; of those 1% had need fully met. *Average percent of need met:* 32% (excluding resources awarded to replace EFC). *Average financial aid package:* $9257 (excluding resources awarded to replace EFC).
GIFT AID (NEED-BASED) *Total amount:* $220,830 (92% federal, 3% state, 1% institutional, 4% external sources). *Receiving aid:* All full-time undergraduates: 41% (49). *Average award:* Undergraduates: $1647. *Scholarships, grants, and awards:* Federal Pell, FSEOG, state, private, college/university gift aid from institutional funds.
GIFT AID (NON-NEED-BASED) *Total amount:* $162,083 (47% federal, 50% state, 3% institutional). *Receiving aid:* Undergraduates: 14% (17). *Scholarships, grants, and awards by category:* Academic Interests/Achievement: 1 award ($5000 total): health fields.
LOANS *Student loans:* $2,496,892 (23% need-based, 77% non-need-based). 95% of past graduating class borrowed through all loan programs. *Average indebtedness per student:* $51,174. *Average need-based loan:* Undergraduates: $4964. *Parent loans:* $53,450 (100% non-need-based). *Programs:* FFEL (Subsidized and Unsubsidized Stafford, PLUS), Perkins, alternative loans.
WORK-STUDY *Federal work-study:* Total amount: $33,411; 21 jobs averaging $3530.
APPLYING FOR FINANCIAL AID *Required financial aid forms:* FAFSA, institution's own form. *Financial aid deadline:* Continuous. *Notification date:* Continuous beginning 6/1. Students must reply within 2 weeks of notification.
CONTACT Lynette Whitcomb, Administrative Assistant, Office of Student Financial Services, Midwestern University, Glendale Campus, 19555 North 59th Avenue, Glendale, AZ 85308, 623-572-3321 or toll-free 888-247-9277 (in-state), 888-247-9271 (out-of-state). Fax: 623-572-3283. E-mail: az_fin_aid@arizona.midwestern.edu.

MIDWIVES COLLEGE OF UTAH
Orem, UT

CONTACT Financial Aid Office, Midwives College of Utah, 560 South State Street, Suite B2, Orem, UT 84058, 801-764-9068 or toll-free 866-764-9068.

MILES COLLEGE
Fairfield, AL

CONTACT P. N. Lanier, Financial Aid Administrator, Miles College, PO Box 3800, Birmingham, AL 35208, 205-929-1663 or toll-free 800-445-0708. Fax: 205-929-1668. E-mail: pnlani@netscape.net.

MILLERSVILLE UNIVERSITY OF PENNSYLVANIA
Millersville, PA

| Tuition & fees (PA res): $6235 | Average undergraduate aid package: $6620 |

ABOUT THE INSTITUTION State-supported, coed. Awards: associate, bachelor's, and master's degrees and post-bachelor's and post-master's certificates. 48 undergraduate majors. Total enrollment: 7,998. Undergraduates: 6,991. Freshmen: 1,409. Federal methodology is used as a basis for awarding need-based institutional aid.
UNDERGRADUATE EXPENSES for 2005–06 *Application fee:* $35. *Tuition, state resident:* full-time $4906; part-time $204 per credit. *Tuition, nonresident:* full-time $12,266; part-time $511 per credit. *Required fees:* full-time $1329; $81 per credit. Part-time tuition and fees vary according to course load. *College room and board:* $5878; *room only:* $3474. Room and board charges vary according to board plan. *Payment plan:* Installment.
FRESHMAN FINANCIAL AID (Fall 2004) 1206 applied for aid; of those 68% were deemed to have need. 97% of freshmen with need received aid; of those 12% had need fully met. *Average percent of need met:* 72% (excluding resources awarded to replace EFC). *Average financial aid package:* $6581 (excluding resources awarded to replace EFC). 2% of all full-time freshmen had no need and received non-need-based gift aid.
UNDERGRADUATE FINANCIAL AID (Fall 2004) 4,795 applied for aid; of those 71% were deemed to have need. 98% of undergraduates with need received aid; of those 21% had need fully met. *Average percent of need met:* 79% (excluding resources awarded to replace EFC). *Average financial aid package:* $6620 (excluding resources awarded to replace EFC). 3% of all full-time undergraduates had no need and received non-need-based gift aid.
GIFT AID (NEED-BASED) *Total amount:* $12,367,053 (92% federal, 5% institutional, 3% external sources). *Receiving aid:* Freshmen: 47% (656); All full-time undergraduates: 39% (2,475). *Average award:* Freshmen: $4380; Undergraduates: $3910. *Scholarships, grants, and awards:* Federal Pell, FSEOG, state, private, college/university gift aid from institutional funds, SICO Scholarships.
GIFT AID (NON-NEED-BASED) *Total amount:* $2,426,889 (16% state, 35% institutional, 49% external sources). *Receiving aid:* Freshmen: 14% (193); Undergraduates: 9% (550). *Average Award:* Freshmen: $2301; Undergraduates: $2432. *Scholarships, grants, and awards by category:* Academic Interests/Achievement: 385 awards ($896,492 total): biological sciences, business, communication, computer science, education, English, foreign languages, general academic interests/achievements, health fields, humanities, mathematics, physical sciences, social sciences. Creative Arts/Performance: 23 awards ($16,123 total): art/fine arts, music. Special Achievements/Activities: 2 awards ($2100 total): community service. Special Characteristics: 126 awards ($514,894 total): children of union members/company employees, international students. *Tuition waivers:* Full or partial for employees or children of employees, senior citizens. *ROTC:* Army.
LOANS *Student loans:* $21,369,253 (51% need-based, 49% non-need-based). 62% of past graduating class borrowed through all loan programs. *Average indebtedness per student:* $16,103. *Average need-based loan:* Freshmen: $2515; Undergraduates: $3557. *Parent loans:* $4,037,473 (100% non-need-based). *Programs:* FFEL (Subsidized and Unsubsidized Stafford, PLUS), Perkins, college/university.
WORK-STUDY *Federal work-study:* Total amount: $352,911; 420 jobs averaging $840. *State or other work-study/employment:* Total amount: $2,069,074 (100% non-need-based). 1,830 part-time jobs averaging $1129.
ATHLETIC AWARDS *Total amount:* $279,480 (23% need-based, 77% non-need-based).
APPLYING FOR FINANCIAL AID *Required financial aid form:* FAFSA. *Financial aid deadline:* 3/15. *Notification date:* Continuous beginning 3/19. Students must reply within 2 weeks of notification.
CONTACT Mr. Dwight Horsey, Director of Financial Aid, Millersville University of Pennsylvania, PO Box 1002, Millersville, PA 17551-0302, 717-872-3026 or toll-free 800-MU-ADMIT (out-of-state). Fax: 717-871-2248. E-mail: dwight.horsey@millersville.edu.

MILLIGAN COLLEGE
Milligan College, TN

| Tuition & fees: $17,240 | Average undergraduate aid package: $10,895 |

ABOUT THE INSTITUTION Independent Christian, coed. Awards: bachelor's and master's degrees. 26 undergraduate majors. Total enrollment: 954. Undergraduates: 753. Freshmen: 168. Federal methodology is used as a basis for awarding need-based institutional aid.
UNDERGRADUATE EXPENSES for 2005–06 *Application fee:* $30. *Comprehensive fee:* $21,990 includes full-time tuition ($16,730), mandatory fees ($510), and room and board ($4750). *College room only:* $2350. Room and board charges vary according to board plan and housing facility. *Part-time tuition:* $290 per credit. Part-time tuition and fees vary according to course load. *Payment plan:* Installment.

FRESHMAN FINANCIAL AID (Fall 2004) 173 applied for aid; of those 94% were deemed to have need. 100% of freshmen with need received aid; of those 38% had need fully met. *Average percent of need met:* 57% (excluding resources awarded to replace EFC). *Average financial aid package:* $11,803 (excluding resources awarded to replace EFC). 14% of all full-time freshmen had no need and received non-need-based gift aid.
UNDERGRADUATE FINANCIAL AID (Fall 2004) 673 applied for aid; of those 98% were deemed to have need. 100% of undergraduates with need received aid; of those 41% had need fully met. *Average percent of need met:* 54% (excluding resources awarded to replace EFC). *Average financial aid package:* $10,895 (excluding resources awarded to replace EFC). 12% of all full-time undergraduates had no need and received non-need-based gift aid.
GIFT AID (NEED-BASED) *Total amount:* $4,804,603 (14% federal, 12% state, 59% institutional, 15% external sources). *Receiving aid:* Freshmen: 57% (99); All full-time undergraduates: 53% (396). *Average award:* Freshmen: $4608; Undergraduates: $3648. *Scholarships, grants, and awards:* Federal Pell, FSEOG, state, private, college/university gift aid from institutional funds.
GIFT AID (NON-NEED-BASED) *Total amount:* $559,401 (17% state, 68% institutional, 15% external sources). *Receiving aid:* Freshmen: 93% (162); Undergraduates: 81% (604). *Average Award:* Freshmen: $5494; Undergraduates: $5636. *Scholarships, grants, and awards by category: Academic Interests/Achievement:* 538 awards ($2,929,572 total): communication, computer science, general academic interests/achievements, health fields, mathematics, religion/biblical studies. *Creative Arts/Performance:* 15 awards ($10,050 total): art/fine arts, music. *Special Achievements/Activities:* 44 awards ($72,500 total): community service. *Special Characteristics:* 16 awards ($189,145 total): children of faculty/staff. *Tuition waivers:* Full or partial for employees or children of employees. *ROTC:* Army cooperative.
LOANS *Student loans:* $3,689,172 (90% need-based, 10% non-need-based). 65% of past graduating class borrowed through all loan programs. *Average indebtedness per student:* $18,769. *Average need-based loan:* Freshmen: $3004; Undergraduates: $4546. *Parent loans:* $1,001,714 (84% need-based, 16% non-need-based). *Programs:* FFEL (Subsidized and Unsubsidized Stafford, PLUS), Perkins, Signature Loans.
WORK-STUDY *Federal work-study:* Total amount: $131,638; 138 jobs averaging $954. *State or other work-study/employment:* Total amount: $195,013 (76% need-based, 24% non-need-based). 180 part-time jobs averaging $1083.
ATHLETIC AWARDS *Total amount:* $1,218,424 (89% need-based, 11% non-need-based).
APPLYING FOR FINANCIAL AID *Required financial aid form:* FAFSA. *Financial aid deadline (priority):* 3/1. *Notification date:* Continuous beginning 3/4. Students must reply within 2 weeks of notification.
CONTACT Becky Brewster, Director of Student Financial Services, Milligan College, PO Box 250, Milligan College, TN 37682, 423-461-8949 or toll-free 800-262-8337 (in-state). *Fax:* 423-929-2368. *E-mail:* rabrewster@milligan.edu.

MILLIKIN UNIVERSITY
Decatur, IL

CONTACT Director of Financial Aid, Millikin University, 1184 West Main Street, Decatur, IL 62522-2084, 217-424-6343 or toll-free 800-373-7733. *Fax:* 217-425-4669.

MILLSAPS COLLEGE
Jackson, MS

Tuition & fees: $20,690	Average undergraduate aid package: $17,774

ABOUT THE INSTITUTION Independent United Methodist, coed. Awards: bachelor's and master's degrees. 27 undergraduate majors. Total enrollment: 1,154. Undergraduates: 1,085. Freshmen: 258. Federal methodology is used as a basis for awarding need-based institutional aid.
UNDERGRADUATE EXPENSES for 2005–06 *Application fee:* $25. *Comprehensive fee:* $28,256 includes full-time tuition ($19,490), mandatory fees ($1200), and room and board ($7566). *College room only:* $4248. Room and board charges vary according to housing facility. *Part-time tuition:* $604 per credit hour. *Part-time fees:* $30 per credit hour. Part-time tuition and fees vary according to course load. *Payment plans:* Installment, deferred payment.
FRESHMAN FINANCIAL AID (Fall 2005, est.) 207 applied for aid; of those 75% were deemed to have need. 100% of freshmen with need received aid; of those 32% had need fully met. *Average percent of need met:* 85% (excluding resources awarded to replace EFC). *Average financial aid package:* $18,185 (excluding resources awarded to replace EFC). 37% of all full-time freshmen had no need and received non-need-based gift aid.
UNDERGRADUATE FINANCIAL AID (Fall 2005, est.) 712 applied for aid; of those 83% were deemed to have need. 99% of undergraduates with need received aid; of those 26% had need fully met. *Average percent of need met:* 80% (excluding resources awarded to replace EFC). *Average financial aid package:* $17,774 (excluding resources awarded to replace EFC). 38% of all full-time undergraduates had no need and received non-need-based gift aid.
GIFT AID (NEED-BASED) *Total amount:* $8,125,509 (12% federal, 3% state, 79% institutional, 6% external sources). *Receiving aid:* Freshmen: 60% (156); All full-time undergraduates: 57% (588). *Average award:* Freshmen: $14,618; Undergraduates: $13,773. *Scholarships, grants, and awards:* Federal Pell, FSEOG, state, private, college/university gift aid from institutional funds.
GIFT AID (NON-NEED-BASED) *Total amount:* $5,240,329 (5% state, 87% institutional, 8% external sources). *Receiving aid:* Freshmen: 17% (44); Undergraduates: 11% (117). *Average Award:* Freshmen: $15,061; Undergraduates: $13,310. *Scholarships, grants, and awards by category: Academic Interests/Achievement:* 845 awards ($7,135,701 total): business, general academic interests/achievements. *Creative Arts/Performance:* 78 awards ($129,516 total): art/fine arts, music, theater/drama. *Special Achievements/Activities:* 837 awards ($7,100,976 total): community service, general special achievements/activities, hobbies/interests, leadership, religious involvement. *Special Characteristics:* 68 awards ($276,268 total): adult students, children of faculty/staff, ethnic background, first-generation college students, members of minority groups, relatives of clergy, religious affiliation. *Tuition waivers:* Full or partial for employees or children of employees. *ROTC:* Army cooperative.
LOANS *Student loans:* $4,239,287 (67% need-based, 33% non-need-based). 63% of past graduating class borrowed through all loan programs. *Average indebtedness per student:* $22,285. *Average need-based loan:* Freshmen: $3544; Undergraduates: $4241. *Parent loans:* $1,360,488 (15% need-based, 85% non-need-based). *Programs:* FFEL (Subsidized and Unsubsidized Stafford, PLUS), Perkins, college/university.
WORK-STUDY *Federal work-study:* Total amount: $426,988; 293 jobs averaging $1256. *State or other work-study/employment:* Part-time jobs available.
APPLYING FOR FINANCIAL AID *Required financial aid forms:* FAFSA, institution's own form. *Financial aid deadline (priority):* 3/1. *Notification date:* Continuous beginning 3/15. Students must reply by 5/1 or within 2 weeks of notification.
CONTACT Patrick James, Director of Financial Aid, Millsaps College, 1701 North State Street, Jackson, MS 39210-0001, 601-974-1220 or toll-free 800-352-1050. *Fax:* 601-974-1224. *E-mail:* jamespg@millsaps.edu.

MILLS COLLEGE
Oakland, CA

CONTACT The M Center/Financial Aid, Mills College, 5000 MacArthur Boulevard, Oakland, CA 94613, 510-430-2000 or toll-free 800-87-MILLS. *E-mail:* mcenter-finaid@mills.edu.

MILWAUKEE INSTITUTE OF ART AND DESIGN
Milwaukee, WI

ABOUT THE INSTITUTION Independent, coed. Awards: bachelor's degrees. 10 undergraduate majors. Total enrollment: 645. Undergraduates: 645. Freshmen: 173.
GIFT AID (NEED-BASED) *Scholarships, grants, and awards:* Federal Pell, FSEOG, state, private, college/university gift aid from institutional funds.
GIFT AID (NON-NEED-BASED) *Scholarships, grants, and awards by category: Creative Arts/Performance:* art/fine arts. *Special Characteristics:* children of faculty/staff, ethnic background, local/state students, members of minority groups.
LOANS *Programs:* FFEL (Subsidized and Unsubsidized Stafford, PLUS), college/university, Norwest Collegiate Loans, Signature Loans.
APPLYING FOR FINANCIAL AID *Required financial aid form:* FAFSA.
CONTACT Mr. Lloyd Mueller, Director of Financial Aid, Milwaukee Institute of Art and Design, 273 East Erie Street, Milwaukee, WI 53202-6003, 414-291-3272 or toll-free 888-749-MIAD. *Fax:* 414-291-8077. *E-mail:* llmuelle@miad.edu.

Milwaukee School of Engineering

MILWAUKEE SCHOOL OF ENGINEERING
Milwaukee, WI

Tuition & fees: $24,960 — **Average undergraduate aid package:** $15,858

ABOUT THE INSTITUTION Independent, coed. Awards: bachelor's and master's degrees. 14 undergraduate majors. Total enrollment: 2,315. Undergraduates: 2,092. Freshmen: 456. Federal methodology is used as a basis for awarding need-based institutional aid.
UNDERGRADUATE EXPENSES for 2006–07 *Application fee:* $25. *Comprehensive fee:* $31,149 includes full-time tuition ($24,960) and room and board ($6189). *College room only:* $3969. *Part-time tuition:* $432 per quarter hour.
FRESHMAN FINANCIAL AID (Fall 2004) 412 applied for aid; of those 90% were deemed to have need. 100% of freshmen with need received aid; of those 14% had need fully met. *Average percent of need met:* 72% (excluding resources awarded to replace EFC). *Average financial aid package:* $16,517 (excluding resources awarded to replace EFC). 17% of all full-time freshmen had no need and received non-need-based gift aid.
UNDERGRADUATE FINANCIAL AID (Fall 2004) 1,678 applied for aid; of those 87% were deemed to have need. 100% of undergraduates with need received aid; of those 16% had need fully met. *Average percent of need met:* 69% (excluding resources awarded to replace EFC). *Average financial aid package:* $15,858 (excluding resources awarded to replace EFC). 14% of all full-time undergraduates had no need and received non-need-based gift aid.
GIFT AID (NEED-BASED) *Total amount:* $19,025,844 (8% federal, 9% state, 80% institutional, 3% external sources). *Receiving aid:* Freshmen: 81% (368); All full-time undergraduates: 80% (1,443). *Average award:* Freshmen: $13,919; Undergraduates: $12,582. *Scholarships, grants, and awards:* Federal Pell, FSEOG, state, private, college/university gift aid from institutional funds.
GIFT AID (NON-NEED-BASED) *Total amount:* $3,011,779 (92% institutional, 8% external sources). *Receiving aid:* Freshmen: 8% (38); Undergraduates: 8% (153). *Average Award:* Freshmen: $11,449; Undergraduates: $12,886. *Scholarships, grants, and awards by category:* Academic Interests/Achievement: 2,118 awards ($13,682,863 total): business, communication, computer science, engineering/technologies, health fields. *Special Characteristics:* 26 awards ($436,755 total): children of faculty/staff. *ROTC:* Army cooperative, Naval cooperative, Air Force cooperative.
LOANS *Student loans:* $14,950,909 (71% need-based, 29% non-need-based). 85% of past graduating class borrowed through all loan programs. *Average indebtedness per student:* $31,808. *Average need-based loan:* Freshmen: $2702; Undergraduates: $3504. *Parent loans:* $2,627,676 (42% need-based, 58% non-need-based). *Programs:* FFEL (Subsidized and Unsubsidized Stafford, PLUS), Perkins, state, college/university.
WORK-STUDY *Federal work-study:* Total amount: $284,273; 198 jobs averaging $1464.
APPLYING FOR FINANCIAL AID *Required financial aid form:* FAFSA. *Financial aid deadline (priority):* 3/15. *Notification date:* Continuous beginning 3/1. Students must reply within 2 weeks of notification.
CONTACT Benjamin P. Dobner, Director of Student Financial Services, Milwaukee School of Engineering, 1025 North Broadway Street, Milwaukee, WI 53202-3109, 800-778-7223 or toll-free 800-332-6763. *Fax:* 414-277-6952. *E-mail:* finaid@msoe.edu.

MINNEAPOLIS COLLEGE OF ART AND DESIGN
Minneapolis, MN

CONTACT Laura Link, Director of Financial Aid, Minneapolis College of Art and Design, 2501 Stevens Avenue South, Minneapolis, MN 55404-4347, 612-874-3733 or toll-free 800-874-6223. *Fax:* 612-874-3701. *E-mail:* laura_link@mead.edu.

MINNESOTA SCHOOL OF BUSINESS
Rochester, MN

CONTACT Financial Aid Office, Minnesota School of Business, 2521 Pennington Drive, NW, Rochester, MN 55901, 507-536-9500 or toll-free 888-662-8772.

MINNESOTA STATE UNIVERSITY MANKATO
Mankato, MN

Tuition & fees (MN res): $5846 — **Average undergraduate aid package:** $6939

ABOUT THE INSTITUTION State-supported, coed. Awards: associate, bachelor's, and master's degrees and post-master's certificates. 127 undergraduate majors. Total enrollment: 14,335. Undergraduates: 12,684. Freshmen: 2,257. Federal methodology is used as a basis for awarding need-based institutional aid.
UNDERGRADUATE EXPENSES for 2005–06 *Application fee:* $20. *Tuition, state resident:* full-time $5104; part-time $204.10 per credit. *Tuition, nonresident:* full-time $10,932; part-time $436 per credit. *Required fees:* full-time $742; $29.89 per credit. Full-time tuition and fees vary according to course load and reciprocity agreements. Part-time tuition and fees vary according to course load and reciprocity agreements. *College room and board:* $5083. Room and board charges vary according to board plan. *Payment plan:* Installment.
FRESHMAN FINANCIAL AID (Fall 2005, est.) 1831 applied for aid; of those 61% were deemed to have need. 98% of freshmen with need received aid; of those 45% had need fully met. *Average percent of need met:* 77% (excluding resources awarded to replace EFC). *Average financial aid package:* $6365 (excluding resources awarded to replace EFC). 10% of all full-time freshmen had no need and received non-need-based gift aid.
UNDERGRADUATE FINANCIAL AID (Fall 2005, est.) 8,423 applied for aid; of those 67% were deemed to have need. 99% of undergraduates with need received aid; of those 46% had need fully met. *Average percent of need met:* 79% (excluding resources awarded to replace EFC). *Average financial aid package:* $6939 (excluding resources awarded to replace EFC). 6% of all full-time undergraduates had no need and received non-need-based gift aid.
GIFT AID (NEED-BASED) *Total amount:* $12,670,931 (56% federal, 39% state, 4% institutional, 1% external sources). *Receiving aid:* Freshmen: 28% (636); All full-time undergraduates: 31% (3,528). *Average award:* Freshmen: $3750; Undergraduates: $3643. *Scholarships, grants, and awards:* Federal Pell, FSEOG, state, private, college/university gift aid from institutional funds.
GIFT AID (NON-NEED-BASED) *Total amount:* $3,987,079 (36% federal, 1% state, 30% institutional, 33% external sources). *Receiving aid:* Freshmen: 17% (390); Undergraduates: 9% (1,024). *Average Award:* Freshmen: $1273; Undergraduates: $1801. *Scholarships, grants, and awards by category:* Academic Interests/Achievement: business, computer science, engineering/technologies, general academic interests/achievements, mathematics, physical sciences. *Creative Arts/Performance:* applied art and design, art/fine arts, creative writing, debating, music, theater/drama. *Special Achievements/Activities:* community service, leadership. *Special Characteristics:* children of union members/company employees, local/state students, out-of-state students. *Tuition waivers:* Full or partial for employees or children of employees, senior citizens. *ROTC:* Army.
LOANS *Student loans:* $58,263,157 (41% need-based, 59% non-need-based). 75% of past graduating class borrowed through all loan programs. *Average indebtedness per student:* $16,500. *Average need-based loan:* Freshmen: $3280; Undergraduates: $3989. *Parent loans:* $3,193,231 (100% non-need-based). *Programs:* FFEL (Subsidized and Unsubsidized Stafford, PLUS), Perkins, state, SELF Loans.
WORK-STUDY *Federal work-study:* Total amount: $1,099,227; 306 jobs averaging $3430. *State or other work-study/employment:* Total amount: $952,054 (100% need-based). 368 part-time jobs averaging $3049.
ATHLETIC AWARDS *Total amount:* $606,750 (100% non-need-based).
APPLYING FOR FINANCIAL AID *Required financial aid forms:* FAFSA, SELF or Alternative Loan Application or PLUS Application. *Financial aid deadline (priority):* 3/15. *Notification date:* Continuous beginning 3/30. Students must reply within 2 weeks of notification.
CONTACT Financial Aid Office, Minnesota State University Mankato, Campus Hub, 117 Centennial Student Union, Mankato, MN 56001, 507-389-1866 or toll-free 800-722-0544. *Fax:* 507-389-2227. *E-mail:* campushub@mnsu.edu.

MINNESOTA STATE UNIVERSITY MOORHEAD
Moorhead, MN

ABOUT THE INSTITUTION State-supported, coed. Awards: associate, bachelor's, and master's degrees and post-master's certificates. 93 undergraduate majors. Total enrollment: 7,652. Undergraduates: 7,242. Freshmen: 1,135.

GIFT AID (NEED-BASED) *Scholarships, grants, and awards:* Federal Pell, FSEOG, state, private, college/university gift aid from institutional funds.
GIFT AID (NON-NEED-BASED) *Scholarships, grants, and awards by category: Academic Interests/Achievement:* general academic interests/achievements. *Creative Arts/Performance:* art/fine arts, creative writing, music, theater/drama. *Special Achievements/Activities:* community service, general special achievements/activities. *Special Characteristics:* children of faculty/staff, members of minority groups.
LOANS *Programs:* Federal Direct (Subsidized and Unsubsidized Stafford, PLUS), Perkins, state, alternative loans.
WORK-STUDY *Federal work-study:* Total amount: $441,601; 232 jobs averaging $1903. *State or other work-study/employment:* Total amount: $2,949,389 (16% need-based, 84% non-need-based). 1,047 part-time jobs averaging $2817.
APPLYING FOR FINANCIAL AID *Required financial aid form:* FAFSA.
CONTACT Ms. Carolyn Zehren, Director of Financial Aid, Minnesota State University Moorhead, 1104 7th Avenue South, Moorhead, MN 56563-0002, 218-477-2251 or toll-free 800-593-7246. *Fax:* 218-477-2058. *E-mail:* zehren@mnstate.edu.

MINOT STATE UNIVERSITY
Minot, ND

ABOUT THE INSTITUTION State-supported, coed. Awards: associate, bachelor's, and master's degrees and post-master's certificates. 58 undergraduate majors. Total enrollment: 3,797. Undergraduates: 3,547. Freshmen: 471.
GIFT AID (NEED-BASED) *Scholarships, grants, and awards:* Federal Pell, FSEOG, state, private, college/university gift aid from institutional funds, Federal Nursing.
GIFT AID (NON-NEED-BASED) *Scholarships, grants, and awards by category: Academic Interests/Achievement:* business, communication, computer science, education, English, general academic interests/achievements, health fields, humanities, mathematics, social sciences. *Creative Arts/Performance:* music, theater/drama. *Special Characteristics:* ethnic background, international students, local/state students, members of minority groups, out-of-state students, veterans, veterans' children.
LOANS *Programs:* FFEL (Subsidized and Unsubsidized Stafford, PLUS), Perkins, Federal Nursing, college/university.
APPLYING FOR FINANCIAL AID *Required financial aid form:* FAFSA.
CONTACT Mr. Dale Gehring, Director of Financial Aid, Minot State University, 500 University Avenue, West, Minot, ND 58707-0002, 701-858-3862 or toll-free 800-777-0750 Ext. 3350. *Fax:* 701-858-4310. *E-mail:* dale.gehring@minotstateu.edu.

MIRRER YESHIVA
Brooklyn, NY

CONTACT Financial Aid Office, Mirrer Yeshiva, 1795 Ocean Parkway, Brooklyn, NY 11223-2010, 718-645-0536.

MISSISSIPPI COLLEGE
Clinton, MS

ABOUT THE INSTITUTION Independent Southern Baptist, coed. Awards: bachelor's, master's, and first professional degrees and post-bachelor's certificates. 60 undergraduate majors. Total enrollment: 3,905. Undergraduates: 2,553. Freshmen: 395.
GIFT AID (NEED-BASED) *Scholarships, grants, and awards:* Federal Pell, FSEOG, state, private, college/university gift aid from institutional funds.
GIFT AID (NON-NEED-BASED) *Scholarships, grants, and awards by category: Academic Interests/Achievement:* general academic interests/achievements. *Creative Arts/Performance:* applied art and design, art/fine arts, music. *Special Achievements/Activities:* general special achievements/activities, leadership, religious involvement. *Special Characteristics:* children and siblings of alumni, children of faculty/staff, general special characteristics, relatives of clergy.
LOANS *Programs:* FFEL (Subsidized and Unsubsidized Stafford, PLUS), Perkins, Federal Nursing, college/university.
APPLYING FOR FINANCIAL AID *Required financial aid form:* FAFSA.
CONTACT Mary Givhan, Director of Financial Aid, Mississippi College, PO Box 4035, Clinton, MS 39058, 601-925-3319 or toll-free 800-738-1236. *E-mail:* givhan@mc.edu.

MISSISSIPPI STATE UNIVERSITY
Mississippi State, MS

Tuition & fees (MS res): $4312   **Average undergraduate aid package: $8916**

ABOUT THE INSTITUTION State-supported, coed. Awards: bachelor's, master's, doctoral, and first professional degrees and post-master's certificates. 71 undergraduate majors. Total enrollment: 16,101. Undergraduates: 12,555. Freshmen: 1,966. Federal methodology is used as a basis for awarding need-based institutional aid.
UNDERGRADUATE EXPENSES for 2005–06 *Tuition, state resident:* full-time $4312; part-time $179.75 per hour. *Tuition, nonresident:* full-time $9772; part-time $407.25 per hour. Part-time tuition and fees vary according to course load. *College room and board:* $5859; *room only:* $2824. Room and board charges vary according to board plan, housing facility, and student level.
FRESHMAN FINANCIAL AID (Fall 2004) 1240 applied for aid; of those 85% were deemed to have need. 96% of freshmen with need received aid; of those 29% had need fully met. *Average percent of need met:* 63% (excluding resources awarded to replace EFC). *Average financial aid package:* $7405 (excluding resources awarded to replace EFC). 19% of all full-time freshmen had no need and received non-need-based gift aid.
UNDERGRADUATE FINANCIAL AID (Fall 2004) 7,546 applied for aid; of those 86% were deemed to have need. 98% of undergraduates with need received aid; of those 41% had need fully met. *Average percent of need met:* 70% (excluding resources awarded to replace EFC). *Average financial aid package:* $8916 (excluding resources awarded to replace EFC). 14% of all full-time undergraduates had no need and received non-need-based gift aid.
GIFT AID (NEED-BASED) *Total amount:* $21,009,874 (56% federal, 10% state, 17% institutional, 17% external sources). *Receiving aid:* Freshmen: 53% (950); All full-time undergraduates: 46% (5,507). *Average award:* Freshmen: $3665; Undergraduates: $3480. *Scholarships, grants, and awards:* Federal Pell, FSEOG, state, private, college/university gift aid from institutional funds, United Negro College Fund.
GIFT AID (NON-NEED-BASED) *Total amount:* $9,023,080 (28% state, 52% institutional, 20% external sources). *Receiving aid:* Freshmen: 8% (148); Undergraduates: 4% (424). *Average Award:* Freshmen: $2595; Undergraduates: $2336. *Scholarships, grants, and awards by category: Academic Interests/Achievement:* agriculture, architecture, area/ethnic studies, biological sciences, business, communication, computer science, education, engineering/technologies, English, foreign languages, general academic interests/achievements, health fields, home economics, humanities, international studies, library science, mathematics, military science, physical sciences, premedicine, religion/biblical studies, social sciences. *Creative Arts/Performance:* applied art and design, art/fine arts, cinema/film/broadcasting, creative writing, dance, debating, general creative arts/performance, journalism/publications, music, performing arts, theater/drama. *Special Achievements/Activities:* cheerleading/drum major, general special achievements/activities, leadership, memberships. *Special Characteristics:* adult students, children and siblings of alumni, children of educators, children of faculty/staff, children of public servants, first-generation college students, handicapped students, local/state students, out-of-state students, previous college experience, spouses of deceased or disabled public servants. *Tuition waivers:* Full or partial for children of alumni, employees or children of employees, senior citizens. *ROTC:* Army, Air Force.
LOANS *Student loans:* $33,516,369 (90% need-based, 10% non-need-based). 49% of past graduating class borrowed through all loan programs. *Average indebtedness per student:* $18,230. *Average need-based loan:* Freshmen: $2651; Undergraduates: $3908. *Parent loans:* $3,633,224 (28% need-based, 72% non-need-based). *Programs:* FFEL (Subsidized and Unsubsidized Stafford, PLUS), Perkins, college/university.
WORK-STUDY *Federal work-study:* Total amount: $2,347,930; 919 jobs averaging $2555.
ATHLETIC AWARDS Total amount: $2,711,243 (100% non-need-based).
APPLYING FOR FINANCIAL AID *Required financial aid forms:* FAFSA, state grant/scholarship application. *Financial aid deadline (priority):* 4/1. *Notification date:* Continuous beginning 12/1. Students must reply by 5/1.
CONTACT Mr. Bruce Crain, Director of Financial Aid, Mississippi State University, PO Box 6035, Mississippi State, MS 39762, 662-325-2450. *Fax:* 662-325-0702. *E-mail:* financialaid@saffairs.msstate.edu.

MISSISSIPPI UNIVERSITY FOR WOMEN
Columbus, MS

ABOUT THE INSTITUTION State-supported, coed, primarily women. Awards: associate, bachelor's, and master's degrees. 39 undergraduate majors. Total enrollment: 2,328. Undergraduates: 2,166.

GIFT AID (NEED-BASED) *Scholarships, grants, and awards:* Federal Pell, FSEOG, state, private, college/university gift aid from institutional funds, United Negro College Fund.

GIFT AID (NON-NEED-BASED) *Scholarships, grants, and awards by category: Academic Interests/Achievement:* biological sciences, business, communication, computer science, education, English, general academic interests/achievements, health fields, home economics, humanities, mathematics, physical sciences. *Creative Arts/Performance:* art/fine arts, dance, journalism/publications, music, performing arts, theater/drama. *Special Achievements/Activities:* junior miss, leadership. *Special Characteristics:* adult students, children and siblings of alumni, children of faculty/staff, ethnic background, international students, members of minority groups, out-of-state students, parents of current students.

LOANS *Programs:* FFEL (Subsidized and Unsubsidized Stafford, PLUS), Perkins.

APPLYING FOR FINANCIAL AID *Required financial aid forms:* FAFSA, state aid form, scholarship application form(s).

CONTACT Don Rainer, Director of Financial Aid, Mississippi University for Women, 1100 College Street, MUW 1614, Columbus, MS 39701-4044, 662-329-7114 or toll-free 877-GO 2 THE W. *Fax:* 662-329-7325. *E-mail:* finaid@muw.edu.

MISSISSIPPI VALLEY STATE UNIVERSITY
Itta Bena, MS

CONTACT Mr. Darrell G. Boyd, Director of Student Financial Aid, Mississippi Valley State University, 14000 Highway 82W #7268, Itta Bena, MS 38941-1400, 662-254-3765 or toll-free 800-844-6885 (in-state). *Fax:* 662-254-3759. *E-mail:* dboyd@mvsu.edu.

MISSOURI BAPTIST UNIVERSITY
St. Louis, MO

ABOUT THE INSTITUTION Independent Southern Baptist, coed. Awards: associate, bachelor's, and master's degrees and post-bachelor's certificates. 33 undergraduate majors. Total enrollment: 4,460. Undergraduates: 3,485. Freshmen: 223.

GIFT AID (NEED-BASED) *Scholarships, grants, and awards:* Federal Pell, FSEOG, state, private, college/university gift aid from institutional funds.

GIFT AID (NON-NEED-BASED) *Scholarships, grants, and awards by category: Academic Interests/Achievement:* general academic interests/achievements, religion/biblical studies. *Creative Arts/Performance:* music, theater/drama. *Special Achievements/Activities:* cheerleading/drum major, religious involvement. *Special Characteristics:* children and siblings of alumni, children of current students, children of faculty/staff, parents of current students, public servants, relatives of clergy, religious affiliation, siblings of current students.

LOANS *Programs:* FFEL (Subsidized and Unsubsidized Stafford, PLUS).

APPLYING FOR FINANCIAL AID *Required financial aid forms:* FAFSA, institution's own form.

CONTACT Bob Miller, Director of Financial Services, Missouri Baptist University, One College Park Drive, St. Louis, MO 63141, 314-392-2366 or toll-free 877-434-1115 Ext. 2290. *Fax:* 314-434-7596. *E-mail:* millerb@mobap.edu.

MISSOURI SOUTHERN STATE UNIVERSITY
Joplin, MO

ABOUT THE INSTITUTION State-supported, coed. Awards: associate, bachelor's, and master's degrees. 57 undergraduate majors. Total enrollment: 5,473. Undergraduates: 5,473. Freshmen: 897.

GIFT AID (NEED-BASED) *Scholarships, grants, and awards:* Federal Pell, FSEOG, state, private, college/university gift aid from institutional funds.

GIFT AID (NON-NEED-BASED) *Scholarships, grants, and awards by category: Academic Interests/Achievement:* general academic interests/achievements. *Creative Arts/Performance:* art/fine arts, debating, journalism/publications, music, theater/drama. *Special Achievements/Activities:* general special achievements/activities, leadership. *Special Characteristics:* children and siblings of alumni, children of faculty/staff, ethnic background, local/state students.

LOANS *Programs:* Federal Direct (Subsidized and Unsubsidized Stafford, PLUS), Perkins, state.

APPLYING FOR FINANCIAL AID *Required financial aid form:* FAFSA.

CONTACT Mr. James E. Gilbert, Director of Financial Aid, Missouri Southern State University, 3950 East Newman Road, Joplin, MO 64801-1595, 417-625-9325 or toll-free 866-818-MSSU. *Fax:* 417-625-3121. *E-mail:* gilbert-j@mssu.edu.

MISSOURI STATE UNIVERSITY
Springfield, MO

Tuition & fees (MO res): $5454   **Average undergraduate aid package:** $6125

ABOUT THE INSTITUTION State-supported, coed. Awards: bachelor's, master's, and doctoral degrees and post-bachelor's and post-master's certificates. 91 undergraduate majors. Total enrollment: 18,928. Undergraduates: 16,157. Freshmen: 2,621. Federal methodology is used as a basis for awarding need-based institutional aid.

UNDERGRADUATE EXPENSES for 2006–07 *Application fee:* $30. *Tuition, state resident:* full-time $4920; part-time $164 per credit hour. *Tuition, nonresident:* full-time $9840; part-time $328 per credit hour. *College room and board:* $5294; *room only:* $3462.

FRESHMAN FINANCIAL AID (Fall 2005, est.) 1888 applied for aid; of those 65% were deemed to have need. 99% of freshmen with need received aid; of those 24% had need fully met. *Average percent of need met:* 62% (excluding resources awarded to replace EFC). *Average financial aid package:* $5748 (excluding resources awarded to replace EFC). 39% of all full-time freshmen had no need and received non-need-based gift aid.

UNDERGRADUATE FINANCIAL AID (Fall 2005, est.) 9,101 applied for aid; of those 74% were deemed to have need. 98% of undergraduates with need received aid; of those 23% had need fully met. *Average percent of need met:* 61% (excluding resources awarded to replace EFC). *Average financial aid package:* $6125 (excluding resources awarded to replace EFC). 33% of all full-time undergraduates had no need and received non-need-based gift aid.

GIFT AID (NEED-BASED) *Total amount:* $19,364,709 (54% federal, 10% state, 28% institutional, 8% external sources). *Receiving aid:* Freshmen: 42% (960); All full-time undergraduates: 41% (4,502). *Average award:* Freshmen: $4595; Undergraduates: $4308. *Scholarships, grants, and awards:* Federal Pell, FSEOG, state, private, college/university gift aid from institutional funds.

GIFT AID (NON-NEED-BASED) *Total amount:* $11,196,437 (1% federal, 11% state, 75% institutional, 13% external sources). *Receiving aid:* Freshmen: 7% (169); Undergraduates: 4% (455). *Average Award:* Freshmen: $7636; Undergraduates: $7328. *Scholarships, grants, and awards by category: Academic Interests/Achievement:* 6,888 awards ($10,500,000 total): agriculture, biological sciences, business, communication, computer science, education, foreign languages, general academic interests/achievements, health fields, home economics, mathematics, military science, physical sciences, premedicine, religion/biblical studies, social sciences. *Creative Arts/Performance:* applied art and design, art/fine arts, dance, debating, general creative arts/performance, journalism/publications, music, performing arts, theater/drama. *Special Achievements/Activities:* cheerleading/drum major, general special achievements/activities, hobbies/interests, memberships, rodeo. *Special Characteristics:* adult students, children and siblings of alumni, children of faculty/staff, ethnic background, first-generation college students, general special characteristics, handicapped students, international students, members of minority groups, out-of-state students, spouses of deceased or disabled public servants, veterans. *ROTC:* Army.

LOANS *Student loans:* $46,354,770 (67% need-based, 33% non-need-based). 54% of past graduating class borrowed through all loan programs. *Average indebtedness per student:* $12,997. *Average need-based loan:* Freshmen: $2708; Undergraduates: $3649. *Parent loans:* $15,997,700 (20% need-based, 80% non-need-based). *Programs:* FFEL (Subsidized and Unsubsidized Stafford, PLUS), Perkins, state, college/university.

WORK-STUDY *Federal work-study:* Total amount: $609,754; 449 jobs averaging $1748. *State or other work-study/employment:* 1,336 part-time jobs averaging $2924.

ATHLETIC AWARDS *Total amount:* $3,389,998 (28% need-based, 72% non-need-based).
APPLYING FOR FINANCIAL AID *Required financial aid form:* FAFSA. *Financial aid deadline (priority):* 3/30. *Notification date:* 4/15.
CONTACT David G. King, Assistant Director of Financial Aid, Missouri State University, 901 South National Avenue, Springfield, MO 65804, 417-836-5262 or toll-free 800-492-7900.

MISSOURI TECH
St. Louis, MO

CONTACT Director of Financial Aid, Missouri Tech, 1167 Corporate Lake Drive, St. Louis, MO 63132-1716, 314-569-3600. *Fax:* 314-569-1167. *E-mail:* contact@motech.edu.

MISSOURI VALLEY COLLEGE
Marshall, MO

ABOUT THE INSTITUTION Independent religious, coed. Awards: associate and bachelor's degrees. 40 undergraduate majors. Total enrollment: 1,623. Undergraduates: 1,623. Freshmen: 405.
GIFT AID (NEED-BASED) *Scholarships, grants, and awards:* Federal Pell, FSEOG, state, private, college/university gift aid from institutional funds.
GIFT AID (NON-NEED-BASED) *Scholarships, grants, and awards by category: Academic Interests/Achievement:* biological sciences, business, communication, computer science, education, English, humanities, mathematics, military science, physical sciences, premedicine, social sciences. *Creative Arts/Performance:* dance, journalism/publications, music, performing arts, theater/drama. *Special Achievements/Activities:* cheerleading/drum major, community service, general special achievements/activities, hobbies/interests, junior miss, leadership, rodeo. *Special Characteristics:* children and siblings of alumni, children of faculty/staff.
LOANS *Programs:* FFEL (Subsidized and Unsubsidized Stafford, PLUS), Perkins.
WORK-STUDY *Federal work-study:* Total amount: $221,349; 146 jobs averaging $1860. *State or other work-study/employment:* Total amount: $810,840 (100% need-based). 530 part-time jobs averaging $1860.
APPLYING FOR FINANCIAL AID *Required financial aid form:* FAFSA.
CONTACT Jennifer Malotte, Director of Financial Aid, Missouri Valley College, 500 East College, Marshall, MO 65340-3197, 660-831-4176. *Fax:* 660-831-4003. *E-mail:* malottej@moval.edu.

MISSOURI WESTERN STATE UNIVERSITY
St. Joseph, MO

CONTACT Angela Beam, Director of Financial Aid, Missouri Western State University, 4525 Downs Drive, St. Joseph, MO 64507-2294, 816-271-4361 or toll-free 800-662-7041 Ext. 60. *Fax:* 816-271-5833.

MITCHELL COLLEGE
New London, CT

ABOUT THE INSTITUTION Independent, coed. Awards: associate and bachelor's degrees. 20 undergraduate majors. Total enrollment: 727. Undergraduates: 727. Freshmen: 245.
GIFT AID (NEED-BASED) *Scholarships, grants, and awards:* Federal Pell, FSEOG, state, college/university gift aid from institutional funds.
LOANS *Programs:* FFEL (Subsidized and Unsubsidized Stafford, PLUS), Perkins, alternative loans.
WORK-STUDY *Federal work-study:* Total amount: $42,230; 44 jobs averaging $1000. *State or other work-study/employment:* Total amount: $2,561,977 (100% need-based).
APPLYING FOR FINANCIAL AID *Required financial aid form:* FAFSA.
CONTACT Jacklyn Stoltz, Director of Financial Aid, Mitchell College, 437 Pequot Avenue, New London, CT 06320-4498, 800-443-2811. *Fax:* 860-444-1209. *E-mail:* stoltz_j@mitchell.edu.

MOLLOY COLLEGE
Rockville Centre, NY

Tuition & fees: $16,460	Average undergraduate aid package: $10,122

ABOUT THE INSTITUTION Independent, coed. Awards: associate, bachelor's, and master's degrees and post-master's certificates. 44 undergraduate majors. Total enrollment: 3,585. Undergraduates: 2,732. Freshmen: 284. Federal methodology is used as a basis for awarding need-based institutional aid.
UNDERGRADUATE EXPENSES for 2005–06 *Application fee:* $30. *Tuition:* full-time $15,760; part-time $525 per credit. *Payment plan:* Installment.
FRESHMAN FINANCIAL AID (Fall 2005, est.) 254 applied for aid; of those 79% were deemed to have need. 100% of freshmen with need received aid; of those 29% had need fully met. *Average percent of need met:* 66% (excluding resources awarded to replace EFC). *Average financial aid package:* $9905 (excluding resources awarded to replace EFC). 20% of all full-time freshmen had no need and received non-need-based gift aid.
UNDERGRADUATE FINANCIAL AID (Fall 2005, est.) 1,601 applied for aid; of those 81% were deemed to have need. 100% of undergraduates with need received aid; of those 18% had need fully met. *Average percent of need met:* 60% (excluding resources awarded to replace EFC). *Average financial aid package:* $10,122 (excluding resources awarded to replace EFC). 18% of all full-time undergraduates had no need and received non-need-based gift aid.
GIFT AID (NEED-BASED) *Total amount:* $7,915,030 (30% federal, 35% state, 34% institutional, 1% external sources). *Receiving aid:* Freshmen: 78% (197); All full-time undergraduates: 74% (1,183). *Average award:* Freshmen: $7389; Undergraduates: $6189. *Scholarships, grants, and awards:* Federal Pell, FSEOG, state, private, college/university gift aid from institutional funds.
GIFT AID (NON-NEED-BASED) *Total amount:* $1,815,058 (49% state, 49% institutional, 2% external sources). *Receiving aid:* Freshmen: 15% (37); Undergraduates: 6% (97). *Average Award:* Freshmen: $10,170; Undergraduates:* $10,788. *Scholarships, grants, and awards by category: Academic Interests/Achievement:* 417 awards ($1,794,759 total): biological sciences, business, general academic interests/achievements, health fields. *Creative Arts/Performance:* 48 awards ($94,598 total): art/fine arts, music, performing arts. *Special Achievements/Activities:* 130 awards ($218,750 total): community service. *Tuition waivers:* Full or partial for employees or children of employees. *ROTC:* Army cooperative, Naval cooperative, Air Force cooperative.
LOANS *Student loans:* $15,513,778 (76% need-based, 24% non-need-based). 70% of past graduating class borrowed through all loan programs. *Average indebtedness per student:* $23,000. *Average need-based loan:* Freshmen: $3267; Undergraduates: $4797. *Parent loans:* $4,101,446 (38% need-based, 62% non-need-based). *Programs:* FFEL (Subsidized Stafford, PLUS), Perkins, Federal Nursing, Alternative Loans.
WORK-STUDY *Federal work-study:* Total amount: $517,304; 487 jobs averaging $1247.
ATHLETIC AWARDS *Total amount:* $1,070,654 (54% need-based, 46% non-need-based).
APPLYING FOR FINANCIAL AID *Required financial aid forms:* FAFSA, state aid form. *Financial aid deadline:* 5/1 (priority: 5/1). *Notification date:* 3/1. Students must reply within 5 weeks of notification.
CONTACT Ana C. Lockward, Director of Financial Aid, Molloy College, 1000 Hempstead Avenue, PO Box 5002, Rockville Centre, NY 11571, 516-678-5000 Ext. 6221 or toll-free 888-4MOLLOY. *Fax:* 516-256-2292. *E-mail:* alockward@molloy.edu.

MONMOUTH COLLEGE
Monmouth, IL

CONTACT Ms. Jayne Whiteside, Director of Financial Aid, Monmouth College, 700 East Broadway, Monmouth, IL 61462-1998, 309-457-2129 or toll-free 800-747-2687. *Fax:* 309-457-2152. *E-mail:* jayne@monm.edu.

MONMOUTH UNIVERSITY
West Long Branch, NJ

Tuition & fees: $20,686	Average undergraduate aid package: $13,765

Monmouth University

ABOUT THE INSTITUTION Independent, coed. Awards: associate, bachelor's, and master's degrees and post-master's certificates. 28 undergraduate majors. Total enrollment: 6,350. Undergraduates: 4,555. Freshmen: 943. Federal methodology is used as a basis for awarding need-based institutional aid.
UNDERGRADUATE EXPENSES for 2005–06 *Application fee:* $35. *Comprehensive fee:* $28,956 includes full-time tuition ($20,066), mandatory fees ($620), and room and board ($8270). *College room only:* $4440. Room and board charges vary according to board plan and housing facility. *Part-time tuition:* $581 per credit hour. *Part-time fees:* $155 per term. *Payment plan:* Installment.
FRESHMAN FINANCIAL AID (Fall 2005, est.) 801 applied for aid; of those 77% were deemed to have need. 100% of freshmen with need received aid; of those 12% had need fully met. *Average percent of need met:* 76% (excluding resources awarded to replace EFC). *Average financial aid package:* $13,575 (excluding resources awarded to replace EFC). 28% of all full-time freshmen had no need and received non-need-based gift aid.
UNDERGRADUATE FINANCIAL AID (Fall 2005, est.) 3,294 applied for aid; of those 81% were deemed to have need. 100% of undergraduates with need received aid; of those 6% had need fully met. *Average percent of need met:* 65% (excluding resources awarded to replace EFC). *Average financial aid package:* $13,765 (excluding resources awarded to replace EFC). 29% of all full-time undergraduates had no need and received non-need-based gift aid.
GIFT AID (NEED-BASED) *Total amount:* $9,330,511 (32% federal, 63% state, 5% institutional). *Receiving aid:* Freshmen: 24% (230); All full-time undergraduates: 27% (1,110). *Average award:* Freshmen: $8203; Undergraduates: $7959. *Scholarships, grants, and awards:* Federal Pell, FSEOG, state, private, college/university gift aid from institutional funds, Federal Nursing.
GIFT AID (NON-NEED-BASED) *Total amount:* $19,147,052 (1% state, 95% institutional, 4% external sources). *Receiving aid:* Freshmen: 61% (580); Undergraduates: 56% (2,325). *Average Award:* Freshmen: $6639; Undergraduates:* $4955. *Scholarships, grants, and awards by category:* Academic Interests/Achievement: 3,731 awards ($20,662,075 total): business, communication, computer science, education, general academic interests/achievements, health fields, humanities, international studies, mathematics, social sciences. *Special Characteristics:* 295 awards ($686,908 total): adult students, children and siblings of alumni, children of faculty/staff, children of public servants, first-generation college students, general special characteristics, international students, local/state students, members of minority groups, out-of-state students, previous college experience, veterans. *Tuition waivers:* Full or partial for employees or children of employees, senior citizens. *ROTC:* Air Force cooperative.
LOANS *Student loans:* $30,098,974 (35% need-based, 65% non-need-based). 66% of past graduating class borrowed through all loan programs. *Average indebtedness per student:* $27,600. *Average need-based loan:* Freshmen: $2877; Undergraduates: $4413. *Parent loans:* $7,022,570 (100% non-need-based). *Programs:* Federal Direct (Subsidized and Unsubsidized Stafford, PLUS), FFEL (PLUS), Perkins, state, college/university.
WORK-STUDY *Federal work-study:* Total amount: $350,000; jobs available (averaging $1200).
ATHLETIC AWARDS *Total amount:* $2,515,895 (100% non-need-based).
APPLYING FOR FINANCIAL AID *Required financial aid form:* FAFSA. *Financial aid deadline:* Continuous. *Notification date:* Continuous beginning 2/1. Students must reply within 2 weeks of notification.
CONTACT Ms. Claire Alasio, Director of Financial Aid, Monmouth University, 400 Cedar Avenue, West Long Branch, NJ 07764-1898, 732-571-3463 or toll-free 800-543-9671. *Fax:* 732-923-4791. *E-mail:* finaid@monmouth.edu.

MONROE COLLEGE
Bronx, NY

Tuition & fees: $9760	Average undergraduate aid package: $9832

ABOUT THE INSTITUTION Proprietary, coed. Awards: associate, bachelor's, and master's degrees. 8 undergraduate majors. Total enrollment: 4,285. Undergraduates: 4,285. Freshmen: 795. Federal methodology is used as a basis for awarding need-based institutional aid.
UNDERGRADUATE EXPENSES for 2005–06 *Application fee:* $35. *Comprehensive fee:* $16,660 includes full-time tuition ($9160), mandatory fees ($600), and room and board ($6900). *Part-time tuition:* $382 per credit hour. *Part-time fees:* $150 per term.
FRESHMAN FINANCIAL AID (Fall 2004) 903 applied for aid; of those 96% were deemed to have need. 100% of freshmen with need received aid; of those 36% had need fully met. *Average percent of need met:* 92% (excluding resources awarded to replace EFC). *Average financial aid package:* $9905 (excluding resources awarded to replace EFC).
UNDERGRADUATE FINANCIAL AID (Fall 2004) 3,436 applied for aid; of those 96% were deemed to have need. 100% of undergraduates with need received aid; of those 40% had need fully met. *Average percent of need met:* 91% (excluding resources awarded to replace EFC). *Average financial aid package:* $9832 (excluding resources awarded to replace EFC).
GIFT AID (NEED-BASED) *Total amount:* $36,790,703 (48% federal, 49% state, 3% institutional). *Receiving aid:* Freshmen: 90% (864); All full-time undergraduates: 87% (3,307). *Average award:* Freshmen: $6300; Undergraduates: $6237. *Scholarships, grants, and awards:* Federal Pell, FSEOG, state, private, college/university gift aid from institutional funds.
GIFT AID (NON-NEED-BASED) *Total amount:* $681,392 (27% institutional, 73% external sources). *Receiving aid:* Freshmen: 1% (10); Undergraduates: 1% (25).
LOANS *Student loans:* $15,621,614 (100% need-based). 86% of past graduating class borrowed through all loan programs. *Average indebtedness per student:* $5307. *Average need-based loan:* Freshmen: $4350; Undergraduates: $4100. *Parent loans:* $315,993 (100% need-based). *Programs:* FFEL (Subsidized and Unsubsidized Stafford, PLUS), college/university.
WORK-STUDY *Federal work-study:* Total amount: $886,237; 132 jobs averaging $3100.
ATHLETIC AWARDS *Total amount:* $136,720 (100% non-need-based).
APPLYING FOR FINANCIAL AID *Required financial aid forms:* FAFSA, state aid form. *Financial aid deadline:* Continuous. *Notification date:* Continuous beginning 3/1.
CONTACT Howard Leslie, Dean of Student Financial Services, Monroe College, 434 Main Street, New Rochelle, NY 10468, 914-740-6864 or toll-free 800-55MONROE. *Fax:* 914-632-5794. *E-mail:* hleslie@monroecollege.edu.

MONROE COLLEGE
New Rochelle, NY

CONTACT Ms. Erdene Kims, Director of Financial Aid Compliance, Monroe College, Monroe College Way, Bronx, NY 10468, 718-933-6700 or toll-free 800-55MONROE. *E-mail:* ekims@monroecoll.edu.

MONTANA STATE UNIVERSITY
Bozeman, MT

Tuition & fees (MT res): $5221	Average undergraduate aid package: $7325

ABOUT THE INSTITUTION State-supported, coed. Awards: bachelor's, master's, and doctoral degrees and post-master's certificates. 55 undergraduate majors. Total enrollment: 12,166. Undergraduates: 10,842. Freshmen: 2,236. Federal methodology is used as a basis for awarding need-based institutional aid.
UNDERGRADUATE EXPENSES for 2005–06 *Application fee:* $30. *Tuition, state resident:* full-time $5221; part-time $171.10 per credit. *Tuition, nonresident:* full-time $14,945; part-time $572.70 per credit. Full-time tuition and fees vary according to course load. Part-time tuition and fees vary according to course load. *College room and board:* $6150. Room and board charges vary according to board plan and housing facility. *Payment plans:* Installment, deferred payment.
FRESHMAN FINANCIAL AID (Fall 2004) 1774 applied for aid; of those 62% were deemed to have need. 97% of freshmen with need received aid; of those 12% had need fully met. *Average percent of need met:* 57% (excluding resources awarded to replace EFC). *Average financial aid package:* $6869 (excluding resources awarded to replace EFC). 9% of all full-time freshmen had no need and received non-need-based gift aid.
UNDERGRADUATE FINANCIAL AID (Fall 2004) 7,174 applied for aid; of those 69% were deemed to have need. 98% of undergraduates with need received aid; of those 12% had need fully met. *Average percent of need met:* 67% (excluding resources awarded to replace EFC). *Average financial aid package:* $7325 (excluding resources awarded to replace EFC). 6% of all full-time undergraduates had no need and received non-need-based gift aid.
GIFT AID (NEED-BASED) *Total amount:* $14,141,979 (64% federal, 5% state, 13% institutional, 18% external sources). *Receiving aid:* Freshmen: 42% (849); All full-time undergraduates: 40% (3,653). *Average award:* Freshmen: $3939;

Undergraduates: $3899. *Scholarships, grants, and awards:* Federal Pell, FSEOG, state, private, college/university gift aid from institutional funds, Federal Nursing. **GIFT AID (NON-NEED-BASED)** *Total amount:* $5,154,023 (100% external sources). *Receiving aid:* Freshmen: 18% (354); Undergraduates: 10% (890). *Average Award:* Freshmen: $2536; Undergraduates: $4611. *Scholarships, grants, and awards by category:* Academic Interests/Achievement: agriculture, architecture, area/ethnic studies, biological sciences, business, communication, computer science, education, engineering/technologies, English, foreign languages, general academic interests/achievements, health fields, home economics, humanities, mathematics, military science, physical sciences, social sciences. Creative Arts/Performance: art/fine arts, cinema/film/broadcasting, dance, music, theater/drama. Special Achievements/Activities: general special achievements/activities. Special Characteristics: general special characteristics. *Tuition waivers:* Full or partial for minority students, employees or children of employees, senior citizens. *ROTC:* Army, Air Force.
LOANS *Student loans:* $33,437,160 (58% need-based, 42% non-need-based). 66% of past graduating class borrowed through all loan programs. *Average indebtedness per student:* $18,081. *Average need-based loan:* Freshmen: $3302; Undergraduates: $4190. *Parent loans:* $7,878,262 (20% need-based, 80% non-need-based). *Programs:* Federal Direct (Subsidized and Unsubsidized Stafford, PLUS), Perkins, Federal Nursing, college/university, Freeborn Loans.
WORK-STUDY *Federal work-study:* Total amount: $510,682; 353 jobs averaging $1781. *State or other work-study/employment:* Total amount: $343,277 (100% need-based). 282 part-time jobs averaging $1792.
ATHLETIC AWARDS *Total amount:* $2,779,661 (86% need-based, 14% non-need-based).
APPLYING FOR FINANCIAL AID *Required financial aid form:* FAFSA. *Financial aid deadline (priority):* 3/1. *Notification date:* Continuous beginning 4/1. Students must reply within 3 weeks of notification.
CONTACT Brandi Payne, Director of Financial Aid Services, Montana State University, Strand Union Building, Room 135, PO Box 174160, Bozeman, MT 59717-4160, 406-994-2845 or toll-free 888-MSU-CATS. *Fax:* 406-994-6962.

MONTANA STATE UNIVERSITY–BILLINGS
Billings, MT

Tuition & fees (MT res): $4856   Average undergraduate aid package: $7566

ABOUT THE INSTITUTION State-supported, coed. Awards: associate, bachelor's, and master's degrees and post-bachelor's and post-master's certificates. 75 undergraduate majors. Total enrollment: 4,872. Undergraduates: 4,407. Freshmen: 963. Federal methodology is used as a basis for awarding need-based institutional aid.
UNDERGRADUATE EXPENSES for 2005–06 *Application fee:* $30. *Tuition, state resident:* full-time $3762; part-time $135 per credit hour. *Tuition, nonresident:* full-time $13,096; part-time $364 per credit hour. Full-time tuition and fees vary according to course load, degree level, and location. Part-time tuition and fees vary according to course load, degree level, and location. *College room and board:* $4050. Room and board charges vary according to board plan and housing facility. *Payment plan:* Installment.
FRESHMAN FINANCIAL AID (Fall 2004) 617 applied for aid; of those 80% were deemed to have need. 95% of freshmen with need received aid; of those 14% had need fully met. *Average percent of need met:* 54% (excluding resources awarded to replace EFC). *Average financial aid package:* $6459 (excluding resources awarded to replace EFC). 4% of all full-time freshmen had no need and received non-need-based gift aid.
UNDERGRADUATE FINANCIAL AID (Fall 2004) 2,724 applied for aid; of those 82% were deemed to have need. 96% of undergraduates with need received aid; of those 21% had need fully met. *Average percent of need met:* 67% (excluding resources awarded to replace EFC). *Average financial aid package:* $7566 (excluding resources awarded to replace EFC). 3% of all full-time undergraduates had no need and received non-need-based gift aid.
GIFT AID (NEED-BASED) *Total amount:* $6,400,640 (82% federal, 5% state, 8% institutional, 5% external sources). *Receiving aid:* Freshmen: 52% (364); All full-time undergraduates: 51% (1,623). *Average award:* Freshmen: $4086; Undergraduates: $4373. *Scholarships, grants, and awards:* Federal Pell, FSEOG, state, private, college/university gift aid from institutional funds.
GIFT AID (NON-NEED-BASED) *Total amount:* $296,312 (74% institutional, 26% external sources). *Receiving aid:* Freshmen: 32% (227); Undergraduates: 25% (813). *Average Award:* Freshmen: $5550; Undergraduates: $9025. *Scholarships, grants, and awards by category:* Academic Interests/Achievement: biological sciences, business, communication, computer science, education, engineering/technologies, English, general academic interests/achievements, health fields, humanities, mathematics, physical sciences, premedicine, social sciences. Creative Arts/Performance: art/fine arts, music, theater/drama. Special Achievements/Activities: cheerleading/drum major, general special achievements/activities. Special Characteristics: adult students, children and siblings of alumni, children of faculty/staff, children of union members/company employees, ethnic background, first-generation college students, local/state students, members of minority groups, out-of-state students, veterans. *Tuition waivers:* Full or partial for minority students, employees or children of employees, senior citizens.
LOANS *Student loans:* $16,017,989 (56% need-based, 44% non-need-based). 68% of past graduating class borrowed through all loan programs. *Average indebtedness per student:* $15,719. *Average need-based loan:* Freshmen: $2414; Undergraduates: $3250. *Parent loans:* $350,741 (23% need-based, 77% non-need-based). *Programs:* FFEL (Subsidized and Unsubsidized Stafford, PLUS), Perkins, college/university.
WORK-STUDY *Federal work-study:* Total amount: $266,504; 184 jobs averaging $1450. *State or other work-study/employment:* Total amount: $108,502 (96% need-based, 4% non-need-based). 77 part-time jobs averaging $1409.
ATHLETIC AWARDS *Total amount:* $736,065 (97% need-based, 3% non-need-based).
APPLYING FOR FINANCIAL AID *Required financial aid form:* FAFSA. *Financial aid deadline (priority):* 3/1. *Notification date:* Continuous beginning 4/1. Students must reply within 3 weeks of notification.
CONTACT Melina Hawkins, Director of Financial Aid, Montana State University–Billings, 1500 University Drive, Billings, MT 59101, 406-657-2188 or toll-free 800-565-6782. *Fax:* 406-657-1789. *E-mail:* mhawkins@msubillings.edu.

MONTANA STATE UNIVERSITY–NORTHERN
Havre, MT

CONTACT Kris Dramstad, Director of Financial Aid, Montana State University–Northern, PO Box 7751, Havre, MT 59501, 406-265-3787 or toll-free 800-662-6132 (in-state).

MONTANA TECH OF THE UNIVERSITY OF MONTANA
Butte, MT

Tuition & fees (MT res): $4816   Average undergraduate aid package: $7000

ABOUT THE INSTITUTION State-supported, coed. Awards: associate, bachelor's, and master's degrees and post-bachelor's certificates. 53 undergraduate majors. Total enrollment: 2,230. Undergraduates: 2,142. Freshmen: 389. Federal methodology is used as a basis for awarding need-based institutional aid.
UNDERGRADUATE EXPENSES for 2005–06 *Application fee:* $30. *Tuition, state resident:* full-time $4816; part-time $233 per credit. *Tuition, nonresident:* full-time $13,807; part-time $607 per credit. *Required fees:* $43 per credit or $49. *College room and board:* $5106; *room only:* $2294.
FRESHMAN FINANCIAL AID (Fall 2005, est.) 200 applied for aid; of those 75% were deemed to have need. 93% of freshmen with need received aid; of those 50% had need fully met. *Average percent of need met:* 50% (excluding resources awarded to replace EFC). *Average financial aid package:* $5000 (excluding resources awarded to replace EFC). 9% of all full-time freshmen had no need and received non-need-based gift aid.
UNDERGRADUATE FINANCIAL AID (Fall 2005, est.) 1,500 applied for aid; of those 87% were deemed to have need. 92% of undergraduates with need received aid; of those 58% had need fully met. *Average percent of need met:* 60% (excluding resources awarded to replace EFC). *Average financial aid package:* $7000 (excluding resources awarded to replace EFC). 5% of all full-time undergraduates had no need and received non-need-based gift aid.
GIFT AID (NEED-BASED) *Total amount:* $1,790,000 (84% federal, 8% state, 6% institutional, 2% external sources). *Receiving aid:* Freshmen: 29% (100); All full-time undergraduates: 47% (900). *Average award:* Freshmen: $1000; Undergraduates: $1000. *Scholarships, grants, and awards:* Federal Pell, FSEOG, state, private, college/university gift aid from institutional funds.
GIFT AID (NON-NEED-BASED) *Total amount:* $1,190,000 (71% institutional, 29% external sources). *Receiving aid:* Freshmen: 9% (30); Undergraduates: 5% (100). *Average Award:* Freshmen: $2500; Undergraduates: $4000. *Scholar-

Montana Tech of The University of Montana

ships, grants, and awards by category: Academic Interests/Achievement: 350 awards ($600,000 total): business, computer science, engineering/technologies, general academic interests/achievements, health fields, mathematics, physical sciences. Special Achievements/Activities: $50,000 total: general special achievements/activities. Special Characteristics: $50,000 total: general special characteristics.
LOANS Student loans: $6,100,000 (57% need-based, 43% non-need-based). 75% of past graduating class borrowed through all loan programs. Average indebtedness per student: $19,000. Average need-based loan: Freshmen: $2500; Undergraduates: $5000. Parent loans: $315,509 (100% need-based). Programs: FFEL (Subsidized and Unsubsidized Stafford, PLUS), Perkins, college/university.
WORK-STUDY Federal work-study: Total amount: $175,000; 100 jobs averaging $2000. State or other work-study/employment: Total amount: $15,000 (100% need-based). 25 part-time jobs averaging $2000.
ATHLETIC AWARDS Total amount: $600,000 (100% non-need-based).
APPLYING FOR FINANCIAL AID Required financial aid forms: FAFSA, institution's own form. Financial aid deadline (priority): 3/1. Notification date: Continuous beginning 3/15. Students must reply within 3 weeks of notification.
CONTACT Mike Richardson, Director of Financial Aid, Montana Tech of The University of Montana, West Park Street, Butte, MT 59701-8997, 406-496-4212 or toll-free 800-445-TECH Ext. 1. Fax: 406-496-4705.

MONTCLAIR STATE UNIVERSITY
Montclair, NJ

Tuition & fees (NJ res): $7709	Average undergraduate aid package: $7826

ABOUT THE INSTITUTION State-supported, coed. Awards: bachelor's, master's, and doctoral degrees and post-bachelor's and post-master's certificates. 46 undergraduate majors. Total enrollment: 16,063. Undergraduates: 12,174. Freshmen: 1,944. Federal methodology is used as a basis for awarding need-based institutional aid.
UNDERGRADUATE EXPENSES for 2005–06 Application fee: $55. Tuition, state resident: full-time $5581; part-time $186.04 per credit. Tuition, nonresident: full-time $10,029; part-time $334.22 per credit. Required fees: full-time $2128; $69.61 per credit or $20 per term part-time. College room and board: $8618; room only: $5768. Room and board charges vary according to board plan and housing facility. Payment plan: Installment.
FRESHMAN FINANCIAL AID (Fall 2005, est.) 1152 applied for aid; of those 82% were deemed to have need. 86% of freshmen with need received aid; of those 29% had need fully met. Average percent of need met: 53% (excluding resources awarded to replace EFC). Average financial aid package: $6376 (excluding resources awarded to replace EFC). 3% of all full-time freshmen had no need and received non-need-based gift aid.
UNDERGRADUATE FINANCIAL AID (Fall 2005, est.) 6,031 applied for aid; of those 80% were deemed to have need. 96% of undergraduates with need received aid; of those 36% had need fully met. Average percent of need met: 54% (excluding resources awarded to replace EFC). Average financial aid package: $7826 (excluding resources awarded to replace EFC). 4% of all full-time undergraduates had no need and received non-need-based gift aid.
GIFT AID (NEED-BASED) Total amount: $19,333,964 (47% federal, 53% state). Receiving aid: Freshmen: 21% (405); All full-time undergraduates: 27% (2,653). Average award: Freshmen: $5603; Undergraduates: $6229. Scholarships, grants, and awards: Federal Pell, FSEOG, state, college/university gift aid from institutional funds.
GIFT AID (NON-NEED-BASED) Total amount: $5,574,138 (20% state, 71% institutional, 9% external sources). Receiving aid: Freshmen: 6% (115); Undergraduates: 5% (448). Average Award: Freshmen: $4438; Undergraduates: $4789. Scholarships, grants, and awards by category: Academic Interests/Achievement: 1,040 awards ($3,382,157 total): biological sciences, business, communication, education, English, foreign languages, general academic interests/achievements, home economics, humanities, mathematics, physical sciences, religion/biblical studies, social sciences. Creative Arts/Performance: 42 awards ($57,824 total): art/fine arts, cinema/film/broadcasting, dance, music, performing arts, theater/drama. Special Achievements/Activities: 120 awards ($523,996 total): community service, general special achievements/activities, leadership. Tuition waivers: Full or partial for employees or children of employees, senior citizens. ROTC: Air Force cooperative.
LOANS Student loans: $40,016,547 (48% need-based, 52% non-need-based). 53% of past graduating class borrowed through all loan programs. Average indebtedness per student: $16,654. Average need-based loan: Freshmen: $2760; Undergraduates: $4078. Parent loans: $5,675,408 (100% non-need-based). Programs: FFEL (Subsidized and Unsubsidized Stafford, PLUS), Perkins, state, private educational loans.
WORK-STUDY Federal work-study: Total amount: $400,789; 394 jobs averaging $1017. State or other work-study/employment: Total amount: $2,729,864 (100% non-need-based). 1,317 part-time jobs averaging $2073.
APPLYING FOR FINANCIAL AID Required financial aid form: FAFSA. Financial aid deadline (priority): 3/1. Notification date: Continuous beginning 4/1. Students must reply within 2 weeks of notification.
CONTACT Frank A. Cuozzo, Director of Financial Aid, Montclair State University, College Hall, Room 222, Upper Montclair, NJ 07043, 973-655-7022 or toll-free 800-331-9205. Fax: 973-655-7712. E-mail: cuozzof@mail.montclair.edu.

MONTREAT COLLEGE
Montreat, NC

Tuition & fees: $15,560	Average undergraduate aid package: $13,417

ABOUT THE INSTITUTION Independent religious, coed. Awards: associate, bachelor's, and master's degrees. 14 undergraduate majors. Total enrollment: 1,035. Undergraduates: 943. Freshmen: 126. Federal methodology is used as a basis for awarding need-based institutional aid.
UNDERGRADUATE EXPENSES for 2005–06 Application fee: $15. Comprehensive fee: $20,568 includes full-time tuition ($15,560) and room and board ($5008). Part-time tuition: $480 per credit hour.
FRESHMAN FINANCIAL AID (Fall 2005, est.) 130 applied for aid; of those 72% were deemed to have need. 100% of freshmen with need received aid; of those 12% had need fully met. Average percent of need met: 82% (excluding resources awarded to replace EFC). Average financial aid package: $11,143 (excluding resources awarded to replace EFC). 35% of all full-time freshmen had no need and received non-need-based gift aid.
UNDERGRADUATE FINANCIAL AID (Fall 2005, est.) 1,012 applied for aid; of those 80% were deemed to have need. 100% of undergraduates with need received aid; of those 22% had need fully met. Average percent of need met: 83% (excluding resources awarded to replace EFC). Average financial aid package: $13,417 (excluding resources awarded to replace EFC). 32% of all full-time undergraduates had no need and received non-need-based gift aid.
GIFT AID (NEED-BASED) Total amount: $3,767,391 (30% federal, 20% state, 43% institutional, 7% external sources). Receiving aid: Freshmen: 69% (93); All full-time undergraduates: 71% (766). Average award: Freshmen: $8012; Undergraduates: $6116. Scholarships, grants, and awards: Federal Pell, FSEOG, state, private, college/university gift aid from institutional funds.
GIFT AID (NON-NEED-BASED) Total amount: $509,000 (100% state). Receiving aid: Freshmen: 6% (8); Undergraduates: 4% (44). Average Award: Freshmen: $5108; Undergraduates: $5219. Scholarships, grants, and awards by category: Academic Interests/Achievement: general academic interests/achievements. Creative Arts/Performance: 13 awards ($12,488 total): art/fine arts, music, theater/drama. Special Achievements/Activities: leadership. Special Characteristics: 58 awards ($130,800 total): children and siblings of alumni, children of faculty/staff, international students, relatives of clergy.
LOANS Student loans: $1,529,406 (100% need-based). 86% of past graduating class borrowed through all loan programs. Average indebtedness per student: $19,166. Average need-based loan: Freshmen: $2546; Undergraduates: $5500. Parent loans: $361,419 (100% need-based). Programs: FFEL (Subsidized and Unsubsidized Stafford, PLUS), Perkins.
WORK-STUDY Federal work-study: Total amount: $111,827; 81 jobs averaging $1510. State or other work-study/employment: Total amount: $37,905 (100% non-need-based). 41 part-time jobs averaging $1360.
ATHLETIC AWARDS Total amount: $402,926 (100% need-based).
APPLYING FOR FINANCIAL AID Required financial aid forms: FAFSA, institution's own form, state aid form (for NC residents only). Financial aid deadline (priority): 3/15. Notification date: Continuous beginning 1/15. Students must reply within 2 weeks of notification.
CONTACT Mrs. Kimberly M. Norton, Director of Financial Aid, Montreat College, PO Box 1267, Montreat, NC 28757-1267, 828-669-8012 Ext. 3795 or toll-free 800-622-6968 (in-state). Fax: 828-669-0120. E-mail: knorton@montreat.edu.

MONTSERRAT COLLEGE OF ART
Beverly, MA

Tuition & fees: $20,679 — **Average undergraduate aid package: $9947**

ABOUT THE INSTITUTION Independent, coed. Awards: bachelor's degrees and post-bachelor's certificates. 10 undergraduate majors. Total enrollment: 308. Undergraduates: 308. Freshmen: 75. Federal methodology is used as a basis for awarding need-based institutional aid.

UNDERGRADUATE EXPENSES for 2005–06 *Application fee:* $40. *One-time required fee:* $725. *Tuition:* full-time $19,934; part-time $831 per credit. *Required fees:* full-time $745; $22 per credit. Full-time tuition and fees vary according to course load. Part-time tuition and fees vary according to course load. Room and board charges vary according to housing facility. *Payment plan:* Installment.

FRESHMAN FINANCIAL AID (Fall 2005, est.) 74 applied for aid; of those 74% were deemed to have need. 100% of freshmen with need received aid. *Average percent of need met:* 26% (excluding resources awarded to replace EFC). *Average financial aid package:* $10,457 (excluding resources awarded to replace EFC). 27% of all full-time freshmen had no need and received non-need-based gift aid.

UNDERGRADUATE FINANCIAL AID (Fall 2005, est.) 281 applied for aid; of those 81% were deemed to have need. 100% of undergraduates with need received aid. *Average financial aid package:* $9947 (excluding resources awarded to replace EFC).

GIFT AID (NEED-BASED) *Total amount:* $1,036,710 (30% federal, 10% state, 55% institutional, 5% external sources). *Receiving aid:* Freshmen: 73% (55); All full-time undergraduates: 69% (207). *Average award:* Freshmen: $4717; Undergraduates: $4548. *Scholarships, grants, and awards:* Federal Pell, FSEOG, state, private, college/university gift aid from institutional funds.

GIFT AID (NON-NEED-BASED) *Total amount:* $696,592 (100% institutional). *Receiving aid:* Freshmen: 68% (51); Undergraduates: 59% (176). *Average Award:* Freshmen: $2350. *Scholarships, grants, and awards by category:* Creative Arts/Performance: 216 awards ($696,592 total): applied art and design, art/fine arts. *Special Characteristics:* siblings of current students. *Tuition waivers:* Full or partial for employees or children of employees. *ROTC:* Air Force cooperative.

LOANS *Student loans:* $2,306,455 (84% need-based, 16% non-need-based). 84% of past graduating class borrowed through all loan programs. *Average need-based loan:* Freshmen: $2928; Undergraduates: $4196. *Parent loans:* $1,235,504 (86% need-based, 14% non-need-based). *Programs:* FFEL (Subsidized and Unsubsidized Stafford, PLUS), state, alternative loans.

WORK-STUDY *Federal work-study:* Total amount: $96,097; 65 jobs averaging $847.

APPLYING FOR FINANCIAL AID *Required financial aid form:* FAFSA. *Financial aid deadline (priority):* 3/1. *Notification date:* Continuous beginning 2/1. Students must reply within 2 weeks of notification.

CONTACT Creda Carney, Director of Financial Aid, Montserrat College of Art, 23 Essex Street, PO Box 26, Beverly, MA 01915, 978-922-8222 Ext. 1155 or toll-free 800-836-0487. *Fax:* 978-922-4268. *E-mail:* finaid@montserrat.edu.

MOODY BIBLE INSTITUTE
Chicago, IL

CONTACT Daniel R. Ward, Director of Financial Aid, Moody Bible Institute, 820 North LaSalle Boulevard, Chicago, IL 60610-3284, 312-329-4178 or toll-free 800-967-4MBI. *Fax:* 312-329-4197. *E-mail:* daniel.ward@moody.edu.

MOORE COLLEGE OF ART & DESIGN
Philadelphia, PA

Tuition & fees: $23,602 — **Average undergraduate aid package: $13,757**

ABOUT THE INSTITUTION Independent, women only. Awards: bachelor's degrees and post-bachelor's certificates. 10 undergraduate majors. Total enrollment: 491. Undergraduates: 491. Freshmen: 80. Federal methodology is used as a basis for awarding need-based institutional aid.

UNDERGRADUATE EXPENSES for 2006–07 *Application fee:* $40. *Comprehensive fee:* $32,256 includes full-time tuition ($22,846), mandatory fees ($756), and room and board ($8654). *College room only:* $5227. *Part-time tuition:* $920 per credit. *Part-time fees:* $189 per term.

FRESHMAN FINANCIAL AID (Fall 2005, est.) 70 applied for aid; of those 89% were deemed to have need. 100% of freshmen with need received aid; of those 6% had need fully met. *Average percent of need met:* 50% (excluding resources awarded to replace EFC). *Average financial aid package:* $13,311 (excluding resources awarded to replace EFC). 27% of all full-time freshmen had no need and received non-need-based gift aid.

UNDERGRADUATE FINANCIAL AID (Fall 2005, est.) 345 applied for aid; of those 91% were deemed to have need. 100% of undergraduates with need received aid; of those 6% had need fully met. *Average percent of need met:* 50% (excluding resources awarded to replace EFC). *Average financial aid package:* $13,757 (excluding resources awarded to replace EFC). 23% of all full-time undergraduates had no need and received non-need-based gift aid.

GIFT AID (NEED-BASED) *Total amount:* $3,215,205 (20% federal, 13% state, 60% institutional, 7% external sources). *Receiving aid:* Freshmen: 70% (62); All full-time undergraduates: 75% (312). *Average award:* Freshmen: $10,162; Undergraduates: $8983. *Scholarships, grants, and awards:* Federal Pell, FSEOG, state, private, college/university gift aid from institutional funds.

GIFT AID (NON-NEED-BASED) *Total amount:* $491,801 (98% institutional, 2% external sources). *Receiving aid:* Freshmen: 3% (3); Undergraduates: 3% (11). *Average Award:* Freshmen: $7933; Undergraduates: $9339. *Scholarships, grants, and awards by category:* Academic Interests/Achievement: 462 awards ($2,000,000 total): general academic interests/achievements. *Special Achievements/Activities:* 29 awards ($2000 total): leadership.

LOANS *Student loans:* $4,389,688 (82% need-based, 18% non-need-based). 83% of past graduating class borrowed through all loan programs. *Average indebtedness per student:* $22,652. *Average need-based loan:* Freshmen: $3144; Undergraduates: $4818. *Parent loans:* $1,619,571 (52% need-based, 48% non-need-based). *Programs:* FFEL (Subsidized and Unsubsidized Stafford, PLUS), Perkins.

WORK-STUDY *Federal work-study:* Total amount: $112,449; 110 jobs averaging $1020. *State or other work-study/employment:* Part-time jobs available.

APPLYING FOR FINANCIAL AID *Required financial aid form:* FAFSA. *Financial aid deadline (priority):* 3/1. *Notification date:* Continuous beginning 3/1. Students must reply within 2 weeks of notification.

CONTACT Rochelle Iannuzzi, Director of Financial Aid, Moore College of Art & Design, 20th and the Parkway, Philadelphia, PA 19103-1179, 215-568-4515 Ext. 4042 or toll-free 800-523-2025. *Fax:* 215-568-8017. *E-mail:* riannuzzi@moore.edu.

MORAVIAN COLLEGE
Bethlehem, PA

Tuition & fees: $25,263 — **Average undergraduate aid package: $17,118**

ABOUT THE INSTITUTION Independent religious, coed. Awards: bachelor's, master's, and first professional degrees and post-bachelor's certificates. 61 undergraduate majors. Total enrollment: 2,030. Undergraduates: 1,792. Freshmen: 382. Both federal and institutional methodology are used as a basis for awarding need-based institutional aid.

UNDERGRADUATE EXPENSES for 2005–06 *Application fee:* $40. *One-time required fee:* $100. *Comprehensive fee:* $32,793 includes full-time tuition ($24,813), mandatory fees ($450), and room and board ($7530). *College room only:* $4230. Room and board charges vary according to board plan and housing facility. *Part-time tuition:* $775 per credit. Part-time tuition and fees vary according to class time. *Payment plan:* Installment.

FRESHMAN FINANCIAL AID (Fall 2005, est.) 343 applied for aid; of those 81% were deemed to have need. 100% of freshmen with need received aid; of those 18% had need fully met. *Average percent of need met:* 76% (excluding resources awarded to replace EFC). *Average financial aid package:* $16,827 (excluding resources awarded to replace EFC). 23% of all full-time freshmen had no need and received non-need-based gift aid.

UNDERGRADUATE FINANCIAL AID (Fall 2005, est.) 1,278 applied for aid; of those 91% were deemed to have need. 95% of undergraduates with need received aid; of those 21% had need fully met. *Average percent of need met:* 74% (excluding resources awarded to replace EFC). *Average financial aid*

Moravian College

package: $17,118 (excluding resources awarded to replace EFC). 22% of all full-time undergraduates had no need and received non-need-based gift aid.
GIFT AID (NEED-BASED) *Total amount:* $13,163,918 (7% federal, 12% state, 78% institutional, 3% external sources). *Receiving aid:* Freshmen: 72% (275); All full-time undergraduates: 73% (1,089). *Average award:* Freshmen: $12,492; Undergraduates: $12,278. *Scholarships, grants, and awards:* Federal Pell, FSEOG, state, private, college/university gift aid from institutional funds.
GIFT AID (NON-NEED-BASED) *Total amount:* $3,050,503 (1% state, 88% institutional, 11% external sources). *Receiving aid:* Freshmen: 9% (33); Undergraduates: 8% (122). *Average Award:* Freshmen: $13,559; Undergraduates:* $13,668. *Scholarships, grants, and awards by category:* Academic Interests/Achievement: 1,260 awards ($7,412,147 total): biological sciences, business, computer science, foreign languages, general academic interests/achievements, health fields, mathematics, physical sciences. *Creative Arts/Performance:* 13 awards ($44,500 total): music. *Special Achievements/Activities:* 23 awards ($43,400 total): religious involvement. *Special Characteristics:* 179 awards ($1,052,626 total): adult students, children and siblings of alumni, children of educators, children of faculty/staff, ethnic background, international students, relatives of clergy, religious affiliation. *Tuition waivers:* Full or partial for children of alumni, employees or children of employees. *ROTC:* Army cooperative.
LOANS *Student loans:* $10,440,852 (62% need-based, 38% non-need-based). *Average need-based loan:* Freshmen: $3307; Undergraduates: $4175. *Parent loans:* $4,214,961 (32% need-based, 68% non-need-based). *Programs:* FFEL (Subsidized and Unsubsidized Stafford, PLUS), Perkins.
WORK-STUDY *Federal work-study:* Total amount: $1,326,080; 905 jobs averaging $1464. *State or other work-study/employment:* Total amount: $288,030 (5% need-based, 95% non-need-based). 269 part-time jobs averaging $1092.
APPLYING FOR FINANCIAL AID *Required financial aid forms:* FAFSA, CSS Financial Aid PROFILE, state aid form, noncustodial (divorced/separated) parent's statement, business/farm supplement. *Financial aid deadline (priority):* 2/15. *Notification date:* 4/1. Students must reply by 5/1 or within 2 weeks of notification.
CONTACT Mr. Stephen C. Cassel, Director of Financial Aid, Moravian College, 1200 Main Street, Bethlehem, PA 18018-6650, 610-861-1330 or toll-free 800-441-3191. *Fax:* 610-861-1346. *E-mail:* cassels@moravian.edu.

MOREHEAD STATE UNIVERSITY
Morehead, KY

Tuition & fees (KY res): $4320	Average undergraduate aid package: $7826

ABOUT THE INSTITUTION State-supported, coed. Awards: associate, bachelor's, and master's degrees and post-master's certificates. 49 undergraduate majors. Total enrollment: 9,062. Undergraduates: 7,544. Freshmen: 1,300. Federal methodology is used as a basis for awarding need-based institutional aid.
UNDERGRADUATE EXPENSES for 2005–06 *Tuition, state resident:* full-time $4320; part-time $180 per credit hour. *Tuition, nonresident:* full-time $11,480; part-time $480 per credit hour. Full-time tuition and fees vary according to course load and reciprocity agreements. *College room and board:* $4830. Room and board charges vary according to board plan and housing facility. *Payment plans:* Installment, deferred payment.
FRESHMAN FINANCIAL AID (Fall 2005, est.) 1137 applied for aid; of those 77% were deemed to have need. 99% of freshmen with need received aid; of those 36% had need fully met. *Average percent of need met:* 88% (excluding resources awarded to replace EFC). *Average financial aid package:* $7449 (excluding resources awarded to replace EFC). 26% of all full-time freshmen had no need and received non-need-based gift aid.
UNDERGRADUATE FINANCIAL AID (Fall 2005, est.) 4,892 applied for aid; of those 83% were deemed to have need. 99% of undergraduates with need received aid; of those 39% had need fully met. *Average percent of need met:* 86% (excluding resources awarded to replace EFC). *Average financial aid package:* $7826 (excluding resources awarded to replace EFC). 18% of all full-time undergraduates had no need and received non-need-based gift aid.
GIFT AID (NEED-BASED) *Total amount:* $14,060,404 (76% federal, 24% state). *Receiving aid:* Freshmen: 48% (613); All full-time undergraduates: 49% (2,937). *Average award:* Freshmen: $4339; Undergraduates: $4263. *Scholarships, grants, and awards:* Federal Pell, FSEOG, state, private, college/university gift aid from institutional funds.
GIFT AID (NON-NEED-BASED) *Total amount:* $7,895,228 (48% state, 43% institutional, 9% external sources). *Receiving aid:* Freshmen: 55% (702); Undergraduates: 34% (2,035). *Average Award:* Freshmen: $4054; Undergraduates:* $3261. *Scholarships, grants, and awards by category:* Academic Interests/Achievement: 1,409 awards ($2,737,897 total): agriculture, biological sciences, business, communication, education, English, general academic interests/achievements, health fields, humanities, physical sciences, social sciences. *Creative Arts/Performance:* 142 awards ($195,107 total): art/fine arts, cinema/film/broadcasting, debating, journalism/publications, music, theater/drama. *Special Achievements/Activities:* 130 awards ($84,613 total): cheerleading/drum major, leadership. *Special Characteristics:* 342 awards ($288,734 total): adult students, children and siblings of alumni, local/state students, members of minority groups, out-of-state students. *Tuition waivers:* Full or partial for children of alumni, employees or children of employees, senior citizens. *ROTC:* Army.
LOANS *Student loans:* $19,255,269 (53% need-based, 47% non-need-based). 59% of past graduating class borrowed through all loan programs. *Average indebtedness per student:* $16,995. *Average need-based loan:* Freshmen: $2570; Undergraduates: $3329. *Parent loans:* $1,667,624 (100% non-need-based). *Programs:* Federal Direct (Subsidized and Unsubsidized Stafford, PLUS), FFEL (Subsidized and Unsubsidized Stafford, PLUS), Perkins, college/university.
WORK-STUDY *Federal work-study:* Total amount: $906,591; 583 jobs averaging $1555. *State or other work-study/employment:* Total amount: $797,720 (100% non-need-based). 552 part-time jobs averaging $1350.
ATHLETIC AWARDS *Total amount:* $1,073,050 (100% non-need-based).
APPLYING FOR FINANCIAL AID *Required financial aid forms:* FAFSA, institution's own form. *Financial aid deadline (priority):* 3/15. *Notification date:* Continuous.
CONTACT Carol Becker, Director of Financial Aid, Morehead State University, 100 Admissions Center, Morehead, KY 40351, 606-783-2011 or toll-free 800-585-6781. *Fax:* 606-783-2293. *E-mail:* c.becker@moreheadstate.edu.

MOREHOUSE COLLEGE
Atlanta, GA

ABOUT THE INSTITUTION Independent, men only. Awards: bachelor's degrees. 33 undergraduate majors. Total enrollment: 3,029. Undergraduates: 3,029. Freshmen: 682.
GIFT AID (NEED-BASED) *Scholarships, grants, and awards:* Federal Pell, FSEOG, state, private, United Negro College Fund.
GIFT AID (NON-NEED-BASED) *Scholarships, grants, and awards by category:* Academic Interests/Achievement: business, general academic interests/achievements, military science. *Creative Arts/Performance:* music. *Special Achievements/Activities:* community service, leadership, religious involvement. *Special Characteristics:* children of faculty/staff.
LOANS *Programs:* Federal Direct (Subsidized and Unsubsidized Stafford, PLUS), FFEL (Subsidized and Unsubsidized Stafford, PLUS), Perkins, state, college/university.
APPLYING FOR FINANCIAL AID *Required financial aid forms:* FAFSA, institution's own form, CSS Financial Aid PROFILE.
CONTACT James A. Stotts, Director of Financial Aid, Morehouse College, 830 Westview Drive, SW, Atlanta, GA 30314, 404-681-2800 Ext. 2638 or toll-free 800-851-1254. *Fax:* 404-215-2711. *E-mail:* jstotts@morehouse.edu.

MORGAN STATE UNIVERSITY
Baltimore, MD

CONTACT Director of Financial Aid, Morgan State University, 1700 East Cold Spring Lane, Baltimore, MD 21251, 443-885-3170 or toll-free 800-332-6674.

MORNINGSIDE COLLEGE
Sioux City, IA

Tuition & fees: $18,080	Average undergraduate aid package: $16,302

ABOUT THE INSTITUTION Independent religious, coed. Awards: bachelor's and master's degrees. 43 undergraduate majors. Total enrollment: 1,440. Undergraduates: 1,149. Freshmen: 309. Federal methodology is used as a basis for awarding need-based institutional aid.
UNDERGRADUATE EXPENSES for 2005–06 *Application fee:* $25. *Comprehensive fee:* $23,704 includes full-time tuition ($17,170), mandatory fees ($910), and room and board ($5624). *College room only:* $2940. Full-time tuition and fees

vary according to program. Room and board charges vary according to housing facility. *Part-time tuition:* $530 per semester hour. Part-time tuition and fees vary according to course load. *Payment plan:* Installment.
FRESHMAN FINANCIAL AID (Fall 2005, est.) 301 applied for aid; of those 93% were deemed to have need. 100% of freshmen with need received aid; of those 64% had need fully met. *Average percent of need met:* 77% (excluding resources awarded to replace EFC). *Average financial aid package:* $16,962 (excluding resources awarded to replace EFC). 9% of all full-time freshmen had no need and received non-need-based gift aid.
UNDERGRADUATE FINANCIAL AID (Fall 2005, est.) 1,012 applied for aid; of those 92% were deemed to have need. 100% of undergraduates with need received aid; of those 62% had need fully met. *Average percent of need met:* 77% (excluding resources awarded to replace EFC). *Average financial aid package:* $16,302 (excluding resources awarded to replace EFC). 12% of all full-time undergraduates had no need and received non-need-based gift aid.
GIFT AID (NEED-BASED) *Total amount:* $4,226,010 (30% federal, 43% state, 27% institutional). *Receiving aid:* Freshmen: 73% (225); All full-time undergraduates: 69% (735). *Average award:* Freshmen: $5939; Undergraduates: $5702. *Scholarships, grants, and awards:* Federal Pell, FSEOG, state, private, college/university gift aid from institutional funds.
GIFT AID (NON-NEED-BASED) *Total amount:* $6,307,329 (2% state, 89% institutional, 9% external sources). *Receiving aid:* Freshmen: 90% (279); Undergraduates: 84% (899). *Average Award:* Freshmen: $7503; Undergraduates: $6130. *Scholarships, grants, and awards by category: Academic Interests/Achievement:* 712 awards ($2,810,469 total): general academic interests/achievements. *Creative Arts/Performance:* 268 awards ($676,925 total): art/fine arts, cinema/film/broadcasting, journalism/publications, music, theater/drama. *Special Achievements/Activities:* 299 awards ($653,809 total): cheerleading/drum major, community service, leadership. *Special Characteristics:* 1,114 awards ($1,733,089 total): children of faculty/staff, international students, out-of-state students. *Tuition waivers:* Full or partial for children of alumni, employees or children of employees, senior citizens. *ROTC:* Army cooperative.
LOANS *Student loans:* $8,393,285 (37% need-based, 63% non-need-based). 91% of past graduating class borrowed through all loan programs. *Average indebtedness per student:* $26,816. *Average need-based loan:* Freshmen: $3228; Undergraduates: $3585. *Parent loans:* $306,056 (100% non-need-based). *Programs:* FFEL (Subsidized and Unsubsidized Stafford, PLUS), Perkins, state, college/university, private loans.
WORK-STUDY *Federal work-study:* Total amount: $348,577; 300 jobs averaging $1161. *State or other work-study/employment:* Total amount: $259,541 (100% non-need-based). 1 part-time job averaging $580.
ATHLETIC AWARDS *Total amount:* $1,257,691 (100% non-need-based).
APPLYING FOR FINANCIAL AID *Required financial aid form:* FAFSA. *Financial aid deadline (priority):* 3/1. *Notification date:* 3/31.
CONTACT Karen Gagnon, Director of Student Financial Planning, Morningside College, 1501 Morningside Avenue, Sioux City, IA 51106, 712-274-5272 or toll-free 800-831-0806 Ext. 5111. *Fax:* 712-274-5605. *E-mail:* gagnon@morningside.edu.

MORRIS COLLEGE
Sumter, SC

ABOUT THE INSTITUTION Independent religious, coed. Awards: bachelor's degrees. 22 undergraduate majors. Total enrollment: 863. Undergraduates: 863. Freshmen: 208.
GIFT AID (NEED-BASED) *Scholarships, grants, and awards:* Federal Pell, FSEOG, state, private, college/university gift aid from institutional funds, United Negro College Fund.
GIFT AID (NON-NEED-BASED) *Scholarships, grants, and awards by category: Academic Interests/Achievement:* biological sciences, business, communication, computer science, education, general academic interests/achievements, humanities, mathematics, military science, physical sciences, premedicine, religion/biblical studies. *Creative Arts/Performance:* art/fine arts, creative writing, journalism/publications, performing arts. *Special Achievements/Activities:* cheerleading/drum major. *Special Characteristics:* first-generation college students, veterans.
LOANS *Programs:* Federal Direct (Subsidized and Unsubsidized Stafford, PLUS), FFEL (PLUS), Perkins.
APPLYING FOR FINANCIAL AID *Required financial aid forms:* FAFSA, institution's own form.

CONTACT Ms. Sandra S. Gibson, Director of Financial Aid, Morris College, 100 West College Street, Sumter, SC 29150-3599, 803-934-3238 or toll-free 866-853-1345. *Fax:* 803-773-3687.

MORRISON UNIVERSITY
Reno, NV

CONTACT Kim Droniak, Financial Aid Administrator, Morrison University, 140 Washington Street, Reno, NV 89503-5600, 775-850-0700 or toll-free 800-369-6144. *Fax:* 775-850-0711.

MOUNTAIN STATE UNIVERSITY
Beckley, WV

Tuition & fees: $7350	Average undergraduate aid package: $6280

ABOUT THE INSTITUTION Independent, coed. Awards: associate, bachelor's, and master's degrees and post-master's certificates. 61 undergraduate majors. Total enrollment: 4,404. Undergraduates: 3,978. Freshmen: 365. Federal methodology is used as a basis for awarding need-based institutional aid.
UNDERGRADUATE EXPENSES for 2005–06 *Application fee:* $25. *Comprehensive fee:* $12,876 includes full-time tuition ($5700), mandatory fees ($1650), and room and board ($5526). *College room only:* $2810. Full-time tuition and fees vary according to program. Room and board charges vary according to board plan. *Part-time tuition:* $190 per credit. *Part-time fees:* $55 per credit. Part-time tuition and fees vary according to program. *Payment plan:* Installment.
FRESHMAN FINANCIAL AID (Fall 2004) 288 applied for aid; of those 77% were deemed to have need. 100% of freshmen with need received aid. *Average percent of need met:* 37% (excluding resources awarded to replace EFC). *Average financial aid package:* $4875 (excluding resources awarded to replace EFC). 1% of all full-time freshmen had no need and received non-need-based gift aid.
UNDERGRADUATE FINANCIAL AID (Fall 2004) 1,941 applied for aid; of those 94% were deemed to have need. 100% of undergraduates with need received aid. *Average percent of need met:* 47% (excluding resources awarded to replace EFC). *Average financial aid package:* $6280 (excluding resources awarded to replace EFC). 1% of all full-time undergraduates had no need and received non-need-based gift aid.
GIFT AID (NEED-BASED) *Total amount:* $6,947,026 (78% federal, 18% state, 2% institutional, 2% external sources). *Receiving aid:* Freshmen: 62% (180); All full-time undergraduates: 50% (1,321). *Average award:* Freshmen: $3319; Undergraduates: $3878. *Scholarships, grants, and awards:* Federal Pell, FSEOG, state, private, college/university gift aid from institutional funds, Federal Nursing.
GIFT AID (NON-NEED-BASED) *Total amount:* $395,636 (58% state, 42% institutional). *Receiving aid:* Freshmen: 4% (12); Undergraduates: 3% (73). *Average Award:* Freshmen: $4047; Undergraduates: $4044. *Scholarships, grants, and awards by category: Academic Interests/Achievement:* 40 awards ($163,208 total): general academic interests/achievements. *Tuition waivers:* Full or partial for employees or children of employees, senior citizens.
LOANS *Student loans:* $18,171,629 (49% need-based, 51% non-need-based). 69% of past graduating class borrowed through all loan programs. *Average indebtedness per student:* $23,570. *Average need-based loan:* Freshmen: $2533; Undergraduates: $3864. *Parent loans:* $277,879 (100% non-need-based). *Programs:* FFEL (Subsidized and Unsubsidized Stafford, PLUS), private education loans.
WORK-STUDY *Federal work-study:* Total amount: $212,140; 156 jobs averaging $1360.
ATHLETIC AWARDS *Total amount:* $295,810 (100% non-need-based).
APPLYING FOR FINANCIAL AID *Required financial aid form:* FAFSA. *Financial aid deadline:* Continuous. *Notification date:* Continuous. Students must reply within 2 weeks of notification.
CONTACT Sandra Richmond, Director of Financial Aid, Mountain State University, PO Box 9003, Beckley, WV 25802-9003, 304-929-1595 or toll-free 800-766-6067 Ext. 1433. *Fax:* 304-929-1390. *E-mail:* srichmond@mountainstate.edu.

MOUNT ALOYSIUS COLLEGE
Cresson, PA

Tuition & fees: $14,650	Average undergraduate aid package: $11,400

Mount Aloysius College

ABOUT THE INSTITUTION Independent Roman Catholic, coed. Awards: associate, bachelor's, and master's degrees. 34 undergraduate majors. Total enrollment: 1,539. Undergraduates: 1,482. Freshmen: 297. Federal methodology is used as a basis for awarding need-based institutional aid.

UNDERGRADUATE EXPENSES for 2005–06 *Application fee:* $30. *Comprehensive fee:* $20,840 includes full-time tuition ($14,220), mandatory fees ($430), and room and board ($6190). *College room only:* $3130. Full-time tuition and fees vary according to class time, course load, and program. Room and board charges vary according to board plan. *Part-time tuition:* $450 per credit. Part-time tuition and fees vary according to class time, course load, and program. *Payment plan:* Installment.

FRESHMAN FINANCIAL AID (Fall 2004) 277 applied for aid; of those 86% were deemed to have need. 100% of freshmen with need received aid. *Average percent of need met:* 23% (excluding resources awarded to replace EFC). *Average financial aid package:* $11,000 (excluding resources awarded to replace EFC). 14% of all full-time freshmen had no need and received non-need-based gift aid.

UNDERGRADUATE FINANCIAL AID (Fall 2004) 1,216 applied for aid; of those 94% were deemed to have need. 100% of undergraduates with need received aid. *Average percent of need met:* 25% (excluding resources awarded to replace EFC). *Average financial aid package:* $11,400 (excluding resources awarded to replace EFC). 6% of all full-time undergraduates had no need and received non-need-based gift aid.

GIFT AID (NEED-BASED) *Total amount:* $7,451,825 (30% federal, 35% state, 33% institutional, 2% external sources). *Receiving aid:* Freshmen: 86% (238); All full-time undergraduates: 94% (1,142). *Average award:* Freshmen: $2800; Undergraduates: $2600. *Scholarships, grants, and awards:* Federal Pell, FSEOG, state, private, college/university gift aid from institutional funds.

GIFT AID (NON-NEED-BASED) *Receiving aid:* Freshmen: 14% (39); Undergraduates: 6% (74). *Average Award:* Freshmen: $2100; Undergraduates: $2000. *Scholarships, grants, and awards by category: Creative Arts/Performance:* 15 awards ($14,000 total): music, performing arts. *Special Achievements/Activities:* 24 awards ($174,000 total): leadership. *Special Characteristics:* 83 awards ($46,500 total): children of current students, parents of current students, religious affiliation, siblings of current students, spouses of current students, twins. *Tuition waivers:* Full or partial for employees or children of employees.

LOANS *Student loans:* $6,617,385 (100% need-based). 79% of past graduating class borrowed through all loan programs. *Average indebtedness per student:* $20,970. *Average need-based loan:* Freshmen: $2600; Undergraduates: $3530. *Parent loans:* $1,420,633 (100% need-based). *Programs:* FFEL (Subsidized and Unsubsidized Stafford, PLUS), Perkins, Federal Nursing, alternative loans.

WORK-STUDY *Federal work-study:* Total amount: $268,749; 189 jobs averaging $1420.

ATHLETIC AWARDS *Total amount:* $11,600 (100% need-based).

APPLYING FOR FINANCIAL AID *Required financial aid form:* FAFSA. *Financial aid deadline (priority):* 2/15. *Notification date:* Continuous beginning 3/15. Students must reply within 4 weeks of notification.

CONTACT Mrs. Stacy L. Schenk, Director of Financial Aid, Mount Aloysius College, 7373 Admiral Peary Highway, Cresson, PA 16630-1900, 814-886-6357 or toll-free 888-823-2220. *Fax:* 814-886-6463. *E-mail:* sschenk@mtaloy.edu.

MOUNT ANGEL SEMINARY
Saint Benedict, OR

CONTACT Dorene Preis, Director of Student Financial Aid/Registrar, Mount Angel Seminary, 1 Abbey Drive, Saint Benedict, OR 97373, 503-845-3951. *Fax:* 503-845-3126. *E-mail:* dpreis@mtangel.edu.

MOUNT CARMEL COLLEGE OF NURSING
Columbus, OH

CONTACT Carol Graham, Director of Financial Aid, Mount Carmel College of Nursing, 127 South Davis Avenue, Columbus, OH 43222, 614-234-5800 Ext. 5177. *E-mail:* cgraham@mchs.com.

MOUNT HOLYOKE COLLEGE
South Hadley, MA

Tuition & fees: $32,598	Average undergraduate aid package: $27,253

ABOUT THE INSTITUTION Independent, women only. Awards: bachelor's and master's degrees and post-bachelor's certificates. 47 undergraduate majors. Total enrollment: 2,127. Undergraduates: 2,125. Freshmen: 497. Both federal and institutional methodology are used as a basis for awarding need-based institutional aid.

UNDERGRADUATE EXPENSES for 2005–06 *Application fee:* $60. *Comprehensive fee:* $42,148 includes full-time tuition ($32,430), mandatory fees ($168), and room and board ($9550). *College room only:* $4670. Room and board charges vary according to board plan and housing facility. *Part-time tuition:* $1015 per credit hour. *Payment plan:* Tuition prepayment.

FRESHMAN FINANCIAL AID (Fall 2005, est.) 370 applied for aid; of those 77% were deemed to have need. 100% of freshmen with need received aid; of those 100% had need fully met. *Average percent of need met:* 100% (excluding resources awarded to replace EFC). *Average financial aid package:* $27,525 (excluding resources awarded to replace EFC). 9% of all full-time freshmen had no need and received non-need-based gift aid.

UNDERGRADUATE FINANCIAL AID (Fall 2005, est.) 1,581 applied for aid; of those 88% were deemed to have need. 100% of undergraduates with need received aid; of those 100% had need fully met. *Average percent of need met:* 100% (excluding resources awarded to replace EFC). *Average financial aid package:* $27,253 (excluding resources awarded to replace EFC). 7% of all full-time undergraduates had no need and received non-need-based gift aid.

GIFT AID (NEED-BASED) *Total amount:* $29,592,691 (5% federal, 1% state, 92% institutional, 2% external sources). *Receiving aid:* Freshmen: 56% (277); All full-time undergraduates: 60% (1,323). *Average award:* Freshmen: $24,079; Undergraduates: $22,500. *Scholarships, grants, and awards:* Federal Pell, FSEOG, state, private, college/university gift aid from institutional funds.

GIFT AID (NON-NEED-BASED) *Total amount:* $2,179,925 (94% institutional, 6% external sources). *Average Award:* Freshmen: $13,422; Undergraduates: $11,981. *Scholarships, grants, and awards by category: Academic Interests/Achievement:* 164 awards ($1,964,884 total): general academic interests/achievements. *Tuition waivers:* Full or partial for employees or children of employees. *ROTC:* Army cooperative, Air Force cooperative.

LOANS *Student loans:* $8,838,896 (78% need-based, 22% non-need-based). 69% of past graduating class borrowed through all loan programs. *Average indebtedness per student:* $19,877. *Average need-based loan:* Freshmen: $2659; Undergraduates: $4470. *Parent loans:* $6,287,171 (100% non-need-based). *Programs:* Federal Direct (Subsidized and Unsubsidized Stafford, PLUS), Perkins, state, college/university.

WORK-STUDY *Federal work-study:* Total amount: $1,331,688; 833 jobs averaging $1580. *State or other work-study/employment:* Total amount: $676,132 (100% need-based). 407 part-time jobs averaging $1625.

APPLYING FOR FINANCIAL AID *Required financial aid forms:* FAFSA, CSS Financial Aid PROFILE, noncustodial (divorced/separated) parent's statement, business/farm supplement, federal income tax form(s), W-2 forms. *Financial aid deadline:* 2/1 (priority: 1/15). *Notification date:* 4/1. Students must reply by 5/1.

CONTACT Ms. Kathy Blaisdell, Director of Student Financial Services, Mount Holyoke College, 50 College Street, South Hadley, MA 01075-1492, 413-538-2291. *Fax:* 413-538-2512. *E-mail:* kblaisde@mtholyoke.edu.

MOUNT IDA COLLEGE
Newton, MA

ABOUT THE INSTITUTION Independent, coed. Awards: associate and bachelor's degrees. 24 undergraduate majors. Total enrollment: 1,297. Undergraduates: 1,297. Freshmen: 378.

GIFT AID (NEED-BASED) *Scholarships, grants, and awards:* Federal Pell, FSEOG, state, private, college/university gift aid from institutional funds.

GIFT AID (NON-NEED-BASED) *Scholarships, grants, and awards by category: Creative Arts/Performance:* applied art and design, art/fine arts, general creative arts/performance. *Special Achievements/Activities:* community service, general special achievements/activities, leadership.

LOANS *Programs:* FFEL (Subsidized and Unsubsidized Stafford, PLUS), state, signature loans.

WORK-STUDY *Federal work-study:* Total amount: $259,837; 290 jobs averaging $896. *State or other work-study/employment:* Part-time jobs available.

APPLYING FOR FINANCIAL AID *Required financial aid form:* FAFSA.

CONTACT Linda Mularczyk, Director of Financial Aid, Mount Ida College, 777 Dedham Street, Newton, MA 02459-3310, 617-928-4099. *Fax:* 617-332-7869. *E-mail:* finserv@mountida.edu.

MOUNT MARTY COLLEGE
Yankton, SD

Tuition & fees: $15,730   **Average undergraduate aid package:** $13,253

ABOUT THE INSTITUTION Independent Roman Catholic, coed. Awards: associate, bachelor's, and master's degrees and post-bachelor's certificates. 31 undergraduate majors. Total enrollment: 1,189. Undergraduates: 1,089. Freshmen: 162. Federal methodology is used as a basis for awarding need-based institutional aid.

UNDERGRADUATE EXPENSES for 2005–06 *Application fee:* $35. *Comprehensive fee:* $20,590 includes full-time tuition ($14,050), mandatory fees ($1680), and room and board ($4860). Full-time tuition and fees vary according to course load and location. *Part-time tuition:* $228 per credit hour. *Part-time fees:* $20 per credit hour. Part-time tuition and fees vary according to course load and location. *Payment plan:* Installment.

FRESHMAN FINANCIAL AID (Fall 2005, est.) 116 applied for aid; of those 94% were deemed to have need. 100% of freshmen with need received aid; of those 17% had need fully met. *Average percent of need met:* 78% (excluding resources awarded to replace EFC). *Average financial aid package:* $14,336 (excluding resources awarded to replace EFC). 8% of all full-time freshmen had no need and received non-need-based gift aid.

UNDERGRADUATE FINANCIAL AID (Fall 2005, est.) 495 applied for aid; of those 92% were deemed to have need. 100% of undergraduates with need received aid; of those 20% had need fully met. *Average percent of need met:* 75% (excluding resources awarded to replace EFC). *Average financial aid package:* $13,253 (excluding resources awarded to replace EFC). 10% of all full-time undergraduates had no need and received non-need-based gift aid.

GIFT AID (NEED-BASED) *Total amount:* $3,386,099 (24% federal, 1% state, 67% institutional, 8% external sources). *Receiving aid:* Freshmen: 92% (108); All full-time undergraduates: 87% (450). *Average award:* Freshmen: $10,431; Undergraduates: $8552. *Scholarships, grants, and awards:* Federal Pell, FSEOG, state, private, college/university gift aid from institutional funds.

GIFT AID (NON-NEED-BASED) *Total amount:* $221,842 (2% state, 82% institutional, 16% external sources). *Receiving aid:* Freshmen: 90% (106); Undergraduates: 79% (405). *Average Award:* Freshmen: $10,402; Undergraduates: $9217. *Scholarships, grants, and awards by category: Academic Interests/Achievement:* 435 awards ($1,126,364 total): general academic interests/achievements. *Creative Arts/Performance:* 64 awards ($36,970 total): creative writing, music, theater/drama. *Special Achievements/Activities:* 141 awards ($256,708 total): leadership, memberships, religious involvement. *Special Characteristics:* 71 awards ($265,056 total): children of current students, children of faculty/staff, international students, parents of current students, religious affiliation, siblings of current students, spouses of current students. *Tuition waivers:* Full or partial for employees or children of employees. *ROTC:* Army cooperative.

LOANS *Student loans:* $3,965,867 (65% need-based, 35% non-need-based). 85% of past graduating class borrowed through all loan programs. *Average indebtedness per student:* $26,304. *Average need-based loan:* Freshmen: $3284; Undergraduates: $4632. *Parent loans:* $1,038,132 (6% need-based, 94% non-need-based). *Programs:* FFEL (Subsidized and Unsubsidized Stafford, PLUS), Perkins, Federal Nursing.

WORK-STUDY *Federal work-study:* Total amount: $267,144; 237 jobs averaging $1000. *State or other work-study/employment:* Total amount: $71,633 (100% non-need-based). 61 part-time jobs averaging $1000.

ATHLETIC AWARDS *Total amount:* $477,565 (25% need-based, 75% non-need-based).

APPLYING FOR FINANCIAL AID *Required financial aid forms:* FAFSA, institution's own form. *Financial aid deadline (priority):* 3/1. *Notification date:* Continuous beginning 3/15. Students must reply within 2 weeks of notification.

CONTACT Mr. Ken Kocer, Director of Financial Assistance, Mount Marty College, 1105 West 8th Street, Yankton, SD 57078-3724, 605-668-1589 or toll-free 800-658-4552. *Fax:* 605-668-1585. *E-mail:* kkocer@mtmc.edu.

MOUNT MARY COLLEGE
Milwaukee, WI

Tuition & fees: $17,105   **Average undergraduate aid package:** $11,550

ABOUT THE INSTITUTION Independent Roman Catholic, undergraduate: women only; graduate: coed. Awards: bachelor's and master's degrees and post-bachelor's certificates. 53 undergraduate majors. Total enrollment: 1,722. Undergraduates: 1,452. Federal methodology is used as a basis for awarding need-based institutional aid.

UNDERGRADUATE EXPENSES for 2005–06 *Application fee:* $25. *Comprehensive fee:* $22,895 includes full-time tuition ($16,925), mandatory fees ($180), and room and board ($5790). Room and board charges vary according to board plan. *Part-time tuition:* $466 per credit. *Part-time fees:* $45 per term. Part-time tuition and fees vary according to course load. *Payment plan:* Installment.

FRESHMAN FINANCIAL AID (Fall 2005, est.) 104 applied for aid; of those 88% were deemed to have need. 100% of freshmen with need received aid; of those 18% had need fully met. *Average percent of need met:* 71% (excluding resources awarded to replace EFC). *Average financial aid package:* $12,026 (excluding resources awarded to replace EFC). 29% of all full-time freshmen had no need and received non-need-based gift aid.

UNDERGRADUATE FINANCIAL AID (Fall 2005, est.) 704 applied for aid; of those 88% were deemed to have need. 100% of undergraduates with need received aid; of those 19% had need fully met. *Average percent of need met:* 68% (excluding resources awarded to replace EFC). *Average financial aid package:* $11,550 (excluding resources awarded to replace EFC). 19% of all full-time undergraduates had no need and received non-need-based gift aid.

GIFT AID (NEED-BASED) *Total amount:* $5,941,053 (21% federal, 21% state, 56% institutional, 2% external sources). *Receiving aid:* Freshmen: 58% (92); All full-time undergraduates: 67% (614). *Average award:* Freshmen: $8764; Undergraduates: $7158. *Scholarships, grants, and awards:* Federal Pell, FSEOG, state, private, college/university gift aid from institutional funds, Metropolitan Milwaukee Association of Commerce Awards.

GIFT AID (NON-NEED-BASED) *Total amount:* $826,220 (1% state, 97% institutional, 2% external sources). *Receiving aid:* Freshmen: 5% (8); Undergraduates: 5% (46). *Average Award:* Freshmen: $5449; Undergraduates: $7287. *Scholarships, grants, and awards by category: Academic Interests/Achievement:* 266 awards ($838,899 total): business, communication, education, English, general academic interests/achievements, health fields, home economics, humanities, mathematics, physical sciences, social sciences. *Creative Arts/Performance:* 23 awards ($18,130 total): applied art and design, art/fine arts, music. *Special Achievements/Activities:* 14 awards ($46,340 total): general special achievements/activities, leadership. *Special Characteristics:* 47 awards ($299,729 total): children of faculty/staff, international students, parents of current students, siblings of current students. *Tuition waivers:* Full or partial for employees or children of employees, senior citizens. *ROTC:* Army cooperative.

LOANS *Student loans:* $6,587,496 (78% need-based, 22% non-need-based). 75% of past graduating class borrowed through all loan programs. *Average indebtedness per student:* $19,040. *Average need-based loan:* Freshmen: $2864; Undergraduates: $4410. *Parent loans:* $911,458 (35% need-based, 65% non-need-based). *Programs:* FFEL (Subsidized and Unsubsidized Stafford, PLUS), Perkins, state.

WORK-STUDY *Federal work-study:* Total amount: $160,000; 268 jobs averaging $1300. *State or other work-study/employment:* Total amount: $80,000 (100% non-need-based). 108 part-time jobs averaging $1200.

APPLYING FOR FINANCIAL AID *Required financial aid form:* FAFSA. *Financial aid deadline (priority):* 3/1. *Notification date:* Continuous. Students must reply within 2 weeks of notification.

CONTACT Debra Duff, Director of Financial Aid, Mount Mary College, 2900 North Menomonee River Parkway, Milwaukee, WI 53222-4597, 414-256-1258. *Fax:* 414-443-3602. *E-mail:* finaid@mtmary.edu.

MOUNT MERCY COLLEGE
Cedar Rapids, IA

Tuition & fees: $18,030   **Average undergraduate aid package:** $14,744

ABOUT THE INSTITUTION Independent Roman Catholic, coed. Awards: bachelor's degrees. 35 undergraduate majors. Total university enrollment: 151. Total unit

Mount Mercy College

enrollment: 1,490. Undergraduates: 1,019. Freshmen: 181. Federal methodology is used as a basis for awarding need-based institutional aid.

UNDERGRADUATE EXPENSES for 2005-06 *Application fee:* $20. *Comprehensive fee:* $23,710 includes full-time tuition ($18,030) and room and board ($5680). Full-time tuition and fees vary according to course load. Room and board charges vary according to board plan and housing facility. *Part-time tuition:* $500 per credit hour. Part-time tuition and fees vary according to course load. *Payment plan:* Installment.

FRESHMAN FINANCIAL AID (Fall 2005, est.) 176 applied for aid; of those 86% were deemed to have need. 100% of freshmen with need received aid; of those 47% had need fully met. *Average percent of need met:* 87% (excluding resources awarded to replace EFC). *Average financial aid package:* $15,850 (excluding resources awarded to replace EFC). 17% of all full-time freshmen had no need and received non-need-based gift aid.

UNDERGRADUATE FINANCIAL AID (Fall 2005, est.) 889 applied for aid; of those 88% were deemed to have need. 100% of undergraduates with need received aid; of those 39% had need fully met. *Average percent of need met:* 81% (excluding resources awarded to replace EFC). *Average financial aid package:* $14,744 (excluding resources awarded to replace EFC). 16% of all full-time undergraduates had no need and received non-need-based gift aid.

GIFT AID (NEED-BASED) *Total amount:* $8,026,680 (11% federal, 27% state, 58% institutional, 4% external sources). *Receiving aid:* Freshmen: 83% (151); All full-time undergraduates: 84% (772). *Average award:* Freshmen: $11,614; Undergraduates: $9678. *Scholarships, grants, and awards:* Federal Pell, FSEOG, state, college/university gift aid from institutional funds.

GIFT AID (NON-NEED-BASED) *Total amount:* $1,526,418 (1% state, 92% institutional, 7% external sources). *Receiving aid:* Freshmen: 8% (14); Undergraduates: 8% (76). *Average Award:* Freshmen: $13,461; Undergraduates: $11,522. *Scholarships, grants, and awards by category: Academic Interests/Achievement:* 848 awards ($4,805,863 total): general academic interests/achievements. *Creative Arts/Performance:* 46 awards ($49,425 total): art/fine arts, music, theater/drama. *Special Achievements/Activities:* 263 awards ($282,877 total): leadership. *Special Characteristics:* 25 awards ($12,875 total): previous college experience. *Tuition waivers:* Full or partial for employees or children of employees.

LOANS *Student loans:* $7,794,878 (63% need-based, 37% non-need-based). 72% of past graduating class borrowed through all loan programs. *Average indebtedness per student:* $22,530. *Average need-based loan:* Freshmen: $3672; Undergraduates: $5041. *Parent loans:* $428,775 (31% need-based, 69% non-need-based). *Programs:* Federal Direct (Subsidized and Unsubsidized Stafford, PLUS), Perkins, state, college/university.

WORK-STUDY *Federal work-study:* Total amount: $483,687; 300 jobs averaging $1460. *State or other work-study/employment:* Total amount: $242,318 (27% need-based, 73% non-need-based). 132 part-time jobs averaging $1466.

APPLYING FOR FINANCIAL AID *Required financial aid form:* FAFSA. *Financial aid deadline (priority):* 3/1. *Notification date:* Continuous beginning 3/15. Students must reply by 5/1 or within 3 weeks of notification.

CONTACT Lois M. Mulbrook, Director of Financial Aid, Mount Mercy College, 1330 Elmhurst Drive, NE, Cedar Rapids, IA 52402-4797, 319-368-6467 or toll-free 800-248-4504. Fax: 319-364-3546. E-mail: lmmulbro@mtmercy.edu.

MOUNT OLIVE COLLEGE
Mount Olive, NC

Tuition & fees: $12,620   **Average undergraduate aid package:** $7091

ABOUT THE INSTITUTION Independent Free Will Baptist, coed. Awards: associate and bachelor's degrees. 22 undergraduate majors. Total enrollment: 2,830. Undergraduates: 2,830. Freshmen: 288. Federal methodology is used as a basis for awarding need-based institutional aid.

UNDERGRADUATE EXPENSES for 2006-07 *Application fee:* $20. *Comprehensive fee:* $17,572 includes full-time tuition ($12,620) and room and board ($4952). *College room only:* $2000. *Part-time tuition:* $215 per credit hour.

FRESHMAN FINANCIAL AID (Fall 2004) 360 applied for aid; of those 55% were deemed to have need. 95% of freshmen with need received aid; of those 20% had need fully met. *Average percent of need met:* 69% (excluding resources awarded to replace EFC). *Average financial aid package:* $7075 (excluding resources awarded to replace EFC). 15% of all full-time freshmen had no need and received non-need-based gift aid.

UNDERGRADUATE FINANCIAL AID (Fall 2004) 1,917 applied for aid; of those 73% were deemed to have need. 95% of undergraduates with need received aid; of those 19% had need fully met. *Average percent of need met:* 67% (excluding resources awarded to replace EFC). *Average financial aid package:* $7091 (excluding resources awarded to replace EFC). 12% of all full-time undergraduates had no need and received non-need-based gift aid.

GIFT AID (NEED-BASED) *Total amount:* $6,682,794 (34% federal, 57% state, 2% institutional, 7% external sources). *Receiving aid:* Freshmen: 34% (188); All full-time undergraduates: 49% (1,309). *Average award:* Freshmen: $5669; Undergraduates: $4983. *Scholarships, grants, and awards:* Federal Pell, FSEOG, state, private, college/university gift aid from institutional funds.

GIFT AID (NON-NEED-BASED) *Total amount:* $1,771,565 (43% state, 2% institutional, 55% external sources). *Receiving aid:* Freshmen: 5% (25); Undergraduates: 4% (102). *Average Award:* Freshmen: $2601; Undergraduates:* $3919. *Scholarships, grants, and awards by category: Academic Interests/Achievement:* 63 awards ($218,526 total): general academic interests/achievements, mathematics. *Creative Arts/Performance:* 53 awards ($84,955 total): art/fine arts, music. *Special Achievements/Activities:* 144 awards ($272,701 total): leadership. *Special Characteristics:* 47 awards ($129,839 total): children of faculty/staff, religious affiliation.

LOANS *Student loans:* $6,895,623 (44% need-based, 56% non-need-based). 57% of past graduating class borrowed through all loan programs. *Average indebtedness per student:* $8901. *Average need-based loan:* Freshmen: $1755; Undergraduates: $2577. *Parent loans:* $154,621 (34% need-based, 66% non-need-based). *Programs:* FFEL (Subsidized Stafford, PLUS), Perkins, Federal Nursing, state.

WORK-STUDY *Federal work-study:* Total amount: $110,108; 120 jobs averaging $719.

ATHLETIC AWARDS *Total amount:* $653,651 (55% need-based, 45% non-need-based).

APPLYING FOR FINANCIAL AID *Required financial aid forms:* FAFSA, state aid form. *Financial aid deadline (priority):* 3/1. *Notification date:* Continuous beginning 2/14. Students must reply within 2 weeks of notification.

CONTACT Ms. Karen Britt Statler, Director of Financial Aid, Mount Olive College, 634 Henderson Street, Mount Olive, NC 28365, 919-658-2502 Ext. 3006 or toll-free 800-653-0854 (in-state). Fax: 919-658-9816.

MOUNT SAINT MARY COLLEGE
Newburgh, NY

ABOUT THE INSTITUTION Independent, coed. Awards: bachelor's and master's degrees. 35 undergraduate majors. Total enrollment: 2,574. Undergraduates: 2,039. Freshmen: 360.

GIFT AID (NEED-BASED) *Scholarships, grants, and awards:* Federal Pell, FSEOG, state, private, college/university gift aid from institutional funds, Federal Nursing.

GIFT AID (NON-NEED-BASED) *Scholarships, grants, and awards by category: Academic Interests/Achievement:* general academic interests/achievements. *Special Characteristics:* children of faculty/staff.

LOANS *Programs:* FFEL (Subsidized and Unsubsidized Stafford, PLUS), Perkins, Federal Nursing.

WORK-STUDY *Federal work-study:* Total amount: $293,046; 219 jobs available. *State or other work-study/employment:* Total amount: $65,000 (100% need-based). 35 part-time jobs available.

APPLYING FOR FINANCIAL AID *Required financial aid forms:* FAFSA, institution's own form.

CONTACT Susan F. Twomey, Director of Financial Aid, Mount Saint Mary College, 330 Powell Avenue, Newburgh, NY 12550-3494, 845-561-0800 or toll-free 888-937-6762. Fax: 845-569-3302. E-mail: twomey@msmc.edu.

MOUNT ST. MARY'S COLLEGE
Los Angeles, CA

Tuition & fees: $24,150   **Average undergraduate aid package:** $17,388

ABOUT THE INSTITUTION Independent Roman Catholic, coed, primarily women. Awards: associate, bachelor's, and master's degrees and post-bachelor's certificates. 40 undergraduate majors. Total enrollment: 2,480. Undergraduates: 1,980. Freshmen: 405. Federal methodology is used as a basis for awarding need-based institutional aid.

UNDERGRADUATE EXPENSES for 2006–07 *Application fee:* $40. *Comprehensive fee:* $32,897 includes full-time tuition ($23,380), mandatory fees ($770), and room and board ($8747). *Part-time tuition:* $900 per unit.
FRESHMAN FINANCIAL AID (Fall 2004) 168 applied for aid; of those 90% were deemed to have need. 100% of freshmen with need received aid; of those 12% had need fully met. *Average percent of need met:* 79% (excluding resources awarded to replace EFC). *Average financial aid package:* $17,925 (excluding resources awarded to replace EFC). 15% of all full-time freshmen had no need and received non-need-based gift aid.
UNDERGRADUATE FINANCIAL AID (Fall 2004) 999 applied for aid; of those 96% were deemed to have need. 98% of undergraduates with need received aid; of those 9% had need fully met. *Average percent of need met:* 65% (excluding resources awarded to replace EFC). *Average financial aid package:* $17,388 (excluding resources awarded to replace EFC). 5% of all full-time undergraduates had no need and received non-need-based gift aid.
GIFT AID (NEED-BASED) *Total amount:* $10,140,584 (16% federal, 47% state, 37% institutional). *Receiving aid:* Freshmen: 71% (127); All full-time undergraduates: 84% (862). *Average award:* Freshmen: $7425. *Scholarships, grants, and awards:* Federal Pell, FSEOG, state, private, college/university gift aid from institutional funds.
GIFT AID (NON-NEED-BASED) *Total amount:* $3,333,300 (92% institutional, 8% external sources). *Receiving aid:* Freshmen: 83% (148); Undergraduates: 34% (355). *Average Award:* Freshmen: $10,760; Undergraduates: $11,847. *Scholarships, grants, and awards by category:* Academic Interests/Achievement: education, general academic interests/achievements. *Special Achievements/Activities:* community service, leadership. *Special Characteristics:* children and siblings of alumni.
LOANS *Student loans:* $3,001,370 (100% need-based). *Average need-based loan:* Freshmen: $2485; Undergraduates: $4097. *Parent loans:* $3,323,296 (100% non-need-based). *Programs:* FFEL (Subsidized and Unsubsidized Stafford, PLUS), Federal Nursing, college/university.
WORK-STUDY *Federal work-study:* Total amount: $932,018; jobs available. *State or other work-study/employment:* Total amount: $52,455 (100% non-need-based). Part-time jobs available.
APPLYING FOR FINANCIAL AID *Required financial aid forms:* FAFSA, institution's own form, state aid form. *Financial aid deadline:* 5/15 (priority: 3/2). *Notification date:* Continuous beginning 12/1. Students must reply by 5/1.
CONTACT La Royce Dodd, Financial Aid Director, Mount St. Mary's College, 12001 Chalon Road, Los Angeles, CA 90049, 310-954-4192 or toll-free 800-999-9893.

MOUNT ST. MARY'S UNIVERSITY
Emmitsburg, MD

Tuition & fees: $24,030   **Average undergraduate aid package: $15,181**

ABOUT THE INSTITUTION Independent Roman Catholic, coed. Awards: bachelor's, master's, and first professional degrees and post-bachelor's and post-master's certificates. 28 undergraduate majors. Total enrollment: 2,176. Undergraduates: 1,656. Freshmen: 439. Federal methodology is used as a basis for awarding need-based institutional aid.
UNDERGRADUATE EXPENSES for 2006–07 *Application fee:* $35. *Comprehensive fee:* $32,720 includes full-time tuition ($23,630), mandatory fees ($400), and room and board ($8690). *College room only:* $4380. *Part-time tuition:* $790 per credit hour. *Part-time fees:* $12 per credit hour.
FRESHMAN FINANCIAL AID (Fall 2005, est.) 378 applied for aid; of those 76% were deemed to have need. 100% of freshmen with need received aid; of those 28% had need fully met. *Average percent of need met:* 80% (excluding resources awarded to replace EFC). *Average financial aid package:* $15,918 (excluding resources awarded to replace EFC). 32% of all full-time freshmen had no need and received non-need-based gift aid.
UNDERGRADUATE FINANCIAL AID (Fall 2005, est.) 1,110 applied for aid; of those 81% were deemed to have need. 100% of undergraduates with need received aid; of those 30% had need fully met. *Average percent of need met:* 77% (excluding resources awarded to replace EFC). *Average financial aid package:* $15,181 (excluding resources awarded to replace EFC). 33% of all full-time undergraduates had no need and received non-need-based gift aid.
GIFT AID (NEED-BASED) *Total amount:* $9,802,640 (8% federal, 11% state, 79% institutional, 2% external sources). *Receiving aid:* Freshmen: 66% (288); All full-time undergraduates: 60% (885). *Average award:* Freshmen: $12,877; Undergraduates: $11,892. *Scholarships, grants, and awards:* Federal Pell, FSEOG, state, private, college/university gift aid from institutional funds.
GIFT AID (NON-NEED-BASED) *Total amount:* $5,698,344 (4% federal, 3% state, 89% institutional, 4% external sources). *Receiving aid:* Freshmen: 15% (66); Undergraduates: 13% (186). *Average Award:* Freshmen: $15,043; Undergraduates: $13,552. *Scholarships, grants, and awards by category:* Academic Interests/Achievement: 1,123 awards ($9,370,233 total): general academic interests/achievements. *Creative Arts/Performance:* 18 awards ($36,100 total): art/fine arts. *Special Characteristics:* 202 awards ($608,435 total): children of educators, children of faculty/staff, members of minority groups, siblings of current students. *ROTC:* Army cooperative.
LOANS *Student loans:* $6,495,362 (56% need-based, 44% non-need-based). 75% of past graduating class borrowed through all loan programs. *Average indebtedness per student:* $15,964. *Average need-based loan:* Freshmen: $3359; Undergraduates: $4056. *Parent loans:* $3,520,397 (22% need-based, 78% non-need-based). *Programs:* FFEL (Subsidized and Unsubsidized Stafford, PLUS), Perkins.
WORK-STUDY *Federal work-study:* Total amount: $290,250; 198 jobs averaging $1465. *State or other work-study/employment:* Total amount: $221,133 (76% need-based, 24% non-need-based). 32 part-time jobs averaging $6910.
ATHLETIC AWARDS *Total amount:* $1,924,418 (34% need-based, 66% non-need-based).
APPLYING FOR FINANCIAL AID *Required financial aid forms:* FAFSA, institution's own form. *Financial aid deadline:* 2/15. *Notification date:* Continuous beginning 2/15. Students must reply by 5/1.
CONTACT Mr. David C. Reeder, Director of Financial Aid, Mount St. Mary's University, 16300 Old Emmitsburg Road, Emmitsburg, MD 21727-7799, 301-447-5207 or toll-free 800-448-4347. *Fax:* 301-447-5755. *E-mail:* reeder@msmary.edu.

MT. SIERRA COLLEGE
Monrovia, CA

CONTACT Financial Aid Office, Mt. Sierra College, 101 East Huntington Drive, Monrovia, CA 91016, 888-828-8800 or toll-free 888-828-8800.

MOUNT UNION COLLEGE
Alliance, OH

Tuition & fees: $19,850   **Average undergraduate aid package: $16,184**

ABOUT THE INSTITUTION Independent United Methodist, coed. Awards: bachelor's degrees. 43 undergraduate majors. Total enrollment: 2,205. Undergraduates: 2,205. Freshmen: 503. Federal methodology is used as a basis for awarding need-based institutional aid.
UNDERGRADUATE EXPENSES for 2005–06 *Comprehensive fee:* $25,840 includes full-time tuition ($19,600), mandatory fees ($250), and room and board ($5990). *College room only:* $2650. Room and board charges vary according to board plan and housing facility. *Part-time tuition:* $820 per semester hour. *Part-time fees:* $50 per term. *Payment plans:* Tuition prepayment, installment.
FRESHMAN FINANCIAL AID (Fall 2005, est.) 462 applied for aid; of those 85% were deemed to have need. 100% of freshmen with need received aid; of those 24% had need fully met. *Average percent of need met:* 86% (excluding resources awarded to replace EFC). *Average financial aid package:* $16,776 (excluding resources awarded to replace EFC). 19% of all full-time freshmen had no need and received non-need-based gift aid.
UNDERGRADUATE FINANCIAL AID (Fall 2005, est.) 1,658 applied for aid; of those 91% were deemed to have need. 100% of undergraduates with need received aid; of those 22% had need fully met. *Average percent of need met:* 83% (excluding resources awarded to replace EFC). *Average financial aid package:* $16,184 (excluding resources awarded to replace EFC). 20% of all full-time undergraduates had no need and received non-need-based gift aid.
GIFT AID (NEED-BASED) *Total amount:* $17,114,510 (8% federal, 13% state, 76% institutional, 3% external sources). *Receiving aid:* Freshmen: 79% (395); All full-time undergraduates: 79% (1,500). *Average award:* Freshmen: $12,088; Undergraduates: $11,209. *Scholarships, grants, and awards:* Federal Pell, FSEOG, state, private, college/university gift aid from institutional funds.
GIFT AID (NON-NEED-BASED) *Total amount:* $2,611,378 (16% state, 79% institutional, 5% external sources). *Receiving aid:* Freshmen: 10% (51);

Mount Union College

Undergraduates: 7% (134). *Average Award:* Freshmen: $9530; Undergraduates: $8759. *Scholarships, grants, and awards by category: Academic Interests/Achievement:* 1,079 awards ($5,932,902 total): general academic interests/achievements. *Creative Arts/Performance:* 131 awards ($360,030 total): art/fine arts, cinema/film/broadcasting, debating, journalism/publications, music, theater/drama. *Special Characteristics:* 163 awards ($905,976 total): children and siblings of alumni, children of faculty/staff, ethnic background, international students, relatives of clergy. *Tuition waivers:* Full or partial for children of alumni, employees or children of employees, adult students. *ROTC:* Army cooperative, Air Force cooperative.
LOANS *Student loans:* $10,461,121 (72% need-based, 28% non-need-based). 86% of past graduating class borrowed through all loan programs. *Average indebtedness per student:* $21,268. *Average need-based loan:* Freshmen: $4716; Undergraduates: $4811. *Parent loans:* $2,504,342 (32% need-based, 68% non-need-based). *Programs:* FFEL (Subsidized and Unsubsidized Stafford, PLUS), Perkins, alternative loans.
WORK-STUDY *Federal work-study:* Total amount: $948,388; 1,164 jobs averaging $1155. *State or other work-study/employment:* Total amount: $222,200 (34% need-based, 66% non-need-based). 124 part-time jobs averaging $1927.
APPLYING FOR FINANCIAL AID *Required financial aid form:* FAFSA. *Financial aid deadline:* Continuous. *Notification date:* Continuous beginning 3/15. Students must reply within 4 weeks of notification.
CONTACT Mrs. Sandra S. Pittenger, Director of Student Financial Services, Mount Union College, 1972 Clark Avenue, Alliance, OH 44601-3993, 330-823-2674 or toll-free 800-334-6682 (in-state), 800-992-6682 (out-of-state). *Fax:* 330-829-2814. *E-mail:* pittenss@muc.edu.

MOUNT VERNON NAZARENE UNIVERSITY
Mount Vernon, OH

Tuition & fees: $16,726 | **Average undergraduate aid package: $12,008**

ABOUT THE INSTITUTION Independent Nazarene, coed. Awards: associate, bachelor's, and master's degrees (Associate). 64 undergraduate majors. Total enrollment: 2,549. Undergraduates: 2,195. Freshmen: 380. Federal methodology is used as a basis for awarding need-based institutional aid.
UNDERGRADUATE EXPENSES for 2006–07 *Application fee:* $25. *Comprehensive fee:* $21,816 includes full-time tuition ($16,216), mandatory fees ($510), and room and board ($5090). *College room only:* $2840. *Part-time tuition:* $585 per semester hour. *Part-time fees:* $18 per semester hour.
FRESHMAN FINANCIAL AID (Fall 2005, est.) 380 applied for aid; of those 84% were deemed to have need. 100% of freshmen with need received aid; of those 17% had need fully met. *Average percent of need met:* 78% (excluding resources awarded to replace EFC). *Average financial aid package:* $12,095 (excluding resources awarded to replace EFC). 11% of all full-time freshmen had no need and received non-need-based gift aid.
UNDERGRADUATE FINANCIAL AID (Fall 2005, est.) 1,307 applied for aid; of those 80% were deemed to have need. 100% of undergraduates with need received aid; of those 18% had need fully met. *Average percent of need met:* 85% (excluding resources awarded to replace EFC). *Average financial aid package:* $12,008 (excluding resources awarded to replace EFC). 7% of all full-time undergraduates had no need and received non-need-based gift aid.
GIFT AID (NEED-BASED) *Total amount:* $7,468,934 (20% federal, 20% state, 51% institutional, 9% external sources). *Receiving aid:* Freshmen: 84% (318); All full-time undergraduates: 54% (1,035). *Average award:* Freshmen: $7600; Undergraduates: $6658. *Scholarships, grants, and awards:* Federal Pell, FSEOG, state, private, college/university gift aid from institutional funds.
GIFT AID (NON-NEED-BASED) *Total amount:* $1,848,069 (51% state, 37% institutional, 12% external sources). *Receiving aid:* Freshmen: 10% (38); Undergraduates: 6% (105). *Average Award:* Freshmen: $3136; Undergraduates: $2893. *Scholarships, grants, and awards by category: Academic Interests/Achievement:* business, computer science, education, general academic interests/achievements, health fields, home economics, religion/biblical studies. *Creative Arts/Performance:* music. *Special Achievements/Activities:* general special achievements/activities, junior miss, religious involvement. *Special Characteristics:* children of faculty/staff, international students, local/state students, relatives of clergy, religious affiliation, siblings of current students, spouses of current students, veterans, veterans' children.
LOANS *Student loans:* $10,864,575 (63% need-based, 37% non-need-based). 79% of past graduating class borrowed through all loan programs. *Average indebtedness per student:* $20,293. *Average need-based loan:* Freshmen: $3228; Undergraduates: $3876. *Parent loans:* $2,504,859 (32% need-based, 68% non-need-based). *Programs:* FFEL (Subsidized and Unsubsidized Stafford, PLUS), Perkins, alternative loans.
WORK-STUDY *Federal work-study:* Total amount: $176,744; 123 jobs averaging $1437. *State or other work-study/employment:* Total amount: $645,657 (45% need-based, 55% non-need-based). 430 part-time jobs averaging $1436.
ATHLETIC AWARDS Total amount: $511,988 (62% need-based, 38% non-need-based).
APPLYING FOR FINANCIAL AID *Required financial aid forms:* FAFSA, institution's own form. *Financial aid deadline (priority):* 3/15. *Notification date:* Continuous beginning 3/1. Students must reply within 2 weeks of notification.
CONTACT Steve Tracht, Director of Student Financial Planning, Mount Vernon Nazarene University, 800 Martinsburg Road, Mount Vernon, OH 43050-9500, 740-392-6868 Ext. 4520 or toll-free 866-462-6868. *Fax:* 740-393-0511. *E-mail:* stracht@mvnu.edu.

MUHLENBERG COLLEGE
Allentown, PA

CONTACT Mr. Greg Mitton, Director of Financial Aid, Muhlenberg College, 2400 Chew Street, Allentown, PA 18104-5586, 484-664-3175. *Fax:* 484-664-3234. *E-mail:* mitton@muhlenberg.edu.

MULTNOMAH BIBLE COLLEGE AND BIBLICAL SEMINARY
Portland, OR

ABOUT THE INSTITUTION Independent interdenominational, coed. Awards: bachelor's, master's, and first professional degrees and post-bachelor's certificates. 13 undergraduate majors. Total enrollment: 803. Undergraduates: 590. Freshmen: 97.
GIFT AID (NEED-BASED) *Scholarships, grants, and awards:* Federal Pell, FSEOG, private, college/university gift aid from institutional funds.
GIFT AID (NON-NEED-BASED) *Scholarships, grants, and awards by category: Academic Interests/Achievement:* communication, general academic interests/achievements, religion/biblical studies. *Special Characteristics:* children of current students, international students, religious affiliation, siblings of current students.
LOANS *Programs:* FFEL (Subsidized and Unsubsidized Stafford, PLUS).
WORK-STUDY *Federal work-study:* Total amount: $165,136; 85 jobs averaging $2000.
APPLYING FOR FINANCIAL AID *Required financial aid forms:* FAFSA, institution's own form.
CONTACT Mr. David Allen, Director of Financial Aid, Multnomah Bible College and Biblical Seminary, 8435 Northeast Glisan Street, Portland, OR 97220-5898, 503-251-5335 or toll-free 800-275-4672. *Fax:* 503-254-1268.

MURRAY STATE UNIVERSITY
Murray, KY

Tuition & fees (KY res): $4428 | **Average undergraduate aid package: $4613**

ABOUT THE INSTITUTION State-supported, coed. Awards: bachelor's and master's degrees and post-master's certificates. 113 undergraduate majors. Total enrollment: 10,266. Undergraduates: 8,577. Freshmen: 1,462. Federal methodology is used as a basis for awarding need-based institutional aid.
UNDERGRADUATE EXPENSES for 2005–06 *Application fee:* $30. *Tuition, state resident:* full-time $3792; part-time $185 per hour. *Tuition, nonresident:* full-time $5464; part-time $240 per hour. *Required fees:* full-time $636; $23 per hour. Full-time tuition and fees vary according to reciprocity agreements. Part-time tuition and fees vary according to reciprocity agreements. *College room and board:* $4472; *room only:* $2366. Room and board charges vary according to board plan. *Payment plan:* Installment.
FRESHMAN FINANCIAL AID (Fall 2005, est.) 1099 applied for aid; of those 60% were deemed to have need. 94% of freshmen with need received aid; of those 94% had need fully met. *Average percent of need met:* 93% (excluding resources awarded to replace EFC). *Average financial aid package:* $4593 (excluding resources awarded to replace EFC). 36% of all full-time freshmen had no need and received non-need-based gift aid.

UNDERGRADUATE FINANCIAL AID (Fall 2005, est.) 6,153 applied for aid; of those 56% were deemed to have need. 92% of undergraduates with need received aid; of those 98% had need fully met. *Average percent of need met:* 88% (excluding resources awarded to replace EFC). *Average financial aid package:* $4613 (excluding resources awarded to replace EFC). 33% of all full-time undergraduates had no need and received non-need-based gift aid.
GIFT AID (NEED-BASED) *Total amount:* $10,865,317 (62% federal, 19% state, 11% institutional, 8% external sources). *Receiving aid:* Freshmen: 34% (464); All full-time undergraduates: 30% (2,156). *Average award:* Freshmen: $2258; Undergraduates: $2182. *Scholarships, grants, and awards:* Federal Pell, FSEOG, state, private, college/university gift aid from institutional funds.
GIFT AID (NON-NEED-BASED) *Total amount:* $8,974,600 (48% state, 35% institutional, 17% external sources). *Receiving aid:* Freshmen: 24% (335); Undergraduates: 21% (1,522). *Average Award:* Freshmen: $2518; Undergraduates: $2552. *Scholarships, grants, and awards by category: Academic Interests/ Achievement:* 4,251 awards ($4,820,800 total): agriculture, biological sciences, business, communication, computer science, education, engineering/technologies, English, foreign languages, general academic interests/achievements, health fields, humanities, international studies, library science, mathematics. *Creative Arts/Performance:* 182 awards ($110,012 total): applied art and design, art/fine arts, creative writing, dance, debating, general creative arts/performance, journalism/publications, music, theater/drama. *Special Achievements/Activities:* 819 awards ($800,959 total): cheerleading/drum major, general special achievements/activities, junior miss, leadership, rodeo. *Special Characteristics:* 2,369 awards ($9,276,858 total): adult students, children and siblings of alumni, children of faculty/staff, general special characteristics, handicapped students, international students, local/state students, members of minority groups, out-of-state students. *Tuition waivers:* Full or partial for children of alumni, employees or children of employees, senior citizens. *ROTC:* Army cooperative.
LOANS *Student loans:* $20,700,000 (58% need-based, 42% non-need-based). 52% of past graduating class borrowed through all loan programs. *Average indebtedness per student:* $17,617. *Average need-based loan:* Freshmen: $1851; Undergraduates: $1955. *Parent loans:* $1,750,000 (100% non-need-based). *Programs:* FFEL (Subsidized and Unsubsidized Stafford, PLUS), Perkins, Federal Nursing, state, college/university.
WORK-STUDY *Federal work-study:* Total amount: $576,900; 462 jobs averaging $1297. *State or other work-study/employment:* Total amount: $3,125,000 (100% non-need-based). 2,035 part-time jobs averaging $1590.
ATHLETIC AWARDS *Total amount:* $2,450,000 (30% need-based, 70% non-need-based).
APPLYING FOR FINANCIAL AID *Required financial aid forms:* FAFSA, institution's own form. *Financial aid deadline (priority):* 4/1. *Notification date:* Continuous beginning 4/15.
CONTACT Charles Vinson, Director of Student Financial Aid, Murray State University, B2 Sparks Hall, Murray, KY 42071-0009, 270-809-2546 or toll-free 800-272-4678. *Fax:* 270-809-3116. *E-mail:* charles.vinson@murraystate.edu.

MUSICIANS INSTITUTE
Hollywood, CA

CONTACT Director of Financial Aid, Musicians Institute, 1655 North McCadden Place, Hollywood, CA 90028, 323-462-1384 or toll-free 800-255-PLAY.

MUSKINGUM COLLEGE
New Concord, OH

ABOUT THE INSTITUTION Independent religious, coed. Awards: bachelor's and master's degrees. 59 undergraduate majors. Total enrollment: 2,142. Undergraduates: 1,622. Freshmen: 386.
GIFT AID (NEED-BASED) *Scholarships, grants, and awards:* Federal Pell, FSEOG, state, private, college/university gift aid from institutional funds.
GIFT AID (NON-NEED-BASED) *Scholarships, grants, and awards by category: Academic Interests/Achievement:* biological sciences, computer science, general academic interests/achievements, mathematics, physical sciences, premedicine. *Creative Arts/Performance:* art/fine arts, debating, journalism/publications, music, theater/drama. *Special Characteristics:* children and siblings of alumni, ethnic background, local/state students, members of minority groups, religious affiliation, siblings of current students.
LOANS *Programs:* FFEL (Subsidized and Unsubsidized Stafford, PLUS), Perkins.
APPLYING FOR FINANCIAL AID *Required financial aid form:* FAFSA.
CONTACT Mr. Jeff Zellers, Dean of Enrollment, Muskingum College, 163 Stormont Street, New Concord, OH 43762, 740-826-8139 or toll-free 800-752-6082. *Fax:* 740-826-8100. *E-mail:* jzellers@muskingum.edu.

NAROPA UNIVERSITY
Boulder, CO

ABOUT THE INSTITUTION Independent, coed. Awards: bachelor's, master's, and first professional degrees. 11 undergraduate majors. Total enrollment: 1,221. Undergraduates: 479. Freshmen: 39.
GIFT AID (NEED-BASED) *Scholarships, grants, and awards:* Federal Pell, FSEOG, private, college/university gift aid from institutional funds.
LOANS *Programs:* FFEL (Subsidized and Unsubsidized Stafford, PLUS), Perkins.
WORK-STUDY *Federal work-study:* Total amount: $748,982; 189 jobs averaging $3963. *State or other work-study/employment:* Total amount: $57,658 (100% need-based). 10 part-time jobs averaging $5766.
APPLYING FOR FINANCIAL AID *Required financial aid form:* FAFSA.
CONTACT Financial Aid Office, Naropa University, 2130 Arapahoe Avenue, Boulder, CO 80302-6697, 303-546-3534 or toll-free 800-772-0410 (out-of-state). *Fax:* 303-442-0792. *E-mail:* finaid@naropa.edu.

NATIONAL AMERICAN UNIVERSITY
Colorado Springs, CO

CONTACT Financial Aid Coordinator, National American University, 2577 North Chelton Road, Colorado Springs, CO 80909, 719-471-4205.

NATIONAL AMERICAN UNIVERSITY
Denver, CO

CONTACT Cheryl Schunneman, Director of Financial Aid, National American University, 321 Kansas City Street, Rapid City, SD 57701, 605-394-4800.

NATIONAL AMERICAN UNIVERSITY
Roseville, MN

CONTACT Financial Aid Office, National American University, 1500 West Highway 36, Roseville, MN 55113-4035, 651-644-1265.

NATIONAL AMERICAN UNIVERSITY
Kansas City, MO

CONTACT Mary Anderson, Coordinator of Financial Aid, National American University, 4200 Blue Ridge, Kansas City, MO 64133, 816-353-4554. *Fax:* 816-353-1176.

NATIONAL AMERICAN UNIVERSITY
Albuquerque, NM

CONTACT Director of Financial Aid, National American University, 321 Kansas City Street, Rapid City, SD 57701, 605-394-4800 or toll-free 800-843-8892.

NATIONAL AMERICAN UNIVERSITY
Rapid City, SD

CONTACT Financial Aid Director, National American University, PO Box 1780, Rapid City, SD 57709-1780, 605-721-5213 or toll-free 800-843-8892.

NATIONAL AMERICAN UNIVERSITY–SIOUX FALLS BRANCH
Sioux Falls, SD

CONTACT Ms. Rhonda Kohnen, Financial Aid Coordinator, National American University–Sioux Falls Branch, 2801 South Kiwanis Avenue, Suite 100, Sioux Falls, SD 57105-4293, 605-334-5430 or toll-free 800-388-5430 (out-of-state). *Fax:* 605-334-1575. *E-mail:* rkohnen@national.edu.

THE NATIONAL HISPANIC UNIVERSITY
San Jose, CA

ABOUT THE INSTITUTION Independent, coed. Awards: associate and bachelor's degrees and post-bachelor's certificates. 5 undergraduate majors. Total enrollment: 469. Undergraduates: 293. Freshmen: 34.
GIFT AID (NEED-BASED) *Scholarships, grants, and awards:* Federal Pell, FSEOG, state, private, college/university gift aid from institutional funds.
GIFT AID (NON-NEED-BASED) *Scholarships, grants, and awards by category: Academic Interests/Achievement:* business, computer science, education. *Special Characteristics:* veterans, veterans' children.
LOANS *Programs:* FFEL (Subsidized and Unsubsidized Stafford, PLUS).
WORK-STUDY *Federal work-study:* Total amount: $12,000; 3 jobs averaging $3000.
APPLYING FOR FINANCIAL AID *Required financial aid form:* FAFSA.
CONTACT Takeo Kubo, Director of Financial Aid and Scholarship, The National Hispanic University, 14271 Story Road, San Jose, CA 95127-3823, 408-273-2708. *Fax:* 408-254-1369. *E-mail:* tkubo@nhu.edu.

NATIONAL-LOUIS UNIVERSITY
Chicago, IL

CONTACT Toni Todd, Student Finance Officer, National-Louis University, 1000 Capitol Drive, Wheeling, IL 60090, 847-465-0575 Ext. 5350 or toll-free 888-NLU-TODAY (in-state), 800-443-5522 (out-of-state).

NATIONAL UNIVERSITY
La Jolla, CA

Tuition & fees: $8352 **Average undergraduate aid package: $5785**

ABOUT THE INSTITUTION Independent, coed. Awards: associate, bachelor's, and master's degrees and post-bachelor's certificates. 45 undergraduate majors. Total enrollment: 26,035. Undergraduates: 6,521. Freshmen: 945. Federal methodology is used as a basis for awarding need-based institutional aid.
UNDERGRADUATE EXPENSES for 2005-06 *Application fee:* $60. *Tuition:* full-time $8352; part-time $1044 per course. Full-time tuition and fees vary according to course load. Part-time tuition and fees vary according to course load.
FRESHMAN FINANCIAL AID (Fall 2004) 20 applied for aid; of those 80% were deemed to have need. 94% of freshmen with need received aid. *Average percent of need met:* 85% (excluding resources awarded to replace EFC). *Average financial aid package:* $3145 (excluding resources awarded to replace EFC).
UNDERGRADUATE FINANCIAL AID (Fall 2004) 1,386 applied for aid; of those 80% were deemed to have need. 93% of undergraduates with need received aid. *Average percent of need met:* 82% (excluding resources awarded to replace EFC). *Average financial aid package:* $5785 (excluding resources awarded to replace EFC).
GIFT AID (NEED-BASED) *Total amount:* $4,657,967 (65% federal, 26% state, 9% institutional). *Receiving aid:* Freshmen: 43% (10); All full-time undergraduates: 13% (209). *Average award:* Freshmen: $1500; Undergraduates: $1325. *Scholarships, grants, and awards:* Federal Pell, FSEOG, state, college/university gift aid from institutional funds.
GIFT AID (NON-NEED-BASED) *Receiving aid:* Freshmen: 9% (2); Undergraduates: 6% (102). *Scholarships, grants, and awards by category: Academic Interests/Achievement:* general academic interests/achievements. *Special Achievements/Activities:* leadership. *Tuition waivers:* Full or partial for employees or children of employees. *ROTC:* Army cooperative, Air Force cooperative.
LOANS *Student loans:* $18,061,859 (78% need-based, 22% non-need-based). 79% of past graduating class borrowed through all loan programs. *Average indebtedness per student:* $23,432. *Average need-based loan:* Freshmen: $2354; Undergraduates: $3574. *Parent loans:* $248,169 (100% need-based). *Programs:* Federal Direct (Subsidized and Unsubsidized Stafford, PLUS), FFEL (Subsidized and Unsubsidized Stafford, PLUS), Perkins, college/university.
APPLYING FOR FINANCIAL AID *Required financial aid forms:* FAFSA, institution's own form. *Financial aid deadline:* Continuous. *Notification date:* Continuous beginning 6/30.
CONTACT Financial Aid Office, National University, 11255 North Torrey Pines Road, La Jolla, CA 92037-1011, 858-642-8500 or toll-free 800-NAT-UNIV. *Fax:* 858-642-8720.

NAZARENE BIBLE COLLEGE
Colorado Springs, CO

ABOUT THE INSTITUTION Independent religious, coed. Awards: associate and bachelor's degrees. 6 undergraduate majors. Total enrollment: 532. Undergraduates: 532. Freshmen: 35.
GIFT AID (NEED-BASED) *Scholarships, grants, and awards:* Federal Pell, FSEOG, college/university gift aid from institutional funds.
GIFT AID (NON-NEED-BASED) *Scholarships, grants, and awards by category: Academic Interests/Achievement:* religion/biblical studies.
LOANS *Programs:* FFEL (Subsidized and Unsubsidized Stafford, PLUS), Perkins, college/university.
APPLYING FOR FINANCIAL AID *Required financial aid form:* FAFSA.
CONTACT Mr. Malcolm Britton, Director of Financial Aid, Nazarene Bible College, 1111 Academy Park Loop, Colorado Springs, CO 80910-3717, 719-884-5051 or toll-free 800-873-3873. *Fax:* 719-884-5199.

NAZARETH COLLEGE OF ROCHESTER
Rochester, NY

Tuition & fees: $19,874 **Average undergraduate aid package: $15,551**

ABOUT THE INSTITUTION Independent, coed. Awards: bachelor's, master's, and doctoral degrees and post-master's certificates. 72 undergraduate majors. Total enrollment: 3,120. Undergraduates: 2,057. Freshmen: 453. Both federal and institutional methodology are used as a basis for awarding need-based institutional aid.
UNDERGRADUATE EXPENSES for 2005-06 *Application fee:* $40. *Comprehensive fee:* $28,234 includes full-time tuition ($19,214), mandatory fees ($660), and room and board ($8360). *College room only:* $4680. Room and board charges vary according to board plan and housing facility. *Part-time tuition:* $460 per credit hour. *Payment plan:* Installment.
FRESHMAN FINANCIAL AID (Fall 2005, est.) 421 applied for aid; of those 82% were deemed to have need. 100% of freshmen with need received aid. *Average percent of need met:* 83% (excluding resources awarded to replace EFC). *Average financial aid package:* $16,383 (excluding resources awarded to replace EFC). 23% of all full-time freshmen had no need and received non-need-based gift aid.
UNDERGRADUATE FINANCIAL AID (Fall 2005, est.) 1,667 applied for aid; of those 87% were deemed to have need. 100% of undergraduates with need received aid. *Average percent of need met:* 76% (excluding resources awarded to replace EFC). *Average financial aid package:* $15,551 (excluding resources awarded to replace EFC). 18% of all full-time undergraduates had no need and received non-need-based gift aid.
GIFT AID (NEED-BASED) *Total amount:* $14,720,189 (11% federal, 18% state, 68% institutional, 3% external sources). *Receiving aid:* Freshmen: 77% (346); All full-time undergraduates: 78% (1,448). *Average award:* Freshmen: $11,818; Undergraduates: $10,299. *Scholarships, grants, and awards:* Federal Pell, FSEOG, state, private, college/university gift aid from institutional funds.
GIFT AID (NON-NEED-BASED) *Total amount:* $3,439,912 (5% state, 85% institutional, 10% external sources). *Receiving aid:* Freshmen: 17% (78); Undergraduates: 10% (180). *Average Award:* Freshmen: $9287; Undergraduates: $7811. *Scholarships, grants, and awards by category: Academic Interests/ Achievement:* 932 awards ($6,750,628 total): general academic interests/ achievements. *Creative Arts/Performance:* 136 awards ($323,950 total): art/fine arts, music, theater/drama. *Special Characteristics:* 28 awards ($493,598 total): children and siblings of alumni, children of faculty/staff, siblings of current students. *Tuition waivers:* Full or partial for minority students, children of alumni, employees or children of employees. *ROTC:* Army cooperative, Air Force cooperative.
LOANS *Student loans:* $12,761,138 (70% need-based, 30% non-need-based). 82% of past graduating class borrowed through all loan programs. *Average indebtedness per student:* $19,785. *Average need-based loan:* Freshmen: $3021; Undergraduates: $4719. *Parent loans:* $4,191,277 (30% need-based, 70% non-need-based). *Programs:* FFEL (Subsidized and Unsubsidized Stafford, PLUS), Perkins.
WORK-STUDY *Federal work-study:* Total amount: $1,048,469; 1,093 jobs averaging $959.

APPLYING FOR FINANCIAL AID *Required financial aid form:* FAFSA. *Financial aid deadline:* 5/1 (priority: 2/15). *Notification date:* Continuous beginning 2/20. Students must reply by 5/1 or within 2 weeks of notification.
CONTACT Dr. Bruce C. Woolley, Director of Financial Aid, Nazareth College of Rochester, 4245 East Avenue, Rochester, NY 14618-3790, 585-389-2310 or toll-free 800-462-3944 (in-state). *Fax:* 585-389-2317. *E-mail:* bwoolle5@naz.edu.

NEBRASKA CHRISTIAN COLLEGE
Norfolk, NE

ABOUT THE INSTITUTION Independent religious, coed. Awards: associate and bachelor's degrees. 10 undergraduate majors. Total enrollment: 167. Undergraduates: 167. Freshmen: 60.
GIFT AID (NEED-BASED) *Scholarships, grants, and awards:* Federal Pell, FSEOG, state, private, college/university gift aid from institutional funds.
GIFT AID (NON-NEED-BASED) *Scholarships, grants, and awards by category: Academic Interests/Achievement:* general academic interests/achievements. *Special Characteristics:* children of faculty/staff, international students, relatives of clergy.
LOANS *Programs:* FFEL (Subsidized and Unsubsidized Stafford, PLUS).
APPLYING FOR FINANCIAL AID *Required financial aid forms:* FAFSA, institution's own form.
CONTACT Linda Bigbee, Director of Financial Aid, Nebraska Christian College, 1800 Syracuse Avenue, Norfolk, NE 68701-2458, 402-379-5017. *Fax:* 402-379-5100. *E-mail:* lbigbee@nechristian.edu.

NEBRASKA METHODIST COLLEGE
Omaha, NE

CONTACT Ms. Brenda Boyd, Financial Aid Coordinator, Nebraska Methodist College, 8501 West Dodge Road, Omaha, NE 68114-3426, 402-354-4874 or toll-free 800-335-5510. *Fax:* 402-354-8893. *E-mail:* bboyd@methodistcollege.edu.

NEBRASKA WESLEYAN UNIVERSITY
Lincoln, NE

Tuition & fees: $18,410   **Average undergraduate aid package: $12,858**

ABOUT THE INSTITUTION Independent United Methodist, coed. Awards: bachelor's and master's degrees and post-master's certificates. 50 undergraduate majors. Total enrollment: 2,016. Undergraduates: 1,842. Freshmen: 406. Federal methodology is used as a basis for awarding need-based institutional aid.
UNDERGRADUATE EXPENSES for 2005–06 *Application fee:* $20. *Comprehensive fee:* $23,425 includes full-time tuition ($18,100), mandatory fees ($310), and room and board ($5015). Room and board charges vary according to board plan and housing facility. *Part-time tuition:* $683 per credit hour. Part-time tuition and fees vary according to class time, course load, degree level, location, and program. *Payment plans:* Installment, deferred payment.
FRESHMAN FINANCIAL AID (Fall 2005, est.) 350 applied for aid; of those 82% were deemed to have need. 100% of freshmen with need received aid; of those 15% had need fully met. *Average percent of need met:* 71% (excluding resources awarded to replace EFC). *Average financial aid package:* $13,361 (excluding resources awarded to replace EFC). 27% of all full-time freshmen had no need and received non-need-based gift aid.
UNDERGRADUATE FINANCIAL AID (Fall 2005, est.) 1,288 applied for aid; of those 84% were deemed to have need. 100% of undergraduates with need received aid; of those 16% had need fully met. *Average percent of need met:* 69% (excluding resources awarded to replace EFC). *Average financial aid package:* $12,858 (excluding resources awarded to replace EFC). 23% of all full-time undergraduates had no need and received non-need-based gift aid.
GIFT AID (NEED-BASED) *Total amount:* $9,120,732 (11% federal, 3% state, 82% institutional, 4% external sources). *Receiving aid:* Freshmen: 69% (283); All full-time undergraduates: 67% (1,065). *Average award:* Freshmen: $9836; Undergraduates: $8532. *Scholarships, grants, and awards:* Federal Pell, FSEOG, state, private, college/university gift aid from institutional funds.
GIFT AID (NON-NEED-BASED) *Total amount:* $2,557,116 (96% institutional, 4% external sources). *Receiving aid:* Freshmen: 7% (30); Undergraduates: 6% (97). *Average Award:* Freshmen: $6250; Undergraduates: $5881. *Scholarships, grants, and awards by category: Academic Interests/Achievement:* 1,239 awards ($6,537,875 total): general academic interests/achievements. *Creative Arts/Performance:* 143 awards ($138,750 total): art/fine arts, music, theater/drama. *Special Characteristics:* 175 awards ($863,595 total): children of faculty/staff, members of minority groups, relatives of clergy, siblings of current students. *Tuition waivers:* Full or partial for employees or children of employees, adult students, senior citizens. *ROTC:* Army cooperative, Air Force cooperative.
LOANS *Student loans:* $5,565,848 (77% need-based, 23% non-need-based). 70% of past graduating class borrowed through all loan programs. *Average indebtedness per student:* $17,100. *Average need-based loan:* Freshmen: $3709; Undergraduates: $4298. *Parent loans:* $3,594,855 (41% need-based, 59% non-need-based). *Programs:* FFEL (Subsidized and Unsubsidized Stafford, PLUS), Perkins.
WORK-STUDY *Federal work-study:* Total amount: $110,000; jobs available. *State or other work-study/employment:* Total amount: $495,000 (66% need-based, 34% non-need-based). Part-time jobs available.
APPLYING FOR FINANCIAL AID *Required financial aid form:* FAFSA. *Financial aid deadline:* Continuous. *Notification date:* Continuous beginning 3/1. Students must reply within 4 weeks of notification.
CONTACT Mr. Thomas J. Ochsner, Director of Scholarships and Financial Aid, Nebraska Wesleyan University, 5000 Saint Paul Avenue, Lincoln, NE 68504, 402-465-2212 or toll-free 800-541-3818. *Fax:* 402-465-2179. *E-mail:* tjo@nebrwesleyan.edu.

NER ISRAEL RABBINICAL COLLEGE
Baltimore, MD

CONTACT Mr. Moshe Pelberg, Financial Aid Administrator, Ner Israel Rabbinical College, 400 Mount Wilson Lane, Baltimore, MD 21208, 410-484-7200.

NEUMANN COLLEGE
Aston, PA

Tuition & fees: $17,920   **Average undergraduate aid package: $17,000**

ABOUT THE INSTITUTION Independent Roman Catholic, coed. Awards: associate, bachelor's, and master's degrees. 18 undergraduate majors. Total enrollment: 2,810. Undergraduates: 2,313. Freshmen: 522. Federal methodology is used as a basis for awarding need-based institutional aid.
UNDERGRADUATE EXPENSES for 2005–06 *Application fee:* $35. *Comprehensive fee:* $25,996 includes full-time tuition ($17,300), mandatory fees ($620), and room and board ($8076). *College room only:* $4796. *Part-time tuition:* $395 per credit.
FRESHMAN FINANCIAL AID (Fall 2005, est.) 470 applied for aid; of those 100% were deemed to have need. 100% of freshmen with need received aid; of those 60% had need fully met. *Average percent of need met:* 65% (excluding resources awarded to replace EFC). *Average financial aid package:* $17,000 (excluding resources awarded to replace EFC).
UNDERGRADUATE FINANCIAL AID (Fall 2005, est.) 1,650 applied for aid; of those 100% were deemed to have need. 100% of undergraduates with need received aid; of those 60% had need fully met. *Average percent of need met:* 65% (excluding resources awarded to replace EFC). *Average financial aid package:* $17,000 (excluding resources awarded to replace EFC).
GIFT AID (NEED-BASED) *Total amount:* $14,971,832 (12% federal, 13% state, 74% institutional, 1% external sources). *Receiving aid:* Freshmen: 77% (400); All full-time undergraduates: 82% (1,500). *Average award:* Freshmen: $17,000; Undergraduates: $17,000. *Scholarships, grants, and awards:* Federal Pell, FSEOG, state, private, college/university gift aid from institutional funds.
GIFT AID (NON-NEED-BASED) *Scholarships, grants, and awards by category: Creative Arts/Performance:* 1 award ($1000 total): music. *Special Characteristics:* 29 awards ($254,386 total): children of faculty/staff. *ROTC:* Army cooperative.
LOANS *Student loans:* $13,347,779 (100% need-based). 80% of past graduating class borrowed through all loan programs. *Average indebtedness per student:* $20,000. *Average need-based loan:* Freshmen: $3000; Undergraduates: $5000. *Parent loans:* $3,763,569 (100% need-based). *Programs:* Federal Direct (Subsidized and Unsubsidized Stafford, PLUS), FFEL (Subsidized and Unsubsidized Stafford, PLUS), Perkins, Federal Nursing.

Neumann College

WORK-STUDY *Federal work-study:* 120 jobs averaging $1200. *State or other work-study/employment:* Total amount: $200,000 (100% need-based). Part-time jobs available.
APPLYING FOR FINANCIAL AID *Required financial aid form:* FAFSA. *Financial aid deadline:* Continuous.
CONTACT Director of Financial Aid, Neumann College, One Neumann Drive, Aston, PA 19014-1298, 610-558-5519 or toll-free 800-963-8626.

NEUMONT UNIVERSITY
Salt Lake City, UT

CONTACT Financial Aid Office, Neumont University, 2755 East Cottonwood Parkway, Suite 600, Salt Lake City, UT 84121, 801-438-1100 or toll-free 866-622-3448.

NEVADA STATE COLLEGE AT HENDERSON
Henderson, NV

CONTACT Financial Aid Office, Nevada State College at Henderson, 1125 Nevada State Drive, Henderson, NV 89015, 702-992-2000.

NEWBERRY COLLEGE
Newberry, SC

Tuition & fees: $19,631 | Average undergraduate aid package: $13,886

ABOUT THE INSTITUTION Independent Evangelical Lutheran, coed. Awards: bachelor's degrees. 36 undergraduate majors. Total enrollment: 841. Undergraduates: 841. Freshmen: 277. Federal methodology is used as a basis for awarding need-based institutional aid.
UNDERGRADUATE EXPENSES for 2006–07 *Application fee:* $30. *Comprehensive fee:* $26,511 includes full-time tuition ($18,900), mandatory fees ($731), and room and board ($6880). *College room only:* $3230. *Part-time tuition:* $350 per hour. *Part-time fees:* $50 per term.
FRESHMAN FINANCIAL AID (Fall 2005, est.) 244 applied for aid; of those 89% were deemed to have need. 100% of freshmen with need received aid; of those 32% had need fully met. *Average percent of need met:* 78% (excluding resources awarded to replace EFC). *Average financial aid package:* $13,857 (excluding resources awarded to replace EFC). 18% of all full-time freshmen had no need and received non-need-based gift aid.
UNDERGRADUATE FINANCIAL AID (Fall 2005, est.) 658 applied for aid; of those 90% were deemed to have need. 100% of undergraduates with need received aid; of those 32% had need fully met. *Average percent of need met:* 79% (excluding resources awarded to replace EFC). *Average financial aid package:* $13,886 (excluding resources awarded to replace EFC). 15% of all full-time undergraduates had no need and received non-need-based gift aid.
GIFT AID (NEED-BASED) *Total amount:* $5,643,478 (16% federal, 32% state, 48% institutional, 4% external sources). *Receiving aid:* Freshmen: 87% (217); All full-time undergraduates: 83% (587). *Average award:* Freshmen: $11,553; Undergraduates: $10,899. *Scholarships, grants, and awards:* Federal Pell, FSEOG, state, private, college/university gift aid from institutional funds.
GIFT AID (NON-NEED-BASED) *Total amount:* $1,428,516 (41% state, 49% institutional, 10% external sources). *Receiving aid:* Freshmen: 22% (54); Undergraduates: 17% (121). *Average Award:* Freshmen: $11,852; Undergraduates: $11,851. *Scholarships, grants, and awards by category:* Academic Interests/Achievement: 3 awards ($3000 total): biological sciences, business, communication, education, foreign languages, general academic interests/achievements, humanities, mathematics, physical sciences, religion/biblical studies, social sciences. Creative Arts/Performance: 39 awards ($135,943 total): music, theater/drama. Special Achievements/Activities: 115 awards ($261,387 total): cheerleading/drum major, religious involvement. Special Characteristics: 72 awards ($60,158 total): children and siblings of alumni, children of faculty/staff, international students, local/state students, relatives of clergy, religious affiliation, siblings of current students. *ROTC:* Army cooperative.
LOANS *Student loans:* $3,363,933 (71% need-based, 29% non-need-based). 98% of past graduating class borrowed through all loan programs. *Average indebtedness per student:* $13,477. *Average need-based loan:* Freshmen: $3058; Undergraduates: $3866. *Parent loans:* $848,759 (35% need-based, 65% non-need-based). *Programs:* FFEL (Subsidized and Unsubsidized Stafford, PLUS), Perkins, state.

WORK-STUDY *Federal work-study:* Total amount: $43,687; 52 jobs averaging $804. *State or other work-study/employment:* Total amount: $23,838 (100% non-need-based). 45 part-time jobs averaging $518.
ATHLETIC AWARDS Total amount: $944,811 (75% need-based, 25% non-need-based).
APPLYING FOR FINANCIAL AID *Required financial aid forms:* FAFSA, institution's own form. *Financial aid deadline (priority):* 3/15. *Notification date:* Continuous beginning 3/15. Students must reply within 2 weeks of notification.
CONTACT Mrs. Susanne Nelson, Director of Financial Aid, Newberry College, 2100 College Street, Newberry, SC 29108, 803-321-5127 or toll-free 800-845-4955 Ext. 5127. *Fax:* 803-321-5627. *E-mail:* susanne.nelson@newberry.edu.

NEWBURY COLLEGE
Brookline, MA

CONTACT Financial Aid Office, Newbury College, 129 Fisher Avenue, Brookline, MA 02445-5796, 617-730-7101 or toll-free 800-NEWBURY. *Fax:* 617-731-9618.

NEW COLLEGE OF CALIFORNIA
San Francisco, CA

CONTACT Director of Student Financial Aid, New College of California, 50 Fell Street, San Francisco, CA 94102-5206, 415-241-1300 Ext. 338 or toll-free 888-437-3460.

NEW COLLEGE OF FLORIDA
Sarasota, FL

Tuition & fees (FL res): $3797 | Average undergraduate aid package: $11,792

ABOUT THE INSTITUTION State-supported, coed. Awards: bachelor's degrees. 38 undergraduate majors. Total enrollment: 761. Undergraduates: 761. Freshmen: 218. Federal methodology is used as a basis for awarding need-based institutional aid.
UNDERGRADUATE EXPENSES for 2006–07 *Application fee:* $30. *Tuition, state resident:* full-time $3797. *Tuition, nonresident:* full-time $20,345. *College room and board:* $6750; *room only:* $4170.
FRESHMAN FINANCIAL AID (Fall 2005, est.) 144 applied for aid; of those 53% were deemed to have need. 100% of freshmen with need received aid; of those 72% had need fully met. *Average percent of need met:* 96% (excluding resources awarded to replace EFC). *Average financial aid package:* $12,085 (excluding resources awarded to replace EFC). 65% of all full-time freshmen had no need and received non-need-based gift aid.
UNDERGRADUATE FINANCIAL AID (Fall 2005, est.) 420 applied for aid; of those 66% were deemed to have need. 100% of undergraduates with need received aid; of those 69% had need fully met. *Average percent of need met:* 94% (excluding resources awarded to replace EFC). *Average financial aid package:* $11,792 (excluding resources awarded to replace EFC). 49% of all full-time undergraduates had no need and received non-need-based gift aid.
GIFT AID (NEED-BASED) *Total amount:* $1,764,031 (25% federal, 32% state, 39% institutional, 4% external sources). *Receiving aid:* Freshmen: 35% (76); All full-time undergraduates: 35% (269). *Average award:* Freshmen: $8439; Undergraduates: $7549. *Scholarships, grants, and awards:* Federal Pell, state, private, college/university gift aid from institutional funds.
GIFT AID (NON-NEED-BASED) *Total amount:* $2,450,732 (54% state, 44% institutional, 2% external sources). *Receiving aid:* Freshmen: 12% (27); Undergraduates: 7% (54). *Average Award:* Freshmen: $3885; Undergraduates: $3580. *Scholarships, grants, and awards by category:* Academic Interests/Achievement: 509 awards ($1,053,443 total): general academic interests/achievements. Special Achievements/Activities: 82 awards ($416,042 total): general special achievements/activities. Special Characteristics: 113 awards ($620,023 total): out-of-state students.
LOANS *Student loans:* $1,225,710 (70% need-based, 30% non-need-based). 38% of past graduating class borrowed through all loan programs. *Average indebtedness per student:* $12,252. *Average need-based loan:* Freshmen: $2215; Undergraduates: $3764. *Parent loans:* $250,676 (11% need-based, 89% non-need-based). *Programs:* FFEL (Subsidized and Unsubsidized Stafford, PLUS).
WORK-STUDY *State or other work-study/employment:* Total amount: $166,731 (100% need-based). 63 part-time jobs averaging $2647.

APPLYING FOR FINANCIAL AID *Required financial aid form:* FAFSA. *Financial aid deadline (priority):* 3/1. *Notification date:* Continuous beginning 3/1. Students must reply by 5/1 or within 4 weeks of notification.
CONTACT Monica Baldwin, Director of Financial Aid, New College of Florida, 5700 North Tamiami Trail, PME 119, Sarasota, FL 34243-2197, 941-359-4255. *Fax:* 941-359-4229. *E-mail:* ncfinaid@ncf.edu.

NEW ENGLAND COLLEGE
Henniker, NH

Tuition & fees: $23,010	Average undergraduate aid package: $22,536

ABOUT THE INSTITUTION Independent, coed. Awards: associate, bachelor's, and master's degrees. 35 undergraduate majors. Total enrollment: 1,380. Undergraduates: 1,041. Freshmen: 356. Federal methodology is used as a basis for awarding need-based institutional aid.
UNDERGRADUATE EXPENSES for 2005–06 *Application fee:* $30. *Comprehensive fee:* $31,466 includes full-time tuition ($22,366), mandatory fees ($644), and room and board ($8456). *College room only:* $4398. Full-time tuition and fees vary according to class time, course load, degree level, location, and program. Room and board charges vary according to board plan and housing facility. *Part-time tuition:* $1065 per credit. *Part-time fees:* $198 per term. Part-time tuition and fees vary according to class time, course load, degree level, location, and program. *Payment plan:* Installment.
FRESHMAN FINANCIAL AID (Fall 2005, est.) 281 applied for aid; of those 89% were deemed to have need. 99% of freshmen with need received aid; of those 61% had need fully met. *Average percent of need met:* 83% (excluding resources awarded to replace EFC). *Average financial aid package:* $20,820 (excluding resources awarded to replace EFC). 11% of all full-time freshmen had no need and received non-need-based gift aid.
UNDERGRADUATE FINANCIAL AID (Fall 2005, est.) 794 applied for aid; of those 84% were deemed to have need. 100% of undergraduates with need received aid; of those 32% had need fully met. *Average percent of need met:* 86% (excluding resources awarded to replace EFC). *Average financial aid package:* $22,536 (excluding resources awarded to replace EFC). 16% of all full-time undergraduates had no need and received non-need-based gift aid.
GIFT AID (NEED-BASED) *Total amount:* $8,166,947 (10% federal, 1% state, 86% institutional, 3% external sources). *Receiving aid:* Freshmen: 71% (247); All full-time undergraduates: 73% (660). *Average award:* Freshmen: $11,375; Undergraduates: $10,140. *Scholarships, grants, and awards:* Federal Pell, FSEOG, state, private, college/university gift aid from institutional funds.
GIFT AID (NON-NEED-BASED) *Total amount:* $1,062,518 (98% institutional, 2% external sources). *Receiving aid:* Freshmen: 8% (28); Undergraduates: 4% (32). *Average Award:* Freshmen: $7099; Undergraduates: $8282. *Scholarships, grants, and awards by category: Academic Interests/Achievement:* 797 awards ($6,306,639 total): biological sciences, business, communication, education, engineering/technologies, English, general academic interests/achievements, humanities, international studies, mathematics, social sciences. *Creative Arts/Performance:* 19 awards ($182,500 total): applied art and design, art/fine arts, creative writing, theater/drama. *Special Achievements/Activities:* 28 awards ($204,650 total): community service, leadership. *Special Characteristics:* 101 awards ($1,005,159 total): children and siblings of alumni, children of educators, children of faculty/staff, ethnic background, international students, local/state students, parents of current students, siblings of current students. *Tuition waivers:* Full or partial for children of alumni, employees or children of employees, adult students, senior citizens. *ROTC:* Army cooperative, Air Force cooperative.
LOANS *Student loans:* $6,642,438 (69% need-based, 31% non-need-based). 74% of past graduating class borrowed through all loan programs. *Average indebtedness per student:* $31,753. *Average need-based loan:* Freshmen: $6810; Undergraduates: $8430. *Parent loans:* $2,296,957 (32% need-based, 68% non-need-based). *Programs:* FFEL (Subsidized and Unsubsidized Stafford, PLUS), Perkins, state.
WORK-STUDY *Federal work-study:* Total amount: $750,623; 453 jobs averaging $1347. *State or other work-study/employment:* Total amount: $34,977 (27% need-based, 73% non-need-based). 23 part-time jobs averaging $1499.
APPLYING FOR FINANCIAL AID *Required financial aid forms:* FAFSA, institution's own form. *Financial aid deadline (priority):* 4/1. *Notification date:* Continuous beginning 1/2. Students must reply within 2 weeks of notification.
CONTACT Ms. Lauren Hughes, Student Financial Services, New England College, 7 Main Street, Henniker, NH 03242-3293, 603-428-2226 or toll-free 800-521-7642. *Fax:* 603-428-2404.

NEW ENGLAND CONSERVATORY OF MUSIC
Boston, MA

ABOUT THE INSTITUTION Independent, coed. Awards: bachelor's, master's, and doctoral degrees and post-bachelor's certificates. 8 undergraduate majors. Total enrollment: 801. Undergraduates: 412. Freshmen: 102.
GIFT AID (NEED-BASED) *Scholarships, grants, and awards:* Federal Pell, FSEOG, state, private, college/university gift aid from institutional funds.
GIFT AID (NON-NEED-BASED) *Scholarships, grants, and awards by category: Creative Arts/Performance:* music, theater/drama.
LOANS *Programs:* FFEL (Subsidized and Unsubsidized Stafford, PLUS), Perkins, state.
WORK-STUDY *Federal work-study:* Total amount: $290,445; 283 jobs averaging $1611. *State or other work-study/employment:* Part-time jobs available.
APPLYING FOR FINANCIAL AID *Required financial aid forms:* FAFSA, institution's own form.
CONTACT Kenneth T. Ferreira Jr., Director of Financial Aid, New England Conservatory of Music, 290 Huntington Avenue, Boston, MA 02115, 617-585-1110. *Fax:* 617-585-1115. *E-mail:* kferreira@newenglandconservatory.edu.

THE NEW ENGLAND INSTITUTE OF ART
Brookline, MA

CONTACT Ms. Merry Kerber, Director of Financial Aid, The New England Institute of Art, 142 Berkeley Street, Boston, MA 02116-5100, 617-267-7910 or toll-free 800-903=4425 (in-state).

NEW ENGLAND SCHOOL OF COMMUNICATIONS
Bangor, ME

Tuition & fees: $9590	Average undergraduate aid package: $7490

ABOUT THE INSTITUTION Independent, coed. Awards: associate and bachelor's degrees. 20 undergraduate majors. Total enrollment: 305. Undergraduates: 305. Freshmen: 112. Federal methodology is used as a basis for awarding need-based institutional aid.
UNDERGRADUATE EXPENSES for 2006–07 *Application fee:* $15. *Comprehensive fee:* $15,620 includes full-time tuition ($8890), mandatory fees ($700), and room and board ($6030). *Part-time tuition:* $275 per credit.
FRESHMAN FINANCIAL AID (Fall 2004) 108 applied for aid; of those 94% were deemed to have need. 100% of freshmen with need received aid; of those 69% had need fully met. *Average percent of need met:* 68% (excluding resources awarded to replace EFC). *Average financial aid package:* $5615 (excluding resources awarded to replace EFC).
UNDERGRADUATE FINANCIAL AID (Fall 2004) 231 applied for aid; of those 97% were deemed to have need. 100% of undergraduates with need received aid; of those 15% had need fully met. *Average percent of need met:* 14% (excluding resources awarded to replace EFC). *Average financial aid package:* $7490 (excluding resources awarded to replace EFC).
GIFT AID (NEED-BASED) *Total amount:* $457,263 (66% federal, 20% state, 5% institutional, 9% external sources). *Receiving aid:* Freshmen: 46% (60); All full-time undergraduates: 44% (124). *Average award:* Freshmen: $3340; Undergraduates: $4400. *Scholarships, grants, and awards:* Federal Pell, state, private, college/university gift aid from institutional funds.
GIFT AID (NON-NEED-BASED) *Receiving aid:* Freshmen: 78% (102); Undergraduates: 80% (225). *Scholarships, grants, and awards by category: Academic Interests/Achievement:* 25 awards ($21,000 total): communication. *Special Achievements/Activities:* general special achievements/activities.
LOANS *Student loans:* $704,120 (75% need-based, 25% non-need-based). 93% of past graduating class borrowed through all loan programs. *Average indebtedness per student:* $30,000. *Average need-based loan:* Freshmen: $2625; Undergraduates: $4500. *Parent loans:* $386,202 (100% need-based). *Programs:* FFEL (Subsidized and Unsubsidized Stafford, PLUS), alternative loans.
WORK-STUDY *State or other work-study/employment:* Total amount: $8360 (100% need-based). 6 part-time jobs averaging $2200.

New England School of Communications

APPLYING FOR FINANCIAL AID *Required financial aid form:* FAFSA. *Financial aid deadline (priority):* 5/1. *Notification date:* Continuous beginning 5/1. Students must reply within 4 weeks of notification.
CONTACT Ms. Nicole Rediker, Director of Financial Aid, New England School of Communications, One College Circle, Bangor, ME 04401, 888-877-1876. *Fax:* 207-947-3987.

NEW HAMPSHIRE INSTITUTE OF ART
Manchester, NH

Tuition & fees: $12,080   Average undergraduate aid package: N/A

ABOUT THE INSTITUTION Proprietary, coed. Awards: bachelor's degrees. 1 undergraduate major. Total enrollment: 180. Undergraduates: 180. Freshmen: 60. Federal methodology is used as a basis for awarding need-based institutional aid.
UNDERGRADUATE EXPENSES for 2005–06 *Application fee:* $25. *Tuition:* full-time $10,950; part-time $365 per credit. *Required fees:* full-time $1130; $466 per year part-time. Room and board charges vary according to housing facility.
GIFT AID (NEED-BASED) *Scholarships, grants, and awards:* Federal Pell, FSEOG, state, private, college/university gift aid from institutional funds.
GIFT AID (NON-NEED-BASED) *Scholarships, grants, and awards by category: Creative Arts/Performance:* art/fine arts. *Tuition waivers:* Full or partial for employees or children of employees.
LOANS *Programs:* FFEL (Subsidized and Unsubsidized Stafford, PLUS), alternative loans.
WORK-STUDY Federal work-study jobs available.
APPLYING FOR FINANCIAL AID *Required financial aid form:* FAFSA. *Financial aid deadline (priority):* 5/1.
CONTACT Linda Lavallee, Director of Financial Aid, New Hampshire Institute of Art, 148 Concord Street, Manchester, NH 03104-4858, 603-623-0313 Ext. 577 or toll-free 866-241-4918 (in-state). *Fax:* 603-647-0658. *E-mail:* llavallee@nhia.edu.

NEW JERSEY CITY UNIVERSITY
Jersey City, NJ

Tuition & fees (NJ res): $7040   Average undergraduate aid package: $7628

ABOUT THE INSTITUTION State-supported, coed. Awards: bachelor's and master's degrees and post-master's certificates. 27 undergraduate majors. Total enrollment: 8,464. Undergraduates: 6,004. Freshmen: 692. Federal methodology is used as a basis for awarding need-based institutional aid.
UNDERGRADUATE EXPENSES for 2005–06 *Application fee:* $35. *Tuition, state resident:* full-time $5190; part-time $173 per credit hour. *Tuition, nonresident:* full-time $10,230; part-time $341 per credit hour. *Required fees:* full-time $1850; $59.95 per credit. *College room and board:* $7306; *room only:* $4630. *Payment plan:* Deferred payment.
FRESHMAN FINANCIAL AID (Fall 2005, est.) 458 applied for aid; of those 85% were deemed to have need. 95% of freshmen with need received aid; of those 11% had need fully met. *Average percent of need met:* 67% (excluding resources awarded to replace EFC). *Average financial aid package:* $7661 (excluding resources awarded to replace EFC). 3% of all full-time freshmen had no need and received non-need-based gift aid.
UNDERGRADUATE FINANCIAL AID (Fall 2005, est.) 2,957 applied for aid; of those 92% were deemed to have need. 96% of undergraduates with need received aid; of those 12% had need fully met. *Average percent of need met:* 65% (excluding resources awarded to replace EFC). *Average financial aid package:* $7628 (excluding resources awarded to replace EFC). 1% of all full-time undergraduates had no need and received non-need-based gift aid.
GIFT AID (NEED-BASED) *Total amount:* $14,342,855 (52% federal, 48% state). *Receiving aid:* Freshmen: 52% (281); All full-time undergraduates: 54% (1,927). *Average award:* Freshmen: $6921; Undergraduates: $6049. *Scholarships, grants, and awards:* Federal Pell, FSEOG, state, private, college/university gift aid from institutional funds, United Negro College Fund.
GIFT AID (NON-NEED-BASED) *Total amount:* $792,974 (9% state, 89% institutional, 2% external sources). *Receiving aid:* Freshmen: 52% (284); Undergraduates: 47% (1,687). *Average Award:* Freshmen: $3029; Undergraduates: $3672. *Scholarships, grants, and awards by category: Academic Interests/Achievement:* biological sciences, business, communication, education, general academic interests/achievements, mathematics. *Creative Arts/Performance:* art/fine arts, dance, music. *Tuition waivers:* Full or partial for senior citizens.
LOANS *Student loans:* $14,316,936 (59% need-based, 41% non-need-based). *Average need-based loan:* Freshmen: $2761; Undergraduates: $3765. *Programs:* FFEL (Subsidized and Unsubsidized Stafford, PLUS), Perkins, state.
WORK-STUDY *Federal work-study:* Total amount: $1,097,873; jobs available.
APPLYING FOR FINANCIAL AID *Required financial aid form:* FAFSA. *Financial aid deadline (priority):* 4/15. *Notification date:* Continuous beginning 4/1.
CONTACT Ms. Carmen Panlilio, Assistant Vice President for Admissions and Financial Aid, New Jersey City University, 2039 Kennedy Boulevard, Jersey City, NJ 07305-1597, 201-200-3173 or toll-free 888-441-NJCU.

NEW JERSEY INSTITUTE OF TECHNOLOGY
Newark, NJ

ABOUT THE INSTITUTION State-supported, coed. Awards: bachelor's, master's, and doctoral degrees and post-bachelor's certificates. 29 undergraduate majors. Total enrollment: 8,058. Undergraduates: 5,263. Freshmen: 762.
GIFT AID (NEED-BASED) *Scholarships, grants, and awards:* Federal Pell, FSEOG, state, private, college/university gift aid from institutional funds.
GIFT AID (NON-NEED-BASED) *Scholarships, grants, and awards by category: Academic Interests/Achievement:* architecture, general academic interests/achievements. *Special Characteristics:* out-of-state students.
LOANS *Programs:* Federal Direct (Subsidized and Unsubsidized Stafford, PLUS), Perkins, state, college/university.
WORK-STUDY *Federal work-study:* Total amount: $558,057; jobs available. *State or other work-study/employment:* Total amount: $404,000 (100% non-need-based). Part-time jobs available.
APPLYING FOR FINANCIAL AID *Required financial aid form:* FAFSA.
CONTACT Ms. Kathy Bialk, Director of Financial Aid, New Jersey Institute of Technology, University Heights, Newark, NJ 07102, 973-596-3478 or toll-free 800-925-NJIT. *Fax:* 973-802-1854. *E-mail:* kathy.j.bialk@njit.edu.

NEW LIFE THEOLOGICAL SEMINARY
Charlotte, NC

CONTACT Financial Aid Office, New Life Theological Seminary, PO Box 790106, Charlotte, NC 28206-7901, 704-334-6882.

NEWMAN UNIVERSITY
Wichita, KS

Tuition & fees: $17,308   Average undergraduate aid package: $10,091

ABOUT THE INSTITUTION Independent Roman Catholic, coed. Awards: associate, bachelor's, and master's degrees. 36 undergraduate majors. Total enrollment: 2,103. Undergraduates: 1,732. Freshmen: 168. Federal methodology is used as a basis for awarding need-based institutional aid.
UNDERGRADUATE EXPENSES for 2006–07 *Application fee:* $20. *Comprehensive fee:* $22,680 includes full-time tuition ($17,008), mandatory fees ($300), and room and board ($5372). *Part-time tuition:* $567 per credit hour. *Part-time fees:* $10 per credit hour.
FRESHMAN FINANCIAL AID (Fall 2004) 231 applied for aid; of those 56% were deemed to have need. 100% of freshmen with need received aid; of those 12% had need fully met. *Average percent of need met:* 64% (excluding resources awarded to replace EFC). *Average financial aid package:* $11,470 (excluding resources awarded to replace EFC). 9% of all full-time freshmen had no need and received non-need-based gift aid.
UNDERGRADUATE FINANCIAL AID (Fall 2004) 1,291 applied for aid; of those 74% were deemed to have need. 100% of undergraduates with need received aid; of those 13% had need fully met. *Average percent of need met:* 58% (excluding resources awarded to replace EFC). *Average financial aid package:* $10,091 (excluding resources awarded to replace EFC). 4% of all full-time undergraduates had no need and received non-need-based gift aid.
GIFT AID (NEED-BASED) *Total amount:* $2,293,971 (63% federal, 37% state). *Receiving aid:* Freshmen: 46% (106); All full-time undergraduates: 58% (771). *Average award:* Freshmen: $3740; Undergraduates: $3891. *Scholarships, grants, and awards:* Federal Pell, FSEOG, state, private, college/university gift aid from institutional funds.

GIFT AID (NON-NEED-BASED) *Total amount:* $3,937,189 (92% institutional, 8% external sources). *Receiving aid:* Freshmen: 55% (127); Undergraduates: 63% (831). *Average Award:* Freshmen: $2839; Undergraduates: $2395. *Scholarships, grants, and awards by category:* Academic Interests/Achievement: 871 awards ($2,306,013 total): general academic interests/achievements. *Creative Arts/Performance:* 45 awards ($95,300 total): art/fine arts, journalism/publications, music, theater/drama. *Special Achievements/Activities:* 123 awards ($339,000 total): community service, leadership, memberships, religious involvement. *Special Characteristics:* 101 awards ($761,373 total): children and siblings of alumni, children of faculty/staff, first-generation college students, international students, out-of-state students, religious affiliation, siblings of current students.
LOANS *Student loans:* $10,420,131 (43% need-based, 57% non-need-based). 70% of past graduating class borrowed through all loan programs. *Average indebtedness per student:* $19,049. *Average need-based loan:* Freshmen: $2429; Undergraduates: $3919. *Parent loans:* $698,713 (100% non-need-based). *Programs:* FFEL (Subsidized and Unsubsidized Stafford, PLUS), Perkins.
WORK-STUDY *Federal work-study:* Total amount: $77,111; 88 jobs averaging $876. *State or other work-study/employment:* Total amount: $209,325 (100% non-need-based). 160 part-time jobs averaging $1308.
ATHLETIC AWARDS *Total amount:* $1,077,363 (100% non-need-based).
APPLYING FOR FINANCIAL AID *Required financial aid forms:* FAFSA, institution's own form. *Financial aid deadline (priority):* 3/1. *Notification date:* Continuous.
CONTACT Victoria Tillotson, Financial Aid Counselor, Newman University, 3100 McCormick Avenue, Wichita, KS 67213, 316-942-4291 Ext. 2103 or toll-free 877-NEWMANU Ext. 2144. *Fax:* 316-942-4483.

NEW MEXICO HIGHLANDS UNIVERSITY
Las Vegas, NM

ABOUT THE INSTITUTION State-supported, coed. Awards: associate, bachelor's, and master's degrees. 45 undergraduate majors. Total enrollment: 3,750. Undergraduates: 1,986. Freshmen: 236.
GIFT AID (NEED-BASED) *Scholarships, grants, and awards:* Federal Pell, FSEOG, state, private, college/university gift aid from institutional funds.
GIFT AID (NON-NEED-BASED) *Scholarships, grants, and awards by category: Academic Interests/Achievement:* biological sciences, business, communication, computer science, education, engineering/technologies, English, foreign languages, general academic interests/achievements, health fields, humanities, mathematics, physical sciences, social sciences. *Creative Arts/Performance:* art/fine arts, music, performing arts, theater/drama. *Special Characteristics:* children of faculty/staff, children with a deceased or disabled parent, first-generation college students, international students.
LOANS *Programs:* FFEL (Subsidized and Unsubsidized Stafford, PLUS), Perkins, state.
APPLYING FOR FINANCIAL AID *Required financial aid form:* FAFSA.
CONTACT Eileen Sedillo, Director, Financial Aid & Scholarship, New Mexico Highlands University, Box 9000, Las Vegas, NM 87701, 505-454-3430 or toll-free 800-338-6648. *Fax:* 505-454-3398. *E-mail:* sedillo_e@nmhu.edu.

NEW MEXICO INSTITUTE OF MINING AND TECHNOLOGY
Socorro, NM

ABOUT THE INSTITUTION State-supported, coed. Awards: associate, bachelor's, master's, and doctoral degrees. 24 undergraduate majors. Total enrollment: 1,891. Undergraduates: 1,388. Freshmen: 281.
GIFT AID (NEED-BASED) *Scholarships, grants, and awards:* Federal Pell, FSEOG, state, private, college/university gift aid from institutional funds, New Mexico Scholar Program, Legislative Endowment Scholarships.
GIFT AID (NON-NEED-BASED) *Scholarships, grants, and awards by category: Academic Interests/Achievement:* communication, engineering/technologies, general academic interests/achievements, physical sciences. *Special Characteristics:* children of faculty/staff.
LOANS *Programs:* FFEL (Subsidized and Unsubsidized Stafford, PLUS), Perkins.
WORK-STUDY *Federal work-study:* Total amount: $268,407; jobs available. *State or other work-study/employment:* Total amount: $132,035 (31% need-based, 69% non-need-based). Part-time jobs available.
APPLYING FOR FINANCIAL AID *Required financial aid forms:* FAFSA, institution's own form.

CONTACT Ms. Annette Kaus, Director of Financial Aid, New Mexico Institute of Mining and Technology, Financial Aid Office, 801 Leroy Place, Socorro, NM 87801, 505-835-5333 or toll-free 800-428-TECH. *Fax:* 505-835-5959. *E-mail:* akaus@admin.nmt.edu.

NEW MEXICO STATE UNIVERSITY
Las Cruces, NM

Tuition & fees (NM res): $3918   **Average undergraduate aid package: $8728**

ABOUT THE INSTITUTION State-supported, coed. Awards: associate, bachelor's, master's, and doctoral degrees and post-master's certificates. 82 undergraduate majors. Total enrollment: 16,072. Undergraduates: 12,656. Freshmen: 2,019. Federal methodology is used as a basis for awarding need-based institutional aid.
UNDERGRADUATE EXPENSES for 2005–06 *Application fee:* $15. *Tuition, state resident:* full-time $2868; part-time $163.25 per credit. *Tuition, nonresident:* full-time $12,156; part-time $550.25 per credit. *College room and board:* $5332; *room only:* $3072. Room and board charges vary according to board plan and gender. *Payment plans:* Installment, deferred payment.
FRESHMAN FINANCIAL AID (Fall 2005, est.) 1471 applied for aid; of those 81% were deemed to have need. 97% of freshmen with need received aid; of those 15% had need fully met. *Average percent of need met:* 61% (excluding resources awarded to replace EFC). *Average financial aid package:* $7745 (excluding resources awarded to replace EFC). 27% of all full-time freshmen had no need and received non-need-based gift aid.
UNDERGRADUATE FINANCIAL AID (Fall 2005, est.) 7,444 applied for aid; of those 88% were deemed to have need. 95% of undergraduates with need received aid; of those 16% had need fully met. *Average percent of need met:* 65% (excluding resources awarded to replace EFC). *Average financial aid package:* $8728 (excluding resources awarded to replace EFC). 20% of all full-time undergraduates had no need and received non-need-based gift aid.
GIFT AID (NEED-BASED) *Total amount:* $27,087,607 (58% federal, 29% state, 7% institutional, 6% external sources). *Receiving aid:* Freshmen: 55% (1,100); All full-time undergraduates: 52% (5,664). *Average award:* Freshmen: $6203; Undergraduates: $5947. *Scholarships, grants, and awards:* Federal Pell, FSEOG, state, private, college/university gift aid from institutional funds.
GIFT AID (NON-NEED-BASED) *Total amount:* $7,864,600 (76% state, 15% institutional, 9% external sources). *Receiving aid:* Freshmen: 5% (104); Undergraduates: 4% (460). *Average Award:* Freshmen: $3161; Undergraduates: $3066. *Scholarships, grants, and awards by category: Academic Interests/Achievement:* agriculture, biological sciences, business, communication, computer science, education, engineering/technologies, English, foreign languages, general academic interests/achievements, health fields, home economics, humanities, mathematics, military science, physical sciences, social sciences. *Creative Arts/Performance:* applied art and design, art/fine arts, general creative arts/performance, journalism/publications, music, performing arts, theater/drama. *Special Achievements/Activities:* leadership, rodeo. *Special Characteristics:* adult students, children and siblings of alumni, children of faculty/staff, children of public servants, children of union members/company employees, children of workers in trades, children with a deceased or disabled parent, ethnic background, handicapped students, international students, local/state students, married students, members of minority groups, out-of-state students, previous college experience, spouses of current students, veterans, veterans' children. *Tuition waivers:* Full or partial for employees or children of employees, senior citizens. *ROTC:* Army, Air Force.
LOANS *Student loans:* $26,586,325 (84% need-based, 16% non-need-based). *Average need-based loan:* Freshmen: $2698; Undergraduates: $4189. *Parent loans:* $905,877 (23% need-based, 77% non-need-based). *Programs:* FFEL (Subsidized and Unsubsidized Stafford, PLUS), Perkins, state.
WORK-STUDY *Federal work-study:* Total amount: $1,153,454; 419 jobs averaging $1957. *State or other work-study/employment:* Total amount: $2,187,169 (75% need-based, 25% non-need-based). 498 part-time jobs averaging $1749.
ATHLETIC AWARDS *Total amount:* $2,469,738 (35% need-based, 65% non-need-based).
APPLYING FOR FINANCIAL AID *Required financial aid forms:* FAFSA, institution's own form. *Financial aid deadline (priority):* 3/1.
CONTACT Tyler Pruett, Director of Financial Aid, New Mexico State University, Box 30001, Department 5100, Las Cruces, NM 88003-8001, 505-646-4105 or toll-free 800-662-6678. *Fax:* 505-646-7381.

NEW ORLEANS BAPTIST THEOLOGICAL SEMINARY
New Orleans, LA

CONTACT Financial Aid Office, New Orleans Baptist Theological Seminary, 3939 Gentilly Boulevard, New Orleans, LA 70126-4858, 504-282-4455 Ext. 3348 or toll-free 800-662-8701. *E-mail:* financialaid@nobts.edu.

NEW SAINT ANDREWS COLLEGE
Moscow, ID

CONTACT Financial Aid Office, New Saint Andrews College, PO Box 9025, Moscow, ID 83843, 208-882-1566.

THE NEW SCHOOL FOR GENERAL STUDIES
New York, NY

CONTACT Financial Aid Counselor, The New School for General Studies, 65 Fifth Avenue, New York, NY 10003, 212-229-8930 or toll-free 800-862-5039 (out-of-state). *Fax:* 212-229-5919.

THE NEW SCHOOL FOR JAZZ AND CONTEMPORARY MUSIC
New York, NY

CONTACT Financial Aid Office, The New School for Jazz and Contemporary Music, 55 West 13th Street, 5th Floor, New York, NY 10011, 212-229-5896.

NEWSCHOOL OF ARCHITECTURE & DESIGN
San Diego, CA

CONTACT Ms. Cara E. Baker, Director of Financial Aid, Newschool of Architecture & Design, 1249 F Street, San Diego, CA 92101-6634, 619-235-4100 Ext. 103. *Fax:* 619-235-4651. *E-mail:* cbaker@newschoolarch.edu.

NEW SCHOOL UNIVERSITY, MANNES COLLEGE OF MUSIC
New York, NY

See Mannes College The New School for Music.

NEW YORK INSTITUTE OF TECHNOLOGY
Old Westbury, NY

Tuition & fees: $19,236 **Average undergraduate aid package:** $13,616

ABOUT THE INSTITUTION Independent, coed. Awards: associate, bachelor's, master's, doctoral, and first professional degrees and post-bachelor's and post-master's certificates. 70 undergraduate majors. Total enrollment: 11,141. Undergraduates: 6,486. Freshmen: 885. Federal methodology is used as a basis for awarding need-based institutional aid.

UNDERGRADUATE EXPENSES for 2005–06 *Application fee:* $50. *Comprehensive fee:* $30,040 includes full-time tuition ($18,696), mandatory fees ($540), and room and board ($10,804). *College room only:* $5600. Full-time tuition and fees vary according to course load and program. Room and board charges vary according to board plan, housing facility, and location. *Part-time tuition:* $630 per credit. *Part-time fees:* $230 per term. Part-time tuition and fees vary according to course load. *Payment plan:* Installment.

FRESHMAN FINANCIAL AID (Fall 2005, est.) 668 applied for aid; of those 88% were deemed to have need. 100% of freshmen with need received aid; of those 14% had need fully met. *Average percent of need met:* 77% (excluding resources awarded to replace EFC). *Average financial aid package:* $13,224 (excluding resources awarded to replace EFC). 19% of all full-time freshmen had no need and received non-need-based gift aid.

UNDERGRADUATE FINANCIAL AID (Fall 2005, est.) 3,582 applied for aid; of those 90% were deemed to have need. 99% of undergraduates with need received aid; of those 23% had need fully met. *Average percent of need met:* 79% (excluding resources awarded to replace EFC). *Average financial aid package:* $13,616 (excluding resources awarded to replace EFC). 13% of all full-time undergraduates had no need and received non-need-based gift aid.

GIFT AID (NEED-BASED) *Total amount:* $14,478,646 (37% federal, 39% state, 24% institutional). *Receiving aid:* Freshmen: 63% (558); All full-time undergraduates: 65% (2,815). *Average award:* Freshmen: $5035; Undergraduates: $5089. *Scholarships, grants, and awards:* Federal Pell, FSEOG, state, private, college/university gift aid from institutional funds.

GIFT AID (NON-NEED-BASED) *Total amount:* $13,240,610 (1% federal, 1% state, 97% institutional, 1% external sources). *Receiving aid:* Freshmen: 55% (485); Undergraduates: 43% (1,857). *Average Award:* Freshmen: $4685; Undergraduates: $4268. *Scholarships, grants, and awards by category: Academic Interests/Achievement:* general academic interests/achievements. *Special Characteristics:* children and siblings of alumni, children of educators, children of faculty/staff, children of public servants, local/state students, previous college experience, public servants, spouses of deceased or disabled public servants, veterans. *Tuition waivers:* Full or partial for employees or children of employees, senior citizens. *ROTC:* Army, Air Force.

LOANS *Student loans:* $17,137,214 (58% need-based, 42% non-need-based). 75% of past graduating class borrowed through all loan programs. *Average indebtedness per student:* $17,125. *Average need-based loan:* Freshmen: $2508; Undergraduates: $3857. *Parent loans:* $7,466,791 (100% non-need-based). *Programs:* FFEL (Subsidized and Unsubsidized Stafford, PLUS), Perkins, Federal Nursing, alternative loans.

WORK-STUDY *Federal work-study:* Total amount: $526,561; jobs available. *State or other work-study/employment:* Total amount: $409,663 (100% non-need-based). Part-time jobs available.

ATHLETIC AWARDS *Total amount:* $1,619,768 (100% non-need-based).

APPLYING FOR FINANCIAL AID *Required financial aid form:* FAFSA. *Financial aid deadline (priority):* 2/1. *Notification date:* Continuous beginning 2/15. Students must reply by 5/1 or within 2 weeks of notification.

CONTACT Doreen Meyer, Director of Financial Aid Office, New York Institute of Technology, PO Box 8000, Old Westbury, NY 11568-8000, 516-686-1085 or toll-free 800-345-NYIT. *Fax:* 516-686-3835. *E-mail:* dmeyer@nyit.edu.

NEW YORK SCHOOL OF INTERIOR DESIGN
New York, NY

Tuition & fees: $18,820 **Average undergraduate aid package:** $8500

ABOUT THE INSTITUTION Independent, coed, primarily women. Awards: associate, bachelor's, and master's degrees. 1 undergraduate major. Total enrollment: 739. Undergraduates: 724. Freshmen: 23. Federal methodology is used as a basis for awarding need-based institutional aid.

UNDERGRADUATE EXPENSES for 2006–07 *Application fee:* $50. *Tuition:* full-time $18,600; part-time $620 per credit. *Required fees:* full-time $220; $110 per term part-time.

FRESHMAN FINANCIAL AID (Fall 2004) 28 applied for aid; of those 100% were deemed to have need. 100% of freshmen with need received aid. *Average percent of need met:* 50% (excluding resources awarded to replace EFC). *Average financial aid package:* $6500 (excluding resources awarded to replace EFC).

UNDERGRADUATE FINANCIAL AID (Fall 2004) 69 applied for aid; of those 100% were deemed to have need. 100% of undergraduates with need received aid. *Average percent of need met:* 50% (excluding resources awarded to replace EFC). *Average financial aid package:* $8500 (excluding resources awarded to replace EFC).

GIFT AID (NEED-BASED) *Total amount:* $402,868 (28% federal, 25% state, 44% institutional, 3% external sources). *Receiving aid:* Freshmen: 44% (21); All full-time undergraduates: 35% (60). *Average award:* Freshmen: $5000; Undergraduates: $5000. *Scholarships, grants, and awards:* Federal Pell, FSEOG, state, college/university gift aid from institutional funds.

GIFT AID (NON-NEED-BASED) *Total amount:* $16,500 (100% institutional). *Receiving aid:* Undergraduates: 1% (2).

LOANS *Student loans:* $983,334 (40% need-based, 60% non-need-based). 15% of past graduating class borrowed through all loan programs. *Average*

indebtedness per student: $13,250. **Average need-based loan:** Freshmen: $2625; Undergraduates: $3000. **Parent loans:** $489,890 (100% need-based). **Programs:** FFEL (Subsidized and Unsubsidized Stafford, PLUS).
WORK-STUDY *Federal work-study:* Total amount: $33,203; 28 jobs averaging $3000.
APPLYING FOR FINANCIAL AID *Required financial aid forms:* FAFSA, institution's own form. *Financial aid deadline (priority):* 5/1. *Notification date:* Continuous. Students must reply within 2 weeks of notification.
CONTACT Nina Bunchuk, Director of Financial Aid, New York School of Interior Design, 170 East 70th Street, New York, NY 10021-5110, 212-472-1500 Ext. 212 or toll-free 800-336-9743 Ext. 204. *Fax:* 212-472-1867. *E-mail:* nina@nysid.edu.

NEW YORK UNIVERSITY
New York, NY

Tuition & fees: $31,690 Average undergraduate aid package: $18,652

ABOUT THE INSTITUTION Independent, coed. Awards: associate, bachelor's, master's, doctoral, and first professional degrees and post-bachelor's, post-master's, and first professional certificates. 116 undergraduate majors. Total enrollment: 40,004. Undergraduates: 20,566. Freshmen: 4,676. Federal methodology is used as a basis for awarding need-based institutional aid.
UNDERGRADUATE EXPENSES for 2005–06 *Application fee:* $65. **Comprehensive fee:** $43,170 includes full-time tuition ($29,890), mandatory fees ($1800), and room and board ($11,480). Full-time tuition and fees vary according to program. Room and board charges vary according to board plan and housing facility. *Part-time tuition:* $881 per credit. *Part-time fees:* $53 per credit; $267 per term. Part-time tuition and fees vary according to program. *Payment plans:* Installment, deferred payment.
FRESHMAN FINANCIAL AID (Fall 2005, est.) 3168 applied for aid; of those 79% were deemed to have need. 99% of freshmen with need received aid. *Average percent of need met:* 68% (excluding resources awarded to replace EFC). *Average financial aid package:* $20,047 (excluding resources awarded to replace EFC). 10% of all full-time freshmen had no need and received non-need-based gift aid.
UNDERGRADUATE FINANCIAL AID (Fall 2005, est.) 11,884 applied for aid; of those 85% were deemed to have need. 99% of undergraduates with need received aid. *Average percent of need met:* 64% (excluding resources awarded to replace EFC). *Average financial aid package:* $18,652 (excluding resources awarded to replace EFC). 10% of all full-time undergraduates had no need and received non-need-based gift aid.
GIFT AID (NEED-BASED) *Total amount:* $127,567,971 (12% federal, 9% state, 75% institutional, 4% external sources). *Receiving aid:* Freshmen: 52% (2,309); All full-time undergraduates: 51% (9,432). *Average award:* Freshmen: $13,275; Undergraduates: $12,592. *Scholarships, grants, and awards:* Federal Pell, FSEOG, state, private, college/university gift aid from institutional funds.
GIFT AID (NON-NEED-BASED) *Total amount:* $16,887,498 (87% institutional, 13% external sources). *Average Award:* Freshmen: $7020; Undergraduates: $6925. *Scholarships, grants, and awards by category:* Academic Interests/Achievement: 1,842 awards ($13,051,532 total): general academic interests/achievements. *Tuition waivers:* Full or partial for employees or children of employees.
LOANS *Student loans:* $93,964,164 (88% need-based, 12% non-need-based). 61% of past graduating class borrowed through all loan programs. *Average indebtedness per student:* $29,480. *Average need-based loan:* Freshmen: $4377; Undergraduates: $5070. *Parent loans:* $95,135,107 (82% need-based, 18% non-need-based). *Programs:* FFEL (Subsidized and Unsubsidized Stafford, PLUS), Perkins, Federal Nursing.
WORK-STUDY *Federal work-study:* Total amount: $6,400,000; 3,075 jobs averaging $2070.
APPLYING FOR FINANCIAL AID *Required financial aid forms:* FAFSA, state aid form. *Financial aid deadline (priority):* 2/15. *Notification date:* 4/1. Students must reply by 5/1.
CONTACT Financial Aid Office, New York University, 25 West Fourth Street, New York, NY 10012-1199, 212-998-4444. *Fax:* 212-995-4661. *E-mail:* financial.aid@nyu.edu.

NIAGARA UNIVERSITY
Niagara Falls, NY

Tuition & fees: $19,800 Average undergraduate aid package: $16,821

ABOUT THE INSTITUTION Independent religious, coed. Awards: associate, bachelor's, and master's degrees and post-master's certificates. 56 undergraduate majors. Total enrollment: 3,853. Undergraduates: 2,942. Freshmen: 735. Federal methodology is used as a basis for awarding need-based institutional aid.
UNDERGRADUATE EXPENSES for 2005–06 *Application fee:* $30. **Comprehensive fee:** $28,250 includes full-time tuition ($19,000), mandatory fees ($800), and room and board ($8450). *Part-time tuition:* $635 per credit hour. *Part-time fees:* $20 per term. *Payment plans:* Installment, deferred payment.
FRESHMAN FINANCIAL AID (Fall 2005, est.) 657 applied for aid; of those 81% were deemed to have need. 98% of freshmen with need received aid; of those 61% had need fully met. *Average percent of need met:* 86% (excluding resources awarded to replace EFC). *Average financial aid package:* $17,285 (excluding resources awarded to replace EFC). 20% of all full-time freshmen had no need and received non-need-based gift aid.
UNDERGRADUATE FINANCIAL AID (Fall 2005, est.) 2,417 applied for aid; of those 87% were deemed to have need. 100% of undergraduates with need received aid; of those 41% had need fully met. *Average percent of need met:* 83% (excluding resources awarded to replace EFC). *Average financial aid package:* $16,821 (excluding resources awarded to replace EFC). 19% of all full-time undergraduates had no need and received non-need-based gift aid.
GIFT AID (NEED-BASED) *Total amount:* $29,718,018 (10% federal, 13% state, 76% institutional, 1% external sources). *Receiving aid:* Freshmen: 71% (520); All full-time undergraduates: 72% (2,037). *Average award:* Freshmen: $10,446; Undergraduates: $9334. *Scholarships, grants, and awards:* Federal Pell, FSEOG, state, private, college/university gift aid from institutional funds.
GIFT AID (NON-NEED-BASED) *Total amount:* $4,622,415 (2% state, 97% institutional, 1% external sources). *Receiving aid:* Freshmen: 19% (136); Undergraduates: 19% (549). *Average Award:* Freshmen: $8600; Undergraduates: $8173. *Scholarships, grants, and awards by category:* Academic Interests/Achievement: 2,648 awards ($19,161,574 total): general academic interests/achievements. Creative Arts/Performance: 48 awards ($178,690 total): theater/drama. Special Achievements/Activities: 10 awards ($20,000 total): community service. Special Characteristics: 95 awards ($1,561,055 total): children of faculty/staff, relatives of clergy. *Tuition waivers:* Full or partial for employees or children of employees, senior citizens. *ROTC:* Army.
LOANS *Student loans:* $12,794,917 (89% need-based, 11% non-need-based). 80% of past graduating class borrowed through all loan programs. *Average indebtedness per student:* $17,163. *Average need-based loan:* Freshmen: $3660; Undergraduates: $4422. *Parent loans:* $3,939,809 (90% need-based, 10% non-need-based). *Programs:* FFEL (Subsidized and Unsubsidized Stafford, PLUS), Perkins, college/university.
WORK-STUDY *Federal work-study:* Total amount: $1,101,809; 444 jobs averaging $2386. *State or other work-study/employment:* Total amount: $147,987 (100% non-need-based). 34 part-time jobs averaging $3758.
ATHLETIC AWARDS *Total amount:* $3,407,018 (36% need-based, 64% non-need-based).
APPLYING FOR FINANCIAL AID *Required financial aid forms:* FAFSA, state aid form. *Financial aid deadline (priority):* 2/15. *Notification date:* Continuous beginning 3/15. Students must reply within 3 weeks of notification.
CONTACT Mrs. Maureen E. Salfi, Director of Financial Aid, Niagara University, Financial Aid Office, Niagara University, NY 14109, 716-286-8686 or toll-free 800-462-2111. *Fax:* 716-286-8678. *E-mail:* finaid@niagara.edu.

NICHOLLS STATE UNIVERSITY
Thibodaux, LA

Tuition & fees (LA res): $3389 Average undergraduate aid package: $5506

ABOUT THE INSTITUTION State-supported, coed. Awards: associate, bachelor's, and master's degrees and post-master's certificates. 52 undergraduate majors. Total enrollment: 7,525. Undergraduates: 6,886. Freshmen: 1,301. Federal methodology is used as a basis for awarding need-based institutional aid.
UNDERGRADUATE EXPENSES for 2005–06 *Application fee:* $20. *Tuition, state resident:* full-time $2230. *Tuition, nonresident:* full-time $7679. Part-time tuition

Nicholls State University

and fees vary according to course load. *College room and board:* $3720; *room only:* $1900. *Payment plans:* Installment, deferred payment.

FRESHMAN FINANCIAL AID (Fall 2004) 1442 applied for aid; of those 64% were deemed to have need. 99% of freshmen with need received aid; of those 65% had need fully met. *Average percent of need met:* 87% (excluding resources awarded to replace EFC). *Average financial aid package:* $5027 (excluding resources awarded to replace EFC). 4% of all full-time freshmen had no need and received non-need-based gift aid.

UNDERGRADUATE FINANCIAL AID (Fall 2004) 4,561 applied for aid; of those 66% were deemed to have need. 99% of undergraduates with need received aid; of those 64% had need fully met. *Average percent of need met:* 87% (excluding resources awarded to replace EFC). *Average financial aid package:* $5506 (excluding resources awarded to replace EFC). 2% of all full-time undergraduates had no need and received non-need-based gift aid.

GIFT AID (NEED-BASED) *Total amount:* $8,123,847 (82% federal, 14% state, 2% institutional, 2% external sources). *Receiving aid:* Freshmen: 51% (810); All full-time undergraduates: 44% (2,466). *Average award:* Freshmen: $3094; Undergraduates: $3107. *Scholarships, grants, and awards:* Federal Pell, FSEOG, state, private, college/university gift aid from institutional funds.

GIFT AID (NON-NEED-BASED) *Total amount:* $4,114,803 (81% state, 10% institutional, 9% external sources). *Receiving aid:* Freshmen: 16% (257); Undergraduates: 10% (544). *Average Award:* Freshmen: $2730; Undergraduates: $2811. *Scholarships, grants, and awards by category: Academic Interests/Achievement:* 183 awards ($434,404 total): general academic interests/achievements. *Creative Arts/Performance:* music. *Special Characteristics:* 384 awards ($508,201 total): children of faculty/staff, public servants. *Tuition waivers:* Full or partial for employees or children of employees.

LOANS *Student loans:* $12,537,177 (41% need-based, 59% non-need-based). 48% of past graduating class borrowed through all loan programs. *Average indebtedness per student:* $12,738. *Average need-based loan:* Freshmen: $2263; Undergraduates: $2973. *Parent loans:* $565,943 (6% need-based, 94% non-need-based). *Programs:* FFEL (Subsidized and Unsubsidized Stafford, PLUS), Perkins.

WORK-STUDY *Federal work-study:* Total amount: $270,847; 240 jobs averaging $989. *State or other work-study/employment:* Total amount: $1,064,910 (4% need-based, 96% non-need-based). 627 part-time jobs averaging $1727.

ATHLETIC AWARDS Total amount: $842,230 (27% need-based, 73% non-need-based).

APPLYING FOR FINANCIAL AID *Required financial aid forms:* FAFSA, institution's own form, state aid form, noncustodial (divorced/separated) parent's statement. *Financial aid deadline:* 4/19 (priority: 4/8). *Notification date:* Continuous. Students must reply within 2 weeks of notification.

CONTACT Colette Lagarde, Office of Financial Aid, Nicholls State University, East Elkins Hall, PO Box 2005, Thibodaux, LA 70310, 985-448-4048 or toll-free 877-NICHOLLS. *Fax:* 985-448-4124. *E-mail:* colette.lagarde@nicholls.edu.

NICHOLS COLLEGE
Dudley, MA

Tuition & fees: N/R	Average undergraduate aid package: $16,326

ABOUT THE INSTITUTION Independent, coed. Awards: associate, bachelor's, and master's degrees. 14 undergraduate majors. Total enrollment: 1,792. Undergraduates: 1,432. Freshmen: 313. Federal methodology is used as a basis for awarding need-based institutional aid.

FRESHMAN FINANCIAL AID (Fall 2005, est.) 266 applied for aid; of those 77% were deemed to have need. 99% of freshmen with need received aid; of those 27% had need fully met. *Average percent of need met:* 72% (excluding resources awarded to replace EFC). *Average financial aid package:* $16,669 (excluding resources awarded to replace EFC). 14% of all full-time freshmen had no need and received non-need-based gift aid.

UNDERGRADUATE FINANCIAL AID (Fall 2005, est.) 978 applied for aid; of those 67% were deemed to have need. 98% of undergraduates with need received aid; of those 32% had need fully met. *Average percent of need met:* 74% (excluding resources awarded to replace EFC). *Average financial aid package:* $16,326 (excluding resources awarded to replace EFC). 19% of all full-time undergraduates had no need and received non-need-based gift aid.

GIFT AID (NEED-BASED) *Total amount:* $6,362,964 (9% federal, 6% state, 79% institutional, 6% external sources). *Receiving aid:* Freshmen: 67% (200); All full-time undergraduates: 63% (627). *Average award:* Freshmen: $11,524; Undergraduates: $9989. *Scholarships, grants, and awards:* Federal Pell, FSEOG, state, private, college/university gift aid from institutional funds.

GIFT AID (NON-NEED-BASED) *Total amount:* $1,302,784 (83% institutional, 17% external sources). *Receiving aid:* Freshmen: 3% (8); Undergraduates: 3% (29). *Average Award:* Freshmen: $11,517; Undergraduates: $11,711. *Scholarships, grants, and awards by category: Academic Interests/Achievement:* 564 awards ($3,534,595 total): general academic interests/achievements. *Special Characteristics:* 46 awards ($262,529 total): children and siblings of alumni, children of faculty/staff, siblings of current students. *Tuition waivers:* Full or partial for employees or children of employees. *ROTC:* Army cooperative.

LOANS *Student loans:* $6,129,940 (68% need-based, 32% non-need-based). 86% of past graduating class borrowed through all loan programs. *Average indebtedness per student:* $26,626. *Average need-based loan:* Freshmen: $5287; Undergraduates: $6610. *Parent loans:* $2,760,091 (39% need-based, 61% non-need-based). *Programs:* FFEL (Subsidized and Unsubsidized Stafford, PLUS), state.

WORK-STUDY *Federal work-study:* Total amount: $424,964; 240 jobs averaging $1771.

APPLYING FOR FINANCIAL AID *Required financial aid form:* FAFSA. *Financial aid deadline (priority):* 3/1. *Notification date:* Continuous beginning 2/25. Students must reply within 2 weeks of notification.

CONTACT Ms. Kathleen A. Goozey, Associate Director of Financial Aid, Nichols College, PO Box 5000, Dudley, MA 01571, 508-213-2276 or toll-free 800-470-3379. *Fax:* 508-943-9885. *E-mail:* kathleen.goozey@nichols.edu.

NORFOLK STATE UNIVERSITY
Norfolk, VA

ABOUT THE INSTITUTION State-supported, coed. Awards: associate, bachelor's, master's, and doctoral degrees. 34 undergraduate majors. Total enrollment: 6,096. Undergraduates: 5,337. Freshmen: 1,001.

GIFT AID (NEED-BASED) *Scholarships, grants, and awards:* Federal Pell, FSEOG, state, private, college/university gift aid from institutional funds.

GIFT AID (NON-NEED-BASED) *Scholarships, grants, and awards by category: Creative Arts/Performance:* music, performing arts. *Special Achievements/Activities:* general special achievements/activities.

LOANS *Programs:* Federal Direct (Subsidized and Unsubsidized Stafford), FFEL (PLUS), Perkins, state, alternative loans.

APPLYING FOR FINANCIAL AID *Required financial aid form:* FAFSA.

CONTACT Mrs. Estherine Harding, Director of Financial Aid, Norfolk State University, 700 Park Avenue, Norfolk, VA 23504-3907, 757-823-8381. *Fax:* 757-823-9059. *E-mail:* ejharding@nsu.edu.

NORTH CAROLINA AGRICULTURAL AND TECHNICAL STATE UNIVERSITY
Greensboro, NC

Tuition & fees (NC res): $3124	Average undergraduate aid package: $5898

ABOUT THE INSTITUTION State-supported, coed. Awards: bachelor's, master's, and doctoral degrees. 59 undergraduate majors. Total enrollment: 11,103. Undergraduates: 9,735. Freshmen: 2,251. Federal methodology is used as a basis for awarding need-based institutional aid.

UNDERGRADUATE EXPENSES for 2006–07 *Application fee:* $45. *Tuition, state resident:* full-time $1769. *Tuition, nonresident:* full-time $11,211. *College room and board:* $5254; *room only:* $2954.

FRESHMAN FINANCIAL AID (Fall 2005, est.) 2717 applied for aid; of those 86% were deemed to have need. 98% of freshmen with need received aid; of those 4% had need fully met. *Average percent of need met:* 50% (excluding resources awarded to replace EFC). *Average financial aid package:* $5720 (excluding resources awarded to replace EFC). 1% of all full-time freshmen had no need and received non-need-based gift aid.

UNDERGRADUATE FINANCIAL AID (Fall 2005, est.) 7,873 applied for aid; of those 87% were deemed to have need. 96% of undergraduates with need received aid; of those 7% had need fully met. *Average percent of need met:* 50% (excluding resources awarded to replace EFC). *Average financial aid package:* $5898 (excluding resources awarded to replace EFC). 3% of all full-time undergraduates had no need and received non-need-based gift aid.

GIFT AID (NEED-BASED) *Total amount:* $23,885,165 (58% federal, 42% state). *Receiving aid:* Freshmen: 61% (1,777); All full-time undergraduates: 54% (4,886). *Average award:* Freshmen: $4181; Undergraduates: $4028. *Scholarships, grants, and awards:* Federal Pell, FSEOG, state, private, college/university gift aid from institutional funds, United Negro College Fund.
GIFT AID (NON-NEED-BASED) *Total amount:* $23,412,049 (1% federal, 14% state, 16% institutional, 69% external sources). *Receiving aid:* Freshmen: 37% (1,065); Undergraduates: 28% (2,588). *Average Award:* Freshmen: $3998; Undergraduates: $4486. *Scholarships, grants, and awards by category: Academic Interests/Achievement:* military science. *Creative Arts/Performance:* music, theater/drama. *Special Characteristics:* ethnic background, handicapped students, members of minority groups. *ROTC:* Army, Air Force.
LOANS *Student loans:* $30,776,581 (100% need-based). 75% of past graduating class borrowed through all loan programs. *Average indebtedness per student:* $20,052. *Average need-based loan:* Freshmen: $4457; Undergraduates: $7202. *Parent loans:* $8,834,537 (100% non-need-based). *Programs:* Federal Direct (Subsidized and Unsubsidized Stafford, PLUS), Perkins, state, Alternative Loans.
WORK-STUDY *Federal work-study:* Total amount: $383,037; jobs available. *State or other work-study/employment:* Part-time jobs available.
ATHLETIC AWARDS *Total amount:* $1,764,816 (100% non-need-based).
APPLYING FOR FINANCIAL AID *Required financial aid form:* FAFSA. *Financial aid deadline (priority):* 3/15. *Notification date:* Continuous beginning 4/1.
CONTACT Mrs. Sherri Avent, Director of Student Financial Aid, North Carolina Agricultural and Technical State University, 1601 East Market Street, Dowdy Administration Building, Greensboro, NC 27411, 336-334-7973 or toll-free 800-443-8964 (in-state). *Fax:* 336-334-7954.

NORTH CAROLINA CENTRAL UNIVERSITY
Durham, NC

CONTACT Sharon J. Oliver, Director of Scholarships and Student Aid, North Carolina Central University, 106 Student Services Building, Durham, NC 27707-3129, 919-530-7412 or toll-free 877-667-7533.

NORTH CAROLINA SCHOOL OF THE ARTS
Winston-Salem, NC

ABOUT THE INSTITUTION State-supported, coed. Awards: bachelor's and master's degrees and post-master's certificates. 9 undergraduate majors. Total enrollment: 827. Undergraduates: 726. Freshmen: 179.
GIFT AID (NEED-BASED) *Scholarships, grants, and awards:* Federal Pell, FSEOG, state, private, college/university gift aid from institutional funds.
GIFT AID (NON-NEED-BASED) *Scholarships, grants, and awards by category: Creative Arts/Performance:* applied art and design, cinema/film/broadcasting, dance, music, performing arts, theater/drama.
LOANS *Programs:* Federal Direct (Subsidized and Unsubsidized Stafford, PLUS), Perkins.
APPLYING FOR FINANCIAL AID *Required financial aid form:* FAFSA.
CONTACT Jane C. Kamiab, Director of Financial Aid, North Carolina School of the Arts, 1533 South Main Street, Winston-Salem, NC 27127, 336-770-3297. *Fax:* 336-770-1489.

NORTH CAROLINA STATE UNIVERSITY
Raleigh, NC

Tuition & fees (NC res): $4784   **Average undergraduate aid package:** $8403

ABOUT THE INSTITUTION State-supported, coed. Awards: associate, bachelor's, master's, doctoral, and first professional degrees and first professional certificates. 121 undergraduate majors. Total enrollment: 30,149. Undergraduates: 22,767. Freshmen: 4,375. Federal methodology is used as a basis for awarding need-based institutional aid.
UNDERGRADUATE EXPENSES for 2006–07 *Application fee:* $60. *Tuition, state resident:* full-time $3530. *Tuition, nonresident:* full-time $15,728. *College room and board:* $7040; *room only:* $4288.
FRESHMAN FINANCIAL AID (Fall 2005, est.) 2911 applied for aid; of those 60% were deemed to have need. 98% of freshmen with need received aid; of those 37% had need fully met. *Average percent of need met:* 83% (excluding resources awarded to replace EFC). *Average financial aid package:* $8162 (excluding resources awarded to replace EFC). 28% of all full-time freshmen had no need and received non-need-based gift aid.
UNDERGRADUATE FINANCIAL AID (Fall 2005, est.) 10,434 applied for aid; of those 71% were deemed to have need. 97% of undergraduates with need received aid; of those 45% had need fully met. *Average percent of need met:* 81% (excluding resources awarded to replace EFC). *Average financial aid package:* $8403 (excluding resources awarded to replace EFC). 23% of all full-time undergraduates had no need and received non-need-based gift aid.
GIFT AID (NEED-BASED) *Total amount:* $41,949,063 (25% federal, 20% state, 47% institutional, 8% external sources). *Receiving aid:* Freshmen: 38% (1,673); All full-time undergraduates: 37% (6,966). *Average award:* Freshmen: $6216; Undergraduates: $5917. *Scholarships, grants, and awards:* Federal Pell, FSEOG, state, private, college/university gift aid from institutional funds.
GIFT AID (NON-NEED-BASED) *Total amount:* $15,841,285 (6% state, 61% institutional, 33% external sources). *Receiving aid:* Freshmen: 4% (178); Undergraduates: 3% (550). *Average Award:* Freshmen: $6597; Undergraduates: $7344. *Scholarships, grants, and awards by category: Academic Interests/Achievement:* agriculture, biological sciences, business, education, engineering/technologies, general academic interests/achievements, humanities, mathematics, physical sciences, social sciences. *ROTC:* Army, Naval, Air Force.
LOANS *Student loans:* $40,351,823 (52% need-based, 48% non-need-based). 52% of past graduating class borrowed through all loan programs. *Average indebtedness per student:* $14,505. *Average need-based loan:* Freshmen: $2208; Undergraduates: $3066. *Parent loans:* $13,407,663 (10% need-based, 90% non-need-based). *Programs:* FFEL (Subsidized and Unsubsidized Stafford, PLUS), Perkins, state, college/university.
WORK-STUDY *Federal work-study:* Total amount: $731,193; 623 jobs averaging $1174. *State or other work-study/employment:* Total amount: $1,357,524 (39% need-based, 61% non-need-based). 224 part-time jobs averaging $6060.
ATHLETIC AWARDS *Total amount:* $5,755,170 (34% need-based, 66% non-need-based).
APPLYING FOR FINANCIAL AID *Required financial aid forms:* FAFSA, institution's own form. *Financial aid deadline (priority):* 3/1. *Notification date:* Continuous beginning 3/1.
CONTACT Ms. Julia Rice Mallette, Director of Scholarships and Financial Aid, North Carolina State University, 2016 Harris Hall, Box 7302, Raleigh, NC 27695-7302, 919-515-2334. *Fax:* 919-515-8422. *E-mail:* julie_mallette@ncsu.edu.

NORTH CAROLINA WESLEYAN COLLEGE
Rocky Mount, NC

CONTACT Director of Financial Aid, North Carolina Wesleyan College, 3400 North Wesleyan Boulevard, Rocky Mount, NC 27804, 252-985-5290 or toll-free 800-488-6292.

NORTH CENTRAL COLLEGE
Naperville, IL

ABOUT THE INSTITUTION Independent United Methodist, coed. Awards: bachelor's and master's degrees and post-bachelor's certificates. 63 undergraduate majors. Total enrollment: 2,472. Undergraduates: 2,133. Freshmen: 425.
GIFT AID (NEED-BASED) *Scholarships, grants, and awards:* Federal Pell, FSEOG, state, private, college/university gift aid from institutional funds.
GIFT AID (NON-NEED-BASED) *Scholarships, grants, and awards by category: Academic Interests/Achievement:* biological sciences, business, communication, computer science, education, English, foreign languages, general academic interests/achievements, humanities, international studies, mathematics, physical sciences, premedicine, religion/biblical studies, social sciences. *Creative Arts/Performance:* art/fine arts, cinema/film/broadcasting, debating, journalism/publications, music, theater/drama. *Special Achievements/Activities:* community service, religious involvement. *Special Characteristics:* adult students, children of faculty/staff, international students, relatives of clergy.
LOANS *Programs:* FFEL (Subsidized and Unsubsidized Stafford, PLUS), Perkins, state, college/university.
WORK-STUDY *Federal work-study:* Total amount: $151,620; 217 jobs averaging $698. *State or other work-study/employment:* Total amount: $184,917 (47% need-based, 53% non-need-based). Part-time jobs available.
APPLYING FOR FINANCIAL AID *Required financial aid forms:* FAFSA, institution's own form, federal income tax form(s).

North Central College

CONTACT Ms. Katherine A. Edmunds, Director of Financial Aid, North Central College, 30 North Brainard Street, PO Box 3065, Naperville, IL 60566-7065, 630-637-5600 or toll-free 800-411-1861. *Fax:* 630-637-5608. *E-mail:* kaedmunds@noctrl.edu.

NORTH CENTRAL UNIVERSITY
Minneapolis, MN

ABOUT THE INSTITUTION Independent religious, coed. Awards: associate and bachelor's degrees. 31 undergraduate majors. Total enrollment: 1,241. Undergraduates: 1,241. Freshmen: 250.
GIFT AID (NEED-BASED) *Scholarships, grants, and awards:* Federal Pell, FSEOG, state, private, college/university gift aid from institutional funds.
GIFT AID (NON-NEED-BASED) *Scholarships, grants, and awards by category: Academic Interests/Achievement:* general academic interests/achievements. *Creative Arts/Performance:* music. *Special Achievements/Activities:* community service, general special achievements/activities, leadership, memberships, religious involvement. *Special Characteristics:* children of faculty/staff, general special characteristics, international students, relatives of clergy, religious affiliation.
LOANS *Programs:* FFEL (Subsidized and Unsubsidized Stafford, PLUS), Perkins, state, alternative loans.
APPLYING FOR FINANCIAL AID *Required financial aid form:* FAFSA.
CONTACT Mrs. Donna Jager, Director of Financial Aid, North Central University, 910 Elliot Avenue, Minneapolis, MN 55404-1322, 612-343-4485 or toll-free 800-289-6222. *Fax:* 612-343-8067. *E-mail:* finaid@northcentral.edu.

NORTH DAKOTA STATE UNIVERSITY
Fargo, ND

ABOUT THE INSTITUTION State-supported, coed. Awards: bachelor's, master's, doctoral, and first professional degrees and post-master's certificates. 95 undergraduate majors. Total enrollment: 12,099. Undergraduates: 10,496.
GIFT AID (NEED-BASED) *Scholarships, grants, and awards:* Federal Pell, FSEOG, state, private, college/university gift aid from institutional funds, diversity waivers.
GIFT AID (NON-NEED-BASED) *Scholarships, grants, and awards by category: Academic Interests/Achievement:* agriculture, architecture, biological sciences, business, communication, computer science, education, engineering/technologies, English, general academic interests/achievements, health fields, home economics, humanities, mathematics, military science, physical sciences, premedicine, social sciences. *Creative Arts/Performance:* art/fine arts, debating, journalism/publications, music, theater/drama. *Special Achievements/Activities:* memberships, religious involvement. *Special Characteristics:* children of faculty/staff, ethnic background.
LOANS *Programs:* FFEL (Subsidized and Unsubsidized Stafford, PLUS), Perkins, Federal Nursing, alternative loans.
WORK-STUDY *Federal work-study:* Total amount: $1,706,669; 853 jobs averaging $1774.
APPLYING FOR FINANCIAL AID *Required financial aid form:* FAFSA.
CONTACT James Kennedy, Director of Financial Aid, North Dakota State University, PO Box 5315, Fargo, ND 58105, 701-231-7536 or toll-free 800-488-NDSU. *Fax:* 701-231-6126. *E-mail:* james.kennedy@ndsu.nodak.edu.

NORTHEASTERN ILLINOIS UNIVERSITY
Chicago, IL

Tuition & fees (IL res): $5646   **Average undergraduate aid package:** $6870

ABOUT THE INSTITUTION State-supported, coed. Awards: bachelor's and master's degrees. 42 undergraduate majors. Total enrollment: 12,227. Undergraduates: 9,418. Freshmen: 1,058. Federal methodology is used as a basis for awarding need-based institutional aid.
UNDERGRADUATE EXPENSES for 2005–06 *Application fee:* $25. *Tuition, state resident:* full-time $4800; part-time $160 per credit hour. *Tuition, nonresident:* full-time $9600; part-time $320 per credit hour. Full-time tuition and fees vary according to student level.
FRESHMAN FINANCIAL AID (Fall 2005, est.) 704 applied for aid; of those 70% were deemed to have need. 99% of freshmen with need received aid; of those 6% had need fully met. *Average percent of need met:* 62% (excluding resources awarded to replace EFC). *Average financial aid package:* $6141 (excluding resources awarded to replace EFC). 2% of all full-time freshmen had no need and received non-need-based gift aid.
UNDERGRADUATE FINANCIAL AID (Fall 2005, est.) 3,249 applied for aid; of those 80% were deemed to have need. 98% of undergraduates with need received aid; of those 14% had need fully met. *Average percent of need met:* 64% (excluding resources awarded to replace EFC). *Average financial aid package:* $6870 (excluding resources awarded to replace EFC). 3% of all full-time undergraduates had no need and received non-need-based gift aid.
GIFT AID (NEED-BASED) *Total amount:* $13,513,266 (62% federal, 38% state). *Receiving aid:* Freshmen: 48% (457); All full-time undergraduates: 43% (2,231). *Average award:* Freshmen: $5674; Undergraduates: $5302. *Scholarships, grants, and awards:* Federal Pell, FSEOG, state, private, college/university gift aid from institutional funds.
GIFT AID (NON-NEED-BASED) *Total amount:* $1,079,997 (53% state, 21% institutional, 26% external sources). *Receiving aid:* Freshmen: 4% (39); Undergraduates: 4% (204). *Average Award:* Freshmen: $1655; Undergraduates:* $1373. *Scholarships, grants, and awards by category: Academic Interests/Achievement:* 326 awards ($388,231 total): biological sciences, business, communication, computer science, education, English, foreign languages, general academic interests/achievements, mathematics, physical sciences, social sciences. *Creative Arts/Performance:* 99 awards ($150,299 total): art/fine arts, creative writing, dance, journalism/publications, music, performing arts, theater/drama. *Special Achievements/Activities:* 4 awards ($9660 total): general special achievements/activities, leadership. *Special Characteristics:* 102 awards ($101,893 total): adult students, children of faculty/staff, general special characteristics.
ROTC: Army cooperative, Air Force cooperative.
LOANS *Student loans:* $8,519,244 (61% need-based, 39% non-need-based). 34% of past graduating class borrowed through all loan programs. *Average indebtedness per student:* $12,284. *Average need-based loan:* Freshmen: $2447; Undergraduates: $3849. *Parent loans:* $90,458 (100% non-need-based). *Programs:* FFEL (Subsidized and Unsubsidized Stafford, PLUS), Perkins.
WORK-STUDY *Federal work-study:* Total amount: $470,530; 250 jobs averaging $1928. *State or other work-study/employment:* Total amount: $994,965 (100% non-need-based). 448 part-time jobs averaging $1863.
APPLYING FOR FINANCIAL AID *Required financial aid forms:* FAFSA, institution's own form. *Financial aid deadline (priority):* 3/1. *Notification date:* Continuous beginning 4/15. Students must reply within 3 weeks of notification.
CONTACT Financial Aid Office, Northeastern Illinois University, 5500 North St. Louis Avenue, Chicago, IL 60625, 773-442-5000. *Fax:* 773-442-5040. *E-mail:* financialaid@neiu.edu.

NORTHEASTERN STATE UNIVERSITY
Tahlequah, OK

ABOUT THE INSTITUTION State-supported, coed. Awards: bachelor's, master's, and first professional degrees. 65 undergraduate majors. Total enrollment: 9,562. Undergraduates: 8,543. Freshmen: 1,302.
GIFT AID (NEED-BASED) *Scholarships, grants, and awards:* Federal Pell, FSEOG, state, private, college/university gift aid from institutional funds.
GIFT AID (NON-NEED-BASED) *Scholarships, grants, and awards by category: Academic Interests/Achievement:* biological sciences, business, communication, computer science, education, English, foreign languages, general academic interests/achievements, health fields, home economics, humanities, library science, mathematics, physical sciences, premedicine, social sciences. *Creative Arts/Performance:* applied art and design, art/fine arts, dance, debating, journalism/publications, music, performing arts, theater/drama. *Special Achievements/Activities:* cheerleading/drum major, community service, junior miss, leadership. *Special Characteristics:* children and siblings of alumni, children of faculty/staff, children with a deceased or disabled parent, spouses of deceased or disabled public servants.
LOANS *Programs:* FFEL (Subsidized and Unsubsidized Stafford, PLUS), Perkins, college/university.
APPLYING FOR FINANCIAL AID *Required financial aid forms:* FAFSA, institution's own form.
CONTACT Teri Cochran, Director of Student Financial Services, Northeastern State University, 715 North Grand Avenue, Tahlequah, OK 74464-2399, 918-456-5511 Ext. 3410 or toll-free 800-722-9614 (in-state). *Fax:* 918-458-2510. *E-mail:* kindlet@nsuok.edu.

NORTHEASTERN UNIVERSITY
Boston, MA

Tuition & fees: $28,792   **Average undergraduate aid package:** $16,085

ABOUT THE INSTITUTION Independent, coed. Awards: bachelor's, master's, doctoral, and first professional degrees and post-master's certificates. 83 undergraduate majors. Total enrollment: 19,541. Undergraduates: 14,730. Freshmen: 2,831. Both federal and institutional methodology are used as a basis for awarding need-based institutional aid.

UNDERGRADUATE EXPENSES for 2005–06 *Application fee:* $75. *Comprehensive fee:* $39,342 includes full-time tuition ($28,400), mandatory fees ($392), and room and board ($10,550). *College room only:* $5620. Room and board charges vary according to board plan and housing facility. *Payment plans:* Installment, deferred payment.

FRESHMAN FINANCIAL AID (Fall 2005, est.) 2244 applied for aid; of those 79% were deemed to have need. 100% of freshmen with need received aid; of those 17% had need fully met. *Average percent of need met:* 64% (excluding resources awarded to replace EFC). *Average financial aid package:* $16,939 (excluding resources awarded to replace EFC). 28% of all full-time freshmen had no need and received non-need-based gift aid.

UNDERGRADUATE FINANCIAL AID (Fall 2005, est.) 10,568 applied for aid; of those 85% were deemed to have need. 99% of undergraduates with need received aid; of those 16% had need fully met. *Average percent of need met:* 61% (excluding resources awarded to replace EFC). *Average financial aid package:* $16,085 (excluding resources awarded to replace EFC). 20% of all full-time undergraduates had no need and received non-need-based gift aid.

GIFT AID (NEED-BASED) *Total amount:* $95,817,679 (8% federal, 2% state, 86% institutional, 4% external sources). *Receiving aid:* Freshmen: 61% (1,716); All full-time undergraduates: 57% (8,440). *Average award:* Freshmen: $13,524; Undergraduates: $11,629. *Scholarships, grants, and awards:* Federal Pell, FSEOG, state, private, college/university gift aid from institutional funds, Federal Nursing.

GIFT AID (NON-NEED-BASED) *Total amount:* $27,350,772 (89% institutional, 11% external sources). *Receiving aid:* Freshmen: 8% (226); Undergraduates: 6% (892). *Average Award:* Freshmen: $13,352; Undergraduates: $13,717. *Scholarships, grants, and awards by category:* Academic Interests/Achievement: 5,093 awards ($42,647,920 total): engineering/technologies, general academic interests/achievements. *Creative Arts/Performance:* 18 awards ($183,337 total): music. *Special Characteristics:* 62 awards ($324,375 total): international students. *Tuition waivers:* Full or partial for employees or children of employees, senior citizens. *ROTC:* Army, Naval cooperative, Air Force cooperative.

LOANS *Student loans:* $104,865,620 (66% need-based, 34% non-need-based). *Average need-based loan:* Freshmen: $3460; Undergraduates: $4746. *Parent loans:* $25,124,063 (40% need-based, 60% non-need-based). *Programs:* FFEL (Subsidized and Unsubsidized Stafford, PLUS), Perkins, Federal Nursing, state, MEFA, TERI, Mass. No Interset Loan (NIL), CitiAssist.

WORK-STUDY *Federal work-study:* Total amount: $5,907,633; 3,479 jobs averaging $1448. *State or other work-study/employment:* Total amount: $1,590,739 (100% need-based).

ATHLETIC AWARDS *Total amount:* $8,640,516 (37% need-based, 63% non-need-based).

APPLYING FOR FINANCIAL AID *Required financial aid forms:* FAFSA, CSS Financial Aid PROFILE. *Financial aid deadline (priority):* 2/15. *Notification date:* Continuous beginning 2/15. Students must reply by 5/1.

CONTACT Mr. M. Seamus Harreys, Dean of Student Financial Services, Northeastern University, 360 Huntington Avenue, Boston, MA 02115, 617-373-3190. *Fax:* 617-373-8735. *E-mail:* sfs@neu.edu.

NORTHERN ARIZONA UNIVERSITY
Flagstaff, AZ

Tuition & fees (AZ res): $4393   **Average undergraduate aid package:** $7995

ABOUT THE INSTITUTION State-supported, coed. Awards: bachelor's, master's, doctoral, and first professional degrees and post-bachelor's and post-master's certificates. 105 undergraduate majors. Total enrollment: 18,779. Undergraduates: 13,252. Freshmen: 2,279. Federal methodology is used as a basis for awarding need-based institutional aid.

UNDERGRADUATE EXPENSES for 2005-06 *Application fee:* $25. *Tuition, state resident:* full-time $4223; part-time $221 per credit. *Tuition, nonresident:* full-time $12,853; part-time $536 per credit. *Required fees:* full-time $170; $85 per term part-time. Full-time tuition and fees vary according to program. Part-time tuition and fees vary according to program. *College room and board:* $5960; *room only:* $3256. Room and board charges vary according to board plan and housing facility. *Payment plan:* Installment.

FRESHMAN FINANCIAL AID (Fall 2004) 1720 applied for aid; of those 64% were deemed to have need. 98% of freshmen with need received aid; of those 19% had need fully met. *Average percent of need met:* 62% (excluding resources awarded to replace EFC). *Average financial aid package:* $6938 (excluding resources awarded to replace EFC). 25% of all full-time freshmen had no need and received non-need-based gift aid.

UNDERGRADUATE FINANCIAL AID (Fall 2004) 8,001 applied for aid; of those 77% were deemed to have need. 98% of undergraduates with need received aid; of those 17% had need fully met. *Average percent of need met:* 62% (excluding resources awarded to replace EFC). *Average financial aid package:* $7995 (excluding resources awarded to replace EFC). 15% of all full-time undergraduates had no need and received non-need-based gift aid.

GIFT AID (NEED-BASED) *Total amount:* $31,241,487 (45% federal, 1% state, 42% institutional, 12% external sources). *Receiving aid:* Freshmen: 28% (634); All full-time undergraduates: 36% (4,133). *Average award:* Freshmen: $4199; Undergraduates: $4386. *Scholarships, grants, and awards:* Federal Pell, FSEOG, state, private, college/university gift aid from institutional funds, Federal Nursing.

GIFT AID (NON-NEED-BASED) *Total amount:* $8,496,565 (4% federal, 79% institutional, 17% external sources). *Receiving aid:* Freshmen: 31% (717); Undergraduates: 24% (2,738). *Average Award:* Freshmen: $3124; Undergraduates:* $3415. *Scholarships, grants, and awards by category:* Academic Interests/Achievement: 655 awards ($795,426 total): biological sciences, business, communication, computer science, education, engineering/technologies, English, foreign languages, general academic interests/achievements, health fields, home economics, humanities, international studies, mathematics, military science, physical sciences, premedicine, religion/biblical studies, social sciences. *Creative Arts/Performance:* 306 awards ($913,495 total): art/fine arts, cinema/film/broadcasting, creative writing, debating, journalism/publications, music, performing arts, theater/drama. *Special Characteristics:* 1,713 awards ($1,559,708 total): children and siblings of alumni, children of educators, children of faculty/staff, children of public servants, first-generation college students, handicapped students, international students, local/state students, out-of-state students, spouses of deceased or disabled public servants. *Tuition waivers:* Full or partial for employees or children of employees. *ROTC:* Army, Air Force.

LOANS *Student loans:* $41,774,837 (85% need-based, 15% non-need-based). 60% of past graduating class borrowed through all loan programs. *Average indebtedness per student:* $16,473. *Average need-based loan:* Freshmen: $2465; Undergraduates: $3690. *Parent loans:* $10,504,471 (73% need-based, 27% non-need-based). *Programs:* Federal Direct (Subsidized and Unsubsidized Stafford, PLUS), Perkins, Federal Nursing, college/university.

WORK-STUDY *Federal work-study:* Total amount: $717,652; 560 jobs averaging $1281. *State or other work-study/employment:* Total amount: $5,287,167 (74% need-based, 26% non-need-based). 3,084 part-time jobs averaging $1714.

ATHLETIC AWARDS *Total amount:* $1,812,350 (38% need-based, 62% non-need-based).

APPLYING FOR FINANCIAL AID *Required financial aid form:* FAFSA. *Financial aid deadline (priority):* 2/14. *Notification date:* Continuous beginning 3/15.

CONTACT Jack Edwards, Director, Financial Aid, Northern Arizona University, Box 4108, Flagstaff, AZ 86011-4108, 928-523-4108 or toll-free 888-MORE-NAU. *Fax:* 928-523-1551.

NORTHERN ILLINOIS UNIVERSITY
De Kalb, IL

Tuition & fees (IL res): $6439   **Average undergraduate aid package:** $9489

ABOUT THE INSTITUTION State-supported, coed. Awards: bachelor's, master's, doctoral, and first professional degrees. 61 undergraduate majors. Total enrollment: 25,208. Undergraduates: 18,467. Freshmen: 3,179. Federal methodology is used as a basis for awarding need-based institutional aid.

UNDERGRADUATE EXPENSES for 2005–06 *Tuition, state resident:* full-time $5061; part-time $169 per credit hour. *Tuition, nonresident:* full-time $10,123; part-time $338 per credit hour. *Required fees:* full-time $1378; $58 per credit hour. Full-time tuition and fees vary according to course load. Part-time tuition

Northern Illinois University

and fees vary according to course load. *College room and board:* $5950. Room and board charges vary according to board plan and housing facility. *Payment plan:* Installment.

FRESHMAN FINANCIAL AID (Fall 2005, est.) 2677 applied for aid; of those 71% were deemed to have need. 96% of freshmen with need received aid; of those 22% had need fully met. *Average percent of need met:* 68% (excluding resources awarded to replace EFC). *Average financial aid package:* $8880 (excluding resources awarded to replace EFC). 2% of all full-time freshmen had no need and received non-need-based gift aid.

UNDERGRADUATE FINANCIAL AID (Fall 2005, est.) 12,574 applied for aid; of those 72% were deemed to have need. 96% of undergraduates with need received aid; of those 19% had need fully met. *Average percent of need met:* 70% (excluding resources awarded to replace EFC). *Average financial aid package:* $9489 (excluding resources awarded to replace EFC). 2% of all full-time undergraduates had no need and received non-need-based gift aid.

GIFT AID (NEED-BASED) *Total amount:* $34,854,943 (41% federal, 59% state). *Receiving aid:* Freshmen: 34% (1,083); All full-time undergraduates: 33% (5,459). *Average award:* Freshmen: $6342; Undergraduates: $5859. *Scholarships, grants, and awards:* Federal Pell, FSEOG, state, private, college/university gift aid from institutional funds, United Negro College Fund, Federal Nursing.

GIFT AID (NON-NEED-BASED) *Total amount:* $7,478,412 (10% federal, 51% state, 19% institutional, 20% external sources). *Receiving aid:* Freshmen: 18% (569); Undergraduates: 15% (2,493). *Average Award:* Freshmen: $982; Undergraduates: $1230. *Scholarships, grants, and awards by category:* Academic Interests/Achievement: biological sciences, business, communication, computer science, education, engineering/technologies, English, foreign languages, general academic interests/achievements, health fields, humanities, international studies, mathematics, physical sciences, social sciences. *Creative Arts/Performance:* applied art and design, art/fine arts, creative writing, dance, debating, journalism/publications, music, performing arts, theater/drama. *Special Achievements/Activities:* leadership. *Special Characteristics:* adult students, children of faculty/staff, ethnic background, international students, members of minority groups, veterans. *Tuition waivers:* Full or partial for minority students, employees or children of employees. *ROTC:* Army, Air Force cooperative.

LOANS *Student loans:* $64,856,543 (51% need-based, 49% non-need-based). 60% of past graduating class borrowed through all loan programs. *Average indebtedness per student:* $17,773. *Average need-based loan:* Freshmen: $2410; Undergraduates: $3968. *Parent loans:* $14,235,329 (100% non-need-based). *Programs:* FFEL (Subsidized and Unsubsidized Stafford, PLUS), Perkins.

WORK-STUDY *Federal work-study:* Total amount: $729,696; 530 jobs averaging $1377. *State or other work-study/employment:* Part-time jobs available.

ATHLETIC AWARDS *Total amount:* $3,945,364 (100% non-need-based).

APPLYING FOR FINANCIAL AID *Required financial aid forms:* FAFSA, institution's own form. *Financial aid deadline (priority):* 3/1. *Notification date:* Continuous beginning 3/9. Students must reply within 2 weeks of notification.

CONTACT Ms. Kathleen D. Brunson, Director of Student Financial Aid, Northern Illinois University, De Kalb, IL 60115-2854, 815-753-1395 or toll-free 800-892-3050 (in-state). *Fax:* 815-753-9475.

NORTHERN KENTUCKY UNIVERSITY
Highland Heights, KY

ABOUT THE INSTITUTION State-supported, coed. Awards: associate, bachelor's, master's, and first professional degrees. 74 undergraduate majors. Total enrollment: 13,908. Undergraduates: 12,057. Freshmen: 2,071.

GIFT AID (NEED-BASED) *Scholarships, grants, and awards:* Federal Pell, FSEOG, state, private.

GIFT AID (NON-NEED-BASED) *Scholarships, grants, and awards by category:* Academic Interests/Achievement: general academic interests/achievements. Creative Arts/Performance: art/fine arts. Special Characteristics: general special characteristics, members of minority groups, spouses of deceased or disabled public servants, veterans' children.

LOANS *Programs:* FFEL (Subsidized and Unsubsidized Stafford, PLUS), Perkins, alternative loans.

APPLYING FOR FINANCIAL AID *Required financial aid form:* FAFSA.

CONTACT Mr. Robert F. Sprague, Director of Student Financial Assistance, Northern Kentucky University, 416 Administrative Center, Nunn Drive, Highland Heights, KY 41099, 859-572-5143 or toll-free 800-637-9948. *Fax:* 859-572-6997. *E-mail:* ofa@nku.edu.

NORTHERN MICHIGAN UNIVERSITY
Marquette, MI

Tuition & fees (MI res): $5958   **Average undergraduate aid package:** $6935

ABOUT THE INSTITUTION State-supported, coed. Awards: associate, bachelor's, and master's degrees and post-bachelor's and post-master's certificates. 110 undergraduate majors. Total enrollment: 9,379. Undergraduates: 8,714. Freshmen: 1,406. Federal methodology is used as a basis for awarding need-based institutional aid.

UNDERGRADUATE EXPENSES for 2005–06 *Application fee:* $30. *One-time required fee:* $150. *Tuition, state resident:* full-time $5328; part-time $222 per credit hour. *Tuition, nonresident:* full-time $9072; part-time $378 per credit hour. *Required fees:* full-time $630; $30 per term part-time. Part-time tuition and fees vary according to location. *College room and board:* $6013. Room and board charges vary according to board plan and housing facility. *Payment plans:* Installment, deferred payment.

FRESHMAN FINANCIAL AID (Fall 2004) 1667 applied for aid; of those 68% were deemed to have need. 98% of freshmen with need received aid; of those 28% had need fully met. *Average percent of need met:* 70% (excluding resources awarded to replace EFC). *Average financial aid package:* $6480 (excluding resources awarded to replace EFC). 14% of all full-time freshmen had no need and received non-need-based gift aid.

UNDERGRADUATE FINANCIAL AID (Fall 2004) 6,695 applied for aid; of those 69% were deemed to have need. 98% of undergraduates with need received aid; of those 23% had need fully met. *Average percent of need met:* 71% (excluding resources awarded to replace EFC). *Average financial aid package:* $6935 (excluding resources awarded to replace EFC). 10% of all full-time undergraduates had no need and received non-need-based gift aid.

GIFT AID (NEED-BASED) *Total amount:* $11,592,490 (74% federal, 10% state, 15% institutional, 1% external sources). *Receiving aid:* Freshmen: 42% (739); All full-time undergraduates: 41% (3,062). *Average award:* Freshmen: $3162; Undergraduates: $3504. *Scholarships, grants, and awards:* Federal Pell, FSEOG, state, private, college/university gift aid from institutional funds, Federal Nursing.

GIFT AID (NON-NEED-BASED) *Total amount:* $10,251,042 (15% state, 50% institutional, 35% external sources). *Receiving aid:* Freshmen: 35% (620); Undergraduates: 22% (1,650). *Average Award:* Freshmen: $2958; Undergraduates: $2670. *Scholarships, grants, and awards by category:* Academic Interests/Achievement: 236 awards ($239,482 total): biological sciences, business, communication, computer science, education, engineering/technologies, English, foreign languages, general academic interests/achievements, health fields, international studies, mathematics, military science, physical sciences, premedicine, social sciences. *Creative Arts/Performance:* 70 awards ($34,290 total): applied art and design, music, theater/drama. *Special Achievements/Activities:* 103 awards ($48,215 total): leadership, memberships. *Special Characteristics:* 823 awards ($2,349,954 total): children of faculty/staff, children of union members/company employees, members of minority groups, out-of-state students. *Tuition waivers:* Full or partial for employees or children of employees, senior citizens. *ROTC:* Army.

LOANS *Student loans:* $30,089,641 (57% need-based, 43% non-need-based). 72% of past graduating class borrowed through all loan programs. *Average indebtedness per student:* $16,829. *Average need-based loan:* Freshmen: $2748; Undergraduates: $3602. *Parent loans:* $2,056,926 (100% non-need-based). *Programs:* Federal Direct (Subsidized and Unsubsidized Stafford, PLUS), Perkins, state, alternative loans.

WORK-STUDY *Federal work-study:* Total amount: $777,440; 756 jobs averaging $1028. *State or other work-study/employment:* Total amount: $276,192 (100% need-based). 123 part-time jobs averaging $2245.

ATHLETIC AWARDS *Total amount:* $1,522,078 (100% non-need-based).

APPLYING FOR FINANCIAL AID *Required financial aid form:* FAFSA. *Financial aid deadline (priority):* 3/1. *Notification date:* Continuous beginning 4/1. Students must reply within 2 weeks of notification.

CONTACT Michael Rotundo, Director of Financial Aid, Northern Michigan University, 1401 Presque Isle Avenue, Marquette, MI 49855, 906-227-1575 or toll-free 800-682-9797 Ext. 1 (in-state), 800-682-9797 (out-of-state). *Fax:* 906-227-2321. *E-mail:* mrotundo@nmu.edu.

NORTHERN STATE UNIVERSITY
Aberdeen, SD

Tuition & fees (SD res): $4699   **Average undergraduate aid package: $6076**

ABOUT THE INSTITUTION State-supported, coed. Awards: associate, bachelor's, and master's degrees and post-bachelor's certificates. 52 undergraduate majors. Total enrollment: 2,631. Undergraduates: 2,425. Freshmen: 381. Federal methodology is used as a basis for awarding need-based institutional aid.
UNDERGRADUATE EXPENSES for 2005–06 *Application fee:* $15. **Tuition, state resident:** full-time $2290; part-time $76.35 per credit hour. **Tuition, nonresident:** full-time $7278; part-time $242.60 per credit hour. **Required fees:** full-time $2409; $80.30 per credit hour. Full-time tuition and fees vary according to course level, course load, and reciprocity agreements. Part-time tuition and fees vary according to course level, course load, and reciprocity agreements. **College room and board:** $3980; **room only:** $2023. Room and board charges vary according to board plan. **Payment plan:** Installment.
FRESHMAN FINANCIAL AID (Fall 2004) 282 applied for aid; of those 78% were deemed to have need. 100% of freshmen with need received aid; of those 100% had need fully met. *Average financial aid package:* $5861 (excluding resources awarded to replace EFC). 10% of all full-time freshmen had no need and received non-need-based gift aid.
UNDERGRADUATE FINANCIAL AID (Fall 2004) 1,215 applied for aid; of those 78% were deemed to have need. 99% of undergraduates with need received aid; of those 100% had need fully met. *Average financial aid package:* $6076 (excluding resources awarded to replace EFC). 7% of all full-time undergraduates had no need and received non-need-based gift aid.
GIFT AID (NEED-BASED) *Total amount:* $2,311,426 (92% federal, 8% state). *Receiving aid:* Freshmen: 51% (185); All full-time undergraduates: 46% (736). *Average award:* Freshmen: $2376; Undergraduates: $2540. *Scholarships, grants, and awards:* Federal Pell, FSEOG, state, private.
GIFT AID (NON-NEED-BASED) *Total amount:* $963,099 (6% state, 61% institutional, 33% external sources). *Receiving aid:* Freshmen: 57% (208); Undergraduates: 54% (850). *Average Award:* Freshmen: $1729; Undergraduates: $1692. *Scholarships, grants, and awards by category: Academic Interests/Achievement:* 204 awards ($124,389 total): biological sciences, business, education, English, foreign languages, general academic interests/achievements, humanities, international studies, mathematics, physical sciences, social sciences. *Creative Arts/Performance:* 117 awards ($58,100 total): art/fine arts, music, theater/drama. *Special Achievements/Activities:* 40 awards ($13,650 total): leadership.
LOANS *Student loans:* $8,639,733 (53% need-based, 47% non-need-based). 80% of past graduating class borrowed through all loan programs. *Average indebtedness per student:* $19,864. *Average need-based loan:* Freshmen: $3140; Undergraduates: $3505. *Parent loans:* $324,022 (100% non-need-based). *Programs:* FFEL (Subsidized and Unsubsidized Stafford, PLUS), Perkins, college/university, SELF Loans, alternative loans.
WORK-STUDY *Federal work-study:* Total amount: $563,000; 352 jobs averaging $1748. *State or other work-study/employment:* Total amount: $467,740 (100% non-need-based). 383 part-time jobs averaging $1221.
ATHLETIC AWARDS *Total amount:* $447,127 (100% non-need-based).
APPLYING FOR FINANCIAL AID *Required financial aid form:* FAFSA. *Financial aid deadline (priority):* 3/1. *Notification date:* 4/15. Students must reply within 2 weeks of notification.
CONTACT Ms. Sharon Kienow, Director of Financial Aid, Northern State University, 1200 South Jay Street, Aberdeen, SD 57401-7198, 605-626-2640 or toll-free 800-678-5330. *Fax:* 605-626-2587. *E-mail:* kienows@northern.edu.

NORTH GEORGIA COLLEGE & STATE UNIVERSITY
Dahlonega, GA

Tuition & fees (GA res): $3068   **Average undergraduate aid package: $6865**

ABOUT THE INSTITUTION State-supported, coed. Awards: associate, bachelor's, and master's degrees and post-bachelor's and post-master's certificates. 48 undergraduate majors. Total enrollment: 4,765. Undergraduates: 4,190. Freshmen: 731. Federal methodology is used as a basis for awarding need-based institutional aid.
UNDERGRADUATE EXPENSES for 2005–06 *Application fee:* $25. **Tuition, state resident:** full-time $2438; part-time $102 per semester hour. **Tuition, nonresident:** full-time $9754; part-time $407 per semester hour. Part-time tuition and fees vary according to course load. **College room and board:** $4596; **room only:** $2292. Room and board charges vary according to board plan and housing facility.
FRESHMAN FINANCIAL AID (Fall 2004) 100% of freshmen with need received aid; of those 53% had need fully met. *Average percent of need met:* 35% (excluding resources awarded to replace EFC). *Average financial aid package:* $6122 (excluding resources awarded to replace EFC). 59% of all full-time freshmen had no need and received non-need-based gift aid.
UNDERGRADUATE FINANCIAL AID (Fall 2004) 100% of undergraduates with need received aid; of those 47% had need fully met. *Average percent of need met:* 47% (excluding resources awarded to replace EFC). *Average financial aid package:* $6865 (excluding resources awarded to replace EFC). 43% of all full-time undergraduates had no need and received non-need-based gift aid.
GIFT AID (NEED-BASED) *Total amount:* $1,716,395 (98% federal, 2% institutional). *Receiving aid:* Freshmen: 16% (112); All full-time undergraduates: 17% (530). *Average award:* Freshmen: $2562; Undergraduates: $2624. *Scholarships, grants, and awards:* Federal Pell, FSEOG, state, private, college/university gift aid from institutional funds.
GIFT AID (NON-NEED-BASED) *Total amount:* $6,842,460 (93% state, 3% institutional, 4% external sources). *Receiving aid:* Freshmen: 26% (188); Undergraduates: 20% (642). *Average Award:* Freshmen: $3482; Undergraduates: $3124. *Scholarships, grants, and awards by category: Academic Interests/Achievement:* biological sciences, business, education, English, general academic interests/achievements, health fields, humanities, mathematics, military science, physical sciences, premedicine. *Creative Arts/Performance:* applied art and design, general creative arts/performance, music. *Special Achievements/Activities:* cheerleading/drum major, community service, general special achievements/activities, leadership. *Special Characteristics:* general special characteristics. *Tuition waivers:* Full or partial for employees or children of employees, senior citizens. *ROTC:* Army.
LOANS *Student loans:* $6,040,499 (36% need-based, 64% non-need-based). *Average need-based loan:* Freshmen: $2009; Undergraduates: $3365. *Parent loans:* $307,384 (100% non-need-based). *Programs:* FFEL (Subsidized and Unsubsidized Stafford, PLUS), Perkins, state, college/university.
WORK-STUDY *Federal work-study:* Total amount: $132,103; jobs available.
ATHLETIC AWARDS *Total amount:* $351,572 (100% non-need-based).
APPLYING FOR FINANCIAL AID *Required financial aid forms:* FAFSA, institution's own form. *Financial aid deadline (priority):* 5/1. *Notification date:* Continuous beginning 5/15. Students must reply within 3 weeks of notification.
CONTACT Charles Hawkins, Director, Institutional Research and Planning, North Georgia College & State University, 110 Barnes Hall, Dahlonega, GA 30597-1001, 706-864-1840 or toll-free 800-498-9581. *Fax:* 706-864-1411. *E-mail:* chawkins@ngcsu.edu.

NORTH GREENVILLE COLLEGE
Tigerville, SC

Tuition & fees: $10,350   **Average undergraduate aid package: N/A**

ABOUT THE INSTITUTION Independent Southern Baptist, coed. Awards: associate and bachelor's degrees. 30 undergraduate majors. Total enrollment: 1,766. Undergraduates: 1,766. Freshmen: 474. Federal methodology is used as a basis for awarding need-based institutional aid.
UNDERGRADUATE EXPENSES for 2005–06 *Application fee:* $25. **Comprehensive fee:** $16,300 includes full-time tuition ($10,350) and room and board ($5950). **Part-time tuition:** $200 per hour. Part-time tuition and fees vary according to course load. **Payment plan:** Installment.
GIFT AID (NEED-BASED) *Total amount:* $10,611,407 (15% federal, 24% state, 57% institutional, 4% external sources). *Scholarships, grants, and awards:* Federal Pell, FSEOG, state, private, college/university gift aid from institutional funds.
GIFT AID (NON-NEED-BASED) *Total amount:* $2,957,375 (100% state). *Scholarships, grants, and awards by category: Academic Interests/Achievement:* communication, education, general academic interests/achievements, military science, religion/biblical studies. *Creative Arts/Performance:* art/fine arts, journalism/publications, music, theater/drama. *Special Achievements/Activities:* $4900 total: cheerleading/drum major, junior miss, religious involvement. *Special Characteristics:*

North Greenville College

$225,000 total: children of faculty/staff, relatives of clergy, siblings of current students. **Tuition waivers:** Full or partial for employees or children of employees. **ROTC:** Army cooperative.

LOANS Student loans: $5,075,143 (64% need-based, 36% non-need-based). 60% of past graduating class borrowed through all loan programs. *Average indebtedness per student:* $10,000. **Parent loans:** $1,227,385 (100% need-based). **Programs:** FFEL (Subsidized and Unsubsidized Stafford, PLUS), Perkins, state, college/university.

WORK-STUDY Federal work-study: Total amount: $150,000; 173 jobs averaging $1000. **State or other work-study/employment:** Total amount: $110,000 (100% need-based). 76 part-time jobs averaging $1000.

ATHLETIC AWARDS Total amount: $925,000 (100% need-based).

APPLYING FOR FINANCIAL AID *Required financial aid form:* FAFSA. *Financial aid deadline (priority):* 6/30. *Notification date:* Continuous.

CONTACT Ms. Shirley Eskew, Assistant Director of Financial Aid, North Greenville College, PO Box 1892, Tigerville, SC 29688-1892, 864-977-7057 or toll-free 800-468-6642 Ext. 7001. *Fax:* 864-977-7177.

NORTHLAND COLLEGE
Ashland, WI

Tuition & fees: $20,789   **Average undergraduate aid package:** $15,302

ABOUT THE INSTITUTION Independent religious, coed. Awards: bachelor's degrees. 54 undergraduate majors. Total enrollment: 739. Undergraduates: 739. Freshmen: 180. Federal methodology is used as a basis for awarding need-based institutional aid.

UNDERGRADUATE EXPENSES for 2006–07 *Comprehensive fee:* $26,680 includes full-time tuition ($20,188), mandatory fees ($601), and room and board ($5891). *College room only:* $2384. *Part-time tuition:* $390 per credit.

FRESHMAN FINANCIAL AID (Fall 2004) 170 applied for aid; of those 88% were deemed to have need. 100% of freshmen with need received aid; of those 17% had need fully met. *Average percent of need met:* 80% (excluding resources awarded to replace EFC). *Average financial aid package:* $15,600 (excluding resources awarded to replace EFC). 13% of all full-time freshmen had no need and received non-need-based gift aid.

UNDERGRADUATE FINANCIAL AID (Fall 2004) 630 applied for aid; of those 91% were deemed to have need. 100% of undergraduates with need received aid; of those 22% had need fully met. *Average percent of need met:* 80% (excluding resources awarded to replace EFC). *Average financial aid package:* $15,302 (excluding resources awarded to replace EFC). 14% of all full-time undergraduates had no need and received non-need-based gift aid.

GIFT AID (NEED-BASED) *Total amount:* $6,099,937 (13% federal, 7% state, 77% institutional, 3% external sources). *Receiving aid:* Freshmen: 79% (147); All full-time undergraduates: 85% (571). *Average award:* Freshmen: $12,851; Undergraduates: $10,783. *Scholarships, grants, and awards:* Federal Pell, FSEOG, state, private, college/university gift aid from institutional funds, Bureau of Indian Affairs Grants.

GIFT AID (NON-NEED-BASED) *Total amount:* $310,894 (94% institutional, 6% external sources). *Receiving aid:* Freshmen: 2% (3); Undergraduates: 1% (8). *Average Award:* Freshmen: $7266; Undergraduates: $10,137. *Scholarships, grants, and awards by category: Academic Interests/Achievement:* 423 awards ($2,273,026 total): general academic interests/achievements. *Creative Arts/Performance:* 41 awards ($12,038 total): music. *Special Achievements/Activities:* 75 awards ($132,800 total): leadership. *Special Characteristics:* 35 awards ($46,100 total): ethnic background.

LOANS Student loans: $3,736,374 (56% need-based, 44% non-need-based). 81% of past graduating class borrowed through all loan programs. *Average indebtedness per student:* $18,983. *Average need-based loan:* Freshmen: $2951; Undergraduates: $4397. **Parent loans:** $1,475,604 (88% need-based, 12% non-need-based). **Programs:** Federal Direct (Subsidized and Unsubsidized Stafford, PLUS), FFEL (Subsidized and Unsubsidized Stafford, PLUS), Perkins.

WORK-STUDY Federal work-study: Total amount: $485,679; 358 jobs averaging $1357. **State or other work-study/employment:** Total amount: $358,516 (82% need-based, 18% non-need-based). 280 part-time jobs averaging $1280.

APPLYING FOR FINANCIAL AID *Required financial aid form:* FAFSA. *Financial aid deadline (priority):* 4/15. *Notification date:* Continuous beginning 3/1. Students must reply by 5/1 or within 4 weeks of notification.

CONTACT Tracy K. Steine, Director of Financial Aid, Northland College, 1411 Ellis Avenue, Ashland, WI 54806, 715-682-1255 or toll-free 800-753-1840 (in-state), 800-753-1040 (out-of-state). *Fax:* 715-682-1308. *E-mail:* tsteine@northland.edu.

NORTH PARK UNIVERSITY
Chicago, IL

CONTACT Dr. Lucy Shaker, Director of Financial Aid, North Park University, 3225 West Foster Avenue, Chicago, IL 60625-4895, 773-244-5526 or toll-free 800-888-NPC8. *Fax:* 773-244-4953.

NORTHWEST CHRISTIAN COLLEGE
Eugene, OR

Tuition & fees: $19,890   **Average undergraduate aid package:** $16,195

ABOUT THE INSTITUTION Independent Christian, coed. Awards: associate, bachelor's, and master's degrees and post-bachelor's certificates. 14 undergraduate majors. Total enrollment: 491. Undergraduates: 402. Freshmen: 47. Federal methodology is used as a basis for awarding need-based institutional aid.

UNDERGRADUATE EXPENSES for 2006–07 *Comprehensive fee:* $26,314 includes full-time tuition ($19,890) and room and board ($6424). *College room only:* $2800. *Part-time tuition:* $663 per credit. *Part-time fees:* $663 per credit.

FRESHMAN FINANCIAL AID (Fall 2005, est.) 46 applied for aid; of those 91% were deemed to have need. 100% of freshmen with need received aid; of those 19% had need fully met. *Average percent of need met:* 74% (excluding resources awarded to replace EFC). *Average financial aid package:* $15,076 (excluding resources awarded to replace EFC). 13% of all full-time freshmen had no need and received non-need-based gift aid.

UNDERGRADUATE FINANCIAL AID (Fall 2005, est.) 253 applied for aid; of those 94% were deemed to have need. 100% of undergraduates with need received aid; of those 20% had need fully met. *Average percent of need met:* 76% (excluding resources awarded to replace EFC). *Average financial aid package:* $16,195 (excluding resources awarded to replace EFC). 8% of all full-time undergraduates had no need and received non-need-based gift aid.

GIFT AID (NEED-BASED) *Total amount:* $2,670,681 (20% federal, 5% state, 52% institutional, 23% external sources). *Receiving aid:* Freshmen: 89% (42); All full-time undergraduates: 90% (235). *Average award:* Freshmen: $11,997; Undergraduates: $11,315. *Scholarships, grants, and awards:* Federal Pell, FSEOG, state, private, college/university gift aid from institutional funds.

GIFT AID (NON-NEED-BASED) *Total amount:* $152,466 (52% institutional, 48% external sources). *Receiving aid:* Freshmen: 9% (4); Undergraduates: 6% (15). *Average Award:* Freshmen: $5892; Undergraduates: $6880. *Scholarships, grants, and awards by category: Academic Interests/Achievement:* general academic interests/achievements. *Creative Arts/Performance:* general creative arts/performance, music. *Special Achievements/Activities:* general special achievements/activities, leadership, religious involvement. *Special Characteristics:* children of faculty/staff, relatives of clergy, religious affiliation. **ROTC:** Army cooperative.

LOANS Student loans: $2,452,413 (79% need-based, 21% non-need-based). 75% of past graduating class borrowed through all loan programs. *Average indebtedness per student:* $17,585. *Average need-based loan:* Freshmen: $2019; Undergraduates: $4198. **Parent loans:** $260,559 (73% need-based, 27% non-need-based). **Programs:** FFEL (Subsidized and Unsubsidized Stafford, PLUS), Perkins.

WORK-STUDY Federal work-study: Total amount: $271,301; jobs available. **State or other work-study/employment:** Total amount: $38,300 (49% need-based, 51% non-need-based). Part-time jobs available.

ATHLETIC AWARDS Total amount: $88,400 (76% need-based, 24% non-need-based).

APPLYING FOR FINANCIAL AID *Required financial aid form:* FAFSA. *Financial aid deadline (priority):* 3/1. *Notification date:* Continuous beginning 4/1.

CONTACT Ms. Jocelyn Hubbs, Associate Director, Financial Aid, Northwest Christian College, 828 East 11th Avenue, Eugene, OR 97401-3727, 541-684-7218 or toll-free 877-463-6622. *Fax:* 541-684-7323. *E-mail:* jocelynh@nwcc.edu.

NORTHWEST COLLEGE OF ART
Poulsbo, WA

ABOUT THE INSTITUTION Proprietary, coed. Awards: bachelor's degrees. 2 undergraduate majors.

GIFT AID (NEED-BASED) *Scholarships, grants, and awards:* Federal Pell, state, private, college/university gift aid from institutional funds.

GIFT AID (NON-NEED-BASED) *Scholarships, grants, and awards by category: Creative Arts/Performance:* applied art and design, art/fine arts.

LOANS *Programs:* FFEL (Subsidized and Unsubsidized Stafford, PLUS), alternative loans.

APPLYING FOR FINANCIAL AID *Required financial aid form:* FAFSA.

CONTACT Ms. Kim Y. Perigard, Director of Financial Aid, Northwest College of Art, 16464 State Highway 305, Poulsbo, WA 98370, 360-779-9993 or toll-free 800-769-ARTS.

NORTHWESTERN COLLEGE
Orange City, IA

ABOUT THE INSTITUTION Independent religious, coed. Awards: bachelor's degrees. 38 undergraduate majors. Total enrollment: 1,273. Undergraduates: 1,273. Freshmen: 374.

GIFT AID (NEED-BASED) *Scholarships, grants, and awards:* Federal Pell, FSEOG, state, private, college/university gift aid from institutional funds.

GIFT AID (NON-NEED-BASED) *Scholarships, grants, and awards by category: Academic Interests/Achievement:* biological sciences, business, communication, computer science, education, engineering/technologies, English, foreign languages, general academic interests/achievements, health fields, humanities, mathematics, physical sciences, premedicine, religion/biblical studies, social sciences. *Creative Arts/Performance:* art/fine arts, journalism/publications, music, theater/drama. *Special Characteristics:* adult students, children and siblings of alumni, children of faculty/staff, ethnic background, first-generation college students, handicapped students, international students, religious affiliation, siblings of current students.

LOANS *Programs:* FFEL (Subsidized and Unsubsidized Stafford, PLUS), Perkins, college/university, alternative loans.

APPLYING FOR FINANCIAL AID *Required financial aid form:* FAFSA.

CONTACT Mr. Gerry Korver, Director of Financial Aid, Northwestern College, 101 Seventh Street, SW, Orange City, IA 51041-1996, 712-707-7131 or toll-free 800-747-4757. *Fax:* 712-707-7164.

NORTHWESTERN COLLEGE
St. Paul, MN

Tuition & fees: $19,100   **Average undergraduate aid package: $14,453**

ABOUT THE INSTITUTION Independent nondenominational, coed. Awards: associate, bachelor's, and master's degrees. 45 undergraduate majors. Total enrollment: 1,785. Undergraduates: 1,767. Freshmen: 468. Federal methodology is used as a basis for awarding need-based institutional aid.

UNDERGRADUATE EXPENSES for 2005–06 *Application fee:* $30. *Comprehensive fee:* $25,220 includes full-time tuition ($19,100) and room and board ($6120). *College room only:* $3400. Full-time tuition and fees vary according to course load. Room and board charges vary according to board plan. *Part-time tuition:* $810 per credit. Part-time tuition and fees vary according to course load. *Payment plan:* Installment.

FRESHMAN FINANCIAL AID (Fall 2005, est.) 459 applied for aid; of those 83% were deemed to have need. 100% of freshmen with need received aid; of those 9% had need fully met. *Average percent of need met:* 71% (excluding resources awarded to replace EFC). *Average financial aid package:* $14,091 (excluding resources awarded to replace EFC). 16% of all full-time freshmen had no need and received non-need-based gift aid.

UNDERGRADUATE FINANCIAL AID (Fall 2005, est.) 1,680 applied for aid; of those 84% were deemed to have need. 100% of undergraduates with need received aid; of those 11% had need fully met. *Average percent of need met:* 75% (excluding resources awarded to replace EFC). *Average financial aid package:* $14,453 (excluding resources awarded to replace EFC). 15% of all full-time undergraduates had no need and received non-need-based gift aid.

GIFT AID (NEED-BASED) *Total amount:* $8,839,028 (18% federal, 22% state, 60% institutional). *Receiving aid:* Freshmen: 82% (382); All full-time undergraduates: 82% (1,406). *Average award:* Freshmen: $11,069; Undergraduates: $10,316. *Scholarships, grants, and awards:* Federal Pell, FSEOG, state, private, college/university gift aid from institutional funds.

GIFT AID (NON-NEED-BASED) *Total amount:* $6,222,675 (93% institutional, 7% external sources). *Receiving aid:* Freshmen: 73% (339); Undergraduates: 69% (1,187). *Average Award:* Freshmen: $4627; Undergraduates: $5089. *Scholarships, grants, and awards by category: Academic Interests/Achievement:* 1,222 awards ($3,406,361 total): biological sciences, general academic interests/achievements. *Creative Arts/Performance:* 108 awards ($180,000 total): music, theater/drama. *Special Achievements/Activities:* 215 awards ($250,000 total): leadership. *Special Characteristics:* 584 awards ($2,463,592 total): children of faculty/staff, ethnic background, international students, relatives of clergy, siblings of current students. *Tuition waivers:* Full or partial for children of alumni, employees or children of employees, senior citizens. *ROTC:* Army cooperative, Air Force cooperative.

LOANS *Student loans:* $9,087,338 (55% need-based, 45% non-need-based). 62% of past graduating class borrowed through all loan programs. *Average indebtedness per student:* $21,778. *Average need-based loan:* Freshmen: $3467; Undergraduates: $4372. *Parent loans:* $3,842,257 (100% non-need-based). *Programs:* FFEL (Subsidized and Unsubsidized Stafford, PLUS), Perkins, state.

WORK-STUDY *Federal work-study:* Total amount: $418,680; 200 jobs averaging $1628. *State or other work-study/employment:* Total amount: $554,560 (100% need-based). 183 part-time jobs averaging $1748.

APPLYING FOR FINANCIAL AID *Required financial aid forms:* FAFSA, institution's own form. *Financial aid deadline:* 6/1 (priority: 3/1). *Notification date:* Continuous. Students must reply within 2 weeks of notification.

CONTACT Mr. Richard L. Blatchley, Director of Financial Aid, Northwestern College, 3003 Snelling Avenue North, St. Paul, MN 55113-1598, 651-631-5321 or toll-free 800-827-6827. *Fax:* 651-628-3332. *E-mail:* rlb@nwc.edu.

NORTHWESTERN OKLAHOMA STATE UNIVERSITY
Alva, OK

Tuition & fees (OK res): $3270   **Average undergraduate aid package: $5598**

ABOUT THE INSTITUTION State-supported, coed. Awards: bachelor's and master's degrees and post-bachelor's and post-master's certificates. 37 undergraduate majors. Total enrollment: 2,102. Undergraduates: 1,864. Freshmen: 283. Both federal and institutional methodology are used as a basis for awarding need-based institutional aid.

UNDERGRADUATE EXPENSES for 2005–06 *Application fee:* $15. *Tuition, state resident:* full-time $3270; part-time $109 per credit hour. *Tuition, nonresident:* full-time $8100; part-time $270 per credit hour. Full-time tuition and fees vary according to course load, degree level, and location. Part-time tuition and fees vary according to course load, degree level, and location. *College room and board:* $2980; *room only:* $1000. Room and board charges vary according to board plan. *Payment plan:* Installment.

FRESHMAN FINANCIAL AID (Fall 2005, est.) 194 applied for aid; of those 65% were deemed to have need. 100% of freshmen with need received aid; of those 43% had need fully met. *Average percent of need met:* 79% (excluding resources awarded to replace EFC). *Average financial aid package:* $5235 (excluding resources awarded to replace EFC). 34% of all full-time freshmen had no need and received non-need-based gift aid.

UNDERGRADUATE FINANCIAL AID (Fall 2005, est.) 1,179 applied for aid; of those 67% were deemed to have need. 100% of undergraduates with need received aid; of those 43% had need fully met. *Average percent of need met:* 75% (excluding resources awarded to replace EFC). *Average financial aid package:* $5598 (excluding resources awarded to replace EFC). 15% of all full-time undergraduates had no need and received non-need-based gift aid.

GIFT AID (NEED-BASED) *Total amount:* $3,062,327 (74% federal, 19% state, 7% institutional). *Receiving aid:* Freshmen: 44% (109); All full-time undergraduates: 48% (663). *Average award:* Freshmen: $4159; Undergraduates: $3531. *Scholarships, grants, and awards:* Federal Pell, FSEOG, state, college/university gift aid from institutional funds.

GIFT AID (NON-NEED-BASED) *Total amount:* $654,672 (21% state, 40% institutional, 39% external sources). *Receiving aid:* Freshmen: 22% (54); Undergraduates: 9% (130). *Average Award:* Freshmen: $1065; Undergradu-

Northwestern Oklahoma State University

ates: $1104. *Scholarships, grants, and awards by category: Academic Interests/ Achievement:* 332 awards ($413,384 total): agriculture, biological sciences, business, communication, computer science, education, English, foreign languages, general academic interests/achievements, health fields, humanities, international studies, library science, mathematics, physical sciences, premedicine, social sciences. *Creative Arts/Performance:* 75 awards ($49,936 total): art/fine arts, cinema/film/broadcasting, dance, debating, general creative arts/performance, journalism/publications, music, theater/drama. *Special Achievements/Activities:* 97 awards ($116,910 total): cheerleading/drum major, general special achievements/activities, leadership, memberships, rodeo. *Special Characteristics:* 50 awards ($53,584 total): children and siblings of alumni, children of faculty/staff. *Tuition waivers:* Full or partial for employees or children of employees, senior citizens.
LOANS *Student loans:* $3,456,435 (61% need-based, 39% non-need-based). 47% of past graduating class borrowed through all loan programs. *Average indebtedness per student:* $9476. *Average need-based loan:* Freshmen: $1925; Undergraduates: $3053. *Parent loans:* $102,830 (100% non-need-based). *Programs:* FFEL (Subsidized and Unsubsidized Stafford, PLUS), Perkins.
WORK-STUDY *Federal work-study:* Total amount: $143,916; 148 jobs averaging $972. *State or other work-study/employment:* Total amount: $186,329 (100% non-need-based). 181 part-time jobs averaging $1029.
ATHLETIC AWARDS Total amount: $253,571 (100% non-need-based).
APPLYING FOR FINANCIAL AID *Required financial aid forms:* FAFSA, institutional scholarship application form. *Financial aid deadline (priority):* 3/1. *Notification date:* Continuous beginning 6/1. Students must reply by 8/15.
CONTACT Irala K. Magee, Director of Financial Aid, Northwestern Oklahoma State University, 709 Oklahoma Boulevard, Alva, OK 73717-2799, 580-327-1700 Ext. 8542. *Fax:* 580-327-8177. *E-mail:* ikmagee@nwosu.edu.

NORTHWESTERN STATE UNIVERSITY OF LOUISIANA
Natchitoches, LA

Tuition & fees (LA res): $3393   **Average undergraduate aid package: $5224**

ABOUT THE INSTITUTION State-supported, coed. Awards: associate, bachelor's, and master's degrees and post-master's certificates. 52 undergraduate majors. Total enrollment: 9,847. Undergraduates: 8,788. Freshmen: 1,533. Institutional methodology is used as a basis for awarding need-based institutional aid.
UNDERGRADUATE EXPENSES for 2005–06 *Application fee:* $20. *Tuition, state resident:* full-time $2240; part-time $240 per credit. *Tuition, nonresident:* full-time $8318; part-time $493 per credit. Full-time tuition and fees vary according to course load. Part-time tuition and fees vary according to course load. *College room and board:* $3626; *room only:* $2050. Room and board charges vary according to board plan, housing facility, and location. *Payment plan:* Installment.
FRESHMAN FINANCIAL AID (Fall 2004) 1490 applied for aid; of those 70% were deemed to have need. 100% of freshmen with need received aid. *Average percent of need met:* 34% (excluding resources awarded to replace EFC). *Average financial aid package:* $4482 (excluding resources awarded to replace EFC). 25% of all full-time freshmen had no need and received non-need-based gift aid.
UNDERGRADUATE FINANCIAL AID (Fall 2004) 5,616 applied for aid; of those 72% were deemed to have need. 100% of undergraduates with need received aid; of those .2% had need fully met. *Average percent of need met:* 36% (excluding resources awarded to replace EFC). *Average financial aid package:* $5224 (excluding resources awarded to replace EFC). 22% of all full-time undergraduates had no need and received non-need-based gift aid.
GIFT AID (NEED-BASED) *Total amount:* $12,232,502 (99% federal, 1% state). *Receiving aid:* Freshmen: 49% (884); All full-time undergraduates: 47% (3,282). *Average award:* Freshmen: $7199; Undergraduates: $8333. *Scholarships, grants, and awards:* Federal Pell, FSEOG, state, private, college/university gift aid from institutional funds, United Negro College Fund, Federal Nursing, third party scholarships.
GIFT AID (NON-NEED-BASED) *Total amount:* $8,224,548 (61% state, 20% institutional, 19% external sources). *Receiving aid:* Freshmen: 21% (386); Undergraduates: 21% (1,430). *Average Award:* Freshmen: $3753; Undergraduates: $3573. *Scholarships, grants, and awards by category: Academic Interests/ Achievement:* 2,088 awards ($1,655,215 total): biological sciences, education, general academic interests/achievements, humanities, mathematics, physical sciences. *Creative Arts/Performance:* 573 awards ($571,852 total): art/fine arts, cinema/film/broadcasting, creative writing, dance, journalism/publications, music, performing arts, theater/drama. *Special Achievements/Activities:* 117 awards ($108,610 total): cheerleading/drum major, general special achievements/activities, leadership, memberships. *Special Characteristics:* 1,441 awards ($2,442,515 total): adult students, children of faculty/staff, children of public servants, general special characteristics, international students, out-of-state students, public servants, veterans, veterans' children. *Tuition waivers:* Full or partial for employees or children of employees, senior citizens. *ROTC:* Army.
LOANS *Student loans:* $25,409,799 (53% need-based, 47% non-need-based). 68% of past graduating class borrowed through all loan programs. *Average indebtedness per student:* $17,442. *Average need-based loan:* Freshmen: $3628; Undergraduates: $4835. *Parent loans:* $352,183 (100% non-need-based). *Programs:* FFEL (Subsidized and Unsubsidized Stafford, PLUS), Perkins, alternative loans.
WORK-STUDY *Federal work-study:* Total amount: $305,537; 415 jobs averaging $736. *State or other work-study/employment:* Total amount: $846,378 (100% non-need-based). 793 part-time jobs averaging $1067.
ATHLETIC AWARDS Total amount: $1,756,258 (100% non-need-based).
APPLYING FOR FINANCIAL AID *Required financial aid forms:* FAFSA, institution's own form. *Financial aid deadline (priority):* 5/1. *Notification date:* Continuous beginning 5/1. Students must reply within 4 weeks of notification.
CONTACT Mrs. Misti Adams, Director of Financial Aid, Northwestern State University of Louisiana, 103 Roy Hall, Natchitoches, LA 71497, 318-357-5961 or toll-free 800-327-1903. *Fax:* 318-357-5488. *E-mail:* nsufinaid@nsula.edu.

NORTHWESTERN UNIVERSITY
Evanston, IL

Tuition & fees: $33,559   **Average undergraduate aid package: $25,831**

ABOUT THE INSTITUTION Independent, coed. Awards: bachelor's, master's, doctoral, and first professional degrees and post-master's certificates. 112 undergraduate majors. Total enrollment: 17,004. Undergraduates: 8,023. Freshmen: 1,952. Both federal and institutional methodology are used as a basis for awarding need-based institutional aid.
UNDERGRADUATE EXPENSES for 2006–07 *Application fee:* $65. *Comprehensive fee:* $43,825 includes full-time tuition ($33,408), mandatory fees ($151), and room and board ($10,266). *College room only:* $5835. *Part-time tuition:* $3963 per course.
FRESHMAN FINANCIAL AID (Fall 2005, est.) 1065 applied for aid; of those 85% were deemed to have need. 100% of freshmen with need received aid; of those 100% had need fully met. *Average percent of need met:* 100% (excluding resources awarded to replace EFC). *Average financial aid package:* $24,912 (excluding resources awarded to replace EFC). 4% of all full-time freshmen had no need and received non-need-based gift aid.
UNDERGRADUATE FINANCIAL AID (Fall 2005, est.) 3,819 applied for aid; of those 89% were deemed to have need. 100% of undergraduates with need received aid; of those 100% had need fully met. *Average percent of need met:* 100% (excluding resources awarded to replace EFC). *Average financial aid package:* $25,831 (excluding resources awarded to replace EFC). 2% of all full-time undergraduates had no need and received non-need-based gift aid.
GIFT AID (NEED-BASED) *Total amount:* $68,698,976 (6% federal, 3% state, 86% institutional, 5% external sources). *Receiving aid:* Freshmen: 44% (863); All full-time undergraduates: 42% (3,269). *Average award:* Freshmen: $21,691; Undergraduates: $21,489. *Scholarships, grants, and awards:* Federal Pell, FSEOG, state, private, college/university gift aid from institutional funds.
GIFT AID (NON-NEED-BASED) *Total amount:* $1,549,368 (26% institutional, 74% external sources). *Average Award:* Freshmen: $2058; Undergraduates: $2353. *Scholarships, grants, and awards by category: Creative Arts/ Performance:* 74 awards ($216,127 total): music. *Special Characteristics:* 10 awards ($393,000 total): international students. *ROTC:* Army cooperative, Naval, Air Force cooperative.
LOANS *Student loans:* $19,447,065 (69% need-based, 31% non-need-based). 46% of past graduating class borrowed through all loan programs. *Average indebtedness per student:* $18,362. *Average need-based loan:* Freshmen: $3284; Undergraduates: $4503. *Parent loans:* $22,795,782 (100% non-need-based). *Programs:* FFEL (Subsidized and Unsubsidized Stafford, PLUS), Perkins, college/university.

WORK-STUDY *Federal work-study:* Total amount: $2,900,000; 1,964 jobs averaging $1629. *State or other work-study/employment:* Total amount: $2,627,026 (100% need-based). Part-time jobs available.

ATHLETIC AWARDS *Total amount:* $9,924,027 (100% non-need-based).

APPLYING FOR FINANCIAL AID *Required financial aid forms:* FAFSA, CSS Financial Aid PROFILE, noncustodial (divorced/separated) parent's statement, business/farm supplement, parent and student federal tax returns. *Financial aid deadline:* 2/1. *Notification date:* 4/15. Students must reply by 5/1 or within 2 weeks of notification.

CONTACT Coordinator of Financial Aid, Northwestern University, PO Box 3060, 1801 Hinman Avenue, Evanston, IL 60204-3060, 847-491-8000. *E-mail:* newstudentaid@northwestern.edu.

NORTHWEST MISSOURI STATE UNIVERSITY
Maryville, MO

CONTACT Mr. Del Morley, Director of Financial Assistance, Northwest Missouri State University, 800 University Drive, Maryville, MO 64468-6001, 660-562-1138 or toll-free 800-633-1175.

NORTHWEST NAZARENE UNIVERSITY
Nampa, ID

Tuition & fees: $18,770   **Average undergraduate aid package: $13,171**

ABOUT THE INSTITUTION Independent religious, coed. Awards: bachelor's and master's degrees. 64 undergraduate majors. Total enrollment: 1,625. Undergraduates: 1,164. Freshmen: 264. Federal methodology is used as a basis for awarding need-based institutional aid.

UNDERGRADUATE EXPENSES for 2006–07 *Application fee:* $25. *Comprehensive fee:* $23,780 includes full-time tuition ($18,430), mandatory fees ($340), and room and board ($5010). *Part-time tuition:* $798 per credit.

FRESHMAN FINANCIAL AID (Fall 2005, est.) 223 applied for aid; of those 83% were deemed to have need. 100% of freshmen with need received aid; of those 19% had need fully met. *Average percent of need met:* 73% (excluding resources awarded to replace EFC). *Average financial aid package:* $12,522 (excluding resources awarded to replace EFC). 16% of all full-time freshmen had no need and received non-need-based gift aid.

UNDERGRADUATE FINANCIAL AID (Fall 2005, est.) 788 applied for aid; of those 88% were deemed to have need. 100% of undergraduates with need received aid; of those 22% had need fully met. *Average percent of need met:* 73% (excluding resources awarded to replace EFC). *Average financial aid package:* $13,171 (excluding resources awarded to replace EFC). 10% of all full-time undergraduates had no need and received non-need-based gift aid.

GIFT AID (NEED-BASED) *Total amount:* $5,140,354 (20% federal, 2% state, 68% institutional, 10% external sources). *Receiving aid:* Freshmen: 55% (138); All full-time undergraduates: 52% (492). *Average award:* Freshmen: $2566; Undergraduates: $2962. *Scholarships, grants, and awards:* Federal Pell, FSEOG, state, private, college/university gift aid from institutional funds.

GIFT AID (NON-NEED-BASED) *Total amount:* $901,152 (1% federal, 1% state, 87% institutional, 11% external sources). *Receiving aid:* Freshmen: 13% (33); Undergraduates: 69% (655). *Average Award:* Freshmen: $7816; Undergraduates: $8480. *Scholarships, grants, and awards by category: Academic Interests/Achievement:* 416 awards ($496,040 total): biological sciences, business, computer science, education, English, general academic interests/achievements, health fields, mathematics, military science, physical sciences, premedicine, religion/biblical studies, social sciences. *Creative Arts/Performance:* 65 awards ($30,875 total): art/fine arts, debating, general creative arts/performance, journalism/publications, music, performing arts, theater/drama. *Special Achievements/Activities:* 6 awards ($733 total): cheerleading/drum major, general special achievements/activities, leadership, religious involvement. *Special Characteristics:* 627 awards ($1,149,081 total): children and siblings of alumni, children of educators, children of faculty/staff, ethnic background, international students, members of minority groups, out-of-state students, relatives of clergy, religious affiliation, siblings of current students, veterans. *ROTC:* Army.

LOANS *Student loans:* $5,869,425 (75% need-based, 25% non-need-based). 94% of past graduating class borrowed through all loan programs. *Average indebtedness per student:* $24,405. *Average need-based loan:* Freshmen: $3751;

Undergraduates: $4960. *Parent loans:* $2,309,972 (85% need-based, 15% non-need-based). *Programs:* FFEL (Subsidized and Unsubsidized Stafford, PLUS), Perkins, college/university.

WORK-STUDY *Federal work-study:* Total amount: $242,007; 168 jobs averaging $1441.

ATHLETIC AWARDS *Total amount:* $875,984 (82% need-based, 18% non-need-based).

APPLYING FOR FINANCIAL AID *Required financial aid forms:* FAFSA, institution's own form. *Financial aid deadline (priority):* 3/1. *Notification date:* Continuous beginning 4/1. Students must reply within 3 weeks of notification.

CONTACT Mr. Wes Maggard, Director of Financial Aid, Northwest Nazarene University, 623 Holly Street, Nampa, ID 83686, 208-467-8774 or toll-free 877-668-4968. *Fax:* 208-467-8375. *E-mail:* mwmaggard@nnu.edu.

NORTHWEST UNIVERSITY
Kirkland, WA

Tuition & fees: $18,144   **Average undergraduate aid package: $12,446**

ABOUT THE INSTITUTION Independent religious, coed. Awards: associate, bachelor's, and master's degrees. 36 undergraduate majors. Total enrollment: 1,260. Undergraduates: 1,153. Freshmen: 198. Federal methodology is used as a basis for awarding need-based institutional aid.

UNDERGRADUATE EXPENSES for 2006–07 *Application fee:* $30. *Comprehensive fee:* $24,594 includes full-time tuition ($17,920), mandatory fees ($224), and room and board ($6450). *Part-time tuition:* $750 per credit. *Part-time fees:* $224 per year.

FRESHMAN FINANCIAL AID (Fall 2005, est.) 163 applied for aid; of those 85% were deemed to have need. 98% of freshmen with need received aid; of those 27% had need fully met. *Average percent of need met:* 70% (excluding resources awarded to replace EFC). *Average financial aid package:* $12,163 (excluding resources awarded to replace EFC). 21% of all full-time freshmen had no need and received non-need-based gift aid.

UNDERGRADUATE FINANCIAL AID (Fall 2005, est.) 915 applied for aid; of those 85% were deemed to have need. 99% of undergraduates with need received aid; of those 16% had need fully met. *Average percent of need met:* 68% (excluding resources awarded to replace EFC). *Average financial aid package:* $12,446 (excluding resources awarded to replace EFC). 17% of all full-time undergraduates had no need and received non-need-based gift aid.

GIFT AID (NEED-BASED) *Total amount:* $5,048,669 (20% federal, 13% state, 61% institutional, 6% external sources). *Receiving aid:* Freshmen: 69% (134); All full-time undergraduates: 71% (749). *Average award:* Freshmen: $8644; Undergraduates: $8054. *Scholarships, grants, and awards:* Federal Pell, FSEOG, state, private, college/university gift aid from institutional funds.

GIFT AID (NON-NEED-BASED) *Total amount:* $720,399 (1% state, 96% institutional, 3% external sources). *Receiving aid:* Freshmen: 10% (19); Undergraduates: 6% (61). *Average Award:* Freshmen: $6243; Undergraduates: $10,199. *Scholarships, grants, and awards by category: Academic Interests/Achievement:* 301 awards ($999,088 total): general academic interests/achievements. *Creative Arts/Performance:* 120 awards ($275,131 total): debating, music, performing arts, theater/drama. *Special Characteristics:* 194 awards ($803,493 total): children of current students, children of faculty/staff, general special characteristics, international students, married students, parents of current students, relatives of clergy, religious affiliation, siblings of current students, spouses of current students. *ROTC:* Army cooperative.

LOANS *Student loans:* $6,891,002 (70% need-based, 30% non-need-based). 88% of past graduating class borrowed through all loan programs. *Average indebtedness per student:* $19,171. *Average need-based loan:* Freshmen: $2931; Undergraduates: $4068. *Parent loans:* $523,745 (100% need-based). *Programs:* FFEL (Subsidized and Unsubsidized Stafford, PLUS), Perkins, state, alternative loans.

WORK-STUDY *Federal work-study:* Total amount: $124,697; 69 jobs averaging $2555. *State or other work-study/employment:* Total amount: $128,333 (100% need-based). 37 part-time jobs averaging $3893.

ATHLETIC AWARDS *Total amount:* $535,988 (44% need-based, 56% non-need-based).

APPLYING FOR FINANCIAL AID *Required financial aid forms:* FAFSA, institution's own form. *Financial aid deadline (priority):* 3/1. *Notification date:* Continuous beginning 3/3. Students must reply within 4 weeks of notification.

Northwest University

CONTACT Ms. Lana J. Walter, Director of Financial Aid, Northwest University, PO Box 579, Kirkland, WA 98083-0579, 425-889-5336 or toll-free 800-669-3781. *Fax:* 425-889-5224. *E-mail:* lana.walter@ncag.edu.

NORTHWOOD UNIVERSITY
Midland, MI

| Tuition & fees: $15,533 | Average undergraduate aid package: $13,063 |

ABOUT THE INSTITUTION Independent, coed. Awards: associate, bachelor's, and master's degrees. 15 undergraduate majors. Total enrollment: 3,888. Undergraduates: 3,577. Freshmen: 493. Both federal and institutional methodology are used as a basis for awarding need-based institutional aid.

UNDERGRADUATE EXPENSES for 2006–07 *Application fee:* $25. *Comprehensive fee:* $22,475 includes full-time tuition ($15,216), mandatory fees ($317), and room and board ($6942). *College room only:* $3567. *Part-time tuition:* $317 per credit hour.

FRESHMAN FINANCIAL AID (Fall 2005, est.) 398 applied for aid; of those 82% were deemed to have need. 100% of freshmen with need received aid; of those 28% had need fully met. *Average percent of need met:* 91% (excluding resources awarded to replace EFC). *Average financial aid package:* $14,645 (excluding resources awarded to replace EFC). 12% of all full-time freshmen had no need and received non-need-based gift aid.

UNDERGRADUATE FINANCIAL AID (Fall 2005, est.) 1,305 applied for aid; of those 83% were deemed to have need. 100% of undergraduates with need received aid; of those 27% had need fully met. *Average percent of need met:* 92% (excluding resources awarded to replace EFC). *Average financial aid package:* $13,063 (excluding resources awarded to replace EFC). 27% of all full-time undergraduates had no need and received non-need-based gift aid.

GIFT AID (NEED-BASED) *Total amount:* $8,479,940 (20% federal, 21% state, 56% institutional, 3% external sources). *Receiving aid:* Freshmen: 60% (294); All full-time undergraduates: 51% (957). *Average award:* Freshmen: $5948; Undergraduates: $5201. *Scholarships, grants, and awards:* Federal Pell, FSEOG, state, private, college/university gift aid from institutional funds.

GIFT AID (NON-NEED-BASED) *Total amount:* $3,540,831 (6% state, 87% institutional, 7% external sources). *Receiving aid:* Freshmen: 24% (119); Undergraduates: 21% (395). *Average Award:* Freshmen: $6602; Undergraduates:* $4884. *Scholarships, grants, and awards by category:* Academic Interests/Achievement: 1,205 awards ($5,489,318 total): business, general academic interests/achievements. Special Achievements/Activities: 372 awards ($449,923 total): cheerleading/drum major, leadership, memberships. Special Characteristics: 115 awards ($498,955 total): children and siblings of alumni, children of faculty/staff, siblings of current students.

LOANS *Student loans:* $8,318,988 (63% need-based, 37% non-need-based). 57% of past graduating class borrowed through all loan programs. *Average indebtedness per student:* $18,389. *Average need-based loan:* Freshmen: $2452; Undergraduates: $3590. *Parent loans:* $1,549,070 (27% need-based, 73% non-need-based). *Programs:* FFEL (Subsidized and Unsubsidized Stafford, PLUS), state.

WORK-STUDY *Federal work-study:* Total amount: $365,092; 204 jobs averaging $1790. *State or other work-study/employment:* Total amount: $555,820 (100% need-based). 316 part-time jobs averaging $1748.

ATHLETIC AWARDS *Total amount:* $1,869,409 (37% need-based, 63% non-need-based).

APPLYING FOR FINANCIAL AID *Required financial aid form:* FAFSA. *Financial aid deadline:* Continuous. *Notification date:* Continuous beginning 3/1.

CONTACT Terri Mieler, Director of Financial Aid, Northwood University, 4000 Whiting Drive, Midland, MI 48640-2398, 989-837-4301 or toll-free 800-457-7878. *Fax:* 989-837-4130. *E-mail:* mieler@northwood.edu.

NORTHWOOD UNIVERSITY, FLORIDA CAMPUS
West Palm Beach, FL

| Tuition & fees: $15,801 | Average undergraduate aid package: $13,127 |

ABOUT THE INSTITUTION Independent, coed. Awards: associate and bachelor's degrees. 12 undergraduate majors. Total enrollment: 923. Undergraduates: 923. Freshmen: 143. Both federal and institutional methodology are used as a basis for awarding need-based institutional aid.

UNDERGRADUATE EXPENSES for 2006–07 *Application fee:* $25. *Comprehensive fee:* $23,316 includes full-time tuition ($15,216), mandatory fees ($585), and room and board ($7515). *College room only:* $3870. *Part-time tuition:* $317 per credit hour.

FRESHMAN FINANCIAL AID (Fall 2005, est.) 97 applied for aid; of those 92% were deemed to have need. 100% of freshmen with need received aid; of those 16% had need fully met. *Average percent of need met:* 67% (excluding resources awarded to replace EFC). *Average financial aid package:* $12,669 (excluding resources awarded to replace EFC). 16% of all full-time freshmen had no need and received non-need-based gift aid.

UNDERGRADUATE FINANCIAL AID (Fall 2005, est.) 353 applied for aid; of those 88% were deemed to have need. 100% of undergraduates with need received aid; of those 17% had need fully met. *Average percent of need met:* 61% (excluding resources awarded to replace EFC). *Average financial aid package:* $13,127 (excluding resources awarded to replace EFC). 18% of all full-time undergraduates had no need and received non-need-based gift aid.

GIFT AID (NEED-BASED) *Total amount:* $2,578,098 (19% federal, 8% state, 70% institutional, 3% external sources). *Receiving aid:* Freshmen: 53% (76); All full-time undergraduates: 36% (250). *Average award:* Freshmen: $6092; Undergraduates: $5989. *Scholarships, grants, and awards:* Federal Pell, FSEOG, state, private, college/university gift aid from institutional funds.

GIFT AID (NON-NEED-BASED) *Total amount:* $1,218,033 (6% state, 87% institutional, 7% external sources). *Receiving aid:* Freshmen: 17% (25); Undergraduates: 17% (119). *Average Award:* Freshmen: $5376; Undergraduates:* $4723. *Scholarships, grants, and awards by category:* Academic Interests/Achievement: 519 awards ($1,456,106 total): business, general academic interests/achievements. Special Achievements/Activities: 51 awards ($58,132 total): memberships. Special Characteristics: 34 awards ($102,251 total): children and siblings of alumni, children of faculty/staff, siblings of current students.

LOANS *Student loans:* $2,235,624 (67% need-based, 33% non-need-based). 45% of past graduating class borrowed through all loan programs. *Average indebtedness per student:* $15,704. *Average need-based loan:* Freshmen: $2555; Undergraduates: $3566. *Parent loans:* $820,232 (26% need-based, 74% non-need-based). *Programs:* FFEL (Subsidized and Unsubsidized Stafford, PLUS).

WORK-STUDY *Federal work-study:* Total amount: $240,800; 112 jobs averaging $2150.

ATHLETIC AWARDS *Total amount:* $781,406 (25% need-based, 75% non-need-based).

APPLYING FOR FINANCIAL AID *Required financial aid form:* FAFSA. *Financial aid deadline:* Continuous. *Notification date:* Continuous beginning 3/1.

CONTACT Ms. Teresa A. Palmer, Director of Financial Aid, Northwood University, Florida Campus, 2600 North Military Trail, West Palm Beach, FL 33409-2911, 561-478-5590 or toll-free 800-458-8325. *Fax:* 561-681-7990. *E-mail:* palmer@northwood.edu.

NORTHWOOD UNIVERSITY, TEXAS CAMPUS
Cedar Hill, TX

| Tuition & fees: $15,801 | Average undergraduate aid package: $14,360 |

ABOUT THE INSTITUTION Independent, coed. Awards: associate and bachelor's degrees. 13 undergraduate majors. Total enrollment: 1,061. Undergraduates: 1,061. Freshmen: 129. Federal methodology is used as a basis for awarding need-based institutional aid.

UNDERGRADUATE EXPENSES for 2006–07 *Application fee:* $25. *Comprehensive fee:* $22,437 includes full-time tuition ($15,216), mandatory fees ($585), and room and board ($6636). *College room only:* $3567. *Part-time tuition:* $317 per credit hour.

FRESHMAN FINANCIAL AID (Fall 2005, est.) 117 applied for aid; of those 86% were deemed to have need. 100% of freshmen with need received aid; of those 17% had need fully met. *Average percent of need met:* 61% (excluding resources awarded to replace EFC). *Average financial aid package:* $14,938 (excluding resources awarded to replace EFC). 5% of all full-time freshmen had no need and received non-need-based gift aid.

UNDERGRADUATE FINANCIAL AID (Fall 2005, est.) 456 applied for aid; of those 87% were deemed to have need. 100% of undergraduates with need received aid; of those 21% had need fully met. *Average percent of need met:* 56% (excluding resources awarded to replace EFC). *Average financial aid package:* $14,360 (excluding resources awarded to replace EFC). 16% of all full-time undergraduates had no need and received non-need-based gift aid.
GIFT AID (NEED-BASED) *Total amount:* $3,223,619 (23% federal, 76% institutional, 1% external sources). *Receiving aid:* Freshmen: 68% (86); All full-time undergraduates: 59% (331). *Average award:* Freshmen: $5709; Undergraduates: $5015. *Scholarships, grants, and awards:* Federal Pell, FSEOG, private, college/university gift aid from institutional funds.
GIFT AID (NON-NEED-BASED) *Total amount:* $777,244 (97% institutional, 3% external sources). *Receiving aid:* Freshmen: 28% (35); Undergraduates: 27% (149). *Average Award:* Freshmen: $6875; Undergraduates: $4726. *Scholarships, grants, and awards by category:* Academic Interests/Achievement: 451 awards ($2,031,391 total): business, general academic interests/achievements. Special Achievements/Activities: 528 awards ($651,485 total): general special achievements/activities, memberships. Special Characteristics: 13 awards ($63,339 total): children and siblings of alumni, children of faculty/staff, siblings of current students.
LOANS *Student loans:* $2,699,456 (78% need-based, 22% non-need-based). 71% of past graduating class borrowed through all loan programs. *Average indebtedness per student:* $16,346. *Average need-based loan:* Freshmen: $2441; Undergraduates: $3721. *Parent loans:* $837,002 (27% need-based, 73% non-need-based). *Programs:* FFEL (Subsidized and Unsubsidized Stafford, PLUS).
WORK-STUDY *Federal work-study:* Total amount: $708,395; 336 jobs averaging $3108.
ATHLETIC AWARDS *Total amount:* $612,848 (56% need-based, 44% non-need-based).
APPLYING FOR FINANCIAL AID *Required financial aid form:* FAFSA. *Financial aid deadline:* Continuous. *Notification date:* Continuous beginning 3/1.
CONTACT Michael Rhodes, Director of Financial Aid, Northwood University, Texas Campus, 1114 West FM 1382, Cedar Hill, TX 75104, 972-293-5479 or toll-free 800-927-9663. *Fax:* 972-293-7196. *E-mail:* rhodes@northwood.edu.

NORWICH UNIVERSITY
Northfield, VT

CONTACT Director of Student Financial Planning, Norwich University, 158 Harmon Drive, Northfield, VT 05663, 802-485-2015 or toll-free 800-468-6679.

NOTRE DAME COLLEGE
South Euclid, OH

CONTACT Ms. Mary E. McCrystal, Financial Aid Director, Notre Dame College, 4545 College Road, South Euclid, OH 44121-4293, 216-381-1680 Ext. 263 or toll-free 800-632-1680. *Fax:* 216-381-3802. *E-mail:* mmccrystal@ndc.edu.

NOTRE DAME DE NAMUR UNIVERSITY
Belmont, CA

CONTACT Ms. Kathleen Kelly, Director of Financial Aid, Notre Dame de Namur University, 1500 Ralston Avenue, Belmont, CA 94002, 650-508-3509 or toll-free 800-263-0545.

NOVA SOUTHEASTERN UNIVERSITY
Fort Lauderdale, FL

Tuition & fees: $17,800 | **Average undergraduate aid package: $10,831**

ABOUT THE INSTITUTION Independent, coed. Awards: associate, bachelor's, master's, doctoral, and first professional degrees and post-master's and first professional certificates. 32 undergraduate majors. Total enrollment: 26,334. Undergraduates: 5,453. Freshmen: 431. Federal methodology is used as a basis for awarding need-based institutional aid.
UNDERGRADUATE EXPENSES for 2005–06 *Application fee:* $50. *Comprehensive fee:* $24,320 includes full-time tuition ($17,250), mandatory fees ($550), and room and board ($6520). *College room only:* $4120. Full-time tuition and fees vary according to class time and program. Room and board charges vary according to board plan and housing facility. *Part-time tuition:* $575 per credit hour. Part-time tuition and fees vary according to class time, course load, and program. *Payment plans:* Installment, deferred payment.
FRESHMAN FINANCIAL AID (Fall 2005, est.) 329 applied for aid; of those 54% were deemed to have need. 99% of freshmen with need received aid; of those 10% had need fully met. *Average financial aid package:* $13,826 (excluding resources awarded to replace EFC). 25% of all full-time freshmen had no need and received non-need-based gift aid.
UNDERGRADUATE FINANCIAL AID (Fall 2005, est.) 2,813 applied for aid; of those 62% were deemed to have need. 100% of undergraduates with need received aid; of those 4% had need fully met. *Average percent of need met:* 59% (excluding resources awarded to replace EFC). *Average financial aid package:* $10,831 (excluding resources awarded to replace EFC). 16% of all full-time undergraduates had no need and received non-need-based gift aid.
GIFT AID (NEED-BASED) *Total amount:* $16,568,386 (84% federal, 9% state, 7% institutional). *Receiving aid:* Freshmen: 25% (100); All full-time undergraduates: 35% (1,192). *Average award:* Freshmen: $5849; Undergraduates: $4823. *Scholarships, grants, and awards:* Federal Pell, FSEOG, state, private, college/university gift aid from institutional funds.
GIFT AID (NON-NEED-BASED) *Total amount:* $12,508,124 (61% state, 38% institutional, 1% external sources). *Receiving aid:* Freshmen: 38% (150); Undergraduates: 27% (900). *Average Award:* Freshmen: $5140; Undergraduates: $6641. *Scholarships, grants, and awards by category:* Academic Interests/Achievement: 1,103 awards ($3,107,972 total): general academic interests/achievements. Special Achievements/Activities: 27 awards ($91,340 total): leadership. Special Characteristics: 42 awards ($309,110 total): children of faculty/staff. *Tuition waivers:* Full or partial for employees or children of employees.
LOANS *Student loans:* $34,657,529 (44% need-based, 56% non-need-based). 69% of past graduating class borrowed through all loan programs. *Average indebtedness per student:* $28,785. *Average need-based loan:* Freshmen: $2988; Undergraduates: $5376. *Parent loans:* $1,302,401 (50% need-based, 50% non-need-based). *Programs:* FFEL (Subsidized and Unsubsidized Stafford, PLUS), Perkins, college/university.
WORK-STUDY *Federal work-study:* Total amount: $3,787,711; 1,043 jobs averaging $3632. *State or other work-study/employment:* Total amount: $737,898 (100% non-need-based). 240 part-time jobs averaging $3075.
ATHLETIC AWARDS *Total amount:* $2,083,411 (100% non-need-based).
APPLYING FOR FINANCIAL AID *Required financial aid forms:* FAFSA, institution's own form. *Financial aid deadline (priority):* 4/15. *Notification date:* Continuous beginning 3/15. Students must reply within 4 weeks of notification.
CONTACT Etta Fleischer, Associate Vice President for Student Financial Services and Registration (Interim), Nova Southeastern University, 3301 College Avenue, Fort Lauderdale, FL 33314, 954-262-7439 or toll-free 800-541-NOVA. *Fax:* 954-262-3967. *E-mail:* ettaf@nova.edu.

NYACK COLLEGE
Nyack, NY

Tuition & fees: $15,400 | **Average undergraduate aid package: $13,931**

ABOUT THE INSTITUTION Independent religious, coed. Awards: associate, bachelor's, master's, and first professional degrees. 28 undergraduate majors. Total enrollment: 3,000. Undergraduates: 2,030. Freshmen: 270. Both federal and institutional methodology are used as a basis for awarding need-based institutional aid.
UNDERGRADUATE EXPENSES for 2006–07 *Application fee:* $25. *Comprehensive fee:* $23,000 includes full-time tuition ($15,400) and room and board ($7600). *Part-time tuition:* $600 per credit.
FRESHMAN FINANCIAL AID (Fall 2004) 231 applied for aid; of those 92% were deemed to have need. 100% of freshmen with need received aid; of those 14% had need fully met. *Average percent of need met:* 63% (excluding resources awarded to replace EFC). *Average financial aid package:* $12,972 (excluding resources awarded to replace EFC). 22% of all full-time freshmen had no need and received non-need-based gift aid.
UNDERGRADUATE FINANCIAL AID (Fall 2004) 1,154 applied for aid; of those 95% were deemed to have need. 100% of undergraduates with need received aid; of those 17% had need fully met. *Average percent of need met:* 64% (excluding resources awarded to replace EFC). *Average financial aid package:*

Nyack College

$13,931 (excluding resources awarded to replace EFC). 15% of all full-time undergraduates had no need and received non-need-based gift aid.
GIFT AID (NEED-BASED) *Total amount:* $10,355,237 (25% federal, 22% state, 51% institutional, 2% external sources). *Receiving aid:* Freshmen: 73% (210); All full-time undergraduates: 82% (1,077). *Average award:* Freshmen: $9110; Undergraduates: $8929. *Scholarships, grants, and awards:* Federal Pell, FSEOG, state, private, college/university gift aid from institutional funds.
GIFT AID (NON-NEED-BASED) *Total amount:* $1,072,064 (2% state, 96% institutional, 2% external sources). *Receiving aid:* Freshmen: 4% (11); Undergraduates: 3% (44). *Average Award:* Freshmen: $6595; Undergraduates: $7076. *Scholarships, grants, and awards by category:* Academic Interests/Achievement: 317 awards ($647,032 total): general academic interests/achievements. Creative Arts/Performance: 88 awards ($196,175 total): journalism/publications, music, performing arts, theater/drama. Special Achievements/Activities: 1,197 awards ($1,519,850 total): general special achievements/activities, leadership, religious involvement. Special Characteristics: 989 awards ($2,284,185 total): children and siblings of alumni, children of faculty/staff, general special characteristics, international students, local/state students, out-of-state students, relatives of clergy, religious affiliation, spouses of current students.
LOANS *Student loans:* $10,105,307 (85% need-based, 15% non-need-based). 76% of past graduating class borrowed through all loan programs. *Average indebtedness per student:* $17,271. *Average need-based loan:* Freshmen: $3615; Undergraduates: $4841. *Parent loans:* $1,613,096 (61% need-based, 39% non-need-based). *Programs:* FFEL (Subsidized and Unsubsidized Stafford, PLUS), Perkins.
WORK-STUDY *Federal work-study:* Total amount: $280,245; 226 jobs averaging $1240. *State or other work-study/employment:* Total amount: $83,760 (99% need-based, 1% non-need-based). 47 part-time jobs averaging $1903.
ATHLETIC AWARDS *Total amount:* $1,094,781 (73% need-based, 27% non-need-based).
APPLYING FOR FINANCIAL AID *Required financial aid forms:* FAFSA, state aid form. *Financial aid deadline (priority):* 3/1. *Notification date:* Continuous. Students must reply by 4/1 or within 4 weeks of notification.
CONTACT Andres Valenzuela, Director of Student Financial Services, Nyack College, 1 South Boulevard, Nyack, NY 10960-3698, 845-358-1710 or toll-free 800-33-NYACK. *Fax:* 845-358-7016. *E-mail:* sfs@nyack.edu.

OAK HILLS CHRISTIAN COLLEGE
Bemidji, MN

CONTACT Daniel Hovestol, Financial Aid Director, Oak Hills Christian College, 1600 Oak Hills Road, SW, Bemidji, MN 56601-8832, 218-751-8671 Ext. 1220 or toll-free 888-751-8670 Ext. 285. *Fax:* 218-444-1311. *E-mail:* ohfinaid@oakhills.edu.

OAKLAND CITY UNIVERSITY
Oakland City, IN

ABOUT THE INSTITUTION Independent General Baptist, coed. Awards: associate, bachelor's, master's, doctoral, and first professional degrees. 60 undergraduate majors. Total enrollment: 1,900. Undergraduates: 1,566. Freshmen: 261.
GIFT AID (NEED-BASED) *Scholarships, grants, and awards:* Federal Pell, FSEOG, state, private, college/university gift aid from institutional funds.
GIFT AID (NON-NEED-BASED) *Scholarships, grants, and awards by category:* Academic Interests/Achievement: general academic interests/achievements. Creative Arts/Performance: art/fine arts, music. Special Achievements/Activities: religious involvement. Special Characteristics: children and siblings of alumni, children of faculty/staff, ethnic background, international students, members of minority groups, religious affiliation.
LOANS *Programs:* FFEL (Subsidized and Unsubsidized Stafford, PLUS), Perkins, college/university.
WORK-STUDY *Federal work-study:* 150 jobs averaging $1600. *State or other work-study/employment:* 4 part-time jobs averaging $1500.
APPLYING FOR FINANCIAL AID *Required financial aid form:* FAFSA.
CONTACT Mrs. Caren K. Richeson, Director of Financial Aid, Oakland City University, 138 North Lucretia Street, Oakland City, IN 47660-1099, 812-749-1224 or toll-free 800-737-5125. *Fax:* 812-749-1438.

OAKLAND UNIVERSITY
Rochester, MI

ABOUT THE INSTITUTION State-supported, coed. Awards: bachelor's, master's, and doctoral degrees and post-bachelor's and post-master's certificates. 58 undergraduate majors. Total enrollment: 17,339. Undergraduates: 13,448. Freshmen: 2,213.
GIFT AID (NEED-BASED) *Scholarships, grants, and awards:* Federal Pell, FSEOG, state, private, college/university gift aid from institutional funds.
GIFT AID (NON-NEED-BASED) *Scholarships, grants, and awards by category:* Academic Interests/Achievement: area/ethnic studies, biological sciences, business, education, engineering/technologies, English, foreign languages, general academic interests/achievements, health fields, humanities. Creative Arts/Performance: dance, music, performing arts. Special Characteristics: adult students, ethnic background, out-of-state students.
LOANS *Programs:* Federal Direct (Subsidized and Unsubsidized Stafford, PLUS), Perkins, state, alternative loans.
APPLYING FOR FINANCIAL AID *Required financial aid form:* FAFSA.
CONTACT Ms. Cindy Hermsen, Director of Financial Aid, Oakland University, 120 North Foundation Hall, Rochester, MI 48309-4481, 248-370-2550 or toll-free 800-OAK-UNIV. *E-mail:* finaid@oakland.edu.

OAKWOOD COLLEGE
Huntsville, AL

CONTACT Financial Aid Director, Oakwood College, 7000 Adventist Boulevard, Huntsville, AL 35896, 256-726-7210 or toll-free 800-358-3978 (in-state).

OBERLIN COLLEGE
Oberlin, OH

ABOUT THE INSTITUTION Independent, coed. Awards: bachelor's and master's degrees and post-bachelor's certificates. 54 undergraduate majors. Total enrollment: 2,864. Undergraduates: 2,845. Freshmen: 741.
GIFT AID (NEED-BASED) *Scholarships, grants, and awards:* Federal Pell, FSEOG, state, private, college/university gift aid from institutional funds.
GIFT AID (NON-NEED-BASED) *Scholarships, grants, and awards by category:* Academic Interests/Achievement: general academic interests/achievements, physical sciences. Creative Arts/Performance: music.
LOANS *Programs:* FFEL (Subsidized and Unsubsidized Stafford, PLUS), Perkins, college/university.
WORK-STUDY *Federal work-study:* Total amount: $2,236,891; jobs available (averaging $1650). *State or other work-study/employment:* Part-time jobs available (averaging $1650).
APPLYING FOR FINANCIAL AID *Required financial aid forms:* FAFSA, CSS Financial Aid PROFILE, noncustodial (divorced/separated) parent's statement.
CONTACT Office of Financial Aid, Oberlin College, Carnegie Building 123, 52 West Lorain Street, Oberlin, OH 44074, 800-693-3173 or toll-free 800-622-OBIE. *Fax:* 440-775-8249. *E-mail:* financial.aid@oberlin.edu.

OCCIDENTAL COLLEGE
Los Angeles, CA

Tuition & fees: $33,644   **Average undergraduate aid package:** $29,089

ABOUT THE INSTITUTION Independent, coed. Awards: bachelor's and master's degrees. 31 undergraduate majors. Total enrollment: 1,839. Undergraduates: 1,819. Freshmen: 436. Institutional methodology is used as a basis for awarding need-based institutional aid.
UNDERGRADUATE EXPENSES for 2006–07 *Application fee:* $50. *Comprehensive fee:* $42,686 includes full-time tuition ($32,800), mandatory fees ($844), and room and board ($9042). *College room only:* $4972. *Part-time tuition:* $1387 per credit.
FRESHMAN FINANCIAL AID (Fall 2005, est.) 272 applied for aid; of those 76% were deemed to have need. 100% of freshmen with need received aid; of those 100% had need fully met. *Average percent of need met:* 100% (excluding resources awarded to replace EFC). *Average financial aid package:* $26,747 (excluding resources awarded to replace EFC). 31% of all full-time freshmen had no need and received non-need-based gift aid.

UNDERGRADUATE FINANCIAL AID (Fall 2005, est.) 1,039 applied for aid; of those 87% were deemed to have need. 99% of undergraduates with need received aid; of those 100% had need fully met. *Average percent of need met:* 100% (excluding resources awarded to replace EFC). *Average financial aid package:* $29,089 (excluding resources awarded to replace EFC). 27% of all full-time undergraduates had no need and received non-need-based gift aid.
GIFT AID (NEED-BASED) *Total amount:* $20,159,018 (7% federal, 12% state, 77% institutional, 4% external sources). *Receiving aid:* Freshmen: 44% (202); All full-time undergraduates: 54% (882). *Average award:* Freshmen: $21,382; Undergraduates: $22,840. *Scholarships, grants, and awards:* Federal Pell, FSEOG, state, private, college/university gift aid from institutional funds.
GIFT AID (NON-NEED-BASED) *Total amount:* $4,665,348 (1% state, 77% institutional, 22% external sources). *Receiving aid:* Freshmen: 5% (23); Undergraduates: 4% (71). *Average Award:* Freshmen: $13,614; Undergraduates: $16,180. *Scholarships, grants, and awards by category:* Academic Interests/Achievement: 452 awards ($4,464,790 total): general academic interests/achievements. Creative Arts/Performance: 38 awards ($24,773 total): music. Special Achievements/Activities: 30 awards ($345,000 total): general special achievements/activities, leadership. Special Characteristics: 21 awards ($607,633 total): children of educators, children of faculty/staff. *ROTC:* Army cooperative, Naval cooperative, Air Force cooperative.
LOANS *Student loans:* $6,488,340 (73% need-based, 27% non-need-based). 52% of past graduating class borrowed through all loan programs. *Average indebtedness per student:* $20,640. *Average need-based loan:* Freshmen: $4824; Undergraduates: $5607. *Parent loans:* $3,584,346 (100% non-need-based). *Programs:* FFEL (Subsidized and Unsubsidized Stafford, PLUS), Perkins, college/university.
WORK-STUDY *Federal work-study:* Total amount: $938,311; 684 jobs averaging $2325. *State or other work-study/employment:* Total amount: $296,115 (38% need-based, 62% non-need-based). 96 part-time jobs averaging $2299.
APPLYING FOR FINANCIAL AID *Required financial aid forms:* FAFSA, CSS Financial Aid PROFILE, state aid form, noncustodial (divorced/separated) parent's statement, business/farm supplement, income tax form(s), W-2 forms. *Financial aid deadline:* 2/1 (priority: 2/1). *Notification date:* 4/1. Students must reply by 5/1.
CONTACT Maureen McRae Levy, Director of Financial Aid, Occidental College, 1600 Campus Road, Los Angeles, CA 90041, 323-259-2548 or toll-free 800-825-5262. *Fax:* 323-341-4961. *E-mail:* finaid@oxy.edu.

OGLALA LAKOTA COLLEGE
Kyle, SD

ABOUT THE INSTITUTION State and locally supported, coed. Awards: associate, bachelor's, and master's degrees. 23 undergraduate majors. Total enrollment: 1,000.
GIFT AID (NEED-BASED) *Scholarships, grants, and awards:* Federal Pell, FSEOG, private, college/university gift aid from institutional funds.
GIFT AID (NON-NEED-BASED) *Scholarships, grants, and awards by category:* Academic Interests/Achievement: business, education, health fields, social sciences.
APPLYING FOR FINANCIAL AID *Required financial aid form:* FAFSA.
CONTACT Financial Aid Director, Oglala Lakota College, 490 Piya Wiconi Road, Kyle, SD 57752-0490, 605-455-6000.

OGLETHORPE UNIVERSITY
Atlanta, GA

Tuition & fees: $22,300 **Average undergraduate aid package: $20,779**

ABOUT THE INSTITUTION Independent, coed. Awards: bachelor's and master's degrees. 33 undergraduate majors. Total enrollment: 1,083. Undergraduates: 1,018. Freshmen: 232. Federal methodology is used as a basis for awarding need-based institutional aid.
UNDERGRADUATE EXPENSES for 2005–06 *Application fee:* $35. *Comprehensive fee:* $30,300 includes full-time tuition ($22,200), mandatory fees ($100), and room and board ($8000). Room and board charges vary according to board plan and housing facility. *Part-time tuition:* $925 per credit hour. Part-time tuition and fees vary according to program. *Payment plans:* Tuition prepayment, installment.
FRESHMAN FINANCIAL AID (Fall 2004) 150 applied for aid; of those 77% were deemed to have need. 100% of freshmen with need received aid; of those 66% had need fully met. *Average percent of need met:* 93% (excluding resources awarded to replace EFC). *Average financial aid package:* $23,190 (excluding resources awarded to replace EFC). 29% of all full-time freshmen had no need and received non-need-based gift aid.
UNDERGRADUATE FINANCIAL AID (Fall 2004) 525 applied for aid; of those 85% were deemed to have need. 100% of undergraduates with need received aid; of those 32% had need fully met. *Average percent of need met:* 86% (excluding resources awarded to replace EFC). *Average financial aid package:* $20,779 (excluding resources awarded to replace EFC). 34% of all full-time undergraduates had no need and received non-need-based gift aid.
GIFT AID (NEED-BASED) *Total amount:* $5,495,303 (12% federal, 15% state, 73% institutional). *Receiving aid:* Freshmen: 69% (115); All full-time undergraduates: 58% (444). *Average award:* Freshmen: $14,140; Undergraduates: $12,198. *Scholarships, grants, and awards:* Federal Pell, FSEOG, state, private, college/university gift aid from institutional funds.
GIFT AID (NON-NEED-BASED) *Total amount:* $4,221,449 (12% state, 76% institutional, 12% external sources). *Receiving aid:* Freshmen: 59% (99); Undergraduates: 58% (444). *Average Award:* Freshmen: $11,336; Undergraduates: $10,542. *Scholarships, grants, and awards by category:* Academic Interests/Achievement: general academic interests/achievements. Creative Arts/Performance: journalism/publications, music, performing arts, theater/drama. Special Achievements/Activities: community service, religious involvement. *Tuition waivers:* Full or partial for employees or children of employees.
LOANS *Student loans:* $3,048,208 (38% need-based, 62% non-need-based). 64% of past graduating class borrowed through all loan programs. *Average indebtedness per student:* $16,273. *Average need-based loan:* Freshmen: $1072; Undergraduates: $2288. *Parent loans:* $569,630 (100% non-need-based). *Programs:* Federal Direct (Subsidized and Unsubsidized Stafford, PLUS), FFEL (Subsidized and Unsubsidized Stafford, PLUS), Perkins.
WORK-STUDY *Federal work-study:* Total amount: $393,499; jobs available. *State or other work-study/employment:* Total amount: $121,015 (100% need-based). Part-time jobs available.
APPLYING FOR FINANCIAL AID *Required financial aid forms:* FAFSA, institution's own form, state aid form, noncustodial (divorced/separated) parent's statement. *Financial aid deadline:* 3/15 (priority: 3/15).
CONTACT Mr. Patrick Bonones, Director of Financial Aid, Oglethorpe University, 4484 Peachtree Road NE, Atlanta, GA 30319, 404-364-8307 or toll-free 800-428-4484.

OHIO DOMINICAN UNIVERSITY
Columbus, OH

CONTACT Ms. Cynthia A. Hahn, Director of Financial Aid, Ohio Dominican University, 1216 Sunbury Road, Columbus, OH 43219, 614-251-4778 or toll-free 800-854-2670. *Fax:* 614-251-4456. *E-mail:* fin-aid@ohiodominican.edu.

OHIO NORTHERN UNIVERSITY
Ada, OH

Tuition & fees: $28,260 **Average undergraduate aid package: $22,130**

ABOUT THE INSTITUTION Independent religious, coed. Awards: bachelor's, master's, and first professional degrees and post-bachelor's certificates. 111 undergraduate majors. Total enrollment: 3,542. Undergraduates: 2,597. Freshmen: 809. Federal methodology is used as a basis for awarding need-based institutional aid.
UNDERGRADUATE EXPENSES for 2006–07 *Application fee:* $30. *Comprehensive fee:* $35,340 includes full-time tuition ($28,050), mandatory fees ($210), and room and board ($7080). *College room only:* $3540.
FRESHMAN FINANCIAL AID (Fall 2005, est.) 773 applied for aid; of those 86% were deemed to have need. 100% of freshmen with need received aid; of those 38% had need fully met. *Average percent of need met:* 91% (excluding resources awarded to replace EFC). *Average financial aid package:* $23,865 (excluding resources awarded to replace EFC). 16% of all full-time freshmen had no need and received non-need-based gift aid.
UNDERGRADUATE FINANCIAL AID (Fall 2005, est.) 2,267 applied for aid; of those 90% were deemed to have need. 100% of undergraduates with need received aid; of those 30% had need fully met. *Average percent of need met:*

Ohio Northern University

85% (excluding resources awarded to replace EFC). *Average financial aid package:* $22,130 (excluding resources awarded to replace EFC). 16% of all full-time undergraduates had no need and received non-need-based gift aid. **GIFT AID (NEED-BASED)** *Total amount:* $30,168,416 (6% federal, 9% state, 83% institutional, 2% external sources). *Receiving aid:* Freshmen: 58% (468); All full-time undergraduates: 54% (1,370). *Average award:* Freshmen: $10,000; Undergraduates: $9754. *Scholarships, grants, and awards:* Federal Pell, FSEOG, state, private, college/university gift aid from institutional funds. **GIFT AID (NON-NEED-BASED)** *Total amount:* $8,774,190 (1% federal, 6% state, 81% institutional, 12% external sources). *Receiving aid:* Freshmen: 80% (650); Undergraduates: 78% (1,958). *Average Award:* Freshmen: $13,477; *Undergraduates:* $12,417. *Scholarships, grants, and awards by category: Academic Interests/Achievement:* 1,368 awards ($15,799,969 total): biological sciences, business, communication, computer science, education, engineering/technologies, English, foreign languages, general academic interests/achievements, health fields, humanities, international studies, mathematics, physical sciences, premedicine, religion/biblical studies, social sciences. *Creative Arts/Performance:* 241 awards ($1,159,851 total): applied art and design, art/fine arts, creative writing, dance, journalism/publications, music, performing arts, theater/drama. *Special Achievements/Activities:* 257 awards ($2,485,500 total): community service, general special achievements/activities, junior miss, leadership. *Special Characteristics:* 163 awards ($2,162,503 total): children of faculty/staff, international students, relatives of clergy, religious affiliation, siblings of current students. *ROTC:* Army cooperative, Air Force cooperative. **LOANS** *Student loans:* $22,192,893 (61% need-based, 39% non-need-based). 78% of past graduating class borrowed through all loan programs. *Average indebtedness per student:* $38,203. *Average need-based loan:* Freshmen: $4410; Undergraduates: $5034. *Parent loans:* $2,199,377 (20% need-based, 80% non-need-based). *Programs:* FFEL (Subsidized and Unsubsidized Stafford, PLUS), Perkins, Federal Nursing, college/university. **WORK-STUDY** *Federal work-study:* Total amount: $2,901,445; 1,349 jobs averaging $2151. *State or other work-study/employment:* Total amount: $220,745 (45% need-based, 55% non-need-based). 96 part-time jobs averaging $2299. **APPLYING FOR FINANCIAL AID** *Required financial aid forms:* FAFSA, institution's own form. *Financial aid deadline (priority):* 4/15. *Notification date:* Continuous beginning 3/1. Students must reply within 2 weeks of notification. **CONTACT** Craig Sneider, Director of Financial Aid, Ohio Northern University, 525 South Main Street, Ada, OH 45810, 419-772-2272 or toll-free 888-408-4ONU. *Fax:* 419-772-2313. *E-mail:* c-sneider@onu.edu.

THE OHIO STATE UNIVERSITY
Columbus, OH

Tuition & fees (OH res): $8082   **Average undergraduate aid package: $9726**

ABOUT THE INSTITUTION State-supported, coed. Awards: associate, bachelor's, master's, doctoral, and first professional degrees and post-bachelor's and post-master's certificates. 170 undergraduate majors. Total enrollment: 50,504. Undergraduates: 37,411. Freshmen: 5,954. Federal methodology is used as a basis for awarding need-based institutional aid. **UNDERGRADUATE EXPENSES for 2005–06** *Application fee:* $40. *Tuition, state resident:* full-time $7929. *Tuition, nonresident:* full-time $19,152. Full-time tuition and fees vary according to course load, program, reciprocity agreements, and student level. Part-time tuition and fees vary according to course load, program, reciprocity agreements, and student level. *College room and board:* $7275. Room and board charges vary according to board plan and housing facility. *Payment plan:* Installment. **FRESHMAN FINANCIAL AID (Fall 2005, est.)** 4783 applied for aid; of those 68% were deemed to have need. 100% of freshmen with need received aid; of those 30% had need fully met. *Average percent of need met:* 72% (excluding resources awarded to replace EFC). *Average financial aid package:* $9588 (excluding resources awarded to replace EFC). 29% of all full-time freshmen had no need and received non-need-based gift aid. **UNDERGRADUATE FINANCIAL AID (Fall 2005, est.)** 22,352 applied for aid; of those 78% were deemed to have need. 100% of undergraduates with need received aid; of those 22% had need fully met. *Average percent of need met:* 69% (excluding resources awarded to replace EFC). *Average financial aid package:* $9726 (excluding resources awarded to replace EFC). 17% of all full-time undergraduates had no need and received non-need-based gift aid. **GIFT AID (NEED-BASED)** *Total amount:* $85,423,400 (26% federal, 12% state, 57% institutional, 5% external sources). *Receiving aid:* Freshmen: 52% (3,087); All full-time undergraduates: 46% (15,344). *Average award:* Freshmen: $7095; Undergraduates: $5713. *Scholarships, grants, and awards:* Federal Pell, FSEOG, state, private, college/university gift aid from institutional funds. **GIFT AID (NON-NEED-BASED)** *Total amount:* $36,252,167 (13% state, 74% institutional, 13% external sources). *Receiving aid:* Freshmen: 4% (234); Undergraduates: 2% (581). *Average Award:* Freshmen: $3645; *Undergraduates:* $4047. *Scholarships, grants, and awards by category: Academic Interests/Achievement:* agriculture, architecture, area/ethnic studies, biological sciences, business, communication, computer science, education, engineering/technologies, English, foreign languages, general academic interests/achievements, health fields, home economics, humanities, international studies, mathematics, military science, physical sciences, premedicine, social sciences. *Creative Arts/Performance:* creative writing, dance, journalism/publications, music, performing arts, theater/drama. *Special Achievements/Activities:* cheerleading/drum major, hobbies/interests, leadership, memberships. *Special Characteristics:* adult students, children and siblings of alumni, children of faculty/staff, children of public servants, children of union members/company employees, children of workers in trades, children with a deceased or disabled parent, ethnic background, handicapped students, members of minority groups, out-of-state students, previous college experience. *Tuition waivers:* Full or partial for employees or children of employees, senior citizens. *ROTC:* Army, Naval, Air Force. **LOANS** *Student loans:* $135,078,194 (67% need-based, 33% non-need-based). 58% of past graduating class borrowed through all loan programs. *Average indebtedness per student:* $17,821. *Average need-based loan:* Freshmen: $2761; Undergraduates: $4085. *Parent loans:* $45,967,676 (100% non-need-based). *Programs:* Federal Direct (Subsidized and Unsubsidized Stafford, PLUS), Perkins, Federal Nursing, college/university. **WORK-STUDY** *Federal work-study:* Total amount: $13,842,114; 4,303 jobs averaging $3322. *State or other work-study/employment:* Total amount: $253,494 (55% need-based, 45% non-need-based). **ATHLETIC AWARDS** *Total amount:* $10,859,872 (100% non-need-based). **APPLYING FOR FINANCIAL AID** *Required financial aid form:* FAFSA. *Financial aid deadline (priority):* 3/1. *Notification date:* 4/5. Students must reply by 5/1 or within 4 weeks of notification. **CONTACT** Ms. Natala Hart, Director of Student Financial Aid, The Ohio State University, 517 Lincoln Tower, 1800 Cannon Drive, Columbus, OH 43210-1230, 614-292-3600. *Fax:* 614-292-9264. *E-mail:* finaid@fa.adm.ohio-state.edu.

OHIO UNIVERSITY
Athens, OH

Tuition & fees (OH res): $8235   **Average undergraduate aid package: $6870**

ABOUT THE INSTITUTION State-supported, coed. Awards: associate, bachelor's, master's, doctoral, and first professional degrees. 173 undergraduate majors. Total enrollment: 20,396. Undergraduates: 17,191. Freshmen: 4,166. Federal methodology is used as a basis for awarding need-based institutional aid. **UNDERGRADUATE EXPENSES for 2005–06** *Application fee:* $45. *Tuition, state resident:* full-time $8235; part-time $262 per quarter hour. *Tuition, nonresident:* full-time $17,199; part-time $557 per quarter hour. *College room and board:* $7686; *room only:* $3855. Room and board charges vary according to board plan. *Payment plan:* Installment. **FRESHMAN FINANCIAL AID (Fall 2005, est.)** 3589 applied for aid; of those 61% were deemed to have need. 98% of freshmen with need received aid; of those 17% had need fully met. *Average percent of need met:* 48% (excluding resources awarded to replace EFC). *Average financial aid package:* $6318 (excluding resources awarded to replace EFC). **UNDERGRADUATE FINANCIAL AID (Fall 2005, est.)** 11,483 applied for aid; of those 69% were deemed to have need. 97% of undergraduates with need received aid; of those 17% had need fully met. *Average percent of need met:* 52% (excluding resources awarded to replace EFC). *Average financial aid package:* $6870 (excluding resources awarded to replace EFC). **GIFT AID (NEED-BASED)** *Total amount:* $12,584,740 (62% federal, 19% state, 19% institutional). *Receiving aid:* Freshmen: 22% (911); All full-time undergraduates: 19% (3,095). *Average award:* Freshmen: $4046; Undergraduates: $4206. *Scholarships, grants, and awards:* Federal Pell, FSEOG, state, private, college/university gift aid from institutional funds. **GIFT AID (NON-NEED-BASED)** *Total amount:* $18,023,182 (7% state, 77% institutional, 16% external sources). *Receiving aid:* Freshmen: 28% (1,143); Undergraduates: 16% (2,636). *Scholarships, grants, and awards by category:*

Academic Interests/Achievement: area/ethnic studies, biological sciences, business, communication, computer science, education, engineering/technologies, English, foreign languages, general academic interests/achievements, health fields, home economics, humanities, international studies, mathematics, military science, physical sciences, premedicine, social sciences. *Creative Arts/Performance:* applied art and design, art/fine arts, cinema/film/broadcasting, dance, debating, journalism/publications, music, performing arts, theater/drama. *Special Characteristics:* children of faculty/staff, members of minority groups. *Tuition waivers:* Full or partial for employees or children of employees.
ROTC: Army, Air Force.
LOANS *Student loans:* $57,283,618 (46% need-based, 54% non-need-based). 62% of past graduating class borrowed through all loan programs. *Average indebtedness per student:* $18,101. *Average need-based loan:* Freshmen: $2658; Undergraduates: $3870. *Parent loans:* $22,895,076 (100% non-need-based). *Programs:* Federal Direct (Subsidized and Unsubsidized Stafford, PLUS), Perkins, state, college/university.
WORK-STUDY *Federal work-study:* Total amount: $1,005,333; jobs available. *State or other work-study/employment:* Total amount: $11,335,684 (100% non-need-based). Part-time jobs available.
ATHLETIC AWARDS Total amount: $5,014,040 (100% non-need-based).
APPLYING FOR FINANCIAL AID *Required financial aid form:* FAFSA. *Financial aid deadline (priority):* 3/15. *Notification date:* 4/1.
CONTACT Ms. Sondra Williams, Director of Financial Aid, Ohio University, 020 Chubb Hall, Athens, OH 45701-2979, 740-593-4141. *Fax:* 740-593-4140. *E-mail:* willias1@ohio.edu.

OHIO UNIVERSITY–CHILLICOTHE
Chillicothe, OH

Tuition & fees: N/R	Average undergraduate aid package: $6923

ABOUT THE INSTITUTION State-supported, coed. Awards: associate, bachelor's, and master's degrees (offers first 2 years of most bachelor's degree programs available at the main campus in Athens; also offers several bachelor's degree programs that can be completed at this campus and several programs exclusive to this campus; also offers some graduate programs). 14 undergraduate majors. Total enrollment: 2,000. Undergraduates: 1,960. Federal methodology is used as a basis for awarding need-based institutional aid.
UNDERGRADUATE EXPENSES for 2005–06 *Application fee:* $20. *Tuition, state resident:* part-time $115 per credit hour. *Tuition, nonresident:* part-time $131 per credit hour. *Required fees:* $16 per credit hour.
FRESHMAN FINANCIAL AID (Fall 2005, est.) 247 applied for aid; of those 85% were deemed to have need. 94% of freshmen with need received aid; of those 13% had need fully met. *Average percent of need met:* 52% (excluding resources awarded to replace EFC). *Average financial aid package:* $5711 (excluding resources awarded to replace EFC).
UNDERGRADUATE FINANCIAL AID (Fall 2005, est.) 1,020 applied for aid; of those 88% were deemed to have need. 97% of undergraduates with need received aid; of those 9% had need fully met. *Average percent of need met:* 54% (excluding resources awarded to replace EFC). *Average financial aid package:* $6923 (excluding resources awarded to replace EFC).
GIFT AID (NEED-BASED) *Total amount:* $3,293,834 (69% federal, 24% state, 7% institutional). *Receiving aid:* Freshmen: 54% (144); All full-time undergraduates: 54% (650). *Average award:* Freshmen: $4389; Undergraduates: $4768. *Scholarships, grants, and awards:* Federal Pell, FSEOG, state, college/university gift aid from institutional funds.
GIFT AID (NON-NEED-BASED) *Total amount:* $326,329 (6% state, 51% institutional, 43% external sources). *Receiving aid:* Freshmen: 11% (29); Undergraduates: 6% (77). *Scholarships, grants, and awards by category:* Academic Interests/Achievement: area/ethnic studies, biological sciences, business, communication, computer science, education, engineering/technologies, English, foreign languages, general academic interests/achievements, health fields, home economics, humanities, international studies, mathematics, military science, physical sciences, premedicine, social sciences. *Creative Arts/Performance:* applied art and design, art/fine arts, cinema/film/broadcasting, dance, debating, journalism/publications, music, performing arts, theater/drama. *Special Characteristics:* children of faculty/staff, members of minority groups. **ROTC:** Army cooperative, Air Force cooperative.
LOANS *Student loans:* $5,856,971 (52% need-based, 48% non-need-based). 62% of past graduating class borrowed through all loan programs. *Average indebtedness per student:* $18,101. *Average need-based loan:* Freshmen: $2577; Undergraduates: $3421. *Parent loans:* $85,622 (100% non-need-based). *Programs:* Federal Direct (Subsidized and Unsubsidized Stafford, PLUS), Perkins, state, college/university.
WORK-STUDY *Federal work-study:* Total amount: $55,620; jobs available. *State or other work-study/employment:* Part-time jobs available.
APPLYING FOR FINANCIAL AID *Required financial aid form:* FAFSA. *Financial aid deadline (priority):* 3/15. *Notification date:* 4/1.
CONTACT Ms. Sondra Williams, Director of Financial Aid, Ohio University–Chillicothe, 020 Chubb Hall, Athens, OH 45701-2979, 740-593-4141 or toll-free 877-462-6824 (in-state). *Fax:* 740-593-4140. *E-mail:* willias1@ohio.edu.

OHIO UNIVERSITY–EASTERN
St. Clairsville, OH

Tuition & fees: N/R	Average undergraduate aid package: $6359

ABOUT THE INSTITUTION State-supported, coed. Awards: associate and bachelor's degrees (also offers some graduate courses). 77 undergraduate majors. Total enrollment: 1,118. Undergraduates: 931. Freshmen: 210. Federal methodology is used as a basis for awarding need-based institutional aid.
UNDERGRADUATE EXPENSES for 2005–06 *Application fee:* $20. *Tuition, area resident:* part-time $115 per credit hour. *Tuition, nonresident:* part-time $131 per credit hour. *Required fees:* $16 per credit hour.
FRESHMAN FINANCIAL AID (Fall 2005, est.) 119 applied for aid; of those 81% were deemed to have need. 93% of freshmen with need received aid; of those 7% had need fully met. *Average percent of need met:* 51% (excluding resources awarded to replace EFC). *Average financial aid package:* $4533 (excluding resources awarded to replace EFC).
UNDERGRADUATE FINANCIAL AID (Fall 2005, est.) 463 applied for aid; of those 84% were deemed to have need. 94% of undergraduates with need received aid; of those 13% had need fully met. *Average percent of need met:* 56% (excluding resources awarded to replace EFC). *Average financial aid package:* $6359 (excluding resources awarded to replace EFC).
GIFT AID (NEED-BASED) *Total amount:* $1,140,844 (70% federal, 21% state, 9% institutional). *Receiving aid:* Freshmen: 48% (63); All full-time undergraduates: 44% (249). *Average award:* Freshmen: $3697; Undergraduates: $4377. *Scholarships, grants, and awards:* Federal Pell, FSEOG, state, private, college/university gift aid from institutional funds.
GIFT AID (NON-NEED-BASED) *Total amount:* $220,984 (8% state, 81% institutional, 11% external sources). *Receiving aid:* Freshmen: 21% (28); Undergraduates: 12% (69). *Scholarships, grants, and awards by category:* Academic Interests/Achievement: area/ethnic studies, biological sciences, business, communication, computer science, education, engineering/technologies, English, foreign languages, general academic interests/achievements, health fields, home economics, humanities, international studies, mathematics, military science, physical sciences, premedicine, social sciences. *Creative Arts/Performance:* applied art and design, art/fine arts, cinema/film/broadcasting, dance, debating, journalism/publications, music, performing arts, theater/drama. *Special Characteristics:* children of faculty/staff, members of minority groups.
LOANS *Student loans:* $2,008,837 (60% need-based, 40% non-need-based). 62% of past graduating class borrowed through all loan programs. *Average indebtedness per student:* $18,101. *Average need-based loan:* Freshmen: $2492; Undergraduates: $3755. *Parent loans:* $31,001 (100% non-need-based). *Programs:* Federal Direct (Subsidized and Unsubsidized Stafford, PLUS), Perkins, state, college/university.
WORK-STUDY *Federal work-study:* Total amount: $37,080; jobs available. *State or other work-study/employment:* Part-time jobs available.
APPLYING FOR FINANCIAL AID *Required financial aid form:* FAFSA. *Financial aid deadline (priority):* 3/15. *Notification date:* 4/1.
CONTACT Ms. Sondra Williams, Director of Financial Aid, Ohio University–Eastern, 020 Chubb Hall, Athens, OH 45701-2979, 740-593-4141 or toll-free 800-648-3331 (in-state). *Fax:* 740-593-4140. *E-mail:* willias1@ohio.edu.

OHIO UNIVERSITY–LANCASTER
Lancaster, OH

Tuition & fees: N/R	Average undergraduate aid package: $6182

Ohio University–Lancaster

ABOUT THE INSTITUTION State-supported, coed. Awards: associate, bachelor's, and master's degrees. 20 undergraduate majors. Total enrollment: 1,744. Undergraduates: 1,617. Freshmen: 308. Federal methodology is used as a basis for awarding need-based institutional aid.

UNDERGRADUATE EXPENSES for 2005–06 *Application fee:* $20. *Tuition, state resident:* part-time $127 per credit hour. *Tuition, nonresident:* part-time $144 per credit hour. *Required fees:* $17 per credit hour.

FRESHMAN FINANCIAL AID (Fall 2005, est.) 262 applied for aid; of those 76% were deemed to have need. 95% of freshmen with need received aid; of those 13% had need fully met. *Average percent of need met:* 54% (excluding resources awarded to replace EFC). *Average financial aid package:* $5182 (excluding resources awarded to replace EFC).

UNDERGRADUATE FINANCIAL AID (Fall 2005, est.) 835 applied for aid; of those 81% were deemed to have need. 96% of undergraduates with need received aid; of those 10% had need fully met. *Average percent of need met:* 54% (excluding resources awarded to replace EFC). *Average financial aid package:* $6182 (excluding resources awarded to replace EFC).

GIFT AID (NEED-BASED) *Total amount:* $1,897,331 (69% federal, 23% state, 8% institutional). *Receiving aid:* Freshmen: 44% (121); All full-time undergraduates: 46% (424). *Average award:* Freshmen: $3872; Undergraduates: $4207. *Scholarships, grants, and awards:* Federal Pell, FSEOG, state, private, college/university gift aid from institutional funds.

GIFT AID (NON-NEED-BASED) *Total amount:* $479,315 (4% state, 74% institutional, 22% external sources). *Receiving aid:* Freshmen: 21% (57); Undergraduates: 11% (97). *Scholarships, grants, and awards by category: Academic Interests/Achievement:* area/ethnic studies, biological sciences, business, communication, computer science, education, engineering/technologies, English, foreign languages, general academic interests/achievements, health fields, home economics, humanities, international studies, mathematics, military science, physical sciences, premedicine, social sciences. *Creative Arts/Performance:* applied art and design, art/fine arts, cinema/film/broadcasting, dance, debating, journalism/publications, music, performing arts, theater/drama. *Special Characteristics:* children of faculty/staff, members of minority groups. *ROTC:* Army cooperative, Air Force cooperative.

LOANS *Student loans:* $4,385,825 (54% need-based, 46% non-need-based). 62% of past graduating class borrowed through all loan programs. *Average indebtedness per student:* $18,101. *Average need-based loan:* Freshmen: $2583; Undergraduates: $3579. *Parent loans:* $76,647 (100% non-need-based). *Programs:* Federal Direct (Subsidized and Unsubsidized Stafford, PLUS), Perkins, state, college/university.

WORK-STUDY *Federal work-study:* Total amount: $45,856; jobs available. *State or other work-study/employment:* Part-time jobs available.

APPLYING FOR FINANCIAL AID *Required financial aid form:* FAFSA. *Financial aid deadline (priority):* 3/15. *Notification date:* 4/1.

CONTACT Ms. Sondra Williams, Director of Financial Aid, Ohio University–Lancaster, 020 Chubb Hall, Athens, OH 45701-2979, 740-593-4141 or toll-free 888-446-4468 Ext. 215. *Fax:* 740-593-4140. *E-mail:* willias1@ohio.edu.

OHIO UNIVERSITY–SOUTHERN CAMPUS
Ironton, OH

Tuition & fees: N/R	Average undergraduate aid package: $7284

ABOUT THE INSTITUTION State-supported, coed. Awards: associate, bachelor's, and master's degrees. 20 undergraduate majors. Total enrollment: 1,746. Undergraduates: 1,630. Freshmen: 348. Federal methodology is used as a basis for awarding need-based institutional aid.

UNDERGRADUATE EXPENSES for 2005–06 *Application fee:* $20. *Tuition, state resident:* part-time $124 per credit hour. *Tuition, nonresident:* part-time $165 per credit hour. *Required fees:* $12 per credit hour. Full-time tuition and fees vary according to student level. Part-time tuition and fees vary according to student level. *Payment plan:* Installment.

FRESHMAN FINANCIAL AID (Fall 2005, est.) 284 applied for aid; of those 86% were deemed to have need. 98% of freshmen with need received aid; of those 11% had need fully met. *Average percent of need met:* 51% (excluding resources awarded to replace EFC). *Average financial aid package:* $6076 (excluding resources awarded to replace EFC).

UNDERGRADUATE FINANCIAL AID (Fall 2005, est.) 1,148 applied for aid; of those 90% were deemed to have need. 98% of undergraduates with need received aid; of those 7% had need fully met. *Average percent of need met:* 55% (excluding resources awarded to replace EFC). *Average financial aid package:* $7284 (excluding resources awarded to replace EFC).

GIFT AID (NEED-BASED) *Total amount:* $3,995,914 (73% federal, 19% state, 8% institutional). *Receiving aid:* Freshmen: 67% (192); All full-time undergraduates: 63% (817). *Average award:* Freshmen: $4354; Undergraduates: $4661. *Scholarships, grants, and awards:* Federal Pell, FSEOG, state, private, college/university gift aid from institutional funds.

GIFT AID (NON-NEED-BASED) *Total amount:* $293,285 (8% state, 74% institutional, 18% external sources). *Receiving aid:* Freshmen: 19% (54); Undergraduates: 12% (157). *Scholarships, grants, and awards by category: Academic Interests/Achievement:* area/ethnic studies, biological sciences, business, communication, computer science, education, engineering/technologies, English, foreign languages, general academic interests/achievements, health fields, home economics, humanities, international studies, mathematics, military science, physical sciences, premedicine, social sciences. *Creative Arts/Performance:* applied art and design, art/fine arts, cinema/film/broadcasting, dance, debating, journalism/publications, music, performing arts, theater/drama. *Special Characteristics:* children of faculty/staff, members of minority groups. *Tuition waivers:* Full or partial for employees or children of employees, senior citizens.

LOANS *Student loans:* $6,337,796 (56% need-based, 44% non-need-based). 62% of past graduating class borrowed through all loan programs. *Average indebtedness per student:* $18,101. *Average need-based loan:* Freshmen: $2586; Undergraduates: $3592. *Parent loans:* $67,632 (100% non-need-based). *Programs:* Federal Direct (Subsidized and Unsubsidized Stafford, PLUS), Perkins, state, college/university.

WORK-STUDY *Federal work-study:* Total amount: $58,710; jobs available. *State or other work-study/employment:* Part-time jobs available.

APPLYING FOR FINANCIAL AID *Required financial aid form:* FAFSA. *Financial aid deadline (priority):* 3/15. *Notification date:* 4/1.

CONTACT Ms. Sondra Williams, Director of Financial Aid, Ohio University–Southern Campus, 020 Chubb Hall, Athens, OH 45701-2979, 740-593-4141 or toll-free 800-626-0513. *Fax:* 740-593-4140. *E-mail:* willias1@ohio.edu.

OHIO UNIVERSITY–ZANESVILLE
Zanesville, OH

Tuition & fees (OH res): $4596	Average undergraduate aid package: $6369

ABOUT THE INSTITUTION State-supported, coed. Awards: associate, bachelor's, and master's degrees (offers first 2 years of most bachelor's degree programs available at the main campus in Athens; also offers several bachelor's degree programs that can be completed at this campus; also offers some graduate courses). 9 undergraduate majors. Total enrollment: 1,904. Undergraduates: 1,849. Freshmen: 356. Federal methodology is used as a basis for awarding need-based institutional aid.

UNDERGRADUATE EXPENSES for 2005–06 *Application fee:* $20. *Tuition, state resident:* full-time $4596; part-time $144 per credit hour. *Tuition, nonresident:* full-time $8919; part-time $275 per credit hour. Full-time tuition and fees vary according to course level. Part-time tuition and fees vary according to course level.

FRESHMAN FINANCIAL AID (Fall 2005, est.) 270 applied for aid; of those 81% were deemed to have need. 96% of freshmen with need received aid; of those 27% had need fully met. *Average percent of need met:* 58% (excluding resources awarded to replace EFC). *Average financial aid package:* $5594 (excluding resources awarded to replace EFC).

UNDERGRADUATE FINANCIAL AID (Fall 2005, est.) 1,029 applied for aid; of those 85% were deemed to have need. 96% of undergraduates with need received aid; of those 14% had need fully met. *Average percent of need met:* 55% (excluding resources awarded to replace EFC). *Average financial aid package:* $6369 (excluding resources awarded to replace EFC).

GIFT AID (NEED-BASED) *Total amount:* $2,683,803 (70% federal, 21% state, 9% institutional). *Receiving aid:* Freshmen: 45% (127); All full-time undergraduates: 50% (574). *Average award:* Freshmen: $4117; Undergraduates: $4326. *Scholarships, grants, and awards:* Federal Pell, FSEOG, state, private, college/university gift aid from institutional funds.

GIFT AID (NON-NEED-BASED) *Total amount:* $852,348 (6% state, 74% institutional, 20% external sources). *Receiving aid:* Freshmen: 34% (96); Undergraduates: 18% (203). *Scholarships, grants, and awards by category: Academic Interests/Achievement:* area/ethnic studies, biological sciences, busi-

ness, communication, computer science, education, engineering/technologies, English, foreign languages, general academic interests/achievements, health fields, home economics, humanities, international studies, mathematics, military science, physical sciences, premedicine, social sciences. *Creative Arts/Performance:* applied art and design, art/fine arts, cinema/film/broadcasting, dance, debating, journalism/publications, music, performing arts, theater/drama. *Special Characteristics:* children of faculty/staff, members of minority groups. *Tuition waivers:* Full or partial for employees or children of employees, senior citizens.
LOANS *Student loans:* $4,734,358 (56% need-based, 44% non-need-based). 62% of past graduating class borrowed through all loan programs. *Average indebtedness per student:* $18,101. *Average need-based loan:* Freshmen $2449; Undergraduates: $3474. *Parent loans:* $40,433 (100% non-need-based). *Programs:* Federal Direct (Subsidized and Unsubsidized Stafford, PLUS), Perkins, state, college/university.
WORK-STUDY *Federal work-study:* Total amount: $74,425; jobs available. *State or other work-study/employment:* Part-time jobs available.
APPLYING FOR FINANCIAL AID *Required financial aid form:* FAFSA. *Financial aid deadline (priority):* 3/15. *Notification date:* 4/1.
CONTACT Ms. Sondra Williams, Director of Financial Aid, Ohio University–Zanesville, 020 Chubb Hall, Athens, OH 45701-2979, 740-593-4141. *Fax:* 740-593-4140. *E-mail:* willias1@ohio.edu.

OHIO VALLEY UNIVERSITY
Vienna, WV

ABOUT THE INSTITUTION Independent religious, coed. Awards: associate and bachelor's degrees. 19 undergraduate majors. Total enrollment: 542. Undergraduates: 542. Freshmen: 86.
GIFT AID (NEED-BASED) *Scholarships, grants, and awards:* Federal Pell, FSEOG, state, private, college/university gift aid from institutional funds.
GIFT AID (NON-NEED-BASED) *Scholarships, grants, and awards by category:* Academic Interests/Achievement: education, English, general academic interests/achievements, religion/biblical studies. *Creative Arts/Performance:* general creative arts/performance, journalism/publications, music, performing arts, theater/drama. *Special Achievements/Activities:* community service, general special achievements/activities, leadership, religious involvement. *Special Characteristics:* adult students, children of faculty/staff, ethnic background, general special characteristics, international students, local/state students, relatives of clergy, religious affiliation.
LOANS *Programs:* FFEL (Subsidized and Unsubsidized Stafford, PLUS), Perkins.
WORK-STUDY *Federal work-study:* Total amount: $121,048; 181 jobs averaging $800. *State or other work-study/employment:* Total amount: $80,778 (100% non-need-based). 102 part-time jobs averaging $800.
APPLYING FOR FINANCIAL AID *Required financial aid form:* FAFSA.
CONTACT Marjorie W. Lyons, Director of Financial Aid, Ohio Valley University, 1 Campus View Drive, Vienna, WV 26105-8000, 304-865-6077 or toll-free 877-446-8668 Ext. 6200 (out-of-state). *Fax:* 304-865-6001. *E-mail:* mlyons@ovc.edu.

OHIO WESLEYAN UNIVERSITY
Delaware, OH

Tuition & fees: $28,280 | **Average undergraduate aid package: $20,854**

ABOUT THE INSTITUTION Independent United Methodist, coed. Awards: bachelor's degrees. 90 undergraduate majors. Total enrollment: 1,976. Undergraduates: 1,976. Freshmen: 594. Federal methodology is used as a basis for awarding need-based institutional aid.
UNDERGRADUATE EXPENSES for 2005–06 *Application fee:* $35. *Comprehensive fee:* $35,830 includes full-time tuition ($27,920), mandatory fees ($360), and room and board ($7550). *College room only:* $3750. Room and board charges vary according to board plan. *Part-time tuition:* $3040 per course. *Payment plan:* Installment.
FRESHMAN FINANCIAL AID (Fall 2005, est.) 420 applied for aid; of those 84% were deemed to have need. 100% of freshmen with need received aid; of those 30% had need fully met. *Average percent of need met:* 85% (excluding resources awarded to replace EFC). *Average financial aid package:* $21,893 (excluding resources awarded to replace EFC). 40% of all full-time freshmen had no need and received non-need-based gift aid.
UNDERGRADUATE FINANCIAL AID (Fall 2005, est.) 1,274 applied for aid; of those 85% were deemed to have need. 100% of undergraduates with need received aid; of those 28% had need fully met. *Average percent of need met:* 82% (excluding resources awarded to replace EFC). *Average financial aid package:* $20,854 (excluding resources awarded to replace EFC). 41% of all full-time undergraduates had no need and received non-need-based gift aid.
GIFT AID (NEED-BASED) *Total amount:* $18,319,286 (7% federal, 7% state, 84% institutional, 2% external sources). *Receiving aid:* Freshmen: 59% (351); All full-time undergraduates: 56% (1,085). *Average award:* Freshmen: $15,595; Undergraduates: $14,473. *Scholarships, grants, and awards:* Federal Pell, FSEOG, state, private, college/university gift aid from institutional funds.
GIFT AID (NON-NEED-BASED) *Total amount:* $10,573,635 (3% state, 96% institutional, 1% external sources). *Receiving aid:* Freshmen: 8% (48); Undergraduates: 6% (123). *Average Award:* Freshmen: $11,747; Undergraduates: $11,439. *Scholarships, grants, and awards by category:* Academic Interests/Achievement: 949 awards ($18,687,367 total): area/ethnic studies, biological sciences, business, communication, computer science, education, engineering/technologies, English, foreign languages, general academic interests/achievements, health fields, humanities, international studies, mathematics, physical sciences, premedicine, religion/biblical studies, social sciences. *Creative Arts/Performance:* 44 awards ($1,232,072 total): art/fine arts, dance, music, theater/drama. *Special Achievements/Activities:* 42 awards ($605,581 total): community service, leadership, religious involvement. *Special Characteristics:* 735 awards ($10,269,965 total): children and siblings of alumni, children of faculty/staff, ethnic background, international students, local/state students, members of minority groups, out-of-state students, relatives of clergy, religious affiliation. *Tuition waivers:* Full or partial for children of alumni, employees or children of employees. *ROTC:* Army cooperative.
LOANS *Student loans:* $6,337,598 (71% need-based, 29% non-need-based). 60% of past graduating class borrowed through all loan programs. *Average indebtedness per student:* $22,619. *Average need-based loan:* Freshmen: $3245; Undergraduates: $3525. *Parent loans:* $3,014,540 (100% non-need-based). *Programs:* FFEL (Subsidized and Unsubsidized Stafford, PLUS), Perkins, state, college/university.
WORK-STUDY *Federal work-study:* Total amount: $1,148,971; 800 jobs averaging $1436. *State or other work-study/employment:* Total amount: $273,725 (30% need-based, 70% non-need-based). 302 part-time jobs averaging $906.
APPLYING FOR FINANCIAL AID *Required financial aid forms:* FAFSA, institution's own form. *Financial aid deadline:* 5/1 (priority: 3/1). *Notification date:* Continuous beginning 2/1. Students must reply by 5/1 or within 2 weeks of notification.
CONTACT Mr. Gregory W. Matthews, Director of Financial Aid, Ohio Wesleyan University, 61 South Sandusky Street, Delaware, OH 43015, 740-368-3050 or toll-free 800-922-8953. *Fax:* 740-368-3066. *E-mail:* owfinaid@owu.edu.

OHR HAMEIR THEOLOGICAL SEMINARY
Peekskill, NY

CONTACT Financial Aid Office, Ohr Hameir Theological Seminary, Furnace Woods Road, Peekskill, NY 10566, 914-736-1500.

OHR SOMAYACH/JOSEPH TANENBAUM EDUCATIONAL CENTER
Monsey, NY

CONTACT Financial Aid Office, Ohr Somayach/Joseph Tanenbaum Educational Center, PO Box 334244, Route 306, Monsey, NY 10952-0334, 914-425-1370.

OKLAHOMA BAPTIST UNIVERSITY
Shawnee, OK

Tuition & fees: $13,846 | **Average undergraduate aid package: $12,278**

ABOUT THE INSTITUTION Independent Southern Baptist, coed. Awards: bachelor's and master's degrees. 100 undergraduate majors. Total enrollment: 1,883. Undergraduates: 1,866. Freshmen: 411. Federal methodology is used as a basis for awarding need-based institutional aid.
UNDERGRADUATE EXPENSES for 2005–06 *Application fee:* $25. *Comprehensive fee:* $17,986 includes full-time tuition ($12,924), mandatory fees ($922), and room and board ($4140). *College room only:* $1840. Full-time tuition and fees

Oklahoma Baptist University

vary according to course load. Room and board charges vary according to board plan and housing facility. Part-time tuition and fees vary according to course load. *Payment plan:* Installment.

FRESHMAN FINANCIAL AID (Fall 2005, est.) 340 applied for aid; of those 73% were deemed to have need. 100% of freshmen with need received aid; of those 62% had need fully met. *Average percent of need met:* 65% (excluding resources awarded to replace EFC). *Average financial aid package:* $12,983 (excluding resources awarded to replace EFC). 25% of all full-time freshmen had no need and received non-need-based gift aid.

UNDERGRADUATE FINANCIAL AID (Fall 2005, est.) 1,305 applied for aid; of those 73% were deemed to have need. 100% of undergraduates with need received aid; of those 52% had need fully met. *Average percent of need met:* 70% (excluding resources awarded to replace EFC). *Average financial aid package:* $12,278 (excluding resources awarded to replace EFC). 21% of all full-time undergraduates had no need and received non-need-based gift aid.

GIFT AID (NEED-BASED) *Total amount:* $1,990,753 (54% federal, 31% state, 15% institutional). *Receiving aid:* Freshmen: 63% (233); All full-time undergraduates: 54% (885). *Average award:* Freshmen: $3843; Undergraduates: $3700. *Scholarships, grants, and awards:* Federal Pell, FSEOG, state, private, college/university gift aid from institutional funds.

GIFT AID (NON-NEED-BASED) *Total amount:* $7,632,988 (1% state, 82% institutional, 17% external sources). *Receiving aid:* Freshmen: 60% (222); Undergraduates: 49% (809). *Average Award:* Freshmen: $5878; Undergraduates: $5240. *Scholarships, grants, and awards by category:* Academic Interests/Achievement: general academic interests/achievements, religion/biblical studies. *Creative Arts/Performance:* art/fine arts, music, performing arts. *Special Achievements/Activities:* leadership, religious involvement. *Special Characteristics:* children and siblings of alumni, children of faculty/staff, general special characteristics, local/state students, out-of-state students, relatives of clergy, religious affiliation. *Tuition waivers:* Full or partial for employees or children of employees, senior citizens. *ROTC:* Air Force cooperative.

LOANS *Student loans:* $4,275,730 (52% need-based, 48% non-need-based). 51% of past graduating class borrowed through all loan programs. *Average indebtedness per student:* $16,614. *Average need-based loan:* Freshmen: $3209; Undergraduates: $3871. *Parent loans:* $1,012,021 (100% non-need-based). *Programs:* FFEL (Subsidized and Unsubsidized Stafford, PLUS), Perkins.

WORK-STUDY *Federal work-study:* Total amount: $196,325; 303 jobs averaging $834. *State or other work-study/employment:* Total amount: $500,000 (100% non-need-based). Part-time jobs available.

ATHLETIC AWARDS *Total amount:* $1,522,122 (100% non-need-based).

APPLYING FOR FINANCIAL AID *Required financial aid form:* FAFSA. *Financial aid deadline (priority):* 3/1. *Notification date:* Continuous. Students must reply by 5/1 or within 2 weeks of notification.

CONTACT Student Financial Services, Oklahoma Baptist University, 500 West University, Shawnee, OK 74804, 405-878-2016 or toll-free 800-654-3285.

OKLAHOMA CHRISTIAN UNIVERSITY
Oklahoma City, OK

CONTACT Missi Bryant, Director of Financial Services, Oklahoma Christian University, Box 11000, Oklahoma City, OK 73136-1100, 405-425-5190 or toll-free 800-877-5010 (in-state). *Fax:* 405-425-5197. *E-mail:* missi.bryant@oc.edu.

OKLAHOMA CITY UNIVERSITY
Oklahoma City, OK

ABOUT THE INSTITUTION Independent United Methodist, coed. Awards: bachelor's, master's, and first professional degrees. 74 undergraduate majors. Total enrollment: 3,688. Undergraduates: 1,911. Freshmen: 370.

GIFT AID (NEED-BASED) *Scholarships, grants, and awards:* Federal Pell, FSEOG, state, private, college/university gift aid from institutional funds, United Negro College Fund, Federal Nursing, Native American Grants.

GIFT AID (NON-NEED-BASED) *Scholarships, grants, and awards by category:* Academic Interests/Achievement: business, communication, education, general academic interests/achievements, health fields, religion/biblical studies. *Creative Arts/Performance:* applied art and design, art/fine arts, dance, music, performing arts, theater/drama. *Special Achievements/Activities:* cheerleading/drum major, general special achievements/activities, junior miss, leadership, religious involvement. *Special Characteristics:* children of faculty/staff, relatives of clergy.

LOANS *Programs:* FFEL (Subsidized and Unsubsidized Stafford, PLUS), Perkins, Federal Nursing.

APPLYING FOR FINANCIAL AID *Required financial aid form:* FAFSA.

CONTACT Denise Flis, Financial Aid Director, Oklahoma City University, 2501 North Blackwelder, Oklahoma City, OK 73106-1493, 405-208-5848 or toll-free 800-633-7242. *Fax:* 405-208-5466. *E-mail:* dflis@okcu.edu.

OKLAHOMA PANHANDLE STATE UNIVERSITY
Goodwell, OK

Tuition & fees (OK res): $3392   **Average undergraduate aid package: N/A**

ABOUT THE INSTITUTION State-supported, coed. Awards: associate and bachelor's degrees. 32 undergraduate majors. Total enrollment: 1,144. Undergraduates: 1,144. Freshmen: 207. Both federal and institutional methodology are used as a basis for awarding need-based institutional aid.

UNDERGRADUATE EXPENSES for 2005–06 *Tuition, state resident:* full-time $2274; part-time $75.80 per hour. *Tuition, nonresident:* full-time $4500; part-time $150 per hour. *Required fees:* full-time $1118; $34.50 per hour or $62 per term part-time. Full-time tuition and fees vary according to course level and program. Part-time tuition and fees vary according to course level. *College room and board:* $4270; *room only:* $2520. Room and board charges vary according to board plan, housing facility, and student level. *Payment plan:* Installment.

GIFT AID (NEED-BASED) *Total amount:* $1,965,587 (69% federal, 12% state, 7% institutional, 12% external sources). *Scholarships, grants, and awards:* Federal Pell, FSEOG, state, private, college/university gift aid from institutional funds.

GIFT AID (NON-NEED-BASED) *Scholarships, grants, and awards by category:* Academic Interests/Achievement: agriculture, education, English, general academic interests/achievements, health fields, mathematics, physical sciences. *Creative Arts/Performance:* art/fine arts, debating, music, performing arts, theater/drama. *Special Achievements/Activities:* cheerleading/drum major, general special achievements/activities, rodeo. *Special Characteristics:* children of faculty/staff, general special characteristics, local/state students, out-of-state students, veterans, veterans' children. *Tuition waivers:* Full or partial for employees or children of employees.

LOANS *Student loans:* $2,022,367 (100% need-based). *Parent loans:* $40,308 (100% need-based). *Programs:* FFEL (Subsidized and Unsubsidized Stafford, PLUS), Perkins.

WORK-STUDY *Federal work-study:* Total amount: $42,116; 36 jobs averaging $1330. *State or other work-study/employment:* Total amount: $264,477 (100% need-based). 241 part-time jobs averaging $1494.

ATHLETIC AWARDS *Total amount:* $217,759 (100% need-based).

APPLYING FOR FINANCIAL AID *Required financial aid form:* FAFSA. *Financial aid deadline (priority):* 3/15. *Notification date:* 5/1. Students must reply by 8/1.

CONTACT Ms. Mary Ellen Riley, Director of Financial Aid, Oklahoma Panhandle State University, PO Box 430, Goodwell, OK 73939-0430, 580-349-2611 Ext. 324 or toll-free 800-664-6778. *E-mail:* mriley@opsu.edu.

OKLAHOMA STATE UNIVERSITY
Stillwater, OK

Tuition & fees (OK res): $4365   **Average undergraduate aid package: $8867**

ABOUT THE INSTITUTION State-supported, coed. Awards: bachelor's, master's, doctoral, and first professional degrees and post-master's certificates. 81 undergraduate majors. Total enrollment: 23,461. Undergraduates: 18,909. Freshmen: 3,315. Federal methodology is used as a basis for awarding need-based institutional aid.

UNDERGRADUATE EXPENSES for 2005–06 *Application fee:* $40. *Tuition, state resident:* full-time $3099; part-time $103.30 per credit hour. *Tuition, nonresident:* full-time $11,122; part-time $370.75 per credit hour. *Required fees:* full-time $1266; $42.21 per credit hour. Full-time tuition and fees vary according to program and student level. Part-time tuition and fees vary according to program and student level. *College room and board:* $5848; *room only:* $2848. Room and board charges vary according to board plan, housing facility, and location. *Payment plan:* Installment.

FRESHMAN FINANCIAL AID (Fall 2005, est.) 2127 applied for aid; of those 69% were deemed to have need. 97% of freshmen with need received aid; of those 19% had need fully met. *Average percent of need met:* 74% (excluding resources awarded to replace EFC). *Average financial aid package:* $8669 (excluding resources awarded to replace EFC). 33% of all full-time freshmen had no need and received non-need-based gift aid.

UNDERGRADUATE FINANCIAL AID (Fall 2005, est.) 11,351 applied for aid; of those 77% were deemed to have need. 97% of undergraduates with need received aid; of those 19% had need fully met. *Average percent of need met:* 73% (excluding resources awarded to replace EFC). *Average financial aid package:* $8867 (excluding resources awarded to replace EFC). 23% of all full-time undergraduates had no need and received non-need-based gift aid.

GIFT AID (NEED-BASED) *Total amount:* $26,459,000 (52% federal, 26% state, 11% institutional, 11% external sources). *Receiving aid:* Freshmen: 33% (1,064); All full-time undergraduates: 36% (5,980). *Average award:* Freshmen: $4326; Undergraduates: $3714. *Scholarships, grants, and awards:* Federal Pell, FSEOG, state, private, college/university gift aid from institutional funds.

GIFT AID (NON-NEED-BASED) *Total amount:* $11,162,000 (29% federal, 16% state, 29% institutional, 26% external sources). *Receiving aid:* Freshmen: 27% (867); Undergraduates: 22% (3,670). *Average Award:* Freshmen: $3321; *Undergraduates:* $3396. *Scholarships, grants, and awards by category: Academic Interests/Achievement:* agriculture, architecture, area/ethnic studies, biological sciences, business, communication, computer science, education, engineering/technologies, English, foreign languages, general academic interests/achievements, home economics, humanities, international studies, mathematics, military science, physical sciences, premedicine, social sciences. *Creative Arts/Performance:* art/fine arts, creative writing, general creative arts/performance, journalism/publications, music, theater/drama. *Special Achievements/Activities:* cheerleading/drum major, community service, general special achievements/activities, leadership, memberships, rodeo. *Special Characteristics:* adult students, children and siblings of alumni, first-generation college students, general special characteristics, handicapped students, out-of-state students, previous college experience. *Tuition waivers:* Full or partial for children of alumni. *ROTC:* Army, Air Force.

LOANS *Student loans:* $53,225,000 (56% need-based, 44% non-need-based). 56% of past graduating class borrowed through all loan programs. *Average indebtedness per student:* $17,844. *Average need-based loan:* Freshmen: $2582; Undergraduates: $4035. *Parent loans:* $26,905,000 (18% need-based, 82% non-need-based). *Programs:* Federal Direct (Subsidized and Unsubsidized Stafford, PLUS), Perkins, college/university.

WORK-STUDY *Federal work-study:* Total amount: $894,000; 430 jobs averaging $2079. *State or other work-study/employment:* Total amount: $8,540,000 (100% non-need-based). 3,730 part-time jobs averaging $2290.

ATHLETIC AWARDS *Total amount:* $2,722,000 (34% need-based, 66% non-need-based).

APPLYING FOR FINANCIAL AID *Required financial aid form:* FAFSA. *Financial aid deadline:* Continuous. *Notification date:* Continuous beginning 3/15. Students must reply within 2 weeks of notification.

CONTACT Office of Scholarships and Financial Aid, Oklahoma State University, 119 Student Union, Stillwater, OK 74078-5061, 405-744-6604 or toll-free 800-233-5019 (in-state), 800-852-1255 (out-of-state). *Fax:* 405-744-6438. *E-mail:* finaid@okstate.edu.

OKLAHOMA WESLEYAN UNIVERSITY
Bartlesville, OK

ABOUT THE INSTITUTION Independent religious, coed. Awards: associate, bachelor's, and master's degrees. 37 undergraduate majors. Total enrollment: 887. Undergraduates: 887. Freshmen: 112.

GIFT AID (NEED-BASED) *Scholarships, grants, and awards:* Federal Pell, FSEOG, state, private, college/university gift aid from institutional funds.

GIFT AID (NON-NEED-BASED) *Scholarships, grants, and awards by category: Academic Interests/Achievement:* biological sciences, computer science, education, general academic interests/achievements, religion/biblical studies. *Creative Arts/Performance:* debating, music. *Special Achievements/Activities:* religious involvement. *Special Characteristics:* children and siblings of alumni, children of educators, children of faculty/staff, international students, relatives of clergy, religious affiliation.

LOANS *Programs:* FFEL (Subsidized and Unsubsidized Stafford, PLUS), Perkins, college/university.

APPLYING FOR FINANCIAL AID *Required financial aid forms:* FAFSA, institution's own form.

CONTACT Lee Kanakis, Director of Financial Aid, Oklahoma Wesleyan University, 2201 Silver Lake Road, Bartlesville, OK 74006, 918-335-6282 or toll-free 866-222-8226 (in-state). *Fax:* 918-335-6811. *E-mail:* financialaid@okwu.edu.

OLD DOMINION UNIVERSITY
Norfolk, VA

ABOUT THE INSTITUTION State-supported, coed. Awards: bachelor's, master's, and doctoral degrees and post-master's certificates. 84 undergraduate majors. Total enrollment: 21,274. Undergraduates: 15,275. Freshmen: 2,094.

GIFT AID (NEED-BASED) *Scholarships, grants, and awards:* Federal Pell, FSEOG, state, private, college/university gift aid from institutional funds, United Negro College Fund, Federal Nursing.

GIFT AID (NON-NEED-BASED) *Scholarships, grants, and awards by category: Academic Interests/Achievement:* biological sciences, business, engineering/technologies, English, general academic interests/achievements, health fields, humanities, military science, physical sciences. *Creative Arts/Performance:* art/fine arts, dance, music, performing arts, theater/drama. *Special Achievements/Activities:* cheerleading/drum major, community service, leadership, memberships. *Special Characteristics:* children of faculty/staff, handicapped students, international students, local/state students, members of minority groups, previous college experience, veterans' children.

LOANS *Programs:* Federal Direct (Subsidized and Unsubsidized Stafford, PLUS), Perkins.

WORK-STUDY *Federal work-study:* Total amount: $1,385,747; jobs available.

APPLYING FOR FINANCIAL AID *Required financial aid form:* FAFSA.

CONTACT Betty Diamond, Director of Student Financial Aid, Old Dominion University, 121 Rollins Hall, Norfolk, VA 23529, 757-683-3690 or toll-free 800-348-7926. *E-mail:* bdiamond@odu.edu.

OLIVET COLLEGE
Olivet, MI

ABOUT THE INSTITUTION Independent religious, coed. Awards: bachelor's and master's degrees. 38 undergraduate majors. Total enrollment: 1,069. Undergraduates: 1,023. Freshmen: 198.

GIFT AID (NEED-BASED) *Scholarships, grants, and awards:* Federal Pell, FSEOG, state, private, college/university gift aid from institutional funds.

GIFT AID (NON-NEED-BASED) *Scholarships, grants, and awards by category: Academic Interests/Achievement:* business, communication, education, English, foreign languages, general academic interests/achievements. *Creative Arts/Performance:* art/fine arts, journalism/publications, music. *Special Achievements/Activities:* community service, leadership, memberships. *Special Characteristics:* children and siblings of alumni, children of faculty/staff, international students, religious affiliation, siblings of current students.

LOANS *Programs:* FFEL (Subsidized and Unsubsidized Stafford, PLUS), Perkins, state, Key Alternative Loans, CitiAssist Loans MI-Loan, Signature Loan.

APPLYING FOR FINANCIAL AID *Required financial aid form:* FAFSA.

CONTACT Mr. Douglas Gilbertson, Director of Admissions, Olivet College, 320 South Main Street, Olivet, MI 49076-9701, 800-456-7189 Ext. 7635 or toll-free 800-456-7189. *Fax:* 269-269-6617.

OLIVET NAZARENE UNIVERSITY
Bourbonnais, IL

Tuition & fees: $16,490	Average undergraduate aid package: $12,033

ABOUT THE INSTITUTION Independent religious, coed. Awards: associate, bachelor's, and master's degrees. 77 undergraduate majors. Total enrollment: 4,364. Undergraduates: 2,633. Freshmen: 703. Federal methodology is used as a basis for awarding need-based institutional aid.

UNDERGRADUATE EXPENSES for 2005–06 *Comprehensive fee:* $22,590 includes full-time tuition ($15,650), mandatory fees ($840), and room and board ($6100). *College room only:* $3050. Full-time tuition and fees vary according to course load. Room and board charges vary according to board

Olivet Nazarene University

plan. *Part-time tuition:* $652 per hour. *Part-time fees:* $10 per term. Part-time tuition and fees vary according to course load. *Payment plan:* Installment.
FRESHMAN FINANCIAL AID (Fall 2005, est.) 575 applied for aid; of those 87% were deemed to have need. 100% of freshmen with need received aid; of those 31% had need fully met. *Average percent of need met:* 81% (excluding resources awarded to replace EFC). *Average financial aid package:* $12,610 (excluding resources awarded to replace EFC). 21% of all full-time freshmen had no need and received non-need-based gift aid.
UNDERGRADUATE FINANCIAL AID (Fall 2005, est.) 1,977 applied for aid; of those 88% were deemed to have need. 100% of undergraduates with need received aid; of those 36% had need fully met. *Average percent of need met:* 84% (excluding resources awarded to replace EFC). *Average financial aid package:* $12,033 (excluding resources awarded to replace EFC). 25% of all full-time undergraduates had no need and received non-need-based gift aid.
GIFT AID (NEED-BASED) *Total amount:* $13,368,750 (14% federal, 17% state, 61% institutional, 8% external sources). *Receiving aid:* Freshmen: 77% (498); All full-time undergraduates: 68% (1,665). *Average award:* Freshmen: $10,056; Undergraduates: $9075. *Scholarships, grants, and awards:* Federal Pell, FSEOG, state, private, college/university gift aid from institutional funds.
GIFT AID (NON-NEED-BASED) *Total amount:* $3,841,512 (13% federal, 4% state, 76% institutional, 7% external sources). *Receiving aid:* Freshmen: 77% (499); Undergraduates: 68% (1,686). *Average Award:* Freshmen: $7156; Undergraduates: $6361. *Scholarships, grants, and awards by category: Academic Interests/Achievement:* 1,407 awards ($4,053,935 total): general academic interests/achievements, military science. *Creative Arts/Performance:* 90 awards ($228,275 total): art/fine arts, music, performing arts, theater/drama. *Special Achievements/Activities:* 1,379 awards ($2,012,451 total): cheerleading/drum major, leadership, religious involvement. *Special Characteristics:* 928 awards ($3,036,989 total): children of current students, children of educators, children of faculty/staff, general special characteristics, international students, parents of current students, relatives of clergy, siblings of current students, spouses of current students. *Tuition waivers:* Full or partial for employees or children of employees. *ROTC:* Army.
LOANS *Student loans:* $13,112,109 (42% need-based, 58% non-need-based). 75% of past graduating class borrowed through all loan programs. *Average indebtedness per student:* $20,062. *Average need-based loan:* Freshmen: $3395; Undergraduates: $4056. *Parent loans:* $4,892,424 (100% non-need-based). *Programs:* FFEL (Subsidized and Unsubsidized Stafford, PLUS), Perkins, alternative loans.
WORK-STUDY *Federal work-study:* Total amount: $225,300; 267 jobs averaging $716. *State or other work-study/employment:* Total amount: $771,716 (100% need-based). 787 part-time jobs averaging $980.
ATHLETIC AWARDS *Total amount:* $1,516,298 (100% need-based).
APPLYING FOR FINANCIAL AID *Financial aid deadline (priority):* 3/1. *Notification date:* Continuous beginning 2/1. Students must reply by 5/1.
CONTACT Mr. Greg Bruner, Financial Aid Director, Olivet Nazarene University, One University Avenue, Bourbonnais, IL 60914, 815-939-5249 or toll-free 800-648-1463. *Fax:* 815-939-5074. *E-mail:* gbruner@olivet.edu.

O'MORE COLLEGE OF DESIGN
Franklin, TN

CONTACT Office of Financial Aid, O'More College of Design, 423 South Margin Street, Franklin, TN 37064-2816, 615-794-4254 Ext. 30.

ORAL ROBERTS UNIVERSITY
Tulsa, OK

Tuition & fees: $15,880	Average undergraduate aid package: $14,950

ABOUT THE INSTITUTION Independent interdenominational, coed. Awards: bachelor's, master's, doctoral, and first professional degrees. 78 undergraduate majors. Total enrollment: 4,086. Undergraduates: 3,265. Federal methodology is used as a basis for awarding need-based institutional aid.
UNDERGRADUATE EXPENSES for 2005–06 *Application fee:* $35. *Comprehensive fee:* $22,650 includes full-time tuition ($15,400), mandatory fees ($480), and room and board ($6770). *College room only:* $3280. Room and board charges vary according to board plan and housing facility. *Part-time tuition:* $642 per credit hour. *Payment plan:* Installment.

FRESHMAN FINANCIAL AID (Fall 2004) 470 applied for aid; of those 86% were deemed to have need. 99% of freshmen with need received aid; of those 53% had need fully met. *Average percent of need met:* 86% (excluding resources awarded to replace EFC). *Average financial aid package:* $13,969 (excluding resources awarded to replace EFC). 22% of all full-time freshmen had no need and received non-need-based gift aid.
UNDERGRADUATE FINANCIAL AID (Fall 2004) 1,978 applied for aid; of those 90% were deemed to have need. 100% of undergraduates with need received aid; of those 45% had need fully met. *Average percent of need met:* 89% (excluding resources awarded to replace EFC). *Average financial aid package:* $14,950 (excluding resources awarded to replace EFC). 18% of all full-time undergraduates had no need and received non-need-based gift aid.
GIFT AID (NEED-BASED) *Total amount:* $10,550,615 (27% federal, 3% state, 64% institutional, 6% external sources). *Receiving aid:* Freshmen: 67% (383); All full-time undergraduates: 64% (1,597). *Average award:* Freshmen: $8414; Undergraduates: $7577. *Scholarships, grants, and awards:* Federal Pell, FSEOG, state, private, college/university gift aid from institutional funds.
GIFT AID (NON-NEED-BASED) *Total amount:* $2,866,534 (2% state, 94% institutional, 4% external sources). *Receiving aid:* Freshmen: 24% (137); Undergraduates: 23% (569). *Average Award:* Freshmen: $7170; Undergraduates: $7029. *Scholarships, grants, and awards by category: Academic Interests/Achievement:* 1,504 awards ($6,526,699 total): biological sciences, business, communication, education, engineering/technologies, general academic interests/achievements, health fields, religion/biblical studies. *Creative Arts/Performance:* 263 awards ($569,637 total): applied art and design, art/fine arts, cinema/film/broadcasting, journalism/publications, music. *Special Achievements/Activities:* 480 awards ($887,157 total): cheerleading/drum major, community service, general special achievements/activities, leadership, memberships, religious involvement. *Special Characteristics:* 1,605 awards ($4,166,293 total): children and siblings of alumni, children of faculty/staff, general special characteristics, international students, relatives of clergy, siblings of current students. *Tuition waivers:* Full or partial for children of alumni, employees or children of employees. *ROTC:* Air Force cooperative.
LOANS *Student loans:* $12,198,663 (76% need-based, 24% non-need-based). 84% of past graduating class borrowed through all loan programs. *Average indebtedness per student:* $27,956. *Average need-based loan:* Freshmen: $6716; Undergraduates: $8629. *Parent loans:* $5,733,187 (62% need-based, 38% non-need-based). *Programs:* FFEL (Subsidized and Unsubsidized Stafford, PLUS), Perkins, college/university.
WORK-STUDY *Federal work-study:* Total amount: $605,610; 313 jobs averaging $1590. *State or other work-study/employment:* Total amount: $723,341 (100% non-need-based). 750 part-time jobs averaging $1500.
ATHLETIC AWARDS *Total amount:* $2,364,056 (31% need-based, 69% non-need-based).
APPLYING FOR FINANCIAL AID *Required financial aid form:* FAFSA. *Financial aid deadline (priority):* 3/15. *Notification date:* Students must reply by 7/15.
CONTACT Scott Carr, Director of Financial Aid, Oral Roberts University, PO Box 700540, Tulsa, OK 74170-0540, 918-495-6510 or toll-free 800-678-8876. *Fax:* 918-495-6803. *E-mail:* finaid@oru.edu.

OREGON COLLEGE OF ART & CRAFT
Portland, OR

CONTACT Lisa Newman, Director of Financial Aid, Oregon College of Art & Craft, 8245 Southwest Barnes Road, Portland, OR 97225, 503-297-5544 Ext. 124 or toll-free 800-390-0632 Ext. 129. *Fax:* 503-297-9651. *E-mail:* lnewman@ocac.edu.

OREGON HEALTH & SCIENCE UNIVERSITY
Portland, OR

Tuition & fees (OR res): $9113	Average undergraduate aid package: $11,440

ABOUT THE INSTITUTION State-related, coed. Awards: bachelor's, master's, doctoral, and first professional degrees and post-bachelor's, post-master's, and first professional certificates. 2 undergraduate majors. Total enrollment: 2,511. Undergraduates: 649. Federal methodology is used as a basis for awarding need-based institutional aid.

UNDERGRADUATE EXPENSES for 2005–06 *Application fee:* $125. *Tuition, state resident:* full-time $7920; part-time $165 per credit. *Tuition, nonresident:* full-time $18,480; part-time $385 per credit.
UNDERGRADUATE FINANCIAL AID (Fall 2005, est.) 403 applied for aid; of those 93% were deemed to have need. 98% of undergraduates with need received aid; of those 8% had need fully met. *Average percent of need met:* 45% (excluding resources awarded to replace EFC). *Average financial aid package:* $11,440 (excluding resources awarded to replace EFC). 1% of all full-time undergraduates had no need and received non-need-based gift aid.
GIFT AID (NEED-BASED) *Total amount:* $1,593,961 (42% federal, 15% state, 13% institutional, 30% external sources). *Receiving aid:* All full-time undergraduates: 34% (162). *Average award:* Undergraduates: $4617. *Scholarships, grants, and awards:* Federal Pell, FSEOG, state, private, college/university gift aid from institutional funds, Health Profession Scholarships.
GIFT AID (NON-NEED-BASED) *Total amount:* $28,979 (26% institutional, 74% external sources). *Receiving aid:* Undergraduates: 27% (129). *Average Award:* Undergraduates: $1500. *Scholarships, grants, and awards by category:* Academic Interests/Achievement: 170 awards ($1,323,087 total): health fields.
ROTC: Army cooperative.
LOANS *Student loans:* $6,030,320 (82% need-based, 18% non-need-based). 71% of past graduating class borrowed through all loan programs. *Average indebtedness per student:* $27,425. *Average need-based loan:* Undergraduates: $7529. *Parent loans:* $716,758 (50% need-based, 50% non-need-based). *Programs:* Federal Direct (Subsidized and Unsubsidized Stafford, PLUS), Perkins, Federal Nursing, state, college/university, alternative loans.
WORK-STUDY *Federal work-study:* Total amount: $17,500; 14 jobs averaging $1250.
APPLYING FOR FINANCIAL AID *Required financial aid form:* OHSU does not have Freshman FA applicants. *Financial aid deadline:* Continuous. *Notification date:* 6/1. Students must reply within 4 weeks of notification.
CONTACT Ms. Cherie Honnell, Director of Financial Aid/Registrar, Oregon Health & Science University, 3181 SW Sam Jackson Park Road, L-109, Portland, OR 97239-3089, 503-494-7800. *Fax:* 503-494-4629. *E-mail:* finaid@ohsu.edu.

OREGON INSTITUTE OF TECHNOLOGY
Klamath Falls, OR

CONTACT Tracey Lehman, Financial Aid Director, Oregon Institute of Technology, 3201 Campus Drive, Klamath Falls, OR 97601-8801, 541-885-1280 or toll-free 800-422-2017 (in-state), 800-343-6653 (out-of-state). *Fax:* 541-885-1024. *E-mail:* marquitt@oit.edu.

OREGON STATE UNIVERSITY
Corvallis, OR

ABOUT THE INSTITUTION State-supported, coed. Awards: bachelor's, master's, doctoral, and first professional degrees and post-bachelor's certificates. 113 undergraduate majors. Total enrollment: 19,236. Undergraduates: 15,747. Freshmen: 2,902.
GIFT AID (NEED-BASED) *Scholarships, grants, and awards:* Federal Pell, FSEOG, state.
GIFT AID (NON-NEED-BASED) *Scholarships, grants, and awards by category:* Academic Interests/Achievement: general academic interests/achievements. Creative Arts/Performance: music. Special Achievements/Activities: general special achievements/activities. Special Characteristics: general special characteristics.
LOANS *Programs:* Federal Direct (Subsidized and Unsubsidized Stafford, PLUS), Perkins, college/university.
WORK-STUDY *Federal work-study:* Total amount: $3,860,325; jobs available.
APPLYING FOR FINANCIAL AID *Required financial aid form:* FAFSA.
CONTACT Kate Peterson, Director, Financial Aid, Oregon State University, 218 Kerr Administration Building, Corvallis, OR 97331-2120, 541-737-2241 or toll-free 800-291-4192 (in-state).

OREGON STATE UNIVERSITY–CASCADES
Bend, OR

CONTACT Financial Aid Office, Oregon State University–Cascades, 2600 NW College Way, Bend, OR 97701, 541-322-3100.

OTIS COLLEGE OF ART AND DESIGN
Los Angeles, CA

Tuition & fees: $27,546 | **Average undergraduate aid package: $14,663**

ABOUT THE INSTITUTION Independent, coed. Awards: bachelor's and master's degrees. 10 undergraduate majors. Total enrollment: 1,098. Undergraduates: 1,040. Freshmen: 169. Federal methodology is used as a basis for awarding need-based institutional aid.
UNDERGRADUATE EXPENSES for 2006–07 *Application fee:* $50. *Tuition:* full-time $26,996; part-time $900 per credit.
FRESHMAN FINANCIAL AID (Fall 2004) 113 applied for aid; of those 94% were deemed to have need. 100% of freshmen with need received aid; of those 1% had need fully met. *Average percent of need met:* 50% (excluding resources awarded to replace EFC). *Average financial aid package:* $12,993 (excluding resources awarded to replace EFC). 9% of all full-time freshmen had no need and received non-need-based gift aid.
UNDERGRADUATE FINANCIAL AID (Fall 2004) 773 applied for aid; of those 97% were deemed to have need. 100% of undergraduates with need received aid; of those 2% had need fully met. *Average percent of need met:* 56% (excluding resources awarded to replace EFC). *Average financial aid package:* $14,663 (excluding resources awarded to replace EFC). 9% of all full-time undergraduates had no need and received non-need-based gift aid.
GIFT AID (NEED-BASED) *Total amount:* $8,037,853 (19% federal, 19% state, 61% institutional, 1% external sources). *Receiving aid:* Freshmen: 86% (106); All full-time undergraduates: 75% (750). *Average award:* Freshmen: $8012; Undergraduates: $8926. *Scholarships, grants, and awards:* Federal Pell, FSEOG, state, private, college/university gift aid from institutional funds.
GIFT AID (NON-NEED-BASED) *Total amount:* $313,336 (89% institutional, 11% external sources). *Receiving aid:* Freshmen: 9% (11); Undergraduates: 9% (91). *Average Award:* Freshmen: $2181; Undergraduates: $2734. *Scholarships, grants, and awards by category:* Academic Interests/Achievement: general academic interests/achievements. Creative Arts/Performance: applied art and design, art/fine arts.
LOANS *Student loans:* $7,531,168 (96% need-based, 4% non-need-based). 78% of past graduating class borrowed through all loan programs. *Average indebtedness per student:* $29,717. *Average need-based loan:* Freshmen: $2958; Undergraduates: $3323. *Parent loans:* $2,932,604 (82% need-based, 18% non-need-based). *Programs:* FFEL (Subsidized and Unsubsidized Stafford, PLUS).
WORK-STUDY *Federal work-study:* Total amount: $2,847,835; 180 jobs averaging $1500. *State or other work-study/employment:* Total amount: $138,746 (58% need-based, 42% non-need-based). 23 part-time jobs averaging $1000.
APPLYING FOR FINANCIAL AID *Required financial aid forms:* FAFSA, institution's own form. *Financial aid deadline (priority):* 2/15. *Notification date:* 3/1. Students must reply within 2 weeks of notification.
CONTACT Nasreen Zia, Associate Director of Financial Aid, Otis College of Art and Design, 9045 Lincoln Boulevard, Los Angeles, CA 90045-9785, 310-665-6883 or toll-free 800-527-OTIS. *Fax:* 310-665-6884. *E-mail:* nzia@otis.edu.

OTTAWA UNIVERSITY
Ottawa, KS

CONTACT Financial Aid Coordinator, Ottawa University, 1001 South Cedar, Ottawa, KS 66067-3399, 785-242-5200 or toll-free 800-755-5200 Ext. 5559. *E-mail:* finaid@ottawa.edu.

OTTERBEIN COLLEGE
Westerville, OH

CONTACT Mr. Thomas V. Yarnell, Director of Financial Aid, Otterbein College, One Otterbein College, Clippinger Hall, Westerville, OH 43081-2006, 614-823-1502 or toll-free 800-488-8144. *Fax:* 614-823-1200. *E-mail:* tyarnell@otterbein.edu.

OUACHITA BAPTIST UNIVERSITY
Arkadelphia, AR

Tuition & fees: $16,990 | **Average undergraduate aid package: $12,992**

Ouachita Baptist University

ABOUT THE INSTITUTION Independent Baptist, coed. Awards: associate and bachelor's degrees. 54 undergraduate majors. Total enrollment: 1,499. Undergraduates: 1,499. Freshmen: 368. Federal methodology is used as a basis for awarding need-based institutional aid.

UNDERGRADUATE EXPENSES for 2006–07 *Application fee:* $50. *Comprehensive fee:* $21,990 includes full-time tuition ($16,650), mandatory fees ($340), and room and board ($5000). *Part-time tuition:* $460 per semester hour.

FRESHMAN FINANCIAL AID (Fall 2005, est.) 268 applied for aid; of those 74% were deemed to have need. 99% of freshmen with need received aid; of those 39% had need fully met. *Average percent of need met:* 70% (excluding resources awarded to replace EFC). *Average financial aid package:* $12,995 (excluding resources awarded to replace EFC). 35% of all full-time freshmen had no need and received non-need-based gift aid.

UNDERGRADUATE FINANCIAL AID (Fall 2005, est.) 882 applied for aid; of those 78% were deemed to have need. 99% of undergraduates with need received aid; of those 30% had need fully met. *Average percent of need met:* 75% (excluding resources awarded to replace EFC). *Average financial aid package:* $12,992 (excluding resources awarded to replace EFC). 33% of all full-time undergraduates had no need and received non-need-based gift aid.

GIFT AID (NEED-BASED) *Total amount:* $6,879,208 (14% federal, 5% state, 78% institutional, 3% external sources). *Receiving aid:* Freshmen: 47% (171); All full-time undergraduates: 45% (625). *Average award:* Freshmen: $8472; Undergraduates: $8419. *Scholarships, grants, and awards:* Federal Pell, FSEOG, state, private, college/university gift aid from institutional funds.

GIFT AID (NON-NEED-BASED) *Total amount:* $4,027,664 (9% state, 80% institutional, 11% external sources). *Receiving aid:* Freshmen: 34% (125); Undergraduates: 33% (459). *Average Award:* Freshmen: $5988; Undergraduates:* $6032. *Scholarships, grants, and awards by category:* Academic Interests/Achievement: 419 awards ($1,103,459 total): area/ethnic studies, biological sciences, business, communication, computer science, education, engineering/technologies, English, foreign languages, general academic interests/achievements, health fields, home economics, humanities, international studies, mathematics, physical sciences, premedicine, religion/biblical studies, social sciences. *Creative Arts/Performance:* 204 awards ($822,900 total): art/fine arts, journalism/publications, music, performing arts, theater/drama. *Special Achievements/Activities:* 801 awards ($3,319,514 total): general special achievements/activities. *Special Characteristics:* 833 awards ($4,622,879 total): children of faculty/staff, ethnic background, first-generation college students, general special characteristics, international students, local/state students, married students, members of minority groups, out-of-state students, relatives of clergy, religious affiliation, twins. *ROTC:* Army.

LOANS *Student loans:* $2,955,523 (57% need-based, 43% non-need-based). 50% of past graduating class borrowed through all loan programs. *Average indebtedness per student:* $14,016. *Average need-based loan:* Freshmen: $2724; Undergraduates: $3709. *Parent loans:* $1,278,591 (20% need-based, 80% non-need-based). *Programs:* FFEL (Subsidized and Unsubsidized Stafford, PLUS), Perkins, college/university.

WORK-STUDY *Federal work-study:* Total amount: $450,296; 313 jobs averaging $1449. *State or other work-study/employment:* Total amount: $369,337 (15% need-based, 85% non-need-based). 232 part-time jobs averaging $1658.

ATHLETIC AWARDS *Total amount:* $2,153,110 (46% need-based, 54% non-need-based).

APPLYING FOR FINANCIAL AID *Required financial aid forms:* FAFSA, institution's own form. *Financial aid deadline:* 6/1 (priority: 2/15). *Notification date:* Continuous beginning 3/31. Students must reply by 5/1.

CONTACT Mr. Lane Smith, Director of Financial Aid, Ouachita Baptist University, Box 3774, Arkadelphia, AR 71998-0001, 870-245-5570 or toll-free 800-342-5628 (in-state). *Fax:* 870-245-5318. *E-mail:* smithl@obu.edu.

OUR LADY OF HOLY CROSS COLLEGE
New Orleans, LA

Tuition & fees: N/R	Average undergraduate aid package: $4259

ABOUT THE INSTITUTION Independent Roman Catholic, coed. Awards: associate, bachelor's, and master's degrees and post-bachelor's certificates. 25 undergraduate majors. Total enrollment: 1,446. Undergraduates: 1,316. Freshmen: 124. Federal methodology is used as a basis for awarding need-based institutional aid.

FRESHMAN FINANCIAL AID (Fall 2005, est.) 863 applied for aid; of those 34% were deemed to have need. 85% of freshmen with need received aid; of those 2% had need fully met. *Average percent of need met:* 15% (excluding resources awarded to replace EFC). *Average financial aid package:* $3753 (excluding resources awarded to replace EFC). 2% of all full-time freshmen had no need and received non-need-based gift aid.

UNDERGRADUATE FINANCIAL AID (Fall 2005, est.) 1,776 applied for aid; of those 85% were deemed to have need. 72% of undergraduates with need received aid; of those 1% had need fully met. *Average percent of need met:* 15% (excluding resources awarded to replace EFC). *Average financial aid package:* $4259 (excluding resources awarded to replace EFC). 3% of all full-time undergraduates had no need and received non-need-based gift aid.

GIFT AID (NEED-BASED) *Total amount:* $3,727,716 (90% federal, 8% state, 2% institutional). *Receiving aid:* Freshmen: 19% (195); All full-time undergraduates: 35% (964). *Average award:* Freshmen: $3325; Undergraduates: $3427. *Scholarships, grants, and awards:* Federal Pell, FSEOG, state, private, college/university gift aid from institutional funds, Federal Nursing.

GIFT AID (NON-NEED-BASED) *Total amount:* $287,317 (53% state, 46% institutional, 1% external sources). *Receiving aid:* Freshmen: 3; Undergraduates: 11. *Average Award:* Freshmen: $3769; Undergraduates: $4943. *Scholarships, grants, and awards by category:* Academic Interests/Achievement: 212 awards: general academic interests/achievements. *Special Characteristics:* 47 awards ($156,509 total): children of faculty/staff, general special characteristics, relatives of clergy, religious affiliation. *Tuition waivers:* Full or partial for employees or children of employees. *ROTC:* Army cooperative, Air Force cooperative.

LOANS *Student loans:* $4,225,366 (92% need-based, 8% non-need-based). 88% of past graduating class borrowed through all loan programs. *Average indebtedness per student:* $13,159. *Average need-based loan:* Freshmen: $2146; Undergraduates: $3129. *Parent loans:* $170,136 (100% need-based). *Programs:* FFEL (Subsidized and Unsubsidized Stafford, PLUS).

WORK-STUDY *Federal work-study:* Total amount: $94,887; 38 jobs averaging $2499.

APPLYING FOR FINANCIAL AID *Required financial aid forms:* FAFSA, institution's own form. *Financial aid deadline (priority):* 4/15. *Notification date:* 5/15. Students must reply within 2 weeks of notification.

CONTACT Mrs. Johnell S. Armer, Director of Financial Aid, Our Lady of Holy Cross College, 4123 Woodland Drive, New Orleans, LA 70131-7399, 504-398-2165 or toll-free 800-259-7744 Ext. 175. *Fax:* 504-391-2421. *E-mail:* jarmer@olhcc.edu.

OUR LADY OF THE LAKE COLLEGE
Baton Rouge, LA

ABOUT THE INSTITUTION Independent Roman Catholic, coed, primarily women. Awards: associate, bachelor's, and master's degrees. 14 undergraduate majors. Total enrollment: 1,990. Undergraduates: 1,990.

GIFT AID (NEED-BASED) *Scholarships, grants, and awards:* Federal Pell, FSEOG, state, private, college/university gift aid from institutional funds.

LOANS *Programs:* FFEL (Subsidized and Unsubsidized Stafford, PLUS).

APPLYING FOR FINANCIAL AID *Required financial aid forms:* FAFSA, institution's own form.

CONTACT Sharon Butler, Director of Financial Aid, Our Lady of the Lake College, 7434 Perkins Road, Baton Rouge, LA 70808, 225-768-1701 or toll-free 877-242-3509. *Fax:* 225-768-1726.

OUR LADY OF THE LAKE UNIVERSITY OF SAN ANTONIO
San Antonio, TX

CONTACT Leah Garza, Director of Financial Aid, Our Lady of the Lake University of San Antonio, 411 Southwest 24th Street, San Antonio, TX 78207-4689, 210-434-6711 Ext. 2299 or toll-free 800-436-6558. *Fax:* 210-431-3958.

OZARK CHRISTIAN COLLEGE
Joplin, MO

CONTACT Jill Kaminsky, Application Processor, Ozark Christian College, 1111 North Main Street, Joplin, MO 64801-4804, 417-624-2518 Ext. 2017 or toll-free 800-299-4622. *Fax:* 417-624-0090. *E-mail:* finaid@occ.edu.

PACE UNIVERSITY
New York, NY
CONTACT Mark Stephens, Pace University, 861 Bedford Road, Pleasantville, NY 10570, 212-773-3501 or toll-free 800-874-7223. *E-mail:* mstephens@pace.edu.

PACIFIC ISLANDS BIBLE COLLEGE
Mangilao, GU
CONTACT Financial Aid Office, Pacific Islands Bible College, PO Box 22619, Guam Main Facility, GU 96921-2619, 671-734-1812.

PACIFIC LUTHERAN UNIVERSITY
Tacoma, WA

Tuition & fees: $22,040	Average undergraduate aid package: $19,269

ABOUT THE INSTITUTION Independent religious, coed. Awards: bachelor's and master's degrees and post-bachelor's and post-master's certificates. 60 undergraduate majors. Total enrollment: 3,680. Undergraduates: 3,369. Freshmen: 690. Federal methodology is used as a basis for awarding need-based institutional aid.
UNDERGRADUATE EXPENSES for 2005–06 *Application fee:* $40. *Comprehensive fee:* $28,805 includes full-time tuition ($22,040) and room and board ($6765). *College room only:* $3330. Full-time tuition and fees vary according to course load. Room and board charges vary according to board plan and housing facility. *Part-time tuition:* $687 per semester hour. Part-time tuition and fees vary according to course load. *Payment plan:* Installment.
FRESHMAN FINANCIAL AID (Fall 2005, est.) 631 applied for aid; of those 81% were deemed to have need. 94% of freshmen with need received aid; of those 44% had need fully met. *Average percent of need met:* 93% (excluding resources awarded to replace EFC). *Average financial aid package:* $19,012 (excluding resources awarded to replace EFC). 16% of all full-time freshmen had no need and received non-need-based gift aid.
UNDERGRADUATE FINANCIAL AID (Fall 2005, est.) 2,586 applied for aid; of those 84% were deemed to have need. 97% of undergraduates with need received aid; of those 35% had need fully met. *Average percent of need met:* 89% (excluding resources awarded to replace EFC). *Average financial aid package:* $19,269 (excluding resources awarded to replace EFC). 20% of all full-time undergraduates had no need and received non-need-based gift aid.
GIFT AID (NEED-BASED) *Total amount:* $21,883,006 (12% federal, 10% state, 71% institutional, 7% external sources). *Receiving aid:* Freshmen: 54% (379); All full-time undergraduates: 51% (1,624). *Average award:* Freshmen: $8528; Undergraduates: $7987. *Scholarships, grants, and awards:* Federal Pell, FSEOG, state, private, college/university gift aid from institutional funds, Federal Nursing.
GIFT AID (NON-NEED-BASED) *Total amount:* $13,428,955 (1% state, 75% institutional, 24% external sources). *Receiving aid:* Freshmen: 37% (258); Undergraduates: 32% (1,017). *Average Award:* Freshmen: $8253; Undergraduates: $8086. *Scholarships, grants, and awards by category: Academic Interests/Achievement:* 1,873 awards ($15,253,352 total): general academic interests/achievements. *Creative Arts/Performance:* 205 awards ($686,160 total): art/fine arts, dance, debating, general creative arts/performance, music, theater/drama. *Special Achievements/Activities:* 27 awards ($48,200 total): leadership. *Special Characteristics:* 581 awards ($1,873,075 total): children and siblings of alumni, children of educators, children of faculty/staff, international students, previous college experience, relatives of clergy. *Tuition waivers:* Full or partial for employees or children of employees, senior citizens. *ROTC:* Army.
LOANS *Student loans:* $14,667,639 (96% need-based, 4% non-need-based). 69% of past graduating class borrowed through all loan programs. *Average indebtedness per student:* $22,372. *Average need-based loan:* Freshmen: $4552; Undergraduates: $7132. *Parent loans:* $6,420,935 (62% need-based, 38% non-need-based). *Programs:* FFEL (Subsidized and Unsubsidized Stafford, PLUS), Perkins, Federal Nursing, state, college/university.
WORK-STUDY *Federal work-study:* Total amount: $862,723; 603 jobs averaging $1435. *State or other work-study/employment:* Total amount: $3,183,857 (31% need-based, 69% non-need-based). 314 part-time jobs averaging $3133.
APPLYING FOR FINANCIAL AID *Required financial aid form:* FAFSA. *Financial aid deadline (priority):* 3/1. *Notification date:* Continuous beginning 3/15. Students must reply by 5/1 or within 4 weeks of notification.

CONTACT Ms. Joan Riley, Associate Director, Systems, Pacific Lutheran University, Tacoma, WA 98447, 253-535-7168 or toll-free 800-274-6758. *Fax:* 253-535-8406. *E-mail:* rileyjo@plu.edu.

PACIFIC NORTHWEST COLLEGE OF ART
Portland, OR
ABOUT THE INSTITUTION Independent, coed. Awards: bachelor's degrees. 9 undergraduate majors. Total enrollment: 293. Undergraduates: 293.
GIFT AID (NEED-BASED) *Scholarships, grants, and awards:* Federal Pell, FSEOG, state, private, college/university gift aid from institutional funds.
GIFT AID (NON-NEED-BASED) *Scholarships, grants, and awards by category: Academic Interests/Achievement:* general academic interests/achievements. *Creative Arts/Performance:* art/fine arts.
LOANS *Programs:* FFEL (Subsidized and Unsubsidized Stafford, PLUS).
APPLYING FOR FINANCIAL AID *Required financial aid form:* FAFSA.
CONTACT Peggy Burgus, Director of Financial Aid, Pacific Northwest College of Art, 1241 Northwest Johnson Street, Portland, OR 97209, 503-821-8976. *Fax:* 503-821-8978.

PACIFIC OAKS COLLEGE
Pasadena, CA

Tuition & fees: $16,380	Average undergraduate aid package: N/A

ABOUT THE INSTITUTION Independent, coed, primarily women. Awards: bachelor's and master's degrees and post-bachelor's and post-master's certificates. 6 undergraduate majors. Total enrollment: 863. Undergraduates: 208. Entering class: . Federal methodology is used as a basis for awarding need-based institutional aid.
UNDERGRADUATE EXPENSES for 2005–06 *Application fee:* $55. *Tuition:* full-time $16,320; part-time $680 per unit. *Required fees:* full-time $60; $30 per term part-time. *Payment plan:* Installment.
GIFT AID (NEED-BASED) *Total amount:* $401,345 (57% federal, 43% state). *Scholarships, grants, and awards:* Federal Pell, FSEOG, state, private, college/university gift aid from institutional funds.
GIFT AID (NON-NEED-BASED) *Tuition waivers:* Full or partial for employees or children of employees.
LOANS *Programs:* FFEL (Subsidized and Unsubsidized Stafford, PLUS), Perkins.
WORK-STUDY *Federal work-study:* Total amount: $37,376; 10 jobs averaging $5000.
APPLYING FOR FINANCIAL AID *Required financial aid forms:* FAFSA, institution's own form. *Financial aid deadline (priority):* 4/15. *Notification date:* Continuous beginning 5/1.
CONTACT Financial Aid Office, Pacific Oaks College, 5 Westmoreland Place, Pasadena, CA 91103, 626-397-1350 or toll-free 800-684-0900. *Fax:* 626-577-6144. *E-mail:* financial@pacificoaks.edu.

PACIFIC UNION COLLEGE
Angwin, CA

Tuition & fees: $19,125	Average undergraduate aid package: $14,150

ABOUT THE INSTITUTION Independent Seventh-day Adventist, coed. Awards: associate, bachelor's, and master's degrees. 67 undergraduate majors. Total enrollment: 1,518. Undergraduates: 1,516. Freshmen: 331. Federal methodology is used as a basis for awarding need-based institutional aid.
UNDERGRADUATE EXPENSES for 2005–06 *Application fee:* $30. *Comprehensive fee:* $24,555 includes full-time tuition ($18,990), mandatory fees ($135), and room and board ($5430). *College room only:* $3312. Full-time tuition and fees vary according to course load. *Part-time tuition:* $550 per quarter hour. *Part-time fees:* $45 per term. Part-time tuition and fees vary according to course load. *Payment plans:* Guaranteed tuition, installment.
FRESHMAN FINANCIAL AID (Fall 2005, est.) 303 applied for aid; of those 68% were deemed to have need. 100% of freshmen with need received aid; of those 41% had need fully met. *Average percent of need met:* 69% (excluding resources awarded to replace EFC). *Average financial aid package:* $14,600 (excluding resources awarded to replace EFC).

Pacific Union College

UNDERGRADUATE FINANCIAL AID (Fall 2005, est.) 1,200 applied for aid; of those 66% were deemed to have need. 100% of undergraduates with need received aid; of those 43% had need fully met. *Average percent of need met:* 67% (excluding resources awarded to replace EFC). *Average financial aid package:* $14,150 (excluding resources awarded to replace EFC).
GIFT AID (NEED-BASED) *Total amount:* $11,749,902 (16% federal, 18% state, 64% institutional, 2% external sources). *Receiving aid:* Freshmen: 67% (205); All full-time undergraduates: 62% (791). *Average award:* Freshmen: $9149; Undergraduates: $6589. *Scholarships, grants, and awards:* Federal Pell, FSEOG, state, private, college/university gift aid from institutional funds.
GIFT AID (NON-NEED-BASED) *Total amount:* $1,598,074 (1% state, 97% institutional, 2% external sources). *Receiving aid:* Freshmen: 65% (199); Undergraduates: 57% (729). *Scholarships, grants, and awards by category: Academic Interests/Achievement:* education. *Special Achievements/Activities:* community service, general special achievements/activities, leadership, religious involvement. *Special Characteristics:* $50,000 total: siblings of current students. *Tuition waivers:* Full or partial for employees or children of employees, senior citizens.
LOANS *Student loans:* $10,263,446 (42% need-based, 58% non-need-based). 90% of past graduating class borrowed through all loan programs. *Average indebtedness per student:* $14,000. *Parent loans:* $953,504 (100% non-need-based). *Programs:* FFEL (Subsidized and Unsubsidized Stafford, PLUS), Perkins, college/university.
WORK-STUDY *Federal work-study:* Total amount: $108,550; 196 jobs averaging $861.
APPLYING FOR FINANCIAL AID *Required financial aid forms:* FAFSA, institution's own form, state aid form. *Financial aid deadline (priority):* 3/2. *Notification date:* Continuous beginning 5/1. Students must reply within 3 weeks of notification.
CONTACT Glen Bobst Jr., Director of Student Financial Services, Pacific Union College, One Angwin Avenue, Angwin, CA 94508, 707-965-7321 or toll-free 800-862-7080. *Fax:* 707-965-6595. *E-mail:* gbobst@puc.edu.

PACIFIC UNIVERSITY
Forest Grove, OR

Tuition & fees: $22,534	Average undergraduate aid package: $17,492

ABOUT THE INSTITUTION Independent, coed. Awards: bachelor's, master's, doctoral, and first professional degrees. 49 undergraduate majors. Total enrollment: 2,563. Undergraduates: 1,232. Freshmen: 324. Federal methodology is used as a basis for awarding need-based institutional aid.
UNDERGRADUATE EXPENSES for 2006–07 *Application fee:* $40. *Comprehensive fee:* $29,002 includes full-time tuition ($21,954), mandatory fees ($580), and room and board ($6468). *College room only:* $3220. *Part-time tuition:* $916 per credit hour.
FRESHMAN FINANCIAL AID (Fall 2005, est.) 304 applied for aid; of those 83% were deemed to have need. 100% of freshmen with need received aid; of those 39% had need fully met. *Average percent of need met:* 89% (excluding resources awarded to replace EFC). *Average financial aid package:* $18,266 (excluding resources awarded to replace EFC). 19% of all full-time freshmen had no need and received non-need-based gift aid.
UNDERGRADUATE FINANCIAL AID (Fall 2005, est.) 1,015 applied for aid; of those 84% were deemed to have need. 100% of undergraduates with need received aid; of those 38% had need fully met. *Average percent of need met:* 86% (excluding resources awarded to replace EFC). *Average financial aid package:* $17,492 (excluding resources awarded to replace EFC). 23% of all full-time undergraduates had no need and received non-need-based gift aid.
GIFT AID (NEED-BASED) *Total amount:* $9,822,908 (12% federal, 3% state, 78% institutional, 7% external sources). *Receiving aid:* Freshmen: 76% (245); All full-time undergraduates: 71% (835). *Average award:* Freshmen: $12,626; Undergraduates: $11,538. *Scholarships, grants, and awards:* Federal Pell, FSEOG, state, private, college/university gift aid from institutional funds.
GIFT AID (NON-NEED-BASED) *Total amount:* $2,849,589 (95% institutional, 5% external sources). *Receiving aid:* Freshmen: 9% (28); Undergraduates: 10% (118). *Average Award:* Freshmen: $9553; Undergraduates: $8645. *Scholarships, grants, and awards by category: Academic Interests/Achievement:* 958 awards ($7,621,904 total): business, education, English, foreign languages, general academic interests/achievements, humanities, mathematics, physical sciences, social sciences. *Creative Arts/Performance:* 108 awards ($195,050 total): art/fine arts, debating, journalism/publications, music, theater/drama. *Special Achievements/Activities:* 13 awards ($16,150 total): community service, memberships. *Special Characteristics:* 73 awards ($1,055,286 total): children and siblings of alumni, children of faculty/staff, general special characteristics, international students, relatives of clergy. *ROTC:* Army cooperative, Air Force cooperative.
LOANS *Student loans:* $7,226,529 (65% need-based, 35% non-need-based). 84% of past graduating class borrowed through all loan programs. *Average indebtedness per student:* $25,581. *Average need-based loan:* Freshmen: $5349; Undergraduates: $5429. *Parent loans:* $2,374,016 (21% need-based, 79% non-need-based). *Programs:* Federal Direct (Subsidized and Unsubsidized Stafford, PLUS), Perkins, alternative loans.
WORK-STUDY *Federal work-study:* Total amount: $1,080,374; 639 jobs averaging $1663. *State or other work-study/employment:* Total amount: $283,080 (38% need-based, 62% non-need-based). 171 part-time jobs averaging $516.
APPLYING FOR FINANCIAL AID *Required financial aid form:* FAFSA. *Financial aid deadline (priority):* 2/15. *Notification date:* Continuous beginning 3/1.
CONTACT Dala Ramsey, Director of Financial Aid, Pacific University, 2043 College Way, Forest Grove, OR 97116-1797, 503-352-2871 or toll-free 877-722-8648. *Fax:* 503-352-2950. *E-mail:* dramsey@pacificu.edu.

PAIER COLLEGE OF ART, INC.
Hamden, CT

CONTACT Mr. John DeRose, Director of Financial Aid, Paier College of Art, Inc., 20 Gorham Avenue, Hamden, CT 06514-3902, 203-287-3034. *Fax:* 203-287-3021. *E-mail:* paier.art@snet.net.

PAINE COLLEGE
Augusta, GA

CONTACT Ms. Gerri Bogan, Director of Financial Aid, Paine College, 1235 15th Street, Augusta, GA 30901, 706-821-8262 or toll-free 800-476-7703. *Fax:* 706-821-8691. *E-mail:* bogang@mail.paine.edu.

PALM BEACH ATLANTIC UNIVERSITY
West Palm Beach, FL

Tuition & fees: $17,350	Average undergraduate aid package: $2448

ABOUT THE INSTITUTION Independent nondenominational, coed. Awards: associate, bachelor's, master's, and first professional degrees. 46 undergraduate majors. Total enrollment: 3,171. Undergraduates: 2,486. Freshmen: 454. Federal methodology is used as a basis for awarding need-based institutional aid.
UNDERGRADUATE EXPENSES for 2005–06 *Application fee:* $25. *Comprehensive fee:* $24,030 includes full-time tuition ($17,130), mandatory fees ($220), and room and board ($6680). *College room only:* $3350. Full-time tuition and fees vary according to course load, degree level, program, and reciprocity agreements. Room and board charges vary according to board plan and housing facility. *Part-time tuition:* $420 per credit. *Part-time fees:* $85 per term. Part-time tuition and fees vary according to course load, degree level, program, and reciprocity agreements. *Payment plan:* Installment.
FRESHMAN FINANCIAL AID (Fall 2005, est.) 380 applied for aid; of those 75% were deemed to have need. 100% of freshmen with need received aid; of those 48% had need fully met. *Average percent of need met:* 66% (excluding resources awarded to replace EFC). *Average financial aid package:* $2540 (excluding resources awarded to replace EFC). 21% of all full-time freshmen had no need and received non-need-based gift aid.
UNDERGRADUATE FINANCIAL AID (Fall 2005, est.) 1,976 applied for aid; of those 43% were deemed to have need. 62% of undergraduates with need received aid; of those 99% had need fully met. *Average percent of need met:* 32% (excluding resources awarded to replace EFC). *Average financial aid package:* $2448 (excluding resources awarded to replace EFC). 15% of all full-time undergraduates had no need and received non-need-based gift aid.
GIFT AID (NEED-BASED) *Total amount:* $3,683,961 (58% federal, 9% state, 33% institutional). *Receiving aid:* Freshmen: 35% (156); All full-time undergraduates: 7% (171). *Average award:* Freshmen: $1911; Undergraduates: $2145. *Scholarships, grants, and awards:* Federal Pell, FSEOG, state, private, college/university gift aid from institutional funds.

GIFT AID (NON-NEED-BASED) *Total amount:* $14,014,228 (40% state, 51% institutional, 9% external sources). *Receiving aid:* Freshmen: 62% (280); Undergraduates: 23% (517). *Average Award:* Freshmen: $4799; *Undergraduates:* $1846. *Scholarships, grants, and awards by category: Academic Interests/Achievement:* 1,588 awards ($4,939,399 total): general academic interests/achievements. *Creative Arts/Performance:* 133 awards ($364,374 total): dance, music, theater/drama. *Special Achievements/Activities:* 339 awards ($329,175 total): religious involvement. *Special Characteristics:* 112 awards ($716,410 total): children and siblings of alumni, children of current students, children of educators, children of faculty/staff, previous college experience, relatives of clergy, siblings of current students, spouses of current students. *Tuition waivers:* Full or partial for employees or children of employees.
LOANS *Student loans:* $10,451,029 (48% need-based, 52% non-need-based). 80% of past graduating class borrowed through all loan programs. *Average indebtedness per student:* $24,393. *Average need-based loan:* Freshmen: $2367; Undergraduates: $3213. *Parent loans:* $3,843,069 (100% non-need-based). *Programs:* FFEL (Subsidized and Unsubsidized Stafford, PLUS), Perkins.
WORK-STUDY *Federal work-study:* Total amount: $522,596; 77 jobs averaging $1830.
ATHLETIC AWARDS Total amount: $626,749 (100% non-need-based).
APPLYING FOR FINANCIAL AID *Required financial aid form:* FAFSA. *Financial aid deadline:* 8/1 (priority: 2/1). *Notification date:* Continuous beginning 2/15. Students must reply within 1 week of notification.
CONTACT Becky Moore, Associate Director, Financial Aid, Palm Beach Atlantic University, PO Box 24708, West Palm Beach, FL 33416-4708, 561-803-2127 or toll-free 800-238-3998. *Fax:* 561-803-2130. *E-mail:* margherite_powell@pba.edu.

PALMER COLLEGE OF CHIROPRACTIC
Davenport, IA

ABOUT THE INSTITUTION Independent, coed. Awards: associate, master's, and first professional degrees. 2 undergraduate majors. Total enrollment: 2,171. Undergraduates: 96. Freshmen: 30.
GIFT AID (NEED-BASED) *Scholarships, grants, and awards:* Federal Pell, FSEOG, state, private, college/university gift aid from institutional funds.
GIFT AID (NON-NEED-BASED) *Scholarships, grants, and awards by category: Academic Interests/Achievement:* biological sciences, general academic interests/achievements, health fields.
LOANS *Programs:* FFEL (Subsidized and Unsubsidized Stafford, PLUS), Perkins, state.
WORK-STUDY *Federal work-study:* Total amount: $13,100; 4 jobs averaging $2200.
APPLYING FOR FINANCIAL AID *Required financial aid form:* FAFSA.
CONTACT Brenda Gran, Financial Planning Office, Palmer College of Chiropractic, 1000 Brady Street, Davenport, IA 52803, 563-884-5888 or toll-free 800-722-3648. *Fax:* 563-884-5299. *E-mail:* gran_b@palmer.edu.

PARK UNIVERSITY
Parkville, MO

ABOUT THE INSTITUTION Independent, coed. Awards: associate, bachelor's, and master's degrees. 51 undergraduate majors. Total university enrollment: 5,448. Total unit enrollment: 13,253. Undergraduates: 12,688. Freshmen: 142.
GIFT AID (NEED-BASED) *Scholarships, grants, and awards:* Federal Pell, FSEOG, state, private, college/university gift aid from institutional funds.
GIFT AID (NON-NEED-BASED) *Scholarships, grants, and awards by category: Academic Interests/Achievement:* general academic interests/achievements. *Creative Arts/Performance:* art/fine arts, theater/drama. *Special Achievements/Activities:* cheerleading/drum major. *Special Characteristics:* children of faculty/staff, religious affiliation, siblings of current students.
LOANS *Programs:* FFEL (Subsidized and Unsubsidized Stafford, PLUS), Perkins, college/university.
APPLYING FOR FINANCIAL AID *Required financial aid forms:* FAFSA, institution's own form.
CONTACT Ms. Cathy Colapietro, Director of Student Financial Services, Park University, 8700 NW River Park Drive, Parkville, MO 64152, 816-584-6728 or toll-free 800-745-7275. *Fax:* 816-741-9668.

PARSONS THE NEW SCHOOL FOR DESIGN
New York, NY

CONTACT Financial Aid Counselor, Parsons The New School for Design, 66 Fifth Avenue, New York, NY 10011, 212-229-8930 or toll-free 877-528-3321.

PATRICK HENRY COLLEGE
Purcellville, VA

CONTACT Financial Aid Office, Patrick Henry College, One Patrick Henry Circle, Purcellville, VA 20132, 540-338-1776.

PATTEN UNIVERSITY
Oakland, CA

CONTACT Mr. Robert A. Olivera, Dean of Enrollment Services, Patten University, 2433 Coolidge Avenue, Oakland, CA 94601-2699, 510-261-8500 Ext. 783. *Fax:* 510-534-8969. *E-mail:* oliverob@patten.edu.

PAUL QUINN COLLEGE
Dallas, TX

CONTACT Khaleelah Ali, Assistant Director of Financial Aid, Paul Quinn College, 3837 Simpson Stuart Road, Dallas, TX 75241, 214-302-3530 or toll-free 800-237-2648. *Fax:* 214-302-3535. *E-mail:* kali@pqc.edu.

PAUL SMITH'S COLLEGE OF ARTS AND SCIENCES
Paul Smiths, NY

Tuition & fees: $18,170 **Average undergraduate aid package: $15,008**

ABOUT THE INSTITUTION Independent, coed. Awards: associate and bachelor's degrees. 13 undergraduate majors. Total enrollment: 846. Undergraduates: 846. Freshmen: 307. Federal methodology is used as a basis for awarding need-based institutional aid.
UNDERGRADUATE EXPENSES for 2006–07 *Application fee:* $30. *Comprehensive fee:* $25,590 includes full-time tuition ($16,910), mandatory fees ($1260), and room and board ($7420). *College room only:* $3710. *Part-time tuition:* $450 per credit hour.
FRESHMAN FINANCIAL AID (Fall 2005, est.) 301 applied for aid; of those 93% were deemed to have need. 100% of freshmen with need received aid; of those 16% had need fully met. *Average percent of need met:* 69% (excluding resources awarded to replace EFC). *Average financial aid package:* $14,752 (excluding resources awarded to replace EFC). 7% of all full-time freshmen had no need and received non-need-based gift aid.
UNDERGRADUATE FINANCIAL AID (Fall 2005, est.) 806 applied for aid; of those 92% were deemed to have need. 100% of undergraduates with need received aid; of those 17% had need fully met. *Average percent of need met:* 71% (excluding resources awarded to replace EFC). *Average financial aid package:* $15,008 (excluding resources awarded to replace EFC). 8% of all full-time undergraduates had no need and received non-need-based gift aid.
GIFT AID (NEED-BASED) *Total amount:* $7,207,566 (13% federal, 18% state, 64% institutional, 5% external sources). *Receiving aid:* Freshmen: 90% (278); All full-time undergraduates: 89% (731). *Average award:* Freshmen: $7316; Undergraduates: $6707. *Scholarships, grants, and awards:* Federal Pell, FSEOG, state, private, college/university gift aid from institutional funds.
GIFT AID (NON-NEED-BASED) *Total amount:* $363,753 (80% institutional, 20% external sources). *Receiving aid:* Freshmen: 8% (24); Undergraduates: 7% (55). *Average Award:* Freshmen: $5695; Undergraduates: $3178. *Scholarships, grants, and awards by category: Academic Interests/Achievement:* general academic interests/achievements.
LOANS *Student loans:* $5,766,387 (83% need-based, 17% non-need-based). 90% of past graduating class borrowed through all loan programs. *Average indebtedness per student:* $6625. *Average need-based loan:* Freshmen: $3227; Undergraduates: $4347. *Parent loans:* $2,719,421 (100% need-based). *Programs:* FFEL (Subsidized and Unsubsidized Stafford, PLUS), Perkins.
WORK-STUDY *Federal work-study:* Total amount: $1,332,615; 735 jobs averaging $1813.

Paul Smith's College of Arts and Sciences

ATHLETIC AWARDS *Total amount:* $4000 (100% need-based).
APPLYING FOR FINANCIAL AID *Required financial aid forms:* FAFSA, state aid form. *Financial aid deadline (priority):* 3/3. *Notification date:* Continuous. Students must reply within 4 weeks of notification.
CONTACT Mary Ellen Chamberlain, Director of Financial Aid, Paul Smith's College of Arts and Sciences, Routes 86 and 30, PO Box 265, Paul Smiths, NY 12970, 518-327-6220 or toll-free 800-421-2605. *Fax:* 518-327-6055. *E-mail:* chambem@paulsmiths.edu.

PEABODY CONSERVATORY OF MUSIC OF THE JOHNS HOPKINS UNIVERSITY
Baltimore, MD

ABOUT THE INSTITUTION Independent, coed. Awards: bachelor's, master's, and doctoral degrees and post-bachelor's certificates. 8 undergraduate majors. Total enrollment: 647. Undergraduates: 323. Freshmen: 76.
GIFT AID (NEED-BASED) *Scholarships, grants, and awards:* Federal Pell, FSEOG, state, private, college/university gift aid from institutional funds.
GIFT AID (NON-NEED-BASED) *Scholarships, grants, and awards by category: Creative Arts/Performance:* music.
LOANS *Programs:* Federal Direct (Subsidized and Unsubsidized Stafford), FFEL (PLUS), Perkins, college/university.
WORK-STUDY *Federal work-study:* Total amount: $218,753; 114 jobs averaging $1919. *State or other work-study/employment:* Total amount: $96,213 (100% non-need-based). 103 part-time jobs averaging $934.
APPLYING FOR FINANCIAL AID *Required financial aid form:* FAFSA.
CONTACT George Tyree, Financial Aid Officer, Peabody Conservatory of Music of The Johns Hopkins University, 1 East Mount Vernon Place, Baltimore, MD 21202-2397, 410-659-8100 Ext. 3023 or toll-free 800-368-2521 (out-of-state). *Fax:* 410-659-8102. *E-mail:* finaid@peabody.jhu.edu.

PEACE COLLEGE
Raleigh, NC

Tuition & fees: $19,250	Average undergraduate aid package: $14,419

ABOUT THE INSTITUTION Independent religious, women only. Awards: bachelor's degrees. 13 undergraduate majors. Total enrollment: 701. Undergraduates: 701. Freshmen: 251. Federal methodology is used as a basis for awarding need-based institutional aid.
UNDERGRADUATE EXPENSES for 2005–06 *Application fee:* $25. *Comprehensive fee:* $26,168 includes full-time tuition ($18,906), mandatory fees ($344), and room and board ($6918). *Part-time tuition:* $400 per credit hour. *Payment plans:* Installment, deferred payment.
FRESHMAN FINANCIAL AID (Fall 2005, est.) 161 applied for aid; of those 84% were deemed to have need. 100% of freshmen with need received aid; of those 12% had need fully met. *Average percent of need met:* 72% (excluding resources awarded to replace EFC). *Average financial aid package:* $14,649 (excluding resources awarded to replace EFC). 28% of all full-time freshmen had no need and received non-need-based gift aid.
UNDERGRADUATE FINANCIAL AID (Fall 2005, est.) 568 applied for aid; of those 84% were deemed to have need. 100% of undergraduates with need received aid; of those 12% had need fully met. *Average percent of need met:* 69% (excluding resources awarded to replace EFC). *Average financial aid package:* $14,419 (excluding resources awarded to replace EFC). 28% of all full-time undergraduates had no need and received non-need-based gift aid.
GIFT AID (NEED-BASED) *Total amount:* $5,204,429 (14% federal, 25% state, 58% institutional, 3% external sources). *Receiving aid:* Freshmen: 67% (136); All full-time undergraduates: 69% (476). *Average award:* Freshmen: $12,327; Undergraduates: $10,965. *Scholarships, grants, and awards:* Federal Pell, FSEOG, state, private, college/university gift aid from institutional funds, Federal Nursing.
GIFT AID (NON-NEED-BASED) *Total amount:* $1,318,711 (25% state, 64% institutional, 11% external sources). *Receiving aid:* Freshmen: 5% (10); Undergraduates: 5% (35). *Average Award:* Freshmen: $9953; Undergraduates: $10,297. *Scholarships, grants, and awards by category: Academic Interests/Achievement:* 656 awards ($2,615,150 total): general academic interests/achievements. *Creative Arts/Performance:* 32 awards ($35,860 total): art/fine arts, music, theater/drama. *Special Characteristics:* 7 awards ($64,427 total):
children of faculty/staff, relatives of clergy. *Tuition waivers:* Full or partial for employees or children of employees. *ROTC:* Army cooperative, Naval cooperative, Air Force cooperative.
LOANS *Student loans:* $3,450,763 (72% need-based, 28% non-need-based). 86% of past graduating class borrowed through all loan programs. *Average need-based loan:* Freshmen: $2175; Undergraduates: $3348. *Parent loans:* $1,620,025 (30% need-based, 70% non-need-based). *Programs:* FFEL (Subsidized and Unsubsidized Stafford, PLUS), alternative loans.
WORK-STUDY *Federal work-study:* Total amount: $266,351; 204 jobs averaging $1306. *State or other work-study/employment:* Total amount: $22,816 (21% need-based, 79% non-need-based). 14 part-time jobs averaging $1630.
APPLYING FOR FINANCIAL AID *Required financial aid form:* FAFSA. *Financial aid deadline:* Continuous. *Notification date:* Continuous.
CONTACT Angela Kirkley, Director of Financial Aid, Peace College, 15 East Peace Street, Raleigh, NC 27604, 919-508-2249 or toll-free 800-PEACE-47. *Fax:* 919-508-2325. *E-mail:* akirkley@peace.edu.

PEIRCE COLLEGE
Philadelphia, PA

ABOUT THE INSTITUTION Independent, coed. Awards: associate and bachelor's degrees and post-bachelor's certificates. 19 undergraduate majors. Total enrollment: 1,971. Undergraduates: 1,971. Freshmen: 294.
GIFT AID (NEED-BASED) *Scholarships, grants, and awards:* Federal Pell, FSEOG, state, private, college/university gift aid from institutional funds.
GIFT AID (NON-NEED-BASED) *Scholarships, grants, and awards by category: Academic Interests/Achievement:* general academic interests/achievements. *Special Achievements/Activities:* community service, leadership, memberships. *Special Characteristics:* children and siblings of alumni, children of public servants, parents of current students, previous college experience, public servants, siblings of current students, spouses of current students.
LOANS *Programs:* FFEL (Subsidized and Unsubsidized Stafford, PLUS).
APPLYING FOR FINANCIAL AID *Required financial aid forms:* FAFSA, institution's own form.
CONTACT Lisa A. Gargiulo, Student Financial Services Manager, Peirce College, 1420 Pine Street, Philadelphia, PA 19102, 215-670-9370 or toll-free 888-467-3472. *Fax:* 215-545-3671. *E-mail:* lagargiulo@peirce.edu.

PENNSYLVANIA COLLEGE OF ART & DESIGN
Lancaster, PA

CONTACT J. David Hershey, Registrar/Director of Financial Aid, Pennsylvania College of Art & Design, 204 North Prince Street, PO Box 59, Lancaster, PA 17608-0059, 717-396-7833 Ext. 13. *Fax:* 717-396-1339. *E-mail:* finaid@psad.edu.

PENNSYLVANIA COLLEGE OF TECHNOLOGY
Williamsport, PA

Tuition & fees (PA res): $10,080	Average undergraduate aid package: N/A

ABOUT THE INSTITUTION State-related, coed. Awards: associate and bachelor's degrees. 108 undergraduate majors. Total enrollment: 6,537. Undergraduates: 6,537. Freshmen: 1,671. Federal methodology is used as a basis for awarding need-based institutional aid.
UNDERGRADUATE EXPENSES for 2005–06 *Application fee:* $50. *Tuition, state resident:* full-time $8580; part-time $286 per credit. *Tuition, nonresident:* full-time $11,160; part-time $372 per credit. Full-time tuition and fees vary according to course load and program. Part-time tuition and fees vary according to course load and program. *College room and board:* $6900; *room only:* $4200. Room and board charges vary according to board plan, housing facility, and location. *Payment plan:* Deferred payment.
GIFT AID (NEED-BASED) *Total amount:* $14,964,800 (38% federal, 52% state, 2% institutional, 8% external sources). *Scholarships, grants, and awards:* Federal Pell, FSEOG, state, private, college/university gift aid from institutional funds.
GIFT AID (NON-NEED-BASED) *Tuition waivers:* Full or partial for employees or children of employees. *ROTC:* Army cooperative.

LOANS *Student loans:* $29,844,516 (100% need-based). *Parent loans:* $8,512,305 (100% need-based). *Programs:* FFEL (Subsidized and Unsubsidized Stafford, PLUS).
WORK-STUDY *Federal work-study:* Total amount: $385,092; 308 jobs averaging $1250. *State or other work-study/employment:* Total amount: $418,449 (100% need-based). 294 part-time jobs averaging $1423.
APPLYING FOR FINANCIAL AID *Required financial aid forms:* FAFSA, institution's own form. *Financial aid deadline (priority):* 4/1. *Notification date:* Continuous beginning 6/1. Students must reply within 2 weeks of notification.
CONTACT Dennis L. Correll, Director of Financial Aid, Pennsylvania College of Technology, One College Avenue, DIF 108, Williamsport, PA 17701, 570-326-4766 Ext. 7048 or toll-free 800-367-9222 (in-state). *Fax:* 570-321-5552. *E-mail:* dcorrell@pct.edu.

THE PENNSYLVANIA STATE UNIVERSITY ABINGTON COLLEGE
Abington, PA

Tuition & fees (PA res): $10,190   Average undergraduate aid package: $10,060

ABOUT THE INSTITUTION State-related, coed. Awards: associate and bachelor's degrees. 119 undergraduate majors. Total enrollment: 3,142. Undergraduates: 3,142. Freshmen: 758. Federal methodology is used as a basis for awarding need-based institutional aid.
UNDERGRADUATE EXPENSES for 2005–06 *Application fee:* $50. *Tuition, state resident:* full-time $9722; part-time $393 per credit hour. *Tuition, nonresident:* full-time $14,854; part-time $619 per credit hour. *Required fees:* full-time $468; $79 per term part-time. Full-time tuition and fees vary according to course level, location, program, and student level. Part-time tuition and fees vary according to course level, course load, location, program, and student level. *Payment plan:* Deferred payment.
FRESHMAN FINANCIAL AID (Fall 2004) 575 applied for aid; of those 77% were deemed to have need. 98% of freshmen with need received aid; of those 5% had need fully met. *Average percent of need met:* 68% (excluding resources awarded to replace EFC). *Average financial aid package:* $9598 (excluding resources awarded to replace EFC). 7% of all full-time freshmen had no need and received non-need-based gift aid.
UNDERGRADUATE FINANCIAL AID (Fall 2004) 1,736 applied for aid; of those 80% were deemed to have need. 98% of undergraduates with need received aid; of those 7% had need fully met. *Average percent of need met:* 67% (excluding resources awarded to replace EFC). *Average financial aid package:* $10,060 (excluding resources awarded to replace EFC). 4% of all full-time undergraduates had no need and received non-need-based gift aid.
GIFT AID (NEED-BASED) *Total amount:* $6,320,305 (46% federal, 35% state, 19% institutional). *Receiving aid:* Freshmen: 50% (347); All full-time undergraduates: 48% (1,100). *Average award:* Freshmen: $5291; Undergraduates: $4985. *Scholarships, grants, and awards:* Federal Pell, FSEOG, state, private, college/university gift aid from institutional funds.
GIFT AID (NON-NEED-BASED) *Total amount:* $1,537,753 (45% institutional, 55% external sources). *Receiving aid:* Freshmen: 38% (264); Undergraduates: 21% (482). *Average Award:* Freshmen: $2537; Undergraduates: $2347. *Scholarships, grants, and awards by category:* Academic Interests/Achievement: general academic interests/achievements. Special Characteristics: general special characteristics. *Tuition waivers:* Full or partial for employees or children of employees, senior citizens. *ROTC:* Army, Air Force cooperative.
LOANS *Student loans:* $7,177,645 (61% need-based, 39% non-need-based). 65% of past graduating class borrowed through all loan programs. *Average indebtedness per student:* $22,400. *Average need-based loan:* Freshmen: $2521; Undergraduates: $3405. *Parent loans:* $1,223,028 (100% non-need-based). *Programs:* Federal Direct (Subsidized and Unsubsidized Stafford, PLUS), FFEL (Subsidized and Unsubsidized Stafford, PLUS), Perkins, college/university, private loans.
WORK-STUDY *Federal work-study:* Total amount: $101,947; 84 jobs averaging $1188. *State or other work-study/employment:* Part-time jobs available.
APPLYING FOR FINANCIAL AID *Required financial aid form:* FAFSA. *Financial aid deadline:* Continuous. *Notification date:* Continuous beginning 2/15.
CONTACT Debbie Meditz, Assistant Student Aid Coordinator, The Pennsylvania State University Abington College, 106 Sutherland Building, 1600 Woodland Road, Abington, PA 19001, 215-881-7348. *Fax:* 215-881-7655. *E-mail:* dlm175@psu.edu.

THE PENNSYLVANIA STATE UNIVERSITY ALTOONA COLLEGE
Altoona, PA

Tuition & fees (PA res): $10,626   Average undergraduate aid package: $12,637

ABOUT THE INSTITUTION State-related, coed. Awards: associate and bachelor's degrees. 123 undergraduate majors. Total enrollment: 3,647. Undergraduates: 3,647. Freshmen: 1,216. Federal methodology is used as a basis for awarding need-based institutional aid.
UNDERGRADUATE EXPENSES for 2005–06 *Application fee:* $50. *Tuition, area resident:* part-time $423 per credit hour. *Tuition, state resident:* full-time $10,148; part-time $423 per credit hour. *Tuition, nonresident:* full-time $15,546; part-time $648 per credit hour. *Required fees:* full-time $478; $80 per term part-time. Full-time tuition and fees vary according to course level, location, program, and student level. Part-time tuition and fees vary according to course level, course load, location, program, and student level. *College room and board:* $6530; *room only:* $3430. Room and board charges vary according to board plan and housing facility. *Payment plan:* Deferred payment.
FRESHMAN FINANCIAL AID (Fall 2004) 1041 applied for aid; of those 80% were deemed to have need. 98% of freshmen with need received aid; of those 6% had need fully met. *Average percent of need met:* 63% (excluding resources awarded to replace EFC). *Average financial aid package:* $11,540 (excluding resources awarded to replace EFC). 3% of all full-time freshmen had no need and received non-need-based gift aid.
UNDERGRADUATE FINANCIAL AID (Fall 2004) 2,738 applied for aid; of those 84% were deemed to have need. 99% of undergraduates with need received aid; of those 8% had need fully met. *Average percent of need met:* 68% (excluding resources awarded to replace EFC). *Average financial aid package:* $12,637 (excluding resources awarded to replace EFC). 3% of all full-time undergraduates had no need and received non-need-based gift aid.
GIFT AID (NEED-BASED) *Total amount:* $8,470,433 (45% federal, 48% state, 7% institutional). *Receiving aid:* Freshmen: 46% (573); All full-time undergraduates: 49% (1,666). *Average award:* Freshmen: $4250; Undergraduates: $4370. *Scholarships, grants, and awards:* Federal Pell, FSEOG, state, private, college/university gift aid from institutional funds.
GIFT AID (NON-NEED-BASED) *Total amount:* $1,640,504 (58% institutional, 42% external sources). *Receiving aid:* Freshmen: 24% (297); Undergraduates: 23% (787). *Average Award:* Freshmen: $2210; Undergraduates: $3659. *Scholarships, grants, and awards by category:* Academic Interests/Achievement: general academic interests/achievements. Special Characteristics: general special characteristics. *Tuition waivers:* Full or partial for employees or children of employees, senior citizens. *ROTC:* Army, Air Force.
LOANS *Student loans:* $11,817,327 (66% need-based, 34% non-need-based). 65% of past graduating class borrowed through all loan programs. *Average indebtedness per student:* $22,400. *Average need-based loan:* Freshmen: $2694; Undergraduates: $3485. *Parent loans:* $5,426,662 (100% non-need-based). *Programs:* Federal Direct (Subsidized and Unsubsidized Stafford, PLUS), FFEL (Subsidized and Unsubsidized Stafford, PLUS), Perkins, college/university, private loans.
WORK-STUDY *Federal work-study:* Total amount: $551,703; 330 jobs averaging $1664. *State or other work-study/employment:* Total amount: $118,486 (100% need-based). 27 part-time jobs averaging $5543.
APPLYING FOR FINANCIAL AID *Required financial aid form:* FAFSA. *Financial aid deadline:* Continuous. *Notification date:* Continuous beginning 2/15.
CONTACT Mr. David Pearlman, Assistant Director of Student Affairs, The Pennsylvania State University Altoona College, W111 Smith Building, Altoona, PA 16601-3760, 814-949-5055 or toll-free 800-848-9843. *Fax:* 814-949-5536. *E-mail:* dpp1@psu.edu.

THE PENNSYLVANIA STATE UNIVERSITY AT ERIE, THE BEHREND COLLEGE
Erie, PA

Tuition & fees (PA res): $10,626   Average undergraduate aid package: $13,042

ABOUT THE INSTITUTION State-related, coed. Awards: associate, bachelor's, and master's degrees. 131 undergraduate majors. Total enrollment: 3,542.

The Pennsylvania State University at Erie, The Behrend College

Undergraduates: 3,382. Freshmen: 838. Federal methodology is used as a basis for awarding need-based institutional aid.

UNDERGRADUATE EXPENSES for 2005–06 *Application fee:* $50. *Tuition, area resident:* part-time $423 per credit hour. *Tuition, state resident:* full-time $10,148; part-time $423 per credit hour. *Tuition, nonresident:* full-time $15,546; part-time $648 per credit hour. *Required fees:* full-time $478; $80 per term part-time. Full-time tuition and fees vary according to course level and student level. Part-time tuition and fees vary according to course level, course load, and student level. *College room and board:* $6530; *room only:* $3430. Room and board charges vary according to board plan and housing facility. *Payment plan:* Deferred payment.

FRESHMAN FINANCIAL AID (Fall 2004) 750 applied for aid; of those 80% were deemed to have need. 98% of freshmen with need received aid; of those 8% had need fully met. *Average percent of need met:* 68% (excluding resources awarded to replace EFC). *Average financial aid package:* $12,337 (excluding resources awarded to replace EFC). 6% of all full-time freshmen had no need and received non-need-based gift aid.

UNDERGRADUATE FINANCIAL AID (Fall 2004) 2,627 applied for aid; of those 84% were deemed to have need. 99% of undergraduates with need received aid; of those 10% had need fully met. *Average percent of need met:* 72% (excluding resources awarded to replace EFC). *Average financial aid package:* $13,042 (excluding resources awarded to replace EFC). 5% of all full-time undergraduates had no need and received non-need-based gift aid.

GIFT AID (NEED-BASED) *Total amount:* $8,516,993 (36% federal, 48% state, 16% institutional). *Receiving aid:* Freshmen: 50% (421); All full-time undergraduates: 50% (1,558). *Average award:* Freshmen: $4511; Undergraduates: $4240. *Scholarships, grants, and awards:* Federal Pell, FSEOG, state, private, college/university gift aid from institutional funds.

GIFT AID (NON-NEED-BASED) *Total amount:* $2,333,040 (59% institutional, 41% external sources). *Receiving aid:* Freshmen: 29% (250); Undergraduates: 27% (842). *Average Award:* Freshmen: $2412; Undergraduates: $3353. *Scholarships, grants, and awards by category:* Academic Interests/Achievement: general academic interests/achievements. Special Characteristics: general special characteristics. *Tuition waivers:* Full or partial for employees or children of employees, senior citizens. *ROTC:* Army cooperative.

LOANS *Student loans:* $11,794,071 (69% need-based, 31% non-need-based). 65% of past graduating class borrowed through all loan programs. *Average indebtedness per student:* $22,400. *Average need-based loan:* Freshmen: $2848; Undergraduates: $3940. *Parent loans:* $5,387,861 (100% non-need-based). *Programs:* Federal Direct (Subsidized and Unsubsidized Stafford, PLUS), FFEL (Subsidized and Unsubsidized Stafford, PLUS), Perkins, college/university, private loans.

WORK-STUDY *Federal work-study:* Total amount: $366,621; 260 jobs averaging $1410. *State or other work-study/employment:* Total amount: $192,552 (100% need-based). 52 part-time jobs averaging $5226.

APPLYING FOR FINANCIAL AID *Required financial aid form:* FAFSA. *Financial aid deadline:* Continuous. *Notification date:* Continuous beginning 2/15.

CONTACT Ms. Jane Brady, Assistant Director of Admissions and Financial Aid, The Pennsylvania State University at Erie, The Behrend College, 5091 Station Road, Erie, PA 16563, 814-898-6162 or toll-free 866-374-3378. *Fax:* 814-898-7595. *E-mail:* jub9@psu.edu.

THE PENNSYLVANIA STATE UNIVERSITY BERKS CAMPUS OF THE BERKS–LEHIGH VALLEY COLLEGE
Reading, PA

Tuition & fees (PA res): $10,626   **Average undergraduate aid package:** $11,476

ABOUT THE INSTITUTION State-related, coed. Awards: associate and bachelor's degrees. 127 undergraduate majors. Total enrollment: 2,488. Undergraduates: 2,444. Freshmen: 856. Federal methodology is used as a basis for awarding need-based institutional aid.

UNDERGRADUATE EXPENSES for 2005–06 *Application fee:* $50. *Tuition, state resident:* full-time $10,148; part-time $423 per credit hour. *Tuition, nonresident:* full-time $15,546; part-time $648 per credit hour. *Required fees:* full-time $478; $80 per term part-time. Full-time tuition and fees vary according to course level, course load, and student level. Part-time tuition and fees vary according to course level and student level. *College room and board:* $7140; *room only:* $4040. Room and board charges vary according to board plan and housing facility. *Payment plan:* Deferred payment.

FRESHMAN FINANCIAL AID (Fall 2004) 637 applied for aid; of those 71% were deemed to have need. 99% of freshmen with need received aid; of those 3% had need fully met. *Average percent of need met:* 61% (excluding resources awarded to replace EFC). *Average financial aid package:* $10,997 (excluding resources awarded to replace EFC). 5% of all full-time freshmen had no need and received non-need-based gift aid.

UNDERGRADUATE FINANCIAL AID (Fall 2004) 1,534 applied for aid; of those 74% were deemed to have need. 99% of undergraduates with need received aid; of those 7% had need fully met. *Average percent of need met:* 66% (excluding resources awarded to replace EFC). *Average financial aid package:* $11,476 (excluding resources awarded to replace EFC). 5% of all full-time undergraduates had no need and received non-need-based gift aid.

GIFT AID (NEED-BASED) *Total amount:* $4,030,834 (37% federal, 47% state, 16% institutional). *Receiving aid:* Freshmen: 37% (292); All full-time undergraduates: 37% (758). *Average award:* Freshmen: $4530; Undergraduates: $4350. *Scholarships, grants, and awards:* Federal Pell, FSEOG, state, private, college/university gift aid from institutional funds.

GIFT AID (NON-NEED-BASED) *Total amount:* $953,497 (51% institutional, 49% external sources). *Receiving aid:* Freshmen: 20% (161); Undergraduates: 20% (404). *Average Award:* Freshmen: $1719; Undergraduates: $2643. *Scholarships, grants, and awards by category:* Academic Interests/Achievement: general academic interests/achievements. Special Characteristics: general special characteristics. *Tuition waivers:* Full or partial for employees or children of employees, senior citizens.

LOANS *Student loans:* $6,057,967 (59% need-based, 41% non-need-based). 65% of past graduating class borrowed through all loan programs. *Average indebtedness per student:* $22,400. *Average need-based loan:* Freshmen: $2612; Undergraduates: $3310. *Parent loans:* $3,357,386 (100% non-need-based). *Programs:* FFEL (Subsidized and Unsubsidized Stafford, PLUS), Perkins, college/university, private loans.

WORK-STUDY *Federal work-study:* Total amount: $91,691; 67 jobs averaging $1358. *State or other work-study/employment:* Total amount: $127,741 (100% need-based). 26 part-time jobs averaging $5853.

APPLYING FOR FINANCIAL AID *Required financial aid form:* FAFSA. *Financial aid deadline:* Continuous. *Notification date:* Continuous beginning 2/15.

CONTACT Maryann Hubick, Financial Aid Coordinator, The Pennsylvania State University Berks Campus of the Berks–Lehigh Valley College, Perkins Student Center, Room 6, Reading, PA 19610-6009, 610-396-6071. *Fax:* 610-396-6077. *E-mail:* mxh61@psu.edu.

THE PENNSYLVANIA STATE UNIVERSITY HARRISBURG CAMPUS
Middletown, PA

Tuition & fees (PA res): $10,616   **Average undergraduate aid package:** $13,028

ABOUT THE INSTITUTION State-related, coed. Awards: associate, bachelor's, master's, and doctoral degrees and post-bachelor's certificates. 33 undergraduate majors. Total enrollment: 3,736. Undergraduates: 2,068. Freshmen: 219. Federal methodology is used as a basis for awarding need-based institutional aid.

UNDERGRADUATE EXPENSES for 2005–06 *Application fee:* $50. *Tuition, state resident:* full-time $10,148; part-time $423 per credit hour. *Tuition, nonresident:* full-time $15,546; part-time $648 per credit hour. *Required fees:* full-time $468; $79 per term part-time. Full-time tuition and fees vary according to course level, location, program, and student level. Part-time tuition and fees vary according to course level, course load, location, program, and student level. *College room and board:* $8030; *room only:* $4930. Room and board charges vary according to board plan and housing facility. *Payment plan:* Deferred payment.

FRESHMAN FINANCIAL AID (Fall 2004) 135 applied for aid; of those 70% were deemed to have need. 98% of freshmen with need received aid; of those 14% had need fully met. *Average percent of need met:* 69% (excluding resources awarded to replace EFC). *Average financial aid package:* $12,828 (excluding resources awarded to replace EFC). 6% of all full-time freshmen had no need and received non-need-based gift aid.

UNDERGRADUATE FINANCIAL AID (Fall 2004) 1,190 applied for aid; of those 84% were deemed to have need. 99% of undergraduates with need received aid; of those 12% had need fully met. *Average percent of need met:* 71% (excluding resources awarded to replace EFC). *Average financial aid package:* $13,028 (excluding resources awarded to replace EFC). 4% of all full-time undergraduates had no need and received non-need-based gift aid.
GIFT AID (NEED-BASED) *Total amount:* $4,242,960 (48% federal, 45% state, 7% institutional). *Receiving aid:* Freshmen: 39% (63); All full-time undergraduates: 50% (732). *Average award:* Freshmen: $5368; Undergraduates: $4515. *Scholarships, grants, and awards:* Federal Pell, FSEOG, state, private, college/university gift aid from institutional funds.
GIFT AID (NON-NEED-BASED) *Total amount:* $694,947 (43% institutional, 57% external sources). *Receiving aid:* Freshmen: 32% (52); Undergraduates: 22% (314). *Average Award: Freshmen:* $4155; *Undergraduates:* $4624. *Scholarships, grants, and awards by category: Academic Interests/Achievement:* general academic interests/achievements. *Special Characteristics:* general special characteristics. *Tuition waivers:* Full or partial for employees or children of employees, senior citizens. *ROTC:* Army cooperative.
LOANS *Student loans:* $8,014,179 (59% need-based, 41% non-need-based). 65% of past graduating class borrowed through all loan programs. *Average indebtedness per student:* $22,400. *Average need-based loan:* Freshmen: $2781; Undergraduates: $4493. *Parent loans:* $975,454 (100% non-need-based). *Programs:* Federal Direct (Subsidized and Unsubsidized Stafford, PLUS), FFEL (Subsidized and Unsubsidized Stafford, PLUS), Perkins, college/university, private loans.
WORK-STUDY *Federal work-study:* Total amount: $85,760; 71 jobs averaging $1187. *State or other work-study/employment:* Total amount: $3840 (100% need-based). 3 part-time jobs averaging $3200.
APPLYING FOR FINANCIAL AID *Required financial aid form:* FAFSA. *Financial aid deadline:* Continuous. *Notification date:* Continuous beginning 2/15.
CONTACT Ms. Carolyn Julian, Student Aid Adviser, The Pennsylvania State University Harrisburg Campus, W112 Olmstead, 777 West Harrisburg Pike, Middletown, PA 17057-4898, 717-948-6307 or toll-free 800-222-2056. *Fax:* 717-948-6008. *E-mail:* czb3@psu.edu.

THE PENNSYLVANIA STATE UNIVERSITY UNIVERSITY PARK CAMPUS
State College, PA

Tuition & fees (PA res): $11,508   **Average undergraduate aid package:** $13,935

ABOUT THE INSTITUTION State-related, coed. Awards: associate, bachelor's, master's, and doctoral degrees and post-bachelor's certificates. 123 undergraduate majors. Total enrollment: 40,709. Undergraduates: 34,637. Freshmen: 6,496. Federal methodology is used as a basis for awarding need-based institutional aid.
UNDERGRADUATE EXPENSES for 2005–06 *Application fee:* $50. *Tuition, state resident:* full-time $11,024; part-time $459 per credit hour. *Tuition, nonresident:* full-time $21,260; part-time $886 per credit hour. *Required fees:* full-time $484; $180 per term part-time. *College room and board:* $6530; *room only:* $3430.
FRESHMAN FINANCIAL AID (Fall 2004) 4424 applied for aid; of those 66% were deemed to have need. 97% of freshmen with need received aid; of those 11% had need fully met. *Average percent of need met:* 68% (excluding resources awarded to replace EFC). *Average financial aid package:* $13,937 (excluding resources awarded to replace EFC). 13% of all full-time freshmen had no need and received non-need-based gift aid.
UNDERGRADUATE FINANCIAL AID (Fall 2004) 21,791 applied for aid; of those 76% were deemed to have need. 98% of undergraduates with need received aid; of those 12% had need fully met. *Average percent of need met:* 70% (excluding resources awarded to replace EFC). *Average financial aid package:* $13,935 (excluding resources awarded to replace EFC). 11% of all full-time undergraduates had no need and received non-need-based gift aid.
GIFT AID (NEED-BASED) *Total amount:* $64,762,256 (34% federal, 36% state, 30% institutional). *Receiving aid:* Freshmen: 26% (1,558); All full-time undergraduates: 30% (9,830). *Average award:* Freshmen: $5033; Undergraduates: $4522. *Scholarships, grants, and awards:* Federal Pell, FSEOG, state, private, college/university gift aid from institutional funds.
GIFT AID (NON-NEED-BASED) *Total amount:* $27,328,440 (68% institutional, 32% external sources). *Receiving aid:* Freshmen: 27% (1,614); Undergraduates: 22% (7,289). *Average Award:* Freshmen: $3880; Undergraduates: $4182.
Scholarships, grants, and awards by category: Academic Interests/Achievement: general academic interests/achievements. *Special Characteristics:* general special characteristics. *ROTC:* Army, Naval, Air Force.
LOANS *Student loans:* $95,642,671 (65% need-based, 35% non-need-based). 65% of past graduating class borrowed through all loan programs. *Average indebtedness per student:* $22,400. *Average need-based loan:* Freshmen: $2756; Undergraduates: $4171. *Parent loans:* $54,961,461 (100% non-need-based). *Programs:* FFEL (Subsidized and Unsubsidized Stafford, PLUS), Perkins, college/university, alternative loans.
WORK-STUDY *Federal work-study:* Total amount: $2,490,073; 1,799 jobs averaging $1371. *State or other work-study/employment:* Total amount: $954,080 (100% need-based). 296 part-time jobs averaging $4876.
ATHLETIC AWARDS *Total amount:* $8,820,578 (100% non-need-based).
APPLYING FOR FINANCIAL AID *Required financial aid form:* FAFSA. *Financial aid deadline:* Continuous. *Notification date:* Continuous beginning 2/15.
CONTACT Ms. Anna Griswold, Assistant Vice Provost for Student Aid, The Pennsylvania State University University Park Campus, 311 Shields Building, University Park, PA 16802, 814-863-0507. *Fax:* 814-863-0322. *E-mail:* amg5@psu.edu.

PEPPERDINE UNIVERSITY
Malibu, CA

Tuition & fees: $32,740   **Average undergraduate aid package:** $30,991

ABOUT THE INSTITUTION Independent religious, coed. Awards: bachelor's, master's, doctoral, and first professional degrees and post-master's certificates. 43 undergraduate majors. Total enrollment: 7,685. Undergraduates: 3,198. Freshmen: 762. Federal methodology is used as a basis for awarding need-based institutional aid.
UNDERGRADUATE EXPENSES for 2006–07 *Application fee:* $65. *Comprehensive fee:* $42,240 includes full-time tuition ($32,620), mandatory fees ($120), and room and board ($9500). *Part-time tuition:* $1010 per unit.
FRESHMAN FINANCIAL AID (Fall 2005, est.) 481 applied for aid; of those 59% were deemed to have need. 99% of freshmen with need received aid; of those 52% had need fully met. *Average percent of need met:* 93% (excluding resources awarded to replace EFC). *Average financial aid package:* $30,500 (excluding resources awarded to replace EFC). 14% of all full-time freshmen had no need and received non-need-based gift aid.
UNDERGRADUATE FINANCIAL AID (Fall 2005, est.) 1,896 applied for aid; of those 71% were deemed to have need. 99% of undergraduates with need received aid; of those 41% had need fully met. *Average percent of need met:* 89% (excluding resources awarded to replace EFC). *Average financial aid package:* $30,991 (excluding resources awarded to replace EFC). 15% of all full-time undergraduates had no need and received non-need-based gift aid.
GIFT AID (NEED-BASED) *Total amount:* $27,908,130 (10% federal, 9% state, 70% institutional, 11% external sources). *Receiving aid:* Freshmen: 35% (265); All full-time undergraduates: 45% (1,225). *Average award:* Freshmen: $21,400; Undergraduates: $20,855. *Scholarships, grants, and awards:* Federal Pell, FSEOG, state, private, college/university gift aid from institutional funds.
GIFT AID (NON-NEED-BASED) *Total amount:* $9,375,043 (87% institutional, 13% external sources). *Receiving aid:* Freshmen: 7% (56); Undergraduates: 12% (328). *Average Award:* Freshmen: $20,064; Undergraduates: $18,720. *Scholarships, grants, and awards by category: Academic Interests/Achievement:* 394 awards ($888,794 total): biological sciences, business, communication, education, general academic interests/achievements, humanities, international studies, religion/biblical studies, social sciences. *Creative Arts/Performance:* 1,049 awards ($1,007,169 total): art/fine arts, debating, journalism/publications, music, performing arts, theater/drama. *Special Characteristics:* general special characteristics. *ROTC:* Army cooperative, Air Force cooperative.
LOANS *Student loans:* $15,692,967 (79% need-based, 21% non-need-based). 62% of past graduating class borrowed through all loan programs. *Average indebtedness per student:* $31,848. *Average need-based loan:* Freshmen: $7712; Undergraduates: $9684. *Parent loans:* $12,035,199 (62% need-based, 38% non-need-based). *Programs:* FFEL (Subsidized and Unsubsidized Stafford, PLUS), Perkins, college/university.
WORK-STUDY *Federal work-study:* Total amount: $1,068,000; 785 jobs averaging $1809. *State or other work-study/employment:* Total amount: $628,590 (15% need-based, 85% non-need-based). 284 part-time jobs averaging $1999.

Pepperdine University

ATHLETIC AWARDS *Total amount:* $4,003,359 (9% need-based, 91% non-need-based).
APPLYING FOR FINANCIAL AID *Required financial aid forms:* FAFSA, institution's own form. *Financial aid deadline:* 2/15 (priority: 2/15). *Notification date:* 4/15. Students must reply within 2 weeks of notification.
CONTACT Janet Lockhart, Director of Financial Assistance, Pepperdine University, 24255 Pacific Coast Highway, Malibu, CA 90263-4301, 310-506-4301. *Fax:* 310-506-4746. *E-mail:* finaid2@pepperdine.edu.

PERU STATE COLLEGE
Peru, NE

ABOUT THE INSTITUTION State-supported, coed. Awards: bachelor's and master's degrees. 41 undergraduate majors. Total enrollment: 1,959. Undergraduates: 1,710. Freshmen: 213.
GIFT AID (NEED-BASED) *Scholarships, grants, and awards:* Federal Pell, FSEOG, state, college/university gift aid from institutional funds.
GIFT AID (NON-NEED-BASED) *Scholarships, grants, and awards by category: Academic Interests/Achievement:* biological sciences, business, computer science, education, English, general academic interests/achievements, humanities, mathematics, physical sciences, premedicine, social sciences. *Creative Arts/Performance:* art/fine arts, music. *Special Achievements/Activities:* cheerleading/drum major, leadership, memberships. *Special Characteristics:* adult students, children of faculty/staff, ethnic background, first-generation college students, international students, local/state students, out-of-state students, previous college experience, veterans, veterans' children.
LOANS *Programs:* FFEL (Subsidized and Unsubsidized Stafford, PLUS).
APPLYING FOR FINANCIAL AID *Required financial aid forms:* FAFSA, institution's own form.
CONTACT Diana Lind, Director of Financial Aid, Peru State College, PO Box 10, Peru, NE 68421, 402-872-2228 or toll-free 800-742-4412 (in-state). *Fax:* 402-872-2419. *E-mail:* finaid@oakmail.peru.edu.

PFEIFFER UNIVERSITY
Misenheimer, NC

ABOUT THE INSTITUTION Independent United Methodist, coed. Awards: bachelor's and master's degrees. 45 undergraduate majors. Total enrollment: 2,150. Undergraduates: 1,202. Freshmen: 198.
GIFT AID (NEED-BASED) *Scholarships, grants, and awards:* Federal Pell, FSEOG, state, private, college/university gift aid from institutional funds, United Negro College Fund.
GIFT AID (NON-NEED-BASED) *Scholarships, grants, and awards by category: Academic Interests/Achievement:* general academic interests/achievements. *Creative Arts/Performance:* music. *Special Achievements/Activities:* leadership, religious involvement. *Special Characteristics:* children and siblings of alumni.
LOANS *Programs:* FFEL (Subsidized and Unsubsidized Stafford, PLUS), Perkins, state, college/university.
APPLYING FOR FINANCIAL AID *Required financial aid forms:* FAFSA, state aid form, noncustodial (divorced/separated) parent's statement.
CONTACT Amy Brown, Director of Financial Aid, Pfeiffer University, PO Box 960, Misenheimer, NC 28109, 704-463-1360 Ext. 2074 or toll-free 800-338-2060. *Fax:* 704-463-1363. *E-mail:* abrown@pfieffer.edu.

PHILADELPHIA BIBLICAL UNIVERSITY
Langhorne, PA

Tuition & fees: $15,875	Average undergraduate aid package: $12,132

ABOUT THE INSTITUTION Independent nondenominational, coed. Awards: bachelor's, master's, and first professional degrees. 11 undergraduate majors. Total enrollment: 1,439. Undergraduates: 1,080. Freshmen: 233. Federal methodology is used as a basis for awarding need-based institutional aid.
UNDERGRADUATE EXPENSES for 2006–07 *Application fee:* $25. *Comprehensive fee:* $22,425 includes full-time tuition ($15,555), mandatory fees ($320), and room and board ($6550). *College room only:* $3400. *Part-time tuition:* $469 per credit.
FRESHMAN FINANCIAL AID (Fall 2005, est.) 197 applied for aid; of those 88% were deemed to have need. 100% of freshmen with need received aid; of those 33% had need fully met. *Average percent of need met:* 79% (excluding resources awarded to replace EFC). *Average financial aid package:* $12,597 (excluding resources awarded to replace EFC). 19% of all full-time freshmen had no need and received non-need-based gift aid.
UNDERGRADUATE FINANCIAL AID (Fall 2005, est.) 783 applied for aid; of those 91% were deemed to have need. 98% of undergraduates with need received aid; of those 25% had need fully met. *Average percent of need met:* 73% (excluding resources awarded to replace EFC). *Average financial aid package:* $12,132 (excluding resources awarded to replace EFC). 17% of all full-time undergraduates had no need and received non-need-based gift aid.
GIFT AID (NEED-BASED) *Total amount:* $6,452,550 (15% federal, 12% state, 70% institutional, 3% external sources). *Receiving aid:* Freshmen: 76% (174); All full-time undergraduates: 67% (657). *Average award:* Freshmen: $10,075; Undergraduates: $8851. *Scholarships, grants, and awards:* Federal Pell, FSEOG, state, private, college/university gift aid from institutional funds.
GIFT AID (NON-NEED-BASED) *Total amount:* $1,274,960 (5% federal, 2% state, 88% institutional, 5% external sources). *Receiving aid:* Freshmen: 10% (23); Undergraduates: 5% (51). *Average Award:* Freshmen: $7670; Undergraduates:* $7417. *Scholarships, grants, and awards by category: Academic Interests/Achievement:* 318 awards ($1,965,837 total): general academic interests/achievements. *Creative Arts/Performance:* 52 awards ($81,000 total): music. *Special Achievements/Activities:* 151 awards ($387,000 total): general special achievements/activities, leadership, religious involvement. *Special Characteristics:* 191 awards ($685,250 total): children and siblings of alumni, children of faculty/staff, international students, relatives of clergy, siblings of current students. *ROTC:* Air Force cooperative.
LOANS *Student loans:* $4,155,280 (76% need-based, 24% non-need-based). 70% of past graduating class borrowed through all loan programs. *Average indebtedness per student:* $15,000. *Average need-based loan:* Freshmen: $3201; Undergraduates: $4474. *Parent loans:* $643,974 (38% need-based, 62% non-need-based). *Programs:* FFEL (Subsidized and Unsubsidized Stafford, PLUS).
WORK-STUDY *Federal work-study:* Total amount: $96,100; 114 jobs averaging $832.
APPLYING FOR FINANCIAL AID *Required financial aid form:* FAFSA. *Financial aid deadline (priority):* 5/1. *Notification date:* Continuous beginning 3/15.
CONTACT William Kellaris, Director of Financial Aid, Philadelphia Biblical University, 200 Manor Avenue, Langhorne, PA 19047-2990, 215-702-4243 or toll-free 800-366-0049. *E-mail:* bkellaris@pbu.edu.

PHILADELPHIA UNIVERSITY
Philadelphia, PA

Tuition & fees: $22,140	Average undergraduate aid package: $15,474

ABOUT THE INSTITUTION Independent, coed. Awards: associate, bachelor's, master's, and doctoral degrees and post-bachelor's and post-master's certificates. 32 undergraduate majors. Total enrollment: 3,193. Undergraduates: 2,707. Freshmen: 687. Federal methodology is used as a basis for awarding need-based institutional aid.
UNDERGRADUATE EXPENSES for 2005–06 *Application fee:* $35. *Comprehensive fee:* $30,076 includes full-time tuition ($22,070), mandatory fees ($70), and room and board ($7936). *College room only:* $3910. Full-time tuition and fees vary according to program. Room and board charges vary according to board plan and housing facility. *Part-time tuition:* $713 per credit. Part-time tuition and fees vary according to class time and program. *Payment plans:* Installment, deferred payment.
FRESHMAN FINANCIAL AID (Fall 2005, est.) 591 applied for aid; of those 86% were deemed to have need. 100% of freshmen with need received aid; of those 15% had need fully met. *Average percent of need met:* 79% (excluding resources awarded to replace EFC). *Average financial aid package:* $16,642 (excluding resources awarded to replace EFC). 24% of all full-time freshmen had no need and received non-need-based gift aid.
UNDERGRADUATE FINANCIAL AID (Fall 2005, est.) 1,930 applied for aid; of those 86% were deemed to have need. 100% of undergraduates with need received aid; of those 11% had need fully met. *Average percent of need met:* 72% (excluding resources awarded to replace EFC). *Average financial aid package:* $15,474 (excluding resources awarded to replace EFC). 26% of all full-time undergraduates had no need and received non-need-based gift aid.
GIFT AID (NEED-BASED) *Total amount:* $15,638,056 (10% federal, 11% state, 77% institutional, 2% external sources). *Receiving aid:* Freshmen: 75% (510);

All full-time undergraduates: 67% (1,625). *Average award:* Freshmen: $11,323; Undergraduates: $9974. *Scholarships, grants, and awards:* Federal Pell, FSEOG, state, private, college/university gift aid from institutional funds, gifts scholarships from outside sources (non-endowed) for which university chooses recipient, also i.
GIFT AID (NON-NEED-BASED) *Total amount:* $2,667,236 (97% institutional, 3% external sources). *Receiving aid:* Freshmen: 7% (47); Undergraduates: 4% (102). *Average Award:* Freshmen: $4660; Undergraduates: $4066. *Scholarships, grants, and awards by category:* Academic Interests/Achievement: 2,165 awards ($8,871,858 total): general academic interests/achievements. *Tuition waivers:* Full or partial for employees or children of employees.
LOANS *Student loans:* $13,020,176 (77% need-based, 23% non-need-based). 74% of past graduating class borrowed through all loan programs. *Average indebtedness per student:* $22,917. *Average need-based loan:* Freshmen: $3113; Undergraduates: $4045. *Parent loans:* $8,294,799 (27% need-based, 73% non-need-based). *Programs:* FFEL (Subsidized and Unsubsidized Stafford, PLUS), Perkins, private loans.
WORK-STUDY *Federal work-study:* Total amount: $1,943,500; 992 jobs averaging $2000. *State or other work-study/employment:* Total amount: $349,987 (82% need-based, 18% non-need-based). Part-time jobs available.
ATHLETIC AWARDS *Total amount:* $1,470,943 (41% need-based, 59% non-need-based).
APPLYING FOR FINANCIAL AID *Required financial aid form:* FAFSA. *Financial aid deadline:* 4/15. *Notification date:* Continuous beginning 2/1. Students must reply within 3 weeks of notification.
CONTACT Ms. Lisa J. Cooper, Director of Financial Aid, Philadelphia University, School House Lane and Henry Avenue, Philadelphia, PA 19144-5497, 215-951-2940. *Fax:* 215-951-2907.

PHILANDER SMITH COLLEGE
Little Rock, AR

CONTACT Director of Financial Aid, Philander Smith College, 812 West 13th Street, Little Rock, AR 72202-3799, 501-370-5270 or toll-free 800-446-6772.

PIEDMONT BAPTIST COLLEGE
Winston-Salem, NC

CONTACT Ronnie Mathis, Director of Financial Aid, Piedmont Baptist College, 716 Franklin Street, Winston-Salem, NC 27101-5197, 336-725-8344 Ext. 2322 or toll-free 800-937-5097. *Fax:* 336-725-5522. *E-mail:* mathisr@pbc.edu.

PIEDMONT COLLEGE
Demorest, GA

ABOUT THE INSTITUTION Independent religious, coed. Awards: bachelor's and master's degrees and post-master's certificates. 32 undergraduate majors. Total enrollment: 1,938. Undergraduates: 939. Freshmen: 166.
GIFT AID (NEED-BASED) *Scholarships, grants, and awards:* Federal Pell, FSEOG, state, private, college/university gift aid from institutional funds.
GIFT AID (NON-NEED-BASED) *Scholarships, grants, and awards by category: Academic Interests/Achievement:* biological sciences, education, English, foreign languages, general academic interests/achievements, health fields, humanities, mathematics, premedicine, religion/biblical studies. *Creative Arts/Performance:* art/fine arts, music, theater/drama. *Special Achievements/Activities:* leadership. *Special Characteristics:* adult students, children of faculty/staff, international students, out-of-state students.
LOANS *Programs:* Federal Direct (Subsidized and Unsubsidized Stafford, PLUS), state.
APPLYING FOR FINANCIAL AID *Required financial aid forms:* FAFSA, state aid form.
CONTACT Mrs. Kim Lovell, Director of Financial Aid, Piedmont College, PO Box 10, Demorest, GA 30535-0010, 706-778-3000 Ext. 1191 or toll-free 800-277-7020. *Fax:* 706-776-2811. *E-mail:* klovell@piedmont.edu.

PIKEVILLE COLLEGE
Pikeville, KY

Tuition & fees: $11,500 **Average undergraduate aid package:** $12,119

ABOUT THE INSTITUTION Independent religious, coed. Awards: associate, bachelor's, and first professional degrees and post-bachelor's certificates. 25 undergraduate majors. Total enrollment: 1,129. Undergraduates: 844. Freshmen: 208. Federal methodology is used as a basis for awarding need-based institutional aid.
UNDERGRADUATE EXPENSES for 2005–06 *Comprehensive fee:* $16,500 includes full-time tuition ($11,500) and room and board ($5000). Full-time tuition and fees vary according to course load. *Part-time tuition:* $479 per credit hour. *Payment plan:* Installment.
FRESHMAN FINANCIAL AID (Fall 2005, est.) 200 applied for aid; of those 100% were deemed to have need. 100% of freshmen with need received aid; of those 65% had need fully met. *Average percent of need met:* 90% (excluding resources awarded to replace EFC). *Average financial aid package:* $11,903 (excluding resources awarded to replace EFC).
UNDERGRADUATE FINANCIAL AID (Fall 2005, est.) 752 applied for aid; of those 99% were deemed to have need. 100% of undergraduates with need received aid; of those 70% had need fully met. *Average percent of need met:* 90% (excluding resources awarded to replace EFC). *Average financial aid package:* $12,119 (excluding resources awarded to replace EFC). 1% of all full-time undergraduates had no need and received non-need-based gift aid.
GIFT AID (NEED-BASED) *Total amount:* $6,330,930 (24% federal, 40% state, 33% institutional, 3% external sources). *Receiving aid:* Freshmen: 97% (199); All full-time undergraduates: 95% (736). *Average award:* Freshmen: $10,040; Undergraduates: $9978. *Scholarships, grants, and awards:* Federal Pell, FSEOG, state, private, college/university gift aid from institutional funds.
GIFT AID (NON-NEED-BASED) *Total amount:* $48,500 (100% institutional). *Average Award:* Undergraduates: $3094. *Scholarships, grants, and awards by category:* Academic Interests/Achievement: 1 award ($1000 total): general academic interests/achievements, health fields. *Creative Arts/Performance:* 43 awards ($39,500 total): music. *Special Characteristics:* 36 awards ($168,670 total): children of faculty/staff, members of minority groups. *Tuition waivers:* Full or partial for employees or children of employees, senior citizens.
LOANS *Student loans:* $2,071,991 (100% need-based). 73% of past graduating class borrowed through all loan programs. *Average indebtedness per student:* $15,208. *Average need-based loan:* Freshmen: $2530; Undergraduates: $3462. *Parent loans:* $51,875 (100% need-based). *Programs:* FFEL (Subsidized and Unsubsidized Stafford, PLUS), Perkins, college/university.
WORK-STUDY *Federal work-study:* Total amount: $381,658; 230 jobs averaging $1659.
ATHLETIC AWARDS *Total amount:* $1,082,782 (91% need-based, 9% non-need-based).
APPLYING FOR FINANCIAL AID *Required financial aid forms:* FAFSA, institution's own form. *Financial aid deadline (priority):* 3/15. *Notification date:* Continuous beginning 1/15. Students must reply by 5/1.
CONTACT Melinda Lynch, Dean of Admissions and Student Financial Services, Pikeville College, 147 Sycamore Street, Pikeville, KY 41501, 606-218-5251 or toll-free 866-232-7700. *Fax:* 606-218-5255. *E-mail:* finaid@pc.edu.

PILLSBURY BAPTIST BIBLE COLLEGE
Owatonna, MN

CONTACT Financial Aid Administrator, Pillsbury Baptist Bible College, 315 South Grove Street, Owatonna, MN 55060-3097, 507-451-2710 or toll-free 800-747-4557. *Fax:* 507-451-6459. *E-mail:* pbbc@pillsbury.edu.

PINE MANOR COLLEGE
Chestnut Hill, MA

ABOUT THE INSTITUTION Independent, women only. Awards: associate and bachelor's degrees. 16 undergraduate majors. Total enrollment: 461. Undergraduates: 461. Freshmen: 138.
GIFT AID (NEED-BASED) *Scholarships, grants, and awards:* Federal Pell, FSEOG, state, private, college/university gift aid from institutional funds.

Pine Manor College

GIFT AID (NON-NEED-BASED) *Scholarships, grants, and awards by category: Academic Interests/Achievement:* biological sciences, education, general academic interests/achievements. *Special Achievements/Activities:* general special achievements/activities, leadership. *Special Characteristics:* children and siblings of alumni, members of minority groups, siblings of current students.
LOANS *Programs:* FFEL (Subsidized and Unsubsidized Stafford, PLUS), state.
WORK-STUDY *Federal work-study:* Total amount: $85,000; 174 jobs averaging $843.
APPLYING FOR FINANCIAL AID *Required financial aid form:* FAFSA.
CONTACT Ms. Nancy Amaral, Director of Financial Aid, Pine Manor College, 400 Heath Street, Chestnut Hill, MA 02467, 617-731-7129 or toll-free 800-762-1357. *Fax:* 617-731-7102. *E-mail:* finaid@pmc.edu.

PITTSBURG STATE UNIVERSITY
Pittsburg, KS

Tuition & fees (KS res): $3562   **Average undergraduate aid package: $6860**

ABOUT THE INSTITUTION State-supported, coed. Awards: bachelor's and master's degrees (associate, specialist in education). 67 undergraduate majors. Total enrollment: 6,628. Undergraduates: 5,543. Freshmen: 976. Federal methodology is used as a basis for awarding need-based institutional aid.
UNDERGRADUATE EXPENSES for 2005–06 *Application fee:* $30. *Tuition, state resident:* full-time $2850; part-time $95 per credit hour. *Tuition, nonresident:* full-time $9732; part-time $324 per credit hour. *Required fees:* full-time $712; $32 per credit hour. *College room and board:* $4550. Room and board charges vary according to board plan and housing facility. *Payment plan:* Installment.
FRESHMAN FINANCIAL AID (Fall 2005, est.) 771 applied for aid; of those 71% were deemed to have need. 98% of freshmen with need received aid; of those 14% had need fully met. *Average percent of need met:* 89% (excluding resources awarded to replace EFC). *Average financial aid package:* $6120 (excluding resources awarded to replace EFC). 8% of all full-time freshmen had no need and received non-need-based gift aid.
UNDERGRADUATE FINANCIAL AID (Fall 2005, est.) 3,682 applied for aid; of those 80% were deemed to have need. 98% of undergraduates with need received aid; of those 14% had need fully met. *Average percent of need met:* 87% (excluding resources awarded to replace EFC). *Average financial aid package:* $6860 (excluding resources awarded to replace EFC). 8% of all full-time undergraduates had no need and received non-need-based gift aid.
GIFT AID (NEED-BASED) *Total amount:* $8,500,543 (59% federal, 7% state, 15% institutional, 19% external sources). *Receiving aid:* Freshmen: 48% (469); All full-time undergraduates: 45% (2,247). *Average award:* Freshmen: $3663; Undergraduates: $3356. *Scholarships, grants, and awards:* Federal Pell, FSEOG, state, private, college/university gift aid from institutional funds.
GIFT AID (NON-NEED-BASED) *Total amount:* $1,415,308 (1% federal, 73% institutional, 26% external sources). *Receiving aid:* Freshmen: 14% (140); Undergraduates: 6% (308). *Average Award:* Freshmen: $1849; Undergraduates: $2385. *Scholarships, grants, and awards by category: Academic Interests/Achievement:* 1,526 awards ($1,744,533 total): biological sciences, business, communication, computer science, education, engineering/technologies, English, foreign languages, general academic interests/achievements, health fields, home economics, mathematics, military science, physical sciences, social sciences. *Creative Arts/Performance:* 213 awards ($203,825 total): music. *Special Characteristics:* 130 awards ($71,012 total): children and siblings of alumni, general special characteristics. *Tuition waivers:* Full or partial for employees or children of employees. *ROTC:* Army.
LOANS *Student loans:* $12,678,974 (73% need-based, 27% non-need-based). 93% of past graduating class borrowed through all loan programs. *Average indebtedness per student:* $10,742. *Average need-based loan:* Freshmen: $2658; Undergraduates: $3856. *Parent loans:* $1,196,599 (2% need-based, 98% non-need-based). *Programs:* FFEL (Subsidized and Unsubsidized Stafford, PLUS), Perkins, Federal Nursing, college/university.
WORK-STUDY *Federal work-study:* Total amount: $430,941; 264 jobs averaging $1053. *State or other work-study/employment:* Total amount: $1,483,089 (24% need-based, 76% non-need-based). 1,027 part-time jobs averaging $1444.
ATHLETIC AWARDS *Total amount:* $833,857 (54% need-based, 46% non-need-based).
APPLYING FOR FINANCIAL AID *Required financial aid form:* FAFSA. *Financial aid deadline (priority):* 3/1. *Notification date:* Continuous. Students must reply within 2 weeks of notification.

CONTACT Marilyn Haverly, Director of Student Financial Assistance, Pittsburg State University, 1701 South Broadway, Pittsburg, KS 66762-5880, 316-235-4238 or toll-free 800-854-7488 Ext. 1. *Fax:* 316-235-4078. *E-mail:* mhaverly@pittstate.edu.

PITZER COLLEGE
Claremont, CA

Tuition & fees: $33,012   **Average undergraduate aid package: $29,002**

ABOUT THE INSTITUTION Independent, coed. Awards: bachelor's degrees. 53 undergraduate majors. Total enrollment: 963. Undergraduates: 963. Freshmen: 241. Both federal and institutional methodology are used as a basis for awarding need-based institutional aid.
UNDERGRADUATE EXPENSES for 2005–06 *Application fee:* $50. *Comprehensive fee:* $41,644 includes full-time tuition ($29,520), mandatory fees ($3492), and room and board ($8632). *College room only:* $5402. Full-time tuition and fees vary according to course load. Room and board charges vary according to board plan. *Part-time tuition:* $3690 per course. Part-time tuition and fees vary according to course load. *Payment plans:* Installment, deferred payment.
FRESHMAN FINANCIAL AID (Fall 2005, est.) 110 applied for aid; of those 85% were deemed to have need. 100% of freshmen with need received aid; of those 100% had need fully met. *Average percent of need met:* 100% (excluding resources awarded to replace EFC). *Average financial aid package:* $28,858 (excluding resources awarded to replace EFC). 6% of all full-time freshmen had no need and received non-need-based gift aid.
UNDERGRADUATE FINANCIAL AID (Fall 2005, est.) 420 applied for aid; of those 88% were deemed to have need. 99% of undergraduates with need received aid; of those 99% had need fully met. *Average percent of need met:* 100% (excluding resources awarded to replace EFC). *Average financial aid package:* $29,002 (excluding resources awarded to replace EFC). 4% of all full-time undergraduates had no need and received non-need-based gift aid.
GIFT AID (NEED-BASED) *Total amount:* $8,892,382 (8% federal, 11% state, 79% institutional, 2% external sources). *Receiving aid:* Freshmen: 39% (94); All full-time undergraduates: 40% (364). *Average award:* Freshmen: $24,317; Undergraduates: $23,424. *Scholarships, grants, and awards:* Federal Pell, FSEOG, state, private, college/university gift aid from institutional funds.
GIFT AID (NON-NEED-BASED) *Total amount:* $415,404 (3% state, 78% institutional, 19% external sources). *Average Award:* Freshmen: $5000; Undergraduates: $8125. *Scholarships, grants, and awards by category: Academic Interests/Achievement:* 64 awards ($640,000 total): general academic interests/achievements. *Special Achievements/Activities:* community service, leadership. *Special Characteristics:* 29 awards ($145,000 total): members of minority groups. *Tuition waivers:* Full or partial for employees or children of employees. *ROTC:* Army cooperative, Air Force cooperative.
LOANS *Student loans:* $1,976,528 (80% need-based, 20% non-need-based). 60% of past graduating class borrowed through all loan programs. *Average indebtedness per student:* $20,900. *Average need-based loan:* Freshmen: $2801; Undergraduates: $4171. *Parent loans:* $1,450,307 (49% need-based, 51% non-need-based). *Programs:* FFEL (Subsidized and Unsubsidized Stafford, PLUS), Perkins, college/university.
WORK-STUDY *Federal work-study:* Total amount: $756,276; 295 jobs averaging $2563.
APPLYING FOR FINANCIAL AID *Required financial aid forms:* FAFSA, CSS Financial Aid PROFILE, state aid form, noncustodial (divorced/separated) parent's statement, business/farm supplement. *Financial aid deadline:* 2/1. *Notification date:* 4/1. Students must reply by 5/1.
CONTACT Margaret Carothers, Director of Financial Aid, Pitzer College, 1050 North Mills Avenue, Claremont, CA 91711-6101, 909-621-8208 or toll-free 800-748-9371. *Fax:* 909-607-1205. *E-mail:* margaret_carothers@pitzer.edu.

PLYMOUTH STATE UNIVERSITY
Plymouth, NH

Tuition & fees (NH res): $7028   **Average undergraduate aid package: $6993**

ABOUT THE INSTITUTION State-supported, coed. Awards: bachelor's and master's degrees and post-bachelor's and post-master's certificates. 43 undergraduate majors. Total enrollment: 5,264. Undergraduates: 4,192. Freshmen: 1,004. Federal methodology is used as a basis for awarding need-based institutional aid.

UNDERGRADUATE EXPENSES for 2005–06 *Application fee:* $35. *Tuition, state resident:* full-time $5410; part-time $226 per credit hour. *Tuition, nonresident:* full-time $12,250; part-time $510 per credit hour. *Required fees:* full-time $1618; $74 per credit hour. Full-time tuition and fees vary according to reciprocity agreements. Part-time tuition and fees vary according to course load and reciprocity agreements. *College room and board:* $6780; *room only:* $4650. Room and board charges vary according to board plan and housing facility. *Payment plan:* Installment.
FRESHMAN FINANCIAL AID (Fall 2004) 904 applied for aid; of those 71% were deemed to have need. 98% of freshmen with need received aid; of those 4% had need fully met. *Average percent of need met:* 57% (excluding resources awarded to replace EFC). *Average financial aid package:* $6411 (excluding resources awarded to replace EFC). 4% of all full-time freshmen had no need and received non-need-based gift aid.
UNDERGRADUATE FINANCIAL AID (Fall 2004) 3,050 applied for aid; of those 67% were deemed to have need. 98% of undergraduates with need received aid; of those 4% had need fully met. *Average percent of need met:* 62% (excluding resources awarded to replace EFC). *Average financial aid package:* $6993 (excluding resources awarded to replace EFC). 7% of all full-time undergraduates had no need and received non-need-based gift aid.
GIFT AID (NEED-BASED) *Total amount:* $5,572,136 (45% federal, 8% state, 47% institutional). *Receiving aid:* Freshmen: 37% (387); All full-time undergraduates: 30% (1,173). *Average award:* Freshmen: $4274; Undergraduates: $4091. *Scholarships, grants, and awards:* Federal Pell, FSEOG, state, private, college/university gift aid from institutional funds.
GIFT AID (NON-NEED-BASED) *Total amount:* $2,137,441 (67% institutional, 33% external sources). *Receiving aid:* Freshmen: 25% (263); Undergraduates: 19% (740). *Average Award:* Freshmen: $2136; Undergraduates: $1792. *Scholarships, grants, and awards by category:* Academic Interests/Achievement: 505 awards ($845,233 total): business, communication, education, English, general academic interests/achievements, health fields, mathematics, physical sciences, social sciences. *Creative Arts/Performance:* 20 awards ($40,000 total): creative writing, dance, music, theater/drama. *Special Characteristics:* 31 awards ($74,346 total): children of faculty/staff, international students. *Tuition waivers:* Full or partial for employees or children of employees, senior citizens. *ROTC:* Army cooperative, Air Force cooperative.
LOANS *Student loans:* $19,142,284 (45% need-based, 55% non-need-based). 73% of past graduating class borrowed through all loan programs. *Average indebtedness per student:* $23,088. *Average need-based loan:* Freshmen: $2554; Undergraduates: $3704. *Parent loans:* $5,675,450 (100% non-need-based). *Programs:* FFEL (Subsidized and Unsubsidized Stafford, PLUS), Perkins.
WORK-STUDY *Federal work-study:* Total amount: $2,129,235; 1,458 jobs averaging $1460.
APPLYING FOR FINANCIAL AID *Required financial aid form:* FAFSA. *Financial aid deadline (priority):* 3/1. *Notification date:* Continuous beginning 3/1. Students must reply by 5/1.
CONTACT June Schlabach, Director of Financial Aid, Plymouth State University, 17 High Street, MSC 18, Plymouth, NH 03264-1595, 603-535-2338 or toll-free 800-842-6900. *Fax:* 603-535-2627. *E-mail:* jlschlabach@plymouth.edu.

POINT LOMA NAZARENE UNIVERSITY
San Diego, CA

CONTACT Student Financial Services, Point Loma Nazarene University, 3900 Lomaland Drive, San Diego, CA 92106, 619-849-2538 or toll-free 800-733-7770. *Fax:* 619-849-7017.

POINT PARK UNIVERSITY
Pittsburgh, PA

ABOUT THE INSTITUTION Independent, coed. Awards: associate, bachelor's, and master's degrees and post-bachelor's and post-master's certificates. 55 undergraduate majors. Total enrollment: 3,407. Undergraduates: 2,962. Freshmen: 472.
GIFT AID (NEED-BASED) *Scholarships, grants, and awards:* Federal Pell, FSEOG, state, private, college/university gift aid from institutional funds.
GIFT AID (NON-NEED-BASED) *Scholarships, grants, and awards by category:* Academic Interests/Achievement: general academic interests/achievements. *Creative Arts/Performance:* cinema/film/broadcasting, dance, journalism/publications, performing arts, theater/drama. *Special Achievements/Activities:* community service, junior miss. *Special Characteristics:* adult students, children and siblings of alumni, children of faculty/staff, international students, members of minority groups, previous college experience, siblings of current students.
LOANS *Programs:* FFEL (Subsidized and Unsubsidized Stafford, PLUS), Perkins.
WORK-STUDY *Federal work-study:* Total amount: $339,061; 213 jobs averaging $2205. *State or other work-study/employment:* Total amount: $2,273,569 (68% need-based, 32% non-need-based). 264 part-time jobs averaging $1965.
APPLYING FOR FINANCIAL AID *Required financial aid form:* FAFSA.
CONTACT Sandra M. Cronin, Director of Financial Aid, Point Park University, 201 Wood Street, Pittsburgh, PA 15222-1984, 412-392-3930 or toll-free 800-321-0129. *E-mail:* scronin@pointpark.edu.

POLYTECHNIC UNIVERSITY, BROOKLYN CAMPUS
Brooklyn, NY

ABOUT THE INSTITUTION Independent, coed. Awards: bachelor's, master's, and doctoral degrees and post-bachelor's certificates. 15 undergraduate majors. Total enrollment: 2,801. Undergraduates: 1,519. Freshmen: 304.
GIFT AID (NEED-BASED) *Scholarships, grants, and awards:* Federal Pell, FSEOG, state, private, college/university gift aid from institutional funds, United Negro College Fund.
GIFT AID (NON-NEED-BASED) *Scholarships, grants, and awards by category:* Academic Interests/Achievement: computer science, engineering/technologies, general academic interests/achievements. *Special Characteristics:* members of minority groups.
LOANS *Programs:* FFEL (Subsidized and Unsubsidized Stafford, PLUS), Perkins, college/university, alternative loans.
WORK-STUDY *Federal work-study:* Total amount: $328,100; 100 jobs averaging $3281.
APPLYING FOR FINANCIAL AID *Required financial aid forms:* FAFSA, state aid form.
CONTACT Mr. Nicholas Simos, Director of Financial Aid Services, Polytechnic University, Brooklyn Campus, 6 Metrotech Center, Brooklyn, NY 11201-2990, 718-260-3025 or toll-free 800-POLYTECH. *Fax:* 718-260-3062.

POLYTECHNIC UNIVERSITY OF PUERTO RICO
Hato Rey, PR

ABOUT THE INSTITUTION Independent, coed. Awards: bachelor's and master's degrees. 12 undergraduate majors. Total enrollment: 5,771. Undergraduates: 5,070. Freshmen: 1,012.
GIFT AID (NEED-BASED) *Scholarships, grants, and awards:* Federal Pell, FSEOG, state.
GIFT AID (NON-NEED-BASED) *Scholarships, grants, and awards by category:* Academic Interests/Achievement: architecture, business, engineering/technologies.
LOANS *Programs:* FFEL (Subsidized and Unsubsidized Stafford, PLUS).
APPLYING FOR FINANCIAL AID *Required financial aid form:* FAFSA.
CONTACT Lidia L. Cruz, Financial Aid Administrator, Polytechnic University of Puerto Rico, 377 Ponce de Leon Avenue, Hato Rey, PR 00919, 787-754-8000 Ext. 253. *Fax:* 787-766-1163.

POMONA COLLEGE
Claremont, CA

Tuition & fees: $29,923   **Average undergraduate aid package:** $29,784

ABOUT THE INSTITUTION Independent, coed. Awards: bachelor's degrees. 53 undergraduate majors. Total enrollment: 1,532. Undergraduates: 1,532. Freshmen: 382. Both federal and institutional methodology are used as a basis for awarding need-based institutional aid.
UNDERGRADUATE EXPENSES for 2005–06 *Application fee:* $60. *Comprehensive fee:* $40,774 includes full-time tuition ($29,650), mandatory fees ($273), and room and board ($10,851). Room and board charges vary according to board plan. *Payment plan:* Installment.
FRESHMAN FINANCIAL AID (Fall 2005, est.) 260 applied for aid; of those 80% were deemed to have need. 100% of freshmen with need received aid; of those

Pomona College

100% had need fully met. *Average percent of need met:* 100% (excluding resources awarded to replace EFC). *Average financial aid package:* $30,474 (excluding resources awarded to replace EFC).
UNDERGRADUATE FINANCIAL AID (Fall 2005, est.) 998 applied for aid; of those 81% were deemed to have need. 100% of undergraduates with need received aid; of those 100% had need fully met. *Average percent of need met:* 100% (excluding resources awarded to replace EFC). *Average financial aid package:* $29,784 (excluding resources awarded to replace EFC).
GIFT AID (NEED-BASED) *Total amount:* $20,590,494 (3% federal, 4% state, 89% institutional, 4% external sources). *Receiving aid:* Freshmen: 54% (208); All full-time undergraduates: 53% (808). *Average award:* Freshmen: $26,674; Undergraduates: $25,484. *Scholarships, grants, and awards:* Federal Pell, FSEOG, state, private, college/university gift aid from institutional funds.
GIFT AID (NON-NEED-BASED) *Total amount:* $742,750 (100% external sources). *Tuition waivers:* Full or partial for employees or children of employees.
LOANS *Student loans:* $2,480,125 (95% need-based, 5% non-need-based). 55% of past graduating class borrowed through all loan programs. *Average indebtedness per student:* $11,250. *Average need-based loan:* Freshmen: $2100; Undergraduates: $2920. *Parent loans:* $2,368,937 (100% non-need-based). *Programs:* FFEL (Subsidized and Unsubsidized Stafford, PLUS), Perkins, college/university.
WORK-STUDY *Federal work-study:* Total amount: $240,000; 203 jobs averaging $1180. *State or other work-study/employment:* Total amount: $1,170,000 (74% need-based, 26% non-need-based). 527 part-time jobs averaging $1650.
APPLYING FOR FINANCIAL AID *Required financial aid forms:* FAFSA, CSS Financial Aid PROFILE, state aid form, noncustodial (divorced/separated) parent's statement, business/farm supplement. *Financial aid deadline:* 2/1. *Notification date:* 4/10. Students must reply by 5/1.
CONTACT Patricia A. Coye, Director of Financial Aid, Pomona College, 550 North College Avenue, Room 117, Claremont, CA 91711, 909-621-8205. *Fax:* 909-607-7941. *E-mail:* financial_aid@pomadm.pomona.edu.

PONTIFICAL CATHOLIC UNIVERSITY OF PUERTO RICO
Ponce, PR

Tuition & fees: $4938   **Average undergraduate aid package:** $6930

ABOUT THE INSTITUTION Independent Roman Catholic, coed. Awards: associate, bachelor's, master's, doctoral, and first professional degrees (branch locations in Arecibo, Guayana, Mayagüez). 65 undergraduate majors. Total enrollment: 7,474. Undergraduates: 5,363. Freshmen: 1,167. Federal methodology is used as a basis for awarding need-based institutional aid.
UNDERGRADUATE EXPENSES for 2005–06 *Application fee:* $15. *Comprehensive fee:* $8078 includes full-time tuition ($4480), mandatory fees ($458), and room and board ($3140). *College room only:* $1100. Full-time tuition and fees vary according to course load. *Part-time tuition:* $140 per credit. Part-time tuition and fees vary according to course load. *Payment plan:* Deferred payment.
FRESHMAN FINANCIAL AID (Fall 2005, est.) 985 applied for aid; of those 97% were deemed to have need. 96% of freshmen with need received aid; of those 3% had need fully met. *Average percent of need met:* 71% (excluding resources awarded to replace EFC). *Average financial aid package:* $6930 (excluding resources awarded to replace EFC).
UNDERGRADUATE FINANCIAL AID (Fall 2005, est.) 6,014 applied for aid; of those 98% were deemed to have need. 97% of undergraduates with need received aid; of those 2% had need fully met. *Average percent of need met:* 71% (excluding resources awarded to replace EFC). *Average financial aid package:* $6930 (excluding resources awarded to replace EFC).
GIFT AID (NEED-BASED) *Total amount:* $24,396,926 (96% federal, 4% state). *Receiving aid:* Freshmen: 88% (901); All full-time undergraduates: 82% (5,152). *Average award:* Freshmen: $4300; Undergraduates: $4500. *Scholarships, grants, and awards:* Federal Pell, FSEOG, state, private, college/university gift aid from institutional funds, Scholarships for Disadvantaged Students (SDS).
GIFT AID (NON-NEED-BASED) *Total amount:* $1,298,914 (97% institutional, 3% external sources). *Scholarships, grants, and awards by category:* Academic Interests/Achievement: 1,045 awards ($402,530 total): general academic interests/achievements. Creative Arts/Performance: 50 awards ($30,000 total): music, performing arts, theater/drama. Special Characteristics: 241 awards ($1,021,082 total): children of faculty/staff, first-generation college students, spouses of current students, veterans, veterans' children. *Tuition waivers:* Full or partial for employees or children of employees. *ROTC:* Army cooperative.
LOANS *Student loans:* $25,667,320 (100% need-based). 70% of past graduating class borrowed through all loan programs. *Average indebtedness per student:* $3500. *Average need-based loan:* Freshmen: $1000; Undergraduates: $1500. *Parent loans:* $20,370 (100% non-need-based). *Programs:* FFEL (Subsidized and Unsubsidized Stafford, PLUS), Perkins.
WORK-STUDY *Federal work-study:* Total amount: $1,445,724; 1,100 jobs averaging $750. *State or other work-study/employment:* Total amount: $40,000 (100% non-need-based). Part-time jobs available.
ATHLETIC AWARDS Total amount: $439,766 (100% non-need-based).
APPLYING FOR FINANCIAL AID *Required financial aid forms:* FAFSA, institution's own form, noncustodial (divorced/separated) parent's statement. *Financial aid deadline (priority):* 5/14. *Notification date:* 6/15. Students must reply within 4 weeks of notification.
CONTACT Mrs. Margaret Alustiza, Director of Financial Aid, Pontifical Catholic University of Puerto Rico, 2250 Las Americas Avenue, Suite 549, Ponce, PR 00717-0777, 787-841-2000 Ext. 1065 or toll-free 800-981-5040. *Fax:* 787-651-2041. *E-mail:* malustiza@pucpr.edu.

PONTIFICAL COLLEGE JOSEPHINUM
Columbus, OH

ABOUT THE INSTITUTION Independent Roman Catholic, coed, primarily men. Awards: bachelor's, master's, and first professional degrees. 6 undergraduate majors. Total enrollment: 133. Undergraduates: 76. Freshmen: 3.
GIFT AID (NEED-BASED) *Scholarships, grants, and awards:* Federal Pell, FSEOG, state, private, college/university gift aid from institutional funds.
GIFT AID (NON-NEED-BASED) *Scholarships, grants, and awards by category:* Special Characteristics: local/state students.
LOANS *Programs:* FFEL (Subsidized and Unsubsidized Stafford, PLUS), Perkins.
APPLYING FOR FINANCIAL AID *Required financial aid forms:* FAFSA, institution's own form.
CONTACT Marky Leichtnam, Financial Aid Director, Pontifical College Josephinum, 7625 North High Street, Columbus, OH 43235-1498, 614-985-2212 or toll-free 888-252-5812. *Fax:* 614-885-2307. *E-mail:* mleichtnam@pcj.edu.

PORTLAND STATE UNIVERSITY
Portland, OR

Tuition & fees (OR res): $4961   **Average undergraduate aid package:** $7576

ABOUT THE INSTITUTION State-supported, coed. Awards: bachelor's, master's, and doctoral degrees and post-bachelor's certificates. 63 undergraduate majors. Total enrollment: 24,120. Undergraduates: 17,971. Freshmen: 1,429. Federal methodology is used as a basis for awarding need-based institutional aid.
UNDERGRADUATE EXPENSES for 2005–06 *Application fee:* $50. *Tuition, state resident:* full-time $3810; part-time $93 per credit. *Tuition, nonresident:* full-time $15,975; part-time $93 per credit. *Required fees:* full-time $1151; $18 per credit or $48.50 per term part-time. Full-time tuition and fees vary according to program. *College room and board:* $8445; *room only:* $6300. Room and board charges vary according to board plan and housing facility. *Payment plan:* Installment.
FRESHMAN FINANCIAL AID (Fall 2005, est.) 804 applied for aid; of those 72% were deemed to have need. 97% of freshmen with need received aid; of those 10% had need fully met. *Average percent of need met:* 48% (excluding resources awarded to replace EFC). *Average financial aid package:* $5526 (excluding resources awarded to replace EFC). 6% of all full-time freshmen had no need and received non-need-based gift aid.
UNDERGRADUATE FINANCIAL AID (Fall 2005, est.) 6,789 applied for aid; of those 86% were deemed to have need. 99% of undergraduates with need received aid; of those 10% had need fully met. *Average percent of need met:* 55% (excluding resources awarded to replace EFC). *Average financial aid package:* $7576 (excluding resources awarded to replace EFC). 1% of all full-time undergraduates had no need and received non-need-based gift aid.
GIFT AID (NEED-BASED) *Total amount:* $22,618,681 (73% federal, 15% state, 7% institutional, 5% external sources). *Receiving aid:* Freshmen: 24% (296); All full-time undergraduates: 35% (3,790). *Average award:* Freshmen: $3983;

Undergraduates: $4420. *Scholarships, grants, and awards:* Federal Pell, FSEOG, state, private, college/university gift aid from institutional funds, United Negro College Fund.
GIFT AID (NON-NEED-BASED) *Total amount:* $1,744,631 (80% institutional, 20% external sources). *Receiving aid:* Freshmen: 14% (167); Undergraduates: 7% (786). *Average Award:* Freshmen: $2143; Undergraduates: $2258. *Scholarships, grants, and awards by category: Academic Interests/Achievement:* architecture, area/ethnic studies, business, computer science, education, engineering/technologies, foreign languages, general academic interests/achievements, humanities, international studies, physical sciences, social sciences. *Creative Arts/Performance:* art/fine arts, general creative arts/performance, music, theater/drama. *Special Achievements/Activities:* community service, general special achievements/activities, leadership, memberships. *Special Characteristics:* adult students, ethnic background, handicapped students, international students, members of minority groups, out-of-state students. *Tuition waivers:* Full or partial for minority students, employees or children of employees, senior citizens. *ROTC:* Army, Air Force cooperative.
LOANS *Student loans:* $53,135,896 (100% need-based). 70% of past graduating class borrowed through all loan programs. *Average indebtedness per student:* $18,085. *Average need-based loan:* Freshmen: $2748; Undergraduates: $4498. *Parent loans:* $4,264,010 (100% need-based). *Programs:* Federal Direct (Subsidized and Unsubsidized Stafford, PLUS), FFEL (Subsidized and Unsubsidized Stafford, PLUS), Perkins.
WORK-STUDY *Federal work-study:* Total amount: $1,283,827; 767 jobs averaging $2337.
ATHLETIC AWARDS *Total amount:* $1,850,533 (100% need-based).
APPLYING FOR FINANCIAL AID *Required financial aid form:* FAFSA. *Financial aid deadline:* Continuous. *Notification date:* Continuous. Students must reply within 4 weeks of notification.
CONTACT Kenneth McGhee, Director of Financial Aid, Portland State University, PO Box 751, Portland, OR 97207-0751, 503-725-5448 or toll-free 800-547-8887. *Fax:* 503-725-4882. *E-mail:* askfa@pdx.edu.

POST UNIVERSITY
Waterbury, CT
ABOUT THE INSTITUTION Independent, coed. Awards: associate and bachelor's degrees and post-bachelor's certificates. 21 undergraduate majors. Total enrollment: 1,101. Undergraduates: 1,101. Freshmen: 205.
GIFT AID (NEED-BASED) *Scholarships, grants, and awards:* Federal Pell, FSEOG, state, private, college/university gift aid from institutional funds.
GIFT AID (NON-NEED-BASED) *Scholarships, grants, and awards by category: Academic Interests/Achievement:* business, international studies. *Special Achievements/Activities:* community service, general special achievements/activities, leadership. *Special Characteristics:* children and siblings of alumni, local/state students, members of minority groups, siblings of current students.
LOANS *Programs:* FFEL (Subsidized and Unsubsidized Stafford, PLUS), Perkins, state, college/university.
WORK-STUDY *Federal work-study:* Total amount: $206,824; 330 jobs averaging $734. *State or other work-study/employment:* Total amount: $20,000 (100% need-based). 10 part-time jobs averaging $1750.
APPLYING FOR FINANCIAL AID *Required financial aid form:* FAFSA.
CONTACT Patricia Del Buono, Associate Director of Financial Aid, Post University, 800 Country Club Road, Waterbury, CT 06723-2540, 203-596-4526 or toll-free 800-345-2562. *Fax:* 203-756-5810. *E-mail:* pdelbuono@teikyopost.edu.

POTOMAC COLLEGE
Washington, DC
CONTACT Phyllis Crews, Financial Aid Counselor, Potomac College, 4000 Chesapeake Street NW, Washington, DC 20016, 202-686-0876 or toll-free 888-686-0876. *Fax:* 202-686-0818. *E-mail:* pcrews@potomac.edu.

PRAIRIE VIEW A&M UNIVERSITY
Prairie View, TX
CONTACT Mr. A. D. James Jr., Executive Director, Student Financial Services and Scholarships, Prairie View A&M University, PO Box 2967, Prairie View, TX 77446-2967, 936-857-2423. *Fax:* 936-857-2425. *E-mail:* ad_james@pvamu.edu.

PRATT INSTITUTE
Brooklyn, NY
CONTACT Karen Price-Scott, Director of Financial Aid, Pratt Institute, 200 Willoughby Avenue, Brooklyn, NY 11205-3899, 718-636-3519 or toll-free 800-331-0834. *Fax:* 718-636-3739. *E-mail:* kpricesc@pratt.edu.

PRESBYTERIAN COLLEGE
Clinton, SC
CONTACT Ms. Judi Gillespie, Director of Financial Aid, Presbyterian College, 503 South Broad Street, Clinton, SC 29325, 864-833-8287 or toll-free 800-476-7272. *Fax:* 864-833-8481. *E-mail:* jgillesp@admin.presby.edu.

PRESCOTT COLLEGE
Prescott, AZ
Tuition & fees: $19,511   **Average undergraduate aid package: $9839**

ABOUT THE INSTITUTION Independent, coed. Awards: bachelor's, master's, and doctoral degrees and post-bachelor's certificates. 49 undergraduate majors. Total enrollment: 1,044. Undergraduates: 793. Freshmen: 53. Federal methodology is used as a basis for awarding need-based institutional aid.
UNDERGRADUATE EXPENSES for 2006–07 *Application fee:* $25. *Tuition:* full-time $18,576; part-time $516 per credit hour.
FRESHMAN FINANCIAL AID (Fall 2004) 25 applied for aid; of those 100% were deemed to have need. 92% of freshmen with need received aid. *Average percent of need met:* 35% (excluding resources awarded to replace EFC). *Average financial aid package:* $7974 (excluding resources awarded to replace EFC).
UNDERGRADUATE FINANCIAL AID (Fall 2004) 486 applied for aid; of those 98% were deemed to have need. 84% of undergraduates with need received aid. *Average percent of need met:* 43% (excluding resources awarded to replace EFC). *Average financial aid package:* $9839 (excluding resources awarded to replace EFC).
GIFT AID (NEED-BASED) *Total amount:* $1,091,653 (58% federal, 3% state, 27% institutional, 12% external sources). *Receiving aid:* Freshmen: 17% (7); All full-time undergraduates: 26% (194). *Average award:* Freshmen: $4627; Undergraduates: $4530. *Scholarships, grants, and awards:* Federal Pell, FSEOG, state, private, college/university gift aid from institutional funds.
LOANS *Student loans:* $2,944,530 (60% need-based, 40% non-need-based). 68% of past graduating class borrowed through all loan programs. *Average indebtedness per student:* $18,235. *Average need-based loan:* Freshmen: $2501; Undergraduates: $3978. *Parent loans:* $1,092,129 (60% need-based, 40% non-need-based). *Programs:* FFEL (Subsidized and Unsubsidized Stafford, PLUS), Perkins, state.
WORK-STUDY *Federal work-study:* Total amount: $153,383; 165 jobs averaging $1373. *State or other work-study/employment:* Total amount: $96,295 (40% need-based, 60% non-need-based). 64 part-time jobs averaging $1010.
APPLYING FOR FINANCIAL AID *Required financial aid form:* FAFSA. *Financial aid deadline:* Continuous. *Notification date:* Continuous beginning 4/1. Students must reply within 3 weeks of notification.
CONTACT Financial Aid Office, Prescott College, 220 Grove Avenue, Prescott, AZ 86301-2990, 928-350-1111 or toll-free 800-628-6364. *Fax:* 928-776-5225. *E-mail:* finaid@prescott.edu.

PRESENTATION COLLEGE
Aberdeen, SD
Tuition & fees: $12,300   **Average undergraduate aid package: $7442**

ABOUT THE INSTITUTION Independent Roman Catholic, coed. Awards: associate and bachelor's degrees. 14 undergraduate majors. Total enrollment: 758. Undergraduates: 758. Freshmen: 81. Federal methodology is used as a basis for awarding need-based institutional aid.
UNDERGRADUATE EXPENSES for 2006–07 *Comprehensive fee:* $17,075 includes full-time tuition ($12,300) and room and board ($4775). *College room only:* $3975. *Part-time tuition:* $450 per credit.
FRESHMAN FINANCIAL AID (Fall 2005, est.) 95 applied for aid; of those 89% were deemed to have need. 100% of freshmen with need received aid; of those

Presentation College

18% had need fully met. *Average percent of need met:* 56% (excluding resources awarded to replace EFC). *Average financial aid package:* $7357 (excluding resources awarded to replace EFC). 7% of all full-time freshmen had no need and received non-need-based gift aid.
UNDERGRADUATE FINANCIAL AID (Fall 2005, est.) 491 applied for aid; of those 94% were deemed to have need. 100% of undergraduates with need received aid; of those 17% had need fully met. *Average percent of need met:* 47% (excluding resources awarded to replace EFC). *Average financial aid package:* $7442 (excluding resources awarded to replace EFC). 4% of all full-time undergraduates had no need and received non-need-based gift aid.
GIFT AID (NEED-BASED) *Total amount:* $1,511,754 (67% federal, 5% state, 21% institutional, 7% external sources). *Receiving aid:* Freshmen: 60% (61); All full-time undergraduates: 64% (328). *Average award:* Freshmen: $3062; Undergraduates: $3127. *Scholarships, grants, and awards:* Federal Pell, FSEOG, private, college/university gift aid from institutional funds.
GIFT AID (NON-NEED-BASED) *Total amount:* $650,633 (100% institutional). *Receiving aid:* Freshmen: 60% (61); Undergraduates: 53% (270). *Average Award:* Freshmen: $2687; Undergraduates: $2692. *Scholarships, grants, and awards by category:* Special Achievements/Activities: 89 awards ($64,964 total): community service, general special achievements/activities, leadership, religious involvement. *Special Characteristics:* children of faculty/staff.
LOANS *Student loans:* $4,988,207 (41% need-based, 59% non-need-based). 96% of past graduating class borrowed through all loan programs. *Average indebtedness per student:* $21,152. *Average need-based loan:* Freshmen: $2940; Undergraduates: $3317. *Parent loans:* $293,512 (100% non-need-based). *Programs:* FFEL (Subsidized and Unsubsidized Stafford, PLUS), Perkins, state, college/university.
WORK-STUDY *Federal work-study:* Total amount: $54,225; 42 jobs averaging $1500. *State or other work-study/employment:* Total amount: $37,634 (100% need-based). 19 part-time jobs averaging $1500.
APPLYING FOR FINANCIAL AID *Required financial aid forms:* FAFSA, state aid form. *Financial aid deadline (priority):* 3/1. *Notification date:* Continuous beginning 4/1. Students must reply within 2 weeks of notification.
CONTACT Ms. Valerie Weisser, Director of Financial Aid, Presentation College, 1500 North Main Street, Aberdeen, SD 57401-1299, 605-229-8427 or toll-free 800-437-6060. *Fax:* 605-229-8537. *E-mail:* weisserv@presentation.edu.

PRINCETON UNIVERSITY
Princeton, NJ

Tuition & fees: $33,000 **Average undergraduate aid package:** $28,368

ABOUT THE INSTITUTION Independent, coed. Awards: bachelor's, master's, and doctoral degrees. 35 undergraduate majors. Total enrollment: 6,916. Undergraduates: 4,906. Freshmen: 1,221. Both federal and institutional methodology are used as a basis for awarding need-based institutional aid.
UNDERGRADUATE EXPENSES for 2006–07 *Application fee:* $65. *Comprehensive fee:* $42,200 includes full-time tuition ($33,000) and room and board ($9200). *College room only:* $4885.
FRESHMAN FINANCIAL AID (Fall 2005, est.) 781 applied for aid; of those 86% were deemed to have need. 100% of freshmen with need received aid; of those 100% had need fully met. *Average percent of need met:* 100% (excluding resources awarded to replace EFC). *Average financial aid package:* $29,692 (excluding resources awarded to replace EFC).
UNDERGRADUATE FINANCIAL AID (Fall 2005, est.) 2,567 applied for aid; of those 94% were deemed to have need. 100% of undergraduates with need received aid; of those 100% had need fully met. *Average percent of need met:* 100% (excluding resources awarded to replace EFC). *Average financial aid package:* $28,368 (excluding resources awarded to replace EFC).
GIFT AID (NEED-BASED) *Total amount:* $65,278,000 (3% federal, 1% state, 91% institutional, 5% external sources). *Receiving aid:* Freshmen: 55% (672); All full-time undergraduates: 51% (2,417). *Average award:* Freshmen: $28,592; Undergraduates: $26,468. *Scholarships, grants, and awards:* Federal Pell, FSEOG, state, private, college/university gift aid from institutional funds.
GIFT AID (NON-NEED-BASED) *ROTC:* Army, Air Force cooperative.
LOANS *Student loans:* 26% of past graduating class borrowed through all loan programs. *Average indebtedness per student:* $4370. *Parent loans:* $2,604,000 (100% non-need-based). *Programs:* FFEL (Subsidized and Unsubsidized Stafford, PLUS), Perkins, college/university.
WORK-STUDY *Federal work-study:* Total amount: $1,054,000; 702 jobs averaging $1500. *State or other work-study/employment:* Total amount: $950,000 (100% need-based). 703 part-time jobs averaging $1350.
APPLYING FOR FINANCIAL AID *Required financial aid forms:* FAFSA, institution's own form. *Financial aid deadline (priority):* 2/1. *Notification date:* 4/1. Students must reply by 5/1.
CONTACT Mr. Don Betterton, Director of Financial Aid, Princeton University, Box 591, Princeton, NJ 08544-1019, 609-258-3330.

PRINCIPIA COLLEGE
Elsah, IL

Tuition & fees: $21,450 **Average undergraduate aid package:** $19,804

ABOUT THE INSTITUTION Independent Christian Science, coed. Awards: bachelor's degrees. 28 undergraduate majors. Total enrollment: 542. Undergraduates: 542. Freshmen: 139. Institutional methodology is used as a basis for awarding need-based institutional aid.
UNDERGRADUATE EXPENSES for 2006–07 *Comprehensive fee:* $29,346 includes full-time tuition ($21,150), mandatory fees ($300), and room and board ($7896). *College room only:* $3831. *Part-time tuition:* $470 per quarter hour.
FRESHMAN FINANCIAL AID (Fall 2005, est.) 93 applied for aid; of those 96% were deemed to have need. 100% of freshmen with need received aid; of those 66% had need fully met. *Average percent of need met:* 95% (excluding resources awarded to replace EFC). *Average financial aid package:* $19,672 (excluding resources awarded to replace EFC). 28% of all full-time freshmen had no need and received non-need-based gift aid.
UNDERGRADUATE FINANCIAL AID (Fall 2005, est.) 338 applied for aid; of those 95% were deemed to have need. 100% of undergraduates with need received aid; of those 63% had need fully met. *Average percent of need met:* 98% (excluding resources awarded to replace EFC). *Average financial aid package:* $19,804 (excluding resources awarded to replace EFC). 24% of all full-time undergraduates had no need and received non-need-based gift aid.
GIFT AID (NEED-BASED) *Total amount:* $5,333,243 (100% institutional). *Receiving aid:* Freshmen: 55% (78); All full-time undergraduates: 54% (298). *Average award:* Freshmen: $13,410; Undergraduates: $13,487. *Scholarships, grants, and awards:* private, college/university gift aid from institutional funds.
GIFT AID (NON-NEED-BASED) *Total amount:* $2,312,102 (100% institutional). *Receiving aid:* Freshmen: 26% (37); Undergraduates: 22% (122). *Average Award:* Freshmen: $10,081; Undergraduates: $8422. *Scholarships, grants, and awards by category:* Academic Interests/Achievement: 105 awards ($2,340,890 total): general academic interests/achievements. *Special Characteristics:* 61 awards ($427,783 total): children and siblings of alumni, children of faculty/staff.
LOANS *Student loans:* $1,041,159 (100% need-based). 65% of past graduating class borrowed through all loan programs. *Average indebtedness per student:* $12,740. *Average need-based loan:* Freshmen: $4111; Undergraduates: $4182. *Programs:* college/university.
WORK-STUDY *State or other work-study/employment:* Total amount: $242,599 (100% need-based). 185 part-time jobs averaging $1368.
APPLYING FOR FINANCIAL AID *Required financial aid forms:* institution's own form, CSS Financial Aid PROFILE, income tax form(s). *Financial aid deadline:* 3/1. *Notification date:* Continuous beginning 3/15. Students must reply by 5/1 or within 4 weeks of notification.
CONTACT Sarah E. McGuigan, Director of Financial Aid, Principia College, 1 Maybeck Place, Elsah, IL 62028-9799, 618-374-5186 or toll-free 800-277-4648 Ext. 2802. *Fax:* 618-374-5906. *E-mail:* finaid@prin.edu.

PROVIDENCE COLLEGE
Providence, RI

ABOUT THE INSTITUTION Independent Roman Catholic, coed. Awards: associate, bachelor's, and master's degrees. 39 undergraduate majors. Total enrollment: 4,832. Undergraduates: 3,912. Freshmen: 1,065.
GIFT AID (NEED-BASED) *Scholarships, grants, and awards:* Federal Pell, FSEOG, state, private, college/university gift aid from institutional funds.
GIFT AID (NON-NEED-BASED) *Scholarships, grants, and awards by category: Academic Interests/Achievement:* business, general academic interests/

achievements, military science, premedicine. *Creative Arts/Performance:* theater/drama. *Special Achievements/Activities:* community service.
LOANS *Programs:* Federal Direct (Subsidized and Unsubsidized Stafford, PLUS), FFEL (Subsidized and Unsubsidized Stafford, PLUS), Perkins.
WORK-STUDY *Federal work-study:* Total amount: $900,000; 700 jobs averaging $1800. *State or other work-study/employment:* Total amount: $993,000 (100% non-need-based). 700 part-time jobs averaging $1800.
APPLYING FOR FINANCIAL AID *Required financial aid forms:* FAFSA, CSS Financial Aid PROFILE.
CONTACT Mr. Herbert J. D'Arcy, Executive Director of Financial Aid, Providence College, River Avenue and Eaton Street, Providence, RI 02918, 401-865-2286 or toll-free 800-721-6444. *Fax:* 401-865-1186. *E-mail:* hdarcy@providence.edu.

PUGET SOUND CHRISTIAN COLLEGE
Everett, WA

CONTACT Carlene Krause, Financial Aid Officer, Puget Sound Christian College, 7011 226th Place SW, Mountlake Terrace, WA 98043, 425-775-8686 Ext. 565 or toll-free 888-775-8699. *Fax:* 425-775-8688. *E-mail:* ckrause@pscc.edu.

PURCHASE COLLEGE, STATE UNIVERSITY OF NEW YORK
Purchase, NY

CONTACT Ms. Emilie B. Devine, Director of Financial Aid and Scholarships, Purchase College, State University of New York, 735 Anderson Hill Road, Purchase, NY 10577-1400, 914-251-6352. *E-mail:* emilie.devine@purchase.edu.

PURDUE UNIVERSITY
West Lafayette, IN

Tuition & fees (IN res): $7096   **Average undergraduate aid package: $11,256**

ABOUT THE INSTITUTION State-supported, coed. Awards: associate, bachelor's, master's, doctoral, and first professional degrees. 84 undergraduate majors. Total enrollment: 38,712. Undergraduates: 30,875. Freshmen: 7,110. Federal methodology is used as a basis for awarding need-based institutional aid.
UNDERGRADUATE EXPENSES for 2006–07 *Application fee:* $30. *Tuition, state resident:* full-time $7096; part-time $254.15 per credit. *Tuition, nonresident:* full-time $21,266; part-time $706.25 per credit.
FRESHMAN FINANCIAL AID (Fall 2005, est.) 5161 applied for aid; of those 60% were deemed to have need. 100% of freshmen with need received aid; of those 33% had need fully met. *Average percent of need met:* 92% (excluding resources awarded to replace EFC). *Average financial aid package:* $11,673 (excluding resources awarded to replace EFC). 18% of all full-time freshmen had no need and received non-need-based gift aid.
UNDERGRADUATE FINANCIAL AID (Fall 2005, est.) 17,854 applied for aid; of those 68% were deemed to have need. 99% of undergraduates with need received aid; of those 36% had need fully met. *Average percent of need met:* 92% (excluding resources awarded to replace EFC). *Average financial aid package:* $11,256 (excluding resources awarded to replace EFC). 14% of all full-time undergraduates had no need and received non-need-based gift aid.
GIFT AID (NEED-BASED) *Total amount:* $64,711,277 (38% federal, 27% state, 35% institutional). *Receiving aid:* Freshmen: 15% (1,029); All full-time undergraduates: 13% (3,928). *Average award:* Freshmen: $9745; Undergraduates: $8293. *Scholarships, grants, and awards:* Federal Pell, FSEOG, state, private, college/university gift aid from institutional funds.
GIFT AID (NON-NEED-BASED) *Total amount:* $9,766,842 (100% external sources). *Receiving aid:* Freshmen: 11% (787); Undergraduates: 6% (1,797). *Average Award:* Freshmen: $14,306; Undergraduates: $11,431. *Scholarships, grants, and awards by category:* Academic Interests/Achievement: agriculture, computer science, education, engineering/technologies, general academic interests/achievements, health fields, humanities, mathematics, military science, physical sciences. *Creative Arts/Performance:* music. *Special Achievements/Activities:* leadership. *Special Characteristics:* children of faculty/staff. *ROTC:* Army, Naval, Air Force.
LOANS *Student loans:* $104,505,178 (54% need-based, 46% non-need-based). 49% of past graduating class borrowed through all loan programs. *Average indebtedness per student:* $18,978. *Average need-based loan:* Freshmen: $3072; Undergraduates: $4107. *Parent loans:* $139,393,457 (16% need-based, 84% non-need-based). *Programs:* FFEL (Subsidized and Unsubsidized Stafford, PLUS), Perkins, college/university.
WORK-STUDY *Federal work-study:* Total amount: $2,054,481; 1,128 jobs averaging $1821.
ATHLETIC AWARDS Total amount: $5,838,658 (100% non-need-based).
APPLYING FOR FINANCIAL AID *Required financial aid form:* FAFSA. *Financial aid deadline (priority):* 3/1. *Notification date:* 4/15.
CONTACT Division of Financial Aid, Purdue University, Schleman Hall of Student Services, Room 305, 475 Stadium Mall Drive, West Lafayette, IN 47907-2050, 765-494-5083. *Fax:* 765-496-3918. *E-mail:* bcjoerschke@purdue.edu.

PURDUE UNIVERSITY CALUMET
Hammond, IN

Tuition & fees (IN res): $4714   **Average undergraduate aid package: $5470**

ABOUT THE INSTITUTION State-supported, coed. Awards: associate, bachelor's, and master's degrees and post-bachelor's certificates. 62 undergraduate majors. Total enrollment: 9,302. Undergraduates: 8,359. Freshmen: 1,325. Federal methodology is used as a basis for awarding need-based institutional aid.
UNDERGRADUATE EXPENSES for 2005–06 *Tuition, state resident:* full-time $4368; part-time $156 per credit hour. *Tuition, nonresident:* full-time $10,260; part-time $366 per credit hour. *Required fees:* full-time $346; $14.80 per credit hour. Full-time tuition and fees vary according to program. Part-time tuition and fees vary according to course load and program. *College room and board: room only:* $3990. Room and board charges vary according to housing facility. *Payment plan:* Deferred payment.
FRESHMAN FINANCIAL AID (Fall 2004) 777 applied for aid; of those 68% were deemed to have need. 90% of freshmen with need received aid. *Average percent of need met:* 18% (excluding resources awarded to replace EFC). *Average financial aid package:* $3420 (excluding resources awarded to replace EFC). 2% of all full-time freshmen had no need and received non-need-based gift aid.
UNDERGRADUATE FINANCIAL AID (Fall 2004) 3,800 applied for aid; of those 73% were deemed to have need. 94% of undergraduates with need received aid; of those 1% had need fully met. *Average percent of need met:* 21% (excluding resources awarded to replace EFC). *Average financial aid package:* $5470 (excluding resources awarded to replace EFC). 3% of all full-time undergraduates had no need and received non-need-based gift aid.
GIFT AID (NEED-BASED) *Total amount:* $10,125,269 (63% federal, 36% state, 1% institutional). *Receiving aid:* Freshmen: 34% (361); All full-time undergraduates: 33% (1,834). *Average award:* Freshmen: $5748; Undergraduates: $8049. *Scholarships, grants, and awards:* Federal Pell, FSEOG, state, private, college/university gift aid from institutional funds.
GIFT AID (NON-NEED-BASED) *Total amount:* $1,640,810 (36% state, 44% institutional, 20% external sources). *Receiving aid:* Freshmen: 6% (58); Undergraduates: 8% (427). *Average Award:* Freshmen: $2898; Undergraduates: $2842. *Scholarships, grants, and awards by category:* Academic Interests/Achievement: 407 awards ($1,279,532 total): general academic interests/achievements. *Tuition waivers:* Full or partial for employees or children of employees, senior citizens. *ROTC:* Army cooperative.
LOANS *Student loans:* $13,629,984 (96% need-based, 4% non-need-based). 38% of past graduating class borrowed through all loan programs. *Average indebtedness per student:* $19,941. *Average need-based loan:* Freshmen: $2763; Undergraduates: $5582. *Parent loans:* $186,996 (100% non-need-based). *Programs:* Federal Direct (Subsidized and Unsubsidized Stafford, PLUS), Perkins.
WORK-STUDY *Federal work-study:* Total amount: $294,758; 138 jobs averaging $1936. *State or other work-study/employment:* Part-time jobs available.
ATHLETIC AWARDS Total amount: $60,550 (100% non-need-based).
APPLYING FOR FINANCIAL AID *Required financial aid form:* FAFSA. *Financial aid deadline (priority):* 3/10. *Notification date:* Continuous beginning 5/1. Students must reply within 2 weeks of notification.
CONTACT Ms. Chris Strug, Assistant Director of Financial Aid, Purdue University Calumet, 2200 169th Street, Hammond, IN 46323-2094, 219-989-2301 or toll-free 800-447-8738 (in-state). *Fax:* 219-989-2141. *E-mail:* finaid@calumet.purdue.edu.

Purdue University North Central

PURDUE UNIVERSITY NORTH CENTRAL
Westville, IN

CONTACT Gerald Lewis, Director of Financial Aid, Purdue University North Central, 1401 South US Highway 421, Westville, IN 46391-9528, 219-785-5279 Ext. 5502 or toll-free 800-872-1231 (in-state). *Fax:* 219-785-5538.

QUEENS COLLEGE OF THE CITY UNIVERSITY OF NEW YORK
Flushing, NY

CONTACT Office of Financial Aid Services, Queens College of the City University of New York, 65-30 Kissena Boulevard, Flushing, NY 11367-1597, 718-997-5100.

QUEENS UNIVERSITY OF CHARLOTTE
Charlotte, NC

CONTACT Lauren H. Mack, Director of Financial Aid, Queens University of Charlotte, 1900 Selwyn Avenue, Charlotte, NC 28274-0002, 704-337-2230 or toll-free 800-849-0202. *Fax:* 704-337-2416. *E-mail:* mackl@queens.edu.

QUINCY UNIVERSITY
Quincy, IL

Tuition & fees: $19,010 | Average undergraduate aid package: $14,145

ABOUT THE INSTITUTION Independent Roman Catholic, coed. Awards: associate, bachelor's, and master's degrees. 40 undergraduate majors. Total enrollment: 1,359. Undergraduates: 1,075. Freshmen: 202. Federal methodology is used as a basis for awarding need-based institutional aid.
UNDERGRADUATE EXPENSES for 2006–07 *Application fee:* $25. *Comprehensive fee:* $25,970 includes full-time tuition ($18,450), mandatory fees ($560), and room and board ($6960). *College room only:* $3740. *Part-time tuition:* $465 per credit hour. *Part-time fees:* $15 per credit hour.
FRESHMAN FINANCIAL AID (Fall 2004) 216 applied for aid; of those 84% were deemed to have need. 100% of freshmen with need received aid; of those 30% had need fully met. *Average percent of need met:* 84% (excluding resources awarded to replace EFC). *Average financial aid package:* $15,162 (excluding resources awarded to replace EFC). 13% of all full-time freshmen had no need and received non-need-based gift aid.
UNDERGRADUATE FINANCIAL AID (Fall 2004) 865 applied for aid; of those 88% were deemed to have need. 99% of undergraduates with need received aid; of those 39% had need fully met. *Average percent of need met:* 80% (excluding resources awarded to replace EFC). *Average financial aid package:* $14,145 (excluding resources awarded to replace EFC). 11% of all full-time undergraduates had no need and received non-need-based gift aid.
GIFT AID (NEED-BASED) *Total amount:* $7,211,181 (16% federal, 21% state, 62% institutional, 1% external sources). *Receiving aid:* Freshmen: 80% (181); All full-time undergraduates: 72% (732). *Average award:* Freshmen: $12,272; Undergraduates: $11,145. *Scholarships, grants, and awards:* Federal Pell, FSEOG, state, private, college/university gift aid from institutional funds.
GIFT AID (NON-NEED-BASED) *Total amount:* $1,077,881 (1% federal, 4% state, 93% institutional, 2% external sources). *Receiving aid:* Freshmen: 14% (31); Undergraduates: 11% (110). *Average Award:* Freshmen: $7276; Undergraduates: $6260. *Scholarships, grants, and awards by category: Academic Interests/Achievement:* 823 awards ($4,515,315 total): biological sciences, business, communication, computer science, education, English, general academic interests/achievements, health fields, international studies, mathematics, premedicine, religion/biblical studies, social sciences. *Creative Arts/Performance:* 44 awards ($56,041 total): art/fine arts, cinema/film/broadcasting, music. *Special Achievements/Activities:* 7 awards ($29,042 total): community service, leadership. *Special Characteristics:* 25 awards ($203,536 total): children of faculty/staff.
LOANS *Student loans:* $4,066,513 (76% need-based, 24% non-need-based). 80% of past graduating class borrowed through all loan programs. *Average indebtedness per student:* $16,837. *Average need-based loan:* Freshmen: $2817; Undergraduates: $4234. *Parent loans:* $1,243,834 (32% need-based, 68% non-need-based). *Programs:* FFEL (Subsidized and Unsubsidized Stafford, PLUS), Perkins.

WORK-STUDY *Federal work-study:* Total amount: $159,895; 569 jobs averaging $2000. *State or other work-study/employment:* Total amount: $25,707 (36% need-based, 64% non-need-based). 35 part-time jobs averaging $3000.
ATHLETIC AWARDS *Total amount:* $1,962,390 (73% need-based, 27% non-need-based).
APPLYING FOR FINANCIAL AID *Required financial aid form:* FAFSA. *Financial aid deadline (priority):* 3/15. *Notification date:* Continuous. Students must reply by 5/1 or within 2 weeks of notification.
CONTACT Shann Doerr, Director of Financial Aid, Quincy University, 1800 College Avenue, Quincy, IL 62301-2699, 217-228-5260 or toll-free 800-688-4295. *Fax:* 217-228-5635. *E-mail:* doerrsh@quincy.edu.

QUINNIPIAC UNIVERSITY
Hamden, CT

Tuition & fees: $26,280 | Average undergraduate aid package: $14,511

ABOUT THE INSTITUTION Independent, coed. Awards: bachelor's, master's, doctoral, and first professional degrees and post-bachelor's certificates. 60 undergraduate majors. Total enrollment: 7,293. Undergraduates: 5,706. Freshmen: 1,361. Federal methodology is used as a basis for awarding need-based institutional aid.
UNDERGRADUATE EXPENSES for 2006–07 *Application fee:* $45. *Comprehensive fee:* $36,980 includes full-time tuition ($25,240), mandatory fees ($1040), and room and board ($10,700). *Part-time tuition:* $625 per credit. *Part-time fees:* $30 per credit.
FRESHMAN FINANCIAL AID (Fall 2005, est.) 1057 applied for aid; of those 76% were deemed to have need. 100% of freshmen with need received aid; of those 12% had need fully met. *Average percent of need met:* 65% (excluding resources awarded to replace EFC). *Average financial aid package:* $14,369 (excluding resources awarded to replace EFC). 11% of all full-time freshmen had no need and received non-need-based gift aid.
UNDERGRADUATE FINANCIAL AID (Fall 2005, est.) 3,707 applied for aid; of those 81% were deemed to have need. 99% of undergraduates with need received aid; of those 13% had need fully met. *Average percent of need met:* 65% (excluding resources awarded to replace EFC). *Average financial aid package:* $14,511 (excluding resources awarded to replace EFC). 10% of all full-time undergraduates had no need and received non-need-based gift aid.
GIFT AID (NEED-BASED) *Total amount:* $21,911,557 (8% federal, 11% state, 76% institutional, 5% external sources). *Receiving aid:* Freshmen: 58% (782); All full-time undergraduates: 55% (2,889). *Average award:* Freshmen: $10,537; Undergraduates: $9613. *Scholarships, grants, and awards:* Federal Pell, FSEOG, state, private, college/university gift aid from institutional funds.
GIFT AID (NON-NEED-BASED) *Total amount:* $9,634,120 (97% institutional, 3% external sources). *Receiving aid:* Freshmen: 20% (265); Undergraduates: 21% (1,119). *Average Award:* Freshmen: $7888; Undergraduates: $6625. *Scholarships, grants, and awards by category: Academic Interests/Achievement:* 1,223 awards ($8,221,658 total): general academic interests/achievements. *Special Achievements/Activities:* 9 awards ($74,000 total): leadership. *Special Characteristics:* 544 awards ($2,480,978 total): children of faculty/staff, international students, members of minority groups, siblings of current students. *ROTC:* Army cooperative, Air Force cooperative.
LOANS *Student loans:* $20,910,999 (73% need-based, 27% non-need-based). 70% of past graduating class borrowed through all loan programs. *Average indebtedness per student:* $25,794. *Average need-based loan:* Freshmen: $2856; Undergraduates: $4207. *Parent loans:* $12,789,324 (100% non-need-based). *Programs:* FFEL (Subsidized and Unsubsidized Stafford, PLUS), Perkins, Federal Nursing.
WORK-STUDY *Federal work-study:* Total amount: $2,949,845; 1,482 jobs averaging $1963. *State or other work-study/employment:* Total amount: $53,051 (100% need-based). 34 part-time jobs averaging $1519.
ATHLETIC AWARDS *Total amount:* $5,048,442 (100% non-need-based).
APPLYING FOR FINANCIAL AID *Required financial aid form:* FAFSA. *Financial aid deadline (priority):* 3/1. *Notification date:* Continuous. Students must reply by 5/1 or within 2 weeks of notification.
CONTACT Mr. Dominic Yoia, Senior Director of Financial Aid, Quinnipiac University, 275 Mount Carmel Avenue, Hamden, CT 06518, 203-582-5224 or toll-free 800-462-1944 (out-of-state). *Fax:* 203-582-5238. *E-mail:* finaid@quinnipiac.edu.

RABBI JACOB JOSEPH SCHOOL
Edison, NJ
CONTACT Financial Aid Office, Rabbi Jacob Joseph School, One Plainfield Ave, Edison, NJ 08817, 908-985-6533.

RABBINICAL ACADEMY MESIVTA RABBI CHAIM BERLIN
Brooklyn, NY
CONTACT Office of Financial Aid, Rabbinical Academy Mesivta Rabbi Chaim Berlin, 1605 Coney Island Avenue, Brooklyn, NY 11230-4715, 718-377-0777.

RABBINICAL COLLEGE BETH SHRAGA
Monsey, NY
CONTACT Financial Aid Office, Rabbinical College Beth Shraga, 28 Saddle River Road, Monsey, NY 10952-3035, 914-356-1980.

RABBINICAL COLLEGE BOBOVER YESHIVA B'NEI ZION
Brooklyn, NY
CONTACT Financial Aid Office, Rabbinical College Bobover Yeshiva B'nei Zion, 1577 48th Street, Brooklyn, NY 11219, 718-438-2018.

RABBINICAL COLLEGE CH'SAN SOFER
Brooklyn, NY
CONTACT Financial Aid Office, Rabbinical College Ch'san Sofer, 1876 50th Street, Brooklyn, NY 11204, 718-236-1171.

RABBINICAL COLLEGE OF AMERICA
Morristown, NJ
CONTACT Financial Aid Office, Rabbinical College of America, 226 Sussex Avenue, Morristown, NJ 07960, 973-267-9404. *Fax:* 973-267-5208.

RABBINICAL COLLEGE OF LONG ISLAND
Long Beach, NY
CONTACT Rabbi Cone, Financial Aid Administrator, Rabbinical College of Long Island, 201 Magnolia Boulevard, Long Beach, NY 11561-3305, 516-431-7414.

RABBINICAL COLLEGE OF OHR SHIMON YISROEL
Brooklyn, NY
CONTACT Financial Aid Office, Rabbinical College of Ohr Shimon Yisroel, 215-217 Hewes Street, Brooklyn, NY 11211, 718-855-4092.

RABBINICAL COLLEGE OF TELSHE
Wickliffe, OH
CONTACT Financial Aid Office, Rabbinical College of Telshe, 28400 Euclid Avenue, Wickliffe, OH 44092-2523, 216-943-5300.

RABBINICAL SEMINARY ADAS YEREIM
Brooklyn, NY
CONTACT Mr. Israel Weingarten, Financial Aid Administrator, Rabbinical Seminary Adas Yereim, 185 Wilson Street, Brooklyn, NY 11211-7206, 718-388-1751.

RABBINICAL SEMINARY M'KOR CHAIM
Brooklyn, NY
CONTACT Financial Aid Office, Rabbinical Seminary M'kor Chaim, 1571 55th Street, Brooklyn, NY 11219, 718-851-0183.

RABBINICAL SEMINARY OF AMERICA
Flushing, NY
CONTACT Ms. Leah Eisenstein, Director of Financial Aid, Rabbinical Seminary of America, 92-15 69th Avenue, Forest Hills, NY 11375, 718-268-4700. *Fax:* 718-268-4684.

RADFORD UNIVERSITY
Radford, VA

Tuition & fees (VA res): $5130   **Average undergraduate aid package: $6990**

ABOUT THE INSTITUTION State-supported, coed. Awards: bachelor's and master's degrees and post-master's certificates. 42 undergraduate majors. Total enrollment: 9,552. Undergraduates: 8,482. Freshmen: 1,896. Federal methodology is used as a basis for awarding need-based institutional aid.

UNDERGRADUATE EXPENSES for 2005–06 *Application fee:* $35. *Tuition, state resident:* full-time $3235; part-time $214 per credit hour. *Tuition, nonresident:* full-time $10,473; part-time $515 per credit hour. *Required fees:* full-time $1895; $78.90 per credit hour. *College room and board:* $6120; *room only:* $3300. Room and board charges vary according to board plan and housing facility. *Payment plan:* Installment.

FRESHMAN FINANCIAL AID (Fall 2005, est.) 1194 applied for aid; of those 61% were deemed to have need. 96% of freshmen with need received aid; of those 70% had need fully met. *Average percent of need met:* 70% (excluding resources awarded to replace EFC). *Average financial aid package:* $6554 (excluding resources awarded to replace EFC). 3% of all full-time freshmen had no need and received non-need-based gift aid.

UNDERGRADUATE FINANCIAL AID (Fall 2005, est.) 4,746 applied for aid; of those 68% were deemed to have need. 96% of undergraduates with need received aid; of those 76% had need fully met. *Average percent of need met:* 74% (excluding resources awarded to replace EFC). *Average financial aid package:* $6990 (excluding resources awarded to replace EFC). 3% of all full-time undergraduates had no need and received non-need-based gift aid.

GIFT AID (NEED-BASED) *Total amount:* $11,375,809 (36% federal, 43% state, 10% institutional, 11% external sources). *Receiving aid:* Freshmen: 24% (454); All full-time undergraduates: 25% (2,024). *Average award:* Freshmen: $4682; Undergraduates: $1529. *Scholarships, grants, and awards:* Federal Pell, FSEOG, state, private, college/university gift aid from institutional funds.

GIFT AID (NON-NEED-BASED) *Total amount:* $1,559,362 (7% state, 39% institutional, 54% external sources). *Receiving aid:* Freshmen: 3% (48); Undergraduates: 4% (310). *Average Award:* Freshmen: $3632; Undergraduates:* $2787. *Scholarships, grants, and awards by category:* Academic Interests/Achievement: 362 awards ($851,112 total): area/ethnic studies, biological sciences, business, communication, computer science, education, English, general academic interests/achievements, health fields, humanities, library science, mathematics, military science, physical sciences, premedicine, social sciences. Creative Arts/Performance: 39 awards ($58,995 total): applied art and design, art/fine arts, cinema/film/broadcasting, dance, music, theater/drama. Special Achievements/Activities: 1 award ($1500 total): leadership. Special Characteristics: 2 awards ($3410 total): children of faculty/staff. *Tuition waivers:* Full or partial for employees or children of employees, senior citizens. *ROTC:* Army, Naval cooperative.

LOANS *Student loans:* $23,328,456 (42% need-based, 58% non-need-based). 63% of past graduating class borrowed through all loan programs. *Average indebtedness per student:* $17,265. *Average need-based loan:* Freshmen: $2654; Undergraduates: $3481. *Parent loans:* $5,357,268 (46% need-based, 54% non-need-based). *Programs:* FFEL (Subsidized and Unsubsidized Stafford, PLUS), Perkins, Federal Nursing, state, college/university.

WORK-STUDY *Federal work-study:* Total amount: $622,899; 506 jobs averaging $1231. *State or other work-study/employment:* Total amount: $1,339,064 (45% need-based, 55% non-need-based). 439 part-time jobs averaging $1682.

ATHLETIC AWARDS *Total amount:* $1,452,116 (34% need-based, 66% non-need-based).

Radford University

APPLYING FOR FINANCIAL AID *Required financial aid form:* FAFSA. *Financial aid deadline (priority):* 3/1. *Notification date:* 4/15. Students must reply within 2 weeks of notification.
CONTACT Mrs. Barbara Porter, Director of Financial Aid, Radford University, PO Box 6905, Radford, VA 24142, 540-831-5408 or toll-free 800-890-4265. *Fax:* 540-831-5138. *E-mail:* bporter@radford.edu.

RAMAPO COLLEGE OF NEW JERSEY
Mahwah, NJ

Tuition & fees (NJ res): $8792	Average undergraduate aid package: $9765

ABOUT THE INSTITUTION State-supported, coed. Awards: bachelor's and master's degrees. 39 undergraduate majors. Total enrollment: 5,538. Undergraduates: 5,233. Freshmen: 748. Federal methodology is used as a basis for awarding need-based institutional aid.
UNDERGRADUATE EXPENSES for 2005–06 *Application fee:* $55. *Tuition, state resident:* full-time $6091; part-time $190.35 per credit. *Tuition, nonresident:* full-time $11,008; part-time $344 per credit. *Required fees:* full-time $2701; $84.40 per credit. *College room and board:* $9464; *room only:* $6840.
FRESHMAN FINANCIAL AID (Fall 2005, est.) 569 applied for aid; of those 69% were deemed to have need. 97% of freshmen with need received aid; of those 16% had need fully met. *Average percent of need met:* 81% (excluding resources awarded to replace EFC). *Average financial aid package:* $10,615 (excluding resources awarded to replace EFC). 11% of all full-time freshmen had no need and received non-need-based gift aid.
UNDERGRADUATE FINANCIAL AID (Fall 2005, est.) 2,932 applied for aid; of those 68% were deemed to have need. 98% of undergraduates with need received aid; of those 17% had need fully met. *Average percent of need met:* 77% (excluding resources awarded to replace EFC). *Average financial aid package:* $9765 (excluding resources awarded to replace EFC). 13% of all full-time undergraduates had no need and received non-need-based gift aid.
GIFT AID (NEED-BASED) *Total amount:* $6,944,088 (39% federal, 50% state, 11% institutional). *Receiving aid:* Freshmen: 25% (190); All full-time undergraduates: 24% (980). *Average award:* Freshmen: $8976; Undergraduates: $6856. *Scholarships, grants, and awards:* Federal Pell, FSEOG, state, private, college/university gift aid from institutional funds.
GIFT AID (NON-NEED-BASED) *Total amount:* $5,204,733 (14% state, 77% institutional, 9% external sources). *Receiving aid:* Freshmen: 23% (174); Undergraduates: 22% (923). *Average Award:* Freshmen: $8332; Undergraduates: $7914. *Scholarships, grants, and awards by category:* Academic Interests/Achievement: 570 awards ($4,315,094 total): general academic interests/achievements. Special Characteristics: 81 awards ($1,199,194 total): international students, out-of-state students. *ROTC:* Air Force cooperative.
LOANS *Student loans:* $16,646,862 (41% need-based, 59% non-need-based). 37% of past graduating class borrowed through all loan programs. *Average indebtedness per student:* $15,937. *Average need-based loan:* Freshmen: $2588; Undergraduates: $3860. *Parent loans:* $4,374,957 (100% non-need-based). *Programs:* Federal Direct (Subsidized and Unsubsidized Stafford, PLUS), Perkins, state.
WORK-STUDY *Federal work-study:* Total amount: $253,106; 168 jobs averaging $1506. *State or other work-study/employment:* Total amount: $1,446,215 (100% non-need-based). 692 part-time jobs averaging $2089.
APPLYING FOR FINANCIAL AID *Required financial aid form:* FAFSA. *Financial aid deadline (priority):* 3/1. *Notification date:* Continuous beginning 4/1. Students must reply by 5/1 or within 2 weeks of notification.
CONTACT Bernice Mulch, Assistant Director of Financial Aid, Ramapo College of New Jersey, 505 Ramapo Valley Road, Mahwah, NJ 07430-1680, 201-684-7252 or toll-free 800-9RAMAPO (in-state). *Fax:* 201-684-7085. *E-mail:* finaid@ramapo.edu.

RANDOLPH-MACON COLLEGE
Ashland, VA

Tuition & fees: $23,945	Average undergraduate aid package: $17,459

ABOUT THE INSTITUTION Independent United Methodist, coed. Awards: bachelor's degrees. 30 undergraduate majors. Total enrollment: 1,125. Undergraduates: 1,125. Freshmen: 305. Federal methodology is used as a basis for awarding need-based institutional aid.
UNDERGRADUATE EXPENSES for 2005–06 *Application fee:* $30. *Comprehensive fee:* $31,250 includes full-time tuition ($23,310), mandatory fees ($635), and room and board ($7305). *College room only:* $4000. Room and board charges vary according to board plan and housing facility. *Part-time tuition:* $863 per credit hour. *Payment plan:* Installment.
FRESHMAN FINANCIAL AID (Fall 2005, est.) 239 applied for aid; of those 79% were deemed to have need. 100% of freshmen with need received aid; of those 25% had need fully met. *Average percent of need met:* 86% (excluding resources awarded to replace EFC). *Average financial aid package:* $19,042 (excluding resources awarded to replace EFC). 36% of all full-time freshmen had no need and received non-need-based gift aid.
UNDERGRADUATE FINANCIAL AID (Fall 2005, est.) 789 applied for aid; of those 83% were deemed to have need. 100% of undergraduates with need received aid; of those 24% had need fully met. *Average percent of need met:* 82% (excluding resources awarded to replace EFC). *Average financial aid package:* $17,459 (excluding resources awarded to replace EFC). 36% of all full-time undergraduates had no need and received non-need-based gift aid.
GIFT AID (NEED-BASED) *Total amount:* $8,159,141 (4% federal, 13% state, 75% institutional, 8% external sources). *Receiving aid:* Freshmen: 62% (189); All full-time undergraduates: 60% (650). *Average award:* Freshmen: $14,629; Undergraduates: $12,821. *Scholarships, grants, and awards:* Federal Pell, FSEOG, state, private, college/university gift aid from institutional funds.
GIFT AID (NON-NEED-BASED) *Total amount:* $4,099,862 (20% state, 69% institutional, 11% external sources). *Receiving aid:* Freshmen: 11% (33); Undergraduates: 9% (103). *Average Award:* Freshmen: $12,714; Undergraduates: $12,987. *Scholarships, grants, and awards by category:* Academic Interests/Achievement: 403 awards ($3,857,123 total): general academic interests/achievements, premedicine. Special Achievements/Activities: 330 awards ($1,290,876 total): general special achievements/activities. Special Characteristics: 157 awards ($622,454 total): children and siblings of alumni, children of faculty/staff, relatives of clergy, siblings of current students. *Tuition waivers:* Full or partial for employees or children of employees. *ROTC:* Army cooperative.
LOANS *Student loans:* $5,011,961 (64% need-based, 36% non-need-based). 70% of past graduating class borrowed through all loan programs. *Average indebtedness per student:* $15,130. *Average need-based loan:* Freshmen: $4645; Undergraduates: $4996. *Parent loans:* $3,239,563 (20% need-based, 80% non-need-based). *Programs:* FFEL (Subsidized and Unsubsidized Stafford, PLUS), Perkins, college/university.
WORK-STUDY *Federal work-study:* Total amount: $351,306; 194 jobs averaging $1811.
APPLYING FOR FINANCIAL AID *Required financial aid forms:* FAFSA, state aid form. *Financial aid deadline (priority):* 2/1. *Notification date:* 3/1. Students must reply by 5/1 or within 2 weeks of notification.
CONTACT Ms. Mary Neal, Director of Financial Aid, Randolph-Macon College, PO Box 5005, Ashland, VA 23005-5505, 804-752-7259 or toll-free 800-888-1762. *Fax:* 804-752-3719. *E-mail:* mneal@rmc.edu.

RANDOLPH-MACON WOMAN'S COLLEGE
Lynchburg, VA

Tuition & fees: $22,930	Average undergraduate aid package: $21,368

ABOUT THE INSTITUTION Independent Methodist, women only. Awards: bachelor's degrees. 37 undergraduate majors. Total enrollment: 712. Undergraduates: 712. Freshmen: 184. Federal methodology is used as a basis for awarding need-based institutional aid.
UNDERGRADUATE EXPENSES for 2005–06 *Application fee:* $35. *Comprehensive fee:* $31,540 includes full-time tuition ($22,550), mandatory fees ($380), and room and board ($8610). *Part-time tuition:* $940 per semester hour. *Part-time fees:* $45 per term. Part-time tuition and fees vary according to course load. *Payment plan:* Installment.
FRESHMAN FINANCIAL AID (Fall 2005, est.) 138 applied for aid; of those 81% were deemed to have need. 100% of freshmen with need received aid; of those 51% had need fully met. *Average percent of need met:* 92% (excluding resources awarded to replace EFC). *Average financial aid package:* $21,686 (excluding resources awarded to replace EFC). 39% of all full-time freshmen had no need and received non-need-based gift aid.
UNDERGRADUATE FINANCIAL AID (Fall 2005, est.) 499 applied for aid; of those 89% were deemed to have need. 100% of undergraduates with need received aid; of those 36% had need fully met. *Average percent of need met:*

88% (excluding resources awarded to replace EFC). *Average financial aid package:* $21,368 (excluding resources awarded to replace EFC). 33% of all full-time undergraduates had no need and received non-need-based gift aid.
GIFT AID (NEED-BASED) *Total amount:* $7,145,514 (8% federal, 6% state, 84% institutional, 2% external sources). *Receiving aid:* Freshmen: 61% (112); All full-time undergraduates: 67% (446). *Average award:* Freshmen: $17,465; Undergraduates: $16,016. *Scholarships, grants, and awards:* Federal Pell, FSEOG, state, private, college/university gift aid from institutional funds.
GIFT AID (NON-NEED-BASED) *Total amount:* $3,649,552 (7% state, 91% institutional, 2% external sources). *Receiving aid:* Freshmen: 12% (23); Undergraduates: 11% (72). *Average Award:* Freshmen: $16,310; Undergraduates: $14,855. *Scholarships, grants, and awards by category:* Academic Interests/Achievement: 425 awards ($5,319,575 total): biological sciences, education, English, general academic interests/achievements, mathematics, physical sciences, premedicine, social sciences. *Creative Arts/Performance:* 10 awards ($23,000 total): art/fine arts, creative writing, music, theater/drama. *Special Achievements/Activities:* 172 awards ($1,305,750 total): community service, general special achievements/activities, leadership, religious involvement. *Special Characteristics:* 134 awards ($1,144,472 total): adult students, children of faculty/staff, international students, local/state students, relatives of clergy, religious affiliation, twins. *Tuition waivers:* Full or partial for employees or children of employees, adult students.
LOANS *Student loans:* $3,895,512 (65% need-based, 35% non-need-based). 70% of past graduating class borrowed through all loan programs. *Average indebtedness per student:* $25,500. *Average need-based loan:* Freshmen: $2526; Undergraduates: $4379. *Parent loans:* $914,951 (21% need-based, 79% non-need-based). *Programs:* FFEL (Subsidized and Unsubsidized Stafford, PLUS), Perkins.
WORK-STUDY *Federal work-study:* Total amount: $146,141; 78 jobs averaging $1860. *State or other work-study/employment:* Total amount: $557,688 (68% need-based, 32% non-need-based). 385 part-time jobs averaging $1070.
APPLYING FOR FINANCIAL AID *Required financial aid forms:* FAFSA, state aid form. *Financial aid deadline (priority):* 3/1. *Notification date:* Continuous beginning 3/1. Students must reply by 5/1 or within 2 weeks of notification.
CONTACT Katherine C Cooper, Director of Financial Planning and Assistance, Randolph-Macon Woman's College, 2500 Rivermont Avenue, Lynchburg, VA 24503-1526, 434-947-8128 or toll-free 800-745-7692. *Fax:* 434-947-8284. *E-mail:* kcooper@rmwc.edu.

REED COLLEGE
Portland, OR

Tuition & fees: $32,590	Average undergraduate aid package: $27,257

ABOUT THE INSTITUTION Independent, coed. Awards: bachelor's and master's degrees. 29 undergraduate majors. Total enrollment: 1,340. Undergraduates: 1,309. Freshmen: 354. Both federal and institutional methodology are used as a basis for awarding need-based institutional aid.
UNDERGRADUATE EXPENSES for 2005–06 *Application fee:* $40. *Comprehensive fee:* $41,106 includes full-time tuition ($32,360), mandatory fees ($230), and room and board ($8516). *College room only:* $4470. Full-time tuition and fees vary according to degree level. Room and board charges vary according to board plan and housing facility. *Part-time tuition:* $5400 per course. Part-time tuition and fees vary according to course level and degree level. *Payment plan:* Installment.
FRESHMAN FINANCIAL AID (Fall 2005, est.) 224 applied for aid; of those 79% were deemed to have need. 93% of freshmen with need received aid; of those 96% had need fully met. *Average percent of need met:* 100% (excluding resources awarded to replace EFC). *Average financial aid package:* $28,205 (excluding resources awarded to replace EFC).
UNDERGRADUATE FINANCIAL AID (Fall 2005, est.) 773 applied for aid; of those 90% were deemed to have need. 95% of undergraduates with need received aid; of those 98% had need fully met. *Average percent of need met:* 100% (excluding resources awarded to replace EFC). *Average financial aid package:* $27,257 (excluding resources awarded to replace EFC).
GIFT AID (NEED-BASED) *Total amount:* $15,154,318 (6% federal, 1% state, 91% institutional, 2% external sources). *Receiving aid:* Freshmen: 43% (153); All full-time undergraduates: 49% (620). *Average award:* Freshmen: $27,387; Undergraduates: $24,493. *Scholarships, grants, and awards:* Federal Pell, FSEOG, state, private, college/university gift aid from institutional funds.

GIFT AID (NON-NEED-BASED) *Total amount:* $51,085 (100% external sources). *Tuition waivers:* Full or partial for employees or children of employees.
LOANS *Student loans:* $3,086,967 (89% need-based, 11% non-need-based). 61% of past graduating class borrowed through all loan programs. *Average indebtedness per student:* $17,175. *Average need-based loan:* Freshmen: $2684; Undergraduates: $4280. *Parent loans:* $2,200,284 (100% non-need-based). *Programs:* FFEL (Subsidized and Unsubsidized Stafford, PLUS), Perkins.
WORK-STUDY *Federal work-study:* Total amount: $285,850; 422 jobs averaging $700. *State or other work-study/employment:* Total amount: $25,900 (100% need-based). 32 part-time jobs averaging $678.
APPLYING FOR FINANCIAL AID *Required financial aid forms:* FAFSA, institution's own form, CSS Financial Aid PROFILE, noncustodial (divorced/separated) parent's statement. *Financial aid deadline:* 2/1 (priority: 1/15). *Notification date:* 4/1. Students must reply by 5/1 or within 2 weeks of notification.
CONTACT Leslie Limper, Financial Aid Director, Reed College, 3203 Southeast Woodstock Boulevard, Portland, OR 97202-8199, 503-777-7223 or toll-free 800-547-4750 (out-of-state). *Fax:* 503-788-6682. *E-mail:* financial.aid@reed.edu.

REGENT UNIVERSITY
Virginia Beach, VA

CONTACT Financial Aid Office, Regent University, 1000 Regent University Drive, Virginia Beach, VA 23464-9800, 757-226-4000 or toll-free 800-373-5504.

REGIS COLLEGE
Weston, MA

Tuition & fees: $21,525	Average undergraduate aid package: $20,003

ABOUT THE INSTITUTION Independent Roman Catholic, undergraduate: women only; graduate: coed. Awards: associate, bachelor's, and master's degrees and post-master's certificates. 23 undergraduate majors. Total enrollment: 1,303. Undergraduates: 843. Freshmen: 161. Both federal and institutional methodology are used as a basis for awarding need-based institutional aid.
UNDERGRADUATE EXPENSES for 2005–06 *Application fee:* $40. *Comprehensive fee:* $31,350 includes full-time tuition ($21,525) and room and board ($9825). *College room only:* $4995. Part-time tuition and fees vary according to class time. *Payment plan:* Installment.
FRESHMAN FINANCIAL AID (Fall 2005, est.) 150 applied for aid; of those 93% were deemed to have need. 100% of freshmen with need received aid; of those 9% had need fully met. *Average percent of need met:* 66% (excluding resources awarded to replace EFC). *Average financial aid package:* $20,803 (excluding resources awarded to replace EFC). 8% of all full-time freshmen had no need and received non-need-based gift aid.
UNDERGRADUATE FINANCIAL AID (Fall 2005, est.) 546 applied for aid; of those 92% were deemed to have need. 100% of undergraduates with need received aid; of those 12% had need fully met. *Average percent of need met:* 62% (excluding resources awarded to replace EFC). *Average financial aid package:* $20,003 (excluding resources awarded to replace EFC). 10% of all full-time undergraduates had no need and received non-need-based gift aid.
GIFT AID (NEED-BASED) *Total amount:* $6,717,187 (13% federal, 7% state, 78% institutional, 2% external sources). *Receiving aid:* Freshmen: 81% (131); All full-time undergraduates: 71% (446). *Average award:* Freshmen: $11,396; Undergraduates: $10,410. *Scholarships, grants, and awards:* Federal Pell, FSEOG, state, private, college/university gift aid from institutional funds.
GIFT AID (NON-NEED-BASED) *Total amount:* $575,805 (100% institutional). *Receiving aid:* Freshmen: 45% (72); Undergraduates: 42% (263). *Average Award:* Freshmen: $8769; Undergraduates: $7940. *Scholarships, grants, and awards by category:* Academic Interests/Achievement: 390 awards ($1,677,000 total): general academic interests/achievements. *Special Achievements/Activities:* 96 awards ($433,000 total): community service. *Special Characteristics:* 50 awards ($259,897 total): adult students, children of faculty/staff, international students, relatives of clergy, religious affiliation, siblings of current students. *Tuition waivers:* Full or partial for employees or children of employees. *ROTC:* Army cooperative.
LOANS *Student loans:* $6,527,808 (100% need-based). 77% of past graduating class borrowed through all loan programs. *Average indebtedness per student:*

Regis College

$24,094. *Average need-based loan:* Freshmen: $4351; Undergraduates: $5166. *Parent loans:* $485,501 (100% non-need-based). *Programs:* FFEL (Subsidized and Unsubsidized Stafford, PLUS), Perkins, state.
WORK-STUDY *Federal work-study:* Total amount: $743,243; 388 jobs averaging $2000. *State or other work-study/employment:* Total amount: $36,000 (100% non-need-based). 37 part-time jobs averaging $1500.
APPLYING FOR FINANCIAL AID *Required financial aid forms:* FAFSA, institution's own form. *Financial aid deadline (priority):* 2/15. *Notification date:* Continuous beginning 3/15. Students must reply by 5/1 or within 2 weeks of notification.
CONTACT Dee J. Ludwick, Director of Financial Aid, Regis College, Box 81, 235 Wellesley Street, Weston, MA 02493, 781-768-7180 or toll-free 866-438-7344. *Fax:* 781-768-7225. *E-mail:* finaid@regiscollege.edu.

REGIS UNIVERSITY
Denver, CO

ABOUT THE INSTITUTION Independent Roman Catholic (Jesuit), coed. Awards: bachelor's, master's, and doctoral degrees. 33 undergraduate majors. Total enrollment: 16,335. Undergraduates: 8,159. Freshmen: 487.
GIFT AID (NEED-BASED) *Scholarships, grants, and awards:* Federal Pell, FSEOG, state, private, college/university gift aid from institutional funds.
GIFT AID (NON-NEED-BASED) *Scholarships, grants, and awards by category: Academic Interests/Achievement:* biological sciences, general academic interests/achievements, physical sciences. *Creative Arts/Performance:* debating. *Special Achievements/Activities:* leadership. *Special Characteristics:* children of faculty/staff, ethnic background, local/state students, members of minority groups.
LOANS *Programs:* FFEL (Subsidized and Unsubsidized Stafford, PLUS), Perkins, Federal Nursing.
WORK-STUDY *Federal work-study:* Total amount: $402,037; 320 jobs averaging $1256. *State or other work-study/employment:* Total amount: $975,914 (41% need-based, 59% non-need-based). 423 part-time jobs averaging $2307.
APPLYING FOR FINANCIAL AID *Required financial aid form:* FAFSA.
CONTACT Ellie Miller, Director of Financial Aid, Regis University, 3333 Regis Boulevard, Denver, CO 80221-1099, 303-964-5758 or toll-free 800-388-2366 Ext. 4900. *Fax:* 303-964-5449. *E-mail:* emiller@regis.edu.

REINHARDT COLLEGE
Waleska, GA

ABOUT THE INSTITUTION Independent religious, coed. Awards: associate and bachelor's degrees. 22 undergraduate majors. Total enrollment: 1,010. Undergraduates: 1,010. Freshmen: 260.
GIFT AID (NEED-BASED) *Scholarships, grants, and awards:* Federal Pell, FSEOG, state, private, college/university gift aid from institutional funds.
GIFT AID (NON-NEED-BASED) *Scholarships, grants, and awards by category: Academic Interests/Achievement:* general academic interests/achievements. *Creative Arts/Performance:* art/fine arts. *Special Characteristics:* children of faculty/staff.
LOANS *Programs:* FFEL (Subsidized and Unsubsidized Stafford, PLUS), alternative loans.
APPLYING FOR FINANCIAL AID *Required financial aid forms:* FAFSA, institution's own form, state aid form.
CONTACT Robert Gregory, Director of Financial Aid, Reinhardt College, 7300 Reinhardt College Circle, Waleska, GA 30183-2981, 770-720-5532 or toll-free 87-REINHARDT. *Fax:* 770-720-9126.

REMINGTON COLLEGE–COLORADO SPRINGS CAMPUS
Colorado Springs, CO

CONTACT Financial Aid Office, Remington College–Colorado Springs Campus, 6050 Erin Park Drive, #250, Colorado Springs, CO 80918, 719-532-1234.

REMINGTON COLLEGE–DENVER CAMPUS
Lakewood, CO

CONTACT Robert J. Lantzy, Director of Financial Services, Remington College–Denver Campus, 11011 West Sixth Avenue, Lakewood, CO 80215, 303-445-0500 or toll-free 800-999-5181. *Fax:* 303-445-0090. *E-mail:* rlantzy@edamerica.com.

REMINGTON COLLEGE–HONOLULU CAMPUS
Honolulu, HI

CONTACT Financial Aid Office, Remington College–Honolulu Campus, 1111 Bishop Street, Suite 400, Honolulu, HI 96813, 808-942-1000.

REMINGTON COLLEGE–SAN DIEGO CAMPUS
San Diego, CA

CONTACT Financial Aid Office, Remington College–San Diego Campus, 123 Camino de la Reina, North Building, Suite 100, San Diego, CA 92108, 619-686-8600 or toll-free 800-214-7001.

REMINGTON COLLEGE–TEMPE CAMPUS
Tempe, AZ

CONTACT Financial Aid Office, Remington College–Tempe Campus, 875 West Elliot Road, Suite 216, Tempe, AZ 85284, 480-834-1000 or toll-free 800-395-4322.

RENSSELAER POLYTECHNIC INSTITUTE
Troy, NY

Tuition & fees: $31,857   **Average undergraduate aid package:** $26,072

ABOUT THE INSTITUTION Independent, coed. Awards: bachelor's, master's, and doctoral degrees. 51 undergraduate majors. Total enrollment: 7,241. Undergraduates: 4,951. Freshmen: 1,240. Federal methodology is used as a basis for awarding need-based institutional aid.
UNDERGRADUATE EXPENSES for 2005–06 *Application fee:* $70. *Comprehensive fee:* $41,288 includes full-time tuition ($31,000), mandatory fees ($857), and room and board ($9431). *College room only:* $5290. Room and board charges vary according to board plan and location. *Part-time tuition:* $969 per credit hour. *Payment plan:* Installment.
FRESHMAN FINANCIAL AID (Fall 2005, est.) 1079 applied for aid; of those 86% were deemed to have need. 100% of freshmen with need received aid; of those 57% had need fully met. *Average percent of need met:* 80% (excluding resources awarded to replace EFC). *Average financial aid package:* $28,075 (excluding resources awarded to replace EFC). 20% of all full-time freshmen had no need and received non-need-based gift aid.
UNDERGRADUATE FINANCIAL AID (Fall 2005, est.) 3,816 applied for aid; of those 90% were deemed to have need. 100% of undergraduates with need received aid; of those 61% had need fully met. *Average percent of need met:* 81% (excluding resources awarded to replace EFC). *Average financial aid package:* $26,072 (excluding resources awarded to replace EFC). 19% of all full-time undergraduates had no need and received non-need-based gift aid.
GIFT AID (NEED-BASED) *Total amount:* $66,126,085 (10% federal, 6% state, 81% institutional, 3% external sources). *Receiving aid:* Freshmen: 75% (926); All full-time undergraduates: 70% (3,426). *Average award:* Freshmen: $22,133; Undergraduates: $19,500. *Scholarships, grants, and awards:* Federal Pell, FSEOG, state, private, college/university gift aid from institutional funds, Gates Millennium Scholarships.
GIFT AID (NON-NEED-BASED) *Total amount:* $15,393,710 (12% federal, 87% institutional, 1% external sources). *Receiving aid:* Freshmen: 22% (275); Undergraduates: 15% (737). *Average Award:* Freshmen: $14,906; Undergraduates: $15,800. *Scholarships, grants, and awards by category: Academic Interests/Achievement:* general academic interests/achievements, humanities, mathematics, military science. *Creative Arts/Performance:* general creative arts/

performance. *Special Achievements/Activities:* general special achievements/activities. *Special Characteristics:* children and siblings of alumni, children of faculty/staff, ethnic background, general special characteristics, members of minority groups. *Tuition waivers:* Full or partial for employees or children of employees. *ROTC:* Army, Naval, Air Force.

LOANS *Student loans:* $32,000,000 (77% need-based, 23% non-need-based). 75% of past graduating class borrowed through all loan programs. *Average indebtedness per student:* $27,235. *Average need-based loan:* Freshmen: $6000; Undergraduates: $7000. *Parent loans:* $8,249,921 (80% need-based, 20% non-need-based). *Programs:* FFEL (Subsidized and Unsubsidized Stafford, PLUS), Perkins, college/university.

WORK-STUDY *Federal work-study:* Total amount: $1,250,000; 1,379 jobs averaging $1978.

ATHLETIC AWARDS *Total amount:* $1,000,000 (100% non-need-based).

APPLYING FOR FINANCIAL AID *Required financial aid forms:* FAFSA, state aid form. *Financial aid deadline (priority):* 2/15. *Notification date:* 3/25.

CONTACT Mr. James Stevenson, Director of Financial Aid, Rensselaer Polytechnic Institute, Financial Aid Building, 110 8th Street, Troy, NY 12180-3590, 518-276-6813 or toll-free 800-448-6562. *Fax:* 518-276-4797. *E-mail:* stevej@rpi.edu.

RESEARCH COLLEGE OF NURSING
Kansas City, MO

ABOUT THE INSTITUTION Independent, coed, primarily women. Awards: bachelor's and master's degrees (bachelor's degree offered jointly with Rockhurst College). 1 undergraduate major. Total enrollment: 213. Undergraduates: 187. Freshmen: 35.

GIFT AID (NEED-BASED) *Scholarships, grants, and awards:* Federal Pell, FSEOG, state, private, college/university gift aid from institutional funds.

GIFT AID (NON-NEED-BASED) *Scholarships, grants, and awards by category: Academic Interests/Achievement:* general academic interests/achievements, health fields. *Special Characteristics:* children and siblings of alumni, children of educators, children of faculty/staff, siblings of current students.

LOANS *Programs:* FFEL (Subsidized and Unsubsidized Stafford, PLUS), Perkins, Federal Nursing, college/university.

APPLYING FOR FINANCIAL AID *Required financial aid form:* FAFSA.

CONTACT Ms. Stacie Withers, Financial Aid Director, Research College of Nursing, 2300 East Meyer Boulevard, Kansas City, MO 64132, 816-276-4728 or toll-free 800-842-6776. *Fax:* 816-276-3526. *E-mail:* stacie.withers@hcamidwest.com.

RHODE ISLAND COLLEGE
Providence, RI

CONTACT Office of Financial Aid, Rhode Island College, 600 Mount Pleasant Avenue, Providence, RI 02908, 401-456-8033 or toll-free 800-669-5760.

RHODE ISLAND SCHOOL OF DESIGN
Providence, RI

ABOUT THE INSTITUTION Independent, coed. Awards: bachelor's, master's, and first professional degrees. 16 undergraduate majors. Total enrollment: 2,258. Undergraduates: 1,878. Freshmen: 405.

GIFT AID (NEED-BASED) *Scholarships, grants, and awards:* Federal Pell, FSEOG, state, private, college/university gift aid from institutional funds.

GIFT AID (NON-NEED-BASED) *Scholarships, grants, and awards by category: Academic Interests/Achievement:* general academic interests/achievements. *Creative Arts/Performance:* applied art and design, art/fine arts.

LOANS *Programs:* FFEL (Subsidized and Unsubsidized Stafford, PLUS), Perkins, college/university.

WORK-STUDY *Federal work-study:* Total amount: $950,000; 511 jobs averaging $1408. *State or other work-study/employment:* Total amount: $975,000 (100% non-need-based). 350 part-time jobs averaging $1400.

APPLYING FOR FINANCIAL AID *Required financial aid forms:* FAFSA, CSS Financial Aid PROFILE.

CONTACT Mr. Peter R. Riefler, Director of Financial Aid, Rhode Island School of Design, 2 College Street, Providence, RI 02903-2784, 401-454-6636 or toll-free 800-364-7473. *Fax:* 401-454-6412.

RHODES COLLEGE
Memphis, TN

CONTACT Forrest M. Stuart, Director of Financial Aid, Rhodes College, 2000 North Parkway, Memphis, TN 38112-1690, 901-843-3810 or toll-free 800-844-5969 (out-of-state). *Fax:* 901-843-3435. *E-mail:* stuart@rhodes.edu.

RICE UNIVERSITY
Houston, TX

Tuition & fees: $23,746 **Average undergraduate aid package: $20,140**

ABOUT THE INSTITUTION Independent, coed. Awards: bachelor's, master's, and doctoral degrees. 59 undergraduate majors. Total enrollment: 5,258. Undergraduates: 3,185. Freshmen: 722. Institutional methodology is used as a basis for awarding need-based institutional aid.

UNDERGRADUATE EXPENSES for 2005–06 *Application fee:* $50. *Comprehensive fee:* $32,726 includes full-time tuition ($23,310), mandatory fees ($436), and room and board ($8980). *College room only:* $5700. Full-time tuition and fees vary according to student level. Room and board charges vary according to board plan. *Payment plan:* Installment.

FRESHMAN FINANCIAL AID (Fall 2005, est.) 533 applied for aid; of those 54% were deemed to have need. 100% of freshmen with need received aid; of those 100% had need fully met. *Average percent of need met:* 100% (excluding resources awarded to replace EFC). *Average financial aid package:* $22,949 (excluding resources awarded to replace EFC). 17% of all full-time freshmen had no need and received non-need-based gift aid.

UNDERGRADUATE FINANCIAL AID (Fall 2005, est.) 1,583 applied for aid; of those 65% were deemed to have need. 100% of undergraduates with need received aid; of those 100% had need fully met. *Average percent of need met:* 100% (excluding resources awarded to replace EFC). *Average financial aid package:* $20,140 (excluding resources awarded to replace EFC). 18% of all full-time undergraduates had no need and received non-need-based gift aid.

GIFT AID (NEED-BASED) *Total amount:* $15,579,363 (6% federal, 16% state, 68% institutional, 10% external sources). *Receiving aid:* Freshmen: 40% (287); All full-time undergraduates: 34% (1,020). *Average award:* Freshmen: $21,157; Undergraduates: $16,889. *Scholarships, grants, and awards:* Federal Pell, FSEOG, state, private, college/university gift aid from institutional funds.

GIFT AID (NON-NEED-BASED) *Total amount:* $5,178,881 (78% institutional, 22% external sources). *Receiving aid:* Freshmen: 8% (56); Undergraduates: 6% (179). *Average Award:* Freshmen: $7052; Undergraduates: $6154. *Scholarships, grants, and awards by category: Academic Interests/Achievement:* architecture, area/ethnic studies, biological sciences, computer science, engineering/technologies, English, foreign languages, general academic interests/achievements, humanities, international studies, mathematics, physical sciences, social sciences. *Creative Arts/Performance:* applied art and design, art/fine arts, creative writing, debating, journalism/publications, music, performing arts. *Special Achievements/Activities:* community service, general special achievements/activities, leadership. *Special Characteristics:* children and siblings of alumni, children of faculty/staff, ethnic background, general special characteristics, international students. *Tuition waivers:* Full or partial for employees or children of employees. *ROTC:* Army cooperative, Naval, Air Force cooperative.

LOANS *Student loans:* $3,018,408 (64% need-based, 36% non-need-based). 28% of past graduating class borrowed through all loan programs. *Average indebtedness per student:* $14,166. *Average need-based loan:* Freshmen: $1276; Undergraduates: $3044. *Parent loans:* $4,514,028 (100% non-need-based). *Programs:* FFEL (Subsidized and Unsubsidized Stafford, PLUS), Perkins, college/university.

WORK-STUDY *Federal work-study:* Total amount: $1,067,252; jobs available (averaging $1800). *State or other work-study/employment:* Total amount: $7200 (100% need-based). Part-time jobs available.

ATHLETIC AWARDS *Total amount:* $6,726,951 (8% need-based, 92% non-need-based).

APPLYING FOR FINANCIAL AID *Required financial aid forms:* FAFSA, CSS Financial Aid PROFILE, noncustodial (divorced/separated) parent's statement, business/farm supplement. *Financial aid deadline:* Continuous. *Notification date:* 4/15. Students must reply by 5/1.

Rice University

CONTACT Office of Student Financial Services, Rice University, 116 Allen Center, MS 12, 6100 Main Street, Houston, TX 77005, 713-348-4958 or toll-free 800-527-OWLS. *Fax:* 713-348-2139.

THE RICHARD STOCKTON COLLEGE OF NEW JERSEY
Pomona, NJ

Tuition & fees (NJ res): $8394	Average undergraduate aid package: $11,022

ABOUT THE INSTITUTION State-supported, coed. Awards: bachelor's and master's degrees and post-bachelor's certificates. 31 undergraduate majors. Total enrollment: 7,034. Undergraduates: 6,570. Freshmen: 812. Federal methodology is used as a basis for awarding need-based institutional aid.

UNDERGRADUATE EXPENSES for 2005–06 *Application fee:* $50. **Tuition, state resident:** full-time $5498; part-time $171.82 per credit. **Tuition, nonresident:** full-time $8896; part-time $278 per credit. **Required fees:** full-time $2896; $90.50 per credit. **College room and board:** $7902; *room only:* $5370. Room and board charges vary according to board plan and housing facility. **Payment plans:** Installment, deferred payment.

FRESHMAN FINANCIAL AID (Fall 2005, est.) 645 applied for aid; of those 71% were deemed to have need. 97% of freshmen with need received aid; of those 59% had need fully met. *Average percent of need met:* 62% (excluding resources awarded to replace EFC). *Average financial aid package:* $12,104 (excluding resources awarded to replace EFC). 9% of all full-time freshmen had no need and received non-need-based gift aid.

UNDERGRADUATE FINANCIAL AID (Fall 2005, est.) 3,940 applied for aid; of those 77% were deemed to have need. 97% of undergraduates with need received aid; of those 51% had need fully met. *Average percent of need met:* 59% (excluding resources awarded to replace EFC). *Average financial aid package:* $11,022 (excluding resources awarded to replace EFC). 6% of all full-time undergraduates had no need and received non-need-based gift aid.

GIFT AID (NEED-BASED) *Total amount:* $11,236,502 (41% federal, 50% state, 8% institutional, 1% external sources). *Receiving aid:* Freshmen: 30% (242); All full-time undergraduates: 29% (1,657). *Average award:* Freshmen: $6512; Undergraduates: $5937. **Scholarships, grants, and awards:** Federal Pell, FSEOG, state, college/university gift aid from institutional funds.

GIFT AID (NON-NEED-BASED) *Total amount:* $1,194,336 (21% state, 59% institutional, 20% external sources). *Receiving aid:* Freshmen: 19% (150); Undergraduates: 9% (490). *Average Award:* Freshmen: $2798; Undergraduates: $2523. **Scholarships, grants, and awards by category:** *Academic Interests/Achievement:* 101 awards ($93,400 total): area/ethnic studies, biological sciences, business, computer science, education, general academic interests/achievements, health fields, humanities, mathematics, physical sciences, social sciences. *Creative Arts/Performance:* 8 awards ($6550 total): applied art and design, art/fine arts, creative writing, dance, journalism/publications, music, performing arts, theater/drama. *Special Achievements/Activities:* 4 awards ($1400 total): community service, general special achievements/activities, leadership. *Special Characteristics:* 25 awards ($17,150 total): adult students, children of faculty/staff, children of union members/company employees, ethnic background, general special characteristics, international students, local/state students, members of minority groups, previous college experience. **Tuition waivers:** Full or partial for employees or children of employees, senior citizens.

LOANS *Student loans:* $25,016,194 (73% need-based, 27% non-need-based). 64% of past graduating class borrowed through all loan programs. *Average indebtedness per student:* $15,875. *Average need-based loan:* Freshmen: $3042; Undergraduates: $3980. *Parent loans:* $5,304,254 (41% need-based, 59% non-need-based). **Programs:** FFEL (Subsidized and Unsubsidized Stafford, PLUS), Perkins, state.

WORK-STUDY *Federal work-study:* Total amount: $639,562; 318 jobs averaging $1586. **State or other work-study/employment:** Total amount: $721,680 (100% non-need-based). 518 part-time jobs averaging $1393.

APPLYING FOR FINANCIAL AID *Required financial aid form:* FAFSA. *Financial aid deadline (priority):* 3/1. *Notification date:* Continuous beginning 4/1. Students must reply within 2 weeks of notification.

CONTACT Ms. Jeanne L. Lewis, Director of Financial Aid, The Richard Stockton College of New Jersey, Jimmie Leeds Road, Pomona, NJ 08240-9988, 609-652-4203. *Fax:* 609-626-5517. *E-mail:* iaprod91@stockton.edu.

RIDER UNIVERSITY
Lawrenceville, NJ

Tuition & fees: $23,470	Average undergraduate aid package: $17,454

ABOUT THE INSTITUTION Independent, coed. Awards: associate, bachelor's, and master's degrees and post-master's certificates. 59 undergraduate majors. Total enrollment: 5,552. Undergraduates: 4,375. Freshmen: 946. Federal methodology is used as a basis for awarding need-based institutional aid.

UNDERGRADUATE EXPENSES for 2005–06 *Application fee:* $45. **Comprehensive fee:** $32,310 includes full-time tuition ($22,910), mandatory fees ($560), and room and board ($8840). **College room only:** $4940. *Part-time tuition:* $432 per credit. *Part-time fees:* $35 per course.

FRESHMAN FINANCIAL AID (Fall 2005, est.) 808 applied for aid; of those 82% were deemed to have need. 100% of freshmen with need received aid; of those 20% had need fully met. *Average percent of need met:* 70% (excluding resources awarded to replace EFC). *Average financial aid package:* $17,925 (excluding resources awarded to replace EFC). 15% of all full-time freshmen had no need and received non-need-based gift aid.

UNDERGRADUATE FINANCIAL AID (Fall 2005, est.) 2,786 applied for aid; of those 86% were deemed to have need. 100% of undergraduates with need received aid; of those 16% had need fully met. *Average percent of need met:* 70% (excluding resources awarded to replace EFC). *Average financial aid package:* $17,454 (excluding resources awarded to replace EFC). 16% of all full-time undergraduates had no need and received non-need-based gift aid.

GIFT AID (NEED-BASED) *Total amount:* $25,088,598 (11% federal, 20% state, 67% institutional, 2% external sources). *Receiving aid:* Freshmen: 68% (638); All full-time undergraduates: 64% (2,300). *Average award:* Freshmen: $12,707; Undergraduates: $11,825. **Scholarships, grants, and awards:** Federal Pell, FSEOG, state, private, college/university gift aid from institutional funds.

GIFT AID (NON-NEED-BASED) *Total amount:* $5,950,423 (93% institutional, 7% external sources). *Receiving aid:* Freshmen: 8% (76); Undergraduates: 8% (293). *Average Award:* Freshmen: $9221; Undergraduates: $8239. **Scholarships, grants, and awards by category:** *Academic Interests/Achievement:* $13,966,281 total: general academic interests/achievements. *Creative Arts/Performance:* 8 awards ($179,804 total): theater/drama. *Special Characteristics:* 14 awards ($186,354 total): members of minority groups. **ROTC:** Army cooperative.

LOANS *Student loans:* $28,316,210 (63% need-based, 37% non-need-based). 72% of past graduating class borrowed through all loan programs. *Average indebtedness per student:* $28,636. *Average need-based loan:* Freshmen: $3214; Undergraduates: $3937. *Parent loans:* $6,674,126 (32% need-based, 68% non-need-based). **Programs:** FFEL (Subsidized and Unsubsidized Stafford, PLUS), Perkins, state, college/university, alternative loans.

WORK-STUDY *Federal work-study:* Total amount: $3,792,721; 1,779 jobs averaging $2087.

ATHLETIC AWARDS *Total amount:* $2,851,309 (45% need-based, 55% non-need-based).

APPLYING FOR FINANCIAL AID *Required financial aid form:* FAFSA. *Financial aid deadline:* 6/1 (priority: 3/1). *Notification date:* Continuous beginning 4/15.

CONTACT John J. Williams, Student Financial Services Office, Rider University, 2083 Lawrenceville Road, Lawrenceville, NJ 08648-3001, 609-896-5360 or toll-free 800-257-9026. *Fax:* 609-219-4487. *E-mail:* finaid@rider.edu.

RINGLING SCHOOL OF ART AND DESIGN
Sarasota, FL

Tuition & fees: $21,400	Average undergraduate aid package: $9533

ABOUT THE INSTITUTION Independent, coed. Awards: bachelor's degrees. 6 undergraduate majors. Total enrollment: 1,088. Undergraduates: 1,088. Freshmen: 217. Federal methodology is used as a basis for awarding need-based institutional aid.

UNDERGRADUATE EXPENSES for 2005–06 *Application fee:* $35. **Comprehensive fee:** $30,565 includes full-time tuition ($21,200), mandatory fees ($200), and room and board ($9165). **College room only:** $4917. Full-time tuition and fees vary according to course load, program, and student level. Room and board charges vary according to board plan and housing facility. *Part-time tuition:* $1000 per credit hour. Part-time tuition and fees vary according to course load, program, and student level. **Payment plan:** Installment.

FRESHMAN FINANCIAL AID (Fall 2005, est.) 153 applied for aid; of those 85% were deemed to have need. 99% of freshmen with need received aid; of those 5% had need fully met. *Average percent of need met:* 30% (excluding resources awarded to replace EFC). *Average financial aid package:* $8319 (excluding resources awarded to replace EFC). 16% of all full-time freshmen had no need and received non-need-based gift aid.
UNDERGRADUATE FINANCIAL AID (Fall 2005, est.) 733 applied for aid; of those 88% were deemed to have need. 99% of undergraduates with need received aid; of those 3% had need fully met. *Average percent of need met:* 30% (excluding resources awarded to replace EFC). *Average financial aid package:* $9533 (excluding resources awarded to replace EFC). 12% of all full-time undergraduates had no need and received non-need-based gift aid.
GIFT AID (NEED-BASED) *Total amount:* $3,815,841 (27% federal, 40% state, 22% institutional, 11% external sources). *Receiving aid:* Freshmen: 54% (108); All full-time undergraduates: 54% (540). *Average award:* Freshmen: $7008; Undergraduates: $6659. *Scholarships, grants, and awards:* Federal Pell, FSEOG, state, private.
GIFT AID (NON-NEED-BASED) *Total amount:* $379,641 (61% state, 15% institutional, 24% external sources). *Receiving aid:* Freshmen: 1% (3); Undergraduates: 1% (9). *Average Award:* Freshmen: $11,508; Undergraduates: $15,759. *Scholarships, grants, and awards by category:* Academic Interests/Achievement: general academic interests/achievements. Creative Arts/Performance: applied art and design, art/fine arts. *Tuition waivers:* Full or partial for employees or children of employees.
LOANS *Student loans:* $7,687,714 (100% need-based). 72% of past graduating class borrowed through all loan programs. *Average indebtedness per student:* $30,558. *Average need-based loan:* Freshmen: $2435; Undergraduates: $3774. *Programs:* FFEL (Subsidized and Unsubsidized Stafford, PLUS), alternative loans.
WORK-STUDY *Federal work-study:* Total amount: $215,753; 144 jobs averaging $1836. *State or other work-study/employment:* Part-time jobs available.
APPLYING FOR FINANCIAL AID *Required financial aid form:* FAFSA. *Financial aid deadline (priority):* 3/1. *Notification date:* Continuous beginning 3/15. Students must reply within 4 weeks of notification.
CONTACT Fran Avenoso, Financial Aid Counselor, Ringling School of Art and Design, 2700 North Tamiami Trail, Sarasota, FL 34243, 941-359-7534 or toll-free 800-255-7695. *Fax:* 941-359-7517. *E-mail:* finaid@ringling.edu.

RIPON COLLEGE
Ripon, WI

Tuition & fees: $22,437	Average undergraduate aid package: $18,534

ABOUT THE INSTITUTION Independent, coed. Awards: bachelor's degrees. 38 undergraduate majors. Total enrollment: 979. Undergraduates: 979. Freshmen: 262. Federal methodology is used as a basis for awarding need-based institutional aid.
UNDERGRADUATE EXPENSES for 2006–07 *Application fee:* $30. *Comprehensive fee:* $28,497 includes full-time tuition ($22,162), mandatory fees ($275), and room and board ($6060). *College room only:* $3030. *Part-time tuition:* $890 per credit.
FRESHMAN FINANCIAL AID (Fall 2004) 247 applied for aid; of those 84% were deemed to have need. 100% of freshmen with need received aid; of those 43% had need fully met. *Average percent of need met:* 94% (excluding resources awarded to replace EFC). *Average financial aid package:* $18,083 (excluding resources awarded to replace EFC). 19% of all full-time freshmen had no need and received non-need-based gift aid.
UNDERGRADUATE FINANCIAL AID (Fall 2004) 892 applied for aid; of those 80% were deemed to have need. 100% of undergraduates with need received aid; of those 41% had need fully met. *Average percent of need met:* 93% (excluding resources awarded to replace EFC). *Average financial aid package:* $18,534 (excluding resources awarded to replace EFC). 18% of all full-time undergraduates had no need and received non-need-based gift aid.
GIFT AID (NEED-BASED) *Total amount:* $10,053,155 (9% federal, 10% state, 62% institutional, 19% external sources). *Receiving aid:* Freshmen: 79% (207); All full-time undergraduates: 75% (706). *Average award:* Freshmen: $14,371; Undergraduates: $14,326. *Scholarships, grants, and awards:* Federal Pell, FSEOG, state, private, college/university gift aid from institutional funds.
GIFT AID (NON-NEED-BASED) *Total amount:* $2,470,047 (66% institutional, 34% external sources). *Receiving aid:* Freshmen: 18% (46); Undergraduates: 14% (128). *Average Award:* Freshmen: $14,539; Undergraduates: $14,807. *Scholarships, grants, and awards by category:* Academic Interests/Achievement: 480 awards ($3,911,715 total): biological sciences, business, computer science, education, English, foreign languages, general academic interests/achievements, humanities, mathematics, military science, physical sciences, premedicine, religion/biblical studies, social sciences. Creative Arts/Performance: 97 awards ($349,000 total): art/fine arts, debating, music, theater/drama. Special Achievements/Activities: 202 awards ($858,000 total): general special achievements/activities, leadership, memberships. Special Characteristics: 326 awards ($1,875,301 total): children and siblings of alumni, children of faculty/staff, general special characteristics, international students, local/state students, members of minority groups, out-of-state students, previous college experience, religious affiliation, siblings of current students. *ROTC:* Army.
LOANS *Student loans:* $4,549,210 (63% need-based, 37% non-need-based). 90% of past graduating class borrowed through all loan programs. *Average indebtedness per student:* $16,492. *Average need-based loan:* Freshmen: $3772; Undergraduates: $4453. *Parent loans:* $1,526,879 (10% need-based, 90% non-need-based). *Programs:* FFEL (Subsidized and Unsubsidized Stafford, PLUS), Perkins, alternative loans.
WORK-STUDY *Federal work-study:* Total amount: $454,380; 314 jobs averaging $1447. *State or other work-study/employment:* Total amount: $713,618 (6% need-based, 94% non-need-based). 419 part-time jobs averaging $1703.
APPLYING FOR FINANCIAL AID *Required financial aid form:* FAFSA. *Financial aid deadline (priority):* 3/1. *Notification date:* Continuous. Students must reply within 2 weeks of notification.
CONTACT Steven M. Schuetz, Dean of Admission and Financial Aid, Ripon College, 300 Seward Street, Ripon, WI 54971, 920-748-8185 or toll-free 800-947-4766. *Fax:* 920-748-8335. *E-mail:* financialaid@ripon.edu.

RIVIER COLLEGE
Nashua, NH

CONTACT Valerie Patnaude, Director of Financial Aid, Rivier College, 420 Main Street, Nashua, NH 03060-5086, 603-897-8533 or toll-free 800-44RIVIER. *Fax:* 603-897-8810. *E-mail:* vpatnaude@rivier.edu.

ROANOKE BIBLE COLLEGE
Elizabeth City, NC

ABOUT THE INSTITUTION Independent Christian, coed. Awards: associate and bachelor's degrees. 3 undergraduate majors. Total enrollment: 182. Undergraduates: 182. Freshmen: 32.
GIFT AID (NEED-BASED) *Scholarships, grants, and awards:* Federal Pell, FSEOG, state, private, college/university gift aid from institutional funds.
GIFT AID (NON-NEED-BASED) *Scholarships, grants, and awards by category:* Academic Interests/Achievement: general academic interests/achievements, religion/biblical studies. Special Achievements/Activities: general special achievements/activities, religious involvement. Special Characteristics: children and siblings of alumni, children of faculty/staff, general special characteristics, handicapped students, international students, married students, spouses of current students.
LOANS *Programs:* FFEL (Subsidized and Unsubsidized Stafford, PLUS), alternative loans.
APPLYING FOR FINANCIAL AID *Required financial aid forms:* FAFSA, institution's own form.
CONTACT Mrs. Julie Ann Fields, Director of Admissions and Financial Aid, Roanoke Bible College, 715 North Poindexter Street, Elizabeth City, NC 27909, 252-334-2019 or toll-free 800-RBC-8980. *Fax:* 252-334-2064. *E-mail:* jaf@roanokebible.edu.

ROANOKE COLLEGE
Salem, VA

Tuition & fees: $23,453	Average undergraduate aid package: $18,931

ABOUT THE INSTITUTION Independent religious, coed. Awards: bachelor's degrees. 31 undergraduate majors. Total enrollment: 1,936. Undergraduates: 1,936. Freshmen: 534. Federal methodology is used as a basis for awarding need-based institutional aid.

Roanoke College

UNDERGRADUATE EXPENSES for 2005–06 *Application fee:* $30. *Comprehensive fee:* $30,748 includes full-time tuition ($22,848), mandatory fees ($605), and room and board ($7295). *College room only:* $3526. Room and board charges vary according to housing facility. *Part-time tuition:* $1084 per course. *Payment plan:* Installment.

FRESHMAN FINANCIAL AID (Fall 2005, est.) 398 applied for aid; of those 99% were deemed to have need. 100% of freshmen with need received aid; of those 23% had need fully met. *Average percent of need met:* 93% (excluding resources awarded to replace EFC). *Average financial aid package:* $19,176 (excluding resources awarded to replace EFC). 21% of all full-time freshmen had no need and received non-need-based gift aid.

UNDERGRADUATE FINANCIAL AID (Fall 2005, est.) 1,441 applied for aid; of those 93% were deemed to have need. 100% of undergraduates with need received aid; of those 30% had need fully met. *Average percent of need met:* 89% (excluding resources awarded to replace EFC). *Average financial aid package:* $18,931 (excluding resources awarded to replace EFC). 23% of all full-time undergraduates had no need and received non-need-based gift aid.

GIFT AID (NEED-BASED) *Total amount:* $16,632,847 (5% federal, 11% state, 81% institutional, 3% external sources). *Receiving aid:* Freshmen: 56% (301); All full-time undergraduates: 61% (1,117). *Average award:* Freshmen: $16,416; Undergraduates: $15,168. *Scholarships, grants, and awards:* Federal Pell, FSEOG, state, private, college/university gift aid from institutional funds.

GIFT AID (NON-NEED-BASED) *Total amount:* $6,284,198 (13% state, 85% institutional, 2% external sources). *Receiving aid:* Freshmen: 67% (357); Undergraduates: 48% (875). *Average Award:* Freshmen: $9150; Undergraduates: $10,255. *Scholarships, grants, and awards by category: Academic Interests/Achievement:* general academic interests/achievements. *Creative Arts/Performance:* art/fine arts, music. *Special Characteristics:* local/state students, members of minority groups, religious affiliation. *Tuition waivers:* Full or partial for employees or children of employees, senior citizens.

LOANS *Student loans:* $7,699,616 (87% need-based, 13% non-need-based). 72% of past graduating class borrowed through all loan programs. *Average indebtedness per student:* $18,543. *Average need-based loan:* Freshmen: $3230; Undergraduates: $4267. *Parent loans:* $2,856,985 (79% need-based, 21% non-need-based). *Programs:* FFEL (Subsidized and Unsubsidized Stafford, PLUS), Perkins, college/university, Alternative Loans.

WORK-STUDY *Federal work-study:* Total amount: $842,713; 620 jobs averaging $1409.

APPLYING FOR FINANCIAL AID *Required financial aid forms:* FAFSA, state aid form. *Financial aid deadline (priority):* 3/1. *Notification date:* Continuous beginning 11/1. Students must reply within 2 weeks of notification.

CONTACT Mr. Thomas S. Blair Jr., Director of Financial Aid, Roanoke College, 221 College Lane, Salem, VA 24153-3794, 540-375-2235 or toll-free 800-388-2276. *E-mail:* finaid@roanoke.edu.

ROBERT MORRIS COLLEGE
Chicago, IL

Tuition & fees: $15,900 | **Average undergraduate aid package:** $11,059

ABOUT THE INSTITUTION Independent, coed. Awards: associate, bachelor's, and master's degrees. 24 undergraduate majors. Total enrollment: 5,418. Undergraduates: 5,418. Freshmen: 977. Federal methodology is used as a basis for awarding need-based institutional aid.

UNDERGRADUATE EXPENSES for 2006–07 *Application fee:* $30. *Tuition:* full-time $15,900.

FRESHMAN FINANCIAL AID (Fall 2005, est.) 867 applied for aid; of those 97% were deemed to have need. 99% of freshmen with need received aid; of those 4% had need fully met. *Average percent of need met:* 50% (excluding resources awarded to replace EFC). *Average financial aid package:* $10,187 (excluding resources awarded to replace EFC). 2% of all full-time freshmen had no need and received non-need-based gift aid.

UNDERGRADUATE FINANCIAL AID (Fall 2005, est.) 4,534 applied for aid; of those 97% were deemed to have need. 99% of undergraduates with need received aid; of those 4% had need fully met. *Average percent of need met:* 47% (excluding resources awarded to replace EFC). *Average financial aid package:* $11,059 (excluding resources awarded to replace EFC). 3% of all full-time undergraduates had no need and received non-need-based gift aid.

GIFT AID (NEED-BASED) *Total amount:* $34,085,389 (29% federal, 37% state, 33% institutional, 1% external sources). *Receiving aid:* Freshmen: 83% (808); All full-time undergraduates: 90% (4,245). *Average award:* Freshmen: $8318; Undergraduates: $8262. *Scholarships, grants, and awards:* Federal Pell, FSEOG, state, private, college/university gift aid from institutional funds.

GIFT AID (NON-NEED-BASED) *Total amount:* $772,196 (100% institutional). *Receiving aid:* Freshmen: 3% (31); Undergraduates: 3% (142). *Average Award:* Freshmen: $12,523; Undergraduates: $9897. *Scholarships, grants, and awards by category: Academic Interests/Achievement:* business, computer science, general academic interests/achievements, health fields. *Creative Arts/Performance:* applied art and design, journalism/publications. *Special Achievements/Activities:* community service, general special achievements/activities. *Special Characteristics:* children of faculty/staff, general special characteristics, out-of-state students, veterans. *ROTC:* Army cooperative.

LOANS *Student loans:* $26,276,894 (92% need-based, 8% non-need-based). 93% of past graduating class borrowed through all loan programs. *Average indebtedness per student:* $18,479. *Average need-based loan:* Freshmen: $2511; Undergraduates: $3620. *Parent loans:* $2,966,589 (63% need-based, 37% non-need-based). *Programs:* FFEL (Subsidized and Unsubsidized Stafford, PLUS), Perkins.

WORK-STUDY *Federal work-study:* Total amount: $133,494; 177 jobs averaging $792.

ATHLETIC AWARDS *Total amount:* $2,159,978 (82% need-based, 18% non-need-based).

APPLYING FOR FINANCIAL AID *Required financial aid form:* FAFSA. *Financial aid deadline:* Continuous. *Notification date:* Continuous.

CONTACT Gabriel Hennessey, Assistant Director of Financial Services, Robert Morris College, 401 South State Street, Suite 140, Chicago, IL 60605, 312-935-4075 or toll-free 800-RMC-5960. *Fax:* 312-935-4074. *E-mail:* ghennessey@robertmorris.edu.

ROBERT MORRIS UNIVERSITY
Moon Township, PA

Tuition & fees: $15,152 | **Average undergraduate aid package:** $12,784

ABOUT THE INSTITUTION Independent, coed. Awards: bachelor's, master's, and doctoral degrees and post-bachelor's certificates. 37 undergraduate majors. Total enrollment: 5,095. Undergraduates: 3,971. Freshmen: 687. Federal methodology is used as a basis for awarding need-based institutional aid.

UNDERGRADUATE EXPENSES for 2005–06 *Application fee:* $30. *Comprehensive fee:* $22,822 includes full-time tuition ($15,152) and room and board ($7670). *College room only:* $4650. Room and board charges vary according to board plan and housing facility. *Part-time tuition:* $505 per credit. Part-time tuition and fees vary according to course load. *Payment plans:* Installment, deferred payment.

FRESHMAN FINANCIAL AID (Fall 2005, est.) 636 applied for aid; of those 84% were deemed to have need. 100% of freshmen with need received aid; of those 29% had need fully met. *Average percent of need met:* 75% (excluding resources awarded to replace EFC). *Average financial aid package:* $13,207 (excluding resources awarded to replace EFC). 20% of all full-time freshmen had no need and received non-need-based gift aid.

UNDERGRADUATE FINANCIAL AID (Fall 2005, est.) 2,550 applied for aid; of those 88% were deemed to have need. 100% of undergraduates with need received aid; of those 24% had need fully met. *Average percent of need met:* 70% (excluding resources awarded to replace EFC). *Average financial aid package:* $12,784 (excluding resources awarded to replace EFC). 19% of all full-time undergraduates had no need and received non-need-based gift aid.

GIFT AID (NEED-BASED) *Total amount:* $13,207,923 (21% federal, 33% state, 43% institutional, 3% external sources). *Receiving aid:* Freshmen: 76% (524); All full-time undergraduates: 68% (2,035). *Average award:* Freshmen: $7960; Undergraduates: $6956. *Scholarships, grants, and awards:* Federal Pell, FSEOG, state, private, college/university gift aid from institutional funds.

GIFT AID (NON-NEED-BASED) *Total amount:* $2,384,101 (3% state, 89% institutional, 8% external sources). *Receiving aid:* Freshmen: 6% (44); Undergraduates: 4% (119). *Average Award:* Freshmen: $8979; Undergraduates: $9451. *Scholarships, grants, and awards by category: Academic Interests/Achievement:* general academic interests/achievements. *Creative Arts/Performance:* general creative arts/performance. *Special Achievements/Activities:* general special achievements/activities. *Special Characteristics:* children of faculty/

Rochester Institute of Technology

staff, ethnic background, members of minority groups, out-of-state students. *Tuition waivers:* Full or partial for employees or children of employees. *ROTC:* Army cooperative, Air Force cooperative.

LOANS *Student loans:* $24,577,354 (74% need-based, 26% non-need-based). *Average need-based loan:* Freshmen: $4528; Undergraduates: $5837. *Parent loans:* $4,447,094 (44% need-based, 56% non-need-based). *Programs:* FFEL (Subsidized and Unsubsidized Stafford, PLUS), Perkins, alternative private loans.

WORK-STUDY *Federal work-study:* Total amount: $2,392,083; jobs available. *State or other work-study/employment:* Part-time jobs available.

ATHLETIC AWARDS *Total amount:* $2,388,746 (59% need-based, 41% non-need-based).

APPLYING FOR FINANCIAL AID *Required financial aid form:* FAFSA. *Financial aid deadline:* Continuous. *Notification date:* Continuous beginning 3/15. Students must reply within 2 weeks of notification.

CONTACT Ms. Shari Payne, Director, Financial Aid, Robert Morris University, 6001 University Boulevard, Moon Township, PA 15108-1189, 412-299-2450 or toll-free 800-762-0097. *Fax:* 412-262-8601. *E-mail:* finaid@rmu.edu.

ROBERTS WESLEYAN COLLEGE
Rochester, NY

Tuition & fees: $20,286   Average undergraduate aid package: $15,545

ABOUT THE INSTITUTION Independent religious, coed. Awards: associate, bachelor's, and master's degrees. 55 undergraduate majors. Total enrollment: 1,948. Undergraduates: 1,408. Freshmen: 224. Federal methodology is used as a basis for awarding need-based institutional aid.

UNDERGRADUATE EXPENSES for 2006-07 *Application fee:* $35. *Comprehensive fee:* $27,734 includes full-time tuition ($19,264), mandatory fees ($1022), and room and board ($7448). *College room only:* $2168. *Part-time tuition:* $422 per credit.

FRESHMAN FINANCIAL AID (Fall 2005, est.) 193 applied for aid; of those 94% were deemed to have need. 100% of freshmen with need received aid; of those 18% had need fully met. *Average percent of need met:* 78% (excluding resources awarded to replace EFC). *Average financial aid package:* $16,898 (excluding resources awarded to replace EFC). 12% of all full-time freshmen had no need and received non-need-based gift aid.

UNDERGRADUATE FINANCIAL AID (Fall 2005, est.) 936 applied for aid; of those 93% were deemed to have need. 100% of undergraduates with need received aid; of those 20% had need fully met. *Average percent of need met:* 75% (excluding resources awarded to replace EFC). *Average financial aid package:* $15,545 (excluding resources awarded to replace EFC). 13% of all full-time undergraduates had no need and received non-need-based gift aid.

GIFT AID (NEED-BASED) *Total amount:* $8,900,491 (15% federal, 18% state, 57% institutional, 10% external sources). *Receiving aid:* Freshmen: 88% (182); All full-time undergraduates: 86% (868). *Average award:* Freshmen: $11,736; Undergraduates: $9830. *Scholarships, grants, and awards:* Federal Pell, FSEOG, state, private, college/university gift aid from institutional funds.

GIFT AID (NON-NEED-BASED) *Total amount:* $1,139,640 (4% state, 62% institutional, 34% external sources). *Receiving aid:* Freshmen: 5% (10); Undergraduates: 6% (59). *Average Award:* Freshmen: $7906; Undergraduates: $8801. *Scholarships, grants, and awards by category:* Creative Arts/Performance: 187 awards ($303,550 total): art/fine arts, music. Special Achievements/Activities: 554 awards ($433,438 total): general special achievements/activities, leadership. Special Characteristics: 646 awards ($1,111,645 total): children and siblings of alumni, children of faculty/staff, international students, out-of-state students, relatives of clergy, religious affiliation, siblings of current students. *ROTC:* Army cooperative, Air Force cooperative.

LOANS *Student loans:* $7,100,186 (82% need-based, 18% non-need-based). 93% of past graduating class borrowed through all loan programs. *Average need-based loan:* Freshmen: $4560; Undergraduates: $5230. *Parent loans:* $2,665,313 (48% need-based, 52% non-need-based). *Programs:* FFEL (Subsidized and Unsubsidized Stafford, PLUS), Perkins.

WORK-STUDY *Federal work-study:* Total amount: $857,906; 703 jobs averaging $980. *State or other work-study/employment:* Total amount: $63,100 (2% need-based, 98% non-need-based). 44 part-time jobs averaging $1700.

ATHLETIC AWARDS *Total amount:* $635,738 (58% need-based, 42% non-need-based).

APPLYING FOR FINANCIAL AID *Required financial aid forms:* FAFSA, state aid form. *Financial aid deadline (priority):* 3/15. *Notification date:* Continuous beginning 3/15. Students must reply by 5/1 or within 2 weeks of notification.

CONTACT Mr. Stephen Field, Director of Student Financial Services, Roberts Wesleyan College, 2301 Westside Drive, Rochester, NY 14624-1997, 585-594-6391 or toll-free 800-777-4RWC. *Fax:* 585-594-6036. *E-mail:* fields@roberts.edu.

ROCHESTER COLLEGE
Rochester Hills, MI

ABOUT THE INSTITUTION Independent religious, coed. Awards: associate, bachelor's, and master's degrees. 31 undergraduate majors. Total university enrollment: 101. Total unit enrollment: 1,055. Undergraduates: 1,047. Freshmen: 137.

GIFT AID (NEED-BASED) *Scholarships, grants, and awards:* Federal Pell, FSEOG, state, private, college/university gift aid from institutional funds.

GIFT AID (NON-NEED-BASED) *Scholarships, grants, and awards by category: Academic Interests/Achievement:* business, computer science, education, general academic interests/achievements, mathematics, religion/biblical studies. *Creative Arts/Performance:* journalism/publications, music, theater/drama. *Special Achievements/Activities:* general special achievements/activities, leadership. *Special Characteristics:* adult students, children and siblings of alumni, children of faculty/staff, first-generation college students, general special characteristics, out-of-state students, previous college experience, relatives of clergy, siblings of current students.

LOANS *Programs:* Federal Direct (Subsidized and Unsubsidized Stafford, PLUS), Perkins.

WORK-STUDY *Federal work-study:* Total amount: $145,934; 93 jobs averaging $1500. *State or other work-study/employment:* Total amount: $75,342 (100% non-need-based). 106 part-time jobs averaging $1000.

APPLYING FOR FINANCIAL AID *Required financial aid forms:* FAFSA, institution's own form.

CONTACT Burt Rutledge, Director of Financial Aid, Rochester College, 800 West Avon Road, Rochester Hills, MI 48307, 248-218-2028 or toll-free 800-521-6010. *Fax:* 248-218-2035. *E-mail:* brutledge@rc.edu.

ROCHESTER INSTITUTE OF TECHNOLOGY
Rochester, NY

Tuition & fees: $23,619   Average undergraduate aid package: $17,100

ABOUT THE INSTITUTION Independent, coed. Awards: associate, bachelor's, master's, and doctoral degrees and post-bachelor's and post-master's certificates. 113 undergraduate majors. Total enrollment: 15,200. Undergraduates: 12,933. Freshmen: 2,217. Both federal and institutional methodology are used as a basis for awarding need-based institutional aid.

UNDERGRADUATE EXPENSES for 2005-06 *Application fee:* $50. *Comprehensive fee:* $32,070 includes full-time tuition ($23,247), mandatory fees ($372), and room and board ($8451). *College room only:* $4863. Full-time tuition and fees vary according to course load, program, and student level. Room and board charges vary according to board plan and housing facility. *Part-time tuition:* $518 per credit hour. *Part-time fees:* $31 per term. Part-time tuition and fees vary according to class time, course load, program, and student level. *Payment plans:* Tuition prepayment, installment, deferred payment.

FRESHMAN FINANCIAL AID (Fall 2005, est.) 1910 applied for aid; of those 83% were deemed to have need. 100% of freshmen with need received aid; of those 83% had need fully met. *Average percent of need met:* 88% (excluding resources awarded to replace EFC). *Average financial aid package:* $17,600 (excluding resources awarded to replace EFC). 11% of all full-time freshmen had no need and received non-need-based gift aid.

UNDERGRADUATE FINANCIAL AID (Fall 2005, est.) 7,950 applied for aid; of those 88% were deemed to have need. 100% of undergraduates with need received aid; of those 83% had need fully met. *Average percent of need met:* 88% (excluding resources awarded to replace EFC). *Average financial aid package:* $17,100 (excluding resources awarded to replace EFC). 8% of all full-time undergraduates had no need and received non-need-based gift aid.

GIFT AID (NEED-BASED) *Total amount:* $76,442,000 (11% federal, 11% state, 75% institutional, 3% external sources). *Receiving aid:* Freshmen: 68% (1,510); All full-time undergraduates: 58% (6,615). *Average award:* Freshmen: $11,500;

Rochester Institute of Technology

Undergraduates: $11,300. *Scholarships, grants, and awards:* Federal Pell, FSEOG, state, private, college/university gift aid from institutional funds, NACME.
GIFT AID (NON-NEED-BASED) *Total amount:* $20,528,000 (9% federal, 29% state, 49% institutional, 13% external sources). *Receiving aid:* Freshmen: 20% (440); Undergraduates: 20% (2,260). *Average Award:* Freshmen: $6500; Undergraduates: $6200. *Scholarships, grants, and awards by category: Academic Interests/Achievement:* 3,000 awards ($19,500,000 total): biological sciences, business, communication, computer science, engineering/technologies, general academic interests/achievements, health fields, international studies, mathematics, military science, physical sciences, premedicine, social sciences. *Creative Arts/Performance:* 300 awards ($2,009,000 total): applied art and design, art/fine arts, cinema/film/broadcasting. *Special Achievements/Activities:* community service, leadership. *Special Characteristics:* children of faculty/staff, international students, members of minority groups, veterans. *Tuition waivers:* Full or partial for employees or children of employees. *ROTC:* Army, Naval cooperative, Air Force.
LOANS *Student loans:* $65,181,000 (57% need-based, 43% non-need-based). 77% of past graduating class borrowed through all loan programs. *Average indebtedness per student:* $22,000. *Average need-based loan:* Freshmen: $5000; Undergraduates: $5400. *Parent loans:* $14,000,000 (40% need-based, 60% non-need-based). *Programs:* Federal Direct (Subsidized and Unsubsidized Stafford, PLUS), Perkins, alternative loans, RIT loans.
WORK-STUDY *Federal work-study:* Total amount: $2,800,000; 2,060 jobs averaging $1330. *State or other work-study/employment:* Total amount: $8,400,000 (100% non-need-based). 4,700 part-time jobs averaging $1780.
APPLYING FOR FINANCIAL AID *Required financial aid form:* FAFSA. *Financial aid deadline (priority):* 3/1. *Notification date:* Continuous beginning 3/15. Students must reply by 5/1 or within 2 weeks of notification.
CONTACT Mrs. Verna Hazen, Assistant Vice President, Financial Aid and Scholarships, Rochester Institute of Technology, Office of Financial Aid and Scholarships, 56 Lomb Drive, Rochester, NY 14623-5604, 585-475-2186. *Fax:* 585-475-7270. *E-mail:* ritaid@rit.edu.

ROCKFORD COLLEGE
Rockford, IL

CONTACT Mrs. Stacey Zimmerman, Financial Aid Specialist, Rockford College, 5050 East State Street, Rockford, IL 61108, 815-226-3396 or toll-free 800-892-2984. *Fax:* 815-394-5174.

ROCKHURST UNIVERSITY
Kansas City, MO

Tuition & fees: $19,210	Average undergraduate aid package: $19,719

ABOUT THE INSTITUTION Independent Roman Catholic (Jesuit), coed. Awards: bachelor's, master's, and doctoral degrees and post-bachelor's certificates. 31 undergraduate majors. Total enrollment: 2,944. Undergraduates: 2,091. Freshmen: 371. Federal methodology is used as a basis for awarding need-based institutional aid.
UNDERGRADUATE EXPENSES for 2005–06 *Application fee:* $25. *One-time required fee:* $60. *Comprehensive fee:* $25,110 includes full-time tuition ($18,500), mandatory fees ($710), and room and board ($5900). Full-time tuition and fees vary according to class time and course load. Room and board charges vary according to board plan and housing facility. *Part-time tuition:* $630 per semester hour. *Part-time fees:* $25 per term. Part-time tuition and fees vary according to class time and course load. *Payment plans:* Installment, deferred payment.
FRESHMAN FINANCIAL AID (Fall 2005, est.) 367 applied for aid; of those 92% were deemed to have need. 99% of freshmen with need received aid; of those 28% had need fully met. *Average percent of need met:* 100% (excluding resources awarded to replace EFC). *Average financial aid package:* $19,921 (excluding resources awarded to replace EFC). 6% of all full-time freshmen had no need and received non-need-based gift aid.
UNDERGRADUATE FINANCIAL AID (Fall 2005, est.) 1,270 applied for aid; of those 84% were deemed to have need. 96% of undergraduates with need received aid; of those 17% had need fully met. *Average percent of need met:* 97% (excluding resources awarded to replace EFC). *Average financial aid package:* $19,719 (excluding resources awarded to replace EFC). 10% of all full-time undergraduates had no need and received non-need-based gift aid.

GIFT AID (NEED-BASED) *Total amount:* $7,611,270 (11% federal, 7% state, 80% institutional, 2% external sources). *Receiving aid:* Freshmen: 57% (212); All full-time undergraduates: 51% (667). *Average award:* Freshmen: $6110; Undergraduates: $5869. *Scholarships, grants, and awards:* Federal Pell, FSEOG, state, private, college/university gift aid from institutional funds.
GIFT AID (NON-NEED-BASED) *Total amount:* $6,561,982 (2% state, 89% institutional, 9% external sources). *Receiving aid:* Freshmen: 90% (333); Undergraduates: 78% (1,026). *Average Award:* Freshmen: $7521; Undergraduates: $8523. *Scholarships, grants, and awards by category: Academic Interests/Achievement:* 1,035 awards ($6,139,580 total): biological sciences, business, communication, computer science, English, foreign languages, general academic interests/achievements, health fields, humanities, mathematics, physical sciences, premedicine, religion/biblical studies, social sciences. *Creative Arts/Performance:* 30 awards ($36,750 total): creative writing, music, performing arts, theater/drama. *Special Achievements/Activities:* 116 awards ($171,500 total): community service, leadership. *Special Characteristics:* 160 awards ($460,325 total): children and siblings of alumni, children of faculty/staff, siblings of current students. *Tuition waivers:* Full or partial for children of alumni, employees or children of employees, senior citizens. *ROTC:* Army cooperative.
LOANS *Student loans:* $5,717,699 (58% need-based, 42% non-need-based). 72% of past graduating class borrowed through all loan programs. *Average indebtedness per student:* $17,890. *Average need-based loan:* Freshmen: $2419; Undergraduates: $3314. *Parent loans:* $1,335,017 (49% need-based, 51% non-need-based). *Programs:* FFEL (Subsidized and Unsubsidized Stafford, PLUS), Perkins.
WORK-STUDY *Federal work-study:* Total amount: $239,202; 139 jobs averaging $1500. *State or other work-study/employment:* Total amount: $79,408 (100% non-need-based). 40 part-time jobs averaging $1200.
ATHLETIC AWARDS *Total amount:* $1,970,106 (28% need-based, 72% non-need-based).
APPLYING FOR FINANCIAL AID *Required financial aid form:* FAFSA. *Financial aid deadline:* 6/1 (priority: 3/1). *Notification date:* Continuous. Students must reply within 4 weeks of notification.
CONTACT Ms. Carla Boren, Director of Financial Aid, Rockhurst University, 1100 Rockhurst Road, Kansas City, MO 64110-2561, 816-501-4100 or toll-free 800-842-6776. *Fax:* 816-501-4241. *E-mail:* carla.boren@rockhurst.edu.

ROCKY MOUNTAIN COLLEGE
Billings, MT

CONTACT Lisa Browning, Financial Aid Director, Rocky Mountain College, 1511 Poly Drive, Billings, MT 59102-1796, 406-657-1031 or toll-free 800-877-6259. *Fax:* 406-238-7351. *E-mail:* browninl@rocky.edu.

ROCKY MOUNTAIN COLLEGE OF ART & DESIGN
Lakewood, CO

Tuition & fees: $17,880	Average undergraduate aid package: $7241

ABOUT THE INSTITUTION Proprietary, coed. Awards: bachelor's degrees. 7 undergraduate majors. Total enrollment: 448. Undergraduates: 448. Freshmen: 62. Federal methodology is used as a basis for awarding need-based institutional aid.
UNDERGRADUATE EXPENSES for 2005–06 *Application fee:* $35. *Tuition:* full-time $17,880; part-time $745 per credit.
FRESHMAN FINANCIAL AID (Fall 2004) 67 applied for aid; of those 82% were deemed to have need. 100% of freshmen with need received aid; of those 25% had need fully met. *Average percent of need met:* 70% (excluding resources awarded to replace EFC). *Average financial aid package:* $6507 (excluding resources awarded to replace EFC). 1% of all full-time freshmen had no need and received non-need-based gift aid.
UNDERGRADUATE FINANCIAL AID (Fall 2004) 382 applied for aid; of those 85% were deemed to have need. 100% of undergraduates with need received aid; of those 13% had need fully met. *Average percent of need met:* 51% (excluding resources awarded to replace EFC). *Average financial aid package:* $7241 (excluding resources awarded to replace EFC). 4% of all full-time undergraduates had no need and received non-need-based gift aid.

GIFT AID (NEED-BASED) *Total amount:* $1,357,404 (35% federal, 10% state, 52% institutional, 3% external sources). *Receiving aid:* Freshmen: 30% (20); All full-time undergraduates: 35% (134). *Average award:* Freshmen: $1876; Undergraduates: $1855. *Scholarships, grants, and awards:* Federal Pell, FSEOG, state, private, college/university gift aid from institutional funds.
GIFT AID (NON-NEED-BASED) *Total amount:* $186,086 (95% institutional, 5% external sources). *Receiving aid:* Freshmen: 48% (32); Undergraduates: 50% (192). *Average Award:* Freshmen: $3750; Undergraduates: $2433. *Scholarships, grants, and awards by category:* Academic Interests/Achievement: 161 awards ($267,371 total): general academic interests/achievements. *Creative Arts/Performance:* 111 awards ($399,996 total): applied art and design, art/fine arts. *Special Characteristics:* children of faculty/staff.
LOANS *Student loans:* $3,384,251 (80% need-based, 20% non-need-based). 75% of past graduating class borrowed through all loan programs. *Average indebtedness per student:* $18,000. *Average need-based loan:* Freshmen: $2107; Undergraduates: $3610. *Parent loans:* $1,418,252 (80% need-based, 20% non-need-based). *Programs:* FFEL (Subsidized and Unsubsidized Stafford, PLUS), alternative loans.
WORK-STUDY *Federal work-study:* Total amount: $45,314; 22 jobs averaging $1951. *State or other work-study/employment:* Total amount: $103,449 (90% need-based, 10% non-need-based). 41 part-time jobs averaging $1978.
APPLYING FOR FINANCIAL AID *Required financial aid forms:* FAFSA, state aid form. *Financial aid deadline (priority):* 4/1. *Notification date:* Continuous beginning 4/1. Students must reply within 2 weeks of notification.
CONTACT David Nelson, Director of Financial Aid, Rocky Mountain College of Art & Design, 1600 Pierce Street, Lakewood, CO 80214, 303-225-8551 or toll-free 800-888-ARTS. *Fax:* 303-567-7200. *E-mail:* dnelson@rmcad.edu.

ROGERS STATE UNIVERSITY
Claremore, OK

CONTACT Cynthia Hoyt, Director of Financial Aid, Rogers State University, 1701 West Will Rogers Boulevard, Claremore, OK 74017-3252, 918-343-7553 or toll-free 800-256-7511. *Fax:* 918-343-7598. *E-mail:* finaid@rsu.edu.

ROGER WILLIAMS UNIVERSITY
Bristol, RI

Tuition & fees: $24,066   **Average undergraduate aid package: $14,600**

ABOUT THE INSTITUTION Independent, coed. Awards: associate, bachelor's, master's, and first professional degrees. 47 undergraduate majors. Total enrollment: 5,214. Undergraduates: 4,359. Freshmen: 1,189. Institutional methodology is used as a basis for awarding need-based institutional aid.
UNDERGRADUATE EXPENSES for 2006–07 *Application fee:* $50. *Comprehensive fee:* $34,759 includes full-time tuition ($22,932), mandatory fees ($1134), and room and board ($10,693). *College room only:* $5569. *Part-time tuition:* $956 per credit.
FRESHMAN FINANCIAL AID (Fall 2005, est.) 935 applied for aid; of those 80% were deemed to have need. 98% of freshmen with need received aid; of those 53% had need fully met. *Average percent of need met:* 78% (excluding resources awarded to replace EFC). *Average financial aid package:* $15,111 (excluding resources awarded to replace EFC). 15% of all full-time freshmen had no need and received non-need-based gift aid.
UNDERGRADUATE FINANCIAL AID (Fall 2005, est.) 2,758 applied for aid; of those 82% were deemed to have need. 99% of undergraduates with need received aid; of those 57% had need fully met. *Average percent of need met:* 83% (excluding resources awarded to replace EFC). *Average financial aid package:* $14,600 (excluding resources awarded to replace EFC). 9% of all full-time undergraduates had no need and received non-need-based gift aid.
GIFT AID (NEED-BASED) *Total amount:* $21,542,482 (7% federal, 2% state, 88% institutional, 3% external sources). *Receiving aid:* Freshmen: 43% (513); All full-time undergraduates: 44% (1,544). *Average award:* Freshmen: $9523; Undergraduates: $7700. *Scholarships, grants, and awards:* Federal Pell, FSEOG, state, private, college/university gift aid from institutional funds.
GIFT AID (NON-NEED-BASED) *Total amount:* $2,003,405 (1% state, 97% institutional, 2% external sources). *Receiving aid:* Freshmen: 31% (372); Undergraduates: 26% (930). *Average Award:* Freshmen: $5840; Undergraduates: $6017. *Scholarships, grants, and awards by category:* Academic Interests/Achievement: 1,468 awards ($11,519,400 total): general academic interests/achievements. *ROTC:* Army.
LOANS *Student loans:* $22,516,092 (90% need-based, 10% non-need-based). 80% of past graduating class borrowed through all loan programs. *Average indebtedness per student:* $28,147. *Average need-based loan:* Freshmen: $3917; Undergraduates: $5100. *Parent loans:* $10,021,495 (82% need-based, 18% non-need-based). *Programs:* FFEL (Subsidized and Unsubsidized Stafford, PLUS), Perkins, state.
WORK-STUDY *Federal work-study:* Total amount: $696,179; 715 jobs averaging $1813. *State or other work-study/employment:* Total amount: $874,300 (92% need-based, 8% non-need-based). 490 part-time jobs averaging $1693.
APPLYING FOR FINANCIAL AID *Required financial aid forms:* FAFSA, CSS Financial Aid PROFILE. *Financial aid deadline:* 2/1. *Notification date:* Continuous beginning 3/15. Students must reply within 2 weeks of notification.
CONTACT Ms. Tracy DaCosta, Associate Dean of Enrollment Management, Roger Williams University, 1 Old Ferry Road, Bristol, RI 02809, 401-254-3100 or toll-free 800-458-7144 (out-of-state). *Fax:* 401-254-5376. *E-mail:* tdacosta@rwu.edu.

ROLLINS COLLEGE
Winter Park, FL

Tuition & fees: $29,224   **Average undergraduate aid package: $27,679**

ABOUT THE INSTITUTION Independent, coed. Awards: bachelor's and master's degrees. 31 undergraduate majors. Total enrollment: 2,493. Undergraduates: 1,719. Freshmen: 464. Federal methodology is used as a basis for awarding need-based institutional aid.
UNDERGRADUATE EXPENSES for 2005–06 *Application fee:* $40. *Comprehensive fee:* $38,366 includes full-time tuition ($28,390), mandatory fees ($834), and room and board ($9142). *College room only:* $5376. *Payment plan:* Installment.
FRESHMAN FINANCIAL AID (Fall 2005, est.) 249 applied for aid; of those 84% were deemed to have need. 100% of freshmen with need received aid; of those 29% had need fully met. *Average percent of need met:* 90% (excluding resources awarded to replace EFC). *Average financial aid package:* $27,618 (excluding resources awarded to replace EFC). 13% of all full-time freshmen had no need and received non-need-based gift aid.
UNDERGRADUATE FINANCIAL AID (Fall 2005, est.) 807 applied for aid; of those 89% were deemed to have need. 100% of undergraduates with need received aid; of those 35% had need fully met. *Average percent of need met:* 90% (excluding resources awarded to replace EFC). *Average financial aid package:* $27,679 (excluding resources awarded to replace EFC). 13% of all full-time undergraduates had no need and received non-need-based gift aid.
GIFT AID (NEED-BASED) *Total amount:* $15,106,375 (7% federal, 16% state, 76% institutional, 1% external sources). *Receiving aid:* Freshmen: 44% (205); All full-time undergraduates: 41% (705). *Average award:* Freshmen: $24,085; Undergraduates: $23,591. *Scholarships, grants, and awards:* Federal Pell, FSEOG, state, private, college/university gift aid from institutional funds.
GIFT AID (NON-NEED-BASED) *Total amount:* $5,401,704 (38% state, 60% institutional, 2% external sources). *Receiving aid:* Freshmen: 7% (34); Undergraduates: 4% (71). *Average Award:* Freshmen: $12,897; Undergraduates: $10,122. *Scholarships, grants, and awards by category:* Academic Interests/Achievement: 495 awards ($4,917,390 total): computer science, engineering/technologies, general academic interests/achievements, mathematics, physical sciences. *Creative Arts/Performance:* 94 awards ($322,692 total): art/fine arts, music, theater/drama. *Tuition waivers:* Full or partial for employees or children of employees.
LOANS *Student loans:* $4,253,316 (70% need-based, 30% non-need-based). 50% of past graduating class borrowed through all loan programs. *Average indebtedness per student:* $15,438. *Average need-based loan:* Freshmen: $3739; Undergraduates: $3986. *Parent loans:* $2,348,892 (11% need-based, 89% non-need-based). *Programs:* Federal Direct (Subsidized and Unsubsidized Stafford, PLUS), Perkins, college/university.
WORK-STUDY *Federal work-study:* Total amount: $360,228; 294 jobs averaging $1225.
ATHLETIC AWARDS *Total amount:* $2,186,554 (11% need-based, 89% non-need-based).

Rollins College

APPLYING FOR FINANCIAL AID *Required financial aid forms:* FAFSA, institution's own form. *Financial aid deadline:* 3/1 (priority: 2/15). *Notification date:* Continuous beginning 3/1.
CONTACT Mr. Phil Asbury, Director of Student Financial Aid, Rollins College, 1000 Holt Avenue, #2721, Winter Park, FL 32789-4499, 407-646-2395. *Fax:* 407-646-2173. *E-mail:* pasbury@rollins.edu.

ROOSEVELT UNIVERSITY
Chicago, IL

Tuition & fees: $14,430 | **Average undergraduate aid package: $13,173**

ABOUT THE INSTITUTION Independent, coed. Awards: bachelor's, master's, and doctoral degrees and post-bachelor's and post-master's certificates. 86 undergraduate majors. Total enrollment: 7,234. Undergraduates: 4,073. Freshmen: 326. Federal methodology is used as a basis for awarding need-based institutional aid.
UNDERGRADUATE EXPENSES for 2005–06 *Application fee:* $25. *Comprehensive fee:* $22,420 includes full-time tuition ($14,180), mandatory fees ($250), and room and board ($7990). *College room only:* $5800. Full-time tuition and fees vary according to course load and program. Room and board charges vary according to board plan, housing facility, and location. *Part-time tuition:* $575 per hour. *Part-time fees:* $125 per term. Part-time tuition and fees vary according to course load and program. *Payment plans:* Installment, deferred payment.
FRESHMAN FINANCIAL AID (Fall 2004) 218 applied for aid; of those 87% were deemed to have need. 94% of freshmen with need received aid; of those 16% had need fully met. *Average percent of need met:* 75% (excluding resources awarded to replace EFC). *Average financial aid package:* $13,142 (excluding resources awarded to replace EFC). 11% of all full-time freshmen had no need and received non-need-based gift aid.
UNDERGRADUATE FINANCIAL AID (Fall 2004) 1,471 applied for aid; of those 87% were deemed to have need. 95% of undergraduates with need received aid; of those 16% had need fully met. *Average percent of need met:* 75% (excluding resources awarded to replace EFC). *Average financial aid package:* $13,173 (excluding resources awarded to replace EFC). 7% of all full-time undergraduates had no need and received non-need-based gift aid.
GIFT AID (NEED-BASED) *Total amount:* $7,061,649 (49% federal, 43% state, 8% institutional). *Receiving aid:* Freshmen: 49% (116); All full-time undergraduates: 49% (887). *Average award:* Freshmen: $5740; Undergraduates: $5579. *Scholarships, grants, and awards:* Federal Pell, FSEOG, state, private, college/university gift aid from institutional funds.
GIFT AID (NON-NEED-BASED) *Total amount:* $4,127,794 (98% institutional, 2% external sources). *Receiving aid:* Freshmen: 55% (132); Undergraduates: 30% (556). *Average Award:* Freshmen: $4420; Undergraduates: $5115. *Scholarships, grants, and awards by category: Academic Interests/Achievement:* general academic interests/achievements. *Creative Arts/Performance:* music, theater/drama. *Special Achievements/Activities:* general special achievements/activities. *Special Characteristics:* general special characteristics. *Tuition waivers:* Full or partial for employees or children of employees, senior citizens.
LOANS *Student loans:* $12,009,164 (100% need-based). *Programs:* FFEL (Subsidized and Unsubsidized Stafford, PLUS).
WORK-STUDY *Federal work-study:* Total amount: $533,624; jobs available.
APPLYING FOR FINANCIAL AID *Required financial aid forms:* FAFSA, institution's own form. *Financial aid deadline (priority):* 4/1. *Notification date:* Continuous beginning 3/15. Students must reply within 2 weeks of notification.
CONTACT Mr. Walter J. H. O'Neill, Director of Financial Aid, Roosevelt University, 430 South Michigan Avenue, Chicago, IL 60605-1394, 312-341-2090 or toll-free 877-APPLYRU. *Fax:* 312-341-3545. *E-mail:* woneill@roosevelt.edu.

ROSE-HULMAN INSTITUTE OF TECHNOLOGY
Terre Haute, IN

Tuition & fees: $27,138 | **Average undergraduate aid package: $19,591**

ABOUT THE INSTITUTION Independent, coed, primarily men. Awards: bachelor's and master's degrees. 16 undergraduate majors. Total enrollment: 1,887. Undergraduates: 1,775. Freshmen: 448. Federal methodology is used as a basis for awarding need-based institutional aid.
UNDERGRADUATE EXPENSES for 2005–06 *Application fee:* $40. *Comprehensive fee:* $34,557 includes full-time tuition ($26,688), mandatory fees ($450), and room and board ($7419). *College room only:* $4236. Full-time tuition and fees vary according to course load. Room and board charges vary according to board plan. *Part-time tuition:* $768 per credit. Part-time tuition and fees vary according to course load. *Payment plans:* Tuition prepayment, installment.
FRESHMAN FINANCIAL AID (Fall 2004) 401 applied for aid; of those 80% were deemed to have need. 100% of freshmen with need received aid; of those 9% had need fully met. *Average percent of need met:* 83% (excluding resources awarded to replace EFC). *Average financial aid package:* $23,161 (excluding resources awarded to replace EFC). 24% of all full-time freshmen had no need and received non-need-based gift aid.
UNDERGRADUATE FINANCIAL AID (Fall 2004) 1,420 applied for aid; of those 86% were deemed to have need. 100% of undergraduates with need received aid; of those 12% had need fully met. *Average percent of need met:* 79% (excluding resources awarded to replace EFC). *Average financial aid package:* $19,591 (excluding resources awarded to replace EFC). 27% of all full-time undergraduates had no need and received non-need-based gift aid.
GIFT AID (NEED-BASED) *Total amount:* $15,975,236 (6% federal, 9% state, 61% institutional, 24% external sources). *Receiving aid:* Freshmen: 71% (317); All full-time undergraduates: 68% (1,192). *Average award:* Freshmen: $15,300; Undergraduates: $13,595. *Scholarships, grants, and awards:* Federal Pell, FSEOG, state, college/university gift aid from institutional funds.
GIFT AID (NON-NEED-BASED) *Total amount:* $5,554,131 (71% institutional, 29% external sources). *Average Award:* Freshmen: $5673; Undergraduates: $6771. *Tuition waivers:* Full or partial for employees or children of employees. *ROTC:* Army, Air Force.
LOANS *Student loans:* $12,612,882 (89% need-based, 11% non-need-based). 79% of past graduating class borrowed through all loan programs. *Average indebtedness per student:* $33,105. *Average need-based loan:* Freshmen: $8104; Undergraduates: $6671. *Parent loans:* $5,699,601 (85% need-based, 15% non-need-based). *Programs:* Federal Direct (Subsidized and Unsubsidized Stafford, PLUS), Perkins.
WORK-STUDY *Federal work-study:* Total amount: $555,152; 352 jobs averaging $1577. *State or other work-study/employment:* Total amount: $994,660 (94% need-based, 6% non-need-based). 636 part-time jobs averaging $1564.
APPLYING FOR FINANCIAL AID *Required financial aid form:* FAFSA. *Financial aid deadline (priority):* 3/1. *Notification date:* 3/10.
CONTACT Melinda L. Middleton, Director of Financial Aid, Rose-Hulman Institute of Technology, 5500 Wabash Avenue, Box #5, Terre Haute, IN 47803, 812-877-8259 or toll-free 800-248-7448. *Fax:* 812-877-8746. *E-mail:* melinda.middleton@rose-hulman.edu.

ROSEMONT COLLEGE
Rosemont, PA

Tuition & fees: $20,550 | **Average undergraduate aid package: $17,513**

ABOUT THE INSTITUTION Independent Roman Catholic, undergraduate: women only; graduate: coed. Awards: bachelor's and master's degrees and post-bachelor's certificates. 24 undergraduate majors. Total enrollment: 1,048. Undergraduates: 644. Freshmen: 120. Federal methodology is used as a basis for awarding need-based institutional aid.
UNDERGRADUATE EXPENSES for 2005–06 *Application fee:* $35. *Comprehensive fee:* $29,350 includes full-time tuition ($19,450), mandatory fees ($1100), and room and board ($8800). Room and board charges vary according to housing facility. *Part-time tuition:* $750 per credit. *Part-time fees:* $310 per term. *Payment plan:* Installment.
FRESHMAN FINANCIAL AID (Fall 2005, est.) 116 applied for aid; of those 87% were deemed to have need. 100% of freshmen with need received aid; of those 24% had need fully met. *Average percent of need met:* 80% (excluding resources awarded to replace EFC). *Average financial aid package:* $19,792 (excluding resources awarded to replace EFC). 19% of all full-time freshmen had no need and received non-need-based gift aid.
UNDERGRADUATE FINANCIAL AID (Fall 2005, est.) 342 applied for aid; of those 87% were deemed to have need. 100% of undergraduates with need

received aid; of those 21% had need fully met. *Average percent of need met:* 76% (excluding resources awarded to replace EFC). *Average financial aid package:* $17,513 (excluding resources awarded to replace EFC). 22% of all full-time undergraduates had no need and received non-need-based gift aid.
GIFT AID (NEED-BASED) *Total amount:* $4,111,050 (14% federal, 13% state, 70% institutional, 3% external sources). *Receiving aid:* Freshmen: 81% (101); All full-time undergraduates: 76% (294). *Average award:* Freshmen: $16,903; Undergraduates: $14,389. *Scholarships, grants, and awards:* Federal Pell, FSEOG, state, private, college/university gift aid from institutional funds.
GIFT AID (NON-NEED-BASED) *Receiving aid:* Freshmen: 15% (18); Undergraduates: 11% (41). *Average Award:* Freshmen: $15,901; Undergraduates: $16,134. *Scholarships, grants, and awards by category: Academic Interests/Achievement:* 104 awards ($807,890 total): general academic interests/achievements. *Creative Arts/Performance:* 1 award ($4000 total): art/fine arts. *Special Achievements/ Activities:* community service, general special achievements/activities. *Special Characteristics:* 16 awards ($148,650 total): children and siblings of alumni, children of educators, children of faculty/staff, relatives of clergy, siblings of current students. *Tuition waivers:* Full or partial for employees or children of employees, senior citizens. *ROTC:* Army cooperative.
LOANS *Student loans:* $2,124,029 (67% need-based, 33% non-need-based). 78% of past graduating class borrowed through all loan programs. *Average indebtedness per student:* $23,091. *Average need-based loan:* Freshmen: $3107; Undergraduates: $3550. *Parent loans:* $701,423 (45% need-based, 55% non-need-based). *Programs:* FFEL (Subsidized and Unsubsidized Stafford, PLUS), Perkins.
WORK-STUDY *Federal work-study:* Total amount: $133,563; 102 jobs averaging $2000. *State or other work-study/employment:* Total amount: $30,000 (100% non-need-based). 29 part-time jobs averaging $1500.
APPLYING FOR FINANCIAL AID *Required financial aid form:* FAFSA. *Financial aid deadline (priority):* 2/15. *Notification date:* Continuous beginning 2/1. Students must reply by 5/1 or within 4 weeks of notification.
CONTACT Melissa Walsh, Director of Financial Aid, Rosemont College, 1400 Montgomery Avenue, Rosemont, PA 19010, 610-527-0200 Ext. 2220 or toll-free 800-331-0708. *Fax:* 610-527-0341. *E-mail:* mwalsh@rosemont.edu.

ROWAN UNIVERSITY
Glassboro, NJ

Tuition & fees (NJ res): $8607	Average undergraduate aid package: $6214

ABOUT THE INSTITUTION State-supported, coed. Awards: bachelor's, master's, and doctoral degrees. 38 undergraduate majors. Total enrollment: 9,762. Undergraduates: 8,484. Freshmen: 1,250. Federal methodology is used as a basis for awarding need-based institutional aid.
UNDERGRADUATE EXPENSES for 2005–06 *Application fee:* $50. *Tuition, state resident:* full-time $6294; part-time $262 per credit hour. *Tuition, nonresident:* full-time $12,588; part-time $524 per credit hour. *Required fees:* full-time $2313; $107.20 per credit hour. Full-time tuition and fees vary according to degree level. Part-time tuition and fees vary according to degree level. *College room and board:* $8242. Room and board charges vary according to board plan and housing facility. *Payment plan:* Deferred payment.
FRESHMAN FINANCIAL AID (Fall 2004) 1128 applied for aid; of those 97% were deemed to have need. 93% of freshmen with need received aid; of those 35% had need fully met. *Average percent of need met:* 66% (excluding resources awarded to replace EFC). *Average financial aid package:* $5716 (excluding resources awarded to replace EFC).
UNDERGRADUATE FINANCIAL AID (Fall 2004) 5,937 applied for aid; of those 98% were deemed to have need. 100% of undergraduates with need received aid; of those 38% had need fully met. *Average percent of need met:* 67% (excluding resources awarded to replace EFC). *Average financial aid package:* $6214 (excluding resources awarded to replace EFC). 1% of all full-time undergraduates had no need and received non-need-based gift aid.
GIFT AID (NEED-BASED) *Total amount:* $19,340,608 (30% federal, 41% state, 23% institutional, 6% external sources). *Receiving aid:* Freshmen: 53% (659); All full-time undergraduates: 48% (3,349). *Average award:* Freshmen: $5722; Undergraduates: $5547. *Scholarships, grants, and awards:* Federal Pell, FSEOG, state, private, college/university gift aid from institutional funds.
GIFT AID (NON-NEED-BASED) *Total amount:* $101,252 (14% state, 55% institutional, 31% external sources). *Receiving aid:* Freshmen: 52% (646); Undergraduates: 45% (3,135). *Average Award:* Undergraduates: $2933. *Scholar-* ships, grants, and awards by category: *Academic Interests/Achievement:* general academic interests/achievements. *Creative Arts/Performance:* general creative arts/performance, music. *Special Characteristics:* handicapped students, international students, members of minority groups. *Tuition waivers:* Full or partial for employees or children of employees. *ROTC:* Army cooperative.
LOANS *Student loans:* $30,840,899 (100% need-based). 97% of past graduating class borrowed through all loan programs. *Average indebtedness per student:* $9575. *Average need-based loan:* Freshmen: $3252; Undergraduates: $3476. *Parent loans:* $16,643,702 (100% need-based). *Programs:* Federal Direct (Subsidized and Unsubsidized Stafford, PLUS), state.
WORK-STUDY *Federal work-study:* Total amount: $941,021; 617 jobs averaging $899. *State or other work-study/employment:* Total amount: $1,631,206 (100% need-based). 537 part-time jobs averaging $1638.
APPLYING FOR FINANCIAL AID *Required financial aid form:* FAFSA. *Financial aid deadline:* Continuous. *Notification date:* Continuous beginning 3/15.
CONTACT Luis Tavarez, Director of Financial Aid, Rowan University, 201 Mullica Hill Road, Savitz Hall, Glassboro, NJ 08028-1701, 856-256-4276 or toll-free 800-447-1165 (in-state). *Fax:* 856-256-4413. *E-mail:* tavarez@rowan.edu.

RUSH UNIVERSITY
Chicago, IL

CONTACT Mr. Robert A. Dame, Director of Student Financial Aid, Rush University, 600 South Paulina Street, Suite 440, Chicago, IL 60612-3832, 312-942-6256. *Fax:* 312-942-2219.

RUSSELL SAGE COLLEGE
Troy, NY

Tuition & fees: $23,520	Average undergraduate aid package: N/A

ABOUT THE INSTITUTION Independent, women only. Awards: bachelor's degrees. 26 undergraduate majors. Total enrollment: 838. Undergraduates: 838. Freshmen: 117. Both federal and institutional methodology are used as a basis for awarding need-based institutional aid.
UNDERGRADUATE EXPENSES for 2005–06 *Application fee:* $30. *Comprehensive fee:* $31,060 includes full-time tuition ($22,650), mandatory fees ($870), and room and board ($7540). *College room only:* $3650. *Part-time tuition:* $755 per credit hour. *Payment plans:* Installment, deferred payment.
FRESHMAN FINANCIAL AID (Fall 2005, est.) 116 applied for aid; of those 92% were deemed to have need. 100% of freshmen with need received aid; of those 3% had need fully met.
UNDERGRADUATE FINANCIAL AID (Fall 2005, est.) 738 applied for aid; of those 88% were deemed to have need. 100% of undergraduates with need received aid; of those .5% had need fully met. 5% of all full-time undergraduates had no need and received non-need-based gift aid.
GIFT AID (NEED-BASED) *Total amount:* $5,272,136 (19% federal, 25% state, 53% institutional, 3% external sources). *Receiving aid:* Freshmen: 60% (70); All full-time undergraduates: 68% (518). *Scholarships, grants, and awards:* Federal Pell, FSEOG, state, private, college/university gift aid from institutional funds, Federal Nursing.
GIFT AID (NON-NEED-BASED) *Total amount:* $4,851,850 (99% institutional, 1% external sources). *Receiving aid:* Freshmen: 74% (87); Undergraduates: 63% (480). *Average Award:* Undergraduates: $10,701. *Scholarships, grants, and awards by category: Academic Interests/Achievement:* 434 awards ($3,804,500 total): general academic interests/achievements. *Special Achievements/ Activities:* 12 awards ($18,000 total): community service, general special achievements/activities, leadership. *Special Characteristics:* 32 awards ($111,415 total): children and siblings of alumni, children of faculty/staff, siblings of current students, spouses of current students. *Tuition waivers:* Full or partial for employees or children of employees. *ROTC:* Army cooperative, Air Force cooperative.
LOANS *Student loans:* $4,586,792 (61% need-based, 39% non-need-based). 90% of past graduating class borrowed through all loan programs. *Average indebtedness per student:* $21,000. *Parent loans:* $2,663,747 (63% need-based, 37% non-need-based). *Programs:* FFEL (Subsidized and Unsubsidized Stafford, PLUS), Perkins.
WORK-STUDY *Federal work-study:* Total amount: $262,500; 329 jobs averaging $1500. *State or other work-study/employment:* Total amount: $201,520 (100% non-need-based). 87 part-time jobs averaging $1200.

Russell Sage College

APPLYING FOR FINANCIAL AID *Required financial aid forms:* FAFSA, state aid form. *Financial aid deadline (priority):* 3/1. *Notification date:* Continuous beginning 3/1. Students must reply within 2 weeks of notification.
CONTACT James Dease, Associate Vice President for Student Services, Russell Sage College, 45 Ferry Street, Troy, NY 12180, 518-244-2062 or toll-free 888-VERY-SAGE (in-state), 888-VERY SAGE (out-of-state). *Fax:* 518-244-2460. *E-mail:* deasej@sage.edu.

RUST COLLEGE
Holly Springs, MS

ABOUT THE INSTITUTION Independent United Methodist, coed. Awards: associate and bachelor's degrees. 19 undergraduate majors. Total enrollment: 1,001. Undergraduates: 1,001. Freshmen: 288.
GIFT AID (NEED-BASED) *Scholarships, grants, and awards:* Federal Pell, FSEOG, state, private, college/university gift aid from institutional funds, United Negro College Fund.
GIFT AID (NON-NEED-BASED) *Scholarships, grants, and awards by category: Academic Interests/Achievement:* general academic interests/achievements. *Creative Arts/Performance:* music, theater/drama. *Special Characteristics:* children of faculty/staff, ethnic background, general special characteristics, international students, local/state students, members of minority groups, relatives of clergy, religious affiliation, siblings of current students, veterans.
LOANS *Programs:* FFEL (Subsidized and Unsubsidized Stafford, PLUS), United Methodist Student Loans.
WORK-STUDY *Federal work-study:* Total amount: $368,600; 492 jobs averaging $714. *State or other work-study/employment:* Total amount: $108,808 (100% non-need-based). 189 part-time jobs averaging $546.
APPLYING FOR FINANCIAL AID *Required financial aid forms:* FAFSA, institution's own form, state aid form, noncustodial (divorced/separated) parent's statement, business/farm supplement.
CONTACT Mrs. Helen L. Street, Director of Financial Aid, Rust College, 150 Rust Avenue, Holly Springs, MS 38635, 662-252-8000 Ext. 4061 or toll-free 888-886-8492 Ext. 4065. *Fax:* 662-252-8895.

RUTGERS, THE STATE UNIVERSITY OF NEW JERSEY, CAMDEN
Camden, NJ

Tuition & fees (NJ res): $9028   **Average undergraduate aid package:** $10,112

ABOUT THE INSTITUTION State-supported, coed. Awards: bachelor's, master's, and first professional degrees. 33 undergraduate majors. Total enrollment: 5,321. Undergraduates: 3,846. Freshmen: 353. Federal methodology is used as a basis for awarding need-based institutional aid.
UNDERGRADUATE EXPENSES for 2005–06 *Application fee:* $50. *Tuition, state resident:* full-time $7336; part-time $236.50 per credit hour. *Tuition, nonresident:* full-time $14,934; part-time $484.05 per credit hour. *College room and board:* $8088; *room only:* $5778.
FRESHMAN FINANCIAL AID (Fall 2005, est.) 295 applied for aid; of those 70% were deemed to have need. 100% of freshmen with need received aid; of those 37% had need fully met. *Average percent of need met:* 74% (excluding resources awarded to replace EFC). *Average financial aid package:* $10,174 (excluding resources awarded to replace EFC). 12% of all full-time freshmen had no need and received non-need-based gift aid.
UNDERGRADUATE FINANCIAL AID (Fall 2005, est.) 2,294 applied for aid; of those 80% were deemed to have need. 99% of undergraduates with need received aid; of those 44% had need fully met. *Average percent of need met:* 74% (excluding resources awarded to replace EFC). *Average financial aid package:* $10,112 (excluding resources awarded to replace EFC). 6% of all full-time undergraduates had no need and received non-need-based gift aid.
GIFT AID (NEED-BASED) *Total amount:* $10,563,142 (30% federal, 53% state, 16% institutional, 1% external sources). *Receiving aid:* Freshmen: 41% (146); All full-time undergraduates: 43% (1,274). *Average award:* Freshmen: $7404; Undergraduates: $7063. *Scholarships, grants, and awards:* Federal Pell, FSEOG, state, private, college/university gift aid from institutional funds, Other Outside Scholarships.
GIFT AID (NON-NEED-BASED) *Total amount:* $821,125 (91% institutional, 9% external sources). *Receiving aid:* Freshmen: 33% (115); Undergraduates: 18% (513). *Average Award:* Freshmen: $4869; Undergraduates: $4624. *Scholarships, grants, and awards by category: Academic Interests/Achievement:* 512 awards ($1,593,836 total): general academic interests/achievements. *Creative Arts/Performance:* general creative arts/performance. *Special Characteristics:* 42 awards ($217,119 total): children of faculty/staff. *ROTC:* Army cooperative, Air Force cooperative.
LOANS *Student loans:* $15,459,473 (79% need-based, 21% non-need-based). 69% of past graduating class borrowed through all loan programs. *Average indebtedness per student:* $17,378. *Average need-based loan:* Freshmen: $2773; Undergraduates: $4023. *Parent loans:* $702,760 (66% need-based, 34% non-need-based). *Programs:* Federal Direct (Subsidized and Unsubsidized Stafford, PLUS), Perkins, state, college/university, alternative loans.
WORK-STUDY *Federal work-study:* Total amount: $542,468; 330 jobs averaging $1780.
ATHLETIC AWARDS Total amount: $2000 (100% need-based).
APPLYING FOR FINANCIAL AID *Required financial aid form:* FAFSA. *Financial aid deadline (priority):* 3/15. *Notification date:* Continuous.
CONTACT Ms. Marlene Martin, Assistant Funds Manager, Rutgers, The State University of New Jersey, Camden, 620 George Street, New Brunswick, NJ 08901, 732-932-7868. *E-mail:* mgmartin@rci.rutgers.edu.

RUTGERS, THE STATE UNIVERSITY OF NEW JERSEY, NEWARK
Newark, NJ

Tuition & fees (NJ res): $8812   **Average undergraduate aid package:** $10,138

ABOUT THE INSTITUTION State-supported, coed. Awards: bachelor's, master's, doctoral, and first professional degrees. 51 undergraduate majors. Total enrollment: 10,246. Undergraduates: 6,513. Freshmen: 704. Federal methodology is used as a basis for awarding need-based institutional aid.
UNDERGRADUATE EXPENSES for 2005–06 *Application fee:* $50. *Tuition, state resident:* full-time $7336; part-time $236.50 per credit hour. *Tuition, nonresident:* full-time $14,934; part-time $484.05 per credit hour. *College room and board:* $8984; *room only:* $5654. Room and board charges vary according to board plan and housing facility. *Payment plan:* Installment.
FRESHMAN FINANCIAL AID (Fall 2005, est.) 549 applied for aid; of those 80% were deemed to have need. 97% of freshmen with need received aid; of those 26% had need fully met. *Average percent of need met:* 81% (excluding resources awarded to replace EFC). *Average financial aid package:* $10,615 (excluding resources awarded to replace EFC). 5% of all full-time freshmen had no need and received non-need-based gift aid.
UNDERGRADUATE FINANCIAL AID (Fall 2005, est.) 3,654 applied for aid; of those 87% were deemed to have need. 98% of undergraduates with need received aid; of those 29% had need fully met. *Average percent of need met:* 72% (excluding resources awarded to replace EFC). *Average financial aid package:* $10,138 (excluding resources awarded to replace EFC). 5% of all full-time undergraduates had no need and received non-need-based gift aid.
GIFT AID (NEED-BASED) *Total amount:* $20,728,362 (32% federal, 51% state, 16% institutional, 1% external sources). *Receiving aid:* Freshmen: 48% (334); All full-time undergraduates: 50% (2,449). *Average award:* Freshmen: $8210; Undergraduates: $7362. *Scholarships, grants, and awards:* Federal Pell, FSEOG, state, private, college/university gift aid from institutional funds, Outside Scholarships.
GIFT AID (NON-NEED-BASED) *Total amount:* $1,157,862 (6% state, 91% institutional, 3% external sources). *Receiving aid:* Freshmen: 22% (151); Undergraduates: 17% (815). *Average Award:* Freshmen: $6922; Undergraduates: $5087. *Scholarships, grants, and awards by category: Academic Interests/Achievement:* 853 awards ($2,738,824 total): general academic interests/achievements. *Creative Arts/Performance:* general creative arts/performance. *Special Characteristics:* 21 awards ($136,843 total): children of faculty/staff. *Tuition waivers:* Full or partial for employees or children of employees. *ROTC:* Army, Air Force.
LOANS *Student loans:* $19,412,339 (84% need-based, 16% non-need-based). 85% of past graduating class borrowed through all loan programs. *Average indebtedness per student:* $16,553. *Average need-based loan:* Freshmen: $2927; Undergraduates: $4151. *Parent loans:* $865,846 (69% need-based, 31% non-need-based). *Programs:* Federal Direct (Subsidized and Unsubsidized Stafford, PLUS), Perkins, state, college/university, Other Educational Loans.

WORK-STUDY *Federal work-study:* Total amount: $965,032; 673 jobs averaging $1930.
ATHLETIC AWARDS *Total amount:* $95,000 (63% need-based, 37% non-need-based).
APPLYING FOR FINANCIAL AID *Required financial aid form:* FAFSA. *Financial aid deadline (priority):* 3/15. *Notification date:* Continuous.
CONTACT Ms. Marlene Martin, Assistant Funds Manager, Rutgers, The State University of New Jersey, Newark, 620 George Street, New Brunswick, NJ 08901, 732-932-7868. *E-mail:* mgmartin@rci.rutgers.edu.

RUTGERS, THE STATE UNIVERSITY OF NEW JERSEY, NEW BRUNSWICK/PISCATAWAY
New Brunswick, NJ

Tuition & fees (NJ res): $9221 **Average undergraduate aid package:** $11,569

ABOUT THE INSTITUTION State-supported, coed. Awards: bachelor's, master's, doctoral, and first professional degrees and post-master's certificates. 122 undergraduate majors. Total enrollment: 34,449. Undergraduates: 26,713. Freshmen: 5,245. Federal methodology is used as a basis for awarding need-based institutional aid.
UNDERGRADUATE EXPENSES for 2005–06 *Application fee:* $50. *Tuition, state resident:* full-time $7336; part-time $236.50 per credit hour. *Tuition, nonresident:* full-time $14,934; part-time $484 per credit hour. Part-time tuition and fees vary according to course level. *College room and board:* $8838; *room only:* $5378. Room and board charges vary according to board plan and housing facility. *Payment plan:* Installment.
FRESHMAN FINANCIAL AID (Fall 2005, est.) 4016 applied for aid; of those 69% were deemed to have need. 98% of freshmen with need received aid; of those 41% had need fully met. *Average percent of need met:* 69% (excluding resources awarded to replace EFC). *Average financial aid package:* $11,555 (excluding resources awarded to replace EFC). 11% of all full-time freshmen had no need and received non-need-based gift aid.
UNDERGRADUATE FINANCIAL AID (Fall 2005, est.) 15,956 applied for aid; of those 78% were deemed to have need. 99% of undergraduates with need received aid; of those 39% had need fully met. *Average percent of need met:* 72% (excluding resources awarded to replace EFC). *Average financial aid package:* $11,569 (excluding resources awarded to replace EFC). 10% of all full-time undergraduates had no need and received non-need-based gift aid.
GIFT AID (NEED-BASED) *Total amount:* $71,357,845 (29% federal, 48% state, 21% institutional, 2% external sources). *Receiving aid:* Freshmen: 32% (1,658); All full-time undergraduates: 33% (7,962). *Average award:* Freshmen: $8579; Undergraduates: $8034. *Scholarships, grants, and awards:* Federal Pell, FSEOG, state, private, college/university gift aid from institutional funds, Outside Scholarships.
GIFT AID (NON-NEED-BASED) *Total amount:* $9,208,436 (13% state, 73% institutional, 14% external sources). *Receiving aid:* Freshmen: 31% (1,611); Undergraduates: 25% (6,154). *Average Award:* Freshmen: $5641; Undergraduates: $5311. *Scholarships, grants, and awards by category:* Academic Interests/Achievement: 5,560 awards ($21,410,325 total): general academic interests/achievements. Creative Arts/Performance: 67 awards ($138,847 total): general creative arts/performance. Special Characteristics: 442 awards ($3,109,869 total): children of faculty/staff. *Tuition waivers:* Full or partial for employees or children of employees. *ROTC:* Army, Air Force.
LOANS *Student loans:* $96,790,894 (78% need-based, 22% non-need-based). 63% of past graduating class borrowed through all loan programs. *Average indebtedness per student:* $15,362. *Average need-based loan:* Freshmen: $3010; Undergraduates: $4170. *Parent loans:* $10,986,718 (64% need-based, 36% non-need-based). *Programs:* Federal Direct (Subsidized and Unsubsidized Stafford, PLUS), Perkins, state, college/university, Other Educational Loans.
WORK-STUDY *Federal work-study:* Total amount: $5,215,274; 2,646 jobs averaging $1903.
ATHLETIC AWARDS *Total amount:* $5,788,515 (49% need-based, 51% non-need-based).
APPLYING FOR FINANCIAL AID *Required financial aid form:* FAFSA. *Financial aid deadline:* Continuous. *Notification date:* Continuous beginning 2/1.

CONTACT Ms. Marlene Martin, Assistant Funds Manager, Rutgers, The State University of New Jersey, New Brunswick/Piscataway, 620 George Street, New Brunswick, NJ 08901, 732-932-7868. *E-mail:* mgmartin@rci.rutgers.edu.

SACRED HEART MAJOR SEMINARY
Detroit, MI

CONTACT Financial Aid Office, Sacred Heart Major Seminary, 2701 Chicago Boulevard, Detroit, MI 48206-1799, 313-883-8500. *Fax:* 313-868-6440.

SACRED HEART UNIVERSITY
Fairfield, CT

Tuition & fees: $23,750 **Average undergraduate aid package:** $14,943

ABOUT THE INSTITUTION Independent Roman Catholic, coed. Awards: associate, bachelor's, master's, and doctoral degrees and post-bachelor's and post-master's certificates (also offers part-time program with significant enrollment not reflected in profile). 67 undergraduate majors. Total enrollment: 5,560. Undergraduates: 4,104. Freshmen: 886. Both federal and institutional methodology are used as a basis for awarding need-based institutional aid.
UNDERGRADUATE EXPENSES for 2005–06 *Application fee:* $50. *Comprehensive fee:* $33,404 includes full-time tuition ($23,750) and room and board ($9654). *College room only:* $7078. Full-time tuition and fees vary according to program. Room and board charges vary according to board plan and housing facility. *Part-time tuition:* $390 per credit. *Part-time fees:* $76 per term. Part-time tuition and fees vary according to program. *Payment plan:* Installment.
FRESHMAN FINANCIAL AID (Fall 2005, est.) 812 applied for aid; of those 78% were deemed to have need. 98% of freshmen with need received aid; of those 29% had need fully met. *Average percent of need met:* 66% (excluding resources awarded to replace EFC). *Average financial aid package:* $13,922 (excluding resources awarded to replace EFC). 24% of all full-time freshmen had no need and received non-need-based gift aid.
UNDERGRADUATE FINANCIAL AID (Fall 2005, est.) 2,778 applied for aid; of those 81% were deemed to have need. 97% of undergraduates with need received aid; of those 31% had need fully met. *Average percent of need met:* 70% (excluding resources awarded to replace EFC). *Average financial aid package:* $14,943 (excluding resources awarded to replace EFC). 19% of all full-time undergraduates had no need and received non-need-based gift aid.
GIFT AID (NEED-BASED) *Total amount:* $17,899,014 (8% federal, 11% state, 73% institutional, 8% external sources). *Receiving aid:* Freshmen: 69% (610); All full-time undergraduates: 66% (2,125). *Average award:* Freshmen: $9266; Undergraduates: $9436. *Scholarships, grants, and awards:* Federal Pell, FSEOG, state, private, college/university gift aid from institutional funds, Federal Nursing.
GIFT AID (NON-NEED-BASED) *Total amount:* $2,538,690 (1% state, 73% institutional, 26% external sources). *Receiving aid:* Freshmen: 7% (62); Undergraduates: 5% (160). *Average Award:* Freshmen: $10,743; Undergraduates: $11,498. *Scholarships, grants, and awards by category:* Academic Interests/Achievement: 1,352 awards ($6,661,293 total): biological sciences, business, computer science, education, English, general academic interests/achievements, health fields, humanities, mathematics, physical sciences, premedicine. Creative Arts/Performance: 78 awards ($97,472 total): applied art and design, art/fine arts, creative writing, music. Special Achievements/Activities: 78 awards ($175,038 total): community service, leadership, religious involvement. Special Characteristics: children of faculty/staff, ethnic background, handicapped students, members of minority groups, religious affiliation, siblings of current students, twins. *Tuition waivers:* Full or partial for employees or children of employees. *ROTC:* Army.
LOANS *Student loans:* $17,503,503 (64% need-based, 36% non-need-based). 93% of past graduating class borrowed through all loan programs. *Average indebtedness per student:* $19,926. *Average need-based loan:* Freshmen: $5051; Undergraduates: $6190. *Parent loans:* $13,137,989 (36% need-based, 64% non-need-based). *Programs:* FFEL (Subsidized and Unsubsidized Stafford, PLUS), Perkins, state.
WORK-STUDY *Federal work-study:* Total amount: $546,868; 248 jobs averaging $1157. *State or other work-study/employment:* Total amount: $1,340,974 (27% need-based, 73% non-need-based).
ATHLETIC AWARDS *Total amount:* $4,465,362 (53% need-based, 47% non-need-based).

Sacred Heart University

APPLYING FOR FINANCIAL AID *Required financial aid forms:* FAFSA, CSS Financial Aid PROFILE. *Financial aid deadline (priority):* 2/15. *Notification date:* Continuous beginning 3/1. Students must reply within 2 weeks of notification.
CONTACT Ms. Julie B. Savino, Dean of University Financial Assistance, Sacred Heart University, 5151 Park Avenue, Fairfield, CT 06825, 203-371-7980. *Fax:* 203-365-7608. *E-mail:* savinoj@sacredheart.edu.

SAGE COLLEGE OF ALBANY
Albany, NY

Tuition & fees: $16,870	Average undergraduate aid package: N/A

ABOUT THE INSTITUTION Independent, coed. Awards: associate and bachelor's degrees. 23 undergraduate majors. Total enrollment: 1,031. Undergraduates: 1,031. Freshmen: 88. Federal methodology is used as a basis for awarding need-based institutional aid.
UNDERGRADUATE EXPENSES for 2005–06 *Application fee:* $30. *Comprehensive fee:* $24,410 includes full-time tuition ($16,000), mandatory fees ($870), and room and board ($7540). *College room only:* $3890. *Part-time tuition:* $535 per credit hour. *Payment plans:* Installment, deferred payment.
FRESHMAN FINANCIAL AID (Fall 2005, est.) 84 applied for aid; of those 95% were deemed to have need. 100% of freshmen with need received aid. 5% of all full-time freshmen had no need and received non-need-based gift aid.
UNDERGRADUATE FINANCIAL AID (Fall 2005, est.) 496 applied for aid; of those 94% were deemed to have need. 100% of undergraduates with need received aid. 7% of all full-time undergraduates had no need and received non-need-based gift aid.
GIFT AID (NEED-BASED) *Total amount:* $2,563,987 (27% federal, 33% state, 40% institutional). *Receiving aid:* Freshmen: 59% (51); All full-time undergraduates: 51% (271). *Scholarships, grants, and awards:* Federal Pell, FSEOG, state, private, college/university gift aid from institutional funds.
GIFT AID (NON-NEED-BASED) *Total amount:* $1,185,053 (98% institutional, 2% external sources). *Receiving aid:* Freshmen: 44% (38); Undergraduates: 49% (261). *Average Award:* Freshmen: $5250; Undergraduates: $4220. *Scholarships, grants, and awards by category:* Academic Interests/Achievement: 311 awards ($760,000 total). Special Achievements/Activities: 5 awards ($13,000 total): community service. Special Characteristics: 11 awards ($107,471 total): children of faculty/staff. *Tuition waivers:* Full or partial for employees or children of employees.
LOANS *Student loans:* $3,676,450 (54% need-based, 46% non-need-based). 91% of past graduating class borrowed through all loan programs. *Average indebtedness per student:* $9200. *Parent loans:* $570,893 (100% non-need-based). *Programs:* FFEL (Subsidized and Unsubsidized Stafford, PLUS), Perkins, alternative loans.
WORK-STUDY *Federal work-study:* Total amount: $128,300; 270 jobs averaging $1500. *State or other work-study/employment:* Total amount: $46,000 (100% non-need-based). 29 part-time jobs averaging $1200.
APPLYING FOR FINANCIAL AID *Required financial aid forms:* FAFSA, state aid form. *Financial aid deadline (priority):* 3/1. *Notification date:* Continuous beginning 3/1. Students must reply within 2 weeks of notification.
CONTACT James K. Dease, Associate Vice President for Student Service, Sage College of Albany, 45 Ferry Street, Troy, NY 12180, 518-244-4525 or toll-free 888-VERY-SAGE. *Fax:* 518-244-2460. *E-mail:* deasej@sage.edu.

SAGINAW VALLEY STATE UNIVERSITY
University Center, MI

CONTACT Robert Lemuel, Director of Scholarships and Financial Aid, Saginaw Valley State University, 7400 Bay Road, University Center, MI 48710, 989-964-4103 or toll-free 800-968-9500. *Fax:* 989-790-0180.

ST. AMBROSE UNIVERSITY
Davenport, IA

ABOUT THE INSTITUTION Independent Roman Catholic, coed. Awards: bachelor's, master's, and doctoral degrees and post-bachelor's and post-master's certificates. 72 undergraduate majors. Total enrollment: 3,623. Undergraduates: 2,698. Freshmen: 472.
GIFT AID (NEED-BASED) *Scholarships, grants, and awards:* Federal Pell, FSEOG, state, private, college/university gift aid from institutional funds.
GIFT AID (NON-NEED-BASED) *Scholarships, grants, and awards by category:* Academic Interests/Achievement: general academic interests/achievements, international studies. Creative Arts/Performance: art/fine arts, dance, music, theater/drama. Special Characteristics: children of faculty/staff, international students, members of minority groups.
LOANS *Programs:* FFEL (Subsidized and Unsubsidized Stafford, PLUS), Perkins, state.
WORK-STUDY *Federal work-study:* Total amount: $964,601; 742 jobs averaging $1300. *State or other work-study/employment:* Total amount: $168,524 (70% need-based, 30% non-need-based). 117 part-time jobs averaging $1441.
APPLYING FOR FINANCIAL AID *Required financial aid form:* FAFSA.
CONTACT Ms. Julie Haack, Director of Financial Aid, St. Ambrose University, 518 West Locust Street, Davenport, IA 52803, 563-333-6314 or toll-free 800-383-2627. *Fax:* 563-333-6243. *E-mail:* haackjuliea@sau.edu.

ST. ANDREWS PRESBYTERIAN COLLEGE
Laurinburg, NC

Tuition & fees: $18,062	Average undergraduate aid package: $12,142

ABOUT THE INSTITUTION Independent Presbyterian, coed. Awards: bachelor's degrees. 23 undergraduate majors. Total enrollment: 781. Undergraduates: 781. Freshmen: 191. Federal methodology is used as a basis for awarding need-based institutional aid.
UNDERGRADUATE EXPENSES for 2005–06 *Application fee:* $30. *Comprehensive fee:* $24,756 includes full-time tuition ($17,162), mandatory fees ($900), and room and board ($6694). *College room only:* $2748. Full-time tuition and fees vary according to location. Room and board charges vary according to housing facility. *Part-time tuition:* $410 per credit. Part-time tuition and fees vary according to location. *Payment plan:* Installment.
FRESHMAN FINANCIAL AID (Fall 2005, est.) 172 applied for aid; of those 74% were deemed to have need. 100% of freshmen with need received aid; of those 28% had need fully met. *Average percent of need met:* 68% (excluding resources awarded to replace EFC). *Average financial aid package:* $10,212 (excluding resources awarded to replace EFC). 39% of all full-time freshmen had no need and received non-need-based gift aid.
UNDERGRADUATE FINANCIAL AID (Fall 2005, est.) 548 applied for aid; of those 79% were deemed to have need. 100% of undergraduates with need received aid; of those 25% had need fully met. *Average percent of need met:* 73% (excluding resources awarded to replace EFC). *Average financial aid package:* $12,142 (excluding resources awarded to replace EFC). 39% of all full-time undergraduates had no need and received non-need-based gift aid.
GIFT AID (NEED-BASED) *Total amount:* $3,411,679 (18% federal, 19% state, 59% institutional, 4% external sources). *Receiving aid:* Freshmen: 60% (127); All full-time undergraduates: 59% (432). *Average award:* Freshmen: $7731; Undergraduates: $8907. *Scholarships, grants, and awards:* Federal Pell, FSEOG, state, private, college/university gift aid from institutional funds.
GIFT AID (NON-NEED-BASED) *Total amount:* $1,961,319 (13% state, 84% institutional, 3% external sources). *Receiving aid:* Freshmen: 14% (29); Undergraduates: 9% (69). *Average Award:* Freshmen: $9056; Undergraduates: $8754. *Scholarships, grants, and awards by category:* Academic Interests/Achievement: general academic interests/achievements. Creative Arts/Performance: 5 awards ($4750 total): performing arts. Special Achievements/Activities: community service, general special achievements/activities, leadership. Special Characteristics: children and siblings of alumni, local/state students. *Tuition waivers:* Full or partial for employees or children of employees, adult students, senior citizens.
LOANS *Student loans:* $2,141,813 (70% need-based, 30% non-need-based). 62% of past graduating class borrowed through all loan programs. *Average indebtedness per student:* $10,591. *Average need-based loan:* Freshmen: $2528; Undergraduates: $3377. *Parent loans:* $2,009,208 (35% need-based, 65% non-need-based). *Programs:* FFEL (Subsidized and Unsubsidized Stafford, PLUS).
WORK-STUDY *Federal work-study:* Total amount: $267,757; 254 jobs averaging $1800. *State or other work-study/employment:* Total amount: $4500 (100% non-need-based). 30 part-time jobs averaging $1800.
ATHLETIC AWARDS *Total amount:* $824,144 (55% need-based, 45% non-need-based).

APPLYING FOR FINANCIAL AID *Required financial aid forms:* FAFSA, state aid form. *Financial aid deadline:* Continuous. *Notification date:* Continuous beginning 2/1. Students must reply within 2 weeks of notification.
CONTACT Kimberly Driggers, Director of Student Financial Planning, St. Andrews Presbyterian College, 1700 Dogwood Mile, Laurinburg, NC 28352, 910-277-5562 or toll-free 800-763-0198. *Fax:* 910-277-5206.

SAINT ANSELM COLLEGE
Manchester, NH

ABOUT THE INSTITUTION Independent Roman Catholic, coed. Awards: bachelor's degrees. 29 undergraduate majors. Total enrollment: 1,986. Undergraduates: 1,986. Freshmen: 519.
GIFT AID (NEED-BASED) *Scholarships, grants, and awards:* Federal Pell, FSEOG, state, private, college/university gift aid from institutional funds.
GIFT AID (NON-NEED-BASED) *Scholarships, grants, and awards by category: Academic Interests/Achievement:* general academic interests/achievements. *Special Characteristics:* children of educators, children of faculty/staff, siblings of current students.
LOANS *Programs:* FFEL (Subsidized and Unsubsidized Stafford, PLUS), Perkins, GATE Loans.
WORK-STUDY *Federal work-study:* Total amount: $1,155,825; 1,173 jobs averaging $987. *State or other work-study/employment:* Total amount: $31,000 (100% non-need-based). 17 part-time jobs averaging $1941.
APPLYING FOR FINANCIAL AID *Required financial aid forms:* FAFSA, CSS Financial Aid PROFILE, federal income tax form(s).
CONTACT Elizabeth Keuffel, Director of Financial Aid, Saint Anselm College, 100 Saint Anselm Drive, Manchester, NH 03102-1310, 603-641-7110 or toll-free 888-4ANSELM. *Fax:* 603-656-6015. *E-mail:* financial_aid@anselm.edu.

SAINT ANTHONY COLLEGE OF NURSING
Rockford, IL

CONTACT Mrs. Lisa Ruch, Financial Aid Officer, Saint Anthony College of Nursing, 5658 East State Street, Rockford, IL 61108-2468, 815-395-5089. *Fax:* 815-395-2275. *E-mail:* lisaruch@sacn.edu.

ST. AUGUSTINE COLLEGE
Chicago, IL

ABOUT THE INSTITUTION Independent, coed. Awards: associate and bachelor's degrees (offers bilingual Spanish/English degree programs). 16 undergraduate majors. Total enrollment: 1,582. Undergraduates: 1,582. Freshmen: 410.
GIFT AID (NEED-BASED) *Scholarships, grants, and awards:* Federal Pell, FSEOG, state, private, college/university gift aid from institutional funds.
GIFT AID (NON-NEED-BASED) *Scholarships, grants, and awards by category: Academic Interests/Achievement:* business, computer science, education, general academic interests/achievements, health fields, humanities, social sciences. *Special Characteristics:* children of faculty/staff.
LOANS *Programs:* Perkins, alternative loans.
APPLYING FOR FINANCIAL AID *Required financial aid forms:* FAFSA, institution's own form.
CONTACT Mrs. Maria Zambonino, Director of Financial Aid, St. Augustine College, 1345 W Angyle, Chicago, IL 60640, 773-878-3813. *Fax:* 773-878-9032. *E-mail:* mzambonino@hotmail.com.

SAINT AUGUSTINE'S COLLEGE
Raleigh, NC

CONTACT Ms. Wanda C. White, Director of Financial Aid, Saint Augustine's College, 1315 Oakwood Avenue, Raleigh, NC 27610-2298, 919-516-4131 or toll-free 800-948-1126. *Fax:* 919-516-4338. *E-mail:* wwhite@es.st-aug.edu.

ST. BONAVENTURE UNIVERSITY
St. Bonaventure, NY

Tuition & fees: $22,515   **Average undergraduate aid package: $16,944**

ABOUT THE INSTITUTION Independent religious, coed. Awards: bachelor's and master's degrees and post-bachelor's and post-master's certificates. 59 undergraduate majors. Total enrollment: 2,614. Undergraduates: 2,141. Freshmen: 478. Federal methodology is used as a basis for awarding need-based institutional aid.
UNDERGRADUATE EXPENSES for 2006–07 *Application fee:* $30. *One-time required fee:* $325. *Comprehensive fee:* $30,275 includes full-time tuition ($21,650), mandatory fees ($865), and room and board ($7760). *College room only:* $3960. *Part-time tuition:* $650 per credit hour.
FRESHMAN FINANCIAL AID (Fall 2005, est.) 417 applied for aid; of those 83% were deemed to have need. 100% of freshmen with need received aid; of those 34% had need fully met. *Average percent of need met:* 87% (excluding resources awarded to replace EFC). *Average financial aid package:* $18,581 (excluding resources awarded to replace EFC). 22% of all full-time freshmen had no need and received non-need-based gift aid.
UNDERGRADUATE FINANCIAL AID (Fall 2005, est.) 1,707 applied for aid; of those 85% were deemed to have need. 100% of undergraduates with need received aid; of those 33% had need fully met. *Average percent of need met:* 82% (excluding resources awarded to replace EFC). *Average financial aid package:* $16,944 (excluding resources awarded to replace EFC). 16% of all full-time undergraduates had no need and received non-need-based gift aid.
GIFT AID (NEED-BASED) *Total amount:* $13,683,502 (13% federal, 16% state, 70% institutional, 1% external sources). *Receiving aid:* Freshmen: 73% (348); All full-time undergraduates: 71% (1,442). *Average award:* Freshmen: $13,301; Undergraduates: $11,762. *Scholarships, grants, and awards:* Federal Pell, FSEOG, state, private, college/university gift aid from institutional funds.
GIFT AID (NON-NEED-BASED) *Total amount:* $6,081,468 (5% federal, 2% state, 91% institutional, 2% external sources). *Receiving aid:* Freshmen: 13% (64); Undergraduates: 12% (250). *Average Award:* Freshmen: $8157; Undergraduates: $6868. *Scholarships, grants, and awards by category: Academic Interests/Achievement:* 1,000 awards ($5,500,000 total): business, general academic interests/achievements. *Creative Arts/Performance:* 40 awards ($40,000 total): journalism/publications, music, performing arts. *Special Characteristics:* children of faculty/staff, local/state students, members of minority groups, relatives of clergy, religious affiliation, siblings of current students. *ROTC:* Army.
LOANS *Student loans:* $13,437,512 (67% need-based, 33% non-need-based). 72% of past graduating class borrowed through all loan programs. *Average indebtedness per student:* $16,900. *Average need-based loan:* Freshmen: $4020; Undergraduates: $4555. *Parent loans:* $4,098,106 (20% need-based, 80% non-need-based). *Programs:* FFEL (Subsidized and Unsubsidized Stafford, PLUS), Perkins, college/university.
WORK-STUDY *Federal work-study:* Total amount: $817,058; 525 jobs averaging $1200. *State or other work-study/employment:* Part-time jobs available.
ATHLETIC AWARDS Total amount: $2,198,043 (31% need-based, 69% non-need-based).
APPLYING FOR FINANCIAL AID *Required financial aid forms:* FAFSA, institution's own form, state aid form. *Financial aid deadline (priority):* 2/1. *Notification date:* Continuous beginning 4/1. Students must reply by 5/1 or within 3 weeks of notification.
CONTACT Ms. Elizabeth T. Rankin, Director of Financial Aid, St. Bonaventure University, Route 417, St. Bonaventure, NY 14778-2284, 716-375-2528 or toll-free 800-462-5050. *Fax:* 716-375-2087. *E-mail:* erankin@sbu.edu.

ST. CHARLES BORROMEO SEMINARY, OVERBROOK
Wynnewood, PA

CONTACT Ms. Bonnie L. Behm, Coordinator of Financial Aid, St. Charles Borromeo Seminary, Overbrook, 100 East Wynnewood Road, Wynnewood, PA 19096-3099, 610-785-6582. *Fax:* 610-667-3971. *E-mail:* finaid.scs@erols.com.

ST. CLOUD STATE UNIVERSITY
St. Cloud, MN

Tuition & fees (MN res): $5322   **Average undergraduate aid package: $9634**

ABOUT THE INSTITUTION State-supported, coed. Awards: associate, bachelor's, and master's degrees and post-bachelor's certificates. 141 undergraduate majors. Total enrollment: 15,964. Undergraduates: 14,486. Freshmen: 2,152. Federal methodology is used as a basis for awarding need-based institutional aid.

St. Cloud State University

UNDERGRADUATE EXPENSES for 2005–06 *Application fee:* $20. *Tuition, state resident:* full-time $4760; part-time $159 per credit. *Tuition, nonresident:* full-time $10,332; part-time $344 per credit. *Required fees:* full-time $562; $23 per credit. Full-time tuition and fees vary according to course load and reciprocity agreements. Part-time tuition and fees vary according to course load and reciprocity agreements. *College room and board:* $4688; *room only:* $3340. Room and board charges vary according to board plan and housing facility. *Payment plan:* Installment.
FRESHMAN FINANCIAL AID (Fall 2005, est.) 1545 applied for aid; of those 68% were deemed to have need. 100% of freshmen with need received aid; of those 71% had need fully met. *Average percent of need met:* 94% (excluding resources awarded to replace EFC). *Average financial aid package:* $10,137 (excluding resources awarded to replace EFC). 10% of all full-time freshmen had no need and received non-need-based gift aid.
UNDERGRADUATE FINANCIAL AID (Fall 2005, est.) 7,433 applied for aid; of those 70% were deemed to have need. 100% of undergraduates with need received aid; of those 60% had need fully met. *Average percent of need met:* 96% (excluding resources awarded to replace EFC). *Average financial aid package:* $9634 (excluding resources awarded to replace EFC). 4% of all full-time undergraduates had no need and received non-need-based gift aid.
GIFT AID (NEED-BASED) *Total amount:* $15,600,220 (53% federal, 37% state, 6% institutional, 4% external sources). *Receiving aid:* Freshmen: 39% (826); All full-time undergraduates: 34% (3,932). *Average award:* Freshmen: $3971; Undergraduates: $3803. *Scholarships, grants, and awards:* Federal Pell, FSEOG, state, private, college/university gift aid from institutional funds.
GIFT AID (NON-NEED-BASED) *Total amount:* $2,816,017 (19% federal, 26% state, 35% institutional, 20% external sources). *Receiving aid:* Freshmen: 4% (83); Undergraduates: 2% (259). *Average Award:* Freshmen: $1639; Undergraduates:* $1812. *Scholarships, grants, and awards by category: Academic Interests/Achievement:* biological sciences, business, communication, computer science, education, engineering/technologies, English, general academic interests/achievements, health fields, international studies, mathematics, physical sciences, social sciences. *Creative Arts/Performance:* applied art and design, art/fine arts, cinema/film/broadcasting, creative writing, journalism/publications, music, performing arts, theater/drama. *Special Achievements/Activities:* community service, general special achievements/activities. *Special Characteristics:* children of faculty/staff, children of union members/company employees, local/state students, members of minority groups, out-of-state students. *Tuition waivers:* Full or partial for employees or children of employees, senior citizens. *ROTC:* Army.
LOANS *Student loans:* $65,030,970 (44% need-based, 56% non-need-based). 52% of past graduating class borrowed through all loan programs. *Average indebtedness per student:* $20,431. *Average need-based loan:* Freshmen: $3874; Undergraduates: $4487. *Parent loans:* $17,675,634 (4% need-based, 96% non-need-based). *Programs:* FFEL (Subsidized and Unsubsidized Stafford, PLUS), Perkins, state.
WORK-STUDY *Federal work-study:* Total amount: $1,439,913; jobs available. *State or other work-study/employment:* Total amount: $2,066,686 (100% need-based). Part-time jobs available.
ATHLETIC AWARDS Total amount: $1,028,894 (21% need-based, 79% non-need-based).
APPLYING FOR FINANCIAL AID *Required financial aid forms:* FAFSA, institution's own form. *Financial aid deadline:* Continuous. *Notification date:* Continuous beginning 6/3.
CONTACT Frank P. Morrissey, Associate Director of Scholarships and Financial Aid, St. Cloud State University, 106 Administrative Services, 720 4th Avenue South, St. Cloud, MN 56301-4498, 320-308-2047 or toll-free 877-654-7278. *Fax:* 320-308-5424. *E-mail:* fpmorrissey@stcloudstate.edu.

ST. EDWARD'S UNIVERSITY
Austin, TX

Tuition & fees: $18,800	Average undergraduate aid package: $14,680

ABOUT THE INSTITUTION Independent Roman Catholic, coed. Awards: bachelor's and master's degrees and post-bachelor's certificates. 49 undergraduate majors. Total enrollment: 4,947. Undergraduates: 3,964. Freshmen: 664. Federal methodology is used as a basis for awarding need-based institutional aid.
UNDERGRADUATE EXPENSES for 2006–07 *Application fee:* $45. *Comprehensive fee:* $25,700 includes full-time tuition ($18,800) and room and board ($6900). *College room only:* $3900. *Part-time tuition:* $628 per hour.
FRESHMAN FINANCIAL AID (Fall 2005, est.) 530 applied for aid; of those 76% were deemed to have need. 100% of freshmen with need received aid; of those 48% had need fully met. *Average percent of need met:* 80% (excluding resources awarded to replace EFC). *Average financial aid package:* $15,124 (excluding resources awarded to replace EFC). 14% of all full-time freshmen had no need and received non-need-based gift aid.
UNDERGRADUATE FINANCIAL AID (Fall 2005, est.) 2,206 applied for aid; of those 82% were deemed to have need. 99% of undergraduates with need received aid; of those 39% had need fully met. *Average percent of need met:* 76% (excluding resources awarded to replace EFC). *Average financial aid package:* $14,680 (excluding resources awarded to replace EFC). 10% of all full-time undergraduates had no need and received non-need-based gift aid.
GIFT AID (NEED-BASED) *Total amount:* $17,684,262 (19% federal, 26% state, 55% institutional). *Receiving aid:* Freshmen: 59% (384); All full-time undergraduates: 55% (1,638). *Average award:* Freshmen: $12,124; Undergraduates: $10,054. *Scholarships, grants, and awards:* Federal Pell, FSEOG, state, private, college/university gift aid from institutional funds, endowed scholarships.
GIFT AID (NON-NEED-BASED) *Total amount:* $3,231,294 (84% institutional, 16% external sources). *Receiving aid:* Freshmen: 32% (207); Undergraduates: 24% (709). *Average Award:* Freshmen: $6216; Undergraduates: $5826. *Scholarships, grants, and awards by category: Academic Interests/Achievement:* 1,062 awards ($5,155,810 total): biological sciences, business, communication, computer science, education, English, foreign languages, general academic interests/achievements, humanities, international studies, mathematics, military science, physical sciences, religion/biblical studies, social sciences. *Creative Arts/Performance:* 38 awards ($88,500 total): theater/drama. *Special Achievements/Activities:* 90 awards ($159,630 total): cheerleading/drum major, community service, general special achievements/activities, leadership. *Special Characteristics:* 60 awards ($589,095 total): adult students, children of faculty/staff, religious affiliation. *ROTC:* Army cooperative, Air Force cooperative.
LOANS *Student loans:* $17,398,621 (42% need-based, 58% non-need-based). 62% of past graduating class borrowed through all loan programs. *Average indebtedness per student:* $24,280. *Average need-based loan:* Freshmen: $3563; Undergraduates: $4324. *Parent loans:* $6,139,670 (100% non-need-based). *Programs:* FFEL (Subsidized and Unsubsidized Stafford, PLUS), Perkins, state, alternative loans.
WORK-STUDY *Federal work-study:* Total amount: $411,023; 210 jobs averaging $1957. *State or other work-study/employment:* Total amount: $33,481 (100% need-based). 20 part-time jobs averaging $1674.
ATHLETIC AWARDS Total amount: $1,404,012 (100% non-need-based).
APPLYING FOR FINANCIAL AID *Required financial aid form:* FAFSA. *Financial aid deadline (priority):* 3/1. *Notification date:* Continuous beginning 2/15. Students must reply by 5/1 or within 2 weeks of notification.
CONTACT Office of Student Financial Services, St. Edward's University, 3001 South Congress Avenue, Austin, TX 78704, 512-448-8523 or toll-free 800-555-0164. *Fax:* 512-416-5837. *E-mail:* seu.finaid@admin.stedwards.edu.

ST. FRANCIS COLLEGE
Brooklyn Heights, NY

Tuition & fees: $12,710	Average undergraduate aid package: $4622

ABOUT THE INSTITUTION Independent Roman Catholic, coed. Awards: associate, bachelor's, and master's degrees. 35 undergraduate majors. Total enrollment: 2,336. Undergraduates: 2,336. Freshmen: 505. Federal methodology is used as a basis for awarding need-based institutional aid.
UNDERGRADUATE EXPENSES for 2005–06 *Application fee:* $35. *Comprehensive fee:* $20,710 includes full-time tuition ($12,450), mandatory fees ($260), and room and board ($8000). *College room only:* $6500. Full-time tuition and fees vary according to course level, course load, degree level, program, and student level. *Part-time tuition:* $440 per credit. *Part-time fees:* $70 per term. Part-time tuition and fees vary according to course level, course load, degree level, program, and student level. *Payment plans:* Installment, deferred payment.
FRESHMAN FINANCIAL AID (Fall 2005, est.) 467 applied for aid; of those 83% were deemed to have need. 100% of freshmen with need received aid; of those 18% had need fully met. *Average percent of need met:* 61% (excluding resources awarded to replace EFC). *Average financial aid package:* $3936 (excluding resources awarded to replace EFC). 11% of all full-time freshmen had no need and received non-need-based gift aid.

UNDERGRADUATE FINANCIAL AID (Fall 2005, est.) 1,725 applied for aid; of those 75% were deemed to have need. 100% of undergraduates with need received aid; of those 31% had need fully met. *Average percent of need met:* 67% (excluding resources awarded to replace EFC). *Average financial aid package:* $4622 (excluding resources awarded to replace EFC). 11% of all full-time undergraduates had no need and received non-need-based gift aid.
GIFT AID (NEED-BASED) *Total amount:* $3,133,066 (45% federal, 55% state). *Receiving aid:* Freshmen: 63% (314); All full-time undergraduates: 55% (1,100). *Average award:* Freshmen: $3523; Undergraduates: $3683. *Scholarships, grants, and awards:* Federal Pell, FSEOG, state, college/university gift aid from institutional funds.
GIFT AID (NON-NEED-BASED) *Total amount:* $2,173,105 (100% institutional). *Receiving aid:* Freshmen: 35% (174); Undergraduates: 31% (623). *Average Award:* Freshmen: $4437; Undergraduates: $3867. *Scholarships, grants, and awards by category:* Academic Interests/Achievement: 827 awards ($4,976,000 total): general academic interests/achievements. *Special Characteristics:* children of public servants, handicapped students, public servants. *Tuition waivers:* Full or partial for employees or children of employees.
LOANS *Student loans:* $2,762,777 (100% need-based). 29% of past graduating class borrowed through all loan programs. *Average need-based loan:* Freshmen: $1290; Undergraduates: $1825. *Parent loans:* $701,955 (100% need-based). *Programs:* FFEL (Subsidized and Unsubsidized Stafford, PLUS), Perkins.
WORK-STUDY *Federal work-study:* Total amount: $156,555; 161 jobs averaging $2200.
ATHLETIC AWARDS *Total amount:* $451,898 (100% need-based).
APPLYING FOR FINANCIAL AID *Required financial aid forms:* FAFSA, state aid form. *Financial aid deadline (priority):* 2/15. *Notification date:* Continuous. Students must reply within 2 weeks of notification.
CONTACT Joseph Cummings, Director of Student Financial Services, St. Francis College, 180 Remsen Street, Brooklyn Heights, NY 11201-4398, 718-489-5390. *Fax:* 718-522-1274. *E-mail:* jcummings@stfranciscollege.edu.

SAINT FRANCIS MEDICAL CENTER COLLEGE OF NURSING
Peoria, IL

Tuition & fees: $10,650   **Average undergraduate aid package: $11,259**

ABOUT THE INSTITUTION Independent Roman Catholic, coed, primarily women. Awards: bachelor's and master's degrees. 1 undergraduate major. Total enrollment: 272. Undergraduates: 220. Federal methodology is used as a basis for awarding need-based institutional aid.
UNDERGRADUATE EXPENSES for 2005–06 *Application fee:* $50. *Tuition:* full-time $10,200; part-time $425 per semester hour. *Required fees:* full-time $450; $225 per term part-time. Full-time tuition and fees vary according to course load. Part-time tuition and fees vary according to course load. *Payment plan:* Installment.
UNDERGRADUATE FINANCIAL AID (Fall 2005, est.) 148 applied for aid; of those 93% were deemed to have need. 100% of undergraduates with need received aid; of those 19% had need fully met. *Average percent of need met:* 81% (excluding resources awarded to replace EFC). *Average financial aid package:* $11,259 (excluding resources awarded to replace EFC). 25% of all full-time undergraduates had no need and received non-need-based gift aid.
GIFT AID (NEED-BASED) *Total amount:* $913,370 (16% federal, 50% state, 27% institutional, 7% external sources). *Receiving aid:* All full-time undergraduates: 53% (100). *Average award:* Undergraduates: $6575. *Scholarships, grants, and awards:* Federal Pell, state, private, college/university gift aid from institutional funds.
GIFT AID (NON-NEED-BASED) *Total amount:* $448,036 (8% state, 80% institutional, 12% external sources). *Receiving aid:* Undergraduates: 3% (5). *Average Award:* Undergraduates: $6974. *Scholarships, grants, and awards by category:* Academic Interests/Achievement: 102 awards ($40,390 total): general academic interests/achievements, health fields. *Tuition waivers:* Full or partial for employees or children of employees.
LOANS *Student loans:* $721,211 (79% need-based, 21% non-need-based). 73% of past graduating class borrowed through all loan programs. *Average indebtedness per student:* $8171. *Average need-based loan:* Undergraduates: $4179. *Parent loans:* $49,655 (27% need-based, 73% non-need-based). *Programs:* FFEL (Subsidized and Unsubsidized Stafford, PLUS), college/university.
APPLYING FOR FINANCIAL AID *Required financial aid forms:* FAFSA, institution's own form. *Financial aid deadline (priority):* 3/1. *Notification date:* Continuous beginning 5/1.
CONTACT Ms. Nancy Perryman, Coordinator Student Finance, Financial Assistance, Saint Francis Medical Center College of Nursing, 511 Northeast Greenleaf Street, Peoria, IL 61603-3783, 309-655-4119. *E-mail:* nancy.s.perryman@osfhealthcare.org.

SAINT FRANCIS UNIVERSITY
Loretto, PA

Tuition & fees: $21,410   **Average undergraduate aid package: $18,573**

ABOUT THE INSTITUTION Independent Roman Catholic, coed. Awards: associate, bachelor's, and master's degrees. 71 undergraduate majors. Total enrollment: 2,065. Undergraduates: 1,461. Freshmen: 364. Federal methodology is used as a basis for awarding need-based institutional aid.
UNDERGRADUATE EXPENSES for 2005–06 *Application fee:* $30. *Comprehensive fee:* $28,978 includes full-time tuition ($20,360), mandatory fees ($1050), and room and board ($7568). *College room only:* $3672. Full-time tuition and fees vary according to course load and program. Room and board charges vary according to board plan. *Part-time tuition:* $636 per credit. *Part-time fees:* $315 per credit hour. *Payment plans:* Installment, deferred payment.
FRESHMAN FINANCIAL AID (Fall 2005, est.) 351 applied for aid; of those 86% were deemed to have need. 100% of freshmen with need received aid; of those 38% had need fully met. *Average percent of need met:* 81% (excluding resources awarded to replace EFC). *Average financial aid package:* $17,141 (excluding resources awarded to replace EFC). 16% of all full-time freshmen had no need and received non-need-based gift aid.
UNDERGRADUATE FINANCIAL AID (Fall 2005, est.) 1,099 applied for aid; of those 89% were deemed to have need. 100% of undergraduates with need received aid; of those 41% had need fully met. *Average percent of need met:* 84% (excluding resources awarded to replace EFC). *Average financial aid package:* $18,573 (excluding resources awarded to replace EFC). 15% of all full-time undergraduates had no need and received non-need-based gift aid.
GIFT AID (NEED-BASED) *Total amount:* $11,882,083 (10% federal, 16% state, 62% institutional, 12% external sources). *Receiving aid:* Freshmen: 83% (300); All full-time undergraduates: 83% (971). *Average award:* Freshmen: $13,366; Undergraduates: $13,427. *Scholarships, grants, and awards:* Federal Pell, FSEOG, state, private, college/university gift aid from institutional funds.
GIFT AID (NON-NEED-BASED) *Total amount:* $1,768,024 (2% state, 72% institutional, 26% external sources). *Receiving aid:* Freshmen: 16% (58); Undergraduates: 12% (145). *Average Award:* Freshmen: $12,836; Undergraduates: $12,433. *Scholarships, grants, and awards by category:* Academic Interests/Achievement: 629 awards ($2,557,176 total): business, general academic interests/achievements, physical sciences. *Creative Arts/Performance:* 28 awards ($26,500 total): music. *Special Achievements/Activities:* 32 awards ($28,500 total): cheerleading/drum major, community service, junior miss, memberships, religious involvement. *Special Characteristics:* 77 awards ($877,781 total): adult students, children of faculty/staff, siblings of current students. *Tuition waivers:* Full or partial for employees or children of employees. *ROTC:* Army cooperative.
LOANS *Student loans:* $8,246,082 (66% need-based, 34% non-need-based). 90% of past graduating class borrowed through all loan programs. *Average indebtedness per student:* $14,100. *Average need-based loan:* Freshmen: $4054; Undergraduates: $5511. *Parent loans:* $2,222,663 (36% need-based, 64% non-need-based). *Programs:* FFEL (Subsidized and Unsubsidized Stafford, PLUS), Perkins, alternative loans.
WORK-STUDY *Federal work-study:* Total amount: $674,992; 724 jobs averaging $1000. *State or other work-study/employment:* Total amount: $29,750 (21% need-based, 79% non-need-based). 30 part-time jobs averaging $991.
ATHLETIC AWARDS *Total amount:* $2,770,893 (64% need-based, 36% non-need-based).
APPLYING FOR FINANCIAL AID *Required financial aid form:* FAFSA. *Financial aid deadline:* Continuous. *Notification date:* Continuous beginning 3/1. Students must reply within 4 weeks of notification.
CONTACT Vincent Frank, Director of Financial Aid, Saint Francis University, PO Box 600, Loretto, PA 15940-0600, 814-472-3010 or toll-free 800-342-5732. *Fax:* 814-472-3999. *E-mail:* vfrank@francis.edu.

ST. GREGORY'S UNIVERSITY
Shawnee, OK

ABOUT THE INSTITUTION Independent Roman Catholic, coed. Awards: associate and bachelor's degrees. 46 undergraduate majors. Total enrollment: 868. Undergraduates: 868. Freshmen: 97.

GIFT AID (NEED-BASED) *Scholarships, grants, and awards:* Federal Pell, FSEOG, state, private, college/university gift aid from institutional funds.

GIFT AID (NON-NEED-BASED) *Scholarships, grants, and awards by category: Academic Interests/Achievement:* general academic interests/achievements. *Creative Arts/Performance:* art/fine arts, dance, journalism/publications, music, theater/drama. *Special Achievements/Activities:* religious involvement. *Special Characteristics:* ethnic background, handicapped students, international students, religious affiliation.

LOANS *Programs:* FFEL (Subsidized and Unsubsidized Stafford, PLUS), Perkins, alternative loans.

APPLYING FOR FINANCIAL AID *Required financial aid forms:* FAFSA, institution's own form.

CONTACT Jonna Raney, Director of Financial Aid, St. Gregory's University, 1900 West MacArthur Drive, Shawnee, OK 74804, 405-878-5412 or toll-free 888-STGREGS. *Fax:* 405-878-5403. *E-mail:* jlraney@stgregorys.edu.

ST. JOHN FISHER COLLEGE
Rochester, NY

Tuition & fees: $19,560 **Average undergraduate aid package: $15,727**

ABOUT THE INSTITUTION Independent religious, coed. Awards: bachelor's and master's degrees and post-bachelor's and post-master's certificates. 37 undergraduate majors. Total enrollment: 3,528. Undergraduates: 2,696. Freshmen: 553. Federal methodology is used as a basis for awarding need-based institutional aid.

UNDERGRADUATE EXPENSES for 2005–06 *Application fee:* $30. *Comprehensive fee:* $27,860 includes full-time tuition ($19,300), mandatory fees ($260), and room and board ($8300). *College room only:* $5400. Room and board charges vary according to board plan. *Part-time tuition:* $525 per credit hour. *Part-time fees:* $25 per term. Part-time tuition and fees vary according to course load. *Payment plans:* Installment, deferred payment.

FRESHMAN FINANCIAL AID (Fall 2005, est.) 527 applied for aid; of those 83% were deemed to have need. 100% of freshmen with need received aid; of those 12% had need fully met. *Average percent of need met:* 86% (excluding resources awarded to replace EFC). *Average financial aid package:* $16,570 (excluding resources awarded to replace EFC). 20% of all full-time freshmen had no need and received non-need-based gift aid.

UNDERGRADUATE FINANCIAL AID (Fall 2005, est.) 2,251 applied for aid; of those 88% were deemed to have need. 100% of undergraduates with need received aid; of those 55% had need fully met. *Average percent of need met:* 79% (excluding resources awarded to replace EFC). *Average financial aid package:* $15,727 (excluding resources awarded to replace EFC). 16% of all full-time undergraduates had no need and received non-need-based gift aid.

GIFT AID (NEED-BASED) *Total amount:* $22,701,721 (9% federal, 16% state, 73% institutional, 2% external sources). *Receiving aid:* Freshmen: 79% (435); All full-time undergraduates: 80% (1,949). *Average award:* Freshmen: $12,476; Undergraduates: $10,103. *Scholarships, grants, and awards:* Federal Pell, FSEOG, state, private, college/university gift aid from institutional funds, Federal Nursing.

GIFT AID (NON-NEED-BASED) *Total amount:* $57,298 (19% state, 81% external sources). *Receiving aid:* Freshmen: 70% (386); Undergraduates: 50% (1,223). *Average Award:* Freshmen: $7015; Undergraduates: $5251. *Scholarships, grants, and awards by category: Academic Interests/Achievement:* 1,150 awards ($6,915,123 total): biological sciences, business, English, foreign languages, general academic interests/achievements, humanities, mathematics, physical sciences. *Special Achievements/Activities:* 127 awards ($1,062,210 total): community service. *Special Characteristics:* 124 awards ($1,025,900 total): children and siblings of alumni, ethnic background, first-generation college students, local/state students, members of minority groups. *Tuition waivers:* Full or partial for employees or children of employees. *ROTC:* Army cooperative, Naval cooperative, Air Force cooperative.

LOANS *Student loans:* $22,535,462 (80% need-based, 20% non-need-based). 85% of past graduating class borrowed through all loan programs. *Average indebtedness per student:* $25,833. *Average need-based loan:* Freshmen: $4124; Undergraduates: $6542. *Parent loans:* $10,177,387 (100% non-need-based). *Programs:* FFEL (Subsidized and Unsubsidized Stafford, PLUS), Perkins.

WORK-STUDY *Federal work-study:* Total amount: $350,000; 1,493 jobs averaging $1638.

APPLYING FOR FINANCIAL AID *Required financial aid forms:* FAFSA, state aid form. *Financial aid deadline (priority):* 2/15. *Notification date:* Continuous beginning 3/21. Students must reply by 5/1 or within 3 weeks of notification.

CONTACT Mrs. Angela Monnat, Director of Financial Aid, St. John Fisher College, 3690 East Avenue, Rochester, NY 14618-3597, 585-385-8042 or toll-free 800-444-4640. *Fax:* 585-385-8044. *E-mail:* amonnat@sjfc.edu.

ST. JOHN'S COLLEGE
Springfield, IL

ABOUT THE INSTITUTION Independent Roman Catholic, coed, primarily women. Awards: bachelor's degrees. 1 undergraduate major. Total enrollment: 82. Undergraduates: 82.

GIFT AID (NEED-BASED) *Scholarships, grants, and awards:* Federal Pell, FSEOG, state, private, college/university gift aid from institutional funds.

GIFT AID (NON-NEED-BASED) *Scholarships, grants, and awards by category: Academic Interests/Achievement:* health fields.

LOANS *Programs:* FFEL (Subsidized and Unsubsidized Stafford, PLUS), Federal Nursing, affiliate hospital offers scholarship/loan in exchange for work after graduation.

APPLYING FOR FINANCIAL AID *Required financial aid forms:* FAFSA, institution's own form.

CONTACT Mary M. Deatherage, Financial Aid Officer, St. John's College, 421 North Ninth Street, Springfield, IL 62702, 217-544-6464 Ext. 44705. *Fax:* 217-757-6870. *E-mail:* mdeather@st-johns.org.

ST. JOHN'S COLLEGE
Annapolis, MD

CONTACT Ms. Caroline Christensen, Director of Financial Aid, St. John's College, PO Box 2800, Annapolis, MD 21404, 410-626-2502 or toll-free 800-727-9238. *Fax:* 410-626-2885. *E-mail:* c-christensen@sjca.edu.

ST. JOHN'S COLLEGE
Santa Fe, NM

CONTACT Michael Rodriguez, Director of Financial Aid, St. John's College, 1160 Camino Cruz Blanca, Santa Fe, NM 87505, 505-984-6058 or toll-free 800-331-5232. *Fax:* 505-984-6003. *E-mail:* faid@mail.sjcsf.edu.

SAINT JOHN'S UNIVERSITY
Collegeville, MN

ABOUT THE INSTITUTION Independent Roman Catholic, coed, primarily men. Awards: bachelor's, master's, and first professional degrees (coordinate with College of Saint Benedict for women). 48 undergraduate majors. Total enrollment: 1,996. Undergraduates: 1,875. Freshmen: 447.

GIFT AID (NEED-BASED) *Scholarships, grants, and awards:* Federal Pell, FSEOG, state, private, college/university gift aid from institutional funds.

GIFT AID (NON-NEED-BASED) *Scholarships, grants, and awards by category: Academic Interests/Achievement:* general academic interests/achievements. *Creative Arts/Performance:* art/fine arts, music, theater/drama. *Special Characteristics:* international students.

LOANS *Programs:* FFEL (Subsidized and Unsubsidized Stafford, PLUS), Perkins, state, SELF Loans, alternative loans.

WORK-STUDY *Federal work-study:* Total amount: $355,381; 157 jobs averaging $2263. *State or other work-study/employment:* Total amount: $1,990,732 (78% need-based, 22% non-need-based). 1,007 part-time jobs averaging $1977.

APPLYING FOR FINANCIAL AID *Required financial aid forms:* FAFSA, institution's own form, federal income tax form(s).

CONTACT Ms. Mary Dehler, Associate Director of Financial Aid, Saint John's University, PO Box 5000, Collegeville, MN 56321-5000, 320-363-3664 or toll-free 800-544-1489. *Fax:* 320-363-3102. *E-mail:* mdehler@csbsju.edu.

ST. JOHN'S UNIVERSITY
Queens, NY

Tuition & fees: $24,970 **Average undergraduate aid package:** $15,807

ABOUT THE INSTITUTION Independent religious, coed. Awards: associate, bachelor's, master's, doctoral, and first professional degrees and post-bachelor's and post-master's certificates. 105 undergraduate majors. Total enrollment: 20,346. Undergraduates: 15,092. Freshmen: 3,159. Federal methodology is used as a basis for awarding need-based institutional aid.

UNDERGRADUATE EXPENSES for 2006–07 *Application fee:* $30. *Comprehensive fee:* $36,440 includes full-time tuition ($24,400), mandatory fees ($570), and room and board ($11,470). *College room only:* $7200. *Part-time tuition:* $813 per credit. *Part-time fees:* $205 per term.

FRESHMAN FINANCIAL AID (Fall 2004) 2723 applied for aid; of those 92% were deemed to have need. 100% of freshmen with need received aid; of those 12% had need fully met. *Average percent of need met:* 71% (excluding resources awarded to replace EFC). *Average financial aid package:* $17,328 (excluding resources awarded to replace EFC). 5% of all full-time freshmen had no need and received non-need-based gift aid.

UNDERGRADUATE FINANCIAL AID (Fall 2004) 10,280 applied for aid; of those 93% were deemed to have need. 100% of undergraduates with need received aid; of those 12% had need fully met. *Average percent of need met:* 65% (excluding resources awarded to replace EFC). *Average financial aid package:* $15,807 (excluding resources awarded to replace EFC). 3% of all full-time undergraduates had no need and received non-need-based gift aid.

GIFT AID (NEED-BASED) *Total amount:* $61,583,007 (27% federal, 31% state, 42% institutional). *Receiving aid:* Freshmen: 77% (2,315); All full-time undergraduates: 71% (8,337). *Average award:* Freshmen: $8753; Undergraduates: $7255. *Scholarships, grants, and awards:* Federal Pell, FSEOG, state, private, college/university gift aid from institutional funds.

GIFT AID (NON-NEED-BASED) *Total amount:* $56,093,832 (1% federal, 1% state, 90% institutional, 8% external sources). *Receiving aid:* Freshmen: 76% (2,287); Undergraduates: 54% (6,350). *Average Award:* Freshmen: $7813; Undergraduates: $8180. *Scholarships, grants, and awards by category: Academic Interests/Achievement:* 4,317 awards ($29,963,574 total): biological sciences, business, communication, computer science, education, general academic interests/achievements, health fields, mathematics, military science. *Creative Arts/Performance:* 132 awards ($141,225 total): art/fine arts, cinema/film/broadcasting, dance, debating, journalism/publications, music. *Special Achievements/Activities:* 136 awards ($182,010 total): cheerleading/drum major, community service, general special achievements/activities, hobbies/interests, leadership, religious involvement. *Special Characteristics:* 4,201 awards ($11,871,107 total): children of faculty/staff, general special characteristics, local/state students, relatives of clergy, religious affiliation. *ROTC:* Army.

LOANS *Student loans:* $60,441,265 (71% need-based, 29% non-need-based). 69% of past graduating class borrowed through all loan programs. *Average indebtedness per student:* $21,122. *Average need-based loan:* Freshmen: $3290; Undergraduates: $4268. *Parent loans:* $25,608,058 (100% non-need-based). *Programs:* FFEL (Subsidized and Unsubsidized Stafford, PLUS), Perkins.

WORK-STUDY *Federal work-study:* Total amount: $2,667,167; 915 jobs averaging $2942.

ATHLETIC AWARDS *Total amount:* $4,267,538 (100% non-need-based).

APPLYING FOR FINANCIAL AID *Required financial aid form:* FAFSA. *Financial aid deadline (priority):* 2/1. *Notification date:* Continuous beginning 3/15. Students must reply within 2 weeks of notification.

CONTACT Mr. Jorge Rodriguez, Assistant Vice President/Executive Director of Financial Aid, St. John's University, 8000 Utopia Parkway, Queens, NY 11439, 718-990-2000 or toll-free 888-9STJOHNS (in-state), 888-9ST JOHNS (out-of-state). *Fax:* 718-990-5945. *E-mail:* financialaid@stjohns.edu.

ST. JOHN VIANNEY COLLEGE SEMINARY
Miami, FL

CONTACT Ms. Bonnie DeAngulo, Director of Financial Aid, St. John Vianney College Seminary, 2900 Southwest 87th Avenue, Miami, FL 33165-3244, 305-223-4561 Ext. 10.

SAINT JOSEPH COLLEGE
West Hartford, CT

ABOUT THE INSTITUTION Independent Roman Catholic, undergraduate: women only; graduate: coed. Awards: bachelor's and master's degrees. 34 undergraduate majors. Total enrollment: 1,858. Undergraduates: 1,159. Freshmen: 253.

GIFT AID (NEED-BASED) *Scholarships, grants, and awards:* Federal Pell, FSEOG, state, private, college/university gift aid from institutional funds.

GIFT AID (NON-NEED-BASED) *Scholarships, grants, and awards by category: Academic Interests/Achievement:* general academic interests/achievements. *Special Characteristics:* siblings of current students.

LOANS *Programs:* FFEL (Subsidized and Unsubsidized Stafford, PLUS), Perkins, state, Connecticut Family Education Loan Program.

APPLYING FOR FINANCIAL AID *Required financial aid form:* FAFSA.

CONTACT Mr. Philip T. Malinoski, Student Financial Services Director, Saint Joseph College, 1678 Asylum Avenue, West Hartford, CT 06117, 860-231-5319 or toll-free 866-442-8752 (out-of-state). *E-mail:* pmalinoski@sjc.edu.

SAINT JOSEPH'S COLLEGE
Rensselaer, IN

Tuition & fees: $19,760 **Average undergraduate aid package:** $18,976

ABOUT THE INSTITUTION Independent Roman Catholic, coed. Awards: associate, bachelor's, and master's degrees. 33 undergraduate majors. Total university enrollment: 9. Total unit enrollment: 1,003. Undergraduates: 1,003. Freshmen: 233. Federal methodology is used as a basis for awarding need-based institutional aid.

UNDERGRADUATE EXPENSES for 2005–06 *Application fee:* $25. *Comprehensive fee:* $26,240 includes full-time tuition ($19,600), mandatory fees ($160), and room and board ($6480). Full-time tuition and fees vary according to reciprocity agreements. Room and board charges vary according to housing facility. *Part-time tuition:* $670 per credit. Part-time tuition and fees vary according to course load and reciprocity agreements. *Payment plan:* Installment.

FRESHMAN FINANCIAL AID (Fall 2005, est.) 227 applied for aid; of those 87% were deemed to have need. 100% of freshmen with need received aid; of those 36% had need fully met. *Average percent of need met:* 82% (excluding resources awarded to replace EFC). *Average financial aid package:* $17,773 (excluding resources awarded to replace EFC). 12% of all full-time freshmen had no need and received non-need-based gift aid.

UNDERGRADUATE FINANCIAL AID (Fall 2005, est.) 763 applied for aid; of those 83% were deemed to have need. 100% of undergraduates with need received aid; of those 36% had need fully met. *Average percent of need met:* 84% (excluding resources awarded to replace EFC). *Average financial aid package:* $18,976 (excluding resources awarded to replace EFC). 14% of all full-time undergraduates had no need and received non-need-based gift aid.

GIFT AID (NEED-BASED) *Total amount:* $6,337,883 (11% federal, 24% state, 63% institutional, 2% external sources). *Receiving aid:* Freshmen: 84% (195); All full-time undergraduates: 71% (626). *Average award:* Freshmen: $12,365; Undergraduates: $12,234. *Scholarships, grants, and awards:* Federal Pell, FSEOG, state, private, college/university gift aid from institutional funds.

GIFT AID (NON-NEED-BASED) *Total amount:* $1,185,468 (89% institutional, 11% external sources). *Receiving aid:* Freshmen: 26% (61); Undergraduates: 18% (159). *Average Award:* Freshmen: $10,386; Undergraduates: $10,042. *Scholarships, grants, and awards by category: Academic Interests/Achievement:* 390 awards ($2,598,164 total): general academic interests/achievements. *Creative Arts/Performance:* 145 awards ($271,987 total): cinema/film/broadcasting, music, theater/drama. *Special Achievements/Activities:* 14 awards ($19,250 total): cheerleading/drum major. *Special Characteristics:* 112 awards ($450,174 total): children and siblings of alumni, children of faculty/staff, siblings of current students. *Tuition waivers:* Full or partial for minority students, children of alumni, employees or children of employees.

LOANS *Student loans:* $4,410,549 (63% need-based, 37% non-need-based). 74% of past graduating class borrowed through all loan programs. *Average indebtedness per student:* $23,417. *Average need-based loan:* Freshmen: $3232; Undergraduates: $4299. *Parent loans:* $1,288,289 (28% need-based, 72% non-need-based). *Programs:* FFEL (Subsidized and Unsubsidized Stafford, PLUS), Perkins.

WORK-STUDY *Federal work-study:* Total amount: $82,328; 111 jobs averaging $742.

Saint Joseph's College

ATHLETIC AWARDS *Total amount:* $2,323,887 (59% need-based, 41% non-need-based).
APPLYING FOR FINANCIAL AID *Required financial aid form:* FAFSA. *Financial aid deadline (priority):* 3/1. *Notification date:* Continuous. Students must reply by 5/1 or within 2 weeks of notification.
CONTACT Debra Sizemore, Director of Student Financial Services, Saint Joseph's College, US Highway 231, PO Box 971, Rensselaer, IN 47978, 219-866-6163 or toll-free 800-447-8781 (out-of-state). *Fax:* 219-866-6144. *E-mail:* debbie@saintjoe.edu.

ST. JOSEPH'S COLLEGE, NEW YORK
Brooklyn, NY

Tuition & fees: $12,236   **Average undergraduate aid package:** $10,000

ABOUT THE INSTITUTION Independent, coed. Awards: bachelor's and master's degrees. 22 undergraduate majors. Total enrollment: 1,318. Undergraduates: 1,122. Freshmen: 158. Federal methodology is used as a basis for awarding need-based institutional aid.
UNDERGRADUATE EXPENSES for 2005–06 *Application fee:* $25. *Tuition:* full-time $11,854; part-time $382 per credit. *Required fees:* full-time $382; $13 per credit or $30 per term part-time. *Payment plan:* Installment.
FRESHMAN FINANCIAL AID (Fall 2005, est.) 141 applied for aid; of those 92% were deemed to have need. 100% of freshmen with need received aid; of those 58% had need fully met. *Average percent of need met:* 86% (excluding resources awarded to replace EFC). *Average financial aid package:* $11,000 (excluding resources awarded to replace EFC). 25% of all full-time freshmen had no need and received non-need-based gift aid.
UNDERGRADUATE FINANCIAL AID (Fall 2005, est.) 550 applied for aid; of those 77% were deemed to have need. 100% of undergraduates with need received aid; of those 71% had need fully met. *Average percent of need met:* 73% (excluding resources awarded to replace EFC). *Average financial aid package:* $10,000 (excluding resources awarded to replace EFC). 18% of all full-time undergraduates had no need and received non-need-based gift aid.
GIFT AID (NEED-BASED) *Total amount:* $3,346,389 (32% federal, 39% state, 29% institutional). *Receiving aid:* Freshmen: 86% (130); All full-time undergraduates: 60% (425). *Average award:* Freshmen: $9000; Undergraduates: $6000. *Scholarships, grants, and awards:* Federal Pell, FSEOG, state, private, college/university gift aid from institutional funds.
GIFT AID (NON-NEED-BASED) *Total amount:* $1,109,752 (2% state, 93% institutional, 5% external sources). *Receiving aid:* Freshmen: 49% (74); Undergraduates: 39% (275). *Average Award:* Freshmen: $5600; Undergraduates: $4600. *Scholarships, grants, and awards by category: Academic Interests/Achievement:* 370 awards ($1,400,000 total): general academic interests/achievements. *Special Characteristics:* 14 awards ($44,093 total): children and siblings of alumni, children of faculty/staff. *Tuition waivers:* Full or partial for employees or children of employees.
LOANS *Student loans:* $3,115,312 (43% need-based, 57% non-need-based). 46% of past graduating class borrowed through all loan programs. *Average indebtedness per student:* $16,805. *Average need-based loan:* Freshmen: $2500; Undergraduates: $3700. *Parent loans:* $352,800 (100% non-need-based). *Programs:* FFEL (Subsidized and Unsubsidized Stafford, PLUS), Perkins.
WORK-STUDY *Federal work-study:* Total amount: $97,629; 67 jobs averaging $1500. *State or other work-study/employment:* Total amount: $6400 (100% non-need-based). 4 part-time jobs averaging $1500.
APPLYING FOR FINANCIAL AID *Required financial aid forms:* FAFSA, institution's own form, state aid form. *Financial aid deadline (priority):* 2/25. *Notification date:* Continuous beginning 4/1. Students must reply by 5/1 or within 3 weeks of notification.
CONTACT Ms. Carol Sullivan, Director of Financial Aid, St. Joseph's College, New York, 245 Clinton Avenue, Brooklyn, NY 11205-3688, 718-636-6808. *Fax:* 718-636-6827. *E-mail:* csullivan@sjcny.edu.

SAINT JOSEPH'S COLLEGE OF MAINE
Standish, ME

Tuition & fees: $20,605   **Average undergraduate aid package:** $16,472

ABOUT THE INSTITUTION Independent religious, coed. Awards: bachelor's and master's degrees (profile does not include enrollment in distance learning master's program). 40 undergraduate majors. Total enrollment: 955. Undergraduates: 955. Freshmen: 268. Both federal and institutional methodology are used as a basis for awarding need-based institutional aid.
UNDERGRADUATE EXPENSES for 2005–06 *Application fee:* $40. *Comprehensive fee:* $29,185 includes full-time tuition ($19,890), mandatory fees ($715), and room and board ($8580). Full-time tuition and fees vary according to program. *Part-time tuition:* $350 per credit. *Part-time fees:* $125 per year. Part-time tuition and fees vary according to course load and program. *Payment plan:* Installment.
FRESHMAN FINANCIAL AID (Fall 2005, est.) 256 applied for aid; of those 86% were deemed to have need. 100% of freshmen with need received aid; of those 43% had need fully met. *Average percent of need met:* 84% (excluding resources awarded to replace EFC). *Average financial aid package:* $16,037 (excluding resources awarded to replace EFC). 18% of all full-time freshmen had no need and received non-need-based gift aid.
UNDERGRADUATE FINANCIAL AID (Fall 2005, est.) 848 applied for aid; of those 89% were deemed to have need. 100% of undergraduates with need received aid; of those 40% had need fully met. *Average percent of need met:* 83% (excluding resources awarded to replace EFC). *Average financial aid package:* $16,472 (excluding resources awarded to replace EFC). 18% of all full-time undergraduates had no need and received non-need-based gift aid.
GIFT AID (NEED-BASED) *Total amount:* $7,835,558 (8% federal, 4% state, 79% institutional, 9% external sources). *Receiving aid:* Freshmen: 81% (220); All full-time undergraduates: 80% (754). *Average award:* Freshmen: $11,566; Undergraduates: $10,328. *Scholarships, grants, and awards:* Federal Pell, FSEOG, state, private, college/university gift aid from institutional funds, Federal Nursing.
GIFT AID (NON-NEED-BASED) *Total amount:* $1,633,856 (85% institutional, 15% external sources). *Receiving aid:* Freshmen: 13% (35); Undergraduates: 9% (88). *Average Award:* Freshmen: $13,493; Undergraduates: $12,702. *Scholarships, grants, and awards by category: Academic Interests/Achievement:* 505 awards ($3,643,167 total): general academic interests/achievements. *Special Achievements/Activities:* 171 awards ($1,181,288 total): community service, religious involvement. *Special Characteristics:* 38 awards ($346,118 total): children of faculty/staff, siblings of current students, spouses of current students. *Tuition waivers:* Full or partial for employees or children of employees. *ROTC:* Army cooperative.
LOANS *Student loans:* $7,390,838 (61% need-based, 39% non-need-based). 96% of past graduating class borrowed through all loan programs. *Average indebtedness per student:* $28,195. *Average need-based loan:* Freshmen: $4524; Undergraduates: $6098. *Parent loans:* $2,123,013 (30% need-based, 70% non-need-based). *Programs:* FFEL (Subsidized and Unsubsidized Stafford, PLUS), Perkins, Federal Nursing, state.
WORK-STUDY *Federal work-study:* Total amount: $554,350; 400 jobs averaging $1386. *State or other work-study/employment:* Total amount: $5,032,932 (100% need-based).
APPLYING FOR FINANCIAL AID *Required financial aid forms:* FAFSA, institution's own form. *Financial aid deadline (priority):* 3/1. *Notification date:* Continuous beginning 3/1. Students must reply within 2 weeks of notification.
CONTACT Office of Financial Aid, Saint Joseph's College of Maine, 278 Whites Bridge Road, Standish, ME 04084-5263, 800-752-1266 or toll-free 800-338-7057. *Fax:* 207-893-6699. *E-mail:* finaid@sjcme.edu.

ST. JOSEPH'S COLLEGE, SUFFOLK CAMPUS
Patchogue, NY

Tuition & fees: $12,766   **Average undergraduate aid package:** $5414

ABOUT THE INSTITUTION Independent, coed. Awards: bachelor's and master's degrees. 34 undergraduate majors. Total enrollment: 4,146. Undergraduates: 3,861. Freshmen: 473. Federal methodology is used as a basis for awarding need-based institutional aid.
UNDERGRADUATE EXPENSES for 2005–06 *Application fee:* $25. *Tuition:* full-time $12,424; part-time $402 per credit. *Required fees:* full-time $342; $13 per credit or $207 per term part-time. Part-time tuition and fees vary according to course load. *Payment plan:* Installment.
FRESHMAN FINANCIAL AID (Fall 2005, est.) 419 applied for aid; of those 93% were deemed to have need. 100% of freshmen with need received aid; of those 74% had need fully met. *Average percent of need met:* 32% (excluding resources

awarded to replace EFC). *Average financial aid package:* $7638 (excluding resources awarded to replace EFC). 28% of all full-time freshmen had no need and received non-need-based gift aid.
UNDERGRADUATE FINANCIAL AID (Fall 2005, est.) 2,497 applied for aid; of those 93% were deemed to have need. 100% of undergraduates with need received aid; of those 80% had need fully met. *Average percent of need met:* 33% (excluding resources awarded to replace EFC). *Average financial aid package:* $5414 (excluding resources awarded to replace EFC). 19% of all full-time undergraduates had no need and received non-need-based gift aid.
GIFT AID (NEED-BASED) *Total amount:* $7,967,627 (20% federal, 41% state, 39% institutional). *Receiving aid:* Freshmen: 83% (388); All full-time undergraduates: 79% (2,317). *Average award:* Freshmen: $5630; Undergraduates: $3439. *Scholarships, grants, and awards:* Federal Pell, FSEOG, state, private, college/university gift aid from institutional funds.
GIFT AID (NON-NEED-BASED) *Total amount:* $3,090,649 (2% state, 95% institutional, 3% external sources). *Receiving aid:* Freshmen: 30% (141); Undergraduates: 22% (648). *Average Award:* Freshmen: $6399; Undergraduates: $5599. *Scholarships, grants, and awards by category: Academic Interests/Achievement:* 751 awards ($4,017,325 total): general academic interests/achievements. *Tuition waivers:* Full or partial for employees or children of employees, senior citizens. *ROTC:* Army cooperative, Air Force cooperative.
LOANS *Student loans:* $11,549,534 (47% need-based, 53% non-need-based). 79% of past graduating class borrowed through all loan programs. *Average indebtedness per student:* $15,014. *Average need-based loan:* Freshmen: $2584; Undergraduates: $1930. *Parent loans:* $4,274,398 (100% non-need-based). *Programs:* FFEL (Subsidized and Unsubsidized Stafford, PLUS), Perkins.
WORK-STUDY *Federal work-study:* Total amount: $105,438; 58 jobs averaging $2441. *State or other work-study/employment:* Total amount: $163,732 (100% non-need-based). 79 part-time jobs averaging $2073.
APPLYING FOR FINANCIAL AID *Required financial aid forms:* FAFSA, institution's own form, state aid form. *Financial aid deadline (priority):* 2/25. *Notification date:* 4/1. Students must reply within 3 weeks of notification.
CONTACT Joan Farley, Associate Director of Financial Aid, St. Joseph's College, Suffolk Campus, 155 West Roe Boulevard, Patchogue, NY 11772-2399, 631-447-3214 or toll-free 866-AT ST JOE (in-state). *Fax:* 631-447-1734.

SAINT JOSEPH SEMINARY COLLEGE
Saint Benedict, LA

CONTACT Betty Anne Burns, Financial Aid Officer, Saint Joseph Seminary College, Saint Benedict, LA 70457, 985-867-2229. *Fax:* 985-867-2270.

SAINT JOSEPH'S UNIVERSITY
Philadelphia, PA

Tuition & fees: $27,455 — Average undergraduate aid package: $13,301

ABOUT THE INSTITUTION Independent Roman Catholic (Jesuit), coed. Awards: associate, bachelor's, master's, and doctoral degrees and post-bachelor's and post-master's certificates. 53 undergraduate majors. Total enrollment: 7,714. Undergraduates: 5,143. Freshmen: 1,140. Federal methodology is used as a basis for awarding need-based institutional aid.
UNDERGRADUATE EXPENSES for 2005–06 *Application fee:* $55. *Comprehensive fee:* $37,428 includes full-time tuition ($27,320), mandatory fees ($135), and room and board ($9973). Full-time tuition and fees vary according to student level. Room and board charges vary according to board plan and housing facility. *Part-time tuition:* $895 per credit. *Payment plans:* Installment, deferred payment.
FRESHMAN FINANCIAL AID (Fall 2005, est.) 793 applied for aid; of those 75% were deemed to have need. 100% of freshmen with need received aid; of those 23% had need fully met. *Average percent of need met:* 79% (excluding resources awarded to replace EFC). *Average financial aid package:* $12,854 (excluding resources awarded to replace EFC). 21% of all full-time freshmen had no need and received non-need-based gift aid.
UNDERGRADUATE FINANCIAL AID (Fall 2005, est.) 2,471 applied for aid; of those 81% were deemed to have need. 100% of undergraduates with need received aid; of those 25% had need fully met. *Average percent of need met:* 80% (excluding resources awarded to replace EFC). *Average financial aid package:* $13,301 (excluding resources awarded to replace EFC). 22% of all full-time undergraduates had no need and received non-need-based gift aid.

GIFT AID (NEED-BASED) *Total amount:* $35,072,459 (5% federal, 4% state, 91% institutional). *Receiving aid:* Freshmen: 40% (449); All full-time undergraduates: 39% (1,624). *Average award:* Freshmen: $8729; Undergraduates: $7706. *Scholarships, grants, and awards:* Federal Pell, FSEOG, state, private, college/university gift aid from institutional funds.
GIFT AID (NON-NEED-BASED) *Total amount:* $913,378 (100% external sources). *Receiving aid:* Freshmen: 35% (390); Undergraduates: 38% (1,613). *Average Award:* Freshmen: $8321; Undergraduates: $7176. *Scholarships, grants, and awards by category: Academic Interests/Achievement:* $18,995,221 total: general academic interests/achievements. *Creative Arts/Performance:* 30 awards ($179,280 total): debating, theater/drama. *Special Characteristics:* 205 awards ($1,345,283 total): members of minority groups. *Tuition waivers:* Full or partial for employees or children of employees. *ROTC:* Army cooperative, Naval cooperative, Air Force.
LOANS *Student loans:* $34,123,292 (100% need-based). 71% of past graduating class borrowed through all loan programs. *Average indebtedness per student:* $16,120. *Average need-based loan:* Freshmen: $4125; Undergraduates: $4890. *Parent loans:* $13,134,320 (100% need-based). *Programs:* FFEL (Subsidized and Unsubsidized Stafford, PLUS), Perkins.
WORK-STUDY *Federal work-study:* Total amount: $500,000; 350 jobs averaging $949.
ATHLETIC AWARDS *Total amount:* $3,411,223 (100% need-based).
APPLYING FOR FINANCIAL AID *Required financial aid form:* FAFSA. *Financial aid deadline:* 5/1 (priority: 2/15). *Notification date:* Continuous beginning 2/15. Students must reply by 5/1.
CONTACT Eileen M. Tucker, Director of Financial Assistance, Saint Joseph's University, 5600 City Avenue, Philadelphia, PA 19131-1395, 610-660-1556 or toll-free 888-BEAHAWK (in-state). *Fax:* 610-660-1342. *E-mail:* tucker@sju.edu.

ST. LAWRENCE UNIVERSITY
Canton, NY

Tuition & fees: $32,150 — Average undergraduate aid package: $30,445

ABOUT THE INSTITUTION Independent, coed. Awards: bachelor's and master's degrees and post-master's certificates. 39 undergraduate majors. Total enrollment: 2,264. Undergraduates: 2,131. Freshmen: 535. Both federal and institutional methodology are used as a basis for awarding need-based institutional aid.
UNDERGRADUATE EXPENSES for 2005–06 *Application fee:* $50. *Comprehensive fee:* $40,330 includes full-time tuition ($31,935), mandatory fees ($215), and room and board ($8180). *College room only:* $4400. Room and board charges vary according to board plan. *Part-time tuition:* $3990 per course. *Payment plans:* Installment, deferred payment.
FRESHMAN FINANCIAL AID (Fall 2005, est.) 415 applied for aid; of those 90% were deemed to have need. 100% of freshmen with need received aid; of those 55% had need fully met. *Average percent of need met:* 95% (excluding resources awarded to replace EFC). *Average financial aid package:* $31,869 (excluding resources awarded to replace EFC). 12% of all full-time freshmen had no need and received non-need-based gift aid.
UNDERGRADUATE FINANCIAL AID (Fall 2005, est.) 1,700 applied for aid; of those 91% were deemed to have need. 90% of undergraduates with need received aid; of those 66% had need fully met. *Average percent of need met:* 92% (excluding resources awarded to replace EFC). *Average financial aid package:* $30,445 (excluding resources awarded to replace EFC). 14% of all full-time undergraduates had no need and received non-need-based gift aid.
GIFT AID (NEED-BASED) *Total amount:* $28,095,426 (6% federal, 6% state, 86% institutional, 2% external sources). *Receiving aid:* Freshmen: 69% (369); All full-time undergraduates: 64% (1,342). *Average award:* Freshmen: $19,303; Undergraduates: $16,983. *Scholarships, grants, and awards:* Federal Pell, FSEOG, state, college/university gift aid from institutional funds.
GIFT AID (NON-NEED-BASED) *Total amount:* $2,974,526 (98% institutional, 2% external sources). *Receiving aid:* Freshmen: 26% (140); Undergraduates: 26% (552). *Average Award:* Freshmen: $13,104; Undergraduates: $13,726. *Scholarships, grants, and awards by category: Academic Interests/Achievement:* 674 awards ($8,231,459 total): general academic interests/achievements. *Special Achievements/Activities:* 36 awards ($266,250 total): community service. *Special Characteristics:* 299 awards ($743,750 total): children and siblings of alumni, siblings of current students. *Tuition waivers:* Full or partial for employees or children of employees. *ROTC:* Army cooperative, Air Force cooperative.

St. Lawrence University

LOANS *Student loans:* $11,940,558 (44% need-based, 56% non-need-based). 76% of past graduating class borrowed through all loan programs. *Average indebtedness per student:* $26,274. *Average need-based loan:* Freshmen: $2878; Undergraduates: $4427. *Parent loans:* $4,392,313 (100% need-based). *Programs:* FFEL (Subsidized and Unsubsidized Stafford, PLUS), Perkins, college/university.
WORK-STUDY *Federal work-study:* Total amount: $1,206,464; 869 jobs averaging $1388. *State or other work-study/employment:* Total amount: $578,636 (100% non-need-based). 420 part-time jobs averaging $1378.
ATHLETIC AWARDS Total amount: $1,246,200 (100% non-need-based).
APPLYING FOR FINANCIAL AID *Required financial aid forms:* FAFSA, institution's own form, noncustodial (divorced/separated) parent's statement, either institution's own financial aid form or CSS/Financial Aid PROFILE, income tax returns/w2s. *Financial aid deadline:* 2/15. *Notification date:* 3/30. Students must reply by 5/1 or within 2 weeks of notification.
CONTACT Mrs. Patricia J. B. Farmer, Director of Financial Aid, St. Lawrence University, Payson Hall, Park Street, Canton, NY 13617-1455, 315-229-5265 or toll-free 800-285-1856. Fax: 315-229-5502. E-mail: pfarmer@stlawu.edu.

SAINT LEO UNIVERSITY
Saint Leo, FL

Tuition & fees: $14,680 | **Average undergraduate aid package: $15,485**

ABOUT THE INSTITUTION Independent Roman Catholic, coed. Awards: associate, bachelor's, and master's degrees. 25 undergraduate majors. Total enrollment: 2,263. Undergraduates: 1,384. Freshmen: 454. Federal methodology is used as a basis for awarding need-based institutional aid.
UNDERGRADUATE EXPENSES for 2005–06 *Application fee:* $35. *Comprehensive fee:* $22,140 includes full-time tuition ($14,250), mandatory fees ($430), and room and board ($7460). *College room only:* $3920. Full-time tuition and fees vary according to location. Room and board charges vary according to board plan and housing facility. Part-time tuition and fees vary according to location. *Payment plan:* Installment.
FRESHMAN FINANCIAL AID (Fall 2004) 398 applied for aid; of those 75% were deemed to have need. 100% of freshmen with need received aid; of those 35% had need fully met. *Average percent of need met:* 85% (excluding resources awarded to replace EFC). *Average financial aid package:* $15,223 (excluding resources awarded to replace EFC). 1% of all full-time freshmen had no need and received non-need-based gift aid.
UNDERGRADUATE FINANCIAL AID (Fall 2004) 1,172 applied for aid; of those 79% were deemed to have need. 99% of undergraduates with need received aid; of those 40% had need fully met. *Average percent of need met:* 86% (excluding resources awarded to replace EFC). *Average financial aid package:* $15,485 (excluding resources awarded to replace EFC). 2% of all full-time undergraduates had no need and received non-need-based gift aid.
GIFT AID (NEED-BASED) *Total amount:* $10,675,206 (12% federal, 22% state, 63% institutional, 3% external sources). *Receiving aid:* Freshmen: 66% (296); All full-time undergraduates: 68% (909). *Average award:* Freshmen: $10,787; Undergraduates: $10,666. *Scholarships, grants, and awards:* Federal Pell, FSEOG, state, private, college/university gift aid from institutional funds, United Negro College Fund.
GIFT AID (NON-NEED-BASED) *Total amount:* $1,306,716 (67% state, 16% institutional, 17% external sources). *Receiving aid:* Freshmen: 8% (36); Undergraduates: 8% (109). *Average Award:* Freshmen: $10,014; Undergraduates: $5845. *Tuition waivers:* Full or partial for employees or children of employees. *ROTC:* Army, Air Force cooperative.
LOANS *Student loans:* $6,501,232 (65% need-based, 35% non-need-based). 67% of past graduating class borrowed through all loan programs. *Average indebtedness per student:* $15,300. *Average need-based loan:* Freshmen: $2740; Undergraduates: $3684. *Parent loans:* $2,045,959 (38% need-based, 62% non-need-based). *Programs:* FFEL (Subsidized and Unsubsidized Stafford, PLUS), Perkins.
WORK-STUDY *Federal work-study:* Total amount: $1,300,708; 560 jobs averaging $2323.
ATHLETIC AWARDS Total amount: $1,063,295 (63% need-based, 37% non-need-based).
APPLYING FOR FINANCIAL AID *Required financial aid form:* FAFSA. *Financial aid deadline (priority):* 4/1. *Notification date:* Continuous beginning 1/31.

CONTACT Office of Student Financial Services, Saint Leo University, PO Box 6665, MC 2228, Saint Leo, FL 33574-6665, 800-240-7658 or toll-free 800-334-5532. Fax: 352-588-8403. E-mail: finaid@saintleo.edu.

ST. LOUIS CHRISTIAN COLLEGE
Florissant, MO

Tuition & fees: $8450 | **Average undergraduate aid package: $10,089**

ABOUT THE INSTITUTION Independent Christian, coed. Awards: associate and bachelor's degrees. 6 undergraduate majors. Total enrollment: 213. Undergraduates: 213. Freshmen: 26. Federal methodology is used as a basis for awarding need-based institutional aid.
UNDERGRADUATE EXPENSES for 2005–06 *Comprehensive fee:* $13,450 includes full-time tuition ($8000), mandatory fees ($450), and room and board ($5000). Room and board charges vary according to housing facility. *Part-time tuition:* $250 per credit. *Part-time fees:* $450 per semester hour.
FRESHMAN FINANCIAL AID (Fall 2005, est.) 35 applied for aid; of those 86% were deemed to have need. 100% of freshmen with need received aid; of those 20% had need fully met. *Average percent of need met:* 88% (excluding resources awarded to replace EFC). *Average financial aid package:* $11,150 (excluding resources awarded to replace EFC). 30% of all full-time freshmen had no need and received non-need-based gift aid.
UNDERGRADUATE FINANCIAL AID (Fall 2005, est.) 178 applied for aid; of those 89% were deemed to have need. 100% of undergraduates with need received aid; of those 23% had need fully met. *Average percent of need met:* 80% (excluding resources awarded to replace EFC). *Average financial aid package:* $10,089 (excluding resources awarded to replace EFC). 25% of all full-time undergraduates had no need and received non-need-based gift aid.
GIFT AID (NEED-BASED) *Total amount:* $1,289,637 (21% federal, 74% institutional, 5% external sources). *Receiving aid:* Freshmen: 70% (30); All full-time undergraduates: 75% (159). *Average award:* Freshmen: $8536; Undergraduates: $7784. *Scholarships, grants, and awards:* Federal Pell, FSEOG, private, college/university gift aid from institutional funds.
GIFT AID (NON-NEED-BASED) *Total amount:* $322,225 (92% institutional, 8% external sources). *Average Award:* Freshmen: $6739; Undergraduates: $5727. *Scholarships, grants, and awards by category:* Academic Interests/Achievement: 14 awards ($21,000 total). Special Characteristics: 3 awards ($14,000 total): children of faculty/staff, general special characteristics. *Tuition waivers:* Full or partial for employees or children of employees.
LOANS *Student loans:* $664,176 (92% need-based, 8% non-need-based). 44% of past graduating class borrowed through all loan programs. *Average indebtedness per student:* $14,585. *Average need-based loan:* Freshmen: $1683; Undergraduates: $2152. *Parent loans:* $45,000 (69% need-based, 31% non-need-based). *Programs:* FFEL (Subsidized and Unsubsidized Stafford, PLUS).
WORK-STUDY *Federal work-study:* Total amount: $14,300; 13 jobs averaging $1100. *State or other work-study/employment:* Total amount: $100,000 (100% non-need-based). 20 part-time jobs averaging $5000.
APPLYING FOR FINANCIAL AID *Required financial aid forms:* FAFSA, institution's own form. *Notification date:* Continuous.
CONTACT Mrs. Catherine Wilhoit, Director of Financial Aid, St. Louis Christian College, 1360 Grandview Drive, Florissant, MO 63033-6499, 314-837-6777 Ext. 1101 or toll-free 800-887-SLCC. Fax: 314-837-8291.

ST. LOUIS COLLEGE OF PHARMACY
St. Louis, MO

Tuition & fees: $19,180 | **Average undergraduate aid package: $10,199**

ABOUT THE INSTITUTION Independent, coed. Awards: master's and first professional degrees. 1 undergraduate major. Total enrollment: 1,093. Federal methodology is used as a basis for awarding need-based institutional aid.
UNDERGRADUATE EXPENSES for 2006–07 *Application fee:* $50. *Comprehensive fee:* $26,690 includes full-time tuition ($18,900), mandatory fees ($280), and room and board ($7510). *Part-time tuition:* $810 per credit.
FRESHMAN FINANCIAL AID (Fall 2005, est.) 216 applied for aid; of those 76% were deemed to have need. 98% of freshmen with need received aid; of those 20% had need fully met. *Average percent of need met:* 61% (excluding resources

awarded to replace EFC). *Average financial aid package:* $11,023 (excluding resources awarded to replace EFC). 36% of all full-time freshmen had no need and received non-need-based gift aid.
UNDERGRADUATE FINANCIAL AID (Fall 2005, est.) 573 applied for aid; of those 82% were deemed to have need. 96% of undergraduates with need received aid; of those 15% had need fully met. *Average percent of need met:* 52% (excluding resources awarded to replace EFC). *Average financial aid package:* $10,199 (excluding resources awarded to replace EFC). 26% of all full-time undergraduates had no need and received non-need-based gift aid.
GIFT AID (NEED-BASED) Total amount: $2,234,099 (17% federal, 66% institutional, 17% external sources). *Receiving aid:* Freshmen: 72% (161); All full-time undergraduates: 59% (372). *Average award:* Freshmen: $7549; Undergraduates: $6547. *Scholarships, grants, and awards:* Federal Pell, FSEOG, state, private, college/university gift aid from institutional funds.
GIFT AID (NON-NEED-BASED) Total amount: $1,502,138 (25% federal, 64% institutional, 11% external sources). *Receiving aid:* Freshmen: 14% (31); Undergraduates: 8% (50). *Average Award:* Freshmen: $12,145; Undergraduates: $12,775. *Scholarships, grants, and awards by category: Academic Interests/Achievement:* 404 awards ($214,556 total): general academic interests/achievements. *Special Achievements/Activities:* community service, leadership. *Special Characteristics:* 24 awards ($57,760 total): children of faculty/staff, local/state students. *ROTC:* Army cooperative, Air Force cooperative.
LOANS Student loans: $5,105,821 (71% need-based, 29% non-need-based). 85% of past graduating class borrowed through all loan programs. *Average indebtedness per student:* $80,000. *Average need-based loan:* Freshmen: $4184; Undergraduates: $5214. *Parent loans:* $2,664,375 (39% need-based, 61% non-need-based). *Programs:* FFEL (Subsidized and Unsubsidized Stafford, PLUS), Perkins, Federal Health Professions Loan.
WORK-STUDY Federal work-study: Total amount: $126,321; 105 jobs averaging $1200.
APPLYING FOR FINANCIAL AID *Required financial aid forms:* FAFSA, institution's own form. *Financial aid deadline (priority):* 3/15. *Notification date:* Continuous beginning 2/1. Students must reply within 2 weeks of notification.
CONTACT Mr. David Rice, Director of Financial Aid, St. Louis College of Pharmacy, 4588 Parkview Place, St. Louis, MO 63110, 314-446-8320 or toll-free 800-278-5267 (in-state). *Fax:* 314-446-8310. *E-mail:* drice@stlcop.edu.

SAINT LOUIS UNIVERSITY
St. Louis, MO

Tuition & fees: $26,448   **Average undergraduate aid package:** $18,858

ABOUT THE INSTITUTION Independent Roman Catholic (Jesuit), coed. Awards: bachelor's, master's, doctoral, and first professional degrees and post-bachelor's and post-master's certificates. 72 undergraduate majors. Total enrollment: 11,823. Undergraduates: 7,421. Freshmen: 1,690. Federal methodology is used as a basis for awarding need-based institutional aid.
UNDERGRADUATE EXPENSES for 2006–07 *Application fee:* $25. *Comprehensive fee:* $34,678 includes full-time tuition ($26,250), mandatory fees ($198), and room and board ($8230). *College room only:* $4700.
FRESHMAN FINANCIAL AID (Fall 2005, est.) 1215 applied for aid; of those 79% were deemed to have need. 100% of freshmen with need received aid; of those 18% had need fully met. *Average percent of need met:* 62% (excluding resources awarded to replace EFC). *Average financial aid package:* $19,543 (excluding resources awarded to replace EFC). 29% of all full-time freshmen had no need and received non-need-based gift aid.
UNDERGRADUATE FINANCIAL AID (Fall 2005, est.) 4,800 applied for aid; of those 83% were deemed to have need. 99% of undergraduates with need received aid; of those 19% had need fully met. *Average percent of need met:* 59% (excluding resources awarded to replace EFC). *Average financial aid package:* $18,858 (excluding resources awarded to replace EFC). 24% of all full-time undergraduates had no need and received non-need-based gift aid.
GIFT AID (NEED-BASED) Total amount: $51,292,929 (10% federal, 5% state, 80% institutional, 5% external sources). *Receiving aid:* Freshmen: 61% (921); All full-time undergraduates: 57% (3,787). *Average award:* Freshmen: $14,325; Undergraduates: $12,875. *Scholarships, grants, and awards:* Federal Pell, FSEOG, state, private, college/university gift aid from institutional funds.
GIFT AID (NON-NEED-BASED) Total amount: $17,610,925 (2% state, 79% institutional, 19% external sources). *Receiving aid:* Freshmen: 7% (107); Undergraduates: 5% (309). *Average Award:* Freshmen: $9972; Undergraduates: $9455. *Scholarships, grants, and awards by category: Academic Interests/Achievement:* 3,956 awards ($28,947,115 total): area/ethnic studies, biological sciences, business, communication, computer science, education, engineering/technologies, English, foreign languages, general academic interests/achievements, health fields, humanities, international studies, mathematics, military science, physical sciences, premedicine, religion/biblical studies, social sciences. *Creative Arts/Performance:* 125 awards ($104,180 total): art/fine arts, music, performing arts, theater/drama. *Special Achievements/Activities:* 440 awards ($4,780,908 total): cheerleading/drum major, community service, general special achievements/activities, leadership, memberships. *Special Characteristics:* 941 awards ($10,692,131 total): children of faculty/staff, first-generation college students, general special characteristics, international students, members of minority groups, previous college experience, siblings of current students. *ROTC:* Army cooperative, Air Force.
LOANS Student loans: $34,363,912 (84% need-based, 16% non-need-based). 67% of past graduating class borrowed through all loan programs. *Average indebtedness per student:* $24,552. *Average need-based loan:* Freshmen: $2599; Undergraduates: $4192. *Parent loans:* $13,251,886 (64% need-based, 36% non-need-based). *Programs:* FFEL (Subsidized and Unsubsidized Stafford, PLUS), Perkins, Federal Nursing.
WORK-STUDY Federal work-study: Total amount: $3,245,812; 846 jobs averaging $3837. *State or other work-study/employment:* Total amount: $225,284 (59% need-based, 41% non-need-based). 69 part-time jobs averaging $1937.
ATHLETIC AWARDS Total amount: $2,835,252 (32% need-based, 68% non-need-based).
APPLYING FOR FINANCIAL AID *Required financial aid form:* FAFSA. *Financial aid deadline (priority):* 3/1. *Notification date:* Continuous beginning 3/1. Students must reply by 5/1 or within 4 weeks of notification.
CONTACT Cari Wickliffe, Director of Scholarship and Financial Aid, Saint Louis University, 221 North Grand Boulevard, Room 121, St. Louis, MO 63103-2097, 314-977-2350 or toll-free 800-758-3678 (out-of-state). *Fax:* 314-977-3437. *E-mail:* wicklics@slu.edu.

SAINT LUKE'S COLLEGE
Kansas City, MO

CONTACT Jeff Gannon, Director of Financial Aid, Saint Luke's College, 8320 Ward Parkway, Suite 300, Kansas City, MO 64114, 816-932-2194. *Fax:* 816-932-9064. *E-mail:* jgannon@saint-lukes.org.

SAINT MARTIN'S UNIVERSITY
Lacey, WA

Tuition & fees: $20,965   **Average undergraduate aid package:** $17,572

ABOUT THE INSTITUTION Independent Roman Catholic, coed. Awards: bachelor's and master's degrees and post-bachelor's certificates. 31 undergraduate majors. Total enrollment: 1,463. Undergraduates: 1,180. Freshmen: 172. Federal methodology is used as a basis for awarding need-based institutional aid.
UNDERGRADUATE EXPENSES for 2006–07 *Application fee:* $35. *Comprehensive fee:* $27,365 includes full-time tuition ($20,675), mandatory fees ($290), and room and board ($6400). *College room only:* $3000. *Part-time tuition:* $689 per credit. *Part-time fees:* $145 per term.
FRESHMAN FINANCIAL AID (Fall 2005, est.) 123 applied for aid; of those 87% were deemed to have need. 100% of freshmen with need received aid; of those 47% had need fully met. *Average percent of need met:* 94% (excluding resources awarded to replace EFC). *Average financial aid package:* $19,549 (excluding resources awarded to replace EFC). 18% of all full-time freshmen had no need and received non-need-based gift aid.
UNDERGRADUATE FINANCIAL AID (Fall 2005, est.) 750 applied for aid; of those 91% were deemed to have need. 100% of undergraduates with need received aid; of those 34% had need fully met. *Average percent of need met:* 85% (excluding resources awarded to replace EFC). *Average financial aid package:* $17,572 (excluding resources awarded to replace EFC). 14% of all full-time undergraduates had no need and received non-need-based gift aid.
GIFT AID (NEED-BASED) Total amount: $8,533,034 (14% federal, 16% state, 46% institutional, 24% external sources). *Receiving aid:* Freshmen: 82% (107); All full-time undergraduates: 83% (659). *Average award:* Freshmen: $14,876; Undergraduates: $11,679. *Scholarships, grants, and awards:* Federal Pell, FSEOG, state, private, college/university gift aid from institutional funds.

Saint Martin's University

GIFT AID (NON-NEED-BASED) *Total amount:* $897,765 (4% state, 70% institutional, 26% external sources). *Receiving aid:* Freshmen: 9% (12); Undergraduates: 8% (64). *Average Award:* Freshmen: $10,207; Undergraduates: $9545. *Scholarships, grants, and awards by category: Academic Interests/Achievement:* business, education, engineering/technologies, general academic interests/achievements, humanities. *Creative Arts/Performance:* music, performing arts, theater/drama. *Special Achievements/Activities:* community service, leadership, memberships. *Special Characteristics:* children and siblings of alumni, children of current students, children of faculty/staff, ethnic background, general special characteristics, international students, local/state students, members of minority groups, religious affiliation, siblings of current students, spouses of current students. *ROTC:* Army cooperative.
LOANS *Student loans:* $7,196,144 (73% need-based, 27% non-need-based). 60% of past graduating class borrowed through all loan programs. *Average indebtedness per student:* $27,846. *Average need-based loan:* Freshmen: $3448; Undergraduates: $5197. *Parent loans:* $802,152 (17% need-based, 83% non-need-based). *Programs:* Federal Direct (Subsidized and Unsubsidized Stafford), FFEL (PLUS), Perkins, college/university.
WORK-STUDY *Federal work-study:* Total amount: $435,168; 191 jobs averaging $1875. *State or other work-study/employment:* Total amount: $964,444 (89% need-based, 11% non-need-based). 175 part-time jobs averaging $1893.
ATHLETIC AWARDS *Total amount:* $460,435 (67% need-based, 33% non-need-based).
APPLYING FOR FINANCIAL AID *Required financial aid forms:* FAFSA, admissions application. *Financial aid deadline (priority):* 3/1. *Notification date:* Continuous beginning 2/15. Students must reply within 3 weeks of notification.
CONTACT Director of Financial Aid (Interim), Saint Martin's University, 5300 Pacific Avenue, SE, Lacey, WA 98503-1297, 360-438-4463 or toll-free 800-368-8803. *Fax:* 360-459-4124. *E-mail:* rwonderly@stmartins.edu.

SAINT MARY-OF-THE-WOODS COLLEGE
Saint Mary-of-the-Woods, IN

CONTACT Ms. Jan Benton, Director of Financial Aid, Saint Mary-of-the-Woods College, 106 Guerin Hall, Saint Mary-of-the-Woods, IN 47876, 812-535-5106 or toll-free 800-926-SMWC. *Fax:* 812-535-4900. *E-mail:* jbenton@smwc.edu.

SAINT MARY'S COLLEGE
Notre Dame, IN

Tuition & fees: $25,580   **Average undergraduate aid package:** $18,964

ABOUT THE INSTITUTION Independent Roman Catholic, women only. Awards: bachelor's degrees. 36 undergraduate majors. Total enrollment: 1,397. Undergraduates: 1,397. Freshmen: 377. Both federal and institutional methodology are used as a basis for awarding need-based institutional aid.
UNDERGRADUATE EXPENSES for 2006–07 *Application fee:* $30. *Comprehensive fee:* $34,005 includes full-time tuition ($25,030), mandatory fees ($550), and room and board ($8425). *College room only:* $5190. *Part-time tuition:* $989 per semester hour.
FRESHMAN FINANCIAL AID (Fall 2005, est.) 306 applied for aid; of those 86% were deemed to have need. 100% of freshmen with need received aid; of those 26% had need fully met. *Average percent of need met:* 80% (excluding resources awarded to replace EFC). *Average financial aid package:* $18,878 (excluding resources awarded to replace EFC). 24% of all full-time freshmen had no need and received non-need-based gift aid.
UNDERGRADUATE FINANCIAL AID (Fall 2005, est.) 1,071 applied for aid; of those 93% were deemed to have need. 100% of undergraduates with need received aid; of those 19% had need fully met. *Average percent of need met:* 77% (excluding resources awarded to replace EFC). *Average financial aid package:* $18,964 (excluding resources awarded to replace EFC). 21% of all full-time undergraduates had no need and received non-need-based gift aid.
GIFT AID (NEED-BASED) *Total amount:* $9,583,819 (7% federal, 10% state, 79% institutional, 4% external sources). *Receiving aid:* Freshmen: 57% (216); All full-time undergraduates: 61% (867). *Average award:* Freshmen: $9557; Undergraduates: $9405. *Scholarships, grants, and awards:* Federal Pell, FSEOG, state, private, college/university gift aid from institutional funds.
GIFT AID (NON-NEED-BASED) *Total amount:* $5,386,337 (1% state, 82% institutional, 17% external sources). *Receiving aid:* Freshmen: 37% (140); Undergraduates: 31% (447). *Average Award:* Freshmen: $8055; Undergraduates: $7845. *Scholarships, grants, and awards by category: Academic Interests/Achievement:* 960 awards ($6,320,760 total): general academic interests/achievements. *Creative Arts/Performance:* 16 awards ($43,500 total): art/fine arts, music, theater/drama. *Special Achievements/Activities:* 1 award ($1875 total): community service. *Special Characteristics:* 119 awards ($1,429,088 total): children of faculty/staff, siblings of current students. *ROTC:* Army cooperative, Naval cooperative, Air Force cooperative.
LOANS *Student loans:* $6,759,287 (52% need-based, 48% non-need-based). 68% of past graduating class borrowed through all loan programs. *Average indebtedness per student:* $24,617. *Average need-based loan:* Freshmen: $2436; Undergraduates: $2961. *Parent loans:* $654,544 (100% need-based). *Programs:* FFEL (Subsidized and Unsubsidized Stafford, PLUS), Perkins, college/university.
WORK-STUDY *Federal work-study:* Total amount: $371,451; 305 jobs averaging $1218. *State or other work-study/employment:* Total amount: $1,073,444 (46% need-based, 54% non-need-based). 671 part-time jobs averaging $1600.
APPLYING FOR FINANCIAL AID *Required financial aid forms:* FAFSA, CSS Financial Aid PROFILE. *Financial aid deadline (priority):* 3/1. *Notification date:* Continuous. Students must reply by 5/1.
CONTACT Kathleen M. Brown, Director of Financial Aid, Saint Mary's College, 141 Le Mans Hall, Notre Dame, IN 46556, 574-284-4557 or toll-free 800-551-7621. *Fax:* 574-284-4707. *E-mail:* kbrown@saintmarys.edu.

SAINT MARY'S COLLEGE OF CALIFORNIA
Moraga, CA

Tuition & fees: $27,280   **Average undergraduate aid package:** $20,858

ABOUT THE INSTITUTION Independent Roman Catholic, coed. Awards: bachelor's, master's, and doctoral degrees. 69 undergraduate majors. Total enrollment: 4,432. Undergraduates: 3,291. Freshmen: 675. Federal methodology is used as a basis for awarding need-based institutional aid.
UNDERGRADUATE EXPENSES for 2005–06 *Application fee:* $55. *Comprehensive fee:* $37,290 includes full-time tuition ($27,130), mandatory fees ($150), and room and board ($10,010). *College room only:* $5590. Full-time tuition and fees vary according to course load. Room and board charges vary according to board plan and housing facility. *Part-time tuition:* $3392 per course. Part-time tuition and fees vary according to course load. *Payment plan:* Installment.
FRESHMAN FINANCIAL AID (Fall 2005, est.) 513 applied for aid; of those 83% were deemed to have need. 100% of freshmen with need received aid; of those 8% had need fully met. *Average percent of need met:* 71% (excluding resources awarded to replace EFC). *Average financial aid package:* $20,109 (excluding resources awarded to replace EFC). 3% of all full-time freshmen had no need and received non-need-based gift aid.
UNDERGRADUATE FINANCIAL AID (Fall 2005, est.) 1,776 applied for aid; of those 90% were deemed to have need. 99% of undergraduates with need received aid; of those 8% had need fully met. *Average percent of need met:* 72% (excluding resources awarded to replace EFC). *Average financial aid package:* $20,858 (excluding resources awarded to replace EFC). 3% of all full-time undergraduates had no need and received non-need-based gift aid.
GIFT AID (NEED-BASED) *Total amount:* $22,570,555 (11% federal, 23% state, 65% institutional, 1% external sources). *Receiving aid:* Freshmen: 58% (392); All full-time undergraduates: 56% (1,404). *Average award:* Freshmen: $16,812; Undergraduates: $16,898. *Scholarships, grants, and awards:* Federal Pell, FSEOG, state, private, college/university gift aid from institutional funds.
GIFT AID (NON-NEED-BASED) *Total amount:* $1,143,355 (77% institutional, 23% external sources). *Receiving aid:* Freshmen: 9% (59); Undergraduates: 9% (215). *Average Award:* Freshmen: $8591; Undergraduates: $7454. *Scholarships, grants, and awards by category: Academic Interests/Achievement:* 330 awards ($2,167,788 total): general academic interests/achievements. *Special Achievements/Activities:* 37 awards ($232,000 total): memberships. *Special Characteristics:* 61 awards ($1,399,235 total): children and siblings of alumni, children of educators, children of faculty/staff, general special characteristics, relatives of clergy. *Tuition waivers:* Full or partial for employees or children of employees. *ROTC:* Army cooperative, Air Force cooperative.
LOANS *Student loans:* $14,841,776 (64% need-based, 36% non-need-based). 62% of past graduating class borrowed through all loan programs. *Average indebtedness per student:* $21,892. *Average need-based loan:* Freshmen: $2986; Undergraduates: $4535. *Parent loans:* $7,115,530 (17% need-based, 83% non-need-based). *Programs:* FFEL (Subsidized and Unsubsidized Stafford, PLUS), Perkins.

WORK-STUDY *Federal work-study:* Total amount: $1,063,408; 478 jobs averaging $2220.
ATHLETIC AWARDS *Total amount:* $3,753,596 (45% need-based, 55% non-need-based).
APPLYING FOR FINANCIAL AID *Required financial aid forms:* FAFSA, state aid form. *Financial aid deadline:* 3/2. *Notification date:* Continuous beginning 3/30. Students must reply by 5/1 or within 2 weeks of notification.
CONTACT Linda Judge, Director of Financial Aid, Saint Mary's College of California, PO Box 4530, Moraga, CA 94575, 925-631-4370 or toll-free 800-800-4SMC. *Fax:* 925-376-2965. *E-mail:* finaid@stmarys-ca.edu.

ST. MARY'S COLLEGE OF MARYLAND
St. Mary's City, MD

ABOUT THE INSTITUTION State-supported, coed. Awards: bachelor's degrees. 23 undergraduate majors. Total enrollment: 1,964. Undergraduates: 1,964. Freshmen: 488.
GIFT AID (NEED-BASED) *Scholarships, grants, and awards:* Federal Pell, FSEOG, state, private, college/university gift aid from institutional funds.
GIFT AID (NON-NEED-BASED) *Scholarships, grants, and awards by category: Academic Interests/Achievement:* general academic interests/achievements. *Special Characteristics:* children and siblings of alumni, children of faculty/staff.
LOANS *Programs:* FFEL (Subsidized and Unsubsidized Stafford, PLUS), Perkins.
WORK-STUDY *Federal work-study:* Total amount: $123,976; 105 jobs averaging $794. *State or other work-study/employment:* Part-time jobs available.
APPLYING FOR FINANCIAL AID *Required financial aid form:* FAFSA.
CONTACT Tim Wolfe, Director of Financial Aid, St. Mary's College of Maryland, 18952 East Fisher Road, St. Mary's City, MD 20686-3001, 240-895-3000 or toll-free 800-492-7181. *Fax:* 240-895-4959. *E-mail:* tawolfe@smcm.edu.

SAINT MARY'S UNIVERSITY OF MINNESOTA
Winona, MN

| Tuition & fees: $20,739 | Average undergraduate aid package: $14,833 |

ABOUT THE INSTITUTION Independent Roman Catholic, coed. Awards: bachelor's, master's, and doctoral degrees and post-bachelor's and post-master's certificates. 61 undergraduate majors. Total enrollment: 5,222. Undergraduates: 1,680. Freshmen: 311. Federal methodology is used as a basis for awarding need-based institutional aid.
UNDERGRADUATE EXPENSES for 2006–07 *Application fee:* $25. *Comprehensive fee:* $26,639 includes full-time tuition ($20,294), mandatory fees ($445), and room and board ($5900). *College room only:* $3300.
FRESHMAN FINANCIAL AID (Fall 2005, est.) 250 applied for aid; of those 85% were deemed to have need. 100% of freshmen with need received aid; of those 61% had need fully met. *Average percent of need met:* 94% (excluding resources awarded to replace EFC). *Average financial aid package:* $13,925 (excluding resources awarded to replace EFC). 19% of all full-time freshmen had no need and received non-need-based gift aid.
UNDERGRADUATE FINANCIAL AID (Fall 2005, est.) 1,115 applied for aid; of those 90% were deemed to have need. 100% of undergraduates with need received aid; of those 61% had need fully met. *Average percent of need met:* 89% (excluding resources awarded to replace EFC). *Average financial aid package:* $14,833 (excluding resources awarded to replace EFC). 15% of all full-time undergraduates had no need and received non-need-based gift aid.
GIFT AID (NEED-BASED) *Total amount:* $9,510,061 (11% federal, 8% state, 79% institutional, 2% external sources). *Receiving aid:* Freshmen: 68% (213); All full-time undergraduates: 79% (1,003). *Average award:* Freshmen: $8350; Undergraduates: $7900. *Scholarships, grants, and awards:* Federal Pell, FSEOG, state.
GIFT AID (NON-NEED-BASED) *Average Award:* Freshmen: $6953; Undergraduates: $7404. *Scholarships, grants, and awards by category: Academic Interests/Achievement:* 607 awards ($3,456,300 total): general academic interests/achievements. *Creative Arts/Performance:* 103 awards ($198,500 total): music, theater/drama. *Special Achievements/Activities:* 320 awards ($531,625 total): leadership. *Special Characteristics:* 170 awards ($933,559 total): children and siblings of alumni, children of faculty/staff, members of minority groups. *ROTC:* Army cooperative.

LOANS *Student loans:* $7,127,719 (100% need-based). 73% of past graduating class borrowed through all loan programs. *Average indebtedness per student:* $26,633. *Average need-based loan:* Freshmen: $4375; Undergraduates: $5633. *Parent loans:* $1,396,254 (100% need-based). *Programs:* FFEL (Subsidized and Unsubsidized Stafford, PLUS), Perkins, state, Signature Loans.
WORK-STUDY *Federal work-study:* Total amount: $276,892; 173 jobs averaging $1051. *State or other work-study/employment:* Total amount: $437,262 (100% need-based). 252 part-time jobs averaging $926.
APPLYING FOR FINANCIAL AID *Required financial aid forms:* FAFSA, Donor form. *Financial aid deadline (priority):* 4/1. *Notification date:* Continuous beginning 1/1. Students must reply within 2 weeks of notification.
CONTACT Ms. Jayne P. Wobig, Director of Financial Aid, Saint Mary's University of Minnesota, 700 Terrace Heights, #5, Winona, MN 55987-1399, 507-457-1437 or toll-free 800-635-5987. *Fax:* 507-457-6698. *E-mail:* jwobig@smumn.edu.

ST. MARY'S UNIVERSITY OF SAN ANTONIO
San Antonio, TX

ABOUT THE INSTITUTION Independent Roman Catholic, coed. Awards: bachelor's, master's, doctoral, and first professional degrees. 46 undergraduate majors. Total enrollment: 3,963. Undergraduates: 2,423. Freshmen: 494.
GIFT AID (NEED-BASED) *Scholarships, grants, and awards:* Federal Pell, FSEOG, state, private, college/university gift aid from institutional funds.
GIFT AID (NON-NEED-BASED) *Scholarships, grants, and awards by category: Academic Interests/Achievement:* general academic interests/achievements, military science. *Creative Arts/Performance:* music. *Special Achievements/Activities:* cheerleading/drum major.
LOANS *Programs:* FFEL (Subsidized and Unsubsidized Stafford, PLUS), Perkins, state, alternative loans.
WORK-STUDY *Federal work-study:* Total amount: $1,509,795; 535 jobs averaging $2822. *State or other work-study/employment:* Total amount: $386,260 (100% non-need-based). 184 part-time jobs averaging $2099.
APPLYING FOR FINANCIAL AID *Required financial aid form:* FAFSA.
CONTACT Mr. David R. Krause, Director of Financial Assistance, St. Mary's University of San Antonio, One Camino Santa Maria, San Antonio, TX 78228-8541, 210-436-3141 or toll-free 800-FOR-STMU. *Fax:* 210-431-2221. *E-mail:* dkrause@alvin.stmarytx.edu.

SAINT MICHAEL'S COLLEGE
Colchester, VT

ABOUT THE INSTITUTION Independent Roman Catholic, coed. Awards: bachelor's and master's degrees and post-bachelor's and post-master's certificates. 35 undergraduate majors. Total enrollment: 2,474. Undergraduates: 2,006. Freshmen: 592.
GIFT AID (NEED-BASED) *Scholarships, grants, and awards:* Federal Pell, FSEOG, state, private, college/university gift aid from institutional funds.
GIFT AID (NON-NEED-BASED) *Scholarships, grants, and awards by category: Academic Interests/Achievement:* general academic interests/achievements. *Creative Arts/Performance:* art/fine arts. *Special Characteristics:* local/state students, members of minority groups, out-of-state students, religious affiliation, siblings of current students.
LOANS *Programs:* FFEL (Subsidized and Unsubsidized Stafford, PLUS), Perkins.
WORK-STUDY *Federal work-study:* Total amount: $400,950; 150 jobs averaging $2000. *State or other work-study/employment:* Total amount: $974,425 (100% need-based). Part-time jobs available (averaging $1500).
APPLYING FOR FINANCIAL AID *Required financial aid form:* federal income tax forms (student and parent).
CONTACT Mrs. Nelberta B. Lunde, Director of Financial Aid, Saint Michael's College, Winooski Park, Colchester, VT 05439, 802-654-3243 or toll-free 800-762-8000. *Fax:* 802-654-2591. *E-mail:* finaid@smcvt.edu.

ST. NORBERT COLLEGE
De Pere, WI

| Tuition & fees: $22,509 | Average undergraduate aid package: $16,729 |

St. Norbert College

ABOUT THE INSTITUTION Independent Roman Catholic, coed. Awards: bachelor's and master's degrees. 31 undergraduate majors. Total enrollment: 2,050. Undergraduates: 1,987. Freshmen: 511. Federal methodology is used as a basis for awarding need-based institutional aid.

UNDERGRADUATE EXPENSES for 2005–06 *Application fee:* $25. *Comprehensive fee:* $28,577 includes full-time tuition ($22,209), mandatory fees ($300), and room and board ($6068). *College room only:* $3212. Full-time tuition and fees vary according to course load. Room and board charges vary according to board plan, housing facility, and student level. *Part-time tuition:* $694 per credit. Part-time tuition and fees vary according to course load. *Payment plans:* Installment, deferred payment.

FRESHMAN FINANCIAL AID (Fall 2004) 416 applied for aid; of those 83% were deemed to have need. 100% of freshmen with need received aid; of those 36% had need fully met. *Average percent of need met:* 88% (excluding resources awarded to replace EFC). *Average financial aid package:* $16,937 (excluding resources awarded to replace EFC). 29% of all full-time freshmen had no need and received non-need-based gift aid.

UNDERGRADUATE FINANCIAL AID (Fall 2004) 1,464 applied for aid; of those 86% were deemed to have need. 100% of undergraduates with need received aid; of those 39% had need fully met. *Average percent of need met:* 86% (excluding resources awarded to replace EFC). *Average financial aid package:* $16,729 (excluding resources awarded to replace EFC). 31% of all full-time undergraduates had no need and received non-need-based gift aid.

GIFT AID (NEED-BASED) *Total amount:* $14,503,885 (9% federal, 10% state, 78% institutional, 3% external sources). *Receiving aid:* Freshmen: 66% (344); All full-time undergraduates: 64% (1,253). *Average award:* Freshmen: $12,740; Undergraduates: $11,568. *Scholarships, grants, and awards:* Federal Pell, FSEOG, state, private, college/university gift aid from institutional funds.

GIFT AID (NON-NEED-BASED) *Total amount:* $3,722,270 (1% federal, 93% institutional, 6% external sources). *Receiving aid:* Freshmen: 9% (49); Undergraduates: 7% (133). *Average Award: Freshmen:* $10,414; *Undergraduates:* $9848. *Scholarships, grants, and awards by category: Academic Interests/Achievement:* 1,469 awards ($7,371,738 total): general academic interests/achievements. *Creative Arts/Performance:* 71 awards ($125,600 total): art/fine arts, music, theater/drama. *Special Characteristics:* 170 awards ($1,545,411 total): children of faculty/staff, children with a deceased or disabled parent, ethnic background, international students. *Tuition waivers:* Full or partial for employees or children of employees. *ROTC:* Army.

LOANS *Student loans:* $9,686,162 (87% need-based, 13% non-need-based). 65% of past graduating class borrowed through all loan programs. *Average indebtedness per student:* $24,808. *Average need-based loan:* Freshmen: $3881; Undergraduates: $5114. *Parent loans:* $1,670,164 (73% need-based, 27% non-need-based). *Programs:* Federal Direct (Subsidized and Unsubsidized Stafford, PLUS), Perkins, college/university.

WORK-STUDY *Federal work-study:* Total amount: $665,531; 502 jobs averaging $828. *State or other work-study/employment:* Total amount: $1,290,290 (56% need-based, 44% non-need-based). 938 part-time jobs averaging $1159.

APPLYING FOR FINANCIAL AID *Required financial aid forms:* FAFSA, institution's own form. *Financial aid deadline (priority):* 3/1. *Notification date:* Continuous beginning 3/15. Students must reply within 2 weeks of notification.

CONTACT Mr. Jeffrey A. Zahn, Director of Financial Aid, St. Norbert College, 100 Grant Street, De Pere, WI 54115-2099, 920-403-3071 or toll-free 800-236-4878. *Fax:* 920-403-3062. *E-mail:* jeff.zahn@snc.edu.

ST. OLAF COLLEGE
Northfield, MN

ABOUT THE INSTITUTION Independent Lutheran, coed. Awards: bachelor's degrees. 50 undergraduate majors. Total enrollment: 3,058. Undergraduates: 3,058. Freshmen: 764.

GIFT AID (NEED-BASED) *Scholarships, grants, and awards:* Federal Pell, FSEOG, state, private, college/university gift aid from institutional funds.

GIFT AID (NON-NEED-BASED) *Scholarships, grants, and awards by category: Academic Interests/Achievement:* general academic interests/achievements. *Creative Arts/Performance:* music. *Special Achievements/Activities:* community service, religious involvement. *Special Characteristics:* international students.

LOANS *Programs:* FFEL (Subsidized and Unsubsidized Stafford, PLUS), Perkins, Federal Nursing, state, college/university.

WORK-STUDY *Federal work-study:* Total amount: $2,123,555; 1,101 jobs averaging $1929. *State or other work-study/employment:* Total amount: $1,516,441 (77% need-based, 23% non-need-based). 949 part-time jobs averaging $1598.

APPLYING FOR FINANCIAL AID *Required financial aid forms:* FAFSA, CSS Financial Aid PROFILE, noncustodial (divorced/separated) parent's statement.

CONTACT Ms. Katharine Ruby, Director of Financial Aid, St. Olaf College, 1520 Saint Olaf Avenue, Northfield, MN 55057-1098, 507-646-3019 or toll-free 800-800-3025. *E-mail:* ruby@stolaf.edu.

SAINT PAUL'S COLLEGE
Lawrenceville, VA

ABOUT THE INSTITUTION Independent Episcopal, coed. Awards: bachelor's degrees. 13 undergraduate majors. Total enrollment: 531. Undergraduates: 531.

GIFT AID (NEED-BASED) *Scholarships, grants, and awards:* Federal Pell, FSEOG, state, private, college/university gift aid from institutional funds, United Negro College Fund.

GIFT AID (NON-NEED-BASED) *Scholarships, grants, and awards by category: Academic Interests/Achievement:* general academic interests/achievements. *Special Achievements/Activities:* general special achievements/activities. *Special Characteristics:* children of faculty/staff, children of union members/company employees.

LOANS *Programs:* Federal Direct (Subsidized and Unsubsidized Stafford, PLUS), Perkins.

WORK-STUDY *Federal work-study:* Total amount: $331,599; 254 jobs averaging $1306.

APPLYING FOR FINANCIAL AID *Required financial aid forms:* FAFSA, state aid form.

CONTACT Office of Financial Aid, Saint Paul's College, 115 College Drive, Lawrenceville, VA 23868-1202, 434-848-6495 or toll-free 800-678-7071. *Fax:* 434-848-6498. *E-mail:* aid@saintpauls.edu.

ST. PETERSBURG THEOLOGICAL SEMINARY
St. Petersburg, FL

CONTACT Financial Aid Office, St. Petersburg Theological Seminary, 10830 Navajo Drive, St. Petersburg, FL 33708, 727-399-0276.

SAINT PETER'S COLLEGE
Jersey City, NJ

CONTACT Director of Financial Aid, Saint Peter's College, 2641 Kennedy Boulevard, Jersey City, NJ 07306, 201-915-4929 or toll-free 888-SPC-9933. *Fax:* 201-434-6878.

ST. THOMAS AQUINAS COLLEGE
Sparkill, NY

CONTACT Margaret McGrail, Director of Financial Aid, St. Thomas Aquinas College, 125 Route 340, Sparkill, NY 10976, 914-398-4097 or toll-free 800-999-STAC.

ST. THOMAS UNIVERSITY
Miami Gardens, FL

Tuition & fees: $17,860   **Average undergraduate aid package:** N/A

ABOUT THE INSTITUTION Independent Roman Catholic, coed. Awards: bachelor's, master's, and first professional degrees and post-bachelor's and post-master's certificates. 28 undergraduate majors. Total enrollment: 2,692. Undergraduates: 1,158. Freshmen: 206. Federal methodology is used as a basis for awarding need-based institutional aid.

UNDERGRADUATE EXPENSES for 2005–06 *Application fee:* $40. *Comprehensive fee:* $23,490 includes full-time tuition ($17,860) and room and board ($5630). Room and board charges vary according to board plan and housing facility. *Part-time tuition:* $595 per credit. *Payment plan:* Installment.

FRESHMAN FINANCIAL AID (Fall 2005, est.) 189 applied for aid; of those 94% were deemed to have need. 100% of freshmen with need received aid; of those 40% had need fully met. 11% of all full-time freshmen had no need and received non-need-based gift aid.
UNDERGRADUATE FINANCIAL AID (Fall 2005, est.) 922 applied for aid; of those 82% were deemed to have need. 100% of undergraduates with need received aid; of those 74% had need fully met. 13% of all full-time undergraduates had no need and received non-need-based gift aid.
GIFT AID (NEED-BASED) *Total amount:* $8,561,217 (19% federal, 29% state, 51% institutional, 1% external sources). *Receiving aid:* Freshmen: 68% (141); All full-time undergraduates: 55% (599). *Average award:* Freshmen: $1820; Undergraduates: $1910. *Scholarships, grants, and awards:* Federal Pell, FSEOG, state, private, college/university gift aid from institutional funds.
GIFT AID (NON-NEED-BASED) *Receiving aid:* Freshmen: 70% (144); Undergraduates: 67% (730). *Average Award:* Freshmen: $6544; Undergraduates: $6332. *Scholarships, grants, and awards by category: Academic Interests/Achievement:* 857 awards ($3,872,588 total): general academic interests/achievements. *Tuition waivers:* Full or partial for minority students, children of alumni, employees or children of employees. *ROTC:* Army cooperative, Air Force cooperative.
LOANS *Student loans:* $4,930,172 (57% need-based, 43% non-need-based). 52% of past graduating class borrowed through all loan programs. *Average indebtedness per student:* $12,000. *Average need-based loan:* Freshmen: $2837; Undergraduates: $3350. *Parent loans:* $553,419 (100% need-based). *Programs:* FFEL (Subsidized and Unsubsidized Stafford, PLUS), Perkins.
WORK-STUDY *Federal work-study:* Total amount: $441,077; 227 jobs averaging $2325. *State or other work-study/employment:* 47 part-time jobs averaging $3277.
ATHLETIC AWARDS *Total amount:* $740,867 (100% need-based).
APPLYING FOR FINANCIAL AID *Required financial aid forms:* FAFSA, state aid form. *Financial aid deadline (priority):* 4/1. *Notification date:* Continuous beginning 3/1. Students must reply within 2 weeks of notification.
CONTACT Ms. Anh Do, Director of Financial Aid, St. Thomas University, 16400 Northwest 32nd Avenue, Miami, FL 33054-6459, 305-628-6547 or toll-free 800-367-9010. *Fax:* 305-628-6754. *E-mail:* ado@stu.edu.

SAINT VINCENT COLLEGE
Latrobe, PA

Tuition & fees: $21,679	Average undergraduate aid package: $16,963

ABOUT THE INSTITUTION Independent Roman Catholic, coed. Awards: bachelor's and master's degrees and post-bachelor's certificates. 44 undergraduate majors. Total enrollment: 1,687. Undergraduates: 1,576. Freshmen: 482. Federal methodology is used as a basis for awarding need-based institutional aid.
UNDERGRADUATE EXPENSES for 2005–06 *Application fee:* $25. *Comprehensive fee:* $28,553 includes full-time tuition ($21,104), mandatory fees ($575), and room and board ($6874). *College room only:* $3500. Room and board charges vary according to board plan and student level. *Part-time tuition:* $660 per credit hour. *Part-time fees:* $45 per term. *Payment plan:* Installment.
FRESHMAN FINANCIAL AID (Fall 2005, est.) 480 applied for aid; of those 82% were deemed to have need. 100% of freshmen with need received aid; of those 25% had need fully met. *Average percent of need met:* 93% (excluding resources awarded to replace EFC). *Average financial aid package:* $15,568 (excluding resources awarded to replace EFC). 17% of all full-time freshmen had no need and received non-need-based gift aid.
UNDERGRADUATE FINANCIAL AID (Fall 2005, est.) 1,425 applied for aid; of those 77% were deemed to have need. 100% of undergraduates with need received aid; of those 21% had need fully met. *Average percent of need met:* 85% (excluding resources awarded to replace EFC). *Average financial aid package:* $16,963 (excluding resources awarded to replace EFC). 20% of all full-time undergraduates had no need and received non-need-based gift aid.
GIFT AID (NEED-BASED) *Total amount:* $13,412,068 (8% federal, 17% state, 73% institutional, 2% external sources). *Receiving aid:* Freshmen: 81% (392); All full-time undergraduates: 8% (111). *Average award:* Freshmen: $12,849; Undergraduates: $12,070. *Scholarships, grants, and awards:* Federal Pell, FSEOG, state, private, college/university gift aid from institutional funds, United Negro College Fund.
GIFT AID (NON-NEED-BASED) *Total amount:* $3,231,207 (97% institutional, 3% external sources). *Receiving aid:* Freshmen: 75% (366); Undergraduates: 63% (920). *Average Award:* Freshmen: $10,956; Undergraduates: $8933. *Scholarships, grants, and awards by category: Academic Interests/Achievement:* 769 awards ($4,615,326 total): biological sciences, business, computer science, general academic interests/achievements, mathematics, physical sciences, social sciences. *Creative Arts/Performance:* 2 awards ($6500 total): music. *Special Achievements/Activities:* 831 awards ($1,291,000 total): leadership. *Special Characteristics:* 76 awards ($248,916 total): international students, members of minority groups. *Tuition waivers:* Full or partial for employees or children of employees, senior citizens. *ROTC:* Air Force cooperative.
LOANS *Student loans:* $6,061,135 (65% need-based, 35% non-need-based). *Average need-based loan:* Freshmen: $1905; Undergraduates: $2905. *Parent loans:* $2,344,851 (100% non-need-based). *Programs:* FFEL (Subsidized and Unsubsidized Stafford, PLUS), Perkins.
WORK-STUDY *Federal work-study:* Total amount: $631,312; 372 jobs averaging $1840. *State or other work-study/employment:* Total amount: $50,742 (100% need-based). 448 part-time jobs averaging $1524.
ATHLETIC AWARDS *Total amount:* $1,673,258 (51% need-based, 49% non-need-based).
APPLYING FOR FINANCIAL AID *Required financial aid forms:* FAFSA, state aid form. *Financial aid deadline:* 5/1 (priority: 3/1). *Notification date:* 3/1. Students must reply within 2 weeks of notification.
CONTACT Thomas Ball, Director of Financial Aid, Saint Vincent College, 300 Fraser Purchase Road, Latrobe, PA 15650, 724-537-4540 or toll-free 800-782-5549. *Fax:* 724-532-5069. *E-mail:* admission@stvincent.edu.

SAINT XAVIER UNIVERSITY
Chicago, IL

Tuition & fees: $18,520	Average undergraduate aid package: $15,408

ABOUT THE INSTITUTION Independent Roman Catholic, coed. Awards: bachelor's and master's degrees and post-bachelor's and post-master's certificates. 39 undergraduate majors. Total enrollment: 5,705. Undergraduates: 3,182. Freshmen: 420. Federal methodology is used as a basis for awarding need-based institutional aid.
UNDERGRADUATE EXPENSES for 2005–06 *Application fee:* $25. *Comprehensive fee:* $25,598 includes full-time tuition ($18,350), mandatory fees ($170), and room and board ($7078). *College room only:* $4428. Full-time tuition and fees vary according to course load. Room and board charges vary according to board plan and housing facility. *Part-time tuition:* $611 per credit hour. *Part-time fees:* $110 per year. Part-time tuition and fees vary according to course load. *Payment plan:* Installment.
FRESHMAN FINANCIAL AID (Fall 2005, est.) 386 applied for aid; of those 88% were deemed to have need. 100% of freshmen with need received aid; of those 20% had need fully met. *Average percent of need met:* 88% (excluding resources awarded to replace EFC). *Average financial aid package:* $17,222 (excluding resources awarded to replace EFC). 17% of all full-time freshmen had no need and received non-need-based gift aid.
UNDERGRADUATE FINANCIAL AID (Fall 2005, est.) 2,140 applied for aid; of those 89% were deemed to have need. 100% of undergraduates with need received aid; of those 22% had need fully met. *Average percent of need met:* 83% (excluding resources awarded to replace EFC). *Average financial aid package:* $15,408 (excluding resources awarded to replace EFC). 18% of all full-time undergraduates had no need and received non-need-based gift aid.
GIFT AID (NEED-BASED) *Total amount:* $18,896,747 (18% federal, 30% state, 48% institutional, 4% external sources). *Receiving aid:* Freshmen: 81% (340); All full-time undergraduates: 79% (1,892). *Average award:* Freshmen: $11,395; Undergraduates: $9018. *Scholarships, grants, and awards:* Federal Pell, FSEOG, state, private, college/university gift aid from institutional funds, United Negro College Fund, Federal Nursing.
GIFT AID (NON-NEED-BASED) *Total amount:* $2,714,105 (1% state, 84% institutional, 15% external sources). *Receiving aid:* Freshmen: 79% (332); Undergraduates: 75% (1,791). *Average Award:* Freshmen: $5465; Undergraduates: $4136. *Scholarships, grants, and awards by category: Academic Interests/Achievement:* 2,433 awards ($8,122,135 total): general academic interests/achievements. *Creative Arts/Performance:* 63 awards ($220,444 total): music. *Special Achievements/Activities:* leadership. *Special Characteristics:* 80 awards ($1,037,564 total): children of faculty/staff. *Tuition waivers:* Full or partial for employees or children of employees, senior citizens. *ROTC:* Air Force cooperative.
LOANS *Student loans:* $16,731,765 (87% need-based, 13% non-need-based). 81% of past graduating class borrowed through all loan programs. *Average*

Saint Xavier University

indebtedness per student: $20,470. **Average need-based loan:** Freshmen: $2571; Undergraduates: $3885. **Parent loans:** $2,410,150 (33% need-based, 67% non-need-based). **Programs:** FFEL (Subsidized and Unsubsidized Stafford, PLUS), Perkins.
WORK-STUDY *Federal work-study:* Total amount: $3,421,620; 1,278 jobs averaging $2624. *State or other work-study/employment:* Total amount: $241,274 (75% need-based, 25% non-need-based). 38 part-time jobs averaging $5867.
ATHLETIC AWARDS *Total amount:* $1,561,450 (68% need-based, 32% non-need-based).
APPLYING FOR FINANCIAL AID *Required financial aid form:* FAFSA. *Financial aid deadline (priority):* 3/1. *Notification date:* Continuous beginning 2/15. Students must reply by 5/1 or within 2 weeks of notification.
CONTACT Ms. Susan Swisher, Assistant Vice President for Student Financial Services, Saint Xavier University, 3700 West 103rd Street, Chicago, IL 60655-3105, 773-298-3070 or toll-free 800-462-9288. *Fax:* 773-779-3084. *E-mail:* swisher@sxu.edu.

SALEM COLLEGE
Winston-Salem, NC

CONTACT Director of Financial Aid, Salem College, PO Box 10548, Winston-Salem, NC 27108, 336-721-2808 or toll-free 800-327-2536. *Fax:* 336-917-5584.

SALEM INTERNATIONAL UNIVERSITY
Salem, WV

| Tuition & fees: N/R | Average undergraduate aid package: $13,116 |

ABOUT THE INSTITUTION Independent, coed. Awards: associate, bachelor's, and master's degrees. 27 undergraduate majors. Total enrollment: 568. Undergraduates: 443. Freshmen: 51. Federal methodology is used as a basis for awarding need-based institutional aid.
FRESHMAN FINANCIAL AID (Fall 2005, est.) 35 applied for aid; of those 89% were deemed to have need. 100% of freshmen with need received aid; of those 58% had need fully met. *Average percent of need met:* 98% (excluding resources awarded to replace EFC). *Average financial aid package:* $11,535 (excluding resources awarded to replace EFC). 73% of all full-time freshmen had no need and received non-need-based gift aid.
UNDERGRADUATE FINANCIAL AID (Fall 2005, est.) 172 applied for aid; of those 85% were deemed to have need. 100% of undergraduates with need received aid; of those 64% had need fully met. *Average percent of need met:* 98% (excluding resources awarded to replace EFC). *Average financial aid package:* $13,116 (excluding resources awarded to replace EFC). 62% of all full-time undergraduates had no need and received non-need-based gift aid.
GIFT AID (NEED-BASED) *Total amount:* $1,007,397 (25% federal, 9% state, 66% institutional). *Receiving aid:* Freshmen: 18% (22); All full-time undergraduates: 25% (98). *Average award:* Freshmen: $4437; Undergraduates: $4489. *Scholarships, grants, and awards:* Federal Pell, FSEOG, state, private, college/university gift aid from institutional funds.
GIFT AID (NON-NEED-BASED) *Total amount:* $1,787,123 (98% institutional, 2% external sources). *Receiving aid:* Freshmen: 8% (10); Undergraduates: 10% (40). *Average Award:* Freshmen: $6277; Undergraduates: $7303. *Scholarships, grants, and awards by category: Academic Interests/Achievement:* 348 awards ($2,304,545 total): business, education, general academic interests/achievements, humanities. *Special Characteristics:* 2 awards ($2489 total): out-of-state students, religious affiliation.
LOANS *Student loans:* $817,842 (63% need-based, 37% non-need-based). 64% of past graduating class borrowed through all loan programs. *Average indebtedness per student:* $15,794. **Average need-based loan:** Freshmen: $3182; Undergraduates: $4288. **Parent loans:** $88,500 (100% non-need-based). **Programs:** FFEL (Subsidized and Unsubsidized Stafford, PLUS), Perkins, Alternative Educational Loans.
WORK-STUDY *Federal work-study:* Total amount: $126,535; 106 jobs averaging $650. *State or other work-study/employment:* Total amount: $22,785 (100% non-need-based). 25 part-time jobs averaging $911.
ATHLETIC AWARDS *Total amount:* $526,741 (36% need-based, 64% non-need-based).

APPLYING FOR FINANCIAL AID *Required financial aid form:* FAFSA. *Financial aid deadline:* Continuous. *Notification date:* Continuous beginning 2/15. Students must reply within 4 weeks of notification.
CONTACT Mrs. Charlotte Lake, Director of Financial Aid, Salem International University, 223 West Main Street, Salem, WV 26426-0500, 304-326-1303 or toll-free 800-283-4562. *Fax:* 304-326-1509. *E-mail:* lake@salemiu.edu.

SALEM STATE COLLEGE
Salem, MA

ABOUT THE INSTITUTION State-supported, coed. Awards: bachelor's and master's degrees and post-master's certificates. 60 undergraduate majors. Total enrollment: 9,863. Undergraduates: 7,296. Freshmen: 1,226.
GIFT AID (NEED-BASED) *Scholarships, grants, and awards:* Federal Pell, FSEOG, state, private, college/university gift aid from institutional funds.
GIFT AID (NON-NEED-BASED) *Scholarships, grants, and awards by category: Academic Interests/Achievement:* general academic interests/achievements. *Creative Arts/Performance:* applied art and design, art/fine arts, creative writing, dance, music, performing arts, theater/drama. *Special Achievements/Activities:* general special achievements/activities, memberships. *Special Characteristics:* adult students, children and siblings of alumni, children of faculty/staff, children of public servants, children of union members/company employees, first-generation college students, general special characteristics, members of minority groups, public servants, veterans, veterans' children.
LOANS *Programs:* Federal Direct (Subsidized and Unsubsidized Stafford), FFEL (PLUS), Perkins, Federal Nursing, state, TERI Loans, MEFA Loans, CitiAssist Loans, Signature Loans.
WORK-STUDY *Federal work-study:* Total amount: $381,822; 726 jobs averaging $2000.
APPLYING FOR FINANCIAL AID *Required financial aid form:* FAFSA.
CONTACT Mary Benda, Director of Financial Aid, Salem State College, 352 Lafayette Street, Salem, MA 01970-5353, 978-542-6139. *Fax:* 978-542-6876.

SALISBURY UNIVERSITY
Salisbury, MD

| Tuition & fees (MD res): $6376 | Average undergraduate aid package: $6052 |

ABOUT THE INSTITUTION State-supported, coed. Awards: bachelor's and master's degrees and post-bachelor's certificates. 42 undergraduate majors. Total enrollment: 7,009. Undergraduates: 6,437. Freshmen: 958. Federal methodology is used as a basis for awarding need-based institutional aid.
UNDERGRADUATE EXPENSES for 2005–06 *Application fee:* $45. *Tuition, state resident:* full-time $4814; part-time $200 per credit hour. *Tuition, nonresident:* full-time $12,492; part-time $520 per credit hour. *Required fees:* full-time $1562; $50 per credit hour. *College room and board:* $6932; room only: $3554. Room and board charges vary according to board plan and housing facility. *Payment plan:* Installment.
FRESHMAN FINANCIAL AID (Fall 2004) 752 applied for aid; of those 50% were deemed to have need. 100% of freshmen with need received aid; of those 18% had need fully met. *Average percent of need met:* 53% (excluding resources awarded to replace EFC). *Average financial aid package:* $5140 (excluding resources awarded to replace EFC). 18% of all full-time freshmen had no need and received non-need-based gift aid.
UNDERGRADUATE FINANCIAL AID (Fall 2004) 3,648 applied for aid; of those 64% were deemed to have need. 100% of undergraduates with need received aid; of those 19% had need fully met. *Average percent of need met:* 57% (excluding resources awarded to replace EFC). *Average financial aid package:* $6052 (excluding resources awarded to replace EFC). 13% of all full-time undergraduates had no need and received non-need-based gift aid.
GIFT AID (NEED-BASED) *Total amount:* $7,422,792 (37% federal, 40% state, 14% institutional, 9% external sources). *Receiving aid:* Freshmen: 27% (268); All full-time undergraduates: 30% (1,674). *Average award:* Freshmen: $4754; Undergraduates: $4351. *Scholarships, grants, and awards:* Federal Pell, FSEOG, state, college/university gift aid from institutional funds.
GIFT AID (NON-NEED-BASED) *Total amount:* $2,130,171 (48% state, 28% institutional, 24% external sources). *Average Award:* Freshmen: $2787; Undergraduates: $3428. *Scholarships, grants, and awards by category: Academic Interests/Achievement:* 931 awards ($1,207,246 total): biological sciences, business, communication, computer science, education, English, foreign

languages, general academic interests/achievements, health fields, humanities, mathematics, physical sciences, premedicine, social sciences. *Tuition waivers:* Full or partial for employees or children of employees, senior citizens. *ROTC:* Army cooperative.

LOANS *Student loans:* $15,691,312 (72% need-based, 28% non-need-based). 63% of past graduating class borrowed through all loan programs. *Average indebtedness per student:* $15,831. *Average need-based loan:* Freshmen: $2020; Undergraduates: $3356. *Parent loans:* $12,252,603 (62% need-based, 38% non-need-based). *Programs:* Federal Direct (Subsidized and Unsubsidized Stafford, PLUS), Perkins.

WORK-STUDY *Federal work-study:* Total amount: $138,566; 71 jobs averaging $3774. *State or other work-study/employment:* Part-time jobs available.

APPLYING FOR FINANCIAL AID *Required financial aid form:* FAFSA. *Financial aid deadline (priority):* 2/1. *Notification date:* Continuous beginning 4/1. Students must reply by 5/1.

CONTACT Ms. Beverly N. Horner, Director of Financial Aid, Salisbury University, 1101 Camden Avenue, Salisbury, MD 21801-6837, 410-543-6165 or toll-free 888-543-0148. *E-mail:* bnhorner@salisbury.edu.

SALVE REGINA UNIVERSITY
Newport, RI

Tuition & fees: $23,950 **Average undergraduate aid package: $16,082**

ABOUT THE INSTITUTION Independent Roman Catholic, coed. Awards: associate, bachelor's, master's, and doctoral degrees and post-bachelor's and post-master's certificates. 47 undergraduate majors. Total enrollment: 2,499. Undergraduates: 2,091. Freshmen: 558. Both federal and institutional methodology are used as a basis for awarding need-based institutional aid.

UNDERGRADUATE EXPENSES for 2005–06 *Application fee:* $40. *Comprehensive fee:* $33,450 includes full-time tuition ($23,500), mandatory fees ($450), and room and board ($9500). Room and board charges vary according to board plan. *Part-time tuition:* $783 per credit. *Part-time fees:* $40 per term. Part-time tuition and fees vary according to course load. *Payment plan:* Installment.

FRESHMAN FINANCIAL AID (Fall 2005, est.) 476 applied for aid; of those 81% were deemed to have need. 99% of freshmen with need received aid; of those 12% had need fully met. *Average percent of need met:* 71% (excluding resources awarded to replace EFC). *Average financial aid package:* $15,523 (excluding resources awarded to replace EFC). 19% of all full-time freshmen had no need and received non-need-based gift aid.

UNDERGRADUATE FINANCIAL AID (Fall 2005, est.) 1,606 applied for aid; of those 86% were deemed to have need. 96% of undergraduates with need received aid; of those 18% had need fully met. *Average percent of need met:* 70% (excluding resources awarded to replace EFC). *Average financial aid package:* $16,082 (excluding resources awarded to replace EFC). 15% of all full-time undergraduates had no need and received non-need-based gift aid.

GIFT AID (NEED-BASED) *Total amount:* $14,054,339 (6% federal, 2% state, 88% institutional, 4% external sources). *Receiving aid:* Freshmen: 64% (365); All full-time undergraduates: 57% (1,226). *Average award:* Freshmen: $12,996; Undergraduates: $11,802. *Scholarships, grants, and awards:* Federal Pell, FSEOG, state, private, college/university gift aid from institutional funds.

GIFT AID (NON-NEED-BASED) *Total amount:* $1,208,687 (85% institutional, 15% external sources). *Receiving aid:* Freshmen: 3% (15); Undergraduates: 2% (51). *Average Award:* Freshmen: $12,255; Undergraduates: $13,553. *Scholarships, grants, and awards by category: Academic Interests/Achievement:* 558 awards ($3,576,217 total): general academic interests/achievements. *Tuition waivers:* Full or partial for employees or children of employees. *ROTC:* Army cooperative.

LOANS *Student loans:* $12,615,018 (63% need-based, 37% non-need-based). 83% of past graduating class borrowed through all loan programs. *Average indebtedness per student:* $27,332. *Average need-based loan:* Freshmen: $2580; Undergraduates: $4635. *Parent loans:* $6,410,742 (29% need-based, 71% non-need-based). *Programs:* FFEL (Subsidized and Unsubsidized Stafford, PLUS), Perkins, Federal Nursing, college/university, alternative loans.

WORK-STUDY *Federal work-study:* Total amount: $350,109; 397 jobs averaging $882. *State or other work-study/employment:* Total amount: $317,261 (100% non-need-based). 265 part-time jobs averaging $1197.

APPLYING FOR FINANCIAL AID *Required financial aid forms:* FAFSA, CSS Financial Aid PROFILE, business/farm supplement, Non-Custodial Statement.

Financial aid deadline (priority): 3/1. *Notification date:* Continuous beginning 2/15. Students must reply by 5/1 or within 2 weeks of notification.

CONTACT Aida Mirante, Director of Financial Aid, Salve Regina University, 100 Ochre Point Avenue, Newport, RI 02840-4192, 401-341-2901 or toll-free 888-GO SALVE. *Fax:* 401-341-2928. *E-mail:* financial_aid@salve.edu.

SAMFORD UNIVERSITY
Birmingham, AL

Tuition & fees: $14,642 **Average undergraduate aid package: $11,879**

ABOUT THE INSTITUTION Independent Baptist, coed. Awards: associate, bachelor's, master's, doctoral, and first professional degrees and post-master's certificates. 68 undergraduate majors. Total enrollment: 4,507. Undergraduates: 2,941. Freshmen: 702. Federal methodology is used as a basis for awarding need-based institutional aid.

UNDERGRADUATE EXPENSES for 2005–06 *Application fee:* $35. *Comprehensive fee:* $20,258 includes full-time tuition ($14,642) and room and board ($5616). *College room only:* $2860. Full-time tuition and fees vary according to course load. Room and board charges vary according to board plan and housing facility. *Part-time tuition:* $486 per semester hour. Part-time tuition and fees vary according to course load.

FRESHMAN FINANCIAL AID (Fall 2004) 457 applied for aid; of those 60% were deemed to have need. 98% of freshmen with need received aid; of those 27% had need fully met. *Average percent of need met:* 76% (excluding resources awarded to replace EFC). *Average financial aid package:* $12,976 (excluding resources awarded to replace EFC). 23% of all full-time freshmen had no need and received non-need-based gift aid.

UNDERGRADUATE FINANCIAL AID (Fall 2004) 1,510 applied for aid; of those 75% were deemed to have need. 99% of undergraduates with need received aid; of those 26% had need fully met. *Average percent of need met:* 72% (excluding resources awarded to replace EFC). *Average financial aid package:* $11,879 (excluding resources awarded to replace EFC). 21% of all full-time undergraduates had no need and received non-need-based gift aid.

GIFT AID (NEED-BASED) *Total amount:* $6,372,813 (20% federal, 1% state, 63% institutional, 16% external sources). *Receiving aid:* Freshmen: 38% (256); All full-time undergraduates: 37% (978). *Average award:* Freshmen: $8149; Undergraduates: $6448. *Scholarships, grants, and awards:* Federal Pell, FSEOG, state, private, college/university gift aid from institutional funds.

GIFT AID (NON-NEED-BASED) *Total amount:* $3,343,579 (1% state, 67% institutional, 32% external sources). *Average Award:* Freshmen: $3664; Undergraduates: $4111. *Scholarships, grants, and awards by category: Academic Interests/Achievement:* 301 awards ($1,107,925 total): general academic interests/achievements. *Creative Arts/Performance:* 36 awards ($57,525 total): music. *Special Characteristics:* 118 awards ($855,495 total): children of faculty/staff, relatives of clergy. *Tuition waivers:* Full or partial for employees or children of employees. *ROTC:* Army cooperative, Air Force.

LOANS *Student loans:* $7,884,646 (53% need-based, 47% non-need-based). 46% of past graduating class borrowed through all loan programs. *Average indebtedness per student:* $17,532. *Average need-based loan:* Freshmen: $3169; Undergraduates: $3955. *Parent loans:* $5,795,378 (100% need-based). *Programs:* FFEL (Subsidized and Unsubsidized Stafford, PLUS), Perkins, college/university.

WORK-STUDY *Federal work-study:* Total amount: $1,059,229; 450 jobs averaging $1800. *State or other work-study/employment:* Total amount: $375,903 (48% need-based, 52% non-need-based). 472 part-time jobs averaging $1800.

ATHLETIC AWARDS *Total amount:* $3,408,386 (31% need-based, 69% non-need-based).

APPLYING FOR FINANCIAL AID *Required financial aid form:* FAFSA. *Financial aid deadline (priority):* 3/1. *Notification date:* 5/1.

CONTACT Ms. Lissa Burkson, Director of Financial Aid, Samford University, 800 Lakeshore Drive, Birmingham, AL 35229-0002, 205-726-2860 or toll-free 800-888-7218. *Fax:* 205-726-2738. *E-mail:* lrburles@samford.edu.

SAM HOUSTON STATE UNIVERSITY
Huntsville, TX

ABOUT THE INSTITUTION State-supported, coed. Awards: bachelor's, master's, and doctoral degrees. 96 undergraduate majors. Total enrollment: 15,000. Undergraduates: 13,013. Freshmen: 6,660.

Sam Houston State University

GIFT AID (NEED-BASED) *Scholarships, grants, and awards:* Federal Pell, FSEOG, state, private, college/university gift aid from institutional funds.
GIFT AID (NON-NEED-BASED) *Scholarships, grants, and awards by category: Academic Interests/Achievement:* agriculture, biological sciences, business, communication, computer science, education, engineering/technologies, English, foreign languages, general academic interests/achievements, home economics, humanities, library science, mathematics, military science, physical sciences, social sciences. *Special Achievements/Activities:* cheerleading/drum major, general special achievements/activities, leadership, rodeo. *Special Characteristics:* general special characteristics, handicapped students.
LOANS *Programs:* FFEL (Subsidized and Unsubsidized Stafford, PLUS), Perkins.
WORK-STUDY *Federal work-study:* Total amount: $162,935; jobs available. *State or other work-study/employment:* Total amount: $69,596 (26% need-based, 74% non-need-based). Part-time jobs available.
APPLYING FOR FINANCIAL AID *Required financial aid forms:* FAFSA, institution's own form.
CONTACT Patricia Mabry, Director of Financial Aid, Sam Houston State University, 1903 University Avenue, Estill Building, 2nd Floor, Huntsville, TX 77341, 936-294-1724 or toll-free 866-232-7528 Ext. 1828.

SAMUEL MERRITT COLLEGE
Oakland, CA

Tuition & fees: $29,576 **Average undergraduate aid package:** $27,500

ABOUT THE INSTITUTION Independent, coed, primarily women. Awards: bachelor's, master's, doctoral, and first professional degrees (bachelor's degree offered jointly with Saint Mary's College of California). 1 undergraduate major. Total enrollment: 1,080. Undergraduates: 363. Federal methodology is used as a basis for awarding need-based institutional aid.
UNDERGRADUATE EXPENSES for 2006-07 *Application fee:* $35. *Tuition:* full-time $29,220; part-time $1214 per unit. *Required fees:* full-time $356; $356 per year part-time.
FRESHMAN FINANCIAL AID (Fall 2004) 8 applied for aid; of those 100% were deemed to have need. 100% of freshmen with need received aid. *Average percent of need met:* 71% (excluding resources awarded to replace EFC). *Average financial aid package:* $21,833 (excluding resources awarded to replace EFC).
UNDERGRADUATE FINANCIAL AID (Fall 2004) 321 applied for aid; of those 99% were deemed to have need. 100% of undergraduates with need received aid; of those 10% had need fully met. *Average percent of need met:* 84% (excluding resources awarded to replace EFC). *Average financial aid package:* $27,500 (excluding resources awarded to replace EFC).
GIFT AID (NEED-BASED) *Total amount:* $3,977,610 (40% federal, 16% state, 40% institutional, 4% external sources). *Receiving aid:* Freshmen: 89% (8); All full-time undergraduates: 91% (319). *Average award:* Freshmen: $13,708; Undergraduates: $12,000. *Scholarships, grants, and awards:* Federal Pell, FSEOG, state, private, college/university gift aid from institutional funds, Federal Nursing.
GIFT AID (NON-NEED-BASED) *Total amount:* $72,247 (32% federal, 11% institutional, 57% external sources). *ROTC:* Army cooperative, Air Force cooperative.
LOANS *Student loans:* $4,369,991 (72% need-based, 28% non-need-based). 98% of past graduating class borrowed through all loan programs. *Average indebtedness per student:* $36,250. *Average need-based loan:* Freshmen: $5125; Undergraduates: $9500. *Parent loans:* $607,541 (67% need-based, 33% non-need-based). *Programs:* FFEL (Subsidized and Unsubsidized Stafford, PLUS), Perkins, Federal Nursing, college/university.
WORK-STUDY *Federal work-study:* Total amount: $120,000; 39 jobs averaging $3300. *State or other work-study/employment:* Total amount: $81,000 (100% non-need-based). 22 part-time jobs averaging $4200.
APPLYING FOR FINANCIAL AID *Required financial aid form:* FAFSA. *Financial aid deadline (priority):* 3/2. *Notification date:* Continuous beginning 4/15. Students must reply within 2 weeks of notification.
CONTACT Anne-Marie Larroque, Assistant Director, Financial Aid Office, Samuel Merritt College, 450 30th Street, Room 2850, Oakland, CA 94609, 510-869-6193 or toll-free 800-607-MERRITT. *Fax:* 510-869-1529. *E-mail:* alarroque@samuelmerritt.edu.

SAN DIEGO CHRISTIAN COLLEGE
El Cajon, CA

Tuition & fees: $17,342 **Average undergraduate aid package:** $14,547

ABOUT THE INSTITUTION Independent nondenominational, coed. Awards: bachelor's degrees and post-bachelor's certificates. 29 undergraduate majors. Total enrollment: 553. Undergraduates: 511. Freshmen: 93. Both federal and institutional methodology are used as a basis for awarding need-based institutional aid.
UNDERGRADUATE EXPENSES for 2006-07 *Application fee:* $25. *Comprehensive fee:* $24,522 includes full-time tuition ($16,476), mandatory fees ($866), and room and board ($7180). *Part-time tuition:* $570 per credit.
FRESHMAN FINANCIAL AID (Fall 2005, est.) 72 applied for aid; of those 88% were deemed to have need. 100% of freshmen with need received aid; of those 70% had need fully met. *Average percent of need met:* 85% (excluding resources awarded to replace EFC). *Average financial aid package:* $12,705 (excluding resources awarded to replace EFC). 26% of all full-time freshmen had no need and received non-need-based gift aid.
UNDERGRADUATE FINANCIAL AID (Fall 2005, est.) 453 applied for aid; of those 85% were deemed to have need. 100% of undergraduates with need received aid; of those 70% had need fully met. *Average percent of need met:* 80% (excluding resources awarded to replace EFC). *Average financial aid package:* $14,547 (excluding resources awarded to replace EFC). 25% of all full-time undergraduates had no need and received non-need-based gift aid.
GIFT AID (NEED-BASED) *Total amount:* $1,679,151 (30% federal, 55% state, 15% institutional). *Receiving aid:* Freshmen: 48% (45); All full-time undergraduates: 56% (254). *Average award:* Freshmen: $6000; Undergraduates: $5500. *Scholarships, grants, and awards:* Federal Pell, FSEOG, state, private, college/university gift aid from institutional funds.
GIFT AID (NON-NEED-BASED) *Total amount:* $1,280,814 (88% institutional, 12% external sources). *Receiving aid:* Freshmen: 61% (57); Undergraduates: 75% (345). *Average Award:* Freshmen: $5720; Undergraduates: $4565. *Scholarships, grants, and awards by category: Academic Interests/Achievement:* 235 awards ($520,445 total): general academic interests/achievements. *Creative Arts/Performance:* 25 awards ($63,910 total): music, performing arts, theater/drama. *Special Achievements/Activities:* 104 awards ($231,287 total): leadership, religious involvement. *Special Characteristics:* 85 awards ($246,084 total): children of faculty/staff, international students, out-of-state students, relatives of clergy, religious affiliation, siblings of current students. *ROTC:* Army cooperative, Air Force cooperative.
LOANS *Student loans:* $2,811,834 (73% need-based, 27% non-need-based). 86% of past graduating class borrowed through all loan programs. *Average indebtedness per student:* $16,000. *Average need-based loan:* Freshmen: $2625; Undergraduates: $3850. *Parent loans:* $990,409 (100% non-need-based). *Programs:* FFEL (Subsidized and Unsubsidized Stafford, PLUS), Perkins.
WORK-STUDY *Federal work-study:* Total amount: $29,908; 20 jobs averaging $1495. *State or other work-study/employment:* Total amount: $19,126 (100% need-based). 12 part-time jobs averaging $1594.
ATHLETIC AWARDS Total amount: $466,672 (100% non-need-based).
APPLYING FOR FINANCIAL AID *Required financial aid forms:* FAFSA, institution's own form, state aid form. *Financial aid deadline (priority):* 3/2. *Notification date:* Continuous. Students must reply by 9/1 or within 4 weeks of notification.
CONTACT Nancy DeMars, Director of Financial Aid, San Diego Christian College, 2100 Greenfield Drive, El Cajon, CA 92019, 619-590-1786 Ext. 3 or toll-free 800-676-2242. *Fax:* 619-590-2186. *E-mail:* ndemars@sdcc.edu.

SAN DIEGO STATE UNIVERSITY
San Diego, CA

Tuition & fees (CA res): $3155 **Average undergraduate aid package:** $7400

ABOUT THE INSTITUTION State-supported, coed. Awards: bachelor's, master's, and doctoral degrees and post-bachelor's and post-master's certificates. 108 undergraduate majors. Total enrollment: 32,936. Undergraduates: 26,853. Freshmen: 4,140. Federal methodology is used as a basis for awarding need-based institutional aid.
UNDERGRADUATE EXPENSES for 2005-06 *Application fee:* $55. *Tuition, state resident:* full-time $0. *Tuition, nonresident:* full-time $10,170; part-time $339 per unit. *Required fees:* full-time $3155; $1033 per term part-time. Full-time

tuition and fees vary according to degree level. Part-time tuition and fees vary according to course load and degree level. **College room and board:** $9849. Room and board charges vary according to board plan and housing facility. **Payment plan:** Installment.

FRESHMAN FINANCIAL AID (Fall 2005, est.) 2800 applied for aid; of those 64% were deemed to have need. 98% of freshmen with need received aid; of those 11% had need fully met. *Average percent of need met:* 66% (excluding resources awarded to replace EFC). *Average financial aid package:* $6100 (excluding resources awarded to replace EFC). 1% of all full-time freshmen had no need and received non-need-based gift aid.

UNDERGRADUATE FINANCIAL AID (Fall 2005, est.) 14,000 applied for aid; of those 79% were deemed to have need. 95% of undergraduates with need received aid; of those 11% had need fully met. *Average percent of need met:* 71% (excluding resources awarded to replace EFC). *Average financial aid package:* $7400 (excluding resources awarded to replace EFC). 2% of all full-time undergraduates had no need and received non-need-based gift aid.

GIFT AID (NEED-BASED) *Total amount:* $47,710,000 (45% federal, 27% state, 28% institutional). *Receiving aid:* Freshmen: 35% (1,200); All full-time undergraduates: 37% (8,000). *Average award:* Freshmen: $5600; Undergraduates: $5700. *Scholarships, grants, and awards:* Federal Pell, FSEOG, state, private, college/university gift aid from institutional funds, Federal Nursing.

GIFT AID (NON-NEED-BASED) *Total amount:* $6,036,700 (37% federal, 18% institutional, 45% external sources). *Receiving aid:* Freshmen: 20% (700); Undergraduates: 7% (1,600). *Average Award:* Freshmen: $2500; Undergraduates: $1700. *Scholarships, grants, and awards by category:* Academic Interests/Achievement: general academic interests/achievements. Creative Arts/Performance: art/fine arts, creative writing, dance, journalism/publications, music, performing arts, theater/drama. Special Achievements/Activities: community service, leadership. Special Characteristics: children and siblings of alumni, children of faculty/staff, children of public servants, handicapped students, local/state students. *Tuition waivers:* Full or partial for employees or children of employees. *ROTC:* Army, Naval, Air Force.

LOANS *Student loans:* $66,333,700 (67% need-based, 33% non-need-based). 49% of past graduating class borrowed through all loan programs. *Average indebtedness per student:* $14,500. *Average need-based loan:* Freshmen: $2300; Undergraduates: $4000. *Parent loans:* $61,820,000 (25% need-based, 75% non-need-based). *Programs:* Federal Direct (Subsidized and Unsubsidized Stafford, PLUS), Perkins, college/university.

WORK-STUDY *Federal work-study:* Total amount: $1,575,900; 840 jobs averaging $1876.

ATHLETIC AWARDS Total amount: $3,798,000 (100% non-need-based).

APPLYING FOR FINANCIAL AID *Required financial aid forms:* FAFSA, state aid form. *Financial aid deadline:* Continuous. *Notification date:* Continuous beginning 2/14.

CONTACT Ms. Chrys Dutton, Director of Financial Aid and Scholarships, San Diego State University, 5500 Campanile Drive, SSW-3605, San Diego, CA 92182-7436, 619-594-6323.

SAN FRANCISCO ART INSTITUTE
San Francisco, CA

CONTACT Director of Financial Aid, San Francisco Art Institute, 800 Chestnut Street, San Francisco, CA 94133-2299, 415-749-4560 or toll-free 800-345-SFAI. *Fax:* 415-351-3503.

SAN FRANCISCO CONSERVATORY OF MUSIC
San Francisco, CA

CONTACT Doris Howard, Financial Aid Manager, San Francisco Conservatory of Music, 1201 Ortega Street, San Francisco, CA 94122-4411, 415-759-3414. *Fax:* 415-759-3499.

SAN FRANCISCO STATE UNIVERSITY
San Francisco, CA

Tuition & fees (CA res): $3370	Average undergraduate aid package: $8441

ABOUT THE INSTITUTION State-supported, coed. Awards: bachelor's, master's, and doctoral degrees and post-bachelor's certificates. 91 undergraduate majors. Total enrollment: 28,950. Undergraduates: 23,074. Freshmen: 3,150. Federal methodology is used as a basis for awarding need-based institutional aid.

UNDERGRADUATE EXPENSES for 2006–07 *Application fee:* $55. *Tuition, state resident:* full-time $0. *Tuition, nonresident:* full-time $13,540; part-time $339 per unit. *College room and board:* $9124; *room only:* $5900.

FRESHMAN FINANCIAL AID (Fall 2005, est.) 2582 applied for aid; of those 78% were deemed to have need. 92% of freshmen with need received aid; of those 8% had need fully met. *Average percent of need met:* 62% (excluding resources awarded to replace EFC). *Average financial aid package:* $7532 (excluding resources awarded to replace EFC). 2% of all full-time freshmen had no need and received non-need-based gift aid.

UNDERGRADUATE FINANCIAL AID (Fall 2005, est.) 9,948 applied for aid; of those 86% were deemed to have need. 95% of undergraduates with need received aid; of those 8% had need fully met. *Average percent of need met:* 65% (excluding resources awarded to replace EFC). *Average financial aid package:* $8441 (excluding resources awarded to replace EFC). 1% of all full-time undergraduates had no need and received non-need-based gift aid.

GIFT AID (NEED-BASED) *Total amount:* $45,670,061 (47% federal, 49% state, 1% institutional, 3% external sources). *Receiving aid:* Freshmen: 35% (1,317); All full-time undergraduates: 36% (6,058). *Average award:* Freshmen: $6341; Undergraduates: $5711. *Scholarships, grants, and awards:* Federal Pell, FSEOG, state, private, college/university gift aid from institutional funds.

GIFT AID (NON-NEED-BASED) *Total amount:* $546,834 (25% institutional, 75% external sources). *Receiving aid:* Freshmen: 8% (295); Undergraduates: 4% (692). *Average Award:* Freshmen: $1939; Undergraduates: $1841. *ROTC:* Army cooperative, Naval cooperative, Air Force cooperative.

LOANS *Student loans:* $43,666,906 (90% need-based, 10% non-need-based). 46% of past graduating class borrowed through all loan programs. *Average indebtedness per student:* $15,376. *Average need-based loan:* Freshmen: $1715; Undergraduates: $2995. *Parent loans:* $14,401,113 (64% need-based, 36% non-need-based). *Programs:* Federal Direct (Subsidized and Unsubsidized Stafford), FFEL (PLUS), Perkins.

WORK-STUDY *Federal work-study:* Total amount: $1,500,000; 600 jobs averaging $2500.

ATHLETIC AWARDS Total amount: $258,277 (44% need-based, 56% non-need-based).

APPLYING FOR FINANCIAL AID *Required financial aid form:* FAFSA. *Financial aid deadline (priority):* 3/2. *Notification date:* Continuous beginning 1/31. Students must reply within 3 weeks of notification.

CONTACT Barbara Hubler, Director of Financial Aid, San Francisco State University, 1600 Holloway Avenue, San Francisco, CA 94132-1722, 415-338-7000. *E-mail:* finaid@sfsu.edu.

SAN JOSE STATE UNIVERSITY
San Jose, CA

Tuition & fees: N/R	Average undergraduate aid package: $6838

ABOUT THE INSTITUTION State-supported, coed. Awards: bachelor's and master's degrees. 89 undergraduate majors. Total enrollment: 29,975. Undergraduates: 22,733. Freshmen: 2,551. Federal methodology is used as a basis for awarding need-based institutional aid.

UNDERGRADUATE EXPENSES for 2005–06 *Application fee:* $55. *Tuition, nonresident:* full-time $10,170; part-time $339 per unit. Full-time tuition and fees vary according to course load. Part-time tuition and fees vary according to course load. *College room and board:* $8718; *room only:* $5412. Room and board charges vary according to board plan and housing facility. *Payment plan:* Installment.

FRESHMAN FINANCIAL AID (Fall 2004) 1555 applied for aid; of those 76% were deemed to have need. 82% of freshmen with need received aid; of those 8% had need fully met. *Average percent of need met:* 60% (excluding resources awarded to replace EFC). *Average financial aid package:* $6329 (excluding resources awarded to replace EFC). 1% of all full-time freshmen had no need and received non-need-based gift aid.

UNDERGRADUATE FINANCIAL AID (Fall 2004) 8,658 applied for aid; of those 87% were deemed to have need. 96% of undergraduates with need received aid; of those 11% had need fully met. *Average percent of need met:* 58% (excluding resources awarded to replace EFC). *Average financial aid package:*

San Jose State University

$6838 (excluding resources awarded to replace EFC). 1% of all full-time undergraduates had no need and received non-need-based gift aid.
GIFT AID (NEED-BASED) *Total amount:* $40,765,502 (46% federal, 49% state, 2% institutional, 3% external sources). *Receiving aid:* Freshmen: 33% (854); All full-time undergraduates: 35% (5,912). *Average award:* Freshmen: $6701; Undergraduates: $5818. *Scholarships, grants, and awards:* Federal Pell, FSEOG, state, private, college/university gift aid from institutional funds.
GIFT AID (NON-NEED-BASED) *Total amount:* $318,530 (38% institutional, 62% external sources). *Receiving aid:* Freshmen: 8; Undergraduates: 64. *Average Award:* Freshmen: $4185; Undergraduates: $7088. *Scholarships, grants, and awards by category: Academic Interests/Achievement:* 115 awards ($120,246 total): general academic interests/achievements. *Tuition waivers:* Full or partial for employees or children of employees. *ROTC:* Army, Air Force.
LOANS *Student loans:* $24,997,357 (88% need-based, 12% non-need-based). 26% of past graduating class borrowed through all loan programs. *Average indebtedness per student:* $5733. *Average need-based loan:* Freshmen: $2420; Undergraduates: $3900. *Parent loans:* $2,666,324 (62% need-based, 38% non-need-based). *Programs:* FFEL (Subsidized and Unsubsidized Stafford, PLUS), Perkins, college/university.
WORK-STUDY *Federal work-study:* Total amount: $1,465,005; 590 jobs averaging $2410.
ATHLETIC AWARDS *Total amount:* $895,942 (88% need-based, 12% non-need-based).
APPLYING FOR FINANCIAL AID *Required financial aid form:* FAFSA. *Financial aid deadline (priority):* 3/2. *Notification date:* Continuous beginning 5/1.
CONTACT Colleen S. Brown, Director of Financial Aid, San Jose State University, One Washington Square, Student Services Center 200, San Jose, CA 95192-0036, 408-924-6060. *E-mail:* brownc@sjsu.edu.

SANTA CLARA UNIVERSITY
Santa Clara, CA

Tuition & fees: $28,899   **Average undergraduate aid package: $19,706**

ABOUT THE INSTITUTION Independent Roman Catholic (Jesuit), coed. Awards: bachelor's, master's, doctoral, and first professional degrees and post-bachelor's, post-master's, and first professional certificates. 43 undergraduate majors. Total enrollment: 8,097. Undergraduates: 4,638. Freshmen: 1,198. Both federal and institutional methodology are used as a basis for awarding need-based institutional aid.
UNDERGRADUATE EXPENSES for 2005–06 *Application fee:* $55. *Comprehensive fee:* $38,931 includes full-time tuition ($28,899) and room and board ($10,032). Room and board charges vary according to board plan, housing facility, and student level. *Part-time tuition:* $925 per unit. Part-time tuition and fees vary according to course load. *Payment plans:* Tuition prepayment, installment, deferred payment.
FRESHMAN FINANCIAL AID (Fall 2005, est.) 735 applied for aid; of those 62% were deemed to have need. 98% of freshmen with need received aid; of those 67% had need fully met. *Average percent of need met:* 71% (excluding resources awarded to replace EFC). *Average financial aid package:* $17,578 (excluding resources awarded to replace EFC). 21% of all full-time freshmen had no need and received non-need-based gift aid.
UNDERGRADUATE FINANCIAL AID (Fall 2005, est.) 3,012 applied for aid; of those 79% were deemed to have need. 84% of undergraduates with need received aid; of those 58% had need fully met. *Average percent of need met:* 70% (excluding resources awarded to replace EFC). *Average financial aid package:* $19,706 (excluding resources awarded to replace EFC). 15% of all full-time undergraduates had no need and received non-need-based gift aid.
GIFT AID (NEED-BASED) *Total amount:* $30,379,517 (7% federal, 16% state, 76% institutional, 1% external sources). *Receiving aid:* Freshmen: 33% (392); All full-time undergraduates: 38% (1,837). *Average award:* Freshmen: $14,253; Undergraduates: $15,990. *Scholarships, grants, and awards:* Federal Pell, FSEOG, state, private, college/university gift aid from institutional funds.
GIFT AID (NON-NEED-BASED) *Total amount:* $12,205,704 (90% institutional, 10% external sources). *Receiving aid:* Freshmen: 11% (133); Undergraduates: 9% (444). *Average Award:* Freshmen: $10,595; Undergraduates: $9259. *Scholarships, grants, and awards by category: Academic Interests/Achievement:* 1,887 awards ($18,437,085 total): business, engineering/technologies, general academic interests/achievements, military science. *Creative Arts/Performance:* 80 awards ($176,202 total): dance, debating, music, theater/drama. *Special Characteristics:* 96 awards ($2,323,352 total): children and siblings of alumni, children of faculty/staff, children with a deceased or disabled parent, handicapped students. *Tuition waivers:* Full or partial for employees or children of employees. *ROTC:* Army, Air Force cooperative.
LOANS *Student loans:* $12,424,409 (53% need-based, 47% non-need-based). 50% of past graduating class borrowed through all loan programs. *Average indebtedness per student:* $17,620. *Average need-based loan:* Freshmen: $3622; Undergraduates: $4963. *Parent loans:* $13,509,234 (100% non-need-based). *Programs:* Federal Direct (Subsidized and Unsubsidized Stafford, PLUS), Perkins, alternative private loans.
WORK-STUDY *Federal work-study:* Total amount: $1,255,568; 322 jobs averaging $2747.
ATHLETIC AWARDS *Total amount:* $2,958,289 (100% non-need-based).
APPLYING FOR FINANCIAL AID *Required financial aid forms:* FAFSA, CSS Financial Aid PROFILE. *Financial aid deadline (priority):* 2/1. *Notification date:* Continuous beginning 4/1. Students must reply by 5/1 or within 2 weeks of notification.
CONTACT Marta I. Chaskelmann, Assistant Director, Technical Services, Santa Clara University, 500 El Camino Real, Santa Clara, CA 95053, 408-551-6088. *Fax:* 408-551-6085. *E-mail:* mchaskelmann@scu.edu.

SARAH LAWRENCE COLLEGE
Bronxville, NY

Tuition & fees: $34,042   **Average undergraduate aid package: $25,032**

ABOUT THE INSTITUTION Independent, coed. Awards: bachelor's and master's degrees. 112 undergraduate majors. Total enrollment: 1,662. Undergraduates: 1,339. Freshmen: 376. Both federal and institutional methodology are used as a basis for awarding need-based institutional aid.
UNDERGRADUATE EXPENSES for 2005–06 *Application fee:* $60. *Comprehensive fee:* $45,506 includes full-time tuition ($33,270), mandatory fees ($772), and room and board ($11,464). *College room only:* $7600. Full-time tuition and fees vary according to course load. Room and board charges vary according to board plan. *Part-time tuition:* $1109 per credit. *Part-time fees:* $386 per term. Part-time tuition and fees vary according to course load. *Payment plan:* Installment.
FRESHMAN FINANCIAL AID (Fall 2005, est.) 229 applied for aid; of those 82% were deemed to have need. 100% of freshmen with need received aid; of those 90% had need fully met. *Average percent of need met:* 92% (excluding resources awarded to replace EFC). *Average financial aid package:* $25,580 (excluding resources awarded to replace EFC). 1% of all full-time freshmen had no need and received non-need-based gift aid.
UNDERGRADUATE FINANCIAL AID (Fall 2005, est.) 724 applied for aid; of those 88% were deemed to have need. 100% of undergraduates with need received aid; of those 80% had need fully met. *Average percent of need met:* 90% (excluding resources awarded to replace EFC). *Average financial aid package:* $25,032 (excluding resources awarded to replace EFC). 1% of all full-time undergraduates had no need and received non-need-based gift aid.
GIFT AID (NEED-BASED) *Total amount:* $12,776,007 (5% federal, 2% state, 92% institutional, 1% external sources). *Receiving aid:* Freshmen: 48% (179); All full-time undergraduates: 47% (593). *Average award:* Freshmen: $22,463; Undergraduates: $21,545. *Scholarships, grants, and awards:* Federal Pell, FSEOG, state, private, college/university gift aid from institutional funds.
GIFT AID (NON-NEED-BASED) *Total amount:* $6000 (100% institutional). *Receiving aid:* Freshmen: 1; Undergraduates: 4. *Average Award:* Freshmen: $500; Undergraduates: $6000. *Tuition waivers:* Full or partial for employees or children of employees.
LOANS *Student loans:* $2,300,692 (92% need-based, 8% non-need-based). 63% of past graduating class borrowed through all loan programs. *Average indebtedness per student:* $13,607. *Average need-based loan:* Freshmen: $2217; Undergraduates: $3061. *Parent loans:* $3,665,418 (77% need-based, 23% non-need-based). *Programs:* FFEL (Subsidized and Unsubsidized Stafford, PLUS), Perkins, college/university, Achiever Loans, Signature Loans, CitiAssist Loans.
WORK-STUDY *Federal work-study:* Total amount: $825,526; 511 jobs averaging $1616. *State or other work-study/employment:* Total amount: $78,177 (93% need-based, 7% non-need-based). 44 part-time jobs averaging $1654.

APPLYING FOR FINANCIAL AID *Required financial aid forms:* FAFSA, CSS Financial Aid PROFILE, state aid form, noncustodial (divorced/separated) parent's statement. *Financial aid deadline:* 2/1. *Notification date:* 4/1. Students must reply by 5/1.
CONTACT Ms. Heather McDonnell, Director of Financial Aid, Sarah Lawrence College, One Mead Way, Bronxville, NY 10708, 914-395-2570 or toll-free 800-888-2858. *Fax:* 914-395-2676. *E-mail:* hmcdonn@sarahlawrence.edu.

SAVANNAH COLLEGE OF ART AND DESIGN
Savannah, GA

| Tuition & fees: $23,450 | Average undergraduate aid package: $9500 |

ABOUT THE INSTITUTION Independent, coed. Awards: bachelor's and master's degrees and post-bachelor's certificates. 21 undergraduate majors. Total enrollment: 7,356. Undergraduates: 6,136. Freshmen: 1,407. Federal methodology is used as a basis for awarding need-based institutional aid.
UNDERGRADUATE EXPENSES for 2006–07 *Application fee:* $50. *Comprehensive fee:* $33,045 includes full-time tuition ($22,950), mandatory fees ($500), and room and board ($9595). *College room only:* $6250. *Part-time tuition:* $2550 per course.
FRESHMAN FINANCIAL AID (Fall 2005, est.) 990 applied for aid; of those 77% were deemed to have need. 98% of freshmen with need received aid; of those 46% had need fully met. *Average percent of need met:* 10% (excluding resources awarded to replace EFC). *Average financial aid package:* $10,400 (excluding resources awarded to replace EFC). 32% of all full-time freshmen had no need and received non-need-based gift aid.
UNDERGRADUATE FINANCIAL AID (Fall 2005, est.) 3,567 applied for aid; of those 81% were deemed to have need. 98% of undergraduates with need received aid; of those 40% had need fully met. *Average percent of need met:* 11% (excluding resources awarded to replace EFC). *Average financial aid package:* $9500 (excluding resources awarded to replace EFC). 3% of all full-time undergraduates had no need and received non-need-based gift aid.
GIFT AID (NEED-BASED) *Total amount:* $3,334,228 (95% federal, 2% state, 3% institutional). *Receiving aid:* Freshmen: 15% (202); All full-time undergraduates: 15% (828). *Average award:* Freshmen: $3200; Undergraduates: $3500. *Scholarships, grants, and awards:* Federal Pell, FSEOG, state, private, college/university gift aid from institutional funds.
GIFT AID (NON-NEED-BASED) *Total amount:* $19,654,611 (9% state, 85% institutional, 6% external sources). *Receiving aid:* Freshmen: 49% (675); Undergraduates: 42% (2,329). *Average Award:* Freshmen: $5100; Undergraduates:* $4400. *Scholarships, grants, and awards by category: Academic Interests/Achievement:* architecture, general academic interests/achievements, humanities. *Creative Arts/Performance:* art/fine arts, general creative arts/performance. *Special Achievements/Activities:* general special achievements/activities. *Special Characteristics:* general special characteristics.
LOANS *Student loans:* $14,929,543 (70% need-based, 30% non-need-based). 93% of past graduating class borrowed through all loan programs. *Average indebtedness per student:* $24,700. *Average need-based loan:* Freshmen: $2600; Undergraduates: $3900. *Parent loans:* $33,978,466 (100% non-need-based). *Programs:* Federal Direct (Subsidized and Unsubsidized Stafford, PLUS), Perkins.
WORK-STUDY *Federal work-study:* Total amount: $185,904; 68 jobs averaging $2734. *State or other work-study/employment:* Total amount: $432,240 (100% non-need-based). 214 part-time jobs averaging $2095.
ATHLETIC AWARDS *Total amount:* $2,838,648 (100% non-need-based).
APPLYING FOR FINANCIAL AID *Required financial aid forms:* FAFSA, institution's own form, state aid form. *Financial aid deadline (priority):* 4/1. *Notification date:* Continuous. Students must reply within 4 weeks of notification.
CONTACT Ms. Cindy Bradley, Director of Financial Aid, Savannah College of Art and Design, PO Box 3146, 342 Bull Street, Savannah, GA 31402-3146, 912-525-6119 or toll-free 800-869-7223. *Fax:* 912-525-6263. *E-mail:* cbradley@scad.edu.

SAVANNAH STATE UNIVERSITY
Savannah, GA

CONTACT Mark Adkins, Director of Financial Aid, Savannah State University, PO Box 20523, Savannah, GA 31404, 912-356-2253 or toll-free 800-788-0478. *Fax:* 912-353-3150. *E-mail:* finaid@savstate.edu.

SCHOOL OF THE ART INSTITUTE OF CHICAGO
Chicago, IL

ABOUT THE INSTITUTION Independent, coed. Awards: bachelor's and master's degrees. 36 undergraduate majors. Total enrollment: 2,679. Undergraduates: 2,099. Freshmen: 354.
GIFT AID (NEED-BASED) *Scholarships, grants, and awards:* Federal Pell, FSEOG, state, private, college/university gift aid from institutional funds.
GIFT AID (NON-NEED-BASED) *Scholarships, grants, and awards by category: Academic Interests/Achievement:* general academic interests/achievements. *Creative Arts/Performance:* art/fine arts.
LOANS *Programs:* FFEL (Subsidized and Unsubsidized Stafford, PLUS), Perkins.
APPLYING FOR FINANCIAL AID *Required financial aid forms:* FAFSA, institution's own form, federal income tax form(s).
CONTACT Financial Aid Office, School of the Art Institute of Chicago, 37 South Wabash, Chicago, IL 60603-3103, 312-899-5106 or toll-free 800-232-SAIC.

SCHOOL OF THE MUSEUM OF FINE ARTS, BOSTON
Boston, MA

| Tuition & fees: $24,760 | Average undergraduate aid package: $15,501 |

ABOUT THE INSTITUTION Independent, coed. Awards: bachelor's and master's degrees and post-bachelor's certificates. 20 undergraduate majors. Total enrollment: 773. Undergraduates: 677. Freshmen: 129. Federal methodology is used as a basis for awarding need-based institutional aid.
UNDERGRADUATE EXPENSES for 2005–06 *Application fee:* $65. *Tuition:* full-time $23,850; part-time $1000 per credit hour. *Required fees:* full-time $910; $455 per term part-time. Full-time tuition and fees vary according to course load, degree level, and program. Part-time tuition and fees vary according to class time, course load, and program. Room and board charges vary according to housing facility. *Payment plan:* Installment.
FRESHMAN FINANCIAL AID (Fall 2005, est.) 85 applied for aid; of those 82% were deemed to have need. 100% of freshmen with need received aid. *Average percent of need met:* 33% (excluding resources awarded to replace EFC). *Average financial aid package:* $14,981 (excluding resources awarded to replace EFC). 4% of all full-time freshmen had no need and received non-need-based gift aid.
UNDERGRADUATE FINANCIAL AID (Fall 2005, est.) 431 applied for aid; of those 94% were deemed to have need. 100% of undergraduates with need received aid. *Average percent of need met:* 35% (excluding resources awarded to replace EFC). *Average financial aid package:* $15,501 (excluding resources awarded to replace EFC). 1% of all full-time undergraduates had no need and received non-need-based gift aid.
GIFT AID (NEED-BASED) *Total amount:* $4,360,059 (13% federal, 2% state, 82% institutional, 3% external sources). *Receiving aid:* Freshmen: 56% (69); All full-time undergraduates: 63% (383). *Average award:* Freshmen: $8164; Undergraduates: $9006. *Scholarships, grants, and awards:* Federal Pell, FSEOG, state, private, college/university gift aid from institutional funds.
GIFT AID (NON-NEED-BASED) *Total amount:* $360,969 (100% institutional). *Receiving aid:* Freshmen: 10% (12); Undergraduates: 6% (38). *Average Award:* Freshmen: $5503; Undergraduates: $4290. *Scholarships, grants, and awards by category: Creative Arts/Performance:* art/fine arts. *Special Characteristics:* general special characteristics. *Tuition waivers:* Full or partial for employees or children of employees.
LOANS *Student loans:* $4,866,216 (100% need-based). 53% of past graduating class borrowed through all loan programs. *Average indebtedness per student:* $23,898. *Average need-based loan:* Freshmen: $2565; Undergraduates: $4019. *Parent loans:* $2,600,855 (100% need-based). *Programs:* FFEL (Subsidized and Unsubsidized Stafford, PLUS), state.
WORK-STUDY *Federal work-study:* Total amount: $253,572; 139 jobs averaging $2173.
APPLYING FOR FINANCIAL AID *Required financial aid forms:* FAFSA, institution's own form. *Financial aid deadline (priority):* 3/15. *Notification date:* 4/1.
CONTACT Ms. Elizabeth Goreham, Director of Financial Aid, School of the Museum of Fine Arts, Boston, 230 The Fenway, Boston, MA 02115, 617-369-3684 or toll-free 800-643-6078 (in-state). *Fax:* 617-369-3041.

School of Visual Arts

SCHOOL OF VISUAL ARTS
New York, NY

ABOUT THE INSTITUTION Proprietary, coed. Awards: bachelor's and master's degrees. 9 undergraduate majors. Total enrollment: 3,575. Undergraduates: 3,163. Freshmen: 586.
GIFT AID (NEED-BASED) *Scholarships, grants, and awards:* Federal Pell, FSEOG, state, private, college/university gift aid from institutional funds.
GIFT AID (NON-NEED-BASED) *Scholarships, grants, and awards by category: Creative Arts/Performance:* art/fine arts.
LOANS *Programs:* FFEL (Subsidized and Unsubsidized Stafford, PLUS), Perkins, alternative loans.
APPLYING FOR FINANCIAL AID *Required financial aid forms:* FAFSA, state aid form.
CONTACT Javier Vega, Director of Financial Aid, School of Visual Arts, 209 East 23rd Street, New York, NY 10010, 212-592-2030 or toll-free 800-436-4204. *Fax:* 212-592-2029. *E-mail:* jvega@sva.edu.

SCHREINER UNIVERSITY
Kerrville, TX

Tuition & fees: $15,142	Average undergraduate aid package: $11,563

ABOUT THE INSTITUTION Independent Presbyterian, coed. Awards: associate, bachelor's, and master's degrees and post-bachelor's certificates. 33 undergraduate majors. Total enrollment: 842. Undergraduates: 793. Freshmen: 212. Federal methodology is used as a basis for awarding need-based institutional aid.
UNDERGRADUATE EXPENSES for 2005–06 *Application fee:* $25. *Comprehensive fee:* $22,474 includes full-time tuition ($14,742), mandatory fees ($400), and room and board ($7332). *College room only:* $3900. Room and board charges vary according to board plan and housing facility. *Part-time tuition:* $629 per credit. *Payment plan:* Installment.
FRESHMAN FINANCIAL AID (Fall 2004) 184 applied for aid; of those 88% were deemed to have need. 99% of freshmen with need received aid; of those 11% had need fully met. *Average percent of need met:* 65% (excluding resources awarded to replace EFC). *Average financial aid package:* $10,366 (excluding resources awarded to replace EFC). 22% of all full-time freshmen had no need and received non-need-based gift aid.
UNDERGRADUATE FINANCIAL AID (Fall 2004) 641 applied for aid; of those 89% were deemed to have need. 99% of undergraduates with need received aid; of those 14% had need fully met. *Average percent of need met:* 72% (excluding resources awarded to replace EFC). *Average financial aid package:* $11,563 (excluding resources awarded to replace EFC). 17% of all full-time undergraduates had no need and received non-need-based gift aid.
GIFT AID (NEED-BASED) *Total amount:* $5,810,921 (19% federal, 21% state, 54% institutional, 6% external sources). *Receiving aid:* Freshmen: 77% (159); All full-time undergraduates: 78% (561). *Average award:* Freshmen: $8566; Undergraduates: $8984. *Scholarships, grants, and awards:* Federal Pell, FSEOG, state, private, college/university gift aid from institutional funds.
GIFT AID (NON-NEED-BASED) *Total amount:* $1,009,338 (4% state, 82% institutional, 14% external sources). *Receiving aid:* Freshmen: 8% (16); Undergraduates: 8% (56). *Average Award:* Freshmen: $12,497; Undergraduates: $12,013. *Scholarships, grants, and awards by category: Academic Interests/Achievement:* 297 awards ($1,261,709 total): biological sciences, business, education, English, general academic interests/achievements, mathematics, physical sciences, religion/biblical studies, social sciences. *Creative Arts/Performance:* 37 awards ($44,750 total): art/fine arts, journalism/publications, music, theater/drama. *Special Achievements/Activities:* 9 awards ($63,000 total): community service, leadership, religious involvement. *Special Characteristics:* 374 awards ($855,073 total): children of faculty/staff, ethnic background, general special characteristics, international students, local/state students, religious affiliation. *Tuition waivers:* Full or partial for employees or children of employees.
LOANS *Student loans:* $4,254,517 (76% need-based, 24% non-need-based). 83% of past graduating class borrowed through all loan programs. *Average indebtedness per student:* $21,455. *Average need-based loan:* Freshmen: $2084; Undergraduates: $2884. *Parent loans:* $1,870,435 (34% need-based, 66% non-need-based). *Programs:* FFEL (Subsidized and Unsubsidized Stafford, PLUS), state, Sallie Mae Signature Loan, alternative loans.
WORK-STUDY *Federal work-study:* Total amount: $80,534; 108 jobs averaging $764. *State or other work-study/employment:* Total amount: $178,260 (54% need-based, 46% non-need-based). 118 part-time jobs averaging $811.
APPLYING FOR FINANCIAL AID *Required financial aid forms:* FAFSA, institution's own form. *Financial aid deadline:* 8/1 (priority: 4/1). *Notification date:* Continuous beginning 2/21. Students must reply within 2 weeks of notification.
CONTACT Toni Bryant, Director of Financial Aid, Schreiner University, 2100 Memorial Boulevard, Kerrville, TX 78028, 830-792-7217 or toll-free 800-343-4919. *Fax:* 830-792-7226. *E-mail:* finaid@schreiner.edu.

SCRIPPS COLLEGE
Claremont, CA

Tuition & fees: $31,500	Average undergraduate aid package: $27,665

ABOUT THE INSTITUTION Independent, women only. Awards: bachelor's degrees and post-bachelor's certificates. 57 undergraduate majors. Total enrollment: 908. Undergraduates: 887. Freshmen: 233. Both federal and institutional methodology are used as a basis for awarding need-based institutional aid.
UNDERGRADUATE EXPENSES for 2005–06 *Application fee:* $50. *Comprehensive fee:* $41,000 includes full-time tuition ($31,332), mandatory fees ($168), and room and board ($9500). *College room only:* $5100. Full-time tuition and fees vary according to program. Room and board charges vary according to board plan. Part-time tuition and fees vary according to program. *Payment plan:* Installment.
FRESHMAN FINANCIAL AID (Fall 2005, est.) 142 applied for aid; of those 70% were deemed to have need. 100% of freshmen with need received aid; of those 100% had need fully met. *Average percent of need met:* 100% (excluding resources awarded to replace EFC). *Average financial aid package:* $26,229 (excluding resources awarded to replace EFC). 9% of all full-time freshmen had no need and received non-need-based gift aid.
UNDERGRADUATE FINANCIAL AID (Fall 2005, est.) 465 applied for aid; of those 80% were deemed to have need. 100% of undergraduates with need received aid; of those 100% had need fully met. *Average percent of need met:* 100% (excluding resources awarded to replace EFC). *Average financial aid package:* $27,665 (excluding resources awarded to replace EFC). 11% of all full-time undergraduates had no need and received non-need-based gift aid.
GIFT AID (NEED-BASED) *Total amount:* $8,917,634 (5% federal, 7% state, 85% institutional, 3% external sources). *Receiving aid:* Freshmen: 43% (100); All full-time undergraduates: 43% (372). *Average award:* Freshmen: $22,305; Undergraduates: $23,122. *Scholarships, grants, and awards:* Federal Pell, FSEOG, state, private, college/university gift aid from institutional funds.
GIFT AID (NON-NEED-BASED) *Total amount:* $1,383,849 (1% state, 89% institutional, 10% external sources). *Receiving aid:* Freshmen: 7% (17); Undergraduates: 5% (43). *Average Award:* Freshmen: $13,626; Undergraduates: $15,715. *Scholarships, grants, and awards by category: Academic Interests/Achievement:* 144 awards ($2,321,478 total): general academic interests/achievements. *Tuition waivers:* Full or partial for employees or children of employees. *ROTC:* Army cooperative, Air Force cooperative.
LOANS *Student loans:* $2,194,082 (50% need-based, 50% non-need-based). 49% of past graduating class borrowed through all loan programs. *Average indebtedness per student:* $12,907. *Average need-based loan:* Freshmen: $2753; Undergraduates: $3872. *Parent loans:* $1,516,726 (100% non-need-based). *Programs:* FFEL (Subsidized and Unsubsidized Stafford, PLUS), Perkins, college/university.
WORK-STUDY *Federal work-study:* Total amount: $502,576; 314 jobs averaging $1626.
APPLYING FOR FINANCIAL AID *Required financial aid forms:* FAFSA, CSS Financial Aid PROFILE, noncustodial (divorced/separated) parent's statement, business/farm supplement, verification worksheet, federal income tax form(s). *Financial aid deadline (priority):* 2/1. *Notification date:* 4/1. Students must reply by 5/1 or within 2 weeks of notification.
CONTACT Sean Smith, Director of Financial Aid, Scripps College, 1030 Columbia Avenue, PMB 1293, Claremont, CA 91711-3948, 909-621-8275 or toll-free 800-770-1333. *Fax:* 909-607-7742. *E-mail:* finaid@scrippscollege.edu.

SEATTLE PACIFIC UNIVERSITY
Seattle, WA

Tuition & fees: $21,783   **Average undergraduate aid package:** $18,525

ABOUT THE INSTITUTION Independent Free Methodist, coed. Awards: bachelor's, master's, and doctoral degrees and post-master's certificates. 54 undergraduate majors. Total enrollment: 3,873. Undergraduates: 3,022. Freshmen: 710. Federal methodology is used as a basis for awarding need-based institutional aid.

UNDERGRADUATE EXPENSES for 2005–06 *Application fee:* $45. *Comprehensive fee:* $29,355 includes full-time tuition ($21,447), mandatory fees ($336), and room and board ($7572). *College room only:* $4071. Room and board charges vary according to board plan and housing facility. *Part-time tuition:* $596 per credit. Part-time tuition and fees vary according to course load. *Payment plan:* Installment.

FRESHMAN FINANCIAL AID (Fall 2005, est.) 578 applied for aid; of those 81% were deemed to have need. 100% of freshmen with need received aid; of those 22% had need fully met. *Average percent of need met:* 81% (excluding resources awarded to replace EFC). *Average financial aid package:* $18,573 (excluding resources awarded to replace EFC). 27% of all full-time freshmen had no need and received non-need-based gift aid.

UNDERGRADUATE FINANCIAL AID (Fall 2005, est.) 2,109 applied for aid; of those 84% were deemed to have need. 99% of undergraduates with need received aid; of those 24% had need fully met. *Average percent of need met:* 82% (excluding resources awarded to replace EFC). *Average financial aid package:* $18,525 (excluding resources awarded to replace EFC). 28% of all full-time undergraduates had no need and received non-need-based gift aid.

GIFT AID (NEED-BASED) *Total amount:* $21,290,784 (9% federal, 8% state, 77% institutional, 6% external sources). *Receiving aid:* Freshmen: 65% (459); All full-time undergraduates: 60% (1,709). *Average award:* Freshmen: $15,431; Undergraduates: $14,723. *Scholarships, grants, and awards:* Federal Pell, FSEOG, state, private, college/university gift aid from institutional funds.

GIFT AID (NON-NEED-BASED) *Total amount:* $5,681,581 (91% institutional, 9% external sources). *Average Award:* Freshmen: $11,096; Undergraduates: $9748. *Scholarships, grants, and awards by category:* Academic Interests/Achievement: 646 awards ($3,190,941 total): engineering/technologies, general academic interests/achievements. Creative Arts/Performance: 29 awards ($37,333 total): art/fine arts, performing arts. Special Characteristics: 221 awards ($755,733 total): children and siblings of alumni, children of faculty/staff, general special characteristics, international students, relatives of clergy, religious affiliation. *Tuition waivers:* Full or partial for employees or children of employees, senior citizens. *ROTC:* Army cooperative, Naval cooperative, Air Force cooperative.

LOANS *Student loans:* $11,181,371 (99% need-based, 1% non-need-based). 68% of past graduating class borrowed through all loan programs. *Average indebtedness per student:* $22,569. *Average need-based loan:* Freshmen: $4778; Undergraduates: $5452. *Parent loans:* $4,122,198 (75% need-based, 25% non-need-based). *Programs:* FFEL (Subsidized and Unsubsidized Stafford, PLUS), Perkins, Federal Nursing, college/university.

WORK-STUDY *Federal work-study:* Total amount: $497,371; 375 jobs averaging $1442. *State or other work-study/employment:* Total amount: $3,215,878 (100% need-based). 413 part-time jobs averaging $1923.

ATHLETIC AWARDS *Total amount:* $1,555,364 (58% need-based, 42% non-need-based).

APPLYING FOR FINANCIAL AID *Required financial aid form:* FAFSA. *Financial aid deadline (priority):* 4/1. *Notification date:* Continuous beginning 3/15. Students must reply by 5/1 or within 4 weeks of notification.

CONTACT Mr. Jordan Grant, Director of Student Financial Services, Seattle Pacific University, 3307 Third Avenue West, Seattle, WA 98119-1997, 206-281-2469 or toll-free 800-366-3344. *E-mail:* grantj@spu.edu.

SEATTLE UNIVERSITY
Seattle, WA

Tuition & fees: $22,905   **Average undergraduate aid package:** $22,535

ABOUT THE INSTITUTION Independent Roman Catholic, coed. Awards: bachelor's, master's, doctoral, and first professional degrees and post-bachelor's, post-master's, and first professional certificates. 56 undergraduate majors. Total enrollment: 7,109. Undergraduates: 4,182. Freshmen: 763. Federal methodology is used as a basis for awarding need-based institutional aid.

UNDERGRADUATE EXPENSES for 2005–06 *Application fee:* $45. *Comprehensive fee:* $30,063 includes full-time tuition ($22,905) and room and board ($7158). *College room only:* $4653. Full-time tuition and fees vary according to course load. Room and board charges vary according to board plan. *Part-time tuition:* $509 per credit. Part-time tuition and fees vary according to course load.

FRESHMAN FINANCIAL AID (Fall 2005, est.) 674 applied for aid; of those 76% were deemed to have need. 99% of freshmen with need received aid; of those 44% had need fully met. *Average percent of need met:* 86% (excluding resources awarded to replace EFC). *Average financial aid package:* $21,431 (excluding resources awarded to replace EFC). 1% of all full-time freshmen had no need and received non-need-based gift aid.

UNDERGRADUATE FINANCIAL AID (Fall 2005, est.) 3,094 applied for aid; of those 83% were deemed to have need. 99% of undergraduates with need received aid; of those 51% had need fully met. *Average percent of need met:* 84% (excluding resources awarded to replace EFC). *Average financial aid package:* $22,535 (excluding resources awarded to replace EFC). 4% of all full-time undergraduates had no need and received non-need-based gift aid.

GIFT AID (NEED-BASED) *Total amount:* $30,625,102 (15% federal, 8% state, 71% institutional, 6% external sources). *Receiving aid:* Freshmen: 64% (489); All full-time undergraduates: 65% (2,473). *Average award:* Freshmen: $19,528; Undergraduates: $17,049. *Scholarships, grants, and awards:* Federal Pell, FSEOG, state, private, college/university gift aid from institutional funds, Federal Nursing.

GIFT AID (NON-NEED-BASED) *Total amount:* $6,854,396 (20% federal, 57% institutional, 23% external sources). *Receiving aid:* Freshmen: 29% (222); Undergraduates: 25% (940). *Average Award:* Freshmen: $6510; Undergraduates: $7847. *Scholarships, grants, and awards by category:* Academic Interests/Achievement: 800 awards ($5,422,207 total): general academic interests/achievements. Creative Arts/Performance: 13 awards ($11,925 total): music. Special Achievements/Activities: 25 awards ($603,074 total): leadership. Special Characteristics: 402 awards ($2,594,224 total): children and siblings of alumni, children of educators, children of faculty/staff, members of minority groups. *Tuition waivers:* Full or partial for employees or children of employees. *ROTC:* Army, Air Force cooperative.

LOANS *Student loans:* $21,704,153 (68% need-based, 32% non-need-based). 68% of past graduating class borrowed through all loan programs. *Average indebtedness per student:* $25,311. *Average need-based loan:* Freshmen: $3464; Undergraduates: $4818. *Parent loans:* $3,799,370 (21% need-based, 79% non-need-based). *Programs:* Federal Direct (Subsidized and Unsubsidized Stafford, PLUS), Perkins, Federal Nursing, alternative loans.

WORK-STUDY *Federal work-study:* Total amount: $2,122,551; 704 jobs averaging $3899. *State or other work-study/employment:* Total amount: $2,686,338 (100% need-based). 830 part-time jobs averaging $5119.

ATHLETIC AWARDS *Total amount:* $1,101,149 (25% need-based, 75% non-need-based).

APPLYING FOR FINANCIAL AID *Required financial aid form:* FAFSA. *Financial aid deadline (priority):* 2/1. *Notification date:* 3/21. Students must reply by 5/1 or within 2 weeks of notification.

CONTACT Mr. James White, Director of Student Financial Services, Seattle University, Broadway & Madison, Seattle, WA 98122-4460, 206-296-2000 or toll-free 800-542-0833 (in-state), 800-426-7123 (out-of-state). *Fax:* 206-296-5755. *E-mail:* financial-aid@seattleu.edu.

SETON HALL UNIVERSITY
South Orange, NJ

ABOUT THE INSTITUTION Independent Roman Catholic, coed. Awards: bachelor's, master's, doctoral, and first professional degrees and post-master's certificates. 48 undergraduate majors. Total enrollment: 9,637. Undergraduates: 5,335. Freshmen: 1,120.

GIFT AID (NEED-BASED) *Scholarships, grants, and awards:* Federal Pell, FSEOG, state, private, college/university gift aid from institutional funds.

GIFT AID (NON-NEED-BASED) *Scholarships, grants, and awards by category:* Academic Interests/Achievement: biological sciences, business, education, general academic interests/achievements, health fields, military science, physical sciences, premedicine. Creative Arts/Performance: art/fine arts, cinema/film/broadcasting, debating, journalism/publications, music. Special Achievements/Activities: community service, leadership. Special Characteristics: children and

Seton Hall University

siblings of alumni, children of faculty/staff, children of union members/company employees, ethnic background, members of minority groups, relatives of clergy, siblings of current students.
LOANS *Programs:* FFEL (Subsidized and Unsubsidized Stafford, PLUS), Perkins, state.
WORK-STUDY *Federal work-study:* Total amount: $1,070,739; 807 jobs averaging $1930. *State or other work-study/employment:* Total amount: $699,459 (36% need-based, 64% non-need-based). 1,116 part-time jobs averaging $1289.
APPLYING FOR FINANCIAL AID *Required financial aid form:* FAFSA.
CONTACT Office of Enrollment Services, Seton Hall University, 400 South Orange Avenue, South Orange, NJ 07079, 973-761-9350 or toll-free 800-THE HALL (out-of-state). *Fax:* 973-275-2040. *E-mail:* thehall@shu.edu.

SETON HILL UNIVERSITY
Greensburg, PA

Tuition & fees: $21,990   **Average undergraduate aid package: $18,903**

ABOUT THE INSTITUTION Independent Roman Catholic, coed. Awards: bachelor's and master's degrees and post-bachelor's and post-master's certificates. 91 undergraduate majors. Total enrollment: 1,863. Undergraduates: 1,526. Freshmen: 336. Federal methodology is used as a basis for awarding need-based institutional aid.
UNDERGRADUATE EXPENSES for 2005–06 *Application fee:* $35. *Comprehensive fee:* $29,020 includes full-time tuition ($21,870), mandatory fees ($120), and room and board ($7030). Room and board charges vary according to board plan and housing facility. *Part-time tuition:* $580 per credit. *Part-time fees:* $60 per term. Part-time tuition and fees vary according to course load. *Payment plans:* Installment, deferred payment.
FRESHMAN FINANCIAL AID (Fall 2005, est.) 334 applied for aid; of those 98% were deemed to have need. 100% of freshmen with need received aid; of those 14% had need fully met. *Average percent of need met:* 83% (excluding resources awarded to replace EFC). *Average financial aid package:* $17,458 (excluding resources awarded to replace EFC). 1% of all full-time freshmen had no need and received non-need-based gift aid.
UNDERGRADUATE FINANCIAL AID (Fall 2005, est.) 973 applied for aid; of those 95% were deemed to have need. 100% of undergraduates with need received aid; of those 20% had need fully met. *Average percent of need met:* 75% (excluding resources awarded to replace EFC). *Average financial aid package:* $18,903 (excluding resources awarded to replace EFC). 5% of all full-time undergraduates had no need and received non-need-based gift aid.
GIFT AID (NEED-BASED) *Total amount:* $11,694,461 (14% federal, 17% state, 66% institutional, 3% external sources). *Receiving aid:* Freshmen: 98% (328); All full-time undergraduates: 85% (923). *Average award:* Freshmen: $13,200; Undergraduates: $12,100. *Scholarships, grants, and awards:* Federal Pell, FSEOG, state, private, college/university gift aid from institutional funds, United Negro College Fund.
GIFT AID (NON-NEED-BASED) *Total amount:* $380,502 (100% institutional). *Receiving aid:* Freshmen: 9% (30); Undergraduates: 7% (77). *Average Award:* Freshmen: $11,214; Undergraduates: $7100. *Scholarships, grants, and awards by category:* Academic Interests/Achievement: 376 awards ($2,492,022 total): biological sciences, business, communication, computer science, education, English, foreign languages, general academic interests/achievements, home economics, humanities, mathematics, physical sciences, premedicine, religion/biblical studies, social sciences. Creative Arts/Performance: 38 awards ($20,175 total): applied art and design, art/fine arts, creative writing, journalism/publications, music, performing arts, theater/drama. Special Achievements/Activities: 364 awards ($526,610 total): community service, general special achievements/activities, leadership, religious involvement. Special Characteristics: 181 awards ($606,018 total): adult students, children and siblings of alumni, children of faculty/staff, children with a deceased or disabled parent, international students, parents of current students, siblings of current students. *Tuition waivers:* Full or partial for employees or children of employees. **ROTC:** Army cooperative.
LOANS *Student loans:* $6,749,621 (50% need-based, 50% non-need-based). 74% of past graduating class borrowed through all loan programs. *Average indebtedness per student:* $26,281. *Average need-based loan:* Freshmen: $3291; Undergraduates: $3895. *Parent loans:* $1,588,110 (81% need-based, 19% non-need-based). *Programs:* FFEL (Subsidized and Unsubsidized Stafford, PLUS), Perkins, college/university, alternative loans.
WORK-STUDY *Federal work-study:* Total amount: $558,161; 452 jobs averaging $1236. *State or other work-study/employment:* Total amount: $401,017 (46% need-based, 54% non-need-based). 267 part-time jobs averaging $1500.
ATHLETIC AWARDS *Total amount:* $3,009,581 (65% need-based, 35% non-need-based).
APPLYING FOR FINANCIAL AID *Required financial aid forms:* FAFSA, institution's own form, state aid form. *Financial aid deadline (priority):* 6/1. *Notification date:* Continuous beginning 11/1. Students must reply within 2 weeks of notification.
CONTACT Maryann Dudas, Director of Financial Aid, Seton Hill University, Seton Hill Drive, Greensburg, PA 15601, 724-838-4293 or toll-free 800-826-6234. *Fax:* 724-830-1194. *E-mail:* dudas@setonhill.edu.

SEWANEE: THE UNIVERSITY OF THE SOUTH
Sewanee, TN

Tuition & fees: $27,095   **Average undergraduate aid package: $19,574**

ABOUT THE INSTITUTION Independent Episcopal, coed. Awards: bachelor's, master's, doctoral, and first professional degrees and post-bachelor's, post-master's, and first professional certificates. 41 undergraduate majors. Total enrollment: 1,528. Undergraduates: 1,432. Freshmen: 421. Both federal and institutional methodology are used as a basis for awarding need-based institutional aid.
UNDERGRADUATE EXPENSES for 2005–06 *Application fee:* $45. *Comprehensive fee:* $34,645 includes full-time tuition ($26,874), mandatory fees ($221), and room and board ($7550). *College room only:* $3860. *Part-time tuition:* $975 per credit hour. *Payment plans:* Installment, deferred payment.
FRESHMAN FINANCIAL AID (Fall 2005, est.) 248 applied for aid; of those 68% were deemed to have need. 100% of freshmen with need received aid; of those 78% had need fully met. *Average percent of need met:* 94% (excluding resources awarded to replace EFC). *Average financial aid package:* $21,576 (excluding resources awarded to replace EFC). 18% of all full-time freshmen had no need and received non-need-based gift aid.
UNDERGRADUATE FINANCIAL AID (Fall 2005, est.) 706 applied for aid; of those 93% were deemed to have need. 100% of undergraduates with need received aid; of those 84% had need fully met. *Average percent of need met:* 97% (excluding resources awarded to replace EFC). *Average financial aid package:* $19,574 (excluding resources awarded to replace EFC). 20% of all full-time undergraduates had no need and received non-need-based gift aid.
GIFT AID (NEED-BASED) *Total amount:* $9,988,903 (6% federal, 5% state, 85% institutional, 4% external sources). *Receiving aid:* Freshmen: 40% (168); All full-time undergraduates: 45% (631). *Average award:* Freshmen: $17,663; Undergraduates: $16,156. *Scholarships, grants, and awards:* Federal Pell, FSEOG, state, private, college/university gift aid from institutional funds.
GIFT AID (NON-NEED-BASED) *Total amount:* $4,098,286 (4% state, 88% institutional, 8% external sources). *Average Award:* Freshmen: $11,712; Undergraduates: $11,581. *Scholarships, grants, and awards by category:* Academic Interests/Achievement: 322 awards ($3,312,177 total): general academic interests/achievements. Special Characteristics: 111 awards ($290,250 total): children of faculty/staff, ethnic background, members of minority groups, relatives of clergy. *Tuition waivers:* Full or partial for employees or children of employees.
LOANS *Student loans:* $2,111,008 (80% need-based, 20% non-need-based). 36% of past graduating class borrowed through all loan programs. *Average indebtedness per student:* $14,926. *Average need-based loan:* Freshmen: $3182; Undergraduates: $3311. *Parent loans:* $3,578,165 (46% need-based, 54% non-need-based). *Programs:* FFEL (Subsidized and Unsubsidized Stafford, PLUS), Perkins, state, college/university, alternative loans.
WORK-STUDY *Federal work-study:* Total amount: $367,523; 327 jobs averaging $1124. *State or other work-study/employment:* Total amount: $70,600 (53% need-based, 47% non-need-based). 65 part-time jobs averaging $1086.
APPLYING FOR FINANCIAL AID *Required financial aid forms:* FAFSA, institution's own form. *Financial aid deadline (priority):* 3/1. *Notification date:* 4/1. Students must reply within 4 weeks of notification.
CONTACT Mr. David R. Gelinas, Director of Financial Aid, Sewanee: The University of the South, 735 University Avenue, Sewanee, TN 37383-1000, 931-598-1312 or toll-free 800-522-2234. *Fax:* 931-598-3273.

SHASTA BIBLE COLLEGE
Redding, CA

Tuition & fees: $6750 | **Average undergraduate aid package: $4275**

ABOUT THE INSTITUTION Independent nondenominational, coed. Awards: associate, bachelor's, and master's degrees. 3 undergraduate majors. Total enrollment: 123. Undergraduates: 90. Freshmen: 9. Both federal and institutional methodology are used as a basis for awarding need-based institutional aid.
UNDERGRADUATE EXPENSES for 2005–06 *Application fee:* $35. *Tuition:* full-time $6400; part-time $200 per unit. *Required fees:* full-time $350; $350 per year part-time. *Payment plan:* Installment.
FRESHMAN FINANCIAL AID (Fall 2004) 12 applied for aid; of those 83% were deemed to have need. 100% of freshmen with need received aid. *Average percent of need met:* 25% (excluding resources awarded to replace EFC). *Average financial aid package:* $4275 (excluding resources awarded to replace EFC).
UNDERGRADUATE FINANCIAL AID (Fall 2004) 76 applied for aid; of those 87% were deemed to have need. 94% of undergraduates with need received aid. *Average percent of need met:* 25% (excluding resources awarded to replace EFC). *Average financial aid package:* $4275 (excluding resources awarded to replace EFC). 5% of all full-time undergraduates had no need and received non-need-based gift aid.
GIFT AID (NEED-BASED) *Total amount:* $207,640 (71% federal, 29% state). *Receiving aid:* Freshmen: 83% (10); All full-time undergraduates: 79% (60). *Scholarships, grants, and awards:* Federal Pell, FSEOG, state, private, college/university gift aid from institutional funds.
GIFT AID (NON-NEED-BASED) *Total amount:* $9500 (63% institutional, 37% external sources). *Receiving aid:* Undergraduates: 3% (2). *Average Award:* Undergraduates: $1100. *Scholarships, grants, and awards by category: Academic Interests/Achievement:* 27 awards ($20,598 total): education. *Creative Arts/Performance:* 11 awards ($7225 total): general creative arts/performance. *Special Achievements/Activities:* general special achievements/activities. *Special Characteristics:* 18 awards ($34,065 total): relatives of clergy, veterans. *Tuition waivers:* Full or partial for employees or children of employees, senior citizens.
WORK-STUDY *Federal work-study:* Total amount: $7758; 10 jobs averaging $1500. *State or other work-study/employment:* Total amount: $20,000 (100% non-need-based). 11 part-time jobs averaging $1000.
APPLYING FOR FINANCIAL AID *Required financial aid forms:* FAFSA, institution's own form, state aid form. *Financial aid deadline:* Continuous. *Notification date:* Continuous beginning 7/2. Students must reply within 3 weeks of notification.
CONTACT Connie Barton, Financial Aid Administrator, Shasta Bible College, 2951 Goodwater Avenue, Redding, CA 96002, 530-221-4275 or toll-free 800-800-45BC (in-state), 800-800-6929 (out-of-state). *Fax:* 530-221-6929. *E-mail:* finaid@shasta.edu.

SHAWNEE STATE UNIVERSITY
Portsmouth, OH

ABOUT THE INSTITUTION State-supported, coed. Awards: associate and bachelor's degrees. 66 undergraduate majors. Total enrollment: 3,820. Undergraduates: 3,820. Freshmen: 506.
GIFT AID (NEED-BASED) *Scholarships, grants, and awards:* Federal Pell, FSEOG, state, private, college/university gift aid from institutional funds.
GIFT AID (NON-NEED-BASED) *Scholarships, grants, and awards by category: Academic Interests/Achievement:* general academic interests/achievements. *Creative Arts/Performance:* art/fine arts, performing arts. *Special Achievements/Activities:* memberships. *Special Characteristics:* ethnic background, first-generation college students, handicapped students, local/state students, members of minority groups, veterans.
LOANS *Programs:* FFEL (Subsidized and Unsubsidized Stafford, PLUS), college/university.
WORK-STUDY *Federal work-study:* Total amount: $209,898; 104 jobs averaging $2018.
APPLYING FOR FINANCIAL AID *Required financial aid forms:* FAFSA, institution's own form.
CONTACT Patricia Moore, Director of Financial Aid, Shawnee State University, 940 Second Street, Portsmouth, OH 45662-4344, 740-351-3245 or toll-free 800-959-2SSU. *E-mail:* pmoore@shawnee.edu.

SHAW UNIVERSITY
Raleigh, NC

ABOUT THE INSTITUTION Independent Baptist, coed. Awards: associate, bachelor's, master's, and first professional degrees. 36 undergraduate majors. Total enrollment: 2,762. Undergraduates: 2,565. Freshmen: 600.
GIFT AID (NEED-BASED) *Scholarships, grants, and awards:* Federal Pell, FSEOG, state, private, college/university gift aid from institutional funds, United Negro College Fund.
GIFT AID (NON-NEED-BASED) *Scholarships, grants, and awards by category: Academic Interests/Achievement:* biological sciences, computer science, education, engineering/technologies, general academic interests/achievements, mathematics, physical sciences. *Creative Arts/Performance:* music, performing arts. *Special Characteristics:* children of faculty/staff, general special characteristics.
LOANS *Programs:* Federal Direct (Subsidized and Unsubsidized Stafford, PLUS), Perkins, college/university, state loans (for Education majors).
APPLYING FOR FINANCIAL AID *Required financial aid forms:* FAFSA, institution's own form, state aid form.
CONTACT Kamesia Ewing, Director of Financial Aid, Shaw University, 118 East South Street, Raleigh, NC 27601-2399, 919-546-8565 or toll-free 800-214-6683. *Fax:* 919-546-8356.

SHELDON JACKSON COLLEGE
Sitka, AK

CONTACT Ms. Louise Driver, Financial Aid Director, Sheldon Jackson College, 801 Lincoln Street, Sitka, AK 99835-7699, 800-747-5206 or toll-free 800-478-4556. *Fax:* 907-747-6366. *E-mail:* ldriver@sj-alaska.edu.

SHENANDOAH UNIVERSITY
Winchester, VA

Tuition & fees: $20,050 | **Average undergraduate aid package: $14,013**

ABOUT THE INSTITUTION Independent United Methodist, coed. Awards: associate, bachelor's, master's, doctoral, and first professional degrees and post-bachelor's and post-master's certificates. 36 undergraduate majors. Total enrollment: 2,998. Undergraduates: 1,606. Freshmen: 370. Federal methodology is used as a basis for awarding need-based institutional aid.
UNDERGRADUATE EXPENSES for 2005–06 *Application fee:* $30. *Comprehensive fee:* $27,600 includes full-time tuition ($19,900), mandatory fees ($150), and room and board ($7550). Full-time tuition and fees vary according to course load and program. Room and board charges vary according to board plan. *Part-time tuition:* $610 per credit hour. Part-time tuition and fees vary according to course load and program. *Payment plan:* Installment.
FRESHMAN FINANCIAL AID (Fall 2005, est.) 304 applied for aid; of those 100% were deemed to have need. 100% of freshmen with need received aid; of those 19% had need fully met. *Average percent of need met:* 85% (excluding resources awarded to replace EFC). *Average financial aid package:* $14,411 (excluding resources awarded to replace EFC). 13% of all full-time freshmen had no need and received non-need-based gift aid.
UNDERGRADUATE FINANCIAL AID (Fall 2005, est.) 1,003 applied for aid; of those 100% were deemed to have need. 100% of undergraduates with need received aid; of those 18% had need fully met. *Average percent of need met:* 85% (excluding resources awarded to replace EFC). *Average financial aid package:* $14,013 (excluding resources awarded to replace EFC). 10% of all full-time undergraduates had no need and received non-need-based gift aid.
GIFT AID (NEED-BASED) *Total amount:* $2,590,004 (40% federal, 2% state, 45% institutional, 13% external sources). *Receiving aid:* Freshmen: 41% (158); All full-time undergraduates: 54% (902). *Average award:* Freshmen: $4905; Undergraduates: $7053. *Scholarships, grants, and awards:* Federal Pell, FSEOG, state, private, college/university gift aid from institutional funds, Federal Nursing.
GIFT AID (NON-NEED-BASED) *Total amount:* $7,835,029 (22% state, 77% institutional, 1% external sources). *Receiving aid:* Freshmen: 30% (116); Undergraduates: 33% (545). *Average Award:* Freshmen: $4500; Undergraduates: $3950. *Scholarships, grants, and awards by category: Academic Interests/Achievement:* 739 awards ($2,699,996 total): business, general academic interests/achievements. *Creative Arts/Performance:* 367 awards ($1,245,435 total): dance, music, performing arts, theater/drama. *Special Characteristics:*

Shenandoah University

217 awards ($909,000 total): children of faculty/staff, local/state students, relatives of clergy, religious affiliation. *Tuition waivers:* Full or partial for employees or children of employees.
LOANS *Student loans:* $7,739,419 (58% need-based, 42% non-need-based). 85% of past graduating class borrowed through all loan programs. *Average indebtedness per student:* $19,518. *Average need-based loan:* Freshmen: $4007; Undergraduates: $5702. *Parent loans:* $4,396,296 (75% need-based, 25% non-need-based). *Programs:* Federal Direct (Subsidized and Unsubsidized Stafford, PLUS), Perkins, Federal Nursing, college/university.
WORK-STUDY *Federal work-study:* Total amount: $588,000; 409 jobs averaging $1475. *State or other work-study/employment:* Total amount: $331,300 (100% non-need-based). 229 part-time jobs averaging $1500.
APPLYING FOR FINANCIAL AID *Required financial aid forms:* FAFSA, state aid form. *Financial aid deadline (priority):* 2/15. *Notification date:* Continuous beginning 3/15. Students must reply within 2 weeks of notification.
CONTACT Nancy Bragg, Director of Financial Aid, Shenandoah University, 1460 University Drive, Winchester, VA 22601-5195, 540-665-4538 or toll-free 800-432-2266. *Fax:* 540-665-4939. *E-mail:* nbragg@su.edu.

SHEPHERD UNIVERSITY
Shepherdstown, WV

Tuition & fees (WV res): $4046   **Average undergraduate aid package:** $8674

ABOUT THE INSTITUTION State-supported, coed. Awards: bachelor's and master's degrees. 22 undergraduate majors. Total enrollment: 3,901. Undergraduates: 3,809. Freshmen: 675. Federal methodology is used as a basis for awarding need-based institutional aid.
UNDERGRADUATE EXPENSES for 2005–06 *Application fee:* $35. *Tuition, state resident:* full-time $4046. *Tuition, nonresident:* full-time $10,618. Full-time tuition and fees vary according to degree level, program, and reciprocity agreements. Part-time tuition and fees vary according to degree level and program. *College room and board:* $6020. Room and board charges vary according to board plan and housing facility. *Payment plan:* Installment.
FRESHMAN FINANCIAL AID (Fall 2005, est.) 571 applied for aid; of those 58% were deemed to have need. 96% of freshmen with need received aid. *Average percent of need met:* 70% (excluding resources awarded to replace EFC). *Average financial aid package:* $7677 (excluding resources awarded to replace EFC). 22% of all full-time freshmen had no need and received non-need-based gift aid.
UNDERGRADUATE FINANCIAL AID (Fall 2005, est.) 2,347 applied for aid; of those 62% were deemed to have need. 96% of undergraduates with need received aid; of those 20% had need fully met. *Average percent of need met:* 74% (excluding resources awarded to replace EFC). *Average financial aid package:* $8674 (excluding resources awarded to replace EFC). 20% of all full-time undergraduates had no need and received non-need-based gift aid.
GIFT AID (NEED-BASED) *Total amount:* $2,961,143 (77% federal, 18% state, 5% institutional). *Receiving aid:* Freshmen: 23% (151); All full-time undergraduates: 25% (743). *Average award:* Freshmen: $3627; Undergraduates: $3529. *Scholarships, grants, and awards:* Federal Pell, FSEOG, state, private, college/university gift aid from institutional funds.
GIFT AID (NON-NEED-BASED) *Total amount:* $3,497,611 (40% state, 52% institutional, 8% external sources). *Receiving aid:* Freshmen: 17% (109); Undergraduates: 11% (327). *Average Award:* Freshmen: $6842; Undergraduates: $7458. *Scholarships, grants, and awards by category:* Academic Interests/Achievement: 307 awards ($396,382 total): biological sciences, business, communication, computer science, education, engineering/technologies, English, foreign languages, general academic interests/achievements, health fields, home economics, humanities, mathematics, physical sciences, premedicine, social sciences. Creative Arts/Performance: 65 awards ($148,024 total): applied art and design, art/fine arts, music, performing arts. Special Achievements/Activities: 52 awards ($34,279 total): leadership. Special Characteristics: 32 awards ($121,211 total): ethnic background, members of minority groups, veterans' children. *Tuition waivers:* Full or partial for minority students, senior citizens.
LOANS *Student loans:* $10,813,806 (42% need-based, 58% non-need-based). 68% of past graduating class borrowed through all loan programs. *Average indebtedness per student:* $14,887. *Average need-based loan:* Freshmen: $2368; Undergraduates: $3584. *Parent loans:* $2,076,666 (100% non-need-based). *Programs:* Federal Direct (Subsidized and Unsubsidized Stafford, PLUS), Perkins.
WORK-STUDY *Federal work-study:* Total amount: $233,698; 183 jobs averaging $1500. *State or other work-study/employment:* Total amount: $682,541 (100% non-need-based). 325 part-time jobs averaging $3000.
ATHLETIC AWARDS Total amount: $606,174 (100% non-need-based).
APPLYING FOR FINANCIAL AID *Required financial aid forms:* FAFSA, state aid form. *Financial aid deadline (priority):* 3/1. *Notification date:* Continuous beginning 3/10. Students must reply within 3 weeks of notification.
CONTACT Financial Aid Office, Shepherd University, PO Box 3210, Shepherdstown, WV 25443-3210, 304-876-5470 or toll-free 800-344-5231. *Fax:* 304-876-5238. *E-mail:* faoweb@shepherd.edu.

SHIMER COLLEGE
Waukegan, IL

Tuition & fees: N/R   **Average undergraduate aid package:** $17,000

ABOUT THE INSTITUTION Independent, coed. Awards: bachelor's degrees and post-bachelor's certificates. 7 undergraduate majors. Total enrollment: 138. Undergraduates: 126. Freshmen: 26. Federal methodology is used as a basis for awarding need-based institutional aid.
UNDERGRADUATE FINANCIAL AID (Fall 2005, est.) 113 applied for aid; of those 100% were deemed to have need. 100% of undergraduates with need received aid. *Average percent of need met:* 75% (excluding resources awarded to replace EFC). *Average financial aid package:* $17,000 (excluding resources awarded to replace EFC). 1% of all full-time undergraduates had no need and received non-need-based gift aid.
GIFT AID (NEED-BASED) *Total amount:* $1,224,992 (13% federal, 12% state, 25% institutional, 50% external sources). *Receiving aid:* All full-time undergraduates: 51% (68). *Average award:* Undergraduates: $4000. *Scholarships, grants, and awards:* Federal Pell, FSEOG, state, private, college/university gift aid from institutional funds.
GIFT AID (NON-NEED-BASED) *Average Award:* Freshmen: $20,760. *Scholarships, grants, and awards by category:* Academic Interests/Achievement: 1 award ($20,760 total): general academic interests/achievements. Creative Arts/Performance: art/fine arts, creative writing, theater/drama. Special Achievements/Activities: hobbies/interests. Special Characteristics: 2 awards ($1500 total): children and siblings of alumni, out-of-state students. *Tuition waivers:* Full or partial for employees or children of employees, adult students, senior citizens.
LOANS *Student loans:* $702,874 (100% need-based). *Average need-based loan:* Undergraduates: $4200. *Parent loans:* $98,219 (100% non-need-based). *Programs:* FFEL (Subsidized and Unsubsidized Stafford, PLUS), Perkins, Sallie Mae Signature Loans, TERI Loans.
WORK-STUDY *Federal work-study:* Total amount: $94,937; 49 jobs averaging $1900. *State or other work-study/employment:* Total amount: $7500 (100% non-need-based). 12 part-time jobs averaging $625.
APPLYING FOR FINANCIAL AID *Required financial aid forms:* FAFSA, institution's own form. *Financial aid deadline:* Continuous. *Notification date:* Continuous.
CONTACT Janet Henthorn, Director of Financial Aid, Shimer College, PO Box 500, Waukegan, IL 60079-0500, 847-249-7180 or toll-free 800-215-7173. *Fax:* 847-249-8798.

SHIPPENSBURG UNIVERSITY OF PENNSYLVANIA
Shippensburg, PA

Tuition & fees (PA res): $6175   **Average undergraduate aid package:** $6256

ABOUT THE INSTITUTION State-supported, coed. Awards: bachelor's and master's degrees and post-master's certificates. 33 undergraduate majors. Total enrollment: 7,485. Undergraduates: 6,459. Freshmen: 1,503. Federal methodology is used as a basis for awarding need-based institutional aid.
UNDERGRADUATE EXPENSES for 2005–06 *Application fee:* $30. *Tuition, state resident:* full-time $4906; part-time $204 per credit hour. *Tuition, nonresident:* full-time $12,266; part-time $511 per credit hour. *Required fees:* full-time $1269; $20 per credit hour or $147 per term part-time. *College room and board:* $5710; *room only:* $3290. Room and board charges vary according to board plan and housing facility. *Payment plan:* Installment.
FRESHMAN FINANCIAL AID (Fall 2005, est.) 1243 applied for aid; of those 65% were deemed to have need. 95% of freshmen with need received aid; of

those 13% had need fully met. *Average percent of need met:* 64% (excluding resources awarded to replace EFC). *Average financial aid package:* $5780 (excluding resources awarded to replace EFC). 10% of all full-time freshmen had no need and received non-need-based gift aid.

UNDERGRADUATE FINANCIAL AID (Fall 2005, est.) 4,407 applied for aid; of those 67% were deemed to have need. 96% of undergraduates with need received aid; of those 22% had need fully met. *Average percent of need met:* 69% (excluding resources awarded to replace EFC). *Average financial aid package:* $6256 (excluding resources awarded to replace EFC). 32% of all full-time undergraduates had no need and received non-need-based gift aid.

GIFT AID (NEED-BASED) *Total amount:* $8,365,919 (38% federal, 55% state, 3% institutional, 4% external sources). *Receiving aid:* Freshmen: 41% (619); All full-time undergraduates: 36% (2,196). *Average award:* Freshmen: $4115; Undergraduates: $3943. *Scholarships, grants, and awards:* Federal Pell, FSEOG, state, private, college/university gift aid from institutional funds.

GIFT AID (NON-NEED-BASED) *Total amount:* $707,216 (5% federal, 2% state, 37% institutional, 56% external sources). *Receiving aid:* Freshmen: 3% (38); Undergraduates: 2% (152). *Average Award: Freshmen:* $2245; *Undergraduates:* $615. *Scholarships, grants, and awards by category: Academic Interests/Achievement:* 386 awards ($751,935 total): biological sciences, business, communication, computer science, education, English, general academic interests/achievements, social sciences. *Tuition waivers:* Full or partial for employees or children of employees, senior citizens. *ROTC:* Army.

LOANS *Student loans:* $20,169,040 (54% need-based, 46% non-need-based). 67% of past graduating class borrowed through all loan programs. *Average indebtedness per student:* $17,976. *Average need-based loan:* Freshmen: $2755; Undergraduates: $3446. *Parent loans:* $6,463,135 (17% need-based, 83% non-need-based). *Programs:* FFEL (Subsidized and Unsubsidized Stafford, PLUS), Perkins, college/university, alternative loans.

WORK-STUDY *Federal work-study:* Total amount: $343,418; 206 jobs averaging $1667. *State or other work-study/employment:* Total amount: $821,584 (19% need-based, 81% non-need-based). 366 part-time jobs averaging $2244.

ATHLETIC AWARDS *Total amount:* $494,036 (45% need-based, 55% non-need-based).

APPLYING FOR FINANCIAL AID *Required financial aid form:* FAFSA. *Financial aid deadline (priority):* 3/15. *Notification date:* Continuous. Students must reply within 2 weeks of notification.

CONTACT Mr. Peter D'Annibale, Director of Financial Aid and Scholarships, Shippensburg University of Pennsylvania, 1871 Old Main Drive, Shippensburg, PA 17257-2299, 717-477-1131 or toll-free 800-822-8028 (in-state). *Fax:* 717-477-4028. *E-mail:* finaid@ship.edu.

SHORTER COLLEGE
Rome, GA

Tuition & fees: $13,500   Average undergraduate aid package: $11,105

ABOUT THE INSTITUTION Independent Baptist, coed. Awards: bachelor's degrees. 38 undergraduate majors. Total enrollment: 967. Undergraduates: 967. Freshmen: 291. Federal methodology is used as a basis for awarding need-based institutional aid.

UNDERGRADUATE EXPENSES for 2005–06 *Application fee:* $25. *Comprehensive fee:* $19,700 includes full-time tuition ($13,200), mandatory fees ($300), and room and board ($6200). *College room only:* $3400. Full-time tuition and fees vary according to course load. Room and board charges vary according to board plan and housing facility. *Part-time tuition:* $285 per semester hour. *Payment plan:* Installment.

FRESHMAN FINANCIAL AID (Fall 2005, est.) 260 applied for aid; of those 83% were deemed to have need. 100% of freshmen with need received aid; of those 22% had need fully met. *Average percent of need met:* 66% (excluding resources awarded to replace EFC). *Average financial aid package:* $11,495 (excluding resources awarded to replace EFC). 30% of all full-time freshmen had no need and received non-need-based gift aid.

UNDERGRADUATE FINANCIAL AID (Fall 2005, est.) 754 applied for aid; of those 83% were deemed to have need. 100% of undergraduates with need received aid; of those 21% had need fully met. *Average percent of need met:* 61% (excluding resources awarded to replace EFC). *Average financial aid package:* $11,105 (excluding resources awarded to replace EFC). 31% of all full-time undergraduates had no need and received non-need-based gift aid.

GIFT AID (NEED-BASED) *Total amount:* $4,209,168 (19% federal, 35% state, 44% institutional, 2% external sources). *Receiving aid:* Freshmen: 74% (215); All full-time undergraduates: 67% (626). *Average award:* Freshmen: $9685; Undergraduates: $8424. *Scholarships, grants, and awards:* Federal Pell, FSEOG, private, college/university gift aid from institutional funds.

GIFT AID (NON-NEED-BASED) *Total amount:* $2,181,385 (45% state, 52% institutional, 3% external sources). *Receiving aid:* Freshmen: 2% (7); Undergraduates: 11% (98). *Average Award:* Freshmen: $8579; Undergraduates: $8685. *Scholarships, grants, and awards by category: Academic Interests/Achievement:* 480 awards ($2,138,700 total): English, foreign languages, general academic interests/achievements, religion/biblical studies. *Creative Arts/Performance:* 117 awards ($205,530 total): art/fine arts, music, theater/drama. *Special Achievements/Activities:* 261 awards ($137,050 total): religious involvement. *Special Characteristics:* 154 awards ($208,827 total): children of faculty/staff, children of union members/company employees, local/state students, out-of-state students, religious affiliation, siblings of current students. *Tuition waivers:* Full or partial for employees or children of employees, senior citizens.

LOANS *Student loans:* $2,857,339 (77% need-based, 23% non-need-based). 59% of past graduating class borrowed through all loan programs. *Average indebtedness per student:* $16,193. *Average need-based loan:* Freshmen: $2470; Undergraduates: $3525. *Parent loans:* $2,285,220 (44% need-based, 56% non-need-based). *Programs:* FFEL (Subsidized and Unsubsidized Stafford, PLUS), Perkins.

WORK-STUDY *Federal work-study:* Total amount: $146,085; 109 jobs averaging $1340. *State or other work-study/employment:* Total amount: $93,865 (4% need-based, 96% non-need-based). 78 part-time jobs averaging $1203.

ATHLETIC AWARDS *Total amount:* $1,504,432 (55% need-based, 45% non-need-based).

APPLYING FOR FINANCIAL AID *Required financial aid forms:* FAFSA, institution's own form, state aid form. *Financial aid deadline (priority):* 4/15. *Notification date:* Students must reply within 2 weeks of notification.

CONTACT Mr. Jared Smith, Director of Financial Aid, Shorter College, 315 Shorter Avenue, Rome, GA 30165, 706-233-7227 or toll-free 800-868-6980. *Fax:* 706-233-7314. *E-mail:* phawkins@shorter.edu.

SH'OR YOSHUV RABBINICAL COLLEGE
Lawrence, NY

CONTACT Office of Financial Aid, Sh'or Yoshuv Rabbinical College, 1526 Central Avenue, Far Rockaway, NY 11691-4002, 718-327-2048.

SIENA COLLEGE
Loudonville, NY

CONTACT Mary K. Lawyer, Assistant Vice President for Financial Aid, Siena College, 515 Loudon Road, Loudonville, NY 12211-1462, 518-783-2427 or toll-free 888-AT-SIENA. *Fax:* 518-783-2410. *E-mail:* aid@siena.edu.

SIENA HEIGHTS UNIVERSITY
Adrian, MI

CONTACT Office of Financial Aid, Siena Heights University, 1247 East Siena Heights Drive, Adrian, MI 49221, 517-264-7130 or toll-free 800-521-0009.

SIERRA NEVADA COLLEGE
Incline Village, NV

ABOUT THE INSTITUTION Independent, coed. Awards: bachelor's and master's degrees. 11 undergraduate majors. Total enrollment: 492. Undergraduates: 302. Freshmen: 67.

GIFT AID (NEED-BASED) *Scholarships, grants, and awards:* Federal Pell, FSEOG, state, private, college/university gift aid from institutional funds.

GIFT AID (NON-NEED-BASED) *Scholarships, grants, and awards by category: Academic Interests/Achievement:* business, education, general academic interests/achievements, humanities. *Creative Arts/Performance:* art/fine arts, music. *Special Characteristics:* ethnic background, local/state students, members of minority groups.

LOANS *Programs:* Federal Direct (Subsidized and Unsubsidized Stafford, PLUS), alternative loans.

Sierra Nevada College

APPLYING FOR FINANCIAL AID *Required financial aid forms:* FAFSA, institution's own form.
CONTACT Dorothy Caruso, Director of Financial Aid, Sierra Nevada College, 999 Tahoe Boulevard, Incline Village, NV 89451, 775-831-1314 Ext. 4066 or toll-free 775-831-1314 (in-state). *Fax:* 775-831-1347. *E-mail:* dcaruso@sierranevada.edu.

SILICON VALLEY UNIVERSITY
San Jose, CA

CONTACT Financial Aid Office, Silicon Valley University, 3590 North First Street, Suite 320, San Jose, CA 95134, 408-435-8989.

SILVER LAKE COLLEGE
Manitowoc, WI

Tuition & fees: $17,108   **Average undergraduate aid package: $12,752**

ABOUT THE INSTITUTION Independent Roman Catholic, coed. Awards: associate, bachelor's, and master's degrees and post-bachelor's certificates. 24 undergraduate majors. Total enrollment: 913. Undergraduates: 629. Freshmen: 33. Federal methodology is used as a basis for awarding need-based institutional aid.
UNDERGRADUATE EXPENSES for 2006–07 *Application fee:* $35. *Tuition:* full-time $17,108; part-time $525 per credit.
FRESHMAN FINANCIAL AID (Fall 2005, est.) 31 applied for aid; of those 87% were deemed to have need. 100% of freshmen with need received aid; of those 11% had need fully met. *Average percent of need met:* 84% (excluding resources awarded to replace EFC). *Average financial aid package:* $16,405 (excluding resources awarded to replace EFC). 15% of all full-time freshmen had no need and received non-need-based gift aid.
UNDERGRADUATE FINANCIAL AID (Fall 2005, est.) 168 applied for aid; of those 90% were deemed to have need. 100% of undergraduates with need received aid; of those 20% had need fully met. *Average percent of need met:* 73% (excluding resources awarded to replace EFC). *Average financial aid package:* $12,752 (excluding resources awarded to replace EFC). 8% of all full-time undergraduates had no need and received non-need-based gift aid.
GIFT AID (NEED-BASED) *Total amount:* $1,522,793 (32% federal, 20% state, 46% institutional, 2% external sources). *Receiving aid:* Freshmen: 82% (27); All full-time undergraduates: 79% (152). *Average award:* Freshmen: $12,279; Undergraduates: $8555. *Scholarships, grants, and awards:* Federal Pell, FSEOG, state, private, college/university gift aid from institutional funds.
GIFT AID (NON-NEED-BASED) *Total amount:* $110,235 (2% federal, 94% institutional, 4% external sources). *Receiving aid:* Freshmen: 3% (1); Undergraduates: 3% (6). *Average Award:* Freshmen: $3300; Undergraduates: $3510. *Scholarships, grants, and awards by category:* Academic Interests/Achievement: 67 awards ($221,053 total): general academic interests/achievements. Creative Arts/Performance: 20 awards ($16,000 total): applied art and design, art/fine arts, music. Special Achievements/Activities: 45 awards ($20,000 total): religious involvement. Special Characteristics: 8 awards ($19,500 total): international students, local/state students.
LOANS *Student loans:* $1,647,031 (97% need-based, 3% non-need-based). 70% of past graduating class borrowed through all loan programs. *Average indebtedness per student:* $18,934. *Average need-based loan:* Freshmen: $2572; Undergraduates: $3688. *Parent loans:* $190,371 (66% need-based, 34% non-need-based). *Programs:* FFEL (Subsidized and Unsubsidized Stafford, PLUS).
WORK-STUDY *Federal work-study:* Total amount: $147,869; 71 jobs averaging $2083.
ATHLETIC AWARDS *Total amount:* $24,000 (75% need-based, 25% non-need-based).
APPLYING FOR FINANCIAL AID *Required financial aid form:* FAFSA. *Financial aid deadline (priority):* 3/15. *Notification date:* Continuous beginning 3/15. Students must reply within 2 weeks of notification.
CONTACT Michelle Leider, Associate Director of Financial Aid, Silver Lake College, 2406 South Alverno Road, Manitowoc, WI 54220-9319, 920-686-6122 or toll-free 800-236-4752 Ext. 175 (in-state). *Fax:* 920-684-7082. *E-mail:* mleider@silver.sl.edu.

SIMMONS COLLEGE
Boston, MA

Tuition & fees: $25,440   **Average undergraduate aid package: $15,085**

ABOUT THE INSTITUTION Independent, undergraduate: women only; graduate: coed. Awards: bachelor's, master's, and doctoral degrees and post-bachelor's and post-master's certificates. 52 undergraduate majors. Total enrollment: 4,805. Undergraduates: 1,965. Freshmen: 410. Federal methodology is used as a basis for awarding need-based institutional aid.
UNDERGRADUATE EXPENSES for 2005–06 *Application fee:* $35. *Comprehensive fee:* $35,640 includes full-time tuition ($24,680), mandatory fees ($760), and room and board ($10,200). Full-time tuition and fees vary according to course load. *Part-time tuition:* $770 per semester hour. Part-time tuition and fees vary according to course load. *Payment plan:* Installment.
FRESHMAN FINANCIAL AID (Fall 2005, est.) 340 applied for aid; of those 89% were deemed to have need. 99% of freshmen with need received aid; of those 6% had need fully met. *Average percent of need met:* 60% (excluding resources awarded to replace EFC). *Average financial aid package:* $17,312 (excluding resources awarded to replace EFC). 4% of all full-time freshmen had no need and received non-need-based gift aid.
UNDERGRADUATE FINANCIAL AID (Fall 2005, est.) 1,353 applied for aid; of those 90% were deemed to have need. 98% of undergraduates with need received aid; of those 4% had need fully met. *Average percent of need met:* 58% (excluding resources awarded to replace EFC). *Average financial aid package:* $15,085 (excluding resources awarded to replace EFC). 2% of all full-time undergraduates had no need and received non-need-based gift aid.
GIFT AID (NEED-BASED) *Total amount:* $16,079,241 (10% federal, 4% state, 86% institutional). *Receiving aid:* Freshmen: 65% (263); All full-time undergraduates: 65% (1,105). *Average award:* Freshmen: $11,751; Undergraduates: $10,829. *Scholarships, grants, and awards:* Federal Pell, FSEOG, state, private, college/university gift aid from institutional funds.
GIFT AID (NON-NEED-BASED) *Total amount:* $3,773,271 (83% institutional, 17% external sources). *Receiving aid:* Freshmen: 30% (121); Undergraduates: 18% (311). *Average Award:* Freshmen: $10,667; Undergraduates: $11,898. *Scholarships, grants, and awards by category:* Academic Interests/Achievement: 57 awards ($778,618 total): general academic interests/achievements. Special Achievements/Activities: 556 awards ($3,798,500 total): community service, general special achievements/activities. Special Characteristics: 82 awards ($274,740 total): children and siblings of alumni, general special characteristics. *Tuition waivers:* Full or partial for employees or children of employees, adult students, senior citizens. *ROTC:* Army cooperative, Naval cooperative, Air Force cooperative.
LOANS *Student loans:* $11,558,297 (51% need-based, 49% non-need-based). 90% of past graduating class borrowed through all loan programs. *Average indebtedness per student:* $26,300. *Average need-based loan:* Freshmen: $3018; Undergraduates: $2908. *Parent loans:* $3,928,155 (100% non-need-based). *Programs:* FFEL (Subsidized and Unsubsidized Stafford, PLUS), Perkins, state, college/university.
WORK-STUDY *Federal work-study:* Total amount: $1,127,373; 451 jobs averaging $2500.
APPLYING FOR FINANCIAL AID *Required financial aid form:* FAFSA. *Financial aid deadline (priority):* 2/15. *Notification date:* 3/15.
CONTACT Diane M. Hallisey, Director of Student Financial Services, Simmons College, 300 The Fenway, Boston, MA 02115, 617-521-2001 or toll-free 800-345-8468 (out-of-state). *Fax:* 617-521-3195. *E-mail:* hallisey@simmons.edu.

SIMON'S ROCK COLLEGE OF BARD
Great Barrington, MA

ABOUT THE INSTITUTION Independent, coed. Awards: associate and bachelor's degrees. 71 undergraduate majors. Total enrollment: 386. Undergraduates: 386. Freshmen: 136.
GIFT AID (NEED-BASED) *Scholarships, grants, and awards:* Federal Pell, FSEOG, state, private, college/university gift aid from institutional funds.
GIFT AID (NON-NEED-BASED) *Scholarships, grants, and awards by category:* Academic Interests/Achievement: general academic interests/achievements, social sciences. Special Characteristics: children of faculty/staff, general special characteristics, local/state students, members of minority groups.

LOANS *Programs:* FFEL (Subsidized and Unsubsidized Stafford, PLUS), Perkins, state, alternative loans.
WORK-STUDY *Federal work-study:* Total amount: $210,000; 96 jobs averaging $1500.
APPLYING FOR FINANCIAL AID *Required financial aid forms:* FAFSA, CSS Financial Aid PROFILE, noncustodial (divorced/separated) parent's statement, business/farm supplement, federal income tax form(s), federal verification worksheet.
CONTACT Ms. Ann Gitto Murtagh, Director of Financial Aid, Simon's Rock College of Bard, 84 Alford Road, Great Barrington, MA 01230-9702, 413-528-0771 or toll-free 800-235-7186. *Fax:* 413-528-7339. *E-mail:* agitto@simons-rock.edu.

SIMPSON COLLEGE
Indianola, IA

Tuition & fees: $20,911 — **Average undergraduate aid package: $18,015**

ABOUT THE INSTITUTION Independent United Methodist, coed. Awards: bachelor's degrees. 50 undergraduate majors. Total enrollment: 2,035. Undergraduates: 2,010. Freshmen: 336. Federal methodology is used as a basis for awarding need-based institutional aid.
UNDERGRADUATE EXPENSES for 2005–06 *Comprehensive fee:* $26,833 includes full-time tuition ($20,693), mandatory fees ($218), and room and board ($5922). *College room only:* $2842. Room and board charges vary according to board plan and housing facility. Part-time tuition and fees vary according to class time and course load. *Payment plan:* Installment.
FRESHMAN FINANCIAL AID (Fall 2005, est.) 336 applied for aid; of those 86% were deemed to have need. 100% of freshmen with need received aid; of those 22% had need fully met. *Average percent of need met:* 87% (excluding resources awarded to replace EFC). *Average financial aid package:* $19,099 (excluding resources awarded to replace EFC). 14% of all full-time freshmen had no need and received non-need-based gift aid.
UNDERGRADUATE FINANCIAL AID (Fall 2005, est.) 1,440 applied for aid; of those 88% were deemed to have need. 100% of undergraduates with need received aid; of those 24% had need fully met. *Average percent of need met:* 85% (excluding resources awarded to replace EFC). *Average financial aid package:* $18,015 (excluding resources awarded to replace EFC). 14% of all full-time undergraduates had no need and received non-need-based gift aid.
GIFT AID (NEED-BASED) *Total amount:* $16,782,867 (7% federal, 18% state, 72% institutional, 3% external sources). *Receiving aid:* Freshmen: 86% (290); All full-time undergraduates: 87% (1,266). *Average award:* Freshmen: $13,935; Undergraduates: $12,280. *Scholarships, grants, and awards:* Federal Pell, FSEOG, state, private, college/university gift aid from institutional funds.
GIFT AID (NON-NEED-BASED) *Total amount:* $2,429,291 (1% state, 93% institutional, 6% external sources). *Receiving aid:* Freshmen: 10% (35); Undergraduates: 9% (129). *Average Award:* Freshmen: $8874; Undergraduates: $9198. *Scholarships, grants, and awards by category:* Academic Interests/Achievement: $4,900,243 total: general academic interests/achievements. Creative Arts/Performance: $614,811 total: art/fine arts, music, theater/drama. Special Achievements/Activities: $287,523 total: leadership, religious involvement. Special Characteristics: $1,442,980 total: adult students, children and siblings of alumni, children of educators, children of faculty/staff, international students, members of minority groups, relatives of clergy, religious affiliation, siblings of current students, twins. *Tuition waivers:* Full or partial for employees or children of employees.
LOANS *Student loans:* $10,926,223 (65% need-based, 35% non-need-based). 87% of past graduating class borrowed through all loan programs. *Average indebtedness per student:* $24,403. *Average need-based loan:* Freshmen: $3209; Undergraduates: $3771. *Parent loans:* $1,329,129 (19% need-based, 81% non-need-based). *Programs:* FFEL (Subsidized and Unsubsidized Stafford, PLUS), Perkins, state, college/university, alternative loans.
WORK-STUDY *Federal work-study:* Total amount: $276,592; 470 jobs averaging $602. *State or other work-study/employment:* Total amount: $499,223 (27% need-based, 73% non-need-based). 630 part-time jobs averaging $753.
APPLYING FOR FINANCIAL AID *Required financial aid form:* FAFSA. *Financial aid deadline:* Continuous. *Notification date:* Continuous beginning 3/15. Students must reply by 5/1 or within 3 weeks of notification.

CONTACT Tracie Pavon, Assistant Vice President of Financial Aid, Simpson College, 701 North C Street, Indianola, IA 50125-1297, 515-961-1630 Ext. 1596 or toll-free 800-362-2454. *Fax:* 515-961-1300. *E-mail:* pavon@simpson.edu.

SIMPSON UNIVERSITY
Redding, CA

Tuition & fees: $17,800 — **Average undergraduate aid package: $7356**

ABOUT THE INSTITUTION Independent religious, coed. Awards: associate, bachelor's, and master's degrees. 20 undergraduate majors. Total enrollment: 1,087. Undergraduates: 923. Freshmen: 219. Federal methodology is used as a basis for awarding need-based institutional aid.
UNDERGRADUATE EXPENSES for 2006–07 *Application fee:* $20. *Comprehensive fee:* $24,000 includes full-time tuition ($17,800) and room and board ($6200). *Part-time tuition:* $750 per credit hour.
FRESHMAN FINANCIAL AID (Fall 2004) 187 applied for aid; of those 88% were deemed to have need. 100% of freshmen with need received aid; of those 7% had need fully met. *Average percent of need met:* 71% (excluding resources awarded to replace EFC). *Average financial aid package:* $8459 (excluding resources awarded to replace EFC). 10% of all full-time freshmen had no need and received non-need-based gift aid.
UNDERGRADUATE FINANCIAL AID (Fall 2004) 777 applied for aid; of those 88% were deemed to have need. 100% of undergraduates with need received aid; of those 2% had need fully met. *Average percent of need met:* 77% (excluding resources awarded to replace EFC). *Average financial aid package:* $7356 (excluding resources awarded to replace EFC). 4% of all full-time undergraduates had no need and received non-need-based gift aid.
GIFT AID (NEED-BASED) *Total amount:* $4,349,453 (30% federal, 61% state, 9% institutional). *Receiving aid:* Freshmen: 77% (149); All full-time undergraduates: 80% (642). *Average award:* Freshmen: $4600; Undergraduates: $4500. *Scholarships, grants, and awards:* Federal Pell, FSEOG, state, private, college/university gift aid from institutional funds.
GIFT AID (NON-NEED-BASED) *Total amount:* $2,819,366 (95% institutional, 5% external sources). *Receiving aid:* Freshmen: 85% (165); Undergraduates: 75% (601). *Average Award:* Freshmen: $5400; Undergraduates: $3780. *Scholarships, grants, and awards by category:* Academic Interests/Achievement: general academic interests/achievements. Creative Arts/Performance: music. Special Achievements/Activities: leadership, religious involvement. Special Characteristics: children of faculty/staff, general special characteristics, members of minority groups, out-of-state students, relatives of clergy, religious affiliation, siblings of current students, spouses of current students.
LOANS *Student loans:* $5,554,034 (51% need-based, 49% non-need-based). 88% of past graduating class borrowed through all loan programs. *Average indebtedness per student:* $17,600. *Average need-based loan:* Freshmen: $2625; Undergraduates: $4900. *Parent loans:* $1,695,623 (100% non-need-based). *Programs:* FFEL (Subsidized and Unsubsidized Stafford, PLUS), Perkins, alternative loans.
WORK-STUDY *Federal work-study:* Total amount: $109,215; jobs available.
APPLYING FOR FINANCIAL AID *Required financial aid forms:* FAFSA, institution's own form, if selected for verification, additional forms such as income tax forms may be required. *Financial aid deadline (priority):* 3/2. *Notification date:* Continuous beginning 3/16. Students must reply within 3 weeks of notification.
CONTACT Mr. James Herberger, Director of Student Financial Services, Simpson University, 2211 College View Drive, Redding, CA 96003-8606, 530-224-5600 or toll-free 800-598-2493. *Fax:* 530-226-4870. *E-mail:* financialaid@simpsonuniveristy.edu.

SINTE GLESKA UNIVERSITY
Rosebud, SD

CONTACT Office of Financial Aid, Sinte Gleska University, PO Box 490, Rosebud, SD 57570-0490, 605-747-4258. *Fax:* 605-747-2098.

SKIDMORE COLLEGE
Saratoga Springs, NY

Tuition & fees: $32,659 — **Average undergraduate aid package: $27,280**

Skidmore College

ABOUT THE INSTITUTION Independent, coed. Awards: bachelor's and master's degrees. 42 undergraduate majors. Total enrollment: 2,828. Undergraduates: 2,773. Freshmen: 694. Both federal and institutional methodology are used as a basis for awarding need-based institutional aid.

UNDERGRADUATE EXPENSES for 2005–06 *Application fee:* $60. *Comprehensive fee:* $41,779 includes full-time tuition ($32,340), mandatory fees ($319), and room and board ($9120). *College room only:* $5100. Full-time tuition and fees vary according to course load. Room and board charges vary according to board plan and housing facility. *Part-time tuition:* $1080 per credit hour. *Part-time fees:* $25 per term. Part-time tuition and fees vary according to course load. *Payment plans:* Tuition prepayment, installment.

FRESHMAN FINANCIAL AID (Fall 2005, est.) 354 applied for aid; of those 79% were deemed to have need. 100% of freshmen with need received aid; of those 84% had need fully met. *Average percent of need met:* 98% (excluding resources awarded to replace EFC). *Average financial aid package:* $26,224 (excluding resources awarded to replace EFC). 1% of all full-time freshmen had no need and received non-need-based gift aid.

UNDERGRADUATE FINANCIAL AID (Fall 2005, est.) 1,182 applied for aid; of those 89% were deemed to have need. 100% of undergraduates with need received aid; of those 86% had need fully met. *Average percent of need met:* 94% (excluding resources awarded to replace EFC). *Average financial aid package:* $27,280 (excluding resources awarded to replace EFC). 1% of all full-time undergraduates had no need and received non-need-based gift aid.

GIFT AID (NEED-BASED) *Total amount:* $22,556,009 (6% federal, 4% state, 90% institutional). *Receiving aid:* Freshmen: 40% (281); All full-time undergraduates: 42% (1,050). *Average award:* Freshmen: $23,032; Undergraduates: $22,810. *Scholarships, grants, and awards:* Federal Pell, FSEOG, state, college/university gift aid from institutional funds.

GIFT AID (NON-NEED-BASED) *Total amount:* $811,098 (8% state, 44% institutional, 48% external sources). *Receiving aid:* Freshmen: 10% (72); Undergraduates: 7% (182). *Average Award:* Freshmen: $10,000; Undergraduates: $10,000. *Scholarships, grants, and awards by category:* Academic Interests/Achievement: 20 awards ($200,000 total): biological sciences, computer science, mathematics, physical sciences. Creative Arts/Performance: 16 awards ($160,000 total): music. Special Characteristics: 34 awards ($737,000 total): children of faculty/staff. *Tuition waivers:* Full or partial for employees or children of employees. *ROTC:* Army cooperative, Air Force cooperative.

LOANS *Student loans:* $5,300,000 (77% need-based, 23% non-need-based). 47% of past graduating class borrowed through all loan programs. *Average indebtedness per student:* $16,078. *Average need-based loan:* Freshmen: $2402; Undergraduates: $3531. *Parent loans:* $7,000,000 (100% non-need-based). *Programs:* FFEL (Subsidized and Unsubsidized Stafford, PLUS), Perkins.

WORK-STUDY *Federal work-study:* Total amount: $540,000; 500 jobs averaging $1080. *State or other work-study/employment:* Total amount: $520,000 (100% non-need-based). 650 part-time jobs averaging $800.

APPLYING FOR FINANCIAL AID *Required financial aid forms:* FAFSA, CSS Financial Aid PROFILE. *Financial aid deadline:* 1/15. *Notification date:* 4/1. Students must reply by 5/1.

CONTACT Mr. Robert D. Shorb, Director of Student Aid and Family Finance, Skidmore College, 815 North Broadway, Saratoga Springs, NY 12866-1632, 518-580-5750 or toll-free 800-867-6007. *Fax:* 518-580-5752. *E-mail:* rshorb@skidmore.edu.

SLIPPERY ROCK UNIVERSITY OF PENNSYLVANIA
Slippery Rock, PA

Tuition & fees (PA res): $6275 | **Average undergraduate aid package: $6938**

ABOUT THE INSTITUTION State-supported, coed. Awards: bachelor's, master's, and doctoral degrees and post-bachelor's certificates. 43 undergraduate majors. Total enrollment: 8,105. Undergraduates: 7,414. Freshmen: 1,465. Federal methodology is used as a basis for awarding need-based institutional aid.

UNDERGRADUATE EXPENSES for 2006–07 *Application fee:* $25. *Tuition, state resident:* full-time $4906; part-time $204 per credit hour. *Tuition, nonresident:* full-time $7360; part-time $511 per credit. *Required fees:* full-time $1369; $47 per credit or $53.25 per term part-time. *College room and board:* $4796; *room only:* $2688.

FRESHMAN FINANCIAL AID (Fall 2005, est.) 1351 applied for aid; of those 69% were deemed to have need. 99% of freshmen with need received aid; of those 63% had need fully met. *Average percent of need met:* 77% (excluding resources awarded to replace EFC). *Average financial aid package:* $6548 (excluding resources awarded to replace EFC). 26% of all full-time freshmen had no need and received non-need-based gift aid.

UNDERGRADUATE FINANCIAL AID (Fall 2005, est.) 6,038 applied for aid; of those 71% were deemed to have need. 97% of undergraduates with need received aid; of those 65% had need fully met. *Average percent of need met:* 81% (excluding resources awarded to replace EFC). *Average financial aid package:* $6938 (excluding resources awarded to replace EFC). 21% of all full-time undergraduates had no need and received non-need-based gift aid.

GIFT AID (NEED-BASED) *Total amount:* $12,241,004 (43% federal, 53% state, 4% external sources). *Receiving aid:* Freshmen: 50% (728); All full-time undergraduates: 46% (3,133). *Average award:* Freshmen: $3300; Undergraduates: $3015. *Scholarships, grants, and awards:* Federal Pell, FSEOG, state, private, college/university gift aid from institutional funds.

GIFT AID (NON-NEED-BASED) *Total amount:* $2,912,893 (24% institutional, 76% external sources). *Receiving aid:* Freshmen: 20% (290); Undergraduates: 13% (915). *Average Award:* Freshmen: $3849; Undergraduates: $5131. *Scholarships, grants, and awards by category:* Academic Interests/Achievement: 443 awards ($431,755 total): biological sciences, business, communication, computer science, education, English, general academic interests/achievements, health fields, physical sciences, social sciences. Creative Arts/Performance: applied art and design, art/fine arts, dance, music, performing arts, theater/drama. Special Achievements/Activities: community service, general special achievements/activities, leadership. Special Characteristics: children and siblings of alumni, children of faculty/staff, children of union members/company employees, ethnic background, general special characteristics, local/state students, members of minority groups, out-of-state students, previous college experience. *ROTC:* Army.

LOANS *Student loans:* $27,163,775 (50% need-based, 50% non-need-based). 76% of past graduating class borrowed through all loan programs. *Average indebtedness per student:* $20,054. *Average need-based loan:* Freshmen: $2352; Undergraduates: $3162. *Parent loans:* $4,825,643 (100% non-need-based). *Programs:* FFEL (Subsidized and Unsubsidized Stafford, PLUS), Perkins.

WORK-STUDY *Federal work-study:* Total amount: $611,689; jobs available. *State or other work-study/employment:* Total amount: $1,257,164 (100% non-need-based). Part-time jobs available.

ATHLETIC AWARDS Total amount: $656,232 (100% non-need-based).

APPLYING FOR FINANCIAL AID *Required financial aid form:* FAFSA. *Financial aid deadline (priority):* 5/1. *Notification date:* Continuous.

CONTACT Ms. Patty A. Hladio, Director of Financial Aid, Slippery Rock University of Pennsylvania, 1 Morrow Way, Slippery Rock, PA 16057, 724-738-2044 or toll-free 800-SRU-9111. *Fax:* 724-738-2922. *E-mail:* financial.aid@sru.edu.

SMITH COLLEGE
Northampton, MA

Tuition & fees: $30,754 | **Average undergraduate aid package: $29,776**

ABOUT THE INSTITUTION Independent, undergraduate: women only; graduate: coed. Awards: bachelor's, master's, and doctoral degrees and post-bachelor's and post-master's certificates. 51 undergraduate majors. Total enrollment: 3,093. Undergraduates: 2,642. Freshmen: 615. Both federal and institutional methodology are used as a basis for awarding need-based institutional aid.

UNDERGRADUATE EXPENSES for 2005–06 *Application fee:* $60. *Comprehensive fee:* $41,474 includes full-time tuition ($30,520), mandatory fees ($234), and room and board ($10,720). *College room only:* $5160. Room and board charges vary according to housing facility. *Part-time tuition:* $955 per credit hour. *Payment plan:* Installment.

FRESHMAN FINANCIAL AID (Fall 2005, est.) 466 applied for aid; of those 79% were deemed to have need. 100% of freshmen with need received aid; of those 100% had need fully met. *Average percent of need met:* 100% (excluding resources awarded to replace EFC). *Average financial aid package:* $29,183 (excluding resources awarded to replace EFC). 10% of all full-time freshmen had no need and received non-need-based gift aid.

UNDERGRADUATE FINANCIAL AID (Fall 2005, est.) 1,834 applied for aid; of those 85% were deemed to have need. 100% of undergraduates with need received aid; of those 100% had need fully met. *Average percent of need met:* 100% (excluding resources awarded to replace EFC). *Average financial aid*

package: $29,776 (excluding resources awarded to replace EFC). 6% of all full-time undergraduates had no need and received non-need-based gift aid.
GIFT AID (NEED-BASED) *Total amount:* $39,871,965 (6% federal, 2% state, 87% institutional, 5% external sources). *Receiving aid:* Freshmen: 60% (366); All full-time undergraduates: 60% (1,555). *Average award:* Freshmen: $25,169; Undergraduates: $23,426. *Scholarships, grants, and awards:* Federal Pell, FSEOG, state, college/university gift aid from institutional funds.
GIFT AID (NON-NEED-BASED) *Total amount:* $1,053,552 (91% institutional, 9% external sources). *Receiving aid:* Freshmen: 2% (11); Undergraduates: 1% (18). *Average Award:* Freshmen: $3465; Undergraduates: $5709. *Scholarships, grants, and awards by category:* Academic Interests/Achievement: 86 awards ($469,250 total): engineering/technologies, general academic interests/achievements. *Special Characteristics:* 13 awards ($147,301 total): local/state students. *Tuition waivers:* Full or partial for employees or children of employees. *ROTC:* Army cooperative.
LOANS *Student loans:* $7,805,668 (81% need-based, 19% non-need-based). 69% of past graduating class borrowed through all loan programs. *Average indebtedness per student:* $25,023. *Average need-based loan:* Freshmen: $2058; Undergraduates: $3772. *Programs:* Federal Direct (Subsidized and Unsubsidized Stafford), FFEL (PLUS), Perkins, state, college/university.
WORK-STUDY *Federal work-study:* Total amount: $2,787,038; jobs available. *State or other work-study/employment:* Total amount: $530,585 (35% need-based, 65% non-need-based). 219 part-time jobs averaging $1961.
APPLYING FOR FINANCIAL AID *Required financial aid forms:* FAFSA, CSS Financial Aid PROFILE, noncustodial (divorced/separated) parent's statement, business/farm supplement. *Financial aid deadline:* 2/1. *Notification date:* 4/1. Students must reply by 5/1 or within 4 weeks of notification.
CONTACT Deborah Luekens, Director of Student Financial Services, Smith College, College Hall, Northampton, MA 01063, 413-585-2530 or toll-free 800-383-3232. *Fax:* 413-585-2566. *E-mail:* sfs@smith.edu.

SOJOURNER-DOUGLASS COLLEGE
Baltimore, MD

Tuition & fees: $6748	Average undergraduate aid package: $7450

ABOUT THE INSTITUTION Independent, coed, primarily women. Awards: bachelor's and master's degrees (offers only evening and weekend programs). 18 undergraduate majors. Total enrollment: 1,124. Undergraduates: 1,060. Freshmen: 169. Federal methodology is used as a basis for awarding need-based institutional aid.
UNDERGRADUATE EXPENSES for 2005–06 *Tuition:* full-time $6540; part-time $363 per credit. *Required fees:* full-time $208; $104 per term part-time. Part-time tuition and fees vary according to course load. *Payment plan:* Installment.
FRESHMAN FINANCIAL AID (Fall 2004) 342 applied for aid; of those 64% were deemed to have need. 91% of freshmen with need received aid. *Average percent of need met:* 85% (excluding resources awarded to replace EFC). *Average financial aid package:* $8290 (excluding resources awarded to replace EFC). 20% of all full-time freshmen had no need and received non-need-based gift aid.
UNDERGRADUATE FINANCIAL AID (Fall 2004) 1,300 applied for aid; of those 66% were deemed to have need. 97% of undergraduates with need received aid. *Average percent of need met:* 85% (excluding resources awarded to replace EFC). *Average financial aid package:* $7450 (excluding resources awarded to replace EFC). 3% of all full-time undergraduates had no need and received non-need-based gift aid.
GIFT AID (NEED-BASED) *Total amount:* $4,243,810 (64% federal, 25% state, 11% institutional). *Receiving aid:* Freshmen: 43% (148); All full-time undergraduates: 43% (562). *Average award:* Freshmen: $4450; Undergraduates: $4350. *Scholarships, grants, and awards:* Federal Pell, FSEOG, state, college/university gift aid from institutional funds.
GIFT AID (NON-NEED-BASED) *Total amount:* $56,960 (30% state, 66% institutional, 4% external sources). *Receiving aid:* Freshmen: 1% (4); Undergraduates: 2% (20). *Average Award:* Freshmen: $2000; Undergraduates: $2000. *Tuition waivers:* Full or partial for employees or children of employees.
LOANS *Student loans:* $4,618,319 (100% need-based). 85% of past graduating class borrowed through all loan programs. *Average need-based loan:* Freshmen: $1706; Undergraduates: $1706. *Parent loans:* $40,585 (100% need-based). *Programs:* FFEL (Subsidized and Unsubsidized Stafford, PLUS), college/university.
WORK-STUDY *Federal work-study:* Total amount: $135,918; 24 jobs averaging $5663.
APPLYING FOR FINANCIAL AID *Required financial aid forms:* FAFSA, institution's own form. *Financial aid deadline:* Continuous.
CONTACT Ms. Rebecca Chalk, Financial Aid Director, Sojourner-Douglass College, 500 North Caroline Street, Baltimore, MD 21205, 410-276-0306 Ext. 260. *Fax:* 410-276-1593.

SOKA UNIVERSITY OF AMERICA
Aliso Viejo, CA

CONTACT Financial Aid Office, Soka University of America, 1 University Drive, Aliso Viejo, CA 92656, 949-480-4000 or toll-free 949-480-4150 (in-state), 888-600-SOKA (out-of-state).

SONOMA STATE UNIVERSITY
Rohnert Park, CA

Tuition & fees (CA res): $3616	Average undergraduate aid package: $7191

ABOUT THE INSTITUTION State-supported, coed. Awards: bachelor's and master's degrees. 64 undergraduate majors. Total enrollment: 7,749. Undergraduates: 6,599. Freshmen: 1,053. Federal methodology is used as a basis for awarding need-based institutional aid.
UNDERGRADUATE EXPENSES for 2005–06 *Application fee:* $55. *Tuition, state resident:* full-time $0. *Tuition, nonresident:* full-time $10,170. Full-time tuition and fees vary according to course load. Part-time tuition and fees vary according to course load. *College room and board:* $8890; *room only:* $6052. Room and board charges vary according to board plan and housing facility.
FRESHMAN FINANCIAL AID (Fall 2004) 671 applied for aid; of those 55% were deemed to have need. 67% of freshmen with need received aid; of those 80% had need fully met. *Average percent of need met:* 80% (excluding resources awarded to replace EFC). *Average financial aid package:* $6400 (excluding resources awarded to replace EFC). 3% of all full-time freshmen had no need and received non-need-based gift aid.
UNDERGRADUATE FINANCIAL AID (Fall 2004) 3,058 applied for aid; of those 75% were deemed to have need. 84% of undergraduates with need received aid; of those 66% had need fully met. *Average percent of need met:* 75% (excluding resources awarded to replace EFC). *Average financial aid package:* $7191 (excluding resources awarded to replace EFC). 4% of all full-time undergraduates had no need and received non-need-based gift aid.
GIFT AID (NEED-BASED) *Total amount:* $8,803,236 (48% federal, 52% state). *Receiving aid:* Freshmen: 16% (192); All full-time undergraduates: 25% (1,455). *Average award:* Freshmen: $6329; Undergraduates: $5211. *Scholarships, grants, and awards:* Federal Pell, FSEOG, state, private, college/university gift aid from institutional funds.
GIFT AID (NON-NEED-BASED) *Total amount:* $1,166,929 (18% state, 22% institutional, 60% external sources). *Receiving aid:* Freshmen: 9% (109); Undergraduates: 8% (469). *Average Award:* Freshmen: $2371; Undergraduates: $2491. *Scholarships, grants, and awards by category:* Academic Interests/Achievement: 164 awards ($135,575 total): area/ethnic studies, biological sciences, business, communication, computer science, education, English, foreign languages, general academic interests/achievements, health fields, humanities, mathematics, physical sciences, premedicine, social sciences. *Creative Arts/Performance:* 36 awards ($32,000 total): applied art and design, art/fine arts, cinema/film/broadcasting, creative writing, dance, journalism/publications, music, performing arts, theater/drama. *Special Achievements/Activities:* 5 awards ($2525 total): community service, leadership, memberships. *Special Characteristics:* 75 awards ($84,377 total): adult students, children and siblings of alumni, children of educators, children of faculty/staff, children of public servants, children of union members/company employees, children of workers in trades, ethnic background, first-generation college students, general special characteristics, handicapped students, international students, local/state students, married students, members of minority groups, out-of-state students, previous college experience, veterans. *Tuition waivers:* Full or partial for employees or children of employees. *ROTC:* Army cooperative, Air Force cooperative.

Sonoma State University

LOANS *Student loans:* $13,961,734 (61% need-based, 39% non-need-based). 71% of past graduating class borrowed through all loan programs. *Average indebtedness per student:* $5030. *Average need-based loan:* Freshmen: $2574; Undergraduates: $4037. *Parent loans:* $6,813,560 (100% non-need-based). *Programs:* Federal Direct (Subsidized and Unsubsidized Stafford, PLUS), Perkins.
WORK-STUDY *Federal work-study:* Total amount: $1,072,660; 401 jobs averaging $2739. *State or other work-study/employment:* Total amount: $1,600,000 (100% non-need-based). 694 part-time jobs averaging $2305.
ATHLETIC AWARDS *Total amount:* $91,123 (100% non-need-based).
APPLYING FOR FINANCIAL AID *Required financial aid form:* FAFSA. *Financial aid deadline (priority):* 1/31. *Notification date:* Continuous beginning 3/15. Students must reply within 4 weeks of notification.
CONTACT Susan Gutierrez, Director of Financial Aid, Sonoma State University, 1801 East Cotati Avenue, Rohnert Park, CA 94928-3609, 707-664-2287. *Fax:* 707-664-4242. *E-mail:* susan.gutierrez@sonoma.edu.

SOUTH CAROLINA STATE UNIVERSITY
Orangeburg, SC

| Tuition & fees (SC res): $6665 | Average undergraduate aid package: N/A |

ABOUT THE INSTITUTION State-supported, coed. Awards: bachelor's, master's, and doctoral degrees and post-bachelor's and post-master's certificates. 49 undergraduate majors. Total enrollment: 4,294. Undergraduates: 3,704. Freshmen: 960. Both federal and institutional methodology are used as a basis for awarding need-based institutional aid.
UNDERGRADUATE EXPENSES for 2005–06 *Application fee:* $25. *Tuition, state resident:* full-time $6480; part-time $270 per credit hour. *Tuition, nonresident:* full-time $13,288; part-time $554 per credit hour. Full-time tuition and fees vary according to course load, degree level, reciprocity agreements, and student level. Part-time tuition and fees vary according to course load, degree level, reciprocity agreements, and student level. *College room and board:* $6028; *room only:* $3642. Room and board charges vary according to board plan and housing facility. *Payment plans:* Installment, deferred payment.
GIFT AID (NEED-BASED) *Total amount:* $8,854,399 (93% federal, 7% state). *Scholarships, grants, and awards:* Federal Pell, FSEOG, state, private, college/university gift aid from institutional funds.
GIFT AID (NON-NEED-BASED) *Total amount:* $6,374,425 (43% state, 27% institutional, 30% external sources). *Scholarships, grants, and awards by category: Academic Interests/Achievement:* general academic interests/achievements. *Creative Arts/Performance:* music. *Tuition waivers:* Full or partial for employees or children of employees, senior citizens. *ROTC:* Army, Air Force cooperative.
LOANS *Student loans:* $22,904,414 (55% need-based, 45% non-need-based). 67% of past graduating class borrowed through all loan programs. *Average indebtedness per student:* $23,580. *Parent loans:* $1,899,039 (100% non-need-based). *Programs:* FFEL (Subsidized and Unsubsidized Stafford, PLUS), Perkins, college/university.
WORK-STUDY *Federal work-study:* Total amount: $359,752; 343 jobs averaging $1048. *State or other work-study/employment:* Total amount: $738,019 (100% non-need-based). 360 part-time jobs averaging $2050.
ATHLETIC AWARDS *Total amount:* $2,337,738 (100% non-need-based).
APPLYING FOR FINANCIAL AID *Required financial aid form:* FAFSA. *Financial aid deadline (priority):* 5/1. *Notification date:* Continuous beginning 4/15. Students must reply within 2 weeks of notification.
CONTACT Sandra S. Davis, Director of Financial Aid, South Carolina State University, 300 College Street Northeast, Orangeburg, SC 29117, 803-536-7067 or toll-free 800-260-5956. *Fax:* 803-536-8420. *E-mail:* sdavis@scsu.edu.

SOUTH DAKOTA SCHOOL OF MINES AND TECHNOLOGY
Rapid City, SD

| Tuition & fees (SD res): $4757 | Average undergraduate aid package: $6899 |

ABOUT THE INSTITUTION State-supported, coed. Awards: associate, bachelor's, master's, and doctoral degrees. 17 undergraduate majors. Total enrollment: 2,313. Undergraduates: 2,057. Freshmen: 365. Federal methodology is used as a basis for awarding need-based institutional aid.
UNDERGRADUATE EXPENSES for 2005–06 *Application fee:* $20. *Tuition, state resident:* full-time $2291; part-time $76.35 per credit hour. *Tuition, nonresident:* full-time $7278; part-time $242.60 per credit hour. *Required fees:* full-time $2466; $82.20 per credit hour. Full-time tuition and fees vary according to course load, program, and reciprocity agreements. Part-time tuition and fees vary according to course load, program, and reciprocity agreements. *College room and board:* $2867; *room only:* $1830. Room and board charges vary according to board plan and housing facility. *Payment plan:* Installment.
FRESHMAN FINANCIAL AID (Fall 2004) 321 applied for aid; of those 56% were deemed to have need. 99% of freshmen with need received aid; of those 44% had need fully met. *Average percent of need met:* 81% (excluding resources awarded to replace EFC). *Average financial aid package:* $6631 (excluding resources awarded to replace EFC). 20% of all full-time freshmen had no need and received non-need-based gift aid.
UNDERGRADUATE FINANCIAL AID (Fall 2004) 1,344 applied for aid; of those 60% were deemed to have need. 100% of undergraduates with need received aid; of those 27% had need fully met. *Average percent of need met:* 70% (excluding resources awarded to replace EFC). *Average financial aid package:* $6899 (excluding resources awarded to replace EFC). 15% of all full-time undergraduates had no need and received non-need-based gift aid.
GIFT AID (NEED-BASED) *Total amount:* $2,117,902 (70% federal, 13% institutional, 17% external sources). *Receiving aid:* Freshmen: 33% (115); All full-time undergraduates: 29% (450). *Average award:* Freshmen: $3520; Undergraduates: $3458. *Scholarships, grants, and awards:* Federal Pell, college/university gift aid from institutional funds, LEAP.
GIFT AID (NON-NEED-BASED) *Total amount:* $613,918 (2% federal, 55% institutional, 43% external sources). *Receiving aid:* Freshmen: 22% (76); Undergraduates: 12% (180). *Average Award:* Freshmen: $2465; Undergraduates: $2620. *Scholarships, grants, and awards by category: Academic Interests/Achievement:* 217 awards ($292,212 total): computer science, engineering/technologies, mathematics. *Tuition waivers:* Full or partial for senior citizens. *ROTC:* Army.
LOANS *Student loans:* $4,753,291 (100% need-based). 21% of past graduating class borrowed through all loan programs. *Average indebtedness per student:* $1623. *Average need-based loan:* Freshmen: $2731; Undergraduates: $3816. *Parent loans:* $635,241 (60% need-based, 40% non-need-based). *Programs:* FFEL (Subsidized and Unsubsidized Stafford, PLUS), Perkins.
WORK-STUDY *Federal work-study:* Total amount: $202,117; jobs available.
ATHLETIC AWARDS *Total amount:* $195,963 (53% need-based, 47% non-need-based).
APPLYING FOR FINANCIAL AID *Required financial aid forms:* FAFSA, freshmen scholarship application form. *Financial aid deadline (priority):* 3/15. *Notification date:* Continuous beginning 5/15. Students must reply within 3 weeks of notification.
CONTACT David W. Martin, Financial Aid Director, South Dakota School of Mines and Technology, 501 East Saint Joseph Street, Rapid City, SD 57701-3995, 605-394-2274 or toll-free 800-544-8162 Ext. 2414. *Fax:* 605-394-1268. *E-mail:* david.martin@sdsmt.edu.

SOUTH DAKOTA STATE UNIVERSITY
Brookings, SD

| Tuition & fees (SD res): $4732 | Average undergraduate aid package: $7550 |

ABOUT THE INSTITUTION State-supported, coed. Awards: associate, bachelor's, master's, doctoral, and first professional degrees and post-bachelor's and post-master's certificates. 80 undergraduate majors. Total enrollment: 10,938. Undergraduates: 9,594. Freshmen: 1,855. Federal methodology is used as a basis for awarding need-based institutional aid.
UNDERGRADUATE EXPENSES for 2005–06 *Application fee:* $20. *Tuition, state resident:* full-time $2291; part-time $76.35 per credit. *Tuition, nonresident:* full-time $7278; part-time $242.60 per credit. *Required fees:* full-time $2441; $81.35 per credit. Full-time tuition and fees vary according to course load, program, and reciprocity agreements. Part-time tuition and fees vary according to course load, program, and reciprocity agreements. *College room and board:* $4769; *room only:* $2113. Room and board charges vary according to board plan and housing facility. *Payment plans:* Installment, deferred payment.
FRESHMAN FINANCIAL AID (Fall 2005, est.) 1559 applied for aid; of those 91% were deemed to have need. 100% of freshmen with need received aid; of those 69% had need fully met. *Average percent of need met:* 86% (excluding

resources awarded to replace EFC). *Average financial aid package:* $6312 (excluding resources awarded to replace EFC). 27% of all full-time freshmen had no need and received non-need-based gift aid.

UNDERGRADUATE FINANCIAL AID (Fall 2005, est.) 6,651 applied for aid; of those 93% were deemed to have need. 99% of undergraduates with need received aid; of those 78% had need fully met. *Average percent of need met:* 83% (excluding resources awarded to replace EFC). *Average financial aid package:* $7550 (excluding resources awarded to replace EFC). 13% of all full-time undergraduates had no need and received non-need-based gift aid.

GIFT AID (NEED-BASED) *Total amount:* $10,608,086 (72% federal, 4% state, 16% institutional, 8% external sources). *Receiving aid:* Freshmen: 40% (716); All full-time undergraduates: 40% (3,124). *Average award:* Freshmen: $3148; Undergraduates: $3128. *Scholarships, grants, and awards:* Federal Pell, FSEOG, state, private, college/university gift aid from institutional funds, United Negro College Fund, Federal Nursing, agency awards.

GIFT AID (NON-NEED-BASED) *Total amount:* $5,196,947 (14% federal, 10% state, 50% institutional, 26% external sources). *Receiving aid:* Freshmen: 54% (958); Undergraduates: 44% (3,416). *Average Award:* Freshmen: $1042; Undergraduates: $1062. *Scholarships, grants, and awards by category: Academic Interests/Achievement:* 2,091 awards ($2,153,162 total): agriculture, area/ethnic studies, biological sciences, business, communication, computer science, education, engineering/technologies, English, foreign languages, general academic interests/achievements, health fields, home economics, humanities, international studies, mathematics, military science, physical sciences, premedicine, social sciences. *Creative Arts/Performance:* 258 awards ($219,410 total): art/fine arts, debating, general creative arts/performance, journalism/publications, music, performing arts, theater/drama. *Special Achievements/Activities:* 80 awards ($60,244 total): community service, general special achievements/activities, hobbies/interests, junior miss, leadership, memberships, rodeo. *Special Characteristics:* 130 awards ($180,124 total): adult students, children of faculty/staff, children of workers in trades, ethnic background, first-generation college students, general special characteristics, handicapped students, international students, members of minority groups, veterans, veterans' children. *Tuition waivers:* Full or partial for children of alumni, employees or children of employees, senior citizens. *ROTC:* Army, Air Force.

LOANS *Student loans:* $43,018,511 (62% need-based, 38% non-need-based). 81% of past graduating class borrowed through all loan programs. *Average indebtedness per student:* $19,520. *Average need-based loan:* Freshmen: $2804; Undergraduates: $4486. *Parent loans:* $2,811,042 (100% non-need-based). *Programs:* FFEL (Subsidized and Unsubsidized Stafford, PLUS), Perkins, Federal Nursing, college/university, alternative loans from private sources.

WORK-STUDY *Federal work-study:* Total amount: $730,964; 659 jobs averaging $1019. *State or other work-study/employment:* Total amount: $2,974,515 (100% non-need-based). 2,180 part-time jobs averaging $1320.

ATHLETIC AWARDS *Total amount:* $1,056,335 (29% need-based, 71% non-need-based).

APPLYING FOR FINANCIAL AID *Required financial aid form:* FAFSA. *Financial aid deadline (priority):* 3/15. *Notification date:* Continuous beginning 4/1. Students must reply within 3 weeks of notification.

CONTACT Mr. Jay Larsen, Director of Financial Aid, South Dakota State University, Box 2201 ADM 106, Brookings, SD 57007, 605-688-4695 or toll-free 800-952-3541. *Fax:* 605-688-5882. *E-mail:* jay.larsen@sdstate.edu.

SOUTHEASTERN BAPTIST COLLEGE
Laurel, MS

CONTACT Financial Aid Officer, Southeastern Baptist College, 4229 Highway 15 North, Laurel, MS 39440-1096, 601-426-6346.

SOUTHEASTERN BAPTIST THEOLOGICAL SEMINARY
Wake Forest, NC

CONTACT H. Allan Moseley, Vice President of Student Services/Dean of Students, Southeastern Baptist Theological Seminary, PO Box 1889, Wake Forest, NC 27588, 919-556-3101 Ext. 306 or toll-free 800-284-6317. *Fax:* 919-556-0998. *E-mail:* deanofstudents@sebts.edu.

SOUTHEASTERN BIBLE COLLEGE
Birmingham, AL

Tuition & fees: N/R **Average undergraduate aid package:** $6457

ABOUT THE INSTITUTION Independent nondenominational, coed. Awards: bachelor's degrees (associate). 8 undergraduate majors. Total enrollment: 232. Undergraduates: 232. Freshmen: 53. Federal methodology is used as a basis for awarding need-based institutional aid.

UNDERGRADUATE EXPENSES for 2006–07 *Application fee:* $20. *Tuition:* part-time $295 per semester hour.

FRESHMAN FINANCIAL AID (Fall 2005, est.) 42 applied for aid; of those 100% were deemed to have need. 100% of freshmen with need received aid. *Average percent of need met:* 70% (excluding resources awarded to replace EFC). *Average financial aid package:* $5125 (excluding resources awarded to replace EFC).

UNDERGRADUATE FINANCIAL AID (Fall 2005, est.) 188 applied for aid; of those 97% were deemed to have need. 100% of undergraduates with need received aid. *Average percent of need met:* 70% (excluding resources awarded to replace EFC). *Average financial aid package:* $6457 (excluding resources awarded to replace EFC).

GIFT AID (NEED-BASED) *Total amount:* $229,136 (100% federal). *Receiving aid:* Freshmen: 100% (42); All full-time undergraduates: 79% (183). *Average award:* Freshmen: $2000; Undergraduates: $4000. *Scholarships, grants, and awards:* Federal Pell, FSEOG.

GIFT AID (NON-NEED-BASED) *Total amount:* $136,000 (85% institutional, 15% external sources). *Receiving aid:* Freshmen: 10% (4); Undergraduates: 12% (27). *Scholarships, grants, and awards by category: Academic Interests/Achievement:* general academic interests/achievements. *Creative Arts/Performance:* 1 award ($2000 total): music. *Special Characteristics:* children of faculty/staff, local/state students, veterans.

LOANS *Student loans:* $1,300,000 (100% need-based). 50% of past graduating class borrowed through all loan programs. *Average indebtedness per student:* $20,000. *Average need-based loan:* Freshmen: $2625; Undergraduates: $4250. *Parent loans:* $144,000 (100% non-need-based). *Programs:* FFEL (Subsidized and Unsubsidized Stafford, PLUS).

WORK-STUDY *Federal work-study:* Total amount: $15,000; 10 jobs averaging $1200. *State or other work-study/employment:* Total amount: $20,000 (100% non-need-based). 10 part-time jobs averaging $2000.

APPLYING FOR FINANCIAL AID *Required financial aid forms:* FAFSA, institution's own form, state aid form. *Financial aid deadline (priority):* 5/1. *Notification date:* Continuous. Students must reply within 2 weeks of notification.

CONTACT Ms. Joanne Belin, Financial Aid Administrator, Southeastern Bible College, 2545 Valleydale Road, Birmingham, AL 35244, 205-970-9215 or toll-free 800-749-8878 (in-state). *E-mail:* jbelin@sebc.edu.

SOUTHEASTERN COLLEGE OF THE ASSEMBLIES OF GOD
Lakeland, FL

See Southeastern University.

SOUTHEASTERN LOUISIANA UNIVERSITY
Hammond, LA

Tuition & fees (LA res): $3341 **Average undergraduate aid package:** $6033

ABOUT THE INSTITUTION State-supported, coed. Awards: associate, bachelor's, and master's degrees. 48 undergraduate majors. Total enrollment: 15,472. Undergraduates: 13,664. Freshmen: 2,539. Federal methodology is used as a basis for awarding need-based institutional aid.

UNDERGRADUATE EXPENSES for 2005–06 *Application fee:* $20. *Tuition, state resident:* full-time $3341; part-time $139 per credit hour. *Tuition, nonresident:* full-time $8669; part-time $361 per credit hour. Full-time tuition and fees vary according to course load. Part-time tuition and fees vary according to course load. *College room and board:* $5180; *room only:* $3150. Room and board charges vary according to board plan and housing facility. *Payment plans:* Installment, deferred payment.

Southeastern Louisiana University

FRESHMAN FINANCIAL AID (Fall 2004) 1956 applied for aid; of those 88% were deemed to have need. 92% of freshmen with need received aid. *Average financial aid package:* $4005 (excluding resources awarded to replace EFC). 44% of all full-time freshmen had no need and received non-need-based gift aid.
UNDERGRADUATE FINANCIAL AID (Fall 2004) 8,727 applied for aid; of those 90% were deemed to have need. 81% of undergraduates with need received aid. *Average financial aid package:* $6033 (excluding resources awarded to replace EFC). 32% of all full-time undergraduates had no need and received non-need-based gift aid.
GIFT AID (NEED-BASED) *Total amount:* $16,897,337 (99% federal, 1% state). *Receiving aid:* Freshmen: 37% (879); All full-time undergraduates: 41% (4,649). *Average award:* Freshmen: $3076; Undergraduates: $3011. *Scholarships, grants, and awards:* Federal Pell, FSEOG, state, private, college/university gift aid from institutional funds, Federal Nursing.
GIFT AID (NON-NEED-BASED) *Total amount:* $5,323,751 (85% state, 12% institutional, 3% external sources). *Receiving aid:* Freshmen: 33% (795); Undergraduates: 12% (1,314). *Average Award:* Freshmen: $2379; Undergraduates: $2307. *Scholarships, grants, and awards by category: Academic Interests/Achievement:* 1,612 awards ($1,022,102 total): biological sciences, business, communication, education, engineering/technologies, English, foreign languages, general academic interests/achievements, health fields, home economics, humanities, international studies, library science, mathematics, physical sciences, premedicine, social sciences. *Creative Arts/Performance:* 302 awards ($201,918 total): art/fine arts, dance, debating, music. *Special Achievements/Activities:* 139 awards ($68,481 total): cheerleading/drum major, leadership, memberships, rodeo. *Special Characteristics:* 531 awards ($1,040,598 total): children of faculty/staff, handicapped students, out-of-state students, veterans' children. *Tuition waivers:* Full or partial for employees or children of employees, senior citizens. *ROTC:* Army cooperative.
LOANS *Student loans:* $32,530,695 (61% need-based, 39% non-need-based). 58% of past graduating class borrowed through all loan programs. *Average indebtedness per student:* $12,527. *Average need-based loan:* Freshmen: $2081; Undergraduates: $3132. *Parent loans:* $653,950 (100% non-need-based). *Programs:* FFEL (Subsidized and Unsubsidized Stafford, PLUS), Perkins, college/university.
WORK-STUDY *Federal work-study:* Total amount: $563,177; 595 jobs averaging $1320. *State or other work-study/employment:* Total amount: $1,695,969 (100% non-need-based). 1,244 part-time jobs averaging $1375.
ATHLETIC AWARDS *Total amount:* $516,717 (100% non-need-based).
APPLYING FOR FINANCIAL AID *Required financial aid form:* FAFSA. *Financial aid deadline (priority):* 5/1. *Notification date:* Continuous. Students must reply within 2 weeks of notification.
CONTACT Rosie Toney, Director of Financial Aid, Southeastern Louisiana University, SLU 10768, Hammond, LA 70402, 985-549-5309 or toll-free 800-222-7358. *Fax:* 985-549-5077. *E-mail:* finaid@selu.edu.

SOUTHEASTERN OKLAHOMA STATE UNIVERSITY
Durant, OK

Tuition & fees (OK res): $3372	Average undergraduate aid package: $1134

ABOUT THE INSTITUTION State-supported, coed. Awards: bachelor's and master's degrees and post-master's certificates. 54 undergraduate majors. Total enrollment: 4,075. Undergraduates: 3,663. Freshmen: 618. Federal methodology is used as a basis for awarding need-based institutional aid.
UNDERGRADUATE EXPENSES for 2005–06 *Application fee:* $20. *Tuition, state resident:* full-time $2195; part-time $73.15 per credit hour. *Tuition, nonresident:* full-time $7016; part-time $233.85 per credit hour. *Required fees:* full-time $1177; $34.70 per credit or $68. Full-time tuition and fees vary according to course level. Part-time tuition and fees vary according to course level and course load. *College room and board:* $3910; *room only:* $1875. Room and board charges vary according to board plan and housing facility.
FRESHMAN FINANCIAL AID (Fall 2004) 245 applied for aid; of those 86% were deemed to have need. 100% of freshmen with need received aid; of those 44% had need fully met. *Average percent of need met:* 60% (excluding resources awarded to replace EFC). *Average financial aid package:* $1059 (excluding resources awarded to replace EFC). 4% of all full-time freshmen had no need and received non-need-based gift aid.
UNDERGRADUATE FINANCIAL AID (Fall 2004) 1,365 applied for aid; of those 89% were deemed to have need. 98% of undergraduates with need received aid; of those 57% had need fully met. *Average percent of need met:* 65% (excluding resources awarded to replace EFC). *Average financial aid package:* $1134 (excluding resources awarded to replace EFC). 1% of all full-time undergraduates had no need and received non-need-based gift aid.
GIFT AID (NEED-BASED) *Total amount:* $5,395,041 (91% federal, 9% state). *Receiving aid:* Freshmen: 40% (124); All full-time undergraduates: 47% (842). *Average award:* Freshmen: $1170; Undergraduates: $1231. *Scholarships, grants, and awards:* Federal Pell, FSEOG, state, private, college/university gift aid from institutional funds.
GIFT AID (NON-NEED-BASED) *Total amount:* $1,738,752 (6% state, 12% institutional, 82% external sources). *Receiving aid:* Freshmen: 34% (105); Undergraduates: 20% (360). *Average Award:* Freshmen: $1446; Undergraduates: $1151. *Scholarships, grants, and awards by category: Academic Interests/Achievement:* 244 awards ($177,180 total): biological sciences, business, computer science, education, engineering/technologies, general academic interests/achievements, mathematics, physical sciences, social sciences. *Creative Arts/Performance:* 28 awards ($24,936 total): music, theater/drama. *Special Achievements/Activities:* 5 awards ($5850 total): cheerleading/drum major. *Special Characteristics:* 1,001 awards ($2,712,409 total): children and siblings of alumni, out-of-state students. *Tuition waivers:* Full or partial for minority students, children of alumni, employees or children of employees, senior citizens.
LOANS *Student loans:* $7,333,827 (77% need-based, 23% non-need-based). 30% of past graduating class borrowed through all loan programs. *Average indebtedness per student:* $6124. *Average need-based loan:* Freshmen: $1183; Undergraduates: $2006. *Parent loans:* $302,946 (100% non-need-based). *Programs:* FFEL (Subsidized and Unsubsidized Stafford, PLUS), Perkins, college/university.
WORK-STUDY *Federal work-study:* Total amount: $242,510; 488 jobs averaging $457. *State or other work-study/employment:* Total amount: $896,811 (100% non-need-based). 849 part-time jobs averaging $939.
ATHLETIC AWARDS *Total amount:* $485,700 (100% non-need-based).
APPLYING FOR FINANCIAL AID *Required financial aid forms:* FAFSA, institution's own form. *Financial aid deadline (priority):* 3/1. *Notification date:* 4/15. Students must reply within 2 weeks of notification.
CONTACT Sherry Foster, Director of Student Financial Aid, Southeastern Oklahoma State University, 1405 North 4th Avenue, PMB 4113, Durant, OK 74701-0609, 580-745-2186 or toll-free 800-435-1327. *Fax:* 580-745-7469. *E-mail:* sfoster@sosu.edu.

SOUTHEASTERN UNIVERSITY
Washington, DC

CONTACT Hope Gibbs, Assistant Director of Financial Aid, Southeastern University, 501 I Street, SW, Washington, DC 20024-2788, 202-488-8162 Ext. 234. *E-mail:* hgibbs@admin.seu.edu.

SOUTHEASTERN UNIVERSITY
Lakeland, FL

Tuition & fees: $11,500	Average undergraduate aid package: $7063

ABOUT THE INSTITUTION Independent religious, coed. Awards: bachelor's degrees. 23 undergraduate majors. Total enrollment: 1,964. Undergraduates: 1,964. Federal methodology is used as a basis for awarding need-based institutional aid.
UNDERGRADUATE EXPENSES for 2005–06 *Application fee:* $40. *Comprehensive fee:* $17,178 includes full-time tuition ($11,040), mandatory fees ($460), and room and board ($5678). Full-time tuition and fees vary according to degree level, program, and reciprocity agreements. Room and board charges vary according to board plan and housing facility. *Part-time tuition:* $460 per credit. Part-time tuition and fees vary according to course load, degree level, program, and reciprocity agreements. *Payment plan:* Installment.
FRESHMAN FINANCIAL AID (Fall 2005, est.) 503 applied for aid; of those 80% were deemed to have need. 97% of freshmen with need received aid; of those 12% had need fully met. *Average percent of need met:* 53% (excluding resources awarded to replace EFC). *Average financial aid package:* $7007 (excluding resources awarded to replace EFC). 30% of all full-time freshmen had no need and received non-need-based gift aid.

UNDERGRADUATE FINANCIAL AID (Fall 2005, est.) 1,949 applied for aid; of those 81% were deemed to have need. 98% of undergraduates with need received aid; of those 12% had need fully met. *Average percent of need met:* 52% (excluding resources awarded to replace EFC). *Average financial aid package:* $7063 (excluding resources awarded to replace EFC). 25% of all full-time undergraduates had no need and received non-need-based gift aid.
GIFT AID (NEED-BASED) *Total amount:* $7,264,742 (27% federal, 43% state, 19% institutional, 11% external sources). *Receiving aid:* Freshmen: 58% (376); All full-time undergraduates: 64% (1,435). *Average award:* Freshmen: $5168; Undergraduates: $4871. *Scholarships, grants, and awards:* Federal Pell, FSEOG, state, private, college/university gift aid from institutional funds.
GIFT AID (NON-NEED-BASED) *Total amount:* $2,647,560 (54% state, 22% institutional, 24% external sources). *Receiving aid:* Freshmen: 6% (37); Undergraduates: 6% (137). *Average Award:* Freshmen: $10,709; Undergraduates: $10,537. *Scholarships, grants, and awards by category: Academic Interests/Achievement:* 748 awards ($966,625 total): communication, general academic interests/achievements, religion/biblical studies. *Creative Arts/Performance:* 181 awards ($211,236 total): journalism/publications, music, theater/drama. *Special Achievements/Activities:* religious involvement. *Special Characteristics:* children of faculty/staff, general special characteristics, siblings of current students. *Tuition waivers:* Full or partial for employees or children of employees. *ROTC:* Army cooperative, Air Force cooperative.
LOANS *Student loans:* $12,256,809 (65% need-based, 35% non-need-based). 92% of past graduating class borrowed through all loan programs. *Average indebtedness per student:* $21,650. *Average need-based loan:* Freshmen: $2268; Undergraduates: $2932. *Parent loans:* $6,294,097 (35% need-based, 65% non-need-based). *Programs:* FFEL (Subsidized and Unsubsidized Stafford, PLUS), Perkins.
WORK-STUDY *Federal work-study:* Total amount: $127,996; 98 jobs averaging $1306.
APPLYING FOR FINANCIAL AID *Required financial aid forms:* FAFSA, institution's own form, state aid form, state aid form (for FL residents only). *Financial aid deadline (priority):* 4/15. *Notification date:* Continuous beginning 3/1. Students must reply by 5/1 or within 4 weeks of notification.
CONTACT Ms. Carol B. Bradley, Financial Aid Director, Southeastern University, 1000 Longfellow Boulevard, Lakeland, FL 33801-6099, 863-667-5000 or toll-free 800-500-8760. *Fax:* 863-667-5200. *E-mail:* cbradly@seuniversity.edu.

SOUTHEAST MISSOURI STATE UNIVERSITY
Cape Girardeau, MO

Tuition & fees (MO res): $5145   **Average undergraduate aid package: $6629**

ABOUT THE INSTITUTION State-supported, coed. Awards: associate, bachelor's, and master's degrees and post-master's certificates. 69 undergraduate majors. Total enrollment: 10,292. Undergraduates: 8,968. Freshmen: 1,679. Federal methodology is used as a basis for awarding need-based institutional aid.
UNDERGRADUATE EXPENSES for 2005–06 *Application fee:* $20. *Tuition, state resident:* full-time $4764; part-time $158.80 per credit hour. *Tuition, nonresident:* full-time $8619; part-time $287.30 per credit hour. *Required fees:* full-time $381; $12.70 per credit hour. Full-time tuition and fees vary according to course load and location. Part-time tuition and fees vary according to course load and location. *College room and board:* $5351; *room only:* $3270. Room and board charges vary according to board plan and housing facility. *Payment plans:* Installment, deferred payment.
FRESHMAN FINANCIAL AID (Fall 2004) 1058 applied for aid; of those 71% were deemed to have need. 100% of freshmen with need received aid; of those 19% had need fully met. *Average percent of need met:* 66% (excluding resources awarded to replace EFC). *Average financial aid package:* $5952 (excluding resources awarded to replace EFC). 20% of all full-time freshmen had no need and received non-need-based gift aid.
UNDERGRADUATE FINANCIAL AID (Fall 2004) 4,466 applied for aid; of those 76% were deemed to have need. 99% of undergraduates with need received aid; of those 21% had need fully met. *Average percent of need met:* 68% (excluding resources awarded to replace EFC). *Average financial aid package:* $6629 (excluding resources awarded to replace EFC). 12% of all full-time undergraduates had no need and received non-need-based gift aid.
GIFT AID (NEED-BASED) *Total amount:* $10,009,789 (58% federal, 9% state, 28% institutional, 5% external sources). *Receiving aid:* Freshmen: 45% (628); All full-time undergraduates: 38% (2,458). *Average award:* Freshmen: $3986; Undergraduates: $4278. *Scholarships, grants, and awards:* Federal Pell, FSEOG, state, private, college/university gift aid from institutional funds.
GIFT AID (NON-NEED-BASED) *Total amount:* $4,277,198 (3% federal, 10% state, 77% institutional, 10% external sources). *Receiving aid:* Freshmen: 5% (73); Undergraduates: 4% (227). *Average Award:* Freshmen: $3383; Undergraduates: $3462. *Scholarships, grants, and awards by category: Academic Interests/Achievement:* 795 awards ($2,822,661 total): agriculture, biological sciences, business, communication, computer science, education, English, foreign languages, general academic interests/achievements, health fields, home economics, humanities, international studies, mathematics, military science, physical sciences, premedicine, religion/biblical studies, social sciences. *Creative Arts/Performance:* 108 awards ($70,755 total): music, theater/drama. *Special Achievements/Activities:* 173 awards ($310,455 total): cheerleading/drum major, general special achievements/activities, leadership. *Special Characteristics:* 219 awards ($591,460 total): adult students, children of faculty/staff, first-generation college students, general special characteristics, international students, members of minority groups, out-of-state students, previous college experience. *Tuition waivers:* Full or partial for employees or children of employees, senior citizens. *ROTC:* Air Force.
LOANS *Student loans:* $21,925,695 (66% need-based, 34% non-need-based). 63% of past graduating class borrowed through all loan programs. *Average indebtedness per student:* $16,006. *Average need-based loan:* Freshmen: $2690; Undergraduates: $3766. *Parent loans:* $6,479,366 (20% need-based, 80% non-need-based). *Programs:* FFEL (Subsidized and Unsubsidized Stafford, PLUS), Perkins, state.
WORK-STUDY *Federal work-study:* Total amount: $426,918; 279 jobs averaging $1530. *State or other work-study/employment:* Total amount: $4,768,155 (15% need-based, 85% non-need-based). 1,675 part-time jobs averaging $2847.
ATHLETIC AWARDS *Total amount:* $2,031,481 (33% need-based, 67% non-need-based).
APPLYING FOR FINANCIAL AID *Required financial aid form:* FAFSA. *Financial aid deadline (priority):* 3/1. *Notification date:* Continuous beginning 4/1. Students must reply within 3 weeks of notification.
CONTACT Barbara Garner, Customer Service Supervisor, Southeast Missouri State University, One University Plaza, Cape Girardeau, MO 63701, 573-651-2840. *Fax:* 573-651-5006.

SOUTHERN ADVENTIST UNIVERSITY
Collegedale, TN

Tuition & fees: $14,784   **Average undergraduate aid package: $12,500**

ABOUT THE INSTITUTION Independent Seventh-day Adventist, coed. Awards: associate, bachelor's, and master's degrees. 62 undergraduate majors. Total enrollment: 2,522. Undergraduates: 2,390. Freshmen: 605. Federal methodology is used as a basis for awarding need-based institutional aid.
UNDERGRADUATE EXPENSES for 2006–07 *Application fee:* $25. *Comprehensive fee:* $19,388 includes full-time tuition ($14,300), mandatory fees ($484), and room and board ($4604). *College room only:* $2604. *Part-time tuition:* $604 per semester hour.
FRESHMAN FINANCIAL AID (Fall 2004) 475 applied for aid; of those 78% were deemed to have need. 100% of freshmen with need received aid; of those 1% had need fully met. *Average percent of need met:* 60% (excluding resources awarded to replace EFC). *Average financial aid package:* $12,000 (excluding resources awarded to replace EFC). 35% of all full-time freshmen had no need and received non-need-based gift aid.
UNDERGRADUATE FINANCIAL AID (Fall 2004) 1,526 applied for aid; of those 86% were deemed to have need. 100% of undergraduates with need received aid; of those .2% had need fully met. *Average percent of need met:* 67% (excluding resources awarded to replace EFC). *Average financial aid package:* $12,500 (excluding resources awarded to replace EFC). 29% of all full-time undergraduates had no need and received non-need-based gift aid.
GIFT AID (NEED-BASED) *Total amount:* $3,681,333 (50% federal, 5% state, 45% institutional). *Receiving aid:* Freshmen: 41% (203); All full-time undergraduates: 42% (798). *Average award:* Freshmen: $2400; Undergraduates: $3000. *Scholarships, grants, and awards:* Federal Pell, FSEOG, state, private, college/university gift aid from institutional funds.
GIFT AID (NON-NEED-BASED) *Total amount:* $9,607,998 (1% federal, 4% state, 42% institutional, 53% external sources). *Receiving aid:* Freshmen: 70% (348); Undergraduates: 52% (990). *Average Award:* Freshmen: $2500;

Southern Adventist University

Undergraduates: $3000. **Scholarships, grants, and awards by category:** *Academic Interests/Achievement:* 1,006 awards ($1,426,168 total): business, communication, education, English, general academic interests/achievements, health fields, mathematics, religion/biblical studies. *Creative Arts/Performance:* 156 awards ($159,556 total): art/fine arts, journalism/publications, music, theater/drama. *Special Achievements/Activities:* 320 awards ($175,719 total): community service, general special achievements/activities, leadership, religious involvement. *Special Characteristics:* 521 awards ($424,212 total): children and siblings of alumni, general special characteristics, international students, local/state students, members of minority groups, out-of-state students, siblings of current students, spouses of current students.
LOANS *Student loans:* $8,602,561 (50% need-based, 50% non-need-based). 67% of past graduating class borrowed through all loan programs. *Average indebtedness per student:* $10,935. *Average need-based loan:* Freshmen: $4700; Undergraduates: $2600. *Parent loans:* $1,402,780 (100% non-need-based). *Programs:* FFEL (Subsidized and Unsubsidized Stafford, PLUS), Perkins, Federal Nursing, college/university.
WORK-STUDY *Federal work-study:* Total amount: $889,021; 396 jobs averaging $2158. *State or other work-study/employment:* Part-time jobs available.
APPLYING FOR FINANCIAL AID *Required financial aid forms:* FAFSA, state aid form. *Financial aid deadline (priority):* 3/1. *Notification date:* Continuous beginning 2/15. Students must reply within 2 weeks of notification.
CONTACT Mr. Marc Grundy, Director of Student Finance Office, Southern Adventist University, PO Box 370, Collegedale, TN 37315-0370, 423-236-2875 or toll-free 800-768-8437. *Fax:* 423-236-1835.

SOUTHERN ARKANSAS UNIVERSITY–MAGNOLIA
Magnolia, AR

Tuition & fees (AR res): $4290 **Average undergraduate aid package:** $4158

ABOUT THE INSTITUTION State-supported, coed. Awards: associate, bachelor's, and master's degrees. 45 undergraduate majors. Total enrollment: 3,057. Undergraduates: 2,803. Freshmen: 651. Federal methodology is used as a basis for awarding need-based institutional aid.
UNDERGRADUATE EXPENSES for 2005–06 *Tuition, state resident:* full-time $3900; part-time $130 per credit hour. *Tuition, nonresident:* full-time $5910; part-time $197 per credit hour. *Required fees:* full-time $390; $390 per year part-time. Full-time tuition and fees vary according to course load. Part-time tuition and fees vary according to course load. *College room and board:* $3790; *room only:* $1960. *Payment plan:* Installment.
FRESHMAN FINANCIAL AID (Fall 2005, est.) 383 applied for aid; of those 87% were deemed to have need. 98% of freshmen with need received aid; of those 82% had need fully met. *Average percent of need met:* 100% (excluding resources awarded to replace EFC). *Average financial aid package:* $1511 (excluding resources awarded to replace EFC). 16% of all full-time freshmen had no need and received non-need-based gift aid.
UNDERGRADUATE FINANCIAL AID (Fall 2005, est.) 1,800 applied for aid; of those 89% were deemed to have need. 97% of undergraduates with need received aid; of those 82% had need fully met. *Average percent of need met:* 100% (excluding resources awarded to replace EFC). *Average financial aid package:* $4158 (excluding resources awarded to replace EFC). 11% of all full-time undergraduates had no need and received non-need-based gift aid.
GIFT AID (NEED-BASED) *Total amount:* $4,995,614 (88% federal, 12% state). *Receiving aid:* Freshmen: 53% (305); All full-time undergraduates: 52% (1,490). *Average award:* Freshmen: $3760; Undergraduates: $2376. **Scholarships, grants, and awards:** Federal Pell, FSEOG, state, private, college/university gift aid from institutional funds.
GIFT AID (NON-NEED-BASED) *Total amount:* $4,080,435 (89% institutional, 11% external sources). *Receiving aid:* Freshmen: 54% (307); Undergraduates: 31% (899). *Average Award:* Freshmen: $4608; Undergraduates: $4557. **Scholarships, grants, and awards by category:** *Academic Interests/Achievement:* 650 awards ($2,442,019 total): agriculture, business, computer science, education, English, foreign languages, general academic interests/achievements, health fields, mathematics, physical sciences, social sciences. *Creative Arts/Performance:* 33 awards ($68,614 total): art/fine arts, dance, music, theater/drama. *Special Achievements/Activities:* 71 awards ($190,497 total): cheerleading/drum major, leadership, rodeo. *Special Characteristics:* 548 awards ($817,035 total): adult students, children and siblings of alumni, children of faculty/staff, members of minority groups, out-of-state students. *Tuition waivers:* Full or partial for children of alumni, employees or children of employees, senior citizens.
LOANS *Student loans:* $7,475,652 (57% need-based, 43% non-need-based). 58% of past graduating class borrowed through all loan programs. *Average indebtedness per student:* $14,162. *Average need-based loan:* Freshmen: $691; Undergraduates: $1283. *Parent loans:* $181,944 (100% non-need-based). *Programs:* FFEL (Subsidized and Unsubsidized Stafford, PLUS), Perkins.
WORK-STUDY *Federal work-study:* Total amount: $2,732,719; 1,095 jobs averaging $2495. *State or other work-study/employment:* Total amount: $1,178,965 (100% non-need-based). 449 part-time jobs averaging $2625.
ATHLETIC AWARDS *Total amount:* $659,303 (100% non-need-based).
APPLYING FOR FINANCIAL AID *Required financial aid form:* FAFSA. *Financial aid deadline (priority):* 7/1. *Notification date:* Continuous beginning 4/1. Students must reply within 2 weeks of notification.
CONTACT Ms. Bronwyn C. Sneed, Director of Student Aid, Southern Arkansas University–Magnolia, PO Box 9344, Magnolia, AR 71754-9344, 870-235-4023 or toll-free 800-332-7286 (in-state). *Fax:* 870-235-4913. *E-mail:* bcsneed@saumag.edu.

SOUTHERN BAPTIST THEOLOGICAL SEMINARY
Louisville, KY

Tuition & fees: N/R **Average undergraduate aid package:** $148

ABOUT THE INSTITUTION Independent Southern Baptist, coed. Awards: associate and bachelor's degrees. Total enrollment: 475. Undergraduates: 475. Institutional methodology is used as a basis for awarding need-based institutional aid.
UNDERGRADUATE FINANCIAL AID (Fall 2004) 163 applied for aid; of those 78% were deemed to have need. 100% of undergraduates with need received aid. *Average percent of need met:* 16% (excluding resources awarded to replace EFC). *Average financial aid package:* $148 (excluding resources awarded to replace EFC).
GIFT AID (NEED-BASED) *Total amount:* $254,354 (7% institutional, 93% external sources). *Receiving aid:* All full-time undergraduates: 17% (127). *Average award:* Undergraduates: $148. *Scholarships, grants, and awards:* state, private, college/university gift aid from institutional funds, all other sources aid as long as the school does not need to participate in Title IV program.
LOANS *Student loans:* $616,904 (100% need-based). *Programs:* college/university, Non-Title IV loan programs such as Sallie Mae "Signature" Loan and Nellie Mae "Excel" loan.
APPLYING FOR FINANCIAL AID *Required financial aid forms:* institution's own form, scholarship application form(s). *Financial aid deadline (priority):* 7/15. *Notification date:* 8/1.
CONTACT Mrs. Teresa M. Crosby, Assistant Director of Student Life, Southern Baptist Theological Seminary, Financial Aid Office, 2825 Lexington Road, Louisville, KY 40280, 502-897-4206. *Fax:* 502-897-4031. *E-mail:* financialaid@sbts.edu.

SOUTHERN CALIFORNIA INSTITUTE OF ARCHITECTURE
Los Angeles, CA

Tuition & fees: N/R **Average undergraduate aid package:** $11,946

ABOUT THE INSTITUTION Independent, coed. Awards: bachelor's, master's, and first professional degrees. 1 undergraduate major. Total enrollment: 447. Undergraduates: 183. Freshmen: 5. Federal methodology is used as a basis for awarding need-based institutional aid.
FRESHMAN FINANCIAL AID (Fall 2005, est.) 53 applied for aid; of those 100% were deemed to have need. 100% of freshmen with need received aid. *Average percent of need met:* 19% (excluding resources awarded to replace EFC). *Average financial aid package:* $8867 (excluding resources awarded to replace EFC). 2% of all full-time freshmen had no need and received non-need-based gift aid.
UNDERGRADUATE FINANCIAL AID (Fall 2005, est.) 173 applied for aid; of those 85% were deemed to have need. 100% of undergraduates with need received aid. *Average percent of need met:* 19% (excluding resources awarded

to replace EFC). *Average financial aid package:* $11,946 (excluding resources awarded to replace EFC). 6% of all full-time undergraduates had no need and received non-need-based gift aid.
GIFT AID (NEED-BASED) *Total amount:* $825,515 (62% federal, 32% state, 5% institutional, 1% external sources). *Receiving aid:* Freshmen: 19% (11); All full-time undergraduates: 60% (122). *Average award:* Freshmen: $4293; Undergraduates: $4271. *Scholarships, grants, and awards:* Federal Pell, FSEOG, state, private, college/university gift aid from institutional funds.
GIFT AID (NON-NEED-BASED) *Total amount:* $24,896 (100% federal). *Receiving aid:* Undergraduates: 2% (4). *Average Award:* Freshmen: $4500; Undergraduates: $2239. *Scholarships, grants, and awards by category:* Academic Interests/Achievement: 35 awards ($137,000 total): architecture.
LOANS *Student loans:* $2,828,911 (27% need-based, 73% non-need-based). 16% of past graduating class borrowed through all loan programs. *Average indebtedness per student:* $33,000. *Average need-based loan:* Freshmen: $4574; Undergraduates: $4589. *Parent loans:* $655,320 (100% non-need-based). *Programs:* FFEL (Subsidized and Unsubsidized Stafford, PLUS), alternative loans.
WORK-STUDY *Federal work-study:* Total amount: $125,852; jobs available (averaging $3000). *State or other work-study/employment:* Total amount: $11,386 (100% non-need-based). Part-time jobs available (averaging $3000).
APPLYING FOR FINANCIAL AID *Required financial aid forms:* FAFSA, institution's own form. *Financial aid deadline (priority):* 3/2. *Notification date:* 4/1. Students must reply within 4 weeks of notification.
CONTACT Lina Johnson, Financial Aid Director, Southern California Institute of Architecture, 960 East 3rd Street, Los Angeles, CA 90013, 213-613-2200 Ext. 345 or toll-free 800-774-7242. *Fax:* 213-613-2260. *E-mail:* financialaid@sciarc.edu.

SOUTHERN CALIFORNIA SEMINARY
El Cajon, CA

CONTACT Financial Aid Office, Southern California Seminary, 2075 East Madison Avenue, El Cajon, CA 92019, 619-442-9841.

SOUTHERN CHRISTIAN UNIVERSITY
Montgomery, AL

ABOUT THE INSTITUTION Independent religious, coed. Awards: bachelor's, master's, doctoral, and first professional degrees. 7 undergraduate majors. Total enrollment: 720. Undergraduates: 371.
GIFT AID (NEED-BASED) *Scholarships, grants, and awards:* Federal Pell, FSEOG, state, private, college/university gift aid from institutional funds.
GIFT AID (NON-NEED-BASED) *Scholarships, grants, and awards by category:* Special Achievements/Activities: religious involvement. Special Characteristics: children of faculty/staff, veterans.
LOANS *Programs:* FFEL (Subsidized and Unsubsidized Stafford, PLUS).
APPLYING FOR FINANCIAL AID *Required financial aid forms:* FAFSA, institution's own form.
CONTACT Rosemary Kennington, Financial Aid Director, Southern Christian University, 1200 Taylor Road, Montgomery, AL 36117, 334-387-3877 Ext. 7527 or toll-free 800-351-4040 Ext. 213. *Fax:* 334-387-3878. *E-mail:* financialaid@southernchristian.edu.

SOUTHERN CONNECTICUT STATE UNIVERSITY
New Haven, CT

Tuition & fees (CT res): $6442   **Average undergraduate aid package: $6629**

ABOUT THE INSTITUTION State-supported, coed. Awards: bachelor's, master's, and doctoral degrees and post-master's certificates. 39 undergraduate majors. Total enrollment: 12,158. Undergraduates: 8,309. Freshmen: 1,340. Federal methodology is used as a basis for awarding need-based institutional aid.
UNDERGRADUATE EXPENSES for 2006–07 *Application fee:* $50. *Tuition, state resident:* full-time $3187; part-time $322 per credit. *Tuition, nonresident:* full-time $10,315; part-time $322 per credit. *Required fees:* full-time $3255; $8 per credit or $55 per term part-time. *College room and board:* $8031; *room only:* $4446.

FRESHMAN FINANCIAL AID (Fall 2005, est.) 1078 applied for aid; of those 60% were deemed to have need. 94% of freshmen with need received aid; of those 39% had need fully met. *Average percent of need met:* 81% (excluding resources awarded to replace EFC). *Average financial aid package:* $6368 (excluding resources awarded to replace EFC). 7% of all full-time freshmen had no need and received non-need-based gift aid.
UNDERGRADUATE FINANCIAL AID (Fall 2005, est.) 5,474 applied for aid; of those 59% were deemed to have need. 95% of undergraduates with need received aid; of those 34% had need fully met. *Average percent of need met:* 79% (excluding resources awarded to replace EFC). *Average financial aid package:* $6629 (excluding resources awarded to replace EFC). 5% of all full-time undergraduates had no need and received non-need-based gift aid.
GIFT AID (NEED-BASED) *Total amount:* $11,056,117 (45% federal, 48% state, 4% institutional, 3% external sources). *Receiving aid:* Freshmen: 33% (434); All full-time undergraduates: 33% (2,238). *Average award:* Freshmen: $4760; Undergraduates: $4409. *Scholarships, grants, and awards:* Federal Pell, FSEOG, state, college/university gift aid from institutional funds.
GIFT AID (NON-NEED-BASED) *Total amount:* $1,085,445 (1% federal, 2% state, 59% institutional, 38% external sources). *Receiving aid:* Freshmen: 11% (141); Undergraduates: 7% (477). *Average Award:* Freshmen: $2816; Undergraduates: $2935. *Scholarships, grants, and awards by category:* Special Characteristics: children of faculty/staff, veterans. *ROTC:* Army cooperative, Air Force cooperative.
LOANS *Student loans:* $15,095,822 (53% need-based, 47% non-need-based). *Average need-based loan:* Freshmen: $2572; Undergraduates: $3383. *Parent loans:* $7,651,474 (51% need-based, 49% non-need-based). *Programs:* FFEL (Subsidized and Unsubsidized Stafford, PLUS), Perkins, alternative loans.
WORK-STUDY *Federal work-study:* Total amount: $275,239; 139 jobs averaging $3086. *State or other work-study/employment:* Total amount: $22,448 (100% need-based). 3 part-time jobs averaging $2589.
ATHLETIC AWARDS *Total amount:* $953,585 (51% need-based, 49% non-need-based).
APPLYING FOR FINANCIAL AID *Required financial aid forms:* FAFSA, institution's own form, federal income tax form(s). *Financial aid deadline (priority):* 4/14. *Notification date:* Continuous. Students must reply within 2 weeks of notification.
CONTACT Avon Dennis, Director of Financial Aid, Southern Connecticut State University, Wintergreen Building, 501 Crescent Street, New Haven, CT 06515-1355, 203-392-5448. *Fax:* 203-392-5229. *E-mail:* dennisa1@southernet.edu.

SOUTHERN ILLINOIS UNIVERSITY CARBONDALE
Carbondale, IL

Tuition & fees (IL res): $6831   **Average undergraduate aid package: $8694**

ABOUT THE INSTITUTION State-supported, coed. Awards: associate, bachelor's, master's, doctoral, and first professional degrees and post-bachelor's and first professional certificates. 89 undergraduate majors. Total enrollment: 21,441. Undergraduates: 16,697. Freshmen: 2,470. Federal methodology is used as a basis for awarding need-based institutional aid.
UNDERGRADUATE EXPENSES for 2005–06 *Application fee:* $30. *Tuition, state resident:* full-time $5310; part-time $177 per semester hour. *Tuition, nonresident:* full-time $13,275; part-time $442.50 per semester hour. *Required fees:* full-time $1521; $654 per term part-time. Full-time tuition and fees vary according to course load and student level. Part-time tuition and fees vary according to course load and student level. *College room and board:* $5560; *room only:* $3058. Room and board charges vary according to board plan and housing facility. *Payment plans:* Guaranteed tuition, installment.
FRESHMAN FINANCIAL AID (Fall 2004) 2126 applied for aid; of those 74% were deemed to have need. 96% of freshmen with need received aid; of those 82% had need fully met. *Average percent of need met:* 94% (excluding resources awarded to replace EFC). *Average financial aid package:* $8397 (excluding resources awarded to replace EFC). 7% of all full-time freshmen had no need and received non-need-based gift aid.
UNDERGRADUATE FINANCIAL AID (Fall 2004) 10,665 applied for aid; of those 82% were deemed to have need. 97% of undergraduates with need received aid; of those 83% had need fully met. *Average percent of need met:* 94% (excluding resources awarded to replace EFC). *Average financial aid package:* $8694 (excluding resources awarded to replace EFC). 8% of all full-time undergraduates had no need and received non-need-based gift aid.

Southern Illinois University Carbondale

GIFT AID (NEED-BASED) *Total amount:* $30,440,276 (50% federal, 45% state, 4% institutional, 1% external sources). *Receiving aid:* Freshmen: 46% (1,233); All full-time undergraduates: 44% (6,674). *Average award:* Freshmen: $4767; Undergraduates: $4620. *Scholarships, grants, and awards:* Federal Pell, FSEOG, state, private, college/university gift aid from institutional funds.
GIFT AID (NON-NEED-BASED) *Total amount:* $13,741,491 (42% federal, 20% state, 29% institutional, 9% external sources). *Receiving aid:* Freshmen: 32% (839); Undergraduates: 27% (4,118). *Average Award:* Freshmen: $3802; Undergraduates: $3529. *Scholarships, grants, and awards by category: Academic Interests/Achievement:* 3,169 awards ($6,562,821 total): agriculture, architecture, area/ethnic studies, biological sciences, business, communication, computer science, education, engineering/technologies, English, foreign languages, general academic interests/achievements, health fields, home economics, humanities, international studies, mathematics, military science, physical sciences, premedicine, religion/biblical studies, social sciences. *Creative Arts/Performance:* 130 awards ($418,903 total): applied art and design, art/fine arts, cinema/film/broadcasting, creative writing, dance, debating, general creative arts/performance, journalism/publications, music, performing arts, theater/drama. *Special Achievements/Activities:* 87 awards ($163,877 total): cheerleading, drum major, community service, general special achievements/activities, leadership. *Special Characteristics:* 206 awards ($284,656 total): children and siblings of alumni, children of educators, children of faculty/staff, children of public servants, children with a deceased or disabled parent, general special characteristics, handicapped students, international students, public servants, spouses of deceased or disabled public servants, veterans. *Tuition waivers:* Full or partial for employees or children of employees, senior citizens. *ROTC:* Army, Air Force.
LOANS *Student loans:* $49,207,346 (63% need-based, 37% non-need-based). 39% of past graduating class borrowed through all loan programs. *Average indebtedness per student:* $14,708. *Average need-based loan:* Freshmen: $3328; Undergraduates: $3708. *Parent loans:* $5,190,096 (13% need-based, 87% non-need-based). *Programs:* Federal Direct (Subsidized and Unsubsidized Stafford, PLUS), Perkins, college/university.
WORK-STUDY *Federal work-study:* Total amount: $2,390,035; 2,010 jobs averaging $1189. *State or other work-study/employment:* Total amount: $7,194,069 (19% need-based, 81% non-need-based). 5,346 part-time jobs averaging $1346.
ATHLETIC AWARDS *Total amount:* $2,694,942 (30% need-based, 70% non-need-based).
APPLYING FOR FINANCIAL AID *Required financial aid form:* FAFSA. *Financial aid deadline (priority):* 4/1. *Notification date:* Continuous. Students must reply within 3 weeks of notification.
CONTACT Billie Jo Hamilton, Director of Financial Aid, Southern Illinois University Carbondale, Woody Hall, Third Floor, B-Wing, Carbondale, IL 62901-4702, 618-453-3102. *Fax:* 618-453-4606. *E-mail:* hamilton@siu.edu.

SOUTHERN ILLINOIS UNIVERSITY EDWARDSVILLE
Edwardsville, IL

Tuition & fees (IL res): $5179 **Average undergraduate aid package: $8483**

ABOUT THE INSTITUTION State-supported, coed. Awards: bachelor's, master's, and first professional degrees and post-bachelor's, post-master's, and first professional certificates. 43 undergraduate majors. Total enrollment: 13,460. Undergraduates: 10,945. Freshmen: 1,748. Federal methodology is used as a basis for awarding need-based institutional aid.
UNDERGRADUATE EXPENSES for 2005–06 *Application fee:* $50. *Tuition, state resident:* full-time $4320; part-time $144 per semester hour. *Tuition, nonresident:* full-time $10,800; part-time $360 per semester hour. *Required fees:* full-time $859; $366.50 per term part-time. Full-time tuition and fees vary according to course load. Part-time tuition and fees vary according to course load. *College room and board:* $5819; *room only:* $3389. Room and board charges vary according to board plan and housing facility. *Payment plan:* Installment.
FRESHMAN FINANCIAL AID (Fall 2004) 1249 applied for aid; of those 68% were deemed to have need. 95% of freshmen with need received aid; of those 23% had need fully met. *Average percent of need met:* 76% (excluding resources awarded to replace EFC). *Average financial aid package:* $8055 (excluding resources awarded to replace EFC). 12% of all full-time freshmen had no need and received non-need-based gift aid.
UNDERGRADUATE FINANCIAL AID (Fall 2004) 6,282 applied for aid; of those 76% were deemed to have need. 96% of undergraduates with need received aid; of those 22% had need fully met. *Average percent of need met:* 76% (excluding resources awarded to replace EFC). *Average financial aid package:* $8483 (excluding resources awarded to replace EFC). 10% of all full-time undergraduates had no need and received non-need-based gift aid.
GIFT AID (NEED-BASED) *Total amount:* $19,282,992 (46% federal, 45% state, 5% institutional, 4% external sources). *Receiving aid:* Freshmen: 35% (607); All full-time undergraduates: 37% (3,408). *Average award:* Freshmen: $5573; Undergraduates: $5279. *Scholarships, grants, and awards:* Federal Pell, FSEOG, state, private, college/university gift aid from institutional funds, Federal Nursing.
GIFT AID (NON-NEED-BASED) *Total amount:* $2,259,362 (4% federal, 50% state, 18% institutional, 28% external sources). *Receiving aid:* Freshmen: 4% (62); Undergraduates: 2% (186). *Average Award:* Freshmen: $3632; Undergraduates: $3459. *Scholarships, grants, and awards by category: Academic Interests/Achievement:* business, education, general academic interests/achievements, health fields. *Creative Arts/Performance:* art/fine arts, dance, music, theater/drama. *Special Characteristics:* children of faculty/staff. *Tuition waivers:* Full or partial for employees or children of employees, senior citizens. *ROTC:* Army, Air Force.
LOANS *Student loans:* $25,142,662 (64% need-based, 36% non-need-based). 20% of past graduating class borrowed through all loan programs. *Average indebtedness per student:* $18,145. *Average need-based loan:* Freshmen: $2369; Undergraduates: $3411. *Parent loans:* $6,621,402 (20% need-based, 80% non-need-based). *Programs:* Federal Direct (Subsidized and Unsubsidized Stafford, PLUS), FFEL (PLUS), Perkins, Federal Nursing, college/university, alternative loans.
WORK-STUDY *Federal work-study:* Total amount: $1,173,444; 679 jobs averaging $1728. *State or other work-study/employment:* Total amount: $9,802,926 (9% need-based, 91% non-need-based). 1,442 part-time jobs averaging $6798.
ATHLETIC AWARDS *Total amount:* $308,334 (33% need-based, 67% non-need-based).
APPLYING FOR FINANCIAL AID *Required financial aid form:* FAFSA. *Financial aid deadline (priority):* 3/1. *Notification date:* Continuous beginning 3/15. Students must reply within 2 weeks of notification.
CONTACT Sharon Berry, Director of Financial Aid, Southern Illinois University Edwardsville, Campus Box 1060, Rendleman Hall, Room 2308, Edwardsville, IL 62026-1060, 618-650-3834 or toll-free 800-447-SIUE. *Fax:* 618-650-3885. *E-mail:* shaberr@siue.edu.

SOUTHERN METHODIST COLLEGE
Orangeburg, SC

Tuition & fees: $5200 **Average undergraduate aid package: $2025**

ABOUT THE INSTITUTION Independent religious, coed. Awards: associate and bachelor's degrees. 2 undergraduate majors. Total enrollment: 77. Undergraduates: 77. Freshmen: 5. Both federal and institutional methodology are used as a basis for awarding need-based institutional aid.
UNDERGRADUATE EXPENSES for 2005–06 *Application fee:* $25. *Comprehensive fee:* $9400 includes full-time tuition ($4600), mandatory fees ($600), and room and board ($4200). Full-time tuition and fees vary according to class time and course load. Room and board charges vary according to housing facility. *Part-time tuition:* $192 per semester hour. *Part-time fees:* $25 per semester hour. Part-time tuition and fees vary according to class time and course load.
FRESHMAN FINANCIAL AID (Fall 2004) 1 applied for aid; of those 100% were deemed to have need. 100% of freshmen with need received aid. *Average percent of need met:* 75% (excluding resources awarded to replace EFC). *Average financial aid package:* $2025 (excluding resources awarded to replace EFC).
UNDERGRADUATE FINANCIAL AID (Fall 2004) 56 applied for aid; of those 100% were deemed to have need. 100% of undergraduates with need received aid. *Average percent of need met:* 75% (excluding resources awarded to replace EFC). *Average financial aid package:* $2025 (excluding resources awarded to replace EFC).
GIFT AID (NEED-BASED) *Total amount:* $9640 (79% institutional, 21% external sources). *Receiving aid:* Freshmen: 100% (1); All full-time undergraduates: 89% (56). *Average award:* Freshmen: $2625; Undergraduates: $5000. *Scholarships, grants, and awards:* Federal Pell, FSEOG, private, college/university gift aid from institutional funds.

GIFT AID (NON-NEED-BASED) *Scholarships, grants, and awards by category:* *Academic Interests/Achievement:* $4000 total: education, religion/biblical studies. *Special Achievements/Activities:* $4600 total: religious involvement. *Special Characteristics:* 5 awards ($9600 total): relatives of clergy. *Tuition waivers:* Full or partial for employees or children of employees, senior citizens.
LOANS *Student loans:* $261,843 (100% need-based). 75% of past graduating class borrowed through all loan programs. *Average indebtedness per student:* $12,600. *Average need-based loan:* Freshmen: $4000; Undergraduates: $4000. *Programs:* Federal Direct (Subsidized and Unsubsidized Stafford, PLUS).
WORK-STUDY *Federal work-study:* Total amount: $9531; 10 jobs averaging $600.
APPLYING FOR FINANCIAL AID *Required financial aid forms:* FAFSA, institution's own form. *Financial aid deadline:* 3/15. *Notification date:* Continuous beginning 4/5. Students must reply within 2 weeks of notification.
CONTACT Terry H. Lynch, Financial Aid Officer, Southern Methodist College, PO Box 1027, 541 Broughton Street, Orangeburg, SC 29116, 803-534-7826 Ext. 1326 or toll-free 800-360-1503. *Fax:* 803-534-7827. *E-mail:* tlynch@smcollege.edu.

SOUTHERN METHODIST UNIVERSITY
Dallas, TX

ABOUT THE INSTITUTION Independent religious, coed. Awards: bachelor's, master's, doctoral, and first professional degrees and post-bachelor's certificates. 77 undergraduate majors. Total enrollment: 11,152. Undergraduates: 6,489. Freshmen: 1,402.
GIFT AID (NEED-BASED) *Scholarships, grants, and awards:* Federal Pell, FSEOG, state, private, college/university gift aid from institutional funds.
GIFT AID (NON-NEED-BASED) *Scholarships, grants, and awards by category:* *Academic Interests/Achievement:* area/ethnic studies, biological sciences, business, communication, computer science, engineering/technologies, English, foreign languages, general academic interests/achievements, humanities, international studies, mathematics, physical sciences, religion/biblical studies, social sciences. *Creative Arts/Performance:* art/fine arts, cinema/film/broadcasting, creative writing, dance, journalism/publications, music, theater/drama. *Special Achievements/Activities:* general special achievements/activities. *Special Characteristics:* children of faculty/staff, relatives of clergy.
LOANS *Programs:* FFEL (Subsidized and Unsubsidized Stafford, PLUS), Perkins, state, college/university.
WORK-STUDY *Federal work-study:* Total amount: $3,195,100; 1,568 jobs averaging $2500. *State or other work-study/employment:* Total amount: $146,064 (38% need-based, 62% non-need-based). 55 part-time jobs averaging $2000.
APPLYING FOR FINANCIAL AID *Required financial aid forms:* FAFSA, CSS Financial Aid PROFILE, noncustodial (divorced/separated) parent's statement, business/farm supplement.
CONTACT Marc Peterson, Director of Financial Aid, Southern Methodist University, PO Box 750181, Dallas, TX 75275, 214-768-1588 or toll-free 800-323-0672.

SOUTHERN NAZARENE UNIVERSITY
Bethany, OK

CONTACT Mr. Chuck Kietzman, Director of Financial Assistance, Southern Nazarene University, 6729 Northwest 39th Expressway, Bethany, OK 73008, 405-491-6310 or toll-free 800-648-9899. *Fax:* 405-717-6271. *E-mail:* ckietzma@snu.edu.

SOUTHERN NEW HAMPSHIRE UNIVERSITY
Manchester, NH

Tuition & fees: $21,714	Average undergraduate aid package: $14,063

ABOUT THE INSTITUTION Independent, coed. Awards: associate, bachelor's, master's, and doctoral degrees and post-bachelor's certificates. 37 undergraduate majors. Total enrollment: 3,887. Undergraduates: 1,844. Freshmen: 403. Federal methodology is used as a basis for awarding need-based institutional aid.
UNDERGRADUATE EXPENSES for 2006–07 *Application fee:* $35. *Comprehensive fee:* $30,194 includes full-time tuition ($21,384), mandatory fees ($330), and room and board ($8480). *College room only:* $6080. *Part-time tuition:* $891 per credit.

FRESHMAN FINANCIAL AID (Fall 2005, est.) 368 applied for aid; of those 86% were deemed to have need. 100% of freshmen with need received aid; of those 11% had need fully met. *Average percent of need met:* 70% (excluding resources awarded to replace EFC). *Average financial aid package:* $14,016 (excluding resources awarded to replace EFC). 15% of all full-time freshmen had no need and received non-need-based gift aid.
UNDERGRADUATE FINANCIAL AID (Fall 2005, est.) 1,334 applied for aid; of those 88% were deemed to have need. 100% of undergraduates with need received aid; of those 12% had need fully met. *Average percent of need met:* 70% (excluding resources awarded to replace EFC). *Average financial aid package:* $14,063 (excluding resources awarded to replace EFC). 17% of all full-time undergraduates had no need and received non-need-based gift aid.
GIFT AID (NEED-BASED) *Total amount:* $10,343,453 (10% federal, 2% state, 85% institutional, 3% external sources). *Receiving aid:* Freshmen: 71% (303); All full-time undergraduates: 67% (1,111). *Average award:* Freshmen: $9740; Undergraduates: $9105. *Scholarships, grants, and awards:* Federal Pell, FSEOG, state, private, college/university gift aid from institutional funds.
GIFT AID (NON-NEED-BASED) *Total amount:* $1,173,474 (96% institutional, 4% external sources). *Receiving aid:* Freshmen: 68% (291); Undergraduates: 69% (1,140). *Average Award:* Freshmen: $4038; Undergraduates: $3426. *Scholarships, grants, and awards by category:* Academic Interests/Achievement: 528 awards ($2,075,313 total): general academic interests/achievements. *Special Achievements/Activities:* 389 awards ($418,750 total): leadership, memberships. *Special Characteristics:* 90 awards ($85,600 total): children and siblings of alumni, children of faculty/staff, general special characteristics, international students, local/state students, previous college experience, siblings of current students, veterans, veterans' children. *ROTC:* Army cooperative, Air Force cooperative.
LOANS *Student loans:* $12,648,582 (54% need-based, 46% non-need-based). *Average indebtedness per student:* $21,138. *Average need-based loan:* Freshmen: $2572; Undergraduates: $3745. *Parent loans:* $4,420,727 (5% need-based, 95% non-need-based). *Programs:* FFEL (Subsidized and Unsubsidized Stafford, PLUS), Perkins.
WORK-STUDY *Federal work-study:* Total amount: $888,931; 568 jobs averaging $695.
ATHLETIC AWARDS Total amount: $1,652,035 (35% need-based, 65% non-need-based).
APPLYING FOR FINANCIAL AID *Required financial aid form:* FAFSA. *Financial aid deadline (priority):* 3/15. *Notification date:* Continuous beginning 3/1. Students must reply within 3 weeks of notification.
CONTACT Financial Aid Office, Southern New Hampshire University, 2500 North River Road, Manchester, NH 03106, 603-645-9645 or toll-free 800-642-4968. *Fax:* 603-645-9639. *E-mail:* finaid@snhu.edu.

SOUTHERN OREGON UNIVERSITY
Ashland, OR

Tuition & fees (OR res): $4986	Average undergraduate aid package: $7980

ABOUT THE INSTITUTION State-supported, coed. Awards: bachelor's and master's degrees and post-bachelor's certificates. 40 undergraduate majors. Total enrollment: 4,977. Undergraduates: 4,436. Freshmen: 770. Federal methodology is used as a basis for awarding need-based institutional aid.
UNDERGRADUATE EXPENSES for 2006–07 *Application fee:* $50. *Tuition, state resident:* full-time $4986; part-time $108 per credit. *Tuition, nonresident:* full-time $14,691; part-time $108 per credit. *Required fees:* $25 per credit. *College room and board:* $6468.
FRESHMAN FINANCIAL AID (Fall 2005, est.) 455 applied for aid; of those 77% were deemed to have need. 100% of freshmen with need received aid; of those 20% had need fully met. *Average percent of need met:* 60% (excluding resources awarded to replace EFC). *Average financial aid package:* $6899 (excluding resources awarded to replace EFC). 17% of all full-time freshmen had no need and received non-need-based gift aid.
UNDERGRADUATE FINANCIAL AID (Fall 2005, est.) 2,319 applied for aid; of those 85% were deemed to have need. 97% of undergraduates with need received aid; of those 13% had need fully met. *Average percent of need met:* 59% (excluding resources awarded to replace EFC). *Average financial aid package:* $7980 (excluding resources awarded to replace EFC). 12% of all full-time undergraduates had no need and received non-need-based gift aid.

Southern Oregon University

GIFT AID (NEED-BASED) *Total amount:* $7,416,235 (52% federal, 13% state, 22% institutional, 13% external sources). *Receiving aid:* Freshmen: 44% (311); All full-time undergraduates: 47% (1,589). *Average award:* Freshmen: $5422; Undergraduates: $5384. *Scholarships, grants, and awards:* Federal Pell, FSEOG, state, private, college/university gift aid from institutional funds.

GIFT AID (NON-NEED-BASED) *Total amount:* $1,004,606 (1% state, 76% institutional, 23% external sources). *Receiving aid:* Freshmen: 6% (40); Undergraduates: 3% (85). *Average Award:* Freshmen: $7208; Undergraduates: $8613. *Scholarships, grants, and awards by category:* Academic Interests/Achievement: 375 awards ($583,109 total): biological sciences, business, education, English, general academic interests/achievements, health fields, mathematics, physical sciences, social sciences. Creative Arts/Performance: 52 awards ($44,225 total): art/fine arts, creative writing, journalism/publications, music, theater/drama. Special Achievements/Activities: 8 awards ($13,300 total): community service, general special achievements/activities, hobbies/interests, leadership, memberships. Special Characteristics: 97 awards ($404,198 total): adult students, international students, members of minority groups.

LOANS *Student loans:* $11,488,392 (82% need-based, 18% non-need-based). 93% of past graduating class borrowed through all loan programs. *Average indebtedness per student:* $22,944. *Average need-based loan:* Freshmen: $2418; Undergraduates: $3835. *Parent loans:* $5,978,441 (38% need-based, 62% non-need-based). *Programs:* Federal Direct (Subsidized and Unsubsidized Stafford, PLUS), Perkins, state, college/university.

WORK-STUDY *Federal work-study:* Total amount: $459,189; 371 jobs averaging $899.

ATHLETIC AWARDS *Total amount:* $245,430 (61% need-based, 39% non-need-based).

APPLYING FOR FINANCIAL AID *Required financial aid form:* FAFSA. *Financial aid deadline (priority):* 3/1. *Notification date:* Continuous beginning 4/1. Students must reply within 2 weeks of notification.

CONTACT Debbie Beck, Associate Director of Financial Aid, Southern Oregon University, 1250 Siskiyou Boulevard, Ashland, OR 97520, 541-552-6162 or toll-free 800-482-7672 (in-state). *Fax:* 541-552-6035. *E-mail:* beck@sou.edu.

SOUTHERN POLYTECHNIC STATE UNIVERSITY
Marietta, GA

Tuition & fees (GA res): $3174 **Average undergraduate aid package: $2667**

ABOUT THE INSTITUTION State-supported, coed. Awards: associate, bachelor's, and master's degrees and post-bachelor's certificates. 23 undergraduate majors. Total enrollment: 3,806. Undergraduates: 3,330. Freshmen: 448. Federal methodology is used as a basis for awarding need-based institutional aid.

UNDERGRADUATE EXPENSES for 2005–06 *Application fee:* $20. *Tuition, state resident:* full-time $2622; part-time $110 per credit hour. *Tuition, nonresident:* full-time $10,486; part-time $437 per credit hour. *College room and board:* $5490; *room only:* $3210.

FRESHMAN FINANCIAL AID (Fall 2005, est.) 342 applied for aid; of those 100% were deemed to have need. 100% of freshmen with need received aid; of those 55% had need fully met. *Average percent of need met:* 68% (excluding resources awarded to replace EFC). *Average financial aid package:* $2284 (excluding resources awarded to replace EFC). 1% of all full-time freshmen had no need and received non-need-based gift aid.

UNDERGRADUATE FINANCIAL AID (Fall 2005, est.) 1,918 applied for aid; of those 73% were deemed to have need. 96% of undergraduates with need received aid; of those 48% had need fully met. *Average percent of need met:* 74% (excluding resources awarded to replace EFC). *Average financial aid package:* $2667 (excluding resources awarded to replace EFC). 1% of all full-time undergraduates had no need and received non-need-based gift aid.

GIFT AID (NEED-BASED) *Total amount:* $2,087,829 (96% federal, 4% external sources). *Receiving aid:* Freshmen: 25% (112); All full-time undergraduates: 26% (806). *Average award:* Freshmen: $2364; Undergraduates: $2352. *Scholarships, grants, and awards:* Federal Pell, FSEOG, state, private, college/university gift aid from institutional funds.

GIFT AID (NON-NEED-BASED) *Total amount:* $3,220,924 (95% state, 5% external sources). *Receiving aid:* Freshmen: 69% (313); Undergraduates: 17% (525). *Average Award:* Freshmen: $1530; Undergraduates: $4097. *ROTC:* Army cooperative, Naval cooperative, Air Force cooperative.

LOANS *Student loans:* $6,043,028 (51% need-based, 49% non-need-based). 60% of past graduating class borrowed through all loan programs. *Average indebtedness per student:* $12,706. *Average need-based loan:* Freshmen: $2531; Undergraduates: $3950. *Parent loans:* $352,711 (100% non-need-based). *Programs:* FFEL (Subsidized and Unsubsidized Stafford, PLUS).

WORK-STUDY *Federal work-study:* Total amount: $53,195; 17 jobs averaging $3239.

ATHLETIC AWARDS *Total amount:* $219,417 (100% non-need-based).

APPLYING FOR FINANCIAL AID *Required financial aid form:* FAFSA. *Financial aid deadline:* Continuous. *Notification date:* Continuous beginning 5/1. Students must reply by 5/1.

CONTACT Gary W. Bush, Director of Financial Aid, Southern Polytechnic State University, 1100 South Marietta Parkway, Marietta, GA 30060-2896, 678-915-7290 or toll-free 800-635-3204. *Fax:* 678-915-4227. *E-mail:* gbush@spsu.edu.

SOUTHERN UNIVERSITY AND AGRICULTURAL AND MECHANICAL COLLEGE
Baton Rouge, LA

Tuition & fees (LA res): $3592 **Average undergraduate aid package: $9516**

ABOUT THE INSTITUTION State-supported, coed. Awards: associate, bachelor's, master's, and doctoral degrees and post-master's certificates. 65 undergraduate majors. Total enrollment: 9,941. Undergraduates: 8,576. Freshmen: 1,485. Federal methodology is used as a basis for awarding need-based institutional aid.

UNDERGRADUATE EXPENSES for 2005–06 *Application fee:* $20. *Tuition, state resident:* full-time $3592. *Tuition, nonresident:* full-time $9384. Full-time tuition and fees vary according to course load and location. Part-time tuition and fees vary according to course load and location. *College room and board:* $4646; *room only:* $2816. Room and board charges vary according to board plan and housing facility.

FRESHMAN FINANCIAL AID (Fall 2005, est.) 1392 applied for aid; of those 94% were deemed to have need. 99% of freshmen with need received aid; of those 12% had need fully met. *Average percent of need met:* 79% (excluding resources awarded to replace EFC). *Average financial aid package:* $8455 (excluding resources awarded to replace EFC). 15% of all full-time freshmen had no need and received non-need-based gift aid.

UNDERGRADUATE FINANCIAL AID (Fall 2005, est.) 7,109 applied for aid; of those 91% were deemed to have need. 97% of undergraduates with need received aid; of those 21% had need fully met. *Average percent of need met:* 78% (excluding resources awarded to replace EFC). *Average financial aid package:* $9516 (excluding resources awarded to replace EFC). 13% of all full-time undergraduates had no need and received non-need-based gift aid.

GIFT AID (NEED-BASED) *Total amount:* $12,599,670 (75% federal, 25% institutional). *Receiving aid:* Freshmen: 56% (836); All full-time undergraduates: 52% (4,107). *Average award:* Freshmen: $1778; Undergraduates: $1808. *Scholarships, grants, and awards:* Federal Pell, FSEOG, state, private, college/university gift aid from institutional funds, Federal work study, LEAP, TOPS, and T.H. Harris.

GIFT AID (NON-NEED-BASED) *Total amount:* $876,175 (100% federal). *Average Award:* Freshmen: $2330; Undergraduates: $2746. *Scholarships, grants, and awards by category:* Academic Interests/Achievement: 1,067 awards ($2,486,110 total): general academic interests/achievements. *Tuition waivers:* Full or partial for children of alumni, employees or children of employees, senior citizens. *ROTC:* Army, Naval, Air Force cooperative.

LOANS *Student loans:* $31,430,082 (94% need-based, 6% non-need-based). 90% of past graduating class borrowed through all loan programs. *Average indebtedness per student:* $23,000. *Average need-based loan:* Freshmen: $2405; Undergraduates: $3997. *Parent loans:* $1,434,540 (100% need-based). *Programs:* Federal Direct (Subsidized and Unsubsidized Stafford, PLUS), FFEL (Subsidized and Unsubsidized Stafford, PLUS), college/university.

WORK-STUDY *Federal work-study:* Total amount: $559,748; 900 jobs averaging $1800. *State or other work-study/employment:* Total amount: $268,286 (100% need-based). 300 part-time jobs averaging $2500.

ATHLETIC AWARDS *Total amount:* $569,416 (100% need-based).

APPLYING FOR FINANCIAL AID *Required financial aid forms:* FAFSA, institution's own form. *Financial aid deadline (priority):* 5/15. *Notification date:* Continuous beginning 6/30. Students must reply within 3 weeks of notification.
CONTACT Mr. Phillip Rodgers Sr., Director of Financial Aid, Southern University and Agricultural and Mechanical College, PO Box 9961, Baton Rouge, LA 70813, 225-771-2790 or toll-free 800-256-1531. *Fax:* 225-771-5898. *E-mail:* phillip_rodgers@cxs.subr.edu.

SOUTHERN UNIVERSITY AT NEW ORLEANS
New Orleans, LA

CONTACT Director of Financial Aid, Southern University at New Orleans, 6400 Press Drive, New Orleans, LA 70126, 504-286-5263. *Fax:* 504-286-5213.

SOUTHERN UTAH UNIVERSITY
Cedar City, UT

ABOUT THE INSTITUTION State-supported, coed. Awards: associate, bachelor's, and master's degrees. 49 undergraduate majors. Total enrollment: 6,859. Undergraduates: 6,465. Freshmen: 1,075.
GIFT AID (NEED-BASED) *Scholarships, grants, and awards:* Federal Pell, FSEOG, state, private, college/university gift aid from institutional funds.
GIFT AID (NON-NEED-BASED) *Scholarships, grants, and awards by category: Academic Interests/Achievement:* business, communication, education, general academic interests/achievements. *Creative Arts/Performance:* dance, general creative arts/performance, journalism/publications, music, performing arts, theater/drama. *Special Achievements/Activities:* cheerleading/drum major, general special achievements/activities, leadership. *Special Characteristics:* ethnic background.
LOANS *Programs:* FFEL (Subsidized and Unsubsidized Stafford, PLUS), Perkins, college/university.
WORK-STUDY *Federal work-study:* Total amount: $284,348; jobs available. *State or other work-study/employment:* Total amount: $148,073 (100% need-based). Part-time jobs available.
APPLYING FOR FINANCIAL AID *Required financial aid forms:* FAFSA, institution's own form, institutional verification form.
CONTACT Paul Morris, Director of Financial Aid, Southern Utah University, 351 West Center Street, Cedar City, UT 84720-2498, 435-586-7734. *Fax:* 435-586-7736. *E-mail:* morris@suu.edu.

SOUTHERN VERMONT COLLEGE
Bennington, VT

Tuition & fees: $14,373	Average undergraduate aid package: $12,862

ABOUT THE INSTITUTION Independent, coed. Awards: associate and bachelor's degrees. 15 undergraduate majors. Total enrollment: 390. Undergraduates: 390. Freshmen: 74. Both federal and institutional methodology are used as a basis for awarding need-based institutional aid.
UNDERGRADUATE EXPENSES for 2005–06 *Application fee:* $30. *Comprehensive fee:* $21,317 includes full-time tuition ($14,373) and room and board ($6944). *College room only:* $3230. *Part-time tuition:* $399 per credit.
FRESHMAN FINANCIAL AID (Fall 2005, est.) 59 applied for aid; of those 86% were deemed to have need. 100% of freshmen with need received aid; of those 27% had need fully met. *Average percent of need met:* 81% (excluding resources awarded to replace EFC). *Average financial aid package:* $11,944 (excluding resources awarded to replace EFC). 4% of all full-time freshmen had no need and received non-need-based gift aid.
UNDERGRADUATE FINANCIAL AID (Fall 2005, est.) 263 applied for aid; of those 88% were deemed to have need. 100% of undergraduates with need received aid; of those 19% had need fully met. *Average percent of need met:* 75% (excluding resources awarded to replace EFC). *Average financial aid package:* $12,862 (excluding resources awarded to replace EFC). 3% of all full-time undergraduates had no need and received non-need-based gift aid.
GIFT AID (NEED-BASED) *Total amount:* $1,895,645 (23% federal, 21% state, 52% institutional, 4% external sources). *Receiving aid:* Freshmen: 68% (49); All full-time undergraduates: 61% (222). *Average award:* Freshmen: $9143; Undergraduates: $8319. *Scholarships, grants, and awards:* Federal Pell, FSEOG, state, private, college/university gift aid from institutional funds.
GIFT AID (NON-NEED-BASED) *Total amount:* $233,611 (91% institutional, 9% external sources). *Receiving aid:* Freshmen: 1% (1); Undergraduates: 1% (5). *Average Award:* Freshmen: $3000; Undergraduates: $3775. *Scholarships, grants, and awards by category: Academic Interests/Achievement:* 101 awards ($270,550 total): general academic interests/achievements. *Special Achievements/Activities:* 20 awards ($34,000 total): community service, leadership. *Special Characteristics:* children of faculty/staff, first-generation college students.
LOANS *Student loans:* $1,957,891 (77% need-based, 23% non-need-based). 54% of past graduating class borrowed through all loan programs. *Average indebtedness per student:* $17,606. *Average need-based loan:* Freshmen: $2778; Undergraduates: $4625. *Parent loans:* $569,703 (33% need-based, 67% non-need-based). *Programs:* FFEL (Subsidized and Unsubsidized Stafford, PLUS).
WORK-STUDY *Federal work-study:* Total amount: $93,616; 63 jobs averaging $1600.
APPLYING FOR FINANCIAL AID *Required financial aid forms:* FAFSA, institution's own form. *Financial aid deadline (priority):* 5/1. *Notification date:* Continuous. Students must reply within 2 weeks of notification.
CONTACT Office of Financial Aid Services, Southern Vermont College, PO Box 2000, Winooski, VT 05404, 877-563-6076 or toll-free 800-378-2782. *Fax:* 802-654-3765. *E-mail:* svc@vsac.org.

SOUTHERN VIRGINIA UNIVERSITY
Buena Vista, VA

Tuition & fees: $15,826	Average undergraduate aid package: $10,652

ABOUT THE INSTITUTION Independent Latter-day Saints, coed. Awards: bachelor's degrees. 15 undergraduate majors. Total enrollment: 685. Undergraduates: 685. Freshmen: 249. Federal methodology is used as a basis for awarding need-based institutional aid.
UNDERGRADUATE EXPENSES for 2006–07 *Application fee:* $35. *Comprehensive fee:* $20,126 includes full-time tuition ($15,826) and room and board ($4300). *College room only:* $2800. *Part-time tuition:* $525 per hour.
FRESHMAN FINANCIAL AID (Fall 2005, est.) 200 applied for aid; of those 74% were deemed to have need. 98% of freshmen with need received aid; of those 18% had need fully met. *Average percent of need met:* 60% (excluding resources awarded to replace EFC). *Average financial aid package:* $8395 (excluding resources awarded to replace EFC). 38% of all full-time freshmen had no need and received non-need-based gift aid.
UNDERGRADUATE FINANCIAL AID (Fall 2005, est.) 563 applied for aid; of those 85% were deemed to have need. 99% of undergraduates with need received aid; of those 18% had need fully met. *Average percent of need met:* 67% (excluding resources awarded to replace EFC). *Average financial aid package:* $10,652 (excluding resources awarded to replace EFC). 28% of all full-time undergraduates had no need and received non-need-based gift aid.
GIFT AID (NEED-BASED) *Total amount:* $3,628,564 (25% federal, 7% state, 60% institutional, 8% external sources). *Receiving aid:* Freshmen: 49% (143); All full-time undergraduates: 66% (472). *Average award:* Freshmen: $6619; Undergraduates: $7981. *Scholarships, grants, and awards:* Federal Pell, FSEOG, state, private, college/university gift aid from institutional funds.
GIFT AID (NON-NEED-BASED) *Total amount:* $1,149,533 (6% state, 88% institutional, 6% external sources). *Receiving aid:* Freshmen: 7% (19); Undergraduates: 8% (58). *Average Award:* Freshmen: $5228; Undergraduates: $5445. *Scholarships, grants, and awards by category: Academic Interests/Achievement:* 711 awards ($2,687,000 total): general academic interests/achievements. *Creative Arts/Performance:* 45 awards ($44,600 total): art/fine arts. *Special Achievements/Activities:* 176 awards ($262,829 total): religious involvement. *Special Characteristics:* 79 awards ($451,236 total): children of faculty/staff, international students. *ROTC:* Army cooperative.
LOANS *Student loans:* $2,731,947 (74% need-based, 26% non-need-based). 94% of past graduating class borrowed through all loan programs. *Average indebtedness per student:* $15,444. *Average need-based loan:* Freshmen: $1958; Undergraduates: $3033. *Parent loans:* $1,627,950 (30% need-based, 70% non-need-based). *Programs:* FFEL (Subsidized and Unsubsidized Stafford, PLUS), alternative loans.
WORK-STUDY *Federal work-study:* Total amount: $112,813; 154 jobs averaging $1000. *State or other work-study/employment:* Total amount: $42,880 (51% need-based, 49% non-need-based).
ATHLETIC AWARDS *Total amount:* $79,150 (60% need-based, 40% non-need-based).

Southern Virginia University

APPLYING FOR FINANCIAL AID *Required financial aid forms:* FAFSA, Virginia Tuition Assistance Grant (VA residents only). *Financial aid deadline (priority):* 4/15. *Notification date:* Continuous beginning 2/1. Students must reply by 5/1 or within 2 weeks of notification.
CONTACT Jessica Massie, Financial Aid Specialist, Southern Virginia University, One University Hill Drive, Buena Vista, VA 24416, 540-261-4351 or toll-free 800-229-8420. *Fax:* 540-261-8559. *E-mail:* finaid@southernvirginia.edu.

SOUTHERN WESLEYAN UNIVERSITY
Central, SC

ABOUT THE INSTITUTION Independent religious, coed. Awards: associate, bachelor's, and master's degrees. 34 undergraduate majors. Total enrollment: 2,632. Undergraduates: 1,995. Freshmen: 172.
GIFT AID (NEED-BASED) *Scholarships, grants, and awards:* Federal Pell, FSEOG, state, private, college/university gift aid from institutional funds.
GIFT AID (NON-NEED-BASED) *Scholarships, grants, and awards by category: Academic Interests/Achievement:* biological sciences, business, computer science, education, English, general academic interests/achievements, humanities, mathematics, physical sciences, premedicine, religion/biblical studies, social sciences. *Creative Arts/Performance:* art/fine arts, creative writing, journalism/publications, music, theater/drama. *Special Achievements/Activities:* community service, leadership, religious involvement. *Special Characteristics:* children of faculty/staff, ethnic background, members of minority groups, relatives of clergy, religious affiliation, siblings of current students.
LOANS *Programs:* FFEL (Subsidized and Unsubsidized Stafford, PLUS), Perkins.
APPLYING FOR FINANCIAL AID *Required financial aid forms:* FAFSA, institution's own form.
CONTACT Mrs. Rita Martin, Financial Aid Associate, Southern Wesleyan University, 907 Wesleyan Drive, Central, SC 29630-1020, 800-289-1292 Ext. 5517 or toll-free 800-289-1292 Ext. 5550. *Fax:* 864-644-5970. *E-mail:* finaid@swu.edu.

SOUTH UNIVERSITY
Montgomery, AL

Tuition & fees: $11,475   **Average undergraduate aid package: $5768**

ABOUT THE INSTITUTION Proprietary, coed. Awards: associate, bachelor's, and master's degrees. 9 undergraduate majors. Total enrollment: 420. Undergraduates: 411. Freshmen: 66. Federal methodology is used as a basis for awarding need-based institutional aid.
UNDERGRADUATE EXPENSES for 2006–07 *Application fee:* $25. *Tuition:* full-time $11,475; part-time $2995 per term.
FRESHMAN FINANCIAL AID (Fall 2004) 47 applied for aid; of those 85% were deemed to have need. 100% of freshmen with need received aid. *Average percent of need met:* 45% (excluding resources awarded to replace EFC). *Average financial aid package:* $5768 (excluding resources awarded to replace EFC).
UNDERGRADUATE FINANCIAL AID (Fall 2004) 221 applied for aid; of those 95% were deemed to have need. 100% of undergraduates with need received aid. *Average percent of need met:* 45% (excluding resources awarded to replace EFC). *Average financial aid package:* $5768 (excluding resources awarded to replace EFC).
GIFT AID (NEED-BASED) *Total amount:* $1,809,061 (100% federal). *Receiving aid:* Freshmen: 85% (40); All full-time undergraduates: 92% (204). *Average award:* Freshmen: $3143; Undergraduates: $3143. *Scholarships, grants, and awards:* Federal Pell, FSEOG, state.
GIFT AID (NON-NEED-BASED) *Total amount:* $81,131 (44% federal, 21% institutional, 35% external sources).
LOANS *Student loans:* $6,112,377 (98% need-based, 2% non-need-based). 95% of past graduating class borrowed through all loan programs. *Average indebtedness per student:* $9600. *Average need-based loan:* Freshmen: $2625; Undergraduates: $2625. *Parent loans:* $626,194 (100% need-based). *Programs:* Federal Direct (Subsidized and Unsubsidized Stafford), FFEL (Subsidized and Unsubsidized Stafford, PLUS), Perkins, college/university.
WORK-STUDY *Federal work-study:* Total amount: $60,921; 21 jobs averaging $2213.
APPLYING FOR FINANCIAL AID *Required financial aid form:* FAFSA. *Financial aid deadline:* Continuous. *Notification date:* Continuous beginning 9/1.

CONTACT James Berry, Director of Financial Aid, South University, 5355 Vaughn Road, Montgomery, AL 36116-1120, 334-395-8800. *Fax:* 334-395-8859. *E-mail:* jberry@southuniversity.edu.

SOUTH UNIVERSITY
Tampa, FL

CONTACT Financial Aid Office, South University, 4401 N. Himes Avenue, Tampa, FL 33614, 813-393-3800.

SOUTH UNIVERSITY
Savannah, GA

ABOUT THE INSTITUTION Proprietary, coed. Awards: associate, bachelor's, master's, and doctoral degrees. 10 undergraduate majors. Total enrollment: 1,037. Undergraduates: 667.
GIFT AID (NEED-BASED) *Scholarships, grants, and awards:* Federal Pell, FSEOG, state, private, college/university gift aid from institutional funds.
GIFT AID (NON-NEED-BASED) *Scholarships, grants, and awards by category: Academic Interests/Achievement:* business, general academic interests/achievements, health fields.
LOANS *Programs:* FFEL (Subsidized and Unsubsidized Stafford, PLUS), Perkins, state.
APPLYING FOR FINANCIAL AID *Required financial aid forms:* FAFSA, state aid form.
CONTACT Ms. Anne Gaglia, Director of Financial Services, South University, 709 Mall Boulevard, Savannah, GA 31406-4881, 912-201-8011 or toll-free 866-629-2901. *Fax:* 912-201-8072. *E-mail:* gaglia@southuniversity.edu.

SOUTH UNIVERSITY
Columbia, SC

CONTACT Sandra Gundlach, Financial Aid Coordinator, South University, 3810 Main Street, Columbia, SC 29203, 803-799-9082 or toll-free 866-629-3031. *Fax:* 803-799-9005.

SOUTHWEST BAPTIST UNIVERSITY
Bolivar, MO

Tuition & fees: $14,100   **Average undergraduate aid package: $10,651**

ABOUT THE INSTITUTION Independent Southern Baptist, coed. Awards: associate, bachelor's, master's, and doctoral degrees and post-master's certificates. 41 undergraduate majors. Total enrollment: 3,440. Undergraduates: 2,701. Freshmen: 398. Federal methodology is used as a basis for awarding need-based institutional aid.
UNDERGRADUATE EXPENSES for 2006–07 *Application fee:* $30. *Comprehensive fee:* $18,300 includes full-time tuition ($13,300), mandatory fees ($800), and room and board ($4200). *College room only:* $2200. *Part-time tuition:* $530 per hour.
FRESHMAN FINANCIAL AID (Fall 2005, est.) 334 applied for aid; of those 78% were deemed to have need. 100% of freshmen with need received aid; of those 25% had need fully met. *Average percent of need met:* 72% (excluding resources awarded to replace EFC). *Average financial aid package:* $11,247 (excluding resources awarded to replace EFC). 25% of all full-time freshmen had no need and received non-need-based gift aid.
UNDERGRADUATE FINANCIAL AID (Fall 2005, est.) 1,459 applied for aid; of those 84% were deemed to have need. 99% of undergraduates with need received aid; of those 22% had need fully met. *Average percent of need met:* 68% (excluding resources awarded to replace EFC). *Average financial aid package:* $10,651 (excluding resources awarded to replace EFC). 23% of all full-time undergraduates had no need and received non-need-based gift aid.
GIFT AID (NEED-BASED) *Total amount:* $2,860,783 (85% federal, 15% state). *Receiving aid:* Freshmen: 34% (127); All full-time undergraduates: 40% (705). *Average award:* Freshmen: $3866; Undergraduates: $3534. *Scholarships, grants, and awards:* Federal Pell, FSEOG, state, private, college/university gift aid from institutional funds.
GIFT AID (NON-NEED-BASED) *Total amount:* $6,727,997 (2% state, 88% institutional, 10% external sources). *Receiving aid:* Freshmen: 64% (237);

Undergraduates: 56% (988). *Average Award: Freshmen:* $5192; *Undergraduates:* $5031. *Scholarships, grants, and awards by category: Academic Interests/Achievement:* 1,617 awards ($3,258,161 total): general academic interests/achievements. *Creative Arts/Performance:* 158 awards ($160,825 total): art/fine arts, debating, general creative arts/performance, music, theater/drama. *Special Achievements/Activities:* 313 awards ($568,000 total): religious involvement. *Special Characteristics:* 2,202 awards ($2,314,021 total): general special characteristics, local/state students, relatives of clergy. *ROTC:* Army cooperative.
LOANS *Student loans:* $8,331,037 (100% need-based). 73% of past graduating class borrowed through all loan programs. *Average indebtedness per student:* $11,268. *Average need-based loan: Freshmen:* $3641; Undergraduates: $4372. *Parent loans:* $1,042,502 (100% need-based). *Programs:* FFEL (Subsidized and Unsubsidized Stafford, PLUS), Perkins, Federal Nursing, state, alternative loans.
WORK-STUDY *Federal work-study:* Total amount: $505,188; 536 jobs averaging $970.
ATHLETIC AWARDS *Total amount:* $1,595,195 (100% non-need-based).
APPLYING FOR FINANCIAL AID *Required financial aid forms:* FAFSA, institution's own form. *Financial aid deadline (priority):* 3/15. *Notification date:* Continuous beginning 3/1. Students must reply within 2 weeks of notification.
CONTACT Mr. Brad Gamble, Director of Financial Aid, Southwest Baptist University, 1600 University Avenue, Bolivar, MO 65613-2597, 417-328-1823 or toll-free 800-526-5859. *Fax:* 417-328-1514. *E-mail:* bgamble@sbuniv.edu.

SOUTHWESTERN ADVENTIST UNIVERSITY
Keene, TX

CONTACT Student Financial Services, Southwestern Adventist University, PO Box 567, Keene, TX 76059, 817-645-3921 Ext. 262 or toll-free 800-433-2240. *Fax:* 817-556-4744.

SOUTHWESTERN ASSEMBLIES OF GOD UNIVERSITY
Waxahachie, TX

CONTACT Financial Aid Office, Southwestern Assemblies of God University, 1200 Sycamore Street, Waxahachie, TX 75165-2397, 972-937-4010 Ext. 1140 or toll-free 888-937-7248. *Fax:* 972-937-4001. *E-mail:* finaid@sagu.edu.

SOUTHWESTERN CHRISTIAN COLLEGE
Terrell, TX

CONTACT Financial Aid Office, Southwestern Christian College, PO Box 10, Terrell, TX 75160, 972-524-3341. *Fax:* 972-563-7133.

SOUTHWESTERN CHRISTIAN UNIVERSITY
Bethany, OK

Tuition & fees: $8250	Average undergraduate aid package: $9000

ABOUT THE INSTITUTION Independent religious, coed. Awards: associate, bachelor's, and master's degrees. 10 undergraduate majors. Total enrollment: 199. Undergraduates: 128. Freshmen: 32. Federal methodology is used as a basis for awarding need-based institutional aid.
UNDERGRADUATE EXPENSES for 2005–06 *Application fee:* $25. *Comprehensive fee:* $12,250 includes full-time tuition ($8250) and room and board ($4000). *Part-time tuition:* $295 per credit hour.
FRESHMAN FINANCIAL AID (Fall 2005, est.) 59 applied for aid; of those 93% were deemed to have need. 100% of freshmen with need received aid; of those 53% had need fully met. *Average percent of need met:* 73% (excluding resources awarded to replace EFC). *Average financial aid package:* $7925 (excluding resources awarded to replace EFC). 12% of all full-time freshmen had no need and received non-need-based gift aid.
UNDERGRADUATE FINANCIAL AID (Fall 2005, est.) 177 applied for aid; of those 96% were deemed to have need. 99% of undergraduates with need received aid; of those 36% had need fully met. *Average percent of need met:* 71% (excluding resources awarded to replace EFC). *Average financial aid package:* $9000 (excluding resources awarded to replace EFC). 6% of all full-time undergraduates had no need and received non-need-based gift aid.

GIFT AID (NEED-BASED) *Total amount:* $660,000 (51% federal, 20% state, 23% institutional, 6% external sources). *Receiving aid: Freshmen:* 73% (49); All full-time undergraduates: 74% (140). *Average award: Freshmen:* $2750; Undergraduates: $2500. *Scholarships, grants, and awards:* Federal Pell, FSEOG, state, private, college/university gift aid from institutional funds.
GIFT AID (NON-NEED-BASED) *Total amount:* $175,000 (18% federal, 14% state, 57% institutional, 11% external sources). *Receiving aid: Freshmen:* 42% (28); Undergraduates: 35% (67). *Average Award: Freshmen:* $1750; *Undergraduates:* $2000. *Scholarships, grants, and awards by category: Academic Interests/Achievement:* 70 awards ($90,000 total): business, education, general academic interests/achievements, religion/biblical studies. *Creative Arts/Performance:* 12 awards ($15,000 total): music, theater/drama. *Special Achievements/Activities:* cheerleading/drum major, religious involvement. *Special Characteristics:* 50 awards ($50,000 total): children and siblings of alumni, children of faculty/staff, relatives of clergy, religious affiliation.
LOANS *Student loans:* $1,000,000 (90% need-based, 10% non-need-based). 74% of past graduating class borrowed through all loan programs. *Average indebtedness per student:* $17,000. *Average need-based loan: Freshmen:* $3000; Undergraduates: $4000. *Parent loans:* $130,000 (100% need-based). *Programs:* FFEL (Subsidized and Unsubsidized Stafford, PLUS).
WORK-STUDY *Federal work-study:* Total amount: $70,000; 60 jobs averaging $1500. *State or other work-study/employment:* Total amount: $15,000 (100% non-need-based). 10 part-time jobs averaging $1000.
APPLYING FOR FINANCIAL AID *Required financial aid form:* FAFSA. *Financial aid deadline (priority):* 8/1. *Notification date:* Continuous.
CONTACT Mr. Mark Arthur, Financial Aid Director, Southwestern Christian University, PO Box 340, Bethany, OK 73008, 405-789-7661 Ext. 3456. *Fax:* 405-495-0078. *E-mail:* mark@swcu.edu.

SOUTHWESTERN COLLEGE
Phoenix, AZ

ABOUT THE INSTITUTION Independent Conservative Baptist, coed. Awards: associate and bachelor's degrees. 7 undergraduate majors. Total enrollment: 267. Undergraduates: 267. Freshmen: 29.
GIFT AID (NEED-BASED) *Scholarships, grants, and awards:* Federal Pell, FSEOG, state, private, college/university gift aid from institutional funds.
GIFT AID (NON-NEED-BASED) *Scholarships, grants, and awards by category: Academic Interests/Achievement:* general academic interests/achievements. *Creative Arts/Performance:* music. *Special Characteristics:* children and siblings of alumni, children of faculty/staff, spouses of current students.
LOANS *Programs:* FFEL (Subsidized and Unsubsidized Stafford, PLUS), Perkins.
WORK-STUDY *Federal work-study:* Total amount: $26,648; 19 jobs averaging $1480.
APPLYING FOR FINANCIAL AID *Required financial aid form:* FAFSA.
CONTACT Mr. Pete Leonard, Director of Enrollment Management, Southwestern College, 2625 East Cactus Road, Phoenix, AZ 85032-7097, 602-992-6101 Ext. 114 or toll-free 800-247-2697. *Fax:* 602-404-2159.

SOUTHWESTERN COLLEGE
Winfield, KS

ABOUT THE INSTITUTION Independent United Methodist, coed. Awards: bachelor's and master's degrees. 37 undergraduate majors. Total enrollment: 1,416. Undergraduates: 1,263. Freshmen: 136.
GIFT AID (NEED-BASED) *Scholarships, grants, and awards:* Federal Pell, FSEOG, state, private, college/university gift aid from institutional funds.
GIFT AID (NON-NEED-BASED) *Scholarships, grants, and awards by category: Academic Interests/Achievement:* biological sciences, business, communication, general academic interests/achievements, health fields, humanities, religion/biblical studies, social sciences. *Creative Arts/Performance:* cinema/film/broadcasting, dance, debating, journalism/publications, music, performing arts, theater/drama. *Special Achievements/Activities:* cheerleading/drum major, community service, general special achievements/activities, leadership, memberships, religious involvement. *Special Characteristics:* children and siblings of alumni, children of current students, children of faculty/staff, ethnic background, international students, local/state students, members of minority groups, relatives of clergy, religious affiliation, siblings of current students, spouses of current students, twins.

Southwestern College

LOANS *Programs:* Federal Direct (Subsidized and Unsubsidized Stafford, PLUS), FFEL (Subsidized and Unsubsidized Stafford, PLUS), Perkins.
WORK-STUDY *Federal work-study:* Total amount: $116,052; 234 jobs averaging $496. *State or other work-study/employment:* Total amount: $86,758 (100% non-need-based). 107 part-time jobs averaging $810.
APPLYING FOR FINANCIAL AID *Required financial aid forms:* FAFSA, institution's own form.
CONTACT Director of Financial Aid, Southwestern College, 100 College Street, Winfield, KS 67156-2499, 620-229-6215 or toll-free 800-846-1543. *Fax:* 620-229-6363. *E-mail:* finaid@sckans.edu.

SOUTHWESTERN OKLAHOMA STATE UNIVERSITY
Weatherford, OK

CONTACT Mr. Thomas M. Ratliff, Director of Student Financial Services, Southwestern Oklahoma State University, 100 Campus Drive, Weatherford, OK 73096-3098, 580-774-3786. *Fax:* 580-774-7066. *E-mail:* ratlift@swosu.edu.

SOUTHWESTERN UNIVERSITY
Georgetown, TX

Tuition & fees: $21,900 **Average undergraduate aid package: $19,315**

ABOUT THE INSTITUTION Independent Methodist, coed. Awards: bachelor's degrees. 45 undergraduate majors. Total enrollment: 1,309. Undergraduates: 1,309. Freshmen: 329. Both federal and institutional methodology are used as a basis for awarding need-based institutional aid.
UNDERGRADUATE EXPENSES for 2005–06 *Application fee:* $40. *Comprehensive fee:* $28,447 includes full-time tuition ($21,900) and room and board ($6547). *College room only:* $3143. Room and board charges vary according to board plan, housing facility, and student level. *Part-time tuition:* $920 per semester hour. *Payment plans:* Installment, deferred payment.
FRESHMAN FINANCIAL AID (Fall 2005, est.) 231 applied for aid; of those 76% were deemed to have need. 100% of freshmen with need received aid; of those 64% had need fully met. *Average percent of need met:* 98% (excluding resources awarded to replace EFC). *Average financial aid package:* $20,426 (excluding resources awarded to replace EFC). 30% of all full-time freshmen had no need and received non-need-based gift aid.
UNDERGRADUATE FINANCIAL AID (Fall 2005, est.) 759 applied for aid; of those 81% were deemed to have need. 100% of undergraduates with need received aid; of those 54% had need fully met. *Average percent of need met:* 97% (excluding resources awarded to replace EFC). *Average financial aid package:* $19,315 (excluding resources awarded to replace EFC). 28% of all full-time undergraduates had no need and received non-need-based gift aid.
GIFT AID (NEED-BASED) *Total amount:* $8,969,875 (8% federal, 16% state, 69% institutional, 7% external sources). *Receiving aid:* Freshmen: 53% (175); All full-time undergraduates: 48% (611). *Average award:* Freshmen: $16,275; Undergraduates: $13,251. *Scholarships, grants, and awards:* Federal Pell, FSEOG, state, private, college/university gift aid from institutional funds.
GIFT AID (NON-NEED-BASED) *Total amount:* $3,368,229 (90% institutional, 10% external sources). *Receiving aid:* Freshmen: 30% (98); Undergraduates: 25% (324). *Average Award:* Freshmen: $8042; Undergraduates: $7935. *Scholarships, grants, and awards by category: Academic Interests/Achievement:* 692 awards ($4,921,508 total): general academic interests/achievements. *Creative Arts/Performance:* 108 awards ($381,480 total): art/fine arts, music, performing arts, theater/drama. *Special Characteristics:* 39 awards ($426,046 total): children of faculty/staff, relatives of clergy. *Tuition waivers:* Full or partial for employees or children of employees.
LOANS *Student loans:* $3,995,876 (88% need-based, 12% non-need-based). 52% of past graduating class borrowed through all loan programs. *Average indebtedness per student:* $18,446. *Average need-based loan:* Freshmen: $2760; Undergraduates: $4530. *Parent loans:* $7,997,222 (53% need-based, 47% non-need-based). *Programs:* FFEL (Subsidized and Unsubsidized Stafford, PLUS), Perkins, state, college/university.
WORK-STUDY *Federal work-study:* Total amount: $363,024; 199 jobs averaging $1824. *State or other work-study/employment:* Total amount: $816,629 (57% need-based, 43% non-need-based). 226 part-time jobs averaging $2065.

APPLYING FOR FINANCIAL AID *Required financial aid form:* FAFSA. *Financial aid deadline:* 3/1 (priority: 3/1). *Notification date:* Continuous beginning 3/25. Students must reply by 5/1 or within 2 weeks of notification.
CONTACT Mr. James P. Gaeta, Director of Financial Aid, Southwestern University, PO Box 770, Georgetown, TX 78627-0770, 512-863-1259 or toll-free 800-252-3166. *E-mail:* gaetaj@southwestern.edu.

SOUTHWEST MINNESOTA STATE UNIVERSITY
Marshall, MN

Tuition & fees: N/R **Average undergraduate aid package: $6736**

ABOUT THE INSTITUTION State-supported, coed. Awards: associate, bachelor's, and master's degrees. 50 undergraduate majors. Total enrollment: 5,636. Undergraduates: 5,167. Freshmen: 1,232. Federal methodology is used as a basis for awarding need-based institutional aid.
FRESHMAN FINANCIAL AID (Fall 2005, est.) 463 applied for aid; of those 75% were deemed to have need. 97% of freshmen with need received aid; of those 22% had need fully met. *Average percent of need met:* 35% (excluding resources awarded to replace EFC). *Average financial aid package:* $6384 (excluding resources awarded to replace EFC). 20% of all full-time freshmen had no need and received non-need-based gift aid.
UNDERGRADUATE FINANCIAL AID (Fall 2005, est.) 1,845 applied for aid; of those 78% were deemed to have need. 99% of undergraduates with need received aid; of those 30% had need fully met. *Average percent of need met:* 40% (excluding resources awarded to replace EFC). *Average financial aid package:* $6736 (excluding resources awarded to replace EFC). 14% of all full-time undergraduates had no need and received non-need-based gift aid.
GIFT AID (NEED-BASED) *Total amount:* $3,803,573 (57% federal, 41% state, 2% institutional). *Receiving aid:* Freshmen: 39% (215); All full-time undergraduates: 42% (979). *Average award:* Freshmen: $3942; Undergraduates: $3680. *Scholarships, grants, and awards:* Federal Pell, FSEOG, state, private, college/university gift aid from institutional funds.
GIFT AID (NON-NEED-BASED) *Total amount:* $1,958,834 (3% federal, 59% institutional, 38% external sources). *Receiving aid:* Freshmen: 38% (207); Undergraduates: 26% (611). *Average Award:* Freshmen: $1947; Undergraduates:* $1798. *Scholarships, grants, and awards by category: Academic Interests/Achievement:* 1,074 awards ($928,120 total): agriculture, biological sciences, business, communication, computer science, education, English, general academic interests/achievements, international studies, library science, mathematics, physical sciences, premedicine, social sciences. *Creative Arts/Performance:* 111 awards ($41,415 total): art/fine arts, creative writing, debating, journalism/publications, music, performing arts, theater/drama. *Special Achievements/Activities:* 334 awards ($508,213 total): general special achievements/activities, hobbies/interests, leadership. *Special Characteristics:* 150 awards ($132,202 total): children and siblings of alumni, children of union members/company employees, ethnic background, first-generation college students, general special characteristics, handicapped students, international students, local/state students, members of minority groups, previous college experience, veterans, veterans' children.
LOANS *Student loans:* $10,161,115 (43% need-based, 57% non-need-based). 83% of past graduating class borrowed through all loan programs. *Average indebtedness per student:* $16,678. *Average need-based loan:* Freshmen: $2417; Undergraduates: $3745. *Parent loans:* $400,937 (100% non-need-based). *Programs:* FFEL (Subsidized and Unsubsidized Stafford, PLUS), Perkins, state.
WORK-STUDY *Federal work-study:* Total amount: $195,909; 88 jobs averaging $2226. *State or other work-study/employment:* Total amount: $291,976 (100% need-based). 142 part-time jobs averaging $2056.
ATHLETIC AWARDS *Total amount:* $457,038 (100% non-need-based).
APPLYING FOR FINANCIAL AID *Required financial aid forms:* FAFSA, institution's own form. *Financial aid deadline (priority):* 3/1. *Notification date:* Continuous beginning 4/1.
CONTACT David Vikander, Director of Financial Aid, Southwest Minnesota State University, 1501 State Street, Marshall, MN 56258, 507-537-6281 or toll-free 800-642-0684. *Fax:* 507-537-6275. *E-mail:* vikander@southwestmsu.edu.

SOUTHWEST MISSOURI STATE UNIVERSITY
Springfield, MO

See Missouri State University.

SPALDING UNIVERSITY
Louisville, KY

CONTACT Director of Student Financial Services, Spalding University, 851 South Fourth Street, Louisville, KY 40203, 502-588-7185 or toll-free 800-896-8941 Ext. 2111. *Fax:* 502-585-7128. *E-mail:* onestop@spalding.edu.

SPELMAN COLLEGE
Atlanta, GA

ABOUT THE INSTITUTION Independent, women only. Awards: bachelor's degrees. 25 undergraduate majors. Total enrollment: 2,318. Undergraduates: 2,318. Freshmen: 531.
GIFT AID (NEED-BASED) *Scholarships, grants, and awards:* Federal Pell, FSEOG, state, private, college/university gift aid from institutional funds, United Negro College Fund.
GIFT AID (NON-NEED-BASED) *Scholarships, grants, and awards by category: Academic Interests/Achievement:* biological sciences, general academic interests/achievements, mathematics, physical sciences. *Creative Arts/Performance:* dance, music, theater/drama. *Special Achievements/Activities:* community service.
LOANS *Programs:* FFEL (Subsidized and Unsubsidized Stafford, PLUS), Perkins.
WORK-STUDY *Federal work-study:* Total amount: $221,802; 172 jobs averaging $882. *State or other work-study/employment:* Total amount: $125,000 (84% need-based, 16% non-need-based). 200 part-time jobs averaging $625.
APPLYING FOR FINANCIAL AID *Required financial aid form:* FAFSA.
CONTACT Lenora J. Jackson, Director, Student Financial Services, Spelman College, 350 Spelman Lane, SW, PO Box 771, Atlanta, GA 30314-4399, 404-270-5212 or toll-free 800-982-2411. *Fax:* 404-270-5220. *E-mail:* lenoraj@spelman.edu.

SPRING ARBOR UNIVERSITY
Spring Arbor, MI

Tuition & fees: $16,666	Average undergraduate aid package: $14,182

ABOUT THE INSTITUTION Independent Free Methodist, coed. Awards: associate, bachelor's, and master's degrees. 32 undergraduate majors. Total enrollment: 3,701. Undergraduates: 2,610. Freshmen: 318. Federal methodology is used as a basis for awarding need-based institutional aid.
UNDERGRADUATE EXPENSES for 2005–06 *Application fee:* $30. *Comprehensive fee:* $22,476 includes full-time tuition ($16,270), mandatory fees ($396), and room and board ($5810). *College room only:* $2730. Room and board charges vary according to board plan, housing facility, and location. *Part-time tuition:* $350 per credit. *Part-time fees:* $306 per year. Part-time tuition and fees vary according to course load and reciprocity agreements. *Payment plans:* Installment, deferred payment.
FRESHMAN FINANCIAL AID (Fall 2004) 306 applied for aid; of those 87% were deemed to have need. 100% of freshmen with need received aid; of those 48% had need fully met. *Average percent of need met:* 93% (excluding resources awarded to replace EFC). *Average financial aid package:* $16,177 (excluding resources awarded to replace EFC). 4% of all full-time freshmen had no need and received non-need-based gift aid.
UNDERGRADUATE FINANCIAL AID (Fall 2004) 1,676 applied for aid; of those 83% were deemed to have need. 98% of undergraduates with need received aid; of those 37% had need fully met. *Average percent of need met:* 82% (excluding resources awarded to replace EFC). *Average financial aid package:* $14,182 (excluding resources awarded to replace EFC). 2% of all full-time undergraduates had no need and received non-need-based gift aid.
GIFT AID (NEED-BASED) *Total amount:* $12,339,918 (16% federal, 18% state, 66% institutional). *Receiving aid:* Freshmen: 81% (265); All full-time undergraduates: 69% (1,311). *Average award:* Freshmen: $9661; Undergraduates: $7965. *Scholarships, grants, and awards:* Federal Pell, FSEOG, state, private, college/university gift aid from institutional funds.
GIFT AID (NON-NEED-BASED) *Total amount:* $509,374 (1% federal, 11% state, 88% external sources). *Receiving aid:* Freshmen: 28% (91); Undergraduates: 13% (246). *Average Award:* Freshmen: $1949; Undergraduates: $2225. *Scholarships, grants, and awards by category: Academic Interests/Achievement:* 824 awards ($2,772,311 total): general academic interests/achievements. *Creative Arts/Performance:* 173 awards ($103,891 total): art/fine arts. *Special Achievements/Activities:* 2 awards ($8000 total): junior miss. *Special Characteristics:* 291 awards ($1,090,909 total): children of faculty/staff, international students, members of minority groups, out-of-state students, relatives of clergy, religious affiliation. *Tuition waivers:* Full or partial for employees or children of employees, senior citizens. *ROTC:* Army cooperative.
LOANS *Student loans:* $15,177,526 (46% need-based, 54% non-need-based). 84% of past graduating class borrowed through all loan programs. *Average indebtedness per student:* $11,989. *Average need-based loan:* Freshmen: $3462; Undergraduates: $4120. *Parent loans:* $1,051,843 (100% need-based). *Programs:* FFEL (Subsidized and Unsubsidized Stafford, PLUS), Perkins, state, Michigan Loan Program and Alternative Loans.
WORK-STUDY *Federal work-study:* Total amount: $73,844; 405 jobs averaging $775. *State or other work-study/employment:* 9 part-time jobs averaging $700.
ATHLETIC AWARDS Total amount: $389,060 (100% need-based).
APPLYING FOR FINANCIAL AID *Required financial aid form:* FAFSA. *Financial aid deadline (priority):* 3/1. *Notification date:* Continuous beginning 4/1. Students must reply within 2 weeks of notification.
CONTACT Lois M. Hardy, Director of Financial Aid, Spring Arbor University, 106 East Main Street, Spring Arbor, MI 49283-9799, 517-750-6468 or toll-free 800-968-0011. *Fax:* 517-750-6620.

SPRINGFIELD COLLEGE
Springfield, MA

CONTACT Edward J. Ciosek, Director of Financial Aid, Springfield College, 263 Alden Street, Springfield, MA 01109-3797, 413-748-3108 or toll-free 800-343-1257 (out-of-state). *Fax:* 413-748-3462. *E-mail:* edward_j_ciosek@spfldcol.edu.

SPRING HILL COLLEGE
Mobile, AL

Tuition & fees: $20,948	Average undergraduate aid package: $18,907

ABOUT THE INSTITUTION Independent Roman Catholic (Jesuit), coed. Awards: associate, bachelor's, and master's degrees and post-bachelor's certificates. 40 undergraduate majors. Total enrollment: 1,497. Undergraduates: 1,299. Freshmen: 276. Federal methodology is used as a basis for awarding need-based institutional aid.
UNDERGRADUATE EXPENSES for 2005–06 *Application fee:* $25. *Comprehensive fee:* $28,678 includes full-time tuition ($19,658), mandatory fees ($1290), and room and board ($7730). *College room only:* $4000. Room and board charges vary according to board plan and housing facility. *Part-time tuition:* $736 per semester hour. *Part-time fees:* $42 per semester hour. *Payment plan:* Installment.
FRESHMAN FINANCIAL AID (Fall 2005, est.) 228 applied for aid; of those 82% were deemed to have need. 100% of freshmen with need received aid; of those 23% had need fully met. *Average percent of need met:* 83% (excluding resources awarded to replace EFC). *Average financial aid package:* $20,217 (excluding resources awarded to replace EFC). 27% of all full-time freshmen had no need and received non-need-based gift aid.
UNDERGRADUATE FINANCIAL AID (Fall 2005, est.) 841 applied for aid; of those 84% were deemed to have need. 100% of undergraduates with need received aid; of those 25% had need fully met. *Average percent of need met:* 80% (excluding resources awarded to replace EFC). *Average financial aid package:* $18,907 (excluding resources awarded to replace EFC). 27% of all full-time undergraduates had no need and received non-need-based gift aid.
GIFT AID (NEED-BASED) *Total amount:* $9,855,064 (11% federal, 3% state, 85% institutional, 1% external sources). *Receiving aid:* Freshmen: 69% (188); All full-time undergraduates: 64% (684). *Average award:* Freshmen: $14,874; Undergraduates: $13,570. *Scholarships, grants, and awards:* Federal Pell, FSEOG, state, private, college/university gift aid from institutional funds.

Spring Hill College

GIFT AID (NON-NEED-BASED) *Total amount:* $3,639,217 (3% state, 95% institutional, 2% external sources). *Receiving aid:* Freshmen: 45% (122); Undergraduates: 46% (498). *Average Award:* Freshmen: $33; Undergraduates: $105. *Scholarships, grants, and awards by category: Academic Interests/Achievement:* 779 awards ($2,289,190 total): general academic interests/achievements. *Special Achievements/Activities:* community service. *Special Characteristics:* children of faculty/staff, siblings of current students. *Tuition waivers:* Full or partial for employees or children of employees. *ROTC:* Army cooperative, Air Force cooperative.
LOANS *Student loans:* $4,855,209 (73% need-based, 27% non-need-based). 80% of past graduating class borrowed through all loan programs. *Average indebtedness per student:* $14,074. *Average need-based loan:* Freshmen: $3583; Undergraduates: $4300. *Parent loans:* $2,335,503 (21% need-based, 79% non-need-based). *Programs:* FFEL (Subsidized and Unsubsidized Stafford, PLUS), Alternative loans (ie, Citiassist, Signature, etc.).
WORK-STUDY *Federal work-study:* Total amount: $285,983; 223 jobs averaging $1200. *State or other work-study/employment:* Total amount: $99,464 (49% need-based, 51% non-need-based). 108 part-time jobs averaging $895.
ATHLETIC AWARDS *Total amount:* $972,486 (38% need-based, 62% non-need-based).
APPLYING FOR FINANCIAL AID *Required financial aid forms:* FAFSA, institution's own form, state aid form. *Financial aid deadline (priority):* 3/1. *Notification date:* Continuous beginning 2/15. Students must reply by 5/1 or within 2 weeks of notification.
CONTACT Ellen Foster, Director, Financial Aid, Spring Hill College, 4000 Dauphin Street, Mobile, AL 36608, 251-380-3460 or toll-free 800-SHC-6704. *Fax:* 251-460-2176. *E-mail:* efoster@shc.edu.

STANFORD UNIVERSITY
Stanford, CA

Tuition & fees: $31,200 **Average undergraduate aid package:** $28,453

ABOUT THE INSTITUTION Independent, coed. Awards: bachelor's, master's, doctoral, and first professional degrees. 68 undergraduate majors. Total enrollment: 19,042. Undergraduates: 6,576. Freshmen: 1,632. Both federal and institutional methodology are used as a basis for awarding need-based institutional aid.
UNDERGRADUATE EXPENSES for 2005–06 *Application fee:* $75. *One-time required fee:* $425. *Comprehensive fee:* $41,132 includes full-time tuition ($31,200) and room and board ($9932). *College room only:* $5275. Room and board charges vary according to board plan.
FRESHMAN FINANCIAL AID (Fall 2004) 958 applied for aid; of those 72% were deemed to have need. 99% of freshmen with need received aid; of those 89% had need fully met. *Average percent of need met:* 100% (excluding resources awarded to replace EFC). *Average financial aid package:* $28,122 (excluding resources awarded to replace EFC). 4% of all full-time freshmen had no need and received non-need-based gift aid.
UNDERGRADUATE FINANCIAL AID (Fall 2004) 3,643 applied for aid; of those 85% were deemed to have need. 99% of undergraduates with need received aid; of those 89% had need fully met. *Average percent of need met:* 100% (excluding resources awarded to replace EFC). *Average financial aid package:* $28,453 (excluding resources awarded to replace EFC). 10% of all full-time undergraduates had no need and received non-need-based gift aid.
GIFT AID (NEED-BASED) *Total amount:* $73,852,154 (6% federal, 7% state, 81% institutional, 6% external sources). *Receiving aid:* Freshmen: 41% (670); All full-time undergraduates: 45% (3,016). *Average award:* Freshmen: $24,631; Undergraduates: $24,244. *Scholarships, grants, and awards:* Federal Pell, FSEOG, state, private, college/university gift aid from institutional funds.
GIFT AID (NON-NEED-BASED) *Total amount:* $9,478,080 (10% federal, 1% state, 29% institutional, 60% external sources). *Receiving aid:* Freshmen: 2% (40); Undergraduates: 2% (138). *Average Award:* Freshmen: $2874; Undergraduates: $3425. *Tuition waivers:* Full or partial for employees or children of employees. *ROTC:* Army cooperative, Naval cooperative, Air Force cooperative.
LOANS *Student loans:* $13,077,662 (83% need-based, 17% non-need-based). 45% of past graduating class borrowed through all loan programs. *Average indebtedness per student:* $15,172. *Average need-based loan:* Freshmen: $2569; Undergraduates: $2664. *Programs:* FFEL (Subsidized and Unsubsidized Stafford, PLUS), Perkins, GATE Loans.
WORK-STUDY *Federal work-study:* Total amount: $2,251,717; 850 jobs averaging $2649. *State or other work-study/employment:* Total amount: $1,240,384 (100% need-based). 801 part-time jobs averaging $1569.
ATHLETIC AWARDS *Total amount:* $12,637,029 (7% need-based, 93% non-need-based).
APPLYING FOR FINANCIAL AID *Required financial aid forms:* FAFSA, CSS Financial Aid PROFILE, noncustodial (divorced/separated) parent's statement. *Financial aid deadline (priority):* 2/1. *Notification date:* Continuous beginning 4/3. Students must reply by 5/1.
CONTACT Financial Aid Office, Stanford University, 355 Galyez Street, Stanford, CA 94305-3021, 650-723-3058. *Fax:* 650-724-2449. *E-mail:* financialaid@lists.stanford.edu.

STATE UNIVERSITY OF NEW YORK AT BINGHAMTON
Binghamton, NY

Tuition & fees (NY res): $5838 **Average undergraduate aid package:** $11,516

ABOUT THE INSTITUTION State-supported, coed. Awards: bachelor's, master's, and doctoral degrees and post-master's certificates. 56 undergraduate majors. Total enrollment: 14,018. Undergraduates: 11,174. Freshmen: 2,215. Federal methodology is used as a basis for awarding need-based institutional aid.
UNDERGRADUATE EXPENSES for 2005–06 *Application fee:* $40. *Tuition, state resident:* full-time $4350; part-time $181 per credit hour. *Tuition, nonresident:* full-time $10,610; part-time $442 per credit hour. *Required fees:* full-time $1488; $133.15 per credit hour. *College room and board:* $8150; *room only:* $4970. Room and board charges vary according to board plan and housing facility. *Payment plan:* Installment.
FRESHMAN FINANCIAL AID (Fall 2005, est.) 1604 applied for aid; of those 56% were deemed to have need. 99% of freshmen with need received aid; of those 90% had need fully met. *Average percent of need met:* 77% (excluding resources awarded to replace EFC). *Average financial aid package:* $11,069 (excluding resources awarded to replace EFC). 4% of all full-time freshmen had no need and received non-need-based gift aid.
UNDERGRADUATE FINANCIAL AID (Fall 2005, est.) 7,143 applied for aid; of those 69% were deemed to have need. 99% of undergraduates with need received aid; of those 77% had need fully met. *Average percent of need met:* 80% (excluding resources awarded to replace EFC). *Average financial aid package:* $11,516 (excluding resources awarded to replace EFC). 3% of all full-time undergraduates had no need and received non-need-based gift aid.
GIFT AID (NEED-BASED) *Total amount:* $23,586,796 (39% federal, 53% state, 2% institutional, 6% external sources). *Receiving aid:* Freshmen: 38% (792); All full-time undergraduates: 42% (4,442). *Average award:* Freshmen: $4874; Undergraduates: $4788. *Scholarships, grants, and awards:* Federal Pell, FSEOG, state, private, college/university gift aid from institutional funds.
GIFT AID (NON-NEED-BASED) *Total amount:* $2,867,452 (23% state, 77% institutional). *Receiving aid:* Freshmen: 10% (212); Undergraduates: 9% (964). *Average Award:* Freshmen: $1305; Undergraduates: $4162. *Scholarships, grants, and awards by category: Academic Interests/Achievement:* 503 awards ($2,072,776 total): biological sciences, business, computer science, engineering/technologies, English, foreign languages, general academic interests/achievements, health fields, international studies, mathematics, physical sciences, premedicine. *Creative Arts/Performance:* 18 awards ($13,300 total): creative writing, general creative arts/performance, music, performing arts, theater/drama. *Special Achievements/Activities:* 32 awards ($64,895 total): community service, general special achievements/activities, leadership, memberships. *Special Characteristics:* 187 awards ($191,400 total): children with a deceased or disabled parent, ethnic background, local/state students, members of minority groups, out-of-state students. *Tuition waivers:* Full or partial for employees or children of employees. *ROTC:* Air Force cooperative.
LOANS *Student loans:* $38,765,095 (100% need-based). 60% of past graduating class borrowed through all loan programs. *Average indebtedness per student:* $14,734. *Average need-based loan:* Freshmen: $2957; Undergraduates: $4345. *Parent loans:* $44,994,177 (100% need-based). *Programs:* Federal Direct (Subsidized and Unsubsidized Stafford), FFEL (PLUS), Perkins, Federal Nursing, college/university.
WORK-STUDY *Federal work-study:* Total amount: $2,162,925; 1,374 jobs averaging $1426.
ATHLETIC AWARDS *Total amount:* $2,132,439 (100% non-need-based).

APPLYING FOR FINANCIAL AID *Required financial aid forms:* FAFSA, state aid form. *Financial aid deadline (priority):* 3/1. *Notification date:* Continuous beginning 3/15. Students must reply within 2 weeks of notification.

CONTACT Mr. Dennis Chavez, Director of Student Financial Aid and Employment, State University of New York at Binghamton, PO Box 6011, Binghamton, NY 13902-6011, 607-777-2428.

STATE UNIVERSITY OF NEW YORK AT BUFFALO
Buffalo, NY

Tuition & fees (NY res): $6068 **Average undergraduate aid package: $6890**

ABOUT THE INSTITUTION State-supported, coed. Awards: bachelor's, master's, doctoral, and first professional degrees and post-master's and first professional certificates. 81 undergraduate majors. Total enrollment: 27,220. Undergraduates: 18,165. Freshmen: 3,230. Federal methodology is used as a basis for awarding need-based institutional aid.

UNDERGRADUATE EXPENSES for 2005–06 *Application fee:* $40. *Tuition, state resident:* full-time $4350; part-time $181 per credit hour. *Tuition, nonresident:* full-time $10,610; part-time $442 per credit hour. *Required fees:* full-time $1718; $76 per credit hour. Part-time tuition and fees vary according to course load. *College room and board:* $7626; *room only:* $4636. Room and board charges vary according to board plan and housing facility. *Payment plan:* Installment.

FRESHMAN FINANCIAL AID (Fall 2005, est.) 2432 applied for aid; of those 70% were deemed to have need. 94% of freshmen with need received aid; of those 48% had need fully met. *Average percent of need met:* 80% (excluding resources awarded to replace EFC). *Average financial aid package:* $5902 (excluding resources awarded to replace EFC). 19% of all full-time freshmen had no need and received non-need-based gift aid.

UNDERGRADUATE FINANCIAL AID (Fall 2005, est.) 11,866 applied for aid; of those 75% were deemed to have need. 95% of undergraduates with need received aid; of those 50% had need fully met. *Average percent of need met:* 70% (excluding resources awarded to replace EFC). *Average financial aid package:* $6890 (excluding resources awarded to replace EFC). 11% of all full-time undergraduates had no need and received non-need-based gift aid.

GIFT AID (NEED-BASED) *Total amount:* $43,038,294 (46% federal, 47% state, 5% institutional, 2% external sources). *Receiving aid:* Freshmen: 31% (983); All full-time undergraduates: 30% (5,031). *Average award:* Freshmen: $3310; Undergraduates: $3237. *Scholarships, grants, and awards:* Federal Pell, FSEOG, state, private, college/university gift aid from institutional funds, Federal Nursing.

GIFT AID (NON-NEED-BASED) *Total amount:* $5,019,885 (100% institutional). *Receiving aid:* Freshmen: 19% (604); Undergraduates: 11% (1,791). *Average Award:* Freshmen: $2772; Undergraduates: $2780. *Scholarships, grants, and awards by category:* Academic Interests/Achievement: general academic interests/achievements. Creative Arts/Performance: music. Special Achievements/Activities: general special achievements/activities. Special Characteristics: local/state students. *Tuition waivers:* Full or partial for minority students. *ROTC:* Army cooperative.

LOANS *Student loans:* $123,037,988 (100% need-based). 63% of past graduating class borrowed through all loan programs. *Average indebtedness per student:* $16,700. *Average need-based loan:* Freshmen: $2253; Undergraduates: $3246. *Parent loans:* $8,211,240 (100% non-need-based). *Programs:* Federal Direct (Subsidized and Unsubsidized Stafford, PLUS), Perkins, Federal Nursing, college/university.

WORK-STUDY *Federal work-study:* Total amount: $2,420,288; 1,296 jobs averaging $1489. *State or other work-study/employment:* Total amount: $5,275,918 (100% non-need-based). 913 part-time jobs averaging $5428.

ATHLETIC AWARDS *Total amount:* $4,421,984 (100% non-need-based).

APPLYING FOR FINANCIAL AID *Required financial aid form:* FAFSA. *Financial aid deadline (priority):* 3/1. *Notification date:* Continuous beginning 5/1.

CONTACT Customer Service Department, State University of New York at Buffalo, 232 Capen Hall, Buffalo, NY 14260, 716-645-2450 or toll-free 888-UB-ADMIT. *Fax:* 716-645-7760. *E-mail:* src@buffalo.edu.

STATE UNIVERSITY OF NEW YORK AT NEW PALTZ
New Paltz, NY

Tuition & fees (NY res): $5360 **Average undergraduate aid package: $2477**

ABOUT THE INSTITUTION State-supported, coed. Awards: bachelor's and master's degrees and post-master's certificates. 73 undergraduate majors. Total enrollment: 7,825. Undergraduates: 6,421. Freshmen: 1,050. Federal methodology is used as a basis for awarding need-based institutional aid.

UNDERGRADUATE EXPENSES for 2006–07 *Application fee:* $40. *Tuition, state resident:* full-time $4350; part-time $181 per credit. *Tuition, nonresident:* full-time $10,610; part-time $442 per credit. *Required fees:* full-time $1010; $28.60 per credit or $160 per term part-time. *College room and board:* $7230; *room only:* $4500.

FRESHMAN FINANCIAL AID (Fall 2004) 690 applied for aid; of those 65% were deemed to have need. 99% of freshmen with need received aid; of those 22% had need fully met. *Average percent of need met:* 71% (excluding resources awarded to replace EFC). *Average financial aid package:* $2092 (excluding resources awarded to replace EFC). 4% of all full-time freshmen had no need and received non-need-based gift aid.

UNDERGRADUATE FINANCIAL AID (Fall 2004) 4,138 applied for aid; of those 72% were deemed to have need. 99% of undergraduates with need received aid; of those 24% had need fully met. *Average percent of need met:* 70% (excluding resources awarded to replace EFC). *Average financial aid package:* $2477 (excluding resources awarded to replace EFC). 3% of all full-time undergraduates had no need and received non-need-based gift aid.

GIFT AID (NEED-BASED) *Total amount:* $12,706,944 (43% federal, 57% state). *Receiving aid:* Freshmen: 50% (402); All full-time undergraduates: 48% (2,610). *Average award:* Freshmen: $2324; Undergraduates: $2361. *Scholarships, grants, and awards:* Federal Pell, FSEOG, state, private, college/university gift aid from institutional funds.

GIFT AID (NON-NEED-BASED) *Total amount:* $1,097,362 (25% federal, 18% state, 12% institutional, 45% external sources). *Receiving aid:* Freshmen: 10% (79); Undergraduates: 5% (273). *Average Award:* Freshmen: $1999; Undergraduates: $1935. *Scholarships, grants, and awards by category:* Academic Interests/Achievement: 91 awards ($135,640 total): computer science, education, engineering/technologies, English, health fields, humanities, mathematics, physical sciences, premedicine. Special Characteristics: members of minority groups.

LOANS *Student loans:* $16,480,103 (62% need-based, 38% non-need-based). 75% of past graduating class borrowed through all loan programs. *Average indebtedness per student:* $18,900. *Average need-based loan:* Freshmen: $1918; Undergraduates: $893. *Parent loans:* $5,282,938 (100% non-need-based). *Programs:* FFEL (Subsidized and Unsubsidized Stafford, PLUS), Perkins, Private.

WORK-STUDY *Federal work-study:* Total amount: $804,171; 986 jobs averaging $852. *State or other work-study/employment:* Total amount: $549,720 (100% non-need-based). 478 part-time jobs averaging $1053.

APPLYING FOR FINANCIAL AID *Required financial aid forms:* FAFSA, state aid form. *Financial aid deadline (priority):* 3/15. *Notification date:* Continuous beginning 4/1. Students must reply within 4 weeks of notification.

CONTACT Mr. Daniel Sistarenik, Director of Financial Aid, State University of New York at New Paltz, 75 South Manheim Boulevard, Suite 2, HAB 603B, New Paltz, NY 12561-2437, 845-257-3250 or toll-free 888-639-7589 (in-state). *Fax:* 845-257-3568. *E-mail:* sistared@newpaltz.edu.

STATE UNIVERSITY OF NEW YORK AT OSWEGO
Oswego, NY

Tuition & fees (NY res): $5322 **Average undergraduate aid package: $8519**

ABOUT THE INSTITUTION State-supported, coed. Awards: bachelor's and master's degrees and post-master's certificates. 63 undergraduate majors. Total enrollment: 8,282. Undergraduates: 7,138. Freshmen: 1,354. Federal methodology is used as a basis for awarding need-based institutional aid.

UNDERGRADUATE EXPENSES for 2005–06 *Application fee:* $40. *Tuition, state resident:* full-time $4350; part-time $181 per credit hour. *Tuition, nonresident:* full-time $10,610; part-time $442 per credit hour. *Required fees:* full-time $972; $30.18 per credit hour. Part-time tuition and fees vary according to class

State University of New York at Oswego

time, course load, and location. **College room and board:** $8340; **room only:** $5090. Room and board charges vary according to board plan and housing facility. **Payment plan:** Installment.

FRESHMAN FINANCIAL AID (Fall 2004) 1228 applied for aid; of those 75% were deemed to have need. 97% of freshmen with need received aid; of those 27% had need fully met. *Average percent of need met:* 75% (excluding resources awarded to replace EFC). *Average financial aid package:* $7771 (excluding resources awarded to replace EFC). 19% of all full-time freshmen had no need and received non-need-based gift aid.

UNDERGRADUATE FINANCIAL AID (Fall 2004) 5,583 applied for aid; of those 79% were deemed to have need. 98% of undergraduates with need received aid; of those 32% had need fully met. *Average percent of need met:* 83% (excluding resources awarded to replace EFC). *Average financial aid package:* $8519 (excluding resources awarded to replace EFC). 16% of all full-time undergraduates had no need and received non-need-based gift aid.

GIFT AID (NEED-BASED) Total amount: $16,301,887 (42% federal, 49% state, 6% institutional, 3% external sources). **Receiving aid:** Freshmen: 63% (852); All full-time undergraduates: 61% (3,976). **Average award:** Freshmen: $4503; Undergraduates: $3705. **Scholarships, grants, and awards:** Federal Pell, FSEOG, state.

GIFT AID (NON-NEED-BASED) Total amount: $1,155,961 (6% federal, 1% state, 78% institutional, 15% external sources). **Receiving aid:** Freshmen: 25% (346); Undergraduates: 14% (927). **Average Award:** Freshmen: $3696; Undergraduates: $5439. **Scholarships, grants, and awards by category:** Academic Interests/Achievement: 1,671 awards ($1,970,432 total): area/ethnic studies, biological sciences, business, communication, computer science, education, English, foreign languages, general academic interests/achievements, humanities, international studies, mathematics, physical sciences, premedicine, social sciences. **ROTC:** Army cooperative.

LOANS Student loans: $30,529,177 (82% need-based, 18% non-need-based). 80% of past graduating class borrowed through all loan programs. *Average indebtedness per student:* $18,917. **Average need-based loan:** Freshmen: $3243. **Parent loans:** $4,917,609 (63% need-based, 37% non-need-based). **Programs:** FFEL (Subsidized and Unsubsidized Stafford, PLUS), Perkins.

WORK-STUDY Federal work-study: Total amount: $595,216; 574 jobs averaging $1083. **State or other work-study/employment:** Total amount: $1,788,908 (78% need-based, 22% non-need-based). 1,260 part-time jobs averaging $1113.

APPLYING FOR FINANCIAL AID Required financial aid forms: FAFSA, state aid form. **Financial aid deadline (priority):** 4/1. **Notification date:** Continuous beginning 3/1. Students must reply by 5/1 or within 3 weeks of notification.

CONTACT Mark C. Humbert, Director of Financial Aid, State University of New York at Oswego, 206 Culkin Hall, Oswego, NY 13126, 315-312-2248. *Fax:* 315-312-3696.

STATE UNIVERSITY OF NEW YORK AT PLATTSBURGH
Plattsburgh, NY

Tuition & fees (NY res): $5296   **Average undergraduate aid package:** $9473

ABOUT THE INSTITUTION State-supported, coed. Awards: bachelor's and master's degrees and post-master's certificates. 47 undergraduate majors. Total enrollment: 6,044. Undergraduates: 5,394. Freshmen: 1,031. Both federal and institutional methodology are used as a basis for awarding need-based institutional aid.

UNDERGRADUATE EXPENSES for 2006–07 Application fee: $40. **Tuition, state resident:** full-time $4350; part-time $181 per credit hour. **Tuition, nonresident:** full-time $10,610; part-time $442 per credit hour. **Required fees:** full-time $946; $39 per credit hour. **College room and board:** $7066; **room only:** $4400.

FRESHMAN FINANCIAL AID (Fall 2005, est.) 854 applied for aid; of those 72% were deemed to have need. 99% of freshmen with need received aid; of those 28% had need fully met. *Average percent of need met:* 85% (excluding resources awarded to replace EFC). *Average financial aid package:* $8628 (excluding resources awarded to replace EFC). 30% of all full-time freshmen had no need and received non-need-based gift aid.

UNDERGRADUATE FINANCIAL AID (Fall 2005, est.) 4,119 applied for aid; of those 76% were deemed to have need. 98% of undergraduates with need received aid; of those 31% had need fully met. *Average percent of need met:* 90% (excluding resources awarded to replace EFC). *Average financial aid package:* $9473 (excluding resources awarded to replace EFC). 26% of all full-time undergraduates had no need and received non-need-based gift aid.

GIFT AID (NEED-BASED) Total amount: $11,616,602 (40% federal, 46% state, 10% institutional, 4% external sources). **Receiving aid:** Freshmen: 57% (587); All full-time undergraduates: 52% (2,744). **Average award:** Freshmen: $5034; Undergraduates: $4226. **Scholarships, grants, and awards:** Federal Pell, FSEOG, state, private, college/university gift aid from institutional funds.

GIFT AID (NON-NEED-BASED) Total amount: $2,514,350 (1% federal, 17% state, 79% institutional, 3% external sources). **Receiving aid:** Freshmen: 25% (254); Undergraduates: 18% (973). **Average Award:** Freshmen: $4199; Undergraduates: $5258. **Scholarships, grants, and awards by category:** Academic Interests/Achievement: 1,905 awards ($3,355,304 total): area/ethnic studies, biological sciences, business, communication, computer science, education, engineering/technologies, English, general academic interests/achievements, health fields, home economics, humanities, international studies, mathematics, physical sciences, premedicine, social sciences. Creative Arts/Performance: 35 awards ($62,898 total): art/fine arts, journalism/publications, music, theater/drama. Special Achievements/Activities: 24 awards ($45,000 total): community service, general special achievements/activities, leadership. Special Characteristics: 885 awards ($1,927,159 total): international students, out-of-state students.

LOANS Student loans: $21,870,875 (79% need-based, 21% non-need-based). 74% of past graduating class borrowed through all loan programs. *Average indebtedness per student:* $17,596. **Average need-based loan:** Freshmen: $3975; Undergraduates: $6184. **Parent loans:** $4,225,180 (63% need-based, 37% non-need-based). **Programs:** Federal Direct (Subsidized and Unsubsidized Stafford, PLUS), Perkins, Federal Nursing, college/university, alternative loans, short-term emergency loans from Student Association.

WORK-STUDY Federal work-study: Total amount: $365,000; 331 jobs averaging $1100.

APPLYING FOR FINANCIAL AID Required financial aid forms: FAFSA, state aid form. **Financial aid deadline (priority):** 2/15. **Notification date:** Continuous beginning 3/15. Students must reply within 6 weeks of notification.

CONTACT Mr. Todd Moravec, Financial Aid Director, State University of New York at Plattsburgh, 101 Broad Street, Kehoe Administration Building 406, Plattsburgh, NY 12901-2681, 518-564-2072 or toll-free 888-673-0012 (in-state). *Fax:* 518-564-4079. *E-mail:* todd.moravec@plattsburgh.edu.

STATE UNIVERSITY OF NEW YORK COLLEGE AT BROCKPORT
Brockport, NY

Tuition & fees: N/R   **Average undergraduate aid package:** $8403

ABOUT THE INSTITUTION State-supported, coed. Awards: bachelor's and master's degrees and post-bachelor's and post-master's certificates. 112 undergraduate majors. Total enrollment: 8,484. Undergraduates: 6,965. Freshmen: 988. Federal methodology is used as a basis for awarding need-based institutional aid.

UNDERGRADUATE EXPENSES for 2006–07 Application fee: $40. **Tuition, state resident:** part-time $181 per credit. **Tuition, nonresident:** part-time $429 per credit.

FRESHMAN FINANCIAL AID (Fall 2004) 906 applied for aid; of those 76% were deemed to have need. 99% of freshmen with need received aid; of those 26% had need fully met. *Average percent of need met:* 83% (excluding resources awarded to replace EFC). *Average financial aid package:* $8461 (excluding resources awarded to replace EFC). 5% of all full-time freshmen had no need and received non-need-based gift aid.

UNDERGRADUATE FINANCIAL AID (Fall 2004) 4,520 applied for aid; of those 79% were deemed to have need. 99% of undergraduates with need received aid; of those 31% had need fully met. *Average percent of need met:* 80% (excluding resources awarded to replace EFC). *Average financial aid package:* $8403 (excluding resources awarded to replace EFC). 2% of all full-time undergraduates had no need and received non-need-based gift aid.

GIFT AID (NEED-BASED) Total amount: $13,705,799 (47% federal, 53% state). **Receiving aid:** Freshmen: 65% (639); All full-time undergraduates: 63% (3,221). **Average award:** Freshmen: $3782; Undergraduates: $3658. **Scholarships, grants, and awards:** Federal Pell, FSEOG, state, private, college/university gift aid from institutional funds.

GIFT AID (NON-NEED-BASED) Total amount: $4,153,841 (19% federal, 4% state, 71% institutional, 6% external sources). **Receiving aid:** Freshmen: 13% (131); Undergraduates: 10% (525). **Average Award:** Freshmen: $4034;

Undergraduates: $4363. ***Scholarships, grants, and awards by category:*** *Academic Interests/Achievement:* 600 awards ($2,000,000 total): biological sciences, business, communication, computer science, education, English, foreign languages, general academic interests/achievements, health fields, international studies, mathematics, military science, physical sciences, social sciences. *Creative Arts/Performance:* 25 awards ($10,000 total): art/fine arts, creative writing, dance, general creative arts/performance, journalism/publications, performing arts, theater/drama. *Special Achievements/Activities:* 3 awards ($2000 total): community service, general special achievements/activities, leadership, religious involvement. *Special Characteristics:* 50 awards ($500,000 total): children and siblings of alumni, ethnic background, first-generation college students, general special characteristics, international students, local/state students, married students, members of minority groups, out-of-state students, religious affiliation, veterans. *ROTC:* Army, Naval cooperative, Air Force cooperative.

LOANS *Student loans:* $32,956,852 (52% need-based, 48% non-need-based). 81% of past graduating class borrowed through all loan programs. *Average indebtedness per student:* $19,082. *Average need-based loan:* Freshmen: $4216; Undergraduates: $4551. *Parent loans:* $2,949,477 (100% non-need-based). *Programs:* Federal Direct (Subsidized and Unsubsidized Stafford, PLUS), Perkins, Federal Nursing, alternative loans.

WORK-STUDY *Federal work-study:* Total amount: $1,154,295; 636 jobs averaging $1280. *State or other work-study/employment:* Total amount: $2,732,704 (100% non-need-based). 1,392 part-time jobs averaging $1378.

APPLYING FOR FINANCIAL AID *Required financial aid forms:* FAFSA, state aid form. *Financial aid deadline (priority):* 3/15. *Notification date:* Continuous.

CONTACT Mr. J. Scott Atkinson, Associate Vice President for Enrollment Management and Student Affairs, State University of New York College at Brockport, 350 New Campus Drive, Brockport, NY 14420-2937, 585-395-2501. *Fax:* 585-395-5445. *E-mail:* satkinso@brockport.edu.

STATE UNIVERSITY OF NEW YORK COLLEGE AT CORTLAND
Cortland, NY

Tuition & fees (NY res): $4350   Average undergraduate aid package: $9372

ABOUT THE INSTITUTION State-supported, coed. Awards: bachelor's and master's degrees and post-bachelor's and post-master's certificates. 57 undergraduate majors. Total enrollment: 7,260. Undergraduates: 5,987. Freshmen: 1,110. Federal methodology is used as a basis for awarding need-based institutional aid.

UNDERGRADUATE EXPENSES for 2006–07 *Application fee:* $40. *Tuition, state resident:* full-time $4350; part-time $181 per credit hour. *Tuition, nonresident:* full-time $10,610; part-time $442 per credit hour. *College room and board:* $7850; *room only:* $4460.

FRESHMAN FINANCIAL AID (Fall 2004) 977 applied for aid; of those 70% were deemed to have need. 98% of freshmen with need received aid; of those 15% had need fully met. *Average percent of need met:* 73% (excluding resources awarded to replace EFC). *Average financial aid package:* $9113 (excluding resources awarded to replace EFC). 18% of all full-time freshmen had no need and received non-need-based gift aid.

UNDERGRADUATE FINANCIAL AID (Fall 2004) 4,841 applied for aid; of those 77% were deemed to have need. 98% of undergraduates with need received aid; of those 20% had need fully met. *Average percent of need met:* 75% (excluding resources awarded to replace EFC). *Average financial aid package:* $9372 (excluding resources awarded to replace EFC). 16% of all full-time undergraduates had no need and received non-need-based gift aid.

GIFT AID (NEED-BASED) *Total amount:* $10,212,045 (41% federal, 58% state, 1% institutional). *Receiving aid:* Freshmen: 55% (600); All full-time undergraduates: 56% (3,213). *Average award:* Freshmen: $3384; Undergraduates: $3550. *Scholarships, grants, and awards:* Federal Pell, FSEOG, state, private, college/university gift aid from institutional funds.

GIFT AID (NON-NEED-BASED) *Receiving aid:* Freshmen: 2% (26); Undergraduates: 4% (212). *Average Award:* Freshmen: $6819; Undergraduates: $6724. *Scholarships, grants, and awards by category:* Academic Interests/Achievement: general academic interests/achievements. Creative Arts/Performance: music, theater/drama. Special Achievements/Activities: general special achievements/activities, leadership. Special Characteristics: children and siblings of alumni, members of minority groups. *ROTC:* Army cooperative, Air Force cooperative.

LOANS *Student loans:* $23,964,338 (51% need-based, 49% non-need-based). *Average need-based loan:* Freshmen: $2624; Undergraduates: $3784. *Parent loans:* $5,238,587 (100% non-need-based). *Programs:* Federal Direct (Subsidized and Unsubsidized Stafford, PLUS), FFEL (Subsidized and Unsubsidized Stafford, PLUS), Perkins.

WORK-STUDY *Federal work-study:* Total amount: $240,436; 609 jobs available. *State or other work-study/employment:* Part-time jobs available.

APPLYING FOR FINANCIAL AID *Required financial aid form:* FAFSA. *Financial aid deadline:* 3/31. *Notification date:* 4/1. Students must reply by 5/1 or within 2 weeks of notification.

CONTACT David Canaski, Financial Aid Office, State University of New York College at Cortland, PO Box 2000, Cortland, NY 13045-0900, 607-753-4717. *Fax:* 607-753-5990. *E-mail:* finaid@em.cortland.edu.

STATE UNIVERSITY OF NEW YORK COLLEGE AT GENESEO
Geneseo, NY

Tuition & fees (NY res): $5520   Average undergraduate aid package: $9339

ABOUT THE INSTITUTION State-supported, coed. Awards: bachelor's and master's degrees. 45 undergraduate majors. Total enrollment: 5,484. Undergraduates: 5,306. Freshmen: 1,029. Federal methodology is used as a basis for awarding need-based institutional aid.

UNDERGRADUATE EXPENSES for 2006–07 *Application fee:* $40. *Tuition, state resident:* full-time $4350; part-time $181 per credit hour. *Tuition, nonresident:* full-time $10,610; part-time $442 per credit hour. *Required fees:* full-time $1170; $48.55 per credit hour. *College room and board:* $7390.

FRESHMAN FINANCIAL AID (Fall 2005, est.) 856 applied for aid; of those 51% were deemed to have need. 100% of freshmen with need received aid; of those 75% had need fully met. *Average percent of need met:* 75% (excluding resources awarded to replace EFC). *Average financial aid package:* $8635 (excluding resources awarded to replace EFC). 4% of all full-time freshmen had no need and received non-need-based gift aid.

UNDERGRADUATE FINANCIAL AID (Fall 2005, est.) 3,877 applied for aid; of those 62% were deemed to have need. 100% of undergraduates with need received aid; of those 85% had need fully met. *Average percent of need met:* 85% (excluding resources awarded to replace EFC). *Average financial aid package:* $9339 (excluding resources awarded to replace EFC). 9% of all full-time undergraduates had no need and received non-need-based gift aid.

GIFT AID (NEED-BASED) *Total amount:* $7,690,251 (37% federal, 63% state). *Receiving aid:* Freshmen: 34% (350); All full-time undergraduates: 39% (2,000). *Average award:* Freshmen: $2450; Undergraduates: $2717. *Scholarships, grants, and awards:* Federal Pell, FSEOG, state, private, college/university gift aid from institutional funds.

GIFT AID (NON-NEED-BASED) *Total amount:* $2,302,118 (26% state, 41% institutional, 33% external sources). *Receiving aid:* Freshmen: 20% (200); Undergraduates: 10% (500). *Average Award:* Freshmen: $2146; Undergraduates: $1900. *Scholarships, grants, and awards by category:* Academic Interests/Achievement: 453 awards ($391,312 total): area/ethnic studies, biological sciences, business, communication, computer science, education, English, foreign languages, general academic interests/achievements, humanities, mathematics, physical sciences, premedicine, social sciences. *Creative Arts/Performance:* 39 awards ($17,249 total): applied art and design, art/fine arts, creative writing, dance, general creative arts/performance, journalism/publications, music, performing arts, theater/drama. *Special Achievements/Activities:* 18 awards ($16,450 total): community service, general special achievements/activities, leadership. *Special Characteristics:* 56 awards ($23,910 total): adult students, local/state students, members of minority groups. *ROTC:* Army cooperative, Air Force cooperative.

LOANS *Student loans:* $18,159,720 (52% need-based, 48% non-need-based). 75% of past graduating class borrowed through all loan programs. *Average indebtedness per student:* $16,000. *Average need-based loan:* Freshmen: $3495; Undergraduates: $5424. *Parent loans:* $3,083,685 (100% non-need-based). *Programs:* FFEL (Subsidized and Unsubsidized Stafford, PLUS), Perkins, state, alternative loans.

WORK-STUDY *Federal work-study:* Total amount: $657,104; 451 jobs averaging $1305.

APPLYING FOR FINANCIAL AID *Required financial aid forms:* FAFSA, state aid form. *Financial aid deadline:* 2/15 (priority: 2/15). *Notification date:* Continuous beginning 3/15. Students must reply by 5/1 or within 3 weeks of notification.

State University of New York College at Geneseo

CONTACT Archie Cureton, Director of Financial Aid, State University of New York College at Geneseo, 1 College Circle, Erwin Hall 104, Geneseo, NY 14454, 585-245-5731 or toll-free 866-245-5211. *Fax:* 585-245-5717. *E-mail:* cureton@geneseo.edu.

STATE UNIVERSITY OF NEW YORK COLLEGE AT OLD WESTBURY
Old Westbury, NY

Tuition & fees (NY res): $5072   **Average undergraduate aid package: $6283**

ABOUT THE INSTITUTION State-supported, coed. Awards: bachelor's and master's degrees. 42 undergraduate majors. Total enrollment: 3,398. Undergraduates: 3,373. Freshmen: 404. Both federal and institutional methodology are used as a basis for awarding need-based institutional aid.

UNDERGRADUATE EXPENSES for 2006–07 *Application fee:* $40. *Tuition, state resident:* full-time $4350; part-time $181 per credit. *Tuition, nonresident:* full-time $10,610; part-time $442 per credit. *College room and board:* $8083; *room only:* $5793.

FRESHMAN FINANCIAL AID (Fall 2005, est.) 350 applied for aid; of those 99% were deemed to have need. *Average percent of need met:* 46% (excluding resources awarded to replace EFC). *Average financial aid package:* $6661 (excluding resources awarded to replace EFC).

UNDERGRADUATE FINANCIAL AID (Fall 2005, est.) 2,043 applied for aid; of those 100% were deemed to have need. *Average percent of need met:* 45% (excluding resources awarded to replace EFC). *Average financial aid package:* $6283 (excluding resources awarded to replace EFC).

GIFT AID (NEED-BASED) *Total amount:* $8,543,739 (48% federal, 51% state, 1% institutional). *Receiving aid:* Freshmen: 75% (307); All full-time undergraduates: 62% (1,679). *Average award:* Freshmen: $5549; Undergraduates: $4677. *Scholarships, grants, and awards:* Federal Pell, FSEOG, state, private, college/university gift aid from institutional funds.

GIFT AID (NON-NEED-BASED) *Total amount:* $27,264 (100% external sources). *Receiving aid:* Freshmen: 3% (14); Undergraduates: 2% (41). *Scholarships, grants, and awards by category: Academic Interests/Achievement:* biological sciences, health fields, physical sciences. *ROTC:* Army cooperative, Air Force cooperative.

LOANS *Student loans:* $5,308,468 (100% need-based). 52% of past graduating class borrowed through all loan programs. *Average indebtedness per student:* $14,532. *Average need-based loan:* Freshmen: $1703; Undergraduates: $2341. *Parent loans:* $975,070 (90% need-based, 10% non-need-based). *Programs:* FFEL (Subsidized and Unsubsidized Stafford, PLUS), Perkins.

WORK-STUDY *Federal work-study:* Total amount: $184,003; 268 jobs averaging $686. *State or other work-study/employment:* Total amount: $113,940 (100% non-need-based). 75 part-time jobs averaging $1519.

APPLYING FOR FINANCIAL AID *Required financial aid forms:* FAFSA, institution's own form, income documentation. *Financial aid deadline (priority):* 4/14. *Notification date:* Continuous beginning 4/25. Students must reply within 2 weeks of notification.

CONTACT Ms. Dee Darrell, Financial Aid Assistant, State University of New York College at Old Westbury, PO Box 210, Old Westbury, NY 11568-0210, 516-876-3222. *Fax:* 516-876-3008. *E-mail:* finaid@oldwestbury.edu.

STATE UNIVERSITY OF NEW YORK COLLEGE AT ONEONTA
Oneonta, NY

Tuition & fees (NY res): $5367   **Average undergraduate aid package: $9244**

ABOUT THE INSTITUTION State-supported, coed. Awards: bachelor's and master's degrees and post-bachelor's and post-master's certificates. 71 undergraduate majors. Total enrollment: 5,860. Undergraduates: 5,649. Freshmen: 1,145. Federal methodology is used as a basis for awarding need-based institutional aid.

UNDERGRADUATE EXPENSES for 2006–07 *Application fee:* $40. *Tuition, state resident:* full-time $4350; part-time $181 per semester hour. *Tuition, nonresident:* full-time $10,610; part-time $442 per semester hour. *Required fees:* full-time $1017; $34.35 per semester hour. *College room and board:* $7538; *room only:* $4378.

FRESHMAN FINANCIAL AID (Fall 2005, est.) 974 applied for aid; of those 68% were deemed to have need. 97% of freshmen with need received aid; of those 15% had need fully met. *Average percent of need met:* 57% (excluding resources awarded to replace EFC). *Average financial aid package:* $7955 (excluding resources awarded to replace EFC). 25% of all full-time freshmen had no need and received non-need-based gift aid.

UNDERGRADUATE FINANCIAL AID (Fall 2005, est.) 4,298 applied for aid; of those 75% were deemed to have need. 97% of undergraduates with need received aid; of those 18% had need fully met. *Average percent of need met:* 64% (excluding resources awarded to replace EFC). *Average financial aid package:* $9244 (excluding resources awarded to replace EFC). 20% of all full-time undergraduates had no need and received non-need-based gift aid.

GIFT AID (NEED-BASED) *Total amount:* $12,243,680 (36% federal, 50% state, 8% institutional, 6% external sources). *Receiving aid:* Freshmen: 50% (572); All full-time undergraduates: 50% (2,722). *Average award:* Freshmen: $3697; Undergraduates: $3666. *Scholarships, grants, and awards:* Federal Pell, FSEOG, state, private, college/university gift aid from institutional funds.

GIFT AID (NON-NEED-BASED) *Total amount:* $240,604 (54% institutional, 46% external sources). *Average Award:* Freshmen: $3835; Undergraduates: $4893. *Scholarships, grants, and awards by category: Academic Interests/Achievement:* 45 awards ($40,000 total): biological sciences, education, general academic interests/achievements, home economics, international studies, physical sciences, premedicine. *Creative Arts/Performance:* 18 awards ($10,000 total): journalism/publications, music. *Special Achievements/Activities:* 37 awards ($31,500 total): community service, general special achievements/activities, leadership. *Special Characteristics:* 33 awards ($37,000 total): adult students, children and siblings of alumni, ethnic background, general special characteristics, handicapped students, international students, local/state students, members of minority groups.

LOANS *Student loans:* $23,258,420 (53% need-based, 47% non-need-based). 68% of past graduating class borrowed through all loan programs. *Average indebtedness per student:* $8308. *Average need-based loan:* Freshmen: $3434; Undergraduates: $4406. *Parent loans:* $8,510,707 (100% need-based). *Programs:* FFEL (Subsidized and Unsubsidized Stafford, PLUS), Perkins.

WORK-STUDY *Federal work-study:* Total amount: $373,113; 378 jobs averaging $1200. *State or other work-study/employment:* Part-time jobs available.

ATHLETIC AWARDS Total amount: $95,500 (21% need-based, 79% non-need-based).

APPLYING FOR FINANCIAL AID *Required financial aid forms:* FAFSA, state aid form. *Financial aid deadline (priority):* 3/15. *Notification date:* Continuous.

CONTACT Mr. Bill Goodhue, Director of Financial Aid, State University of New York College at Oneonta, Ravine Parkway, Oneonta, NY 13820, 607-436-2992 or toll-free 800-SUNY-123. *Fax:* 607-436-2659. *E-mail:* goodhucw@oneonta.edu.

STATE UNIVERSITY OF NEW YORK COLLEGE AT POTSDAM
Potsdam, NY

Tuition & fees (NY res): $5289   **Average undergraduate aid package: $11,771**

ABOUT THE INSTITUTION State-supported, coed. Awards: bachelor's and master's degrees. 37 undergraduate majors. Total enrollment: 4,329. Undergraduates: 3,619. Freshmen: 739. Federal methodology is used as a basis for awarding need-based institutional aid.

UNDERGRADUATE EXPENSES for 2005–06 *Application fee:* $40. *Tuition, state resident:* full-time $4350; part-time $181 per credit hour. *Tuition, nonresident:* full-time $10,610; part-time $442 per credit hour. *Required fees:* full-time $939; $43.95 per credit hour. *College room and board:* $7670; *room only:* $4420. Room and board charges vary according to board plan and housing facility. *Payment plan:* Installment.

FRESHMAN FINANCIAL AID (Fall 2005, est.) 660 applied for aid; of those 74% were deemed to have need. 100% of freshmen with need received aid; of those 80% had need fully met. *Average percent of need met:* 80% (excluding resources awarded to replace EFC). *Average financial aid package:* $12,295 (excluding resources awarded to replace EFC). 18% of all full-time freshmen had no need and received non-need-based gift aid.

UNDERGRADUATE FINANCIAL AID (Fall 2005, est.) 2,932 applied for aid; of those 78% were deemed to have need. 99% of undergraduates with need received aid; of those 78% had need fully met. *Average percent of need met:*

State University of New York College of Environmental Science and Forestry

78% (excluding resources awarded to replace EFC). *Average financial aid package:* $11,771 (excluding resources awarded to replace EFC). 11% of all full-time undergraduates had no need and received non-need-based gift aid.
GIFT AID (NEED-BASED) *Total amount:* $9,964,983 (38% federal, 48% state, 11% institutional, 3% external sources). *Receiving aid:* Freshmen: 63% (464); All full-time undergraduates: 61% (2,098). *Average award:* Freshmen: $5992; Undergraduates: $4518. *Scholarships, grants, and awards:* Federal Pell, FSEOG, state, private, college/university gift aid from institutional funds, VESID Awards, Veterans Administration Rehabilitation Awards, Bureau of Indian Affairs Grant.
GIFT AID (NON-NEED-BASED) *Total amount:* $2,225,960 (22% federal, 6% state, 65% institutional, 7% external sources). *Receiving aid:* Freshmen: 35% (257); Undergraduates: 29% (1,014). *Average Award:* Freshmen: $2730; Undergraduates: $3637. *Scholarships, grants, and awards by category: Academic Interests/Achievement:* 381 awards ($999,097 total): biological sciences, business, communication, computer science, education, engineering/technologies, English, foreign languages, general academic interests/achievements, humanities, mathematics, physical sciences, social sciences. *Creative Arts/Performance:* 113 awards ($141,105 total): art/fine arts, dance, music, performing arts, theater/drama. *Special Achievements/Activities:* 239 awards ($378,299 total): community service, general special activities/activities, leadership. *Special Characteristics:* 159 awards ($157,350 total): adult students, children and siblings of alumni, children of faculty/staff, ethnic background, handicapped students, local/state students, members of minority groups, previous college experience. *Tuition waivers:* Full or partial for minority students, employees or children of employees. *ROTC:* Army cooperative, Air Force cooperative.
LOANS *Student loans:* $15,416,653 (53% need-based, 47% non-need-based). 82% of past graduating class borrowed through all loan programs. *Average indebtedness per student:* $16,117. *Average need-based loan:* Freshmen: $3314; Undergraduates: $4175. *Parent loans:* $7,006,621 (100% non-need-based). *Programs:* Federal Direct (Subsidized and Unsubsidized Stafford, PLUS), Perkins, college/university, alternative loans.
WORK-STUDY *Federal work-study:* Total amount: $407,279; 342 jobs averaging $1200.
APPLYING FOR FINANCIAL AID *Required financial aid forms:* FAFSA, state aid form. *Financial aid deadline:* 5/1 (priority: 3/1). *Notification date:* Continuous beginning 2/1. Students must reply within 18 weeks of notification.
CONTACT Susan C. Aldrich, Director of Financial Aid, State University of New York College at Potsdam, 44 Pierrepont Avenue, Potsdam, NY 13676, 315-267-2162 or toll-free 877-POTSDAM. *Fax:* 315-267-3067. *E-mail:* aldricsc@potsdam.edu.

STATE UNIVERSITY OF NEW YORK COLLEGE OF AGRICULTURE AND TECHNOLOGY AT COBLESKILL
Cobleskill, NY

Tuition & fees (NY res): $5345   **Average undergraduate aid package:** $6976

ABOUT THE INSTITUTION State-supported, coed. Awards: associate and bachelor's degrees. 46 undergraduate majors. Total enrollment: 2,482. Undergraduates: 2,482. Freshmen: 909. Federal methodology is used as a basis for awarding need-based institutional aid.
UNDERGRADUATE EXPENSES for 2005–06 *Application fee:* $40. *Tuition, state resident:* full-time $4350; part-time $181 per credit hour. *Tuition, nonresident:* full-time $7210; part-time $300 per credit hour. *Required fees:* full-time $995; $59.12 per credit hour. Full-time tuition and fees vary according to course level and degree level. Part-time tuition and fees vary according to course level and degree level. *College room and board:* $7270; *room only:* $4300. Room and board charges vary according to board plan and housing facility. *Payment plan:* Installment.
FRESHMAN FINANCIAL AID (Fall 2004) 914 applied for aid; of those 80% were deemed to have need. 99% of freshmen with need received aid; of those 4% had need fully met. *Average percent of need met:* 59% (excluding resources awarded to replace EFC). *Average financial aid package:* $6675 (excluding resources awarded to replace EFC).
UNDERGRADUATE FINANCIAL AID (Fall 2004) 1,916 applied for aid; of those 83% were deemed to have need. 99% of undergraduates with need received aid; of those 4% had need fully met. *Average percent of need met:* 61% (excluding resources awarded to replace EFC). *Average financial aid package:* $6976 (excluding resources awarded to replace EFC).
GIFT AID (NEED-BASED) *Total amount:* $6,446,566 (43% federal, 57% state). *Receiving aid:* Freshmen: 59% (650); All full-time undergraduates: 62% (1,435). *Average award:* Freshmen: $4515; Undergraduates: $4467. *Scholarships, grants, and awards:* Federal Pell, FSEOG, state, private, college/university gift aid from institutional funds.
GIFT AID (NON-NEED-BASED) *Total amount:* $245,681 (100% institutional). *Receiving aid:* Freshmen: 7% (80); Undergraduates: 5% (125). *Tuition waivers:* Full or partial for employees or children of employees.
LOANS *Student loans:* $8,329,671 (100% need-based). 77% of past graduating class borrowed through all loan programs. *Average indebtedness per student:* $6300. *Average need-based loan:* Freshmen: $2794; Undergraduates: $3190. *Parent loans:* $5,730,844 (54% need-based, 46% non-need-based). *Programs:* FFEL (Subsidized and Unsubsidized Stafford, PLUS), Perkins.
WORK-STUDY *Federal work-study:* Total amount: $167,850; 208 jobs averaging $915. *State or other work-study/employment:* Part-time jobs available.
APPLYING FOR FINANCIAL AID *Required financial aid forms:* FAFSA, state aid form. *Financial aid deadline:* 3/15. *Notification date:* 4/15. Students must reply within 2 weeks of notification.
CONTACT Richard Young, Director of Financial Aid, State University of New York College of Agriculture and Technology at Cobleskill, Knapp Hall, Cobleskill, NY 12043, 518-255-5623 or toll-free 800-295-8988. *Fax:* 518-255-5844.

STATE UNIVERSITY OF NEW YORK COLLEGE OF ENVIRONMENTAL SCIENCE AND FORESTRY
Syracuse, NY

Tuition & fees (NY res): $5032   **Average undergraduate aid package:** $12,150

ABOUT THE INSTITUTION State-supported, coed. Awards: associate, bachelor's, master's, and doctoral degrees. 44 undergraduate majors. Total enrollment: 1,934. Undergraduates: 1,392. Freshmen: 260. Federal methodology is used as a basis for awarding need-based institutional aid.
UNDERGRADUATE EXPENSES for 2006–07 *Application fee:* $40. *Tuition, state resident:* full-time $4350; part-time $181 per credit hour. *Tuition, nonresident:* full-time $10,610; part-time $442 per credit hour. *Required fees:* full-time $682; $32.85 per credit hour or $19.10 per year part-time. *College room and board:* $10,180; *room only:* $5090.
FRESHMAN FINANCIAL AID (Fall 2005, est.) 210 applied for aid; of those 90% were deemed to have need. 100% of freshmen with need received aid; of those 100% had need fully met. *Average percent of need met:* 100% (excluding resources awarded to replace EFC). *Average financial aid package:* $10,850 (excluding resources awarded to replace EFC). 8% of all full-time freshmen had no need and received non-need-based gift aid.
UNDERGRADUATE FINANCIAL AID (Fall 2005, est.) 1,058 applied for aid; of those 93% were deemed to have need. 100% of undergraduates with need received aid; of those 100% had need fully met. *Average percent of need met:* 100% (excluding resources awarded to replace EFC). *Average financial aid package:* $12,150 (excluding resources awarded to replace EFC). 3% of all full-time undergraduates had no need and received non-need-based gift aid.
GIFT AID (NEED-BASED) *Total amount:* $4,256,000 (42% federal, 38% state, 15% institutional, 5% external sources). *Receiving aid:* Freshmen: 48% (108); All full-time undergraduates: 45% (501). *Average award:* Freshmen: $4500; Undergraduates: $5200. *Scholarships, grants, and awards:* Federal Pell, FSEOG, state, private, college/university gift aid from institutional funds.
GIFT AID (NON-NEED-BASED) *Total amount:* $508,000 (20% federal, 11% state, 49% institutional, 20% external sources). *Receiving aid:* Freshmen: 8% (18); Undergraduates: 3% (33). *Average Award:* Freshmen: $2500; Undergraduates: $2000. *Scholarships, grants, and awards by category: Academic Interests/Achievement:* 108 awards ($150,000 total): agriculture, architecture, biological sciences, engineering/technologies, physical sciences, premedicine. *Special Achievements/Activities:* leadership. *Special Characteristics:* 42 awards ($90,000 total): members of minority groups. *ROTC:* Army cooperative, Air Force cooperative.
LOANS *Student loans:* $8,000,000 (54% need-based, 46% non-need-based). 92% of past graduating class borrowed through all loan programs. *Average*

State University of New York College of Environmental Science and Forestry

indebtedness per student: $19,000. **Average need-based loan:** Freshmen: $4625; Undergraduates: $6400. **Parent loans:** $8,800,000 (18% need-based, 82% non-need-based). **Programs:** FFEL (Subsidized and Unsubsidized Stafford, PLUS), Perkins, college/university.

WORK-STUDY *Federal work-study:* Total amount: $350,000; 310 jobs averaging $1129. **State or other work-study/employment:** Total amount: $200,000 (100% non-need-based). 120 part-time jobs averaging $1667.

APPLYING FOR FINANCIAL AID *Required financial aid forms:* FAFSA, state aid form. **Financial aid deadline (priority):** 3/1. **Notification date:** 4/1. Students must reply within 2 weeks of notification.

CONTACT Mr. John E. View, Director of Financial Aid, State University of New York College of Environmental Science and Forestry, One Forestry Drive, 115 Bray Hall, Syracuse, NY 13210-2779, 315-470-6671 or toll-free 800-777-7373. *Fax:* 315-470-4734. *E-mail:* jeview@esf.edu.

STATE UNIVERSITY OF NEW YORK DOWNSTATE MEDICAL CENTER
Brooklyn, NY

CONTACT Office of Financial Aid, State University of New York Downstate Medical Center, 450 Clarkson Avenue, Brooklyn, NY 11203-2098, 718-270-2488.

STATE UNIVERSITY OF NEW YORK, FREDONIA
Fredonia, NY

Tuition & fees (NY res): $5441   **Average undergraduate aid package:** $7024

ABOUT THE INSTITUTION State-supported, coed. Awards: bachelor's and master's degrees. 74 undergraduate majors. Total enrollment: 5,432. Undergraduates: 4,843. Freshmen: 1,038. Federal methodology is used as a basis for awarding need-based institutional aid.

UNDERGRADUATE EXPENSES for 2005–06 *Application fee:* $40. **Tuition, state resident:** full-time $4350; part-time $181 per credit hour. **Tuition, nonresident:** full-time $10,610; part-time $442 per credit hour. **Required fees:** full-time $1091; $43.15 per credit hour. **College room and board:** $6940; *room only:* $4350. Room and board charges vary according to board plan and housing facility. **Payment plan:** Installment.

FRESHMAN FINANCIAL AID (Fall 2005, est.) 927 applied for aid; of those 65% were deemed to have need. 99% of freshmen with need received aid; of those 22% had need fully met. *Average percent of need met:* 68% (excluding resources awarded to replace EFC). *Average financial aid package:* $6751 (excluding resources awarded to replace EFC). 11% of all full-time freshmen had no need and received non-need-based gift aid.

UNDERGRADUATE FINANCIAL AID (Fall 2005, est.) 4,154 applied for aid; of those 71% were deemed to have need. 100% of undergraduates with need received aid; of those 29% had need fully met. *Average percent of need met:* 77% (excluding resources awarded to replace EFC). *Average financial aid package:* $7024 (excluding resources awarded to replace EFC). 6% of all full-time undergraduates had no need and received non-need-based gift aid.

GIFT AID (NEED-BASED) *Total amount:* $10,643,835 (35% federal, 52% state, 8% institutional, 5% external sources). *Receiving aid:* Freshmen: 55% (564); All full-time undergraduates: 57% (2,714). *Average award:* Freshmen: $3541; Undergraduates: $3187. *Scholarships, grants, and awards:* Federal Pell, FSEOG, state, private, college/university gift aid from institutional funds.

GIFT AID (NON-NEED-BASED) *Receiving aid:* Freshmen: 15% (154); Undergraduates: 9% (438). *Average Award:* Freshmen: $1661; Undergraduates: $1671. *Scholarships, grants, and awards by category: Academic Interests/Achievement:* 266 awards ($425,100 total): biological sciences, business, communication, computer science, education, English, foreign languages, general academic interests/achievements, humanities, international studies, mathematics, physical sciences, social sciences. *Creative Arts/Performance:* 60 awards ($88,000 total): applied art and design, dance, music, performing arts, theater/drama. *Special Achievements/Activities:* 20 awards ($30,000 total): general special achievements/activities, leadership. *Special Characteristics:* 60 awards ($90,000 total): children and siblings of alumni, ethnic background, general special characteristics, international students, local/state students, members of minority groups, out-of-state students, previous college experience, veterans, veterans' children.

LOANS *Student loans:* $29,000,000 (51% need-based, 49% non-need-based). 81% of past graduating class borrowed through all loan programs. *Average indebtedness per student:* $12,500. **Average need-based loan:** Freshmen: $2888; Undergraduates: $3756. **Parent loans:** $360,000 (100% non-need-based). **Programs:** FFEL (Subsidized and Unsubsidized Stafford, PLUS), Perkins, alternative (private) loans.

WORK-STUDY *Federal work-study:* Total amount: $360,548; 260 jobs averaging $1387. **State or other work-study/employment:** 850 part-time jobs averaging $1950.

APPLYING FOR FINANCIAL AID *Required financial aid forms:* FAFSA, state aid form. **Financial aid deadline:** 5/15 (priority: 1/31). **Notification date:** Continuous beginning 3/10. Students must reply within 4 weeks of notification.

CONTACT Amy Beers, Financial Aid Advisor, State University of New York, Fredonia, 2nd Floor Maytum Hall, Fredonia, NY 14063, 716-673-3253 or toll-free 800-252-1212. *Fax:* 716-673-3785. *E-mail:* tramuta@fredonia.edu.

STATE UNIVERSITY OF NEW YORK INSTITUTE OF TECHNOLOGY
Utica, NY

Tuition & fees (NY res): $5285   **Average undergraduate aid package:** $8343

ABOUT THE INSTITUTION State-supported, coed. Awards: bachelor's and master's degrees and post-master's certificates. 19 undergraduate majors. Total enrollment: 2,590. Undergraduates: 2,019. Freshmen: 159. Federal methodology is used as a basis for awarding need-based institutional aid.

UNDERGRADUATE EXPENSES for 2005–06 *Application fee:* $40. **Tuition, state resident:** full-time $4350; part-time $181 per credit hour. **Tuition, nonresident:** full-time $10,610; part-time $442 per credit hour. **Required fees:** full-time $935; $36.70 per credit hour. **College room and board:** $7290.

FRESHMAN FINANCIAL AID (Fall 2005, est.) 139 applied for aid; of those 76% were deemed to have need. 97% of freshmen with need received aid; of those 28% had need fully met. *Average percent of need met:* 83% (excluding resources awarded to replace EFC). *Average financial aid package:* $8354 (excluding resources awarded to replace EFC). 5% of all full-time freshmen had no need and received non-need-based gift aid.

UNDERGRADUATE FINANCIAL AID (Fall 2005, est.) 1,005 applied for aid; of those 85% were deemed to have need. 97% of undergraduates with need received aid; of those 46% had need fully met. *Average percent of need met:* 79% (excluding resources awarded to replace EFC). *Average financial aid package:* $8343 (excluding resources awarded to replace EFC). 4% of all full-time undergraduates had no need and received non-need-based gift aid.

GIFT AID (NEED-BASED) *Total amount:* $3,389,051 (51% federal, 46% state, 3% institutional). *Receiving aid:* Freshmen: 60% (96); All full-time undergraduates: 62% (769). *Average award:* Freshmen: $1068; Undergraduates: $1480. *Scholarships, grants, and awards:* Federal Pell, FSEOG, state.

GIFT AID (NON-NEED-BASED) *Total amount:* $931,080 (6% federal, 14% state, 50% institutional, 30% external sources). *Receiving aid:* Freshmen: 24% (38); Undergraduates: 20% (254). *Average Award:* Freshmen: $1359; Undergraduates: $1589. *Scholarships, grants, and awards by category: Academic Interests/Achievement:* computer science, engineering/technologies, general academic interests/achievements. *Special Characteristics:* local/state students, members of minority groups, previous college experience. **ROTC:** Army cooperative, Air Force cooperative.

LOANS *Student loans:* $7,735,105 (70% need-based, 30% non-need-based). 74% of past graduating class borrowed through all loan programs. *Average indebtedness per student:* $16,318. **Average need-based loan:** Freshmen: $2039; Undergraduates: $3474. **Parent loans:** $1,167,439 (80% need-based, 20% non-need-based). **Programs:** Federal Direct (Subsidized and Unsubsidized Stafford, PLUS), Perkins, Federal Nursing.

WORK-STUDY *Federal work-study:* Total amount: $161,000; 100 jobs averaging $1400.

APPLYING FOR FINANCIAL AID *Required financial aid forms:* FAFSA, state aid form. **Financial aid deadline:** Continuous. **Notification date:** Continuous beginning 3/15. Students must reply within 2 weeks of notification.

CONTACT Director of Financial Aid, State University of New York Institute of Technology, PO Box 3050, Utica, NY 13504-3050, 315-792-7210 or toll-free 800-SUNYTEC. *Fax:* 315-792-7220. *E-mail:* @sunyit.edu.

STATE UNIVERSITY OF NEW YORK MARITIME COLLEGE
Throggs Neck, NY

CONTACT Ms. Madeline Aponte, Director of Financial Aid, State University of New York Maritime College, 6 Pennyfield Avenue, Throgs Neck, NY 10465-4198, 718-409-7267 or toll-free 800-654-1874 (in-state), 800-642-1874 (out-of-state). *Fax:* 718-409-7275. *E-mail:* finaid@sunymaritime.edu.

STATE UNIVERSITY OF NEW YORK UPSTATE MEDICAL UNIVERSITY
Syracuse, NY

Tuition & fees (NY res): $9166   **Average undergraduate aid package:** $19,250

ABOUT THE INSTITUTION State-supported, coed. Awards: bachelor's, master's, doctoral, and first professional degrees and post-master's certificates. 8 undergraduate majors. Total enrollment: 1,235. Undergraduates: 243. Entering class: . Federal methodology is used as a basis for awarding need-based institutional aid.
UNDERGRADUATE EXPENSES for 2005–06 *Application fee:* $40. *Tuition, state resident:* full-time $8700; part-time $181 per credit. *Tuition, nonresident:* full-time $21,200; part-time $422 per credit. *College room and board: room only:* $3585.
UNDERGRADUATE FINANCIAL AID (Fall 2004) 170 applied for aid; of those 100% were deemed to have need. 100% of undergraduates with need received aid; of those 98% had need fully met. *Average percent of need met:* 100% (excluding resources awarded to replace EFC). *Average financial aid package:* $19,250 (excluding resources awarded to replace EFC).
GIFT AID (NEED-BASED) *Total amount:* $566,352 (47% federal, 28% state, 9% institutional, 16% external sources). *Receiving aid:* All full-time undergraduates: 56% (146). *Average award:* Undergraduates: $3200. *Scholarships, grants, and awards:* Federal Pell, FSEOG, college/university gift aid from institutional funds, State Grants.
GIFT AID (NON-NEED-BASED) *Total amount:* $133,873 (5% federal, 8% state, 87% institutional). *Receiving aid:* Undergraduates: 14% (36). *Scholarships, grants, and awards by category: Academic Interests/Achievement:* health fields.
LOANS *Student loans:* $1,117,530 (68% need-based, 32% non-need-based). 46% of past graduating class borrowed through all loan programs. *Average indebtedness per student:* $9970. *Average need-based loan:* Undergraduates: $8400. *Programs:* FFEL (Subsidized and Unsubsidized Stafford, PLUS), Perkins.
WORK-STUDY *Federal work-study:* Total amount: $123,433; jobs available.
APPLYING FOR FINANCIAL AID *Required financial aid form:* FAFSA. *Financial aid deadline:* 4/1 (priority: 3/1). *Notification date:* Continuous beginning 5/1. Students must reply within 3 weeks of notification.
CONTACT Office of Financial Aid, State University of New York Upstate Medical University, 155 Elizabeth Blackwell Street, Syracuse, NY 13210-2375, 315-464-4329 or toll-free 800-736-2171. *E-mail:* finaid@upstate.edu.

STEPHEN F. AUSTIN STATE UNIVERSITY
Nacogdoches, TX

Tuition & fees (TX res): $4718   **Average undergraduate aid package:** $4549

ABOUT THE INSTITUTION State-supported, coed. Awards: bachelor's, master's, and doctoral degrees. 73 undergraduate majors. Total enrollment: 11,435. Undergraduates: 9,806. Freshmen: 1,921. Federal methodology is used as a basis for awarding need-based institutional aid.
UNDERGRADUATE EXPENSES for 2005–06 *Application fee:* $25. *Tuition, state resident:* full-time $4718; part-time $126 per credit hour. *Tuition, nonresident:* full-time $12,998; part-time $402 per credit hour. *Required fees:* $60.50 per credit hour or $9 per term part-time. Full-time tuition and fees vary according to course load. Part-time tuition and fees vary according to course load. *College room and board:* $5459. Room and board charges vary according to board plan and housing facility. *Payment plan:* Installment.
FRESHMAN FINANCIAL AID (Fall 2004) 1208 applied for aid; of those 66% were deemed to have need. 98% of freshmen with need received aid; of those 27% had need fully met. *Average percent of need met:* 75% (excluding resources awarded to replace EFC). *Average financial aid package:* $4394 (excluding resources awarded to replace EFC). 11% of all full-time freshmen had no need and received non-need-based gift aid.
UNDERGRADUATE FINANCIAL AID (Fall 2004) 5,345 applied for aid; of those 76% were deemed to have need. 97% of undergraduates with need received aid; of those 23% had need fully met. *Average percent of need met:* 74% (excluding resources awarded to replace EFC). *Average financial aid package:* $4549 (excluding resources awarded to replace EFC). 5% of all full-time undergraduates had no need and received non-need-based gift aid.
GIFT AID (NEED-BASED) *Total amount:* $16,579,369 (60% federal, 25% state, 15% institutional). *Receiving aid:* Freshmen: 39% (600); All full-time undergraduates: 45% (3,254). *Average award:* Freshmen: $2425; Undergraduates: $2209. *Scholarships, grants, and awards:* Federal Pell, FSEOG, state, private, college/university gift aid from institutional funds.
GIFT AID (NON-NEED-BASED) *Total amount:* $8,580,780 (2% state, 51% institutional, 47% external sources). *Receiving aid:* Freshmen: 28% (425); Undergraduates: 20% (1,468). *Average Award:* Freshmen: $3120; Undergraduates: $2852. *Scholarships, grants, and awards by category: Academic Interests/Achievement:* agriculture, biological sciences, business, communication, computer science, education, general academic interests/achievements, health fields, home economics, mathematics, military science, physical sciences, premedicine. *Creative Arts/Performance:* applied art and design, art/fine arts, journalism/publications, music, theater/drama. *Special Achievements/Activities:* cheerleading/drum major, general special achievements/activities, hobbies/interests, leadership, rodeo. *Special Characteristics:* adult students, children of union members/company employees, first-generation college students, general special characteristics, local/state students, previous college experience, religious affiliation. *Tuition waivers:* Full or partial for employees or children of employees. *ROTC:* Army.
LOANS *Student loans:* $41,659,444 (50% need-based, 50% non-need-based). 62% of past graduating class borrowed through all loan programs. *Average indebtedness per student:* $17,243. *Average need-based loan:* Freshmen: $1262; Undergraduates: $2126. *Parent loans:* $5,782,828 (100% non-need-based). *Programs:* FFEL (Subsidized and Unsubsidized Stafford, PLUS), Perkins, state, college/university, alternative loans.
WORK-STUDY *Federal work-study:* Total amount: $708,157; 493 jobs averaging $1436. *State or other work-study/employment:* Total amount: $100,227 (100% need-based). 72 part-time jobs averaging $1392.
ATHLETIC AWARDS Total amount: $1,740,149 (100% non-need-based).
APPLYING FOR FINANCIAL AID *Required financial aid forms:* FAFSA, institution's own form. *Financial aid deadline:* 5/15 (priority: 4/1). *Notification date:* Continuous beginning 4/10. Students must reply within 3 weeks of notification.
CONTACT Office of Financial Aid, Stephen F. Austin State University, PO Box 13052, SFA Station, Nacogdoches, TX 75962, 936-468-2403 or toll-free 800-731-2902. *Fax:* 936-468-1048. *E-mail:* finaid@sfasu.edu.

STEPHENS COLLEGE
Columbia, MO

Tuition & fees: $20,500   **Average undergraduate aid package:** $16,894

ABOUT THE INSTITUTION Independent, undergraduate: women only; graduate: coed. Awards: bachelor's and master's degrees and post-bachelor's certificates. 35 undergraduate majors. Total enrollment: 824. Undergraduates: 754. Freshmen: 203. Federal methodology is used as a basis for awarding need-based institutional aid.
UNDERGRADUATE EXPENSES for 2006–07 *Application fee:* $25. *Comprehensive fee:* $28,475 includes full-time tuition ($20,500) and room and board ($7975). *College room only:* $4760. *Part-time tuition:* $220 per hour.
FRESHMAN FINANCIAL AID (Fall 2005, est.) 181 applied for aid; of those 87% were deemed to have need. 100% of freshmen with need received aid; of those 28% had need fully met. *Average percent of need met:* 82% (excluding resources awarded to replace EFC). *Average financial aid package:* $17,252 (excluding resources awarded to replace EFC). 20% of all full-time freshmen had no need and received non-need-based gift aid.
UNDERGRADUATE FINANCIAL AID (Fall 2005, est.) 485 applied for aid; of those 88% were deemed to have need. 100% of undergraduates with need received aid; of those 21% had need fully met. *Average percent of need met:*

Stephens College

83% (excluding resources awarded to replace EFC). *Average financial aid package:* $16,894 (excluding resources awarded to replace EFC). 21% of all full-time undergraduates had no need and received non-need-based gift aid.
GIFT AID (NEED-BASED) *Total amount:* $4,742,526 (12% federal, 5% state, 81% institutional, 2% external sources). *Receiving aid:* Freshmen: 64% (129); All full-time undergraduates: 54% (314). *Average award:* Freshmen: $6755; Undergraduates: $6533. *Scholarships, grants, and awards:* Federal Pell, FSEOG, state, private, college/university gift aid from institutional funds.
GIFT AID (NON-NEED-BASED) *Total amount:* $1,728,840 (1% state, 97% institutional, 2% external sources). *Receiving aid:* Freshmen: 76% (154); Undergraduates: 71% (413). *Average Award:* Freshmen: $7892; Undergraduates:* $7714. *Scholarships, grants, and awards by category:* Academic Interests/Achievement: 457 awards ($2,945,580 total): general academic interests/achievements. *Creative Arts/Performance:* 75 awards ($314,030 total): dance, performing arts, theater/drama. *Special Achievements/Activities:* 339 awards ($602,326 total): leadership. *Special Characteristics:* 152 awards ($355,822 total): children of faculty/staff, local/state students, out-of-state students, siblings of current students. *ROTC:* Army cooperative, Air Force cooperative.
LOANS *Student loans:* $2,084,325 (62% need-based, 38% non-need-based). 63% of past graduating class borrowed through all loan programs. *Average indebtedness per student:* $19,396. *Average need-based loan:* Freshmen: $2735; Undergraduates: $3907. *Parent loans:* $1,150,217 (15% need-based, 85% non-need-based). *Programs:* FFEL (Subsidized and Unsubsidized Stafford, PLUS), Perkins, alternative loans.
WORK-STUDY *Federal work-study:* Total amount: $60,085; 43 jobs averaging $1397. *State or other work-study/employment:* Total amount: $196,255 (100% non-need-based). 141 part-time jobs averaging $1392.
ATHLETIC AWARDS Total amount: $150,898 (66% need-based, 34% non-need-based).
APPLYING FOR FINANCIAL AID *Required financial aid form:* FAFSA. *Financial aid deadline (priority):* 3/15. *Notification date:* Continuous beginning 3/1.
CONTACT Mrs. Rachel Touchatt, Financial Aid Director, Stephens College, 1200 East Broadway, Campus Box 2124, Columbia, MO 65215-0002, 800-876-7207. *Fax:* 573-876-2320. *E-mail:* finaid@stephens.edu.

STERLING COLLEGE
Sterling, KS

ABOUT THE INSTITUTION Independent Presbyterian, coed. Awards: bachelor's degrees. 19 undergraduate majors. Total enrollment: 516. Undergraduates: 494. Freshmen: 127.
GIFT AID (NEED-BASED) *Scholarships, grants, and awards:* Federal Pell, FSEOG, state, private, college/university gift aid from institutional funds.
GIFT AID (NON-NEED-BASED) *Scholarships, grants, and awards by category:* Academic Interests/Achievement: general academic interests/achievements. Creative Arts/Performance: art/fine arts, debating, general creative arts/performance, music, theater/drama. *Special Characteristics:* children and siblings of alumni, siblings of current students, twins.
LOANS *Programs:* FFEL (Subsidized and Unsubsidized Stafford, PLUS), Perkins, college/university.
WORK-STUDY *Federal work-study:* Total amount: $216,238; 169 jobs averaging $501. *State or other work-study/employment:* Total amount: $203,123 (100% need-based). 196 part-time jobs averaging $808.
APPLYING FOR FINANCIAL AID *Required financial aid form:* FAFSA.
CONTACT Ms. Jodi Lightner, Director of Financial Aid, Sterling College, PO Box 98, Sterling, KS 67579-0098, 620-278-4207 or toll-free 800-346-1017. *Fax:* 620-278-4416. *E-mail:* jlightner@sterling.edu.

STERLING COLLEGE
Craftsbury Common, VT

Tuition & fees: $16,950 **Average undergraduate aid package:** $14,345

ABOUT THE INSTITUTION Independent, coed. Awards: associate and bachelor's degrees. 85 undergraduate majors. Total enrollment: 98. Undergraduates: 98. Freshmen: 17. Both federal and institutional methodology are used as a basis for awarding need-based institutional aid.
UNDERGRADUATE EXPENSES for 2005–06 *Application fee:* $35. *Comprehensive fee:* $23,286 includes full-time tuition ($16,600), mandatory fees ($350), and room and board ($6336). *College room only:* $2860. Full-time tuition and fees vary according to course load. Room and board charges vary according to board plan. *Part-time tuition:* $520 per credit. Part-time tuition and fees vary according to course load. *Payment plan:* Installment.
FRESHMAN FINANCIAL AID (Fall 2004) 17 applied for aid; of those 82% were deemed to have need. 100% of freshmen with need received aid. *Average percent of need met:* 77% (excluding resources awarded to replace EFC). *Average financial aid package:* $13,979 (excluding resources awarded to replace EFC). 11% of all full-time freshmen had no need and received non-need-based gift aid.
UNDERGRADUATE FINANCIAL AID (Fall 2004) 67 applied for aid; of those 90% were deemed to have need. 100% of undergraduates with need received aid; of those 3% had need fully met. *Average percent of need met:* 75% (excluding resources awarded to replace EFC). *Average financial aid package:* $14,345 (excluding resources awarded to replace EFC). 6% of all full-time undergraduates had no need and received non-need-based gift aid.
GIFT AID (NEED-BASED) *Total amount:* $546,028 (23% federal, 10% state, 64% institutional, 3% external sources). *Receiving aid:* Freshmen: 78% (14); All full-time undergraduates: 69% (60). *Average award:* Freshmen: $9255; Undergraduates: $9033. *Scholarships, grants, and awards:* Federal Pell, FSEOG, state, private, college/university gift aid from institutional funds.
GIFT AID (NON-NEED-BASED) *Total amount:* $6000 (100% institutional). *Average Award:* Freshmen: $1000; Undergraduates: $1200. *Scholarships, grants, and awards by category:* Academic Interests/Achievement: 6 awards ($14,500 total): general academic interests/achievements. *Special Achievements/Activities:* 11 awards ($13,000 total): general special achievements/activities. *Special Characteristics:* 30 awards ($29,375 total): general special characteristics, local/state students, previous college experience. *Tuition waivers:* Full or partial for employees or children of employees.
LOANS *Student loans:* $363,618 (97% need-based, 3% non-need-based). 57% of past graduating class borrowed through all loan programs. *Average indebtedness per student:* $28,251. *Average need-based loan:* Freshmen: $2625; Undergraduates: $3347. *Parent loans:* $207,983 (35% need-based, 65% non-need-based). *Programs:* FFEL (Subsidized and Unsubsidized Stafford, PLUS).
WORK-STUDY *Federal work-study:* Total amount: $9832; 29 jobs averaging $339. *State or other work-study/employment:* Total amount: $102,902 (80% need-based, 20% non-need-based). 71 part-time jobs averaging $1449.
APPLYING FOR FINANCIAL AID *Required financial aid forms:* FAFSA, institution's own form, state aid form. *Financial aid deadline:* Continuous. *Notification date:* Continuous beginning 1/31. Students must reply by 5/1 or within 2 weeks of notification.
CONTACT Barbara Stuart, Associate Director of Financial Aid, Sterling College, PO Box 72, Craftsbury Common, VT 05827, 800-648-3591 Ext. 2 or toll-free 800-648-3591 Ext. 100. *Fax:* 802-586-2596. *E-mail:* bstuart@sterlingcollege.edu.

STETSON UNIVERSITY
DeLand, FL

Tuition & fees: $25,450 **Average undergraduate aid package:** $21,991

ABOUT THE INSTITUTION Independent, coed. Awards: bachelor's, master's, and first professional degrees and post-master's and first professional certificates. 60 undergraduate majors. Total enrollment: 3,665. Undergraduates: 2,234. Freshmen: 550. Federal methodology is used as a basis for awarding need-based institutional aid.
UNDERGRADUATE EXPENSES for 2005–06 *Application fee:* $40. *Comprehensive fee:* $32,725 includes full-time tuition ($23,975), mandatory fees ($1475), and room and board ($7275). *College room only:* $4075. Full-time tuition and fees vary according to course load and student level. Room and board charges vary according to board plan and housing facility. *Part-time tuition:* $760 per credit hour. Part-time tuition and fees vary according to course load. *Payment plan:* Installment.
FRESHMAN FINANCIAL AID (Fall 2005, est.) 436 applied for aid; of those 81% were deemed to have need. 100% of freshmen with need received aid; of those 43% had need fully met. *Average percent of need met:* 90% (excluding resources awarded to replace EFC). *Average financial aid package:* $22,588 (excluding resources awarded to replace EFC). 28% of all full-time freshmen had no need and received non-need-based gift aid.
UNDERGRADUATE FINANCIAL AID (Fall 2005, est.) 1,345 applied for aid; of those 85% were deemed to have need. 100% of undergraduates with need

received aid; of those 38% had need fully met. *Average percent of need met:* 86% (excluding resources awarded to replace EFC). *Average financial aid package:* $21,991 (excluding resources awarded to replace EFC). 35% of all full-time undergraduates had no need and received non-need-based gift aid.
GIFT AID (NEED-BASED) *Total amount:* $13,363,008 (11% federal, 4% state, 85% institutional). *Receiving aid:* Freshmen: 64% (350); All full-time undergraduates: 53% (1,132). *Average award:* Freshmen: $19,028; Undergraduates: $16,755. *Scholarships, grants, and awards:* Federal Pell, FSEOG, state, private, college/university gift aid from institutional funds.
GIFT AID (NON-NEED-BASED) *Total amount:* $16,093,623 (45% state, 51% institutional, 4% external sources). *Receiving aid:* Freshmen: 64% (349); Undergraduates: 53% (1,119). *Average Award:* Freshmen: $11,309; Undergraduates:* $9975. *Scholarships, grants, and awards by category: Academic Interests/Achievement:* area/ethnic studies, biological sciences, business, communication, computer science, education, English, foreign languages, general academic interests/achievements, humanities, mathematics, military science, physical sciences, premedicine, religion/biblical studies, social sciences. *Creative Arts/Performance:* applied art and design, art/fine arts, music, theater/drama. *Special Achievements/Activities:* cheerleading/drum major, community service, general special achievements/activities, leadership, religious involvement. *Special Characteristics:* children and siblings of alumni, children of faculty/staff, ethnic background, general special characteristics, international students, local/state students, members of minority groups. *Tuition waivers:* Full or partial for employees or children of employees. *ROTC:* Army cooperative.
LOANS *Student loans:* $7,854,304 (64% need-based, 36% non-need-based). 55% of past graduating class borrowed through all loan programs. *Average indebtedness per student:* $21,500. *Average need-based loan:* Freshmen: $3607; Undergraduates: $4983. *Parent loans:* $2,168,014 (75% need-based, 25% non-need-based). *Programs:* FFEL (Subsidized and Unsubsidized Stafford, PLUS), Perkins, college/university.
WORK-STUDY *Federal work-study:* Total amount: $1,361,333; 576 jobs averaging $2363. *State or other work-study/employment:* Total amount: $820,900 (50% need-based, 50% non-need-based). 314 part-time jobs averaging $2614.
ATHLETIC AWARDS *Total amount:* $2,630,585 (33% need-based, 67% non-need-based).
APPLYING FOR FINANCIAL AID *Required financial aid forms:* FAFSA, institution's own form. *Financial aid deadline (priority):* 3/15. *Notification date:* Continuous beginning 2/15. Students must reply within 2 weeks of notification.
CONTACT Terry Whittum, Dean of Admissions and Financial Aid, Stetson University, 421 North Woodland Boulevard, DeLand, FL 32723, 386-822-7120 or toll-free 800-688-0101. *Fax:* 386-822-7126. *E-mail:* finaid@stetson.edu.

STEVENS-HENAGER COLLEGE
Boise, ID

CONTACT Financial Aid Office, Stevens-Henager College, 730 Americana Boulevard, Boise, ID 83702, 801-345-0700.

STEVENS INSTITUTE OF TECHNOLOGY
Hoboken, NJ

Tuition & fees: $31,835   **Average undergraduate aid package: $21,139**

ABOUT THE INSTITUTION Independent, coed. Awards: bachelor's, master's, and doctoral degrees and post-bachelor's certificates. 26 undergraduate majors. Total enrollment: 4,689. Undergraduates: 1,789. Freshmen: 484. Federal methodology is used as a basis for awarding need-based institutional aid.
UNDERGRADUATE EXPENSES for 2005–06 *Application fee:* $55. *Comprehensive fee:* $41,335 includes full-time tuition ($30,240), mandatory fees ($1595), and room and board ($9500). *College room only:* $4800. Full-time tuition and fees vary according to student level. Room and board charges vary according to board plan and housing facility. *Part-time tuition:* $1008 per credit. *Part-time fees:* $528 per term. *Payment plan:* Installment.
FRESHMAN FINANCIAL AID (Fall 2005, est.) 430 applied for aid; of those 81% were deemed to have need. 100% of freshmen with need received aid; of those 27% had need fully met. *Average percent of need met:* 86% (excluding resources awarded to replace EFC). *Average financial aid package:* $25,792 (excluding resources awarded to replace EFC). 9% of all full-time freshmen had no need and received non-need-based gift aid.

UNDERGRADUATE FINANCIAL AID (Fall 2005, est.) 1,645 applied for aid; of those 87% were deemed to have need. 86% of undergraduates with need received aid; of those 20% had need fully met. *Average percent of need met:* 85% (excluding resources awarded to replace EFC). *Average financial aid package:* $21,139 (excluding resources awarded to replace EFC). 16% of all full-time undergraduates had no need and received non-need-based gift aid.
GIFT AID (NEED-BASED) *Total amount:* $12,050,000 (10% federal, 15% state, 75% institutional). *Receiving aid:* Freshmen: 55% (279); All full-time undergraduates: 53% (961). *Average award:* Freshmen: $15,021; Undergraduates: $12,871. *Scholarships, grants, and awards:* Federal Pell, FSEOG, state, private, college/university gift aid from institutional funds.
GIFT AID (NON-NEED-BASED) *Total amount:* $11,910,000 (2% state, 92% institutional, 6% external sources). *Receiving aid:* Freshmen: 57% (292); Undergraduates: 49% (886). *Average Award:* Freshmen: $11,909; Undergraduates:* $9973. *Scholarships, grants, and awards by category: Academic Interests/Achievement:* 1,450 awards ($10,800,000 total): business, computer science, engineering/technologies, general academic interests/achievements, humanities, mathematics, physical sciences, premedicine. *Creative Arts/Performance:* 52 awards ($154,500 total): art/fine arts, journalism/publications, music, performing arts, theater/drama. *Special Characteristics:* 85 awards ($920,000 total): children and siblings of alumni, children of educators, children of faculty/staff, international students, local/state students, members of minority groups. *Tuition waivers:* Full or partial for employees or children of employees. *ROTC:* Army cooperative, Air Force cooperative.
LOANS *Student loans:* $6,500,000 (72% need-based, 28% non-need-based). 68% of past graduating class borrowed through all loan programs. *Average indebtedness per student:* $14,113. *Average need-based loan:* Freshmen: $3655; Undergraduates: $4203. *Parent loans:* $3,100,000 (100% non-need-based). *Programs:* Federal Direct (Subsidized and Unsubsidized Stafford, PLUS), Perkins, state, Sallie Mae Signature Loans, TERI Loans, NJ Class Loans, CitiAssist Loans.
WORK-STUDY *Federal work-study:* Total amount: $500,000; 818 jobs averaging $1269.
APPLYING FOR FINANCIAL AID *Required financial aid form:* FAFSA. *Financial aid deadline (priority):* 2/15. *Notification date:* Continuous beginning 3/30. Students must reply by 5/1.
CONTACT Ms. Adrienne Hynek, Associate Director of Financial Aid, Stevens Institute of Technology, Castle Point on Hudson, Hoboken, NJ 07030, 201-216-5555 or toll-free 800-458-5323. *Fax:* 201-216-8050. *E-mail:* ahynek@stevens.edu.

STILLMAN COLLEGE
Tuscaloosa, AL

CONTACT Jacqueline S. Morris, Director of Financial Aid, Stillman College, PO Box 1430, Tuscaloosa, AL 35403, 205-366-8950 or toll-free 800-841-5722. *Fax:* 205-247-8106.

STONEHILL COLLEGE
Easton, MA

Tuition & fees: $25,540   **Average undergraduate aid package: $17,828**

ABOUT THE INSTITUTION Independent Roman Catholic, coed. Awards: bachelor's and master's degrees. 32 undergraduate majors. Total enrollment: 2,443. Undergraduates: 2,431. Freshmen: 619. Both federal and institutional methodology are used as a basis for awarding need-based institutional aid.
UNDERGRADUATE EXPENSES for 2005–06 *Application fee:* $50. *Comprehensive fee:* $36,104 includes full-time tuition ($25,540) and room and board ($10,564). *Part-time tuition:* $840 per course. *Part-time fees:* $25 per term. Part-time tuition and fees vary according to course load. *Payment plans:* Tuition prepayment, installment.
FRESHMAN FINANCIAL AID (Fall 2005, est.) 519 applied for aid; of those 77% were deemed to have need. 100% of freshmen with need received aid; of those 28% had need fully met. *Average percent of need met:* 82% (excluding resources awarded to replace EFC). *Average financial aid package:* $17,917 (excluding resources awarded to replace EFC). 28% of all full-time freshmen had no need and received non-need-based gift aid.
UNDERGRADUATE FINANCIAL AID (Fall 2005, est.) 1,733 applied for aid; of those 82% were deemed to have need. 100% of undergraduates with need

Stonehill College

received aid; of those 21% had need fully met. *Average percent of need met:* 88% (excluding resources awarded to replace EFC). *Average financial aid package:* $17,828 (excluding resources awarded to replace EFC). 24% of all full-time undergraduates had no need and received non-need-based gift aid. **GIFT AID (NEED-BASED)** *Total amount:* $17,049,050 (4% federal, 5% state, 86% institutional, 5% external sources). *Receiving aid:* Freshmen: 62% (385); All full-time undergraduates: 61% (1,367). *Average award:* Freshmen: $13,594; Undergraduates: $12,896. *Scholarships, grants, and awards:* Federal Pell, FSEOG, state, private, college/university gift aid from institutional funds. **GIFT AID (NON-NEED-BASED)** *Total amount:* $3,319,479 (83% institutional, 17% external sources). *Receiving aid:* Freshmen: 8% (48); Undergraduates: 6% (142). *Average Award:* Freshmen: $11,272; Undergraduates: $1325. *Scholarships, grants, and awards by category: Academic Interests/Achievement:* 1,224 awards ($7,152,377 total): general academic interests/achievements. *Special Characteristics:* 141 awards ($1,638,254 total): children of faculty/staff, members of minority groups, relatives of clergy, siblings of current students. *Tuition waivers:* Full or partial for employees or children of employees. *ROTC:* Army. **LOANS** *Student loans:* $12,105,617 (65% need-based, 35% non-need-based). 75% of past graduating class borrowed through all loan programs. *Average indebtedness per student:* $19,712. *Average need-based loan:* Freshmen: $4798; Undergraduates: $5337. *Parent loans:* $7,727,719 (28% need-based, 72% non-need-based). *Programs:* Federal Direct (Subsidized and Unsubsidized Stafford, PLUS), Perkins, state. **WORK-STUDY** *Federal work-study:* Total amount: $1,568,544; 857 jobs averaging $1830. *State or other work-study/employment:* Total amount: $317,516 (2% need-based, 98% non-need-based). 256 part-time jobs averaging $1240. **ATHLETIC AWARDS** *Total amount:* $1,417,723 (56% need-based, 44% non-need-based). **APPLYING FOR FINANCIAL AID** *Required financial aid forms:* FAFSA, CSS Financial Aid PROFILE, noncustodial (divorced/separated) parent's statement, business/farm supplement. *Financial aid deadline (priority):* 2/1. *Notification date:* 4/1. Students must reply by 5/1. **CONTACT** Rhonda Nickley, Staff Assistant, Stonehill College, 320 Washington Street, Easton, MA 02357, 508-565-1088. *Fax:* 508-565-1426. *E-mail:* finaid@stonehill.edu.

STONY BROOK UNIVERSITY, STATE UNIVERSITY OF NEW YORK
Stony Brook, NY

Tuition & fees (NY res): $5575 **Average undergraduate aid package:** $8331

ABOUT THE INSTITUTION State-supported, coed. Awards: bachelor's, master's, doctoral, and first professional degrees and post-bachelor's, post-master's, and first professional certificates. 58 undergraduate majors. Total enrollment: 22,011. Undergraduates: 14,287. Freshmen: 2,508. Federal methodology is used as a basis for awarding need-based institutional aid.
UNDERGRADUATE EXPENSES for 2005–06 *Application fee:* $40. *Tuition, state resident:* full-time $4350; part-time $181 per credit. *Tuition, nonresident:* full-time $10,610; part-time $442 per credit. *Required fees:* full-time $1225; $59.30 per credit. *College room and board:* $8050. Room and board charges vary according to board plan and housing facility. *Payment plan:* Installment.
FRESHMAN FINANCIAL AID (Fall 2004) 1702 applied for aid; of those 72% were deemed to have need. 98% of freshmen with need received aid; of those 10% had need fully met. *Average percent of need met:* 67% (excluding resources awarded to replace EFC). *Average financial aid package:* $8066 (excluding resources awarded to replace EFC). 18% of all full-time freshmen had no need and received non-need-based gift aid.
UNDERGRADUATE FINANCIAL AID (Fall 2004) 9,057 applied for aid; of those 82% were deemed to have need. 98% of undergraduates with need received aid; of those 10% had need fully met. *Average percent of need met:* 68% (excluding resources awarded to replace EFC). *Average financial aid package:* $8331 (excluding resources awarded to replace EFC). 10% of all full-time undergraduates had no need and received non-need-based gift aid.
GIFT AID (NEED-BASED) *Total amount:* $35,927,898 (44% federal, 51% state, 3% institutional, 2% external sources). *Receiving aid:* Freshmen: 54% (1,141); All full-time undergraduates: 53% (6,621). *Average award:* Freshmen: $5979; Undergraduates: $5323. *Scholarships, grants, and awards:* Federal Pell, FSEOG, state, private, college/university gift aid from institutional funds.
GIFT AID (NON-NEED-BASED) *Total amount:* $3,248,318 (6% federal, 12% state, 64% institutional, 18% external sources). *Receiving aid:* Freshmen: 5% (109); Undergraduates: 5% (596). *Average Award:* Freshmen: $2487; Undergraduates: $2385. *Scholarships, grants, and awards by category: Academic Interests/Achievement:* 1,122 awards ($3,171,433 total): area/ethnic studies, biological sciences, business, computer science, engineering/technologies, English, general academic interests/achievements, health fields, physical sciences, social sciences. *Creative Arts/Performance:* 9 awards ($17,200 total): music, theater/drama. *Special Achievements/Activities:* general special achievements/activities. *ROTC:* Army cooperative, Air Force cooperative.
LOANS *Student loans:* $40,362,420 (75% need-based, 25% non-need-based). 61% of past graduating class borrowed through all loan programs. *Average indebtedness per student:* $14,437. *Average need-based loan:* Freshmen: $2763; Undergraduates: $4019. *Parent loans:* $5,618,259 (34% need-based, 66% non-need-based). *Programs:* FFEL (Subsidized and Unsubsidized Stafford, PLUS), Perkins.
WORK-STUDY *Federal work-study:* Total amount: $686,584; 419 jobs averaging $1639. *State or other work-study/employment:* Total amount: $4,004,606 (40% need-based, 60% non-need-based). 1,719 part-time jobs averaging $2330.
ATHLETIC AWARDS *Total amount:* $2,456,125 (33% need-based, 67% non-need-based).
APPLYING FOR FINANCIAL AID *Required financial aid form:* FAFSA. *Financial aid deadline (priority):* 3/1. *Notification date:* Continuous beginning 3/7. Students must reply within 2 weeks of notification.
CONTACT Jacqueline Pascariello, Director of Financial Aid and Student Employment, Stony Brook University, State University of New York, 180 Administration Building, Stony Brook, NY 11794-0851, 631-632-6840 or toll-free 800-872-7869 (out-of-state). *Fax:* 631-632-9525.

STRATFORD UNIVERSITY
Falls Church, VA

CONTACT Financial Aid Office, Stratford University, 7777 Leesburg Pike, Suite 100 South, Falls Church, VA 22043, 703-821-8570 or toll-free 800-444-0804.

STRAYER UNIVERSITY
Washington, DC

CONTACT Ms. Marjorie Arrington, Director of Financial Aid, Strayer University, 1133 15th Street, NW, Washington, DC 20005-2603, 703-558-7020 or toll-free 888-4-STRAYER. *Fax:* 703-741-3710. *E-mail:* ma@strayer.edu.

SUFFOLK UNIVERSITY
Boston, MA

Tuition & fees: $21,220 **Average undergraduate aid package:** $13,162

ABOUT THE INSTITUTION Independent, coed. Awards: associate, bachelor's, master's, doctoral, and first professional degrees and post-bachelor's, post-master's, and first professional certificates (doctoral degree in law). 61 undergraduate majors. Total enrollment: 8,474. Undergraduates: 4,784. Freshmen: 1,136. Both federal and institutional methodology are used as a basis for awarding need-based institutional aid.
UNDERGRADUATE EXPENSES for 2005–06 *Application fee:* $50. *Comprehensive fee:* $33,160 includes full-time tuition ($21,140), mandatory fees ($80), and room and board ($11,940). *College room only:* $10,020. Room and board charges vary according to board plan and housing facility. *Part-time tuition:* $526 per credit. *Part-time fees:* $10 per term. *Payment plans:* Installment, deferred payment.
FRESHMAN FINANCIAL AID (Fall 2005, est.) 862 applied for aid; of those 74% were deemed to have need. 100% of freshmen with need received aid; of those 15% had need fully met. *Average percent of need met:* 63% (excluding resources awarded to replace EFC). *Average financial aid package:* $12,025 (excluding resources awarded to replace EFC). 9% of all full-time freshmen had no need and received non-need-based gift aid.
UNDERGRADUATE FINANCIAL AID (Fall 2005, est.) 2,789 applied for aid; of those 79% were deemed to have need. 100% of undergraduates with need received aid; of those 14% had need fully met. *Average percent of need met:* 65% (excluding resources awarded to replace EFC). *Average financial aid*

package: $13,162 (excluding resources awarded to replace EFC). 9% of all full-time undergraduates had no need and received non-need-based gift aid.
GIFT AID (NEED-BASED) *Total amount:* $13,292,637 (21% federal, 10% state, 65% institutional, 4% external sources). *Receiving aid:* Freshmen: 47% (530); All full-time undergraduates: 35% (1,416). *Average award:* Freshmen: $6685; Undergraduates: $6828. *Scholarships, grants, and awards:* Federal Pell, FSEOG, state, private, college/university gift aid from institutional funds.
GIFT AID (NON-NEED-BASED) *Total amount:* $4,602,511 (99% institutional, 1% external sources). *Receiving aid:* Freshmen: 14% (160); Undergraduates: 16% (662). *Average Award:* Freshmen: $6978; Undergraduates: $5557. *Scholarships, grants, and awards by category: Academic Interests/Achievement:* 715 awards ($3,984,220 total): general academic interests/achievements. *Special Achievements/Activities:* 3 awards ($9000 total): community service. *Special Characteristics:* 138 awards ($96,425 total): children and siblings of alumni, children of faculty/staff, siblings of current students. *Tuition waivers:* Full or partial for employees or children of employees, senior citizens. *ROTC:* Army cooperative.
LOANS *Student loans:* $28,364,359 (40% need-based, 60% non-need-based). 61% of past graduating class borrowed through all loan programs. *Average indebtedness per student:* $19,012. *Average need-based loan:* Freshmen: $3768; Undergraduates: $4660. *Parent loans:* $9,805,108 (100% non-need-based). *Programs:* Federal Direct (Subsidized and Unsubsidized Stafford, PLUS), Perkins, state, college/university.
WORK-STUDY *Federal work-study:* Total amount: $1,675,135; 721 jobs averaging $2066. *State or other work-study/employment:* Total amount: $572,028 (100% non-need-based). 255 part-time jobs averaging $2256.
APPLYING FOR FINANCIAL AID *Required financial aid forms:* FAFSA, institution's own form. *Financial aid deadline:* 4/1 (priority: 3/1). *Notification date:* Continuous. Students must reply within 2 weeks of notification.
CONTACT Ms. Christine A. Perry, Director of Financial Aid, Suffolk University, 8 Ashburton Place, Boston, MA 02108, 617-573-8470 or toll-free 800-6-SUFFOLK. *Fax:* 617-720-3579. *E-mail:* finaid@suffolk.edu.

SULLIVAN UNIVERSITY
Louisville, KY

CONTACT Charlene Geiser, Financial Planning Office, Sullivan University, 3101 Bardstown Road, Louisville, KY 40205, 502-456-6504 Ext. 311 or toll-free 800-844-1354. *Fax:* 502-456-0040. *E-mail:* cgeiser@sullivan.edu.

SUL ROSS STATE UNIVERSITY
Alpine, TX

CONTACT Ms. Rena Gallego, Director of Financial Assistance and Recruiting, Sul Ross State University, PO Box C-113, Alpine, TX 79832, 915-837-8059 or toll-free 888-722-7778.

SUSQUEHANNA UNIVERSITY
Selinsgrove, PA

ABOUT THE INSTITUTION Independent religious, coed. Awards: bachelor's degrees (also offers evening associate degree program limited to local adult students). 54 undergraduate majors. Total enrollment: 1,989. Undergraduates: 1,989. Freshmen: 512.
GIFT AID (NEED-BASED) *Scholarships, grants, and awards:* Federal Pell, FSEOG, state, private, college/university gift aid from institutional funds.
GIFT AID (NON-NEED-BASED) *Scholarships, grants, and awards by category: Academic Interests/Achievement:* biological sciences, business, general academic interests/achievements, mathematics, physical sciences, premedicine. *Creative Arts/Performance:* creative writing, music. *Special Achievements/Activities:* general special achievements/activities. *Special Characteristics:* children of educators, children of faculty/staff, members of minority groups, relatives of clergy.
LOANS *Programs:* FFEL (Subsidized and Unsubsidized Stafford, PLUS), Perkins, college/university.
WORK-STUDY *Federal work-study:* Total amount: $1,424,825; 905 jobs averaging $1574. *State or other work-study/employment:* Total amount: $244,195 (46% need-based, 54% non-need-based). 64 part-time jobs averaging $3816.
APPLYING FOR FINANCIAL AID *Required financial aid forms:* FAFSA, CSS Financial Aid PROFILE, business/farm supplement, income tax form(s).

CONTACT Helen S. Nunn, Director of Financial Aid, Susquehanna University, 514 University Avenue, Selinsgrove, PA 17870, 570-372-4450 or toll-free 800-326-9672. *Fax:* 570-372-2722. *E-mail:* nunn@susqu.edu.

SWARTHMORE COLLEGE
Swarthmore, PA

Tuition & fees: $31,516   **Average undergraduate aid package: $28,914**

ABOUT THE INSTITUTION Independent, coed. Awards: bachelor's degrees. 44 undergraduate majors. Total enrollment: 1,479. Undergraduates: 1,479. Freshmen: 389. Institutional methodology is used as a basis for awarding need-based institutional aid.
UNDERGRADUATE EXPENSES for 2005–06 *Application fee:* $60. *Comprehensive fee:* $41,280 includes full-time tuition ($31,196), mandatory fees ($320), and room and board ($9764). *College room only:* $5006. Room and board charges vary according to board plan. *Payment plan:* Installment.
FRESHMAN FINANCIAL AID (Fall 2005, est.) 257 applied for aid; of those 78% were deemed to have need. 100% of freshmen with need received aid; of those 100% had need fully met. *Average percent of need met:* 100% (excluding resources awarded to replace EFC). *Average financial aid package:* $29,935 (excluding resources awarded to replace EFC). 1% of all full-time freshmen had no need and received non-need-based gift aid.
UNDERGRADUATE FINANCIAL AID (Fall 2005, est.) 798 applied for aid; of those 89% were deemed to have need. 100% of undergraduates with need received aid; of those 100% had need fully met. *Average percent of need met:* 100% (excluding resources awarded to replace EFC). *Average financial aid package:* $28,914 (excluding resources awarded to replace EFC). 1% of all full-time undergraduates had no need and received non-need-based gift aid.
GIFT AID (NEED-BASED) *Total amount:* $17,699,426 (4% federal, 1% state, 92% institutional, 3% external sources). *Receiving aid:* Freshmen: 51% (200); All full-time undergraduates: 48% (708). *Average award:* Freshmen: $26,824; Undergraduates: $24,980. *Scholarships, grants, and awards:* Federal Pell, FSEOG, state, private, college/university gift aid from institutional funds.
GIFT AID (NON-NEED-BASED) *Total amount:* $681,072 (1% state, 55% institutional, 44% external sources). *Average Award:* Freshmen: $31,196; Undergraduates: $31,196. *Scholarships, grants, and awards by category: Academic Interests/Achievement:* 12 awards ($374,352 total): general academic interests/achievements. *Tuition waivers:* Full or partial for employees or children of employees. *ROTC:* Army cooperative, Air Force cooperative.
LOANS *Student loans:* $1,880,888 (89% need-based, 11% non-need-based). 36% of past graduating class borrowed through all loan programs. *Average indebtedness per student:* $12,413. *Average need-based loan:* Freshmen: $2199; Undergraduates: $3179. *Parent loans:* $2,568,713 (100% non-need-based). *Programs:* FFEL (Subsidized and Unsubsidized Stafford, PLUS), Perkins, state, college/university.
WORK-STUDY *Federal work-study:* Total amount: $650,392; 632 jobs averaging $1574. *State or other work-study/employment:* Total amount: $613,578 (76% need-based, 24% non-need-based). Part-time jobs available.
APPLYING FOR FINANCIAL AID *Required financial aid forms:* FAFSA, institution's own form, CSS Financial Aid PROFILE, state aid form, noncustodial (divorced/separated) parent's statement, business/farm supplement, federal tax return, W2 statement, year-end paycheck stub. *Financial aid deadline:* 2/15. *Notification date:* 4/1. Students must reply by 5/1.
CONTACT Laura Talbot, Director of Financial Aid, Swarthmore College, 500 College Avenue, Swarthmore, PA 19081-1397, 610-328-8358 or toll-free 800-667-3110. *Fax:* 610-328-8673. *E-mail:* finaid@swarthmore.edu.

SWEDISH INSTITUTE, COLLEGE OF HEALTH SCIENCES
New York, NY

CONTACT Financial Aid Office, Swedish Institute, College of Health Sciences, 226 West 26th Street, New York, NY 10001-6700, 212-924-5900.

Sweet Briar College

SWEET BRIAR COLLEGE
Sweet Briar, VA

Tuition & fees: $23,340 | **Average undergraduate aid package: $15,293**

ABOUT THE INSTITUTION Independent, women only. Awards: bachelor's and master's degrees. 34 undergraduate majors. Total enrollment: 752. Undergraduates: 739. Freshmen: 182. Federal methodology is used as a basis for awarding need-based institutional aid.
UNDERGRADUATE EXPENSES for 2006–07 *Application fee:* $40. *Comprehensive fee:* $32,820 includes full-time tuition ($23,340) and room and board ($9480). *College room only:* $3810. *Part-time tuition:* $775 per credit hour.
FRESHMAN FINANCIAL AID (Fall 2005, est.) 123 applied for aid; of those 100% were deemed to have need. 99% of freshmen with need received aid; of those 95% had need fully met. *Average percent of need met:* 36% (excluding resources awarded to replace EFC). *Average financial aid package:* $14,480 (excluding resources awarded to replace EFC). 47% of all full-time freshmen had no need and received non-need-based gift aid.
UNDERGRADUATE FINANCIAL AID (Fall 2005, est.) 346 applied for aid; of those 100% were deemed to have need. 99% of undergraduates with need received aid; of those 100% had need fully met. *Average percent of need met:* 39% (excluding resources awarded to replace EFC). *Average financial aid package:* $15,293 (excluding resources awarded to replace EFC). 46% of all full-time undergraduates had no need and received non-need-based gift aid.
GIFT AID (NEED-BASED) *Total amount:* $3,802,492 (7% federal, 16% state, 73% institutional, 4% external sources). *Receiving aid:* Freshmen: 46% (83); All full-time undergraduates: 46% (246). *Average award:* Freshmen: $14,320; Undergraduates: $13,706. *Scholarships, grants, and awards:* Federal Pell, FSEOG, state, private, college/university gift aid from institutional funds.
GIFT AID (NON-NEED-BASED) *Total amount:* $3,041,545 (9% state, 90% institutional, 1% external sources). *Receiving aid:* Freshmen: 47% (85); Undergraduates: 46% (246). *Average Award:* Freshmen: $10,826; Undergraduates: $11,213. *Scholarships, grants, and awards by category:* Academic Interests/Achievement: 420 awards ($4,019,337 total): general academic interests/achievements, premedicine. Creative Arts/Performance: 1 award ($1000 total): art/fine arts, general creative arts/performance, music. *Special Characteristics:* 169 awards ($1,354,408 total): adult students, general special characteristics, international students, local/state students.
LOANS *Student loans:* $623,329 (85% need-based, 15% non-need-based). 56% of past graduating class borrowed through all loan programs. *Average indebtedness per student:* $17,808. *Average need-based loan:* Freshmen: $3848; Undergraduates: $4755. *Parent loans:* $1,269,215 (65% need-based, 35% non-need-based). *Programs:* Federal Direct (Subsidized and Unsubsidized Stafford, PLUS), Perkins, college/university.
WORK-STUDY *Federal work-study:* Total amount: $21,457; 63 jobs averaging $960. *State or other work-study/employment:* Total amount: $25,385 (100% need-based). 79 part-time jobs averaging $915.
APPLYING FOR FINANCIAL AID *Required financial aid form:* FAFSA. *Financial aid deadline (priority):* 3/1. *Notification date:* Continuous beginning 3/1. Students must reply by 5/1 or within 2 weeks of notification.
CONTACT Bobbi Carpenter, Director of Financial Aid, Sweet Briar College, Box AS, Sweet Briar, VA 24595, 800-381-6156 or toll-free 800-381-6142. *Fax:* 434-381-6450. *E-mail:* bcarpenter@sbc.edu.

SYRACUSE UNIVERSITY
Syracuse, NY

Tuition & fees: $28,285 | **Average undergraduate aid package: $20,716**

ABOUT THE INSTITUTION Independent, coed. Awards: bachelor's, master's, doctoral, and first professional degrees and post-master's certificates. 147 undergraduate majors. Total enrollment: 17,266. Undergraduates: 11,441. Freshmen: 3,248. Both federal and institutional methodology are used as a basis for awarding need-based institutional aid.
UNDERGRADUATE EXPENSES for 2005–06 *Application fee:* $60. *Comprehensive fee:* $38,655 includes full-time tuition ($27,210), mandatory fees ($1075), and room and board ($10,370). *College room only:* $5620. Room and board charges vary according to board plan and housing facility. *Part-time tuition:* $1120 per credit hour. *Payment plan:* Installment.
FRESHMAN FINANCIAL AID (Fall 2005, est.) 2377 applied for aid; of those 81% were deemed to have need. 100% of freshmen with need received aid; of those 65% had need fully met. *Average percent of need met:* 84% (excluding resources awarded to replace EFC). *Average financial aid package:* $21,135 (excluding resources awarded to replace EFC). 14% of all full-time freshmen had no need and received non-need-based gift aid.
UNDERGRADUATE FINANCIAL AID (Fall 2005, est.) 7,589 applied for aid; of those 87% were deemed to have need. 100% of undergraduates with need received aid; of those 65% had need fully met. *Average percent of need met:* 80% (excluding resources awarded to replace EFC). *Average financial aid package:* $20,716 (excluding resources awarded to replace EFC). 16% of all full-time undergraduates had no need and received non-need-based gift aid.
GIFT AID (NEED-BASED) *Total amount:* $105,544,718 (8% federal, 7% state, 82% institutional, 3% external sources). *Receiving aid:* Freshmen: 54% (1,738); All full-time undergraduates: 52% (5,914). *Average award:* Freshmen: $16,600; Undergraduates: $15,020. *Scholarships, grants, and awards:* Federal Pell, FSEOG, state, college/university gift aid from institutional funds.
GIFT AID (NON-NEED-BASED) *Total amount:* $16,926,682 (94% institutional, 6% external sources). *Receiving aid:* Freshmen: 3% (99); Undergraduates: 3% (294). *Average Award:* Freshmen: $8600; Undergraduates: $8840. *Scholarships, grants, and awards by category:* Academic Interests/Achievement: general academic interests/achievements. Creative Arts/Performance: art/fine arts, music. *Tuition waivers:* Full or partial for employees or children of employees. *ROTC:* Army, Air Force.
LOANS *Student loans:* $47,200,359 (89% need-based, 11% non-need-based). 70% of past graduating class borrowed through all loan programs. *Average indebtedness per student:* $19,200. *Average need-based loan:* Freshmen: $3800; Undergraduates: $5300. *Parent loans:* $30,127,903 (73% need-based, 27% non-need-based). *Programs:* FFEL (Subsidized and Unsubsidized Stafford, PLUS), Perkins.
WORK-STUDY *Federal work-study:* Total amount: $3,294,722; jobs available (averaging $1500). *State or other work-study/employment:* Part-time jobs available.
ATHLETIC AWARDS *Total amount:* $10,073,734 (41% need-based, 59% non-need-based).
APPLYING FOR FINANCIAL AID *Required financial aid forms:* FAFSA, CSS Financial Aid PROFILE, noncustodial (divorced/separated) parent's statement, business/farm supplement. *Financial aid deadline:* 2/1. *Notification date:* 4/1. Students must reply by 5/1.
CONTACT Mr. Christopher Walsh, Executive Director of Financial Aid, Syracuse University, 200 Archbold Gymnasium, Syracuse, NY 13244-1140, 315-443-1513. *E-mail:* finmail@syr.edu.

TABOR COLLEGE
Hillsboro, KS

Tuition & fees: $15,934 | **Average undergraduate aid package: $15,751**

ABOUT THE INSTITUTION Independent Mennonite Brethren, coed. Awards: associate, bachelor's, and master's degrees. 53 undergraduate majors. Total enrollment: 606. Undergraduates: 586. Freshmen: 139. Federal methodology is used as a basis for awarding need-based institutional aid.
UNDERGRADUATE EXPENSES for 2005–06 *Application fee:* $20. *Comprehensive fee:* $21,604 includes full-time tuition ($15,574), mandatory fees ($360), and room and board ($5670). *College room only:* $2215. Full-time tuition and fees vary according to course load. Room and board charges vary according to board plan, housing facility, and location. Part-time tuition and fees vary according to course load. *Payment plan:* Installment.
FRESHMAN FINANCIAL AID (Fall 2005, est.) 116 applied for aid; of those 83% were deemed to have need. 100% of freshmen with need received aid; of those 25% had need fully met. *Average percent of need met:* 88% (excluding resources awarded to replace EFC). *Average financial aid package:* $16,198 (excluding resources awarded to replace EFC). 18% of all full-time freshmen had no need and received non-need-based gift aid.
UNDERGRADUATE FINANCIAL AID (Fall 2005, est.) 511 applied for aid; of those 77% were deemed to have need. 100% of undergraduates with need received aid; of those 35% had need fully met. *Average percent of need met:* 89% (excluding resources awarded to replace EFC). *Average financial aid package:* $15,751 (excluding resources awarded to replace EFC). 20% of all full-time undergraduates had no need and received non-need-based gift aid.

GIFT AID (NEED-BASED) *Total amount:* $972,175 (58% federal, 42% state). *Receiving aid:* Freshmen: 71% (83); All full-time undergraduates: 58% (314). *Average award:* Freshmen: $3826; Undergraduates: $3477. *Scholarships, grants, and awards:* Federal Pell, FSEOG, state, private, college/university gift aid from institutional funds.
GIFT AID (NON-NEED-BASED) *Total amount:* $2,602,755 (90% institutional, 10% external sources). *Receiving aid:* Freshmen: 81% (95); Undergraduates: 67% (359). *Average Award:* Freshmen: $4418; Undergraduates: $5075. *Scholarships, grants, and awards by category:* Academic Interests/Achievement: 303 awards ($1,152,022 total): biological sciences, business, communication, computer science, education, English, general academic interests/achievements, humanities, mathematics, premedicine, religion/biblical studies, social sciences. *Creative Arts/Performance:* 73 awards ($103,488 total): music, performing arts, theater/drama. *Special Achievements/Activities:* 280,457 awards ($458,973 total): cheerleading/drum major, general special achievements/activities, religious involvement. *Special Characteristics:* children and siblings of alumni, children of faculty/staff, general special characteristics, international students, local/state students, out-of-state students, religious affiliation. *Tuition waivers:* Full or partial for employees or children of employees.
LOANS *Student loans:* $3,191,028 (100% need-based). 82% of past graduating class borrowed through all loan programs. *Average indebtedness per student:* $20,181. *Average need-based loan:* Freshmen: $5768; Undergraduates: $7036. *Parent loans:* $456,651 (100% need-based). *Programs:* FFEL (Subsidized and Unsubsidized Stafford, PLUS), Perkins.
WORK-STUDY *Federal work-study:* Total amount: $98,109; 147 jobs averaging $667. *State or other work-study/employment:* Part-time jobs available.
ATHLETIC AWARDS *Total amount:* $884,943 (100% non-need-based).
APPLYING FOR FINANCIAL AID *Required financial aid forms:* FAFSA, state aid form, admissions application. *Financial aid deadline:* 8/15 (priority: 3/1). *Notification date:* Continuous beginning 3/15. Students must reply within 4 weeks of notification.
CONTACT Mr. Bruce Jost, Director of Student Financial Assistance, Tabor College, 400 South Jefferson, Hillsboro, KS 67063, 620-947-3121 Ext. 1726 or toll-free 800-822-6799. *Fax:* 620-947-6276. *E-mail:* brucej@tabor.edu.

TALLADEGA COLLEGE
Talladega, AL

ABOUT THE INSTITUTION Independent, coed. Awards: bachelor's degrees. 35 undergraduate majors. Total enrollment: 368. Undergraduates: 368. Freshmen: 182.
GIFT AID (NEED-BASED) *Scholarships, grants, and awards:* Federal Pell, FSEOG, state, private, college/university gift aid from institutional funds, United Negro College Fund.
GIFT AID (NON-NEED-BASED) *Scholarships, grants, and awards by category:* Academic Interests/Achievement: general academic interests/achievements.
LOANS *Programs:* Federal Direct (Subsidized and Unsubsidized Stafford, PLUS), FFEL (Subsidized and Unsubsidized Stafford, PLUS), Perkins, college/university.
APPLYING FOR FINANCIAL AID *Required financial aid forms:* FAFSA, institution's own form.
CONTACT K. Michael Francois, Director of Financial Aid, Talladega College, 627 West Battle Street, Talladega, AL 35160, 256-761-6341 or toll-free 800-762-2468 (in-state), 800-633-2440 (out-of-state). *Fax:* 256-761-6462.

TALMUDICAL ACADEMY OF NEW JERSEY
Adelphia, NJ

CONTACT Office of Financial Aid, Talmudical Academy of New Jersey, Route 524, Adelphia, NJ 07710, 732-431-1600.

TALMUDICAL INSTITUTE OF UPSTATE NEW YORK
Rochester, NY

CONTACT Mrs. Ella Berenstein, Financial Aid Administrator, Talmudical Institute of Upstate New York, 769 Park Avenue, Rochester, NY 14607-3046, 716-473-2810.

TALMUDICAL SEMINARY OHOLEI TORAH
Brooklyn, NY

CONTACT Financial Aid Administrator, Talmudical Seminary Oholei Torah, 667 Eastern Parkway, Brooklyn, NY 11213-3310, 718-774-5050.

TALMUDICAL YESHIVA OF PHILADELPHIA
Philadelphia, PA

CONTACT Rabbi Uri Mandelbaum, Director of Student Financial Aid/Registrar, Talmudical Yeshiva of Philadelphia, 6063 Drexel Road, Philadelphia, PA 19131-1296, 215-473-1212. *E-mail:* typp@juno.com.

TALMUDIC COLLEGE OF FLORIDA
Miami Beach, FL

CONTACT Rabbi Ira Hill, Director of Financial Aid, Talmudic College of Florida, 1910 Alton Road, Miami Beach, FL 33139, 305-534-7050 or toll-free 888-825-6834. *Fax:* 305-534-8444.

TARLETON STATE UNIVERSITY
Stephenville, TX

ABOUT THE INSTITUTION State-supported, coed. Awards: associate, bachelor's, master's, and doctoral degrees. 77 undergraduate majors. Total enrollment: 9,144. Undergraduates: 7,613. Freshmen: 1,116.
GIFT AID (NEED-BASED) *Scholarships, grants, and awards:* Federal Pell, FSEOG, state, private, college/university gift aid from institutional funds.
GIFT AID (NON-NEED-BASED) *Scholarships, grants, and awards by category:* Academic Interests/Achievement: general academic interests/achievements. *Creative Arts/Performance:* music, theater/drama. *Special Achievements/Activities:* rodeo. *Special Characteristics:* children of faculty/staff.
LOANS *Programs:* FFEL (Subsidized and Unsubsidized Stafford, PLUS), college/university.
APPLYING FOR FINANCIAL AID *Required financial aid forms:* FAFSA, institution's own form.
CONTACT Ms. Betty Murray, Director of Student Financial Aid, Tarleton State University, Box T-0310, Stephenville, TX 76402, 254-968-9070 or toll-free 800-687-8236 (in-state). *Fax:* 254-968-9600. *E-mail:* finaid@tarleton.edu.

TAYLOR UNIVERSITY
Upland, IN

Tuition & fees: $20,746	Average undergraduate aid package: $14,069

ABOUT THE INSTITUTION Independent interdenominational, coed. Awards: associate, bachelor's, and master's degrees. 74 undergraduate majors. Total enrollment: 1,865. Undergraduates: 1,851. Freshmen: 461. Both federal and institutional methodology are used as a basis for awarding need-based institutional aid.
UNDERGRADUATE EXPENSES for 2005–06 *Application fee:* $25. *Comprehensive fee:* $26,376 includes full-time tuition ($20,520), mandatory fees ($226), and room and board ($5630). *College room only:* $2732. Full-time tuition and fees vary according to course load. Room and board charges vary according to housing facility. *Part-time tuition:* $696 per credit. *Part-time fees:* $64 per year. Part-time tuition and fees vary according to course load. *Payment plan:* Installment.
FRESHMAN FINANCIAL AID (Fall 2005, est.) 361 applied for aid; of those 74% were deemed to have need. 100% of freshmen with need received aid; of those 26% had need fully met. *Average percent of need met:* 74% (excluding resources awarded to replace EFC). *Average financial aid package:* $13,886 (excluding resources awarded to replace EFC). 24% of all full-time freshmen had no need and received non-need-based gift aid.
UNDERGRADUATE FINANCIAL AID (Fall 2005, est.) 1,248 applied for aid; of those 81% were deemed to have need. 100% of undergraduates with need received aid; of those 26% had need fully met. *Average percent of need met:* 77% (excluding resources awarded to replace EFC). *Average financial aid package:* $14,069 (excluding resources awarded to replace EFC). 23% of all full-time undergraduates had no need and received non-need-based gift aid.

Taylor University

GIFT AID (NEED-BASED) *Total amount:* $8,813,867 (9% federal, 12% state, 68% institutional, 11% external sources). *Receiving aid:* Freshmen: 55% (250); All full-time undergraduates: 52% (934). *Average award:* Freshmen: $10,644; Undergraduates: $10,631. *Scholarships, grants, and awards:* Federal Pell, FSEOG, state, private, college/university gift aid from institutional funds.
GIFT AID (NON-NEED-BASED) *Total amount:* $2,462,725 (2% state, 74% institutional, 24% external sources). *Receiving aid:* Freshmen: 7% (32); Undergraduates: 6% (109). *Average Award:* Freshmen: $4078; Undergraduates:* $3898. *Scholarships, grants, and awards by category:* Academic Interests/Achievement: 774 awards ($2,388,904 total): general academic interests/achievements. Creative Arts/Performance: 101 awards ($164,692 total): music, theater/drama. Special Achievements/Activities: 87 awards ($396,614 total): leadership. Special Characteristics: 592 awards ($1,825,186 total): children and siblings of alumni, children of faculty/staff, ethnic background, international students, religious affiliation. *Tuition waivers:* Full or partial for employees or children of employees, senior citizens.
LOANS *Student loans:* $6,937,129 (64% need-based, 36% non-need-based). 60% of past graduating class borrowed through all loan programs. *Average indebtedness per student:* $17,910. *Average need-based loan:* Freshmen: $4260; Undergraduates: $4537. *Parent loans:* $13,629,836 (25% need-based, 75% non-need-based). *Programs:* FFEL (Subsidized and Unsubsidized Stafford, PLUS), Perkins, college/university.
WORK-STUDY *Federal work-study:* Total amount: $313,812; 755 jobs averaging $416.
ATHLETIC AWARDS *Total amount:* $1,001,020 (55% need-based, 45% non-need-based).
APPLYING FOR FINANCIAL AID *Required financial aid forms:* FAFSA, institution's own form. *Financial aid deadline:* 3/10. *Notification date:* Continuous beginning 3/1. Students must reply by 5/1.
CONTACT Mr. Timothy A. Nace, Director of Financial Aid, Taylor University, 236 West Reade Avenue, Upland, IN 46989-1001, 765-998-5358 or toll-free 800-882-3456. *Fax:* 765-998-4910. *E-mail:* tmnace@taylor.edu.

TAYLOR UNIVERSITY FORT WAYNE
Fort Wayne, IN

| Tuition & fees: $17,714 | Average undergraduate aid package: $15,627 |

ABOUT THE INSTITUTION Independent interdenominational, coed. Awards: associate, bachelor's, and master's degrees and post-bachelor's certificates. 16 undergraduate majors. Total enrollment: 595. Undergraduates: 544. Freshmen: 83. Both federal and institutional methodology are used as a basis for awarding need-based institutional aid.
UNDERGRADUATE EXPENSES for 2005–06 *Application fee:* $20. *Comprehensive fee:* $22,674 includes full-time tuition ($17,600), mandatory fees ($114), and room and board ($4960). *College room only:* $2160. Room and board charges vary according to board plan. *Part-time tuition:* $250 per credit hour. *Part-time fees:* $52 per year. Part-time tuition and fees vary according to course load. *Payment plan:* Installment.
FRESHMAN FINANCIAL AID (Fall 2005, est.) 59 applied for aid; of those 90% were deemed to have need. 100% of freshmen with need received aid; of those 42% had need fully met. *Average percent of need met:* 86% (excluding resources awarded to replace EFC). *Average financial aid package:* $15,850 (excluding resources awarded to replace EFC). 14% of all full-time freshmen had no need and received non-need-based gift aid.
UNDERGRADUATE FINANCIAL AID (Fall 2005, est.) 301 applied for aid; of those 91% were deemed to have need. 100% of undergraduates with need received aid; of those 32% had need fully met. *Average percent of need met:* 85% (excluding resources awarded to replace EFC). *Average financial aid package:* $15,627 (excluding resources awarded to replace EFC). 13% of all full-time undergraduates had no need and received non-need-based gift aid.
GIFT AID (NEED-BASED) *Total amount:* $3,116,424 (15% federal, 30% state, 52% institutional, 3% external sources). *Receiving aid:* Freshmen: 73% (53); All full-time undergraduates: 80% (268). *Average award:* Freshmen: $11,573; Undergraduates: $11,286. *Scholarships, grants, and awards:* Federal Pell, FSEOG, state, private, college/university gift aid from institutional funds, endowed-donor scholarships.
GIFT AID (NON-NEED-BASED) *Total amount:* $301,105 (9% state, 86% institutional, 5% external sources). *Receiving aid:* Freshmen: 12% (9); Undergraduates: 7% (25). *Average Award:* Freshmen: $4552; Undergraduates: $4375. *Scholarships, grants, and awards by category:* Academic Interests/Achievement: 143 awards ($508,141 total): business, general academic interests/achievements. Creative Arts/Performance: 3 awards ($7600 total): music. Special Achievements/Activities: 31 awards ($54,000 total): leadership. Special Characteristics: 340 awards ($541,903 total): children and siblings of alumni, children of faculty/staff, general special characteristics, local/state students, relatives of clergy, spouses of current students. *Tuition waivers:* Full or partial for children of alumni, employees or children of employees, senior citizens.
LOANS *Student loans:* $1,991,998 (75% need-based, 25% non-need-based). 87% of past graduating class borrowed through all loan programs. *Average indebtedness per student:* $15,650. *Average need-based loan:* Freshmen: $4083; Undergraduates: $4196. *Parent loans:* $414,320 (28% need-based, 72% non-need-based). *Programs:* FFEL (Subsidized and Unsubsidized Stafford, PLUS), Perkins, college/university.
WORK-STUDY *Federal work-study:* Total amount: $251,595; 162 jobs averaging $1553.
ATHLETIC AWARDS *Total amount:* $10,372 (47% need-based, 53% non-need-based).
APPLYING FOR FINANCIAL AID *Required financial aid forms:* FAFSA, institution's own form. *Financial aid deadline (priority):* 3/1. *Notification date:* Continuous beginning 3/1. Students must reply by 5/1 or within 2 weeks of notification.
CONTACT Mr. Paul Johnston, Director of Financial Aid, Taylor University Fort Wayne, 1025 West Rudisill Boulevard, Fort Wayne, IN 46807-2197, 260-744-8691 or toll-free 800-233-3922. *Fax:* 260-744-8850. *E-mail:* pljohnston@taylor u.edu.

TEIKYO LORETTO HEIGHTS UNIVERSITY
Denver, CO

CONTACT Financial Aid Office, Teikyo Loretto Heights University, 3001 South Federal Boulevard, Denver, CO 80236, 303-936-4200.

TELSHE YESHIVA–CHICAGO
Chicago, IL

CONTACT Office of Financial Aid, Telshe Yeshiva–Chicago, 3535 West Foster Avenue, Chicago, IL 60625-5598, 773-463-7738.

TEMPLE BAPTIST COLLEGE
Cincinnati, OH

CONTACT Financial Aid Office, Temple Baptist College, 11965 Kenn Road, Cincinnati, OH 45240, 513-851-3800.

TEMPLE UNIVERSITY
Philadelphia, PA

| Tuition & fees (PA res): $9640 | Average undergraduate aid package: $12,927 |

ABOUT THE INSTITUTION State-related, coed. Awards: associate, bachelor's, master's, doctoral, and first professional degrees and post-master's and first professional certificates. 118 undergraduate majors. Total enrollment: 33,693. Undergraduates: 24,194. Freshmen: 3,871. Federal methodology is used as a basis for awarding need-based institutional aid.
UNDERGRADUATE EXPENSES for 2005–06 *Application fee:* $35. *Tuition, state resident:* full-time $9140; part-time $354 per credit hour. *Tuition, nonresident:* full-time $16,736; part-time $596 per credit hour. *Required fees:* full-time $500; $109 per term part-time. Full-time tuition and fees vary according to course load, location, program, and reciprocity agreements. Part-time tuition and fees vary according to course load, location, program, and reciprocity agreements. *College room and board:* $7794; *room only:* $5054. Room and board charges vary according to board plan and housing facility. *Payment plan:* Installment.
FRESHMAN FINANCIAL AID (Fall 2004) 3380 applied for aid; of those 80% were deemed to have need. 98% of freshmen with need received aid; of those 31% had need fully met. *Average percent of need met:* 87% (excluding resources awarded to replace EFC). *Average financial aid package:* $13,429 (excluding resources awarded to replace EFC). 26% of all full-time freshmen had no need and received non-need-based gift aid.

UNDERGRADUATE FINANCIAL AID (Fall 2004) 18,090 applied for aid; of those 78% were deemed to have need. 94% of undergraduates with need received aid; of those 36% had need fully met. *Average percent of need met:* 88% (excluding resources awarded to replace EFC). *Average financial aid package:* $12,927 (excluding resources awarded to replace EFC). 21% of all full-time undergraduates had no need and received non-need-based gift aid.
GIFT AID (NEED-BASED) *Total amount:* $63,489,578 (37% federal, 28% state, 35% institutional). *Receiving aid:* Freshmen: 73% (2,636); All full-time undergraduates: 71% (13,282). *Average award:* Freshmen: $5116; Undergraduates: $4653. *Scholarships, grants, and awards:* Federal Pell, FSEOG, state, private, college/university gift aid from institutional funds, Federal Nursing.
GIFT AID (NON-NEED-BASED) *Total amount:* $42,390,024 (15% institutional, 85% external sources). *Receiving aid:* Freshmen: 44% (1,569); Undergraduates: 33% (6,300). *Average Award:* Freshmen: $4066; Undergraduates: $4397. *Scholarships, grants, and awards by category: Academic Interests/Achievement:* general academic interests/achievements. *Creative Arts/Performance:* art/fine arts, general creative arts/performance, music, performing arts. *Special Achievements/Activities:* cheerleading/drum major. *Special Characteristics:* general special characteristics. *Tuition waivers:* Full or partial for employees or children of employees. *ROTC:* Army, Naval cooperative, Air Force cooperative.
LOANS *Student loans:* $92,097,540 (66% need-based, 34% non-need-based). 71% of past graduating class borrowed through all loan programs. *Average indebtedness per student:* $25,493. *Average need-based loan:* Freshmen: $2881; Undergraduates: $3676. *Parent loans:* $644,871 (100% non-need-based). *Programs:* FFEL (Subsidized and Unsubsidized Stafford, PLUS), Perkins, Federal Nursing, college/university.
WORK-STUDY *Federal work-study:* Total amount: $2,849,324; jobs available.
ATHLETIC AWARDS Total amount: $5,610,154 (100% non-need-based).
APPLYING FOR FINANCIAL AID *Required financial aid form:* FAFSA. *Financial aid deadline (priority):* 3/1. *Notification date:* Continuous beginning 2/15. Students must reply by 5/1 or within 3 weeks of notification.
CONTACT Dr. John F. Morris, Director, Student Financial Services, Temple University, Conwell Hall, Ground Floor, 1801 North Broad Street, Philadelphia, PA 19122-6096, 215-204-8760 or toll-free 888-340-2222. Fax: 215-204-2016. E-mail: john.morris@temple.edu.

TENNESSEE STATE UNIVERSITY
Nashville, TN

Tuition & fees (TN res): $4639   **Average undergraduate aid package:** $3687

ABOUT THE INSTITUTION State-supported, coed. Awards: associate, bachelor's, master's, and doctoral degrees. 59 undergraduate majors. Total enrollment: 8,880. Undergraduates: 7,036. Freshmen: 1,016. Federal methodology is used as a basis for awarding need-based institutional aid.
UNDERGRADUATE EXPENSES for 2005–06 *Application fee:* $15. *Tuition, state resident:* full-time $4414; part-time $336 per hour. *Tuition, nonresident:* full-time $13,726; part-time $740 per hour. Full-time tuition and fees vary according to course load and program. Part-time tuition and fees vary according to course load. *College room and board:* $4270; *room only:* $2460. Room and board charges vary according to board plan and housing facility.
FRESHMAN FINANCIAL AID (Fall 2004) 1264 applied for aid; of those 87% were deemed to have need. 99% of freshmen with need received aid; of those 8% had need fully met. *Average percent of need met:* 85% (excluding resources awarded to replace EFC). *Average financial aid package:* $6075 (excluding resources awarded to replace EFC).
UNDERGRADUATE FINANCIAL AID (Fall 2004) 5,171 applied for aid; of those 84% were deemed to have need. 99% of undergraduates with need received aid; of those 12% had need fully met. *Average percent of need met:* 81% (excluding resources awarded to replace EFC). *Average financial aid package:* $3687 (excluding resources awarded to replace EFC). 6% of all full-time undergraduates had no need and received non-need-based gift aid.
GIFT AID (NEED-BASED) *Total amount:* $15,100,715 (88% federal, 12% state). *Receiving aid:* Freshmen: 785; All full-time undergraduates: 51% (3,017). *Average award:* Freshmen: $719; Undergraduates: $1208. *Scholarships, grants, and awards:* Federal Pell, FSEOG, state, private, college/university gift aid from institutional funds.
GIFT AID (NON-NEED-BASED) *Total amount:* $4,665,189 (100% institutional). *Receiving aid:* Freshmen: 100; Undergraduates: 6% (364). *Average Award:* Freshmen: $8640; Undergraduates: $6004. *Scholarships, grants, and awards by category: Academic Interests/Achievement:* general academic interests/achievements. *Creative Arts/Performance:* music. *Special Achievements/Activities:* general special achievements/activities. *Special Characteristics:* local/state students, members of minority groups. *Tuition waivers:* Full or partial for minority students, employees or children of employees, senior citizens. *ROTC:* Army cooperative, Naval cooperative, Air Force.
LOANS *Student loans:* $42,385,180 (56% need-based, 44% non-need-based). 76% of past graduating class borrowed through all loan programs. *Average indebtedness per student:* $22,517. *Parent loans:* $5,390,626 (100% non-need-based). *Programs:* Federal Direct (Subsidized and Unsubsidized Stafford), FFEL (Subsidized and Unsubsidized Stafford, PLUS), Perkins, college/university.
WORK-STUDY *Federal work-study:* Total amount: $2,018,268; 915 jobs averaging $2000. *State or other work-study/employment:* Part-time jobs available.
ATHLETIC AWARDS Total amount: $1,173,758 (100% non-need-based).
APPLYING FOR FINANCIAL AID *Required financial aid form:* FAFSA. *Financial aid deadline (priority):* 4/1. *Notification date:* Continuous beginning 4/15. Students must reply within 2 weeks of notification.
CONTACT Michael Jones, Director of Financial Aid, Tennessee State University, 3500 John Merritt Boulevard, Nashville, TN 37209-1561, 615-963-5701. Fax: 615-963-5108.

TENNESSEE TECHNOLOGICAL UNIVERSITY
Cookeville, TN

Tuition & fees (TN res): $4660   **Average undergraduate aid package:** $3502

ABOUT THE INSTITUTION State-supported, coed. Awards: bachelor's, master's, and doctoral degrees and post-bachelor's certificates. 67 undergraduate majors. Total enrollment: 9,313. Undergraduates: 7,255. Freshmen: 1,424. Federal methodology is used as a basis for awarding need-based institutional aid.
UNDERGRADUATE EXPENSES for 2006–07 *Application fee:* $15. *Tuition, state resident:* full-time $4660. *Tuition, nonresident:* full-time $14,620. *College room and board:* $6650; *room only:* $3096.
FRESHMAN FINANCIAL AID (Fall 2004) 770 applied for aid; of those 68% were deemed to have need. 100% of freshmen with need received aid; of those 28% had need fully met. *Average percent of need met:* 86% (excluding resources awarded to replace EFC). *Average financial aid package:* $6849 (excluding resources awarded to replace EFC). 15% of all full-time freshmen had no need and received non-need-based gift aid.
UNDERGRADUATE FINANCIAL AID (Fall 2004) 5,309 applied for aid; of those 62% were deemed to have need. 99% of undergraduates with need received aid; of those 27% had need fully met. *Average percent of need met:* 80% (excluding resources awarded to replace EFC). *Average financial aid package:* $3502 (excluding resources awarded to replace EFC). 22% of all full-time undergraduates had no need and received non-need-based gift aid.
GIFT AID (NEED-BASED) *Total amount:* $7,590,162 (78% federal, 22% state). *Receiving aid:* Freshmen: 20% (297); All full-time undergraduates: 29% (1,847). *Average award:* Freshmen: $3063; Undergraduates: $2632. *Scholarships, grants, and awards:* Federal Pell, FSEOG, state, private, college/university gift aid from institutional funds, United Negro College Fund.
GIFT AID (NON-NEED-BASED) *Total amount:* $11,338,413 (1% federal, 52% state, 33% institutional, 14% external sources). *Receiving aid:* Freshmen: 29% (422); Undergraduates: 25% (1,619). *Average Award:* Freshmen: $4341; Undergraduates: $3481. *Scholarships, grants, and awards by category: Academic Interests/Achievement:* 2,061 awards ($2,428,329 total): agriculture, biological sciences, business, communication, computer science, education, engineering/technologies, English, foreign languages, general academic interests/achievements, health fields, home economics, humanities, international studies, mathematics, military science, physical sciences, premedicine, social sciences. *Creative Arts/Performance:* 176 awards ($231,466 total): art/fine arts, debating, music. *Special Achievements/Activities:* 2,654 awards ($5,251,527 total): cheerleading/drum major, general special achievements/activities. *Special Characteristics:* 1,330 awards ($2,038,958 total): children and siblings of alumni, children of educators, children of faculty/staff, children of public servants, ethnic background, first-generation college students, local/state students, members of minority groups, out-of-state students, public servants. *ROTC:* Army, Air Force cooperative.
LOANS *Student loans:* $17,749,183 (67% need-based, 33% non-need-based). 35% of past graduating class borrowed through all loan programs. *Average indebtedness per student:* $14,164. *Average need-based loan:* Freshmen: $1482;

Tennessee Technological University

Undergraduates: $3223. **Parent loans:** $1,074,946 (100% non-need-based). **Programs:** Federal Direct (Subsidized and Unsubsidized Stafford), FFEL (PLUS), Perkins, college/university.
WORK-STUDY *Federal work-study:* Total amount: $877,598; 561 jobs averaging $877. *State or other work-study/employment:* Total amount: $2,004,790 (100% non-need-based). 1,114 part-time jobs averaging $1800.
ATHLETIC AWARDS *Total amount:* $2,867,069 (100% non-need-based).
APPLYING FOR FINANCIAL AID *Required financial aid form:* FAFSA. *Financial aid deadline (priority):* 3/15. *Notification date:* Continuous beginning 4/1. Students must reply within 2 weeks of notification.
CONTACT Lester McKenzie, Director of Financial Aid, Tennessee Technological University, Box 5076, 1000 North Dixie Avenue, Cookeville, TN 38501, 931-372-3073 or toll-free 800-255-8881. *Fax:* 931-372-6309. *E-mail:* lmckenzie@tntech.edu.

TENNESSEE TEMPLE UNIVERSITY
Chattanooga, TN

CONTACT Mr. Michael Sapienza, Director of Financial Aid, Tennessee Temple University, 1815 Union Avenue, Chattanooga, TN 37404-3587, 423-493-4208 or toll-free 800-553-4050. *Fax:* 423-493-4497. *E-mail:* michaels@mail.tntemple.edu.

TENNESSEE WESLEYAN COLLEGE
Athens, TN

ABOUT THE INSTITUTION Independent United Methodist, coed. Awards: bachelor's degrees (profile includes information for both the main and branch campuses). 40 undergraduate majors. Total enrollment: 815. Undergraduates: 815. Freshmen: 166.
GIFT AID (NEED-BASED) *Scholarships, grants, and awards:* Federal Pell, FSEOG, state, private, college/university gift aid from institutional funds, Federal Nursing.
GIFT AID (NON-NEED-BASED) *Scholarships, grants, and awards by category: Academic Interests/Achievement:* biological sciences, business, communication, computer science, education, English, foreign languages, general academic interests/achievements, health fields, humanities, international studies, mathematics, physical sciences, premedicine, religion/biblical studies, social sciences. *Creative Arts/Performance:* music. *Special Achievements/Activities:* cheerleading/drum major, general special achievements/activities, junior miss, memberships, religious involvement. *Special Characteristics:* children of faculty/staff, general special characteristics, international students, members of minority groups, relatives of clergy, religious affiliation.
LOANS *Programs:* FFEL (Subsidized and Unsubsidized Stafford, PLUS), Perkins, state, United Methodist Student Loans.
WORK-STUDY *Federal work-study:* Total amount: $70,481; 103 jobs averaging $678. *State or other work-study/employment:* Total amount: $24,856 (7% need-based, 93% non-need-based). 39 part-time jobs averaging $837.
APPLYING FOR FINANCIAL AID *Required financial aid forms:* FAFSA, institution's own form.
CONTACT Ms. Bobbie Pennington, Financial Aid Officer, Tennessee Wesleyan College, PO Box 40, Athens, TN 37371-0040, 423-746-5215 or toll-free 800-PICK-TWC. *Fax:* 423-744-9968. *E-mail:* bpennington@twcnet.edu.

TEXAS A&M INTERNATIONAL UNIVERSITY
Laredo, TX

CONTACT Laura Elizondo, Director of Financial Aid, Texas A&M International University, 5201 University Boulevard, Laredo, TX 78041, 956-326-2225 or toll-free 888-489-2648. *Fax:* 956-326-2224. *E-mail:* laura@tamiu.edu.

TEXAS A&M UNIVERSITY
College Station, TX

Tuition & fees (TX res): $6399   **Average undergraduate aid package:** $10,747

ABOUT THE INSTITUTION State-supported, coed. Awards: bachelor's, master's, doctoral, and first professional degrees and post-bachelor's certificates. 107 undergraduate majors. Total enrollment: 44,910. Undergraduates: 36,368. Freshmen: 7,147. Federal methodology is used as a basis for awarding need-based institutional aid.
UNDERGRADUATE EXPENSES for 2005–06 *Application fee:* $50. *Tuition, state resident:* full-time $4110; part-time $137 per semester hour. *Tuition, nonresident:* full-time $12,390; part-time $413 per semester hour. Full-time tuition and fees vary according to course load, location, and program. *College room and board:* $6952; *room only:* $3704. Room and board charges vary according to board plan, housing facility, and location. *Payment plan:* Installment.
FRESHMAN FINANCIAL AID (Fall 2005, est.) 4292 applied for aid; of those 60% were deemed to have need. 98% of freshmen with need received aid; of those 66% had need fully met. *Average percent of need met:* 90% (excluding resources awarded to replace EFC). *Average financial aid package:* $11,418 (excluding resources awarded to replace EFC). 33% of all full-time freshmen had no need and received non-need-based gift aid.
UNDERGRADUATE FINANCIAL AID (Fall 2005, est.) 17,553 applied for aid; of those 70% were deemed to have need. 98% of undergraduates with need received aid; of those 56% had need fully met. *Average percent of need met:* 87% (excluding resources awarded to replace EFC). *Average financial aid package:* $10,747 (excluding resources awarded to replace EFC). 23% of all full-time undergraduates had no need and received non-need-based gift aid.
GIFT AID (NEED-BASED) *Total amount:* $68,412,244 (27% federal, 32% state, 26% institutional, 15% external sources). *Receiving aid:* Freshmen: 34% (2,314); All full-time undergraduates: 30% (9,981). *Average award:* Freshmen: $8723; Undergraduates: $6795. *Scholarships, grants, and awards:* Federal Pell, FSEOG, state, private, college/university gift aid from institutional funds.
GIFT AID (NON-NEED-BASED) *Total amount:* $37,192,916 (4% federal, 2% state, 36% institutional, 58% external sources). *Receiving aid:* Freshmen: 6% (374); Undergraduates: 3% (943). *Average Award:* Freshmen: $4805; Undergraduates: $4406. *Scholarships, grants, and awards by category: Academic Interests/Achievement:* agriculture, architecture, biological sciences, business, computer science, education, engineering/technologies, general academic interests/achievements, health fields, physical sciences. *Creative Arts/Performance:* journalism/publications, performing arts, theater/drama. *Special Achievements/Activities:* general special achievements/activities, leadership, memberships, rodeo. *Special Characteristics:* children of faculty/staff, veterans, veterans' children.
ROTC: Army, Naval, Air Force.
LOANS *Student loans:* $81,005,796 (55% need-based, 45% non-need-based). 32% of past graduating class borrowed through all loan programs. *Average indebtedness per student:* $16,027. *Average need-based loan:* Freshmen: $3726; Undergraduates: $4984. *Parent loans:* $31,193,326 (12% need-based, 88% non-need-based). *Programs:* FFEL (Subsidized and Unsubsidized Stafford, PLUS), Perkins, state, college/university.
WORK-STUDY *Federal work-study:* Total amount: $2,409,192; 1,068 jobs averaging $2256. *State or other work-study/employment:* Total amount: $524,142 (100% need-based). 225 part-time jobs averaging $2330.
ATHLETIC AWARDS *Total amount:* $4,252,977 (34% need-based, 66% non-need-based).
APPLYING FOR FINANCIAL AID *Required financial aid form:* FAFSA. *Financial aid deadline:* Continuous. *Notification date:* Continuous beginning 4/1. Students must reply within 4 weeks of notification.
CONTACT Financial Aid Office, Texas A&M University, Department of Student Financial Aid, PO Box 30016, College Station, TX 77842-3016, 979-845-3236. *Fax:* 979-847-9061. *E-mail:* financialaid@tamu.edu.

TEXAS A&M UNIVERSITY AT GALVESTON
Galveston, TX

Tuition & fees (TX res): $5118   **Average undergraduate aid package:** $10,288

ABOUT THE INSTITUTION State-supported, coed. Awards: bachelor's and master's degrees. 12 undergraduate majors. Total enrollment: 1,677. Undergraduates: 1,636. Freshmen: 466. Federal methodology is used as a basis for awarding need-based institutional aid.
UNDERGRADUATE EXPENSES for 2005–06 *Application fee:* $35. *Tuition, state resident:* full-time $4110; part-time $137 per hour. *Tuition, nonresident:* full-time $12,390; part-time $413 per hour. *Required fees:* full-time $1008; $504 per term part-time. Full-time tuition and fees vary according to course load and program. Part-time tuition and fees vary according to course load and program.

College room and board: $4870; *room only:* $1958. Room and board charges vary according to board plan and housing facility. *Payment plan:* Installment.
FRESHMAN FINANCIAL AID (Fall 2005, est.) 277 applied for aid; of those 83% were deemed to have need. 94% of freshmen with need received aid; of those 27% had need fully met. *Average percent of need met:* 19% (excluding resources awarded to replace EFC). *Average financial aid package:* $10,122 (excluding resources awarded to replace EFC). 2% of all full-time freshmen had no need and received non-need-based gift aid.
UNDERGRADUATE FINANCIAL AID (Fall 2005, est.) 864 applied for aid; of those 91% were deemed to have need. 94% of undergraduates with need received aid; of those 30% had need fully met. *Average percent of need met:* 22% (excluding resources awarded to replace EFC). *Average financial aid package:* $10,288 (excluding resources awarded to replace EFC). 2% of all full-time undergraduates had no need and received non-need-based gift aid.
GIFT AID (NEED-BASED) *Total amount:* $1,362,287 (70% federal, 20% state, 10% institutional). *Receiving aid:* Freshmen: 26% (120); All full-time undergraduates: 29% (431). *Average award:* Freshmen: $4380; Undergraduates: $4413. *Scholarships, grants, and awards:* Federal Pell, FSEOG, state, private, college/university gift aid from institutional funds.
GIFT AID (NON-NEED-BASED) *Total amount:* $189,337 (1% federal, 18% state, 78% institutional, 3% external sources). *Receiving aid:* Freshmen: 3% (16); Undergraduates: 6% (95). *Average Award:* Freshmen: $6112; Undergraduates: $7103. *Scholarships, grants, and awards by category:* Academic Interests/Achievement: 100 awards ($100,000 total): general academic interests/achievements. Special Achievements/Activities: 35 awards ($42,000 total): leadership. *ROTC:* Naval.
LOANS *Student loans:* $5,841,798 (32% need-based, 68% non-need-based). 73% of past graduating class borrowed through all loan programs. *Average indebtedness per student:* $11,156. *Average need-based loan:* Freshmen: $2646; Undergraduates: $3102. *Parent loans:* $2,188,929 (3% need-based, 97% non-need-based). *Programs:* FFEL (Subsidized and Unsubsidized Stafford, PLUS), Perkins, college/university, alternative loans.
WORK-STUDY *Federal work-study:* Total amount: $28,895; jobs available (averaging $1871). *State or other work-study/employment:* Total amount: $12,105 (100% non-need-based).
APPLYING FOR FINANCIAL AID *Required financial aid form:* FAFSA. *Financial aid deadline:* Continuous. *Notification date:* 3/15. Students must reply within 3 weeks of notification.
CONTACT Dennis Carlton, Director for Financial Aid, Texas A&M University at Galveston, PO Box 1675, Galveston, TX 77553-1675, 409-740-4500 or toll-free 87—SEAAGGIE. *Fax:* 409-740-4959. *E-mail:* carltond@tamug.tamu.edu.

TEXAS A&M UNIVERSITY–COMMERCE
Commerce, TX

Tuition & fees (TX res): $3834 **Average undergraduate aid package:** $7254

ABOUT THE INSTITUTION State-supported, coed. Awards: bachelor's, master's, and doctoral degrees. 67 undergraduate majors. Total enrollment: 8,787. Undergraduates: 5,271. Federal methodology is used as a basis for awarding need-based institutional aid.
UNDERGRADUATE EXPENSES for 2005–06 *Application fee:* $25. *One-time required fee:* $990. *Tuition, state resident:* full-time $3834; part-time $278.50 per credit. *Tuition, nonresident:* full-time $11,574; part-time $554.50 per credit. Full-time tuition and fees vary according to course load. Part-time tuition and fees vary according to course load. *College room and board:* $5740. Room and board charges vary according to board plan and housing facility. *Payment plan:* Installment.
FRESHMAN FINANCIAL AID (Fall 2005, est.) 252 applied for aid; of those 83% were deemed to have need. 97% of freshmen with need received aid; of those 15% had need fully met. *Average percent of need met:* 66% (excluding resources awarded to replace EFC). *Average financial aid package:* $6769 (excluding resources awarded to replace EFC). 18% of all full-time freshmen had no need and received non-need-based gift aid.
UNDERGRADUATE FINANCIAL AID (Fall 2005, est.) 2,960 applied for aid; of those 86% were deemed to have need. 98% of undergraduates with need received aid; of those 19% had need fully met. *Average percent of need met:* 68% (excluding resources awarded to replace EFC). *Average financial aid package:* $7254 (excluding resources awarded to replace EFC). 13% of all full-time undergraduates had no need and received non-need-based gift aid.

GIFT AID (NEED-BASED) *Total amount:* $10,451,696 (64% federal, 23% state, 10% institutional, 3% external sources). *Receiving aid:* Freshmen: 58% (184); All full-time undergraduates: 58% (2,209). *Average award:* Freshmen: $5724; Undergraduates: $4697. *Scholarships, grants, and awards:* Federal Pell, FSEOG, state, private, college/university gift aid from institutional funds.
GIFT AID (NON-NEED-BASED) *Total amount:* $1,024,567 (2% state, 78% institutional, 20% external sources). *Average Award:* Freshmen: $1574; Undergraduates: $1953. *Scholarships, grants, and awards by category:* Academic Interests/Achievement: agriculture, general academic interests/achievements. Creative Arts/Performance: art/fine arts, journalism/publications, music, theater/drama. Special Achievements/Activities: cheerleading/drum major, general special achievements/activities, leadership. *Tuition waivers:* Full or partial for senior citizens.
LOANS *Student loans:* $15,905,433 (88% need-based, 12% non-need-based). 66% of past graduating class borrowed through all loan programs. *Average indebtedness per student:* $18,182. *Average need-based loan:* Freshmen: $2145; Undergraduates: $3599. *Parent loans:* $844,120 (60% need-based, 40% non-need-based). *Programs:* Federal Direct (Subsidized and Unsubsidized Stafford), FFEL (Subsidized and Unsubsidized Stafford, PLUS), Perkins, state.
WORK-STUDY *Federal work-study:* Total amount: $382,406; 185 jobs averaging $1864. *State or other work-study/employment:* Total amount: $55,177 (100% need-based). 83 part-time jobs averaging $636.
ATHLETIC AWARDS *Total amount:* $47,812 (84% need-based, 16% non-need-based).
APPLYING FOR FINANCIAL AID *Required financial aid forms:* FAFSA, institution's own form. *Financial aid deadline (priority):* 4/1. *Notification date:* Continuous. Students must reply within 2 weeks of notification.
CONTACT Ms. Smithenia Harris, Interim Director of Financial Aid, Texas A&M University–Commerce, PO Box 3011, Commerce, TX 75429, 903-886-5096 or toll-free 800-331-3878.

TEXAS A&M UNIVERSITY–CORPUS CHRISTI
Corpus Christi, TX

CONTACT Financial Aid Adviser, Texas A&M University–Corpus Christi, 6300 Ocean Drive, Corpus Christi, TX 78412-5503, 361-825-2338 or toll-free 800-482-6822. *Fax:* 361-825-6095. *E-mail:* faoweb@mail.tamucc.edu.

TEXAS A&M UNIVERSITY–KINGSVILLE
Kingsville, TX

CONTACT Roel M. Villarreal, Director, Financial Aid, Texas A&M University–Kingsville, 700 University Boulevard, Kingsville, TX 78363, 361-593-2174 or toll-free 800-687-6000. *Fax:* 361-593-3026.

TEXAS A&M UNIVERSITY–TEXARKANA
Texarkana, TX

ABOUT THE INSTITUTION State-supported, coed. Awards: bachelor's and master's degrees. 19 undergraduate majors. Total enrollment: 1,653. Undergraduates: 1,003.
GIFT AID (NEED-BASED) *Scholarships, grants, and awards:* Federal Pell, FSEOG, state, private, college/university gift aid from institutional funds.
GIFT AID (NON-NEED-BASED) *Scholarships, grants, and awards by category:* Academic Interests/Achievement: business, education, English, general academic interests/achievements, mathematics, social sciences. Special Achievements/Activities: community service, general special achievements/activities, leadership, memberships.
LOANS *Programs:* FFEL (Subsidized and Unsubsidized Stafford, PLUS), college/university.
APPLYING FOR FINANCIAL AID *Required financial aid forms:* FAFSA, institution's own form, state aid form.
CONTACT Marilyn Raney, Director of Financial Aid and Veterans' Services, Texas A&M University–Texarkana, 2600 North Robison Road, Texarkana, TX 75505, 903-223-3060. *Fax:* 903-223-3118. *E-mail:* marilyn.raney@tamut.edu.

Texas Chiropractic College

TEXAS CHIROPRACTIC COLLEGE
Pasadena, TX

CONTACT Arthur Goudeau, Financial Aid Director, Texas Chiropractic College, 5912 Spencer Highway, Pasadena, TX 77505, 281-998-6022 or toll-free 800-468-6839. *Fax:* 281-991-5237. *E-mail:* agoudeau@txchiro.edu.

TEXAS CHRISTIAN UNIVERSITY
Fort Worth, TX

Tuition & fees: $21,320   **Average undergraduate aid package: $14,589**

ABOUT THE INSTITUTION Independent religious, coed. Awards: bachelor's, master's, doctoral, and first professional degrees and post-bachelor's and first professional certificates. 86 undergraduate majors. Total enrollment: 8,749. Undergraduates: 7,171. Freshmen: 1,610. Federal methodology is used as a basis for awarding need-based institutional aid.
UNDERGRADUATE EXPENSES for 2005–06 *Application fee:* $40. *Comprehensive fee:* $28,300 includes full-time tuition ($21,280), mandatory fees ($40), and room and board ($6980). *College room only:* $4180. Room and board charges vary according to board plan and housing facility. *Payment plan:* Installment.
FRESHMAN FINANCIAL AID (Fall 2005, est.) 875 applied for aid; of those 70% were deemed to have need. 100% of freshmen with need received aid; of those 47% had need fully met. *Average percent of need met:* 71% (excluding resources awarded to replace EFC). *Average financial aid package:* $14,193 (excluding resources awarded to replace EFC). 25% of all full-time freshmen had no need and received non-need-based gift aid.
UNDERGRADUATE FINANCIAL AID (Fall 2005, est.) 3,654 applied for aid; of those 80% were deemed to have need. 99% of undergraduates with need received aid; of those 42% had need fully met. *Average percent of need met:* 67% (excluding resources awarded to replace EFC). *Average financial aid package:* $14,589 (excluding resources awarded to replace EFC). 22% of all full-time undergraduates had no need and received non-need-based gift aid.
GIFT AID (NEED-BASED) *Total amount:* $23,332,092 (11% federal, 23% state, 59% institutional, 7% external sources). *Receiving aid:* Freshmen: 34% (551); All full-time undergraduates: 37% (2,485). *Average award:* Freshmen: $10,246; Undergraduates: $10,253. *Scholarships, grants, and awards:* Federal Pell, FSEOG, state, private, college/university gift aid from institutional funds, United Negro College Fund.
GIFT AID (NON-NEED-BASED) *Total amount:* $20,322,040 (79% institutional, 21% external sources). *Receiving aid:* Freshmen: 19% (308); Undergraduates: 17% (1,124). *Average Award:* Freshmen: $8117; Undergraduates: $8800. *Scholarships, grants, and awards by category:* Academic Interests/Achievement: 2,071 awards ($12,097,000 total): education, engineering/technologies, general academic interests/achievements, international studies, military science, premedicine, religion/biblical studies. Creative Arts/Performance: 244 awards ($1,470,000 total): art/fine arts, cinema/film/broadcasting, dance, journalism/publications, music, performing arts, theater/drama. Special Achievements/Activities: 400 awards ($2,264,000 total): general special achievements/activities, leadership. Special Characteristics: 722 awards ($7,311,000 total): adult students, children of faculty/staff, children of union members/company employees, international students, local/state students, relatives of clergy, religious affiliation. *Tuition waivers:* Full or partial for employees or children of employees.
ROTC: Army, Air Force.
LOANS *Student loans:* $27,438,664 (75% need-based, 25% non-need-based). *Average need-based loan:* Freshmen: $4809; Undergraduates: $5957. *Parent loans:* $26,883,189 (39% need-based, 61% non-need-based). *Programs:* FFEL (Subsidized and Unsubsidized Stafford, PLUS), Perkins, Federal Nursing, state.
WORK-STUDY *Federal work-study:* Total amount: $2,906,540; 1,296 jobs averaging $2313. *State or other work-study/employment:* Total amount: $43,134 (100% need-based). 25 part-time jobs averaging $2400.
ATHLETIC AWARDS *Total amount:* $7,795,366 (39% need-based, 61% non-need-based).
APPLYING FOR FINANCIAL AID *Required financial aid forms:* FAFSA, institution's own form. *Financial aid deadline:* 5/1 (priority: 5/1). *Notification date:* Continuous.
CONTACT Michael Scott, Director, Scholarships and Student Financial Aid, Texas Christian University, PO Box 297012, Fort Worth, TX 76129-0002, 817-257-7858 or toll-free 800-828-3764. *Fax:* 817-257-7462. *E-mail:* m.scott@tcu.edu.

TEXAS COLLEGE
Tyler, TX

CONTACT Mrs. Ruth Jordan, Financial Aid Office, Texas College, 2404 North Grand Avenue, Tyler, TX 75702, 903-593-8311 Ext. 2210 or toll-free 800-306-6299 (out-of-state). *Fax:* 903-596-0001. *E-mail:* rjordanW@texascollege.edu.

TEXAS LUTHERAN UNIVERSITY
Seguin, TX

Tuition & fees: $18,840   **Average undergraduate aid package: $12,726**

ABOUT THE INSTITUTION Independent religious, coed. Awards: bachelor's degrees and post-bachelor's certificates. 42 undergraduate majors. Total enrollment: 1,435. Undergraduates: 1,435. Freshmen: 381. Federal methodology is used as a basis for awarding need-based institutional aid.
UNDERGRADUATE EXPENSES for 2006–07 *Application fee:* $25. *Comprehensive fee:* $24,440 includes full-time tuition ($18,720), mandatory fees ($120), and room and board ($5600). *College room only:* $2600. *Part-time tuition:* $630 per credit hour. *Part-time fees:* $60 per term.
FRESHMAN FINANCIAL AID (Fall 2004) 356 applied for aid; of those 80% were deemed to have need. 100% of freshmen with need received aid; of those 25% had need fully met. *Average percent of need met:* 72% (excluding resources awarded to replace EFC). *Average financial aid package:* $12,748 (excluding resources awarded to replace EFC). 26% of all full-time freshmen had no need and received non-need-based gift aid.
UNDERGRADUATE FINANCIAL AID (Fall 2004) 1,098 applied for aid; of those 86% were deemed to have need. 100% of undergraduates with need received aid; of those 20% had need fully met. *Average percent of need met:* 70% (excluding resources awarded to replace EFC). *Average financial aid package:* $12,726 (excluding resources awarded to replace EFC). 25% of all full-time undergraduates had no need and received non-need-based gift aid.
GIFT AID (NEED-BASED) *Total amount:* $8,848,337 (15% federal, 26% state, 54% institutional, 5% external sources). *Receiving aid:* Freshmen: 69% (267); All full-time undergraduates: 64% (826). *Average award:* Freshmen: $5700; Undergraduates: $5540. *Scholarships, grants, and awards:* Federal Pell, FSEOG, state, private, college/university gift aid from institutional funds.
GIFT AID (NON-NEED-BASED) *Total amount:* $2,066,183 (90% institutional, 10% external sources). *Receiving aid:* Freshmen: 73% (282); Undergraduates: 71% (917). *Average Award:* Freshmen: $6183; Undergraduates: $5651. *Scholarships, grants, and awards by category:* Academic Interests/Achievement: 717 awards ($3,477,945 total): general academic interests/achievements. Creative Arts/Performance: 250 awards ($453,608 total): journalism/publications, music, theater/drama. Special Achievements/Activities: 236 awards ($455,529 total): general special achievements/activities, leadership, religious involvement. Special Characteristics: 666 awards ($925,093 total): children and siblings of alumni, children of faculty/staff, first-generation college students, general special characteristics, international students, religious affiliation. *ROTC:* Army cooperative, Air Force cooperative.
LOANS *Student loans:* $7,533,541 (87% need-based, 13% non-need-based). 68% of past graduating class borrowed through all loan programs. *Average indebtedness per student:* $28,300. *Average need-based loan:* Freshmen: $3148; Undergraduates: $4166. *Parent loans:* $8,268,098 (34% need-based, 66% non-need-based). *Programs:* FFEL (Subsidized and Unsubsidized Stafford, PLUS), Perkins, alternative loans.
WORK-STUDY *Federal work-study:* Total amount: $110,626; 342 jobs averaging $1000. *State or other work-study/employment:* Total amount: $338,911 (5% need-based, 95% non-need-based). 16 part-time jobs averaging $1029.
APPLYING FOR FINANCIAL AID *Required financial aid form:* FAFSA. *Financial aid deadline (priority):* 4/1. *Notification date:* Continuous beginning 3/1. Students must reply within 2 weeks of notification.
CONTACT Debbie Mattke, Assistant Director Financial Aid, Texas Lutheran University, 1000 West Court Street, Seguin, TX 78155-5999, 830-372-8075 or toll-free 800-771-8521. *Fax:* 830-372-8096. *E-mail:* dmattke@tlu.edu.

TEXAS SOUTHERN UNIVERSITY
Houston, TX

Tuition & fees (TX res): $3772   **Average undergraduate aid package: $14,065**

ABOUT THE INSTITUTION State-supported, coed. Awards: bachelor's, master's, doctoral, and first professional degrees. 106 undergraduate majors. Total enrollment: 11,903. Undergraduates: 9,760. Freshmen: 2,001. Federal methodology is used as a basis for awarding need-based institutional aid.

UNDERGRADUATE EXPENSES for 2005–06 *Application fee:* $42. *Tuition, state resident:* full-time $1200; part-time $50 per hour. *Tuition, nonresident:* full-time $7824; part-time $326 per hour. *Required fees:* full-time $2572; $817 per term part-time. Full-time tuition and fees vary according to course load and program. Part-time tuition and fees vary according to course load and program. *College room and board:* $6056. Room and board charges vary according to board plan and housing facility. *Payment plan:* Installment.

FRESHMAN FINANCIAL AID (Fall 2005, est.) 1785 applied for aid; of those 94% were deemed to have need. 93% of freshmen with need received aid; of those 29% had need fully met. *Average percent of need met:* 42% (excluding resources awarded to replace EFC). *Average financial aid package:* $14,065 (excluding resources awarded to replace EFC).

UNDERGRADUATE FINANCIAL AID (Fall 2005, est.) 7,047 applied for aid; of those 81% were deemed to have need. 80% of undergraduates with need received aid; of those 35% had need fully met. *Average percent of need met:* 48% (excluding resources awarded to replace EFC). *Average financial aid package:* $14,065 (excluding resources awarded to replace EFC).

GIFT AID (NEED-BASED) *Total amount:* $91,805,981 (88% federal, 5% state, 6% institutional, 1% external sources). *Receiving aid:* Freshmen: 63% (1,327); All full-time undergraduates: 45% (3,881). *Average award:* Freshmen: $9050; Undergraduates: $9050. *Scholarships, grants, and awards:* Federal Pell, FSEOG, state, private, college/university gift aid from institutional funds, United Negro College Fund, Federal Nursing.

GIFT AID (NON-NEED-BASED) *Scholarships, grants, and awards by category: Academic Interests/Achievement:* 254 awards ($351,422 total): business, communication, engineering/technologies, general academic interests/achievements. *Tuition waivers:* Full or partial for minority students, senior citizens. *ROTC:* Army cooperative, Naval cooperative.

LOANS *Student loans:* $57,781,263 (100% need-based). 65% of past graduating class borrowed through all loan programs. *Average indebtedness per student:* $25,310. *Average need-based loan:* Freshmen: $6625; Undergraduates: $6625. *Parent loans:* $1,798,471 (100% need-based). *Programs:* FFEL (Subsidized and Unsubsidized Stafford, PLUS), Perkins.

WORK-STUDY *Federal work-study:* Total amount: $729,525; 225 jobs averaging $4000. *State or other work-study/employment:* Total amount: $22,046 (100% need-based). 29 part-time jobs averaging $4000.

ATHLETIC AWARDS *Total amount:* $1,388,518 (100% need-based).

APPLYING FOR FINANCIAL AID *Required financial aid forms:* FAFSA, institution's own form. *Financial aid deadline (priority):* 4/15. *Notification date:* Continuous.

CONTACT Financial Aid Office, Texas Southern University, 3100 Cleburne, Houston, TX 77004-4584, 713-313-7011. *Fax:* 713-313-1858.

TEXAS STATE UNIVERSITY-SAN MARCOS
San Marcos, TX

| Tuition & fees (TX res): $5252 | Average undergraduate aid package: $9274 |

ABOUT THE INSTITUTION State-supported, coed. Awards: bachelor's, master's, and doctoral degrees and post-bachelor's certificates. 94 undergraduate majors. Total enrollment: 27,129. Undergraduates: 22,986. Freshmen: 3,073. Federal methodology is used as a basis for awarding need-based institutional aid.

UNDERGRADUATE EXPENSES for 2005–06 *Application fee:* $40. *Tuition, state resident:* full-time $3780; part-time $126 per semester hour. *Tuition, nonresident:* full-time $12,060; part-time $402 per semester hour. *Required fees:* full-time $1472; $37 per semester hour or $267 per term part-time. Full-time tuition and fees vary according to course load. Part-time tuition and fees vary according to course load. *College room and board:* $5610; *room only:* $3524. Room and board charges vary according to board plan and housing facility. *Payment plan:* Installment.

FRESHMAN FINANCIAL AID (Fall 2005, est.) 2003 applied for aid; of those 68% were deemed to have need. 89% of freshmen with need received aid; of those 13% had need fully met. *Average percent of need met:* 70% (excluding resources awarded to replace EFC). *Average financial aid package:* $9827 (excluding resources awarded to replace EFC). 5% of all full-time freshmen had no need and received non-need-based gift aid.

UNDERGRADUATE FINANCIAL AID (Fall 2005, est.) 12,566 applied for aid; of those 77% were deemed to have need. 96% of undergraduates with need received aid; of those 15% had need fully met. *Average percent of need met:* 67% (excluding resources awarded to replace EFC). *Average financial aid package:* $9274 (excluding resources awarded to replace EFC). 2% of all full-time undergraduates had no need and received non-need-based gift aid.

GIFT AID (NEED-BASED) *Total amount:* $30,364,303 (53% federal, 47% state). *Receiving aid:* Freshmen: 30% (898); All full-time undergraduates: 36% (6,729). *Average award:* Freshmen: $4781; Undergraduates: $4057. *Scholarships, grants, and awards:* Federal Pell, FSEOG, state, college/university gift aid from institutional funds.

GIFT AID (NON-NEED-BASED) *Total amount:* $6,316,767 (34% institutional, 66% external sources). *Receiving aid:* Freshmen: 3% (100); Undergraduates: 3% (479). *Average Award:* Freshmen: $2069; Undergraduates: $2165. *Scholarships, grants, and awards by category: Academic Interests/Achievement:* agriculture, business, education, English, general academic interests/achievements, home economics, international studies, military science. *Creative Arts/Performance:* applied art and design, journalism/publications, music, theater/drama. *Special Characteristics:* children and siblings of alumni, first-generation college students, handicapped students. *Tuition waivers:* Full or partial for employees or children of employees. *ROTC:* Army, Air Force.

LOANS *Student loans:* $72,975,544 (50% need-based, 50% non-need-based). 59% of past graduating class borrowed through all loan programs. *Average indebtedness per student:* $16,863. *Average need-based loan:* Freshmen: $2911; Undergraduates: $3890. *Parent loans:* $12,423,148 (100% non-need-based). *Programs:* Federal Direct (Subsidized and Unsubsidized Stafford, PLUS), FFEL (Subsidized and Unsubsidized Stafford, PLUS), Perkins, state, college/university.

WORK-STUDY *Federal work-study:* Total amount: $1,093,708; 773 jobs averaging $1484. *State or other work-study/employment:* Total amount: $208,352 (100% need-based). 157 part-time jobs averaging $885.

ATHLETIC AWARDS *Total amount:* $2,210,044 (100% non-need-based).

APPLYING FOR FINANCIAL AID *Required financial aid form:* FAFSA. *Financial aid deadline (priority):* 4/1. *Notification date:* Continuous. Students must reply within 3 weeks of notification.

CONTACT Ms. Mariko Gomez, Director of Financial Aid, Texas State University-San Marcos, 601 University Drive, San Marcos, TX 78666-4602, 512-245-2315. *Fax:* 512-245-7920. *E-mail:* mg01@txstate.edu.

TEXAS TECH UNIVERSITY
Lubbock, TX

| Tuition & fees (TX res): $6152 | Average undergraduate aid package: $7080 |

ABOUT THE INSTITUTION State-supported, coed. Awards: bachelor's, master's, doctoral, and first professional degrees. 111 undergraduate majors. Total enrollment: 28,001. Undergraduates: 23,002. Freshmen: 3,779. Federal methodology is used as a basis for awarding need-based institutional aid.

UNDERGRADUATE EXPENSES for 2005–06 *Application fee:* $50. *Tuition, state resident:* full-time $3870; part-time $129 per credit hour. *Tuition, nonresident:* full-time $12,150; part-time $405 per credit hour. *Required fees:* full-time $2282; $58.75 per credit hour or $291. Full-time tuition and fees vary according to course load, program, and reciprocity agreements. Part-time tuition and fees vary according to course load, program, and reciprocity agreements. *College room and board:* $6875; *room only:* $3663. Room and board charges vary according to board plan and housing facility. *Payment plan:* Installment.

FRESHMAN FINANCIAL AID (Fall 2004) 2676 applied for aid; of those 58% were deemed to have need. 97% of freshmen with need received aid; of those 6% had need fully met. *Average percent of need met:* 62% (excluding resources awarded to replace EFC). *Average financial aid package:* $5824 (excluding resources awarded to replace EFC). 4% of all full-time freshmen had no need and received non-need-based gift aid.

UNDERGRADUATE FINANCIAL AID (Fall 2004) 13,152 applied for aid; of those 67% were deemed to have need. 98% of undergraduates with need received aid; of those 4% had need fully met. *Average percent of need met:* 63% (excluding resources awarded to replace EFC). *Average financial aid package:* $7080 (excluding resources awarded to replace EFC). 2% of all full-time undergraduates had no need and received non-need-based gift aid.

GIFT AID (NEED-BASED) *Total amount:* $26,090,052 (52% federal, 44% state, 4% institutional). *Receiving aid:* Freshmen: 23% (855); All full-time undergradu-

Texas Tech University

ates: 28% (5,943). *Average award:* Freshmen: $4809; Undergraduates: $4228. *Scholarships, grants, and awards:* Federal Pell, FSEOG, state, private, college/university gift aid from institutional funds.

GIFT AID (NON-NEED-BASED) *Total amount:* $10,458,604 (62% institutional, 38% external sources). *Receiving aid:* Freshmen: 17% (634); Undergraduates: 10% (2,110). *Average Award: Freshmen:* $1899; *Undergraduates:* $1640. *Scholarships, grants, and awards by category: Academic Interests/Achievement:* agriculture, architecture, biological sciences, business, communication, computer science, education, engineering/technologies, English, foreign languages, general academic interests/achievements, home economics, humanities, international studies, mathematics, military science, physical sciences, premedicine, social sciences. *Creative Arts/Performance:* applied art and design, art/fine arts, dance, journalism/publications, music, performing arts, theater/drama. *Special Achievements/Activities:* community service, memberships, rodeo. *Special Characteristics:* children of faculty/staff, first-generation college students, handicapped students, out-of-state students, veterans, veterans' children. *Tuition waivers:* Full or partial for employees or children of employees, senior citizens. *ROTC:* Army, Air Force.

LOANS *Student loans:* $62,354,556 (46% need-based, 54% non-need-based). 57% of past graduating class borrowed through all loan programs. *Average indebtedness per student:* $19,972. *Average need-based loan:* Freshmen: $3083; Undergraduates: $3901. *Parent loans:* $14,304,790 (100% non-need-based). *Programs:* FFEL (Subsidized and Unsubsidized Stafford, PLUS), Perkins, state, college/university.

WORK-STUDY *Federal work-study:* Total amount: $714,881.

ATHLETIC AWARDS *Total amount:* $3,598,990 (100% non-need-based).

APPLYING FOR FINANCIAL AID *Required financial aid form:* FAFSA. *Financial aid deadline (priority):* 4/15. *Notification date:* Continuous. Students must reply within 2 weeks of notification.

CONTACT Becky Wilson, Director of Financial Aid, Interim, Texas Tech University, PO Box 45011, Lubbock, TX 79409-5011, 806-742-3681. *Fax:* 806-742-0880.

TEXAS WESLEYAN UNIVERSITY
Fort Worth, TX

ABOUT THE INSTITUTION Independent United Methodist, coed. Awards: bachelor's, master's, and first professional degrees. 70 undergraduate majors. Total enrollment: 2,742. Undergraduates: 1,491. Freshmen: 161.

GIFT AID (NEED-BASED) *Scholarships, grants, and awards:* Federal Pell, FSEOG, state, private, college/university gift aid from institutional funds.

GIFT AID (NON-NEED-BASED) *Scholarships, grants, and awards by category: Academic Interests/Achievement:* general academic interests/achievements. *Creative Arts/Performance:* art/fine arts, general creative arts/performance. *Special Achievements/Activities:* cheerleading/drum major, general special achievements/activities, leadership, religious involvement. *Special Characteristics:* relatives of clergy, religious affiliation.

LOANS *Programs:* FFEL (Subsidized and Unsubsidized Stafford, PLUS), state, college/university.

WORK-STUDY *Federal work-study:* Total amount: $250,000; jobs available (averaging $2400). *State or other work-study/employment:* Total amount: $32,779 (100% need-based). Part-time jobs available (averaging $2400).

APPLYING FOR FINANCIAL AID *Required financial aid forms:* FAFSA, institution's own form.

CONTACT Mrs. Dean Carpenter, Director of Financial Aid, Texas Wesleyan University, 1201 Wesleyan Street, Fort Worth, TX 76105-1536, 817-531-4420 or toll-free 800-580-8980 (in-state). *Fax:* 817-531-4231. *E-mail:* finaid@txwes.edu.

TEXAS WOMAN'S UNIVERSITY
Denton, TX

Tuition & fees (TX res): $5010 | **Average undergraduate aid package: $9718**

ABOUT THE INSTITUTION State-supported, coed, primarily women. Awards: bachelor's, master's, and doctoral degrees and post-master's certificates. 37 undergraduate majors. Total enrollment: 11,344. Undergraduates: 6,266. Freshmen: 702. Federal methodology is used as a basis for awarding need-based institutional aid.

UNDERGRADUATE EXPENSES for 2006–07 *Application fee:* $30. *Tuition, state resident:* full-time $3690; part-time $123 per hour. *Tuition, nonresident:* full-time $11,970; part-time $399 per hour. *College room and board:* $5598; *room only:* $2804.

FRESHMAN FINANCIAL AID (Fall 2005, est.) 538 applied for aid; of those 75% were deemed to have need. 98% of those with need received aid; of those 87% had need fully met. *Average percent of need met:* 98% (excluding resources awarded to replace EFC). *Average financial aid package:* $9312 (excluding resources awarded to replace EFC). 11% of all full-time freshmen had no need and received non-need-based gift aid.

UNDERGRADUATE FINANCIAL AID (Fall 2005, est.) 3,339 applied for aid; of those 80% were deemed to have need. 99% of undergraduates with need received aid; of those 89% had need fully met. *Average percent of need met:* 95% (excluding resources awarded to replace EFC). *Average financial aid package:* $9718 (excluding resources awarded to replace EFC). 5% of all full-time undergraduates had no need and received non-need-based gift aid.

GIFT AID (NEED-BASED) *Total amount:* $13,030,300 (53% federal, 13% state, 34% institutional). *Receiving aid:* Freshmen: 40% (281); All full-time undergraduates: 42% (1,909). *Average award:* Freshmen: $4206; Undergraduates: $4011. *Scholarships, grants, and awards:* Federal Pell, FSEOG, state, private, college/university gift aid from institutional funds.

GIFT AID (NON-NEED-BASED) *Total amount:* $2,656,779 (72% institutional, 28% external sources). *Receiving aid:* Freshmen: 24% (169); Undergraduates: 18% (816). *Average Award: Freshmen:* $3339; *Undergraduates:* $2705. *Scholarships, grants, and awards by category: Academic Interests/Achievement:* 1,651 awards ($1,830,415 total): biological sciences, business, communication, computer science, education, English, foreign languages, general academic interests/achievements, health fields, home economics, humanities, library science, mathematics, physical sciences, premedicine, social sciences. *Creative Arts/Performance:* 80 awards ($82,470 total): applied art and design, art/fine arts, cinema/film/broadcasting, dance, journalism/publications, music, theater/drama. *Special Characteristics:* 61 awards ($109,800 total): international students. *ROTC:* Army cooperative, Air Force cooperative.

LOANS *Student loans:* $28,285,026 (41% need-based, 59% non-need-based). 54% of past graduating class borrowed through all loan programs. *Average indebtedness per student:* $18,125. *Average need-based loan:* Freshmen: $2230; Undergraduates: $3775. *Parent loans:* $725,737 (11% need-based, 89% non-need-based). *Programs:* FFEL (Subsidized and Unsubsidized Stafford, PLUS), Perkins, Federal Nursing, state, college/university, alternative loans.

WORK-STUDY *Federal work-study:* Total amount: $154,822; 86 jobs averaging $1800. *State or other work-study/employment:* Total amount: $1,442,492 (4% need-based, 96% non-need-based). 432 part-time jobs averaging $3200.

ATHLETIC AWARDS *Total amount:* $365,663 (100% non-need-based).

APPLYING FOR FINANCIAL AID *Required financial aid form:* FAFSA. *Financial aid deadline (priority):* 4/1. *Notification date:* 5/1. Students must reply within 3 weeks of notification.

CONTACT Mr. Governor Jackson, Director of Financial Aid, Texas Woman's University, PO Box 425408, Denton, TX 76204-5408, 940-898-3051 or toll-free 888-948-9984. *Fax:* 940-898-3068. *E-mail:* gjackson@twu.edu.

THIEL COLLEGE
Greenville, PA

Tuition & fees: $17,590 | **Average undergraduate aid package: $13,265**

ABOUT THE INSTITUTION Independent religious, coed. Awards: associate and bachelor's degrees. 40 undergraduate majors. Total enrollment: 1,320. Undergraduates: 1,320. Freshmen: 427. Federal methodology is used as a basis for awarding need-based institutional aid.

UNDERGRADUATE EXPENSES for 2005–06 *Application fee:* $25. *Comprehensive fee:* $24,580 includes full-time tuition ($16,200), mandatory fees ($1390), and room and board ($6990). *College room only:* $3566. Full-time tuition and fees vary according to course load. Room and board charges vary according to board plan and housing facility. *Part-time tuition:* $400 per credit hour. *Part-time fees:* $21 per credit hour. Part-time tuition and fees vary according to course load. *Payment plan:* Installment.

FRESHMAN FINANCIAL AID (Fall 2005, est.) 415 applied for aid; of those 85% were deemed to have need. 100% of freshmen with need received aid; of those 20% had need fully met. *Average percent of need met:* 78% (excluding resources

awarded to replace EFC). *Average financial aid package:* $14,960 (excluding resources awarded to replace EFC). 17% of all full-time freshmen had no need and received non-need-based gift aid.
UNDERGRADUATE FINANCIAL AID (Fall 2005, est.) 1,215 applied for aid; of those 90% were deemed to have need. 100% of undergraduates with need received aid; of those 20% had need fully met. *Average percent of need met:* 75% (excluding resources awarded to replace EFC). *Average financial aid package:* $13,265 (excluding resources awarded to replace EFC). 13% of all full-time undergraduates had no need and received non-need-based gift aid.
GIFT AID (NEED-BASED) *Total amount:* $10,105,185 (15% federal, 19% state, 64% institutional, 2% external sources). *Receiving aid:* Freshmen: 83% (353); All full-time undergraduates: 87% (1,094). *Average award:* Freshmen: $11,135; Undergraduates: $9236. *Scholarships, grants, and awards:* Federal Pell, FSEOG, state, private, college/university gift aid from institutional funds.
GIFT AID (NON-NEED-BASED) *Total amount:* $1,149,448 (100% institutional). *Receiving aid:* Freshmen: 83% (353); Undergraduates: 87% (1,094). *Average Award:* Freshmen: $6293; Undergraduates: $7229. *Scholarships, grants, and awards by category: Academic Interests/Achievement:* biological sciences, business, computer science, education, English, general academic interests/achievements, mathematics, physical sciences, religion/biblical studies. *Creative Arts/Performance:* 10 awards ($5750 total): music. *Special Achievements/Activities:* leadership. *Special Characteristics:* children and siblings of alumni, children of faculty/staff, relatives of clergy, religious affiliation, siblings of current students. *Tuition waivers:* Full or partial for employees or children of employees, senior citizens.
LOANS *Student loans:* $6,978,358 (55% need-based, 45% non-need-based). 87% of past graduating class borrowed through all loan programs. *Average indebtedness per student:* $20,000. *Average need-based loan:* Freshmen: $3662; Undergraduates: $3508. *Parent loans:* $2,034,192 (77% need-based, 23% non-need-based). *Programs:* FFEL (Subsidized and Unsubsidized Stafford, PLUS), Perkins, college/university.
WORK-STUDY *Federal work-study:* Total amount: $118,594; 154 jobs averaging $1013. *State or other work-study/employment:* Total amount: $505,406 (83% need-based, 17% non-need-based). 416 part-time jobs averaging $1014.
APPLYING FOR FINANCIAL AID *Required financial aid forms:* FAFSA, state aid form. *Financial aid deadline (priority):* 3/15. *Notification date:* Continuous beginning 2/15. Students must reply within 2 weeks of notification.
CONTACT Ms. Cynthia H. Farrell, Director of Financial Aid, Thiel College, 75 College Avenue, Greenville, PA 16125-2181, 724-589-2178 or toll-free 800-248-4435. *Fax:* 724-589-2850. *E-mail:* cfarrell@thiel.edu.

THOMAS AQUINAS COLLEGE
Santa Paula, CA

Tuition & fees: $19,300 | **Average undergraduate aid package: $16,479**

ABOUT THE INSTITUTION Independent Roman Catholic, coed. Awards: bachelor's degrees. 4 undergraduate majors. Total enrollment: 359. Undergraduates: 359. Freshmen: 102. Both federal and institutional methodology are used as a basis for awarding need-based institutional aid.
UNDERGRADUATE EXPENSES for 2006–07 *Comprehensive fee:* $25,300 includes full-time tuition ($19,300) and room and board ($6000).
FRESHMAN FINANCIAL AID (Fall 2005, est.) 81 applied for aid; of those 95% were deemed to have need. 100% of freshmen with need received aid; of those 100% had need fully met. *Average percent of need met:* 100% (excluding resources awarded to replace EFC). *Average financial aid package:* $15,806 (excluding resources awarded to replace EFC).
UNDERGRADUATE FINANCIAL AID (Fall 2005, est.) 254 applied for aid; of those 94% were deemed to have need. 100% of undergraduates with need received aid; of those 100% had need fully met. *Average percent of need met:* 100% (excluding resources awarded to replace EFC). *Average financial aid package:* $16,479 (excluding resources awarded to replace EFC).
GIFT AID (NEED-BASED) *Total amount:* $2,541,531 (9% federal, 15% state, 73% institutional, 3% external sources). *Receiving aid:* Freshmen: 67% (68); All full-time undergraduates: 59% (212). *Average award:* Freshmen: $11,949; Undergraduates: $11,955. *Scholarships, grants, and awards:* Federal Pell, state, private, college/university gift aid from institutional funds.
GIFT AID (NON-NEED-BASED) *Total amount:* $39,365 (8% state, 92% external sources). *Receiving aid:* Freshmen: 1% (1); Undergraduates: 3% (10).
LOANS *Student loans:* $855,337 (84% need-based, 16% non-need-based). 85% of past graduating class borrowed through all loan programs. *Average indebtedness per student:* $14,000. *Average need-based loan:* Freshmen: $2519; Undergraduates: $3297. *Parent loans:* $168,628 (21% need-based, 79% non-need-based). *Programs:* FFEL (Subsidized and Unsubsidized Stafford, PLUS), college/university, Canada Student Loans.
WORK-STUDY *State or other work-study/employment:* Total amount: $672,000 (98% need-based, 2% non-need-based). 214 part-time jobs averaging $3140.
APPLYING FOR FINANCIAL AID *Required financial aid forms:* FAFSA, institution's own form, state aid form, noncustodial (divorced/separated) parent's statement, income tax returns. *Financial aid deadline:* 3/2. *Notification date:* Continuous beginning 1/1. Students must reply within 2 weeks of notification.
CONTACT Mr. Gregory Becher, Director of Financial Aid, Thomas Aquinas College, 10000 North Ojai Road, Santa Paula, CA 93060-9980, 805-525-4419 Ext. 235 or toll-free 800-634-9797. *Fax:* 805-525-9342. *E-mail:* gbecher@thomasaquinas.edu.

THOMAS COLLEGE
Waterville, ME

Tuition & fees: $17,730 | **Average undergraduate aid package: $15,198**

ABOUT THE INSTITUTION Independent, coed. Awards: associate, bachelor's, and master's degrees (associate). 16 undergraduate majors. Total enrollment: 875. Undergraduates: 731. Freshmen: 197. Federal methodology is used as a basis for awarding need-based institutional aid.
UNDERGRADUATE EXPENSES for 2006–07 *Application fee:* $50. *Comprehensive fee:* $25,160 includes full-time tuition ($17,280), mandatory fees ($450), and room and board ($7430). *Part-time tuition:* $720 per credit hour.
FRESHMAN FINANCIAL AID (Fall 2005, est.) 183 applied for aid; of those 90% were deemed to have need. 100% of freshmen with need received aid; of those 19% had need fully met. *Average percent of need met:* 85% (excluding resources awarded to replace EFC). *Average financial aid package:* $16,464 (excluding resources awarded to replace EFC). 21% of all full-time freshmen had no need and received non-need-based gift aid.
UNDERGRADUATE FINANCIAL AID (Fall 2005, est.) 555 applied for aid; of those 93% were deemed to have need. 100% of undergraduates with need received aid; of those 19% had need fully met. *Average percent of need met:* 85% (excluding resources awarded to replace EFC). *Average financial aid package:* $15,198 (excluding resources awarded to replace EFC). 14% of all full-time undergraduates had no need and received non-need-based gift aid.
GIFT AID (NEED-BASED) *Total amount:* $4,841,386 (21% federal, 7% state, 72% institutional). *Receiving aid:* Freshmen: 85% (165); All full-time undergraduates: 90% (516). *Average award:* Freshmen: $11,129; Undergraduates: $9382. *Scholarships, grants, and awards:* Federal Pell, FSEOG, state, private, college/university gift aid from institutional funds.
GIFT AID (NON-NEED-BASED) *Total amount:* $618,972 (60% institutional, 40% external sources). *Receiving aid:* Freshmen: 12% (23); Undergraduates: 11% (61). *Average Award:* Freshmen: $4060; Undergraduates: $4619. *Scholarships, grants, and awards by category: Academic Interests/Achievement:* 183 awards ($979,624 total): general academic interests/achievements.
LOANS *Student loans:* $4,339,307 (48% need-based, 52% non-need-based). 78% of past graduating class borrowed through all loan programs. *Average indebtedness per student:* $19,125. *Average need-based loan:* Freshmen: $3405; Undergraduates: $4274. *Parent loans:* $512,638 (100% non-need-based). *Programs:* Federal Direct (Subsidized and Unsubsidized Stafford, PLUS), Perkins.
WORK-STUDY *Federal work-study:* Total amount: $198,931; 108 jobs averaging $1700. *State or other work-study/employment:* Total amount: $12,000 (100% need-based).
APPLYING FOR FINANCIAL AID *Required financial aid form:* FAFSA. *Financial aid deadline (priority):* 2/15. *Notification date:* Continuous beginning 3/15. Students must reply within 2 weeks of notification.
CONTACT Jeannine Bosse, Associate Director of Student Financial Services, Thomas College, 180 West River Road, Waterville, ME 04901-5097, 800-339-7001. *Fax:* 207-859-1114. *E-mail:* sfsassistant@thomas.edu.

THOMAS EDISON STATE COLLEGE
Trenton, NJ

| Tuition & fees: N/R | Average undergraduate aid package: N/A |

ABOUT THE INSTITUTION State-supported, coed. Awards: associate, bachelor's, and master's degrees (offers only distance learning degree programs). Total enrollment: 11,224. Undergraduates: 10,904. Federal methodology is used as a basis for awarding need-based institutional aid.

UNDERGRADUATE EXPENSES for 2005–06 *Application fee:* $75. *Tuition, state resident:* part-time $3780 per year. *Tuition, nonresident:* part-time $5400 per year.

GIFT AID (NEED-BASED) *Total amount:* $1,309,797 (91% federal, 9% state). *Scholarships, grants, and awards:* Federal Pell, state, private.

GIFT AID (NON-NEED-BASED) *Total amount:* $13,332 (100% external sources). *Tuition waivers:* Full or partial for employees or children of employees.

LOANS *Student loans:* $4,754,139 (100% need-based). *Programs:* FFEL (Subsidized and Unsubsidized Stafford, PLUS), private educational loans.

APPLYING FOR FINANCIAL AID *Required financial aid forms:* FAFSA, institution's own form. *Financial aid deadline:* Continuous. *Notification date:* Continuous.

CONTACT Financial Aid Office, Thomas Edison State College, 101 West State Street, Trenton, NJ 08608, 609-633-9658 or toll-free 888-442-8372. *Fax:* 609-633-6489.

THOMAS JEFFERSON UNIVERSITY
Philadelphia, PA

| Tuition & fees: $21,975 | Average undergraduate aid package: N/A |

ABOUT THE INSTITUTION Independent, coed. Awards: bachelor's, master's, and doctoral degrees and post-bachelor's certificates. 8 undergraduate majors. Total enrollment: 2,681. Undergraduates: 988. Freshmen: 103. Both federal and institutional methodology are used as a basis for awarding need-based institutional aid.

UNDERGRADUATE EXPENSES for 2005–06 *Application fee:* $50. *Tuition:* full-time $21,975.

FRESHMAN FINANCIAL AID (Fall 2005, est.) 53 applied for aid; of those 92% were deemed to have need. 100% of freshmen with need received aid; of those 4% had need fully met.

UNDERGRADUATE FINANCIAL AID (Fall 2005, est.) 525 applied for aid; of those 93% were deemed to have need. 100% of undergraduates with need received aid; of those 6% had need fully met. 2% of all full-time undergraduates had no need and received non-need-based gift aid.

GIFT AID (NEED-BASED) *Total amount:* $3,254,558 (23% federal, 19% state, 15% institutional, 43% external sources). *Receiving aid:* Freshmen: 57% (33); All full-time undergraduates: 45% (253). *Scholarships, grants, and awards:* Federal Pell, FSEOG, state, private, college/university gift aid from institutional funds, Scholarships for Disadvantaged Students (SDS).

GIFT AID (NON-NEED-BASED) *Total amount:* $438,000 (11% institutional, 89% external sources). *Receiving aid:* Freshmen: 2% (1); Undergraduates: 2% (10). *Average Award:* Undergraduates: $5000. *Scholarships, grants, and awards by category: Academic Interests/Achievement:* 75 awards ($270,000 total): general academic interests/achievements, health fields. *Special Characteristics:* members of minority groups, veterans. *ROTC:* Air Force cooperative.

LOANS *Student loans:* $10,160,165 (90% need-based, 10% non-need-based). 75% of past graduating class borrowed through all loan programs. *Average indebtedness per student:* $25,975. *Average need-based loan:* Undergraduates: $10,993. *Parent loans:* $669,769 (100% non-need-based). *Programs:* FFEL (Subsidized and Unsubsidized Stafford, PLUS), Perkins, Federal Nursing, college/university.

WORK-STUDY *Federal work-study:* Total amount: $107,286; 120 jobs averaging $2000.

APPLYING FOR FINANCIAL AID *Required financial aid forms:* FAFSA, institution's own form, parent and student income tax returns. *Financial aid deadline (priority):* 4/1. *Notification date:* Continuous beginning 4/1. Students must reply within 2 weeks of notification.

CONTACT Susan Batchelor, University Director of Financial Aid, Thomas Jefferson University, 1025 Walnut Street, Room G-1, College Building, Philadelphia, PA 19107, 215-955-2867 or toll-free 877-533-3247. *E-mail:* financial.aid@jefferson.edu.

THOMAS MORE COLLEGE
Crestview Hills, KY

| Tuition & fees: $18,320 | Average undergraduate aid package: $17,432 |

ABOUT THE INSTITUTION Independent Roman Catholic, coed. Awards: associate, bachelor's, and master's degrees. 42 undergraduate majors. Total enrollment: 1,434. Undergraduates: 1,343. Federal methodology is used as a basis for awarding need-based institutional aid.

UNDERGRADUATE EXPENSES for 2005–06 *Application fee:* $25. *Comprehensive fee:* $24,470 includes full-time tuition ($17,600), mandatory fees ($720), and room and board ($6150). *College room only:* $2900. Full-time tuition and fees vary according to program. Room and board charges vary according to board plan and housing facility. *Part-time tuition:* $450 per credit hour. *Part-time fees:* $30 per credit hour; $15 per term. Part-time tuition and fees vary according to course load and program. *Payment plans:* Installment, deferred payment.

FRESHMAN FINANCIAL AID (Fall 2005, est.) 190 applied for aid; of those 100% were deemed to have need. 100% of freshmen with need received aid; of those 100% had need fully met. *Average percent of need met:* 90% (excluding resources awarded to replace EFC). *Average financial aid package:* $17,950 (excluding resources awarded to replace EFC). 5% of all full-time freshmen had no need and received non-need-based gift aid.

UNDERGRADUATE FINANCIAL AID (Fall 2005, est.) 828 applied for aid; of those 100% were deemed to have need. 100% of undergraduates with need received aid; of those 100% had need fully met. *Average percent of need met:* 82% (excluding resources awarded to replace EFC). *Average financial aid package:* $17,432 (excluding resources awarded to replace EFC). 13% of all full-time undergraduates had no need and received non-need-based gift aid.

GIFT AID (NEED-BASED) *Total amount:* $1,960,180 (39% federal, 57% state, 4% institutional). *Receiving aid:* Freshmen: 79% (179); All full-time undergraduates: 65% (727). *Average award:* Freshmen: $4709; Undergraduates: $4608. *Scholarships, grants, and awards:* Federal Pell, FSEOG, state, private, college/university gift aid from institutional funds.

GIFT AID (NON-NEED-BASED) *Total amount:* $6,141,241 (9% state, 76% institutional, 15% external sources). *Receiving aid:* Freshmen: 83% (190); Undergraduates: 73% (818). *Average Award:* Freshmen: $7088; Undergraduates: $6804. *Scholarships, grants, and awards by category: Academic Interests/Achievement:* 293 awards ($1,652,367 total): general academic interests/achievements. *Creative Arts/Performance:* 10 awards ($11,130 total): art/fine arts, theater/drama. *Special Achievements/Activities:* religious involvement. *Special Characteristics:* 212 awards ($620,207 total): adult students, children and siblings of alumni, children of faculty/staff, religious affiliation. *Tuition waivers:* Full or partial for children of alumni, employees or children of employees. *ROTC:* Army cooperative, Air Force cooperative.

LOANS *Student loans:* $5,262,861 (38% need-based, 62% non-need-based). 70% of past graduating class borrowed through all loan programs. *Average indebtedness per student:* $25,779. *Average need-based loan:* Freshmen: $1756; Undergraduates: $2281. *Parent loans:* $1,160,176 (100% non-need-based). *Programs:* FFEL (Subsidized and Unsubsidized Stafford, PLUS), Perkins, Federal Nursing, college/university.

WORK-STUDY *Federal work-study:* Total amount: $171,922; 86 jobs averaging $2100. *State or other work-study/employment:* Total amount: $215,497 (100% non-need-based). 130 part-time jobs averaging $2100.

APPLYING FOR FINANCIAL AID *Required financial aid forms:* FAFSA, institution's own form. *Financial aid deadline (priority):* 3/15. *Notification date:* Continuous beginning 3/1. Students must reply by 5/1.

CONTACT Ms. Linda Hayes, Director of Financial Aid, Thomas More College, 333 Thomas More Parkway, Crestview Hills, KY 41017-3495, 859-344-3531 or toll-free 800-825-4557. *Fax:* 859-344-3638. *E-mail:* linda.hayes@thomasmore.edu.

THOMAS MORE COLLEGE OF LIBERAL ARTS
Merrimack, NH

Tuition & fees: $10,650	Average undergraduate aid package: $10,499

ABOUT THE INSTITUTION Independent religious, coed. Awards: bachelor's degrees. 4 undergraduate majors. Total enrollment: 86. Undergraduates: 86. Freshmen: 21. Federal methodology is used as a basis for awarding need-based institutional aid.

UNDERGRADUATE EXPENSES for 2005–06 *Comprehensive fee:* $18,650 includes full-time tuition ($10,600), mandatory fees ($50), and room and board ($8000). *Part-time tuition:* $175 per credit hour. *Payment plan:* Installment.

FRESHMAN FINANCIAL AID (Fall 2005, est.) 18 applied for aid; of those 50% were deemed to have need. 100% of freshmen with need received aid. *Average percent of need met:* 70% (excluding resources awarded to replace EFC). *Average financial aid package:* $11,229 (excluding resources awarded to replace EFC). 47% of all full-time freshmen had no need and received non-need-based gift aid.

UNDERGRADUATE FINANCIAL AID (Fall 2005, est.) 84 applied for aid; of those 40% were deemed to have need. 100% of undergraduates with need received aid; of those 6% had need fully met. *Average percent of need met:* 70% (excluding resources awarded to replace EFC). *Average financial aid package:* $10,499 (excluding resources awarded to replace EFC). 55% of all full-time undergraduates had no need and received non-need-based gift aid.

GIFT AID (NEED-BASED) *Total amount:* $237,960 (24% federal, 3% state, 72% institutional, 1% external sources). *Receiving aid:* Freshmen: 47% (9); All full-time undergraduates: 36% (31). *Average award:* Freshmen: $4564; Undergraduates: $5491. *Scholarships, grants, and awards:* Federal Pell, FSEOG, state, private, college/university gift aid from institutional funds.

GIFT AID (NON-NEED-BASED) *Total amount:* $202,810 (100% institutional). *Receiving aid:* Freshmen: 11% (2). *Average Award:* Freshmen: $5433; Undergraduates: $4315. *Scholarships, grants, and awards by category:* Academic Interests/Achievement: 47 awards ($202,810 total): general academic interests/achievements. *Tuition waivers:* Full or partial for employees or children of employees.

LOANS *Student loans:* $326,305 (43% need-based, 57% non-need-based). 80% of past graduating class borrowed through all loan programs. *Average indebtedness per student:* $17,878. *Average need-based loan:* Freshmen: $2438; Undergraduates: $4142. *Parent loans:* $104,469 (49% need-based, 51% non-need-based). *Programs:* FFEL (Subsidized and Unsubsidized Stafford, PLUS).

WORK-STUDY *State or other work-study/employment:* Total amount: $68,688 (56% need-based, 44% non-need-based). 50 part-time jobs averaging $1374.

APPLYING FOR FINANCIAL AID *Required financial aid form:* FAFSA. *Financial aid deadline:* Continuous. *Notification date:* Continuous beginning 5/15. Students must reply within 2 weeks of notification.

CONTACT Mrs. Pamela Bernstein, Business Manager, Thomas More College of Liberal Arts, 6 Manchester Street, Merrimack, NH 03054-4818, 603-880-8308 or toll-free 800-880-8308. *Fax:* 603-546-0034. *E-mail:* thomasmorecollege@hotmail.com.

THOMAS UNIVERSITY
Thomasville, GA

ABOUT THE INSTITUTION Independent, coed. Awards: associate, bachelor's, and master's degrees and post-bachelor's certificates. 23 undergraduate majors. Total enrollment: 739. Undergraduates: 635. Freshmen: 11.

GIFT AID (NEED-BASED) *Scholarships, grants, and awards:* Federal Pell, FSEOG, state, private, college/university gift aid from institutional funds.

GIFT AID (NON-NEED-BASED) *Scholarships, grants, and awards by category:* Academic Interests/Achievement: biological sciences, business, education, English, general academic interests/achievements, health fields, international studies, physical sciences, social sciences. *Creative Arts/Performance:* art/fine arts, music, performing arts. *Special Achievements/Activities:* junior miss. *Special Characteristics:* children of faculty/staff, out-of-state students, veterans.

LOANS *Programs:* FFEL (Subsidized and Unsubsidized Stafford, PLUS), state, alternative loans.

APPLYING FOR FINANCIAL AID *Required financial aid forms:* FAFSA, institution's own form, state aid form.

CONTACT Ms. Angela Keys, Director of Financial Aid, Thomas University, 1501 Millpond Road, Thomasville, GA 31792-7499, 229-226-1621 Ext. 216 or toll-free 800-538-9784. *Fax:* 229-227-6919. *E-mail:* akeys@thomasu.edu.

TIFFIN UNIVERSITY
Tiffin, OH

Tuition & fees: $15,870	Average undergraduate aid package: $12,053

ABOUT THE INSTITUTION Independent, coed. Awards: associate, bachelor's, and master's degrees. 21 undergraduate majors. Total enrollment: 1,605. Undergraduates: 1,235. Freshmen: 284. Federal methodology is used as a basis for awarding need-based institutional aid.

UNDERGRADUATE EXPENSES for 2006–07 *Application fee:* $20. *Comprehensive fee:* $22,645 includes full-time tuition ($15,870) and room and board ($6775). *College room only:* $3525. *Part-time tuition:* $529 per credit hour.

FRESHMAN FINANCIAL AID (Fall 2004) 269 applied for aid; of those 90% were deemed to have need. 100% of freshmen with need received aid; of those 19% had need fully met. *Average percent of need met:* 11% (excluding resources awarded to replace EFC). *Average financial aid package:* $14,383 (excluding resources awarded to replace EFC). 9% of all full-time freshmen had no need and received non-need-based gift aid.

UNDERGRADUATE FINANCIAL AID (Fall 2004) *Average percent of need met:* 17% (excluding resources awarded to replace EFC). *Average financial aid package:* $12,053 (excluding resources awarded to replace EFC). 8% of all full-time undergraduates had no need and received non-need-based gift aid.

GIFT AID (NEED-BASED) *Total amount:* $6,777,270 (23% federal, 27% state, 49% institutional, 1% external sources). *Receiving aid:* Freshmen: 38% (107); All full-time undergraduates: 56% (611). *Average award:* Freshmen: $4397; Undergraduates: $4569. *Scholarships, grants, and awards:* Federal Pell, FSEOG, state, private, college/university gift aid from institutional funds.

GIFT AID (NON-NEED-BASED) *Receiving aid:* Freshmen: 85% (240); Undergraduates: 87% (950). *Average Award:* Freshmen: $7199; Undergraduates: $10,062. *Scholarships, grants, and awards by category:* Academic Interests/Achievement: 519 awards ($2,016,785 total): business, general academic interests/achievements, international studies. *Creative Arts/Performance:* 70 awards ($173,250 total): music. *Special Achievements/Activities:* 43 awards ($180,500 total): cheerleading/drum major, general special achievements/activities, leadership. *Special Characteristics:* 128 awards ($236,177 total): children and siblings of alumni, children of faculty/staff, general special characteristics, international students, local/state students, out-of-state students, public servants, veterans' children. *ROTC:* Army cooperative, Air Force cooperative.

LOANS *Student loans:* $7,164,467 (100% need-based). 82% of past graduating class borrowed through all loan programs. *Average indebtedness per student:* $19,994. *Average need-based loan:* Freshmen: $2467; Undergraduates: $3818. *Parent loans:* $1,318,303 (100% need-based). *Programs:* Federal Direct (Subsidized and Unsubsidized Stafford, PLUS), Perkins, college/university, alternative loans.

WORK-STUDY *Federal work-study:* Total amount: $480,114; 148 jobs averaging $895.

ATHLETIC AWARDS *Total amount:* $1,690,871 (100% need-based).

APPLYING FOR FINANCIAL AID *Required financial aid form:* FAFSA. *Financial aid deadline:* Continuous. *Notification date:* Continuous beginning 2/15. Students must reply within 2 weeks of notification.

CONTACT Ms. Judy Gardner, Director of Financial Aid, Tiffin University, 155 Miami Street, Tiffin, OH 44883-2161, 419-448-3420 or toll-free 800-968-6446. *Fax:* 419-443-5006. *E-mail:* jgardner@tiffin.edu.

TOCCOA FALLS COLLEGE
Toccoa Falls, GA

Tuition & fees: $12,050	Average undergraduate aid package: $9653

ABOUT THE INSTITUTION Independent interdenominational, coed. Awards: associate and bachelor's degrees. 22 undergraduate majors. Total enrollment: 922. Undergraduates: 922. Freshmen: 271. Federal methodology is used as a basis for awarding need-based institutional aid.

UNDERGRADUATE EXPENSES for 2005–06 *Application fee:* $20. *One-time required fee:* $475. *Comprehensive fee:* $16,650 includes full-time tuition ($12,050) and room and board ($4600). Full-time tuition and fees vary accord-

Toccoa Falls College

ing to course load. Room and board charges vary according to board plan. *Part-time tuition:* $502 per credit hour. Part-time tuition and fees vary according to course load. *Payment plan:* Installment.

FRESHMAN FINANCIAL AID (Fall 2005, est.) 211 applied for aid; of those 85% were deemed to have need. 99% of freshmen with need received aid; of those 13% had need fully met. *Average percent of need met:* 61% (excluding resources awarded to replace EFC). *Average financial aid package:* $9336 (excluding resources awarded to replace EFC). 19% of all full-time freshmen had no need and received non-need-based gift aid.

UNDERGRADUATE FINANCIAL AID (Fall 2005, est.) 765 applied for aid; of those 88% were deemed to have need. 99% of undergraduates with need received aid; of those 12% had need fully met. *Average percent of need met:* 60% (excluding resources awarded to replace EFC). *Average financial aid package:* $9653 (excluding resources awarded to replace EFC). 20% of all full-time undergraduates had no need and received non-need-based gift aid.

GIFT AID (NEED-BASED) *Total amount:* $4,212,253 (25% federal, 19% state, 55% institutional, 1% external sources). *Receiving aid:* Freshmen: 80% (178); All full-time undergraduates: 77% (664). *Average award:* Freshmen: $6920; Undergraduates: $6486. *Scholarships, grants, and awards:* Federal Pell, FSEOG, state, private, college/university gift aid from institutional funds.

GIFT AID (NON-NEED-BASED) *Total amount:* $1,119,340 (31% state, 67% institutional, 2% external sources). *Receiving aid:* Freshmen: 9% (20); Undergraduates: 6% (53). *Average Award:* Freshmen: $7682; Undergraduates: $7595. *Scholarships, grants, and awards by category: Academic Interests/Achievement:* 315 awards ($1,360,675 total): business, communication, education, general academic interests/achievements, religion/biblical studies. *Creative Arts/Performance:* 45 awards ($107,570 total): music. *Special Achievements/Activities:* 62 awards ($181,715 total): leadership. *Special Characteristics:* 269 awards ($502,235 total): children of faculty/staff, ethnic background, general special characteristics, international students, married students, relatives of clergy, religious affiliation, siblings of current students. *Tuition waivers:* Full or partial for employees or children of employees.

LOANS *Student loans:* $3,325,631 (82% need-based, 18% non-need-based). 71% of past graduating class borrowed through all loan programs. *Average indebtedness per student:* $17,273. *Average need-based loan:* Freshmen: $2085; Undergraduates: $3110. *Parent loans:* $1,158,668 (48% need-based, 52% non-need-based). *Programs:* FFEL (Subsidized and Unsubsidized Stafford, PLUS), Perkins, college/university.

WORK-STUDY *Federal work-study:* Total amount: $492,805; 369 jobs averaging $1336. *State or other work-study/employment:* Total amount: $208,120 (100% non-need-based). 154 part-time jobs averaging $1351.

APPLYING FOR FINANCIAL AID *Required financial aid forms:* FAFSA, institution's own form. *Financial aid deadline (priority):* 5/1. *Notification date:* Continuous beginning 3/15. Students must reply within 2 weeks of notification.

CONTACT Vince Welch, Director of Financial Aid, Toccoa Falls College, PO Box 800900, Toccoa Falls, GA 30598, 706-886-7299 Ext. 5234. *Fax:* 706-282-6041. *E-mail:* vwelch@tfc.edu.

TORAH TEMIMAH TALMUDICAL SEMINARY
Brooklyn, NY

CONTACT Financial Aid Office, Torah Temimah Talmudical Seminary, 507 Ocean Parkway, Brooklyn, NY 11218-5913, 718-853-8500.

TOUGALOO COLLEGE
Tougaloo, MS

CONTACT Director of Financial Aid, Tougaloo College, 500 West County Line Road, Tougaloo, MS 39174, 601-977-6134 or toll-free 888-42GALOO. *Fax:* 601-977-6164.

TOURO COLLEGE
New York, NY

CONTACT Office of Financial Aid, Touro College, 27 West 23rd Street, New York, NY 10010, 212-463-0400.

TOURO UNIVERSITY INTERNATIONAL
Cypress, CA

CONTACT Financial Aid Office, Touro University International, 5665 Plaza Drive, 3rd Floor, Cypress, CA 90630, 714-816-0366.

TOWSON UNIVERSITY
Towson, MD

Tuition & fees (MD res): $7096	Average undergraduate aid package: $7203

ABOUT THE INSTITUTION State-supported, coed. Awards: bachelor's, master's, and doctoral degrees and post-bachelor's and post-master's certificates. 50 undergraduate majors. Total enrollment: 18,011. Undergraduates: 14,495. Freshmen: 2,327. Federal methodology is used as a basis for awarding need-based institutional aid.

UNDERGRADUATE EXPENSES for 2005–06 *Application fee:* $45. *Tuition, state resident:* full-time $5180; part-time $225 per credit. *Tuition, nonresident:* full-time $14,114; part-time $528 per credit. *Required fees:* full-time $1916; $74 per credit. Full-time tuition and fees vary according to course load. *College room and board:* $6828; *room only:* $3968. Room and board charges vary according to board plan and housing facility. *Payment plan:* Installment.

FRESHMAN FINANCIAL AID (Fall 2005, est.) 1401 applied for aid; of those 59% were deemed to have need. 95% of freshmen with need received aid; of those 23% had need fully met. *Average percent of need met:* 62% (excluding resources awarded to replace EFC). *Average financial aid package:* $5816 (excluding resources awarded to replace EFC). 10% of all full-time freshmen had no need and received non-need-based gift aid.

UNDERGRADUATE FINANCIAL AID (Fall 2005, est.) 6,315 applied for aid; of those 69% were deemed to have need. 96% of undergraduates with need received aid; of those 22% had need fully met. *Average percent of need met:* 66% (excluding resources awarded to replace EFC). *Average financial aid package:* $7203 (excluding resources awarded to replace EFC). 4% of all full-time undergraduates had no need and received non-need-based gift aid.

GIFT AID (NEED-BASED) *Total amount:* $21,876,354 (32% federal, 33% state, 33% institutional, 2% external sources). *Receiving aid:* Freshmen: 20% (471); All full-time undergraduates: 18% (2,564). *Average award:* Freshmen: $4122; Undergraduates: $4734. *Scholarships, grants, and awards:* Federal Pell, FSEOG, state, private, college/university gift aid from institutional funds.

GIFT AID (NON-NEED-BASED) *Total amount:* $12,596,368 (1% federal, 13% state, 73% institutional, 13% external sources). *Receiving aid:* Freshmen: 17% (398); Undergraduates: 9% (1,230). *Average Award:* Freshmen: $3321; Undergraduates: $3772. *Scholarships, grants, and awards by category: Academic Interests/Achievement:* general academic interests/achievements. *Creative Arts/Performance:* art/fine arts, dance, music, theater/drama. *Tuition waivers:* Full or partial for employees or children of employees, senior citizens. *ROTC:* Army cooperative, Air Force cooperative.

LOANS *Student loans:* $36,945,475 (66% need-based, 34% non-need-based). 53% of past graduating class borrowed through all loan programs. *Average indebtedness per student:* $14,808. *Average need-based loan:* Freshmen: $2472; Undergraduates: $3651. *Parent loans:* $26,043,145 (17% need-based, 83% non-need-based). *Programs:* Federal Direct (Subsidized and Unsubsidized Stafford, PLUS), Perkins.

WORK-STUDY *Federal work-study:* Total amount: $2,357,899; jobs available. *State or other work-study/employment:* Part-time jobs available.

ATHLETIC AWARDS *Total amount:* $3,350,928 (14% need-based, 86% non-need-based).

APPLYING FOR FINANCIAL AID *Required financial aid form:* FAFSA. *Financial aid deadline:* 3/1 (priority: 1/31). *Notification date:* Continuous beginning 3/21. Students must reply within 2 weeks of notification.

CONTACT Vince Pecora, Director of Financial Aid, Towson University, 8000 York Road, Towson, MD 21252-0001, 410-704-4236 or toll-free 888-4TOWSON. *E-mail:* finaid@towson.edu.

TRANSYLVANIA UNIVERSITY
Lexington, KY

Tuition & fees: $19,650	Average undergraduate aid package: $16,537

ABOUT THE INSTITUTION Independent religious, coed. Awards: bachelor's degrees. 31 undergraduate majors. Total enrollment: 1,151. Undergraduates: 1,151. Freshmen: 326. Federal methodology is used as a basis for awarding need-based institutional aid.
UNDERGRADUATE EXPENSES for 2005–06 *Application fee:* $30. *Comprehensive fee:* $26,240 includes full-time tuition ($19,650) and room and board ($6590). Room and board charges vary according to board plan and location. *Part-time tuition:* $2100 per course. *Part-time fees:* $84 per course. *Payment plan:* Installment.
FRESHMAN FINANCIAL AID (Fall 2005, est.) 275 applied for aid; of those 81% were deemed to have need. 100% of freshmen with need received aid; of those 31% had need fully met. *Average percent of need met:* 88% (excluding resources awarded to replace EFC). *Average financial aid package:* $15,892 (excluding resources awarded to replace EFC). 33% of all full-time freshmen had no need and received non-need-based gift aid.
UNDERGRADUATE FINANCIAL AID (Fall 2005, est.) 811 applied for aid; of those 84% were deemed to have need. 100% of undergraduates with need received aid; of those 27% had need fully met. *Average percent of need met:* 87% (excluding resources awarded to replace EFC). *Average financial aid package:* $16,537 (excluding resources awarded to replace EFC). 38% of all full-time undergraduates had no need and received non-need-based gift aid.
GIFT AID (NEED-BASED) *Total amount:* $8,481,598 (7% federal, 27% state, 63% institutional, 3% external sources). *Receiving aid:* Freshmen: 66% (221); All full-time undergraduates: 60% (680). *Average award:* Freshmen: $12,719; Undergraduates: $12,598. *Scholarships, grants, and awards:* Federal Pell, FSEOG, state, private, college/university gift aid from institutional funds.
GIFT AID (NON-NEED-BASED) *Total amount:* $4,742,773 (16% state, 79% institutional, 5% external sources). *Receiving aid:* Freshmen: 13% (42); Undergraduates: 9% (104). *Average Award:* Freshmen: $11,890; Undergraduates: $11,584. *Scholarships, grants, and awards by category:* Academic Interests/Achievement: 1,085 awards ($7,227,152 total): computer science, general academic interests/achievements. Creative Arts/Performance: 48 awards ($117,850 total): art/fine arts, music. Special Achievements/Activities: 281 awards ($533,724 total): general special achievements/activities, religious involvement. Special Characteristics: 141 awards ($680,798 total): children of faculty/staff, members of minority groups, out-of-state students, relatives of clergy, religious affiliation. *Tuition waivers:* Full or partial for employees or children of employees. *ROTC:* Army cooperative, Air Force cooperative.
LOANS *Student loans:* $3,488,474 (66% need-based, 34% non-need-based). 59% of past graduating class borrowed through all loan programs. *Average indebtedness per student:* $15,673. *Average need-based loan:* Freshmen: $3080; Undergraduates: $3829. *Parent loans:* $1,490,387 (15% need-based, 85% non-need-based). *Programs:* FFEL (Subsidized and Unsubsidized Stafford, PLUS), Perkins, college/university.
WORK-STUDY *Federal work-study:* Total amount: $491,625; 367 jobs averaging $1201. *State or other work-study/employment:* Total amount: $312,580 (28% need-based, 72% non-need-based). 50 part-time jobs averaging $5928.
APPLYING FOR FINANCIAL AID *Required financial aid form:* FAFSA. *Financial aid deadline (priority):* 3/1. *Notification date:* Continuous beginning 3/15. Students must reply within 2 weeks of notification.
CONTACT Mr. Dave Cecil, Director of Financial Aid, Transylvania University, 300 North Broadway, Lexington, KY 40508-1797, 859-233-8239 or toll-free 800-872-6798. *Fax:* 859-281-3650. *E-mail:* dcecil@transy.edu.

TREVECCA NAZARENE UNIVERSITY
Nashville, TN

Tuition & fees: $14,774	Average undergraduate aid package: $8846

ABOUT THE INSTITUTION Independent Nazarene, coed. Awards: associate, bachelor's, master's, and doctoral degrees and post-master's certificates. 36 undergraduate majors. Total enrollment: 2,196. Undergraduates: 1,245. Freshmen: 241. Federal methodology is used as a basis for awarding need-based institutional aid.
UNDERGRADUATE EXPENSES for 2006–07 *Application fee:* $25. *Comprehensive fee:* $21,244 includes full-time tuition ($14,774) and room and board ($6470). *College room only:* $2920. *Part-time tuition:* $569 per semester hour.
FRESHMAN FINANCIAL AID (Fall 2004) 180 applied for aid; of those 86% were deemed to have need. 66% of freshmen with need received aid; of those 26% had need fully met. *Average percent of need met:* 47% (excluding resources awarded to replace EFC). *Average financial aid package:* $10,502 (excluding resources awarded to replace EFC). 52% of all full-time freshmen had no need and received non-need-based gift aid.
UNDERGRADUATE FINANCIAL AID (Fall 2004) 893 applied for aid; of those 86% were deemed to have need. 82% of undergraduates with need received aid; of those 17% had need fully met. *Average percent of need met:* 52% (excluding resources awarded to replace EFC). *Average financial aid package:* $8846 (excluding resources awarded to replace EFC). 28% of all full-time undergraduates had no need and received non-need-based gift aid.
GIFT AID (NEED-BASED) *Total amount:* $1,443,921 (85% federal, 15% state). *Receiving aid:* Freshmen: 41% (97); All full-time undergraduates: 53% (540). *Average award:* Freshmen: $8176; Undergraduates: $6388. *Scholarships, grants, and awards:* Federal Pell, FSEOG, state, private, college/university gift aid from institutional funds.
GIFT AID (NON-NEED-BASED) *Total amount:* $4,936,682 (7% state, 87% institutional, 6% external sources). *Receiving aid:* Freshmen: 9% (21); Undergraduates: 7% (73). *Average Award:* Freshmen: $8486; Undergraduates: $8622. *Scholarships, grants, and awards by category:* Academic Interests/Achievement: business, communication, education, general academic interests/achievements, physical sciences, religion/biblical studies, social sciences. Creative Arts/Performance: music, theater/drama. Special Achievements/Activities: general special achievements/activities, memberships. Special Characteristics: children and siblings of alumni, general special characteristics, handicapped students, relatives of clergy, religious affiliation. *ROTC:* Army cooperative.
LOANS *Student loans:* $5,647,511 (60% need-based, 40% non-need-based). 73% of past graduating class borrowed through all loan programs. *Average indebtedness per student:* $24,000. *Average need-based loan:* Freshmen: $3820; Undergraduates: $4342. *Parent loans:* $1,577,889 (100% non-need-based). *Programs:* FFEL (Subsidized and Unsubsidized Stafford, PLUS), Perkins.
WORK-STUDY *Federal work-study:* Total amount: $119,908; jobs available. *State or other work-study/employment:* Part-time jobs available.
ATHLETIC AWARDS *Total amount:* $841,537 (100% non-need-based).
APPLYING FOR FINANCIAL AID *Required financial aid form:* FAFSA. *Financial aid deadline (priority):* 3/1. *Notification date:* Continuous beginning 3/15.
CONTACT Eddie White, Assistant Director of Financial Aid, Trevecca Nazarene University, 333 Murfreesboro Road, Nashville, TN 37210-2834, 615-248-1242 or toll-free 888-210-4TNU. *Fax:* 615-248-7728. *E-mail:* ewhite@trevecca.edu.

TRINITY BAPTIST COLLEGE
Jacksonville, FL

CONTACT Mr. Donald Schaffer, Financial Aid Administrator, Trinity Baptist College, 800 Hammond Boulevard, Jacksonville, FL 32221, 904-596-2445 or toll-free 800-786-2206 (out-of-state). *Fax:* 904-596-2531. *E-mail:* financialaid@tbc.edu.

TRINITY BIBLE COLLEGE
Ellendale, ND

CONTACT Rhonda Miller, Financial Aid Associate, Trinity Bible College, 50 South 6th Avenue, Ellendale, ND 58436-7150, 888-822-2329 Ext. 2781 or toll-free 888-TBC-2DAY. *Fax:* 701-349-5786. *E-mail:* financialaid@trinitybiblecollege.edu.

TRINITY CHRISTIAN COLLEGE
Palos Heights, IL

CONTACT L. Denise Coleman, Director of Financial Aid, Trinity Christian College, 6601 West College Drive, Palos Heights, IL 60463-0929, 708-239-4706 or toll-free 800-748-0085. *E-mail:* financial.aid@trnty.edu.

TRINITY COLLEGE
Washington, DC

See Trinity (Washington) University.

Trinity College

TRINITY COLLEGE
Hartford, CT

| Tuition & fees: $33,630 | Average undergraduate aid package: $25,590 |

ABOUT THE INSTITUTION Independent, coed. Awards: bachelor's and master's degrees. 44 undergraduate majors. Total enrollment: 2,526. Undergraduates: 2,343. Freshmen: 573. Both federal and institutional methodology are used as a basis for awarding need-based institutional aid.

UNDERGRADUATE EXPENSES for 2005–06 *Application fee:* $60. *Comprehensive fee:* $42,220 includes full-time tuition ($32,000), mandatory fees ($1630), and room and board ($8590). *College room only:* $5550. Full-time tuition and fees vary according to program. Room and board charges vary according to board plan. *Part-time tuition:* $1185 per credit hour. Part-time tuition and fees vary according to program. *Payment plan:* Installment.

FRESHMAN FINANCIAL AID (Fall 2004) 322 applied for aid; of those 86% were deemed to have need. 100% of freshmen with need received aid; of those 100% had need fully met. *Average percent of need met:* 100% (excluding resources awarded to replace EFC). *Average financial aid package:* $27,916 (excluding resources awarded to replace EFC). 1% of all full-time freshmen had no need and received non-need-based gift aid.

UNDERGRADUATE FINANCIAL AID (Fall 2004) 1,068 applied for aid; of those 85% were deemed to have need. 100% of undergraduates with need received aid; of those 100% had need fully met. *Average percent of need met:* 100% (excluding resources awarded to replace EFC). *Average financial aid package:* $25,590 (excluding resources awarded to replace EFC). 1% of all full-time undergraduates had no need and received non-need-based gift aid.

GIFT AID (NEED-BASED) *Total amount:* $20,974,387 (5% federal, 3% state, 90% institutional, 2% external sources). *Receiving aid:* Freshmen: 46% (264); All full-time undergraduates: 42% (833). *Average award:* Freshmen: $25,914; Undergraduates: $23,183. *Scholarships, grants, and awards:* Federal Pell, FSEOG, state, private, college/university gift aid from institutional funds.

GIFT AID (NON-NEED-BASED) *Total amount:* $387,670 (100% institutional). *Receiving aid:* Freshmen: 1% (6); Undergraduates: 1% (14). *Average Award:* Freshmen: $30,380; Undergraduates: $27,442. *Scholarships, grants and awards by category:* Academic Interests/Achievement: 3 awards ($3000 total): general academic interests/achievements. Special Achievements/Activities: 2 awards ($57,480 total): leadership. *Tuition waivers:* Full or partial for employees or children of employees, adult students. *ROTC:* Army cooperative.

LOANS *Student loans:* $5,760,601 (56% need-based, 44% non-need-based). 42% of past graduating class borrowed through all loan programs. *Average indebtedness per student:* $18,122. *Average need-based loan:* Freshmen: $2669; Undergraduates: $4250. *Parent loans:* $4,631,747 (100% non-need-based). *Programs:* FFEL (Subsidized and Unsubsidized Stafford, PLUS), Perkins, college/university, alternative loans.

WORK-STUDY *Federal work-study:* Total amount: $976,290; 713 jobs averaging $1530. *State or other work-study/employment:* 12 part-time jobs averaging $838.

APPLYING FOR FINANCIAL AID *Required financial aid forms:* FAFSA, CSS Financial Aid PROFILE, noncustodial (divorced/separated) parent's statement, business/farm supplement, federal income tax form(s). *Financial aid deadline:* 3/1 (priority: 2/1). *Notification date:* 4/1. Students must reply by 5/1 or within 2 weeks of notification.

CONTACT Ms. Kelly O'Brien, Director of Financial Aid, Trinity College, 300 Summit Street, Hartford, CT 06106-3100, 860-297-2046. *Fax:* 860-987-6296.

TRINITY COLLEGE OF FLORIDA
New Port Richey, FL

| Tuition & fees: N/R | Average undergraduate aid package: $7500 |

ABOUT THE INSTITUTION Independent nondenominational, coed. Awards: associate and bachelor's degrees. 8 undergraduate majors. Total enrollment: 203. Undergraduates: 203. Freshmen: 34. Federal methodology is used as a basis for awarding need-based institutional aid.

FRESHMAN FINANCIAL AID (Fall 2004) 36 applied for aid; of those 94% were deemed to have need. 100% of freshmen with need received aid; of those 50% had need fully met. *Average percent of need met:* 50% (excluding resources awarded to replace EFC). *Average financial aid package:* $6900 (excluding resources awarded to replace EFC). 14% of all full-time freshmen had no need and received non-need-based gift aid.

UNDERGRADUATE FINANCIAL AID (Fall 2004) 138 applied for aid; of those 95% were deemed to have need. 100% of undergraduates with need received aid; of those 50% had need fully met. *Average percent of need met:* 50% (excluding resources awarded to replace EFC). *Average financial aid package:* $7500 (excluding resources awarded to replace EFC). 6% of all full-time undergraduates had no need and received non-need-based gift aid.

GIFT AID (NEED-BASED) *Total amount:* $378,752 (76% federal, 11% state, 7% institutional, 6% external sources). *Receiving aid:* Freshmen: 86% (31); All full-time undergraduates: 87% (120). *Average award:* Freshmen: $3105; Undergraduates: $3375. *Scholarships, grants, and awards:* Federal Pell, FSEOG, state, private, college/university gift aid from institutional funds.

GIFT AID (NON-NEED-BASED) *Total amount:* $153,211 (60% state, 20% institutional, 20% external sources). *Receiving aid:* Freshmen: 69% (25); Undergraduates: 71% (98). *Average Award:* Freshmen: $500; Undergraduates: $500. *Scholarships, grants, and awards by category:* Academic Interests/Achievement: religion/biblical studies. Special Achievements/Activities: community service, leadership, religious involvement. *Tuition waivers:* Full or partial for children of alumni, employees or children of employees, senior citizens.

LOANS *Student loans:* $508,670 (100% need-based). *Average need-based loan:* Freshmen: $4500; Undergraduates: $4500. *Parent loans:* $61,044 (100% need-based). *Programs:* FFEL (Subsidized and Unsubsidized Stafford, PLUS).

WORK-STUDY *Federal work-study:* Total amount: $76,121; 27 jobs averaging $2819. *State or other work-study/employment:* Part-time jobs available.

APPLYING FOR FINANCIAL AID *Required financial aid forms:* FAFSA, institution's own form. *Financial aid deadline (priority):* 4/1. *Notification date:* Continuous.

CONTACT Sue Wayne, Director of Financial Aid, Trinity College of Florida, 2430 Welbilt Boulevard, New Port Richey, FL 34655, 727-376-6911 Ext. 310 or toll-free 800-388-0869. *Fax:* 727-376-0781.

TRINITY COLLEGE OF NURSING AND HEALTH SCIENCES
Rock Island, IL

| Tuition & fees: N/R | Average undergraduate aid package: N/A |

ABOUT THE INSTITUTION Independent, coed. Awards: associate and bachelor's degrees (general education requirements are taken off campus, usually at Black Hawk College, Eastern Iowa Community College District and Western Illinois University). 5 undergraduate majors. Total enrollment: 165. Undergraduates: 165. Freshmen: 5. Federal methodology is used as a basis for awarding need-based institutional aid.

FRESHMAN FINANCIAL AID (Fall 2005, est.) 3 applied for aid; of those 100% were deemed to have need. 100% of freshmen with need received aid. 60% of all full-time freshmen had no need and received non-need-based gift aid.

UNDERGRADUATE FINANCIAL AID (Fall 2005, est.) 87 applied for aid; of those 46% were deemed to have need. 100% of undergraduates with need received aid; of those 5% had need fully met. 29% of all full-time undergraduates had no need and received non-need-based gift aid.

GIFT AID (NEED-BASED) *Total amount:* $248,658 (41% federal, 59% state). *Receiving aid:* Freshmen: 20% (1); All full-time undergraduates: 40% (40). *Scholarships, grants, and awards:* Federal Pell, FSEOG, state, college/university gift aid from institutional funds.

GIFT AID (NON-NEED-BASED) *Total amount:* $28,158 (77% institutional, 23% external sources). *Receiving aid:* Freshmen: 40% (2); Undergraduates: 28% (28). *Average Award:* Freshmen: $500; Undergraduates: $750.

LOANS *Student loans:* $409,489 (69% need-based, 31% non-need-based). *Average indebtedness per student:* $5000. *Parent loans:* $3250 (100% need-based). *Programs:* FFEL (Subsidized and Unsubsidized Stafford, PLUS), Federal Nursing.

WORK-STUDY *Federal work-study:* 5 jobs averaging $1500.

APPLYING FOR FINANCIAL AID *Required financial aid forms:* FAFSA, institution's own form. *Financial aid deadline:* Continuous. *Notification date:* Continuous beginning 6/1. Students must reply within 4 weeks of notification.

CONTACT Angela Sumpler, Assistant Director of Learner Services, Trinity College of Nursing and Health Sciences, 2122 25th Avenue, Rock Island, IL 61201, 309-779-7733. *Fax:* 309-779-7796. *E-mail:* sumplera@trinityqc.com.

TRINITY INTERNATIONAL UNIVERSITY
Deerfield, IL

Tuition & fees: $19,366   **Average undergraduate aid package:** $14,846

ABOUT THE INSTITUTION Independent religious, coed. Awards: bachelor's, master's, doctoral, and first professional degrees and post-bachelor's certificates. 38 undergraduate majors. Total enrollment: 2,836. Undergraduates: 1,263. Freshmen: 202. Federal methodology is used as a basis for awarding need-based institutional aid.

UNDERGRADUATE EXPENSES for 2005–06 *Application fee:* $25. *Comprehensive fee:* $25,686 includes full-time tuition ($19,080), mandatory fees ($286), and room and board ($6320). *College room only:* $3430. Full-time tuition and fees vary according to location. Room and board charges vary according to board plan. *Part-time tuition:* $796 per hour. *Part-time fees:* $143 per term. Part-time tuition and fees vary according to location. *Payment plan:* Installment.

FRESHMAN FINANCIAL AID (Fall 2005, est.) 183 applied for aid; of those 84% were deemed to have need. 100% of freshmen with need received aid; of those 5% had need fully met. *Average percent of need met:* 16% (excluding resources awarded to replace EFC). *Average financial aid package:* $14,902 (excluding resources awarded to replace EFC). 8% of all full-time freshmen had no need and received non-need-based gift aid.

UNDERGRADUATE FINANCIAL AID (Fall 2005, est.) 869 applied for aid; of those 84% were deemed to have need. 100% of undergraduates with need received aid; of those 5% had need fully met. *Average percent of need met:* 26% (excluding resources awarded to replace EFC). *Average financial aid package:* $14,846 (excluding resources awarded to replace EFC). 6% of all full-time undergraduates had no need and received non-need-based gift aid.

GIFT AID (NEED-BASED) *Total amount:* $4,255,360 (24% federal, 26% state, 50% institutional). *Receiving aid:* Freshmen: 46% (92); All full-time undergraduates: 45% (484). *Average award:* Freshmen: $5897; Undergraduates: $5894. *Scholarships, grants, and awards:* Federal Pell, FSEOG, state, private, college/university gift aid from institutional funds.

GIFT AID (NON-NEED-BASED) *Total amount:* $1,588,422 (95% institutional, 5% external sources). *Receiving aid:* Freshmen: 58% (117); Undergraduates: 48% (522). *Average Award:* Freshmen: $3469; Undergraduates: $4005. *Scholarships, grants, and awards by category:* Academic Interests/Achievement: 205 awards ($617,500 total): general academic interests/achievements. *Creative Arts/Performance:* 72 awards ($522,835 total): music. *Special Achievements/Activities:* $30,050 total: religious involvement. *Special Characteristics:* $122,500 total: children and siblings of alumni, children of current students, members of minority groups, religious affiliation. *Tuition waivers:* Full or partial for employees or children of employees.

LOANS *Student loans:* $4,691,778 (56% need-based, 44% non-need-based). 78% of past graduating class borrowed through all loan programs. *Average indebtedness per student:* $17,129. *Average need-based loan:* Freshmen: $3121; Undergraduates: $3517. *Parent loans:* $1,091,286 (100% need-based). *Programs:* Federal Direct (Subsidized and Unsubsidized Stafford, PLUS), Perkins.

WORK-STUDY *Federal work-study:* Total amount: $743,088; 385 jobs averaging $1906.

ATHLETIC AWARDS *Total amount:* $2,290,872 (100% non-need-based).

APPLYING FOR FINANCIAL AID *Required financial aid form:* FAFSA. *Financial aid deadline (priority):* 4/1. *Notification date:* Continuous beginning 2/15. Students must reply within 4 weeks of notification.

CONTACT Mr. Ron Campbell, Director of Enrollment Services for Financial Aid and Undergraduate Admission, Trinity International University, 2065 Half Day Road, Deerfield, IL 60015-1284, 847-317-8060 or toll-free 800-822-3225 (out-of-state). *Fax:* 847-317-7081. *E-mail:* finaid@tiu.edu.

TRINITY LIFE BIBLE COLLEGE
Sacramento, CA

CONTACT Financial Aid Office, Trinity Life Bible College, 5225 Hillsdale Boulevard, Sacramento, CA 95842, 916-348-4689.

TRINITY LUTHERAN COLLEGE
Issaquah, WA

Tuition & fees: $21,582   **Average undergraduate aid package:** N/A

ABOUT THE INSTITUTION Independent Lutheran, coed. Awards: associate and bachelor's degrees and post-bachelor's certificates. 3 undergraduate majors. Total enrollment: 156. Undergraduates: 156. Freshmen: 19. Federal methodology is used as a basis for awarding need-based institutional aid.

UNDERGRADUATE EXPENSES for 2005–06 *Application fee:* $30. *Comprehensive fee:* $30,307 includes full-time tuition ($21,432), mandatory fees ($150), and room and board ($8725). *College room only:* $5815. Full-time tuition and fees vary according to course load. Room and board charges vary according to board plan. *Part-time tuition:* $893 per semester hour. Part-time tuition and fees vary according to course load. *Payment plan:* Installment.

GIFT AID (NEED-BASED) *Total amount:* $189,351 (55% federal, 44% institutional, 1% external sources). *Scholarships, grants, and awards:* Federal Pell, FSEOG, college/university gift aid from institutional funds.

GIFT AID (NON-NEED-BASED) *Total amount:* $106,559 (100% institutional). *Scholarships, grants, and awards by category:* Academic Interests/Achievement: general academic interests/achievements, religion/biblical studies. *Creative Arts/Performance:* general creative arts/performance, music. *Special Achievements/Activities:* leadership, religious involvement. *Special Characteristics:* children of faculty/staff, international students, religious affiliation. *Tuition waivers:* Full or partial for employees or children of employees.

LOANS *Student loans:* $554,079 (100% need-based). *Parent loans:* $108,660 (100% need-based). *Programs:* FFEL (Subsidized and Unsubsidized Stafford, PLUS), college/university.

WORK-STUDY *Federal work-study:* Total amount: $25,103; 27 jobs averaging $1240.

APPLYING FOR FINANCIAL AID *Required financial aid forms:* FAFSA, institution's own form. *Financial aid deadline (priority):* 3/1. *Notification date:* Continuous. Students must reply within 4 weeks of notification.

CONTACT Ms. Susan Dalgleish, Director of Financial Aid, Trinity Lutheran College, 4221 228th Avenue SE, Issaquah, WA 98029-9299, 425-961-5514 or toll-free 800-843-5659. *Fax:* 425-392-0404. *E-mail:* finaid@tlc.edu.

TRINITY UNIVERSITY
San Antonio, TX

ABOUT THE INSTITUTION Independent religious, coed. Awards: bachelor's and master's degrees. 49 undergraduate majors. Total enrollment: 2,756. Undergraduates: 2,524. Freshmen: 651.

GIFT AID (NEED-BASED) *Scholarships, grants, and awards:* Federal Pell, FSEOG, state, private, college/university gift aid from institutional funds.

GIFT AID (NON-NEED-BASED) *Scholarships, grants, and awards by category:* Academic Interests/Achievement: general academic interests/achievements. Creative Arts/Performance: music. Special Achievements/Activities: general special achievements/activities.

LOANS *Programs:* FFEL (Subsidized and Unsubsidized Stafford, PLUS), Perkins, state, college/university.

WORK-STUDY *Federal work-study:* Total amount: $637,721; jobs available. *State or other work-study/employment:* Total amount: $19,686 (100% need-based). 10 part-time jobs averaging $1435.

APPLYING FOR FINANCIAL AID *Required financial aid form:* FAFSA.

CONTACT Director of Financial Aid, Trinity University, 715 Stadium Drive, San Antonio, TX 78212-7200, 210-999-8315 or toll-free 800-TRINITY. *Fax:* 210-999-8316. *E-mail:* financialaid@trinity.edu.

TRINITY (WASHINGTON) UNIVERSITY
Washington, DC

ABOUT THE INSTITUTION Independent Roman Catholic, undergraduate: women only; graduate: coed. Awards: bachelor's and master's degrees and post-bachelor's certificates. 27 undergraduate majors. Total enrollment: 1,672. Undergraduates: 968. Freshmen: 182.

GIFT AID (NEED-BASED) *Scholarships, grants, and awards:* Federal Pell, FSEOG, state, private, college/university gift aid from institutional funds.

Trinity (Washington) University

GIFT AID (NON-NEED-BASED) *Scholarships, grants, and awards by category: Academic Interests/Achievement:* biological sciences, general academic interests/achievements. *Special Achievements/Activities:* memberships. *Special Characteristics:* children and siblings of alumni, siblings of current students.
LOANS *Programs:* FFEL (Subsidized and Unsubsidized Stafford, PLUS), Perkins.
WORK-STUDY *Federal work-study:* Total amount: $163,075; 122 jobs averaging $1300. *State or other work-study/employment:* Total amount: $16,925 (100% non-need-based).
APPLYING FOR FINANCIAL AID *Required financial aid form:* FAFSA.
CONTACT Catherine H. Geier, Director of Student Financial Services, Trinity (Washington) University, 125 Michigan Avenue, NE, Washington, DC 20017-1094, 202-884-9530 or toll-free 800-IWANTTC. *Fax:* 202-884-9524. *E-mail:* financialaid@trinitydc.edu.

TRI-STATE BIBLE COLLEGE
South Point, OH

CONTACT Financial Aid Office, Tri-State Bible College, 506 Margaret Street, PO Box 445, South Point, OH 45680-8402, 740-377-2520.

TRI-STATE UNIVERSITY
Angola, IN

Tuition & fees: $21,210   **Average undergraduate aid package:** $13,327

ABOUT THE INSTITUTION Independent, coed. Awards: associate, bachelor's, and master's degrees. 42 undergraduate majors. Total enrollment: 1,172. Undergraduates: 1,168. Freshmen: 305. Federal methodology is used as a basis for awarding need-based institutional aid.
UNDERGRADUATE EXPENSES for 2006–07 *Application fee:* $20. *Comprehensive fee:* $27,450 includes full-time tuition ($21,210) and room and board ($6240). *Part-time tuition:* $663 per credit hour.
FRESHMAN FINANCIAL AID (Fall 2005, est.) 297 applied for aid; of those 73% were deemed to have need. 100% of freshmen with need received aid; of those 100% had need fully met. *Average percent of need met:* 90% (excluding resources awarded to replace EFC). *Average financial aid package:* $15,043 (excluding resources awarded to replace EFC). 25% of all full-time freshmen had no need and received non-need-based gift aid.
UNDERGRADUATE FINANCIAL AID (Fall 2005, est.) 1,000 applied for aid; of those 73% were deemed to have need. 100% of undergraduates with need received aid; of those 100% had need fully met. *Average percent of need met:* 90% (excluding resources awarded to replace EFC). *Average financial aid package:* $13,327 (excluding resources awarded to replace EFC). 31% of all full-time undergraduates had no need and received non-need-based gift aid.
GIFT AID (NEED-BASED) *Total amount:* $3,767,096 (23% federal, 45% state, 32% institutional). *Receiving aid:* Freshmen: 50% (150); All full-time undergraduates: 34% (336). *Average award:* Freshmen: $3832; Undergraduates: $3552. *Scholarships, grants, and awards:* Federal Pell, FSEOG, state, private, college/university gift aid from institutional funds.
GIFT AID (NON-NEED-BASED) *Total amount:* $6,456,340 (86% institutional, 14% external sources). *Receiving aid:* Freshmen: 66% (198); Undergraduates: 53% (531). *Average Award:* Freshmen: $7864; Undergraduates: $6758. *Scholarships, grants, and awards by category: Academic Interests/Achievement:* general academic interests/achievements. *Special Characteristics:* children and siblings of alumni, children of faculty/staff, members of minority groups.
LOANS *Student loans:* $3,607,486 (70% need-based, 30% non-need-based). 61% of past graduating class borrowed through all loan programs. *Average indebtedness per student:* $15,400. *Average need-based loan:* Freshmen: $2290; Undergraduates: $3753. *Parent loans:* $3,355,680 (100% non-need-based). *Programs:* FFEL (Subsidized and Unsubsidized Stafford, PLUS), alternative loans.
WORK-STUDY *Federal work-study:* Total amount: $98,185; jobs available.
APPLYING FOR FINANCIAL AID *Required financial aid form:* FAFSA. *Financial aid deadline:* 3/10 (priority: 3/10). *Notification date:* Continuous beginning 2/1. Students must reply by 4/15 or within 2 weeks of notification.
CONTACT Kim Bennett, Director of Financial Aid, Tri-State University, 1 University Avenue, Angola, IN 46703-1764, 260-665-4175 or toll-free 800-347-4TSU. *Fax:* 260-665-4511. *E-mail:* admit@tristate.edu.

TROY UNIVERSITY
Troy, AL

ABOUT THE INSTITUTION State-supported, coed. Awards: associate, bachelor's, and master's degrees and post-master's certificates. 50 undergraduate majors. Total enrollment: 26,880. Undergraduates: 18,778. Freshmen: 2,250.
GIFT AID (NEED-BASED) *Scholarships, grants, and awards:* Federal Pell, FSEOG, state, private, college/university gift aid from institutional funds.
GIFT AID (NON-NEED-BASED) *Scholarships, grants, and awards by category: Academic Interests/Achievement:* general academic interests/achievements. *Creative Arts/Performance:* music, theater/drama. *Special Achievements/Activities:* leadership. *Special Characteristics:* general special characteristics.
LOANS *Programs:* FFEL (Subsidized and Unsubsidized Stafford, PLUS), Perkins.
WORK-STUDY *Federal work-study:* Total amount: $633,180.
APPLYING FOR FINANCIAL AID *Required financial aid forms:* FAFSA, institution's own form.
CONTACT Ms. Carol Supri, Director of Financial Aid, Troy University, 131 Adams Administration Bldg., Troy, AL 36082, 334-670-3186 or toll-free 800-551-9716. *Fax:* 334-670-3702. *E-mail:* csupri@troy.edu.

TRUMAN STATE UNIVERSITY
Kirksville, MO

Tuition & fees (MO res): $5812   **Average undergraduate aid package:** $6056

ABOUT THE INSTITUTION State-supported, coed. Awards: bachelor's and master's degrees. 56 undergraduate majors. Total enrollment: 5,803. Undergraduates: 5,571. Freshmen: 1,448. Federal methodology is used as a basis for awarding need-based institutional aid.
UNDERGRADUATE EXPENSES for 2005–06 *One-time required fee:* $150. *Tuition, state resident:* full-time $5740; part-time $239 per credit hour. *Tuition, nonresident:* full-time $9920; part-time $413 per credit hour. Part-time tuition and fees vary according to course load. *College room and board:* $5380. Room and board charges vary according to housing facility. *Payment plan:* Installment.
FRESHMAN FINANCIAL AID (Fall 2005, est.) 1072 applied for aid; of those 52% were deemed to have need. 100% of freshmen with need received aid; of those 65% had need fully met. *Average percent of need met:* 85% (excluding resources awarded to replace EFC). *Average financial aid package:* $6682 (excluding resources awarded to replace EFC). 61% of all full-time freshmen had no need and received non-need-based gift aid.
UNDERGRADUATE FINANCIAL AID (Fall 2005, est.) 3,747 applied for aid; of those 70% were deemed to have need. 100% of undergraduates with need received aid; of those 63% had need fully met. *Average percent of need met:* 83% (excluding resources awarded to replace EFC). *Average financial aid package:* $6056 (excluding resources awarded to replace EFC). 44% of all full-time undergraduates had no need and received non-need-based gift aid.
GIFT AID (NEED-BASED) *Total amount:* $2,692,809 (69% federal, 15% state, 16% institutional). *Receiving aid:* Freshmen: 20% (282); All full-time undergraduates: 17% (937). *Average award:* Freshmen: $2751; Undergraduates: $2960. *Scholarships, grants, and awards:* Federal Pell, FSEOG, state, private, college/university gift aid from institutional funds.
GIFT AID (NON-NEED-BASED) *Total amount:* $22,800,874 (11% state, 82% institutional, 7% external sources). *Receiving aid:* Freshmen: 36% (522); Undergraduates: 36% (1,980). *Average Award:* Freshmen: $4273; Undergraduates: $4262. *Scholarships, grants, and awards by category: Academic Interests/Achievement:* 3,923 awards ($17,950,253 total): biological sciences, business, communication, education, English, foreign languages, general academic interests/achievements, mathematics, military science, physical sciences, premedicine, social sciences. *Creative Arts/Performance:* 115 awards ($104,924 total): art/fine arts, debating, music, theater/drama. *Special Achievements/Activities:* 375 awards ($832,864 total): leadership. *Special Characteristics:* 269 awards ($1,095,354 total): children and siblings of alumni, children of faculty/staff, ethnic background, international students. *Tuition waivers:* Full or partial for employees or children of employees, senior citizens. *ROTC:* Army.
LOANS *Student loans:* $12,523,976 (49% need-based, 51% non-need-based). 46% of past graduating class borrowed through all loan programs. *Average indebtedness per student:* $16,656. *Average need-based loan:* Freshmen: $3202; Undergraduates: $4050. *Parent loans:* $2,243,649 (100% non-need-based). *Programs:* FFEL (Subsidized and Unsubsidized Stafford, PLUS), Perkins, Federal Nursing, state, college/university.

WORK-STUDY *Federal work-study:* Total amount: $414,424; 346 jobs averaging $886. *State or other work-study/employment:* Total amount: $1,614,051 (100% non-need-based). 1,733 part-time jobs averaging $904.

ATHLETIC AWARDS *Total amount:* $1,178,604 (100% non-need-based).

APPLYING FOR FINANCIAL AID *Required financial aid forms:* FAFSA, institution's own form. *Financial aid deadline (priority):* 4/1. *Notification date:* Continuous beginning 4/1. Students must reply within 4 weeks of notification.

CONTACT Ms. Melinda Wood, Director of Financial Aid, Truman State University, 103 McClain Hall, Kirksville, MO 63501-4221, 660-785-4130 or toll-free 800-892-7792 (in-state). *Fax:* 660-785-7389. *E-mail:* mwood@truman.edu.

TUFTS UNIVERSITY
Medford, MA

Tuition & fees: $32,621   Average undergraduate aid package: $25,749

ABOUT THE INSTITUTION Independent, coed. Awards: bachelor's, master's, doctoral, and first professional degrees and post-master's certificates. 64 undergraduate majors. Total enrollment: 9,780. Undergraduates: 5,078. Freshmen: 1,363. Both federal and institutional methodology are used as a basis for awarding need-based institutional aid.

UNDERGRADUATE EXPENSES for 2005–06 *Application fee:* $70. *Comprehensive fee:* $42,018 includes full-time tuition ($31,828), mandatory fees ($793), and room and board ($9397). *College room only:* $4827. Room and board charges vary according to board plan. *Payment plans:* Tuition prepayment, installment.

FRESHMAN FINANCIAL AID (Fall 2005, est.) 753 applied for aid; of those 71% were deemed to have need. 100% of freshmen with need received aid; of those 100% had need fully met. *Average percent of need met:* 100% (excluding resources awarded to replace EFC). *Average financial aid package:* $25,199 (excluding resources awarded to replace EFC). 2% of all full-time freshmen had no need and received non-need-based gift aid.

UNDERGRADUATE FINANCIAL AID (Fall 2005, est.) 2,244 applied for aid; of those 86% were deemed to have need. 100% of undergraduates with need received aid; of those 100% had need fully met. *Average percent of need met:* 100% (excluding resources awarded to replace EFC). *Average financial aid package:* $25,749 (excluding resources awarded to replace EFC). 2% of all full-time undergraduates had no need and received non-need-based gift aid.

GIFT AID (NEED-BASED) *Total amount:* $39,974,215 (6% federal, 2% state, 88% institutional, 4% external sources). *Receiving aid:* Freshmen: 36% (495); All full-time undergraduates: 36% (1,785). *Average award:* Freshmen: $23,271; Undergraduates: $22,465. *Scholarships, grants, and awards:* Federal Pell, FSEOG, state, private, college/university gift aid from institutional funds.

GIFT AID (NON-NEED-BASED) *Total amount:* $236,425 (25% federal, 19% institutional, 56% external sources). *Average Award:* Freshmen: $500; Undergraduates: $500. *Scholarships, grants, and awards by category:* Academic Interests/Achievement: 159 awards ($177,750 total): general academic interests/achievements. Special Characteristics: children of faculty/staff. *Tuition waivers:* Full or partial for employees or children of employees. *ROTC:* Army cooperative, Naval cooperative, Air Force cooperative.

LOANS *Student loans:* $7,658,993 (88% need-based, 12% non-need-based). 40% of past graduating class borrowed through all loan programs. *Average indebtedness per student:* $14,400. *Average need-based loan:* Freshmen: $3025; Undergraduates: $4287. *Parent loans:* $10,470,711 (100% non-need-based). *Programs:* FFEL (Subsidized and Unsubsidized Stafford, PLUS), Perkins, state, college/university.

WORK-STUDY *Federal work-study:* Total amount: $2,698,890; 1,888 jobs averaging $1403. *State or other work-study/employment:* Total amount: $68,400 (100% need-based). 36 part-time jobs averaging $1900.

APPLYING FOR FINANCIAL AID *Required financial aid forms:* FAFSA, CSS Financial Aid PROFILE, noncustodial (divorced/separated) parent's statement, business/farm supplement, federal income tax form(s). *Financial aid deadline:* 2/15. *Notification date:* 4/5. Students must reply by 5/1.

CONTACT Patricia C. Reilly, Director of Financial Aid, Tufts University, Dowling Hall, Medford, MA 02155, 617-627-2000. *Fax:* 617-627-3987. *E-mail:* patricia.reilly@tufts.edu.

TULANE UNIVERSITY
New Orleans, LA

CONTACT Ms. Elaine Rivera, Director of Financial Aid, Tulane University, 6823 St. Charles Avenue, New Orleans, LA 70118-5669, 504-865-5723 or toll-free 800-873-9283. *E-mail:* finaid@tulane.edu.

TUSCULUM COLLEGE
Greeneville, TN

Tuition & fees: $16,215   Average undergraduate aid package: $9092

ABOUT THE INSTITUTION Independent Presbyterian, coed. Awards: bachelor's and master's degrees. 27 undergraduate majors. Total enrollment: 2,656. Undergraduates: 2,289. Freshmen: 307. Federal methodology is used as a basis for awarding need-based institutional aid.

UNDERGRADUATE EXPENSES for 2006–07 *Comprehensive fee:* $22,715 includes full-time tuition ($15,900), mandatory fees ($315), and room and board ($6500). *Part-time tuition:* $695 per semester hour.

FRESHMAN FINANCIAL AID (Fall 2005, est.) 301 applied for aid; of those 80% were deemed to have need. 99% of freshmen with need received aid; of those 4% had need fully met. *Average percent of need met:* 59% (excluding resources awarded to replace EFC). *Average financial aid package:* $10,336 (excluding resources awarded to replace EFC). 12% of all full-time freshmen had no need and received non-need-based gift aid.

UNDERGRADUATE FINANCIAL AID (Fall 2005, est.) 2,117 applied for aid; of those 75% were deemed to have need. 99% of undergraduates with need received aid; of those 10% had need fully met. *Average percent of need met:* 61% (excluding resources awarded to replace EFC). *Average financial aid package:* $9092 (excluding resources awarded to replace EFC). 12% of all full-time undergraduates had no need and received non-need-based gift aid.

GIFT AID (NEED-BASED) *Total amount:* $8,659,594 (28% federal, 13% state, 59% institutional). *Receiving aid:* Freshmen: 57% (173); All full-time undergraduates: 28% (649). *Average award:* Freshmen: $6976; Undergraduates: $6313. *Scholarships, grants, and awards:* Federal Pell, FSEOG, state, private, college/university gift aid from institutional funds.

GIFT AID (NON-NEED-BASED) *Total amount:* $3,171,964 (19% state, 72% institutional, 9% external sources). *Receiving aid:* Freshmen: 26% (81); Undergraduates: 13% (309). *Average Award:* Freshmen: $5621; Undergraduates: $6043. *Scholarships, grants, and awards by category:* Academic Interests/Achievement: general academic interests/achievements. Creative Arts/Performance: music. Special Achievements/Activities: cheerleading/drum major, community service, leadership. Special Characteristics: adult students, children of faculty/staff, local/state students.

LOANS *Student loans:* $14,369,356 (45% need-based, 55% non-need-based). 72% of past graduating class borrowed through all loan programs. *Average indebtedness per student:* $20,928. *Average need-based loan:* Freshmen: $2314; Undergraduates: $3863. *Parent loans:* $1,051,654 (100% non-need-based). *Programs:* FFEL (Subsidized and Unsubsidized Stafford, PLUS), Perkins.

WORK-STUDY *Federal work-study:* Total amount: $270,136; 259 jobs averaging $1040. *State or other work-study/employment:* Total amount: $291,788 (100% non-need-based). 220 part-time jobs averaging $1332.

ATHLETIC AWARDS *Total amount:* $879,341 (100% non-need-based).

APPLYING FOR FINANCIAL AID *Required financial aid form:* FAFSA. *Financial aid deadline (priority):* 2/15. *Notification date:* Continuous beginning 3/1. Students must reply within 3 weeks of notification.

CONTACT Mr. J. Pat Shannon, Director of Financial Aid, Tusculum College, 5049 Tusculum Station, Greeneville, TN 37743-9997, 423-636-7377 or toll-free 800-729-0256. *Fax:* 615-250-4968. *E-mail:* pshannon@tusculum.edu.

TUSKEGEE UNIVERSITY
Tuskegee, AL

Tuition & fees: $12,700   Average undergraduate aid package: $13,824

ABOUT THE INSTITUTION Independent, coed. Awards: bachelor's, master's, doctoral, and first professional degrees. 43 undergraduate majors. Total enrollment: 2,880. Undergraduates: 2,510. Freshmen: 737. Federal methodology is used as a basis for awarding need-based institutional aid.

Tuskegee University

UNDERGRADUATE EXPENSES for 2006–07 *Application fee:* $25. *Comprehensive fee:* $20,587 includes full-time tuition ($12,400), mandatory fees ($300), and room and board ($7887). *Part-time tuition:* $490 per credit hour.
FRESHMAN FINANCIAL AID (Fall 2004) 635 applied for aid; of those 85% were deemed to have need. 92% of freshmen with need received aid; of those 70% had need fully met. *Average percent of need met:* 85% (excluding resources awarded to replace EFC). *Average financial aid package:* $13,824 (excluding resources awarded to replace EFC). 36% of all full-time freshmen had no need and received non-need-based gift aid.
UNDERGRADUATE FINANCIAL AID (Fall 2004) 2,519 applied for aid; of those 85% were deemed to have need. 92% of undergraduates with need received aid; of those 70% had need fully met. *Average percent of need met:* 85% (excluding resources awarded to replace EFC). *Average financial aid package:* $13,824 (excluding resources awarded to replace EFC). 32% of all full-time undergraduates had no need and received non-need-based gift aid.
GIFT AID (NEED-BASED) *Total amount:* $5,459,147 (98% federal, 2% institutional). *Receiving aid:* Freshmen: 56% (422); All full-time undergraduates: 61% (1,675). *Average award:* Freshmen: $8000; Undergraduates: $8000. *Scholarships, grants, and awards:* Federal Pell, FSEOG, state, private, college/university gift aid from institutional funds, United Negro College Fund, Federal Nursing.
GIFT AID (NON-NEED-BASED) *Total amount:* $3,408,097 (45% institutional, 55% external sources). *Receiving aid:* Freshmen: 36% (273); Undergraduates: 35% (951). *Average Award:* Freshmen: $6000; Undergraduates: $6000. *Scholarships, grants, and awards by category:* Academic Interests/Achievement: 1,714 awards ($9,086,319 total): general academic interests/achievements. *Creative Arts/Performance:* 108 awards ($68,400 total): music. *Special Characteristics:* 36 awards ($157,002 total): children of faculty/staff, local/state students. *ROTC:* Army, Air Force.
LOANS *Student loans:* $16,456,358 (53% need-based, 47% non-need-based). 91% of past graduating class borrowed through all loan programs. *Average indebtedness per student:* $30,000. *Average need-based loan:* Freshmen: $5625; Undergraduates: $6006. *Parent loans:* $3,098,631 (100% non-need-based). *Programs:* FFEL (Subsidized and Unsubsidized Stafford, PLUS), Perkins.
WORK-STUDY *Federal work-study:* Total amount: $830,097; 525 jobs averaging $1879. *State or other work-study/employment:* Total amount: $1,318,823 (100% non-need-based). 425 part-time jobs averaging $4739.
ATHLETIC AWARDS *Total amount:* $1,145,218 (100% non-need-based).
APPLYING FOR FINANCIAL AID *Required financial aid forms:* FAFSA, institution's own form. *Financial aid deadline (priority):* 3/31. *Notification date:* Continuous beginning 4/15. Students must reply within 2 weeks of notification.
CONTACT Mr. A. D. James Jr., Director of Student Financial Services, Tuskegee University, Office of Student Financial Services, Tuskegee, AL 36088, 334-727-8201 or toll-free 800-622-6531. *Fax:* 334-724-4227. *E-mail:* jamesad@tuskegee.edu.

UNION COLLEGE
Barbourville, KY

Tuition & fees: $15,290	Average undergraduate aid package: $12,612

ABOUT THE INSTITUTION Independent United Methodist, coed. Awards: bachelor's and master's degrees. 21 undergraduate majors. Total enrollment: 1,224. Undergraduates: 611. Freshmen: 181. Federal methodology is used as a basis for awarding need-based institutional aid.
UNDERGRADUATE EXPENSES for 2006–07 *Application fee:* $20. *One-time required fee:* $800. *Comprehensive fee:* $19,890 includes full-time tuition ($14,950), mandatory fees ($340), and room and board ($4600). *College room only:* $1700. *Part-time tuition:* $260 per hour. *Part-time fees:* $15 per semester hour.
FRESHMAN FINANCIAL AID (Fall 2005, est.) 177 applied for aid; of those 97% were deemed to have need. 99% of freshmen with need received aid; of those 18% had need fully met. *Average percent of need met:* 73% (excluding resources awarded to replace EFC). *Average financial aid package:* $12,928 (excluding resources awarded to replace EFC). 25% of all full-time freshmen had no need and received non-need-based gift aid.
UNDERGRADUATE FINANCIAL AID (Fall 2005, est.) 548 applied for aid; of those 98% were deemed to have need. 99% of undergraduates with need received aid; of those 24% had need fully met. *Average percent of need met:* 75% (excluding resources awarded to replace EFC). *Average financial aid package:* $12,612 (excluding resources awarded to replace EFC). 12% of all full-time undergraduates had no need and received non-need-based gift aid.
GIFT AID (NEED-BASED) *Total amount:* $3,337,345 (33% federal, 44% state, 18% institutional, 5% external sources). *Receiving aid:* Freshmen: 97% (171); All full-time undergraduates: 96% (532). *Average award:* Freshmen: $9226; Undergraduates: $8298. *Scholarships, grants, and awards:* Federal Pell, FSEOG, state, college/university gift aid from institutional funds.
GIFT AID (NON-NEED-BASED) *Total amount:* $283,079 (100% state). *Receiving aid:* Freshmen: 12% (21); Undergraduates: 11% (60). *Average Award:* Freshmen: $8516; Undergraduates: $9800. *Scholarships, grants, and awards by category:* Academic Interests/Achievement: 282 awards ($589,201 total): general academic interests/achievements. *Creative Arts/Performance:* 15 awards ($35,000 total): music. *Special Achievements/Activities:* 13 awards ($41,987 total): cheerleading/drum major. *Special Characteristics:* 24 awards ($20,850 total): children and siblings of alumni, religious affiliation. *ROTC:* Army cooperative.
LOANS *Student loans:* $3,344,907 (73% need-based, 27% non-need-based). 95% of past graduating class borrowed through all loan programs. *Average indebtedness per student:* $14,626. *Average need-based loan:* Freshmen: $3488; Undergraduates: $4218. *Parent loans:* $286,226 (100% need-based). *Programs:* FFEL (Subsidized and Unsubsidized Stafford, PLUS), Perkins, college/university.
WORK-STUDY *Federal work-study:* Total amount: $186,166; 139 jobs averaging $1339. *State or other work-study/employment:* Part-time jobs available.
ATHLETIC AWARDS *Total amount:* $1,774,234 (100% need-based).
APPLYING FOR FINANCIAL AID *Required financial aid form:* FAFSA. *Financial aid deadline (priority):* 3/15. *Notification date:* Continuous beginning 4/1. Students must reply within 2 weeks of notification.
CONTACT Mrs. Sue Buttery, Associate Dean of Financial Aid and Admission, Union College, 310 College Street, Barbourville, KY 40906-1499, 606-546-1224 or toll-free 800-489-8646. *Fax:* 606-546-1556. *E-mail:* sbuttery@unionky.edu.

UNION COLLEGE
Lincoln, NE

CONTACT Mr. John C. Burdick, IV, Director of Financial Aid, Union College, 3800 South 48th Street, Lincoln, NE 68506-4300, 800-228-4600. *Fax:* 402-486-2895. *E-mail:* financialaid@ucollege.edu.

UNION COLLEGE
Schenectady, NY

Comprehensive fee: $41,595	Average undergraduate aid package: $26,330

ABOUT THE INSTITUTION Independent, coed. Awards: bachelor's degrees. 28 undergraduate majors. Total enrollment: 2,252. Undergraduates: 2,252. Freshmen: 581. Both federal and institutional methodology are used as a basis for awarding need-based institutional aid.
UNDERGRADUATE EXPENSES for 2005–06 *Application fee:* $50. *Comprehensive fee:* $41,595. *Payment plan:* Installment.
FRESHMAN FINANCIAL AID (Fall 2004) 330 applied for aid; of those 77% were deemed to have need. 100% of freshmen with need received aid; of those 100% had need fully met. *Average percent of need met:* 100% (excluding resources awarded to replace EFC). *Average financial aid package:* $26,636 (excluding resources awarded to replace EFC). 11% of all full-time freshmen had no need and received non-need-based gift aid.
UNDERGRADUATE FINANCIAL AID (Fall 2004) 1,142 applied for aid; of those 89% were deemed to have need. 100% of undergraduates with need received aid; of those 96% had need fully met. *Average percent of need met:* 100% (excluding resources awarded to replace EFC). *Average financial aid package:* $26,330 (excluding resources awarded to replace EFC). 5% of all full-time undergraduates had no need and received non-need-based gift aid.
GIFT AID (NEED-BASED) *Total amount:* $21,758,642 (6% federal, 5% state, 87% institutional, 2% external sources). *Receiving aid:* Freshmen: 46% (254); All full-time undergraduates: 48% (1,017). *Average award:* Freshmen: $23,287; Undergraduates: $21,368. *Scholarships, grants, and awards:* Federal Pell, FSEOG, state, private, college/university gift aid from institutional funds.
GIFT AID (NON-NEED-BASED) *Total amount:* $2,932,518 (4% federal, 4% state, 92% institutional). *Receiving aid:* Freshmen: 3% (19); Undergraduates: 1% (28). *Average Award:* Freshmen: $10,850; Undergraduates: $12,200. *Scholarships, grants, and awards by category:* Academic Interests/Achievement: 85

awards ($900,000 total): general academic interests/achievements. *Tuition waivers:* Full or partial for employees or children of employees, senior citizens. *ROTC:* Army cooperative, Air Force cooperative.
LOANS *Student loans:* $4,713,539 (86% need-based, 14% non-need-based). 50% of past graduating class borrowed through all loan programs. *Average indebtedness per student:* $16,705. *Average need-based loan:* Freshmen: $2967; Undergraduates: $4596. *Parent loans:* $3,351,399 (100% non-need-based). *Programs:* FFEL (Subsidized and Unsubsidized Stafford, PLUS), Perkins, college/university.
WORK-STUDY *Federal work-study:* Total amount: $854,196; 542 jobs averaging $1680. *State or other work-study/employment:* Total amount: $53,247 (100% need-based). 36 part-time jobs averaging $1800.
APPLYING FOR FINANCIAL AID *Required financial aid forms:* FAFSA, CSS Financial Aid PROFILE, state aid form, business/farm supplement, Non custodial (divorced/separated) parent's statement. *Financial aid deadline:* 2/1. *Notification date:* 4/1. Students must reply by 5/1.
CONTACT Ms. Beth Post, Director of Financial Aid and Family Financing, Union College, Grant Hall, Schenectady, NY 12308-2311, 518-388-6123 or toll-free 888-843-6688 (in-state). *Fax:* 518-388-8052. *E-mail:* financialaid@union.edu.

UNION INSTITUTE & UNIVERSITY
Cincinnati, OH

CONTACT Ms. Rebecca Zackerman, Director of Financial Aid, Union Institute & University, 440 East McMillan Street, Cincinnati, OH 45206-1925, 513-861-6400 or toll-free 800-486-3116. *Fax:* 513-861-0779. *E-mail:* bzackerman@tui.edu.

UNION UNIVERSITY
Jackson, TN

Tuition & fees: $16,450	Average undergraduate aid package: $12,200

ABOUT THE INSTITUTION Independent Southern Baptist, coed. Awards: associate, bachelor's, master's, and doctoral degrees and post-master's certificates. 66 undergraduate majors. Total enrollment: 2,866. Undergraduates: 2,086. Freshmen: 412. Federal methodology is used as a basis for awarding need-based institutional aid.
UNDERGRADUATE EXPENSES for 2005–06 *Application fee:* $25. *Comprehensive fee:* $21,920 includes full-time tuition ($15,900), mandatory fees ($550), and room and board ($5470). *College room only:* $3290. Full-time tuition and fees vary according to class time, course load, location, and program. Room and board charges vary according to board plan and location. *Part-time tuition:* $530 per credit hour. *Payment plans:* Installment, deferred payment.
FRESHMAN FINANCIAL AID (Fall 2005, est.) 352 applied for aid; of those 82% were deemed to have need. 100% of freshmen with need received aid. *Average financial aid package:* $12,200 (excluding resources awarded to replace EFC). 22% of all full-time freshmen had no need and received non-need-based gift aid.
UNDERGRADUATE FINANCIAL AID (Fall 2005, est.) 1,280 applied for aid; of those 89% were deemed to have need. 100% of undergraduates with need received aid. *Average financial aid package:* $12,200 (excluding resources awarded to replace EFC). 11% of all full-time undergraduates had no need and received non-need-based gift aid.
GIFT AID (NEED-BASED) *Total amount:* $3,341,093 (36% federal, 18% state, 43% institutional, 3% external sources). *Receiving aid:* Freshmen: 73% (272); All full-time undergraduates: 66% (1,050). *Average award:* Freshmen: $8010; Undergraduates: $7312. *Scholarships, grants, and awards:* Federal Pell, FSEOG, state, private, college/university gift aid from institutional funds.
GIFT AID (NON-NEED-BASED) *Total amount:* $8,002,495 (17% state, 79% institutional, 4% external sources). *Receiving aid:* Freshmen: 27% (101); Undergraduates: 32% (512). *Average Award:* Freshmen: $11,210; Undergraduates: $11,485. *Scholarships, grants, and awards by category:* Academic Interests/Achievement: 1,050 awards ($3,386,984 total): business, communication, education, general academic interests/achievements, mathematics, premedicine, religion/biblical studies. Creative Arts/Performance: 102 awards ($147,300 total): art/fine arts, cinema/film/broadcasting, journalism/publications, music, theater/drama. Special Achievements/Activities: 640 awards ($704,254 total): cheerleading/drum major, leadership. Special Characteristics: 433 awards ($1,546,126 total): children and siblings of alumni, children of faculty/staff, ethnic background,

relatives of clergy, religious affiliation, siblings of current students. *Tuition waivers:* Full or partial for employees or children of employees.
LOANS *Student loans:* $8,790,086 (48% need-based, 52% non-need-based). 52% of past graduating class borrowed through all loan programs. *Average indebtedness per student:* $17,645. *Average need-based loan:* Freshmen: $3316; Undergraduates: $4410. *Parent loans:* $1,829,613 (100% non-need-based). *Programs:* FFEL (Subsidized and Unsubsidized Stafford, PLUS), Perkins, college/university, alternative loans.
WORK-STUDY *Federal work-study:* Total amount: $206,737; 127 jobs averaging $985. *State or other work-study/employment:* Total amount: $280,000 (100% non-need-based). 111 part-time jobs averaging $1440.
ATHLETIC AWARDS *Total amount:* $1,340,487 (100% non-need-based).
APPLYING FOR FINANCIAL AID *Required financial aid forms:* FAFSA, institution's own form. *Financial aid deadline (priority):* 3/1. *Notification date:* Continuous beginning 2/15. Students must reply by 5/1 or within 2 weeks of notification.
CONTACT John Brandt, Director of Financial Aid, Union University, 1050 Union University Drive, Jackson, TN 38305-3697, 731-661-5015 or toll-free 800-33-UNION. *Fax:* 731-661-5570. *E-mail:* jbrandt@uu.edu.

UNITED TALMUDICAL SEMINARY
Brooklyn, NY

CONTACT Financial Aid Office, United Talmudical Seminary, 82 Lee Avenue, Brooklyn, NY 11211-7900, 718-963-9770 Ext. 309.

UNITY COLLEGE
Unity, ME

Tuition & fees: $17,680	Average undergraduate aid package: $12,589

ABOUT THE INSTITUTION Independent, coed. Awards: associate and bachelor's degrees. 14 undergraduate majors. Total enrollment: 521. Undergraduates: 521. Freshmen: 159. Federal methodology is used as a basis for awarding need-based institutional aid.
UNDERGRADUATE EXPENSES for 2005–06 *Application fee:* $25. *Comprehensive fee:* $24,310 includes full-time tuition ($16,740), mandatory fees ($940), and room and board ($6630). Room and board charges vary according to board plan. *Part-time tuition:* $630 per credit hour. Part-time tuition and fees vary according to course load. *Payment plan:* Installment.
FRESHMAN FINANCIAL AID (Fall 2005, est.) 142 applied for aid; of those 86% were deemed to have need. 100% of freshmen with need received aid; of those 33% had need fully met. *Average percent of need met:* 76% (excluding resources awarded to replace EFC). *Average financial aid package:* $13,934 (excluding resources awarded to replace EFC). 17% of all full-time freshmen had no need and received non-need-based gift aid.
UNDERGRADUATE FINANCIAL AID (Fall 2005, est.) 463 applied for aid; of those 88% were deemed to have need. 100% of undergraduates with need received aid; of those 27% had need fully met. *Average percent of need met:* 76% (excluding resources awarded to replace EFC). *Average financial aid package:* $12,589 (excluding resources awarded to replace EFC). 15% of all full-time undergraduates had no need and received non-need-based gift aid.
GIFT AID (NEED-BASED) *Total amount:* $2,971,234 (23% federal, 5% state, 66% institutional, 6% external sources). *Receiving aid:* Freshmen: 81% (122); All full-time undergraduates: 70% (407). *Average award:* Freshmen: $8580; Undergraduates: $7300. *Scholarships, grants, and awards:* Federal Pell, FSEOG, state, private, college/university gift aid from institutional funds.
GIFT AID (NON-NEED-BASED) *Total amount:* $316,986 (92% institutional, 8% external sources). *Receiving aid:* Freshmen: 5% (7); Undergraduates: 3% (17). *Average Award:* Freshmen: $8646; Undergraduates: $8753. *Scholarships, grants, and awards by category:* Academic Interests/Achievement: 215 awards ($836,375 total): general academic interests/achievements. Special Achievements/Activities: 99 awards ($97,500 total): community service, leadership. Special Characteristics: 54 awards ($121,500 total): children of educators, general special characteristics, local/state students, members of minority groups. *Tuition waivers:* Full or partial for employees or children of employees. *ROTC:* Army cooperative.
LOANS *Student loans:* $3,954,204 (71% need-based, 29% non-need-based). *Average need-based loan:* Freshmen: $5115; Undergraduates: $5751. *Parent loans:* $747,543 (40% need-based, 60% non-need-based). *Programs:* FFEL (Subsidized and Unsubsidized Stafford, PLUS), Perkins.

Unity College

WORK-STUDY *Federal work-study:* Total amount: $484,790; 331 jobs averaging $1594. *State or other work-study/employment:* Total amount: $17,200 (8% need-based, 92% non-need-based). 13 part-time jobs averaging $1323.
APPLYING FOR FINANCIAL AID *Required financial aid form:* FAFSA. *Financial aid deadline:* Continuous. *Notification date:* Continuous beginning 3/10. Students must reply within 2 weeks of notification.
CONTACT Mr. Rand E. Newell, Director of Financial Aid, Unity College, 90 Quaker Hill Road, Unity, ME 04988, 207-948-3131 Ext. 201. *Fax:* 207-948-6277. *E-mail:* rnewell@unity.edu.

UNIVERSIDAD ADVENTISTA DE LAS ANTILLAS
Mayagüez, PR

CONTACT Mr. Heriberto Juarbe, Director of Financial Aid, Universidad Adventista de las Antillas, Box 118, Mayagüez, PR 00681-0118, 787-834-9595 Ext. 2200. *Fax:* 787-834-9597.

UNIVERSIDAD DEL ESTE
Carolina, PR

CONTACT Mr. Clotilde Santiago, Director of Financial Aid, Universidad del Este, Apartado 2010, Carolina, PR 00928, 787-257-7373 Ext. 3300.

UNIVERSIDAD DEL TURABO
Gurabo, PR

CONTACT Ms. Ivette Vázquez Ríos, Directora Oficina de Asistencia Económica, Universidad del Turabo, Apartado 3030, Gurabo, PR 00778-3030, 787-743-7979 Ext. 4352. *Fax:* 787-743-7979.

UNIVERSIDAD FLET
Miami, FL

CONTACT Financial Aid Office, Universidad FLET, 14540 SW 136th Street, Suite 200, Miami, FL 33186, 305-232-5880 or toll-free 888-376-3538.

UNIVERSIDAD METROPOLITANA
San Juan, PR

CONTACT Economic Assistant Director, Universidad Metropolitana, Call Box 21150, Rio Piedras, PR 00928-1150, 787-766-1717 Ext. 6586 or toll-free 800-747-8362 (out-of-state).

UNIVERSITY AT ALBANY, STATE UNIVERSITY OF NEW YORK
Albany, NY

Tuition & fees (NY res): $5887	Average undergraduate aid package: $8258

ABOUT THE INSTITUTION State-supported, coed. Awards: bachelor's, master's, and doctoral degrees and post-master's certificates. 69 undergraduate majors. Total enrollment: 17,040. Undergraduates: 12,013. Freshmen: 2,560. Federal methodology is used as a basis for awarding need-based institutional aid.
UNDERGRADUATE EXPENSES for 2005–06 *Application fee:* $40. *Tuition, state resident:* full-time $4350; part-time $181 per credit. *Tuition, nonresident:* full-time $10,610; part-time $442 per credit. Part-time tuition and fees vary according to course load. *College room and board:* $8050; *room only:* $4834. Room and board charges vary according to board plan and housing facility. *Payment plan:* Installment.
FRESHMAN FINANCIAL AID (Fall 2005, est.) 2082 applied for aid; of those 67% were deemed to have need. 99% of freshmen with need received aid; of those 13% had need fully met. *Average percent of need met:* 72% (excluding resources awarded to replace EFC). *Average financial aid package:* $8071 (excluding resources awarded to replace EFC). 11% of all full-time freshmen had no need and received non-need-based gift aid.
UNDERGRADUATE FINANCIAL AID (Fall 2005, est.) 8,460 applied for aid; of those 72% were deemed to have need. 99% of undergraduates with need received aid; of those 18% had need fully met. *Average percent of need met:* 73% (excluding resources awarded to replace EFC). *Average financial aid package:* $8258 (excluding resources awarded to replace EFC). 7% of all full-time undergraduates had no need and received non-need-based gift aid.
GIFT AID (NEED-BASED) *Total amount:* $26,083,404 (39% federal, 52% state, 7% institutional, 2% external sources). *Receiving aid:* Freshmen: 51% (1,299); All full-time undergraduates: 51% (5,636). *Average award:* Freshmen: $4728; Undergraduates: $4673. *Scholarships, grants, and awards:* Federal Pell, FSEOG, state.
GIFT AID (NON-NEED-BASED) *Total amount:* $4,106,275 (1% federal, 29% state, 61% institutional, 9% external sources). *Receiving aid:* Freshmen: 2% (53); Undergraduates: 2% (218). *Average Award:* Freshmen: $2023; Undergraduates: $3073. *Scholarships, grants, and awards by category:* Academic Interests/Achievement: 1,494 awards ($4,112,199 total): general academic interests/achievements. *Tuition waivers:* Full or partial for senior citizens. *ROTC:* Army, Air Force cooperative.
LOANS *Student loans:* $41,064,688 (52% need-based, 48% non-need-based). 74% of past graduating class borrowed through all loan programs. *Average indebtedness per student:* $14,392. *Average need-based loan:* Freshmen: $3390; Undergraduates: $4154. *Parent loans:* $8,688,548 (100% non-need-based). *Programs:* FFEL (Subsidized and Unsubsidized Stafford, PLUS), Perkins.
WORK-STUDY *Federal work-study:* Total amount: $1,673,065; 1,127 jobs averaging $1485. *State or other work-study/employment:* Total amount: $1,072,523 (59% need-based, 41% non-need-based). 232 part-time jobs averaging $4623.
ATHLETIC AWARDS *Total amount:* $2,526,413 (31% need-based, 69% non-need-based).
APPLYING FOR FINANCIAL AID *Required financial aid forms:* FAFSA, NY state residents should apply for TAP online at www.tapweb.org. *Financial aid deadline:* 4/15. *Notification date:* Continuous beginning 3/15. Students must reply by 5/1 or within 2 weeks of notification.
CONTACT Brenda Wright, Assistant Director of Financial Aid, University at Albany, State University of New York, 1400 Washington Avenue, Campus Center B52, Albany, NY 12222-0001, 518-442-5757 or toll-free 800-293-7869 (in-state). *Fax:* 518-442-5295. *E-mail:* faoweb@albany.edu.

UNIVERSITY AT BUFFALO, THE STATE UNIVERSITY OF NEW YORK
Buffalo, NY

See State University of New York at Buffalo.

UNIVERSITY OF ADVANCING TECHNOLOGY
Tempe, AZ

CONTACT Director of Financial Aid, University of Advancing Technology, 2625 West Baseline Road, Tempe, AZ 85283-1042, 602-383-8228 or toll-free 800-658-5744 (out-of-state).

THE UNIVERSITY OF AKRON
Akron, OH

Tuition & fees (OH res): $7958	Average undergraduate aid package: $6798

ABOUT THE INSTITUTION State-supported, coed. Awards: bachelor's, master's, doctoral, and first professional degrees and post-bachelor's and first professional certificates (associate). 234 undergraduate majors. Total enrollment: 21,049. Undergraduates: 17,140. Freshmen: 3,086. Federal methodology is used as a basis for awarding need-based institutional aid.
UNDERGRADUATE EXPENSES for 2005–06 *Application fee:* $30. *Tuition, state resident:* full-time $6810; part-time $284 per credit. *Tuition, nonresident:* full-time $15,535; part-time $575 per credit. *Required fees:* full-time $1148; $47 per credit. Full-time tuition and fees vary according to course load, degree level, and location. Part-time tuition and fees vary according to course load, degree level, and location. *College room and board:* $7208; *room only:* $4494. Room and board charges vary according to board plan and housing facility. *Payment plan:* Installment.
FRESHMAN FINANCIAL AID (Fall 2005, est.) 2300 applied for aid; of those 80% were deemed to have need. 100% of freshmen with need received aid; of those 5% had need fully met. *Average percent of need met:* 47% (excluding

resources awarded to replace EFC). *Average financial aid package:* $6168 (excluding resources awarded to replace EFC). 7% of all full-time freshmen had no need and received non-need-based gift aid.
UNDERGRADUATE FINANCIAL AID (Fall 2005, est.) 9,765 applied for aid; of those 81% were deemed to have need. 100% of undergraduates with need received aid; of those 5% had need fully met. *Average percent of need met:* 49% (excluding resources awarded to replace EFC). *Average financial aid package:* $6798 (excluding resources awarded to replace EFC). 5% of all full-time undergraduates had no need and received non-need-based gift aid.
GIFT AID (NEED-BASED) *Total amount:* $25,019,137 (76% federal, 24% state). *Receiving aid:* Freshmen: 33% (961); All full-time undergraduates: 34% (4,258). *Average award:* Freshmen: $4513; Undergraduates: $4427. *Scholarships, grants, and awards:* Federal Pell, FSEOG.
GIFT AID (NON-NEED-BASED) *Total amount:* $12,484,691 (9% state, 73% institutional, 18% external sources). *Receiving aid:* Freshmen: 34% (989); Undergraduates: 26% (3,320). *Average Award:* Freshmen: $3238; Undergraduates: $3419. *Scholarships, grants, and awards by category:* Academic Interests/Achievement: 2,380 awards ($5,911,541 total): biological sciences, business, communication, computer science, education, engineering/technologies, English, foreign languages, general academic interests/achievements, health fields, home economics, humanities, international studies, mathematics, military science, physical sciences, premedicine, social sciences. Creative Arts/Performance: 245 awards ($350,622 total): applied art and design, art/fine arts, creative writing, dance, debating, general creative arts/performance, journalism/publications, music, performing arts, theater/drama. Special Achievements/Activities: 193 awards ($362,137 total): community service, general special achievements/activities, leadership, memberships. Special Characteristics: 967 awards ($2,603,734 total): adult students, general special characteristics, handicapped students, international students, local/state students, members of minority groups, out-of-state students. *Tuition waivers:* Full or partial for employees or children of employees, senior citizens. *ROTC:* Army, Air Force.
LOANS *Student loans:* $76,066,571 (47% need-based, 53% non-need-based). 58% of past graduating class borrowed through all loan programs. *Average indebtedness per student:* $15,036. *Average need-based loan:* Freshmen: $2519; Undergraduates: $3415. *Parent loans:* $10,115,801 (100% non-need-based). *Programs:* FFEL (Subsidized and Unsubsidized Stafford, PLUS), Perkins, Federal Nursing, college/university.
WORK-STUDY *Federal work-study:* Total amount: $1,560,091; 787 jobs averaging $1982. *State or other work-study/employment:* Total amount: $4,948,629 (100% non-need-based). 2,638 part-time jobs averaging $1876.
ATHLETIC AWARDS *Total amount:* $4,663,210 (100% non-need-based).
APPLYING FOR FINANCIAL AID *Required financial aid forms:* FAFSA, institution's own form. *Financial aid deadline (priority):* 2/1. *Notification date:* Continuous beginning 4/15. Students must reply within 2 weeks of notification.
CONTACT Mr. Doug McNutt, Director of Financial Aid, The University of Akron, Office of Student Financial Aid, Akron, OH 44325-6211, 330-972-6334 or toll-free 800-655-4884. *Fax:* 330-972-7139. *E-mail:* mcnuttd@uakron.edu.

THE UNIVERSITY OF ALABAMA
Tuscaloosa, AL

Tuition & fees (AL res): $4864   **Average undergraduate aid package:** $7980

ABOUT THE INSTITUTION State-supported, coed. Awards: bachelor's, master's, doctoral, and first professional degrees and post-bachelor's and post-master's certificates. 78 undergraduate majors. Total enrollment: 21,835. Undergraduates: 17,553. Freshmen: 3,735. Federal methodology is used as a basis for awarding need-based institutional aid.
UNDERGRADUATE EXPENSES for 2005–06 *Application fee:* $30. *Tuition, state resident:* full-time $4864. *Tuition, nonresident:* full-time $13,516. Full-time tuition and fees vary according to course load. Part-time tuition and fees vary according to course load. *College room and board:* $5024; *room only:* $3120. Room and board charges vary according to board plan and housing facility. *Payment plans:* Installment, deferred payment.
FRESHMAN FINANCIAL AID (Fall 2004) 2547 applied for aid; of those 48% were deemed to have need. 98% of freshmen with need received aid; of those 34% had need fully met. *Average percent of need met:* 67% (excluding resources awarded to replace EFC). *Average financial aid package:* $7887 (excluding resources awarded to replace EFC). 36% of all full-time freshmen had no need and received non-need-based gift aid.

The University of Alabama at Birmingham

UNDERGRADUATE FINANCIAL AID (Fall 2004) 10,886 applied for aid; of those 53% were deemed to have need. 99% of undergraduates with need received aid; of those 31% had need fully met. *Average percent of need met:* 70% (excluding resources awarded to replace EFC). *Average financial aid package:* $7980 (excluding resources awarded to replace EFC). 29% of all full-time undergraduates had no need and received non-need-based gift aid.
GIFT AID (NEED-BASED) *Total amount:* $11,642,422 (96% federal, 4% institutional). *Receiving aid:* Freshmen: 19% (647); All full-time undergraduates: 23% (3,391). *Average award:* Freshmen: $3847; Undergraduates: $3732. *Scholarships, grants, and awards:* Federal Pell, FSEOG, state, private, college/university gift aid from institutional funds, Federal Nursing.
GIFT AID (NON-NEED-BASED) *Total amount:* $22,249,185 (38% institutional, 62% external sources). *Receiving aid:* Freshmen: 10% (343); Undergraduates: 8% (1,212). *Average Award:* Freshmen: $5431; Undergraduates: $5151. *Scholarships, grants, and awards by category:* Academic Interests/Achievement: 4,899 awards ($9,042,252 total): area/ethnic studies, biological sciences, business, communication, computer science, education, engineering/technologies, English, foreign languages, general academic interests/achievements, home economics, library science, mathematics, military science, physical sciences, premedicine, social sciences. Creative Arts/Performance: 679 awards ($743,073 total): art/fine arts, cinema/film/broadcasting, creative writing, dance, debating, journalism/publications, music, theater/drama. Special Achievements/Activities: 233 awards ($942,896 total): cheerleading/drum major, community service, general special achievements/activities, hobbies/interests, junior miss. Special Characteristics: 169 awards ($307,024 total): children of union members/company employees, general special characteristics, international students, out-of-state students, spouses of deceased or disabled public servants. *Tuition waivers:* Full or partial for employees or children of employees. *ROTC:* Army, Air Force.
LOANS *Student loans:* $50,499,164 (41% need-based, 59% non-need-based). 50% of past graduating class borrowed through all loan programs. *Average indebtedness per student:* $18,545. *Average need-based loan:* Freshmen: $3367; Undergraduates: $4895. *Parent loans:* $9,525,240 (100% non-need-based). *Programs:* Federal Direct (Subsidized and Unsubsidized Stafford, PLUS), Perkins, college/university.
WORK-STUDY *Federal work-study:* Total amount: $1,952,434; 655 jobs averaging $2981.
ATHLETIC AWARDS *Total amount:* $4,451,873 (100% non-need-based).
APPLYING FOR FINANCIAL AID *Required financial aid form:* FAFSA. *Financial aid deadline (priority):* 3/1. *Notification date:* 4/1. Students must reply within 3 weeks of notification.
CONTACT Helen Leathers, Assistant Director of Financial Aid, The University of Alabama, Box 870162, Tuscaloosa, AL 35487-0162, 205-348-6756 or toll-free 800-933-BAMA. *Fax:* 205-348-2989. *E-mail:* helen.leathers@ua.edu.

THE UNIVERSITY OF ALABAMA AT BIRMINGHAM
Birmingham, AL

Tuition & fees (AL res): $4792   **Average undergraduate aid package:** $13,600

ABOUT THE INSTITUTION State-supported, coed. Awards: bachelor's, master's, doctoral, and first professional degrees and post-bachelor's and post-master's certificates. 48 undergraduate majors. Total enrollment: 16,572. Undergraduates: 11,470. Freshmen: 1,587. Institutional methodology is used as a basis for awarding need-based institutional aid.
UNDERGRADUATE EXPENSES for 2005–06 *Application fee:* $30. *Tuition, state resident:* full-time $3960; part-time $132 per credit hour. *Tuition, nonresident:* full-time $9900; part-time $330 per credit hour. Full-time tuition and fees vary according to program. Part-time tuition and fees vary according to program. *College room and board: room only:* $3390. Room and board charges vary according to board plan, housing facility, and student level.
FRESHMAN FINANCIAL AID (Fall 2004) 1226 applied for aid; of those 66% were deemed to have need. 99% of freshmen with need received aid; of those 13% had need fully met. *Average percent of need met:* 39% (excluding resources awarded to replace EFC). *Average financial aid package:* $10,410 (excluding resources awarded to replace EFC). 22% of all full-time freshmen had no need and received non-need-based gift aid.
UNDERGRADUATE FINANCIAL AID (Fall 2004) 5,812 applied for aid; of those 73% were deemed to have need. 98% of undergraduates with need received aid; of those 13% had need fully met. *Average percent of need met:* 42%

The University of Alabama at Birmingham

(excluding resources awarded to replace EFC). *Average financial aid package:* $13,600 (excluding resources awarded to replace EFC). 16% of all full-time undergraduates had no need and received non-need-based gift aid.
GIFT AID (NEED-BASED) *Total amount:* $11,606,591 (98% federal, 2% institutional). *Receiving aid:* Freshmen: 32% (501); All full-time undergraduates: 34% (2,682). *Average award:* Freshmen: $3204; Undergraduates: $3345. *Scholarships, grants, and awards:* Federal Pell, FSEOG, state, private, college/university gift aid from institutional funds, United Negro College Fund.
GIFT AID (NON-NEED-BASED) *Total amount:* $4,472,949 (1% federal, 2% state, 69% institutional, 28% external sources). *Receiving aid:* Freshmen: 17% (256); Undergraduates: 14% (1,125). *Average Award: Freshmen:* $7335; *Undergraduates:* $8392. *Scholarships, grants, and awards by category: Academic Interests/Achievement:* business, communication, computer science, engineering/technologies, general academic interests/achievements, health fields, mathematics. *Creative Arts/Performance:* art/fine arts, music, performing arts, theater/drama. *Special Achievements/Activities:* cheerleading/drum major, junior miss, leadership, memberships, religious involvement. *Special Characteristics:* adult students, children and siblings of alumni, children of current students, children of educators, children of faculty/staff, children of public servants, children of union members/company employees, children of workers in trades, children with a deceased or disabled parent, ethnic background, first-generation college students, general special characteristics, handicapped students, local/state students, married students, members of minority groups, out-of-state students, parents of current students, previous college experience, public servants, relatives of clergy, religious affiliation, siblings of current students, spouses of current students, spouses of deceased or disabled public servants, twins, veterans, veterans' children. *Tuition waivers:* Full or partial for employees or children of employees. *ROTC:* Army, Air Force cooperative.
LOANS *Student loans:* $30,788,289 (70% need-based, 30% non-need-based). 54% of past graduating class borrowed through all loan programs. *Average indebtedness per student:* $17,594. *Average need-based loan:* Freshmen: $2962; Undergraduates: $4163. *Parent loans:* $4,621,761 (100% non-need-based). *Programs:* Federal Direct (Subsidized and Unsubsidized Stafford, PLUS), Perkins, state, college/university.
WORK-STUDY *Federal work-study:* Total amount: $2,120,284; jobs available.
ATHLETIC AWARDS *Total amount:* $3,671,711 (100% non-need-based).
APPLYING FOR FINANCIAL AID *Required financial aid forms:* FAFSA, institution's own form. *Financial aid deadline (priority):* 4/1. *Notification date:* Continuous beginning 4/1. Students must reply within 4 weeks of notification.
CONTACT Ms. Janet B. May, Financial Aid Director, The University of Alabama at Birmingham, Hill University Center 317, 1530 3rd Avenue South, Birmingham, AL 35294-1150, 205-934-8132 or toll-free 800-421-8743.

THE UNIVERSITY OF ALABAMA IN HUNTSVILLE
Huntsville, AL

Tuition & fees (AL res): $4688   **Average undergraduate aid package: $5917**

ABOUT THE INSTITUTION State-supported, coed. Awards: bachelor's, master's, and doctoral degrees and post-bachelor's and post-master's certificates. 29 undergraduate majors. Total enrollment: 7,084. Undergraduates: 5,690. Freshmen: 660. Both federal and institutional methodology are used as a basis for awarding need-based institutional aid.
UNDERGRADUATE EXPENSES for 2005–06 *Application fee:* $30. *Tuition, state resident:* full-time $4688. *Tuition, nonresident:* full-time $9886. Full-time tuition and fees vary according to course load. Part-time tuition and fees vary according to course load. *College room and board:* $5320; *room only:* $3720. Room and board charges vary according to board plan and housing facility. *Payment plan:* Deferred payment.
FRESHMAN FINANCIAL AID (Fall 2004) 590 applied for aid; of those 45% were deemed to have need. 97% of freshmen with need received aid; of those 16% had need fully met. *Average percent of need met:* 51% (excluding resources awarded to replace EFC). *Average financial aid package:* $5324 (excluding resources awarded to replace EFC). 40% of all full-time freshmen had no need and received non-need-based gift aid.
UNDERGRADUATE FINANCIAL AID (Fall 2004) 3,179 applied for aid; of those 55% were deemed to have need. 94% of undergraduates with need received aid; of those 16% had need fully met. *Average percent of need met:* 52% (excluding resources awarded to replace EFC). *Average financial aid package:* $5917 (excluding resources awarded to replace EFC). 22% of all full-time undergraduates had no need and received non-need-based gift aid.
GIFT AID (NEED-BASED) *Total amount:* $4,668,208 (76% federal, 1% state, 15% institutional, 8% external sources). *Receiving aid:* Freshmen: 21% (131); All full-time undergraduates: 24% (977). *Average award:* Freshmen: $2866; Undergraduates: $3080. *Scholarships, grants, and awards:* Federal Pell, FSEOG, state, private, college/university gift aid from institutional funds, Federal Nursing.
GIFT AID (NON-NEED-BASED) *Total amount:* $2,253,844 (2% state, 71% institutional, 27% external sources). *Receiving aid:* Freshmen: 30% (187); Undergraduates: 15% (616). *Average Award: Freshmen:* $2647; *Undergraduates:* $2194. *Scholarships, grants, and awards by category: Academic Interests/Achievement:* 2,078 awards ($3,294,938 total): business, computer science, education, engineering/technologies, English, general academic interests/achievements, health fields, humanities, physical sciences, social sciences. *Creative Arts/Performance:* 70 awards ($32,125 total): art/fine arts, music. *Special Achievements/Activities:* 644 awards ($1,255,846 total): cheerleading/drum major, community service, general special achievements/activities, junior miss, leadership. *Special Characteristics:* 48 awards ($71,700 total): general special characteristics, local/state students, members of minority groups. *Tuition waivers:* Full or partial for employees or children of employees. *ROTC:* Army cooperative.
LOANS *Student loans:* $10,363,982 (100% need-based). 52% of past graduating class borrowed through all loan programs. *Average indebtedness per student:* $17,272. *Average need-based loan:* Freshmen: $2247; Undergraduates: $3595. *Parent loans:* $1,213,922 (100% need-based). *Programs:* Federal Direct (Subsidized and Unsubsidized Stafford, PLUS).
WORK-STUDY *Federal work-study:* Total amount: $336,797; 122 jobs averaging $2608.
ATHLETIC AWARDS *Total amount:* $1,197,771 (18% need-based, 82% non-need-based).
APPLYING FOR FINANCIAL AID *Required financial aid forms:* FAFSA, institution's own form. *Financial aid deadline:* 7/31 (priority: 4/1). *Notification date:* Continuous beginning 4/1. Students must reply within 2 weeks of notification.
CONTACT Mr. Andrew Weaver, Director of Student Financial Services, The University of Alabama in Huntsville, Office of Financial Aid, 301 Sparkman Drive, Huntsville, AL 35899, 256-824-6241 or toll-free 800-UAH-CALL. *Fax:* 256-824-6212. *E-mail:* finaid@email.uah.edu.

UNIVERSITY OF ALASKA ANCHORAGE
Anchorage, AK

ABOUT THE INSTITUTION State-supported, coed. Awards: associate, bachelor's, and master's degrees. 67 undergraduate majors. Total enrollment: 16,261. Undergraduates: 15,481. Freshmen: 1,417.
GIFT AID (NEED-BASED) *Scholarships, grants, and awards:* Federal Pell, FSEOG, state, private, college/university gift aid from institutional funds.
GIFT AID (NON-NEED-BASED) *Scholarships, grants, and awards by category: Academic Interests/Achievement:* biological sciences, business, communication, computer science, education, engineering/technologies, English, general academic interests/achievements, health fields, humanities, mathematics, social sciences. *Special Achievements/Activities:* general special achievements/activities.
LOANS *Programs:* FFEL (Subsidized and Unsubsidized Stafford, PLUS), state.
APPLYING FOR FINANCIAL AID *Required financial aid form:* FAFSA.
CONTACT Theodore E. Malone, Director of Student Financial Aid, University of Alaska Anchorage, PO Box 141608, Anchorage, AK 99514-1608, 907-786-1520. *Fax:* 907-786-6122.

UNIVERSITY OF ALASKA FAIRBANKS
Fairbanks, AK

Tuition & fees (AK res): $4518   **Average undergraduate aid package: $8899**

ABOUT THE INSTITUTION State-supported, coed. Awards: associate, bachelor's, master's, and doctoral degrees. 68 undergraduate majors. Total enrollment: 8,230. Undergraduates: 7,136. Freshmen: 1,000. Federal methodology is used as a basis for awarding need-based institutional aid.
UNDERGRADUATE EXPENSES for 2006–07 *Application fee:* $40. *Tuition, state resident:* full-time $3825; part-time $128 per credit. *Tuition, nonresident:* full-time $12,195; part-time $407 per credit. *College room and board:* $5580; *room only:* $2990.

FRESHMAN FINANCIAL AID (Fall 2005, est.) 806 applied for aid; of those 39% were deemed to have need. 93% of freshmen with need received aid; of those 28% had need fully met. *Average percent of need met:* 66% (excluding resources awarded to replace EFC). *Average financial aid package:* $7830 (excluding resources awarded to replace EFC). 16% of all full-time freshmen had no need and received non-need-based gift aid.
UNDERGRADUATE FINANCIAL AID (Fall 2005, est.) 3,462 applied for aid; of those 42% were deemed to have need. 94% of undergraduates with need received aid; of those 28% had need fully met. *Average percent of need met:* 69% (excluding resources awarded to replace EFC). *Average financial aid package:* $8899 (excluding resources awarded to replace EFC). 16% of all full-time undergraduates had no need and received non-need-based gift aid.
GIFT AID (NEED-BASED) *Total amount:* $3,866,731 (84% federal, 12% institutional, 4% external sources). *Receiving aid:* Freshmen: 26% (207); All full-time undergraduates: 26% (909). *Average award:* Freshmen: $4074; Undergraduates: $4354. *Scholarships, grants, and awards:* Federal Pell, FSEOG, private, college/university gift aid from institutional funds, Native Non-Profit Corporations.
GIFT AID (NON-NEED-BASED) *Total amount:* $1,833,411 (1% federal, 84% institutional, 15% external sources). *Receiving aid:* Freshmen: 3% (25); Undergraduates: 4% (124). *Average Award:* Freshmen: $2947; Undergraduates:* $3362. *Scholarships, grants, and awards by category: Academic Interests/Achievement:* 524 awards ($1,354,375 total): general academic interests/achievements. *Creative Arts/Performance:* art/fine arts, creative writing, music, theater/drama. *Special Achievements/Activities:* 57 awards ($194,160 total): community service, general special achievements/activities. *Special Characteristics:* $749,084 total: children and siblings of alumni, children of faculty/staff. *ROTC:* Army.
LOANS *Student loans:* $15,321,567 (71% need-based, 29% non-need-based). 49% of past graduating class borrowed through all loan programs. *Average indebtedness per student:* $13,432. *Average need-based loan:* Freshmen: $5377; Undergraduates: $6256. *Parent loans:* $239,849 (24% need-based, 76% non-need-based). *Programs:* Federal Direct (Subsidized and Unsubsidized Stafford, PLUS), FFEL (Subsidized and Unsubsidized Stafford, PLUS), state, college/university.
WORK-STUDY *Federal work-study:* Total amount: $324,615; 118 jobs averaging $2100.
ATHLETIC AWARDS *Total amount:* $664,523 (12% need-based, 88% non-need-based).
APPLYING FOR FINANCIAL AID *Required financial aid form:* FAFSA. *Financial aid deadline (priority):* 7/1. *Notification date:* Continuous beginning 3/1. Students must reply within 2 weeks of notification.
CONTACT Tamara Hornbuckle, Financial Aid Officer, University of Alaska Fairbanks, 101 Eielson Building, PO Box 756360, Fairbanks, AK 99775-6360, 907-474-6628 or toll-free 800-478-1823. *Fax:* 907-474-7065. *E-mail:* fntmh@uaf.edu.

UNIVERSITY OF ALASKA SOUTHEAST
Juneau, AK

Tuition & fees (AK res): $3856	Average undergraduate aid package: $6967

ABOUT THE INSTITUTION State-supported, coed. Awards: associate, bachelor's, and master's degrees. 17 undergraduate majors. Total enrollment: 3,126. Undergraduates: 2,914. Freshmen: 190. Federal methodology is used as a basis for awarding need-based institutional aid.
UNDERGRADUATE EXPENSES for 2006–07 *Application fee:* $40. *Tuition, state resident:* full-time $3060; part-time $135 per credit hour. *Tuition, nonresident:* full-time $9756; part-time $414 per credit hour. *College room and board:* $6714; *room only:* $4177.
FRESHMAN FINANCIAL AID (Fall 2005, est.) 122 applied for aid; of those 53% were deemed to have need. 97% of freshmen with need received aid; of those 19% had need fully met. *Average percent of need met:* 53% (excluding resources awarded to replace EFC). *Average financial aid package:* $6134 (excluding resources awarded to replace EFC). 1% of all full-time freshmen had no need and received non-need-based gift aid.
UNDERGRADUATE FINANCIAL AID (Fall 2005, est.) 565 applied for aid; of those 63% were deemed to have need. 92% of undergraduates with need received aid; of those 19% had need fully met. *Average percent of need met:* 56% (excluding resources awarded to replace EFC). *Average financial aid package:* $6967 (excluding resources awarded to replace EFC). 4% of all full-time undergraduates had no need and received non-need-based gift aid.
GIFT AID (NEED-BASED) *Total amount:* $972,989 (74% federal, 10% institutional, 16% external sources). *Receiving aid:* Freshmen: 24% (38); All full-time undergraduates: 28% (206). *Average award:* Freshmen: $3352; Undergraduates: $3413. *Scholarships, grants, and awards:* Federal Pell, FSEOG, state, private, college/university gift aid from institutional funds.
GIFT AID (NON-NEED-BASED) *Total amount:* $296,935 (3% federal, 57% institutional, 40% external sources). *Receiving aid:* Freshmen: 1% (2); Undergraduates: 3% (19). *Average Award:* Freshmen: $2750; Undergraduates: $2608. *Scholarships, grants, and awards by category: Academic Interests/Achievement:* 508 awards ($598,055 total): biological sciences, business, communication, computer science, education, general academic interests/achievements, humanities, mathematics, social sciences. *Creative Arts/Performance:* 1 award ($500 total): performing arts. *Special Achievements/Activities:* 17 awards ($9200 total): general special achievements/activities, leadership. *Special Characteristics:* 45 awards ($251,300 total): ethnic background, first-generation college students.
LOANS *Student loans:* $3,673,327 (68% need-based, 32% non-need-based). 44% of past graduating class borrowed through all loan programs. *Average indebtedness per student:* $19,979. *Average need-based loan:* Freshmen: $4457; Undergraduates: $4778. *Parent loans:* $456,322 (29% need-based, 71% non-need-based). *Programs:* FFEL (Subsidized and Unsubsidized Stafford, PLUS), state.
WORK-STUDY *Federal work-study:* Total amount: $76,829; 36 jobs averaging $2134.
APPLYING FOR FINANCIAL AID *Required financial aid form:* FAFSA. *Financial aid deadline (priority):* 6/1. *Notification date:* Continuous beginning 2/15. Students must reply within 3 weeks of notification.
CONTACT Ms. Barbara Carlson Burnett, Financial Aid Director, University of Alaska Southeast, 11120 Glacier Highway, Juneau, AK 99801-8680, 907-796-6296 or toll-free 877-796-4827. *Fax:* 907-796-6250. *E-mail:* barbara.burnett@uas.alaska.edu.

THE UNIVERSITY OF ARIZONA
Tucson, AZ

ABOUT THE INSTITUTION State-supported, coed. Awards: bachelor's, master's, doctoral, and first professional degrees and post-bachelor's certificates. 128 undergraduate majors. Total enrollment: 37,036. Undergraduates: 28,462. Freshmen: 5,974.
GIFT AID (NEED-BASED) *Scholarships, grants, and awards:* Federal Pell, FSEOG, state, private, college/university gift aid from institutional funds, Federal Nursing.
GIFT AID (NON-NEED-BASED) *Scholarships, grants, and awards by category: Academic Interests/Achievement:* agriculture, architecture, biological sciences, business, education, engineering/technologies, general academic interests/achievements, humanities, military science, physical sciences, religion/biblical studies. *Creative Arts/Performance:* art/fine arts, dance, music, performing arts, theater/drama. *Special Achievements/Activities:* leadership. *Special Characteristics:* children of faculty/staff, ethnic background, international students.
LOANS *Programs:* FFEL (Subsidized and Unsubsidized Stafford, PLUS), Perkins, Federal Nursing, college/university.
APPLYING FOR FINANCIAL AID *Required financial aid form:* FAFSA.
CONTACT Student Financial Aid Office, The University of Arizona, PO Box 210066, Tucson, AZ 85721-0066, 520-621-1858. *Fax:* 520-621-9473. *E-mail:* askaid@arizona.edu.

UNIVERSITY OF ARKANSAS
Fayetteville, AR

Tuition & fees (AR res): $5494	Average undergraduate aid package: $8798

ABOUT THE INSTITUTION State-supported, coed. Awards: bachelor's, master's, doctoral, and first professional degrees and post-bachelor's and post-master's certificates. 75 undergraduate majors. Total enrollment: 17,821. Undergraduates: 14,281. Freshmen: 2,752. Federal methodology is used as a basis for awarding need-based institutional aid.
UNDERGRADUATE EXPENSES for 2005–06 *Application fee:* $40. *Tuition, state resident:* full-time $4361; part-time $145.38 per credit hour. *Tuition, nonresident:*

University of Arkansas

full-time $12,089; part-time $402.96 per credit hour. *College room and board:* $6365; *room only:* $3782. Room and board charges vary according to board plan and housing facility. *Payment plan:* Installment.
FRESHMAN FINANCIAL AID (Fall 2005, est.) 1467 applied for aid; of those 71% were deemed to have need. 99% of freshmen with need received aid; of those 28% had need fully met. *Average percent of need met:* 70% (excluding resources awarded to replace EFC). *Average financial aid package:* $9405 (excluding resources awarded to replace EFC). 19% of all full-time freshmen had no need and received non-need-based gift aid.
UNDERGRADUATE FINANCIAL AID (Fall 2005, est.) 5,957 applied for aid; of those 78% were deemed to have need. 97% of undergraduates with need received aid; of those 18% had need fully met. *Average percent of need met:* 64% (excluding resources awarded to replace EFC). *Average financial aid package:* $8798 (excluding resources awarded to replace EFC). 19% of all full-time undergraduates had no need and received non-need-based gift aid.
GIFT AID (NEED-BASED) *Total amount:* $12,634,184 (67% federal, 23% state, 10% institutional). *Receiving aid:* Freshmen: 22% (602); All full-time undergraduates: 24% (2,747). *Average award:* Freshmen: $3744; Undergraduates: $3630. *Scholarships, grants, and awards:* Federal Pell, FSEOG, state, private, college/university gift aid from institutional funds.
GIFT AID (NON-NEED-BASED) *Total amount:* $23,980,929 (18% state, 73% institutional, 9% external sources). *Receiving aid:* Freshmen: 24% (649); Undergraduates: 16% (1,800). *Average Award:* Freshmen: $6024; Undergraduates:* $5796. *Scholarships, grants, and awards by category:* Academic Interests/Achievement: general academic interests/achievements. Creative Arts/Performance: music, theater/drama. Special Achievements/Activities: community service, general special achievements/activities, leadership. Special Characteristics: children and siblings of alumni, children of faculty/staff, ethnic background, international students, out-of-state students, previous college experience. *Tuition waivers:* Full or partial for employees or children of employees, senior citizens.
ROTC: Army, Air Force.
LOANS *Student loans:* $33,049,297 (52% need-based, 48% non-need-based). 50% of past graduating class borrowed through all loan programs. *Average indebtedness per student:* $19,862. *Average need-based loan:* Freshmen: $2864; Undergraduates: $4276. *Parent loans:* $6,363,167 (100% non-need-based). *Programs:* FFEL (Subsidized and Unsubsidized Stafford, PLUS), Perkins, state, college/university, Alternative Loans.
WORK-STUDY *Federal work-study:* Total amount: $2,516,566; jobs available.
ATHLETIC AWARDS *Total amount:* $3,858,247 (100% non-need-based).
APPLYING FOR FINANCIAL AID *Required financial aid form:* FAFSA. *Financial aid deadline (priority):* 3/15. *Notification date:* Continuous beginning 4/1. Students must reply within 4 weeks of notification.
CONTACT Kattie Wing, Director of Financial Aid, University of Arkansas, 114 Silas H. Hunt Hall, Fayetteville, AR 72701-1201, 479-575-3806 or toll-free 800-377-5346 (in-state), 800-377-8632 (out-of-state). *E-mail:* kattie@uark.edu.

UNIVERSITY OF ARKANSAS AT FORT SMITH
Fort Smith, AR

ABOUT THE INSTITUTION State and locally supported, coed. Awards: associate and bachelor's degrees. 34 undergraduate majors. Total enrollment: 6,787. Undergraduates: 6,787. Freshmen: 1,278.
GIFT AID (NEED-BASED) *Scholarships, grants, and awards:* Federal Pell, FSEOG, state, private, college/university gift aid from institutional funds.
GIFT AID (NON-NEED-BASED) *Scholarships, grants, and awards by category:* Academic Interests/Achievement: biological sciences, business, computer science, education, engineering/technologies, English, health fields, mathematics, military science, social sciences. Creative Arts/Performance: music. Special Achievements/Activities: cheerleading/drum major, general special achievements/activities, leadership. Special Characteristics: adult students, children of faculty/staff, children of workers in trades, general special characteristics, local/state students.
LOANS *Programs:* FFEL (Subsidized and Unsubsidized Stafford, PLUS), state.
WORK-STUDY *Federal work-study:* Total amount: $633,531; 110 jobs averaging $3000. *State or other work-study/employment:* Total amount: $117,787 (61% need-based, 39% non-need-based). 94 part-time jobs averaging $3000.
APPLYING FOR FINANCIAL AID *Required financial aid forms:* FAFSA, institution's own form.

CONTACT Tammy Malone, Interim Financial Aid Director, University of Arkansas at Fort Smith, 5210 Grand Avenue, Fort Smith, AR 72913, 479-788-7099 or toll-free 888-512-5466. *Fax:* 479-788-7095. *E-mail:* tmalone@uafortsmith.edu.

UNIVERSITY OF ARKANSAS AT LITTLE ROCK
Little Rock, AR

CONTACT Financial Aid Office, University of Arkansas at Little Rock, 2801 South University Avenue, Little Rock, AR 72204-1099, 501-569-3127 or toll-free 800-482-8892 (in-state).

UNIVERSITY OF ARKANSAS AT MONTICELLO
Monticello, AR

Tuition & fees: N/R	Average undergraduate aid package: N/A

ABOUT THE INSTITUTION State-supported, coed. Awards: associate, bachelor's, and master's degrees and post-bachelor's certificates. 33 undergraduate majors. Total enrollment: 2,875. Undergraduates: 2,694. Freshmen: 751. Federal methodology is used as a basis for awarding need-based institutional aid.
GIFT AID (NEED-BASED) *Total amount:* $7,751,010 (70% federal, 14% state, 13% institutional, 3% external sources). *Scholarships, grants, and awards:* Federal Pell, FSEOG, state, private, college/university gift aid from institutional funds.
GIFT AID (NON-NEED-BASED) *Total amount:* $1,477,100 (11% state, 79% institutional, 10% external sources). *Scholarships, grants, and awards by category:* Academic Interests/Achievement: 296 awards ($944,736 total): general academic interests/achievements. Creative Arts/Performance: 187 awards ($391,692 total): debating, music. Special Achievements/Activities: 116 awards ($108,296 total): cheerleading/drum major, general special achievements/activities, leadership, rodeo. Special Characteristics: 259 awards ($773,929 total): children of faculty/staff, out-of-state students. *Tuition waivers:* Full or partial for employees or children of employees, senior citizens.
LOANS *Student loans:* $7,379,684 (69% need-based, 31% non-need-based). *Average indebtedness per student:* $13,599. *Parent loans:* $234,983 (100% non-need-based). *Programs:* FFEL (Subsidized and Unsubsidized Stafford, PLUS), Perkins.
WORK-STUDY *Federal work-study:* Total amount: $174,072; 205 jobs averaging $849. *State or other work-study/employment:* Total amount: $353,878 (100% non-need-based). 393 part-time jobs averaging $901.
ATHLETIC AWARDS *Total amount:* $580,999 (68% need-based, 32% non-need-based).
APPLYING FOR FINANCIAL AID *Required financial aid forms:* FAFSA, institution's own form. *Financial aid deadline:* Continuous. *Notification date:* Continuous beginning 3/1. Students must reply within 2 weeks of notification.
CONTACT Susan Brewer, Director of Financial Aid, University of Arkansas at Monticello, PO Box 3470, Monticello, AR 71656, 870-460-1050 or toll-free 800-844-1826 (in-state). *Fax:* 870-460-1450. *E-mail:* brewers@uamont.edu.

UNIVERSITY OF ARKANSAS AT PINE BLUFF
Pine Bluff, AR

Tuition & fees: N/R	Average undergraduate aid package: $8121

ABOUT THE INSTITUTION State-supported, coed. Awards: associate, bachelor's, and master's degrees. 52 undergraduate majors. Total enrollment: 3,303. Undergraduates: 3,200. Freshmen: 699. Federal methodology is used as a basis for awarding need-based institutional aid.
FRESHMAN FINANCIAL AID (Fall 2005, est.) 714 applied for aid; of those 100% were deemed to have need. 95% of freshmen with need received aid; of those 44% had need fully met. *Average percent of need met:* 65% (excluding resources awarded to replace EFC). *Average financial aid package:* $7569 (excluding resources awarded to replace EFC).
UNDERGRADUATE FINANCIAL AID (Fall 2005, est.) 2,825 applied for aid; of those 100% were deemed to have need. 96% of undergraduates with need

received aid; of those 44% had need fully met. *Average percent of need met:* 70% (excluding resources awarded to replace EFC). *Average financial aid package:* $8121 (excluding resources awarded to replace EFC).
GIFT AID (NEED-BASED) *Total amount:* $9,068,041 (77% federal, 2% state, 21% institutional). *Receiving aid:* Freshmen: 70% (500); All full-time undergraduates: 75% (2,132). *Average award:* Freshmen: $1000; Undergraduates: $1000. *Scholarships, grants, and awards:* Federal Pell, FSEOG, state.
GIFT AID (NON-NEED-BASED) *Total amount:* $1,165,854 (100% external sources). *Receiving aid:* Freshmen: 19% (136); Undergraduates: 74% (2,100). *Scholarships, grants, and awards by category: Academic Interests/Achievement:* agriculture, biological sciences, business, education, English, general academic interests/achievements, mathematics. *Creative Arts/Performance:* art/fine arts, music. *Special Achievements/Activities:* leadership. *Tuition waivers:* Full or partial for employees or children of employees, senior citizens. *ROTC:* Army.
LOANS *Student loans:* $13,283,672 (53% need-based, 47% non-need-based). *Average need-based loan:* Freshmen: $2625; Undergraduates: $4500. *Parent loans:* $586,034 (100% non-need-based). *Programs:* FFEL (Subsidized and Unsubsidized Stafford, PLUS), signature loans.
WORK-STUDY *Federal work-study:* Total amount: $328,969; 328 jobs averaging $1000. *State or other work-study/employment:* Total amount: $9720 (100% non-need-based).
ATHLETIC AWARDS Total amount: $1,132,311 (100% need-based).
APPLYING FOR FINANCIAL AID *Required financial aid forms:* FAFSA, institution's own form, verification worksheet. *Financial aid deadline (priority):* 4/1. *Notification date:* Continuous beginning 1/1. Students must reply within 2 weeks of notification.
CONTACT Mrs. Carolyn Iverson, Director of Financial Aid, University of Arkansas at Pine Bluff, 1200 North University Drive, PO Box 4985, Pine Bluff, AR 71601, 870-575-8303 or toll-free 800-264-6585. *Fax:* 870-575-4622. *E-mail:* iverson_c@uapb.edu.

UNIVERSITY OF ARKANSAS FOR MEDICAL SCIENCES
Little Rock, AR

Tuition & fees: N/R	Average undergraduate aid package: $3000

ABOUT THE INSTITUTION State-supported, coed. Awards: associate, bachelor's, master's, doctoral, and first professional degrees (bachelor's degree is upper-level). 10 undergraduate majors. Total enrollment: 2,016. Undergraduates: 683. Federal methodology is used as a basis for awarding need-based institutional aid.
GIFT AID (NEED-BASED) *Total amount:* $1,186,450 (65% federal, 26% state, 6% institutional, 3% external sources). *Average award:* Undergraduates: $500. *Scholarships, grants, and awards:* Federal Pell, FSEOG, state, private, college/university gift aid from institutional funds.
GIFT AID (NON-NEED-BASED) *ROTC:* Army cooperative.
LOANS *Student loans:* $2,877,259 (100% need-based). 73% of past graduating class borrowed through all loan programs. *Average indebtedness per student:* $7000. *Average need-based loan:* Undergraduates: $4000. *Parent loans:* $283,834 (100% non-need-based). *Programs:* FFEL (Subsidized and Unsubsidized Stafford, PLUS), Perkins, Federal Nursing.
APPLYING FOR FINANCIAL AID *Required financial aid form:* FAFSA. *Financial aid deadline:* Continuous. *Notification date:* Continuous beginning 4/1. Students must reply within 2 weeks of notification.
CONTACT Mr. Paul Carter, Director of Financial Aid, University of Arkansas for Medical Sciences, 4301 West Markham Street, MS 601, Little Rock, AR 72205, 501-686-5454. *Fax:* 501-686-5661. *E-mail:* pvcarter@uams.edu.

UNIVERSITY OF BALTIMORE
Baltimore, MD

Tuition & fees (MD res): $6793	Average undergraduate aid package: $8738

ABOUT THE INSTITUTION State-supported, coed. Awards: bachelor's, master's, doctoral, and first professional degrees and post-bachelor's and post-master's certificates. 30 undergraduate majors. Total enrollment: 4,987. Undergraduates: 2,117. Federal methodology is used as a basis for awarding need-based institutional aid.

University of California, Berkeley

UNDERGRADUATE EXPENSES for 2005–06 *Application fee:* $35. *Tuition, state resident:* full-time $5324; part-time $243 per credit. *Tuition, nonresident:* full-time $16,904; part-time $704 per credit. *Required fees:* full-time $1469; $27 per credit. Full-time tuition and fees vary according to class time, course load, and degree level. Part-time tuition and fees vary according to class time, course load, and degree level. *Payment plans:* Installment, deferred payment.
UNDERGRADUATE FINANCIAL AID (Fall 2005, est.) 827 applied for aid; of those 90% were deemed to have need. 91% of undergraduates with need received aid; of those 11% had need fully met. *Average percent of need met:* 31% (excluding resources awarded to replace EFC). *Average financial aid package:* $8738 (excluding resources awarded to replace EFC). 3% of all full-time undergraduates had no need and received non-need-based gift aid.
GIFT AID (NEED-BASED) *Total amount:* $2,438,525 (61% federal, 29% state, 10% institutional). *Receiving aid:* All full-time undergraduates: 40% (420). *Average award:* Undergraduates: $2392. *Scholarships, grants, and awards:* Federal Pell, FSEOG, state, private, college/university gift aid from institutional funds.
GIFT AID (NON-NEED-BASED) *Total amount:* $2,609,582 (5% state, 94% institutional, 1% external sources). *Receiving aid:* Undergraduates: 24% (255). *Average Award:* Undergraduates: $3143. *Scholarships, grants, and awards by category: Academic Interests/Achievement:* business, English, general academic interests/achievements. *Special Achievements/Activities:* community service, memberships. *Special Characteristics:* handicapped students. *Tuition waivers:* Full or partial for employees or children of employees, senior citizens. *ROTC:* Army cooperative, Air Force cooperative.
LOANS *Student loans:* $35,445,254 (46% need-based, 54% non-need-based). 6% of past graduating class borrowed through all loan programs. *Average indebtedness per student:* $18,050. *Average need-based loan:* Undergraduates: $4078. *Parent loans:* $38,600 (100% non-need-based). *Programs:* FFEL (Subsidized and Unsubsidized Stafford, PLUS), Perkins, college/university.
WORK-STUDY *Federal work-study:* Total amount: $385,606; 105 jobs averaging $3672. *State or other work-study/employment:* Total amount: $72,319 (100% non-need-based).
APPLYING FOR FINANCIAL AID *Required financial aid forms:* FAFSA, institution's own form. *Financial aid deadline (priority):* 3/1. *Notification date:* Continuous beginning 4/1. Students must reply within 4 weeks of notification.
CONTACT Financial Aid Office, University of Baltimore, 1420 North Charles Street, CH 123, Baltimore, MD 21201-5779, 410-837-4763 or toll-free 877-APPLYUB. *Fax:* 410-837-5493.

UNIVERSITY OF BRIDGEPORT
Bridgeport, CT

ABOUT THE INSTITUTION Independent, coed. Awards: associate, bachelor's, master's, doctoral, and first professional degrees and post-master's certificates. 32 undergraduate majors. Total enrollment: 3,626. Undergraduates: 1,676. Freshmen: 365.
GIFT AID (NEED-BASED) *Scholarships, grants, and awards:* Federal Pell, FSEOG, state, college/university gift aid from institutional funds.
GIFT AID (NON-NEED-BASED) *Scholarships, grants, and awards by category: Academic Interests/Achievement:* general academic interests/achievements. *Creative Arts/Performance:* music. *Special Achievements/Activities:* leadership. *Special Characteristics:* children of faculty/staff, local/state students, parents of current students, siblings of current students, spouses of current students.
LOANS *Programs:* FFEL (Subsidized and Unsubsidized Stafford, PLUS), Perkins.
WORK-STUDY *Federal work-study:* Total amount: $532,892; jobs available.
APPLYING FOR FINANCIAL AID *Required financial aid forms:* FAFSA, institution's own form.
CONTACT Kathleen A. Gailor, Director of Financial Aid, University of Bridgeport, 126 Park Avenue, Bridgeport, CT 06604, 203-576-4568 or toll-free 800-EXCEL-UB (in-state), 800-243-9496 (out-of-state). *Fax:* 203-576-4570. *E-mail:* finaid@bridgeport.edu.

UNIVERSITY OF CALIFORNIA, BERKELEY
Berkeley, CA

Tuition & fees (CA res): $6558	Average undergraduate aid package: $15,203

ABOUT THE INSTITUTION State-supported, coed. Awards: bachelor's, master's, doctoral, and first professional degrees. 93 undergraduate majors. Total enroll-

University of California, Berkeley

ment: 33,558. Undergraduates: 23,482. Freshmen: 4,101. Both federal and institutional methodology are used as a basis for awarding need-based institutional aid.

UNDERGRADUATE EXPENSES for 2006–07 *Application fee:* $60. *Tuition, state resident:* full-time $0. *Tuition, nonresident:* full-time $18,684. *College room and board:* $13,074.

FRESHMAN FINANCIAL AID (Fall 2005, est.) 3168 applied for aid; of those 63% were deemed to have need. 97% of freshmen with need received aid; of those 51% had need fully met. *Average percent of need met:* 90% (excluding resources awarded to replace EFC). *Average financial aid package:* $16,460 (excluding resources awarded to replace EFC). 9% of all full-time freshmen had no need and received non-need-based gift aid.

UNDERGRADUATE FINANCIAL AID (Fall 2005, est.) 13,862 applied for aid; of those 80% were deemed to have need. 98% of undergraduates with need received aid; of those 56% had need fully met. *Average percent of need met:* 89% (excluding resources awarded to replace EFC). *Average financial aid package:* $15,203 (excluding resources awarded to replace EFC). 7% of all full-time undergraduates had no need and received non-need-based gift aid.

GIFT AID (NEED-BASED) *Total amount:* $114,043,488 (21% federal, 29% state, 46% institutional, 4% external sources). *Receiving aid:* Freshmen: 44% (1,786); All full-time undergraduates: 45% (10,124). *Average award:* Freshmen: $12,021; Undergraduates: $10,937. *Scholarships, grants, and awards:* Federal Pell, FSEOG, state, private, college/university gift aid from institutional funds.

GIFT AID (NON-NEED-BASED) *Total amount:* $11,652,407 (7% federal, 17% state, 46% institutional, 30% external sources). *Receiving aid:* Freshmen: 1% (44); Undergraduates: 1% (136). *Average Award:* Freshmen: $2958; Undergraduates: $3402. *Scholarships, grants, and awards by category:* Academic Interests/Achievement: engineering/technologies, general academic interests/achievements. *ROTC:* Army, Naval, Air Force.

LOANS *Student loans:* $45,259,812 (77% need-based, 23% non-need-based). 47% of past graduating class borrowed through all loan programs. *Average indebtedness per student:* $13,171. *Average need-based loan:* Freshmen: $4254; Undergraduates: $5058. *Parent loans:* $29,796,185 (12% need-based, 88% non-need-based). *Programs:* Federal Direct (Subsidized and Unsubsidized Stafford, PLUS), Perkins.

WORK-STUDY *Federal work-study:* Total amount: $13,250,028; jobs available. *State or other work-study/employment:* Total amount: $3,447,108 (100% need-based). Part-time jobs available.

ATHLETIC AWARDS *Total amount:* $7,336,213 (23% need-based, 77% non-need-based).

APPLYING FOR FINANCIAL AID *Required financial aid forms:* FAFSA, state aid form. *Financial aid deadline:* 3/2 (priority: 3/2). *Notification date:* 4/15.

CONTACT Sandy Jensen, Administrative Services Coordinator, University of California, Berkeley, 225 Sproul Hall, Berkeley, CA 94720-1960, 510-642-0649. *Fax:* 510-643-5526.

UNIVERSITY OF CALIFORNIA, DAVIS
Davis, CA

Tuition & fees (CA res): $7593 **Average undergraduate aid package:** $11,697

ABOUT THE INSTITUTION State-supported, coed. Awards: bachelor's, master's, doctoral, and first professional degrees and post-bachelor's and post-master's certificates. 83 undergraduate majors. Total enrollment: 28,815. Undergraduates: 22,735. Freshmen: 4,381. Both federal and institutional methodology are used as a basis for awarding need-based institutional aid.

UNDERGRADUATE EXPENSES for 2006–07 *Application fee:* $60. *Tuition, state resident:* full-time $0. *Tuition, nonresident:* full-time $18,168. *College room and board:* $11,239.

FRESHMAN FINANCIAL AID (Fall 2005, est.) 2439 applied for aid; of those 69% were deemed to have need. 95% of freshmen with need received aid; of those 16% had need fully met. *Average percent of need met:* 73% (excluding resources awarded to replace EFC). *Average financial aid package:* $12,281 (excluding resources awarded to replace EFC). 13% of all full-time freshmen had no need and received non-need-based gift aid.

UNDERGRADUATE FINANCIAL AID (Fall 2005, est.) 12,601 applied for aid; of those 83% were deemed to have need. 96% of undergraduates with need received aid; of those 18% had need fully met. *Average percent of need met:* 75% (excluding resources awarded to replace EFC). *Average financial aid package:* $11,697 (excluding resources awarded to replace EFC). 6% of all full-time undergraduates had no need and received non-need-based gift aid.

GIFT AID (NEED-BASED) *Total amount:* $92,902,189 (23% federal, 38% state, 37% institutional, 2% external sources). *Receiving aid:* Freshmen: 48% (1,529); All full-time undergraduates: 44% (9,079). *Average award:* Freshmen: $9555; Undergraduates: $9072. *Scholarships, grants, and awards:* Federal Pell, FSEOG, state, private, college/university gift aid from institutional funds, Federal Nursing.

GIFT AID (NON-NEED-BASED) *Total amount:* $8,284,152 (3% federal, 11% state, 74% institutional, 12% external sources). *Receiving aid:* Freshmen: 1% (33); Undergraduates: 101. *Average Award:* Freshmen: $2557; Undergraduates: $4342. *Scholarships, grants, and awards by category:* Academic Interests/Achievement: agriculture, general academic interests/achievements. *ROTC:* Army, Naval cooperative, Air Force cooperative.

LOANS *Student loans:* $39,648,737 (85% need-based, 15% non-need-based). 50% of past graduating class borrowed through all loan programs. *Average indebtedness per student:* $12,701. *Average need-based loan:* Freshmen: $4425; Undergraduates: $4515. *Parent loans:* $15,348,858 (15% need-based, 85% non-need-based). *Programs:* Federal Direct (Subsidized and Unsubsidized Stafford, PLUS), Perkins, college/university.

WORK-STUDY *Federal work-study:* Total amount: $1,833,566; jobs available. *State or other work-study/employment:* Total amount: $275,003 (100% need-based).

APPLYING FOR FINANCIAL AID *Required financial aid forms:* FAFSA, state aid form. *Financial aid deadline (priority):* 3/2. *Notification date:* Continuous beginning 3/15.

CONTACT Lora Jo Bossio, Director of Financial Aid, University of California, Davis, One Shields Avenue, 1100 Dutton Hall, Davis, CA 95616, 530-752-2396. *Fax:* 530-752-7339.

UNIVERSITY OF CALIFORNIA, IRVINE
Irvine, CA

Tuition & fees (CA res): $6141 **Average undergraduate aid package:** $12,914

ABOUT THE INSTITUTION State-supported, coed. Awards: bachelor's, master's, doctoral, and first professional degrees and post-bachelor's certificates. 66 undergraduate majors. Total enrollment: 24,362. Undergraduates: 19,930. Freshmen: 4,338. Federal methodology is used as a basis for awarding need-based institutional aid.

UNDERGRADUATE EXPENSES for 2006–07 *Application fee:* $60. *Tuition, state resident:* full-time $0. *Tuition, nonresident:* full-time $17,820. *College room and board:* $9875.

FRESHMAN FINANCIAL AID (Fall 2005, est.) 3231 applied for aid; of those 66% were deemed to have need. 91% of freshmen with need received aid; of those 52% had need fully met. *Average percent of need met:* 85% (excluding resources awarded to replace EFC). *Average financial aid package:* $12,377 (excluding resources awarded to replace EFC). 4% of all full-time freshmen had no need and received non-need-based gift aid.

UNDERGRADUATE FINANCIAL AID (Fall 2005, est.) 12,071 applied for aid; of those 80% were deemed to have need. 95% of undergraduates with need received aid; of those 45% had need fully met. *Average percent of need met:* 85% (excluding resources awarded to replace EFC). *Average financial aid package:* $12,914 (excluding resources awarded to replace EFC). 4% of all full-time undergraduates had no need and received non-need-based gift aid.

GIFT AID (NEED-BASED) *Total amount:* $79,807,821 (20% federal, 38% state, 40% institutional, 2% external sources). *Receiving aid:* Freshmen: 37% (1,626); All full-time undergraduates: 41% (7,861). *Average award:* Freshmen: $4603; Undergraduates: $10,067. *Scholarships, grants, and awards:* Federal Pell, FSEOG, state, private, college/university gift aid from institutional funds.

GIFT AID (NON-NEED-BASED) *Total amount:* $8,345,568 (2% federal, 11% state, 78% institutional, 9% external sources). *Receiving aid:* Freshmen: 1% (31); Undergraduates: 92. *Average Award:* Freshmen: $8268; Undergraduates: $7381. *Scholarships, grants, and awards by category:* Academic Interests/Achievement: 639 awards ($4,640,685 total): computer science, general academic interests/achievements, humanities. Creative Arts/Performance: 67 awards ($111,123 total): art/fine arts, dance, general creative arts/performance, music. *ROTC:* Army cooperative, Air Force cooperative.

LOANS *Student loans:* $37,337,481 (77% need-based, 23% non-need-based). 55% of past graduating class borrowed through all loan programs. *Average indebtedness per student:* $13,587. *Average need-based loan:* Freshmen: $5465;

Undergraduates: $5633. **Parent loans:** $33,733,888 (21% need-based, 79% non-need-based). **Programs:** Federal Direct (Subsidized and Unsubsidized Stafford, PLUS), Perkins, college/university, Private loans.
WORK-STUDY Federal work-study: Total amount: $3,652,030; 2,843 jobs averaging $1737. **State or other work-study/employment:** Part-time jobs available.
ATHLETIC AWARDS Total amount: $2,258,649 (20% need-based, 80% non-need-based).
APPLYING FOR FINANCIAL AID Required financial aid forms: FAFSA, state aid form. **Financial aid deadline:** 5/1 (priority: 3/2). **Notification date:** Continuous beginning 4/1.
CONTACT Penny Harrell, Associate Director of Student Services, University of California, Irvine, Office of Financial Aid and Scholarships, 102 Administration Building, Irvine, CA 92697-2825, 949-824-8262. *Fax:* 949-824-4876. *E-mail:* finaid@uci.edu.

UNIVERSITY OF CALIFORNIA, LOS ANGELES
Los Angeles, CA

Tuition & fees (CA res): $6504   Average undergraduate aid package: $14,036

ABOUT THE INSTITUTION State-supported, coed. Awards: bachelor's, master's, doctoral, and first professional degrees. 150 undergraduate majors. Total enrollment: 37,221. Undergraduates: 24,811. Freshmen: 4,422. Both federal and institutional methodology are used as a basis for awarding need-based institutional aid.
UNDERGRADUATE EXPENSES for 2005–06 Application fee: $60. **Tuition, state resident:** full-time $0. **Tuition, nonresident:** full-time $17,457. **College room and board:** $11,928. Room and board charges vary according to board plan and housing facility.
FRESHMAN FINANCIAL AID (Fall 2005, est.) 2908 applied for aid; of those 81% were deemed to have need. 100% of freshmen with need received aid; of those 36% had need fully met. *Average percent of need met:* 83% (excluding resources awarded to replace EFC). *Average financial aid package:* $14,748 (excluding resources awarded to replace EFC). 5% of all full-time freshmen had no need and received non-need-based gift aid.
UNDERGRADUATE FINANCIAL AID (Fall 2005, est.) 14,143 applied for aid; of those 90% were deemed to have need. 100% of undergraduates with need received aid; of those 40% had need fully met. *Average percent of need met:* 83% (excluding resources awarded to replace EFC). *Average financial aid package:* $14,036 (excluding resources awarded to replace EFC). 4% of all full-time undergraduates had no need and received non-need-based gift aid.
GIFT AID (NEED-BASED) *Total amount:* $133,294,933 (19% federal, 34% state, 43% institutional, 4% external sources). *Receiving aid:* Freshmen: 52% (2,282); All full-time undergraduates: 51% (12,140). *Average award:* Freshmen: $11,802; Undergraduates: $10,888. *Scholarships, grants, and awards:* Federal Pell, FSEOG, state, private, college/university gift aid from institutional funds, United Negro College Fund, Federal Nursing, National Merit.
GIFT AID (NON-NEED-BASED) *Total amount:* $6,804,627 (5% federal, 19% state, 54% institutional, 22% external sources). *Receiving aid:* Freshmen: 1% (46); Undergraduates: 109. *Average Award:* Freshmen: $3837; Undergraduates: $3412. *Scholarships, grants, and awards by category:* Academic Interests/Achievement: general academic interests/achievements. *Special Achievements/Activities:* general special achievements/activities. *Special Characteristics:* general special characteristics. *ROTC:* Army, Naval, Air Force.
LOANS *Student loans:* $49,975,073 (83% need-based, 17% non-need-based). 52% of past graduating class borrowed through all loan programs. *Average indebtedness per student:* $14,431. *Average need-based loan:* Freshmen: $4744; Undergraduates: $4948. *Parent loans:* $19,998,251 (17% need-based, 83% non-need-based). *Programs:* FFEL (Subsidized and Unsubsidized Stafford, PLUS), Perkins, Federal Nursing, state, college/university.
WORK-STUDY Federal work-study: Total amount: $6,414,286; 3,043 jobs averaging $2108. **State or other work-study/employment:** Total amount: $715,722 (100% need-based). 656 part-time jobs averaging $1091.
ATHLETIC AWARDS Total amount: $6,722,038 (24% need-based, 76% non-need-based).
APPLYING FOR FINANCIAL AID Required financial aid form: FAFSA. **Financial aid deadline (priority):** 3/2. **Notification date:** Continuous beginning 3/15.

CONTACT Ms. Yolanda Tan, Administrative Assistant, University of California, Los Angeles, Financial Aid Office, A-129 Murphy Hall, 405 Hilgard Avenue, Los Angeles, CA 90095-1435, 310-206-0404. *E-mail:* finaid@saonet.ucla.edu.

UNIVERSITY OF CALIFORNIA, RIVERSIDE
Riverside, CA

Tuition & fees (CA res): $7250   Average undergraduate aid package: $13,538

ABOUT THE INSTITUTION State-supported, coed. Awards: bachelor's, master's, and doctoral degrees. 59 undergraduate majors. Total enrollment: 16,622. Undergraduates: 14,571. Freshmen: 2,988. Federal methodology is used as a basis for awarding need-based institutional aid.
UNDERGRADUATE EXPENSES for 2005–06 Application fee: $60. **Tuition, state resident:** full-time $0. **Tuition, nonresident:** full-time $17,820. **College room and board:** $10,200. Room and board charges vary according to board plan and housing facility. **Payment plan:** Deferred payment.
FRESHMAN FINANCIAL AID (Fall 2005, est.) 2411 applied for aid; of those 78% were deemed to have need. 97% of freshmen with need received aid; of those 56% had need fully met. *Average percent of need met:* 89% (excluding resources awarded to replace EFC). *Average financial aid package:* $14,746 (excluding resources awarded to replace EFC). 3% of all full-time freshmen had no need and received non-need-based gift aid.
UNDERGRADUATE FINANCIAL AID (Fall 2005, est.) 10,244 applied for aid; of those 86% were deemed to have need. 97% of undergraduates with need received aid; of those 44% had need fully met. *Average percent of need met:* 84% (excluding resources awarded to replace EFC). *Average financial aid package:* $13,538 (excluding resources awarded to replace EFC). 1% of all full-time undergraduates had no need and received non-need-based gift aid.
GIFT AID (NEED-BASED) *Total amount:* $74,459,004 (25% federal, 41% state, 33% institutional, 1% external sources). *Receiving aid:* Freshmen: 55% (1,616); All full-time undergraduates: 53% (7,520). *Average award:* Freshmen: $11,017; Undergraduates: $7852. *Scholarships, grants, and awards:* Federal Pell, FSEOG, state, private, college/university gift aid from institutional funds.
GIFT AID (NON-NEED-BASED) *Total amount:* $4,486,730 (4% federal, 5% state, 82% institutional, 9% external sources). *Receiving aid:* Freshmen: 1% (44); Undergraduates: 1% (103). *Average Award:* Freshmen: $5449; Undergraduates:* $5606. *Scholarships, grants, and awards by category:* Academic Interests/Achievement: agriculture, area/ethnic studies, biological sciences, business, education, engineering/technologies, English, general academic interests/achievements, humanities, mathematics, physical sciences, premedicine, social sciences. *Creative Arts/Performance:* art/fine arts, creative writing, dance, music, theater/drama. *ROTC:* Army cooperative, Air Force cooperative.
LOANS *Student loans:* $33,454,583 (85% need-based, 15% non-need-based). 65% of past graduating class borrowed through all loan programs. *Average indebtedness per student:* $14,814. *Average need-based loan:* Freshmen: $4596; Undergraduates: $5618. *Parent loans:* $19,065,831 (41% need-based, 59% non-need-based). *Programs:* Federal Direct (Subsidized and Unsubsidized Stafford, PLUS), Perkins, college/university.
WORK-STUDY Federal work-study: Total amount: $4,616,336; 1,701 jobs averaging $2766. **State or other work-study/employment:** Part-time jobs available.
ATHLETIC AWARDS Total amount: $1,806,781 (32% need-based, 68% non-need-based).
APPLYING FOR FINANCIAL AID Required financial aid forms: FAFSA, state aid form. **Financial aid deadline:** 3/2 (priority: 3/2). **Notification date:** Continuous beginning 3/1. Students must reply by 5/1 or within 3 weeks of notification.
CONTACT Ms. Sheryl Hayes, Director of Financial Aid, University of California, Riverside, 1156 Hinderaker Hall, Riverside, CA 92521-0209, 909-787-3878. *E-mail:* finaid@ucr.edu.

UNIVERSITY OF CALIFORNIA, SAN DIEGO
La Jolla, CA

Tuition & fees (CA res): $6681   Average undergraduate aid package: $13,342

ABOUT THE INSTITUTION State-supported, coed. Awards: bachelor's, master's, doctoral, and first professional degrees. 76 undergraduate majors. Total enrollment: 24,645. Undergraduates: 20,339. Freshmen: 3,874. Federal methodology is used as a basis for awarding need-based institutional aid.

University of California, San Diego

UNDERGRADUATE EXPENSES for 2005–06 *Application fee:* $60. *Tuition, state resident:* full-time $0. *Tuition, nonresident:* full-time $17,820. Full-time tuition and fees vary according to location. *College room and board:* $9421. Room and board charges vary according to board plan and location. *Payment plans:* Installment, deferred payment.
FRESHMAN FINANCIAL AID (Fall 2005, est.) 2737 applied for aid; of those 69% were deemed to have need. 94% of freshmen with need received aid; of those 28% had need fully met. *Average percent of need met:* 84% (excluding resources awarded to replace EFC). *Average financial aid package:* $13,479 (excluding resources awarded to replace EFC). 1% of all full-time freshmen had no need and received non-need-based gift aid.
UNDERGRADUATE FINANCIAL AID (Fall 2005, est.) 12,535 applied for aid; of those 83% were deemed to have need. 96% of undergraduates with need received aid; of those 28% had need fully met. *Average percent of need met:* 84% (excluding resources awarded to replace EFC). *Average financial aid package:* $13,342 (excluding resources awarded to replace EFC). 3% of all full-time undergraduates had no need and received non-need-based gift aid.
GIFT AID (NEED-BASED) *Total amount:* $92,421,560 (23% federal, 41% state, 33% institutional, 3% external sources). *Receiving aid:* Freshmen: 48% (1,657); All full-time undergraduates: 47% (9,244). *Average award:* Freshmen: $9633; Undergraduates: $9540. *Scholarships, grants, and awards:* Federal Pell, FSEOG, state, private, college/university gift aid from institutional funds.
GIFT AID (NON-NEED-BASED) *Total amount:* $7,344,610 (7% federal, 15% state, 60% institutional, 18% external sources). *Receiving aid:* Freshmen: 1% (38); Undergraduates: 97. *Average Award:* Freshmen: $7744; Undergraduates: $6824. *Scholarships, grants, and awards by category: Academic Interests/Achievement:* 708 awards ($1,937,941 total): biological sciences, business, communication, computer science, engineering/technologies, general academic interests/achievements, mathematics, physical sciences, premedicine, social sciences. *Creative Arts/Performance:* 14 awards ($15,400 total): applied art and design, cinema/film/broadcasting, dance, journalism/publications, performing arts. *Special Achievements/Activities:* 1 award ($1000 total): community service, leadership. *Special Characteristics:* 63 awards ($112,380 total): ethnic background, first-generation college students, handicapped students, members of minority groups, veterans' children. *ROTC:* Army cooperative.
LOANS *Student loans:* $44,654,958 (81% need-based, 19% non-need-based). 49% of past graduating class borrowed through all loan programs. *Average indebtedness per student:* $14,689. *Average need-based loan:* Freshmen: $4541; Undergraduates: $5109. *Parent loans:* $16,194,152 (21% need-based, 79% non-need-based). *Programs:* FFEL (Subsidized and Unsubsidized Stafford, PLUS), Perkins, college/university, alternative loans.
WORK-STUDY *Federal work-study:* Total amount: $6,643,455; 5,053 jobs averaging $1610.
APPLYING FOR FINANCIAL AID *Required financial aid forms:* FAFSA, state aid form. *Financial aid deadline (priority):* 3/2. *Notification date:* Continuous beginning 3/15.
CONTACT Mr. Vincent De Anda, Director of Financial Aid Office, University of California, San Diego, 9500 Gilman Drive-0013, La Jolla, CA 92093-0013, 858-534-3800. *Fax:* 858-534-5459. *E-mail:* vdeanda@ucsd.edu.

UNIVERSITY OF CALIFORNIA, SANTA BARBARA
Santa Barbara, CA

Tuition & fees (CA res): $6993 **Average undergraduate aid package:** $12,280

ABOUT THE INSTITUTION State-supported, coed. Awards: bachelor's, master's, and doctoral degrees and first professional certificates. 71 undergraduate majors. Total enrollment: 21,016. Undergraduates: 18,077. Freshmen: 3,821. Both federal and institutional methodology are used as a basis for awarding need-based institutional aid.
UNDERGRADUATE EXPENSES for 2005–06 *Application fee:* $40. *Tuition, state resident:* full-time $0. *Tuition, nonresident:* full-time $17,820. *College room and board:* $10,577; *room only:* $8110.
FRESHMAN FINANCIAL AID (Fall 2004) 2846 applied for aid; of those 70% were deemed to have need. 89% of freshmen with need received aid; of those 50% had need fully met. *Average percent of need met:* 83% (excluding resources awarded to replace EFC). *Average financial aid package:* $13,502 (excluding resources awarded to replace EFC). 2% of all full-time freshmen had no need and received non-need-based gift aid.
UNDERGRADUATE FINANCIAL AID (Fall 2004) 10,681 applied for aid; of those 80% were deemed to have need. 93% of undergraduates with need received aid; of those 38% had need fully met. *Average percent of need met:* 82% (excluding resources awarded to replace EFC). *Average financial aid package:* $12,280 (excluding resources awarded to replace EFC). 2% of all full-time undergraduates had no need and received non-need-based gift aid.
GIFT AID (NEED-BASED) *Total amount:* $61,746,601 (25% federal, 41% state, 32% institutional, 2% external sources). *Receiving aid:* Freshmen: 39% (1,528); All full-time undergraduates: 38% (6,635). *Average award:* Freshmen: $10,641; Undergraduates: $9210. *Scholarships, grants, and awards:* Federal Pell, FSEOG, state, college/university gift aid from institutional funds, endowed scholarships.
GIFT AID (NON-NEED-BASED) *Total amount:* $3,722,301 (4% federal, 25% state, 55% institutional, 16% external sources). *Receiving aid:* Freshmen: 1% (44); Undergraduates: 1% (105). *Average Award:* Freshmen: $5365; Undergraduates:* $5099. *Scholarships, grants, and awards by category: Academic Interests/Achievement:* general academic interests/achievements. *Tuition waivers:* Full or partial for employees or children of employees. *ROTC:* Army.
LOANS *Student loans:* $39,734,392 (81% need-based, 19% non-need-based). *Average need-based loan:* Freshmen: $5621; Undergraduates: $6092. *Parent loans:* $28,005,580 (26% need-based, 74% non-need-based). *Programs:* Federal Direct (Subsidized and Unsubsidized Stafford, PLUS), Perkins.
WORK-STUDY *Federal work-study:* Total amount: $2,009,331; jobs available.
ATHLETIC AWARDS *Total amount:* $2,169,804 (27% need-based, 73% non-need-based).
APPLYING FOR FINANCIAL AID *Required financial aid form:* FAFSA. *Financial aid deadline (priority):* 3/2. *Notification date:* Continuous beginning 3/15. Students must reply by 8/15.
CONTACT Office of Financial Aid, University of California, Santa Barbara, Santa Barbara, CA 93106, 805-893-2432. *Fax:* 805-893-8793.

UNIVERSITY OF CALIFORNIA, SANTA CRUZ
Santa Cruz, CA

Tuition & fees (CA res): $7603 **Average undergraduate aid package:** $14,285

ABOUT THE INSTITUTION State-supported, coed. Awards: bachelor's, master's, and doctoral degrees and post-bachelor's certificates. 76 undergraduate majors. Total enrollment: 15,012. Undergraduates: 13,625. Freshmen: 2,996. Both federal and institutional methodology are used as a basis for awarding need-based institutional aid.
UNDERGRADUATE EXPENSES for 2005–06 *Application fee:* $65. *Tuition, state resident:* full-time $0. *Tuition, nonresident:* full-time $17,820. *College room and board:* $11,571. Room and board charges vary according to board plan and housing facility. *Payment plans:* Installment, deferred payment.
FRESHMAN FINANCIAL AID (Fall 2005, est.) 2184 applied for aid; of those 66% were deemed to have need. 95% of freshmen with need received aid; of those 49% had need fully met. *Average percent of need met:* 89% (excluding resources awarded to replace EFC). *Average financial aid package:* $14,307 (excluding resources awarded to replace EFC). 2% of all full-time freshmen had no need and received non-need-based gift aid.
UNDERGRADUATE FINANCIAL AID (Fall 2005, est.) 8,125 applied for aid; of those 78% were deemed to have need. 95% of undergraduates with need received aid; of those 51% had need fully met. *Average percent of need met:* 89% (excluding resources awarded to replace EFC). *Average financial aid package:* $14,285 (excluding resources awarded to replace EFC). 2% of all full-time undergraduates had no need and received non-need-based gift aid.
GIFT AID (NEED-BASED) *Total amount:* $57,195,500 (18% federal, 31% state, 49% institutional, 2% external sources). *Receiving aid:* Freshmen: 41% (1,207); All full-time undergraduates: 41% (5,404). *Average award:* Freshmen: $10,307; Undergraduates: $10,340. *Scholarships, grants, and awards:* Federal Pell, FSEOG, state, private, college/university gift aid from institutional funds.
GIFT AID (NON-NEED-BASED) *Total amount:* $3,207,079 (2% federal, 14% state, 69% institutional, 15% external sources). *Receiving aid:* Freshmen: 9; Undergraduates: 57. *Average Award:* Freshmen: $8706; Undergraduates: $6851. *Scholarships, grants, and awards by category: Creative Arts/Performance:* music. *Tuition waivers:* Full or partial for employees or children of employees. *ROTC:* Army cooperative, Naval cooperative, Air Force cooperative.
LOANS *Student loans:* $29,001,759 (76% need-based, 24% non-need-based). 51% of past graduating class borrowed through all loan programs. *Average indebtedness per student:* $13,374. *Average need-based loan:* Freshmen: $4225;

Undergraduates: $4656. *Parent loans:* $16,744,367 (7% need-based, 93% non-need-based). *Programs:* Federal Direct (Subsidized and Unsubsidized Stafford, PLUS), Perkins.
WORK-STUDY *Federal work-study:* Total amount: $7,314,375. *State or other work-study/employment:* Total amount: $2600 (100% need-based).
APPLYING FOR FINANCIAL AID *Required financial aid forms:* FAFSA, state aid form. *Financial aid deadline:* 6/1 (priority: 3/17). *Notification date:* Continuous beginning 4/1. Students must reply within 4 weeks of notification.
CONTACT Ms. Ann Draper, Interim Director of Financial Aid, University of California, Santa Cruz, 201 Hahn Student Services Building, Santa Cruz, CA 95064, 831-459-4358. *Fax:* 831-459-4631. *E-mail:* ann@ucsc.edu.

UNIVERSITY OF CENTRAL ARKANSAS
Conway, AR

CONTACT Cheryl Lyons, Director of Student Aid, University of Central Arkansas, 201 Donaghey Avenue, Conway, AR 72035, 501-450-3140 or toll-free 800-243-8245 (in-state). *Fax:* 501-450-5168. *E-mail:* clyons@uca.edu.

UNIVERSITY OF CENTRAL FLORIDA
Orlando, FL

ABOUT THE INSTITUTION State-supported, coed. Awards: associate, bachelor's, master's, and doctoral degrees and post-bachelor's certificates. 81 undergraduate majors. Total enrollment: 44,953. Undergraduates: 37,796. Freshmen: 6,359.
GIFT AID (NEED-BASED) *Scholarships, grants, and awards:* Federal Pell, FSEOG, state, private, college/university gift aid from institutional funds.
GIFT AID (NON-NEED-BASED) *Scholarships, grants, and awards by category:* Academic Interests/Achievement: general academic interests/achievements. Creative Arts/Performance: music, theater/drama. Special Achievements/Activities: general special achievements/activities, leadership. Special Characteristics: members of minority groups.
LOANS *Programs:* FFEL (Subsidized and Unsubsidized Stafford, PLUS), Perkins.
APPLYING FOR FINANCIAL AID *Required financial aid form:* FAFSA.
CONTACT Mr. Thomas S. Silarek, Coordinator, Student Financial Assistance, University of Central Florida, 4000 Central Florida Boulevard, Orlando, FL 32816-0113, 407-823-2827. *Fax:* 407-823-5241. *E-mail:* tsilarek@mail.ucf.edu.

UNIVERSITY OF CENTRAL OKLAHOMA
Edmond, OK

Tuition & fees (OK res): $3618   Average undergraduate aid package: $5314

ABOUT THE INSTITUTION State-supported, coed. Awards: bachelor's and master's degrees. 86 undergraduate majors. Total enrollment: 15,953. Undergraduates: 14,629. Freshmen: 2,169. Federal methodology is used as a basis for awarding need-based institutional aid.
UNDERGRADUATE EXPENSES for 2005–06 *Application fee:* $25. *Tuition, state resident:* full-time $2811; part-time $93.70 per semester hour. *Tuition, nonresident:* full-time $7821; part-time $260.70 per semester hour. *Required fees:* full-time $807; $26.90 per semester hour. Full-time tuition and fees vary according to course load, degree level, program, and student level. Part-time tuition and fees vary according to course load, degree level, program, and student level. *College room and board:* $4476; *room only:* $2166. Room and board charges vary according to board plan and housing facility. *Payment plans:* Installment, deferred payment.
FRESHMAN FINANCIAL AID (Fall 2004) 1202 applied for aid; of those 75% were deemed to have need. 92% of freshmen with need received aid; of those 42% had need fully met. *Average percent of need met:* 29% (excluding resources awarded to replace EFC). *Average financial aid package:* $3762 (excluding resources awarded to replace EFC). 20% of all full-time freshmen had no need and received non-need-based gift aid.
UNDERGRADUATE FINANCIAL AID (Fall 2004) 5,903 applied for aid; of those 82% were deemed to have need. 92% of undergraduates with need received aid; of those 10% had need fully met. *Average percent of need met:* 46% (excluding resources awarded to replace EFC). *Average financial aid package:* $5314 (excluding resources awarded to replace EFC). 11% of all full-time undergraduates had no need and received non-need-based gift aid.

GIFT AID (NEED-BASED) *Total amount:* $14,629,779 (70% federal, 19% state, 2% institutional, 9% external sources). *Receiving aid:* Freshmen: 62% (791); All full-time undergraduates: 42% (4,172). *Average award:* Freshmen: $6506; Undergraduates: $6973. *Scholarships, grants, and awards:* Federal Pell, FSEOG, state, private, college/university gift aid from institutional funds.
GIFT AID (NON-NEED-BASED) *Total amount:* $2,357,903 (20% state, 23% institutional, 57% external sources). *Receiving aid:* Freshmen: 3% (33); Undergraduates: 3% (280). *Average Award:* Freshmen: $1604; Undergraduates: $1874. *Scholarships, grants, and awards by category:* Academic Interests/Achievement: biological sciences, business, computer science, education, foreign languages, general academic interests/achievements, health fields, home economics, mathematics, military science, physical sciences, social sciences. Creative Arts/Performance: applied art and design, art/fine arts, journalism/publications, music, theater/drama. Special Achievements/Activities: general special achievements/activities, leadership. Special Characteristics: ethnic background, members of minority groups. *Tuition waivers:* Full or partial for employees or children of employees. *ROTC:* Army.
LOANS *Student loans:* $34,444,506 (89% need-based, 11% non-need-based). 46% of past graduating class borrowed through all loan programs. *Average indebtedness per student:* $14,142. *Average need-based loan:* Freshmen: $5727; Undergraduates: $5314. *Parent loans:* $1,130,940 (63% need-based, 37% non-need-based). *Programs:* FFEL (Subsidized and Unsubsidized Stafford, PLUS), Perkins.
WORK-STUDY *Federal work-study:* Total amount: $520,002; jobs available.
ATHLETIC AWARDS Total amount: $619,906 (55% need-based, 45% non-need-based).
APPLYING FOR FINANCIAL AID *Required financial aid forms:* FAFSA, institution's own form. *Financial aid deadline:* Continuous. *Notification date:* Continuous beginning 5/1. Students must reply by 6/30 or within 4 weeks of notification.
CONTACT Ms. Becky Garrett, Assistant Director, Technical Services, University of Central Oklahoma, 100 North University Drive, Edmond, OK 73034-5209, 405-974-3334 or toll-free 800-254-4215. *Fax:* 405-340-7658. *E-mail:* bgarrett@ucok.edu.

UNIVERSITY OF CHARLESTON
Charleston, WV

ABOUT THE INSTITUTION Independent, coed. Awards: associate, bachelor's, and master's degrees. 27 undergraduate majors. Total enrollment: 1,006. Undergraduates: 987. Freshmen: 279.
GIFT AID (NEED-BASED) *Scholarships, grants, and awards:* Federal Pell, FSEOG, state, private, college/university gift aid from institutional funds, Council of Independent Colleges Tuition Exchange grants, Tuition Exchange Inc. grants.
GIFT AID (NON-NEED-BASED) *Scholarships, grants, and awards by category:* Academic Interests/Achievement: general academic interests/achievements, military science. Creative Arts/Performance: music. Special Achievements/Activities: cheerleading/drum major, community service, general special achievements/activities, leadership. Special Characteristics: children and siblings of alumni, children of educators, children of faculty/staff, international students, local/state students.
LOANS *Programs:* FFEL (Subsidized and Unsubsidized Stafford, PLUS), Perkins, Federal Nursing, alternative loans.
WORK-STUDY *Federal work-study:* Total amount: $142,000; jobs available (averaging $975). *State or other work-study/employment:* Part-time jobs available (averaging $850).
APPLYING FOR FINANCIAL AID *Required financial aid forms:* FAFSA, institution's own form.
CONTACT Ms. Janet M. Ruge, Director of Financial Aid, University of Charleston, 2300 MacCorkle Avenue SE, Charleston, WV 25304-1099, 304-357-4759 or toll-free 800-995-GOUC. *Fax:* 304-357-4769. *E-mail:* janetruge@ucwv.edu.

THE UNIVERSITY OF CHICAGO
Chicago, IL

CONTACT Office of College Aid, University of Chicago, 1116 East 59th Street, Room 203, Chicago, IL 60637, 773-702-8666. *Fax:* 773-702-5846.

University of Cincinnati

UNIVERSITY OF CINCINNATI
Cincinnati, OH

Tuition & fees (OH res): $8883 **Average undergraduate aid package: $7787**

ABOUT THE INSTITUTION State-supported, coed. Awards: associate, bachelor's, master's, doctoral, and first professional degrees and post-bachelor's certificates. 142 undergraduate majors. Total enrollment: 27,932. Undergraduates: 19,512. Freshmen: 3,914. Federal methodology is used as a basis for awarding need-based institutional aid.

UNDERGRADUATE EXPENSES for 2005–06 *Application fee:* $40. *Tuition, state resident:* full-time $7458; part-time $247 per credit hour. *Tuition, nonresident:* full-time $21,210; part-time $629 per credit hour. Full-time tuition and fees vary according to course load, degree level, location, program, and reciprocity agreements. Part-time tuition and fees vary according to course load, degree level, location, program, and reciprocity agreements. *College room and board:* $7890; *room only:* $4680. Room and board charges vary according to board plan and housing facility. *Payment plan:* Installment.

FRESHMAN FINANCIAL AID (Fall 2005, est.) 2921 applied for aid; of those 79% were deemed to have need. 98% of freshmen with need received aid; of those 6% had need fully met. *Average percent of need met:* 63% (excluding resources awarded to replace EFC). *Average financial aid package:* $7618 (excluding resources awarded to replace EFC). 16% of all full-time freshmen had no need and received non-need-based gift aid.

UNDERGRADUATE FINANCIAL AID (Fall 2005, est.) 10,602 applied for aid; of those 83% were deemed to have need. 96% of undergraduates with need received aid; of those 7% had need fully met. *Average percent of need met:* 59% (excluding resources awarded to replace EFC). *Average financial aid package:* $7787 (excluding resources awarded to replace EFC). 15% of all full-time undergraduates had no need and received non-need-based gift aid.

GIFT AID (NEED-BASED) *Total amount:* $30,459,437 (44% federal, 15% state, 35% institutional, 6% external sources). *Receiving aid:* Freshmen: 28% (1,084); All full-time undergraduates: 26% (4,078). *Average award:* Freshmen: $5393; Undergraduates: $10,602. *Scholarships, grants, and awards:* Federal Pell, FSEOG, state, private, college/university gift aid from institutional funds, Federal Nursing.

GIFT AID (NON-NEED-BASED) *Total amount:* $13,389,946 (4% state, 81% institutional, 15% external sources). *Receiving aid:* Freshmen: 25% (963); Undergraduates: 17% (2,707). *Average Award:* Freshmen: $4734; Undergraduates: $4696. *Scholarships, grants, and awards by category: Academic Interests/Achievement:* architecture, area/ethnic studies, biological sciences, business, communication, computer science, education, engineering/technologies, English, foreign languages, general academic interests/achievements, health fields, humanities, mathematics, military science, physical sciences, premedicine, social sciences. *Creative Arts/Performance:* applied art and design, art/fine arts, music. *Special Achievements/Activities:* general special achievements/activities. *Special Characteristics:* children of faculty/staff, members of minority groups, out-of-state students. *Tuition waivers:* Full or partial for employees or children of employees. *ROTC:* Army, Air Force.

LOANS *Student loans:* $71,301,643 (50% need-based, 50% non-need-based). 66% of past graduating class borrowed through all loan programs. *Average indebtedness per student:* $16,794. *Average need-based loan:* Freshmen: $3408; Undergraduates: $3783. *Parent loans:* $57,346,290 (9% need-based, 91% non-need-based). *Programs:* Federal Direct (Subsidized and Unsubsidized Stafford, PLUS), FFEL (Subsidized and Unsubsidized Stafford, PLUS), Perkins, Federal Nursing, state, college/university.

WORK-STUDY *Federal work-study:* Total amount: $3,714,943; jobs available.

ATHLETIC AWARDS Total amount: $5,369,617 (35% need-based, 65% non-need-based).

APPLYING FOR FINANCIAL AID *Required financial aid form:* FAFSA. *Financial aid deadline:* Continuous. *Notification date:* Continuous beginning 3/10. Students must reply within 2 weeks of notification.

CONTACT Mrs. Martha Geiger, Student Financial Aid Associate Director, University of Cincinnati, 2624 Clifton Avenue, Cincinnati, OH 45221, 513-556-2441. *Fax:* 513-556-9171. *E-mail:* martha.geiger@uc.edu.

UNIVERSITY OF COLORADO AT BOULDER
Boulder, CO

Tuition & fees (CO res): $5372 **Average undergraduate aid package: $9973**

ABOUT THE INSTITUTION State-supported, coed. Awards: bachelor's, master's, doctoral, and first professional degrees. 60 undergraduate majors. Total enrollment: 31,068. Undergraduates: 25,842. Freshmen: 5,051. Federal methodology is used as a basis for awarding need-based institutional aid.

UNDERGRADUATE EXPENSES for 2005–06 *Application fee:* $50. *One-time required fee:* $108. *Tuition, state resident:* full-time $4446. *Tuition, nonresident:* full-time $21,900. Full-time tuition and fees vary according to program. Part-time tuition and fees vary according to course load and program. *College room and board:* $7980. Room and board charges vary according to board plan, location, and student level. *Payment plan:* Deferred payment.

FRESHMAN FINANCIAL AID (Fall 2005, est.) 4187 applied for aid; of those 48% were deemed to have need. 98% of freshmen with need received aid; of those 74% had need fully met. *Average percent of need met:* 91% (excluding resources awarded to replace EFC). *Average financial aid package:* $7964 (excluding resources awarded to replace EFC). 40% of all full-time freshmen had no need and received non-need-based gift aid.

UNDERGRADUATE FINANCIAL AID (Fall 2005, est.) 18,452 applied for aid; of those 43% were deemed to have need. 97% of undergraduates with need received aid; of those 67% had need fully met. *Average percent of need met:* 90% (excluding resources awarded to replace EFC). *Average financial aid package:* $9973 (excluding resources awarded to replace EFC). 37% of all full-time undergraduates had no need and received non-need-based gift aid.

GIFT AID (NEED-BASED) *Total amount:* $34,388,760 (33% federal, 13% state, 46% institutional, 8% external sources). *Receiving aid:* Freshmen: 36% (1,790); All full-time undergraduates: 30% (6,989). *Average award:* Freshmen: $3923; Undergraduates: $4411. *Scholarships, grants, and awards:* Federal Pell, FSEOG, state, private, college/university gift aid from institutional funds.

GIFT AID (NON-NEED-BASED) *Total amount:* $11,195,639 (21% federal, 1% state, 66% institutional, 12% external sources). *Receiving aid:* Freshmen: 1% (69); Undergraduates: 1% (279). *Average Award:* Freshmen: $2486; Undergraduates: $2667. *Scholarships, grants, and awards by category: Academic Interests/Achievement:* architecture, area/ethnic studies, biological sciences, business, communication, computer science, education, engineering/technologies, English, foreign languages, general academic interests/achievements, health fields, humanities, international studies, mathematics, military science, physical sciences, premedicine, social sciences. *Creative Arts/Performance:* art/fine arts, cinema/film/broadcasting, creative writing, dance, journalism/publications, music, performing arts, theater/drama. *Special Achievements/Activities:* community service, general special achievements/activities, leadership. *Special Characteristics:* first-generation college students, general special characteristics, local/state students. *Tuition waivers:* Full or partial for senior citizens. *ROTC:* Army, Naval, Air Force.

LOANS *Student loans:* $56,180,465 (66% need-based, 34% non-need-based). 44% of past graduating class borrowed through all loan programs. *Average indebtedness per student:* $17,225. *Average need-based loan:* Freshmen: $3660; Undergraduates: $5039. *Parent loans:* $90,636,018 (41% need-based, 59% non-need-based). *Programs:* Federal Direct (Subsidized and Unsubsidized Stafford, PLUS), Perkins, college/university, private lenders.

WORK-STUDY *Federal work-study:* Total amount: $1,721,814; 1,253 jobs averaging $1838. *State or other work-study/employment:* Total amount: $2,489,537 (98% need-based, 2% non-need-based). 960 part-time jobs averaging $2045.

ATHLETIC AWARDS Total amount: $4,486,946 (32% need-based, 68% non-need-based).

APPLYING FOR FINANCIAL AID *Required financial aid forms:* FAFSA, income tax form(s). *Financial aid deadline (priority):* 4/1. *Notification date:* Continuous beginning 2/1. Students must reply within 3 weeks of notification.

CONTACT Gwen Eberhard, Director of Financial Aid, University of Colorado at Boulder, University Campus Box 77, Boulder, CO 80309, 303-492-8223. *Fax:* 303-492-0838. *E-mail:* finaid@colorado.edu.

UNIVERSITY OF COLORADO AT COLORADO SPRINGS
Colorado Springs, CO

Tuition & fees (CO res): $4888   **Average undergraduate aid package:** $6456

ABOUT THE INSTITUTION State-supported, coed. Awards: bachelor's, master's, and doctoral degrees and post-bachelor's certificates. 34 undergraduate majors. Total enrollment: 8,437. Undergraduates: 6,271. Freshmen: 939. Federal methodology is used as a basis for awarding need-based institutional aid.

UNDERGRADUATE EXPENSES for 2005–06 *Application fee:* $50. *Tuition, state resident:* full-time $3966; part-time $178 per credit hour. *Tuition, nonresident:* full-time $15,260; part-time $763 per credit hour. *College room and board:* $6418; *room only:* $4878.

FRESHMAN FINANCIAL AID (Fall 2005, est.) 630 applied for aid; of those 53% were deemed to have need. 92% of freshmen with need received aid; of those 12% had need fully met. *Average percent of need met:* 52% (excluding resources awarded to replace EFC). *Average financial aid package:* $5756 (excluding resources awarded to replace EFC). 18% of all full-time freshmen had no need and received non-need-based gift aid.

UNDERGRADUATE FINANCIAL AID (Fall 2005, est.) 3,803 applied for aid; of those 68% were deemed to have need. 94% of undergraduates with need received aid; of those 12% had need fully met. *Average percent of need met:* 53% (excluding resources awarded to replace EFC). *Average financial aid package:* $6456 (excluding resources awarded to replace EFC). 7% of all full-time undergraduates had no need and received non-need-based gift aid.

GIFT AID (NEED-BASED) *Total amount:* $10,027,310 (40% federal, 18% state, 31% institutional, 11% external sources). *Receiving aid:* Freshmen: 35% (242); All full-time undergraduates: 34% (1,638). *Average award:* Freshmen: $4813; Undergraduates: $4965. *Scholarships, grants, and awards:* Federal Pell, FSEOG, state, private, college/university gift aid from institutional funds.

GIFT AID (NON-NEED-BASED) *Average Award:* Freshmen: $1240; Undergraduates: $1698. *Scholarships, grants, and awards by category:* Academic Interests/Achievement: biological sciences, business, computer science, education, engineering/technologies, English, general academic interests/achievements, health fields, mathematics, military science, physical sciences, premedicine. *Special Achievements/Activities:* community service, leadership. *Special Characteristics:* children and siblings of alumni, ethnic background, first-generation college students, general special characteristics, handicapped students, out-of-state students. *ROTC:* Army.

LOANS *Student loans:* $14,503,223 (100% need-based). 48% of past graduating class borrowed through all loan programs. *Average indebtedness per student:* $12,438. *Average need-based loan:* Freshmen: $2459; Undergraduates: $3591. *Parent loans:* $3,366,169 (100% need-based). *Programs:* FFEL (Subsidized and Unsubsidized Stafford, PLUS), Perkins, college/university.

WORK-STUDY *Federal work-study:* Total amount: $257,554; 72 jobs averaging $3577. *State or other work-study/employment:* Total amount: $787,747 (84% need-based, 16% non-need-based). 220 part-time jobs averaging $3580.

ATHLETIC AWARDS *Total amount:* $145,069 (100% need-based).

APPLYING FOR FINANCIAL AID *Required financial aid form:* FAFSA. *Financial aid deadline (priority):* 4/1. *Notification date:* Continuous beginning 4/15. Students must reply within 3 weeks of notification.

CONTACT Ms. Lee Ingalls-Noble, Director of Financial Aid, University of Colorado at Colorado Springs, 1420 Austin Bluffs Parkway, Colorado Springs, CO 80933-7150, 719-262-3466 or toll-free 800-990-8227 Ext. 3383.

UNIVERSITY OF COLORADO AT DENVER AND HEALTH SCIENCES CENTER— DOWNTOWN DENVER CAMPUS
Denver, CO

Tuition & fees (CO res): $5021   **Average undergraduate aid package:** $7837

ABOUT THE INSTITUTION State-supported, coed. Awards: bachelor's, master's, doctoral, and first professional degrees and post-master's certificates. 30 undergraduate majors. Total enrollment: 19,755. Undergraduates: 10,242. Freshmen: 808. Federal methodology is used as a basis for awarding need-based institutional aid.

UNDERGRADUATE EXPENSES for 2006–07 *Application fee:* $50. *Tuition, state resident:* full-time $4224; part-time $210 per semester hour. *Tuition, nonresident:* full-time $15,394; part-time $924 per semester hour. *Required fees:* full-time $797; $14 per semester hour or $377.

FRESHMAN FINANCIAL AID (Fall 2004) 451 applied for aid; of those 71% were deemed to have need. 89% of freshmen with need received aid; of those 9% had need fully met. *Average percent of need met:* 61% (excluding resources awarded to replace EFC). *Average financial aid package:* $5362 (excluding resources awarded to replace EFC). 3% of all full-time freshmen had no need and received non-need-based gift aid.

UNDERGRADUATE FINANCIAL AID (Fall 2004) 3,289 applied for aid; of those 82% were deemed to have need. 93% of undergraduates with need received aid; of those 8% had need fully met. *Average percent of need met:* 71% (excluding resources awarded to replace EFC). *Average financial aid package:* $7837 (excluding resources awarded to replace EFC). 2% of all full-time undergraduates had no need and received non-need-based gift aid.

GIFT AID (NEED-BASED) *Total amount:* $8,556,800 (58% federal, 19% state, 16% institutional, 7% external sources). *Receiving aid:* Freshmen: 33% (230); All full-time undergraduates: 31% (1,695). *Average award:* Freshmen: $4295; Undergraduates: $4421. *Scholarships, grants, and awards:* Federal Pell, FSEOG, state, private, college/university gift aid from institutional funds.

GIFT AID (NON-NEED-BASED) *Total amount:* $713,188 (4% federal, 28% state, 30% institutional, 38% external sources). *Receiving aid:* Freshmen: 1% (10); Undergraduates: 1% (38). *Average Award:* Freshmen: $1733; Undergraduates: $1367. *Scholarships, grants, and awards by category:* Academic Interests/Achievement: 696 awards ($869,864 total): business, engineering/technologies, general academic interests/achievements. *Creative Arts/Performance:* 7 awards ($5100 total): general creative arts/performance. *Special Achievements/Activities:* 51 awards ($101,500 total): leadership. *Special Characteristics:* 317 awards ($509,671 total): children of faculty/staff, first-generation college students, general special characteristics, handicapped students, members of minority groups. *ROTC:* Army, Air Force cooperative.

LOANS *Student loans:* $19,329,318 (74% need-based, 26% non-need-based). 41% of past graduating class borrowed through all loan programs. *Average indebtedness per student:* $16,933. *Average need-based loan:* Freshmen: $2264; Undergraduates: $4013. *Parent loans:* $758,620 (50% need-based, 50% non-need-based). *Programs:* FFEL (Subsidized and Unsubsidized Stafford, PLUS), Perkins, Federal Nursing, alternative loans.

WORK-STUDY *Federal work-study:* Total amount: $596,222; 165 jobs averaging $3613. *State or other work-study/employment:* Total amount: $679,630 (90% need-based, 10% non-need-based). 176 part-time jobs averaging $3862.

APPLYING FOR FINANCIAL AID *Required financial aid forms:* FAFSA, institution's own form. *Financial aid deadline (priority):* 4/1. *Notification date:* Continuous beginning 5/1.

CONTACT Patrick McTee, Director of Financial Aid, University of Colorado at Denver and Health Sciences Center—Downtown Denver Campus, PO Box 173364, Denver, CO 80217-3364, 303-556-2886. *Fax:* 303-556-2325. *E-mail:* patrick.mctee@cudenver.edu.

UNIVERSITY OF CONNECTICUT
Storrs, CT

Tuition & fees (CT res): $8362   **Average undergraduate aid package:** $9070

ABOUT THE INSTITUTION State-supported, coed. Awards: associate, bachelor's, master's, doctoral, and first professional degrees and post-bachelor's and post-master's certificates. 96 undergraduate majors. Total enrollment: 23,185. Undergraduates: 16,112. Freshmen: 3,260. Federal methodology is used as a basis for awarding need-based institutional aid.

UNDERGRADUATE EXPENSES for 2006–07 *Application fee:* $70. *Tuition, state resident:* full-time $6456; part-time $269 per credit. *Tuition, nonresident:* full-time $19,656; part-time $819 per credit. *Required fees:* full-time $1906; $635 per term part-time. *College room and board:* $8266; *room only:* $4350.

FRESHMAN FINANCIAL AID (Fall 2005, est.) 2628 applied for aid; of those 62% were deemed to have need. 96% of freshmen with need received aid; of those 15% had need fully met. *Average percent of need met:* 70% (excluding resources awarded to replace EFC). *Average financial aid package:* $9035 (excluding resources awarded to replace EFC). 8% of all full-time freshmen had no need and received non-need-based gift aid.

University of Connecticut

UNDERGRADUATE FINANCIAL AID (Fall 2005, est.) 10,371 applied for aid; of those 72% were deemed to have need. 96% of undergraduates with need received aid; of those 18% had need fully met. *Average percent of need met:* 69% (excluding resources awarded to replace EFC). *Average financial aid package:* $9070 (excluding resources awarded to replace EFC). 7% of all full-time undergraduates had no need and received non-need-based gift aid.
GIFT AID (NEED-BASED) *Total amount:* $36,792,785 (20% federal, 21% state, 53% institutional, 6% external sources). *Receiving aid:* Freshmen: 38% (1,231); All full-time undergraduates: 36% (5,489). *Average award:* Freshmen: $6393; Undergraduates: $5958. *Scholarships, grants, and awards:* Federal Pell, FSEOG, state, private, college/university gift aid from institutional funds.
GIFT AID (NON-NEED-BASED) *Total amount:* $8,321,064 (78% institutional, 22% external sources). *Receiving aid:* Freshmen: 30% (967); Undergraduates: 20% (2,987). *Average Award:* Freshmen: $5118; Undergraduates: $4787. *Scholarships, grants, and awards by category:* Academic Interests/Achievement: 2,272 awards ($12,068,051 total): agriculture, biological sciences, business, computer science, education, engineering/technologies, English, foreign languages, general academic interests/achievements, health fields, humanities, international studies, mathematics, physical sciences, premedicine, religion/biblical studies, social sciences. *Creative Arts/Performance:* 96 awards ($185,000 total): art/fine arts, music, theater/drama. *Special Achievements/Activities:* 435 awards ($3,223,374 total): community service, leadership. *Special Characteristics:* 329 awards ($1,792,298 total): adult students, children of faculty/staff, veterans. *ROTC:* Army, Air Force.
LOANS *Student loans:* $51,147,791 (81% need-based, 19% non-need-based). 60% of past graduating class borrowed through all loan programs. *Average indebtedness per student:* $19,410. *Average need-based loan:* Freshmen: $3212; Undergraduates: $5122. *Parent loans:* $17,446,558 (40% need-based, 60% non-need-based). *Programs:* FFEL (Subsidized and Unsubsidized Stafford, PLUS), Perkins, state.
WORK-STUDY *Federal work-study:* Total amount: $2,563,052; 1,528 jobs averaging $1677. *State or other work-study/employment:* Total amount: $10,400,000 (100% non-need-based). 5,502 part-time jobs averaging $1890.
ATHLETIC AWARDS *Total amount:* $6,814,817 (8% need-based, 92% non-need-based).
APPLYING FOR FINANCIAL AID *Required financial aid form:* FAFSA. *Financial aid deadline (priority):* 3/1. *Notification date:* Continuous. Students must reply within 4 weeks of notification.
CONTACT Client Service Staff, University of Connecticut, 233 Glenbrook Road, Unit 4116, Storrs, CT 06269-4116, 860-486-2819.

UNIVERSITY OF DALLAS
Irving, TX

Tuition & fees: $21,805	Average undergraduate aid package: $14,101

ABOUT THE INSTITUTION Independent Roman Catholic, coed. Awards: bachelor's, master's, and doctoral degrees and post-bachelor's and post-master's certificates. 32 undergraduate majors. Total enrollment: 3,021. Undergraduates: 1,166. Freshmen: 256. Federal methodology is used as a basis for awarding need-based institutional aid.
UNDERGRADUATE EXPENSES for 2006–07 *Application fee:* $40. *Comprehensive fee:* $29,137 includes full-time tuition ($20,780), mandatory fees ($1025), and room and board ($7332). *College room only:* $4116. *Part-time tuition:* $900 per credit hour. *Part-time fees:* $1025 per year.
GIFT AID (NEED-BASED) *Total amount:* $7,206,124 (12% federal, 14% state, 72% institutional, 2% external sources). *Receiving aid:* Freshmen: 66% (160); All full-time undergraduates: 63% (667). *Average award:* Freshmen: $11,388; Undergraduates: $10,648. *Scholarships, grants, and awards:* Federal Pell, FSEOG, state, private, college/university gift aid from institutional funds.
GIFT AID (NON-NEED-BASED) *Total amount:* $3,405,353 (1% federal, 94% institutional, 5% external sources). *Receiving aid:* Freshmen: 12% (30); Undergraduates: 11% (116). *Average Award:* Freshmen: $7971; Undergraduates: $9435. *Scholarships, grants, and awards by category:* Academic Interests/Achievement: 1,288 awards ($7,269,483 total): biological sciences, business, computer science, education, foreign languages, general academic interests/achievements, mathematics, physical sciences, religion/biblical studies. *Creative Arts/Performance:* 61 awards ($94,878 total): art/fine arts, performing arts. *Special Achievements/Activities:* 240 awards ($360,000 total): leadership, religious involvement. *Special Characteristics:* 153 awards ($492,968 total): children of faculty/staff, members of minority groups, siblings of current students. *ROTC:* Army cooperative, Air Force cooperative.
LOANS *Student loans:* $4,541,160 (71% need-based, 29% non-need-based). 70% of past graduating class borrowed through all loan programs. *Average indebtedness per student:* $21,700. *Average need-based loan:* Freshmen: $2638; Undergraduates: $3830. *Parent loans:* $1,530,704 (28% need-based, 72% non-need-based). *Programs:* FFEL (Subsidized and Unsubsidized Stafford, PLUS), Perkins, state.
APPLYING FOR FINANCIAL AID *Required financial aid forms:* FAFSA, institution's own form. *Financial aid deadline (priority):* 3/1. *Notification date:* Continuous. Students must reply by 5/1 or within 2 weeks of notification.
CONTACT Curt Eley, Dean of Enrollment Management, University of Dallas, 1845 East Northgate Drive, Irving, TX 75062, 972-721-5266 or toll-free 800-628-6999. *Fax:* 972-721-5017. *E-mail:* ugadmis@udallas.edu.

UNIVERSITY OF DAYTON
Dayton, OH

Tuition & fees: $22,846	Average undergraduate aid package: $13,532

ABOUT THE INSTITUTION Independent Roman Catholic, coed. Awards: bachelor's, master's, doctoral, and first professional degrees and post-master's certificates. 74 undergraduate majors. Total enrollment: 10,572. Undergraduates: 7,426. Freshmen: 1,966. Both federal and institutional methodology are used as a basis for awarding need-based institutional aid.
UNDERGRADUATE EXPENSES for 2005–06 *Comprehensive fee:* $29,626 includes full-time tuition ($22,046), mandatory fees ($800), and room and board ($6780). *College room only:* $4000. Full-time tuition and fees vary according to program. Room and board charges vary according to board plan, housing facility, and student level. *Part-time tuition:* $708 per credit hour. *Part-time fees:* $25 per term. Part-time tuition and fees vary according to course load and program. *Payment plan:* Deferred payment.
FRESHMAN FINANCIAL AID (Fall 2004) 1442 applied for aid; of those 76% were deemed to have need. 100% of freshmen with need received aid; of those 50% had need fully met. *Average percent of need met:* 94% (excluding resources awarded to replace EFC). *Average financial aid package:* $13,473 (excluding resources awarded to replace EFC). 36% of all full-time freshmen had no need and received non-need-based gift aid.
UNDERGRADUATE FINANCIAL AID (Fall 2004) 5,038 applied for aid; of those 82% were deemed to have need. 97% of undergraduates with need received aid; of those 59% had need fully met. *Average percent of need met:* 88% (excluding resources awarded to replace EFC). *Average financial aid package:* $13,532 (excluding resources awarded to replace EFC). 33% of all full-time undergraduates had no need and received non-need-based gift aid.
GIFT AID (NEED-BASED) *Total amount:* $35,629,277 (10% federal, 11% state, 75% institutional, 4% external sources). *Receiving aid:* Freshmen: 59% (1,070); All full-time undergraduates: 58% (3,853). *Average award:* Freshmen: $9185; Undergraduates: $8603. *Scholarships, grants, and awards:* Federal Pell, FSEOG, state, private, college/university gift aid from institutional funds.
GIFT AID (NON-NEED-BASED) *Total amount:* $14,543,301 (6% federal, 11% state, 77% institutional, 6% external sources). *Receiving aid:* Freshmen: 59% (1,069); Undergraduates: 57% (3,820). *Average Award:* Freshmen: $5320; Undergraduates: $5159. *Scholarships, grants, and awards by category:* Academic Interests/Achievement: 5,000 awards ($22,744,139 total): business, education, engineering/technologies, general academic interests/achievements, humanities. *Creative Arts/Performance:* 95 awards ($336,993 total): art/fine arts, music. *Special Achievements/Activities:* 140 awards ($241,630 total): general special achievements/activities. *Special Characteristics:* 10 awards ($101,010 total): religious affiliation. *Tuition waivers:* Full or partial for employees or children of employees, senior citizens. *ROTC:* Army, Air Force cooperative.
LOANS *Student loans:* $20,416,444 (79% need-based, 21% non-need-based). 67% of past graduating class borrowed through all loan programs. *Average indebtedness per student:* $20,151. *Average need-based loan:* Freshmen: $3145; Undergraduates: $3620. *Parent loans:* $7,105,811 (73% need-based, 27% non-need-based). *Programs:* FFEL (Subsidized and Unsubsidized Stafford, PLUS), Perkins, state, college/university.
WORK-STUDY *Federal work-study:* Total amount: $1,208,937; 930 jobs averaging $1343. *State or other work-study/employment:* Total amount: $4,448,645 (100% non-need-based). 3,093 part-time jobs averaging $1677.

ATHLETIC AWARDS *Total amount:* $2,187,547 (45% need-based, 55% non-need-based).
APPLYING FOR FINANCIAL AID *Required financial aid form:* FAFSA. *Financial aid deadline (priority):* 3/31. *Notification date:* Continuous beginning 3/1.
CONTACT Jeff Daniels, Director of Scholarships and Financial Aid, University of Dayton, 300 College Park Drive, Dayton, OH 45469-1305, 937-229-4311 or toll-free 800-837-7433. *Fax:* 937-229-4338. *E-mail:* jdaniels@udayton.edu.

UNIVERSITY OF DELAWARE
Newark, DE

Tuition & fees (DE res): $7318   **Average undergraduate aid package: $11,100**

ABOUT THE INSTITUTION State-related, coed. Awards: associate, bachelor's, master's, and doctoral degrees. 133 undergraduate majors. Total enrollment: 20,373. Undergraduates: 16,939. Freshmen: 3,404. Federal methodology is used as a basis for awarding need-based institutional aid.
UNDERGRADUATE EXPENSES for 2005–06 *Application fee:* $60. *Tuition, state resident:* full-time $6614; part-time $276 per credit. *Tuition, nonresident:* full-time $16,770; part-time $699 per credit. *Required fees:* full-time $704; $25 per term part-time. *College room and board:* $6824; *room only:* $3924. Room and board charges vary according to housing facility. *Payment plan:* Installment.
FRESHMAN FINANCIAL AID (Fall 2005, est.) 2597 applied for aid; of those 54% were deemed to have need. 100% of freshmen with need received aid; of those 48% had need fully met. *Average percent of need met:* 77% (excluding resources awarded to replace EFC). *Average financial aid package:* $10,400 (excluding resources awarded to replace EFC). 26% of all full-time freshmen had no need and received non-need-based gift aid.
UNDERGRADUATE FINANCIAL AID (Fall 2005, est.) 8,856 applied for aid; of those 64% were deemed to have need. 100% of undergraduates with need received aid; of those 51% had need fully met. *Average percent of need met:* 79% (excluding resources awarded to replace EFC). *Average financial aid package:* $11,100 (excluding resources awarded to replace EFC). 22% of all full-time undergraduates had no need and received non-need-based gift aid.
GIFT AID (NEED-BASED) *Total amount:* $24,400,000 (16% federal, 26% state, 40% institutional, 18% external sources). *Receiving aid:* Freshmen: 31% (1,086); All full-time undergraduates: 28% (4,216). *Average award:* Freshmen: $6600; Undergraduates: $6300. *Scholarships, grants, and awards:* Federal Pell, FSEOG, state, private, college/university gift aid from institutional funds.
GIFT AID (NON-NEED-BASED) *Total amount:* $14,100,000 (4% state, 76% institutional, 20% external sources). *Receiving aid:* Freshmen: 12% (431); Undergraduates: 10% (1,521). *Average Award:* Freshmen: $4500; Undergraduates: $4400. *Scholarships, grants, and awards by category:* Academic Interests/Achievement: agriculture, biological sciences, business, communication, computer science, education, engineering/technologies, English, foreign languages, general academic interests/achievements, health fields, humanities, international studies, mathematics, military science, physical sciences, premedicine, religion/biblical studies, social sciences. *Creative Arts/Performance:* applied art and design, art/fine arts, music, theater/drama. *Special Achievements/Activities:* cheerleading/drum major, community service, general special achievements/activities, leadership. *Special Characteristics:* children and siblings of alumni, children of faculty/staff, children of public servants, ethnic background, first-generation college students, general special characteristics, local/state students, members of minority groups. *Tuition waivers:* Full or partial for employees or children of employees, senior citizens. *ROTC:* Army, Air Force.
LOANS *Student loans:* $34,715,000 (70% need-based, 30% non-need-based). 40% of past graduating class borrowed through all loan programs. *Average indebtedness per student:* $15,200. *Average need-based loan:* Freshmen: $4000; Undergraduates: $4900. *Parent loans:* $19,200,000 (60% need-based, 40% non-need-based). *Programs:* Federal Direct (Subsidized and Unsubsidized Stafford, PLUS), Perkins, Federal Nursing.
WORK-STUDY *Federal work-study:* Total amount: $2,400,000; jobs available. *State or other work-study/employment:* Total amount: $221,000 (79% need-based, 21% non-need-based). Part-time jobs available.
ATHLETIC AWARDS *Total amount:* $5,400,000 (33% need-based, 67% non-need-based).
APPLYING FOR FINANCIAL AID *Required financial aid form:* FAFSA. *Financial aid deadline:* 3/15 (priority: 2/1). *Notification date:* Continuous beginning 3/15. Students must reply by 5/1 or within 3 weeks of notification.

CONTACT Mr. Johnie A. Burton, Director of Scholarships and Financial Aid, University of Delaware, 224 Hullihen Hall, Newark, DE 19716, 302-831-8081. *E-mail:* jburton@udel.edu.

UNIVERSITY OF DENVER
Denver, CO

Tuition & fees: $28,410   **Average undergraduate aid package: $19,329**

ABOUT THE INSTITUTION Independent, coed. Awards: bachelor's, master's, doctoral, and first professional degrees. 68 undergraduate majors. Total enrollment: 10,374. Undergraduates: 4,877. Freshmen: 1,103. Federal methodology is used as a basis for awarding need-based institutional aid.
UNDERGRADUATE EXPENSES for 2005–06 *Application fee:* $50. *Comprehensive fee:* $37,159 includes full-time tuition ($27,756), mandatory fees ($654), and room and board ($8749). *College room only:* $5355. Full-time tuition and fees vary according to class time, course load, and program. Room and board charges vary according to board plan and housing facility. *Part-time tuition:* $771 per quarter hour. Part-time tuition and fees vary according to class time, course load, and program. *Payment plan:* Deferred payment.
FRESHMAN FINANCIAL AID (Fall 2004) 681 applied for aid; of those 74% were deemed to have need. 100% of freshmen with need received aid; of those 15% had need fully met. *Average percent of need met:* 78% (excluding resources awarded to replace EFC). *Average financial aid package:* $21,710 (excluding resources awarded to replace EFC). 36% of all full-time freshmen had no need and received non-need-based gift aid.
UNDERGRADUATE FINANCIAL AID (Fall 2004) 2,212 applied for aid; of those 82% were deemed to have need. 100% of undergraduates with need received aid; of those 10% had need fully met. *Average percent of need met:* 67% (excluding resources awarded to replace EFC). *Average financial aid package:* $19,329 (excluding resources awarded to replace EFC). 31% of all full-time undergraduates had no need and received non-need-based gift aid.
GIFT AID (NEED-BASED) *Total amount:* $29,082,962 (9% federal, 4% state, 86% institutional, 1% external sources). *Receiving aid:* Freshmen: 44% (494); All full-time undergraduates: 42% (1,771). *Average award:* Freshmen: $16,913; Undergraduates: $14,471. *Scholarships, grants, and awards:* Federal Pell, FSEOG, state, private, college/university gift aid from institutional funds.
GIFT AID (NON-NEED-BASED) *Total amount:* $13,424,849 (87% institutional, 13% external sources). *Receiving aid:* Freshmen: 6% (64); Undergraduates: 4% (155). *Average Award:* Freshmen: $9210; Undergraduates: $8489. *Scholarships, grants, and awards by category:* Academic Interests/Achievement: business. *Creative Arts/Performance:* art/fine arts, debating, music, theater/drama. *Special Achievements/Activities:* community service, leadership. *Special Characteristics:* children of faculty/staff, local/state students. *Tuition waivers:* Full or partial for employees or children of employees. *ROTC:* Army cooperative, Air Force cooperative.
LOANS *Student loans:* $13,141,673 (78% need-based, 22% non-need-based). 43% of past graduating class borrowed through all loan programs. *Average indebtedness per student:* $22,633. *Average need-based loan:* Freshmen: $4265; Undergraduates: $4263. *Parent loans:* $6,530,537 (31% need-based, 69% non-need-based). *Programs:* Federal Direct (Subsidized and Unsubsidized Stafford, PLUS), FFEL (Subsidized and Unsubsidized Stafford, PLUS), Perkins, college/university.
WORK-STUDY *Federal work-study:* Total amount: $441,293; 263 jobs averaging $1670. *State or other work-study/employment:* Total amount: $416,692 (56% need-based, 44% non-need-based). 239 part-time jobs averaging $1743.
ATHLETIC AWARDS *Total amount:* $5,281,650 (16% need-based, 84% non-need-based).
APPLYING FOR FINANCIAL AID *Required financial aid form:* FAFSA. *Financial aid deadline (priority):* 3/1. *Notification date:* Continuous beginning 3/15. Students must reply within 4 weeks of notification.
CONTACT Ms. Barbara McFall, Director of Financial Aid, University of Denver, Office of Financial Aid, 2197 S. University Boulevard, Denver, CO 80208, 303-871-2342 or toll-free 800-525-9495 (out-of-state). *Fax:* 303-871-2341. *E-mail:* bmcfall@du.edu.

University of Detroit Mercy

UNIVERSITY OF DETROIT MERCY
Detroit, MI

ABOUT THE INSTITUTION Independent Roman Catholic (Jesuit), coed. Awards: associate, bachelor's, master's, doctoral, and first professional degrees and post-bachelor's, post-master's, and first professional certificates. 64 undergraduate majors. Total enrollment: 5,521. Undergraduates: 3,311. Freshmen: 461.
GIFT AID (NEED-BASED) *Scholarships, grants, and awards:* Federal Pell, FSEOG, state, private, college/university gift aid from institutional funds.
GIFT AID (NON-NEED-BASED) *Scholarships, grants, and awards by category: Academic Interests/Achievement:* general academic interests/achievements. *Creative Arts/Performance:* theater/drama. *Special Achievements/Activities:* religious involvement. *Special Characteristics:* children and siblings of alumni, children of faculty/staff, members of minority groups.
LOANS *Programs:* FFEL (Subsidized and Unsubsidized Stafford, PLUS), Perkins, Federal Nursing.
APPLYING FOR FINANCIAL AID *Required financial aid form:* FAFSA.
CONTACT Sandy Ross, Director of Financial Aid and Scholarships, University of Detroit Mercy, 4001 West McNichols Road, PO Box 19900, Detroit, MI 48219-0900, 313-993-3350 or toll-free 800-635-5020 (out-of-state). *Fax:* 313-993-3347.

UNIVERSITY OF DUBUQUE
Dubuque, IA

ABOUT THE INSTITUTION Independent Presbyterian, coed. Awards: associate, bachelor's, master's, doctoral, and first professional degrees. 32 undergraduate majors. Total enrollment: 1,441. Undergraduates: 1,179. Freshmen: 309.
GIFT AID (NEED-BASED) *Scholarships, grants, and awards:* Federal Pell, FSEOG, state, private, college/university gift aid from institutional funds.
GIFT AID (NON-NEED-BASED) *Scholarships, grants, and awards by category: Academic Interests/Achievement:* general academic interests/achievements. *Special Characteristics:* children and siblings of alumni, children of educators, children of faculty/staff, ethnic background, members of minority groups, out-of-state students, relatives of clergy, religious affiliation, siblings of current students.
LOANS *Programs:* FFEL (Subsidized and Unsubsidized Stafford, PLUS), Perkins, state, college/university.
WORK-STUDY *Federal work-study:* Total amount: $166,894; 175 jobs averaging $1500. *State or other work-study/employment:* Total amount: $150,000 (100% need-based). 150 part-time jobs averaging $1500.
APPLYING FOR FINANCIAL AID *Required financial aid form:* FAFSA.
CONTACT Mr. Timothy Kremer, Director of Financial Aid, University of Dubuque, 2000 University Avenue, Dubuque, IA 52001-5050, 563-589-3170 or toll-free 800-722-5583 (in-state). *Fax:* 563-589-3690.

UNIVERSITY OF EVANSVILLE
Evansville, IN

Tuition & fees: $21,660 | **Average undergraduate aid package:** $19,847

ABOUT THE INSTITUTION Independent religious, coed. Awards: associate, bachelor's, and master's degrees. 86 undergraduate majors. Total enrollment: 2,836. Undergraduates: 2,767. Freshmen: 670. Federal methodology is used as a basis for awarding need-based institutional aid.
UNDERGRADUATE EXPENSES for 2005–06 *Application fee:* $35. *Comprehensive fee:* $28,320 includes full-time tuition ($21,120), mandatory fees ($540), and room and board ($6660). *College room only:* $3280. Room and board charges vary according to board plan and housing facility. *Part-time tuition:* $580 per hour. *Part-time fees:* $35 per term. Part-time tuition and fees vary according to course load. *Payment plan:* Installment.
FRESHMAN FINANCIAL AID (Fall 2005, est.) 580 applied for aid; of those 85% were deemed to have need. 100% of freshmen with need received aid; of those 81% had need fully met. *Average percent of need met:* 96% (excluding resources awarded to replace EFC). *Average financial aid package:* $20,635 (excluding resources awarded to replace EFC). 22% of all full-time freshmen had no need and received non-need-based gift aid.
UNDERGRADUATE FINANCIAL AID (Fall 2005, est.) 2,048 applied for aid; of those 85% were deemed to have need. 100% of undergraduates with need received aid; of those 71% had need fully met. *Average percent of need met:* 93% (excluding resources awarded to replace EFC). *Average financial aid package:* $19,847 (excluding resources awarded to replace EFC). 23% of all full-time undergraduates had no need and received non-need-based gift aid.
GIFT AID (NEED-BASED) *Total amount:* $24,080,638 (8% federal, 20% state, 65% institutional, 7% external sources). *Receiving aid:* Freshmen: 73% (491); All full-time undergraduates: 71% (1,733). *Average award:* Freshmen: $16,730; Undergraduates: $15,028. *Scholarships, grants, and awards:* Federal Pell, FSEOG, state, private, college/university gift aid from institutional funds.
GIFT AID (NON-NEED-BASED) *Total amount:* $6,243,168 (91% institutional, 9% external sources). *Receiving aid:* Freshmen: 57% (385); Undergraduates: 50% (1,212). *Average Award:* Freshmen: $9757; Undergraduates: $10,137. *Scholarships, grants, and awards by category: Academic Interests/Achievement:* 805 awards ($5,300,229 total): biological sciences, business, communication, computer science, education, engineering/technologies, English, foreign languages, general academic interests/achievements, health fields, humanities, international studies, mathematics, physical sciences, premedicine, religion/biblical studies, social sciences. *Creative Arts/Performance:* 224 awards ($1,672,376 total): art/fine arts, music, theater/drama. *Special Achievements/Activities:* 144 awards ($608,100 total): leadership. *Special Characteristics:* 307 awards ($3,052,529 total): children and siblings of alumni, children of faculty/staff, international students, members of minority groups, religious affiliation, siblings of current students. *Tuition waivers:* Full or partial for minority students, children of alumni, employees or children of employees, senior citizens.
LOANS *Student loans:* $8,255,967 (91% need-based, 9% non-need-based). 67% of past graduating class borrowed through all loan programs. *Average indebtedness per student:* $21,142. *Average need-based loan:* Freshmen: $3835; Undergraduates: $4760. *Parent loans:* $4,805,393 (82% need-based, 18% non-need-based). *Programs:* FFEL (Subsidized and Unsubsidized Stafford, PLUS), Perkins, Federal Nursing, college/university.
WORK-STUDY *Federal work-study:* Total amount: $504,050; 390 jobs averaging $1292. *State or other work-study/employment:* Total amount: $97,500 (1% need-based, 99% non-need-based). 77 part-time jobs averaging $1266.
ATHLETIC AWARDS Total amount: $2,866,888 (39% need-based, 61% non-need-based).
APPLYING FOR FINANCIAL AID *Required financial aid form:* FAFSA. *Financial aid deadline (priority):* 3/10. *Notification date:* Continuous beginning 3/21. Students must reply by 5/1.
CONTACT Ms. JoAnn E. Laugel, Director of Financial Aid, University of Evansville, 1800 Lincoln Avenue, Evansville, IN 47722, 812-488-2364 or toll-free 800-423-8633 Ext. 2468. *Fax:* 812-488-2028. *E-mail:* jl25@evansville.edu.

THE UNIVERSITY OF FINDLAY
Findlay, OH

Tuition & fees: $21,746 | **Average undergraduate aid package:** $14,300

ABOUT THE INSTITUTION Independent religious, coed. Awards: associate, bachelor's, and master's degrees. 58 undergraduate majors. Total enrollment: 4,743. Undergraduates: 3,601. Freshmen: 606. Federal methodology is used as a basis for awarding need-based institutional aid.
UNDERGRADUATE EXPENSES for 2005–06 *Comprehensive fee:* $29,238 includes full-time tuition ($20,796), mandatory fees ($950), and room and board ($7492). *College room only:* $3756. Full-time tuition and fees vary according to location and program. Room and board charges vary according to housing facility. *Part-time tuition:* $458 per semester hour. *Part-time fees:* $125 per term. Part-time tuition and fees vary according to location and program. *Payment plan:* Installment.
FRESHMAN FINANCIAL AID (Fall 2004) 412 applied for aid; of those 100% were deemed to have need. 100% of freshmen with need received aid; of those 20% had need fully met. *Average percent of need met:* 87% (excluding resources awarded to replace EFC). *Average financial aid package:* $16,059 (excluding resources awarded to replace EFC). 17% of all full-time freshmen had no need and received non-need-based gift aid.
UNDERGRADUATE FINANCIAL AID (Fall 2004) 1,915 applied for aid; of those 98% were deemed to have need. 100% of undergraduates with need received aid; of those 19% had need fully met. *Average percent of need met:* 84% (excluding resources awarded to replace EFC). *Average financial aid package:* $14,300 (excluding resources awarded to replace EFC). 15% of all full-time undergraduates had no need and received non-need-based gift aid.

University of Georgia

GIFT AID (NEED-BASED) *Total amount:* $14,848,701 (15% federal, 8% state, 77% institutional). *Receiving aid:* Freshmen: 70% (410); All full-time undergraduates: 69% (1,820). *Average award:* Freshmen: $9959; Undergraduates: $9200. *Scholarships, grants, and awards:* Federal Pell, FSEOG, state, college/university gift aid from institutional funds.
GIFT AID (NON-NEED-BASED) *Total amount:* $9,793,292 (19% state, 75% institutional, 6% external sources). *Receiving aid:* Freshmen: 12% (71); Undergraduates: 22% (577). *Average Award:* Freshmen: $8400; Undergraduates: $7200. *Scholarships, grants, and awards by category: Academic Interests/Achievement:* general academic interests/achievements. *Creative Arts/Performance:* music, theater/drama. *Special Characteristics:* children of faculty/staff. *Tuition waivers:* Full or partial for children of alumni, employees or children of employees, senior citizens. *ROTC:* Army cooperative, Air Force cooperative.
LOANS *Student loans:* $14,712,000 (43% need-based, 57% non-need-based). 85% of past graduating class borrowed through all loan programs. *Average indebtedness per student:* $17,000. *Average need-based loan:* Freshmen: $2500; Undergraduates: $4000. *Parent loans:* $2,324,600 (100% non-need-based). *Programs:* FFEL (Subsidized and Unsubsidized Stafford, PLUS), Perkins, college/university.
WORK-STUDY *Federal work-study:* Total amount: $350,000; 420 jobs averaging $830. *State or other work-study/employment:* Total amount: $340,000 (100% non-need-based). 300 part-time jobs averaging $850.
ATHLETIC AWARDS *Total amount:* $2,303,000 (100% non-need-based).
APPLYING FOR FINANCIAL AID *Required financial aid form:* FAFSA. *Financial aid deadline:* Continuous. *Notification date:* Continuous beginning 3/1.
CONTACT Mr. Arman Habegger, Director of Financial Aid, The University of Findlay, 1000 North Main Street, Findlay, OH 45840-3695, 419-434-4791 or toll-free 800-548-0932. *Fax:* 419-434-4898. *E-mail:* finaid@findlay.edu.

UNIVERSITY OF FLORIDA
Gainesville, FL

Tuition & fees (FL res): $3094   **Average undergraduate aid package: $10,566**

ABOUT THE INSTITUTION State-supported, coed. Awards: bachelor's, master's, doctoral, and first professional degrees. 98 undergraduate majors. Total enrollment: 49,693. Undergraduates: 34,668. Freshmen: 7,241. Federal methodology is used as a basis for awarding need-based institutional aid.
UNDERGRADUATE EXPENSES for 2005–06 *Application fee:* $30. *Tuition, state resident:* full-time $3,094; part-time $103.12 per credit hour. *Tuition, nonresident:* full-time $17,222; part-time $574.08 per credit hour. *College room and board:* $6260; *room only:* $3940. Room and board charges vary according to board plan and housing facility. *Payment plan:* Tuition prepayment.
FRESHMAN FINANCIAL AID (Fall 2004) 4136 applied for aid; of those 62% were deemed to have need. 100% of freshmen with need received aid; of those 36% had need fully met. *Average percent of need met:* 85% (excluding resources awarded to replace EFC). *Average financial aid package:* $9763 (excluding resources awarded to replace EFC). 57% of all full-time freshmen had no need and received non-need-based gift aid.
UNDERGRADUATE FINANCIAL AID (Fall 2004) 16,565 applied for aid; of those 80% were deemed to have need. 99% of undergraduates with need received aid; of those 30% had need fully met. *Average percent of need met:* 84% (excluding resources awarded to replace EFC). *Average financial aid package:* $10,566 (excluding resources awarded to replace EFC). 49% of all full-time undergraduates had no need and received non-need-based gift aid.
GIFT AID (NEED-BASED) *Total amount:* $32,638,997 (64% federal, 17% state, 18% institutional, 1% external sources). *Receiving aid:* Freshmen: 21% (1,403); All full-time undergraduates: 25% (8,364). *Average award:* Freshmen: $4317; Undergraduates: $4302. *Scholarships, grants, and awards:* Federal Pell, FSEOG, state, private, college/university gift aid from institutional funds.
GIFT AID (NON-NEED-BASED) *Total amount:* $114,153,360 (58% state, 16% institutional, 26% external sources). *Receiving aid:* Freshmen: 35% (2,386); Undergraduates: 28% (9,361). *Average Award:* Freshmen: $5065; Undergraduates: $4261. *Scholarships, grants, and awards by category: Academic Interests/Achievement:* agriculture, architecture, business, communication, computer science, education, engineering/technologies, general academic interests/achievements, health fields, military science. *Creative Arts/Performance:* art/fine arts, dance, general creative arts/performance, journalism/publications, music, performing arts, theater/drama. *Special Achievements/Activities:* community service, general special achievements/activities, leadership. *Special Characteristics:* children of faculty/staff, members of minority groups, out-of-state students. *Tuition waivers:* Full or partial for employees or children of employees, senior citizens. *ROTC:* Army, Air Force.
LOANS *Student loans:* $53,761,136 (54% need-based, 46% non-need-based). 41% of past graduating class borrowed through all loan programs. *Average indebtedness per student:* $14,835. *Average need-based loan:* Freshmen: $2792; Undergraduates: $4116. *Parent loans:* $4,615,336 (100% non-need-based). *Programs:* Federal Direct (Subsidized and Unsubsidized Stafford, PLUS), Perkins, college/university.
WORK-STUDY *Federal work-study:* Total amount: $5,124,557; 2,588 jobs averaging $1980. *State or other work-study/employment:* Total amount: $11,176,417 (100% non-need-based). 4,397 part-time jobs averaging $2542.
ATHLETIC AWARDS *Total amount:* $3,665,729 (100% non-need-based).
APPLYING FOR FINANCIAL AID *Required financial aid form:* FAFSA. *Financial aid deadline (priority):* 3/15. *Notification date:* Continuous beginning 4/1.
CONTACT Ms. Karen L. Fooks, Director of Student Financial Affairs, University of Florida, S-107 Criser Hall, PO Box 114025, Gainesville, FL 32611-4025, 352-392-1271. *Fax:* 352-392-2861. *E-mail:* kfooks@ufl.edu.

UNIVERSITY OF GEORGIA
Athens, GA

Tuition & fees (GA res): $4628   **Average undergraduate aid package: $7058**

ABOUT THE INSTITUTION State-supported, coed. Awards: associate, bachelor's, master's, doctoral, and first professional degrees. 144 undergraduate majors. Total enrollment: 33,660. Undergraduates: 25,204. Freshmen: 4,696. Federal methodology is used as a basis for awarding need-based institutional aid.
UNDERGRADUATE EXPENSES for 2005–06 *Application fee:* $50. *Tuition, state resident:* full-time $3638; part-time $152 per credit. *Tuition, nonresident:* full-time $15,858; part-time $661 per credit. *Required fees:* full-time $990; $495 per term part-time. Full-time tuition and fees vary according to course load, location, program, and reciprocity agreements. Part-time tuition and fees vary according to course load, location, program, and reciprocity agreements. *College room and board:* $6376; *room only:* $3436. Room and board charges vary according to board plan and housing facility.
FRESHMAN FINANCIAL AID (Fall 2005, est.) 2836 applied for aid; of those 45% were deemed to have need. 99% of freshmen with need received aid; of those 39% had need fully met. *Average percent of need met:* 81% (excluding resources awarded to replace EFC). *Average financial aid package:* $7290 (excluding resources awarded to replace EFC). 8% of all full-time freshmen had no need and received non-need-based gift aid.
UNDERGRADUATE FINANCIAL AID (Fall 2005, est.) 10,201 applied for aid; of those 57% were deemed to have need. 97% of undergraduates with need received aid; of those 33% had need fully met. *Average percent of need met:* 74% (excluding resources awarded to replace EFC). *Average financial aid package:* $7058 (excluding resources awarded to replace EFC). 6% of all full-time undergraduates had no need and received non-need-based gift aid.
GIFT AID (NEED-BASED) *Total amount:* $27,096,699 (33% federal, 61% state, 2% institutional, 4% external sources). *Receiving aid:* Freshmen: 26% (1,218); All full-time undergraduates: 21% (4,804). *Average award:* Freshmen: $6148; Undergraduates: $5731. *Scholarships, grants, and awards:* Federal Pell, FSEOG, state, private, college/university gift aid from institutional funds.
GIFT AID (NON-NEED-BASED) *Total amount:* $63,790,196 (1% federal, 91% state, 4% institutional, 4% external sources). *Receiving aid:* Freshmen: 8% (383); Undergraduates: 4% (988). *Average Award:* Freshmen: $1656; Undergraduates: $1870. *Scholarships, grants, and awards by category: Academic Interests/Achievement:* 20,643 awards ($81,473,699 total): agriculture, business, education, general academic interests/achievements. *Creative Arts/Performance:* 114 awards ($134,345 total): music. *Special Characteristics:* 67 awards ($96,500 total): local/state students. *Tuition waivers:* Full or partial for senior citizens. *ROTC:* Army, Air Force.
LOANS *Student loans:* $37,349,164 (49% need-based, 51% non-need-based). 43% of past graduating class borrowed through all loan programs. *Average indebtedness per student:* $13,422. *Average need-based loan:* Freshmen: $2558; Undergraduates: $3683. *Parent loans:* $10,239,625 (17% need-based, 83% non-need-based). *Programs:* Federal Direct (Subsidized and Unsubsidized Stafford, PLUS), Perkins, state, college/university.

University of Georgia

WORK-STUDY *Federal work-study:* Total amount: $961,284; 359 jobs averaging $2678.
ATHLETIC AWARDS Total amount: $5,091,856 (25% need-based, 75% non-need-based).
APPLYING FOR FINANCIAL AID *Required financial aid form:* FAFSA. *Financial aid deadline (priority):* 3/1. *Notification date:* Continuous beginning 3/1. Students must reply within 2 weeks of notification.
CONTACT Ms. Susan D. Little, Director of Student Affairs, University of Georgia, 220 Holmes/Hunter Academic Building, Athens, GA 30602-6114, 706-542-8208. *Fax:* 706-542-8217. *E-mail:* slittle@uga.edu.

UNIVERSITY OF GREAT FALLS
Great Falls, MT

Tuition & fees: $15,220   **Average undergraduate aid package: $10,989**

ABOUT THE INSTITUTION Independent Roman Catholic, coed. Awards: associate, bachelor's, and master's degrees. 76 undergraduate majors. Total enrollment: 778. Undergraduates: 673. Freshmen: 122. Federal methodology is used as a basis for awarding need-based institutional aid.
UNDERGRADUATE EXPENSES for 2006–07 *Application fee:* $35. *Comprehensive fee:* $20,720 includes full-time tuition ($14,600), mandatory fees ($620), and room and board ($5500). *College room only:* $2400. *Part-time tuition:* $460 per credit. *Part-time fees:* $15 per credit.
FRESHMAN FINANCIAL AID (Fall 2005, est.) 103 applied for aid; of those 93% were deemed to have need. 100% of freshmen with need received aid; of those 5% had need fully met. *Average percent of need met:* 46% (excluding resources awarded to replace EFC). *Average financial aid package:* $10,541 (excluding resources awarded to replace EFC). 3% of all full-time freshmen had no need and received non-need-based gift aid.
UNDERGRADUATE FINANCIAL AID (Fall 2005, est.) 420 applied for aid; of those 95% were deemed to have need. 100% of undergraduates with need received aid; of those 4% had need fully met. *Average percent of need met:* 41% (excluding resources awarded to replace EFC). *Average financial aid package:* $10,989 (excluding resources awarded to replace EFC). 3% of all full-time undergraduates had no need and received non-need-based gift aid.
GIFT AID (NEED-BASED) *Total amount:* $1,056,848 (92% federal, 8% state). *Receiving aid:* Freshmen: 47% (55); All full-time undergraduates: 53% (252). *Average award:* Freshmen: $3410; Undergraduates: $3719. *Scholarships, grants, and awards:* Federal Pell, FSEOG, state, private, college/university gift aid from institutional funds.
GIFT AID (NON-NEED-BASED) *Total amount:* $1,443,489 (87% institutional, 13% external sources). *Receiving aid:* Freshmen: 78% (90); Undergraduates: 78% (376). *Average Award:* Freshmen: $5667; Undergraduates: $3933. *Scholarships, grants, and awards by category:* Academic Interests/Achievement: 359 awards ($939,268 total): biological sciences, business, computer science, education, general academic interests/achievements, humanities, mathematics, physical sciences, premedicine, religion/biblical studies, social sciences. Creative Arts/Performance: 5 awards ($14,500 total): art/fine arts, music. Special Characteristics: 91 awards ($290,988 total): children of current students, children of faculty/staff, ethnic background, first-generation college students, international students, parents of current students, religious affiliation, siblings of current students, spouses of current students.
LOANS *Student loans:* $3,108,251 (56% need-based, 44% non-need-based). 83% of past graduating class borrowed through all loan programs. *Average indebtedness per student:* $26,450. *Average need-based loan:* Freshmen: $2704; Undergraduates: $4024. *Parent loans:* $456,562 (100% non-need-based). *Programs:* FFEL (Subsidized and Unsubsidized Stafford, PLUS), Perkins.
WORK-STUDY *Federal work-study:* Total amount: $138,692; 142 jobs averaging $1992. *State or other work-study/employment:* Total amount: $8006 (100% non-need-based). Part-time jobs available.
ATHLETIC AWARDS Total amount: $577,220 (100% non-need-based).
APPLYING FOR FINANCIAL AID *Required financial aid form:* FAFSA. *Financial aid deadline (priority):* 3/1. *Notification date:* Continuous beginning 2/15.
CONTACT Chris Steckmann, Director of Financial Aid, University of Great Falls, 1301 20th Street South, Great Falls, MT 59405, 406-791-5237 or toll-free 800-856-9544. *Fax:* 406-791-5242. *E-mail:* lhabel@ugf.edu.

UNIVERSITY OF GUAM
Mangilao, GU

CONTACT Office of Financial Aid, University of Guam, UOG Station, Mangilao, GU 96923, 671-735-2280.

UNIVERSITY OF HARTFORD
West Hartford, CT

Tuition & fees: $25,766   **Average undergraduate aid package: $15,565**

ABOUT THE INSTITUTION Independent, coed. Awards: associate, bachelor's, master's, and doctoral degrees and post-bachelor's and post-master's certificates. 78 undergraduate majors. Total enrollment: 7,260. Undergraduates: 5,592. Freshmen: 1,469. Federal methodology is used as a basis for awarding need-based institutional aid.
UNDERGRADUATE EXPENSES for 2006–07 *Application fee:* $35. *Comprehensive fee:* $35,688 includes full-time tuition ($24,576), mandatory fees ($1190), and room and board ($9922). *College room only:* $6118. *Part-time tuition:* $360 per credit. *Part-time fees:* $360 per credit.
FRESHMAN FINANCIAL AID (Fall 2004) 991 applied for aid; of those 87% were deemed to have need. 100% of freshmen with need received aid; of those 10% had need fully met. *Average percent of need met:* 45% (excluding resources awarded to replace EFC). *Average financial aid package:* $14,471 (excluding resources awarded to replace EFC). 29% of all full-time freshmen had no need and received non-need-based gift aid.
UNDERGRADUATE FINANCIAL AID (Fall 2004) 3,246 applied for aid; of those 90% were deemed to have need. 99% of undergraduates with need received aid; of those 8% had need fully met. *Average percent of need met:* 64% (excluding resources awarded to replace EFC). *Average financial aid package:* $15,565 (excluding resources awarded to replace EFC). 29% of all full-time undergraduates had no need and received non-need-based gift aid.
GIFT AID (NEED-BASED) *Total amount:* $33,507,014 (9% federal, 7% state, 82% institutional, 2% external sources). *Receiving aid:* Freshmen: 64% (837); All full-time undergraduates: 61% (2,773). *Average award:* Freshmen: $11,833; Undergraduates: $12,022. *Scholarships, grants, and awards:* Federal Pell, FSEOG, state, private, college/university gift aid from institutional funds.
GIFT AID (NON-NEED-BASED) *Total amount:* $8,703,669 (99% institutional, 1% external sources). *Receiving aid:* Freshmen: 63% (830); Undergraduates: 60% (2,735). *Average Award:* Freshmen: $6557; Undergraduates: $6499. *Scholarships, grants, and awards by category:* Academic Interests/Achievement: 3,223 awards ($19,939,596 total): general academic interests/achievements, health fields, premedicine. Creative Arts/Performance: 542 awards ($5,143,375 total): art/fine arts, dance, music, performing arts, theater/drama. Special Achievements/Activities: community service. Special Characteristics: adult students, children of current students, children of faculty/staff, children of union members/company employees, children with a deceased or disabled parent, ethnic background, first-generation college students, handicapped students, international students, local/state students, members of minority groups, parents of current students, previous college experience, religious affiliation, siblings of current students, twins. *ROTC:* Army cooperative, Air Force cooperative.
LOANS *Student loans:* $26,923,213 (88% need-based, 12% non-need-based). 66% of past graduating class borrowed through all loan programs. *Average indebtedness per student:* $25,553. *Average need-based loan:* Freshmen: $3061; Undergraduates: $4702. *Parent loans:* $10,609,112 (100% need-based). *Programs:* FFEL (Subsidized and Unsubsidized Stafford, PLUS), Perkins.
WORK-STUDY *Federal work-study:* Total amount: $569,883; 372 jobs averaging $1532. *State or other work-study/employment:* Total amount: $861,367 (81% need-based, 19% non-need-based). 86 part-time jobs averaging $9197.
ATHLETIC AWARDS Total amount: $3,258,946 (28% need-based, 72% non-need-based).
APPLYING FOR FINANCIAL AID *Required financial aid form:* FAFSA. *Financial aid deadline (priority):* 2/1. *Notification date:* Continuous beginning 3/1. Students must reply by 5/1.
CONTACT Financial Aid Office, University of Hartford, 200 Bloomfield Avenue, West Hartford, CT 06117-1599, 860-768-4296 or toll-free 800-947-4303. *Fax:* 860-768-4961. *E-mail:* finaid@hartford.edu.

UNIVERSITY OF HAWAII AT HILO
Hilo, HI

Tuition & fees (HI res): $2604   **Average undergraduate aid package:** $6252

ABOUT THE INSTITUTION State-supported, coed. Awards: bachelor's and master's degrees and post-bachelor's certificates. 29 undergraduate majors. Total enrollment: 3,288. Undergraduates: 3,081. Federal methodology is used as a basis for awarding need-based institutional aid.
UNDERGRADUATE EXPENSES for 2005–06 *Application fee:* $40. *Tuition, state resident:* full-time $2472; part-time $103 per credit hour. *Tuition, nonresident:* full-time $8040; part-time $335 per credit hour. *College room and board:* $5374; *room only:* $2774.
FRESHMAN FINANCIAL AID (Fall 2005, est.) 284 applied for aid; of those 71% were deemed to have need. 100% of freshmen with need received aid; of those 22% had need fully met. *Average percent of need met:* 63% (excluding resources awarded to replace EFC). *Average financial aid package:* $5008 (excluding resources awarded to replace EFC). 1% of all full-time freshmen had no need and received non-need-based gift aid.
UNDERGRADUATE FINANCIAL AID (Fall 2005, est.) 1,752 applied for aid; of those 86% were deemed to have need. 100% of undergraduates with need received aid; of those 18% had need fully met. *Average percent of need met:* 82% (excluding resources awarded to replace EFC). *Average financial aid package:* $6252 (excluding resources awarded to replace EFC). 1% of all full-time undergraduates had no need and received non-need-based gift aid.
GIFT AID (NEED-BASED) *Total amount:* $3,715,478 (97% federal, 1% state, 2% institutional). *Receiving aid:* Freshmen: 44% (175); All full-time undergraduates: 59% (1,270). *Average award:* Freshmen: $3532; Undergraduates: $3440. *Scholarships, grants, and awards:* Federal Pell, FSEOG, state, private, college/university gift aid from institutional funds.
GIFT AID (NON-NEED-BASED) *Total amount:* $2,120,394 (15% institutional, 85% external sources). *Receiving aid:* Freshmen: 8% (31); Undergraduates: 10% (212). *Average Award:* Freshmen: $850; Undergraduates: $850. *Scholarships, grants, and awards by category:* Academic Interests/Achievement: 10 awards ($6500 total): agriculture, business, computer science, English, general academic interests/achievements, health fields, social sciences. *Creative Arts/Performance:* art/fine arts, music, performing arts, theater/drama. *Special Achievements/Activities:* 5 awards ($4125 total): community service, leadership.
LOANS *Student loans:* $6,943,250 (56% need-based, 44% non-need-based). 43% of past graduating class borrowed through all loan programs. *Average indebtedness per student:* $14,145. *Average need-based loan:* Freshmen: $1923; Undergraduates: $3502. *Parent loans:* $511,115 (100% non-need-based). *Programs:* FFEL (Subsidized and Unsubsidized Stafford, PLUS), Perkins, state.
WORK-STUDY *Federal work-study:* Total amount: $388,086; 133 jobs averaging $1996. *State or other work-study/employment:* Total amount: $1,008,744 (100% non-need-based). 339 part-time jobs averaging $2221.
ATHLETIC AWARDS *Total amount:* $140,691 (100% non-need-based).
APPLYING FOR FINANCIAL AID *Required financial aid form:* FAFSA. *Financial aid deadline (priority):* 3/1. *Notification date:* Continuous beginning 4/1. Students must reply within 3 weeks of notification.
CONTACT Financial Aid Coordinator, University of Hawaii at Hilo, 200 West Kawili Street, Hilo, HI 96720-4091, 808-974-7324 or toll-free 808-974-7414 (in-state), 800-897-4456 (out-of-state). *Fax:* 808-933-0861.

UNIVERSITY OF HAWAII AT MANOA
Honolulu, HI

Tuition & fees (HI res): $4513   **Average undergraduate aid package:** $5956

ABOUT THE INSTITUTION State-supported, coed. Awards: bachelor's, master's, doctoral, and first professional degrees and post-bachelor's certificates. 87 undergraduate majors. Total enrollment: 20,644. Undergraduates: 14,351. Freshmen: 2,022. Federal methodology is used as a basis for awarding need-based institutional aid.
UNDERGRADUATE EXPENSES for 2005–06 *Application fee:* $50. *Tuition, state resident:* full-time $4320; part-time $180 per credit hour. *Tuition, nonresident:* full-time $12,942; part-time $508 per credit hour. Full-time tuition and fees vary according to class time, course load, program, and reciprocity agreements. Part-time tuition and fees vary according to class time, course load, program, and reciprocity agreements. *College room and board:* $6690; *room only:* $4232. Room and board charges vary according to board plan and housing facility.
FRESHMAN FINANCIAL AID (Fall 2005, est.) 1236 applied for aid; of those 49% were deemed to have need. 90% of freshmen with need received aid; of those 24% had need fully met. *Average percent of need met:* 64% (excluding resources awarded to replace EFC). *Average financial aid package:* $5334 (excluding resources awarded to replace EFC). 11% of all full-time freshmen had no need and received non-need-based gift aid.
UNDERGRADUATE FINANCIAL AID (Fall 2005, est.) 6,682 applied for aid; of those 61% were deemed to have need. 93% of undergraduates with need received aid; of those 23% had need fully met. *Average percent of need met:* 65% (excluding resources awarded to replace EFC). *Average financial aid package:* $5956 (excluding resources awarded to replace EFC). 8% of all full-time undergraduates had no need and received non-need-based gift aid.
GIFT AID (NEED-BASED) *Total amount:* $9,329,749 (87% federal, 1% state, 7% institutional, 5% external sources). *Receiving aid:* Freshmen: 23% (428); All full-time undergraduates: 24% (2,826). *Average award:* Freshmen: $3665; Undergraduates: $3596. *Scholarships, grants, and awards:* Federal Pell, FSEOG, state, private, college/university gift aid from institutional funds, Federal Nursing.
GIFT AID (NON-NEED-BASED) *Total amount:* $1,920,601 (14% institutional, 86% external sources). *Receiving aid:* Freshmen: 4% (83); Undergraduates: 3% (411). *Average Award:* Freshmen: $2398; Undergraduates: $2376. *Scholarships, grants, and awards by category:* Academic Interests/Achievement: general academic interests/achievements. *Creative Arts/Performance:* art/fine arts, dance, journalism/publications, music, performing arts, theater/drama. *Tuition waivers:* Full or partial for minority students, employees or children of employees. *ROTC:* Army, Air Force.
LOANS *Student loans:* $19,762,995 (58% need-based, 42% non-need-based). 33% of past graduating class borrowed through all loan programs. *Average indebtedness per student:* $12,459. *Average need-based loan:* Freshmen: $2300; Undergraduates: $3624. *Parent loans:* $7,649,950 (100% non-need-based). *Programs:* FFEL (Subsidized and Unsubsidized Stafford, PLUS), Perkins, Federal Nursing, state, college/university.
WORK-STUDY *Federal work-study:* Total amount: $1,336,450; 691 jobs averaging $1934.
ATHLETIC AWARDS *Total amount:* $3,519,024 (1% need-based, 99% non-need-based).
APPLYING FOR FINANCIAL AID *Required financial aid forms:* FAFSA, institution's own form. *Financial aid deadline (priority):* 3/1. *Notification date:* Continuous beginning 3/28. Students must reply within 2 weeks of notification.
CONTACT Jamie Uyehara, Interim Director of Financial Aid Services, University of Hawaii at Manoa, 2600 Campus Road, Suite 112, Honolulu, HI 96822, 808-956-3989 or toll-free 800-823-9771. *Fax:* 808-956-3985. *E-mail:* finaid@hawaii.edu.

UNIVERSITY OF HAWAII–WEST OAHU
Pearl City, HI

CONTACT Student Services Office, University of Hawaii–West Oahu, 96-129 Ala Ike, Pearl City, HI 96782-3366, 808-454-4700 or toll-free 808-454 Ext. 4700 (in-state). *Fax:* 808-453-6075.

UNIVERSITY OF HOUSTON
Houston, TX

CONTACT Financial Aid Office, University of Houston, 4800 Calhoun Road, Houston, TX 77204-2160, 713-743-1010. *Fax:* 713-743-9098.

UNIVERSITY OF HOUSTON–CLEAR LAKE
Houston, TX

CONTACT Lynda McKendree, Director of Financial Aid and Veterans' Affairs, University of Houston–Clear Lake, 2700 Bay Area Boulevard, Houston, TX 77058-1098, 281-283-2485. *Fax:* 281-283-2502. *E-mail:* mckendree@cl.uh.edu.

University of Houston–Downtown

UNIVERSITY OF HOUSTON–DOWNTOWN
Houston, TX

ABOUT THE INSTITUTION State-supported, coed. Awards: bachelor's and master's degrees. 28 undergraduate majors. Total enrollment: 11,484. Undergraduates: 11,359. Freshmen: 1,029.

GIFT AID (NEED-BASED) *Scholarships, grants, and awards:* Federal Pell, FSEOG, state, private, college/university gift aid from institutional funds.

GIFT AID (NON-NEED-BASED) *Scholarships, grants, and awards by category: Academic Interests/Achievement:* general academic interests/achievements. *Special Achievements/Activities:* community service, general special achievements/activities, leadership. *Special Characteristics:* general special characteristics.

LOANS *Programs:* FFEL (Subsidized and Unsubsidized Stafford, PLUS), state.

APPLYING FOR FINANCIAL AID *Required financial aid forms:* FAFSA, institution's own form.

CONTACT Office of Scholarships and Financial Aid, University of Houston–Downtown, One Main Street, Suite 330 South, Houston, TX 77002-1001, 713-221-8041. *Fax:* 713-221-8468. *E-mail:* uhd.finaid@dt.uh.edu.

UNIVERSITY OF HOUSTON–VICTORIA
Victoria, TX

Tuition & fees: N/R   **Average undergraduate aid package:** $6669

ABOUT THE INSTITUTION State-supported, coed. Awards: bachelor's and master's degrees and post-bachelor's and post-master's certificates. 10 undergraduate majors. Total enrollment: 2,491. Undergraduates: 1,229. Federal methodology is used as a basis for awarding need-based institutional aid.

UNDERGRADUATE EXPENSES for 2005–06 *Tuition, state resident:* part-time $150 per semester hour. *Tuition, nonresident:* part-time $426 per semester hour.

UNDERGRADUATE FINANCIAL AID (Fall 2004) 313 applied for aid; of those 84% were deemed to have need. 92% of undergraduates with need received aid; of those 1% had need fully met. *Average percent of need met:* 53% (excluding resources awarded to replace EFC). *Average financial aid package:* $6669 (excluding resources awarded to replace EFC). 10% of all full-time undergraduates had no need and received non-need-based gift aid.

GIFT AID (NEED-BASED) *Total amount:* $2,357,012 (56% federal, 16% state, 12% institutional, 16% external sources). *Receiving aid:* All full-time undergraduates: 65% (223). *Average award:* Undergraduates: $3681. *Scholarships, grants, and awards:* Federal Pell, FSEOG, state, private, college/university gift aid from institutional funds.

GIFT AID (NON-NEED-BASED) *Total amount:* $182,366 (1% federal, 64% institutional, 35% external sources). *Receiving aid:* Undergraduates: 1. *Average Award:* Undergraduates: $5638. *Scholarships, grants, and awards by category: Academic Interests/Achievement:* 190 awards ($215,811 total): biological sciences, business, communication, computer science, education, general academic interests/achievements, humanities, mathematics, social sciences. *Special Achievements/Activities:* 12 awards ($13,800 total): community service, leadership, memberships. *Special Characteristics:* 2 awards ($3800 total): first-generation college students.

LOANS *Student loans:* $4,045,930 (77% need-based, 23% non-need-based). 54% of past graduating class borrowed through all loan programs. *Average indebtedness per student:* $18,145. *Average need-based loan:* Undergraduates: $4095. *Parent loans:* $21,776 (100% non-need-based). *Programs:* FFEL (Subsidized and Unsubsidized Stafford, PLUS), state.

WORK-STUDY *Federal work-study:* Total amount: $54,324; 30 jobs averaging $1871. *State or other work-study/employment:* Total amount: $12,559 (100% need-based). 5 part-time jobs averaging $2512.

APPLYING FOR FINANCIAL AID *Required financial aid form:* FAFSA. *Financial aid deadline (priority):* 4/15. *Notification date:* Continuous beginning 5/20. Students must reply within 3 weeks of notification.

CONTACT Carolyn Mallory, Financial Aid Director, University of Houston–Victoria, 3007 North Ben Wilson, Victoria, TX 77901-5731, 361-570-4131 or toll-free 877-970-4848 Ext. 110. *Fax:* 361-570-4132. *E-mail:* malloryc@uhv.edu.

UNIVERSITY OF IDAHO
Moscow, ID

Tuition & fees (ID res): $3968   **Average undergraduate aid package:** $9506

ABOUT THE INSTITUTION State-supported, coed. Awards: bachelor's, master's, doctoral, and first professional degrees and post-master's certificates. 109 undergraduate majors. Total enrollment: 12,476. Undergraduates: 9,503. Freshmen: 1,733. Federal methodology is used as a basis for awarding need-based institutional aid.

UNDERGRADUATE EXPENSES for 2005–06 *Application fee:* $40. *Tuition, state resident:* full-time $0. *Tuition, nonresident:* full-time $8770; part-time $130 per credit. *Required fees:* full-time $3968; $190 per credit. Full-time tuition and fees vary according to degree level and program. Part-time tuition and fees vary according to course load, degree level, and program. *College room and board:* $5342. Room and board charges vary according to board plan and housing facility. *Payment plans:* Installment, deferred payment.

FRESHMAN FINANCIAL AID (Fall 2004) 1303 applied for aid; of those 73% were deemed to have need. 99% of freshmen with need received aid; of those 31% had need fully met. *Average percent of need met:* 80% (excluding resources awarded to replace EFC). *Average financial aid package:* $8151 (excluding resources awarded to replace EFC). 37% of all full-time freshmen had no need and received non-need-based gift aid.

UNDERGRADUATE FINANCIAL AID (Fall 2004) 6,378 applied for aid; of those 81% were deemed to have need. 98% of undergraduates with need received aid; of those 28% had need fully met. *Average percent of need met:* 78% (excluding resources awarded to replace EFC). *Average financial aid package:* $9506 (excluding resources awarded to replace EFC). 25% of all full-time undergraduates had no need and received non-need-based gift aid.

GIFT AID (NEED-BASED) *Total amount:* $11,543,348 (88% federal, 12% institutional). *Receiving aid:* Freshmen: 33% (542); All full-time undergraduates: 39% (3,339). *Average award:* Freshmen: $3263; Undergraduates: $3161. *Scholarships, grants, and awards:* Federal Pell, FSEOG, state, private, college/university gift aid from institutional funds.

GIFT AID (NON-NEED-BASED) *Total amount:* $8,231,051 (2% state, 78% institutional, 20% external sources). *Receiving aid:* Freshmen: 51% (849); Undergraduates: 44% (3,734). *Average Award:* Freshmen: $3286; Undergraduates: $3777. *Scholarships, grants, and awards by category: Academic Interests/Achievement:* 7,500 awards ($15,000,000 total): agriculture, architecture, biological sciences, business, communication, computer science, education, engineering/technologies, English, foreign languages, general academic interests/achievements, home economics, humanities, mathematics, military science, physical sciences, premedicine, social sciences. *Creative Arts/Performance:* 300 awards ($500,000 total): applied art and design, art/fine arts, creative writing, dance, general creative arts/performance, journalism/publications, music, performing arts, theater/drama. *Special Achievements/Activities:* 70 awards ($100,000 total): cheerleading/drum major, general special achievements/activities, junior miss, leadership, rodeo. *Special Characteristics:* 400 awards ($250,000 total): children and siblings of alumni, children of faculty/staff, ethnic background, first-generation college students, general special characteristics, handicapped students, international students, local/state students, members of minority groups, out-of-state students. *Tuition waivers:* Full or partial for minority students, children of alumni, employees or children of employees, senior citizens. *ROTC:* Army, Naval, Air Force cooperative.

LOANS *Student loans:* $34,942,893 (59% need-based, 41% non-need-based). 69% of past graduating class borrowed through all loan programs. *Average indebtedness per student:* $20,002. *Average need-based loan:* Freshmen: $3337; Undergraduates: $5923. *Parent loans:* $2,813,061 (100% non-need-based). *Programs:* Federal Direct (Subsidized and Unsubsidized Stafford, PLUS), Perkins, college/university.

WORK-STUDY *Federal work-study:* Total amount: $793,391; 500 jobs averaging $1400. *State or other work-study/employment:* Total amount: $366,113 (100% need-based). 171 part-time jobs averaging $1400.

ATHLETIC AWARDS *Total amount:* $3,525,999 (100% non-need-based).

APPLYING FOR FINANCIAL AID *Required financial aid form:* FAFSA. *Financial aid deadline (priority):* 2/15. *Notification date:* Continuous beginning 3/30. Students must reply within 4 weeks of notification.

CONTACT Mr. Dan Davenport, Director of Admissions and Financial Aid, University of Idaho, Financial Aid Office, Moscow, ID 83844-4291, 208-885-6312 or toll-free 888-884-3246. *Fax:* 208-885-5592. *E-mail:* dand@uidaho.edu.

UNIVERSITY OF ILLINOIS AT CHICAGO
Chicago, IL

ABOUT THE INSTITUTION State-supported, coed. Awards: bachelor's, master's, doctoral, and first professional degrees and first professional certificates. 76 undergraduate majors. Total enrollment: 24,812. Undergraduates: 15,150. Freshmen: 2,776.
GIFT AID (NEED-BASED) *Scholarships, grants, and awards:* Federal Pell, FSEOG, state, private, college/university gift aid from institutional funds.
GIFT AID (NON-NEED-BASED) *Scholarships, grants, and awards by category: Academic Interests/Achievement:* architecture, general academic interests/achievements. *Creative Arts/Performance:* applied art and design, art/fine arts, music, performing arts, theater/drama. *Special Achievements/Activities:* general special achievements/activities. *Special Characteristics:* children of faculty/staff, general special characteristics, members of minority groups, veterans, veterans' children.
LOANS *Programs:* Federal Direct (Subsidized and Unsubsidized Stafford, PLUS), Perkins, Federal Nursing, college/university.
APPLYING FOR FINANCIAL AID *Required financial aid form:* FAFSA.
CONTACT Ms. Agnes Roche, Associate Director of Financial Aid, University of Illinois at Chicago, 1200 West Harrison, M/C 334, Chicago, IL 60607-7128, 312-996-5563. *Fax:* 312-996-3385. *E-mail:* aroche@uic.edu.

UNIVERSITY OF ILLINOIS AT SPRINGFIELD
Springfield, IL

Tuition & fees (IL res): $5335 **Average undergraduate aid package: $7761**

ABOUT THE INSTITUTION State-supported, coed. Awards: bachelor's, master's, and doctoral degrees and post-bachelor's and post-master's certificates. 19 undergraduate majors. Total enrollment: 4,517. Undergraduates: 2,634. Freshmen: 138. Federal methodology is used as a basis for awarding need-based institutional aid.
UNDERGRADUATE EXPENSES for 2005–06 *Application fee:* $40. *Tuition, state resident:* full-time $3953; part-time $132 per credit hour. *Tuition, nonresident:* full-time $11,858; part-time $396 per credit hour. *Required fees:* full-time $1382; $586 per term part-time. Full-time tuition and fees vary according to program. *College room and board:* $7110; *room only:* $3270. Room and board charges vary according to housing facility. *Payment plans:* Guaranteed tuition, installment.
FRESHMAN FINANCIAL AID (Fall 2004) 87 applied for aid; of those 63% were deemed to have need. 100% of freshmen with need received aid; of those 62% had need fully met. *Average percent of need met:* 88% (excluding resources awarded to replace EFC). *Average financial aid package:* $7946 (excluding resources awarded to replace EFC). 38% of all full-time freshmen had no need and received non-need-based gift aid.
UNDERGRADUATE FINANCIAL AID (Fall 2004) 1,107 applied for aid; of those 81% were deemed to have need. 96% of undergraduates with need received aid; of those 37% had need fully met. *Average percent of need met:* 82% (excluding resources awarded to replace EFC). *Average financial aid package:* $7761 (excluding resources awarded to replace EFC). 14% of all full-time undergraduates had no need and received non-need-based gift aid.
GIFT AID (NEED-BASED) *Total amount:* $3,839,694 (48% federal, 44% state, 8% institutional). *Receiving aid:* Freshmen: 34% (31); All full-time undergraduates: 40% (596). *Average award:* Freshmen: $4719; Undergraduates: $4917. *Scholarships, grants, and awards:* Federal Pell, FSEOG, state, private, college/university gift aid from institutional funds.
GIFT AID (NON-NEED-BASED) *Total amount:* $1,719,912 (2% federal, 33% state, 56% institutional, 9% external sources). *Receiving aid:* Freshmen: 61% (55); Undergraduates: 22% (323). *Average Award:* Freshmen: $4188; Undergraduates: $3493. *Scholarships, grants, and awards by category: Academic Interests/Achievement:* 593 awards ($1,282,055 total): agriculture, biological sciences, business, communication, computer science, education, engineering/technologies, English, foreign languages, general academic interests/achievements, health fields, humanities, international studies, mathematics, physical sciences, social sciences. *Creative Arts/Performance:* 4 awards ($2750 total): applied art and design, art/fine arts, general creative arts/performance, journalism/publications, music, performing arts. *Special Achievements/Activities:* 15 awards ($14,850 total): community service, general special achievements/activities, leadership, memberships. *Special Characteristics:* 79 awards ($214,176 total): adult students, children of educators, children of faculty/staff, children of union members/company employees, children of workers in trades, children with a deceased or disabled parent, ethnic background, first-generation college students, general special characteristics, international students, local/state students, members of minority groups, out-of-state students, public servants, veterans, veterans' children. *Tuition waivers:* Full or partial for senior citizens.
LOANS *Student loans:* $6,325,001 (60% need-based, 40% non-need-based). 47% of past graduating class borrowed through all loan programs. *Average indebtedness per student:* $11,069. *Average need-based loan:* Freshmen: $2361; Undergraduates: $3942. *Parent loans:* $525,809 (100% non-need-based). *Programs:* FFEL (Subsidized and Unsubsidized Stafford, PLUS), Perkins, college/university.
WORK-STUDY *Federal work-study:* Total amount: $185,745; 90 jobs averaging $2064. *State or other work-study/employment:* Total amount: $702,835 (100% non-need-based). 284 part-time jobs averaging $2475.
ATHLETIC AWARDS *Total amount:* $380,567 (100% non-need-based).
APPLYING FOR FINANCIAL AID *Required financial aid form:* FAFSA. *Financial aid deadline:* 11/15 (priority: 4/1). *Notification date:* Continuous beginning 1/1. Students must reply within 3 weeks of notification.
CONTACT Mr. Gerard Joseph, Director of Financial Aid, University of Illinois at Springfield, One University Plaza, MS UHB 1015, Financial Aid Office, Room 1015, Springfield, IL 627-5407, 217-206-6724 or toll-free 888-977-4847. *Fax:* 217-206-7376. *E-mail:* finaid@uis.edu.

UNIVERSITY OF ILLINOIS AT URBANA–CHAMPAIGN
Champaign, IL

Tuition & fees (IL res): $8624 **Average undergraduate aid package: $9714**

ABOUT THE INSTITUTION State-supported, coed. Awards: bachelor's, master's, doctoral, and first professional degrees and post-master's certificates. 156 undergraduate majors. Total enrollment: 41,938. Undergraduates: 30,909. Freshmen: 7,580. Federal methodology is used as a basis for awarding need-based institutional aid.
UNDERGRADUATE EXPENSES for 2005–06 *Application fee:* $40. *Tuition, state resident:* full-time $7042. *Tuition, nonresident:* full-time $21,128. Full-time tuition and fees vary according to course load, program, and student level. *College room and board:* $7176; *room only:* $2970. Room and board charges vary according to board plan and housing facility. *Payment plans:* Guaranteed tuition, installment.
FRESHMAN FINANCIAL AID (Fall 2004) 4994 applied for aid; of those 62% were deemed to have need. 95% of freshmen with need received aid; of those 51% had need fully met. *Average percent of need met:* 90% (excluding resources awarded to replace EFC). *Average financial aid package:* $9050 (excluding resources awarded to replace EFC). 27% of all full-time freshmen had no need and received non-need-based gift aid.
UNDERGRADUATE FINANCIAL AID (Fall 2004) 16,335 applied for aid; of those 73% were deemed to have need. 97% of undergraduates with need received aid; of those 54% had need fully met. *Average percent of need met:* 90% (excluding resources awarded to replace EFC). *Average financial aid package:* $9714 (excluding resources awarded to replace EFC). 18% of all full-time undergraduates had no need and received non-need-based gift aid.
GIFT AID (NEED-BASED) *Total amount:* $56,878,280 (24% federal, 41% state, 28% institutional, 7% external sources). *Receiving aid:* Freshmen: 23% (1,733); All full-time undergraduates: 25% (7,410). *Average award:* Freshmen: $6680; Undergraduates: $6234. *Scholarships, grants, and awards:* Federal Pell, FSEOG, state, private, college/university gift aid from institutional funds, United Negro College Fund.
GIFT AID (NON-NEED-BASED) *Total amount:* $10,348,212 (2% federal, 19% state, 49% institutional, 30% external sources). *Receiving aid:* Freshmen: 29% (2,162); Undergraduates: 23% (6,878). *Average Award:* Freshmen: $2706; Undergraduates: $3583. *Scholarships, grants, and awards by category: Academic Interests/Achievement:* agriculture, architecture, area/ethnic studies, biological sciences, business, communication, computer science, education, engineering/technologies, English, foreign languages, general academic interests/achievements, health fields, humanities, international studies, library science, mathematics, military science, physical sciences, social sciences. *Creative Arts/Performance:* applied art and design, art/fine arts, cinema/film/broadcasting, creative writing, dance, general creative arts/performance, journalism/publications,

University of Illinois at Urbana–Champaign

music, performing arts, theater/drama. *Special Achievements/Activities:* community service, general special achievements/activities, leadership, memberships. *Special Characteristics:* children and siblings of alumni, children of faculty/staff, children with a deceased or disabled parent, ethnic background, first-generation college students, general special characteristics, handicapped students, local/state students, members of minority groups, out-of-state students, veterans, veterans' children. *Tuition waivers:* Full or partial for employees or children of employees, senior citizens. *ROTC:* Army, Naval, Air Force.

LOANS *Student loans:* $61,669,305 (94% need-based, 6% non-need-based). 46% of past graduating class borrowed through all loan programs. *Average indebtedness per student:* $15,526. *Average need-based loan:* Freshmen: $3290; Undergraduates: $4114. *Parent loans:* $32,387,228 (57% need-based, 43% non-need-based). *Programs:* Federal Direct (Subsidized and Unsubsidized Stafford, PLUS), Perkins, college/university, alternative loans.

WORK-STUDY *Federal work-study:* Total amount: $2,372,692; 1,877 jobs averaging $1274. *State or other work-study/employment:* Total amount: $13,713,011 (47% need-based, 53% non-need-based). 8,507 part-time jobs averaging $1901.

ATHLETIC AWARDS Total amount: $4,947,118 (30% need-based, 70% non-need-based).

APPLYING FOR FINANCIAL AID *Required financial aid form:* FAFSA. *Financial aid deadline (priority):* 3/15. *Notification date:* 3/15.

CONTACT Daniel Mann, Director of Student Financial Aid, University of Illinois at Urbana–Champaign, Student Services Arcade Building, 620 East John Street, Champaign, IL 61820-5711, 217-333-0100.

UNIVERSITY OF INDIANAPOLIS
Indianapolis, IN

ABOUT THE INSTITUTION Independent religious, coed. Awards: associate, bachelor's, master's, and doctoral degrees. 69 undergraduate majors. Total enrollment: 4,462. Undergraduates: 3,361. Freshmen: 776.

GIFT AID (NEED-BASED) *Scholarships, grants, and awards:* Federal Pell, FSEOG, state, private, college/university gift aid from institutional funds.

GIFT AID (NON-NEED-BASED) *Scholarships, grants, and awards by category: Academic Interests/Achievement:* business, communication, general academic interests/achievements, health fields, physical sciences, religion/biblical studies. *Creative Arts/Performance:* art/fine arts, music, theater/drama. *Special Achievements/Activities:* community service, memberships. *Special Characteristics:* children of faculty/staff, ethnic background, international students, out-of-state students, relatives of clergy, religious affiliation.

LOANS *Programs:* FFEL (Subsidized and Unsubsidized Stafford, PLUS), Perkins, Federal Nursing.

APPLYING FOR FINANCIAL AID *Required financial aid forms:* FAFSA, institution's own form.

CONTACT Ms. Linda B. Handy, Director of Financial Aid, University of Indianapolis, 1400 East Hanna Avenue, Indianapolis, IN 46227-3697, 317-788-3217 or toll-free 800-232-8634 Ext. 3216. *Fax:* 317-788-6136. *E-mail:* handy@uindy.edu.

THE UNIVERSITY OF IOWA
Iowa City, IA

Tuition & fees (IA res): $5935   **Average undergraduate aid package:** $7445

ABOUT THE INSTITUTION State-supported, coed. Awards: bachelor's, master's, doctoral, and first professional degrees and post-master's and first professional certificates. 144 undergraduate majors. Total enrollment: 28,426. Undergraduates: 20,300. Freshmen: 3,849. Federal methodology is used as a basis for awarding need-based institutional aid.

UNDERGRADUATE EXPENSES for 2006–07 *Application fee:* $40. *Tuition, state resident:* full-time $5110; part-time $213 per semester hour. *Tuition, nonresident:* full-time $17,334; part-time $757 per semester hour. *Required fees:* full-time $825; $413 per term part-time. *College room and board:* $6912.

FRESHMAN FINANCIAL AID (Fall 2005, est.) 2983 applied for aid; of those 66% were deemed to have need. 95% of freshmen with need received aid; of those 100% had need fully met. *Average percent of need met:* 99% (excluding resources awarded to replace EFC). *Average financial aid package:* $7213 (excluding resources awarded to replace EFC). 19% of all full-time freshmen had no need and received non-need-based gift aid.

UNDERGRADUATE FINANCIAL AID (Fall 2005, est.) 12,960 applied for aid; of those 74% were deemed to have need. 94% of undergraduates with need received aid; of those 97% had need fully met. *Average percent of need met:* 97% (excluding resources awarded to replace EFC). *Average financial aid package:* $7445 (excluding resources awarded to replace EFC). 14% of all full-time undergraduates had no need and received non-need-based gift aid.

GIFT AID (NEED-BASED) *Total amount:* $24,311,378 (37% federal, 5% state, 53% institutional, 5% external sources). *Receiving aid:* Freshmen: 28% (1,153); All full-time undergraduates: 30% (5,445). *Average award:* Freshmen: $4529; Undergraduates: $4459. *Scholarships, grants, and awards:* Federal Pell, FSEOG, state, private, college/university gift aid from institutional funds.

GIFT AID (NON-NEED-BASED) *Total amount:* $11,341,765 (13% federal, 7% state, 55% institutional, 25% external sources). *Receiving aid:* Freshmen: 24% (978); Undergraduates: 15% (2,730). *Average Award:* Freshmen: $1788; Undergraduates: $1950. *Scholarships, grants, and awards by category: Academic Interests/Achievement:* business, engineering/technologies, general academic interests/achievements. *Creative Arts/Performance:* music, performing arts, theater/drama. *Special Achievements/Activities:* general special achievements/activities. *Special Characteristics:* general special characteristics. *ROTC:* Army, Air Force.

LOANS *Student loans:* $46,117,012 (62% need-based, 38% non-need-based). 58% of past graduating class borrowed through all loan programs. *Average indebtedness per student:* $19,886. *Average need-based loan:* Freshmen: $2845; Undergraduates: $3847. *Parent loans:* $28,578,267 (100% non-need-based). *Programs:* Federal Direct (Subsidized and Unsubsidized Stafford, PLUS), Perkins, Federal Nursing, college/university.

WORK-STUDY *Federal work-study:* Total amount: $2,744,048; 1,200 jobs averaging $2500. *State or other work-study/employment:* Part-time jobs available.

ATHLETIC AWARDS Total amount: $6,094,575 (100% non-need-based).

APPLYING FOR FINANCIAL AID *Required financial aid forms:* FAFSA, institution's own form. *Financial aid deadline:* Continuous. *Notification date:* Continuous beginning 3/1.

CONTACT Mark Warner, Director of Student Financial Aid, The University of Iowa, 208 Calvin Hall, Iowa City, IA 52242, 319-335-1449 or toll-free 800-553-4692.

UNIVERSITY OF JUDAISM
Bel Air, CA

Tuition & fees: $19,330   **Average undergraduate aid package:** $19,860

ABOUT THE INSTITUTION Independent Jewish, coed. Awards: bachelor's and master's degrees. 8 undergraduate majors. Total enrollment: 114. Undergraduates: 114. Both federal and institutional methodology are used as a basis for awarding need-based institutional aid.

UNDERGRADUATE EXPENSES for 2005–06 *Application fee:* $35. *Comprehensive fee:* $32,376 includes full-time tuition ($18,480), mandatory fees ($850), and room and board ($13,046). *College room only:* $7964. Room and board charges vary according to board plan. *Part-time tuition:* $770 per credit. *Payment plan:* Installment.

FRESHMAN FINANCIAL AID (Fall 2004) 16 applied for aid; of those 100% were deemed to have need. 100% of freshmen with need received aid; of those 100% had need fully met. *Average percent of need met:* 100% (excluding resources awarded to replace EFC). *Average financial aid package:* $19,860 (excluding resources awarded to replace EFC). 11% of all full-time freshmen had no need and received non-need-based gift aid.

UNDERGRADUATE FINANCIAL AID (Fall 2004) 119 applied for aid; of those 100% were deemed to have need. 100% of undergraduates with need received aid; of those 100% had need fully met. *Average percent of need met:* 100% (excluding resources awarded to replace EFC). *Average financial aid package:* $19,860 (excluding resources awarded to replace EFC). 5% of all full-time undergraduates had no need and received non-need-based gift aid.

GIFT AID (NEED-BASED) *Total amount:* $836,485 (22% federal, 26% state, 52% institutional). *Receiving aid:* Freshmen: 79% (15); All full-time undergraduates: 54% (71). *Average award:* Freshmen: $6330; Undergraduates: $6499. *Scholarships, grants, and awards:* Federal Pell, FSEOG, state, private, college/university gift aid from institutional funds.

GIFT AID (NON-NEED-BASED) *Total amount:* $60,722 (100% institutional). *Receiving aid:* Freshmen: 11% (2); Undergraduates: 8% (10). *Average Award:* Freshmen: $6370; Undergraduates: $4269. *Scholarships, grants, and awards*

by category: Academic Interests/Achievement: 10 awards ($41,435 total): general academic interests/achievements, premedicine. *Special Achievements/Activities:* 2 awards ($2000 total): leadership.
LOANS *Student loans:* $542,343 (44% need-based, 56% non-need-based). 41% of past graduating class borrowed through all loan programs. *Average indebtedness per student:* $17,000. *Average need-based loan:* Freshmen: $2406; Undergraduates: $4386. *Parent loans:* $213,821 (100% non-need-based). *Programs:* FFEL (Subsidized and Unsubsidized Stafford, PLUS), alternative loans.
WORK-STUDY *Federal work-study:* Total amount: $54,370; 26 jobs averaging $2091. *State or other work-study/employment:* Part-time jobs available.
APPLYING FOR FINANCIAL AID *Required financial aid forms:* FAFSA, institution's own form, parent and student income tax returns. *Financial aid deadline (priority):* 3/2. *Notification date:* Continuous beginning 3/15. Students must reply within 3 weeks of notification.
CONTACT Larisa Zadoyen, Director of Financial Aid, University of Judaism, 15600 Mulholland Drive, Bel Air, CA 90077-1599, 310-476-9777 Ext. 252 or toll-free 888-853-6763. *Fax:* 310-476-4613. *E-mail:* finaid@uj.edu.

UNIVERSITY OF KANSAS
Lawrence, KS

Tuition & fees (KS res): $5413 **Average undergraduate aid package: $7025**

ABOUT THE INSTITUTION State-supported, coed. Awards: bachelor's, master's, doctoral, and first professional degrees and post-master's certificates (University of Kansas is a single institution with academic programs and facilities at two primary locations: Lawrence and Kansas City.). 103 undergraduate majors. Total enrollment: 28,949. Undergraduates: 21,391. Freshmen: 4,201. Federal methodology is used as a basis for awarding need-based institutional aid.
UNDERGRADUATE EXPENSES for 2005–06 *Application fee:* $30. *Tuition, state resident:* full-time $4824; part-time $160.80 per credit hour. *Tuition, nonresident:* full-time $13,277; part-time $442.55 per credit hour. *Required fees:* full-time $589; $49.08 per credit hour. Full-time tuition and fees vary according to program and reciprocity agreements. Part-time tuition and fees vary according to program and reciprocity agreements. *College room and board:* $5502; *room only:* $2752. Room and board charges vary according to board plan and housing facility. *Payment plan:* Installment.
FRESHMAN FINANCIAL AID (Fall 2004) 2598 applied for aid; of those 61% were deemed to have need. 95% of freshmen with need received aid; of those 23% had need fully met. *Average percent of need met:* 62% (excluding resources awarded to replace EFC). *Average financial aid package:* $5933 (excluding resources awarded to replace EFC). 10% of all full-time freshmen had no need and received non-need-based gift aid.
UNDERGRADUATE FINANCIAL AID (Fall 2004) 9,771 applied for aid; of those 70% were deemed to have need. 96% of undergraduates with need received aid; of those 26% had need fully met. *Average percent of need met:* 69% (excluding resources awarded to replace EFC). *Average financial aid package:* $7025 (excluding resources awarded to replace EFC). 9% of all full-time undergraduates had no need and received non-need-based gift aid.
GIFT AID (NEED-BASED) *Total amount:* $17,972,152 (49% federal, 8% state, 29% institutional, 14% external sources). *Receiving aid:* Freshmen: 30% (1,263); All full-time undergraduates: 28% (5,027). *Average award:* Freshmen: $3752; Undergraduates: $3660. *Scholarships, grants, and awards:* Federal Pell, FSEOG, state, private, college/university gift aid from institutional funds.
GIFT AID (NON-NEED-BASED) *Total amount:* $5,971,340 (86% institutional, 14% external sources). *Receiving aid:* Freshmen: 19; Undergraduates: 53. *Average Award:* Freshmen: $2538; Undergraduates: $4001. *Scholarships, grants, and awards by category: Academic Interests/Achievement:* architecture, area/ethnic studies, biological sciences, business, communication, computer science, education, engineering/technologies, English, foreign languages, general academic interests/achievements, health fields, humanities, international studies, library science, mathematics, military science, physical sciences, premedicine, religion/biblical studies, social sciences. *Creative Arts/Performance:* applied art and design, art/fine arts, cinema/film/broadcasting, creative writing, dance, debating, general creative arts/performance, journalism/publications, music, performing arts, theater/drama. *Special Achievements/Activities:* community service, general special achievements/activities, leadership. *Special Characteristics:* adult students, children of faculty/staff, ethnic background, first-generation college students, general special characteristics, international students, local/state students, married students, members of minority groups, out-of-state students, previous college experience. *Tuition waivers:* Full or partial for employees or children of employees. *ROTC:* Army, Naval, Air Force.
LOANS *Student loans:* $45,639,791 (53% need-based, 47% non-need-based). 42% of past graduating class borrowed through all loan programs. *Average indebtedness per student:* $17,243. *Average need-based loan:* Freshmen: $2067; Undergraduates: $3723. *Parent loans:* $22,399,849 (100% non-need-based). *Programs:* Federal Direct (Subsidized and Unsubsidized Stafford, PLUS), Perkins, college/university.
WORK-STUDY *Federal work-study:* Total amount: $826,388; 396 jobs averaging $2087. *State or other work-study/employment:* Total amount: $454,120 (100% non-need-based). 106 part-time jobs averaging $3783.
ATHLETIC AWARDS *Total amount:* $5,189,280 (39% need-based, 61% non-need-based).
APPLYING FOR FINANCIAL AID *Required financial aid form:* FAFSA. *Financial aid deadline (priority):* 3/1. *Notification date:* Continuous beginning 4/1. Students must reply within 2 weeks of notification.
CONTACT Ms. Brenda Maigaard, Director of Student Financial Aid, University of Kansas, Office of Student Financial Aid, 50 Strong Hall, 1450 Jayhawk Boulevard, Lawrence, KS 66045-7535, 785-864-4700 or toll-free 888-686-7323 (in-state). *Fax:* 785-864-5469. *E-mail:* osfa@ku.edu.

UNIVERSITY OF KENTUCKY
Lexington, KY

Tuition & fees (KY res): $5812 **Average undergraduate aid package: $7861**

ABOUT THE INSTITUTION State-supported, coed. Awards: bachelor's, master's, doctoral, and first professional degrees and post-master's certificates. 80 undergraduate majors. Total enrollment: 25,672. Undergraduates: 18,702. Freshmen: 3,835. Federal methodology is used as a basis for awarding need-based institutional aid.
UNDERGRADUATE EXPENSES for 2005–06 *Application fee:* $40. *Tuition, state resident:* full-time $5162; part-time $216 per credit hour. *Tuition, nonresident:* full-time $12,148; part-time $507 per credit hour. *Required fees:* full-time $650; $16.25 per credit hour. Full-time tuition and fees vary according to degree level, program, reciprocity agreements, and student level. Part-time tuition and fees vary according to degree level, program, reciprocity agreements, and student level. *College room and board:* $5129; *room only:* $3363. Room and board charges vary according to board plan and housing facility. *Payment plan:* Installment.
FRESHMAN FINANCIAL AID (Fall 2005, est.) 2387 applied for aid; of those 64% were deemed to have need. 99% of freshmen with need received aid; of those 45% had need fully met. *Average percent of need met:* 79% (excluding resources awarded to replace EFC). *Average financial aid package:* $7252 (excluding resources awarded to replace EFC). 9% of all full-time freshmen had no need and received non-need-based gift aid.
UNDERGRADUATE FINANCIAL AID (Fall 2005, est.) 9,067 applied for aid; of those 73% were deemed to have need. 99% of undergraduates with need received aid; of those 45% had need fully met. *Average percent of need met:* 81% (excluding resources awarded to replace EFC). *Average financial aid package:* $7861 (excluding resources awarded to replace EFC). 3% of all full-time undergraduates had no need and received non-need-based gift aid.
GIFT AID (NEED-BASED) *Total amount:* $54,808,033 (17% federal, 37% state, 40% institutional, 6% external sources). *Receiving aid:* Freshmen: 20% (777); All full-time undergraduates: 24% (4,012). *Average award:* Freshmen: $5743; Undergraduates: $4854. *Scholarships, grants, and awards:* Federal Pell, FSEOG, state, private, college/university gift aid from institutional funds.
GIFT AID (NON-NEED-BASED) *Receiving aid:* Freshmen: 35% (1,328); Undergraduates: 25% (4,305). *Average Award:* Freshmen: $3225; Undergraduates: $2821. *Scholarships, grants, and awards by category: Academic Interests/Achievement:* agriculture, architecture, biological sciences, business, communication, education, engineering/technologies, foreign languages, general academic interests/achievements, health fields, home economics, mathematics, military science, physical sciences. *Creative Arts/Performance:* applied art and design, art/fine arts, debating, general creative arts/performance, journalism/publications, music, performing arts. *Special Achievements/Activities:* cheerleading/drum major, general special achievements/activities, leadership. *Special Characteristics:* adult students, children and siblings of alumni, children of educators, children of faculty/staff, children of public servants, children of union members/company employees, children of workers in trades, children with a deceased or disabled parent, ethnic background, first-generation college students, general special

University of Kentucky

characteristics, handicapped students, international students, members of minority groups, spouses of deceased or disabled public servants, veterans, veterans' children. **Tuition waivers:** Full or partial for employees or children of employees, senior citizens. **ROTC:** Army, Air Force.
LOANS Student loans: $39,252,611 (100% need-based). 68% of past graduating class borrowed through all loan programs. *Average indebtedness per student:* $17,692. *Average need-based loan:* Freshmen: $2599; Undergraduates: $3765. *Parent loans:* $10,167,588 (100% need-based). *Programs:* Federal Direct (Subsidized and Unsubsidized Stafford, PLUS), FFEL (Subsidized and Unsubsidized Stafford, PLUS), Perkins, Federal Nursing, college/university.
WORK-STUDY *Federal work-study:* Total amount: $964,642; 489 jobs averaging $2038. *State or other work-study/employment:* Part-time jobs available.
ATHLETIC AWARDS *Total amount:* $4,653,214 (100% need-based).
APPLYING FOR FINANCIAL AID *Required financial aid form:* FAFSA. *Financial aid deadline (priority):* 2/15. *Notification date:* Continuous beginning 4/1. Students must reply within 3 weeks of notification.
CONTACT Ms. Lynda S. George, Director of Financial Aid, University of Kentucky, 128 Funkhouser Building, Lexington, KY 40506-0054, 859-257-3172 Ext. 241 or toll-free 800-432-0967 (in-state). *Fax:* 859-257-4398. *E-mail:* lgeorge@email.uky.edu.

UNIVERSITY OF LA VERNE
La Verne, CA

ABOUT THE INSTITUTION Independent, coed. Awards: associate, bachelor's, master's, doctoral, and first professional degrees and post-bachelor's and post-master's certificates (also offers continuing education program with significant enrollment not reflected in profile). 48 undergraduate majors. Total enrollment: 4,000. Undergraduates: 1,685. Freshmen: 339.
GIFT AID (NEED-BASED) *Scholarships, grants, and awards:* Federal Pell, FSEOG, state, private, college/university gift aid from institutional funds.
GIFT AID (NON-NEED-BASED) *Scholarships, grants, and awards by category: Academic Interests/Achievement:* general academic interests/achievements. *Creative Arts/Performance:* art/fine arts, debating, journalism/publications, music, theater/drama. *Special Achievements/Activities:* community service, leadership. *Special Characteristics:* children and siblings of alumni, children of faculty/staff, ethnic background, first-generation college students, general special characteristics, international students, religious affiliation.
LOANS *Programs:* FFEL (Subsidized and Unsubsidized Stafford, PLUS), Perkins, college/university, alternative loans.
WORK-STUDY *Federal work-study:* Total amount: $616,481; 752 jobs averaging $1997. *State or other work-study/employment:* Part-time jobs available.
APPLYING FOR FINANCIAL AID *Required financial aid forms:* FAFSA, state aid form.
CONTACT Leatha Webster, Director of Financial Aid, University of La Verne, 1950 3rd Street, La Verne, CA 91750-4443, 909-593-3511 Ext. 4180 or toll-free 800-876-4858. *Fax:* 909-392-2751. *E-mail:* websterl@ulv.edu.

UNIVERSITY OF LOUISIANA AT LAFAYETTE
Lafayette, LA

Tuition & fees (LA res): $3324   **Average undergraduate aid package:** $5562

ABOUT THE INSTITUTION State-supported, coed. Awards: bachelor's, master's, and doctoral degrees and post-master's certificates. 89 undergraduate majors. Total enrollment: 17,075. Undergraduates: 15,564. Freshmen: 2,943. Federal methodology is used as a basis for awarding need-based institutional aid.
UNDERGRADUATE EXPENSES for 2005–06 *Application fee:* $25. *Tuition, state resident:* full-time $3324; part-time $92.75 per credit hour. *Tuition, nonresident:* full-time $9504; part-time $350.25 per credit hour. Full-time tuition and fees vary according to course load. Part-time tuition and fees vary according to course load. *College room and board:* $3478. Room and board charges vary according to board plan and housing facility. *Payment plan:* Deferred payment.
FRESHMAN FINANCIAL AID (Fall 2004) 2328 applied for aid; of those 67% were deemed to have need. 97% of freshmen with need received aid; of those 13% had need fully met. *Average percent of need met:* 55% (excluding resources awarded to replace EFC). *Average financial aid package:* $4800 (excluding resources awarded to replace EFC). 23% of all full-time freshmen had no need and received non-need-based gift aid.
UNDERGRADUATE FINANCIAL AID (Fall 2004) 9,264 applied for aid; of those 73% were deemed to have need. 97% of undergraduates with need received aid; of those 9% had need fully met. *Average percent of need met:* 53% (excluding resources awarded to replace EFC). *Average financial aid package:* $5562 (excluding resources awarded to replace EFC). 12% of all full-time undergraduates had no need and received non-need-based gift aid.
GIFT AID (NEED-BASED) *Total amount:* $13,455,310 (99% federal, 1% state). *Receiving aid:* Freshmen: 53% (1,394); All full-time undergraduates: 45% (5,586). *Average award:* Freshmen: $3796; Undergraduates: $3679. *Scholarships, grants, and awards:* Federal Pell, FSEOG, state, college/university gift aid from institutional funds.
GIFT AID (NON-NEED-BASED) *Total amount:* $13,878,542 (73% state, 19% institutional, 8% external sources). *Receiving aid:* Freshmen: 7% (185); Undergraduates: 4% (490). *Average Award:* Freshmen: $1549; Undergraduates: $1744. *Scholarships, grants, and awards by category: Academic Interests/Achievement:* 1,478 awards ($2,578,852 total): general academic interests/achievements. *Creative Arts/Performance:* general creative arts/performance. *Special Achievements/Activities:* general special achievements/activities. *Tuition waivers:* Full or partial for children of alumni, employees or children of employees, senior citizens. *ROTC:* Army.
LOANS *Student loans:* $26,527,473 (66% need-based, 34% non-need-based). *Average need-based loan:* Freshmen: $2250; Undergraduates: $3663. *Parent loans:* $1,082,306 (100% non-need-based). *Programs:* FFEL (Subsidized and Unsubsidized Stafford, PLUS), Perkins, Federal Nursing.
WORK-STUDY *Federal work-study:* Total amount: $922,932; 660 jobs averaging $1504. *State or other work-study/employment:* Total amount: $293,132 (100% non-need-based). 234 part-time jobs averaging $1253.
ATHLETIC AWARDS *Total amount:* $1,600,866 (100% non-need-based).
APPLYING FOR FINANCIAL AID *Required financial aid form:* FAFSA. *Financial aid deadline (priority):* 5/1. *Notification date:* Continuous beginning 5/1. Students must reply within 2 weeks of notification.
CONTACT Cindy S. Perez, Director of Financial Aid, University of Louisiana at Lafayette, PO Box 41206, Lafayette, LA 70504-1206, 337-482-6497 or toll-free 800-752-6553 (in-state). *Fax:* 337-482-6502. *E-mail:* cperez@louisiana.edu.

UNIVERSITY OF LOUISIANA AT MONROE
Monroe, LA

CONTACT Roslynn Pogue, Assistant Director, Financial Aid, University of Louisiana at Monroe, 700 University Avenue, Monroe, LA 71209, 318-342-5320 or toll-free 800-372-5272 (in-state), 800-372-5127 (out-of-state). *Fax:* 318-342-3539. *E-mail:* sspogue@ulm.edu.

UNIVERSITY OF LOUISVILLE
Louisville, KY

Tuition & fees (KY res): $5532   **Average undergraduate aid package:** $8175

ABOUT THE INSTITUTION State-supported, coed. Awards: associate, bachelor's, master's, doctoral, and first professional degrees and post-bachelor's and post-master's certificates. 50 undergraduate majors. Total enrollment: 20,734. Undergraduates: 14,933. Freshmen: 2,313. Federal methodology is used as a basis for awarding need-based institutional aid.
UNDERGRADUATE EXPENSES for 2005–06 *Application fee:* $30. *Tuition, state resident:* full-time $5532; part-time $231 per hour. *Tuition, nonresident:* full-time $15,092; part-time $629 per hour. Full-time tuition and fees vary according to reciprocity agreements. Part-time tuition and fees vary according to course load and reciprocity agreements. *College room and board:* $6036; *room only:* $4490. Room and board charges vary according to board plan and housing facility. *Payment plan:* Installment.
FRESHMAN FINANCIAL AID (Fall 2005, est.) 1564 applied for aid; of those 82% were deemed to have need. 99% of freshmen with need received aid; of those 17% had need fully met. *Average percent of need met:* 56% (excluding resources awarded to replace EFC). *Average financial aid package:* $8229 (excluding resources awarded to replace EFC). 22% of all full-time freshmen had no need and received non-need-based gift aid.
UNDERGRADUATE FINANCIAL AID (Fall 2005, est.) 6,867 applied for aid; of those 87% were deemed to have need. 97% of undergraduates with need received aid; of those 12% had need fully met. *Average percent of need met:* 55% (excluding resources awarded to replace EFC). *Average financial aid*

package: $8175 (excluding resources awarded to replace EFC). 16% of all full-time undergraduates had no need and received non-need-based gift aid. **GIFT AID (NEED-BASED)** *Total amount:* $29,945,200 (32% federal, 26% state, 35% institutional, 7% external sources). *Receiving aid:* Freshmen: 52% (1,188); All full-time undergraduates: 43% (4,872). *Average award:* Freshmen: $5876; Undergraduates: $5473. *Scholarships, grants, and awards:* Federal Pell, FSEOG, state, private, college/university gift aid from institutional funds. **GIFT AID (NON-NEED-BASED)** *Total amount:* $17,584,423 (33% state, 59% institutional, 8% external sources). *Receiving aid:* Freshmen: 7% (164); Undergraduates: 3% (371). *Average Award:* Freshmen: $5541; Undergraduates: $5184. *Scholarships, grants, and awards by category:* Academic Interests/Achievement: general academic interests/achievements. Creative Arts/Performance: general creative arts/performance. Special Achievements/Activities: general special achievements/activities, memberships. Special Characteristics: general special characteristics. *Tuition waivers:* Full or partial for employees or children of employees, senior citizens. *ROTC:* Army, Air Force. **LOANS** *Student loans:* $26,575,303 (86% need-based, 14% non-need-based). 42% of past graduating class borrowed through all loan programs. *Average indebtedness per student:* $15,128. *Average need-based loan:* Freshmen: $2618; Undergraduates: $3976. *Parent loans:* $2,142,672 (49% need-based, 51% non-need-based). *Programs:* FFEL (Subsidized and Unsubsidized Stafford, PLUS), Perkins, Federal Nursing, college/university. **WORK-STUDY** *Federal work-study:* Total amount: $1,395,988; jobs available. **ATHLETIC AWARDS** *Total amount:* $5,347,253 (34% need-based, 66% non-need-based). **APPLYING FOR FINANCIAL AID** *Required financial aid form:* FAFSA. *Financial aid deadline (priority):* 3/15. *Notification date:* Continuous beginning 4/1. Students must reply by 5/1. **CONTACT** Ms. Patricia O. Arauz, Director of Financial Aid, University of Louisville, 2301 South Third Street, Louisville, KY 40292-0001, 502-852-6145 or toll-free 502-852-6531 (in-state), 800-334-8635 (out-of-state). *Fax:* 502-852-0182. *E-mail:* finaid@louisville.edu.

UNIVERSITY OF MAINE
Orono, ME

Tuition & fees (ME res): $6910   Average undergraduate aid package: $9147

ABOUT THE INSTITUTION State-supported, coed. Awards: bachelor's, master's, and doctoral degrees and post-master's certificates. 105 undergraduate majors. Total enrollment: 11,435. Undergraduates: 9,179. Freshmen: 1,753. Federal methodology is used as a basis for awarding need-based institutional aid. **UNDERGRADUATE EXPENSES for 2005–06** *Application fee:* $40. *Tuition, state resident:* full-time $5520; part-time $184 per credit hour. *Tuition, nonresident:* full-time $15,660; part-time $522 per credit hour. Full-time tuition and fees vary according to reciprocity agreements. Part-time tuition and fees vary according to reciprocity agreements. *College room and board:* $6732; room only: $3390. Room and board charges vary according to board plan and housing facility. *Payment plan:* Installment. **FRESHMAN FINANCIAL AID (Fall 2005, est.)** 1710 applied for aid; of those 76% were deemed to have need. 98% of freshmen with need received aid; of those 26% had need fully met. *Average percent of need met:* 83% (excluding resources awarded to replace EFC). *Average financial aid package:* $9170 (excluding resources awarded to replace EFC). 20% of all full-time freshmen had no need and received non-need-based gift aid. **UNDERGRADUATE FINANCIAL AID (Fall 2005, est.)** 6,848 applied for aid; of those 80% were deemed to have need. 98% of undergraduates with need received aid; of those 28% had need fully met. *Average percent of need met:* 84% (excluding resources awarded to replace EFC). *Average financial aid package:* $9147 (excluding resources awarded to replace EFC). 22% of all full-time undergraduates had no need and received non-need-based gift aid. **GIFT AID (NEED-BASED)** *Total amount:* $20,022,710 (42% federal, 13% state, 35% institutional, 10% external sources). *Receiving aid:* Freshmen: 50% (1,083); All full-time undergraduates: 55% (4,144). *Average award:* Freshmen: $5766; Undergraduates: $4890. *Scholarships, grants, and awards:* Federal Pell, FSEOG, state, private, college/university gift aid from institutional funds. **GIFT AID (NON-NEED-BASED)** *Total amount:* $5,203,989 (1% state, 19% institutional, 80% external sources). *Receiving aid:* Freshmen: 4% (94); Undergraduates: 4% (319). *Average Award:* Freshmen: $4533; Undergraduates: $5625. *Scholarships, grants, and awards by category:* Academic Interests/

University of Maine at Farmington

Achievement: 786 awards ($1,980,211 total): biological sciences, business, communication, computer science, education, engineering/technologies, English, general academic interests/achievements, humanities, mathematics, military science, physical sciences, social sciences. Creative Arts/Performance: applied art and design, art/fine arts, creative writing, journalism/publications, music, performing arts, theater/drama. Special Achievements/Activities: community service, general special achievements/activities, leadership, memberships. Special Characteristics: children and siblings of alumni, children of faculty/staff, children of union members/company employees, children with a deceased or disabled parent, ethnic background, international students, local/state students, members of minority groups, out-of-state students, previous college experience, public servants, veterans, veterans' children. *Tuition waivers:* Full or partial for employees or children of employees. *ROTC:* Army, Naval. **LOANS** *Student loans:* $29,556,563 (65% need-based, 35% non-need-based). 72% of past graduating class borrowed through all loan programs. *Average indebtedness per student:* $20,700. *Average need-based loan:* Freshmen: $3007; Undergraduates: $4094. *Parent loans:* $5,447,590 (100% non-need-based). *Programs:* FFEL (Subsidized and Unsubsidized Stafford, PLUS, Perkins, state, college/university. **WORK-STUDY** *Federal work-study:* Total amount: $3,539,397; 1,916 jobs averaging $1755. **ATHLETIC AWARDS** *Total amount:* $2,168,947 (25% need-based, 75% non-need-based). **APPLYING FOR FINANCIAL AID** *Required financial aid form:* FAFSA. *Financial aid deadline (priority):* 3/1. *Notification date:* Continuous beginning 3/15. Students must reply by 5/1 or within 2 weeks of notification. **CONTACT** Ms. Peggy L. Crawford, Director of Student Aid, University of Maine, 5781 Wingate Hall, Orono, ME 04469, 207-581-1324 or toll-free 877-486-2364. *Fax:* 207-581-3261. *E-mail:* peggy.crawford@umit.maine.edu.

THE UNIVERSITY OF MAINE AT AUGUSTA
Augusta, ME

ABOUT THE INSTITUTION State-supported, coed. Awards: associate and bachelor's degrees and post-bachelor's certificates (also offers some graduate courses and continuing education programs with significant enrollment not reflected in profile). 26 undergraduate majors. Total enrollment: 5,494. Undergraduates: 5,494. Freshmen: 526. **GIFT AID (NEED-BASED)** *Scholarships, grants, and awards:* Federal Pell, FSEOG, state, private, college/university gift aid from institutional funds. **GIFT AID (NON-NEED-BASED)** *Scholarships, grants, and awards by category:* Academic Interests/Achievement: biological sciences, business, general academic interests/achievements, mathematics. Creative Arts/Performance: music. Special Achievements/Activities: general special achievements/activities, leadership. Special Characteristics: children of faculty/staff, ethnic background, international students, local/state students, veterans' children. **LOANS** *Programs:* Federal Direct (Subsidized and Unsubsidized Stafford), FFEL (Subsidized and Unsubsidized Stafford, PLUS), Perkins, Federal Nursing. **WORK-STUDY** *Federal work-study:* Total amount: $363,232; 241 jobs averaging $1507. **APPLYING FOR FINANCIAL AID** *Required financial aid form:* FAFSA. **CONTACT** Sherry McCollett, Financial Aid Counselor, The University of Maine at Augusta, 46 University Drive, Augusta, ME 04330-9410, 207-621-3455 or toll-free 877-862-1234 Ext. 3185 (in-state). *Fax:* 207-621-3116. *E-mail:* sherrym@maine.edu.

UNIVERSITY OF MAINE AT FARMINGTON
Farmington, ME

Tuition & fees (ME res): $5631   Average undergraduate aid package: $8156

ABOUT THE INSTITUTION State-supported, coed. Awards: bachelor's degrees. 40 undergraduate majors. Total enrollment: 2,452. Undergraduates: 2,452. Freshmen: 555. Federal methodology is used as a basis for awarding need-based institutional aid. **UNDERGRADUATE EXPENSES for 2005–06** *Application fee:* $40. *Tuition, state resident:* full-time $5010; part-time $167 per credit hour. *Tuition, nonresident:* full-time $12,240; part-time $408 per credit hour. *Required fees:* full-time $621; $75 per term part-time. Full-time tuition and fees vary according to course load, reciprocity agreements, and student level. Part-time tuition and

University of Maine at Farmington

fees vary according to course load, reciprocity agreements, and student level. *College room and board:* $5984; *room only:* $3200. Room and board charges vary according to board plan and housing facility. *Payment plan:* Installment.

FRESHMAN FINANCIAL AID (Fall 2005, est.) 519 applied for aid; of those 76% were deemed to have need. 99% of freshmen with need received aid; of those 15% had need fully met. *Average percent of need met:* 79% (excluding resources awarded to replace EFC). *Average financial aid package:* $8398 (excluding resources awarded to replace EFC). 4% of all full-time freshmen had no need and received non-need-based gift aid.

UNDERGRADUATE FINANCIAL AID (Fall 2005, est.) 1,767 applied for aid; of those 80% were deemed to have need. 99% of undergraduates with need received aid; of those 22% had need fully met. *Average percent of need met:* 79% (excluding resources awarded to replace EFC). *Average financial aid package:* $8156 (excluding resources awarded to replace EFC). 4% of all full-time undergraduates had no need and received non-need-based gift aid.

GIFT AID (NEED-BASED) *Total amount:* $5,136,260 (50% federal, 17% state, 32% institutional, 1% external sources). *Receiving aid:* Freshmen: 60% (329); All full-time undergraduates: 54% (1,136). *Average award:* Freshmen: $4641; Undergraduates: $4007. *Scholarships, grants, and awards:* Federal Pell, FSEOG, state, private, college/university gift aid from institutional funds.

GIFT AID (NON-NEED-BASED) *Total amount:* $1,714,865 (28% institutional, 72% external sources). *Receiving aid:* Freshmen: 48% (263); Undergraduates: 26% (554). *Average Award:* Freshmen: $1457; Undergraduates: $1647. *Scholarships, grants, and awards by category:* Academic Interests/Achievement: general academic interests/achievements. Special Characteristics: children of faculty/staff, members of minority groups, out-of-state students, veterans' children. *Tuition waivers:* Full or partial for minority students, employees or children of employees, senior citizens.

LOANS *Student loans:* $9,840,408 (54% need-based, 46% non-need-based). 80% of past graduating class borrowed through all loan programs. *Average indebtedness per student:* $16,289. *Average need-based loan:* Freshmen: $3199; Undergraduates: $3671. *Parent loans:* $6,902,049 (82% need-based, 18% non-need-based). *Programs:* FFEL (Subsidized and Unsubsidized Stafford, PLUS), Perkins, college/university, Educators For Maine Loans.

WORK-STUDY *Federal work-study:* Total amount: $766,961; 525 jobs averaging $1013. *State or other work-study/employment:* Total amount: $1,178,325 (100% non-need-based). 529 part-time jobs available.

APPLYING FOR FINANCIAL AID *Required financial aid form:* FAFSA. *Financial aid deadline (priority):* 3/1. *Notification date:* Continuous beginning 3/15. Students must reply within 2 weeks of notification.

CONTACT Mr. Ronald P. Milliken, Director of Financial Aid, University of Maine at Farmington, 224 Main Street, Farmington, ME 04938-1990, 207-778-7105. *Fax:* 207-788-8178. *E-mail:* milliken@maine.edu.

UNIVERSITY OF MAINE AT FORT KENT
Fort Kent, ME

ABOUT THE INSTITUTION State-supported, coed. Awards: associate and bachelor's degrees. 25 undergraduate majors. Total enrollment: 1,076. Undergraduates: 1,076.

GIFT AID (NEED-BASED) *Scholarships, grants, and awards:* Federal Pell, FSEOG, state, private, college/university gift aid from institutional funds.

GIFT AID (NON-NEED-BASED) *Scholarships, grants, and awards by category:* Academic Interests/Achievement: business, computer science, education, English, foreign languages, general academic interests/achievements, health fields, humanities, mathematics, social sciences. Creative Arts/Performance: general creative arts/performance, performing arts. Special Achievements/Activities: general special achievements/activities. Special Characteristics: adult students, children of faculty/staff, general special characteristics, international students, members of minority groups.

LOANS *Programs:* FFEL (Subsidized and Unsubsidized Stafford, PLUS), Perkins, state.

WORK-STUDY *Federal work-study:* Total amount: $140,363; 119 jobs averaging $1500. *State or other work-study/employment:* Total amount: $48,687 (8% need-based, 92% non-need-based). 44 part-time jobs averaging $1500.

APPLYING FOR FINANCIAL AID *Required financial aid form:* FAFSA.

CONTACT Ellen Cost, Director of Financial Aid, University of Maine at Fort Kent, 23 University Drive, Fort Kent, ME 04743-1292, 207-834-7606 or toll-free 888-TRY-UMFK. *Fax:* 207-834-7841. *E-mail:* ecost@maine.edu.

UNIVERSITY OF MAINE AT MACHIAS
Machias, ME

CONTACT Ms. Stephanie Larrabee, Director of Financial Aid, University of Maine at Machias, 9 O'Brien Avenue, Machias, ME 04654, 207-255-1203 or toll-free 888-GOTOUMM. *Fax:* 207-255-4864.

UNIVERSITY OF MAINE AT PRESQUE ISLE
Presque Isle, ME

Tuition & fees (ME res): $4820   **Average undergraduate aid package:** $7248

ABOUT THE INSTITUTION State-supported, coed. Awards: associate and bachelor's degrees. 28 undergraduate majors. Total enrollment: 1,548. Undergraduates: 1,548. Freshmen: 211. Federal methodology is used as a basis for awarding need-based institutional aid.

UNDERGRADUATE EXPENSES for 2005–06 *Application fee:* $40. *Tuition, state resident:* full-time $4290; part-time $143 per credit hour. *Tuition, nonresident:* full-time $10,680; part-time $356 per credit hour. *Required fees:* full-time $530; $19 per credit hour. Full-time tuition and fees vary according to course load and reciprocity agreements. Part-time tuition and fees vary according to course load and reciprocity agreements. *College room and board:* $5246; *room only:* $3000. Room and board charges vary according to board plan. *Payment plans:* Installment, deferred payment.

FRESHMAN FINANCIAL AID (Fall 2005, est.) 187 applied for aid; of those 86% were deemed to have need. 86% of freshmen with need received aid; of those 41% had need fully met. *Average percent of need met:* 89% (excluding resources awarded to replace EFC). *Average financial aid package:* $6790 (excluding resources awarded to replace EFC). 10% of all full-time freshmen had no need and received non-need-based gift aid.

UNDERGRADUATE FINANCIAL AID (Fall 2005, est.) 800 applied for aid; of those 87% were deemed to have need. 91% of undergraduates with need received aid; of those 42% had need fully met. *Average percent of need met:* 89% (excluding resources awarded to replace EFC). *Average financial aid package:* $7248 (excluding resources awarded to replace EFC). 8% of all full-time undergraduates had no need and received non-need-based gift aid.

GIFT AID (NEED-BASED) *Total amount:* $2,814,357 (68% federal, 14% state, 10% institutional, 8% external sources). *Receiving aid:* Freshmen: 66% (124); All full-time undergraduates: 52% (576). *Average award:* Freshmen: $5288; Undergraduates: $4509. *Scholarships, grants, and awards:* Federal Pell, FSEOG, state, private, college/university gift aid from institutional funds.

GIFT AID (NON-NEED-BASED) *Total amount:* $144,096 (1% federal, 35% institutional, 64% external sources). *Receiving aid:* Freshmen: 5% (9); Undergraduates: 3% (30). *Average Award:* Freshmen: $4390; Undergraduates: $4046. *Scholarships, grants, and awards by category:* Academic Interests/Achievement: general academic interests/achievements. Creative Arts/Performance: art/fine arts. Special Achievements/Activities: community service. Special Characteristics: children of faculty/staff, ethnic background, international students, veterans' children. *Tuition waivers:* Full or partial for minority students, employees or children of employees, senior citizens.

LOANS *Student loans:* $2,545,840 (63% need-based, 37% non-need-based). 33% of past graduating class borrowed through all loan programs. *Average indebtedness per student:* $11,181. *Average need-based loan:* Freshmen: $2499; Undergraduates: $3323. *Parent loans:* $174,692 (100% non-need-based). *Programs:* Federal Direct (Subsidized and Unsubsidized Stafford, PLUS), Perkins, state, college/university.

WORK-STUDY *Federal work-study:* Total amount: $450,200; 283 jobs averaging $1318.

APPLYING FOR FINANCIAL AID *Required financial aid form:* FAFSA. *Financial aid deadline (priority):* 4/1. *Notification date:* Continuous beginning 3/1. Students must reply within 2 weeks of notification.

CONTACT Christopher A. R. Bill, (Acting) Director of Financial Aid, University of Maine at Presque Isle, 181 Main Street, Presque Isle, ME 04769-2888, 207-768-9511. *Fax:* 207-768-9608. *E-mail:* chris@maine.edu.

UNIVERSITY OF MANAGEMENT AND TECHNOLOGY
Arlington, VA

CONTACT Financial Aid Office, University of Management and Technology, 1901 North Fort Myer Drive, Arlington, VA 22209, 703-516-0035 or toll-free 800-924-4885 (in-state). *E-mail:* info@umtweb.edu.

UNIVERSITY OF MARY
Bismarck, ND

Tuition & fees: $11,324   **Average undergraduate aid package: N/A**

ABOUT THE INSTITUTION Independent Roman Catholic, coed. Awards: associate, bachelor's, master's, and doctoral degrees. 37 undergraduate majors. Total enrollment: 2,758. Undergraduates: 2,197. Freshmen: 352. Federal methodology is used as a basis for awarding need-based institutional aid.

UNDERGRADUATE EXPENSES for 2006-07 *Application fee:* $25. *Comprehensive fee:* $15,374 includes full-time tuition ($11,100), mandatory fees ($224), and room and board ($4050). *College room only:* $1750. *Part-time tuition:* $350 per credit. *Part-time fees:* $7 per credit.

FRESHMAN FINANCIAL AID (Fall 2004) 404 applied for aid; of those 67% were deemed to have need. 100% of freshmen with need received aid; of those 19% had need fully met.

GIFT AID (NEED-BASED) *Total amount:* $7,498,400 (29% federal, 3% state, 62% institutional, 6% external sources). *Receiving aid:* Freshmen: 63% (271). *Scholarships, grants, and awards:* Federal Pell, FSEOG, state, private, college/university gift aid from institutional funds.

GIFT AID (NON-NEED-BASED) *Receiving aid:* Freshmen: 63% (271). *Scholarships, grants, and awards by category: Academic Interests/Achievement:* 1,539 awards ($4,362,950 total): general academic interests/achievements. *Creative Arts/Performance:* 52 awards ($277,865 total): debating, music, theater/drama. *Special Characteristics:* 94 awards ($310,385 total): children of faculty/staff.

LOANS *Student loans:* $12,525,493 (54% need-based, 46% non-need-based). *Parent loans:* $1,359,703 (100% need-based). *Programs:* FFEL (Subsidized and Unsubsidized Stafford, PLUS), Perkins, Federal Nursing, college/university.

WORK-STUDY *Federal work-study:* Total amount: $309,873; 295 jobs averaging $1050. *State or other work-study/employment:* Total amount: $73,248 (100% non-need-based). 132 part-time jobs averaging $555.

ATHLETIC AWARDS Total amount: $1,617,665 (100% need-based).

APPLYING FOR FINANCIAL AID *Required financial aid form:* FAFSA. *Financial aid deadline (priority):* 5/1. *Notification date:* Continuous. Students must reply within 2 weeks of notification.

CONTACT Dave Hanson, Director of Financial Aid, University of Mary, 7500 University Drive, Bismarck, ND 58504-9652, 701-255-7500 Ext. 8079 or toll-free 800-288-6279. *Fax:* 701-255-7687.

UNIVERSITY OF MARY HARDIN-BAYLOR
Belton, TX

Tuition & fees: $15,710   **Average undergraduate aid package: $12,511**

ABOUT THE INSTITUTION Independent Southern Baptist, coed. Awards: bachelor's and master's degrees. 52 undergraduate majors. Total enrollment: 2,727. Undergraduates: 2,591. Freshmen: 499. Federal methodology is used as a basis for awarding need-based institutional aid.

UNDERGRADUATE EXPENSES for 2006-07 *Application fee:* $35. *Comprehensive fee:* $19,910 includes full-time tuition ($14,250), mandatory fees ($1460), and room and board ($4200). *Part-time tuition:* $475 per semester hour. *Part-time fees:* $47 per semester hour; $30 per term.

FRESHMAN FINANCIAL AID (Fall 2005, est.) 472 applied for aid; of those 76% were deemed to have need. 98% of freshmen with need received aid; of those 24% had need fully met. *Average percent of need met:* 64% (excluding resources awarded to replace EFC). *Average financial aid package:* $10,113 (excluding resources awarded to replace EFC). 25% of all full-time freshmen had no need and received non-need-based gift aid.

UNDERGRADUATE FINANCIAL AID (Fall 2005, est.) 2,111 applied for aid; of those 81% were deemed to have need. 98% of undergraduates with need received aid; of those 22% had need fully met. *Average percent of need met:* 73% (excluding resources awarded to replace EFC). *Average financial aid package:* $12,511 (excluding resources awarded to replace EFC). 23% of all full-time undergraduates had no need and received non-need-based gift aid.

GIFT AID (NEED-BASED) *Total amount:* $8,130,155 (33% federal, 52% state, 15% institutional). *Receiving aid:* Freshmen: 62% (311); All full-time undergraduates: 61% (1,382). *Average award:* Freshmen: $5334; Undergraduates: $5134. *Scholarships, grants, and awards:* Federal Pell, FSEOG, state, private, college/university gift aid from institutional funds.

GIFT AID (NON-NEED-BASED) *Total amount:* $4,217,329 (1% federal, 88% institutional, 11% external sources). *Receiving aid:* Freshmen: 58% (287); Undergraduates: 55% (1,243). *Average Award:* Freshmen: $3314; Undergraduates: $3314. *Scholarships, grants, and awards by category: Academic Interests/Achievement:* 567 awards ($1,104,670 total): biological sciences, business, communication, computer science, education, English, foreign languages, general academic interests/achievements, health fields, humanities, international studies, mathematics, physical sciences, premedicine, religion/biblical studies, social sciences. *Creative Arts/Performance:* 148 awards ($206,375 total): art/fine arts, music. *Special Achievements/Activities:* 82 awards ($200,265 total): cheerleading/drum major, community service, leadership, religious involvement. *Special Characteristics:* 341 awards ($1,143,036 total): children and siblings of alumni, children of faculty/staff, ethnic background, handicapped students, international students, local/state students, members of minority groups, out-of-state students, relatives of clergy, religious affiliation. *ROTC:* Air Force cooperative.

LOANS *Student loans:* $13,140,292 (56% need-based, 44% non-need-based). 80% of past graduating class borrowed through all loan programs. *Average indebtedness per student:* $15,819. *Average need-based loan:* Freshmen: $2514; Undergraduates: $4948. *Parent loans:* $2,629,863 (100% need-based). *Programs:* FFEL (Subsidized and Unsubsidized Stafford, PLUS), Perkins, state, college/university.

WORK-STUDY *Federal work-study:* Total amount: $412,981; 209 jobs averaging $2300. *State or other work-study/employment:* Total amount: $378,837 (27% need-based, 73% non-need-based). 201 part-time jobs averaging $2300.

APPLYING FOR FINANCIAL AID *Required financial aid form:* FAFSA. *Financial aid deadline (priority):* 3/1. *Notification date:* Continuous beginning 2/1. Students must reply within 2 weeks of notification.

CONTACT Ms. Kelly Graves, Assistant Director of Financial Aid, University of Mary Hardin-Baylor, Box 8080, UMHB Station, Belton, TX 76513, 254-295-4517 or toll-free 800-727-8642. *Fax:* 254-295-5049. *E-mail:* kgraves@umhb.edu.

UNIVERSITY OF MARYLAND, BALTIMORE COUNTY
Baltimore, MD

Tuition & fees (MD res): $8520   **Average undergraduate aid package: $9527**

ABOUT THE INSTITUTION State-supported, coed. Awards: bachelor's, master's, and doctoral degrees and post-bachelor's certificates. 57 undergraduate majors. Total enrollment: 11,650. Undergraduates: 9,406. Freshmen: 1,429. Federal methodology is used as a basis for awarding need-based institutional aid.

UNDERGRADUATE EXPENSES for 2005-06 *Application fee:* $50. *Tuition, state resident:* full-time $6484; part-time $270 per credit hour. *Tuition, nonresident:* full-time $14,560; part-time $606 per credit hour. *Required fees:* full-time $2036; $5 per credit hour. *College room and board:* $8090; *room only:* $4930.

FRESHMAN FINANCIAL AID (Fall 2005, est.) 925 applied for aid; of those 68% were deemed to have need. 100% of freshmen with need received aid; of those 27% had need fully met. *Average percent of need met:* 77% (excluding resources awarded to replace EFC). *Average financial aid package:* $9335 (excluding resources awarded to replace EFC). 20% of all full-time freshmen had no need and received non-need-based gift aid.

UNDERGRADUATE FINANCIAL AID (Fall 2005, est.) 4,661 applied for aid; of those 80% were deemed to have need. 100% of undergraduates with need received aid; of those 30% had need fully met. *Average percent of need met:* 71% (excluding resources awarded to replace EFC). *Average financial aid package:* $9527 (excluding resources awarded to replace EFC). 7% of all full-time undergraduates had no need and received non-need-based gift aid.

GIFT AID (NEED-BASED) *Total amount:* $11,660,710 (50% federal, 41% state, 9% institutional). *Receiving aid:* Freshmen: 30% (420); All full-time undergraduates: 31% (2,536). *Average award:* Freshmen: $4761; Undergraduates: $5090. *Scholarships, grants, and awards:* Federal Pell, FSEOG, state, private, college/university gift aid from institutional funds.

University of Maryland, Baltimore County

GIFT AID (NON-NEED-BASED) *Total amount:* $17,169,867 (13% state, 82% institutional, 5% external sources). *Receiving aid:* Freshmen: 41% (580); Undergraduates: 31% (2,492). *Average Award:* Freshmen: $3839; Undergraduates: $3268. *Scholarships, grants, and awards by category: Academic Interests/Achievement:* 878 awards ($4,687,479 total): biological sciences, computer science, engineering/technologies, English, foreign languages, general academic interests/achievements, humanities, mathematics, physical sciences. *Creative Arts/Performance:* 87 awards ($485,297 total): art/fine arts, cinema/film/broadcasting, creative writing, dance, music, performing arts, theater/drama. *ROTC:* Army cooperative.

LOANS *Student loans:* $22,459,393 (49% need-based, 51% non-need-based). 48% of past graduating class borrowed through all loan programs. *Average indebtedness per student:* $19,018. *Average need-based loan:* Freshmen: $3060; Undergraduates: $4304. *Parent loans:* $8,013,253 (100% non-need-based). *Programs:* FFEL (Subsidized and Unsubsidized Stafford, PLUS), Perkins.

WORK-STUDY *Federal work-study:* Total amount: $297,686; jobs available (averaging $2000). *State or other work-study/employment:* Total amount: $731,850 (100% non-need-based).

ATHLETIC AWARDS Total amount: $1,820,620 (100% non-need-based).

APPLYING FOR FINANCIAL AID *Required financial aid form:* FAFSA. *Financial aid deadline (priority):* 2/15. *Notification date:* Continuous beginning 3/15. Students must reply within 2 weeks of notification.

CONTACT Stephanie Johnson, Director of Financial Aid, University of Maryland, Baltimore County, 1000 Hilltop Circle, Baltimore, MD 21250, 410-455-2387 or toll-free 800-UMBC-4U2 (in-state), 800-862-2402 (out-of-state). *Fax:* 410-455-1094. *E-mail:* finaid@umbc.edu.

UNIVERSITY OF MARYLAND, COLLEGE PARK
College Park, MD

Tuition & fees (MD res): $7821	Average undergraduate aid package: $12,132

ABOUT THE INSTITUTION State-supported, coed. Awards: bachelor's, master's, doctoral, and first professional degrees and post-bachelor's and post-master's certificates. 92 undergraduate majors. Total enrollment: 35,300. Undergraduates: 25,373. Freshmen: 4,211. Federal methodology is used as a basis for awarding need-based institutional aid.

UNDERGRADUATE EXPENSES for 2005-06 *Application fee:* $55. *Tuition, state resident:* full-time $6566; part-time $273 per credit hour. *Tuition, nonresident:* full-time $18,890; part-time $787 per credit hour. *Required fees:* full-time $1255; $288 per term part-time. Part-time tuition and fees vary according to course load. *College room and board:* $8075; *room only:* $4784. Room and board charges vary according to board plan. *Payment plans:* Installment, deferred payment.

FRESHMAN FINANCIAL AID (Fall 2004) 3337 applied for aid; of those 54% were deemed to have need. 92% of freshmen with need received aid; of those 31% had need fully met. *Average percent of need met:* 71% (excluding resources awarded to replace EFC). *Average financial aid package:* $11,800 (excluding resources awarded to replace EFC). 22% of all full-time freshmen had no need and received non-need-based gift aid.

UNDERGRADUATE FINANCIAL AID (Fall 2004) 15,238 applied for aid; of those 63% were deemed to have need. 94% of undergraduates with need received aid; of those 26% had need fully met. *Average percent of need met:* 68% (excluding resources awarded to replace EFC). *Average financial aid package:* $12,132 (excluding resources awarded to replace EFC). 15% of all full-time undergraduates had no need and received non-need-based gift aid.

GIFT AID (NEED-BASED) *Total amount:* $29,131,632 (41% federal, 28% state, 31% institutional). *Receiving aid:* Freshmen: 26% (1,054); All full-time undergraduates: 27% (6,156). *Average award:* Freshmen: $5762; Undergraduates: $4722. *Scholarships, grants, and awards:* Federal Pell, FSEOG, state, private, college/university gift aid from institutional funds.

GIFT AID (NON-NEED-BASED) *Total amount:* $28,678,390 (24% state, 52% institutional, 24% external sources). *Receiving aid:* Freshmen: 22% (884); Undergraduates: 14% (3,118). *Average Award:* Freshmen: $5145; Undergraduates: $5889. *Scholarships, grants, and awards by category: Academic Interests/Achievement:* 2,849 awards ($16,531,151 total): agriculture, architecture, biological sciences, business, communication, computer science, education, engineering/technologies, English, foreign languages, general academic interests/achievements, health fields, humanities, international studies, library science, mathematics, military science, physical sciences, premedicine, social sciences. *Creative Arts/Performance:* 58 awards ($420,115 total): applied art and design, art/fine arts, dance, music, performing arts, theater/drama. *Special Achievements/Activities:* 41 awards ($157,037 total): cheerleading/drum major, leadership. *Special Characteristics:* 395 awards ($1,701,500 total): adult students, out-of-state students. *Tuition waivers:* Full or partial for employees or children of employees. *ROTC:* Army, Naval cooperative, Air Force.

LOANS *Student loans:* $54,864,755 (73% need-based, 27% non-need-based). 34% of past graduating class borrowed through all loan programs. *Average indebtedness per student:* $14,076. *Average need-based loan:* Freshmen: $2437; Undergraduates: $3845. *Parent loans:* $19,571,516 (40% need-based, 60% non-need-based). *Programs:* FFEL (Subsidized and Unsubsidized Stafford, PLUS), Perkins, college/university.

WORK-STUDY *Federal work-study:* Total amount: $1,150,533; 1,340 jobs averaging $1198.

ATHLETIC AWARDS Total amount: $7,277,356 (100% non-need-based).

APPLYING FOR FINANCIAL AID *Required financial aid form:* FAFSA. *Financial aid deadline (priority):* 2/15. *Notification date:* Continuous beginning 4/1.

CONTACT Sarah Bauder, Director of Financial Aid, University of Maryland, College Park, 0102 Lee Building, College Park, MD 20742, 301-314-8279 or toll-free 800-422-5867. *Fax:* 301-314-9587. *E-mail:* sbauder@umd.edu.

UNIVERSITY OF MARYLAND EASTERN SHORE
Princess Anne, MD

ABOUT THE INSTITUTION State-supported, coed. Awards: bachelor's, master's, and doctoral degrees. 53 undergraduate majors. Total enrollment: 3,762. Undergraduates: 3,326. Freshmen: 846.

GIFT AID (NEED-BASED) *Scholarships, grants, and awards:* Federal Pell, FSEOG, state, college/university gift aid from institutional funds.

GIFT AID (NON-NEED-BASED) *Scholarships, grants, and awards by category: Academic Interests/Achievement:* agriculture, business, computer science, education, engineering/technologies, English, general academic interests/achievements, health fields, home economics, mathematics, physical sciences, social sciences. *Creative Arts/Performance:* art/fine arts, music, performing arts, theater/drama. *Special Characteristics:* adult students, children of faculty/staff, first-generation college students, veterans.

LOANS *Programs:* Federal Direct (Subsidized and Unsubsidized Stafford, PLUS), Perkins.

APPLYING FOR FINANCIAL AID *Required financial aid form:* FAFSA.

CONTACT Mr. James W. Kellam, Director of Financial Aid, University of Maryland Eastern Shore, Backbone Road, Princess Anne, MD 21853-1299, 410-651-6172. *Fax:* 410-651-7670. *E-mail:* jwkellam@umes.edu.

UNIVERSITY OF MARYLAND UNIVERSITY COLLEGE
Adelphi, MD

ABOUT THE INSTITUTION State-supported, coed. Awards: associate, bachelor's, master's, and doctoral degrees and post-bachelor's certificates (offers primarily part-time evening and weekend degree programs at more than 30 off-campus locations in Maryland and the Washington, DC area, and more than 180 military communities in Europe and Asia with military enrollment not reflected in this profile; associate of arts program available to military students only). 19 undergraduate majors. Total enrollment: 28,374. Undergraduates: 19,857. Freshmen: 558.

GIFT AID (NEED-BASED) *Scholarships, grants, and awards:* Federal Pell, FSEOG, state, private, college/university gift aid from institutional funds.

GIFT AID (NON-NEED-BASED) *Scholarships, grants, and awards by category: Academic Interests/Achievement:* general academic interests/achievements. *Special Achievements/Activities:* general special achievements/activities.

LOANS *Programs:* Federal Direct (Subsidized and Unsubsidized Stafford, PLUS), Perkins.

APPLYING FOR FINANCIAL AID *Required financial aid forms:* FAFSA, institution's own form.

CONTACT Financial Aid Counselor, University of Maryland University College, 3501 University Boulevard East, Adelphi, MD 20783, 301-985-7510 or toll-free 800-888-8682 (in-state). *Fax:* 301-985-7462. *E-mail:* finaid@umuc.edu.

UNIVERSITY OF MARY WASHINGTON
Fredericksburg, VA

Tuition & fees (VA res): $5634   **Average undergraduate aid package: $5300**

ABOUT THE INSTITUTION State-supported, coed. Awards: bachelor's and master's degrees and post-bachelor's certificates. 40 undergraduate majors. Total enrollment: 4,734. Undergraduates: 4,085. Freshmen: 880. Federal methodology is used as a basis for awarding need-based institutional aid.
UNDERGRADUATE EXPENSES for 2005–06 *Application fee:* $45. *Tuition, state resident:* full-time $5634; part-time $199 per credit. *Tuition, nonresident:* full-time $14,776; part-time $579 per credit. Part-time tuition and fees vary according to course load. *College room and board:* $6002; *room only:* $3484. Room and board charges vary according to board plan and housing facility. *Payment plan:* Installment.
FRESHMAN FINANCIAL AID (Fall 2004) 650 applied for aid; of those 63% were deemed to have need. 94% of freshmen with need received aid; of those 9% had need fully met. *Average percent of need met:* 60% (excluding resources awarded to replace EFC). *Average financial aid package:* $4450 (excluding resources awarded to replace EFC). 16% of all full-time freshmen had no need and received non-need-based gift aid.
UNDERGRADUATE FINANCIAL AID (Fall 2004) 2,501 applied for aid; of those 64% were deemed to have need. 88% of undergraduates with need received aid; of those 6% had need fully met. *Average percent of need met:* 56% (excluding resources awarded to replace EFC). *Average financial aid package:* $5300 (excluding resources awarded to replace EFC). 12% of all full-time undergraduates had no need and received non-need-based gift aid.
GIFT AID (NEED-BASED) *Total amount:* $3,057,000 (33% federal, 38% state, 18% institutional, 11% external sources). *Receiving aid:* Freshmen: 40% (350); All full-time undergraduates: 36% (1,292). *Average award:* Freshmen: $2825; Undergraduates: $3200. *Scholarships, grants, and awards:* Federal Pell, FSEOG, state, college/university gift aid from institutional funds.
GIFT AID (NON-NEED-BASED) *Total amount:* $771,900 (1% state, 60% institutional, 39% external sources). *Receiving aid:* Freshmen: 16% (140); Undergraduates: 8% (270). *Average Award:* Freshmen: $1080; Undergraduates: $1180. *Scholarships, grants, and awards by category: Academic Interests/Achievement:* 750 awards ($905,000 total): business, computer science, education, English, foreign languages, general academic interests/achievements, humanities, mathematics, physical sciences, religion/biblical studies, social sciences. *Creative Arts/Performance:* 65 awards ($120,000 total): art/fine arts, dance, journalism/publications, music, theater/drama. *Special Achievements/Activities:* 2 awards ($13,500 total): leadership. *Special Characteristics:* 15 awards ($36,000 total): adult students, children and siblings of alumni, children of faculty/staff, local/state students. *Tuition waivers:* Full or partial for senior citizens.
LOANS *Student loans:* $8,190,000 (47% need-based, 53% non-need-based). 72% of past graduating class borrowed through all loan programs. *Average indebtedness per student:* $12,665. *Average need-based loan:* Freshmen: $2515; Undergraduates: $4000. *Parent loans:* $4,100,000 (100% non-need-based). *Programs:* FFEL (Subsidized and Unsubsidized Stafford, PLUS), Perkins.
WORK-STUDY *Federal work-study:* Total amount: $52,600; 45 jobs averaging $1600. *State or other work-study/employment:* Total amount: $1,243,000 (100% non-need-based). 751 part-time jobs averaging $1480.
APPLYING FOR FINANCIAL AID *Required financial aid form:* FAFSA. *Financial aid deadline (priority):* 3/1. *Notification date:* 4/15. Students must reply by 5/1 or within 2 weeks of notification.
CONTACT Ms. Debra J. Harber, Associate Dean for Financial Aid, University of Mary Washington, 1301 College Avenue, Fredericksburg, VA 22401-5358, 540-654-2468 or toll-free 800-468-5614. *Fax:* 540-654-1858. *E-mail:* dharber@umw.edu.

UNIVERSITY OF MASSACHUSETTS AMHERST
Amherst, MA

Tuition & fees (MA res): $9595   **Average undergraduate aid package: $10,865**

ABOUT THE INSTITUTION State-supported, coed. Awards: associate, bachelor's, master's, and doctoral degrees and post-master's certificates. 85 undergraduate majors. Total enrollment: 25,093. Undergraduates: 19,394. Freshmen: 4,486. Federal methodology is used as a basis for awarding need-based institutional aid.
UNDERGRADUATE EXPENSES for 2006–07 *Application fee:* $40. *Tuition, state resident:* full-time $2031. *Tuition, nonresident:* full-time $10,857.
FRESHMAN FINANCIAL AID (Fall 2004) 2581 applied for aid; of those 69% were deemed to have need. 94% of freshmen with need received aid; of those 13% had need fully met. *Average percent of need met:* 81% (excluding resources awarded to replace EFC). *Average financial aid package:* $9590 (excluding resources awarded to replace EFC). 1% of all full-time freshmen had no need and received non-need-based gift aid.
UNDERGRADUATE FINANCIAL AID (Fall 2004) 12,037 applied for aid; of those 77% were deemed to have need. 96% of undergraduates with need received aid; of those 27% had need fully met. *Average percent of need met:* 87% (excluding resources awarded to replace EFC). *Average financial aid package:* $10,865 (excluding resources awarded to replace EFC). 2% of all full-time undergraduates had no need and received non-need-based gift aid.
GIFT AID (NEED-BASED) *Total amount:* $42,614,715 (32% federal, 15% state, 45% institutional, 8% external sources). *Receiving aid:* Freshmen: 28% (1,190); All full-time undergraduates: 38% (6,608). *Average award:* Freshmen: $6366; Undergraduates: $7033. *Scholarships, grants, and awards:* Federal Pell, FSEOG, state, private, college/university gift aid from institutional funds.
GIFT AID (NON-NEED-BASED) *Total amount:* $4,423,640 (1% federal, 3% state, 36% institutional, 60% external sources). *Receiving aid:* Freshmen: 1% (50); Undergraduates: 2% (354). *Average Award:* Freshmen: $4829; Undergraduates:* $4934. *Scholarships, grants, and awards by category: Academic Interests/Achievement:* agriculture, architecture, biological sciences, business, communication, computer science, education, engineering/technologies, English, general academic interests/achievements, health fields, humanities, mathematics, military science, physical sciences, premedicine, social sciences. *Creative Arts/Performance:* art/fine arts, dance, journalism/publications, music, theater/drama. *Special Achievements/Activities:* cheerleading/drum major, general special achievements/activities, leadership. *Special Characteristics:* children and siblings of alumni, children of faculty/staff, handicapped students, veterans. *ROTC:* Army, Air Force.
LOANS *Student loans:* $65,545,120 (62% need-based, 38% non-need-based). 61% of past graduating class borrowed through all loan programs. *Average indebtedness per student:* $14,672. *Average need-based loan:* Freshmen: $1281; Undergraduates: $4099. *Parent loans:* $20,733,845 (21% need-based, 79% non-need-based). *Programs:* Federal Direct (Subsidized and Unsubsidized Stafford, PLUS), Perkins, state.
WORK-STUDY *Federal work-study:* Total amount: $8,712,500; 4,940 jobs averaging $1684.
ATHLETIC AWARDS *Total amount:* $4,280,657 (36% need-based, 64% non-need-based).
APPLYING FOR FINANCIAL AID *Required financial aid form:* FAFSA. *Financial aid deadline (priority):* 3/1. *Notification date:* Continuous beginning 4/1.
CONTACT Office of Financial Aid Services, University of Massachusetts Amherst, 255 Whitmore Administration Building, Amherst, MA 01003, 413-545-0801.

UNIVERSITY OF MASSACHUSETTS BOSTON
Boston, MA

ABOUT THE INSTITUTION State-supported, coed. Awards: bachelor's, master's, and doctoral degrees and post-bachelor's and post-master's certificates. 41 undergraduate majors. Total enrollment: 11,862. Undergraduates: 8,958. Freshmen: 781.
GIFT AID (NEED-BASED) *Scholarships, grants, and awards:* Federal Pell, FSEOG, state, private, college/university gift aid from institutional funds.
GIFT AID (NON-NEED-BASED) *Scholarships, grants, and awards by category: Academic Interests/Achievement:* general academic interests/achievements. *Special Achievements/Activities:* general special achievements/activities.
LOANS *Programs:* Federal Direct (Subsidized and Unsubsidized Stafford, PLUS), Perkins, state.
APPLYING FOR FINANCIAL AID *Required financial aid form:* FAFSA.
CONTACT Judy L. Keyes, Director of Financial Aid Services, University of Massachusetts Boston, 100 Morrissey Boulevard, Boston, MA 02125-3393, 617-287-6300. *Fax:* 617-287-6323. *E-mail:* judy.keyes@umb.edu.

University of Massachusetts Dartmouth

UNIVERSITY OF MASSACHUSETTS DARTMOUTH
North Dartmouth, MA

Tuition & fees (MA res): $8036 — Average undergraduate aid package: $10,805

ABOUT THE INSTITUTION State-supported, coed. Awards: bachelor's, master's, and doctoral degrees and post-bachelor's and post-master's certificates. 48 undergraduate majors. Total enrollment: 8,549. Undergraduates: 7,519. Freshmen: 1,740. Federal methodology is used as a basis for awarding need-based institutional aid.

UNDERGRADUATE EXPENSES for 2005–06 *Application fee:* $35; $55 for nonresidents. *Tuition, state resident:* full-time $1417; part-time $59.04 per credit. *Tuition, nonresident:* full-time $8099; part-time $454.88 per credit. *Required fees:* full-time $6619; $275.79 per credit. Full-time tuition and fees vary according to reciprocity agreements. Part-time tuition and fees vary according to course load and reciprocity agreements. *College room and board:* $7634; *room only:* $4460. Room and board charges vary according to board plan and housing facility. *Payment plan:* Installment.

FRESHMAN FINANCIAL AID (Fall 2005, est.) 1005 applied for aid; of those 81% were deemed to have need. 97% of freshmen with need received aid; of those 68% had need fully met. *Average percent of need met:* 95% (excluding resources awarded to replace EFC). *Average financial aid package:* $10,700 (excluding resources awarded to replace EFC). 2% of all full-time freshmen had no need and received non-need-based gift aid.

UNDERGRADUATE FINANCIAL AID (Fall 2005, est.) 4,986 applied for aid; of those 80% were deemed to have need. 97% of undergraduates with need received aid; of those 66% had need fully met. *Average percent of need met:* 95% (excluding resources awarded to replace EFC). *Average financial aid package:* $10,805 (excluding resources awarded to replace EFC). 5% of all full-time undergraduates had no need and received non-need-based gift aid.

GIFT AID (NEED-BASED) *Total amount:* $18,445,272 (27% federal, 19% state, 49% institutional, 5% external sources). *Receiving aid:* Freshmen: 39% (650); All full-time undergraduates: 54% (3,275). *Average award:* Freshmen: $5600; Undergraduates: $5500. *Scholarships, grants, and awards:* Federal Pell, FSEOG, state, private, college/university gift aid from institutional funds.

GIFT AID (NON-NEED-BASED) *Total amount:* $2,156,008 (93% institutional, 7% external sources). *Receiving aid:* Freshmen: 3% (45); Undergraduates: 5% (292). *Average Award:* Freshmen: $3000; Undergraduates: $2500. *Scholarships, grants, and awards by category: Academic Interests/Achievement:* 600 awards ($1,400,000 total): general academic interests/achievements. *Special Achievements/Activities:* 185 awards ($150,000 total): community service. *Special Characteristics:* 300 awards ($450,000 total): adult students, children of faculty/staff, children with a deceased or disabled parent, first-generation college students, members of minority groups, veterans. *Tuition waivers:* Full or partial for employees or children of employees, senior citizens. *ROTC:* Army cooperative.

LOANS *Student loans:* $29,000,000 (69% need-based, 31% non-need-based). 65% of past graduating class borrowed through all loan programs. *Average indebtedness per student:* $16,214. *Average need-based loan:* Freshmen: $6050; Undergraduates: $6375. *Parent loans:* $3,450,000 (64% need-based, 36% non-need-based). *Programs:* Federal Direct (Subsidized and Unsubsidized Stafford, PLUS), Perkins, Federal Nursing, state.

WORK-STUDY *Federal work-study:* Total amount: $850,000; 825 jobs averaging $1030. *State or other work-study/employment:* Total amount: $4,100,000 (76% need-based, 24% non-need-based). 1,300 part-time jobs averaging $3153.

APPLYING FOR FINANCIAL AID *Required financial aid form:* FAFSA. *Financial aid deadline (priority):* 3/1. *Notification date:* Continuous beginning 3/25.

CONTACT Bruce Palmer, Director of Financial Aid, University of Massachusetts Dartmouth, 285 Old Westport Road, North Dartmouth, MA 02747-2300, 508-999-8643. Fax: 508-999-8935. E-mail: financialaid@umassd.edu.

UNIVERSITY OF MASSACHUSETTS LOWELL
Lowell, MA

Tuition & fees (MA res): $8166 — Average undergraduate aid package: $8590

ABOUT THE INSTITUTION State-supported, coed. Awards: associate, bachelor's, master's, and doctoral degrees and post-master's dertificates. 38 undergraduate majors. Total enrollment: 10,666. Undergraduates: 8,301. Federal methodology is used as a basis for awarding need-based institutional aid.

UNDERGRADUATE EXPENSES for 2005–06 *Application fee:* $20. *Tuition, state resident:* full-time $1454; part-time $60.58 per credit. *Tuition, nonresident:* full-time $8567; part-time $356.96 per credit. *Required fees:* full-time $6712; $291.33 per credit. *College room and board:* $6311; *room only:* $3810. Room and board charges vary according to board plan and housing facility. *Payment plan:* Installment.

FRESHMAN FINANCIAL AID (Fall 2004) 745 applied for aid; of those 65% were deemed to have need. 97% of freshmen with need received aid; of those 74% had need fully met. *Average percent of need met:* 94% (excluding resources awarded to replace EFC). *Average financial aid package:* $8192 (excluding resources awarded to replace EFC). 3% of all full-time freshmen had no need and received non-need-based gift aid.

UNDERGRADUATE FINANCIAL AID (Fall 2004) 3,904 applied for aid; of those 74% were deemed to have need. 98% of undergraduates with need received aid; of those 75% had need fully met. *Average percent of need met:* 94% (excluding resources awarded to replace EFC). *Average financial aid package:* $8590 (excluding resources awarded to replace EFC). 4% of all full-time undergraduates had no need and received non-need-based gift aid.

GIFT AID (NEED-BASED) *Total amount:* $8,102,883 (53% federal, 26% state, 21% institutional). *Receiving aid:* Freshmen: 44% (434); All full-time undergraduates: 42% (2,395). *Average award:* Freshmen: $3720; Undergraduates: $3589. *Scholarships, grants, and awards:* Federal Pell, FSEOG, state, private, college/university gift aid from institutional funds.

GIFT AID (NON-NEED-BASED) *Total amount:* $2,579,857 (1% state, 61% institutional, 38% external sources). *Receiving aid:* Freshmen: 8% (78); Undergraduates: 10% (570). *Average Award:* Freshmen: $3298; Undergraduates: $4089. *Scholarships, grants, and awards by category: Academic Interests/Achievement:* computer science, engineering/technologies, general academic interests/achievements, health fields, humanities. *Creative Arts/Performance:* music. *Special Achievements/Activities:* community service, general special achievements/activities. *Special Characteristics:* general special characteristics. *Tuition waivers:* Full or partial for employees or children of employees, senior citizens. *ROTC:* Air Force.

LOANS *Student loans:* $21,164,236 (44% need-based, 56% non-need-based). 62% of past graduating class borrowed through all loan programs. *Average indebtedness per student:* $15,167. *Average need-based loan:* Freshmen: $2545; Undergraduates: $3500. *Parent loans:* $4,195,033 (100% non-need-based). *Programs:* Federal Direct (Subsidized and Unsubsidized Stafford, PLUS), Perkins, state.

WORK-STUDY *Federal work-study:* Total amount: $183,398; 74 jobs averaging $3316. *State or other work-study/employment:* Total amount: $2,144,716 (100% need-based). 682 part-time jobs averaging $3154.

ATHLETIC AWARDS *Total amount:* $1,031,525 (100% non-need-based).

APPLYING FOR FINANCIAL AID *Required financial aid form:* FAFSA. *Financial aid deadline (priority):* 3/1. *Notification date:* Continuous beginning 3/24.

CONTACT Mr. Richard Barrett, Director of Financial Aid, University of Massachusetts Lowell, 883 Broadway Street, Room 102, Lowell, MA 01854, 978-934-4226 or toll-free 800-410-4607. E-mail: richard_barrett@uml.edu.

UNIVERSITY OF MEMPHIS
Memphis, TN

Tuition & fees (TN res): $5084 — Average undergraduate aid package: $4557

ABOUT THE INSTITUTION State-supported, coed. Awards: bachelor's, master's, doctoral, and first professional degrees and post-bachelor's, post-master's, and first professional certificates. 66 undergraduate majors. Total enrollment: 20,465. Undergraduates: 15,765. Freshmen: 2,073. Federal methodology is used as a basis for awarding need-based institutional aid.

UNDERGRADUATE EXPENSES for 2005–06 *Application fee:* $25. *Tuition, state resident:* full-time $4216; part-time $178 per credit hour. *Tuition, nonresident:* full-time $14,030; part-time $588 per credit hour. *Required fees:* full-time $868; $62 per credit hour. Full-time tuition and fees vary according to program and reciprocity agreements. Part-time tuition and fees vary according to course load and program. *College room and board:* $6069; *room only:* $2950. Room and board charges vary according to housing facility. *Payment plan:* Installment.

FRESHMAN FINANCIAL AID (Fall 2004) 1445 applied for aid; of those 75% were deemed to have need. 98% of freshmen with need received aid; of those

12% had need fully met. *Average percent of need met:* 81% (excluding resources awarded to replace EFC). *Average financial aid package:* $6073 (excluding resources awarded to replace EFC). 2% of all full-time freshmen had no need and received non-need-based gift aid.
UNDERGRADUATE FINANCIAL AID (Fall 2004) 9,103 applied for aid; of those 72% were deemed to have need. 94% of undergraduates with need received aid; of those 19% had need fully met. *Average percent of need met:* 78% (excluding resources awarded to replace EFC). *Average financial aid package:* $4557 (excluding resources awarded to replace EFC). 6% of all full-time undergraduates had no need and received non-need-based gift aid.
GIFT AID (NEED-BASED) *Total amount:* $27,874,238 (65% federal, 16% state, 18% institutional, 1% external sources). *Receiving aid:* Freshmen: 49% (963); All full-time undergraduates: 40% (4,654). *Average award:* Freshmen: $4433; Undergraduates: $2975. *Scholarships, grants, and awards:* Federal Pell, FSEOG, state, college/university gift aid from institutional funds.
GIFT AID (NON-NEED-BASED) *Total amount:* $10,669,449 (58% state, 39% institutional, 3% external sources). *Receiving aid:* Freshmen: 18% (354); Undergraduates: 16% (1,824). *Average Award:* Freshmen: $3691; Undergraduates: $4144. *Scholarships, grants, and awards by category: Academic Interests/Achievement:* biological sciences, business, communication, education, engineering/technologies, English, general academic interests/achievements, health fields, humanities, international studies, mathematics, military science, physical sciences, premedicine, social sciences. *Creative Arts/Performance:* art/fine arts, cinema/film/broadcasting, dance, journalism/publications, music. *Special Achievements/Activities:* cheerleading/drum major, general special achievements/activities, leadership. *Special Characteristics:* adult students, children of educators, children of faculty/staff, children of public servants, handicapped students, members of minority groups, public servants. *Tuition waivers:* Full or partial for employees or children of employees, senior citizens. *ROTC:* Army, Naval, Air Force.
LOANS *Student loans:* $49,420,024 (54% need-based, 46% non-need-based). 28% of past graduating class borrowed through all loan programs. *Average indebtedness per student:* $21,908. *Average need-based loan:* Freshmen: $1715; Undergraduates: $3463. *Parent loans:* $2,176,987 (100% non-need-based). *Programs:* Federal Direct (Subsidized and Unsubsidized Stafford, PLUS), Perkins, college/university.
WORK-STUDY *Federal work-study:* Total amount: $707,401; 419 jobs averaging $1919.
ATHLETIC AWARDS *Total amount:* $4,217,452 (68% need-based, 32% non-need-based).
APPLYING FOR FINANCIAL AID *Required financial aid form:* FAFSA. *Financial aid deadline (priority):* 3/1. *Notification date:* Continuous. Students must reply by 8/1.
CONTACT Richard Ritzman, Director of Student Financial Aid, University of Memphis, Wilder Tower 103, Memphis, TN 38152, 901-678-2832 or toll-free 800-669-2678 (out-of-state). *Fax:* 901-678-3590. *E-mail:* rritzman@memphis.edu.

UNIVERSITY OF MIAMI
Coral Gables, FL

Tuition & fees: $29,020   **Average undergraduate aid package:** $23,709

ABOUT THE INSTITUTION Independent, coed. Awards: bachelor's, master's, doctoral, and first professional degrees and post-bachelor's and post-master's certificates. 125 undergraduate majors. Total enrollment: 15,674. Undergraduates: 10,537. Freshmen: 2,277. Both federal and institutional methodology are used as a basis for awarding need-based institutional aid.
UNDERGRADUATE EXPENSES for 2005–06 *Application fee:* $65. *Comprehensive fee:* $37,926 includes full-time tuition ($29,020) and room and board ($8906). *College room only:* $5224. Full-time tuition and fees vary according to course load, location, and program. Room and board charges vary according to board plan and housing facility. *Part-time tuition:* $1208 per credit. Part-time tuition and fees vary according to course load, location, and program. *Payment plans:* Guaranteed tuition, tuition prepayment, installment, deferred payment.
FRESHMAN FINANCIAL AID (Fall 2005, est.) 1496 applied for aid; of those 78% were deemed to have need. 100% of freshmen with need received aid; of those 34% had need fully met. *Average percent of need met:* 80% (excluding resources awarded to replace EFC). *Average financial aid package:* $23,188 (excluding resources awarded to replace EFC). 22% of all full-time freshmen had no need and received non-need-based gift aid.

UNDERGRADUATE FINANCIAL AID (Fall 2005, est.) 5,801 applied for aid; of those 86% were deemed to have need. 100% of undergraduates with need received aid; of those 30% had need fully met. *Average percent of need met:* 78% (excluding resources awarded to replace EFC). *Average financial aid package:* $23,709 (excluding resources awarded to replace EFC). 22% of all full-time undergraduates had no need and received non-need-based gift aid.
GIFT AID (NEED-BASED) *Total amount:* $77,104,943 (9% federal, 18% state, 70% institutional, 3% external sources). *Receiving aid:* Freshmen: 50% (1,132); All full-time undergraduates: 51% (4,863). *Average award:* Freshmen: $17,512; Undergraduates: $17,257. *Scholarships, grants, and awards:* Federal Pell, FSEOG, state, private, college/university gift aid from institutional funds, Federal Nursing.
GIFT AID (NON-NEED-BASED) *Total amount:* $50,363,966 (1% federal, 27% state, 68% institutional, 4% external sources). *Receiving aid:* Freshmen: 16% (372); Undergraduates: 14% (1,359). *Average Award:* Freshmen: $14,846; Undergraduates: $14,784. *Scholarships, grants, and awards by category: Academic Interests/Achievement:* 812 awards ($4,735,624 total): architecture, area/ethnic studies, biological sciences, business, communication, computer science, education, engineering/technologies, English, foreign languages, general academic interests/achievements, health fields, international studies, mathematics, physical sciences, social sciences. *Creative Arts/Performance:* 469 awards ($6,135,914 total): art/fine arts, cinema/film/broadcasting, debating, music, performing arts, theater/drama. *Special Characteristics:* 885 awards ($19,206,609 total): children of faculty/staff, international students. *Tuition waivers:* Full or partial for employees or children of employees. *ROTC:* Army, Air Force.
LOANS *Student loans:* $54,568,570 (67% need-based, 33% non-need-based). 56% of past graduating class borrowed through all loan programs. *Average indebtedness per student:* $19,140. *Average need-based loan:* Freshmen: $3534; Undergraduates: $5104. *Parent loans:* $14,137,020 (27% need-based, 73% non-need-based). *Programs:* FFEL (Subsidized and Unsubsidized Stafford, PLUS), Perkins, Federal Nursing, Private Alternative Education Loans.
WORK-STUDY *Federal work-study:* Total amount: $4,678,933; 2,241 jobs averaging $2088. *State or other work-study/employment:* Total amount: $1,033,926 (26% need-based, 74% non-need-based). 224 part-time jobs averaging $4616.
ATHLETIC AWARDS *Total amount:* $8,103,652 (34% need-based, 66% non-need-based).
APPLYING FOR FINANCIAL AID *Required financial aid form:* FAFSA. *Financial aid deadline (priority):* 2/1. *Notification date:* Continuous beginning 3/1.
CONTACT Mr. James M. Bauer, Director, Financial Assistance, University of Miami, Rhodes House, Building 37R, Coral Gables, FL 33124-5240, 305-284-2270. *Fax:* 305-284-4491. *E-mail:* jbauer@miami.edu.

UNIVERSITY OF MICHIGAN
Ann Arbor, MI

Tuition & fees (MI res): $9400   **Average undergraduate aid package:** $10,234

ABOUT THE INSTITUTION State-supported, coed. Awards: bachelor's, master's, doctoral, and first professional degrees and post-bachelor's and post-master's certificates. 124 undergraduate majors. Total enrollment: 39,993. Undergraduates: 25,467. Freshmen: 6,113. Federal methodology is used as a basis for awarding need-based institutional aid.
UNDERGRADUATE EXPENSES for 2005–06 *Application fee:* $40. *Tuition, state resident:* full-time $9213; part-time $349 per hour. *Tuition, nonresident:* full-time $27,602; part-time $1115 per hour. *Required fees:* full-time $187; $94.69 per term part-time. Full-time tuition and fees vary according to course load, degree level, location, program, and student level. Part-time tuition and fees vary according to course load, degree level, location, program, and student level. *College room and board:* $7374. Room and board charges vary according to board plan and housing facility. *Payment plan:* Installment.
FRESHMAN FINANCIAL AID (Fall 2004) 3320 applied for aid; of those 88% were deemed to have need. 100% of freshmen with need received aid; of those 90% had need fully met. *Average percent of need met:* 90% (excluding resources awarded to replace EFC). *Average financial aid package:* $8079 (excluding resources awarded to replace EFC). 33% of all full-time freshmen had no need and received non-need-based gift aid.
UNDERGRADUATE FINANCIAL AID (Fall 2004) 13,282 applied for aid; of those 83% were deemed to have need. 100% of undergraduates with need received aid; of those 90% had need fully met. *Average percent of need met:* 90% (excluding resources awarded to replace EFC). *Average financial aid package:*

University of Michigan

$10,234 (excluding resources awarded to replace EFC). 25% of all full-time undergraduates had no need and received non-need-based gift aid. **GIFT AID (NEED-BASED)** *Total amount:* $43,981,318 (24% federal, 1% state, 75% institutional). *Receiving aid:* Freshmen: 26% (1,578); All full-time undergraduates: 25% (6,252). *Average award:* Freshmen: $6886; Undergraduates: $7035. *Scholarships, grants, and awards:* Federal Pell, FSEOG, state, private, college/university gift aid from institutional funds. **GIFT AID (NON-NEED-BASED)** *Total amount:* $66,644,169 (7% federal, 19% state, 50% institutional, 24% external sources). *Receiving aid:* Freshmen: 41% (2,423); Undergraduates: 29% (7,289). *Average Award: Freshmen:* $4475; *Undergraduates:* $5418. *Scholarships, grants, and awards by category: Academic Interests/Achievement:* architecture, area/ethnic studies, biological sciences, business, communication, computer science, education, engineering/technologies, English, foreign languages, general academic interests/achievements, health fields, humanities, international studies, library science, mathematics, military science, physical sciences, premedicine, social sciences. *Creative Arts/Performance:* journalism/publications, music, theater/drama. *Special Achievements/Activities:* community service, general special achievements/activities, leadership. *Special Characteristics:* children of faculty/staff, children of workers in trades, handicapped students, international students, local/state students, members of minority groups, out-of-state students. *Tuition waivers:* Full or partial for senior citizens. *ROTC:* Army, Air Force.
LOANS *Student loans:* $80,858,654 (56% need-based, 44% non-need-based). 42% of past graduating class borrowed through all loan programs. *Average indebtedness per student:* $22,312. *Average need-based loan:* Freshmen: $4305; Undergraduates: $5695. *Parent loans:* $17,121,510 (100% non-need-based). *Programs:* Federal Direct (Subsidized and Unsubsidized Stafford, PLUS), Perkins, Federal Nursing, state, college/university, MI-Loan Program, Health Professions Student Loans (HPSL).
WORK-STUDY *Federal work-study:* Total amount: $11,631,793; 4,740 jobs averaging $2454. *State or other work-study/employment:* Total amount: $1,273,317 (100% need-based). 492 part-time jobs averaging $2226.
ATHLETIC AWARDS *Total amount:* $11,222,687 (100% non-need-based).
APPLYING FOR FINANCIAL AID *Required financial aid forms:* FAFSA, CSS Financial Aid PROFILE, federal income tax form(s). *Financial aid deadline:* 4/30. *Notification date:* Continuous beginning 3/15.
CONTACT Financial Aid Counseling and Advising Office, University of Michigan, 2011 Student Activities Building, Ann Arbor, MI 48109-1316, 734-763-6600. *Fax:* 734-647-3081. *E-mail:* financial.aid@umich.edu.

UNIVERSITY OF MICHIGAN–DEARBORN
Dearborn, MI

Tuition & fees (MI res): $6841 **Average undergraduate aid package:** $4847

ABOUT THE INSTITUTION State-supported, coed. Awards: bachelor's and master's degrees and post-bachelor's certificates. 53 undergraduate majors. Total enrollment: 8,613. Undergraduates: 6,571. Freshmen: 840. Federal methodology is used as a basis for awarding need-based institutional aid.
UNDERGRADUATE EXPENSES for 2005–06 *Application fee:* $30. *Tuition, state resident:* full-time $6718; part-time $256.10 per credit hour. *Tuition, nonresident:* full-time $14,858; part-time $581.50 per credit hour. *Required fees:* full-time $123; $123.50 per term part-time. Full-time tuition and fees vary according to course level, course load, program, and student level. Part-time tuition and fees vary according to course level, course load, program, and student level. *Payment plan:* Installment.
FRESHMAN FINANCIAL AID (Fall 2005, est.) 553 applied for aid; of those 66% were deemed to have need. 100% of freshmen with need received aid; of those 14% had need fully met. *Average percent of need met:* 46% (excluding resources awarded to replace EFC). *Average financial aid package:* $4011 (excluding resources awarded to replace EFC). 78% of all full-time freshmen had no need and received non-need-based gift aid.
UNDERGRADUATE FINANCIAL AID (Fall 2005, est.) 2,796 applied for aid; of those 78% were deemed to have need. 99% of undergraduates with need received aid; of those 8% had need fully met. *Average percent of need met:* 43% (excluding resources awarded to replace EFC). *Average financial aid package:* $4847 (excluding resources awarded to replace EFC). 33% of all full-time undergraduates had no need and received non-need-based gift aid.
GIFT AID (NEED-BASED) *Total amount:* $6,229,828 (70% federal, 7% state, 23% institutional). *Receiving aid:* Freshmen: 28% (229); All full-time undergraduates: 30% (1,432). *Average award:* Freshmen: $4107; Undergraduates: $3863. *Scholarships, grants, and awards:* Federal Pell, FSEOG, state, private, college/university gift aid from institutional funds.
GIFT AID (NON-NEED-BASED) *Total amount:* $4,901,553 (30% state, 43% institutional, 27% external sources). *Receiving aid:* Freshmen: 36% (296); Undergraduates: 16% (743). *Average Award:* Freshmen: $3007; Undergraduates: $2921. *Scholarships, grants, and awards by category: Academic Interests/Achievement:* 298 awards ($884,545 total): biological sciences, business, computer science, engineering/technologies, general academic interests/achievements, international studies, mathematics, physical sciences, social sciences. *Creative Arts/Performance:* 41 awards ($54,496 total): art/fine arts, cinema/film/broadcasting, creative writing, debating, general creative arts/performance, journalism/publications. *Special Achievements/Activities:* 142 awards ($648,469 total): community service, general special achievements/activities, leadership, memberships. *Special Characteristics:* 177 awards ($739,980 total): children and siblings of alumni, children of current students, children of workers in trades, ethnic background, general special characteristics, handicapped students, members of minority groups, out-of-state students, previous college experience. *Tuition waivers:* Full or partial for employees or children of employees, senior citizens. *ROTC:* Army cooperative, Naval cooperative, Air Force cooperative.
LOANS *Student loans:* $19,635,002 (55% need-based, 45% non-need-based). 51% of past graduating class borrowed through all loan programs. *Average indebtedness per student:* $20,509. *Average need-based loan:* Freshmen: $2423; Undergraduates: $4015. *Parent loans:* $571,331 (100% non-need-based). *Programs:* Federal Direct (Subsidized and Unsubsidized Stafford, PLUS), Perkins, state, college/university, Alternative Loans.
WORK-STUDY *Federal work-study:* Total amount: $130,000; 75 jobs averaging $1750. *State or other work-study/employment:* Total amount: $40,483 (100% need-based). 30 part-time jobs averaging $1350.
ATHLETIC AWARDS *Total amount:* $68,250 (100% non-need-based).
APPLYING FOR FINANCIAL AID *Required financial aid form:* FAFSA. *Financial aid deadline (priority):* 2/14. *Notification date:* Continuous beginning 3/15. Students must reply within 3 weeks of notification.
CONTACT Mr. John A. Mason, Director of Financial Aid, University of Michigan–Dearborn, 4901 Evergreen Road, 1183 UC, Dearborn, MI 48128-1491, 313-593-5300. *Fax:* 313-593-5313. *E-mail:* jamason@umd.umich.edu.

UNIVERSITY OF MICHIGAN–FLINT
Flint, MI

Tuition & fees (MI res): $6398 **Average undergraduate aid package:** $6893

ABOUT THE INSTITUTION State-supported, coed. Awards: bachelor's, master's, and first professional degrees. 77 undergraduate majors. Total enrollment: 6,423. Undergraduates: 5,671. Freshmen: 579. Federal methodology is used as a basis for awarding need-based institutional aid.
UNDERGRADUATE EXPENSES for 2005–06 *Application fee:* $30. *Tuition, state resident:* full-time $6082; part-time $240 per credit. *Tuition, nonresident:* full-time $11,834; part-time $480 per credit. *Required fees:* full-time $316; $124 per term part-time. Full-time tuition and fees vary according to program. Part-time tuition and fees vary according to program.
FRESHMAN FINANCIAL AID (Fall 2004) 342 applied for aid; of those 69% were deemed to have need. 98% of freshmen with need received aid; of those 3% had need fully met. *Average financial aid package:* $5621 (excluding resources awarded to replace EFC). 4% of all full-time freshmen had no need and received non-need-based gift aid.
UNDERGRADUATE FINANCIAL AID (Fall 2004) 2,367 applied for aid; of those 81% were deemed to have need. 98% of undergraduates with need received aid; of those 3% had need fully met. *Average financial aid package:* $6893 (excluding resources awarded to replace EFC). 1% of all full-time undergraduates had no need and received non-need-based gift aid.
GIFT AID (NEED-BASED) *Total amount:* $8,321,845 (55% federal, 4% state, 38% institutional, 3% external sources). *Receiving aid:* Freshmen: 28% (134); All full-time undergraduates: 35% (1,148). *Average award:* Freshmen: $3674; Undergraduates: $4327. *Scholarships, grants, and awards:* Federal Pell, FSEOG, state, private, college/university gift aid from institutional funds.
GIFT AID (NON-NEED-BASED) *Total amount:* $924,006 (100% state). *Receiving aid:* Freshmen: 35% (167); Undergraduates: 17% (571). *Average Award: Freshmen:* $2772; *Undergraduates:* $2100. *Scholarships, grants, and awards by category: Academic Interests/Achievement:* biological sciences, business,

communication, computer science, education, engineering/technologies, English, foreign languages, general academic interests/achievements, health fields, humanities, international studies, mathematics, physical sciences, premedicine, social sciences. *Creative Arts/Performance:* art/fine arts, music, theater/drama. *Special Achievements/Activities:* community service, general special achievements/activities, hobbies/interests, leadership. *Special Characteristics:* adult students, children and siblings of alumni, children of union members/company employees, ethnic background, first-generation college students, general special characteristics, handicapped students, international students, local/state students, members of minority groups. *Tuition waivers:* Full or partial for employees or children of employees, senior citizens.
LOANS *Student loans:* $18,433,306 (51% need-based, 49% non-need-based). 66% of past graduating class borrowed through all loan programs. *Average indebtedness per student:* $21,888. *Average need-based loan:* Freshmen: $2800; Undergraduates: $3977. *Parent loans:* $218,081 (100% non-need-based). *Programs:* Federal Direct (Subsidized and Unsubsidized Stafford, PLUS), Perkins.
WORK-STUDY *Federal work-study:* Total amount: $391,488; 428 jobs averaging $2000. *State or other work-study/employment:* Total amount: $173,192 (100% need-based). 59 part-time jobs averaging $2000.
APPLYING FOR FINANCIAL AID *Required financial aid form:* FAFSA. *Financial aid deadline (priority):* 3/1. *Notification date:* Continuous beginning 3/15. Students must reply within 4 weeks of notification.
CONTACT Financial Aid Office, University of Michigan–Flint, Room 277 UPAV, Flint, MI 48502-1950, 810-762-3444 or toll-free 800-942-5636 (in-state). *Fax:* 810-766-6757. *E-mail:* financial_aid@list.flint.umich.edu.

UNIVERSITY OF MINNESOTA, CROOKSTON
Crookston, MN

CONTACT Associate Director of Financial Aid, University of Minnesota, Crookston, 170 Owen Hall, Crookston, MN 56716-5001, 218-281-8576 or toll-free 800-862-6466. *Fax:* 218-281-8575.

UNIVERSITY OF MINNESOTA, DULUTH
Duluth, MN

Tuition & fees (MN res): $8928   **Average undergraduate aid package:** $8139

ABOUT THE INSTITUTION State-supported, coed. Awards: bachelor's, master's, and first professional degrees. 70 undergraduate majors. Total enrollment: 10,496. Undergraduates: 9,538. Freshmen: 2,164. Federal methodology is used as a basis for awarding need-based institutional aid.
UNDERGRADUATE EXPENSES for 2005–06 *Application fee:* $35. *Tuition, state resident:* full-time $7170; part-time $239 per credit. *Tuition, nonresident:* full-time $18,270; part-time $609 per credit. Full-time tuition and fees vary according to course load, degree level, program, and reciprocity agreements. Part-time tuition and fees vary according to course load, degree level, program, and reciprocity agreements. *College room and board:* $5546. *Payment plan:* Installment.
FRESHMAN FINANCIAL AID (Fall 2005, est.) 1722 applied for aid; of those 63% were deemed to have need. 99% of freshmen with need received aid; of those 56% had need fully met. *Average percent of need met:* 60% (excluding resources awarded to replace EFC). *Average financial aid package:* $7122 (excluding resources awarded to replace EFC). 20% of all full-time freshmen had no need and received non-need-based gift aid.
UNDERGRADUATE FINANCIAL AID (Fall 2005, est.) 6,287 applied for aid; of those 71% were deemed to have need. 98% of undergraduates with need received aid; of those 64% had need fully met. *Average percent of need met:* 66% (excluding resources awarded to replace EFC). *Average financial aid package:* $8139 (excluding resources awarded to replace EFC). 10% of all full-time undergraduates had no need and received non-need-based gift aid.
GIFT AID (NEED-BASED) *Total amount:* $18,203,981 (25% federal, 35% state, 27% institutional, 13% external sources). *Receiving aid:* Freshmen: 41% (871); All full-time undergraduates: 38% (3,203). *Average award:* Freshmen: $5438; Undergraduates: $5751. *Scholarships, grants, and awards:* Federal Pell, FSEOG, state, private, college/university gift aid from institutional funds.
GIFT AID (NON-NEED-BASED) *Total amount:* $1,715,669 (1% state, 34% institutional, 65% external sources). *Receiving aid:* Freshmen: 4% (86); Undergraduates: 2% (188). *Average Award:* Freshmen: $1700; Undergraduates: $2275. *Tuition waivers:* Full or partial for children of alumni. *ROTC:* Air Force.
LOANS *Student loans:* $52,778,245 (92% need-based, 8% non-need-based). 71% of past graduating class borrowed through all loan programs. *Average indebtedness per student:* $20,205. *Average need-based loan:* Freshmen: $2811; Undergraduates: $3739. *Parent loans:* $15,958,424 (100% non-need-based). *Programs:* Federal Direct (Subsidized and Unsubsidized Stafford, PLUS), Perkins, state, college/university, Primary Care Loans.
WORK-STUDY *Federal work-study:* Total amount: $386,521; 159 jobs averaging $2431. *State or other work-study/employment:* Total amount: $522,572 (100% need-based). 249 part-time jobs averaging $2099.
ATHLETIC AWARDS Total amount: $1,678,929 (25% need-based, 75% non-need-based).
APPLYING FOR FINANCIAL AID *Required financial aid form:* FAFSA. *Financial aid deadline (priority):* 3/1. *Notification date:* Continuous beginning 3/1. Students must reply within 2 weeks of notification.
CONTACT Ms. Brenda Herzig, Director of Financial Aid, University of Minnesota, Duluth, 10 University Drive, 184 Darland Administration Building, Duluth, MN 55812-2496, 218-726-8000 or toll-free 800-232-1339. *Fax:* 218-726-8219.

UNIVERSITY OF MINNESOTA, MORRIS
Morris, MN

Tuition & fees (MN res): $9721   **Average undergraduate aid package:** $12,660

ABOUT THE INSTITUTION State-supported, coed. Awards: bachelor's degrees. 42 undergraduate majors. Total enrollment: 1,678. Undergraduates: 1,678. Freshmen: 357. Federal methodology is used as a basis for awarding need-based institutional aid.
UNDERGRADUATE EXPENSES for 2005–06 *Application fee:* $35. *Tuition, state resident:* full-time $8204; part-time $273.47 per credit. *Tuition, nonresident:* full-time $8204; part-time $273.47 per credit. Full-time tuition and fees vary according to reciprocity agreements. Part-time tuition and fees vary according to course load and reciprocity agreements. *College room and board:* $5750; *room only:* $2730. Room and board charges vary according to board plan and housing facility. *Payment plan:* Installment.
FRESHMAN FINANCIAL AID (Fall 2005, est.) 312 applied for aid; of those 76% were deemed to have need. 98% of freshmen with need received aid; of those 44% had need fully met. *Average percent of need met:* 83% (excluding resources awarded to replace EFC). *Average financial aid package:* $12,676 (excluding resources awarded to replace EFC). 23% of all full-time freshmen had no need and received non-need-based gift aid.
UNDERGRADUATE FINANCIAL AID (Fall 2005, est.) 1,238 applied for aid; of those 82% were deemed to have need. 99% of undergraduates with need received aid; of those 44% had need fully met. *Average percent of need met:* 82% (excluding resources awarded to replace EFC). *Average financial aid package:* $12,660 (excluding resources awarded to replace EFC). 20% of all full-time undergraduates had no need and received non-need-based gift aid.
GIFT AID (NEED-BASED) *Total amount:* $5,078,855 (35% federal, 37% state, 12% institutional, 16% external sources). *Receiving aid:* Freshmen: 59% (209); All full-time undergraduates: 58% (869). *Average award:* Freshmen: $6613; Undergraduates: $5885. *Scholarships, grants, and awards:* Federal Pell, FSEOG, state, private, college/university gift aid from institutional funds.
GIFT AID (NON-NEED-BASED) *Total amount:* $1,429,593 (50% institutional, 50% external sources). *Receiving aid:* Freshmen: 23% (82); Undergraduates: 22% (323). *Average Award:* Freshmen: $3251; Undergraduates: $3052. *Scholarships, grants, and awards by category:* Academic Interests/Achievement: 719 awards ($1,000,042 total): general academic interests/achievements. *Creative Arts/Performance:* 9 awards ($5950 total): music. *Special Achievements/Activities:* 41 awards ($33,925 total): general special achievements/activities. *Special Characteristics:* 100 awards ($243,398 total): ethnic background, international students, members of minority groups, veterans, veterans' children. *Tuition waivers:* Full or partial for senior citizens.
LOANS *Student loans:* $8,649,774 (42% need-based, 58% non-need-based). 75% of past graduating class borrowed through all loan programs. *Average indebtedness per student:* $15,490. *Average need-based loan:* Freshmen: $6423; Undergraduates: $7333. *Parent loans:* $259,806 (100% non-need-based). *Programs:* Federal Direct (Subsidized and Unsubsidized Stafford, PLUS), Perkins, state, college/university.

University of Minnesota, Morris

WORK-STUDY *Federal work-study:* Total amount: $395,617; 432 jobs averaging $916. *State or other work-study/employment:* Total amount: $445,766 (44% need-based, 56% non-need-based). 516 part-time jobs averaging $863.
ATHLETIC AWARDS *Total amount:* $14,100 (100% non-need-based).
APPLYING FOR FINANCIAL AID *Required financial aid form:* FAFSA. *Notification date:* Continuous. Students must reply within 3 weeks of notification.
CONTACT Ms. Pam Engebretson, Director of Financial Aid, University of Minnesota, Morris, 600 East 4th Street, Morris, MN 56267, 320-589-6035 or toll-free 800-992-8863. *Fax:* 320-589-1673. *E-mail:* finaid@morris.umn.edu.

UNIVERSITY OF MINNESOTA, TWIN CITIES CAMPUS
Minneapolis, MN

Tuition & fees (MN res): $8622   **Average undergraduate aid package: $11,007**

ABOUT THE INSTITUTION State-supported, coed. Awards: bachelor's, master's, doctoral, and first professional degrees and post-bachelor's, post-master's, and first professional certificates. 132 undergraduate majors. Total enrollment: 51,175. Undergraduates: 32,817. Freshmen: 5,305. Both federal and institutional methodology are used as a basis for awarding need-based institutional aid.
UNDERGRADUATE EXPENSES for 2005-06 *Application fee:* $45. *Tuition, state resident:* full-time $7140; part-time $275 per credit. *Tuition, nonresident:* full-time $19,670; part-time $722 per credit. Full-time tuition and fees vary according to program and reciprocity agreements. Part-time tuition and fees vary according to course load, program, and reciprocity agreements. *College room and board:* $6722; *room only:* $3886. Room and board charges vary according to board plan, housing facility, and location. *Payment plans:* Guaranteed tuition, installment.
FRESHMAN FINANCIAL AID (Fall 2005, est.) 4095 applied for aid; of those 63% were deemed to have need. 97% of freshmen with need received aid; of those 51% had need fully met. *Average percent of need met:* 85% (excluding resources awarded to replace EFC). *Average financial aid package:* $11,075 (excluding resources awarded to replace EFC). 17% of all full-time freshmen had no need and received non-need-based gift aid.
UNDERGRADUATE FINANCIAL AID (Fall 2005, est.) 17,614 applied for aid; of those 73% were deemed to have need. 98% of undergraduates with need received aid; of those 47% had need fully met. *Average percent of need met:* 83% (excluding resources awarded to replace EFC). *Average financial aid package:* $11,007 (excluding resources awarded to replace EFC). 11% of all full-time undergraduates had no need and received non-need-based gift aid.
GIFT AID (NEED-BASED) *Total amount:* $62,492,831 (28% federal, 31% state, 36% institutional, 5% external sources). *Receiving aid:* Freshmen: 36% (1,903); All full-time undergraduates: 35% (9,052). *Average award:* Freshmen: $6842; Undergraduates: $6663. *Scholarships, grants, and awards:* Federal Pell, FSEOG, state, private, college/university gift aid from institutional funds, Federal Nursing.
GIFT AID (NON-NEED-BASED) *Total amount:* $12,869,034 (86% institutional, 14% external sources). *Receiving aid:* Freshmen: 12% (641); Undergraduates: 9% (2,389). *Average Award:* Freshmen: $3981; Undergraduates: $4363. *Scholarships, grants, and awards by category: Academic Interests/Achievement:* agriculture, architecture, area/ethnic studies, biological sciences, business, communication, computer science, education, engineering/technologies, English, foreign languages, general academic interests/achievements, health fields, home economics, humanities, international studies, library science, mathematics, military science, physical sciences, premedicine, religion/biblical studies, social sciences. *Creative Arts/Performance:* general creative arts/performance. *Special Achievements/Activities:* hobbies/interests, leadership. *Special Characteristics:* general special characteristics. *Tuition waivers:* Full or partial for senior citizens.
ROTC: Army, Air Force.
LOANS *Student loans:* $104,234,206 (76% need-based, 24% non-need-based). *Average need-based loan:* Freshmen: $6058; Undergraduates: $7369. *Parent loans:* $51,564,236 (50% need-based, 50% non-need-based). *Programs:* Federal Direct (Subsidized and Unsubsidized Stafford, PLUS), Perkins, Federal Nursing, state, college/university, Health Professions Loans, alternative loans.
WORK-STUDY *Federal work-study:* Total amount: $4,888,226; jobs available. *State or other work-study/employment:* Total amount: $7,004,528 (100% need-based). Part-time jobs available.
ATHLETIC AWARDS *Total amount:* $13,116,580 (50% need-based, 50% non-need-based).
APPLYING FOR FINANCIAL AID *Required financial aid forms:* FAFSA, institution's own form. *Financial aid deadline (priority):* 1/15. *Notification date:* Continuous.
CONTACT Mr. John Kellogg, Institutional Research and Reporting, University of Minnesota, Twin Cities Campus, 318 Morrill Hall, 100 Church Street SE, Minneapolis, MN 55455, 612-625-3387 or toll-free 800-752-1000. *E-mail:* j-kell@umn.edu.

UNIVERSITY OF MISSISSIPPI
Oxford, MS

ABOUT THE INSTITUTION State-supported, coed. Awards: bachelor's, master's, doctoral, and first professional degrees. 63 undergraduate majors. Total enrollment: 14,901. Undergraduates: 12,197. Freshmen: 2,192.
GIFT AID (NEED-BASED) *Scholarships, grants, and awards:* Federal Pell, FSEOG, state, private, college/university gift aid from institutional funds.
GIFT AID (NON-NEED-BASED) *Scholarships, grants, and awards by category: Academic Interests/Achievement:* business, education, engineering/technologies, general academic interests/achievements, international studies, military science. *Creative Arts/Performance:* art/fine arts, journalism/publications, music, theater/drama. *Special Achievements/Activities:* cheerleading/drum major, general special achievements/activities, leadership. *Special Characteristics:* children and siblings of alumni, children of faculty/staff, handicapped students, local/state students, out-of-state students, spouses of current students.
LOANS *Programs:* FFEL (Subsidized and Unsubsidized Stafford, PLUS), Perkins, college/university.
APPLYING FOR FINANCIAL AID *Required financial aid form:* FAFSA.
CONTACT Ms. Laura Diven-Brown, Director of Financial Aid, University of Mississippi, 257 Martindale Center, University, MS 38677, 662-915-5788 or toll-free 800-653-6477 (in-state). *Fax:* 662-915-1164. *E-mail:* ldivenbr@olemiss.edu.

UNIVERSITY OF MISSISSIPPI MEDICAL CENTER
Jackson, MS

CONTACT Minetta Veazey, Administrative Secretary, University of Mississippi Medical Center, 2500 North State Street, Jackson, MS 39216, 601-984-1117. *Fax:* 601-984-6984. *E-mail:* mveazey@registrar.umsmed.edu.

UNIVERSITY OF MISSOURI–COLUMBIA
Columbia, MO

Tuition & fees (MO res): $7745   **Average undergraduate aid package: $10,676**

ABOUT THE INSTITUTION State-supported, coed. Awards: bachelor's, master's, doctoral, and first professional degrees and post-master's and first professional certificates. 124 undergraduate majors. Total enrollment: 27,985. Undergraduates: 21,375. Freshmen: 4,718. Federal methodology is used as a basis for awarding need-based institutional aid.
UNDERGRADUATE EXPENSES for 2005-06 *Application fee:* $35. *Tuition, state resident:* full-time $6495; part-time $216.50 per credit hour. *Tuition, nonresident:* full-time $16,272; part-time $542.40 per credit hour. *Required fees:* full-time $1250; $32.07 per credit hour. Full-time tuition and fees vary according to course load, program, and reciprocity agreements. Part-time tuition and fees vary according to course load, program, and reciprocity agreements. *College room and board:* $6245. Room and board charges vary according to board plan and housing facility. *Payment plan:* Installment.
FRESHMAN FINANCIAL AID (Fall 2005, est.) 3303 applied for aid; of those 63% were deemed to have need. 99% of freshmen with need received aid; of those 25% had need fully met. *Average percent of need met:* 89% (excluding resources awarded to replace EFC). *Average financial aid package:* $11,955 (excluding resources awarded to replace EFC). 28% of all full-time freshmen had no need and received non-need-based gift aid.
UNDERGRADUATE FINANCIAL AID (Fall 2005, est.) 12,482 applied for aid; of those 68% were deemed to have need. 99% of undergraduates with need received aid; of those 24% had need fully met. *Average percent of need met:* 85% (excluding resources awarded to replace EFC). *Average financial aid package:* $10,676 (excluding resources awarded to replace EFC). 23% of all full-time undergraduates had no need and received non-need-based gift aid.

GIFT AID (NEED-BASED) *Total amount:* $37,753,643 (30% federal, 12% state, 43% institutional, 15% external sources). *Receiving aid:* Freshmen: 39% (1,832); All full-time undergraduates: 36% (7,175). *Average award:* Freshmen: $6005; Undergraduates: $5404. *Scholarships, grants, and awards:* Federal Pell, FSEOG, state, private, college/university gift aid from institutional funds, Federal Nursing.
GIFT AID (NON-NEED-BASED) *Total amount:* $20,611,801 (4% federal, 15% state, 49% institutional, 32% external sources). *Receiving aid:* Freshmen: 4% (187); Undergraduates: 3% (563). *Average Award:* Freshmen: $4181; Undergraduates: $4170. *Scholarships, grants, and awards by category: Academic Interests/Achievement:* agriculture, biological sciences, business, communication, computer science, education, engineering/technologies, English, foreign languages, general academic interests/achievements, health fields, home economics, mathematics, premedicine, religion/biblical studies, social sciences. *Creative Arts/Performance:* journalism/publications, music, theater/drama. *Special Achievements/Activities:* general special achievements/activities. *Special Characteristics:* children and siblings of alumni, international students, members of minority groups, out-of-state students. *Tuition waivers:* Full or partial for employees or children of employees, senior citizens. *ROTC:* Army, Naval, Air Force.
LOANS *Student loans:* $64,703,365 (60% need-based, 40% non-need-based). 50% of past graduating class borrowed through all loan programs. *Average indebtedness per student:* $17,907. *Average need-based loan:* Freshmen: $3609; Undergraduates: $4177. *Parent loans:* $31,649,286 (43% need-based, 57% non-need-based). *Programs:* Federal Direct (Subsidized and Unsubsidized Stafford, PLUS), Perkins, Federal Nursing, state, college/university, Health Professions Loans, Primary Care Loans, alternative loans.
WORK-STUDY *Federal work-study:* Total amount: $1,835,867; 1,276 jobs averaging $1460.
ATHLETIC AWARDS Total amount: $5,041,534 (29% need-based, 71% non-need-based).
APPLYING FOR FINANCIAL AID *Required financial aid form:* FAFSA. *Financial aid deadline (priority):* 3/1. *Notification date:* Continuous beginning 4/1. Students must reply within 4 weeks of notification.
CONTACT Lori A. Hartman, Associate Director, Student Financial Aid, University of Missouri–Columbia, 11 Jesse Hall, Columbia, MO 65211, 573-882-3569 or toll-free 800-225-6075 (in-state). *Fax:* 573-884-5335. *E-mail:* hartmanlo@missouri.edu.

UNIVERSITY OF MISSOURI–KANSAS CITY
Kansas City, MO

Tuition & fees (MO res): $6819   **Average undergraduate aid package:** $9859

ABOUT THE INSTITUTION State-supported, coed. Awards: bachelor's, master's, doctoral, and first professional degrees and post-master's and first professional certificates. 50 undergraduate majors. Total enrollment: 14,310. Undergraduates: 9,491. Freshmen: 1,028. Federal methodology is used as a basis for awarding need-based institutional aid.
UNDERGRADUATE EXPENSES for 2006–07 *Application fee:* $35. *Tuition, state resident:* full-time $6819; part-time $227.30 per credit hour. *Tuition, nonresident:* full-time $17,085; part-time $569.50 per credit hour.
FRESHMAN FINANCIAL AID (Fall 2005, est.) 950 applied for aid; of those 68% were deemed to have need. 100% of freshmen with need received aid; of those 60% had need fully met. *Average percent of need met:* 56% (excluding resources awarded to replace EFC). *Average financial aid package:* $11,089 (excluding resources awarded to replace EFC). 21% of all full-time freshmen had no need and received non-need-based gift aid.
UNDERGRADUATE FINANCIAL AID (Fall 2005, est.) 4,961 applied for aid; of those 73% were deemed to have need. 100% of undergraduates with need received aid; of those 44% had need fully met. *Average percent of need met:* 51% (excluding resources awarded to replace EFC). *Average financial aid package:* $9859 (excluding resources awarded to replace EFC). 13% of all full-time undergraduates had no need and received non-need-based gift aid.
GIFT AID (NEED-BASED) *Total amount:* $13,485,497 (50% federal, 6% state, 37% institutional, 7% external sources). *Receiving aid:* Freshmen: 44% (445); All full-time undergraduates: 41% (2,296). *Average award:* Freshmen: $6941; Undergraduates: $5428. *Scholarships, grants, and awards:* Federal Pell, FSEOG, state, private, college/university gift aid from institutional funds, United Negro College Fund, Federal Nursing.
GIFT AID (NON-NEED-BASED) *Total amount:* $5,642,950 (3% federal, 9% state, 80% institutional, 8% external sources). *Receiving aid:* Freshmen: 38% (379); Undergraduates: 22% (1,216). *Average Award:* Freshmen: $3997; Undergraduates: $4223. *Scholarships, grants, and awards by category: Academic Interests/Achievement:* general academic interests/achievements. *Creative Arts/Performance:* debating, general creative arts/performance, music, performing arts. *Special Achievements/Activities:* general special achievements/activities. *Special Characteristics:* ethnic background, members of minority groups, out-of-state students. *ROTC:* Army, Air Force cooperative.
LOANS *Student loans:* $37,445,671 (72% need-based, 28% non-need-based). 87% of past graduating class borrowed through all loan programs. *Average indebtedness per student:* $16,387. *Average need-based loan:* Freshmen: $3666; Undergraduates: $6311. *Parent loans:* $1,920,672 (15% need-based, 85% non-need-based). *Programs:* FFEL (Subsidized and Unsubsidized Stafford, PLUS), Perkins, Federal Nursing, state, college/university.
WORK-STUDY *Federal work-study:* Total amount: $1,757,524; jobs available.
ATHLETIC AWARDS Total amount: $1,701,687 (17% need-based, 83% non-need-based).
APPLYING FOR FINANCIAL AID *Required financial aid form:* FAFSA. *Financial aid deadline (priority):* 3/1. *Notification date:* Continuous beginning 4/1.
CONTACT Jan Brandow, Financial Aid and Scholarships Office, University of Missouri–Kansas City, 5100 Rockhill Road, Kansas City, MO 64110-2499, 816-235-1154 or toll-free 800-775-8652 (out-of-state). *Fax:* 816-235-5511.

UNIVERSITY OF MISSOURI–ROLLA
Rolla, MO

CONTACT Mr. Robert W. Whites, Director of Student Financial Assistance, University of Missouri–Rolla, G1 Parker Hall, Rolla, MO 65409, 573-341-4282 or toll-free 800-522-0938. *Fax:* 573-341-4274. *E-mail:* bobw@umr.edu.

UNIVERSITY OF MISSOURI–ST. LOUIS
St. Louis, MO

Tuition & fees (MO res): $7618   **Average undergraduate aid package:** $9633

ABOUT THE INSTITUTION State-supported, coed. Awards: bachelor's, master's, doctoral, and first professional degrees and post-bachelor's certificates. 71 undergraduate majors. Total enrollment: 15,561. Undergraduates: 12,619. Freshmen: 532. Federal methodology is used as a basis for awarding need-based institutional aid.
UNDERGRADUATE EXPENSES for 2005–06 *Application fee:* $35. *Tuition, state resident:* full-time $6495; part-time $216.50 per credit hour. *Tuition, nonresident:* full-time $16,272; part-time $542.40 per credit hour. *Required fees:* full-time $1123; $43.20 per credit hour. Full-time tuition and fees vary according to course load, program, and reciprocity agreements. Part-time tuition and fees vary according to course load, program, and reciprocity agreements. *College room and board:* $6428; room only: $4561. Room and board charges vary according to board plan and housing facility. *Payment plan:* Installment.
FRESHMAN FINANCIAL AID (Fall 2005, est.) 340 applied for aid; of those 77% were deemed to have need. 98% of freshmen with need received aid; of those 15% had need fully met. *Average percent of need met:* 64% (excluding resources awarded to replace EFC). *Average financial aid package:* $8802 (excluding resources awarded to replace EFC). 18% of all full-time freshmen had no need and received non-need-based gift aid.
UNDERGRADUATE FINANCIAL AID (Fall 2005, est.) 3,619 applied for aid; of those 86% were deemed to have need. 99% of undergraduates with need received aid; of those 8% had need fully met. *Average percent of need met:* 65% (excluding resources awarded to replace EFC). *Average financial aid package:* $9633 (excluding resources awarded to replace EFC). 10% of all full-time undergraduates had no need and received non-need-based gift aid.
GIFT AID (NEED-BASED) *Total amount:* $10,880,205 (66% federal, 8% state, 22% institutional, 4% external sources). *Receiving aid:* Freshmen: 41% (203); All full-time undergraduates: 33% (1,925). *Average award:* Freshmen: $5836; Undergraduates: $4137. *Scholarships, grants, and awards:* Federal Pell, FSEOG, state, private, college/university gift aid from institutional funds, Federal Nursing.
GIFT AID (NON-NEED-BASED) *Total amount:* $3,374,919 (2% federal, 6% state, 86% institutional, 6% external sources). *Receiving aid:* Freshmen: 11% (56); Undergraduates: 3% (184). *Average Award:* Freshmen: $4261; Undergraduates: $4701. *Scholarships, grants, and awards by category: Academic Interests/Achievement:* biological sciences, business, communication, computer science, education, engineering/technologies, English, foreign languages, general academic

University of Missouri–St. Louis

interests/achievements, health fields, humanities, international studies, mathematics. *Creative Arts/Performance:* art/fine arts, music. *Special Achievements/Activities:* memberships. *Special Characteristics:* ethnic background, general special characteristics, local/state students, members of minority groups. *Tuition waivers:* Full or partial for employees or children of employees, senior citizens. *ROTC:* Army cooperative, Air Force cooperative.

LOANS *Student loans:* $34,423,247 (88% need-based, 12% non-need-based). 47% of past graduating class borrowed through all loan programs. *Average indebtedness per student:* $19,435. *Average need-based loan:* Freshmen: $2595; Undergraduates: $4371. *Parent loans:* $3,219,794 (57% need-based, 43% non-need-based). *Programs:* FFEL (Subsidized and Unsubsidized Stafford, PLUS), Perkins, Federal Nursing, state, college/university.

WORK-STUDY *Federal work-study:* Total amount: $625,100; 97 jobs averaging $3242.

ATHLETIC AWARDS *Total amount:* $626,302 (35% need-based, 65% non-need-based).

APPLYING FOR FINANCIAL AID *Required financial aid form:* FAFSA. *Financial aid deadline (priority):* 4/1. *Notification date:* Continuous beginning 4/1. Students must reply within 2 weeks of notification.

CONTACT Samantha Ruffini, Senior Associate Director, Student Financial Aid, University of Missouri–St. Louis, One University Boulevard, 327 MSC, St. Louis, MO 63121-4400, 314-516-6893 or toll-free 888-GO2-UMSL (in-state). *Fax:* 314-516-5408. *E-mail:* ruffinis@umsl.edu.

UNIVERSITY OF MOBILE
Mobile, AL

CONTACT Marie Thomas, Director of Financial Aid, University of Mobile, PO Box 13220, Mobile, AL 36663-0220, 251-442-2370 or toll-free 800-946-7267. *Fax:* 251-442-2498.

THE UNIVERSITY OF MONTANA–MISSOULA
Missoula, MT

CONTACT Mick Hanson, Director of Financial Aid, The University of Montana–Missoula, Enrollment Services, Missoula, MT 59812-0002, 406-243-5373 or toll-free 800-462-8636. *Fax:* 406-243-4930. *E-mail:* faid@mso.umt.edu.

THE UNIVERSITY OF MONTANA–WESTERN
Dillon, MT

ABOUT THE INSTITUTION State-supported, coed. Awards: associate and bachelor's degrees. 41 undergraduate majors. Total enrollment: 1,159. Undergraduates: 1,159. Freshmen: 230.

GIFT AID (NEED-BASED) *Scholarships, grants, and awards:* Federal Pell, FSEOG, state, private, college/university gift aid from institutional funds.

GIFT AID (NON-NEED-BASED) *Scholarships, grants, and awards by category: Academic Interests/Achievement:* business, education, English, general academic interests/achievements, social sciences. *Creative Arts/Performance:* art/fine arts. *Special Achievements/Activities:* rodeo. *Special Characteristics:* members of minority groups.

LOANS *Programs:* FFEL (Subsidized and Unsubsidized Stafford, PLUS), Perkins, college/university.

WORK-STUDY *Federal work-study:* Total amount: $247,405; 210 jobs averaging $1178. *State or other work-study/employment:* Total amount: $312,464 (10% need-based, 90% non-need-based). 187 part-time jobs averaging $1671.

APPLYING FOR FINANCIAL AID *Required financial aid form:* FAFSA.

CONTACT Arlene Williams, Financial Aid Director, The University of Montana–Western, 710 South Atlantic Street, Dillon, MT 59725, 406-683-7511 or toll-free 866-869-6668. *Fax:* 406-683-7493. *E-mail:* a_williams@umwestern.edu.

UNIVERSITY OF MONTEVALLO
Montevallo, AL

CONTACT Ms. Maria Parker, Director of Student Financial Aid, University of Montevallo, Station 6050, Montevallo, AL 35115, 205-665-6050 or toll-free 800-292-4349. *Fax:* 205-665-6047. *E-mail:* finaid@montevallo.edu.

UNIVERSITY OF NEBRASKA AT KEARNEY
Kearney, NE

Tuition & fees (NE res): $4493   **Average undergraduate aid package:** $6823

ABOUT THE INSTITUTION State-supported, coed. Awards: bachelor's and master's degrees and post-master's certificates. 41 undergraduate majors. Total enrollment: 6,445. Undergraduates: 5,381. Freshmen: 1,062. Federal methodology is used as a basis for awarding need-based institutional aid.

UNDERGRADUATE EXPENSES for 2005–06 *Application fee:* $45. *Tuition, state resident:* full-time $3668; part-time $122.25 per hour. *Tuition, nonresident:* full-time $7508; part-time $250.25 per hour. *Required fees:* full-time $825; $16.25 per hour. Full-time tuition and fees vary according to course load and degree level. Part-time tuition and fees vary according to course load and degree level. *College room and board:* $5326. Room and board charges vary according to board plan and housing facility. *Payment plan:* Installment.

FRESHMAN FINANCIAL AID (Fall 2004) 924 applied for aid; of those 75% were deemed to have need. 99% of freshmen with need received aid; of those 56% had need fully met. *Average percent of need met:* 78% (excluding resources awarded to replace EFC). *Average financial aid package:* $6994 (excluding resources awarded to replace EFC). 16% of all full-time freshmen had no need and received non-need-based gift aid.

UNDERGRADUATE FINANCIAL AID (Fall 2004) 3,588 applied for aid; of those 83% were deemed to have need. 98% of undergraduates with need received aid; of those 42% had need fully met. *Average percent of need met:* 78% (excluding resources awarded to replace EFC). *Average financial aid package:* $6823 (excluding resources awarded to replace EFC). 27% of all full-time undergraduates had no need and received non-need-based gift aid.

GIFT AID (NEED-BASED) *Total amount:* $8,792,874 (51% federal, 7% state, 29% institutional, 13% external sources). *Receiving aid:* Freshmen: 59% (608); All full-time undergraduates: 48% (2,382). *Average award:* Freshmen: $4668; Undergraduates: $4179. *Scholarships, grants, and awards:* Federal Pell, FSEOG, state, private, college/university gift aid from institutional funds.

GIFT AID (NON-NEED-BASED) *Average Award:* Freshmen: $2990; Undergraduates: $1450. *Scholarships, grants, and awards by category: Academic Interests/Achievement:* 3 awards ($2200 total): communication. *Creative Arts/Performance:* 89 awards ($63,874 total): applied art and design, art/fine arts, debating, journalism/publications, music. *Special Achievements/Activities:* 15 awards ($3120 total): cheerleading/drum major. *Special Characteristics:* 469 awards ($812,191 total): children of faculty/staff, ethnic background, first-generation college students, international students, out-of-state students, veterans, veterans' children. *Tuition waivers:* Full or partial for employees or children of employees.

LOANS *Student loans:* $13,265,445 (63% need-based, 37% non-need-based). 72% of past graduating class borrowed through all loan programs. *Average indebtedness per student:* $16,808. *Average need-based loan:* Freshmen: $2472; Undergraduates: $3486. *Parent loans:* $2,249,010 (100% non-need-based). *Programs:* FFEL (Subsidized and Unsubsidized Stafford, PLUS), Perkins.

WORK-STUDY *Federal work-study:* Total amount: $371,353; 325 jobs averaging $1088.

ATHLETIC AWARDS *Total amount:* $636,577 (100% need-based).

APPLYING FOR FINANCIAL AID *Required financial aid forms:* FAFSA, institution's own form. *Financial aid deadline (priority):* 4/1. *Notification date:* Continuous beginning 3/15.

CONTACT Financial Aid Office, University of Nebraska at Kearney, Memorial Student Affairs Building, 905 West 25th Street, Kearney, NE 68849-0001, 308-865-8520 or toll-free 800-532-7639. *Fax:* 308-865-8096.

UNIVERSITY OF NEBRASKA AT OMAHA
Omaha, NE

Tuition & fees (NE res): $4825   **Average undergraduate aid package:** N/A

ABOUT THE INSTITUTION State-supported, coed. Awards: bachelor's, master's, and doctoral degrees and post-bachelor's and post-master's certificates. 73 undergraduate majors. Total enrollment: 14,093. Undergraduates: 11,329. Freshmen: 1,758. Federal methodology is used as a basis for awarding need-based institutional aid.

UNDERGRADUATE EXPENSES for 2005–06 *Application fee:* $45. *Tuition, state resident:* full-time $4133; part-time $137.75 per semester hour. *Tuition, nonresident:* full-time $12,180; part-time $406 per semester hour. *Required*

fees: full-time $692; $19.55 per semester hour or $81.50 per term part-time. Full-time tuition and fees vary according to course load and student level. Part-time tuition and fees vary according to course load and student level. **College room and board:** $6140; **room only:** $3690. Room and board charges vary according to board plan. **Payment plans:** Installment, deferred payment.
FRESHMAN FINANCIAL AID (Fall 2005, est.) 1310 applied for aid; of those 65% were deemed to have need. 100% of freshmen with need received aid.
UNDERGRADUATE FINANCIAL AID (Fall 2005, est.) 5,792 applied for aid; of those 71% were deemed to have need. 100% of undergraduates with need received aid.
GIFT AID (NEED-BASED) *Total amount:* $8,938,149 (77% federal, 9% state, 14% institutional). *Receiving aid:* Freshmen: 28% (519); All full-time undergraduates: 33% (3,100). *Scholarships, grants, and awards:* Federal Pell, FSEOG, state, private, college/university gift aid from institutional funds.
GIFT AID (NON-NEED-BASED) *Total amount:* $8,772,120 (2% federal, 2% state, 71% institutional, 25% external sources). *Receiving aid:* Freshmen: 36% (669); Undergraduates: 32% (2,962). *Scholarships, grants, and awards by category:* Academic Interests/Achievement: biological sciences, business, communication, computer science, education, engineering/technologies, English, foreign languages, general academic interests/achievements, home economics, mathematics, physical sciences, premedicine, social sciences. *Creative Arts/Performance:* art/fine arts, creative writing, debating, journalism/publications, music, performing arts, theater/drama. *Special Achievements/Activities:* general special achievements/activities, leadership, memberships. *Special Characteristics:* adult students, children and siblings of alumni, children of faculty/staff, ethnic background, first-generation college students, handicapped students, international students, members of minority groups, out-of-state students, veterans' children. *Tuition waivers:* Full or partial for employees or children of employees. *ROTC:* Army cooperative, Air Force.
LOANS *Student loans:* $34,950,000 (50% need-based, 50% non-need-based). 48% of past graduating class borrowed through all loan programs. *Average indebtedness per student:* $16,900. *Parent loans:* $1,300,000 (100% non-need-based). *Programs:* FFEL (Subsidized and Unsubsidized Stafford, PLUS), Perkins, college/university.
WORK-STUDY *Federal work-study:* Total amount: $437,000; 283 jobs averaging $1325.
ATHLETIC AWARDS *Total amount:* $685,378 (100% non-need-based).
APPLYING FOR FINANCIAL AID *Required financial aid form:* FAFSA. *Financial aid deadline (priority):* 3/1. *Notification date:* Continuous beginning 4/1. Students must reply within 2 weeks of notification.
CONTACT Office of Financial Aid, University of Nebraska at Omaha, 103 Eppley Administration Building, 6001 Dodge Street, Omaha, NE 68182-0187, 402-554-2327 or toll-free 800-858-8648 (in-state). *Fax:* 402-554-3472. *E-mail:* finaid@unomaha.edu.

UNIVERSITY OF NEBRASKA–LINCOLN
Lincoln, NE

Tuition & fees (NE res): $5540   **Average undergraduate aid package:** $8245

ABOUT THE INSTITUTION State-supported, coed. Awards: associate, bachelor's, master's, doctoral, and first professional degrees and post-bachelor's and post-master's certificates. 128 undergraduate majors. Total enrollment: 21,675. Undergraduates: 17,037. Freshmen: 3,560. Both federal and institutional methodology are used as a basis for awarding need-based institutional aid.
UNDERGRADUATE EXPENSES for 2005–06 *Application fee:* $45. *Tuition, state resident:* full-time $4530; part-time $151 per credit hour. *Tuition, nonresident:* full-time $13,440; part-time $448 per credit hour. *Required fees:* full-time $1010; $8.50 per credit hour or $202.10 per term part-time. Full-time tuition and fees vary according to course load. Part-time tuition and fees vary according to course load. **College room and board:** $6008; **room only:** $3239. Room and board charges vary according to board plan and housing facility. **Payment plan:** Installment.
FRESHMAN FINANCIAL AID (Fall 2004) 2222 applied for aid; of those 69% were deemed to have need. 98% of freshmen with need received aid; of those 28% had need fully met. *Average percent of need met:* 88% (excluding resources awarded to replace EFC). *Average financial aid package:* $8606 (excluding resources awarded to replace EFC). 13% of all full-time freshmen had no need and received non-need-based gift aid.

University of Nebraska Medical Center

UNDERGRADUATE FINANCIAL AID (Fall 2004) 9,785 applied for aid; of those 76% were deemed to have need. 97% of undergraduates with need received aid; of those 28% had need fully met. *Average percent of need met:* 85% (excluding resources awarded to replace EFC). *Average financial aid package:* $8245 (excluding resources awarded to replace EFC). 6% of all full-time undergraduates had no need and received non-need-based gift aid.
GIFT AID (NEED-BASED) *Total amount:* $26,785,048 (37% federal, 5% state, 48% institutional, 10% external sources). *Receiving aid:* Freshmen: 41% (1,323); All full-time undergraduates: 36% (5,637). *Average award:* Freshmen: $5512; Undergraduates: $4867. *Scholarships, grants, and awards:* Federal Pell, FSEOG, state, private, college/university gift aid from institutional funds.
GIFT AID (NON-NEED-BASED) *Total amount:* $17,592,375 (6% federal, 76% institutional, 18% external sources). *Receiving aid:* Freshmen: 5% (155); Undergraduates: 3% (420). *Average Award:* Freshmen: $5030; Undergraduates:* $4999. *Scholarships, grants, and awards by category:* Academic Interests/Achievement: agriculture, architecture, biological sciences, business, computer science, education, engineering/technologies, English, foreign languages, general academic interests/achievements, health fields, home economics, humanities, international studies, mathematics, physical sciences, premedicine, social sciences. *Creative Arts/Performance:* art/fine arts, cinema/film/broadcasting, dance, journalism/publications, music, performing arts, theater/drama. *Special Achievements/Activities:* cheerleading/drum major, community service, leadership. *Special Characteristics:* children and siblings of alumni, ethnic background, handicapped students, international students, members of minority groups, out-of-state students, veterans' children. *Tuition waivers:* Full or partial for employees or children of employees. *ROTC:* Army, Naval, Air Force.
LOANS *Student loans:* $41,643,175 (71% need-based, 29% non-need-based). 61% of past graduating class borrowed through all loan programs. *Average indebtedness per student:* $16,909. *Average need-based loan:* Freshmen: $3066; Undergraduates: $4011. *Parent loans:* $14,758,570 (28% need-based, 72% non-need-based). *Programs:* Federal Direct (Subsidized and Unsubsidized Stafford, PLUS), Perkins, college/university.
WORK-STUDY *Federal work-study:* Total amount: $2,110,073; 1,364 jobs averaging $2121.
ATHLETIC AWARDS *Total amount:* $5,027,951 (100% non-need-based).
APPLYING FOR FINANCIAL AID *Required financial aid form:* FAFSA. *Financial aid deadline:* Continuous. *Notification date:* Continuous beginning 3/15.
CONTACT Ms. Jo Tederman, Assistant Director of Scholarships and Financial Aid, University of Nebraska–Lincoln, 16 Canfield Administration Building, PO Box 880411, Lincoln, NE 68588-0411, 402-472-2030 or toll-free 800-742-8800. *Fax:* 402-472-9826.

UNIVERSITY OF NEBRASKA MEDICAL CENTER
Omaha, NE

Tuition & fees (NE res): $7418   **Average undergraduate aid package:** $8209

ABOUT THE INSTITUTION State-supported, coed. Awards: bachelor's, master's, doctoral, and first professional degrees and post-bachelor's, post-master's, and first professional certificates. 7 undergraduate majors. Total enrollment: 2,995. Undergraduates: 851. Federal methodology is used as a basis for awarding need-based institutional aid.
UNDERGRADUATE EXPENSES for 2005–06 *Application fee:* $45. *Tuition, state resident:* full-time $6685; part-time $191 per credit hour. *Tuition, nonresident:* full-time $16,591; part-time $559.75 per credit hour. Full-time tuition and fees vary according to course level, course load, and program. Part-time tuition and fees vary according to program.
UNDERGRADUATE FINANCIAL AID (Fall 2004) 796 applied for aid; of those 85% were deemed to have need. 98% of undergraduates with need received aid; of those 16% had need fully met. *Average percent of need met:* 68% (excluding resources awarded to replace EFC). *Average financial aid package:* $8209 (excluding resources awarded to replace EFC). 2% of all full-time undergraduates had no need and received non-need-based gift aid.
GIFT AID (NEED-BASED) *Total amount:* $2,409,450 (29% federal, 22% state, 35% institutional, 14% external sources). *Receiving aid:* All full-time undergraduates: 60% (565). *Average award:* Undergraduates: $4406. *Scholarships, grants, and awards:* Federal Pell, FSEOG, state, private, college/university gift aid from institutional funds.

University of Nebraska Medical Center

GIFT AID (NON-NEED-BASED) *Receiving aid:* Undergraduates: 3% (28). *Average Award:* Undergraduates: $7912. *Tuition waivers:* Full or partial for children of alumni, employees or children of employees. *ROTC:* Army cooperative, Air Force cooperative.

LOANS *Student loans:* $5,626,475 (100% need-based). 94% of past graduating class borrowed through all loan programs. *Average indebtedness per student:* $24,192. *Average need-based loan:* Undergraduates: $4810. *Parent loans:* $984,459 (100% need-based). *Programs:* FFEL (Subsidized and Unsubsidized Stafford, PLUS), Perkins, Federal Nursing, state, college/university.

WORK-STUDY *Federal work-study:* Total amount: $33,573; 37 jobs averaging $955.

APPLYING FOR FINANCIAL AID *Required financial aid forms:* FAFSA, institution's own form. *Financial aid deadline (priority):* 3/15. *Notification date:* Continuous beginning 4/1. Students must reply within 2 weeks of notification.

CONTACT Judi Walker, Director of Financial Aid, University of Nebraska Medical Center, 984265 Nebraska Medical Center, Omaha, NE 68198-4265, 402-559-6409 or toll-free 800-626-8431 Ext. 6468. *Fax:* 402-559-6796. *E-mail:* jdwalker@unmc.edu.

UNIVERSITY OF NEVADA, LAS VEGAS
Las Vegas, NV

Tuition & fees (NV res): $3818   **Average undergraduate aid package:** $6416

ABOUT THE INSTITUTION State-supported, coed. Awards: bachelor's, master's, doctoral, and first professional degrees and post-bachelor's and post-master's certificates. 86 undergraduate majors. Total enrollment: 27,344. Undergraduates: 21,783. Freshmen: 3,271. Federal methodology is used as a basis for awarding need-based institutional aid.

UNDERGRADUATE EXPENSES for 2006–07 *Application fee:* $60. *Tuition, state resident:* full-time $3278; part-time $105.25 per credit hour. *Tuition, nonresident:* full-time $13,189; part-time $225 per credit hour. *College room and board:* $8326; *room only:* $5278.

FRESHMAN FINANCIAL AID (Fall 2005, est.) 2505 applied for aid; of those 58% were deemed to have need. 99% of freshmen with need received aid; of those 50% had need fully met. *Average percent of need met:* 65% (excluding resources awarded to replace EFC). *Average financial aid package:* $5801 (excluding resources awarded to replace EFC). 44% of all full-time freshmen had no need and received non-need-based gift aid.

UNDERGRADUATE FINANCIAL AID (Fall 2005, est.) 12,050 applied for aid; of those 56% were deemed to have need. 97% of undergraduates with need received aid; of those 44% had need fully met. *Average percent of need met:* 70% (excluding resources awarded to replace EFC). *Average financial aid package:* $6416 (excluding resources awarded to replace EFC). 22% of all full-time undergraduates had no need and received non-need-based gift aid.

GIFT AID (NEED-BASED) *Total amount:* $20,500,000 (66% federal, 29% state, 2% institutional, 3% external sources). *Receiving aid:* Freshmen: 20% (577); All full-time undergraduates: 21% (3,198). *Average award:* Freshmen: $2909; Undergraduates: $3117. *Scholarships, grants, and awards:* Federal Pell, FSEOG, state, private, college/university gift aid from institutional funds.

GIFT AID (NON-NEED-BASED) *Total amount:* $22,150,000 (18% federal, 67% state, 1% institutional, 14% external sources). *Receiving aid:* Freshmen: 30% (865); Undergraduates: 16% (2,488). *Average Award:* Freshmen: $1120; Undergraduates: $2473. *Scholarships, grants, and awards by category: Academic Interests/Achievement:* architecture, biological sciences, business, communication, computer science, education, engineering/technologies, English, general academic interests/achievements, health fields, humanities, international studies, mathematics, physical sciences, premedicine, social sciences. *Creative Arts/Performance:* applied art and design, art/fine arts, cinema/film/broadcasting, dance, journalism/publications, music, performing arts, theater/drama. *Special Achievements/Activities:* cheerleading/drum major, community service, general special achievements/activities, hobbies/interests, leadership, memberships, rodeo. *Special Characteristics:* children and siblings of alumni, children of faculty/staff, children of public servants, children of workers in trades, ethnic background, first-generation college students, general special characteristics, handicapped students, international students, local/state students, members of minority groups, out-of-state students.

LOANS *Student loans:* $66,000,000 (61% need-based, 39% non-need-based). 40% of past graduating class borrowed through all loan programs. *Average indebtedness per student:* $17,394. *Average need-based loan:* Freshmen: $2619; Undergraduates: $4104. *Parent loans:* $10,300,000 (71% need-based, 29% non-need-based). *Programs:* Federal Direct (Subsidized and Unsubsidized Stafford, PLUS), Perkins, state, college/university.

WORK-STUDY *Federal work-study:* Total amount: $1,100,000; 300 jobs averaging $3100. *State or other work-study/employment:* Total amount: $5,800,000 (28% need-based, 72% non-need-based). 300 part-time jobs averaging $3000.

ATHLETIC AWARDS *Total amount:* $5,600,000 (100% non-need-based).

APPLYING FOR FINANCIAL AID *Required financial aid forms:* FAFSA, institution's own form. *Financial aid deadline (priority):* 2/1. *Notification date:* Students must reply within 2 weeks of notification.

CONTACT Director of Student Financial Services, University of Nevada, Las Vegas, 4505 Maryland Parkway, Box 452016, Las Vegas, NV 89154-2016, 702-895-3424. *Fax:* 702-895-1353.

UNIVERSITY OF NEVADA, RENO
Reno, NV

Tuition & fees (NV res): $3270   **Average undergraduate aid package:** $6571

ABOUT THE INSTITUTION State-supported, coed. Awards: bachelor's, master's, doctoral, and first professional degrees and post-bachelor's, post-master's, and first professional certificates. 97 undergraduate majors. Total enrollment: 16,336. Undergraduates: 12,937. Freshmen: 2,432. Federal methodology is used as a basis for awarding need-based institutional aid.

UNDERGRADUATE EXPENSES for 2005–06 *Application fee:* $60. *Tuition, state resident:* full-time $3060; part-time $102 per credit. *Tuition, nonresident:* full-time $11,735; part-time $209.75 per credit. Full-time tuition and fees vary according to course load. Part-time tuition and fees vary according to course load. *College room and board:* $7785; *room only:* $4190. Room and board charges vary according to board plan and housing facility. *Payment plan:* Deferred payment.

FRESHMAN FINANCIAL AID (Fall 2004) 1018 applied for aid; of those 66% were deemed to have need. 98% of freshmen with need received aid; of those 14% had need fully met. *Average percent of need met:* 47% (excluding resources awarded to replace EFC). *Average financial aid package:* $4802 (excluding resources awarded to replace EFC). 59% of all full-time freshmen had no need and received non-need-based gift aid.

UNDERGRADUATE FINANCIAL AID (Fall 2004) 4,242 applied for aid; of those 77% were deemed to have need. 96% of undergraduates with need received aid; of those 15% had need fully met. *Average percent of need met:* 57% (excluding resources awarded to replace EFC). *Average financial aid package:* $6571 (excluding resources awarded to replace EFC). 46% of all full-time undergraduates had no need and received non-need-based gift aid.

GIFT AID (NEED-BASED) *Total amount:* $13,557,273 (36% federal, 34% state, 23% institutional, 7% external sources). *Receiving aid:* Freshmen: 27% (567); All full-time undergraduates: 28% (2,783). *Average award:* Freshmen: $4238; Undergraduates: $4567. *Scholarships, grants, and awards:* Federal Pell, FSEOG, private, college/university gift aid from institutional funds.

GIFT AID (NON-NEED-BASED) *Total amount:* $12,606,864 (2% federal, 69% state, 20% institutional, 9% external sources). *Receiving aid:* Freshmen: 30% (636); Undergraduates: 31% (3,005). *Average Award:* Freshmen: $2582; Undergraduates: $2559. *Scholarships, grants, and awards by category: Academic Interests/Achievement:* agriculture, biological sciences, business, computer science, education, engineering/technologies, English, foreign languages, general academic interests/achievements, health fields, humanities, international studies, mathematics, military science, physical sciences, premedicine, social sciences. *Creative Arts/Performance:* applied art and design, art/fine arts, creative writing, dance, debating, general creative arts/performance, journalism/publications, music, performing arts, theater/drama. *Special Achievements/Activities:* cheerleading/drum major. *Special Characteristics:* adult students, children and siblings of alumni, ethnic background, first-generation college students, local/state students, married students, members of minority groups. *Tuition waivers:* Full or partial for children of alumni, employees or children of employees, senior citizens. *ROTC:* Army.

LOANS *Student loans:* $16,399,026 (82% need-based, 18% non-need-based). 42% of past graduating class borrowed through all loan programs. *Average indebtedness per student:* $15,696. *Average need-based loan:* Freshmen: $2465; Undergraduates: $4216. *Parent loans:* $1,935,757 (43% need-based, 57% non-need-based). *Programs:* FFEL (Subsidized and Unsubsidized Stafford, PLUS), Perkins, Federal Nursing, college/university.

WORK-STUDY *Federal work-study:* Total amount: $379,987; 210 jobs averaging $2464. *State or other work-study/employment:* Total amount: $32,017 (38% need-based, 62% non-need-based). 16 part-time jobs averaging $2115.
ATHLETIC AWARDS *Total amount:* $4,145,008 (17% need-based, 83% non-need-based).
APPLYING FOR FINANCIAL AID *Required financial aid form:* FAFSA. *Financial aid deadline (priority):* 2/1. *Notification date:* Continuous beginning 4/1. Students must reply within 2 weeks of notification.
CONTACT Dr. Nancee Langley, Director of Student Financial Aid, University of Nevada, Reno, Student Services Building, Room 316, Mail Stop 076, Reno, NV 89557, 775-784-4666 Ext. 3009 or toll-free 866-263-8232. *Fax:* 775-784-1025. *E-mail:* langley@unr.edu.

UNIVERSITY OF NEW ENGLAND
Biddeford, ME

Tuition & fees: $22,275   **Average undergraduate aid package: $20,171**

ABOUT THE INSTITUTION Independent, coed. Awards: associate, bachelor's, master's, and first professional degrees and post-bachelor's and post-master's certificates. 38 undergraduate majors. Total enrollment: 3,312. Undergraduates: 1,736. Freshmen: 468. Federal methodology is used as a basis for awarding need-based institutional aid.
UNDERGRADUATE EXPENSES for 2005–06 *Application fee:* $40. *Comprehensive fee:* $31,005 includes full-time tuition ($21,540), mandatory fees ($735), and room and board ($8730). Room and board charges vary according to housing facility. *Part-time tuition:* $775 per credit. *Payment plan:* Installment.
FRESHMAN FINANCIAL AID (Fall 2005, est.) 440 applied for aid; of those 88% were deemed to have need. 100% of freshmen with need received aid; of those 21% had need fully met. *Average percent of need met:* 76% (excluding resources awarded to replace EFC). *Average financial aid package:* $18,574 (excluding resources awarded to replace EFC). 16% of all full-time freshmen had no need and received non-need-based gift aid.
UNDERGRADUATE FINANCIAL AID (Fall 2005, est.) 1,343 applied for aid; of those 92% were deemed to have need. 100% of undergraduates with need received aid; of those 14% had need fully met. *Average percent of need met:* 70% (excluding resources awarded to replace EFC). *Average financial aid package:* $20,171 (excluding resources awarded to replace EFC). 16% of all full-time undergraduates had no need and received non-need-based gift aid.
GIFT AID (NEED-BASED) *Total amount:* $12,952,801 (10% federal, 3% state, 83% institutional, 4% external sources). *Receiving aid:* Freshmen: 83% (387); All full-time undergraduates: 83% (1,225). *Average award:* Freshmen: $11,382; Undergraduates: $10,475. *Scholarships, grants, and awards:* Federal Pell, FSEOG, state, private, college/university gift aid from institutional funds.
GIFT AID (NON-NEED-BASED) *Total amount:* $2,111,395 (96% institutional, 4% external sources). *Receiving aid:* Freshmen: 9% (43); Undergraduates: 5% (80). *Average Award:* Freshmen: $8169; Undergraduates: $7523. *Scholarships, grants, and awards by category:* Academic Interests/Achievement: 1,682 awards ($7,782,848 total): biological sciences, business, education, English, general academic interests/achievements, health fields, humanities, international studies, mathematics, physical sciences, premedicine, social sciences. *Special Achievements/Activities:* 16 awards ($13,500 total): community service, general special achievements/activities, leadership. *Special Characteristics:* 11 awards ($12,750 total): children and siblings of alumni, siblings of current students. *Tuition waivers:* Full or partial for children of alumni, employees or children of employees. *ROTC:* Army cooperative.
LOANS *Student loans:* $14,927,089 (78% need-based, 22% non-need-based). 88% of past graduating class borrowed through all loan programs. *Average indebtedness per student:* $37,507. *Average need-based loan:* Freshmen: $4294; Undergraduates: $5227. *Parent loans:* $3,476,421 (44% need-based, 56% non-need-based). *Programs:* FFEL (Subsidized and Unsubsidized Stafford, PLUS), Perkins, Federal Nursing, state, college/university.
WORK-STUDY *Federal work-study:* Total amount: $1,158,044; 678 jobs averaging $1708. *State or other work-study/employment:* Total amount: $372,006 (100% non-need-based).
APPLYING FOR FINANCIAL AID *Required financial aid form:* FAFSA. *Financial aid deadline (priority):* 5/1. *Notification date:* Continuous beginning 1/25.
CONTACT John R. Bowie, Director of Financial Aid, University of New England, 11 Hills Beach Road, Biddeford, ME 04005, 207-602-2342 or toll-free 800-477-4UNE. *Fax:* 207-602-5946. *E-mail:* finaid@une.edu.

UNIVERSITY OF NEW HAMPSHIRE
Durham, NH

Tuition & fees (NH res): $10,401   **Average undergraduate aid package: $14,888**

ABOUT THE INSTITUTION State-supported, coed. Awards: associate, bachelor's, master's, and doctoral degrees and post-master's certificates. 143 undergraduate majors. Total enrollment: 14,564. Undergraduates: 11,529. Freshmen: 2,798. Federal methodology is used as a basis for awarding need-based institutional aid.
UNDERGRADUATE EXPENSES for 2006–07 *Application fee:* $45. *Tuition, state resident:* full-time $8240. *Tuition, nonresident:* full-time $20,690. *College room and board:* $7584; *room only:* $4606.
FRESHMAN FINANCIAL AID (Fall 2004) 1961 applied for aid; of those 76% were deemed to have need. 98% of freshmen with need received aid; of those 25% had need fully met. *Average percent of need met:* 82% (excluding resources awarded to replace EFC). *Average financial aid package:* $15,275 (excluding resources awarded to replace EFC). 22% of all full-time freshmen had no need and received non-need-based gift aid.
UNDERGRADUATE FINANCIAL AID (Fall 2004) 7,360 applied for aid; of those 81% were deemed to have need. 99% of undergraduates with need received aid; of those 20% had need fully met. *Average percent of need met:* 78% (excluding resources awarded to replace EFC). *Average financial aid package:* $14,888 (excluding resources awarded to replace EFC). 21% of all full-time undergraduates had no need and received non-need-based gift aid.
GIFT AID (NEED-BASED) *Total amount:* $27,142,692 (25% federal, 4% state, 52% institutional, 19% external sources). *Receiving aid:* Freshmen: 42% (1,020); All full-time undergraduates: 37% (3,814). *Average award:* Freshmen: $2708; Undergraduates: $2293. *Scholarships, grants, and awards:* Federal Pell, FSEOG, state, private, college/university gift aid from institutional funds.
GIFT AID (NON-NEED-BASED) *Total amount:* $12,442,905 (100% institutional). *Receiving aid:* Freshmen: 6% (149); Undergraduates: 3% (352). *Average Award:* Freshmen: $5427; Undergraduates: $5827. *Scholarships, grants, and awards by category:* Academic Interests/Achievement: agriculture, business, education, engineering/technologies, English, general academic interests/achievements, health fields, humanities, mathematics, military science. *Creative Arts/Performance:* art/fine arts, dance, music, theater/drama. *Special Achievements/Activities:* community service. *Special Characteristics:* children and siblings of alumni, children of faculty/staff, handicapped students, international students, local/state students. *ROTC:* Army, Air Force.
LOANS *Student loans:* $59,692,379 (50% need-based, 50% non-need-based). 72% of past graduating class borrowed through all loan programs. *Average indebtedness per student:* $21,459. *Average need-based loan:* Freshmen: $2345; Undergraduates: $3385. *Parent loans:* $14,329,980 (100% non-need-based). *Programs:* FFEL (Subsidized and Unsubsidized Stafford, PLUS), Perkins, state, college/university.
WORK-STUDY *Federal work-study:* Total amount: $6,430,657; 3,176 jobs averaging $1763. *State or other work-study/employment:* Total amount: $4,863,727 (100% non-need-based). 2,764 part-time jobs averaging $1773.
ATHLETIC AWARDS *Total amount:* $5,147,934 (100% non-need-based).
APPLYING FOR FINANCIAL AID *Required financial aid form:* FAFSA. *Financial aid deadline (priority):* 3/1. *Notification date:* Continuous beginning 3/1.
CONTACT Susan K. Allen, Director of Financial Aid, University of New Hampshire, 11 Garrison Avenue, Stoke Hall, Durham, NH 03824, 603-862-3600. *Fax:* 603-862-1947. *E-mail:* financial.aid@unh.edu.

UNIVERSITY OF NEW HAMPSHIRE AT MANCHESTER
Manchester, NH

Tuition & fees (NH res): $7163   **Average undergraduate aid package: $7666**

ABOUT THE INSTITUTION State-supported, coed. Awards: associate, bachelor's, and master's degrees. 13 undergraduate majors. Total enrollment: 1,165. Undergraduates: 998. Freshmen: 121. Federal methodology is used as a basis for awarding need-based institutional aid.
UNDERGRADUATE EXPENSES for 2005–06 *Application fee:* $35. *Tuition, state resident:* full-time $6960; part-time $290 per credit. *Tuition, nonresident:*

University of New Hampshire at Manchester

full-time $17,610; part-time $734 per credit. Full-time tuition and fees vary according to course load and program. Part-time tuition and fees vary according to course load and program.
FRESHMAN FINANCIAL AID (Fall 2004) 72 applied for aid; of those 62% were deemed to have need. 100% of freshmen with need received aid; of those 11% had need fully met. *Average percent of need met:* 50% (excluding resources awarded to replace EFC). *Average financial aid package:* $6262 (excluding resources awarded to replace EFC).
UNDERGRADUATE FINANCIAL AID (Fall 2004) 474 applied for aid; of those 76% were deemed to have need. 96% of undergraduates with need received aid; of those 11% had need fully met. *Average percent of need met:* 56% (excluding resources awarded to replace EFC). *Average financial aid package:* $7666 (excluding resources awarded to replace EFC).
GIFT AID (NEED-BASED) *Total amount:* $579,439 (58% federal, 9% state, 8% institutional, 25% external sources). *Receiving aid:* Freshmen: 20% (21); All full-time undergraduates: 13% (105). *Average award:* Freshmen: $590; Undergraduates: $498. *Scholarships, grants, and awards:* Federal Pell, FSEOG, state, private, college/university gift aid from institutional funds.
GIFT AID (NON-NEED-BASED) *Total amount:* $42,305 (100% institutional). *Scholarships, grants, and awards by category: Academic Interests/Achievement:* general academic interests/achievements. *Special Characteristics:* children of faculty/staff. *Tuition waivers:* Full or partial for employees or children of employees, senior citizens. *ROTC:* Army cooperative, Air Force cooperative.
LOANS *Student loans:* $2,445,145 (51% need-based, 49% non-need-based). 64% of past graduating class borrowed through all loan programs. *Average indebtedness per student:* $16,437. *Average need-based loan:* Freshmen: $1855; Undergraduates: $3323. *Parent loans:* $54,816 (100% non-need-based). *Programs:* FFEL (Subsidized and Unsubsidized Stafford, PLUS), Perkins, state, college/university.
WORK-STUDY *Federal work-study:* Total amount: $146,457; 81 jobs averaging $1808.
APPLYING FOR FINANCIAL AID *Required financial aid form:* FAFSA. *Financial aid deadline (priority):* 5/1. *Notification date:* Continuous beginning 4/1.
CONTACT Jodi Abad, Assistant Director of Financial Aid, University of New Hampshire at Manchester, French Hall, 400 Commercial Street, Manchester, NH 03101-1113, 603-641-4146. *Fax:* 603-641-4125.

UNIVERSITY OF NEW HAVEN
West Haven, CT

Tuition & fees: $22,982	Average undergraduate aid package: $14,751

ABOUT THE INSTITUTION Independent, coed. Awards: associate, bachelor's, and master's degrees and post-bachelor's and post-master's certificates. 48 undergraduate majors. Total enrollment: 4,466. Undergraduates: 2,788. Freshmen: 664. Federal methodology is used as a basis for awarding need-based institutional aid.
UNDERGRADUATE EXPENSES for 2005–06 *Application fee:* $50. *Comprehensive fee:* $32,532 includes full-time tuition ($22,380), mandatory fees ($602), and room and board ($9550). *College room only:* $5796. Full-time tuition and fees vary according to course load and program. Room and board charges vary according to board plan and housing facility. *Part-time tuition:* $746 per credit hour. Part-time tuition and fees vary according to class time, course load, location, and program. *Payment plan:* Installment.
FRESHMAN FINANCIAL AID (Fall 2005, est.) 577 applied for aid; of those 88% were deemed to have need. 100% of freshmen with need received aid; of those 17% had need fully met. *Average percent of need met:* 68% (excluding resources awarded to replace EFC). *Average financial aid package:* $15,093 (excluding resources awarded to replace EFC). 17% of all full-time freshmen had no need and received non-need-based gift aid.
UNDERGRADUATE FINANCIAL AID (Fall 2005, est.) 1,920 applied for aid; of those 89% were deemed to have need. 100% of undergraduates with need received aid; of those 18% had need fully met. *Average percent of need met:* 67% (excluding resources awarded to replace EFC). *Average financial aid package:* $14,751 (excluding resources awarded to replace EFC). 13% of all full-time undergraduates had no need and received non-need-based gift aid.
GIFT AID (NEED-BASED) *Total amount:* $17,361,298 (9% federal, 9% state, 79% institutional, 3% external sources). *Receiving aid:* Freshmen: 75% (492); All full-time undergraduates: 71% (1,640). *Average award:* Freshmen: $12,317;

Undergraduates: $11,257. *Scholarships, grants, and awards:* Federal Pell, FSEOG, state, college/university gift aid from institutional funds.
GIFT AID (NON-NEED-BASED) *Total amount:* $1,634,458 (100% institutional). *Receiving aid:* Freshmen: 8% (51); Undergraduates: 7% (152). *Average Award:* Freshmen: $15,049; Undergraduates: $15,347. *Scholarships, grants, and awards by category: Special Achievements/Activities:* general special achievements/activities. *Tuition waivers:* Full or partial for employees or children of employees.
LOANS *Student loans:* $20,579,770 (30% need-based, 70% non-need-based). 62% of past graduating class borrowed through all loan programs. *Average indebtedness per student:* $30,399. *Average need-based loan:* Freshmen: $3320; Undergraduates: $4174. *Parent loans:* $4,734,690 (100% non-need-based). *Programs:* FFEL (Subsidized and Unsubsidized Stafford, PLUS), Perkins.
WORK-STUDY *Federal work-study:* Total amount: $182,433.
ATHLETIC AWARDS *Total amount:* $1,466,925 (49% need-based, 51% non-need-based).
APPLYING FOR FINANCIAL AID *Required financial aid forms:* FAFSA, institution's own form. *Financial aid deadline:* 3/1 (priority: 3/1). *Notification date:* Continuous beginning 3/15. Students must reply by 5/1 or within 2 weeks of notification.
CONTACT Mr. Christopher Hourigan, Director of Institutional Research, University of New Haven, 300 Boston Post Road, West Haven, CT 06516-1916, 203-932-7139 or toll-free 800-DIAL-UNH. *Fax:* 203-931-6050. *E-mail:* finaid@newhaven.edu.

UNIVERSITY OF NEW MEXICO
Albuquerque, NM

CONTACT Office of Student Financial Aid, University of New Mexico, Mesa Vista Hall North, Albuquerque, NM 87131, 505-277-2041 or toll-free 800-CALLUNM (in-state). *Fax:* 505-277-6326. *E-mail:* finaid@unm.edu.

UNIVERSITY OF NEW ORLEANS
New Orleans, LA

Tuition & fees (LA res): $3810	Average undergraduate aid package: $5910

ABOUT THE INSTITUTION State-supported, coed. Awards: bachelor's, master's, and doctoral degrees and post-bachelor's certificates. 50 undergraduate majors. Total enrollment: 17,350. Undergraduates: 13,225. Freshmen: 2,079. Federal methodology is used as a basis for awarding need-based institutional aid.
UNDERGRADUATE EXPENSES for 2005–06 *Application fee:* $20. *Tuition, state resident:* full-time $3292; part-time $133 per hour. *Tuition, nonresident:* full-time $10,336; part-time $426 per hour. Part-time tuition and fees vary according to course load. *College room and board: room only:* $4590. Room and board charges vary according to board plan and housing facility. *Payment plan:* Deferred payment.
FRESHMAN FINANCIAL AID (Fall 2004) 1767 applied for aid; of those 100% were deemed to have need. 72% of freshmen with need received aid; of those 11% had need fully met. *Average percent of need met:* 64% (excluding resources awarded to replace EFC). *Average financial aid package:* $5331 (excluding resources awarded to replace EFC). 6% of all full-time freshmen had no need and received non-need-based gift aid.
UNDERGRADUATE FINANCIAL AID (Fall 2004) 7,565 applied for aid; of those 100% were deemed to have need. 74% of undergraduates with need received aid; of those 11% had need fully met. *Average percent of need met:* 70% (excluding resources awarded to replace EFC). *Average financial aid package:* $5910 (excluding resources awarded to replace EFC). 2% of all full-time undergraduates had no need and received non-need-based gift aid.
GIFT AID (NEED-BASED) *Total amount:* $13,695,884 (99% federal, 1% state). *Receiving aid:* Freshmen: 43% (839); All full-time undergraduates: 38% (3,650). *Average award:* Freshmen: $3231; Undergraduates: $3118. *Scholarships, grants, and awards:* Federal Pell, FSEOG, state, private, college/university gift aid from institutional funds.
GIFT AID (NON-NEED-BASED) *Total amount:* $6,642,105 (100% state). *Receiving aid:* Freshmen: 31% (606); Undergraduates: 16% (1,579). *Average Award:* Freshmen: $1471; Undergraduates: $1486. *Scholarships, grants, and awards by category: Academic Interests/Achievement:* 234 awards ($542,219 total): communication, computer science, education, foreign languages, general academic interests/achievements, international studies, mathematics, military science, physical sciences. *Creative Arts/Performance:* 62 awards ($244,951 total): general creative arts/performance, music. *Special Achievements/Activities:*

23 awards ($12,042 total). *Special Characteristics:* 2,528 awards ($6,834,854 total): adult students, children and siblings of alumni, children of public servants, children with a deceased or disabled parent, local/state students, out-of-state students, previous college experience, public servants, veterans' children. *Tuition waivers:* Full or partial for employees or children of employees, senior citizens. *ROTC:* Army cooperative, Naval cooperative, Air Force cooperative.

LOANS *Student loans:* $44,030,324 (54% need-based, 46% non-need-based). 36% of past graduating class borrowed through all loan programs. *Average indebtedness per student:* $22,272. *Average need-based loan:* Freshmen: $2477; Undergraduates: $3570. *Parent loans:* $875,237 (100% non-need-based). *Programs:* FFEL (Subsidized and Unsubsidized Stafford, PLUS), Perkins, college/university.

WORK-STUDY *Federal work-study:* Total amount: $417,646; 289 jobs averaging $1445. *State or other work-study/employment:* Total amount: $2,351,204 (100% non-need-based). 1,351 part-time jobs averaging $1741.

ATHLETIC AWARDS *Total amount:* $1,013,087 (100% non-need-based).

APPLYING FOR FINANCIAL AID *Required financial aid forms:* FAFSA, institution's own form. *Financial aid deadline (priority):* 5/15. *Notification date:* Continuous beginning 4/20. Students must reply within 4 weeks of notification.

CONTACT Ms. Emily London-Jones, Director of Student Financial Aid, University of New Orleans, Administration Building, Room 1005, New Orleans, LA 70148, 504-280-6687 or toll-free 800-256-5866 (out-of-state). *Fax:* 504-280-3973. *E-mail:* elondon@uno.edu.

UNIVERSITY OF NORTH ALABAMA
Florence, AL

Tuition & fees (AL res): $4366 **Average undergraduate aid package: $3690**

ABOUT THE INSTITUTION State-supported, coed. Awards: bachelor's and master's degrees and post-master's certificates. 38 undergraduate majors. Total enrollment: 6,415. Undergraduates: 5,417. Freshmen: 931. Federal methodology is used as a basis for awarding need-based institutional aid.

UNDERGRADUATE EXPENSES for 2005–06 *Application fee:* $25. *Tuition, state resident:* full-time $3648; part-time $143 per credit hour. *Tuition, nonresident:* full-time $7296; part-time $286 per credit hour. Part-time tuition and fees vary according to course load. *College room and board:* $4170; *room only:* $1960. Room and board charges vary according to board plan and housing facility. *Payment plan:* Installment.

FRESHMAN FINANCIAL AID (Fall 2005, est.) 560 applied for aid; of those 77% were deemed to have need. 97% of freshmen with need received aid; of those 28% had need fully met. *Average percent of need met:* 45% (excluding resources awarded to replace EFC). *Average financial aid package:* $3722 (excluding resources awarded to replace EFC).

UNDERGRADUATE FINANCIAL AID (Fall 2005, est.) 3,322 applied for aid; of those 82% were deemed to have need. 93% of undergraduates with need received aid; of those 39% had need fully met. *Average percent of need met:* 61% (excluding resources awarded to replace EFC). *Average financial aid package:* $3690 (excluding resources awarded to replace EFC).

GIFT AID (NEED-BASED) *Total amount:* $4,437,918 (100% federal). *Receiving aid:* Freshmen: 27% (256); All full-time undergraduates: 36% (1,601). *Average award:* Freshmen: $3584; Undergraduates: $2832. *Scholarships, grants, and awards:* Federal Pell, FSEOG, state, private, college/university gift aid from institutional funds.

GIFT AID (NON-NEED-BASED) *Total amount:* $2,270,349 (82% institutional, 18% external sources). *Scholarships, grants, and awards by category: Academic Interests/Achievement:* general academic interests/achievements. *Creative Arts/Performance:* art/fine arts, journalism/publications, music. *Special Achievements/Activities:* cheerleading/drum major, general special achievements/activities, leadership. *Special Characteristics:* children of faculty/staff, first-generation college students, general special characteristics, out-of-state students. *Tuition waivers:* Full or partial for employees or children of employees, senior citizens. *ROTC:* Army.

LOANS *Student loans:* $12,734,790 (55% need-based, 45% non-need-based). *Average need-based loan:* Freshmen: $3263; Undergraduates: $5068. *Parent loans:* $641,156 (100% non-need-based). *Programs:* FFEL (Subsidized and Unsubsidized Stafford, PLUS), Perkins.

WORK-STUDY *Federal work-study:* Total amount: $303,008; 214 jobs averaging $1240.

ATHLETIC AWARDS *Total amount:* $1,108,048 (100% non-need-based).

APPLYING FOR FINANCIAL AID *Required financial aid form:* FAFSA. *Financial aid deadline (priority):* 4/1. *Notification date:* 5/31. Students must reply within 2 weeks of notification.

CONTACT Mr. Ben Baker, Director of Student Financial Services, University of North Alabama, UNA Box 5014, Florence, AL 35632-0001, 256-765-4278 or toll-free 800-TALKUNA. *Fax:* 256-765-4920. *E-mail:* bjbaker@una.edu.

THE UNIVERSITY OF NORTH CAROLINA AT ASHEVILLE
Asheville, NC

Tuition & fees (NC res): $3525 **Average undergraduate aid package: $7873**

ABOUT THE INSTITUTION State-supported, coed. Awards: bachelor's and master's degrees and post-bachelor's certificates. 29 undergraduate majors. Total enrollment: 3,513. Undergraduates: 3,476. Freshmen: 472. Federal methodology is used as a basis for awarding need-based institutional aid.

UNDERGRADUATE EXPENSES for 2005–06 *Application fee:* $50. *Tuition, state resident:* full-time $1897. *Tuition, nonresident:* full-time $11,697. Part-time tuition and fees vary according to course load. *College room and board:* $5712; *room only:* $3122. Room and board charges vary according to housing facility.

FRESHMAN FINANCIAL AID (Fall 2004) 503 applied for aid; of those 57% were deemed to have need. 98% of freshmen with need received aid; of those 29% had need fully met. *Average percent of need met:* 73% (excluding resources awarded to replace EFC). *Average financial aid package:* $5984 (excluding resources awarded to replace EFC). 14% of all full-time freshmen had no need and received non-need-based gift aid.

UNDERGRADUATE FINANCIAL AID (Fall 2004) 1,916 applied for aid; of those 65% were deemed to have need. 97% of undergraduates with need received aid; of those 38% had need fully met. *Average percent of need met:* 78% (excluding resources awarded to replace EFC). *Average financial aid package:* $7873 (excluding resources awarded to replace EFC). 10% of all full-time undergraduates had no need and received non-need-based gift aid.

GIFT AID (NEED-BASED) *Total amount:* $4,287,226 (49% federal, 30% state, 16% institutional, 5% external sources). *Receiving aid:* Freshmen: 38% (267); All full-time undergraduates: 38% (1,088). *Average award:* Freshmen: $2825; Undergraduates: $3430. *Scholarships, grants, and awards:* Federal Pell, FSEOG, state, private, college/university gift aid from institutional funds.

GIFT AID (NON-NEED-BASED) *Total amount:* $1,252,445 (14% federal, 33% state, 36% institutional, 17% external sources). *Receiving aid:* Freshmen: 14% (101); Undergraduates: 10% (283). *Average Award:* Freshmen: $2365; Undergraduates: $3001. *Scholarships, grants, and awards by category: Academic Interests/Achievement:* 297 awards ($749,644 total): biological sciences, business, communication, computer science, education, engineering/technologies, English, general academic interests/achievements, health fields, mathematics, physical sciences, premedicine, social sciences. *Creative Arts/Performance:* 37 awards ($19,158 total): art/fine arts, general creative arts/performance, music, theater/drama. *Special Achievements/Activities:* 89 awards ($163,373 total): community service, general special achievements/activities, junior miss, leadership. *Special Characteristics:* 42 awards ($143,027 total): adult students, children and siblings of alumni, children of faculty/staff, ethnic background, first-generation college students, general special characteristics, handicapped students, international students, local/state students, members of minority groups, veterans, veterans' children. *Tuition waivers:* Full or partial for employees or children of employees, senior citizens.

LOANS *Student loans:* $6,479,633 (73% need-based, 27% non-need-based). 51% of past graduating class borrowed through all loan programs. *Average indebtedness per student:* $15,309. *Average need-based loan:* Freshmen: $2338; Undergraduates: $3685. *Parent loans:* $1,249,264 (22% need-based, 78% non-need-based). *Programs:* Federal Direct (Subsidized and Unsubsidized Stafford, PLUS), Perkins, state, college/university.

WORK-STUDY *Federal work-study:* Total amount: $148,530; 79 jobs averaging $1880. *State or other work-study/employment:* Total amount: $1,058,349 (14% need-based, 86% non-need-based). 767 part-time jobs averaging $1203.

ATHLETIC AWARDS *Total amount:* $822,755 (31% need-based, 69% non-need-based).

APPLYING FOR FINANCIAL AID *Required financial aid form:* FAFSA. *Financial aid deadline (priority):* 3/1. *Notification date:* Continuous beginning 3/15. Students must reply within 2 weeks of notification.

The University of North Carolina at Asheville

CONTACT Ms. Elizabeth D. Bartlett, Associate Director of Financial Aid, The University of North Carolina at Asheville, 1 University Heights, Asheville, NC 28804-8510, 828-232-6535 or toll-free 800-531-9842. *Fax:* 828-251-2294. *E-mail:* bbartlett@unca.edu.

THE UNIVERSITY OF NORTH CAROLINA AT CHAPEL HILL
Chapel Hill, NC

Tuition & fees (NC res): $4613   **Average undergraduate aid package: $9687**

ABOUT THE INSTITUTION State-supported, coed. Awards: bachelor's, master's, doctoral, and first professional degrees and post-master's certificates. 60 undergraduate majors. Total enrollment: 26,878. Undergraduates: 16,525. Freshmen: 3,589. Both federal and institutional methodology are used as a basis for awarding need-based institutional aid.

UNDERGRADUATE EXPENSES for 2005–06 *Application fee:* $60. *Tuition, state resident:* full-time $3205. *Tuition, nonresident:* full-time $17,003. Full-time tuition and fees vary according to program. Part-time tuition and fees vary according to course load and program. *College room and board:* $6516; *room only:* $3630. Room and board charges vary according to board plan, housing facility, and location. *Payment plans:* Installment, deferred payment.

FRESHMAN FINANCIAL AID (Fall 2004) 2716 applied for aid; of those 45% were deemed to have need. 99% of freshmen with need received aid; of those 82% had need fully met. *Average percent of need met:* 100% (excluding resources awarded to replace EFC). *Average financial aid package:* $9801 (excluding resources awarded to replace EFC). 21% of all full-time freshmen had no need and received non-need-based gift aid.

UNDERGRADUATE FINANCIAL AID (Fall 2004) 9,951 applied for aid; of those 53% were deemed to have need. 99% of undergraduates with need received aid; of those 74% had need fully met. *Average percent of need met:* 100% (excluding resources awarded to replace EFC). *Average financial aid package:* $9687 (excluding resources awarded to replace EFC). 15% of all full-time undergraduates had no need and received non-need-based gift aid.

GIFT AID (NEED-BASED) *Total amount:* $37,838,960 (20% federal, 17% state, 54% institutional, 9% external sources). *Receiving aid:* Freshmen: 34% (1,212); All full-time undergraduates: 33% (5,164). *Average award:* Freshmen: $8158; Undergraduates: $7170. *Scholarships, grants, and awards:* Federal Pell, FSEOG, state, private, college/university gift aid from institutional funds, state grants.

GIFT AID (NON-NEED-BASED) *Total amount:* $14,308,405 (7% federal, 13% state, 36% institutional, 44% external sources). *Receiving aid:* Freshmen: 17% (595); Undergraduates: 9% (1,467). *Average Award:* Freshmen: $4170; Undergraduates: $5308. *Scholarships, grants, and awards by category: Academic Interests/Achievement:* business, communication, education, English, general academic interests/achievements, health fields, mathematics. *Creative Arts/Performance:* applied art and design, art/fine arts, journalism/publications, music, theater/drama. *Special Achievements/Activities:* community service, general special achievements/activities, leadership. *Special Characteristics:* children of faculty/staff, international students, out-of-state students, relatives of clergy, religious affiliation. *Tuition waivers:* Full or partial for employees or children of employees, senior citizens. *ROTC:* Army, Naval, Air Force.

LOANS *Student loans:* $26,365,090 (71% need-based, 29% non-need-based). 34% of past graduating class borrowed through all loan programs. *Average indebtedness per student:* $13,801. *Average need-based loan:* Freshmen: $2444; Undergraduates: $3840. *Parent loans:* $8,958,434 (36% need-based, 64% non-need-based). *Programs:* FFEL (Subsidized and Unsubsidized Stafford, PLUS), Perkins, state, college/university, alternative loans.

WORK-STUDY *Federal work-study:* Total amount: $1,447,024; 803 jobs averaging $1802.

ATHLETIC AWARDS Total amount: $6,216,889 (31% need-based, 69% non-need-based).

APPLYING FOR FINANCIAL AID *Required financial aid forms:* FAFSA, CSS Financial Aid PROFILE. *Financial aid deadline (priority):* 3/1. *Notification date:* Continuous beginning 3/15. Students must reply by 5/1.

CONTACT Ms. Shirley A. Ort, Associate Provost and Director, Office of Scholarships and Student Aid, The University of North Carolina at Chapel Hill, PO Box 1080, Chapel Hill, NC 27514, 919-962-9246. *E-mail:* sao@unc.edu.

THE UNIVERSITY OF NORTH CAROLINA AT CHARLOTTE
Charlotte, NC

ABOUT THE INSTITUTION State-supported, coed. Awards: bachelor's, master's, and doctoral degrees and post-master's certificates. 71 undergraduate majors. Total enrollment: 20,772. Undergraduates: 16,555. Freshmen: 2,890.

GIFT AID (NEED-BASED) *Scholarships, grants, and awards:* Federal Pell, FSEOG, state, private, college/university gift aid from institutional funds.

GIFT AID (NON-NEED-BASED) *Scholarships, grants, and awards by category: Academic Interests/Achievement:* architecture, business, computer science, education, engineering/technologies, general academic interests/achievements, health fields, humanities, mathematics, military science. *Creative Arts/Performance:* music, performing arts. *Special Characteristics:* adult students.

LOANS *Programs:* FFEL (Subsidized and Unsubsidized Stafford, PLUS), Perkins, state, college/university.

WORK-STUDY *Federal work-study:* Total amount: $679,643; 530 jobs averaging $1282. *State or other work-study/employment:* Total amount: $2,298,246 (100% non-need-based). 1,825 part-time jobs averaging $1611.

APPLYING FOR FINANCIAL AID *Required financial aid form:* FAFSA.

CONTACT Anthony D. Carter, Director of Financial Aid, The University of North Carolina at Charlotte, 9201 University City Boulevard, Charlotte, NC 28223-0001, 704-687-2461. *Fax:* 704-687-3132. *E-mail:* finaid@email.uncc.edu.

THE UNIVERSITY OF NORTH CAROLINA AT GREENSBORO
Greensboro, NC

Tuition & fees (NC res): $3813   **Average undergraduate aid package: $7008**

ABOUT THE INSTITUTION State-supported, coed. Awards: bachelor's, master's, and doctoral degrees. 76 undergraduate majors. Total enrollment: 16,060. Undergraduates: 12,291. Freshmen: 2,424. Federal methodology is used as a basis for awarding need-based institutional aid.

UNDERGRADUATE EXPENSES for 2006–07 *Application fee:* $45. *Tuition, state resident:* full-time $2308. *Tuition, nonresident:* full-time $13,576. *College room and board:* $5706; *room only:* $3232.

FRESHMAN FINANCIAL AID (Fall 2005, est.) 1806 applied for aid; of those 91% were deemed to have need. 97% of freshmen with need received aid; of those 23% had need fully met. *Average percent of need met:* 53% (excluding resources awarded to replace EFC). *Average financial aid package:* $6113 (excluding resources awarded to replace EFC). 6% of all full-time freshmen had no need and received non-need-based gift aid.

UNDERGRADUATE FINANCIAL AID (Fall 2005, est.) 7,213 applied for aid; of those 98% were deemed to have need. 97% of undergraduates with need received aid; of those 23% had need fully met. *Average percent of need met:* 60% (excluding resources awarded to replace EFC). *Average financial aid package:* $7008 (excluding resources awarded to replace EFC). 5% of all full-time undergraduates had no need and received non-need-based gift aid.

GIFT AID (NEED-BASED) *Total amount:* $12,059,907 (85% federal, 8% state, 7% institutional). *Receiving aid:* Freshmen: 30% (712); All full-time undergraduates: 31% (3,269). *Average award:* Freshmen: $3558; Undergraduates: $3814. *Scholarships, grants, and awards:* Federal Pell, FSEOG, state, private, college/university gift aid from institutional funds.

GIFT AID (NON-NEED-BASED) *Total amount:* $10,623,087 (66% state, 34% institutional). *Receiving aid:* Freshmen: 38% (924); Undergraduates: 33% (3,509). *Average Award:* Freshmen: $2650; Undergraduates: $3909. *Scholarships, grants, and awards by category: Academic Interests/Achievement:* 320 awards ($600,000 total): biological sciences, business, communication, education, English, foreign languages, general academic interests/achievements, health fields, home economics, humanities, library science, mathematics, physical sciences, premedicine, religion/biblical studies, social sciences. *Creative Arts/Performance:* 100 awards ($350,000 total): art/fine arts, cinema/film/broadcasting, dance, music, performing arts, theater/drama. *Special Achievements/Activities:* 25 awards ($30,000 total): community service, general special achievements/activities, junior miss, leadership, religious involvement. *Special Characteristics:* 500 awards ($500,000 total): adult students, ethnic background, general special

characteristics, handicapped students, members of minority groups, out-of-state students, religious affiliation, veterans, veterans' children. *ROTC:* Army cooperative, Air Force cooperative.
LOANS *Student loans:* $36,342,308 (49% need-based, 51% non-need-based). 60% of past graduating class borrowed through all loan programs. *Average indebtedness per student:* $13,661. *Average need-based loan:* Freshmen: $2446; Undergraduates: $3654. *Parent loans:* $11,691,002 (100% non-need-based). *Programs:* FFEL (Subsidized and Unsubsidized Stafford, PLUS), Perkins, college/university.
WORK-STUDY *Federal work-study:* Total amount: $593,020; 313 jobs averaging $1895.
ATHLETIC AWARDS *Total amount:* $1,620,346 (100% non-need-based).
APPLYING FOR FINANCIAL AID *Required financial aid form:* FAFSA. *Financial aid deadline (priority):* 3/1. *Notification date:* Continuous beginning 3/15. Students must reply within 3 weeks of notification.
CONTACT Mr. Bruce Cabiness, Associate Director of Financial Aid, The University of North Carolina at Greensboro, PO Box 26170, Greensboro, NC 27402-6170, 336-334-5702. *Fax:* 336-334-3010. *E-mail:* bruce_cabiness@uncg.edu.

THE UNIVERSITY OF NORTH CAROLINA AT PEMBROKE
Pembroke, NC

Tuition & fees (NC res): $2980 | **Average undergraduate aid package: $6446**

ABOUT THE INSTITUTION State-supported, coed. Awards: bachelor's and master's degrees. 42 undergraduate majors. Total enrollment: 5,732. Undergraduates: 5,063. Freshmen: 984. Federal methodology is used as a basis for awarding need-based institutional aid.
UNDERGRADUATE EXPENSES for 2005–06 *Application fee:* $40. *Tuition, state resident:* full-time $1689. *Tuition, nonresident:* full-time $11,129. Full-time tuition and fees vary according to course load and location. Part-time tuition and fees vary according to course load and location. *College room and board:* $4890; *room only:* $2700. Room and board charges vary according to board plan and housing facility. *Payment plan:* Installment.
FRESHMAN FINANCIAL AID (Fall 2005, est.) 848 applied for aid; of those 83% were deemed to have need. 96% of freshmen with need received aid; of those 10% had need fully met. *Average percent of need met:* 56% (excluding resources awarded to replace EFC). *Average financial aid package:* $5943 (excluding resources awarded to replace EFC). 6% of all full-time freshmen had no need and received non-need-based gift aid.
UNDERGRADUATE FINANCIAL AID (Fall 2005, est.) 3,100 applied for aid; of those 92% were deemed to have need. 90% of undergraduates with need received aid; of those 12% had need fully met. *Average percent of need met:* 62% (excluding resources awarded to replace EFC). *Average financial aid package:* $6446 (excluding resources awarded to replace EFC). 4% of all full-time undergraduates had no need and received non-need-based gift aid.
GIFT AID (NEED-BASED) *Total amount:* $9,939,299 (57% federal, 33% state, 4% institutional, 6% external sources). *Receiving aid:* Freshmen: 63% (607); All full-time undergraduates: 61% (2,226). *Average award:* Freshmen: $4279; Undergraduates: $4136. *Scholarships, grants, and awards:* Federal Pell, FSEOG, state, private, college/university gift aid from institutional funds.
GIFT AID (NON-NEED-BASED) *Total amount:* $172,134 (100% institutional). *Receiving aid:* Freshmen: 5% (46); Undergraduates: 3% (100). *Average Award:* Freshmen: $1190; Undergraduates: $1208. *Scholarships, grants and awards by category:* Academic Interests/Achievement: 92 awards ($137,321 total): business, communication, education, English, general academic interests/achievements, health fields, physical sciences. *Creative Arts/Performance:* 43 awards ($19,513 total): journalism/publications, music. *Special Characteristics:* 4 awards ($13,800 total): children and siblings of alumni, general special characteristics. *Tuition waivers:* Full or partial for senior citizens. *ROTC:* Army, Air Force.
LOANS *Student loans:* $13,706,289 (58% need-based, 42% non-need-based). 70% of past graduating class borrowed through all loan programs. *Average indebtedness per student:* $14,766. *Average need-based loan:* Freshmen: $2410; Undergraduates: $3357. *Parent loans:* $1,129,897 (100% non-need-based). *Programs:* FFEL (Subsidized and Unsubsidized Stafford, PLUS), Perkins, college/university.

WORK-STUDY *Federal work-study:* Total amount: $355,768; 402 jobs averaging $959. *State or other work-study/employment:* Total amount: $30,100 (100% need-based). 55 part-time jobs averaging $668.
ATHLETIC AWARDS *Total amount:* $965,279 (100% need-based).
APPLYING FOR FINANCIAL AID *Required financial aid form:* FAFSA. *Financial aid deadline:* Continuous. *Notification date:* 4/15.
CONTACT Mildred Weber, Assistant Director of Financial Aid, The University of North Carolina at Pembroke, PO Box 1510, Pembroke, NC 28372, 910-521-6612 or toll-free 800-949-UNCP. *Fax:* 910-775-4159. *E-mail:* mildred.weber@uncp.edu.

THE UNIVERSITY OF NORTH CAROLINA WILMINGTON
Wilmington, NC

Tuition & fees (NC res): $3695 | **Average undergraduate aid package: $6527**

ABOUT THE INSTITUTION State-supported, coed. Awards: bachelor's, master's, and doctoral degrees. 62 undergraduate majors. Total enrollment: 11,653. Undergraduates: 10,581. Freshmen: 1,943. Federal methodology is used as a basis for awarding need-based institutional aid.
UNDERGRADUATE EXPENSES for 2005–06 *Application fee:* $45. *Tuition, state resident:* full-time $1928. *Tuition, nonresident:* full-time $11,863. Full-time tuition and fees vary according to course load. Part-time tuition and fees vary according to course load. *College room and board:* $6412. Room and board charges vary according to board plan and housing facility. *Payment plan:* Installment.
FRESHMAN FINANCIAL AID (Fall 2005, est.) 1047 applied for aid; of those 55% were deemed to have need. 100% of freshmen with need received aid; of those 70% had need fully met. *Average percent of need met:* 89% (excluding resources awarded to replace EFC). *Average financial aid package:* $5611 (excluding resources awarded to replace EFC). 1% of all full-time freshmen had no need and received non-need-based gift aid.
UNDERGRADUATE FINANCIAL AID (Fall 2005, est.) 5,499 applied for aid; of those 64% were deemed to have need. 100% of undergraduates with need received aid; of those 64% had need fully met. *Average percent of need met:* 87% (excluding resources awarded to replace EFC). *Average financial aid package:* $6527 (excluding resources awarded to replace EFC). 2% of all full-time undergraduates had no need and received non-need-based gift aid.
GIFT AID (NEED-BASED) *Total amount:* $12,294,621 (44% federal, 35% state, 5% institutional, 16% external sources). *Receiving aid:* Freshmen: 24% (460); All full-time undergraduates: 30% (2,916). *Average award:* Freshmen: $3761; Undergraduates: $3554. *Scholarships, grants, and awards:* Federal Pell, FSEOG, state, private, college/university gift aid from institutional funds.
GIFT AID (NON-NEED-BASED) *Total amount:* $2,673,445 (34% state, 21% institutional, 45% external sources). *Receiving aid:* Freshmen: 2; Undergraduates: 15. *Average Award:* Freshmen: $1602; Undergraduates: $1625. *Scholarships, grants, and awards by category:* Academic Interests/Achievement: 133 awards ($275,315 total): biological sciences, business, communication, computer science, education, English, foreign languages, general academic interests/achievements, health fields, humanities, international studies, mathematics, physical sciences, social sciences. *Creative Arts/Performance:* 21 awards ($14,500 total): art/fine arts, creative writing, music, theater/drama. *Special Achievements/Activities:* 63 awards ($14,430 total): cheerleading/drum major, general special achievements/activities, leadership. *Special Characteristics:* local/state students. *Tuition waivers:* Full or partial for employees or children of employees, senior citizens.
LOANS *Student loans:* $24,197,822 (52% need-based, 48% non-need-based). 52% of past graduating class borrowed through all loan programs. *Average indebtedness per student:* $15,620. *Average need-based loan:* Freshmen: $2836; Undergraduates: $4006. *Parent loans:* $16,092,573 (100% non-need-based). *Programs:* Federal Direct (Subsidized and Unsubsidized Stafford, PLUS), Perkins, state, college/university.
WORK-STUDY *Federal work-study:* Total amount: $695,179; 279 jobs averaging $3000.
ATHLETIC AWARDS *Total amount:* $1,551,572 (29% need-based, 71% non-need-based).
APPLYING FOR FINANCIAL AID *Required financial aid form:* FAFSA. *Financial aid deadline:* Continuous. *Notification date:* Continuous beginning 4/1. Students must reply within 3 weeks of notification.

The University of North Carolina Wilmington

CONTACT Emily Bliss, Director of Financial Aid and Veterans' Services Office, The University of North Carolina Wilmington, 601 South College Road, Wilmington, NC 28403-5951, 910-962-3177 or toll-free 800-228-5571 (out-of-state). *Fax:* 910-962-3851. *E-mail:* finaid@uncw.edu.

UNIVERSITY OF NORTH DAKOTA
Grand Forks, ND

| Tuition & fees (ND res): $5327 | Average undergraduate aid package: $10,311 |

ABOUT THE INSTITUTION State-supported, coed. Awards: bachelor's, master's, doctoral, and first professional degrees and post-master's certificates. 88 undergraduate majors. Total enrollment: 12,954. Undergraduates: 10,498. Freshmen: 1,884. Federal methodology is used as a basis for awarding need-based institutional aid.

UNDERGRADUATE EXPENSES for 2005–06 *Application fee:* $35. *Tuition, state resident:* full-time $4390. *Tuition, nonresident:* full-time $11,722. Full-time tuition and fees vary according to degree level, program, and reciprocity agreements. Part-time tuition and fees vary according to course load, degree level, program, and reciprocity agreements. *College room and board:* $4787; *room only:* $1979. Room and board charges vary according to board plan and housing facility. *Payment plan:* Deferred payment.

FRESHMAN FINANCIAL AID (Fall 2004) 2125 applied for aid; of those 66% were deemed to have need. 100% of freshmen with need received aid; of those 39% had need fully met. *Average percent of need met:* 83% (excluding resources awarded to replace EFC). *Average financial aid package:* $9175 (excluding resources awarded to replace EFC). 7% of all full-time freshmen had no need and received non-need-based gift aid.

UNDERGRADUATE FINANCIAL AID (Fall 2004) 6,706 applied for aid; of those 69% were deemed to have need. 100% of undergraduates with need received aid; of those 43% had need fully met. *Average percent of need met:* 86% (excluding resources awarded to replace EFC). *Average financial aid package:* $10,311 (excluding resources awarded to replace EFC). 4% of all full-time undergraduates had no need and received non-need-based gift aid.

GIFT AID (NEED-BASED) *Total amount:* $13,542,600 (55% federal, 4% state, 23% institutional, 18% external sources). *Receiving aid:* Freshmen: 20% (548); All full-time undergraduates: 24% (2,014). *Average award:* Freshmen: $2967; Undergraduates: $3098. *Scholarships, grants, and awards:* Federal Pell, FSEOG, state, private, college/university gift aid from institutional funds, Federal Nursing.

GIFT AID (NON-NEED-BASED) *Total amount:* $1,830,691 (10% federal, 2% state, 58% institutional, 30% external sources). *Receiving aid:* Freshmen: 26% (688); Undergraduates: 18% (1,506). *Average Award:* Freshmen: $2960; Undergraduates: $2924. *Scholarships, grants, and awards by category: Academic Interests/Achievement:* 2,634 awards ($3,118,021 total): biological sciences, business, communication, computer science, education, engineering/technologies, English, foreign languages, general academic interests/achievements, health fields, humanities, international studies, mathematics, military science, physical sciences, premedicine, social sciences. *Creative Arts/Performance:* 113 awards ($70,185 total): art/fine arts, debating, music, theater/drama. *Special Achievements/Activities:* 590 awards ($1,571,474 total): general special achievements/activities, leadership, memberships. *Special Characteristics:* 302 awards ($985,693 total): children of faculty/staff, ethnic background, general special characteristics, handicapped students, international students, members of minority groups, veterans' children. *Tuition waivers:* Full or partial for minority students, employees or children of employees, senior citizens. *ROTC:* Army, Air Force.

LOANS *Student loans:* $38,802,090 (80% need-based, 20% non-need-based). 70% of past graduating class borrowed through all loan programs. *Average indebtedness per student:* $26,225. *Average need-based loan:* Freshmen: $3309; Undergraduates: $4260. *Parent loans:* $2,149,986 (62% need-based, 38% non-need-based). *Programs:* FFEL (Subsidized and Unsubsidized Stafford, PLUS), Perkins, Federal Nursing, Alternative Commercial Loans.

WORK-STUDY *Federal work-study:* Total amount: $1,315,000; 1,048 jobs averaging $1035.

ATHLETIC AWARDS Total amount: $1,220,513 (30% need-based, 70% non-need-based).

APPLYING FOR FINANCIAL AID *Required financial aid form:* FAFSA. *Financial aid deadline (priority):* 3/15. *Notification date:* Continuous beginning 5/15. Students must reply within 4 weeks of notification.

CONTACT Ms. Robin Holden, Director of Student Financial Aid, University of North Dakota, Box 8371, Grand Forks, ND 58202, 701-777-3121 or toll-free 800-CALL UND. *Fax:* 701-777-2040. *E-mail:* robin.holden@mail.und.nodak.edu.

UNIVERSITY OF NORTHERN COLORADO
Greeley, CO

| Tuition & fees (CO res): $3837 | Average undergraduate aid package: $9640 |

ABOUT THE INSTITUTION State-supported, coed. Awards: bachelor's, master's, and doctoral degrees (specialist). 42 undergraduate majors. Total enrollment: 13,156. Undergraduates: 10,811. Freshmen: 2,441. Federal methodology is used as a basis for awarding need-based institutional aid.

UNDERGRADUATE EXPENSES for 2005–06 *Application fee:* $40. *Tuition, state resident:* full-time $3192; part-time $133 per credit hour. *Tuition, nonresident:* full-time $11,736; part-time $489 per credit hour. *Required fees:* full-time $645; $32.25 per credit hour. *College room and board:* $6412; *room only:* $3150. Room and board charges vary according to board plan and housing facility. *Payment plan:* Deferred payment.

FRESHMAN FINANCIAL AID (Fall 2005, est.) 2003 applied for aid; of those 53% were deemed to have need. 99% of freshmen with need received aid; of those 46% had need fully met. *Average percent of need met:* 95% (excluding resources awarded to replace EFC). *Average financial aid package:* $7928 (excluding resources awarded to replace EFC). 11% of all full-time freshmen had no need and received non-need-based gift aid.

UNDERGRADUATE FINANCIAL AID (Fall 2005, est.) 7,567 applied for aid; of those 58% were deemed to have need. 99% of undergraduates with need received aid; of those 57% had need fully met. *Average percent of need met:* 100% (excluding resources awarded to replace EFC). *Average financial aid package:* $9640 (excluding resources awarded to replace EFC). 9% of all full-time undergraduates had no need and received non-need-based gift aid.

GIFT AID (NEED-BASED) *Total amount:* $9,080,444 (68% federal, 25% state, 7% institutional). *Receiving aid:* Freshmen: 22% (525); All full-time undergraduates: 24% (2,308). *Average award:* Freshmen: $3379; Undergraduates: $3721. *Scholarships, grants, and awards:* Federal Pell, FSEOG, state, private, college/university gift aid from institutional funds.

GIFT AID (NON-NEED-BASED) *Total amount:* $8,275,942 (17% state, 22% institutional, 61% external sources). *Receiving aid:* Freshmen: 20% (492); Undergraduates: 17% (1,625). *Average Award:* Freshmen: $2395; Undergraduates: $2602. *Scholarships, grants, and awards by category: Academic Interests/Achievement:* 720 awards ($774,232 total): biological sciences, business, communication, education, English, general academic interests/achievements, health fields, home economics, mathematics, military science, physical sciences, social sciences. *Creative Arts/Performance:* 228 awards ($103,057 total): dance, music, performing arts, theater/drama. *Special Characteristics:* 3,613 awards ($6,784,591 total): adult students, children and siblings of alumni, children of faculty/staff, children of union members/company employees, ethnic background, general special characteristics, handicapped students, international students, local/state students, members of minority groups, out-of-state students, veterans. *ROTC:* Army, Air Force.

LOANS *Student loans:* $32,615,984 (47% need-based, 53% non-need-based). *Average need-based loan:* Freshmen: $3134; Undergraduates: $3813. *Parent loans:* $35,777,242 (100% non-need-based). *Programs:* FFEL (Subsidized and Unsubsidized Stafford, PLUS), Perkins, college/university.

WORK-STUDY *Federal work-study:* Total amount: $777,591; 366 jobs averaging $2125. *State or other work-study/employment:* Total amount: $9,139,763 (18% need-based, 82% non-need-based). 855 part-time jobs averaging $1966.

ATHLETIC AWARDS Total amount: $775,642 (100% non-need-based).

APPLYING FOR FINANCIAL AID *Required financial aid form:* FAFSA. *Financial aid deadline (priority):* 3/1. *Notification date:* Continuous beginning 4/15. Students must reply within 4 weeks of notification.

CONTACT Donni Clark, Director of Student Financial Resources, University of Northern Colorado, Carter Hall 1005, Campus Box 33, Greeley, CO 80639, 970-351-2502 or toll-free 888-700-4UNC (in-state). *Fax:* 970-351-3737. *E-mail:* sfr@unco.edu.

UNIVERSITY OF NORTHERN IOWA
Cedar Falls, IA

Tuition & fees (IA res): $5602 **Average undergraduate aid package:** $6738

ABOUT THE INSTITUTION State-supported, coed. Awards: bachelor's, master's, and doctoral degrees. 112 undergraduate majors. Total enrollment: 12,622. Undergraduates: 10,994. Freshmen: 1,737. Federal methodology is used as a basis for awarding need-based institutional aid.
UNDERGRADUATE EXPENSES for 2005–06 *Application fee:* $30. *Tuition, state resident:* full-time $4890; part-time $204 per hour. *Tuition, nonresident:* full-time $12,502; part-time $521 per hour. *Required fees:* full-time $712; $313.75 per term part-time. Full-time tuition and fees vary according to course load. Part-time tuition and fees vary according to course load. *College room and board:* $5531; *room only:* $2588. Room and board charges vary according to board plan and housing facility. *Payment plan:* Installment.
FRESHMAN FINANCIAL AID (Fall 2005, est.) 1460 applied for aid; of those 65% were deemed to have need. 96% of freshmen with need received aid; of those 23% had need fully met. *Average percent of need met:* 65% (excluding resources awarded to replace EFC). *Average financial aid package:* $6011 (excluding resources awarded to replace EFC). 17% of all full-time freshmen had no need and received non-need-based gift aid.
UNDERGRADUATE FINANCIAL AID (Fall 2005, est.) 7,623 applied for aid; of those 74% were deemed to have need. 97% of undergraduates with need received aid; of those 22% had need fully met. *Average percent of need met:* 66% (excluding resources awarded to replace EFC). *Average financial aid package:* $6738 (excluding resources awarded to replace EFC). 9% of all full-time undergraduates had no need and received non-need-based gift aid.
GIFT AID (NEED-BASED) *Total amount:* $10,579,183 (66% federal, 7% state, 27% institutional). *Receiving aid:* Freshmen: 38% (647); All full-time undergraduates: 34% (3,343). *Average award:* Freshmen: $2556; Undergraduates: $2690. *Scholarships, grants, and awards:* Federal Pell, FSEOG, state, private, college/university gift aid from institutional funds.
GIFT AID (NON-NEED-BASED) *Total amount:* $6,550,666 (5% state, 72% institutional, 23% external sources). *Receiving aid:* Freshmen: 26% (439); Undergraduates: 14% (1,401). *Average Award:* Freshmen: $2331; Undergraduates: $2900. *Scholarships, grants, and awards by category: Academic Interests/Achievement:* biological sciences, business, education, general academic interests/achievements, mathematics, physical sciences, social sciences. *Creative Arts/Performance:* applied art and design, art/fine arts, music, theater/drama. *Special Achievements/Activities:* leadership. *Special Characteristics:* general special characteristics, members of minority groups. *ROTC:* Army.
LOANS *Student loans:* $51,194,514 (46% need-based, 54% non-need-based). 77% of past graduating class borrowed through all loan programs. *Average indebtedness per student:* $20,239. *Average need-based loan:* Freshmen: $2701; Undergraduates: $4121. *Parent loans:* $11,125,790 (100% non-need-based). *Programs:* Federal Direct (Subsidized and Unsubsidized Stafford, PLUS), Perkins, state, alternative loans.
WORK-STUDY *Federal work-study:* Total amount: $958,186; 423 jobs averaging $1852. *State or other work-study/employment:* Total amount: $216,273 (54% need-based, 46% non-need-based). 123 part-time jobs averaging $1953.
ATHLETIC AWARDS *Total amount:* $2,726,470 (100% non-need-based).
APPLYING FOR FINANCIAL AID *Required financial aid form:* FAFSA. *Financial aid deadline:* Continuous. *Notification date:* Continuous beginning 3/1.
CONTACT Joyce Morrow, Associate Director Enrollment Services, University of Northern Iowa, 255 Gilchrist Hall, Cedar Falls, IA 50614-0024, 319-273-2700 or toll-free 800-772-2037. *Fax:* 319-273-6950. *E-mail:* joyce.morrow@uni.edu.

UNIVERSITY OF NORTHERN VIRGINIA
Manassas, VA

CONTACT Financial Aid Office, University of Northern Virginia, 10021 Balls Ford Road, Manassas, VA 20109, 703-392-0771.

UNIVERSITY OF NORTH FLORIDA
Jacksonville, FL

Tuition & fees (FL res): $3269 **Average undergraduate aid package:** $1485

ABOUT THE INSTITUTION State-supported, coed. Awards: associate, bachelor's, master's, and doctoral degrees and post-bachelor's and post-master's certificates (doctoral degree in education only). 50 undergraduate majors. Total enrollment: 15,234. Undergraduates: 13,410. Freshmen: 2,378. Federal methodology is used as a basis for awarding need-based institutional aid.
UNDERGRADUATE EXPENSES for 2005–06 *Application fee:* $30. *Tuition, state resident:* full-time $3269; part-time $108.95 per semester hour. *Tuition, nonresident:* full-time $14,911; part-time $497.02 per semester hour. *College room and board:* $6640; *room only:* $3810. Room and board charges vary according to board plan and housing facility. *Payment plan:* Deferred payment.
FRESHMAN FINANCIAL AID (Fall 2005, est.) 1328 applied for aid; of those 25% were deemed to have need. 99% of freshmen with need received aid; of those 39% had need fully met. *Average percent of need met:* 89% (excluding resources awarded to replace EFC). *Average financial aid package:* $1441 (excluding resources awarded to replace EFC). 10% of all full-time freshmen had no need and received non-need-based gift aid.
UNDERGRADUATE FINANCIAL AID (Fall 2005, est.) 4,928 applied for aid; of those 29% were deemed to have need. 98% of undergraduates with need received aid; of those 29% had need fully met. *Average percent of need met:* 88% (excluding resources awarded to replace EFC). *Average financial aid package:* $1485 (excluding resources awarded to replace EFC). 9% of all full-time undergraduates had no need and received non-need-based gift aid.
GIFT AID (NEED-BASED) *Total amount:* $13,319,574 (55% federal, 24% state, 20% institutional, 1% external sources). *Receiving aid:* Freshmen: 8% (171); All full-time undergraduates: 9% (839). *Average award:* Freshmen: $1018; Undergraduates: $1052. *Scholarships, grants, and awards:* Federal Pell, FSEOG, state, college/university gift aid from institutional funds, 2+2 Scholarships (jointly sponsored with Florida Community College at Jacksonville).
GIFT AID (NON-NEED-BASED) *Total amount:* $16,970,765 (81% state, 15% institutional, 4% external sources). *Receiving aid:* Freshmen: 12% (260); Undergraduates: 7% (681). *Average Award:* Freshmen: $1356; Undergraduates: $1297. *Scholarships, grants, and awards by category: Academic Interests/Achievement:* 647 awards ($1,820,982 total): business, computer science, education, engineering/technologies, general academic interests/achievements, health fields, international studies. *Creative Arts/Performance:* 66 awards ($64,020 total): art/fine arts, music. *Special Achievements/Activities:* 48 awards ($53,478 total): community service, general special achievements/activities, leadership. *Special Characteristics:* 13 awards ($24,000 total): first-generation college students, general special characteristics, international students, members of minority groups, out-of-state students. *Tuition waivers:* Full or partial for employees or children of employees, senior citizens. *ROTC:* Naval cooperative.
LOANS *Student loans:* $22,173,613 (63% need-based, 37% non-need-based). 46% of past graduating class borrowed through all loan programs. *Average indebtedness per student:* $16,707. *Average need-based loan:* Freshmen: $778; Undergraduates: $1561. *Parent loans:* $1,711,257 (17% need-based, 83% non-need-based). *Programs:* FFEL (Subsidized and Unsubsidized Stafford, PLUS), Perkins.
WORK-STUDY *Federal work-study:* Total amount: $342,379; 122 jobs averaging $2806.
ATHLETIC AWARDS *Total amount:* $186,273 (48% need-based, 52% non-need-based).
APPLYING FOR FINANCIAL AID *Required financial aid forms:* FAFSA, financial aid transcript (for transfers). *Financial aid deadline (priority):* 4/1. *Notification date:* Continuous. Students must reply within 2 weeks of notification.
CONTACT Mrs. Janice Nowak, Director of Financial Aid, University of North Florida, 4567 St. Johns Bluff Road, South, Jacksonville, FL 32224-2645, 904-620-2604. *E-mail:* jnowak@unf.edu.

UNIVERSITY OF NORTH TEXAS
Denton, TX

ABOUT THE INSTITUTION State-supported, coed. Awards: bachelor's, master's, and doctoral degrees and post-bachelor's certificates. 103 undergraduate majors. Total enrollment: 32,047. Undergraduates: 25,308. Freshmen: 3,635.
GIFT AID (NEED-BASED) *Scholarships, grants, and awards:* Federal Pell, FSEOG, state, college/university gift aid from institutional funds.
GIFT AID (NON-NEED-BASED) *Scholarships, grants, and awards by category: Academic Interests/Achievement:* general academic interests/achievements. *Creative Arts/Performance:* dance, music, theater/drama.

University of North Texas

LOANS *Programs:* FFEL (Subsidized and Unsubsidized Stafford, PLUS), Perkins, state, college/university.
WORK-STUDY *Federal work-study:* Total amount: $2,825,012; jobs available. *State or other work-study/employment:* Total amount: $203,348 (100% need-based). Part-time jobs available.
APPLYING FOR FINANCIAL AID *Required financial aid form:* FAFSA.
CONTACT Mrs. Carolyn Cunningham, Director of Financial Aid, University of North Texas, PO Box 311370, Denton, TX 76203-1370, 940-565-2302 or toll-free 800-868-8211 (in-state). *Fax:* 940-565-2738.

UNIVERSITY OF NOTRE DAME
Notre Dame, IN

ABOUT THE INSTITUTION Independent Roman Catholic, coed. Awards: bachelor's, master's, doctoral, and first professional degrees. 55 undergraduate majors. Total enrollment: 11,417. Undergraduates: 8,275. Freshmen: 1,966.
GIFT AID (NEED-BASED) *Scholarships, grants, and awards:* Federal Pell, FSEOG, state, college/university gift aid from institutional funds.
GIFT AID (NON-NEED-BASED) *Scholarships, grants, and awards by category: Special Characteristics:* children of faculty/staff.
LOANS *Programs:* FFEL (Subsidized and Unsubsidized Stafford, PLUS), Perkins, private student loans.
WORK-STUDY *Federal work-study:* Total amount: $3,411,105; 1,752 jobs averaging $1947. *State or other work-study/employment:* Total amount: $7,651,390 (3% need-based, 97% non-need-based). 3,164 part-time jobs averaging $2418.
APPLYING FOR FINANCIAL AID *Required financial aid forms:* FAFSA, CSS Financial Aid PROFILE, noncustodial (divorced/separated) parent's statement, business/farm supplement, income tax form(s), W-2 forms.
CONTACT Mr. Joseph A. Russo, Director of Financial Aid, University of Notre Dame, 115 Main Building, Notre Dame, IN 46556, 574-631-6436. *Fax:* 574-631-6899. *E-mail:* finaid.1@nd.edu.

UNIVERSITY OF OKLAHOMA
Norman, OK

Tuition & fees (OK res): $4408   **Average undergraduate aid package: $8745**

ABOUT THE INSTITUTION State-supported, coed. Awards: bachelor's, master's, doctoral, and first professional degrees and post-master's certificates. 104 undergraduate majors. Total enrollment: 26,968. Undergraduates: 20,398. Freshmen: 3,245. Federal methodology is used as a basis for awarding need-based institutional aid.
UNDERGRADUATE EXPENSES for 2005–06 *Application fee:* $40. *Tuition, state resident:* full-time $2862; part-time $95.40 per credit hour. *Tuition, nonresident:* full-time $10,755; part-time $358.50 per credit hour. *Required fees:* full-time $1546; $44.10 per credit hour or $111.50 per term part-time. Full-time tuition and fees vary according to course load, location, program, and reciprocity agreements. Part-time tuition and fees vary according to course load, location, program, and reciprocity agreements. *College room and board:* $6361; *room only:* $3355. Room and board charges vary according to board plan and housing facility. *Payment plan:* Installment.
FRESHMAN FINANCIAL AID (Fall 2004) 2054 applied for aid; of those 86% were deemed to have need. 100% of freshmen with need received aid; of those 47% had need fully met. *Average percent of need met:* 85% (excluding resources awarded to replace EFC). *Average financial aid package:* $8492 (excluding resources awarded to replace EFC). 9% of all full-time freshmen had no need and received non-need-based gift aid.
UNDERGRADUATE FINANCIAL AID (Fall 2004) 9,628 applied for aid; of those 92% were deemed to have need. 100% of undergraduates with need received aid; of those 47% had need fully met. *Average percent of need met:* 85% (excluding resources awarded to replace EFC). *Average financial aid package:* $8745 (excluding resources awarded to replace EFC). 9% of all full-time undergraduates had no need and received non-need-based gift aid.
GIFT AID (NEED-BASED) *Total amount:* $24,702,262 (58% federal, 23% state, 11% institutional, 8% external sources). *Receiving aid:* Freshmen: 11% (377); All full-time undergraduates: 16% (2,836). *Average award:* Freshmen: $3984; Undergraduates: $3741. *Scholarships, grants, and awards:* Federal Pell, FSEOG, state, private, college/university gift aid from institutional funds, United Negro College Fund.
GIFT AID (NON-NEED-BASED) *Total amount:* $8,528,608 (10% federal, 53% state, 21% institutional, 16% external sources). *Receiving aid:* Freshmen: 31% (1,095); Undergraduates: 23% (4,152). *Average Award:* Freshmen: $1008; Undergraduates: $1049. *Scholarships, grants, and awards by category: Academic Interests/Achievement:* 7,984 awards ($16,798,800 total): architecture, area/ethnic studies, biological sciences, business, communication, computer science, education, engineering/technologies, foreign languages, general academic interests/achievements, humanities, international studies, mathematics, physical sciences, social sciences. *Creative Arts/Performance:* 114 awards ($1,166,416 total): art/fine arts, dance, journalism/publications, music, performing arts, theater/drama. *Special Achievements/Activities:* 56 awards ($75,596 total): leadership. *Special Characteristics:* 782 awards ($1,660,660 total): children and siblings of alumni, members of minority groups, previous college experience. *Tuition waivers:* Full or partial for employees or children of employees, senior citizens. *ROTC:* Army, Naval, Air Force.
LOANS *Student loans:* $48,944,703 (98% need-based, 2% non-need-based). 49% of past graduating class borrowed through all loan programs. *Average indebtedness per student:* $18,494. *Average need-based loan:* Freshmen: $3110; Undergraduates: $4432. *Parent loans:* $11,299,796 (84% need-based, 16% non-need-based). *Programs:* FFEL (Subsidized and Unsubsidized Stafford, PLUS), Perkins, college/university, alternative loans.
WORK-STUDY *Federal work-study:* Total amount: $1,500,458; 649 jobs averaging $2312.
ATHLETIC AWARDS *Total amount:* $4,355,558 (40% need-based, 60% non-need-based).
APPLYING FOR FINANCIAL AID *Required financial aid form:* FAFSA. *Financial aid deadline:* Continuous. *Notification date:* Continuous beginning 3/15. Students must reply within 6 weeks of notification.
CONTACT Financial Aid Assistant, University of Oklahoma, 1000 Asp Avenue, Room 216, Norman, OK 73019-4078, 405-325-4521 or toll-free 800-234-6868. *Fax:* 405-325-0819. *E-mail:* financialaid@ou.edu.

UNIVERSITY OF OREGON
Eugene, OR

Tuition & fees (OR res): $5613   **Average undergraduate aid package: $7656**

ABOUT THE INSTITUTION State-supported, coed. Awards: bachelor's, master's, doctoral, and first professional degrees and post-bachelor's and post-master's certificates. 95 undergraduate majors. Total enrollment: 20,347. Undergraduates: 16,473. Freshmen: 3,207. Federal methodology is used as a basis for awarding need-based institutional aid.
UNDERGRADUATE EXPENSES for 2005–06 *Application fee:* $50. *Tuition, state resident:* full-time $4164; part-time $104 per credit hour. *Tuition, nonresident:* full-time $15,996; part-time $420 per credit hour. *Required fees:* full-time $1449; $427 per term part-time. Full-time tuition and fees vary according to class time, course level, course load, degree level, program, and reciprocity agreements. Part-time tuition and fees vary according to class time, course level, course load, degree level, and program. *College room and board:* $7496. Room and board charges vary according to board plan and housing facility. *Payment plan:* Installment.
FRESHMAN FINANCIAL AID (Fall 2005, est.) 2008 applied for aid; of those 58% were deemed to have need. 94% of freshmen with need received aid; of those 18% had need fully met. *Average percent of need met:* 55% (excluding resources awarded to replace EFC). *Average financial aid package:* $7138 (excluding resources awarded to replace EFC). 12% of all full-time freshmen had no need and received non-need-based gift aid.
UNDERGRADUATE FINANCIAL AID (Fall 2005, est.) 9,009 applied for aid; of those 71% were deemed to have need. 95% of undergraduates with need received aid; of those 18% had need fully met. *Average percent of need met:* 64% (excluding resources awarded to replace EFC). *Average financial aid package:* $7656 (excluding resources awarded to replace EFC). 6% of all full-time undergraduates had no need and received non-need-based gift aid.
GIFT AID (NEED-BASED) *Total amount:* $14,545,418 (79% federal, 20% state, 1% institutional). *Receiving aid:* Freshmen: 16% (518); All full-time undergraduates: 22% (3,338). *Average award:* Freshmen: $4005; Undergraduates: $4034. *Scholarships, grants, and awards:* Federal Pell, FSEOG, state, private, college/university gift aid from institutional funds.
GIFT AID (NON-NEED-BASED) *Total amount:* $9,151,715 (85% institutional, 15% external sources). *Receiving aid:* Freshmen: 19% (585); Undergraduates: 12% (1,724). *Average Award:* Freshmen: $1579; Undergraduates: $1701.

Scholarships, grants, and awards by category: Academic Interests/Achievement: architecture, biological sciences, business, education, foreign languages, general academic interests/achievements, physical sciences, social sciences. *Creative Arts/Performance:* art/fine arts, dance, journalism/publications, music, performing arts, theater/drama. *Special Achievements/Activities:* general special achievements/activities. *Special Characteristics:* general special characteristics, international students, local/state students. *Tuition waivers:* Full or partial for employees or children of employees. *ROTC:* Army, Air Force cooperative.
LOANS *Student loans:* $43,266,135 (57% need-based, 43% non-need-based). 60% of past graduating class borrowed through all loan programs. *Average indebtedness per student:* $18,029. *Average need-based loan:* Freshmen: $3669; Undergraduates: $4489. *Parent loans:* $27,469,837 (22% need-based, 78% non-need-based). *Programs:* Federal Direct (Subsidized and Unsubsidized Stafford, PLUS), Perkins, college/university.
WORK-STUDY *Federal work-study:* Total amount: $3,752,957; jobs available. *State or other work-study/employment:* Total amount: $340,966 (100% need-based). Part-time jobs available.
APPLYING FOR FINANCIAL AID *Required financial aid form:* FAFSA. *Financial aid deadline (priority):* 3/1. *Notification date:* Continuous beginning 4/1. Students must reply within 4 weeks of notification.
CONTACT Elizabeth Bickford, Director of Financial Aid, University of Oregon, 1278 University of Oregon, 260 Oregon Hall, Eugene, OR 97403-1278, 541-346-3221 or toll-free 800-232-3825 (in-state). *Fax:* 541-346-1175. *E-mail:* ebick@uoregon.edu.

UNIVERSITY OF PENNSYLVANIA
Philadelphia, PA

Tuition & fees: $32,364 — **Average undergraduate aid package: $27,011**

ABOUT THE INSTITUTION Independent, coed. Awards: associate, bachelor's, master's, doctoral, and first professional degrees and post-bachelor's, post-master's, and first professional certificates (also offers evening program with significant enrollment not reflected in profile). 95 undergraduate majors. Total enrollment: 18,814. Undergraduates: 9,841. Freshmen: 2,543. Institutional methodology is used as a basis for awarding need-based institutional aid.
UNDERGRADUATE EXPENSES for 2005–06 *Application fee:* $70. *Comprehensive fee:* $41,766 includes full-time tuition ($29,030), mandatory fees ($3334), and room and board ($9402). *College room only:* $5730. Room and board charges vary according to board plan and housing facility. *Part-time tuition:* $3708 per course. *Part-time fees:* $389 per course. Part-time tuition and fees vary according to course load. *Payment plan:* Installment.
FRESHMAN FINANCIAL AID (Fall 2004) 1285 applied for aid; of those 78% were deemed to have need. 100% of freshmen with need received aid; of those 100% had need fully met. *Average percent of need met:* 100% (excluding resources awarded to replace EFC). *Average financial aid package:* $26,978 (excluding resources awarded to replace EFC).
UNDERGRADUATE FINANCIAL AID (Fall 2004) 4,869 applied for aid; of those 88% were deemed to have need. 100% of undergraduates with need received aid; of those 100% had need fully met. *Average percent of need met:* 100% (excluding resources awarded to replace EFC). *Average financial aid package:* $27,011 (excluding resources awarded to replace EFC).
GIFT AID (NEED-BASED) *Total amount:* $86,255,000 (7% federal, 1% state, 87% institutional, 5% external sources). *Receiving aid:* Freshmen: 37% (938); All full-time undergraduates: 41% (3,950). *Average award:* Freshmen: $22,051; Undergraduates: $21,716. *Scholarships, grants, and awards:* Federal Pell, FSEOG, state, private, college/university gift aid from institutional funds.
GIFT AID (NON-NEED-BASED) *Total amount:* $5,578,911 (1% federal, 99% external sources). *Tuition waivers:* Full or partial for employees or children of employees. *ROTC:* Army cooperative, Naval, Air Force cooperative.
LOANS *Student loans:* $32,637,631 (80% need-based, 20% non-need-based). 41% of past graduating class borrowed through all loan programs. *Average indebtedness per student:* $21,133. *Average need-based loan:* Freshmen: $3028; Undergraduates: $3935. *Parent loans:* $14,002,727 (58% need-based, 42% non-need-based). *Programs:* FFEL (Subsidized and Unsubsidized Stafford, PLUS), Perkins, Federal Nursing, college/university, supplemental third-party loans (guaranteed by institution).
WORK-STUDY *Federal work-study:* Total amount: $14,595,000; 3,942 jobs averaging $3702.

APPLYING FOR FINANCIAL AID *Required financial aid forms:* FAFSA, institution's own form, CSS Financial Aid PROFILE, state aid form, noncustodial (divorced/separated) parent's statement, business/farm supplement, federal income tax form(s). *Financial aid deadline (priority):* 2/15. *Notification date:* Continuous beginning 4/1. Students must reply by 5/1.
CONTACT Mr. William Schilling, Director of Financial Aid, University of Pennsylvania, 212 Franklin Building, 3451 Walnut Street, Philadelphia, PA 19104-6270, 215-898-6784. *Fax:* 215-573-2208. *E-mail:* schilling@sfs.upenn.edu.

UNIVERSITY OF PHOENIX–ATLANTA CAMPUS
Atlanta, GA

Tuition & fees: $11,150 — **Average undergraduate aid package: $4406**

ABOUT THE INSTITUTION Proprietary, coed. Awards: bachelor's and master's degrees. 6 undergraduate majors. Total enrollment: 2,495. Undergraduates: 1,741. Freshmen: 95. Both federal and institutional methodology are used as a basis for awarding need-based institutional aid.
UNDERGRADUATE EXPENSES for 2005–06 *Application fee:* $110. *Tuition:* full-time $10,590; part-time $353 per credit. *Required fees:* full-time $560; $70 per course. *Payment plan:* Deferred payment.
UNDERGRADUATE FINANCIAL AID (Fall 2004) *Average financial aid package:* $4406 (excluding resources awarded to replace EFC).
GIFT AID (NEED-BASED) *Total amount:* $9,134,306 (100% federal). *Receiving aid:* All full-time undergraduates: 1,916. *Scholarships, grants, and awards:* Federal Pell, FSEOG, state, private, college/university gift aid from institutional funds, Academic Competitiveness Grant and National Science and Mathematics Access to Retain Talent (SMART).
GIFT AID (NON-NEED-BASED) *Total amount:* $9,902,423 (100% federal). *Receiving aid:* Undergraduates: 1,864. *Scholarships, grants, and awards by category: Academic Interests/Achievement:* business, computer science, health fields. *Tuition waivers:* Full or partial for employees or children of employees.
LOANS *Programs:* FFEL (Subsidized and Unsubsidized Stafford, PLUS), Perkins.
APPLYING FOR FINANCIAL AID *Required financial aid form:* institution's own form. *Financial aid deadline:* Continuous. *Notification date:* Continuous beginning 7/1.
CONTACT ACS/AFS, University of Phoenix–Atlanta Campus, 875 West Elliot Road, Suite 116, Tempe, AZ 85284, 480-735-3000 or toll-free 800-776-4867 (in-state), 800-228-7240 (out-of-state). *Fax:* 480-940-2060.

UNIVERSITY OF PHOENIX–BAY AREA CAMPUS
Pleasanton, CA

Tuition & fees: $13,550 — **Average undergraduate aid package: $3673**

ABOUT THE INSTITUTION Proprietary, coed. Awards: associate, bachelor's, and master's degrees. 10 undergraduate majors. Total enrollment: 3,681. Undergraduates: 2,581. Freshmen: 86. Both federal and institutional methodology are used as a basis for awarding need-based institutional aid.
UNDERGRADUATE EXPENSES for 2005–06 *Application fee:* $110. *Tuition:* full-time $12,990; part-time $444 per credit. *Required fees:* full-time $560; $70 per course. *Payment plan:* Deferred payment.
UNDERGRADUATE FINANCIAL AID (Fall 2004) *Average financial aid package:* $3673 (excluding resources awarded to replace EFC).
GIFT AID (NEED-BASED) *Total amount:* $11,172,396 (100% federal). *Receiving aid:* All full-time undergraduates: 2,700. *Scholarships, grants, and awards:* Federal Pell, FSEOG, state, private, college/university gift aid from institutional funds, Academic Competitiveness Grant and National Science and Mathematics Access to Retain Talent (SMART).
GIFT AID (NON-NEED-BASED) *Total amount:* $15,995,807 (95% federal, 5% state). *Receiving aid:* Undergraduates: 2,921. *Scholarships, grants, and awards by category: Academic Interests/Achievement:* business, computer science, health fields, social sciences. *Tuition waivers:* Full or partial for employees or children of employees.
LOANS *Programs:* FFEL (Subsidized and Unsubsidized Stafford, PLUS), Perkins.

University of Phoenix–Bay Area Campus

APPLYING FOR FINANCIAL AID *Required financial aid form:* institution's own form. *Financial aid deadline:* Continuous. *Notification date:* Continuous beginning 7/1.
CONTACT ACS/AFS, University of Phoenix–Bay Area Campus, 875 West Elliot Road, Suite 116, Tempe, AZ 85284, 480-735-3000 or toll-free 877-4-STUDENT. *Fax:* 480-940-2060.

UNIVERSITY OF PHOENIX–BOSTON CAMPUS
Braintree, MA

Tuition & fees: $13,580 — **Average undergraduate aid package: $3600**

ABOUT THE INSTITUTION Proprietary, coed. Awards: bachelor's and master's degrees. 2 undergraduate majors. Total enrollment: 628. Undergraduates: 421. Freshmen: 23. Both federal and institutional methodology are used as a basis for awarding need-based institutional aid.
UNDERGRADUATE EXPENSES for 2005–06 *Application fee:* $110. *Tuition:* full-time $13,020; part-time $434 per credit. *Required fees:* full-time $560; $70 per course. *Payment plan:* Deferred payment.
UNDERGRADUATE FINANCIAL AID (Fall 2004) *Average financial aid package:* $3600 (excluding resources awarded to replace EFC).
GIFT AID (NEED-BASED) *Total amount:* $1,555,167 (100% federal). *Receiving aid:* All full-time undergraduates: 380. *Scholarships, grants, and awards:* Federal Pell, FSEOG, state, private, college/university gift aid from institutional funds, Academic Competitiveness Grant and National Science and Mathematics Access to Retain Talent (SMART).
GIFT AID (NON-NEED-BASED) *Total amount:* $1,855,669 (100% federal). *Receiving aid:* Undergraduates: 364. *Scholarships, grants, and awards by category: Academic Interests/Achievement:* business, computer science, health fields. *Tuition waivers:* Full or partial for employees or children of employees.
LOANS *Programs:* FFEL (Subsidized and Unsubsidized Stafford, PLUS), Perkins.
APPLYING FOR FINANCIAL AID *Required financial aid form:* institution's own form. *Financial aid deadline:* Continuous. *Notification date:* Continuous beginning 7/1.
CONTACT ACS/AFS, University of Phoenix–Boston Campus, 875 West Elliot Road, Suite 116, Tempe, AZ 85284, 480-735-3000 or toll-free 800-228-7240. *Fax:* 480-940-2060.

UNIVERSITY OF PHOENIX–CENTRAL FLORIDA CAMPUS
Maitland, FL

Tuition & fees: $10,520 — **Average undergraduate aid package: $4430**

ABOUT THE INSTITUTION Proprietary, coed. Awards: bachelor's and master's degrees. 9 undergraduate majors. Total enrollment: 2,267. Undergraduates: 1,654. Freshmen: 46. Both federal and institutional methodology are used as a basis for awarding need-based institutional aid.
UNDERGRADUATE EXPENSES for 2005–06 *Application fee:* $110. *Tuition:* full-time $9960; part-time $332 per credit. *Required fees:* full-time $560; $70 per course. Full-time tuition and fees vary according to program. *Payment plan:* Deferred payment.
UNDERGRADUATE FINANCIAL AID (Fall 2004) *Average financial aid package:* $4430 (excluding resources awarded to replace EFC).
GIFT AID (NEED-BASED) *Total amount:* $8,725,167 (100% federal). *Receiving aid:* All full-time undergraduates: 1,814. *Scholarships, grants, and awards:* Federal Pell, FSEOG, state, private, college/university gift aid from institutional funds, Academic Competitiveness Grant and National Science and Mathematics Access to Retain Talent (SMART).
GIFT AID (NON-NEED-BASED) *Total amount:* $9,390,910 (100% federal). *Receiving aid:* Undergraduates: 1,810. *Scholarships, grants, and awards by category: Academic Interests/Achievement:* business, computer science, health fields, social sciences. *Tuition waivers:* Full or partial for employees or children of employees.
LOANS *Programs:* FFEL (Subsidized and Unsubsidized Stafford, PLUS), Perkins.
APPLYING FOR FINANCIAL AID *Required financial aid form:* institution's own form. *Financial aid deadline:* Continuous. *Notification date:* Continuous beginning 7/1.
CONTACT ACS/AFS, University of Phoenix–Central Florida Campus, 875 West Elliot Road, Suite 116, Tempe, AZ 85284, 480-735-3000 or toll-free 800-776-4867 (in-state), 800-228-7240 (out-of-state). *Fax:* 480-940-2060.

UNIVERSITY OF PHOENIX–CENTRAL MASSACHUSETTS CAMPUS
Westborough, MA

Tuition & fees: $13,580 — **Average undergraduate aid package: $3761**

ABOUT THE INSTITUTION Proprietary, coed. Awards: bachelor's and master's degrees. 3 undergraduate majors. Total enrollment: 339. Undergraduates: 233. Freshmen: 24. Both federal and institutional methodology are used as a basis for awarding need-based institutional aid.
UNDERGRADUATE EXPENSES for 2005–06 *Application fee:* $110. *Tuition:* full-time $13,020; part-time $434 per credit. *Required fees:* full-time $560; $70 per course. *Payment plan:* Deferred payment.
UNDERGRADUATE FINANCIAL AID (Fall 2004) *Average financial aid package:* $3761 (excluding resources awarded to replace EFC).
GIFT AID (NEED-BASED) *Total amount:* $639,347 (100% federal). *Receiving aid:* All full-time undergraduates: 151. *Scholarships, grants, and awards:* Federal Pell, FSEOG, state, private, college/university gift aid from institutional funds, Academic Competitiveness Grant and National Science and Mathematics Access to retain talent (Smart).
GIFT AID (NON-NEED-BASED) *Total amount:* $810,771 (100% federal). *Receiving aid:* Undergraduates: 154. *Tuition waivers:* Full or partial for employees or children of employees.
LOANS *Programs:* FFEL (Subsidized and Unsubsidized Stafford, PLUS), Perkins.
APPLYING FOR FINANCIAL AID *Required financial aid form:* institution's own form. *Financial aid deadline:* Continuous. *Notification date:* Continuous beginning 7/1.
CONTACT ACS/AFS, University of Phoenix–Central Massachusetts Campus, 875 West Elliot Road, Suite 116, Tempe, AZ 85284, 480-735-3000 or toll-free 800-776-4867 (in-state), 800-228-7240 (out-of-state). *Fax:* 480-940-2060.

UNIVERSITY OF PHOENIX–CENTRAL VALLEY CAMPUS
Fresno, CA

Tuition & fees: $12,335 — **Average undergraduate aid package: $5626**

ABOUT THE INSTITUTION Proprietary, coed. Awards: bachelor's and master's degrees and post-bachelor's certificates. 8 undergraduate majors. Total enrollment: 1,887. Undergraduates: 1,606. Freshmen: 36. Both federal and institutional methodology are used as a basis for awarding need-based institutional aid.
UNDERGRADUATE EXPENSES for 2005–06 *Application fee:* $110. *Tuition:* full-time $11,775; part-time $392.50 per credit. *Required fees:* full-time $560; $70 per course. Full-time tuition and fees vary according to program. *Payment plan:* Deferred payment.
UNDERGRADUATE FINANCIAL AID (Fall 2004) *Average financial aid package:* $5626 (excluding resources awarded to replace EFC).
GIFT AID (NEED-BASED) *Total amount:* $8,273,683 (100% federal). *Receiving aid:* All full-time undergraduates: 1,677. *Scholarships, grants, and awards:* Federal Pell, FSEOG, state, private, college/university gift aid from institutional funds, Academic Competitiveness Grant and National Science and Mathematics Access to Retain Talent (SMART).
GIFT AID (NON-NEED-BASED) *Total amount:* $8,840,702 (79% federal, 21% state). *Receiving aid:* Undergraduates: 1,610. *Scholarships, grants, and awards by category: Academic Interests/Achievement:* business, computer science. *Tuition waivers:* Full or partial for employees or children of employees.
LOANS *Programs:* FFEL (Subsidized and Unsubsidized Stafford, PLUS), Perkins.
APPLYING FOR FINANCIAL AID *Required financial aid form:* institution's own form. *Financial aid deadline:* Continuous. *Notification date:* Continuous beginning 7/1.
CONTACT ACS/AFS, University of Phoenix–Central Valley Campus, 875 West Elliott Road, Suite 116, Tempe, AZ 85284, 480-735-3000 or toll-free 888-776-4867 (in-state), 888-228-7240 (out-of-state). *Fax:* 480-940-2060.

University of Phoenix–Cleveland Campus

UNIVERSITY OF PHOENIX–CHARLOTTE CAMPUS
Charlotte, NC

Tuition & fees: $10,730   **Average undergraduate aid package:** $4337

ABOUT THE INSTITUTION Proprietary, coed. Awards: bachelor's and master's degrees. Total enrollment: 1,301. Undergraduates: 854. Freshmen: 43. Both federal and institutional methodology are used as a basis for awarding need-based institutional aid.

UNDERGRADUATE EXPENSES for 2005–06 *Application fee:* $110. *Tuition:* full-time $10,170; part-time $339 per credit. *Required fees:* full-time $560; $70 per course. *Payment plan:* Deferred payment.

UNDERGRADUATE FINANCIAL AID (Fall 2004) *Average financial aid package:* $4337 (excluding resources awarded to replace EFC).

GIFT AID (NEED-BASED) *Total amount:* $4,289,747 (100% federal). *Receiving aid:* All full-time undergraduates: 918. *Scholarships, grants, and awards:* Federal Pell, FSEOG, state, private, college/university gift aid from institutional funds, Academic Competitiveness Grant and National Science and Mathematics Access to Retain Talent (SMART).

GIFT AID (NON-NEED-BASED) *Total amount:* $4,900,310 (100% federal). *Receiving aid:* Undergraduates: 890. *Scholarships, grants, and awards by category: Academic Interests/Achievement:* business, computer science. *Tuition waivers:* Full or partial for employees or children of employees.

LOANS *Programs:* FFEL (Subsidized and Unsubsidized Stafford, PLUS), Perkins.

APPLYING FOR FINANCIAL AID *Required financial aid form:* institution's own form. *Financial aid deadline:* Continuous. *Notification date:* Continuous beginning 7/1.

CONTACT ACS/AFS, University of Phoenix–Charlotte Campus, 875 West Elliott Road, Suite 116, Tempe, AZ 85284, 480-735-3000 or toll-free 800-776-4867 (in-state), 800-228-7240 (out-of-state). *Fax:* 480-940-2060.

UNIVERSITY OF PHOENIX–CHICAGO CAMPUS
Schaumburg, IL

Tuition & fees: $11,705   **Average undergraduate aid package:** $3743

ABOUT THE INSTITUTION Proprietary, coed. Awards: bachelor's and master's degrees. 7 undergraduate majors. Total enrollment: 1,602. Undergraduates: 1,279. Freshmen: 65. Both federal and institutional methodology are used as a basis for awarding need-based institutional aid.

UNDERGRADUATE EXPENSES for 2005–06 *Application fee:* $110. *Tuition:* full-time $11,145; part-time $371.50 per credit. *Required fees:* full-time $560; $70 per course. *Payment plan:* Deferred payment.

FRESHMAN FINANCIAL AID (Fall 2004) *Average financial aid package:* $1274 (excluding resources awarded to replace EFC).

UNDERGRADUATE FINANCIAL AID (Fall 2004) *Average financial aid package:* $3743 (excluding resources awarded to replace EFC).

GIFT AID (NEED-BASED) *Total amount:* $5,090,560 (100% federal). *Receiving aid:* Freshmen: 3; All full-time undergraduates: 1,207. *Scholarships, grants, and awards:* Federal Pell, FSEOG, state, private, college/university gift aid from institutional funds, Academic Competitiveness Grant and National Science and Mathematics Access to Retain Talent (SMART).

GIFT AID (NON-NEED-BASED) *Total amount:* $6,066,983 (100% federal). *Receiving aid:* Freshmen: 3; Undergraduates: 1,201. *Scholarships, grants, and awards by category: Academic Interests/Achievement:* business, computer science. *Tuition waivers:* Full or partial for employees or children of employees.

LOANS *Programs:* FFEL (Subsidized and Unsubsidized Stafford, PLUS), Perkins.

APPLYING FOR FINANCIAL AID *Required financial aid form:* institution's own form. *Financial aid deadline:* Continuous. *Notification date:* Continuous beginning 7/1.

CONTACT ACS/AFS, University of Phoenix–Chicago Campus, 875 West Elliott Road, Suite 116, Tempe, AZ 85284, 480-735-3000 or toll-free 800-776-4867 (in-state), 800-228-7240 (out-of-state). *Fax:* 480-940-2060.

UNIVERSITY OF PHOENIX–CINCINNATI CAMPUS
West Chester, OH

Tuition & fees: $12,110   **Average undergraduate aid package:** $3979

ABOUT THE INSTITUTION Proprietary, coed. Awards: bachelor's and master's degrees. 2 undergraduate majors. Total enrollment: 619. Undergraduates: 407. Freshmen: 33. Both federal and institutional methodology are used as a basis for awarding need-based institutional aid.

UNDERGRADUATE EXPENSES for 2005–06 *Application fee:* $110. *Tuition:* full-time $11,550; part-time $385 per credit. *Required fees:* full-time $560; $70 per course. *Payment plan:* Deferred payment.

UNDERGRADUATE FINANCIAL AID (Fall 2004) *Average financial aid package:* $3979 (excluding resources awarded to replace EFC).

GIFT AID (NEED-BASED) *Total amount:* $1,595,649 (100% federal). *Receiving aid:* All full-time undergraduates: 364. *Scholarships, grants, and awards:* Federal Pell, FSEOG, state, private, college/university gift aid from institutional funds, Academic Competitiveness Grant and National Science and Mathematics Access to Retain Talent (SMART).

GIFT AID (NON-NEED-BASED) *Total amount:* $1,870,411 (100% federal). *Receiving aid:* Undergraduates: 352. *Scholarships, grants, and awards by category: Academic Interests/Achievement:* business, computer science. *Tuition waivers:* Full or partial for employees or children of employees.

LOANS *Programs:* FFEL (Subsidized and Unsubsidized Stafford, PLUS), Perkins.

APPLYING FOR FINANCIAL AID *Required financial aid form:* institution's own form. *Financial aid deadline:* Continuous. *Notification date:* Continuous beginning 7/1.

CONTACT ACS/AFS, University of Phoenix–Cincinnati Campus, 875 West Elliot Road, Suite 116, Tempe, AZ 85284, 480-735-3000 or toll-free 800-776-4867 (in-state), 800-228-7240 (out-of-state). *Fax:* 480-940-2060.

UNIVERSITY OF PHOENIX–CLEVELAND CAMPUS
Independence, OH

Tuition & fees: $12,110   **Average undergraduate aid package:** $4196

ABOUT THE INSTITUTION Proprietary, coed. Awards: bachelor's and master's degrees. 3 undergraduate majors. Total enrollment: 882. Undergraduates: 675. Freshmen: 32. Both federal and institutional methodology are used as a basis for awarding need-based institutional aid.

UNDERGRADUATE EXPENSES for 2005–06 *Application fee:* $110. *Tuition:* full-time $11,550; part-time $385 per credit. *Required fees:* full-time $560; $70 per course. *Payment plan:* Deferred payment.

FRESHMAN FINANCIAL AID (Fall 2004) *Average financial aid package:* $7055 (excluding resources awarded to replace EFC).

UNDERGRADUATE FINANCIAL AID (Fall 2004) *Average financial aid package:* $4196 (excluding resources awarded to replace EFC).

GIFT AID (NEED-BASED) *Total amount:* $3,207,840 (100% federal). *Receiving aid:* Freshmen: 1; All full-time undergraduates: 707. *Scholarships, grants, and awards:* Federal Pell, FSEOG, state, private, college/university gift aid from institutional funds, Academic Competitiveness Grant and National Science and Mathematics Access to Retain Talent (SMART).

GIFT AID (NON-NEED-BASED) *Total amount:* $3,214,526 (100% federal). *Receiving aid:* Freshmen: 1; Undergraduates: 649. *Scholarships, grants, and awards by category: Academic Interests/Achievement:* business, computer science, health fields, social sciences. *Tuition waivers:* Full or partial for employees or children of employees.

LOANS *Programs:* FFEL (Subsidized and Unsubsidized Stafford, PLUS), Perkins.

APPLYING FOR FINANCIAL AID *Required financial aid form:* institution's own form. *Financial aid deadline:* Continuous. *Notification date:* Continuous beginning 7/1.

CONTACT ACS/AFS, University of Phoenix–Cleveland Campus, 875 West Elliott Road, Suite 116, Tempe, AZ 85284, 480-735-3000 or toll-free 800-776-4867 (in-state), 800-228-7240 (out-of-state). *Fax:* 480-940-2060.

University of Phoenix–Columbus Georgia Campus

UNIVERSITY OF PHOENIX–COLUMBUS GEORGIA CAMPUS
Columbus, GA

Tuition & fees: $10,880   **Average undergraduate aid package:** $4053

ABOUT THE INSTITUTION Proprietary, coed. Awards: bachelor's and master's degrees. 7 undergraduate majors. Total enrollment: 676. Undergraduates: 581. Freshmen: 32. Both federal and institutional methodology are used as a basis for awarding need-based institutional aid.

UNDERGRADUATE EXPENSES for 2005–06 *Application fee:* $110. *Tuition:* full-time $10,320; part-time $344 per credit. *Required fees:* full-time $560; $70 per course. *Payment plan:* Deferred payment.

FRESHMAN FINANCIAL AID (Fall 2004) *Average financial aid package:* $1137 (excluding resources awarded to replace EFC).

UNDERGRADUATE FINANCIAL AID (Fall 2004) *Average financial aid package:* $4053 (excluding resources awarded to replace EFC).

GIFT AID (NEED-BASED) *Total amount:* $2,330,531 (100% federal). *Receiving aid:* Freshmen: 67% (2); All full-time undergraduates: 559. *Scholarships, grants, and awards:* Federal Pell, FSEOG, state, private, college/university gift aid from institutional funds, Academic Competitiveness Grant and National Science and Mathematics Access to Retain Talent (SMART).

GIFT AID (NON-NEED-BASED) *Total amount:* $1,713,569 (100% federal). *Receiving aid:* Freshmen: 33% (1); Undergraduates: 465. *Scholarships, grants, and awards by category:* Academic Interests/Achievement: business, computer science. *Tuition waivers:* Full or partial for employees or children of employees.

LOANS *Programs:* FFEL (Subsidized and Unsubsidized Stafford, PLUS), Perkins.

APPLYING FOR FINANCIAL AID *Required financial aid form:* institution's own form. *Financial aid deadline:* Continuous. *Notification date:* Continuous beginning 7/1.

CONTACT ACS/AFS, University of Phoenix–Columbus Georgia Campus, 875 West Elliot Road, Suite 116, Tempe, AZ 85284, 480-735-3000 or toll-free 800-776-4867 (in-state), 800-228-7240 (out-of-state). *Fax:* 480-940-2060.

UNIVERSITY OF PHOENIX–DALLAS CAMPUS
Dallas, TX

Tuition & fees: $11,345   **Average undergraduate aid package:** $4227

ABOUT THE INSTITUTION Proprietary, coed. Awards: bachelor's and master's degrees. 4 undergraduate majors. Total enrollment: 2,972. Undergraduates: 2,303. Freshmen: 113. Both federal and institutional methodology are used as a basis for awarding need-based institutional aid.

UNDERGRADUATE EXPENSES for 2005–06 *Application fee:* $110. *Tuition:* full-time $10,785; part-time $359.50 per credit. *Required fees:* full-time $560; $70 per course. *Payment plan:* Deferred payment.

FRESHMAN FINANCIAL AID (Fall 2004) *Average financial aid package:* $999 (excluding resources awarded to replace EFC).

UNDERGRADUATE FINANCIAL AID (Fall 2004) *Average financial aid package:* $4227 (excluding resources awarded to replace EFC).

GIFT AID (NEED-BASED) *Total amount:* $10,178,806 (100% federal). *Receiving aid:* Freshmen: 2; All full-time undergraduates: 2,184. *Scholarships, grants, and awards:* Federal Pell, FSEOG, state, private, college/university gift aid from institutional funds, Academic Competitiveness Grant and National Science and Mathematics Access to Retain Talent (SMART).

GIFT AID (NON-NEED-BASED) *Total amount:* $10,781,644 (100% federal). *Receiving aid:* Freshmen: 1; Undergraduates: 2,155. *Scholarships, grants, and awards by category:* Academic Interests/Achievement: business, computer science, health fields, social sciences. *Tuition waivers:* Full or partial for employees or children of employees.

LOANS *Programs:* FFEL (Subsidized and Unsubsidized Stafford, PLUS), Perkins.

APPLYING FOR FINANCIAL AID *Required financial aid form:* institution's own form. *Financial aid deadline:* Continuous. *Notification date:* Continuous beginning 7/1.

CONTACT ACS/AFS, University of Phoenix–Dallas Campus, 875 West Elliot Road, Suite 116, Tempe, AZ 85284, 480-735-3000 or toll-free 800-776-4867 (in-state), 800-228-7240 (out-of-state). *Fax:* 480-940-2060.

UNIVERSITY OF PHOENIX–COLUMBUS OHIO CAMPUS
Columbus, OH

Tuition & fees: $12,110   **Average undergraduate aid package:** $3824

ABOUT THE INSTITUTION Proprietary, coed. Awards: bachelor's and master's degrees. 1 undergraduate major. Total enrollment: 493. Undergraduates: 332. Freshmen: 16. Both federal and institutional methodology are used as a basis for awarding need-based institutional aid.

UNDERGRADUATE EXPENSES for 2005–06 *Application fee:* $110. *Tuition:* full-time $11,550; part-time $385 per credit. *Required fees:* full-time $560; $70 per course. *Payment plan:* Deferred payment.

UNDERGRADUATE FINANCIAL AID (Fall 2004) *Average financial aid package:* $3824 (excluding resources awarded to replace EFC).

GIFT AID (NEED-BASED) *Total amount:* $1,521,873 (100% federal). *Receiving aid:* All full-time undergraduates: 359. *Scholarships, grants, and awards:* Federal Pell, FSEOG, state, private, college/university gift aid from institutional funds, Academic Competitiveness Grant and National Science and Mathematics Access to Retain Talent (SMART).

GIFT AID (NON-NEED-BASED) *Total amount:* $1,826,858 (100% federal). *Receiving aid:* Undergraduates: 343. *Scholarships, grants, and awards by category:* Academic Interests/Achievement: business, computer science. *Tuition waivers:* Full or partial for employees or children of employees.

LOANS *Programs:* FFEL (Subsidized and Unsubsidized Stafford, PLUS), Perkins.

APPLYING FOR FINANCIAL AID *Required financial aid form:* institution's own form. *Financial aid deadline:* Continuous. *Notification date:* Continuous beginning 7/1.

CONTACT ACS/AFS, University of Phoenix–Columbus Ohio Campus, 875 West Elliot Road, Suite 116, Tempe, AZ 85284, 480-735-3000 or toll-free 800-776-4867 (in-state), 800-228-7240 (out-of-state). *Fax:* 480-940-2060.

UNIVERSITY OF PHOENIX–DENVER CAMPUS
Lone Tree, CO

Tuition & fees: $10,040   **Average undergraduate aid package:** $4444

ABOUT THE INSTITUTION Proprietary, coed. Awards: bachelor's and master's degrees and post-master's certificates. 8 undergraduate majors. Total enrollment: 3,420. Undergraduates: 2,010. Freshmen: 74. Both federal and institutional methodology are used as a basis for awarding need-based institutional aid.

UNDERGRADUATE EXPENSES for 2005–06 *Application fee:* $110. *Tuition:* full-time $9480; part-time $316 per credit. *Required fees:* full-time $560; $70 per course. *Payment plan:* Deferred payment.

FRESHMAN FINANCIAL AID (Fall 2004) *Average financial aid package:* $2471 (excluding resources awarded to replace EFC).

UNDERGRADUATE FINANCIAL AID (Fall 2004) *Average financial aid package:* $4444 (excluding resources awarded to replace EFC).

GIFT AID (NEED-BASED) *Total amount:* $13,000,418 (100% federal). *Receiving aid:* Freshmen: 3; All full-time undergraduates: 2,568. *Scholarships, grants, and awards:* Federal Pell, FSEOG, state, private, college/university gift aid from institutional funds, Academic Competitiveness Grant and National Science and Mathematics Access to Retain Talent (SMART).

GIFT AID (NON-NEED-BASED) *Total amount:* $16,674,902 (100% federal). *Receiving aid:* Freshmen: 3; Undergraduates: 2,758. *Tuition waivers:* Full or partial for employees or children of employees.

LOANS *Programs:* FFEL (Subsidized and Unsubsidized Stafford, PLUS), Perkins.

APPLYING FOR FINANCIAL AID *Required financial aid form:* institution's own form. *Financial aid deadline:* Continuous. *Notification date:* Continuous beginning 7/1.

CONTACT ACS/AFS, University of Phoenix–Denver Campus, 875 West Elliot Road, Suite 116, Tempe, AZ 85284, 480-735-3000 or toll-free 800-776-4867 (in-state), 800-228-7240 (out-of-state). *Fax:* 480-940-2060.

UNIVERSITY OF PHOENIX–HAWAII CAMPUS
Honolulu, HI

Tuition & fees: $12,110 | **Average undergraduate aid package:** $4638

ABOUT THE INSTITUTION Proprietary, coed. Awards: bachelor's and master's degrees (courses conducted at 121 campuses and learning centers in 25 states). 12 undergraduate majors. Total enrollment: 1,348. Undergraduates: 907. Freshmen: 18. Both federal and institutional methodology are used as a basis for awarding need-based institutional aid.
UNDERGRADUATE EXPENSES for 2005–06 *Application fee:* $110. *Tuition:* full-time $11,550; part-time $385 per credit. *Required fees:* full-time $560; $70 per course. *Payment plan:* Deferred payment.
UNDERGRADUATE FINANCIAL AID (Fall 2004) *Average financial aid package:* $4638 (excluding resources awarded to replace EFC).
GIFT AID (NEED-BASED) *Total amount:* $6,164,710 (100% federal). *Receiving aid:* All full-time undergraduates: 1,267. *Scholarships, grants, and awards:* Federal Pell, FSEOG, state, private, college/university gift aid from institutional funds, Academic Competitiveness Grant and National Science and Mathematics Access to Retain Talent (SMART).
GIFT AID (NON-NEED-BASED) *Total amount:* $6,245,010 (99% federal, 1% state). *Receiving aid:* Undergraduates: 1,234. *Tuition waivers:* Full or partial for employees or children of employees.
LOANS *Programs:* FFEL (Subsidized and Unsubsidized Stafford, PLUS), Perkins.
APPLYING FOR FINANCIAL AID *Required financial aid form:* institution's own form. *Financial aid deadline:* Continuous. *Notification date:* Continuous beginning 7/1.
CONTACT ACS/AFS, University of Phoenix–Hawaii Campus, 875 West Elliot Road, Suite 116, Tempe, AZ 85284, 480-735-3000 or toll-free 800-776-4867 (in-state), 800-228-7240 (out-of-state). *Fax:* 480-940-2060.

UNIVERSITY OF PHOENIX–HOUSTON CAMPUS
Houston, TX

Tuition & fees: $11,345 | **Average undergraduate aid package:** $4732

ABOUT THE INSTITUTION Proprietary, coed. Awards: bachelor's and master's degrees. 4 undergraduate majors. Total enrollment: 4,808. Undergraduates: 3,914. Freshmen: 169. Both federal and institutional methodology are used as a basis for awarding need-based institutional aid.
UNDERGRADUATE EXPENSES for 2005–06 *Application fee:* $110. *Tuition:* full-time $10,785; part-time $359.50 per credit. *Required fees:* full-time $560; $70 per course. *Payment plan:* Deferred payment.
FRESHMAN FINANCIAL AID (Fall 2004) *Average financial aid package:* $3606 (excluding resources awarded to replace EFC).
UNDERGRADUATE FINANCIAL AID (Fall 2004) *Average financial aid package:* $4732 (excluding resources awarded to replace EFC).
GIFT AID (NEED-BASED) *Total amount:* $18,359,124 (100% federal). *Receiving aid:* Freshmen: 3; All full-time undergraduates: 3,583. *Scholarships, grants, and awards:* Federal Pell, FSEOG, state, private, college/university gift aid from institutional funds, Academic Competitiveness Grant and National Science and Mathematics Access to Retain Talent (SMART).
GIFT AID (NON-NEED-BASED) *Total amount:* $18,575,045 (100% federal). *Receiving aid:* Freshmen: 2; Undergraduates: 3,589. *Scholarships, grants, and awards by category:* Academic Interests/Achievement: business, computer science, health fields, social sciences. *Tuition waivers:* Full or partial for employees or children of employees.
LOANS *Programs:* FFEL (Subsidized and Unsubsidized Stafford, PLUS), Perkins.
APPLYING FOR FINANCIAL AID *Required financial aid form:* institution's own form. *Financial aid deadline:* Continuous. *Notification date:* Continuous beginning 7/1.
CONTACT ACS/AFS, University of Phoenix–Houston Campus, 875 West Elliot Road, Suite 116, Tempe, AZ 85284, 480-735-3000 or toll-free 800-776-4867 (in-state), 800-228-7240 (out-of-state). *Fax:* 480-940-2060.

UNIVERSITY OF PHOENIX–IDAHO CAMPUS
Meridian, ID

Tuition & fees: $10,460 | **Average undergraduate aid package:** $4106

ABOUT THE INSTITUTION Proprietary, coed. Awards: bachelor's and master's degrees. 6 undergraduate majors. Total enrollment: 767. Undergraduates: 656. Freshmen: 21. Both federal and institutional methodology are used as a basis for awarding need-based institutional aid.
UNDERGRADUATE EXPENSES for 2005–06 *Application fee:* $110. *Tuition:* full-time $9900; part-time $330 per credit. *Required fees:* full-time $560; $70 per course. *Payment plan:* Deferred payment.
UNDERGRADUATE FINANCIAL AID (Fall 2004) *Average financial aid package:* $4106 (excluding resources awarded to replace EFC).
GIFT AID (NEED-BASED) *Total amount:* $2,787,673 (100% federal). *Receiving aid:* All full-time undergraduates: 644. *Scholarships, grants, and awards:* Federal Pell, FSEOG, state, private, college/university gift aid from institutional funds, Academic Competitiveness Grant and National Science and Mathematics Access to Retain Talent (SMART).
GIFT AID (NON-NEED-BASED) *Total amount:* $2,489,116 (100% federal). *Receiving aid:* Undergraduates: 606. *Scholarships, grants, and awards by category:* Academic Interests/Achievement: business, computer science. *Tuition waivers:* Full or partial for employees or children of employees.
LOANS *Programs:* FFEL (Subsidized and Unsubsidized Stafford, PLUS), Perkins.
APPLYING FOR FINANCIAL AID *Required financial aid form:* institution's own form. *Financial aid deadline:* Continuous. *Notification date:* Continuous beginning 7/1.
CONTACT ACS/AFS, University of Phoenix–Idaho Campus, 875 West Elliot Road, Suite 116, Tempe, AZ 85284, 480-735-3000 or toll-free 800-776-4867 (in-state), 800-228-7240 (out-of-state). *Fax:* 480-940-2060.

UNIVERSITY OF PHOENIX–INDIANAPOLIS CAMPUS
Indianapolis, IN

Tuition & fees: $10,340 | **Average undergraduate aid package:** $3604

ABOUT THE INSTITUTION Proprietary, coed. Awards: bachelor's and master's degrees. 6 undergraduate majors. Total enrollment: 616. Undergraduates: 474. Freshmen: 61. Both federal and institutional methodology are used as a basis for awarding need-based institutional aid.
UNDERGRADUATE EXPENSES for 2005–06 *Application fee:* $110. *Tuition:* full-time $9780; part-time $326 per credit. *Required fees:* full-time $560; $70 per course. *Payment plan:* Deferred payment.
FRESHMAN FINANCIAL AID (Fall 2004) *Average financial aid package:* $2025 (excluding resources awarded to replace EFC).
UNDERGRADUATE FINANCIAL AID (Fall 2004) *Average financial aid package:* $3604 (excluding resources awarded to replace EFC).
GIFT AID (NEED-BASED) *Total amount:* $1,575,030 (100% federal). *Receiving aid:* Freshmen: 1; All full-time undergraduates: 399. *Scholarships, grants, and awards:* Federal Pell, FSEOG, state, private, college/university gift aid from institutional funds, Academic Competitiveness Grant and National Science and Mathematics Access to Retain Talent (SMART).
GIFT AID (NON-NEED-BASED) *Total amount:* $1,709,775 (100% federal). *Receiving aid:* Undergraduates: 365. *Scholarships, grants, and awards by category:* Academic Interests/Achievement: business, computer science. *Tuition waivers:* Full or partial for employees or children of employees.
LOANS *Programs:* FFEL (Subsidized and Unsubsidized Stafford, PLUS), Perkins.
APPLYING FOR FINANCIAL AID *Required financial aid form:* institution's own form. *Financial aid deadline:* Continuous. *Notification date:* Continuous beginning 7/1.
CONTACT ACS/AFS, University of Phoenix–Indianapolis Campus, 875 West Elliot Road, Suite 116, Tempe, AZ 85284, 480-735-3000 or toll-free 800-776-4867 (in-state), 800-228-7240 (out-of-state). *Fax:* 480-940-2060.

University of Phoenix–Kansas City Campus

UNIVERSITY OF PHOENIX–KANSAS CITY CAMPUS
Kansas City, MO

Tuition & fees: $11,705 | Average undergraduate aid package: $4057

ABOUT THE INSTITUTION Proprietary, coed. Awards: bachelor's and master's degrees. 6 undergraduate majors. Total enrollment: 1,297. Undergraduates: 1,020. Freshmen: 57. Both federal and institutional methodology are used as a basis for awarding need-based institutional aid.

UNDERGRADUATE EXPENSES for 2005–06 *Application fee:* $110. *Tuition:* full-time $11,145; part-time $371.50 per credit. *Payment plan:* Deferred payment.

UNDERGRADUATE FINANCIAL AID (Fall 2004) *Average financial aid package:* $4057 (excluding resources awarded to replace EFC).

GIFT AID (NEED-BASED) *Total amount:* $4,444,415 (100% federal). *Receiving aid:* All full-time undergraduates: 1,024. *Scholarships, grants, and awards:* Federal Pell, FSEOG, state, private, college/university gift aid from institutional funds, Academic Competitiveness Grant and National Science and Mathematics Access to Retain Talent (SMART).

GIFT AID (NON-NEED-BASED) *Total amount:* $4,361,099 (100% federal). *Receiving aid:* Undergraduates: 929. *Scholarships, grants, and awards by category: Academic Interests/Achievement:* business, computer science. *Tuition waivers:* Full or partial for employees or children of employees.

LOANS *Programs:* FFEL (Subsidized and Unsubsidized Stafford, PLUS), Perkins.

APPLYING FOR FINANCIAL AID *Required financial aid form:* institution's own form. *Financial aid deadline:* Continuous. *Notification date:* Continuous beginning 7/1.

CONTACT ACS/AFS, University of Phoenix–Kansas City Campus, 875 West Elliot Road, Suite 116, Tempe, AZ 85284, 480-735-3000 or toll-free 800-776-4867 (in-state), 800-228-7240 (out-of-state). *Fax:* 480-940-2060.

UNIVERSITY OF PHOENIX–LITTLE ROCK CAMPUS
Little Rock, AR

Tuition & fees: $10,100 | Average undergraduate aid package: $3985

ABOUT THE INSTITUTION Proprietary, coed. Awards: bachelor's and master's degrees. 3 undergraduate majors. Total enrollment: 499. Undergraduates: 327. Freshmen: 36. Both federal and institutional methodology are used as a basis for awarding need-based institutional aid.

UNDERGRADUATE EXPENSES for 2005–06 *Application fee:* $110. *Tuition:* full-time $9540; part-time $318 per credit. *Required fees:* full-time $560; $70 per course. *Payment plan:* Deferred payment.

FRESHMAN FINANCIAL AID (Fall 2004) *Average financial aid package:* $1666 (excluding resources awarded to replace EFC).

UNDERGRADUATE FINANCIAL AID (Fall 2004) *Average financial aid package:* $3985 (excluding resources awarded to replace EFC).

GIFT AID (NEED-BASED) *Total amount:* $1,675,887 (100% federal). *Receiving aid:* Freshmen: 1; All full-time undergraduates: 405. *Scholarships, grants, and awards:* Federal Pell, FSEOG, state, private, college/university gift aid from institutional funds, Academic Competitiveness Grant and National Science and Mathematics Access to Retain Talent (SMART).

GIFT AID (NON-NEED-BASED) *Total amount:* $1,468,373 (100% federal). *Receiving aid:* Undergraduates: 385. *Scholarships, grants, and awards by category: Academic Interests/Achievement:* business, computer science. *Tuition waivers:* Full or partial for employees or children of employees.

LOANS *Programs:* FFEL (Subsidized and Unsubsidized Stafford, PLUS), Perkins.

APPLYING FOR FINANCIAL AID *Required financial aid form:* institution's own form. *Financial aid deadline:* Continuous. *Notification date:* Continuous beginning 7/1.

CONTACT ACS/AFS, University of Phoenix–Little Rock Campus, 875 West Elliot Road, Suite 116, Tempe, AZ 85284, 480-735-3000 or toll-free 800-776-4867 (in-state), 800-228-7240 (out-of-state). *Fax:* 480-940-2060.

UNIVERSITY OF PHOENIX–LOUISIANA CAMPUS
Metairie, LA

Tuition & fees: $9680 | Average undergraduate aid package: $5011

ABOUT THE INSTITUTION Proprietary, coed. Awards: bachelor's and master's degrees. 7 undergraduate majors. Total enrollment: 2,747. Undergraduates: 2,085. Freshmen: 114. Both federal and institutional methodology are used as a basis for awarding need-based institutional aid.

UNDERGRADUATE EXPENSES for 2005–06 *Application fee:* $110. *Tuition:* full-time $9120; part-time $304 per credit. *Required fees:* full-time $560; $70 per course. Full-time tuition and fees vary according to program. *Payment plan:* Deferred payment.

FRESHMAN FINANCIAL AID (Fall 2004) *Average financial aid package:* $8954 (excluding resources awarded to replace EFC).

UNDERGRADUATE FINANCIAL AID (Fall 2004) *Average financial aid package:* $5011 (excluding resources awarded to replace EFC).

GIFT AID (NEED-BASED) *Total amount:* $13,811,040 (100% federal). *Receiving aid:* Freshmen: 4; All full-time undergraduates: 2,629. *Scholarships, grants, and awards:* Federal Pell, FSEOG, state, private, college/university gift aid from institutional funds, Academic Competitiveness Grant and National Science and Mathematics Access to Retain Talent (SMART).

GIFT AID (NON-NEED-BASED) *Total amount:* $12,187,624 (100% federal). *Receiving aid:* Freshmen: 4; Undergraduates: 2,504. *Scholarships, grants, and awards by category: Academic Interests/Achievement:* business, computer science, health fields, social sciences. *Tuition waivers:* Full or partial for employees or children of employees.

LOANS *Programs:* FFEL (Subsidized and Unsubsidized Stafford, PLUS), Perkins.

APPLYING FOR FINANCIAL AID *Required financial aid form:* institution's own form. *Financial aid deadline:* Continuous. *Notification date:* Continuous beginning 7/1.

CONTACT ACS/AFS, University of Phoenix–Louisiana Campus, 875 West Elliot Road, Suite 116, Tempe, AZ 85284, 480-735-3000 or toll-free 800-776-4867 (in-state), 800-228-7240 (out-of-state). *Fax:* 480-940-2060.

UNIVERSITY OF PHOENIX–MARYLAND CAMPUS
Columbia, MD

Tuition & fees: $12,510 | Average undergraduate aid package: $3932

ABOUT THE INSTITUTION Proprietary, coed. Awards: bachelor's and master's degrees. 4 undergraduate majors. Total enrollment: 2,028. Undergraduates: 1,586. Freshmen: 136. Both federal and institutional methodology are used as a basis for awarding need-based institutional aid.

UNDERGRADUATE EXPENSES for 2005–06 *Application fee:* $110. *Tuition:* full-time $11,950; part-time $398 per credit. *Required fees:* full-time $560; $70 per course. Full-time tuition and fees vary according to program. *Payment plan:* Deferred payment.

UNDERGRADUATE FINANCIAL AID (Fall 2004) *Average financial aid package:* $3932 (excluding resources awarded to replace EFC).

GIFT AID (NEED-BASED) *Total amount:* $5,569,721 (100% federal). *Receiving aid:* All full-time undergraduates: 1,277. *Scholarships, grants, and awards:* Federal Pell, FSEOG, state, private, college/university gift aid from institutional funds, Academic Competitiveness Grant and National Science and Mathematics Access to Retain Talent (SMART).

GIFT AID (NON-NEED-BASED) *Total amount:* $6,298,748 (100% federal). *Receiving aid:* Undergraduates: 1,258. *Scholarships, grants, and awards by category: Academic Interests/Achievement:* business, computer science. *Tuition waivers:* Full or partial for employees or children of employees.

LOANS *Programs:* FFEL (Subsidized and Unsubsidized Stafford, PLUS), Perkins.

APPLYING FOR FINANCIAL AID *Required financial aid form:* institution's own form. *Financial aid deadline:* Continuous. *Notification date:* Continuous beginning 7/1.

CONTACT ACS/AFS, University of Phoenix–Maryland Campus, 875 West Elliot Road, Suite 116, Tempe, AZ 85284, 480-735-3000 or toll-free 800-776-4867 (in-state), 800-228-7240 (out-of-state). *Fax:* 480-940-2060.

UNIVERSITY OF PHOENIX–METRO DETROIT CAMPUS
Troy, MI

Tuition & fees: $11,900   **Average undergraduate aid package:** $4252

ABOUT THE INSTITUTION Proprietary, coed. Awards: bachelor's and master's degrees. 8 undergraduate majors. Total enrollment: 3,993. Undergraduates: 2,970. Freshmen: 202. Both federal and institutional methodology are used as a basis for awarding need-based institutional aid.
UNDERGRADUATE EXPENSES for 2005–06 Application fee: $110. **Tuition:** full-time $11,340; part-time $378 per credit. **Required fees:** full-time $560; $70 per course. **Payment plan:** Deferred payment.
FRESHMAN FINANCIAL AID (Fall 2004) Average financial aid package: $1341 (excluding resources awarded to replace EFC).
UNDERGRADUATE FINANCIAL AID (Fall 2004) Average financial aid package: $4252 (excluding resources awarded to replace EFC).
GIFT AID (NEED-BASED) Total amount: $15,536,290 (100% federal). **Receiving aid:** Freshmen: 1; All full-time undergraduates: 3,374. **Scholarships, grants, and awards:** Federal Pell, FSEOG, state, private, college/university gift aid from institutional funds, Academic Competitiveness Grant and National Science and Mathematics Access to Retain Talent (SMART).
GIFT AID (NON-NEED-BASED) Total amount: $15,999,175 (100% federal). **Receiving aid:** Undergraduates: 3,210. **Scholarships, grants, and awards by category:** Academic Interests/Achievement: business, computer science, health fields, social sciences. **Tuition waivers:** Full or partial for employees or children of employees.
LOANS Programs: FFEL (Subsidized and Unsubsidized Stafford, PLUS), Perkins.
APPLYING FOR FINANCIAL AID Required financial aid form: institution's own form. **Financial aid deadline:** Continuous. **Notification date:** Continuous beginning 7/1.
CONTACT ACS/AFS, University of Phoenix–Metro Detroit Campus, 875 West Elliot Road, Suite 116, Tempe, AZ 85284, 480-735-3000 or toll-free 800-776-4867 (in-state), 800-228-7240 (out-of-state). Fax: 480-940-2060.

UNIVERSITY OF PHOENIX–NASHVILLE CAMPUS
Nashville, TN

Tuition & fees: $10,730   **Average undergraduate aid package:** $3969

ABOUT THE INSTITUTION Proprietary, coed. Awards: bachelor's and master's degrees. 7 undergraduate majors. Total enrollment: 1,291. Undergraduates: 909. Freshmen: 61. Both federal and institutional methodology are used as a basis for awarding need-based institutional aid.
UNDERGRADUATE EXPENSES for 2005–06 Application fee: $110. **Tuition:** full-time $10,170; part-time $339 per credit. **Required fees:** full-time $560; $70 per course. **Payment plan:** Deferred payment.
UNDERGRADUATE FINANCIAL AID (Fall 2004) Average financial aid package: $3969 (excluding resources awarded to replace EFC).
GIFT AID (NEED-BASED) Total amount: $4,287,288 (100% federal). **Receiving aid:** All full-time undergraduates: 981. **Scholarships, grants, and awards:** Federal Pell, FSEOG, state, private, college/university gift aid from institutional funds, Academic Competitiveness Grant and National Science and Mathematics Access to Retain Talent (SMART).
GIFT AID (NON-NEED-BASED) Total amount: $4,666,872 (100% federal). **Receiving aid:** Undergraduates: 944. **Scholarships, grants, and awards by category:** Academic Interests/Achievement: business, computer science. **Tuition waivers:** Full or partial for employees or children of employees.
LOANS Programs: FFEL (Subsidized and Unsubsidized Stafford, PLUS), Perkins.
APPLYING FOR FINANCIAL AID Required financial aid form: institution's own form. **Financial aid deadline:** Continuous. **Notification date:** Continuous beginning 7/1.
CONTACT ACS/AFS, University of Phoenix–Nashville Campus, 875 West Elliot Road, Suite 116, Tempe, AZ 85284, 480-735-3000 or toll-free 800-776-4867 (in-state), 800-228-7240 (out-of-state). Fax: 480-940-2060.

UNIVERSITY OF PHOENIX–NEVADA CAMPUS
Las Vegas, NV

ABOUT THE INSTITUTION Proprietary, coed. Awards: bachelor's and master's degrees and post-master's certificates. 6 undergraduate majors. Total enrollment: 4,238. Undergraduates: 2,976. Freshmen: 104.
GIFT AID (NEED-BASED) Scholarships, grants, and awards: Federal Pell, FSEOG, state.
GIFT AID (NON-NEED-BASED) Scholarships, grants, and awards by category: Academic Interests/Achievement: business, computer science, social sciences.
LOANS Programs: Federal Direct (Unsubsidized Stafford, PLUS), Perkins.
APPLYING FOR FINANCIAL AID Required financial aid form: FAFSA.
CONTACT ACS/AFS, University of Phoenix–Nevada Campus, 875 West Elliot Road, Suite 116, Tempe, AZ 85284, 480-735-3000 or toll-free 800-776-4867 (in-state), 800-228-7240 (out-of-state). Fax: 480-940-2060.

UNIVERSITY OF PHOENIX–NEW MEXICO CAMPUS
Albuquerque, NM

Tuition & fees: $9950   **Average undergraduate aid package:** $5428

ABOUT THE INSTITUTION Proprietary, coed. Awards: bachelor's and master's degrees. 11 undergraduate majors. Total enrollment: 4,724. Undergraduates: 3,669. Freshmen: 172. Both federal and institutional methodology are used as a basis for awarding need-based institutional aid.
UNDERGRADUATE EXPENSES for 2005–06 Application fee: $110. **Tuition:** full-time $9390; part-time $313 per credit. **Required fees:** full-time $560; $70 per course. **Payment plan:** Deferred payment.
FRESHMAN FINANCIAL AID (Fall 2004) Average financial aid package: $3788 (excluding resources awarded to replace EFC).
UNDERGRADUATE FINANCIAL AID (Fall 2004) Average financial aid package: $5428 (excluding resources awarded to replace EFC).
GIFT AID (NEED-BASED) Total amount: $25,290,065 (100% federal). **Receiving aid:** Freshmen: 7; All full-time undergraduates: 4,491. **Scholarships, grants, and awards:** Federal Pell, FSEOG, state, private, college/university gift aid from institutional funds, Academic Competitiveness Grant and National Science and Mathematics Access to Retain Talent (SMART).
GIFT AID (NON-NEED-BASED) Total amount: $20,981,751 (100% federal). **Receiving aid:** Freshmen: 5; Undergraduates: 4,250. **Scholarships, grants, and awards by category:** Academic Interests/Achievement: business, computer science, health fields, social sciences. **Tuition waivers:** Full or partial for employees or children of employees.
LOANS Programs: FFEL (Subsidized and Unsubsidized Stafford, PLUS), Perkins.
APPLYING FOR FINANCIAL AID Required financial aid form: institution's own form. **Financial aid deadline:** Continuous. **Notification date:** Continuous beginning 7/1.
CONTACT ACS/AFS, University of Phoenix–New Mexico Campus, 875 West Elliot Road, Suite 116, Tempe, AZ 85284, 480-735-3000 or toll-free 800-776-4867 (in-state), 800-228-7240 (out-of-state). Fax: 480-940-2060.

UNIVERSITY OF PHOENIX–NORTHERN VIRGINIA CAMPUS
Reston, VA

Tuition & fees: $12,365   **Average undergraduate aid package:** $3562

ABOUT THE INSTITUTION Proprietary, coed. Awards: bachelor's and master's degrees. 3 undergraduate majors. Total enrollment: 1,377. Undergraduates: 1,020. Freshmen: 80. Both federal and institutional methodology are used as a basis for awarding need-based institutional aid.
UNDERGRADUATE EXPENSES for 2005–06 Application fee: $110. **Tuition:** full-time $11,805; part-time $393.50 per credit. **Required fees:** full-time $560; $70 per course. **Payment plan:** Deferred payment.
FRESHMAN FINANCIAL AID (Fall 2004) Average financial aid package: $9733 (excluding resources awarded to replace EFC).

University of Phoenix–Northern Virginia Campus

UNDERGRADUATE FINANCIAL AID (Fall 2004) *Average financial aid package:* $3562 (excluding resources awarded to replace EFC).
GIFT AID (NEED-BASED) *Total amount:* $2,728,350 (100% federal). *Receiving aid:* Freshmen: 1; All full-time undergraduates: 631. *Scholarships, grants, and awards:* Federal Pell, FSEOG, state, private, college/university gift aid from institutional funds, Academic Competitiveness Grant and National Science and Mathematics Access to Retain Talent (SMART).
GIFT AID (NON-NEED-BASED) *Total amount:* $3,908,213 (100% federal). *Receiving aid:* Freshmen: 1; Undergraduates: 675. *Scholarships, grants, and awards by category: Academic Interests/Achievement:* business, computer science, health fields, social sciences. *Tuition waivers:* Full or partial for employees or children of employees.
LOANS *Programs:* FFEL (Subsidized and Unsubsidized Stafford, PLUS).
APPLYING FOR FINANCIAL AID *Required financial aid form:* institution's own form. *Financial aid deadline:* Continuous. *Notification date:* Continuous beginning 7/1.
CONTACT ACS/AFS, University of Phoenix–Northern Virginia Campus, 875 W. Elliott Road, Suite 116, Tempe, AZ 85284, 480-735-3000 or toll-free 800-776-4867 (in-state), 800-228-7240 (out-of-state). *Fax:* 480-940-2060.

UNIVERSITY OF PHOENIX–NORTH FLORIDA CAMPUS
Jacksonville, FL

| Tuition & fees: $10,520 | Average undergraduate aid package: $4442 |

ABOUT THE INSTITUTION Proprietary, coed. Awards: bachelor's and master's degrees. 10 undergraduate majors. Total enrollment: 2,380. Undergraduates: 1,784. Freshmen: 91. Both federal and institutional methodology are used as a basis for awarding need-based institutional aid.
UNDERGRADUATE EXPENSES for 2005–06 *Application fee:* $110. *Tuition:* full-time $9960; part-time $332 per credit. *Required fees:* full-time $560; $70 per course. *Payment plan:* Deferred payment.
FRESHMAN FINANCIAL AID (Fall 2004) *Average financial aid package:* $2525 (excluding resources awarded to replace EFC).
UNDERGRADUATE FINANCIAL AID (Fall 2004) *Average financial aid package:* $4442 (excluding resources awarded to replace EFC).
GIFT AID (NEED-BASED) *Total amount:* $8,888,551 (100% federal). *Receiving aid:* Freshmen: 1; All full-time undergraduates: 1,824. *Scholarships, grants, and awards:* Federal Pell, FSEOG, state, private, college/university gift aid from institutional funds, Academic Competitiveness Grant and National Science and Mathematics Access to Retain Talent (SMART).
GIFT AID (NON-NEED-BASED) *Total amount:* $9,390,927 (100% federal). *Receiving aid:* Undergraduates: 1,789. *Scholarships, grants, and awards by category: Academic Interests/Achievement:* business, computer science, health fields, social sciences. *Tuition waivers:* Full or partial for employees or children of employees.
LOANS *Programs:* FFEL (Subsidized and Unsubsidized Stafford, PLUS), Perkins.
APPLYING FOR FINANCIAL AID *Required financial aid form:* institution's own form. *Financial aid deadline:* Continuous. *Notification date:* Continuous beginning 7/1.
CONTACT ACS/AFS, University of Phoenix–North Florida Campus, 875 West Elliot Road, Suite 116, Tempe, AZ 85284, 480-735-3000 or toll-free 800-776-4867 (in-state), 800-894-1758 (out-of-state). *Fax:* 480-940-2060.

UNIVERSITY OF PHOENIX–OKLAHOMA CITY CAMPUS
Oklahoma City, OK

| Tuition & fees: $9920 | Average undergraduate aid package: $4830 |

ABOUT THE INSTITUTION Proprietary, coed. Awards: bachelor's and master's degrees. 8 undergraduate majors. Total enrollment: 1,051. Undergraduates: 876. Freshmen: 37. Both federal and institutional methodology are used as a basis for awarding need-based institutional aid.
UNDERGRADUATE EXPENSES for 2005–06 *Application fee:* $110. *Tuition:* full-time $9360; part-time $312 per credit. *Required fees:* full-time $560; $70 per course. *Payment plan:* Deferred payment.
FRESHMAN FINANCIAL AID (Fall 2004) *Average financial aid package:* $1857 (excluding resources awarded to replace EFC).
UNDERGRADUATE FINANCIAL AID (Fall 2004) *Average financial aid package:* $4830 (excluding resources awarded to replace EFC).
GIFT AID (NEED-BASED) *Total amount:* $5,178,663 (100% federal). *Receiving aid:* Freshmen: 3; All full-time undergraduates: 1,017. *Scholarships, grants, and awards:* Federal Pell, FSEOG, state, private, college/university gift aid from institutional funds, Academic Competitiveness Grant and National Science and Mathematics Access to Retain Talent (SMART).
GIFT AID (NON-NEED-BASED) *Total amount:* $4,299,565 (100% federal). *Receiving aid:* Freshmen: 2; Undergraduates: 930. *Scholarships, grants, and awards by category: Academic Interests/Achievement:* business, computer science, health fields, social sciences. *Tuition waivers:* Full or partial for employees or children of employees.
LOANS *Programs:* FFEL (Subsidized and Unsubsidized Stafford, PLUS), Perkins.
APPLYING FOR FINANCIAL AID *Required financial aid form:* institution's own form. *Financial aid deadline:* Continuous. *Notification date:* Continuous beginning 7/1.
CONTACT ACS/AFS, University of Phoenix–Oklahoma City Campus, 875 West Elliot Road, Suite 116, Tempe, AZ 85284, 480-735-3000 or toll-free 800-776-4867 (in-state), 800-228-7240 (out-of-state). *Fax:* 480-940-2060.

UNIVERSITY OF PHOENIX ONLINE CAMPUS
Phoenix, AZ

| Tuition & fees: $13,880 | Average undergraduate aid package: $3903 |

ABOUT THE INSTITUTION Proprietary, coed. Awards: associate, bachelor's, master's, and doctoral degrees and post-bachelor's and post-master's certificates. 8 undergraduate majors. Total enrollment: 117,259. Undergraduates: 70,820. Freshmen: 699. Both federal and institutional methodology are used as a basis for awarding need-based institutional aid.
UNDERGRADUATE EXPENSES for 2005–06 *Application fee:* $110. *Tuition:* full-time $13,320; part-time $444 per credit. Full-time tuition and fees vary according to program. *Payment plan:* Deferred payment.
FRESHMAN FINANCIAL AID (Fall 2004) *Average financial aid package:* $4697 (excluding resources awarded to replace EFC).
UNDERGRADUATE FINANCIAL AID (Fall 2004) *Average financial aid package:* $3903 (excluding resources awarded to replace EFC).
GIFT AID (NEED-BASED) *Total amount:* $361,020,159 (100% federal). *Receiving aid:* Freshmen: 23; All full-time undergraduates: 84,868. *Scholarships, grants, and awards:* Federal Pell, FSEOG, state, private, college/university gift aid from institutional funds, Academic Competitiveness Grant and National Science and Mathematics Access to Retain Talent (SMART).
GIFT AID (NON-NEED-BASED) *Total amount:* $401,813,270 (99% federal, 1% state). *Receiving aid:* Freshmen: 23; Undergraduates: 78,987. *Scholarships, grants, and awards by category: Academic Interests/Achievement:* business, computer science, health fields, social sciences. *Tuition waivers:* Full or partial for employees or children of employees.
LOANS *Programs:* FFEL (Subsidized and Unsubsidized Stafford, PLUS), Perkins.
APPLYING FOR FINANCIAL AID *Required financial aid form:* institution's own form. *Financial aid deadline:* Continuous. *Notification date:* Continuous beginning 7/1.
CONTACT ACS/AFS, University of Phoenix Online Campus, 875 West Elliot Road, Suite 116, Tempe, AZ 85284, 480-735-3000 or toll-free 800-776-4867 (in-state), 800-228-7240 (out-of-state). *Fax:* 480-940-2060.

UNIVERSITY OF PHOENIX–OREGON CAMPUS
Portland, OR

| Tuition & fees: $10,970 | Average undergraduate aid package: $4109 |

ABOUT THE INSTITUTION Proprietary, coed. Awards: bachelor's and master's degrees. 5 undergraduate majors. Total enrollment: 2,053. Undergraduates: 1,686. Freshmen: 42. Both federal and institutional methodology are used as a basis for awarding need-based institutional aid.

UNDERGRADUATE EXPENSES for 2005–06 *Application fee:* $110. *Tuition:* full-time $10,410; part-time $347 per credit. *Required fees:* full-time $560; $70 per course. *Payment plan:* Deferred payment.
UNDERGRADUATE FINANCIAL AID (Fall 2004) *Average financial aid package:* $4109 (excluding resources awarded to replace EFC).
GIFT AID (NEED-BASED) *Total amount:* $7,365,909 (100% federal). *Receiving aid:* All full-time undergraduates: 1,638. *Scholarships, grants, and awards:* Federal Pell, FSEOG, state, private, college/university gift aid from institutional funds, Academic Competitiveness Grant and National Science and Mathematics Access to Retain Talent (SMART).
GIFT AID (NON-NEED-BASED) *Total amount:* $7,707,577 (100% federal). *Receiving aid:* Undergraduates: 1,623. *Scholarships, grants, and awards by category:* Academic Interests/Achievement: business, computer science, health fields, social sciences. *Tuition waivers:* Full or partial for employees or children of employees.
LOANS *Programs:* FFEL (Subsidized and Unsubsidized Stafford, PLUS), Perkins.
APPLYING FOR FINANCIAL AID *Required financial aid form:* institution's own form. *Financial aid deadline:* Continuous. *Notification date:* Continuous.
CONTACT ACS/AFS, University of Phoenix–Oregon Campus, 875 West Elliot Road, Suite 116, Tempe, AZ 85284, 480-735-3000 or toll-free 800-776-4867 (in-state), 800-228-7240 (out-of-state). *Fax:* 480-940-2060.

UNIVERSITY OF PHOENIX–PHILADELPHIA CAMPUS
Wayne, PA

Tuition & fees: $13,610 | Average undergraduate aid package: $4021

ABOUT THE INSTITUTION Proprietary, coed. Awards: bachelor's and master's degrees. 4 undergraduate majors. Total enrollment: 1,694. Undergraduates: 1,282. Freshmen: 97. Both federal and institutional methodology are used as a basis for awarding need-based institutional aid.
UNDERGRADUATE EXPENSES for 2005–06 *Application fee:* $110. *Tuition:* full-time $13,050; part-time $435 per credit. *Required fees:* full-time $560; $70 per course. *Payment plan:* Deferred payment.
FRESHMAN FINANCIAL AID (Fall 2004) *Average financial aid package:* $2008 (excluding resources awarded to replace EFC).
UNDERGRADUATE FINANCIAL AID (Fall 2004) *Average financial aid package:* $4021 (excluding resources awarded to replace EFC).
GIFT AID (NEED-BASED) *Total amount:* $5,530,075 (100% federal). *Receiving aid:* Freshmen: 3; All full-time undergraduates: 1,284. *Scholarships, grants, and awards:* Federal Pell, FSEOG, state, private, college/university gift aid from institutional funds, Academic Competitiveness Grant and National Science and Mathematics Access to Retain Talent (SMART).
GIFT AID (NON-NEED-BASED) *Total amount:* $5,860,646 (99% federal, 1% state). *Receiving aid:* Freshmen: 1; Undergraduates: 1,156. *Scholarships, grants, and awards by category:* Academic Interests/Achievement: business, computer science. *Tuition waivers:* Full or partial for employees or children of employees.
LOANS *Programs:* FFEL (Subsidized and Unsubsidized Stafford, PLUS), Perkins.
APPLYING FOR FINANCIAL AID *Required financial aid form:* institution's own form. *Financial aid deadline:* Continuous. *Notification date:* Continuous beginning 7/1.
CONTACT ACS/AFS, University of Phoenix–Philadelphia Campus, 875 West Elliot Road, Suite 116, Tempe, AZ 85284, 480-735-3000 or toll-free 800-776-4867 (in-state), 800-228-7240 (out-of-state). *Fax:* 480-940-2060.

UNIVERSITY OF PHOENIX–PHOENIX CAMPUS
Phoenix, AZ

Tuition & fees: $10,325 | Average undergraduate aid package: $4348

ABOUT THE INSTITUTION Proprietary, coed. Awards: bachelor's and master's degrees and post-bachelor's and post-master's certificates. 10 undergraduate majors. Total enrollment: 9,408. Undergraduates: 5,898. Freshmen: 169. Both federal and institutional methodology are used as a basis for awarding need-based institutional aid.
UNDERGRADUATE EXPENSES for 2005–06 *Application fee:* $110. *Tuition:* full-time $9765; part-time $323 per credit. *Required fees:* full-time $560; $70 per course. *Payment plan:* Deferred payment.
FRESHMAN FINANCIAL AID (Fall 2004) *Average financial aid package:* $4030 (excluding resources awarded to replace EFC).
UNDERGRADUATE FINANCIAL AID (Fall 2004) *Average financial aid package:* $4348 (excluding resources awarded to replace EFC).
GIFT AID (NEED-BASED) *Total amount:* $31,121,984 (100% federal). *Receiving aid:* Freshmen: 6; All full-time undergraduates: 6,544. *Scholarships, grants, and awards:* Federal Pell, FSEOG, state, private, college/university gift aid from institutional funds, Academic Competitiveness Grant and National Science and Mathematics Access to Retain Talent (SMART).
GIFT AID (NON-NEED-BASED) *Total amount:* $34,187,851 (99% federal, 1% state). *Receiving aid:* Freshmen: 7; Undergraduates: 6,518. *Scholarships, grants, and awards by category:* Academic Interests/Achievement: business, computer science, health fields, social sciences. *Tuition waivers:* Full or partial for employees or children of employees.
LOANS *Programs:* FFEL (Subsidized and Unsubsidized Stafford, PLUS), Perkins.
APPLYING FOR FINANCIAL AID *Required financial aid form:* institution's own form. *Financial aid deadline:* Continuous. *Notification date:* Continuous beginning 7/1.
CONTACT ACS/AFS, University of Phoenix–Phoenix Campus, 875 West Elliot Road, Suite 116, Tempe, AZ 85284, 480-735-3000 or toll-free 800-776-4867 (in-state), 800-228-7240 (out-of-state). *Fax:* 480-940-2060.

UNIVERSITY OF PHOENIX–PITTSBURGH CAMPUS
Pittsburgh, PA

Tuition & fees: $13,610 | Average undergraduate aid package: $3806

ABOUT THE INSTITUTION Proprietary, coed. Awards: bachelor's and master's degrees. 5 undergraduate majors. Total enrollment: 645. Undergraduates: 497. Freshmen: 36. Both federal and institutional methodology are used as a basis for awarding need-based institutional aid.
UNDERGRADUATE EXPENSES for 2005–06 *Application fee:* $110. *Tuition:* full-time $13,050; part-time $435 per credit. *Required fees:* full-time $560; $70 per course. *Payment plan:* Deferred payment.
UNDERGRADUATE FINANCIAL AID (Fall 2004) *Average financial aid package:* $3806 (excluding resources awarded to replace EFC).
GIFT AID (NEED-BASED) *Total amount:* $2,141,853 (100% federal). *Receiving aid:* All full-time undergraduates: 528. *Scholarships, grants, and awards:* Federal Pell, FSEOG, state, private, college/university gift aid from institutional funds, Academic Competitiveness Grant and National Science and Mathematics Access to Retain Talent (SMART).
GIFT AID (NON-NEED-BASED) *Total amount:* $2,189,726 (99% federal, 1% state). *Receiving aid:* Undergraduates: 449. *Scholarships, grants, and awards by category:* Academic Interests/Achievement: business, computer science. *Tuition waivers:* Full or partial for employees or children of employees.
LOANS *Programs:* FFEL (Subsidized and Unsubsidized Stafford, PLUS), Perkins.
APPLYING FOR FINANCIAL AID *Required financial aid form:* institution's own form. *Financial aid deadline:* Continuous. *Notification date:* Continuous beginning 7/1.
CONTACT ACS/AFS, University of Phoenix–Pittsburgh Campus, 875 West Elliot Road, Suite 116, Tempe, AZ 85284, 480-735-3000 or toll-free 800-776-4867 (in-state), 800-228-7240 (out-of-state). *Fax:* 480-940-2060.

UNIVERSITY OF PHOENIX–PUERTO RICO CAMPUS
Guaynabo, PR

Tuition & fees: $6200 | Average undergraduate aid package: $5913

ABOUT THE INSTITUTION Proprietary, coed. Awards: bachelor's and master's degrees (courses conducted at 121 campuses and learning centers in 25 states). 2 undergraduate majors. Total enrollment: 2,714. Undergraduates: 832. Freshmen: 42. Both federal and institutional methodology are used as a basis for awarding need-based institutional aid.

University of Phoenix–Puerto Rico Campus

UNDERGRADUATE EXPENSES for 2005–06 *Application fee:* $110. *Tuition:* full-time $5640; part-time $188 per credit. *Required fees:* full-time $560; $70 per course. *Payment plan:* Deferred payment.
UNDERGRADUATE FINANCIAL AID (Fall 2004) *Average financial aid package:* $5913 (excluding resources awarded to replace EFC).
GIFT AID (NEED-BASED) *Total amount:* $9,692,942 (100% federal). *Receiving aid:* All full-time undergraduates: 1,617. *Scholarships, grants, and awards:* Federal Pell, FSEOG, state, private, college/university gift aid from institutional funds, Academic Competitiveness Grant and National Science and Mathematics Access to Retain Talent (SMART).
GIFT AID (NON-NEED-BASED) *Total amount:* $8,400,522 (100% federal). *Receiving aid:* Undergraduates: 1,368. *Scholarships, grants, and awards by category: Academic Interests/Achievement:* business, computer science, social sciences. *Tuition waivers:* Full or partial for employees or children of employees.
LOANS *Programs:* FFEL (Subsidized and Unsubsidized Stafford, PLUS), Perkins.
APPLYING FOR FINANCIAL AID *Required financial aid form:* institution's own form. *Financial aid deadline:* Continuous. *Notification date:* Continuous beginning 7/1.
CONTACT ACS/AFS, University of Phoenix–Puerto Rico Campus, 875 West Elliot Road, Suite 116, Tempe, AZ 85284, 480-735-3000 or toll-free 800-776-4867 (in-state), 800-228-7240 (out-of-state). *Fax:* 480-940-2060.

UNIVERSITY OF PHOENIX–RALEIGH CAMPUS
Raleigh, NC

Tuition & fees: $10,730 | **Average undergraduate aid package: $3028**

ABOUT THE INSTITUTION Proprietary, coed. Awards: bachelor's and master's degrees. 5 undergraduate majors. Total enrollment: 221. Undergraduates: 134. Freshmen: 16. Both federal and institutional methodology are used as a basis for awarding need-based institutional aid.
UNDERGRADUATE EXPENSES for 2005–06 *Application fee:* $110. *Tuition:* full-time $10,170; part-time $339 per credit. *Required fees:* full-time $560; $70 per course. *Payment plan:* Deferred payment.
FRESHMAN FINANCIAL AID (Fall 2004) *Average financial aid package:* $867 (excluding resources awarded to replace EFC).
UNDERGRADUATE FINANCIAL AID (Fall 2004) *Average financial aid package:* $3028 (excluding resources awarded to replace EFC).
GIFT AID (NEED-BASED) *Total amount:* $230,142 (100% federal). *Receiving aid:* Freshmen: 1; All full-time undergraduates: 73. *Scholarships, grants, and awards:* Federal Pell, FSEOG, state, private, college/university gift aid from institutional funds, Academic Competitiveness Grant and National Science and Mathematics Access to Retain Talent (SMART).
GIFT AID (NON-NEED-BASED) *Total amount:* $249,171 (100% federal). *Receiving aid:* Freshmen: 1; Undergraduates: 69. *Scholarships, grants, and awards by category: Academic Interests/Achievement:* business, computer science, health fields, social sciences. *Tuition waivers:* Full or partial for employees or children of employees.
LOANS *Programs:* FFEL (Subsidized and Unsubsidized Stafford, PLUS), Perkins.
APPLYING FOR FINANCIAL AID *Required financial aid form:* institution's own form. *Financial aid deadline:* Continuous. *Notification date:* Continuous beginning 7/1.
CONTACT ACS/AFS, University of Phoenix–Raleigh Campus, 875 West Elliott Road, Suite 116, Tempe, AZ 85284, 480-735-3000 or toll-free 800-776-4867 (in-state), 800-228-7240 (out-of-state). *Fax:* 480-940-2060.

UNIVERSITY OF PHOENIX–RICHMOND CAMPUS
Richmond, VA

Tuition & fees: $11,930 | **Average undergraduate aid package: $2403**

ABOUT THE INSTITUTION Proprietary, coed. Awards: bachelor's and master's degrees. 2 undergraduate majors. Total enrollment: 383. Undergraduates: 301. Freshmen: 45. Both federal and institutional methodology are used as a basis for awarding need-based institutional aid.

UNDERGRADUATE EXPENSES for 2005–06 *Application fee:* $110. *Tuition:* full-time $11,370; part-time $379 per credit. *Required fees:* full-time $560; $70 per course. *Payment plan:* Deferred payment.
UNDERGRADUATE FINANCIAL AID (Fall 2004) *Average financial aid package:* $2403 (excluding resources awarded to replace EFC).
GIFT AID (NEED-BASED) *Total amount:* $334,001 (100% federal). *Receiving aid:* All full-time undergraduates: 128. *Scholarships, grants, and awards:* Federal Pell, FSEOG, state, private, college/university gift aid from institutional funds, Academic Competitiveness Grant and National Science and Mathematics Access to Retain Talent (SMART).
GIFT AID (NON-NEED-BASED) *Total amount:* $311,142 (100% federal). *Receiving aid:* Undergraduates: 103. *Scholarships, grants, and awards by category: Academic Interests/Achievement:* business, computer science. *Tuition waivers:* Full or partial for employees or children of employees.
LOANS *Programs:* FFEL (Subsidized and Unsubsidized Stafford, PLUS), Perkins, Academic Competitiveness Grant and National Science and Mathematics Access to Retain Talent (SMART).
APPLYING FOR FINANCIAL AID *Required financial aid form:* institution's own form. *Financial aid deadline:* Continuous. *Notification date:* Continuous beginning 7/1.
CONTACT ACS/AFS, University of Phoenix–Richmond Campus, 875 West Elliott Road, Suite 116, Tempe, AZ 85284, 480-735-3000 or toll-free 800-776-4867 (in-state), 800-228-7240 (out-of-state). *Fax:* 480-940-2060.

UNIVERSITY OF PHOENIX–SACRAMENTO VALLEY CAMPUS
Sacramento, CA

Tuition & fees: $12,785 | **Average undergraduate aid package: $4856**

ABOUT THE INSTITUTION Proprietary, coed. Awards: bachelor's and master's degrees. 11 undergraduate majors. Total enrollment: 4,629. Undergraduates: 3,506. Freshmen: 111. Both federal and institutional methodology are used as a basis for awarding need-based institutional aid.
UNDERGRADUATE EXPENSES for 2005–06 *Application fee:* $110. *Tuition:* full-time $12,225; part-time $407.50 per credit. *Required fees:* full-time $560; $70 per course. *Payment plan:* Deferred payment.
UNDERGRADUATE FINANCIAL AID (Fall 2004) *Average financial aid package:* $4856 (excluding resources awarded to replace EFC).
GIFT AID (NEED-BASED) *Total amount:* $16,972,417 (100% federal). *Receiving aid:* All full-time undergraduates: 3,613. *Scholarships, grants, and awards:* Federal Pell, FSEOG, state, private, college/university gift aid from institutional funds, Academic Competitiveness Grant and National Science and Mathematics Access to Retain Talent (SMART).
GIFT AID (NON-NEED-BASED) *Total amount:* $20,947,141 (87% federal, 13% state). *Receiving aid:* Undergraduates: 3,599. *Scholarships, grants, and awards by category: Academic Interests/Achievement:* business, computer science, health fields, social sciences. *Tuition waivers:* Full or partial for employees or children of employees.
LOANS *Programs:* FFEL (Subsidized and Unsubsidized Stafford, PLUS), Perkins.
APPLYING FOR FINANCIAL AID *Required financial aid form:* institution's own form. *Financial aid deadline:* Continuous. *Notification date:* Continuous beginning 7/1.
CONTACT ACS/AFS, University of Phoenix–Sacramento Valley Campus, 875 West Elliott Road, Suite 116, Tempe, AZ 85284, 480-735-3000 or toll-free 800-776-4867 (in-state), 800-228-7240 (out-of-state). *Fax:* 480-940-2060.

UNIVERSITY OF PHOENIX–ST. LOUIS CAMPUS
St. Louis, MO

Tuition & fees: $12,110 | **Average undergraduate aid package: $3798**

ABOUT THE INSTITUTION Proprietary, coed. Awards: bachelor's and master's degrees. 3 undergraduate majors. Total enrollment: 1,026. Undergraduates: 869. Freshmen: 57. Both federal and institutional methodology are used as a basis for awarding need-based institutional aid.

UNDERGRADUATE EXPENSES for 2005–06 *Application fee:* $110. *Tuition:* full-time $11,550; part-time $385 per credit. *Required fees:* full-time $560; $70 per course. *Payment plan:* Deferred payment.
FRESHMAN FINANCIAL AID (Fall 2004) *Average financial aid package:* $1274 (excluding resources awarded to replace EFC).
UNDERGRADUATE FINANCIAL AID (Fall 2004) *Average financial aid package:* $3798 (excluding resources awarded to replace EFC).
GIFT AID (NEED-BASED) *Total amount:* $3,687,755 (100% federal). *Receiving aid:* Freshmen: 1; All full-time undergraduates: 911. *Scholarships, grants, and awards:* Federal Pell, FSEOG, state, private, college/university gift aid from institutional funds, Academic Competitiveness Grant and National Science and Mathematics Access to Retain Talent (SMART).
GIFT AID (NON-NEED-BASED) *Total amount:* $3,177,668 (100% federal). *Receiving aid:* Freshmen: 1; Undergraduates: 811. *Scholarships, grants, and awards by category:* Academic Interests/Achievement: business, computer science. *Tuition waivers:* Full or partial for employees or children of employees.
LOANS *Programs:* FFEL (Subsidized and Unsubsidized Stafford, PLUS), Perkins.
APPLYING FOR FINANCIAL AID *Required financial aid form:* institution's own form. *Financial aid deadline:* Continuous. *Notification date:* Continuous beginning 7/1.
CONTACT ACS/AFS, University of Phoenix–St. Louis Campus, 875 West Elliot Road, Suite 116, Tempe, AZ 85284, 480-735-3000 or toll-free 800-776-4867 (in-state), 800-228-7240 (out-of-state). *Fax:* 480-940-2060.

UNIVERSITY OF PHOENIX–SAN DIEGO CAMPUS
San Diego, CA

Tuition & fees: $12,500	Average undergraduate aid package: $4280

ABOUT THE INSTITUTION Proprietary, coed. Awards: bachelor's and master's degrees. 10 undergraduate majors. Total enrollment: 4,563. Undergraduates: 3,459. Freshmen: 113. Both federal and institutional methodology are used as a basis for awarding need-based institutional aid.
UNDERGRADUATE EXPENSES for 2005–06 *Application fee:* $110. *Tuition:* full-time $11,940; part-time $398 per credit. *Required fees:* full-time $560; $70 per course. *Payment plan:* Deferred payment.
FRESHMAN FINANCIAL AID (Fall 2004) *Average financial aid package:* $8245 (excluding resources awarded to replace EFC).
UNDERGRADUATE FINANCIAL AID (Fall 2004) *Average financial aid package:* $4280 (excluding resources awarded to replace EFC).
GIFT AID (NEED-BASED) *Total amount:* $17,367,901 (100% federal). *Receiving aid:* Freshmen: 2; All full-time undergraduates: 3,803. *Scholarships, grants, and awards:* Federal Pell, FSEOG, state, private, college/university gift aid from institutional funds, Academic Competitiveness Grant and National Science and Mathematics Access to Retain Talent (SMART).
GIFT AID (NON-NEED-BASED) *Total amount:* $20,246,863 (96% federal, 4% state). *Receiving aid:* Freshmen: 2; Undergraduates: 3,830. *Scholarships, grants, and awards by category:* Academic Interests/Achievement: business, computer science, health fields, social sciences. *Tuition waivers:* Full or partial for employees or children of employees.
LOANS *Programs:* FFEL (Subsidized and Unsubsidized Stafford, PLUS), Perkins.
APPLYING FOR FINANCIAL AID *Required financial aid form:* institution's own form. *Financial aid deadline:* Continuous. *Notification date:* Continuous beginning 7/1.
CONTACT ACS/AFS, University of Phoenix–San Diego Campus, 875 West Elliot Road, Suite 116, Tempe, AZ 85284, 480-735-3000 or toll-free 888-776-4867 (in-state), 888-228-7240 (out-of-state). *Fax:* 480-940-2060.

UNIVERSITY OF PHOENIX–SOUTHERN ARIZONA CAMPUS
Tucson, AZ

Tuition & fees: $10,235	Average undergraduate aid package: $4731

ABOUT THE INSTITUTION Proprietary, coed. Awards: bachelor's and master's degrees and post-master's certificates. 12 undergraduate majors. Total enrollment: 3,392. Undergraduates: 2,431. Freshmen: 64. Both federal and institutional methodology are used as a basis for awarding need-based institutional aid.
UNDERGRADUATE EXPENSES for 2005–06 *Application fee:* $110. *Tuition:* full-time $9675; part-time $322.50 per credit. *Required fees:* full-time $560; $70 per course. *Payment plan:* Deferred payment.
FRESHMAN FINANCIAL AID (Fall 2004) *Average financial aid package:* $4839 (excluding resources awarded to replace EFC).
UNDERGRADUATE FINANCIAL AID (Fall 2004) *Average financial aid package:* $4731 (excluding resources awarded to replace EFC).
GIFT AID (NEED-BASED) *Total amount:* $12,412,765 (100% federal). *Receiving aid:* Freshmen: 3; All full-time undergraduates: 2,494. *Scholarships, grants, and awards:* Federal Pell, FSEOG, state, private, college/university gift aid from institutional funds, Academic Competitiveness Grant and National Science and Mathematics Access to Retain Talent (SMART).
GIFT AID (NON-NEED-BASED) *Total amount:* $11,765,971 (99% federal, 1% state). *Receiving aid:* Freshmen: 3; Undergraduates: 2,406. *Tuition waivers:* Full or partial for employees or children of employees.
LOANS *Programs:* FFEL (Subsidized and Unsubsidized Stafford, PLUS), Perkins.
APPLYING FOR FINANCIAL AID *Required financial aid form:* institution's own form. *Financial aid deadline:* Continuous. *Notification date:* Continuous beginning 7/1.
CONTACT ACS/AFS, University of Phoenix–Southern Arizona Campus, 875 West Elliot Road, Suite 116, Tempe, AZ 85284, 480-735-3000 or toll-free 800-776-4867 (in-state), 800-228-7240 (out-of-state). *Fax:* 480-940-2060.

UNIVERSITY OF PHOENIX–SOUTHERN CALIFORNIA CAMPUS
Costa Mesa, CA

Tuition & fees: $13,685	Average undergraduate aid package: $4755

ABOUT THE INSTITUTION Proprietary, coed. Awards: bachelor's and master's degrees. 6 undergraduate majors. Total enrollment: 16,134. Undergraduates: 12,476. Freshmen: 373. Both federal and institutional methodology are used as a basis for awarding need-based institutional aid.
UNDERGRADUATE EXPENSES for 2005–06 *Application fee:* $110. *Tuition:* full-time $13,125; part-time $437.50 per credit. *Required fees:* full-time $560; $70 per course. *Payment plan:* Deferred payment.
FRESHMAN FINANCIAL AID (Fall 2004) *Average financial aid package:* $4250 (excluding resources awarded to replace EFC).
UNDERGRADUATE FINANCIAL AID (Fall 2004) *Average financial aid package:* $4755 (excluding resources awarded to replace EFC).
GIFT AID (NEED-BASED) *Total amount:* $62,963,709 (100% federal). *Receiving aid:* Freshmen: 1; All full-time undergraduates: 13,541. *Scholarships, grants, and awards:* Federal Pell, FSEOG, state, private, college/university gift aid from institutional funds, Academic Competitiveness Grant and National Science and Mathematics Access to Retain Talent (SMART).
GIFT AID (NON-NEED-BASED) *Total amount:* $72,910,583 (89% federal, 11% state). *Receiving aid:* Freshmen: 1; Undergraduates: 13,246. *Tuition waivers:* Full or partial for employees or children of employees.
LOANS *Programs:* FFEL (Subsidized and Unsubsidized Stafford, PLUS), Perkins.
APPLYING FOR FINANCIAL AID *Required financial aid form:* institution's own form. *Financial aid deadline:* Continuous. *Notification date:* Continuous beginning 7/1.
CONTACT ACS/AFS, University of Phoenix–Southern California Campus, 875 West Elliot Road, Suite 116, Tempe, AZ 85284, 480-735-3000 or toll-free 800-776-4867 (in-state), 800-228-7240 (out-of-state). *Fax:* 480-940-2060.

UNIVERSITY OF PHOENIX–SOUTHERN COLORADO CAMPUS
Colorado Springs, CO

Tuition & fees: $10,049	Average undergraduate aid package: $4860

ABOUT THE INSTITUTION Proprietary, coed. Awards: bachelor's and master's degrees. 7 undergraduate majors. Total enrollment: 1,294. Undergraduates: 775. Freshmen: 23. Both federal and institutional methodology are used as a basis for awarding need-based institutional aid.

University of Phoenix–Southern Colorado Campus

UNDERGRADUATE EXPENSES for 2005–06 *Application fee:* $110. *Tuition:* full-time $9489; part-time $316 per credit. *Required fees:* full-time $560; $70 per course. *Payment plan:* Deferred payment.

UNDERGRADUATE FINANCIAL AID (Fall 2004) *Average financial aid package:* $4860 (excluding resources awarded to replace EFC).

GIFT AID (NEED-BASED) *Total amount:* $5,166,369 (100% federal). *Receiving aid:* All full-time undergraduates: 984. *Scholarships, grants, and awards:* Federal Pell, FSEOG, state, private, college/university gift aid from institutional funds, Academic Competitiveness Grant and National Science and Mathematics Access to Retain Talent (SMART).

GIFT AID (NON-NEED-BASED) *Total amount:* $5,641,988 (100% federal). *Receiving aid:* Undergraduates: 984. *Scholarships, grants, and awards by category: Academic Interests/Achievement:* business, computer science, health fields, social sciences. *Tuition waivers:* Full or partial for employees or children of employees.

LOANS *Programs:* FFEL (Subsidized and Unsubsidized Stafford, PLUS), Perkins.

APPLYING FOR FINANCIAL AID *Required financial aid form:* institution's own form. *Financial aid deadline:* Continuous. *Notification date:* Continuous beginning 7/1.

CONTACT ACS/AFS, University of Phoenix–Southern Colorado Campus, 875 West Elliot Road, Suite 116, Tempe, AZ 85284, 480-735-3000 or toll-free 800-776-4867 (in-state), 800-228-7240 (out-of-state). *Fax:* 480-940-2060.

UNIVERSITY OF PHOENIX–SOUTH FLORIDA CAMPUS
Fort Lauderdale, FL

Tuition & fees: $10,520   **Average undergraduate aid package:** $4230

ABOUT THE INSTITUTION Proprietary, coed. Awards: bachelor's and master's degrees. 7 undergraduate majors. Total enrollment: 2,791. Undergraduates: 2,043. Freshmen: 92. Both federal and institutional methodology are used as a basis for awarding need-based institutional aid.

UNDERGRADUATE EXPENSES for 2005–06 *Application fee:* $110. *Tuition:* full-time $9960; part-time $332 per credit. *Required fees:* full-time $560; $70 per course. *Payment plan:* Deferred payment.

FRESHMAN FINANCIAL AID (Fall 2004) *Average financial aid package:* $500 (excluding resources awarded to replace EFC).

UNDERGRADUATE FINANCIAL AID (Fall 2004) *Average financial aid package:* $4230 (excluding resources awarded to replace EFC).

GIFT AID (NEED-BASED) *Total amount:* $10,261,274 (100% federal). *Receiving aid:* Freshmen: 1; All full-time undergraduates: 2,203. *Scholarships, grants, and awards:* Federal Pell, FSEOG, state, private, college/university gift aid from institutional funds, Academic Competitiveness Grant and National Science and Mathematics Access to Retain Talent (SMART).

GIFT AID (NON-NEED-BASED) *Total amount:* $11,143,387 (100% federal). *Receiving aid:* Undergraduates: 2,214. *Scholarships, grants, and awards by category: Academic Interests/Achievement:* business, computer science, health fields, social sciences. *Tuition waivers:* Full or partial for employees or children of employees.

LOANS *Programs:* FFEL (Subsidized and Unsubsidized Stafford, PLUS), Perkins.

APPLYING FOR FINANCIAL AID *Required financial aid form:* institution's own form. *Financial aid deadline:* Continuous. *Notification date:* Continuous beginning 7/1.

CONTACT ACS/AFS, University of Phoenix–South Florida Campus, 875 West Elliot Road, Suite 116, Tempe, AZ 85284, 480-735-3000 or toll-free 800-228-7240. *Fax:* 480-940-2060.

UNIVERSITY OF PHOENIX–SPOKANE CAMPUS
Spokane Valley, WA

Tuition & fees: $10,310   **Average undergraduate aid package:** $3574

ABOUT THE INSTITUTION Proprietary, coed. Awards: bachelor's and master's degrees. 4 undergraduate majors. Total enrollment: 343. Undergraduates: 284. Freshmen: 13. Both federal and institutional methodology are used as a basis for awarding need-based institutional aid.

UNDERGRADUATE EXPENSES for 2005–06 *Application fee:* $110. *Tuition:* full-time $9750; part-time $325 per credit. *Required fees:* full-time $560; $70 per course. *Payment plan:* Deferred payment.

UNDERGRADUATE FINANCIAL AID (Fall 2004) *Average financial aid package:* $3574 (excluding resources awarded to replace EFC).

GIFT AID (NEED-BASED) *Total amount:* $1,039,989 (100% federal). *Receiving aid:* All full-time undergraduates: 273. *Scholarships, grants, and awards:* Federal Pell, FSEOG, state, private, college/university gift aid from institutional funds, Academic Competitiveness Grant and National Science and Mathematics Access to Retain Talent (SMART).

GIFT AID (NON-NEED-BASED) *Total amount:* $982,422 (100% federal). *Receiving aid:* Undergraduates: 232. *Scholarships, grants, and awards by category: Academic Interests/Achievement:* business, computer science. *Tuition waivers:* Full or partial for employees or children of employees.

LOANS *Programs:* FFEL (Subsidized and Unsubsidized Stafford, PLUS), Perkins.

APPLYING FOR FINANCIAL AID *Required financial aid form:* institution's own form. *Financial aid deadline:* Continuous. *Notification date:* Continuous beginning 7/1.

CONTACT ACS/AFS, University of Phoenix–Spokane Campus, 875 West Elliott Road, Suite 116, Tempe, AZ 85284, 480-735-3000 or toll-free 800-697-8223 (in-state), 800-228-7240 (out-of-state). *Fax:* 480-940-2060.

UNIVERSITY OF PHOENIX–SPRINGFIELD CAMPUS
Springfield, MO

Tuition & fees: $10,010   **Average undergraduate aid package:** $3093

ABOUT THE INSTITUTION Proprietary, coed. Awards: bachelor's and master's degrees. 2 undergraduate majors. Total enrollment: 259. Undergraduates: 220. Freshmen: 34. Both federal and institutional methodology are used as a basis for awarding need-based institutional aid.

UNDERGRADUATE EXPENSES for 2005–06 *Application fee:* $110. *Tuition:* full-time $9450; part-time $315 per credit. *Required fees:* full-time $560; $70 per course. *Payment plan:* Deferred payment.

UNDERGRADUATE FINANCIAL AID (Fall 2004) *Average financial aid package:* $3093 (excluding resources awarded to replace EFC).

GIFT AID (NEED-BASED) *Total amount:* $479,449 (100% federal). *Receiving aid:* All full-time undergraduates: 148. *Scholarships, grants, and awards:* Federal Pell, FSEOG, state, private, college/university gift aid from institutional funds, Academic Competitiveness Grant and National Science and Mathematics Access to Retain Talent (SMART).

GIFT AID (NON-NEED-BASED) *Total amount:* $411,214 (100% federal). *Receiving aid:* Undergraduates: 118. *Scholarships, grants, and awards by category: Academic Interests/Achievement:* business, computer science. *Tuition waivers:* Full or partial for employees or children of employees.

LOANS *Programs:* FFEL (Subsidized and Unsubsidized Stafford, PLUS), Perkins.

APPLYING FOR FINANCIAL AID *Required financial aid form:* institution's own form. *Financial aid deadline:* Continuous. *Notification date:* Continuous beginning 7/1.

CONTACT ACS/AFS, University of Phoenix–Springfield Campus, 875 West Elliott Road, Suite 116, Tempe, AZ 85284, 480-735-3000 or toll-free 800-776-4867 (in-state), 800-228-7240 (out-of-state). *Fax:* 480-940-2060.

UNIVERSITY OF PHOENIX–TULSA CAMPUS
Tulsa, OK

Tuition & fees: $9920   **Average undergraduate aid package:** $4519

ABOUT THE INSTITUTION Proprietary, coed. Awards: bachelor's and master's degrees. 9 undergraduate majors. Total enrollment: 1,302. Undergraduates: 1,114. Freshmen: 75. Both federal and institutional methodology are used as a basis for awarding need-based institutional aid.

UNDERGRADUATE EXPENSES for 2005–06 *Application fee:* $110. *Tuition:* full-time $9360; part-time $312 per credit. *Required fees:* full-time $560; $70 per course. *Payment plan:* Deferred payment.

FRESHMAN FINANCIAL AID (Fall 2004) *Average financial aid package:* $1265 (excluding resources awarded to replace EFC).

UNDERGRADUATE FINANCIAL AID (Fall 2004) *Average financial aid package:* $4519 (excluding resources awarded to replace EFC).
GIFT AID (NEED-BASED) *Total amount:* $6,453,652 (100% federal). *Receiving aid:* Freshmen: 11; All full-time undergraduates: 1,382. *Scholarships, grants, and awards:* Federal Pell, FSEOG, state, private, college/university gift aid from institutional funds, Academic Competitiveness Grant and National Science and Mathematics Access to Retain Talent (SMART).
GIFT AID (NON-NEED-BASED) *Total amount:* $5,289,613 (100% federal). *Receiving aid:* Freshmen: 3; Undergraduates: 1,225. *Scholarships, grants, and awards by category:* Academic Interests/Achievement: business, computer science, health fields, social sciences. *Tuition waivers:* Full or partial for employees or children of employees.
LOANS *Programs:* FFEL (Subsidized and Unsubsidized Stafford, PLUS), Perkins.
APPLYING FOR FINANCIAL AID *Required financial aid form:* institution's own form. *Financial aid deadline:* Continuous. *Notification date:* Continuous beginning 7/1.
CONTACT ACS/AFS, University of Phoenix–Tulsa Campus, 875 West Elliot Road, Suite 116, Tempe, AZ 85284, 480-735-3000 or toll-free 800-776-4867 (in-state), 800-228-7240 (out-of-state). *Fax:* 480-940-2060.

UNIVERSITY OF PHOENIX–UTAH CAMPUS
Salt Lake City, UT

Tuition & fees: $10,580	Average undergraduate aid package: $4853

ABOUT THE INSTITUTION Proprietary, coed. Awards: bachelor's and master's degrees. 11 undergraduate majors. Total enrollment: 4,135. Undergraduates: 2,663. Freshmen: 88. Both federal and institutional methodology are used as a basis for awarding need-based institutional aid.
UNDERGRADUATE EXPENSES for 2005–06 *Application fee:* $110. *Tuition:* full-time $10,020; part-time $344 per credit. *Required fees:* full-time $560; $70 per course. *Payment plan:* Deferred payment.
FRESHMAN FINANCIAL AID (Fall 2004) *Average financial aid package:* $1801 (excluding resources awarded to replace EFC).
UNDERGRADUATE FINANCIAL AID (Fall 2004) *Average financial aid package:* $4853 (excluding resources awarded to replace EFC).
GIFT AID (NEED-BASED) *Total amount:* $15,636,862 (100% federal). *Receiving aid:* Freshmen: 7; All full-time undergraduates: 3,086. *Scholarships, grants, and awards:* Federal Pell, FSEOG, state, private, college/university gift aid from institutional funds, Academic Competitiveness Grant and National Science and Mathematics Access to Retain Talent (SMART).
GIFT AID (NON-NEED-BASED) *Total amount:* $14,344,281 (100% federal). *Receiving aid:* Freshmen: 3; Undergraduates: 2,867. *Scholarships, grants, and awards by category:* Academic Interests/Achievement: business, computer science, health fields, social sciences. *Tuition waivers:* Full or partial for employees or children of employees.
LOANS *Programs:* FFEL (Subsidized and Unsubsidized Stafford, PLUS), Perkins.
APPLYING FOR FINANCIAL AID *Required financial aid form:* institution's own form. *Financial aid deadline:* Continuous. *Notification date:* Continuous beginning 7/1.
CONTACT ACS/AFS, University of Phoenix–Utah Campus, 875 West Elliot Road, Suite 116, Tempe, AZ 85284, 480-735-3000 or toll-free 800-776-4867 (in-state), 800-228-7240 (out-of-state). *Fax:* 480-940-2060.

UNIVERSITY OF PHOENIX–WASHINGTON CAMPUS
Seattle, WA

Tuition & fees: $11,615	Average undergraduate aid package: $3913

ABOUT THE INSTITUTION Proprietary, coed. Awards: bachelor's and master's degrees. 7 undergraduate majors. Total enrollment: 2,172. Undergraduates: 1,678. Freshmen: 47. Both federal and institutional methodology are used as a basis for awarding need-based institutional aid.
UNDERGRADUATE EXPENSES for 2005–06 *Application fee:* $110. *Tuition:* full-time $11,055; part-time $368.50. *Required fees:* full-time $560; $70 per course. *Payment plan:* Deferred payment.
UNDERGRADUATE FINANCIAL AID (Fall 2004) *Average financial aid package:* $3913 (excluding resources awarded to replace EFC).

GIFT AID (NEED-BASED) *Total amount:* $6,843,759 (100% federal). *Receiving aid:* All full-time undergraduates: 1,533. *Scholarships, grants, and awards:* Federal Pell, FSEOG, state, private, college/university gift aid from institutional funds, Academic Competitiveness Grant and National Science and Mathematics Access to Retain Talent (SMART).
GIFT AID (NON-NEED-BASED) *Total amount:* $7,973,313 (100% federal). *Receiving aid:* Undergraduates: 1,611. *Scholarships, grants, and awards by category:* Academic Interests/Achievement: business, computer science, health fields, social sciences. *Tuition waivers:* Full or partial for employees or children of employees.
LOANS *Programs:* FFEL (Subsidized and Unsubsidized Stafford, PLUS), Perkins.
APPLYING FOR FINANCIAL AID *Required financial aid form:* institution's own form. *Financial aid deadline:* Continuous. *Notification date:* Continuous beginning 7/1.
CONTACT ACS/AFS, University of Phoenix–Washington Campus, 875 West Elliot Road, Suite 116, Tempe, AZ 85284, 480-735-3000 or toll-free 800-776-4867 (in-state), 800-228-7240 (out-of-state). *Fax:* 480-940-2060.

UNIVERSITY OF PHOENIX–WEST FLORIDA CAMPUS
Temple Terrace, FL

Tuition & fees: $10,520	Average undergraduate aid package: $4104

ABOUT THE INSTITUTION Proprietary, coed. Awards: bachelor's and master's degrees. 10 undergraduate majors. Total enrollment: 2,755. Undergraduates: 2,064. Freshmen: 99. Both federal and institutional methodology are used as a basis for awarding need-based institutional aid.
UNDERGRADUATE EXPENSES for 2005–06 *Application fee:* $110. *Tuition:* full-time $9960; part-time $332 per credit. *Required fees:* full-time $560; $70 per course. *Payment plan:* Deferred payment.
FRESHMAN FINANCIAL AID (Fall 2004) *Average financial aid package:* $500 (excluding resources awarded to replace EFC).
UNDERGRADUATE FINANCIAL AID (Fall 2004) *Average financial aid package:* $4104 (excluding resources awarded to replace EFC).
GIFT AID (NEED-BASED) *Total amount:* $9,764,536 (100% federal). *Receiving aid:* Freshmen: 1; All full-time undergraduates: 2,178. *Scholarships, grants, and awards:* Federal Pell, FSEOG, state, private, college/university gift aid from institutional funds, Academic Competitiveness Grant and National Science and Mathematics Access to Retain Talent (SMART).
GIFT AID (NON-NEED-BASED) *Total amount:* $11,106,115 (100% federal). *Receiving aid:* Undergraduates: 2,121. *Scholarships, grants, and awards by category:* Academic Interests/Achievement: business, computer science, health fields, social sciences. *Tuition waivers:* Full or partial for employees or children of employees.
LOANS *Programs:* FFEL (Subsidized and Unsubsidized Stafford, PLUS), Perkins.
APPLYING FOR FINANCIAL AID *Required financial aid form:* institution's own form. *Financial aid deadline:* Continuous. *Notification date:* Continuous beginning 7/1.
CONTACT ACS/AFS, University of Phoenix–West Florida Campus, 875 West Elliot Road, Suite 116, Tempe, AZ 85284, 480-735-3000 or toll-free 800-776-4867 (in-state), 800-228-7240 (out-of-state). *Fax:* 480-940-2060.

UNIVERSITY OF PHOENIX–WEST MICHIGAN CAMPUS
Grand Rapids, MI

Tuition & fees: $11,660	Average undergraduate aid package: $4187

ABOUT THE INSTITUTION Proprietary, coed. Awards: bachelor's and master's degrees. 9 undergraduate majors. Total enrollment: 1,156. Undergraduates: 959. Freshmen: 42. Both federal and institutional methodology are used as a basis for awarding need-based institutional aid.
UNDERGRADUATE EXPENSES for 2005–06 *Application fee:* $110. *Tuition:* full-time $11,100; part-time $370 per credit. *Required fees:* full-time $560; $70 per course. *Payment plan:* Deferred payment.
UNDERGRADUATE FINANCIAL AID (Fall 2004) *Average financial aid package:* $4187 (excluding resources awarded to replace EFC).

University of Phoenix–West Michigan Campus

GIFT AID (NEED-BASED) *Total amount:* $4,685,554 (100% federal). *Receiving aid:* All full-time undergraduates: 1,041. *Scholarships, grants, and awards:* Federal Pell, FSEOG, state, private, college/university gift aid from institutional funds, Academic Competitiveness Grant and National Science and Mathematics Access to Retain Talent (SMART).
GIFT AID (NON-NEED-BASED) *Total amount:* $4,380,784 (100% federal). *Receiving aid:* Undergraduates: 946. *Scholarships, grants, and awards by category: Academic Interests/Achievement:* business, computer science, health fields, social sciences. *Tuition waivers:* Full or partial for employees or children of employees.
LOANS *Programs:* FFEL (Subsidized and Unsubsidized Stafford, PLUS), Perkins.
APPLYING FOR FINANCIAL AID *Required financial aid form:* institution's own form. *Financial aid deadline:* Continuous. *Notification date:* Continuous beginning 7/1.
CONTACT ACS/AFS, University of Phoenix–West Michigan Campus, 875 West Elliot Road, Suite 116, Tempe, AZ 85284, 480-735-3000 or toll-free 800-776-4867 (in-state), 800-228-7240 (out-of-state). *Fax:* 480-940-2060.

UNIVERSITY OF PHOENIX–WICHITA CAMPUS
Wichita, KS

Tuition & fees: $11,000   **Average undergraduate aid package:** $3590

ABOUT THE INSTITUTION Proprietary, coed. Awards: bachelor's and master's degrees. 2 undergraduate majors. Total enrollment: 400. Undergraduates: 331. Freshmen: 29. Both federal and institutional methodology are used as a basis for awarding need-based institutional aid.
UNDERGRADUATE EXPENSES for 2005–06 *Application fee:* $110. *Tuition:* full-time $10,440; part-time $348 per credit. *Required fees:* full-time $560; $70 per course. *Payment plan:* Deferred payment.
UNDERGRADUATE FINANCIAL AID (Fall 2004) *Average financial aid package:* $3590 (excluding resources awarded to replace EFC).
GIFT AID (NEED-BASED) *Total amount:* $1,332,070 (100% federal). *Receiving aid:* All full-time undergraduates: 344. *Scholarships, grants, and awards:* Federal Pell, FSEOG, state, private, college/university gift aid from institutional funds, Academic Competitiveness Grant and National Science and Mathematics Access to Retain Talent (SMART).
GIFT AID (NON-NEED-BASED) *Total amount:* $1,247,216 (100% federal). *Receiving aid:* Undergraduates: 283. *Scholarships, grants, and awards by category: Academic Interests/Achievement:* business, computer science. *Tuition waivers:* Full or partial for employees or children of employees.
LOANS *Programs:* FFEL (Subsidized and Unsubsidized Stafford, PLUS), Perkins.
APPLYING FOR FINANCIAL AID *Required financial aid form:* institution's own form. *Financial aid deadline:* Continuous. *Notification date:* Continuous beginning 7/1.
CONTACT ACS/AFS, University of Phoenix–Wichita Campus, 875 West Elliot Road, Suite 116, Tempe, AZ 85284, 480-735-3000 or toll-free 800-776-4867 (in-state), 800-228-7240 (out-of-state). *Fax:* 480-940-2060.

UNIVERSITY OF PHOENIX–WISCONSIN CAMPUS
Brookfield, WI

Tuition & fees: $11,345   **Average undergraduate aid package:** $4011

ABOUT THE INSTITUTION Proprietary, coed. Awards: bachelor's and master's degrees. 3 undergraduate majors. Total enrollment: 1,357. Undergraduates: 1,067. Freshmen: 64. Both federal and institutional methodology are used as a basis for awarding need-based institutional aid.
UNDERGRADUATE EXPENSES for 2005–06 *Application fee:* $110. *Tuition:* full-time $10,785; part-time $359.50 per credit. *Required fees:* full-time $560; $70 per course. *Payment plan:* Deferred payment.
UNDERGRADUATE FINANCIAL AID (Fall 2004) *Average financial aid package:* $4011 (excluding resources awarded to replace EFC).
GIFT AID (NEED-BASED) *Total amount:* $5,142,240 (100% federal). *Receiving aid:* All full-time undergraduates: 1,185. *Scholarships, grants, and awards:* Federal Pell, FSEOG, state, private, college/university gift aid from institutional funds, Academic Competitiveness Grant and National Science and Mathematics Access to Retain Talent (SMART).
GIFT AID (NON-NEED-BASED) *Total amount:* $5,014,465 (100% federal). *Receiving aid:* Undergraduates: 1,082. *Tuition waivers:* Full or partial for employees or children of employees.
LOANS *Programs:* FFEL (Subsidized and Unsubsidized Stafford, PLUS), Perkins.
APPLYING FOR FINANCIAL AID *Required financial aid form:* institution's own form. *Financial aid deadline:* Continuous. *Notification date:* Continuous beginning 7/1.
CONTACT ACS/AFS, University of Phoenix–Wisconsin Campus, 875 West Elliot Road, Suite 116, Tempe, AZ 85284, 480-735-3000 or toll-free 800-776-4867 (in-state), 800-228-7240 (out-of-state). *Fax:* 480-940-2060.

UNIVERSITY OF PITTSBURGH
Pittsburgh, PA

Tuition & fees (PA res): $11,436   **Average undergraduate aid package:** $11,605

ABOUT THE INSTITUTION State-related, coed. Awards: bachelor's, master's, doctoral, and first professional degrees and post-bachelor's and post-master's certificates. 86 undergraduate majors. Total enrollment: 26,559. Undergraduates: 17,024. Freshmen: 3,224. Federal methodology is used as a basis for awarding need-based institutional aid.
UNDERGRADUATE EXPENSES for 2005–06 *Application fee:* $35. *Tuition, state resident:* full-time $10,736; part-time $412 per credit. *Tuition, nonresident:* full-time $20,084; part-time $772 per credit. *Required fees:* full-time $700; $164 per term part-time. Full-time tuition and fees vary according to degree level and program. Part-time tuition and fees vary according to degree level and program. *College room and board:* $7430; *room only:* $4510. Room and board charges vary according to board plan and housing facility. *Payment plans:* Installment, deferred payment.
FRESHMAN FINANCIAL AID (Fall 2005, est.) 2641 applied for aid; of those 69% were deemed to have need. 92% of freshmen with need received aid; of those 44% had need fully met. *Average percent of need met:* 79% (excluding resources awarded to replace EFC). *Average financial aid package:* $12,085 (excluding resources awarded to replace EFC). 7% of all full-time freshmen had no need and received non-need-based gift aid.
UNDERGRADUATE FINANCIAL AID (Fall 2005, est.) 10,690 applied for aid; of those 80% were deemed to have need. 95% of undergraduates with need received aid; of those 37% had need fully met. *Average percent of need met:* 76% (excluding resources awarded to replace EFC). *Average financial aid package:* $11,605 (excluding resources awarded to replace EFC). 7% of all full-time undergraduates had no need and received non-need-based gift aid.
GIFT AID (NEED-BASED) *Total amount:* $24,977,615 (34% federal, 52% state, 14% institutional). *Receiving aid:* Freshmen: 35% (1,132); All full-time undergraduates: 34% (5,286). *Average award:* Freshmen: $4749; Undergraduates: $4486. *Scholarships, grants, and awards:* Federal Pell, FSEOG, state, private, college/university gift aid from institutional funds.
GIFT AID (NON-NEED-BASED) *Total amount:* $20,198,278 (3% state, 97% institutional). *Average Award:* Freshmen: $12,115; Undergraduates: $9699. *Scholarships, grants, and awards by category: Academic Interests/Achievement:* 3,578 awards ($19,509,968 total): general academic interests/achievements. *Special Characteristics:* children of faculty/staff. *Tuition waivers:* Full or partial for employees or children of employees. *ROTC:* Army, Naval cooperative, Air Force.
LOANS *Student loans:* $70,001,751 (48% need-based, 52% non-need-based). 63% of past graduating class borrowed through all loan programs. *Average indebtedness per student:* $17,051. *Average need-based loan:* Freshmen: $3761; Undergraduates: $4542. *Parent loans:* $18,247,988 (100% non-need-based). *Programs:* FFEL (Subsidized and Unsubsidized Stafford, PLUS), Perkins, Federal Nursing, college/university.
WORK-STUDY *Federal work-study:* Total amount: $2,300,000; jobs available.
ATHLETIC AWARDS *Total amount:* $5,810,325 (100% non-need-based).
APPLYING FOR FINANCIAL AID *Required financial aid forms:* FAFSA, institution's own form. *Financial aid deadline:* 6/1 (priority: 3/1). *Notification date:* Continuous beginning 3/15.
CONTACT Dr. Betsy A. Porter, Director, Office of Admissions and Financial Aid, University of Pittsburgh, 4227 Fifth Avenue, First Floor, Alumni Hall, Pittsburgh, PA 15260, 412-624-7488. *Fax:* 412-648-8815. *E-mail:* oafa@pitt.edu.

UNIVERSITY OF PITTSBURGH AT BRADFORD
Bradford, PA

Tuition & fees (PA res): $10,538   **Average undergraduate aid package:** $12,000

ABOUT THE INSTITUTION State-related, coed. Awards: associate and bachelor's degrees. 25 undergraduate majors. Total enrollment: 1,301. Undergraduates: 1,301. Freshmen: 239. Federal methodology is used as a basis for awarding need-based institutional aid.
UNDERGRADUATE EXPENSES for 2005–06 *Application fee:* $35. *Tuition, state resident:* full-time $9888; part-time $380 per credit. *Tuition, nonresident:* full-time $19,776; part-time $760 per credit. *Required fees:* full-time $650; $95 per term part-time. Full-time tuition and fees vary according to course load and program. Part-time tuition and fees vary according to course load and program. *College room and board:* $6470. Room and board charges vary according to board plan and housing facility. *Payment plan:* Installment.
FRESHMAN FINANCIAL AID (Fall 2005, est.) 217 applied for aid; of those 87% were deemed to have need. 100% of freshmen with need received aid; of those 18% had need fully met. *Average percent of need met:* 76% (excluding resources awarded to replace EFC). *Average financial aid package:* $11,400 (excluding resources awarded to replace EFC). 17% of all full-time freshmen had no need and received non-need-based gift aid.
UNDERGRADUATE FINANCIAL AID (Fall 2005, est.) 892 applied for aid; of those 87% were deemed to have need. 100% of undergraduates with need received aid; of those 22% had need fully met. *Average percent of need met:* 78% (excluding resources awarded to replace EFC). *Average financial aid package:* $12,000 (excluding resources awarded to replace EFC). 12% of all full-time undergraduates had no need and received non-need-based gift aid.
GIFT AID (NEED-BASED) *Total amount:* $3,101,305 (46% federal, 54% state). *Receiving aid:* Freshmen: 58% (138); All full-time undergraduates: 59% (551). *Average award:* Freshmen: $4000; Undergraduates: $4000. *Scholarships, grants, and awards:* Federal Pell, FSEOG, state, private, college/university gift aid from institutional funds.
GIFT AID (NON-NEED-BASED) *Total amount:* $3,943,169 (10% state, 64% institutional, 26% external sources). *Receiving aid:* Freshmen: 61% (146); Undergraduates: 58% (543). *Average Award:* Freshmen: $4000; Undergraduates: $4000. *Scholarships, grants, and awards by category:* Academic Interests/Achievement: biological sciences, business, communication, computer science, education, engineering/technologies, English, general academic interests/achievements, health fields, humanities, mathematics, physical sciences, social sciences. *Tuition waivers:* Full or partial for employees or children of employees. *ROTC:* Army cooperative.
LOANS *Student loans:* $7,350,047 (47% need-based, 53% non-need-based). 85% of past graduating class borrowed through all loan programs. *Average indebtedness per student:* $19,313. *Average need-based loan:* Freshmen: $2625; Undergraduates: $4281. *Parent loans:* $978,035 (100% non-need-based). *Programs:* FFEL (Subsidized and Unsubsidized Stafford, PLUS), Perkins.
WORK-STUDY *Federal work-study:* Total amount: $144,829; 200 jobs averaging $1400. *State or other work-study/employment:* Total amount: $100,000 (100% non-need-based). 10 part-time jobs averaging $1400.
APPLYING FOR FINANCIAL AID *Required financial aid form:* FAFSA. *Financial aid deadline (priority):* 3/1. *Notification date:* Continuous beginning 4/1. Students must reply within 2 weeks of notification.
CONTACT Melissa Ibañez, Director of Financial Aid, University of Pittsburgh at Bradford, 300 Campus Drive, Bradford, PA 16701-2812, 814-362-7550 or toll-free 800-872-1787. Fax: 814-362-7578. E-mail: ibanez@exchange.upb.pitt.edu.

UNIVERSITY OF PITTSBURGH AT GREENSBURG
Greensburg, PA

Tuition & fees (PA res): $10,562   **Average undergraduate aid package:** $7063

ABOUT THE INSTITUTION State-related, coed. Awards: bachelor's degrees. 22 undergraduate majors. Total enrollment: 1,796. Undergraduates: 1,796. Freshmen: 424. Federal methodology is used as a basis for awarding need-based institutional aid.
UNDERGRADUATE EXPENSES for 2005–06 *Application fee:* $45. *Tuition, state resident:* full-time $9888; part-time $380 per credit. *Tuition, nonresident:* full-time $19,776; part-time $760 per credit. *Required fees:* full-time $674; $113 per term part-time. *College room and board:* $7210; *room only:* $4910.
FRESHMAN FINANCIAL AID (Fall 2005, est.) 424 applied for aid; of those 81% were deemed to have need. 84% of freshmen with need received aid; of those 41% had need fully met. *Average percent of need met:* 54% (excluding resources awarded to replace EFC). *Average financial aid package:* $6840 (excluding resources awarded to replace EFC). 5% of all full-time freshmen had no need and received non-need-based gift aid.
UNDERGRADUATE FINANCIAL AID (Fall 2005, est.) 1,641 applied for aid; of those 84% were deemed to have need. 91% of undergraduates with need received aid; of those 33% had need fully met. *Average percent of need met:* 54% (excluding resources awarded to replace EFC). *Average financial aid package:* $7063 (excluding resources awarded to replace EFC). 2% of all full-time undergraduates had no need and received non-need-based gift aid.
GIFT AID (NEED-BASED) *Total amount:* $3,201,032 (33% federal, 67% state). *Receiving aid:* Freshmen: 48% (202); All full-time undergraduates: 51% (836). *Average award:* Freshmen: $4042; Undergraduates: $3970. *Scholarships, grants, and awards:* Federal Pell, FSEOG, state, private, college/university gift aid from institutional funds, United Negro College Fund.
GIFT AID (NON-NEED-BASED) *Total amount:* $865,000 (64% institutional, 36% external sources). *Receiving aid:* Freshmen: 24% (101); Undergraduates: 17% (284). *Average Award:* Freshmen: $2928; Undergraduates: $2676. *Scholarships, grants, and awards by category:* Academic Interests/Achievement: 68 awards ($230,000 total): general academic interests/achievements. *Special Achievements/Activities:* 5 awards ($5000 total): general special achievements/activities, leadership. *ROTC:* Army cooperative, Air Force cooperative.
LOANS *Student loans:* $12,005,884 (27% need-based, 73% non-need-based). 85% of past graduating class borrowed through all loan programs. *Average indebtedness per student:* $17,125. *Average need-based loan:* Freshmen: $2721; Undergraduates: $3666. *Parent loans:* $2,067,211 (100% non-need-based). *Programs:* FFEL (Subsidized and Unsubsidized Stafford, PLUS), Perkins.
WORK-STUDY *Federal work-study:* Total amount: $291,181; 95 jobs averaging $2175.
APPLYING FOR FINANCIAL AID *Required financial aid forms:* FAFSA, institution's own form, state aid form. *Financial aid deadline (priority):* 3/1. *Notification date:* Continuous beginning 4/15. Students must reply within 3 weeks of notification.
CONTACT Ms. Brandi S. Darr, Director of Admissions and Financial Aid, University of Pittsburgh at Greensburg, 1150 Mount Pleasant Road, Greensburg, PA 15601-5860, 724-836-7167. E-mail: upgadmit@pitt.edu.

UNIVERSITY OF PITTSBURGH AT JOHNSTOWN
Johnstown, PA

Tuition & fees (PA res): $10,500   **Average undergraduate aid package:** $9093

ABOUT THE INSTITUTION State-related, coed. Awards: associate and bachelor's degrees. 50 undergraduate majors. Total enrollment: 3,173. Undergraduates: 3,173. Freshmen: 772. Federal methodology is used as a basis for awarding need-based institutional aid.
UNDERGRADUATE EXPENSES for 2005–06 *Application fee:* $35. *Tuition, state resident:* full-time $9888; part-time $380 per credit. *Tuition, nonresident:* full-time $19,776; part-time $760 per credit. *Required fees:* full-time $612; $77 per term part-time. Full-time tuition and fees vary according to program and student level. Part-time tuition and fees vary according to program and student level. *College room and board:* $6100; *room only:* $3700. Room and board charges vary according to board plan and housing facility. *Payment plan:* Installment.
FRESHMAN FINANCIAL AID (Fall 2004) 775 applied for aid; of those 86% were deemed to have need. 93% of freshmen with need received aid; of those 10% had need fully met. *Average percent of need met:* 44% (excluding resources awarded to replace EFC). *Average financial aid package:* $8013 (excluding resources awarded to replace EFC). 5% of all full-time freshmen had no need and received non-need-based gift aid.
UNDERGRADUATE FINANCIAL AID (Fall 2004) 2,794 applied for aid; of those 78% were deemed to have need. 93% of undergraduates with need received aid; of those 7% had need fully met. *Average percent of need met:* 51%

University of Pittsburgh at Johnstown

(excluding resources awarded to replace EFC). *Average financial aid package:* $9093 (excluding resources awarded to replace EFC). 3% of all full-time undergraduates had no need and received non-need-based gift aid.
GIFT AID (NEED-BASED) *Total amount:* $6,801,780 (35% federal, 55% state, 7% institutional, 3% external sources). *Receiving aid:* Freshmen: 66% (570); All full-time undergraduates: 55% (1,623). *Average award:* Freshmen: $4061; Undergraduates: $4064. *Scholarships, grants, and awards:* Federal Pell, FSEOG, state, private, college/university gift aid from institutional funds.
GIFT AID (NON-NEED-BASED) *Total amount:* $1,641,467 (15% state, 65% institutional, 20% external sources). *Receiving aid:* Freshmen: 40% (348); Undergraduates: 22% (649). *Average Award:* Freshmen: $2438; Undergraduates: $2591. *Scholarships, grants, and awards by category:* Academic Interests/Achievement: 166 awards ($541,734 total): general academic interests/achievements. Special Achievements/Activities: 144 awards ($179,750 total): leadership. Special Characteristics: 157 awards ($1,227,116 total): children of faculty/staff. *Tuition waivers:* Full or partial for employees or children of employees.
LOANS *Student loans:* $10,736,867 (61% need-based, 39% non-need-based). 83% of past graduating class borrowed through all loan programs. *Average indebtedness per student:* $18,962. *Average need-based loan:* Freshmen: $2355; Undergraduates: $2459. *Parent loans:* $3,131,985 (100% non-need-based). *Programs:* FFEL (Subsidized and Unsubsidized Stafford, PLUS), Perkins.
WORK-STUDY *Federal work-study:* Total amount: $589,853; 372 jobs averaging $1661. *State or other work-study/employment:* Total amount: $296,514 (100% non-need-based). 332 part-time jobs averaging $941.
ATHLETIC AWARDS *Total amount:* $387,803 (100% non-need-based).
APPLYING FOR FINANCIAL AID *Required financial aid form:* FAFSA. *Financial aid deadline (priority):* 4/1. *Notification date:* Continuous beginning 3/15. Students must reply within 2 weeks of notification.
CONTACT Ms. Julie A. Salem, Director of Student Financial Aid, University of Pittsburgh at Johnstown, 125 Biddle Hall, Johnstown, PA 15904-2990, 814-269-7045 or toll-free 800-765-4875. *Fax:* 814-269-7061. *E-mail:* jasalem@pitt.edu.

UNIVERSITY OF PORTLAND
Portland, OR

Tuition & fees: $24,900	Average undergraduate aid package: $21,821

ABOUT THE INSTITUTION Independent Roman Catholic, coed. Awards: bachelor's and master's degrees and post-master's certificates. 42 undergraduate majors. Total enrollment: 3,413. Undergraduates: 2,920. Freshmen: 724. Federal methodology is used as a basis for awarding need-based institutional aid.
UNDERGRADUATE EXPENSES for 2005–06 *Application fee:* $50. *Comprehensive fee:* $32,300 includes full-time tuition ($24,580), mandatory fees ($320), and room and board ($7400). *College room only:* $3700. Full-time tuition and fees vary according to program. Room and board charges vary according to board plan and housing facility. *Part-time tuition:* $778 per credit hour. Part-time tuition and fees vary according to program. *Payment plans:* Installment, deferred payment.
FRESHMAN FINANCIAL AID (Fall 2005, est.) 597 applied for aid; of those 65% were deemed to have need. 100% of freshmen with need received aid; of those 25% had need fully met. *Average percent of need met:* 89% (excluding resources awarded to replace EFC). *Average financial aid package:* $20,356 (excluding resources awarded to replace EFC). 41% of all full-time freshmen had no need and received non-need-based gift aid.
UNDERGRADUATE FINANCIAL AID (Fall 2005, est.) 1,999 applied for aid; of those 73% were deemed to have need. 99% of undergraduates with need received aid; of those 27% had need fully met. *Average percent of need met:* 94% (excluding resources awarded to replace EFC). *Average financial aid package:* $21,821 (excluding resources awarded to replace EFC). 43% of all full-time undergraduates had no need and received non-need-based gift aid.
GIFT AID (NEED-BASED) *Total amount:* $18,615,472 (8% federal, 2% state, 84% institutional, 6% external sources). *Receiving aid:* Freshmen: 53% (386); All full-time undergraduates: 51% (1,435). *Average award:* Freshmen: $13,838; Undergraduates: $14,249. *Scholarships, grants, and awards:* Federal Pell, FSEOG, state, private, college/university gift aid from institutional funds.
GIFT AID (NON-NEED-BASED) *Total amount:* $18,625,400 (1% federal, 82% institutional, 17% external sources). *Receiving aid:* Freshmen: 37% (268); Undergraduates: 27% (766). *Average Award:* Freshmen: $12,245; Undergraduates: $16,651. *Scholarships, grants, and awards by category:* Academic Interests/Achievement: biological sciences, business, communication, computer science, education, engineering/technologies, English, foreign languages, general academic interests/achievements, health fields, humanities, mathematics, military science, physical sciences, premedicine, religion/biblical studies, social sciences. Creative Arts/Performance: music, performing arts, theater/drama. Special Achievements/Activities: community service. Special Characteristics: children of faculty/staff, relatives of clergy. *Tuition waivers:* Full or partial for employees or children of employees. *ROTC:* Army, Air Force.
LOANS *Student loans:* $7,326,658 (81% need-based, 19% non-need-based). 64% of past graduating class borrowed through all loan programs. *Average indebtedness per student:* $22,253. *Average need-based loan:* Freshmen: $2912; Undergraduates: $5511. *Parent loans:* $5,746,039 (31% need-based, 69% non-need-based). *Programs:* FFEL (Subsidized and Unsubsidized Stafford, PLUS), Perkins, Federal Nursing, college/university.
WORK-STUDY *Federal work-study:* Total amount: $1,408,167; 848 jobs averaging $1819. *State or other work-study/employment:* Total amount: $14,940 (78% need-based, 22% non-need-based). 9 part-time jobs averaging $1660.
ATHLETIC AWARDS *Total amount:* $3,389,125 (14% need-based, 86% non-need-based).
APPLYING FOR FINANCIAL AID *Required financial aid forms:* FAFSA, institution's own form. *Financial aid deadline (priority):* 3/1. *Notification date:* Continuous beginning 3/15. Students must reply within 3 weeks of notification.
CONTACT Ms. Tracy Reisinger, Director of Financial Aid, University of Portland, 5000 North Willamette Boulevard, Portland, OR 97203-5798, 503-943-7311 or toll-free 888-627-5601 (out-of-state). *Fax:* 503-943-7508. *E-mail:* reisinge@up.edu.

UNIVERSITY OF PUERTO RICO, AGUADILLA UNIVERSITY COLLEGE
Aguadilla, PR

CONTACT Director of Financial Aid, University of Puerto Rico, Aguadilla University College, PO Box 250-160, Aguadilla, PR 00604-0160, 787-890-2681 Ext. 273.

UNIVERSITY OF PUERTO RICO AT ARECIBO
Arecibo, PR

CONTACT Mr. Luis Rodriguez, Director of Financial Aid, University of Puerto Rico at Arecibo, PO Box 4010, Arecibo, PR 00613, 787-878-2830 Ext. 2008.

UNIVERSITY OF PUERTO RICO AT BAYAMÓN
Bayamón, PR

CONTACT Financial Aid Director, University of Puerto Rico at Bayamón, 170 Carr 174 Parque Indust Minillas, Bayamon, PR 00959-1919, 787-786-2885 Ext. 2434.

UNIVERSITY OF PUERTO RICO AT HUMACAO
Humacao, PR

CONTACT Larry Cruz, Director of Financial Aid, University of Puerto Rico at Humacao, HUC Station, Humacao, PR 00791-4300, 787-850-9342.

UNIVERSITY OF PUERTO RICO AT PONCE
Ponce, PR

CONTACT Carmelo Vega Montes, Director of Financial Aid, University of Puerto Rico at Ponce, Box 7186, Ponce, PR 00732-7186, 787-844-8181. *Fax:* 787-840-8108.

UNIVERSITY OF PUERTO RICO AT UTUADO
Utuado, PR

CONTACT Edgar Salva, Director of Student Financial Assistance, University of Puerto Rico at Utuado, Call Box 2500, Utuado, PR 00641, 787-894-2828. *Fax:* 787-894-2891.

UNIVERSITY OF PUERTO RICO, CAYEY UNIVERSITY COLLEGE
Cayey, PR

CONTACT Mr. Hector Maldonado Otero, Director of Financial Aid, University of Puerto Rico, Cayey University College, Antonio Barcelo, Cayey, PR 00736, 787-738-2161. *Fax:* 787-263-0676.

UNIVERSITY OF PUERTO RICO, MAYAGÜEZ CAMPUS
Mayagüez, PR

Tuition & fees: N/R	Average undergraduate aid package: $4293

ABOUT THE INSTITUTION Commonwealth-supported, coed. Awards: bachelor's, master's, and doctoral degrees. 50 undergraduate majors. Total enrollment: 12,108. Undergraduates: 11,032. Freshmen: 2,158. Federal methodology is used as a basis for awarding need-based institutional aid.

UNDERGRADUATE EXPENSES for 2005–06 *Application fee:* $15.

FRESHMAN FINANCIAL AID (Fall 2004) 1821 applied for aid; of those 82% were deemed to have need. 100% of freshmen with need received aid. *Average percent of need met:* 38% (excluding resources awarded to replace EFC). *Average financial aid package:* $4293 (excluding resources awarded to replace EFC).

UNDERGRADUATE FINANCIAL AID (Fall 2004) 7,756 applied for aid; of those 85% were deemed to have need. 100% of undergraduates with need received aid. *Average percent of need met:* 38% (excluding resources awarded to replace EFC). *Average financial aid package:* $4293 (excluding resources awarded to replace EFC).

GIFT AID (NEED-BASED) *Total amount:* $25,110,458 (86% federal, 12% state, 2% external sources). *Receiving aid:* Freshmen: 65% (1,494); All full-time undergraduates: 54% (6,629). *Average award:* Freshmen: $4293; Undergraduates: $4293. *Scholarships, grants, and awards:* Federal Pell, FSEOG, state, private, college/university gift aid from institutional funds.

GIFT AID (NON-NEED-BASED) *Total amount:* $117,000 (100% external sources). *Receiving aid:* Freshmen: 2% (45); Undergraduates: 2% (249). *Scholarships, grants, and awards by category: Academic Interests/Achievement:* military science. *Creative Arts/Performance:* 251 awards ($341,360 total): dance, music. *Special Achievements/Activities:* 295 awards ($26,220 total): cheerleading/drum major. *ROTC:* Army, Air Force.

LOANS *Student loans:* $6,703,436 (94% need-based, 6% non-need-based). 52% of past graduating class borrowed through all loan programs. *Average indebtedness per student:* $6400. *Average need-based loan:* Freshmen: $2625; Undergraduates: $3875. *Programs:* FFEL (Subsidized and Unsubsidized Stafford), college/university.

WORK-STUDY *Federal work-study:* Total amount: $730,280; 420 jobs averaging $1560. *State or other work-study/employment:* 425 part-time jobs available.

ATHLETIC AWARDS *Total amount:* $382,500 (100% non-need-based).

APPLYING FOR FINANCIAL AID *Required financial aid forms:* FAFSA, institution's own form, noncustodial (divorced/separated) parent's statement, business/farm supplement. *Financial aid deadline:* Continuous. *Notification date:* Continuous beginning 5/1. Students must reply within 2 weeks of notification.

CONTACT Ms. Ana I. Rodríguez, Director of Financial Aid, University of Puerto Rico, Mayagüez Campus, PO Box 9000, Mayagüez, PR 00681-9000, 787-265-3863. *Fax:* 787-265-1920. *E-mail:* a_rodriguez@rumad.uprm.edu.

UNIVERSITY OF PUERTO RICO, MEDICAL SCIENCES CAMPUS
San Juan, PR

ABOUT THE INSTITUTION Commonwealth-supported, coed, primarily women. Awards: associate, bachelor's, master's, doctoral, and first professional degrees and post-bachelor's and first professional certificates (bachelor's degree is upper-level). 14 undergraduate majors. Total enrollment: 2,334. Undergraduates: 474.

GIFT AID (NEED-BASED) *Scholarships, grants, and awards:* Federal Pell, FSEOG, state, college/university gift aid from institutional funds, Department of Health and Human Services Scholarships.

LOANS *Programs:* Perkins, alternative loans.

APPLYING FOR FINANCIAL AID *Required financial aid forms:* FAFSA, institution's own form.

CONTACT Zoraida Figueroa, Financial Aid Director, University of Puerto Rico, Medical Sciences Campus, Terreno Centro Médico-Edificio Decanato Farmacia y Estudiantes, PO Box 365067, Rio Piedras, PR 00936-5067, 787-763-2525. *Fax:* 787-282-7117. *E-mail:* zfigueroa@rcm.upr.edu.

UNIVERSITY OF PUERTO RICO, RÍO PIEDRAS
San Juan, PR

CONTACT Mr. Efraim Williams, EDP Manager, University of Puerto Rico, Río Piedras, PO Box 23353, San Juan, PR 00931, 787-764-0000 Ext. 5573.

UNIVERSITY OF PUGET SOUND
Tacoma, WA

Tuition & fees: $28,460	Average undergraduate aid package: $20,466

ABOUT THE INSTITUTION Independent, coed. Awards: bachelor's, master's, and first professional degrees and post-master's certificates. 40 undergraduate majors. Total enrollment: 2,887. Undergraduates: 2,604. Freshmen: 670. Federal methodology is used as a basis for awarding need-based institutional aid.

UNDERGRADUATE EXPENSES for 2005–06 *Application fee:* $40. *Comprehensive fee:* $35,600 includes full-time tuition ($28,270), mandatory fees ($190), and room and board ($7140). *College room only:* $3900. Full-time tuition and fees vary according to course load. Room and board charges vary according to board plan and housing facility. *Part-time tuition:* $3570 per unit. Part-time tuition and fees vary according to course load. *Payment plans:* Installment, deferred payment.

FRESHMAN FINANCIAL AID (Fall 2005, est.) 491 applied for aid; of those 80% were deemed to have need. 100% of freshmen with need received aid; of those 27% had need fully met. *Average percent of need met:* 82% (excluding resources awarded to replace EFC). *Average financial aid package:* $20,591 (excluding resources awarded to replace EFC). 24% of all full-time freshmen had no need and received non-need-based gift aid.

UNDERGRADUATE FINANCIAL AID (Fall 2005, est.) 1,733 applied for aid; of those 87% were deemed to have need. 100% of undergraduates with need received aid; of those 23% had need fully met. *Average percent of need met:* 80% (excluding resources awarded to replace EFC). *Average financial aid package:* $20,466 (excluding resources awarded to replace EFC). 27% of all full-time undergraduates had no need and received non-need-based gift aid.

GIFT AID (NEED-BASED) *Total amount:* $21,991,884 (8% federal, 3% state, 85% institutional, 4% external sources). *Receiving aid:* Freshmen: 58% (387); All full-time undergraduates: 57% (1,474). *Average award:* Freshmen: $16,270; Undergraduates: $15,106. *Scholarships, grants, and awards:* Federal Pell, FSEOG, state, private, college/university gift aid from institutional funds.

GIFT AID (NON-NEED-BASED) *Total amount:* $5,335,152 (1% state, 94% institutional, 5% external sources). *Receiving aid:* Freshmen: 26% (173); Undergraduates: 28% (720). *Average Award:* Freshmen: $6943; Undergraduates: $7210. *Scholarships, grants, and awards by category: Academic Interests/Achievement:* 789 awards ($400,942 total): biological sciences, business, communication, computer science, English, foreign languages, general academic interests/achievements, humanities, international studies, mathematics, physical sciences, premedicine, social sciences. *Creative Arts/Performance:* 65 awards ($199,250 total): art/fine arts, debating, music, theater/drama. *Special Achievements/*

University of Puget Sound

Activities: 7 awards ($19,500 total): leadership, religious involvement. *Special Characteristics:* 24 awards ($516,719 total): children of faculty/staff, international students. *Tuition waivers:* Full or partial for employees or children of employees. *ROTC:* Army cooperative.
LOANS *Student loans:* $10,371,863 (90% need-based, 10% non-need-based). 60% of past graduating class borrowed through all loan programs. *Average indebtedness per student:* $25,842. *Average need-based loan:* Freshmen: $3699; Undergraduates: $5274. *Parent loans:* $5,456,626 (73% need-based, 27% non-need-based). *Programs:* FFEL (Subsidized and Unsubsidized Stafford, PLUS), Perkins, Alaska Loans.
WORK-STUDY *Federal work-study:* Total amount: $1,262,000; 552 jobs averaging $2286. *State or other work-study/employment:* Total amount: $2,023,896 (100% need-based). 809 part-time jobs averaging $2502.
APPLYING FOR FINANCIAL AID *Required financial aid form:* FAFSA. *Financial aid deadline (priority):* 2/1. *Notification date:* Continuous beginning 3/15. Students must reply by 5/1.
CONTACT Maggie A. Mittuch, Associate Director for Student Financial Services, University of Puget Sound, 1500 North Warner Street, Tacoma, WA 98416-1039, 253-879-3214 or toll-free 800-396-7191. *Fax:* 253-879-8508. *E-mail:* mmittuch@ups.edu.

UNIVERSITY OF REDLANDS
Redlands, CA

Tuition & fees: $27,164 **Average undergraduate aid package: $25,071**

ABOUT THE INSTITUTION Independent, coed. Awards: bachelor's and master's degrees and post-bachelor's and post-master's certificates. 42 undergraduate majors. Total enrollment: 2,454. Undergraduates: 2,362. Freshmen: 612. Federal methodology is used as a basis for awarding need-based institutional aid.
UNDERGRADUATE EXPENSES for 2005–06 *Application fee:* $45. *Comprehensive fee:* $36,164 includes full-time tuition ($26,864), mandatory fees ($300), and room and board ($9000). *College room only:* $5020. Room and board charges vary according to board plan and housing facility. *Part-time tuition:* $840 per credit. *Part-time fees:* $150 per term. Part-time tuition and fees vary according to course load. *Payment plan:* Installment.
FRESHMAN FINANCIAL AID (Fall 2005, est.) 514 applied for aid; of those 78% were deemed to have need. 100% of freshmen with need received aid; of those 54% had need fully met. *Average percent of need met:* 91% (excluding resources awarded to replace EFC). *Average financial aid package:* $25,155 (excluding resources awarded to replace EFC). 21% of all full-time freshmen had no need and received non-need-based gift aid.
UNDERGRADUATE FINANCIAL AID (Fall 2005, est.) 1,939 applied for aid; of those 83% were deemed to have need. 100% of undergraduates with need received aid; of those 43% had need fully met. *Average percent of need met:* 89% (excluding resources awarded to replace EFC). *Average financial aid package:* $25,071 (excluding resources awarded to replace EFC). 19% of all full-time undergraduates had no need and received non-need-based gift aid.
GIFT AID (NEED-BASED) *Total amount:* $29,071,753 (8% federal, 16% state, 74% institutional, 2% external sources). *Receiving aid:* Freshmen: 64% (390); All full-time undergraduates: 66% (1,549). *Average award:* Freshmen: $19,703; Undergraduates: $18,517. *Scholarships, grants, and awards:* Federal Pell, FSEOG, state, private, college/university gift aid from institutional funds.
GIFT AID (NON-NEED-BASED) *Total amount:* $4,514,225 (98% institutional, 2% external sources). *Receiving aid:* Freshmen: 43% (264); Undergraduates: 38% (881). *Average Award:* Freshmen: $11,187; Undergraduates: $9816. *Scholarships, grants, and awards by category: Academic Interests/Achievement:* general academic interests/achievements. *Creative Arts/Performance:* art/fine arts, creative writing, debating, music. *Special Achievements/Activities:* general special achievements/activities. *Special Characteristics:* international students. *Tuition waivers:* Full or partial for employees or children of employees.
LOANS *Student loans:* $10,153,695 (93% need-based, 7% non-need-based). 78% of past graduating class borrowed through all loan programs. *Average indebtedness per student:* $15,024. *Average need-based loan:* Freshmen: $4770; Undergraduates: $5377. *Parent loans:* $4,586,782 (77% need-based, 23% non-need-based). *Programs:* FFEL (Subsidized and Unsubsidized Stafford, PLUS), Perkins, college/university, alternative loans.
WORK-STUDY *Federal work-study:* Total amount: $2,110,300; jobs available. *State or other work-study/employment:* Total amount: $936,201 (73% need-based, 27% non-need-based). Part-time jobs available.
APPLYING FOR FINANCIAL AID *Required financial aid forms:* FAFSA, state aid form. *Financial aid deadline (priority):* 2/15. *Notification date:* Continuous beginning 2/28. Students must reply by 5/1.
CONTACT Mr. Craig Slaughter, Director of Financial Aid, University of Redlands, PO Box 3080, Redlands, CA 92373-0999, 909-335-4047 or toll-free 800-455-5064. *Fax:* 909-335-4089. *E-mail:* bethann_corey@redlands.edu.

UNIVERSITY OF RHODE ISLAND
Kingston, RI

Tuition & fees (RI res): $7284 **Average undergraduate aid package: $11,659**

ABOUT THE INSTITUTION State-supported, coed. Awards: bachelor's, master's, doctoral, and first professional degrees and post-bachelor's certificates. 76 undergraduate majors. Total enrollment: 15,095. Undergraduates: 11,546. Freshmen: 2,366. Federal methodology is used as a basis for awarding need-based institutional aid.
UNDERGRADUATE EXPENSES for 2005–06 *Application fee:* $50. *Tuition, state resident:* full-time $5258; part-time $219 per credit. *Tuition, nonresident:* full-time $17,900; part-time $746 per credit. *Required fees:* full-time $2026; $74 per credit or $48 per term part-time. Full-time tuition and fees vary according to reciprocity agreements. Part-time tuition and fees vary according to reciprocity agreements. *College room and board:* $8114; *room only:* $4620. Room and board charges vary according to board plan and housing facility. *Payment plan:* Installment.
FRESHMAN FINANCIAL AID (Fall 2005, est.) 2134 applied for aid; of those 78% were deemed to have need. 80% of freshmen with need received aid; of those 83% had need fully met. *Average percent of need met:* 67% (excluding resources awarded to replace EFC). *Average financial aid package:* $12,009 (excluding resources awarded to replace EFC). 8% of all full-time freshmen had no need and received non-need-based gift aid.
UNDERGRADUATE FINANCIAL AID (Fall 2005, est.) 8,089 applied for aid; of those 83% were deemed to have need. 75% of undergraduates with need received aid; of those 70% had need fully met. *Average percent of need met:* 61% (excluding resources awarded to replace EFC). *Average financial aid package:* $11,659 (excluding resources awarded to replace EFC). 4% of all full-time undergraduates had no need and received non-need-based gift aid.
GIFT AID (NEED-BASED) *Total amount:* $33,261,377 (21% federal, 9% state, 62% institutional, 8% external sources). *Receiving aid:* Freshmen: 54% (1,244); All full-time undergraduates: 49% (4,830). *Average award:* Freshmen: $6353; Undergraduates: $5883. *Scholarships, grants, and awards:* Federal Pell, FSEOG, state, private, college/university gift aid from institutional funds.
GIFT AID (NON-NEED-BASED) *Total amount:* $2,327,146 (1% state, 85% institutional, 14% external sources). *Receiving aid:* Freshmen: 9% (207); Undergraduates: 5% (481). *Average Award:* Freshmen: $4711; Undergraduates: $4607. *Scholarships, grants, and awards by category: Academic Interests/Achievement:* general academic interests/achievements. *Creative Arts/Performance:* music. *Special Achievements/Activities:* general special achievements/activities. *Special Characteristics:* general special characteristics. *Tuition waivers:* Full or partial for minority students, employees or children of employees, senior citizens. *ROTC:* Army.
LOANS *Student loans:* $45,475,590 (79% need-based, 21% non-need-based). 56% of past graduating class borrowed through all loan programs. *Average indebtedness per student:* $16,200. *Average need-based loan:* Freshmen: $6184; Undergraduates: $6713. *Parent loans:* $16,265,402 (66% need-based, 34% non-need-based). *Programs:* Federal Direct (Subsidized and Unsubsidized Stafford, PLUS), Perkins, Federal Nursing, state, college/university.
WORK-STUDY *Federal work-study:* Total amount: $960,000; jobs available. *State or other work-study/employment:* Part-time jobs available.
ATHLETIC AWARDS *Total amount:* $3,911,180 (98% need-based, 2% non-need-based).
APPLYING FOR FINANCIAL AID *Required financial aid form:* FAFSA. *Financial aid deadline (priority):* 3/1. *Notification date:* Continuous beginning 3/31. Students must reply by 5/1 or within 2 weeks of notification.
CONTACT Mr. Horace J. Amaral Jr., Director of Enrollment Services, University of Rhode Island, Green Hall, Kingston, RI 02881, 401-874-9500.

UNIVERSITY OF RICHMOND
Richmond, VA

Tuition & fees: $36,550   **Average undergraduate aid package:** $23,258

ABOUT THE INSTITUTION Independent, coed. Awards: associate, bachelor's, master's, and first professional degrees and post-bachelor's certificates. 53 undergraduate majors. Total enrollment: 3,685. Undergraduates: 2,920. Freshmen: 775. Federal methodology is used as a basis for awarding need-based institutional aid.

UNDERGRADUATE EXPENSES for 2006–07 *Application fee:* $50. *Comprehensive fee:* $42,610 includes full-time tuition ($36,550) and room and board ($6060). *College room only:* $2710. *Part-time tuition:* $1460 per semester hour.

FRESHMAN FINANCIAL AID (Fall 2005, est.) 423 applied for aid; of those 71% were deemed to have need. 100% of freshmen with need received aid; of those 97% had need fully met. *Average percent of need met:* 100% (excluding resources awarded to replace EFC). *Average financial aid package:* $27,202 (excluding resources awarded to replace EFC). 10% of all full-time freshmen had no need and received non-need-based gift aid.

UNDERGRADUATE FINANCIAL AID (Fall 2005, est.) 1,405 applied for aid; of those 74% were deemed to have need. 100% of undergraduates with need received aid; of those 93% had need fully met. *Average percent of need met:* 100% (excluding resources awarded to replace EFC). *Average financial aid package:* $23,258 (excluding resources awarded to replace EFC). 14% of all full-time undergraduates had no need and received non-need-based gift aid.

GIFT AID (NEED-BASED) *Total amount:* $19,627,398 (4% federal, 3% state, 91% institutional, 2% external sources). *Receiving aid:* Freshmen: 38% (292); All full-time undergraduates: 33% (1,010). *Average award:* Freshmen: $23,594; Undergraduates: $20,314. *Scholarships, grants, and awards:* Federal Pell, FSEOG, state, private, college/university gift aid from institutional funds.

GIFT AID (NON-NEED-BASED) *Total amount:* $8,751,960 (6% federal, 7% state, 82% institutional, 5% external sources). *Receiving aid:* Freshmen: 5% (36); Undergraduates: 3% (94). *Average Award:* Freshmen: $24,345; Undergraduates: $15,469. *Scholarships, grants, and awards by category: Academic Interests/Achievement:* 210 awards ($4,587,840 total): biological sciences, computer science, general academic interests/achievements, mathematics, physical sciences. *Creative Arts/Performance:* 13 awards ($41,250 total): art/fine arts, dance, music, performing arts, theater/drama. *Special Achievements/Activities:* 16 awards ($33,600 total): community service. *Special Characteristics:* 58 awards ($1,167,120 total): members of minority groups. *ROTC:* Army.

LOANS *Student loans:* $7,920,931 (28% need-based, 72% non-need-based). 41% of past graduating class borrowed through all loan programs. *Average indebtedness per student:* $18,500. *Average need-based loan:* Freshmen: $2829; Undergraduates: $2755. *Parent loans:* $4,093,552 (2% need-based, 98% non-need-based). *Programs:* Federal Direct (Subsidized and Unsubsidized Stafford, PLUS), Perkins.

WORK-STUDY *Federal work-study:* Total amount: $342,655; 215 jobs averaging $1590.

ATHLETIC AWARDS Total amount: $6,073,021 (13% need-based, 87% non-need-based).

APPLYING FOR FINANCIAL AID *Required financial aid forms:* FAFSA, institution's own form. *Financial aid deadline:* 2/25. *Notification date:* 4/1. Students must reply within 4 weeks of notification.

CONTACT Financial Aid Office, University of Richmond, Sarah Brunet Hall, 28 Westhampton Way, University of Richmond, VA 23173, 804-289-8438 or toll-free 800-700-1662. *Fax:* 804-287-6003. *E-mail:* finaid@richmond.edu.

UNIVERSITY OF RIO GRANDE
Rio Grande, OH

ABOUT THE INSTITUTION Independent, coed. Awards: associate, bachelor's, and master's degrees. 71 undergraduate majors. Total enrollment: 2,376. Undergraduates: 2,141. Freshmen: 375.

GIFT AID (NEED-BASED) *Scholarships, grants, and awards:* Federal Pell, FSEOG, state, private, college/university gift aid from institutional funds.

GIFT AID (NON-NEED-BASED) *Scholarships, grants, and awards by category: Academic Interests/Achievement:* biological sciences, business, communication, computer science, education, English, general academic interests/achievements, health fields, humanities, mathematics, physical sciences, social sciences. *Creative Arts/Performance:* art/fine arts, music. *Special Achievements/Activities:* cheerleading/drum major. *Special Characteristics:* children and siblings of alumni, children of faculty/staff, local/state students, out-of-state students.

LOANS *Programs:* Federal Direct (Subsidized and Unsubsidized Stafford, PLUS), Perkins.

APPLYING FOR FINANCIAL AID *Required financial aid form:* FAFSA.

CONTACT Dr. John Hill, Director of Financial Aid, University of Rio Grande, 218 North College Avenue, Rio Grande, OH 45674, 740-245-7218 or toll-free 800-282-7201 (in-state). *Fax:* 740-245-7102.

UNIVERSITY OF ROCHESTER
Rochester, NY

Tuition & fees: $31,297   **Average undergraduate aid package:** $24,474

ABOUT THE INSTITUTION Independent, coed. Awards: bachelor's, master's, doctoral, and first professional degrees and post-bachelor's, post-master's, and first professional certificates. 50 undergraduate majors. Total enrollment: 8,588. Undergraduates: 4,696. Freshmen: 1,107. Institutional methodology is used as a basis for awarding need-based institutional aid.

UNDERGRADUATE EXPENSES for 2005–06 *Application fee:* $50. *Comprehensive fee:* $41,485 includes full-time tuition ($30,540), mandatory fees ($757), and room and board ($10,188). *College room only:* $5710. Room and board charges vary according to board plan. *Part-time tuition:* $534 per credit hour. Part-time tuition and fees vary according to course load. *Payment plans:* Tuition prepayment, installment.

FRESHMAN FINANCIAL AID (Fall 2005, est.) 778 applied for aid; of those 73% were deemed to have need. 100% of freshmen with need received aid; of those 100% had need fully met. *Average percent of need met:* 100% (excluding resources awarded to replace EFC). *Average financial aid package:* $25,741 (excluding resources awarded to replace EFC). 33% of all full-time freshmen had no need and received non-need-based gift aid.

UNDERGRADUATE FINANCIAL AID (Fall 2005, est.) 2,600 applied for aid; of those 83% were deemed to have need. 100% of undergraduates with need received aid; of those 41% had need fully met. *Average percent of need met:* 87% (excluding resources awarded to replace EFC). *Average financial aid package:* $24,474 (excluding resources awarded to replace EFC). 33% of all full-time undergraduates had no need and received non-need-based gift aid.

GIFT AID (NEED-BASED) *Total amount:* $48,632,188 (6% federal, 6% state, 84% institutional, 4% external sources). *Receiving aid:* Freshmen: 57% (566); All full-time undergraduates: 56% (2,139). *Average award:* Freshmen: $21,544; Undergraduates: $19,585. *Scholarships, grants, and awards:* Federal Pell, FSEOG, state, college/university gift aid from institutional funds.

GIFT AID (NON-NEED-BASED) *Total amount:* $4,100,174 (3% state, 93% institutional, 4% external sources). *Receiving aid:* Freshmen: 8% (80); Undergraduates: 7% (275). *Average Award:* Freshmen: $7814; Undergraduates:* $8773. *Scholarships, grants, and awards by category: Academic Interests/Achievement:* biological sciences, engineering/technologies, general academic interests/achievements, humanities, mathematics, physical sciences, social sciences. *Creative Arts/Performance:* general creative arts/performance. *Special Achievements/Activities:* general special achievements/activities, leadership. *Special Characteristics:* children and siblings of alumni, children of faculty/staff, international students, local/state students. *Tuition waivers:* Full or partial for children of alumni, employees or children of employees. *ROTC:* Naval, Air Force cooperative.

LOANS *Student loans:* $18,860,127 (86% need-based, 14% non-need-based). 56% of past graduating class borrowed through all loan programs. *Average indebtedness per student:* $26,100. *Average need-based loan:* Freshmen: $4023; Undergraduates: $5076. *Parent loans:* $7,461,653 (70% need-based, 30% non-need-based). *Programs:* Federal Direct (Subsidized and Unsubsidized Stafford, PLUS), Perkins, Federal Nursing, college/university, alternative loans.

WORK-STUDY *Federal work-study:* Total amount: $3,121,880; 1,250 jobs averaging $2498. *State or other work-study/employment:* Total amount: $516,450 (82% need-based, 18% non-need-based).

APPLYING FOR FINANCIAL AID *Required financial aid forms:* FAFSA, CSS Financial Aid PROFILE, state aid form, noncustodial (divorced/separated) parent's statement, business/farm supplement. *Financial aid deadline (priority):* 2/1. *Notification date:* 4/1. Students must reply by 5/1.

University of Rochester

CONTACT Charles W. Puls, Director of Financial Aid, University of Rochester, Office of Financial Aid, 314 Meliora Hall, Box 270261, Rochester, NY 14627, 585-275-3226 or toll-free 888-822-2256. *Fax:* 585-756-7664. *E-mail:* cpuls@finaid.rochester.edu.

UNIVERSITY OF ST. FRANCIS
Joliet, IL

Tuition & fees: $19,150	Average undergraduate aid package: $15,359

ABOUT THE INSTITUTION Independent Roman Catholic, coed. Awards: bachelor's and master's degrees. 43 undergraduate majors. Total enrollment: 2,062. Undergraduates: 1,276. Freshmen: 190. Federal methodology is used as a basis for awarding need-based institutional aid.
UNDERGRADUATE EXPENSES for 2006–07 *Application fee:* $30. *Comprehensive fee:* $26,430 includes full-time tuition ($19,150) and room and board ($7280). *Part-time tuition:* $625 per credit hour.
FRESHMAN FINANCIAL AID (Fall 2005, est.) 175 applied for aid; of those 82% were deemed to have need. 100% of freshmen with need received aid; of those 92% had need fully met. *Average percent of need met:* 91% (excluding resources awarded to replace EFC). *Average financial aid package:* $16,007 (excluding resources awarded to replace EFC). 16% of all full-time freshmen had no need and received non-need-based gift aid.
UNDERGRADUATE FINANCIAL AID (Fall 2005, est.) 961 applied for aid; of those 84% were deemed to have need. 100% of undergraduates with need received aid; of those 72% had need fully met. *Average percent of need met:* 73% (excluding resources awarded to replace EFC). *Average financial aid package:* $15,359 (excluding resources awarded to replace EFC). 12% of all full-time undergraduates had no need and received non-need-based gift aid.
GIFT AID (NEED-BASED) *Total amount:* $6,381,637 (15% federal, 28% state, 56% institutional, 1% external sources). *Receiving aid:* Freshmen: 42% (80); All full-time undergraduates: 47% (532). *Average award:* Freshmen: $7030; Undergraduates: $6894. *Scholarships, grants, and awards:* Federal Pell, FSEOG, state, private, college/university gift aid from institutional funds.
GIFT AID (NON-NEED-BASED) *Total amount:* $2,478,209 (2% federal, 4% state, 93% institutional, 1% external sources). *Receiving aid:* Freshmen: 75% (142); Undergraduates: 64% (734). *Average Award:* Freshmen: $6098; Undergraduates: $5793. *Scholarships, grants, and awards by category:* Academic Interests/Achievement: 980 awards ($4,229,389 total): biological sciences, education, general academic interests/achievements, health fields, social sciences. Creative Arts/Performance: 22 awards ($16,750 total): applied art and design, art/fine arts, music. *Special Achievements/Activities:* 502 awards ($2,884,638 total): community service, leadership, religious involvement. *Special Characteristics:* 230 awards ($196,777 total): children and siblings of alumni, children of educators, ethnic background, religious affiliation, siblings of current students.
LOANS *Student loans:* $5,668,346 (49% need-based, 51% non-need-based). 76% of past graduating class borrowed through all loan programs. *Average indebtedness per student:* $15,662. *Average need-based loan:* Freshmen: $2692; Undergraduates: $4413. *Parent loans:* $1,831,125 (57% need-based, 43% non-need-based). *Programs:* Federal Direct (Subsidized and Unsubsidized Stafford, PLUS), Perkins, alternative loans.
WORK-STUDY *Federal work-study:* Total amount: $485,743; 252 jobs averaging $1928. *State or other work-study/employment:* Total amount: $422,575 (100% non-need-based). 266 part-time jobs averaging $1589.
ATHLETIC AWARDS *Total amount:* $3,272,813 (40% need-based, 60% non-need-based).
APPLYING FOR FINANCIAL AID *Required financial aid forms:* FAFSA, institution's own form. *Financial aid deadline (priority):* 4/1. *Notification date:* Continuous beginning 3/5. Students must reply within 3 weeks of notification.
CONTACT Mrs. Mary V. Shaw, Director of Financial Aid Services, University of St. Francis, 500 North Wilcox Street, Joliet, IL 60435-6188, 815-740-3403 or toll-free 800-735-3500. *Fax:* 815-740-3822. *E-mail:* mshaw@stfrancis.edu.

UNIVERSITY OF SAINT FRANCIS
Fort Wayne, IN

Tuition & fees: $18,478	Average undergraduate aid package: $12,457

ABOUT THE INSTITUTION Independent Roman Catholic, coed. Awards: associate, bachelor's, and master's degrees and post-bachelor's certificates. 52 undergraduate majors. Total enrollment: 2,003. Undergraduates: 1,768. Freshmen: 312. Federal methodology is used as a basis for awarding need-based institutional aid.
UNDERGRADUATE EXPENSES for 2006–07 *Application fee:* $20. *Comprehensive fee:* $24,312 includes full-time tuition ($17,760), mandatory fees ($718), and room and board ($5834). *Part-time tuition:* $560 per hour. *Part-time fees:* $17 per hour.
FRESHMAN FINANCIAL AID (Fall 2004) 280 applied for aid; of those 86% were deemed to have need. 100% of freshmen with need received aid; of those 30% had need fully met. *Average percent of need met:* 75% (excluding resources awarded to replace EFC). *Average financial aid package:* $12,237 (excluding resources awarded to replace EFC). 14% of all full-time freshmen had no need and received non-need-based gift aid.
UNDERGRADUATE FINANCIAL AID (Fall 2004) 1,120 applied for aid; of those 88% were deemed to have need. 100% of undergraduates with need received aid; of those 26% had need fully met. *Average percent of need met:* 74% (excluding resources awarded to replace EFC). *Average financial aid package:* $12,457 (excluding resources awarded to replace EFC). 12% of all full-time undergraduates had no need and received non-need-based gift aid.
GIFT AID (NEED-BASED) *Total amount:* $8,824,973 (16% federal, 38% state, 33% institutional, 13% external sources). *Receiving aid:* Freshmen: 83% (242); All full-time undergraduates: 85% (982). *Average award:* Freshmen: $9470; Undergraduates: $8927. *Scholarships, grants, and awards:* Federal Pell, FSEOG, state, private, college/university gift aid from institutional funds.
GIFT AID (NON-NEED-BASED) *Total amount:* $1,037,641 (2% state, 57% institutional, 41% external sources). *Receiving aid:* Freshmen: 14% (41); Undergraduates: 10% (118). *Average Award:* Freshmen: $9848; Undergraduates: $9793. *Scholarships, grants, and awards by category:* Academic Interests/Achievement: 583 awards ($2,050,795 total): biological sciences, business, communication, education, English, general academic interests/achievements, health fields, mathematics, physical sciences, premedicine, religion/biblical studies, social sciences. *Creative Arts/Performance:* 198 awards ($558,492 total): art/fine arts, dance, debating, music. *Special Achievements/Activities:* 69 awards ($66,991 total): cheerleading/drum major, religious involvement. *Special Characteristics:* 104 awards ($411,994 total): children and siblings of alumni, children of faculty/staff, siblings of current students, spouses of current students.
LOANS *Student loans:* $8,685,326 (73% need-based, 27% non-need-based). 85% of past graduating class borrowed through all loan programs. *Average indebtedness per student:* $22,709. *Average need-based loan:* Freshmen: $2354; Undergraduates: $3130. *Parent loans:* $1,594,321 (38% need-based, 62% non-need-based). *Programs:* FFEL (Subsidized and Unsubsidized Stafford, PLUS), Perkins.
WORK-STUDY *Federal work-study:* Total amount: $1,177,071; 889 jobs averaging $1515. *State or other work-study/employment:* Part-time jobs available.
ATHLETIC AWARDS *Total amount:* $2,028,821 (78% need-based, 22% non-need-based).
APPLYING FOR FINANCIAL AID *Required financial aid form:* FAFSA. *Financial aid deadline:* 6/30 (priority: 3/10). *Notification date:* Continuous beginning 3/1. Students must reply within 2 weeks of notification.
CONTACT James McGrath, Director of Financial Aid, University of Saint Francis, 2701 Spring Street, Fort Wayne, IN 46808, 260-434-3283 or toll-free 800-729-4732. *Fax:* 260-434-7526.

UNIVERSITY OF SAINT MARY
Leavenworth, KS

CONTACT Mrs. Judy Wiedower, Financial Aid Director, University of Saint Mary, 4100 South Fourth Street, Leavenworth, KS 66048, 913-758-6314 or toll-free 800-752-7043 (out-of-state). *Fax:* 913-758-6146. *E-mail:* wiedower@hub.smcks.edu.

UNIVERSITY OF ST. THOMAS
St. Paul, MN

Comprehensive fee: $30,380	Average undergraduate aid package: $18,218

ABOUT THE INSTITUTION Independent Roman Catholic, coed. Awards: bachelor's, master's, doctoral, and first professional degrees and post-bachelor's and post-master's certificates. 83 undergraduate majors. Total enrollment: 10,474. Undergraduates: 5,302. Freshmen: 1,162. Both federal and institutional methodology are used as a basis for awarding need-based institutional aid.

UNDERGRADUATE EXPENSES for 2005–06 *Comprehensive fee:* $30,380. Full-time tuition and fees vary according to class time, course load, and program. Room and board charges vary according to board plan, housing facility, and student level. *Part-time tuition:* $715 per credit hour. Part-time tuition and fees vary according to class time, course load, and program. *Payment plans:* Installment, deferred payment.

FRESHMAN FINANCIAL AID (Fall 2005, est.) 891 applied for aid; of those 71% were deemed to have need. 100% of freshmen with need received aid; of those 49% had need fully met. *Average percent of need met:* 78% (excluding resources awarded to replace EFC). *Average financial aid package:* $17,103 (excluding resources awarded to replace EFC). 19% of all full-time freshmen had no need and received non-need-based gift aid.

UNDERGRADUATE FINANCIAL AID (Fall 2005, est.) 3,109 applied for aid; of those 76% were deemed to have need. 100% of undergraduates with need received aid; of those 49% had need fully met. *Average percent of need met:* 78% (excluding resources awarded to replace EFC). *Average financial aid package:* $18,218 (excluding resources awarded to replace EFC). 12% of all full-time undergraduates had no need and received non-need-based gift aid.

GIFT AID (NEED-BASED) *Total amount:* $33,598,280 (8% federal, 25% state, 65% institutional, 2% external sources). *Receiving aid:* Freshmen: 48% (631); All full-time undergraduates: 44% (2,279). *Average award:* Freshmen: $10,124; Undergraduates: $9049. *Scholarships, grants, and awards:* Federal Pell, FSEOG, state, private, college/university gift aid from institutional funds.

GIFT AID (NON-NEED-BASED) *Total amount:* $7,435,071 (1% state, 88% institutional, 11% external sources). *Receiving aid:* Freshmen: 10% (130); Undergraduates: 6% (328). *Average Award:* Freshmen: $9511; Undergraduates: $7920. *Scholarships, grants, and awards by category:* Academic Interests/Achievement: 1,564 awards ($8,870,534 total): biological sciences, business, education, English, general academic interests/achievements, humanities, international studies, mathematics, physical sciences, religion/biblical studies, social sciences. Creative Arts/Performance: 42 awards ($134,198 total): journalism/publications, music. Special Characteristics: 216 awards ($2,704,253 total): general special characteristics. *Tuition waivers:* Full or partial for employees or children of employees, senior citizens. *ROTC:* Army cooperative, Air Force.

LOANS *Student loans:* $27,239,069 (66% need-based, 34% non-need-based). 66% of past graduating class borrowed through all loan programs. *Average indebtedness per student:* $26,621. *Average need-based loan:* Freshmen: $2763; Undergraduates: $4408. *Parent loans:* $7,337,940 (34% need-based, 66% non-need-based). *Programs:* FFEL (Subsidized and Unsubsidized Stafford, PLUS), Perkins, state, alternative loans.

WORK-STUDY *Federal work-study:* Total amount: $2,178,515; 770 jobs averaging $2869. *State or other work-study/employment:* Total amount: $4,509,855 (100% need-based). 1,618 part-time jobs averaging $2786.

APPLYING FOR FINANCIAL AID *Required financial aid form:* FAFSA. *Financial aid deadline:* Continuous. *Notification date:* Continuous beginning 3/1. Students must reply within 3 weeks of notification.

CONTACT Ms. Ginny Reese, Associate Director, Student Financial Services, University of St. Thomas, 2115 Summit Avenue, FOL100, St. Paul, MN 55105-1096, 651-962-6557 or toll-free 800-328-6819 Ext. 26150. *Fax:* 651-962-6599. *E-mail:* vmreese@stthomas.edu.

UNIVERSITY OF ST. THOMAS
Houston, TX

Tuition & fees: $17,110   **Average undergraduate aid package: $12,487**

ABOUT THE INSTITUTION Independent Roman Catholic, coed. Awards: bachelor's, master's, doctoral, and first professional degrees. 36 undergraduate majors. Total enrollment: 3,776. Undergraduates: 1,884. Freshmen: 295. Federal methodology is used as a basis for awarding need-based institutional aid.

UNDERGRADUATE EXPENSES for 2005–06 *Application fee:* $35. *Comprehensive fee:* $23,810 includes full-time tuition ($16,950), mandatory fees ($160), and room and board ($6700). *College room only:* $4000. Full-time tuition and fees vary according to course load. Room and board charges vary according to board plan and housing facility. *Part-time tuition:* $565 per credit hour. *Part-time fees:* $80 per term. Part-time tuition and fees vary according to course load. *Payment plans:* Installment, deferred payment.

FRESHMAN FINANCIAL AID (Fall 2005, est.) 203 applied for aid; of those 85% were deemed to have need. 99% of freshmen with need received aid; of those 12% had need fully met. *Average percent of need met:* 68% (excluding resources awarded to replace EFC). *Average financial aid package:* $12,985 (excluding resources awarded to replace EFC). 3% of all full-time freshmen had no need and received non-need-based gift aid.

UNDERGRADUATE FINANCIAL AID (Fall 2005, est.) 876 applied for aid; of those 88% were deemed to have need. 99% of undergraduates with need received aid; of those 12% had need fully met. *Average percent of need met:* 64% (excluding resources awarded to replace EFC). *Average financial aid package:* $12,487 (excluding resources awarded to replace EFC). 18% of all full-time undergraduates had no need and received non-need-based gift aid.

GIFT AID (NEED-BASED) *Total amount:* $6,656,030 (24% federal, 30% state, 46% institutional). *Receiving aid:* Freshmen: 58% (167); All full-time undergraduates: 54% (727). *Average award:* Freshmen: $9958; Undergraduates: $8653. *Scholarships, grants, and awards:* Federal Pell, FSEOG, state, college/university gift aid from institutional funds.

GIFT AID (NON-NEED-BASED) *Total amount:* $2,105,609 (86% institutional, 14% external sources). *Receiving aid:* Freshmen: 18% (53); Undergraduates: 10% (132). *Average Award:* Freshmen: $8829; Undergraduates: $6613. *Scholarships, grants, and awards by category:* Academic Interests/Achievement: 298 awards ($1,802,930 total): biological sciences, English, foreign languages, general academic interests/achievements, mathematics, physical sciences, social sciences. Creative Arts/Performance: debating, music, theater/drama. Special Achievements/Activities: community service. Special Characteristics: children of educators, children of faculty/staff, general special characteristics, international students, members of minority groups, relatives of clergy, religious affiliation. *Tuition waivers:* Full or partial for employees or children of employees, senior citizens. *ROTC:* Army cooperative.

LOANS *Student loans:* $5,726,663 (56% need-based, 44% non-need-based). 63% of past graduating class borrowed through all loan programs. *Average indebtedness per student:* $21,626. *Average need-based loan:* Freshmen: $2815; Undergraduates: $4199. *Parent loans:* $1,477,858 (100% non-need-based). *Programs:* FFEL (Subsidized and Unsubsidized Stafford, PLUS), Perkins.

WORK-STUDY *Federal work-study:* Total amount: $53,082; 20 jobs averaging $2654. *State or other work-study/employment:* Total amount: $9000 (100% need-based). 3 part-time jobs averaging $3000.

APPLYING FOR FINANCIAL AID *Required financial aid form:* FAFSA. *Financial aid deadline (priority):* 3/1. *Notification date:* Continuous. Students must reply within 4 weeks of notification.

CONTACT Scott Moore, Dean of Scholarships and Financial Aid, University of St. Thomas, 3800 Montrose Boulevard, Houston, TX 77006-4696, 713-942-3465 or toll-free 800-856-8565. *Fax:* 713-525-2142. *E-mail:* finaid@stthom.edu.

UNIVERSITY OF SAN DIEGO
San Diego, CA

Tuition & fees: $30,704   **Average undergraduate aid package: $20,484**

ABOUT THE INSTITUTION Independent Roman Catholic, coed. Awards: bachelor's, master's, doctoral, and first professional degrees and post-bachelor's, post-master's, and first professional certificates. 35 undergraduate majors. Total enrollment: 7,548. Undergraduates: 4,970. Freshmen: 1,136. Federal methodology is used as a basis for awarding need-based institutional aid.

UNDERGRADUATE EXPENSES for 2006–07 *Application fee:* $55. *Comprehensive fee:* $41,664 includes full-time tuition ($30,480), mandatory fees ($224), and room and board ($10,960). *Part-time tuition:* $1050 per unit. *Part-time fees:* $38.

FRESHMAN FINANCIAL AID (Fall 2004) 781 applied for aid; of those 71% were deemed to have need. 100% of freshmen with need received aid; of those 37% had need fully met. *Average percent of need met:* 62% (excluding resources awarded to replace EFC). *Average financial aid package:* $16,603 (excluding resources awarded to replace EFC). 10% of all full-time freshmen had no need and received non-need-based gift aid.

UNDERGRADUATE FINANCIAL AID (Fall 2004) 2,960 applied for aid; of those 77% were deemed to have need. 100% of undergraduates with need received aid; of those 39% had need fully met. *Average percent of need met:* 83% (excluding resources awarded to replace EFC). *Average financial aid package:* $20,484 (excluding resources awarded to replace EFC). 10% of all full-time undergraduates had no need and received non-need-based gift aid.

University of San Diego

GIFT AID (NEED-BASED) *Total amount:* $36,381,686 (12% federal, 15% state, 70% institutional, 3% external sources). *Receiving aid:* Freshmen: 45% (525); All full-time undergraduates: 46% (2,247). *Average award:* Freshmen: $13,137; Undergraduates: $16,123. *Scholarships, grants, and awards:* Federal Pell, FSEOG, state, private.

GIFT AID (NON-NEED-BASED) *Total amount:* $7,046,311 (37% federal, 56% institutional, 7% external sources). *Receiving aid:* Freshmen: 21% (250); Undergraduates: 15% (733). *Average Award:* Freshmen: $7000; Undergraduates: $6477. *Scholarships, grants, and awards by category:* Academic Interests/Achievement: 973 awards ($7,493,591 total): general academic interests/achievements. *Creative Arts/Performance:* 9 awards ($60,750 total): music. *Special Characteristics:* 56 awards ($1,215,825 total): children of faculty/staff. *ROTC:* Army cooperative, Naval, Air Force cooperative.

LOANS *Student loans:* $15,436,401 (91% need-based, 9% non-need-based). 43% of past graduating class borrowed through all loan programs. *Average indebtedness per student:* $27,722. *Average need-based loan:* Freshmen: $3997; Undergraduates: $4972. *Parent loans:* $21,780,185 (72% need-based, 28% non-need-based). *Programs:* FFEL (Subsidized and Unsubsidized Stafford, PLUS), Perkins, Federal Nursing, state, college/university, Non-Federal Loan Programs.

WORK-STUDY *Federal work-study:* Total amount: $1,632,469; jobs available. *State or other work-study/employment:* Total amount: $3,011,374 (14% need-based, 86% non-need-based). Part-time jobs available.

ATHLETIC AWARDS *Total amount:* $3,213,483 (23% need-based, 77% non-need-based).

APPLYING FOR FINANCIAL AID *Required financial aid form:* FAFSA. *Financial aid deadline (priority):* 2/20. *Notification date:* Continuous beginning 3/1. Students must reply within 3 weeks of notification.

CONTACT Judith Lewis Logue, Director of Financial Aid Services, University of San Diego, 5998 Alcala Park, San Diego, CA 92110-2492, 619-260-4514 or toll-free 800-248-4873.

UNIVERSITY OF SAN FRANCISCO
San Francisco, CA

ABOUT THE INSTITUTION Independent Roman Catholic (Jesuit), coed. Awards: bachelor's, master's, doctoral, and first professional degrees and post-master's certificates. 64 undergraduate majors. Total enrollment: 8,457. Undergraduates: 5,212. Freshmen: 934.

GIFT AID (NEED-BASED) *Scholarships, grants, and awards:* Federal Pell, FSEOG, state, private, college/university gift aid from institutional funds.

GIFT AID (NON-NEED-BASED) *Scholarships, grants, and awards by category:* Academic Interests/Achievement: general academic interests/achievements, military science. *Creative Arts/Performance:* general creative arts/performance. *Special Achievements/Activities:* general special achievements/activities.

LOANS *Programs:* Federal Direct (Subsidized and Unsubsidized Stafford, PLUS), Perkins, Federal Nursing, college/university.

WORK-STUDY *Federal work-study:* Total amount: $2,342,460; 680 jobs averaging $3441. *State or other work-study/employment:* Total amount: $694,000 (100% non-need-based). 202 part-time jobs averaging $3428.

APPLYING FOR FINANCIAL AID *Required financial aid form:* FAFSA.

CONTACT Ms. Susan Murphy, Director of Financial Aid, University of San Francisco, 2130 Fulton Street, San Francisco, CA 94117-1080, 415-422-2620 or toll-free 415-422-6563 (in-state), 800-CALL USF (out-of-state). *Fax:* 415-422-6084. *E-mail:* murphy@usfca.edu.

UNIVERSITY OF SCIENCE AND ARTS OF OKLAHOMA
Chickasha, OK

Tuition & fees (OK res): $3480	Average undergraduate aid package: $6799

ABOUT THE INSTITUTION State-supported, coed. Awards: bachelor's degrees. 25 undergraduate majors. Total enrollment: 1,430. Undergraduates: 1,430. Freshmen: 282. Federal methodology is used as a basis for awarding need-based institutional aid.

UNDERGRADUATE EXPENSES for 2005–06 *Application fee:* $15. *Tuition, state resident:* full-time $2490; part-time $83 per hour. *Tuition, nonresident:* full-time $7230; part-time $241 per hour. *Required fees:* full-time $990; $33 per hour. *College room and board:* $4170; *room only:* $2180. Room and board charges vary according to board plan and housing facility. *Payment plan:* Installment.

FRESHMAN FINANCIAL AID (Fall 2005, est.) 224 applied for aid; of those 77% were deemed to have need. 98% of freshmen with need received aid; of those 22% had need fully met. *Average percent of need met:* 67% (excluding resources awarded to replace EFC). *Average financial aid package:* $6034 (excluding resources awarded to replace EFC). 21% of all full-time freshmen had no need and received non-need-based gift aid.

UNDERGRADUATE FINANCIAL AID (Fall 2005, est.) 851 applied for aid; of those 84% were deemed to have need. 98% of undergraduates with need received aid; of those 19% had need fully met. *Average percent of need met:* 68% (excluding resources awarded to replace EFC). *Average financial aid package:* $6799 (excluding resources awarded to replace EFC). 18% of all full-time undergraduates had no need and received non-need-based gift aid.

GIFT AID (NEED-BASED) *Total amount:* $2,744,649 (59% federal, 19% state, 7% institutional, 15% external sources). *Receiving aid:* Freshmen: 61% (162); All full-time undergraduates: 61% (648). *Average award:* Freshmen: $4948; Undergraduates: $4866. *Scholarships, grants, and awards:* Federal Pell, FSEOG, state, private, college/university gift aid from institutional funds, USAO Foundation Grants.

GIFT AID (NON-NEED-BASED) *Total amount:* $397,311 (40% state, 32% institutional, 28% external sources). *Receiving aid:* Freshmen: 8% (22); Undergraduates: 5% (50). *Average Award:* Freshmen: $3957; Undergraduates: $3857. *Scholarships, grants, and awards by category:* Academic Interests/Achievement: 130 awards ($158,509 total): general academic interests/achievements. *Creative Arts/Performance:* 24 awards ($25,750 total): art/fine arts, music, theater/drama. *Special Achievements/Activities:* 16 awards ($9100 total): cheerleading/drum major, leadership. *Special Characteristics:* 64 awards ($171,059 total): international students, out-of-state students, previous college experience. *Tuition waivers:* Full or partial for employees or children of employees, senior citizens.

LOANS *Student loans:* $2,349,373 (75% need-based, 25% non-need-based). 67% of past graduating class borrowed through all loan programs. *Average indebtedness per student:* $11,378. *Average need-based loan:* Freshmen: $2227; Undergraduates: $2884. *Parent loans:* $195,903 (8% need-based, 92% non-need-based). *Programs:* FFEL (Subsidized and Unsubsidized Stafford, PLUS), Perkins.

WORK-STUDY *Federal work-study:* Total amount: $244,186; 191 jobs averaging $1279.

ATHLETIC AWARDS *Total amount:* $556,650 (53% need-based, 47% non-need-based).

APPLYING FOR FINANCIAL AID *Required financial aid forms:* FAFSA, institution's own form. *Financial aid deadline (priority):* 3/15. *Notification date:* Continuous beginning 3/15. Students must reply within 4 weeks of notification.

CONTACT Nancy Moats, Director of Financial Aid, University of Science and Arts of Oklahoma, 1727 West Alabama, Chickasha, OK 73018-5322, 405-574-1251 or toll-free 800-933-8726 Ext. 1212. *Fax:* 405-574-1220.

THE UNIVERSITY OF SCRANTON
Scranton, PA

ABOUT THE INSTITUTION Independent Roman Catholic (Jesuit), coed. Awards: associate, bachelor's, master's, and doctoral degrees and post-bachelor's and post-master's certificates. 55 undergraduate majors. Total enrollment: 5,160. Undergraduates: 4,084. Freshmen: 949.

GIFT AID (NEED-BASED) *Scholarships, grants, and awards:* Federal Pell, FSEOG, state, private, college/university gift aid from institutional funds.

GIFT AID (NON-NEED-BASED) *Scholarships, grants, and awards by category:* Academic Interests/Achievement: general academic interests/achievements, military science. *Special Characteristics:* children of educators, children of faculty/staff, members of minority groups, siblings of current students.

LOANS *Programs:* FFEL (Subsidized and Unsubsidized Stafford, PLUS), Perkins, Federal Nursing.

WORK-STUDY *Federal work-study:* Total amount: $1,744,021; 1,005 jobs averaging $1800. *State or other work-study/employment:* Total amount: $396,382 (16% need-based, 84% non-need-based). 255 part-time jobs averaging $1500.

APPLYING FOR FINANCIAL AID *Required financial aid form:* FAFSA.

CONTACT Mr. William R. Burke, Director of Financial Aid, The University of Scranton, St. Thomas Hall 401, Scranton, PA 18510, 570-941-7887 or toll-free 888-SCRANTON. *Fax:* 570-941-4370. *E-mail:* finaid@scranton.edu.

UNIVERSITY OF SIOUX FALLS
Sioux Falls, SD

ABOUT THE INSTITUTION Independent American Baptist Churches in the USA, coed. Awards: associate, bachelor's, master's, and doctoral degrees. 57 undergraduate majors. Total enrollment: 1,606. Undergraduates: 1,262. Freshmen: 224.

GIFT AID (NEED-BASED) *Scholarships, grants, and awards:* Federal Pell, FSEOG, private, college/university gift aid from institutional funds.

GIFT AID (NON-NEED-BASED) *Scholarships, grants, and awards by category: Academic Interests/Achievement:* biological sciences, business, communication, computer science, education, engineering/technologies, English, general academic interests/achievements, humanities, mathematics, physical sciences, premedicine, religion/biblical studies, social sciences. *Creative Arts/Performance:* art/fine arts, music, theater/drama. *Special Achievements/Activities:* cheerleading/drum major, leadership. *Special Characteristics:* children and siblings of alumni, children of faculty/staff, international students, local/state students, out-of-state students, religious affiliation, siblings of current students, spouses of current students.

LOANS *Programs:* FFEL (Subsidized and Unsubsidized Stafford, PLUS), Perkins, alternative loans.

WORK-STUDY *Federal work-study:* Total amount: $229,471; 130 jobs averaging $1200.

APPLYING FOR FINANCIAL AID *Required financial aid form:* FAFSA.

CONTACT Rachel Gunn, Financial Aid Counselor, University of Sioux Falls, 1101 West 22nd Street, Sioux Falls, SD 57105-1699, 605-331-6623 or toll-free 800-888-1047. *Fax:* 605-331-6615. *E-mail:* rachel.gunn@usiouxfalls.edu.

UNIVERSITY OF SOUTH ALABAMA
Mobile, AL

CONTACT Financial Aid Office, University of South Alabama, 307 University Boulevard, Mobile, AL 36688-0002, 251-460-6231 or toll-free 800-872-5247. *Fax:* 251-460-6517.

UNIVERSITY OF SOUTH CAROLINA
Columbia, SC

Tuition & fees (SC res): $6914   Average undergraduate aid package: $9501

ABOUT THE INSTITUTION State-supported, coed. Awards: bachelor's, master's, doctoral, and first professional degrees and post-bachelor's and post-master's certificates. 65 undergraduate majors. Total enrollment: 27,065. Undergraduates: 18,362. Freshmen: 3,734. Federal methodology is used as a basis for awarding need-based institutional aid.

UNDERGRADUATE EXPENSES for 2005–06 *Application fee:* $50. *Tuition, state resident:* full-time $6914; part-time $324 per credit hour. *Tuition, nonresident:* full-time $18,556; part-time $844 per credit hour. Full-time tuition and fees vary according to program. *College room and board:* $6080. Room and board charges vary according to board plan, housing facility, and location. *Payment plans:* Installment, deferred payment.

FRESHMAN FINANCIAL AID (Fall 2004) 2293 applied for aid; of those 69% were deemed to have need. 99% of freshmen with need received aid; of those 30% had need fully met. *Average percent of need met:* 74% (excluding resources awarded to replace EFC). *Average financial aid package:* $9067 (excluding resources awarded to replace EFC). 42% of all full-time freshmen had no need and received non-need-based gift aid.

UNDERGRADUATE FINANCIAL AID (Fall 2004) 9,506 applied for aid; of those 78% were deemed to have need. 99% of undergraduates with need received aid; of those 24% had need fully met. *Average percent of need met:* 71% (excluding resources awarded to replace EFC). *Average financial aid package:* $9501 (excluding resources awarded to replace EFC). 32% of all full-time undergraduates had no need and received non-need-based gift aid.

GIFT AID (NEED-BASED) *Total amount:* $33,811,705 (34% federal, 50% state, 9% institutional, 7% external sources). *Receiving aid:* Freshmen: 22% (743); All full-time undergraduates: 26% (3,957). *Average award:* Freshmen: $3529; Undergraduates: $3426. *Scholarships, grants, and awards:* Federal Pell, FSEOG, state, private, college/university gift aid from institutional funds, United Negro College Fund, Federal Nursing.

GIFT AID (NON-NEED-BASED) *Total amount:* $33,821,152 (61% state, 26% institutional, 13% external sources). *Receiving aid:* Freshmen: 43% (1,407); Undergraduates: 27% (4,122). *Average Award:* Freshmen: $5654; Undergraduates: $5950. *Scholarships, grants, and awards by category: Academic Interests/Achievement:* 4,479 awards ($9,044,812 total): area/ethnic studies, biological sciences, business, communication, computer science, education, engineering/technologies, English, foreign languages, general academic interests/achievements, health fields, humanities, international studies, library science, mathematics, military science, physical sciences, premedicine, religion/biblical studies, social sciences. *Creative Arts/Performance:* 115 awards ($482,848 total): art/fine arts, debating, journalism/publications, music, theater/drama. *Special Achievements/Activities:* 170 awards ($87,300 total): cheerleading/drum major, community service, general special achievements/activities, leadership, religious involvement. *Special Characteristics:* 3,409 awards ($7,454,077 total): adult students, children and siblings of alumni, children of faculty/staff, children of union members/company employees, children of workers in trades, children with a deceased or disabled parent, ethnic background, first-generation college students, general special characteristics, handicapped students, international students, local/state students, members of minority groups, out-of-state students, relatives of clergy, religious affiliation, spouses of deceased or disabled public servants. *Tuition waivers:* Full or partial for employees or children of employees, senior citizens. *ROTC:* Army, Air Force.

LOANS *Student loans:* $47,092,279 (69% need-based, 31% non-need-based). 50% of past graduating class borrowed through all loan programs. *Average indebtedness per student:* $18,699. *Average need-based loan:* Freshmen: $1860; Undergraduates: $3486. *Parent loans:* $9,185,797 (28% need-based, 72% non-need-based). *Programs:* FFEL (Subsidized and Unsubsidized Stafford, PLUS), Perkins, Federal Nursing.

WORK-STUDY *Federal work-study:* Total amount: $1,298,515; 667 jobs averaging $2171. *State or other work-study/employment:* Total amount: $4,719,459 (100% non-need-based). Part-time jobs available.

ATHLETIC AWARDS *Total amount:* $5,094,202 (38% need-based, 62% non-need-based).

APPLYING FOR FINANCIAL AID *Required financial aid form:* FAFSA. *Financial aid deadline (priority):* 4/1. *Notification date:* Continuous beginning 4/1.

CONTACT Dr. Ed Miller, Financial Aid Director, University of South Carolina, 1714 College Street, Columbia, SC 29208, 803-777-8134 or toll-free 800-868-5872 (in-state). *Fax:* 803-777-0941.

UNIVERSITY OF SOUTH CAROLINA AIKEN
Aiken, SC

CONTACT Financial Aid Office, University of South Carolina Aiken, 471 University Parkway, Aiken, SC 29801, 803-641-3476 or toll-free 888-WOW-USCA.

UNIVERSITY OF SOUTH CAROLINA BEAUFORT
Beaufort, SC

CONTACT Sally Maybin, Financial Aid Director, University of South Carolina Beaufort, 801 Carteret Street, Beaufort, SC 29902, 843-521-3104. *Fax:* 843-521-4194. *E-mail:* smaybin@gwm.sc.edu.

UNIVERSITY OF SOUTH CAROLINA UPSTATE
Spartanburg, SC

Tuition & fees (SC res): $6762   Average undergraduate aid package: $7400

ABOUT THE INSTITUTION State-supported, coed. Awards: associate, bachelor's, and master's degrees. 20 undergraduate majors. Total enrollment: 4,484. Undergraduates: 4,409. Freshmen: 749. Federal methodology is used as a basis for awarding need-based institutional aid.

UNDERGRADUATE EXPENSES for 2005–06 *Application fee:* $40. *Tuition, state resident:* full-time $6436; part-time $282 per hour. *Tuition, nonresident:* full-time $13,274; part-time $583 per hour. *Required fees:* full-time $326; $11 per

University of South Carolina Upstate

hour or $25 per term part-time. Full-time tuition and fees vary according to course load. Part-time tuition and fees vary according to course load. **College room and board:** $5160; **room only:** $3200. Room and board charges vary according to board plan and housing facility. **Payment plan:** Deferred payment.
FRESHMAN FINANCIAL AID (Fall 2005, est.) 579 applied for aid; of those 77% were deemed to have need. 100% of freshmen with need received aid; of those 21% had need fully met. *Average percent of need met:* 36% (excluding resources awarded to replace EFC). *Average financial aid package:* $7846 (excluding resources awarded to replace EFC). 3% of all full-time freshmen had no need and received non-need-based gift aid.
UNDERGRADUATE FINANCIAL AID (Fall 2005, est.) 2,712 applied for aid; of those 84% were deemed to have need. 99% of undergraduates with need received aid; of those 14% had need fully met. *Average percent of need met:* 42% (excluding resources awarded to replace EFC). *Average financial aid package:* $7400 (excluding resources awarded to replace EFC). 2% of all full-time undergraduates had no need and received non-need-based gift aid.
GIFT AID (NEED-BASED) *Total amount:* $5,207,637 (86% federal, 14% state). *Receiving aid:* Freshmen: 39% (277); All full-time undergraduates: 41% (1,431). *Average award:* Freshmen: $3425; Undergraduates: $3340. *Scholarships, grants, and awards:* Federal Pell, FSEOG, state, private, college/university gift aid from institutional funds.
GIFT AID (NON-NEED-BASED) *Total amount:* $6,472,956 (87% state, 6% institutional, 7% external sources). *Receiving aid:* Freshmen: 50% (362); Undergraduates: 24% (831). *Average Award:* Freshmen: $3091; Undergraduates: $3003. *Scholarships, grants, and awards by category:* Academic Interests/Achievement: 175 awards ($419,266 total): general academic interests/achievements. Special Characteristics: 74 awards ($32,775 total): first-generation college students. *Tuition waivers:* Full or partial for senior citizens. *ROTC:* Army cooperative.
LOANS *Student loans:* $15,805,295 (49% need-based, 51% non-need-based). 67% of past graduating class borrowed through all loan programs. *Average indebtedness per student:* $17,238. *Average need-based loan:* Freshmen: $2408; Undergraduates: $3610. *Parent loans:* $884,385 (100% non-need-based). *Programs:* FFEL (Subsidized and Unsubsidized Stafford, PLUS), Perkins, state.
WORK-STUDY *Federal work-study:* Total amount: $166,675; 91 jobs averaging $1992. *State or other work-study/employment:* Total amount: $322,975 (100% non-need-based). 383 part-time jobs averaging $1028.
ATHLETIC AWARDS *Total amount:* $736,850 (100% non-need-based).
APPLYING FOR FINANCIAL AID *Required financial aid form:* FAFSA. *Financial aid deadline (priority):* 3/1. *Notification date:* Continuous beginning 4/1. Students must reply within 2 weeks of notification.
CONTACT Kim Jenerette, Director of Financial Aid, University of South Carolina Upstate, 800 University Way, Spartanburg, SC 29303, 864-503-5340 or toll-free 800-277-8727. *Fax:* 864-503-5974. *E-mail:* kjenerette@uscupstate.edu.

THE UNIVERSITY OF SOUTH DAKOTA
Vermillion, SD

Tuition & fees (SD res): $4829	Average undergraduate aid package: $5545

ABOUT THE INSTITUTION State-supported, coed. Awards: associate, bachelor's, master's, doctoral, and first professional degrees and post-bachelor's and post-master's certificates. 61 undergraduate majors. Total enrollment: 8,641. Undergraduates: 6,408. Freshmen: 1,165. Federal methodology is used as a basis for awarding need-based institutional aid.
UNDERGRADUATE EXPENSES for 2005–06 *Application fee:* $20. *Tuition, state resident:* full-time $2291; part-time $76.35 per credit hour. *Tuition, nonresident:* full-time $7278; part-time $242.60 per credit hour. *Required fees:* full-time $2538; $84.60 per credit hour. Full-time tuition and fees vary according to course load and reciprocity agreements. Part-time tuition and fees vary according to course load and reciprocity agreements. *College room and board:* $4240; *room only:* $2253. Room and board charges vary according to board plan and housing facility. *Payment plan:* Deferred payment.
FRESHMAN FINANCIAL AID (Fall 2004) 786 applied for aid; of those 70% were deemed to have need. 89% of freshmen with need received aid; of those 85% had need fully met. *Average percent of need met:* 75% (excluding resources awarded to replace EFC). *Average financial aid package:* $4339 (excluding resources awarded to replace EFC). 27% of all full-time freshmen had no need and received non-need-based gift aid.
UNDERGRADUATE FINANCIAL AID (Fall 2004) 3,450 applied for aid; of those 78% were deemed to have need. 95% of undergraduates with need received aid; of those 68% had need fully met. *Average percent of need met:* 75% (excluding resources awarded to replace EFC). *Average financial aid package:* $5545 (excluding resources awarded to replace EFC). 17% of all full-time undergraduates had no need and received non-need-based gift aid.
GIFT AID (NEED-BASED) *Total amount:* $5,025,691 (100% federal). *Receiving aid:* Freshmen: 26% (246); All full-time undergraduates: 31% (1,314). *Average award:* Freshmen: $2996; Undergraduates: $3061. *Scholarships, grants, and awards:* Federal Pell, FSEOG, private, college/university gift aid from institutional funds, Federal Nursing.
GIFT AID (NON-NEED-BASED) *Total amount:* $5,273,186 (12% federal, 3% state, 64% institutional, 21% external sources). *Receiving aid:* Freshmen: 28% (266); Undergraduates: 17% (717). *Average Award:* Freshmen: $2983; Undergraduates: $2954. *Scholarships, grants, and awards by category:* Academic Interests/Achievement: biological sciences, business, communication, computer science, education, English, foreign languages, general academic interests/achievements, humanities, mathematics, military science, premedicine, social sciences. Creative Arts/Performance: art/fine arts, creative writing, debating, music, theater/drama. *Tuition waivers:* Full or partial for employees or children of employees, senior citizens. *ROTC:* Army.
LOANS *Student loans:* $19,183,607 (57% need-based, 43% non-need-based). 80% of past graduating class borrowed through all loan programs. *Average indebtedness per student:* $19,535. *Average need-based loan:* Freshmen: $2694; Undergraduates: $3790. *Parent loans:* $1,502,668 (100% non-need-based). *Programs:* FFEL (Subsidized and Unsubsidized Stafford, PLUS), Perkins, Federal Nursing, alternative loans.
WORK-STUDY *Federal work-study:* Total amount: $773,653; 650 jobs averaging $1200. *State or other work-study/employment:* Total amount: $1,090,809 (100% non-need-based).
ATHLETIC AWARDS *Total amount:* $901,935 (100% non-need-based).
APPLYING FOR FINANCIAL AID *Required financial aid form:* FAFSA. *Financial aid deadline (priority):* 3/15. *Notification date:* Continuous beginning 4/1. Students must reply within 3 weeks of notification.
CONTACT Julie Pier, Director of Student Financial Aid, The University of South Dakota, Belbas Center, 414 East Clark Street, Vermillion, SD 57069-2390, 605-677-5446 or toll-free 877-269-6837. *Fax:* 605-677-5238.

UNIVERSITY OF SOUTHERN CALIFORNIA
Los Angeles, CA

Tuition & fees: $32,008	Average undergraduate aid package: $28,459

ABOUT THE INSTITUTION Independent, coed. Awards: bachelor's, master's, doctoral, and first professional degrees and post-bachelor's, post-master's, and first professional certificates. 111 undergraduate majors. Total enrollment: 32,836. Undergraduates: 16,897. Freshmen: 2,741. Both federal and institutional methodology are used as a basis for awarding need-based institutional aid.
UNDERGRADUATE EXPENSES for 2005–06 *Application fee:* $65. *Comprehensive fee:* $41,618 includes full-time tuition ($31,458), mandatory fees ($550), and room and board ($9610). *College room only:* $5260. Full-time tuition and fees vary according to program. Room and board charges vary according to board plan and housing facility. *Part-time tuition:* $1059 per credit hour. *Part-time fees:* $685 per year. Part-time tuition and fees vary according to course load and program. *Payment plans:* Tuition prepayment, installment, deferred payment.
FRESHMAN FINANCIAL AID (Fall 2004) 1805 applied for aid; of those 67% were deemed to have need. 100% of freshmen with need received aid; of those 95% had need fully met. *Average percent of need met:* 100% (excluding resources awarded to replace EFC). *Average financial aid package:* $28,371 (excluding resources awarded to replace EFC). 24% of all full-time freshmen had no need and received non-need-based gift aid.
UNDERGRADUATE FINANCIAL AID (Fall 2004) 8,810 applied for aid; of those 80% were deemed to have need. 100% of undergraduates with need received aid; of those 93% had need fully met. *Average percent of need met:* 100% (excluding resources awarded to replace EFC). *Average financial aid package:* $28,459 (excluding resources awarded to replace EFC). 19% of all full-time undergraduates had no need and received non-need-based gift aid.
GIFT AID (NEED-BASED) *Total amount:* $147,204,148 (9% federal, 13% state, 74% institutional, 4% external sources). *Receiving aid:* Freshmen: 39% (1,067); All full-time undergraduates: 41% (6,422). *Average award:* Freshmen: $18,919;

Undergraduates: $18,481. *Scholarships, grants, and awards:* Federal Pell, FSEOG, state, private, college/university gift aid from institutional funds.
GIFT AID (NON-NEED-BASED) *Total amount:* $39,037,824 (75% institutional, 25% external sources). *Receiving aid:* Freshmen: 27% (757); Undergraduates: 20% (3,175). *Average Award:* Freshmen: $12,134; Undergraduates: $12,874. *Scholarships, grants, and awards by category: Academic Interests/Achievement:* 4,929 awards ($49,438,305 total): general academic interests/achievements. *Creative Arts/Performance:* 19 awards ($345,855 total): debating. *Special Achievements/Activities:* 158 awards ($1,544,497 total): leadership. *Special Characteristics:* 853 awards ($12,879,763 total): children and siblings of alumni, children of faculty/staff, international students, members of minority groups. *Tuition waivers:* Full or partial for employees or children of employees. *ROTC:* Army, Air Force.
LOANS *Student loans:* $97,780,049 (38% need-based, 62% non-need-based). 48% of past graduating class borrowed through all loan programs. *Average indebtedness per student:* $19,131. *Average need-based loan:* Freshmen: $3767; Undergraduates: $6181. *Parent loans:* $38,036,237 (51% need-based, 49% non-need-based). *Programs:* FFEL (Subsidized and Unsubsidized Stafford, PLUS), Perkins, 'Credit Ready' and 'Credit Based' loans.
WORK-STUDY *Federal work-study:* Total amount: $12,487,943; 4,632 jobs averaging $2696.
ATHLETIC AWARDS *Total amount:* $11,866,253 (23% need-based, 77% non-need-based).
APPLYING FOR FINANCIAL AID *Required financial aid forms:* FAFSA, CSS Financial Aid PROFILE, For 2006-2007; 2005 parent and student federal income tax forms and all schedules and W-2s, USC non-filing terms for tho. *Financial aid deadline (priority):* 1/20. *Notification date:* Continuous beginning 3/15. Students must reply by 5/1 or within 2 weeks of notification.
CONTACT Catherine C. Thomas, Associate Dean of Admission and Financial Aid, University of Southern California, University Park Campus, Los Angeles, CA 90089-0914, 213-740-1111. *Fax:* 213-740-0680. *E-mail:* fao@usc.edu.

UNIVERSITY OF SOUTHERN INDIANA
Evansville, IN

Tuition & fees (IN res): $4304   **Average undergraduate aid package: $5393**

ABOUT THE INSTITUTION State-supported, coed. Awards: associate, bachelor's, and master's degrees and post-bachelor's certificates. 55 undergraduate majors. Total enrollment: 10,004. Undergraduates: 9,252. Freshmen: 2,148. Federal methodology is used as a basis for awarding need-based institutional aid.
UNDERGRADUATE EXPENSES for 2006–07 *Application fee:* $25. *Tuition, state resident:* full-time $4244; part-time $141.45 per credit hour. *Tuition, nonresident:* full-time $10,118; part-time $337.25 per credit hour. *Required fees:* full-time $60; $22.75 per term part-time. *College room and board:* $6368; *room only:* $3170.
FRESHMAN FINANCIAL AID (Fall 2005, est.) 1772 applied for aid; of those 69% were deemed to have need. 90% of freshmen with need received aid; of those 14% had need fully met. *Average percent of need met:* 55% (excluding resources awarded to replace EFC). *Average financial aid package:* $4985 (excluding resources awarded to replace EFC). 10% of all full-time freshmen had no need and received non-need-based gift aid.
UNDERGRADUATE FINANCIAL AID (Fall 2005, est.) 5,960 applied for aid; of those 74% were deemed to have need. 87% of undergraduates with need received aid; of those 15% had need fully met. *Average percent of need met:* 54% (excluding resources awarded to replace EFC). *Average financial aid package:* $5393 (excluding resources awarded to replace EFC). 7% of all full-time undergraduates had no need and received non-need-based gift aid.
GIFT AID (NEED-BASED) *Total amount:* $12,680,065 (48% federal, 38% state, 10% institutional, 4% external sources). *Receiving aid:* Freshmen: 40% (813); All full-time undergraduates: 37% (2,763). *Average award:* Freshmen: $4506; Undergraduates: $4509. *Scholarships, grants, and awards:* Federal Pell, FSEOG, state, private, college/university gift aid from institutional funds.
GIFT AID (NON-NEED-BASED) *Total amount:* $2,192,301 (78% institutional, 22% external sources). *Receiving aid:* Freshmen: 8% (158); Undergraduates: 9% (687). *Average Award:* Freshmen: $1994; Undergraduates: $2140. *Scholarships, grants, and awards by category: Academic Interests/Achievement:* 756 awards ($1,022,014 total): biological sciences, business, education, engineering/technologies, general academic interests/achievements, health fields, humanities, mathematics, premedicine, social sciences. *Creative Arts/Performance:* 27 awards ($23,300 total): art/fine arts, creative writing, theater/drama. *Special Achievements/Activities:* leadership. *Special Characteristics:* 279 awards ($651,287 total): children of faculty/staff, members of minority groups, out-of-state students, spouses of current students, veterans' children. *ROTC:* Army.
LOANS *Student loans:* $15,473,668 (71% need-based, 29% non-need-based). 60% of past graduating class borrowed through all loan programs. *Average indebtedness per student:* $15,724. *Average need-based loan:* Freshmen: $2412; Undergraduates: $3260. *Parent loans:* $4,700,553 (58% need-based, 42% non-need-based). *Programs:* FFEL (Subsidized and Unsubsidized Stafford, PLUS), Perkins.
WORK-STUDY *Federal work-study:* Total amount: $163,800; 90 jobs averaging $1820.
ATHLETIC AWARDS *Total amount:* $651,637 (38% need-based, 62% non-need-based).
APPLYING FOR FINANCIAL AID *Required financial aid forms:* FAFSA, institution's own form. *Financial aid deadline:* 3/1. *Notification date:* Continuous beginning 4/15.
CONTACT Financial Aid Counselor, University of Southern Indiana, 8600 University Boulevard, Evansville, IN 47712-3590, 812-464-1767 or toll-free 800-467-1965. *Fax:* 812-465-7154. *E-mail:* finaid@usi.edu.

UNIVERSITY OF SOUTHERN MAINE
Portland, ME

Tuition & fees (ME res): $5906   **Average undergraduate aid package: $8754**

ABOUT THE INSTITUTION State-supported, coed. Awards: associate, bachelor's, master's, doctoral, and first professional degrees and post-master's certificates. 46 undergraduate majors. Total enrollment: 10,944. Undergraduates: 8,622. Freshmen: 984. Federal methodology is used as a basis for awarding need-based institutional aid.
UNDERGRADUATE EXPENSES for 2005–06 *Application fee:* $40. *Tuition, state resident:* full-time $4980; part-time $166 per credit hour. *Tuition, nonresident:* full-time $13,800; part-time $460 per credit hour. Full-time tuition and fees vary according to course load, degree level, and reciprocity agreements. Part-time tuition and fees vary according to course load, degree level, and reciprocity agreements. *College room and board:* $6755; *room only:* $3586. Room and board charges vary according to board plan, housing facility, and location. *Payment plan:* Installment.
FRESHMAN FINANCIAL AID (Fall 2005, est.) 707 applied for aid; of those 79% were deemed to have need. 96% of freshmen with need received aid; of those 20% had need fully met. *Average percent of need met:* 69% (excluding resources awarded to replace EFC). *Average financial aid package:* $7333 (excluding resources awarded to replace EFC). 13% of all full-time freshmen had no need and received non-need-based gift aid.
UNDERGRADUATE FINANCIAL AID (Fall 2005, est.) 3,814 applied for aid; of those 83% were deemed to have need. 97% of undergraduates with need received aid; of those 28% had need fully met. *Average percent of need met:* 76% (excluding resources awarded to replace EFC). *Average financial aid package:* $8754 (excluding resources awarded to replace EFC). 12% of all full-time undergraduates had no need and received non-need-based gift aid.
GIFT AID (NEED-BASED) *Total amount:* $10,751,594 (61% federal, 12% state, 13% institutional, 14% external sources). *Receiving aid:* Freshmen: 47% (428); All full-time undergraduates: 50% (2,328). *Average award:* Freshmen: $4116; Undergraduates: $3913. *Scholarships, grants, and awards:* Federal Pell, FSEOG, state, college/university gift aid from institutional funds.
GIFT AID (NON-NEED-BASED) *Total amount:* $1,727,186 (34% institutional, 66% external sources). *Receiving aid:* Freshmen: 3% (25); Undergraduates: 2% (95). *Average Award:* Freshmen: $3267; Undergraduates: $4410. *Scholarships, grants, and awards by category: Academic Interests/Achievement:* general academic interests/achievements. *Creative Arts/Performance:* music, theater/drama. *Special Achievements/Activities:* community service. *Special Characteristics:* children of faculty/staff, general special characteristics, local/state students, out-of-state students. *Tuition waivers:* Full or partial for minority students, employees or children of employees. *ROTC:* Army cooperative, Air Force cooperative.
LOANS *Student loans:* $21,034,671 (63% need-based, 37% non-need-based). 61% of past graduating class borrowed through all loan programs. *Average indebtedness per student:* $21,800. *Average need-based loan:* Freshmen: $2816;

University of Southern Maine

Undergraduates: $4085. *Parent loans:* $3,497,843 (100% non-need-based). *Programs:* FFEL (Subsidized and Unsubsidized Stafford, PLUS), Perkins, Federal Nursing, college/university.
WORK-STUDY *Federal work-study:* Total amount: $4,213,334; jobs available.
APPLYING FOR FINANCIAL AID *Required financial aid form:* FAFSA. *Financial aid deadline (priority):* 2/15. *Notification date:* Continuous beginning 3/15. Students must reply within 2 weeks of notification.
CONTACT Mr. Keith P. Dubois, Director of Student Financial Aid, University of Southern Maine, 96 Falmouth Street, PO Box 9300, Portland, ME 04104-9300, 207-780-5122 or toll-free 800-800-4USM Ext. 5670. *Fax:* 207-780-5143. *E-mail:* dubois@maine.edu.

UNIVERSITY OF SOUTHERN MISSISSIPPI
Hattiesburg, MS

Tuition & fees (MS res): $4342 — Average undergraduate aid package: $7204

ABOUT THE INSTITUTION State-supported, coed. Awards: bachelor's, master's, and doctoral degrees. 66 undergraduate majors. Total enrollment: 15,030. Undergraduates: 12,468. Freshmen: 1,346. Federal methodology is used as a basis for awarding need-based institutional aid.
UNDERGRADUATE EXPENSES for 2006–07 *Tuition, state resident:* full-time $4312; part-time $180 per credit hour. *Tuition, nonresident:* full-time $9742; part-time $407 per credit hour. *College room and board:* $5800; *room only:* $2620.
FRESHMAN FINANCIAL AID (Fall 2004) 1227 applied for aid; of those 80% were deemed to have need. 98% of freshmen with need received aid; of those 20% had need fully met. *Average percent of need met:* 77% (excluding resources awarded to replace EFC). *Average financial aid package:* $6156 (excluding resources awarded to replace EFC). 12% of all full-time freshmen had no need and received non-need-based gift aid.
UNDERGRADUATE FINANCIAL AID (Fall 2004) 7,611 applied for aid; of those 85% were deemed to have need. 99% of undergraduates with need received aid; of those 31% had need fully met. *Average percent of need met:* 84% (excluding resources awarded to replace EFC). *Average financial aid package:* $7204 (excluding resources awarded to replace EFC). 8% of all full-time undergraduates had no need and received non-need-based gift aid.
GIFT AID (NEED-BASED) *Total amount:* $18,372,603 (77% federal, 8% state, 9% institutional, 6% external sources). *Receiving aid:* Freshmen: 41% (646); All full-time undergraduates: 44% (4,420). *Average award:* Freshmen: $3296; Undergraduates: $3205. *Scholarships, grants, and awards:* Federal Pell, FSEOG, state, private, college/university gift aid from institutional funds.
GIFT AID (NON-NEED-BASED) *Total amount:* $8,923,960 (2% federal, 34% state, 43% institutional, 21% external sources). *Receiving aid:* Freshmen: 34% (527); Undergraduates: 29% (2,915). *Average Award:* Freshmen: $2910; Undergraduates: $2408. *Scholarships, grants, and awards by category: Academic Interests/Achievement:* 1,768 awards ($2,205,627 total): general academic interests/achievements. *Creative Arts/Performance:* 509 awards ($620,457 total): art/fine arts, dance, music, theater/drama. *Special Achievements/Activities:* 178 awards ($241,050 total): cheerleading/drum major, leadership. *Special Characteristics:* 4,553 awards ($5,572,227 total): children and siblings of alumni, children of faculty/staff, ethnic background, local/state students, out-of-state students, veterans. *ROTC:* Army, Air Force.
LOANS *Student loans:* $39,800,417 (66% need-based, 34% non-need-based). 65% of past graduating class borrowed through all loan programs. *Average indebtedness per student:* $15,776. *Average need-based loan:* Freshmen: $2851; Undergraduates: $4307. *Parent loans:* $2,810,368 (23% need-based, 77% non-need-based). *Programs:* FFEL (Subsidized and Unsubsidized Stafford, PLUS), Perkins, Federal Nursing, college/university.
WORK-STUDY *Federal work-study:* Total amount: $175,168; 97 jobs averaging $1834.
ATHLETIC AWARDS *Total amount:* $2,222,465 (36% need-based, 64% non-need-based).
APPLYING FOR FINANCIAL AID *Required financial aid forms:* FAFSA, institution's own form, state aid form. *Financial aid deadline (priority):* 3/15. *Notification date:* Continuous. Students must reply within 2 weeks of notification.
CONTACT Kristi Motter, Director of Financial Aid, University of Southern Mississippi, Box 5101, Hattiesburg, MS 39406-5101, 601-266-4774. *E-mail:* kristi.motter@usm.edu.

UNIVERSITY OF SOUTH FLORIDA
Tampa, FL

Tuition & fees (FL res): $3384 — Average undergraduate aid package: $9365

ABOUT THE INSTITUTION State-supported, coed. Awards: associate, bachelor's, master's, doctoral, and first professional degrees and post-bachelor's certificates. 84 undergraduate majors. Total enrollment: 42,660. Undergraduates: 33,703. Freshmen: 4,307. Federal methodology is used as a basis for awarding need-based institutional aid.
UNDERGRADUATE EXPENSES for 2005–06 *Application fee:* $30. *Tuition, state resident:* full-time $3310; part-time $108 per credit hour. *Tuition, nonresident:* full-time $16,076; part-time $533 per credit hour. *Required fees:* full-time $74; $37 per term part-time. Full-time tuition and fees vary according to course level, course load, and location. Part-time tuition and fees vary according to course level, course load, and location. *College room and board:* $6900; *room only:* $3563. Room and board charges vary according to board plan, housing facility, and location. *Payment plan:* Installment.
FRESHMAN FINANCIAL AID (Fall 2004) 2554 applied for aid; of those 73% were deemed to have need. 99% of freshmen with need received aid; of those 5% had need fully met. *Average percent of need met:* 31% (excluding resources awarded to replace EFC). *Average financial aid package:* $7824 (excluding resources awarded to replace EFC). 15% of all full-time freshmen had no need and received non-need-based gift aid.
UNDERGRADUATE FINANCIAL AID (Fall 2004) 12,793 applied for aid; of those 83% were deemed to have need. 98% of undergraduates with need received aid; of those 4% had need fully met. *Average percent of need met:* 33% (excluding resources awarded to replace EFC). *Average financial aid package:* $9365 (excluding resources awarded to replace EFC). 6% of all full-time undergraduates had no need and received non-need-based gift aid.
GIFT AID (NEED-BASED) *Total amount:* $33,608,121 (73% federal, 18% state, 9% institutional). *Receiving aid:* Freshmen: 22% (928); All full-time undergraduates: 26% (6,190). *Average award:* Freshmen: $4020; Undergraduates: $4261. *Scholarships, grants, and awards:* Federal Pell, FSEOG, state, private, college/university gift aid from institutional funds.
GIFT AID (NON-NEED-BASED) *Total amount:* $50,067,704 (1% federal, 71% state, 22% institutional, 6% external sources). *Receiving aid:* Freshmen: 20% (855); Undergraduates: 13% (3,175). *Average Award:* Freshmen: $4038; Undergraduates: $2022. *Scholarships, grants, and awards by category: Academic Interests/Achievement:* 1,651 awards ($2,200,130 total): architecture, biological sciences, business, communication, computer science, education, engineering/technologies, English, foreign languages, general academic interests/achievements, health fields, humanities, international studies, library science, mathematics, military science, physical sciences, premedicine, religion/biblical studies, social sciences. *Creative Arts/Performance:* 110 awards ($110,680 total): applied art and design, art/fine arts, cinema/film/broadcasting, creative writing, dance, debating, journalism/publications, music, performing arts, theater/drama. *Special Achievements/Activities:* general special achievements/activities. *Special Characteristics:* general special characteristics. *Tuition waivers:* Full or partial for senior citizens. *ROTC:* Army, Naval, Air Force.
LOANS *Student loans:* $79,385,030 (55% need-based, 45% non-need-based). 54% of past graduating class borrowed through all loan programs. *Average indebtedness per student:* $17,434. *Average need-based loan:* Freshmen: $2440; Undergraduates: $4914. *Parent loans:* $4,999,845 (100% non-need-based). *Programs:* FFEL (Subsidized and Unsubsidized Stafford, PLUS), Perkins, college/university.
WORK-STUDY *Federal work-study:* Total amount: $2,869,503; 905 jobs averaging $3600.
ATHLETIC AWARDS *Total amount:* $2,424,133 (100% non-need-based).
APPLYING FOR FINANCIAL AID *Required financial aid form:* FAFSA. *Financial aid deadline (priority):* 3/1. *Notification date:* Continuous beginning 3/28. Students must reply within 4 weeks of notification.
CONTACT Mr. Leonard Gude, Director of Student Financial Aid, University of South Florida, 4202 East Fowler Avenue, SVC 1102, Tampa, FL 33620-6960, 813-974-4700 or toll-free 877-USF-BULLS. *Fax:* 813-974-5144. *E-mail:* lgude@admin.usf.edu.

THE UNIVERSITY OF TAMPA
Tampa, FL

Tuition & fees: $18,848 **Average undergraduate aid package:** $14,640

ABOUT THE INSTITUTION Independent, coed. Awards: associate, bachelor's, and master's degrees. 45 undergraduate majors. Total enrollment: 5,202. Undergraduates: 4,636. Freshmen: 1,015. Federal methodology is used as a basis for awarding need-based institutional aid.

UNDERGRADUATE EXPENSES for 2005–06 *Application fee:* $35. *Comprehensive fee:* $25,784 includes full-time tuition ($17,906), mandatory fees ($942), and room and board ($6936). *College room only:* $3710. Full-time tuition and fees vary according to class time. Room and board charges vary according to board plan and housing facility. *Part-time tuition:* $380 per hour. *Part-time fees:* $35 per term. Part-time tuition and fees vary according to class time. *Payment plan:* Installment.

FRESHMAN FINANCIAL AID (Fall 2005, est.) 699 applied for aid; of those 78% were deemed to have need. 100% of freshmen with need received aid; of those 22% had need fully met. *Average percent of need met:* 82% (excluding resources awarded to replace EFC). *Average financial aid package:* $14,268 (excluding resources awarded to replace EFC). 13% of all full-time freshmen had no need and received non-need-based gift aid.

UNDERGRADUATE FINANCIAL AID (Fall 2005, est.) 2,721 applied for aid; of those 83% were deemed to have need. 100% of undergraduates with need received aid; of those 18% had need fully met. *Average percent of need met:* 81% (excluding resources awarded to replace EFC). *Average financial aid package:* $14,640 (excluding resources awarded to replace EFC). 9% of all full-time undergraduates had no need and received non-need-based gift aid.

GIFT AID (NEED-BASED) *Total amount:* $22,693,063 (13% federal, 15% state, 67% institutional, 5% external sources). *Receiving aid:* Freshmen: 53% (529); All full-time undergraduates: 51% (2,113). *Average award:* Freshmen: $7185; Undergraduates: $6758. *Scholarships, grants, and awards:* Federal Pell, FSEOG, state, private, college/university gift aid from institutional funds.

GIFT AID (NON-NEED-BASED) *Total amount:* $10,056,076 (22% state, 69% institutional, 9% external sources). *Receiving aid:* Freshmen: 48% (485); Undergraduates: 39% (1,591). *Average Award:* Freshmen: $6283; Undergraduates: $6087. *Scholarships, grants, and awards by category: Academic Interests/Achievement:* biological sciences, business, communication, education, general academic interests/achievements, health fields, military science, social sciences. *Creative Arts/Performance:* art/fine arts, creative writing, journalism/publications, music, performing arts. *Special Achievements/Activities:* general special achievements/activities, leadership. *Special Characteristics:* children and siblings of alumni, children of faculty/staff, international students. *Tuition waivers:* Full or partial for employees or children of employees. *ROTC:* Army, Air Force cooperative.

LOANS *Student loans:* $19,819,396 (63% need-based, 37% non-need-based). 71% of past graduating class borrowed through all loan programs. *Average indebtedness per student:* $23,051. *Average need-based loan:* Freshmen: $3612; Undergraduates: $5036. *Parent loans:* $7,325,519 (71% need-based, 29% non-need-based). *Programs:* FFEL (Subsidized and Unsubsidized Stafford, PLUS), Perkins, state, college/university.

WORK-STUDY *Federal work-study:* Total amount: $497,612; jobs available (averaging $2000).

ATHLETIC AWARDS *Total amount:* $998,778 (49% need-based, 51% non-need-based).

APPLYING FOR FINANCIAL AID *Required financial aid forms:* FAFSA, state aid form. *Financial aid deadline:* Continuous. *Notification date:* Continuous beginning 2/1. Students must reply within 3 weeks of notification.

CONTACT Financial Aid Office, The University of Tampa, 401 West Kennedy Boulevard, Tampa, FL 33606-1490, 813-253-6219 or toll-free 888-646-2438 (in-state), 888-MINARET (out-of-state). *Fax:* 813-254-4955. *E-mail:* finaid@ut.edu.

THE UNIVERSITY OF TENNESSEE
Knoxville, TN

CONTACT Office of Financial Aid and Scholarships, The University of Tennessee, 115 Student Services Building, Knoxville, TN 37996-0210, 865-974-3131 or toll-free 800-221-8657 (in-state). *Fax:* 865-974-2175. *E-mail:* finaid@utk.edu.

THE UNIVERSITY OF TENNESSEE AT CHATTANOOGA
Chattanooga, TN

ABOUT THE INSTITUTION State-supported, coed. Awards: bachelor's, master's, doctoral, and first professional degrees and post-bachelor's and post-master's certificates. 44 undergraduate majors. Total enrollment: 8,656. Undergraduates: 7,277. Freshmen: 1,456.

GIFT AID (NEED-BASED) *Scholarships, grants, and awards:* Federal Pell, FSEOG, state, private, college/university gift aid from institutional funds, Federal Nursing.

GIFT AID (NON-NEED-BASED) *Scholarships, grants, and awards by category: Academic Interests/Achievement:* general academic interests/achievements. *Creative Arts/Performance:* art/fine arts, music, theater/drama. *Special Achievements/Activities:* cheerleading/drum major, leadership. *Special Characteristics:* members of minority groups.

LOANS *Programs:* FFEL (Subsidized and Unsubsidized Stafford, PLUS), Perkins.

WORK-STUDY *Federal work-study:* Total amount: $395,000; 220 jobs averaging $1795. *State or other work-study/employment:* Total amount: $750,000 (100% non-need-based). 400 part-time jobs averaging $1875.

APPLYING FOR FINANCIAL AID *Required financial aid forms:* FAFSA, institution's own form.

CONTACT Jonathan Looney, Financial Aid Director, The University of Tennessee at Chattanooga, 615 McCallie Avenue, Chattanooga, TN 37403-2598, 423-425-4677 or toll-free 800-UTC-MOCS (in-state). *Fax:* 423-425-2292. *E-mail:* jonathan-looney@utc.edu.

THE UNIVERSITY OF TENNESSEE AT MARTIN
Martin, TN

Tuition & fees (TN res): $4493 **Average undergraduate aid package:** $8443

ABOUT THE INSTITUTION State-supported, coed. Awards: bachelor's and master's degrees. 103 undergraduate majors. Total enrollment: 6,484. Undergraduates: 5,942. Freshmen: 1,250. Federal methodology is used as a basis for awarding need-based institutional aid.

UNDERGRADUATE EXPENSES for 2005–06 *Application fee:* $25. *Tuition, state resident:* full-time $3744; part-time $156 per credit hour. *Tuition, nonresident:* full-time $12,798; part-time $534 per credit hour. *Required fees:* full-time $749; $33 per credit hour. *College room and board:* $4220; *room only:* $2000. Room and board charges vary according to board plan and housing facility. *Payment plan:* Deferred payment.

FRESHMAN FINANCIAL AID (Fall 2005, est.) 1758 applied for aid; of those 67% were deemed to have need. 98% of freshmen with need received aid; of those 39% had need fully met. *Average percent of need met:* 75% (excluding resources awarded to replace EFC). *Average financial aid package:* $8275 (excluding resources awarded to replace EFC). 25% of all full-time freshmen had no need and received non-need-based gift aid.

UNDERGRADUATE FINANCIAL AID (Fall 2005, est.) 4,643 applied for aid; of those 65% were deemed to have need. 97% of undergraduates with need received aid; of those 39% had need fully met. *Average percent of need met:* 77% (excluding resources awarded to replace EFC). *Average financial aid package:* $8443 (excluding resources awarded to replace EFC). 24% of all full-time undergraduates had no need and received non-need-based gift aid.

GIFT AID (NEED-BASED) *Total amount:* $8,088,083 (73% federal, 19% state, 5% institutional, 3% external sources). *Receiving aid:* Freshmen: 39% (721); All full-time undergraduates: 37% (1,879). *Average award:* Freshmen: $4493; Undergraduates: $4252. *Scholarships, grants, and awards:* Federal Pell, FSEOG, state, private, TN minority: Teaching fellowships; TN teachers; Sc.

GIFT AID (NON-NEED-BASED) *Total amount:* $9,247,753 (68% state, 28% institutional, 4% external sources). *Receiving aid:* Freshmen: 40% (745); Undergraduates: 29% (1,443). *Average Award:* Freshmen: $4398; Undergraduates: $4449. *Scholarships, grants, and awards by category: Academic Interests/Achievement:* 1,356 awards ($1,811,550 total): agriculture, biological sciences, business, communication, computer science, education, engineering/technologies, English, general academic interests/achievements, health fields, home economics, humanities, mathematics, military science, physical sciences, premedicine, social sciences. *Creative Arts/Performance:* 175 awards ($127,130 total): art/

The University of Tennessee at Martin

fine arts, journalism/publications, music, theater/drama. *Special Achievements/Activities:* 454 awards ($566,410 total): cheerleading/drum major, general special achievements/activities, leadership, rodeo. *Special Characteristics:* 1,362 awards ($1,899,264 total): adult students, children of educators, children of faculty/staff, ethnic background, handicapped students, members of minority groups, out-of-state students. *Tuition waivers:* Full or partial for employees or children of employees, senior citizens. *ROTC:* Army.
LOANS *Student loans:* $13,201,156 (54% need-based, 46% non-need-based). 57% of past graduating class borrowed through all loan programs. *Average indebtedness per student:* $16,749. *Average need-based loan:* Freshmen: $2680; Undergraduates: $3613. *Parent loans:* $1,314,691 (100% non-need-based). *Programs:* FFEL (Subsidized and Unsubsidized Stafford, PLUS), Perkins.
WORK-STUDY *Federal work-study:* Total amount: $521,514; 265 jobs averaging $2019.
ATHLETIC AWARDS Total amount: $2,110,331 (100% non-need-based).
APPLYING FOR FINANCIAL AID *Required financial aid form:* FAFSA. *Financial aid deadline:* Continuous.
CONTACT Sandra J. Neel, Director of Student Financial Assistance, The University of Tennessee at Martin, 205 Administration Building, Martin, TN 38238-1000, 731-881-7040 or toll-free 800-829-8861. *Fax:* 731-881-7036. *E-mail:* bmcclain@utm.edu.

THE UNIVERSITY OF TEXAS AT ARLINGTON
Arlington, TX

Tuition & fees (TX res): $5563   **Average undergraduate aid package:** $9016

ABOUT THE INSTITUTION State-supported, coed. Awards: bachelor's, master's, and doctoral degrees and post-bachelor's and post-master's certificates. 60 undergraduate majors. Total enrollment: 25,432. Undergraduates: 19,649. Freshmen: 1,835. Federal methodology is used as a basis for awarding need-based institutional aid.
UNDERGRADUATE EXPENSES for 2005–06 *Application fee:* $35. *Tuition, state resident:* full-time $3893; part-time $134.50 per credit hour. *Tuition, nonresident:* full-time $12,173; part-time $410.50 per credit hour. *Required fees:* full-time $1670; $59.58 per credit hour or $102.50 per term part-time. Full-time tuition and fees vary according to course level, course load, and program. Part-time tuition and fees vary according to course level, course load, and program. *College room and board:* $5345. Room and board charges vary according to board plan and housing facility. *Payment plan:* Installment.
FRESHMAN FINANCIAL AID (Fall 2005, est.) 1180 applied for aid; of those 88% were deemed to have need. 100% of freshmen with need received aid; of those 16% had need fully met. *Average percent of need met:* 71% (excluding resources awarded to replace EFC). *Average financial aid package:* $7898 (excluding resources awarded to replace EFC). 24% of all full-time freshmen had no need and received non-need-based gift aid.
UNDERGRADUATE FINANCIAL AID (Fall 2005, est.) 9,428 applied for aid; of those 77% were deemed to have need. 100% of undergraduates with need received aid; of those 19% had need fully met. *Average percent of need met:* 74% (excluding resources awarded to replace EFC). *Average financial aid package:* $9016 (excluding resources awarded to replace EFC). 13% of all full-time undergraduates had no need and received non-need-based gift aid.
GIFT AID (NEED-BASED) *Total amount:* $30,504,858 (53% federal, 26% state, 14% institutional, 7% external sources). *Receiving aid:* Freshmen: 40% (718); All full-time undergraduates: 37% (5,120). *Average award:* Freshmen: $3998; Undergraduates: $4229. *Scholarships, grants, and awards:* Federal Pell, FSEOG, state, private, college/university gift aid from institutional funds, United Negro College Fund.
GIFT AID (NON-NEED-BASED) *Total amount:* $4,440,818 (60% institutional, 40% external sources). *Receiving aid:* Freshmen: 32% (575); Undergraduates: 20% (2,772). *Average Award:* Freshmen: $2032; Undergraduates: $2323. *Scholarships, grants, and awards by category: Academic Interests/Achievement:* 4,135 awards ($5,409,352 total): architecture, biological sciences, business, communication, computer science, education, engineering/technologies, English, foreign languages, general academic interests/achievements, health fields, humanities, international studies, mathematics, military science, physical sciences, social sciences. *Creative Arts/Performance:* 260 awards ($194,067 total): journalism/publications, music, theater/drama. *Special Achievements/Activities:* 183 awards ($211,060 total): cheerleading/drum major, community service, general special achievements/activities, leadership. *Special Characteristics:* 76 awards ($119,406 total): children with a deceased or disabled parent, first-generation college students, general special characteristics, handicapped students, public servants. *Tuition waivers:* Full or partial for employees or children of employees. *ROTC:* Army, Air Force cooperative.
LOANS *Student loans:* $52,603,698 (82% need-based, 18% non-need-based). 42% of past graduating class borrowed through all loan programs. *Average indebtedness per student:* $16,780. *Average need-based loan:* Freshmen: $4096; Undergraduates: $5798. *Parent loans:* $3,603,387 (40% need-based, 60% non-need-based). *Programs:* FFEL (Subsidized and Unsubsidized Stafford, PLUS), Perkins, state.
WORK-STUDY *Federal work-study:* Total amount: $4,153,507; 718 jobs averaging $1827.
ATHLETIC AWARDS Total amount: $1,407,830 (26% need-based, 74% non-need-based).
APPLYING FOR FINANCIAL AID *Required financial aid form:* FAFSA. *Financial aid deadline (priority):* 5/15. *Notification date:* Continuous beginning 4/1. Students must reply within 3 weeks of notification.
CONTACT Karen Krause, Director of Financial Aid, The University of Texas at Arlington, PO Box 19199, Arlington, TX 76019, 817-272-3568. *Fax:* 817-272-3555. *E-mail:* kkrause@uta.edu.

THE UNIVERSITY OF TEXAS AT AUSTIN
Austin, TX

Tuition & fees (TX res): $6972   **Average undergraduate aid package:** $9085

ABOUT THE INSTITUTION State-supported, coed. Awards: bachelor's, master's, doctoral, and first professional degrees. 104 undergraduate majors. Total enrollment: 49,696. Undergraduates: 36,878. Freshmen: 6,836. Federal methodology is used as a basis for awarding need-based institutional aid.
UNDERGRADUATE EXPENSES for 2005–06 *Application fee:* $60. *Tuition, state resident:* full-time $6972. *Tuition, nonresident:* full-time $16,310. Full-time tuition and fees vary according to course load and program. Part-time tuition and fees vary according to course load and program. *College room and board:* $7638. Room and board charges vary according to board plan, housing facility, and location. *Payment plan:* Installment.
FRESHMAN FINANCIAL AID (Fall 2005, est.) 4590 applied for aid; of those 85% were deemed to have need. 98% of freshmen with need received aid; of those 91% had need fully met. *Average percent of need met:* 95% (excluding resources awarded to replace EFC). *Average financial aid package:* $9175 (excluding resources awarded to replace EFC). 26% of all full-time freshmen had no need and received non-need-based gift aid.
UNDERGRADUATE FINANCIAL AID (Fall 2005, est.) 22,700 applied for aid; of those 80% were deemed to have need. 97% of undergraduates with need received aid; of those 86% had need fully met. *Average percent of need met:* 94% (excluding resources awarded to replace EFC). *Average financial aid package:* $9085 (excluding resources awarded to replace EFC). 30% of all full-time undergraduates had no need and received non-need-based gift aid.
GIFT AID (NEED-BASED) *Total amount:* $74,059,200 (31% federal, 22% state, 38% institutional, 9% external sources). *Receiving aid:* Freshmen: 48% (3,295); All full-time undergraduates: 37% (12,320). *Average award:* Freshmen: $6700; Undergraduates: $6250. *Scholarships, grants, and awards:* Federal Pell, FSEOG, state, private, college/university gift aid from institutional funds, Federal Nursing.
GIFT AID (NON-NEED-BASED) *Total amount:* $46,545,000 (1% federal, 1% state, 80% institutional, 18% external sources). *Average Award:* Freshmen: $3700; Undergraduates: $4935. *Scholarships, grants, and awards by category: Academic Interests/Achievement:* general academic interests/achievements. *Creative Arts/Performance:* general creative arts/performance. *Special Achievements/Activities:* general special achievements/activities. *Special Characteristics:* general special characteristics. *Tuition waivers:* Full or partial for employees or children of employees, senior citizens. *ROTC:* Army, Naval, Air Force.
LOANS *Student loans:* $103,201,000 (78% need-based, 22% non-need-based). 38% of past graduating class borrowed through all loan programs. *Average indebtedness per student:* $16,000. *Average need-based loan:* Freshmen: $3600; Undergraduates: $4700. *Parent loans:* $43,319,000 (30% need-based, 70% non-need-based). *Programs:* FFEL (Subsidized and Unsubsidized Stafford, PLUS), Perkins, state.
WORK-STUDY *Federal work-study:* Total amount: $2,378,000; 1,500 jobs averaging $1585. *State or other work-study/employment:* Total amount: $15,023,600 (2% need-based, 98% non-need-based). 290 part-time jobs averaging $1202.

APPLYING FOR FINANCIAL AID *Required financial aid form:* FAFSA. *Financial aid deadline (priority):* 4/1. *Notification date:* Continuous beginning 4/1. Students must reply within 4 weeks of notification.
CONTACT Don C. Davis, Associate Director of Student Financial Services, The University of Texas at Austin, PO Box 7758, UT Station, Austin, TX 78713-7758, 512-475-6282. *Fax:* 512-475-6296. *E-mail:* dondavis@mail.utexas.edu.

THE UNIVERSITY OF TEXAS AT BROWNSVILLE
Brownsville, TX

ABOUT THE INSTITUTION State-supported, coed. Awards: associate, bachelor's, and master's degrees. 35 undergraduate majors. Total enrollment: 13,316. Undergraduates: 12,467. Entering class: 1,395.
GIFT AID (NEED-BASED) *Scholarships, grants, and awards:* Federal Pell, FSEOG, state, private, college/university gift aid from institutional funds.
GIFT AID (NON-NEED-BASED) *Scholarships, grants, and awards by category: Academic Interests/Achievement:* biological sciences, education, engineering/technologies, general academic interests/achievements, health fields, mathematics. *Creative Arts/Performance:* art/fine arts, music. *Special Characteristics:* general special characteristics.
LOANS *Programs:* FFEL (Subsidized and Unsubsidized Stafford, PLUS), state, college/university.
WORK-STUDY *Federal work-study:* Total amount: $198,981; jobs available. *State or other work-study/employment:* Total amount: $84,735 (100% need-based). Part-time jobs available.
APPLYING FOR FINANCIAL AID *Required financial aid form:* FAFSA.
CONTACT Ms. Georgiana M. Velarde, Assistant Director of Financial Aid, The University of Texas at Brownsville, 80 Fort Brown, Tandy Building, Suite 206, Brownsville, TX 78520-4991, 956-544-8830 or toll-free 800-850-0160 (in-state). *Fax:* 956-544-8229. *E-mail:* gvelarde@utb.edu.

THE UNIVERSITY OF TEXAS AT DALLAS
Richardson, TX

Tuition & fees (TX res): $6831 **Average undergraduate aid package: $9016**

ABOUT THE INSTITUTION State-supported, coed. Awards: bachelor's, master's, and doctoral degrees. 35 undergraduate majors. Total enrollment: 14,480. Undergraduates: 9,412. Freshmen: 1,057. Both federal and institutional methodology are used as a basis for awarding need-based institutional aid.
UNDERGRADUATE EXPENSES for 2005–06 *Application fee:* $50. *Tuition, state resident:* full-time $6831; part-time $198 per credit. *Tuition, nonresident:* full-time $15,111; part-time $474 per credit. Full-time tuition and fees vary according to course load, degree level, and program. Part-time tuition and fees vary according to course load, degree level, and program. *College room and board:* $6244. Room and board charges vary according to board plan and housing facility. *Payment plan:* Installment.
FRESHMAN FINANCIAL AID (Fall 2005, est.) 863 applied for aid; of those 40% were deemed to have need. 100% of freshmen with need received aid; of those 45% had need fully met. *Average percent of need met:* 80% (excluding resources awarded to replace EFC). *Average financial aid package:* $11,115 (excluding resources awarded to replace EFC). 38% of all full-time freshmen had no need and received non-need-based gift aid.
UNDERGRADUATE FINANCIAL AID (Fall 2005, est.) 4,477 applied for aid; of those 59% were deemed to have need. 100% of undergraduates with need received aid; of those 29% had need fully met. *Average percent of need met:* 72% (excluding resources awarded to replace EFC). *Average financial aid package:* $9016 (excluding resources awarded to replace EFC). 19% of all full-time undergraduates had no need and received non-need-based gift aid.
GIFT AID (NEED-BASED) *Total amount:* $12,578,189 (60% federal, 30% state, 10% institutional). *Receiving aid:* Freshmen: 23% (242); All full-time undergraduates: 30% (2,002). *Average award:* Freshmen: $5103; Undergraduates: $4208. *Scholarships, grants, and awards:* Federal Pell, FSEOG, state, private, college/university gift aid from institutional funds.
GIFT AID (NON-NEED-BASED) *Total amount:* $18,041,653 (85% institutional, 15% external sources). *Receiving aid:* Freshmen: 18% (195); Undergraduates: 7% (471). *Average Award:* Freshmen: $8005; Undergraduates: $8114. *Scholarships, grants, and awards by category: Academic Interests/Achievement:* biological sciences, business, computer science, engineering/technologies, general academic interests/achievements, mathematics, physical sciences. *Special Achievements/Activities:* general special achievements/activities, leadership. *Special Characteristics:* adult students, children of public servants, general special characteristics, handicapped students, international students, local/state students, members of minority groups, out-of-state students, public servants, veterans, veterans' children. *Tuition waivers:* Full or partial for senior citizens. **ROTC:** Army cooperative, Air Force cooperative.
LOANS *Student loans:* $38,400,453 (44% need-based, 56% non-need-based). *Average need-based loan:* Freshmen: $3199; Undergraduates: $4670. *Parent loans:* $25,812,223 (100% non-need-based). *Programs:* FFEL (Subsidized and Unsubsidized Stafford, PLUS), Perkins, state, college/university.
WORK-STUDY *Federal work-study:* Total amount: $2,345,788; 466 jobs averaging $5027. *State or other work-study/employment:* Total amount: $101,096 (36% need-based, 64% non-need-based). 22 part-time jobs averaging $4558.
APPLYING FOR FINANCIAL AID *Required financial aid form:* FAFSA. *Financial aid deadline (priority):* 4/12. *Notification date:* Continuous beginning 3/1. Students must reply within 3 weeks of notification.
CONTACT Maria Ramos, Director of Financial Aid, The University of Texas at Dallas, 2601 North Floyd Road, MC12, PO Box 830688, MC12, Richardson, TX 75083, 972-883-2941 or toll-free 800-889-2443. *Fax:* 972-883-2947. *E-mail:* ramos@utdallas.edu.

THE UNIVERSITY OF TEXAS AT EL PASO
El Paso, TX

Tuition & fees (TX res): $5064 **Average undergraduate aid package: $9043**

ABOUT THE INSTITUTION State-supported, coed. Awards: bachelor's, master's, and doctoral degrees. 61 undergraduate majors. Total enrollment: 19,268. Undergraduates: 16,037. Freshmen: 2,493. Federal methodology is used as a basis for awarding need-based institutional aid.
UNDERGRADUATE EXPENSES for 2005–06 *Tuition, state resident:* full-time $3930; part-time $131 per credit hour. *Tuition, nonresident:* full-time $12,210. Part-time tuition and fees vary according to course load. *College room and board: room only:* $4095. Room and board charges vary according to housing facility. *Payment plan:* Installment.
FRESHMAN FINANCIAL AID (Fall 2004) 1950 applied for aid; of those 79% were deemed to have need. 99% of freshmen with need received aid; of those 14% had need fully met. *Average percent of need met:* 71% (excluding resources awarded to replace EFC). *Average financial aid package:* $7823 (excluding resources awarded to replace EFC). 8% of all full-time freshmen had no need and received non-need-based gift aid.
UNDERGRADUATE FINANCIAL AID (Fall 2004) 7,737 applied for aid; of those 80% were deemed to have need. 98% of undergraduates with need received aid; of those 27% had need fully met. *Average percent of need met:* 76% (excluding resources awarded to replace EFC). *Average financial aid package:* $9043 (excluding resources awarded to replace EFC). 7% of all full-time undergraduates had no need and received non-need-based gift aid.
GIFT AID (NEED-BASED) *Total amount:* $36,787,046 (71% federal, 19% state, 10% institutional). *Receiving aid:* Freshmen: 58% (1,381); All full-time undergraduates: 56% (5,267). *Average award:* Freshmen: $5068; Undergraduates: $4732. *Scholarships, grants, and awards:* Federal Pell, FSEOG, state, college/university gift aid from institutional funds, Federal Nursing.
GIFT AID (NON-NEED-BASED) *Total amount:* $4,530,028 (1% federal, 9% state, 71% institutional, 19% external sources). *Receiving aid:* Freshmen: 9% (214); Undergraduates: 7% (631). *Average Award:* Freshmen: $1208; Undergraduates: $1673. *Scholarships, grants, and awards by category: Academic Interests/Achievement:* biological sciences, business, communication, computer science, education, engineering/technologies, English, general academic interests/achievements, health fields, humanities, international studies, mathematics, military science, physical sciences. *Creative Arts/Performance:* applied art and design, art/fine arts, journalism/publications, music, performing arts, theater/drama. *Special Achievements/Activities:* cheerleading/drum major, leadership. *Special Characteristics:* ethnic background, international students, local/state students, members of minority groups, out-of-state students. **ROTC:** Army, Air Force.
LOANS *Student loans:* $46,929,132 (100% need-based). 47% of past graduating class borrowed through all loan programs. *Average indebtedness per student:* $6538. *Average need-based loan:* Freshmen: $2773; Undergraduates: $4800.

The University of Texas at El Paso

Parent loans: $4,960,045 (100% non-need-based). *Programs:* FFEL (Subsidized and Unsubsidized Stafford, PLUS), Perkins, Federal Nursing, state, college/university.

WORK-STUDY *Federal work-study:* Total amount: $1,870,535; 854 jobs averaging $2097. *State or other work-study/employment:* Total amount: $197,268 (100% need-based). 63 part-time jobs averaging $2563.

ATHLETIC AWARDS Total amount: $3,064,172 (100% non-need-based).

APPLYING FOR FINANCIAL AID *Required financial aid forms:* FAFSA, institution's own form. *Financial aid deadline (priority):* 3/15. *Notification date:* 6/30. Students must reply within 2 weeks of notification.

CONTACT Mr. Raul Lerma, Director of Financial Aid, The University of Texas at El Paso, 500 West University Avenue, El Paso, TX 79968-0001, 915-747-7378 or toll-free 877-746-4636.

THE UNIVERSITY OF TEXAS AT SAN ANTONIO
San Antonio, TX

Tuition & fees (TX res): $5858   **Average undergraduate aid package:** $6381

ABOUT THE INSTITUTION State-supported, coed. Awards: bachelor's, master's, and doctoral degrees. 56 undergraduate majors. Total enrollment: 27,337. Undergraduates: 23,431. Freshmen: 4,482. Federal methodology is used as a basis for awarding need-based institutional aid.

UNDERGRADUATE EXPENSES for 2005–06 *Application fee:* $30. *Tuition, state resident:* full-time $3,968; part-time $132.25 per hour. *Tuition, nonresident:* full-time $12,248; part-time $408.25 per hour. *College room and board:* $7190; *room only:* $4770. *Payment plans:* Installment, deferred payment.

FRESHMAN FINANCIAL AID (Fall 2004) 3518 applied for aid; of those 74% were deemed to have need. 95% of freshmen with need received aid; of those 10% had need fully met. *Average percent of need met:* 54% (excluding resources awarded to replace EFC). *Average financial aid package:* $5624 (excluding resources awarded to replace EFC). 5% of all full-time freshmen had no need and received non-need-based gift aid.

UNDERGRADUATE FINANCIAL AID (Fall 2004) 15,273 applied for aid; of those 81% were deemed to have need. 97% of undergraduates with need received aid; of those 11% had need fully met. *Average percent of need met:* 52% (excluding resources awarded to replace EFC). *Average financial aid package:* $6381 (excluding resources awarded to replace EFC). 3% of all full-time undergraduates had no need and received non-need-based gift aid.

GIFT AID (NEED-BASED) *Total amount:* $35,399,375 (72% federal, 28% state). *Receiving aid:* Freshmen: 42% (1,926); All full-time undergraduates: 46% (9,177). *Average award:* Freshmen: $4198; Undergraduates: $3807. *Scholarships, grants, and awards:* Federal Pell, FSEOG, state, private, college/university gift aid from institutional funds.

GIFT AID (NON-NEED-BASED) *Total amount:* $9,912,234 (4% state, 65% institutional, 31% external sources). *Receiving aid:* Freshmen: 15% (706); Undergraduates: 10% (1,936). *Average Award:* Freshmen: $1308; Undergraduates: $1539. *Scholarships, grants, and awards by category:* Academic Interests/Achievement: agriculture, architecture, area/ethnic studies, biological sciences, business, communication, computer science, education, engineering/technologies, English, foreign languages, general academic interests/achievements, humanities, mathematics, physical sciences, social sciences. *Creative Arts/Performance:* art/fine arts, debating, music. *Special Achievements/Activities:* general special achievements/activities. *Special Characteristics:* ethnic background, general special characteristics, handicapped students, local/state students, out-of-state students. *ROTC:* Army, Air Force.

LOANS *Student loans:* $85,139,784 (57% need-based, 43% non-need-based). 66% of past graduating class borrowed through all loan programs. *Average indebtedness per student:* $16,054. *Average need-based loan:* Freshmen: $2388; Undergraduates: $3669. *Parent loans:* $4,331,148 (100% non-need-based). *Programs:* FFEL (Subsidized and Unsubsidized Stafford, PLUS), Perkins, state, college/university.

WORK-STUDY *Federal work-study:* Total amount: $1,219,026; 542 jobs averaging $4000. *State or other work-study/employment:* Total amount: $451,305 (100% need-based). 330 part-time jobs averaging $4000.

ATHLETIC AWARDS Total amount: $1,585,366 (100% non-need-based).

APPLYING FOR FINANCIAL AID *Required financial aid forms:* FAFSA, institution's own form. *Financial aid deadline (priority):* 3/31. *Notification date:* Continuous beginning 4/1. Students must reply within 4 weeks of notification.

CONTACT Kim Canady, Assistant Director of Student Financial Aid, The University of Texas at San Antonio, 6900 North Loop 1604 West, San Antonio, TX 78249, 210-458-8000 or toll-free 800-669-0919. *Fax:* 210-458-4638. *E-mail:* financialaid@utsa.edu.

THE UNIVERSITY OF TEXAS AT TYLER
Tyler, TX

Tuition & fees (TX res): $4250   **Average undergraduate aid package:** $7270

ABOUT THE INSTITUTION State-supported, coed. Awards: bachelor's and master's degrees. 38 undergraduate majors. Total enrollment: 5,748. Undergraduates: 4,657. Freshmen: 547. Federal methodology is used as a basis for awarding need-based institutional aid.

UNDERGRADUATE EXPENSES for 2005–06 *Tuition, state resident:* full-time $3450; part-time $115 per semester hour. *Tuition, nonresident:* full-time $11,730; part-time $391 per semester hour. Full-time tuition and fees vary according to course load and degree level. *College room and board:* $7010. Room and board charges vary according to housing facility. *Payment plan:* Installment.

FRESHMAN FINANCIAL AID (Fall 2005, est.) 350 applied for aid; of those 63% were deemed to have need. 100% of freshmen with need received aid; of those 26% had need fully met. *Average percent of need met:* 55% (excluding resources awarded to replace EFC). *Average financial aid package:* $7054 (excluding resources awarded to replace EFC). 28% of all full-time freshmen had no need and received non-need-based gift aid.

UNDERGRADUATE FINANCIAL AID (Fall 2005, est.) 2,276 applied for aid; of those 79% were deemed to have need. 100% of undergraduates with need received aid; of those 21% had need fully met. *Average percent of need met:* 68% (excluding resources awarded to replace EFC). *Average financial aid package:* $7270 (excluding resources awarded to replace EFC). 11% of all full-time undergraduates had no need and received non-need-based gift aid.

GIFT AID (NEED-BASED) *Total amount:* $7,398,650 (60% federal, 16% state, 18% institutional, 6% external sources). *Receiving aid:* Freshmen: 34% (193); All full-time undergraduates: 42% (1,509). *Average award:* Freshmen: $5500; Undergraduates: $4160. *Scholarships, grants, and awards:* Federal Pell, FSEOG, state, private, college/university gift aid from institutional funds, Texas Grant, Teach for Texas Conditional Prog, Institutional Grants (Education Affordability Prog).

GIFT AID (NON-NEED-BASED) *Total amount:* $2,624,514 (1% state, 70% institutional, 29% external sources). *Receiving aid:* Freshmen: 9% (50); Undergraduates: 4% (134). *Average Award:* Freshmen: $3230; Undergraduates: $2496. *Scholarships, grants, and awards by category:* Academic Interests/Achievement: 7,325 awards ($9,022,790 total): engineering/technologies, general academic interests/achievements. *Tuition waivers:* Full or partial for employees or children of employees, senior citizens.

LOANS *Student loans:* $16,695,708 (67% need-based, 33% non-need-based). 55% of past graduating class borrowed through all loan programs. *Average indebtedness per student:* $14,581. *Average need-based loan:* Freshmen: $2087; Undergraduates: $3512. *Parent loans:* $5,497,564 (18% need-based, 82% non-need-based). *Programs:* FFEL (Subsidized and Unsubsidized Stafford, PLUS), state.

WORK-STUDY *Federal work-study:* Total amount: $250,698; 102 jobs averaging $2458. *State or other work-study/employment:* Total amount: $155,382 (59% need-based, 41% non-need-based). 38 part-time jobs averaging $2379.

APPLYING FOR FINANCIAL AID *Required financial aid form:* FAFSA. *Financial aid deadline (priority):* 4/1. *Notification date:* Continuous beginning 4/15. Students must reply within 2 weeks of notification.

CONTACT Candice A. Lindsey, Associate Dean for Enrollment Management, Financial Aid, and Registrar's Office, The University of Texas at Tyler, 3900 University Boulevard Adm 213, Tyler, TX 75799-0001, 903-566-7221 or toll-free 800-UTTYLER (in-state). *Fax:* 903-566-7183. *E-mail:* cgarner@uttyler.edu.

THE UNIVERSITY OF TEXAS HEALTH SCIENCE CENTER AT HOUSTON
Houston, TX

Tuition & fees (TX res): $5602   **Average undergraduate aid package:** $15,838

ABOUT THE INSTITUTION State-supported, coed. Awards: bachelor's, master's, doctoral, and first professional degrees and post-master's certificates. 2

undergraduate majors. Total enrollment: 3,399. Undergraduates: 381. Federal methodology is used as a basis for awarding need-based institutional aid.

UNDERGRADUATE EXPENSES for 2005–06 *Application fee:* $30. *Tuition, state resident:* full-time $4905; part-time $105 per hour. *Tuition, nonresident:* full-time $16,571; part-time $364.50 per hour. Part-time tuition and fees vary according to course load. *Payment plan:* Installment.

UNDERGRADUATE FINANCIAL AID (Fall 2004) 265 applied for aid; of those 82% were deemed to have need. 100% of undergraduates with need received aid. *Average percent of need met:* 95% (excluding resources awarded to replace EFC). *Average financial aid package:* $15,838 (excluding resources awarded to replace EFC).

GIFT AID (NEED-BASED) *Total amount:* $774,860 (39% federal, 19% state, 32% institutional, 10% external sources). *Receiving aid:* Entering class: 38% (160); All full-time undergraduates: 39% (148). *Average award:* Freshmen: $5750; Undergraduates: $5059. *Scholarships, grants, and awards:* Federal Pell, FSEOG, state, private, college/university gift aid from institutional funds.

GIFT AID (NON-NEED-BASED) *ROTC:* Army cooperative.

LOANS *Student loans:* $3,220,734 (100% need-based). 95% of past graduating class borrowed through all loan programs. *Average indebtedness per student:* $19,235. *Average need-based loan:* Freshmen: $6850; Undergraduates: $6200. *Parent loans:* $402,686 (100% need-based). *Programs:* FFEL (Subsidized and Unsubsidized Stafford, PLUS), Perkins, state, college/university, alternative loans.

APPLYING FOR FINANCIAL AID *Required financial aid forms:* FAFSA, institution's own form. *Financial aid deadline:* Continuous. *Notification date:* Continuous.

CONTACT Ms. Wanda Williams, Administrative Services Officer, The University of Texas Health Science Center at Houston, PO Box 20036, Houston, TX 77225, 713-500-3860. *Fax:* 713-500-3863. *E-mail:* wanta.k.williams@uth.tmc.edu.

THE UNIVERSITY OF TEXAS HEALTH SCIENCE CENTER AT SAN ANTONIO
San Antonio, TX

CONTACT Robert T. Lawson, Financial Aid Administrator, The University of Texas Health Science Center at San Antonio, 7703 Floyd Curl Drive, MSC 7708, San Antonio, TX 78284, 210-567-0025. *Fax:* 210-567-6643.

THE UNIVERSITY OF TEXAS MEDICAL BRANCH
Galveston, TX

Tuition & fees (TX res): $2690　　**Average undergraduate aid package:** N/A

ABOUT THE INSTITUTION State-supported, coed. Awards: bachelor's, master's, doctoral, and first professional degrees. 3 undergraduate majors. Total enrollment: 2,198. Undergraduates: 499. Entering class: . Federal methodology is used as a basis for awarding need-based institutional aid.

UNDERGRADUATE EXPENSES for 2005–06 *Application fee:* $25. *Tuition, state resident:* full-time $2160; part-time $90 per credit hour. *Tuition, nonresident:* full-time $8784; part-time $366 per credit hour. *College room and board: room only:* $2322.

GIFT AID (NEED-BASED) *Total amount:* $843,806 (41% federal, 33% state, 20% institutional, 6% external sources). *Scholarships, grants, and awards:* Federal Pell, FSEOG, state, private, college/university gift aid from institutional funds.

GIFT AID (NON-NEED-BASED) *Total amount:* $5800 (52% institutional, 48% external sources). *Scholarships, grants, and awards by category:* Academic Interests/Achievement: 16 awards ($177,762 total): health fields.

LOANS *Student loans:* $5,125,971 (97% need-based, 3% non-need-based). *Parent loans:* $27,000 (100% need-based). *Programs:* Federal Direct (Subsidized and Unsubsidized Stafford, PLUS), Perkins, Federal Nursing, state, college/university.

WORK-STUDY *Federal work-study:* Total amount: $61,748; 33 jobs averaging $1871.

APPLYING FOR FINANCIAL AID *Required financial aid form:* FAFSA. *Financial aid deadline:* Continuous. *Notification date:* Continuous. Students must reply within 4 weeks of notification.

CONTACT Mr. Carl Gordon, University Financial Aid Officer, The University of Texas Medical Branch, 301 University Boulevard, Galveston, TX 77555-1305, 409-772-1215. *Fax:* 409-772-4466. *E-mail:* enrollment.services@utmb.edu.

The University of Texas–Pan American

THE UNIVERSITY OF TEXAS OF THE PERMIAN BASIN
Odessa, TX

Tuition & fees: N/R　　**Average undergraduate aid package:** $3302

ABOUT THE INSTITUTION State-supported, coed. Awards: bachelor's and master's degrees. 24 undergraduate majors. Total enrollment: 2,695. Undergraduates: 2,012. Freshmen: 226. Federal methodology is used as a basis for awarding need-based institutional aid.

FRESHMAN FINANCIAL AID (Fall 2005, est.) 241 applied for aid; of those 83% were deemed to have need. 100% of freshmen with need received aid; of those 43% had need fully met. *Average percent of need met:* 89% (excluding resources awarded to replace EFC). *Average financial aid package:* $3212 (excluding resources awarded to replace EFC). 7% of all full-time freshmen had no need and received non-need-based gift aid.

UNDERGRADUATE FINANCIAL AID (Fall 2005, est.) 1,440 applied for aid; of those 88% were deemed to have need. 100% of undergraduates with need received aid; of those 13% had need fully met. *Average percent of need met:* 51% (excluding resources awarded to replace EFC). *Average financial aid package:* $3302 (excluding resources awarded to replace EFC). 7% of all full-time undergraduates had no need and received non-need-based gift aid.

GIFT AID (NEED-BASED) *Total amount:* $5,358,295 (60% federal, 10% state, 25% institutional, 5% external sources). *Receiving aid:* Freshmen: 26% (79); All full-time undergraduates: 37% (695). *Average award:* Freshmen: $3150; Undergraduates: $2327. *Scholarships, grants, and awards:* Federal Pell, FSEOG, state, private, college/university gift aid from institutional funds.

GIFT AID (NON-NEED-BASED) *Total amount:* $1,308,177 (11% federal, 21% state, 57% institutional, 11% external sources). *Receiving aid:* Freshmen: 7% (22); Undergraduates: 14% (262). *Average Award:* Freshmen: $1000; Undergraduates: $765. *Scholarships, grants, and awards by category:* Academic Interests/Achievement: 1,389 awards ($1,334,000 total): general academic interests/achievements. Creative Arts/Performance: 16 awards ($2000 total): art/fine arts, dance, general creative arts/performance, music.

LOANS *Student loans:* $7,830,458 (55% need-based, 45% non-need-based). *Average need-based loan:* Freshmen: $2818; Undergraduates: $1105. *Parent loans:* $113,604 (100% non-need-based). *Programs:* FFEL (Subsidized and Unsubsidized Stafford, PLUS), state.

WORK-STUDY *Federal work-study:* Total amount: $130,000; 84 jobs averaging $2300. *State or other work-study/employment:* Total amount: $19,339 (100% need-based). 12 part-time jobs averaging $650.

ATHLETIC AWARDS *Total amount:* $302,960 (100% non-need-based).

APPLYING FOR FINANCIAL AID *Required financial aid form:* FAFSA. *Financial aid deadline (priority):* 5/1. *Notification date:* Continuous beginning 5/1. Students must reply within 2 weeks of notification.

CONTACT Mr. Robert L. Vasquez, Director, Office of Student Financial Aid, The University of Texas of the Permian Basin, 4901 East University Blvd., Odessa, TX 79762, 432-552-2620 or toll-free 866-552-UTPB. *Fax:* 432-552-2621. *E-mail:* finaid@utpb.edu.

THE UNIVERSITY OF TEXAS–PAN AMERICAN
Edinburg, TX

Tuition & fees (TX res): $4160　　**Average undergraduate aid package:** $7835

ABOUT THE INSTITUTION State-supported, coed. Awards: bachelor's, master's, and doctoral degrees and post-bachelor's and post-master's certificates. 58 undergraduate majors. Total enrollment: 17,048. Undergraduates: 14,942. Freshmen: 2,434. Federal methodology is used as a basis for awarding need-based institutional aid.

UNDERGRADUATE EXPENSES for 2006–07 *Tuition, state resident:* full-time $3348; part-time $116 per semester hour. *Tuition, nonresident:* full-time $11,598; part-time $391 per semester hour. *Required fees:* full-time $812; $98 per semester hour. *College room and board:* $4333; *room only:* $2406.

FRESHMAN FINANCIAL AID (Fall 2004) 1404 applied for aid; of those 96% were deemed to have need. 97% of freshmen with need received aid; of those 3% had need fully met. *Average percent of need met:* 57% (excluding resources

The University of Texas–Pan American

awarded to replace EFC). *Average financial aid package:* $7271 (excluding resources awarded to replace EFC). 7% of all full-time freshmen had no need and received non-need-based gift aid.

UNDERGRADUATE FINANCIAL AID (Fall 2004) 7,903 applied for aid; of those 97% were deemed to have need. 96% of undergraduates with need received aid; of those 3% had need fully met. *Average percent of need met:* 67% (excluding resources awarded to replace EFC). *Average financial aid package:* $7835 (excluding resources awarded to replace EFC). 5% of all full-time undergraduates had no need and received non-need-based gift aid.

GIFT AID (NEED-BASED) *Total amount:* $44,326,980 (52% federal, 41% state, 5% institutional, 2% external sources). *Receiving aid:* Freshmen: 81% (1,247); All full-time undergraduates: 77% (6,921). *Average award:* Freshmen: $7435; Undergraduates: $8004. *Scholarships, grants, and awards:* Federal Pell, FSEOG, state, private, college/university gift aid from institutional funds.

GIFT AID (NON-NEED-BASED) *Total amount:* $1,641,538 (7% federal, 63% institutional, 30% external sources). *Receiving aid:* Freshmen: 2% (28); Undergraduates: 1% (100). *Average Award:* Freshmen: $4932; Undergraduates: $4609. *Scholarships, grants, and awards by category: Academic Interests/Achievement:* 1,286 awards ($2,713,027 total): biological sciences, business, communication, computer science, education, engineering/technologies, English, general academic interests/achievements, health fields, mathematics, military science, premedicine, social sciences. *Creative Arts/Performance:* 83 awards ($39,735 total): art/fine arts, dance, journalism/publications, music, theater/drama. *Special Achievements/Activities:* 193 awards ($241,280 total): cheerleading/drum major, community service, general special achievements/activities, leadership, memberships. *Special Characteristics:* 160 awards ($313,341 total): ethnic background, general special characteristics, international students, local/state students, out-of-state students, veterans. *ROTC:* Army.

LOANS *Student loans:* $19,617,850 (100% need-based). 87% of past graduating class borrowed through all loan programs. *Average indebtedness per student:* $11,499. *Average need-based loan:* Freshmen: $2077; Undergraduates: $3823. *Parent loans:* $168,884 (56% need-based, 44% non-need-based). *Programs:* FFEL (Subsidized and Unsubsidized Stafford, PLUS), Perkins, college/university.

WORK-STUDY *Federal work-study:* Total amount: $2,062,145; 822 jobs averaging $2509. *State or other work-study/employment:* Total amount: $147,933 (99% need-based, 1% non-need-based). 112 part-time jobs averaging $1321.

ATHLETIC AWARDS *Total amount:* $761,769 (40% need-based, 60% non-need-based).

APPLYING FOR FINANCIAL AID *Required financial aid form:* FAFSA. *Financial aid deadline (priority):* 3/1. *Notification date:* Continuous beginning 3/15. Students must reply within 2 weeks of notification.

CONTACT Mrs. Elaine Rivera, Executive Director of Student Financial Services, The University of Texas–Pan American, 1201 West University Drive, Edinburg, TX 78541, 956-381-2190. *Fax:* 956-381-2396. *E-mail:* eriverall@panam.edu.

THE UNIVERSITY OF TEXAS SOUTHWESTERN MEDICAL CENTER AT DALLAS
Dallas, TX

ABOUT THE INSTITUTION State-supported, coed. Awards: bachelor's, master's, doctoral, and first professional degrees and post-bachelor's certificates. 4 undergraduate majors. Total enrollment: 2,393. Undergraduates: 121.

GIFT AID (NEED-BASED) *Scholarships, grants, and awards:* Federal Pell, FSEOG, state, private, college/university gift aid from institutional funds.

GIFT AID (NON-NEED-BASED) *Scholarships, grants, and awards by category: Special Achievements/Activities:* community service.

LOANS *Programs:* FFEL (Subsidized and Unsubsidized Stafford, PLUS), Perkins, state, college/university, alternative loans.

APPLYING FOR FINANCIAL AID *Required financial aid forms:* FAFSA, we do not enroll freshmen, they must have 60-90 hours prior to attending U T Southwestern.

CONTACT Ms. June M. Perry, Associate Director of Student Financial Aid, The University of Texas Southwestern Medical Center at Dallas, 5323 Harry Hines Boulevard, Dallas, TX 75390-9064, 214-648-3611. *Fax:* 214-648-3289. *E-mail:* june.perry@utsouthwestern.edu.

THE UNIVERSITY OF THE ARTS
Philadelphia, PA

CONTACT Office of Financial Aid, The University of the Arts, 320 South Broad Street, Philadelphia, PA 19102-4944, 800-616-ARTS Ext. 6170 or toll-free 800-616-ARTS. *E-mail:* finaid@uarts.edu.

UNIVERSITY OF THE CUMBERLANDS
Williamsburg, KY

Tuition & fees: $13,658 | **Average undergraduate aid package: $13,277**

ABOUT THE INSTITUTION Independent Kentucky Baptist, coed. Awards: associate, bachelor's, and master's degrees. 34 undergraduate majors. Total enrollment: 1,843. Undergraduates: 1,633. Freshmen: 433. Federal methodology is used as a basis for awarding need-based institutional aid.

UNDERGRADUATE EXPENSES for 2006–07 *Application fee:* $30. *Comprehensive fee:* $19,984 includes full-time tuition ($13,298), mandatory fees ($360), and room and board ($6326). *Part-time tuition:* $410 per hour. *Part-time fees:* $48.75 per term.

FRESHMAN FINANCIAL AID (Fall 2005, est.) 402 applied for aid; of those 88% were deemed to have need. 100% of freshmen with need received aid; of those 59% had need fully met. *Average percent of need met:* 93% (excluding resources awarded to replace EFC). *Average financial aid package:* $14,014 (excluding resources awarded to replace EFC). 5% of all full-time freshmen had no need and received non-need-based gift aid.

UNDERGRADUATE FINANCIAL AID (Fall 2005, est.) 1,289 applied for aid; of those 91% were deemed to have need. 100% of undergraduates with need received aid; of those 60% had need fully met. *Average percent of need met:* 94% (excluding resources awarded to replace EFC). *Average financial aid package:* $13,277 (excluding resources awarded to replace EFC). 4% of all full-time undergraduates had no need and received non-need-based gift aid.

GIFT AID (NEED-BASED) *Total amount:* $5,270,205 (40% federal, 45% state, 14% institutional, 1% external sources). *Receiving aid:* Freshmen: 57% (243); All full-time undergraduates: 61% (860). *Average award:* Freshmen: $6538; Undergraduates: $6032. *Scholarships, grants, and awards:* Federal Pell, FSEOG, state, private, college/university gift aid from institutional funds.

GIFT AID (NON-NEED-BASED) *Total amount:* $6,046,420 (16% state, 80% institutional, 4% external sources). *Receiving aid:* Freshmen: 83% (353); Undergraduates: 72% (1,021). *Average Award:* Freshmen: $5989; Undergraduates: $6136. *Scholarships, grants, and awards by category: Academic Interests/Achievement:* 855 awards ($2,835,010 total): general academic interests/achievements. *Creative Arts/Performance:* 119 awards ($198,531 total): art/fine arts, debating, music, theater/drama. *Special Achievements/Activities:* 281 awards ($178,463 total): cheerleading/drum major, community service, religious involvement. *Special Characteristics:* 318 awards ($377,864 total): children and siblings of alumni, children of faculty/staff, relatives of clergy, siblings of current students. *ROTC:* Army.

LOANS *Student loans:* $4,909,607 (60% need-based, 40% non-need-based). 58% of past graduating class borrowed through all loan programs. *Average indebtedness per student:* $16,083. *Average need-based loan:* Freshmen: $3319; Undergraduates: $3796. *Parent loans:* $810,788 (100% non-need-based). *Programs:* FFEL (Subsidized and Unsubsidized Stafford, PLUS), Perkins, college/university.

WORK-STUDY *Federal work-study:* Total amount: $790,470; 449 jobs averaging $1761. *State or other work-study/employment:* Total amount: $396,542 (100% need-based). 213 part-time jobs averaging $1862.

ATHLETIC AWARDS *Total amount:* $2,212,751 (100% non-need-based).

APPLYING FOR FINANCIAL AID *Required financial aid form:* FAFSA. *Financial aid deadline (priority):* 3/1. *Notification date:* Continuous beginning 4/1. Students must reply within 2 weeks of notification.

CONTACT Mr. Steve Allen, Director of Student Financial Planning, University of the Cumberlands, 6190 College Station Drive, Williamsburg, KY 40769-1372, 606-549-2200 Ext. 4220 or toll-free 800-343-1609. *Fax:* 606-539-4220. *E-mail:* finplan@ucumberlands.edu.

UNIVERSITY OF THE DISTRICT OF COLUMBIA
Washington, DC

Tuition & fees (area res): $2070 **Average undergraduate aid package: $6010**

ABOUT THE INSTITUTION District-supported, coed. Awards: associate, bachelor's, and master's degrees. 102 undergraduate majors. Total enrollment: 5,364. Undergraduates: 5,170. Freshmen: 1,137. Federal methodology is used as a basis for awarding need-based institutional aid.

UNDERGRADUATE EXPENSES for 2005–06 *Application fee:* $20. *Tuition, area resident:* full-time $1800; part-time $75 per credit. *Tuition, nonresident:* full-time $4440; part-time $185 per credit. *Required fees:* full-time $270; $135 per term part-time. Part-time tuition and fees vary according to course load. *Payment plans:* Installment, deferred payment.

FRESHMAN FINANCIAL AID (Fall 2004) 387 applied for aid; of those 80% were deemed to have need. 95% of freshmen with need received aid; of those 27% had need fully met. *Average percent of need met:* 72% (excluding resources awarded to replace EFC). *Average financial aid package:* $4930 (excluding resources awarded to replace EFC). 6% of all full-time freshmen had no need and received non-need-based gift aid.

UNDERGRADUATE FINANCIAL AID (Fall 2004) 1,812 applied for aid; of those 89% were deemed to have need. 77% of undergraduates with need received aid; of those 30% had need fully met. *Average financial aid package:* $6010 (excluding resources awarded to replace EFC). 4% of all full-time undergraduates had no need and received non-need-based gift aid.

GIFT AID (NEED-BASED) *Total amount:* $5,528,777 (90% federal, 5% state, 5% institutional). *Receiving aid:* Freshmen: 26% (130); All full-time undergraduates: 36% (710). *Average award:* Freshmen: $2875; Undergraduates: $2917. *Scholarships, grants, and awards:* Federal Pell, FSEOG, state, college/university gift aid from institutional funds.

GIFT AID (NON-NEED-BASED) *Total amount:* $221,560 (40% institutional, 60% external sources). *Receiving aid:* Freshmen: 14% (71); Undergraduates: 7% (133). *Average Award:* Freshmen: $3412; Undergraduates: $2252. *Scholarships, grants, and awards by category:* Academic Interests/Achievement: general academic interests/achievements. Creative Arts/Performance: music. Special Characteristics: children of faculty/staff. *Tuition waivers:* Full or partial for employees or children of employees, senior citizens. *ROTC:* Army cooperative, Air Force cooperative.

LOANS *Student loans:* $5,926,522 (81% need-based, 19% non-need-based). 74% of past graduating class borrowed through all loan programs. *Average indebtedness per student:* $16,270. *Average need-based loan:* Freshmen: $2951; Undergraduates: $4587. *Parent loans:* $25,486 (53% need-based, 47% non-need-based). *Programs:* FFEL (Subsidized and Unsubsidized Stafford, PLUS), Perkins, college/university.

WORK-STUDY *Federal work-study:* Total amount: $239,796; 110 jobs averaging $3000. *State or other work-study/employment:* Total amount: $116,978 (100% non-need-based). Part-time jobs available.

ATHLETIC AWARDS Total amount: $1,313,837 (100% non-need-based).

APPLYING FOR FINANCIAL AID *Required financial aid forms:* FAFSA, district aid form, loan request form. *Financial aid deadline (priority):* 3/31. *Notification date:* Continuous beginning 4/1. Students must reply within 2 weeks of notification.

CONTACT Henry Anderson, Director, Officer of Financial Aid, University of the District of Columbia, 4200 Connecticut Avenue NW, Washington, DC 20008-1175, 202-274-6053. *E-mail:* henderson@udc.edu.

UNIVERSITY OF THE INCARNATE WORD
San Antonio, TX

ABOUT THE INSTITUTION Independent Roman Catholic, coed. Awards: associate, bachelor's, master's, doctoral, and first professional degrees. 69 undergraduate majors. Total enrollment: 5,217. Undergraduates: 4,370. Freshmen: 578.

GIFT AID (NEED-BASED) *Scholarships, grants, and awards:* Federal Pell, FSEOG, state, private, college/university gift aid from institutional funds, United Negro College Fund, Federal Nursing.

GIFT AID (NON-NEED-BASED) *Scholarships, grants, and awards by category:* Academic Interests/Achievement: general academic interests/achievements. Creative Arts/Performance: art/fine arts, dance, music, theater/drama. Special Achievements/Activities: religious involvement. Special Characteristics: children of union members/company employees.

LOANS *Programs:* FFEL (Subsidized and Unsubsidized Stafford, PLUS), Perkins, Federal Nursing, state, alternative loans.

WORK-STUDY *Federal work-study:* Total amount: $704,017; 471 jobs averaging $1526. *State or other work-study/employment:* Total amount: $42,383 (100% need-based). 27 part-time jobs averaging $1569.

APPLYING FOR FINANCIAL AID *Required financial aid form:* FAFSA.

CONTACT Ms. Amy Carcanagues, Director of Financial Assistance, University of the Incarnate Word, 4301 Broadway, Box 308, San Antonio, TX 78209, 210-829-6008 or toll-free 800-749-WORD. *Fax:* 210-283-5053. *E-mail:* amyc@universe.uiwtx.edu.

UNIVERSITY OF THE OZARKS
Clarksville, AR

Tuition & fees: $14,950 **Average undergraduate aid package: $16,375**

ABOUT THE INSTITUTION Independent Presbyterian, coed. Awards: bachelor's degrees. 35 undergraduate majors. Total enrollment: 628. Undergraduates: 628. Freshmen: 170. Both federal and institutional methodology are used as a basis for awarding need-based institutional aid.

UNDERGRADUATE EXPENSES for 2006–07 *Comprehensive fee:* $20,210 includes full-time tuition ($14,470), mandatory fees ($480), and room and board ($5260). *Part-time tuition:* $605 per credit hour.

FRESHMAN FINANCIAL AID (Fall 2005, est.) 124 applied for aid; of those 92% were deemed to have need. 100% of freshmen with need received aid; of those 16% had need fully met. *Average percent of need met:* 72% (excluding resources awarded to replace EFC). *Average financial aid package:* $16,008 (excluding resources awarded to replace EFC). 22% of all full-time freshmen had no need and received non-need-based gift aid.

UNDERGRADUATE FINANCIAL AID (Fall 2005, est.) 335 applied for aid; of those 92% were deemed to have need. 100% of undergraduates with need received aid; of those 15% had need fully met. *Average percent of need met:* 70% (excluding resources awarded to replace EFC). *Average financial aid package:* $16,375 (excluding resources awarded to replace EFC). 44% of all full-time undergraduates had no need and received non-need-based gift aid.

GIFT AID (NEED-BASED) *Total amount:* $3,223,300 (20% federal, 7% state, 69% institutional, 4% external sources). *Receiving aid:* Freshmen: 67% (114); All full-time undergraduates: 52% (307). *Average award:* Freshmen: $14,135; Undergraduates: $13,862. *Scholarships, grants, and awards:* Federal Pell, FSEOG, state, private, college/university gift aid from institutional funds.

GIFT AID (NON-NEED-BASED) *Total amount:* $2,650,816 (3% state, 94% institutional, 3% external sources). *Receiving aid:* Freshmen: 62% (106); Undergraduates: 45% (265). *Average Award:* Freshmen: $15,565; Undergraduates: $12,092. *Scholarships, grants, and awards by category:* Academic Interests/Achievement: 324 awards ($1,490,955 total): biological sciences, business, communication, education, English, general academic interests/achievements, humanities, mathematics, premedicine, religion/biblical studies, social sciences. Creative Arts/Performance: 41 awards ($122,562 total): art/fine arts, music, theater/drama. Special Achievements/Activities: 170 awards ($440,569 total): leadership. Special Characteristics: 220 awards ($721,211 total): children and siblings of alumni, children of faculty/staff, general special characteristics, international students, members of minority groups, relatives of clergy, religious affiliation, siblings of current students.

LOANS *Student loans:* $1,683,602 (92% need-based, 8% non-need-based). 50% of past graduating class borrowed through all loan programs. *Average indebtedness per student:* $12,866. *Average need-based loan:* Freshmen: $1271; Undergraduates: $3025. *Parent loans:* $670,924 (54% need-based, 46% non-need-based). *Programs:* FFEL (Subsidized and Unsubsidized Stafford, PLUS), Perkins, college/university.

WORK-STUDY *Federal work-study:* Total amount: $125,510; 122 jobs averaging $806. *State or other work-study/employment:* Total amount: $194,662 (19% need-based, 81% non-need-based). 209 part-time jobs averaging $1494.

APPLYING FOR FINANCIAL AID *Required financial aid form:* FAFSA. *Financial aid deadline (priority):* 2/15. *Notification date:* Continuous beginning 3/15. Students must reply within 2 weeks of notification.

University of the Ozarks

CONTACT Ms. Jana D. Hart, Director of Financial Aid, University of the Ozarks, 415 North College Avenue, Clarksville, AR 72830-2880, 479-979-1221 or toll-free 800-264-8636. *Fax:* 479-979-1355. *E-mail:* jhart@ozarks.edu.

UNIVERSITY OF THE PACIFIC
Stockton, CA

| Tuition & fees: $26,088 | Average undergraduate aid package: $23,050 |

ABOUT THE INSTITUTION Independent, coed. Awards: bachelor's, master's, doctoral, and first professional degrees. 54 undergraduate majors. Total enrollment: 6,196. Undergraduates: 3,457. Freshmen: 800. Federal methodology is used as a basis for awarding need-based institutional aid.

UNDERGRADUATE EXPENSES for 2005–06 *Application fee:* $60. *Comprehensive fee:* $34,566 includes full-time tuition ($25,658), mandatory fees ($430), and room and board ($8478). *College room only:* $5760. Room and board charges vary according to board plan and housing facility. *Part-time tuition:* $886 per unit. Part-time tuition and fees vary according to course load. *Payment plan:* Deferred payment.

FRESHMAN FINANCIAL AID (Fall 2005, est.) 657 applied for aid; of those 100% were deemed to have need. 82% of freshmen with need received aid; of those 29% had need fully met. *Average financial aid package:* $21,946 (excluding resources awarded to replace EFC). 19% of all full-time freshmen had no need and received non-need-based gift aid.

UNDERGRADUATE FINANCIAL AID (Fall 2005, est.) 2,546 applied for aid; of those 88% were deemed to have need. 100% of undergraduates with need received aid; of those 25% had need fully met. *Average financial aid package:* $23,050 (excluding resources awarded to replace EFC). 13% of all full-time undergraduates had no need and received non-need-based gift aid.

GIFT AID (NEED-BASED) *Total amount:* $36,391,602 (11% federal, 24% state, 65% institutional). *Receiving aid:* Freshmen: 66% (529); All full-time undergraduates: 64% (2,152). *Average award:* Freshmen: $17,574; Undergraduates: $17,486. *Scholarships, grants, and awards:* Federal Pell, FSEOG, state, private, college/university gift aid from institutional funds.

GIFT AID (NON-NEED-BASED) *Total amount:* $3,712,784 (100% institutional). *Average Award:* Freshmen: $8388; Undergraduates: $8140. *Scholarships, grants, and awards by category:* Academic Interests/Achievement: 1,257 awards ($10,038,679 total): general academic interests/achievements. *Creative Arts/Performance:* 105 awards ($599,300 total): music. *Special Achievements/Activities:* 24 awards ($60,000 total): religious involvement. *Tuition waivers:* Full or partial for employees or children of employees.

LOANS *Student loans:* $12,713,930 (92% need-based, 8% non-need-based). *Average need-based loan:* Freshmen: $3814; Undergraduates: $5628. *Parent loans:* $6,904,393 (78% need-based, 22% non-need-based). *Programs:* Federal Direct (Subsidized and Unsubsidized Stafford, PLUS), FFEL (Subsidized and Unsubsidized Stafford, PLUS), Perkins, state.

WORK-STUDY *Federal work-study:* Total amount: $3,080,142; 2,290 jobs averaging $1917. *State or other work-study/employment:* Part-time jobs available.

ATHLETIC AWARDS *Total amount:* $3,901,458 (41% need-based, 59% non-need-based).

APPLYING FOR FINANCIAL AID *Required financial aid form:* FAFSA. *Financial aid deadline (priority):* 2/15. *Notification date:* Continuous beginning 3/15.

CONTACT Director of Financial Aid, University of the Pacific, 3601 Pacific Avenue, Stockton, CA 95211-0197, 209-946-2421 or toll-free 800-959-2867.

UNIVERSITY OF THE SACRED HEART
San Juan, PR

CONTACT Ms. Maria Torres, Director of Financial Aid, University of the Sacred Heart, PO Box 12383, San Juan, PR 00914-0383, 787-728-1515 Ext. 3605.

UNIVERSITY OF THE SCIENCES IN PHILADELPHIA
Philadelphia, PA

CONTACT Mr. Nick Flocco, Director of Financial Aid, University of the Sciences in Philadelphia, 600 South 43rd Street, Philadelphia, PA 19104-4495, 215-596-8894 or toll-free 888-996-8747 (in-state). *Fax:* 215-596-8554.

UNIVERSITY OF THE SOUTH
Sewanee, TN

See Sewanee: The University of the South.

UNIVERSITY OF THE VIRGIN ISLANDS
Saint Thomas, VI

| Tuition & fees (VI res): $3726 | Average undergraduate aid package: $4263 |

ABOUT THE INSTITUTION Territory-supported, coed. Awards: associate, bachelor's, and master's degrees. 23 undergraduate majors. Total enrollment: 2,392. Undergraduates: 2,185. Freshmen: 361. Federal methodology is used as a basis for awarding need-based institutional aid.

UNDERGRADUATE EXPENSES for 2005–06 *Application fee:* $25. *Tuition, state resident:* full-time $3300; part-time $110 per credit. *Tuition, nonresident:* full-time $9900; part-time $330 per credit. *Required fees:* full-time $426; $276 per year part-time. Full-time tuition and fees vary according to course load, degree level, and program. Part-time tuition and fees vary according to course load, degree level, and program. *College room and board:* $7550; *room only:* $1100. Room and board charges vary according to board plan and housing facility.

FRESHMAN FINANCIAL AID (Fall 2005, est.) 247 applied for aid; of those 85% were deemed to have need. 96% of freshmen with need received aid; of those 3% had need fully met. *Average percent of need met:* 60% (excluding resources awarded to replace EFC). *Average financial aid package:* $4026 (excluding resources awarded to replace EFC). 3% of all full-time freshmen had no need and received non-need-based gift aid.

UNDERGRADUATE FINANCIAL AID (Fall 2005, est.) 1,118 applied for aid; of those 92% were deemed to have need. 92% of undergraduates with need received aid; of those 2% had need fully met. *Average percent of need met:* 45% (excluding resources awarded to replace EFC). *Average financial aid package:* $4263 (excluding resources awarded to replace EFC). 1% of all full-time undergraduates had no need and received non-need-based gift aid.

GIFT AID (NEED-BASED) *Total amount:* $2,724,665 (91% federal, 9% institutional). *Receiving aid:* Freshmen: 62% (189); All full-time undergraduates: 77% (908). *Average award:* Freshmen: $3454; Undergraduates: $3277. *Scholarships, grants, and awards:* Federal Pell, FSEOG, state, college/university gift aid from institutional funds, Federal Nursing.

GIFT AID (NON-NEED-BASED) *Total amount:* $511,200 (100% institutional). *Receiving aid:* Freshmen: 9% (26); Undergraduates: 8% (93). *Average Award:* Freshmen: $4322; Undergraduates: $4384. *Scholarships, grants, and awards by category:* Academic Interests/Achievement: 125 awards ($511,200 total). *Special Characteristics:* $145,000 total: children of faculty/staff, veterans. *Tuition waivers:* Full or partial for employees or children of employees, senior citizens.

ROTC: Army.

LOANS *Student loans:* $1,452,707 (81% need-based, 19% non-need-based). 21% of past graduating class borrowed through all loan programs. *Average indebtedness per student:* $3380. *Average need-based loan:* Freshmen: $1523; Undergraduates: $2387. *Parent loans:* $204,205 (100% need-based). *Programs:* Federal Direct (Subsidized and Unsubsidized Stafford, PLUS), Perkins, college/university.

WORK-STUDY *Federal work-study:* Total amount: $17,179; 17 jobs averaging $1010. *State or other work-study/employment:* Total amount: $11,509 (100% need-based). 8 part-time jobs averaging $1440.

ATHLETIC AWARDS *Total amount:* $23,869 (100% non-need-based).

APPLYING FOR FINANCIAL AID *Required financial aid form:* FAFSA. *Financial aid deadline (priority):* 3/1. *Notification date:* Continuous beginning 5/15. Students must reply within 2 weeks of notification.

CONTACT Mavis M. Gilchrist, Director of Financial Aid, University of the Virgin Islands, RR #2, Box 10,000, Kingshill, St. Croix, VI 00850, 340-692-4186. *Fax:* 340-692-4145. *E-mail:* mgilchr@uvi.edu.

UNIVERSITY OF THE WEST
Rosemead, CA

CONTACT Dr. Teresa Ku, Director of Student Services, University of the West, 1409 Walnut Grove Avenue, Rosemead, CA 91770, 626-571-8811 Ext. 355. *Fax:* 626-571-1413. *E-mail:* naikuangk@hlu.edu.

THE UNIVERSITY OF TOLEDO
Toledo, OH

Tuition & fees (OH res): $7494 **Average undergraduate aid package: $6979**

ABOUT THE INSTITUTION State-supported, coed. Awards: associate, bachelor's, master's, doctoral, and first professional degrees and post-bachelor's and post-master's certificates. 173 undergraduate majors. Total enrollment: 19,480. Undergraduates: 16,366. Freshmen: 3,025. Federal methodology is used as a basis for awarding need-based institutional aid.

UNDERGRADUATE EXPENSES for 2005–06 *Application fee:* $40. *Tuition, state resident:* full-time $6430; part-time $311 per semester hour. *Tuition, nonresident:* full-time $15,241; part-time $679 per semester hour. Full-time tuition and fees vary according to course load, program, and reciprocity agreements. Part-time tuition and fees vary according to course load, program, and reciprocity agreements. *College room and board:* $8312. Room and board charges vary according to board plan, housing facility, and location. *Payment plan:* Installment.

FRESHMAN FINANCIAL AID (Fall 2005, est.) 2307 applied for aid; of those 75% were deemed to have need. 100% of freshmen with need received aid; of those 10% had need fully met. *Average percent of need met:* 48% (excluding resources awarded to replace EFC). *Average financial aid package:* $6364 (excluding resources awarded to replace EFC). 18% of all full-time freshmen had no need and received non-need-based gift aid.

UNDERGRADUATE FINANCIAL AID (Fall 2005, est.) 9,788 applied for aid; of those 79% were deemed to have need. 100% of undergraduates with need received aid; of those 10% had need fully met. *Average percent of need met:* 54% (excluding resources awarded to replace EFC). *Average financial aid package:* $6979 (excluding resources awarded to replace EFC). 15% of all full-time undergraduates had no need and received non-need-based gift aid.

GIFT AID (NEED-BASED) *Total amount:* $29,325,503 (44% federal, 16% state, 35% institutional, 5% external sources). *Receiving aid:* Freshmen: 53% (1,435); All full-time undergraduates: 45% (5,852). *Average award:* Freshmen: $4901; Undergraduates: $4746. *Scholarships, grants, and awards:* Federal Pell, FSEOG, state, private, college/university gift aid from institutional funds.

GIFT AID (NON-NEED-BASED) *Total amount:* $7,655,759 (11% state, 82% institutional, 7% external sources). *Receiving aid:* Freshmen: 20% (539); Undergraduates: 17% (2,240). *Average Award:* Freshmen: $3019; Undergraduates: $3120. *Scholarships, grants, and awards by category: Academic Interests/Achievement:* 5,412 awards ($13,835,648 total): biological sciences, business, communication, education, engineering/technologies, English, foreign languages, general academic interests/achievements, health fields, humanities, international studies, library science, mathematics, physical sciences, premedicine, social sciences. *Creative Arts/Performance:* 99 awards ($142,445 total): art/fine arts, general creative arts/performance, music, performing arts, theater/drama. *Special Achievements/Activities:* 237 awards ($318,720 total): cheerleading/drum major, general special achievements/activities, hobbies/interests, leadership, memberships, religious involvement. *Special Characteristics:* 1,264 awards ($2,339,615 total): adult students, children and siblings of alumni, children of faculty/staff, children of public servants, children of union members/company employees, ethnic background, general special characteristics, handicapped students, international students, members of minority groups, previous college experience, public servants, religious affiliation, veterans, veterans' children. *Tuition waivers:* Full or partial for employees or children of employees. *ROTC:* Army, Air Force cooperative.

LOANS *Student loans:* $62,361,912 (82% need-based, 18% non-need-based). 66% of past graduating class borrowed through all loan programs. *Average indebtedness per student:* $21,531. *Average need-based loan:* Freshmen: $2587; Undergraduates: $3434. *Parent loans:* $21,888,565 (73% need-based, 27% non-need-based). *Programs:* Federal Direct (Subsidized and Unsubsidized Stafford, PLUS), Perkins, alternative loans.

WORK-STUDY *Federal work-study:* Total amount: $1,468,920; 470 jobs averaging $1705.

ATHLETIC AWARDS *Total amount:* $3,113,053 (44% need-based, 56% non-need-based).

APPLYING FOR FINANCIAL AID *Required financial aid form:* FAFSA. *Financial aid deadline (priority):* 4/1. *Notification date:* Continuous beginning 4/1. Students must reply within 4 weeks of notification.

CONTACT Lisa Hasselschwert, Interim Director, The University of Toledo, 2801 West Bancroft Street, 1200 Rocket Hall, MS-314, Toledo, OH 43606, 419-530-8700 or toll-free 800-5TOLEDO (in-state). *Fax:* 419-530-5835. *E-mail:* lhassel@utnet.utoledo.edu.

UNIVERSITY OF TULSA
Tulsa, OK

Tuition & fees: $20,738 **Average undergraduate aid package: $15,335**

ABOUT THE INSTITUTION Independent religious, coed. Awards: bachelor's, master's, doctoral, and first professional degrees and post-bachelor's and first professional certificates. 54 undergraduate majors. Total enrollment: 4,084. Undergraduates: 2,796. Freshmen: 631. Federal methodology is used as a basis for awarding need-based institutional aid.

UNDERGRADUATE EXPENSES for 2006–07 *Application fee:* $35. *Comprehensive fee:* $27,790 includes full-time tuition ($20,658), mandatory fees ($80), and room and board ($7052). *College room only:* $3896. *Part-time tuition:* $741 per credit hour. *Part-time fees:* $3 per credit hour.

FRESHMAN FINANCIAL AID (Fall 2005, est.) 631 applied for aid; of those 57% were deemed to have need. 100% of freshmen with need received aid; of those 56% had need fully met. *Average percent of need met:* 83% (excluding resources awarded to replace EFC). *Average financial aid package:* $16,030 (excluding resources awarded to replace EFC). 35% of all full-time freshmen had no need and received non-need-based gift aid.

UNDERGRADUATE FINANCIAL AID (Fall 2005, est.) 2,273 applied for aid; of those 56% were deemed to have need. 100% of undergraduates with need received aid; of those 52% had need fully met. *Average percent of need met:* 77% (excluding resources awarded to replace EFC). *Average financial aid package:* $15,335 (excluding resources awarded to replace EFC). 30% of all full-time undergraduates had no need and received non-need-based gift aid.

GIFT AID (NEED-BASED) *Total amount:* $3,074,649 (64% federal, 16% state, 20% institutional). *Receiving aid:* Freshmen: 23% (154); All full-time undergraduates: 28% (729). *Average award:* Freshmen: $4736; Undergraduates: $4157. *Scholarships, grants, and awards:* Federal Pell, FSEOG, state, private, college/university gift aid from institutional funds.

GIFT AID (NON-NEED-BASED) *Total amount:* $14,254,235 (2% federal, 9% state, 82% institutional, 7% external sources). *Receiving aid:* Freshmen: 50% (340); Undergraduates: 41% (1,046). *Average Award:* Freshmen: $9243; Undergraduates: $9756. *Scholarships, grants, and awards by category: Academic Interests/Achievement:* 1,446 awards ($10,319,921 total): biological sciences, business, communication, computer science, education, engineering/technologies, English, foreign languages, general academic interests/achievements, health fields, international studies, mathematics, physical sciences, premedicine, religion/biblical studies, social sciences. *Creative Arts/Performance:* 179 awards ($936,813 total): art/fine arts, music, performing arts, theater/drama. *Special Achievements/Activities:* 175 awards ($439,091 total): cheerleading/drum major, community service, leadership. *Special Characteristics:* 493 awards ($3,396,006 total): children and siblings of alumni, children of faculty/staff, relatives of clergy, religious affiliation, siblings of current students. *ROTC:* Air Force cooperative.

LOANS *Student loans:* $9,453,385 (52% need-based, 48% non-need-based). 59% of past graduating class borrowed through all loan programs. *Average indebtedness per student:* $23,824. *Average need-based loan:* Freshmen: $4457; Undergraduates: $5570. *Parent loans:* $3,485,514 (100% non-need-based). *Programs:* FFEL (Subsidized and Unsubsidized Stafford, PLUS), Perkins.

WORK-STUDY *Federal work-study:* Total amount: $1,751,413; 654 jobs averaging $2678. *State or other work-study/employment:* Total amount: $22,030 (100% non-need-based). 17 part-time jobs averaging $1296.

ATHLETIC AWARDS *Total amount:* $5,495,923 (100% non-need-based).

APPLYING FOR FINANCIAL AID *Required financial aid forms:* FAFSA, institution's own form. *Financial aid deadline (priority):* 4/1. *Notification date:* Continuous beginning 3/1. Students must reply by 5/1 or within 2 weeks of notification.

CONTACT Ms. Vicki Hendrickson, Director of Student Financial Services, University of Tulsa, 600 South College, Tulsa, OK 74104-3189, 918-631-2526 or toll-free 800-331-3050. *Fax:* 918-631-5105. *E-mail:* vicki-hendrickson@utulsa.edu.

University of Utah

UNIVERSITY OF UTAH
Salt Lake City, UT

Tuition & fees (UT res): $4342   **Average undergraduate aid package: $8086**

ABOUT THE INSTITUTION State-supported, coed. Awards: bachelor's, master's, doctoral, and first professional degrees and post-bachelor's and post-master's certificates. 128 undergraduate majors. Total enrollment: 29,012. Undergraduates: 22,661. Freshmen: 2,821. Federal methodology is used as a basis for awarding need-based institutional aid.

UNDERGRADUATE EXPENSES for 2005–06 *Application fee:* $35. *Tuition, state resident:* full-time $3672; part-time $102 per credit. *Tuition, nonresident:* full-time $12,860; part-time $351 per credit. Full-time tuition and fees vary according to course level, course load, degree level, and student level. Part-time tuition and fees vary according to course level, course load, degree level, and student level. *College room and board:* $5422; *room only:* $2704. Room and board charges vary according to board plan and housing facility. *Payment plan:* Installment.

FRESHMAN FINANCIAL AID (Fall 2005, est.) 1301 applied for aid; of those 55% were deemed to have need. 99% of freshmen with need received aid; of those 16% had need fully met. *Average percent of need met:* 47% (excluding resources awarded to replace EFC). *Average financial aid package:* $7506 (excluding resources awarded to replace EFC). 11% of all full-time freshmen had no need and received non-need-based gift aid.

UNDERGRADUATE FINANCIAL AID (Fall 2005, est.) 8,773 applied for aid; of those 70% were deemed to have need. 99% of undergraduates with need received aid; of those 11% had need fully met. *Average percent of need met:* 50% (excluding resources awarded to replace EFC). *Average financial aid package:* $8086 (excluding resources awarded to replace EFC). 4% of all full-time undergraduates had no need and received non-need-based gift aid.

GIFT AID (NEED-BASED) *Total amount:* $21,670,000 (72% federal, 5% state, 7% institutional, 16% external sources). *Receiving aid:* Freshmen: 23% (529); All full-time undergraduates: 30% (4,527). *Average award:* Freshmen: $4414; Undergraduates: $3970. *Scholarships, grants, and awards:* Federal Pell, FSEOG, state, private, college/university gift aid from institutional funds.

GIFT AID (NON-NEED-BASED) *Total amount:* $2,950,000 (6% institutional, 94% external sources). *Receiving aid:* Freshmen: 1% (29); Undergraduates: 1% (93). *Average Award:* Freshmen: $2819; Undergraduates: $3471. *Scholarships, grants, and awards by category:* Academic Interests/Achievement: architecture, area/ethnic studies, biological sciences, business, communication, computer science, education, engineering/technologies, English, foreign languages, general academic interests/achievements, health fields, humanities, international studies, mathematics, military science, physical sciences, social sciences. *Creative Arts/Performance:* art/fine arts, cinema/film/broadcasting, creative writing, dance, journalism/publications, music, performing arts, theater/drama. *Special Achievements/Activities:* cheerleading/drum major, general special achievements/activities, leadership. *Special Characteristics:* children of faculty/staff, children of public servants, children with a deceased or disabled parent, ethnic background, first-generation college students, handicapped students, out-of-state students, spouses of deceased or disabled public servants. *Tuition waivers:* Full or partial for employees or children of employees, senior citizens. *ROTC:* Army, Naval, Air Force.

LOANS *Student loans:* $41,000,000 (78% need-based, 22% non-need-based). 45% of past graduating class borrowed through all loan programs. *Average indebtedness per student:* $12,806. *Average need-based loan:* Freshmen: $2903; Undergraduates: $4622. *Parent loans:* $1,320,000 (32% need-based, 68% non-need-based). *Programs:* FFEL (Subsidized and Unsubsidized Stafford, PLUS), Perkins, Federal Nursing, college/university, alternative loans.

WORK-STUDY *Federal work-study:* Total amount: $1,500,000; 427 jobs averaging $3500.

ATHLETIC AWARDS Total amount: $3,899,000 (2% need-based, 98% non-need-based).

APPLYING FOR FINANCIAL AID *Required financial aid forms:* FAFSA, institution's own form. *Financial aid deadline (priority):* 3/15. *Notification date:* Continuous beginning 4/15. Students must reply within 6 weeks of notification.

CONTACT Amy Capps, Assistant Director, University of Utah, 201 South 1460 East, Room 105, Salt Lake City, UT 84112-9055, 801-581-6211 or toll-free 800-444-8638. *Fax:* 801-585-6350. *E-mail:* fawin1@saff.utah.edu.

UNIVERSITY OF VERMONT
Burlington, VT

Tuition & fees (VT res): $10,748   **Average undergraduate aid package: $15,786**

ABOUT THE INSTITUTION State-supported, coed. Awards: bachelor's, master's, doctoral, and first professional degrees and post-bachelor's and post-master's certificates. 99 undergraduate majors. Total enrollment: 11,597. Undergraduates: 9,859. Freshmen: 2,394. Federal methodology is used as a basis for awarding need-based institutional aid.

UNDERGRADUATE EXPENSES for 2005–06 *Application fee:* $45. *Tuition, state resident:* full-time $9452; part-time $394 per credit. *Tuition, nonresident:* full-time $23,638; part-time $985 per credit. Part-time tuition and fees vary according to course load. *College room and board:* $7332; *room only:* $4936. Room and board charges vary according to board plan. *Payment plans:* Installment, deferred payment.

FRESHMAN FINANCIAL AID (Fall 2004) 1395 applied for aid; of those 79% were deemed to have need. 99% of freshmen with need received aid; of those 98% had need fully met. *Average percent of need met:* 87% (excluding resources awarded to replace EFC). *Average financial aid package:* $17,342 (excluding resources awarded to replace EFC). 16% of all full-time freshmen had no need and received non-need-based gift aid.

UNDERGRADUATE FINANCIAL AID (Fall 2004) 5,258 applied for aid; of those 85% were deemed to have need. 99% of undergraduates with need received aid; of those 91% had need fully met. *Average percent of need met:* 82% (excluding resources awarded to replace EFC). *Average financial aid package:* $15,786 (excluding resources awarded to replace EFC). 11% of all full-time undergraduates had no need and received non-need-based gift aid.

GIFT AID (NEED-BASED) *Total amount:* $44,158,953 (15% federal, 8% state, 72% institutional, 5% external sources). *Receiving aid:* Freshmen: 50% (966); All full-time undergraduates: 51% (3,957). *Average award:* Freshmen: $12,913; Undergraduates: $10,766. *Scholarships, grants, and awards:* Federal Pell, FSEOG, state, private, college/university gift aid from institutional funds, Federal Nursing.

GIFT AID (NON-NEED-BASED) *Total amount:* $3,088,848 (79% institutional, 21% external sources). *Receiving aid:* Freshmen: 3% (52); Undergraduates: 2% (189). *Average Award:* Freshmen: $2684; Undergraduates: $2340. *Scholarships, grants, and awards by category:* Academic Interests/Achievement: 3,183 awards ($7,290,618 total): agriculture, business, engineering/technologies, general academic interests/achievements, humanities, mathematics, military science, social sciences. *Creative Arts/Performance:* 15 awards ($40,583 total): music, theater/drama. *Special Achievements/Activities:* 67 awards ($170,136 total): community service. *Special Characteristics:* 57 awards ($217,750 total): ethnic background, first-generation college students. *Tuition waivers:* Full or partial for employees or children of employees, senior citizens. *ROTC:* Army.

LOANS *Student loans:* $35,158,805 (65% need-based, 35% non-need-based). 60% of past graduating class borrowed through all loan programs. *Average indebtedness per student:* $20,142. *Average need-based loan:* Freshmen: $5455; Undergraduates: $6108. *Parent loans:* $31,542,456 (100% non-need-based). *Programs:* FFEL (Subsidized and Unsubsidized Stafford, PLUS), Perkins, Federal Nursing, state, college/university.

WORK-STUDY *Federal work-study:* Total amount: $3,993,185; 1,886 jobs averaging $2117.

ATHLETIC AWARDS Total amount: $2,875,104 (27% need-based, 73% non-need-based).

APPLYING FOR FINANCIAL AID *Required financial aid form:* FAFSA. *Financial aid deadline (priority):* 2/10. *Notification date:* Continuous beginning 3/15. Students must reply within 4 weeks of notification.

CONTACT Student Financial Services, University of Vermont, 330 Waterman, South Prospect Street, Burlington, VT 05405-0160, 802-656-5700. *Fax:* 802-656-4076. *E-mail:* financialaid@uvm.edu.

UNIVERSITY OF VIRGINIA
Charlottesville, VA

Tuition & fees (VA res): $7370   **Average undergraduate aid package: $14,974**

ABOUT THE INSTITUTION State-supported, coed. Awards: bachelor's, master's, doctoral, and first professional degrees and post-master's certificates. 52

undergraduate majors. Total enrollment: 23,765. Undergraduates: 14,213. Freshmen: 3,112. Federal methodology is used as a basis for awarding need-based institutional aid.

UNDERGRADUATE EXPENSES for 2005–06 *Application fee:* $60. **Tuition, state resident:** full-time $5602. **Tuition, nonresident:** full-time $22,346. Part-time tuition and fees vary according to course load. **College room and board:** $6389; *room only:* $3289. Room and board charges vary according to board plan and housing facility. *Payment plan:* Installment.

FRESHMAN FINANCIAL AID (Fall 2005, est.) 1692 applied for aid; of those 44% were deemed to have need. 100% of freshmen with need received aid; of those 100% had need fully met. *Average percent of need met:* 100% (excluding resources awarded to replace EFC). *Average financial aid package:* $15,251 (excluding resources awarded to replace EFC). 14% of all full-time freshmen had no need and received non-need-based gift aid.

UNDERGRADUATE FINANCIAL AID (Fall 2005, est.) 5,433 applied for aid; of those 59% were deemed to have need. 100% of undergraduates with need received aid; of those 100% had need fully met. *Average percent of need met:* 100% (excluding resources awarded to replace EFC). *Average financial aid package:* $14,974 (excluding resources awarded to replace EFC). 14% of all full-time undergraduates had no need and received non-need-based gift aid.

GIFT AID (NEED-BASED) *Total amount:* $28,268,189 (11% federal, 15% state, 67% institutional, 7% external sources). *Receiving aid:* Freshmen: 22% (679); All full-time undergraduates: 20% (2,679). *Average award:* Freshmen: $11,960; Undergraduates: $10,916. *Scholarships, grants, and awards:* Federal Pell, FSEOG, state, private, college/university gift aid from institutional funds.

GIFT AID (NON-NEED-BASED) *Total amount:* $6,483,264 (6% state, 30% institutional, 64% external sources). *Receiving aid:* Freshmen: 4% (122); Undergraduates: 2% (320). *Average Award:* Freshmen: $7792; Undergraduates: $8535. *Scholarships, grants, and awards by category:* Academic Interests/Achievement: general academic interests/achievements. *Tuition waivers:* Full or partial for employees or children of employees, senior citizens. *ROTC:* Army, Naval, Air Force.

LOANS *Student loans:* $22,925,366 (45% need-based, 55% non-need-based). 30% of past graduating class borrowed through all loan programs. *Average indebtedness per student:* $15,176. *Average need-based loan:* Freshmen: $3882; Undergraduates: $4617. *Parent loans:* $8,975,846 (1% need-based, 99% non-need-based). *Programs:* Federal Direct (Subsidized and Unsubsidized Stafford, PLUS), Perkins, Federal Nursing, college/university.

WORK-STUDY *Federal work-study:* Total amount: $1,133,352; 597 jobs averaging $1898.

ATHLETIC AWARDS *Total amount:* $7,731,720 (27% need-based, 73% non-need-based).

APPLYING FOR FINANCIAL AID *Required financial aid forms:* FAFSA, institution's own form. *Financial aid deadline (priority):* 3/1. *Notification date:* 4/5. Students must reply by 5/1.

CONTACT Ms. Yvonne B. Hubbard, Director, Student Financial Services, University of Virginia, PO Box 400207, Charlottesville, VA 22904-4207, 434-982-6000. *E-mail:* faid@virginia.edu.

THE UNIVERSITY OF VIRGINIA'S COLLEGE AT WISE
Wise, VA

ABOUT THE INSTITUTION State-supported, coed. Awards: bachelor's degrees and post-bachelor's certificates. 24 undergraduate majors. Total enrollment: 1,836. Undergraduates: 1,836. Freshmen: 374.

GIFT AID (NEED-BASED) *Scholarships, grants, and awards:* Federal Pell, FSEOG, state, private, college/university gift aid from institutional funds.

GIFT AID (NON-NEED-BASED) *Scholarships, grants, and awards by category:* Academic Interests/Achievement: agriculture, biological sciences, business, computer science, education, English, general academic interests/achievements, health fields, humanities, mathematics, physical sciences, premedicine, social sciences. *Creative Arts/Performance:* creative writing, general creative arts/performance, journalism/publications, music, performing arts, theater/drama. *Special Achievements/Activities:* community service, religious involvement. *Special Characteristics:* children with a deceased or disabled parent, ethnic background, local/state students, veterans, veterans' children.

LOANS *Programs:* FFEL (Subsidized and Unsubsidized Stafford, PLUS), Perkins, state, college/university.

APPLYING FOR FINANCIAL AID *Required financial aid form:* FAFSA.

CONTACT Bill Wendle, Director of Financial Aid, The University of Virginia's College at Wise, 1 College Avenue, Wise, VA 24293, 276-328-0103 or toll-free 888-282-9324. *Fax:* 276-328-0251. *E-mail:* wdw8m@uvawise.edu.

UNIVERSITY OF WASHINGTON
Seattle, WA

ABOUT THE INSTITUTION State-supported, coed. Awards: bachelor's, master's, doctoral, and first professional degrees and first professional certificates. 155 undergraduate majors. Total enrollment: 39,251. Undergraduates: 27,488. Freshmen: 4,922.

GIFT AID (NEED-BASED) *Scholarships, grants, and awards:* Federal Pell, FSEOG, state, private, college/university gift aid from institutional funds.

GIFT AID (NON-NEED-BASED) *Scholarships, grants, and awards by category:* Academic Interests/Achievement: architecture, biological sciences, business, communication, engineering/technologies, English, foreign languages, general academic interests/achievements, health fields, humanities, mathematics, physical sciences, social sciences. *Creative Arts/Performance:* art/fine arts, creative writing, dance, general creative arts/performance, journalism/publications, music, performing arts, theater/drama. *Special Achievements/Activities:* community service, general special achievements/activities, leadership. *Special Characteristics:* international students.

LOANS *Programs:* Federal Direct (Subsidized and Unsubsidized Stafford, PLUS), Perkins, Federal Nursing, college/university.

WORK-STUDY *Federal work-study:* Total amount: $2,300,000; 855 jobs averaging $2690. *State or other work-study/employment:* Total amount: $470,000 (100% need-based). 156 part-time jobs averaging $3000.

APPLYING FOR FINANCIAL AID *Required financial aid form:* FAFSA.

CONTACT Office of Student Financial Aid, University of Washington, Box 355880, Seattle, WA 98195-5880, 206-543-6101. *E-mail:* osfa@u.washington.edu.

UNIVERSITY OF WASHINGTON, BOTHELL
Bothell, WA

CONTACT Financial Aid Office, University of Washington, Bothell, 18115 Campus Way NE, Bothell, WA 98011-8246, 425-352-5000.

UNIVERSITY OF WASHINGTON, TACOMA
Tacoma, WA

CONTACT Financial Aid Office, University of Washington, Tacoma, 1900 Commerce Street, Tacoma, WA 98402-3100, 253-692-4000 or toll-free 800-736-7750 (out-of-state).

THE UNIVERSITY OF WEST ALABAMA
Livingston, AL

Tuition & fees (AL res): $4326	Average undergraduate aid package: $10,765

ABOUT THE INSTITUTION State-supported, coed. Awards: associate, bachelor's, and master's degrees. 19 undergraduate majors. Total enrollment: 2,667. Undergraduates: 1,637. Freshmen: 264. Federal methodology is used as a basis for awarding need-based institutional aid.

UNDERGRADUATE EXPENSES for 2005–06 *Application fee:* $20. **Tuition, state resident:** full-time $3838; part-time $162 per semester hour. **Tuition, nonresident:** full-time $7676; part-time $324 per semester hour. *Required fees:* full-time $488; $235 per term part-time. Part-time tuition and fees vary according to course level. **College room and board:** $3285; *room only:* $1746. Room and board charges vary according to board plan and housing facility. *Payment plan:* Deferred payment.

UNDERGRADUATE FINANCIAL AID (Fall 2005, est.) 1,856 applied for aid; of those 84% were deemed to have need. 96% of undergraduates with need received aid; of those 86% had need fully met. *Average financial aid package:* $10,765 (excluding resources awarded to replace EFC).

GIFT AID (NEED-BASED) *Total amount:* $2,781,129 (99% federal, 1% state). *Receiving aid:* All full-time undergraduates: 38% (976). *Average award:* Undergraduates: $4400. *Scholarships, grants, and awards:* Federal Pell, FSEOG, state, private, college/university gift aid from institutional funds.

The University of West Alabama

GIFT AID (NON-NEED-BASED) *Total amount:* $995,881 (74% institutional, 26% external sources). *Scholarships, grants, and awards by category:* Academic Interests/Achievement: business, computer science, education, English, general academic interests/achievements. *Creative Arts/Performance:* creative writing, dance, journalism/publications, music. *Special Achievements/Activities:* cheerleading/drum major, rodeo. *Special Characteristics:* children of faculty/staff, first-generation college students. *Tuition waivers:* Full or partial for employees or children of employees. *ROTC:* Army cooperative, Air Force cooperative.
LOANS *Student loans:* $8,785,575 (100% need-based). 62% of past graduating class borrowed through all loan programs. *Average indebtedness per student:* $16,043. *Average need-based loan:* Undergraduates: $4915. *Parent loans:* $1,548,366 (18% need-based, 82% non-need-based). *Programs:* FFEL (Subsidized and Unsubsidized Stafford, PLUS), Perkins.
WORK-STUDY *Federal work-study:* Total amount: $222,851; 176 jobs averaging $1221.
ATHLETIC AWARDS Total amount: $780,150 (100% non-need-based).
APPLYING FOR FINANCIAL AID *Required financial aid form:* FAFSA. *Financial aid deadline (priority):* 4/1. *Notification date:* Continuous beginning 5/1. Students must reply within 4 weeks of notification.
CONTACT Mr. Don Rainer, Director of Financial Aid, The University of West Alabama, Station 3, Livingston, AL 35470, 205-652-3576 or toll-free 800-621-7742 (in-state), 800-621-8044 (out-of-state).

UNIVERSITY OF WEST FLORIDA
Pensacola, FL

ABOUT THE INSTITUTION State-supported, coed. Awards: associate, bachelor's, master's, and doctoral degrees (specialists). 55 undergraduate majors. Total enrollment: 9,632. Undergraduates: 8,168. Freshmen: 934.
GIFT AID (NEED-BASED) *Scholarships, grants, and awards:* Federal Pell, FSEOG, state, college/university gift aid from institutional funds.
GIFT AID (NON-NEED-BASED) *Scholarships, grants, and awards by category:* Academic Interests/Achievement: general academic interests/achievements. *Creative Arts/Performance:* applied art and design, art/fine arts, music, theater/drama. *Special Characteristics:* members of minority groups.
LOANS *Programs:* Federal Direct (Subsidized and Unsubsidized Stafford, PLUS), Perkins, college/university.
WORK-STUDY *Federal work-study:* Total amount: $245,584; 178 jobs averaging $2350. *State or other work-study/employment:* 1,545 part-time jobs available.
APPLYING FOR FINANCIAL AID *Required financial aid forms:* FAFSA, institution's own form.
CONTACT Ms. Georganne E. Major, Program Manager, University of West Florida, 11000 University Parkway, Pensacola, FL 32514-5750, 850-474-2397 or toll-free 800-263-1074. *E-mail:* gmajor@uwf.edu.

UNIVERSITY OF WEST GEORGIA
Carrollton, GA

Tuition & fees (GA res): $3270	Average undergraduate aid package: $6441

ABOUT THE INSTITUTION State-supported, coed. Awards: bachelor's, master's, and doctoral degrees and post-master's certificates. 51 undergraduate majors. Total enrollment: 10,155. Undergraduates: 8,346. Freshmen: 1,983. Federal methodology is used as a basis for awarding need-based institutional aid.
UNDERGRADUATE EXPENSES for 2005–06 *Application fee:* $20. *Tuition, state resident:* full-time $2438; part-time $102 per semester hour. *Tuition, nonresident:* full-time $9754; part-time $407 per semester hour. *Required fees:* full-time $832; $25.17 per semester hour or $114 per term part-time. Full-time tuition and fees vary according to course load. Part-time tuition and fees vary according to course load. *College room and board:* $5568; *room only:* $3540. Room and board charges vary according to board plan and housing facility.
FRESHMAN FINANCIAL AID (Fall 2005, est.) 1872 applied for aid; of those 69% were deemed to have need. 99% of freshmen with need received aid; of those 19% had need fully met. *Average percent of need met:* 66% (excluding resources awarded to replace EFC). *Average financial aid package:* $6478 (excluding resources awarded to replace EFC). 2% of all full-time freshmen had no need and received non-need-based gift aid.
UNDERGRADUATE FINANCIAL AID (Fall 2005, est.) 4,251 applied for aid; of those 82% were deemed to have need. 97% of undergraduates with need received aid; of those 23% had need fully met. *Average percent of need met:* 78% (excluding resources awarded to replace EFC). *Average financial aid package:* $6441 (excluding resources awarded to replace EFC). 2% of all full-time undergraduates had no need and received non-need-based gift aid.
GIFT AID (NEED-BASED) *Total amount:* $13,054,051 (47% federal, 50% state, 2% institutional, 1% external sources). *Receiving aid:* Freshmen: 51% (1,248); All full-time undergraduates: 39% (2,682). *Average award:* Freshmen: $4348; Undergraduates: $4346. *Scholarships, grants, and awards:* Federal Pell, FSEOG, state, private, college/university gift aid from institutional funds.
GIFT AID (NON-NEED-BASED) *Total amount:* $4,964,252 (91% state, 5% institutional, 4% external sources). *Receiving aid:* Freshmen: 34% (833); Undergraduates: 29% (1,978). *Average Award:* Freshmen: $1735; Undergraduates: $1635. *Scholarships, grants, and awards by category:* Academic Interests/Achievement: biological sciences, business, communication, computer science, education, English, foreign languages, general academic interests/achievements, health fields, humanities, mathematics, physical sciences, social sciences. *Creative Arts/Performance:* art/fine arts, debating, journalism/publications, music, theater/drama. *Special Achievements/Activities:* community service, memberships, religious involvement. *Special Characteristics:* adult students, children and siblings of alumni, children of union members/company employees, ethnic background, handicapped students, international students, local/state students, members of minority groups, previous college experience. *Tuition waivers:* Full or partial for minority students, employees or children of employees, adult students, senior citizens. *ROTC:* Army.
LOANS *Student loans:* $15,470,805 (57% need-based, 43% non-need-based). 61% of past graduating class borrowed through all loan programs. *Average indebtedness per student:* $14,555. *Average need-based loan:* Freshmen: $2121; Undergraduates: $3025. *Parent loans:* $1,479,061 (100% non-need-based). *Programs:* Federal Direct (Subsidized and Unsubsidized Stafford, PLUS), Perkins, state, college/university.
WORK-STUDY *Federal work-study:* Total amount: $2,364,900; 634 jobs averaging $1835. *State or other work-study/employment:* Part-time jobs available.
ATHLETIC AWARDS Total amount: $743,588 (43% need-based, 57% non-need-based).
APPLYING FOR FINANCIAL AID *Required financial aid form:* FAFSA. *Financial aid deadline (priority):* 4/1. *Notification date:* Continuous beginning 3/1. Students must reply by 5/1.
CONTACT Kimberly Jordan, Director of Financial Aid, University of West Georgia, Aycock Hall, Carrollton, GA 30118, 678-839-6421. *Fax:* 678-839-6422. *E-mail:* kjordan@westga.edu.

UNIVERSITY OF WEST LOS ANGELES
Inglewood, CA

CONTACT Roberto Quinones, Assistant Director of Financial Aid, University of West Los Angeles, 1155 West Arbor Vitae Street, Inglewood, CA 90301-2902, 310-342-5268. *Fax:* 310-342-5294.

UNIVERSITY OF WISCONSIN–EAU CLAIRE
Eau Claire, WI

Tuition & fees (WI res): $5178	Average undergraduate aid package: $6967

ABOUT THE INSTITUTION State-supported, coed. Awards: associate, bachelor's, and master's degrees and post-bachelor's and post-master's certificates. 48 undergraduate majors. Total enrollment: 10,566. Undergraduates: 10,063. Freshmen: 2,068. Federal methodology is used as a basis for awarding need-based institutional aid.
UNDERGRADUATE EXPENSES for 2005–06 *Application fee:* $35. *Tuition, state resident:* full-time $5178; part-time $215.59 per credit. *Tuition, nonresident:* full-time $15,224; part-time $634.18 per credit. Full-time tuition and fees vary according to reciprocity agreements. Part-time tuition and fees vary according to reciprocity agreements. *College room and board:* $4737; *room only:* $2540. Room and board charges vary according to board plan. *Payment plan:* Installment.
FRESHMAN FINANCIAL AID (Fall 2004) 1524 applied for aid; of those 55% were deemed to have need. 99% of freshmen with need received aid; of those 69% had need fully met. *Average percent of need met:* 95% (excluding resources awarded to replace EFC). *Average financial aid package:* $6570 (excluding resources awarded to replace EFC). 16% of all full-time freshmen had no need and received non-need-based gift aid.

UNDERGRADUATE FINANCIAL AID (Fall 2004) 6,144 applied for aid; of those 66% were deemed to have need. 99% of undergraduates with need received aid; of those 74% had need fully met. *Average percent of need met:* 94% (excluding resources awarded to replace EFC). *Average financial aid package:* $6967 (excluding resources awarded to replace EFC). 9% of all full-time undergraduates had no need and received non-need-based gift aid.
GIFT AID (NEED-BASED) *Total amount:* $9,933,676 (61% federal, 27% state, 4% institutional, 8% external sources). *Receiving aid:* Freshmen: 24% (494); All full-time undergraduates: 24% (2,244). *Average award:* Freshmen: $3643; Undergraduates: $4168. *Scholarships, grants, and awards:* Federal Pell, FSEOG, state, private, college/university gift aid from institutional funds, Federal Nursing.
GIFT AID (NON-NEED-BASED) *Total amount:* $1,502,312 (7% federal, 6% state, 34% institutional, 53% external sources). *Average Award:* Freshmen: $1525; Undergraduates: $1704. *Scholarships, grants, and awards by category: Academic Interests/Achievement:* biological sciences, business, communication, computer science, education, English, foreign languages, general academic interests/achievements, health fields, international studies, mathematics, physical sciences, premedicine, social sciences. *Creative Arts/Performance:* debating, music, theater/drama. *Special Achievements/Activities:* community service, general special achievements/activities, hobbies/interests, leadership, memberships. *Special Characteristics:* adult students, ethnic background, first-generation college students, general special characteristics, international students, local/state students, members of minority groups, previous college experience. *Tuition waivers:* Full or partial for minority students, senior citizens.
LOANS *Student loans:* $25,113,350 (63% need-based, 37% non-need-based). 65% of past graduating class borrowed through all loan programs. *Average indebtedness per student:* $16,953. *Average need-based loan:* Freshmen: $3516; Undergraduates: $4020. *Parent loans:* $1,590,665 (100% non-need-based). *Programs:* Federal Direct (Subsidized and Unsubsidized Stafford, PLUS), Perkins, college/university, alternative loans.
WORK-STUDY *Federal work-study:* Total amount: $3,675,849; 1,956 jobs averaging $1879. *State or other work-study/employment:* Total amount: $2,355,101 (41% need-based, 59% non-need-based). 1,894 part-time jobs averaging $1243.
APPLYING FOR FINANCIAL AID *Required financial aid form:* FAFSA. *Financial aid deadline (priority):* 4/15. *Notification date:* Continuous beginning 4/15. Students must reply within 3 weeks of notification.
CONTACT Ms. Kathleen Sahlhoff, Director of Financial Aid, University of Wisconsin–Eau Claire, 115 Schofield Hall, Eau Claire, WI 54701, 715-836-3373. *Fax:* 715-836-3846.

UNIVERSITY OF WISCONSIN–GREEN BAY
Green Bay, WI

Tuition & fees (WI res): $5425   **Average undergraduate aid package: $7839**

ABOUT THE INSTITUTION State-supported, coed. Awards: associate, bachelor's, and master's degrees and post-bachelor's certificates. 35 undergraduate majors. Total enrollment: 5,826. Undergraduates: 5,622. Freshmen: 910. Federal methodology is used as a basis for awarding need-based institutional aid.
UNDERGRADUATE EXPENSES for 2005–06 *Application fee:* $35. *Tuition, state resident:* full-time $4277; part-time $178 per credit hour. *Tuition, nonresident:* full-time $14,323; part-time $597 per credit hour. *Required fees:* full-time $1148; $38 per credit hour. Full-time tuition and fees vary according to reciprocity agreements. Part-time tuition and fees vary according to reciprocity agreements. *College room and board:* $4698; *room only:* $2772. Room and board charges vary according to board plan and housing facility. *Payment plan:* Installment.
FRESHMAN FINANCIAL AID (Fall 2005, est.) 773 applied for aid; of those 64% were deemed to have need. 93% of freshmen with need received aid; of those 34% had need fully met. *Average percent of need met:* 74% (excluding resources awarded to replace EFC). *Average financial aid package:* $7360 (excluding resources awarded to replace EFC). 4% of all full-time freshmen had no need and received non-need-based gift aid.
UNDERGRADUATE FINANCIAL AID (Fall 2005, est.) 3,509 applied for aid; of those 73% were deemed to have need. 96% of undergraduates with need received aid; of those 41% had need fully met. *Average percent of need met:* 79% (excluding resources awarded to replace EFC). *Average financial aid package:* $7839 (excluding resources awarded to replace EFC). 2% of all full-time undergraduates had no need and received non-need-based gift aid.
GIFT AID (NEED-BASED) *Total amount:* $6,672,850 (49% federal, 35% state, 2% institutional, 14% external sources). *Receiving aid:* Freshmen: 33% (299);

All full-time undergraduates: 31% (1,402). *Average award:* Freshmen: $4125; Undergraduates: $4609. *Scholarships, grants, and awards:* Federal Pell, FSEOG, state, private, college/university gift aid from institutional funds.
GIFT AID (NON-NEED-BASED) *Total amount:* $612,809 (11% state, 20% institutional, 69% external sources). *Receiving aid:* Freshmen: 17% (150); Undergraduates: 18% (792). *Average Award:* Freshmen: $2399; Undergraduates: $2890. *Scholarships, grants, and awards by category: Academic Interests/Achievement:* 200 awards ($250,000 total): area/ethnic studies, biological sciences, business, communication, engineering/technologies, general academic interests/achievements, physical sciences, social sciences. *Creative Arts/Performance:* 30 awards ($20,400 total): art/fine arts, dance, music, theater/drama. *Special Achievements/Activities:* community service, leadership. *Special Characteristics:* adult students, children of public servants, ethnic background, veterans. *Tuition waivers:* Full or partial for senior citizens. *ROTC:* Army.
LOANS *Student loans:* $14,632,692 (56% need-based, 44% non-need-based). 61% of past graduating class borrowed through all loan programs. *Average indebtedness per student:* $12,222. *Average need-based loan:* Freshmen: $3030; Undergraduates: $4030. *Parent loans:* $1,439,942 (100% non-need-based). *Programs:* FFEL (Subsidized and Unsubsidized Stafford, PLUS), Perkins.
WORK-STUDY *Federal work-study:* Total amount: $441,180; jobs available. *State or other work-study/employment:* Part-time jobs available.
ATHLETIC AWARDS Total amount: $1,806,146 (77% need-based, 23% non-need-based).
APPLYING FOR FINANCIAL AID *Required financial aid form:* FAFSA. *Financial aid deadline (priority):* 4/15. *Notification date:* Continuous. Students must reply within 3 weeks of notification.
CONTACT Mr. Ron Ronnenberg, Director of Financial Aid, University of Wisconsin–Green Bay, 2420 Nicolet Drive, Green Bay, WI 54311-7001, 920-465-2073 or toll-free 888-367-8942 (out-of-state). *E-mail:* ronnenbr@uwgb.edu.

UNIVERSITY OF WISCONSIN–LA CROSSE
La Crosse, WI

Tuition & fees (WI res): $5225   **Average undergraduate aid package: $6210**

ABOUT THE INSTITUTION State-supported, coed. Awards: associate, bachelor's, and master's degrees. 42 undergraduate majors. Total enrollment: 9,397. Undergraduates: 8,133. Freshmen: 1,753. Federal methodology is used as a basis for awarding need-based institutional aid.
UNDERGRADUATE EXPENSES for 2005–06 *Application fee:* $35. *Tuition, state resident:* full-time $5225; part-time $230 per credit hour. *Tuition, nonresident:* full-time $15,271; part-time $649 per credit hour. Full-time tuition and fees vary according to program and reciprocity agreements. Part-time tuition and fees vary according to course load, program, and reciprocity agreements. *College room and board:* $4820; *room only:* $2720. Room and board charges vary according to board plan. *Payment plan:* Installment.
FRESHMAN FINANCIAL AID (Fall 2004) 1122 applied for aid; of those 79% were deemed to have need. 96% of freshmen with need received aid; of those 87% had need fully met. *Average percent of need met:* 80% (excluding resources awarded to replace EFC). *Average financial aid package:* $4874 (excluding resources awarded to replace EFC). 4% of all full-time freshmen had no need and received non-need-based gift aid.
UNDERGRADUATE FINANCIAL AID (Fall 2004) 5,610 applied for aid; of those 79% were deemed to have need. 97% of undergraduates with need received aid; of those 87% had need fully met. *Average percent of need met:* 81% (excluding resources awarded to replace EFC). *Average financial aid package:* $6210 (excluding resources awarded to replace EFC). 6% of all full-time undergraduates had no need and received non-need-based gift aid.
GIFT AID (NEED-BASED) *Total amount:* $7,211,973 (55% federal, 34% state, 7% institutional, 4% external sources). *Receiving aid:* Freshmen: 26% (401); All full-time undergraduates: 28% (2,025). *Average award:* Freshmen: $1609; Undergraduates: $2050. *Scholarships, grants, and awards:* Federal Pell, FSEOG, state, private, college/university gift aid from institutional funds.
GIFT AID (NON-NEED-BASED) *Total amount:* $1,854,126 (7% federal, 19% state, 7% institutional, 67% external sources). *Receiving aid:* Freshmen: 6% (85); Undergraduates: 6% (461). *Average Award:* Freshmen: $447; Undergraduates: $801. *Scholarships, grants, and awards by category: Academic Interests/Achievement:* 172 awards ($185,032 total): biological sciences, business, communication, computer science, education, English, foreign languages, general academic interests/achievements, health fields, mathematics, military science,

University of Wisconsin–La Crosse

physical sciences, social sciences. *Creative Arts/Performance:* 35 awards ($21,012 total): art/fine arts, music, theater/drama. *Special Characteristics:* 42 awards ($74,110 total): adult students, children and siblings of alumni, ethnic background, general special characteristics, members of minority groups, out-of-state students. *ROTC:* Army.
LOANS *Student loans:* $27,558,965 (51% need-based, 49% non-need-based). 70% of past graduating class borrowed through all loan programs. *Average indebtedness per student:* $13,948. *Average need-based loan:* Freshmen: $3265; Undergraduates: $3726. *Parent loans:* $1,820,333 (100% non-need-based). *Programs:* FFEL (Subsidized and Unsubsidized Stafford, PLUS), Perkins, state, college/university.
WORK-STUDY *Federal work-study:* Total amount: $456,683; 598 jobs averaging $768. *State or other work-study/employment:* Total amount: $2,449,362 (100% non-need-based). 1,072 part-time jobs averaging $2415.
APPLYING FOR FINANCIAL AID *Required financial aid forms:* FAFSA, institution's own form. *Financial aid deadline (priority):* 3/15. *Notification date:* Continuous beginning 3/10. Students must reply by 5/10 or within 3 weeks of notification.
CONTACT Mr. James E. Finn, Director of Financial Aid, University of Wisconsin–La Crosse, 1725 State Street, La Crosse, WI 54601-3742, 608-785-8604. *Fax:* 608-785-8843. *E-mail:* finn.jame@uwlax.edu.

UNIVERSITY OF WISCONSIN–MADISON
Madison, WI

Tuition & fees (WI res): $6617	Average undergraduate aid package: $11,310

ABOUT THE INSTITUTION State-supported, coed. Awards: bachelor's, master's, doctoral, and first professional degrees and post-master's and first professional certificates. 136 undergraduate majors. Total enrollment: 41,480. Undergraduates: 30,106. Freshmen: 6,141. Both federal and institutional methodology are used as a basis for awarding need-based institutional aid.
UNDERGRADUATE EXPENSES for 2005–06 *Application fee:* $35. *Tuition, state resident:* full-time $6284; part-time $264 per credit. *Tuition, nonresident:* full-time $20,284; part-time $847 per credit. *Required fees:* full-time $333; $30 per credit. Full-time tuition and fees vary according to degree level and reciprocity agreements. Part-time tuition and fees vary according to course load, degree level, and reciprocity agreements. *College room and board:* $6500. Room and board charges vary according to board plan, housing facility, and location.
FRESHMAN FINANCIAL AID (Fall 2005, est.) 4361 applied for aid; of those 45% were deemed to have need. 89% of freshmen with need received aid; of those 41% had need fully met. *Average financial aid package:* $11,240 (excluding resources awarded to replace EFC). 22% of all full-time freshmen had no need and received non-need-based gift aid.
UNDERGRADUATE FINANCIAL AID (Fall 2005, est.) 19,071 applied for aid; of those 57% were deemed to have need. 92% of undergraduates with need received aid; of those 53% had need fully met. *Average financial aid package:* $11,310 (excluding resources awarded to replace EFC). 16% of all full-time undergraduates had no need and received non-need-based gift aid.
GIFT AID (NEED-BASED) *Total amount:* $22,198,706 (51% federal, 27% state, 22% institutional). *Receiving aid:* Freshmen: 18% (1,043); All full-time undergraduates: 23% (5,898). *Average award:* Freshmen: $3592; Undergraduates: $3854. *Scholarships, grants, and awards:* Federal Pell, FSEOG, state, private, college/university gift aid from institutional funds.
GIFT AID (NON-NEED-BASED) *Total amount:* $23,968,415 (9% federal, 19% state, 41% institutional, 31% external sources). *Receiving aid:* Freshmen: 17% (959); Undergraduates: 20% (5,168). *Average Award:* Freshmen: $2635; Undergraduates: $2992. *Scholarships, grants, and awards by category: Academic Interests/Achievement:* general academic interests/achievements. *Creative Arts/Performance:* general creative arts/performance. *Special Achievements/Activities:* general special achievements/activities. *Special Characteristics:* general special characteristics. *ROTC:* Army, Naval, Air Force.
LOANS *Student loans:* $72,342,402 (54% need-based, 46% non-need-based). 45% of past graduating class borrowed through all loan programs. *Average indebtedness per student:* $18,630. *Average need-based loan:* Freshmen: $4359; Undergraduates: $3707. *Parent loans:* $12,875,103 (100% non-need-based). *Programs:* FFEL (Subsidized and Unsubsidized Stafford, PLUS), Perkins, Federal Nursing, state, college/university.
WORK-STUDY *Federal work-study:* Total amount: $8,360,006; 3,894 jobs averaging $2640.
ATHLETIC AWARDS *Total amount:* $5,944,268 (100% non-need-based).

APPLYING FOR FINANCIAL AID *Required financial aid forms:* FAFSA, institution's own form. *Financial aid deadline:* Continuous. *Notification date:* Continuous beginning 4/1. Students must reply within 3 weeks of notification.
CONTACT Office of Student Financial Services, University of Wisconsin–Madison, 432 North Murray Street, Madison, WI 53706-1380, 608-262-3060. *Fax:* 608-262-9068. *E-mail:* finaid@das.wisc.edu.

UNIVERSITY OF WISCONSIN–MILWAUKEE
Milwaukee, WI

ABOUT THE INSTITUTION State-supported, coed. Awards: bachelor's, master's, and doctoral degrees and post-bachelor's and post-master's certificates. 105 undergraduate majors. Total enrollment: 27,502. Undergraduates: 22,916. Freshmen: 4,340.
GIFT AID (NEED-BASED) *Scholarships, grants, and awards:* Federal Pell, FSEOG, state, private.
GIFT AID (NON-NEED-BASED) *Scholarships, grants, and awards by category: Academic Interests/Achievement:* general academic interests/achievements. *Creative Arts/Performance:* general creative arts/performance. *Special Achievements/Activities:* general special achievements/activities. *Special Characteristics:* general special characteristics.
LOANS *Programs:* Federal Direct (Subsidized and Unsubsidized Stafford, PLUS), Perkins, Federal Nursing, Alternative loans.
APPLYING FOR FINANCIAL AID *Required financial aid form:* FAFSA.
CONTACT Ms. Jane Hojan-Clark, Director of Financial Aid and Student Employment Services, University of Wisconsin–Milwaukee, Mellencamp Hall 162, Milwaukee, WI 53201, 414-229-6300. *E-mail:* jhojan@uwm.edu.

UNIVERSITY OF WISCONSIN–OSHKOSH
Oshkosh, WI

ABOUT THE INSTITUTION State-supported, coed. Awards: associate, bachelor's, and master's degrees. 56 undergraduate majors. Total enrollment: 10,997. Undergraduates: 9,740. Freshmen: 1,634.
GIFT AID (NEED-BASED) *Scholarships, grants, and awards:* Federal Pell, FSEOG, state, private, college/university gift aid from institutional funds, Federal Nursing.
GIFT AID (NON-NEED-BASED) *Scholarships, grants, and awards by category: Academic Interests/Achievement:* business, computer science, general academic interests/achievements, mathematics, physical sciences. *Creative Arts/Performance:* art/fine arts, debating, music, theater/drama. *Special Achievements/Activities:* general special achievements/activities. *Special Characteristics:* children and siblings of alumni, local/state students, members of minority groups.
LOANS *Programs:* FFEL (Subsidized and Unsubsidized Stafford, PLUS), Perkins, Federal Nursing, state.
APPLYING FOR FINANCIAL AID *Required financial aid form:* FAFSA.
CONTACT Ms. Sheila Denney, Financial Aid Counselor, University of Wisconsin–Oshkosh, 800 Algoma Boulevard, Oshkosh, WI 54901, 920-424-3377. *E-mail:* denney@uwosh.edu.

UNIVERSITY OF WISCONSIN–PARKSIDE
Kenosha, WI

Tuition & fees (WI res): $5001	Average undergraduate aid package: $5420

ABOUT THE INSTITUTION State-supported, coed. Awards: bachelor's and master's degrees. 37 undergraduate majors. Total enrollment: 4,944. Undergraduates: 4,853. Freshmen: 877. Federal methodology is used as a basis for awarding need-based institutional aid.
UNDERGRADUATE EXPENSES for 2005–06 *Application fee:* $35. *Tuition, state resident:* full-time $5001. *Tuition, nonresident:* full-time $15,047. Full-time tuition and fees vary according to course load and reciprocity agreements. Part-time tuition and fees vary according to course load. *College room and board:* $5500; *room only:* $3250. Room and board charges vary according to board plan and housing facility. *Payment plan:* Installment.
FRESHMAN FINANCIAL AID (Fall 2004) 580 applied for aid; of those 78% were deemed to have need. 94% of freshmen with need received aid; of those 91% had need fully met. *Average percent of need met:* 87% (excluding resources awarded to replace EFC). *Average financial aid package:* $4780 (excluding resources awarded to replace EFC).

UNDERGRADUATE FINANCIAL AID (Fall 2004) 2,588 applied for aid; of those 81% were deemed to have need. 100% of undergraduates with need received aid; of those 53% had need fully met. *Average percent of need met:* 84% (excluding resources awarded to replace EFC). *Average financial aid package:* $5420 (excluding resources awarded to replace EFC).
GIFT AID (NEED-BASED) *Total amount:* $7,508,374 (68% federal, 32% state). *Receiving aid:* Freshmen: 46% (405); All full-time undergraduates: 47% (1,666). *Average award:* Freshmen: $3108; Undergraduates: $3212. **Scholarships, grants, and awards:** Federal Pell, FSEOG, state, private, college/university gift aid from institutional funds, Federal Nursing.
GIFT AID (NON-NEED-BASED) *Total amount:* $960,620 (5% state, 53% institutional, 42% external sources). *Receiving aid:* Freshmen: 19% (168); Undergraduates: 9% (318). *Scholarships, grants, and awards by category: Academic Interests/Achievement:* biological sciences, business, communication, education, engineering/technologies, English, foreign languages, general academic interests/achievements, health fields, mathematics, physical sciences, premedicine. *Creative Arts/Performance:* applied art and design, art/fine arts, music, theater/drama. *Special Achievements/Activities:* community service, leadership. *Special Characteristics:* adult students, children of union members/company employees, children of workers in trades, ethnic background, general special characteristics, international students, local/state students, members of minority groups. *Tuition waivers:* Full or partial for senior citizens. *ROTC:* Army cooperative.
LOANS *Student loans:* $12,034,877 (53% need-based, 47% non-need-based). 56% of past graduating class borrowed through all loan programs. *Average indebtedness per student:* $17,158. *Average need-based loan:* Freshmen: $2666; Undergraduates: $3347. *Parent loans:* $1,137,944 (100% non-need-based). *Programs:* FFEL (Subsidized and Unsubsidized Stafford, PLUS), Perkins, state.
WORK-STUDY *Federal work-study:* Total amount: $316,986; 212 jobs averaging $1495.
ATHLETIC AWARDS *Total amount:* $75,350 (100% non-need-based).
APPLYING FOR FINANCIAL AID *Required financial aid form:* FAFSA. *Financial aid deadline:* Continuous. *Notification date:* Continuous beginning 4/1. Students must reply within 2 weeks of notification.
CONTACT Dr. Randall McCready, Director of Financial Aid and Scholarships, University of Wisconsin–Parkside, 900 Wood Road, Kenosha, WI 53141-2000, 262-595-2574. *Fax:* 262-595-2216. *E-mail:* randall.mccready@uwp.edu.

UNIVERSITY OF WISCONSIN–PLATTEVILLE
Platteville, WI

CONTACT Elizabeth Tucker, Director of Financial Aid, University of Wisconsin–Platteville, 1 University Plaza, Platteville, WI 53818-3099, 608-342-1836 or toll-free 800-362-5515. *Fax:* 608-342-1281. *E-mail:* tucker@uwplatt.edu.

UNIVERSITY OF WISCONSIN–RIVER FALLS
River Falls, WI

CONTACT Mr. David Woodward, Director of Financial Aid, University of Wisconsin–River Falls, 410 South Third Street, River Falls, WI 54022-5001, 715-425-3272. *Fax:* 715-425-0708.

UNIVERSITY OF WISCONSIN–STEVENS POINT
Stevens Point, WI

Tuition & fees (WI res): $5062   **Average undergraduate aid package: $6673**

ABOUT THE INSTITUTION State-supported, coed. Awards: associate, bachelor's, and master's degrees. 55 undergraduate majors. Total enrollment: 8,577. Undergraduates: 8,353. Freshmen: 1,523. Federal methodology is used as a basis for awarding need-based institutional aid.
UNDERGRADUATE EXPENSES for 2005–06 *Application fee:* $35. *Tuition, state resident:* full-time $4277; part-time $178 per credit. *Tuition, nonresident:* full-time $14,323; part-time $596 per credit. *Required fees:* full-time $785; $70 per credit. Full-time tuition and fees vary according to course load and reciprocity agreements. Part-time tuition and fees vary according to course load and reciprocity agreements. *College room and board:* $4322; *room only:* $2574. Room and board charges vary according to housing facility. *Payment plan:* Installment.

FRESHMAN FINANCIAL AID (Fall 2004) 1284 applied for aid; of those 59% were deemed to have need. 95% of freshmen with need received aid; of those 65% had need fully met. *Average percent of need met:* 93% (excluding resources awarded to replace EFC). *Average financial aid package:* $5301 (excluding resources awarded to replace EFC). 6% of all full-time freshmen had no need and received non-need-based gift aid.
UNDERGRADUATE FINANCIAL AID (Fall 2004) 7,047 applied for aid; of those 59% were deemed to have need. 97% of undergraduates with need received aid; of those 63% had need fully met. *Average percent of need met:* 89% (excluding resources awarded to replace EFC). *Average financial aid package:* $6673 (excluding resources awarded to replace EFC). 5% of all full-time undergraduates had no need and received non-need-based gift aid.
GIFT AID (NEED-BASED) *Total amount:* $10,021,384 (65% federal, 30% state, 3% institutional, 2% external sources). *Receiving aid:* Freshmen: 22% (333); All full-time undergraduates: 26% (2,131). *Average award:* Freshmen: $4078; Undergraduates: $4413. **Scholarships, grants, and awards:** Federal Pell, FSEOG, state, college/university gift aid from institutional funds.
GIFT AID (NON-NEED-BASED) *Total amount:* $1,345,462 (7% state, 51% institutional, 42% external sources). *Receiving aid:* Freshmen: 4% (67); Undergraduates: 5% (398). *Average Award:* Freshmen: $2072; Undergraduates: $1863. *Scholarships, grants, and awards by category: Academic Interests/Achievement:* 998 awards ($662,360 total): agriculture, architecture, biological sciences, business, communication, computer science, education, engineering/technologies, English, foreign languages, general academic interests/achievements, health fields, home economics, humanities, international studies, mathematics, military science, physical sciences, premedicine, social sciences. *Creative Arts/Performance:* 87 awards ($44,144 total): applied art and design, creative writing, dance, music, performing arts, theater/drama. *Special Achievements/Activities:* 20 awards ($28,183 total): general special achievements/activities, leadership. *Special Characteristics:* 17 awards ($39,309 total): adult students, ethnic background, general special characteristics, international students, members of minority groups, out-of-state students, veterans. *Tuition waivers:* Full or partial for senior citizens. *ROTC:* Army.
LOANS *Student loans:* $22,724,522 (70% need-based, 30% non-need-based). 67% of past graduating class borrowed through all loan programs. *Average indebtedness per student:* $14,975. *Average need-based loan:* Freshmen: $3206; Undergraduates: $4178. *Parent loans:* $1,367,230 (4% need-based, 96% non-need-based). *Programs:* Perkins, college/university.
WORK-STUDY *Federal work-study:* Total amount: $2,247,959; 903 jobs averaging $1267.
APPLYING FOR FINANCIAL AID *Required financial aid form:* FAFSA. *Financial aid deadline (priority):* 6/15. *Notification date:* Continuous. Students must reply within 4 weeks of notification.
CONTACT Mr. Paul Watson, Interim Director of Financial Aid, University of Wisconsin–Stevens Point, 105 Student Services Center, Stevens Point, WI 54481-3897, 715-346-4771. *Fax:* 715-346-3526. *E-mail:* pwatson@uwsp.edu.

UNIVERSITY OF WISCONSIN–STOUT
Menomonie, WI

Tuition & fees (WI res): $6592   **Average undergraduate aid package: $7467**

ABOUT THE INSTITUTION State-supported, coed. Awards: bachelor's and master's degrees and post-master's certificates. 30 undergraduate majors. Total enrollment: 7,891. Undergraduates: 7,337. Freshmen: 1,694. Federal methodology is used as a basis for awarding need-based institutional aid.
UNDERGRADUATE EXPENSES for 2005–06 *Application fee:* $35. *Tuition, state resident:* full-time $4745; part-time $158 per credit. *Tuition, nonresident:* full-time $15,078; part-time $503 per credit. *Required fees:* full-time $1847; $62 per credit. Full-time tuition and fees vary according to reciprocity agreements. Part-time tuition and fees vary according to reciprocity agreements. *College room and board:* $4572; *room only:* $2814. Room and board charges vary according to board plan and housing facility. *Payment plan:* Installment.
FRESHMAN FINANCIAL AID (Fall 2005, est.) 1305 applied for aid; of those 63% were deemed to have need. 100% of freshmen with need received aid; of those 45% had need fully met. *Average percent of need met:* 83% (excluding resources awarded to replace EFC). *Average financial aid package:* $6893 (excluding resources awarded to replace EFC). 12% of all full-time freshmen had no need and received non-need-based gift aid.
UNDERGRADUATE FINANCIAL AID (Fall 2005, est.) 4,869 applied for aid; of those 68% were deemed to have need. 100% of undergraduates with need

University of Wisconsin–Stout

received aid; of those 50% had need fully met. *Average percent of need met:* 85% (excluding resources awarded to replace EFC). *Average financial aid package:* $7467 (excluding resources awarded to replace EFC). 7% of all full-time undergraduates had no need and received non-need-based gift aid.
GIFT AID (NEED-BASED) *Total amount:* $7,347,822 (62% federal, 35% state, 1% institutional, 2% external sources). *Receiving aid:* Freshmen: 24% (404); All full-time undergraduates: 25% (1,670). *Average award:* Freshmen: $3811; Undergraduates: $4177. *Scholarships, grants, and awards:* Federal Pell, FSEOG, state, private, college/university gift aid from institutional funds, Bureau of Indian Affairs Grants, GEAR UP grants.
GIFT AID (NON-NEED-BASED) *Total amount:* $2,023,231 (5% federal, 2% state, 19% institutional, 74% external sources). *Receiving aid:* Freshmen: 24% (412); Undergraduates: 11% (744). *Average Award:* Freshmen: $1370; Undergraduates: $2087. *Scholarships, grants, and awards by category: Academic Interests/Achievement:* 242 awards ($208,035 total): business, education, engineering/technologies, general academic interests/achievements, home economics, international studies, mathematics, physical sciences. *Creative Arts/Performance:* 14 awards ($3600 total): applied art and design, art/fine arts, music. *Special Achievements/Activities:* 20 awards ($10,475 total): community service, general special achievements/activities, memberships. *Special Characteristics:* 36 awards ($26,450 total): adult students, first-generation college students, handicapped students, international students, local/state students, members of minority groups, out-of-state students, previous college experience, veterans, veterans' children.
LOANS *Student loans:* $26,576,368 (48% need-based, 52% non-need-based). 73% of past graduating class borrowed through all loan programs. *Average indebtedness per student:* $18,496. *Average need-based loan:* Freshmen: $3170; Undergraduates: $3880. *Parent loans:* $3,362,954 (100% non-need-based). *Programs:* FFEL (Subsidized and Unsubsidized Stafford, PLUS), Perkins, alternative loans.
WORK-STUDY *Federal work-study:* Total amount: $2,082,507; 1,249 jobs averaging $1493.
APPLYING FOR FINANCIAL AID *Required financial aid form:* FAFSA. *Financial aid deadline (priority):* 3/15. *Notification date:* Continuous beginning 4/1. Students must reply within 4 weeks of notification.
CONTACT Beth A. Resech, Director of Financial Aid, University of Wisconsin–Stout, 210 Bowman Hall, Menomonie, WI 54751, 715-232-1363 or toll-free 800-HI-STOUT (in-state). *Fax:* 715-232-5246. *E-mail:* resechb@uwstout.edu.

UNIVERSITY OF WISCONSIN–SUPERIOR
Superior, WI

ABOUT THE INSTITUTION State-supported, coed. Awards: bachelor's and master's degrees (associate, educational specialist). 63 undergraduate majors. Total enrollment: 2,872. Undergraduates: 2,583. Freshmen: 346.
GIFT AID (NEED-BASED) *Scholarships, grants, and awards:* Federal Pell, FSEOG, state, private, college/university gift aid from institutional funds.
GIFT AID (NON-NEED-BASED) *Scholarships, grants, and awards by category: Academic Interests/Achievement:* biological sciences, business, communication, computer science, education, English, general academic interests/achievements, health fields, humanities, mathematics, physical sciences, social sciences. *Special Characteristics:* general special characteristics.
LOANS *Programs:* Federal Direct (Subsidized and Unsubsidized Stafford, PLUS), Perkins, state, college/university.
WORK-STUDY *Federal work-study:* Total amount: $362,871; 260 jobs averaging $1320. *State or other work-study/employment:* Part-time jobs available.
APPLYING FOR FINANCIAL AID *Required financial aid form:* FAFSA.
CONTACT Financial Aid Office, University of Wisconsin–Superior, Belknap and Catlin, PO Box 2000, Superior, WI 54880-4500, 715-394-8200 or toll-free 715-394-8230 (in-state).

UNIVERSITY OF WISCONSIN–WHITEWATER
Whitewater, WI

Tuition & fees (WI res): $5080	Average undergraduate aid package: $6527

ABOUT THE INSTITUTION State-supported, coed. Awards: associate, bachelor's, and master's degrees. 56 undergraduate majors. Total enrollment: 10,750. Undergraduates: 9,387. Freshmen: 1,712. Federal methodology is used as a basis for awarding need-based institutional aid.
UNDERGRADUATE EXPENSES for 2005–06 *Application fee:* $35. *One-time required fee:* $100. *Tuition, state resident:* full-time $4370; part-time $186 per credit. *Tuition, nonresident:* full-time $14,965; part-time $663 per credit. *Required fees:* full-time $710; $28.75 per credit. Full-time tuition and fees vary according to degree level and reciprocity agreements. *College room and board:* $4210; *room only:* $2460. Room and board charges vary according to board plan. *Payment plan:* Installment.
FRESHMAN FINANCIAL AID (Fall 2005, est.) 1427 applied for aid; of those 67% were deemed to have need. 93% of freshmen with need received aid; of those 44% had need fully met. *Average percent of need met:* 70% (excluding resources awarded to replace EFC). *Average financial aid package:* $5866 (excluding resources awarded to replace EFC). 11% of all full-time freshmen had no need and received non-need-based gift aid.
UNDERGRADUATE FINANCIAL AID (Fall 2005, est.) 5,770 applied for aid; of those 69% were deemed to have need. 94% of undergraduates with need received aid; of those 53% had need fully met. *Average percent of need met:* 75% (excluding resources awarded to replace EFC). *Average financial aid package:* $6527 (excluding resources awarded to replace EFC). 7% of all full-time undergraduates had no need and received non-need-based gift aid.
GIFT AID (NEED-BASED) *Total amount:* $8,900,000 (58% federal, 42% state). *Receiving aid:* Freshmen: 22% (380); All full-time undergraduates: 20% (1,751). *Average award:* Freshmen: $4860; Undergraduates: $4739. *Scholarships, grants, and awards:* Federal Pell, FSEOG, state, private, college/university gift aid from institutional funds.
GIFT AID (NON-NEED-BASED) *Total amount:* $2,466,000 (3% federal, 4% state, 32% institutional, 61% external sources). *Receiving aid:* Freshmen: 13% (222); Undergraduates: 5% (466). *Average Award:* Freshmen: $2264; Undergraduates: $2091. *Scholarships, grants, and awards by category: Academic Interests/Achievement:* biological sciences, business, communication, computer science, education, English, foreign languages, general academic interests/achievements, humanities, mathematics, physical sciences, premedicine, social sciences. *Creative Arts/Performance:* art/fine arts, cinema/film/broadcasting, creative writing, journalism/publications, music, theater/drama. *Special Achievements/Activities:* leadership. *Special Characteristics:* adult students, ethnic background, handicapped students, international students, local/state students, members of minority groups, out-of-state students. *Tuition waivers:* Full or partial for children of alumni, senior citizens. *ROTC:* Army, Air Force.
LOANS *Student loans:* $32,000,000 (50% need-based, 50% non-need-based). 63% of past graduating class borrowed through all loan programs. *Average indebtedness per student:* $17,394. *Average need-based loan:* Freshmen: $3014; Undergraduates: $3822. *Parent loans:* $3,500,000 (100% non-need-based). *Programs:* Federal Direct (Subsidized and Unsubsidized Stafford, PLUS), Perkins.
WORK-STUDY *Federal work-study:* Total amount: $670,000; 515 jobs averaging $1300. *State or other work-study/employment:* Total amount: $3,000,000 (100% non-need-based). 2,100 part-time jobs averaging $1660.
APPLYING FOR FINANCIAL AID *Required financial aid form:* FAFSA. *Financial aid deadline (priority):* 3/15. *Notification date:* Continuous beginning 4/1. Students must reply within 2 weeks of notification.
CONTACT Ms. Carol Miller, Director of Financial Aid, University of Wisconsin–Whitewater, 800 West Main Street, Whitewater, WI 53190-1790, 262-472-1130. *Fax:* 262-472-5655.

UNIVERSITY OF WYOMING
Laramie, WY

Tuition & fees (WY res): $3426	Average undergraduate aid package: $7017

ABOUT THE INSTITUTION State-supported, coed. Awards: bachelor's, master's, doctoral, and first professional degrees and post-master's certificates. 78 undergraduate majors. Total enrollment: 13,126. Undergraduates: 9,510. Freshmen: 1,421. Federal methodology is used as a basis for awarding need-based institutional aid.
UNDERGRADUATE EXPENSES for 2005–06 *Application fee:* $30. *Tuition, state resident:* full-time $2760; part-time $92 per credit hour. *Tuition, nonresident:* full-time $9150; part-time $305 per credit hour. *Required fees:* full-time $666; $162 per term part-time. Full-time tuition and fees vary according to course load, location, program, and reciprocity agreements. Part-time tuition and fees vary according to course load, location, program, and reciprocity agreements. *College room and board:* $6240; *room only:* $2709. Room and board charges vary according to board plan and housing facility. *Payment plans:* Installment, deferred payment.

FRESHMAN FINANCIAL AID (Fall 2004) 1297 applied for aid; of those 79% were deemed to have need. 98% of freshmen with need received aid; of those 22% had need fully met. *Average percent of need met:* 76% (excluding resources awarded to replace EFC). *Average financial aid package:* $6512 (excluding resources awarded to replace EFC). 20% of all full-time freshmen had no need and received non-need-based gift aid.

UNDERGRADUATE FINANCIAL AID (Fall 2004) 5,250 applied for aid; of those 76% were deemed to have need. 98% of undergraduates with need received aid; of those 23% had need fully met. *Average percent of need met:* 75% (excluding resources awarded to replace EFC). *Average financial aid package:* $7017 (excluding resources awarded to replace EFC). 17% of all full-time undergraduates had no need and received non-need-based gift aid.

GIFT AID (NEED-BASED) *Total amount:* $8,170,649 (88% federal, 1% state, 3% institutional, 8% external sources). *Receiving aid:* Freshmen: 34% (476); All full-time undergraduates: 28% (2,497). *Average award:* Freshmen: $2656; Undergraduates: $3272. *Scholarships, grants, and awards:* Federal Pell, FSEOG, state, private, college/university gift aid from institutional funds.

GIFT AID (NON-NEED-BASED) *Total amount:* $14,840,288 (12% federal, 50% state, 16% institutional, 22% external sources). *Receiving aid:* Freshmen: 52% (726); Undergraduates: 16% (1,470). *Average Award:* Freshmen: $1574; Undergraduates: $1434. *Scholarships, grants, and awards by category: Academic Interests/Achievement:* 2,532 awards ($5,440,298 total): agriculture, business, communication, computer science, education, engineering/technologies, English, foreign languages, general academic interests/achievements, health fields, home economics, international studies, mathematics, military science, physical sciences, social sciences. *Creative Arts/Performance:* 476 awards ($529,292 total): dance, debating, music, theater/drama. *Special Achievements/Activities:* 202 awards ($240,857 total): cheerleading/drum major, junior miss, leadership, rodeo. *Special Characteristics:* adult students, children and siblings of alumni, ethnic background, first-generation college students, handicapped students, international students, local/state students, out-of-state students, veterans. *Tuition waivers:* Full or partial for children of alumni, employees or children of employees, senior citizens. *ROTC:* Army, Air Force.

LOANS *Student loans:* $21,807,201 (60% need-based, 40% non-need-based). 45% of past graduating class borrowed through all loan programs. *Average indebtedness per student:* $16,741. *Average need-based loan:* Freshmen: $2030; Undergraduates: $4022. *Parent loans:* $2,424,974 (100% non-need-based). *Programs:* FFEL (Subsidized and Unsubsidized Stafford, PLUS), Perkins, alternative loans.

WORK-STUDY *Federal work-study:* Total amount: $520,085; 450 jobs averaging $1197.

ATHLETIC AWARDS *Total amount:* $2,762,801 (100% non-need-based).

APPLYING FOR FINANCIAL AID *Required financial aid form:* FAFSA. *Financial aid deadline (priority):* 2/1. *Notification date:* Continuous beginning 3/15. Students must reply within 3 weeks of notification.

CONTACT Mr. David Gruen, Director of Student Financial Aid, University of Wyoming, Department 3335, 1000 East University Avenue, Laramie, WY 82071-3335, 307-766-2116 or toll-free 800-342-5996. *Fax:* 307-766-3800. *E-mail:* finaid@uwyo.edu.

UPPER IOWA UNIVERSITY
Fayette, IA

CONTACT Jobyna Johnston, Director of Financial Aid, Upper Iowa University, Parker Fox Hall, Box 1859, Fayette, IA 52142-1859, 563-425-5393 or toll-free 800-553-4150 Ext. 2. *Fax:* 563-425-5277. *E-mail:* jobyna@uiu.edu.

URBANA UNIVERSITY
Urbana, OH

Tuition & fees: $16,254 **Average undergraduate aid package:** $12,617

ABOUT THE INSTITUTION Independent, coed. Awards: associate, bachelor's, and master's degrees. 28 undergraduate majors. Total enrollment: 1,551. Undergraduates: 1,461. Freshmen: 279. Federal methodology is used as a basis for awarding need-based institutional aid.

UNDERGRADUATE EXPENSES for 2006–07 *Application fee:* $25. *Comprehensive fee:* $22,866 includes full-time tuition ($16,254) and room and board ($6612). *College room only:* $2234. *Part-time tuition:* $337 per semester hour.

FRESHMAN FINANCIAL AID (Fall 2005, est.) 287 applied for aid; of those 97% were deemed to have need. 100% of freshmen with need received aid; of those 66% had need fully met. *Average percent of need met:* 32% (excluding resources awarded to replace EFC). *Average financial aid package:* $10,412 (excluding resources awarded to replace EFC).

UNDERGRADUATE FINANCIAL AID (Fall 2005, est.) 693 applied for aid; of those 97% were deemed to have need. 100% of undergraduates with need received aid; of those 80% had need fully met. *Average percent of need met:* 40% (excluding resources awarded to replace EFC). *Average financial aid package:* $12,617 (excluding resources awarded to replace EFC).

GIFT AID (NEED-BASED) *Total amount:* $1,732,045 (63% federal, 37% state). *Receiving aid:* Freshmen: 44% (142); All full-time undergraduates: 75% (538). *Average award:* Freshmen: $1641; Undergraduates: $2106. *Scholarships, grants, and awards:* Federal Pell, FSEOG, state, private, college/university gift aid from institutional funds.

GIFT AID (NON-NEED-BASED) *Total amount:* $2,140,965 (25% state, 68% institutional, 7% external sources). *Receiving aid:* Freshmen: 87% (279); Undergraduates: 93% (673). *Scholarships, grants, and awards by category: Academic Interests/Achievement:* 304 awards ($1,002,034 total): general academic interests/achievements. *Creative Arts/Performance:* 37 awards ($151,380 total): music. *Special Achievements/Activities:* community service, leadership, religious involvement. *Special Characteristics:* 51 awards ($246,631 total): children and siblings of alumni, children of faculty/staff, religious affiliation, spouses of current students.

LOANS *Student loans:* $5,735,381 (100% need-based). 86% of past graduating class borrowed through all loan programs. *Average indebtedness per student:* $20,462. *Average need-based loan:* Freshmen: $3082; Undergraduates: $4861. *Parent loans:* $11,718,403 (100% need-based). *Programs:* FFEL (Subsidized and Unsubsidized Stafford, PLUS), Perkins.

WORK-STUDY *Federal work-study:* Total amount: $145,205; 267 jobs averaging $1200.

ATHLETIC AWARDS *Total amount:* $2,705,220 (100% non-need-based).

APPLYING FOR FINANCIAL AID *Required financial aid forms:* FAFSA, institution's own form. *Financial aid deadline (priority):* 4/1. *Notification date:* Continuous beginning 2/15. Students must reply within 4 weeks of notification.

CONTACT Mrs. Amy M. Barnhart, Director of Student Financial Services, Urbana University, 579 College Way, Urbana, OH 43078-2091, 937-484-1359 or toll-free 800-7-URBANA. *Fax:* 937-652-6870. *E-mail:* abarnhart@urbana.edu.

URSINUS COLLEGE
Collegeville, PA

Tuition & fees: $31,600 **Average undergraduate aid package:** $23,938

ABOUT THE INSTITUTION Independent, coed. Awards: bachelor's degrees. 36 undergraduate majors. Total enrollment: 1,571. Undergraduates: 1,571. Freshmen: 415. Both federal and institutional methodology are used as a basis for awarding need-based institutional aid.

UNDERGRADUATE EXPENSES for 2005–06 *Application fee:* $50. *Comprehensive fee:* $38,950 includes full-time tuition ($31,450), mandatory fees ($150), and room and board ($7350). *Part-time tuition:* $1048 per credit. *Payment plan:* Installment.

FRESHMAN FINANCIAL AID (Fall 2005, est.) 411 applied for aid; of those 79% were deemed to have need. 100% of freshmen with need received aid; of those 75% had need fully met. *Average percent of need met:* 85% (excluding resources awarded to replace EFC). *Average financial aid package:* $24,927 (excluding resources awarded to replace EFC). 20% of all full-time freshmen had no need and received non-need-based gift aid.

UNDERGRADUATE FINANCIAL AID (Fall 2005, est.) 1,521 applied for aid; of those 85% were deemed to have need. 100% of undergraduates with need received aid; of those 65% had need fully met. *Average percent of need met:* 85% (excluding resources awarded to replace EFC). *Average financial aid package:* $23,938 (excluding resources awarded to replace EFC). 15% of all full-time undergraduates had no need and received non-need-based gift aid.

GIFT AID (NEED-BASED) *Total amount:* $22,035,107 (6% federal, 6% state, 88% institutional). *Receiving aid:* Freshmen: 78% (326); All full-time undergraduates: 83% (1,291). *Average award:* Freshmen: $20,043; Undergraduates: $18,558. *Scholarships, grants, and awards:* Federal Pell, FSEOG, state, private, college/university gift aid from institutional funds, Office of Vocational Rehabilitation Awards.

Ursinus College

GIFT AID (NON-NEED-BASED) *Total amount:* $3,993,359 (86% institutional, 14% external sources). *Receiving aid:* Freshmen: 8% (35); Undergraduates: 8% (118). *Average Award:* Freshmen: $10,000; Undergraduates: $9000. *Scholarships, grants, and awards by category: Academic Interests/Achievement:* 118 awards ($3,993,359 total): general academic interests/achievements. *Creative Arts/Performance:* 12 awards ($100,000 total): art/fine arts, creative writing, music, theater/drama. *Special Achievements/Activities:* 60 awards ($350,000 total): leadership. *Special Characteristics:* 60 awards ($527,000 total): children of faculty/staff, international students, siblings of current students. *Tuition waivers:* Full or partial for employees or children of employees, senior citizens.
LOANS *Student loans:* $10,799,770 (100% need-based). 78% of past graduating class borrowed through all loan programs. *Average indebtedness per student:* $18,000. *Average need-based loan:* Freshmen: $3649; Undergraduates: $4607. *Parent loans:* $3,462,544 (100% need-based). *Programs:* FFEL (Subsidized and Unsubsidized Stafford, PLUS), Perkins, college/university.
WORK-STUDY *Federal work-study:* Total amount: $1,262,000; 637 jobs averaging $1540.
APPLYING FOR FINANCIAL AID *Required financial aid forms:* FAFSA, institution's own form, CSS Financial Aid PROFILE. *Financial aid deadline (priority):* 2/15. *Notification date:* 4/1. Students must reply by 5/1.
CONTACT Ms. Suzanne B. Sparrow, Financial Aid Officer, Ursinus College, PO Box 1000, Collegeville, PA 19426-1000, 610-409-3600 Ext. 2242. *Fax:* 610-409-3662. *E-mail:* ssparrowui@ursinus.edu.

URSULINE COLLEGE
Pepper Pike, OH

ABOUT THE INSTITUTION Independent Roman Catholic, undergraduate: women only; graduate: coed. Awards: bachelor's and master's degrees and post-master's certificates (applications from men are also accepted). 47 undergraduate majors. Total enrollment: 1,494. Undergraduates: 1,152. Freshmen: 141.
GIFT AID (NEED-BASED) *Scholarships, grants, and awards:* Federal Pell, FSEOG, state, private, college/university gift aid from institutional funds, United Negro College Fund.
GIFT AID (NON-NEED-BASED) *Scholarships, grants, and awards by category: Academic Interests/Achievement:* general academic interests/achievements. *Special Achievements/Activities:* community service, leadership. *Special Characteristics:* children and siblings of alumni, children of faculty/staff, relatives of clergy, religious affiliation, siblings of current students.
LOANS *Programs:* FFEL (Subsidized and Unsubsidized Stafford, PLUS), Perkins, college/university.
APPLYING FOR FINANCIAL AID *Required financial aid forms:* FAFSA, institution's own form.
CONTACT Ms. Mary Lynn Perri, Director of Financial Aid and Enrollment Services, Ursuline College, 2550 Lander Road, Mullen Building, Room 202b, Pepper Pike, OH 44124-4398, 440-646-8330 or toll-free 888-URSULINE.

UTAH STATE UNIVERSITY
Logan, UT

Tuition & fees (UT res): $3672	Average undergraduate aid package: $5000

ABOUT THE INSTITUTION State-supported, coed. Awards: associate, bachelor's, master's, and doctoral degrees and post-bachelor's and post-master's certificates. 121 undergraduate majors. Total enrollment: 14,458. Undergraduates: 12,737. Freshmen: 2,054. Federal methodology is used as a basis for awarding need-based institutional aid.
UNDERGRADUATE EXPENSES for 2005–06 *Application fee:* $40. *Tuition, state resident:* full-time $3128. *Tuition, nonresident:* full-time $10,072. Full-time tuition and fees vary according to course load and student level. Part-time tuition and fees vary according to course load and student level. *College room and board:* $4330; *room only:* $1550. Room and board charges vary according to board plan and housing facility. *Payment plan:* Deferred payment.
FRESHMAN FINANCIAL AID (Fall 2004) 899 applied for aid; of those 83% were deemed to have need. 95% of freshmen with need received aid; of those 13% had need fully met. *Average percent of need met:* 60% (excluding resources awarded to replace EFC). *Average financial aid package:* $3400 (excluding resources awarded to replace EFC). 16% of all full-time freshmen had no need and received non-need-based gift aid.
UNDERGRADUATE FINANCIAL AID (Fall 2004) 5,812 applied for aid; of those 92% were deemed to have need. 97% of undergraduates with need received aid; of those 13% had need fully met. *Average percent of need met:* 59% (excluding resources awarded to replace EFC). *Average financial aid package:* $5000 (excluding resources awarded to replace EFC). 9% of all full-time undergraduates had no need and received non-need-based gift aid.
GIFT AID (NEED-BASED) *Total amount:* $14,661,252 (98% federal, 2% state). *Receiving aid:* Freshmen: 22% (446); All full-time undergraduates: 36% (4,063). *Average award:* Freshmen: $2800; Undergraduates: $3100. *Scholarships, grants, and awards:* Federal Pell, FSEOG, state, private, college/university gift aid from institutional funds.
GIFT AID (NON-NEED-BASED) *Total amount:* $5,669,907 (87% institutional, 13% external sources). *Receiving aid:* Freshmen: 13% (266); Undergraduates: 12% (1,324). *Average Award:* Freshmen: $2550; Undergraduates: $2900. *Scholarships, grants, and awards by category: Academic Interests/Achievement:* 6,994 awards ($10,863,860 total): agriculture, architecture, biological sciences, business, communication, computer science, education, engineering/technologies, English, foreign languages, general academic interests/achievements, health fields, home economics, humanities, international studies, library science, mathematics, physical sciences, premedicine, social sciences. *Creative Arts/Performance:* 158 awards ($174,225 total): applied art and design, art/fine arts, general creative arts/performance, journalism/publications, music, performing arts, theater/drama. *Tuition waivers:* Full or partial for minority students, children of alumni, employees or children of employees, adult students, senior citizens.
ROTC: Army, Air Force.
LOANS *Student loans:* $19,376,365 (76% need-based, 24% non-need-based). 50% of past graduating class borrowed through all loan programs. *Average indebtedness per student:* $12,430. *Average need-based loan:* Freshmen: $2600; Undergraduates: $3800. *Parent loans:* $947,848 (100% non-need-based). *Programs:* FFEL (Subsidized and Unsubsidized Stafford, PLUS), Perkins, college/university.
WORK-STUDY *Federal work-study:* Total amount: $969,604; 458 jobs averaging $2406. *State or other work-study/employment:* Total amount: $231,204 (100% need-based). 113 part-time jobs averaging $2406.
ATHLETIC AWARDS *Total amount:* $1,955,100 (100% non-need-based).
APPLYING FOR FINANCIAL AID *Required financial aid forms:* FAFSA, institution's own form. *Financial aid deadline:* Continuous. *Notification date:* Continuous beginning 4/1. Students must reply within 4 weeks of notification.
CONTACT Steve Sharp, Associate Director of Financial Aid, Utah State University, Old Main Hill, Logan, UT 84322, 435-797-1455 or toll-free 800-488-8108. *Fax:* 435-797-0654. *E-mail:* sjsharp@cc.usu.edu.

UTAH VALLEY STATE COLLEGE
Orem, UT

ABOUT THE INSTITUTION State-supported, coed. Awards: associate and bachelor's degrees. 77 undergraduate majors. Total enrollment: 24,487. Undergraduates: 24,487. Freshmen: 3,713.
GIFT AID (NEED-BASED) *Scholarships, grants, and awards:* Federal Pell, FSEOG, state, private, college/university gift aid from institutional funds.
LOANS *Programs:* FFEL (Subsidized and Unsubsidized Stafford, PLUS), Perkins, college/university.
APPLYING FOR FINANCIAL AID *Required financial aid forms:* FAFSA, institution's own form.
CONTACT Mr. Michael H. Johnson, Director of Financial Aid, Utah Valley State College, Mail Code—164, 800 West 1200 South Street, Orem, UT 84058-0001, 801-222-8442. *Fax:* 801-222-8448.

U.T.A. MESIVTA OF KIRYAS JOEL
Monroe, NY

CONTACT Financial Aid Office, U.T.A. Mesivta of Kiryas Joel, 33 Forest Road, Suite 101, Monroe, NY 10950, 845-873-9901.

UTICA COLLEGE
Utica, NY

Tuition & fees: $22,340	Average undergraduate aid package: $18,190

ABOUT THE INSTITUTION Independent, coed. Awards: bachelor's, master's, and first professional degrees. 44 undergraduate majors. Total enrollment: 2,888. Undergraduates: 2,413. Freshmen: 470. Federal methodology is used as a basis for awarding need-based institutional aid.
UNDERGRADUATE EXPENSES for 2005–06 *Application fee:* $40. *Comprehensive fee:* $31,396 includes full-time tuition ($22,030), mandatory fees ($310), and room and board ($9056). *College room only:* $4750. Full-time tuition and fees vary according to class time and course load. Room and board charges vary according to board plan and housing facility. *Part-time tuition:* $750 per credit hour. *Part-time fees:* $50 per term. Part-time tuition and fees vary according to class time and course load. *Payment plans:* Installment, deferred payment.
FRESHMAN FINANCIAL AID (Fall 2005, est.) 417 applied for aid; of those 93% were deemed to have need. 100% of freshmen with need received aid; of those 9% had need fully met. *Average percent of need met:* 78% (excluding resources awarded to replace EFC). *Average financial aid package:* $19,483 (excluding resources awarded to replace EFC). 7% of all full-time freshmen had no need and received non-need-based gift aid.
UNDERGRADUATE FINANCIAL AID (Fall 2005, est.) 1,859 applied for aid; of those 93% were deemed to have need. 100% of undergraduates with need received aid; of those 18% had need fully met. *Average percent of need met:* 73% (excluding resources awarded to replace EFC). *Average financial aid package:* $18,190 (excluding resources awarded to replace EFC). 7% of all full-time undergraduates had no need and received non-need-based gift aid.
GIFT AID (NEED-BASED) *Total amount:* $23,618,873 (11% federal, 16% state, 71% institutional, 2% external sources). *Receiving aid:* Freshmen: 90% (387); All full-time undergraduates: 90% (1,733). *Average award:* Freshmen: $9859; Undergraduates: $7451. *Scholarships, grants, and awards:* Federal Pell, FSEOG, state, private, college/university gift aid from institutional funds, Federal Nursing.
GIFT AID (NON-NEED-BASED) *Total amount:* $970,096 (1% federal, 3% state, 95% institutional, 1% external sources). *Receiving aid:* Freshmen: 7% (28); Undergraduates: 6% (119). *Average Award:* Freshmen: $5945; Undergraduates: $6004. *Scholarships, grants, and awards by category:* Academic Interests/Achievement: 107 awards ($504,317 total): general academic interests/achievements. *Tuition waivers:* Full or partial for employees or children of employees, senior citizens. *ROTC:* Army, Air Force cooperative.
LOANS *Student loans:* $9,734,488 (94% need-based, 6% non-need-based). 89% of past graduating class borrowed through all loan programs. *Average indebtedness per student:* $25,565. *Average need-based loan:* Freshmen: $3722; Undergraduates: $4447. *Parent loans:* $3,688,604 (93% need-based, 7% non-need-based). *Programs:* Federal Direct (Subsidized and Unsubsidized Stafford, PLUS), Perkins, GATE Loans.
WORK-STUDY *Federal work-study:* Total amount: $1,400,403; 872 jobs averaging $1512. *State or other work-study/employment:* Total amount: $546,126 (80% need-based, 20% non-need-based). 367 part-time jobs averaging $1540.
APPLYING FOR FINANCIAL AID *Required financial aid forms:* FAFSA, state aid form. *Financial aid deadline (priority):* 2/15. *Notification date:* Continuous beginning 2/1. Students must reply by 5/1 or within 4 weeks of notification.
CONTACT Mrs. Elizabeth C. Wilson, Director of Financial Aid, Utica College, 1600 Burrstone Road, Utica, NY 13502-4892, 800-782-8884. *Fax:* 315-792-3368.

VALDOSTA STATE UNIVERSITY
Valdosta, GA

Tuition & fees (GA res): $3278	Average undergraduate aid package: $12,672

ABOUT THE INSTITUTION State-supported, coed. Awards: associate, bachelor's, master's, and doctoral degrees and post-master's certificates. 49 undergraduate majors. Total enrollment: 10,503. Undergraduates: 9,093. Freshmen: 1,812. Federal methodology is used as a basis for awarding need-based institutional aid.
UNDERGRADUATE EXPENSES for 2005–06 *Application fee:* $20. *Tuition, state resident:* full-time $2438; part-time $102 per semester hour. *Tuition, nonresident:* full-time $9754; part-time $407 per semester hour. *Required fees:* full-time $840; $38. Part-time tuition and fees vary according to course load. *College room and board:* $5524; *room only:* $2904. Room and board charges vary according to board plan and housing facility.
FRESHMAN FINANCIAL AID (Fall 2004) 1681 applied for aid; of those 56% were deemed to have need. 100% of freshmen with need received aid; of those 83% had need fully met. *Average percent of need met:* 82% (excluding resources awarded to replace EFC). *Average financial aid package:* $8244 (excluding resources awarded to replace EFC). 7% of all full-time freshmen had no need and received non-need-based gift aid.
UNDERGRADUATE FINANCIAL AID (Fall 2004) 6,070 applied for aid; of those 59% were deemed to have need. 100% of undergraduates with need received aid; of those 71% had need fully met. *Average percent of need met:* 91% (excluding resources awarded to replace EFC). *Average financial aid package:* $12,672 (excluding resources awarded to replace EFC). 2% of all full-time undergraduates had no need and received non-need-based gift aid.
GIFT AID (NEED-BASED) *Total amount:* $17,308,069 (48% federal, 48% state, 1% institutional, 3% external sources). *Receiving aid:* Freshmen: 51% (877); All full-time undergraduates: 30% (2,095). *Average award:* Freshmen: $4413; Undergraduates: $4631. *Scholarships, grants, and awards:* Federal Pell, FSEOG, state, private, college/university gift aid from institutional funds.
GIFT AID (NON-NEED-BASED) *Total amount:* $9,144,639 (95% state, 2% institutional, 3% external sources). *Receiving aid:* Freshmen: 44% (759); Undergraduates: 27% (1,882). *Average Award:* Freshmen: $1843; Undergraduates: $1445. *Scholarships, grants, and awards by category:* Academic Interests/Achievement: 412 awards ($217,374 total): biological sciences, business, communication, computer science, education, engineering/technologies, English, foreign languages, general academic interests/achievements, health fields, humanities, library science, mathematics, military science, physical sciences, premedicine, social sciences. Creative Arts/Performance: 71 awards ($59,255 total): art/fine arts, music, theater/drama. Special Achievements/Activities: 86 awards ($89,610 total): community service, general special achievements/activities, hobbies/interests. Special Characteristics: 38 awards ($34,800 total): children of public servants, general special characteristics, international students, members of minority groups. *Tuition waivers:* Full or partial for employees or children of employees, senior citizens. *ROTC:* Air Force.
LOANS *Student loans:* $34,634,189 (55% need-based, 45% non-need-based). 61% of past graduating class borrowed through all loan programs. *Average indebtedness per student:* $16,220. *Average need-based loan:* Freshmen: $2176; Undergraduates: $3873. *Parent loans:* $22,103,847 (25% need-based, 75% non-need-based). *Programs:* Federal Direct (Subsidized and Unsubsidized Stafford, PLUS), college/university.
WORK-STUDY *Federal work-study:* Total amount: $594,621; 345 jobs averaging $1723.
ATHLETIC AWARDS Total amount: $732,867 (42% need-based, 58% non-need-based).
APPLYING FOR FINANCIAL AID *Required financial aid form:* FAFSA. *Financial aid deadline (priority):* 5/1. *Notification date:* Continuous beginning 5/15.
CONTACT Mr. Douglas R. Tanner, Director of Financial Aid, Valdosta State University, 1500 North Patterson Street, Valdosta, GA 31698, 229-333-5935 or toll-free 800-618-1878 Ext. 1. *Fax:* 229-333-5430.

VALLEY CITY STATE UNIVERSITY
Valley City, ND

Tuition & fees (ND res): $5160	Average undergraduate aid package: $6401

ABOUT THE INSTITUTION State-supported, coed. Awards: bachelor's degrees. 40 undergraduate majors. Total enrollment: 1,035. Undergraduates: 1,013. Freshmen: 173. Federal methodology is used as a basis for awarding need-based institutional aid.
UNDERGRADUATE EXPENSES for 2005–06 *Application fee:* $35. *Tuition, state resident:* full-time $3656; part-time $114.25 per semester hour. *Tuition, nonresident:* full-time $9761; part-time $305.05 per semester hour. *College room and board:* $4694; *room only:* $2080. Room and board charges vary according to board plan.
FRESHMAN FINANCIAL AID (Fall 2005, est.) 122 applied for aid; of those 85% were deemed to have need. 98% of freshmen with need received aid; of those 27% had need fully met. *Average percent of need met:* 72% (excluding resources awarded to replace EFC). *Average financial aid package:* $5194 (excluding resources awarded to replace EFC). 17% of all full-time freshmen had no need and received non-need-based gift aid.
UNDERGRADUATE FINANCIAL AID (Fall 2005, est.) 579 applied for aid; of those 82% were deemed to have need. 99% of undergraduates with need received aid; of those 19% had need fully met. *Average percent of need met:* 69% (excluding resources awarded to replace EFC). *Average financial aid*

Valley City State University

package: $6401 (excluding resources awarded to replace EFC). 14% of all full-time undergraduates had no need and received non-need-based gift aid. **GIFT AID (NEED-BASED)** *Total amount:* $1,109,928 (70% federal, 7% state, 18% institutional, 5% external sources). *Receiving aid:* Freshmen: 57% (98); All full-time undergraduates: 50% (391). *Average award:* Freshmen: $4309; Undergraduates: $3534. *Scholarships, grants, and awards:* Federal Pell, FSEOG, state, private, college/university gift aid from institutional funds.
GIFT AID (NON-NEED-BASED) *Total amount:* $73,277 (78% institutional, 22% external sources). *Receiving aid:* Freshmen: 52% (90); Undergraduates: 37% (289). *Average Award:* Freshmen: $1278; Undergraduates: $1204. *Scholarships, grants, and awards by category: Academic Interests/Achievement:* 374 awards ($558,400 total): biological sciences, business, communication, computer science, education, English, general academic interests/achievements, library science, mathematics, physical sciences, social sciences. *Creative Arts/Performance:* 90 awards ($26,700 total): applied art and design, art/fine arts, journalism/publications, music, theater/drama. *Special Achievements/Activities:* 154 awards ($135,240 total): general special achievements/activities. *Special Characteristics:* 14 awards ($24,020 total): children of faculty/staff. *Tuition waivers:* Full or partial for children of alumni, employees or children of employees.
LOANS *Student loans:* $3,283,678 (46% need-based, 54% non-need-based). 60% of past graduating class borrowed through all loan programs. *Average indebtedness per student:* $18,394. *Average need-based loan:* Freshmen: $2820; Undergraduates: $3626. *Parent loans:* $110,516 (70% need-based, 30% non-need-based). *Programs:* FFEL (Subsidized and Unsubsidized Stafford, PLUS), Perkins, college/university.
WORK-STUDY *Federal work-study:* Total amount: $95,775; 70 jobs averaging $1368. *State or other work-study/employment:* Total amount: $195,384 (100% non-need-based). 155 part-time jobs averaging $1261.
ATHLETIC AWARDS *Total amount:* $122,925 (53% need-based, 47% non-need-based).
APPLYING FOR FINANCIAL AID *Required financial aid form:* FAFSA. *Financial aid deadline (priority):* 3/15. *Notification date:* Continuous beginning 2/1. Students must reply within 4 weeks of notification.
CONTACT Betty Kuss Schumacher, Director of Financial Aid, Valley City State University, 101 College Street SW, Valley City, ND 58072, 701-845-7412 or toll-free 800-532-8641 Ext. 37101. *Fax:* 701-845-7410. *E-mail:* betty.schumacher@vcsu.edu.

VALLEY FORGE CHRISTIAN COLLEGE
Phoenixville, PA

Tuition & fees: $11,700 — **Average undergraduate aid package:** $7325

ABOUT THE INSTITUTION Independent Assemblies of God, coed. Awards: associate and bachelor's degrees. 6 undergraduate majors. Total enrollment: 934. Undergraduates: 934. Freshmen: 212. Federal methodology is used as a basis for awarding need-based institutional aid.
UNDERGRADUATE EXPENSES for 2006-07 *Application fee:* $25. *Comprehensive fee:* $17,550 includes full-time tuition ($10,750), mandatory fees ($950), and room and board ($5850). *College room only:* $2650. *Part-time tuition:* $414 per credit.
FRESHMAN FINANCIAL AID (Fall 2005, est.) 215 applied for aid; of those 87% were deemed to have need. 98% of freshmen with need received aid; of those 5% had need fully met. *Average percent of need met:* 45% (excluding resources awarded to replace EFC). *Average financial aid package:* $6455 (excluding resources awarded to replace EFC). 37% of all full-time freshmen had no need and received non-need-based gift aid.
UNDERGRADUATE FINANCIAL AID (Fall 2005, est.) 826 applied for aid; of those 88% were deemed to have need. 99% of undergraduates with need received aid; of those 4% had need fully met. *Average percent of need met:* 53% (excluding resources awarded to replace EFC). *Average financial aid package:* $7325 (excluding resources awarded to replace EFC). 21% of all full-time undergraduates had no need and received non-need-based gift aid.
GIFT AID (NEED-BASED) *Total amount:* $3,824,383 (26% federal, 21% state, 41% institutional, 12% external sources). *Receiving aid:* Freshmen: 54% (163); All full-time undergraduates: 65% (609). *Average award:* Freshmen: $4667; Undergraduates: $4763. *Scholarships, grants, and awards:* Federal Pell, FSEOG, state, private, college/university gift aid from institutional funds.
GIFT AID (NON-NEED-BASED) *Receiving aid:* Freshmen: 14% (44); Undergraduates: 17% (160). *Average Award:* Freshmen: $4193; Undergraduates: $6512.

Scholarships, grants, and awards by category: Academic Interests/Achievement: 163 awards ($326,608 total): general academic interests/achievements. *Creative Arts/Performance:* 376 awards ($429,963 total): art/fine arts, music. *Special Achievements/Activities:* 403 awards ($347,833 total): general special achievements/activities, leadership. *Special Characteristics:* 215 awards ($257,170 total): children of current students, children of faculty/staff, general special characteristics, married students, relatives of clergy, siblings of current students, spouses of current students.
LOANS *Student loans:* $6,428,316 (39% need-based, 61% non-need-based). 96% of past graduating class borrowed through all loan programs. *Average indebtedness per student:* $27,186. *Average need-based loan:* Freshmen: $2414; Undergraduates: $3345. *Parent loans:* $1,181,541 (100% non-need-based). *Programs:* FFEL (Subsidized and Unsubsidized Stafford, PLUS), Perkins, state.
WORK-STUDY *Federal work-study:* Total amount: $76,109; 76 jobs averaging $1001.
APPLYING FOR FINANCIAL AID *Required financial aid form:* FAFSA. *Financial aid deadline (priority):* 5/1. *Notification date:* Continuous beginning 3/1. Students must reply within 3 weeks of notification.
CONTACT Mrs. Evie Meyer, Director of Financial Aid, Valley Forge Christian College, 1401 Charlestown Road, Phoenixville, PA 19460-2399, 610-917-1417 or toll-free 800-432-8322. *Fax:* 610-917-2069. *E-mail:* eemeyer@vfcc.edu.

VALPARAISO UNIVERSITY
Valparaiso, IN

Tuition & fees: $22,750 — **Average undergraduate aid package:** $17,707

ABOUT THE INSTITUTION Independent religious, coed. Awards: associate, bachelor's, master's, and first professional degrees and post-bachelor's and post-master's certificates. 86 undergraduate majors. Total enrollment: 3,864. Undergraduates: 2,964. Freshmen: 673. Both federal and institutional methodology are used as a basis for awarding need-based institutional aid.
UNDERGRADUATE EXPENSES for 2005-06 *Application fee:* $30. *Comprehensive fee:* $28,970 includes full-time tuition ($22,000), mandatory fees ($750), and room and board ($6220). *College room only:* $3910. Room and board charges vary according to housing facility and student level. *Part-time tuition:* $1000 per credit hour. *Part-time fees:* $20 per credit hour. Part-time tuition and fees vary according to course load. *Payment plans:* Installment, deferred payment.
FRESHMAN FINANCIAL AID (Fall 2005, est.) 599 applied for aid; of those 80% were deemed to have need. 100% of freshmen with need received aid; of those 27% had need fully met. *Average percent of need met:* 92% (excluding resources awarded to replace EFC). *Average financial aid package:* $18,070 (excluding resources awarded to replace EFC). 25% of all full-time freshmen had no need and received non-need-based gift aid.
UNDERGRADUATE FINANCIAL AID (Fall 2005, est.) 2,294 applied for aid; of those 84% were deemed to have need. 100% of undergraduates with need received aid; of those 31% had need fully met. *Average percent of need met:* 90% (excluding resources awarded to replace EFC). *Average financial aid package:* $17,707 (excluding resources awarded to replace EFC). 25% of all full-time undergraduates had no need and received non-need-based gift aid.
GIFT AID (NEED-BASED) *Total amount:* $23,013,000 (11% federal, 10% state, 73% institutional, 6% external sources). *Receiving aid:* Freshmen: 71% (482); All full-time undergraduates: 67% (1,896). *Average award:* Freshmen: $13,799; Undergraduates: $12,137. *Scholarships, grants, and awards:* Federal Pell, FSEOG, state, private, college/university gift aid from institutional funds.
GIFT AID (NON-NEED-BASED) *Total amount:* $7,500,000 (93% institutional, 7% external sources). *Receiving aid:* Freshmen: 11% (75); Undergraduates: 10% (279). *Average Award:* Freshmen: $7145; Undergraduates: $7888. *Scholarships, grants, and awards by category: Academic Interests/Achievement:* 1,900 awards ($13,300,000 total): business, engineering/technologies, foreign languages, general academic interests/achievements, health fields, physical sciences, religion/biblical studies. *Creative Arts/Performance:* 200 awards ($200,000 total): art/fine arts, music, performing arts, theater/drama. *Special Achievements/Activities:* 400 awards ($1,100,000 total): general special achievements/activities, religious involvement. *Special Characteristics:* 1,910 awards ($4,700,000 total): children and siblings of alumni, children of faculty/staff, international students, relatives of clergy, religious affiliation. *Tuition waivers:* Full or partial for employees or children of employees. *ROTC:* Air Force.
LOANS *Student loans:* $14,220,000 (53% need-based, 47% non-need-based). 71% of past graduating class borrowed through all loan programs. *Average*

indebtedness per student: $23,853. **Average need-based loan:** Freshmen: $4660; Undergraduates: $4988. **Parent loans:** $3,300,000 (100% non-need-based). **Programs:** Federal Direct (Subsidized and Unsubsidized Stafford, PLUS), Perkins, college/university.
WORK-STUDY *Federal work-study:* Total amount: $600,000; 500 jobs averaging $1200. **State or other work-study/employment:** Total amount: $1,000,000 (20% need-based, 80% non-need-based). 750 part-time jobs averaging $1333.
ATHLETIC AWARDS *Total amount:* $2,375,000 (46% need-based, 54% non-need-based).
APPLYING FOR FINANCIAL AID *Required financial aid form:* FAFSA. **Financial aid deadline (priority):** 3/1. **Notification date:** Continuous beginning 3/1. Students must reply by 5/1.
CONTACT Mr. David Fevig, Director of Financial Aid, Valparaiso University, 1700 Chapel Drive, Valparaiso, IN 46383-6493, 219-464-5015 or toll-free 888-GO-VALPO. *Fax:* 219-464-5012. *E-mail:* david.fevig@valpo.edu.

VANDERBILT UNIVERSITY
Nashville, TN

Tuition & fees: $31,700   **Average undergraduate aid package: $31,935**

ABOUT THE INSTITUTION Independent, coed. Awards: bachelor's, master's, doctoral, and first professional degrees. 56 undergraduate majors. Total enrollment: 11,481. Undergraduates: 6,402. Freshmen: 1,622. Both federal and institutional methodology are used as a basis for awarding need-based institutional aid.
UNDERGRADUATE EXPENSES for 2005–06 *Application fee:* $50. **Comprehensive fee:** $41,986 includes full-time tuition ($30,920), mandatory fees ($780), and room and board ($10,286). **College room only:** $6760.
FRESHMAN FINANCIAL AID (Fall 2005, est.) 864 applied for aid; of those 87% were deemed to have need. 100% of freshmen with need received aid; of those 99% had need fully met. *Average percent of need met:* 100% (excluding resources awarded to replace EFC). *Average financial aid package:* $32,265 (excluding resources awarded to replace EFC). 14% of all full-time freshmen had no need and received non-need-based gift aid.
UNDERGRADUATE FINANCIAL AID (Fall 2005, est.) 2,775 applied for aid; of those 93% were deemed to have need. 100% of undergraduates with need received aid; of those 95% had need fully met. *Average percent of need met:* 99% (excluding resources awarded to replace EFC). *Average financial aid package:* $31,935 (excluding resources awarded to replace EFC). 13% of all full-time undergraduates had no need and received non-need-based gift aid.
GIFT AID (NEED-BASED) *Total amount:* $73,797,317 (4% federal, 3% state, 90% institutional, 3% external sources). *Receiving aid:* Freshmen: 41% (667); All full-time undergraduates: 38% (2,409). **Average award:** Freshmen: $25,749; Undergraduates: $25,074. **Scholarships, grants, and awards:** Federal Pell, FSEOG, state, private, college/university gift aid from institutional funds.
GIFT AID (NON-NEED-BASED) *Total amount:* $14,318,005 (5% state, 93% institutional, 2% external sources). *Receiving aid:* Freshmen: 28% (451); Undergraduates: 19% (1,207). **Average Award:** Freshmen: $13,216; Undergraduates: $17,542. **Scholarships, grants, and awards by category:** Academic Interests/Achievement: education, engineering/technologies, general academic interests/achievements, humanities. Creative Arts/Performance: 52 awards ($344,234 total): journalism/publications, music. Special Characteristics: 144 awards ($3,191,412 total): local/state students, members of minority groups. **ROTC:** Army, Naval, Air Force cooperative.
LOANS *Student loans:* $11,892,689 (89% need-based, 11% non-need-based). 31% of past graduating class borrowed through all loan programs. *Average indebtedness per student:* $19,585. **Average need-based loan:** Freshmen: $3096; Undergraduates: $3801. **Parent loans:** $10,392,879 (41% need-based, 59% non-need-based). **Programs:** FFEL (Subsidized and Unsubsidized Stafford, PLUS), Perkins, Federal Nursing, college/university, Undergrad Education Loan.
WORK-STUDY *Federal work-study:* Total amount: $1,815,595; jobs available.
ATHLETIC AWARDS *Total amount:* $7,681,492 (36% need-based, 64% non-need-based).
APPLYING FOR FINANCIAL AID *Required financial aid forms:* FAFSA, CSS Financial Aid PROFILE, noncustodial (divorced/separated) parent's statement. **Financial aid deadline (priority):** 2/1. **Notification date:** 4/1. Students must reply by 5/1.

CONTACT David Mohning, Director of Financial Aid, Vanderbilt University, 2309 West End Avenue, Nashville, TN 37235, 615-322-3591 or toll-free 800-288-0432. *Fax:* 615-343-8512. *E-mail:* finaid@vanderbilt.edu.

VANDERCOOK COLLEGE OF MUSIC
Chicago, IL

Tuition & fees: $17,890   **Average undergraduate aid package: N/A**

ABOUT THE INSTITUTION Independent, coed. Awards: bachelor's and master's degrees. 1 undergraduate major. Total enrollment: 227. Undergraduates: 150. Freshmen: 22. Federal methodology is used as a basis for awarding need-based institutional aid.
UNDERGRADUATE EXPENSES for 2006–07 *Application fee:* $35. **Comprehensive fee:** $25,940 includes full-time tuition ($17,120), mandatory fees ($770), and room and board ($8050). **Part-time tuition:** $590 per credit hour.
GIFT AID (NEED-BASED) *Total amount:* $346,999 (34% federal, 55% state, 11% institutional). **Scholarships, grants, and awards:** Federal Pell, state, private, college/university gift aid from institutional funds.
GIFT AID (NON-NEED-BASED) *Total amount:* $640,192 (29% state, 64% institutional, 7% external sources). **Scholarships, grants, and awards by category:** Academic Interests/Achievement: education, general academic interests/achievements. Creative Arts/Performance: music. Special Characteristics: ethnic background.
LOANS *Student loans:* $717,298 (59% need-based, 41% non-need-based). *Parent loans:* $457,419 (100% non-need-based). **Programs:** FFEL (Subsidized and Unsubsidized Stafford, PLUS), alternative loans.
WORK-STUDY *State or other work-study/employment:* Total amount: $40,820 (100% need-based). Part-time jobs available.
APPLYING FOR FINANCIAL AID *Required financial aid form:* FAFSA. **Financial aid deadline:** 4/1. **Notification date:** Continuous beginning 5/15. Students must reply within 2 weeks of notification.
CONTACT Ms. D. Denny, Director of Financial Aid, VanderCook College of Music, 3140 South Federal Street, Chicago, IL 60616, 312-225-6288 Ext. 241 or toll-free 800-448-2655. *Fax:* 312-225-5211. *E-mail:* finaid@vandercook.edu.

VANGUARD UNIVERSITY OF SOUTHERN CALIFORNIA
Costa Mesa, CA

Tuition & fees: $20,315   **Average undergraduate aid package: $13,406**

ABOUT THE INSTITUTION Independent religious, coed. Awards: bachelor's and master's degrees. 37 undergraduate majors. Total enrollment: 2,246. Undergraduates: 1,900. Freshmen: 402. Federal methodology is used as a basis for awarding need-based institutional aid.
UNDERGRADUATE EXPENSES for 2005–06 *Application fee:* $45. **Comprehensive fee:** $27,071 includes full-time tuition ($19,900), mandatory fees ($415), and room and board ($6756). **College room only:** $3366. Room and board charges vary according to board plan and housing facility. **Part-time tuition:** $829 per credit hour. **Part-time fees:** $25 per term. **Payment plan:** Installment.
FRESHMAN FINANCIAL AID (Fall 2005, est.) 345 applied for aid; of those 81% were deemed to have need. 100% of freshmen with need received aid; of those 14% had need fully met. *Average percent of need met:* 69% (excluding resources awarded to replace EFC). *Average financial aid package:* $15,502 (excluding resources awarded to replace EFC). 11% of all full-time freshmen had no need and received non-need-based gift aid.
UNDERGRADUATE FINANCIAL AID (Fall 2005, est.) 1,329 applied for aid; of those 88% were deemed to have need. 100% of undergraduates with need received aid; of those 15% had need fully met. *Average percent of need met:* 68% (excluding resources awarded to replace EFC). *Average financial aid package:* $13,406 (excluding resources awarded to replace EFC). 12% of all full-time undergraduates had no need and received non-need-based gift aid.
GIFT AID (NEED-BASED) *Total amount:* $10,929,626 (11% federal, 25% state, 61% institutional, 3% external sources). *Receiving aid:* Freshmen: 54% (225); All full-time undergraduates: 58% (780). **Average award:** Freshmen: $8850; Undergraduates: $7892. **Scholarships, grants, and awards:** Federal Pell, FSEOG, state, private, college/university gift aid from institutional funds.

Vanguard University of Southern California

GIFT AID (NON-NEED-BASED) *Total amount:* $1,000,646 (90% institutional, 10% external sources). *Receiving aid:* Freshmen: 61% (253); Undergraduates: 74% (991). *Average Award:* Freshmen: $7190; Undergraduates: $5028. *Scholarships, grants, and awards by category:* Academic Interests/Achievement: 739 awards ($4,086,316 total): general academic interests/achievements. *Creative Arts/Performance:* 207 awards ($506,753 total): debating, music, theater/drama. *Special Characteristics:* 20 awards ($316,457 total): children of faculty/staff. *Tuition waivers:* Full or partial for employees or children of employees. *ROTC:* Air Force cooperative.

LOANS *Student loans:* $6,958,395 (74% need-based, 26% non-need-based). 76% of past graduating class borrowed through all loan programs. *Average indebtedness per student:* $16,979. *Average need-based loan:* Freshmen: $2614; Undergraduates: $3190. *Parent loans:* $3,115,490 (38% need-based, 62% non-need-based). *Programs:* FFEL (Subsidized and Unsubsidized Stafford, PLUS), Perkins, college/university.

WORK-STUDY *Federal work-study:* Total amount: $151,103; 69 jobs averaging $2179. *State or other work-study/employment:* Total amount: $90,882 (67% need-based, 33% non-need-based). 26 part-time jobs averaging $3495.

ATHLETIC AWARDS *Total amount:* $745,901 (69% need-based, 31% non-need-based).

APPLYING FOR FINANCIAL AID *Required financial aid forms:* FAFSA, state aid form. *Financial aid deadline:* 3/2. *Notification date:* 3/15. Students must reply within 3 weeks of notification.

CONTACT Ms. Jennifer Purga, Director of Undergraduate Admissions, Vanguard University of Southern California, 55 Fair Drive, Costa Mesa, CA 92626-6597, 800-722-6279. *Fax:* 714-966-5471. *E-mail:* admissions@vanguard.edu.

VASSAR COLLEGE
Poughkeepsie, NY

Tuition & fees: $33,800	Average undergraduate aid package: $27,982

ABOUT THE INSTITUTION Independent, coed. Awards: bachelor's and master's degrees. 51 undergraduate majors. Total enrollment: 2,378. Undergraduates: 2,378. Freshmen: 647. Institutional methodology is used as a basis for awarding need-based institutional aid.

UNDERGRADUATE EXPENSES for 2005–06 *Application fee:* $60. *Comprehensive fee:* $41,700 includes full-time tuition ($33,310), mandatory fees ($490), and room and board ($7900). *College room only:* $4190. Room and board charges vary according to board plan and housing facility. *Part-time tuition:* $3920 per course. *Part-time fees:* $240 per year. Part-time tuition and fees vary according to course load. *Payment plan:* Installment.

FRESHMAN FINANCIAL AID (Fall 2005, est.) 422 applied for aid; of those 72% were deemed to have need. 100% of freshmen with need received aid; of those 100% had need fully met. *Average percent of need met:* 100% (excluding resources awarded to replace EFC). *Average financial aid package:* $27,803 (excluding resources awarded to replace EFC).

UNDERGRADUATE FINANCIAL AID (Fall 2005, est.) 1,489 applied for aid; of those 84% were deemed to have need. 100% of undergraduates with need received aid; of those 100% had need fully met. *Average percent of need met:* 100% (excluding resources awarded to replace EFC). *Average financial aid package:* $27,982 (excluding resources awarded to replace EFC).

GIFT AID (NEED-BASED) *Total amount:* $27,697,888 (4% federal, 2% state, 92% institutional, 2% external sources). *Receiving aid:* Freshmen: 46% (302); All full-time undergraduates: 53% (1,228). *Average award:* Freshmen: $23,920; Undergraduates: $22,754. *Scholarships, grants, and awards:* Federal Pell, FSEOG, state, private, college/university gift aid from institutional funds.

GIFT AID (NON-NEED-BASED) *Total amount:* $221,297 (5% federal, 20% state, 75% external sources). *Tuition waivers:* Full or partial for employees or children of employees.

LOANS *Student loans:* $6,993,834 (60% need-based, 40% non-need-based). 56% of past graduating class borrowed through all loan programs. *Average indebtedness per student:* $19,038. *Average need-based loan:* Freshmen: $2283; Undergraduates: $3378. *Parent loans:* $4,888,907 (100% non-need-based). *Programs:* FFEL (Subsidized and Unsubsidized Stafford, PLUS), Perkins, college/university.

WORK-STUDY *Federal work-study:* Total amount: $1,519,107; 852 jobs averaging $1746. *State or other work-study/employment:* Total amount: $594,508 (98% need-based, 2% non-need-based). 331 part-time jobs averaging $1740.

APPLYING FOR FINANCIAL AID *Required financial aid forms:* FAFSA, institution's own form, CSS Financial Aid PROFILE, state aid form, noncustodial (divorced/separated) parent's statement, business/farm supplement. *Financial aid deadline:* 2/1. *Notification date:* 3/29. Students must reply by 5/1.

CONTACT Mr. Daniel J. Giannini, Registrar and Director of Institutional Research, Vassar College, 124 Raymond Avenue, Poughkeepsie, NY 12604, 845-437-5276 or toll-free 800-827-7270. *Fax:* 845-437-7060. *E-mail:* dagiannini@vassar.edu.

VAUGHN COLLEGE OF AERONAUTICS AND TECHNOLOGY
Flushing, NY

Tuition & fees: $13,680	Average undergraduate aid package: $4900

ABOUT THE INSTITUTION Independent, coed, primarily men. Awards: associate and bachelor's degrees. 9 undergraduate majors. Total enrollment: 1,126. Undergraduates: 1,126. Freshmen: 214.

UNDERGRADUATE EXPENSES for 2005–06 *Application fee:* $45. *Tuition:* full-time $13,400; part-time $450 per credit. Full-time tuition and fees vary according to course load, degree level, and program. *Payment plan:* Installment.

FRESHMAN FINANCIAL AID (Fall 2005, est.) 187 applied for aid; of those 93% were deemed to have need. 100% of freshmen with need received aid; of those 12% had need fully met. *Average percent of need met:* 80% (excluding resources awarded to replace EFC). *Average financial aid package:* $5600 (excluding resources awarded to replace EFC). 4% of all full-time freshmen had no need and received non-need-based gift aid.

UNDERGRADUATE FINANCIAL AID (Fall 2005, est.) 798 applied for aid; of those 97% were deemed to have need. 100% of undergraduates with need received aid; of those 10% had need fully met. *Average percent of need met:* 80% (excluding resources awarded to replace EFC). *Average financial aid package:* $4900 (excluding resources awarded to replace EFC). 2% of all full-time undergraduates had no need and received non-need-based gift aid.

GIFT AID (NEED-BASED) *Total amount:* $1,572,877 (32% federal, 36% state, 29% institutional, 3% external sources). *Receiving aid:* Freshmen: 88% (173); All full-time undergraduates: 92% (772). *Average award:* Freshmen: $1000; Undergraduates: $1000. *Scholarships, grants, and awards:* Federal Pell, FSEOG, state, private, college/university gift aid from institutional funds.

GIFT AID (NON-NEED-BASED) *Receiving aid:* Freshmen: 41% (80); Undergraduates: 46% (386). *Average Award:* Freshmen: $500; Undergraduates: $500. *Tuition waivers:* Full or partial for employees or children of employees. *ROTC:* Army cooperative, Air Force cooperative.

LOANS *Student loans:* $652,075 (100% need-based). 72% of past graduating class borrowed through all loan programs. *Average indebtedness per student:* $17,125. *Average need-based loan:* Freshmen: $1313; Undergraduates: $1750. *Parent loans:* $280,000 (100% need-based).

WORK-STUDY *Federal work-study:* Total amount: $55,000; jobs available. *State or other work-study/employment:* Part-time jobs available.

APPLYING FOR FINANCIAL AID *Required financial aid forms:* FAFSA, state aid form. *Financial aid deadline (priority):* 3/1. *Notification date:* Continuous.

CONTACT Sinu Jacob, Acting Director of Financial Aid, Vaughn College of Aeronautics and Technology, 8601 23rd Avenue, Flushing, NY 11369-1037, 718-429-6600 Ext. 187 or toll-free 800-776-2376 Ext. 145 (in-state).

VENNARD COLLEGE
University Park, IA

ABOUT THE INSTITUTION Independent interdenominational, coed. Awards: associate and bachelor's degrees. 18 undergraduate majors. Total enrollment: 72. Undergraduates: 72. Freshmen: 10.

GIFT AID (NEED-BASED) *Scholarships, grants, and awards:* Federal Pell, FSEOG, state, college/university gift aid from institutional funds.

APPLYING FOR FINANCIAL AID *Required financial aid forms:* FAFSA, institution's own form, scholarship application form(s).

CONTACT Office of Financial Aid, Vennard College, PO Box 29, University Park, IA 52595, 641-673-8391 or toll-free 800-686-8391.

VERMONT TECHNICAL COLLEGE
Randolph Center, VT

Tuition & fees (area res): $7926 **Average undergraduate aid package:** $9400

ABOUT THE INSTITUTION State-supported, coed. Awards: associate and bachelor's degrees. 20 undergraduate majors. Total enrollment: 1,356. Undergraduates: 1,356. Freshmen: 258. Federal methodology is used as a basis for awarding need-based institutional aid.

UNDERGRADUATE EXPENSES for 2005–06 *Application fee:* $35. *Tuition, area resident:* full-time $7680. *Tuition, state resident:* full-time $11,544; part-time $320 per credit. *Tuition, nonresident:* full-time $14,640; part-time $610 per credit. *Required fees:* full-time $246; $50 per term part-time. Full-time tuition and fees vary according to course load and program. Part-time tuition and fees vary according to program. *College room and board:* $6674; *room only:* $3974. Room and board charges vary according to board plan. *Payment plans:* Installment, deferred payment.

FRESHMAN FINANCIAL AID (Fall 2005, est.) 212 applied for aid; of those 85% were deemed to have need. 99% of freshmen with need received aid; of those 13% had need fully met. *Average percent of need met:* 68% (excluding resources awarded to replace EFC). *Average financial aid package:* $8400 (excluding resources awarded to replace EFC). 2% of all full-time freshmen had no need and received non-need-based gift aid.

UNDERGRADUATE FINANCIAL AID (Fall 2005, est.) 812 applied for aid; of those 90% were deemed to have need. 98% of undergraduates with need received aid; of those 13% had need fully met. *Average percent of need met:* 70% (excluding resources awarded to replace EFC). *Average financial aid package:* $9400 (excluding resources awarded to replace EFC). 1% of all full-time undergraduates had no need and received non-need-based gift aid.

GIFT AID (NEED-BASED) *Total amount:* $3,130,802 (39% federal, 26% state, 15% institutional, 20% external sources). *Receiving aid:* Freshmen: 61% (145); All full-time undergraduates: 65% (600). *Average award:* Freshmen: $4104; Undergraduates: $4100. *Scholarships, grants, and awards:* Federal Pell, FSEOG, state, private, college/university gift aid from institutional funds.

GIFT AID (NON-NEED-BASED) *Total amount:* $215,668 (38% institutional, 62% external sources). *Receiving aid:* Freshmen: 4% (10); Undergraduates: 7% (62). *Average Award:* Freshmen: $7186; Undergraduates: $5209. *Scholarships, grants, and awards by category:* Academic Interests/Achievement: 24 awards ($132,490 total): general academic interests/achievements. *Tuition waivers:* Full or partial for employees or children of employees. *ROTC:* Army cooperative.

LOANS *Student loans:* $5,581,170 (89% need-based, 11% non-need-based). 80% of past graduating class borrowed through all loan programs. *Average indebtedness per student:* $12,600. *Average need-based loan:* Freshmen: $2856; Undergraduates: $3171. *Parent loans:* $1,545,791 (80% need-based, 20% non-need-based). *Programs:* Federal Direct (Subsidized and Unsubsidized Stafford, PLUS), FFEL (Subsidized and Unsubsidized Stafford, PLUS), Perkins.

WORK-STUDY *Federal work-study:* Total amount: $149,795; 184 jobs averaging $814. *State or other work-study/employment:* Part-time jobs available.

APPLYING FOR FINANCIAL AID *Required financial aid forms:* FAFSA, state aid form. *Financial aid deadline (priority):* 3/1. *Notification date:* 4/1. Students must reply within 2 weeks of notification.

CONTACT Catherine R. McCullough, Director of Financial Aid, Vermont Technical College, PO Box 500, Randolph Center, VT 05061-0500, 802-728-1248 or toll-free 800-442-VTC1. *Fax:* 802-728-1390.

VILLA JULIE COLLEGE
Stevenson, MD

Tuition & fees: $15,674 **Average undergraduate aid package:** $10,438

ABOUT THE INSTITUTION Independent, coed. Awards: associate, bachelor's, and master's degrees. 50 undergraduate majors. Total enrollment: 2,956. Undergraduates: 2,807. Freshmen: 543. Both federal and institutional methodology are used as a basis for awarding need-based institutional aid.

UNDERGRADUATE EXPENSES for 2005–06 *Application fee:* $25. *Comprehensive fee:* $25,222 includes full-time tuition ($14,674), mandatory fees ($1000), and room and board ($9548). *College room only:* $6550. Room and board charges vary according to board plan and housing facility. *Part-time tuition:* $415 per credit. *Part-time fees:* $75 per term. *Payment plans:* Installment, deferred payment.

FRESHMAN FINANCIAL AID (Fall 2005, est.) 431 applied for aid; of those 78% were deemed to have need. 100% of freshmen with need received aid; of those 25% had need fully met. *Average percent of need met:* 68% (excluding resources awarded to replace EFC). *Average financial aid package:* $10,876 (excluding resources awarded to replace EFC). 28% of all full-time freshmen had no need and received non-need-based gift aid.

UNDERGRADUATE FINANCIAL AID (Fall 2005, est.) 1,595 applied for aid; of those 79% were deemed to have need. 99% of undergraduates with need received aid; of those 27% had need fully met. *Average percent of need met:* 71% (excluding resources awarded to replace EFC). *Average financial aid package:* $10,438 (excluding resources awarded to replace EFC). 24% of all full-time undergraduates had no need and received non-need-based gift aid.

GIFT AID (NEED-BASED) *Total amount:* $9,253,106 (15% federal, 30% state, 55% institutional). *Receiving aid:* Freshmen: 59% (318); All full-time undergraduates: 53% (1,179). *Average award:* Freshmen: $9145; Undergraduates: $7876. *Scholarships, grants, and awards:* Federal Pell, FSEOG, state, private, college/university gift aid from institutional funds.

GIFT AID (NON-NEED-BASED) *Total amount:* $4,905,800 (12% state, 73% institutional, 15% external sources). *Receiving aid:* Freshmen: 50% (270); Undergraduates: 36% (813). *Average Award:* Freshmen: $5828; Undergraduates: $5720. *Scholarships, grants, and awards by category:* Academic Interests/Achievement: 1,771 awards ($5,611,947 total): business, computer science, general academic interests/achievements. Creative Arts/Performance: 23 awards ($136,022 total): art/fine arts, cinema/film/broadcasting. Special Achievements/Activities: 211 awards ($984,698 total): community service, general special achievements/activities, leadership. *Tuition waivers:* Full or partial for employees or children of employees. *ROTC:* Army cooperative.

LOANS *Student loans:* $9,036,385 (43% need-based, 57% non-need-based). 68% of past graduating class borrowed through all loan programs. *Average indebtedness per student:* $15,580. *Average need-based loan:* Freshmen: $2486; Undergraduates: $3586. *Parent loans:* $6,360,203 (100% non-need-based). *Programs:* FFEL (Subsidized and Unsubsidized Stafford, PLUS), Perkins.

WORK-STUDY *Federal work-study:* Total amount: $220,426; 156 jobs averaging $1407.

APPLYING FOR FINANCIAL AID *Required financial aid form:* FAFSA. *Financial aid deadline (priority):* 2/15. *Notification date:* Continuous beginning 3/15. Students must reply by 5/1 or within 2 weeks of notification.

CONTACT Ms. Debra Bottomms, Director of Financial Aid, Villa Julie College, 1525 Greenspring Valley Road, Stevenson, MD 21153, 443-334-2559 or toll-free 877-468-6852 (in-state), 877-468-3852 (out-of-state). *Fax:* 443-334-2600. *E-mail:* fa-deb1@mail.vjc.edu.

VILLANOVA UNIVERSITY
Villanova, PA

Tuition & fees: $29,435 **Average undergraduate aid package:** $20,503

ABOUT THE INSTITUTION Independent Roman Catholic, coed. Awards: associate, bachelor's, master's, doctoral, and first professional degrees. 44 undergraduate majors. Total enrollment: 10,450. Undergraduates: 7,208. Freshmen: 1,628. Federal methodology is used as a basis for awarding need-based institutional aid.

UNDERGRADUATE EXPENSES for 2005–06 *Application fee:* $70. *Comprehensive fee:* $38,797 includes full-time tuition ($28,760), mandatory fees ($675), and room and board ($9362). *College room only:* $4962. Full-time tuition and fees vary according to program and student level. Room and board charges vary according to board plan and housing facility. *Part-time tuition:* $624 per credit hour. *Part-time fees:* $280 per term. Part-time tuition and fees vary according to class time, course level, and program. *Payment plan:* Installment.

FRESHMAN FINANCIAL AID (Fall 2005, est.) 1054 applied for aid; of those 70% were deemed to have need. 99% of freshmen with need received aid; of those 23% had need fully met. *Average percent of need met:* 85% (excluding resources awarded to replace EFC). *Average financial aid package:* $22,149 (excluding resources awarded to replace EFC). 6% of all full-time freshmen had no need and received non-need-based gift aid.

UNDERGRADUATE FINANCIAL AID (Fall 2005, est.) 3,654 applied for aid; of those 79% were deemed to have need. 99% of undergraduates with need

Villanova University

received aid; of those 18% had need fully met. *Average percent of need met:* 78% (excluding resources awarded to replace EFC). *Average financial aid package:* $20,503 (excluding resources awarded to replace EFC). 5% of all full-time undergraduates had no need and received non-need-based gift aid.
GIFT AID (NEED-BASED) *Total amount:* $41,263,801 (9% federal, 4% state, 83% institutional, 4% external sources). *Receiving aid:* Freshmen: 41% (665); All full-time undergraduates: 39% (2,534). *Average award:* Freshmen: $18,878; Undergraduates: $16,202. *Scholarships, grants, and awards:* Federal Pell, FSEOG, state, private, college/university gift aid from institutional funds, endowed and restricted grants.
GIFT AID (NON-NEED-BASED) *Total amount:* $6,842,713 (34% federal, 57% institutional, 9% external sources). *Receiving aid:* Freshmen: 15% (239); Undergraduates: 13% (849). *Average Award:* Freshmen: $11,028; Undergraduates: $10,971. *Scholarships, grants, and awards by category:* Academic Interests/Achievement: 567 awards ($4,387,293 total): general academic interests/achievements, international studies, military science. Special Achievements/Activities: 17 awards ($15,000 total): general special achievements/activities. Special Characteristics: 284 awards ($7,158,944 total): children of educators, children of faculty/staff, general special characteristics, members of minority groups, religious affiliation. *Tuition waivers:* Full or partial for employees or children of employees, senior citizens. *ROTC:* Army cooperative, Naval, Air Force cooperative.
LOANS *Student loans:* $25,558,516 (81% need-based, 19% non-need-based). 51% of past graduating class borrowed through all loan programs. *Average indebtedness per student:* $28,549. *Average need-based loan:* Freshmen: $3110; Undergraduates: $4698. *Parent loans:* $18,207,342 (78% need-based, 22% non-need-based). *Programs:* FFEL (Subsidized and Unsubsidized Stafford, PLUS), Perkins, Federal Nursing, Villanova Loan.
WORK-STUDY *Federal work-study:* Total amount: $3,342,674; 1,586 jobs averaging $2108. *State or other work-study/employment:* Total amount: $16,000 (100% need-based). 8 part-time jobs averaging $2000.
ATHLETIC AWARDS *Total amount:* $6,940,334 (28% need-based, 72% non-need-based).
APPLYING FOR FINANCIAL AID *Required financial aid forms:* FAFSA, institution's own form, W-2 forms, federal income tax forms. *Financial aid deadline (priority):* 2/7. *Notification date:* 4/1. Students must reply by 5/1.
CONTACT Bonnie Lee Behm, Director of Financial Assistance, Villanova University, 800 Lancaster Avenue, Villanova, PA 19085-1699, 610-519-4010. *Fax:* 610-519-7599.

VIRGINIA COLLEGE AT BIRMINGHAM
Birmingham, AL

CONTACT Vice President, Campus Administration, Virginia College at Birmingham, 65 Bagby Drive, Birmingham, AL 35209, 205-802-1200. *Fax:* 205-271-8273.

VIRGINIA COMMONWEALTH UNIVERSITY
Richmond, VA

Tuition & fees (VA res): $5385	Average undergraduate aid package: $7257

ABOUT THE INSTITUTION State-supported, coed. Awards: bachelor's, master's, doctoral, and first professional degrees and post-bachelor's, post-master's, and first professional certificates. 55 undergraduate majors. Total enrollment: 29,349. Undergraduates: 20,508. Freshmen: 3,540. Federal methodology is used as a basis for awarding need-based institutional aid.
UNDERGRADUATE EXPENSES for 2005–06 *Application fee:* $30. *Tuition, state resident:* full-time $5385; part-time $165.40 per credit. *Tuition, nonresident:* full-time $17,440; part-time $668 per credit. *Required fees:* $52.05 per credit. *College room and board:* $7042; *room only:* $4102. Room and board charges vary according to board plan. *Payment plan:* Installment.
FRESHMAN FINANCIAL AID (Fall 2004) 2445 applied for aid; of those 72% were deemed to have need. 96% of freshmen with need received aid; of those 5% had need fully met. *Average percent of need met:* 42% (excluding resources awarded to replace EFC). *Average financial aid package:* $6845 (excluding resources awarded to replace EFC). 6% of all full-time freshmen had no need and received non-need-based gift aid.
UNDERGRADUATE FINANCIAL AID (Fall 2004) 10,421 applied for aid; of those 75% were deemed to have need. 98% of undergraduates with need received aid; of those 7% had need fully met. *Average percent of need met:* 47% (excluding resources awarded to replace EFC). *Average financial aid package:* $7257 (excluding resources awarded to replace EFC). 5% of all full-time undergraduates had no need and received non-need-based gift aid.
GIFT AID (NEED-BASED) *Total amount:* $23,789,090 (53% federal, 46% state, 1% external sources). *Receiving aid:* Freshmen: 38% (1,318); All full-time undergraduates: 35% (5,563). *Average award:* Freshmen: $3959; Undergraduates: $3814. *Scholarships, grants, and awards:* Federal Pell, FSEOG, state, private, college/university gift aid from institutional funds, Federal Nursing.
GIFT AID (NON-NEED-BASED) *Total amount:* $9,452,376 (35% federal, 1% state, 24% institutional, 40% external sources). *Receiving aid:* Freshmen: 15% (527); Undergraduates: 9% (1,432). *Average Award:* Freshmen: $4105; Undergraduates: $4189. *Scholarships, grants, and awards by category:* Academic Interests/Achievement: business, engineering/technologies, foreign languages, general academic interests/achievements, health fields, mathematics, military science. Creative Arts/Performance: applied art and design, art/fine arts, dance, music, performing arts, theater/drama. Special Characteristics: children of union members/company employees, general special characteristics, veterans' children. *Tuition waivers:* Full or partial for employees or children of employees, senior citizens. *ROTC:* Army cooperative.
LOANS *Student loans:* $51,772,841 (56% need-based, 44% non-need-based). 66% of past graduating class borrowed through all loan programs. *Average indebtedness per student:* $20,069. *Average need-based loan:* Freshmen: $2857; Undergraduates: $3804. *Parent loans:* $9,470,712 (100% non-need-based). *Programs:* Federal Direct (Subsidized and Unsubsidized Stafford, PLUS), Perkins, Federal Nursing, college/university.
WORK-STUDY *Federal work-study:* Total amount: $1,770,204; 884 jobs averaging $2002.
ATHLETIC AWARDS *Total amount:* $2,117,442 (100% non-need-based).
APPLYING FOR FINANCIAL AID *Required financial aid form:* FAFSA. *Financial aid deadline (priority):* 3/1. *Notification date:* 3/15. Students must reply by 5/1 or within 2 weeks of notification.
CONTACT Susan Kadir, Director of Financial Aid, Virginia Commonwealth University, PO Box 843026, 901 W. Franklin Street, Richmond, VA 23284-3026, 804-828-6669 or toll-free 800-841-3638. *Fax:* 804-828-6186. *E-mail:* faidmail@vcu.edu.

VIRGINIA INTERMONT COLLEGE
Bristol, VA

Tuition & fees: $16,450	Average undergraduate aid package: $10,961

ABOUT THE INSTITUTION Independent religious, coed. Awards: associate and bachelor's degrees. 41 undergraduate majors. Total enrollment: 1,138. Undergraduates: 1,138. Freshmen: 114. Federal methodology is used as a basis for awarding need-based institutional aid.
UNDERGRADUATE EXPENSES for 2005–06 *Application fee:* $15. *Comprehensive fee:* $22,200 includes full-time tuition ($15,500), mandatory fees ($950), and room and board ($5750). *College room only:* $2750. Full-time tuition and fees vary according to class time and program. Room and board charges vary according to housing facility. *Part-time tuition:* $220 per credit. *Part-time fees:* $50 per credit. Part-time tuition and fees vary according to class time, course level, course load, and program. *Payment plan:* Installment.
FRESHMAN FINANCIAL AID (Fall 2005, est.) 133 applied for aid; of those 83% were deemed to have need. 100% of freshmen with need received aid; of those 7% had need fully met. *Average percent of need met:* 58% (excluding resources awarded to replace EFC). *Average financial aid package:* $12,445 (excluding resources awarded to replace EFC). 23% of all full-time freshmen had no need and received non-need-based gift aid.
UNDERGRADUATE FINANCIAL AID (Fall 2005, est.) 752 applied for aid; of those 92% were deemed to have need. 100% of undergraduates with need received aid; of those 9% had need fully met. *Average percent of need met:* 55% (excluding resources awarded to replace EFC). *Average financial aid package:* $10,961 (excluding resources awarded to replace EFC). 16% of all full-time undergraduates had no need and received non-need-based gift aid.
GIFT AID (NEED-BASED) *Total amount:* $3,909,423 (27% federal, 24% state, 43% institutional, 6% external sources). *Receiving aid:* Freshmen: 65% (108); All full-time undergraduates: 70% (650). *Average award:* Freshmen: $10,186; Undergraduates: $7767. *Scholarships, grants, and awards:* Federal Pell, FSEOG, state, private, college/university gift aid from institutional funds.

GIFT AID (NON-NEED-BASED) *Total amount:* $908,692 (15% state, 82% institutional, 3% external sources). *Receiving aid:* Freshmen: 4% (6); Undergraduates: 4% (34). *Average Award: Freshmen:* $9360; *Undergraduates:* $8508. *Scholarships, grants, and awards by category:* Academic Interests/Achievement: general academic interests/achievements. *Creative Arts/Performance:* applied art and design, art/fine arts, dance, general creative arts/performance, music, performing arts, theater/drama. *Special Achievements/Activities:* cheerleading/drum major. *Special Characteristics:* children and siblings of alumni, children of current students, children of faculty/staff, first-generation college students, members of minority groups, religious affiliation, siblings of current students. *Tuition waivers:* Full or partial for employees or children of employees, senior citizens.
LOANS *Student loans:* $4,623,699 (87% need-based, 13% non-need-based). 83% of past graduating class borrowed through all loan programs. *Average indebtedness per student:* $18,700. *Average need-based loan:* Freshmen: $2516; Undergraduates: $3855. *Parent loans:* $1,445,791 (53% need-based, 47% non-need-based). *Programs:* FFEL (Subsidized and Unsubsidized Stafford, PLUS), Perkins, alternative loans.
WORK-STUDY *Federal work-study:* Total amount: $198,175; 220 jobs averaging $750.
ATHLETIC AWARDS *Total amount:* $2,059,810 (49% need-based, 51% non-need-based).
APPLYING FOR FINANCIAL AID *Required financial aid forms:* FAFSA, state aid form. *Financial aid deadline (priority):* 3/1. *Notification date:* Continuous beginning 2/15. Students must reply within 3 weeks of notification.
CONTACT Ms. Denise Posey, Director of Financial Aid, Virginia Intermont College, 1013 Moore Street, Bristol, VA 24201-4298, 276-466-7872 or toll-free 800-451-1842. *Fax:* 276-669-5763.

VIRGINIA MILITARY INSTITUTE
Lexington, VA

Tuition & fees (VA res): $6988 **Average undergraduate aid package:** $13,114

ABOUT THE INSTITUTION State-supported, coed, primarily men. Awards: bachelor's degrees. 14 undergraduate majors. Total enrollment: 1,362. Undergraduates: 1,362. Freshmen: 363. Federal methodology is used as a basis for awarding need-based institutional aid.
UNDERGRADUATE EXPENSES for 2005–06 *Application fee:* $35. *One-time required fee:* $1678. *Tuition, state resident:* full-time $4382. *Tuition, nonresident:* full-time $18,582. *College room and board:* $5666. *Payment plan:* Installment.
FRESHMAN FINANCIAL AID (Fall 2004) 262 applied for aid; of those 70% were deemed to have need. 98% of freshmen with need received aid; of those 37% had need fully met. *Average percent of need met:* 88% (excluding resources awarded to replace EFC). *Average financial aid package:* $11,017 (excluding resources awarded to replace EFC). 14% of all full-time freshmen had no need and received non-need-based gift aid.
UNDERGRADUATE FINANCIAL AID (Fall 2004) 765 applied for aid; of those 76% were deemed to have need. 99% of undergraduates with need received aid; of those 32% had need fully met. *Average percent of need met:* 90% (excluding resources awarded to replace EFC). *Average financial aid package:* $13,114 (excluding resources awarded to replace EFC). 17% of all full-time undergraduates had no need and received non-need-based gift aid.
GIFT AID (NEED-BASED) *Total amount:* $4,216,514 (13% federal, 15% state, 68% institutional, 4% external sources). *Receiving aid:* Freshmen: 45% (173); All full-time undergraduates: 40% (561). *Average award:* Freshmen: $9343; Undergraduates: $10,972. *Scholarships, grants, and awards:* Federal Pell, FSEOG, state, private, college/university gift aid from institutional funds.
GIFT AID (NON-NEED-BASED) *Total amount:* $4,390,256 (69% federal, 28% institutional, 3% external sources). *Receiving aid:* Freshmen: 4% (15); Undergraduates: 5% (67). *Average Award: Freshmen:* $3158; *Undergraduates:* $5284. *Scholarships, grants, and awards by category:* Academic Interests/Achievement: 150 awards ($1,000,000 total): biological sciences, business, computer science, engineering/technologies, English, general academic interests/achievements, international studies, mathematics, military science, premedicine. *Creative Arts/Performance:* 12 awards ($6000 total): music. *Special Achievements/Activities:* 15 awards ($75,000 total): general special achievements/activities, leadership. *Special Characteristics:* 300 awards ($1,250,000 total): children and siblings of alumni, children of faculty/staff, general special characteristics, local/state students, out-of-state students. *ROTC:* Army, Naval, Air Force.
LOANS *Student loans:* $2,940,601 (44% need-based, 56% non-need-based). 41% of past graduating class borrowed through all loan programs. *Average indebtedness per student:* $14,367. *Average need-based loan:* Freshmen: $3432; Undergraduates: $3657. *Parent loans:* $1,956,128 (100% non-need-based). *Programs:* Federal Direct (Subsidized and Unsubsidized Stafford, PLUS), Perkins.
WORK-STUDY *Federal work-study:* Total amount: $38,474; 52 jobs averaging $740.
ATHLETIC AWARDS *Total amount:* $2,090,300 (33% need-based, 67% non-need-based).
APPLYING FOR FINANCIAL AID *Required financial aid forms:* FAFSA, institution's own form. *Financial aid deadline (priority):* 3/1. *Notification date:* Continuous beginning 3/15. Students must reply by 5/1.
CONTACT Col. Timothy P. Golden, Director of Financial Aid, Virginia Military Institute, 306 Carroll Hall, Lexington, VA 24450, 540-464-7208 or toll-free 800-767-4207. *Fax:* 540-464-7629. *E-mail:* goldentp@vmi.edu.

VIRGINIA POLYTECHNIC INSTITUTE AND STATE UNIVERSITY
Blacksburg, VA

Tuition & fees (VA res): $6378 **Average undergraduate aid package:** $7710

ABOUT THE INSTITUTION State-supported, coed. Awards: associate, bachelor's, master's, doctoral, and first professional degrees. 66 undergraduate majors. Total enrollment: 27,979. Undergraduates: 21,627. Freshmen: 5,049. Institutional methodology is used as a basis for awarding need-based institutional aid.
UNDERGRADUATE EXPENSES for 2005–06 *Application fee:* $40. *Tuition, state resident:* full-time $4959; part-time $206.75 per credit hour. *Tuition, nonresident:* full-time $16,298; part-time $679 per credit hour. *Required fees:* full-time $1419; $169 per term part-time. *College room and board:* $4400; *room only:* $2346. Room and board charges vary according to board plan and location. *Payment plan:* Installment.
FRESHMAN FINANCIAL AID (Fall 2004) 3426 applied for aid; of those 67% were deemed to have need. 80% of freshmen with need received aid; of those 3% had need fully met. *Average percent of need met:* 71% (excluding resources awarded to replace EFC). *Average financial aid package:* $7999 (excluding resources awarded to replace EFC). 8% of all full-time freshmen had no need and received non-need-based gift aid.
UNDERGRADUATE FINANCIAL AID (Fall 2004) 12,884 applied for aid; of those 66% were deemed to have need. 90% of undergraduates with need received aid; of those 4% had need fully met. *Average percent of need met:* 77% (excluding resources awarded to replace EFC). *Average financial aid package:* $7710 (excluding resources awarded to replace EFC). 5% of all full-time undergraduates had no need and received non-need-based gift aid.
GIFT AID (NON-NEED-BASED) *Total amount:* $14,944,566 (100% external sources). *Receiving aid:* Freshmen: 8% (374); Undergraduates: 5% (1,136). *Average Award: Freshmen:* $1773; *Undergraduates:* $1714. *Scholarships, grants, and awards by category:* Academic Interests/Achievement: agriculture, architecture, area/ethnic studies, biological sciences, business, communication, computer science, education, engineering/technologies, English, foreign languages, general academic interests/achievements, health fields, home economics, humanities, international studies, mathematics, military science, physical sciences, premedicine, religion/biblical studies, social sciences. *Creative Arts/Performance:* applied art and design, art/fine arts, cinema/film/broadcasting, creative writing, journalism/publications, music, performing arts, theater/drama. *Special Achievements/Activities:* cheerleading/drum major, community service, general special achievements/activities, leadership, memberships, religious involvement. *Special Characteristics:* children of faculty/staff, first-generation college students, local/state students, members of minority groups, out-of-state students, twins, veterans' children. *ROTC:* Army, Naval, Air Force.
LOANS *Student loans:* $51,792,722 (48% need-based, 52% non-need-based). 54% of past graduating class borrowed through all loan programs. *Average indebtedness per student:* $18,385. *Average need-based loan:* Freshmen: $3240; Undergraduates: $3680. *Parent loans:* $19,738,291 (100% non-need-based).
WORK-STUDY *Federal work-study:* Total amount: $1,015,544; 917 jobs averaging $1107. *State or other work-study/employment:* Total amount: $6,013,343 (100% non-need-based). 4,074 part-time jobs averaging $1476.
ATHLETIC AWARDS *Total amount:* $4,230,680 (100% non-need-based).

Virginia Polytechnic Institute and State University

APPLYING FOR FINANCIAL AID *Financial aid deadline (priority):* 3/11. *Notification date:* Continuous beginning 3/30. Students must reply by 5/1 or within 4 weeks of notification.
CONTACT Dr. Barry Simmons, Director, Virginia Polytechnic Institute and State University, 300 Student Service Building, Virginia Tech, Blacksburg, VA 24061, 540-231-5179. *Fax:* 540-231-9139. *E-mail:* simmonsb@vt.edu.

VIRGINIA STATE UNIVERSITY
Petersburg, VA

CONTACT Sylvia Blizzard, Interim Assistant Director of Student Services, Virginia State University, 102 Gandy Hall, PO Box 9031, Petersburg, VA 23806-2096, 804-524-5565 or toll-free 800-871-7611. *Fax:* 804-524-6818. *E-mail:* sblizzard@vsu.edu.

VIRGINIA UNION UNIVERSITY
Richmond, VA

Tuition & fees: $12,770	Average undergraduate aid package: $12,687

ABOUT THE INSTITUTION Independent Baptist, coed. Awards: bachelor's, master's, doctoral, and first professional degrees. 22 undergraduate majors. Total enrollment: 1,700. Undergraduates: 1,344. Freshmen: 341. Federal methodology is used as a basis for awarding need-based institutional aid.
UNDERGRADUATE EXPENSES for 2005–06 *Application fee:* $25. *Comprehensive fee:* $18,432 includes full-time tuition ($11,600), mandatory fees ($1170), and room and board ($5662). *College room only:* $2662. Full-time tuition and fees vary according to course level and course load. *Part-time tuition:* $483 per credit hour. *Part-time fees:* $370 per term. Part-time tuition and fees vary according to course level and course load. *Payment plans:* Installment, deferred payment.
FRESHMAN FINANCIAL AID (Fall 2005, est.) 329 applied for aid; of those 91% were deemed to have need. 99% of freshmen with need received aid; of those 32% had need fully met. *Average percent of need met:* 81% (excluding resources awarded to replace EFC). *Average financial aid package:* $12,207 (excluding resources awarded to replace EFC). 5% of all full-time freshmen had no need and received non-need-based gift aid.
UNDERGRADUATE FINANCIAL AID (Fall 2005, est.) 1,193 applied for aid; of those 91% were deemed to have need. 100% of undergraduates with need received aid; of those 28% had need fully met. *Average percent of need met:* 67% (excluding resources awarded to replace EFC). *Average financial aid package:* $12,687 (excluding resources awarded to replace EFC). 8% of all full-time undergraduates had no need and received non-need-based gift aid.
GIFT AID (NEED-BASED) *Total amount:* $2,831,653 (91% federal, 7% state, 2% external sources). *Receiving aid:* Freshmen: 52% (174); All full-time undergraduates: 55% (719). *Average award:* Freshmen: $3959; Undergraduates: $3681. *Scholarships, grants, and awards:* Federal Pell, FSEOG, state, private, college/university gift aid from institutional funds.
GIFT AID (NON-NEED-BASED) *Total amount:* $3,208,592 (42% state, 34% institutional, 24% external sources). *Receiving aid:* Freshmen: 88% (297); Undergraduates: 50% (660). *Average Award:* Freshmen: $9468; Undergraduates:* $8482. *Scholarships, grants, and awards by category: Academic Interests/Achievement:* 114 awards ($818,306 total): general academic interests/achievements. *Tuition waivers:* Full or partial for employees or children of employees. *ROTC:* Army cooperative.
LOANS *Student loans:* $6,424,036 (56% need-based, 44% non-need-based). 98% of past graduating class borrowed through all loan programs. *Average indebtedness per student:* $17,568. *Average need-based loan:* Freshmen: $3642; Undergraduates: $3968. *Parent loans:* $3,882,832 (100% non-need-based). *Programs:* Federal Direct (Subsidized and Unsubsidized Stafford), FFEL (PLUS), Perkins.
WORK-STUDY *Federal work-study:* Total amount: $459,270; 260 jobs averaging $1678.
ATHLETIC AWARDS *Total amount:* $1,041,295 (100% non-need-based).
APPLYING FOR FINANCIAL AID *Required financial aid forms:* FAFSA, state aid form. *Financial aid deadline (priority):* 5/1. *Notification date:* Continuous. Students must reply within 2 weeks of notification.
CONTACT Mrs. Phenie Golatt, Director of Financial Aid, Virginia Union University, 1500 North Lombardy Street, Richmond, VA 23220-1170, 804-257-5882 or toll-free 800-368-3227 (out-of-state). *E-mail:* pgolatt@vuu.edu.

VIRGINIA UNIVERSITY OF LYNCHBURG
Lynchburg, VA

CONTACT Financial Aid Office, Virginia University of Lynchburg, 2058 Garfield Avenue, Lynchburg, VA 24501-6417, 804-528-5276.

VIRGINIA WESLEYAN COLLEGE
Norfolk, VA

Tuition & fees: $23,136	Average undergraduate aid package: $14,385

ABOUT THE INSTITUTION Independent United Methodist, coed. Awards: bachelor's degrees. 44 undergraduate majors. Total enrollment: 1,392. Undergraduates: 1,392. Freshmen: 323. Federal methodology is used as a basis for awarding need-based institutional aid.
UNDERGRADUATE EXPENSES for 2006–07 *Application fee:* $40. *Comprehensive fee:* $29,986 includes full-time tuition ($22,976), mandatory fees ($160), and room and board ($6850). *Part-time tuition:* $957 per semester hour.
FRESHMAN FINANCIAL AID (Fall 2005, est.) 219 applied for aid; of those 100% were deemed to have need. 100% of freshmen with need received aid; of those 5% had need fully met. *Average percent of need met:* 67% (excluding resources awarded to replace EFC). *Average financial aid package:* $14,326 (excluding resources awarded to replace EFC). 31% of all full-time freshmen had no need and received non-need-based gift aid.
UNDERGRADUATE FINANCIAL AID (Fall 2005, est.) 764 applied for aid; of those 100% were deemed to have need. 97% of undergraduates with need received aid; of those 5% had need fully met. *Average percent of need met:* 66% (excluding resources awarded to replace EFC). *Average financial aid package:* $14,385 (excluding resources awarded to replace EFC). 22% of all full-time undergraduates had no need and received non-need-based gift aid.
GIFT AID (NEED-BASED) *Total amount:* $1,040,970 (89% federal, 5% state, 6% institutional). *Receiving aid:* Freshmen: 25% (80); All full-time undergraduates: 26% (304). *Average award:* Freshmen: $3091; Undergraduates: $3239. *Scholarships, grants, and awards:* Federal Pell, FSEOG, state, private, college/university gift aid from institutional funds, United Negro College Fund.
GIFT AID (NON-NEED-BASED) *Total amount:* $9,066,676 (19% state, 77% institutional, 4% external sources). *Receiving aid:* Freshmen: 68% (218); Undergraduates: 63% (737). *Average Award:* Freshmen: $4594; Undergraduates:* $5992. *Scholarships, grants, and awards by category: Academic Interests/Achievement:* general academic interests/achievements. *Creative Arts/Performance:* music. *Special Achievements/Activities:* leadership, religious involvement. *Special Characteristics:* children of faculty/staff, relatives of clergy, religious affiliation. *ROTC:* Army cooperative.
LOANS *Student loans:* $6,750,136 (43% need-based, 57% non-need-based). 79% of past graduating class borrowed through all loan programs. *Average indebtedness per student:* $20,386. *Average need-based loan:* Freshmen: $3107; Undergraduates: $4077. *Parent loans:* $3,497,100 (100% non-need-based). *Programs:* FFEL (Subsidized and Unsubsidized Stafford, PLUS), Perkins, alternative loans.
WORK-STUDY *Federal work-study:* Total amount: $177,855; 129 jobs averaging $1378.
APPLYING FOR FINANCIAL AID *Required financial aid forms:* FAFSA, state aid form. *Financial aid deadline (priority):* 3/1. *Notification date:* Continuous beginning 2/1. Students must reply by 5/1 or within 2 weeks of notification.
CONTACT Ms. Eugenia F. Hickman, Director of Financial Aid, Virginia Wesleyan College, 1584 Wesleyan Drive, Norfolk, VA 23502-5599, 757-455-3207 or toll-free 800-737-8684. *Fax:* 757-455-6779. *E-mail:* dhickman@vwc.edu.

VITERBO UNIVERSITY
La Crosse, WI

CONTACT Ms. Terry Norman, Director of Financial Aid, Viterbo University, 900 Viterbo Drive, La Crosse, WI 54601-4797, 608-796-3900 or toll-free 800-VITERBO Ext. 3010. *Fax:* 608-796-3050. *E-mail:* twnorman@viterbo.edu.

VOORHEES COLLEGE
Denmark, SC

ABOUT THE INSTITUTION Independent Episcopal, coed. Awards: bachelor's degrees. 16 undergraduate majors. Total enrollment: 847. Undergraduates: 847. Freshmen: 156.
GIFT AID (NEED-BASED) *Scholarships, grants, and awards:* Federal Pell, FSEOG, state, private, college/university gift aid from institutional funds, United Negro College Fund.
GIFT AID (NON-NEED-BASED) *Scholarships, grants, and awards by category: Special Characteristics:* children of faculty/staff.
LOANS *Programs:* FFEL (Subsidized and Unsubsidized Stafford, PLUS).
WORK-STUDY *Federal work-study:* Total amount: $321,361; 223 jobs averaging $2000. *State or other work-study/employment:* Part-time jobs available.
APPLYING FOR FINANCIAL AID *Required financial aid forms:* FAFSA, institution's own form.
CONTACT Augusta L. Kitchen, Director of Financial Aid, Voorhees College, PO Box 678, Denmark, SC 29042, 803-703-7109 Ext. 7106 or toll-free 800-446-6250. *Fax:* 803-793-0831. *E-mail:* akitchen@voorhees.edu.

WABASH COLLEGE
Crawfordsville, IN

Tuition & fees: $23,388   **Average undergraduate aid package:** $22,192

ABOUT THE INSTITUTION Independent, men only. Awards: bachelor's degrees. 24 undergraduate majors. Total enrollment: 877. Undergraduates: 877. Freshmen: 249. Both federal and institutional methodology are used as a basis for awarding need-based institutional aid.
UNDERGRADUATE EXPENSES for 2005–06 *Application fee:* $30. *Comprehensive fee:* $30,116 includes full-time tuition ($22,964), mandatory fees ($424), and room and board ($6728). *College room only:* $2740. Room and board charges vary according to board plan and housing facility. *Part-time tuition:* $3827 per course. Part-time tuition and fees vary according to course load. *Payment plans:* Tuition prepayment, installment.
FRESHMAN FINANCIAL AID (Fall 2005, est.) 217 applied for aid; of those 82% were deemed to have need. 100% of freshmen with need received aid; of those 100% had need fully met. *Average percent of need met:* 100% (excluding resources awarded to replace EFC). *Average financial aid package:* $22,859 (excluding resources awarded to replace EFC). 23% of all full-time freshmen had no need and received non-need-based gift aid.
UNDERGRADUATE FINANCIAL AID (Fall 2005, est.) 695 applied for aid; of those 88% were deemed to have need. 100% of undergraduates with need received aid; of those 100% had need fully met. *Average percent of need met:* 100% (excluding resources awarded to replace EFC). *Average financial aid package:* $22,192 (excluding resources awarded to replace EFC). 26% of all full-time undergraduates had no need and received non-need-based gift aid.
GIFT AID (NEED-BASED) *Total amount:* $9,044,001 (5% federal, 12% state, 79% institutional, 4% external sources). *Receiving aid:* Freshmen: 71% (178); All full-time undergraduates: 70% (606). *Average award:* Freshmen: $17,396; Undergraduates: $15,660. *Scholarships, grants, and awards:* Federal Pell, state, private, college/university gift aid from institutional funds.
GIFT AID (NON-NEED-BASED) *Total amount:* $3,559,474 (1% state, 80% institutional, 19% external sources). *Receiving aid:* Freshmen: 15% (38); Undergraduates: 12% (102). *Average Award:* Freshmen: $12,915; Undergraduates:* $11,150. *Scholarships, grants, and awards by category: Academic Interests/Achievement:* 619 awards ($5,504,429 total): education, general academic interests/achievements. *Creative Arts/Performance:* 54 awards ($185,235 total): art/fine arts, creative writing, journalism/publications, music, theater/drama. *Special Achievements/Activities:* 17 awards ($489,985 total): community service, leadership. *Special Characteristics:* 38 awards ($607,220 total): children of faculty/staff, international students. *Tuition waivers:* Full or partial for employees or children of employees. *ROTC:* Army cooperative.
LOANS *Student loans:* $3,845,887 (37% need-based, 63% non-need-based). 65% of past graduating class borrowed through all loan programs. *Average indebtedness per student:* $17,328. *Average need-based loan:* Freshmen: $1506; Undergraduates: $2353. *Programs:* FFEL (Subsidized and Unsubsidized Stafford, PLUS), college/university.
WORK-STUDY *State or other work-study/employment:* Total amount: $743,258 (52% need-based, 48% non-need-based). 820 part-time jobs averaging $2037.

APPLYING FOR FINANCIAL AID *Required financial aid forms:* FAFSA, CSS Financial Aid PROFILE, federal income tax form(s), W-2 forms. *Financial aid deadline:* 3/1 (priority: 2/15). *Notification date:* 4/1. Students must reply by 5/1 or within 2 weeks of notification.
CONTACT Mr. Clint Gasaway, Financial Aid Director, Wabash College, PO Box 352, Crawfordsville, IN 47933-0352, 800-718-9746 or toll-free 800-345-5385. *Fax:* 765-361-6166. *E-mail:* financialaid@wabash.edu.

WAGNER COLLEGE
Staten Island, NY

CONTACT Mr. Angelo Araimo, Vice President for Enrollment and Planning, Wagner College, One Campus Road, Staten Island, NY 10301, 718-390-3411 or toll-free 800-221-1010 (out-of-state). *Fax:* 718-390-3105.

WAKE FOREST UNIVERSITY
Winston-Salem, NC

Tuition & fees: $32,140   **Average undergraduate aid package:** $22,581

ABOUT THE INSTITUTION Independent, coed. Awards: bachelor's, master's, doctoral, and first professional degrees. 37 undergraduate majors. Total enrollment: 6,716. Undergraduates: 4,263. Freshmen: 1,119. Both federal and institutional methodology are used as a basis for awarding need-based institutional aid.
UNDERGRADUATE EXPENSES for 2006–07 *Application fee:* $40. *Comprehensive fee:* $40,940 includes full-time tuition ($32,040), mandatory fees ($100), and room and board ($8800). *College room only:* $5500. *Part-time tuition:* $1250 per credit hour.
FRESHMAN FINANCIAL AID (Fall 2005, est.) 585 applied for aid; of those 72% were deemed to have need. 99% of freshmen with need received aid; of those 39% had need fully met. *Average percent of need met:* 90% (excluding resources awarded to replace EFC). *Average financial aid package:* $22,513 (excluding resources awarded to replace EFC). 31% of all full-time freshmen had no need and received non-need-based gift aid.
UNDERGRADUATE FINANCIAL AID (Fall 2005, est.) 1,795 applied for aid; of those 82% were deemed to have need. 100% of undergraduates with need received aid; of those 32% had need fully met. *Average percent of need met:* 87% (excluding resources awarded to replace EFC). *Average financial aid package:* $22,581 (excluding resources awarded to replace EFC). 29% of all full-time undergraduates had no need and received non-need-based gift aid.
GIFT AID (NEED-BASED) *Total amount:* $20,300,581 (7% federal, 11% state, 76% institutional, 6% external sources). *Receiving aid:* Freshmen: 37% (408); All full-time undergraduates: 33% (1,376). *Average award:* Freshmen: $17,826; Undergraduates: $16,797. *Scholarships, grants, and awards:* Federal Pell, FSEOG, state, private, college/university gift aid from institutional funds.
GIFT AID (NON-NEED-BASED) *Total amount:* $7,899,404 (15% state, 57% institutional, 28% external sources). *Receiving aid:* Freshmen: 10% (113); Undergraduates: 6% (251). *Average Award:* Freshmen: $8621; Undergraduates:* $10,520. *Scholarships, grants, and awards by category: Academic Interests/Achievement:* 619 awards ($3,151,247 total): biological sciences, business, education, English, foreign languages, general academic interests/achievements, international studies, mathematics, military science, physical sciences, premedicine, religion/biblical studies. *Creative Arts/Performance:* 109 awards ($816,465 total): art/fine arts, debating, general creative arts/performance, journalism/publications, music, theater/drama. *Special Achievements/Activities:* 21 awards ($40,220 total): cheerleading/drum major, community service, memberships. *Special Characteristics:* 495 awards ($5,740,272 total): children of faculty/staff, general special characteristics, members of minority groups, relatives of clergy, religious affiliation. *ROTC:* Army.
LOANS *Student loans:* $15,651,488 (64% need-based, 36% non-need-based). 39% of past graduating class borrowed through all loan programs. *Average indebtedness per student:* $22,831. *Average need-based loan:* Freshmen: $5404; Undergraduates: $6643. *Parent loans:* $9,510,795 (9% need-based, 91% non-need-based). *Programs:* FFEL (Subsidized and Unsubsidized Stafford, PLUS), Perkins, state, college/university, private alternative loans.
WORK-STUDY *Federal work-study:* Total amount: $1,825,377; 983 jobs averaging $1818. *State or other work-study/employment:* Part-time jobs available.
ATHLETIC AWARDS *Total amount:* $7,958,186 (29% need-based, 71% non-need-based).

Wake Forest University

APPLYING FOR FINANCIAL AID *Required financial aid forms:* FAFSA, CSS Financial Aid PROFILE, state aid form, noncustodial (divorced/separated) parent's statement. *Financial aid deadline:* 3/1 (priority: 2/1). *Notification date:* 4/1. Students must reply by 5/1 or within 4 weeks of notification.
CONTACT Adam Shick, Assistant Director, Wake Forest University, PO Box 7373, Reynolda Station, Winston-Salem, NC 27109-7373, 336-758-5154. *Fax:* 336-758-4924. *E-mail:* shickaw@wfu.edu.

WALDEN UNIVERSITY
Minneapolis, MN

CONTACT Financial Aid Office, Walden University, 155 Fifth Avenue South, Minneapolis, MN 55401, 800-444-6795 or toll-free 866-492-5336 (out-of-state). *Fax:* 410-843-6211. *E-mail:* finaid@waldenu.edu.

WALDORF COLLEGE
Forest City, IA

Tuition & fees: $15,520 **Average undergraduate aid package: $14,436**

ABOUT THE INSTITUTION Independent Lutheran, coed. Awards: bachelor's degrees. 31 undergraduate majors. Total enrollment: 629. Undergraduates: 629. Freshmen: 197. Federal methodology is used as a basis for awarding need-based institutional aid.
UNDERGRADUATE EXPENSES for 2005–06 *Comprehensive fee:* $20,140 includes full-time tuition ($14,785), mandatory fees ($735), and room and board ($4620). *College room only:* $2150. Full-time tuition and fees vary according to class time, course load, and program. Room and board charges vary according to board plan and housing facility. *Part-time tuition:* $180 per credit. *Part-time fees:* $200 per credit. *Payment plans:* Installment, deferred payment.
FRESHMAN FINANCIAL AID (Fall 2004) 168 applied for aid; of those 91% were deemed to have need. 99% of freshmen with need received aid; of those 32% had need fully met. *Average percent of need met:* 85% (excluding resources awarded to replace EFC). *Average financial aid package:* $12,494 (excluding resources awarded to replace EFC). 19% of all full-time freshmen had no need and received non-need-based gift aid.
UNDERGRADUATE FINANCIAL AID (Fall 2004) 491 applied for aid; of those 92% were deemed to have need. 100% of undergraduates with need received aid; of those 32% had need fully met. *Average percent of need met:* 86% (excluding resources awarded to replace EFC). *Average financial aid package:* $14,436 (excluding resources awarded to replace EFC). 15% of all full-time undergraduates had no need and received non-need-based gift aid.
GIFT AID (NEED-BASED) *Total amount:* $3,883,953 (19% federal, 23% state, 48% institutional, 10% external sources). *Receiving aid:* Freshmen: 76% (152); All full-time undergraduates: 81% (452). *Average award:* Freshmen: $9126; Undergraduates: $10,020. *Scholarships, grants, and awards:* Federal Pell, FSEOG, state, private, college/university gift aid from institutional funds.
GIFT AID (NON-NEED-BASED) *Total amount:* $549,678 (75% institutional, 25% external sources). *Receiving aid:* Freshmen: 10% (20); Undergraduates: 10% (53). *Average Award:* Freshmen: $8358; Undergraduates: $9532. *Scholarships, grants, and awards by category:* Academic Interests/Achievement: 363 awards ($1,114,881 total): communication, general academic interests/achievements. Creative Arts/Performance: 197 awards ($196,707 total): music, theater/drama. Special Achievements/Activities: 126 awards ($235,269 total): cheerleading/drum major, junior miss, leadership. Special Characteristics: 125 awards ($228,384 total): children of faculty/staff, religious affiliation. *Tuition waivers:* Full or partial for employees or children of employees.
LOANS *Student loans:* $2,798,402 (76% need-based, 24% non-need-based). 63% of past graduating class borrowed through all loan programs. *Average indebtedness per student:* $14,782. *Average need-based loan:* Freshmen: $3421; Undergraduates: $4615. *Parent loans:* $1,922,216 (36% need-based, 64% non-need-based). *Programs:* Federal Direct (Subsidized and Unsubsidized Stafford, PLUS), Perkins, state, alternative loans.
WORK-STUDY *Federal work-study:* Total amount: $187,196; 389 jobs averaging $1289. *State or other work-study/employment:* Total amount: $73,354 (5% need-based, 95% non-need-based). 85 part-time jobs averaging $845.
ATHLETIC AWARDS *Total amount:* $891,796 (83% need-based, 17% non-need-based).

APPLYING FOR FINANCIAL AID *Required financial aid form:* FAFSA. *Financial aid deadline (priority):* 3/1. *Notification date:* Continuous beginning 3/1. Students must reply within 2 weeks of notification.
CONTACT Duane Polsdofer, Director of Financial Aid, Waldorf College, 106 South 6th Street, Forest City, IA 50436, 641-585-8120 or toll-free 800-292-1903. *Fax:* 641-585-8125.

WALLA WALLA COLLEGE
College Place, WA

Tuition & fees: $19,917 **Average undergraduate aid package: $17,349**

ABOUT THE INSTITUTION Independent Seventh-day Adventist, coed. Awards: associate, bachelor's, and master's degrees. 64 undergraduate majors. Total enrollment: 1,942. Undergraduates: 1,670. Freshmen: 292. Both federal and institutional methodology are used as a basis for awarding need-based institutional aid.
UNDERGRADUATE EXPENSES for 2006–07 *Application fee:* $40. *Comprehensive fee:* $24,489 includes full-time tuition ($19,725), mandatory fees ($192), and room and board ($4572). *College room only:* $2472. *Part-time tuition:* $516 per credit.
FRESHMAN FINANCIAL AID (Fall 2004) 336 applied for aid; of those 68% were deemed to have need. 100% of freshmen with need received aid; of those 24% had need fully met. *Average percent of need met:* 88% (excluding resources awarded to replace EFC). *Average financial aid package:* $16,018 (excluding resources awarded to replace EFC). 29% of all full-time freshmen had no need and received non-need-based gift aid.
UNDERGRADUATE FINANCIAL AID (Fall 2004) 1,373 applied for aid; of those 75% were deemed to have need. 100% of undergraduates with need received aid; of those 17% had need fully met. *Average percent of need met:* 86% (excluding resources awarded to replace EFC). *Average financial aid package:* $17,349 (excluding resources awarded to replace EFC). 18% of all full-time undergraduates had no need and received non-need-based gift aid.
GIFT AID (NEED-BASED) *Total amount:* $9,902,403 (19% federal, 6% state, 50% institutional, 25% external sources). *Receiving aid:* Freshmen: 54% (188); All full-time undergraduates: 58% (847). *Average award:* Freshmen: $5632; Undergraduates: $6500. *Scholarships, grants, and awards:* Federal Pell, FSEOG, state, private, college/university gift aid from institutional funds.
GIFT AID (NON-NEED-BASED) *Total amount:* $2,231,550 (42% institutional, 58% external sources). *Receiving aid:* Freshmen: 60% (208); Undergraduates: 54% (795). *Average Award:* Freshmen: $4036; Undergraduates: $3308. *Scholarships, grants, and awards by category:* Academic Interests/Achievement: 751 awards ($1,232,843 total): biological sciences, education, general academic interests/achievements, social sciences. Creative Arts/Performance: 62 awards ($39,798 total): general creative arts/performance, music. Special Achievements/Activities: 200 awards ($285,179 total): community service, leadership. Special Characteristics: 184 awards ($843,840 total): children of faculty/staff, ethnic background.
LOANS *Student loans:* $8,406,264 (89% need-based, 11% non-need-based). 72% of past graduating class borrowed through all loan programs. *Average indebtedness per student:* $23,668. *Average need-based loan:* Freshmen: $5219; Undergraduates: $5751. *Parent loans:* $1,812,864 (47% need-based, 53% non-need-based). *Programs:* FFEL (Subsidized and Unsubsidized Stafford, PLUS), Perkins, Federal Nursing, college/university.
WORK-STUDY *Federal work-study:* Total amount: $1,818,519; 747 jobs averaging $2564. *State or other work-study/employment:* Total amount: $127,442 (100% need-based). 86 part-time jobs averaging $2519.
APPLYING FOR FINANCIAL AID *Required financial aid forms:* FAFSA, institution's own form. *Financial aid deadline:* Continuous. *Notification date:* Continuous beginning 3/15.
CONTACT Ms. Nancy Caldera, Associate Director of Financial Aid, Walla Walla College, 204 South College Avenue, College Place, WA 99324-1198, 509-527-2315 or toll-free 800-541-8900. *Fax:* 509-527-2556. *E-mail:* caldna@wwc.edu.

WALSH COLLEGE OF ACCOUNTANCY AND BUSINESS ADMINISTRATION
Troy, MI

Tuition & fees: $9230 **Average undergraduate aid package: $10,763**

ABOUT THE INSTITUTION Independent, coed. Awards: bachelor's and master's degrees. 5 undergraduate majors. Total enrollment: 3,105. Undergraduates: 909. Federal methodology is used as a basis for awarding need-based institutional aid.
UNDERGRADUATE EXPENSES for 2005–06 *Application fee:* $25. *Tuition:* full-time $9000; part-time $250 per credit. *Required fees:* full-time $230; $115 per term part-time. *Payment plan:* Deferred payment.
UNDERGRADUATE FINANCIAL AID (Fall 2004) 141 applied for aid; of those 90% were deemed to have need. 99% of undergraduates with need received aid. *Average percent of need met:* 52% (excluding resources awarded to replace EFC). *Average financial aid package:* $10,763 (excluding resources awarded to replace EFC). 28% of all full-time undergraduates had no need and received non-need-based gift aid.
GIFT AID (NEED-BASED) *Total amount:* $639,855 (46% federal, 33% state, 21% institutional). *Receiving aid:* All full-time undergraduates: 27% (83). *Average award:* Undergraduates: $4232. *Scholarships, grants, and awards:* Federal Pell, FSEOG, state, private, college/university gift aid from institutional funds.
GIFT AID (NON-NEED-BASED) *Total amount:* $210,028 (2% state, 95% institutional, 3% external sources). *Receiving aid:* Undergraduates: 12% (38). *Average Award:* Undergraduates: $2292. *Scholarships, grants, and awards by category:* Academic Interests/Achievement: business. *Special Characteristics:* $127,000 total: previous college experience.
LOANS *Student loans:* $2,117,923 (94% need-based, 6% non-need-based). 45% of past graduating class borrowed through all loan programs. *Average indebtedness per student:* $10,306. *Average need-based loan:* Undergraduates: $7430. *Parent loans:* $19,369 (100% need-based). *Programs:* FFEL (Subsidized and Unsubsidized Stafford, PLUS), alternative loans.
WORK-STUDY Federal work-study jobs available. *State or other work-study/employment:* Total amount: $5204 (100% need-based). Part-time jobs available.
APPLYING FOR FINANCIAL AID *Required financial aid forms:* FAFSA, institution's own form. *Financial aid deadline:* Continuous. *Notification date:* Continuous beginning 6/1.
CONTACT Howard Thomas, Director of Student Financial Resources, Walsh College of Accountancy and Business Administration, 3838 Livernois Road, PO Box 7006, Troy, MI 48007-7006, 248-823-1285 or toll-free 800-925-7401 (in-state). *Fax:* 248-524-2520. *E-mail:* hthomas@walshcollege.edu.

WALSH UNIVERSITY
North Canton, OH

CONTACT Holly Van Gilder, Director of Financial Aid, Walsh University, 2020 East Maple NW, North Canton, OH 44720-3396, 330-490-7147 or toll-free 800-362-9846 (in-state), 800-362-8846 (out-of-state). *Fax:* 330-490-7372. *E-mail:* hvangilder@walsh.edu.

WARNER PACIFIC COLLEGE
Portland, OR

Tuition & fees: N/R	Average undergraduate aid package: $14,227

ABOUT THE INSTITUTION Independent religious, coed. Awards: associate, bachelor's, and master's degrees and post-bachelor's certificates. 34 undergraduate majors. Total enrollment: 575. Undergraduates: 567. Federal methodology is used as a basis for awarding need-based institutional aid.
FRESHMAN FINANCIAL AID (Fall 2005, est.) 67 applied for aid; of those 94% were deemed to have need. 100% of freshmen with need received aid; of those 10% had need fully met. *Average percent of need met:* 73% (excluding resources awarded to replace EFC). *Average financial aid package:* $13,600 (excluding resources awarded to replace EFC). 3% of all full-time freshmen had no need and received non-need-based gift aid.
UNDERGRADUATE FINANCIAL AID (Fall 2005, est.) 359 applied for aid; of those 92% were deemed to have need. 100% of undergraduates with need received aid; of those 11% had need fully met. *Average percent of need met:* 75% (excluding resources awarded to replace EFC). *Average financial aid package:* $14,227 (excluding resources awarded to replace EFC). 5% of all full-time undergraduates had no need and received non-need-based gift aid.
GIFT AID (NEED-BASED) *Total amount:* $1,365,906 (37% federal, 9% state, 54% institutional). *Receiving aid:* Freshmen: 77% (53); All full-time undergraduates: 76% (285). *Average award:* Freshmen: $5056; Undergraduates: $4758. *Scholarships, grants, and awards:* Federal Pell, FSEOG, state, private, college/university gift aid from institutional funds.
GIFT AID (NON-NEED-BASED) *Total amount:* $1,690,777 (1% state, 90% institutional, 9% external sources). *Receiving aid:* Freshmen: 71% (49); Undergraduates: 72% (269). *Average Award:* Freshmen: $15,090; Undergraduates: $7176. *Scholarships, grants, and awards by category:* Academic Interests/Achievement: 201 awards ($976,955 total): biological sciences, general academic interests/achievements, religion/biblical studies. Creative Arts/Performance: 45 awards ($90,000 total): music, theater/drama. Special Achievements/Activities: 48 awards ($79,875 total): leadership. Special Characteristics: 206 awards ($277,460 total): children and siblings of alumni, members of minority groups, religious affiliation. *Tuition waivers:* Full or partial for children of alumni, employees or children of employees. *ROTC:* Army cooperative, Air Force cooperative.
LOANS *Student loans:* $2,460,941 (50% need-based, 50% non-need-based). 86% of past graduating class borrowed through all loan programs. *Average indebtedness per student:* $18,591. *Average need-based loan:* Freshmen: $3155; Undergraduates: $4103. *Parent loans:* $470,427 (100% non-need-based). *Programs:* FFEL (Subsidized and Unsubsidized Stafford, PLUS), Perkins.
WORK-STUDY *Federal work-study:* Total amount: $234,205; 197 jobs averaging $1189. *State or other work-study/employment:* Part-time jobs available.
ATHLETIC AWARDS Total amount: $514,434 (100% non-need-based).
APPLYING FOR FINANCIAL AID *Required financial aid form:* FAFSA. *Financial aid deadline:* Continuous. *Notification date:* Continuous beginning 3/1. Students must reply within 2 weeks of notification.
CONTACT Cynthia Pollard, Director of Financial Aid, Warner Pacific College, 2219 Southeast 68th Avenue, Portland, OR 97215-4099, 503-517-1018 or toll-free 800-582-7885 (in-state), 800-804-1510 (out-of-state). *E-mail:* cpollard@warnerpacific.edu.

WARNER SOUTHERN COLLEGE
Lake Wales, FL

ABOUT THE INSTITUTION Independent religious, coed. Awards: associate, bachelor's, and master's degrees. 24 undergraduate majors. Total enrollment: 970. Undergraduates: 921. Freshmen: 108.
GIFT AID (NEED-BASED) *Scholarships, grants, and awards:* Federal Pell, FSEOG, state, private, college/university gift aid from institutional funds.
GIFT AID (NON-NEED-BASED) *Scholarships, grants, and awards by category:* Academic Interests/Achievement: business, communication, education, English, general academic interests/achievements, humanities. Creative Arts/Performance: music. Special Achievements/Activities: leadership, religious involvement. Special Characteristics: children and siblings of alumni, children of educators, children of faculty/staff, international students, out-of-state students, previous college experience, relatives of clergy, siblings of current students, veterans, veterans' children.
LOANS *Programs:* FFEL (Subsidized and Unsubsidized Stafford, PLUS), Perkins, alternative loans.
APPLYING FOR FINANCIAL AID *Required financial aid forms:* FAFSA, state aid form, verification form.
CONTACT Student Financial Services, Warner Southern College, 13895 Highway 27, Lake Wales, FL 33859, 863-638-7202 or toll-free 800-949-7248 (in-state). *Fax:* 863-638-7603. *E-mail:* financialaid@warner.edu.

WARREN WILSON COLLEGE
Swannanoa, NC

Tuition & fees: $20,126	Average undergraduate aid package: $11,365

ABOUT THE INSTITUTION Independent religious, coed. Awards: bachelor's and master's degrees. 27 undergraduate majors. Total enrollment: 901. Undergraduates: 832. Freshmen: 244. Both federal and institutional methodology are used as a basis for awarding need-based institutional aid.
UNDERGRADUATE EXPENSES for 2006–07 *Comprehensive fee:* $26,126 includes full-time tuition ($20,126) and room and board ($6000).
FRESHMAN FINANCIAL AID (Fall 2005, est.) 207 applied for aid; of those 74% were deemed to have need. 100% of freshmen with need received aid; of those 15% had need fully met. *Average percent of need met:* 69% (excluding resources

Warren Wilson College

awarded to replace EFC). *Average financial aid package:* $10,382 (excluding resources awarded to replace EFC). 13% of all full-time freshmen had no need and received non-need-based gift aid.

UNDERGRADUATE FINANCIAL AID (Fall 2005, est.) 607 applied for aid; of those 83% were deemed to have need. 100% of undergraduates with need received aid; of those 17% had need fully met. *Average percent of need met:* 75% (excluding resources awarded to replace EFC). *Average financial aid package:* $11,365 (excluding resources awarded to replace EFC). 11% of all full-time undergraduates had no need and received non-need-based gift aid.

GIFT AID (NEED-BASED) *Total amount:* $4,142,952 (14% federal, 5% state, 75% institutional, 6% external sources). *Receiving aid:* Freshmen: 47% (132); All full-time undergraduates: 49% (431). *Average award:* Freshmen: $8805; Undergraduates: $8908. *Scholarships, grants, and awards:* Federal Pell, FSEOG, state, college/university gift aid from institutional funds.

GIFT AID (NON-NEED-BASED) *Total amount:* $688,146 (14% state, 58% institutional, 28% external sources). *Receiving aid:* Freshmen: 19% (52); Undergraduates: 16% (142). *Average Award:* Freshmen: $2340; Undergraduates: $2203. *Scholarships, grants, and awards by category: Academic Interests/Achievement:* 132 awards ($257,750 total): general academic interests/achievements. *Creative Arts/Performance:* 23 awards ($14,250 total): art/fine arts, creative writing. *Special Achievements/Activities:* 39 awards ($54,750 total): community service, general special achievements/activities, leadership. *Special Characteristics:* 82 awards ($227,760 total): children of faculty/staff, general special characteristics, local/state students, previous college experience, religious affiliation.

LOANS *Student loans:* $2,258,295 (88% need-based, 12% non-need-based). 59% of past graduating class borrowed through all loan programs. *Average indebtedness per student:* $16,211. *Average need-based loan:* Freshmen: $2581; Undergraduates: $3419. *Parent loans:* $1,561,617 (70% need-based, 30% non-need-based). *Programs:* FFEL (Subsidized and Unsubsidized Stafford, PLUS), Perkins, college/university.

WORK-STUDY *Federal work-study:* Total amount: $800,000; 370 jobs averaging $2162. *State or other work-study/employment:* Total amount: $800,000 (31% need-based, 69% non-need-based). 400 part-time jobs averaging $2000.

APPLYING FOR FINANCIAL AID *Required financial aid forms:* FAFSA, institution's own form, state aid form. *Financial aid deadline (priority):* 4/1. *Notification date:* Continuous beginning 3/1. Students must reply by 5/1 or within 3 weeks of notification.

CONTACT Admissions Office, Warren Wilson College, PO Box 9000, Asheville, NC 28815-9000, 800-934-3536. *Fax:* 828-298-1440.

WARTBURG COLLEGE
Waverly, IA

Tuition & fees: $21,130   **Average undergraduate aid package: $17,098**

ABOUT THE INSTITUTION Independent Lutheran, coed. Awards: bachelor's degrees. 52 undergraduate majors. Total enrollment: 1,811. Undergraduates: 1,811. Freshmen: 519. Federal methodology is used as a basis for awarding need-based institutional aid.

UNDERGRADUATE EXPENSES for 2005–06 *Application fee:* $20. *Comprehensive fee:* $26,895 includes full-time tuition ($20,500), mandatory fees ($630), and room and board ($5765). *College room only:* $2815. Room and board charges vary according to board plan and housing facility. *Part-time tuition:* $760 per credit. *Part-time fees:* $50 per term. Part-time tuition and fees vary according to course load. *Payment plan:* Installment.

FRESHMAN FINANCIAL AID (Fall 2005, est.) 464 applied for aid; of those 86% were deemed to have need. 100% of freshmen with need received aid; of those 36% had need fully met. *Average percent of need met:* 90% (excluding resources awarded to replace EFC). *Average financial aid package:* $17,853 (excluding resources awarded to replace EFC). 22% of all full-time freshmen had no need and received non-need-based gift aid.

UNDERGRADUATE FINANCIAL AID (Fall 2005, est.) 1,568 applied for aid; of those 87% were deemed to have need. 100% of undergraduates with need received aid; of those 29% had need fully met. *Average percent of need met:* 85% (excluding resources awarded to replace EFC). *Average financial aid package:* $17,098 (excluding resources awarded to replace EFC). 23% of all full-time undergraduates had no need and received non-need-based gift aid.

GIFT AID (NEED-BASED) *Total amount:* $16,921,407 (6% federal, 15% state, 69% institutional, 10% external sources). *Receiving aid:* Freshmen: 77% (398); All full-time undergraduates: 78% (1,354). *Average award:* Freshmen: $13,851; Undergraduates: $12,455. *Scholarships, grants, and awards:* Federal Pell, FSEOG, state, private, college/university gift aid from institutional funds.

GIFT AID (NON-NEED-BASED) *Total amount:* $4,903,335 (83% institutional, 17% external sources). *Receiving aid:* Freshmen: 12% (61); Undergraduates: 9% (163). *Average Award:* Freshmen: $14,105; Undergraduates: $12,721. *Scholarships, grants, and awards by category: Academic Interests/Achievement:* biological sciences, business, communication, computer science, education, English, general academic interests/achievements, international studies, mathematics, physical sciences, religion/biblical studies. *Creative Arts/Performance:* art/fine arts, journalism/publications, music. *Special Achievements/Activities:* junior miss. *Special Characteristics:* children and siblings of alumni, children of faculty/staff, ethnic background, international students, members of minority groups, out-of-state students, religious affiliation, siblings of current students. *Tuition waivers:* Full or partial for employees or children of employees, senior citizens.

LOANS *Student loans:* $10,351,141 (58% need-based, 42% non-need-based). 84% of past graduating class borrowed through all loan programs. *Average indebtedness per student:* $22,122. *Average need-based loan:* Freshmen: $3966; Undergraduates: $4786. *Parent loans:* $1,212,455 (50% need-based, 50% non-need-based). *Programs:* FFEL (Subsidized and Unsubsidized Stafford, PLUS), Perkins, alternative loans.

WORK-STUDY *Federal work-study:* Total amount: $687,975; 382 jobs averaging $1801. *State or other work-study/employment:* Total amount: $1,200,733 (100% non-need-based). 628 part-time jobs averaging $1911.

APPLYING FOR FINANCIAL AID *Required financial aid form:* FAFSA. *Financial aid deadline (priority):* 3/1. *Notification date:* Continuous beginning 3/21. Students must reply within 2 weeks of notification.

CONTACT Ms. Jennifer Sassman, Director of Financial Aid, Wartburg College, 100 Wartburg Boulevard, PO Box 1003, Waverly, IA 50677-0903, 319-352-8262 or toll-free 800-772-2085. *Fax:* 319-352-8514. *E-mail:* jennifer.sassman@wartburg.edu.

WASHBURN UNIVERSITY
Topeka, KS

CONTACT Annita Huff, Director of Financial Aid, Washburn University, 1700 SW College Avenue, Topeka, KS 66621, 785-231-1151 or toll-free 800-332-0291 (in-state). *E-mail:* zzahuff@washburn.edu.

WASHINGTON & JEFFERSON COLLEGE
Washington, PA

Tuition & fees: $26,330   **Average undergraduate aid package: $19,096**

ABOUT THE INSTITUTION Independent, coed. Awards: associate and bachelor's degrees. 27 undergraduate majors. Total enrollment: 1,418. Undergraduates: 1,418. Freshmen: 388. Both federal and institutional methodology are used as a basis for awarding need-based institutional aid.

UNDERGRADUATE EXPENSES for 2005–06 *Application fee:* $25. *Comprehensive fee:* $33,490 includes full-time tuition ($25,930), mandatory fees ($400), and room and board ($7160). *College room only:* $4150. Room and board charges vary according to board plan and housing facility. *Part-time tuition:* $810 per credit hour. *Payment plans:* Installment, deferred payment.

FRESHMAN FINANCIAL AID (Fall 2005, est.) 353 applied for aid; of those 85% were deemed to have need. 100% of freshmen with need received aid; of those 22% had need fully met. *Average percent of need met:* 80% (excluding resources awarded to replace EFC). *Average financial aid package:* $19,380 (excluding resources awarded to replace EFC). 19% of all full-time freshmen had no need and received non-need-based gift aid.

UNDERGRADUATE FINANCIAL AID (Fall 2005, est.) 1,169 applied for aid; of those 88% were deemed to have need. 99% of undergraduates with need received aid; of those 29% had need fully met. *Average percent of need met:* 74% (excluding resources awarded to replace EFC). *Average financial aid package:* $19,096 (excluding resources awarded to replace EFC). 20% of all full-time undergraduates had no need and received non-need-based gift aid.

GIFT AID (NEED-BASED) *Total amount:* $13,904,862 (6% federal, 11% state, 80% institutional, 3% external sources). *Receiving aid:* Freshmen: 76% (296); All full-time undergraduates: 71% (997). *Average award:* Freshmen: $14,800; Undergraduates: $14,301. *Scholarships, grants, and awards:* Federal Pell, FSEOG, state, private, college/university gift aid from institutional funds.

GIFT AID (NON-NEED-BASED) *Total amount:* $3,104,950 (98% institutional, 2% external sources). *Receiving aid:* Freshmen: 9% (34); Undergraduates: 6% (87). *Average Award: Freshmen:* $9519; *Undergraduates:* $9297. *Scholarships, grants, and awards by category: Academic Interests/Achievement:* 1,006 awards ($9,284,700 total): business, general academic interests/achievements. *Special Characteristics:* 54 awards ($1,380,690 total): children and siblings of alumni, children of faculty/staff. *Tuition waivers:* Full or partial for employees or children of employees. *ROTC:* Army cooperative, Air Force cooperative.

LOANS *Student loans:* $9,359,550 (63% need-based, 37% non-need-based). 75% of past graduating class borrowed through all loan programs. *Average indebtedness per student:* $17,000. *Average need-based loan:* Freshmen: $2696; Undergraduates: $3725. *Parent loans:* $1,547,346 (48% need-based, 52% non-need-based). *Programs:* FFEL (Subsidized and Unsubsidized Stafford, PLUS), Perkins, college/university.

WORK-STUDY *Federal work-study:* Total amount: $863,981; 530 jobs averaging $1630. *State or other work-study/employment:* Total amount: $200,000 (100% non-need-based). 175 part-time jobs averaging $1140.

APPLYING FOR FINANCIAL AID *Required financial aid form:* FAFSA. *Financial aid deadline (priority):* 2/15. *Notification date:* Continuous beginning 3/1. Students must reply by 5/1.

CONTACT Michelle Vettorel, Director of Financial Aid, Washington & Jefferson College, 60 South Lincoln Street, Washington, PA 15301-4801, 724-223-6528 or toll-free 888-WANDJAY. *Fax:* 724-223-6534. *E-mail:* mvettorel@washjeff.edu.

WASHINGTON AND LEE UNIVERSITY
Lexington, VA

Tuition & fees: $28,635	Average undergraduate aid package: $25,106

ABOUT THE INSTITUTION Independent, coed. Awards: bachelor's, master's, and first professional degrees. 39 undergraduate majors. Total enrollment: 2,179. Undergraduates: 1,770. Freshmen: 465. Both federal and institutional methodology are used as a basis for awarding need-based institutional aid.

UNDERGRADUATE EXPENSES for 2005–06 *Application fee:* $50. *Comprehensive fee:* $35,860 includes full-time tuition ($27,960), mandatory fees ($675), and room and board ($7225). *College room only:* $3425. Room and board charges vary according to housing facility and student level. *Part-time tuition:* $935 per credit.

FRESHMAN FINANCIAL AID (Fall 2005, est.) 244 applied for aid; of those 70% were deemed to have need. 98% of freshmen with need received aid; of those 87% had need fully met. *Average percent of need met:* 99% (excluding resources awarded to replace EFC). *Average financial aid package:* $25,256 (excluding resources awarded to replace EFC). 6% of all full-time freshmen had no need and received non-need-based gift aid.

UNDERGRADUATE FINANCIAL AID (Fall 2005, est.) 683 applied for aid; of those 85% were deemed to have need. 99% of undergraduates with need received aid; of those 86% had need fully met. *Average percent of need met:* 99% (excluding resources awarded to replace EFC). *Average financial aid package:* $25,106 (excluding resources awarded to replace EFC). 13% of all full-time undergraduates had no need and received non-need-based gift aid.

GIFT AID (NEED-BASED) *Total amount:* $10,164,463 (3% federal, 2% state, 91% institutional, 4% external sources). *Receiving aid:* Freshmen: 31% (144); All full-time undergraduates: 27% (463). *Average award:* Freshmen: $21,071; Undergraduates: $19,019. *Scholarships, grants, and awards:* Federal Pell, FSEOG, state, private, college/university gift aid from institutional funds.

GIFT AID (NON-NEED-BASED) *Total amount:* $6,804,432 (1% federal, 6% state, 89% institutional, 4% external sources). *Receiving aid:* Freshmen: 10% (46); Undergraduates: 10% (181). *Average Award: Freshmen:* $19,217; *Undergraduates:* $13,805. *Scholarships, grants, and awards by category: Academic Interests/Achievement:* general academic interests/achievements. *Special Characteristics:* local/state students. *Tuition waivers:* Full or partial for employees or children of employees. *ROTC:* Army cooperative.

LOANS *Student loans:* $2,987,960 (71% need-based, 29% non-need-based). 25% of past graduating class borrowed through all loan programs. *Average indebtedness per student:* $17,105. *Average need-based loan:* Freshmen: $4170; Undergraduates: $4708. *Parent loans:* $3,990,370 (58% need-based, 42% non-need-based). *Programs:* FFEL (Subsidized and Unsubsidized Stafford, PLUS), Perkins, college/university.

WORK-STUDY *Federal work-study:* Total amount: $202,260; 141 jobs averaging $1434. *State or other work-study/employment:* Total amount: $553,200 (77% need-based, 23% non-need-based). 394 part-time jobs averaging $1076.

APPLYING FOR FINANCIAL AID *Required financial aid forms:* FAFSA, CSS Financial Aid PROFILE, noncustodial (divorced/separated) parent's statement, business/farm supplement. *Financial aid deadline (priority):* 2/1. *Notification date:* 4/3. Students must reply by 5/1.

CONTACT John DeCourcy, Director, Financial Aid, Washington and Lee University, Gilliam House, Letcher Avenue, Lexington, VA 24450, 540-458-8729. *Fax:* 540-458-8614.

WASHINGTON BIBLE COLLEGE
Lanham, MD

ABOUT THE INSTITUTION Independent nondenominational, coed. Awards: associate and bachelor's degrees. 8 undergraduate majors. Total enrollment: 331. Undergraduates: 331.

GIFT AID (NEED-BASED) *Scholarships, grants, and awards:* Federal Pell, FSEOG, state, private, college/university gift aid from institutional funds.

GIFT AID (NON-NEED-BASED) *Scholarships, grants, and awards by category: Academic Interests/Achievement:* general academic interests/achievements. *Special Achievements/Activities:* general special achievements/activities, leadership, religious involvement. *Special Characteristics:* children of faculty/staff, international students, relatives of clergy, religious affiliation, spouses of current students.

LOANS *Programs:* FFEL (Subsidized and Unsubsidized Stafford, PLUS).

APPLYING FOR FINANCIAL AID *Required financial aid forms:* FAFSA, institution's own form, CSS Financial Aid PROFILE, verification worksheet.

CONTACT Nancy Minton, Director of Financial Aid, Washington Bible College, 6511 Princess Garden Parkway, Lanham, MD 20706-3599, 301-552-1400 Ext. 1243 or toll-free 877-793-7227 Ext. 1212. *Fax:* 301-614-1051. *E-mail:* nminton@bible.edu.

WASHINGTON COLLEGE
Chestertown, MD

Tuition & fees: $28,790	Average undergraduate aid package: $16,314

ABOUT THE INSTITUTION Independent, coed. Awards: bachelor's and master's degrees. 34 undergraduate majors. Total enrollment: 1,412. Undergraduates: 1,341. Freshmen: 343. Both federal and institutional methodology are used as a basis for awarding need-based institutional aid.

UNDERGRADUATE EXPENSES for 2005–06 *Application fee:* $45. *Comprehensive fee:* $34,990 includes full-time tuition ($28,230), mandatory fees ($560), and room and board ($6200). *College room only:* $3000. Full-time tuition and fees vary according to program and reciprocity agreements. Room and board charges vary according to board plan and housing facility. *Part-time tuition:* $4705 per course. Part-time tuition and fees vary according to course load and program. *Payment plans:* Tuition prepayment, installment.

FRESHMAN FINANCIAL AID (Fall 2005, est.) 202 applied for aid; of those 63% were deemed to have need. 100% of freshmen with need received aid; of those 70% had need fully met. *Average percent of need met:* 85% (excluding resources awarded to replace EFC). *Average financial aid package:* $15,528 (excluding resources awarded to replace EFC). 35% of all full-time freshmen had no need and received non-need-based gift aid.

UNDERGRADUATE FINANCIAL AID (Fall 2005, est.) 753 applied for aid; of those 74% were deemed to have need. 100% of undergraduates with need received aid; of those 73% had need fully met. *Average percent of need met:* 90% (excluding resources awarded to replace EFC). *Average financial aid package:* $16,314 (excluding resources awarded to replace EFC). 40% of all full-time undergraduates had no need and received non-need-based gift aid.

GIFT AID (NEED-BASED) *Total amount:* $7,146,777 (6% federal, 11% state, 83% institutional). *Receiving aid:* Freshmen: 36% (123); All full-time undergraduates: 43% (545). *Average award:* Freshmen: $13,881; Undergraduates: $14,939. *Scholarships, grants, and awards:* Federal Pell, FSEOG, state, private, college/university gift aid from institutional funds.

GIFT AID (NON-NEED-BASED) *Total amount:* $6,180,803 (5% state, 86% institutional, 9% external sources). *Receiving aid:* Freshmen: 26% (90); Undergraduates: 32% (400). *Average Award: Freshmen:* $9266; *Undergraduates:* $10,743. *Scholarships, grants, and awards by category: Academic

Washington College

Interests/Achievement: general academic interests/achievements. *Creative Arts/Performance:* 12 awards ($18,000 total): creative writing. *Special Achievements/Activities:* 580 awards ($5,800,000 total): memberships. *Special Characteristics:* 54 awards ($1,394,736 total): children of faculty/staff, children of union members/company employees, international students. *Tuition waivers:* Full or partial for minority students, employees or children of employees.

LOANS *Student loans:* $4,917,689 (37% need-based, 63% non-need-based). 60% of past graduating class borrowed through all loan programs. *Average indebtedness per student:* $20,483. *Average need-based loan:* Freshmen: $3219; Undergraduates: $4583. *Parent loans:* $5,151,756 (100% non-need-based). *Programs:* FFEL (Subsidized and Unsubsidized Stafford, PLUS), Perkins, college/university.

WORK-STUDY *Federal work-study:* Total amount: $298,401; 238 jobs averaging $1455.

APPLYING FOR FINANCIAL AID *Required financial aid forms:* FAFSA, institution's own form, federal income tax form(s). *Financial aid deadline (priority):* 2/15. *Notification date:* Continuous beginning 3/1. Students must reply by 5/1.

CONTACT Ms. Jean M. Narcum, Director of Financial Aid, Washington College, 300 Washington Avenue, Chestertown, MD 21620-1197, 410-778-7214 or toll-free 800-422-1782. *Fax:* 410-778-7287. *E-mail:* jnarcum2@washcoll.edu.

WASHINGTON STATE UNIVERSITY
Pullman, WA

Tuition & fees (WA res): $5432 **Average undergraduate aid package:** $9886

ABOUT THE INSTITUTION State-supported, coed. Awards: bachelor's, master's, doctoral, and first professional degrees and post-bachelor's and post-master's certificates. 131 undergraduate majors. Total enrollment: 23,544. Undergraduates: 19,585. Freshmen: 2,886. Federal methodology is used as a basis for awarding need-based institutional aid.

UNDERGRADUATE EXPENSES for 2006–07 *Application fee:* $50. *Tuition, state resident:* full-time $5432. *Tuition, nonresident:* full-time $15,072.

FRESHMAN FINANCIAL AID (Fall 2004) 2201 applied for aid; of those 64% were deemed to have need. 99% of freshmen with need received aid; of those 31% had need fully met. *Average percent of need met:* 95% (excluding resources awarded to replace EFC). *Average financial aid package:* $8846 (excluding resources awarded to replace EFC). 11% of all full-time freshmen had no need and received non-need-based gift aid.

UNDERGRADUATE FINANCIAL AID (Fall 2004) 11,045 applied for aid; of those 77% were deemed to have need. 100% of undergraduates with need received aid; of those 33% had need fully met. *Average percent of need met:* 95% (excluding resources awarded to replace EFC). *Average financial aid package:* $9886 (excluding resources awarded to replace EFC). 5% of all full-time undergraduates had no need and received non-need-based gift aid.

GIFT AID (NEED-BASED) *Total amount:* $31,257,289 (45% federal, 44% state, 11% institutional). *Receiving aid:* Freshmen: 26% (798); All full-time undergraduates: 34% (5,620). *Average award:* Freshmen: $4771; Undergraduates: $5404. *Scholarships, grants, and awards:* Federal Pell, FSEOG, state, private, college/university gift aid from institutional funds.

GIFT AID (NON-NEED-BASED) *Total amount:* $13,394,756 (10% state, 30% institutional, 60% external sources). *Receiving aid:* Freshmen: 29% (893); Undergraduates: 19% (3,055). *Average Award:* Freshmen: $4018; Undergraduates: $3606. *Scholarships, grants, and awards by category:* Academic Interests/Achievement: agriculture, architecture, area/ethnic studies, biological sciences, business, communication, computer science, education, engineering/technologies, English, foreign languages, general academic interests/achievements, health fields, home economics, humanities, international studies, mathematics, military science, physical sciences, premedicine, social sciences. *Creative Arts/Performance:* applied art and design, art/fine arts, cinema/film/broadcasting, creative writing, general creative arts/performance, journalism/publications, music, performing arts, theater/drama. *Special Achievements/Activities:* community service, general special achievements/activities, junior miss, leadership, memberships, religious involvement, rodeo. *Special Characteristics:* children and siblings of alumni, children of faculty/staff, children of public servants, children with a deceased or disabled parent, first-generation college students, handicapped students, international students, out-of-state students, public servants, religious affiliation, veterans. *ROTC:* Army, Naval, Air Force.

LOANS *Student loans:* $57,472,798 (56% need-based, 44% non-need-based). 49% of past graduating class borrowed through all loan programs. *Average indebtedness per student:* $21,201. *Average need-based loan:* Freshmen: $3042;

Undergraduates: $4525. *Parent loans:* $26,053,759 (100% non-need-based). *Programs:* FFEL (Subsidized and Unsubsidized Stafford, PLUS), Perkins, Federal Nursing, college/university, alternative loans.

WORK-STUDY *Federal work-study:* Total amount: $700,989; 529 jobs averaging $1308. *State or other work-study/employment:* Total amount: $1,540,453 (100% need-based). 1,022 part-time jobs averaging $1440.

ATHLETIC AWARDS Total amount: $4,469,107 (100% non-need-based).

APPLYING FOR FINANCIAL AID *Required financial aid form:* FAFSA. *Financial aid deadline (priority):* 3/1. *Notification date:* 4/15.

CONTACT Financial Aid Office, Washington State University, Office of Student Financial Aid, PO Box 641068, Pullman, WA 99164-1068, 509-335-9711 or toll-free 888-468-6978. *E-mail:* finaid@wsu.edu.

WASHINGTON UNIVERSITY IN ST. LOUIS
St. Louis, MO

Tuition & fees: $33,788 **Average undergraduate aid package:** $25,653

ABOUT THE INSTITUTION Independent, coed. Awards: bachelor's, master's, doctoral, and first professional degrees and post-bachelor's certificates. 167 undergraduate majors. Total enrollment: 13,383. Undergraduates: 7,466. Freshmen: 1,388. Both federal and institutional methodology are used as a basis for awarding need-based institutional aid.

UNDERGRADUATE EXPENSES for 2006–07 *Application fee:* $55. *Comprehensive fee:* $44,240 includes full-time tuition ($32,800), mandatory fees ($988), and room and board ($10,452). *College room only:* $6402.

FRESHMAN FINANCIAL AID (Fall 2005, est.) 915 applied for aid; of those 60% were deemed to have need. 98% of freshmen with need received aid; of those 100% had need fully met. *Average percent of need met:* 100% (excluding resources awarded to replace EFC). *Average financial aid package:* $25,347 (excluding resources awarded to replace EFC). 18% of all full-time freshmen had no need and received non-need-based gift aid.

UNDERGRADUATE FINANCIAL AID (Fall 2005, est.) 4,321 applied for aid; of those 61% were deemed to have need. 99% of undergraduates with need received aid; of those 100% had need fully met. *Average percent of need met:* 100% (excluding resources awarded to replace EFC). *Average financial aid package:* $25,653 (excluding resources awarded to replace EFC). 13% of all full-time undergraduates had no need and received non-need-based gift aid.

GIFT AID (NEED-BASED) *Total amount:* $54,269,766 (3% federal, 2% state, 89% institutional, 6% external sources). *Receiving aid:* Freshmen: 38% (518); All full-time undergraduates: 42% (2,561). *Average award:* Freshmen: $21,653; Undergraduates: $21,191. *Scholarships, grants, and awards:* Federal Pell, FSEOG, state, private, college/university gift aid from institutional funds, United Negro College Fund.

GIFT AID (NON-NEED-BASED) *Total amount:* $5,329,980 (3% federal, 7% state, 77% institutional, 13% external sources). *Receiving aid:* Freshmen: 5% (63); Undergraduates: 3% (173). *Average Award:* Freshmen: $9186; Undergraduates: $7090. *Scholarships, grants, and awards by category:* Academic Interests/Achievement: architecture, biological sciences, business, communication, computer science, education, engineering/technologies, English, foreign languages, general academic interests/achievements, health fields, humanities, international studies, mathematics, military science, physical sciences, premedicine, religion/biblical studies, social sciences. *Creative Arts/Performance:* applied art and design, art/fine arts, cinema/film/broadcasting, creative writing, dance, music, performing arts, theater/drama. *ROTC:* Army, Air Force cooperative.

LOANS *Student loans:* $14,117,877 (93% need-based, 7% non-need-based). 43% of past graduating class borrowed through all loan programs. *Average need-based loan:* Freshmen: $4461; Undergraduates: $5884. *Parent loans:* $4,807,327 (69% need-based, 31% non-need-based). *Programs:* FFEL (Subsidized and Unsubsidized Stafford, PLUS), Perkins, state, college/university.

WORK-STUDY *Federal work-study:* Total amount: $2,075,081; 1,108 jobs averaging $1873.

APPLYING FOR FINANCIAL AID *Required financial aid forms:* FAFSA, CSS Financial Aid PROFILE, noncustodial (divorced/separated) parent's statement, student and parent 1040 tax return or signed waiver if there is no tax return. *Financial aid deadline:* 2/15. *Notification date:* 4/1. Students must reply by 5/1 or within 2 weeks of notification.

CONTACT Mr. William Witbrodt, Director of Financial Aid, Washington University in St. Louis, Campus Box 1041, One Brookings Drive, St. Louis, MO 63130-4899, 314-935-5900 or toll-free 800-638-0700. *Fax:* 314-935-4037. *E-mail:* financial@wustl.edu.

WATKINS COLLEGE OF ART AND DESIGN
Nashville, TN

Tuition & fees: $12,720	Average undergraduate aid package: $9000

ABOUT THE INSTITUTION Independent, coed. Awards: bachelor's degrees. 5 undergraduate majors. Total enrollment: 393. Undergraduates: 375. Freshmen: 40. Federal methodology is used as a basis for awarding need-based institutional aid.
UNDERGRADUATE EXPENSES for 2006–07 *Application fee:* $50. *Tuition:* full-time $12,000; part-time $500 per hour. *Required fees:* full-time $720; $30 per hour.
FRESHMAN FINANCIAL AID (Fall 2005, est.) 29 applied for aid; of those 100% were deemed to have need. 100% of freshmen with need received aid. *Average percent of need met:* 60% (excluding resources awarded to replace EFC). *Average financial aid package:* $7500 (excluding resources awarded to replace EFC).
UNDERGRADUATE FINANCIAL AID (Fall 2005, est.) 123 applied for aid; of those 100% were deemed to have need. 98% of undergraduates with need received aid. *Average percent of need met:* 60% (excluding resources awarded to replace EFC). *Average financial aid package:* $9000 (excluding resources awarded to replace EFC).
GIFT AID (NEED-BASED) *Total amount:* $531,824 (40% federal, 35% state, 24% institutional, 1% external sources). *Receiving aid:* Freshmen: 34% (14); All full-time undergraduates: 30% (60). *Average award:* Freshmen: $1500; Undergraduates: $1500. *Scholarships, grants, and awards:* Federal Pell, FSEOG, state, college/university gift aid from institutional funds.
GIFT AID (NON-NEED-BASED) *Receiving aid:* Freshmen: 56% (23). *Scholarships, grants, and awards by category: Creative Arts/Performance:* 4 awards ($8500 total): applied art and design, art/fine arts, cinema/film/broadcasting.
LOANS *Student loans:* $1,617,105 (45% need-based, 55% non-need-based). 21% of past graduating class borrowed through all loan programs. *Average indebtedness per student:* $18,000. *Average need-based loan:* Freshmen: $2625; Undergraduates: $4000. *Parent loans:* $430,657 (100% non-need-based). *Programs:* FFEL (Subsidized and Unsubsidized Stafford, PLUS), Private Alternative Loans.
WORK-STUDY *Federal work-study:* Total amount: $19,000; 15 jobs averaging $1500. *State or other work-study/employment:* Total amount: $20,000 (100% need-based). 15 part-time jobs averaging $1500.
APPLYING FOR FINANCIAL AID *Required financial aid forms:* FAFSA, institution's own form. *Financial aid deadline (priority):* 4/1. *Notification date:* Continuous beginning 5/15. Students must reply within 2 weeks of notification.
CONTACT Regina Gilbert, Financial Aid Director, Watkins College of Art and Design, 2298 Metrocenter Boulevard, Nashville, TN 37228, 615-383-4848. *Fax:* 615-383-4849. *E-mail:* rgilbert@watkins.edu.

WAYLAND BAPTIST UNIVERSITY
Plainview, TX

Tuition & fees: $9900	Average undergraduate aid package: $9012

ABOUT THE INSTITUTION Independent Baptist, coed. Awards: associate, bachelor's, and master's degrees (branch locations in Anchorage, AK; Amarillo, TX; Luke Airforce Base, AZ; Glorieta, NM; Aiea, HI; Lubbock, TX; San Antonio, TX; Wichita Falls, TX). 27 undergraduate majors. Total enrollment: 1,124. Undergraduates: 1,004. Freshmen: 226. Federal methodology is used as a basis for awarding need-based institutional aid.
UNDERGRADUATE EXPENSES for 2005–06 *Application fee:* $35. *Comprehensive fee:* $13,484 includes full-time tuition ($9450), mandatory fees ($450), and room and board ($3584). *College room only:* $1276. Full-time tuition and fees vary according to course load and location. Room and board charges vary according to board plan and housing facility. *Part-time tuition:* $315 per credit hour. *Part-time fees:* $50 per term. Part-time tuition and fees vary according to course load and location. *Payment plan:* Installment.
FRESHMAN FINANCIAL AID (Fall 2005, est.) 175 applied for aid; of those 83% were deemed to have need. 100% of freshmen with need received aid; of those 21% had need fully met. *Average percent of need met:* 77% (excluding resources awarded to replace EFC). *Average financial aid package:* $9200 (excluding resources awarded to replace EFC). 22% of all full-time freshmen had no need and received non-need-based gift aid.
UNDERGRADUATE FINANCIAL AID (Fall 2005, est.) 773 applied for aid; of those 81% were deemed to have need. 100% of undergraduates with need received aid; of those 23% had need fully met. *Average percent of need met:* 76% (excluding resources awarded to replace EFC). *Average financial aid package:* $9012 (excluding resources awarded to replace EFC). 20% of all full-time undergraduates had no need and received non-need-based gift aid.
GIFT AID (NEED-BASED) *Total amount:* $4,149,267 (35% federal, 28% state, 33% institutional, 4% external sources). *Receiving aid:* Freshmen: 64% (142); All full-time undergraduates: 71% (596). *Average award:* Freshmen: $7632; Undergraduates: $6770. *Scholarships, grants, and awards:* Federal Pell, FSEOG, state, private, college/university gift aid from institutional funds.
GIFT AID (NON-NEED-BASED) *Total amount:* $872,286 (1% state, 90% institutional, 9% external sources). *Receiving aid:* Freshmen: 8% (17); Undergraduates: 6% (54). *Average Award:* Freshmen: $8192; Undergraduates: $8514. *Scholarships, grants, and awards by category: Academic Interests/Achievement:* 554 awards ($1,228,616 total): biological sciences, business, communication, education, English, general academic interests/achievements, mathematics, physical sciences, religion/biblical studies, social sciences. *Creative Arts/Performance:* 156 awards ($199,219 total): art/fine arts, journalism/publications, music, theater/drama. *Special Achievements/Activities:* 9 awards ($3750 total): cheerleading/drum major, leadership, memberships, religious involvement. *Special Characteristics:* 260 awards ($253,290 total): children and siblings of alumni, children of faculty/staff, ethnic background, general special characteristics, local/state students, members of minority groups, relatives of clergy. *Tuition waivers:* Full or partial for employees or children of employees.
ROTC: Army cooperative, Air Force cooperative.
LOANS *Student loans:* $3,702,718 (73% need-based, 27% non-need-based). 78% of past graduating class borrowed through all loan programs. *Average indebtedness per student:* $13,972. *Average need-based loan:* Freshmen: $2037; Undergraduates: $3037. *Parent loans:* $338,108 (11% need-based, 89% non-need-based). *Programs:* FFEL (Subsidized and Unsubsidized Stafford, PLUS), Perkins, state.
WORK-STUDY *Federal work-study:* Total amount: $129,720; 169 jobs averaging $1311. *State or other work-study/employment:* Total amount: $13,236 (100% non-need-based). 33 part-time jobs averaging $871.
ATHLETIC AWARDS *Total amount:* $958,575 (18% need-based, 82% non-need-based).
APPLYING FOR FINANCIAL AID *Required financial aid forms:* FAFSA, institution's own form. *Financial aid deadline (priority):* 5/1. *Notification date:* Continuous beginning 2/15. Students must reply within 4 weeks of notification.
CONTACT Karen LaQuey, Director of Financial Aid, Wayland Baptist University, 1900 West 7th Street, Plainview, TX 79072-6998, 806-291-3520 or toll-free 800-588-1928. *Fax:* 806-291-1956. *E-mail:* laquey@wbu.edu.

WAYNESBURG COLLEGE
Waynesburg, PA

Tuition & fees: $14,810	Average undergraduate aid package: $11,952

ABOUT THE INSTITUTION Independent religious, coed. Awards: associate, bachelor's, and master's degrees. 50 undergraduate majors. Total enrollment: 2,159. Undergraduates: 1,616. Freshmen: 380. Federal methodology is used as a basis for awarding need-based institutional aid.
UNDERGRADUATE EXPENSES for 2005–06 *Application fee:* $20. *Comprehensive fee:* $20,890 includes full-time tuition ($14,810) and room and board ($6080). *College room only:* $3100. Full-time tuition and fees vary according to class time. Room and board charges vary according to board plan. *Part-time tuition:* $620 per credit. *Part-time fees:* $15 per credit. Part-time tuition and fees vary according to class time, course load, and location. *Payment plans:* Installment, deferred payment.
FRESHMAN FINANCIAL AID (Fall 2005, est.) 336 applied for aid; of those 90% were deemed to have need. 100% of freshmen with need received aid; of those 26% had need fully met. *Average percent of need met:* 81% (excluding resources

Waynesburg College

awarded to replace EFC). *Average financial aid package:* $12,338 (excluding resources awarded to replace EFC). 13% of all full-time freshmen had no need and received non-need-based gift aid.
UNDERGRADUATE FINANCIAL AID (Fall 2005, est.) 1,278 applied for aid; of those 89% were deemed to have need. 100% of undergraduates with need received aid; of those 29% had need fully met. *Average percent of need met:* 80% (excluding resources awarded to replace EFC). *Average financial aid package:* $11,952 (excluding resources awarded to replace EFC). 12% of all full-time undergraduates had no need and received non-need-based gift aid.
GIFT AID (NEED-BASED) *Total amount:* $10,042,283 (14% federal, 24% state, 58% institutional, 4% external sources). *Receiving aid:* Freshmen: 85% (299); All full-time undergraduates: 83% (1,104). *Average award:* Freshmen: $9720; Undergraduates: $8902. *Scholarships, grants, and awards:* Federal Pell, FSEOG, state, private, college/university gift aid from institutional funds.
GIFT AID (NON-NEED-BASED) *Total amount:* $980,894 (5% state, 90% institutional, 5% external sources). *Receiving aid:* Freshmen: 5% (17); Undergraduates: 6% (81). *Average Award:* Freshmen: $11,515; Undergraduates: $10,405. *Scholarships, grants, and awards by category: Academic Interests/Achievement:* 60 awards ($2000 total): biological sciences, business, communication, computer science, education, English, general academic interests/achievements, international studies, mathematics, religion/biblical studies. *Creative Arts/Performance:* 4 awards ($2000 total): music. *Special Achievements/Activities:* 65 awards ($2100 total): community service. *Special Characteristics:* 50 awards ($500,000 total): children of faculty/staff. *Tuition waivers:* Full or partial for employees or children of employees. *ROTC:* Army cooperative.
LOANS *Student loans:* $8,907,221 (63% need-based, 37% non-need-based). 87% of past graduating class borrowed through all loan programs. *Average indebtedness per student:* $20,000. *Average need-based loan:* Freshmen: $2732; Undergraduates: $3608. *Parent loans:* $1,656,370 (22% need-based, 78% non-need-based). *Programs:* FFEL (Subsidized and Unsubsidized Stafford, PLUS), Perkins, Federal Nursing.
WORK-STUDY *Federal work-study:* Total amount: $176,890; 270 jobs averaging $1200.
APPLYING FOR FINANCIAL AID *Required financial aid form:* FAFSA. *Financial aid deadline:* Continuous. *Notification date:* Continuous beginning 2/15. Students must reply within 2 weeks of notification.
CONTACT Matthew C. Stokan, Director of Financial Aid, Waynesburg College, 51 West College Street, Waynesburg, PA 15370-1222, 724-852-3208 or toll-free 800-225-7393. *Fax:* 724-627-6416. *E-mail:* mstokan@waynesburg.edu.

WAYNE STATE COLLEGE
Wayne, NE

Tuition & fees (NE res): $3803   **Average undergraduate aid package:** $3264

ABOUT THE INSTITUTION State-supported, coed. Awards: bachelor's and master's degrees and post-master's certificates. 75 undergraduate majors. Total enrollment: 3,322. Undergraduates: 2,706. Freshmen: 593. Federal methodology is used as a basis for awarding need-based institutional aid.
UNDERGRADUATE EXPENSES for 2005–06 *Application fee:* $30. *Tuition, state resident:* full-time $2933; part-time $97.75 per credit hour. *Tuition, nonresident:* full-time $5865; part-time $195.50 per credit hour. *Required fees:* full-time $870; $34.75 per credit hour. Full-time tuition and fees vary according to course level and course load. Part-time tuition and fees vary according to course level and course load. *College room and board:* $4300; *room only:* $2080. Room and board charges vary according to board plan and housing facility. *Payment plan:* Installment.
FRESHMAN FINANCIAL AID (Fall 2005, est.) 500 applied for aid; of those 70% were deemed to have need. 99% of freshmen with need received aid; of those 26% had need fully met. *Average percent of need met:* 32% (excluding resources awarded to replace EFC). *Average financial aid package:* $3209 (excluding resources awarded to replace EFC).
UNDERGRADUATE FINANCIAL AID (Fall 2005, est.) 2,045 applied for aid; of those 76% were deemed to have need. 99% of undergraduates with need received aid; of those 31% had need fully met. *Average percent of need met:* 37% (excluding resources awarded to replace EFC). *Average financial aid package:* $3264 (excluding resources awarded to replace EFC).
GIFT AID (NEED-BASED) *Total amount:* $3,336,162 (83% federal, 16% state, 1% institutional). *Receiving aid:* Freshmen: 40% (233); All full-time undergraduates: 42% (1,040). *Average award:* Freshmen: $1479; Undergraduates: $1574. *Scholarships, grants, and awards:* Federal Pell, FSEOG, state, college/university gift aid from institutional funds.
GIFT AID (NON-NEED-BASED) *Total amount:* $1,217,859 (51% institutional, 49% external sources). *Receiving aid:* Freshmen: 20% (119); Undergraduates: 19% (468). *Scholarships, grants, and awards by category: Academic Interests/Achievement:* biological sciences, business, communication, computer science, education, English, foreign languages, general academic interests/achievements, health fields, home economics, humanities, mathematics, physical sciences, premedicine, social sciences. *Creative Arts/Performance:* applied art and design, art/fine arts, creative writing, debating, general creative arts/performance, journalism/publications, music, performing arts, theater/drama. *Special Achievements/Activities:* general special achievements/activities, leadership. *Special Characteristics:* children of faculty/staff, children with a deceased or disabled parent, ethnic background, general special characteristics, local/state students, members of minority groups, out-of-state students, veterans, veterans' children. *Tuition waivers:* Full or partial for minority students, employees or children of employees. *ROTC:* Army cooperative.
LOANS *Student loans:* $9,553,584 (58% need-based, 42% non-need-based). *Average need-based loan:* Freshmen: $1516; Undergraduates: $1912. *Parent loans:* $831,642 (100% non-need-based). *Programs:* FFEL (Subsidized and Unsubsidized Stafford, PLUS), Perkins.
WORK-STUDY *Federal work-study:* Total amount: $138,553; 186 jobs averaging $1200.
ATHLETIC AWARDS Total amount: $278,300 (100% non-need-based).
APPLYING FOR FINANCIAL AID *Required financial aid forms:* FAFSA, institution's own form. *Financial aid deadline (priority):* 5/1. *Notification date:* Continuous beginning 3/15. Students must reply within 4 weeks of notification.
CONTACT Mrs. Kyle M. Rose, Director of Financial Aid, Wayne State College, 1111 Main Street, Wayne, NE 68787, 402-375-7230 or toll-free 800-228-9972 (in-state). *Fax:* 402-375-7204. *E-mail:* kyrose1@wsc.edu.

WAYNE STATE UNIVERSITY
Detroit, MI

Tuition & fees (MI res): $6439   **Average undergraduate aid package:** $6958

ABOUT THE INSTITUTION State-supported, coed. Awards: bachelor's, master's, doctoral, and first professional degrees and post-bachelor's and post-master's certificates. 83 undergraduate majors. Total enrollment: 33,137. Undergraduates: 20,737. Freshmen: 2,878. Federal methodology is used as a basis for awarding need-based institutional aid.
UNDERGRADUATE EXPENSES for 2005–06 *Application fee:* $30. *Tuition, state resident:* full-time $5682; part-time $189.40 per semester hour. *Tuition, nonresident:* full-time $13,014; part-time $433.80 per semester hour. *Required fees:* full-time $757; $15.80 per semester hour or $141.70 per term part-time. Full-time tuition and fees vary according to student level. Part-time tuition and fees vary according to student level. *College room and board:* $5350. Room and board charges vary according to housing facility. *Payment plan:* Installment.
FRESHMAN FINANCIAL AID (Fall 2005, est.) 1851 applied for aid; of those 79% were deemed to have need. 99% of freshmen with need received aid; of those 7% had need fully met. *Average percent of need met:* 50% (excluding resources awarded to replace EFC). *Average financial aid package:* $6233 (excluding resources awarded to replace EFC). 6% of all full-time freshmen had no need and received non-need-based gift aid.
UNDERGRADUATE FINANCIAL AID (Fall 2005, est.) 7,660 applied for aid; of those 85% were deemed to have need. 98% of undergraduates with need received aid; of those 7% had need fully met. *Average percent of need met:* 64% (excluding resources awarded to replace EFC). *Average financial aid package:* $6958 (excluding resources awarded to replace EFC). 2% of all full-time undergraduates had no need and received non-need-based gift aid.
GIFT AID (NEED-BASED) *Total amount:* $23,088,205 (91% federal, 4% state, 5% institutional). *Receiving aid:* Freshmen: 43% (1,051); All full-time undergraduates: 38% (4,469). *Average award:* Freshmen: $3716; Undergraduates: $3484. *Scholarships, grants, and awards:* Federal Pell, FSEOG, state, private, college/university gift aid from institutional funds.
GIFT AID (NON-NEED-BASED) *Total amount:* $16,786,014 (11% state, 85% institutional, 4% external sources). *Receiving aid:* Freshmen: 31% (755); Undergraduates: 26% (3,056). *Average Award:* Freshmen: $3778; Undergraduates: $2030. *Scholarships, grants, and awards by category: Academic Interests/*

Achievement: 1,373 awards ($7,337,108 total): general academic interests/achievements. *Creative Arts/Performance:* 305 awards ($586,818 total): art/fine arts, dance, debating, journalism/publications, music, theater/drama. *Special Achievements/Activities:* 38 awards ($16,208 total): general special achievements/activities. **Tuition waivers:** Full or partial for employees or children of employees, senior citizens. **ROTC:** Air Force cooperative.
LOANS *Student loans:* $62,820,809 (94% need-based, 6% non-need-based). 50% of past graduating class borrowed through all loan programs. *Average indebtedness per student:* $19,329. **Average need-based loan:** Freshmen: $2586; Undergraduates: $3756. *Parent loans:* $1,331,274 (100% need-based). *Programs:* FFEL (Subsidized and Unsubsidized Stafford, PLUS), Perkins, Federal Nursing, state, college/university.
WORK-STUDY *Federal work-study:* Total amount: $570,161; 375 jobs averaging $2954. *State or other work-study/employment:* Total amount: $201,822 (100% need-based). 189 part-time jobs averaging $1754.
ATHLETIC AWARDS *Total amount:* $1,986,187 (100% non-need-based).
APPLYING FOR FINANCIAL AID *Required financial aid forms:* FAFSA, income tax forms, W-2 forms. *Financial aid deadline (priority):* 3/1. *Notification date:* Continuous beginning 4/15. Students must reply within 2 weeks of notification.
CONTACT Catherine Kay, Interim Director of Scholarships and Financial Aid, Wayne State University, 3W HNJ Student Services Building, Detroit, MI 48202, 313-577-3378 or toll-free 877-978 Ext. 4636 (in-state), 800-WSU-INFO (out-of-state). *Fax:* 313-577-6648.

WEBBER INTERNATIONAL UNIVERSITY
Babson Park, FL

Tuition & fees: $14,390   Average undergraduate aid package: $12,660

ABOUT THE INSTITUTION Independent, coed. Awards: associate, bachelor's, and master's degrees. 11 undergraduate majors. Total enrollment: 616. Undergraduates: 557. Freshmen: 143. Federal methodology is used as a basis for awarding need-based institutional aid.
UNDERGRADUATE EXPENSES for 2006–07 *Application fee:* $35. *Comprehensive fee:* $19,090 includes full-time tuition ($14,390) and room and board ($4700).
FRESHMAN FINANCIAL AID (Fall 2005, est.) 99 applied for aid; of those 83% were deemed to have need. 100% of freshmen with need received aid; of those 24% had need fully met. *Average percent of need met:* 69% (excluding resources awarded to replace EFC). *Average financial aid package:* $12,470 (excluding resources awarded to replace EFC). 37% of all full-time freshmen had no need and received non-need-based gift aid.
UNDERGRADUATE FINANCIAL AID (Fall 2005, est.) 353 applied for aid; of those 85% were deemed to have need. 100% of undergraduates with need received aid; of those 22% had need fully met. *Average percent of need met:* 68% (excluding resources awarded to replace EFC). *Average financial aid package:* $12,660 (excluding resources awarded to replace EFC). 35% of all full-time undergraduates had no need and received non-need-based gift aid.
GIFT AID (NEED-BASED) *Total amount:* $1,865,154 (35% federal, 45% state, 15% institutional, 5% external sources). *Receiving aid:* Freshmen: 58% (82); All full-time undergraduates: 59% (300). *Average award:* Freshmen: $10,647; Undergraduates: $9515. *Scholarships, grants, and awards:* Federal Pell, FSEOG, state, private, college/university gift aid from institutional funds.
GIFT AID (NON-NEED-BASED) *Total amount:* $983,496 (40% state, 48% institutional, 12% external sources). *Receiving aid:* Freshmen: 57% (81); Undergraduates: 36% (182). *Average Award:* Freshmen: $5534; Undergraduates: $5266. *Scholarships, grants, and awards by category:* Academic Interests/Achievement: 201 awards ($316,950 total): business, general academic interests/achievements. *Creative Arts/Performance:* 53 awards ($45,750 total): general creative arts/performance, journalism/publications. *Special Achievements/Activities:* 529 awards ($1,819,351 total): cheerleading/drum major, community service, general special achievements/activities, leadership, memberships. *Special Characteristics:* 84 awards ($169,859 total): children and siblings of alumni, children of faculty/staff, first-generation college students, general special characteristics, international students, local/state students, siblings of current students.
LOANS *Student loans:* $2,429,488 (81% need-based, 19% non-need-based). 64% of past graduating class borrowed through all loan programs. *Average indebtedness per student:* $16,329. **Average need-based loan:** Freshmen: $2455; Undergraduates: $3531. *Parent loans:* $308,565 (85% need-based, 15% non-need-based). *Programs:* FFEL (Subsidized and Unsubsidized Stafford, PLUS), Perkins, alternative loans.
WORK-STUDY *Federal work-study:* Total amount: $32,429; 44 jobs averaging $836. *State or other work-study/employment:* Total amount: $61,249 (24% need-based, 76% non-need-based). 48 part-time jobs averaging $752.
ATHLETIC AWARDS *Total amount:* $1,606,490 (58% need-based, 42% non-need-based).
APPLYING FOR FINANCIAL AID *Required financial aid forms:* FAFSA, state aid form. *Financial aid deadline:* 8/1 (priority: 5/1). *Notification date:* Continuous. Students must reply within 4 weeks of notification.
CONTACT Ms. Kathleen Wilson, Director of Financial Aid, Webber International University, PO Box 96, Babson Park, FL 33827-0096, 863-638-2930 or toll-free 800-741-1844. *Fax:* 863-638-1317. *E-mail:* wilson@webber.edu.

WEBB INSTITUTE
Glen Cove, NY

Tuition & fees: Average undergraduate aid package: $2797

ABOUT THE INSTITUTION Independent, coed. Awards: bachelor's degrees. 1 undergraduate major. Total enrollment: 80. Undergraduates: 80. Freshmen: 20. Federal methodology is used as a basis for awarding need-based institutional aid.
UNDERGRADUATE EXPENSES for 2006–07 *Application fee:* $25. includes room and board ($8340).
FRESHMAN FINANCIAL AID (Fall 2005, est.) 7 applied for aid; of those 86% were deemed to have need. 100% of freshmen with need received aid; of those 33% had need fully met. *Average percent of need met:* 81% (excluding resources awarded to replace EFC). *Average financial aid package:* $2626 (excluding resources awarded to replace EFC). 10% of all full-time freshmen had no need and received non-need-based gift aid.
UNDERGRADUATE FINANCIAL AID (Fall 2005, est.) 16 applied for aid; of those 56% were deemed to have need. 100% of undergraduates with need received aid; of those 44% had need fully met. *Average percent of need met:* 85% (excluding resources awarded to replace EFC). *Average financial aid package:* $2797 (excluding resources awarded to replace EFC). 8% of all full-time undergraduates had no need and received non-need-based gift aid.
GIFT AID (NEED-BASED) *Total amount:* $9334 (48% federal, 52% state). *Receiving aid:* Freshmen: 5% (1); All full-time undergraduates: 2% (2). *Average award:* Freshmen: $4050; Undergraduates: $2225. *Scholarships, grants, and awards:* Federal Pell, private, college/university gift aid from institutional funds.
GIFT AID (NON-NEED-BASED) *Total amount:* $3,643,100 (2% state, 16% institutional, 82% external sources). *Receiving aid:* Freshmen: 15% (3); Undergraduates: 10% (8). *Average Award:* Freshmen: $1500; Undergraduates: $1160.
LOANS *Student loans:* $54,875 (40% need-based, 60% non-need-based). 17% of past graduating class borrowed through all loan programs. *Average indebtedness per student:* $11,612. *Average need-based loan:* Freshmen: $2389; Undergraduates: $2769. *Parent loans:* $30,825 (100% need-based). *Programs:* FFEL (Subsidized and Unsubsidized Stafford, PLUS).
APPLYING FOR FINANCIAL AID *Required financial aid form:* FAFSA. *Financial aid deadline (priority):* 7/1. *Notification date:* Continuous beginning 8/15.
CONTACT Stephen P Ostendorff, Director of Financial Aid, Webb Institute, Crescent Beach Road, Glen Cove, NY 11542-1398, 516-671-2213 Ext. 104. *Fax:* 516-674-9838. *E-mail:* sostendo@webb-institute.edu.

WEBER STATE UNIVERSITY
Ogden, UT

CONTACT Mr. Richard O. Effiong, Financial Aid Director, Weber State University, 120 Student Service Center, 1136 University Circle, Ogden, UT 84408-1136, 801-626-7569 or toll-free 800-634-6568 (in-state), 800-848-7770 (out-of-state). *E-mail:* finaid@weber.edu.

Webster University

WEBSTER UNIVERSITY
St. Louis, MO

Tuition & fees: $17,210   **Average undergraduate aid package:** $17,299

ABOUT THE INSTITUTION Independent, coed. Awards: bachelor's, master's, and doctoral degrees and post-bachelor's and post-master's certificates. 56 undergraduate majors. Total enrollment: 7,327. Undergraduates: 3,523. Freshmen: 445. Federal methodology is used as a basis for awarding need-based institutional aid.

UNDERGRADUATE EXPENSES for 2005–06 *Application fee:* $25. *Comprehensive fee:* $23,947 includes full-time tuition ($17,210) and room and board ($6737). *College room only:* $3586. Full-time tuition and fees vary according to program. Room and board charges vary according to board plan and housing facility. *Part-time tuition:* $445 per credit hour. Part-time tuition and fees vary according to location. *Payment plan:* Installment.

FRESHMAN FINANCIAL AID (Fall 2005, est.) 362 applied for aid; of those 80% were deemed to have need. 100% of freshmen with need received aid. *Average financial aid package:* $17,548 (excluding resources awarded to replace EFC). 27% of all full-time freshmen had no need and received non-need-based gift aid.

UNDERGRADUATE FINANCIAL AID (Fall 2005, est.) 2,039 applied for aid; of those 85% were deemed to have need. 100% of undergraduates with need received aid. *Average financial aid package:* $17,299 (excluding resources awarded to replace EFC). 22% of all full-time undergraduates had no need and received non-need-based gift aid.

GIFT AID (NEED-BASED) *Total amount:* $16,398,542 (12% federal, 7% state, 60% institutional, 21% external sources). *Receiving aid:* Freshmen: 56% (247); All full-time undergraduates: 57% (1,466). *Average award:* Freshmen: $5188; Undergraduates: $4900. *Scholarships, grants, and awards:* Federal Pell, FSEOG, state, private, college/university gift aid from institutional funds.

GIFT AID (NON-NEED-BASED) *Total amount:* $3,942,118 (2% state, 74% institutional, 24% external sources). *Receiving aid:* Freshmen: 47% (208); Undergraduates: 42% (1,085). *Average Award:* Freshmen: $10,111; Undergraduates:* $9204. *Scholarships, grants, and awards by category:* Academic Interests/Achievement: 1,523 awards ($7,860,000 total): education, general academic interests/achievements, humanities, international studies. Creative Arts/Performance: 120 awards ($127,000 total): art/fine arts, creative writing, debating, music, theater/drama. Special Achievements/Activities: 60 awards ($90,000 total): leadership. *Tuition waivers:* Full or partial for employees or children of employees. *ROTC:* Army cooperative, Air Force cooperative.

LOANS *Student loans:* $13,784,880 (89% need-based, 11% non-need-based). 49% of past graduating class borrowed through all loan programs. *Average indebtedness per student:* $18,690. *Average need-based loan:* Freshmen: $2565; Undergraduates: $4121. *Parent loans:* $2,194,798 (69% need-based, 31% non-need-based). *Programs:* FFEL (Subsidized and Unsubsidized Stafford, PLUS), Perkins.

WORK-STUDY *Federal work-study:* Total amount: $995,030; 484 jobs averaging $2113. *State or other work-study/employment:* Total amount: $1,043,843 (68% need-based, 32% non-need-based). 338 part-time jobs averaging $2170.

APPLYING FOR FINANCIAL AID *Required financial aid forms:* FAFSA, institution's own form. *Financial aid deadline (priority):* 4/1. *Notification date:* Continuous beginning 2/10. Students must reply within 2 weeks of notification.

CONTACT Marilynn Shelton, Financial Aid Counselor, Webster University, Financial Aid Office, 470 East Lockwood Avenue, St. Louis, MO 63119, 314-968-6992 Ext. 7671 or toll-free 800-75-ENROL. *Fax:* 314-968-7125. *E-mail:* sheltoma@webster.edu.

WELLESLEY COLLEGE
Wellesley, MA

Tuition & fees: $31,348   **Average undergraduate aid package:** $27,907

ABOUT THE INSTITUTION Independent, women only. Awards: bachelor's degrees (double bachelor's degree with Massachusetts Institute of Technology). 54 undergraduate majors. Total enrollment: 2,331. Undergraduates: 2,331. Freshmen: 604. Both federal and institutional methodology are used as a basis for awarding need-based institutional aid.

UNDERGRADUATE EXPENSES for 2005–06 *Application fee:* $50. *Comprehensive fee:* $41,030 includes full-time tuition ($30,696), mandatory fees ($652), and room and board ($9682). *College room only:* $4906. Room and board charges vary according to board plan. *Payment plans:* Tuition prepayment, installment.

FRESHMAN FINANCIAL AID (Fall 2005, est.) 454 applied for aid; of those 80% were deemed to have need. 100% of freshmen with need received aid; of those 100% had need fully met. *Average percent of need met:* 100% (excluding resources awarded to replace EFC). *Average financial aid package:* $27,999 (excluding resources awarded to replace EFC).

UNDERGRADUATE FINANCIAL AID (Fall 2005, est.) 1,520 applied for aid; of those 87% were deemed to have need. 100% of undergraduates with need received aid; of those 100% had need fully met. *Average percent of need met:* 100% (excluding resources awarded to replace EFC). *Average financial aid package:* $27,907 (excluding resources awarded to replace EFC).

GIFT AID (NEED-BASED) *Total amount:* $32,235,826 (5% federal, 1% state, 91% institutional, 3% external sources). *Receiving aid:* Freshmen: 58% (350); All full-time undergraduates: 58% (1,275). *Average award:* Freshmen: $26,239; Undergraduates: $25,283. *Scholarships, grants, and awards:* Federal Pell, FSEOG, state, private, college/university gift aid from institutional funds.

GIFT AID (NON-NEED-BASED) *Total amount:* $784,261 (100% external sources). *Tuition waivers:* Full or partial for employees or children of employees. *ROTC:* Army cooperative, Air Force cooperative.

LOANS *Student loans:* $4,543,974 (76% need-based, 24% non-need-based). 51% of past graduating class borrowed through all loan programs. *Average indebtedness per student:* $11,821. *Average need-based loan:* Freshmen: $2463; Undergraduates: $3197. *Parent loans:* $5,523,052 (100% non-need-based). *Programs:* FFEL (Subsidized and Unsubsidized Stafford, PLUS), Perkins, state, college/university.

WORK-STUDY *Federal work-study:* Total amount: $863,274; 740 jobs averaging $1167. *State or other work-study/employment:* Total amount: $434,032 (100% need-based). 357 part-time jobs averaging $1216.

APPLYING FOR FINANCIAL AID *Required financial aid forms:* FAFSA, institution's own form, CSS Financial Aid PROFILE, noncustodial (divorced/separated) parent's statement, business/farm supplement, federal income tax form(s), W-2 forms. *Financial aid deadline (priority):* 1/15. *Notification date:* 4/1. Students must reply by 5/1.

CONTACT Ms. Kathryn Osmond, Director of Financial Aid, Wellesley College, 106 Central Street, Wellesley, MA 02481-8203, 781-283-2360. *Fax:* 781-283-3946. *E-mail:* finaid@wellesley.edu.

WELLS COLLEGE
Aurora, NY

Tuition & fees: $16,680   **Average undergraduate aid package:** $17,290

ABOUT THE INSTITUTION Independent, coed, primarily women. Awards: bachelor's degrees. 40 undergraduate majors. Total enrollment: 417. Undergraduates: 417. Freshmen: 130. Federal methodology is used as a basis for awarding need-based institutional aid.

UNDERGRADUATE EXPENSES for 2006–07 *Application fee:* $40. *Comprehensive fee:* $24,180 includes full-time tuition ($15,580), mandatory fees ($1100), and room and board ($7500). *College room only:* $3750.

FRESHMAN FINANCIAL AID (Fall 2005, est.) 122 applied for aid; of those 81% were deemed to have need. 100% of freshmen with need received aid; of those 29% had need fully met. *Average percent of need met:* 92% (excluding resources awarded to replace EFC). *Average financial aid package:* $16,897 (excluding resources awarded to replace EFC). 10% of all full-time freshmen had no need and received non-need-based gift aid.

UNDERGRADUATE FINANCIAL AID (Fall 2005, est.) 349 applied for aid; of those 85% were deemed to have need. 100% of undergraduates with need received aid; of those 25% had need fully met. *Average percent of need met:* 92% (excluding resources awarded to replace EFC). *Average financial aid package:* $17,290 (excluding resources awarded to replace EFC). 14% of all full-time undergraduates had no need and received non-need-based gift aid.

GIFT AID (NEED-BASED) *Total amount:* $3,465,429 (15% federal, 14% state, 68% institutional, 3% external sources). *Receiving aid:* Freshmen: 76% (99); All full-time undergraduates: 74% (297). *Average award:* Freshmen: $12,620; Undergraduates: $11,668. *Scholarships, grants, and awards:* Federal Pell, FSEOG, state, private, college/university gift aid from institutional funds.

GIFT AID (NON-NEED-BASED) *Total amount:* $328,266 (3% state, 86% institutional, 11% external sources). *Average Award:* Freshmen: $4972; Undergraduates: $4960. *Scholarships, grants, and awards by category:*

Academic Interests/Achievement: 25 awards ($117,500 total): general academic interests/achievements. *Special Achievements/Activities:* 17 awards ($85,000 total): leadership. *Special Characteristics:* 5 awards ($12,500 total): children and siblings of alumni. *ROTC:* Air Force cooperative.

LOANS *Student loans:* $1,674,874 (75% need-based, 25% non-need-based). 91% of past graduating class borrowed through all loan programs. *Average indebtedness per student:* $17,125. *Average need-based loan:* Freshmen: $3407; Undergraduates: $4737. *Parent loans:* $538,305 (100% non-need-based). *Programs:* FFEL (Subsidized and Unsubsidized Stafford, PLUS), Perkins.

WORK-STUDY *Federal work-study:* Total amount: $110,000; 78 jobs averaging $1400. *State or other work-study/employment:* Total amount: $364,023 (84% need-based, 16% non-need-based). 260 part-time jobs averaging $1400.

APPLYING FOR FINANCIAL AID *Required financial aid form:* FAFSA. *Financial aid deadline (priority):* 2/15. *Notification date:* 3/1. Students must reply by 5/1.

CONTACT Ms. Cathleen A. Bellomo, Director of Financial Aid, Wells College, Route 90, Aurora, NY 13026, 315-364-3289 or toll-free 800-952-9355. *Fax:* 315-364-3227. *E-mail:* cpatella@wells.edu.

WENTWORTH INSTITUTE OF TECHNOLOGY
Boston, MA

Tuition & fees: $18,500 **Average undergraduate aid package: $7625**

ABOUT THE INSTITUTION Independent, coed. Awards: associate and bachelor's degrees. 21 undergraduate majors. Total enrollment: 3,636. Undergraduates: 3,636. Freshmen: 863. Federal methodology is used as a basis for awarding need-based institutional aid.

UNDERGRADUATE EXPENSES for 2005–06 *Application fee:* $30. *Comprehensive fee:* $27,500 includes full-time tuition ($18,500) and room and board ($9000). *Payment plan:* Installment.

FRESHMAN FINANCIAL AID (Fall 2004) 852 applied for aid; of those 67% were deemed to have need. 100% of freshmen with need received aid; of those 4% had need fully met. *Average percent of need met:* 40% (excluding resources awarded to replace EFC). *Average financial aid package:* $8443 (excluding resources awarded to replace EFC). 19% of all full-time freshmen had no need and received non-need-based gift aid.

UNDERGRADUATE FINANCIAL AID (Fall 2004) 3,192 applied for aid; of those 42% were deemed to have need. 100% of undergraduates with need received aid; of those 5% had need fully met. *Average percent of need met:* 46% (excluding resources awarded to replace EFC). *Average financial aid package:* $7625 (excluding resources awarded to replace EFC). 13% of all full-time undergraduates had no need and received non-need-based gift aid.

GIFT AID (NEED-BASED) *Total amount:* $4,240,713 (49% federal, 18% state, 15% institutional, 18% external sources). *Receiving aid:* Freshmen: 23% (195); All full-time undergraduates: 13% (412). *Average award:* Freshmen: $2163; Undergraduates: $2163. *Scholarships, grants, and awards:* Federal Pell, FSEOG, state, private, college/university gift aid from institutional funds.

GIFT AID (NON-NEED-BASED) *Total amount:* $8,387,446 (100% institutional). *Receiving aid:* Freshmen: 62% (528); Undergraduates: 3% (82). *Average Award:* Freshmen: $3657; Undergraduates: $3657. *Tuition waivers:* Full or partial for employees or children of employees. *ROTC:* Army cooperative, Air Force cooperative.

LOANS *Student loans:* $20,807,211 (38% need-based, 62% non-need-based). 80% of past graduating class borrowed through all loan programs. *Average indebtedness per student:* $20,928. *Average need-based loan:* Freshmen: $3076; Undergraduates: $4156. *Parent loans:* $3,634,699 (100% non-need-based). *Programs:* Federal Direct (Subsidized and Unsubsidized Stafford, PLUS), Perkins, state.

WORK-STUDY *Federal work-study:* Total amount: $1,281,374; 800 jobs averaging $1600.

APPLYING FOR FINANCIAL AID *Required financial aid forms:* FAFSA, state aid form. *Financial aid deadline (priority):* 3/1. *Notification date:* Continuous beginning 3/15. Students must reply within 2 weeks of notification.

CONTACT Shelle Riehl, Director of Financial Aid, Wentworth Institute of Technology, 550 Huntington Avenue, Boston, MA 02115-5998, 617-989-4033 or toll-free 800-556-0610. *Fax:* 617-989-4201. *E-mail:* shahanriehlr@wir.edu.

WESLEYAN COLLEGE
Macon, GA

Tuition & fees: $12,110 **Average undergraduate aid package: $10,758**

ABOUT THE INSTITUTION Independent United Methodist, undergraduate: women only; graduate: coed. Awards: bachelor's and master's degrees. 31 undergraduate majors. Total enrollment: 640. Undergraduates: 551. Freshmen: 113. Federal methodology is used as a basis for awarding need-based institutional aid.

UNDERGRADUATE EXPENSES for 2005–06 *Application fee:* $30. *Comprehensive fee:* $19,560 includes full-time tuition ($11,260), mandatory fees ($850), and room and board ($7450). Full-time tuition and fees vary according to class time, course load, and program. Room and board charges vary according to board plan and housing facility. *Part-time tuition:* $355 per semester hour. Part-time tuition and fees vary according to class time, course load, and program.

FRESHMAN FINANCIAL AID (Fall 2005, est.) 86 applied for aid; of those 81% were deemed to have need. 100% of freshmen with need received aid; of those 27% had need fully met. *Average percent of need met:* 82% (excluding resources awarded to replace EFC). *Average financial aid package:* $11,641 (excluding resources awarded to replace EFC). 34% of all full-time freshmen had no need and received non-need-based gift aid.

UNDERGRADUATE FINANCIAL AID (Fall 2005, est.) 296 applied for aid; of those 83% were deemed to have need. 99% of undergraduates with need received aid; of those 28% had need fully met. *Average percent of need met:* 79% (excluding resources awarded to replace EFC). *Average financial aid package:* $10,758 (excluding resources awarded to replace EFC). 38% of all full-time undergraduates had no need and received non-need-based gift aid.

GIFT AID (NEED-BASED) *Total amount:* $2,149,032 (26% federal, 20% state, 49% institutional, 5% external sources). *Receiving aid:* Freshmen: 65% (70); All full-time undergraduates: 60% (235). *Average award:* Freshmen: $9408; Undergraduates: $7913. *Scholarships, grants, and awards:* Federal Pell, FSEOG, state, private, college/university gift aid from institutional funds.

GIFT AID (NON-NEED-BASED) *Total amount:* $1,881,990 (16% state, 74% institutional, 10% external sources). *Receiving aid:* Freshmen: 14% (15); Undergraduates: 13% (50). *Average Award:* Freshmen: $13,235; Undergraduates: $13,943. *Scholarships, grants, and awards by category:* Academic Interests/Achievement: 413 awards ($2,414,669 total): biological sciences, business, communication, education, English, foreign languages, general academic interests/achievements, humanities, mathematics, premedicine, religion/biblical studies, social sciences. *Creative Arts/Performance:* $130,169 total: art/fine arts, music, theater/drama. *Special Achievements/Activities:* 67 awards ($116,788 total): community service, general special achievements/activities, leadership, religious involvement. *Special Characteristics:* 99 awards ($395,265 total): adult students, children and siblings of alumni, children of current students, children of faculty/staff, ethnic background, first-generation college students, general special characteristics, handicapped students, international students, out-of-state students, parents of current students, relatives of clergy, religious affiliation, siblings of current students, spouses of current students. *Tuition waivers:* Full or partial for employees or children of employees, senior citizens.

LOANS *Student loans:* $2,246,901 (64% need-based, 36% non-need-based). 80% of past graduating class borrowed through all loan programs. *Average indebtedness per student:* $20,988. *Average need-based loan:* Freshmen: $2654; Undergraduates: $3799. *Parent loans:* $360,015 (17% need-based, 83% non-need-based). *Programs:* FFEL (Subsidized and Unsubsidized Stafford, PLUS), Perkins, college/university, various Alternative or Private Education Loans.

WORK-STUDY *Federal work-study:* Total amount: $51,804; 97 jobs averaging $1200. *State or other work-study/employment:* Total amount: $90,689 (8% need-based, 92% non-need-based). 147 part-time jobs averaging $1200.

APPLYING FOR FINANCIAL AID *Required financial aid forms:* FAFSA, institution's own form, state aid form. *Financial aid deadline (priority):* 4/1. *Notification date:* Continuous beginning 3/1. Students must reply by 5/1 or within 2 weeks of notification.

CONTACT Quintress L. Hollis, Director of Financial Aid, Wesleyan College, 4760 Forsyth Road, Macon, GA 31210-4462, 478-757-5205 or toll-free 800-447-6610. *Fax:* 478-757-4030. *E-mail:* sjones@wesleyancollege.edu.

Wesleyan University

WESLEYAN UNIVERSITY
Middletown, CT

Tuition & fees: $35,230 **Average undergraduate aid package:** $28,880

ABOUT THE INSTITUTION Independent, coed. Awards: bachelor's, master's, and doctoral degrees and post-master's certificates. 48 undergraduate majors. Total enrollment: 3,207. Undergraduates: 2,764. Freshmen: 705. Both federal and institutional methodology are used as a basis for awarding need-based institutional aid.
UNDERGRADUATE EXPENSES for 2006–07 *Application fee:* $55. *Comprehensive fee:* $44,770 includes full-time tuition ($34,930), mandatory fees ($300), and room and board ($9540). *College room only:* $5808.
FRESHMAN FINANCIAL AID (Fall 2004) 403 applied for aid; of those 81% were deemed to have need. 100% of freshmen with need received aid; of those 100% had need fully met. *Average percent of need met:* 100% (excluding resources awarded to replace EFC). *Average financial aid package:* $28,280 (excluding resources awarded to replace EFC).
UNDERGRADUATE FINANCIAL AID (Fall 2004) 1,483 applied for aid; of those 89% were deemed to have need. 100% of undergraduates with need received aid; of those 100% had need fully met. *Average percent of need met:* 100% (excluding resources awarded to replace EFC). *Average financial aid package:* $28,880 (excluding resources awarded to replace EFC).
GIFT AID (NEED-BASED) *Total amount:* $27,777,297 (1% federal, 1% state, 94% institutional, 4% external sources). *Receiving aid:* Freshmen: 43% (313); All full-time undergraduates: 45% (1,248). *Average award:* Freshmen: $23,568; Undergraduates: $23,443. *Scholarships, grants, and awards:* Federal Pell, FSEOG, state, private, college/university gift aid from institutional funds.
GIFT AID (NON-NEED-BASED) *ROTC:* Air Force cooperative.
LOANS *Student loans:* $6,296,872 (100% need-based). 41% of past graduating class borrowed through all loan programs. *Average indebtedness per student:* $22,395. *Average need-based loan:* Freshmen: $2595; Undergraduates: $4777. *Programs:* FFEL (Subsidized and Unsubsidized Stafford, PLUS), Perkins, college/university.
WORK-STUDY *Federal work-study:* Total amount: $1,857,451; 1,010 jobs averaging $1838. *State or other work-study/employment:* Total amount: $340,168 (100% need-based). 193 part-time jobs averaging $1756.
APPLYING FOR FINANCIAL AID *Required financial aid forms:* FAFSA, CSS Financial Aid PROFILE, noncustodial (divorced/separated) parent's statement, business/farm supplement. *Financial aid deadline:* 2/15. *Notification date:* 4/1. Students must reply by 5/1 or within 2 weeks of notification.
CONTACT Ms. Karen Hook, Associate Director of Financial Aid, Wesleyan University, 237 High Street, Middletown, CT 06459-0260, 860-685-2800. *Fax:* 860-685-2801. *E-mail:* finaid@wesleyan.edu.

WESLEY COLLEGE
Dover, DE

ABOUT THE INSTITUTION Independent United Methodist, coed. Awards: associate, bachelor's, and master's degrees and post-bachelor's and post-master's certificates. 18 undergraduate majors. Total enrollment: 2,282. Undergraduates: 2,116. Freshmen: 528.
GIFT AID (NEED-BASED) *Scholarships, grants, and awards:* Federal Pell, FSEOG, state, private, college/university gift aid from institutional funds.
GIFT AID (NON-NEED-BASED) *Scholarships, grants, and awards by category: Academic Interests/Achievement:* general academic interests/achievements. *Special Achievements/Activities:* community service, general special achievements/activities, leadership, religious involvement.
LOANS *Programs:* Federal Direct (Subsidized and Unsubsidized Stafford, PLUS), FFEL (Subsidized and Unsubsidized Stafford, PLUS), Perkins, state, college/university.
WORK-STUDY *Federal work-study:* Total amount: $128,700; 225 jobs averaging $2200. *State or other work-study/employment:* Part-time jobs available.
APPLYING FOR FINANCIAL AID *Required financial aid forms:* FAFSA, institution's own form.
CONTACT James Marks, Director of Student Financial Planning, Wesley College, 120 North State Street, Dover, DE 19901-3875, 302-736-2334 or toll-free 800-937-5398 Ext. 2400 (out-of-state). *Fax:* 302-736-2594. *E-mail:* marksja@wesley.edu.

WESLEY COLLEGE
Florence, MS

Tuition & fees: $7600 **Average undergraduate aid package:** $6300

ABOUT THE INSTITUTION Independent Congregational Methodist, coed. Awards: bachelor's degrees. 2 undergraduate majors. Total enrollment: 80. Undergraduates: 80. Freshmen: 19. Federal methodology is used as a basis for awarding need-based institutional aid.
UNDERGRADUATE EXPENSES for 2006–07 *Application fee:* $20. *Comprehensive fee:* $10,980 includes full-time tuition ($6900), mandatory fees ($700), and room and board ($3380). *Part-time tuition:* $230 per credit hour.
FRESHMAN FINANCIAL AID (Fall 2005, est.) 18 applied for aid; of those 78% were deemed to have need. 100% of freshmen with need received aid. *Average percent of need met:* 60% (excluding resources awarded to replace EFC). *Average financial aid package:* $5400 (excluding resources awarded to replace EFC). 11% of all full-time freshmen had no need and received non-need-based gift aid.
UNDERGRADUATE FINANCIAL AID (Fall 2005, est.) 51 applied for aid; of those 80% were deemed to have need. 100% of undergraduates with need received aid. *Average percent of need met:* 75% (excluding resources awarded to replace EFC). *Average financial aid package:* $6300 (excluding resources awarded to replace EFC). 11% of all full-time undergraduates had no need and received non-need-based gift aid.
GIFT AID (NEED-BASED) *Total amount:* $137,081 (98% federal, 2% state). *Receiving aid:* Freshmen: 17% (3); All full-time undergraduates: 16% (9). *Average award:* Freshmen: $200; Undergraduates: $200. *Scholarships, grants, and awards:* Federal Pell, FSEOG, state, college/university gift aid from institutional funds.
GIFT AID (NON-NEED-BASED) *Total amount:* $16,000 (62% institutional, 38% external sources). *Average Award:* Freshmen: $500; Undergraduates: $500. *Scholarships, grants, and awards by category: Academic Interests/Achievement:* 2 awards ($4800 total): general academic interests/achievements. *Creative Arts/Performance:* 8 awards ($500 total): music. *Special Achievements/Activities:* 17 awards ($350 total): leadership, religious involvement.
LOANS *Student loans:* $322,500 (57% need-based, 43% non-need-based). 85% of past graduating class borrowed through all loan programs. *Average indebtedness per student:* $15,000. *Average need-based loan:* Freshmen: $900; Undergraduates: $1600. *Parent loans:* $5200 (100% need-based). *Programs:* Federal Direct (Subsidized and Unsubsidized Stafford, PLUS).
WORK-STUDY *Federal work-study:* Total amount: $25,296; 18 jobs averaging $700.
APPLYING FOR FINANCIAL AID *Required financial aid form:* FAFSA. *Financial aid deadline (priority):* 8/20. *Notification date:* Continuous beginning 5/1. Students must reply within 2 weeks of notification.
CONTACT William Devore Jr., Director of Financial Aid, Wesley College, PO Box 1070, Florence, MS 39073-1070, 601-845-4086 or toll-free 800-748-9972. *Fax:* 601-845-2266. *E-mail:* wdevore@wesleycollege.edu.

WEST CHESTER UNIVERSITY OF PENNSYLVANIA
West Chester, PA

CONTACT Financial Aid Office, West Chester University of Pennsylvania, 138 E.O. Bull Center, West Chester, PA 19383, 610-436-2627 or toll-free 877-315-2165 (in-state). *Fax:* 610-436-2574.

WESTERN BAPTIST COLLEGE
Salem, OR

See Corban College.

WESTERN CAROLINA UNIVERSITY
Cullowhee, NC

Tuition & fees: N/R **Average undergraduate aid package:** $6648

ABOUT THE INSTITUTION State-supported, coed. Awards: bachelor's, master's, and doctoral degrees and post-master's certificates. 66 undergraduate majors. Total enrollment: 8,665. Undergraduates: 6,980. Freshmen: 1,557. Federal methodology is used as a basis for awarding need-based institutional aid.

UNDERGRADUATE EXPENSES for 2006–07 *Application fee:* $40. *Tuition, state resident:* part-time $278.03 per hour. *Tuition, nonresident:* part-time $1,457.53 per hour.

FRESHMAN FINANCIAL AID (Fall 2005, est.) 1125 applied for aid; of those 63% were deemed to have need. 99% of freshmen with need received aid; of those 41% had need fully met. *Average percent of need met:* 76% (excluding resources awarded to replace EFC). *Average financial aid package:* $6321 (excluding resources awarded to replace EFC). 14% of all full-time freshmen had no need and received non-need-based gift aid.

UNDERGRADUATE FINANCIAL AID (Fall 2005, est.) 3,226 applied for aid; of those 89% were deemed to have need. 99% of undergraduates with need received aid; of those 42% had need fully met. *Average percent of need met:* 79% (excluding resources awarded to replace EFC). *Average financial aid package:* $6648 (excluding resources awarded to replace EFC). 12% of all full-time undergraduates had no need and received non-need-based gift aid.

GIFT AID (NEED-BASED) *Total amount:* $9,735,858 (47% federal, 39% state, 8% institutional, 6% external sources). *Receiving aid:* Freshmen: 44% (690); All full-time undergraduates: 46% (2,757). *Average award:* Freshmen: $4136; Undergraduates: $3843. *Scholarships, grants, and awards:* Federal Pell, FSEOG, state, private, college/university gift aid from institutional funds.

GIFT AID (NON-NEED-BASED) *Total amount:* $3,072,989 (35% state, 36% institutional, 29% external sources). *Receiving aid:* Freshmen: 3% (41); Undergraduates: 3% (185). *Average Award:* Freshmen: $2550; Undergraduates: $2487. *Scholarships, grants, and awards by category: Academic Interests/Achievement:* 719 awards ($911,801 total): biological sciences, business, communication, education, English, general academic interests/achievements, health fields, mathematics, social sciences. *Creative Arts/Performance:* 213 awards ($61,010 total): art/fine arts, music, theater/drama. *Special Characteristics:* 120 awards ($95,974 total): ethnic background, handicapped students, local/state students, members of minority groups.

LOANS *Student loans:* $15,410,728 (70% need-based, 30% non-need-based). 49% of past graduating class borrowed through all loan programs. *Average indebtedness per student:* $17,782. *Average need-based loan:* Freshmen: $2441; Undergraduates: $3136. *Parent loans:* $6,835,603 (48% need-based, 52% non-need-based). *Programs:* Federal Direct (Subsidized and Unsubsidized Stafford, PLUS), Perkins.

WORK-STUDY *Federal work-study:* Total amount: $773,839; jobs available (averaging $1256).

ATHLETIC AWARDS *Total amount:* $1,663,448 (46% need-based, 54% non-need-based).

APPLYING FOR FINANCIAL AID *Required financial aid forms:* FAFSA, institution's own form. *Financial aid deadline (priority):* 3/31. *Notification date:* Continuous beginning 4/1.

CONTACT Ms. Nancy B. Dillard, Director of Financial Aid, Western Carolina University, 224 Killian Annex, Cullowhee, NC 28723, 828-227-7292 or toll-free 877-WCU4YOU. *Fax:* 828-227-7042. *E-mail:* dillard@wcu.edu.

WESTERN CONNECTICUT STATE UNIVERSITY
Danbury, CT

ABOUT THE INSTITUTION State-supported, coed. Awards: associate, bachelor's, master's, and doctoral degrees. 39 undergraduate majors. Total enrollment: 5,907. Undergraduates: 5,195. Freshmen: 787.

GIFT AID (NEED-BASED) *Scholarships, grants, and awards:* Federal Pell, FSEOG, state, private, college/university gift aid from institutional funds.

GIFT AID (NON-NEED-BASED) *Scholarships, grants, and awards by category: Academic Interests/Achievement:* general academic interests/achievements.

LOANS *Programs:* FFEL (Subsidized and Unsubsidized Stafford, PLUS), Perkins.

APPLYING FOR FINANCIAL AID *Required financial aid forms:* FAFSA, institution's own form.

CONTACT Nancy Barton, Director of Financial Aid, Western Connecticut State University, 181 White Street, Danbury, CT 06810-6860, 203-837-8580 or toll-free 877-837-9278. *Fax:* 203-837-8528. *E-mail:* bartonn@wcsu.edu.

WESTERN GOVERNORS UNIVERSITY
Salt Lake City, UT

CONTACT Stacey Ludwig-Hardman, Director of Academic Services, Western Governors University, 2040 East Murray Holladay Road, Suite #106, Salt Lake City, UT 84117, 801-274-3280 or toll-free 877-435-7948. *Fax:* 801-274-3305. *E-mail:* shardman@wgu.edu.

WESTERN ILLINOIS UNIVERSITY
Macomb, IL

Tuition & fees (IL res): $6899   **Average undergraduate aid package: $7891**

ABOUT THE INSTITUTION State-supported, coed. Awards: bachelor's, master's, and doctoral degrees and post-bachelor's and post-master's certificates. 53 undergraduate majors. Total enrollment: 13,404. Undergraduates: 11,284. Freshmen: 1,816. Federal methodology is used as a basis for awarding need-based institutional aid.

UNDERGRADUATE EXPENSES for 2005–06 *Application fee:* $30. *Tuition, state resident:* full-time $4968; part-time $213.69 per semester hour. *Tuition, nonresident:* full-time $7452; part-time $296.49 per semester hour. *Required fees:* full-time $1931; $48.09 per semester hour. Full-time tuition and fees vary according to location and student level. Part-time tuition and fees vary according to location and student level. *College room and board:* $6143; *room only:* $3693. Room and board charges vary according to housing facility and student level. *Payment plan:* Guaranteed tuition.

FRESHMAN FINANCIAL AID (Fall 2005, est.) 1341 applied for aid; of those 74% were deemed to have need. 96% of freshmen with need received aid; of those 33% had need fully met. *Average percent of need met:* 63% (excluding resources awarded to replace EFC). *Average financial aid package:* $6643 (excluding resources awarded to replace EFC). 6% of all full-time freshmen had no need and received non-need-based gift aid.

UNDERGRADUATE FINANCIAL AID (Fall 2005, est.) 7,261 applied for aid; of those 80% were deemed to have need. 97% of undergraduates with need received aid; of those 37% had need fully met. *Average percent of need met:* 67% (excluding resources awarded to replace EFC). *Average financial aid package:* $7891 (excluding resources awarded to replace EFC). 5% of all full-time undergraduates had no need and received non-need-based gift aid.

GIFT AID (NEED-BASED) *Total amount:* $24,916,564 (42% federal, 50% state, 6% institutional, 2% external sources). *Receiving aid:* Freshmen: 35% (635); All full-time undergraduates: 38% (3,902). *Average award:* Freshmen: $6423; Undergraduates: $5776. *Scholarships, grants, and awards:* Federal Pell, FSEOG, state, private, college/university gift aid from institutional funds.

GIFT AID (NON-NEED-BASED) *Total amount:* $4,032,697 (32% federal, 32% state, 30% institutional, 6% external sources). *Average Award:* Freshmen: $3039; Undergraduates: $2306. *Scholarships, grants, and awards by category: Academic Interests/Achievement:* 2,250 awards ($1,971,655 total): agriculture, biological sciences, business, education, foreign languages, general academic interests/achievements, home economics, mathematics, physical sciences, social sciences. *Creative Arts/Performance:* 490 awards ($453,312 total): applied art and design, cinema/film/broadcasting, dance, debating, journalism/publications, music, performing arts, theater/drama. *Special Achievements/Activities:* 292 awards ($153,808 total): community service, leadership. *Special Characteristics:* 1,124 awards ($1,646,569 total): children of faculty/staff, general special characteristics, international students, members of minority groups, veterans' children. *Tuition waivers:* Full or partial for employees or children of employees, senior citizens. *ROTC:* Army.

LOANS *Student loans:* $35,263,843 (64% need-based, 36% non-need-based). 62% of past graduating class borrowed through all loan programs. *Average indebtedness per student:* $14,850. *Average need-based loan:* Freshmen: $2517; Undergraduates: $3573. *Parent loans:* $8,898,736 (69% need-based, 31% non-need-based). *Programs:* FFEL (Subsidized and Unsubsidized Stafford, PLUS), Perkins, college/university.

WORK-STUDY *Federal work-study:* Total amount: $384,610; 203 jobs averaging $1895. *State or other work-study/employment:* Total amount: $1,383,575 (64% need-based, 36% non-need-based). 1,569 part-time jobs averaging $855.

ATHLETIC AWARDS *Total amount:* $1,930,944 (46% need-based, 54% non-need-based).

APPLYING FOR FINANCIAL AID *Required financial aid form:* FAFSA. *Financial aid deadline (priority):* 2/15. *Notification date:* Continuous beginning 1/15.

Western Illinois University

CONTACT Financial Aid Office, Western Illinois University, 1 University Circle, 127 Sherman Hall, Macomb, IL 61455-1390, 309-298-2446 or toll-free 877-742-5948. *Fax:* 309-298-2353. *E-mail:* financial_aid@doss.wiu.edu.

WESTERN KENTUCKY UNIVERSITY
Bowling Green, KY

Tuition & fees (KY res): $5316	Average undergraduate aid package: $7926

ABOUT THE INSTITUTION State-supported, coed. Awards: associate, bachelor's, and master's degrees and post-bachelor's, post-master's, and first professional certificates. 85 undergraduate majors. Total enrollment: 18,634. Undergraduates: 15,967. Freshmen: 3,150. Federal methodology is used as a basis for awarding need-based institutional aid.

UNDERGRADUATE EXPENSES for 2005–06 *Application fee:* $35. *Tuition, state resident:* full-time $5316; part-time $228 per hour. *Tuition, nonresident:* full-time $12,732; part-time $537 per hour. Full-time tuition and fees vary according to course load, location, program, and reciprocity agreements. Part-time tuition and fees vary according to course load, location, program, and reciprocity agreements. *College room and board:* $4876; *room only:* $2800. Room and board charges vary according to board plan and housing facility. *Payment plans:* Tuition prepayment, installment.

FRESHMAN FINANCIAL AID (Fall 2004) 2275 applied for aid; of those 74% were deemed to have need. 98% of freshmen with need received aid; of those 28% had need fully met. *Average percent of need met:* 28% (excluding resources awarded to replace EFC). *Average financial aid package:* $7012 (excluding resources awarded to replace EFC). 9% of all full-time freshmen had no need and received non-need-based gift aid.

UNDERGRADUATE FINANCIAL AID (Fall 2004) 9,293 applied for aid; of those 76% were deemed to have need. 98% of undergraduates with need received aid; of those 29% had need fully met. *Average percent of need met:* 29% (excluding resources awarded to replace EFC). *Average financial aid package:* $7926 (excluding resources awarded to replace EFC). 8% of all full-time undergraduates had no need and received non-need-based gift aid.

GIFT AID (NEED-BASED) *Total amount:* $19,102,646 (72% federal, 28% state). *Receiving aid:* Freshmen: 35% (1,014); All full-time undergraduates: 35% (4,498). *Average award:* Freshmen: $3728; Undergraduates: $3790. *Scholarships, grants, and awards:* Federal Pell, FSEOG, state, private, college/university gift aid from institutional funds, United Negro College Fund.

GIFT AID (NON-NEED-BASED) *Total amount:* $19,133,316 (11% federal, 43% state, 33% institutional, 13% external sources). *Receiving aid:* Freshmen: 46% (1,328); Undergraduates: 30% (3,866). *Average Award:* Freshmen: $3313; Undergraduates: $3109. *Scholarships, grants, and awards by category: Academic Interests/Achievement:* 1,931 awards ($4,456,227 total): agriculture, biological sciences, business, communication, education, engineering/technologies, English, foreign languages, general academic interests/achievements, health fields, home economics, library science, mathematics, military science, physical sciences, premedicine, social sciences. *Creative Arts/Performance:* 343 awards ($465,190 total): art/fine arts, cinema/film/broadcasting, dance, debating, general creative arts/performance, journalism/publications, music, theater/drama. *Special Achievements/Activities:* 238 awards ($139,285 total): general special achievements/activities, leadership, memberships. *Special Characteristics:* 1,489 awards ($1,587,080 total): adult students, children of union members/company employees, ethnic background, general special characteristics, handicapped students, international students, local/state students, members of minority groups, out-of-state students, religious affiliation, veterans, veterans' children. *Tuition waivers:* Full or partial for employees or children of employees, senior citizens. *ROTC:* Army, Air Force cooperative.

LOANS *Student loans:* $31,508,397 (58% need-based, 42% non-need-based). 54% of past graduating class borrowed through all loan programs. *Average indebtedness per student:* $12,946. *Average need-based loan:* Freshmen: $2307; Undergraduates: $3342. *Parent loans:* $4,162,230 (100% non-need-based). *Programs:* FFEL (Subsidized and Unsubsidized Stafford, PLUS), Perkins, alternative loans.

WORK-STUDY *Federal work-study:* Total amount: $1,113,579; 816 jobs averaging $1365. *State or other work-study/employment:* Total amount: $3,227,578 (100% non-need-based). 1,576 part-time jobs averaging $2048.

ATHLETIC AWARDS *Total amount:* $2,630,806 (100% non-need-based).

APPLYING FOR FINANCIAL AID *Required financial aid form:* FAFSA. *Financial aid deadline (priority):* 4/1. *Notification date:* Continuous beginning 3/1.

CONTACT Cindy Burnette, Student Financial Assistance Director, Western Kentucky University, Potter Hall, Room 317, 1906 College Heights Blvd., Bowling Green, KY 42101-1018, 270-745-2758 or toll-free 800-495-8463 (in-state). *Fax:* 270-745-6586. *E-mail:* cindy.burnette@wku.edu.

WESTERN MICHIGAN UNIVERSITY
Kalamazoo, MI

CONTACT Mr. David Ladd, Associate Director of Student Financial Aid, Western Michigan University, 1903 West Michigan Avenue, Faunce Student Services Building, Room 3306, Kalamazoo, MI 49008-5337, 269-387-6000. *E-mail:* david.ladd@wmich.edu.

WESTERN NEW ENGLAND COLLEGE
Springfield, MA

Tuition & fees: $23,164	Average undergraduate aid package: $13,646

ABOUT THE INSTITUTION Independent, coed. Awards: associate, bachelor's, master's, and first professional degrees. 35 undergraduate majors. Total enrollment: 3,729. Undergraduates: 2,840. Freshmen: 676. Federal methodology is used as a basis for awarding need-based institutional aid.

UNDERGRADUATE EXPENSES for 2005–06 *Application fee:* $50. *Comprehensive fee:* $32,054 includes full-time tuition ($21,600), mandatory fees ($1564), and room and board ($8890). Full-time tuition and fees vary according to program and student level. Room and board charges vary according to board plan and housing facility. *Part-time tuition:* $452 per credit hour. *Part-time fees:* $21 per term. Part-time tuition and fees vary according to program. *Payment plans:* Tuition prepayment, installment.

FRESHMAN FINANCIAL AID (Fall 2005, est.) 618 applied for aid; of those 80% were deemed to have need. 99% of freshmen with need received aid; of those 9% had need fully met. *Average percent of need met:* 70% (excluding resources awarded to replace EFC). *Average financial aid package:* $14,994 (excluding resources awarded to replace EFC). 10% of all full-time freshmen had no need and received non-need-based gift aid.

UNDERGRADUATE FINANCIAL AID (Fall 2005, est.) 2,155 applied for aid; of those 80% were deemed to have need. 98% of undergraduates with need received aid; of those 13% had need fully met. *Average percent of need met:* 68% (excluding resources awarded to replace EFC). *Average financial aid package:* $13,646 (excluding resources awarded to replace EFC). 9% of all full-time undergraduates had no need and received non-need-based gift aid.

GIFT AID (NEED-BASED) *Total amount:* $15,680,099 (8% federal, 4% state, 83% institutional, 5% external sources). *Receiving aid:* Freshmen: 74% (488); All full-time undergraduates: 70% (1,647). *Average award:* Freshmen: $9868; Undergraduates: $8462. *Scholarships, grants, and awards:* Federal Pell, FSEOG, state, private, college/university gift aid from institutional funds.

GIFT AID (NON-NEED-BASED) *Total amount:* $1,676,199 (91% institutional, 9% external sources). *Receiving aid:* Freshmen: 2% (16); Undergraduates: 3% (71). *Average Award:* Freshmen: $7538; Undergraduates: $6851. *Scholarships, grants, and awards by category: Academic Interests/Achievement:* business, engineering/technologies, general academic interests/achievements. *Creative Arts/Performance:* 1 award ($500 total): music. *Special Achievements/Activities:* community service, leadership. *Special Characteristics:* children of faculty/staff, children of union members/company employees, international students, local/state students, members of minority groups, out-of-state students, siblings of current students. *Tuition waivers:* Full or partial for employees or children of employees, senior citizens. *ROTC:* Army, Air Force cooperative.

LOANS *Student loans:* $18,659,172 (37% need-based, 63% non-need-based). 85% of past graduating class borrowed through all loan programs. *Average need-based loan:* Freshmen: $3321; Undergraduates: $3948. *Parent loans:* $5,437,712 (100% non-need-based). *Programs:* Federal Direct (Subsidized and Unsubsidized Stafford, PLUS), FFEL (PLUS), Perkins, state.

WORK-STUDY *Federal work-study:* Total amount: $1,510,890; 825 jobs averaging $1831. *State or other work-study/employment:* Total amount: $600,000 (100% non-need-based). Part-time jobs available.

APPLYING FOR FINANCIAL AID *Required financial aid forms:* FAFSA, federal income tax form(s) and W2's. *Financial aid deadline (priority):* 4/15. *Notification date:* Continuous beginning 3/15. Students must reply by 5/1 or within 2 weeks of notification.

CONTACT Mrs. Kathy M. Chambers, Associate Director of Student Administrative Services, Western New England College, 1215 Wilbraham Road, Springfield, MA 01119-2684, 413-796-2080 or toll-free 800-325-1122 Ext. 1321. *Fax:* 413-796-2081. *E-mail:* finaid@wnec.edu.

WESTERN NEW MEXICO UNIVERSITY
Silver City, NM

ABOUT THE INSTITUTION State-supported, coed. Awards: associate, bachelor's, and master's degrees. 53 undergraduate majors. Total enrollment: 3,074. Undergraduates: 2,555.

GIFT AID (NEED-BASED) *Scholarships, grants, and awards:* Federal Pell, FSEOG, state, private, college/university gift aid from institutional funds.

GIFT AID (NON-NEED-BASED) *Scholarships, grants, and awards by category: Academic Interests/Achievement:* general academic interests/achievements. *Creative Arts/Performance:* performing arts. *Special Achievements/Activities:* general special achievements/activities. *Special Characteristics:* general special characteristics, veterans.

LOANS *Programs:* FFEL (Subsidized and Unsubsidized Stafford, PLUS), Perkins, state, college/university.

APPLYING FOR FINANCIAL AID *Required financial aid forms:* FAFSA, institution's own form.

CONTACT Debra Reyes, Grant Counselor, Western New Mexico University, PO Box 680, Silver City, NM 88062, 505-538-6173 or toll-free 800-872-WNMU (in-state).

WESTERN OREGON UNIVERSITY
Monmouth, OR

Tuition & fees (OR res): $4332   **Average undergraduate aid package: $6412**

ABOUT THE INSTITUTION State-supported, coed. Awards: associate, bachelor's, and master's degrees and post-bachelor's certificates. 35 undergraduate majors. Total enrollment: 4,520. Undergraduates: 4,261. Freshmen: 834. Federal methodology is used as a basis for awarding need-based institutional aid.

UNDERGRADUATE EXPENSES for 2005–06 *Application fee:* $50. *Tuition, state resident:* full-time $3240; part-time $90 per credit. *Tuition, nonresident:* full-time $11,685; part-time $325 per credit. *College room and board:* $6276. Room and board charges vary according to board plan and housing facility. *Payment plan:* Deferred payment.

FRESHMAN FINANCIAL AID (Fall 2005, est.) 640 applied for aid; of those 73% were deemed to have need. 100% of freshmen with need received aid; of those 11% had need fully met. *Average percent of need met:* 63% (excluding resources awarded to replace EFC). *Average financial aid package:* $5929 (excluding resources awarded to replace EFC). 23% of all full-time freshmen had no need and received non-need-based gift aid.

UNDERGRADUATE FINANCIAL AID (Fall 2005, est.) 2,839 applied for aid; of those 79% were deemed to have need. 100% of undergraduates with need received aid; of those 11% had need fully met. *Average percent of need met:* 65% (excluding resources awarded to replace EFC). *Average financial aid package:* $6412 (excluding resources awarded to replace EFC). 22% of all full-time undergraduates had no need and received non-need-based gift aid.

GIFT AID (NEED-BASED) *Total amount:* $6,682,948 (56% federal, 16% state, 5% institutional, 23% external sources). *Receiving aid:* Freshmen: 55% (382); All full-time undergraduates: 53% (1,642). *Average award:* Freshmen: $4451; Undergraduates: $4261. *Scholarships, grants, and awards:* Federal Pell, FSEOG, state, private, college/university gift aid from institutional funds.

GIFT AID (NON-NEED-BASED) *Total amount:* $859,348 (2% state, 25% institutional, 73% external sources). *Receiving aid:* Freshmen: 5% (36); Undergraduates: 3% (107). *Average Award:* Freshmen: $6789; Undergraduates: $7544. *Scholarships, grants, and awards by category: Academic Interests/Achievement:* 209 awards ($341,934 total): biological sciences, business, computer science, education, foreign languages, general academic interests/achievements, international studies, mathematics, physical sciences, social sciences. *Creative Arts/Performance:* 7 awards ($5834 total): art/fine arts, dance, music, performing arts. *Special Achievements/Activities:* 168 awards ($1142 total): general special achievements/activities. *Tuition waivers:* Full or partial for employees or children of employees. *ROTC:* Army, Air Force cooperative.

LOANS *Student loans:* $15,854,013 (70% need-based, 30% non-need-based). 51% of past graduating class borrowed through all loan programs. *Average indebtedness per student:* $19,422. *Average need-based loan:* Freshmen: $2475; Undergraduates: $3535. *Parent loans:* $6,335,952 (28% need-based, 72% non-need-based). *Programs:* Federal Direct (Subsidized and Unsubsidized Stafford, PLUS), Perkins, college/university.

WORK-STUDY *Federal work-study:* Total amount: $206,345; 321 jobs averaging $850.

ATHLETIC AWARDS *Total amount:* $204,531 (64% need-based, 36% non-need-based).

APPLYING FOR FINANCIAL AID *Required financial aid form:* FAFSA. *Financial aid deadline (priority):* 3/1. *Notification date:* Continuous beginning 3/20. Students must reply within 2 weeks of notification.

CONTACT Ms. Donna Fossum, Director of Financial Aid, Western Oregon University, 345 North Monmouth Avenue, Monmouth, OR 97361, 503-838-8475 or toll-free 877-877-1593. *Fax:* 503-838-8200. *E-mail:* finaid@wou.edu.

WESTERN STATE COLLEGE OF COLORADO
Gunnison, CO

Tuition & fees (CO res): $3207   **Average undergraduate aid package: $8800**

ABOUT THE INSTITUTION State-supported, coed. Awards: bachelor's degrees. 75 undergraduate majors. Total enrollment: 2,177. Undergraduates: 2,177. Freshmen: 474. Federal methodology is used as a basis for awarding need-based institutional aid.

UNDERGRADUATE EXPENSES for 2006–07 *Application fee:* $30. *Tuition, state resident:* full-time $2,411; part-time $100.45 per credit hour. *Tuition, nonresident:* full-time $10,968; part-time $457 per credit hour. *Required fees:* full-time $796; $26.05 per credit hour. *College room and board:* $6976; *room only:* $3794.

FRESHMAN FINANCIAL AID (Fall 2005, est.) 354 applied for aid; of those 80% were deemed to have need. 85% of freshmen with need received aid; of those 15% had need fully met. *Average percent of need met:* 50% (excluding resources awarded to replace EFC). *Average financial aid package:* $6625 (excluding resources awarded to replace EFC). 35% of all full-time freshmen had no need and received non-need-based gift aid.

UNDERGRADUATE FINANCIAL AID (Fall 2005, est.) 1,368 applied for aid; of those 65% were deemed to have need. 85% of undergraduates with need received aid; of those 9% had need fully met. *Average percent of need met:* 40% (excluding resources awarded to replace EFC). *Average financial aid package:* $8800 (excluding resources awarded to replace EFC). 25% of all full-time undergraduates had no need and received non-need-based gift aid.

GIFT AID (NEED-BASED) *Total amount:* $2,420,000 (68% federal, 17% state, 10% institutional, 5% external sources). *Receiving aid:* Freshmen: 25% (120); All full-time undergraduates: 19% (378). *Average award:* Freshmen: $2500; Undergraduates: $2500. *Scholarships, grants, and awards:* Federal Pell, FSEOG, state, private, college/university gift aid from institutional funds.

GIFT AID (NON-NEED-BASED) *Total amount:* $935,000 (2% state, 72% institutional, 26% external sources). *Receiving aid:* Freshmen: 15% (72); Undergraduates: 7% (133). *Average Award:* Freshmen: $1750; Undergraduates: $1500. *Scholarships, grants, and awards by category: Academic Interests/Achievement:* 175 awards ($150,000 total): general academic interests/achievements. *Creative Arts/Performance:* 75 awards ($35,000 total): art/fine arts, music. *Special Achievements/Activities:* 50 awards ($75,000 total): leadership. *Special Characteristics:* 7 awards ($3500 total): children and siblings of alumni.

LOANS *Student loans:* $5,750,000 (48% need-based, 52% non-need-based). 67% of past graduating class borrowed through all loan programs. *Average indebtedness per student:* $16,000. *Average need-based loan:* Freshmen: $2625; Undergraduates: $5000. *Parent loans:* $1,800,000 (100% non-need-based). *Programs:* FFEL (Subsidized and Unsubsidized Stafford, PLUS), Perkins.

WORK-STUDY *Federal work-study:* Total amount: $210,000; 200 jobs averaging $1050. *State or other work-study/employment:* Total amount: $605,000 (34% need-based, 66% non-need-based). 161 part-time jobs averaging $1273.

ATHLETIC AWARDS *Total amount:* $500,000 (15% need-based, 85% non-need-based).

APPLYING FOR FINANCIAL AID *Required financial aid form:* FAFSA. *Financial aid deadline (priority):* 4/1. *Notification date:* Continuous beginning 4/1. Students must reply within 3 weeks of notification.

Western State College of Colorado

CONTACT Marty Somero, Director, Financial Aid, Western State College of Colorado, Room 207, Taylor Hall, Gunnison, CO 81231, 970-943-3026 or toll-free 800-876-5309. *Fax:* 970-943-3086. *E-mail:* msomero@western.edu.

WESTERN WASHINGTON UNIVERSITY
Bellingham, WA

Tuition & fees (WA res): $4738   **Average undergraduate aid package: $8981**

ABOUT THE INSTITUTION State-supported, coed. Awards: bachelor's and master's degrees and post-bachelor's certificates. 99 undergraduate majors. Total enrollment: 14,247. Undergraduates: 13,002. Freshmen: 2,382. Federal methodology is used as a basis for awarding need-based institutional aid.

UNDERGRADUATE EXPENSES for 2005–06 *Application fee:* $50. *Tuition, state resident:* full-time $3673; part-time $137 per credit. *Tuition, nonresident:* full-time $13,623; part-time $469 per credit. Full-time tuition and fees vary according to location. Part-time tuition and fees vary according to location. *College room and board:* $6524; *room only:* $4209. Room and board charges vary according to board plan and housing facility. *Payment plan:* Installment.

FRESHMAN FINANCIAL AID (Fall 2004) 1651 applied for aid; of those 51% were deemed to have need. 97% of freshmen with need received aid; of those 24% had need fully met. *Average percent of need met:* 87% (excluding resources awarded to replace EFC). *Average financial aid package:* $8542 (excluding resources awarded to replace EFC). 2% of all full-time freshmen had no need and received non-need-based gift aid.

UNDERGRADUATE FINANCIAL AID (Fall 2004) 7,104 applied for aid; of those 67% were deemed to have need. 97% of undergraduates with need received aid; of those 33% had need fully met. *Average percent of need met:* 87% (excluding resources awarded to replace EFC). *Average financial aid package:* $8981 (excluding resources awarded to replace EFC). 2% of all full-time undergraduates had no need and received non-need-based gift aid.

GIFT AID (NEED-BASED) *Total amount:* $19,507,602 (38% federal, 45% state, 9% institutional, 8% external sources). *Receiving aid:* Freshmen: 28% (674); All full-time undergraduates: 31% (3,690). *Average award:* Freshmen: $5608; Undergraduates: $5602. *Scholarships, grants, and awards:* Federal Pell, FSEOG, state, private, college/university gift aid from institutional funds.

GIFT AID (NON-NEED-BASED) *Total amount:* $2,064,856 (4% federal, 16% state, 28% institutional, 52% external sources). *Receiving aid:* Freshmen: 2% (45); Undergraduates: 1% (126). *Average Award:* Freshmen: $1566; Undergraduates: $1586. *Scholarships, grants, and awards by category: Academic Interests/Achievement:* biological sciences, business, communication, computer science, education, engineering/technologies, English, foreign languages, general academic interests/achievements, health fields, humanities, library science, mathematics, physical sciences, premedicine, social sciences. *Creative Arts/Performance:* applied art and design, art/fine arts, cinema/film/broadcasting, creative writing, dance, general creative arts/performance, journalism/publications, music, performing arts, theater/drama. *Special Achievements/Activities:* community service, leadership, memberships. *Special Characteristics:* children of public servants, children of union members/company employees, ethnic background, general special characteristics, international students, local/state students, members of minority groups, previous college experience, veterans. *Tuition waivers:* Full or partial for employees or children of employees.

LOANS *Student loans:* $29,076,091 (60% need-based, 40% non-need-based). 58% of past graduating class borrowed through all loan programs. *Average indebtedness per student:* $15,784. *Average need-based loan:* Freshmen: $2895; Undergraduates: $4150. *Parent loans:* $19,078,391 (13% need-based, 87% non-need-based). *Programs:* Federal Direct (Subsidized and Unsubsidized Stafford, PLUS), FFEL (PLUS), Perkins, college/university, alternative loans.

WORK-STUDY *Federal work-study:* Total amount: $779,062; 274 jobs averaging $2843. *State or other work-study/employment:* Total amount: $1,137,216 (100% need-based). 364 part-time jobs averaging $3124.

ATHLETIC AWARDS *Total amount:* $754,060 (30% need-based, 70% non-need-based).

APPLYING FOR FINANCIAL AID *Required financial aid form:* FAFSA. *Financial aid deadline (priority):* 2/15. *Notification date:* 5/1. Students must reply within 3 weeks of notification.

CONTACT Ms. Fidele Dent, Office Support Supervisor II, Student Financial Resources, Western Washington University, OM 255 MS 9006, Bellingham, WA 98225-9006, 360-650-3470. *E-mail:* financialaid@wwu.edu.

WESTFIELD STATE COLLEGE
Westfield, MA

Tuition & fees (MA res): $5657   **Average undergraduate aid package: $5743**

ABOUT THE INSTITUTION State-supported, coed. Awards: bachelor's and master's degrees and post-bachelor's and post-master's certificates. 49 undergraduate majors. Total enrollment: 5,345. Undergraduates: 4,667. Freshmen: 1,185. Federal methodology is used as a basis for awarding need-based institutional aid.

UNDERGRADUATE EXPENSES for 2006–07 *Application fee:* $25. *Tuition, state resident:* full-time $970. *Tuition, nonresident:* full-time $7050. *College room and board:* $6470.

FRESHMAN FINANCIAL AID (Fall 2004) 705 applied for aid; of those 98% were deemed to have need. 100% of freshmen with need received aid; of those 23% had need fully met. *Average percent of need met:* 73% (excluding resources awarded to replace EFC). *Average financial aid package:* $5548 (excluding resources awarded to replace EFC). 2% of all full-time freshmen had no need and received non-need-based gift aid.

UNDERGRADUATE FINANCIAL AID (Fall 2004) 2,639 applied for aid; of those 92% were deemed to have need. 100% of undergraduates with need received aid; of those 26% had need fully met. *Average percent of need met:* 77% (excluding resources awarded to replace EFC). *Average financial aid package:* $5743 (excluding resources awarded to replace EFC). 2% of all full-time undergraduates had no need and received non-need-based gift aid.

GIFT AID (NEED-BASED) *Total amount:* $5,560,193 (39% federal, 37% state, 20% institutional, 4% external sources). *Receiving aid:* Freshmen: 39% (324); All full-time undergraduates: 34% (1,282). *Average award:* Freshmen: $4125; Undergraduates: $3688. *Scholarships, grants, and awards:* Federal Pell, FSEOG, state, private.

GIFT AID (NON-NEED-BASED) *Total amount:* $502,148 (23% state, 46% institutional, 31% external sources). *Receiving aid:* Freshmen: 21% (174); Undergraduates: 9% (334). *Average Award:* Freshmen: $3745; Undergraduates: $3728. *Scholarships, grants, and awards by category: Academic Interests/Achievement:* $123,784 total: general academic interests/achievements. *Special Achievements/Activities:* community service. *ROTC:* Army cooperative, Air Force cooperative.

LOANS *Student loans:* $9,943,276 (58% need-based, 42% non-need-based). *Average need-based loan:* Freshmen: $2458; Undergraduates: $3272. *Parent loans:* $1,798,086 (28% need-based, 72% non-need-based). *Programs:* FFEL (Subsidized and Unsubsidized Stafford, PLUS), Perkins, state.

WORK-STUDY *Federal work-study:* Total amount: $359,834; 339 jobs averaging $1126.

APPLYING FOR FINANCIAL AID *Required financial aid form:* FAFSA. *Financial aid deadline (priority):* 3/1. *Notification date:* 4/15.

CONTACT Catherine Ryan, Financial Aid Director, Westfield State College, 333 Western Avenue, Westfield, MA 01086, 413-572-5218 or toll-free 800-322-8401 (in-state).

WEST LIBERTY STATE COLLEGE
West Liberty, WV

ABOUT THE INSTITUTION State-supported, coed. Awards: associate and bachelor's degrees. 35 undergraduate majors. Total enrollment: 2,246. Undergraduates: 2,241. Freshmen: 421.

GIFT AID (NEED-BASED) *Scholarships, grants, and awards:* Federal Pell, FSEOG, state, private, college/university gift aid from institutional funds.

GIFT AID (NON-NEED-BASED) *Scholarships, grants, and awards by category: Academic Interests/Achievement:* business, communication, education, English, general academic interests/achievements, health fields, mathematics, physical sciences. *Creative Arts/Performance:* art/fine arts, music, theater/drama. *Special Achievements/Activities:* cheerleading/drum major. *Special Characteristics:* children and siblings of alumni, children of faculty/staff.

LOANS *Programs:* Federal Direct (Subsidized and Unsubsidized Stafford, PLUS), Perkins, Federal Nursing, alternative loans.

WORK-STUDY *Federal work-study:* Total amount: $133,700; 142 jobs averaging $941. *State or other work-study/employment:* Total amount: $215,541 (100% non-need-based). 61 part-time jobs averaging $3533.

APPLYING FOR FINANCIAL AID *Required financial aid form:* FAFSA.

CONTACT Mr. Scott A. Cook, Director of Financial Aid, West Liberty State College, PO Box 295, West Liberty, WV 26074-0295, 304-336-8016 or toll-free 800-732-6204 Ext. 8076. *Fax:* 304-336-8088. *E-mail:* cookscot@wlsc.edu.

WESTMINSTER CHOIR COLLEGE OF RIDER UNIVERSITY
Princeton, NJ

CONTACT Student Financial Services, Westminster Choir College of Rider University, 2083 Lawrenceville Road, Lawrenceville, NJ 08648, 609-896-5360 or toll-free 800-96-CHOIR. *Fax:* 609-219-4487. *E-mail:* finaid@rider.edu.

WESTMINSTER COLLEGE
Fulton, MO

Tuition & fees: $15,030   **Average undergraduate aid package: $16,226**

ABOUT THE INSTITUTION Independent religious, coed. Awards: bachelor's degrees. 28 undergraduate majors. Total enrollment: 918. Undergraduates: 918. Freshmen: 270. Federal methodology is used as a basis for awarding need-based institutional aid.
UNDERGRADUATE EXPENSES for 2006–07 *Comprehensive fee:* $21,170 includes full-time tuition ($14,600), mandatory fees ($430), and room and board ($6140). *College room only:* $3170. *Part-time tuition:* $750 per credit hour.
FRESHMAN FINANCIAL AID (Fall 2005, est.) 235 applied for aid; of those 78% were deemed to have need. 100% of freshmen with need received aid; of those 36% had need fully met. *Average percent of need met:* 87% (excluding resources awarded to replace EFC). *Average financial aid package:* $15,325 (excluding resources awarded to replace EFC). 49% of all full-time freshmen had no need and received non-need-based gift aid.
UNDERGRADUATE FINANCIAL AID (Fall 2005, est.) 620 applied for aid; of those 84% were deemed to have need. 100% of undergraduates with need received aid; of those 44% had need fully met. *Average percent of need met:* 89% (excluding resources awarded to replace EFC). *Average financial aid package:* $16,226 (excluding resources awarded to replace EFC). 41% of all full-time undergraduates had no need and received non-need-based gift aid.
GIFT AID (NEED-BASED) *Total amount:* $8,810,010 (8% federal, 5% state, 80% institutional, 7% external sources). *Receiving aid:* Freshmen: 68% (183); All full-time undergraduates: 58% (518). *Average award:* Freshmen: $10,896; Undergraduates: $11,001. *Scholarships, grants, and awards:* Federal Pell, FSEOG, state, private, college/university gift aid from institutional funds.
GIFT AID (NON-NEED-BASED) *Average Award:* Freshmen: $10,319; Undergraduates: $8946. *Scholarships, grants, and awards by category: Academic Interests/Achievement:* 574 awards ($3,797,317 total): general academic interests/achievements. *Special Achievements/Activities:* 230 awards ($503,636 total): general special achievements/activities, leadership. *Special Characteristics:* 270 awards ($1,614,902 total): children and siblings of alumni, children of faculty/staff, ethnic background, international students, local/state students, relatives of clergy, religious affiliation, siblings of current students, twins. *ROTC:* Army cooperative, Air Force cooperative.
LOANS *Student loans:* $2,575,958 (52% need-based, 48% non-need-based). 66% of past graduating class borrowed through all loan programs. *Average indebtedness per student:* $17,534. *Average need-based loan:* Freshmen: $1707; Undergraduates: $2631. *Parent loans:* $1,187,823 (100% non-need-based). *Programs:* FFEL (Subsidized and Unsubsidized Stafford, PLUS), Perkins.
WORK-STUDY *Federal work-study:* Total amount: $90,000; 147 jobs averaging $612. *State or other work-study/employment:* Total amount: $181,250 (100% non-need-based). 111 part-time jobs averaging $1633.
APPLYING FOR FINANCIAL AID *Required financial aid form:* FAFSA. *Financial aid deadline (priority):* 2/15. *Notification date:* Continuous beginning 2/28. Students must reply within 3 weeks of notification.
CONTACT Ms. Aimee Bristow, Director of Financial Aid, Westminster College, 501 Westminster Avenue, Fulton, MO 65251-1299, 800-475-3361. *Fax:* 573-592-5255. *E-mail:* bristoa@westminster-mo.edu.

WESTMINSTER COLLEGE
New Wilmington, PA

Tuition & fees: $24,325   **Average undergraduate aid package: $18,665**

ABOUT THE INSTITUTION Independent religious, coed. Awards: bachelor's and master's degrees. 52 undergraduate majors. Total enrollment: 1,593. Undergraduates: 1,464. Freshmen: 359. Federal methodology is used as a basis for awarding need-based institutional aid.
UNDERGRADUATE EXPENSES for 2006–07 *Application fee:* $35. *Comprehensive fee:* $31,395 includes full-time tuition ($23,220), mandatory fees ($1105), and room and board ($7070). *Part-time tuition:* $730 per semester hour.
FRESHMAN FINANCIAL AID (Fall 2005, est.) 325 applied for aid; of those 89% were deemed to have need. 100% of freshmen with need received aid; of those 28% had need fully met. *Average percent of need met:* 88% (excluding resources awarded to replace EFC). *Average financial aid package:* $17,951 (excluding resources awarded to replace EFC). 20% of all full-time freshmen had no need and received non-need-based gift aid.
UNDERGRADUATE FINANCIAL AID (Fall 2005, est.) 1,170 applied for aid; of those 92% were deemed to have need. 100% of undergraduates with need received aid; of those 33% had need fully met. *Average percent of need met:* 89% (excluding resources awarded to replace EFC). *Average financial aid package:* $18,665 (excluding resources awarded to replace EFC). 20% of all full-time undergraduates had no need and received non-need-based gift aid.
GIFT AID (NEED-BASED) *Total amount:* $15,531,559 (7% federal, 12% state, 76% institutional, 5% external sources). *Receiving aid:* Freshmen: 80% (287); All full-time undergraduates: 78% (1,069). *Average award:* Freshmen: $14,550; Undergraduates: $14,511. *Scholarships, grants, and awards:* Federal Pell, FSEOG, state, private, college/university gift aid from institutional funds.
GIFT AID (NON-NEED-BASED) *Total amount:* $2,461,383 (1% state, 97% institutional, 2% external sources). *Receiving aid:* Freshmen: 78% (281); Undergraduates: 73% (1,009). *Average Award:* Freshmen: $9928; Undergraduates: $8818. *Scholarships, grants, and awards by category: Academic Interests/Achievement:* 1,265 awards ($9,699,531 total): general academic interests/achievements. *Creative Arts/Performance:* 166 awards ($172,901 total): cinema/film/broadcasting, general creative arts/performance, music, theater/drama. *Special Characteristics:* 331 awards ($1,069,789 total): children and siblings of alumni, general special characteristics, international students, religious affiliation. *ROTC:* Army cooperative.
LOANS *Student loans:* $6,447,789 (94% need-based, 6% non-need-based). 83% of past graduating class borrowed through all loan programs. *Average indebtedness per student:* $20,386. *Average need-based loan:* Freshmen: $3255; Undergraduates: $4031. *Parent loans:* $2,164,165 (85% need-based, 15% non-need-based). *Programs:* FFEL (Subsidized and Unsubsidized Stafford, PLUS), Perkins, Resource Loans.
WORK-STUDY *Federal work-study:* Total amount: $563,292; 355 jobs averaging $1587. *State or other work-study/employment:* Total amount: $278,639 (70% need-based, 30% non-need-based). 162 part-time jobs averaging $1720.
APPLYING FOR FINANCIAL AID *Required financial aid forms:* FAFSA, institution's own form. *Financial aid deadline (priority):* 5/1. *Notification date:* Continuous. Students must reply within 3 weeks of notification.
CONTACT Mr. Robert A. Latta, Director of Financial Aid, Westminster College, South Market Street, New Wilmington, PA 16172-0001, 724-946-7102 or toll-free 800-942-8033 (in-state). *Fax:* 724-946-6171. *E-mail:* lattara@westminster.edu.

WESTMINSTER COLLEGE
Salt Lake City, UT

ABOUT THE INSTITUTION Independent, coed. Awards: bachelor's and master's degrees and post-bachelor's certificates. 33 undergraduate majors. Total enrollment: 2,455. Undergraduates: 1,878. Freshmen: 350.
GIFT AID (NEED-BASED) *Scholarships, grants, and awards:* Federal Pell, FSEOG, state, private, college/university gift aid from institutional funds, United Negro College Fund, Federal Nursing.
GIFT AID (NON-NEED-BASED) *Scholarships, grants, and awards by category: Academic Interests/Achievement:* biological sciences, business, communication, computer science, education, English, general academic interests/achievements, health fields, humanities, international studies, mathematics, military science, physical sciences, premedicine, social sciences. *Creative Arts/*

Westminster College

Performance: art/fine arts, journalism/publications, music, theater/drama. *Special Characteristics:* adult students, children and siblings of alumni, children of faculty/staff, children of public servants, ethnic background, first-generation college students, handicapped students, international students, local/state students, members of minority groups, public servants, relatives of clergy, religious affiliation, siblings of current students, spouses of current students, veterans, veterans' children.

LOANS *Programs:* FFEL (Subsidized and Unsubsidized Stafford, PLUS), Perkins.

WORK-STUDY *Federal work-study:* Total amount: $508,400; 248 jobs averaging $2050. *State or other work-study/employment:* Total amount: $455,500 (100% non-need-based). Part-time jobs available.

APPLYING FOR FINANCIAL AID *Required financial aid form:* FAFSA.

CONTACT Ruth Henneman, Director of Financial Aid, Westminster College, 1840 South 1300 East, Salt Lake City, UT 84105, 801-832-2500 or toll-free 800-748-4753 (out-of-state). *Fax:* 801-832-2506. *E-mail:* rhenneman@westminstercollege.edu.

WESTMONT COLLEGE
Santa Barbara, CA

Tuition & fees: $27,806　　**Average undergraduate aid package: $18,521**

ABOUT THE INSTITUTION Independent nondenominational, coed. Awards: bachelor's degrees and post-bachelor's certificates. 43 undergraduate majors. Total enrollment: 1,379. Undergraduates: 1,373. Federal methodology is used as a basis for awarding need-based institutional aid.

UNDERGRADUATE EXPENSES for 2005–06 *Application fee:* $50. *Comprehensive fee:* $36,672 includes full-time tuition ($27,076), mandatory fees ($730), and room and board ($8866). *College room only:* $5376. Room and board charges vary according to board plan. *Payment plan:* Installment.

FRESHMAN FINANCIAL AID (Fall 2005, est.) 256 applied for aid; of those 77% were deemed to have need. 100% of freshmen with need received aid; of those 11% had need fully met. *Average percent of need met:* 64% (excluding resources awarded to replace EFC). *Average financial aid package:* $16,502 (excluding resources awarded to replace EFC). 32% of all full-time freshmen had no need and received non-need-based gift aid.

UNDERGRADUATE FINANCIAL AID (Fall 2005, est.) 892 applied for aid; of those 85% were deemed to have need. 99% of undergraduates with need received aid; of those 10% had need fully met. *Average percent of need met:* 67% (excluding resources awarded to replace EFC). *Average financial aid package:* $18,521 (excluding resources awarded to replace EFC). 32% of all full-time undergraduates had no need and received non-need-based gift aid.

GIFT AID (NEED-BASED) *Total amount:* $9,251,975 (7% federal, 18% state, 70% institutional, 5% external sources). *Receiving aid:* Freshmen: 57% (192); All full-time undergraduates: 54% (740). *Average award:* Freshmen: $12,941; Undergraduates: $13,480. *Scholarships, grants, and awards:* Federal Pell, FSEOG, state, private, college/university gift aid from institutional funds.

GIFT AID (NON-NEED-BASED) *Total amount:* $3,204,173 (1% state, 94% institutional, 5% external sources). *Receiving aid:* Freshmen: 5% (17); Undergraduates: 4% (51). *Average Award:* Freshmen: $11,168; Undergraduates: $9990. *Scholarships, grants, and awards by category:* Academic Interests/Achievement: 802 awards ($5,054,079 total): general academic interests/achievements. *Creative Arts/Performance:* 71 awards ($72,475 total): art/fine arts, music, theater/drama. *Special Achievements/Activities:* 29 awards ($40,500 total): general special achievements/activities, leadership. *Special Characteristics:* 255 awards ($1,525,916 total): children of faculty/staff, ethnic background, international students. *Tuition waivers:* Full or partial for employees or children of employees. *ROTC:* Army cooperative, Air Force cooperative.

LOANS *Student loans:* $5,521,983 (77% need-based, 23% non-need-based). 74% of past graduating class borrowed through all loan programs. *Average indebtedness per student:* $16,999. *Average need-based loan:* Freshmen: $3922; Undergraduates: $5461. *Parent loans:* $4,578,176 (39% need-based, 61% non-need-based). *Programs:* FFEL (Subsidized and Unsubsidized Stafford, PLUS), Perkins, college/university, Alternative Loans.

WORK-STUDY *Federal work-study:* Total amount: $201,140; 138 jobs averaging $1458.

ATHLETIC AWARDS *Total amount:* $662,480 (49% need-based, 51% non-need-based).

APPLYING FOR FINANCIAL AID *Required financial aid form:* FAFSA. *Financial aid deadline (priority):* 3/1. *Notification date:* 3/1. Students must reply by 5/1 or within 2 weeks of notification.

CONTACT Mrs. Diane L. Horvath, Director of Financial Aid, Westmont College, 955 La Paz Road, Santa Barbara, CA 93108, 888-963-4624 or toll-free 800-777-9011. *Fax:* 805-565-7157. *E-mail:* dhorvath@westmont.edu.

WEST SUBURBAN COLLEGE OF NURSING
Oak Park, IL

CONTACT Ms. Ruth Rehwadt, Director of Financial Aid, West Suburban College of Nursing, 3 Erie Court, Oak Park, IL 60302, 708-287-8100.

WEST TEXAS A&M UNIVERSITY
Canyon, TX

Tuition & fees (TX res): $3756　　**Average undergraduate aid package: $6215**

ABOUT THE INSTITUTION State-supported, coed. Awards: bachelor's, master's, and doctoral degrees. 59 undergraduate majors. Total enrollment: 8,667. Undergraduates: 5,795. Freshmen: 780. Federal methodology is used as a basis for awarding need-based institutional aid.

UNDERGRADUATE EXPENSES for 2005–06 *Application fee:* $25. *Tuition, state resident:* full-time $2760. *Tuition, nonresident:* full-time $11,040. *College room and board:* $4916; *room only:* $2300.

FRESHMAN FINANCIAL AID (Fall 2004) 621 applied for aid; of those 74% were deemed to have need. 98% of freshmen with need received aid; of those 100% had need fully met. *Average percent of need met:* 77% (excluding resources awarded to replace EFC). *Average financial aid package:* $5958 (excluding resources awarded to replace EFC). 18% of all full-time freshmen had no need and received non-need-based gift aid.

UNDERGRADUATE FINANCIAL AID (Fall 2004) 3,541 applied for aid; of those 82% were deemed to have need. 98% of undergraduates with need received aid; of those 100% had need fully met. *Average percent of need met:* 67% (excluding resources awarded to replace EFC). *Average financial aid package:* $6215 (excluding resources awarded to replace EFC). 11% of all full-time undergraduates had no need and received non-need-based gift aid.

GIFT AID (NEED-BASED) *Total amount:* $8,941,351 (62% federal, 35% state, 3% institutional). *Receiving aid:* Freshmen: 39% (319); All full-time undergraduates: 45% (2,263). *Average award:* Freshmen: $4562; Undergraduates: $3616. *Scholarships, grants, and awards:* Federal Pell, FSEOG, state, college/university gift aid from institutional funds.

GIFT AID (NON-NEED-BASED) *Total amount:* $2,529,562 (69% institutional, 31% external sources). *Receiving aid:* Freshmen: 51% (416); Undergraduates: 15% (770). *Average Award:* Freshmen: $3236; Undergraduates: $4303. *Scholarships, grants, and awards by category:* Academic Interests/Achievement: 732 awards ($794,920 total): agriculture, biological sciences, business, communication, computer science, education, English, foreign languages, general academic interests/achievements, health fields, humanities, mathematics, physical sciences, social sciences. *Creative Arts/Performance:* 167 awards ($79,977 total): art/fine arts, dance, debating, journalism/publications, music, theater/drama. *Special Achievements/Activities:* 110 awards ($69,980 total): cheerleading/drum major, leadership, memberships, rodeo. *Special Characteristics:* 130 awards ($67,948 total): children of faculty/staff, first-generation college students, handicapped students.

LOANS *Student loans:* $15,613,276 (53% need-based, 47% non-need-based). 34% of past graduating class borrowed through all loan programs. *Average indebtedness per student:* $13,136. *Average need-based loan:* Freshmen: $2123; Undergraduates: $3524. *Parent loans:* $519,244 (100% non-need-based). *Programs:* FFEL (Subsidized and Unsubsidized Stafford, PLUS), Perkins, state, college/university.

WORK-STUDY *Federal work-study:* Total amount: $202,987; 149 jobs averaging $1288. *State or other work-study/employment:* Total amount: $49,819 (100% need-based). 97 part-time jobs averaging $557.

ATHLETIC AWARDS *Total amount:* $683,914 (100% non-need-based).

APPLYING FOR FINANCIAL AID *Required financial aid forms:* FAFSA, scholarship application form(s). *Financial aid deadline (priority):* 5/1. *Notification date:* Continuous. Students must reply within 2 weeks of notification.

CONTACT Mr. Jim Reed, Director of Financial Aid, West Texas A&M University, WTAMU Box 60939, Canyon, TX 79016-0001, 806-651-2055 or toll-free 800-99-WTAMU. *Fax:* 806-651-2924. *E-mail:* jreed@mail.wtamu.edu.

WEST VIRGINIA STATE UNIVERSITY
Institute, WV

CONTACT Mrs. Mary Blizzard, Director, Office of Student Financial Assistance, West Virginia State University, PO Box 1000, Ferrell Hall 324, Institute, WV 25112-1000, 304-766-3131 or toll-free 800-987-2112.

WEST VIRGINIA UNIVERSITY
Morgantown, WV

Tuition & fees (WV res): $4164   **Average undergraduate aid package: $7011**

ABOUT THE INSTITUTION State-supported, coed. Awards: bachelor's, master's, doctoral, and first professional degrees. 75 undergraduate majors. Total enrollment: 26,051. Undergraduates: 19,510. Freshmen: 4,574. Federal methodology is used as a basis for awarding need-based institutional aid.
UNDERGRADUATE EXPENSES for 2005–06 *Application fee:* $25. *Tuition, state resident:* full-time $4164; part-time $176 per credit hour. *Tuition, nonresident:* full-time $12,874; part-time $538 per credit hour. Full-time tuition and fees vary according to location, program, and reciprocity agreements. Part-time tuition and fees vary according to course load, location, program, and reciprocity agreements. *College room and board:* $6342; *room only:* $3348. Room and board charges vary according to board plan, housing facility, and location. *Payment plan:* Deferred payment.
FRESHMAN FINANCIAL AID (Fall 2005, est.) 2525 applied for aid; of those 80% were deemed to have need. 95% of freshmen with need received aid; of those 45% had need fully met. *Average percent of need met:* 87% (excluding resources awarded to replace EFC). *Average financial aid package:* $6379 (excluding resources awarded to replace EFC). 27% of all full-time freshmen had no need and received non-need-based gift aid.
UNDERGRADUATE FINANCIAL AID (Fall 2005, est.) 13,274 applied for aid; of those 75% were deemed to have need. 92% of undergraduates with need received aid; of those 26% had need fully met. *Average percent of need met:* 88% (excluding resources awarded to replace EFC). *Average financial aid package:* $7011 (excluding resources awarded to replace EFC). 37% of all full-time undergraduates had no need and received non-need-based gift aid.
GIFT AID (NEED-BASED) *Total amount:* $20,811,864 (65% federal, 24% state, 11% institutional). *Receiving aid:* Freshmen: 21% (962); All full-time undergraduates: 35% (6,453). *Average award:* Freshmen: $3149; Undergraduates: $3225. *Scholarships, grants, and awards:* Federal Pell, FSEOG, state, private, college/university gift aid from institutional funds.
GIFT AID (NON-NEED-BASED) *Total amount:* $20,060,825 (1% federal, 69% state, 22% institutional, 8% external sources). *Receiving aid:* Freshmen: 24% (1,090); Undergraduates: 26% (4,736). *Average Award:* Freshmen: $5096; Undergraduates: $3036. *Scholarships, grants, and awards by category:* Academic Interests/Achievement: 3,000 awards ($5,000,000 total): agriculture, architecture, area/ethnic studies, biological sciences, business, communication, computer science, education, engineering/technologies, English, foreign languages, general academic interests/achievements, health fields, home economics, humanities, international studies, library science, mathematics, military science, physical sciences, premedicine, religion/biblical studies, social sciences. *Creative Arts/Performance:* 100 awards ($660,000 total): art/fine arts, debating, music, theater/drama. *Special Achievements/Activities:* 12 awards ($35,000 total): general special achievements/activities, leadership. *Special Characteristics:* 500 awards ($1,100,000 total): children of faculty/staff, children of union members/company employees, children of workers in trades, ethnic background, general special characteristics, international students, local/state students, members of minority groups. *Tuition waivers:* Full or partial for employees or children of employees, senior citizens. *ROTC:* Army, Air Force.
LOANS *Student loans:* $57,634,473 (52% need-based, 48% non-need-based). 62% of past graduating class borrowed through all loan programs. *Average indebtedness per student:* $13,798. *Average need-based loan:* Freshmen: $3493; Undergraduates: $4034. *Parent loans:* $28,312,343 (100% non-need-based). *Programs:* Federal Direct (Subsidized and Unsubsidized Stafford, PLUS), Perkins, college/university.

WORK-STUDY *Federal work-study:* Total amount: $1,651,972; 1,656 jobs averaging $1000. *State or other work-study/employment:* Total amount: $1,314,789 (100% non-need-based). 1,230 part-time jobs averaging $1070.
ATHLETIC AWARDS *Total amount:* $4,539,579 (100% non-need-based).
APPLYING FOR FINANCIAL AID *Required financial aid form:* FAFSA. *Financial aid deadline:* 3/1. *Notification date:* Continuous beginning 3/15. Students must reply within 4 weeks of notification.
CONTACT Kaye Widney, Director of Financial Aid, West Virginia University, PO Box 6004, Morgantown, WV 26506-6004, 304-293-5242 or toll-free 800-344-9881. *Fax:* 304-293-4890. *E-mail:* kaye.widney@mail.wvu.edu.

WEST VIRGINIA UNIVERSITY INSTITUTE OF TECHNOLOGY
Montgomery, WV

CONTACT Nina M. Morton, Director of Financial Aid, West Virginia University Institute of Technology, 405 Fayette Pike, Montgomery, WV 25136, 304-442-3032 or toll-free 888-554-8324.

WEST VIRGINIA WESLEYAN COLLEGE
Buckhannon, WV

Tuition & fees: $21,250   **Average undergraduate aid package: $21,518**

ABOUT THE INSTITUTION Independent religious, coed. Awards: bachelor's and master's degrees. 64 undergraduate majors. Total enrollment: 1,408. Undergraduates: 1,366. Freshmen: 348. Federal methodology is used as a basis for awarding need-based institutional aid.
UNDERGRADUATE EXPENSES for 2005–06 *Application fee:* $35. *Comprehensive fee:* $26,800 includes full-time tuition ($20,250), mandatory fees ($1000), and room and board ($5550). Full-time tuition and fees vary according to course load. Room and board charges vary according to board plan and housing facility. Part-time tuition and fees vary according to course load.
FRESHMAN FINANCIAL AID (Fall 2005, est.) 268 applied for aid; of those 89% were deemed to have need. 100% of freshmen with need received aid; of those 35% had need fully met. *Average percent of need met:* 88% (excluding resources awarded to replace EFC). *Average financial aid package:* $21,577 (excluding resources awarded to replace EFC). 19% of all full-time freshmen had no need and received non-need-based gift aid.
UNDERGRADUATE FINANCIAL AID (Fall 2005, est.) 1,024 applied for aid; of those 94% were deemed to have need. 100% of undergraduates with need received aid; of those 38% had need fully met. *Average percent of need met:* 88% (excluding resources awarded to replace EFC). *Average financial aid package:* $21,518 (excluding resources awarded to replace EFC). 23% of all full-time undergraduates had no need and received non-need-based gift aid.
GIFT AID (NEED-BASED) *Total amount:* $13,445,655 (9% federal, 3% state, 88% institutional). *Receiving aid:* Freshmen: 78% (239); All full-time undergraduates: 74% (966). *Average award:* Freshmen: $17,169; Undergraduates: $16,286. *Scholarships, grants, and awards:* Federal Pell, FSEOG, state, private, college/university gift aid from institutional funds.
GIFT AID (NON-NEED-BASED) *Total amount:* $5,708,566 (23% state, 63% institutional, 14% external sources). *Receiving aid:* Freshmen: 18% (54); Undergraduates: 13% (168). *Average Award:* Freshmen: $11,746; Undergraduates: $11,945. *Scholarships, grants, and awards by category:* Academic Interests/Achievement: general academic interests/achievements. *Creative Arts/Performance:* art/fine arts, music, theater/drama. *Special Achievements/Activities:* community service, leadership, religious involvement. *Special Characteristics:* children of faculty/staff, general special characteristics, international students, members of minority groups, relatives of clergy. *Tuition waivers:* Full or partial for employees or children of employees.
LOANS *Student loans:* $5,239,281 (93% need-based, 7% non-need-based). 63% of past graduating class borrowed through all loan programs. *Average indebtedness per student:* $19,750. *Average need-based loan:* Freshmen: $2935; Undergraduates: $3562. *Parent loans:* $1,926,362 (100% non-need-based). *Programs:* FFEL (Subsidized and Unsubsidized Stafford, PLUS), Perkins, college/university.
WORK-STUDY *Federal work-study:* Total amount: $807,400; jobs available. *State or other work-study/employment:* Total amount: $925,150 (100% non-need-based). Part-time jobs available.

West Virginia Wesleyan College

ATHLETIC AWARDS *Total amount:* $2,095,244 (58% need-based, 42% non-need-based).
APPLYING FOR FINANCIAL AID *Required financial aid form:* FAFSA. *Financial aid deadline (priority):* 2/15. *Notification date:* Continuous beginning 3/15. Students must reply within 4 weeks of notification.
CONTACT Ms. Tammy Crites, Director of Financial Aid, West Virginia Wesleyan College, 59 College Avenue, Buckhannon, WV 26201, 304-473-8510 or toll-free 800-722-9933 (out-of-state). *Fax:* 304-472-2571.

WESTWOOD COLLEGE–ARLINGTON BALLSTON CAMPUS
Arlington, VA

CONTACT Financial Aid Office, Westwood College–Arlington Ballston Campus, 1901 North Ft. Myer Drive, Arlington, VA 22209, 800-281-2978.

WESTWOOD COLLEGE–ATLANTA NORTHLAKE
Atlanta, GA

CONTACT Financial Aid Office, Westwood College–Atlanta Northlake, 2220 Parklake Drive, Suite 175, Atlanta, GA 30345, 404-962-2999.

WHEATON COLLEGE
Wheaton, IL

Tuition & fees: $21,100 **Average undergraduate aid package: $18,445**

ABOUT THE INSTITUTION Independent nondenominational, coed. Awards: bachelor's, master's, and doctoral degrees and post-bachelor's certificates. 38 undergraduate majors. Total enrollment: 2,932. Undergraduates: 2,417. Freshmen: 578. Institutional methodology is used as a basis for awarding need-based institutional aid.
UNDERGRADUATE EXPENSES for 2005–06 *Application fee:* $50. *Comprehensive fee:* $27,700 includes full-time tuition ($21,100) and room and board ($6600). *College room only:* $3900. Room and board charges vary according to board plan and housing facility. *Part-time tuition:* $586 per credit hour. Part-time tuition and fees vary according to course load. *Payment plans:* Installment, deferred payment.
FRESHMAN FINANCIAL AID (Fall 2005, est.) 466 applied for aid; of those 61% were deemed to have need. 99% of freshmen with need received aid; of those 29% had need fully met. *Average percent of need met:* 87% (excluding resources awarded to replace EFC). *Average financial aid package:* $18,867 (excluding resources awarded to replace EFC). 28% of all full-time freshmen had no need and received non-need-based gift aid.
UNDERGRADUATE FINANCIAL AID (Fall 2005, est.) 1,756 applied for aid; of those 67% were deemed to have need. 99% of undergraduates with need received aid; of those 25% had need fully met. *Average percent of need met:* 85% (excluding resources awarded to replace EFC). *Average financial aid package:* $18,445 (excluding resources awarded to replace EFC). 20% of all full-time undergraduates had no need and received non-need-based gift aid.
GIFT AID (NEED-BASED) *Total amount:* $14,181,595 (9% federal, 3% state, 81% institutional, 7% external sources). *Receiving aid:* Freshmen: 40% (232); All full-time undergraduates: 41% (961). *Average award:* Freshmen: $13,272; Undergraduates: $12,568. *Scholarships, grants, and awards:* Federal Pell, FSEOG, state, college/university gift aid from institutional funds.
GIFT AID (NON-NEED-BASED) *Total amount:* $1,296,659 (4% federal, 1% state, 71% institutional, 24% external sources). *Receiving aid:* Freshmen: 19% (111); Undergraduates: 18% (418). *Average Award:* Freshmen: $3732; Undergraduates: $3756. *Scholarships, grants, and awards by category:* Academic Interests/Achievement: 19 awards ($50,447 total): English, general academic interests/achievements, physical sciences, premedicine. *Creative Arts/Performance:* 26 awards ($152,552 total): music. *Special Characteristics:* 1 award ($5500 total): handicapped students. *Tuition waivers:* Full or partial for employees or children of employees. *ROTC:* Army, Air Force cooperative.
LOANS *Student loans:* $7,690,916 (84% need-based, 16% non-need-based). 55% of past graduating class borrowed through all loan programs. *Average indebtedness per student:* $18,717. *Average need-based loan:* Freshmen: $4758;

Undergraduates: $5397. *Parent loans:* $3,815,382 (61% need-based, 39% non-need-based). *Programs:* FFEL (Subsidized and Unsubsidized Stafford, PLUS), Perkins.
WORK-STUDY *Federal work-study:* Total amount: $535,999; 774 jobs averaging $972.
APPLYING FOR FINANCIAL AID *Required financial aid forms:* FAFSA, institution's own form. *Financial aid deadline (priority):* 2/15. *Notification date:* Continuous beginning 3/1.
CONTACT Mrs. Donna Peltz, Director of Financial Aid, Wheaton College, 501 College Avenue, Wheaton, IL 60187-5593, 630-752-5021 or toll-free 800-222-2419 (out-of-state). *E-mail:* finaid@wheaton.edu.

WHEATON COLLEGE
Norton, MA

Tuition & fees: $32,350 **Average undergraduate aid package: $23,155**

ABOUT THE INSTITUTION Independent, coed. Awards: bachelor's degrees. 37 undergraduate majors. Total enrollment: 1,568. Undergraduates: 1,568. Freshmen: 466. Institutional methodology is used as a basis for awarding need-based institutional aid.
UNDERGRADUATE EXPENSES for 2005–06 *Application fee:* $55. *Comprehensive fee:* $40,180 includes full-time tuition ($32,115), mandatory fees ($235), and room and board ($7830). *College room only:* $4130. *Payment plans:* Tuition prepayment, installment.
FRESHMAN FINANCIAL AID (Fall 2005, est.) 270 applied for aid; of those 84% were deemed to have need. 100% of freshmen with need received aid; of those 41% had need fully met. *Average percent of need met:* 94% (excluding resources awarded to replace EFC). *Average financial aid package:* $22,540 (excluding resources awarded to replace EFC). 14% of all full-time freshmen had no need and received non-need-based gift aid.
UNDERGRADUATE FINANCIAL AID (Fall 2005, est.) 886 applied for aid; of those 91% were deemed to have need. 100% of undergraduates with need received aid; of those 38% had need fully met. *Average percent of need met:* 94% (excluding resources awarded to replace EFC). *Average financial aid package:* $23,155 (excluding resources awarded to replace EFC). 12% of all full-time undergraduates had no need and received non-need-based gift aid.
GIFT AID (NEED-BASED) *Total amount:* $14,497,406 (6% federal, 3% state, 87% institutional, 4% external sources). *Receiving aid:* Freshmen: 46% (216); All full-time undergraduates: 47% (771). *Average award:* Freshmen: $19,030; Undergraduates: $18,303. *Scholarships, grants, and awards:* Federal Pell, FSEOG, state, private, college/university gift aid from institutional funds.
GIFT AID (NON-NEED-BASED) *Total amount:* $2,585,046 (89% institutional, 11% external sources). *Receiving aid:* Freshmen: 1; Undergraduates: 2. *Average Award:* Freshmen: $12,523; Undergraduates: $10,760. *Scholarships, grants, and awards by category:* Academic Interests/Achievement: 453 awards ($3,855,750 total): general academic interests/achievements. *Tuition waivers:* Full or partial for employees or children of employees. *ROTC:* Army cooperative.
LOANS *Student loans:* $5,161,801 (66% need-based, 34% non-need-based). 61% of past graduating class borrowed through all loan programs. *Average indebtedness per student:* $22,380. *Average need-based loan:* Freshmen: $3566; Undergraduates: $4667. *Parent loans:* $4,798,756 (100% non-need-based). *Programs:* FFEL (Subsidized and Unsubsidized Stafford, PLUS), Perkins, state, college/university, MEFA, TERI, Citi Assist, Signature, alternative loans.
WORK-STUDY *Federal work-study:* Total amount: $1,133,733; 660 jobs averaging $1718. *State or other work-study/employment:* Total amount: $549,850 (38% need-based, 62% non-need-based). 251 part-time jobs averaging $2191.
APPLYING FOR FINANCIAL AID *Required financial aid forms:* FAFSA, CSS Financial Aid PROFILE, noncustodial (divorced/separated) parent's statement, business/farm supplement, federal income tax form(s). *Financial aid deadline:* 2/1. *Notification date:* 4/1. Students must reply by 5/1.
CONTACT Ms. Susan Beard, Director of Financial Aid Programs, Wheaton College, East Main Street, Norton, MA 02766, 508-286-8232 or toll-free 800-394-6003. *Fax:* 508-286-3787. *E-mail:* sfs@wheatonma.edu.

WHEELING JESUIT UNIVERSITY
Wheeling, WV

Tuition & fees: $21,350 **Average undergraduate aid package: $17,903**

ABOUT THE INSTITUTION Independent Roman Catholic (Jesuit), coed. Awards: bachelor's, master's, and doctoral degrees. 54 undergraduate majors. Total enrollment: 1,699. Undergraduates: 1,232. Freshmen: 288. Both federal and institutional methodology are used as a basis for awarding need-based institutional aid.
UNDERGRADUATE EXPENSES for 2005–06 *Application fee:* $25. *Comprehensive fee:* $27,800 includes full-time tuition ($20,890), mandatory fees ($460), and room and board ($6450). *College room only:* $3070. Full-time tuition and fees vary according to course load and program. Room and board charges vary according to board plan, gender, and housing facility. *Part-time tuition:* $540 per credit hour. *Part-time fees:* $465 per term. Part-time tuition and fees vary according to class time and program. *Payment plan:* Installment.
FRESHMAN FINANCIAL AID (Fall 2005, est.) 267 applied for aid; of those 87% were deemed to have need. 100% of freshmen with need received aid; of those 45% had need fully met. *Average percent of need met:* 96% (excluding resources awarded to replace EFC). *Average financial aid package:* $19,113 (excluding resources awarded to replace EFC). 18% of all full-time freshmen had no need and received non-need-based gift aid.
UNDERGRADUATE FINANCIAL AID (Fall 2005, est.) 952 applied for aid; of those 85% were deemed to have need. 100% of undergraduates with need received aid; of those 38% had need fully met. *Average percent of need met:* 87% (excluding resources awarded to replace EFC). *Average financial aid package:* $17,903 (excluding resources awarded to replace EFC). 18% of all full-time undergraduates had no need and received non-need-based gift aid.
GIFT AID (NEED-BASED) *Total amount:* $3,402,341 (29% federal, 6% state, 65% institutional). *Receiving aid:* Freshmen: 71% (203); All full-time undergraduates: 58% (611). *Average award:* Freshmen: $7041; Undergraduates: $5449. *Scholarships, grants, and awards:* Federal Pell, FSEOG, state, private, college/university gift aid from institutional funds, Federal Nursing.
GIFT AID (NON-NEED-BASED) *Total amount:* $8,319,872 (1% federal, 6% state, 89% institutional, 4% external sources). *Receiving aid:* Freshmen: 82% (233); Undergraduates: 71% (743). *Average Award:* Freshmen: $10,306; Undergraduates: $10,318. *Scholarships, grants, and awards by category: Academic Interests/Achievement:* 858 awards ($6,760,104 total): biological sciences, business, communication, computer science, education, engineering/technologies, English, foreign languages, general academic interests/achievements, health fields, humanities, international studies, mathematics, physical sciences, premedicine, religion/biblical studies, social sciences. *Creative Arts/Performance:* 43 awards ($74,100 total): music. *Special Achievements/Activities:* 93 awards ($251,655 total): community service, general special achievements/activities. *Special Characteristics:* 427 awards ($1,241,687 total): children and siblings of alumni, children of faculty/staff, children of union members/company employees, general special characteristics, international students, religious affiliation. *Tuition waivers:* Full or partial for employees or children of employees, senior citizens.
LOANS *Student loans:* $6,056,801 (43% need-based, 57% non-need-based). 67% of past graduating class borrowed through all loan programs. *Average indebtedness per student:* $16,309. *Average need-based loan:* Freshmen: $2582; Undergraduates: $3757. *Parent loans:* $1,093,562 (100% non-need-based). *Programs:* Federal Direct (Subsidized and Unsubsidized Stafford, PLUS), Perkins, Federal Nursing, alternative loans.
WORK-STUDY *Federal work-study:* Total amount: $374,243; 253 jobs averaging $1479. *State or other work-study/employment:* Total amount: $368,597 (100% non-need-based). 256 part-time jobs averaging $1440.
ATHLETIC AWARDS *Total amount:* $650,013 (100% non-need-based).
APPLYING FOR FINANCIAL AID *Required financial aid forms:* FAFSA, institution's own form. *Financial aid deadline (priority):* 3/1. *Notification date:* Continuous beginning 3/15. Students must reply within 2 weeks of notification.
CONTACT Christie Tomczyk, Director of Financial Aid, Wheeling Jesuit University, 316 Washington Avenue, Wheeling, WV 26003-6295, 304-243-2304 or toll-free 800-624-6992 Ext. 2359. *Fax:* 304-243-4397. *E-mail:* finaid@wju.edu.

WHEELOCK COLLEGE
Boston, MA

CONTACT Joseph L. Chillo, Vice President for Enrollment Management, Wheelock College, 200 The Riverway, Boston, MA 02215-4176, 617-879-2205 or toll-free 800-734-5212 (out-of-state).

WHITMAN COLLEGE
Walla Walla, WA

Tuition & fees: $28,640 **Average undergraduate aid package:** $22,050

ABOUT THE INSTITUTION Independent, coed. Awards: bachelor's degrees. 27 undergraduate majors. Total enrollment: 1,512. Undergraduates: 1,512. Freshmen: 361. Both federal and institutional methodology are used as a basis for awarding need-based institutional aid.
UNDERGRADUATE EXPENSES for 2005–06 *Application fee:* $45. *Comprehensive fee:* $36,110 includes full-time tuition ($28,400), mandatory fees ($240), and room and board ($7470). *College room only:* $3430. Room and board charges vary according to board plan and housing facility. *Part-time tuition:* $1190 per credit. *Payment plan:* Deferred payment.
FRESHMAN FINANCIAL AID (Fall 2005, est.) 258 applied for aid; of those 70% were deemed to have need. 100% of freshmen with need received aid; of those 78% had need fully met. *Average percent of need met:* 98% (excluding resources awarded to replace EFC). *Average financial aid package:* $21,400 (excluding resources awarded to replace EFC). 28% of all full-time freshmen had no need and received non-need-based gift aid.
UNDERGRADUATE FINANCIAL AID (Fall 2005, est.) 835 applied for aid; of those 85% were deemed to have need. 100% of undergraduates with need received aid; of those 78% had need fully met. *Average percent of need met:* 89% (excluding resources awarded to replace EFC). *Average financial aid package:* $22,050 (excluding resources awarded to replace EFC). 38% of all full-time undergraduates had no need and received non-need-based gift aid.
GIFT AID (NEED-BASED) *Total amount:* $10,760,450 (6% federal, 2% state, 92% institutional). *Receiving aid:* Freshmen: 58% (180); All full-time undergraduates: 55% (707). *Average award:* Freshmen: $17,400; Undergraduates: $16,850. *Scholarships, grants, and awards:* Federal Pell, FSEOG, state, private, college/university gift aid from institutional funds.
GIFT AID (NON-NEED-BASED) *Total amount:* $5,853,300 (4% state, 84% institutional, 12% external sources). *Receiving aid:* Freshmen: 34% (104); Undergraduates: 30% (385). *Average Award:* Freshmen: $8700; Undergraduates:* $8250. *Scholarships, grants, and awards by category: Academic Interests/Achievement:* 634 awards ($4,884,675 total): general academic interests/achievements. *Creative Arts/Performance:* 53 awards ($284,769 total): art/fine arts, debating, music, theater/drama. *Special Characteristics:* 152 awards ($3,500,574 total): ethnic background, international students. *Tuition waivers:* Full or partial for employees or children of employees.
LOANS *Student loans:* $3,164,550 (79% need-based, 21% non-need-based). 45% of past graduating class borrowed through all loan programs. *Average indebtedness per student:* $16,200. *Average need-based loan:* Freshmen: $3450; Undergraduates: $4250. *Parent loans:* $2,457,850 (100% non-need-based). *Programs:* FFEL (Subsidized and Unsubsidized Stafford, PLUS), Perkins, alternative loans.
WORK-STUDY *Federal work-study:* Total amount: $1,001,300; 521 jobs averaging $1922. *State or other work-study/employment:* Total amount: $1,288,850 (76% need-based, 24% non-need-based). 204 part-time jobs averaging $1543.
APPLYING FOR FINANCIAL AID *Required financial aid forms:* FAFSA, CSS Financial Aid PROFILE. *Financial aid deadline (priority):* 11/15. *Notification date:* Continuous beginning 12/19. Students must reply within 3 weeks of notification.
CONTACT Tyson Hailow, Financial Aid Assistant, Whitman College, 515 Boyer Avenue, Walla Walla, WA 99362-2046, 509-527-5178 or toll-free 877-462-9448. *Fax:* 509-527-4967.

WHITTIER COLLEGE
Whittier, CA

Tuition & fees: $26,138 **Average undergraduate aid package:** $23,742

ABOUT THE INSTITUTION Independent, coed. Awards: bachelor's, master's, and first professional degrees. 25 undergraduate majors. Total enrollment: 1,307. Undergraduates: 1,307. Freshmen: 394. Both federal and institutional methodology are used as a basis for awarding need-based institutional aid.
UNDERGRADUATE EXPENSES for 2005–06 *Application fee:* $50. *Comprehensive fee:* $34,066 includes full-time tuition ($25,838), mandatory fees ($300), and room and board ($7928).

Whittier College

FRESHMAN FINANCIAL AID (Fall 2005, est.) 351 applied for aid; of those 72% were deemed to have need. 100% of freshmen with need received aid; of those 31% had need fully met. *Average percent of need met:* 73% (excluding resources awarded to replace EFC). *Average financial aid package:* $22,027 (excluding resources awarded to replace EFC). 11% of all full-time freshmen had no need and received non-need-based gift aid.
UNDERGRADUATE FINANCIAL AID (Fall 2005, est.) 1,200 applied for aid; of those 70% were deemed to have need. 99% of undergraduates with need received aid; of those 35% had need fully met. *Average percent of need met:* 71% (excluding resources awarded to replace EFC). *Average financial aid package:* $23,742 (excluding resources awarded to replace EFC). 17% of all full-time undergraduates had no need and received non-need-based gift aid.
GIFT AID (NEED-BASED) *Total amount:* $10,949,810 (12% federal, 18% state, 70% institutional). *Receiving aid:* Freshmen: 65% (229); All full-time undergraduates: 58% (694). *Average award:* Freshmen: $12,535; Undergraduates: $11,316. *Scholarships, grants, and awards:* Federal Pell, FSEOG, state, private, college/university gift aid from institutional funds.
GIFT AID (NON-NEED-BASED) *Total amount:* $856,338 (63% institutional, 37% external sources). *Receiving aid:* Freshmen: 30% (104); Undergraduates: 43% (516). *Average Award:* Freshmen: $7480; Undergraduates: $11,219. *Scholarships, grants, and awards by category: Academic Interests/Achievement:* general academic interests/achievements. *Creative Arts/Performance:* art/fine arts, music, theater/drama. *Special Characteristics:* children and siblings of alumni, children of faculty/staff, international students. *ROTC:* Army cooperative, Air Force cooperative.
LOANS *Student loans:* $7,767,447 (100% need-based). 78% of past graduating class borrowed through all loan programs. *Average indebtedness per student:* $27,335. *Average need-based loan:* Freshmen: $6296; Undergraduates: $7579. *Parent loans:* $2,052,100 (100% need-based). *Programs:* Federal Direct (PLUS), FFEL (Subsidized and Unsubsidized Stafford, PLUS), Perkins, alternative financing loans.
WORK-STUDY *Federal work-study:* Total amount: $1,414,331; jobs available. *State or other work-study/employment:* Total amount: $732,684 (72% need-based, 28% non-need-based). Part-time jobs available.
APPLYING FOR FINANCIAL AID *Required financial aid forms:* FAFSA, CSS Financial Aid PROFILE. *Financial aid deadline:* 6/30 (priority: 3/1). *Notification date:* Continuous beginning 3/1. Students must reply within 2 weeks of notification.
CONTACT Mr. Vernon Bridges, Director of Student Financing, Whittier College, 13406 East Philadelphia Street, PO Box 634, Whittier, CA 90608-0634, 562-907-4285. *Fax:* 562-464-4560. *E-mail:* vbridges@whittier.edu.

WHITWORTH COLLEGE
Spokane, WA

Tuition & fees: $24,154 | **Average undergraduate aid package: $17,441**

ABOUT THE INSTITUTION Independent Presbyterian, coed. Awards: bachelor's and master's degrees. 43 undergraduate majors. Total enrollment: 2,441. Undergraduates: 2,179. Freshmen: 451. Federal methodology is used as a basis for awarding need-based institutional aid.
UNDERGRADUATE EXPENSES for 2006–07 *Comprehensive fee:* $31,184 includes full-time tuition ($23,850), mandatory fees ($304), and room and board ($7030). *Part-time tuition:* $994 per credit.
FRESHMAN FINANCIAL AID (Fall 2005, est.) 399 applied for aid; of those 79% were deemed to have need. 100% of freshmen with need received aid; of those 23% had need fully met. *Average percent of need met:* 83% (excluding resources awarded to replace EFC). *Average financial aid package:* $16,733 (excluding resources awarded to replace EFC). 25% of all full-time freshmen had no need and received non-need-based gift aid.
UNDERGRADUATE FINANCIAL AID (Fall 2005, est.) 1,608 applied for aid; of those 87% were deemed to have need. 100% of undergraduates with need received aid; of those 17% had need fully met. *Average percent of need met:* 79% (excluding resources awarded to replace EFC). *Average financial aid package:* $17,441 (excluding resources awarded to replace EFC). 23% of all full-time undergraduates had no need and received non-need-based gift aid.
GIFT AID (NEED-BASED) *Total amount:* $16,917,603 (10% federal, 12% state, 72% institutional, 6% external sources). *Receiving aid:* Freshmen: 69% (312); All full-time undergraduates: 71% (1,343). *Average award:* Freshmen: $12,851; Undergraduates: $12,423. *Scholarships, grants, and awards:* Federal Pell, FSEOG, state, private, college/university gift aid from institutional funds.
GIFT AID (NON-NEED-BASED) *Total amount:* $4,364,632 (3% federal, 2% state, 84% institutional, 11% external sources). *Receiving aid:* Freshmen: 13% (58); Undergraduates: 7% (127). *Average Award:* Freshmen: $8604; Undergraduates: $7382. *Scholarships, grants, and awards by category: Academic Interests/Achievement:* 1,550 awards ($10,273,247 total): biological sciences, computer science, general academic interests/achievements, military science, physical sciences. *Creative Arts/Performance:* 148 awards ($266,643 total): art/fine arts, journalism/publications, music, theater/drama. *Special Achievements/Activities:* 395 awards ($474,678 total): religious involvement. *Special Characteristics:* 390 awards ($706,601 total): children and siblings of alumni, ethnic background, international students, relatives of clergy, siblings of current students. *ROTC:* Army cooperative.
LOANS *Student loans:* $8,722,401 (79% need-based, 21% non-need-based). 73% of past graduating class borrowed through all loan programs. *Average indebtedness per student:* $18,246. *Average need-based loan:* Freshmen: $3757; Undergraduates: $4572. *Parent loans:* $2,736,015 (37% need-based, 63% non-need-based). *Programs:* Federal Direct (Subsidized and Unsubsidized Stafford, PLUS), Perkins, college/university.
WORK-STUDY *Federal work-study:* Total amount: $1,044,880; 456 jobs averaging $2190. *State or other work-study/employment:* Total amount: $836,223 (96% need-based, 4% non-need-based). 260 part-time jobs averaging $3050.
APPLYING FOR FINANCIAL AID *Required financial aid form:* FAFSA. *Financial aid deadline (priority):* 3/1. *Notification date:* Continuous beginning 3/1. Students must reply by 5/1 or within 4 weeks of notification.
CONTACT Ms. Wendy Z. Olson, Director of Financial Aid, Whitworth College, 300 West Hawthorne Road, Spokane, WA 99251-0001, 509-777-4306 or toll-free 800-533-4668 (out-of-state). *Fax:* 509-777-3725. *E-mail:* wolson@whitworth.edu.

WICHITA STATE UNIVERSITY
Wichita, KS

Tuition & fees (KS res): $4231 | **Average undergraduate aid package: $5885**

ABOUT THE INSTITUTION State-supported, coed. Awards: associate, bachelor's, master's, and doctoral degrees and post-bachelor's and post-master's certificates. 56 undergraduate majors. Total enrollment: 14,076. Undergraduates: 10,975. Freshmen: 1,241. Federal methodology is used as a basis for awarding need-based institutional aid.
UNDERGRADUATE EXPENSES for 2005–06 *Application fee:* $30. *Tuition, state resident:* full-time $3434; part-time $114.45 per credit hour. *Tuition, nonresident:* full-time $10,887; part-time $362.90 per credit hour. *Required fees:* full-time $797; $25.45 per credit hour or $17 per term part-time. Full-time tuition and fees vary according to course load. Part-time tuition and fees vary according to course load. *College room and board:* $5070. Room and board charges vary according to board plan and housing facility. *Payment plan:* Installment.
FRESHMAN FINANCIAL AID (Fall 2004) 902 applied for aid; of those 98% were deemed to have need. 85% of freshmen with need received aid; of those 12% had need fully met. *Average percent of need met:* 43% (excluding resources awarded to replace EFC). *Average financial aid package:* $2514 (excluding resources awarded to replace EFC). 20% of all full-time freshmen had no need and received non-need-based gift aid.
UNDERGRADUATE FINANCIAL AID (Fall 2004) 5,667 applied for aid; of those 99% were deemed to have need. 93% of undergraduates with need received aid; of those 12% had need fully met. *Average percent of need met:* 47% (excluding resources awarded to replace EFC). *Average financial aid package:* $5885 (excluding resources awarded to replace EFC). 14% of all full-time undergraduates had no need and received non-need-based gift aid.
GIFT AID (NEED-BASED) *Total amount:* $10,098,591 (87% federal, 12% state, 1% external sources). *Receiving aid:* Freshmen: 27% (353); All full-time undergraduates: 33% (2,783). *Average award:* Freshmen: $2897; Undergraduates: $2664. *Scholarships, grants, and awards:* Federal Pell, FSEOG, state, private, college/university gift aid from institutional funds, Bureau of Indian Affairs Grants.
GIFT AID (NON-NEED-BASED) *Total amount:* $4,309,722 (85% institutional, 15% external sources). *Receiving aid:* Freshmen: 27% (350); Undergraduates: 16% (1,370). *Average Award:* Freshmen: $2150; Undergraduates: $2205. *Scholarships, grants, and awards by category: Academic Interests/Achievement:* area/ethnic studies, biological sciences, business, communication, computer

science, education, engineering/technologies, English, foreign languages, general academic interests/achievements, health fields, humanities, international studies, mathematics, physical sciences, premedicine, social sciences. *Creative Arts/Performance:* applied art and design, art/fine arts, dance, debating, journalism/publications, music, performing arts, theater/drama. *Special Achievements/Activities:* general special achievements/activities, leadership. *Special Characteristics:* adult students, first-generation college students, international students, members of minority groups. *Tuition waivers:* Full or partial for employees or children of employees, senior citizens.
LOANS *Student loans:* $42,532,930 (56% need-based, 44% non-need-based). 55% of past graduating class borrowed through all loan programs. *Average indebtedness per student:* $18,840. *Average need-based loan:* Freshmen: $2186; Undergraduates: $2583. *Parent loans:* $761,781 (100% non-need-based). *Programs:* FFEL (Subsidized and Unsubsidized Stafford, PLUS), Perkins, college/university.
WORK-STUDY *Federal work-study:* Total amount: $431,016; 195 jobs averaging $2576. *State or other work-study/employment:* Total amount: $98,140 (100% need-based). Part-time jobs available.
ATHLETIC AWARDS *Total amount:* $1,226,691 (100% non-need-based).
APPLYING FOR FINANCIAL AID *Required financial aid forms:* FAFSA, state aid form, scholarship application form(s). *Financial aid deadline (priority):* 3/15. *Notification date:* Continuous beginning 4/1. Students must reply within 2 weeks of notification.
CONTACT Deborah D. Byers, Director of Financial Aid, Wichita State University, 1845 Fairmount, Wichita, KS 67260-0024, 316-978-3430 or toll-free 800-362-2594. *Fax:* 316-978-3396.

WIDENER UNIVERSITY
Chester, PA

| Tuition & fees: $24,970 | Average undergraduate aid package: $20,192 |

ABOUT THE INSTITUTION Independent, coed. Awards: associate, bachelor's, master's, doctoral, and first professional degrees. 70 undergraduate majors. Total enrollment: 5,793. Undergraduates: 2,516. Freshmen: 649. Both federal and institutional methodology are used as a basis for awarding need-based institutional aid.
UNDERGRADUATE EXPENSES for 2005–06 *Application fee:* $35. *Comprehensive fee:* $33,490 includes full-time tuition ($24,620), mandatory fees ($350), and room and board ($8520). *College room only:* $3900. Full-time tuition and fees vary according to class time, course load, and program. Room and board charges vary according to board plan and housing facility. *Part-time tuition:* $821 per credit. *Part-time fees:* $65. *Payment plan:* Installment.
FRESHMAN FINANCIAL AID (Fall 2005, est.) 597 applied for aid; of those 91% were deemed to have need. 100% of freshmen with need received aid; of those 19% had need fully met. *Average percent of need met:* 79% (excluding resources awarded to replace EFC). *Average financial aid package:* $21,490 (excluding resources awarded to replace EFC). 12% of all full-time freshmen had no need and received non-need-based gift aid.
UNDERGRADUATE FINANCIAL AID (Fall 2005, est.) 2,164 applied for aid; of those 91% were deemed to have need. 100% of undergraduates with need received aid; of those 48% had need fully met. *Average percent of need met:* 77% (excluding resources awarded to replace EFC). *Average financial aid package:* $20,192 (excluding resources awarded to replace EFC). 12% of all full-time undergraduates had no need and received non-need-based gift aid.
GIFT AID (NEED-BASED) *Total amount:* $26,703,541 (12% federal, 11% state, 72% institutional, 5% external sources). *Receiving aid:* Freshmen: 78% (506); All full-time undergraduates: 73% (1,790). *Average award:* Freshmen: $12,330; Undergraduates: $10,799. *Scholarships, grants, and awards:* Federal Pell, FSEOG, state, private, college/university gift aid from institutional funds, Federal Nursing.
GIFT AID (NON-NEED-BASED) *Total amount:* $2,991,344 (2% federal, 1% state, 82% institutional, 15% external sources). *Receiving aid:* Freshmen: 57% (371); Undergraduates: 52% (1,272). *Average Award:* Freshmen: $8812; Undergraduates: $8201. *Scholarships, grants, and awards by category: Academic Interests/Achievement:* 2,139 awards ($12,269,615 total): biological sciences, business, communication, computer science, education, engineering/technologies, English, foreign languages, general academic interests/achievements, health fields, humanities, international studies, mathematics, military science, physical sciences, premedicine, social sciences. *Creative Arts/Performance:* 38 awards ($74,000 total): music. *Special Achievements/Activities:* 156 awards ($511,677 total): community service, general special achievements/activities, leadership. *Special Characteristics:* 144 awards ($2,561,045 total): adult students, children and siblings of alumni, children of faculty/staff, ethnic background, international students, siblings of current students, veterans. *Tuition waivers:* Full or partial for employees or children of employees, senior citizens. *ROTC:* Army, Naval cooperative, Air Force cooperative.
LOANS *Student loans:* $19,858,765 (92% need-based, 8% non-need-based). 79% of past graduating class borrowed through all loan programs. *Average indebtedness per student:* $26,348. *Average need-based loan:* Freshmen: $3763; Undergraduates: $4705. *Parent loans:* $6,734,459 (90% need-based, 10% non-need-based). *Programs:* FFEL (Subsidized and Unsubsidized Stafford, PLUS), Perkins.
WORK-STUDY *Federal work-study:* Total amount: $3,363,923; 1,573 jobs averaging $2139. *State or other work-study/employment:* Total amount: $185,583 (64% need-based, 36% non-need-based). 171 part-time jobs averaging $1085.
APPLYING FOR FINANCIAL AID *Required financial aid form:* FAFSA. *Financial aid deadline (priority):* 2/15. *Notification date:* Continuous beginning 3/15. Students must reply within 4 weeks of notification.
CONTACT Thomas K Malloy, Director of Financial Aid, Widener University, One University Place, Chester, PA 19013-5792, 610-499-4174 or toll-free 888-WIDENER. *Fax:* 610-499-4687. *E-mail:* finaidmc@mail.widener.edu.

WILBERFORCE UNIVERSITY
Wilberforce, OH

CONTACT Director of Financial Aid, Wilberforce University, 1055 North Bickett Road, Wilberforce, OH 45384, 937-708-5727 or toll-free 800-367-8568. *Fax:* 937-376-4752.

WILEY COLLEGE
Marshall, TX

CONTACT Cecelia Jones, Interim Director of Financial Aid, Wiley College, 711 Wiley Avenue, Marshall, TX 75670-5199, 903-927-3210 or toll-free 800-658-6889. *Fax:* 903-927-3366.

WILKES UNIVERSITY
Wilkes-Barre, PA

| Tuition & fees: $21,646 | Average undergraduate aid package: $16,882 |

ABOUT THE INSTITUTION Independent, coed. Awards: bachelor's, master's, and first professional degrees. 36 undergraduate majors. Total enrollment: 4,480. Undergraduates: 2,188. Freshmen: 572. Federal methodology is used as a basis for awarding need-based institutional aid.
UNDERGRADUATE EXPENSES for 2005–06 *Application fee:* $35. *Comprehensive fee:* $30,886 includes full-time tuition ($20,592), mandatory fees ($1054), and room and board ($9240). *College room only:* $5600. Room and board charges vary according to board plan and housing facility. *Part-time tuition:* $569 per credit. *Part-time fees:* $43 per credit. *Payment plans:* Installment, deferred payment.
FRESHMAN FINANCIAL AID (Fall 2005, est.) 547 applied for aid; of those 88% were deemed to have need. 100% of freshmen with need received aid; of those 18% had need fully met. *Average percent of need met:* 81% (excluding resources awarded to replace EFC). *Average financial aid package:* $17,438 (excluding resources awarded to replace EFC). 15% of all full-time freshmen had no need and received non-need-based gift aid.
UNDERGRADUATE FINANCIAL AID (Fall 2005, est.) 1,951 applied for aid; of those 89% were deemed to have need. 95% of undergraduates with need received aid; of those 26% had need fully met. *Average percent of need met:* 82% (excluding resources awarded to replace EFC). *Average financial aid package:* $16,882 (excluding resources awarded to replace EFC). 13% of all full-time undergraduates had no need and received non-need-based gift aid.
GIFT AID (NEED-BASED) *Total amount:* $21,217,895 (8% federal, 16% state, 74% institutional, 2% external sources). *Receiving aid:* Freshmen: 84% (478); All full-time undergraduates: 78% (1,633). *Average award:* Freshmen: $13,439; Undergraduates: $12,315. *Scholarships, grants, and awards:* Federal Pell, FSEOG, state, private, college/university gift aid from institutional funds.
GIFT AID (NON-NEED-BASED) *Total amount:* $2,469,835 (5% federal, 94% institutional, 1% external sources). *Receiving aid:* Freshmen: 71% (401);

Wilkes University

Undergraduates: 71% (1,492). *Average Award:* Freshmen: $9538; Undergraduates: $8838. *Scholarships, grants, and awards by category:* Academic Interests/Achievement: biological sciences, business, communication, education, engineering/technologies, English, general academic interests/achievements, health fields, humanities, international studies, mathematics, premedicine, social sciences. *Creative Arts/Performance:* dance, journalism/publications, music, performing arts, theater/drama. *Special Achievements/Activities:* general special achievements/activities, leadership. *Special Characteristics:* adult students, children of faculty/staff. *Tuition waivers:* Full or partial for employees or children of employees. *ROTC:* Army cooperative, Air Force.
LOANS *Student loans:* $12,094,230 (93% need-based, 7% non-need-based). 84% of past graduating class borrowed through all loan programs. *Average indebtedness per student:* $25,164. *Average need-based loan:* Freshmen: $2664; Undergraduates: $3787. *Parent loans:* $1,945,085 (89% need-based, 11% non-need-based). *Programs:* FFEL (Subsidized and Unsubsidized Stafford, PLUS), Perkins, Federal Nursing, state, college/university, Gulf Oil Loan Fund, Rulison Evans Loan Fund.
WORK-STUDY *Federal work-study:* Total amount: $1,677,490; 1,017 jobs averaging $1649. *State or other work-study/employment:* Total amount: $174,850 (64% need-based, 36% non-need-based). 91 part-time jobs averaging $1921.
APPLYING FOR FINANCIAL AID *Required financial aid forms:* FAFSA, institution's own form. *Financial aid deadline (priority):* 3/1. *Notification date:* Continuous.
CONTACT Mrs. Rachael L. Lohman, Director of Financial Aid, Wilkes University, 84 W South Street, Wilkes-Barre, PA 18766, 570-408-4346 or toll-free 800-945-5378 Ext. 4400. *Fax:* 570-408-7808. *E-mail:* rachael.lohman@wilkes.edu.

WILLAMETTE UNIVERSITY
Salem, OR

Tuition & fees: $28,416   **Average undergraduate aid package: $24,448**

ABOUT THE INSTITUTION Independent United Methodist, coed. Awards: bachelor's, master's, and first professional degrees and post-bachelor's and first professional certificates. 40 undergraduate majors. Total enrollment: 2,642. Undergraduates: 1,954. Freshmen: 444. Federal methodology is used as a basis for awarding need-based institutional aid.
UNDERGRADUATE EXPENSES for 2005–06 *Application fee:* $50. *Comprehensive fee:* $35,416 includes full-time tuition ($28,250), mandatory fees ($166), and room and board ($7000). Full-time tuition and fees vary according to course load. Room and board charges vary according to board plan and housing facility. *Part-time tuition:* $3531 per course. Part-time tuition and fees vary according to course load. *Payment plan:* Installment.
FRESHMAN FINANCIAL AID (Fall 2005, est.) 353 applied for aid; of those 84% were deemed to have need. 100% of freshmen with need received aid; of those 39% had need fully met. *Average percent of need met:* 92% (excluding resources awarded to replace EFC). *Average financial aid package:* $23,382 (excluding resources awarded to replace EFC). 28% of all full-time freshmen had no need and received non-need-based gift aid.
UNDERGRADUATE FINANCIAL AID (Fall 2005, est.) 1,244 applied for aid; of those 89% were deemed to have need. 100% of undergraduates with need received aid; of those 41% had need fully met. *Average percent of need met:* 93% (excluding resources awarded to replace EFC). *Average financial aid package:* $24,448 (excluding resources awarded to replace EFC). 32% of all full-time undergraduates had no need and received non-need-based gift aid.
GIFT AID (NEED-BASED) *Total amount:* $20,817,010 (8% federal, 2% state, 85% institutional, 5% external sources). *Receiving aid:* Freshmen: 67% (297); All full-time undergraduates: 62% (1,108). *Average award:* Freshmen: $18,666; Undergraduates: $13,131. *Scholarships, grants, and awards:* Federal Pell, FSEOG, state, private, college/university gift aid from institutional funds, United Negro College Fund.
GIFT AID (NON-NEED-BASED) *Total amount:* $6,791,926 (95% institutional, 5% external sources). *Receiving aid:* Freshmen: 7% (30); Undergraduates: 8% (136). *Average Award:* Freshmen: $8340; Undergraduates: $10,235. *Scholarships, grants, and awards by category:* Academic Interests/Achievement: general academic interests/achievements. *Creative Arts/Performance:* debating, music, theater/drama. *Special Achievements/Activities:* community service, leadership. *Special Characteristics:* international students, members of minority groups. *Tuition waivers:* Full or partial for employees or children of employees. *ROTC:* Air Force cooperative.
LOANS *Student loans:* $6,886,948 (100% need-based). 79% of past graduating class borrowed through all loan programs. *Average indebtedness per student:* $18,756. *Average need-based loan:* Freshmen: $3797; Undergraduates: $4506. *Parent loans:* $6,484,589 (100% need-based). *Programs:* FFEL (Subsidized and Unsubsidized Stafford, PLUS), Perkins, state, alternative loans.
WORK-STUDY *Federal work-study:* Total amount: $1,296,589; 769 jobs averaging $1856.
APPLYING FOR FINANCIAL AID *Required financial aid forms:* FAFSA, CSS Financial Aid PROFILE. *Financial aid deadline (priority):* 2/1. *Notification date:* 4/1. Students must reply by 5/1 or within 2 weeks of notification.
CONTACT Patricia Hoban, Director of Financial Aid, Willamette University, 900 State Street, Salem, OR 97301-3931, 503-370-6273 or toll-free 877-542-2787. *Fax:* 503-370-6588. *E-mail:* phoban@willamette.edu.

WILLIAM CAREY COLLEGE
Hattiesburg, MS

Tuition & fees: $8415   **Average undergraduate aid package: $12,000**

ABOUT THE INSTITUTION Independent Southern Baptist, coed. Awards: bachelor's and master's degrees. 32 undergraduate majors. Total enrollment: 2,758. Undergraduates: 1,853. Freshmen: 125. Federal methodology is used as a basis for awarding need-based institutional aid.
UNDERGRADUATE EXPENSES for 2005–06 *Application fee:* $20. *Comprehensive fee:* $11,880 includes full-time tuition ($8100), mandatory fees ($315), and room and board ($3465). *College room only:* $1305. Full-time tuition and fees vary according to degree level and location. Room and board charges vary according to board plan, housing facility, and location. *Part-time tuition:* $270 per hour. *Part-time fees:* $105 per term. Part-time tuition and fees vary according to degree level and location. *Payment plan:* Deferred payment.
UNDERGRADUATE FINANCIAL AID (Fall 2005, est.) 2,001 applied for aid; of those 99% were deemed to have need. 100% of undergraduates with need received aid; of those 97% had need fully met. *Average percent of need met:* 85% (excluding resources awarded to replace EFC). *Average financial aid package:* $12,000 (excluding resources awarded to replace EFC). 11% of all full-time undergraduates had no need and received non-need-based gift aid.
GIFT AID (NEED-BASED) *Total amount:* $3,800,000 (66% federal, 26% state, 8% external sources). *Receiving aid:* All full-time undergraduates: 96% (1,974). *Average award:* Undergraduates: $6000. *Scholarships, grants, and awards:* Federal Pell, FSEOG, state, private, college/university gift aid from institutional funds.
GIFT AID (NON-NEED-BASED) *Total amount:* $4,000,000 (100% institutional). *Receiving aid:* Undergraduates: 48% (981). *Average Award:* Undergraduates: $6000. *Scholarships, grants, and awards by category:* Academic Interests/Achievement: 850 awards ($3,500,000 total): general academic interests/achievements. *Creative Arts/Performance:* 75 awards ($350,000 total): art/fine arts, debating, journalism/publications, music, theater/drama. *Special Achievements/Activities:* 200 awards ($150,000 total): cheerleading/drum major, junior miss, leadership, religious involvement. *Special Characteristics:* 180 awards ($250,000 total): children and siblings of alumni, children of educators, children of faculty/staff, first-generation college students, international students, relatives of clergy, religious affiliation, veterans. *Tuition waivers:* Full or partial for employees or children of employees. *ROTC:* Army cooperative, Air Force cooperative.
LOANS *Student loans:* $16,000,000 (100% need-based). 85% of past graduating class borrowed through all loan programs. *Average indebtedness per student:* $16,000. *Average need-based loan:* Undergraduates: $5000. *Parent loans:* $200,000 (100% need-based). *Programs:* FFEL (Subsidized and Unsubsidized Stafford, PLUS), Perkins, Federal Nursing, college/university.
WORK-STUDY *Federal work-study:* Total amount: $370,000; 250 jobs averaging $1700. *State or other work-study/employment:* Total amount: $85,000 (100% non-need-based). 45 part-time jobs averaging $1700.
ATHLETIC AWARDS *Total amount:* $750,000 (100% non-need-based).
APPLYING FOR FINANCIAL AID *Required financial aid form:* FAFSA. *Financial aid deadline (priority):* 4/1. *Notification date:* Continuous beginning 5/1. Students must reply within 2 weeks of notification.
CONTACT Ms. Brenda Pittman, Associate Director of Financial Aid, William Carey College, 498 Tuscan Avenue, Hattiesburg, MS 39401-5499, 601-318-6153 or toll-free 800-962-5991 (in-state).

WILLIAM JESSUP UNIVERSITY
Rocklin, CA

CONTACT Kristi Kindberg, Financial Aid Administrator, William Jessup University, 790 South 12th Street, San Jose, CA 95112-2381, 408-278-4328 or toll-free 800-355-7522. *Fax:* 408-293-9299. *E-mail:* finaid@sjchristian.edu.

WILLIAM JEWELL COLLEGE
Liberty, MO

Tuition & fees: $20,150	Average undergraduate aid package: $15,288

ABOUT THE INSTITUTION Independent Baptist, coed. Awards: bachelor's degrees (also offers evening program with significant enrollment not reflected in profile). 42 undergraduate majors. Total enrollment: 1,331. Undergraduates: 1,331. Freshmen: 302. Federal methodology is used as a basis for awarding need-based institutional aid.

UNDERGRADUATE EXPENSES for 2006–07 *Application fee:* $25. *Comprehensive fee:* $25,660 includes full-time tuition ($20,150) and room and board ($5510). *College room only:* $2320.

FRESHMAN FINANCIAL AID (Fall 2005, est.) 249 applied for aid; of those 68% were deemed to have need. 100% of freshmen with need received aid. *Average financial aid package:* $16,295 (excluding resources awarded to replace EFC).

UNDERGRADUATE FINANCIAL AID (Fall 2005, est.) 1,029 applied for aid; of those 71% were deemed to have need. 100% of undergraduates with need received aid. *Average financial aid package:* $15,288 (excluding resources awarded to replace EFC).

GIFT AID (NEED-BASED) *Total amount:* $6,788,518 (14% federal, 8% state, 71% institutional, 7% external sources). *Receiving aid:* Freshmen: 56% (170); All full-time undergraduates: 56% (721). *Average award:* Freshmen: $12,773; Undergraduates: $11,260. *Scholarships, grants, and awards:* Federal Pell, FSEOG, state, college/university gift aid from institutional funds.

GIFT AID (NON-NEED-BASED) *Total amount:* $3,444,266 (4% state, 87% institutional, 9% external sources). *Receiving aid:* Freshmen: 45% (135); Undergraduates: 45% (577). *Scholarships, grants, and awards by category:* Academic Interests/Achievement: 222 awards ($1,168,442 total): education, general academic interests/achievements. Creative Arts/Performance: 78 awards ($173,525 total): art/fine arts, cinema/film/broadcasting, debating, journalism/publications, music, theater/drama. Special Achievements/Activities: 34 awards ($69,600 total): cheerleading/drum major, religious involvement. Special Characteristics: 187 awards ($400,861 total): children and siblings of alumni, children of faculty/staff, members of minority groups, out-of-state students, relatives of clergy, religious affiliation, siblings of current students.

LOANS *Student loans:* $5,580,003 (74% need-based, 26% non-need-based). 71% of past graduating class borrowed through all loan programs. *Average indebtedness per student:* $17,133. *Average need-based loan:* Freshmen: $3777; Undergraduates: $4502. *Parent loans:* $2,748,609 (63% need-based, 37% non-need-based). *Programs:* FFEL (Subsidized and Unsubsidized Stafford, PLUS), Perkins, Federal Nursing, non-Federal alternative loans (non-college).

WORK-STUDY *Federal work-study:* Total amount: $740,733; 529 jobs averaging $1629. *State or other work-study/employment:* Total amount: $144,960 (100% non-need-based). 63 part-time jobs averaging $1224.

ATHLETIC AWARDS *Total amount:* $2,100,172 (59% need-based, 41% non-need-based).

APPLYING FOR FINANCIAL AID *Required financial aid form:* FAFSA. *Financial aid deadline (priority):* 3/1. *Notification date:* Continuous beginning 1/31.

CONTACT Susan Arbo, Director of Financial Aid and Scholarship Services, William Jewell College, 500 College Hill, Box 2005, T38, Brown Hall, Liberty, MO 64068, 816-415-7681 or toll-free 888-2JEWELL. *Fax:* 816-415-5006. *E-mail:* arbos@william.jewell.edu.

WILLIAM PATERSON UNIVERSITY OF NEW JERSEY
Wayne, NJ

Tuition & fees (NJ res): $8740	Average undergraduate aid package: $10,130

ABOUT THE INSTITUTION State-supported, coed. Awards: bachelor's and master's degrees and post-bachelor's and post-master's certificates. 53 undergraduate majors. Total enrollment: 10,970. Undergraduates: 9,110. Freshmen: 1,412. Federal methodology is used as a basis for awarding need-based institutional aid.

UNDERGRADUATE EXPENSES for 2005–06 *Application fee:* $50. *Tuition, state resident:* full-time $5358; part-time $172.16 per credit. *Tuition, nonresident:* full-time $10,474; part-time $339.16 per credit. *Required fees:* full-time $3382; $108.84 per credit. *College room and board:* $9070; *room only:* $6040. Room and board charges vary according to board plan and housing facility. *Payment plan:* Installment.

FRESHMAN FINANCIAL AID (Fall 2005, est.) 1015 applied for aid; of those 73% were deemed to have need. 95% of freshmen with need received aid; of those 28% had need fully met. *Average percent of need met:* 82% (excluding resources awarded to replace EFC). *Average financial aid package:* $9845 (excluding resources awarded to replace EFC). 4% of all full-time freshmen had no need and received non-need-based gift aid.

UNDERGRADUATE FINANCIAL AID (Fall 2005, est.) 5,010 applied for aid; of those 78% were deemed to have need. 94% of undergraduates with need received aid; of those 25% had need fully met. *Average percent of need met:* 83% (excluding resources awarded to replace EFC). *Average financial aid package:* $10,130 (excluding resources awarded to replace EFC). 1% of all full-time undergraduates had no need and received non-need-based gift aid.

GIFT AID (NEED-BASED) *Total amount:* $12,800,000 (44% federal, 51% state, 5% institutional). *Receiving aid:* Freshmen: 29% (404); All full-time undergraduates: 23% (2,049). *Average award:* Freshmen: $6412; Undergraduates: $5955. *Scholarships, grants, and awards:* Federal Pell, FSEOG, state, college/university gift aid from institutional funds.

GIFT AID (NON-NEED-BASED) *Total amount:* $6,300,000 (6% state, 90% institutional, 4% external sources). *Receiving aid:* Freshmen: 21% (296); Undergraduates: 12% (1,073). *Average Award:* Freshmen: $5790; Undergraduates: $4694. *Scholarships, grants, and awards by category:* Academic Interests/Achievement: 844 awards ($4,959,434 total): general academic interests/achievements. Creative Arts/Performance: 12 awards ($3300 total): music. Special Characteristics: general special characteristics. *Tuition waivers:* Full or partial for employees or children of employees, senior citizens. *ROTC:* Air Force cooperative.

LOANS *Student loans:* $30,000,000 (42% need-based, 58% non-need-based). 50% of past graduating class borrowed through all loan programs. *Average indebtedness per student:* $11,483. *Average need-based loan:* Freshmen: $2584; Undergraduates: $3800. *Parent loans:* $4,800,000 (100% non-need-based). *Programs:* FFEL (Subsidized and Unsubsidized Stafford, PLUS), Perkins.

WORK-STUDY *Federal work-study:* Total amount: $300,000; 220 jobs averaging $1136. *State or other work-study/employment:* Total amount: $275,000 (100% non-need-based). 192 part-time jobs averaging $1300.

APPLYING FOR FINANCIAL AID *Required financial aid form:* FAFSA. *Financial aid deadline:* 4/1 (priority: 4/1). *Notification date:* Continuous beginning 3/1. Students must reply within 2 weeks of notification.

CONTACT Robert Baumel, Director of Financial Aid, William Paterson University of New Jersey, 300 Pompton Road, Raubinger Hall, Wayne, NJ 07470, 973-720-2928 or toll-free 877-WPU-EXCEL (in-state). *E-mail:* baumelr@wpunj.edu.

WILLIAM PENN UNIVERSITY
Oskaloosa, IA

Tuition & fees: $15,945	Average undergraduate aid package: $17,782

ABOUT THE INSTITUTION Independent religious, coed. Awards: associate and bachelor's degrees. 39 undergraduate majors. Total enrollment: 1,892. Undergraduates: 1,892. Freshmen: 462. Federal methodology is used as a basis for awarding need-based institutional aid.

UNDERGRADUATE EXPENSES for 2006–07 *Application fee:* $20. *Comprehensive fee:* $20,927 includes full-time tuition ($15,575), mandatory fees ($370), and room and board ($4982).

FRESHMAN FINANCIAL AID (Fall 2005, est.) 149 applied for aid; of those 95% were deemed to have need. 100% of freshmen with need received aid; of those 31% had need fully met. *Average percent of need met:* 82% (excluding resources awarded to replace EFC). *Average financial aid package:* $17,782 (excluding resources awarded to replace EFC). 1% of all full-time freshmen had no need and received non-need-based gift aid.

UNDERGRADUATE FINANCIAL AID (Fall 2005, est.) 808 applied for aid; of those 95% were deemed to have need. 100% of undergraduates with need

William Penn University

received aid; of those 31% had need fully met. *Average percent of need met:* 82% (excluding resources awarded to replace EFC). *Average financial aid package:* $17,782 (excluding resources awarded to replace EFC). 1% of all full-time undergraduates had no need and received non-need-based gift aid.

GIFT AID (NEED-BASED) *Total amount:* $5,610,299 (58% federal, 23% state, 18% institutional, 1% external sources). *Receiving aid:* Freshmen: 94% (142); All full-time undergraduates: 94% (768). *Average award:* Freshmen: $11,300; Undergraduates: $11,300. *Scholarships, grants, and awards:* Federal Pell, FSEOG, state, private, college/university gift aid from institutional funds.

GIFT AID (NON-NEED-BASED) *Total amount:* $117,162 (3% federal, 94% institutional, 3% external sources). *Receiving aid:* Freshmen: 86% (130); Undergraduates: 87% (707). *Average Award:* Freshmen: $4500; Undergraduates: $4500. *Scholarships, grants, and awards by category:* Academic Interests/Achievement: 85 awards ($378,610 total): general academic interests/achievements. *Creative Arts/Performance:* 37 awards ($119,111 total): dance, journalism/publications, music, theater/drama. *Special Achievements/Activities:* 582 awards ($3,564,697 total): cheerleading/drum major, general special achievements/activities, junior miss, leadership, religious involvement. *Special Characteristics:* 62 awards ($116,107 total): children and siblings of alumni, children of faculty/staff, general special characteristics, international students.

LOANS *Student loans:* $4,586,413 (81% need-based, 19% non-need-based). 96% of past graduating class borrowed through all loan programs. *Average indebtedness per student:* $22,169. *Average need-based loan:* Freshmen: $4125; Undergraduates: $4600. *Parent loans:* $1,366,492 (63% need-based, 37% non-need-based). *Programs:* FFEL (Subsidized and Unsubsidized Stafford, PLUS), Perkins, state, college/university.

WORK-STUDY *Federal work-study:* Total amount: $657,564; 511 jobs averaging $1287. *State or other work-study/employment:* Total amount: $1103 (100% need-based). 1 part-time job averaging $1103.

ATHLETIC AWARDS *Total amount:* $3,417,480 (95% need-based, 5% non-need-based).

APPLYING FOR FINANCIAL AID *Required financial aid form:* FAFSA. *Financial aid deadline (priority):* 4/15. *Notification date:* Continuous beginning 3/1. Students must reply within 3 weeks of notification.

CONTACT Cyndi Peiffer, Director of Financial Aid, William Penn University, 201 Trueblood Avenue, Oskaloosa, IA 52577-1799, 641-673-1060 or toll-free 800-779-7366. *Fax:* 641-673-1115. *E-mail:* peifferc@wmpenn.edu.

WILLIAMS BAPTIST COLLEGE
Walnut Ridge, AR

Tuition & fees: N/R	Average undergraduate aid package: $9494

ABOUT THE INSTITUTION Independent Southern Baptist, coed. Awards: associate and bachelor's degrees. 26 undergraduate majors. Total enrollment: 653. Undergraduates: 653. Freshmen: 121. Federal methodology is used as a basis for awarding need-based institutional aid.

FRESHMAN FINANCIAL AID (Fall 2004) 133 applied for aid; of those 72% were deemed to have need. 100% of freshmen with need received aid. *Average financial aid package:* $7954 (excluding resources awarded to replace EFC). 30% of all full-time freshmen had no need and received non-need-based gift aid.

UNDERGRADUATE FINANCIAL AID (Fall 2004) 447 applied for aid; of those 81% were deemed to have need. 100% of undergraduates with need received aid. *Average financial aid package:* $9494 (excluding resources awarded to replace EFC). 23% of all full-time undergraduates had no need and received non-need-based gift aid.

GIFT AID (NEED-BASED) *Total amount:* $1,159,987 (77% federal, 23% state). *Receiving aid:* Freshmen: 46% (66); All full-time undergraduates: 58% (278). *Average award:* Freshmen: $2540; Undergraduates: $2880. *Scholarships, grants, and awards:* Federal Pell, FSEOG, state, private, college/university gift aid from institutional funds.

GIFT AID (NON-NEED-BASED) *Total amount:* $1,536,488 (9% state, 82% institutional, 9% external sources). *Receiving aid:* Freshmen: 46% (65); Undergraduates: 69% (329). *Average Award:* Freshmen: $3730; Undergraduates: $3551. *Scholarships, grants, and awards by category:* Academic Interests/Achievement: 406 awards ($945,987 total): biological sciences, business, education, general academic interests/achievements, humanities, religion/biblical studies. *Creative Arts/Performance:* 33 awards ($40,175 total): art/fine arts, music. *Special Achievements/Activities:* 8 awards ($2800 total): cheerleading/drum major. *Special Characteristics:* 179 awards ($153,815 total): children of faculty/staff, international students, members of minority groups, relatives of clergy, religious affiliation. *Tuition waivers:* Full or partial for employees or children of employees, senior citizens. *ROTC:* Army cooperative.

LOANS *Student loans:* $1,667,429 (69% need-based, 31% non-need-based). 81% of past graduating class borrowed through all loan programs. *Average indebtedness per student:* $14,768. *Average need-based loan:* Freshmen: $1903; Undergraduates: $3416. *Parent loans:* $130,066 (100% non-need-based). *Programs:* Federal Direct (Subsidized and Unsubsidized Stafford, PLUS).

WORK-STUDY *Federal work-study:* Total amount: $244,040; 213 jobs averaging $1008. *State or other work-study/employment:* Total amount: $35,107 (100% non-need-based). 28 part-time jobs averaging $940.

ATHLETIC AWARDS *Total amount:* $397,154 (100% non-need-based).

APPLYING FOR FINANCIAL AID *Required financial aid form:* FAFSA. *Financial aid deadline:* Continuous. *Notification date:* Continuous beginning 4/1. Students must reply within 2 weeks of notification.

CONTACT Barbara Turner, Director of Financial Aid, Williams Baptist College, 60 West Fulbright Avenue, PO Box 3734, Walnut Ridge, AR 72476, 870-759-4112 or toll-free 800-722-4434. *Fax:* 870-759-4209. *E-mail:* financialaid@wbcoll.edu.

WILLIAMS COLLEGE
Williamstown, MA

ABOUT THE INSTITUTION Independent, coed. Awards: bachelor's and master's degrees. 33 undergraduate majors. Total enrollment: 2,070. Undergraduates: 2,017. Freshmen: 536.

GIFT AID (NEED-BASED) *Scholarships, grants, and awards:* Federal Pell, FSEOG, state, private, college/university gift aid from institutional funds.

LOANS *Programs:* Federal Direct (Subsidized and Unsubsidized Stafford, PLUS), Perkins, college/university.

WORK-STUDY *Federal work-study:* Total amount: $681,279; 444 jobs averaging $1572. *State or other work-study/employment:* Total amount: $530,404 (91% need-based, 9% non-need-based). 338 part-time jobs averaging $1589.

APPLYING FOR FINANCIAL AID *Required financial aid forms:* FAFSA, CSS Financial Aid PROFILE.

CONTACT Paul J. Boyer, Director of Financial Aid, Williams College, PO Box 37, Williamstown, MA 01267, 413-597-4181. *Fax:* 413-597-2999. *E-mail:* paul.j.boyer@williams.edu.

WILLIAMSON CHRISTIAN COLLEGE
Franklin, TN

CONTACT Jeanie Maguire, Director of Financial Aid, Williamson Christian College, 200 Seaboard Lane, Franklin, TN 37067, 615-771-7821. *Fax:* 615-771-7810. *E-mail:* info@williamsoncc.edu.

WILLIAM WOODS UNIVERSITY
Fulton, MO

Tuition & fees: $15,120	Average undergraduate aid package: $12,617

ABOUT THE INSTITUTION Independent religious, coed. Awards: associate, bachelor's, and master's degrees and post-master's certificates. 46 undergraduate majors. Total enrollment: 3,047. Undergraduates: 1,173. Freshmen: 258. Federal methodology is used as a basis for awarding need-based institutional aid.

UNDERGRADUATE EXPENSES for 2005–06 *Application fee:* $25. *Comprehensive fee:* $21,020 includes full-time tuition ($14,700), mandatory fees ($420), and room and board ($5900). Full-time tuition and fees vary according to program. Room and board charges vary according to board plan and housing facility. *Part-time tuition:* $490 per credit. *Part-time fees:* $15 per term. Part-time tuition and fees vary according to course load and program. *Payment plan:* Installment.

FRESHMAN FINANCIAL AID (Fall 2005, est.) 194 applied for aid; of those 73% were deemed to have need. 100% of freshmen with need received aid; of those 30% had need fully met. *Average percent of need met:* 77% (excluding resources awarded to replace EFC). *Average financial aid package:* $12,541 (excluding resources awarded to replace EFC). 33% of all full-time freshmen had no need and received non-need-based gift aid.

UNDERGRADUATE FINANCIAL AID (Fall 2005, est.) 733 applied for aid; of those 70% were deemed to have need. 98% of undergraduates with need received aid; of those 32% had need fully met. *Average percent of need met:* 79% (excluding resources awarded to replace EFC). *Average financial aid package:* $12,617 (excluding resources awarded to replace EFC). 34% of all full-time undergraduates had no need and received non-need-based gift aid.
GIFT AID (NEED-BASED) *Total amount:* $3,639,687 (19% federal, 5% state, 72% institutional, 4% external sources). *Receiving aid:* Freshmen: 56% (142); All full-time undergraduates: 61% (491). *Average award:* Freshmen: $9626; Undergraduates: $9235. *Scholarships, grants, and awards:* Federal Pell, FSEOG, state, college/university gift aid from institutional funds.
GIFT AID (NON-NEED-BASED) *Total amount:* $2,084,591 (1% state, 93% institutional, 6% external sources). *Receiving aid:* Freshmen: 13% (33); Undergraduates: 11% (92). *Average Award:* Freshmen: $9449; Undergraduates:* $9356. *Scholarships, grants, and awards by category: Academic Interests/Achievement:* 806 awards ($1,319,451 total): general academic interests/achievements, health fields. *Creative Arts/Performance:* 22 awards ($68,700 total): art/fine arts, journalism/publications, performing arts, theater/drama. *Special Achievements/Activities:* 888 awards ($3,979,977 total): general special achievements/activities, leadership. *Special Characteristics:* 111 awards ($298,900 total): children and siblings of alumni, children of faculty/staff, relatives of clergy, religious affiliation, siblings of current students. *Tuition waivers:* Full or partial for children of alumni, employees or children of employees, senior citizens. *ROTC:* Army cooperative, Naval cooperative, Air Force cooperative.
LOANS *Student loans:* $3,088,846 (62% need-based, 38% non-need-based). 85% of past graduating class borrowed through all loan programs. *Average indebtedness per student:* $13,865. *Average need-based loan:* Freshmen: $3035; Undergraduates: $3931. *Parent loans:* $1,507,128 (28% need-based, 72% non-need-based). *Programs:* FFEL (Subsidized and Unsubsidized Stafford, PLUS), Perkins, college/university.
WORK-STUDY *Federal work-study:* Total amount: $274,233; 302 jobs averaging $1278. *State or other work-study/employment:* Total amount: $192,474 (16% need-based, 84% non-need-based). 169 part-time jobs averaging $847.
ATHLETIC AWARDS *Total amount:* $305,600 (55% need-based, 45% non-need-based).
APPLYING FOR FINANCIAL AID *Required financial aid forms:* FAFSA, institution's own form. *Financial aid deadline:* Continuous. *Notification date:* Continuous beginning 3/15. Students must reply within 2 weeks of notification.
CONTACT Deana Ready, Director of Student Financial Services, William Woods University, One University Avenue, Fulton, MO 65251, 573-592-4232 or toll-free 800-995-3159 Ext. 4221. *Fax:* 573-592-1180.

WILMINGTON COLLEGE
New Castle, DE

ABOUT THE INSTITUTION Independent, coed. Awards: associate, bachelor's, master's, and doctoral degrees and post-bachelor's and post-master's certificates. 23 undergraduate majors. Total enrollment: 7,511. Undergraduates: 4,570. Freshmen: 367.
GIFT AID (NEED-BASED) *Scholarships, grants, and awards:* Federal Pell, FSEOG, state, college/university gift aid from institutional funds, Federal Nursing.
GIFT AID (NON-NEED-BASED) *Scholarships, grants, and awards by category: Academic Interests/Achievement:* education.
LOANS *Programs:* FFEL (Subsidized and Unsubsidized Stafford, PLUS), alternative loans.
WORK-STUDY *Federal work-study:* Total amount: $134,000; 25 jobs averaging $2000.
APPLYING FOR FINANCIAL AID *Required financial aid form:* FAFSA.
CONTACT J. Lynn Iocono, Director of Financial Aid, Wilmington College, 320 DuPont Highway, New Castle, DE 19720, 302-328-9437 or toll-free 877-967-5464. *Fax:* 302-328-5902.

WILMINGTON COLLEGE
Wilmington, OH

ABOUT THE INSTITUTION Independent Friends, coed. Awards: bachelor's and master's degrees. 42 undergraduate majors. Total enrollment: 1,764. Undergraduates: 1,723. Freshmen: 386.
GIFT AID (NEED-BASED) *Scholarships, grants, and awards:* Federal Pell, FSEOG, state, college/university gift aid from institutional funds.
GIFT AID (NON-NEED-BASED) *Scholarships, grants, and awards by category: Academic Interests/Achievement:* agriculture, biological sciences, business, communication, education, general academic interests/achievements, international studies, mathematics, physical sciences, premedicine, religion/biblical studies. *Creative Arts/Performance:* theater/drama. *Special Achievements/Activities:* leadership. *Special Characteristics:* children and siblings of alumni, members of minority groups, religious affiliation, siblings of current students.
LOANS *Programs:* FFEL (Subsidized and Unsubsidized Stafford, PLUS), Perkins.
APPLYING FOR FINANCIAL AID *Required financial aid form:* FAFSA.
CONTACT Donna Barton, Coordinator of Financial Aid, Wilmington College, Pyle Center Box 1184, Wilmington, OH 45177, 937-382-6661 Ext. 466 or toll-free 800-341-9318. *Fax:* 937-383-8564.

WILSON COLLEGE
Chambersburg, PA

Tuition & fees: $20,050   **Average undergraduate aid package:** $16,276

ABOUT THE INSTITUTION Independent religious, women only. Awards: associate and bachelor's degrees. 23 undergraduate majors. Total enrollment: 732. Undergraduates: 732. Freshmen: 76. Both federal and institutional methodology are used as a basis for awarding need-based institutional aid.
UNDERGRADUATE EXPENSES for 2005–06 *Application fee:* $35. *Comprehensive fee:* $27,660 includes full-time tuition ($19,570), mandatory fees ($480), and room and board ($7610). *College room only:* $3920. Room and board charges vary according to board plan. *Part-time tuition:* $1960 per course. *Part-time fees:* $30 per course; $35 per term. Part-time tuition and fees vary according to course load. *Payment plan:* Installment.
FRESHMAN FINANCIAL AID (Fall 2005, est.) 67 applied for aid; of those 87% were deemed to have need. 98% of freshmen with need received aid; of those 21% had need fully met. *Average percent of need met:* 74% (excluding resources awarded to replace EFC). *Average financial aid package:* $15,252 (excluding resources awarded to replace EFC). 19% of all full-time freshmen had no need and received non-need-based gift aid.
UNDERGRADUATE FINANCIAL AID (Fall 2005, est.) 280 applied for aid; of those 88% were deemed to have need. 99% of undergraduates with need received aid; of those 19% had need fully met. *Average percent of need met:* 78% (excluding resources awarded to replace EFC). *Average financial aid package:* $16,276 (excluding resources awarded to replace EFC). 23% of all full-time undergraduates had no need and received non-need-based gift aid.
GIFT AID (NEED-BASED) *Total amount:* $3,285,891 (14% federal, 16% state, 68% institutional, 2% external sources). *Receiving aid:* Freshmen: 77% (57); All full-time undergraduates: 71% (238). *Average award:* Freshmen: $12,296; Undergraduates: $12,461. *Scholarships, grants, and awards:* Federal Pell, FSEOG, state, private, college/university gift aid from institutional funds.
GIFT AID (NON-NEED-BASED) *Total amount:* $1,054,009 (2% federal, 11% state, 81% institutional, 6% external sources). *Receiving aid:* Freshmen: 15% (11); Undergraduates: 10% (32). *Average Award:* Freshmen: $18,667; Undergraduates:* $14,532. *Scholarships, grants, and awards by category: Academic Interests/Achievement:* 207 awards ($830,000 total): biological sciences, business, communication, computer science, education, English, foreign languages, general academic interests/achievements, humanities, international studies, mathematics, physical sciences, premedicine, religion/biblical studies, social sciences. *Creative Arts/Performance:* 1 award ($1800 total): music. *Special Achievements/Activities:* 20 awards ($93,997 total): community service, leadership. *Special Characteristics:* 76 awards ($300,000 total): adult students, children and siblings of alumni, children of current students, children of faculty/staff, international students, local/state students, relatives of clergy, religious affiliation, veterans. *Tuition waivers:* Full or partial for children of alumni, employees or children of employees. *ROTC:* Army cooperative.
LOANS *Student loans:* $2,809,158 (69% need-based, 31% non-need-based). 91% of past graduating class borrowed through all loan programs. *Average indebtedness per student:* $25,534. *Average need-based loan:* Freshmen: $3236; Undergraduates: $4439. *Parent loans:* $901,332 (32% need-based, 68% non-need-based). *Programs:* FFEL (Subsidized and Unsubsidized Stafford, PLUS), Perkins, college/university.
WORK-STUDY *Federal work-study:* Total amount: $31,442; 60 jobs averaging $1340. *State or other work-study/employment:* Total amount: $130,625 (31% need-based, 69% non-need-based). 101 part-time jobs averaging $1340.

Wilson College

APPLYING FOR FINANCIAL AID *Required financial aid forms:* FAFSA, institution's own form. *Financial aid deadline (priority):* 4/30. *Notification date:* Continuous beginning 3/1. Students must reply within 2 weeks of notification.
CONTACT Linda Brittain, Associate Dean of Enrollment, Wilson College, 1015 Philadelphia Avenue, Chambersburg, PA 17201-1285, 717-262-2016 or toll-free 800-421-8402. *Fax:* 717-262-2546. *E-mail:* finaid@wilson.edu.

WINGATE UNIVERSITY
Wingate, NC

Tuition & fees: $16,850	Average undergraduate aid package: $12,528

ABOUT THE INSTITUTION Independent Baptist, coed. Awards: bachelor's, master's, and first professional degrees. 39 undergraduate majors. Total enrollment: 1,632. Undergraduates: 1,341. Freshmen: 371. Both federal and institutional methodology are used as a basis for awarding need-based institutional aid.
UNDERGRADUATE EXPENSES for 2005–06 *Application fee:* $30. *Comprehensive fee:* $23,300 includes full-time tuition ($15,800), mandatory fees ($1050), and room and board ($6450). *Part-time tuition:* $525 per credit hour. *Part-time fees:* $175 per term. *Payment plan:* Installment.
FRESHMAN FINANCIAL AID (Fall 2005, est.) 301 applied for aid; of those 78% were deemed to have need. 100% of freshmen with need received aid; of those 24% had need fully met. *Average percent of need met:* 77% (excluding resources awarded to replace EFC). *Average financial aid package:* $11,582 (excluding resources awarded to replace EFC). 32% of all full-time freshmen had no need and received non-need-based gift aid.
UNDERGRADUATE FINANCIAL AID (Fall 2005, est.) 982 applied for aid; of those 84% were deemed to have need. 100% of undergraduates with need received aid; of those 26% had need fully met. *Average percent of need met:* 76% (excluding resources awarded to replace EFC). *Average financial aid package:* $12,528 (excluding resources awarded to replace EFC). 29% of all full-time undergraduates had no need and received non-need-based gift aid.
GIFT AID (NEED-BASED) *Total amount:* $3,089,891 (31% federal, 28% state, 41% institutional). *Receiving aid:* Freshmen: 56% (208); All full-time undergraduates: 51% (674). *Average award:* Freshmen: $3021; Undergraduates: $2971. *Scholarships, grants, and awards:* Federal Pell, FSEOG, state, private, college/university gift aid from institutional funds.
GIFT AID (NON-NEED-BASED) *Total amount:* $7,054,668 (18% state, 76% institutional, 6% external sources). *Receiving aid:* Freshmen: 63% (232); Undergraduates: 61% (798). *Average Award:* Freshmen: $4881; Undergraduates: $4955. *Scholarships, grants, and awards by category:* Academic Interests/Achievement: 1,108 awards ($5,079,500 total): general academic interests/achievements. *Creative Arts/Performance:* 28 awards ($51,000 total): music. *Special Achievements/Activities:* 56 awards ($26,041 total): religious involvement. *Special Characteristics:* 14 awards ($6250 total): children and siblings of alumni, relatives of clergy, religious affiliation. *Tuition waivers:* Full or partial for employees or children of employees. *ROTC:* Army cooperative, Air Force cooperative.
LOANS *Student loans:* $5,338,359 (44% need-based, 56% non-need-based). 79% of past graduating class borrowed through all loan programs. *Average indebtedness per student:* $21,971. *Average need-based loan:* Freshmen: $2538; Undergraduates: $3966. *Parent loans:* $2,442,456 (100% non-need-based). *Programs:* FFEL (Subsidized and Unsubsidized Stafford, PLUS)
WORK-STUDY *Federal work-study:* Total amount: $104,477; 192 jobs averaging $657. *State or other work-study/employment:* Total amount: $300,000 (100% non-need-based). 373 part-time jobs averaging $560.
ATHLETIC AWARDS *Total amount:* $1,771,138 (100% non-need-based).
APPLYING FOR FINANCIAL AID *Required financial aid form:* FAFSA. *Financial aid deadline (priority):* 5/1. *Notification date:* Continuous. Students must reply within 4 weeks of notification.
CONTACT Teresa G. Williams, Director of Financial Planning, Wingate University, Campus Box 3001, Wingate, NC 28174, 704-233-8209 or toll-free 800-755-5550. *Fax:* 704-233-9396. *E-mail:* tgwilliam@wingate.edu.

WINONA STATE UNIVERSITY
Winona, MN

Tuition & fees (MN res): $7727	Average undergraduate aid package: $5946

ABOUT THE INSTITUTION State-supported, coed. Awards: associate, bachelor's, and master's degrees and post-master's certificates. 104 undergraduate majors. Total enrollment: 8,236. Undergraduates: 7,569. Freshmen: 1,552. Federal methodology is used as a basis for awarding need-based institutional aid.
UNDERGRADUATE EXPENSES for 2005–06 *Application fee:* $20. *Tuition, state resident:* full-time $5877. *Tuition, nonresident:* full-time $10,297. *College room and board:* $5000. Room and board charges vary according to board plan and housing facility.
FRESHMAN FINANCIAL AID (Fall 2004) 1157 applied for aid; of those 67% were deemed to have need. 98% of freshmen with need received aid; of those 13% had need fully met. *Average percent of need met:* 51% (excluding resources awarded to replace EFC). *Average financial aid package:* $4657 (excluding resources awarded to replace EFC). 25% of all full-time freshmen had no need and received non-need-based gift aid.
UNDERGRADUATE FINANCIAL AID (Fall 2004) 4,874 applied for aid; of those 73% were deemed to have need. 98% of undergraduates with need received aid; of those 16% had need fully met. *Average percent of need met:* 56% (excluding resources awarded to replace EFC). *Average financial aid package:* $5946 (excluding resources awarded to replace EFC). 15% of all full-time undergraduates had no need and received non-need-based gift aid.
GIFT AID (NEED-BASED) *Total amount:* $6,710,294 (57% federal, 41% state, 2% institutional). *Receiving aid:* Freshmen: 24% (355); All full-time undergraduates: 29% (1,941). *Average award:* Freshmen: $3186; Undergraduates: $3122. *Scholarships, grants, and awards:* Federal Pell, FSEOG, state, private, college/university gift aid from institutional funds.
GIFT AID (NON-NEED-BASED) *Total amount:* $4,682,124 (55% institutional, 45% external sources). *Receiving aid:* Freshmen: 26% (383); Undergraduates: 16% (1,056). *Average Award:* Freshmen: $1608; Undergraduates: $2356. *Scholarships, grants, and awards by category:* Academic Interests/Achievement: 1,229 awards ($1,780,814 total): general academic interests/achievements. *Creative Arts/Performance:* 12 awards ($4650 total): art/fine arts, debating, music, theater/drama. *Special Characteristics:* 1,095 awards ($1,898,210 total): children and siblings of alumni, children of faculty/staff, local/state students, members of minority groups, out-of-state students. *ROTC:* Army cooperative.
LOANS *Student loans:* $29,971,174 (40% need-based, 60% non-need-based). 66% of past graduating class borrowed through all loan programs. *Average indebtedness per student:* $16,588. *Average need-based loan:* Freshmen: $2286; Undergraduates: $3448. *Parent loans:* $1,935,541 (100% non-need-based). *Programs:* FFEL (Subsidized and Unsubsidized Stafford, PLUS), Perkins, state, college/university.
WORK-STUDY *Federal work-study:* Total amount: $414,225; 230 jobs averaging $1801. *State or other work-study/employment:* Total amount: $836,954 (68% need-based, 32% non-need-based). 288 part-time jobs averaging $1986.
ATHLETIC AWARDS *Total amount:* $328,490 (100% non-need-based).
APPLYING FOR FINANCIAL AID *Required financial aid form:* FAFSA. *Financial aid deadline:* Continuous. *Notification date:* 5/1. Students must reply within 3 weeks of notification.
CONTACT Cindy Groth, Counselor, Winona State University, PO Box 5838, Winona, MN 55987-5838, 507-457-5090 Ext. 5561 or toll-free 800-DIAL WSU.

WINSTON-SALEM BIBLE COLLEGE
Winston-Salem, NC

CONTACT Financial Aid Office, Winston-Salem Bible College, 4117 Northampton Drive, PO Box 777, Winston-Salem, NC 27102-0777, 336-744-0900.

WINSTON-SALEM STATE UNIVERSITY
Winston-Salem, NC

Tuition & fees (NC res): $2805	Average undergraduate aid package: $3392

ABOUT THE INSTITUTION State-supported, coed. Awards: bachelor's and master's degrees. 41 undergraduate majors. Total enrollment: 5,566. Undergraduates: 5,264. Freshmen: 1,083. Federal methodology is used as a basis for awarding need-based institutional aid.
UNDERGRADUATE EXPENSES for 2005–06 *Application fee:* $30. *Tuition, state resident:* full-time $1451. *Tuition, nonresident:* full-time $10,090. Full-time tuition and fees vary according to degree level. Part-time tuition and fees vary

according to course load and location. *College room and board:* $5298; *room only:* $3122. Room and board charges vary according to board plan and housing facility. *Payment plan:* Installment.
FRESHMAN FINANCIAL AID (Fall 2004) 761 applied for aid; of those 98% were deemed to have need. 94% of freshmen with need received aid. *Average percent of need met:* 71% (excluding resources awarded to replace EFC). *Average financial aid package:* $3606 (excluding resources awarded to replace EFC). 1% of all full-time freshmen had no need and received non-need-based gift aid.
UNDERGRADUATE FINANCIAL AID (Fall 2004) 3,859 applied for aid; of those 98% were deemed to have need. 99% of undergraduates with need received aid. *Average percent of need met:* 80% (excluding resources awarded to replace EFC). *Average financial aid package:* $3392 (excluding resources awarded to replace EFC). 2% of all full-time undergraduates had no need and received non-need-based gift aid.
GIFT AID (NEED-BASED) *Total amount:* $11,535,635 (80% federal, 20% state). *Receiving aid:* Freshmen: 72% (639); All full-time undergraduates: 92% (3,601). *Average award:* Freshmen: $2878; Undergraduates: $2762. **Scholarships, grants, and awards:** Federal Pell, FSEOG, state, private, college/university gift aid from institutional funds, United Negro College Fund.
GIFT AID (NON-NEED-BASED) *Total amount:* $2,230,577 (16% state, 40% institutional, 44% external sources). *Receiving aid:* Freshmen: 9% (81); Undergraduates: 5% (203). *Average Award:* Freshmen: $3089; Undergraduates: $3239. **Scholarships, grants, and awards by category:** Academic Interests/Achievement: 353 awards ($1,492,580 total): business, computer science, education, general academic interests/achievements, health fields, mathematics. Creative Arts/Performance: 54 awards ($92,004 total): music. Special Achievements/Activities: 17 awards ($2075 total): cheerleading/drum major. Special Characteristics: 41 awards ($25,100 total): adult students, first-generation college students. **Tuition waivers:** Full or partial for employees or children of employees, senior citizens. **ROTC:** Army, Air Force.
LOANS *Student loans:* $18,730,247 (58% need-based, 42% non-need-based). 83% of past graduating class borrowed through all loan programs. *Average indebtedness per student:* $10,200. *Average need-based loan:* Freshmen: $2499; Undergraduates: $3375. *Parent loans:* $2,328,307 (100% non-need-based). **Programs:** FFEL (Subsidized and Unsubsidized Stafford, PLUS), Perkins, state, college/university.
WORK-STUDY *Federal work-study:* Total amount: $548,447; jobs available. *State or other work-study/employment:* Total amount: $366,694 (100% non-need-based). Part-time jobs available.
ATHLETIC AWARDS *Total amount:* $455,325 (100% non-need-based).
APPLYING FOR FINANCIAL AID *Required financial aid form:* FAFSA. *Financial aid deadline:* 4/1 (priority: 3/1). *Notification date:* 5/15. Students must reply within 2 weeks of notification.
CONTACT Deborah Colbert, Director of Financial Aid Office, Winston-Salem State University, 601 Martin Luther King Jr. Drive, PO Box 19524, Winston-Salem, NC 27110-0003, 336-750-3280 or toll-free 800-257-4052. *Fax:* 336-750-3297.

WINTHROP UNIVERSITY
Rock Hill, SC

Tuition & fees (SC res): $8756   **Average undergraduate aid package:** $8522

ABOUT THE INSTITUTION State-supported, coed. Awards: bachelor's and master's degrees. 32 undergraduate majors. Total enrollment: 6,480. Undergraduates: 5,187. Freshmen: 1,017. Federal methodology is used as a basis for awarding need-based institutional aid.
UNDERGRADUATE EXPENSES for 2005–06 *Application fee:* $40. *Tuition, state resident:* full-time $8756; part-time $364 per semester hour. *Tuition, nonresident:* full-time $16,150; part-time $673 per semester hour. Full-time tuition and fees vary according to degree level. Part-time tuition and fees vary according to degree level. *College room and board:* $5352; *room only:* $3420. Room and board charges vary according to board plan and housing facility. *Payment plan:* Installment.
FRESHMAN FINANCIAL AID (Fall 2005, est.) 812 applied for aid; of those 74% were deemed to have need. 100% of freshmen with need received aid; of those 24% had need fully met. *Average percent of need met:* 75% (excluding resources awarded to replace EFC). *Average financial aid package:* $9675 (excluding resources awarded to replace EFC). 17% of all full-time freshmen had no need and received non-need-based gift aid.

UNDERGRADUATE FINANCIAL AID (Fall 2005, est.) 3,354 applied for aid; of those 81% were deemed to have need. 99% of undergraduates with need received aid; of those 22% had need fully met. *Average percent of need met:* 64% (excluding resources awarded to replace EFC). *Average financial aid package:* $8522 (excluding resources awarded to replace EFC). 11% of all full-time undergraduates had no need and received non-need-based gift aid.
GIFT AID (NEED-BASED) *Total amount:* $14,293,195 (30% federal, 48% state, 19% institutional, 3% external sources). *Receiving aid:* Freshmen: 59% (594); All full-time undergraduates: 48% (2,219). *Average award:* Freshmen: $7599; Undergraduates: $6350. **Scholarships, grants, and awards:** Federal Pell, FSEOG, state, private, college/university gift aid from institutional funds.
GIFT AID (NON-NEED-BASED) *Total amount:* $7,740,814 (51% state, 36% institutional, 13% external sources). *Receiving aid:* Freshmen: 10% (97); Undergraduates: 5% (233). *Average Award:* Freshmen: $3027; Undergraduates: $5409. **Scholarships, grants, and awards by category:** Academic Interests/Achievement: 572 awards ($2,290,903 total): general academic interests/achievements. Creative Arts/Performance: 136 awards ($129,400 total): art/fine arts, dance, music, performing arts, theater/drama. Special Characteristics: 6 awards ($4200 total): children of faculty/staff. **Tuition waivers:** Full or partial for employees or children of employees, senior citizens.
LOANS *Student loans:* $19,813,874 (46% need-based, 54% non-need-based). 63% of past graduating class borrowed through all loan programs. *Average indebtedness per student:* $18,793. *Average need-based loan:* Freshmen: $2769; Undergraduates: $3970. *Parent loans:* $2,938,610 (100% non-need-based). **Programs:** Federal Direct (Subsidized and Unsubsidized Stafford), FFEL (PLUS), Perkins.
WORK-STUDY *Federal work-study:* Total amount: $240,000; 260 jobs averaging $925. *State or other work-study/employment:* Total amount: $1,470,958 (100% non-need-based). Part-time jobs available (averaging $1000).
ATHLETIC AWARDS *Total amount:* $1,470,958 (40% need-based, 60% non-need-based).
APPLYING FOR FINANCIAL AID *Required financial aid form:* FAFSA. *Financial aid deadline (priority):* 3/1. *Notification date:* Continuous beginning 3/15. Students must reply within 4 weeks of notification.
CONTACT Ms. Geneva Drakeford, Assistant Director, Office of Financial Aid, Winthrop University, 119 Tillman Hall, Rock Hill, SC 29733, 803-323-2189 or toll-free 800-763-0230. *Fax:* 803-323-2557. *E-mail:* finaid@winthrop.edu.

WISCONSIN LUTHERAN COLLEGE
Milwaukee, WI

CONTACT Mrs. Linda Loeffel, Director of Financial Aid, Wisconsin Lutheran College, 8800 West Bluemound Road, Milwaukee, WI 53226-4699, 414-443-8842 or toll-free 888-WIS LUTH. *Fax:* 414-443-8514. *E-mail:* linda_loeffel@wlc.edu.

WITTENBERG UNIVERSITY
Springfield, OH

Tuition & fees: $29,280   **Average undergraduate aid package:** $21,098

ABOUT THE INSTITUTION Independent religious, coed. Awards: bachelor's and master's degrees. 38 undergraduate majors. Total enrollment: 2,093. Undergraduates: 2,078. Freshmen: 496. Federal methodology is used as a basis for awarding need-based institutional aid.
UNDERGRADUATE EXPENSES for 2006–07 *Application fee:* $40. *Comprehensive fee:* $36,778 includes full-time tuition ($29,080), mandatory fees ($200), and room and board ($7498). *College room only:* $3890. *Part-time tuition:* $969 per credit hour.
FRESHMAN FINANCIAL AID (Fall 2005, est.) 427 applied for aid; of those 84% were deemed to have need. 100% of freshmen with need received aid; of those 46% had need fully met. *Average percent of need met:* 92% (excluding resources awarded to replace EFC). *Average financial aid package:* $23,495 (excluding resources awarded to replace EFC). 29% of all full-time freshmen had no need and received non-need-based gift aid.
UNDERGRADUATE FINANCIAL AID (Fall 2005, est.) 1,235 applied for aid; of those 88% were deemed to have need. 100% of undergraduates with need received aid; of those 40% had need fully met. *Average percent of need met:* 87% (excluding resources awarded to replace EFC). *Average financial aid*

Wittenberg University

package: $21,098 (excluding resources awarded to replace EFC). 18% of all full-time undergraduates had no need and received non-need-based gift aid.
GIFT AID (NEED-BASED) *Total amount:* $23,642,916 (6% federal, 8% state, 83% institutional, 3% external sources). *Receiving aid:* Freshmen: 72% (355); All full-time undergraduates: 56% (1,082). *Average award:* Freshmen: $18,312; Undergraduates: $16,197. *Scholarships, grants, and awards:* Federal Pell, FSEOG, state, private, college/university gift aid from institutional funds.
GIFT AID (NON-NEED-BASED) *Total amount:* $6,205,384 (5% state, 93% institutional, 2% external sources). *Average Award:* Freshmen: $11,241; Undergraduates: $9776. *Scholarships, grants, and awards by category: Academic Interests/Achievement:* general academic interests/achievements. *Creative Arts/Performance:* art/fine arts, dance, music, theater/drama. *Special Achievements/Activities:* community service, general special achievements/activities, leadership. *Special Characteristics:* adult students, children and siblings of alumni, children of faculty/staff, ethnic background, international students, local/state students, members of minority groups, relatives of clergy, religious affiliation. *ROTC:* Army cooperative, Air Force cooperative.
LOANS *Student loans:* $9,398,005 (72% need-based, 28% non-need-based). 69% of past graduating class borrowed through all loan programs. *Average indebtedness per student:* $21,615. *Average need-based loan:* Freshmen: $3046; Undergraduates: $3465. *Parent loans:* $5,317,597 (87% need-based, 13% non-need-based). *Programs:* FFEL (Subsidized and Unsubsidized Stafford, PLUS), Perkins, college/university, alternative loans.
WORK-STUDY *Federal work-study:* Total amount: $904,952; 529 jobs averaging $1711. *State or other work-study/employment:* Total amount: $2,246,895 (39% need-based, 61% non-need-based). 865 part-time jobs averaging $2598.
APPLYING FOR FINANCIAL AID *Required financial aid form:* FAFSA. *Financial aid deadline (priority):* 3/15. *Notification date:* Continuous beginning 3/1. Students must reply by 5/1 or within 2 weeks of notification.
CONTACT Mr. J. Randy Green, Director of Financial Aid, Wittenberg University, PO Box 720, Springfield, OH 45501-0720, 937-327-7321 or toll-free 800-677-7558 Ext. 6314. *Fax:* 937-327-6379. *E-mail:* jgreen@wittenberg.edu.

WOFFORD COLLEGE
Spartanburg, SC

Tuition & fees: $24,130	Average undergraduate aid package: $22,401

ABOUT THE INSTITUTION Independent religious, coed. Awards: bachelor's degrees. 30 undergraduate majors. Total enrollment: 1,173. Undergraduates: 1,173. Freshmen: 321. Federal methodology is used as a basis for awarding need-based institutional aid.
UNDERGRADUATE EXPENSES for 2005–06 *Application fee:* $40. *Comprehensive fee:* $30,935 includes full-time tuition ($24,130) and room and board ($6805). *Part-time tuition:* $875 per hour. *Payment plan:* Installment.
FRESHMAN FINANCIAL AID (Fall 2005, est.) 224 applied for aid; of those 72% were deemed to have need. 100% of freshmen with need received aid; of those 54% had need fully met. *Average percent of need met:* 85% (excluding resources awarded to replace EFC). *Average financial aid package:* $21,456 (excluding resources awarded to replace EFC). 26% of all full-time freshmen had no need and received non-need-based gift aid.
UNDERGRADUATE FINANCIAL AID (Fall 2005, est.) 746 applied for aid; of those 80% were deemed to have need. 100% of undergraduates with need received aid; of those 56% had need fully met. *Average percent of need met:* 89% (excluding resources awarded to replace EFC). *Average financial aid package:* $22,401 (excluding resources awarded to replace EFC). 25% of all full-time undergraduates had no need and received non-need-based gift aid.
GIFT AID (NEED-BASED) *Total amount:* $8,625,799 (7% federal, 28% state, 62% institutional, 3% external sources). *Receiving aid:* Freshmen: 50% (162); All full-time undergraduates: 52% (599). *Average award:* Freshmen: $16,532; Undergraduates: $16,648. *Scholarships, grants, and awards:* Federal Pell, FSEOG, state, private, college/university gift aid from institutional funds.
GIFT AID (NON-NEED-BASED) *Total amount:* $5,710,013 (34% state, 60% institutional, 6% external sources). *Receiving aid:* Freshmen: 29% (93); Undergraduates: 29% (336). *Average Award:* Freshmen: $10,466; Undergraduates: $9884. *Scholarships, grants, and awards by category: Academic Interests/Achievement:* general academic interests/achievements. *Creative Arts/Performance:* music. *Special Achievements/Activities:* cheerleading/drum major, community service, general special achievements/activities, leadership, religious involvement. *Special Characteristics:* children of faculty/staff, general special characteristics, relatives of clergy. *Tuition waivers:* Full or partial for employees or children of employees. *ROTC:* Army.
LOANS *Student loans:* $2,422,491 (57% need-based, 43% non-need-based). 47% of past graduating class borrowed through all loan programs. *Average indebtedness per student:* $10,242. *Average need-based loan:* Freshmen: $2942; Undergraduates: $4391. *Parent loans:* $1,519,766 (20% need-based, 80% non-need-based). *Programs:* FFEL (Subsidized and Unsubsidized Stafford, PLUS), Perkins, state.
WORK-STUDY *Federal work-study:* Total amount: $283,559; jobs available. *State or other work-study/employment:* Part-time jobs available.
ATHLETIC AWARDS *Total amount:* $3,088,445 (41% need-based, 59% non-need-based).
APPLYING FOR FINANCIAL AID *Required financial aid form:* FAFSA. *Financial aid deadline (priority):* 3/15. *Notification date:* Continuous beginning 3/31. Students must reply by 5/1.
CONTACT Donna D. Hawkins, Director of Financial Aid, Wofford College, Campus PO Box 171, 429 North Church Street, Spartanburg, SC 29303-3663, 864-597-4160. *Fax:* 864-597-4149. *E-mail:* hawkinsdd@wofford.edu.

WOODBURY COLLEGE
Montpelier, VT

Tuition & fees: N/R	Average undergraduate aid package: $8436

ABOUT THE INSTITUTION Independent, coed. Awards: associate and bachelor's degrees. 4 undergraduate majors. Total enrollment: 138. Undergraduates: 138. Freshmen: 11. Federal methodology is used as a basis for awarding need-based institutional aid.
FRESHMAN FINANCIAL AID (Fall 2005, est.) 7 applied for aid; of those 100% were deemed to have need. 100% of freshmen with need received aid; of those 14% had need fully met. *Average percent of need met:* 51% (excluding resources awarded to replace EFC). *Average financial aid package:* $8580 (excluding resources awarded to replace EFC).
UNDERGRADUATE FINANCIAL AID (Fall 2005, est.) 81 applied for aid; of those 91% were deemed to have need. 100% of undergraduates with need received aid; of those 8% had need fully met. *Average percent of need met:* 52% (excluding resources awarded to replace EFC). *Average financial aid package:* $8436 (excluding resources awarded to replace EFC). 4% of all full-time undergraduates had no need and received non-need-based gift aid.
GIFT AID (NEED-BASED) *Total amount:* $457,334 (37% federal, 41% state, 19% institutional, 3% external sources). *Receiving aid:* Freshmen: 100% (7); All full-time undergraduates: 81% (66). *Average award:* Freshmen: $6157; Undergraduates: $5603. *Scholarships, grants, and awards:* Federal Pell, FSEOG, state, private, college/university gift aid from institutional funds.
GIFT AID (NON-NEED-BASED) *Total amount:* $6368 (100% institutional). *Receiving aid:* Undergraduates: 4% (3). *Average Award:* Undergraduates: $2897. *Tuition waivers:* Full or partial for employees or children of employees.
LOANS *Student loans:* $854,258 (82% need-based, 18% non-need-based). 80% of past graduating class borrowed through all loan programs. *Average indebtedness per student:* $21,879. *Average need-based loan:* Freshmen: $2423; Undergraduates: $3631. *Parent loans:* $10,397 (90% need-based, 10% non-need-based). *Programs:* Federal Direct (Subsidized and Unsubsidized Stafford, PLUS).
WORK-STUDY *Federal work-study:* Total amount: $2248; jobs available.
APPLYING FOR FINANCIAL AID *Required financial aid forms:* FAFSA, institution's own form, state aid form. *Financial aid deadline:* Continuous. *Notification date:* Continuous.
CONTACT Marcy Spaulding, Financial Aid Director, Woodbury College, 660 Elm Street, Montpelier, VT 05602, 800-639-6039 Ext. 245 or toll-free 800-639-6039 (in-state). *E-mail:* admissions@woodbury-college.edu.

WOODBURY UNIVERSITY
Burbank, CA

Tuition & fees: $23,474	Average undergraduate aid package: $16,383

ABOUT THE INSTITUTION Independent, coed. Awards: bachelor's and master's degrees. 17 undergraduate majors. Total enrollment: 1,436. Undergraduates: 1,267. Freshmen: 131. Federal methodology is used as a basis for awarding need-based institutional aid.
UNDERGRADUATE EXPENSES for 2006–07 *Application fee:* $35. *Comprehensive fee:* $31,672 includes full-time tuition ($23,234), mandatory fees ($240), and room and board ($8198). *College room only:* $5000. *Part-time tuition:* $758 per unit.
FRESHMAN FINANCIAL AID (Fall 2005, est.) 109 applied for aid; of those 94% were deemed to have need. 100% of freshmen with need received aid; of those 5% had need fully met. *Average percent of need met:* 61% (excluding resources awarded to replace EFC). *Average financial aid package:* $17,279 (excluding resources awarded to replace EFC). 15% of all full-time freshmen had no need and received non-need-based gift aid.
UNDERGRADUATE FINANCIAL AID (Fall 2005, est.) 874 applied for aid; of those 93% were deemed to have need. 100% of undergraduates with need received aid; of those 6% had need fully met. *Average percent of need met:* 58% (excluding resources awarded to replace EFC). *Average financial aid package:* $16,383 (excluding resources awarded to replace EFC). 14% of all full-time undergraduates had no need and received non-need-based gift aid.
GIFT AID (NEED-BASED) *Total amount:* $10,931,492 (18% federal, 32% state, 48% institutional, 2% external sources). *Receiving aid:* Freshmen: 40% (103); All full-time undergraduates: 70% (772). *Average award:* Freshmen: $14,953; Undergraduates: $12,862. *Scholarships, grants, and awards:* Federal Pell, FSEOG, state, private, college/university gift aid from institutional funds.
GIFT AID (NON-NEED-BASED) *Total amount:* $831,289 (1% state, 91% institutional, 8% external sources). *Receiving aid:* Freshmen: 2% (4); Undergraduates: 2% (17). *Average Award:* Freshmen: $8808; Undergraduates: $12,259. *Scholarships, grants, and awards by category:* Academic Interests/Achievement: 883 awards ($3,832,082 total): general academic interests/achievements. Creative Arts/Performance: applied art and design.
LOANS *Student loans:* $9,662,449 (86% need-based, 14% non-need-based). 91% of past graduating class borrowed through all loan programs. *Average indebtedness per student:* $20,134. *Average need-based loan:* Freshmen: $2753; Undergraduates: $4422. *Parent loans:* $3,511,514 (52% need-based, 48% non-need-based). *Programs:* FFEL (Subsidized and Unsubsidized Stafford, PLUS), Perkins, alternative loans.
WORK-STUDY *Federal work-study:* Total amount: $111,799; 100 jobs averaging $1500.
APPLYING FOR FINANCIAL AID *Required financial aid forms:* FAFSA, institution's own form. *Financial aid deadline:* Continuous. *Notification date:* Continuous beginning 3/15. Students must reply within 2 weeks of notification.
CONTACT Celeastia Williams, Director of Enrollment Services, Woodbury University, 7500 Glenoaks Boulevard, Burbank, CA 91510, 818-767-0888 Ext. 273 or toll-free 800-784-WOOD. Fax: 818-767-4816.

WORCESTER POLYTECHNIC INSTITUTE
Worcester, MA

| Tuition & fees: $33,270 | Average undergraduate aid package: $20,928 |

ABOUT THE INSTITUTION Independent, coed. Awards: bachelor's, master's, and doctoral degrees and post-bachelor's and post-master's certificates. 48 undergraduate majors. Total enrollment: 3,910. Undergraduates: 2,892. Freshmen: 733. Both federal and institutional methodology are used as a basis for awarding need-based institutional aid.
UNDERGRADUATE EXPENSES for 2006–07 *Application fee:* $60. *Comprehensive fee:* $43,110 includes full-time tuition ($32,850), mandatory fees ($420), and room and board ($9840). *College room only:* $5720. *Part-time tuition:* $2738 per unit.
FRESHMAN FINANCIAL AID (Fall 2004) 695 applied for aid; of those 80% were deemed to have need. 99% of freshmen with need received aid; of those 42% had need fully met. *Average percent of need met:* 76% (excluding resources awarded to replace EFC). *Average financial aid package:* $20,979 (excluding resources awarded to replace EFC). 15% of all full-time freshmen had no need and received non-need-based gift aid.
UNDERGRADUATE FINANCIAL AID (Fall 2004) 2,187 applied for aid; of those 91% were deemed to have need. 99% of undergraduates with need received aid; of those 30% had need fully met. *Average percent of need met:* 72% (excluding resources awarded to replace EFC). *Average financial aid package:* $20,928 (excluding resources awarded to replace EFC). 11% of all full-time undergraduates had no need and received non-need-based gift aid.
GIFT AID (NEED-BASED) *Total amount:* $34,177,684 (5% federal, 3% state, 84% institutional, 8% external sources). *Receiving aid:* Freshmen: 73% (543); All full-time undergraduates: 71% (1,888). *Average award:* Freshmen: $17,390; Undergraduates: $15,925. *Scholarships, grants, and awards:* Federal Pell, FSEOG, state, private, college/university gift aid from institutional funds.
GIFT AID (NON-NEED-BASED) *Total amount:* $4,966,569 (78% institutional, 22% external sources). *Receiving aid:* Freshmen: 25% (185); Undergraduates: 15% (393). *Average Award:* Freshmen: $18,461; Undergraduates: $19,318. *Scholarships, grants, and awards by category:* Academic Interests/Achievement: 642 awards ($7,965,287 total): general academic interests/achievements, premedicine. *Special Characteristics:* 28 awards ($119,460 total): children of workers in trades. *ROTC:* Army, Naval cooperative, Air Force.
LOANS *Student loans:* $18,418,791 (60% need-based, 40% non-need-based). 94% of past graduating class borrowed through all loan programs. *Average indebtedness per student:* $27,384. *Average need-based loan:* Freshmen: $4558; Undergraduates: $6089. *Parent loans:* $5,659,931 (100% non-need-based). *Programs:* FFEL (Subsidized and Unsubsidized Stafford, PLUS), Perkins, state, college/university.
WORK-STUDY *Federal work-study:* Total amount: $459,266; 555 jobs averaging $1103. *State or other work-study/employment:* Part-time jobs available.
APPLYING FOR FINANCIAL AID *Required financial aid forms:* FAFSA, CSS Financial Aid PROFILE, noncustodial (divorced/separated) parent's statement, federal income tax form(s) and W-2 statements. *Financial aid deadline:* 2/1 (priority: 2/1). *Notification date:* 4/1. Students must reply by 5/1.
CONTACT Office of Financial Aid, Worcester Polytechnic Institute, 100 Institute Road, Worcester, MA 01609-2280, 508-831-5469. Fax: 508-831-5039. E-mail: finaid@wpi.edu.

WORCESTER STATE COLLEGE
Worcester, MA

| Tuition & fees (MA res): $5079 | Average undergraduate aid package: $6868 |

ABOUT THE INSTITUTION State-supported, coed. Awards: bachelor's and master's degrees and post-bachelor's certificates. 23 undergraduate majors. Total enrollment: 5,471. Undergraduates: 4,598. Freshmen: 648. Federal methodology is used as a basis for awarding need-based institutional aid.
UNDERGRADUATE EXPENSES for 2005–06 *Application fee:* $20. *Tuition, state resident:* full-time $970; part-time $40.42 per credit. *Tuition, nonresident:* full-time $7050; part-time $293.75 per credit. *Required fees:* full-time $4109; $167.04 per credit. Full-time tuition and fees vary according to class time, course load, and reciprocity agreements. Part-time tuition and fees vary according to class time, course load, and reciprocity agreements. *College room and board:* $7420; *room only:* $4730. Room and board charges vary according to board plan and housing facility. *Payment plan:* Installment.
FRESHMAN FINANCIAL AID (Fall 2004) 477 applied for aid; of those 66% were deemed to have need. 96% of freshmen with need received aid; of those 45% had need fully met. *Average percent of need met:* 75% (excluding resources awarded to replace EFC). *Average financial aid package:* $5494 (excluding resources awarded to replace EFC). 3% of all full-time freshmen had no need and received non-need-based gift aid.
UNDERGRADUATE FINANCIAL AID (Fall 2004) 1,920 applied for aid; of those 72% were deemed to have need. 95% of undergraduates with need received aid; of those 48% had need fully met. *Average percent of need met:* 79% (excluding resources awarded to replace EFC). *Average financial aid package:* $6868 (excluding resources awarded to replace EFC). 1% of all full-time undergraduates had no need and received non-need-based gift aid.
GIFT AID (NEED-BASED) *Total amount:* $3,746,794 (62% federal, 38% state). *Receiving aid:* Freshmen: 42% (259); All full-time undergraduates: 34% (1,052). *Average award:* Freshmen: $1717; Undergraduates: $1836. *Scholarships, grants, and awards:* Federal Pell, FSEOG, state, private, college/university gift aid from institutional funds.
GIFT AID (NON-NEED-BASED) *Total amount:* $1,426,093 (11% federal, 7% state, 54% institutional, 28% external sources). *Receiving aid:* Freshmen: 12% (75); Undergraduates: 7% (222). *Average Award:* Freshmen: $2199; Undergraduates: $1541. *Scholarships, grants, and awards by category:* Academic Interests/Achievement: biological sciences, business, education, English, foreign languages, health fields. Creative Arts/Performance: art/fine arts. Special Achievements/

Worcester State College

Activities: community service, general special achievements/activities. *Special Characteristics:* children and siblings of alumni, children of faculty/staff, children with a deceased or disabled parent, general special characteristics, handicapped students, local/state students, veterans. *Tuition waivers:* Full or partial for employees or children of employees, senior citizens. *ROTC:* Army cooperative, Naval cooperative, Air Force cooperative.
LOANS *Student loans:* $3,366,260 (42% need-based, 58% non-need-based). *Average indebtedness per student:* $11,843. *Average need-based loan:* Freshmen: $1022; Undergraduates: $1532. *Parent loans:* $589,747 (100% non-need-based). *Programs:* FFEL (Subsidized and Unsubsidized Stafford, PLUS), Perkins, Massachusetts No-Interest Loans (NIL).
WORK-STUDY *Federal work-study:* Total amount: $240,160; jobs available.
APPLYING FOR FINANCIAL AID *Required financial aid forms:* FAFSA, institution's own form. *Financial aid deadline (priority):* 3/1. *Notification date:* Continuous. Students must reply within 2 weeks of notification.
CONTACT Jayne McGinn, Director of Financial Aid, Worcester State College, 486 Chandler Street, Worcester, MA 01602, 508-929-8058 or toll-free 866-WSC-CALL. *Fax:* 508-929-8194. *E-mail:* jmcginn@worcester.edu.

WRIGHT STATE UNIVERSITY
Dayton, OH

CONTACT Mr. David R. Darr, Director of Financial Aid, Wright State University, Colonel Glenn Highway, Dayton, OH 45435, 937-873-5721 or toll-free 800-247-1770.

XAVIER UNIVERSITY
Cincinnati, OH

Tuition & fees: $22,430   **Average undergraduate aid package: $14,510**

ABOUT THE INSTITUTION Independent Roman Catholic, coed. Awards: associate, bachelor's, master's, and doctoral degrees and post-bachelor's and post-master's certificates. 56 undergraduate majors. Total enrollment: 6,665. Undergraduates: 3,879. Freshmen: 765. Federal methodology is used as a basis for awarding need-based institutional aid.
UNDERGRADUATE EXPENSES for 2005–06 *Application fee:* $35. *Comprehensive fee:* $31,070 includes full-time tuition ($21,850), mandatory fees ($580), and room and board ($8640). *College room only:* $4860. Full-time tuition and fees vary according to program and student level. Room and board charges vary according to board plan and housing facility. *Part-time tuition:* $425 per credit hour. Part-time tuition and fees vary according to course load. *Payment plans:* Installment, deferred payment.
FRESHMAN FINANCIAL AID (Fall 2005, est.) 612 applied for aid; of those 72% were deemed to have need. 100% of freshmen with need received aid; of those 29% had need fully met. *Average percent of need met:* 79% (excluding resources awarded to replace EFC). *Average financial aid package:* $15,226 (excluding resources awarded to replace EFC). 30% of all full-time freshmen had no need and received non-need-based gift aid.
UNDERGRADUATE FINANCIAL AID (Fall 2005, est.) 2,272 applied for aid; of those 79% were deemed to have need. 100% of undergraduates with need received aid; of those 26% had need fully met. *Average percent of need met:* 75% (excluding resources awarded to replace EFC). *Average financial aid package:* $14,510 (excluding resources awarded to replace EFC). 29% of all full-time undergraduates had no need and received non-need-based gift aid.
GIFT AID (NEED-BASED) *Total amount:* $17,387,051 (9% federal, 9% state, 76% institutional, 6% external sources). *Receiving aid:* Freshmen: 56% (427); All full-time undergraduates: 52% (1,722). *Average award:* Freshmen: $10,809; Undergraduates: $9872. *Scholarships, grants, and awards:* Federal Pell, FSEOG, state, private, college/university gift aid from institutional funds.
GIFT AID (NON-NEED-BASED) *Total amount:* $11,167,129 (7% state, 82% institutional, 11% external sources). *Receiving aid:* Freshmen: 12% (92); Undergraduates: 9% (295). *Average Award:* Freshmen: $9385; Undergraduates: $8158. *Scholarships, grants, and awards by category: Academic Interests/Achievement:* 2,309 awards ($15,306,870 total): foreign languages, general academic interests/achievements, mathematics, military science, physical sciences, social sciences. *Creative Arts/Performance:* 130 awards ($427,200 total): art/fine arts, music, performing arts, theater/drama. *Special Characteristics:* 298 awards ($1,100,540 total): international students, members of minority groups, siblings of current students. *Tuition waivers:* Full or partial for employees or children of employees, senior citizens. *ROTC:* Army, Air Force cooperative.
LOANS *Student loans:* $15,115,799 (67% need-based, 33% non-need-based). 58% of past graduating class borrowed through all loan programs. *Average indebtedness per student:* $19,300. *Average need-based loan:* Freshmen: $3447; Undergraduates: $4426. *Parent loans:* $6,209,035 (30% need-based, 70% non-need-based). *Programs:* FFEL (Subsidized and Unsubsidized Stafford, PLUS), Perkins.
WORK-STUDY *Federal work-study:* Total amount: $1,208,019; 616 jobs averaging $1961. *State or other work-study/employment:* Total amount: $157,338 (8% need-based, 92% non-need-based). 93 part-time jobs averaging $1692.
ATHLETIC AWARDS *Total amount:* $2,854,315 (34% need-based, 66% non-need-based).
APPLYING FOR FINANCIAL AID *Required financial aid form:* FAFSA. *Financial aid deadline (priority):* 2/15. *Notification date:* Continuous beginning 2/15. Students must reply by 5/1.
CONTACT Office of Financial Aid, Xavier University, 3800 Victory Parkway, Cincinnati, OH 45207-5411, 513-745-3142 or toll-free 800-344-4698. *Fax:* 513-745-2806.

XAVIER UNIVERSITY OF LOUISIANA
New Orleans, LA

Tuition & fees: $13,100   **Average undergraduate aid package: $4551**

ABOUT THE INSTITUTION Independent Roman Catholic, coed. Awards: bachelor's, master's, and first professional degrees. 54 undergraduate majors. Total enrollment: 4,121. Undergraduates: 3,290. Freshmen: 1,001. Federal methodology is used as a basis for awarding need-based institutional aid.
UNDERGRADUATE EXPENSES for 2005–06 *Application fee:* $25. *Comprehensive fee:* $20,200 includes full-time tuition ($12,100), mandatory fees ($1000), and room and board ($7100). Room and board charges vary according to location. *Part-time tuition:* $500 per credit hour. *Payment plan:* Installment.
FRESHMAN FINANCIAL AID (Fall 2004) 947 applied for aid; of those 84% were deemed to have need. 100% of freshmen with need received aid; of those 1% had need fully met. *Average percent of need met:* 74% (excluding resources awarded to replace EFC). *Average financial aid package:* $3921 (excluding resources awarded to replace EFC). 7% of all full-time freshmen had no need and received non-need-based gift aid.
UNDERGRADUATE FINANCIAL AID (Fall 2004) 3,128 applied for aid; of those 87% were deemed to have need. 99% of undergraduates with need received aid; of those .4% had need fully met. *Average percent of need met:* 77% (excluding resources awarded to replace EFC). *Average financial aid package:* $4551 (excluding resources awarded to replace EFC). 3% of all full-time undergraduates had no need and received non-need-based gift aid.
GIFT AID (NEED-BASED) *Total amount:* $7,675,345 (88% federal, 12% state). *Scholarships, grants, and awards:* Federal Pell, FSEOG, state, private, college/university gift aid from institutional funds, United Negro College Fund.
GIFT AID (NON-NEED-BASED) *Total amount:* $8,652,494 (96% institutional, 4% external sources). *Receiving aid:* Freshmen: 35% (345); Undergraduates: 23% (806). *Average Award:* Freshmen: $3215; Undergraduates: $3152. *Scholarships, grants, and awards by category: Academic Interests/Achievement:* biological sciences, business, computer science, education, engineering/technologies, foreign languages, general academic interests/achievements, humanities, mathematics, physical sciences, premedicine, social sciences. *Creative Arts/Performance:* art/fine arts, music, performing arts. *Special Achievements/Activities:* religious involvement. *Special Characteristics:* children of faculty/staff. *Tuition waivers:* Full or partial for employees or children of employees. *ROTC:* Army cooperative, Naval cooperative, Air Force cooperative.
LOANS *Student loans:* $23,217,790 (56% need-based, 44% non-need-based). 74% of past graduating class borrowed through all loan programs. *Average indebtedness per student:* $20,083. *Average need-based loan:* Freshmen: $2340; Undergraduates: $5241. *Parent loans:* $9,854,660 (100% non-need-based). *Programs:* Federal Direct (Subsidized and Unsubsidized Stafford, PLUS), FFEL (Subsidized and Unsubsidized Stafford, PLUS), Perkins.
WORK-STUDY *Federal work-study:* Total amount: $289,318; jobs available.
ATHLETIC AWARDS *Total amount:* $943,439 (100% non-need-based).
APPLYING FOR FINANCIAL AID *Required financial aid form:* FAFSA. *Financial aid deadline (priority):* 1/1. *Notification date:* Continuous beginning 4/1.

CONTACT Mrs. Mildred Higgins, Financial Aid Director, Xavier University of Louisiana, One Drexel Drive, New Orleans, LA 70125-1098, 504-520-7517 or toll-free 877-XAVIERU.

YALE UNIVERSITY
New Haven, CT

Tuition & fees: $31,460   Average undergraduate aid package: $30,129

ABOUT THE INSTITUTION Independent, coed. Awards: bachelor's, master's, doctoral, and first professional degrees and post-master's certificates. 67 undergraduate majors. Total enrollment: 11,483. Undergraduates: 5,409. Freshmen: 1,321. Both federal and institutional methodology are used as a basis for awarding need-based institutional aid.

UNDERGRADUATE EXPENSES for 2005–06 *Application fee:* $75. *Comprehensive fee:* $41,000 includes full-time tuition ($31,460) and room and board ($9540).

FRESHMAN FINANCIAL AID (Fall 2005, est.) 803 applied for aid; of those 74% were deemed to have need. 100% of freshmen with need received aid; of those 100% had need fully met. *Average percent of need met:* 100% (excluding resources awarded to replace EFC). *Average financial aid package:* $30,125 (excluding resources awarded to replace EFC).

UNDERGRADUATE FINANCIAL AID (Fall 2005, est.) 2,486 applied for aid; of those 91% were deemed to have need. 100% of undergraduates with need received aid; of those 100% had need fully met. *Average percent of need met:* 100% (excluding resources awarded to replace EFC). *Average financial aid package:* $30,129 (excluding resources awarded to replace EFC).

GIFT AID (NEED-BASED) *Total amount:* $58,272,394 (6% federal, 1% state, 84% institutional, 9% external sources). *Receiving aid:* Freshmen: 45% (589); All full-time undergraduates: 42% (2,232). *Average award:* Freshmen: $27,902; Undergraduates: $27,932. *Scholarships, grants, and awards:* Federal Pell, FSEOG, state, private, college/university gift aid from institutional funds, United Negro College Fund, Alumni Club awards.

GIFT AID (NON-NEED-BASED) *Total amount:* $64,264,264 (5% federal, 1% state, 87% institutional, 7% external sources). *ROTC:* Army cooperative, Air Force cooperative.

LOANS *Student loans:* $11,615,130 (52% need-based, 48% non-need-based). 40% of past graduating class borrowed through all loan programs. *Average indebtedness per student:* $14,306. *Average need-based loan:* Freshmen: $1530; Undergraduates: $1994. *Parent loans:* $23,075,291 (48% need-based, 52% non-need-based). *Programs:* FFEL (Subsidized and Unsubsidized Stafford, PLUS), Perkins, state, college/university.

WORK-STUDY *Federal work-study:* Total amount: $2,633,720; 991 jobs averaging $2042. *State or other work-study/employment:* Total amount: $3,157,815 (40% need-based, 60% non-need-based). 612 part-time jobs averaging $2663.

APPLYING FOR FINANCIAL AID *Required financial aid forms:* FAFSA, CSS Financial Aid PROFILE, noncustodial (divorced/separated) parent's statement, business/farm supplement. *Financial aid deadline:* 3/1 (priority: 3/1). *Notification date:* 4/1. Students must reply by 5/1.

CONTACT Mr. Caesar Storlazzi, University Director of Student Financial Services and Chief Financial Aid Officer, Yale University, PO Box 208288, New Haven, CT 06520-8288, 203-432-0371. *Fax:* 203-432-0359. *E-mail:* caesar.storlazzi@yale.edu.

YESHIVA AND KOLEL BAIS MEDRASH ELYON
Monsey, NY

CONTACT Financial Aid Office, Yeshiva and Kolel Bais Medrash Elyon, 73 Main Street, Monsey, NY 10952, 845-356-7064.

YESHIVA AND KOLLEL HARBOTZAS TORAH
Brooklyn, NY

CONTACT Financial Aid Office, Yeshiva And Kollel Harbotzas Torah, 1049 East 15th Street, Brooklyn, NY 11230, 718-692-0208.

YESHIVA BETH MOSHE
Scranton, PA

CONTACT Financial Aid Office, Yeshiva Beth Moshe, 930 Hickory Street, Scranton, PA 18505-2124, 717-346-1747.

YESHIVA COLLEGE OF THE NATION'S CAPITAL
Silver Spring, MD

CONTACT Financial Aid Office, Yeshiva College of the Nation's Capital, 1216 Arcola Avenue, Silver Spring, MD 20902, 301-593-2534.

YESHIVA DERECH CHAIM
Brooklyn, NY

CONTACT Financial Aid Office, Yeshiva Derech Chaim, 1573 39th Street, Brooklyn, NY 11218, 718-438-5426.

YESHIVA D'MONSEY RABBINICAL COLLEGE
Monsey, NY

CONTACT Financial Aid Office, Yeshiva D'Monsey Rabbinical College, 2 Roman Boulevard, Monsey, NY 10952, 914-352-5852.

YESHIVA GEDDOLAH OF GREATER DETROIT RABBINICAL COLLEGE
Oak Park, MI

CONTACT Rabbi P. Rushnawitz, Executive Administrator, Yeshiva Geddolah of Greater Detroit Rabbinical College, 24600 Greenfield Road, Oak Park, MI 48237-1544, 810-968-3360. *Fax:* 810-968-8613.

YESHIVA GEDOLAH IMREI YOSEF D'SPINKA
Brooklyn, NY

CONTACT Financial Aid Office, Yeshiva Gedolah Imrei Yosef D'Spinka, 1466 56th Street, Brooklyn, NY 11219, 718-851-8721.

YESHIVA GEDOLAH RABBINICAL COLLEGE
Miami Beach, FL

CONTACT Financial Aid Office, Yeshiva Gedolah Rabbinical College, 1140 Alton Road, Miami Beach, FL 33139, 305-673-5664.

YESHIVA KARLIN STOLIN RABBINICAL INSTITUTE
Brooklyn, NY

CONTACT Mr. Daniel Ross, Financial Aid Administrator, Yeshiva Karlin Stolin Rabbinical Institute, 1818 Fifty-fourth Street, Brooklyn, NY 11204, 718-232-7800 Ext. 116. *Fax:* 718-331-4833.

YESHIVA OF NITRA RABBINICAL COLLEGE
Mount Kisco, NY

CONTACT Mr. Yosef Rosen, Financial Aid Administrator, Yeshiva of Nitra Rabbinical College, 194 Division Avenue, Mount Kisco, NY 10549, 718-384-5460. *Fax:* 718-387-9400.

YESHIVA OF THE TELSHE ALUMNI
Riverdale, NY

CONTACT Financial Aid Office, Yeshiva of the Telshe Alumni, 4904 Independence Avenue, Riverdale, NY 10471, 718-601-3523.

YESHIVA OHR ELCHONON CHABAD/WEST COAST TALMUDICAL SEMINARY
Los Angeles, CA

CONTACT Ms. Hendy Tauber, Director of Financial Aid, Yeshiva Ohr Elchonon Chabad/West Coast Talmudical Seminary, 7215 Waring Avenue, Los Angeles, CA 90046-7660, 213-937-3763. *Fax:* 213-937-9456.

YESHIVA SHAAREI TORAH OF ROCKLAND
Suffern, NY

CONTACT Financial Aid Office, Yeshiva Shaarei Torah of Rockland, 91 West Carlton Road, Suffern, NY 10901, 845-352-3431.

YESHIVA SHAAR HATORAH TALMUDIC RESEARCH INSTITUTE
Kew Gardens, NY

CONTACT Mr. Yoel Yankelewitz, Executive Director, Financial Aid, Yeshiva Shaar Hatorah Talmudic Research Institute, 117-06 84th Avenue, Kew Gardens, NY 11418-1469, 718-846-1940.

YESHIVAS NOVOMINSK
Brooklyn, NY

CONTACT Financial Aid Office, Yeshivas Novominsk, 1569 47th Street, Brooklyn, NY 11219, 718-438-2727.

YESHIVATH VIZNITZ
Monsey, NY

CONTACT Financial Aid Office, Yeshivath Viznitz, Phyllis Terrace, PO Box 446, Monsey, NY 10952, 914-356-1010.

YESHIVATH ZICHRON MOSHE
South Fallsburg, NY

CONTACT Ms. Miryom R. Miller, Director of Financial Aid, Yeshivath Zichron Moshe, Laurel Park Road, South Fallsburg, NY 12779, 914-434-5240. *Fax:* 914-434-1009. *E-mail:* lehus@aol.com.

YESHIVAT MIKDASH MELECH
Brooklyn, NY

CONTACT Financial Aid Office, Yeshivat Mikdash Melech, 1326 Ocean Parkway, Brooklyn, NY 11230-5601, 718-339-1090.

YESHIVA TORAS CHAIM TALMUDICAL SEMINARY
Denver, CO

CONTACT Office of Financial Aid, Yeshiva Toras Chaim Talmudical Seminary, 1400 Quitman Street, Denver, CO 80204-1415, 303-629-8200.

YESHIVA UNIVERSITY
New York, NY

CONTACT Jean Belmont, Director of Student Finances, Yeshiva University, 500 West 185th Street, Room 121, New York, NY 10033-3201, 212-960-5269. *Fax:* 212-960-0037. *E-mail:* jbelmont@ymail.yu.edu.

YORK COLLEGE
York, NE

ABOUT THE INSTITUTION Independent religious, coed. Awards: associate and bachelor's degrees. 38 undergraduate majors. Total enrollment: 450. Undergraduates: 450. Freshmen: 119.

GIFT AID (NEED-BASED) *Scholarships, grants, and awards:* Federal Pell, FSEOG, state, private, college/university gift aid from institutional funds.
GIFT AID (NON-NEED-BASED) *Scholarships, grants, and awards by category: Academic Interests/Achievement:* biological sciences, business, communication, computer science, education, English, general academic interests/achievements, mathematics, premedicine, religion/biblical studies. *Creative Arts/Performance:* music, theater/drama. *Special Achievements/Activities:* leadership. *Special Characteristics:* children and siblings of alumni, children of faculty/staff, previous college experience, siblings of current students.
LOANS *Programs:* FFEL (Subsidized and Unsubsidized Stafford, PLUS), Perkins, alternative loans.
WORK-STUDY *Federal work-study:* Total amount: $78,774; 160 jobs averaging $820. *State or other work-study/employment:* Total amount: $44,228 (100% non-need-based).
APPLYING FOR FINANCIAL AID *Required financial aid form:* FAFSA.
CONTACT Deb Lowry, Director of Financial Aid, York College, 1125 East 8th Street, York, NE 68467, 402-363-5624 or toll-free 800-950-9675. *Fax:* 402-363-5623.

YORK COLLEGE OF PENNSYLVANIA
York, PA

Tuition & fees: $10,050 **Average undergraduate aid package: $7015**

ABOUT THE INSTITUTION Independent, coed. Awards: associate, bachelor's, and master's degrees. 59 undergraduate majors. Total enrollment: 5,316. Undergraduates: 5,170. Freshmen: 1,098. Federal methodology is used as a basis for awarding need-based institutional aid.
UNDERGRADUATE EXPENSES for 2005–06 *Application fee:* $30. *Comprehensive fee:* $16,550 includes full-time tuition ($9350), mandatory fees ($700), and room and board ($6500). *College room only:* $3625. Full-time tuition and fees vary according to course load and program. Room and board charges vary according to housing facility. *Part-time tuition:* $285 per credit hour. Part-time tuition and fees vary according to course load and program. *Payment plans:* Tuition prepayment, installment.
FRESHMAN FINANCIAL AID (Fall 2005, est.) 933 applied for aid; of those 60% were deemed to have need. 99% of freshmen with need received aid; of those 20% had need fully met. *Average percent of need met:* 71% (excluding resources awarded to replace EFC). *Average financial aid package:* $6708 (excluding resources awarded to replace EFC). 14% of all full-time freshmen had no need and received non-need-based gift aid.
UNDERGRADUATE FINANCIAL AID (Fall 2005, est.) 3,418 applied for aid; of those 66% were deemed to have need. 99% of undergraduates with need received aid; of those 25% had need fully met. *Average percent of need met:* 71% (excluding resources awarded to replace EFC). *Average financial aid package:* $7015 (excluding resources awarded to replace EFC). 9% of all full-time undergraduates had no need and received non-need-based gift aid.
GIFT AID (NEED-BASED) *Total amount:* $8,480,414 (25% federal, 34% state, 36% institutional, 5% external sources). *Receiving aid:* Freshmen: 38% (407); All full-time undergraduates: 35% (1,580). *Average award:* Freshmen: $4225; Undergraduates: $4138. *Scholarships, grants, and awards:* Federal Pell, FSEOG, state, private, college/university gift aid from institutional funds.
GIFT AID (NON-NEED-BASED) *Total amount:* $1,242,902 (2% state, 86% institutional, 12% external sources). *Receiving aid:* Freshmen: 17% (179); Undergraduates: 11% (492). *Average Award:* Freshmen: $3341; Undergraduates: $3090. *Scholarships, grants, and awards by category: Academic Interests/Achievement:* 565 awards ($1,837,002 total): general academic interests/achievements. *Creative Arts/Performance:* 21 awards ($16,268 total): music. *Special Achievements/Activities:* 13 awards ($38,963 total): community service, memberships. *Special Characteristics:* 33 awards ($49,794 total): children and siblings of alumni, children of union members/company employees, international students, members of minority groups. *Tuition waivers:* Full or partial for employees or children of employees. *ROTC:* Army cooperative.
LOANS *Student loans:* $19,831,233 (38% need-based, 62% non-need-based). 68% of past graduating class borrowed through all loan programs. *Average indebtedness per student:* $18,198. *Average need-based loan:* Freshmen: $2512; Undergraduates: $3569. *Parent loans:* $4,123,667 (56% need-based, 44% non-need-based). *Programs:* Federal Direct (Subsidized and Unsubsidized Stafford, PLUS), FFEL (Subsidized and Unsubsidized Stafford, PLUS), Perkins, Federal Nursing, college/university.

WORK-STUDY *Federal work-study:* Total amount: $325,863; 251 jobs averaging $1313. *State or other work-study/employment:* Total amount: $65,200 (21% need-based, 79% non-need-based). 55 part-time jobs averaging $1149.
APPLYING FOR FINANCIAL AID *Required financial aid form:* FAFSA. *Financial aid deadline (priority):* 3/1. *Notification date:* Continuous beginning 3/1. Students must reply within 4 weeks of notification.
CONTACT Calvin Williams, Director of Financial Aid, York College of Pennsylvania, Country Club Road, York, PA 17405-7199, 717-849-1682 or toll-free 800-455-8018. *Fax:* 717-849-1607. *E-mail:* financialaid@ycp.edu.

YORK COLLEGE OF THE CITY UNIVERSITY OF NEW YORK
Jamaica, NY

Tuition & fees (NY res): $4000   **Average undergraduate aid package: $3482**

ABOUT THE INSTITUTION State and locally supported, coed. Awards: bachelor's degrees. 36 undergraduate majors. Total enrollment: 5,900. Undergraduates: 5,900. Freshmen: 781. Federal methodology is used as a basis for awarding need-based institutional aid.
UNDERGRADUATE EXPENSES for 2006–07 *Application fee:* $65. *Tuition, state resident:* full-time $4000. *Tuition, nonresident:* full-time $8640.
FRESHMAN FINANCIAL AID (Fall 2005, est.) 619 applied for aid; of those 89% were deemed to have need. 97% of freshmen with need received aid; of those .2% had need fully met. *Average percent of need met:* 32% (excluding resources awarded to replace EFC). *Average financial aid package:* $3313 (excluding resources awarded to replace EFC).
UNDERGRADUATE FINANCIAL AID (Fall 2005, est.) 3,030 applied for aid; of those 92% were deemed to have need. 96% of undergraduates with need received aid; of those 3% had need fully met. *Average percent of need met:* 30% (excluding resources awarded to replace EFC). *Average financial aid package:* $3482 (excluding resources awarded to replace EFC).
GIFT AID (NEED-BASED) *Total amount:* $8,730,568 (51% federal, 48% state, 1% institutional). *Receiving aid:* Freshmen: 71% (533); All full-time undergraduates: 67% (2,605). *Average award:* Freshmen: $3017; Undergraduates: $2976. *Scholarships, grants, and awards:* Federal Pell, FSEOG, state, private.
GIFT AID (NON-NEED-BASED) *Receiving aid:* Freshmen: 10% (74); Undergraduates: 2% (93). *ROTC:* Army cooperative, Air Force cooperative.
LOANS *Student loans:* $1,996,082 (100% need-based). *Average need-based loan:* Freshmen: $1791; Undergraduates: $3623. *Programs:* Federal Direct (Subsidized and Unsubsidized Stafford, PLUS), Perkins, college/university.
WORK-STUDY *Federal work-study:* Total amount: $627,550; jobs available.
APPLYING FOR FINANCIAL AID *Required financial aid forms:* FAFSA, state aid form. *Financial aid deadline:* Continuous. *Notification date:* Continuous beginning 3/1.
CONTACT Ms. Cathy Tsiapanos, Director of Student Financial Services, York College of the City University of New York, 94-20 Guy R. Brewer Boulevard, Jamaica, NY 11451-0001, 718-262-2238. *E-mail:* ctsia@york.cuny.edu.

YOUNGSTOWN STATE UNIVERSITY
Youngstown, OH

Tuition & fees (OH res): $6333   **Average undergraduate aid package: N/A**

ABOUT THE INSTITUTION State-supported, coed. Awards: associate, bachelor's, master's, and doctoral degrees and post-bachelor's certificates. 121 undergraduate majors. Total enrollment: 12,809. Undergraduates: 11,700. Freshmen: 2,154. Federal methodology is used as a basis for awarding need-based institutional aid.
UNDERGRADUATE EXPENSES for 2005–06 *Application fee:* $30. *Tuition, state resident:* full-time $6104; part-time $254.33 per credit. *Tuition, nonresident:* full-time $11,312; part-time $471.33 per credit. *Required fees:* full-time $229; $9.54 per credit. Full-time tuition and fees vary according to course load. Part-time tuition and fees vary according to course load. *College room and board:* $6280. Room and board charges vary according to board plan and housing facility. *Payment plan:* Installment.
GIFT AID (NEED-BASED) *Total amount:* $18,347,284 (73% federal, 21% state, 6% institutional). *Scholarships, grants, and awards:* Federal Pell, FSEOG, state, private, college/university gift aid from institutional funds.
GIFT AID (NON-NEED-BASED) *Total amount:* $10,355,021 (2% federal, 23% state, 45% institutional, 30% external sources). *Scholarships, grants, and awards by category: Academic Interests/Achievement:* business, computer science, education, engineering/technologies, English, general academic interests/achievements, health fields, humanities, military science. *Creative Arts/Performance:* music, theater/drama. *Special Achievements/Activities:* cheerleading/drum major, leadership. *Special Characteristics:* adult students, children and siblings of alumni, children of faculty/staff, children of union members/company employees, children of workers in trades, children with a deceased or disabled parent, handicapped students, members of minority groups, spouses of deceased or disabled public servants, veterans, veterans' children. *Tuition waivers:* Full or partial for employees or children of employees, senior citizens. *ROTC:* Army, Air Force cooperative.
LOANS *Student loans:* $48,231,270 (92% need-based, 8% non-need-based). *Parent loans:* $4,891,522 (100% non-need-based). *Programs:* FFEL (Subsidized and Unsubsidized Stafford, PLUS), Perkins, state, Charles E. Schell Foundation Loans.
WORK-STUDY *Federal work-study:* Total amount: $657,335; 322 jobs averaging $2142. *State or other work-study/employment:* Part-time jobs available.
ATHLETIC AWARDS *Total amount:* $2,547,150 (100% non-need-based).
APPLYING FOR FINANCIAL AID *Required financial aid forms:* FAFSA, institution's own form. *Financial aid deadline (priority):* 2/15. *Notification date:* 5/1. Students must reply within 4 weeks of notification.
CONTACT Ms. Beth Bartlett, Administrative Assistant, Youngstown State University, One University Plaza, Youngstown, OH 44555, 330-941-3504 or toll-free 877-468-6978. *Fax:* 330-941-1659. *E-mail:* babartlett@ysu.edu.

ZION BIBLE INSTITUTE
Barrington, RI

CONTACT Financial Aid Office, Zion Bible Institute, 27 Middle Highway, Barrington, RI 02806, 401-246-0900 or toll-free 800-356-4014.

Appendix

State Scholarship and Grant Programs

Each state government has established one or more state-administered financial aid programs for qualified students. In many instances, these state programs are restricted to legal residents of the state. However, they often are available to out-of-state students who will be or are attending colleges or universities within the state. In addition to residential status, other qualifications frequently exist.

Gift aid and forgivable loan programs open to undergraduate students for all states and the District of Columbia are described on the following pages. They are arranged in alphabetical order, first by state name, then by program name. The annotation for each program provides information about the program, eligibility, and the contact addresses for applications or further information. Unless otherwise stated, this information refers to awards for 2005-06. Information is provided by the state-sponsoring agency in response to *Thomson Peterson's Annual Survey of Non-institutional Aid*, which was conducted between November 2005 and March 2006. Information is accurate when Peterson's receives it. However, it is always advisable to check with the sponsor to ascertain that the information remains correct.

You should write to the address given for each program to request that award details for 2006-07 be sent to you as soon as they are available. Descriptive information, brochures, and application forms for state scholarship programs are usually available from the financial aid offices of public colleges or universities within the specific state. High school guidance offices often have information and relevant forms for awards for which high school seniors may be eligible. Increasingly, state government agencies are putting state scholarship information on state government agency Web sites. In searching state government Web sites, however, you should be aware that the higher education agency in many states is separate from the state's general education office, which is often responsible only for elementary and secondary education. Also, the page at public university Web sites that provides information about student financial aid frequently has a list of state-sponsored scholarships and financial aid programs. College and university Web sites can be easily accessed through www.petersons.com.

Names of scholarship programs are frequently used inconsistently or become abbreviated in popular usage. Many programs have variant names by which they are known. The program's sponsor has approved the title of the program that Peterson's uses in this guide, yet this name may differ from the program's official name or from its most commonly used name.

In addition to the grant aid and forgivable loan programs listed on the following pages, states may also offer internship or work-study programs, graduate fellowships and grants, or low-interest loans. If you are interested in learning more about these other kinds of programs, the state education office that supplies information or applications for the undergraduate scholarship programs listed here should be able to provide information about other kinds of higher education financial aid programs that are sponsored by the state.

State Scholarship and Grant Programs
Alaska

ALABAMA

Air Force ROTC College Scholarship. Air Force ROTC offers college scholarships in both technical and non-technical majors that cover tuition, books, fees and up to $400 spending cash per academic month. Air Force ROTC college scholarships can be used at over 1000 college and universities across the U.S. and Puerto Rico. Please use online application: http://www.afrotc.com *Award:* Scholarship for use in freshman, sophomore, junior, or senior year; renewable. *Award amount:* $9000–$15,000. *Number of awards:* 2000–4000. *Eligibility Requirements:* Applicant must be age 17-30 and enrolled or expecting to enroll full-time at a four-year institution or university. Applicant must have 3.0 GPA or higher. Available to U.S. citizens. Applicant must have served in the Air Force. *Application Requirements:* Application, interview, test scores, transcript. *Deadline:* December 1.

Contact Ty Christian, Chief Air Force ROTC Advertising Manager, Air Force Reserve Officer Training Corps, 551 East Maxwell Boulevard, Maxwell Air Force Base, AL 36112-6106. *E-mail:* ty.christian@maxwell.af.mil. *Phone:* 334-953-2278. *Fax:* 334-953-6167. *Web site:* www.afrotc.com.

Alabama National Guard Educational Assistance Program. Renewable award aids Alabama residents who are members of the Alabama National Guard and are enrolled in an accredited college in Alabama. Forms must be signed by a representative of the Alabama Military Department and financial aid officer. Recipient must be in a degree-seeking program. *Award:* Grant for use in freshman, sophomore, junior, senior, or graduate year; renewable. *Award amount:* up to $1000. *Number of awards:* varies. *Eligibility Requirements:* Applicant must be enrolled or expecting to enroll full or part-time at a two-year, four-year, or technical institution or university; resident of Alabama and studying in Alabama. Available to U.S. citizens. Applicant must have served in the Air Force National Guard or Army National Guard. *Application Requirements:* Application. *Deadline:* continuous.

Contact William Wall, Associate Executive Director for Student Assistance, Alabama Commission on Higher Education, PO Box 302000, Montgomery, AL 36130-2000. *E-mail:* wwall@ache.state.al.us. *Phone:* 334-242-2271. *Fax:* 334-242-0268. *Web site:* www.ache.state.al.us.

Math and Science Scholarship Program for Alabama Teachers. For students pursuing teaching certificates in mathematics, general science, biology, or physics. Applicants must agree to teach for five years (if a position is offered) in a targeted system with critical needs. Renewable if recipient continues to meet the requirements. Minimum 2.5 GPA required. Must attend school in Alabama. *Academic Fields/Career Goals:* Biology; Earth Science; Meteorology/Atmospheric Science; Natural Sciences; Physical Sciences and Math. *Award:* Forgivable loan for use in junior, senior, or graduate year; renewable. *Award amount:* $2000–$12,000. *Eligibility Requirements:* Applicant must be enrolled or expecting to enroll full or part-time at a four-year institution or university and studying in Alabama. Applicant must have 2.5 GPA or higher. Available to U.S. citizens. *Application Requirements:* Application. *Deadline:* varies.

Contact Alabama State Department of Education, PO Box 302101, Montgomery, AL 36130-2101. *Phone:* 334-242-9935. *Web site:* www.alsde.edu.

Alabama G.I. Dependents Scholarship Program. Full scholarship for dependents of Alabama disabled, prisoner of war, or missing-in-action veterans. Child or stepchild must initiate training before 26th birthday; age 30 deadline may apply in certain situations. No age deadline for spouses or widows. Contact for application procedures and deadline. *Award:* Scholarship for use in freshman, sophomore, junior, senior, or graduate year; renewable. *Award amount:* varies. *Number of awards:* varies. *Eligibility Requirements:* Applicant must be enrolled or expecting to enroll full or part-time at a four-year, or technical institution or university; resident of Alabama and studying in Alabama. Available to U.S. and non-U.S. citizens. Applicant or parent must meet one or more of the following requirements: general military experience; retired from active duty; disabled or killed as a result of military service; prisoner of war; or missing in action. *Application Requirements:* Application. *Deadline:* varies.

Contact Willie E. Moore, Scholarship Administrator, Alabama Department of Veterans Affairs, PO Box 1509, Montgomery, AL 36102-1509. *E-mail:* wmoore@va.state.al.us. *Phone:* 334-242-5077. *Fax:* 334-242-5102. *Web site:* www.va.state.al.us.

Police Officers and Firefighters Survivors Education Assistance Program-Alabama. Provides tuition, fees, books, and supplies to dependents of full-time police officers and firefighters killed in the line of duty. Must attend any Alabama public college as an undergraduate. Must be Alabama resident. Renewable. *Award:* Grant for use in freshman, sophomore, junior, or senior year; renewable. *Award amount:* $2000–$5000. *Number of awards:* 15–30. *Eligibility Requirements:* Applicant must be enrolled or expecting to enroll full or part-time at a two-year, four-year, or technical institution or university; single; resident of Alabama and studying in Alabama. Applicant or parent of applicant must have employment or volunteer experience in police/firefighting. Available to U.S. citizens. *Application Requirements:* Application, transcript. *Deadline:* continuous.

Contact William Wall, Associate Executive Director for Student Assistance, ACHE, Alabama Commission on Higher Education, PO Box 302000, Montgomery, AL 36130-2000. *E-mail:* wwall@ache.state.al.us. *Phone:* 334-242-2273. *Fax:* 334-242-0268. *Web site:* www.ache.state.al.us.

Alabama Student Grant Program. Renewable awards available to Alabama residents for undergraduate study at certain independent colleges within the state. Both full and half-time students are eligible. Deadlines: September 15, January 15, and February 15. *Award:* Grant for use in freshman, sophomore, junior, or senior year; renewable. *Award amount:* up to $1200. *Number of awards:* varies. *Eligibility Requirements:* Applicant must be enrolled or expecting to enroll full or part-time at a four-year institution or university; resident of Alabama and studying in Alabama. Available to U.S. citizens. *Application Requirements:* Application. *Deadline:* varies.

Contact William Wall, Associate Executive Director for Student Assistance, ACHE, Alabama Commission on Higher Education, PO Box 302000, Montgomery, AL 36130-2000. *E-mail:* wwall@ache.state.al.us. *Phone:* 334-242-2271. *Fax:* 334-242-0268. *Web site:* www.ache.state.al.us.

ALASKA

GEAR UP Alaska Scholarship. Scholarship provides up to $7000 each year for up to four years of undergraduate study (up to $3,500 each year for half-time study). The federal government funds the scholarships. Alaska GEAR UP scholarships are available to students who have participated in GEAR UP Programs in 6th, 7th, and 8th grade and have met the academic milestones established by their district. *Award:* Scholarship for use in freshman, sophomore, junior, or senior year. *Award amount:* $3500–$7000. *Eligibility Requirements:* Applicant must be age 21 or under; enrolled or expecting to enroll full or part-time at a four-year institution or university and resident of Alaska. Available to U.S. citizens. *Application Requirements:* Application, references, transcript. *Deadline:* May 31.

Contact Alaska State Department of Education, 801 West 10th Street, Suite 200, Goldbelt

State Scholarship and Grant Programs

Alaska

Place, PO Box 110500, Juneau, AK 99811-0500. *Phone:* 907-465-2800. *Fax:* 907-465-4156. *Web site:* www.eed.state.ak.us.

ARIZONA

Arizona Private Postsecondary Education Student Financial Assistance Program. Provides grants to financially needy Arizona Community College graduates, to attend a private postsecondary baccalaureate degree-granting institution. *Award:* Forgivable loan for use in freshman, sophomore, junior, or senior year; renewable. *Award amount:* up to $1000. *Number of awards:* varies. *Eligibility Requirements:* Applicant must be enrolled or expecting to enroll full-time at a four-year institution or university; resident of Arizona and studying in Arizona. Available to U.S. citizens. *Application Requirements:* Financial need analysis, transcript, promissory note. *Deadline:* June 30.

Contact Danny Lee, PFAP Program Manager, Arizona Commission for Postsecondary Education, 2020 North Central Avenue, Suite 550, Phoenix, AZ 85004-4503. *E-mail:* dan_lee@azhighered.org. *Phone:* 602-258-2435 Ext. 103. *Fax:* 602-258-2483. *Web site:* www.azhighered.org/.

Robert C. Byrd Honors Scholarship-Arizona. Federally funded program for high school graduates who show academic excellence and the promise of continued postsecondary education. A Byrd Scholar receives $1500 for each academic year for a maximum of four years to be applied toward undergraduate study at any accredited college or university in the United States. The number of scholarships awarded each year is subject to change due to funding. Deadline is March 27. *Award:* Scholarship for use in freshman, sophomore, junior, or senior year; renewable. *Award amount:* $3000–$6000. *Number of awards:* 50–100. *Eligibility Requirements:* Applicant must be high school student and planning to enroll or expecting to enroll full or part-time at a two-year, four-year, or technical institution or university. Available to U.S. citizens. *Application Requirements:* Application, transcript. *Deadline:* March 27.

Contact Jessica Enders, Robert C. Byrd Scholarship Coordinator, Arizona State Department of Education, 1535 West Jefferson, Phoenix, AZ 85007. *E-mail:* jenders@ade.az.gov. *Phone:* 602-542-3710. *Fax:* 602-364-1532. *Web site:* www.ade.state.az.us.

Leveraging Educational Assistance Partnership. LEAP provides grants to financially needy students, who enroll in and attend postsecondary education or training in Arizona schools. LEAP Program was formerly known as the State Student Incentive Grant or SSIG Program. *Award:* Grant for use in freshman, sophomore, junior, senior, or graduate year; not renewable. *Award amount:* $100–$2500. *Number of awards:* varies. *Eligibility Requirements:* Applicant must be enrolled or expecting to enroll full or part-time at a two-year, four-year, or technical institution or university; resident of Arizona and studying in Arizona. Available to U.S. citizens. *Application Requirements:* Financial need analysis. *Deadline:* April 30.

Contact Mila A. Zaporteza, Business Manager/LEAP Financial Aid Manager, Arizona Commission for Postsecondary Education, 2020 North Central Avenue, Suite 550, Phoenix, AZ 85004-4503. *E-mail:* mila@azhighered.org. *Phone:* 602-258-2435 Ext. 102. *Fax:* 602-258-2483. *Web site:* www.azhighered.org/.

ARKANSAS

Governor's Scholars-Arkansas. Awards for outstanding Arkansas high school seniors. Must be an Arkansas resident and have a high school GPA of at least 3.5 or have scored at least 27 on the ACT. Award is $4000 per year for four years of full-time undergraduate study. Applicants who attain 32 or above on ACT, 1410 or above on SAT and have an academic 3.50 GPA, or are selected as National Merit or National Achievement finalists may receive an award equal to tuition, mandatory fees, room, and board up to $10,000 per year at any Arkansas institution. *Award:* Scholarship for use in freshman, sophomore, junior, or senior year; renewable. *Award amount:* $4000–$10,000. *Number of awards:* 75–250. *Eligibility Requirements:* Applicant must be high school student; planning to enroll or expecting to enroll full-time at a two-year or four-year institution or university; resident of Arkansas and studying in Arkansas. Applicant must have 3.5 GPA or higher. Available to U.S. citizens. *Application Requirements:* Application, test scores, transcript. *Deadline:* February 1.

Contact Philip Axelroth, Assistant Coordinator of Financial Aid, Arkansas Department of Higher Education, 114 East Capitol, Little Rock, AR 72201. *E-mail:* phila@adhe.arknet.edu. *Phone:* 501-371-2050. *Fax:* 501-371-2001. *Web site:* www.arkansashighered.com.

Second Effort Scholarship. Awarded to those scholars who achieved one of the 10 highest scores on the Arkansas High School Diploma Test (GED). Must be at least age 18 and not have graduated from high school. Students do not apply for this award, they are contacted by the Arkansas Department of Higher Education. *Award:* Scholarship for use in freshman, sophomore, junior, or senior year; renewable. *Award amount:* up to $1000. *Number of awards:* 10. *Eligibility Requirements:* Applicant must be age 18; enrolled or expecting to enroll full or part-time at a two-year or four-year institution or university; resident of Arkansas and studying in Arkansas. Applicant must have 2.5 GPA or higher. Available to U.S. citizens. *Application Requirements:* Application.

Contact Arkansas Department of Higher Education. *Phone:* 501-371-2050. *Fax:* 501-371-2001. *Web site:* www.arkansashighered.com.

Arkansas Academic Challenge Scholarship Program. Awards for Arkansas residents who are graduating high school seniors to study at an Arkansas institution. Must have at least a 2.75 GPA, meet minimum ACT composite score standards, and have financial need. Renewable up to three additional years. *Award:* Scholarship for use in freshman, sophomore, junior, or senior year; renewable. *Award amount:* $2000–$3000. *Eligibility Requirements:* Applicant must be high school student; planning to enroll or expecting to enroll full-time at a two-year or four-year institution or university; resident of Arkansas and studying in Arkansas. Available to U.S. citizens. *Application Requirements:* Application, financial need analysis, test scores, transcript. *Deadline:* June 1.

Contact Elyse Price, Assistant Coordinator, Arkansas Department of Higher Education, 114 East Capitol, Little Rock, AR 72201. *Phone:* 501-371-2050. *Fax:* 501-371-2001. *Web site:* www.arkansashighered.com.

Emergency Secondary Education Loan Program. Must be Arkansas resident enrolled full-time in approved Arkansas institution. Renewable award for students majoring in secondary math, chemistry, physics, biology, physical science, general science, special education, or foreign language. Must teach in Arkansas at least five years. Must rank in upper half of class or have a minimum 2.5 GPA. *Academic Fields/Career Goals:* Biology; Education; Foreign Language; Physical Sciences and Math; Special Education. *Award:* Forgivable loan for use in sophomore, junior, senior, or graduate year; renewable. *Award amount:* up to $2500. *Number of awards:* up to 50. *Eligibility Requirements:* Applicant must be enrolled or expecting to enroll full-time at a two-year or four-year institution or university; resident of Arkansas and studying in Arkansas. Applicant must have 2.5 GPA or higher. Available to U.S. citizens.

State Scholarship and Grant Programs
California

Application Requirements: Application, transcript. *Deadline:* April 1.

Contact Lillian K. Williams, Assistant Coordinator, Arkansas Department of Higher Education, 114 East Capitol, Little Rock, AR 72201. *Phone:* 501-371-2050. *Fax:* 501-371-2001. *Web site:* www.arkansashighered.com.

Arkansas Minority Teacher Scholars Program. Renewable award for Native-American, African-American, Hispanic and Asian-American students who have completed at least sixty semester hours and are enrolled full-time in a teacher education program in Arkansas. Award may be renewed for one year. Must be Arkansas resident with minimum 2.5 GPA. Must teach for three to five years in Arkansas to repay scholarship funds received. Must pass PPST exam. *Academic Fields/Career Goals:* Education. *Award:* Forgivable loan for use in junior or senior year; renewable. *Award amount:* up to $5000. *Number of awards:* up to 100. *Eligibility Requirements:* Applicant must be American Indian/Alaska Native, Asian/Pacific Islander, Black (non-Hispanic), or Hispanic; enrolled or expecting to enroll full-time at a four-year institution or university; resident of Arkansas and studying in Arkansas. Applicant must have 2.5 GPA or higher. Available to U.S. citizens. *Application Requirements:* Application, transcript. *Deadline:* June 1.

Contact Lillian Williams, Assistant Coordinator, Arkansas Department of Higher Education, 114 East Capitol, Little Rock, AR 72201. *Phone:* 501-371-2050. *Fax:* 501-371-2001. *Web site:* www.arkansashighered.com.

Arkansas Student Assistance Grant Program. Award for Arkansas residents attending a college within the state. Must be enrolled full-time, have financial need, and maintain satisfactory progress. One-time award for undergraduate use only. Application is the FAFSA that each student submits as soon as possible after January 1 of each year. *Award:* Grant for use in freshman, sophomore, junior, or senior year; not renewable. *Award amount:* $600. *Number of awards:* 600–5500. *Eligibility Requirements:* Applicant must be enrolled or expecting to enroll full-time at a two-year, four-year, or technical institution or university; resident of Arkansas and studying in Arkansas. Available to U.S. citizens. *Application Requirements:* Application, financial need analysis, FAFSA. *Deadline:* April 1.

Contact Philip Axelroth, Assistant Coordinator, Arkansas Department of Higher Education, 114 East Capitol, Little Rock, AR 72201. *Phone:* 501-371-2050. *Fax:* 501-371-2001. *Web site:* www.arkansashighered.com.

Law Enforcement Officers' Dependents Scholarship-Arkansas. For dependents, under 23 years old, of Arkansas law-enforcement officers killed or permanently disabled in the line of duty. Renewable award is a waiver of tuition, fees, and room at two- or four-year Arkansas institution. Submit birth certificate, death certificate, and claims commission report of findings of fact. Proof of disability from State Claims Commission may also be submitted. *Award:* Scholarship for use in freshman, sophomore, junior, or senior year; renewable. *Award amount:* $2000–$2500. *Number of awards:* 27–32. *Eligibility Requirements:* Applicant must be age 22 or under; enrolled or expecting to enroll full or part-time at a two-year, four-year, or technical institution or university; resident of Arkansas and studying in Arkansas. Applicant or parent of applicant must have employment or volunteer experience in police/firefighting. Available to U.S. citizens. *Application Requirements:* Application. *Deadline:* continuous.

Contact Lillian Williams, Assistant Coordinator, Arkansas Department of Higher Education, 114 East Capitol, Little Rock, AR 72201. *E-mail:* lillianw@adhe.arknet.edu. *Phone:* 501-371-2050. *Fax:* 501-371-2001. *Web site:* www.arkansashighered.com.

Arkansas Health Education Grant Program (ARHEG). Award provides assistance to Arkansas residents pursuing professional degrees in dentistry, optometry, veterinary medicine, podiatry, chiropractic medicine, or osteopathic medicine at out-of-state, accredited institutions (programs that are unavailable in Arkansas). *Academic Fields/Career Goals:* Animal/Veterinary Sciences; Dental Health/Services; Health and Medical Sciences. *Award:* Grant for use in sophomore, junior, senior, or graduate year; renewable. *Award amount:* $5000–$14,600. *Number of awards:* 258–288. *Eligibility Requirements:* Applicant must be enrolled or expecting to enroll full-time at a four-year institution or university and resident of Arkansas. Available to U.S. citizens. *Application Requirements:* Application, affidavit of Arkansas residency. *Deadline:* continuous.

Contact Judy McAinsh, Coordinator, Arkansas Health Education Grant Program, Arkansas Department of Higher Education, 114 East Capitol, Little Rock, AR 72201-3818. *E-mail:* judym@adhe.arknet.edu. *Phone:* 501-371-2013. *Fax:* 501-371-2002. *Web site:* www.arkansashighered.com.

Missing in Action/Killed in Action Dependent's Scholarship-Arkansas. Available to Arkansas residents whose parent or spouse was classified either as missing in action, killed in action, or a prisoner-of-war. Must attend state-supported institution in Arkansas. Renewable waiver of tuition, fees, room and board. Submit proof of casualty. *Award:* Scholarship for use in freshman, sophomore, junior, or senior year; renewable. *Award amount:* up to $2500. *Eligibility Requirements:* Applicant must be enrolled or expecting to enroll full-time at a two-year, four-year, or technical institution or university; resident of Arkansas and studying in Arkansas. Available to U.S. citizens. Applicant or parent must meet one or more of the following requirements: general military experience; retired from active duty; disabled or killed as a result of military service; prisoner of war; or missing in action. *Application Requirements:* Application, report of casualty. *Deadline:* continuous.

Contact Lillian K. Williams, Assistant Coordinator, Arkansas Department of Higher Education, 114 East Capitol, Little Rock, AR 72201. *Phone:* 501-371-2050. *Fax:* 501-371-2001. *Web site:* www.arkansashighered.com.

Robert C. Byrd Honors Scholarship-Arkansas. Federally funded program for high school graduates who show academic excellence and the promise of continued postsecondary education. Award is $1500 for each academic year for a maximum of four years to be applied toward undergraduate study at any accredited college or university in the United States. The number of scholarships awarded each year is subject to change due to funding. Deadline is February 17. *Award:* Scholarship for use in freshman, sophomore, junior, or senior year; renewable. *Award amount:* $3000–$6000. *Number of awards:* 62–100. *Eligibility Requirements:* Applicant must be enrolled or expecting to enroll full or part-time at a two-year, four-year, or technical institution or university. Available to U.S. and non-Canadian citizens. *Application Requirements:* Application, transcript. *Deadline:* February 17.

Contact Margaret Amps, Program Coordinator, Arkansas State Department of Education, 4 State Capitol Mall, Room 107A, Little Rock, AR 72201. *E-mail:* mcrank@arkedu.k12.ar.us. *Phone:* 501-682-4396. *Web site:* arkedu.state.ar.us.

CALIFORNIA

Cooperative Agencies Resources for Education Program. Renewable award available to California resident attending a two-year California community college. Must have no more than 70 degree-applicable units, currently receive CALWORKS/TANF, and have at least one child under fourteen years of age. Must be

State Scholarship and Grant Programs
California

in EOPS, single head of household, and 18 or older. Contact local college EOPS-CARE office. *Award:* Grant for use in freshman or sophomore year; renewable. *Number of awards:* up to 10,000. *Eligibility Requirements:* Applicant must be age 18; enrolled or expecting to enroll full-time at a two-year institution; single; resident of California and studying in California. Available to U.S. citizens. *Application Requirements:* Application, financial need analysis, test scores, transcript. *Deadline:* continuous.

Contact Cheryl Fong, CARE Coordinator, California Community Colleges, 1102 Q Street, Sacramento, CA 95814-6511. *E-mail:* cfong@cccco.edu. *Phone:* 916-323-5954. *Fax:* 916-327-8232. *Web site:* www.cccco.edu/.

Entitlement Cal Grant B. Award for California residents who are high school graduates attending an approved college or university within the state. Must show financial need and meet the minimum 2.0 GPA requirement. *Award:* Grant for use in freshman, sophomore, junior, or senior year; renewable. *Award amount:* $700–$11,259. *Number of awards:* varies. *Eligibility Requirements:* Applicant must be age 23 or under; enrolled or expecting to enroll full or part-time at a two-year, four-year, or technical institution or university; resident of California and studying in California. Available to U.S. citizens. *Application Requirements:* Application, financial need analysis. *Deadline:* March 2.

Contact Student Support Services Branch, California Student Aid Commission, PO Box 419027, Rancho Cordova, CA 95741-9027. *E-mail:* custsvcs@csac.ca.gov. *Phone:* 916-526-7590. *Fax:* 916-526-8002. *Web site:* www.csac.ca.gov.

Cal Grant C. Award for California residents who are enrolled in a short-term vocational training program. Program must lead to a recognized degree or certificate. Course length must be a minimum of 4 months and no longer than 24 months. Students must be attending an approved California institution and show financial need. *Award:* Grant for use in freshman, sophomore, junior, or senior year; renewable. *Award amount:* $576–$3168. *Number of awards:* up to 7761. *Eligibility Requirements:* Applicant must be enrolled or expecting to enroll full or part-time at a two-year or technical institution; resident of California and studying in California. Available to U.S. citizens. *Application Requirements:* Application, financial need analysis, GPA verification. *Deadline:* March 2.

Contact Student Support Services Branch, California Student Aid Commission, PO Box 419027, Rancho Cordova, CA 95741-9027. *E-mail:* custsvcs@csac.ca.gov. *Phone:* 916-526-7590. *Fax:* 916-526-8002. *Web site:* www.csac.ca.gov.

Entitlement Cal Grant A. Award is for California residents who are recent high school graduates attending an approved college or university within the state. Must show financial need and meet the minimum 3.0 GPA requirement. *Award:* Grant for use in freshman, sophomore, junior, or senior year; renewable. *Award amount:* $2046–$9708. *Number of awards:* varies. *Eligibility Requirements:* Applicant must be enrolled or expecting to enroll full or part-time at a two-year, four-year, or technical institution or university; resident of California and studying in California. Applicant must have 3.0 GPA or higher. Available to U.S. citizens. *Application Requirements:* Application, financial need analysis, GPA verification. *Deadline:* March 2.

Contact Student Support Services Branch, California Student Aid Commission, PO Box 419027, Rancho Cordova, CA 95741-9027. *E-mail:* custsvcs@csac.ca.gov. *Phone:* 916-526-7590. *Fax:* 916-526-8002. *Web site:* www.csac.ca.gov.

Competitive Cal Grant B. Award is for California residents who are not recent high school graduates attending an approved college or university within the state. Must show financial need and meet the minimum 2.0 GPA requirement. *Award:* Grant for use in freshman, sophomore, or junior year; renewable. *Award amount:* $700–$11,259. *Number of awards:* up to 22,500. *Eligibility Requirements:* Applicant must be age 23 or under; enrolled or expecting to enroll full or part-time at a two-year, four-year, or technical institution or university; resident of California and studying in California. Available to U.S. citizens. *Application Requirements:* Application, financial need analysis, GPA verification. *Deadline:* March 2.

Contact Student Support Services Branch, California Student Aid Commission, PO Box 419027, Rancho Cordova, CA 95741-9027. *E-mail:* custsvcs@csac.ca.gov. *Phone:* 916-526-7590. *Fax:* 916-526-8002. *Web site:* www.csac.ca.gov.

Child Development Teacher and Supervisor Grant Program. Award is for those students pursuing an approved course of study leading to a Child Development Permit issued by the California Commission on Teacher Credentialing. In exchange for each year funding is received, recipients agree to provide one year of service in a licensed childcare center. *Award:* Grant for use in freshman, sophomore, junior, or senior year; renewable. *Award amount:* $1000–$2000. *Number of awards:* up to 300. *Eligibility Requirements:* Applicant must be enrolled or expecting to enroll full or part-time at a two-year, four-year, or technical institution or university; resident of California and studying in California. Available to U.S. citizens. *Application Requirements:* Application, financial need analysis, references, FAFSA. *Deadline:* June 1.

Contact California Student Aid Commission, PO Box 419027, Rancho Cordova, CA 95741-9027. *E-mail:* custsvcs@csac.ca.gov. *Phone:* 916-526-7590. *Fax:* 916-526-8002. *Web site:* www.csac.ca.gov.

Competitive Cal Grant A. Award for California residents who are not recent high school graduates attending an approved college or university within the state. Must show financial need and meet minimum 3.0 GPA requirement. *Award:* Grant for use in freshman, sophomore, junior, or senior year; renewable. *Award amount:* $2046–$9708. *Number of awards:* up to 22,500. *Eligibility Requirements:* Applicant must be enrolled or expecting to enroll full or part-time at a two-year, four-year, or technical institution or university; resident of California and studying in California. Applicant must have 3.0 GPA or higher. Available to U.S. citizens. *Application Requirements:* Application, financial need analysis, GPA verification. *Deadline:* March 2.

Contact Student Support Services Branch, California Student Aid Commission, PO Box 419027, Rancho Cordova, CA 95741-9027. *E-mail:* custsvcs@csac.ca.gov. *Phone:* 916-526-7590. *Fax:* 916-526-8002. *Web site:* www.csac.ca.gov.

COLORADO

Western Undergraduate Exchange Program. Residents of Alaska, Arizona, Colorado, Hawaii, Idaho, Montana, Nevada, New Mexico, North Dakota, Oregon, South Dakota, Utah, Washington and Wyoming can enroll in designated two- and four-year undergraduate programs at public institutions in participating states at reduced tuition level (resident tuition plus half). Contact Western Interstate Commission for Higher Education for list and deadlines. *Award:* Scholarship for use in freshman, sophomore, junior, or senior year; renewable. *Eligibility Requirements:* Applicant must be enrolled or expecting to enroll full or part-time at a two-year or four-year institution; resident of Alaska, Arizona, Colorado, Hawaii, Idaho, Montana, Nevada, New Mexico, North Dakota, Oregon, South

State Scholarship and Grant Programs
Connecticut

Dakota, Utah, Washington, or Wyoming and studying in Alaska, Arizona, Colorado, Hawaii, Idaho, Montana, Nevada, New Mexico, North Dakota, Oregon, South Dakota, or Utah. Available to U.S. citizens. *Application Requirements:* Application.

Contact Sandy Jackson, Program Coordinator, Western Interstate Commission for Higher Education, PO Box 9752, Boulder, CO 80301-9752. *E-mail:* info-sep@wiche.edu. *Phone:* 303-541-0214. *Fax:* 303-541-0291. *Web site:* www.wiche.edu/.

Governor's Opportunity Scholarship. Scholarship available for the most needy first-time freshmen whose parents' adjusted gross income is less than $26,000. Must be U.S. citizen or permanent legal resident. Work-study is part of the program. *Award:* Scholarship for use in freshman year; renewable. *Award amount:* up to $10,700. *Number of awards:* 250. *Eligibility Requirements:* Applicant must be high school student; planning to enroll or expecting to enroll full-time at a two-year, four-year, or technical institution or university; resident of Colorado and studying in Colorado. Available to U.S. citizens. *Application Requirements:* Application, financial need analysis, test scores, transcript. *Deadline:* continuous.

Contact Governor's Opportunity Scholarship Program, Colorado Commission on Higher Education. *E-mail:* gos@cche.state.co.us. *Phone:* 303-866-2723. *Fax:* 303-866-4266. *Web site:* www.state.co.us/cche.

Colorado Student Grant. Assists Colorado residents attending eligible public, private, or vocational institutions within the state. Application deadlines vary by institution. Renewable award for undergraduates. Contact the financial aid office at the college/institution for more information and an application. *Award:* Grant for use in freshman, sophomore, junior, or senior year; renewable. *Award amount:* $1500–$3000. *Number of awards:* varies. *Eligibility Requirements:* Applicant must be enrolled or expecting to enroll full or part-time at a two-year, four-year, or technical institution or university; resident of Colorado and studying in Colorado. Available to U.S. citizens. *Application Requirements:* Application, financial need analysis. *Deadline:* varies.

Contact Financial Aid Office at college/institution, Colorado Commission on Higher Education, 1380 Lawrence Street, Suite 1200, Denver, CO 80204-2059. *E-mail:* cche@state.co.us. *Phone:* 303-866-2723. *Web site:* www.state.co.us/cche.

Colorado Undergraduate Merit Scholarships. Renewable awards for students attending Colorado state-supported institutions at the undergraduate level. Must demonstrate superior scholarship or talent. Contact college financial aid office for complete information and deadlines. *Award:* Scholarship for use in freshman, sophomore, junior, or senior year; renewable. *Award amount:* $1230. *Number of awards:* 10,823. *Eligibility Requirements:* Applicant must be enrolled or expecting to enroll full or part-time at a two-year, four-year, or technical institution or university; resident of Colorado and studying in Colorado. Applicant must have 3.0 GPA or higher. Available to U.S. citizens. *Application Requirements:* Application, test scores, transcript. *Deadline:* varies.

Contact Financial Aid Office at college/institution, Colorado Commission on Higher Education, 1380 Lawrence Street, Suite 1200, Denver, CO 80204-2059. *E-mail:* cche@state.co.us. *Phone:* 303-866-2723. *Web site:* www.state.co.us/cche.

Colorado Leveraging Educational Assistance Partnership (CLEAP) and SLEAP. Renewable awards for Colorado residents who are attending Colorado state-supported postsecondary institutions at the undergraduate level. Must document financial need. Contact colleges for complete information and deadlines. *Award:* Grant for use in freshman, sophomore, junior, or senior year; not renewable. *Award amount:* $50–$900. *Number of awards:* 5000. *Eligibility Requirements:* Applicant must be enrolled or expecting to enroll full or part-time at a two-year, four-year, or technical institution or university; resident of Colorado and studying in Colorado. Available to U.S. citizens. *Application Requirements:* Application, financial need analysis. *Deadline:* varies.

Contact Financial Aid Office at college/institution, Colorado Commission on Higher Education, 1380 Lawrence Street, Suite 1200, Denver, CO 80204-2059. *E-mail:* cche@state.co.us. *Phone:* 303-866-2723. *Web site:* www.state.co.us/cche.

CONNECTICUT

Connecticut Army National Guard 100% Tuition Waiver. 100% Tuition Waiver Program is for any active member of the Connecticut Army National Guard in good standing. Must be a resident of Connecticut attending any Connecticut state (public) university, community-technical college or regional vocational-technical school. *Award:* Scholarship for use in freshman, sophomore, junior, or senior year; not renewable. *Award amount:* varies. *Number of awards:* varies. *Eligibility Requirements:* Applicant must be age 17-65; enrolled or expecting to enroll full or part-time at a two-year, four-year, or technical institution or university; resident of Connecticut and studying in Connecticut. Available to U.S. and non-U.S. citizens. Applicant must have served in the Army National Guard. *Application Requirements:* Application. *Deadline:* July 1.

Contact Capt. Jeremy Lingenfelser, Education Services Officer, Connecticut Army National Guard. *E-mail:* education@ct.ngb.army.mil. *Phone:* 860-524-4816. *Fax:* 860-524-4904. *Web site:* www.ct.ngb.army.mil.

Connecticut Independent College Student Grants. Award for Connecticut residents attending an independent college or university within the state on at least a half-time basis. Renewable awards based on financial need. Application deadline varies by institution. Apply at college financial aid office. *Award:* Grant for use in freshman, sophomore, junior, or senior year; renewable. *Award amount:* $7700–$8500. *Number of awards:* varies. *Eligibility Requirements:* Applicant must be enrolled or expecting to enroll full or part-time at a two-year or four-year institution or university; resident of Connecticut and studying in Connecticut. Available to U.S. citizens. *Application Requirements:* Application, financial need analysis, transcript. *Deadline:* varies.

Contact John Siegrist, Financial Aid Office, Connecticut Department of Higher Education, 61 Woodland Street, Hartford, CT 06105-2326. *Phone:* 860-947-1855. *Fax:* 860-947-1311. *Web site:* www.ctdhe.org.

Connecticut Special Education Teacher Incentive Grant. Renewable award for upper-level undergraduates or graduate students in special education programs. Must be in a program at a Connecticut college or university, or be a Connecticut resident enrolled in an approved out-of-state program. Priority is placed on minority and bilingual candidates. Application deadline is October 1. Must be nominated by the education dean of institution attended. *Academic Fields/Career Goals:* Special Education. *Award:* Grant for use in junior, senior, or graduate year; renewable. *Award amount:* $2000–$5000. *Number of awards:* varies. *Eligibility Requirements:* Applicant must be enrolled or expecting to enroll full or part-time at a four-year institution or university; resident of Connecticut and studying in Connecticut. Available to U.S. citizens. *Application Requirements:* Application. *Deadline:* October 1.

Contact John Siegrist, Director, Financial Aid Office, Connecticut Department of Higher Education, 61 Woodland Street, Hartford, CT 06105-2326. *E-mail:* jsiegrist@ctdhe.org.

State Scholarship and Grant Programs
Connecticut

Phone: 860-947-1855. *Fax:* 860-947-1311. *Web site:* www.ctdhe.org.

Capitol Scholarship Program. Award for Connecticut residents attending eligible institutions in Connecticut or in a state with reciprocity with Connecticut (Delaware, Maine, Massachusetts, New Hampshire, Pennsylvania, Rhode Island, Vermont, or Washington, D.C). Must be U.S. citizen or permanent resident alien who is a high school senior or graduate. Must rank in top 20% of class or score at least 1200 on SAT. Must show financial need. *Award:* Scholarship for use in freshman, sophomore, junior, or senior year; renewable. *Award amount:* $500–$3000. *Number of awards:* varies. *Eligibility Requirements:* Applicant must be enrolled or expecting to enroll at a two-year institution; resident of Connecticut and studying in Connecticut, Delaware, District of Columbia, Maine, Massachusetts, New Hampshire, Pennsylvania, Rhode Island, or Vermont. Applicant must have 3.5 GPA or higher. Available to U.S. citizens. *Application Requirements:* Application, financial need analysis, test scores. *Deadline:* February 15.

Contact John Siegrist, Financial Aid Office, Connecticut Department of Higher Education, 61 Woodland Street, Hartford, CT 06105-2326. *Phone:* 860-947-1855. *Fax:* 860-947-1311. *Web site:* www.ctdhe.org.

Minority Teacher Incentive Grant Program. Program provides up to $5000 a year for two years of full-time study in a teacher preparation program, for the junior or senior year at a Connecticut college or university. Applicant must be African American, Hispanic/Latino, Asian American or Native American heritage, and be nominated by the Education Dean. *Academic Fields/Career Goals:* Education. *Award:* Grant for use in junior or senior year; not renewable. *Award amount:* $5000. *Eligibility Requirements:* Applicant must be American Indian/Alaska Native, Asian/Pacific Islander, Black (non-Hispanic), or Hispanic and enrolled or expecting to enroll full-time at a four-year institution or university. Available to U.S. citizens. *Application Requirements:* Application, transcript. *Deadline:* October 1.

Contact John Siegrist, Director, Financial Aid Office, Connecticut Department of Higher Education, 61 Woodland Street, Hartford, CT 06105-2326. *E-mail:* jsiegrist@ctdhe.org. *Phone:* 860-947-1855. *Fax:* 860-947-1311. *Web site:* www.ctdhe.org.

DELAWARE

State Tuition Assistance. Award providing tuition assistance for any member of the Air or Army National Guard attending a Delaware two-year or four-year college. Awards are renewable. Applicant's minimum GPA must be 2.0. For full- or part-time study. Amount of award varies. *Award:* Scholarship for use in freshman, sophomore, junior, or senior year; renewable. *Award amount:* varies. *Number of awards:* varies. *Eligibility Requirements:* Applicant must be enrolled or expecting to enroll full or part-time at a two-year or four-year institution or university and studying in Delaware. Applicant must have 2.5 GPA or higher. Available to U.S. citizens. Applicant must have served in the Air Force National Guard or Army National Guard. *Application Requirements:* Application, transcript. *Deadline:* varies.

Contact Robert Csizmadia, State Tuition Assistance Manager, Delaware National Guard, 1st Regiment Road, Wilmington, DE 19808-2191. *E-mail:* robert.csizmadi@de.ngb.army.mil. *Phone:* 302-326-7012. *Fax:* 302-326-7029. *Web site:* www.delawarenationalguard.com.

Scholarship Incentive Program (ScIP). Award for legal residents of Delaware who plan to enroll full-time in an undergraduate degree program at a non-profit regionally accredited institution college in Delaware or Pennsylvania. Must have a minimum cumulative, unweighted GPA of 2.5. Graduate students attending the University of Delaware or Delaware State University are not eligible. Award for undergraduate is $700 to $2200, depending on GPA and for graduate is $1000. Deadline is April 15. *Award:* Grant for use in freshman, sophomore, junior, or senior year; not renewable. *Award amount:* $700–$2250. *Number of awards:* up to 2. *Eligibility Requirements:* Applicant must be enrolled or expecting to enroll full-time at a two-year or four-year institution or university; resident of Delaware and studying in Delaware or Pennsylvania. Applicant must have 2.5 GPA or higher. Available to U.S. citizens. *Application Requirements:* Application, transcript. *Deadline:* April 15.

Contact Maureen Laffey, Director, Delaware Department of Education, Carvel State Office Building, 820 North French Street, Wilmington, DE 19801. *E-mail:* dedoe@doe.k12.de.us. *Phone:* 302-577-5240. *Fax:* 302-577-6765. *Web site:* www.doe.k12.de.us.

Charles L. Hebner Memorial Scholarship. Award for legal residents of Delaware who plan to enroll full-time at the University of Delaware or Delaware State University. Must pursue their career in humanities or social sciences. Must have combined score of 1350 on the SAT. Full tuition, fees, room, board, and books at the University of Delaware or Delaware State University. Renewable for up to three additional years. One award every year per school. Deadline is March 13. *Academic Fields/Career Goals:* Humanities; Social Sciences. *Award:* Scholarship for use in freshman, sophomore, junior, senior, graduate, or postgraduate years; renewable. *Number of awards:* 1. *Eligibility Requirements:* Applicant must be enrolled or expecting to enroll full-time at a two-year, four-year, or technical institution or university; resident of Delaware and studying in Delaware. Available to U.S. citizens. *Application Requirements:* Application, transcript. *Deadline:* March 13.

Contact Maureen Laffey, Director, Delaware Department of Education, Carvel State Office Building, 820 North French Street, Wilmington, DE 19801. *E-mail:* dedoe@doe.k12.de.us. *Phone:* 302-577-5240. *Fax:* 302-577-6765. *Web site:* www.doe.k12.de.us.

Educational Benefits for Children of Deceased Veterans and Others. Award for legal residents of Delaware. Must be a child of deceased U.S. military veterans or state police officers whose cause of death was service related or of military veterans held prisoner of war or declared missing in action. Must be 16 to 24 years old. Must attain full- or part-time undergraduate student admission at a public institution in Delaware. Award must not exceed tuition and fees at a Delaware public institution adjusted for other colleges. *Award:* Grant for use in freshman, sophomore, junior, or senior year; renewable. *Number of awards:* 4. *Eligibility Requirements:* Applicant must be age 16-24; enrolled or expecting to enroll full or part-time at a two-year or four-year institution or university and resident of Delaware. Available to U.S. citizens. Applicant or parent must meet one or more of the following requirements: general military experience; retired from active duty; disabled or killed as a result of military service; prisoner of war; or missing in action. *Application Requirements:* Application, transcript. *Deadline:* varies.

Contact Maureen Laffey, Director, Delaware Department of Education, Carvel State Office Building, 820 North French Street, Wilmington, DE 19801. *E-mail:* dedoe@doe.k12.de.us. *Phone:* 302-577-5240. *Fax:* 302-577-6765. *Web site:* www.doe.k12.de.us.

Legislative Essay Scholarship. Award for high school seniors from Delaware in public or private schools or in home school programs, who plan to enroll full-time at a nonprofit, regionally accredited college. Must submit an essay of between 500-2000 words. See Web site for essay topic and more information: http://www.doe.k12.

State Scholarship and Grant Programs
Delaware

de.us/ Deadline is December 1. Three statewide, nonrenewable awards of $7500, $3750, and $2250. *Award:* Scholarship for use in freshman year; not renewable. *Award amount:* $2250–$7500. *Number of awards:* 3. *Eligibility Requirements:* Applicant must be high school student; planning to enroll or expecting to enroll full-time at an institution or university and resident of Delaware. Available to U.S. citizens. *Application Requirements:* Application, essay. *Deadline:* December 1.

Contact Maureen Laffey, Director, Delaware Department of Education, Carvel State Office Building, 820 North French Street, Wilmington, DE 19801. *E-mail:* dedoe@doe.k12.de.us. *Phone:* 302-577-5240. *Fax:* 302-577-6765. *Web site:* www.doe.k12.de.us.

Legislative Essay Scholarship. Must be a senior in high school and Delaware resident. Submit an essay of 500 to 2000 words on a designated historical topic (changes annually). For more information visit: http://www.doe.state.de.us/high-ed *Award:* Scholarship for use in freshman year; not renewable. *Award amount:* $750–$7500. *Number of awards:* 62–65. *Eligibility Requirements:* Applicant must be high school student; planning to enroll or expecting to enroll full or part-time at a two-year, four-year, or technical institution or university and resident of Delaware. Available to U.S. citizens. *Application Requirements:* Application, applicant must enter a contest, essay. *Deadline:* varies.

Contact Donna Myers, Field Agent/Program Administrator, Delaware Higher Education Commission, 820 North French Street, 5th Floor, Wilmington, DE 19711-3509. *E-mail:* dmyers@doe.k12.de.us. *Phone:* 302-577-3240. *Fax:* 302-577-6765. *Web site:* www.doe.k12.de.us.

Michael C. Ferguson Achievement Award. Merit-based awards for eighth and tenth grade students who demonstrate superior performance on the Delaware Student Testing Program (DSPT) in reading, writing, and mathematics. Annual award of $1,000. *Award:* Scholarship for use in freshman year; not renewable. *Award amount:* $1000. *Eligibility Requirements:* Applicant must be enrolled or expecting to enroll at an institution or university and resident of Delaware. Available to U.S. citizens. *Application Requirements:* Application, transcript. *Deadline:* varies.

Contact Tony J. Marchio, Superintendent, Delaware Department of Education, 118 South Sixth Street, PO Box 4010, Odessa, DE 19730-4010. *Web site:* www.doe.k12.de.us.

Governor's Workforce Development Grant. Award for residents of Delaware and a U.S. citizen. Must be employed by a company in Delaware that contributes to the Blue Collar Training Fund Program. Must attend a participating college in Delaware on a part-time basis. Individual income must not exceed $32,417 annually. Full-time students are not eligible. The maximum Governor's Workforce Development Grant for one academic year is $2000 for part-time undergraduate study. Applications are due by the end of the free drop/add period each term. *Award:* Grant for use in freshman, sophomore, junior, or senior year; not renewable. *Award amount:* $2000. *Number of awards:* 1. *Eligibility Requirements:* Applicant must be age 18; enrolled or expecting to enroll part-time at a two-year or four-year institution or university; resident of Delaware and studying in Delaware. Available to U.S. citizens. *Application Requirements:* Application, transcript. *Deadline:* varies.

Contact Maureen Laffey, Director, Delaware Department of Education, Carvel State Office Building, 820 North French Street, Wilmington, DE 19801. *E-mail:* dedoe@doe.k12.de.us. *Phone:* 302-577-5240. *Fax:* 302-577-6765. *Web site:* www.doe.k12.de.us.

Christa McAuliffe Teacher Scholarship Loan-Delaware. Award for Delaware residents who are pursuing teaching careers. Must agree to teach in Delaware public schools as repayment of loan. Minimum award is $1000 and is renewable for up to four years. Available only at Delaware colleges. Based on academic merit. Must be ranked in upper half of class, and have a score of 1050 on SAT or 25 on the ACT. *Academic Fields/Career Goals:* Education. *Award:* Forgivable loan for use in freshman, sophomore, junior, or senior year; renewable. *Award amount:* $1000–$5000. *Number of awards:* 1–60. *Eligibility Requirements:* Applicant must be enrolled or expecting to enroll full-time at a four-year institution or university; resident of Delaware and studying in Delaware. Applicant must have 2.5 GPA or higher. Available to U.S. citizens. *Application Requirements:* Application, essay, test scores, transcript. *Deadline:* March 31.

Contact Donna Myers, Field Agent/Program Administrator, Delaware Higher Education Commission, 820 North French Street, 5th Floor, Wilmington, DE 19711-3509. *E-mail:* dmyers@doe.k12.de.us. *Phone:* 302-577-3240. *Fax:* 302-577-6765. *Web site:* www.doe.k12.de.us.

Educational Benefits for Children of Deceased Military and State Police. Renewable award for Delaware residents who are children of state or military police who were killed in the line of duty. Must attend a Delaware institution unless program of study is not available. Funds cover tuition and fees at Delaware institutions. The amount varies at non-Delaware institutions. Must submit proof of service and related death. Must be ages 16-24 at time of application. Deadline is three weeks before classes begin. *Award:* Grant for use in freshman, sophomore, junior, or senior year; renewable. *Award amount:* $6255. *Number of awards:* 1–10. *Eligibility Requirements:* Applicant must be age 16-24; enrolled or expecting to enroll full-time at a two-year or four-year institution or university and resident of Delaware. Applicant or parent of applicant must have employment or volunteer experience in police/firefighting. Available to U.S. citizens. Applicant or parent must meet one or more of the following requirements: general military experience; retired from active duty; disabled or killed as a result of military service; prisoner of war; or missing in action. *Application Requirements:* Application, verification of service-related death. *Deadline:* continuous.

Contact Donna Myers, Field Agent/Program Administrator, Delaware Higher Education Commission, 820 North French Street, 5th Floor, Wilmington, DE 19711-3509. *E-mail:* dmyers@doe.k12.de.us. *Phone:* 302-577-3240. *Fax:* 302-577-6765. *Web site:* www.doe.k12.de.us.

Delaware Solid Waste Authority John P. "Pat" Healy Scholarship. Scholarships given to residents of Delaware who are high school seniors or freshmen or sophomores in college. Must be majoring in either environmental engineering or environmental sciences in a Delaware college. Must file the Free Application for Federal Student Aid (FAFSA). Scholarships are automatically renewed for three years if a 3.0 GPA is maintained. Deadline: March 15. *Academic Fields/Career Goals:* Environmental Health. *Award:* Scholarship for use in freshman or sophomore year; renewable. *Award amount:* $2000. *Number of awards:* 1. *Eligibility Requirements:* Applicant must be enrolled or expecting to enroll full-time at a two-year or four-year institution or university; resident of Delaware and studying in Delaware. Applicant must have 3.0 GPA or higher. Available to U.S. citizens. *Application Requirements:* Application, financial need analysis, FAFSA. *Deadline:* March 15.

Contact Donna Myers, Field Agent/Program Administrator, Delaware Higher Education Commission, 820 North French Street, 5th Floor, Wilmington, DE 19711-3509. *E-mail:* dmyers@doe.k12.de.us. *Phone:* 302-577-3240. *Fax:* 302-577-6765. *Web site:* www.doe.k12.de.us.

State Scholarship and Grant Programs
Delaware

Diamond State Scholarship. Renewable award for Delaware high school seniors enrolling full-time at an accredited college or university. Must be ranked in upper quarter of class and score 1200 on SAT or 27 on the ACT. *Award:* Scholarship for use in freshman year; renewable. *Award amount:* $1250. *Number of awards:* 50–200. *Eligibility Requirements:* Applicant must be high school student; planning to enroll or expecting to enroll full-time at a four-year institution or university and resident of Delaware. Applicant must have 3.5 GPA or higher. Available to U.S. citizens. *Application Requirements:* Application, essay, test scores, transcript. *Deadline:* March 31.

Contact Donna Myers, Field Agent/Program Administrator, Delaware Higher Education Commission, 820 North French Street, 5th Floor, Wilmington, DE 19711-3509. *E-mail:* dmyers@doe.k12.de.us. *Phone:* 302-577-3240. *Fax:* 302-577-6765. *Web site:* www.doe.k12.de.us.

Diamond State Scholarship. Award of $1250 per year and renewable for up to three additional years. Must be a legal residents of Delaware. The deadline is March 31. *Award:* Scholarship for use in freshman, sophomore, junior, or senior year; renewable. *Award amount:* $1250–$5000. *Number of awards:* 50. *Eligibility Requirements:* Applicant must be high school student; planning to enroll or expecting to enroll full-time at a two-year, four-year, or technical institution or university and resident of Delaware. Available to U.S. citizens. *Application Requirements:* Application, transcript. *Deadline:* March 31.

Contact Maureen Laffey, Director, Delaware Department of Education, Carvel State Office Building, 820 North French Street, Wilmington, DE 19801. *E-mail:* dedoe@doe.k12.de.us. *Phone:* 302-577-5240. *Fax:* 302-577-6765. *Web site:* www.doe.k12.de.us.

Scholarship Incentive Program-Delaware. One-time award for Delaware residents with financial need. May be used at an institution in Delaware or Pennsylvania, or at another out-of-state institution if a program is not available at a publicly-supported school in Delaware. Must have minimum 2.5 GPA. *Award:* Grant for use in freshman, sophomore, junior, senior, or graduate year; not renewable. *Award amount:* $700–$2200. *Number of awards:* 1000–1300. *Eligibility Requirements:* Applicant must be enrolled or expecting to enroll full-time at a two-year or four-year institution or university; resident of Delaware and studying in Delaware or Pennsylvania. Applicant must have 2.5 GPA or higher. Available to U.S. citizens. *Application Requirements:* Application, financial need analysis, transcript. *Deadline:* April 15.

Contact Donna Myers, Field Agent/Program Administrator, Delaware Higher Education Commission, 820 North French Street, 5th Floor, Wilmington, DE 19711-3509. *E-mail:* dmyers@doe.k12.de.us. *Phone:* 302-577-3240. *Fax:* 302-577-6765. *Web site:* www.doe.k12.de.us.

DISTRICT OF COLUMBIA

Carville M. Akehurst Memorial Scholarship. Scholarship is available to resident of Maryland, Virginia, or West Virginia. Applicant must be enrolled in an accredited undergraduate or graduate landscape/ horticulture program or related discipline at a two- or four-year institution and must have minimum 3.0 GPA. Application deadline April 1. *Academic Fields/Career Goals:* Horticulture/Floriculture; Landscape Architecture. *Award:* Scholarship for use in junior, senior, or graduate year; not renewable. *Award amount:* $1000. *Number of awards:* 1–2. *Eligibility Requirements:* Applicant must be enrolled or expecting to enroll full-time at a two-year or four-year institution or university and resident of Maryland, Virginia, or West Virginia. Applicant must have 3.0 GPA or higher. Available to U.S. citizens. *Application Requirements:* Application, essay, financial need analysis, resume, references, transcript. *Deadline:* April 1.

Contact Teresa Jodon, Endowment Program Administrator, American Nursery and Landscape Association, 1000 Vermont Avenue, NW, Suite 300, Washington, DC 20005. *E-mail:* tjodon@anla.org. *Phone:* 202-789-5980 Ext. 3014. *Fax:* 202-789-1893. *Web site:* www.anla.org/research.

ANLA National Scholarship Endowment-Usrey Family Scholarship. Award for students accredited undergraduate or graduate landscape horticulture program or related discipline at a two- or four-year institution. The applicant must be a student enrolled in a California state university or college. Preference given to applicants who plan to work within the industry. Must have a minimum 2.5 GPA. *Academic Fields/Career Goals:* Horticulture/Floriculture; Landscape Architecture. *Award:* Scholarship for use in sophomore, junior, senior, graduate, or postgraduate years; not renewable. *Award amount:* $1000–$1500. *Number of awards:* 1. *Eligibility Requirements:* Applicant must be enrolled or expecting to enroll full-time at a two-year, four-year, or technical institution or university and studying in California. Applicant must have 2.5 GPA or higher. Available to U.S. and non-U.S. citizens. *Application Requirements:* Application, essay, financial need analysis, references, transcript. *Deadline:* April 1.

Contact Teresa Jodon, Endowment Program Administrator, American Nursery and Landscape Association, 1000 Vermont Avenue, NW, Suite 300, Washington, DC 20005. *E-mail:* hriresearch@anla.org. *Phone:* 202-789-2900 Ext. 3014. *Fax:* 202-789-1893. *Web site:* www.anla.org/research.

Robert C. Byrd Scholarship-District of Columbia. Federally-funded, state-administered program to recognize exceptionally able high school seniors who show promise of continued excellence in postsecondary education. Must be a U.S. citizen and permanent resident of District of Columbia. *Award:* Scholarship for use in freshman year; renewable. *Award amount:* $1500–$6000. *Number of awards:* 28. *Eligibility Requirements:* Applicant must be enrolled or expecting to enroll full-time at a two-year, four-year, or technical institution or university and resident of District of Columbia. Available to U.S. citizens. *Application Requirements:* Application, transcript. *Deadline:* varies.

Contact Michon Peck, Scholarship Coordinator, District of Columbia Public Schools, 825 North Capitol Street, NE, 6th Floor, Room 6077, Washington, DC 20002. *E-mail:* michon.peck@k12.dc.us. *Phone:* 202-442-5110. *Fax:* 202-442-5303.

DC Leveraging Educational Assistance Partnership Program (LEAP). Available to Washington, D.C. residents who have financial need. Must also apply for the Federal Pell Grant. Must attend an eligible college at least half time. Contact financial aid office or local library for more information. Proof of residency may be required. Deadline is last Friday in June. *Award:* Grant for use in freshman, sophomore, junior, or senior year; renewable. *Award amount:* $250–$1500. *Number of awards:* 2274–2300. *Eligibility Requirements:* Applicant must be enrolled or expecting to enroll full or part-time at a two-year, four-year, or technical institution or university and resident of District of Columbia. Available to U.S. citizens. *Application Requirements:* Application, financial need analysis, transcript, Student Aid Report (SAR), FASFA. *Deadline:* June 28.

Contact Miss. Carol Talley, District of Columbia State Education Office, 441 4th Street, NW, 350 North, Washington, DC 20001. *Phone:* 202-724-7784. *Web site:* www.seo.dc.gov.

American Council of the Blind Scholarships. Merit-based award available to undergraduate, graduate, vocational or technical students who are legally blind

State Scholarship and Grant Programs
Florida

in both eyes. Submit certificate of legal blindness and proof of acceptance at an accredited postsecondary institution. *Award:* Scholarship for use in freshman, sophomore, junior, senior, or graduate year; renewable. *Award amount:* $500–$3000. *Number of awards:* 26. *Eligibility Requirements:* Applicant must be enrolled or expecting to enroll full-time at a four-year, or technical institution or university. Applicant must be visually impaired. Applicant must have 3.5 GPA or higher. Available to U.S. citizens. *Application Requirements:* Application, autobiography, essay, references, transcript, evidence of legal blindness. *Deadline:* March 1.

Contact Terry Pacheco, Affiliate and Membership Services, American Council of the Blind, 1155 15th Street, NW, Suite 1004, Washington, DC 20005. *E-mail:* info@acb.org. *Phone:* 202-467-5081. *Fax:* 202-467-5085. *Web site:* www.acb.org.

Spring Meadow Nursery Scholarship. Scholarship for the full-time study of horticulture or landscape architecture students in undergraduate or graduate landscape horticulture program or related discipline at a two- or four-year institution. Applicant must have minimum 2.5 GPA. Application deadline is April 1. *Academic Fields/Career Goals:* Horticulture/Floriculture; Landscape Architecture. *Award:* Scholarship for use in freshman, sophomore, junior, senior, or graduate year; not renewable. *Award amount:* $1000–$1500. *Number of awards:* 1–2. *Eligibility Requirements:* Applicant must be enrolled or expecting to enroll full-time at a two-year, four-year, or technical institution or university. Applicant must have 2.5 GPA or higher. Available to U.S. and Canadian citizens. *Application Requirements:* Application, essay, financial need analysis, resume, references, transcript. *Deadline:* April 1.

Contact Teresa Jodon, Endowment Program Administrator, American Nursery and Landscape Association, 1000 Vermont Avenue, NW, Suite 300, Washington, DC 20005-4914. *E-mail:* tjodon@anla.org. *Phone:* 202-789-5980 Ext. 3014. *Fax:* 202-789-1893. *Web site:* www.anla.org/research.

FLORIDA

Rosewood Family Scholarship Fund. Renewable award for eligible minority students to attend a Florida public postsecondary institution on a full-time basis. Preference given to direct descendants of African-American Rosewood families affected by the incidents of January 1923. Must be Black, Hispanic, Asian, Pacific Islander, American-Indian, or Alaska Native. Free Application for Federal Student Aid (and Student Aid Report for nonresidents of Florida) must be processed by May 15. *Award:* Scholarship for use in freshman, sophomore, junior, or senior year; renewable. *Award amount:* up to $4000. *Number of awards:* up to 25. *Eligibility Requirements:* Applicant must be American Indian/Alaska Native, Asian/Pacific Islander, Black (non-Hispanic), or Hispanic; enrolled or expecting to enroll full-time at a two-year, four-year, or technical institution or university and studying in Florida. Available to U.S. citizens. *Application Requirements:* Application, financial need analysis. *Deadline:* April 1.

Contact Barb Dombrowski, Education Director, Policy and Training, Florida Department of Education, Office of Student Financial Assistance, 1940 North Monroe, Suite 70, Tallahassee, FL 32303-4759. *E-mail:* barb.dombrowski@fldoe.org. *Phone:* 850-410-5191. *Fax:* 850-488-5966. *Web site:* www.floridastudentfinancialaid.org.

Critical Teacher Shortage Student Loan Forgiveness Program-Florida. Eligible Florida teachers may receive up to $5000 for repayment of undergraduate and graduate educational loans, which lead to certification in critical teacher shortage subject area. Must teach full-time at a Florida public school in a critical area for a minimum of ninety days to be eligible. Visit Web site for further information. *Award:* Forgivable loan for use in freshman, sophomore, junior, senior, or graduate year; renewable. *Award amount:* $2500–$5000. *Number of awards:* varies. *Eligibility Requirements:* Applicant must be enrolled or expecting to enroll at a two-year or four-year institution or university; resident of Florida and studying in Florida. Applicant or parent of applicant must have employment or volunteer experience in teaching. Available to U.S. citizens. *Application Requirements:* Application, transcript. *Deadline:* July 15.

Contact Barb Dombrowski, Education Director, Policy and Training, Florida Department of Education, Office of Student Financial Assistance, 1940 North Monroe, Suite 70, Tallahassee, FL 32303-4759. *E-mail:* barb.dombrowski@fldoe.org. *Phone:* 850-410-5191. *Fax:* 850-488-5966. *Web site:* www.floridastudentfinancialaid.org.

William L. Boyd IV Florida Resident Access Grant. Awards given to Florida residents attending an independent non-profit college or university in Florida for undergraduate study. Cannot have previously received bachelor's degree. Must enroll minimum 12 credit hours. Deadline set by eligible postsecondary financial aid offices. Contact financial aid administrator for application information. Reapply for renewal. *Award:* Grant for use in freshman, sophomore, junior, or senior year; not renewable. *Award amount:* up to $2850. *Number of awards:* varies. *Eligibility Requirements:* Applicant must be enrolled or expecting to enroll full-time at a four-year institution or university; resident of Florida and studying in Florida. Available to U.S. citizens. *Application Requirements:* Application. *Deadline:* April 1.

Contact Barb Dombrowski, Education Director, Policy and Training, Florida Department of Education, Office of Student Financial Assistance, 1940 North Monroe, Suite 70, Tallahassee, FL 32303-4759. *E-mail:* barb.dombrowski@fldoe.org. *Phone:* 850-410-5191. *Fax:* 850-488-5966. *Web site:* www.floridastudentfinancialaid.org.

Florida Work Experience Program. Program is offered at participating state public universities and community colleges and eligible private, non-profit postsecondary institutions. Contact the financial aid administrator for application deadlines and student eligibility requirements. *Award:* Grant for use in freshman, sophomore, junior, or senior year. *Eligibility Requirements:* Applicant must be enrolled or expecting to enroll full or part-time at a two-year or four-year institution or university. Available to U.S. citizens. *Application Requirements:* Application, financial need analysis, FAFSA. *Deadline:* varies.

Contact Barb Dombrowski, Education Director, Policy and Training, Florida Department of Education, Office of Student Financial Assistance, 1940 North Monroe, Suite 70, Tallahassee, FL 32303-4759. *E-mail:* barb.dombrowski@fldoe.org. *Phone:* 850-410-5191. *Fax:* 850-488-5966. *Web site:* www.floridastudentfinancialaid.org.

Ethics in Business Scholarship. Provides assistance to undergraduate college students who enroll at community colleges and eligible Florida colleges or universities. Scholarships are funded by private and state contributions. Awards are dependent on private matching funds. For more information contact the financial aid office at participating institutions, which are listed on the Florida Department of Education Web site at http://www.firn.edu/doe/ofsa *Award:* Scholarship for use in freshman, sophomore, junior, or senior year; not renewable. *Number of awards:* varies. *Eligibility Requirements:* Applicant must be enrolled or expecting to enroll at a two-year or four-year institution or university and studying in Florida. Available to U.S. citizens. *Application Requirements:* Application. *Deadline:* varies.

State Scholarship and Grant Programs
Florida

Contact Barb Dombrowski, Education Director, Policy and Training, Florida Department of Education, Office of Student Financial Assistance, 1940 North Monroe, Suite 70, Tallahassee, FL 32303-4759. *E-mail:* barb.dombrowski@fldoe.org. *Phone:* 850-410-5191. *Fax:* 850-488-5966. *Web site:* www.floridastudentfinancialaid.org.

Critical Teacher Shortage Tuition Reimbursement-Florida. One-time awards for full-time Florida public school employees who are certified to teach in Florida and are teaching, or preparing to teach, in critical teacher shortage subject areas. Must earn minimum grade of 3.0 in approved courses. May receive tuition reimbursement up to 9 semester hours or equivalent per academic year, not to exceed $78 per semester hour, for maximum 36 hours. Must be resident of Florida. *Academic Fields/Career Goals:* Education. *Award:* Scholarship for use in freshman, sophomore, junior, senior, or graduate year; not renewable. *Award amount:* $702–$2808. *Eligibility Requirements:* Applicant must be enrolled or expecting to enroll at a two-year or four-year institution or university; resident of Florida and studying in Florida. Applicant or parent of applicant must have employment or volunteer experience in teaching. Applicant must have 3.0 GPA or higher. Available to U.S. citizens. *Application Requirements:* Application. *Deadline:* September 15.

Contact Barb Dombrowski, Education Director, Policy and Training, Florida Department of Education, Office of Student Financial Assistance, 1940 North Monroe, Suite 70, Tallahassee, FL 32303-4759. *E-mail:* barb.dombrowski@fldoe.org. *Phone:* 850-410-5191. *Fax:* 850-488-5966. *Web site:* www.floridastudentfinancialaid.org.

Florida/NASA Matching Grant Program. One-time award for aerospace and technology research. Grant is for research in Florida only. Submit research proposal with budget. Applicants must be from a university, college, or industry in Florida. Deadline varies. *Award:* Grant for use in freshman, sophomore, junior, senior, graduate, or postgraduate years; not renewable. *Number of awards:* 9–12. *Eligibility Requirements:* Applicant must be enrolled or expecting to enroll full or part-time at a two-year, four-year, or technical institution or university and studying in Florida. Available to U.S. citizens. *Application Requirements:* Proposal with budget. *Deadline:* March 5.

Contact Dr. Jaydeep Mukherjee, FSGC Administrator, NASA Florida Space Grant Consortium, Mail Code: FSGC, Kennedy Space Center, FL 32899. *E-mail:* fsgc@mail.ucf.edu. *Phone:* 321-452-4301. *Fax:* 321-449-0739. *Web site:* fsgc.engr.ucf.edu.

Scholarships for Children of Deceased or Disabled Veterans or Children of Servicemen Classified as POW or MIA. Scholarship provides full tuition assistance for children of deceased or disabled veterans or of servicemen classified as POW or MIA who are in full-time attendance at eligible public or non-public Florida institutions. Service connection must be as specified under Florida statute. Amount of payment to non-public institutions is equal to cost at public institutions at the comparable level. Must be between 16 and 22. Qualified veteran and applicant must meet residency requirements. *Award:* Scholarship for use in freshman, sophomore, junior, or senior year; renewable. *Number of awards:* 160. *Eligibility Requirements:* Applicant must be age 17-21; enrolled or expecting to enroll full or part-time at a two-year, four-year, or technical institution or university; resident of Florida and studying in Florida. Available to U.S. citizens. Applicant or parent must meet one or more of the following requirements: general military experience; retired from active duty; disabled or killed as a result of military service; prisoner of war; or missing in action. *Application Requirements:* Application. *Deadline:* April 1.

Contact Barb Dombrowski, Education Director, Policy and Training, Florida Department of Education, Office of Student Financial Assistance, 1940 North Monroe, Suite 70, Tallahassee, FL 32303-4759. *E-mail:* barb.dombrowski@fldoe.org. *Phone:* 850-410-5191. *Fax:* 850-488-5966. *Web site:* www.floridastudentfinancialaid.org.

Jose Marti Scholarship Challenge Grant Fund. Award available to Hispanic-American students who were born in, or whose parent was born in a Hispanic country. Must have lived in Florida for one year, be enrolled full-time in Florida at an eligible school, and have a GPA of 3.0 or above. Must be U.S. citizen or eligible non-citizen. Renewable award of $2000. Application must be postmarked by April 1. Free Application for Federal Student Aid must be processed by May 15. *Award:* Scholarship for use in freshman, sophomore, junior, senior, or graduate year; renewable. *Award amount:* $2000. *Number of awards:* 63. *Eligibility Requirements:* Applicant must be of Hispanic heritage; enrolled or expecting to enroll full-time at a two-year, four-year, or technical institution or university; resident of Florida and studying in Florida. Applicant must have 3.0 GPA or higher. Available to U.S. citizens. *Application Requirements:* Application, financial need analysis, FAFSA. *Deadline:* April 1.

Contact Barb Dombrowski, Education Director, Policy and Training, Florida Department of Education, Office of Student Financial Assistance, 1940 North Monroe, Suite 70, Tallahassee, FL 32303-4759. *E-mail:* barb.dombrowski@fldoe.org. *Phone:* 850-410-5191. *Fax:* 850-488-5966. *Web site:* www.floridastudentfinancialaid.org.

Florida Public Student Assistance Grant. Grants for Florida residents, U.S. citizens, or eligible non-citizens attending a Florida public college or university full-time. Based on financial need. Renewable up to 9 semesters, 14 quarters, or until receipt of bachelor's degree. Deadline set by eligible participating institutions. *Award:* Grant for use in freshman, sophomore, junior, or senior year; renewable. *Award amount:* $200–$1672. *Number of awards:* varies. *Eligibility Requirements:* Applicant must be enrolled or expecting to enroll full or part-time at a two-year or four-year institution or university; resident of Florida and studying in Florida. Available to U.S. citizens. *Application Requirements:* Application, financial need analysis, FAFSA. *Deadline:* varies.

Contact Barb Dombrowski, Education Director, Policy and Training, Florida Department of Education, Office of Student Financial Assistance, 1940 North Monroe, Suite 70, Tallahassee, FL 32303-4759. *E-mail:* barb.dombrowski@fldoe.org. *Phone:* 850-410-5191. *Fax:* 850-488-5966. *Web site:* www.floridastudentfinancialaid.org.

Mary McLeod Bethune Scholarship. Available to Florida students with a GPA of 3.0 or above who will attend Florida Agricultural and Mechanical University, Edward Waters College, Bethune-Cookman College, or Florida Memorial College. Based on need and merit. Further information, deadlines, and applications available at the financial aid office at the school. *Award:* Scholarship for use in freshman, sophomore, junior, or senior year; renewable. *Award amount:* $3000. *Eligibility Requirements:* Applicant must be enrolled or expecting to enroll full-time at a two-year or four-year institution or university; resident of Florida and studying in Florida. Applicant must have 3.0 GPA or higher. Available to U.S. citizens. *Application Requirements:* Application, financial need analysis. *Deadline:* varies.

Contact Barb Dombrowski, Education Director, Policy and Training, Florida Department of Education, Office of Student Financial Assistance, 1940 North Monroe, Suite 70, Tallahassee, FL 32303-4759. *E-mail:* barb.dombrowski@fldoe.org. *Phone:* 850-410-5191. *Fax:* 850-488-5966. *Web site:* www.floridastudentfinancialaid.org.

State Scholarship and Grant Programs
Georgia

Access to Better Learning and Education Grant. Provides tuition assistance to Florida undergraduates enrolled full-time in degree programs at eligible independent postsecondary institutions in Florida. Students must be US citizens or eligible non-citizens and must meet Florida residency requirements. Contact the financial aid administrator for application deadlines and student eligibility requirements. *Award:* Grant for use in freshman, sophomore, junior, or senior year. *Eligibility Requirements:* Applicant must be enrolled or expecting to enroll full-time at a four-year institution or university; resident of Florida and studying in Florida. Available to U.S. citizens. *Application Requirements:* Application. *Deadline:* varies.

Contact Barb Dombrowski, Education Director, Policy and Training, Florida Department of Education, Office of Student Financial Assistance, 1940 North Monroe, Suite 70, Tallahassee, FL 32303-4759. *E-mail:* barb.dombrowski@fldoe.org. *Phone:* 850-410-5191. *Fax:* 850-488-5966. *Web site:* www.floridastudentfinancialaid.org.

Florida Private Student Assistance Grant. Grants for Florida residents who are U.S. citizens or eligible non-citizens attending eligible independent nonprofit colleges or universities in Florida. Must be full-time student and demonstrate substantial financial need. Renewable for up to nine semesters, fourteen quarters, or until receipt of bachelor's degree. Deadline to be determined by individual eligible institutions. *Award:* Grant for use in freshman, sophomore, junior, or senior year; renewable. *Award amount:* $200–$1672. *Number of awards:* varies. *Eligibility Requirements:* Applicant must be enrolled or expecting to enroll full-time at a two-year or four-year institution or university; resident of Florida and studying in Florida. Available to U.S. citizens. *Application Requirements:* Application, financial need analysis, FAFSA. *Deadline:* varies.

Contact Barb Dombrowski, Education Director, Policy and Training, Florida Department of Education, Office of Student Financial Assistance, 1940 North Monroe, Suite 70, Tallahassee, FL 32303-4759. *E-mail:* barb.dombrowski@fldoe.org. *Phone:* 850-410-5191. *Fax:* 850-488-5966. *Web site:* www.floridastudentfinancialaid.org.

GEORGIA

GAE GFIE Scholarship for Aspiring Teachers. Scholarships will be awarded to graduating seniors who currently attend a fully accredited public Georgia high school and will attend a fully accredited Georgia college or university within the next 12 months. Must have a 3.0 GPA. Must submit three letters of recommendation. Must have plans to enter the teaching profession. *Academic Fields/Career Goals:* Education. *Award:* Scholarship for use in freshman year; not renewable. *Award amount:* $1000. *Number of awards:* 10–20. *Eligibility Requirements:* Applicant must be high school student; planning to enroll or expecting to enroll at a two-year or four-year institution or university; resident of Georgia and studying in Georgia. Applicant must have 3.0 GPA or higher. Available to U.S. citizens. *Application Requirements:* Application, transcript. *Deadline:* March 15.

Contact Sally Bennett, Professional Development Specialist, Georgia Association of Educators, 100 Crescent Centre Parkway Suite 500, Tucker, GA 30084-7049. *E-mail:* sally.bennett@gae.org. *Phone:* 678-837-1103. *Web site:* www.gae.org.

Georgia Leveraging Educational Assistance Partnership Grant Program. Based on financial need. Recipients must be eligible for the Federal Pell Grant. Renewable award for Georgia residents enrolled in a state postsecondary institution. Must be U.S. citizen. *Award:* Grant for use in freshman, sophomore, junior, or senior year; renewable. *Award amount:* up to $2000. *Number of awards:* 3000–3500. *Eligibility Requirements:* Applicant must be enrolled or expecting to enroll full or part-time at a two-year, four-year, or technical institution or university; resident of Georgia and studying in Georgia. Available to U.S. citizens. *Application Requirements:* Application, financial need analysis. *Deadline:* continuous.

Contact William Flook, Director of Scholarships and Grants, Georgia Student Finance Commission, 2082 East Exchange Place, Suite 100, Tucker, GA 30084. *E-mail:* billf@gsfc.org. *Phone:* 770-724-9052. *Fax:* 770-724-9031. *Web site:* www.doe.k12.ga.us.

Georgia PROMISE Teacher Scholarship Program. Renewable, forgivable loans for junior undergraduates at Georgia colleges who have been accepted for enrollment into a teacher education program leading to initial certification. Minimum cumulative 3.0 GPA required. Recipient must teach at a Georgia public school for one year for each $1500 awarded. Available to seniors for renewal only. Write for deadlines. *Academic Fields/Career Goals:* Education. *Award:* Forgivable loan for use in junior or senior year; renewable. *Award amount:* $3000–$6000. *Number of awards:* 700–1400. *Eligibility Requirements:* Applicant must be enrolled or expecting to enroll full or part-time at a four-year institution or university and studying in Georgia. Applicant must have 3.0 GPA or higher. Available to U.S. citizens. *Application Requirements:* Application, transcript, Selective Service registration, official certification to be admitted into an approved teacher education program in Georgia. *Deadline:* continuous.

Contact Stan DeWitt, Manager of Teacher Scholarships, Georgia Student Finance Commission, 2082 East Exchange Place, Suite 100, Tucker, GA 30084. *E-mail:* stand@gsfc.org. *Phone:* 770-724-9060. *Fax:* 770-724-9031. *Web site:* www.doe.k12.ga.us.

Georgia Public Safety Memorial Grant/ Law Enforcement Personnel Department Grant. Award for children of Georgia law enforcement officers, prison guards, or fire fighters killed or permanently disabled in the line of duty. Must attend an accredited postsecondary Georgia school. Complete the Law Enforcement Personnel Dependents application. *Award:* Grant for use in freshman, sophomore, junior, or senior year; renewable. *Award amount:* $1000–$8000. *Number of awards:* 20–40. *Eligibility Requirements:* Applicant must be enrolled or expecting to enroll full-time at a two-year, four-year, or technical institution or university; resident of Georgia and studying in Georgia. Applicant or parent of applicant must have employment or volunteer experience in police/firefighting. Available to U.S. citizens. *Application Requirements:* Application, financial need analysis, Selective Service registration. *Deadline:* continuous.

Contact William Flook, Director of Scholarships and Grants Division, Georgia Student Finance Commission, 2082 East Exchange Place, Suite 100, Tucker, GA 30084. *E-mail:* billf@gsfc.org. *Phone:* 770-724-9052. *Fax:* 770-724-9031. *Web site:* www.doe.k12.ga.us.

Robert C. Byrd Honors Scholarship-Georgia. Complete the application provided by the Georgia Department of Education. Renewable awards for outstanding graduating Georgia high school seniors to be used for full-time undergraduate study at eligible U.S. institution. Must a legal resident of Georgia and a U.S. citizen. *Award:* Scholarship for use in freshman, sophomore, junior, or senior year; renewable. *Award amount:* up to $1500. *Number of awards:* 600–720. *Eligibility Requirements:* Applicant must be high school student and planning to enroll or expecting to enroll full-time at a two-year or four-year institution or university. Available to U.S. citizens. *Application Requirements:* Application, transcript. *Deadline:* February 1.

Contact William Flook, Director of Scholarships and Grants Division, Georgia Student

State Scholarship and Grant Programs

Georgia

Finance Commission, 2082 East Exchange Place, Suite 100, Tucker, GA 30084. *E-mail:* billf@gsfc.org. *Phone:* 770-724-9052. *Fax:* 770-724-9031. *Web site:* www.doe.k12.ga.us.

HOPE—Helping Outstanding Pupils Educationally. Grant program for Georgia residents who are college undergraduates to attend an accredited two or four-year Georgia institution. Tuition and fees may be covered by the grant. Minimum 3.0 GPA required. Renewable if student maintains grades and reapplies. Write for deadlines. *Award:* Scholarship for use in freshman, sophomore, junior, or senior year; renewable. *Award amount:* $300–$3900. *Number of awards:* 140,000–170,000. *Eligibility Requirements:* Applicant must be enrolled or expecting to enroll full or part-time at a two-year or four-year institution or university; resident of Georgia and studying in Georgia. Applicant must have 3.0 GPA or higher. Available to U.S. citizens. *Application Requirements:* Application. *Deadline:* continuous.

Contact William Flook, Director of Scholarships and Grants Division, Georgia Student Finance Commission, 2082 East Exchange Place, Suite 100, Tucker, GA 30084. *E-mail:* billf@gsfc.org. *Phone:* 770-724-9052. *Fax:* 770-724-9031. *Web site:* www.doe.k12.ga.us.

Georgia Tuition Equalization Grant (GTEG). Award for Georgia residents pursuing undergraduate study at an accredited two- or four-year Georgia private institution. Complete the Georgia Student Grant Application. Available to residents of Georgia who live near the State borders to attend certain four-year public colleges out-of-state, so that a four-year public college. Award is $909 per academic year *Award:* Grant for use in freshman, sophomore, junior, or senior year; renewable. *Eligibility Requirements:* Applicant must be enrolled or expecting to enroll full-time at a two-year or four-year institution or university; resident of Georgia and studying in Alabama, Florida, Georgia, or Tennessee. Available to U.S. citizens. *Application Requirements:* Application, Social Security number. *Deadline:* continuous.

Contact William Flook, Grants Director, Georgia Student Finance Commission, 2082 East Exchange Place, Suite 100, Tucker, GA 30084. *E-mail:* billf@gsfc.org. *Phone:* 770-724-9052. *Fax:* 770-724-9031. *Web site:* www.doe.k12.ga.us.

Governor's Scholarship-Georgia. Award to assist students selected as Georgia scholars, STAR students, valedictorians, and salutatorians. For use at two- and four-year colleges and universities in Georgia. Recipients are selected as entering freshmen. Renewable award of up to $1000. Minimum 3.0 GPA required. *Award:* Scholarship for use in freshman, sophomore, junior, or senior year; renewable. *Award amount:* up to $1000. *Number of awards:* 900–3000. *Eligibility Requirements:* Applicant must be high school student; planning to enroll or expecting to enroll full-time at a two-year or four-year institution or university; resident of Georgia and studying in Georgia. Applicant must have 3.0 GPA or higher. Available to U.S. citizens. *Application Requirements:* Application, transcript. *Deadline:* continuous.

Contact William Flook, Director of Scholarships and Grants Division, Georgia Student Finance Commission, 2082 East Exchange Place, Suite 100, Tucker, GA 30084. *E-mail:* billf@gsfc.org. *Phone:* 770-724-9052. *Fax:* 770-724-9031. *Web site:* www.doe.k12.ga.us.

HAWAII

Hawaii State Student Incentive Grant. Grants are given to residents of Hawaii who are enrolled in a participating Hawaiian state school. Funds are for undergraduate tuition only. Applicants must submit a financial need analysis. *Award:* Grant for use in freshman, sophomore, junior, or senior year; renewable. *Award amount:* $200–$2000. *Number of awards:* up to 470. *Eligibility Requirements:* Applicant must be enrolled or expecting to enroll full or part-time at a two-year, four-year, or technical institution or university; resident of Hawaii and studying in Hawaii. Available to U.S. citizens. *Application Requirements:* Financial need analysis. *Deadline:* continuous.

Contact Janine Oyama, Financial Aid Specialist, Hawaii State Postsecondary Education Commission, University of Hawaii, Honolulu, HI 96822. *Phone:* 808-956-6066.

Robert C. Byrd Scholarship-Hawaii. The Robert C. Byrd Honors Scholarship is available to students planning to attend college. The scholarship is federally funded, state-administered and recognizes exceptional high school seniors who show promise of continued excellence in the postsecondary educational system. Award of $1500 renewable for four years. Must have a minimum GPA of 3.2 and 1270 SAT. Deadline is March 17. *Award:* Scholarship for use in freshman year; renewable. *Award amount:* $1500–$6000. *Number of awards:* 28. *Eligibility Requirements:* Applicant must be enrolled or expecting to enroll full-time at an institution or university. Applicant must have 3.0 GPA or higher. Available to U.S. citizens. *Application Requirements:* Application, transcript, community service. *Deadline:* March 17.

Contact Deanna Helber, Education Specialist, Hawaii Department of Education, 641 18th Avenue, Building V, Room 201, Honolulu, HI 96816-4444. *E-mail:* dee_helber@notes.k12.hi.us. *Phone:* 808-735-6222. *Fax:* 808-733-9890. *Web site:* doe.k12.hi.us.

Kumu Kahua Theater/UHM Theater Department Playwriting Contest, Pacific Rim Prize. Contest for residents and non-residents of Hawaii. Play must be set in or deal with the Pacific Islands, the Pacific Rim, or the Pacific/Asian-American experience. Restricted to full-length plays of a minimum of 50 pages in standard form. Write for details. *Award:* Prize for use in freshman, sophomore, junior, senior, graduate, or postgraduate years; not renewable. *Award amount:* $450. *Number of awards:* 1. *Eligibility Requirements:* Applicant must be enrolled or expecting to enroll at an institution or university and must have an interest in writing. Available to U.S. and non-U.S. citizens. *Application Requirements:* Applicant must enter a contest, 3 copies of manuscript. *Deadline:* January 2.

Contact Kuma Kahua Playwriting Contest, Kumu Kahua Theatre, 46 Merchant Street, Honolulu, HI 96813. *E-mail:* info@kumukahua.com. *Web site:* kumukahua.org/.

IDAHO

Idaho Promise Category A Scholarship Program. Renewable award available to Idaho residents who are graduating high school seniors. Must attend an approved Idaho institute of higher education full-time. Based on class rank (must be verified by school official), GPA, and ACT scores. Professional-technical student applicants must take COMPASS. *Award:* Scholarship for use in freshman, sophomore, junior, or senior year; renewable. *Award amount:* $3000. *Number of awards:* 25–30. *Eligibility Requirements:* Applicant must be high school student; planning to enroll or expecting to enroll full-time at a two-year, four-year, or technical institution or university; resident of Idaho and studying in Idaho. Applicant must have 3.5 GPA or higher. Available to U.S. citizens. *Application Requirements:* Application, test scores. *Deadline:* December 15.

Contact Lynn Humphrey, Manager, Student Aid Programs, Idaho State Board of Education, PO Box 83720, Boise, ID 83720-0037. *E-mail:* lhumphre@osbe.state.id.us. *Phone:* 208-334-2270. *Fax:* 208-334-2632. *Web site:* www.boardofed.idaho.gov.

State Scholarship and Grant Programs
Illinois

Idaho Minority and "At Risk" Student Scholarship. Renewable award for Idaho residents who are disabled or members of a minority group and have financial need. Must attend one of eight postsecondary institutions in the state for undergraduate study. Deadlines vary by institution. Must be a U.S. citizen and be a graduate of an Idaho high school. Contact college financial aid office. *Award:* Scholarship for use in freshman, sophomore, junior, or senior year; renewable. *Award amount:* $3000. *Number of awards:* 35–40. *Eligibility Requirements:* Applicant must be American Indian/Alaska Native, Black (non-Hispanic), or Hispanic; enrolled or expecting to enroll full-time at a two-year, four-year, or technical institution or university; resident of Idaho and studying in Idaho. Applicant must be hearing impaired, physically disabled, or visually impaired. Available to U.S. citizens. *Application Requirements:* Application, financial need analysis, transcript. *Deadline:* varies.

Contact Dana Kelly, Program Manager, Idaho State Board of Education, PO Box 83720, Boise, ID 83720-0037. *E-mail:* dana.kelly@osbe.idaho.gov. *Phone:* 208-332-1574. *Web site:* www.boardofed.idaho.gov.

Freedom Scholarship. Scholarship for children of Idaho citizens determined by the federal government to have been prisoners of war, missing in action, or killed in action or died of injuries or wounds sustained in action in southeast Asia, including Korea, or who shall become so hereafter, in any area of armed conflict in which the United States is a party. Applicant must attend an Idaho public college or university and meet all requirements for regular admission. *Award:* Scholarship for use in freshman, sophomore, junior, senior, graduate, or postgraduate years; not renewable. *Award amount:* $1000. *Eligibility Requirements:* Applicant must be enrolled or expecting to enroll at a two-year, four-year, or technical institution or university; resident of Idaho and studying in Idaho. Available to U.S. citizens. Applicant or parent must meet one or more of the following requirements: general military experience; retired from active duty; disabled or killed as a result of military service; prisoner of war; or missing in action. *Application Requirements:* Application.

Contact Dana Kelly, Program Manager, Idaho State Board of Education, PO Box 83720, Boise, ID 83720-0037. *E-mail:* dana.kelly@osbe.idaho.gov. *Phone:* 208-332-1574. *Web site:* www.boardofed.idaho.gov.

Public Safety Officer Dependent Scholarship. Scholarship for dependents of full-time Idaho public safety officers who were killed or disabled in the line of duty. Recipients will attend an Idaho postsecondary institution with a full waiver of fees. *Award:* Scholarship for use in freshman year; renewable. *Award amount:* $1000. *Eligibility Requirements:* Applicant must be enrolled or expecting to enroll at an institution or university; resident of Idaho and studying in Idaho. Applicant or parent of applicant must have employment or volunteer experience in police/firefighting. Available to U.S. citizens. *Application Requirements:* Application.

Contact Dana Kelly, Program Manager, Idaho State Board of Education, PO Box 83720, Boise, ID 83720-0037. *E-mail:* dana.kelly@osbe.idaho.gov. *Phone:* 208-332-1574. *Web site:* www.boardofed.idaho.gov.

Education Incentive Loan Forgiveness Contract-Idaho. Renewable award assists Idaho residents enrolling in teacher education or nursing programs within state. Must rank in top 15% of high school graduating class, have a 3.0 GPA or above, and agree to work in Idaho for two years. Deadlines vary. Contact financial aid office at institution of choice. *Academic Fields/Career Goals:* Education; Nursing. *Award:* Forgivable loan for use in freshman, sophomore, junior, or senior year; renewable. *Award amount:* varies. *Number of awards:* 13–45. *Eligibility Requirements:* Applicant must be enrolled or expecting to enroll full-time at a two-year or four-year institution or university; resident of Idaho and studying in Idaho. Applicant must have 3.0 GPA or higher. Available to U.S. citizens. *Application Requirements:* Application, test scores, transcript. *Deadline:* varies.

Contact Dana Kelly, Program Manager, Idaho State Board of Education, PO Box 83720, Boise, ID 83720-0037. *E-mail:* dana.kelly@osbe.idaho.gov. *Phone:* 208-332-1574. *Web site:* www.boardofed.idaho.gov.

Leveraging Educational Assistance State Partnership Program (LEAP). One-time award assists students attending participating Idaho trade schools, colleges, and universities majoring in any field except theology or divinity. Must be U.S. citizen or permanent resident, and show financial need. Application deadlines vary by institution. *Award:* Grant for use in freshman, sophomore, junior, senior, or graduate year; not renewable. *Award amount:* $400–$5000. *Number of awards:* varies. *Eligibility Requirements:* Applicant must be enrolled or expecting to enroll full or part-time at a two-year, four-year, or technical institution or university; resident of Idaho and studying in Idaho. Available to U.S. citizens. *Application Requirements:* Application, financial need analysis, self-addressed stamped envelope. *Deadline:* varies.

Contact Lynn Humphrey, Manager, Student Aid Programs, Idaho State Board of Education, PO Box 83720, Boise, ID 83720-0037. *Phone:* 208-334-2270. *Fax:* 208-334-2632. *Web site:* www.boardofed.idaho.gov.

Idaho Promise Category B Scholarship Program. Available to Idaho residents entering college for the first time prior to the age of 22. Must have completed high school or its equivalent in Idaho and have a minimum GPA of 3.0 or an ACT score of 20 or higher. Scholarship limited to two years or 4 semesters. *Award:* Scholarship for use in freshman or sophomore year; renewable. *Award amount:* $500. *Number of awards:* varies. *Eligibility Requirements:* Applicant must be age 21 or under; enrolled or expecting to enroll full-time at a two-year, four-year, or technical institution or university; resident of Idaho and studying in Idaho. Applicant must have 3.0 GPA or higher. Available to U.S. citizens. *Application Requirements:* Application, transcript. *Deadline:* continuous.

Contact Lynn Humphrey, Manager, Student Aid Programs, Idaho State Board of Education, PO Box 83720, Boise, ID 83720-0037. *Phone:* 208-334-2270. *Fax:* 208-334-2632. *Web site:* www.boardofed.idaho.gov.

ILLINOIS

Higher Education License Plate Program—HELP. Need-based grants for students at Illinois institutions participating in program whose funds are raised by sale of special license plates commemorating the institutions. Must be Illinois resident. May be eligible to receive the grant for the equivalent of 10 semesters of full-time enrollment. *Award:* Grant for use in freshman, sophomore, junior, or senior year; not renewable. *Award amount:* $1000–$2000. *Number of awards:* 175–200. *Eligibility Requirements:* Applicant must be enrolled or expecting to enroll full or part-time at a two-year or four-year institution or university; resident of Illinois and studying in Illinois. Available to U.S. citizens. *Application Requirements:* Financial need analysis, FAFSA. *Deadline:* June 30.

Contact College Zone Counselor, Illinois Student Assistance Commission (ISAC), 1755 Lake Cook Road, Deerfield, IL 60015-5209. *E-mail:* collegezone@isac.org. *Phone:* 800-899-4722. *Web site:* www.collegezone.org.

Illinois General Assembly Scholarship. Scholarships available for Illinois students enrolled at an Illinois four-year state-supported college. Must contact the General

State Scholarship and Grant Programs
Illinois

Assembly member from your district for eligibility criteria. *Award:* Scholarship for use in freshman, sophomore, junior, or senior year. *Award amount:* varies. *Number of awards:* 1. *Eligibility Requirements:* Applicant must be enrolled or expecting to enroll at a four-year institution or university; resident of Illinois and studying in Illinois. Available to U.S. citizens. *Application Requirements:* Application. *Deadline:* continuous.

Contact College Zone Counselor, Illinois Student Assistance Commission (ISAC), 1755 Lake Cook Road, Deerfield, IL 60015-5209. *E-mail:* collegezone@isac.org. *Phone:* 800-899-4722. *Web site:* www.collegezone.org.

Illinois Future Teachers Corps Program. Scholarships available for students planning to become teachers in Illinois. Students must be Illinois residents, enrolled or accepted as a junior or above in a Teacher Education Program at an Illinois college or university. By receiving award, students agree to teach for 5 years at either a public, private, or parochial Illinois preschool, or at a public elementary or secondary school. For an application and further information, visit http://www.collegezone.com *Academic Fields/Career Goals:* Education. *Award:* Forgivable loan for use in junior, senior, or graduate year; renewable. *Award amount:* up to $15,000. *Number of awards:* 1150. *Eligibility Requirements:* Applicant must be enrolled or expecting to enroll full or part-time at a four-year institution or university; resident of Illinois and studying in Illinois. Applicant must have 2.5 GPA or higher. Available to U.S. citizens. *Application Requirements:* Application, financial need analysis, FAFSA. *Deadline:* March 1.

Contact College Zone Counselor, Illinois Student Assistance Commission (ISAC), 1755 Lake Cook Road, Deerfield, IL 60015-5209. *E-mail:* collegezone@isac.org. *Phone:* 800-899-4722. *Web site:* www.collegezone.org.

Illinois Department of Public Health Center for Rural Health Allied Health Care Professional Scholarship Program. Scholarship for Illinois students studying to be a nurse practitioner, physician assistant, or certified nurse midwife. Funding available for up to two years. Must fulfill an obligation to practice full-time in a designated shortage area as an allied healthcare professional in Illinois for one year for each year of scholarship funding. Failure to fulfill the obligation will require repayment to the state three times the amount of the scholarship received for each unfulfilled year of obligation plus 7% interest per year. *Academic Fields/Career Goals:* Health and Medical Sciences. *Award:* Scholarship for use in freshman, sophomore, junior, or senior year; renewable. *Award amount:* $7500–$15,000. *Number of awards:* 20. *Eligibility Requirements:* Applicant must be enrolled or expecting to enroll full or part-time at a two-year or four-year institution or university and resident of Illinois. Available to U.S. citizens. *Application Requirements:* Application, copy of Student Aid Report (SAR), letter of acceptance. *Deadline:* June 30.

Contact Marcia Franklin, Department of Public Health, Illinois Student Assistance Commission (ISAC), 535 West Jefferson Street, Springfield, IL 62761. *Phone:* 217-782-1624. *Web site:* www.collegezone.org.

Silas Purnell Illinois Incentive for Access Program. Award for eligible first-time freshmen enrolling in approved Illinois institutions. One-time grant of up to $500 may be used for any educational expense. Using the FAFSA, applicants are encouraged to apply as quickly as possible after January 1st preceding the academic year. *Award:* Grant for use in freshman year; not renewable. *Award amount:* $500. *Number of awards:* 19,000–22,000. *Eligibility Requirements:* Applicant must be enrolled or expecting to enroll full or part-time at a two-year, four-year, or technical institution or university; resident of Illinois and studying in Illinois. Available to U.S. citizens. *Application Requirements:* Financial need analysis, FAFSA online. *Deadline:* continuous.

Contact College Zone Counselor, Illinois Student Assistance Commission (ISAC), 1755 Lake Cook Road, Deerfield, IL 60015-5209. *E-mail:* collegezone@isac.org. *Phone:* 800-899-4722. *Web site:* www.collegezone.org.

Illinois Veteran Grant Program—IVG. Award for qualified veterans for tuition and fees at Illinois public universities and community colleges. Must provide documentation of service (DD214). Deadlines for submission of applications are January 15, September 15, and May 25. *Award:* Grant for use in freshman, sophomore, junior, senior, or graduate year; renewable. *Award amount:* $1400–$1600. *Number of awards:* 11,000–13,000. *Eligibility Requirements:* Applicant must be enrolled or expecting to enroll full or part-time at a two-year or four-year institution or university; resident of Illinois and studying in Illinois. Available to U.S. citizens. Applicant must have general military experience. *Application Requirements:* Application, documentation of service. *Deadline:* continuous.

Contact College Zone Counselor, Illinois Student Assistance Commission (ISAC), 1755 Lake Cook Road, Deerfield, IL 60015-5209. *E-mail:* collegezone@isac.org. *Phone:* 800-899-4722. *Web site:* www.collegezone.org.

Illinois Department of Public Health Center for Rural Health Nursing Education Scholarship Program. Scholarship for Illinois students pursuing a certificate, diploma, or degree in nursing and demonstrating financial need. Scholarship provides up to four years of financial aid in return for full-or part-time employment as a licensed practical or registered nurse in Illinois upon graduation. Must remain employed in Illinois for a period equivalent to the educational time that was supported by the scholarship. Application deadline is May 31. *Academic Fields/Career Goals:* Health and Medical Sciences; Nursing. *Award:* Scholarship for use in freshman, sophomore, junior, or senior year; renewable. *Award amount:* $1500–$6000. *Number of awards:* varies. *Eligibility Requirements:* Applicant must be enrolled or expecting to enroll full or part-time at a two-year or four-year institution or university and resident of Illinois. Available to U.S. citizens. *Application Requirements:* Application, financial need analysis, transcript. *Deadline:* May 31.

Contact Nursing Education Scholarship Program, Illinois Student Assistance Commission (ISAC), 535 West Jefferson Street, Springfield, IL 62761-0001. *Phone:* 212-782-1624. *Web site:* www.collegezone.org.

Illinois Monetary Award Program. Award for eligible students attending Illinois public universities, private colleges and universities, community colleges, and some proprietary institutions. Applicable only to tuition and fees. Based on financial need. Deadline dates are August 15 for renewal and September 30 for new applications. *Award:* Grant for use in freshman, sophomore, junior, or senior year; renewable. *Award amount:* up to $4968. *Number of awards:* 135,000–145,000. *Eligibility Requirements:* Applicant must be enrolled or expecting to enroll full-time at a two-year, four-year, or technical institution or university; resident of Illinois and studying in Illinois. Available to U.S. citizens. *Application Requirements:* Financial need analysis, FAFSA online. *Deadline:* September 30.

Contact College Zone Counselor, Illinois Student Assistance Commission (ISAC), 1755 Lake Cook Road, Deerfield, IL 60015-5209. *E-mail:* collegezone@isac.org. *Phone:* 800-899-4722. *Web site:* www.collegezone.org.

Grant Program for Dependents of Police, Fire, or Correctional Officers. Award for dependents of police, fire, and corrections officers killed or disabled in line of duty. Provides for tuition and fees at approved Illinois institutions. Must be resident of Illinois. Continuous deadline. Provide proof

State Scholarship and Grant Programs
Illinois

of status. For information and application, go to Web site: http://www.collegezone. *Award:* Grant for use in freshman, sophomore, junior, senior, graduate, or postgraduate years; renewable. *Award amount:* $3000–$4000. *Number of awards:* 50–55. *Eligibility Requirements:* Applicant must be enrolled or expecting to enroll at a two-year, four-year, or technical institution or university; resident of Illinois and studying in Illinois. Applicant or parent of applicant must have employment or volunteer experience in police/firefighting. Available to U.S. citizens. *Application Requirements:* Application, proof of status. *Deadline:* continuous.

Contact College Zone Counselor, Illinois Student Assistance Commission (ISAC), 1755 Lake Cook Road, Deerfield, IL 60015-5209. *E-mail:* collegezone@isac.org. *Phone:* 800-899-4722. *Web site:* www.collegezone.org.

Illinois College Savings Bond Bonus Incentive Grant Program. Program offers holders of Illinois College Savings Bonds a $20 grant for each year of bond maturity payable upon bond redemption if at least 70% of proceeds are used to attend college in Illinois. May not be used by students attending religious or divinity schools. *Award:* Grant for use in freshman, sophomore, junior, senior, graduate, or postgraduate years; not renewable. *Award amount:* $40–$440. *Number of awards:* 1200–1400. *Eligibility Requirements:* Applicant must be enrolled or expecting to enroll full or part-time at a two-year, four-year, or technical institution or university and studying in Illinois. Available to U.S. citizens. *Application Requirements:* Application. *Deadline:* May 30.

Contact College Zone Counselor, Illinois Student Assistance Commission (ISAC), 1755 Lake Cook Road, Deerfield, IL 60015-5209. *E-mail:* collegezone@isac.org. *Phone:* 800-899-4722. *Web site:* www.collegezone.org.

Minority Teachers of Illinois Scholarship Program. Award for minority students planning to teach at an approved Illinois preschool, elementary, or secondary school. Deadline: March 1. Must be Illinois resident. *Academic Fields/Career Goals:* Education; Special Education. *Award:* Forgivable loan for use in freshman, sophomore, junior, senior, graduate, or postgraduate years; renewable. *Award amount:* up to $5000. *Number of awards:* 450–550. *Eligibility Requirements:* Applicant must be American Indian/Alaska Native, Asian/Pacific Islander, Black (non-Hispanic), or Hispanic; enrolled or expecting to enroll full or part-time at a two-year or four-year institution or university; resident of Illinois and studying in Illinois. Applicant must

have 2.5 GPA or higher. Available to U.S. citizens. *Application Requirements:* Application. *Deadline:* March 1.

Contact College Zone Counselor, Illinois Student Assistance Commission (ISAC), 1755 Lake Cook Road, Deerfield, IL 60015-5209. *E-mail:* collegezone@isac.org. *Phone:* 800-899-4722. *Web site:* www.collegezone.org.

Merit Recognition Scholarship (MRS) Program. Award for Illinois high school seniors graduating in the top 4% of their class and attending Illinois post secondary institution or one of the nation's four approved Military Service Academies. Students scoring in the top 4% in one of the college entrance tests among Illinois residents are also eligible. Contact for application procedures. *Award:* Scholarship for use in freshman year; not renewable. *Award amount:* up to $1000. *Number of awards:* 5000–6000. *Eligibility Requirements:* Applicant must be high school student; planning to enroll or expecting to enroll full or part-time at a two-year or four-year institution or university; resident of Illinois and studying in Illinois. Applicant must have 3.5 GPA or higher. Available to U.S. citizens. *Application Requirements:* Application. *Deadline:* August 1.

Contact College Zone Counselor, Illinois Student Assistance Commission (ISAC), 1755 Lake Cook Road, Deerfield, IL 60015-5209. *E-mail:* collegezone@isac.org. *Phone:* 800-899-4722. *Web site:* www.collegezone.org.

Illinois National Guard Grant Program. Award for qualified National Guard personnel which pays tuition and fees at Illinois public universities and community colleges. Must provide documentation of service. Applications are due October 1 of the academic year for full year, March 1 for second/third term, or June 15 for the summer term. Deadline dates are October 5, March 6, and June 15. *Award:* Grant for use in freshman, sophomore, junior, senior, graduate, or postgraduate years; renewable. *Award amount:* $1300–$1700. *Number of awards:* 2000–3000. *Eligibility Requirements:* Applicant must be enrolled or expecting to enroll full or part-time at a two-year or four-year institution or university and studying in Illinois. Available to U.S. citizens. Applicant must have served in the Air Force National Guard or Army National Guard. *Application Requirements:* Application, documentation of service. *Deadline:* continuous.

Contact College Zone Counselor, Illinois Student Assistance Commission (ISAC), 1755 Lake Cook Road, Deerfield, IL 60015-5209. *E-mail:* collegezone@isac.org. *Phone:* 800-899-4722. *Web site:* www.collegezone.org.

Veterans' Children Educational Opportunities. Award is provided to each child age 18 or younger of a veteran who died or became totally disabled as a result of service during World War I, World War II, Korean, or Vietnam War. Must be studying in Illinois. Death must be service-connected. Disability must be rated 100% for two or more years. *Award:* Grant for use in freshman year; not renewable. *Award amount:* up to $250. *Number of awards:* varies. *Eligibility Requirements:* Applicant must be age 10-18; enrolled or expecting to enroll at an institution or university and resident of Illinois. Available to U.S. citizens. Applicant or parent must meet one or more of the following requirements: general military experience; retired from active duty; disabled or killed as a result of military service; prisoner of war; or missing in action. *Application Requirements:* Application. *Deadline:* June 30.

Contact Tracy Mahan, Grants Section, Illinois Department of Veterans Affairs, 833 South Spring Street, Springfield, IL 62794-9432. *Phone:* 217-782-3564. *Fax:* 217-782-4161. *Web site:* www.state.il.us/agency/dva.

Paul Douglas Teacher Scholarship (PDTS) Program. Program enables and encourages outstanding high school graduates to pursue teaching careers at the preschool, elementary or secondary school level by providing financial assistance. *Academic Fields/Career Goals:* Education. *Award:* Scholarship for use in freshman year; not renewable. *Award amount:* $1666–$5000. *Eligibility Requirements:* Applicant must be enrolled or expecting to enroll full-time at an institution or university. Available to U.S. citizens. *Application Requirements:* Application, financial need analysis. *Deadline:* August 1.

Contact College Zone Counselor, Illinois Student Assistance Commission (ISAC), 1755 Lake Cook Road, Deerfield, IL 60015-5209. *E-mail:* collegezone@isac.org. *Phone:* 800-899-4722. *Web site:* www.collegezone.org.

Illinois Special Education Teacher Tuition Waiver. Tuition waiver for up to four years for Illinois teacher or student pursuing a career in special education. Must be enrolled in an eligible Illinois institution and seeking certification in any area of special education. Must teach in Illinois for two years upon gaining certification. *Academic Fields/Career Goals:* Special Education. *Award:* Forgivable loan for use in freshman, sophomore, junior, senior, or graduate year; renewable. *Number of awards:* up to 250. *Eligibility Requirements:* Applicant must be enrolled or expecting to enroll at a four-year institution or university; resident of Illinois and studying in Illinois. Avail-

State Scholarship and Grant Programs
Illinois

able to U.S. citizens. *Application Requirements:* Application. *Deadline:* March 1.

Contact College Zone Counselor, Illinois Student Assistance Commission (ISAC), 1755 Lake Cook Road, Deerfield, IL 60015-5209. *E-mail:* collegezone@isac.org. *Phone:* 800-899-4722. *Web site:* www.collegezone.org.

Illinois Student-to-Student Program of Matching Grants. Award provides matching funds for need-based grants at participating Illinois public universities and community colleges. Contact financial aid office at the institution in which you are enrolled for eligibility. Deadline dates are October 15, February 15, April 15, and June 15. *Award:* Grant for use in freshman, sophomore, junior, or senior year; not renewable. *Award amount:* $300–$1000. *Number of awards:* 2000–4000. *Eligibility Requirements:* Applicant must be enrolled or expecting to enroll full or part-time at a two-year or four-year institution or university; resident of Illinois and studying in Illinois. Available to U.S. citizens. *Application Requirements:* Application, financial need analysis. *Deadline:* continuous.

Contact College Zone Counselor, Illinois Student Assistance Commission (ISAC), 1755 Lake Cook Road, Deerfield, IL 60015-5209. *E-mail:* collegezone@isac.org. *Phone:* 800-899-4722. *Web site:* www.collegezone.org.

Golden Apple Scholars of Illinois. 100 scholars are selected annually. Scholars receive $7,000 a year for four years. Applicants must be between 17 and 21 and maintain a GPA of 2.5. Eligible applicants must be residents of Illinois studying in Illinois. The deadline is December 1. Recipients must agree to teach in high-need Illinois schools. *Academic Fields/Career Goals:* Education. *Award:* Forgivable loan for use in freshman, sophomore, junior, or senior year; not renewable. *Award amount:* $7000. *Number of awards:* up to 100. *Eligibility Requirements:* Applicant must be age 17-21; enrolled or expecting to enroll full-time at a four-year institution or university; resident of Illinois and studying in Illinois. Applicant must have 2.5 GPA or higher. Available to U.S. and non-U.S. citizens. *Application Requirements:* Application, autobiography, essay, interview, photo, references, test scores, transcript. *Deadline:* December 1.

Contact Pat Kilduff, Director of Recruitment and Placement, Golden Apple Foundation, 8 South Michigan Avenue, Suite 700, Chicago, IL 60603-3318. *E-mail:* kilduff@goldenapple.org. *Phone:* 312-407-0006. *Fax:* 312-407-0344. *Web site:* www.goldenapple.org.

INDIANA

Hoosier Scholar Award. The Hoosier Scholar Award is a $500 nonrenewable award. Based on the size of the senior class, one to three scholars are selected by the guidance counselor(s) of each accredited high school in Indiana. The award is based on academic merit and may be used for any educational expense at an eligible Indiana institution of higher education. *Award:* Scholarship for use in freshman year; not renewable. *Award amount:* $500. *Number of awards:* 790–840. *Eligibility Requirements:* Applicant must be high school student; planning to enroll or expecting to enroll full-time at a two-year or four-year institution or university; resident of Indiana and studying in Indiana. Applicant must have 3.5 GPA or higher. Available to U.S. citizens. *Application Requirements:* Application, references. *Deadline:* March 10.

Contact Ada Sparkman, Program Coordinator, State Student Assistance Commission of Indiana (SSACI), 150 West Market Street, Suite 500, Indianapolis, IN 46204-2805. *Phone:* 317-232-2350. *Fax:* 317-232-3260. *Web site:* www.in.gov/ssaci.

Indiana Nursing Scholarship Fund. Need-based tuition funding for nursing students enrolled full- or part-time at an eligible Indiana institution. Must be a U.S. citizen and an Indiana resident and have a minimum 2.0 GPA or meet the minimum requirements for the nursing program. Upon graduation, recipients must practice as a nurse in an Indiana health care setting for two years. *Academic Fields/Career Goals:* Nursing. *Award:* Scholarship for use in freshman, sophomore, junior, or senior year; not renewable. *Award amount:* $200–$5000. *Number of awards:* 490–690. *Eligibility Requirements:* Applicant must be enrolled or expecting to enroll full or part-time at a two-year or four-year institution or university; resident of Indiana and studying in Indiana. Available to U.S. citizens. *Application Requirements:* Application, financial need analysis, FAFSA. *Deadline:* continuous.

Contact Yvonne Heflin, Director, Special Programs, State Student Assistance Commission of Indiana (SSACI), 150 West Market Street, Suite 500, Indianapolis, IN 46204-2805. *Phone:* 317-232-2350. *Fax:* 317-232-3260. *Web site:* www.in.gov/ssaci.

Charles A. Holt Indiana Wildlife Federation Endowment Scholarship. A $1000 scholarship will be awarded to an Indiana resident accepted for the study or already enrolled for the study of resource conservation or environmental education at the undergraduate level. For more details see Web site: http://www.indianawildlife.org.

Academic Fields/Career Goals: Natural Resources. *Award:* Scholarship for use in sophomore, junior, or senior year; not renewable. *Award amount:* $1000. *Number of awards:* 1. *Eligibility Requirements:* Applicant must be enrolled or expecting to enroll full-time at a four-year institution or university; resident of Indiana and studying in Indiana. Available to U.S. citizens. *Application Requirements:* Application, essay, references. *Deadline:* April 30.

Contact Application available at Web site., Indiana Wildlife Federation Endowment. *Web site:* indianawildlife.org/.

Part-time Grant Program. Program is designed to encourage part-time undergraduates to start and complete their associate or baccalaureate degrees or certificates by subsidizing part-time tuition costs. It is a term-based award that is based on need. State residency requirements must be met and a FAFSA must be filed. Eligibility is determined at the institutional level subject to approval by SSACI. *Award:* Grant for use in freshman, sophomore, junior, or senior year; not renewable. *Award amount:* $50–$4000. *Number of awards:* 4680–6700. *Eligibility Requirements:* Applicant must be enrolled or expecting to enroll part-time at a two-year, four-year, or technical institution or university; resident of Indiana and studying in Indiana. Available to U.S. citizens. *Application Requirements:* Application, financial need analysis. *Deadline:* continuous.

Contact Grants Counselor, State Student Assistance Commission of Indiana (SSACI), 150 West Market Street, Suite 500, Indianapolis, IN 46204-2805. *E-mail:* grants@ssaci.state.in.us. *Phone:* 317-232-2350. *Fax:* 317-232-3260. *Web site:* www.in.gov/ssaci.

Twenty-first Century Scholars Gear Up Summer Scholarship. Grant of up to $1500 that pays for summer school tuition and regularly assessed course fees (but it does not cover other costs such as text books or room and board). *Award:* Scholarship for use in freshman, sophomore, junior, or senior year. *Award amount:* up to $1500. *Eligibility Requirements:* Applicant must be enrolled or expecting to enroll full-time at a two-year or four-year institution or university; resident of Indiana and studying in Indiana. Available to U.S. citizens. *Application Requirements:* Application. *Deadline:* varies.

Contact GEAR UP Coordinator, Office of Twenty-first Century Scholars, State Student Assistance Commission of Indiana (SSACI), 150 West Market Street, Suite 500, Indianapolis, IN 46204. *E-mail:* 21stscholars@ssaci.in.gov. *Phone:* 317-234-1394. *Web site:* www.in.gov/ssaci.

State Scholarship and Grant Programs
Iowa

Frank O'Bannon Grant Program. The Higher Education Award is a need-based, tuition-restricted program for students attending Indiana public, private, or proprietary institutions seeking a first undergraduate degree. Students (and parents of dependent students) who are U.S. citizens and Indiana residents must file the FAFSA yearly by the March 10 deadline. *Award:* Grant for use in freshman, sophomore, junior, or senior year; not renewable. *Award amount:* $200–$4700. *Number of awards:* 38,000–43,660. *Eligibility Requirements:* Applicant must be enrolled or expecting to enroll full-time at a two-year, four-year, or technical institution or university; resident of Indiana and studying in Indiana. Available to U.S. citizens. *Application Requirements:* Application, financial need analysis, FAFSA. *Deadline:* March 10.

Contact Grants Counselor, State Student Assistance Commission of Indiana (SSACI), 150 West Market Street, Suite 500, Indianapolis, IN 46204-2805. *E-mail:* grants@ssaci.state.in.us. *Phone:* 317-232-2350. *Fax:* 317-232-3260. *Web site:* www.in.gov/ssaci.

Child of Disabled Veteran Grant or Purple Heart Recipient Grant. Free tuition at Indiana state-supported colleges or universities for children of disabled veterans or Purple Heart recipients. Must submit Form DD214 or service record. *Award:* Grant for use in freshman, sophomore, junior, senior, graduate, or postgraduate years; renewable. *Award amount:* varies. *Number of awards:* varies. *Eligibility Requirements:* Applicant must be enrolled or expecting to enroll full or part-time at a two-year or four-year institution or university; resident of Indiana and studying in Indiana. Available to U.S. citizens. Applicant or parent must meet one or more of the following requirements: general military experience; retired from active duty; disabled or killed as a result of military service; prisoner of war; or missing in action. *Application Requirements:* Application. *Deadline:* continuous.

Contact Jon Brinkley, State Service Officer, Indiana Department of Veterans Affairs, 302 West Washington Street, Room E-120, Indianapolis, IN 46204-2738. *E-mail:* jbrinkley@dva.state.in.us. *Phone:* 317-232-3910. *Fax:* 317-232-7721. *Web site:* www.ai.org/veteran/index.html.

Department of Veterans Affairs Free Tuition for Children of POW/MIA's in Vietnam. Renewable award for residents of Indiana who are the children of veterans declared missing in action or prisoner-of-war after January 1, 1960. Provides tuition at Indiana state-supported institutions for undergraduate study. *Award:* Grant for use in freshman, sophomore, junior, senior, graduate, or postgraduate years; renewable. *Award amount:* varies. *Number of awards:* varies. *Eligibility Requirements:* Applicant must be age 24 or under; enrolled or expecting to enroll at a two-year or four-year institution or university; resident of Indiana and studying in Indiana. Available to U.S. citizens. Applicant or parent must meet one or more of the following requirements: general military experience; retired from active duty; disabled or killed as a result of military service; prisoner of war; or missing in action. *Application Requirements:* Application. *Deadline:* March 10.

Contact Jon Brinkley, State Service Officer, Indiana Department of Veterans Affairs, 302 West Washington Street, Room E-120, Indianapolis, IN 46204-2738. *E-mail:* jbrinkley@dva.state.in.us. *Phone:* 317-232-3910. *Fax:* 317-232-7721. *Web site:* www.ai.org/veteran/index.html.

Culture Connection Foundation Scholarship. Scholarships available for students in single parent families. May be used for undergraduate or graduate study. Those interested in foreign languages, culture, and ethnic studies are encouraged to apply. Application deadline is August 1. *Academic Fields/Career Goals:* African Studies; Anthropology; Area/Ethnic Studies; Art History; Asian Studies; Education; European Studies; Foreign Language; International Studies; Law/Legal Services. *Award:* Scholarship for use in freshman, sophomore, junior, senior, or graduate year; renewable. *Award amount:* up to $4700. *Number of awards:* 1000. *Eligibility Requirements:* Applicant must be enrolled or expecting to enroll full or part-time at a two-year, four-year, or technical institution or university and single. Applicant must have 2.5 GPA or higher. Available to U.S. and non-U.S. citizens. *Application Requirements:* Application, essay, financial need analysis, interview, references, self-addressed stamped envelope, test scores, transcript, birth certificate, divorce decree. *Deadline:* August 1.

Contact Anna Leis, National Program Director, Culture Connection, 8888 Keystone Crossing, Suite 1300, Indianapolis, IN 46240. *E-mail:* annaleis@thecultureconnection.com. *Phone:* 317-547-7055. *Web site:* www.thecultureconnection.com.

Indiana National Guard Supplemental Grant. The award is a supplement to the Indiana Higher Education Grant program. Applicants must be members of the Indiana National Guard. All Guard paperwork must be completed prior to the start of each semester. The FAFSA must be received by March 10. Award covers certain tuition and fees at select public colleges. *Award:* Grant for use in freshman, sophomore, junior, or senior year; not renewable. *Award amount:* $200–$6516. *Number of awards:* 503–925. *Eligibility Requirements:* Applicant must be enrolled or expecting to enroll full or part-time at a two-year or four-year institution or university; resident of Indiana and studying in Indiana. Available to U.S. citizens. Applicant must have served in the Air Force National Guard or Army National Guard. *Application Requirements:* Application. *Deadline:* March 10.

Contact Grants Counselor, State Student Assistance Commission of Indiana (SSACI), 150 West Market Street, Suite 500, Indianapolis, IN 46204-2805. *E-mail:* grants@ssaci.state.in.us. *Phone:* 317-232-2350. *Fax:* 317-232-2360. *Web site:* www.in.gov/ssaci.

IOWA

Iowa Vocational Rehabilitation. Provides vocational rehabilitation services to individuals with disabilities who need these services in order to maintain, retain, or obtain employment compatible with their disabilities. Must be Iowa resident. *Award:* Grant for use in freshman, sophomore, junior, senior, graduate, or postgraduate years; renewable. *Award amount:* $500–$4000. *Number of awards:* up to 5000. *Eligibility Requirements:* Applicant must be enrolled or expecting to enroll full or part-time at a two-year, four-year, or technical institution or university and resident of Iowa. Applicant must be hearing impaired, learning disabled, physically disabled, or visually impaired. Available to U.S. and non-U.S. citizens. *Application Requirements:* Application, interview. *Deadline:* continuous.

Contact Ralph Childers, Policy and Workforce Initiatives Coordinator, Iowa Division of Vocational Rehabilitation Services, Division of Vocational Rehabilitation Services, 510 East 12th Street, Des Moines, IA 50319. *E-mail:* ralph.childers@iowa.gov. *Phone:* 515-281-4151. *Fax:* 515-281-4703. *Web site:* www.ivrs.iowa.gov.

State of Iowa Scholarship Program. Program provides recognition and financial honorarium to Iowa's academically talented high school seniors. Honorary scholarships are presented to all qualified candidates. Approximately 1700 top-ranking candidates are designated State of Iowa Scholars every March, from an applicant pool of nearly 5000 high school seniors. Must be used at an Iowa post secondary institution. Minimum 3.5 GPA required. *Award:* Scholarship for use in freshman year; not renewable. *Award amount:* up to $400. *Number of awards:* up to 1700. *Eligibility Requirements:*

State Scholarship and Grant Programs
Iowa

Applicant must be high school student; planning to enroll or expecting to enroll full-time at a two-year, four-year, or technical institution or university; resident of Iowa and studying in Iowa. Applicant must have 3.5 GPA or higher. Available to U.S. citizens. *Application Requirements:* Application, test scores. *Deadline:* November 1.

Contact Julie Leeper, Director, State Student Aid Programs, Iowa College Student Aid Commission, 200 10th Street, 4th Floor, Des Moines, IA 50309-3609. *E-mail:* icsac@max.state.ia.us. *Phone:* 515-242-3370. *Fax:* 515-242-3388. *Web site:* www.iowacollegeaid.org.

Governor Terry E. Branstad Iowa State Fair Scholarship. Up to four scholarships ranging from $500 to $1000 will be awarded to students graduating from an Iowa high school. Must actively participate at the Iowa State Fair. For more details see Web site: http://www.iowacollegeaid.org. *Award:* Scholarship for use in freshman year; not renewable. *Award amount:* $500–$1000. *Number of awards:* up to 4. *Eligibility Requirements:* Applicant must be high school student; planning to enroll or expecting to enroll at an institution or university; resident of Iowa and studying in Iowa. Available to U.S. citizens. *Application Requirements:* Application, essay, financial need analysis, references, transcript. *Deadline:* May 1.

Contact Brenda Easter, Director, Special Programs, Iowa College Student Aid Commission, 200 10th Street, 4th Floor, Des Moines, IA 50309-3609. *Phone:* 515-242-3380. *Fax:* 515-242-3388. *Web site:* www.iowacollegeaid.org.

Iowa Grants. Statewide need-based program to assist high-need Iowa residents. Recipients must demonstrate a high level of financial need to receive awards ranging from $100 to $1,000. Awards are prorated for students enrolled for less than full-time. Awards must be used at Iowa postsecondary institutions. *Award:* Grant for use in freshman, sophomore, junior, or senior year; not renewable. *Award amount:* $100–$1000. *Number of awards:* varies. *Eligibility Requirements:* Applicant must be enrolled or expecting to enroll full or part-time at a two-year, four-year, or technical institution or university; resident of Iowa and studying in Iowa. Available to U.S. citizens. *Application Requirements:* Application, financial need analysis. *Deadline:* continuous.

Contact Julie Leeper, Director, State Student Aid Programs, Iowa College Student Aid Commission, 200 10th Street, 4th Floor, Des Moines, IA 50309-3609. *E-mail:* icsac@max.state.ia.us. *Phone:* 515-242-3370. *Fax:* 515-242-3388. *Web site:* www.iowacollegeaid.org.

Iowa National Guard Education Assistance Program. Program provides postsecondary tuition assistance to members of Iowa National Guard Units. Must study at a postsecondary institution in Iowa. Contact for additional information. *Award:* Grant for use in freshman, sophomore, junior, or senior year; not renewable. *Award amount:* up to $1200. *Number of awards:* varies. *Eligibility Requirements:* Applicant must be enrolled or expecting to enroll full or part-time at a two-year, four-year, or technical institution or university; resident of Iowa and studying in Iowa. Available to U.S. citizens. Applicant must have served in the Air Force National Guard or Army National Guard. *Application Requirements:* Application. *Deadline:* continuous.

Contact Julie Leeper, Director, State Student Aid Programs, Iowa College Student Aid Commission, 200 10th Street, 4th Floor, Des Moines, IA 50309-3609. *E-mail:* icsac@max.state.ia.us. *Phone:* 515-242-3370. *Fax:* 515-242-3388. *Web site:* www.iowacollegeaid.org.

Iowa Teacher Forgivable Loan Program. Forgivable loan assists students who will teach in Iowa secondary schools. Must be an Iowa resident attending an Iowa postsecondary institution. Contact for additional information. *Academic Fields/Career Goals:* Education. *Award:* Forgivable loan for use in freshman, sophomore, junior, or senior year; not renewable. *Award amount:* $2686. *Number of awards:* varies. *Eligibility Requirements:* Applicant must be enrolled or expecting to enroll full or part-time at a four-year institution or university; resident of Iowa and studying in Iowa. Applicant or parent of applicant must have employment or volunteer experience in teaching. Available to U.S. citizens. *Application Requirements:* Application, financial need analysis. *Deadline:* continuous.

Contact Brenda Easter, Special Programs Administrator, Iowa College Student Aid Commission, 200 10th Street, 4th Floor, Des Moines, IA 50309-3609. *E-mail:* icsac@max.state.ia.us. *Phone:* 515-242-3380. *Fax:* 515-242-3388. *Web site:* www.iowacollegeaid.org.

Iowa Foster Child Grants. Grants renewable up to four years will be awarded to students graduating from an Iowa high school who are in Iowa foster care under the care and custody of the Iowa Department of Human Service. Must have a minimum GPA of 2.25 and have applied to an accredited Iowa college or university. For more details see Web site: http://www.iowacollegeaid.org. *Award:* Grant for use in freshman year; renewable. *Award amount:* $2000–$4200. *Number of awards:* varies. *Eligibility Requirements:* Applicant must be high school student; planning to enroll or expecting to enroll at a two-year or four-year institution or university; resident of Iowa and studying in Iowa. Available to U.S. citizens. *Application Requirements:* Application. *Deadline:* April 15.

Contact Brenda Easter, Director, Special Programs, Iowa College Student Aid Commission, 200 10th Street, 4th Floor, Des Moines, IA 50309-3609. *Phone:* 515-242-3380. *Fax:* 515-242-3388. *Web site:* www.iowacollegeaid.org.

Iowa Vocational-Technical Tuition Grant Program. Program provides need-based financial assistance to Iowa residents enrolled in career education (vocational-technical), and career option programs at Iowa area community colleges. Grants range from $150 to $650, depending on the length of program, financial need, and available funds. *Award:* Grant for use in freshman or sophomore year; not renewable. *Award amount:* $150–$650. *Number of awards:* varies. *Eligibility Requirements:* Applicant must be enrolled or expecting to enroll full or part-time at a technical institution; resident of Iowa and studying in Iowa. Available to U.S. citizens. *Application Requirements:* Application, financial need analysis. *Deadline:* July 1.

Contact Julie Leeper, Director, State Student Aid Programs, Iowa College Student Aid Commission, 200 10th Street, 4th Floor, Des Moines, IA 50309-3609. *E-mail:* icsac@max.state.ia.us. *Phone:* 515-242-3370. *Fax:* 515-242-3388. *Web site:* www.iowacollegeaid.org.

Iowa Tuition Grant Program. Program assists students who attend independent postsecondary institutions in Iowa. Iowa residents currently enrolled, or planning to enroll, for at least three semester hours at one of the eligible Iowa postsecondary institutions may apply. Awards currently range from $100 to $4000. Grants may not exceed the difference between independent college and university tuition and fees and the average tuition and fees at the three public Regent universities. *Award:* Grant for use in freshman, sophomore, junior, or senior year; not renewable. *Award amount:* $100–$4000. *Number of awards:* varies. *Eligibility Requirements:* Applicant must be enrolled or expecting to enroll full or part-time at a two-year or four-year institution or university; resident of Iowa and studying in Iowa. Available to U.S. citizens.

State Scholarship and Grant Programs
Kentucky

Application Requirements: Application, financial need analysis. *Deadline:* July 1.

Contact Julie Leeper, Director, State Student Aid Programs, Iowa College Student Aid Commission, 200 10th Street, 4th Floor, Des Moines, IA 50309-3609. *E-mail:* icsac@max.state.ia.us. *Phone:* 515-242-3370. *Fax:* 515-242-3388. *Web site:* www.iowacollegeaid.org.

KANSAS

Kansas National Guard Tuition Assistance Award Program. Service scholarship for enlisted soldiers in the Kansas National Guard. Pays up to 100% of tuition and fees based on funding. Must attend a state-supported institution. Recipients will be required to serve in the KNG for three months for every semester of benefits after the last payment of state tuition assistance. Must not have over 15 years of service at time of application. Deadlines are February 1 and September 1. Contact KNG Education Services Specialist for further information. Must be Kansas resident. *Award:* Scholarship for use in freshman, sophomore, junior, or senior year; renewable. *Award amount:* $250–$3500. *Number of awards:* up to 400. *Eligibility Requirements:* Applicant must be enrolled or expecting to enroll full or part-time at a two-year, four-year, or technical institution or university; resident of Kansas and studying in Kansas. Available to U.S. citizens. Applicant must have served in the Air Force National Guard or Army National Guard. *Application Requirements:* Application. *Deadline:* varies.

Contact Ray Bergman, Education Services Officer, Kansas National Guard Educational Assistance Program, 2800 South West Topeka Boulevard, Topeka, KS 66611-1287. *E-mail:* ray.bergman@ng.army.mil. *Phone:* 785-274-1081. *Fax:* 785-274-1609.

Kansas Educational Benefits for Children of MIA, POW, and Deceased Veterans of the Vietnam War. Full-tuition scholarship awarded to students who are children of veterans. Must show proof of parent's status as missing in action, prisoner of war, or killed in action in the Vietnam War. Kansas residence required of veteran at time of entry to service. Must attend a state-supported postsecondary school. *Award:* Scholarship for use in freshman, sophomore, junior, or senior year; not renewable. *Number of awards:* 1. *Eligibility Requirements:* Applicant must be enrolled or expecting to enroll at a two-year, four-year, or technical institution or university and studying in Kansas. Available to U.S. citizens. Applicant or parent must meet one or more of the following requirements: general military experience; retired from active duty; disabled or killed as a result of military service; prisoner of war; or missing in action. *Application Requirements:* Application, report of casualty, birth certificate, school acceptance letter, Military discharge of veteran. *Deadline:* continuous.

Contact Wayne Bollig, Program Director, Kansas Commission on Veterans Affairs, 700 Southwest Jackson Street, Room 701, Topeka, KS 66603. *E-mail:* kcva004@ink.org. *Phone:* 785-291-3422. *Fax:* 785-296-1462. *Web site:* www.kcva.org.

KENTUCKY

Women in Rural Electrification (WIRE) Scholarships. Scholarship available to Kentucky students who are juniors or seniors in a Kentucky college or university and have 60 credit hours by fall semester. Immediate family of student must be served by one of the state's 24 rural electric distribution cooperatives. Awards based on academic achievement, extracurricular activities, career goals, recommendations. *Award:* Scholarship for use in freshman, sophomore, junior, senior, graduate, or postgraduate years. *Award amount:* $1000. *Number of awards:* 3. *Eligibility Requirements:* Applicant must be enrolled or expecting to enroll full or part-time at a two-year, four-year, or technical institution or university. Available to U.S. citizens. *Application Requirements:* Application. *Deadline:* June 15.

Contact Ellie Hobgood, W.I.R.E. Scholarships, South Kentucky Rural Electric Cooperative Corporation, PO Box 32170, Louisville, KY 40232. *Phone:* 800-264-5112. *Web site:* www.skrecc.com.

Senior Scholarships. Twelve $1000 scholarships to be awarded to Kentucky high school seniors in counties where more than 500 people are served by the South Kentucky Rural Electric Cooperative. Students from Adair, Casey, Clinton, Lincoln, McCreary, Pulaski, Russell, and Wayne County High Schools and Monticello, Somerset, and Southwestern high schools are eligible to apply. In addition, one scholarship will be given to a senior attending a private school or being home-schooled in one of these counties. *Award:* Scholarship for use in freshman year. *Award amount:* $1000. *Number of awards:* up to 12. *Eligibility Requirements:* Applicant must be high school student; planning to enroll or expecting to enroll at a four-year institution and resident of Kentucky. Available to U.S. citizens. *Application Requirements:* Application, essay. *Deadline:* April 20.

Contact Scholarship Coordinator, South Kentucky Rural Electric Cooperative Corporation, Senior Scholarships, PO Box 910, Somerset, KY 42501. *Phone:* 800-264-5112. *Fax:* 606-679-8279. *Web site:* www.skrecc.com.

Touchstone Energy All "A" Classic Scholarship. Award of $1000 for senior student in good standing at a Kentucky high school. Applicant must plan to attend a postsecondary institution in Kentucky in the upcoming year as a full-time student and be drug free. Deadline is December 2. *Award:* Scholarship for use in freshman year; not renewable. *Award amount:* $1000. *Number of awards:* 12. *Eligibility Requirements:* Applicant must be high school student; planning to enroll or expecting to enroll full-time at a two-year or four-year institution or university; resident of Kentucky and studying in Kentucky. Available to U.S. citizens. *Application Requirements:* Application, essay, photo, references, transcript. *Deadline:* December 2.

Contact H.D. Cowden, Coordinator, Kentucky Touchstone Energy Cooperatives, Hancock County High School, 80 State Route 271 South, Lewisport, KY 42351. *Phone:* 859-744-4812.

Kentucky Tuition Grant (KTG). Available to Kentucky residents who are full-time undergraduates at an independent college within the state. Must not be enrolled in a religion program. Based on financial need. Submit Free Application for Federal Student Aid. Priority deadline is March 15. *Award:* Grant for use in freshman, sophomore, junior, or senior year; not renewable. *Award amount:* $200–$2800. *Number of awards:* 10,000–12,000. *Eligibility Requirements:* Applicant must be enrolled or expecting to enroll full-time at a two-year or four-year institution or university; resident of Kentucky and studying in Kentucky. Available to U.S. citizens. *Application Requirements:* Application, financial need analysis, FAFSA. *Deadline:* continuous.

Contact Tim Phelps, Student Aid Branch Manager, Kentucky Higher Education Assistance Authority (KHEAA), PO Box 798, Frankfort, KY 40602-0798. *E-mail:* tphelps@kheaa.com. *Phone:* 502-696-7393. *Fax:* 502-696-7496. *Web site:* www.kheaa.com.

Kentucky Department of Vocational Rehabilitation. Kentucky Department of Vocational Rehabilitation provides services necessary to secure employment. Eligible individual must possess physical or mental impairment that results in a substantial impediment to employment; benefit from vocational rehabilitation services in terms of an employment outcome; and require

State Scholarship and Grant Programs
Kentucky

vocational rehabilitation services to prepare for, enter, or retain employment. *Award:* Grant for use in freshman, sophomore, junior, senior, graduate, or postgraduate years; renewable. *Award amount:* varies. *Number of awards:* varies. *Eligibility Requirements:* Applicant must be enrolled or expecting to enroll full or part-time at a two-year, four-year, or technical institution or university. Applicant must be learning disabled or physically disabled. Available to U.S. and non-U.S. citizens. *Application Requirements:* Application, financial need analysis, interview, transcript. *Deadline:* continuous.

Contact Charles Tuckett, Program Administrator, Kentucky Department of Vocational Rehabilitation, 209 Street Clair Street, Frankfort, KY 40601. *E-mail:* marianu.spencer@mail.state.ky.us. *Phone:* 502-595-3423. *Fax:* 502-564-6745. *Web site:* ovr.ky.gov/index.htm.

Kentucky Transportation Cabinet Civil Engineering Scholarship Program. Scholarships are available to eligible applicants at 4 universities in Kentucky. Our mission is to continually pursue statewide recruitment and retention of bright, motivated civil engineers in the Kentucky Transportation Cabinet. *Academic Fields/Career Goals:* Civil Engineering. *Award:* Scholarship for use in freshman, sophomore, junior, senior, or graduate year; renewable. *Award amount:* $4000–$4400. *Number of awards:* 10–20. *Eligibility Requirements:* Applicant must be enrolled or expecting to enroll full-time at a four-year institution or university; resident of Kentucky and studying in Kentucky. Applicant must have 2.5 GPA or higher. Available to U.S. and non-U.S. citizens. *Application Requirements:* Application, essay, interview, references, test scores, transcript. *Deadline:* March 1.

Contact Jo Anne Tingle, Scholarship Program Manager, Kentucky Transportation Cabinet, Attention: Scholarship Program Manager, SHE's Office, Suite E6-S1-00, 200 Metro Street, Frankfort, KY 40622. *E-mail:* jo.tingle@ky.gov. *Phone:* 502-564-3730. *Fax:* 502-564-2277. *Web site:* www.transportation.ky.gov.

College Access Program (CAP) Grant. Award for U.S. citizen and Kentucky resident with no previous college degree. Applicants seeking degrees in religion are not eligible. Applicants seeking degrees in religion are not eligible. Must demonstrate financial need and submit Free Application for Federal Student Aid. Priority deadline is March 15. *Award:* Grant for use in freshman, sophomore, junior, or senior year; not renewable. *Award amount:* up to $1700. *Number of awards:* 35,000–40,000. *Eligibility Requirements:* Applicant must be enrolled or expecting to enroll full or part-time at a two-year, four-year, or technical institution or university; resident of Kentucky and studying in Kentucky. Available to U.S. citizens. *Application Requirements:* Financial need analysis.

Contact Michael D. Morgan, Program Coordinator, Kentucky Higher Education Assistance Authority (KHEAA), PO Box 798, Frankfort, KY 40602-0798. *E-mail:* mmorgan@kheaa.com. *Phone:* 502-696-7394. *Fax:* 502-696-7373. *Web site:* www.kheaa.com.

Kentucky National Guard Tuition Award Program. Tuition award available to all members of the Kentucky National Guard. Award is for study at state institutions. Members must be in good standing to be eligible for awards. Applications deadlines are April 1 and October 1. Completed AGO-18-7 required. Undergraduate study given priority. *Award:* Scholarship for use in freshman, sophomore, junior, senior, or graduate year; not renewable. *Award amount:* varies. *Number of awards:* varies. *Eligibility Requirements:* Applicant must be enrolled or expecting to enroll full or part-time at a two-year, four-year, or technical institution or university and studying in Kentucky. Available to U.S. citizens. Applicant must have served in the Air Force National Guard or Army National Guard. *Application Requirements:* AGO-18-7. *Deadline:* varies.

Contact Michelle Kelley, Administration Specialist, Kentucky National Guard, Education Office, 100 Minuteman Parkway, Frankfort, KY 40601. *E-mail:* kelleyam@bng.dma.state.ky.us. *Phone:* 502-607-1039. *Fax:* 502-607-1264. *Web site:* www.kyloui.ang.af.mil.

Kentucky Air National Guard Educational Assistance. Students receive up to $272 each month toward an undergraduate degree. May attend any college and receive up to 36 months of benefits and a maximum of $9792. Must have a high school diploma or GED and be a member of the Kentucky Air National Guard. For additional information see Web site: http://www.kyloui.ang.af.mil. *Award:* Grant for use in freshman, sophomore, junior, or senior year; renewable. *Award amount:* up to $3312. *Number of awards:* varies. *Eligibility Requirements:* Applicant must be enrolled or expecting to enroll at a two-year, four-year, or technical institution or university. Available to U.S. citizens. Applicant must have served in the Air Force National Guard. *Application Requirements:* Application. *Deadline:* continuous.

Contact MSGT. Scott Crimm, Relation Office Manager, Kentucky National Guard, 1101 Grade Lane, Louisville, KY 40213-2616. *E-mail:* scott.crimm@kyloui.ang.af.mil. *Phone:* 502-364-9604. *Web site:* www.kyloui.ang.af.mil.

Kentucky Minority Educator Recruitment and Retention (KMERR) Scholarship. Scholarship for minority teacher candidates who rank in the upper half of their class or have a minimum 2.5 GPA. Must be a U.S. citizen and Kentucky resident enrolled in one of Kentucky's eight public institutions. Must teach one semester in Kentucky for each semester the scholarship is received. *Academic Fields/Career Goals:* Education. *Award:* Forgivable loan for use in freshman, sophomore, junior, senior, or graduate year; renewable. *Award amount:* $2500–$5000. *Number of awards:* 300. *Eligibility Requirements:* Applicant must be American Indian/Alaska Native, Asian/Pacific Islander, Black (non-Hispanic), or Hispanic; enrolled or expecting to enroll full-time at a two-year or four-year institution or university; resident of Kentucky and studying in Kentucky. Applicant must have 2.5 GPA or higher. Available to U.S. citizens. *Application Requirements:* Application, essay, references, test scores, transcript. *Deadline:* continuous.

Contact Robby Morton, Director, Kentucky Department of Education, 500 Mero Street, 17th Floor, Frankfort, KY 40601. *E-mail:* rmorton@kde.state.ky.us. *Phone:* 502-564-1479. *Fax:* 502-564-6952. *Web site:* www.kde.state.ky.us.

Kentucky Teacher Scholarship Program. Award for Kentucky resident attending Kentucky institutions and pursuing initial teacher certification. Must teach one semester for each semester of award received. In critical shortage areas, must teach one semester for every two semesters of award received. Repayment obligation if teaching requirement not met. Submit Free Application for Federal Student Aid and Teacher Scholarship Application by May 1. *Academic Fields/Career Goals:* Education. *Award:* Forgivable loan for use in freshman, sophomore, junior, senior, or graduate year; renewable. *Award amount:* $250–$5000. *Number of awards:* 600–700. *Eligibility Requirements:* Applicant must be enrolled or expecting to enroll full-time at a two-year or four-year institution or university; resident of Kentucky and studying in Kentucky. Available to U.S. citizens. *Application Requirements:* Application, financial need analysis. *Deadline:* May 1.

Contact Tim Phelps, Student Aid Branch Manager, Kentucky Higher Education Assistance Authority (KHEAA), PO Box 798, Frankfort, KY 40602. *E-mail:* tphelps@kheaa.

com. *Phone:* 502-696-7393. *Fax:* 502-696-7496. *Web site:* www.kheaa.com.

George R. Crafton Scholarship. Scholarship available for a high school student applying for enrollment in a Kentucky public institution in the forthcoming year in an area related to agriculture and conservation of natural resources. Must be a Kentucky resident. *Academic Fields/Career Goals:* Agriculture; Environmental Science; Natural Resources. *Award:* Scholarship for use in freshman year; not renewable. *Award amount:* $1000. *Number of awards:* 1. *Eligibility Requirements:* Applicant must be high school student; planning to enroll or expecting to enroll at a two-year or four-year institution or university; resident of Kentucky and studying in Kentucky. Available to U.S. citizens. *Application Requirements:* Application, essay, references, transcript. *Deadline:* March 31.

Contact Kentucky Association of Conservation, Kentucky Natural Resources and Environmental Protection Cabinet, 375 Versailles Road, Frankfort, KY 40601. *E-mail:* steve.coleman@mail.state.ky.us. *Phone:* 502-573-3080. *Web site:* www.uky.edu/waterresources.

Conservation of Natural Resources Scholarship. Scholarship available for a student currently enrolled in college in a Kentucky public institution who has declared a major in the field of agriculture or conservation of natural resources. Must be Kentucky resident. *Academic Fields/Career Goals:* Agriculture; Environmental Science; Natural Resources. *Award:* Scholarship for use in freshman, sophomore, junior, or senior year; not renewable. *Award amount:* $1000. *Number of awards:* 1. *Eligibility Requirements:* Applicant must be enrolled or expecting to enroll at a four-year institution or university; resident of Kentucky and studying in Kentucky. Available to U.S. citizens. *Application Requirements:* Application, essay, references, transcript. *Deadline:* March 31.

Contact Kentucky Division of Conservation, Kentucky Natural Resources and Environmental Protection Cabinet, 375 Versailles Road, Frankfort, KY 40601. *E-mail:* steve.coleman@mail.state.ky.us. *Phone:* 502-573-3080. *Web site:* www.uky.edu/waterresources.

Conservation of Natural Resources Scholarship for Nontraditional Students. Scholarship available for student at least age 25 pursuing an undergraduate degree in agriculture or a related natural resources field. Must be enrolled in a Kentucky public institution and be a resident of Kentucky. *Academic Fields/Career Goals:* Agriculture; Environmental Science; Natural Resources. *Award:* Scholarship for use in freshman, sophomore, junior, or senior year; not renewable. *Award amount:* $1000. *Number of awards:* 1. *Eligibility Requirements:* Applicant must be age 25; enrolled or expecting to enroll at a two-year or four-year institution or university; resident of Kentucky and studying in Kentucky. Available to U.S. citizens. *Application Requirements:* Application, essay, references, transcript. *Deadline:* March 31.

Contact Kentucky Association of Conservation, Kentucky Natural Resources and Environmental Protection Cabinet, 375 Versailles Road, Frankfort, KY 40601. *E-mail:* steve.coleman@mail.state.ky.us. *Phone:* 502-573-3080. *Web site:* www.uky.edu/waterresources.

Environmental Protection Scholarships. Renewable awards for college juniors, seniors, and graduate students for tuition, fees, and room and board at a Kentucky state university. Minimum 2.5 GPA required. Must agree to work full-time for the Kentucky Natural Resources and Environmental Protection Cabinet upon graduation. Interview is required. *Academic Fields/Career Goals:* Chemical Engineering; Civil Engineering; Earth Science; Materials Science, Engineering, and Metallurgy. *Award:* Scholarship for use in junior, senior, or graduate year; renewable. *Award amount:* $4750–$7600. *Number of awards:* 3–5. *Eligibility Requirements:* Applicant must be enrolled or expecting to enroll full-time at a four-year institution or university and studying in Kentucky. Applicant must have 2.5 GPA or higher. Available to U.S. and non-U.S. citizens. *Application Requirements:* Application, essay, interview, references, transcript, non-U.S. citizens must have valid work permit. *Deadline:* February 15.

Contact James Kipp, Scholarship Program Coordinator, Kentucky Natural Resources and Environmental Protection Cabinet, 233 Mining/Mineral Resources Building, Lexington, KY 40506-0107. *E-mail:* kipp@uky.edu. *Phone:* 859-257-1299. *Fax:* 859-323-1049. *Web site:* www.uky.edu/waterresources.

Robert C. Byrd Honors Scholarship–Kentucky. Scholarship available to high school seniors who show past high achievement and potential for continued academic success. Must have applied for admission or have been accepted for enrollment at a public or private nonprofit postsecondary school. Must be a Kentucky resident. Deadline for applications is the second Friday in March. *Award:* Scholarship for use in freshman, sophomore, junior, or senior year; renewable. *Award amount:* up to $1500. *Number of awards:* varies. *Eligibility Requirements:* Applicant must be high school student; planning to enroll or expecting to enroll full-time at a two-year or four-year institution or university and resident of Kentucky. Applicant must have 3.5 GPA or higher. Available to U.S. citizens. *Application Requirements:* Application, test scores. *Deadline:* varies.

Contact Donna Melton, Kentucky Department of Education, 500 Mero Street, 19th Floor, Frankfort, KY 40601. *E-mail:* dmelton@kde.state.ky.us. *Phone:* 502-564-1479. *Web site:* www.kde.state.ky.us.

Early Childhood Development Scholarship. Scholarship with conditional service commitment for part-time students currently employed by participating ECD facility or providing training in ECD for an approved organization. *Academic Fields/Career Goals:* Child and Family Studies; Education. *Award:* Scholarship for use in freshman, sophomore, junior, or senior year; not renewable. *Award amount:* up to $1400. *Number of awards:* 900–1000. *Eligibility Requirements:* Applicant must be enrolled or expecting to enroll part-time at a four-year institution or university; resident of Kentucky and studying in Kentucky. Available to U.S. citizens. *Application Requirements:* Application, resume. *Deadline:* continuous.

Contact Early Childhood Development Authority, Kentucky Higher Education Assistance Authority (KHEAA), 275 East Main Street, 2W-E, Frankfort, KY 40621. *Phone:* 502-564-8099. *Web site:* www.kheaa.com.

LOUISIANA

Louisiana Department of Veterans Affairs State Aid Program. Tuition exemption at any state supported college, university, or technical institute for children (dependents between the ages of 18-25) of veterans that are rated 90% or above service connected disabled by the U.S. Department of Veterans Affairs. Tuition exemption also available for the surviving spouse and children (dependents between the ages of 18-25) of veterans who died on active duty, in line of duty, or where death was the result of a disability incurred in or aggravated by military service. For residents of Louisiana who are attending a Louisiana institution. *Award:* Grant for use in freshman, sophomore, junior, senior, graduate, or postgraduate years; renewable. *Award amount:* varies. *Number of awards:* 1. *Eligibility Requirements:* Applicant must be age 16-25; enrolled or expecting to enroll full-time at a two-year, four-year, or techni-

State Scholarship and Grant Programs
Louisiana

cal institution or university; resident of Louisiana and studying in Louisiana. Available to U.S. citizens. Applicant or parent must meet one or more of the following requirements: general military experience; retired from active duty; disabled or killed as a result of military service; prisoner of war; or missing in action. *Application Requirements:* Application. *Deadline:* continuous.

Contact Richard Blackwell, Veterans Affairs Regional Manager, Louisiana Department of Veterans Affairs, PO Box 94095, Capitol Station, Baton Rouge, LA 70804-4095. *E-mail:* rblackwell@vetaffairs.com. *Phone:* 225-922-0500 Ext. 203. *Fax:* 225-922-0511. *Web site:* www.vetaffairs.com/VAMain.htm.

TOPS Tech Award. Program awards an amount equal to tuition for up to two years of technical training at a Louisiana postsecondary institution that offers a vocational or technical education certificate or diploma program, or a non-academic degree program. Must have a 2.5 high school GPA based on TOPS Tech core curriculum, an ACT score of 17, and complete the TOPS-Tech core curriculum. Must be a Louisiana resident. *Award:* Scholarship for use in freshman or sophomore year; renewable. *Award amount:* $741–$1592. *Number of awards:* varies. *Eligibility Requirements:* Applicant must be enrolled or expecting to enroll full-time at a technical institution; resident of Louisiana and studying in Louisiana. Applicant must have 2.5 GPA or higher. Available to U.S. citizens. *Application Requirements:* Application, test scores, FAFSA. *Deadline:* July 1.

Contact Public Information, Louisiana Office of Student Financial Assistance, PO Box 91202, Baton Rouge, LA 70821-9202. *E-mail:* custserv@osfa.state.la.us. *Phone:* 800-259-5626 Ext. 1012. *Fax:* 225-922-0790. *Web site:* www.osfa.state.la.us.

Rockefeller State Wildlife Scholarship. Awarded to high school graduates, college undergraduates and graduate students majoring in forestry, wildlife or marine science. Renewable up to five years as an undergraduate and two years as a graduate. Must have at least a 2.5 GPA and have taken the ACT or SAT. *Academic Fields/Career Goals:* Animal/Veterinary Sciences; Applied Sciences; Marine Biology; Natural Resources. *Award:* Scholarship for use in freshman, sophomore, junior, senior, or graduate year; renewable. *Award amount:* $1000. *Number of awards:* 60. *Eligibility Requirements:* Applicant must be enrolled or expecting to enroll full-time at a four-year institution or university; resident of Louisiana and studying in Louisiana. Applicant must have 2.5 GPA or higher. Available to U.S. citizens.

Application Requirements: Application, test scores, transcript, FAFSA. *Deadline:* July 1.

Contact Public Information, Louisiana Office of Student Financial Assistance, PO Box 91202, Baton Rouge, LA 70821-9202. *E-mail:* custserv@osfa.state.la.us. *Phone:* 800-259-5626 Ext. 1012. *Fax:* 225-922-0790. *Web site:* www.osfa.state.la.us.

TOPS Honors Award. Program awards an amount equal to tuition plus an $800 per year stipend to students attending a Louisiana public institution, or an amount equal to the weighted average public tuition plus an $800 per year stipend to students attending a LAICU private institution. Must have a minimum high school GPA of 3.5 based on TOPS core curriculum, ACT score of 27, and complete a 16.5 unit core curriculum. Must be resident of Louisiana. *Award:* Scholarship for use in freshman, sophomore, junior, or senior year; renewable. *Award amount:* varies. *Number of awards:* varies. *Eligibility Requirements:* Applicant must be high school student; planning to enroll or expecting to enroll full-time at a two-year, four-year, or technical institution or university; resident of Louisiana and studying in Louisiana. Applicant must have 3.5 GPA or higher. Available to U.S. citizens. *Application Requirements:* Application, test scores. *Deadline:* July 1.

Contact Public Information, Louisiana Office of Student Financial Assistance, PO Box 91202, Baton Rouge, LA 70821-9202. *E-mail:* custserv@osfa.state.la.us. *Phone:* 800-259-5626 Ext. 1012. *Fax:* 225-922-0790. *Web site:* www.osfa.state.la.us.

TOPS Performance Award. Program awards an amount equal to tuition plus a $400 annual stipend to students attending a Louisiana public institution, or an amount equal to the weighted average public tuition plus a $400 annual stipend to students attending a LAICU private institution. Must have a minimum high school GPA of 3.5 based on the TOPS core curriculum, an ACT score of 23 and completion of a 16.5 unit core curriculum. Must be a Louisiana resident. *Award:* Scholarship for use in freshman, sophomore, junior, or senior year; renewable. *Award amount:* varies. *Number of awards:* varies. *Eligibility Requirements:* Applicant must be high school student; planning to enroll or expecting to enroll full-time at a two-year, four-year, or technical institution or university; resident of Louisiana and studying in Louisiana. Applicant must have 3.5 GPA or higher. Available to U.S. citizens. *Application Requirements:* Application, test scores. *Deadline:* July 1.

Contact Public Information, Louisiana Office of Student Financial Assistance, PO Box 91202, Baton Rouge, LA 70821-9202. *E-mail:* custserv@osfa.state.la.us. *Phone:* 800-259-5626 Ext. 1012. *Fax:* 225-922-0790. *Web site:* www.osfa.state.la.us.

TOPS Alternate Performance Award. Program awards an amount equal to tuition plus a $400 annual stipend to students attending a Louisiana public institution, or an amount equal to the weighted average public tuition plus a $400 annual stipend to students attending a LAICU private institution. Must have a minimum high school GPA of 3.0 based on TOPS core curriculum, ACT score of 24, completion of 10 honors courses, and completion of a 16.5 unit core curriculum. Must be a resident of Louisiana. *Award:* Scholarship for use in freshman, sophomore, junior, or senior year; renewable. *Award amount:* varies. *Number of awards:* varies. *Eligibility Requirements:* Applicant must be enrolled or expecting to enroll full-time at a two-year, four-year, or technical institution or university; resident of Louisiana and studying in Louisiana. Applicant must have 3.0 GPA or higher. Available to U.S. citizens. *Application Requirements:* Application, test scores. *Deadline:* July 1.

Contact Public Information Representative, Louisiana Office of Student Financial Assistance, PO Box 91202, Baton Rouge, LA 70821-9202. *E-mail:* custserv@osfa.state.la.us. *Phone:* 800-259-5626 Ext. 1012. *Fax:* 225-922-0790. *Web site:* www.osfa.state.la.us.

Leveraging Educational Assistance Program (LEAP). LEAP program provides federal and state funds to provide need-based grants to academically qualified students. Individual award determined by Financial Aid Office and governed by number of applicants and availability of funds. File FAFSA by school deadline to apply each year. For Louisiana students attending Louisiana postsecondary institutions. Required GPA is 2.0 and above. *Award:* Grant for use in freshman, sophomore, junior, or senior year; not renewable. *Award amount:* $200–$2000. *Number of awards:* 3000–4000. *Eligibility Requirements:* Applicant must be enrolled or expecting to enroll full or part-time at a two-year, four-year, or technical institution or university; resident of Louisiana and studying in Louisiana. Available to U.S. citizens. *Application Requirements:* Application, financial need analysis. *Deadline:* varies.

Contact Public Information, Louisiana Office of Student Financial Assistance, PO Box 91202, Baton Rouge, LA 70821-9202. *E-mail:* custserv@osfa.state.la.us. *Phone:* 800-

259-5626 Ext. 1012. *Fax:* 225-922-0790. *Web site:* www.osfa.state.la.us.

TOPS Opportunity Award. Program awards an amount equal to tuition to students attending a Louisiana public institution, or an amount equal to the weighted average public tuition to students attending a LAICU private institution. Must have a minimum high school GPA of 2.5 based on the TOPS core curriculum, the prior year's state average ACT score, and complete a 16.5 unit core curriculum. Must be a Louisiana resident. *Award:* Scholarship for use in freshman, sophomore, junior, or senior year; renewable. *Award amount:* $741–$3094. *Number of awards:* varies. *Eligibility Requirements:* Applicant must be enrolled or expecting to enroll full-time at a two-year, four-year, or technical institution or university; resident of Louisiana and studying in Louisiana. Applicant must have 2.5 GPA or higher. Available to U.S. citizens. *Application Requirements:* Application, test scores. *Deadline:* July 1.

Contact Public Information, Louisiana Office of Student Financial Assistance, PO Box 91202, Baton Rouge, LA 70821-9202. *E-mail:* custserv@osfa.state.la.us. *Phone:* 800-259-5626 Ext. 1012. *Fax:* 225-922-0790. *Web site:* www.osfa.state.la.us.

Robert C. Byrd Honors Scholarship-Louisiana. Applicant must have earned a diploma from a public or private secondary school or received the recognized equivalent of a high school diploma (GED) in the State of Louisiana in the same academic year in which the scholarship is to be awarded. Must have a GPA of 3.5. Must be a U.S. citizen and legal resident of Louisiana. Total number of awards varies each year. Deadline is March 10. *Award:* Scholarship for use in senior year; not renewable. *Award amount:* up to $6000. *Eligibility Requirements:* Applicant must be enrolled or expecting to enroll full-time at an institution or university and resident of Louisiana. Applicant must have 3.5 GPA or higher. Available to U.S. citizens. *Application Requirements:* Application, essay, test scores, transcript, selective service form. *Deadline:* March 10.

Contact Melissa Hollins, Scholarship Coordinator, Louisiana State Department of Education, PO Box 94064, Baton Rouge, LA 70804. *E-mail:* melissa.hollins@la.gov. *Phone:* 225-342-2098. *Web site:* www.doe.state.la.us.

Louisiana National Guard State Tuition Exemption Program. Renewable award for college undergraduates to receive tuition exemption upon satisfactory performance in the Louisiana National Guard. Applicant must attend a state-funded institution in Louisiana, be a resident and registered voter in Louisiana, meet the academic and residency requirements of the university attended, and provide documentation of Louisiana National Guard enlistment. The exemption can be used for up to 15 semesters. Minimum 2.5 GPA required. *Award:* Scholarship for use in freshman, sophomore, junior, or senior year; renewable. *Award amount:* varies. *Number of awards:* 1. *Eligibility Requirements:* Applicant must be enrolled or expecting to enroll full or part-time at a two-year, four-year, or technical institution or university; resident of Louisiana and studying in Louisiana. Applicant must have 2.5 GPA or higher. Available to U.S. citizens. Applicant must have served in the Air Force National Guard or Army National Guard. *Application Requirements: Deadline:* continuous.

Contact Jona M. Hughes, Education Services Officers, Louisiana National Guard—State of Louisiana, Joint Task Force LA, Building 35, Jackson Barracks, JI-PD, New Orleans, LA 70146-0330. *E-mail:* hughesj@la-arng.ngb.army.mil. *Phone:* 504-278-8531 Ext. 8304. *Fax:* 504-278-8025. *Web site:* www.la.ngb.army.mil.

MAINE

Tuition Waiver Programs. Provides tuition waivers for children and spouses of EMS personnel, firefighters, and law enforcement officers who have been killed in the line of duty and for students who were foster children under the custody of the Department of Human Services when they graduated from high school. Waivers valid at the University of Maine System, the Maine Technical College System, and Maine Maritime Academy. *Award:* Grant for use in freshman, sophomore, junior, or senior year; not renewable. *Award amount:* varies. *Number of awards:* 1. *Eligibility Requirements:* Applicant must be enrolled or expecting to enroll at an institution or university; resident of Maine and studying in Maine. Applicant or parent of applicant must have employment or volunteer experience in designated career field or police/firefighting. Available to U.S. citizens. *Application Requirements:* Application, letter from the Department of Human Services documenting that applicant is in their custody and residing in foster care at the time of graduation from high school or its equivalent. *Deadline:* continuous.

Contact Trisha Malloy, Program Officer, Finance Authority of Maine, 5 Community Drive, Augusta, ME 04332. *E-mail:* trisha@famemaine.com. *Phone:* 207-623-3263. *Fax:* 207-623-0095. *Web site:* www.famemaine.com.

George J. Mitchell Peace Scholarship. An annual exchange and scholarship to Ireland for students from the Maine Community College System and the University of Maine System. Scholarship will provide opportunity for student to study at a university or institute of technology in Ireland. Refer to Web site for details: http://www.mccs.me.edu *Award:* Scholarship for use in freshman, sophomore, junior, or senior year. *Award amount:* varies. *Number of awards:* 1. *Eligibility Requirements:* Applicant must be age 18; enrolled or expecting to enroll full-time at a two-year institution or university and resident of Maine. Applicant must have 3.0 GPA or higher. Available to U.S. citizens. *Application Requirements: Deadline:* February 15.

Contact Center for Career Development-Peace Exchange, Maine Community College System, Center for Career Development-Peace Exchange, 2 Fort Road, South Portland, ME 04106. *Phone:* 207-767-5210 Ext. 4117. *Web site:* www.mccs.me.edu.

Veterans Dependents Educational Benefits-Maine. Tuition waiver award for dependents or spouses of veterans who were prisoners of war, missing in action, or permanently disabled as a result of service. Veteran must have been Maine resident at service entry for five years preceding application. For use at Maine University system, technical colleges and Maine Maritime. Must be high school graduate. Must submit birth certificate and proof of VA disability of veteran. Award renewable for eight semesters for those under 22 years of age. *Award:* Scholarship for use in freshman, sophomore, junior, or senior year; renewable. *Award amount:* varies. *Number of awards:* varies. *Eligibility Requirements:* Applicant must be age 21-25; enrolled or expecting to enroll full or part-time at a technical institution or university; resident of Maine and studying in Maine. Available to U.S. citizens. Applicant or parent must meet one or more of the following requirements: general military experience; retired from active duty; disabled or killed as a result of military service; prisoner of war; or missing in action. *Application Requirements:* Application. *Deadline:* continuous.

Contact Roland Lapointe, Director, Maine Bureau of Veterans Services, State House Station 117, Augusta, ME 04333-0117. *E-mail:* mvs@me.ngb.army.mil. *Phone:* 207-626-4464. *Fax:* 207-626-4471. *Web site:* www.state.me.us.

State Scholarship and Grant Programs

Maine

Early College Program. For high school students who have not made plans for college but are academically capable of success in college. Recipients are selected by their school principal or director. Refer to Web site: http://www.mccs.me.edu/scholarships.html. Students must be entering a Maine Community College. *Award:* Scholarship for use in freshman year; not renewable. *Award amount:* up to $2000. *Number of awards:* up to 200. *Eligibility Requirements:* Applicant must be high school student; planning to enroll or expecting to enroll full-time at a two-year institution; resident of Maine and studying in Maine. Available to U.S. citizens. *Application Requirements:* Application. *Deadline:* varies.

Contact Scholarship Coordinator, Maine Community College System, 323 State Street, Augusta, ME 04330. *Phone:* 207-629-4000. *Fax:* 207-629-4048. *Web site:* www.mccs.me.edu.

NextGen Access Scholarship Program. Students attending Maine institutions are eligible for up to $1000 with a minimum award of $250. Students attending out-of-state-institutions are eligible for up to $500 with a minimum award of $250. The financial aid officer at each institution selects recipients. Applicant must be first year attendees. *Award:* Scholarship for use in freshman, sophomore, junior, senior, graduate, or postgraduate years. *Award amount:* $250–$1000. *Eligibility Requirements:* Applicant must be enrolled or expecting to enroll at a two-year, four-year, or technical institution or university and resident of Maine. Available to U.S. citizens. *Application Requirements:* Application.

Contact Cathy Kimball, Manager of Education Finance Programs, Finance Authority of Maine, 5 Community Drive, PO Box 949, Augusta, ME 04332-0949. *E-mail:* cathy@famemaine.com. *Phone:* 800-228-3734. *Fax:* 207-623-0095. *Web site:* www.famemaine.com.

Maine Community College Scholarship. Participating high schools and technical centers/regions identify students to apply for the scholarship during their junior year. Students must be both nominated by their school and accepted into a Maine community college program of study. Award is $500 per semester, $1000 per year for a one-year program and a maximum of $2000 for a two-year program, so long as student meets program requirements. For details see Web site: http://www.ccd.me.edu/scholarship *Award:* Scholarship for use in freshman or sophomore year; renewable. *Award amount:* $200–$2000. *Number of awards:* varies. *Eligibility Requirements:* Applicant must be high school student; planning to enroll or expecting to enroll at a two-year or technical institution; resident of Maine and studying in Maine. Available to U.S. citizens. *Application Requirements:* Deadline: varies.

Contact Dorry French, Career Assistant, Maine Community College System, 2 Fort Road, South Portland, ME 04106. *E-mail:* dfrench@ccd.me.edu. *Phone:* 207-767-5210 Ext. 4117. *Web site:* www.mccs.me.edu.

NextGen Student Grant Program. Need-based grant program available to undergraduate students who are Maine residents. Students can apply for this grant by filing the (FAFSA) by May 1st each year. *Award:* Grant for use in freshman, sophomore, junior, or senior year. *Award amount:* $400–$1000. *Eligibility Requirements:* Applicant must be enrolled or expecting to enroll full-time at a four-year institution or university and resident of Maine. Available to U.S. citizens. *Application Requirements:* Application.

Contact Cathy Kimball, Manager of Education Finance Programs, Finance Authority of Maine, 5 Community Drive, PO Box 949, Augusta, ME 04332-0949. *E-mail:* cathy@famemaine.com. *Phone:* 800-228-3734. *Fax:* 207-623-0095. *Web site:* www.famemaine.com.

MARYLAND

Tuition Reduction for Non-Resident Nursing Students. Forgivable loan is available to nonresidents of Maryland who attend a two-year or four-year public institution in Maryland. The loan will be renewed provided student maintains academic requirements designated by institution attended. Loan recipient must agree to serve as a full-time nurse in a hospital or related institution for an equal amount of years as tuition was paid by Maryland Higher Education Commission. Loan recipient will pay tuition of Maryland resident. *Academic Fields/Career Goals:* Nursing. *Award:* Forgivable loan for use in freshman, sophomore, junior, or senior year; renewable. *Award amount:* varies. *Number of awards:* 1. *Eligibility Requirements:* Applicant must be enrolled or expecting to enroll full or part-time at a two-year or four-year institution and studying in Maryland. Available to U.S. citizens. *Application Requirements:* Application. *Deadline:* varies.

Contact Financial Aid Office of your school, Maryland Higher Education Commission. *Web site:* www.mhec.state.md.us.

Distinguished Scholar Award-Maryland. Renewable award for Maryland students enrolled full-time at Maryland institutions. National Merit Scholar Finalists automatically offered award. Others may qualify for the award in satisfying criteria of a minimum 3.7 GPA or in combination with high test scores, or for Talent in Arts competition in categories of music, drama, dance, or visual arts. Must maintain annual 3.0 GPA in college for award to be renewed. Contact for further details. *Award:* Scholarship for use in freshman, sophomore, junior, or senior year; renewable. *Award amount:* up to $3000. *Number of awards:* up to 2000. *Eligibility Requirements:* Applicant must be high school student; planning to enroll or expecting to enroll full-time at a two-year or four-year institution or university; resident of Maryland and studying in Maryland. Available to U.S. citizens. *Application Requirements:* Application, test scores, transcript. *Deadline:* varies.

Contact Monica Tipton, Office of Student Financial Assistance, Maryland Higher Education Commission, 839 Bestgate Road, Suite 400, Annapolis, MD 21401-3013. *E-mail:* ofsamail@mhec.state.md.us. *Phone:* 410-260-4568. *Fax:* 410-260-3200. *Web site:* www.mhec.state.md.us.

Distinguished Scholar-Teacher Education Awards. Up to $3,000 award for Maryland high school seniors who have received the Distinguished Scholar Award. Recipient must enroll as a full-time undergraduate in a Maryland institution and pursue a program of study leading to a Maryland teaching certificate. Must maintain annual 3.0 GPA for renewal. Must teach in a Maryland public school one year for each year award is received. *Academic Fields/Career Goals:* Education. *Award:* Forgivable loan for use in freshman, sophomore, junior, or senior year; renewable. *Award amount:* up to $3000. *Number of awards:* 20–80. *Eligibility Requirements:* Applicant must be high school student; planning to enroll or expecting to enroll full-time at a two-year or four-year institution or university; resident of Maryland and studying in Maryland. Applicant must have 3.0 GPA or higher. Available to U.S. citizens. *Application Requirements:* Application, test scores, transcript, must be recipient of the Distinguished Scholar Award. *Deadline:* July 1.

Contact Monica Tipton, Office of Student Financial Assistance, Maryland Higher Education Commission, 839 Bestgate Road, Suite 400, Annapolis, MD 21401-3013. *E-mail:* ofsamail@mhec.state.md.us. *Phone:* 410-260-4568. *Fax:* 410-260-3200. *Web site:* www.mhec.state.md.us.

State Scholarship and Grant Programs
Maryland

Maryland State Nursing Scholarship and Living Expenses Grant. Renewable grant for Maryland residents enrolled in a two or four-year Maryland institution nursing degree program. Recipients must agree to serve as a full-time nurse in a Maryland shortage area and must maintain a 3.0 GPA in college. Application deadline is June 30. Submit Free Application for Federal Student Aid. *Academic Fields/Career Goals:* Nursing. *Award:* Forgivable loan for use in freshman, sophomore, junior, senior, or graduate year; renewable. *Award amount:* $200–$3000. *Number of awards:* up to 600. *Eligibility Requirements:* Applicant must be enrolled or expecting to enroll full-time at a two-year or four-year institution or university; resident of Maryland and studying in Maryland. Applicant must have 3.0 GPA or higher. Available to U.S. citizens. *Application Requirements:* Application, financial need analysis, transcript, FAFSA. *Deadline:* June 30.

Contact Marie Janiszewski, Office of Student Financial Assistance, Maryland Higher Education Commission, 839 Bestgate Road, Suite 400, Annapolis, MD 21401-3013. *E-mail:* ofsamail@mhec.state.md.us. *Phone:* 410-260-4569. *Fax:* 410-260-3203. *Web site:* www.mhec.state.md.us.

William Donald Schaefer Scholarship. Scholarship for current high school seniors, full-time degree seeking undergraduate and graduate students who are accepted for admission or are currently enrolled at an eligible institution in Maryland that offers courses of study, training, or other educational activities that are designed to prepare individuals for a career in public service. *Academic Fields/Career Goals:* Public Policy and Administration. *Award:* Scholarship for use in freshman, sophomore, junior, senior, or graduate year; renewable. *Award amount:* up to $8500. *Eligibility Requirements:* Applicant must be enrolled or expecting to enroll full-time at a two-year or four-year institution or university; resident of Maryland and studying in Maryland. Available to U.S. citizens. *Application Requirements:* Application, financial need analysis, FAFSA. *Deadline:* March 1.

Contact Office of Student Financial Assistance, Maryland Higher Education Commission, 839 Bestgate Road, Suite 400, Annapolis, MD 21401-3013. *E-mail:* lasplin@mhec.state.md.us. *Phone:* 410-260-4565. *Web site:* www.mhec.state.md.us.

Delegate Scholarship Program-Maryland. Delegate scholarships help Maryland residents attending Maryland degree-granting institutions, certain career schools, or nursing diploma schools. May attend out-of-state institution if Maryland Higher Education Commission deems major to be unique and not offered at a Maryland institution. Free Application for Federal Student Aid may be required. Students interested in this program should apply by contacting their legislative district delegate. *Award:* Scholarship for use in freshman, sophomore, junior, senior, or graduate year; not renewable. *Award amount:* $200–$7950. *Number of awards:* up to 3500. *Eligibility Requirements:* Applicant must be enrolled or expecting to enroll full or part-time at a two-year, four-year, or technical institution or university; resident of Maryland and studying in Maryland. Available to U.S. citizens. *Application Requirements:* Application, financial need analysis. *Deadline:* continuous.

Contact Barbara Fantom, Office of Student Financial Assistance, Maryland Higher Education Commission, 839 Bestgate Road, Suite 400, Annapolis, MD 21401-3013. *E-mail:* osfamail@mhec.state.md.us. *Phone:* 410-260-4547. *Fax:* 410-260-3200. *Web site:* www.mhec.state.md.us.

Robert C. Byrd Honors Scholarship-Maryland. Scholarship amount changes each year, however, it has ranged from $1000-1500. Amount received by the students is based on the total cost of attendance at each institution of higher education, awarded on merit basis. *Award:* Scholarship for use in freshman, sophomore, junior, or senior year. *Award amount:* $1000–$1500. *Eligibility Requirements:* Applicant must be enrolled or expecting to enroll full-time at a two-year, four-year, or technical institution or university. Available to U.S. citizens. *Application Requirements:* Application. *Deadline:* varies.

Contact William Cappe, Maryland State Department of Education, 200 West Baltimore Street, Baltimore, MD 21201. *E-mail:* wcappe@msde.state.md.us. *Phone:* 888-246-0016. *Web site:* www.msde.state.md.us/.

Senatorial Scholarships-Maryland. Renewable award for Maryland residents attending a Maryland degree-granting institution, nursing diploma school, or certain private career schools. May be used out-of-state only if Maryland Higher Education Commission deems major to be unique and not offered at Maryland institution. *Award:* Scholarship for use in freshman, sophomore, junior, senior, or graduate year; renewable. *Award amount:* $200–$2000. *Number of awards:* up to 7000. *Eligibility Requirements:* Applicant must be enrolled or expecting to enroll full or part-time at a two-year, four-year, or technical institution or university; resident of Maryland and studying in Maryland. Available to U.S. citizens. *Application Requirements:* Application, financial need analysis, test scores, application to Legislative District Senator. *Deadline:* March 1.

Contact Barbara Fantom, Office of Student Financial Assistance, Maryland Higher Education Commission, 839 Bestgate Road, Suite 400, Annapolis, MD 21401-3013. *E-mail:* osfamail@mhec.state.md.us. *Phone:* 410-260-4547. *Fax:* 410-260-3202. *Web site:* www.mhec.state.md.us.

Tuition Waiver for Foster Care Recipients. Applicant must be a high school graduate or recipient of a GED under the age of 21. Applicant must either have resided in a foster care home in Maryland at time of high school graduation or GED reception, or until 14th birthday and had been adopted after 14th birthday. Applicant, if status approved, will be exempt from paying tuition and mandatory fees at a public college in Maryland. *Award:* Scholarship for use in freshman, sophomore, junior, senior, or graduate year; renewable. *Award amount:* varies. *Number of awards:* 1. *Eligibility Requirements:* Applicant must be age 20 or under; enrolled or expecting to enroll full or part-time at a two-year or four-year institution or university and studying in Maryland. Available to U.S. citizens. *Application Requirements:* Application, financial need analysis. *Deadline:* March 1.

Contact Inquire at financial aid office of your school., Maryland Higher Education Commission. *Web site:* www.mhec.state.md.us.

Child Care Provider Program-Maryland. Forgivable loan provides assistance for Maryland undergraduates attending a Maryland institution and pursuing studies in a child development program or an early childhood education program. Must serve as a professional day care provider in Maryland for one year for each year award received. Must maintain minimum 2.0 GPA. Contact for further information. *Academic Fields/Career Goals:* Education. *Award:* Forgivable loan for use in freshman, sophomore, junior, or senior year; renewable. *Award amount:* $500–$2000. *Number of awards:* 100–150. *Eligibility Requirements:* Applicant must be enrolled or expecting to enroll full or part-time at a two-year or four-year institution or university; resident of Maryland and studying in Maryland. Available to U.S. citizens. *Application Requirements:* Application, transcript. *Deadline:* June 15.

Contact Margaret Crutchley, Office of Student Financial Assistance, Maryland Higher Education Commission, 839 Bestgate Road, Suite 400, Annapolis, MD 21401-3013. *E-mail:* ofsamail@mhec.state.md.us. *Phone:*

State Scholarship and Grant Programs
Maryland

410-260-4545. *Fax:* 410-260-3203. *Web site:* www.mhec.state.md.us.

Janet L. Hoffmann Loan Assistance Repayment Program. Provides assistance for repayment of loan debt to Maryland residents working full-time in nonprofit organizations and state or local governments. Must submit Employment Verification Form and Lender Verification Form. *Academic Fields/Career Goals:* Education; Law/Legal Services; Nursing; Social Services; Therapy/Rehabilitation. *Award:* Grant for use in freshman, sophomore, junior, senior, or graduate year; not renewable. *Award amount:* up to $7500. *Number of awards:* up to 400. *Eligibility Requirements:* Applicant must be enrolled or expecting to enroll at an institution or university; resident of Maryland and studying in Maryland. Available to U.S. citizens. *Application Requirements:* Application, transcript, IRS 1040 form. *Deadline:* September 30.

Contact Marie Janiszewski, Office of Student Financial Assistance, Maryland Higher Education Commission, 839 Bestgate Road, Suite 400, Annapolis, MD 21401. *E-mail:* osfamail@mhec.state.md.us. *Phone:* 410-260-4569. *Fax:* 410-260-3203. *Web site:* www.mhec.state.md.us.

Physical and Occupational Therapists and Assistants Grant Program. For Maryland residents training as physical, occupational therapists or therapy assistants at Maryland postsecondary institutions. Recipients must provide one year of service for each full, or partial, year of award. Service must be to handicapped children in a Maryland facility that has, or accommodates and provides services to, such children. Minimum 2.0 GPA. *Academic Fields/Career Goals:* Therapy/Rehabilitation. *Award:* Forgivable loan for use in freshman, sophomore, junior, senior, or graduate year; renewable. *Award amount:* up to $2000. *Number of awards:* up to 10. *Eligibility Requirements:* Applicant must be enrolled or expecting to enroll full-time at a two-year or four-year institution or university; resident of Maryland and studying in Maryland. Available to U.S. citizens. *Application Requirements:* Application, transcript. *Deadline:* July 1.

Contact Gerrie Rogers, Office of Student Financial Assistance, Maryland Higher Education Commission, 839 Bestgate Road, Suite 400, Annapolis, MD 21401. *E-mail:* ssamail@mhec.state.md.us. *Phone:* 410-260-4574. *Fax:* 410-260-3203. *Web site:* www.mhec.state.md.us.

William Kapell International Piano Competition and Festival. Quadrennial international piano competition for ages 18-31. $80 application fee. Competition takes place at the Clarice Smith Performing Arts Center at the University of Maryland. Next competition will be in 2007. *Academic Fields/Career Goals:* Performing Arts. *Award:* Prize for use in freshman, sophomore, junior, senior, graduate, or postgraduate years; not renewable. *Award amount:* $1000–$20,000. *Number of awards:* up to 12. *Eligibility Requirements:* Applicant must be age 18-31; enrolled or expecting to enroll at an institution or university and must have an interest in music. Available to U.S. and non-U.S. citizens. *Application Requirements:* Application, applicant must enter a contest, autobiography, photo, portfolio, references, CD of performance. *Fee:* $80. *Deadline:* December 1.

Contact Christopher Patton, Coordinator, Clarice Smith Performing Arts Center at Maryland, Suite 3800, University of Maryland, College Park, MD 20742-1625. *E-mail:* kapell@deans.umd.edu. *Phone:* 301-405-8174. *Fax:* 301-405-5977. *Web site:* www.claricesmithcenter.umd.edu.

Graduate and Professional Scholarship Program-Maryland. Graduate and professional scholarships provide need-based financial assistance to students attending a Maryland school of medicine, dentistry, law, pharmacy, social work, or nursing. Funds are provided to specific Maryland colleges and universities. Students must demonstrate financial need and be Maryland residents. Contact institution financial aid office for more information. *Academic Fields/Career Goals:* Dental Health/Services; Health and Medical Sciences; Law/Legal Services; Nursing; Social Services. *Award:* Scholarship for use in freshman, sophomore, junior, senior, graduate, or postgraduate years; renewable. *Award amount:* $1000–$5000. *Number of awards:* 40–200. *Eligibility Requirements:* Applicant must be enrolled or expecting to enroll full or part-time at a four-year institution or university; resident of Maryland and studying in Maryland. Available to U.S. citizens. *Application Requirements:* Application, financial need analysis. *Deadline:* March 1.

Contact institution financial aid office, Maryland Higher Education Commission. *Web site:* www.mhec.state.md.us.

J.F. Tolbert Memorial Student Grant Program. Available to Maryland residents attending a private career school in Maryland with at least 18 clock hours per week. *Award:* Grant for use in freshman or sophomore year; not renewable. *Award amount:* up to $400. *Number of awards:* 400. *Eligibility Requirements:* Applicant must be enrolled or expecting to enroll at a technical institution; resident of Maryland and studying in Maryland. Available to U.S. citizens. *Application Requirements:* Application, financial need analysis. *Deadline:* continuous.

Contact Carla Rich, Office of Student Financial Assistance, Maryland Higher Education Commission, 839 Bestgate Road, Suite 400, Annapolis, MD 21401-3013. *E-mail:* osfamail@mhec.state.md.us. *Phone:* 410-260-4513. *Fax:* 410-260-3200. *Web site:* www.mhec.state.md.us.

Sharon Christa McAuliffe Teacher Education-Critical Shortage Grant Program. Renewable awards for Maryland residents who are college juniors, seniors, or graduate students enrolled in a Maryland teacher education program. Must agree to enter profession in a subject designated as a critical shortage area. Must teach in Maryland for one year for each award year. Renewable for one year. *Academic Fields/Career Goals:* Education. *Award:* Forgivable loan for use in junior, senior, or graduate year; renewable. *Award amount:* $200–$17,000. *Number of awards:* up to 137. *Eligibility Requirements:* Applicant must be enrolled or expecting to enroll full or part-time at a four-year institution or university; resident of Maryland and studying in Maryland. Applicant must have 3.0 GPA or higher. Available to U.S. citizens. *Application Requirements:* Application, essay, resume, transcript. *Deadline:* December 31.

Contact Margaret Crutchley, Office of Student Financial Assistance, Maryland Higher Education Commission, 839 Bestgate Road, Suite 400, Annapolis, MD 21401-3013. *E-mail:* ofsamail@mhec.state.md.us. *Phone:* 410-260-4545. *Fax:* 410-260-3203. *Web site:* www.mhec.state.md.us.

Firefighter, Ambulance, and Rescue Squad Member Tuition Reimbursement Program-Maryland. Award intended to reimburse members of rescue organizations serving Maryland communities for tuition costs of course work towards a degree or certificate in fire service or medical technology. Must attend a two- or four-year school in Maryland. Minimum 2.0 GPA. *Academic Fields/Career Goals:* Fire Sciences; Health and Medical Sciences; Trade/Technical Specialties. *Award:* Scholarship for use in freshman, sophomore, junior, or senior year; not renewable. *Award amount:* $200–$4000. *Number of awards:* 100–300. *Eligibility Requirements:* Applicant must be enrolled or expecting to enroll full or part-time at a two-year or four-year institution or university; resident of Maryland and studying in Maryland. Applicant or parent of applicant must have employment or volunteer experience in police/

State Scholarship and Grant Programs
Massachusetts

firefighting. Available to U.S. citizens. *Application Requirements:* Application, transcript. *Deadline:* July 1.

Contact Gerrie Rogers, Office of Student Financial Assistance, Maryland Higher Education Commission, 839 Bestgate Road, Suite 400, Annapolis, MD 21401-3013. *E-mail:* ofsamai@mhec.state.md.us. *Phone:* 410-260-4574. *Fax:* 410-260-3203. *Web site:* www.mhec.state.md.us.

Educational Assistance Grants-Maryland. Award for Maryland residents accepted or enrolled in a full-time undergraduate degree or certificate program at a Maryland institution or hospital nursing school. Must submit financial aid form by March 1. Must earn 2.0 GPA in college to maintain award. *Award:* Grant for use in freshman, sophomore, junior, or senior year; renewable. *Award amount:* $400–$2700. *Number of awards:* 11,000–20,000. *Eligibility Requirements:* Applicant must be enrolled or expecting to enroll full-time at a two-year or four-year institution or university; resident of Maryland and studying in Maryland. Available to U.S. citizens. *Application Requirements:* Application, financial need analysis. *Deadline:* March 1.

Contact Barbara Fantom, Office of Student Financial Assistance, Maryland Higher Education Commission, 839 Bestgate Road, Suite 400, Annapolis, MD 21401-3013. *E-mail:* osfamail@mhec.state.md.us. *Phone:* 410-260-4547. *Fax:* 410-260-3200. *Web site:* www.mhec.state.md.us.

Guaranteed Access Grant-Maryland. Award for Maryland resident enrolling full-time in an undergraduate program at a Maryland institution. Must be under 22 at time of first award and begin college within one year of completing high school in Maryland with a minimum 2.5 GPA. Must have an annual family income less than 130% of the federal poverty level guideline. *Award:* Grant for use in freshman, sophomore, junior, senior, or graduate year; renewable. *Award amount:* $400–$13,800. *Number of awards:* up to 1000. *Eligibility Requirements:* Applicant must be age 21 or under; enrolled or expecting to enroll full-time at a two-year or four-year institution or university; resident of Maryland and studying in Maryland. Applicant must have 2.5 GPA or higher. Available to U.S. citizens. *Application Requirements:* Application, financial need analysis, transcript. *Deadline:* continuous.

Contact Theresa Lowe, Office of Student Financial Assistance, Maryland Higher Education Commission, 839 Bestgate Road, Suite 400, Annapolis, MD 21401-3013. *E-mail:* osfamail@mhec.state.md.us. *Phone:* 410-260-4555. *Fax:* 410-260-3200. *Web site:* www.mhec.state.md.us.

Edward T. Conroy Memorial Scholarship Program. Scholarship for dependents of deceased or 100% disabled U.S. Armed Forces personnel; the son, daughter, or surviving spouse of a victim of the September 11, 2001, terrorist attacks who died as a result of the attacks on the World Trade Center in New York City, the attack on the Pentagon in Virginia, or the crash of United Airlines Flight 93 in Pennsylvania; a POW/MIA of the Vietnam Conflict or his/her son or daughter; the son, daughter or surviving spouse (who has not remarried), of a state or local public safety employee or volunteer who died in the line of duty; or a state or local public safety employee or volunteer who was 100% disabled in the line of duty. Must be Maryland resident at time of disability. Submit applicable VA certification. Must be at least 16 years of age and attend Maryland institution. *Award:* Scholarship for use in freshman, sophomore, junior, senior, or graduate year; renewable. *Award amount:* $7200–$8550. *Number of awards:* up to 70. *Eligibility Requirements:* Applicant must be age 16-24; enrolled or expecting to enroll full or part-time at a two-year or four-year institution or university; resident of Maryland and studying in Maryland. Available to U.S. citizens. Applicant or parent must meet one or more of the following requirements: Army experience; retired from active duty; disabled or killed as a result of military service; prisoner of war; or missing in action. *Application Requirements:* Application, birth and death certificate, and disability papers. *Deadline:* July 30.

Contact Margaret Crutchley, Office of Student Financial Assistance, Maryland Higher Education Commission, 839 Bestgate Road, Suite 400, Annapolis, MD 21401-3013. *E-mail:* osfamail@mhec.state.md.us. *Phone:* 410-260-4545. *Fax:* 410-260-3203. *Web site:* www.mhec.state.md.us.

Part-time Grant Program-Maryland. Funds provided to Maryland colleges and universities. Eligible students must be enrolled on a part-time basis (6-11 credits) in an undergraduate degree program. Must demonstrate financial need and also be Maryland resident. Contact financial aid office at institution for more information. *Award:* Grant for use in freshman, sophomore, junior, or senior year; renewable. *Award amount:* $200–$1000. *Number of awards:* 1800–9000. *Eligibility Requirements:* Applicant must be enrolled or expecting to enroll part-time at a two-year or four-year institution or university; resident of Maryland and studying in Maryland. Available to U.S. citizens. *Application Requirements:* Application, financial need analysis. *Deadline:* March 1.

Contact Andrea E. Hunt, Director, Maryland Higher Education Commission, 839 Bestgate Road, Suite 400, Annapolis, MD 21401-3013. *E-mail:* ahunt@mhec.state.md.us. *Phone:* 410-260-4558. *Fax:* 410-260-3202. *Web site:* www.mhec.state.md.us.

MASSACHUSETTS

Massachusetts Cash Grant Program. A need-based grant to assist with mandatory fees and non-state supported tuition, this supplemental award is available to Massachusetts residents who are undergraduates at public two-year colleges, four-year colleges and universities in Massachusetts. Must file FAFSA before May 1. Contact college financial aid office for information. *Award:* Grant for use in freshman, sophomore, junior, or senior year; not renewable. *Award amount:* $150–$1900. *Number of awards:* varies. *Eligibility Requirements:* Applicant must be enrolled or expecting to enroll full-time at a two-year or four-year institution or university; resident of Massachusetts and studying in Massachusetts. Available to U.S. citizens. *Application Requirements:* Financial need analysis, FAFSA. *Deadline:* continuous.

Contact College Financial Aid Office, Massachusetts Office of Student Financial Assistance. *Web site:* www.osfa.mass.edu.

Performance Bonus Grant Program. One-time award to residents of Massachusetts enrolled in a Massachusetts postsecondary institution. Minimum 3.0 GPA required. Timely filing of FAFSA required. Must be sophomore-, junior-, or senior-level undergraduate. *Award:* Grant for use in sophomore, junior, or senior year; not renewable. *Award amount:* $350–$500. *Number of awards:* varies. *Eligibility Requirements:* Applicant must be enrolled or expecting to enroll full-time at a two-year or four-year institution or university; resident of Massachusetts and studying in Massachusetts. Applicant must have 3.0 GPA or higher. Available to U.S. citizens. *Application Requirements:* Financial need analysis, FAFSA. *Deadline:* May 1.

Contact Scholarship Information, Massachusetts Office of Student Financial Assistance, 454 Broadway, Suite 200, Revere, MA 02151. *Phone:* 617-727-9420. *Fax:* 617-727-0667. *Web site:* www.osfa.mass.edu.

Massachusetts Gilbert Matching Student Grant Program. Must be permanent Massachusetts resident for at least one year and attending an independent, regionally

State Scholarship and Grant Programs
Massachusetts

accredited Massachusetts school or school of nursing full time. File the Free Application for Federal Student Aid after January 1. Contact college financial aid office for complete details and deadlines. *Academic Fields/Career Goals:* Nursing. *Award:* Grant for use in freshman, sophomore, junior, or senior year; not renewable. *Award amount:* $200–$2500. *Number of awards:* varies. *Eligibility Requirements:* Applicant must be enrolled or expecting to enroll full-time at a four-year institution or university; resident of Massachusetts and studying in Massachusetts. Available to U.S. citizens. *Application Requirements:* Financial need analysis, FAFSA. *Deadline:* varies.

Contact College Financial Aid Office, Massachusetts Office of Student Financial Assistance. *Web site:* www.osfa.mass.edu.

Tomorrow's Teachers Scholarship Program. Tuition waver for graduating high school senior ranking in top 25% of class. Must be a resident of Massachusetts and pursue a bachelor's degree at a public college or university in the Commonwealth. Must commit to teach for four years in a Massachusetts public school. Scholarship Program provides payment of full tuition and required fees at eligible public colleges and universities. *Academic Fields/Career Goals:* Education. *Award:* Scholarship for use in freshman, sophomore, junior, or senior year; renewable. *Award amount:* varies. *Number of awards:* varies. *Eligibility Requirements:* Applicant must be high school student; planning to enroll or expecting to enroll full-time at a four-year institution or university; resident of Massachusetts and studying in Massachusetts. Applicant must have 3.5 GPA or higher. Available to U.S. citizens. *Application Requirements:* Application, essay, references, transcript. *Deadline:* February 15.

Contact Alison Leary, Massachusetts Office of Student Financial Assistance, 454 Broadway, Suite 200, Revere, MA 02151. *E-mail:* osfa@osfa.mass.edu. *Phone:* 617-727-9420. *Fax:* 617-727-0667. *Web site:* www.osfa.mass.edu.

Paraprofessional Teacher Preparation Grant. Grant providing financial aid assistance to Massachusetts residents who are currently employed as paraprofessionals in Massachusetts public schools and wish to obtain higher education and become certified as full time teachers. *Academic Fields/Career Goals:* Education. *Award:* Grant for use in freshman, sophomore, junior, or senior year. *Award amount:* $250–$7500. *Number of awards:* varies. *Eligibility Requirements:* Applicant must be enrolled or expecting to enroll full or part-time at a two-year or four-year institution or university and resident of Massachusetts. Available to U.S. citizens. *Application Requirements:* Application. *Deadline:* varies.

Contact Clantha McCurdy, Associate Vice Chancellor, Massachusetts Office of Student Financial Assistance, 454 Broadway, Suite 200, Revere, MA 02151. *E-mail:* cmccurdy@osfa.mass.edu. *Phone:* 617-727-9420. *Fax:* 617-727-0667. *Web site:* www.osfa.mass.edu.

Massachusetts Assistance for Student Success Program. Provides need-based financial assistance to Massachusetts residents to attend undergraduate postsecondary institutions in Connecticut, Maine, Massachusetts, New Hampshire, Pennsylvania, Rhode Island, Vermont, and District of Columbia. High school seniors may apply. Timely filing of FAFSA required. *Award:* Grant for use in freshman, sophomore, junior, or senior year; not renewable. *Award amount:* $300–$2300. *Number of awards:* 25,000–30,000. *Eligibility Requirements:* Applicant must be enrolled or expecting to enroll full-time at a two-year, four-year, or technical institution or university; resident of Massachusetts and studying in Connecticut, District of Columbia, Maine, Massachusetts, New Hampshire, Pennsylvania, Rhode Island, or Vermont. Available to U.S. citizens. *Application Requirements:* Financial need analysis, FAFSA. *Deadline:* May 1.

Contact Robert Brun, Director of Scholarships and Grants, Massachusetts Office of Student Financial Assistance, 454 Broadway, Suite 200, Revere, MA 02151. *Phone:* 617-727-9420. *Fax:* 617-727-0667. *Web site:* www.osfa.mass.edu.

Christian A. Herter Memorial Scholarship. Renewable award for Massachusetts residents who are in the tenth-eleventh grades and whose socio-economic backgrounds and environment may inhibit their ability to attain educational goals. Must exhibit severe personal or family-related difficulties, medical problems, or have overcome a personal obstacle. Provides up to 50% of the student's calculated need, as determined by Federal methodology, at the college of their choice within the continental U.S. *Award:* Scholarship for use in freshman, sophomore, junior, or senior year; renewable. *Award amount:* up to $15,000. *Number of awards:* 25. *Eligibility Requirements:* Applicant must be high school student; planning to enroll or expecting to enroll full-time at a two-year, four-year, or technical institution or university and resident of Massachusetts. Applicant must have 2.5 GPA or higher. Available to U.S. citizens. *Application Requirements:* Application, autobiography, financial need analysis, interview, references. *Deadline:* March 31.

Contact Ken Smith, Massachusetts Office of Student Financial Assistance, 454 Broadway, Suite 200, Revere, MA 02151. *E-mail:* osfa@osfa.mass.edu. *Phone:* 617-727-9420. *Fax:* 617-727-0667. *Web site:* www.osfa.mass.edu.

Massachusetts Public Service Grant Program. Scholarships for children and/or spouses of deceased members of fire, police, and corrections departments who were killed in the line of duty. For Massachusetts residents attending Massachusetts institutions. Applicant should have not received a prior bachelor's degree or its equivalent *Award:* Grant for use in freshman, sophomore, junior, or senior year; not renewable. *Award amount:* $720–$2500. *Number of awards:* varies. *Eligibility Requirements:* Applicant must be enrolled or expecting to enroll full-time at a four-year institution or university; resident of Massachusetts and studying in Massachusetts. Applicant or parent of applicant must have employment or volunteer experience in police/firefighting. Available to U.S. citizens. *Application Requirements:* Application, financial need analysis, FAFSA. *Deadline:* May 1.

Contact Alison Leary, Massachusetts Office of Student Financial Assistance, 454 Broadway, Suite 200, Revere, MA 02151. *E-mail:* osfa@osfa.mass.edu. *Phone:* 617-727-9420. *Fax:* 617-727-0667. *Web site:* www.osfa.mass.edu.

New England Regional Student Program (New England Board of Higher Education). For residents of Connecticut, Maine, Massachusetts, New Hampshire, Rhode Island, and Vermont. Through Regional Student Program, students pay reduced out-of-state tuition at public colleges or universities in other New England states when enrolling in certain majors not offered at public institutions in home state. Deadline: College application deadline. *Award:* Scholarship for use in freshman, sophomore, junior, senior, or graduate year; renewable. *Award amount:* varies. *Number of awards:* 1. *Eligibility Requirements:* Applicant must be enrolled or expecting to enroll full or part-time at a two-year or four-year institution or university; resident of Connecticut, Maine, Massachusetts, New Hampshire, Rhode Island, or Vermont and studying in Connecticut, Maine, Massachusetts, New Hampshire, Rhode Island, or Vermont. Available to U.S. citizens. *Application Requirements:* College application. *Deadline:* continuous.

Contact Wendy Lindsay, Director of Regional Student Program, New England Board of Higher Education, 45 Temple Place, Boston, MA 02111-1305. *E-mail:* tuitionbreak@nebhe.org. *Phone:* 617-357-9620 Ext. 111. *Fax:* 617-338-1577. *Web site:* www.nebhe.org.

State Scholarship and Grant Programs
Michigan

Massachusetts Part-time Grant Program. Award for permanent Massachusetts resident for at least one year enrolled part-time in a state-approved postsecondary school. Recipient must not have first bachelor's degree. FAFSA must be filed before May 1. Contact college financial aid office for further information. *Award:* Grant for use in freshman, sophomore, junior, or senior year; not renewable. *Award amount:* $200–$1150. *Number of awards:* 200. *Eligibility Requirements:* Applicant must be enrolled or expecting to enroll part-time at a two-year, four-year, or technical institution or university; resident of Massachusetts and studying in Massachusetts. Available to U.S. citizens. *Application Requirements:* Financial need analysis, FAFSA. *Deadline:* May 1.

Contact College Financial Aid Office, Massachusetts Office of Student Financial Assistance. *Web site:* www.osfa.mass.edu.

Hemophilia Federation of America. Person with hemophilia or VWD attending any accredited two- or four-year college, university or vocation/technical school in the U.S. *Award:* Scholarship for use in freshman, sophomore, junior, or senior year. *Award amount:* $1500. *Number of awards:* 1–3. *Eligibility Requirements:* Applicant must be enrolled or expecting to enroll full or part-time at a two-year, four-year, or technical institution or university. Applicant must be physically disabled. Available to U.S. citizens. *Application Requirements:* Application. *Deadline:* April 1.

Contact Sandy Aultman, LA Kelley Communications, 1045 West Pinhook Road, Suite 101, Lafayette, LA 70503. *Phone:* 337-261-9787. *Fax:* 337-261-1787. *Web site:* www.kelleycom.com.

Department of Education Scholarship for Programs in China. Scholarships offered to students who are pursuing Chinese language programs in China. Must be a U.S. citizen enrolled in a CIEE program. Students must have the equivalent of two years study in Chinese language documented. Deadlines are April 1 and November 1. For more details see Web site: http://www.ciee.org/study/scholarships.aspx#china *Academic Fields/Career Goals:* Education. *Award:* Scholarship for use in junior, senior, or graduate year; not renewable. *Award amount:* $500–$8000. *Number of awards:* 10–20. *Eligibility Requirements:* Applicant must be enrolled or expecting to enroll full-time at a two-year or four-year institution or university and must have an interest in foreign language. Applicant must have 3.0 GPA or higher. Available to U.S. citizens. *Application Requirements:* Application, essay, financial need analysis, references, transcript. *Deadline:* varies.

Contact Kate Dunkerley, Senior Program Coordinator-Grants Program, Council for International Educational Exchange, 3 Copley Place, 2nd Floor, Boston, MA 02116. *E-mail:* kdunkerley@ciee.org. *Phone:* 800-448-9944 Ext. 368. *Fax:* 617-247-2911. *Web site:* www.ciee.org/study.

MICHIGAN

Michigan Tuition Grant. Need-based program. Students must attend a Michigan private, nonprofit, degree-granting college. Must file the Free Application for Federal Student Aid and meet the college's academic progress requirements. Deadline: March 1. Must be Michigan resident. Renewable award of $2000. *Award:* Grant for use in freshman, sophomore, junior, senior, or graduate year; renewable. *Award amount:* $100–$2000. *Number of awards:* varies. *Eligibility Requirements:* Applicant must be enrolled or expecting to enroll full or part-time at a two-year or four-year institution or university; resident of Michigan and studying in Michigan. Available to U.S. citizens. *Application Requirements:* Financial need analysis. *Deadline:* March 1.

Contact Scholarship and Grant Director, Michigan Bureau of Student Financial Assistance, PO Box 30462, Lansing, MI 48909-7962. *Web site:* www.michigan.gov/studentaid.

Michigan Competitive Scholarship. Awards limited to tuition. Must maintain a C average and meet the college's academic progress requirements. Must file Free Application for Federal Student Aid. Deadline: March 1. Must be Michigan resident. Renewable award of $1300 for undergraduate study at a Michigan institution. *Award:* Scholarship for use in freshman, sophomore, junior, or senior year; renewable. *Award amount:* $100–$1300. *Number of awards:* varies. *Eligibility Requirements:* Applicant must be enrolled or expecting to enroll at a two-year or four-year institution or university; resident of Michigan and studying in Michigan. Available to U.S. citizens. *Application Requirements:* Application, financial need analysis, test scores, FAFSA. *Deadline:* March 1.

Contact Scholarship and Grant Director, Michigan Bureau of Student Financial Assistance, PO Box 30466, Lansing, MI 48909. *Web site:* www.michigan.gov/studentaid.

Michigan Adult Part-Time Grant. Grant for part-time, needy, independent undergraduates at an approved, degree-granting Michigan college or university. Eligibility is limited to two years. Must be Michigan resident. Deadlines determined by college. *Award:* Grant for use in freshman, sophomore, junior, or senior year; not renewable. *Award amount:* up to $600. *Number of awards:* varies. *Eligibility Requirements:* Applicant must be enrolled or expecting to enroll part-time at a two-year or four-year institution or university; resident of Michigan and studying in Michigan. Available to U.S. citizens. *Application Requirements:* Financial need analysis. *Deadline:* varies.

Contact Program Director, Michigan Bureau of Student Financial Assistance, PO Box 30462, Lansing, MI 48909-7962. *E-mail:* osg@michigan.gov. *Phone:* 888-447-2687. *Web site:* www.michigan.gov/studentaid.

Michigan Educational Opportunity Grant. Need-based program for Michigan residents who are at least half-time undergraduates attending public Michigan colleges. Must maintain good academic standing. Deadline determined by college. Award of up to $1000. *Award:* Grant for use in freshman, sophomore, junior, or senior year; not renewable. *Award amount:* up to $1000. *Number of awards:* varies. *Eligibility Requirements:* Applicant must be enrolled or expecting to enroll full or part-time at a two-year institution or university; resident of Michigan and studying in Michigan. Available to U.S. citizens. *Application Requirements:* Financial need analysis. *Deadline:* varies.

Contact Program Director, Michigan Bureau of Student Financial Assistance, PO Box 30462, Lansing, MI 48909-7962. *E-mail:* osg@michigan.gov. *Phone:* 888-447-2687. *Web site:* www.michigan.gov/studentaid.

Michigan Indian Tuition Waiver. Renewable award provides free tuition for Native-American of one-quarter or more blood degree who attend a Michigan public college or university. Must be a Michigan resident for at least one year. The tuition waiver program covers part-time and summer school students, as well as Masters and Doctoral work. For more details and deadlines contact college financial aid office. *Award:* Scholarship for use in freshman, sophomore, junior, senior, graduate, or postgraduate years; renewable. *Award amount:* varies. *Number of awards:* 1. *Eligibility Requirements:* Applicant must be American Indian/Alaska Native; enrolled or expecting to enroll full or part-time at a two-year or four-year institution or university; resident of Michigan and studying in Michigan. Available to U.S. and Canadian citizens. *Application Requirements:* Application, driver's license, tribal certification. *Deadline:* continuous.

State Scholarship and Grant Programs
Michigan

Contact Christin McKerchie, Executive Assistant to Programs, Inter-Tribal Council of Michigan, Inc., 2956 Ashmun Street, Sault Ste. Marie, MI 49783. *Phone:* 906-632-6896 Ext. 136. *Fax:* 906-632-6878. *Web site:* www.itcmi.org.

Michigan Nursing Scholarship. For students enrolled in an LPN, associate degree in nursing, or bachelor of science in nursing programs. Colleges determine application procedure and select recipients. Recipients must fulfill in-state work commitment or repay scholarship. *Academic Fields/Career Goals:* Nursing. *Award:* Scholarship for use in freshman, sophomore, junior, or senior year; renewable. *Award amount:* up to $4000. *Number of awards:* varies. *Eligibility Requirements:* Applicant must be enrolled or expecting to enroll full or part-time at a two-year or four-year institution or university; resident of Michigan and studying in Michigan. Available to U.S. citizens. *Application Requirements: Deadline:* varies.

Contact Program Director, Michigan Bureau of Student Financial Assistance, PO Box 30462, Lansing, MI 48909-7962. *E-mail:* osg@michigan.gov. *Phone:* 888-447-2687. *Web site:* www.michigan.gov/studentaid.

Tuition Incentive Program (TIP). Award for Michigan residents who receive or have received Medicaid for required period of time through the Family Independence Agency. Scholarship provides two years tuition towards an associate's degree at a Michigan college or university. Apply before graduating from high school or earning General Education Development diploma. *Award:* Grant for use in freshman, sophomore, junior, or senior year; renewable. *Number of awards:* varies. *Eligibility Requirements:* Applicant must be high school student; planning to enroll or expecting to enroll full or part-time at a two-year or four-year institution or university; resident of Michigan and studying in Michigan. Available to U.S. citizens. *Application Requirements:* Application, Medicaid eligibility for specified period of time. *Deadline:* continuous.

Contact Program Director, Michigan Bureau of Student Financial Assistance, PO Box 30462, Lansing, MI 48909-7962. *E-mail:* osg@michigan.gov. *Phone:* 888-447-2687. *Web site:* www.michigan.gov/studentaid.

Michigan Merit Award. Scholarship for students scoring well on state's standardized assessment tests. Students will have four years from high school graduation to use the award. *Award:* Scholarship for use in freshman, sophomore, junior, or senior year; not renewable. *Award amount:* $1000–$2500. *Number of awards:* varies. *Eligibility Requirements:* Applicant must be high school student; planning to enroll or expecting to enroll full or part-time at a two-year, four-year, or technical institution or university and resident of Michigan. Available to U.S. citizens. *Application Requirements:* Test scores.

Contact Program Director, Michigan Bureau of Student Financial Assistance, PO Box 30466, Lansing, MI 48909-7962. *E-mail:* osg@michigan.gov. *Phone:* 888-447-2687. *Web site:* www.michigan.gov/studentaid.

Michigan Veterans Trust Fund Tuition Grant Program. Tuition grant of $2,800 for children of Michigan veterans who died on active duty or subsequently declared 100% disabled as the result of service-connected illness or injury. Must be 17 to 25 years old, be a Michigan resident, and attend a private or public institution in Michigan. *Award:* Grant for use in freshman, sophomore, junior, or senior year; renewable. *Award amount:* up to $2800. *Number of awards:* varies. *Eligibility Requirements:* Applicant must be age 17-25; enrolled or expecting to enroll full-time at a two-year, four-year, or technical institution or university; resident of Michigan and studying in Michigan. Available to U.S. citizens. Applicant or parent must meet one or more of the following requirements: general military experience; retired from active duty; disabled or killed as a result of military service; prisoner of war; or missing in action. *Application Requirements:* Application. *Deadline:* continuous.

Contact Phyllis Ochis, Department of Military and Veterans Affairs, Michigan Veterans Trust Fund, 2500 South Washington Avenue, Lansing, MI 48913. *Phone:* 517-483-5469. *Web site:* www.michigan.gov/dmva.

MINNESOTA

Postsecondary Child Care Grant Program-Minnesota. One-time grant available for students not receiving MFIP. Based on financial need. Cannot exceed actual child care costs or maximum award chart (based on income). Must be Minnesota resident. For use at Minnesota two- or four-year school, including public technical colleges. *Award:* Grant for use in freshman, sophomore, junior, or senior year; not renewable. *Award amount:* $100–$2300. *Number of awards:* varies. *Eligibility Requirements:* Applicant must be enrolled or expecting to enroll full or part-time at a two-year, four-year, or technical institution or university; resident of Minnesota and studying in Minnesota. Available to U.S. citizens. *Application Requirements:* Application, financial need analysis. *Deadline:* continuous.

Contact Minnesota Higher Education Services Office, 1450 Energy Park Drive, Suite 350, St. Paul, MN 55108-5227. *Phone:* 651-642-0567 Ext. 1. *Web site:* www.getreadyforcollege.org.

Donaldson Company, Inc. Scholarship Program. Scholarships for children of U.S. employees of Donaldson Company, Inc. Any form of accredited postsecondary education is eligible. Application deadline is March 15. *Award:* Scholarship for use in freshman, sophomore, junior, or senior year; renewable. *Award amount:* $1000–$3000. *Eligibility Requirements:* Applicant must be enrolled or expecting to enroll full-time at a two-year, four-year, or technical institution or university. Applicant or parent of applicant must be affiliated with Donaldson Company. Available to U.S. citizens. *Application Requirements:* Application, essay, financial need analysis, references, transcript. *Deadline:* March 15.

Contact Norm Linnell, Vice President, General Counsel, and Secretary, Donaldson Company, PO Box 1299, Minneapolis, MN 55440. *E-mail:* nlinnell@mail.donaldson.com. *Phone:* 952-887-3631. *Fax:* 952-887-3005. *Web site:* www.donaldson.com.

Safety Officers' Survivor Grant Program. Grant for eligible survivors of Minnesota public safety officers killed in the line of duty. Safety officers who have been permanently or totally disabled in the line of duty are also eligible. Must be used at a Minnesota institution participating in State Grant Program. Write for details. Must submit proof of death or disability and Public Safety Officers Benefit Fund Certificate. Must apply each year. Can be renewed for four years. *Award:* Grant for use in freshman, sophomore, junior, or senior year; renewable. *Award amount:* up to $9208. *Eligibility Requirements:* Applicant must be age 23 or under; enrolled or expecting to enroll full or part-time at a two-year, four-year, or technical institution or university; resident of Minnesota and studying in Minnesota. Applicant or parent of applicant must have employment or volunteer experience in police/firefighting. Available to U.S. citizens. *Application Requirements:* Application, proof of death/disability. *Deadline:* continuous.

Contact Minnesota Higher Education Services Office, 1450 Energy Park Drive, Suite 350, St. Paul, MN 55108-5227. *Phone:* 651-642-0567 Ext. 1. *Web site:* www.getreadyforcollege.org.

State Scholarship and Grant Programs
Mississippi

Minnesota State Grant Program. Need-based grant program available for Minnesota residents attending Minnesota colleges. Student covers 46% of cost with remainder covered by Pell Grant, parent contribution and state grant. Students apply with FAFSA and college administers the program on campus. *Award:* Grant for use in freshman, sophomore, junior, or senior year; not renewable. *Award amount:* $100–$7861. *Number of awards:* 71,000–75,000. *Eligibility Requirements:* Applicant must be age 17; enrolled or expecting to enroll full or part-time at a two-year, four-year, or technical institution or university; resident of Minnesota and studying in Minnesota. Available to U.S. citizens. *Application Requirements:* Application, financial need analysis. *Deadline:* varies.

Contact Minnesota Higher Education Services Office, 1450 Energy Park Drive, Suite 350, St. Paul, MN 55108. *Phone:* 651-642-0567 Ext. 1. *Web site:* www.getreadyforcollege.org.

Leadership, Excellence and Dedicated Service Scholarship. Awarded to high school seniors who enlist in the Minnesota National Guard. The award recognizes demonstrated leadership, community services and potential for success in the Minnesota National Guard. For more information, applicant may contact any Minnesota army national guard recruiter at 1-800-go-guard or visit the Web site http://www.dma.state.mn.us. *Award:* Scholarship for use in freshman year; not renewable. *Award amount:* $1000. *Number of awards:* 30. *Eligibility Requirements:* Applicant must be high school student and planning to enroll or expecting to enroll full or part-time at a two-year, four-year, or technical institution or university. Available to U.S. and non-U.S. citizens. Applicant must have served in the Air Force National Guard or Army National Guard. *Application Requirements:* Essay, resume, references, transcript. *Deadline:* March 15.

Contact Barbara O'Reilly, Education Services Officer, Minnesota Department of Military Affairs, Veterans Services Building, 20 West 12th Street, St. Paul, MN 55155-2098. *E-mail:* barbara.oreilly@mn.ngb.army.mil. *Phone:* 651-282-4508. *Web site:* www.dma.state.mn.us.

Minnesota Indian Scholarship Program. One-time award for Minnesota Native-American. Applicant must be one quarter Native-American and a resident of Minnesota. Must re-apply for scholarship annually. *Award:* Scholarship for use in freshman, sophomore, junior, or senior year; not renewable. *Award amount:* $3300–$6600. *Number of awards:* varies. *Eligibility Requirements:* Applicant must be American Indian/Alaska Native; enrolled or expecting to enroll full or part-time at a two-year, four-year, or technical institution or university; resident of Minnesota and studying in Minnesota. Available to U.S. citizens. *Application Requirements:* Application, financial need analysis. *Deadline:* July 1.

Contact Lea Perkins, Director, Minnesota Indian Scholarship Office, Minnesota Department of Education, 1500 Highway 36W, Roseville, MN 55113-4266. *E-mail:* cfl.indianeducation@state.mn.us. *Phone:* 800-657-3927. *Web site:* www.mheso.state.mn.us.

Minnesota Nurses Loan Forgiveness Program. This program offers loan repayment to registered nurse and licensed practical nurse students who agree to practice in a Minnesota nursing home or an Intermediate Care Facility for persons with mental retardation for a minimum 3-year/4-year service obligation after completion of training. Candidates must apply while still in school. *Academic Fields/Career Goals:* Health and Medical Sciences; Nursing. *Award:* Forgivable loan for use in freshman, sophomore, junior, or senior year; not renewable. *Award amount:* $3000–$3500. *Number of awards:* 25–35. *Eligibility Requirements:* Applicant must be enrolled or expecting to enroll full or part-time at a two-year, four-year, or technical institution or university. Available to U.S. citizens. *Application Requirements:* Application, essay, resume. *Deadline:* December 1.

Contact Karen Welter, Minnesota Department of Health, 121 East Seventh Place, Suite 460, PO Box 64975, St. Paul, MN 55164-0975. *E-mail:* karen.welter@health.state.mn.us. *Phone:* 651-282-6302. *Fax:* 651-297-5808. *Web site:* www.health.state.mn.us.

Minnesota State Veterans' Dependents Assistance Program. Tuition assistance to dependents of persons considered to be prisoner-of-war or missing in action after August 1, 1958. Must be Minnesota resident attending Minnesota two- or four-year school. *Award:* Scholarship for use in freshman, sophomore, junior, or senior year; renewable. *Award amount:* varies. *Number of awards:* 1. *Eligibility Requirements:* Applicant must be enrolled or expecting to enroll at a two-year or four-year institution; resident of Minnesota and studying in Minnesota. Available to U.S. citizens. Applicant or parent must meet one or more of the following requirements: general military experience; retired from active duty; disabled or killed as a result of military service; prisoner of war; or missing in action. *Application Requirements:* Application. *Deadline:* continuous.

Contact Minnesota Higher Education Services Office, 1450 Energy Park Drive, Suite 350, St. Paul, MN 55108-5227. *Web site:* www.getreadyforcollege.org.

Minnesota Reciprocal Agreement. Renewable tuition waiver for Minnesota residents. Waives all or part of non-resident tuition surcharge at public institutions in Iowa, Kansas, Michigan, Missouri, Nebraska, North Dakota, South Dakota, and Wisconsin. Deadline is last day of academic term. *Award:* Scholarship for use in freshman, sophomore, junior, senior, graduate, or postgraduate years; renewable. *Award amount:* varies. *Number of awards:* 1. *Eligibility Requirements:* Applicant must be enrolled or expecting to enroll full or part-time at a two-year, four-year, or technical institution or university; resident of Minnesota and studying in Iowa, Kansas, Michigan, Missouri, Nebraska, North Dakota, South Dakota, or Wisconsin. Available to U.S. citizens. *Application Requirements:* Application. *Deadline:* varies.

Contact Minnesota Higher Education Services Office, 1450 Energy Park Drive, Suite 350, St. Paul, MN 55108-5227. *Phone:* 651-642-0567 Ext. 1. *Web site:* www.getreadyforcollege.org.

MISSISSIPPI

Mississippi Health Care Professions Loan/Scholarship Program. Renewable award for junior and senior undergraduates studying psychology, speech pathology or occupational therapy. Must be Mississippi residents attending four-year universities in Mississippi. Must fulfill work obligation in Mississippi or pay back as loan. Renewable award for graduate student enrolled in physical therapy. *Academic Fields/Career Goals:* Health and Medical Sciences; Psychology; Therapy/Rehabilitation. *Award:* Forgivable loan for use in junior, senior, or graduate year; renewable. *Award amount:* $1500–$6000. *Number of awards:* varies. *Eligibility Requirements:* Applicant must be enrolled or expecting to enroll full-time at a four-year institution or university; resident of Mississippi and studying in Mississippi. Available to U.S. citizens. *Application Requirements:* Application, driver's license, references, transcript. *Deadline:* March 31.

Contact Susan Eckels, Program Administrator, Mississippi State Student Financial Aid, 3825 Ridgewood Road, Jackson, MS 39211-6453. *E-mail:* sme@ihl.state.ms.us. *Phone:* 601-432-6997. *Web site:* www.mississippiuniversities.com.

William Winter Teacher Scholar Loan. Scholarship available to a junior or senior

State Scholarship and Grant Programs
Mississippi

student at a four year Mississippi college or university. Applicants must enroll in a program of study leading to a Class "A" teacher educator license. *Award:* Scholarship for use in junior or senior year; renewable. *Award amount:* up to $4000. *Eligibility Requirements:* Applicant must be enrolled or expecting to enroll full-time at a four-year institution or university. Applicant must have 2.5 GPA or higher. Available to U.S. citizens. *Application Requirements:* Application. *Deadline:* March 31.

Contact Mississippi Student Financial Aid, Mississippi State Student Financial Aid, 3825 Ridgewood Road, Jackson, MS 39211-6453. *E-mail:* sfa@ihl.state.ms.us. *Phone:* 800-327-2980. *Web site:* www.mississippiuniversities.com.

William Winter Teacher Scholar Loan Program. Awarded to Mississippi residents pursuing a teaching career. Must be enrolled full-time in a program leading to a Class A certification and maintain a 2.5 GPA. Must agree to teach one year for each year award is received. *Academic Fields/Career Goals:* Education. *Award:* Forgivable loan for use in junior or senior year; renewable. *Award amount:* $500–$4000. *Number of awards:* varies. *Eligibility Requirements:* Applicant must be enrolled or expecting to enroll full-time at a two-year or four-year institution or university; resident of Mississippi and studying in Mississippi. Applicant must have 2.5 GPA or higher. Available to U.S. citizens. *Application Requirements:* Application, driver's license, references, transcript. *Deadline:* March 31.

Contact Board of Trustees, Mississippi State Student Financial Aid, 3825 Ridgewood Road, Jackson, MS 39211-6453. *Web site:* www.mississippiuniversities.com.

Gulf Coast Research Laboratory Minority Summer Grant. Grants to minority freshmen, sophomore, junior, or senior student at a Mississippi college or university majoring in marine and environmental sciences. *Academic Fields/Career Goals:* Environmental Science. *Award:* Grant for use in freshman, sophomore, junior, or senior year. *Number of awards:* 1. *Eligibility Requirements:* Applicant must be American Indian/Alaska Native, Asian/Pacific Islander, Black (non-Hispanic), or Hispanic; enrolled or expecting to enroll full-time at a four-year institution or university; resident of Mississippi and studying in Mississippi. Available to U.S. citizens. *Application Requirements:* Application, transcript. *Deadline:* March 31.

Contact Mississippi Student Financial Aid, Mississippi State Student Financial Aid, 3825 Ridgewood Road, Jackson, MS 39211-6453. *E-mail:* sfa@ihl.state.ms.us. *Phone:* 800-327-2980. *Web site:* www.mississippiuniversities.com.

Mississippi Eminent Scholars Grant. Award for high-school seniors who are residents of Mississippi. Applicants must achieve a grade point average of 3.5 after a minimum of seven semesters in high school and must have scored 29 on the ACT. Must enroll full-time at an eligible Mississippi college or university. *Award:* Grant for use in freshman, sophomore, junior, or senior year; renewable. *Award amount:* up to $2500. *Number of awards:* varies. *Eligibility Requirements:* Applicant must be enrolled or expecting to enroll full-time at a two-year or four-year institution or university; resident of Mississippi and studying in Mississippi. Applicant must have 3.5 GPA or higher. Available to U.S. citizens. *Application Requirements:* Application, test scores, transcript. *Deadline:* September 15.

Contact Mississippi Student Financial Aid, Mississippi State Student Financial Aid, 3825 Ridgewood Road, Jackson, MS 39211-6453. *E-mail:* sfa@ihl.state.ms.us. *Phone:* 800-327-2980. *Web site:* www.mississippiuniversities.com.

Critical Needs Teacher Loan/Scholarship. Eligible applicants will agree to employment immediately upon degree completion as a full-time classroom teacher in a public school located in a critical teacher shortage area in the state of Mississippi. Must verify the intention to pursue a first bachelor's degree in teacher education. Award covers tuition and required fees, average cost of room and meals plus a $500 allowance for books. Must be enrolled at a Mississippi college or university. *Academic Fields/Career Goals:* Education; Psychology; Therapy/Rehabilitation. *Award:* Forgivable loan for use in junior or senior year; not renewable. *Number of awards:* 1. *Eligibility Requirements:* Applicant must be enrolled or expecting to enroll full or part-time at a four-year institution or university and studying in Mississippi. Applicant must have 2.5 GPA or higher. Available to U.S. citizens. *Application Requirements:* Application, test scores, transcript. *Deadline:* March 31.

Contact Mississippi Student Financial Aid, Mississippi State Student Financial Aid, 3825 Ridgewood Road, Jackson, MS 39211-6453. *E-mail:* sfa@ihl.state.ms.us. *Phone:* 800-327-2980. *Web site:* www.mississippiuniversities.com.

Higher Education Legislative Plan (HELP). Eligible applicant must be resident of Mississippi and be freshmen and/or sophomore student who graduated from high school within the immediate past two years. Must demonstrate need as determined by the results of the Free Application for Federal Student Aid, documenting an average family adjusted gross income of $36,500 or less over the prior two years. Must be enrolled full-time at a Mississippi college or university, have a cumulative grade point average of 2.5 and have scored 20 on the ACT. *Award:* Scholarship for use in freshman or sophomore year; renewable. *Number of awards:* 1. *Eligibility Requirements:* Applicant must be enrolled or expecting to enroll full-time at a four-year institution or university; resident of Mississippi and studying in Mississippi. Applicant must have 2.5 GPA or higher. Available to U.S. citizens. *Application Requirements:* Application, financial need analysis, test scores, transcript, FAFSA. *Deadline:* March 31.

Contact Mississippi Student Financial Aid, Mississippi State Student Financial Aid, 3825 Ridgewood Road, Jackson, MS 39211-6453. *E-mail:* sfa@ihl.state.ms.us. *Phone:* 800-327-2980. *Web site:* www.mississippiuniversities.com.

Mississippi Resident Tuition Assistance Grant. Must be a resident of Mississippi enrolled full-time at an eligible Mississippi college or university. Must maintain a minimum 2.5 GPA each semester. MTAG awards may be up to $500 per academic year for freshmen and sophomores and $1,000 per academic year for juniors and seniors. Funds will be made available to eligible participants for eight semesters or the normal time required to complete the degree program, whichever comes first. Refer to Web site for application information http://www.mississippiuniversities.com *Award:* Grant for use in freshman, sophomore, junior, or senior year; renewable. *Award amount:* $500–$1000. *Eligibility Requirements:* Applicant must be enrolled or expecting to enroll full-time at a two-year or four-year institution or university; resident of Mississippi and studying in Mississippi. Applicant must have 2.5 GPA or higher. Available to U.S. citizens. *Application Requirements:* Application, test scores, transcript. *Deadline:* September 15.

Contact Mississippi Student Financial Aid, Mississippi State Student Financial Aid, 3825 Ridgewood Road, Jackson, MS 39211-6453. *E-mail:* sfa@ihl.state.ms.us. *Phone:* 800-327-2980. *Web site:* www.mississippiuniversities.com.

Nursing Education Loan/Scholarship-BSN. Renewable award for Mississippi undergraduates in junior or senior year pursuing nursing programs in Mississippi in order to earn BSN degree. Include transcript and references with application.

Must agree to employment in professional nursing (patient care) in Mississippi. *Academic Fields/Career Goals:* Nursing. *Award:* Forgivable loan for use in junior or senior year; renewable. *Award amount:* $4000–$8000. *Number of awards:* varies. *Eligibility Requirements:* Applicant must be enrolled or expecting to enroll full or part-time at a four-year institution or university; resident of Mississippi and studying in Mississippi. Applicant must have 2.5 GPA or higher. Available to U.S. citizens. *Application Requirements:* Application, driver's license, financial need analysis, references, transcript. *Deadline:* March 31.

Contact Board of Trustees, Mississippi State Student Financial Aid, 3825 Ridgewood Road, Jackson, MS 39211-6453. *Web site:* www.mississippiuniversities.com.

MISSOURI

Missouri College Guarantee Program. Available to Missouri residents attending Missouri colleges full-time. Minimum 2.5 GPA required. Must have participated in high school extracurricular activities. *Award:* Scholarship for use in freshman, sophomore, junior, or senior year; not renewable. *Award amount:* $100–$4900. *Number of awards:* varies. *Eligibility Requirements:* Applicant must be enrolled or expecting to enroll full-time at a two-year or four-year institution or university; resident of Missouri and studying in Missouri. Applicant must have 2.5 GPA or higher. Available to U.S. citizens. *Application Requirements:* Financial need analysis, test scores, FAFSA. *Deadline:* April 1.

Contact MDHE Information Center, Missouri Department of Higher Education, 3515 Amazonas Drive, Jefferson City, MO 65109. *E-mail:* icweb@dhe.mo.gov. *Phone:* 800-473-6757 Ext. 1. *Fax:* 573-751-6635. *Web site:* www.dhe.mo.gov.

Robert C. Byrd Honors Scholarship-Missouri. Award for Missouri high school seniors who are residents of Missouri. The amount of the award per student each year depends on the amount the state is allotted by the U.S. Department of Education. The highest amount of award per student is $1500. Students must rank in top 10% of high school class and score in top 10% of ACT test. *Award:* Scholarship for use in freshman year; renewable. *Award amount:* $1100–$1500. *Number of awards:* 100–150. *Eligibility Requirements:* Applicant must be high school student; planning to enroll or expecting to enroll full-time at a two-year, four-year, or technical institution or university and resident of Missouri. Applicant must have 3.5 GPA or higher.

Available to U.S. citizens. *Application Requirements:* Application, test scores, transcript, 7th semester transcripts. *Deadline:* April 15.

Contact Laura Harrison, Administrative Assistant II, Missouri Department of Elementary and Secondary Education, PO Box 480, Jefferson City, MO 65102-0480. *E-mail:* laura.harrison@dese.mo.gov. *Phone:* 573-751-1668. *Fax:* 573-526-3580. *Web site:* www.dese.mo.gov.

Missouri Minority Teaching Scholarship. Award may be used any year up to four years at an approved, participating Missouri institution. Scholarship is for minority Missouri residents in teaching programs. Recipients must commit to teach for five years in a Missouri public elementary or secondary school. Graduate students must teach math or science. Otherwise, award must be repaid. *Academic Fields/Career Goals:* Education. *Award:* Scholarship for use in freshman, sophomore, junior, senior, or graduate year; renewable. *Award amount:* up to $3000. *Number of awards:* 100. *Eligibility Requirements:* Applicant must be American Indian/Alaska Native, Asian/Pacific Islander, Black (non-Hispanic), or Hispanic; enrolled or expecting to enroll full-time at a two-year or four-year institution or university; resident of Missouri and studying in Missouri. Applicant must have 3.0 GPA or higher. Available to U.S. citizens. *Application Requirements:* Application, essay, financial need analysis, resume, references, test scores, transcript. *Deadline:* February 15.

Contact Laura Harrison, Administrative Assistant, Missouri Department of Elementary and Secondary Education, PO Box 480, Jefferson City, MO 65102-0480. *E-mail:* laura.harrison@dese.mo.gov. *Phone:* 573-751-1668. *Fax:* 573-526-3580. *Web site:* www.dese.mo.gov.

Missouri Teacher Education Scholarship (General). Nonrenewable award for Missouri high school seniors or Missouri resident college students. Must attend approved teacher training program at a participating Missouri institution. Must rank in top 15 % of high school class on ACT/SAT. Merit-based award. Recipients must commit to teach in Missouri for five years at a public elementary or secondary school or award must be repaid. *Academic Fields/Career Goals:* Education. *Award:* Scholarship for use in freshman, sophomore, junior, or senior year; not renewable. *Award amount:* up to $2000. *Number of awards:* 200–240. *Eligibility Requirements:* Applicant must be enrolled or expecting to enroll full-time at a two-year or four-year institution or university; resident of Missouri and studying in Missouri. Applicant must have 3.5 GPA or higher. Available to U.S. citizens. *Application Requirements:* Application, essay, resume, references, test scores, transcript. *Deadline:* February 15.

Contact Laura Harrison, Administrative Assistant II, Missouri Department of Elementary and Secondary Education, PO Box 480, Jefferson City, MO 65102-0480. *E-mail:* laura.harrison@dese.mo.gov. *Phone:* 573-751-1668. *Fax:* 573-526-3580. *Web site:* www.dese.mo.gov.

Marguerite Ross Barnett Memorial Scholarship. Applicant must be employed (at least 20 hours per week) and attending school part-time. Must be Missouri resident and enrolled at a participating Missouri post secondary school. Awards not available during summer term. Minimum age is 18. Scholarships can be renewed annually. *Award:* Scholarship for use in freshman, sophomore, junior, or senior year; renewable. *Award amount:* $900–$1700. *Number of awards:* varies. *Eligibility Requirements:* Applicant must be age 18; enrolled or expecting to enroll part-time at a two-year or four-year institution or university; resident of Missouri and studying in Missouri. Available to U.S. citizens. *Application Requirements:* Application, financial need analysis, FAFSA. *Deadline:* April 1.

Contact MDHE Information Center, Missouri Department of Higher Education, 3515 Amazonas Drive, Jefferson City, MO 65109. *E-mail:* icweb@dhe.mo.gov. *Phone:* 800-473-6757 Ext. 1. *Fax:* 573-751-6635. *Web site:* www.dhe.mo.gov.

Missouri Higher Education Academic Scholarship (Bright Flight). Awards of $2000 for Missouri high school seniors. Must be in top 3% of Missouri SAT or ACT scorers. Must attend Missouri institution as full-time undergraduate. Must be Missouri resident and U.S. citizen. *Award:* Scholarship for use in freshman, sophomore, junior, or senior year; not renewable. *Award amount:* $2000. *Number of awards:* varies. *Eligibility Requirements:* Applicant must be high school student; planning to enroll or expecting to enroll full-time at a two-year, four-year, or technical institution or university; resident of Missouri and studying in Missouri. Available to U.S. citizens. *Application Requirements:* Test scores. *Deadline:* July 31.

Contact MDHE Information Center, Missouri Department of Higher Education, 3515 Amazonas Drive, Jefferson City, MO 65109. *E-mail:* icweb@dhe.mo.gov. *Phone:* 800-473-6757 Ext. 1. *Fax:* 573-751-6635. *Web site:* www.dhe.mo.gov.

Charles Gallagher Student Assistance Program. Available to Missouri residents

State Scholarship and Grant Programs
Missouri

attending Missouri colleges or universities full-time. Must be undergraduates with financial need. Free Application for Federal Student Aid (FAFSA) or a renewal must be received by the federal processor by April 1 to be considered. *Award:* Grant for use in freshman, sophomore, junior, or senior year; not renewable. *Award amount:* $100–$1500. *Number of awards:* varies. *Eligibility Requirements:* Applicant must be enrolled or expecting to enroll full-time at a two-year, four-year, or technical institution or university; resident of Missouri and studying in Missouri. Available to U.S. citizens. *Application Requirements:* Financial need analysis, FAFSA. *Deadline:* April 1.

Contact MDHE Information Center, Missouri Department of Higher Education, 3515 Amazonas Drive, Jefferson City, MO 65109. *E-mail:* icweb@dhe.mo.gov. *Phone:* 800-473-6757. *Fax:* 573-751-6635. *Web site:* www.dhe.mo.gov.

Primary Care Resource Initiative for Missouri Loan Program. Forgivable loans for Missouri residents attending Missouri institutions pursuing a degree as a primary care physician or dentist, studying for a bachelor's degree as a dental hygienist, or a master of science degree in nursing leading to certification as an Advanced Practice Nurse. To be forgiven participant must work in a Missouri health professional shortage area. *Academic Fields/Career Goals:* Dental Health/Services; Health and Medical Sciences; Nursing. *Award:* Forgivable loan for use in freshman, sophomore, junior, senior, graduate, or postgraduate years; not renewable. *Award amount:* $3000–$25,000. *Number of awards:* varies. *Eligibility Requirements:* Applicant must be enrolled or expecting to enroll full or part-time at a four-year institution or university; resident of Missouri and studying in Missouri. Available to U.S. citizens. *Application Requirements:* Application, driver's license. *Deadline:* July 1.

Contact Kristie Frank, Health Program Representative, Missouri Department of Health and Senior Services, PO Box 570, Jefferson City, MO 65102-0570. *E-mail:* frank@dhss.mo.gov. *Phone:* 800-891-7415. *Fax:* 573-522-8146. *Web site:* www.dhss.mo.gov.

ACES/PRIMO Program. Program of the Missouri Area Health Education Centers (MAHEC) And the Primary Care Resource Initiative for Missouri students interested in Primary Care. Applicant should have a minimum GPA of 3.0 *Academic Fields/Career Goals:* Health and Medical Sciences. *Award:* Forgivable loan for use in freshman, sophomore, junior, or senior year; not renewable. *Award amount:* up to $5000. *Eligibility Requirements:* Applicant must be enrolled or expecting to enroll full-time at an institution or university. Applicant must have 3.0 GPA or higher. Available to U.S. citizens. *Application Requirements:* Application. *Deadline:* July 1.

Contact Jan Shipley, Programs Director, Missouri Department of Health and Senior Services, 1101 Yuane Ave, Rolla, MO 65401. *Phone:* 573-364-4797. *Fax:* 573-364-8972. *Web site:* www.dhss.mo.gov.

MONTANA

Montana Tuition Assistance Program-Baker Grant. Need-based grant for Montana residents attending participating Montana schools who have earned at least $2575 during the previous calendar year. Must be enrolled full time. Grant does not need to be repaid. Award covers the first undergraduate degree or certificate. Apply by filing a free application for Federal Student Aid by March 1 and contacting the financial aid office at the admitting college. *Award:* Grant for use in freshman, sophomore, junior, or senior year; not renewable. *Award amount:* $100–$1000. *Number of awards:* 1000–3000. *Eligibility Requirements:* Applicant must be enrolled or expecting to enroll full-time at a two-year or four-year institution or university; resident of Montana and studying in Montana. Available to U.S. citizens. *Application Requirements:* Application, financial need analysis, FAFSA. *Deadline:* March 1.

Contact Jamie Bushin, Scholarship Coordinator, Montana Guaranteed Student Loan Program, Office of Commissioner of Higher Education, PO Box 203101, Helena, MT 59620-3101. *E-mail:* jbushin@mgslp.state.mt.us. *Phone:* 406-444-0364. *Fax:* 406-444-1869. *Web site:* www.mgslp.state.mt.us.

Montana Higher Education Opportunity Grant. This grant is awarded based on need to undergraduate students attending either part-time or full-time who are residents of Montana and attending participating Montana schools. Awards are limited to the most needy students. A specific major or program of study is not required. This grant does not need to be repaid, and students may apply each year. Apply by filing a free application for Federal Student Aid by March 1 and contacting the financial aid office at the admitting college. *Award:* Grant for use in freshman, sophomore, junior, or senior year; not renewable. *Award amount:* $400–$600. *Number of awards:* up to 800. *Eligibility Requirements:* Applicant must be enrolled or expecting to enroll full or part-time at a two-year or four-year institution or university; resident of Montana and studying in Montana. Available to U.S. citizens. *Application Requirements:* Application, financial need analysis, FAFSA. *Deadline:* March 1.

Contact Jamie Bushin, Scholarship Coordinator, Montana Guaranteed Student Loan Program, Office of Commissioner of Higher Education, PO Box 203101, Helena, MT 59620-3101. *E-mail:* jbushin@mgslp.state.mt.us. *Phone:* 406-444-0364. *Fax:* 406-444-1869. *Web site:* www.mgslp.state.mt.us.

Indian Student Fee Waiver. Fee waiver awarded by the Montana University System to undergraduate and graduate students meeting the criteria. Amount varies depending upon the tuition and registration fee at each participating college. Students must provide documentation of 1/4 Indian blood or more; must be a resident of Montana for at least one year prior to enrolling in school and must demonstrate financial need. Full-or part-time study qualifies. Complete and submit the FAFSA by March 1 and a Montana Indian Fee Waiver application form. Contact the financial aid office at the college of attendance to determine eligibility. *Award:* Scholarship for use in freshman, sophomore, junior, senior, or graduate year; renewable. *Award amount:* $2000. *Number of awards:* 600. *Eligibility Requirements:* Applicant must be American Indian/Alaska Native; enrolled or expecting to enroll full or part-time at a two-year or four-year institution or university; resident of Montana and studying in Montana. Available to U.S. citizens. *Application Requirements:* Application, financial need analysis, FAFSA, documentation of Indian blood. *Deadline:* March 1.

Contact Ellen Swaney, Scholarship Coordinator, Montana Guaranteed Student Loan Program, Office of Commissioner of Higher Education, PO Box 203101, Helena, MT 59620-3101. *Phone:* 406-444-0332. *Web site:* www.mgslp.state.mt.us.

Montana University System Honor Scholarship. Scholarship provides a four-year renewable fee waiver of tuition and registration and is awarded to graduating high school seniors from accredited high schools in Montana. 300-400 scholarships are awarded each year averaging $2000-$3000 per recipient. The value of the award varies, depending on the tuition and registration fee at each participating Montana university or college. Must have a minimum 3.5 GPA, meet all college preparatory requirements, and be enrolled in an accredited high school for at least three years prior to graduation. Awarded to highest-ranking student in class attending a participating school. Contact high school counselor to apply. Deadline: January 31. *Award:* Scholarship for use in freshman, sophomore, junior,

State Scholarship and Grant Programs
Nevada

or senior year; renewable. *Award amount:* $2000–$3000. *Number of awards:* 300–400. *Eligibility Requirements:* Applicant must be high school student; planning to enroll or expecting to enroll full or part-time at a two-year or four-year institution or university; resident of Montana and studying in Montana. Applicant must have 3.5 GPA or higher. Available to U.S. citizens. *Application Requirements:* Application, transcript. *Deadline:* January 31.

Contact Janice Kirkpatrick, Grant and Scholarship Coordinator, Montana Guaranteed Student Loan Program, Office of Commissioner of Higher Education, PO Box 203101, Helena, MT 59620-3101. *E-mail:* jkirkpatrick@mgslp.state.mt.us. *Phone:* 406-444-0638. *Fax:* 406-444-1869. *Web site:* www.mgslp.state.mt.us.

Life Member Montana Federation of Garden Clubs Scholarship. Applicant must be at least a sophomore, majoring in conservation, horticulture, park or forestry, floriculture, greenhouse management, land management, or related subjects. Must be in need of assistance. Must have a potential for a successful future. Must be ranked in upper half of class or have a minimum 2.7 GPA. Must be a Montana resident and all study must be done in Montana. Deadline: May 1. *Academic Fields/Career Goals:* Biology; Earth Science; Horticulture/Floriculture; Landscape Architecture. *Award:* Scholarship for use in sophomore, junior, or senior year; not renewable. *Award amount:* $1000. *Number of awards:* 1. *Eligibility Requirements:* Applicant must be enrolled or expecting to enroll full-time at a four-year institution or university; resident of Montana and studying in Montana. Available to U.S. citizens. *Application Requirements:* Autobiography, financial need analysis, photo, references, transcript. *Deadline:* May 1.

Contact Joyce Backa, Montana Federation of Garden Clubs, 50 Leonard Street, Craig, MT 59648-8712. *Phone:* 406-235-4229. *Web site:* www.mtfgc.org.

NEBRASKA

Nebraska State Grant. Available to undergraduates attending a participating postsecondary institution in Nebraska. Available to Pell Grant recipients only. Nebraska residency required. Awards determined by each participating institution. Contact financial aid office at institution for application and additional information. *Award:* Grant for use in freshman, sophomore, junior, or senior year; not renewable. *Award amount:* $100–$1032. *Number of awards:* varies. *Eligibility Requirements:* Applicant must be enrolled or expecting to enroll full or part-time at a two-year, four-year, or technical institution or university; resident of Nebraska and studying in Nebraska. Available to U.S. citizens. *Application Requirements:* Application, financial need analysis. *Deadline:* continuous.

Contact J. Ritchie Morrow, Financial Aid Coordinator, State of Nebraska Coordinating Commission for Postsecondary Education, 140 North 8th Street, Suite 300, PO Box 95005, Lincoln, NE 68509-5005. *E-mail:* rmorrow@ccpe.st.ne.us. *Phone:* 402-471-0032. *Fax:* 402-471-2886. *Web site:* www.ccpe.state.ne.us.

Nebraska National Guard Tuition Credit. Renewable award for members of the Nebraska National Guard. Pays 75% of enlisted soldier's tuition until he or she has received a baccalaureate degree. *Award:* Scholarship for use in freshman, sophomore, junior, or senior year; renewable. *Number of awards:* up to 1200. *Eligibility Requirements:* Applicant must be enrolled or expecting to enroll full or part-time at a four-year, or technical institution or university; resident of Nebraska and studying in Nebraska. Available to U.S. citizens. Applicant must have served in the Air Force National Guard or Army National Guard. *Application Requirements:* Application. *Deadline:* continuous.

Contact Cindy York, Administrative Assistant, Nebraska National Guard, 1300 Military Road, Lincoln, NE 68508-1090. *Phone:* 402-309-7143. *Fax:* 402-309-7128. *Web site:* www.neguard.com.

Rural Health Student Loan Program. Must be enrolled or accepted for enrollment in medical or dental school at Creighton University or University of Nebraska Medical Center, or in Physician Assistant Program at a Nebraska college. Students must agree to practice one year in a shortage area for each year a scholarship is awarded, and to specialize in family practice, general surgery, internal medicine, pediatrics, obstetrics/gynecology, or psychiatry. Applications accepted April 1 to June 1. Must be a Nebraska resident. *Academic Fields/Career Goals:* Dental Health/Services; Health and Medical Sciences. *Award:* Forgivable loan for use in freshman, sophomore, junior, senior, or graduate year; not renewable. *Award amount:* $5000–$20,000. *Eligibility Requirements:* Applicant must be enrolled or expecting to enroll at a four-year institution or university; resident of Nebraska and studying in Nebraska. Applicant or parent of applicant must have employment or volunteer experience in designated career field. Available to U.S. citizens. *Application Requirements:* Application, interview. *Deadline:* varies.

Contact Nebraska Health and Human Services System, Office of Rural Health, 301 Centennial Mall South, PO Box 95044, Lincoln, NE 68509. *Phone:* 402-471-2337. *Fax:* 402-471-0180. *Web site:* www.hhs.state.ne.us.

NEVADA

Governor Guinn Millennium Scholarship. Scholarship for high school graduates with a diploma from a Nevada public or private high school in the graduating class of the year 2000 or later. Must complete high school with at least a 3.10 GPA for 2005 and 2006. 3.25 GPA for 2007 and later. A student attending a university who is enrolled in 12 semester credit hours would be eligible to receive $960 or a student attending a community college who is enrolled in 9 semester credit hours would be eligible to receive $360. *Award:* Scholarship for use in freshman, sophomore, junior, or senior year. *Number of awards:* 1. *Eligibility Requirements:* Applicant must be enrolled or expecting to enroll full-time at a two-year or four-year institution and resident of Nevada. Available to U.S. citizens. *Application Requirements:* Application, financial need analysis, references, test scores. *Deadline:* varies.

Contact Susan K. Moore, Director, Nevada Office of the State Treasurer. *E-mail:* millennium@NevadaTreasurer.gov. *Phone:* 702-486-3383. *Fax:* 702-486-3246. *Web site:* nevadatreasurer.gov/millennium/programinfo.asp.

Nevada Student Incentive Grant. Award available to Nevada residents for use at an accredited Nevada college or university. Must show financial need. Any field of study eligible. High school students may not apply. One-time award of up to $5000. Contact financial aid office at local college. *Award:* Grant for use in freshman, sophomore, junior, or senior year; not renewable. *Award amount:* $100–$5000. *Number of awards:* 400–800. *Eligibility Requirements:* Applicant must be enrolled or expecting to enroll full or part-time at a two-year, four-year, or technical institution or university; resident of Nevada and studying in Nevada. Available to U.S. citizens. *Application Requirements:* Application, financial need analysis. *Deadline:* continuous.

Contact Wendi Skibinski, Program Coordinator, Nevada Department of Education, 700 East 5th Street, Carson City, NV 89701. *E-mail:* wendi@nsn.k12.nv.us. *Phone:* 775-687-9228. *Fax:* 775-687-9101. *Web site:* www.doe.nv.gov/index.html.

State Scholarship and Grant Programs
New Hampshire

NEW HAMPSHIRE

Scholarships for Orphans of Veterans-New Hampshire. Awards for New Hampshire residents whose parent died as a result of service in WWI, WWII, the Korean Conflict, or the Southeast Asian Conflict. Parent must have been a New Hampshire resident at time of death. Possible full tuition and $1000 per year with automatic renewal on reapplication. Contact department for application deadlines. Must be under 26. Must include proof of eligibility and proof of parent's death. *Award:* Scholarship for use in freshman, sophomore, junior, or senior year; renewable. *Award amount:* varies. *Number of awards:* 1–10. *Eligibility Requirements:* Applicant must be age 16-25; enrolled or expecting to enroll full-time at a two-year or four-year institution or university and resident of New Hampshire. Available to U.S. citizens. Applicant or parent must meet one or more of the following requirements: general military experience; retired from active duty; disabled or killed as a result of military service; prisoner of war; or missing in action. *Application Requirements:* Application, VA approval. *Deadline:* varies.

Contact Melanie K. Deshaies, Program Assistant, New Hampshire Postsecondary Education Commission, 3 Barrell Court, Suite 300, Concord, NH 03301-8543. E-mail: mdeshaies@pec.state.nh.us. Phone: 603-271-2555 Ext. 356. Fax: 603-271-2696. Web site: www.state.nh.us/postsecondary.

New Hampshire Incentive Program (NHIP). One-time grants for New Hampshire residents attending school in New England. Must have financial need. Deadline is May 1. Complete Free Application for Federal Student Aid. Grant is not automatically renewable. Applicant must reapply. *Award:* Grant for use in freshman, sophomore, junior, or senior year; renewable. *Award amount:* $125–$1000. *Number of awards:* 3000–4300. *Eligibility Requirements:* Applicant must be enrolled or expecting to enroll full or part-time at a two-year, four-year, or technical institution or university; resident of New Hampshire and studying in Connecticut, Maine, Massachusetts, New Hampshire, Rhode Island, or Vermont. Available to U.S. citizens. *Application Requirements:* Application, financial need analysis, FAFSA. *Deadline:* May 1.

Contact Sherrie Tucker, Program Assistant, New Hampshire Postsecondary Education Commission, 3 Barrell Court, Suite 300, Concord, NH 03301-8512. E-mail: stucker@pec.state.nh.us. Phone: 603-271-2555 Ext. 355. Fax: 603-271-2696. Web site: www.state.nh.us/postsecondary.

Workforce Incentive Program. The Workforce Incentive Program links higher education with critical workforce needs. There are two components to the program: an incentive for students to study in particular areas (forgivable loan) and assistance for employees in critical workforce shortage areas (loan repayment). Critical shortage areas are: nursing, special education, and foreign language education. Please refer to Web site for further details: http://www.state.nh.us/postsecondary *Academic Fields/Career Goals:* Education; Foreign Language; Nursing; Special Education. *Award:* Forgivable loan for use in freshman, sophomore, junior, senior, graduate, or postgraduate years. *Award amount:* varies. *Number of awards:* varies. *Eligibility Requirements:* Applicant must be enrolled or expecting to enroll at an institution or university and studying in New Hampshire. Available to U.S. citizens. *Application Requirements:* Application. *Deadline:* varies.

Contact Judith A Knapp, Scholarship Coordinator, New Hampshire Postsecondary Education Commission, 3 Barrell Court, Suite 300, Concord, NH 03301-8543. E-mail: jknapp@pec.state.nh.us. Phone: 603-271-2555. Fax: 603-271-2696. Web site: www.state.nh.us/postsecondary.

Leveraged Incentive Grant Program. Award open to New Hampshire residents attending school in New Hampshire. Must be in sophomore, junior, or senior year. Award based on financial need and merit. Contact financial aid office for more information and deadline. *Award:* Grant for use in sophomore, junior, or senior year; not renewable. *Award amount:* $200–$7500. *Number of awards:* varies. *Eligibility Requirements:* Applicant must be enrolled or expecting to enroll full-time at a two-year, four-year, or technical institution or university; resident of New Hampshire and studying in New Hampshire. Available to U.S. citizens. *Application Requirements:* Application, financial need analysis. *Deadline:* varies.

Contact Judith A Knapp, Scholarship Coordinator, New Hampshire Postsecondary Education Commission, 3 Barrell Court, Suite 300, Concord, NH 03301-8543. E-mail: jknapp@pec.state.nh.us. Phone: 603-271-2555. Fax: 603-271-2696. Web site: www.state.nh.us/postsecondary.

NEW JERSEY

Richard G. McCormick Prize. Award to the author of an outstanding book on New Jersey history published during the preceding two years. Offered only in odd-numbered years. Nomination form is on the Web site. Must be nominated. *Academic Fields/Career Goals:* History. *Award:* Prize for use in freshman, sophomore, junior, senior, graduate, or postgraduate years; not renewable. *Award amount:* $1000. *Number of awards:* 1. *Eligibility Requirements:* Applicant must be enrolled or expecting to enroll at an institution or university. Available to U.S. citizens. *Application Requirements:* Application, nomination, 1 copy of book. *Deadline:* January 2.

Contact Mary R. Murrin, Director, Grants Program, New Jersey Historical Commission, Attention: Grants and Prizes, 225 W State Street, PO Box 305, Trenton, NJ 08625-0305. E-mail: mary.murrin@sos.state.nj.us. Phone: 609-984-0954. Fax: 609-633-8168. Web site: www.state.nj.us/state/history/grants.html.

Urban Scholars. Renewable scholarship to high achieving students attending public secondary schools in the State's urban and economically distressed areas of New Jersey. Students must rank in the top 10% of their class and have a GPA of at least 3.0 at the end of their junior year. Must be New Jersey resident. Must attend a New Jersey two-year college, four-year college or university, or approved programs at proprietary institutions. Students do not apply directly for scholarship consideration. Secondary schools forward to HESAA the names and class standing for all nominees. *Award:* Scholarship for use in freshman, sophomore, junior, or senior year; renewable. *Award amount:* $1000. *Number of awards:* varies. *Eligibility Requirements:* Applicant must be high school student; planning to enroll or expecting to enroll full-time at a two-year or four-year institution or university; resident of New Jersey and studying in New Jersey. Applicant must have 3.0 GPA or higher. Available to U.S. citizens. *Application Requirements:* Test scores, nominated by school. *Deadline:* varies.

Contact Carol Muka, Assistant Director of Grants and Scholarships, New Jersey Higher Education Student Assistance Authority, PO Box 540, Trenton, NJ 08625. Phone: 800-792-8670. Fax: 609-588-2228. Web site: www.hesaa.org.

Law Enforcement Officer Memorial Scholarship. Scholarships for full-time undergraduate study at approved New Jersey institutions for the dependent children of New Jersey law enforcement officers killed in the line of duty. Value of scholarship established annually. *Award:* Scholarship for use in freshman, sophomore, junior, or senior year; renewable. *Award amount:* varies. *Number of awards:* 1. *Eligibility Requirements:* Applicant must be enrolled or expecting to enroll full-time at a four-

State Scholarship and Grant Programs
New Jersey

year institution or university; resident of New Jersey and studying in New Jersey. Applicant or parent of applicant must have employment or volunteer experience in police/firefighting. Available to U.S. citizens. *Application Requirements:* Application. *Deadline:* varies.

Contact Carol Muka, Assistant Director of Grants and Scholarships, New Jersey Higher Education Student Assistance Authority, PO Box 540, Trenton, NJ 08625. *Phone:* 800-792-8670. *Fax:* 609-588-2228. *Web site:* www.hesaa.org.

Part-time Tuition Aid Grant (TAG) for County Colleges. Provides financial aid to eligible part-time undergraduate students enrolled for 6-11 credits at participating NJ community colleges. Deadline varies: March 1 for Fall, October 1 for Spring. *Award:* Grant for use in freshman, sophomore, junior, or senior year; renewable. *Award amount:* $116–$375. *Number of awards:* varies. *Eligibility Requirements:* Applicant must be enrolled or expecting to enroll part-time at a two-year or four-year institution or university; resident of New Jersey and studying in New Jersey. Available to U.S. citizens. *Application Requirements:* Application, financial need analysis. *Deadline:* varies.

Contact Sherri Fox, Acting Director of Grants and Scholarships, New Jersey Higher Education Student Assistance Authority, PO Box 540, Trenton, NJ 08625. *Phone:* 800-792-8670. *Fax:* 609-588-2228. *Web site:* www.hesaa.org.

NJ Student Tuition Assistance Reward Scholarship. Scholarship for students who graduate in the top 20% of their high school class. Recipients may be awarded up to 5 semesters of tuition (up to 15 credits per term) and approved fees at one of New Jersey's 19 county colleges. *Award:* Scholarship for use in freshman or sophomore year; renewable. *Number of awards:* 1. *Eligibility Requirements:* Applicant must be high school student; planning to enroll or expecting to enroll full-time at a two-year institution; resident of New Jersey and studying in New Jersey. Applicant must have 3.0 GPA or higher. Available to U.S. citizens. *Application Requirements:* Application, transcript. *Deadline:* varies.

Contact Carol Muka, Assistant Director of Grants and Scholarships, New Jersey Higher Education Student Assistance Authority, PO Box 540, Trenton, NJ 08625. *E-mail:* cmuka@hessa.org. *Phone:* 800-792-8670. *Fax:* 609-588-2228. *Web site:* www.hesaa.org.

New Jersey World Trade Center Scholarship. Established by the legislature to aid the dependent children and surviving spouses of NJ residents who were killed in the terrorist attacks, or who are missing and officially presumed dead as a direct result of the attacks; applies to in-state and out-of-state institutions for students seeking undergraduate degrees. Deadline varies: March 1 for Fall, October 1 for Spring. *Award:* Scholarship for use in freshman, sophomore, junior, or senior year; renewable. *Award amount:* up to $6500. *Number of awards:* varies. *Eligibility Requirements:* Applicant must be enrolled or expecting to enroll full-time at a four-year institution or university and resident of New Jersey. Available to U.S. citizens. *Application Requirements:* Application. *Deadline:* varies.

Contact Giselle Joachim, Director of Financial Aid Services, New Jersey Higher Education Student Assistance Authority, PO Box 540, Trenton, NJ 08625. *Phone:* 800-792-8670. *Fax:* 609-588-7389. *Web site:* www.hesaa.org.

Martin Luther King Physician/Dentist Scholarships. Renewable award available to New Jersey residents enrolled full-time in a medical or dental program. Several scholarships are available. Dollar amount varies. Must be a former or current EOF recipient, a minority or from a disadvantaged background. Applicant must attend a New Jersey institution and apply for financial aid. *Academic Fields/Career Goals:* Dental Health/Services; Health and Medical Sciences. *Award:* Scholarship for use in freshman, sophomore, junior, senior, or graduate year; renewable. *Award amount:* varies. *Number of awards:* varies. *Eligibility Requirements:* Applicant must be enrolled or expecting to enroll full-time at a four-year institution or university; resident of New Jersey and studying in New Jersey. Available to U.S. citizens. *Application Requirements:* Application, financial need analysis. *Deadline:* continuous.

Contact Glenn Lang, EOF Executive Director, University of Medicine and Dentistry of NJ School of Osteopathic Medicine, 20 West State Street, 7th Floor, PO Box 542, Trenton, NJ 08625-0542. *E-mail:* glang@che.state.nj.us. *Phone:* 609-984-2709. *Fax:* 609-633-8420. *Web site:* www.umdnj.edu.

Tuition Assistance for Children of POW/MIAs. Assists children of military service personnel declared missing in action or prisoner-of-war after January 1, 1960. Must be a resident of New Jersey. Renewable grants provide tuition for undergraduate study in New Jersey. Apply by October 1 for fall, March 1 for spring. Must be high school senior to apply. *Award:* Scholarship for use in freshman, sophomore, or junior year; renewable. *Award amount:* $500. *Number of awards:* varies. *Eligibility Requirements:* Applicant must be high school student; planning to enroll or expecting to enroll full-time at a two-year or four-year institution or university; resident of New Jersey and studying in New Jersey. Applicant must have 2.5 GPA or higher. Available to U.S. citizens. Applicant or parent must meet one or more of the following requirements: general military experience; retired from active duty; disabled or killed as a result of military service; prisoner of war; or missing in action. *Application Requirements:* Application, transcript. *Deadline:* varies.

Contact Patricia Richter, Grants Manager, New Jersey Department of Military and Veterans Affairs, PO Box 340, Trenton, NJ 08625-0340. *E-mail:* patricia.richter@njdmava.state.nj.us. *Phone:* 609-530-6854. *Fax:* 609-530-6970. *Web site:* www.state.nj.us/military.

New Jersey Educational Opportunity Fund Grants. Grants up to $4350 per year. Must be a New Jersey resident for at least twelve consecutive months and attend a New Jersey institution. Must be from a disadvantaged background as defined by EOF guidelines. EOF grant applicants must also apply for financial aid. EOF recipients may qualify for the Martin Luther King Physician/Dentistry Scholarships for graduate study at a professional institution. *Academic Fields/Career Goals:* Dental Health/Services; Health and Medical Sciences. *Award:* Grant for use in freshman, sophomore, junior, senior, or graduate year; renewable. *Award amount:* $200–$4350. *Number of awards:* varies. *Eligibility Requirements:* Applicant must be enrolled or expecting to enroll full-time at a four-year institution or university; resident of New Jersey and studying in New Jersey. Available to U.S. citizens. *Application Requirements:* Application, financial need analysis. *Deadline:* continuous.

Contact Glenn Lang, EOF Executive Director, University of Medicine and Dentistry of NJ School of Osteopathic Medicine, 40 East Laurel Road, Primary Care Center 119, PO Box 542, Trenton, NJ 08625-0542. *E-mail:* glang@che.state.nj.us. *Phone:* 609-984-2709. *Fax:* 609-292-7225. *Web site:* www.umdnj.edu.

Outstanding Scholar Recruitment Program. Students who meet the eligibility criteria and enrolled as first-time freshmen at participating New Jersey institutions receive annual scholarship awards of $2500 to $7500. The award amounts vary on a sliding scale depending on class rank and combined SAT scores. Must maintain a B average for renewal. Deadline: October 1 for Fall and March 1 for Spring. *Award:* Scholarship for use in freshman, sophomore,

State Scholarship and Grant Programs
New Jersey

junior, or senior year; renewable. *Award amount:* $2500–$7500. *Number of awards:* varies. *Eligibility Requirements:* Applicant must be enrolled or expecting to enroll at a four-year institution or university; resident of New Jersey and studying in New Jersey. Available to U.S. citizens. *Application Requirements:* Test scores. *Deadline:* varies.

Contact Carol Muka, Assistant Director of Grants and Scholarships, New Jersey Higher Education Student Assistance Authority, PO Box 540, Trenton, NJ 08625. *Phone:* 800-792-8670. *Fax:* 609-588-2228. *Web site:* www.hesaa.org.

Edward J. Bloustein Distinguished Scholars. Renewable scholarship for students who place in top 10% of their classes and have a minimum combined SAT score of 1260, or are ranked first, second or third in their class as of end of junior year. Must be New Jersey resident. Must attend a New Jersey two-year college, four-year college or university, or approved programs at proprietary institutions. Secondary schools forward to HESAA, names and class standings for all nominees. Deadline: October 1 for Fall and March 1 for Spring. *Award:* Scholarship for use in freshman, sophomore, junior, senior, or graduate year; renewable. *Award amount:* $1000. *Number of awards:* varies. *Eligibility Requirements:* Applicant must be high school student; planning to enroll or expecting to enroll full-time at a two-year or four-year institution or university; resident of New Jersey and studying in New Jersey. Available to U.S. citizens. *Application Requirements:* Test scores, nominated by high school. *Deadline:* varies.

Contact Carol Muka, Assistant Director of Grants and Scholarships, New Jersey Higher Education Student Assistance Authority, PO Box 540, Trenton, NJ 08625. *Phone:* 800-792-8670. *Fax:* 609-588-2228. *Web site:* www.hesaa.org.

Tuition Aid Grant. The Tuition Aid Grant (TAG) program provides financial aid to eligible undergraduate students attending participating in-state institutions. Deadline varies: March 1 for Fall, October 1 for Spring. *Award:* Grant for use in freshman, sophomore, junior, or senior year; renewable. *Award amount:* $868–$7272. *Number of awards:* varies. *Eligibility Requirements:* Applicant must be enrolled or expecting to enroll full-time at a two-year or four-year institution or university; resident of New Jersey and studying in New Jersey. Available to U.S. citizens. *Application Requirements:* Application, financial need analysis. *Deadline:* varies.

Contact Sherri Fox, Acting Director of Grants and Scholarships, New Jersey Higher Education Student Assistance Authority, PO Box 540, Trenton, NJ 08625. *Phone:* 800-792-8670. *Fax:* 609-588-2228. *Web site:* www.hesaa.org.

Dana Christmas Scholarship for Heroism. Honors young New Jersey residents for acts of heroism. Scholarship is a non-renewable award of up to $10,000 for up to five recipients. This scholarship may be used for undergraduate or graduate study. Deadline: October 1 for Fall and March 1 for Spring. *Award:* Scholarship for use in freshman, sophomore, junior, senior, or graduate year; not renewable. *Award amount:* up to $10,000. *Number of awards:* up to 5. *Eligibility Requirements:* Applicant must be age 21 or under; enrolled or expecting to enroll full or part-time at a four-year institution or university and resident of New Jersey. Available to U.S. citizens. *Application Requirements:* Application. *Deadline:* varies.

Contact Gisele Joachim, Director of Financial Aid Services, New Jersey Higher Education Student Assistance Authority, PO Box 540, Trenton, NJ 08625. *Phone:* 800-792-8670. *Fax:* 609-588-7389. *Web site:* www.hesaa.org.

Survivor Tuition Benefits Program. Program will pay the full tuition for eligible applicants attending two and four-year public colleges and universities as either half-time or full-time students. Eligibility for this program is limited to a period of 8 years from the date of death of the member in the case of a surviving spouse, and 8 years following graduation from high school in the case of a child. Deadline: October 1 for Fall and March 1 for Spring. *Award:* Scholarship for use in freshman, sophomore, junior, or senior year; renewable. *Number of awards:* varies. *Eligibility Requirements:* Applicant must be enrolled or expecting to enroll full or part-time at a two-year or four-year institution or university; resident of New Jersey and studying in New Jersey. Applicant or parent of applicant must have employment or volunteer experience in police/firefighting. Available to U.S. citizens. *Application Requirements:* Application. *Deadline:* varies.

Contact Carol Muka, Scholarship Coordinator, New Jersey Higher Education Student Assistance Authority, PO Box 540, Trenton, NJ 08625. *Phone:* 800-792-8670. *Fax:* 609-588-2228. *Web site:* www.hesaa.org.

New Jersey War Orphans Tuition Assistance. Renewable award for New Jersey residents who are high school seniors ages 16-21 and who are children of veterans killed or disabled in duty, missing in action, or prisoner-of-war. For use at a two- or four-year college or university. Write for more information. Deadlines: October 1 for Fall semester and March 1 for Spring semester. *Award:* Scholarship for use in freshman, sophomore, junior, or senior year; renewable. *Award amount:* $2000–$8000. *Number of awards:* varies. *Eligibility Requirements:* Applicant must be high school student; age 16-21; planning to enroll or expecting to enroll full-time at a two-year or four-year institution or university and resident of New Jersey. Available to U.S. citizens. Applicant or parent must meet one or more of the following requirements: general military experience; retired from active duty; disabled or killed as a result of military service; prisoner of war; or missing in action. *Application Requirements:* Application, transcript. *Deadline:* varies.

Contact Patricia Richter, Grants Manager, New Jersey Department of Military and Veterans Affairs, PO Box 340, Trenton, NJ 08625-0340. *E-mail:* patricia.richter@njdmava.state.nj.us. *Phone:* 609-530-6854. *Fax:* 609-530-6970. *Web site:* www.state.nj.us/military.

Veterans' Tuition Credit Program-New Jersey. Award for veterans who served in the armed forces between December 31, 1960, and May 7, 1975. Must have been a New Jersey resident at time of induction or discharge or for one year prior to application. Apply by October 1 for fall, March 1 for spring. Renewable award of $200-$400. *Award:* Scholarship for use in freshman, sophomore, junior, or senior year; renewable. *Award amount:* $200–$400. *Number of awards:* varies. *Eligibility Requirements:* Applicant must be enrolled or expecting to enroll full or part-time at a two-year, four-year, or technical institution or university. Available to U.S. citizens. Applicant must have general military experience. *Application Requirements:* Application. *Deadline:* varies.

Contact Patricia Richter, Grants Manager, New Jersey Department of Military and Veterans Affairs, PO Box 340, Trenton, NJ 08625-0340. *E-mail:* patricia.richter@njdmava.state.nj.us. *Phone:* 609-530-6854. *Fax:* 609-530-6970. *Web site:* www.state.nj.us/military.

NEW MEXICO

Lottery Success Scholarships. Awards equal to 100% of tuition at New Mexico public postsecondary institution. Must have New Mexico high school degree and be enrolled at New Mexico public college or university in first regular semester following high school graduation. Must obtain 2.5 GPA during this semester. May be eligible for up to eight consecutive semesters of support. Deadlines vary by institution. Apply through financial aid office of any

State Scholarship and Grant Programs
New Mexico

New Mexico public postsecondary institution. *Award:* Scholarship for use in freshman, sophomore, junior, or senior year; renewable. *Number of awards:* 1. *Eligibility Requirements:* Applicant must be enrolled or expecting to enroll full-time at a two-year or four-year institution; resident of New Mexico and studying in New Mexico. Applicant must have 2.5 GPA or higher. Available to U.S. citizens. *Application Requirements:* Application. *Deadline:* varies.

Contact Ofelia Morales, Director of Financial Aid, New Mexico Commission on Higher Education, 1068 Cerrillos Road, PO Box 15910, Santa Fe, NM 87505. *E-mail:* ofelia.morales@state.nm.us. *Phone:* 505-476-6506. *Web site:* www.hed.state.nm.us.

3% Scholarship Program. Award equal to tuition and required fees for New Mexico residents who are undergraduate students attending public postsecondary institutions in New Mexico. Contact financial aid office of any public postsecondary institution in New Mexico for deadline. *Award:* Scholarship for use in freshman, sophomore, junior, senior, or graduate year; not renewable. *Number of awards:* 1. *Eligibility Requirements:* Applicant must be enrolled or expecting to enroll full or part-time at a two-year or four-year institution or university; resident of New Mexico and studying in New Mexico. Available to U.S. citizens. *Application Requirements:* Application. *Deadline:* varies.

Contact Ofelia Morales, Director of Financial Aid, New Mexico Commission on Higher Education, 1068 Cerrillos Road, PO Box 15910, Santa Fe, NM 87505. *E-mail:* ofelia.morales@state.nm.us. *Phone:* 505-476-6506. *Web site:* www.hed.state.nm.us.

New Mexico Scholars' Program. Several scholarships to encourage New Mexico high school graduates to enroll in college at a public or selected private nonprofit postsecondary institution in New Mexico before their 22nd birthday. Selected private colleges are College of Santa Fe, St. John's College in Santa Fe, and College of the Southwest. Must have graduated in top 5% of their class or obtained an ACT score of 25 or SAT score of 1140. One-time scholarship for tuition, books, and fees. Contact financial aid office at college to apply. *Award:* Scholarship for use in freshman, sophomore, junior, or senior year; not renewable. *Number of awards:* 1. *Eligibility Requirements:* Applicant must be age 22 or under; enrolled or expecting to enroll full or part-time at a two-year or four-year institution; resident of New Mexico and studying in New Mexico. Available to U.S. citizens. *Application Requirements:* Application, financial need analysis, test scores, FAFSA. *Deadline:* varies.

Contact Ofelia Morales, Director of Financial Aid, New Mexico Commission on Higher Education, 1068 Cerrillos Road, PO Box 15910, Santa Fe, NM 87505. *E-mail:* ofelia.morales@state.nm.us. *Phone:* 505-476-6506. *Web site:* www.hed.state.nm.us.

New Mexico Competitive Scholarship. Scholarship available to encourage out-of-state students who have demonstrated high academic achievement to enroll in public institutions of higher education in New Mexico. One-time award for undergraduate students. Deadlines set by each institution. Contact financial aid office of any New Mexico public postsecondary institution to apply. *Award:* Scholarship for use in freshman, sophomore, junior, or senior year; not renewable. *Award amount:* $100. *Eligibility Requirements:* Applicant must be enrolled or expecting to enroll full or part-time at a two-year or four-year institution or university and studying in New Mexico. Applicant must have 3.0 GPA or higher. Available to U.S. citizens. *Application Requirements:* Application, essay, references, test scores. *Deadline:* varies.

Contact Ofelia Morales, Director of Financial Aid, New Mexico Commission on Higher Education, 1068 Cerrillos Road, Santa Fe, NM 87505. *E-mail:* ofelia.morales@state.nm.us. *Phone:* 505-476-6506. *Fax:* 505-827-7392. *Web site:* www.hed.state.nm.us.

Nursing Student Loan-For-Service Program. Award for New Mexico residents accepted or enrolled in nursing program at New Mexico public postsecondary institution. Must practice as nurse in designated health professional shortage area in New Mexico. Award dependent upon financial need but may not exceed $12,000. Deadline: July 1. *Academic Fields/Career Goals:* Nursing. *Award:* Forgivable loan for use in freshman, sophomore, junior, or senior year; not renewable. *Award amount:* up to $12,000. *Eligibility Requirements:* Applicant must be enrolled or expecting to enroll full or part-time at a two-year or four-year institution; resident of New Mexico and studying in New Mexico. Available to U.S. citizens. *Application Requirements:* Application, financial need analysis, transcript, FAFSA, letter of acceptance. *Deadline:* July 1.

Contact Ofelia Morales, Director of Financial Aid, New Mexico Commission on Higher Education, 1068 Cerrillos Road, PO Box 15910, Santa Fe, NM 87505. *E-mail:* ofelia.morales@state.nm.us. *Phone:* 505-476-6506. *Web site:* www.hed.state.nm.us.

Allied Health Student Loan Program-New Mexico. Renewable loans for New Mexico residents enrolled in an undergraduate allied health program. Loans can be forgiven through service in a medically underserved area or can be repaid. Penalties apply for failure to provide service. May borrow up to $12,000 per year for four years. *Academic Fields/Career Goals:* Dental Health/Services; Health and Medical Sciences; Nursing; Social Sciences; Therapy/Rehabilitation. *Award:* Forgivable loan for use in freshman, sophomore, junior, or senior year; renewable. *Award amount:* up to $12,000. *Number of awards:* 1–40. *Eligibility Requirements:* Applicant must be enrolled or expecting to enroll full or part-time at a two-year or four-year institution or university; resident of New Mexico and studying in New Mexico. Available to U.S. citizens. *Application Requirements:* Application, financial need analysis, transcript, FAFSA. *Deadline:* July 1.

Contact Ofelia Morales, Director of Financial Aid, New Mexico Commission on Higher Education, 1068 Cerrillos Road, PO Box 15910, Santa Fe, NM 87505. *E-mail:* ofelia.morales@state.nm.us. *Phone:* 505-476-6506. *Web site:* www.hed.state.nm.us.

Legislative Endowment Scholarships. Awards for undergraduate students with substantial financial need who are attending public postsecondary institutions in New Mexico. Preference given to returning adult students at two-year and four-year institutions and students transferring from two-year to four-year institutions. Deadline set by each institution. Must be resident of New Mexico. Contact financial aid office of any New Mexico public postsecondary institution to apply. *Award:* Scholarship for use in freshman, sophomore, junior, or senior year; not renewable. *Award amount:* $1000–$2500. *Eligibility Requirements:* Applicant must be enrolled or expecting to enroll full or part-time at a two-year, four-year, or technical institution or university; resident of New Mexico and studying in New Mexico. Available to U.S. citizens. *Application Requirements:* Application, financial need analysis, FAFSA. *Deadline:* varies.

Contact Ofelia Morales, Director of Financial Aid, New Mexico Commission on Higher Education, 1068 Cerrillos Road, PO Box 15910, Santa Fe, NM 87505. *E-mail:* ofelia.morales@state.nm.us. *Phone:* 505-476-6506. *Web site:* www.hed.state.nm.us.

New Mexico Vietnam Veterans' Scholarship. Renewable award for Vietnam veterans who are New Mexico residents attending state-sponsored schools. Must have been awarded the Vietnam Campaign medal. Submit DD214. Must include discharge papers. *Award:* Scholarship for use in freshman, sophomore, junior, or

State Scholarship and Grant Programs
New Mexico

senior year; renewable. *Award amount:* up to $2020. *Eligibility Requirements:* Applicant must be enrolled or expecting to enroll full or part-time at an institution or university; resident of New Mexico and studying in New Mexico. Available to U.S. citizens. Applicant must have general military experience. *Application Requirements:* Application, copy of DD214. *Deadline:* continuous.

Contact Alan Martinez, Director, State Benefits Division, New Mexico Veterans Service Commission, PO Box 2324, Sante Fe, NM 87504. *E-mail:* alan.martinez@state.nm.us. *Phone:* 505-827-6300. *Fax:* 505-827-6372. *Web site:* www.state.nm.us/veterans.

Children of Deceased Veterans Scholarship-New Mexico. Award for New Mexico residents who are children of veterans killed or disabled as a result of service, prisoner of war, or veterans missing-in-action. Must be between ages 16 to 26. For use at New Mexico schools for undergraduate study. Submit parent's death certificate and DD form 214. *Award:* Scholarship for use in freshman, sophomore, junior, or senior year; renewable. *Eligibility Requirements:* Applicant must be age 16-26; enrolled or expecting to enroll full or part-time at an institution or university; resident of New Mexico and studying in New Mexico. Available to U.S. citizens. Applicant or parent must meet one or more of the following requirements: general military experience; retired from active duty; disabled or killed as a result of military service; prisoner of war; or missing in action. *Application Requirements:* Application, transcript, death certificate or notice of casualty. *Deadline:* continuous.

Contact Alan Martinez, Director, State Benefits Division, New Mexico Veterans Service Commission, PO Box 2324, Sante Fe, NM 87504. *Phone:* 505-827-6300. *Fax:* 505-827-6372. *Web site:* www.state.nm.us/veterans.

Vietnam Veterans' Scholarship Program. Award for New Mexico residents who are Vietnam veterans enrolled in undergraduate or master's-level course work at public or selected private New Mexico postsecondary institutions. Award may include tuition, required fees, and book allowance. Contact financial aid office of any public or eligible private New Mexico postsecondary institution for deadline. *Award:* Scholarship for use in freshman, sophomore, junior, senior, or graduate year; not renewable. *Number of awards:* 1. *Eligibility Requirements:* Applicant must be enrolled or expecting to enroll full or part-time at a two-year or four-year institution; resident of New Mexico and studying in New Mexico. Available to U.S. citizens. Applicant must have general military experience. *Application Requirements:* Application, certification by the NM Veteran's commission. *Deadline:* varies.

Contact Ofelia Morales, Director of Financial Aid, New Mexico Commission on Higher Education, 1068 Cerrillos Road, PO Box 15910, Santa Fe, NM 87505. *E-mail:* ofelia.morales@state.nm.us. *Phone:* 505-476-6506. *Web site:* www.hed.state.nm.us.

New Mexico Student Incentive Grant. Several grants available for resident undergraduate students attending public and selected private nonprofit institutions in New Mexico. Must demonstrate financial need. To apply contact financial aid office at any public or private nonprofit postsecondary institution in New Mexico. *Award:* Grant for use in freshman, sophomore, junior, or senior year; not renewable. *Award amount:* $200–$2500. *Eligibility Requirements:* Applicant must be enrolled or expecting to enroll full or part-time at a two-year, four-year, or technical institution or university; resident of New Mexico and studying in New Mexico. Available to U.S. citizens. *Application Requirements:* Application, financial need analysis, FAFSA. *Deadline:* varies.

Contact Ofelia Morales, Director of Financial Aid, New Mexico Commission on Higher Education, 1068 Cerrillos Road, PO Box 15910, Santa Fe, NM 87505. *E-mail:* ofelia.morales@state.nm.us. *Phone:* 505-476-6506. *Web site:* www.hed.state.nm.us.

NEW YORK

Regents Professional Opportunity Scholarship. Scholarship for New York residents beginning or already enrolled in an approved degree-bearing program of study in New York that leads to licensure in a particular profession. See the Web site for the list of eligible professions. Must be U.S. citizen or permanent resident. Award recipients must agree to practice upon licensure in their profession in New York for 12 months for each annual payment received. Priority given to economically disadvantaged members of minority groups underrepresented in the professions. *Academic Fields/Career Goals:* Accounting; Architecture; Dental Health/Services; Engineering/Technology; Health and Medical Sciences; Interior Design; Landscape Architecture; Law/Legal Services; Nursing; Pharmacy; Psychology; Social Services. *Award:* Scholarship for use in freshman, sophomore, junior, senior, or graduate year. *Award amount:* $1000–$5000. *Number of awards:* 220. *Eligibility Requirements:* Applicant must be enrolled or expecting to enroll full-time at a two-year or four-year institution or university; resident of New York and studying in New York. Available to U.S. citizens. *Application Requirements:* Deadline: May 3.

Contact Lewis J. Hall, Coordinator, New York State Education Department, Room 1078 EBA, Albany, NY 12234. *Phone:* 518-486-1319. *Fax:* 518-486-5346. *Web site:* www.highered.nysed.gov.

Broome and Allen Boys Camp and Scholarship Fund. The Broome and Allen Scholarship is awarded to students of Sephardic origin or those working in Sephardic studies. Both graduate and undergraduate degree candidates as well as those doing research projects will be considered. It is awarded for one year and must be renewed for successive years. Enclose copy of tax returns with application. Deadline is May 15. *Award:* Scholarship for use in freshman, sophomore, junior, senior, graduate, or postgraduate years; not renewable. *Award amount:* $500–$2000. *Number of awards:* 25–60. *Eligibility Requirements:* Applicant must be Jewish and enrolled or expecting to enroll full or part-time at a two-year, four-year, or technical institution or university. Available to U.S. and non-U.S. citizens. *Application Requirements:* Application, essay, financial need analysis, references, transcript, copy of tax returns. *Deadline:* May 15.

Contact Esme Berg, Director, American Sephardi Foundation, 15 West 16th Street, New York, NY 10011. *E-mail:* eberg@asf.cjh.org. *Phone:* 212-294-8350. *Fax:* 212-294-8348. *Web site:* www.asfonline.org.

New York Lottery Leaders of Tomorrow (Lot) Scholarship. The goal of this program is to reinforce the lottery's education mission by awarding four-year scholarships, $1000 per year for up to four years. One scholarship is available to every New York high school, public or private, that awards a high school diploma. *Award:* Scholarship for use in freshman, sophomore, junior, or senior year; renewable. *Award amount:* $1000. *Number of awards:* varies. *Eligibility Requirements:* Applicant must be high school student; planning to enroll or expecting to enroll full-time at a two-year, four-year, or technical institution or university; resident of New York and studying in New York. Applicant must have 3.0 GPA or higher. Available to U.S. citizens. *Application Requirements:* Application, essay, transcript. *Deadline:* March 19.

Contact Betsey Morgan, Program Coordinator, CASDA-LOT (Capital Area School Development Association), The University at Albany East Campus, 1 University Place A-409, Rensselaer, NY 12144-3456. *E-mail:*

State Scholarship and Grant Programs
North Carolina

casdalot@uamail.albany.edu. *Phone:* 518-525-2788. *Fax:* 518-525-2797. *Web site:* www.nylottery.org/lot.

American-Scandinavian Foundation Translation Prize. Two prizes are awarded for outstanding English translations of poetry, fiction, drama or literary prose originally written in Danish, Finnish, Icelandic, Norwegian or Swedish. One-time award of $2000. *Award:* Prize for use in freshman, sophomore, junior, senior, graduate, or postgraduate years; not renewable. *Award amount:* $2000. *Number of awards:* 2. *Eligibility Requirements:* Applicant must be enrolled or expecting to enroll at an institution or university and must have an interest in Scandinavian language. Available to U.S. citizens. *Application Requirements:* Application, applicant must enter a contest, resume. *Deadline:* June 1.

Contact Ellen McKey, Director of Fellowships and Grants, American-Scandinavian Foundation, 58 Park Avenue, New York, NY 10016. *E-mail:* info@amscan.org. *Phone:* 212-879-9779. *Fax:* 212-686-2115. *Web site:* www.amscan.org.

New York Aid for Part-time Study (APTS). Renewable scholarship provides tuition assistance to part-time undergraduate students who are New York residents attending New York accredited institutions. Deadline varies. Must be U.S. citizen. *Award:* Grant for use in freshman, sophomore, junior, or senior year; renewable. *Award amount:* up to $2000. *Number of awards:* varies. *Eligibility Requirements:* Applicant must be enrolled or expecting to enroll part-time at a two-year or four-year institution or university; resident of New York and studying in New York. Available to U.S. citizens. *Application Requirements:* Application. *Deadline:* varies.

Contact Student Information, New York State Higher Education Services Corporation, 99 Washington Avenue, Room 1320, Albany, NY 12255. *Phone:* 518-473-3887. *Fax:* 518-474-2839. *Web site:* www.hesc.com/.

New York State Aid to Native Americans. Award for enrolled members of a New York State tribe and their children who are attending or planning to attend a New York State college and who are New York State residents. Award for full-time-students up to $1550 annually; part-time awards approximately $85 per credit hour. Application deadline: July 15 for the Fall semester; December 31 for the Spring semester; and by May 20 for Summer session. *Award:* Scholarship for use in freshman, sophomore, junior or senior year; not renewable. *Award amount:* up to $1550. *Number of awards:* varies. *Eligibility Requirements:* Applicant must be American Indian/Alaska Native; enrolled or expecting to enroll full or part-time at a two-year, four-year, or technical institution or university; resident of New York and studying in New York. Available to U.S. citizens. *Application Requirements:* Application.

Contact Native American Education Unit, New York State Education Department, New York State Higher Education Services Corporation, EBA Room 374, Albany, NY 12234. *Phone:* 518-474-0537. *Web site:* www.hesc.com/.

Regents Professional Opportunity Scholarships. Award for New York State residents pursuing career in certain licensed professions. Must attend New York State college. Priority given to economically disadvantaged members of minority group underrepresented in chosen profession and graduates of SEEK, College Discovery, EOP, and HEOP. Must work in New York State in chosen profession one year for each annual payment. Scholarships are awarded to undergraduate or graduate students, depending on the program. *Award:* Scholarship for use in freshman, sophomore, junior, senior, or graduate year; not renewable. *Award amount:* $1000–$5000. *Number of awards:* 220. *Eligibility Requirements:* Applicant must be enrolled or expecting to enroll full-time at a two-year or four-year institution or university; resident of New York and studying in New York. Available to U.S. citizens. *Application Requirements:* Application. *Deadline:* May 3.

Contact New York State Education Department, Bureau of HEOP/VATEA/Scholarships, New York State Higher Education Services Corporation, Education Building Addition Room 1071, Albany, NY 12234. *Phone:* 518-486-1319. *Web site:* www.hesc.com/.

World Trade Center Memorial Scholarship. Renewable awards of up to the average cost of attendance at a State University of New York four-year college. Available to the families and financial dependents of victims who died or were severely and permanently disabled as a result of the September 11, 2001 terrorist attacks on the U.S. and the rescue and recovery efforts. *Award:* Scholarship for use in freshman, sophomore, junior, or senior year; renewable. *Award amount:* varies. *Number of awards:* 1. *Eligibility Requirements:* Applicant must be enrolled or expecting to enroll full-time at a two-year or four-year institution or university; resident of New York and studying in New York. Available to U.S. citizens. *Application Requirements:* Application. *Deadline:* May 1.

Contact HESC Scholarship Unit, New York State Higher Education Services Corporation, 99 Washington Avenue, Room 1320, Albany, NY 12255. *Phone:* 518-402-6494. *Web site:* www.hesc.com/.

Scholarship for Academic Excellence. Renewable award for New York residents. Scholarship winners must attend a college or university in New York. 2000 scholarships are for $1500 and 6000 are for $500. The selection criteria used are based on Regents test scores and rank in class. Must be U.S. citizen or permanent resident. *Award:* Scholarship for use in freshman, sophomore, junior, or senior year; renewable. *Award amount:* $500–$1500. *Number of awards:* up to 8000. *Eligibility Requirements:* Applicant must be high school student; planning to enroll or expecting to enroll full-time at a two-year or four-year institution or university; resident of New York and studying in New York. Applicant must have 3.5 GPA or higher. Available to U.S. citizens. *Application Requirements:* Application. *Deadline:* December 19.

Contact Lewis J. Hall, Coordinator, New York State Education Department, Room 1078 EBA, Albany, NY 12234. *Phone:* 518-486-1319. *Fax:* 518-486-5346. *Web site:* www.highered.nysed.gov.

New York State Tuition Assistance Program. Award for New York state residents attending a New York postsecondary institution. Must be full-time student in approved program with tuition over $200 per year. Must show financial need and not be in default in any other state program. Renewable award of $500-$5000. *Award:* Grant for use in freshman, sophomore, junior, or senior year; renewable. *Award amount:* $500–$5000. *Number of awards:* 350,000–360,000. *Eligibility Requirements:* Applicant must be enrolled or expecting to enroll full-time at a two-year or four-year institution or university; resident of New York and studying in New York. Available to U.S. citizens. *Application Requirements:* Application, financial need analysis. *Deadline:* May 1.

Contact Student Information, New York State Higher Education Services Corporation, 99 Washington Avenue, Room 1320, Albany, NY 12255. *Web site:* www.hesc.com/.

NORTH CAROLINA

North Carolina National Guard Tuition Assistance Program. Scholarship for members of the North Carolina Air and

State Scholarship and Grant Programs
North Carolina

Army National Guard who will remain in the service for two years following the period for which assistance is provided. Applicants must reapply for each academic period. For use at approved North Carolina institutions. Deadline: last day of late registration period set by the school. Applicant must currently be serving in the Air National Guard or Army National Guard. Annual maximum (July 1 through June 30) of $2000. Career maximum of $8000. *Award:* Grant for use in freshman, sophomore, junior, senior, or graduate year; not renewable. *Award amount:* up to $2000. *Number of awards:* varies. *Eligibility Requirements:* Applicant must be enrolled or expecting to enroll full or part-time at a two-year, four-year, or technical institution or university and studying in North Carolina. Available to U.S. citizens. Applicant must have served in the Air Force National Guard or Army National Guard. *Application Requirements:* Application. *Deadline:* varies.

Contact Capt. Miriam Gray, Education Services Officer, North Carolina National Guard, 4105 Reedy Creek Road, Raleigh, NC 27607-6410. *E-mail:* miriam.gray@nc.ngb.army.mil. *Phone:* 800-621-4136 Ext. 6272. *Fax:* 919-664-6520. *Web site:* www.nc.ngb.army.mil/education.

North Carolina Police Corps Scholarship. Selected participants must attend a four-year institution full-time. May receive up to $6667 per year with a maximum of $30,000. Must complete 24-week training course receiving $450 per week while in residence and serve four years in selected law enforcement agency. Must have physical, background investigation, drug test, and psychological evaluation. *Academic Fields/Career Goals:* Criminal Justice/Criminology; Law Enforcement/Police Administration. *Award:* Scholarship for use in freshman, sophomore, junior, senior, or graduate year; renewable. *Number of awards:* 15–30. *Eligibility Requirements:* Applicant must be enrolled or expecting to enroll full-time at a four-year institution or university. Available to U.S. citizens. *Application Requirements:* Application, autobiography, essay, interview, photo, references, test scores, transcript. *Deadline:* varies.

Contact Pat Watson, North Carolina Police Corps, NC Department of Crime Control and Public Safety, 309 Chapanoke Road, Raleigh, NC 27603. *Phone:* 919-773-2823. *Fax:* 919-773-2845. *Web site:* www.ncpolicecorps.org.

North Carolina Sheriffs' Association Undergraduate Criminal Justice Scholarships. One-time award for full-time North Carolina resident undergraduate students majoring in criminal justice at a University of North Carolina school. Priority given to child of any North Carolina law enforcement officer. Letter of recommendation from county sheriff required. *Academic Fields/Career Goals:* Criminal Justice/Criminology; Law Enforcement/Police Administration. *Award:* Scholarship for use in freshman, sophomore, junior, or senior year; not renewable. *Award amount:* $1000–$2000. *Number of awards:* up to 10. *Eligibility Requirements:* Applicant must be enrolled or expecting to enroll full-time at a two-year or four-year institution or university; resident of North Carolina and studying in North Carolina. Applicant or parent of applicant must have employment or volunteer experience in police/firefighting. Available to U.S. citizens. *Application Requirements:* Application, financial need analysis, references, transcript, statement of career goals. *Deadline:* continuous.

Contact Bill Carswell, Manager of Scholarship and Grant Division, North Carolina State Education Assistance Authority, PO Box 14103, Research Triangle Park, NC 27709. *E-mail:* carswellb@ncseaa.edu. *Phone:* 919-549-8614. *Fax:* 919-248-4687. *Web site:* www.ncseaa.edu.

North Carolina Veterans Scholarships Class III. Renewable awards for children of a veteran who died or was, at time of death, drawing a pension for total and permanent disability as rated by U.S. DVA, was honorably discharged and does not qualify for Class I, II, or IV, scholarships, or served in a combat zone or waters adjacent to a combat zone and received a campaign badge or medal and does not qualify under Class I, II, IV, or V. Parent must have been a North Carolina resident at time of entry into service. Duration of the scholarship is four academic years (8 semesters) if used within eight years. Free tuition and exemption from certain mandatory fees as set forth in the law in Public, Community & Technical Colleges/Institutions. $4500 per nine month academic year in Private Colleges & Junior Colleges. See Web site for details and where to procure an application. Up to 100 awarded each year. Deadline is March 31. *Award:* Scholarship for use in freshman, sophomore, junior, or senior year; renewable. *Award amount:* up to $4500. *Number of awards:* up to 100. *Eligibility Requirements:* Applicant must be enrolled or expecting to enroll full or part-time at a two-year, four-year, or technical institution or university and studying in North Carolina. Available to U.S. citizens. Applicant or parent must meet one or more of the following requirements: general military experience; retired from active duty; disabled or killed as a result of military service; prisoner of war; or missing in action. *Application Requirements:* Application, financial need analysis, interview, transcript. *Deadline:* March 31.

Contact Charles Smith, Assistant Secretary, North Carolina Division of Veterans Affairs, 325 North Salisbury Street, Raleigh, NC 27603. *Phone:* 919-733-3851. *Fax:* 919-733-2834. *Web site:* www.doa.state.nc.us/doa/vets/va.htm.

North Carolina Division of Services for the Blind Rehabilitation Services. Financial assistance is available for North Carolina residents who are blind or visually impaired and who require vocational rehabilitation to help find employment. Tuition and other assistance provided based on need. Open to U.S. citizens and legal residents of United States. Applicants goal must be to work after receiving vocational services. To apply, contact the local DSB office and apply for vocational rehabilitation services. *Award:* Scholarship for use in freshman, sophomore, junior, or senior year; renewable. *Award amount:* varies. *Number of awards:* 1. *Eligibility Requirements:* Applicant must be enrolled or expecting to enroll full or part-time at a two-year, four-year, or technical institution or university and resident of North Carolina. Applicant must be visually impaired. Available to U.S. citizens. *Application Requirements:* Application, financial need analysis, interview, proof of eligibility. *Deadline:* continuous.

Contact JoAnn Strader, Chief of Rehabilitation Field Services, North Carolina Division of Services for the Blind, 2601 Mail Service Center, Raleigh, NC 27699-2601. *E-mail:* joann.strader@ncmail.net. *Phone:* 919-733-9700. *Fax:* 919-715-8771.

North Carolina Teaching Fellows Scholarship Program. Renewable award for North Carolina high school seniors pursuing teaching careers. Must agree to teach in a North Carolina public or government school for four years or repay award. Must attend one of the 14 approved schools in North Carolina. Merit-based. Must interview at the local level and at the regional level as a finalist. Application available online only: http://www.teachingfellows.org. *Academic Fields/Career Goals:* Education. *Award:* Forgivable loan for use in freshman, sophomore, junior, or senior year; renewable. *Award amount:* $6500. *Number of awards:* up to 500. *Eligibility Requirements:* Applicant must be high school student; planning to enroll or expecting to enroll full-time at a four-year institution; resident of North Carolina and studying in North Carolina. Applicant must have 3.5 GPA or higher.

State Scholarship and Grant Programs
North Carolina

Available to U.S. citizens. *Application Requirements:* Application, essay, interview, references, test scores, transcript. *Deadline:* varies.

Contact Sherry Woodruff, Program Officer, North Carolina Teaching Fellows Commission, 3739 National Drive, Suite 210, Raleigh, NC 27612. *E-mail:* tfellows@ncforum.org. *Phone:* 919-781-6833 Ext. 103. *Fax:* 919-781-6527. *Web site:* www.teachingfellows.org.

Nurse Education Scholarship Loan Program (NESLP). Must be U.S. citizen and North Carolina resident. Award available through financial aid offices of North Carolina colleges and universities that offer nurse education programs to prepare students for licensure in the state as LPN or RN. Recipients enter contract with the State of North Carolina to work full time as a licensed nurse. Loans not repaid through service must be repaid in cash. Award based upon financial need. Maximum award for students enrolled in Associate Degree Nursing and Practical Nurse Education programs is $3000. Maximum award for students enrolled in a Baccalaureate program is $5000. *Academic Fields/Career Goals:* Nursing. *Award:* Forgivable loan for use in freshman, sophomore, junior, or senior year; renewable. *Award amount:* $400–$5000. *Number of awards:* varies. *Eligibility Requirements:* Applicant must be enrolled or expecting to enroll at a four-year institution or university; resident of North Carolina and studying in North Carolina. Available to U.S. citizens. *Application Requirements:* Application, financial need analysis. *Deadline:* continuous.

Contact Bill Carswell, Manager of Scholarship and Grant Division, North Carolina State Education Assistance Authority, PO Box 14103, Research Triangle Park, NC 27709. *E-mail:* carswellb@ncseaa.edu. *Phone:* 919-549-8614. *Fax:* 919-248-4687. *Web site:* www.ncseaa.edu.

North Carolina Student Loan Program for Health, Science, and Mathematics. Renewable award for North Carolina residents studying health-related fields, or science or math education. Based on merit, need, and promise of service as a health professional or educator in an underserved area of North Carolina. Need two co-signers. Submit surety statement. *Academic Fields/Career Goals:* Dental Health/Services; Health Administration; Health and Medical Sciences; Nursing; Physical Sciences and Math; Therapy/Rehabilitation. *Award:* Forgivable loan for use in freshman, junior, senior, or graduate year; renewable. *Award amount:* $3000–$8500. *Eligibility Requirements:* Applicant must be enrolled or expecting to enroll full-time at a two-year or four-year institution or university and resident of North Carolina. Available to U.S. citizens. *Application Requirements:* Application, financial need analysis, transcript. *Deadline:* June 1.

Contact Edna Williams, Manager, Selection and Origination, HSM Loan Program, North Carolina State Education Assistance Authority, PO Box 14223, Research Triangle Park, NC 27709. *E-mail:* eew@ncseaa.edu. *Phone:* 800-700-1775 Ext. 313. *Web site:* www.ncseaa.edu.

North Carolina Legislative Tuition Grant Program (NCLTG). Renewable aid for North Carolina residents attending approved private colleges or universities within the state. Must be enrolled full-time in an undergraduate program not leading to a religious vocation. Contact college financial aid office for deadlines. *Award:* Grant for use in freshman, sophomore, junior, or senior year; renewable. *Award amount:* $1500–$1800. *Number of awards:* varies. *Eligibility Requirements:* Applicant must be enrolled or expecting to enroll full-time at a two-year or four-year institution or university; resident of North Carolina and studying in North Carolina. Available to U.S. citizens. *Application Requirements:* Application. *Deadline:* varies.

Contact Bill Carswell, Manager of Scholarship and Grant Division, North Carolina State Education Assistance Authority, PO Box 14103, Research Triangle Park, NC 27709. *E-mail:* carswellb@ncseaa.edu. *Phone:* 919-549-8614. *Fax:* 919-248-4687. *Web site:* www.ncseaa.edu.

North Carolina Community College Grant Program. Annual award for North Carolina residents enrolled at least part-time in a North Carolina community college curriculum program. Priority given to those enrolled in college transferable curriculum programs, persons seeking new job skills, women in non-traditional curricula, and those participating in an ABE, GED, or high school diploma program. Contact financial aid office of institution the student attends for information and deadline. Must complete Free Application for Federal Student Aid. *Award:* Grant for use in freshman or sophomore year; renewable. *Award amount:* $683. *Number of awards:* up to 13,000. *Eligibility Requirements:* Applicant must be enrolled or expecting to enroll full or part-time at a two-year or technical institution; resident of North Carolina and studying in North Carolina. Available to U.S. citizens. *Application Requirements:* Application, financial need analysis, FAFSA. *Deadline:* varies.

Contact Bill Carswell, Manager, Scholarship and Grants Division, North Carolina State Education Assistance Authority, PO Box 14103, Research Triangle Park, NC 27709. *E-mail:* carswellb@ncseaa.edu. *Phone:* 919-549-8614. *Fax:* 919-248-4687. *Web site:* www.ncseaa.edu.

State Contractual Scholarship Fund Program-North Carolina. Renewable award for North Carolina residents already attending an approved private college or university in the state in pursuit of an undergraduate degree. Must have financial need. Contact college financial aid office for deadline and information. May not be enrolled in a program leading to a religious vocation. *Award:* Scholarship for use in freshman, sophomore, junior, or senior year; renewable. *Award amount:* up to $1100. *Number of awards:* varies. *Eligibility Requirements:* Applicant must be enrolled or expecting to enroll full or part-time at a two-year or four-year institution or university; resident of North Carolina and studying in North Carolina. Available to U.S. citizens. *Application Requirements:* Application, financial need analysis. *Deadline:* varies.

Contact Bill Carswell, Manager of Scholarship and Grant Division, North Carolina State Education Assistance Authority, PO Box 14103, Research Triangle Park, NC 27709. *E-mail:* carswellb@ncseaa.edu. *Phone:* 919-549-8614. *Fax:* 919-248-4687. *Web site:* www.ncseaa.edu.

Teacher Assistant Scholarship Program. Funding to attend a public or private four-year college or university in North Carolina with an approved teacher education program. Applicant must be employed full-time as a teacher assistant in an instructional area while pursuing licensure and maintain employment to remain eligible. Refer to Web site for further details: http://www.ncseaa.edu/tas.htm *Academic Fields/Career Goals:* Education. *Award:* Scholarship for use in freshman, sophomore, junior, or senior year; renewable. *Award amount:* $1200–$3600. *Number of awards:* varies. *Eligibility Requirements:* Applicant must be enrolled or expecting to enroll full-time at a four-year institution or university; resident of North Carolina and studying in North Carolina. Applicant must have 2.5 GPA or higher. Available to U.S. citizens. *Application Requirements:* Application, FAFSA. *Deadline:* March 31.

Contact Bill Carswell, Manager of Scholarship and Grant Division, North Carolina State Education Assistance Authority, PO Box 14103, Research Triangle Park, NC 27709. *E-mail:* carswellb@ncseaa.edu. *Phone:* 919-549-8614. *Fax:* 919-248-4687. *Web site:* www.ncseaa.edu.

State Scholarship and Grant Programs
North Carolina

North Carolina Veterans Scholarships Class IV. Renewable awards for children of a veteran who was a POW or MIA. Parent must have been a North Carolina resident at time of entry into service. Duration of the scholarship is four academic years (8 semesters) if used within eight years. No limit on number awarded per year. The student receives free tuition, a room allowance, a board allowance, and exemption from certain mandatory fees as set forth in the law in public, community and technical colleges or institutions. The scholarship is $4500 per nine-month academic year in private colleges and junior colleges. *Award:* Scholarship for use in freshman, sophomore, junior, or senior year; renewable. *Award amount:* up to $4500. *Number of awards:* varies. *Eligibility Requirements:* Applicant must be enrolled or expecting to enroll full or part-time at a two-year, four-year, or technical institution or university and studying in North Carolina. Available to U.S. citizens. Applicant or parent must meet one or more of the following requirements: general military experience; retired from active duty; disabled or killed as a result of military service; prisoner of war; or missing in action. *Application Requirements:* Application, financial need analysis, interview, transcript. *Deadline:* March 31.

Contact Charles Smith, Assistant Secretary, North Carolina Division of Veterans Affairs, 325 North Salisbury Street, Raleigh, NC 27603. *Phone:* 919-733-3851. *Fax:* 919-733-2834. *Web site:* www.doa.state.nc.us/doa/vets/va.htm.

North Carolina Veterans Scholarships Class I-B. Renewable awards for children of veterans rated by U.S. DVA as 100% disabled due to wartime service as defined in the law, and currently or at time of death drawing compensation for such disability. Parent must have been a North Carolina resident at time of entry into service. Duration of the scholarship is four academic years (8 semesters) if used within 8 years. Free tuition and exemption from certain mandatory fees as set forth in the law in Public, Community & Technical Colleges/Institutions. No limit on number awarded each year. *Award:* Scholarship for use in freshman, sophomore, junior, or senior year; renewable. *Award amount:* $1500. *Number of awards:* varies. *Eligibility Requirements:* Applicant must be enrolled or expecting to enroll full or part-time at a two-year, four-year, or technical institution or university and studying in North Carolina. Available to U.S. citizens. Applicant or parent must meet one or more of the following requirements: general military experience; retired from active duty; disabled or killed as a result of military service; prisoner of war; or missing in action. *Application Requirements:* Application, financial need analysis, interview, transcript. *Deadline:* continuous.

Contact Charles Smith, Assistant Secretary, North Carolina Division of Veterans Affairs, 325 North Salisbury Street, Raleigh, NC 27603. *Phone:* 919-733-3851. *Fax:* 919-733-2834. *Web site:* www.doa.state.nc.us/doa/vets/va.htm.

North Carolina Veterans Scholarships Class II. Renewable awards for children of veterans rated by U.S. DVA as much as 20% but less than 100% disabled due to wartime service as defined in the law, or awarded Purple Heart Medal for wounds received. Parent must have been a North Carolina resident at time of entry into service. Duration of the scholarship is four academic years (8 semesters) if used within 8 years. Free tuition and exemption from certain mandatory fees as set forth in the law in Public, Community & Technical Colleges/Institutions. $4500 per nine month academic year in Private Colleges & Junior Colleges. Up to 100 awarded each year. Deadline is March 31. *Award:* Scholarship for use in freshman, sophomore, junior, or senior year; renewable. *Award amount:* up to $4500. *Number of awards:* up to 100. *Eligibility Requirements:* Applicant must be enrolled or expecting to enroll full or part-time at a two-year, four-year, or technical institution or university and studying in North Carolina. Available to U.S. citizens. Applicant or parent must meet one or more of the following requirements: general military experience; retired from active duty; disabled or killed as a result of military service; prisoner of war; or missing in action. *Application Requirements:* Application, financial need analysis, interview, transcript. *Deadline:* March 31.

Contact Charles Smith, Assistant Secretary, North Carolina Division of Veterans Affairs, 325 North Salisbury Street, Raleigh, NC 27603. *Phone:* 919-733-3851. *Fax:* 919-733-2834. *Web site:* www.doa.state.nc.us/doa/vets/va.htm.

University of North Carolina Need-Based Grant. Must be enrolled in at least 6 credit hours at one of 16 UNC system universities. Eligibility based on need; applicant must have submitted Free Application for Federal Student Aid. Award varies, consideration for grant automatic when FAFSA is filed. Late applications may be denied due to insufficient funds. *Award:* Grant for use in freshman, sophomore, junior, or senior year; renewable. *Award amount:* varies. *Number of awards:* varies. *Eligibility Requirements:* Applicant must be enrolled or expecting to enroll full or part-time at an institution or university and studying in North Carolina. Available to U.S. citizens. *Application Requirements:* Application, financial need analysis, FAFSA. *Deadline:* varies.

Contact Bill Carswell, Manager of Scholarship and Grant Division, North Carolina State Education Assistance Authority, PO Box 14103, Research Triangle Park, NC 27709. *E-mail:* carswellb@ncseaa.edu. *Phone:* 919-549-8614. *Fax:* 919-248-4687. *Web site:* www.ncseaa.edu.

NORTH DAKOTA

North Dakota Scholars Program. Provides scholarships equal to cost of tuition at the public colleges in North Dakota for North Dakota residents. Must score at or above the 95th percentile on ACT and rank in top twenty percent of high school graduation class. Must take ACT in fall. For high school seniors with a minimum 3.5 GPA. Application deadline is the October or June ACT test date. *Award:* Scholarship for use in freshman year; renewable. *Award amount:* varies. *Number of awards:* 15–20. *Eligibility Requirements:* Applicant must be high school student; planning to enroll or expecting to enroll full-time at a two-year or four-year institution or university; resident of North Dakota and studying in North Dakota. Applicant must have 3.5 GPA or higher. Available to U.S. citizens. *Application Requirements:* Test scores. *Deadline:* varies.

Contact Peggy Wipf, Director of Financial Aid, State of North Dakota, 600 East Boulevard Avenue, Department 215, Bismarck, ND 58505-0230. *Phone:* 701-328-4114. *Web site:* www.ndus.nodak.edu.

North Dakota State Student Incentive Grant Program. Grants to North Dakota residents pursuing their undergraduate degree who attend North Dakota's public, private (not-for-profit), and tribal colleges. *Award:* Grant for use in freshman, sophomore, junior, or senior year. *Award amount:* $600–$1000. *Number of awards:* 2500. *Eligibility Requirements:* Applicant must be enrolled or expecting to enroll full-time at a four-year institution or university and resident of North Dakota. Available to U.S. citizens. *Application Requirements:* Application. *Deadline:* March 15.

Contact State of North Dakota. *E-mail:* peggy.wipf@ndus.nodak.edu. *Phone:* 701-328-4114. *Web site:* www.ndus.nodak.edu.

North Dakota Indian Scholarship Program. Assists Native-American North Dakota residents in obtaining a college education. Priority given to full-time undergraduate students and those having a 3.5 GPA or higher. Certification of tribal enrollment required. For use at North Dakota institution. *Award:* Scholarship for use in freshman, sophomore, junior, senior, or graduate year; renewable. *Award amount:* $500–$2000. *Number of awards:* 150–170. *Eligibility Requirements:* Applicant must be American Indian/Alaska Native; enrolled or expecting to enroll at a two-year or four-year institution or university; resident of North Dakota and studying in North Dakota. Applicant must have 3.5 GPA or higher. Available to U.S. citizens. *Application Requirements:* Application, financial need analysis, transcript, proof of tribal enrollment, budget completed by a financial aid officer at the institution being attended. *Deadline:* July 15.

Contact Rhonda Schauer, Coordinator of American Indian Higher Education, State of North Dakota, 600 East Boulevard Avenue, Department 215, Bismarck, ND 58505-0230. *Phone:* 701-328-9661. *Web site:* www.ndus.nodak.edu.

North Dakota Teacher Shortage Loan Forgiveness Program. Forgivable loan for individuals who received their education degree from a North Dakota public institution and teach in North Dakota at grade levels and/or content areas identified by the Department of Public Instruction as having a teacher shortage. Funding recipients are eligible to have indebtedness reduced for up to $1000 per year for every consecutive year they teach in a teacher shortage area for up to three years. Applications are available on Web site: http://www.ndus.nodak.edu/students/financial-aid *Academic Fields/Career Goals:* Education. *Award:* Forgivable loan for use in freshman, sophomore, junior, or senior year; renewable. *Award amount:* up to $1000. *Number of awards:* 100–175. *Eligibility Requirements:* Applicant must be enrolled or expecting to enroll at a four-year institution or university; resident of North Dakota and studying in North Dakota. Applicant or parent of applicant must have employment or volunteer experience in teaching. Available to U.S. citizens. *Application Requirements:* Application, financial need analysis. *Deadline:* April 1.

Contact Peggy Wipf, North Dakota University System, 600 East Boulevard Avenue, Department 215, Bismarck, ND 58505-0230. *Phone:* 701-328-4114. *Web site:* www.ndus.nodak.edu.

North Dakota State Student Incentive Grant Program. Aids North Dakota residents attending an approved college or university in North Dakota. Must be enrolled in a program of at least nine months in length. *Award:* Grant for use in freshman, sophomore, junior, or senior year; not renewable. *Award amount:* up to $600. *Number of awards:* 2500–2600. *Eligibility Requirements:* Applicant must be enrolled or expecting to enroll full-time at a two-year or four-year institution or university; resident of North Dakota and studying in North Dakota. Available to U.S. and non-U.S. citizens. *Application Requirements:* Financial need analysis, FAFSA. *Deadline:* March 15.

Contact Peggy Wipf, Director of Financial Aid, State of North Dakota, 600 East Boulevard Avenue, Department 215, Bismarck, ND 58505-0230. *Phone:* 701-328-4114. *Web site:* www.ndus.nodak.edu.

OHIO

Robert C. Byrd Honors Scholarship-Ohio. Renewable award for graduating high school seniors who demonstrate outstanding academic achievement. Each Ohio high school receives applications by January of each year. School can submit one application for every 200 students in the senior class. Application deadline is the second Friday in March. *Award:* Scholarship for use in freshman, sophomore, junior, or senior year; renewable. *Award amount:* up to $1500. *Number of awards:* varies. *Eligibility Requirements:* Applicant must be high school student; planning to enroll or expecting to enroll at a two-year or four-year institution or university and resident of Ohio. Applicant must have 3.5 GPA or higher. Available to U.S. citizens. *Application Requirements:* Application, test scores. *Deadline:* varies.

Contact Ohio Department of Education, Ohio Department of Education, 25 South Front Street, Second Floor, Columbus, OH 43215. *Phone:* 614-466-4590. *Web site:* www.ode.state.oh.us.

Ohio Missing in Action and Prisoners of War Orphans Scholarship. Renewable award aids children of Vietnam conflict servicemen who have been classified as missing in action or prisoner of war. Must be an Ohio resident, be 16-21, and be enrolled full-time at an Ohio college. Full tuition awards. *Award:* Scholarship for use in freshman, sophomore, junior, or senior year; renewable. *Award amount:* varies. *Number of awards:* 1–5. *Eligibility Requirements:* Applicant must be age 16-21; enrolled or expecting to enroll full-time at a four-year institution or university; resident of Ohio and studying in Ohio. Available to U.S. citizens. Applicant or parent must meet one or more of the following requirements: general military experience; retired from active duty; disabled or killed as a result of military service; prisoner of war; or missing in action. *Application Requirements:* Application. *Deadline:* July 1.

Contact Sarina Wilks, Program Administrator, Ohio Board of Regents, 30 East Broad Street, 36th Floor, PO Box 182452, Columbus, OH 43215-3414. *E-mail:* swilks@regents.state.oh.us. *Phone:* 614-752-9528. *Fax:* 614-752-5903. *Web site:* www.regents.state.oh.us.

Ohio Instructional Grant. Award for low- and middle-income Ohio residents attending an approved college or school in Ohio or Pennsylvania. Must be enrolled full-time and have financial need. Average award is $630. May be used for any course of study except theology. *Award:* Grant for use in freshman, sophomore, junior, or senior year; renewable. *Award amount:* $78–$5466. *Number of awards:* varies. *Eligibility Requirements:* Applicant must be enrolled or expecting to enroll full-time at a two-year or four-year institution or university; resident of Ohio and studying in Ohio or Pennsylvania. Available to U.S. citizens. *Application Requirements:* Application, financial need analysis. *Deadline:* October 1.

Contact Lamar Burch, Program Administrator, Ohio Board of Regents, 30 East Broad Street, 36th Floor, PO Box 182452, Columbus, OH 43215-3414. *E-mail:* lburch@regents.state.oh.us. *Phone:* 614-752-9489. *Fax:* 614-752-5903. *Web site:* www.regents.state.oh.us.

Ohio Academic Scholarship Program. Award for academically outstanding Ohio residents planning to attend an approved Ohio college. Must be a high school senior intending to enroll full-time. Award is renewable for up to four years. Must rank in upper quarter of class or have a minimum GPA of 3.5. *Award:* Scholarship for use in freshman, sophomore, junior, or senior year; renewable. *Award amount:* $2205. *Number of awards:* 1000. *Eligibility Requirements:* Applicant must be high school student; planning to enroll or expecting to enroll full-time at a two-year or four-year institution; resident of Ohio and studying in Ohio. Applicant must have 3.5 GPA or higher. Available to U.S. citizens. *Application Requirements:* Application, test scores, transcript. *Deadline:* February 23.

Contact Sarina Wilks, Program Administrator, Ohio Board of Regents, 30 East Broad Street, 36th Floor, PO Box 182452, Columbus, OH 43215-3414. *E-mail:* swilks@regents.state.oh.us. *Phone:* 614-752-9528. *Fax:* 614-752-5903. *Web site:* www.regents.state.oh.us.

Ohio Safety Officers College Memorial Fund. Renewable award covering up to full tuition is available to children and surviving spouses of peace officers and

State Scholarship and Grant Programs
Ohio

fire fighters killed in the line of duty in any state. Children must be under 26 years of age. Must be an Ohio resident and enroll full-time or part-time at an Ohio college or university. *Award:* Scholarship for use in freshman, sophomore, junior, or senior year; renewable. *Award amount:* varies. *Number of awards:* 50–65. *Eligibility Requirements:* Applicant must be age 25 or under; enrolled or expecting to enroll full or part-time at a two-year or four-year institution or university; resident of Ohio and studying in Ohio. Applicant or parent of applicant must have employment or volunteer experience in police/firefighting. Available to U.S. citizens. *Application Requirements: Deadline:* continuous.

Contact Barbara Metheney, Program Administrator, Ohio Board of Regents, 30 East Broad Street, 36th Floor, Columbus, OH 43215-3414. *E-mail:* bmethene@regents.state.oh.us. *Phone:* 614-752-9535. *Fax:* 614-752-5903. *Web site:* www.regents.state.oh.us.

Ohio War Orphans Scholarship. Aids Ohio residents attending an eligible college in Ohio. Must be between the ages of 16-21, the child of a disabled or deceased veteran, and enrolled full-time. Renewable up to five years. Amount of award varies. Must include Form DD214. *Award:* Scholarship for use in freshman, sophomore, junior, or senior year; renewable. *Award amount:* varies. *Number of awards:* 300–450. *Eligibility Requirements:* Applicant must be age 16-21; enrolled or expecting to enroll full-time at a two-year or four-year institution or university; resident of Ohio and studying in Ohio. Available to U.S. citizens. Applicant or parent must meet one or more of the following requirements: general military experience; retired from active duty; disabled or killed as a result of military service; prisoner of war; or missing in action. *Application Requirements:* Application. *Deadline:* July 1.

Contact Sarina Wilks, Program Administrator, Ohio Board of Regents, 30 East Broad Street, 36th Floor, Columbus, OH 43215-3414. *E-mail:* swilks@regents.state.oh.us. *Phone:* 614-752-9528. *Fax:* 614-752-5903. *Web site:* www.regents.state.oh.us.

Ohio National Guard Scholarship Program. Scholarships are for undergraduate studies at an approved Ohio postsecondary institution. Applicants must enlist for six years of Selective Service Reserve Duty in the Ohio National Guard. Scholarship pays 100% instructional and general fees for public institutions and an average of cost of public schools is available for private schools. Must be 18 years of age or older. Award is renewable. Deadlines: July 1, November 1, February 1, April 1. *Award:* Scholarship for use in freshman, sophomore, junior, or senior year; renewable. *Award amount:* up to $3000. *Number of awards:* 3500–8000. *Eligibility Requirements:* Applicant must be age 18; enrolled or expecting to enroll full or part-time at a two-year, four-year, or technical institution or university and studying in Ohio. Available to U.S. citizens. Applicant must have served in the Air Force National Guard or Army National Guard. *Application Requirements:* Application. *Deadline:* varies.

Contact Toni Davis, Grants Administrator, Ohio National Guard, 2825 West Dublin Granville Road, Columbus, OH 43235-2789. *E-mail:* toni.davis@tagoh.org. *Phone:* 614-336-7032. *Fax:* 614-336-7318. *Web site:* www.ongsp.org.

Student Workforce Development Grant Program. Provides tuition assistance to Ohio students. Students must be pursuing an associate or bachelor's degree and must not have been enrolled full-time in a private career school prior to July 1, 2000. *Award:* Grant for use in freshman, sophomore, junior, or senior year. *Award amount:* $300. *Eligibility Requirements:* Applicant must be enrolled or expecting to enroll full-time at a four-year institution or university; resident of Ohio and studying in Ohio. Available to U.S. citizens.

Contact Barbara Metheney, Program Administrator, Ohio Board of Regents. *E-mail:* bmethene@regents.state.oh.us. *Phone:* 614-752-9535. *Fax:* 614-752-5903. *Web site:* www.regents.state.oh.us.

Ohio Environmental Science & Engineering Scholarships. Merit-based, non-renewable, tuition-only scholarships given to undergraduate students admitted to Ohio state or private colleges and universities who can demonstrate their knowledge and commitment to careers in environmental sciences or environmental engineering. Must be in their final year of a program in a two-year or four-year institution. Sophomores in a four-year institution are not eligible. Deadline is June 1. *Academic Fields/Career Goals:* Environmental Science. *Award:* Scholarship for use in senior year; not renewable. *Award amount:* $1250–$2500. *Number of awards:* 18. *Eligibility Requirements:* Applicant must be enrolled or expecting to enroll full or part-time at a two-year or four-year institution or university; resident of Ohio and studying in Ohio. Applicant must have 3.0 GPA or higher. Available to U.S. citizens. *Application Requirements:* Application, essay, resume, references, self-addressed stamped envelope, transcript. *Deadline:* June 1.

Contact Mr. Lynn E. Elfner, CEO, Ohio Academy of Science/Ohio Environmental Education Fund, 1500 West Third Avenue, Suite 228, Columbus, OH 43212-2817. *E-mail:* oas@iwaynet.net. *Phone:* 614-488-2228. *Fax:* 614-488-7629. *Web site:* www.ohiosci.org.

Accountancy Board of Ohio Educational Assistance Program. Program intended for minority students or students with financial need. Applicant must be enrolled as accounting major at an accredited Ohio college or university in a five-year degree program. Applicant must be an Ohio resident. Please refer to Web site for further details: http://acc.ohio.gov/educasst.html *Academic Fields/Career Goals:* Accounting. *Award:* Scholarship for use in sophomore, junior, or senior year; not renewable. *Award amount:* $7700. *Number of awards:* varies. *Eligibility Requirements:* Applicant must be enrolled or expecting to enroll at a four-year institution or university; resident of Ohio and studying in Ohio. Available to U.S. citizens. *Application Requirements:* Application, financial need analysis, transcript, FAFSA. *Deadline:* November 15.

Contact Kay Sedgmer, Scholarship Secretary, Accountancy Board of Ohio, Accountancy Board of Ohio, 77 South High Street, 18th Floor, Columbus, OH 43266-0301. *E-mail:* kay.sedgmer@acc.state.oh.us. *Phone:* 614-466-4135. *Fax:* 614-466-2628. *Web site:* acc.ohio.gov.

Part-time Student Instructional Grant. Renewable grants for part-time undergraduates who are Ohio residents. Award amounts vary. Must attend an Ohio institution. *Award:* Grant for use in freshman, sophomore, junior, or senior year; renewable. *Award amount:* varies. *Number of awards:* varies. *Eligibility Requirements:* Applicant must be enrolled or expecting to enroll part-time at a two-year or four-year institution or university; resident of Ohio and studying in Ohio. Available to U.S. citizens. *Application Requirements:* Application, financial need analysis. *Deadline:* continuous.

Contact Barbara Metheney, Program Administrator, Ohio Board of Regents, 30 East Broad Street, 36th Floor, Columbus, OH 43215-3414. *E-mail:* bmethene@regents.state.oh.us. *Phone:* 614-752-9535. *Fax:* 614-752-5903. *Web site:* www.regents.state.oh.us.

Ohio Student Choice Grant Program. Renewable award available to Ohio residents attending private colleges within the state. Must be enrolled full-time in a bachelor's degree program. Do not apply to state. Check with financial aid office of college. *Award:* Grant for use in freshman, sophomore, junior, or senior year; renewable. *Award amount:* up to $900. *Number of awards:* varies. *Eligibility Requirements:* Applicant must be enrolled or expecting to

State Scholarship and Grant Programs
Oregon

enroll full-time at a four-year institution or university; resident of Ohio and studying in Ohio. Available to U.S. citizens. *Application Requirements: Deadline:* continuous.

Contact Barbara Metheney, Program Administrator, Ohio Board of Regents, 30 East Broad Street, 36th Floor, PO Box 182452, Columbus, OH 43215-3414. *E-mail:* bmethene@regents.state.oh.us. *Phone:* 614-752-9535. *Fax:* 614-752-5903. *Web site:* www.regents.state.oh.us.

OKLAHOMA

Regional University Baccalaureate Scholarship. Renewable award for Oklahoma residents attending one of 11 participating Oklahoma public universities. Must have an ACT composite score of at least 30 or be a National Merit semifinalist or commended student. In addition to the award amount, each recipient will receive a resident tuition waiver from the institution. Must maintain a 3.25 GPA. Deadlines vary depending upon the institution attended. *Award:* Scholarship for use in freshman, sophomore, junior, or senior year; renewable. *Award amount:* $3000. *Number of awards:* up to 165. *Eligibility Requirements:* Applicant must be enrolled or expecting to enroll full-time at an institution or university; resident of Oklahoma and studying in Oklahoma. Available to U.S. citizens. *Application Requirements:* Application. *Deadline:* varies.

Contact Alicia Harris, Scholarship Programs Coordinator, Oklahoma State Regents for Higher Education, PO Box 108850, Oklahoma City, OK 73101-8850. *E-mail:* aharris@osrhe.edu. *Phone:* 405-225-9131. *Fax:* 405-225-9230. *Web site:* www.okighered.org.

Academic Scholars Program. Encourages students of high academic ability to attend institutions in Oklahoma. Renewable up to four years. ACT or SAT scores must fall between 99.5 and 100th percentiles, or applicant must be designated as a National Merit scholar or finalist. *Award:* Scholarship for use in freshman, sophomore, junior, or senior year; renewable. *Award amount:* $1800–$2800. *Number of awards:* varies. *Eligibility Requirements:* Applicant must be high school student; planning to enroll or expecting to enroll full-time at a two-year or four-year institution or university and studying in Oklahoma. Available to U.S. citizens. *Application Requirements:* Application, test scores, transcript. *Deadline:* continuous.

Contact Scholarship Programs Coordinator, Oklahoma State Regents for Higher Education, PO Box 108850, Oklahoma City, OK 73101-8850. *E-mail:* studentinfo@osrhe.edu. *Phone:* 800-858-1840. *Fax:* 405-225-9230. *Web site:* www.okighered.org.

Future Teacher Scholarship-Oklahoma. Open to outstanding Oklahoma high school graduates who agree to teach in shortage areas. Must rank in top 15% of graduating class or score above 85th percentile on ACT or similar test, or be accepted in an educational program. Students nominated by institution. Reapply to renew. Must attend college/university in Oklahoma. Contact institution's financial aid office for application deadline. *Academic Fields/Career Goals:* Education. *Award:* Scholarship for use in freshman, sophomore, junior, senior, or graduate year; renewable. *Award amount:* $500–$1500. *Number of awards:* varies. *Eligibility Requirements:* Applicant must be enrolled or expecting to enroll full or part-time at a two-year or four-year institution or university; resident of Oklahoma and studying in Oklahoma. Available to U.S. citizens. *Application Requirements:* Application, essay, test scores, transcript.

Contact Scholarship Programs Coordinator, Oklahoma State Regents for Higher Education, PO Box 108850, Oklahoma City, OK 73101-8850. *Phone:* 800-858-1840. *Fax:* 405-225-9230. *Web site:* www.okighered.org.

Oklahoma Tuition Aid Grant. Award for Oklahoma residents enrolled at an Oklahoma institution at least part time each semester in a degree program. May be enrolled in two or four-year or approved vocational-technical institution. Award of up to $1000 per year. Application is made through FAFSA. *Award:* Grant for use in freshman, sophomore, junior, senior, or graduate year; renewable. *Award amount:* $200–$1000. *Number of awards:* 23,000. *Eligibility Requirements:* Applicant must be enrolled or expecting to enroll full or part-time at a two-year, four-year, or technical institution or university; resident of Oklahoma and studying in Oklahoma. Available to U.S. citizens. *Application Requirements:* Application, financial need analysis, FAFSA. *Deadline:* April 30.

Contact Oklahoma State Regents for Higher Education, PO Box 3020, Oklahoma City, OK 73101-3020. *E-mail:* otaginfo@otag.org. *Phone:* 405-225-9456. *Fax:* 405-225-9392. *Web site:* www.okighered.org.

OREGON

Oregon Veterans' Education Aid. To be eligible, veteran must have served in U.S. armed forces 90 days and been discharged under honorable conditions; U.S. citizen and Oregon resident; Korean War veteran or received campaign or expeditionary medal or ribbon awarded by U.S. armed forces for services after June 30, 1958. Full-time students receive $50/month, part-time students receive $35/month. *Award:* Grant for use in freshman, sophomore, junior, senior, graduate, or postgraduate years; not renewable. *Award amount:* varies. *Number of awards:* varies. *Eligibility Requirements:* Applicant must be enrolled or expecting to enroll full-time at a two-year, four-year, or technical institution or university; resident of Oregon and studying in Oregon. Available to U.S. citizens. Applicant must have general military experience. *Application Requirements:* Application, certified copy of DD Form 214. *Deadline:* continuous.

Contact Mary Kluver, Educational Aid Coordinator, Oregon Department of Veterans Affairs, 700 Summer Street, NE, Salem, OR 97301-1289. *Phone:* 503-373-2085. *Fax:* 503-373-2392. *Web site:* www.odva.state.or.us.

American Ex-Prisoner of War Scholarships: Peter Connacher Memorial Scholarship. Renewable award for American prisoners-of-war and their descendants. Written proof of prisoner-of-war status and discharge papers from the U.S. Armed Forces must accompany application. Statement of relationship between applicant and former prisoner-of-war is required. See Web site at http://www.osac.state.or.us for details. *Award:* Scholarship for use in freshman, sophomore, junior, or senior year; renewable. *Award amount:* $1150. *Number of awards:* 4. *Eligibility Requirements:* Applicant must be enrolled or expecting to enroll at a two-year or four-year institution and resident of Oregon. Available to U.S. citizens. Applicant or parent must meet one or more of the following requirements: general military experience; retired from active duty; disabled or killed as a result of military service; prisoner of war; or missing in action. *Application Requirements:* Application, essay, financial need analysis, transcript, activities chart. *Deadline:* March 1.

Contact Director of Grant Programs, Oregon Student Assistance Commission, 1500 Valley River Drive, Suite 100, Eugene, OR 97401-7020. *Phone:* 800-452-8807 Ext. 7395. *Web site:* www.osac.state.or.us.

Oregon Trucking Association Scholarship. One scholarship available to a child of an Oregon Trucking Association member, or child of employee of member. Applicants must be Oregon residents who are graduating high school seniors from an Oregon high school. One-time award. *Award:* Scholarship for use in freshman year; not renewable. *Award amount:* $750. *Number of awards:* 4. *Eligibility Requirements:* Applicant must be high school

State Scholarship and Grant Programs
Oregon

student; planning to enroll or expecting to enroll at a four-year institution and resident of Oregon. Applicant or parent of applicant must be affiliated with Oregon Trucking Association. Applicant or parent of applicant must have employment or volunteer experience in designated career field. Available to U.S. citizens. *Application Requirements:* Application, essay, financial need analysis, references, transcript, activity chart. *Deadline:* March 1.

Contact Director of Grant Programs, Oregon Student Assistance Commission, 1500 Valley River Drive, Suite 100, Eugene, OR 97401-7020. *Phone:* 800-452-8807 Ext. 7395. *Web site:* www.osac.state.or.us.

Oregon Student Assistance Commission Employee and Dependent Scholarship. One-time award for current permanent employee of the Oregon Student Assistance Commission or legally dependent children of employee. Also available to dependent children of an employee who retires, is permanently disabled, or deceased directly from employment at OSAC. Dependent must enroll full time. Employee may enroll part time. *Award:* Scholarship for use in freshman, sophomore, junior, or senior year; renewable. *Award amount:* $500. *Number of awards:* 7. *Eligibility Requirements:* Applicant must be enrolled or expecting to enroll full or part-time at an institution or university and resident of Oregon. Available to U.S. citizens. *Application Requirements:* Application, essay, transcript, activities chart. *Deadline:* March 1.

Contact Director of Grant Programs, Oregon Student Assistance Commission, 1500 Valley River Drive, Suite 100, Eugene, OR 97401-7020. *Phone:* 800-452-8807 Ext. 7395. *Web site:* www.osac.state.or.us.

Oregon Scholarship Fund Transfer Student Award. Award open to Oregon residents who are currently enrolled in their second year at a community college and are planning to transfer to a four-year college in Oregon. Prior recipients may apply for one additional year. *Award:* Scholarship for use in junior or senior year; renewable. *Award amount:* $500. *Number of awards:* varies. *Eligibility Requirements:* Applicant must be enrolled or expecting to enroll full-time at a four-year institution or university; resident of Oregon and studying in Oregon. Available to U.S. citizens. *Application Requirements:* Application, essay, financial need analysis, transcript, activity chart. *Deadline:* March 1.

Contact Director of Grant Programs, Oregon Student Assistance Commission, 1500 Valley River Drive, Suite 100, Eugene, OR 97401-7020. *Phone:* 800-452-8807 Ext. 7395. *Web site:* www.osac.state.or.us.

Glenn Jackson Scholars Scholarships (OCF). Award for graduating high school seniors who are dependents of employees or retirees of Oregon Department of Transportation or Parks and Recreation Department. Employees must have worked in their department at least three years. Award for maximum twelve undergraduate quarters or six quarters at a two-year institution. Must be U.S. citizen or permanent resident. Visit Web site (http://www.osac.state.or.us) for more details. *Award:* Scholarship for use in freshman, sophomore, junior, or senior year; renewable. *Award amount:* $2500. *Number of awards:* 2. *Eligibility Requirements:* Applicant must be high school student; planning to enroll or expecting to enroll at a four-year institution and resident of Oregon. Applicant or parent of applicant must be affiliated with Oregon Department of Transportation Parks and Recreation. Applicant or parent of applicant must have employment or volunteer experience in designated career field. Available to U.S. citizens. *Application Requirements:* Application, essay, financial need analysis, references, transcript, activity chart. *Deadline:* March 1.

Contact Director of Grant Programs, Oregon Student Assistance Commission, 1500 Valley River Drive, Suite 100, Eugene, OR 97401-7020. *Phone:* 800-452-8807 Ext. 7395. *Web site:* www.osac.state.or.us.

Dorothy Campbell Memorial Scholarship. Renewable award for female Oregon high school graduates with a minimum 2.75 GPA. Must submit essay describing strong, continuing interest in golf and the contribution that sport has made to applicant's development. *Award:* Scholarship for use in freshman, sophomore, junior, or senior year; renewable. *Award amount:* $1500. *Number of awards:* 2. *Eligibility Requirements:* Applicant must be high school student; planning to enroll or expecting to enroll full-time at a four-year institution or university; female; resident of Oregon; studying in Oregon and must have an interest in golf. Available to U.S. citizens. *Application Requirements:* Application, essay, financial need analysis, transcript, activity chart. *Deadline:* March 1.

Contact Director of Grant Programs, Oregon Student Assistance Commission, 1500 Valley River Drive, Suite 100, Eugene, OR 97401-7020. *Phone:* 800-452-8807 Ext. 7395. *Web site:* www.osac.state.or.us.

Lawrence R. Foster Memorial Scholarship. One-time award to students enrolled or planning to enroll in a public health degree program. First preference given to those working in the public health field and those pursuing a graduate degree in public health. Undergraduates entering junior or senior year health programs may apply if seeking a public health career, and not private practice. Prefer applicants from diverse cultures. Must provide 3 references. Additional essay required. Must be resident of Oregon. *Academic Fields/Career Goals:* Health and Medical Sciences. *Award:* Scholarship for use in junior, senior, graduate, or postgraduate years; renewable. *Award amount:* $4167. *Number of awards:* 6. *Eligibility Requirements:* Applicant must be enrolled or expecting to enroll full or part-time at a four-year institution or university and resident of Oregon. Available to U.S. citizens. *Application Requirements:* Application, essay, financial need analysis, references, transcript, activity chart. *Deadline:* March 1.

Contact Director of Grant Programs, Oregon Student Assistance Commission, 1500 Valley River Drive, Suite 100, Eugene, OR 97401-7020. *Phone:* 800-452-8807 Ext. 7395. *Web site:* www.osac.state.or.us.

Oregon Occupational Safety and Health Division Workers Memorial Scholarship. Available to Oregon residents who are the dependents or spouses of an Oregon worker who was killed or permanently disabled on the job. Submit essay of 500 words or less titled "How has the injury or death of your parent or spouse affected or influenced your decision to further your education?" See Web site for more details. (http://www.osac.state.or.us) *Award:* Scholarship for use in freshman, sophomore, junior, senior, or graduate year; renewable. *Award amount:* $4786. *Number of awards:* 1. *Eligibility Requirements:* Applicant must be enrolled or expecting to enroll full-time at a four-year institution or university and resident of Oregon. Applicant or parent of applicant must have employment or volunteer experience in designated career field. Available to U.S. citizens. *Application Requirements:* Application, essay, financial need analysis, test scores, transcript, workers compensation claim number. *Deadline:* March 1.

Contact Director of Grant Programs, Oregon Student Assistance Commission, 1500 Valley River Drive, Suite 100, Eugene, OR 97401-7020. *Phone:* 800-452-8807 Ext. 7395. *Web site:* www.osac.state.or.us.

Children, Adult, and Family Services Scholarship. One-time award for graduating high school seniors, GED recipients, and college students currently or formerly in foster care or an Independent Living Program (ILP) financially supported through the Oregon State Office for Services to Children and Families. Must attend an Oregon public college. Visit Web site for more details (http://www.osac.state.or.us).

State Scholarship and Grant Programs
Pennsylvania

Award varies between $500-$5000. *Award:* Scholarship for use in freshman, sophomore, junior, senior, or graduate year; renewable. *Award amount:* $500–$5000. *Number of awards:* varies. *Eligibility Requirements:* Applicant must be enrolled or expecting to enroll full-time at a two-year or four-year institution; resident of Oregon and studying in Oregon. Available to U.S. citizens. *Application Requirements:* Application, essay, financial need analysis, references, transcript, activity chart. *Deadline:* March 1.

Contact Director of Grant Programs, Oregon Student Assistance Commission, 1500 Valley River Drive, Suite 100, Eugene, OR 97401-7020. *Phone:* 800-452-8807 Ext. 7395. *Web site:* www.osac.state.or.us.

Oregon Scholarship Fund Community College Student Award. Scholarship open to Oregon residents enrolled or planning to enroll in Oregon community college programs. May apply for one additional year. *Award:* Scholarship for use in freshman or sophomore year; renewable. *Award amount:* $500. *Number of awards:* varies. *Eligibility Requirements:* Applicant must be enrolled or expecting to enroll full-time at a two-year institution; resident of Oregon and studying in Oregon. Available to U.S. citizens. *Application Requirements:* Application, essay, financial need analysis, transcript, activity chart. *Deadline:* March 1.

Contact Director of Grant Programs, Oregon Student Assistance Commission, 1500 Valley River Drive, Suite 100, Eugene, OR 97401-7020. *Phone:* 800-452-8807 Ext. 7395. *Web site:* www.osac.state.or.us.

PENNSYLVANIA

Pennsylvania State Grants. Award for Pennsylvania residents attending an approved postsecondary institution as undergraduates in a program of at least two years duration. Renewable for up to eight semesters if applicants show continued need and academic progress. Submit Free Application for Federal Student Aid. Deadline is May 1 for renewal applicants and new applicants who plan to enroll in an undergraduate baccalaureate degree and August 1 for new applicants in specific school given in research URL *Award:* Grant for use in freshman, sophomore, junior, or senior year; renewable. *Award amount:* $300–$3300. *Number of awards:* up to 151,000. *Eligibility Requirements:* Applicant must be enrolled or expecting to enroll full or part-time at a two-year, four-year, or technical institution or university and resident of Pennsylvania. Available to U.S. and Canadian citizens. *Application Requirements:* Application, financial need analysis. *Deadline:* varies.

Contact Keith New, Director of Communications and Press Office, Pennsylvania Higher Education Assistance Agency, 1200 North Seventh Street, Harrisburg, PA 17102-1444. *Phone:* 717-720-2509. *Fax:* 717-720-3903. *Web site:* www.pheaa.org.

Educational Gratuity Program. This program is for eligible dependents of 100% disabled or deceased veterans whose disability was incurred during a period of war or armed conflict. Must be a Pennsylvania resident attending a Pennsylvania school. Up to $500 per semester may be awarded. *Award:* Grant for use in freshman, sophomore, junior, or senior year; renewable. *Award amount:* $500. *Number of awards:* varies. *Eligibility Requirements:* Applicant must be age 16-23; enrolled or expecting to enroll full-time at a two-year, four-year, or technical institution or university; resident of Pennsylvania and studying in Pennsylvania. Available to U.S. citizens. Applicant or parent must meet one or more of the following requirements: general military experience; retired from active duty; disabled or killed as a result of military service; prisoner of war; or missing in action. *Application Requirements:* Application, driver's license, financial need analysis, transcript, birth certificate. *Deadline:* continuous.

Contact Sophie Matukewicz, Program Manager, Pennsylvania Bureau for Veterans Affairs, Department of Military and Veterans Affairs, Building S-0-47, Ft. Indiantown Gap, Annville, PA 17003-5003. *E-mail:* smatukewic@state.pa.us. *Phone:* 717-861-8610. *Fax:* 717-861-8589.

Quality Early Education Loan Forgiveness program. Forgivable loan available to graduates working in Pennsylvania in the field of Early Childhood Education. Applicants must be employed full-time by a Pennsylvania Department of Public Welfare-approved child daycare center or group child daycare home. Applicants cannot have a gross annual income of more than $23,000 from employment in a Pennsylvania Department of Public Welfare-approved child daycare center or group child daycare home. *Academic Fields/Career Goals:* Education. *Award:* Forgivable loan for use in freshman, sophomore, junior, or senior year. *Award amount:* up to $3300. *Eligibility Requirements:* Applicant must be enrolled or expecting to enroll at a two-year, four-year, or technical institution or university and resident of Pennsylvania. Available to U.S. citizens. *Application Requirements:* Application.

Contact Keith New, Director of Communications and Press Office, Pennsylvania Higher Education Assistance Agency, 1200 N 7th Street, Harrisburg, PA 17102-1444. *E-mail:* knew@pheaa.org. *Phone:* 717-720-2509. *Fax:* 717-720-3903. *Web site:* www.pheaa.org.

Armed Forces Loan Forgiveness Program. Loan forgiveness for nonresidents of Pennsylvania who served in Armed Forces in an active duty status between September 11, 2001 and June 30, 2006. Student either left a PA approved institution of postsecondary education due to call to active duty, or was living in PA at time of enlistment, or enlisted in military immediately after attending a PA approved institution of postsecondary education. Must have an eligible, non-default loan. *Award:* Forgivable loan for use in freshman, sophomore, junior, or senior year; not renewable. *Award amount:* up to $2500. *Eligibility Requirements:* Applicant must be enrolled or expecting to enroll at a two-year, four-year, or technical institution or university and resident of Pennsylvania. Available to U.S. citizens. Applicant or parent must meet one or more of the following requirements: general military experience; retired from active duty; disabled or killed as a result of military service; prisoner of war; or missing in action. *Application Requirements:* Application. *Deadline:* December 31.

Contact Pennsylvania Higher Education Assistance Agency, AES Lender School Team, PO Box 2461, Harrisburg, PA 17105-2461. *Web site:* www.pheaa.org.

Loan Forgiveness Program for State Veterans Homes Nurses. Forgivable loans for nursing education. Must have full-time employment as a direct care nurse, within three months of graduation, at one of State Veterans Homes. Applicants must complete qualifying program of study between November 17, 2005 and December 31, 2006 leading to certification as a Licensed Practical Nurse within PA Registered Nurse within PA. *Academic Fields/Career Goals:* Nursing. *Award:* Forgivable loan for use in senior year. *Award amount:* up to $10,000. *Eligibility Requirements:* Applicant must be enrolled or expecting to enroll at an institution or university and resident of Pennsylvania. Available to U.S. citizens. *Application Requirements:* Application. *Deadline:* December 31.

Contact Pennsylvania Higher Education Assistance Agency, AES Lender School Team, PO Box 2461, Harrisburg, PA 17105-2461. *Web site:* www.pheaa.org.

State Scholarship and Grant Programs
Pennsylvania

New Economy Technology Scholarship (NETS)-SciTech Scholarships. Scholarship for undergraduate studying in approved science or technology fields. Recipients of these scholarships must agree to work full-time in Pennsylvania following graduation, one year for each year that a scholarship award is received. Funds under this program will be awarded on a first-come, first-served basis. *Academic Fields/Career Goals:* Science, Technology, and Society. *Award:* Scholarship for use in sophomore, junior, or senior year; renewable. *Award amount:* up to $3000. *Eligibility Requirements:* Applicant must be enrolled or expecting to enroll full-time at a four-year institution or university; resident of Pennsylvania and studying in Pennsylvania. Applicant must have 3.0 GPA or higher. Available to U.S. citizens. *Application Requirements:* Application. *Deadline:* varies.

Contact Pennsylvania Higher Education Assistance Agency, New Economy Technology Scholarship Program, PHEAA State Grant and Special Programs, 1200 North 7th St, Harrisburg, PA 17102-1444. *Phone:* 800-692-7392. *Web site:* www.pheaa.org.

New Economy Technology Scholarship-Technology Scholarships. Scholarships make financial aid available if you are an undergraduate studying in approved science or technology fields. Recipients of these scholarships must agree to work full-time in Pennsylvania following graduation, one year for each year that a scholarship award is received. funds under this program will be awarded on a first-come, first-served basis. *Academic Fields/Career Goals:* Science, Technology, and Society. *Award:* Scholarship for use in freshman, sophomore, junior, or senior year. *Award amount:* up to $1000. *Eligibility Requirements:* Applicant must be enrolled or expecting to enroll full or part-time at a two-year or four-year institution; resident of Pennsylvania and studying in Pennsylvania. Applicant must have 3.0 GPA or higher. Available to U.S. citizens. *Application Requirements:* Application. *Deadline:* varies.

Contact Pennsylvania Higher Education Assistance Agency, New Economy Technology Scholarship Program, PHEAA State Grant and Special Programs, 1200 North 7th St, Harrisburg, PA 17102-1444. *Phone:* 800-692-7392. *Web site:* www.pheaa.org.

Postsecondary Education Gratuity Program. Waiver of tuition and fees for children of Pennsylvania police officers, firefighters, rescue or ambulance squad members, corrections facility employees, or National Guard members who died in line of duty after January 1, 1976. child by birth or adoption of a deceased sheriff, deputy sheriff, National Guard member or other individual who was on federal or state active military duty who died since September 11, 2001, as a direct result of performing official duties. *Award:* Grant for use in freshman, sophomore, junior, or senior year; renewable. *Award amount:* varies. *Number of awards:* 1. *Eligibility Requirements:* Applicant must be age 25 or under; enrolled or expecting to enroll full-time at a two-year or four-year institution or university; resident of Pennsylvania and studying in Pennsylvania. Available to U.S. citizens. Applicant or parent must meet one or more of the following requirements: general military experience; retired from active duty; disabled or killed as a result of military service; prisoner of war; or missing in action. *Application Requirements:* Application. *Deadline:* March 31.

Contact PHEAA State Grant and Special Programs Division, Pennsylvania Higher Education Assistance Agency, 1200 North Seventh Street, Harrisburg, PA 17102-1444. *Phone:* 800-692-7392. *Web site:* www.pheaa.org.

Nursing Loan Forgiveness for Healthier Futures Program. Forgivable loans for nursing education. Applicants must pass the Pennsylvania State Board of Nursing examination, and begin full-time employment within three months of graduation as a direct patient care nurse at an approved, participating Pennsylvania facility, or within one year, as a nurse educator in an approved participating Pennsylvania postsecondary education program. *Academic Fields/Career Goals:* Nursing. *Award:* Forgivable loan for use in freshman, sophomore, junior, or senior year. *Award amount:* up to $12,500. *Eligibility Requirements:* Applicant must be enrolled or expecting to enroll at an institution or university and resident of Pennsylvania. Available to U.S. citizens. *Application Requirements:* Application. *Deadline:* December 31.

Contact Pennsylvania Higher Education Assistance Agency, American Education Services, Nursing Loan Forgiveness for Healthier Futures Program, Lender School Team, PO Box 2461, Harrisburg, PA 17105-2461. *Phone:* 800-859-5442. *Fax:* 717-720-3916. *Web site:* www.pheaa.org.

PUERTO RICO

Robert C. Byrd Honor Scholarship-Puerto Rico. This grant is sponsored by the Puerto Rico Department of Education and is granted to gifted students. These are students chosen from public and private schools who graduate from high school and are admitted to an accredited university in Puerto Rico or in the United States and who show promise to complete a college career. It is granted for a period of four years if the student maintains a satisfactory academic progress. Must be a U.S. citizen and rank in the upper quarter of class or have a minimum 3.5 GPA. *Award:* Scholarship for use in freshman, sophomore, junior, or senior year; renewable. *Award amount:* up to $1500. *Number of awards:* 74–85. *Eligibility Requirements:* Applicant must be high school student and planning to enroll or expecting to enroll full-time at a four-year institution or university. Applicant must have 3.5 GPA or higher. Available to U.S. citizens. *Application Requirements:* Application, financial need analysis, interview, portfolio, references, test scores, transcript. *Deadline:* May 30.

Contact Marta Colon-Rivera, Coordinator, Puerto Rico Department of Education, PO Box 19900, San Juan, PR 00910-1900. *E-mail:* hernandez_eli@de.gobierno.pr. *Phone:* 787-759-8313. *Fax:* 787-758-2281.

RHODE ISLAND

Rhode Island Higher Education Grant Program. Grants for residents of Rhode Island attending an approved school in the U.S., Canada, or Mexico. Based on need. Renewable for up to four years if in good academic standing. Applications accepted January 1 through March 1. Several awards of variable amounts. Must be U.S. citizen or registered alien. *Award:* Grant for use in freshman, sophomore, junior, or senior year; renewable. *Award amount:* $300–$1400. *Number of awards:* 10,000–12,900. *Eligibility Requirements:* Applicant must be enrolled or expecting to enroll full or part-time at an institution or university and resident of Rhode Island. Available to U.S. citizens. *Application Requirements:* Application, financial need analysis. *Deadline:* March 1.

Contact Ms. Mary Ann Welch, Director of Program Administration, Rhode Island Higher Education Assistance Authority, 560 Jefferson Boulevard, Warwick, RI 02886. *E-mail:* mawelch@riheaa.org. *Phone:* 401-736-1171. *Fax:* 401-736-1178. *Web site:* www.riheaa.org.

SOUTH CAROLINA

South Carolina Teacher Loan Program. One-time awards for South Carolina residents attending four-year postsecondary institutions in South Carolina. Recipients must teach in the South Carolina public school system in a critical-need area after graduation. 20% of loan forgiven for each year of service. Write for additional requirements.

Academic Fields/Career Goals: Education; Special Education. *Award:* Forgivable loan for use in freshman, sophomore, junior, senior, or graduate year; not renewable. *Award amount:* $2500–$5000. *Number of awards:* up to 1121. *Eligibility Requirements:* Applicant must be enrolled or expecting to enroll full or part-time at a four-year institution or university; resident of South Carolina and studying in South Carolina. Applicant must have 3.0 GPA or higher. Available to U.S. citizens. *Application Requirements:* Application, test scores. *Deadline:* June 1.

Contact Jennifer Jones-Gaddy, Vice President, South Carolina Student Loan Corporation, PO Box 21487, Columbia, SC 29221. *E-mail:* jgaddy@slc.sc.edu. *Phone:* 803-798-0916. *Fax:* 803-772-9410. *Web site:* www.slc.sc.edu.

Legislative Incentives for Future Excellence Program. Scholarship for students from South Carolina to attend an institution of higher education in South Carolina. For students attending a four-year institution, two of the following three criteria must be met: 1) minimum 3.0 GPA, 2) 1100 SAT or 24 ACT, or 3) graduate in the top 30% of class. Students attending a two-year or technical college must have a 3.0 GPA (SAT and class rank requirements are waived). *Award:* Scholarship for use in freshman, sophomore, junior, senior, or graduate year; renewable. *Award amount:* $2000–$5000. *Number of awards:* varies. *Eligibility Requirements:* Applicant must be enrolled or expecting to enroll full-time at a two-year, four-year, or technical institution or university; resident of South Carolina and studying in South Carolina. Applicant must have 3.0 GPA or higher. Available to U.S. citizens. *Application Requirements:* Test scores, transcript. *Deadline:* continuous.

Contact Bichevia Green, LIFE Scholarship Coordinator, South Carolina Commission on Higher Education, 1333 Main Street, Suite 200, Columbia, SC 29201. *E-mail:* bgreen@che.sc.gov. *Phone:* 803-737-2280. *Fax:* 803-737-2297. *Web site:* www.che.sc.gov.

South Carolina Need-Based Grants Program. Award based on results of Free Application for Federal Student Aid. A student may receive up to $2500 annually for full-time and up to $1250 annually for part-time study. The grant must be applied toward the cost of attendance at a South Carolina college for up to eight full-time equivalent terms. Student must be degree-seeking. *Award:* Grant for use in freshman, sophomore, junior, senior, or graduate year; renewable. *Award amount:* $1250–$2500. *Number of awards:* 1–23,485. *Eligibility Requirements:* Applicant must be enrolled or expecting to enroll full or part-time at a two-year, four-year, or technical institution or university; resident of South Carolina and studying in South Carolina. Available to U.S. citizens. *Application Requirements:* Application, financial need analysis. *Deadline:* continuous.

Contact Sherry Hubbard, Coordinator, South Carolina Commission on Higher Education, 1333 Main Street, Suite 200, Columbia, SC 29201. *E-mail:* shubbard@che.sc.gov. *Phone:* 803-737-2260. *Fax:* 803-737-2297. *Web site:* www.che.sc.gov.

South Carolina Tuition Grants Program. Assists South Carolina residents attending one of twenty approved South Carolina independent colleges. Freshmen must be in upper 3/4 of high school class or have SAT score of at least 900. Upper-class students must complete 24 semester hours per year to be eligible. *Award:* Grant for use in freshman, sophomore, junior, or senior year; renewable. *Award amount:* $100–$3240. *Number of awards:* up to 11,000. *Eligibility Requirements:* Applicant must be enrolled or expecting to enroll full-time at a two-year or four-year institution or university; resident of South Carolina and studying in South Carolina. Available to U.S. citizens. *Application Requirements:* Application, financial need analysis, test scores, transcript, FAFSA. *Deadline:* June 30.

Contact Toni Cave, Financial Aid Counselor, South Carolina Tuition Grants Commission, 101 Business Park Boulevard, Suite 2100, Columbia, SC 29203-9498. *E-mail:* toni@sctuitiongrants.org. *Phone:* 803-896-1120. *Fax:* 803-896-1126. *Web site:* www.sctuitiongrants.com.

SOUTH DAKOTA

Haines Memorial Scholarship. One-time scholarship for South Dakota public university students who are sophomores, juniors, or seniors having at least a 2.5 GPA and majoring in a teacher education program. Include resume with application. Must be South Dakota resident. *Academic Fields/Career Goals:* Education. *Award:* Scholarship for use in sophomore, junior, or senior year; not renewable. *Award amount:* $2150. *Number of awards:* 1. *Eligibility Requirements:* Applicant must be enrolled or expecting to enroll at an institution or university; resident of South Dakota and studying in South Dakota. Applicant must have 2.5 GPA or higher. Available to U.S. citizens. *Application Requirements:* Application, autobiography, essay, resume. *Deadline:* February 9.

Contact Scholarship Committee, South Dakota Board of Regents, 306 East Capitol Avenue, Suite 200, Pierre, SD 57501-3159. *Web site:* www.sdbor.edu.

TENNESSEE

Tennessee Education Lottery Scholarship Program Tennessee HOPE Scholarship. Award of $3000 per year for students at Four-year colleges or $1500 per year for students at Two-year colleges. *Award:* Scholarship for use in freshman, sophomore, junior, or senior year; renewable. *Award amount:* $1650–$3300. *Number of awards:* varies. *Eligibility Requirements:* Applicant must be enrolled or expecting to enroll full or part-time at a two-year, four-year, or technical institution or university; resident of Tennessee and studying in Tennessee. Applicant must have 3.0 GPA or higher. Available to U.S. citizens. *Application Requirements:* Application, financial need analysis. *Deadline:* May 1.

Contact Robert Biggers, Lottery Scholarship Program Administrator, Tennessee Student Assistance Corporation, 404 James Robertson Parkway, Suite 1950, Nashville, TN 37243-0820. *E-mail:* tsac.aidinfo@state.tn.us. *Phone:* 800-342-1663. *Fax:* 615-253-3867. *Web site:* www.state.tn.us/tsac.

Christa McAuliffe Scholarship Program. Scholarship to assist and support Tennessee students who have demonstrated a commitment to a career in educating the youth of Tennessee. The scholarship is offered to college seniors for a period of one academic year. *Academic Fields/Career Goals:* Education. *Award:* Scholarship for use in senior year. *Award amount:* up to $1000. *Eligibility Requirements:* Applicant must be enrolled or expecting to enroll at a four-year institution or university and studying in Tennessee. Available to U.S. citizens. *Application Requirements:* Application. *Deadline:* April 1.

Contact Naomi Derryberry, Grant and Scholarship Administrator, Tennessee Student Assistance Corporation, 404 James Robertson Parkway, Suite 1950, Parkway Towers, Nashville, TN 37243-0820. *E-mail:* tsac.aidinfo@state.tn.us. *Phone:* 800-342-1663. *Fax:* 615-741-6101. *Web site:* www.state.tn.us/tsac.

Tennessee Education Lottery Scholarship Program Tennessee HOPE Access Grant. Non-renewable award of $2000 for students at Four-year colleges or $1250 for students at Two-year colleges. Entering freshmen must have a minimum GPA of 2.75 and parents income must be $36,000 or less. Recipients will be eligible for Tennessee HOPE Scholarship by meeting

State Scholarship and Grant Programs
Tennessee

HOPE Scholarship renewal criteria. *Award:* Grant for use in freshman, sophomore, junior, or senior year; not renewable. *Award amount:* $1575–$2400. *Number of awards:* varies. *Eligibility Requirements:* Applicant must be enrolled or expecting to enroll full or part-time at a two-year, four-year, or technical institution or university; resident of Tennessee and studying in Tennessee. Available to U.S. citizens. *Application Requirements:* Application, financial need analysis. *Deadline:* May 1.

Contact Robert Biggers, Lottery Scholarship Program Administrator, Tennessee Student Assistance Corporation, 404 James Robertson Parkway, Suite 1950, Nashville, TN 37243-0820. *E-mail:* tsac.aidinfo@state.tn.us. *Phone:* 800-342-1663. *Fax:* 615-253-3867. *Web site:* www.state.tn.us/tsac.

Dependent Children Scholarship Program. Scholarship aid for Tennessee residents who are dependent children of a Tennessee law enforcement officer, fireman, or an emergency medical service technician who has been killed or totally and permanently disabled while performing duties within the scope of such employment. The scholarship awarded to full-time undergraduate students for a maximum of four academic years or the period required for the completion of the program of study. *Award:* Scholarship for use in freshman, sophomore, junior, or senior year. *Number of awards:* 1. *Eligibility Requirements:* Applicant must be enrolled or expecting to enroll at a four-year institution or university and resident of Tennessee. Applicant or parent of applicant must have employment or volunteer experience in police/firefighting. Available to U.S. citizens. *Application Requirements:* Application, FAFSA. *Deadline:* July 15.

Contact Naomi Derryberry, Grant and Scholarship Administrator, Tennessee Student Assistance Corporation, 404 James Robertson Parkway, Suite 1950, Parkway Towers, Nashville, TN 37243-0820. *E-mail:* tsac.aidinfo@state.tn.us. *Phone:* 800-342-1663. *Fax:* 615-741-6101. *Web site:* www.state.tn.us/tsac.

Tennessee Student Assistance Award Program. Assists Tennessee residents attending an approved college or university within the state. Complete a Free Application for Federal Student Aid form. Apply by January 1. FAFSA must be processed by May 1 for priority consideration. *Award:* Grant for use in freshman, sophomore, junior, or senior year; renewable. *Award amount:* $100–$2130. *Number of awards:* 26,000. *Eligibility Requirements:* Applicant must be enrolled or expecting to enroll full or part-time at a two-year, four-year, or technical institution or university; resident of Tennessee and studying in Tennessee. Available to U.S. citizens. *Application Requirements:* Application, financial need analysis. *Deadline:* May 1.

Contact Naomi Derryberry, Grant and Scholarship Administrator, Tennessee Student Assistance Corporation, 404 James Robertson Parkway, Suite 1950, Parkway Towers, Nashville, TN 37243-0820. *E-mail:* naomi.derryberry@state.tn.us. *Phone:* 615-741-1346. *Fax:* 615-741-6101. *Web site:* www.state.tn.us/tsac.

Tennessee Education Lottery Scholarship Program Wilder-Naifeh Technical Skills Grant. Award of $1300 for students enrolled in Tennessee Technology Centers. Cannot be prior recipient of Tennessee HOPE Scholarship. *Award:* Grant for use in freshman, sophomore, junior, or senior year. *Award amount:* $1300. *Number of awards:* varies. *Eligibility Requirements:* Applicant must be enrolled or expecting to enroll full or part-time at a technical institution; resident of Tennessee and studying in Tennessee. Available to U.S. citizens. *Application Requirements:* Application, financial need analysis. *Deadline:* May 1.

Contact Robert Biggers, Lottery Scholarship Program Administrator, Tennessee Student Assistance Corporation, 404 James Robertson Parkway, Suite 1950, Nashville, TN 37243-0820. *E-mail:* tsac.aidinfo@state.tn.us. *Phone:* 800-342-1663. *Fax:* 615-253-3867. *Web site:* www.state.tn.us/tsac.

Tennessee Teaching Scholars Program. Forgivable loan for college juniors, seniors, and college graduates admitted to an education program in Tennessee with a minimum GPA of 2.75. Students must commit to teach in a Tennessee public school one year for each year of the award. *Academic Fields/Career Goals:* Education. *Award:* Forgivable loan for use in junior, senior, or graduate year; not renewable. *Award amount:* $1000–$4200. *Number of awards:* 30–250. *Eligibility Requirements:* Applicant must be enrolled or expecting to enroll full or part-time at a four-year institution or university; resident of Tennessee and studying in Tennessee. Available to U.S. citizens. *Application Requirements:* Application, references, test scores, transcript, letter of intent. *Deadline:* April 15.

Contact Mike McCormack, Scholarship Administrator, Tennessee Student Assistance Corporation, Parkway Towers, Suite 1950, Nashville, TN 37243-0820. *E-mail:* mike.mccormack@state.tn.us. *Phone:* 615-741-1346. *Fax:* 615-741-6101. *Web site:* www.state.tn.us/tsac.

TEXAS

Tuition Equalization Grant (TEG) Program. Renewable award for Texas residents enrolled at least half-time at an independent college or university within the state. Based on financial need. Maintain an overall college GPA of at least 2.5 on a 4.0 scale. Deadlines vary by institution. Must not be receiving athletic scholarship. Contact college/university financial aid office for application information. *Award:* Grant for use in freshman, sophomore, junior, or senior year; renewable. *Award amount:* up to $3444. *Number of awards:* varies. *Eligibility Requirements:* Applicant must be enrolled or expecting to enroll full or part-time at a two-year or four-year institution or university; resident of Texas and studying in Texas. Available to U.S. citizens. *Application Requirements:* Financial need analysis, FAFSA. *Deadline:* varies.

Contact Financial Aid Office, Texas Higher Education Coordinating Board, PO Box 12788, Austin, TX 78711-2788. *E-mail:* grantinfo@thecb.state.tx.us. *Phone:* 512-427-6101. *Fax:* 512-427-6127. *Web site:* www.collegefortexans.com.

Jere W. Thompson, Jr., Scholarship Fund. Renewable scholarships awarded to full-time undergraduate juniors or seniors with a disadvantaged backgrounds, pursuing a degree in civil engineering and closely related disciplines at Texas public colleges and universities. Up to $2000 awarded each semester, beginning with junior year. Must maintain 2.5 GPA. Special consideration given to students from Collin, Dallas, Denton, and Tarrant Counties, Texas Deadline is April 1. *Academic Fields/Career Goals:* Civil Engineering. *Award:* Scholarship for use in junior or senior year; renewable. *Award amount:* up to $2000. *Number of awards:* 2. *Eligibility Requirements:* Applicant must be enrolled or expecting to enroll full-time at a four-year institution or university and resident of Texas. Applicant must have 2.5 GPA or higher. Available to U.S. citizens. *Application Requirements:* Application. *Deadline:* April 1.

Contact Cathy McNally, Scholarship Coordinator, Dallas Architectural Foundation-HKS/John Humphries Minority Scholarship, 900 Jackson Street, Suite 150, Dallas, TX 75202. *E-mail:* cmcnally@dallasfoundation.org. *Phone:* 214-741-9898. *Fax:* 214-741-9848. *Web site:* www.dallasfoundation.org.

Conditional Grant Program. Grants available for up to $6000 ($3000 per semester). Students must be considered economically disadvantaged based on federal guidelines. Must be pursuing a degree in Civil Engineering, Computer Science, Computer Informa-

State Scholarship and Grant Programs
Utah

tion Systems or Management Information Systems. Must be a Texas resident and study in Texas. *Academic Fields/Career Goals:* Civil Engineering; Computer Science/Data Processing. *Award:* Grant for use in freshman, sophomore, junior, or senior year; renewable. *Award amount:* up to $6000. *Number of awards:* varies. *Eligibility Requirements:* Applicant must be American Indian/Alaska Native, Asian/Pacific Islander, Black (non-Hispanic), or Hispanic; enrolled or expecting to enroll full-time at a four-year institution or university; female; resident of Texas and studying in Texas. Applicant must have 2.5 GPA or higher. Available to U.S. citizens. *Application Requirements:* Application, essay, interview, references, test scores, transcript. *Deadline:* March 1.

Contact Minnie Brown, Program Coordinator, Texas Department of Transportation, 125 East 11th Street, Austin, TX 78701-2483. *E-mail:* mbrown2@dot.state.tx.us. *Phone:* 512-416-4979. *Fax:* 512-416-4980. *Web site:* www.dot.state.tx.us.

Academic Common Market Waiver. For Texas residents who are students pursuing a degree in a field of study not offered in Texas. May qualify for special tuition rates. Deadlines vary by institution. Must be studying in the South. *Award:* Scholarship for use in freshman, sophomore, junior, senior, or graduate year; renewable. *Award amount:* varies. *Number of awards:* 1. *Eligibility Requirements:* Applicant must be enrolled or expecting to enroll full or part-time at a four-year institution or university; resident of Texas and studying in Alabama, Arkansas, Florida, Georgia, Kentucky, Louisiana, Mississippi, Missouri, Oklahoma, South Carolina, Tennessee, or Virginia. Available to U.S. citizens. *Application Requirements:* Application. *Deadline:* varies.

Contact Linda McDonough, ACM Coordinator, Texas Higher Education Coordinating Board, PO Box 12788, Austin, TX 78711-2788. *Phone:* 512-427-6525. *Web site:* www.collegefortexans.com.

Texas National Guard Tuition Assistance Program. Provides exemption from the payment of tuition to certain members of the Texas National Guard, Texas Air Guard or the State Guard. Must be Texas resident and attend school in Texas. Visit the TNG Web site at: http://www.agd.state.tx.us/education_office/state_tuition.htm. *Award:* Scholarship for use in freshman, sophomore, junior, or senior year; renewable. *Award amount:* varies. *Number of awards:* varies. *Eligibility Requirements:* Applicant must be enrolled or expecting to enroll at a four-year institution or university; resident of Texas and studying in Texas. Available to U.S. citizens. Applicant must have served in the Air Force National Guard or Army National Guard. *Application Requirements:* Application. *Deadline:* varies.

Contact State Adjutant General's Office, Texas Higher Education Coordinating Board, PO Box 5218, Austin, TX 78763-5218. *E-mail:* education.office@tx.ngb.army.mil. *Phone:* 512-465-5515. *Web site:* www.collegefortexans.com.

Toward Excellence, Access and Success (TEXAS Grant). Renewable aid for students enrolled in a public or private non-profit, college or university in Texas. Based on need. Amount of award is determined by the financial aid office of each school. Deadlines vary. Contact the college/university financial aid office for application information. *Award:* Grant for use in freshman, sophomore, junior, or senior year; renewable. *Award amount:* $1552–$4392. *Number of awards:* varies. *Eligibility Requirements:* Applicant must be enrolled or expecting to enroll full or part-time at a two-year, four-year, or technical institution or university; resident of Texas and studying in Texas. Applicant must have 2.5 GPA or higher. Available to U.S. citizens. *Application Requirements:* Application, financial need analysis, transcript. *Deadline:* varies.

Contact Financial Aid Office, Texas Higher Education Coordinating Board, PO Box 12788, Austin, TX 78711-2788. *E-mail:* grantinfo@thecb.state.tx.us. *Phone:* 512-427-6101. *Fax:* 512-427-6127. *Web site:* www.collegefortexans.com.

Dallas Architectural Foundation—Harrell and Hamilton Scholarship Fund. This program is established to assist students in their final year at one of eight accredited Texas architecture schools, on a rotating basis. Must be a U.S. citizen and permanent resident of Dallas-Fort Worth area. Deadline is March 28. *Academic Fields/Career Goals:* Architecture. *Award:* Scholarship for use in sophomore year; not renewable. *Award amount:* $2500. *Eligibility Requirements:* Applicant must be enrolled or expecting to enroll at a four-year institution or university and resident of Texas. Available to U.S. citizens. *Application Requirements:* Application. *Deadline:* March 28.

Contact Dallas Architectural Foundation-HKS/John Humphries Minority Scholarship, 1444 Oak Lawn Avenue, Suite 600, Dallas, TX 75207. *Phone:* 214-742-3242. *Web site:* www.dallasfoundation.org.

Scholarship For Service (SFS) Program. Scholarships for undergraduate and graduate students. Fully funds the typical costs that students pay for books, tuition, and room and board while attending an approved institution of higher learning. Additionally, participants receive stipends of up to $8000 for undergraduate and $12,000 for graduate students. *Award:* Scholarship for use in junior, senior, or graduate year; renewable. *Award amount:* $8000. *Eligibility Requirements:* Applicant must be enrolled or expecting to enroll full-time at a four-year institution or university. Available to U.S. citizens. *Application Requirements:* *Deadline:* varies.

Contact Scholarship For Service Program Office, Office of Personnel Management, 8610 Broadway, Suite 305, San Antonio, TX 78217-6352. *Web site:* www.sfs.opm.gov.

Outstanding Rural Scholar Program. Award enables rural communities to sponsor a student going into health professions. The students must agree to work in that community once they receive their degree. Must be Texas resident entering a Texas institution on a full-time basis. Must demonstrate financial need. *Academic Fields/Career Goals:* Health and Medical Sciences. *Award:* Scholarship for use in freshman, sophomore, junior, or senior year; renewable. *Award amount:* varies. *Number of awards:* 1. *Eligibility Requirements:* Applicant must be enrolled or expecting to enroll full-time at a four-year institution or university; resident of Texas and studying in Texas. Applicant must have 3.0 GPA or higher. Available to U.S. citizens. *Application Requirements:* Application, financial need analysis, transcript, nomination. *Deadline:* varies.

Contact Office of Rural Community Affairs, Texas Higher Education Coordinating Board, PO Drawer 1708, Austin, TX 78767. *E-mail:* grantinfo@thecb.state.tx.us. *Phone:* 512-479-8891. *Web site:* www.collegefortexans.com.

UTAH

Terrill H. Bell Teaching Incentive Loan. Designed to provide financial assistance to outstanding Utah students pursuing a degree in education. The incentive loan funds full-time tuition and general fees for eight semesters. After graduation/certification the loan may be forgiven if the recipient teaches in a Utah public school or accredited private school (K-12). Loan forgiveness is done on a year-for-year basis. For more details see Web site: http://www.utahsbr.edu *Academic Fields/Career Goals:* Education. *Award:* Forgivable loan for use in freshman, sophomore, junior, senior, or graduate year; renewable. *Award amount:* $900–$2500. *Number of awards:* 365. *Eligibility Requirements:* Applicant must be enrolled or expecting to enroll full-time at a two-

State Scholarship and Grant Programs
Utah

year or four-year institution or university; resident of Utah and studying in Utah. Available to U.S. citizens. *Application Requirements:* Application, essay, references, test scores, transcript. *Deadline:* varies.

Contact Charles Downer, Compliance Officer, Utah State Board of Regents, Board of Regents Building, the Gateway, 60 South 400 West, Salt Lake City, UT 84101-1284. *E-mail:* cdowner@utahsbr.edu. *Phone:* 801-321-7221. *Fax:* 801-366-8470. *Web site:* www.utahsbr.edu/.

Leveraging Educational Assistance Partnership (LEAP). Available to students with substantial financial need for use at participating Utah schools. Contact Financial Aid Office of specific school for application requirements and deadlines. Must be Utah resident. *Award:* Grant for use in freshman, sophomore, junior, or senior year; not renewable. *Award amount:* $300–$2500. *Number of awards:* up to 4008. *Eligibility Requirements:* Applicant must be enrolled or expecting to enroll full or part-time at a two-year, four-year, or technical institution or university; resident of Utah and studying in Utah. Available to U.S. citizens. *Application Requirements:* Application, financial need analysis. *Deadline:* continuous.

Contact Financial Aid Office, Utah Higher Education Assistance Authority. *Phone:* 801-321-7207. *Fax:* 801-366-8470. *Web site:* www.uheaa.org.

Utah Centennial Opportunity Program for Education. Renewable awards for undergraduate college student in Utah institution. Must be a Utah resident. Contact financial aid office at participating institutions for more information. *Award:* Grant for use in freshman, sophomore, junior, or senior year; not renewable. *Award amount:* $300–$5000. *Number of awards:* up to 2807. *Eligibility Requirements:* Applicant must be enrolled or expecting to enroll full or part-time at a two-year, four-year, or technical institution or university; resident of Utah and studying in Utah. Available to U.S. citizens. *Application Requirements:* Application, financial need analysis. *Deadline:* continuous.

Contact Financial Aid Office, Utah Higher Education Assistance Authority. *Phone:* 801-321-7207. *Fax:* 801-366-8470. *Web site:* www.uheaa.org.

New Century Scholarship. Scholarship for qualified high school graduates of Utah. Must attend Utah state-operated college. Award depends on number of hours student enrolled. Please contact for further eligibility requirements. Eligible recipients receive an award equal to 75% of tuition for 60 credit hours toward the completion of a bachelor's degree. For more details see Web site: http://www.utahsbr.edu. *Award:* Scholarship for use in freshman, sophomore, junior, or senior year; renewable. *Award amount:* $1060–$3400. *Number of awards:* 145. *Eligibility Requirements:* Applicant must be enrolled or expecting to enroll full or part-time at a four-year institution or university; resident of Utah and studying in Utah. Available to U.S. citizens. *Application Requirements:* Application, transcript, GPA/copy of enrollment verification from an eligible Utah 4-year institution, verification from Registrar of completion of requirements for associate's degree. *Deadline:* continuous.

Contact Charles Downer, Compliance Officer, Utah State Board of Regents, Board of Regents Building, the Gateway, 60 South 400 West, Salt Lake City, UT 84101-1284. *E-mail:* cdowner@utahsbr.edu. *Phone:* 801-321-7221. *Fax:* 801-366-8470. *Web site:* www.utahsbr.edu/.

VERMONT

Vermont Teacher Diversity Scholarship Program. Loan forgiveness program for students from diverse racial and ethnic backgrounds who attend college in Vermont with a goal of becoming public school teachers. After three years of teaching in the Vermont public school system, they may receive up to $12,000 in loan forgiveness. Preference will be given to residents of Vermont. Application and information available on Web site: http://templeton.vsc.edu/teacherdiversity. Applications are due in April or November. *Academic Fields/Career Goals:* Education. *Award:* Forgivable loan for use in freshman, sophomore, junior, senior, or graduate year; not renewable. *Award amount:* up to $4000. *Number of awards:* up to 4. *Eligibility Requirements:* Applicant must be American Indian/Alaska Native, Asian/Pacific Islander, Black (non-Hispanic), or Hispanic; enrolled or expecting to enroll full or part-time at a four-year institution or university and studying in Vermont. Available to U.S. citizens. *Application Requirements:* Application, resume, references, transcript. *Deadline:* April 6.

Contact Ms. Phyl Newbeck, Director, Vermont Teacher Diversity Scholarship Program, PO Box 359, Waterbury, VT 05676-0359. *Phone:* 802-241-3379. *Fax:* 802-241-3369. *Web site:* www.templeton.vsc.edu/teacherdiversity/.

Vermont Incentive Grants. Renewable grants for Vermont residents based on financial need. Must meet needs test. Must be college undergraduate or graduate student enrolled full-time at an approved post secondary institution. Only available to U.S. citizens or permanent residents. *Award:* Grant for use in freshman, sophomore, junior, senior, or graduate year; renewable. *Award amount:* $500–$9800. *Number of awards:* varies. *Eligibility Requirements:* Applicant must be enrolled or expecting to enroll full-time at a two-year, four-year, or technical institution or university and resident of Vermont. Available to U.S. citizens. *Application Requirements:* Application, financial need analysis, FAFSA. *Deadline:* continuous.

Contact Grant Program, Vermont Student Assistance Corporation, PO Box 2000, Winooski, VT 05404-2000. *Phone:* 802-655-9602. *Fax:* 802-654-3765. *Web site:* services.vsac.org/ilwwcm/connect/VSAC.

Vermont Part-time Student Grants. For undergraduates carrying less than twelve credits per semester who have not received a bachelor's degree. Must be Vermont resident. Based on financial need. Complete Vermont Financial Aid Packet to apply. May be used at any approved post secondary institution. *Award:* Grant for use in freshman, sophomore, junior, or senior year; renewable. *Award amount:* $250–$7350. *Number of awards:* varies. *Eligibility Requirements:* Applicant must be enrolled or expecting to enroll part-time at a four-year institution or university and resident of Vermont. Available to U.S. citizens. *Application Requirements:* Application, financial need analysis. *Deadline:* continuous.

Contact Grant Program, Vermont Student Assistance Corporation, PO Box 2000, Winooski, VT 05404-2000. *Phone:* 802-655-9602. *Fax:* 802-654-3765. *Web site:* services.vsac.org/ilwwcm/connect/VSAC.

VIRGINIA

State Department Federal Credit Union Annual Scholarship Program. Scholarships available to members who are currently enrolled in a degree program and have completed 12 credit hours of coursework at an accredited college or university. Must have an account in good standing in their name with SDFCU, have a minimum 2.5 GPA, submit official cumulative transcripts, and describe need for financial assistance to continue their education. *Award:* Scholarship for use in freshman, sophomore, junior, or senior year; renewable. *Eligibility Requirements:* Applicant must be enrolled or expecting to enroll at a four-year institution or university. Applicant must have 2.5 GPA or higher. Available to U.S.

State Scholarship and Grant Programs
Virginia

citizens. *Application Requirements:* Application, financial need analysis, transcript. *Deadline:* April 14.

Contact Scholarship Coordinator, State Department Federal Credit Union Annual Scholarship Program, SDFCU, 1630 King Street, Alexandria, VA 22314. *E-mail:* marketing@sdfcu.org. *Phone:* 703-706-5019. *Web site:* www.sdfcu.org/youth/scholar.html.

Virginia Commonwealth Award. Need-based award for undergraduate or graduate study at a Virginia public two- or four-year college, or university. Undergraduates must be Virginia residents. The application and awards process are administered by the financial aid office at the Virginia public institution where student is enrolled. Contact financial aid office for application and deadlines. *Award:* Grant for use in freshman, sophomore, junior, senior, or graduate year; renewable. *Award amount:* varies. *Number of awards:* varies. *Eligibility Requirements:* Applicant must be enrolled or expecting to enroll full or part-time at a two-year or four-year institution or university; resident of Virginia and studying in Virginia. Available to U.S. citizens. *Application Requirements:* Application, financial need analysis, FAFSA.

Contact Lee Andes, Assistant Director for Financial Aid, State Council of Higher Education for Virginia, James Monroe Building, 10th Floor, 101 North 14th Street, Richmond, VA 23219. *E-mail:* leeandes@schev.edu. *Phone:* 804-225-2614. *Fax:* 804-225-2604. *Web site:* www.schev.edu.

Mary Marshall Practical Nursing Scholarships. Award for practical nursing students who are Virginia residents. Must attend a nursing program in Virginia. Recipient must agree to work in Virginia after graduation. Minimum 3.0 GPA required. Recipients may reapply up to three years for an award. *Academic Fields/Career Goals:* Nursing. *Award:* Scholarship for use in freshman, sophomore, junior, or senior year; not renewable. *Award amount:* $100–$1200. *Number of awards:* varies. *Eligibility Requirements:* Applicant must be enrolled or expecting to enroll full or part-time at a two-year or technical institution; resident of Virginia and studying in Virginia. Applicant must have 3.0 GPA or higher. Available to U.S. citizens. *Application Requirements:* Application, financial need analysis, references, transcript. *Deadline:* June 30.

Contact Norma Marrin, Business Manager/Policy Analyst, Virginia Department of Health, Office of Health Policy and Planning, PO Box 2448, Richmond, VA 23218-2448. *E-mail:* norma.marrin@vdh.virginia.gov. *Phone:* 804-864-7433. *Fax:* 804-864-7440. *Web site:* www.vdh.virginia.gov.

Vice Admiral Robert L. Walters Scholarship. Scholarship for a child, stepchild, ward, or spouse of a Surface Navy Association member. The member must be in their second or subsequent consecutive year of membership. *Award:* Scholarship for use in freshman, sophomore, junior, or senior year; renewable. *Award amount:* $2000. *Eligibility Requirements:* Applicant must be enrolled or expecting to enroll at a four-year institution or university. Applicant must have 3.0 GPA or higher. Available to U.S. citizens. *Application Requirements:* Application, essay, references, transcript. *Deadline:* March 15.

Contact Surface Navy Association, 2550 Huntington Avenue, Suite 202, Alexandria, VA 22303. *Web site:* www.navysna.org.

Gheens Foundation Scholarship. This scholarship supports students from Louisville, Kentucky, who are enrolled in a HBCU participating school. Please visit Web site for more information: http://www.uncf.org *Award:* Scholarship for use in freshman, sophomore, junior, senior, or graduate year. *Award amount:* up to $2000. *Number of awards:* varies. *Eligibility Requirements:* Applicant must be Black (non-Hispanic); enrolled or expecting to enroll at a four-year institution or university and resident of Kentucky. Applicant must have 2.5 GPA or higher. Available to U.S. citizens. *Application Requirements:* Application, financial need analysis, transcript. *Deadline:* varies.

Contact Rebecca Bennett, Director, Program Services, United Negro College Fund, 8260 Willow Oaks Corporate Drive, Fairfax, VA 22031-8044. *E-mail:* rbennett@uncf.org. *Phone:* 800-331-2244. *Web site:* www.uncf.org.

Virginia War Orphans Education Program. Scholarships for postsecondary students between ages 16 and 25 to attend Virginia state supported institutions. Must be child or surviving child of veteran who has either been permanently or totally disabled due to war or other armed conflict; died as a result of war or other armed conflict; or been listed as a POW or MIA. Parent must also meet Virginia residency requirements. Contact for application procedures and deadline. *Award:* Scholarship for use in freshman, sophomore, junior, senior, or graduate year; renewable. *Award amount:* varies. *Number of awards:* varies. *Eligibility Requirements:* Applicant must be age 16-25; enrolled or expecting to enroll full-time at a two-year, four-year, or technical institution or university; resident of Virginia and studying in Virginia. Available to U.S. citizens. Applicant or parent must meet one or more of the following requirements: general military experience; retired from active duty; disabled or killed as a result of military service; prisoner of war; or missing in action. *Application Requirements:* Application. *Deadline:* varies.

Contact Doris Marie Sullivan, Coordinator, Virginia Department of Veterans Services, Poff Federal Building, 270 Franklin Road SW, Room 503, Roanoke, VA 24011-2215. *Phone:* 540-857-7101 Ext. 213. *Fax:* 540-857-7573. *Web site:* www.vdva.vipnet.org/education_benefits.htm.

College Scholarship Assistance Program. Need-based scholarship for undergraduate study by a Virginia resident at a participating Virginia two- or four-year college, or university. Contact financial aid office at the participating institution. *Award:* Grant for use in freshman, sophomore, junior, or senior year; renewable. *Award amount:* $400–$5000. *Number of awards:* varies. *Eligibility Requirements:* Applicant must be enrolled or expecting to enroll full or part-time at a two-year or four-year institution or university; resident of Virginia and studying in Virginia. Available to U.S. citizens. *Application Requirements:* Application, financial need analysis, FAFSA.

Contact Lee Andes, Assistant Director for Financial Aid, State Council of Higher Education for Virginia, James Monroe Building, 10th Floor, 101 North 14th Street, Richmond, VA 23219. *E-mail:* leeandes@schev.edu. *Phone:* 804-225-2614. *Fax:* 804-225-2604. *Web site:* www.schev.edu.

Walter Reed Smith Scholarship. Award for full-time female undergraduate student who is a descendant of a Confederate soldier, studying nutrition, home economics, nursing, business administration, or computer science. Must carry a minimum of 12 credit hours each semester and have a minimum 3.0 GPA. Submit letter of endorsement from sponsoring chapter of the United Daughters of the Confederacy. Scholarship amount for the entire academic year will be sent to college/university. *Academic Fields/Career Goals:* Business/Consumer Services; Computer Science/Data Processing; Food Science/Nutrition; Home Economics; Nursing. *Award:* Scholarship for use in freshman, sophomore, junior, or senior year; renewable. *Award amount:* $800–$1000. *Number of awards:* 1–2. *Eligibility Requirements:* Applicant must be enrolled or expecting to enroll full-time at a four-year institution or university and female. Applicant or parent of applicant must be member of United Daughters of the Confederacy. Applicant must have 3.0 GPA or higher. Available to U.S. citizens. *Application Requirements:* Application, essay, financial need analysis, photo, refer-

State Scholarship and Grant Programs
Virginia

ences, self-addressed stamped envelope, transcript, confederate ancestor's proof of service. *Deadline:* March 15.

Contact Robert C. Kraus, Second Vice President General, United Daughters of the Confederacy, 328 North Boulevard, Richmond, VA 23220-4057. *Phone:* 804-355-1636. *Web site:* www.hqudc.org.

Mary Marshall Registered Nursing Program Scholarships. Award for registered nursing students who are Virginia residents. Must attend a nursing program in Virginia. Recipient must agree to work in Virginia after graduation. Minimum 3.0 GPA required. Recipient may reapply up to three years for an award. *Academic Fields/Career Goals:* Nursing. *Award:* Scholarship for use in freshman, sophomore, junior, or senior year; not renewable. *Award amount:* $100–$1200. *Number of awards:* 60–100. *Eligibility Requirements:* Applicant must be enrolled or expecting to enroll full or part-time at a two-year or four-year institution or university; resident of Virginia and studying in Virginia. Applicant must have 3.0 GPA or higher. Available to U.S. citizens. *Application Requirements:* Application, financial need analysis, references, transcript. *Deadline:* June 30.

Contact Norma Marrin, Business Manager/Policy Analyst, Virginia Department of Health, Office of Health Policy and Planning, PO Box 2448, Richmond, VA 23218-2448. *E-mail:* norma.marrin@vdh.virginia.gov. *Phone:* 804-864-7433. *Fax:* 804-864-7440. *Web site:* www.vdh.virginia.gov.

Southside Virginia Tobacco Teacher Scholarship/Loan. Need-based scholarship for Southside Virginia natives to pursue a degree in K-12 teacher education in any four-year U.S. institution and then return to the Southside region to live and work. Must teach in Southside Virginia public school for scholarship/loan forgiveness. *Academic Fields/Career Goals:* Education. *Award:* Forgivable loan for use in freshman, sophomore, junior, or senior year; renewable. *Award amount:* up to $4000. *Number of awards:* varies. *Eligibility Requirements:* Applicant must be enrolled or expecting to enroll full or part-time at a two-year or four-year institution or university and resident of Virginia. Available to U.S. citizens. *Application Requirements:* Application, financial need analysis, FAFSA.

Contact Christine Fields, State Council of Higher Education for Virginia, PO Box 1987, Abingdon, VA 24212. *Phone:* 276-619-4376 Ext. 4002. *Web site:* www.schev.edu.

Virginia Guaranteed Assistance Program. Awards to undergraduate students proportional to their need, up to full tuition, fees and book allowance. Must be a graduate of a Virginia high school, not homeschooled. High school GPA of 2.5 required. Must be enrolled full-time in a Virginia 2- or 4-year institution and demonstrate financial need. Contact financial aid office of your institution for application process and deadlines. Must maintain minimum college GPA of 2.0 for renewal awards. *Award:* Scholarship for use in freshman, sophomore, junior, or senior year; renewable. *Award amount:* varies. *Number of awards:* varies. *Eligibility Requirements:* Applicant must be enrolled or expecting to enroll full-time at a two-year or four-year institution or university; resident of Virginia and studying in Virginia. Applicant must have 2.5 GPA or higher. Available to U.S. citizens. *Application Requirements:* Application, financial need analysis, transcript, FAFSA.

Contact Lee Andes, Assistant Director for Financial Aid, State Council of Higher Education for Virginia, James Monroe Building, 10th Floor, 101 North 14th Street, Richmond, VA 23219. *E-mail:* leeandes@schev.edu. *Phone:* 804-225-2614. *Fax:* 804-225-2604. *Web site:* www.schev.edu.

Virginia Tuition Assistance Grant Program (Private Institutions). Renewable awards of approximately $1900-$2500 each for undergraduate, graduate, and first professional degree students attending an approved private, non-profit college within Virginia. Must be a Virginia resident and be enrolled full-time. Not to be used for religious study. Preferred deadline July 31. Others are waitlisted. Information and application available from participating Virginia colleges' financial aid office. *Award:* Grant for use in freshman, sophomore, junior, senior, or graduate year; renewable. *Award amount:* $1900–$2500. *Number of awards:* 18,600. *Eligibility Requirements:* Applicant must be enrolled or expecting to enroll full-time at a four-year institution or university; resident of Virginia and studying in Virginia. Available to U.S. citizens. *Application Requirements:* Application. *Deadline:* July 31.

Contact Lee Andes, Financial Aid Manager, State Council of Higher Education for Virginia, James Monroe Building, 10th Floor, 101 North 14th Street, Richmond, VA 23219. *E-mail:* fainfo@schev.edu. *Phone:* 804-225-2614. *Web site:* www.schev.edu.

WASHINGTON

Washington Award for Vocational Excellence (WAVE). Award to honor three vocational students from each of the state's 49 legislative districts. Grants for up to two years of undergraduate resident tuition. Must be enrolled in Washington high school, skills center, or technical college at time of application. Complete 360 hours in single vocational program in high school or one year at technical college. Contact principal or guidance counselor for more information. *Award:* Grant for use in freshman, sophomore, junior, or senior year; renewable. *Award amount:* varies. *Number of awards:* up to 147. *Eligibility Requirements:* Applicant must be enrolled or expecting to enroll full-time at a two-year, four-year, or technical institution or university; resident of Washington and studying in Washington. Available to U.S. citizens. *Application Requirements:* *Deadline:* continuous.

Contact Ann Lee, Program Manager, Washington Higher Education Coordinating Board, 917 Lakeridge Way, SW, PO Box 43430, Olympia, WA 98504-3430. *E-mail:* annl@hecb.wa.gov. *Phone:* 360-753-7843. *Fax:* 360-753-7808. *Web site:* www.hecb.wa.gov.

Washington Award for Vocational Excellence. Tuition-only award for those completing a vocational education program as graduating seniors or community/technical college students who have completed first year of a two-year program. The scholarship is for 6 quarters or 4 semesters. Three are awarded in each of 49 legislative districts in the state. Must be a Washington State resident attending a postsecondary institution in Washington State. *Award:* Grant for use in freshman, sophomore, junior, or senior year; renewable. *Award amount:* $2445–$5506. *Number of awards:* 147. *Eligibility Requirements:* Applicant must be enrolled or expecting to enroll full or part-time at a two-year, four-year, or technical institution or university; resident of Washington and studying in Washington. Available to U.S. and non-U.S. citizens. *Application Requirements:* Application, essay, references. *Deadline:* March 1.

Contact Lee Williams, Program Administrator, Washington State Workforce Training and Education Coordinating Board, 128 10th Avenue SW, PO Box 43105, Olympia, WA 98504-3105. *E-mail:* lwilliams@wtb.wa.gov. *Phone:* 360-586-3321. *Fax:* 360-586-5862. *Web site:* www.wtb.wa.gov/.

Washington National Guard Scholarship Program. A state funded retention incentive/loan program for both Washington Army and Air Guard members meeting all eligibility requirements. The loans are forgiven if the soldier/airman completes their service requirements. Failure to meet/complete service obligations incurs the requirement to repay the loan plus 8% interest. Minimum 2.5 GPA required.

State Scholarship and Grant Programs
Washington

Deadline is April 30. *Award:* Forgivable loan for use in freshman, sophomore, junior, or senior year; not renewable. *Award amount:* $200–$4000. *Number of awards:* varies. *Eligibility Requirements:* Applicant must be enrolled or expecting to enroll full or part-time at a two-year, four-year, or technical institution or university and resident of Washington. Applicant must have 2.5 GPA or higher. Available to U.S. and non-U.S. citizens. Applicant must have served in the Air Force National Guard or Army National Guard. *Application Requirements:* Application, transcript, enlistment/extension documents. *Deadline:* April 30.

Contact Mark M. Rhoden, Educational Services Officer, Washington National Guard, Building 15, Camp Murray, Tacoma, WA 98430-5073. *E-mail:* mark.rhoden@wa.ngb.army.mil. *Phone:* 253-512-8899. *Fax:* 253-512-8936. *Web site:* www.washingtonguard.com.

State Need Grant. Grants for undergraduate students with significant financial need. Must be Washington resident and attend school in Washington. Must have family income equal or less than 55% of state median. The financial aid office at each school makes awards to eligible students. *Award:* Grant for use in freshman, sophomore, junior, or senior year; renewable. *Award amount:* $2200–$4300. *Number of awards:* 55,000. *Eligibility Requirements:* Applicant must be enrolled or expecting to enroll full or part-time at a two-year, four-year, or technical institution or university; resident of Washington and studying in Washington. Available to U.S. citizens. *Application Requirements:* Application, financial need analysis, FAFSA. *Deadline:* continuous.

Contact Financial Aid Director of school to which you are applying, Washington Higher Education Coordinating Board. *Web site:* www.hecb.wa.gov.

Washington Promise Scholarship. College scholarships to low- and middle-income students in high school. Must either rank in top 15 percent of senior class or score a combined 1200 on SAT or 27 on ACT on first attempt. Family income cannot exceed 135% of state median family income. Must be Washington resident, attend a Washington school. School must identify applicants. Contact principal or guidance counselor for more information. *Award:* Scholarship for use in freshman or sophomore year; renewable. *Award amount:* up to $1000. *Number of awards:* varies. *Eligibility Requirements:* Applicant must be high school student; planning to enroll or expecting to enroll full or part-time at a two-year, four-year, or technical institution or university; resident of Washington and studying in Washington. Available to U.S. citizens. *Application Requirements:* Financial need analysis. *Deadline:* continuous.

Contact John Klacik, Washington Higher Education Coordinating Board, 917 Lakeridge Way, SW, PO Box 43430, Olympia, WA 98504-3430. *E-mail:* johnk@hecb.wa.gov. *Phone:* 360-753-7851. *Fax:* 360-753-7808. *Web site:* www.hecb.wa.gov.

American Indian Endowed Scholarship. Awarded to financially needy undergraduate and graduate students with close social and cultural ties to a Native-American community. Must be Washington resident, enrolled full time at Washington School. Deadline is May 15. *Award:* Scholarship for use in freshman, sophomore, junior, senior, or graduate year; renewable. *Award amount:* $500–$2000. *Number of awards:* up to 15. *Eligibility Requirements:* Applicant must be American Indian/Alaska Native; enrolled or expecting to enroll full-time at a two-year, four-year, or technical institution or university; resident of Washington and studying in Washington. Available to U.S. citizens. *Application Requirements:* Application, financial need analysis. *Deadline:* May 15.

Contact Ann Lee, Washington Higher Education Coordinating Board, 917 Lakeridge Way, SW, PO Box 43430, Olympia, WA 98504-3430. *E-mail:* annl@hecb.wa.gov. *Phone:* 360-755-7843. *Fax:* 360-753-7808. *Web site:* www.hecb.wa.gov.

Future Teachers Conditional Scholarship and Loan Repayment Program. This program is designed to encourage outstanding students and paraprofessionals to become teachers. In return for conditional scholarships or loan repayments, participants agree to teach in Washington K-12 schools. Additional consideration is given to individuals seeking certification or additional endorsements in teacher subject shortage areas, as well as to individuals with demonstrated bilingual ability. Must be residents of Washington and attend an institution in Washington. *Academic Fields/Career Goals:* Education. *Award:* Forgivable loan for use in freshman, sophomore, junior, or senior year; renewable. *Award amount:* $600–$5000. *Number of awards:* 50. *Eligibility Requirements:* Applicant must be enrolled or expecting to enroll full or part-time at a two-year or four-year institution or university; resident of Washington and studying in Washington. Available to U.S. citizens. *Application Requirements:* Application, essay, references, transcript, bilingual verification (if applicable). *Deadline:* October 15.

Contact Mary Knutson, Program Coordinator, Washington Higher Education Coordinating Board, 917 Lakeridge Way, SW, PO Box 43430, Olympia, WA 98504-3430. *E-mail:* futureteachers@hecb.wa.gov. *Phone:* 360-753-7800. *Fax:* 360-753-7808. *Web site:* www.hecb.wa.gov.

Educational Opportunity Grant. Annual grants of $2500 to encourage financially needy, place bound students to complete bachelor's degree. Must be unable to continue education due to family or work commitments, health concerns, financial needs or similar. Must be Washington residents, live in one of 13 designated counties, and have completed two years of college. Grant only used at eligible four-year colleges in Washington. Applications accepted beginning in April and following months until funds are depleted. *Award:* Grant for use in freshman, sophomore, junior, or senior year; renewable. *Award amount:* $2500. *Number of awards:* 1350. *Eligibility Requirements:* Applicant must be enrolled or expecting to enroll full-time at a four-year institution or university; resident of Washington and studying in Washington. Available to U.S. citizens. *Application Requirements:* Application, financial need analysis. *Deadline:* continuous.

Contact Dawn Cypriano-McAferty, Program Manager, Washington Higher Education Coordinating Board, 917 Lakeridge Way, SW, PO Box 43430, Olympia, WA 98504-3430. *E-mail:* eog@hecb.wa.gov. *Phone:* 360-753-7800. *Fax:* 360-753-7808. *Web site:* www.hecb.wa.gov.

Washington Scholars Program. Awarded to three high school students from each of the 49 state legislative districts. Must be Washington resident and enroll in college or university in Washington. Scholarships equal up to four years of full-time resident undergraduate tuition and fees. Contact principal or guidance counselor for more information. *Award:* Grant for use in freshman, sophomore, junior, or senior year; renewable. *Award amount:* varies. *Number of awards:* varies. *Eligibility Requirements:* Applicant must be high school student; planning to enroll or expecting to enroll full-time at a four-year institution or university; resident of Washington and studying in Washington. Available to U.S. citizens. *Application Requirements:* *Deadline:* continuous.

Contact Ann Lee, Program Manager, Washington Higher Education Coordinating Board, 917 Lakeridge Way, SW, PO Box 43430, Olympia, WA 98504-3430. *E-mail:* annl@hecb.wa.gov. *Phone:* 360-753-7843. *Fax:* 360-753-7808. *Web site:* www.hecb.wa.gov.

State Scholarship and Grant Programs
West Virginia

WEST VIRGINIA

Higher Education Adult Part-time Student Grant Program. Program to assist needy adult students to continue their education on a part-time basis. Also has a component in which 25% of the funding may be utilized for students enrolled in workforce and skill development programs. Contact institution financial aid office for more information and deadlines. *Award:* Grant for use in freshman, sophomore, junior, or senior year; not renewable. *Number of awards:* varies. *Eligibility Requirements:* Applicant must be enrolled or expecting to enroll full or part-time at a two-year, four-year, or technical institution or university; resident of West Virginia and studying in West Virginia. Available to U.S. citizens. *Application Requirements:* Application, financial need analysis. *Deadline:* varies.

Contact: Judy Kee, Financial Aid Manager, West Virginia Higher Education Policy Commission-Office of Financial Aid and Outreach Services, 1018 Kanawha Boulevard East, Suite 700, Charleston, WV 25301. *E-mail:* kee@hepc.wvnet.edu. *Phone:* 304-558-4618. *Fax:* 304-558-4622. *Web site:* www.hepc.wvnet.edu.

Promise Scholarship. Renewable award for West Virginia residents. Minimum 3.0 GPA, ACT composite of 21, with 19 on each subtest, and combined SAT score of 1000, with no less than 470 verbal and 460 math. Provides full tuition scholarship to a state college or university in West Virginia or an equivalent scholarship to an in-state private college. Financial resources are not a factor. *Award:* Scholarship for use in freshman, sophomore, junior, or senior year; renewable. *Award amount:* $3000. *Number of awards:* 3500. *Eligibility Requirements:* Applicant must be high school student; planning to enroll or expecting to enroll full-time at a two-year or four-year institution or university; resident of West Virginia and studying in West Virginia. Applicant must have 3.0 GPA or higher. Available to U.S. citizens. *Application Requirements:* Application, financial need analysis, test scores, transcript. *Deadline:* January 31.

Contact: Lisa DeFrank-Cole, Executive Director, West Virginia Higher Education Policy Commission-Office of Financial Aid and Outreach Services, 1018 Kanawha Boulevard East, Suite 700, Charleston, WV 25301. *Phone:* 304-558-4417. *Fax:* 304-558-3264. *Web site:* www.hepc.wvnet.edu.

Underwood-Smith Teacher Scholarship Program. For West Virginia residents at West Virginia institutions pursuing teaching careers. Must have a 3.25 GPA after completion of two years of course work. Must teach two years in West Virginia public schools for each year the award is received. Recipients will be required to sign an agreement acknowledging an understanding of the program's requirements and their willingness to repay the award if appropriate teaching service is not rendered. *Academic Fields/Career Goals:* Education. *Award:* Scholarship for use in junior, senior, or graduate year; renewable. *Award amount:* $1620–$5000. *Number of awards:* 53. *Eligibility Requirements:* Applicant must be enrolled or expecting to enroll full-time at a four-year institution or university; resident of West Virginia and studying in West Virginia. Available to U.S. citizens. *Application Requirements:* Application, essay, references. *Deadline:* March 1.

Contact: Michelle Wicks, Scholarship Coordinator, West Virginia Higher Education Policy Commission-Office of Financial Aid and Outreach Services, 1018 Kanawha Boulevard East, Suite 700, Charleston, WV 25301. *E-mail:* wicks@hepc.wvnet.edu. *Phone:* 304-558-4618. *Fax:* 304-558-4622. *Web site:* www.hepc.wvnet.edu.

West Virginia Division of Veterans' Affairs War Orphans Education Program. Renewable waiver of tuition award for West Virginia residents who are children of deceased veterans. Parent must have died of war related service-connected disability. Must be ages 16-23. Minimum 2.0 GPA required. Must attend a state-supported West Virginia postsecondary institution. Deadline: July 1 and December 1. *Award:* Scholarship for use in freshman, sophomore, junior, senior, or graduate year; renewable. *Award amount:* varies. *Number of awards:* varies. *Eligibility Requirements:* Applicant must be age 16-23; enrolled or expecting to enroll full or part-time at a two-year, four-year, or technical institution or university; resident of West Virginia and studying in West Virginia. Available to U.S. citizens. Applicant or parent must meet one or more of the following requirements: general military experience; retired from active duty; disabled or killed as a result of military service; prisoner of war; or missing in action. *Application Requirements:* Application, references. *Deadline:* varies.

Contact: Ms. Linda Walker, Administrative Secretary, West Virginia Division of Veterans' Affairs, 1321 Plaza East, Suite 101, Charleston, WV 25301-1400. *E-mail:* wvdva@state.wv.us. *Phone:* 304-558-3661. *Fax:* 304-558-3662. *Web site:* www.state.wv.us/va.

West Virginia Engineering, Science & Technology Scholarship Program. For students attending West Virginia institutions full-time pursuing a career in engineering, science, or technology. Must have a 3.0 GPA on a 4.0 scale. Must work in the fields of engineering, science, or technology in West Virginia one year for each year the award is received. *Academic Fields/Career Goals:* Electrical Engineering/Electronics; Engineering/Technology; Engineering-Related Technologies; Science, Technology, and Society. *Award:* Scholarship for use in freshman, sophomore, junior, or senior year; renewable. *Award amount:* up to $3000. *Number of awards:* 250. *Eligibility Requirements:* Applicant must be enrolled or expecting to enroll full-time at a two-year, four-year, or technical institution or university and studying in West Virginia. Applicant must have 3.0 GPA or higher. Available to U.S. citizens. *Application Requirements:* Application, essay, test scores, transcript. *Deadline:* March 1.

Contact: Michelle Wicks, Scholarship Coordinator, West Virginia Higher Education Policy Commission-Office of Financial Aid and Outreach Services, 1018 Kanawha Boulevard East, Suite 700, Charleston, WV 25301. *E-mail:* wicks@hepc.wvnet.edu. *Phone:* 304-558-4618. *Fax:* 304-558-4622. *Web site:* www.hepc.wvnet.edu.

West Virginia Higher Education Grant Program. For West Virginia residents attending an approved nonprofit degree granting college or university in West Virginia or Pennsylvania. Must be enrolled full-time. Based on financial need and academic merit. Award covers tuition and fees. *Award:* Grant for use in freshman, sophomore, junior, or senior year; renewable. *Award amount:* $350–$2846. *Number of awards:* 10,755–11,000. *Eligibility Requirements:* Applicant must be enrolled or expecting to enroll full-time at a two-year or four-year institution or university; resident of West Virginia and studying in Pennsylvania or West Virginia. Available to U.S. citizens. *Application Requirements:* Application, financial need analysis, test scores, transcript. *Deadline:* March 1.

Contact: Daniel Crockett, Director of Student and Educational Services, West Virginia Higher Education Policy Commission-Office of Financial Aid and Outreach Services, 1018 Kanawha Boulevard East, Suite 700, Charleston, WV 25301-2827. *E-mail:* crockett@hepc.wvnet.edu. *Phone:* 888-825-5707. *Fax:* 304-558-4618. *Web site:* www.hepc.wvnet.edu.

WISCONSIN

Wisconsin Department of Veterans Affairs Retraining Grants. Renewable award for veterans, unmarried spouses of deceased veterans, or dependents of deceased veterans. Must be resident of Wisconsin and attend an institution in Wisconsin. Veteran must be recently unemployed and show financial need. Must enroll in a vocational or technical program that can reasonably be expected to lead to employment. Course work at four-year colleges or universities does not qualify as retraining. *Award:* Grant for use in freshman or sophomore year; renewable. *Award amount:* up to $3000. *Number of awards:* varies. *Eligibility Requirements:* Applicant must be enrolled or expecting to enroll full or part-time at a technical institution; resident of Wisconsin and studying in Wisconsin. Available to U.S. citizens. Applicant or parent must meet one or more of the following requirements: general military experience; retired from active duty; disabled or killed as a result of military service; prisoner of war; or missing in action. *Application Requirements:* Application, financial need analysis. *Deadline:* varies.

Contact Mike Keatley, Grants Coordinator, Wisconsin Department of Veterans Affairs, PO Box 7843, Madison, WI 53707-7843. *E-mail:* mike.keatley@dva.state.wi.us. *Phone:* 608-266-1311. *Web site:* www.dva.state.wi.us.

Wisconsin Veterans Part-time Study Reimbursement Grant. Open only to Wisconsin veterans. Renewable for continuing study. Contact office for more details. Application deadline is no later than sixty days after the course completion. Veterans may be reimbursed up to 100% of tuition and fees. *Award:* Grant for use in freshman, sophomore, junior, or senior year; renewable. *Award amount:* $300–$2000. *Number of awards:* varies. *Eligibility Requirements:* Applicant must be enrolled or expecting to enroll part-time at a four-year, or technical institution or university; resident of Wisconsin and studying in Wisconsin. Available to U.S. citizens. Applicant or parent must meet one or more of the following requirements: general military experience; retired from active duty; disabled or killed as a result of military service; prisoner of war; or missing in action. *Application Requirements:* Application. *Deadline:* varies.

Contact Mike Keatley, Grants Coordinator, Wisconsin Department of Veterans Affairs, PO Box 7843, Madison, WI 53707-7843. *Phone:* 608-266-1311. *Web site:* www.dva.state.wi.us.

Minority Undergraduate Retention Grant-Wisconsin. Provides financial assistance to African-American, Native-American, Hispanic, and former citizens of Laos, Vietnam, and Cambodia, for study in Wisconsin. Must be Wisconsin resident, enrolled at least half-time in a two-year or four-year nonprofit college, and must show financial need. Please refer to Web site for further details: http://www.heab.state.wi.us *Award:* Grant for use in freshman, sophomore, junior, senior, or graduate year; not renewable. *Award amount:* $250–$2500. *Number of awards:* varies. *Eligibility Requirements:* Applicant must be American Indian/Alaska Native, Asian/Pacific Islander, Black (non-Hispanic), or Hispanic; enrolled or expecting to enroll full or part-time at a two-year, four-year, or technical institution or university; resident of Wisconsin and studying in Wisconsin. Available to U.S. and non-U.S. citizens. *Application Requirements:* Application, financial need analysis. *Deadline:* continuous.

Contact Mary Lou Kuzdas, Program Coordinator, Wisconsin Higher Educational Aids Board, PO Box 7885, Madison, WI 53707-7885. *E-mail:* mary.kuzdas@heab.state.wi.us. *Phone:* 608-267-2212. *Fax:* 608-267-2808. *Web site:* www.heab.state.wi.us.

Nursing Student Loan Program. Provides forgivable loans to students enrolled in a nursing program. Must be a Wisconsin resident studying in Wisconsin. Application deadline is last day on which student is enrolled. Please refer to Web site for further details: http://www.heab.state.wi.us *Academic Fields/Career Goals:* Nursing. *Award:* Forgivable loan for use in freshman, sophomore, junior, or senior year; renewable. *Award amount:* $250–$3000. *Number of awards:* 150–1800. *Eligibility Requirements:* Applicant must be enrolled or expecting to enroll full or part-time at a two-year, four-year, or technical institution or university; resident of Wisconsin and studying in Wisconsin. Available to U.S. citizens. *Application Requirements:* Application, financial need analysis.

Contact Cindy Lehrman, Program Coordinator, Wisconsin Higher Educational Aids Board, PO Box 7885, Madison, WI 53707-7885. *E-mail:* cindy.lehrman@heab.state.wi.us. *Phone:* 608-267-2209. *Fax:* 608-267-2808. *Web site:* www.heab.state.wi.us.

Talent Incentive Program Grant. Assists residents of Wisconsin who are attending a nonprofit institution in Wisconsin and have substantial financial need. Must meet income criteria, be considered economically and educationally disadvantaged and be enrolled at least half-time. Please refer to Web site for further details: http://www.heab.state.wi.us *Award:* Grant for use in freshman, sophomore, junior, or senior year; renewable. *Award amount:* $250–$1800. *Number of awards:* varies. *Eligibility Requirements:* Applicant must be enrolled or expecting to enroll full or part-time at a two-year, four-year, or technical institution or university; resident of Wisconsin and studying in Wisconsin. Available to U.S. citizens. *Application Requirements:* Financial need analysis, nomination. *Deadline:* continuous.

Contact John Whitt, Program Coordinator, Wisconsin Higher Educational Aids Board, PO Box 7885, Madison, WI 53707-7885. *E-mail:* john.whitt@heab.state.wi.us. *Phone:* 608-266-1665. *Fax:* 608-267-2808. *Web site:* www.heab.state.wi.us.

Handicapped Student Grant-Wisconsin. One-time award available to residents of Wisconsin who have severe or profound hearing or visual impairment. Must be enrolled at least half-time at a nonprofit institution. If the handicap prevents the student from attending a Wisconsin school, the award may be used out-of-state in a specialized college. Please refer to Web site for further details: http://www.heab.state.wi.us *Award:* Grant for use in freshman, sophomore, junior, or senior year; not renewable. *Award amount:* $250–$1800. *Number of awards:* varies. *Eligibility Requirements:* Applicant must be enrolled or expecting to enroll full or part-time at a two-year, four-year, or technical institution or university and resident of Wisconsin. Applicant must be hearing impaired or visually impaired. Available to U.S. citizens. *Application Requirements:* Application, financial need analysis. *Deadline:* continuous.

Contact Sandy Thomas, Program Coordinator, Wisconsin Higher Educational Aids Board, PO Box 7885, Madison, WI 53707-7885. *E-mail:* sandy.thomas@heab.state.wi.us. *Phone:* 608-266-0888. *Fax:* 608-267-2808. *Web site:* www.heab.state.wi.us.

Wisconsin Higher Education Grants (WHEG). Grants for residents of Wisconsin attending a campus of the University of Wisconsin or Wisconsin Technical College. Must be enrolled at least half-time and show financial need. Please refer to Web site for further details: http://www.heab.state.wi.us *Award:* Grant for use in freshman, sophomore, junior, or senior year; not renewable. *Award amount:* $250–$2500. *Number of awards:* varies. *Eligibility Requirements:* Applicant must be enrolled or expecting to enroll full or part-time at a two-year, four-year, or technical institution or university; resident of Wisconsin and studying in Wisconsin. Available to U.S. citizens. *Application Requirements:* Application, financial need analysis. *Deadline:* continuous.

Contact Sandra Thomas, Program Coordinator, Wisconsin Higher Educational Aids Board, PO Box 7885, Madison, WI 53707-7885. *E-mail:* sandy.thomas@heab.state.wi.us. *Phone:* 608-266-0888. *Fax:* 608-267-2808. *Web site:* www.heab.state.wi.us.

State Scholarship and Grant Programs
Wisconsin

Wisconsin Academic Excellence Scholarship. Renewable award for high school seniors with the highest GPA in graduating class. Must be a Wisconsin resident. Award covers tuition for up to four years. Must maintain 3.0 GPA for renewal. Scholarships of up to $2250 each. Must attend a nonprofit Wisconsin institution full-time. Please refer to Web site for further details: http://www.heab.state.wi.us *Award:* Scholarship for use in freshman, sophomore, junior, or senior year; renewable. *Award amount:* up to $2250. *Number of awards:* 3445. *Eligibility Requirements:* Applicant must be enrolled or expecting to enroll full-time at a two-year, four-year, or technical institution or university; resident of Wisconsin and studying in Wisconsin. Applicant must have 3.5 GPA or higher. Available to U.S. citizens. *Application Requirements:* Transcript. *Deadline:* continuous.

Contact Alice Winters, Program Coordinator, Wisconsin Higher Educational Aids Board, PO Box 7885, Madison, WI 53707-7885. *E-mail:* alice.winters@heab.state.wi.us. *Phone:* 608-267-2213. *Fax:* 608-267-2808. *Web site:* www.heab.state.wi.us.

Wisconsin Native American/ Indian Student Assistance Grant. Grants for Wisconsin residents who are at least one-quarter American-Indian. Must be attending a college or university within the state. Please refer to Web site for further details: http://www.heab.state.wi.us *Award:* Grant for use in freshman, sophomore, junior, senior, graduate, or postgraduate years; not renewable. *Award amount:* $250–$1100. *Number of awards:* varies. *Eligibility Requirements:* Applicant must be American Indian/Alaska Native; enrolled or expecting to enroll full or part-time at a two-year, four-year, or technical institution or university; resident of Wisconsin and studying in Wisconsin. Available to U.S. citizens. *Application Requirements:* Application, financial need analysis. *Deadline:* continuous.

Contact Sandra Thomas, Program Coordinator, Wisconsin Higher Educational Aids Board, PO Box 7885, Madison, WI 53707-7885. *E-mail:* sandy.thomas@heab.state.wi.us. *Phone:* 608-266-0888. *Fax:* 608-267-2808. *Web site:* www.heab.state.wi.us.

WYOMING

Vietnam Veterans Award/Wyoming. Available to Wyoming residents who served in the armed forces between August 5, 1964, and May 7, 1975, and received a Vietnam service medal. Award is free tuition at the University of Wyoming or a state (WY) community college. *Award:* Scholarship for use in freshman, sophomore, junior, or senior year; renewable. *Award amount:* varies. *Number of awards:* varies. *Eligibility Requirements:* Applicant must be enrolled or expecting to enroll full or part-time at a two-year or four-year institution or university; resident of Wyoming and studying in Wyoming. Available to U.S. citizens. Applicant must have general military experience. *Application Requirements:* Application. *Deadline:* continuous.

Contact Joel Anne Berrigan, Assistant Director, Scholarships, State of Wyoming, administered by University of Wyoming, Student Financial Aid, Department 3335, 1000 East University Avenue, Laramie, WY 82071-3335. *E-mail:* finaid@uwyo.edu. *Phone:* 307-766-2117. *Fax:* 307-766-3800. *Web site:* www.uwyo.edu/scholarships.

Superior Student in Education Scholarship-Wyoming. Available to Wyoming high school graduates who have demonstrated high academic achievement and plan to teach in Wyoming public schools. Award is for tuition at Wyoming institutions. Must maintain 3.0 GPA. *Academic Fields/Career Goals:* Education. *Award:* Scholarship for use in freshman, sophomore, junior, or senior year; renewable. *Award amount:* varies. *Number of awards:* 16–80. *Eligibility Requirements:* Applicant must be enrolled or expecting to enroll full-time at a two-year or four-year institution or university; resident of Wyoming and studying in Wyoming. Applicant must have 3.0 GPA or higher. Available to U.S. citizens. *Application Requirements:* Application, references, test scores, transcript. *Deadline:* October 31.

Contact Joel Anne Berrigan, Assistant Director, Scholarships, State of Wyoming, administered by University of Wyoming, Student Financial Aid, Department 3335, 1000 East University Avenue, Laramie, WY 82071-3335. *E-mail:* finaid@uwyo.edu. *Phone:* 307-766-2117. *Fax:* 307-766-3800. *Web site:* www.uwyo.edu/scholarships.

Douvas Memorial Scholarship. Available to Wyoming residents who are first-generation Americans. Must be between 18-22 years old. Must be used at any Wyoming public institution of higher education for study in freshman year. *Award:* Scholarship for use in freshman year; not renewable. *Award amount:* up to $500. *Number of awards:* 1. *Eligibility Requirements:* Applicant must be age 18-22; enrolled or expecting to enroll at a two-year or four-year institution; resident of Wyoming and studying in Wyoming. Available to U.S. citizens. *Application Requirements:* Application. *Deadline:* March 24.

Contact Bruce Hayes, Consultant, Wyoming Department of Education, 2300 Capitol Avenue, Hathaway Building, 2nd Floor, Cheyenne, WY 82002-0050. *Phone:* 307-777-7690. *Fax:* 307-777-6234.

Hathaway Scholarship. Scholarship for Wyoming students to pursue postsecondary education within the state. *Award:* Scholarship for use in freshman, sophomore, junior, or senior year. *Number of awards:* 1. *Eligibility Requirements:* Applicant must be enrolled or expecting to enroll full-time at an institution or university and resident of Wyoming. Available to U.S. citizens. *Application Requirements:* Application.

Contact Gerry Mass, Wyoming Department of Education. *Phone:* 307-777-6282.

Indexes

Non-Need Scholarships for Undergraduates

Academic Interests/Achievements

Agriculture
Abilene Christian University, TX
Arkansas State University, AR
Arkansas Tech University, AR
Auburn University, AL
Berry College, GA
California Polytechnic State University, San Luis Obispo, CA
California State University, Chico, CA
California State University, Fresno, CA
California State University, Stanislaus, CA
Central Missouri State University, MO
Clemson University, SC
Dickinson State University, ND
Dordt College, IA
Eastern Michigan University, MI
Florida Agricultural and Mechanical University, FL
Florida Southern College, FL
Fort Hays State University, KS
Fort Lewis College, CO
Illinois State University, IL
Kansas State University, KS
Lincoln University, MO
Louisiana State University and Agricultural and Mechanical College, LA
Louisiana Tech University, LA
Lubbock Christian University, TX
Michigan State University, MI
MidAmerica Nazarene University, KS
Middle Tennessee State University, TN
Midway College, KY
Mississippi State University, MS
Missouri State University, MO
Montana State University, MT
Morehead State University, KY
Murray State University, KY
New Mexico State University, NM
North Carolina State University, NC
Northwestern Oklahoma State University, OK
The Ohio State University, OH
Oklahoma Panhandle State University, OK
Oklahoma State University, OK
Purdue University, IN
South Dakota State University, SD
Southeast Missouri State University, MO
Southern Arkansas University–Magnolia, AR
Southern Illinois University Carbondale, IL
Southwest Minnesota State University, MN
State University of New York College of Environmental Science and Forestry, NY
Stephen F. Austin State University, TX
Tennessee Technological University, TN
Texas A&M University, TX
Texas A&M University–Commerce, TX
Texas State University–San Marcos, TX
Texas Tech University, TX
University of Arkansas at Pine Bluff, AR
University of California, Davis, CA
University of California, Riverside, CA
University of Connecticut, CT
University of Delaware, DE
University of Florida, FL
University of Georgia, GA
University of Hawaii at Hilo, HI
University of Idaho, ID
University of Illinois at Springfield, IL
University of Illinois at Urbana–Champaign, IL
University of Kentucky, KY
University of Maryland, College Park, MD
University of Massachusetts Amherst, MA
University of Minnesota, Twin Cities Campus, MN
University of Missouri–Columbia, MO
University of Nebraska–Lincoln, NE
University of Nevada, Reno, NV
University of New Hampshire, NH
The University of Tennessee at Martin, TN
The University of Texas at San Antonio, TX
University of Vermont, VT
University of Wisconsin–Stevens Point, WI
University of Wyoming, WY
Utah State University, UT
Virginia Polytechnic Institute and State University, VA
Washington State University, WA
Western Illinois University, IL
Western Kentucky University, KY
West Texas A&M University, TX
West Virginia University, WV

Architecture
Arizona State University, AZ
Auburn University, AL
Ball State University, IN
California Polytechnic State University, San Luis Obispo, CA
California State University, Bakersfield, CA
City College of the City University of New York, NY
Clemson University, SC
Cooper Union for the Advancement of Science and Art, NY
Eastern Michigan University, MI
Fairmont State University, WV
Georgia Institute of Technology, GA
James Madison University, VA
Kansas State University, KS
Kent State University, OH
Lawrence Technological University, MI
Louisiana State University and Agricultural and Mechanical College, LA
Louisiana Tech University, LA
Miami University, OH
Michigan State University, MI
Mississippi State University, MS
Montana State University, MT
The Ohio State University, OH
Oklahoma State University, OK
Portland State University, OR
Rice University, TX
Savannah College of Art and Design, GA
Southern California Institute of Architecture, CA
Southern Illinois University Carbondale, IL
State University of New York College of Environmental Science and Forestry, NY
Texas A&M University, TX
Texas Tech University, TX
University of Cincinnati, OH
University of Colorado at Boulder, CO
University of Florida, FL
University of Idaho, ID
University of Illinois at Urbana–Champaign, IL
University of Kansas, KS
University of Kentucky, KY
University of Maryland, College Park, MD
University of Massachusetts Amherst, MA
University of Miami, FL
University of Michigan, MI
University of Minnesota, Twin Cities Campus, MN
University of Nebraska–Lincoln, NE
University of Nevada, Las Vegas, NV
University of Oklahoma, OK
University of Oregon, OR
University of South Florida, FL
The University of Texas at Arlington, TX
The University of Texas at San Antonio, TX
University of Utah, UT
University of Wisconsin–Stevens Point, WI
Utah State University, UT
Virginia Polytechnic Institute and State University, VA

Non-Need Scholarships for Undergraduates
Academic Interests/Achievements

Washington State University, WA
Washington University in St. Louis, MO
West Virginia University, WV

Area/Ethnic Studies
Arizona State University, AZ
Brigham Young University–Hawaii, HI
California State University, Chico, CA
California State University, Fresno, CA
California State University, Stanislaus, CA
Central Missouri State University, MO
City College of the City University of New York, NY
Felician College, NJ
Fort Lewis College, CO
Furman University, SC
Hamline University, MN
Indiana University of Pennsylvania, PA
Kent State University, OH
Marian College, IN
Mississippi State University, MS
Montana State University, MT
The Ohio State University, OH
Ohio University, OH
Ohio University–Chillicothe, OH
Ohio University–Eastern, OH
Ohio University–Lancaster, OH
Ohio University–Southern Campus, OH
Ohio University–Zanesville, OH
Ohio Wesleyan University, OH
Oklahoma State University, OK
Ouachita Baptist University, AR
Portland State University, OR
Radford University, VA
Rice University, TX
The Richard Stockton College of New Jersey, NJ
Saint Louis University, MO
Sonoma State University, CA
South Dakota State University, SD
Southern Illinois University Carbondale, IL
State University of New York at Oswego, NY
State University of New York at Plattsburgh, NY
State University of New York College at Geneseo, NY
Stetson University, FL
Stony Brook University, State University of New York, NY
The University of Alabama, AL
University of California, Riverside, CA
University of Cincinnati, OH
University of Colorado at Boulder, CO
University of Illinois at Urbana–Champaign, IL
University of Kansas, KS
University of Miami, FL
University of Michigan, MI
University of Minnesota, Twin Cities Campus, MN
University of Oklahoma, OK
University of South Carolina, SC
The University of Texas at San Antonio, TX
University of Utah, UT

University of Wisconsin–Green Bay, WI
Virginia Polytechnic Institute and State University, VA
Washington State University, WA
West Virginia University, WV
Wichita State University, KS

Biological Sciences
Abilene Christian University, TX
Alaska Pacific University, AK
Albertson College of Idaho, ID
Albertus Magnus College, CT
Alderson-Broaddus College, WV
Alfred University, NY
Antioch College, OH
Arizona State University, AZ
Arkansas State University, AR
Armstrong Atlantic State University, GA
Athens State University, AL
Auburn University, AL
Augsburg College, MN
Augustana College, SD
Augusta State University, GA
Austin College, TX
Austin Peay State University, TN
Averett University, VA
Avila University, MO
Azusa Pacific University, CA
Ball State University, IN
Bard College, NY
Barton College, NC
Belhaven College, MS
Black Hills State University, SD
Bloomfield College, NJ
Bloomsburg University of Pennsylvania, PA
Blue Mountain College, MS
Bowling Green State University, OH
Brenau University, GA
Brevard College, NC
Brewton-Parker College, GA
Brigham Young University–Hawaii, HI
Bryan College, TN
Buena Vista University, IA
Butler University, IN
California Lutheran University, CA
California Polytechnic State University, San Luis Obispo, CA
California State University, Bakersfield, CA
California State University, Chico, CA
California State University, Fresno, CA
California State University, Stanislaus, CA
Calvin College, MI
Campbellsville University, KY
Carroll College, WI
Carson-Newman College, TN
Carthage College, WI
Cascade College, OR
Case Western Reserve University, OH
Centenary College of Louisiana, LA
Central College, IA
Central Michigan University, MI
Central Missouri State University, MO
Chapman University, CA
The Citadel, The Military College of South Carolina, SC

City College of the City University of New York, NY
Clarkson University, NY
Clemson University, SC
Coastal Carolina University, SC
Coe College, IA
College of Charleston, SC
College of Staten Island of the City University of New York, NY
The College of Wooster, OH
The Colorado College, CO
Columbia College, SC
Columbus State University, GA
Concordia University, NE
Concordia University, St. Paul, MN
Davidson College, NC
Davis & Elkins College, WV
Defiance College, OH
Denison University, OH
DePaul University, IL
DePauw University, IN
Dickinson State University, ND
Dordt College, IA
East Carolina University, NC
Eastern Michigan University, MI
Eastern Washington University, WA
East Stroudsburg University of Pennsylvania, PA
East Tennessee State University, TN
East Texas Baptist University, TX
Edinboro University of Pennsylvania, PA
Elizabethtown College, PA
Elmhurst College, IL
Elon University, NC
Emmanuel College, MA
Emporia State University, KS
Erskine College, SC
Fairfield University, CT
Felician College, NJ
Fitchburg State College, MA
Florida Gulf Coast University, FL
Florida Southern College, FL
Fort Hays State University, KS
Fort Lewis College, CO
Francis Marion University, SC
Freed-Hardeman University, TN
Friends University, KS
Frostburg State University, MD
Furman University, SC
Gannon University, PA
Georgia Institute of Technology, GA
Georgia Southern University, GA
Glenville State College, WV
Grambling State University, LA
Greenville College, IL
Grove City College, PA
Guilford College, NC
Hamline University, MN
Hampden-Sydney College, VA
Hardin-Simmons University, TX
Hawai'i Pacific University, HI
Hillsdale College, MI
Idaho State University, ID
Illinois State University, IL
Indiana University of Pennsylvania, PA

Peterson's College Money Handbook 2007 www.petersons.com **681**

Non-Need Scholarships for Undergraduates
Academic Interests/Achievements

Indiana University–Purdue University Fort Wayne, IN
Jacksonville State University, AL
James Madison University, VA
Jefferson College of Health Sciences, VA
Kansas State University, KS
Kennesaw State University, GA
Kent State University, OH
King's College, PA
LaGrange College, GA
Lake Forest College, IL
Lebanon Valley College, PA
Lee University, TN
Limestone College, SC
Lincoln University, PA
Lindenwood University, MO
Lock Haven University of Pennsylvania, PA
Louisiana State University and Agricultural and Mechanical College, LA
Louisiana Tech University, LA
Lycoming College, PA
MacMurray College, IL
Maine Maritime Academy, ME
Malone College, OH
Manhattan College, NY
Mansfield University of Pennsylvania, PA
Marquette University, WI
Marymount Manhattan College, NY
The Master's College and Seminary, CA
Mayville State University, ND
McKendree College, IL
Mercer University, GA
Meredith College, NC
Mesa State College, CO
Metropolitan State College of Denver, CO
Michigan State University, MI
Michigan Technological University, MI
Middle Tennessee State University, TN
Millersville University of Pennsylvania, PA
Mississippi State University, MS
Missouri State University, MO
Molloy College, NY
Montana State University, MT
Montana State University–Billings, MT
Montclair State University, NJ
Moravian College, PA
Morehead State University, KY
Murray State University, KY
Newberry College, SC
New England College, NH
New Jersey City University, NJ
New Mexico State University, NM
North Carolina State University, NC
Northeastern Illinois University, IL
Northern Arizona University, AZ
Northern Illinois University, IL
Northern Michigan University, MI
Northern State University, SD
North Georgia College & State University, GA
Northwestern College, MN
Northwestern Oklahoma State University, OK
Northwestern State University of Louisiana, LA
Northwest Nazarene University, ID

Ohio Northern University, OH
The Ohio State University, OH
Ohio University, OH
Ohio University–Chillicothe, OH
Ohio University–Eastern, OH
Ohio University–Lancaster, OH
Ohio University–Southern Campus, OH
Ohio University–Zanesville, OH
Ohio Wesleyan University, OH
Oklahoma State University, OK
Oral Roberts University, OK
Ouachita Baptist University, AR
Pepperdine University, CA
Pittsburg State University, KS
Quincy University, IL
Radford University, VA
Randolph-Macon Woman's College, VA
Rice University, TX
The Richard Stockton College of New Jersey, NJ
Ripon College, WI
Rochester Institute of Technology, NY
Rockhurst University, MO
Sacred Heart University, CT
St. Cloud State University, MN
St. Edward's University, TX
St. John Fisher College, NY
St. John's University, NY
Saint Louis University, MO
Saint Vincent College, PA
Salisbury University, MD
Schreiner University, TX
Seton Hill University, PA
Shepherd University, WV
Shippensburg University of Pennsylvania, PA
Skidmore College, NY
Slippery Rock University of Pennsylvania, PA
Sonoma State University, CA
South Dakota State University, SD
Southeastern Louisiana University, LA
Southeastern Oklahoma State University, OK
Southeast Missouri State University, MO
Southern Illinois University Carbondale, IL
Southern Oregon University, OR
Southwest Minnesota State University, MN
State University of New York at Binghamton, NY
State University of New York at Oswego, NY
State University of New York at Plattsburgh, NY
State University of New York College at Brockport, NY
State University of New York College at Geneseo, NY
State University of New York College at Old Westbury, NY
State University of New York College at Oneonta, NY
State University of New York College at Potsdam, NY
State University of New York College of Environmental Science and Forestry, NY

State University of New York, Fredonia, NY
Stephen F. Austin State University, TX
Stetson University, FL
Stony Brook University, State University of New York, NY
Tabor College, KS
Tennessee Technological University, TN
Texas A&M University, TX
Texas Tech University, TX
Texas Woman's University, TX
Thiel College, PA
Truman State University, MO
The University of Akron, OH
The University of Alabama, AL
University of Alaska Southeast, AK
University of Arkansas at Pine Bluff, AR
University of California, Riverside, CA
University of California, San Diego, CA
University of Central Oklahoma, OK
University of Cincinnati, OH
University of Colorado at Boulder, CO
University of Colorado at Colorado Springs, CO
University of Connecticut, CT
University of Dallas, TX
University of Delaware, DE
University of Evansville, IN
University of Great Falls, MT
University of Houston–Victoria, TX
University of Idaho, ID
University of Illinois at Springfield, IL
University of Illinois at Urbana–Champaign, IL
University of Kansas, KS
University of Kentucky, KY
University of Maine, ME
University of Mary Hardin-Baylor, TX
University of Maryland, Baltimore County, MD
University of Maryland, College Park, MD
University of Massachusetts Amherst, MA
University of Memphis, TN
University of Miami, FL
University of Michigan, MI
University of Michigan–Dearborn, MI
University of Michigan–Flint, MI
University of Minnesota, Twin Cities Campus, MN
University of Missouri–Columbia, MO
University of Missouri–St. Louis, MO
University of Nebraska at Omaha, NE
University of Nebraska–Lincoln, NE
University of Nevada, Las Vegas, NV
University of Nevada, Reno, NV
University of New England, ME
The University of North Carolina at Asheville, NC
The University of North Carolina at Greensboro, NC
The University of North Carolina Wilmington, NC
University of North Dakota, ND
University of Northern Colorado, CO
University of Northern Iowa, IA
University of Oklahoma, OK

Non-Need Scholarships for Undergraduates
Academic Interests/Achievements

University of Oregon, OR
University of Pittsburgh at Bradford, PA
University of Portland, OR
University of Puget Sound, WA
University of Richmond, VA
University of Rochester, NY
University of St. Francis, IL
University of Saint Francis, IN
University of St. Thomas, MN
University of St. Thomas, TX
University of South Carolina, SC
The University of South Dakota, SD
University of Southern Indiana, IN
University of South Florida, FL
The University of Tampa, FL
The University of Tennessee at Martin, TN
The University of Texas at Arlington, TX
The University of Texas at Dallas, TX
The University of Texas at El Paso, TX
The University of Texas at San Antonio, TX
The University of Texas–Pan American, TX
University of the Ozarks, AR
The University of Toledo, OH
University of Tulsa, OK
University of Utah, UT
University of West Georgia, GA
University of Wisconsin–Eau Claire, WI
University of Wisconsin–Green Bay, WI
University of Wisconsin–La Crosse, WI
University of Wisconsin–Parkside, WI
University of Wisconsin–Stevens Point, WI
University of Wisconsin–Whitewater, WI
Utah State University, UT
Valdosta State University, GA
Valley City State University, ND
Virginia Military Institute, VA
Virginia Polytechnic Institute and State University, VA
Wake Forest University, NC
Walla Walla College, WA
Warner Pacific College, OR
Wartburg College, IA
Washington State University, WA
Washington University in St. Louis, MO
Wayland Baptist University, TX
Waynesburg College, PA
Wayne State College, NE
Wesleyan College, GA
Western Carolina University, NC
Western Illinois University, IL
Western Kentucky University, KY
Western Oregon University, OR
Western Washington University, WA
West Texas A&M University, TX
West Virginia University, WV
Wheeling Jesuit University, WV
Whitworth College, WA
Wichita State University, KS
Widener University, PA
Wilkes University, PA
Williams Baptist College, AR
Wilson College, PA
Worcester State College, MA
Xavier University of Louisiana, LA

Business

Abilene Christian University, TX
Adrian College, MI
Alaska Pacific University, AK
Albertus Magnus College, CT
Albion College, MI
Alderson-Broaddus College, WV
Alfred University, NY
Alliant International University, CA
Arizona State University, AZ
Arkansas State University, AR
Athens State University, AL
Atlantic Union College, MA
Auburn University, AL
Augsburg College, MN
Augustana College, SD
Augusta State University, GA
Austin College, TX
Austin Peay State University, TN
Averett University, VA
Ball State University, IN
Barton College, NC
Baylor University, TX
Beacon University, GA
Belhaven College, MS
Bennett College For Women, NC
Black Hills State University, SD
Bloomfield College, NJ
Bloomsburg University of Pennsylvania, PA
Blue Mountain College, MS
Bowling Green State University, OH
Brenau University, GA
Brevard College, NC
Brewton-Parker College, GA
Brigham Young University–Hawaii, HI
Bryan College, TN
Bucknell University, PA
Buena Vista University, IA
Butler University, IN
California Lutheran University, CA
California Polytechnic State University, San Luis Obispo, CA
California State University, Bakersfield, CA
California State University, Chico, CA
California State University, Fresno, CA
California State University, Fullerton, CA
California State University, Stanislaus, CA
Calvin College, MI
Campbellsville University, KY
Carroll College, WI
Carson-Newman College, TN
Cascade College, OR
Case Western Reserve University, OH
Centenary College of Louisiana, LA
Central College, IA
Central Michigan University, MI
Central Missouri State University, MO
Central Washington University, WA
Champlain College, VT
Christopher Newport University, VA
The Citadel, The Military College of South Carolina, SC
Clarkson University, NY
Clearwater Christian College, FL
Clemson University, SC
Coastal Carolina University, SC

Coe College, IA
College Misericordia, PA
College of Charleston, SC
College of St. Catherine, MN
The College of Saint Rose, NY
College of Staten Island of the City University of New York, NY
College of the Southwest, NM
Colorado School of Mines, CO
Columbia College, SC
Columbus State University, GA
Concordia University, NE
Concordia University, St. Paul, MN
Cornerstone University, MI
Creighton University, NE
Dakota State University, SD
Dallas Baptist University, TX
Dalton State College, GA
Daniel Webster College, NH
David N. Myers University, OH
Davis & Elkins College, WV
Defiance College, OH
DePaul University, IL
DePauw University, IN
Dickinson State University, ND
Dordt College, IA
Dowling College, NY
East Carolina University, NC
Eastern Michigan University, MI
Eastern Washington University, WA
East Stroudsburg University of Pennsylvania, PA
East Tennessee State University, TN
East Texas Baptist University, TX
Edinboro University of Pennsylvania, PA
Elizabethtown College, PA
Elmhurst College, IL
Elon University, NC
Emporia State University, KS
Endicott College, MA
Erskine College, SC
Evangel University, MO
Fairfield University, CT
Fairmont State University, WV
Felician College, NJ
Fitchburg State College, MA
Five Towns College, NY
Flagler College, FL
Florida Agricultural and Mechanical University, FL
Florida Atlantic University, FL
Florida Gulf Coast University, FL
Florida Metropolitan University–Pinellas Campus, FL
Florida Southern College, FL
Fort Hays State University, KS
Fort Lewis College, CO
Francis Marion University, SC
Freed-Hardeman University, TN
Friends University, KS
Frostburg State University, MD
Furman University, SC
Gannon University, PA
Georgia College & State University, GA
Georgia Southern University, GA
Gonzaga University, WA

Non-Need Scholarships for Undergraduates
Academic Interests/Achievements

Goshen College, IN
Grambling State University, LA
Greenville College, IL
Grove City College, PA
Hardin-Simmons University, TX
Hawai'i Pacific University, HI
Hillsdale College, MI
Husson College, ME
Idaho State University, ID
Illinois State University, IL
Indiana University of Pennsylvania, PA
Indiana University–Purdue University Fort Wayne, IN
Jacksonville State University, AL
Jacksonville University, FL
James Madison University, VA
Juniata College, PA
Kansas State University, KS
Kean University, NJ
Kennesaw State University, GA
Kent State University, OH
Kentucky Christian University, KY
Kettering University, MI
King's College, PA
LaGrange College, GA
Lakeland College, WI
Lawrence Technological University, MI
Lee University, TN
Lewis-Clark State College, ID
Limestone College, SC
Lincoln University, PA
Lindenwood University, MO
Louisiana State University and Agricultural and Mechanical College, LA
Louisiana Tech University, LA
Lubbock Christian University, TX
Lycoming College, PA
Lynn University, FL
Maine Maritime Academy, ME
Malone College, OH
Manchester College, IN
Manhattan College, NY
Maranatha Baptist Bible College, WI
Marquette University, WI
Marymount Manhattan College, NY
Marywood University, PA
The Master's College and Seminary, CA
Mayville State University, ND
McKendree College, IL
Mercer University, GA
Mesa State College, CO
Metropolitan State College of Denver, CO
Michigan State University, MI
Michigan Technological University, MI
Middle Tennessee State University, TN
Midway College, KY
Midwestern State University, TX
Millersville University of Pennsylvania, PA
Millsaps College, MS
Milwaukee School of Engineering, WI
Minnesota State University Mankato, MN
Mississippi State University, MS
Missouri State University, MO
Molloy College, NY
Monmouth University, NJ
Montana State University, MT
Montana State University–Billings, MT
Montana Tech of The University of Montana, MT
Montclair State University, NJ
Moravian College, PA
Morehead State University, KY
Mount Mary College, WI
Mount Vernon Nazarene University, OH
Murray State University, KY
Newberry College, SC
New England College, NH
New Jersey City University, NJ
New Mexico State University, NM
North Carolina State University, NC
Northeastern Illinois University, IL
Northern Arizona University, AZ
Northern Illinois University, IL
Northern Michigan University, MI
Northern State University, SD
North Georgia College & State University, GA
Northwestern Oklahoma State University, OK
Northwest Nazarene University, ID
Northwood University, MI
Northwood University, Florida Campus, FL
Northwood University, Texas Campus, TX
Ohio Northern University, OH
The Ohio State University, OH
Ohio University, OH
Ohio University–Chillicothe, OH
Ohio University–Eastern, OH
Ohio University–Lancaster, OH
Ohio University–Southern Campus, OH
Ohio University–Zanesville, OH
Ohio Wesleyan University, OH
Oklahoma State University, OK
Oral Roberts University, OK
Ouachita Baptist University, AR
Pacific University, OR
Pepperdine University, CA
Pittsburg State University, KS
Plymouth State University, NH
Portland State University, OR
Quincy University, IL
Radford University, VA
The Richard Stockton College of New Jersey, NJ
Ripon College, WI
Robert Morris College, IL
Rochester Institute of Technology, NY
Rockhurst University, MO
Sacred Heart University, CT
St. Bonaventure University, NY
St. Cloud State University, MN
St. Edward's University, TX
Saint Francis University, PA
St. John Fisher College, NY
St. John's University, NY
Saint Louis University, MO
Saint Martin's University, WA
Saint Vincent College, PA
Salem International University, WV
Salisbury University, MD
Santa Clara University, CA
Schreiner University, TX
Seton Hill University, PA
Shenandoah University, VA
Shepherd University, WV
Shippensburg University of Pennsylvania, PA
Slippery Rock University of Pennsylvania, PA
Sonoma State University, CA
South Dakota State University, SD
Southeastern Louisiana University, LA
Southeastern Oklahoma State University, OK
Southeast Missouri State University, MO
Southern Adventist University, TN
Southern Arkansas University–Magnolia, AR
Southern Illinois University Carbondale, IL
Southern Illinois University Edwardsville, IL
Southern Oregon University, OR
Southwestern Christian University, OK
Southwest Minnesota State University, MN
State University of New York at Binghamton, NY
State University of New York at Oswego, NY
State University of New York at Plattsburgh, NY
State University of New York College at Brockport, NY
State University of New York College at Geneseo, NY
State University of New York College at Potsdam, NY
State University of New York, Fredonia, NY
Stephen F. Austin State University, TX
Stetson University, FL
Stevens Institute of Technology, NJ
Stony Brook University, State University of New York, NY
Tabor College, KS
Taylor University Fort Wayne, IN
Tennessee Technological University, TN
Texas A&M University, TX
Texas Southern University, TX
Texas State University–San Marcos, TX
Texas Tech University, TX
Texas Woman's University, TX
Thiel College, PA
Tiffin University, OH
Toccoa Falls College, GA
Trevecca Nazarene University, TN
Truman State University, MO
Union University, TN
The University of Akron, OH
The University of Alabama, AL
The University of Alabama at Birmingham, AL
The University of Alabama in Huntsville, AL
University of Alaska Southeast, AK
University of Arkansas at Pine Bluff, AR
University of Baltimore, MD
University of California, Riverside, CA
University of California, San Diego, CA

Non-Need Scholarships for Undergraduates
Academic Interests/Achievements

University of Central Oklahoma, OK
University of Cincinnati, OH
University of Colorado at Boulder, CO
University of Colorado at Colorado Springs, CO
University of Colorado at Denver and Health Sciences Center—Downtown Denver Campus, CO
University of Connecticut, CT
University of Dallas, TX
University of Dayton, OH
University of Delaware, DE
University of Denver, CO
University of Evansville, IN
University of Florida, FL
University of Georgia, GA
University of Great Falls, MT
University of Hawaii at Hilo, HI
University of Houston–Victoria, TX
University of Idaho, ID
University of Illinois at Springfield, IL
University of Illinois at Urbana–Champaign, IL
The University of Iowa, IA
University of Kansas, KS
University of Kentucky, KY
University of Maine, ME
University of Mary Hardin-Baylor, TX
University of Maryland, College Park, MD
University of Mary Washington, VA
University of Massachusetts Amherst, MA
University of Memphis, TN
University of Miami, FL
University of Michigan, MI
University of Michigan–Dearborn, MI
University of Michigan–Flint, MI
University of Minnesota, Twin Cities Campus, MN
University of Missouri–Columbia, MO
University of Missouri–St. Louis, MO
University of Nebraska at Omaha, NE
University of Nebraska–Lincoln, NE
University of Nevada, Las Vegas, NV
University of Nevada, Reno, NV
University of New England, ME
University of New Hampshire, NH
The University of North Carolina at Asheville, NC
The University of North Carolina at Chapel Hill, NC
The University of North Carolina at Greensboro, NC
The University of North Carolina at Pembroke, NC
The University of North Carolina Wilmington, NC
University of North Dakota, ND
University of Northern Colorado, CO
University of Northern Iowa, IA
University of North Florida, FL
University of Oklahoma, OK
University of Oregon, OR
University of Phoenix–Atlanta Campus, GA
University of Phoenix–Bay Area Campus, CA
University of Phoenix–Boston Campus, MA

University of Phoenix–Central Florida Campus, FL
University of Phoenix–Central Valley Campus, CA
University of Phoenix–Charlotte Campus, NC
University of Phoenix–Chicago Campus, IL
University of Phoenix–Cincinnati Campus, OH
University of Phoenix–Cleveland Campus, OH
University of Phoenix–Columbus Georgia Campus, GA
University of Phoenix–Columbus Ohio Campus, OH
University of Phoenix–Dallas Campus, TX
University of Phoenix–Houston Campus, TX
University of Phoenix–Idaho Campus, ID
University of Phoenix–Indianapolis Campus, IN
University of Phoenix–Kansas City Campus, MO
University of Phoenix–Little Rock Campus, AR
University of Phoenix–Louisiana Campus, LA
University of Phoenix–Maryland Campus, MD
University of Phoenix–Metro Detroit Campus, MI
University of Phoenix–Nashville Campus, TN
University of Phoenix–New Mexico Campus, NM
University of Phoenix–Northern Virginia Campus, VA
University of Phoenix–North Florida Campus, FL
University of Phoenix–Oklahoma City Campus, OK
University of Phoenix Online Campus, AZ
University of Phoenix–Oregon Campus, OR
University of Phoenix–Philadelphia Campus, PA
University of Phoenix–Phoenix Campus, AZ
University of Phoenix–Pittsburgh Campus, PA
University of Phoenix–Puerto Rico Campus, PR
University of Phoenix–Raleigh Campus, NC
University of Phoenix–Richmond Campus, VA
University of Phoenix–Sacramento Valley Campus, CA
University of Phoenix–St. Louis Campus, MO
University of Phoenix–San Diego Campus, CA
University of Phoenix–Southern Colorado Campus, CO
University of Phoenix–South Florida Campus, FL
University of Phoenix–Spokane Campus, WA

University of Phoenix–Springfield Campus, MO
University of Phoenix–Tulsa Campus, OK
University of Phoenix–Utah Campus, UT
University of Phoenix–Washington Campus, WA
University of Phoenix–West Florida Campus, FL
University of Phoenix–West Michigan Campus, MI
University of Phoenix–Wichita Campus, KS
University of Pittsburgh at Bradford, PA
University of Portland, OR
University of Puget Sound, WA
University of Saint Francis, IN
University of St. Thomas, MN
University of South Carolina, SC
The University of South Dakota, SD
University of Southern Indiana, IN
University of South Florida, FL
The University of Tampa, FL
The University of Tennessee at Martin, TN
The University of Texas at Arlington, TX
The University of Texas at Dallas, TX
The University of Texas at El Paso, TX
The University of Texas at San Antonio, TX
The University of Texas–Pan American, TX
University of the Ozarks, AR
The University of Toledo, OH
University of Tulsa, OK
University of Utah, UT
University of Vermont, VT
The University of West Alabama, AL
University of West Georgia, GA
University of Wisconsin–Eau Claire, WI
University of Wisconsin–Green Bay, WI
University of Wisconsin–La Crosse, WI
University of Wisconsin–Parkside, WI
University of Wisconsin–Stevens Point, WI
University of Wisconsin–Stout, WI
University of Wisconsin–Whitewater, WI
University of Wyoming, WY
Utah State University, UT
Valdosta State University, GA
Valley City State University, ND
Valparaiso University, IN
Villa Julie College, MD
Virginia Commonwealth University, VA
Virginia Military Institute, VA
Virginia Polytechnic Institute and State University, VA
Wake Forest University, NC
Walsh College of Accountancy and Business Administration, MI
Wartburg College, IA
Washington & Jefferson College, PA
Washington State University, WA
Washington University in St. Louis, MO
Wayland Baptist University, TX
Waynesburg College, PA
Wayne State College, NE
Webber International University, FL
Wesleyan College, GA
Western Carolina University, NC
Western Illinois University, IL

Peterson's College Money Handbook 2007   *www.petersons.com*   **685**

Non-Need Scholarships for Undergraduates
Academic Interests/Achievements

Western Kentucky University, KY
Western New England College, MA
Western Oregon University, OR
Western Washington University, WA
West Texas A&M University, TX
West Virginia University, WV
Wheeling Jesuit University, WV
Wichita State University, KS
Widener University, PA
Wilkes University, PA
Williams Baptist College, AR
Wilson College, PA
Winston-Salem State University, NC
Worcester State College, MA
Xavier University of Louisiana, LA
Youngstown State University, OH

Communication

Abilene Christian University, TX
Adelphi University, NY
Albertus Magnus College, CT
Albion College, MI
Alderson-Broaddus College, WV
Alfred University, NY
Alliant International University, CA
Arizona State University, AZ
Arkansas State University, AR
Auburn University, AL
Augsburg College, MN
Augustana College, SD
Augusta State University, GA
Austin College, TX
Avila University, MO
Ball State University, IN
Barton College, NC
Baylor University, TX
Belhaven College, MS
Berry College, GA
Biola University, CA
Black Hills State University, SD
Bloomsburg University of Pennsylvania, PA
Bowling Green State University, OH
Brenau University, GA
Brewton-Parker College, GA
Brigham Young University–Hawaii, HI
Bryan College, TN
Butler University, IN
California Lutheran University, CA
California Polytechnic State University, San Luis Obispo, CA
California State University, Bakersfield, CA
California State University, Chico, CA
California State University, Fresno, CA
California State University, Fullerton, CA
California State University, Stanislaus, CA
Calvin College, MI
Campbellsville University, KY
Cascade College, OR
Case Western Reserve University, OH
Centenary College of Louisiana, LA
Central College, IA
Central Michigan University, MI
Central Missouri State University, MO
Central Washington University, WA
Champlain College, VT
Christopher Newport University, VA

City College of the City University of New York, NY
Clemson University, SC
College of Charleston, SC
Columbia College, SC
Columbus State University, GA
Concordia University, NE
Concordia University, St. Paul, MN
Dakota State University, SD
Dallas Baptist University, TX
Defiance College, OH
Denison University, OH
DePauw University, IN
Dickinson State University, ND
Dordt College, IA
East Central University, OK
Eastern Michigan University, MI
East Stroudsburg University of Pennsylvania, PA
East Texas Baptist University, TX
Edinboro University of Pennsylvania, PA
Elizabethtown College, PA
Elmhurst College, IL
Elon University, NC
Emporia State University, KS
Evangel University, MO
Fairmont State University, WV
Fitchburg State College, MA
Flagler College, FL
Florida Southern College, FL
Fordham University, NY
Fort Hays State University, KS
Fort Lewis College, CO
Franklin Pierce College, NH
Friends University, KS
Frostburg State University, MD
Furman University, SC
Georgia Southern University, GA
Goshen College, IN
Grambling State University, LA
Grove City College, PA
Hamline University, MN
Hardin-Simmons University, TX
Hawai'i Pacific University, HI
Hofstra University, NY
Idaho State University, ID
Illinois State University, IL
Indiana University of Pennsylvania, PA
Indiana University–Purdue University Fort Wayne, IN
Ithaca College, NY
Jacksonville State University, AL
Johnson Bible College, TN
Kansas State University, KS
Kennesaw State University, GA
Kent State University, OH
King's College, PA
Lee University, TN
Lehigh University, PA
Limestone College, SC
Lincoln University, PA
Lindenwood University, MO
Lock Haven University of Pennsylvania, PA
Long Island University, Brooklyn Campus, NY

Louisiana State University and Agricultural and Mechanical College, LA
Lubbock Christian University, TX
Lycoming College, PA
Lynn University, FL
Malone College, OH
Mansfield University of Pennsylvania, PA
Marquette University, WI
Marymount Manhattan College, NY
Marywood University, PA
Mesa State College, CO
Metropolitan State College of Denver, CO
Michigan State University, MI
Michigan Technological University, MI
Middle Tennessee State University, TN
Millersville University of Pennsylvania, PA
Milligan College, TN
Milwaukee School of Engineering, WI
Mississippi State University, MS
Missouri State University, MO
Monmouth University, NJ
Montana State University, MT
Montana State University–Billings, MT
Montclair State University, NJ
Morehead State University, KY
Mount Mary College, WI
Murray State University, KY
Newberry College, SC
New England College, NH
New England School of Communications, ME
New Jersey City University, NJ
New Mexico State University, NM
Northeastern Illinois University, IL
Northern Arizona University, AZ
Northern Illinois University, IL
Northern Michigan University, MI
North Greenville College, SC
Northwestern Oklahoma State University, OK
Ohio Northern University, OH
The Ohio State University, OH
Ohio University, OH
Ohio University–Chillicothe, OH
Ohio University–Eastern, OH
Ohio University–Lancaster, OH
Ohio University–Southern Campus, OH
Ohio University–Zanesville, OH
Ohio Wesleyan University, OH
Oklahoma State University, OK
Oral Roberts University, OK
Ouachita Baptist University, AR
Pepperdine University, CA
Pittsburg State University, KS
Plymouth State University, NH
Quincy University, IL
Radford University, VA
Rochester Institute of Technology, NY
Rockhurst University, MO
St. Cloud State University, MN
St. Edward's University, TX
St. John's University, NY
Saint Louis University, MO
Salisbury University, MD
Seton Hill University, PA
Shepherd University, WV

Non-Need Scholarships for Undergraduates
Academic Interests/Achievements

Shippensburg University of Pennsylvania, PA
Slippery Rock University of Pennsylvania, PA
Sonoma State University, CA
South Dakota State University, SD
Southeastern Louisiana University, LA
Southeastern University, FL
Southeast Missouri State University, MO
Southern Adventist University, TN
Southern Illinois University Carbondale, IL
Southwest Minnesota State University, MN
State University of New York at Oswego, NY
State University of New York at Plattsburgh, NY
State University of New York College at Brockport, NY
State University of New York College at Geneseo, NY
State University of New York College at Potsdam, NY
State University of New York, Fredonia, NY
Stephen F. Austin State University, TX
Stetson University, FL
Tabor College, KS
Tennessee Technological University, TN
Texas Southern University, TX
Texas Tech University, TX
Texas Woman's University, TX
Toccoa Falls College, GA
Trevecca Nazarene University, TN
Truman State University, MO
Union University, TN
The University of Akron, OH
The University of Alabama, AL
The University of Alabama at Birmingham, AL
University of Alaska Southeast, AK
University of California, San Diego, CA
University of Cincinnati, OH
University of Colorado at Boulder, CO
University of Delaware, DE
University of Evansville, IN
University of Florida, FL
University of Houston–Victoria, TX
University of Idaho, ID
University of Illinois at Springfield, IL
University of Illinois at Urbana–Champaign, IL
University of Kansas, KS
University of Kentucky, KY
University of Maine, ME
University of Mary Hardin-Baylor, TX
University of Maryland, College Park, MD
University of Massachusetts Amherst, MA
University of Memphis, TN
University of Miami, FL
University of Michigan, MI
University of Michigan–Flint, MI
University of Minnesota, Twin Cities Campus, MN
University of Missouri–Columbia, MO
University of Missouri–St. Louis, MO
University of Nebraska at Kearney, NE

University of Nebraska at Omaha, NE
University of Nevada, Las Vegas, NV
University of New Orleans, LA
The University of North Carolina at Asheville, NC
The University of North Carolina at Chapel Hill, NC
The University of North Carolina at Greensboro, NC
The University of North Carolina at Pembroke, NC
The University of North Carolina Wilmington, NC
University of North Dakota, ND
University of Northern Colorado, CO
University of Oklahoma, OK
University of Pittsburgh at Bradford, PA
University of Portland, OR
University of Puget Sound, WA
University of Saint Francis, IN
University of South Carolina, SC
The University of South Dakota, SD
University of South Florida, FL
The University of Tampa, FL
The University of Tennessee at Martin, TN
The University of Texas at Arlington, TX
The University of Texas at El Paso, TX
The University of Texas at San Antonio, TX
The University of Texas–Pan American, TX
University of the Ozarks, AR
The University of Toledo, OH
University of Tulsa, OK
University of Utah, UT
University of West Georgia, GA
University of Wisconsin–Eau Claire, WI
University of Wisconsin–Green Bay, WI
University of Wisconsin–La Crosse, WI
University of Wisconsin–Parkside, WI
University of Wisconsin–Stevens Point, WI
University of Wisconsin–Whitewater, WI
University of Wyoming, WY
Utah State University, UT
Valdosta State University, GA
Valley City State University, ND
Virginia Polytechnic Institute and State University, VA
Waldorf College, IA
Wartburg College, IA
Washington State University, WA
Washington University in St. Louis, MO
Wayland Baptist University, TX
Waynesburg College, PA
Wayne State College, NE
Wesleyan College, GA
Western Carolina University, NC
Western Kentucky University, KY
Western Washington University, WA
West Texas A&M University, TX
West Virginia University, WV
Wheeling Jesuit University, WV
Wichita State University, KS
Widener University, PA
Wilkes University, PA
Wilson College, PA

Computer Science

Albertus Magnus College, CT
Alderson-Broaddus College, WV
Alfred University, NY
Alliant International University, CA
Arizona State University, AZ
Arkansas State University, AR
Armstrong Atlantic State University, GA
Athens State University, AL
Atlantic Union College, MA
Auburn University, AL
Augsburg College, MN
Augustana College, SD
Augusta State University, GA
Azusa Pacific University, CA
Barton College, NC
Baylor University, TX
Belhaven College, MS
Black Hills State University, SD
Bloomfield College, NJ
Bloomsburg University of Pennsylvania, PA
Bowling Green State University, OH
Brigham Young University–Hawaii, HI
Bryan College, TN
Buena Vista University, IA
Butler University, IN
California Lutheran University, CA
California Polytechnic State University, San Luis Obispo, CA
California State University, Chico, CA
California State University, Stanislaus, CA
Calvin College, MI
Campbellsville University, KY
Carroll College, WI
Carthage College, WI
Case Western Reserve University, OH
Central College, IA
Central Michigan University, MI
Central Missouri State University, MO
Central Washington University, WA
Christopher Newport University, VA
City College of the City University of New York, NY
Clarke College, IA
Clarkson University, NY
Clemson University, SC
College Misericordia, PA
College of Charleston, SC
College of Staten Island of the City University of New York, NY
Colorado School of Mines, CO
Columbus State University, GA
Concordia University, NE
Dakota State University, SD
Dallas Baptist University, TX
Daniel Webster College, NH
Davis & Elkins College, WV
Defiance College, OH
DePaul University, IL
DePauw University, IN
Dickinson State University, ND
Dordt College, IA
Eastern Michigan University, MI
Eastern Washington University, WA
East Stroudsburg University of Pennsylvania, PA

Non-Need Scholarships for Undergraduates
Academic Interests/Achievements

East Tennessee State University, TN
East Texas Baptist University, TX
Edinboro University of Pennsylvania, PA
Elizabethtown College, PA
Elmhurst College, IL
Elon University, NC
Emporia State University, KS
Evangel University, MO
Fairmont State University, WV
Felician College, NJ
Fitchburg State College, MA
Florida Metropolitan University–Pinellas Campus, FL
Fort Hays State University, KS
Fort Lewis College, CO
Freed-Hardeman University, TN
Friends University, KS
Frostburg State University, MD
Furman University, SC
Georgia College & State University, GA
Georgia Institute of Technology, GA
Graceland University, IA
Grambling State University, LA
Husson College, ME
Idaho State University, ID
Illinois State University, IL
Indiana University of Pennsylvania, PA
Indiana University–Purdue University Fort Wayne, IN
Jacksonville State University, AL
James Madison University, VA
Kansas State University, KS
Kennesaw State University, GA
Kent State University, OH
Kettering University, MI
King's College, PA
LaGrange College, GA
Lawrence Technological University, MI
Limestone College, SC
Lincoln University, PA
Lindenwood University, MO
Louisiana State University and Agricultural and Mechanical College, LA
Louisiana Tech University, LA
Lubbock Christian University, TX
Lycoming College, PA
Malone College, OH
Manhattan College, NY
Meredith College, NC
Mesa State College, CO
Metropolitan State College of Denver, CO
Michigan State University, MI
Michigan Technological University, MI
Middle Tennessee State University, TN
Midwestern State University, TX
Millersville University of Pennsylvania, PA
Milligan College, TN
Milwaukee School of Engineering, WI
Minnesota State University Mankato, MN
Mississippi State University, MS
Missouri State University, MO
Monmouth University, NJ
Montana State University, MT
Montana State University–Billings, MT
Montana Tech of The University of Montana, MT

Moravian College, PA
Mount Vernon Nazarene University, OH
Murray State University, KY
New Mexico State University, NM
Northeastern Illinois University, IL
Northern Arizona University, AZ
Northern Illinois University, IL
Northern Michigan University, MI
Northwestern Oklahoma State University, OK
Northwest Nazarene University, ID
Ohio Northern University, OH
The Ohio State University, OH
Ohio University, OH
Ohio University–Chillicothe, OH
Ohio University–Eastern, OH
Ohio University–Lancaster, OH
Ohio University–Southern Campus, OH
Ohio University–Zanesville, OH
Ohio Wesleyan University, OH
Oklahoma State University, OK
Ouachita Baptist University, AR
Pittsburg State University, KS
Portland State University, OR
Purdue University, IN
Quincy University, IL
Radford University, VA
Rice University, TX
The Richard Stockton College of New Jersey, NJ
Ripon College, WI
Robert Morris College, IL
Rochester Institute of Technology, NY
Rockhurst University, MO
Rollins College, FL
Sacred Heart University, CT
St. Cloud State University, MN
St. Edward's University, TX
St. John's University, NY
Saint Louis University, MO
Saint Vincent College, PA
Salisbury University, MD
Seton Hill University, PA
Shepherd University, WV
Shippensburg University of Pennsylvania, PA
Skidmore College, NY
Slippery Rock University of Pennsylvania, PA
Sonoma State University, CA
South Dakota School of Mines and Technology, SD
South Dakota State University, SD
Southeastern Oklahoma State University, OK
Southeast Missouri State University, MO
Southern Arkansas University–Magnolia, AR
Southern Illinois University Carbondale, IL
Southwest Minnesota State University, MN
State University of New York at Binghamton, NY
State University of New York at New Paltz, NY
State University of New York at Oswego, NY

State University of New York at Plattsburgh, NY
State University of New York College at Brockport, NY
State University of New York College at Geneseo, NY
State University of New York College at Potsdam, NY
State University of New York, Fredonia, NY
State University of New York Institute of Technology, NY
Stephen F. Austin State University, TX
Stetson University, FL
Stevens Institute of Technology, NJ
Stony Brook University, State University of New York, NY
Tabor College, KS
Tennessee Technological University, TN
Texas A&M University, TX
Texas Tech University, TX
Texas Woman's University, TX
Thiel College, PA
Transylvania University, KY
The University of Akron, OH
The University of Alabama, AL
The University of Alabama at Birmingham, AL
The University of Alabama in Huntsville, AL
University of Alaska Southeast, AK
University of California, Irvine, CA
University of California, San Diego, CA
University of Central Oklahoma, OK
University of Cincinnati, OH
University of Colorado at Boulder, CO
University of Colorado at Colorado Springs, CO
University of Connecticut, CT
University of Dallas, TX
University of Delaware, DE
University of Evansville, IN
University of Florida, FL
University of Great Falls, MT
University of Hawaii at Hilo, HI
University of Houston–Victoria, TX
University of Idaho, ID
University of Illinois at Springfield, IL
University of Illinois at Urbana–Champaign, IL
University of Kansas, KS
University of Maine, ME
University of Mary Hardin-Baylor, TX
University of Maryland, Baltimore County, MD
University of Maryland, College Park, MD
University of Mary Washington, VA
University of Massachusetts Amherst, MA
University of Massachusetts Lowell, MA
University of Miami, FL
University of Michigan, MI
University of Michigan–Dearborn, MI
University of Michigan–Flint, MI
University of Minnesota, Twin Cities Campus, MN
University of Missouri–Columbia, MO

Non-Need Scholarships for Undergraduates
Academic Interests/Achievements

University of Missouri–St. Louis, MO
University of Nebraska at Omaha, NE
University of Nebraska–Lincoln, NE
University of Nevada, Las Vegas, NV
University of Nevada, Reno, NV
University of New Orleans, LA
The University of North Carolina at Asheville, NC
The University of North Carolina Wilmington, NC
University of North Dakota, ND
University of North Florida, FL
University of Oklahoma, OK
University of Phoenix–Atlanta Campus, GA
University of Phoenix–Bay Area Campus, CA
University of Phoenix–Boston Campus, MA
University of Phoenix–Central Florida Campus, FL
University of Phoenix–Central Valley Campus, CA
University of Phoenix–Charlotte Campus, NC
University of Phoenix–Chicago Campus, IL
University of Phoenix–Cincinnati Campus, OH
University of Phoenix–Cleveland Campus, OH
University of Phoenix–Columbus Georgia Campus, GA
University of Phoenix–Columbus Ohio Campus, OH
University of Phoenix–Dallas Campus, TX
University of Phoenix–Houston Campus, TX
University of Phoenix–Idaho Campus, ID
University of Phoenix–Indianapolis Campus, IN
University of Phoenix–Kansas City Campus, MO
University of Phoenix–Little Rock Campus, AR
University of Phoenix–Louisiana Campus, LA
University of Phoenix–Maryland Campus, MD
University of Phoenix–Metro Detroit Campus, MI
University of Phoenix–Nashville Campus, TN
University of Phoenix–New Mexico Campus, NM
University of Phoenix–Northern Virginia Campus, VA
University of Phoenix–North Florida Campus, FL
University of Phoenix–Oklahoma City Campus, OK
University of Phoenix Online Campus, AZ
University of Phoenix–Oregon Campus, OR
University of Phoenix–Philadelphia Campus, PA
University of Phoenix–Phoenix Campus, AZ
University of Phoenix–Pittsburgh Campus, PA

University of Phoenix–Puerto Rico Campus, PR
University of Phoenix–Raleigh Campus, NC
University of Phoenix–Richmond Campus, VA
University of Phoenix–Sacramento Valley Campus, CA
University of Phoenix–St. Louis Campus, MO
University of Phoenix–San Diego Campus, CA
University of Phoenix–Southern Colorado Campus, CO
University of Phoenix–South Florida Campus, FL
University of Phoenix–Spokane Campus, WA
University of Phoenix–Springfield Campus, MO
University of Phoenix–Tulsa Campus, OK
University of Phoenix–Utah Campus, UT
University of Phoenix–Washington Campus, WA
University of Phoenix–West Florida Campus, FL
University of Phoenix–West Michigan Campus, MI
University of Phoenix–Wichita Campus, KS
University of Pittsburgh at Bradford, PA
University of Portland, OR
University of Puget Sound, WA
University of Richmond, VA
University of South Carolina, SC
The University of South Dakota, SD
University of South Florida, FL
The University of Tennessee at Martin, TN
The University of Texas at Arlington, TX
The University of Texas at Dallas, TX
The University of Texas at El Paso, TX
The University of Texas at San Antonio, TX
The University of Texas–Pan American, TX
University of Tulsa, OK
University of Utah, UT
The University of West Alabama, AL
University of West Georgia, GA
University of Wisconsin–Eau Claire, WI
University of Wisconsin–La Crosse, WI
University of Wisconsin–Stevens Point, WI
University of Wisconsin–Whitewater, WI
University of Wyoming, WY
Utah State University, UT
Valdosta State University, GA
Valley City State University, ND
Villa Julie College, MD
Virginia Military Institute, VA
Virginia Polytechnic Institute and State University, VA
Wartburg College, IA
Washington State University, WA
Washington University in St. Louis, MO
Waynesburg College, PA
Wayne State College, NE
Western Oregon University, OR
Western Washington University, WA
West Texas A&M University, TX

West Virginia University, WV
Wheeling Jesuit University, WV
Whitworth College, WA
Wichita State University, KS
Widener University, PA
Wilson College, PA
Winston-Salem State University, NC
Xavier University of Louisiana, LA
Youngstown State University, OH

Education

Abilene Christian University, TX
Alaska Pacific University, AK
Albertson College of Idaho, ID
Albertus Magnus College, CT
Albion College, MI
Alderson-Broaddus College, WV
Alfred University, NY
Alliant International University, CA
Antioch College, OH
Arizona State University, AZ
Arkansas State University, AR
Armstrong Atlantic State University, GA
Athens State University, AL
Atlantic Union College, MA
Auburn University, AL
Augsburg College, MN
Augustana College, SD
Augusta State University, GA
Aurora University, IL
Austin College, TX
Austin Peay State University, TN
Averett University, VA
Ball State University, IN
The Baptist College of Florida, FL
Barton College, NC
Baylor University, TX
Belhaven College, MS
Berry College, GA
Black Hills State University, SD
Bloomfield College, NJ
Bloomsburg University of Pennsylvania, PA
Blue Mountain College, MS
Boston University, MA
Bowling Green State University, OH
Brenau University, GA
Brewton-Parker College, GA
Brigham Young University–Hawaii, HI
Bryan College, TN
Buena Vista University, IA
Butler University, IN
California Lutheran University, CA
California Polytechnic State University, San Luis Obispo, CA
California State University, Bakersfield, CA
California State University, Chico, CA
California State University, Fresno, CA
California State University, Stanislaus, CA
Calvin College, MI
Campbellsville University, KY
Carroll College, WI
Carson-Newman College, TN
Cascade College, OR
Catawba College, NC
Centenary College of Louisiana, LA
Central College, IA

Non-Need Scholarships for Undergraduates
Academic Interests/Achievements

Central Michigan University, MI
Central Missouri State University, MO
Central Washington University, WA
Christopher Newport University, VA
City College of the City University of New York, NY
Clearwater Christian College, FL
Clemson University, SC
Coastal Carolina University, SC
College Misericordia, PA
College of Charleston, SC
College of St. Catherine, MN
The College of Saint Rose, NY
College of Staten Island of the City University of New York, NY
College of the Southwest, NM
Columbia College, SC
Columbus State University, GA
Concordia University, NE
Cornerstone University, MI
Creighton University, NE
Dakota State University, SD
Dallas Baptist University, TX
Dallas Christian College, TX
Dalton State College, GA
Davidson College, NC
Davis & Elkins College, WV
Defiance College, OH
DePaul University, IL
Dickinson State University, ND
Dordt College, IA
Dowling College, NY
East Carolina University, NC
Eastern Michigan University, MI
Eastern Washington University, WA
East Stroudsburg University of Pennsylvania, PA
East Tennessee State University, TN
East Texas Baptist University, TX
Edinboro University of Pennsylvania, PA
Elizabethtown College, PA
Elmhurst College, IL
Elon University, NC
Emmanuel College, MA
Emporia State University, KS
Endicott College, MA
Erskine College, SC
Evangel University, MO
Fairfield University, CT
Fairmont State University, WV
Felician College, NJ
Fitchburg State College, MA
Five Towns College, NY
Flagler College, FL
Florida Christian College, FL
Florida Gulf Coast University, FL
Florida Southern College, FL
Fort Hays State University, KS
Fort Lewis College, CO
Francis Marion University, SC
Freed-Hardeman University, TN
Friends University, KS
Frostburg State University, MD
Furman University, SC
Gannon University, PA
Georgia College & State University, GA

Georgia Southern University, GA
Glenville State College, WV
Goshen College, IN
Grambling State University, LA
Greenville College, IL
Grove City College, PA
Hampden-Sydney College, VA
Hardin-Simmons University, TX
Hillsdale College, MI
Husson College, ME
Idaho State University, ID
Illinois State University, IL
Indiana University of Pennsylvania, PA
Indiana University–Purdue University Fort Wayne, IN
Jacksonville State University, AL
James Madison University, VA
Johnson Bible College, TN
Kansas State University, KS
Kean University, NJ
Kennesaw State University, GA
Kent State University, OH
Kentucky Christian University, KY
King's College, PA
LaGrange College, GA
Laura and Alvin Siegal College of Judaic Studies, OH
Lawrence Technological University, MI
Lee University, TN
Lewis-Clark State College, ID
Limestone College, SC
Lincoln University, MO
Lincoln University, PA
Lindenwood University, MO
Lock Haven University of Pennsylvania, PA
Long Island University, Brooklyn Campus, NY
Louisiana State University and Agricultural and Mechanical College, LA
Louisiana Tech University, LA
Lubbock Christian University, TX
Lycoming College, PA
MacMurray College, IL
Malone College, OH
Mansfield University of Pennsylvania, PA
Marymount Manhattan College, NY
Maryville University of Saint Louis, MO
Marywood University, PA
The Master's College and Seminary, CA
Mayville State University, ND
Mercer University, GA
Meredith College, NC
Mesa State College, CO
Messenger College, MO
Metropolitan State College of Denver, CO
Miami University, OH
Michigan State University, MI
Michigan Technological University, MI
Middle Tennessee State University, TN
Midwestern State University, TX
Millersville University of Pennsylvania, PA
Mississippi State University, MS
Missouri State University, MO
Monmouth University, NJ
Montana State University, MT
Montana State University–Billings, MT

Montclair State University, NJ
Morehead State University, KY
Mount Mary College, WI
Mount St. Mary's College, CA
Mount Vernon Nazarene University, OH
Murray State University, KY
Newberry College, SC
New England College, NH
New Jersey City University, NJ
New Mexico State University, NM
North Carolina State University, NC
Northeastern Illinois University, IL
Northern Arizona University, AZ
Northern Illinois University, IL
Northern Michigan University, MI
Northern State University, SD
North Georgia College & State University, GA
North Greenville College, SC
Northwestern Oklahoma State University, OK
Northwestern State University of Louisiana, LA
Northwest Nazarene University, ID
Ohio Northern University, OH
The Ohio State University, OH
Ohio University, OH
Ohio University–Chillicothe, OH
Ohio University–Eastern, OH
Ohio University–Lancaster, OH
Ohio University–Southern Campus, OH
Ohio University–Zanesville, OH
Ohio Wesleyan University, OH
Oklahoma Panhandle State University, OK
Oklahoma State University, OK
Oral Roberts University, OK
Ouachita Baptist University, AR
Pacific Union College, CA
Pacific University, OR
Pepperdine University, CA
Pittsburg State University, KS
Plymouth State University, NH
Portland State University, OR
Purdue University, IN
Quincy University, IL
Radford University, VA
Randolph-Macon Woman's College, VA
The Richard Stockton College of New Jersey, NJ
Ripon College, WI
Sacred Heart University, CT
St. Cloud State University, MN
St. Edward's University, TX
St. John's University, NY
Saint Louis University, MO
Saint Martin's University, WA
Salem International University, WV
Salisbury University, MD
Schreiner University, TX
Seton Hill University, PA
Shasta Bible College, CA
Shepherd University, WV
Shippensburg University of Pennsylvania, PA
Slippery Rock University of Pennsylvania, PA

Non-Need Scholarships for Undergraduates
Academic Interests/Achievements

Sonoma State University, CA
South Dakota State University, SD
Southeastern Louisiana University, LA
Southeastern Oklahoma State University, OK
Southeast Missouri State University, MO
Southern Adventist University, TN
Southern Arkansas University–Magnolia, AR
Southern Illinois University Carbondale, IL
Southern Illinois University Edwardsville, IL
Southern Methodist College, SC
Southern Oregon University, OR
Southwestern Christian University, OK
Southwest Minnesota State University, MN
State University of New York at New Paltz, NY
State University of New York at Oswego, NY
State University of New York at Plattsburgh, NY
State University of New York College at Brockport, NY
State University of New York College at Geneseo, NY
State University of New York College at Oneonta, NY
State University of New York College at Potsdam, NY
State University of New York, Fredonia, NY
Stephen F. Austin State University, TX
Stetson University, FL
Tabor College, KS
Tennessee Technological University, TN
Texas A&M University, TX
Texas Christian University, TX
Texas State University-San Marcos, TX
Texas Tech University, TX
Texas Woman's University, TX
Thiel College, PA
Toccoa Falls College, GA
Trevecca Nazarene University, TN
Truman State University, MO
Union University, TN
The University of Akron, OH
The University of Alabama, AL
The University of Alabama in Huntsville, AL
University of Alaska Southeast, AK
University of Arkansas at Pine Bluff, AR
University of California, Riverside, CA
University of Central Oklahoma, OK
University of Cincinnati, OH
University of Colorado at Boulder, CO
University of Colorado at Colorado Springs, CO
University of Connecticut, CT
University of Dallas, TX
University of Dayton, OH
University of Delaware, DE
University of Evansville, IN
University of Florida, FL
University of Georgia, GA
University of Great Falls, MT

University of Houston–Victoria, TX
University of Idaho, ID
University of Illinois at Springfield, IL
University of Illinois at Urbana–Champaign, IL
University of Kansas, KS
University of Kentucky, KY
University of Maine, ME
University of Mary Hardin-Baylor, TX
University of Maryland, College Park, MD
University of Mary Washington, VA
University of Massachusetts Amherst, MA
University of Memphis, TN
University of Miami, FL
University of Michigan, MI
University of Michigan–Flint, MI
University of Minnesota, Twin Cities Campus, MN
University of Missouri–Columbia, MO
University of Missouri–St. Louis, MO
University of Nebraska at Omaha, NE
University of Nebraska–Lincoln, NE
University of Nevada, Las Vegas, NV
University of Nevada, Reno, NV
University of New England, ME
University of New Hampshire, NH
University of New Orleans, LA
The University of North Carolina at Asheville, NC
The University of North Carolina at Chapel Hill, NC
The University of North Carolina at Greensboro, NC
The University of North Carolina at Pembroke, NC
The University of North Carolina Wilmington, NC
University of North Dakota, ND
University of Northern Colorado, CO
University of Northern Iowa, IA
University of North Florida, FL
University of Oklahoma, OK
University of Oregon, OR
University of Pittsburgh at Bradford, PA
University of Portland, OR
University of St. Francis, IL
University of Saint Francis, IN
University of St. Thomas, MN
University of South Carolina, SC
The University of South Dakota, SD
University of Southern Indiana, IN
University of South Florida, FL
The University of Tampa, FL
The University of Tennessee at Martin, TN
The University of Texas at Arlington, TX
The University of Texas at El Paso, TX
The University of Texas at San Antonio, TX
The University of Texas–Pan American, TX
University of the Ozarks, AR
The University of Toledo, OH
University of Tulsa, OK
University of Utah, UT
The University of West Alabama, AL
University of West Georgia, GA
University of Wisconsin–Eau Claire, WI

University of Wisconsin–La Crosse, WI
University of Wisconsin–Parkside, WI
University of Wisconsin–Stevens Point, WI
University of Wisconsin–Stout, WI
University of Wisconsin–Whitewater, WI
University of Wyoming, WY
Utah State University, UT
Valdosta State University, GA
Valley City State University, ND
Vanderbilt University, TN
VanderCook College of Music, IL
Virginia Polytechnic Institute and State University, VA
Wabash College, IN
Wake Forest University, NC
Walla Walla College, WA
Wartburg College, IA
Washington State University, WA
Washington University in St. Louis, MO
Wayland Baptist University, TX
Waynesburg College, PA
Wayne State College, NE
Webster University, MO
Wesleyan College, GA
Western Carolina University, NC
Western Illinois University, IL
Western Kentucky University, KY
Western Oregon University, OR
Western Washington University, WA
West Texas A&M University, TX
West Virginia University, WV
Wheeling Jesuit University, WV
Wichita State University, KS
Widener University, PA
Wilkes University, PA
William Jewell College, MO
Williams Baptist College, AR
Wilson College, PA
Winston-Salem State University, NC
Worcester State College, MA
Xavier University of Louisiana, LA
Youngstown State University, OH

Engineering/Technologies
Alfred University, NY
Arizona State University, AZ
Arkansas State University, AR
Arkansas Tech University, AR
Armstrong Atlantic State University, GA
Auburn University, AL
Austin College, TX
Averett University, VA
Baylor University, TX
Bluefield State College, WV
Boston University, MA
Bowling Green State University, OH
Bryant University, RI
Bucknell University, PA
Butler University, IN
California Polytechnic State University, San Luis Obispo, CA
California State University, Chico, CA
California State University, Fresno, CA
California State University, Fullerton, CA
Calvin College, MI
Carthage College, WI

Non-Need Scholarships for Undergraduates
Academic Interests/Achievements

Case Western Reserve University, OH
Centenary College of Louisiana, LA
Central Michigan University, MI
Central Missouri State University, MO
Central Washington University, WA
Christian Brothers University, TN
The Citadel, The Military College of South Carolina, SC
City College of the City University of New York, NY
Clarkson University, NY
Clemson University, SC
Cleveland State University, OH
College of Charleston, SC
The College of New Jersey, NJ
The College of Saint Rose, NY
College of Staten Island of the City University of New York, NY
Colorado School of Mines, CO
Cooper Union for the Advancement of Science and Art, NY
Dalton State College, GA
Daniel Webster College, NH
Davis & Elkins College, WV
Dordt College, IA
Eastern Michigan University, MI
Eastern Washington University, WA
East Tennessee State University, TN
Edinboro University of Pennsylvania, PA
Elizabethtown College, PA
Elon University, NC
Emmanuel College, MA
Emporia State University, KS
Evangel University, MO
Fairfield University, CT
Fairmont State University, WV
Florida Agricultural and Mechanical University, FL
Florida Atlantic University, FL
Florida Gulf Coast University, FL
Fort Hays State University, KS
Freed-Hardeman University, TN
Frostburg State University, MD
Furman University, SC
Gannon University, PA
Geneva College, PA
Georgia Institute of Technology, GA
Georgia Southern University, GA
Gonzaga University, WA
Graceland University, IA
Grambling State University, LA
Greenville College, IL
Grove City College, PA
Idaho State University, ID
Illinois State University, IL
Indiana University of Pennsylvania, PA
Indiana University–Purdue University Fort Wayne, IN
James Madison University, VA
The Johns Hopkins University, MD
Kansas State University, KS
Kettering University, MI
Lakeland College, WI
Lawrence Technological University, MI
Lindenwood University, MO
Loras College, IA
Louisiana State University and Agricultural and Mechanical College, LA
Louisiana Tech University, LA
Maine Maritime Academy, ME
Marquette University, WI
Mercer University, GA
Mesa State College, CO
Metropolitan State College of Denver, CO
Miami University, OH
Michigan State University, MI
Michigan Technological University, MI
Middle Tennessee State University, TN
Milwaukee School of Engineering, WI
Minnesota State University Mankato, MN
Mississippi State University, MS
Montana State University, MT
Montana State University–Billings, MT
Montana Tech of The University of Montana, MT
Murray State University, KY
New England College, NH
New Mexico State University, NM
North Carolina State University, NC
Northeastern University, MA
Northern Arizona University, AZ
Northern Illinois University, IL
Northern Michigan University, MI
Ohio Northern University, OH
The Ohio State University, OH
Ohio University, OH
Ohio University–Chillicothe, OH
Ohio University–Eastern, OH
Ohio University–Lancaster, OH
Ohio University–Southern Campus, OH
Ohio University–Zanesville, OH
Ohio Wesleyan University, OH
Oklahoma State University, OK
Oral Roberts University, OK
Ouachita Baptist University, AR
Pittsburg State University, KS
Portland State University, OR
Purdue University, IN
Rice University, TX
Rochester Institute of Technology, NY
Rollins College, FL
St. Cloud State University, MN
Saint Louis University, MO
Saint Martin's University, WA
Santa Clara University, CA
Seattle Pacific University, WA
Shepherd University, WV
Smith College, MA
South Dakota School of Mines and Technology, SD
South Dakota State University, SD
Southeastern Louisiana University, LA
Southeastern Oklahoma State University, OK
Southern Illinois University Carbondale, IL
State University of New York at Binghamton, NY
State University of New York at New Paltz, NY
State University of New York at Plattsburgh, NY
State University of New York College at Potsdam, NY
State University of New York College of Environmental Science and Forestry, NY
State University of New York Institute of Technology, NY
Stevens Institute of Technology, NJ
Stony Brook University, State University of New York, NY
Tennessee Technological University, TN
Texas A&M University, TX
Texas Christian University, TX
Texas Southern University, TX
Texas Tech University, TX
The University of Akron, OH
The University of Alabama, AL
The University of Alabama at Birmingham, AL
The University of Alabama in Huntsville, AL
University of California, Berkeley, CA
University of California, Riverside, CA
University of California, San Diego, CA
University of Cincinnati, OH
University of Colorado at Boulder, CO
University of Colorado at Colorado Springs, CO
University of Colorado at Denver and Health Sciences Center—Downtown Denver Campus, CO
University of Connecticut, CT
University of Dayton, OH
University of Delaware, DE
University of Evansville, IN
University of Florida, FL
University of Idaho, ID
University of Illinois at Springfield, IL
University of Illinois at Urbana–Champaign, IL
The University of Iowa, IA
University of Kansas, KS
University of Kentucky, KY
University of Maine, ME
University of Maryland, Baltimore County, MD
University of Maryland, College Park, MD
University of Massachusetts Amherst, MA
University of Massachusetts Lowell, MA
University of Memphis, TN
University of Miami, FL
University of Michigan, MI
University of Michigan–Dearborn, MI
University of Michigan–Flint, MI
University of Minnesota, Twin Cities Campus, MN
University of Missouri–Columbia, MO
University of Missouri–St. Louis, MO
University of Nebraska at Omaha, NE
University of Nebraska–Lincoln, NE
University of Nevada, Las Vegas, NV
University of Nevada, Reno, NV
University of New Hampshire, NH
The University of North Carolina at Asheville, NC
University of North Dakota, ND
University of North Florida, FL

Non-Need Scholarships for Undergraduates
Academic Interests/Achievements

University of Oklahoma, OK
University of Pittsburgh at Bradford, PA
University of Portland, OR
University of Rochester, NY
University of South Carolina, SC
University of Southern Indiana, IN
University of South Florida, FL
The University of Tennessee at Martin, TN
The University of Texas at Arlington, TX
The University of Texas at Dallas, TX
The University of Texas at El Paso, TX
The University of Texas at San Antonio, TX
The University of Texas at Tyler, TX
The University of Texas–Pan American, TX
The University of Toledo, OH
University of Tulsa, OK
University of Utah, UT
University of Vermont, VT
University of Wisconsin–Green Bay, WI
University of Wisconsin–Parkside, WI
University of Wisconsin–Stevens Point, WI
University of Wisconsin–Stout, WI
University of Wyoming, WY
Utah State University, UT
Valdosta State University, GA
Valparaiso University, IN
Vanderbilt University, TN
Virginia Commonwealth University, VA
Virginia Military Institute, VA
Virginia Polytechnic Institute and State University, VA
Washington State University, WA
Washington University in St. Louis, MO
Western Kentucky University, KY
Western New England College, MA
Western Washington University, WA
West Virginia University, WV
Wheeling Jesuit University, WV
Wichita State University, KS
Widener University, PA
Wilkes University, PA
Xavier University of Louisiana, LA
Youngstown State University, OH

English

Abilene Christian University, TX
Albertus Magnus College, CT
Alfred University, NY
Alliant International University, CA
Arizona State University, AZ
Arkansas State University, AR
Armstrong Atlantic State University, GA
Athens State University, AL
Atlantic Union College, MA
Auburn University, AL
Augsburg College, MN
Augustana College, SD
Augusta State University, GA
Austin College, TX
Averett University, VA
Ball State University, IN
Barton College, NC
Baylor University, TX
Belhaven College, MS
Berry College, GA

Black Hills State University, SD
Bloomfield College, NJ
Bloomsburg University of Pennsylvania, PA
Blue Mountain College, MS
Bowling Green State University, OH
Brevard College, NC
Brigham Young University–Hawaii, HI
Bryan College, TN
Butler University, IN
California Lutheran University, CA
California Polytechnic State University, San Luis Obispo, CA
California State University, Chico, CA
California State University, Fresno, CA
California State University, Stanislaus, CA
Calvin College, MI
Campbellsville University, KY
Cascade College, OR
Case Western Reserve University, OH
Centenary College of Louisiana, LA
Central Michigan University, MI
Central Missouri State University, MO
Central Washington University, WA
Christopher Newport University, VA
City College of the City University of New York, NY
Clemson University, SC
College of Charleston, SC
College of St. Catherine, MN
The College of Saint Rose, NY
College of the Southwest, NM
Columbia College, SC
Columbus State University, GA
Concordia University, NE
Concordia University, St. Paul, MN
Dakota State University, SD
Denison University, OH
Dickinson State University, ND
Dordt College, IA
Eastern Michigan University, MI
Eastern Washington University, WA
East Stroudsburg University of Pennsylvania, PA
East Tennessee State University, TN
East Texas Baptist University, TX
Edinboro University of Pennsylvania, PA
Elizabethtown College, PA
Elmhurst College, IL
Emporia State University, KS
Erskine College, SC
Evangel University, MO
Fairmont State University, WV
Felician College, NJ
Fitchburg State College, MA
Flagler College, FL
Fort Hays State University, KS
Fort Lewis College, CO
Francis Marion University, SC
Freed-Hardeman University, TN
Friends University, KS
Frostburg State University, MD
Furman University, SC
Gannon University, PA
Georgia College & State University, GA
Georgia Southern University, GA
Glenville State College, WV

Graceland University, IA
Grambling State University, LA
Grove City College, PA
Hamline University, MN
Hardin-Simmons University, TX
Hillsdale College, MI
Idaho State University, ID
Illinois State University, IL
Indiana University of Pennsylvania, PA
Indiana University–Purdue University Fort Wayne, IN
Jacksonville State University, AL
James Madison University, VA
Kansas State University, KS
Kennesaw State University, GA
Kent State University, OH
King's College, PA
LaGrange College, GA
Lakeland College, WI
Lewis-Clark State College, ID
Limestone College, SC
Lindenwood University, MO
Lock Haven University of Pennsylvania, PA
Louisiana State University and Agricultural and Mechanical College, LA
Louisiana Tech University, LA
Lubbock Christian University, TX
Lycoming College, PA
MacMurray College, IL
Malone College, OH
Manchester College, IN
Marymount Manhattan College, NY
Mayville State University, ND
Mercer University, GA
Mesa State College, CO
Methodist College, NC
Metropolitan State College of Denver, CO
Michigan State University, MI
Middle Tennessee State University, TN
Midwestern State University, TX
Millersville University of Pennsylvania, PA
Mississippi State University, MS
Montana State University, MT
Montana State University–Billings, MT
Montclair State University, NJ
Morehead State University, KY
Mount Mary College, WI
Murray State University, KY
New England College, NH
New Mexico State University, NM
Northeastern Illinois University, IL
Northern Arizona University, AZ
Northern Illinois University, IL
Northern Michigan University, MI
Northern State University, SD
North Georgia College & State University, GA
Northwestern Oklahoma State University, OK
Northwest Nazarene University, ID
Ohio Northern University, OH
The Ohio State University, OH
Ohio University, OH
Ohio University–Chillicothe, OH
Ohio University–Eastern, OH
Ohio University–Lancaster, OH

Non-Need Scholarships for Undergraduates
Academic Interests/Achievements

Ohio University–Southern Campus, OH
Ohio University–Zanesville, OH
Ohio Wesleyan University, OH
Oklahoma Panhandle State University, OK
Oklahoma State University, OK
Ouachita Baptist University, AR
Pacific University, OR
Pittsburg State University, KS
Plymouth State University, NH
Quincy University, IL
Radford University, VA
Randolph-Macon Woman's College, VA
Rice University, TX
Ripon College, WI
Rockhurst University, MO
Sacred Heart University, CT
St. Cloud State University, MN
St. Edward's University, TX
St. John Fisher College, NY
Saint Louis University, MO
Salisbury University, MD
Schreiner University, TX
Seton Hill University, PA
Shepherd University, WV
Shippensburg University of Pennsylvania, PA
Shorter College, GA
Slippery Rock University of Pennsylvania, PA
Sonoma State University, CA
South Dakota State University, SD
Southeastern Louisiana University, LA
Southeast Missouri State University, MO
Southern Adventist University, TN
Southern Arkansas University–Magnolia, AR
Southern Illinois University Carbondale, IL
Southern Oregon University, OR
Southwest Minnesota State University, MN
State University of New York at Binghamton, NY
State University of New York at New Paltz, NY
State University of New York at Oswego, NY
State University of New York at Plattsburgh, NY
State University of New York College at Brockport, NY
State University of New York College at Geneseo, NY
State University of New York College at Potsdam, NY
State University of New York, Fredonia, NY
Stetson University, FL
Stony Brook University, State University of New York, NY
Tabor College, KS
Tennessee Technological University, TN
Texas State University-San Marcos, TX
Texas Tech University, TX
Texas Woman's University, TX
Thiel College, PA
Truman State University, MO
The University of Akron, OH

The University of Alabama, AL
The University of Alabama in Huntsville, AL
University of Arkansas at Pine Bluff, AR
University of Baltimore, MD
University of California, Riverside, CA
University of Cincinnati, OH
University of Colorado at Boulder, CO
University of Colorado at Colorado Springs, CO
University of Connecticut, CT
University of Delaware, DE
University of Evansville, IN
University of Hawaii at Hilo, HI
University of Idaho, ID
University of Illinois at Springfield, IL
University of Illinois at Urbana–Champaign, IL
University of Kansas, KS
University of Maine, ME
University of Mary Hardin-Baylor, TX
University of Maryland, Baltimore County, MD
University of Maryland, College Park, MD
University of Mary Washington, VA
University of Massachusetts Amherst, MA
University of Memphis, TN
University of Miami, FL
University of Michigan, MI
University of Michigan–Flint, MI
University of Minnesota, Twin Cities Campus, MN
University of Missouri–Columbia, MO
University of Missouri–St. Louis, MO
University of Nebraska at Omaha, NE
University of Nebraska–Lincoln, NE
University of Nevada, Las Vegas, NV
University of Nevada, Reno, NV
University of New England, ME
University of New Hampshire, NH
The University of North Carolina at Asheville, NC
The University of North Carolina at Chapel Hill, NC
The University of North Carolina at Greensboro, NC
The University of North Carolina at Pembroke, NC
The University of North Carolina Wilmington, NC
University of North Dakota, ND
University of Northern Colorado, CO
University of Pittsburgh at Bradford, PA
University of Portland, OR
University of Puget Sound, WA
University of Saint Francis, IN
University of St. Thomas, MN
University of St. Thomas, TX
University of South Carolina, SC
The University of South Dakota, SD
University of South Florida, FL
The University of Tennessee at Martin, TN
The University of Texas at Arlington, TX
The University of Texas at El Paso, TX
The University of Texas at San Antonio, TX

The University of Texas–Pan American, TX
University of the Ozarks, AR
The University of Toledo, OH
University of Tulsa, OK
University of Utah, UT
The University of West Alabama, AL
University of West Georgia, GA
University of Wisconsin–Eau Claire, WI
University of Wisconsin–La Crosse, WI
University of Wisconsin–Parkside, WI
University of Wisconsin–Stevens Point, WI
University of Wisconsin–Whitewater, WI
University of Wyoming, WY
Utah State University, UT
Valdosta State University, GA
Valley City State University, ND
Virginia Military Institute, VA
Virginia Polytechnic Institute and State University, VA
Wake Forest University, NC
Wartburg College, IA
Washington State University, WA
Washington University in St. Louis, MO
Wayland Baptist University, TX
Waynesburg College, PA
Wayne State College, NE
Wesleyan College, GA
Western Carolina University, NC
Western Kentucky University, KY
Western Washington University, WA
West Texas A&M University, TX
West Virginia University, WV
Wheaton College, IL
Wheeling Jesuit University, WV
Wichita State University, KS
Widener University, PA
Wilkes University, PA
Wilson College, PA
Worcester State College, MA
Youngstown State University, OH

Foreign Languages

Abilene Christian University, TX
Adelphi University, NY
Albertus Magnus College, CT
Alfred University, NY
Alliant International University, CA
Arizona State University, AZ
Armstrong Atlantic State University, GA
Auburn University, AL
Augsburg College, MN
Augustana College, SD
Austin College, TX
Averett University, VA
Ball State University, IN
Baylor University, TX
Belhaven College, MS
Black Hills State University, SD
Bloomsburg University of Pennsylvania, PA
Boston University, MA
Bowling Green State University, OH
Brigham Young University–Hawaii, HI
Bryan College, TN
Butler University, IN
California Lutheran University, CA

Non-Need Scholarships for Undergraduates
Academic Interests/Achievements

California Polytechnic State University, San Luis Obispo, CA
California State University, Chico, CA
California State University, Fresno, CA
California State University, Stanislaus, CA
Calvin College, MI
Carthage College, WI
Centenary College of Louisiana, LA
Central College, IA
Central Michigan University, MI
Central Missouri State University, MO
Central Washington University, WA
Christopher Newport University, VA
City College of the City University of New York, NY
Clarke College, IA
Clemson University, SC
Coe College, IA
College of Charleston, SC
College of St. Catherine, MN
The College of Saint Rose, NY
Columbia College, SC
Davidson College, NC
Denison University, OH
DePauw University, IN
Dickinson State University, ND
Dordt College, IA
Eastern Michigan University, MI
Eastern Washington University, WA
East Stroudsburg University of Pennsylvania, PA
East Texas Baptist University, TX
Edinboro University of Pennsylvania, PA
Elizabethtown College, PA
Elmhurst College, IL
Emmanuel College, MA
Emporia State University, KS
Erskine College, SC
Evangel University, MO
Fairfield University, CT
Fairmont State University, WV
Flagler College, FL
Fordham University, NY
Fort Hays State University, KS
Friends University, KS
Frostburg State University, MD
Furman University, SC
Gannon University, PA
Georgia College & State University, GA
Georgia Southern University, GA
Grambling State University, LA
Grove City College, PA
Hamline University, MN
Hardin-Simmons University, TX
Hillsdale College, MI
Idaho State University, ID
Illinois State University, IL
Indiana University of Pennsylvania, PA
Indiana University–Purdue University Fort Wayne, IN
Kansas State University, KS
Kennesaw State University, GA
King's College, PA
Lake Forest College, IL
Lindenwood University, MO
Lock Haven University of Pennsylvania, PA

Louisiana State University and Agricultural and Mechanical College, LA
Louisiana Tech University, LA
Lubbock Christian University, TX
Lycoming College, PA
MacMurray College, IL
Malone College, OH
Manchester College, IN
Manhattan College, NY
Marquette University, WI
Marywood University, PA
Mercer University, GA
Metropolitan State College of Denver, CO
Michigan State University, MI
Middle Tennessee State University, TN
Millersville University of Pennsylvania, PA
Mississippi State University, MS
Missouri State University, MO
Montana State University, MT
Montclair State University, NJ
Moravian College, PA
Murray State University, KY
Newberry College, SC
New Mexico State University, NM
Northeastern Illinois University, IL
Northern Arizona University, AZ
Northern Illinois University, IL
Northern Michigan University, MI
Northern State University, SD
Northwestern Oklahoma State University, OK
Ohio Northern University, OH
The Ohio State University, OH
Ohio University, OH
Ohio University–Chillicothe, OH
Ohio University–Eastern, OH
Ohio University–Lancaster, OH
Ohio University–Southern Campus, OH
Ohio University–Zanesville, OH
Ohio Wesleyan University, OH
Oklahoma State University, OK
Ouachita Baptist University, AR
Pacific University, OR
Pittsburg State University, KS
Portland State University, OR
Rice University, TX
Ripon College, WI
Rockhurst University, MO
St. Edward's University, TX
St. John Fisher College, NY
Saint Louis University, MO
Salisbury University, MD
Seton Hill University, PA
Shepherd University, WV
Shorter College, GA
Sonoma State University, CA
South Dakota State University, SD
Southeastern Louisiana University, LA
Southeast Missouri State University, MO
Southern Arkansas University–Magnolia, AR
Southern Illinois University Carbondale, IL
State University of New York at Binghamton, NY
State University of New York at Oswego, NY

State University of New York College at Brockport, NY
State University of New York College at Geneseo, NY
State University of New York College at Potsdam, NY
State University of New York, Fredonia, NY
Stetson University, FL
Tennessee Technological University, TN
Texas Tech University, TX
Texas Woman's University, TX
Truman State University, MO
The University of Akron, OH
The University of Alabama, AL
University of Central Oklahoma, OK
University of Cincinnati, OH
University of Colorado at Boulder, CO
University of Connecticut, CT
University of Dallas, TX
University of Delaware, DE
University of Evansville, IN
University of Idaho, ID
University of Illinois at Springfield, IL
University of Illinois at Urbana–Champaign, IL
University of Kansas, KS
University of Kentucky, KY
University of Mary Hardin-Baylor, TX
University of Maryland, Baltimore County, MD
University of Maryland, College Park, MD
University of Mary Washington, VA
University of Miami, FL
University of Michigan, MI
University of Michigan–Flint, MI
University of Minnesota, Twin Cities Campus, MN
University of Missouri–Columbia, MO
University of Missouri–St. Louis, MO
University of Nebraska at Omaha, NE
University of Nebraska–Lincoln, NE
University of Nevada, Reno, NV
University of New Orleans, LA
The University of North Carolina at Greensboro, NC
The University of North Carolina Wilmington, NC
University of North Dakota, ND
University of Oklahoma, OK
University of Oregon, OR
University of Portland, OR
University of Puget Sound, WA
University of St. Thomas, TX
University of South Carolina, SC
The University of South Dakota, SD
University of South Florida, FL
The University of Texas at Arlington, TX
The University of Texas at San Antonio, TX
The University of Toledo, OH
University of Tulsa, OK
University of Utah, UT
University of West Georgia, GA
University of Wisconsin–Eau Claire, WI
University of Wisconsin–La Crosse, WI

Non-Need Scholarships for Undergraduates
Academic Interests/Achievements

University of Wisconsin–Parkside, WI
University of Wisconsin–Stevens Point, WI
University of Wisconsin–Whitewater, WI
University of Wyoming, WY
Utah State University, UT
Valdosta State University, GA
Valparaiso University, IN
Virginia Commonwealth University, VA
Virginia Polytechnic Institute and State University, VA
Wake Forest University, NC
Washington State University, WA
Washington University in St. Louis, MO
Wayne State College, NE
Wesleyan College, GA
Western Illinois University, IL
Western Kentucky University, KY
Western Oregon University, OR
Western Washington University, WA
West Texas A&M University, TX
West Virginia University, WV
Wheeling Jesuit University, WV
Wichita State University, KS
Widener University, PA
Wilson College, PA
Worcester State College, MA
Xavier University, OH
Xavier University of Louisiana, LA

Health Fields

Alderson-Broaddus College, WV
Allen College, IA
Arizona State University, AZ
Arkansas State University, AR
Armstrong Atlantic State University, GA
Atlantic Union College, MA
Auburn University, AL
Augsburg College, MN
Augustana College, SD
Augusta State University, GA
Austin College, TX
Averett University, VA
Azusa Pacific University, CA
Ball State University, IN
Barton College, NC
Bastyr University, WA
Baylor University, TX
Biola University, CA
Black Hills State University, SD
Bloomfield College, NJ
Bloomsburg University of Pennsylvania, PA
Bowling Green State University, OH
Brenau University, GA
Brevard College, NC
California Polytechnic State University, San Luis Obispo, CA
California State University, Bakersfield, CA
California State University, Chico, CA
California State University, Fresno, CA
California State University, Stanislaus, CA
Calvin College, MI
Carroll College, WI
Carthage College, WI
Case Western Reserve University, OH
Centenary College of Louisiana, LA
Central College, IA

Central Michigan University, MI
Central Missouri State University, MO
Central Washington University, WA
Champlain College, VT
Clemson University, SC
College Misericordia, PA
College of Charleston, SC
College of St. Catherine, MN
College of Staten Island of the City University of New York, NY
Columbus State University, GA
Concordia University, NE
Dalton State College, GA
Davis & Elkins College, WV
Dickinson State University, ND
East Carolina University, NC
Eastern Michigan University, MI
Eastern Washington University, WA
East Stroudsburg University of Pennsylvania, PA
East Tennessee State University, TN
East Texas Baptist University, TX
Edinboro University of Pennsylvania, PA
Elizabethtown College, PA
Elmhurst College, IL
Emmanuel College, MA
Emporia State University, KS
Endicott College, MA
Fairmont State University, WV
Felician College, NJ
Fitchburg State College, MA
Florida Agricultural and Mechanical University, FL
Florida Gulf Coast University, FL
Florida Metropolitan University–Pinellas Campus, FL
Fort Hays State University, KS
Francis Marion University, SC
Friends University, KS
Frostburg State University, MD
Furman University, SC
Georgia College & State University, GA
Georgia Southern University, GA
Grambling State University, LA
Hamline University, MN
Hampden-Sydney College, VA
Hardin-Simmons University, TX
Hawai'i Pacific University, HI
Hillsdale College, MI
Houston Baptist University, TX
Husson College, ME
Idaho State University, ID
Illinois State University, IL
Indiana University of Pennsylvania, PA
Indiana University–Purdue University Fort Wayne, IN
Jacksonville State University, AL
James Madison University, VA
Jefferson College of Health Sciences, VA
Kansas State University, KS
Kean University, NJ
Kennesaw State University, GA
Kent State University, OH
King's College, PA
LaGrange College, GA
Lewis-Clark State College, ID

Lindenwood University, MO
Long Island University, Brooklyn Campus, NY
Louisiana Tech University, LA
Lycoming College, PA
MacMurray College, IL
Malone College, OH
Mansfield University of Pennsylvania, PA
Marquette University, WI
Maryville University of Saint Louis, MO
Marywood University, PA
Medcenter One College of Nursing, ND
Medical College of Georgia, GA
Mesa State College, CO
Metropolitan State College of Denver, CO
Michigan State University, MI
MidAmerica Nazarene University, KS
Middle Tennessee State University, TN
Midway College, KY
Midwestern State University, TX
Midwestern University, Glendale Campus, AZ
Millersville University of Pennsylvania, PA
Milligan College, TN
Milwaukee School of Engineering, WI
Mississippi State University, MS
Missouri State University, MO
Molloy College, NY
Monmouth University, NJ
Montana State University, MT
Montana State University–Billings, MT
Montana Tech of The University of Montana, MT
Moravian College, PA
Morehead State University, KY
Mount Mary College, WI
Mount Vernon Nazarene University, OH
Murray State University, KY
New Mexico State University, NM
Northern Arizona University, AZ
Northern Illinois University, IL
Northern Michigan University, MI
North Georgia College & State University, GA
Northwestern Oklahoma State University, OK
Northwest Nazarene University, ID
Ohio Northern University, OH
The Ohio State University, OH
Ohio University, OH
Ohio University–Chillicothe, OH
Ohio University–Eastern, OH
Ohio University–Lancaster, OH
Ohio University–Southern Campus, OH
Ohio University–Zanesville, OH
Ohio Wesleyan University, OH
Oklahoma Panhandle State University, OK
Oral Roberts University, OK
Oregon Health & Science University, OR
Ouachita Baptist University, AR
Pikeville College, KY
Pittsburg State University, KS
Plymouth State University, NH
Purdue University, IN
Quincy University, IL
Radford University, VA

Non-Need Scholarships for Undergraduates
Academic Interests/Achievements

The Richard Stockton College of New Jersey, NJ
Robert Morris College, IL
Rochester Institute of Technology, NY
Rockhurst University, MO
Sacred Heart University, CT
St. Cloud State University, MN
Saint Francis Medical Center College of Nursing, IL
St. John's University, NY
Saint Louis University, MO
Salisbury University, MD
Shepherd University, WV
Slippery Rock University of Pennsylvania, PA
Sonoma State University, CA
South Dakota State University, SD
Southeastern Louisiana University, LA
Southeast Missouri State University, MO
Southern Adventist University, TN
Southern Arkansas University–Magnolia, AR
Southern Illinois University Carbondale, IL
Southern Illinois University Edwardsville, IL
Southern Oregon University, OR
State University of New York at Binghamton, NY
State University of New York at New Paltz, NY
State University of New York at Plattsburgh, NY
State University of New York College at Brockport, NY
State University of New York College at Old Westbury, NY
State University of New York Upstate Medical University, NY
Stephen F. Austin State University, TX
Stony Brook University, State University of New York, NY
Tennessee Technological University, TN
Texas A&M University, TX
Texas Woman's University, TX
Thomas Jefferson University, PA
The University of Akron, OH
The University of Alabama at Birmingham, AL
The University of Alabama in Huntsville, AL
University of Central Oklahoma, OK
University of Cincinnati, OH
University of Colorado at Boulder, CO
University of Colorado at Colorado Springs, CO
University of Connecticut, CT
University of Delaware, DE
University of Evansville, IN
University of Florida, FL
University of Hartford, CT
University of Hawaii at Hilo, HI
University of Illinois at Springfield, IL
University of Illinois at Urbana–Champaign, IL
University of Kansas, KS
University of Kentucky, KY

University of Mary Hardin-Baylor, TX
University of Maryland, College Park, MD
University of Massachusetts Amherst, MA
University of Massachusetts Lowell, MA
University of Memphis, TN
University of Miami, FL
University of Michigan, MI
University of Michigan–Flint, MI
University of Minnesota, Twin Cities Campus, MN
University of Missouri–Columbia, MO
University of Missouri–St. Louis, MO
University of Nebraska–Lincoln, NE
University of Nevada, Las Vegas, NV
University of Nevada, Reno, NV
University of New England, ME
University of New Hampshire, NH
The University of North Carolina at Asheville, NC
The University of North Carolina at Chapel Hill, NC
The University of North Carolina at Greensboro, NC
The University of North Carolina at Pembroke, NC
The University of North Carolina Wilmington, NC
University of North Dakota, ND
University of Northern Colorado, CO
University of North Florida, FL
University of Phoenix–Atlanta Campus, GA
University of Phoenix–Bay Area Campus, CA
University of Phoenix–Boston Campus, MA
University of Phoenix–Central Florida Campus, FL
University of Phoenix–Cleveland Campus, OH
University of Phoenix–Dallas Campus, TX
University of Phoenix–Houston Campus, TX
University of Phoenix–Louisiana Campus, LA
University of Phoenix–Metro Detroit Campus, MI
University of Phoenix–New Mexico Campus, NM
University of Phoenix–Northern Virginia Campus, VA
University of Phoenix–North Florida Campus, FL
University of Phoenix–Oklahoma City Campus, OK
University of Phoenix Online Campus, AZ
University of Phoenix–Oregon Campus, OR
University of Phoenix–Phoenix Campus, AZ
University of Phoenix–Raleigh Campus, NC
University of Phoenix–Sacramento Valley Campus, CA
University of Phoenix–San Diego Campus, CA
University of Phoenix–Southern Colorado Campus, CO
University of Phoenix–South Florida Campus, FL

University of Phoenix–Tulsa Campus, OK
University of Phoenix–Utah Campus, UT
University of Phoenix–Washington Campus, WA
University of Phoenix–West Florida Campus, FL
University of Phoenix–West Michigan Campus, MI
University of Pittsburgh at Bradford, PA
University of Portland, OR
University of St. Francis, IL
University of Saint Francis, IN
University of South Carolina, SC
University of Southern Indiana, IN
University of South Florida, FL
The University of Tampa, FL
The University of Tennessee at Martin, TN
The University of Texas at Arlington, TX
The University of Texas at El Paso, TX
The University of Texas Medical Branch, TX
The University of Texas–Pan American, TX
The University of Toledo, OH
University of Tulsa, OK
University of Utah, UT
University of West Georgia, GA
University of Wisconsin–Eau Claire, WI
University of Wisconsin–La Crosse, WI
University of Wisconsin–Parkside, WI
University of Wisconsin–Stevens Point, WI
University of Wyoming, WY
Utah State University, UT
Valdosta State University, GA
Valparaiso University, IN
Virginia Commonwealth University, VA
Virginia Polytechnic Institute and State University, VA
Washington State University, WA
Washington University in St. Louis, MO
Wayne State College, NE
Western Carolina University, NC
Western Kentucky University, KY
Western Washington University, WA
West Texas A&M University, TX
West Virginia University, WV
Wheeling Jesuit University, WV
Wichita State University, KS
Widener University, PA
Wilkes University, PA
William Woods University, MO
Winston-Salem State University, NC
Worcester State College, MA
Youngstown State University, OH

Home Economics
Arizona State University, AZ
Auburn University, AL
Averett University, VA
Baylor University, TX
Bowling Green State University, OH
California Polytechnic State University, San Luis Obispo, CA
Carson-Newman College, TN
Central Missouri State University, MO
College of St. Catherine, MN
East Carolina University, NC

Non-Need Scholarships for Undergraduates
Academic Interests/Achievements

Eastern Michigan University, MI
Fairmont State University, WV
Grambling State University, LA
Idaho State University, ID
Illinois State University, IL
Indiana University of Pennsylvania, PA
Jacksonville State University, AL
Kansas State University, KS
Louisiana State University and Agricultural and Mechanical College, LA
Louisiana Tech University, LA
Middle Tennessee State University, TN
Mississippi State University, MS
Missouri State University, MO
Montana State University, MT
Montclair State University, NJ
Mount Mary College, WI
Mount Vernon Nazarene University, OH
New Mexico State University, NM
Northern Arizona University, AZ
The Ohio State University, OH
Ohio University, OH
Ohio University–Chillicothe, OH
Ohio University–Eastern, OH
Ohio University–Lancaster, OH
Ohio University–Southern Campus, OH
Ohio University–Zanesville, OH
Oklahoma State University, OK
Ouachita Baptist University, AR
Pittsburg State University, KS
Seton Hill University, PA
Shepherd University, WV
South Dakota State University, SD
Southeastern Louisiana University, LA
Southeast Missouri State University, MO
Southern Illinois University Carbondale, IL
State University of New York at Plattsburgh, NY
State University of New York College at Oneonta, NY
Stephen F. Austin State University, TX
Tennessee Technological University, TN
Texas State University-San Marcos, TX
Texas Tech University, TX
Texas Woman's University, TX
The University of Akron, OH
The University of Alabama, AL
University of Central Oklahoma, OK
University of Idaho, ID
University of Kentucky, KY
University of Minnesota, Twin Cities Campus, MN
University of Missouri–Columbia, MO
University of Nebraska at Omaha, NE
University of Nebraska–Lincoln, NE
The University of North Carolina at Greensboro, NC
University of Northern Colorado, CO
The University of Tennessee at Martin, TN
University of Wisconsin–Stevens Point, WI
University of Wisconsin–Stout, WI
University of Wyoming, WY
Utah State University, UT
Virginia Polytechnic Institute and State University, VA
Washington State University, WA

Wayne State College, NE
Western Illinois University, IL
Western Kentucky University, KY
West Virginia University, WV

Humanities

Alaska Pacific University, AK
Albertus Magnus College, CT
Alderson-Broaddus College, WV
Alfred University, NY
Alliant International University, CA
Antioch College, OH
Arizona State University, AZ
Arkansas State University, AR
Armstrong Atlantic State University, GA
Athens State University, AL
Auburn University, AL
Augustana College, SD
Austin College, TX
Austin Peay State University, TN
Averett University, VA
Avila University, MO
Barton College, NC
Baylor University, TX
Belhaven College, MS
Berry College, GA
Black Hills State University, SD
Bloomfield College, NJ
Bloomsburg University of Pennsylvania, PA
Bowling Green State University, OH
Brenau University, GA
Brigham Young University–Hawaii, HI
Bryan College, TN
Buena Vista University, IA
Butler University, IN
California Lutheran University, CA
California Polytechnic State University, San Luis Obispo, CA
California State University, Chico, CA
California State University, Fresno, CA
California State University, Fullerton, CA
California State University, Stanislaus, CA
Calvin College, MI
Campbellsville University, KY
Carroll College, WI
Case Western Reserve University, OH
Centenary College of Louisiana, LA
Central College, IA
Central Michigan University, MI
Central Missouri State University, MO
Christopher Newport University, VA
The Citadel, The Military College of South Carolina, SC
City College of the City University of New York, NY
Clarkson University, NY
Clemson University, SC
Coastal Carolina University, SC
College of Charleston, SC
College of St. Catherine, MN
College of the Holy Cross, MA
Columbia College, SC
Columbus State University, GA
Concordia University, NE
Dallas Baptist University, TX
Dalton State College, GA

Defiance College, OH
Denison University, OH
DePauw University, IN
Dickinson State University, ND
Dordt College, IA
East Carolina University, NC
Eastern Michigan University, MI
Edinboro University of Pennsylvania, PA
Elizabethtown College, PA
Elmhurst College, IL
Emmanuel College, MA
Emporia State University, KS
Evangel University, MO
Fairmont State University, WV
Flagler College, FL
Florida Gulf Coast University, FL
Fort Hays State University, KS
Fort Lewis College, CO
Francis Marion University, SC
Freed-Hardeman University, TN
Fresno Pacific University, CA
Friends University, KS
Frostburg State University, MD
Furman University, SC
Georgia College & State University, GA
Georgia Southern University, GA
Grambling State University, LA
Hardin-Simmons University, TX
Hillsdale College, MI
Idaho State University, ID
Illinois State University, IL
Indiana University of Pennsylvania, PA
Indiana University–Purdue University Fort Wayne, IN
Jacksonville State University, AL
James Madison University, VA
Kansas State University, KS
Kean University, NJ
Kennesaw State University, GA
King's College, PA
Lawrence Technological University, MI
Lewis-Clark State College, ID
Limestone College, SC
Lincoln University, PA
Lindenwood University, MO
Louisiana State University and Agricultural and Mechanical College, LA
Louisiana Tech University, LA
Lubbock Christian University, TX
Lycoming College, PA
Malone College, OH
Manchester College, IN
Marymount Manhattan College, NY
Mesa State College, CO
Metropolitan State College of Denver, CO
Michigan Technological University, MI
Middle Tennessee State University, TN
Millersville University of Pennsylvania, PA
Mississippi State University, MS
Monmouth University, NJ
Montana State University, MT
Montana State University–Billings, MT
Montclair State University, NJ
Morehead State University, KY
Mount Mary College, WI
Murray State University, KY

Non-Need Scholarships for Undergraduates
Academic Interests/Achievements

Newberry College, SC
New England College, NH
New Mexico State University, NM
North Carolina State University, NC
Northern Arizona University, AZ
Northern Illinois University, IL
Northern State University, SD
North Georgia College & State University, GA
Northwestern Oklahoma State University, OK
Northwestern State University of Louisiana, LA
Ohio Northern University, OH
The Ohio State University, OH
Ohio University, OH
Ohio University–Chillicothe, OH
Ohio University–Eastern, OH
Ohio University–Lancaster, OH
Ohio University–Southern Campus, OH
Ohio University–Zanesville, OH
Ohio Wesleyan University, OH
Oklahoma State University, OK
Ouachita Baptist University, AR
Pacific University, OR
Pepperdine University, CA
Portland State University, OR
Purdue University, IN
Radford University, VA
Rensselaer Polytechnic Institute, NY
Rice University, TX
The Richard Stockton College of New Jersey, NJ
Ripon College, WI
Rockhurst University, MO
Sacred Heart University, CT
St. Edward's University, TX
St. John Fisher College, NY
Saint Louis University, MO
Saint Martin's University, WA
Salem International University, WV
Salisbury University, MD
Savannah College of Art and Design, GA
Seton Hill University, PA
Shepherd University, WV
Sonoma State University, CA
South Dakota State University, SD
Southeastern Louisiana University, LA
Southeast Missouri State University, MO
Southern Illinois University Carbondale, IL
State University of New York at New Paltz, NY
State University of New York at Oswego, NY
State University of New York at Plattsburgh, NY
State University of New York College at Geneseo, NY
State University of New York College at Potsdam, NY
State University of New York, Fredonia, NY
Stetson University, FL
Stevens Institute of Technology, NJ
Tabor College, KS
Tennessee Technological University, TN
Texas Tech University, TX
Texas Woman's University, TX
The University of Akron, OH
The University of Alabama in Huntsville, AL
University of Alaska Southeast, AK
University of California, Irvine, CA
University of California, Riverside, CA
University of Cincinnati, OH
University of Colorado at Boulder, CO
University of Connecticut, CT
University of Dayton, OH
University of Delaware, DE
University of Evansville, IN
University of Great Falls, MT
University of Houston–Victoria, TX
University of Idaho, ID
University of Illinois at Springfield, IL
University of Illinois at Urbana–Champaign, IL
University of Kansas, KS
University of Maine, ME
University of Mary Hardin-Baylor, TX
University of Maryland, Baltimore County, MD
University of Maryland, College Park, MD
University of Mary Washington, VA
University of Massachusetts Amherst, MA
University of Massachusetts Lowell, MA
University of Memphis, TN
University of Michigan, MI
University of Michigan–Flint, MI
University of Minnesota, Twin Cities Campus, MN
University of Missouri–St. Louis, MO
University of Nebraska–Lincoln, NE
University of Nevada, Las Vegas, NV
University of Nevada, Reno, NV
University of New England, ME
University of New Hampshire, NH
The University of North Carolina at Greensboro, NC
The University of North Carolina Wilmington, NC
University of North Dakota, ND
University of Oklahoma, OK
University of Pittsburgh at Bradford, PA
University of Portland, OR
University of Puget Sound, WA
University of Rochester, NY
University of St. Thomas, MN
University of South Carolina, SC
The University of South Dakota, SD
University of Southern Indiana, IN
University of South Florida, FL
The University of Tennessee at Martin, TN
The University of Texas at Arlington, TX
The University of Texas at El Paso, TX
The University of Texas at San Antonio, TX
University of the Ozarks, AR
The University of Toledo, OH
University of Utah, UT
University of Vermont, VT
University of West Georgia, GA
University of Wisconsin–Stevens Point, WI
University of Wisconsin–Whitewater, WI
Utah State University, UT
Valdosta State University, GA
Vanderbilt University, TN
Virginia Polytechnic Institute and State University, VA
Washington State University, WA
Washington University in St. Louis, MO
Wayne State College, NE
Webster University, MO
Wesleyan College, GA
Western Washington University, WA
West Texas A&M University, TX
West Virginia University, WV
Wheeling Jesuit University, WV
Wichita State University, KS
Widener University, PA
Wilkes University, PA
Williams Baptist College, AR
Wilson College, PA
Xavier University of Louisiana, LA
Youngstown State University, OH

International Studies

Albertus Magnus College, CT
Alfred University, NY
Alliant International University, CA
Antioch College, OH
Armstrong Atlantic State University, GA
Athens State University, AL
Auburn University, AL
Augsburg College, MN
Augustana College, SD
Austin College, TX
Baylor University, TX
Bloomsburg University of Pennsylvania, PA
Bowling Green State University, OH
Brigham Young University–Hawaii, HI
Buena Vista University, IA
Butler University, IN
California Lutheran University, CA
California Polytechnic State University, San Luis Obispo, CA
California State University, Chico, CA
Calvin College, MI
Carroll College, WI
Cascade College, OR
Case Western Reserve University, OH
Central College, IA
Central Washington University, WA
City College of the City University of New York, NY
Clemson University, SC
College of Staten Island of the City University of New York, NY
Columbus State University, GA
Culver-Stockton College, MO
DePauw University, IN
Elizabethtown College, PA
Emory & Henry College, VA
Fort Hays State University, KS
Frostburg State University, MD
Furman University, SC
Gannon University, PA
Georgia College & State University, GA
Georgia Southern University, GA

Non-Need Scholarships for Undergraduates
Academic Interests/Achievements

Hampshire College, MA
Hillsdale College, MI
Idaho State University, ID
Illinois State University, IL
Indiana University of Pennsylvania, PA
James Madison University, VA
Kennesaw State University, GA
Kent State University, OH
Lawrence Technological University, MI
Lindenwood University, MO
Lock Haven University of Pennsylvania, PA
Lycoming College, PA
Malone College, OH
Marymount Manhattan College, NY
Mercer University, GA
Michigan State University, MI
Middle Tennessee State University, TN
Mississippi State University, MS
Monmouth University, NJ
Murray State University, KY
New England College, NH
Northern Arizona University, AZ
Northern Illinois University, IL
Northern Michigan University, MI
Northern State University, SD
Northwestern Oklahoma State University, OK
Ohio Northern University, OH
The Ohio State University, OH
Ohio University, OH
Ohio University–Chillicothe, OH
Ohio University–Eastern, OH
Ohio University–Lancaster, OH
Ohio University–Southern Campus, OH
Ohio University–Zanesville, OH
Ohio Wesleyan University, OH
Oklahoma State University, OK
Ouachita Baptist University, AR
Pepperdine University, CA
Portland State University, OR
Quincy University, IL
Rice University, TX
Rochester Institute of Technology, NY
St. Cloud State University, MN
St. Edward's University, TX
Saint Louis University, MO
South Dakota State University, SD
Southeastern Louisiana University, LA
Southeast Missouri State University, MO
Southern Illinois University Carbondale, IL
Southwest Minnesota State University, MN
State University of New York at Binghamton, NY
State University of New York at Oswego, NY
State University of New York at Plattsburgh, NY
State University of New York College at Brockport, NY
State University of New York College at Oneonta, NY
State University of New York, Fredonia, NY
Tennessee Technological University, TN
Texas Christian University, TX
Texas State University-San Marcos, TX

Texas Tech University, TX
Tiffin University, OH
The University of Akron, OH
University of Colorado at Boulder, CO
University of Connecticut, CT
University of Delaware, DE
University of Evansville, IN
University of Illinois at Springfield, IL
University of Illinois at Urbana–Champaign, IL
University of Kansas, KS
University of Mary Hardin-Baylor, TX
University of Maryland, College Park, MD
University of Memphis, TN
University of Miami, FL
University of Michigan, MI
University of Michigan–Dearborn, MI
University of Michigan–Flint, MI
University of Minnesota, Twin Cities Campus, MN
University of Missouri–St. Louis, MO
University of Nebraska–Lincoln, NE
University of Nevada, Las Vegas, NV
University of Nevada, Reno, NV
University of New England, ME
University of New Orleans, LA
The University of North Carolina Wilmington, NC
University of North Dakota, ND
University of North Florida, FL
University of Oklahoma, OK
University of Puget Sound, WA
University of St. Thomas, MN
University of South Carolina, SC
University of South Florida, FL
The University of Texas at Arlington, TX
The University of Texas at El Paso, TX
The University of Toledo, OH
University of Tulsa, OK
University of Utah, UT
University of Wisconsin–Eau Claire, WI
University of Wisconsin–Stevens Point, WI
University of Wisconsin–Stout, WI
University of Wyoming, WY
Utah State University, UT
Villanova University, PA
Virginia Military Institute, VA
Virginia Polytechnic Institute and State University, VA
Wake Forest University, NC
Wartburg College, IA
Washington State University, WA
Washington University in St. Louis, MO
Waynesburg College, PA
Webster University, MO
Western Oregon University, OR
West Virginia University, WV
Wheeling Jesuit University, WV
Wichita State University, KS
Widener University, PA
Wilkes University, PA
Wilson College, PA

Library Science
Arkansas State University, AR

California Polytechnic State University, San Luis Obispo, CA
Central Missouri State University, MO
Emporia State University, KS
Fort Hays State University, KS
Illinois State University, IL
Kent State University, OH
Lindenwood University, MO
Lock Haven University of Pennsylvania, PA
Louisiana Tech University, LA
Mayville State University, ND
Mississippi State University, MS
Murray State University, KY
Northwestern Oklahoma State University, OK
Radford University, VA
Southeastern Louisiana University, LA
Southwest Minnesota State University, MN
Texas Woman's University, TX
The University of Alabama, AL
University of Illinois at Urbana–Champaign, IL
University of Kansas, KS
University of Maryland, College Park, MD
University of Michigan, MI
University of Minnesota, Twin Cities Campus, MN
The University of North Carolina at Greensboro, NC
University of South Carolina, SC
University of South Florida, FL
The University of Toledo, OH
Utah State University, UT
Valdosta State University, GA
Valley City State University, ND
Western Kentucky University, KY
Western Washington University, WA
West Virginia University, WV

Mathematics
Abilene Christian University, TX
Albertus Magnus College, CT
Albion College, MI
Alderson-Broaddus College, WV
Alfred University, NY
Antioch College, OH
Arizona State University, AZ
Arkansas State University, AR
Armstrong Atlantic State University, GA
Ashland University, OH
Athens State University, AL
Atlantic Union College, MA
Auburn University, AL
Augsburg College, MN
Augustana College, SD
Augusta State University, GA
Aurora University, IL
Austin Peay State University, TN
Averett University, VA
Ball State University, IN
Bard College, NY
Barton College, NC
Baylor University, TX
Belhaven College, MS
Bennett College For Women, NC
Black Hills State University, SD

Non-Need Scholarships for Undergraduates
Academic Interests/Achievements

Bloomsburg University of Pennsylvania, PA
Blue Mountain College, MS
Bowling Green State University, OH
Brevard College, NC
Brewton-Parker College, GA
Brigham Young University–Hawaii, HI
Bryan College, TN
Buena Vista University, IA
Butler University, IN
California Lutheran University, CA
California Polytechnic State University, San Luis Obispo, CA
California State University, Bakersfield, CA
California State University, Chico, CA
California State University, Fresno, CA
California State University, Fullerton, CA
California State University, San Marcos, CA
California State University, Stanislaus, CA
Calvin College, MI
Campbellsville University, KY
Carroll College, WI
Carson-Newman College, TN
Carthage College, WI
Case Western Reserve University, OH
Centenary College of Louisiana, LA
Central College, IA
Central Michigan University, MI
Central Missouri State University, MO
Central Washington University, WA
Christopher Newport University, VA
City College of the City University of New York, NY
Clarkson University, NY
Clemson University, SC
Coastal Carolina University, SC
College of Charleston, SC
College of St. Catherine, MN
The College of Saint Rose, NY
College of Staten Island of the City University of New York, NY
College of the Southwest, NM
The College of Wooster, OH
The Colorado College, CO
Colorado School of Mines, CO
Columbia College, SC
Concordia University, NE
Concordia University, St. Paul, MN
Dakota State University, SD
Dallas Baptist University, TX
Davidson College, NC
Defiance College, OH
DePauw University, IN
Dickinson State University, ND
Dordt College, IA
Duke University, NC
Eastern Michigan University, MI
Eastern Washington University, WA
East Stroudsburg University of Pennsylvania, PA
East Tennessee State University, TN
East Texas Baptist University, TX
Edinboro University of Pennsylvania, PA
Elizabethtown College, PA
Elmhurst College, IL
Elon University, NC

Emmanuel College, MA
Emporia State University, KS
Erskine College, SC
Evangel University, MO
Fairmont State University, WV
Felician College, NJ
Fitchburg State College, MA
Florida Gulf Coast University, FL
Fort Hays State University, KS
Fort Lewis College, CO
Francis Marion University, SC
Freed-Hardeman University, TN
Friends University, KS
Frostburg State University, MD
Furman University, SC
Gannon University, PA
Georgia College & State University, GA
Georgia Southern University, GA
Glenville State College, WV
Grambling State University, LA
Greenville College, IL
Hardin-Simmons University, TX
Heidelberg College, OH
Hillsdale College, MI
Idaho State University, ID
Illinois State University, IL
Indiana University of Pennsylvania, PA
Indiana University–Purdue University Fort Wayne, IN
Jacksonville State University, AL
James Madison University, VA
Kansas State University, KS
Kennesaw State University, GA
Kent State University, OH
Kentucky State University, KY
Kettering University, MI
King's College, PA
Knox College, IL
Lawrence Technological University, MI
Lewis-Clark State College, ID
Limestone College, SC
Lincoln University, PA
Lindenwood University, MO
Lock Haven University of Pennsylvania, PA
Louisiana State University and Agricultural and Mechanical College, LA
Louisiana Tech University, LA
Lycoming College, PA
Malone College, OH
Manhattan College, NY
Mansfield University of Pennsylvania, PA
Marquette University, WI
Marywood University, PA
The Master's College and Seminary, CA
Mayville State University, ND
Meredith College, NC
Mesa State College, CO
Metropolitan State College of Denver, CO
Michigan State University, MI
Michigan Technological University, MI
Middle Tennessee State University, TN
Midwestern State University, TX
Millersville University of Pennsylvania, PA
Milligan College, TN
Minnesota State University Mankato, MN
Mississippi State University, MS

Missouri State University, MO
Monmouth University, NJ
Montana State University, MT
Montana State University–Billings, MT
Montana Tech of The University of Montana, MT
Montclair State University, NJ
Moravian College, PA
Mount Mary College, WI
Mount Olive College, NC
Murray State University, KY
Newberry College, SC
New England College, NH
New Jersey City University, NJ
New Mexico State University, NM
North Carolina State University, NC
Northeastern Illinois University, IL
Northern Arizona University, AZ
Northern Illinois University, IL
Northern Michigan University, MI
Northern State University, SD
North Georgia College & State University, GA
Northwestern Oklahoma State University, OK
Northwestern State University of Louisiana, LA
Northwest Nazarene University, ID
Ohio Northern University, OH
The Ohio State University, OH
Ohio University, OH
Ohio University–Chillicothe, OH
Ohio University–Eastern, OH
Ohio University–Lancaster, OH
Ohio University–Southern Campus, OH
Ohio University–Zanesville, OH
Ohio Wesleyan University, OH
Oklahoma Panhandle State University, OK
Oklahoma State University, OK
Ouachita Baptist University, AR
Pacific University, OR
Pittsburg State University, KS
Plymouth State University, NH
Purdue University, IN
Quincy University, IL
Radford University, VA
Randolph-Macon Woman's College, VA
Rensselaer Polytechnic Institute, NY
Rice University, TX
The Richard Stockton College of New Jersey, NJ
Ripon College, WI
Rochester Institute of Technology, NY
Rockhurst University, MO
Rollins College, FL
Sacred Heart University, CT
St. Cloud State University, MN
St. Edward's University, TX
St. John Fisher College, NY
St. John's University, NY
Saint Louis University, MO
Saint Vincent College, PA
Salisbury University, MD
Schreiner University, TX
Seton Hill University, PA
Shepherd University, WV

Non-Need Scholarships for Undergraduates
Academic Interests/Achievements

Skidmore College, NY
Sonoma State University, CA
South Dakota School of Mines and Technology, SD
South Dakota State University, SD
Southeastern Louisiana University, LA
Southeastern Oklahoma State University, OK
Southeast Missouri State University, MO
Southern Adventist University, TN
Southern Arkansas University–Magnolia, AR
Southern Illinois University Carbondale, IL
Southern Oregon University, OR
Southwest Minnesota State University, MN
State University of New York at Binghamton, NY
State University of New York at New Paltz, NY
State University of New York at Oswego, NY
State University of New York at Plattsburgh, NY
State University of New York College at Brockport, NY
State University of New York College at Geneseo, NY
State University of New York College at Potsdam, NY
State University of New York, Fredonia, NY
Stephen F. Austin State University, TX
Stetson University, FL
Stevens Institute of Technology, NJ
Tabor College, KS
Tennessee Technological University, TN
Texas Tech University, TX
Texas Woman's University, TX
Thiel College, PA
Truman State University, MO
Union University, TN
The University of Akron, OH
The University of Alabama, AL
The University of Alabama at Birmingham, AL
University of Alaska Southeast, AK
University of Arkansas at Pine Bluff, AR
University of California, Riverside, CA
University of California, San Diego, CA
University of Central Oklahoma, OK
University of Cincinnati, OH
University of Colorado at Boulder, CO
University of Colorado at Colorado Springs, CO
University of Connecticut, CT
University of Dallas, TX
University of Delaware, DE
University of Evansville, IN
University of Great Falls, MT
University of Houston–Victoria, TX
University of Idaho, ID
University of Illinois at Springfield, IL
University of Illinois at Urbana–Champaign, IL
University of Kansas, KS
University of Kentucky, KY
University of Maine, ME
University of Mary Hardin-Baylor, TX
University of Maryland, Baltimore County, MD
University of Maryland, College Park, MD
University of Mary Washington, VA
University of Massachusetts Amherst, MA
University of Memphis, TN
University of Miami, FL
University of Michigan, MI
University of Michigan–Dearborn, MI
University of Michigan–Flint, MI
University of Minnesota, Twin Cities Campus, MN
University of Missouri–Columbia, MO
University of Missouri–St. Louis, MO
University of Nebraska at Omaha, NE
University of Nebraska–Lincoln, NE
University of Nevada, Las Vegas, NV
University of Nevada, Reno, NV
University of New England, ME
University of New Hampshire, NH
University of New Orleans, LA
The University of North Carolina at Asheville, NC
The University of North Carolina at Chapel Hill, NC
The University of North Carolina at Greensboro, NC
The University of North Carolina Wilmington, NC
University of North Dakota, ND
University of Northern Colorado, CO
University of Northern Iowa, IA
University of Oklahoma, OK
University of Pittsburgh at Bradford, PA
University of Portland, OR
University of Puget Sound, WA
University of Richmond, VA
University of Rochester, NY
University of Saint Francis, IN
University of St. Thomas, MN
University of St. Thomas, TX
University of South Carolina, SC
The University of South Dakota, SD
University of Southern Indiana, IN
University of South Florida, FL
The University of Tennessee at Martin, TN
The University of Texas at Arlington, TX
The University of Texas at Dallas, TX
The University of Texas at El Paso, TX
The University of Texas at San Antonio, TX
The University of Texas–Pan American, TX
University of the Ozarks, AR
The University of Toledo, OH
University of Tulsa, OK
University of Utah, UT
University of Vermont, VT
University of West Georgia, GA
University of Wisconsin–Eau Claire, WI
University of Wisconsin–La Crosse, WI
University of Wisconsin–Parkside, WI
University of Wisconsin–Stevens Point, WI
University of Wisconsin–Stout, WI
University of Wisconsin–Whitewater, WI
University of Wyoming, WY
Utah State University, UT
Valdosta State University, GA
Valley City State University, ND
Virginia Commonwealth University, VA
Virginia Military Institute, VA
Virginia Polytechnic Institute and State University, VA
Wake Forest University, NC
Wartburg College, IA
Washington State University, WA
Washington University in St. Louis, MO
Wayland Baptist University, TX
Waynesburg College, PA
Wayne State College, NE
Wesleyan College, GA
Western Carolina University, NC
Western Illinois University, IL
Western Kentucky University, KY
Western Oregon University, OR
Western Washington University, WA
West Texas A&M University, TX
West Virginia University, WV
Wheeling Jesuit University, WV
Wichita State University, KS
Widener University, PA
Wilkes University, PA
Wilson College, PA
Winston-Salem State University, NC
Xavier University, OH
Xavier University of Louisiana, LA

Military Science
Alfred University, NY
Arizona State University, AZ
Arkansas State University, AR
Armstrong Atlantic State University, GA
Augusta State University, GA
Austin Peay State University, TN
Baylor University, TX
Black Hills State University, SD
Boston College, MA
Bowling Green State University, OH
California Polytechnic State University, San Luis Obispo, CA
California State University, Fullerton, CA
Carson-Newman College, TN
Central Michigan University, MI
Central Missouri State University, MO
Central Washington University, WA
Christopher Newport University, VA
The Citadel, The Military College of South Carolina, SC
Clarkson University, NY
Clemson University, SC
College of Saint Benedict, MN
College of the Holy Cross, MA
Colorado School of Mines, CO
Columbus State University, GA
Creighton University, NE
Dickinson College, PA
East Carolina University, NC
East Tennessee State University, TN
Edinboro University of Pennsylvania, PA
Elon University, NC
Florida Institute of Technology, FL

Non-Need Scholarships for Undergraduates
Academic Interests/Achievements

Furman University, SC
Georgia Southern University, GA
Grambling State University, LA
Idaho State University, ID
Illinois State University, IL
Jacksonville State University, AL
James Madison University, VA
Kansas State University, KS
Kent State University, OH
Lawrence Technological University, MI
Lehigh University, PA
Lincoln University, MO
Lindenwood University, MO
Louisiana State University and Agricultural and Mechanical College, LA
Louisiana Tech University, LA
Manhattan College, NY
Mercer University, GA
Michigan State University, MI
Middle Tennessee State University, TN
Mississippi State University, MS
Missouri State University, MO
Montana State University, MT
New Mexico State University, NM
North Carolina Agricultural and Technical State University, NC
Northern Arizona University, AZ
Northern Michigan University, MI
North Georgia College & State University, GA
North Greenville College, SC
Northwest Nazarene University, ID
The Ohio State University, OH
Ohio University, OH
Ohio University–Chillicothe, OH
Ohio University–Eastern, OH
Ohio University–Lancaster, OH
Ohio University–Southern Campus, OH
Ohio University–Zanesville, OH
Oklahoma State University, OK
Olivet Nazarene University, IL
Pittsburg State University, KS
Purdue University, IN
Radford University, VA
Rensselaer Polytechnic Institute, NY
Ripon College, WI
Rochester Institute of Technology, NY
St. Edward's University, TX
St. John's University, NY
Saint Louis University, MO
Santa Clara University, CA
South Dakota State University, SD
Southeast Missouri State University, MO
Southern Illinois University Carbondale, IL
State University of New York College at Brockport, NY
Stephen F. Austin State University, TX
Stetson University, FL
Tennessee Technological University, TN
Texas Christian University, TX
Texas State University-San Marcos, TX
Texas Tech University, TX
Truman State University, MO
The University of Akron, OH
The University of Alabama, AL
University of Central Oklahoma, OK

University of Cincinnati, OH
University of Colorado at Boulder, CO
University of Colorado at Colorado Springs, CO
University of Delaware, DE
University of Florida, FL
University of Idaho, ID
University of Illinois at Urbana–Champaign, IL
University of Kansas, KS
University of Kentucky, KY
University of Maine, ME
University of Maryland, College Park, MD
University of Massachusetts Amherst, MA
University of Memphis, TN
University of Michigan, MI
University of Minnesota, Twin Cities Campus, MN
University of Nevada, Reno, NV
University of New Hampshire, NH
University of New Orleans, LA
University of North Dakota, ND
University of Northern Colorado, CO
University of Portland, OR
University of Puerto Rico, Mayagüez Campus, PR
University of South Carolina, SC
The University of South Dakota, SD
University of South Florida, FL
The University of Tampa, FL
The University of Tennessee at Martin, TN
The University of Texas at Arlington, TX
The University of Texas at El Paso, TX
The University of Texas–Pan American, TX
University of Utah, UT
University of Vermont, VT
University of Wisconsin–La Crosse, WI
University of Wisconsin–Stevens Point, WI
University of Wyoming, WY
Valdosta State University, GA
Villanova University, PA
Virginia Commonwealth University, VA
Virginia Military Institute, VA
Virginia Polytechnic Institute and State University, VA
Wake Forest University, NC
Washington State University, WA
Washington University in St. Louis, MO
Western Kentucky University, KY
West Virginia University, WV
Whitworth College, WA
Widener University, PA
Xavier University, OH
Youngstown State University, OH

Physical Sciences
Abilene Christian University, TX
Alaska Pacific University, AK
Albertus Magnus College, CT
Alderson-Broaddus College, WV
Alfred University, NY
Antioch College, OH
Arizona State University, AZ
Arkansas State University, AR
Armstrong Atlantic State University, GA
Ashland University, OH

Athens State University, AL
Auburn University, AL
Augsburg College, MN
Augustana College, SD
Augusta State University, GA
Austin College, TX
Averett University, VA
Bard College, NY
Barton College, NC
Baylor University, TX
Black Hills State University, SD
Bloomfield College, NJ
Bloomsburg University of Pennsylvania, PA
Bowling Green State University, OH
Brevard College, NC
Brigham Young University–Hawaii, HI
Bryan College, TN
Bucknell University, PA
Butler University, IN
California Lutheran University, CA
California Polytechnic State University, San Luis Obispo, CA
California State University, Bakersfield, CA
California State University, Chico, CA
California State University, Stanislaus, CA
Calvin College, MI
Campbellsville University, KY
Carroll College, WI
Carthage College, WI
Case Western Reserve University, OH
Centenary College of Louisiana, LA
Central College, IA
Central Michigan University, MI
Central Missouri State University, MO
Central Washington University, WA
Chapman University, CA
Clarkson University, NY
Clemson University, SC
Coe College, IA
College of Charleston, SC
The College of New Jersey, NJ
College of St. Catherine, MN
College of Staten Island of the City University of New York, NY
The College of Wooster, OH
The Colorado College, CO
Colorado School of Mines, CO
Columbus State University, GA
Concordia University, NE
Concordia University, St. Paul, MN
Davidson College, NC
Davis & Elkins College, WV
Defiance College, OH
Denison University, OH
DePauw University, IN
Dickinson State University, ND
Dominican University, IL
Dordt College, IA
Eastern Michigan University, MI
Eastern Washington University, WA
East Stroudsburg University of Pennsylvania, PA
East Texas Baptist University, TX
Edinboro University of Pennsylvania, PA
Elizabethtown College, PA
Elmhurst College, IL

Non-Need Scholarships for Undergraduates
Academic Interests/Achievements

Elon University, NC
Emmanuel College, MA
Emporia State University, KS
Evangel University, MO
Fairfield University, CT
Fairmont State University, WV
Florida Atlantic University, FL
Florida Gulf Coast University, FL
Florida Southern College, FL
Fort Hays State University, KS
Fort Lewis College, CO
Freed-Hardeman University, TN
Friends University, KS
Frostburg State University, MD
Furman University, SC
Georgia College & State University, GA
Georgia Institute of Technology, GA
Graceland University, IA
Grambling State University, LA
Greenville College, IL
Grove City College, PA
Hamline University, MN
Hampshire College, MA
Hardin-Simmons University, TX
Heidelberg College, OH
Hillsdale College, MI
Idaho State University, ID
Illinois State University, IL
Indiana University of Pennsylvania, PA
Indiana University–Purdue University Fort Wayne, IN
Jacksonville State University, AL
James Madison University, VA
Jamestown College, ND
Kansas State University, KS
Kennesaw State University, GA
Kent State University, OH
Kettering University, MI
King's College, PA
LaGrange College, GA
Lake Forest College, IL
Lawrence Technological University, MI
Limestone College, SC
Lincoln University, PA
Lindenwood University, MO
Lock Haven University of Pennsylvania, PA
Loras College, IA
Louisiana State University and Agricultural and Mechanical College, LA
Louisiana Tech University, LA
Lubbock Christian University, TX
Lycoming College, PA
MacMurray College, IL
Malone College, OH
Mansfield University of Pennsylvania, PA
The Master's College and Seminary, CA
Mayville State University, ND
Mercyhurst College, PA
Meredith College, NC
Mesa State College, CO
Metropolitan State College of Denver, CO
Michigan State University, MI
Michigan Technological University, MI
Middle Tennessee State University, TN
Millersville University of Pennsylvania, PA
Minnesota State University Mankato, MN

Mississippi State University, MS
Missouri State University, MO
Montana State University, MT
Montana State University–Billings, MT
Montana Tech of The University of Montana, MT
Montclair State University, NJ
Moravian College, PA
Morehead State University, KY
Mount Mary College, WI
Newberry College, SC
New Mexico State University, NM
North Carolina State University, NC
Northeastern Illinois University, IL
Northern Arizona University, AZ
Northern Illinois University, IL
Northern Michigan University, MI
Northern State University, SD
North Georgia College & State University, GA
Northwestern Oklahoma State University, OK
Northwestern State University of Louisiana, LA
Northwest Nazarene University, ID
Ohio Northern University, OH
The Ohio State University, OH
Ohio University, OH
Ohio University–Chillicothe, OH
Ohio University–Eastern, OH
Ohio University–Lancaster, OH
Ohio University–Southern Campus, OH
Ohio University–Zanesville, OH
Ohio Wesleyan University, OH
Oklahoma Panhandle State University, OK
Oklahoma State University, OK
Ouachita Baptist University, AR
Pacific University, OR
Pittsburg State University, KS
Plymouth State University, NH
Portland State University, OR
Purdue University, IN
Radford University, VA
Randolph-Macon Woman's College, VA
Rice University, TX
The Richard Stockton College of New Jersey, NJ
Ripon College, WI
Rochester Institute of Technology, NY
Rockhurst University, MO
Rollins College, FL
Sacred Heart University, CT
St. Cloud State University, MN
St. Edward's University, TX
Saint Francis University, PA
St. John Fisher College, NY
Saint Louis University, MO
Saint Vincent College, PA
Salisbury University, MD
Schreiner University, TX
Seton Hill University, PA
Shepherd University, WV
Skidmore College, NY
Slippery Rock University of Pennsylvania, PA
Sonoma State University, CA

South Dakota State University, SD
Southeastern Louisiana University, LA
Southeastern Oklahoma State University, OK
Southeast Missouri State University, MO
Southern Arkansas University–Magnolia, AR
Southern Illinois University Carbondale, IL
Southern Oregon University, OR
Southwest Minnesota State University, MN
State University of New York at Binghamton, NY
State University of New York at New Paltz, NY
State University of New York at Oswego, NY
State University of New York at Plattsburgh, NY
State University of New York College at Brockport, NY
State University of New York College at Geneseo, NY
State University of New York College at Old Westbury, NY
State University of New York College at Oneonta, NY
State University of New York College at Potsdam, NY
State University of New York College of Environmental Science and Forestry, NY
State University of New York, Fredonia, NY
Stephen F. Austin State University, TX
Stetson University, FL
Stevens Institute of Technology, NJ
Stony Brook University, State University of New York, NY
Tennessee Technological University, TN
Texas A&M University, TX
Texas Tech University, TX
Texas Woman's University, TX
Thiel College, PA
Trevecca Nazarene University, TN
Truman State University, MO
The University of Akron, OH
The University of Alabama, AL
The University of Alabama in Huntsville, AL
University of California, Riverside, CA
University of California, San Diego, CA
University of Central Oklahoma, OK
University of Cincinnati, OH
University of Colorado at Boulder, CO
University of Colorado at Colorado Springs, CO
University of Connecticut, CT
University of Dallas, TX
University of Delaware, DE
University of Evansville, IN
University of Great Falls, MT
University of Idaho, ID
University of Illinois at Springfield, IL
University of Illinois at Urbana–Champaign, IL
University of Kansas, KS
University of Kentucky, KY

Non-Need Scholarships for Undergraduates
Academic Interests/Achievements

University of Maine, ME
University of Mary Hardin-Baylor, TX
University of Maryland, Baltimore County, MD
University of Maryland, College Park, MD
University of Mary Washington, VA
University of Massachusetts Amherst, MA
University of Memphis, TN
University of Miami, FL
University of Michigan, MI
University of Michigan–Dearborn, MI
University of Michigan–Flint, MI
University of Minnesota, Twin Cities Campus, MN
University of Nebraska at Omaha, NE
University of Nebraska–Lincoln, NE
University of Nevada, Las Vegas, NV
University of Nevada, Reno, NV
University of New England, ME
University of New Orleans, LA
The University of North Carolina at Asheville, NC
The University of North Carolina at Greensboro, NC
The University of North Carolina at Pembroke, NC
The University of North Carolina Wilmington, NC
University of North Dakota, ND
University of Northern Colorado, CO
University of Northern Iowa, IA
University of Oklahoma, OK
University of Oregon, OR
University of Pittsburgh at Bradford, PA
University of Portland, OR
University of Puget Sound, WA
University of Richmond, VA
University of Rochester, NY
University of Saint Francis, IN
University of St. Thomas, MN
University of St. Thomas, TX
University of South Carolina, SC
University of South Florida, FL
The University of Tennessee at Martin, TN
The University of Texas at Arlington, TX
The University of Texas at Dallas, TX
The University of Texas at El Paso, TX
The University of Texas at San Antonio, TX
The University of Toledo, OH
University of Tulsa, OK
University of Utah, UT
University of West Georgia, GA
University of Wisconsin–Eau Claire, WI
University of Wisconsin–Green Bay, WI
University of Wisconsin–La Crosse, WI
University of Wisconsin–Parkside, WI
University of Wisconsin–Stevens Point, WI
University of Wisconsin–Stout, WI
University of Wisconsin–Whitewater, WI
University of Wyoming, WY
Utah State University, UT
Valdosta State University, GA
Valley City State University, ND
Valparaiso University, IN

Virginia Polytechnic Institute and State University, VA
Wake Forest University, NC
Wartburg College, IA
Washington State University, WA
Washington University in St. Louis, MO
Wayland Baptist University, TX
Wayne State College, NE
Western Illinois University, IL
Western Kentucky University, KY
Western Oregon University, OR
Western Washington University, WA
West Texas A&M University, TX
West Virginia University, WV
Wheaton College, IL
Wheeling Jesuit University, WV
Whitworth College, WA
Wichita State University, KS
Widener University, PA
Wilson College, PA
Xavier University, OH
Xavier University of Louisiana, LA

Premedicine

Albertus Magnus College, CT
Albion College, MI
Alderson-Broaddus College, WV
Alfred University, NY
Arizona State University, AZ
Arkansas State University, AR
Atlantic Union College, MA
Auburn University, AL
Augustana College, SD
Austin College, TX
Averett University, VA
Avila University, MO
Baylor University, TX
Belhaven College, MS
Blue Mountain College, MS
Brevard College, NC
Bryan College, TN
California State University, Stanislaus, CA
Calvin College, MI
Campbellsville University, KY
Carroll College, WI
Carthage College, WI
Case Western Reserve University, OH
Centenary College of Louisiana, LA
Central Missouri State University, MO
Central Washington University, WA
City College of the City University of New York, NY
Clearwater Christian College, FL
Clemson University, SC
Coe College, IA
College of Charleston, SC
College of St. Catherine, MN
The College of Saint Rose, NY
College of Staten Island of the City University of New York, NY
Concordia University, NE
Dallas Baptist University, TX
Davidson College, NC
Defiance College, OH
Dickinson State University, ND
Dordt College, IA

Edinboro University of Pennsylvania, PA
Elizabethtown College, PA
Elmhurst College, IL
Elon University, NC
Emory & Henry College, VA
Emporia State University, KS
Erskine College, SC
Evangel University, MO
Felician College, NJ
Fort Hays State University, KS
Francis Marion University, SC
Freed-Hardeman University, TN
Friends University, KS
Frostburg State University, MD
Furman University, SC
Gannon University, PA
Grambling State University, LA
Hamline University, MN
Hampden-Sydney College, VA
Hardin-Simmons University, TX
Hillsdale College, MI
Idaho State University, ID
Illinois State University, IL
Indiana University of Pennsylvania, PA
Indiana University–Purdue University Fort Wayne, IN
James Madison University, VA
Juniata College, PA
Kansas State University, KS
Kennesaw State University, GA
King's College, PA
Lindenwood University, MO
Louisiana State University and Agricultural and Mechanical College, LA
Lycoming College, PA
Malone College, OH
Marymount Manhattan College, NY
Mercyhurst College, PA
Michigan Technological University, MI
Middle Tennessee State University, TN
Midway College, KY
Mississippi State University, MS
Missouri State University, MO
Montana State University–Billings, MT
Northern Arizona University, AZ
Northern Michigan University, MI
North Georgia College & State University, GA
Northwestern Oklahoma State University, OK
Northwest Nazarene University, ID
Ohio Northern University, OH
The Ohio State University, OH
Ohio University, OH
Ohio University–Chillicothe, OH
Ohio University–Eastern, OH
Ohio University–Lancaster, OH
Ohio University–Southern Campus, OH
Ohio University–Zanesville, OH
Ohio Wesleyan University, OH
Oklahoma State University, OK
Ouachita Baptist University, AR
Quincy University, IL
Radford University, VA
Randolph-Macon College, VA
Randolph-Macon Woman's College, VA

Non-Need Scholarships for Undergraduates
Academic Interests/Achievements

Ripon College, WI
Rochester Institute of Technology, NY
Rockhurst University, MO
Sacred Heart University, CT
Saint Louis University, MO
Salisbury University, MD
Seton Hill University, PA
Shepherd University, WV
Sonoma State University, CA
South Dakota State University, SD
Southeastern Louisiana University, LA
Southeast Missouri State University, MO
Southern Illinois University Carbondale, IL
Southwest Minnesota State University, MN
State University of New York at Binghamton, NY
State University of New York at New Paltz, NY
State University of New York at Oswego, NY
State University of New York at Plattsburgh, NY
State University of New York College at Geneseo, NY
State University of New York College at Oneonta, NY
State University of New York College of Environmental Science and Forestry, NY
Stephen F. Austin State University, TX
Stetson University, FL
Stevens Institute of Technology, NJ
Sweet Briar College, VA
Tabor College, KS
Tennessee Technological University, TN
Texas Christian University, TX
Texas Tech University, TX
Texas Woman's University, TX
Truman State University, MO
Union University, TN
The University of Akron, OH
The University of Alabama, AL
University of California, Riverside, CA
University of California, San Diego, CA
University of Cincinnati, OH
University of Colorado at Boulder, CO
University of Colorado at Colorado Springs, CO
University of Connecticut, CT
University of Delaware, DE
University of Evansville, IN
University of Great Falls, MT
University of Hartford, CT
University of Idaho, ID
University of Judaism, CA
University of Kansas, KS
University of Mary Hardin-Baylor, TX
University of Maryland, College Park, MD
University of Massachusetts Amherst, MA
University of Memphis, TN
University of Michigan, MI
University of Michigan–Flint, MI
University of Minnesota, Twin Cities Campus, MN
University of Missouri–Columbia, MO
University of Nebraska at Omaha, NE
University of Nebraska–Lincoln, NE

University of Nevada, Las Vegas, NV
University of Nevada, Reno, NV
University of New England, ME
The University of North Carolina at Asheville, NC
The University of North Carolina at Greensboro, NC
University of North Dakota, ND
University of Portland, OR
University of Puget Sound, WA
University of Saint Francis, IN
University of South Carolina, SC
The University of South Dakota, SD
University of Southern Indiana, IN
University of South Florida, FL
The University of Tennessee at Martin, TN
The University of Texas–Pan American, TX
University of the Ozarks, AR
The University of Toledo, OH
University of Tulsa, OK
University of Wisconsin–Eau Claire, WI
University of Wisconsin–Parkside, WI
University of Wisconsin–Stevens Point, WI
University of Wisconsin–Whitewater, WI
Utah State University, UT
Valdosta State University, GA
Virginia Military Institute, VA
Virginia Polytechnic Institute and State University, VA
Wake Forest University, NC
Washington State University, WA
Washington University in St. Louis, MO
Wayne State College, NE
Wesleyan College, GA
Western Kentucky University, KY
Western Washington University, WA
West Virginia University, WV
Wheaton College, IL
Wheeling Jesuit University, WV
Wichita State University, KS
Widener University, PA
Wilkes University, PA
Wilson College, PA
Worcester Polytechnic Institute, MA
Xavier University of Louisiana, LA

Religion/Biblical Studies

Abilene Christian University, TX
Alaska Bible College, AK
Albertus Magnus College, CT
Albright College, PA
Alderson-Broaddus College, WV
Athens State University, AL
Atlantic Union College, MA
Augsburg College, MN
Augustana College, SD
Austin College, TX
Averett University, VA
Azusa Pacific University, CA
The Baptist College of Florida, FL
Barton College, NC
Baylor University, TX
Beacon University, GA
Belhaven College, MS
Belmont University, TN
Berry College, GA

Bloomsburg University of Pennsylvania, PA
Blue Mountain College, MS
Brewton-Parker College, GA
Brigham Young University–Hawaii, HI
Bryan College, TN
California Baptist University, CA
California Lutheran University, CA
Calvin College, MI
Campbellsville University, KY
Carson-Newman College, TN
Cascade College, OR
Case Western Reserve University, OH
Centenary College of Louisiana, LA
Central Christian College of the Bible, MO
Central College, IA
Central Missouri State University, MO
Christopher Newport University, VA
The Citadel, The Military College of South Carolina, SC
Clearwater Christian College, FL
Columbia College, SC
Concordia University, CA
Concordia University, MI
Concordia University, NE
Concordia University, St. Paul, MN
Cornerstone University, MI
Dallas Baptist University, TX
Dallas Christian College, TX
Davis & Elkins College, WV
Defiance College, OH
Dordt College, IA
Eastern Michigan University, MI
East Texas Baptist University, TX
Edinboro University of Pennsylvania, PA
Elizabethtown College, PA
Elmhurst College, IL
Elon University, NC
Emmanuel College, MA
Emory & Henry College, VA
Erskine College, SC
Eugene Bible College, OR
Evangel University, MO
Faulkner University, AL
Felician College, NJ
Flagler College, FL
Florida Christian College, FL
Florida Gulf Coast University, FL
Florida Southern College, FL
Freed-Hardeman University, TN
Fresno Pacific University, CA
Friends University, KS
Furman University, SC
Gannon University, PA
Geneva College, PA
Greenville College, IL
Grove City College, PA
Hampden-Sydney College, VA
Hannibal-LaGrange College, MO
Hardin-Simmons University, TX
Hillsdale College, MI
Houston Baptist University, TX
Idaho State University, ID
James Madison University, VA
Johnson Bible College, TN
Kentucky Christian University, KY
King's College, PA

Non-Need Scholarships for Undergraduates
Academic Interests/Achievements

LaGrange College, GA
Lakeland College, WI
Laura and Alvin Siegal College of Judaic Studies, OH
Lee University, TN
Limestone College, SC
Lipscomb University, TN
Lubbock Christian University, TX
Lycoming College, PA
MacMurray College, IL
Malone College, OH
Manhattan Christian College, KS
Maranatha Baptist Bible College, WI
Marian College, IN
Marywood University, PA
The Master's College and Seminary, CA
McKendree College, IL
Mercer University, GA
Meredith College, NC
Messenger College, MO
Milligan College, TN
Mississippi State University, MS
Missouri State University, MO
Montclair State University, NJ
Mount Vernon Nazarene University, OH
Newberry College, SC
Northern Arizona University, AZ
North Greenville College, SC
Northwest Nazarene University, ID
Ohio Northern University, OH
Ohio Wesleyan University, OH
Oklahoma Baptist University, OK
Oral Roberts University, OK
Ouachita Baptist University, AR
Pepperdine University, CA
Quincy University, IL
Ripon College, WI
Rockhurst University, MO
St. Edward's University, TX
Saint Louis University, MO
Schreiner University, TX
Seton Hill University, PA
Shorter College, GA
Southeastern University, FL
Southeast Missouri State University, MO
Southern Adventist University, TN
Southern Illinois University Carbondale, IL
Southern Methodist College, SC
Southwestern Christian University, OK
Stetson University, FL
Tabor College, KS
Texas Christian University, TX
Thiel College, PA
Toccoa Falls College, GA
Trevecca Nazarene University, TN
Trinity College of Florida, FL
Trinity Lutheran College, WA
Union University, TN
University of Connecticut, CT
University of Dallas, TX
University of Delaware, DE
University of Evansville, IN
University of Great Falls, MT
University of Kansas, KS
University of Mary Hardin-Baylor, TX
University of Mary Washington, VA

University of Minnesota, Twin Cities Campus, MN
University of Missouri–Columbia, MO
The University of North Carolina at Greensboro, NC
University of Portland, OR
University of Saint Francis, IN
University of St. Thomas, MN
University of South Carolina, SC
University of South Florida, FL
University of the Ozarks, AR
University of Tulsa, OK
Valparaiso University, IN
Virginia Polytechnic Institute and State University, VA
Wake Forest University, NC
Warner Pacific College, OR
Wartburg College, IA
Washington University in St. Louis, MO
Wayland Baptist University, TX
Waynesburg College, PA
Wesleyan College, GA
West Virginia University, WV
Wheeling Jesuit University, WV
Williams Baptist College, AR
Wilson College, PA

Social Sciences

Abilene Christian University, TX
Alaska Pacific University, AK
Albertus Magnus College, CT
Alderson-Broaddus College, WV
Alfred University, NY
Alliant International University, CA
Antioch College, OH
Arizona State University, AZ
Arkansas State University, AR
Ashland University, OH
Athens State University, AL
Auburn University, AL
Augsburg College, MN
Augustana College, SD
Augusta State University, GA
Austin College, TX
Austin Peay State University, TN
Ball State University, IN
Barton College, NC
Baylor University, TX
Beacon University, GA
Belhaven College, MS
Black Hills State University, SD
Bloomfield College, NJ
Bloomsburg University of Pennsylvania, PA
Blue Mountain College, MS
Bowling Green State University, OH
Brevard College, NC
Brigham Young University–Hawaii, HI
Bryan College, TN
Butler University, IN
California Lutheran University, CA
California Polytechnic State University, San Luis Obispo, CA
California State University, Bakersfield, CA
California State University, Chico, CA
California State University, Fresno, CA
California State University, Fullerton, CA

California State University, Stanislaus, CA
Calvin College, MI
Campbellsville University, KY
Carroll College, WI
Case Western Reserve University, OH
Centenary College of Louisiana, LA
Central Michigan University, MI
Central Missouri State University, MO
City College of the City University of New York, NY
Clemson University, SC
College Misericordia, PA
College of Charleston, SC
College of St. Catherine, MN
The College of Saint Rose, NY
College of the Southwest, NM
The College of Wooster, OH
Concordia University, NE
Concordia University, St. Paul, MN
Daniel Webster College, NH
Defiance College, OH
Dickinson State University, ND
Dordt College, IA
Eastern Michigan University, MI
Eastern Washington University, WA
East Stroudsburg University of Pennsylvania, PA
East Tennessee State University, TN
Edinboro University of Pennsylvania, PA
Elizabethtown College, PA
Elon University, NC
Emmanuel College, MA
Emporia State University, KS
Erskine College, SC
Evangel University, MO
Fairmont State University, WV
Felician College, NJ
Fitchburg State College, MA
Flagler College, FL
Florida Atlantic University, FL
Florida Gulf Coast University, FL
Florida Southern College, FL
Fort Hays State University, KS
Fort Lewis College, CO
Francis Marion University, SC
Fresno Pacific University, CA
Friends University, KS
Frostburg State University, MD
Furman University, SC
Georgia College & State University, GA
Georgia Southern University, GA
Grambling State University, LA
Grove City College, PA
Hampshire College, MA
Hardin-Simmons University, TX
Hawai'i Pacific University, HI
Idaho State University, ID
Illinois State University, IL
Indiana University of Pennsylvania, PA
Indiana University–Purdue University Fort Wayne, IN
Jacksonville State University, AL
James Madison University, VA
Kansas State University, KS
Kennesaw State University, GA
Kent State University, OH

Peterson's College Money Handbook 2007 *www.petersons.com* **707**

Non-Need Scholarships for Undergraduates
Academic Interests/Achievements

King's College, PA
LaGrange College, GA
Lewis-Clark State College, ID
Limestone College, SC
Lincoln University, PA
Lindenwood University, MO
Lock Haven University of Pennsylvania, PA
Louisiana Tech University, LA
Lubbock Christian University, TX
Lycoming College, PA
MacMurray College, IL
Malone College, OH
Marymount Manhattan College, NY
The Master's College and Seminary, CA
Mercyhurst College, PA
Mesa State College, CO
Metropolitan State College of Denver, CO
Michigan State University, MI
Michigan Technological University, MI
Middle Tennessee State University, TN
Midwestern State University, TX
Millersville University of Pennsylvania, PA
Mississippi State University, MS
Missouri State University, MO
Monmouth University, NJ
Montana State University, MT
Montana State University–Billings, MT
Montclair State University, NJ
Morehead State University, KY
Mount Mary College, WI
Newberry College, SC
New England College, NH
New Mexico State University, NM
North Carolina State University, NC
Northeastern Illinois University, IL
Northern Arizona University, AZ
Northern Illinois University, IL
Northern Michigan University, MI
Northern State University, SD
Northwestern Oklahoma State University, OK
Northwest Nazarene University, ID
Ohio Northern University, OH
The Ohio State University, OH
Ohio University, OH
Ohio University–Chillicothe, OH
Ohio University–Eastern, OH
Ohio University–Lancaster, OH
Ohio University–Southern Campus, OH
Ohio University–Zanesville, OH
Ohio Wesleyan University, OH
Oklahoma State University, OK
Ouachita Baptist University, AR
Pacific University, OR
Pepperdine University, CA
Pittsburg State University, KS
Plymouth State University, NH
Portland State University, OR
Quincy University, IL
Radford University, VA
Randolph-Macon Woman's College, VA
Rice University, TX
The Richard Stockton College of New Jersey, NJ
Ripon College, WI
Rochester Institute of Technology, NY

Rockhurst University, MO
St. Cloud State University, MN
St. Edward's University, TX
Saint Louis University, MO
Saint Vincent College, PA
Salisbury University, MD
Schreiner University, TX
Seton Hill University, PA
Shepherd University, WV
Shippensburg University of Pennsylvania, PA
Slippery Rock University of Pennsylvania, PA
Sonoma State University, CA
South Dakota State University, SD
Southeastern Louisiana University, LA
Southeastern Oklahoma State University, OK
Southeast Missouri State University, MO
Southern Arkansas University–Magnolia, AR
Southern Illinois University Carbondale, IL
Southern Oregon University, OR
Southwest Minnesota State University, MN
State University of New York at Oswego, NY
State University of New York at Plattsburgh, NY
State University of New York College at Brockport, NY
State University of New York College at Geneseo, NY
State University of New York College at Potsdam, NY
State University of New York, Fredonia, NY
Stetson University, FL
Stony Brook University, State University of New York, NY
Tabor College, KS
Tennessee Technological University, TN
Texas Tech University, TX
Texas Woman's University, TX
Trevecca Nazarene University, TN
Truman State University, MO
The University of Akron, OH
The University of Alabama, AL
The University of Alabama in Huntsville, AL
University of Alaska Southeast, AK
University of California, Riverside, CA
University of California, San Diego, CA
University of Central Oklahoma, OK
University of Cincinnati, OH
University of Colorado at Boulder, CO
University of Connecticut, CT
University of Delaware, DE
University of Evansville, IN
University of Great Falls, MT
University of Hawaii at Hilo, HI
University of Houston–Victoria, TX
University of Idaho, ID
University of Illinois at Springfield, IL
University of Illinois at Urbana–Champaign, IL
University of Kansas, KS

University of Maine, ME
University of Mary Hardin-Baylor, TX
University of Maryland, College Park, MD
University of Mary Washington, VA
University of Massachusetts Amherst, MA
University of Memphis, TN
University of Miami, FL
University of Michigan, MI
University of Michigan–Dearborn, MI
University of Michigan–Flint, MI
University of Minnesota, Twin Cities Campus, MN
University of Missouri–Columbia, MO
University of Nebraska at Omaha, NE
University of Nebraska–Lincoln, NE
University of Nevada, Las Vegas, NV
University of Nevada, Reno, NV
University of New England, ME
The University of North Carolina at Asheville, NC
The University of North Carolina at Greensboro, NC
The University of North Carolina Wilmington, NC
University of North Dakota, ND
University of Northern Colorado, CO
University of Northern Iowa, IA
University of Oklahoma, OK
University of Oregon, OR
University of Phoenix–Bay Area Campus, CA
University of Phoenix–Central Florida Campus, FL
University of Phoenix–Cleveland Campus, OH
University of Phoenix–Dallas Campus, TX
University of Phoenix–Houston Campus, TX
University of Phoenix–Louisiana Campus, LA
University of Phoenix–Metro Detroit Campus, MI
University of Phoenix–New Mexico Campus, NM
University of Phoenix–Northern Virginia Campus, VA
University of Phoenix–North Florida Campus, FL
University of Phoenix–Oklahoma City Campus, OK
University of Phoenix Online Campus, AZ
University of Phoenix–Oregon Campus, OR
University of Phoenix–Phoenix Campus, AZ
University of Phoenix–Puerto Rico Campus, PR
University of Phoenix–Raleigh Campus, NC
University of Phoenix–Sacramento Valley Campus, CA
University of Phoenix–San Diego Campus, CA
University of Phoenix–Southern Colorado Campus, CO
University of Phoenix–South Florida Campus, FL
University of Phoenix–Tulsa Campus, OK

Non-Need Scholarships for Undergraduates
Creative Arts/Performance

University of Phoenix–Utah Campus, UT
University of Phoenix–Washington Campus, WA
University of Phoenix–West Florida Campus, FL
University of Phoenix–West Michigan Campus, MI
University of Pittsburgh at Bradford, PA
University of Portland, OR
University of Puget Sound, WA
University of Rochester, NY
University of St. Francis, IL
University of Saint Francis, IN
University of St. Thomas, MN
University of St. Thomas, TX
University of South Carolina, SC
The University of South Dakota, SD
University of Southern Indiana, IN
University of South Florida, FL
The University of Tampa, FL
The University of Tennessee at Martin, TN
The University of Texas at Arlington, TX
The University of Texas at San Antonio, TX
The University of Texas–Pan American, TX
University of the Ozarks, AR
The University of Toledo, OH
University of Tulsa, OK
University of Utah, UT
University of Vermont, VT
University of West Georgia, GA
University of Wisconsin–Eau Claire, WI
University of Wisconsin–Green Bay, WI
University of Wisconsin–La Crosse, WI
University of Wisconsin–Stevens Point, WI
University of Wisconsin–Whitewater, WI
University of Wyoming, WY
Utah State University, UT
Valdosta State University, GA
Valley City State University, ND
Virginia Polytechnic Institute and State University, VA
Walla Walla College, WA
Washington State University, WA
Washington University in St. Louis, MO
Wayland Baptist University, TX
Wayne State College, NE
Wesleyan College, GA
Western Carolina University, NC
Western Illinois University, IL
Western Kentucky University, KY
Western Oregon University, OR
Western Washington University, WA
West Texas A&M University, TX
West Virginia University, WV
Wheeling Jesuit University, WV
Wichita State University, KS
Widener University, PA
Wilkes University, PA
Wilson College, PA
Xavier University, OH
Xavier University of Louisiana, LA

Creative Arts/Performance

Applied Art and Design
Arizona State University, AZ
Auburn University, AL
Belhaven College, MS
Brenau University, GA
California Institute of the Arts, CA
California Polytechnic State University, San Luis Obispo, CA
California State University, Chico, CA
Carthage College, WI
Central Michigan University, MI
Central Missouri State University, MO
Central Washington University, WA
Chester College of New England, NH
City College of the City University of New York, NY
Clemson University, SC
College for Creative Studies, MI
College of Santa Fe, NM
Collins College: A School of Design and Technology, AZ
Columbia College, SC
Concordia University, CA
Converse College, SC
Corcoran College of Art and Design, DC
East Carolina University, NC
Eastern Michigan University, MI
East Stroudsburg University of Pennsylvania, PA
The Evergreen State College, WA
Fashion Institute of Technology, NY
Flagler College, FL
Fort Hays State University, KS
Friends University, KS
Georgia College & State University, GA
Graceland University, IA
Greenville College, IL
Illinois State University, IL
Indiana University of Pennsylvania, PA
Kean University, NJ
Keene State College, NH
LaGrange College, GA
Lindenwood University, MO
Louisiana State University and Agricultural and Mechanical College, LA
Marian College, IN
Marshall University, WV
Memphis College of Art, TN
Mercyhurst College, PA
Meredith College, NC
Minnesota State University Mankato, MN
Mississippi State University, MS
Missouri State University, MO
Montserrat College of Art, MA
Mount Mary College, WI
Murray State University, KY
New England College, NH
New Mexico State University, NM
Northern Illinois University, IL
Northern Michigan University, MI
North Georgia College & State University, GA
Ohio Northern University, OH
Ohio University, OH

Ohio University–Chillicothe, OH
Ohio University–Eastern, OH
Ohio University–Lancaster, OH
Ohio University–Southern Campus, OH
Ohio University–Zanesville, OH
Oral Roberts University, OK
Otis College of Art and Design, CA
Radford University, VA
Rice University, TX
The Richard Stockton College of New Jersey, NJ
Ringling School of Art and Design, FL
Robert Morris College, IL
Rochester Institute of Technology, NY
Rocky Mountain College of Art & Design, CO
Sacred Heart University, CT
St. Cloud State University, MN
Seton Hill University, PA
Shepherd University, WV
Silver Lake College, WI
Slippery Rock University of Pennsylvania, PA
Sonoma State University, CA
Southern Illinois University Carbondale, IL
State University of New York College at Geneseo, NY
State University of New York, Fredonia, NY
Stephen F. Austin State University, TX
Stetson University, FL
Texas State University-San Marcos, TX
Texas Tech University, TX
Texas Woman's University, TX
The University of Akron, OH
University of California, San Diego, CA
University of Central Oklahoma, OK
University of Cincinnati, OH
University of Delaware, DE
University of Idaho, ID
University of Illinois at Springfield, IL
University of Illinois at Urbana–Champaign, IL
University of Kansas, KS
University of Kentucky, KY
University of Maine, ME
University of Maryland, College Park, MD
University of Nebraska at Kearney, NE
University of Nevada, Las Vegas, NV
University of Nevada, Reno, NV
The University of North Carolina at Chapel Hill, NC
University of Northern Iowa, IA
University of St. Francis, IL
University of South Florida, FL
The University of Texas at El Paso, TX
University of Wisconsin–Parkside, WI
University of Wisconsin–Stevens Point, WI
University of Wisconsin–Stout, WI
Utah State University, UT
Valley City State University, ND
Virginia Commonwealth University, VA
Virginia Intermont College, VA
Virginia Polytechnic Institute and State University, VA
Washington State University, WA

Non-Need Scholarships for Undergraduates
Creative Arts/Performance

Washington University in St. Louis, MO
Watkins College of Art and Design, TN
Wayne State College, NE
Western Illinois University, IL
Western Washington University, WA
Wichita State University, KS
Woodbury University, CA

Art/Fine Arts
Abilene Christian University, TX
Adelphi University, NY
Adrian College, MI
Albertson College of Idaho, ID
Albertus Magnus College, CT
Albion College, MI
Albright College, PA
Alderson-Broaddus College, WV
Alfred University, NY
Alma College, MI
Alverno College, WI
Arizona State University, AZ
Arkansas State University, AR
Armstrong Atlantic State University, GA
Art Center College of Design, CA
Ashland University, OH
Athens State University, AL
Auburn University, AL
Augustana College, SD
Augusta State University, GA
Austin College, TX
Austin Peay State University, TN
Averett University, VA
Avila University, MO
Ball State University, IN
Barton College, NC
Baylor University, TX
Belhaven College, MS
Berry College, GA
Bethany College, KS
Bethany Lutheran College, MN
Bethel College, KS
Bethel University, MN
Biola University, CA
Black Hills State University, SD
Bloomfield College, NJ
Bluffton University, OH
Boston University, MA
Bowling Green State University, OH
Bradley University, IL
Brenau University, GA
Brevard College, NC
Brewton-Parker College, GA
Brigham Young University–Hawaii, HI
Bryan College, TN
Bucknell University, PA
Buena Vista University, IA
Butler University, IN
California Baptist University, CA
California Institute of the Arts, CA
California Lutheran University, CA
California Polytechnic State University, San Luis Obispo, CA
California State University, Bakersfield, CA
California State University, Chico, CA
California State University, Fresno, CA
California State University, Fullerton, CA

California State University, Stanislaus, CA
Calvin College, MI
Campbellsville University, KY
Campbell University, NC
Carnegie Mellon University, PA
Carroll College, WI
Carson-Newman College, TN
Carthage College, WI
Case Western Reserve University, OH
Cedar Crest College, PA
Centenary College of Louisiana, LA
Central College, IA
Central Michigan University, MI
Central Missouri State University, MO
Central Washington University, WA
Chapman University, CA
Chester College of New England, NH
Christopher Newport University, VA
City College of the City University of New York, NY
Clarke College, IA
Clemson University, SC
The Cleveland Institute of Art, OH
Cleveland State University, OH
Coastal Carolina University, SC
Coe College, IA
College for Creative Studies, MI
College of Charleston, SC
College of Mount St. Joseph, OH
The College of New Jersey, NJ
College of Notre Dame of Maryland, MD
College of Saint Benedict, MN
College of St. Catherine, MN
The College of Saint Rose, NY
College of Santa Fe, NM
College of Staten Island of the City University of New York, NY
College of Visual Arts, MN
The College of William and Mary, VA
Colorado State University, CO
Columbia College, SC
Columbus College of Art & Design, OH
Columbus State University, GA
Concordia University, MI
Concordia University, NE
Concordia University, St. Paul, MN
Cooper Union for the Advancement of Science and Art, NY
Cornell College, IA
Creighton University, NE
Culver-Stockton College, MO
Daemen College, NY
Davidson College, NC
Davis & Elkins College, WV
Denison University, OH
DePaul University, IL
DePauw University, IN
Dickinson State University, ND
Doane College, NE
Drake University, IA
East Carolina University, NC
Eastern Michigan University, MI
Eastern Washington University, WA
East Tennessee State University, TN
Eckerd College, FL
Edinboro University of Pennsylvania, PA

Elizabethtown College, PA
Elmhurst College, IL
Elon University, NC
Emporia State University, KS
Endicott College, MA
Eureka College, IL
Evangel University, MO
The Evergreen State College, WA
Fairfield University, CT
Fairmont State University, WV
Ferrum College, VA
Finlandia University, MI
Flagler College, FL
Florida Gulf Coast University, FL
Florida Southern College, FL
Fort Hays State University, KS
Fort Lewis College, CO
Francis Marion University, SC
Freed-Hardeman University, TN
Fresno Pacific University, CA
Friends University, KS
Frostburg State University, MD
Furman University, SC
Georgetown College, KY
Georgia College & State University, GA
Georgia Southern University, GA
Georgia Southwestern State University, GA
Goucher College, MD
Grace College, IN
Grand Valley State University, MI
Grand View College, IA
Green Mountain College, VT
Greenville College, IL
Hamline University, MN
Hannibal-LaGrange College, MO
Hardin-Simmons University, TX
Hendrix College, AR
Hillsdale College, MI
Hobart and William Smith Colleges, NY
Hofstra University, NY
Hollins University, VA
Hope College, MI
Houghton College, NY
Houston Baptist University, TX
Howard University, DC
Huntington University, IN
Idaho State University, ID
Illinois College, IL
Illinois State University, IL
Illinois Wesleyan University, IL
Indiana State University, IN
Indiana University of Pennsylvania, PA
Indiana University–Purdue University Fort Wayne, IN
Iowa Wesleyan College, IA
Jacksonville State University, AL
James Madison University, VA
Jamestown College, ND
Johnson Bible College, TN
Judson College, AL
Kansas City Art Institute, MO
Kansas State University, KS
Kean University, NJ
Keene State College, NH
Kent State University, OH
Kentucky State University, KY

Non-Need Scholarships for Undergraduates
Creative Arts/Performance

Kentucky Wesleyan College, KY
Knox College, IL
LaGrange College, GA
Lake Forest College, IL
Lakeland College, WI
Lesley University, MA
Lewis-Clark State College, ID
Limestone College, SC
Lincoln University, MO
Lindenwood University, MO
Lipscomb University, TN
Lock Haven University of Pennsylvania, PA
Long Island University, Brooklyn Campus, NY
Louisiana State University and Agricultural and Mechanical College, LA
Loyola University Chicago, IL
Lubbock Christian University, TX
Lycoming College, PA
Lyme Academy College of Fine Arts, CT
Lyon College, AR
MacMurray College, IL
Mansfield University of Pennsylvania, PA
Marian College, IN
Marshall University, WV
Maryville College, TN
Maryville University of Saint Louis, MO
Marywood University, PA
Memphis College of Art, TN
Mercer University, GA
Mercyhurst College, PA
Meredith College, NC
Mesa State College, CO
Messiah College, PA
Metropolitan State College of Denver, CO
Miami University, OH
Midland Lutheran College, NE
Midway College, KY
Midwestern State University, TX
Millersville University of Pennsylvania, PA
Milligan College, TN
Millsaps College, MS
Minnesota State University Mankato, MN
Mississippi State University, MS
Missouri State University, MO
Molloy College, NY
Montana State University, MT
Montana State University–Billings, MT
Montclair State University, NJ
Montreat College, NC
Montserrat College of Art, MA
Morehead State University, KY
Morningside College, IA
Mount Mary College, WI
Mount Mercy College, IA
Mount Olive College, NC
Mount St. Mary's University, MD
Mount Union College, OH
Murray State University, KY
Nazareth College of Rochester, NY
Nebraska Wesleyan University, NE
New England College, NH
New Hampshire Institute of Art, NH
New Jersey City University, NJ
Newman University, KS
New Mexico State University, NM

Northeastern Illinois University, IL
Northern Arizona University, AZ
Northern Illinois University, IL
Northern State University, SD
North Greenville College, SC
Northwestern Oklahoma State University, OK
Northwestern State University of Louisiana, LA
Northwest Nazarene University, ID
Ohio Northern University, OH
Ohio University, OH
Ohio University–Chillicothe, OH
Ohio University–Eastern, OH
Ohio University–Lancaster, OH
Ohio University–Southern Campus, OH
Ohio University–Zanesville, OH
Ohio Wesleyan University, OH
Oklahoma Baptist University, OK
Oklahoma Panhandle State University, OK
Oklahoma State University, OK
Olivet Nazarene University, IL
Oral Roberts University, OK
Otis College of Art and Design, CA
Ouachita Baptist University, AR
Pacific Lutheran University, WA
Pacific University, OR
Peace College, NC
Pepperdine University, CA
Portland State University, OR
Quincy University, IL
Radford University, VA
Randolph-Macon Woman's College, VA
Rice University, TX
The Richard Stockton College of New Jersey, NJ
Ringling School of Art and Design, FL
Ripon College, WI
Roanoke College, VA
Roberts Wesleyan College, NY
Rochester Institute of Technology, NY
Rocky Mountain College of Art & Design, CO
Rollins College, FL
Rosemont College, PA
Sacred Heart University, CT
St. Cloud State University, MN
St. John's University, NY
Saint Louis University, MO
Saint Mary's College, IN
St. Norbert College, WI
San Diego State University, CA
Savannah College of Art and Design, GA
School of the Museum of Fine Arts, Boston, MA
Schreiner University, TX
Seattle Pacific University, WA
Seton Hill University, PA
Shepherd University, WV
Shimer College, IL
Shorter College, GA
Silver Lake College, WI
Simpson College, IA
Slippery Rock University of Pennsylvania, PA
Sonoma State University, CA

South Dakota State University, SD
Southeastern Louisiana University, LA
Southern Adventist University, TN
Southern Arkansas University–Magnolia, AR
Southern Illinois University Carbondale, IL
Southern Illinois University Edwardsville, IL
Southern Oregon University, OR
Southern Virginia University, VA
Southwest Baptist University, MO
Southwestern University, TX
Southwest Minnesota State University, MN
Spring Arbor University, MI
State University of New York at Plattsburgh, NY
State University of New York College at Brockport, NY
State University of New York College at Geneseo, NY
State University of New York College at Potsdam, NY
Stephen F. Austin State University, TX
Stetson University, FL
Stevens Institute of Technology, NJ
Sweet Briar College, VA
Syracuse University, NY
Temple University, PA
Tennessee Technological University, TN
Texas A&M University–Commerce, TX
Texas Christian University, TX
Texas Tech University, TX
Texas Woman's University, TX
Thomas More College, KY
Towson University, MD
Transylvania University, KY
Truman State University, MO
Union University, TN
The University of Akron, OH
The University of Alabama, AL
The University of Alabama at Birmingham, AL
The University of Alabama in Huntsville, AL
University of Alaska Fairbanks, AK
University of Arkansas at Pine Bluff, AR
University of California, Irvine, CA
University of California, Riverside, CA
University of Central Oklahoma, OK
University of Cincinnati, OH
University of Colorado at Boulder, CO
University of Connecticut, CT
University of Dallas, TX
University of Dayton, OH
University of Delaware, DE
University of Denver, CO
University of Evansville, IN
University of Florida, FL
University of Great Falls, MT
University of Hartford, CT
University of Hawaii at Hilo, HI
University of Hawaii at Manoa, HI
University of Idaho, ID
University of Illinois at Springfield, IL
University of Illinois at Urbana–Champaign, IL

Non-Need Scholarships for Undergraduates
Creative Arts/Performance

University of Kansas, KS
University of Kentucky, KY
University of Maine, ME
University of Maine at Presque Isle, ME
University of Mary Hardin-Baylor, TX
University of Maryland, Baltimore County, MD
University of Maryland, College Park, MD
University of Mary Washington, VA
University of Massachusetts Amherst, MA
University of Memphis, TN
University of Miami, FL
University of Michigan–Dearborn, MI
University of Michigan–Flint, MI
University of Missouri–St. Louis, MO
University of Nebraska at Kearney, NE
University of Nebraska at Omaha, NE
University of Nebraska–Lincoln, NE
University of Nevada, Las Vegas, NV
University of Nevada, Reno, NV
University of New Hampshire, NH
University of North Alabama, AL
The University of North Carolina at Asheville, NC
The University of North Carolina at Chapel Hill, NC
The University of North Carolina at Greensboro, NC
The University of North Carolina Wilmington, NC
University of North Dakota, ND
University of Northern Iowa, IA
University of North Florida, FL
University of Oklahoma, OK
University of Oregon, OR
University of Puget Sound, WA
University of Redlands, CA
University of Richmond, VA
University of St. Francis, IL
University of Saint Francis, IN
University of Science and Arts of Oklahoma, OK
University of South Carolina, SC
The University of South Dakota, SD
University of Southern Indiana, IN
University of Southern Mississippi, MS
University of South Florida, FL
The University of Tampa, FL
The University of Tennessee at Martin, TN
The University of Texas at El Paso, TX
The University of Texas at San Antonio, TX
The University of Texas of the Permian Basin, TX
The University of Texas–Pan American, TX
University of the Cumberlands, KY
University of the Ozarks, AR
The University of Toledo, OH
University of Tulsa, OK
University of Utah, UT
University of West Georgia, GA
University of Wisconsin–Green Bay, WI
University of Wisconsin–La Crosse, WI
University of Wisconsin–Parkside, WI
University of Wisconsin–Stout, WI
University of Wisconsin–Whitewater, WI

Ursinus College, PA
Utah State University, UT
Valdosta State University, GA
Valley City State University, ND
Valley Forge Christian College, PA
Valparaiso University, IN
Villa Julie College, MD
Virginia Commonwealth University, VA
Virginia Intermont College, VA
Virginia Polytechnic Institute and State University, VA
Wabash College, IN
Wake Forest University, NC
Warren Wilson College, NC
Wartburg College, IA
Washington State University, WA
Washington University in St. Louis, MO
Watkins College of Art and Design, TN
Wayland Baptist University, TX
Wayne State College, NE
Wayne State University, MI
Webster University, MO
Wesleyan College, GA
Western Carolina University, NC
Western Kentucky University, KY
Western Oregon University, OR
Western State College of Colorado, CO
Western Washington University, WA
Westmont College, CA
West Texas A&M University, TX
West Virginia University, WV
West Virginia Wesleyan College, WV
Whitman College, WA
Whittier College, CA
Whitworth College, WA
Wichita State University, KS
William Carey College, MS
William Jewell College, MO
Williams Baptist College, AR
William Woods University, MO
Winona State University, MN
Winthrop University, SC
Wittenberg University, OH
Worcester State College, MA
Xavier University, OH
Xavier University of Louisiana, LA

Cinema/Film/Broadcasting

Arizona State University, AZ
Arkansas State University, AR
Auburn University, AL
Baylor University, TX
Bowling Green State University, OH
Brenau University, GA
Butler University, IN
California Institute of the Arts, CA
California Polytechnic State University, San Luis Obispo, CA
California State University, Chico, CA
Central Michigan University, MI
Central Missouri State University, MO
Chapman University, CA
City College of the City University of New York, NY
College of Santa Fe, NM
DePauw University, IN

Eastern Michigan University, MI
Eastern Washington University, WA
Edinboro University of Pennsylvania, PA
Five Towns College, NY
Flagler College, FL
Fort Hays State University, KS
Freed-Hardeman University, TN
Georgia Southern University, GA
Illinois State University, IL
James Madison University, VA
Keene State College, NH
Lindenwood University, MO
Long Island University, Brooklyn Campus, NY
Marshall University, WV
Marywood University, PA
MidAmerica Nazarene University, KS
Mississippi State University, MS
Montana State University, MT
Montclair State University, NJ
Morehead State University, KY
Morningside College, IA
Mount Union College, OH
Northern Arizona University, AZ
Northwestern Oklahoma State University, OK
Northwestern State University of Louisiana, LA
Ohio University, OH
Ohio University–Chillicothe, OH
Ohio University–Eastern, OH
Ohio University–Lancaster, OH
Ohio University–Southern Campus, OH
Ohio University–Zanesville, OH
Oral Roberts University, OK
Quincy University, IL
Radford University, VA
Rochester Institute of Technology, NY
St. Cloud State University, MN
St. John's University, NY
Saint Joseph's College, IN
Sonoma State University, CA
Southern Illinois University Carbondale, IL
Texas Christian University, TX
Texas Woman's University, TX
Union University, TN
The University of Alabama, AL
University of California, San Diego, CA
University of Colorado at Boulder, CO
University of Illinois at Urbana–Champaign, IL
University of Kansas, KS
University of Maryland, Baltimore County, MD
University of Memphis, TN
University of Miami, FL
University of Michigan–Dearborn, MI
University of Nebraska–Lincoln, NE
University of Nevada, Las Vegas, NV
The University of North Carolina at Greensboro, NC
University of South Florida, FL
University of Utah, UT
University of Wisconsin–Whitewater, WI
Villa Julie College, MD

Non-Need Scholarships for Undergraduates
Creative Arts/Performance

Virginia Polytechnic Institute and State University, VA
Washington State University, WA
Washington University in St. Louis, MO
Watkins College of Art and Design, TN
Western Illinois University, IL
Western Kentucky University, KY
Western Washington University, WA
Westminster College, PA
William Jewell College, MO

Creative Writing
Alderson-Broaddus College, WV
Arizona State University, AZ
Arkansas Tech University, AR
Auburn University, AL
Augusta State University, GA
Austin Peay State University, TN
Belhaven College, MS
Bowling Green State University, OH
Brenau University, GA
Brigham Young University–Hawaii, HI
California Institute of the Arts, CA
California Lutheran University, CA
California Polytechnic State University, San Luis Obispo, CA
California State University, Chico, CA
Campbell University, NC
Case Western Reserve University, OH
Central Michigan University, MI
Central Missouri State University, MO
Chapman University, CA
Chester College of New England, NH
City College of the City University of New York, NY
Cleveland State University, OH
Coe College, IA
College of Santa Fe, NM
Colorado State University, CO
Creighton University, NE
Davidson College, NC
Dickinson State University, ND
Duke University, NC
Eastern Michigan University, MI
Eastern Washington University, WA
Eckerd College, FL
Emporia State University, KS
The Evergreen State College, WA
Fort Hays State University, KS
Frostburg State University, MD
Furman University, SC
Georgia College & State University, GA
Graceland University, IA
Grove City College, PA
Hamline University, MN
Hampshire College, MA
Hardin-Simmons University, TX
Hobart and William Smith Colleges, NY
Hollins University, VA
Hope College, MI
Illinois State University, IL
Knox College, IL
Lake Forest College, IL
Lakeland College, WI
Lewis-Clark State College, ID
Lycoming College, PA

Maharishi University of Management, IA
Marshall University, WV
Meredith College, NC
Mesa State College, CO
Michigan State University, MI
Minnesota State University Mankato, MN
Mississippi State University, MS
Mount Marty College, SD
Murray State University, KY
New England College, NH
Northeastern Illinois University, IL
Northern Arizona University, AZ
Northern Illinois University, IL
Northwestern State University of Louisiana, LA
Ohio Northern University, OH
The Ohio State University, OH
Oklahoma State University, OK
Plymouth State University, NH
Randolph-Macon Woman's College, VA
Rice University, TX
The Richard Stockton College of New Jersey, NJ
Rockhurst University, MO
Sacred Heart University, CT
St. Cloud State University, MN
San Diego State University, CA
Seton Hill University, PA
Shimer College, IL
Sonoma State University, CA
Southern Illinois University Carbondale, IL
Southern Oregon University, OR
Southwest Minnesota State University, MN
State University of New York at Binghamton, NY
State University of New York College at Brockport, NY
State University of New York College at Geneseo, NY
The University of Akron, OH
The University of Alabama, AL
University of Alaska Fairbanks, AK
University of California, Riverside, CA
University of Colorado at Boulder, CO
University of Idaho, ID
University of Illinois at Urbana–Champaign, IL
University of Kansas, KS
University of Maine, ME
University of Maryland, Baltimore County, MD
University of Michigan–Dearborn, MI
University of Nebraska at Omaha, NE
University of Nevada, Reno, NV
The University of North Carolina Wilmington, NC
University of Redlands, CA
The University of South Dakota, SD
University of Southern Indiana, IN
University of South Florida, FL
The University of Tampa, FL
University of Utah, UT
The University of West Alabama, AL
University of Wisconsin–Stevens Point, WI
University of Wisconsin–Whitewater, WI
Ursinus College, PA

Virginia Polytechnic Institute and State University, VA
Wabash College, IN
Warren Wilson College, NC
Washington College, MD
Washington State University, WA
Washington University in St. Louis, MO
Wayne State College, NE
Webster University, MO
Western Washington University, WA

Dance
Adelphi University, NY
Alma College, MI
Arizona State University, AZ
Ball State University, IN
Belhaven College, MS
The Boston Conservatory, MA
Bowling Green State University, OH
Brenau University, GA
Butler University, IN
California Institute of the Arts, CA
California Polytechnic State University, San Luis Obispo, CA
California State University, Bakersfield, CA
California State University, Chico, CA
Case Western Reserve University, OH
Cedar Crest College, PA
Centenary College of Louisiana, LA
Central Michigan University, MI
Chapman University, CA
Cleveland State University, OH
College of Santa Fe, NM
The College of Wooster, OH
Colorado State University, CO
Columbia College, SC
Denison University, OH
Drexel University, PA
Duquesne University, PA
Eastern Michigan University, MI
Friends University, KS
Frostburg State University, MD
Goucher College, MD
Grambling State University, LA
Hawai'i Pacific University, HI
Hendrix College, AR
Hobart and William Smith Colleges, NY
Hofstra University, NY
Hollins University, VA
Hope College, MI
Howard University, DC
Indiana University of Pennsylvania, PA
Ithaca College, NY
James Madison University, VA
Keene State College, NH
Knox College, IL
Lindenwood University, MO
Long Island University, Brooklyn Campus, NY
Marshall University, WV
Marymount Manhattan College, NY
Mercyhurst College, PA
Middle Tennessee State University, TN
Mississippi State University, MS
Missouri State University, MO
Montana State University, MT

Non-Need Scholarships for Undergraduates
Creative Arts/Performance

Montclair State University, NJ
Murray State University, KY
New Jersey City University, NJ
Northeastern Illinois University, IL
Northern Illinois University, IL
Northwestern Oklahoma State University, OK
Northwestern State University of Louisiana, LA
Ohio Northern University, OH
The Ohio State University, OH
Ohio University, OH
Ohio University–Chillicothe, OH
Ohio University–Eastern, OH
Ohio University–Lancaster, OH
Ohio University–Southern Campus, OH
Ohio University–Zanesville, OH
Ohio Wesleyan University, OH
Pacific Lutheran University, WA
Palm Beach Atlantic University, FL
Plymouth State University, NH
Radford University, VA
The Richard Stockton College of New Jersey, NJ
St. John's University, NY
San Diego State University, CA
Santa Clara University, CA
Shenandoah University, VA
Slippery Rock University of Pennsylvania, PA
Sonoma State University, CA
Southeastern Louisiana University, LA
Southern Arkansas University–Magnolia, AR
Southern Illinois University Carbondale, IL
Southern Illinois University Edwardsville, IL
State University of New York College at Brockport, NY
State University of New York College at Geneseo, NY
State University of New York College at Potsdam, NY
State University of New York, Fredonia, NY
Stephens College, MO
Texas Christian University, TX
Texas Tech University, TX
Texas Woman's University, TX
Towson University, MD
The University of Akron, OH
The University of Alabama, AL
University of California, Irvine, CA
University of California, Riverside, CA
University of California, San Diego, CA
University of Colorado at Boulder, CO
University of Florida, FL
University of Hartford, CT
University of Hawaii at Manoa, HI
University of Idaho, ID
University of Illinois at Urbana–Champaign, IL
University of Kansas, KS
University of Maryland, Baltimore County, MD
University of Maryland, College Park, MD

University of Mary Washington, VA
University of Massachusetts Amherst, MA
University of Memphis, TN
University of Nebraska–Lincoln, NE
University of Nevada, Las Vegas, NV
University of Nevada, Reno, NV
University of New Hampshire, NH
The University of North Carolina at Greensboro, NC
University of Northern Colorado, CO
University of Oklahoma, OK
University of Oregon, OR
University of Puerto Rico, Mayagüez Campus, PR
University of Richmond, VA
University of Saint Francis, IN
University of Southern Mississippi, MS
University of South Florida, FL
The University of Texas of the Permian Basin, TX
The University of Texas–Pan American, TX
University of Utah, UT
The University of West Alabama, AL
University of Wisconsin–Green Bay, WI
University of Wisconsin–Stevens Point, WI
University of Wyoming, WY
Virginia Commonwealth University, VA
Virginia Intermont College, VA
Washington University in St. Louis, MO
Wayne State University, MI
Western Illinois University, IL
Western Kentucky University, KY
Western Oregon University, OR
Western Washington University, WA
West Texas A&M University, TX
Wichita State University, KS
Wilkes University, PA
William Penn University, IA
Winthrop University, SC
Wittenberg University, OH

Debating

Abilene Christian University, TX
Albertson College of Idaho, ID
Alderson-Broaddus College, WV
Arizona State University, AZ
Arkansas State University, AR
Austin Peay State University, TN
Azusa Pacific University, CA
Baylor University, TX
Berry College, GA
Bethany Lutheran College, MN
Bethel College, KS
Bethel University, MN
Biola University, CA
Bowling Green State University, OH
California Polytechnic State University, San Luis Obispo, CA
California State University, Chico, CA
Carroll College, MT
Carson-Newman College, TN
Cedarville University, OH
Central Missouri State University, MO
Concordia University, CA
Creighton University, NE
Culver-Stockton College, MO

DePaul University, IL
Doane College, NE
Eastern Michigan University, MI
Emory University, GA
Emporia State University, KS
Evangel University, MO
Fairmont State University, WV
Ferris State University, MI
Florida College, FL
Fort Hays State University, KS
Georgia College & State University, GA
Gonzaga University, WA
Hillsdale College, MI
Idaho State University, ID
Illinois State University, IL
Kansas State University, KS
Kentucky Christian University, KY
King's College, PA
Lewis & Clark College, OR
Lindsey Wilson College, KY
Linfield College, OR
Louisiana Tech University, LA
Loyola University Chicago, IL
Malone College, OH
Marist College, NY
Marshall University, WV
Mercer University, GA
Methodist College, NC
Michigan State University, MI
Middle Tennessee State University, TN
Midland Lutheran College, NE
Minnesota State University Mankato, MN
Mississippi State University, MS
Missouri State University, MO
Morehead State University, KY
Mount Union College, OH
Murray State University, KY
Northern Arizona University, AZ
Northern Illinois University, IL
Northwestern Oklahoma State University, OK
Northwest Nazarene University, ID
Northwest University, WA
Ohio University, OH
Ohio University–Chillicothe, OH
Ohio University–Eastern, OH
Ohio University–Lancaster, OH
Ohio University–Southern Campus, OH
Ohio University–Zanesville, OH
Oklahoma Panhandle State University, OK
Pacific Lutheran University, WA
Pacific University, OR
Pepperdine University, CA
Rice University, TX
Ripon College, WI
St. John's University, NY
Saint Joseph's University, PA
Santa Clara University, CA
South Dakota State University, SD
Southeastern Louisiana University, LA
Southern Illinois University Carbondale, IL
Southwest Baptist University, MO
Southwest Minnesota State University, MN
Tennessee Technological University, TN
Truman State University, MO
The University of Akron, OH

Non-Need Scholarships for Undergraduates
Creative Arts/Performance

The University of Alabama, AL
University of Arkansas at Monticello, AR
University of Denver, CO
University of Kansas, KS
University of Kentucky, KY
University of Mary, ND
University of Miami, FL
University of Michigan–Dearborn, MI
University of Missouri–Kansas City, MO
University of Nebraska at Kearney, NE
University of Nebraska at Omaha, NE
University of Nevada, Reno, NV
University of North Dakota, ND
University of Puget Sound, WA
University of Redlands, CA
University of Saint Francis, IN
University of St. Thomas, TX
University of South Carolina, SC
The University of South Dakota, SD
University of Southern California, CA
University of South Florida, FL
The University of Texas at San Antonio, TX
University of the Cumberlands, KY
University of West Georgia, GA
University of Wisconsin–Eau Claire, WI
University of Wyoming, WY
Vanguard University of Southern California, CA
Wake Forest University, NC
Wayne State College, NE
Wayne State University, MI
Webster University, MO
Western Illinois University, IL
Western Kentucky University, KY
West Texas A&M University, TX
West Virginia University, WV
Whitman College, WA
Wichita State University, KS
Willamette University, OR
William Carey College, MS
William Jewell College, MO
Winona State University, MN

Journalism/Publications

Abilene Christian University, TX
Alderson-Broaddus College, WV
Arizona State University, AZ
Arkansas State University, AR
Athens State University, AL
Auburn University, AL
Austin Peay State University, TN
Averett University, VA
Ball State University, IN
Baylor University, TX
Belhaven College, MS
Berry College, GA
Bethany Lutheran College, MN
Biola University, CA
Bowling Green State University, OH
Brenau University, GA
Brevard College, NC
Brewton-Parker College, GA
Brigham Young University–Hawaii, HI
Bryan College, TN
California Lutheran University, CA

California Polytechnic State University, San Luis Obispo, CA
California State University, Chico, CA
California State University, Fresno, CA
Campbellsville University, KY
Campbell University, NC
Carroll College, WI
Carson-Newman College, TN
Cascade College, OR
Central Michigan University, MI
Central Missouri State University, MO
Central Washington University, WA
The Citadel, The Military College of South Carolina, SC
College of Santa Fe, NM
Concordia University, St. Paul, MN
DePauw University, IN
Dickinson State University, ND
Dordt College, IA
Eastern Washington University, WA
East Tennessee State University, TN
Edinboro University of Pennsylvania, PA
Elon University, NC
Faulkner University, AL
Ferris State University, MI
Florida College, FL
Fort Hays State University, KS
Freed-Hardeman University, TN
Fresno Pacific University, CA
Frostburg State University, MD
Georgia College & State University, GA
Hannibal-LaGrange College, MO
Hardin-Simmons University, TX
Hawai'i Pacific University, HI
Hillsdale College, MI
Huntington University, IN
Indiana University of Pennsylvania, PA
Ithaca College, NY
Jacksonville State University, AL
James Madison University, VA
John Brown University, AR
Kent State University, OH
King's College, PA
Lakeland College, WI
LeMoyne-Owen College, TN
Lincoln University, MO
Lock Haven University of Pennsylvania, PA
Louisiana State University and Agricultural and Mechanical College, LA
Louisiana Tech University, LA
Loyola University Chicago, IL
Lubbock Christian University, TX
Malone College, OH
Mansfield University of Pennsylvania, PA
Marshall University, WV
Marywood University, PA
Mesa State College, CO
Michigan State University, MI
Middle Tennessee State University, TN
Midland Lutheran College, NE
Mississippi State University, MS
Missouri State University, MO
Morehead State University, KY
Morningside College, IA
Mount Union College, OH
Murray State University, KY

Newman University, KS
New Mexico State University, NM
Northeastern Illinois University, IL
Northern Arizona University, AZ
Northern Illinois University, IL
North Greenville College, SC
Northwestern Oklahoma State University, OK
Northwestern State University of Louisiana, LA
Northwest Nazarene University, ID
Nyack College, NY
Oglethorpe University, GA
Ohio Northern University, OH
The Ohio State University, OH
Ohio University, OH
Ohio University–Chillicothe, OH
Ohio University–Eastern, OH
Ohio University–Lancaster, OH
Ohio University–Southern Campus, OH
Ohio University–Zanesville, OH
Oklahoma State University, OK
Oral Roberts University, OK
Ouachita Baptist University, AR
Pacific University, OR
Pepperdine University, CA
Rice University, TX
The Richard Stockton College of New Jersey, NJ
Robert Morris College, IL
St. Bonaventure University, NY
St. Cloud State University, MN
St. John's University, NY
San Diego State University, CA
Schreiner University, TX
Seton Hill University, PA
Sonoma State University, CA
South Dakota State University, SD
Southeastern University, FL
Southern Adventist University, TN
Southern Illinois University Carbondale, IL
Southern Oregon University, OR
Southwest Minnesota State University, MN
State University of New York at Plattsburgh, NY
State University of New York College at Brockport, NY
State University of New York College at Geneseo, NY
State University of New York College at Oneonta, NY
Stephen F. Austin State University, TX
Stevens Institute of Technology, NJ
Texas A&M University, TX
Texas A&M University–Commerce, TX
Texas Christian University, TX
Texas Lutheran University, TX
Texas State University-San Marcos, TX
Texas Tech University, TX
Texas Woman's University, TX
Union University, TN
The University of Akron, OH
The University of Alabama, AL
University of California, San Diego, CA
University of Central Oklahoma, OK
University of Colorado at Boulder, CO

Non-Need Scholarships for Undergraduates
Creative Arts/Performance

University of Florida, FL
University of Hawaii at Manoa, HI
University of Idaho, ID
University of Illinois at Springfield, IL
University of Illinois at Urbana–Champaign, IL
University of Kansas, KS
University of Kentucky, KY
University of Maine, ME
University of Mary Washington, VA
University of Massachusetts Amherst, MA
University of Memphis, TN
University of Michigan, MI
University of Michigan–Dearborn, MI
University of Missouri–Columbia, MO
University of Nebraska at Kearney, NE
University of Nebraska at Omaha, NE
University of Nebraska–Lincoln, NE
University of Nevada, Las Vegas, NV
University of Nevada, Reno, NV
University of North Alabama, AL
The University of North Carolina at Chapel Hill, NC
The University of North Carolina at Pembroke, NC
University of Oklahoma, OK
University of Oregon, OR
University of St. Thomas, MN
University of South Carolina, SC
University of South Florida, FL
The University of Tampa, FL
The University of Tennessee at Martin, TN
The University of Texas at Arlington, TX
The University of Texas at El Paso, TX
The University of Texas–Pan American, TX
University of Utah, UT
The University of West Alabama, AL
University of West Georgia, GA
University of Wisconsin–Whitewater, WI
Utah State University, UT
Valley City State University, ND
Vanderbilt University, TN
Virginia Polytechnic Institute and State University, VA
Wabash College, IN
Wake Forest University, NC
Wartburg College, IA
Washington State University, WA
Wayland Baptist University, TX
Wayne State College, NE
Wayne State University, MI
Webber International University, FL
Western Illinois University, IL
Western Kentucky University, KY
Western Washington University, WA
West Texas A&M University, TX
Whitworth College, WA
Wichita State University, KS
Wilkes University, PA
William Carey College, MS
William Jewell College, MO
William Penn University, IA
William Woods University, MO

Music

Abilene Christian University, TX
Adelphi University, NY
Adrian College, MI
Agnes Scott College, GA
Alabama Agricultural and Mechanical University, AL
Alaska Bible College, AK
Albertson College of Idaho, ID
Albion College, MI
Albright College, PA
Alderson-Broaddus College, WV
Alma College, MI
Alverno College, WI
Andrews University, MI
Anna Maria College, MA
Arizona State University, AZ
Arkansas State University, AR
Arkansas Tech University, AR
Armstrong Atlantic State University, GA
Asbury College, KY
Ashland University, OH
Atlantic Union College, MA
Auburn University, AL
Augsburg College, MN
Augustana College, SD
Augusta State University, GA
Austin College, TX
Austin Peay State University, TN
Averett University, VA
Avila University, MO
Azusa Pacific University, CA
Baldwin-Wallace College, OH
Ball State University, IN
The Baptist College of Florida, FL
Barton College, NC
Baylor University, TX
Belhaven College, MS
Belmont University, TN
Beloit College, WI
Benedictine College, KS
Benedictine University, IL
Berry College, GA
Bethany College, KS
Bethany Lutheran College, MN
Bethel College, KS
Bethel University, MN
Biola University, CA
Black Hills State University, SD
Blue Mountain College, MS
Bluffton University, OH
The Boston Conservatory, MA
Boston University, MA
Bowling Green State University, OH
Bradley University, IL
Brenau University, GA
Brevard College, NC
Brewton-Parker College, GA
Bridgewater College, VA
Brigham Young University–Hawaii, HI
Bryan College, TN
Bucknell University, PA
Buena Vista University, IA
Butler University, IN
California Baptist University, CA
California Institute of the Arts, CA

California Lutheran University, CA
California Polytechnic State University, San Luis Obispo, CA
California State University, Bakersfield, CA
California State University, Chico, CA
California State University, East Bay, CA
California State University, Fresno, CA
California State University, Fullerton, CA
California State University, Stanislaus, CA
Calvin College, MI
Campbellsville University, KY
Campbell University, NC
Carleton College, MN
Carnegie Mellon University, PA
Carroll College, WI
Carson-Newman College, TN
Carthage College, WI
Cascade College, OR
Case Western Reserve University, OH
Catawba College, NC
The Catholic University of America, DC
Cedarville University, OH
Centenary College of Louisiana, LA
Central College, IA
Central Michigan University, MI
Central Missouri State University, MO
Central Washington University, WA
Centre College, KY
Chapman University, CA
Chowan University, NC
Christopher Newport University, VA
Cincinnati Christian University, OH
The Citadel, The Military College of South Carolina, SC
City College of the City University of New York, NY
Clark Atlanta University, GA
Clarke College, IA
Clear Creek Baptist Bible College, KY
Clearwater Christian College, FL
Cleveland Institute of Music, OH
Cleveland State University, OH
Coastal Carolina University, SC
Coe College, IA
College of Charleston, SC
College of Mount St. Joseph, OH
The College of New Jersey, NJ
College of Saint Benedict, MN
College of St. Catherine, MN
College of Saint Mary, NE
The College of Saint Rose, NY
The College of St. Scholastica, MN
College of Santa Fe, NM
College of Staten Island of the City University of New York, NY
College of the Holy Cross, MA
College of the Southwest, NM
The College of William and Mary, VA
The College of Wooster, OH
Colorado State University, CO
Columbia College, SC
Columbus State University, GA
Concordia University, CA
Concordia University, MI
Concordia University, NE
Concordia University at Austin, TX

Non-Need Scholarships for Undergraduates
Creative Arts/Performance

Concordia University, St. Paul, MN
Concordia University Wisconsin, WI
Converse College, SC
Corban College, OR
Cornell College, IA
Cornerstone University, MI
Crown College, MN
Culver-Stockton College, MO
The Curtis Institute of Music, PA
Dakota State University, SD
Dallas Baptist University, TX
Dallas Christian College, TX
Davidson College, NC
Davis & Elkins College, WV
Delaware Valley College, PA
Denison University, OH
DePaul University, IL
DePauw University, IN
Dickinson State University, ND
Doane College, NE
Dominican University of California, CA
Dordt College, IA
Drake University, IA
Drexel University, PA
Duquesne University, PA
East Carolina University, NC
East Central University, OK
Eastern Michigan University, MI
Eastern Washington University, WA
East Stroudsburg University of Pennsylvania, PA
East Tennessee State University, TN
East Texas Baptist University, TX
Eckerd College, FL
Edinboro University of Pennsylvania, PA
Elizabethtown College, PA
Elmhurst College, IL
Elon University, NC
Emmaus Bible College, IA
Emory University, GA
Emporia State University, KS
Erskine College, SC
Eugene Bible College, OR
Evangel University, MO
Fairfield University, CT
Fairmont State University, WV
Faith Baptist Bible College and Theological Seminary, IA
Faulkner University, AL
Ferris State University, MI
Five Towns College, NY
Florida Atlantic University, FL
Florida Christian College, FL
Florida College, FL
Florida Gulf Coast University, FL
Florida Southern College, FL
Florida State University, FL
Fordham University, NY
Fort Hays State University, KS
Fort Lewis College, CO
Francis Marion University, SC
Franklin and Marshall College, PA
Freed-Hardeman University, TN
Fresno Pacific University, CA
Friends University, KS
Frostburg State University, MD

Furman University, SC
Gannon University, PA
Geneva College, PA
Georgetown College, KY
Georgia College & State University, GA
Georgia Southern University, GA
Georgia Southwestern State University, GA
Gettysburg College, PA
Glenville State College, WV
Gonzaga University, WA
Gordon College, MA
Goshen College, IN
Goucher College, MD
Grace Bible College, MI
Grace College, IN
Graceland University, IA
Grambling State University, LA
Grand Valley State University, MI
Grand View College, IA
Green Mountain College, VT
Greenville College, IL
Grove City College, PA
Guilford College, NC
Gustavus Adolphus College, MN
Hamline University, MN
Hampden-Sydney College, VA
Hampton University, VA
Hannibal-LaGrange College, MO
Hanover College, IN
Harding University, AR
Hardin-Simmons University, TX
Harris-Stowe State University, MO
Hawai'i Pacific University, HI
Heidelberg College, OH
Hendrix College, AR
Hillsdale College, MI
Hobart and William Smith Colleges, NY
Hofstra University, NY
Hollins University, VA
Holy Names University, CA
Hope College, MI
Houghton College, NY
Houston Baptist University, TX
Howard University, DC
Huntington University, IN
Idaho State University, ID
Illinois College, IL
Illinois State University, IL
Illinois Wesleyan University, IL
Indiana University of Pennsylvania, PA
Indiana University–Purdue University Fort Wayne, IN
Iona College, NY
Iowa Wesleyan College, IA
Ithaca College, NY
Jacksonville State University, AL
James Madison University, VA
John Brown University, AR
Johnson Bible College, TN
Judson College, AL
Kansas State University, KS
Kean University, NJ
Keene State College, NH
Kennesaw State University, GA
Kent State University, OH
Kentucky Christian University, KY

Kentucky State University, KY
Kentucky Wesleyan College, KY
King College, TN
Knox College, IL
LaGrange College, GA
Lake Forest College, IL
Lakeland College, WI
Lancaster Bible College, PA
La Sierra University, CA
Lawrence University, WI
Lebanon Valley College, PA
Lee University, TN
Lehigh University, PA
LeMoyne-Owen College, TN
Lewis & Clark College, OR
Lewis-Clark State College, ID
Limestone College, SC
Lincoln University, MO
Lincoln University, PA
Lindenwood University, MO
Linfield College, OR
Lipscomb University, TN
Lock Haven University of Pennsylvania, PA
Long Island University, Brooklyn Campus, NY
Loras College, IA
Louisiana State University and Agricultural and Mechanical College, LA
Louisiana Tech University, LA
Loyola University Chicago, IL
Lubbock Christian University, TX
Luther College, IA
Lycoming College, PA
Lynchburg College, VA
Lynn University, FL
Lyon College, AR
MacMurray College, IL
Maharishi University of Management, IA
Malone College, OH
Manhattan Christian College, KS
Manhattan College, NY
Manhattan School of Music, NY
Mannes College The New School for Music, NY
Mansfield University of Pennsylvania, PA
Marian College, IN
Marian College of Fond du Lac, WI
Marist College, NY
Marshall University, WV
Maryville College, TN
Marywood University, PA
The Master's College and Seminary, CA
Mayville State University, ND
McKendree College, IL
Mercer University, GA
Mercyhurst College, PA
Meredith College, NC
Mesa State College, CO
Messiah College, PA
Methodist College, NC
Metropolitan State College of Denver, CO
Miami University, OH
Michigan State University, MI
MidAmerica Nazarene University, KS
Middle Tennessee State University, TN
Midland Lutheran College, NE

Non-Need Scholarships for Undergraduates
Creative Arts/Performance

Midway College, KY
Midwestern State University, TX
Millersville University of Pennsylvania, PA
Milligan College, TN
Millsaps College, MS
Minnesota State University Mankato, MN
Mississippi State University, MS
Missouri State University, MO
Molloy College, NY
Montana State University, MT
Montana State University–Billings, MT
Montclair State University, NJ
Montreat College, NC
Moravian College, PA
Morehead State University, KY
Morningside College, IA
Mount Aloysius College, PA
Mount Marty College, SD
Mount Mary College, WI
Mount Mercy College, IA
Mount Olive College, NC
Mount Union College, OH
Mount Vernon Nazarene University, OH
Murray State University, KY
Nazareth College of Rochester, NY
Nebraska Wesleyan University, NE
Neumann College, PA
Newberry College, SC
New Jersey City University, NJ
Newman University, KS
New Mexico State University, NM
Nicholls State University, LA
North Carolina Agricultural and Technical State University, NC
Northeastern Illinois University, IL
Northeastern University, MA
Northern Arizona University, AZ
Northern Illinois University, IL
Northern Michigan University, MI
Northern State University, SD
North Georgia College & State University, GA
North Greenville College, SC
Northland College, WI
Northwest Christian College, OR
Northwestern College, MN
Northwestern Oklahoma State University, OK
Northwestern State University of Louisiana, LA
Northwestern University, IL
Northwest Nazarene University, ID
Northwest University, WA
Nyack College, NY
Occidental College, CA
Oglethorpe University, GA
Ohio Northern University, OH
The Ohio State University, OH
Ohio University, OH
Ohio University–Chillicothe, OH
Ohio University–Eastern, OH
Ohio University–Lancaster, OH
Ohio University–Southern Campus, OH
Ohio University–Zanesville, OH
Ohio Wesleyan University, OH
Oklahoma Baptist University, OK

Oklahoma Panhandle State University, OK
Oklahoma State University, OK
Olivet Nazarene University, IL
Oral Roberts University, OK
Ouachita Baptist University, AR
Pacific Lutheran University, WA
Pacific University, OR
Palm Beach Atlantic University, FL
Peace College, NC
Pepperdine University, CA
Philadelphia Biblical University, PA
Pikeville College, KY
Pittsburg State University, KS
Plymouth State University, NH
Pontifical Catholic University of Puerto Rico, PR
Portland State University, OR
Purdue University, IN
Quincy University, IL
Radford University, VA
Randolph-Macon Woman's College, VA
Rice University, TX
The Richard Stockton College of New Jersey, NJ
Ripon College, WI
Roanoke College, VA
Roberts Wesleyan College, NY
Rockhurst University, MO
Rollins College, FL
Roosevelt University, IL
Rowan University, NJ
Sacred Heart University, CT
St. Bonaventure University, NY
St. Cloud State University, MN
Saint Francis University, PA
St. John's University, NY
Saint Joseph's College, IN
Saint Louis University, MO
Saint Martin's University, WA
Saint Mary's College, IN
Saint Mary's University of Minnesota, MN
St. Norbert College, WI
Saint Vincent College, PA
Saint Xavier University, IL
Samford University, AL
San Diego Christian College, CA
San Diego State University, CA
Santa Clara University, CA
Schreiner University, TX
Seattle University, WA
Seton Hill University, PA
Shenandoah University, VA
Shepherd University, WV
Shorter College, GA
Silver Lake College, WI
Simpson College, IA
Simpson University, CA
Skidmore College, NY
Slippery Rock University of Pennsylvania, PA
Sonoma State University, CA
South Carolina State University, SC
South Dakota State University, SD
Southeastern Bible College, AL
Southeastern Louisiana University, LA

Southeastern Oklahoma State University, OK
Southeastern University, FL
Southeast Missouri State University, MO
Southern Adventist University, TN
Southern Arkansas University–Magnolia, AR
Southern Illinois University Carbondale, IL
Southern Illinois University Edwardsville, IL
Southern Oregon University, OR
Southwest Baptist University, MO
Southwestern Christian University, OK
Southwestern University, TX
Southwest Minnesota State University, MN
State University of New York at Binghamton, NY
State University of New York at Buffalo, NY
State University of New York at Plattsburgh, NY
State University of New York College at Cortland, NY
State University of New York College at Geneseo, NY
State University of New York College at Oneonta, NY
State University of New York College at Potsdam, NY
State University of New York, Fredonia, NY
Stephen F. Austin State University, TX
Stetson University, FL
Stevens Institute of Technology, NJ
Stony Brook University, State University of New York, NY
Sweet Briar College, VA
Syracuse University, NY
Tabor College, KS
Taylor University, IN
Taylor University Fort Wayne, IN
Temple University, PA
Tennessee State University, TN
Tennessee Technological University, TN
Texas A&M University–Commerce, TX
Texas Christian University, TX
Texas Lutheran University, TX
Texas State University-San Marcos, TX
Texas Tech University, TX
Texas Woman's University, TX
Thiel College, PA
Tiffin University, OH
Toccoa Falls College, GA
Towson University, MD
Transylvania University, KY
Trevecca Nazarene University, TN
Trinity International University, IL
Trinity Lutheran College, WA
Truman State University, MO
Tusculum College, TN
Tuskegee University, AL
Union College, KY
Union University, TN
The University of Akron, OH
The University of Alabama, AL

Non-Need Scholarships for Undergraduates
Creative Arts/Performance

The University of Alabama at Birmingham, AL
The University of Alabama in Huntsville, AL
University of Alaska Fairbanks, AK
University of Arkansas, AR
University of Arkansas at Monticello, AR
University of Arkansas at Pine Bluff, AR
University of California, Irvine, CA
University of California, Riverside, CA
University of California, Santa Cruz, CA
University of Central Oklahoma, OK
University of Cincinnati, OH
University of Colorado at Boulder, CO
University of Connecticut, CT
University of Dayton, OH
University of Delaware, DE
University of Denver, CO
University of Evansville, IN
The University of Findlay, OH
University of Florida, FL
University of Georgia, GA
University of Great Falls, MT
University of Hartford, CT
University of Hawaii at Hilo, HI
University of Hawaii at Manoa, HI
University of Idaho, ID
University of Illinois at Springfield, IL
University of Illinois at Urbana–Champaign, IL
The University of Iowa, IA
University of Kansas, KS
University of Kentucky, KY
University of Maine, ME
University of Mary, ND
University of Mary Hardin-Baylor, TX
University of Maryland, Baltimore County, MD
University of Maryland, College Park, MD
University of Mary Washington, VA
University of Massachusetts Amherst, MA
University of Massachusetts Lowell, MA
University of Memphis, TN
University of Miami, FL
University of Michigan, MI
University of Michigan–Flint, MI
University of Minnesota, Morris, MN
University of Missouri–Columbia, MO
University of Missouri–Kansas City, MO
University of Missouri–St. Louis, MO
University of Nebraska at Kearney, NE
University of Nebraska at Omaha, NE
University of Nebraska–Lincoln, NE
University of Nevada, Las Vegas, NV
University of Nevada, Reno, NV
University of New Hampshire, NH
University of New Orleans, LA
University of North Alabama, AL
The University of North Carolina at Asheville, NC
The University of North Carolina at Chapel Hill, NC
The University of North Carolina at Greensboro, NC
The University of North Carolina at Pembroke, NC

The University of North Carolina Wilmington, NC
University of North Dakota, ND
University of Northern Colorado, CO
University of Northern Iowa, IA
University of North Florida, FL
University of Oklahoma, OK
University of Oregon, OR
University of Portland, OR
University of Puerto Rico, Mayagüez Campus, PR
University of Puget Sound, WA
University of Redlands, CA
University of Rhode Island, RI
University of Richmond, VA
University of St. Francis, IL
University of Saint Francis, IN
University of St. Thomas, MN
University of St. Thomas, TX
University of San Diego, CA
University of Science and Arts of Oklahoma, OK
University of South Carolina, SC
The University of South Dakota, SD
University of Southern Maine, ME
University of Southern Mississippi, MS
University of South Florida, FL
The University of Tampa, FL
The University of Tennessee at Martin, TN
The University of Texas at Arlington, TX
The University of Texas at El Paso, TX
The University of Texas at San Antonio, TX
The University of Texas of the Permian Basin, TX
The University of Texas–Pan American, TX
University of the Cumberlands, KY
University of the District of Columbia, DC
University of the Ozarks, AR
University of the Pacific, CA
The University of Toledo, OH
University of Tulsa, OK
University of Utah, UT
University of Vermont, VT
The University of West Alabama, AL
University of West Georgia, GA
University of Wisconsin–Eau Claire, WI
University of Wisconsin–Green Bay, WI
University of Wisconsin–La Crosse, WI
University of Wisconsin–Parkside, WI
University of Wisconsin–Stevens Point, WI
University of Wisconsin–Stout, WI
University of Wisconsin–Whitewater, WI
University of Wyoming, WY
Urbana University, OH
Ursinus College, PA
Utah State University, UT
Valdosta State University, GA
Valley City State University, ND
Valley Forge Christian College, PA
Valparaiso University, IN
Vanderbilt University, TN
VanderCook College of Music, IL
Vanguard University of Southern California, CA
Virginia Commonwealth University, VA

Virginia Intermont College, VA
Virginia Military Institute, VA
Virginia Polytechnic Institute and State University, VA
Virginia Wesleyan College, VA
Wabash College, IN
Wake Forest University, NC
Waldorf College, IA
Walla Walla College, WA
Warner Pacific College, OR
Wartburg College, IA
Washington State University, WA
Washington University in St. Louis, MO
Wayland Baptist University, TX
Waynesburg College, PA
Wayne State College, NE
Wayne State University, MI
Webster University, MO
Wesleyan College, GA
Wesley College, MS
Western Carolina University, NC
Western Illinois University, IL
Western Kentucky University, KY
Western New England College, MA
Western Oregon University, OR
Western State College of Colorado, CO
Western Washington University, WA
Westminster College, PA
Westmont College, CA
West Texas A&M University, TX
West Virginia University, WV
West Virginia Wesleyan College, WV
Wheaton College, IL
Wheeling Jesuit University, WV
Whitman College, WA
Whittier College, CA
Whitworth College, WA
Wichita State University, KS
Widener University, PA
Wilkes University, PA
Willamette University, OR
William Carey College, MS
William Jewell College, MO
William Paterson University of New Jersey, NJ
William Penn University, IA
Williams Baptist College, AR
Wilson College, PA
Wingate University, NC
Winona State University, MN
Winston-Salem State University, NC
Winthrop University, SC
Wittenberg University, OH
Wofford College, SC
Xavier University, OH
Xavier University of Louisiana, LA
York College of Pennsylvania, PA
Youngstown State University, OH

Performing Arts
Adelphi University, NY
Albertus Magnus College, CT
Albion College, MI
Alderson-Broaddus College, WV
Alfred University, NY
Arizona State University, AZ

Non-Need Scholarships for Undergraduates
Creative Arts/Performance

Arkansas State University, AR
Auburn University, AL
Augsburg College, MN
Augustana College, SD
Augusta State University, GA
Avila University, MO
Belhaven College, MS
Biola University, CA
Bowling Green State University, OH
Bryan College, TN
Bucknell University, PA
California Institute of the Arts, CA
California Lutheran University, CA
California Polytechnic State University, San Luis Obispo, CA
California State University, Chico, CA
Calvin College, MI
Carroll College, WI
Cedar Crest College, PA
Centenary College of Louisiana, LA
Central Michigan University, MI
Central Missouri State University, MO
Central Washington University, WA
Chapman University, CA
City College of the City University of New York, NY
Clemson University, SC
Coe College, IA
College of Charleston, SC
College of Santa Fe, NM
Columbus State University, GA
Concordia University, MI
Concordia University Wisconsin, WI
Corban College, OR
Davis & Elkins College, WV
DePaul University, IL
Drexel University, PA
Eastern Michigan University, MI
Elizabethtown College, PA
Elon University, NC
Emerson College, MA
Emory University, GA
Eureka College, IL
Fairfield University, CT
Ferrum College, VA
Flagler College, FL
Florida Atlantic University, FL
Fort Hays State University, KS
Fort Lewis College, CO
Franklin Pierce College, NH
Freed-Hardeman University, TN
Friends University, KS
Frostburg State University, MD
Georgetown College, KY
Georgia College & State University, GA
Goucher College, MD
Grambling State University, LA
Green Mountain College, VT
Greenville College, IL
Hannibal-LaGrange College, MO
Hobart and William Smith Colleges, NY
Idaho State University, ID
Illinois State University, IL
Indiana State University, IN
Indiana University of Pennsylvania, PA
Ithaca College, NY

Kennesaw State University, GA
Kentucky Christian University, KY
King College, TN
Lakeland College, WI
Lehigh University, PA
Limestone College, SC
Lindenwood University, MO
Louisiana State University and Agricultural and Mechanical College, LA
Louisiana Tech University, LA
Lubbock Christian University, TX
Marian College, IN
Marshall University, WV
Marywood University, PA
Michigan State University, MI
Mississippi State University, MS
Missouri State University, MO
Molloy College, NY
Montclair State University, NJ
Mount Aloysius College, PA
New Mexico State University, NM
Northeastern Illinois University, IL
Northern Arizona University, AZ
Northern Illinois University, IL
Northwestern State University of Louisiana, LA
Northwest Nazarene University, ID
Northwest University, WA
Nyack College, NY
Oglethorpe University, GA
Ohio Northern University, OH
The Ohio State University, OH
Ohio University, OH
Ohio University–Chillicothe, OH
Ohio University–Eastern, OH
Ohio University–Lancaster, OH
Ohio University–Southern Campus, OH
Ohio University–Zanesville, OH
Oklahoma Baptist University, OK
Oklahoma Panhandle State University, OK
Olivet Nazarene University, IL
Ouachita Baptist University, AR
Pepperdine University, CA
Pontifical Catholic University of Puerto Rico, PR
Rice University, TX
The Richard Stockton College of New Jersey, NJ
Rockhurst University, MO
St. Andrews Presbyterian College, NC
St. Bonaventure University, NY
St. Cloud State University, MN
Saint Louis University, MO
Saint Martin's University, WA
San Diego Christian College, CA
San Diego State University, CA
Seattle Pacific University, WA
Seton Hill University, PA
Shenandoah University, VA
Shepherd University, WV
Slippery Rock University of Pennsylvania, PA
Sonoma State University, CA
South Dakota State University, SD
Southern Illinois University Carbondale, IL
Southwestern University, TX

Southwest Minnesota State University, MN
State University of New York at Binghamton, NY
State University of New York College at Brockport, NY
State University of New York College at Geneseo, NY
State University of New York College at Potsdam, NY
State University of New York, Fredonia, NY
Stephens College, MO
Stevens Institute of Technology, NJ
Tabor College, KS
Temple University, PA
Texas A&M University, TX
Texas Christian University, TX
Texas Tech University, TX
The University of Akron, OH
The University of Alabama at Birmingham, AL
University of Alaska Southeast, AK
University of California, San Diego, CA
University of Colorado at Boulder, CO
University of Dallas, TX
University of Florida, FL
University of Hartford, CT
University of Hawaii at Hilo, HI
University of Hawaii at Manoa, HI
University of Idaho, ID
University of Illinois at Springfield, IL
University of Illinois at Urbana–Champaign, IL
The University of Iowa, IA
University of Kansas, KS
University of Kentucky, KY
University of Maine, ME
University of Maryland, Baltimore County, MD
University of Maryland, College Park, MD
University of Miami, FL
University of Missouri–Kansas City, MO
University of Nebraska at Omaha, NE
University of Nebraska–Lincoln, NE
University of Nevada, Las Vegas, NV
University of Nevada, Reno, NV
The University of North Carolina at Greensboro, NC
University of Northern Colorado, CO
University of Oklahoma, OK
University of Oregon, OR
University of Portland, OR
University of Richmond, VA
University of South Florida, FL
The University of Tampa, FL
The University of Texas at El Paso, TX
The University of Toledo, OH
University of Tulsa, OK
University of Utah, UT
University of Wisconsin–Stevens Point, WI
Utah State University, UT
Valparaiso University, IN
Virginia Commonwealth University, VA
Virginia Intermont College, VA
Virginia Polytechnic Institute and State University, VA

Non-Need Scholarships for Undergraduates
Creative Arts/Performance

Washington State University, WA
Washington University in St. Louis, MO
Wayne State College, NE
Western Illinois University, IL
Western Oregon University, OR
Western Washington University, WA
Wichita State University, KS
Wilkes University, PA
William Woods University, MO
Winthrop University, SC
Xavier University, OH
Xavier University of Louisiana, LA

Theater/Drama
Abilene Christian University, TX
Adelphi University, NY
Adrian College, MI
Alabama Agricultural and Mechanical University, AL
Albertson College of Idaho, ID
Albertus Magnus College, CT
Albion College, MI
Albright College, PA
Alderson-Broaddus College, WV
Alma College, MI
Arizona State University, AZ
Arkansas State University, AR
Ashland University, OH
Auburn University, AL
Augsburg College, MN
Augustana College, SD
Augusta State University, GA
Austin College, TX
Austin Peay State University, TN
Averett University, VA
Avila University, MO
Azusa Pacific University, CA
Ball State University, IN
Barton College, NC
Baylor University, TX
Belhaven College, MS
Belmont Abbey College, NC
Benedictine College, KS
Berry College, GA
Bethany College, KS
Bethany Lutheran College, MN
Bethel College, KS
Bethel University, MN
Biola University, CA
Black Hills State University, SD
Blue Mountain College, MS
The Boston Conservatory, MA
Boston University, MA
Bowling Green State University, OH
Bradley University, IL
Brenau University, GA
Brevard College, NC
Brewton-Parker College, GA
Brigham Young University–Hawaii, HI
Bryan College, TN
Buena Vista University, IA
Butler University, IN
California Baptist University, CA
California Institute of the Arts, CA
California Lutheran University, CA

California Polytechnic State University, San Luis Obispo, CA
California State University, Bakersfield, CA
California State University, Chico, CA
California State University, Fresno, CA
Calvin College, MI
Campbellsville University, KY
Campbell University, NC
Carnegie Mellon University, PA
Carroll College, MT
Carroll College, WI
Carthage College, WI
Cascade College, OR
Case Western Reserve University, OH
Catawba College, NC
The Catholic University of America, DC
Cedar Crest College, PA
Centenary College of Louisiana, LA
Central College, IA
Central Michigan University, MI
Central Missouri State University, MO
Central Washington University, WA
Centre College, KY
Chapman University, CA
Christopher Newport University, VA
Clarke College, IA
Clemson University, SC
Cleveland State University, OH
Coastal Carolina University, SC
Coe College, IA
College of Charleston, SC
College of Saint Benedict, MN
College of Santa Fe, NM
College of Staten Island of the City University of New York, NY
College of the Southwest, NM
The College of Wooster, OH
Colorado State University, CO
Columbus State University, GA
Concordia University, CA
Concordia University, MI
Concordia University, NE
Concordia University, St. Paul, MN
Converse College, SC
Cornell College, IA
Culver-Stockton College, MO
Davidson College, NC
Davis & Elkins College, WV
Denison University, OH
DePaul University, IL
Dickinson State University, ND
Doane College, NE
Dordt College, IA
Drake University, IA
Drexel University, PA
East Central University, OK
Eastern Michigan University, MI
Eastern Washington University, WA
East Stroudsburg University of Pennsylvania, PA
East Tennessee State University, TN
East Texas Baptist University, TX
Eckerd College, FL
Elizabethtown College, PA
Elmhurst College, IL
Elon University, NC

Emporia State University, KS
Erskine College, SC
Fairmont State University, WV
Faulkner University, AL
Ferris State University, MI
Ferrum College, VA
Five Towns College, NY
Flagler College, FL
Florida College, FL
Florida Southern College, FL
Fort Hays State University, KS
Fort Lewis College, CO
Francis Marion University, SC
Franklin Pierce College, NH
Freed-Hardeman University, TN
Fresno Pacific University, CA
Friends University, KS
Frostburg State University, MD
Furman University, SC
Gannon University, PA
Georgetown College, KY
Georgia College & State University, GA
Georgia Southern University, GA
Goucher College, MD
Grace College, IN
Graceland University, IA
Grambling State University, LA
Grand Valley State University, MI
Grand View College, IA
Green Mountain College, VT
Guilford College, NC
Gustavus Adolphus College, MN
Hamline University, MN
Hannibal-LaGrange College, MO
Hanover College, IN
Hardin-Simmons University, TX
Harris-Stowe State University, MO
Hendrix College, AR
Hillsdale College, MI
Hofstra University, NY
Hope College, MI
Huntington University, IN
Idaho State University, ID
Illinois College, IL
Illinois State University, IL
Illinois Wesleyan University, IL
Indiana University of Pennsylvania, PA
Indiana University–Purdue University Fort Wayne, IN
Ithaca College, NY
Jacksonville State University, AL
James Madison University, VA
Kansas State University, KS
Kean University, NJ
Keene State College, NH
Kennesaw State University, GA
Kent State University, OH
Kentucky Christian University, KY
Kentucky Wesleyan College, KY
King College, TN
Knox College, IL
LaGrange College, GA
Lake Forest College, IL
La Sierra University, CA
Lee University, TN
Lehigh University, PA

Non-Need Scholarships for Undergraduates
Creative Arts/Performance

Lewis-Clark State College, ID
Limestone College, SC
Lindenwood University, MO
Lindsey Wilson College, KY
Lipscomb University, TN
Louisiana State University and Agricultural and Mechanical College, LA
Louisiana Tech University, LA
Loyola University Chicago, IL
Lubbock Christian University, TX
Lycoming College, PA
Lyon College, AR
MacMurray College, IL
Malone College, OH
Marian College, IN
Marshall University, WV
Marymount Manhattan College, NY
Maryville College, TN
Marywood University, PA
Massachusetts Maritime Academy, MA
Mercer University, GA
Merrimack College, MA
Mesa State College, CO
Messiah College, PA
Methodist College, NC
Metropolitan State College of Denver, CO
Miami University, OH
Michigan State University, MI
Middle Tennessee State University, TN
Midland Lutheran College, NE
Midwestern State University, TX
Millsaps College, MS
Minnesota State University Mankato, MN
Mississippi State University, MS
Missouri State University, MO
Montana State University, MT
Montana State University–Billings, MT
Montclair State University, NJ
Montreat College, NC
Morehead State University, KY
Morningside College, IA
Mount Marty College, SD
Mount Mercy College, IA
Mount Union College, OH
Murray State University, KY
Nazareth College of Rochester, NY
Nebraska Wesleyan University, NE
Newberry College, SC
New England College, NH
Newman University, KS
New Mexico State University, NM
Niagara University, NY
North Carolina Agricultural and Technical State University, NC
Northeastern Illinois University, IL
Northern Arizona University, AZ
Northern Illinois University, IL
Northern Michigan University, MI
Northern State University, SD
North Greenville College, SC
Northwestern College, MN
Northwestern Oklahoma State University, OK
Northwestern State University of Louisiana, LA
Northwest Nazarene University, ID

Northwest University, WA
Nyack College, NY
Oglethorpe University, GA
Ohio Northern University, OH
The Ohio State University, OH
Ohio University, OH
Ohio University–Chillicothe, OH
Ohio University–Eastern, OH
Ohio University–Lancaster, OH
Ohio University–Southern Campus, OH
Ohio University–Zanesville, OH
Ohio Wesleyan University, OH
Oklahoma Panhandle State University, OK
Oklahoma State University, OK
Olivet Nazarene University, IL
Ouachita Baptist University, AR
Pacific Lutheran University, WA
Pacific University, OR
Palm Beach Atlantic University, FL
Peace College, NC
Pepperdine University, CA
Plymouth State University, NH
Pontifical Catholic University of Puerto Rico, PR
Portland State University, OR
Radford University, VA
Randolph-Macon Woman's College, VA
The Richard Stockton College of New Jersey, NJ
Rider University, NJ
Ripon College, WI
Rockhurst University, MO
Rollins College, FL
Roosevelt University, IL
St. Cloud State University, MN
St. Edward's University, TX
Saint Joseph's College, IN
Saint Joseph's University, PA
Saint Louis University, MO
Saint Martin's University, WA
Saint Mary's College, IN
Saint Mary's University of Minnesota, MN
St. Norbert College, WI
San Diego Christian College, CA
San Diego State University, CA
Santa Clara University, CA
Schreiner University, TX
Seton Hill University, PA
Shenandoah University, VA
Shimer College, IL
Shorter College, GA
Simpson College, IA
Slippery Rock University of Pennsylvania, PA
Sonoma State University, CA
South Dakota State University, SD
Southeastern Oklahoma State University, OK
Southeastern University, FL
Southeast Missouri State University, MO
Southern Adventist University, TN
Southern Arkansas University–Magnolia, AR
Southern Illinois University Carbondale, IL
Southern Illinois University Edwardsville, IL

Southern Oregon University, OR
Southwest Baptist University, MO
Southwestern Christian University, OK
Southwestern University, TX
Southwest Minnesota State University, MN
State University of New York at Binghamton, NY
State University of New York at Plattsburgh, NY
State University of New York College at Brockport, NY
State University of New York College at Cortland, NY
State University of New York College at Geneseo, NY
State University of New York College at Potsdam, NY
State University of New York, Fredonia, NY
Stephen F. Austin State University, TX
Stephens College, MO
Stetson University, FL
Stevens Institute of Technology, NJ
Stony Brook University, State University of New York, NY
Tabor College, KS
Taylor University, IN
Texas A&M University, TX
Texas A&M University–Commerce, TX
Texas Christian University, TX
Texas Lutheran University, TX
Texas State University-San Marcos, TX
Texas Tech University, TX
Texas Woman's University, TX
Thomas More College, KY
Towson University, MD
Trevecca Nazarene University, TN
Truman State University, MO
Union University, TN
The University of Akron, OH
The University of Alabama, AL
The University of Alabama at Birmingham, AL
University of Alaska Fairbanks, AK
University of Arkansas, AR
University of California, Riverside, CA
University of Central Oklahoma, OK
University of Colorado at Boulder, CO
University of Connecticut, CT
University of Delaware, DE
University of Denver, CO
University of Evansville, IN
The University of Findlay, OH
University of Florida, FL
University of Hartford, CT
University of Hawaii at Hilo, HI
University of Hawaii at Manoa, HI
University of Idaho, ID
University of Illinois at Urbana–Champaign, IL
The University of Iowa, IA
University of Kansas, KS
University of Maine, ME
University of Mary, ND
University of Maryland, Baltimore County, MD

Non-Need Scholarships for Undergraduates
Special Achievements/Activities

University of Maryland, College Park, MD
University of Mary Washington, VA
University of Massachusetts Amherst, MA
University of Miami, FL
University of Michigan, MI
University of Michigan–Flint, MI
University of Missouri–Columbia, MO
University of Nebraska at Omaha, NE
University of Nebraska–Lincoln, NE
University of Nevada, Las Vegas, NV
University of Nevada, Reno, NV
University of New Hampshire, NH
The University of North Carolina at Asheville, NC
The University of North Carolina at Chapel Hill, NC
The University of North Carolina at Greensboro, NC
The University of North Carolina Wilmington, NC
University of North Dakota, ND
University of Northern Colorado, CO
University of Northern Iowa, IA
University of Oklahoma, OK
University of Oregon, OR
University of Portland, OR
University of Puget Sound, WA
University of Richmond, VA
University of St. Thomas, TX
University of Science and Arts of Oklahoma, OK
University of South Carolina, SC
The University of South Dakota, SD
University of Southern Indiana, IN
University of Southern Maine, ME
University of Southern Mississippi, MS
University of South Florida, FL
The University of Tennessee at Martin, TN
The University of Texas at Arlington, TX
The University of Texas at El Paso, TX
The University of Texas–Pan American, TX
University of the Cumberlands, KY
University of the Ozarks, AR
The University of Toledo, OH
University of Tulsa, OK
University of Utah, UT
University of Vermont, VT
University of West Georgia, GA
University of Wisconsin–Eau Claire, WI
University of Wisconsin–Green Bay, WI
University of Wisconsin–La Crosse, WI
University of Wisconsin–Parkside, WI
University of Wisconsin–Stevens Point, WI
University of Wisconsin–Whitewater, WI
University of Wyoming, WY
Ursinus College, PA
Utah State University, UT
Valdosta State University, GA
Valley City State University, ND
Valparaiso University, IN
Vanguard University of Southern California, CA
Virginia Commonwealth University, VA
Virginia Intermont College, VA
Virginia Polytechnic Institute and State University, VA

Wabash College, IN
Wake Forest University, NC
Waldorf College, IA
Warner Pacific College, OR
Washington State University, WA
Washington University in St. Louis, MO
Wayland Baptist University, TX
Wayne State College, NE
Wayne State University, MI
Webster University, MO
Wesleyan College, GA
Western Carolina University, NC
Western Illinois University, IL
Western Kentucky University, KY
Western Washington University, WA
Westminster College, PA
Westmont College, CA
West Texas A&M University, TX
West Virginia University, WV
West Virginia Wesleyan College, WV
Whitman College, WA
Whittier College, CA
Whitworth College, WA
Wichita State University, KS
Wilkes University, PA
Willamette University, OR
William Carey College, MS
William Jewell College, MO
William Penn University, IA
William Woods University, MO
Winona State University, MN
Winthrop University, SC
Wittenberg University, OH
Xavier University, OH
Youngstown State University, OH

Special Achievements/Activities

Cheerleading/Drum Major
Abilene Christian University, TX
Arkansas State University, AR
Athens State University, AL
Auburn University, AL
Azusa Pacific University, CA
Belhaven College, MS
Bethany College, KS
Bluefield State College, WV
Brevard College, NC
Brewton-Parker College, GA
Brigham Young University–Hawaii, HI
Bryan College, TN
Campbellsville University, KY
Campbell University, NC
Central Missouri State University, MO
Columbus State University, GA
Culver-Stockton College, MO
Dickinson State University, ND
Drexel University, PA
East Central University, OK
East Texas Baptist University, TX
Evangel University, MO
Fairmont State University, WV
Faulkner University, AL
Fort Hays State University, KS

Francis Marion University, SC
Graceland University, IA
Grambling State University, LA
Harding University, AR
Hawai'i Pacific University, HI
Houston Baptist University, TX
Huntington University, IN
Iowa Wesleyan College, IA
James Madison University, VA
John Brown University, AR
Lee University, TN
Limestone College, SC
Lindenwood University, MO
Lipscomb University, TN
Long Island University, Brooklyn Campus, NY
Louisiana Tech University, LA
Lubbock Christian University, TX
McKendree College, IL
Methodist College, NC
MidAmerica Nazarene University, KS
Middle Tennessee State University, TN
Midwestern State University, TX
Mississippi State University, MS
Missouri State University, MO
Montana State University–Billings, MT
Morehead State University, KY
Morningside College, IA
Murray State University, KY
Newberry College, SC
North Georgia College & State University, GA
North Greenville College, SC
Northwestern Oklahoma State University, OK
Northwestern State University of Louisiana, LA
Northwest Nazarene University, ID
Northwood University, MI
The Ohio State University, OH
Oklahoma Panhandle State University, OK
Oklahoma State University, OK
Olivet Nazarene University, IL
Oral Roberts University, OK
St. Edward's University, TX
Saint Francis University, PA
St. John's University, NY
Saint Joseph's College, IN
Saint Louis University, MO
Southeastern Louisiana University, LA
Southeastern Oklahoma State University, OK
Southeast Missouri State University, MO
Southern Arkansas University–Magnolia, AR
Southern Illinois University Carbondale, IL
Southwestern Christian University, OK
Stephen F. Austin State University, TX
Stetson University, FL
Tabor College, KS
Temple University, PA
Tennessee Technological University, TN
Texas A&M University–Commerce, TX
Tiffin University, OH
Tusculum College, TN
Union College, KY

Non-Need Scholarships for Undergraduates
Special Achievements/Activities

Union University, TN
The University of Alabama, AL
The University of Alabama at Birmingham, AL
The University of Alabama in Huntsville, AL
University of Arkansas at Monticello, AR
University of Delaware, DE
University of Idaho, ID
University of Kentucky, KY
University of Mary Hardin-Baylor, TX
University of Maryland, College Park, MD
University of Massachusetts Amherst, MA
University of Memphis, TN
University of Nebraska at Kearney, NE
University of Nebraska–Lincoln, NE
University of Nevada, Las Vegas, NV
University of Nevada, Reno, NV
University of North Alabama, AL
The University of North Carolina Wilmington, NC
University of Puerto Rico, Mayagüez Campus, PR
University of Saint Francis, IN
University of Science and Arts of Oklahoma, OK
University of South Carolina, SC
University of Southern Mississippi, MS
The University of Tennessee at Martin, TN
The University of Texas at Arlington, TX
The University of Texas at El Paso, TX
The University of Texas–Pan American, TX
University of the Cumberlands, KY
The University of Toledo, OH
University of Tulsa, OK
University of Utah, UT
The University of West Alabama, AL
University of Wyoming, WY
Virginia Intermont College, VA
Virginia Polytechnic Institute and State University, VA
Wake Forest University, NC
Waldorf College, IA
Wayland Baptist University, TX
Webber International University, FL
West Texas A&M University, TX
William Carey College, MS
William Jewell College, MO
William Penn University, IA
Williams Baptist College, AR
Winston-Salem State University, NC
Wofford College, SC
Youngstown State University, OH

Community Service
Adelphi University, NY
Agnes Scott College, GA
Alaska Pacific University, AK
Albertus Magnus College, CT
Allen College, IA
Alliant International University, CA
Alvernia College, PA
Alverno College, WI
Arkansas State University, AR
Armstrong Atlantic State University, GA
Augsburg College, MN

Augusta State University, GA
Baylor University, TX
Beloit College, WI
Bentley College, MA
Berry College, GA
Bethel University, MN
Biola University, CA
Bloomfield College, NJ
Bradley University, IL
Brevard College, NC
Brigham Young University–Hawaii, HI
Bryan College, TN
California Lutheran University, CA
California Polytechnic State University, San Luis Obispo, CA
California State University, Bakersfield, CA
California State University, Chico, CA
California State University, Fresno, CA
California State University, Stanislaus, CA
Calvin College, MI
Cedar Crest College, PA
Centenary College of Louisiana, LA
Central Washington University, WA
The Citadel, The Military College of South Carolina, SC
City College of the City University of New York, NY
Clark University, MA
Clemson University, SC
College Misericordia, PA
College of Mount St. Joseph, OH
College of Notre Dame of Maryland, MD
College of St. Catherine, MN
College of St. Joseph, VT
College of Saint Mary, NE
The College of Saint Rose, NY
College of the Atlantic, ME
The College of Wooster, OH
Columbus State University, GA
Cornell College, IA
Dallas Baptist University, TX
Davidson College, NC
Defiance College, OH
DePaul University, IL
DePauw University, IN
Dominican University of California, CA
Eckerd College, FL
Elmhurst College, IL
Elon University, NC
Emmanuel College, MA
Endicott College, MA
Eugene Bible College, OR
The Evergreen State College, WA
Ferrum College, VA
Finlandia University, MI
Florida Gulf Coast University, FL
Florida Southern College, FL
Frostburg State University, MD
Furman University, SC
Gannon University, PA
Georgia College & State University, GA
Georgia Southern University, GA
Green Mountain College, VT
Gustavus Adolphus College, MN
Hampshire College, MA
Hillsdale College, MI

Hollins University, VA
Holy Names University, CA
Illinois State University, IL
Illinois Wesleyan University, IL
Indiana University of Pennsylvania, PA
Iowa Wesleyan College, IA
Jacksonville University, FL
Johnson Bible College, TN
Juniata College, PA
Kean University, NJ
Kennesaw State University, GA
Kent State University, OH
Kentucky Christian University, KY
King College, TN
King's College, PA
Knox College, IL
LaGrange College, GA
Lakeland College, WI
Lasell College, MA
Lewis & Clark College, OR
Lincoln Christian College, IL
Lincoln University, PA
Lindenwood University, MO
Loyola University Chicago, IL
Lynchburg College, VA
Malone College, OH
Manhattan College, NY
Marian College, IN
Marlboro College, VT
Marymount University, VA
Maryville College, TN
Maryville University of Saint Louis, MO
Marywood University, PA
McKendree College, IL
Menlo College, CA
Mercer University, GA
Mercyhurst College, PA
Meredith College, NC
Michigan State University, MI
Midland Lutheran College, NE
Millersville University of Pennsylvania, PA
Milligan College, TN
Millsaps College, MS
Minnesota State University Mankato, MN
Molloy College, NY
Montclair State University, NJ
Morningside College, IA
Mount St. Mary's College, CA
New England College, NH
Newman University, KS
Niagara University, NY
North Georgia College & State University, GA
Oglethorpe University, GA
Ohio Northern University, OH
Ohio Wesleyan University, OH
Oklahoma State University, OK
Oral Roberts University, OK
Pacific Union College, CA
Pacific University, OR
Pitzer College, CA
Portland State University, OR
Presentation College, SD
Quincy University, IL
Randolph-Macon Woman's College, VA
Regis College, MA

Non-Need Scholarships for Undergraduates
Special Achievements/Activities

Rice University, TX
The Richard Stockton College of New Jersey, NJ
Robert Morris College, IL
Rochester Institute of Technology, NY
Rockhurst University, MO
Rosemont College, PA
Russell Sage College, NY
Sacred Heart University, CT
Sage College of Albany, NY
St. Andrews Presbyterian College, NC
St. Cloud State University, MN
St. Edward's University, TX
Saint Francis University, PA
St. John Fisher College, NY
St. John's University, NY
Saint Joseph's College of Maine, ME
St. Lawrence University, NY
St. Louis College of Pharmacy, MO
Saint Louis University, MO
Saint Martin's University, WA
Saint Mary's College, IN
San Diego State University, CA
Schreiner University, TX
Seton Hill University, PA
Simmons College, MA
Slippery Rock University of Pennsylvania, PA
Sonoma State University, CA
South Dakota State University, SD
Southern Adventist University, TN
Southern Illinois University Carbondale, IL
Southern Oregon University, OR
Southern Vermont College, VT
Spring Hill College, AL
State University of New York at Binghamton, NY
State University of New York at Plattsburgh, NY
State University of New York College at Brockport, NY
State University of New York College at Geneseo, NY
State University of New York College at Oneonta, NY
State University of New York College at Potsdam, NY
Stetson University, FL
Suffolk University, MA
Texas Tech University, TX
Trinity College of Florida, FL
Tusculum College, TN
Unity College, ME
The University of Akron, OH
The University of Alabama, AL
The University of Alabama in Huntsville, AL
University of Alaska Fairbanks, AK
University of Arkansas, AR
University of Baltimore, MD
University of California, San Diego, CA
University of Colorado at Boulder, CO
University of Colorado at Colorado Springs, CO
University of Connecticut, CT
University of Delaware, DE
University of Denver, CO
University of Florida, FL
University of Hartford, CT
University of Hawaii at Hilo, HI
University of Houston–Victoria, TX
University of Illinois at Springfield, IL
University of Illinois at Urbana–Champaign, IL
University of Kansas, KS
University of Maine, ME
University of Maine at Presque Isle, ME
University of Mary Hardin-Baylor, TX
University of Massachusetts Dartmouth, MA
University of Massachusetts Lowell, MA
University of Michigan, MI
University of Michigan–Dearborn, MI
University of Michigan–Flint, MI
University of Nebraska–Lincoln, NE
University of Nevada, Las Vegas, NV
University of New England, ME
University of New Hampshire, NH
The University of North Carolina at Asheville, NC
The University of North Carolina at Chapel Hill, NC
The University of North Carolina at Greensboro, NC
University of North Florida, FL
University of Portland, OR
University of Richmond, VA
University of St. Francis, IL
University of St. Thomas, TX
University of South Carolina, SC
University of Southern Maine, ME
The University of Texas at Arlington, TX
The University of Texas–Pan American, TX
University of the Cumberlands, KY
University of Tulsa, OK
University of Vermont, VT
University of West Georgia, GA
University of Wisconsin–Eau Claire, WI
University of Wisconsin–Green Bay, WI
University of Wisconsin–Parkside, WI
University of Wisconsin–Stout, WI
Urbana University, OH
Valdosta State University, GA
Villa Julie College, MD
Virginia Polytechnic Institute and State University, VA
Wabash College, IN
Wake Forest University, NC
Walla Walla College, WA
Warren Wilson College, NC
Washington State University, WA
Waynesburg College, PA
Webber International University, FL
Wesleyan College, GA
Western Illinois University, IL
Western New England College, MA
Western Washington University, WA
Westfield State College, MA
West Virginia Wesleyan College, WV
Wheeling Jesuit University, WV
Widener University, PA
Willamette University, OR
Wilson College, PA
Wittenberg University, OH
Wofford College, SC
Worcester State College, MA
York College of Pennsylvania, PA

Hobbies/Interests
Augusta State University, GA
Brevard College, NC
California State University, Chico, CA
Central Washington University, WA
Corban College, OR
Dalton State College, GA
Eugene Bible College, OR
Hawai'i Pacific University, HI
Illinois Wesleyan University, IL
Indiana University of Pennsylvania, PA
Mesa State College, CO
Michigan State University, MI
Millsaps College, MS
Missouri State University, MO
The Ohio State University, OH
St. John's University, NY
Shimer College, IL
South Dakota State University, SD
Southern Oregon University, OR
Southwest Minnesota State University, MN
Stephen F. Austin State University, TX
The University of Alabama, AL
University of Michigan–Flint, MI
University of Minnesota, Twin Cities Campus, MN
University of Nevada, Las Vegas, NV
The University of Toledo, OH
University of Wisconsin–Eau Claire, WI
Valdosta State University, GA

Junior Miss
Albertson College of Idaho, ID
Albright College, PA
Alvernia College, PA
Augsburg College, MN
Belhaven College, MS
Bethel University, MN
Bluefield State College, WV
Brigham Young University–Hawaii, HI
Campbellsville University, KY
Campbell University, NC
Carroll College, WI
Cedar Crest College, PA
College of Saint Benedict, MN
Georgetown College, KY
Georgia Southern University, GA
Grambling State University, LA
Grand View College, IA
Hamline University, MN
Hardin-Simmons University, TX
Idaho State University, ID
Judson College, AL
Kentucky Wesleyan College, KY
Lebanon Valley College, PA
Lewis-Clark State College, ID
Lindenwood University, MO
Lindsey Wilson College, KY
Malone College, OH
McDaniel College, MD
Mercer University, GA

Non-Need Scholarships for Undergraduates
Special Achievements/Activities

Michigan State University, MI
Midway College, KY
Mount Vernon Nazarene University, OH
Murray State University, KY
North Greenville College, SC
Ohio Northern University, OH
Saint Francis University, PA
South Dakota State University, SD
Spring Arbor University, MI
The University of Alabama, AL
The University of Alabama at Birmingham, AL
The University of Alabama in Huntsville, AL
University of Idaho, ID
The University of North Carolina at Asheville, NC
The University of North Carolina at Greensboro, NC
University of Wyoming, WY
Waldorf College, IA
Wartburg College, IA
Washington State University, WA
William Carey College, MS
William Penn University, IA

Leadership
Abilene Christian University, TX
Agnes Scott College, GA
Alaska Pacific University, AK
Albertus Magnus College, CT
Alderson-Broaddus College, WV
Alfred University, NY
Allen College, IA
Alliant International University, CA
Alma College, MI
Alvernia College, PA
American University, DC
Andrews University, MI
Arkansas Tech University, AR
Asbury College, KY
Athens State University, AL
Atlantic Union College, MA
Auburn University, AL
Augsburg College, MN
Augustana College, SD
Augusta State University, GA
Austin College, TX
Austin Peay State University, TN
Averett University, VA
Azusa Pacific University, CA
Babson College, MA
Baldwin-Wallace College, OH
Ball State University, IN
Bard College, NY
Barton College, NC
Baylor University, TX
Becker College, MA
Belhaven College, MS
Bethel University, MN
Bluefield State College, WV
Blue Mountain College, MS
Bluffton University, OH
Boston University, MA
Bowdoin College, ME
Bowling Green State University, OH

Bradley University, IL
Brenau University, GA
Brevard College, NC
Brewton-Parker College, GA
Brigham Young University–Hawaii, HI
Bryan College, TN
Buena Vista University, IA
California Lutheran University, CA
California Polytechnic State University, San Luis Obispo, CA
California State University, Chico, CA
California State University, Fullerton, CA
California State University, Stanislaus, CA
Campbellsville University, KY
Carroll College, WI
Carson-Newman College, TN
Carthage College, WI
Cascade College, OR
Case Western Reserve University, OH
Cedar Crest College, PA
Cedarville University, OH
Centenary College, NJ
Centenary College of Louisiana, LA
Central Michigan University, MI
Central Missouri State University, MO
Central Washington University, WA
Chestnut Hill College, PA
Chowan University, NC
Christian Brothers University, TN
Christopher Newport University, VA
The Citadel, The Military College of South Carolina, SC
City College of the City University of New York, NY
Clark Atlanta University, GA
Clarke College, IA
Clarkson University, NY
Clearwater Christian College, FL
Clemson University, SC
College Misericordia, PA
College of Mount St. Joseph, OH
College of Mount Saint Vincent, NY
College of Notre Dame of Maryland, MD
College of St. Catherine, MN
College of St. Joseph, VT
College of Saint Mary, NE
College of the Atlantic, ME
The College of Wooster, OH
Columbia College, SC
Columbus State University, GA
Concordia University Wisconsin, WI
Converse College, SC
Corban College, OR
Cornerstone University, MI
Crown College, MN
Culver-Stockton College, MO
Dallas Baptist University, TX
Dallas Christian College, TX
Daniel Webster College, NH
David N. Myers University, OH
Davidson College, NC
Davis & Elkins College, WV
Defiance College, OH
Denison University, OH
DePauw University, IN
Dickinson College, PA

Dickinson State University, ND
Dominican University, IL
Dordt College, IA
Duke University, NC
East Carolina University, NC
Eastern Michigan University, MI
East Tennessee State University, TN
East Texas Baptist University, TX
Eckerd College, FL
Elmira College, NY
Elon University, NC
Embry-Riddle Aeronautical University, AZ
Embry-Riddle Aeronautical University, FL
Embry-Riddle Aeronautical University, Extended Campus, FL
Emmaus Bible College, IA
Endicott College, MA
Erskine College, SC
Eugene Bible College, OR
Eureka College, IL
Evangel University, MO
Faith Baptist Bible College and Theological Seminary, IA
Faulkner University, AL
Ferrum College, VA
Finlandia University, MI
Fitchburg State College, MA
Flagler College, FL
Florida Gulf Coast University, FL
Florida Southern College, FL
Fort Lewis College, CO
Freed-Hardeman University, TN
Fresno Pacific University, CA
Friends University, KS
Frostburg State University, MD
Furman University, SC
Gannon University, PA
Georgetown College, KY
Georgia College & State University, GA
Georgia Institute of Technology, GA
Georgia Southern University, GA
Georgia Southwestern State University, GA
Gonzaga University, WA
Gordon College, MA
Graceland University, IA
Grambling State University, LA
Green Mountain College, VT
Greenville College, IL
Grove City College, PA
Hampden-Sydney College, VA
Hampshire College, MA
Hardin-Simmons University, TX
Hawai'i Pacific University, HI
Hendrix College, AR
Hilbert College, NY
Hillsdale College, MI
Hobart and William Smith Colleges, NY
Hofstra University, NY
Hollins University, VA
Husson College, ME
Idaho State University, ID
Illinois State University, IL
Illinois Wesleyan University, IL
Indiana University of Pennsylvania, PA
Iowa Wesleyan College, IA
Ithaca College, NY

Non-Need Scholarships for Undergraduates
Special Achievements/Activities

Jacksonville University, FL
James Madison University, VA
Jamestown College, ND
John Brown University, AR
Johnson Bible College, TN
Juniata College, PA
Kansas State University, KS
Kean University, NJ
Kennesaw State University, GA
Kent State University, OH
Kentucky Christian University, KY
Kentucky Wesleyan College, KY
King's College, PA
Kuyper College, MI
LaGrange College, GA
Lake Forest College, IL
Lakeland College, WI
Lancaster Bible College, PA
La Sierra University, CA
Lee University, TN
Le Moyne College, NY
Lewis-Clark State College, ID
Limestone College, SC
Lincoln Christian College, IL
Lindenwood University, MO
Lindsey Wilson College, KY
Linfield College, OR
Lipscomb University, TN
Lock Haven University of Pennsylvania, PA
Long Island University, Brooklyn Campus, NY
Louisiana State University and Agricultural and Mechanical College, LA
Loyola University Chicago, IL
Lubbock Christian University, TX
Lycoming College, PA
Lynchburg College, VA
Lynn University, FL
Lyon College, AR
MacMurray College, IL
Malone College, OH
Manhattan Christian College, KS
Manhattan College, NY
Mary Baldwin College, VA
Marymount Manhattan College, NY
Marymount University, VA
Maryville College, TN
Maryville University of Saint Louis, MO
Marywood University, PA
Massachusetts Maritime Academy, MA
The Master's College and Seminary, CA
Mayville State University, ND
McDaniel College, MD
McKendree College, IL
Mercyhurst College, PA
Meredith College, NC
Merrimack College, MA
Messiah College, PA
Methodist College, NC
Miami University, OH
Michigan State University, MI
Michigan Technological University, MI
MidAmerica Nazarene University, KS
Middle Tennessee State University, TN
Midland Lutheran College, NE
Midway College, KY

Midwestern State University, TX
Millsaps College, MS
Minnesota State University Mankato, MN
Mississippi State University, MS
Montclair State University, NJ
Montreat College, NC
Moore College of Art & Design, PA
Morehead State University, KY
Morningside College, IA
Mount Aloysius College, PA
Mount Marty College, SD
Mount Mary College, WI
Mount Mercy College, IA
Mount Olive College, NC
Mount St. Mary's College, CA
Murray State University, KY
National University, CA
New England College, NH
Newman University, KS
New Mexico State University, NM
Northeastern Illinois University, IL
Northern Illinois University, IL
Northern Michigan University, MI
Northern State University, SD
North Georgia College & State University, GA
Northland College, WI
Northwest Christian College, OR
Northwestern College, MN
Northwestern Oklahoma State University, OK
Northwestern State University of Louisiana, LA
Northwest Nazarene University, ID
Northwood University, MI
Nova Southeastern University, FL
Nyack College, NY
Occidental College, CA
Ohio Northern University, OH
The Ohio State University, OH
Ohio Wesleyan University, OH
Oklahoma Baptist University, OK
Oklahoma State University, OK
Olivet Nazarene University, IL
Oral Roberts University, OK
Pacific Lutheran University, WA
Pacific Union College, CA
Philadelphia Biblical University, PA
Pitzer College, CA
Portland State University, OR
Presentation College, SD
Purdue University, IN
Quincy University, IL
Quinnipiac University, CT
Radford University, VA
Randolph-Macon Woman's College, VA
Rice University, TX
The Richard Stockton College of New Jersey, NJ
Ripon College, WI
Roberts Wesleyan College, NY
Rochester Institute of Technology, NY
Rockhurst University, MO
Russell Sage College, NY
Sacred Heart University, CT
St. Andrews Presbyterian College, NC

St. Edward's University, TX
St. John's University, NY
St. Louis College of Pharmacy, MO
Saint Louis University, MO
Saint Martin's University, WA
Saint Mary's University of Minnesota, MN
Saint Vincent College, PA
Saint Xavier University, IL
San Diego Christian College, CA
San Diego State University, CA
Schreiner University, TX
Seattle University, WA
Seton Hill University, PA
Shepherd University, WV
Simpson College, IA
Simpson University, CA
Slippery Rock University of Pennsylvania, PA
Sonoma State University, CA
South Dakota State University, SD
Southeastern Louisiana University, LA
Southeast Missouri State University, MO
Southern Adventist University, TN
Southern Arkansas University–Magnolia, AR
Southern Illinois University Carbondale, IL
Southern New Hampshire University, NH
Southern Oregon University, OR
Southern Vermont College, VT
Southwest Minnesota State University, MN
State University of New York at Binghamton, NY
State University of New York at Plattsburgh, NY
State University of New York College at Brockport, NY
State University of New York College at Cortland, NY
State University of New York College at Geneseo, NY
State University of New York College at Oneonta, NY
State University of New York College at Potsdam, NY
State University of New York College of Environmental Science and Forestry, NY
State University of New York, Fredonia, NY
Stephen F. Austin State University, TX
Stephens College, MO
Stetson University, FL
Taylor University, IN
Taylor University Fort Wayne, IN
Texas A&M University, TX
Texas A&M University at Galveston, TX
Texas A&M University–Commerce, TX
Texas Christian University, TX
Texas Lutheran University, TX
Thiel College, PA
Tiffin University, OH
Toccoa Falls College, GA
Trinity College, CT
Trinity College of Florida, FL
Trinity Lutheran College, WA
Truman State University, MO
Tusculum College, TN

Non-Need Scholarships for Undergraduates
Special Achievements/Activities

Union University, TN
Unity College, ME
The University of Akron, OH
The University of Alabama at Birmingham, AL
The University of Alabama in Huntsville, AL
University of Alaska Southeast, AK
University of Arkansas, AR
University of Arkansas at Monticello, AR
University of Arkansas at Pine Bluff, AR
University of California, San Diego, CA
University of Central Oklahoma, OK
University of Colorado at Boulder, CO
University of Colorado at Colorado Springs, CO
University of Colorado at Denver and Health Sciences Center—Downtown Denver Campus, CO
University of Connecticut, CT
University of Dallas, TX
University of Delaware, DE
University of Denver, CO
University of Evansville, IN
University of Florida, FL
University of Hawaii at Hilo, HI
University of Houston–Victoria, TX
University of Idaho, ID
University of Illinois at Springfield, IL
University of Illinois at Urbana–Champaign, IL
University of Judaism, CA
University of Kansas, KS
University of Kentucky, KY
University of Maine, ME
University of Mary Hardin-Baylor, TX
University of Maryland, College Park, MD
University of Mary Washington, VA
University of Massachusetts Amherst, MA
University of Memphis, TN
University of Michigan, MI
University of Michigan–Dearborn, MI
University of Michigan–Flint, MI
University of Minnesota, Twin Cities Campus, MN
University of Nebraska at Omaha, NE
University of Nebraska–Lincoln, NE
University of Nevada, Las Vegas, NV
University of New England, ME
University of North Alabama, AL
The University of North Carolina at Asheville, NC
The University of North Carolina at Chapel Hill, NC
The University of North Carolina at Greensboro, NC
The University of North Carolina Wilmington, NC
University of North Dakota, ND
University of Northern Iowa, IA
University of North Florida, FL
University of Oklahoma, OK
University of Pittsburgh at Greensburg, PA
University of Pittsburgh at Johnstown, PA
University of Puget Sound, WA
University of Rochester, NY
University of St. Francis, IL
University of Science and Arts of Oklahoma, OK
University of South Carolina, SC
University of Southern California, CA
University of Southern Indiana, IN
University of Southern Mississippi, MS
The University of Tampa, FL
The University of Tennessee at Martin, TN
The University of Texas at Arlington, TX
The University of Texas at Dallas, TX
The University of Texas at El Paso, TX
The University of Texas–Pan American, TX
University of the Ozarks, AR
The University of Toledo, OH
University of Tulsa, OK
University of Utah, UT
University of Wisconsin–Eau Claire, WI
University of Wisconsin–Green Bay, WI
University of Wisconsin–Parkside, WI
University of Wisconsin–Stevens Point, WI
University of Wisconsin–Whitewater, WI
University of Wyoming, WY
Urbana University, OH
Ursinus College, PA
Valley Forge Christian College, PA
Villa Julie College, MD
Virginia Military Institute, VA
Virginia Polytechnic Institute and State University, VA
Virginia Wesleyan College, VA
Wabash College, IN
Waldorf College, IA
Walla Walla College, WA
Warner Pacific College, OR
Warren Wilson College, NC
Washington State University, WA
Wayland Baptist University, TX
Wayne State College, NE
Webber International University, FL
Webster University, MO
Wells College, NY
Wesleyan College, GA
Wesley College, MS
Western Illinois University, IL
Western Kentucky University, KY
Western New England College, MA
Western State College of Colorado, CO
Western Washington University, WA
Westminster College, MO
Westmont College, CA
West Texas A&M University, TX
West Virginia University, WV
West Virginia Wesleyan College, WV
Wichita State University, KS
Widener University, PA
Wilkes University, PA
Willamette University, OR
William Carey College, MS
William Penn University, IA
William Woods University, MO
Wilson College, PA
Wittenberg University, OH
Wofford College, SC
Youngstown State University, OH

Memberships

Adelphi University, NY
Albright College, PA
American University, DC
Auburn University, AL
Averett University, VA
Blue Mountain College, MS
Boston University, MA
California State University, Chico, CA
California State University, Stanislaus, CA
Carroll College, WI
Carson-Newman College, TN
Cascade College, OR
Cedar Crest College, PA
Central Washington University, WA
College of Notre Dame of Maryland, MD
College of Saint Benedict, MN
College of St. Catherine, MN
Concordia University, NE
Corban College, OR
Dallas Baptist University, TX
Dalton State College, GA
Delaware Valley College, PA
Eastern Michigan University, MI
East Tennessee State University, TN
Emory University, GA
Emporia State University, KS
Erskine College, SC
Flagler College, FL
Fresno Pacific University, CA
Georgia Southern University, GA
Greenville College, IL
Grove City College, PA
Hawai'i Pacific University, HI
Idaho State University, ID
Johnson & Wales University, CO
Johnson & Wales University, FL
Johnson & Wales University, NC
Johnson & Wales University, RI
Kennesaw State University, GA
Kettering University, MI
Lock Haven University of Pennsylvania, PA
Loras College, IA
Loyola University Chicago, IL
Marymount University, VA
Medcenter One College of Nursing, ND
Mercer University, GA
Michigan State University, MI
Midwestern State University, TX
Mississippi State University, MS
Missouri State University, MO
Mount Marty College, SD
Newman University, KS
Northern Michigan University, MI
Northwestern Oklahoma State University, OK
Northwestern State University of Louisiana, LA
Northwood University, MI
Northwood University, Florida Campus, FL
Northwood University, Texas Campus, TX
The Ohio State University, OH
Oklahoma State University, OK
Oral Roberts University, OK
Pacific University, OR
Portland State University, OR

Non-Need Scholarships for Undergraduates
Special Achievements/Activities

Ripon College, WI
Saint Francis University, PA
Saint Louis University, MO
Saint Martin's University, WA
Saint Mary's College of California, CA
Sonoma State University, CA
South Dakota State University, SD
Southeastern Louisiana University, LA
Southern New Hampshire University, NH
Southern Oregon University, OR
State University of New York at Binghamton, NY
Texas A&M University, TX
Texas Tech University, TX
Trevecca Nazarene University, TN
The University of Akron, OH
The University of Alabama at Birmingham, AL
University of Baltimore, MD
University of Houston–Victoria, TX
University of Illinois at Springfield, IL
University of Illinois at Urbana–Champaign, IL
University of Louisville, KY
University of Maine, ME
University of Michigan–Dearborn, MI
University of Missouri–St. Louis, MO
University of Nebraska at Omaha, NE
University of Nevada, Las Vegas, NV
University of North Dakota, ND
The University of Texas–Pan American, TX
The University of Toledo, OH
University of West Georgia, GA
University of Wisconsin–Eau Claire, WI
University of Wisconsin–Stout, WI
Virginia Polytechnic Institute and State University, VA
Wake Forest University, NC
Washington College, MD
Washington State University, WA
Wayland Baptist University, TX
Webber International University, FL
Western Kentucky University, KY
Western Washington University, WA
West Texas A&M University, TX
York College of Pennsylvania, PA

Religious Involvement
Adrian College, MI
Alaska Bible College, AK
Alaska Pacific University, AK
Alvernia College, PA
Andrews University, MI
Anna Maria College, MA
Augsburg College, MN
Austin College, TX
Averett University, VA
Azusa Pacific University, CA
Barton College, NC
Baylor University, TX
Belmont Abbey College, NC
Berry College, GA
Bethel University, MN
Blue Mountain College, MS
Brigham Young University–Hawaii, HI
Bryan College, TN

California Lutheran University, CA
Calvary Bible College and Theological Seminary, MO
Calvin College, MI
Campbellsville University, KY
Campbell University, NC
Carroll College, MT
Carroll College, WI
Carthage College, WI
Cedar Crest College, PA
Centenary College of Louisiana, LA
Central College, IA
The Citadel, The Military College of South Carolina, SC
College of Notre Dame of Maryland, MD
The College of Wooster, OH
Concordia University, NE
Concordia University at Austin, TX
Corban College, OR
Cornell College, IA
Cornerstone University, MI
Dallas Baptist University, TX
Davidson College, NC
Davis & Elkins College, WV
Defiance College, OH
Eastern Michigan University, MI
East Texas Baptist University, TX
Elizabethtown College, PA
Elon University, NC
Emmaus Bible College, IA
Endicott College, MA
Eugene Bible College, OR
Evangel University, MO
Fairfield University, CT
Faulkner University, AL
Ferrum College, VA
Finlandia University, MI
Flagler College, FL
Fresno Pacific University, CA
Furman University, SC
Georgetown College, KY
Graceland University, IA
Green Mountain College, VT
Greenville College, IL
Grove City College, PA
Guilford College, NC
Harding University, AR
Hawai'i Pacific University, HI
Heidelberg College, OH
Hendrix College, AR
Houghton College, NY
Iowa Wesleyan College, IA
Johnson Bible College, TN
Kentucky Christian University, KY
Kuyper College, MI
Lakeland College, WI
Lancaster Bible College, PA
Lee University, TN
Limestone College, SC
Lindsey Wilson College, KY
Lipscomb University, TN
Loras College, IA
Lynn University, FL
MacMurray College, IL
Malone College, OH
Marian College, IN

Mercyhurst College, PA
Messenger College, MO
Midland Lutheran College, NE
Midway College, KY
Millsaps College, MS
Moravian College, PA
Mount Marty College, SD
Mount Vernon Nazarene University, OH
Newberry College, SC
Newman University, KS
North Greenville College, SC
Northwest Christian College, OR
Northwest Nazarene University, ID
Nyack College, NY
Oglethorpe University, GA
Ohio Wesleyan University, OH
Oklahoma Baptist University, OK
Olivet Nazarene University, IL
Oral Roberts University, OK
Pacific Union College, CA
Palm Beach Atlantic University, FL
Philadelphia Biblical University, PA
Presentation College, SD
Randolph-Macon Woman's College, VA
Sacred Heart University, CT
Saint Francis University, PA
St. John's University, NY
Saint Joseph's College of Maine, ME
San Diego Christian College, CA
Schreiner University, TX
Seton Hill University, PA
Shorter College, GA
Silver Lake College, WI
Simpson College, IA
Simpson University, CA
Southeastern University, FL
Southern Adventist University, TN
Southern Methodist College, SC
Southern Virginia University, VA
Southwest Baptist University, MO
Southwestern Christian University, OK
State University of New York College at Brockport, NY
Stetson University, FL
Tabor College, KS
Texas Lutheran University, TX
Thomas More College, KY
Transylvania University, KY
Trinity College of Florida, FL
Trinity International University, IL
Trinity Lutheran College, WA
The University of Alabama at Birmingham, AL
University of Dallas, TX
University of Mary Hardin-Baylor, TX
The University of North Carolina at Greensboro, NC
University of Puget Sound, WA
University of St. Francis, IL
University of Saint Francis, IN
University of South Carolina, SC
University of the Cumberlands, KY
University of the Pacific, CA
The University of Toledo, OH
University of West Georgia, GA
Urbana University, OH

Non-Need Scholarships for Undergraduates
Special Achievements/Activities

Valparaiso University, IN
Virginia Polytechnic Institute and State University, VA
Virginia Wesleyan College, VA
Washington State University, WA
Wayland Baptist University, TX
Wesleyan College, GA
Wesley College, MS
West Virginia Wesleyan College, WV
Whitworth College, WA
William Carey College, MS
William Jewell College, MO
William Penn University, IA
Wingate University, NC
Wofford College, SC
Xavier University of Louisiana, LA

Rodeo
California Polytechnic State University, San Luis Obispo, CA
Dickinson State University, ND
Fort Hays State University, KS
Idaho State University, ID
Lewis-Clark State College, ID
Michigan State University, MI
Missouri State University, MO
Murray State University, KY
New Mexico State University, NM
Northwestern Oklahoma State University, OK
Oklahoma Panhandle State University, OK
Oklahoma State University, OK
South Dakota State University, SD
Southeastern Louisiana University, LA
Southern Arkansas University–Magnolia, AR
Stephen F. Austin State University, TX
Texas A&M University, TX
Texas Tech University, TX
University of Arkansas at Monticello, AR
University of Idaho, ID
University of Nevada, Las Vegas, NV
The University of Tennessee at Martin, TN
The University of West Alabama, AL
University of Wyoming, WY
Washington State University, WA
West Texas A&M University, TX

Special Characteristics

Adult Students
Agnes Scott College, GA
Allegheny College, PA
American University, DC
Arkansas State University, AR
Arkansas Tech University, AR
Atlantic Union College, MA
Averett University, VA
Barton College, NC
Berry College, GA
Biola University, CA
Bloomfield College, NJ
California Baptist University, CA
California Lutheran University, CA
California State University, Bakersfield, CA
California State University, Chico, CA
Campbellsville University, KY
Carroll College, WI
The Catholic University of America, DC
Cedar Crest College, PA
Central Missouri State University, MO
Central Washington University, WA
Coe College, IA
College of Mount St. Joseph, OH
College of St. Catherine, MN
The College of Saint Rose, NY
The Culinary Institute of America, NY
Dalton State College, GA
Dominican University of California, CA
East Carolina University, NC
East Stroudsburg University of Pennsylvania, PA
Edinboro University of Pennsylvania, PA
The Evergreen State College, WA
Faulkner University, AL
Ferrum College, VA
Fitchburg State College, MA
Florida Gulf Coast University, FL
Fort Hays State University, KS
Francis Marion University, SC
Franklin Pierce College, NH
Freed-Hardeman University, TN
Frostburg State University, MD
Gannon University, PA
Indiana University of Pennsylvania, PA
Juniata College, PA
Kansas State University, KS
Kent State University, OH
Kentucky State University, KY
Lancaster Bible College, PA
La Sierra University, CA
Lipscomb University, TN
Loyola University Chicago, IL
Marian College, IN
Marywood University, PA
Mercer University, GA
Mercyhurst College, PA
Meredith College, NC
Messiah College, PA
Middle Tennessee State University, TN
Millsaps College, MS
Mississippi State University, MS
Missouri State University, MO
Monmouth University, NJ
Montana State University–Billings, MT
Moravian College, PA
Morehead State University, KY
Murray State University, KY
New Mexico State University, NM
Northeastern Illinois University, IL
Northern Illinois University, IL
Northwestern State University of Louisiana, LA
The Ohio State University, OH
Oklahoma State University, OK
Portland State University, OR
Randolph-Macon Woman's College, VA
Regis College, MA
The Richard Stockton College of New Jersey, NJ
St. Edward's University, TX
Saint Francis University, PA
Seton Hill University, PA
Simpson College, IA
Sonoma State University, CA
South Dakota State University, SD
Southeast Missouri State University, MO
Southern Arkansas University–Magnolia, AR
Southern Oregon University, OR
State University of New York College at Geneseo, NY
State University of New York College at Oneonta, NY
State University of New York College at Potsdam, NY
Stephen F. Austin State University, TX
Sweet Briar College, VA
Texas Christian University, TX
Thomas More College, KY
Tusculum College, TN
The University of Akron, OH
The University of Alabama at Birmingham, AL
University of Connecticut, CT
University of Hartford, CT
University of Illinois at Springfield, IL
University of Kansas, KS
University of Kentucky, KY
University of Maryland, College Park, MD
University of Mary Washington, VA
University of Massachusetts Dartmouth, MA
University of Memphis, TN
University of Michigan–Flint, MI
University of Nebraska at Omaha, NE
University of Nevada, Reno, NV
University of New Orleans, LA
The University of North Carolina at Asheville, NC
The University of North Carolina at Greensboro, NC
University of Northern Colorado, CO
University of South Carolina, SC
The University of Tennessee at Martin, TN
The University of Texas at Dallas, TX
The University of Toledo, OH
University of West Georgia, GA
University of Wisconsin–Eau Claire, WI
University of Wisconsin–Green Bay, WI
University of Wisconsin–La Crosse, WI
University of Wisconsin–Parkside, WI
University of Wisconsin–Stevens Point, WI
University of Wisconsin–Stout, WI
University of Wisconsin–Whitewater, WI
University of Wyoming, WY
Wesleyan College, GA
Western Kentucky University, KY
Wichita State University, KS
Widener University, PA
Wilkes University, PA
Wilson College, PA
Winston-Salem State University, NC
Wittenberg University, OH
Youngstown State University, OH

Non-Need Scholarships for Undergraduates
Special Characteristics

Children and Siblings of Alumni

Adelphi University, NY
Adrian College, MI
Alaska Pacific University, AK
Albertson College of Idaho, ID
Albion College, MI
Albright College, PA
Alliant International University, CA
Alma College, MI
Alvernia College, PA
Alverno College, WI
American University, DC
Anna Maria College, MA
Arkansas State University, AR
Asbury College, KY
Ashland University, OH
Athens State University, AL
Auburn University, AL
Augsburg College, MN
Augustana College, SD
Aurora University, IL
Averett University, VA
Avila University, MO
Baldwin-Wallace College, OH
Ball State University, IN
Barton College, NC
Bemidji State University, MN
Benedictine University, IL
Bethel College, KS
Bethel University, MN
Bloomfield College, NJ
Blue Mountain College, MS
Boston University, MA
Bowling Green State University, OH
Bradley University, IL
Brigham Young University–Hawaii, HI
Bryan College, TN
Bryant University, RI
Cabrini College, PA
California Baptist University, CA
California Lutheran University, CA
Calvary Bible College and Theological Seminary, MO
Calvin College, MI
Carroll College, WI
Carson-Newman College, TN
Carthage College, WI
Cascade College, OR
Cedar Crest College, PA
Cedarville University, OH
Centenary College, NJ
Central College, IA
Central Michigan University, MI
Central Missouri State University, MO
Central Washington University, WA
Centre College, KY
Chapman University, CA
Chestnut Hill College, PA
Christian Brothers University, TN
The Citadel, The Military College of South Carolina, SC
Clarke College, IA
Clearwater Christian College, FL
Coe College, IA
College Misericordia, PA
College of Mount St. Joseph, OH
College of Mount Saint Vincent, NY
College of St. Catherine, MN
The College of Saint Rose, NY
The College of St. Scholastica, MN
College of Santa Fe, NM
Colorado School of Mines, CO
Concordia University, MI
Concordia University, NE
Concordia University at Austin, TX
Converse College, SC
Corban College, OR
Cornerstone University, MI
The Culinary Institute of America, NY
Culver-Stockton College, MO
Daemen College, NY
Dakota State University, SD
Dalton State College, GA
DePauw University, IN
Dickinson College, PA
Dominican University, IL
Dominican University of California, CA
Dordt College, IA
Dowling College, NY
Drake University, IA
Drexel University, PA
Duke University, NC
Duquesne University, PA
Eastern Michigan University, MI
Eastern Washington University, WA
East Texas Baptist University, TX
Edinboro University of Pennsylvania, PA
Elmhurst College, IL
Embry-Riddle Aeronautical University, AZ
Embry-Riddle Aeronautical University, FL
Emmanuel College, MA
Emporia State University, KS
Endicott College, MA
Erskine College, SC
Fairfield University, CT
Fairmont State University, WV
Faulkner University, AL
Ferrum College, VA
Fitchburg State College, MA
Florida Christian College, FL
Florida Institute of Technology, FL
Florida Southern College, FL
Fordham University, NY
Francis Marion University, SC
Franklin Pierce College, NH
Friends University, KS
Frostburg State University, MD
Georgia Southern University, GA
Gonzaga University, WA
Gordon College, MA
Graceland University, IA
Grambling State University, LA
Grand View College, IA
Green Mountain College, VT
Greenville College, IL
Gustavus Adolphus College, MN
Gwynedd-Mercy College, PA
Hanover College, IN
Heritage Christian University, AL
Hilbert College, NY
Hollins University, VA
Holy Names University, CA
Houghton College, NY
Huntington University, IN
Idaho State University, ID
Indiana State University, IN
Indiana University–Purdue University Fort Wayne, IN
Iona College, NY
Iowa Wesleyan College, IA
Ithaca College, NY
Jacksonville University, FL
James Madison University, VA
John Brown University, AR
Juniata College, PA
Kansas State University, KS
Kennesaw State University, GA
Kent State University, OH
Kentucky Christian University, KY
Kentucky Wesleyan College, KY
Kettering University, MI
Lake Forest College, IL
Lancaster Bible College, PA
Lasell College, MA
Lawrence University, WI
Lebanon Valley College, PA
Le Moyne College, NY
Limestone College, SC
Lincoln University, PA
Long Island University, Brooklyn Campus, NY
Loras College, IA
Louisiana State University and Agricultural and Mechanical College, LA
Luther College, IA
MacMurray College, IL
Malone College, OH
Manchester College, IN
Maranatha Baptist Bible College, WI
Marian College, IN
Marymount University, VA
Maryville College, TN
Marywood University, PA
Massachusetts Maritime Academy, MA
The Master's College and Seminary, CA
Medcenter One College of Nursing, ND
Mercyhurst College, PA
Merrimack College, MA
Messiah College, PA
Methodist College, NC
Michigan State University, MI
Michigan Technological University, MI
Midland Lutheran College, NE
Midway College, KY
Mississippi State University, MS
Missouri State University, MO
Monmouth University, NJ
Montana State University–Billings, MT
Montreat College, NC
Moravian College, PA
Morehead State University, KY
Mount St. Mary's College, CA
Mount Union College, OH
Murray State University, KY
Nazareth College of Rochester, NY
Newberry College, SC
New England College, NH
Newman University, KS

Non-Need Scholarships for Undergraduates
Special Characteristics

New Mexico State University, NM
New York Institute of Technology, NY
Nichols College, MA
Northern Arizona University, AZ
Northwestern Oklahoma State University, OK
Northwest Nazarene University, ID
Northwood University, MI
Northwood University, Florida Campus, FL
Northwood University, Texas Campus, TX
Nyack College, NY
The Ohio State University, OH
Ohio Wesleyan University, OH
Oklahoma Baptist University, OK
Oklahoma State University, OK
Oral Roberts University, OK
Pacific Lutheran University, WA
Pacific University, OR
Palm Beach Atlantic University, FL
Philadelphia Biblical University, PA
Pittsburg State University, KS
Principia College, IL
Randolph-Macon College, VA
Rensselaer Polytechnic Institute, NY
Rice University, TX
Ripon College, WI
Roberts Wesleyan College, NY
Rockhurst University, MO
Rosemont College, PA
Russell Sage College, NY
St. Andrews Presbyterian College, NC
St. John Fisher College, NY
Saint Joseph's College, IN
St. Joseph's College, New York, NY
St. Lawrence University, NY
Saint Martin's University, WA
Saint Mary's College of California, CA
Saint Mary's University of Minnesota, MN
San Diego State University, CA
Santa Clara University, CA
Seattle Pacific University, WA
Seattle University, WA
Seton Hill University, PA
Shimer College, IL
Simmons College, MA
Simpson College, IA
Slippery Rock University of Pennsylvania, PA
Sonoma State University, CA
Southeastern Oklahoma State University, OK
Southern Adventist University, TN
Southern Arkansas University–Magnolia, AR
Southern Illinois University Carbondale, IL
Southern New Hampshire University, NH
Southwestern Christian University, OK
Southwest Minnesota State University, MN
State University of New York College at Brockport, NY
State University of New York College at Cortland, NY
State University of New York College at Oneonta, NY
State University of New York College at Potsdam, NY

State University of New York, Fredonia, NY
Stetson University, FL
Stevens Institute of Technology, NJ
Suffolk University, MA
Tabor College, KS
Taylor University, IN
Taylor University Fort Wayne, IN
Tennessee Technological University, TN
Texas Lutheran University, TX
Texas State University-San Marcos, TX
Thiel College, PA
Thomas More College, KY
Tiffin University, OH
Trevecca Nazarene University, TN
Trinity International University, IL
Tri-State University, IN
Truman State University, MO
Union College, KY
Union University, TN
The University of Alabama at Birmingham, AL
University of Alaska Fairbanks, AK
University of Arkansas, AR
University of Colorado at Colorado Springs, CO
University of Delaware, DE
University of Evansville, IN
University of Idaho, ID
University of Illinois at Urbana–Champaign, IL
University of Kentucky, KY
University of Maine, ME
University of Mary Hardin-Baylor, TX
University of Mary Washington, VA
University of Massachusetts Amherst, MA
University of Michigan–Dearborn, MI
University of Michigan–Flint, MI
University of Missouri–Columbia, MO
University of Nebraska at Omaha, NE
University of Nebraska-Lincoln, NE
University of Nevada, Las Vegas, NV
University of Nevada, Reno, NV
University of New England, ME
University of New Hampshire, NH
University of New Orleans, LA
The University of North Carolina at Asheville, NC
The University of North Carolina at Pembroke, NC
University of Northern Colorado, CO
University of Oklahoma, OK
University of Rochester, NY
University of St. Francis, IL
University of Saint Francis, IN
University of South Carolina, SC
University of Southern California, CA
University of Southern Mississippi, MS
The University of Tampa, FL
University of the Cumberlands, KY
University of the Ozarks, AR
The University of Toledo, OH
University of Tulsa, OK
University of West Georgia, GA
University of Wisconsin–La Crosse, WI
University of Wyoming, WY

Urbana University, OH
Valparaiso University, IN
Virginia Intermont College, VA
Virginia Military Institute, VA
Warner Pacific College, OR
Wartburg College, IA
Washington & Jefferson College, PA
Washington State University, WA
Wayland Baptist University, TX
Webber International University, FL
Wells College, NY
Wesleyan College, GA
Western State College of Colorado, CO
Westminster College, MO
Westminster College, PA
Wheeling Jesuit University, WV
Whittier College, CA
Whitworth College, WA
Widener University, PA
William Carey College, MS
William Jewell College, MO
William Penn University, IA
William Woods University, MO
Wilson College, PA
Wingate University, NC
Winona State University, MN
Wittenberg University, OH
Worcester State College, MA
York College of Pennsylvania, PA
Youngstown State University, OH

Children of Current Students

Alliant International University, CA
Atlantic Union College, MA
Augustana College, SD
Avila University, MO
Blue Mountain College, MS
Bryan College, TN
Carroll College, WI
Cascade College, OR
Central College, IA
Cincinnati Christian University, OH
College Misericordia, PA
Elmhurst College, IL
Finlandia University, MI
Franklin Pierce College, NH
Green Mountain College, VT
Huntington University, IN
Jacksonville University, FL
Johnson Bible College, TN
Lancaster Bible College, PA
Marymount University, VA
Maryville University of Saint Louis, MO
Marywood University, PA
Mount Aloysius College, PA
Mount Marty College, SD
Northwest University, WA
Olivet Nazarene University, IL
Palm Beach Atlantic University, FL
Saint Martin's University, WA
Trinity International University, IL
The University of Alabama at Birmingham, AL
University of Great Falls, MT
University of Hartford, CT
University of Michigan–Dearborn, MI

Non-Need Scholarships for Undergraduates
Special Characteristics

Valley Forge Christian College, PA
Virginia Intermont College, VA
Wesleyan College, GA
Wilson College, PA

Children of Educators
Agnes Scott College, GA
Alfred University, NY
Allegheny College, PA
Aurora University, IL
Austin Peay State University, TN
Bard College, NY
Benedictine College, KS
Bennington College, VT
Brigham Young University–Hawaii, HI
Bryan College, TN
Calvary Bible College and Theological Seminary, MO
Campbellsville University, KY
Carthage College, WI
Centenary College of Louisiana, LA
College of St. Catherine, MN
Columbus College of Art & Design, OH
Concordia University, NE
Cornell College, IA
Dowling College, NY
East Texas Baptist University, TX
Emmanuel College, MA
Emory & Henry College, VA
Endicott College, MA
Ferrum College, VA
Florida College, FL
Franklin Pierce College, NH
Gallaudet University, DC
Grand View College, IA
Hampden-Sydney College, VA
Heritage Christian University, AL
John Brown University, AR
Johnson Bible College, TN
Judson College, AL
King's College, PA
Lipscomb University, TN
Lycoming College, PA
Maranatha Baptist Bible College, WI
Mary Baldwin College, VA
Mississippi State University, MS
Moravian College, PA
Mount St. Mary's University, MD
New England College, NH
New York Institute of Technology, NY
Northern Arizona University, AZ
Northwest Nazarene University, ID
Occidental College, CA
Olivet Nazarene University, IL
Pacific Lutheran University, WA
Palm Beach Atlantic University, FL
Rosemont College, PA
Saint Mary's College of California, CA
Seattle University, WA
Simpson College, IA
Sonoma State University, CA
Southern Illinois University Carbondale, IL
Stevens Institute of Technology, NJ
Tennessee Technological University, TN
Unity College, ME

The University of Alabama at Birmingham, AL
University of Illinois at Springfield, IL
University of Kentucky, KY
University of Memphis, TN
University of St. Francis, IL
University of St. Thomas, TX
The University of Tennessee at Martin, TN
Villanova University, PA
William Carey College, MS

Children of Faculty/Staff
Abilene Christian University, TX
Adelphi University, NY
Adrian College, MI
Agnes Scott College, GA
Alabama Agricultural and Mechanical University, AL
Alaska Bible College, AK
Alaska Pacific University, AK
Albertson College of Idaho, ID
Alderson-Broaddus College, WV
Alfred University, NY
Allegheny College, PA
Alliant International University, CA
Alma College, MI
Alvernia College, PA
American University, DC
Andrews University, MI
Anna Maria College, MA
Arkansas State University, AR
Arkansas Tech University, AR
Arlington Baptist College, TX
Asbury College, KY
Ashford University, IA
Ashland University, OH
Athens State University, AL
Atlantic Union College, MA
Auburn University, AL
Augustana College, SD
Aurora University, IL
Austin College, TX
Austin Peay State University, TN
Avila University, MO
Azusa Pacific University, CA
Ball State University, IN
Bard College, NY
Barton College, NC
Baylor University, TX
Becker College, MA
Belhaven College, MS
Belmont Abbey College, NC
Belmont University, TN
Bemidji State University, MN
Bennett College For Women, NC
Bennington College, VT
Berry College, GA
Bethany Lutheran College, MN
Bethel College, KS
Bethel University, MN
Beulah Heights Bible College, GA
Biola University, CA
Bloomsburg University of Pennsylvania, PA
Blue Mountain College, MS
Bluffton University, OH
Bowdoin College, ME

Bowling Green State University, OH
Bradley University, IL
Brenau University, GA
Brevard College, NC
Brewton-Parker College, GA
Brigham Young University–Hawaii, HI
Bryan College, TN
Buena Vista University, IA
Cabrini College, PA
California Baptist University, CA
California Lutheran University, CA
California State University, Bakersfield, CA
California State University, Chico, CA
California State University, Stanislaus, CA
Calvary Bible College and Theological Seminary, MO
Calvin College, MI
Campbell University, NC
Carroll College, MT
Carroll College, WI
Carthage College, WI
Cascade College, OR
Case Western Reserve University, OH
Catawba College, NC
The Catholic University of America, DC
Cedarville University, OH
Centenary College, NJ
Centenary College of Louisiana, LA
Central College, IA
Central Michigan University, MI
Central Missouri State University, MO
Centre College, KY
Chowan University, NC
Christian Brothers University, TN
Cincinnati Christian University, OH
Clarke College, IA
Clarkson University, NY
Clemson University, SC
Coe College, IA
College Misericordia, PA
College of Mount St. Joseph, OH
College of Mount Saint Vincent, NY
College of St. Catherine, MN
The College of St. Scholastica, MN
College of the Holy Cross, MA
College of the Southwest, NM
College of Visual Arts, MN
The College of Wooster, OH
Colorado State University, CO
Columbia College, SC
Columbus College of Art & Design, OH
Concordia University, CA
Concordia University, MI
Concordia University, NE
Concordia University, St. Paul, MN
Concordia University Wisconsin, WI
Converse College, SC
Corban College, OR
Cornell College, IA
Cornerstone University, MI
Creighton University, NE
Crown College, MN
The Culinary Institute of America, NY
Culver-Stockton College, MO
Daemen College, NY
Dallas Baptist University, TX

Non-Need Scholarships for Undergraduates
Special Characteristics

Dallas Christian College, TX
Dalton State College, GA
Davenport University, MI
Davidson College, NC
Davis & Elkins College, WV
Defiance College, OH
DePaul University, IL
DePauw University, IN
Dickinson College, PA
Dickinson State University, ND
Dominican University, IL
Dominican University of California, CA
Dordt College, IA
Dowling College, NY
Duquesne University, PA
East Carolina University, NC
East Central University, OK
East Texas Baptist University, TX
Eckerd College, FL
Edinboro University of Pennsylvania, PA
Elizabethtown College, PA
Elmira College, NY
Elms College, MA
Elon University, NC
Embry-Riddle Aeronautical University, AZ
Embry-Riddle Aeronautical University, FL
Embry-Riddle Aeronautical University, Extended Campus, FL
Emmanuel College, MA
Emmaus Bible College, IA
Emory & Henry College, VA
Emory University, GA
Emporia State University, KS
Erskine College, SC
Eureka College, IL
Evangel University, MO
Faith Baptist Bible College and Theological Seminary, IA
Faulkner University, AL
Ferris State University, MI
Ferrum College, VA
Finlandia University, MI
Flagler College, FL
Florida Christian College, FL
Florida College, FL
Florida Institute of Technology, FL
Florida Southern College, FL
Fordham University, NY
Fort Lewis College, CO
Francis Marion University, SC
Franklin and Marshall College, PA
Franklin Pierce College, NH
Freed-Hardeman University, TN
Free Will Baptist Bible College, TN
Fresno Pacific University, CA
Furman University, SC
Gallaudet University, DC
Geneva College, PA
Georgetown College, KY
Georgetown University, DC
Georgia College & State University, GA
Georgia Institute of Technology, GA
Gonzaga University, WA
Grace Bible College, MI
Grace College, IN
Graceland University, IA

Grambling State University, LA
Grand Valley State University, MI
Grand View College, IA
Greenville College, IL
Guilford College, NC
Hampden-Sydney College, VA
Hampshire College, MA
Hannibal-LaGrange College, MO
Hanover College, IN
Hardin-Simmons University, TX
Heidelberg College, OH
Hendrix College, AR
Heritage Christian University, AL
Hillsdale College, MI
Houston Baptist University, TX
Huntington University, IN
Idaho State University, ID
Illinois College, IL
Illinois State University, IL
Illinois Wesleyan University, IL
Indiana State University, IN
Indiana University of Pennsylvania, PA
Indiana University–Purdue University Fort Wayne, IN
Iona College, NY
Iowa Wesleyan College, IA
Jacksonville University, FL
James Madison University, VA
Jamestown College, ND
John Brown University, AR
The Johns Hopkins University, MD
Johnson & Wales University, CO
Johnson & Wales University, FL
Johnson & Wales University, NC
Johnson & Wales University, RI
Johnson Bible College, TN
Judson College, AL
Juniata College, PA
Kent State University, OH
Kentucky Christian University, KY
Kentucky Wesleyan College, KY
Kettering University, MI
King College, TN
King's College, PA
Kuyper College, MI
LaGrange College, GA
Lakeland College, WI
Lancaster Bible College, PA
Lasell College, MA
La Sierra University, CA
Lawrence Technological University, MI
Lebanon Valley College, PA
Lee University, TN
LeMoyne-Owen College, TN
LeTourneau University, TX
Limestone College, SC
Lincoln Christian College, IL
Lincoln University, PA
Lindsey Wilson College, KY
Linfield College, OR
Lipscomb University, TN
Long Island University, Brooklyn Campus, NY
Louisiana Tech University, LA
Loyola University New Orleans, LA
Lubbock Christian University, TX

Lycoming College, PA
Lynchburg College, VA
Lynn University, FL
Lyon College, AR
MacMurray College, IL
Maharishi University of Management, IA
Maine Maritime Academy, ME
Malone College, OH
Manhattan Christian College, KS
Manhattan College, NY
Maranatha Baptist Bible College, WI
Marian College, IN
Marian College of Fond du Lac, WI
Marquette University, WI
Marshall University, WV
Mary Baldwin College, VA
Marymount University, VA
Maryville College, TN
Marywood University, PA
Massachusetts College of Art, MA
Massachusetts College of Pharmacy and Health Sciences, MA
Massachusetts Maritime Academy, MA
The Master's College and Seminary, CA
Mayville State University, ND
McKendree College, IL
Mercer University, GA
Mercyhurst College, PA
Meredith College, NC
Merrimack College, MA
Messiah College, PA
Methodist College, NC
Miami University, OH
Michigan State University, MI
Michigan Technological University, MI
MidAmerica Nazarene University, KS
Midway College, KY
Midwestern State University, TX
Milligan College, TN
Millsaps College, MS
Milwaukee School of Engineering, WI
Mississippi State University, MS
Missouri State University, MO
Monmouth University, NJ
Montana State University–Billings, MT
Montreat College, NC
Moravian College, PA
Morningside College, IA
Mount Marty College, SD
Mount Mary College, WI
Mount Olive College, NC
Mount St. Mary's University, MD
Mount Union College, OH
Mount Vernon Nazarene University, OH
Murray State University, KY
Nazareth College of Rochester, NY
Nebraska Wesleyan University, NE
Neumann College, PA
Newberry College, SC
New England College, NH
Newman University, KS
New Mexico State University, NM
New York Institute of Technology, NY
Niagara University, NY
Nicholls State University, LA
Nichols College, MA

Non-Need Scholarships for Undergraduates
Special Characteristics

Northeastern Illinois University, IL
Northern Arizona University, AZ
Northern Illinois University, IL
Northern Michigan University, MI
North Greenville College, SC
Northwest Christian College, OR
Northwestern College, MN
Northwestern Oklahoma State University, OK
Northwestern State University of Louisiana, LA
Northwest Nazarene University, ID
Northwest University, WA
Northwood University, MI
Northwood University, Florida Campus, FL
Northwood University, Texas Campus, TX
Nova Southeastern University, FL
Nyack College, NY
Occidental College, CA
Ohio Northern University, OH
The Ohio State University, OH
Ohio University, OH
Ohio University–Chillicothe, OH
Ohio University–Eastern, OH
Ohio University–Lancaster, OH
Ohio University–Southern Campus, OH
Ohio University–Zanesville, OH
Ohio Wesleyan University, OH
Oklahoma Baptist University, OK
Oklahoma Panhandle State University, OK
Olivet Nazarene University, IL
Oral Roberts University, OK
Ouachita Baptist University, AR
Our Lady of Holy Cross College, LA
Pacific Lutheran University, WA
Pacific University, OR
Palm Beach Atlantic University, FL
Peace College, NC
Philadelphia Biblical University, PA
Pikeville College, KY
Plymouth State University, NH
Pontifical Catholic University of Puerto Rico, PR
Presentation College, SD
Principia College, IL
Purdue University, IN
Quincy University, IL
Quinnipiac University, CT
Radford University, VA
Randolph-Macon College, VA
Randolph-Macon Woman's College, VA
Regis College, MA
Rensselaer Polytechnic Institute, NY
Rice University, TX
The Richard Stockton College of New Jersey, NJ
Ripon College, WI
Robert Morris College, IL
Robert Morris University, PA
Roberts Wesleyan College, NY
Rochester Institute of Technology, NY
Rockhurst University, MO
Rocky Mountain College of Art & Design, CO
Rosemont College, PA
Russell Sage College, NY

Rutgers, The State University of New Jersey, Camden, NJ
Rutgers, The State University of New Jersey, Newark, NJ
Rutgers, The State University of New Jersey, New Brunswick/Piscataway, NJ
Sacred Heart University, CT
Sage College of Albany, NY
St. Bonaventure University, NY
St. Cloud State University, MN
St. Edward's University, TX
Saint Francis University, PA
St. John's University, NY
Saint Joseph's College, IN
St. Joseph's College, New York, NY
Saint Joseph's College of Maine, ME
St. Louis Christian College, MO
St. Louis College of Pharmacy, MO
Saint Louis University, MO
Saint Martin's University, WA
Saint Mary's College, IN
Saint Mary's College of California, CA
Saint Mary's University of Minnesota, MN
St. Norbert College, WI
Saint Xavier University, IL
Samford University, AL
San Diego Christian College, CA
San Diego State University, CA
Santa Clara University, CA
Schreiner University, TX
Seattle Pacific University, WA
Seattle University, WA
Seton Hill University, PA
Sewanee: The University of the South, TN
Shenandoah University, VA
Shorter College, GA
Simpson College, IA
Simpson University, CA
Skidmore College, NY
Slippery Rock University of Pennsylvania, PA
Sonoma State University, CA
South Dakota State University, SD
Southeastern Bible College, AL
Southeastern Louisiana University, LA
Southeastern University, FL
Southeast Missouri State University, MO
Southern Arkansas University–Magnolia, AR
Southern Connecticut State University, CT
Southern Illinois University Carbondale, IL
Southern Illinois University Edwardsville, IL
Southern New Hampshire University, NH
Southern Vermont College, VT
Southern Virginia University, VA
Southwestern Christian University, OK
Southwestern University, TX
Spring Arbor University, MI
Spring Hill College, AL
State University of New York College at Potsdam, NY
Stephens College, MO
Stetson University, FL
Stevens Institute of Technology, NJ
Stonehill College, MA

Suffolk University, MA
Tabor College, KS
Taylor University, IN
Taylor University Fort Wayne, IN
Tennessee Technological University, TN
Texas A&M University, TX
Texas Christian University, TX
Texas Lutheran University, TX
Texas Tech University, TX
Thiel College, PA
Thomas More College, KY
Tiffin University, OH
Toccoa Falls College, GA
Transylvania University, KY
Trinity Lutheran College, WA
Tri-State University, IN
Truman State University, MO
Tufts University, MA
Tusculum College, TN
Tuskegee University, AL
Union University, TN
The University of Alabama at Birmingham, AL
University of Alaska Fairbanks, AK
University of Arkansas, AR
University of Arkansas at Monticello, AR
University of Cincinnati, OH
University of Colorado at Denver and Health Sciences Center—Downtown Denver Campus, CO
University of Connecticut, CT
University of Dallas, TX
University of Delaware, DE
University of Denver, CO
University of Evansville, IN
The University of Findlay, OH
University of Florida, FL
University of Great Falls, MT
University of Hartford, CT
University of Idaho, ID
University of Illinois at Springfield, IL
University of Illinois at Urbana–Champaign, IL
University of Kansas, KS
University of Kentucky, KY
University of Maine, ME
University of Maine at Farmington, ME
University of Maine at Presque Isle, ME
University of Mary, ND
University of Mary Hardin-Baylor, TX
University of Mary Washington, VA
University of Massachusetts Amherst, MA
University of Massachusetts Dartmouth, MA
University of Memphis, TN
University of Miami, FL
University of Michigan, MI
University of Nebraska at Kearney, NE
University of Nebraska at Omaha, NE
University of Nevada, Las Vegas, NV
University of New Hampshire, NH
University of New Hampshire at Manchester, NH
University of North Alabama, AL
The University of North Carolina at Asheville, NC

Non-Need Scholarships for Undergraduates
Special Characteristics

The University of North Carolina at Chapel Hill, NC
University of North Dakota, ND
University of Northern Colorado, CO
University of Pittsburgh, PA
University of Pittsburgh at Johnstown, PA
University of Portland, OR
University of Puget Sound, WA
University of Rochester, NY
University of Saint Francis, IN
University of St. Thomas, TX
University of San Diego, CA
University of South Carolina, SC
University of Southern California, CA
University of Southern Indiana, IN
University of Southern Maine, ME
University of Southern Mississippi, MS
The University of Tampa, FL
The University of Tennessee at Martin, TN
University of the Cumberlands, KY
University of the District of Columbia, DC
University of the Ozarks, AR
University of the Virgin Islands, VI
The University of Toledo, OH
University of Tulsa, OK
University of Utah, UT
The University of West Alabama, AL
Urbana University, OH
Ursinus College, PA
Valley City State University, ND
Valley Forge Christian College, PA
Valparaiso University, IN
Vanguard University of Southern California, CA
Villanova University, PA
Virginia Intermont College, VA
Virginia Military Institute, VA
Virginia Polytechnic Institute and State University, VA
Virginia Wesleyan College, VA
Wabash College, IN
Wake Forest University, NC
Waldorf College, IA
Walla Walla College, WA
Warren Wilson College, NC
Wartburg College, IA
Washington & Jefferson College, PA
Washington College, MD
Washington State University, WA
Wayland Baptist University, TX
Waynesburg College, PA
Wayne State College, NE
Webber International University, FL
Wesleyan College, GA
Western Illinois University, IL
Western New England College, MA
Westminster College, MO
Westmont College, CA
West Texas A&M University, TX
West Virginia University, WV
West Virginia Wesleyan College, WV
Wheeling Jesuit University, WV
Whittier College, CA
Widener University, PA
Wilkes University, PA
William Carey College, MS
William Jewell College, MO
William Penn University, IA
Williams Baptist College, AR
William Woods University, MO
Wilson College, PA
Winona State University, MN
Winthrop University, SC
Wittenberg University, OH
Wofford College, SC
Worcester State College, MA
Xavier University of Louisiana, LA
Youngstown State University, OH

Children of Public Servants
Carthage College, WI
College of Staten Island of the City University of New York, NY
Dowling College, NY
Georgia Southern University, GA
Graceland University, IA
Grambling State University, LA
Mercer University, GA
Mississippi State University, MS
Monmouth University, NJ
New Mexico State University, NM
New York Institute of Technology, NY
Northern Arizona University, AZ
Northwestern State University of Louisiana, LA
The Ohio State University, OH
St. Francis College, NY
San Diego State University, CA
Sonoma State University, CA
Southern Illinois University Carbondale, IL
Tennessee Technological University, TN
The University of Alabama at Birmingham, AL
University of Delaware, DE
University of Kentucky, KY
University of Memphis, TN
University of Nevada, Las Vegas, NV
University of New Orleans, LA
The University of Texas at Dallas, TX
The University of Toledo, OH
University of Utah, UT
University of Wisconsin–Green Bay, WI
Valdosta State University, GA
Washington State University, WA
Western Washington University, WA

Children of Union Members/Company Employees
Adrian College, MI
Auburn University, AL
Averett University, VA
California State University, Bakersfield, CA
Calvin College, MI
Carroll College, MT
Central Michigan University, MI
The College of Saint Rose, NY
Cornerstone University, MI
Dowling College, NY
Eastern Washington University, WA
East Tennessee State University, TN
Edinboro University of Pennsylvania, PA
Emmanuel College, MA
Emporia State University, KS
Fordham University, NY
Frostburg State University, MD
Georgia Institute of Technology, GA
Grand Valley State University, MI
Husson College, ME
Illinois State University, IL
Kennesaw State University, GA
Kent State University, OH
Kentucky Wesleyan College, KY
Massachusetts College of Art, MA
Mercer University, GA
Michigan State University, MI
Millersville University of Pennsylvania, PA
Minnesota State University Mankato, MN
Montana State University–Billings, MT
New Mexico State University, NM
Northern Michigan University, MI
The Ohio State University, OH
The Richard Stockton College of New Jersey, NJ
St. Cloud State University, MN
Shorter College, GA
Slippery Rock University of Pennsylvania, PA
Sonoma State University, CA
Southwest Minnesota State University, MN
Stephen F. Austin State University, TX
Texas Christian University, TX
The University of Alabama, AL
The University of Alabama at Birmingham, AL
University of Hartford, CT
University of Illinois at Springfield, IL
University of Kentucky, KY
University of Maine, ME
University of Michigan–Flint, MI
University of Northern Colorado, CO
University of South Carolina, SC
The University of Toledo, OH
University of West Georgia, GA
University of Wisconsin–Parkside, WI
Virginia Commonwealth University, VA
Washington College, MD
Western Kentucky University, KY
Western New England College, MA
Western Washington University, WA
West Virginia University, WV
Wheeling Jesuit University, WV
York College of Pennsylvania, PA
Youngstown State University, OH

Children of Workers in Trades
Blue Mountain College, MS
Dowling College, NY
Kennesaw State University, GA
Marywood University, PA
New Mexico State University, NM
The Ohio State University, OH
Sonoma State University, CA
South Dakota State University, SD
The University of Alabama at Birmingham, AL
University of Illinois at Springfield, IL
University of Kentucky, KY
University of Michigan, MI

Non-Need Scholarships for Undergraduates
Special Characteristics

University of Michigan–Dearborn, MI
University of Nevada, Las Vegas, NV
University of South Carolina, SC
University of Wisconsin–Parkside, WI
West Virginia University, WV
Worcester Polytechnic Institute, MA
Youngstown State University, OH

Children with a Deceased or Disabled Parent
Anna Maria College, MA
The Baptist College of Florida, FL
The Citadel, The Military College of South Carolina, SC
Clarke College, IA
The College of New Jersey, NJ
College of Staten Island of the City University of New York, NY
Defiance College, OH
Dickinson State University, ND
Edinboro University of Pennsylvania, PA
Erskine College, SC
Fordham University, NY
Georgia College & State University, GA
Hamline University, MN
Harding University, AR
Illinois State University, IL
Indiana State University, IN
Indiana University–Purdue University Fort Wayne, IN
Kent State University, OH
Kentucky State University, KY
Lipscomb University, TN
Louisiana State University and Agricultural and Mechanical College, LA
Louisiana Tech University, LA
Marian College of Fond du Lac, WI
New Mexico State University, NM
The Ohio State University, OH
St. Norbert College, WI
Santa Clara University, CA
Seton Hill University, PA
Southern Illinois University Carbondale, IL
State University of New York at Binghamton, NY
The University of Alabama at Birmingham, AL
University of Hartford, CT
University of Illinois at Springfield, IL
University of Illinois at Urbana–Champaign, IL
University of Kentucky, KY
University of Maine, ME
University of Massachusetts Dartmouth, MA
University of New Orleans, LA
University of South Carolina, SC
The University of Texas at Arlington, TX
University of Utah, UT
Washington State University, WA
Wayne State College, NE
Worcester State College, MA
Youngstown State University, OH

Ethnic Background
Abilene Christian University, TX
Alaska Pacific University, AK
Albertson College of Idaho, ID
Alderson-Broaddus College, WV
Alliant International University, CA
American University, DC
Arkansas State University, AR
Arkansas Tech University, AR
Asbury College, KY
Auburn University, AL
Augustana College, SD
Austin College, TX
Azusa Pacific University, CA
Benedictine College, KS
Berry College, GA
Bethel University, MN
Biola University, CA
Bridgewater College, VA
Brigham Young University–Hawaii, HI
Buena Vista University, IA
Cabarrus College of Health Sciences, NC
Cabrini College, PA
California Lutheran University, CA
California State University, Chico, CA
California State University, Dominguez Hills, CA
California State University, Stanislaus, CA
Calvin College, MI
The Catholic University of America, DC
Cedarville University, OH
Centenary College, NJ
Centenary College of Louisiana, LA
Central Missouri State University, MO
Centre College, KY
Claremont McKenna College, CA
Clearwater Christian College, FL
Clemson University, SC
College of Saint Benedict, MN
College of St. Catherine, MN
The College of Saint Rose, NY
Concordia University, CA
Concordia University, MI
Cornell College, IA
Cornerstone University, MI
Dakota State University, SD
DePauw University, IN
Dickinson State University, ND
Dominican University of California, CA
Drake University, IA
Duke University, NC
East Carolina University, NC
Eastern Michigan University, MI
Eastern Washington University, WA
Elmhurst College, IL
Emmanuel College, MA
Emory & Henry College, VA
Erskine College, SC
Fairfield University, CT
Flagler College, FL
Florida Gulf Coast University, FL
Fort Lewis College, CO
Fresno Pacific University, CA
Furman University, SC
Gannon University, PA
Georgia Institute of Technology, GA
Grambling State University, LA
Grove City College, PA
Hamline University, MN
Hardin-Simmons University, TX
Hawai'i Pacific University, HI
Holy Names University, CA
Illinois College, IL
Indiana University of Pennsylvania, PA
John Brown University, AR
Johnson Bible College, TN
Juniata College, PA
Kennesaw State University, GA
Kent State University, OH
Kenyon College, OH
LaGrange College, GA
Lebanon Valley College, PA
Lesley University, MA
Lewis-Clark State College, ID
Long Island University, Brooklyn Campus, NY
Lyon College, AR
Macalester College, MN
Maharishi University of Management, IA
Manchester College, IN
Marywood University, PA
Meredith College, NC
Michigan State University, MI
Michigan Technological University, MI
Millsaps College, MS
Missouri State University, MO
Montana State University–Billings, MT
Moravian College, PA
Mount Union College, OH
New England College, NH
New Mexico State University, NM
North Carolina Agricultural and Technical State University, NC
Northern Illinois University, IL
Northland College, WI
Northwestern College, MN
Northwest Nazarene University, ID
The Ohio State University, OH
Ohio Wesleyan University, OH
Ouachita Baptist University, AR
Portland State University, OR
Rensselaer Polytechnic Institute, NY
Rice University, TX
The Richard Stockton College of New Jersey, NJ
Robert Morris University, PA
Sacred Heart University, CT
St. John Fisher College, NY
Saint Martin's University, WA
St. Norbert College, WI
Schreiner University, TX
Sewanee: The University of the South, TN
Shepherd University, WV
Slippery Rock University of Pennsylvania, PA
Sonoma State University, CA
South Dakota State University, SD
Southwest Minnesota State University, MN
State University of New York at Binghamton, NY
State University of New York College at Brockport, NY
State University of New York College at Oneonta, NY

Non-Need Scholarships for Undergraduates
Special Characteristics

State University of New York College at Potsdam, NY
State University of New York, Fredonia, NY
Stetson University, FL
Taylor University, IN
Tennessee Technological University, TN
Toccoa Falls College, GA
Truman State University, MO
Union University, TN
The University of Alabama at Birmingham, AL
University of Alaska Southeast, AK
University of Arkansas, AR
University of California, San Diego, CA
University of Central Oklahoma, OK
University of Colorado at Colorado Springs, CO
University of Delaware, DE
University of Great Falls, MT
University of Hartford, CT
University of Idaho, ID
University of Illinois at Springfield, IL
University of Illinois at Urbana–Champaign, IL
University of Kansas, KS
University of Kentucky, KY
University of Maine, ME
University of Maine at Presque Isle, ME
University of Mary Hardin-Baylor, TX
University of Michigan–Dearborn, MI
University of Michigan–Flint, MI
University of Minnesota, Morris, MN
University of Missouri–Kansas City, MO
University of Missouri–St. Louis, MO
University of Nebraska at Kearney, NE
University of Nebraska at Omaha, NE
University of Nebraska–Lincoln, NE
University of Nevada, Las Vegas, NV
University of Nevada, Reno, NV
The University of North Carolina at Asheville, NC
The University of North Carolina at Greensboro, NC
University of North Dakota, ND
University of Northern Colorado, CO
University of St. Francis, IL
University of South Carolina, SC
University of Southern Mississippi, MS
The University of Tennessee at Martin, TN
The University of Texas at El Paso, TX
The University of Texas at San Antonio, TX
The University of Texas–Pan American, TX
The University of Toledo, OH
University of Utah, UT
University of Vermont, VT
University of West Georgia, GA
University of Wisconsin–Eau Claire, WI
University of Wisconsin–Green Bay, WI
University of Wisconsin–La Crosse, WI
University of Wisconsin–Parkside, WI
University of Wisconsin–Stevens Point, WI
University of Wisconsin–Whitewater, WI
University of Wyoming, WY
VanderCook College of Music, IL

Walla Walla College, WA
Wartburg College, IA
Wayland Baptist University, TX
Wayne State College, NE
Wesleyan College, GA
Western Carolina University, NC
Western Kentucky University, KY
Western Washington University, WA
Westminster College, MO
Westmont College, CA
West Virginia University, WV
Whitman College, WA
Whitworth College, WA
Widener University, PA
Wittenberg University, OH

First-Generation College Students

Abilene Christian University, TX
American University, DC
Appalachian State University, NC
Arkansas State University, AR
Austin College, TX
Averett University, VA
Brenau University, GA
Brewton-Parker College, GA
Cabarrus College of Health Sciences, NC
California Lutheran University, CA
California State University, Bakersfield, CA
California State University, Chico, CA
California State University, Stanislaus, CA
The Catholic University of America, DC
Central Michigan University, MI
Centre College, KY
Chowan University, NC
College of the Southwest, NM
Colorado State University, CO
Creighton University, NE
Davis & Elkins College, WV
Defiance College, OH
Dominican University of California, CA
Dowling College, NY
Edinboro University of Pennsylvania, PA
Elon University, NC
Erskine College, SC
The Evergreen State College, WA
Fairfield University, CT
Finlandia University, MI
Flagler College, FL
Fort Lewis College, CO
Georgia Southern University, GA
Glenville State College, WV
Graceland University, IA
Guilford College, NC
Idaho State University, ID
Illinois State University, IL
LaGrange College, GA
Lewis-Clark State College, ID
Limestone College, SC
Long Island University, Brooklyn Campus, NY
Meredith College, NC
Mesa State College, CO
Michigan State University, MI
Millsaps College, MS
Mississippi State University, MS
Missouri State University, MO

Monmouth University, NJ
Montana State University–Billings, MT
Newman University, KS
Northern Arizona University, AZ
Oklahoma State University, OK
Ouachita Baptist University, AR
Pontifical Catholic University of Puerto Rico, PR
St. John Fisher College, NY
Saint Louis University, MO
Sonoma State University, CA
South Dakota State University, SD
Southeast Missouri State University, MO
Southern Vermont College, VT
Southwest Minnesota State University, MN
State University of New York College at Brockport, NY
Stephen F. Austin State University, TX
Tennessee Technological University, TN
Texas Lutheran University, TX
Texas State University-San Marcos, TX
Texas Tech University, TX
The University of Alabama at Birmingham, AL
University of Alaska Southeast, AK
University of California, San Diego, CA
University of Colorado at Boulder, CO
University of Colorado at Colorado Springs, CO
University of Colorado at Denver and Health Sciences Center—Downtown Denver Campus, CO
University of Delaware, DE
University of Great Falls, MT
University of Hartford, CT
University of Houston–Victoria, TX
University of Idaho, ID
University of Illinois at Springfield, IL
University of Illinois at Urbana–Champaign, IL
University of Kansas, KS
University of Kentucky, KY
University of Massachusetts Dartmouth, MA
University of Michigan–Flint, MI
University of Nebraska at Kearney, NE
University of Nebraska at Omaha, NE
University of Nevada, Las Vegas, NV
University of Nevada, Reno, NV
University of North Alabama, AL
The University of North Carolina at Asheville, NC
University of North Florida, FL
University of South Carolina, SC
University of South Carolina Upstate, SC
The University of Texas at Arlington, TX
University of Utah, UT
University of Vermont, VT
The University of West Alabama, AL
University of Wisconsin–Eau Claire, WI
University of Wisconsin–Stout, WI
University of Wyoming, WY
Virginia Intermont College, VA
Virginia Polytechnic Institute and State University, VA
Washington State University, WA

Non-Need Scholarships for Undergraduates
Special Characteristics

Webber International University, FL
Wesleyan College, GA
West Texas A&M University, TX
Wichita State University, KS
William Carey College, MS
Winston-Salem State University, NC

Handicapped Students

Albertson College of Idaho, ID
Appalachian State University, NC
Arkansas State University, AR
Augusta State University, GA
Austin College, TX
Bryan College, TN
California State University, Bakersfield, CA
California State University, Chico, CA
California State University, Fresno, CA
Calvin College, MI
The Catholic University of America, DC
Central College, IA
Central Washington University, WA
Clear Creek Baptist Bible College, KY
College of Staten Island of the City University of New York, NY
Creighton University, NE
The Culinary Institute of America, NY
Delaware Valley College, PA
Dordt College, IA
East Carolina University, NC
Eastern Washington University, WA
East Stroudsburg University of Pennsylvania, PA
Edinboro University of Pennsylvania, PA
Emmanuel College, MA
Emporia State University, KS
Florida Gulf Coast University, FL
Fordham University, NY
Fort Lewis College, CO
Francis Marion University, SC
Gallaudet University, DC
Georgia College & State University, GA
Georgia Institute of Technology, GA
Georgia Southern University, GA
Grand Valley State University, MI
Idaho State University, ID
Indiana University–Purdue University Fort Wayne, IN
James Madison University, VA
Kennesaw State University, GA
Kent State University, OH
Kentucky State University, KY
Lock Haven University of Pennsylvania, PA
Michigan State University, MI
Midland Lutheran College, NE
Midwestern State University, TX
Mississippi State University, MS
Missouri State University, MO
Murray State University, KY
New Mexico State University, NM
North Carolina Agricultural and Technical State University, NC
Northern Arizona University, AZ
The Ohio State University, OH
Oklahoma State University, OK
Portland State University, OR
Rowan University, NJ

Sacred Heart University, CT
St. Francis College, NY
San Diego State University, CA
Santa Clara University, CA
Sonoma State University, CA
South Dakota State University, SD
Southeastern Louisiana University, LA
Southern Illinois University Carbondale, IL
Southwest Minnesota State University, MN
State University of New York College at Oneonta, NY
State University of New York College at Potsdam, NY
Texas State University–San Marcos, TX
Texas Tech University, TX
Trevecca Nazarene University, TN
The University of Akron, OH
The University of Alabama at Birmingham, AL
University of Baltimore, MD
University of California, San Diego, CA
University of Colorado at Colorado Springs, CO
University of Colorado at Denver and Health Sciences Center—Downtown Denver Campus, CO
University of Hartford, CT
University of Idaho, ID
University of Illinois at Urbana–Champaign, IL
University of Kentucky, KY
University of Mary Hardin-Baylor, TX
University of Massachusetts Amherst, MA
University of Memphis, TN
University of Michigan, MI
University of Michigan–Dearborn, MI
University of Michigan–Flint, MI
University of Nebraska at Omaha, NE
University of Nebraska–Lincoln, NE
University of Nevada, Las Vegas, NV
University of New Hampshire, NH
The University of North Carolina at Asheville, NC
The University of North Carolina at Greensboro, NC
University of North Dakota, ND
University of Northern Colorado, CO
University of South Carolina, SC
The University of Tennessee at Martin, TN
The University of Texas at Arlington, TX
The University of Texas at Dallas, TX
The University of Texas at San Antonio, TX
The University of Toledo, OH
University of Utah, UT
University of West Georgia, GA
University of Wisconsin–Stout, WI
University of Wisconsin–Whitewater, WI
University of Wyoming, WY
Washington State University, WA
Wesleyan College, GA
Western Carolina University, NC
Western Kentucky University, KY
West Texas A&M University, TX
Wheaton College, IL
Worcester State College, MA
Youngstown State University, OH

International Students

Adrian College, MI
Agnes Scott College, GA
Alaska Pacific University, AK
Albertson College of Idaho, ID
Albright College, PA
Alderson-Broaddus College, WV
Alfred University, NY
Allegheny College, PA
Alliant International University, CA
Alvernia College, PA
Andrews University, MI
Arkansas Tech University, AR
Armstrong Atlantic State University, GA
Asbury College, KY
Ashford University, IA
Ashland University, OH
Atlantic Union College, MA
Augsburg College, MN
Augustana College, SD
Austin College, TX
Averett University, VA
Azusa Pacific University, CA
Barton College, NC
Belhaven College, MS
Bemidji State University, MN
Benedictine College, KS
Bethany College, KS
Bethel College, KS
Bethel University, MN
Beulah Heights Bible College, GA
Biola University, CA
Bloomsburg University of Pennsylvania, PA
Bluffton University, OH
Bowling Green State University, OH
Brenau University, GA
Brewton-Parker College, GA
Bridgewater College, VA
Brigham Young University–Hawaii, HI
Bryan College, TN
Buena Vista University, IA
California Lutheran University, CA
California State University, Chico, CA
Calvin College, MI
Campbellsville University, KY
Carroll College, MT
Carroll College, WI
Cascade College, OR
Centenary College of Louisiana, LA
Central College, IA
Central Michigan University, MI
Chestnut Hill College, PA
Chowan University, NC
Cincinnati Christian University, OH
Clarke College, IA
Clarkson University, NY
Clear Creek Baptist Bible College, KY
Coastal Carolina University, SC
Coe College, IA
College of Notre Dame of Maryland, MD
College of Saint Benedict, MN
College of St. Catherine, MN
The College of St. Scholastica, MN
College of Staten Island of the City University of New York, NY
The College of Wooster, OH

Non-Need Scholarships for Undergraduates
Special Characteristics

The Colorado College, CO
Concordia University, NE
Corban College, OR
Cornell College, IA
Cornerstone University, MI
Crown College, MN
The Culinary Institute of America, NY
Culver-Stockton College, MO
Defiance College, OH
DePauw University, IN
Dickinson College, PA
Dickinson State University, ND
Dominican University, IL
Dominican University of California, CA
Dordt College, IA
Duquesne University, PA
Eastern Michigan University, MI
East Stroudsburg University of Pennsylvania, PA
East Texas Baptist University, TX
Eckerd College, FL
Edinboro University of Pennsylvania, PA
Elizabethtown College, PA
Elmira College, NY
Emmanuel College, MA
Emporia State University, KS
Endicott College, MA
Eugene Bible College, OR
Fairmont State University, WV
Ferrum College, VA
Finlandia University, MI
Florida Gulf Coast University, FL
Fort Lewis College, CO
Francis Marion University, SC
Franklin Pierce College, NH
Free Will Baptist Bible College, TN
Fresno Pacific University, CA
Friends University, KS
Frostburg State University, MD
Furman University, SC
Gallaudet University, DC
Gannon University, PA
Georgia College & State University, GA
Goshen College, IN
Graceland University, IA
Grambling State University, LA
Green Mountain College, VT
Greenville College, IL
Hamline University, MN
Hampton University, VA
Hanover College, IN
Harding University, AR
Hawai'i Pacific University, HI
Hendrix College, AR
Hillsdale College, MI
Hollins University, VA
Holy Names University, CA
Huntington University, IN
Illinois College, IL
Illinois Wesleyan University, IL
Indiana University of Pennsylvania, PA
Iowa Wesleyan College, IA
Jacksonville University, FL
James Madison University, VA
Jamestown College, ND
John Brown University, AR

Johnson Bible College, TN
Juniata College, PA
Kennesaw State University, GA
Kent State University, OH
Kentucky Christian University, KY
King's College, PA
Kuyper College, MI
Lancaster Bible College, PA
Lebanon Valley College, PA
LeTourneau University, TX
Lincoln University, PA
Lipscomb University, TN
Long Island University, Brooklyn Campus, NY
MacMurray College, IL
Malone College, OH
Manchester College, IN
Marian College, IN
Marywood University, PA
Massachusetts Maritime Academy, MA
The Master's College and Seminary, CA
Mayville State University, ND
Mercer University, GA
Meredith College, NC
Mesa State College, CO
Michigan State University, MI
Michigan Technological University, MI
Midland Lutheran College, NE
Midwestern State University, TX
Millersville University of Pennsylvania, PA
Missouri State University, MO
Monmouth University, NJ
Montreat College, NC
Moravian College, PA
Morningside College, IA
Mount Marty College, SD
Mount Mary College, WI
Mount Union College, OH
Mount Vernon Nazarene University, OH
Murray State University, KY
Newberry College, SC
New England College, NH
Newman University, KS
New Mexico State University, NM
Northeastern University, MA
Northern Arizona University, AZ
Northern Illinois University, IL
Northwestern College, MN
Northwestern State University of Louisiana, LA
Northwestern University, IL
Northwest Nazarene University, ID
Northwest University, WA
Nyack College, NY
Ohio Northern University, OH
Ohio Wesleyan University, OH
Olivet Nazarene University, IL
Oral Roberts University, OK
Ouachita Baptist University, AR
Pacific Lutheran University, WA
Pacific University, OR
Philadelphia Biblical University, PA
Plymouth State University, NH
Portland State University, OR
Quinnipiac University, CT
Ramapo College of New Jersey, NJ

Randolph-Macon Woman's College, VA
Regis College, MA
Rice University, TX
The Richard Stockton College of New Jersey, NJ
Ripon College, WI
Roberts Wesleyan College, NY
Rochester Institute of Technology, NY
Rowan University, NJ
Saint Louis University, MO
Saint Martin's University, WA
St. Norbert College, WI
Saint Vincent College, PA
San Diego Christian College, CA
Schreiner University, TX
Seattle Pacific University, WA
Seton Hill University, PA
Silver Lake College, WI
Simpson College, IA
Sonoma State University, CA
South Dakota State University, SD
Southeast Missouri State University, MO
Southern Adventist University, TN
Southern Illinois University Carbondale, IL
Southern New Hampshire University, NH
Southern Oregon University, OR
Southern Virginia University, VA
Southwest Minnesota State University, MN
Spring Arbor University, MI
State University of New York at Plattsburgh, NY
State University of New York College at Brockport, NY
State University of New York College at Oneonta, NY
State University of New York, Fredonia, NY
Stetson University, FL
Stevens Institute of Technology, NJ
Sweet Briar College, VA
Tabor College, KS
Taylor University, IN
Texas Christian University, TX
Texas Lutheran University, TX
Texas Woman's University, TX
Tiffin University, OH
Toccoa Falls College, GA
Trinity Lutheran College, WA
Truman State University, MO
The University of Akron, OH
The University of Alabama, AL
University of Arkansas, AR
University of Evansville, IN
University of Great Falls, MT
University of Hartford, CT
University of Idaho, ID
University of Illinois at Springfield, IL
University of Kansas, KS
University of Kentucky, KY
University of Maine, ME
University of Maine at Presque Isle, ME
University of Mary Hardin-Baylor, TX
University of Miami, FL
University of Michigan, MI
University of Michigan–Flint, MI
University of Minnesota, Morris, MN
University of Missouri–Columbia, MO

Non-Need Scholarships for Undergraduates
Special Characteristics

University of Nebraska at Kearney, NE
University of Nebraska at Omaha, NE
University of Nebraska–Lincoln, NE
University of Nevada, Las Vegas, NV
University of New Hampshire, NH
The University of North Carolina at Asheville, NC
The University of North Carolina at Chapel Hill, NC
University of North Dakota, ND
University of Northern Colorado, CO
University of North Florida, FL
University of Oregon, OR
University of Puget Sound, WA
University of Redlands, CA
University of Rochester, NY
University of St. Thomas, TX
University of Science and Arts of Oklahoma, OK
University of South Carolina, SC
University of Southern California, CA
The University of Tampa, FL
The University of Texas at Dallas, TX
The University of Texas at El Paso, TX
The University of Texas–Pan American, TX
University of the Ozarks, AR
The University of Toledo, OH
University of West Georgia, GA
University of Wisconsin–Eau Claire, WI
University of Wisconsin–Parkside, WI
University of Wisconsin–Stevens Point, WI
University of Wisconsin–Stout, WI
University of Wisconsin–Whitewater, WI
University of Wyoming, WY
Ursinus College, PA
Valdosta State University, GA
Valparaiso University, IN
Wabash College, IN
Wartburg College, IA
Washington College, MD
Washington State University, WA
Webber International University, FL
Wesleyan College, GA
Western Illinois University, IL
Western Kentucky University, KY
Western New England College, MA
Western Washington University, WA
Westminster College, MO
Westminster College, PA
Westmont College, CA
West Virginia University, WV
West Virginia Wesleyan College, WV
Wheeling Jesuit University, WV
Whitman College, WA
Whittier College, CA
Whitworth College, WA
Wichita State University, KS
Widener University, PA
Willamette University, OR
William Carey College, MS
William Penn University, IA
Williams Baptist College, AR
Wilson College, PA
Wittenberg University, OH
Xavier University, OH
York College of Pennsylvania, PA

Local/State Students

Abilene Christian University, TX
Agnes Scott College, GA
Alaska Bible College, AK
Alaska Pacific University, AK
Albertson College of Idaho, ID
Allen College, IA
Alliant International University, CA
Alvernia College, PA
American University, DC
Anna Maria College, MA
Antioch College, OH
Arkansas State University, AR
Auburn University, AL
Augustana College, SD
Augusta State University, GA
Austin College, TX
Averett University, VA
Barton College, NC
Belhaven College, MS
Benedictine College, KS
Berry College, GA
Boston University, MA
Brevard College, NC
Brewton-Parker College, GA
Brigham Young University–Hawaii, HI
Bryan College, TN
Bryant University, RI
California State University, Chico, CA
California State University, Fresno, CA
California State University, Stanislaus, CA
Carthage College, WI
The Catholic University of America, DC
Centenary College, NJ
Centenary College of Louisiana, LA
Central Michigan University, MI
Central Washington University, WA
Chowan University, NC
The Citadel, The Military College of South Carolina, SC
Clarke College, IA
Clarkson University, NY
Clemson University, SC
Coastal Carolina University, SC
College of St. Catherine, MN
College of St. Joseph, VT
The College of Wooster, OH
Columbus College of Art & Design, OH
Concordia University, NE
Cornell College, IA
Creighton University, NE
Culver-Stockton College, MO
Dakota State University, SD
Davis & Elkins College, WV
Defiance College, OH
Dominican University of California, CA
Dordt College, IA
Dowling College, NY
Duke University, NC
East Carolina University, NC
Eastern Washington University, WA
East Texas Baptist University, TX
Eckerd College, FL
Edinboro University of Pennsylvania, PA
Elizabethtown College, PA
Elmira College, NY

Emmanuel College, MA
Emory University, GA
Endicott College, MA
Fairmont State University, WV
Ferrum College, VA
Flagler College, FL
Florida Gulf Coast University, FL
Florida Southern College, FL
Florida State University, FL
Fort Lewis College, CO
Franklin Pierce College, NH
Frostburg State University, MD
Furman University, SC
Georgetown College, KY
Georgia College & State University, GA
Georgia Institute of Technology, GA
Graceland University, IA
Grambling State University, LA
Grand Valley State University, MI
Green Mountain College, VT
Greenville College, IL
Guilford College, NC
Hamline University, MN
Hardin-Simmons University, TX
Hawai'i Pacific University, HI
Heidelberg College, OH
Hollins University, VA
Idaho State University, ID
Indiana University–Purdue University Fort Wayne, IN
Jefferson College of Health Sciences, VA
Kennesaw State University, GA
Lee University, TN
Lesley University, MA
LeTourneau University, TX
Lewis-Clark State College, ID
Limestone College, SC
Lock Haven University of Pennsylvania, PA
Lyon College, AR
Mansfield University of Pennsylvania, PA
Maryville College, TN
Marywood University, PA
Mayville State University, ND
McDaniel College, MD
Medcenter One College of Nursing, ND
Mercer University, GA
Mercyhurst College, PA
Mesa State College, CO
Miami University, OH
Michigan State University, MI
Michigan Technological University, MI
Middle Tennessee State University, TN
Minnesota State University Mankato, MN
Mississippi State University, MS
Monmouth University, NJ
Montana State University–Billings, MT
Morehead State University, KY
Mount Vernon Nazarene University, OH
Murray State University, KY
Newberry College, SC
New England College, NH
New Mexico State University, NM
New York Institute of Technology, NY
Northern Arizona University, AZ
Nyack College, NY
Ohio Wesleyan University, OH

Non-Need Scholarships for Undergraduates
Special Characteristics

Oklahoma Baptist University, OK
Oklahoma Panhandle State University, OK
Ouachita Baptist University, AR
Randolph-Macon Woman's College, VA
The Richard Stockton College of New Jersey, NJ
Ripon College, WI
Roanoke College, VA
St. Andrews Presbyterian College, NC
St. Bonaventure University, NY
St. Cloud State University, MN
St. John Fisher College, NY
St. John's University, NY
St. Louis College of Pharmacy, MO
Saint Martin's University, WA
San Diego State University, CA
Schreiner University, TX
Shenandoah University, VA
Shorter College, GA
Silver Lake College, WI
Slippery Rock University of Pennsylvania, PA
Smith College, MA
Sonoma State University, CA
Southeastern Bible College, AL
Southern Adventist University, TN
Southern New Hampshire University, NH
Southwest Baptist University, MO
Southwest Minnesota State University, MN
State University of New York at Binghamton, NY
State University of New York at Buffalo, NY
State University of New York College at Brockport, NY
State University of New York College at Geneseo, NY
State University of New York College at Oneonta, NY
State University of New York College at Potsdam, NY
State University of New York, Fredonia, NY
State University of New York Institute of Technology, NY
Stephen F. Austin State University, TX
Stephens College, MO
Sterling College, VT
Stetson University, FL
Stevens Institute of Technology, NJ
Sweet Briar College, VA
Tabor College, KS
Taylor University Fort Wayne, IN
Tennessee State University, TN
Tennessee Technological University, TN
Texas Christian University, TX
Tiffin University, OH
Tusculum College, TN
Tuskegee University, AL
Unity College, ME
The University of Akron, OH
The University of Alabama at Birmingham, AL
The University of Alabama in Huntsville, AL
University of Colorado at Boulder, CO
University of Delaware, DE
University of Denver, CO
University of Georgia, GA
University of Hartford, CT
University of Idaho, ID
University of Illinois at Springfield, IL
University of Illinois at Urbana–Champaign, IL
University of Kansas, KS
University of Maine, ME
University of Mary Hardin-Baylor, TX
University of Mary Washington, VA
University of Michigan, MI
University of Michigan–Flint, MI
University of Missouri–St. Louis, MO
University of Nevada, Las Vegas, NV
University of Nevada, Reno, NV
University of New Hampshire, NH
University of New Orleans, LA
The University of North Carolina at Asheville, NC
The University of North Carolina Wilmington, NC
University of Northern Colorado, CO
University of Oregon, OR
University of Rochester, NY
University of South Carolina, SC
University of Southern Maine, ME
University of Southern Mississippi, MS
The University of Texas at Dallas, TX
The University of Texas at El Paso, TX
The University of Texas at San Antonio, TX
The University of Texas–Pan American, TX
University of West Georgia, GA
University of Wisconsin–Eau Claire, WI
University of Wisconsin–Parkside, WI
University of Wisconsin–Stout, WI
University of Wisconsin–Whitewater, WI
University of Wyoming, WY
Vanderbilt University, TN
Virginia Military Institute, VA
Virginia Polytechnic Institute and State University, VA
Warren Wilson College, NC
Washington and Lee University, VA
Wayland Baptist University, TX
Wayne State College, NE
Webber International University, FL
Western Carolina University, NC
Western Kentucky University, KY
Western New England College, MA
Western Washington University, WA
Westminster College, MO
West Virginia University, WV
Wilson College, PA
Winona State University, MN
Wittenberg University, OH
Worcester State College, MA

Married Students
Auburn University, AL
Beulah Heights Bible College, GA
Blue Mountain College, MS
Brigham Young University–Hawaii, HI
California State University, Chico, CA
Cincinnati Christian University, OH
Eugene Bible College, OR
Franklin Pierce College, NH
Free Will Baptist Bible College, TN
Georgia Southern University, GA
Johnson Bible College, TN
Lancaster Bible College, PA
New Mexico State University, NM
Northwest University, WA
Ouachita Baptist University, AR
Sonoma State University, CA
State University of New York College at Brockport, NY
Toccoa Falls College, GA
The University of Alabama at Birmingham, AL
University of Kansas, KS
University of Nevada, Reno, NV
Valley Forge Christian College, PA

Members of Minority Groups
Abilene Christian University, TX
Alaska Pacific University, AK
Albertson College of Idaho, ID
Albright College, PA
Alice Lloyd College, KY
Allen College, IA
Alliant International University, CA
American University, DC
Appalachian State University, NC
Arkansas State University, AR
Augsburg College, MN
Augustana College, SD
Austin Peay State University, TN
Baldwin-Wallace College, OH
Beloit College, WI
Benedictine College, KS
Bentley College, MA
Berry College, GA
Bethel University, MN
Bluffton University, OH
Bowling Green State University, OH
Bradley University, IL
Brigham Young University–Hawaii, HI
Bryant University, RI
California State University, Chico, CA
California State University, Dominguez Hills, CA
California State University, Stanislaus, CA
Calvin College, MI
Carson-Newman College, TN
Carthage College, WI
Centenary College of Louisiana, LA
Central College, IA
Central Connecticut State University, CT
Central Michigan University, MI
Central Missouri State University, MO
Clarke College, IA
Clarkson University, NY
Clemson University, SC
The College of New Jersey, NJ
The College of Saint Rose, NY
The College of St. Scholastica, MN
College of Staten Island of the City University of New York, NY
The College of Wooster, OH

Non-Need Scholarships for Undergraduates
Special Characteristics

Concordia University, NE
Cornerstone University, MI
Creighton University, NE
Crown College, MN
The Culinary Institute of America, NY
Dakota State University, SD
Defiance College, OH
Denison University, OH
DePauw University, IN
Dickinson State University, ND
Dominican University of California, CA
Dordt College, IA
Drake University, IA
Duquesne University, PA
East Central University, OK
Eastern Michigan University, MI
East Stroudsburg University of Pennsylvania, PA
East Tennessee State University, TN
Edinboro University of Pennsylvania, PA
Elizabethtown College, PA
Elmhurst College, IL
Emporia State University, KS
Erskine College, SC
The Evergreen State College, WA
Fairfield University, CT
Fairmont State University, WV
Flagler College, FL
Florida Gulf Coast University, FL
Fort Hays State University, KS
Franklin and Marshall College, PA
Fresno Pacific University, CA
Gannon University, PA
Georgia College & State University, GA
Georgia Institute of Technology, GA
Georgia Southern University, GA
Gonzaga University, WA
Graceland University, IA
Grambling State University, LA
Grand Valley State University, MI
Grove City College, PA
Hamline University, MN
Hampton University, VA
Hanover College, IN
Hilbert College, NY
Idaho State University, ID
Illinois College, IL
Illinois State University, IL
Indiana State University, IN
John Brown University, AR
Johnson Bible College, TN
Kennesaw State University, GA
Kent State University, OH
Kentucky Christian University, KY
Kettering University, MI
King College, TN
King's College, PA
Kuyper College, MI
Lawrence Technological University, MI
Lawrence University, WI
Le Moyne College, NY
Lesley University, MA
Lewis-Clark State College, ID
Lindsey Wilson College, KY
Lipscomb University, TN
Lock Haven University of Pennsylvania, PA

Loyola College in Maryland, MD
Luther College, IA
Lyon College, AR
Manchester College, IN
Mansfield University of Pennsylvania, PA
Marian College, IN
Maryville College, TN
Maryville University of Saint Louis, MO
Mayville State University, ND
Mercer University, GA
Meredith College, NC
Mesa State College, CO
Miami University, OH
Michigan State University, MI
Michigan Technological University, MI
Middle Tennessee State University, TN
Midland Lutheran College, NE
Midway College, KY
Millsaps College, MS
Missouri State University, MO
Monmouth University, NJ
Montana State University–Billings, MT
Morehead State University, KY
Mount St. Mary's University, MD
Murray State University, KY
Nebraska Wesleyan University, NE
New Mexico State University, NM
North Carolina Agricultural and Technical State University, NC
Northern Illinois University, IL
Northern Michigan University, MI
Northwest Nazarene University, ID
The Ohio State University, OH
Ohio University, OH
Ohio University–Chillicothe, OH
Ohio University–Eastern, OH
Ohio University–Lancaster, OH
Ohio University–Southern Campus, OH
Ohio University–Zanesville, OH
Ohio Wesleyan University, OH
Ouachita Baptist University, AR
Pikeville College, KY
Pitzer College, CA
Portland State University, OR
Quinnipiac University, CT
Rensselaer Polytechnic Institute, NY
The Richard Stockton College of New Jersey, NJ
Rider University, NJ
Ripon College, WI
Roanoke College, VA
Robert Morris University, PA
Rochester Institute of Technology, NY
Rowan University, NJ
Sacred Heart University, CT
St. Bonaventure University, NY
St. Cloud State University, MN
St. John Fisher College, NY
Saint Joseph's University, PA
Saint Louis University, MO
Saint Martin's University, WA
Saint Mary's University of Minnesota, MN
Saint Vincent College, PA
Seattle University, WA
Sewanee: The University of the South, TN
Shepherd University, WV

Simpson College, IA
Simpson University, CA
Slippery Rock University of Pennsylvania, PA
Sonoma State University, CA
South Dakota State University, SD
Southeast Missouri State University, MO
Southern Adventist University, TN
Southern Arkansas University–Magnolia, AR
Southern Oregon University, OR
Southwest Minnesota State University, MN
Spring Arbor University, MI
State University of New York at Binghamton, NY
State University of New York at New Paltz, NY
State University of New York College at Brockport, NY
State University of New York College at Cortland, NY
State University of New York College at Geneseo, NY
State University of New York College at Oneonta, NY
State University of New York College at Potsdam, NY
State University of New York College of Environmental Science and Forestry, NY
State University of New York, Fredonia, NY
State University of New York Institute of Technology, NY
Stetson University, FL
Stevens Institute of Technology, NJ
Stonehill College, MA
Tennessee State University, TN
Tennessee Technological University, TN
Thomas Jefferson University, PA
Transylvania University, KY
Trinity International University, IL
Tri-State University, IN
Unity College, ME
The University of Akron, OH
The University of Alabama at Birmingham, AL
The University of Alabama in Huntsville, AL
University of California, San Diego, CA
University of Central Oklahoma, OK
University of Cincinnati, OH
University of Colorado at Denver and Health Sciences Center—Downtown Denver Campus, CO
University of Dallas, TX
University of Delaware, DE
University of Evansville, IN
University of Florida, FL
University of Hartford, CT
University of Idaho, ID
University of Illinois at Springfield, IL
University of Illinois at Urbana–Champaign, IL
University of Kansas, KS
University of Kentucky, KY
University of Maine, ME

Peterson's College Money Handbook 2007

Non-Need Scholarships for Undergraduates
Special Characteristics

University of Maine at Farmington, ME
University of Mary Hardin-Baylor, TX
University of Massachusetts Dartmouth, MA
University of Memphis, TN
University of Michigan, MI
University of Michigan–Dearborn, MI
University of Michigan–Flint, MI
University of Minnesota, Morris, MN
University of Missouri–Columbia, MO
University of Missouri–Kansas City, MO
University of Missouri–St. Louis, MO
University of Nebraska at Omaha, NE
University of Nebraska–Lincoln, NE
University of Nevada, Las Vegas, NV
University of Nevada, Reno, NV
The University of North Carolina at Asheville, NC
The University of North Carolina at Greensboro, NC
University of North Dakota, ND
University of Northern Colorado, CO
University of Northern Iowa, IA
University of North Florida, FL
University of Oklahoma, OK
University of Richmond, VA
University of St. Thomas, TX
University of South Carolina, SC
University of Southern California, CA
University of Southern Indiana, IN
The University of Tennessee at Martin, TN
The University of Texas at Dallas, TX
The University of Texas at El Paso, TX
University of the Ozarks, AR
The University of Toledo, OH
University of West Georgia, GA
University of Wisconsin–Eau Claire, WI
University of Wisconsin–La Crosse, WI
University of Wisconsin–Parkside, WI
University of Wisconsin–Stevens Point, WI
University of Wisconsin–Stout, WI
University of Wisconsin–Whitewater, WI
Valdosta State University, GA
Vanderbilt University, TN
Villanova University, PA
Virginia Intermont College, VA
Virginia Polytechnic Institute and State University, VA
Wake Forest University, NC
Warner Pacific College, OR
Wartburg College, IA
Wayland Baptist University, TX
Wayne State College, NE
Western Carolina University, NC
Western Illinois University, IL
Western Kentucky University, KY
Western New England College, MA
Western Washington University, WA
West Virginia University, WV
West Virginia Wesleyan College, WV
Wichita State University, KS
Willamette University, OR
William Jewell College, MO
Williams Baptist College, AR
Winona State University, MN
Wittenberg University, OH
Xavier University, OH
York College of Pennsylvania, PA
Youngstown State University, OH

Out-of-State Students

Abilene Christian University, TX
Alaska Pacific University, AK
Allen College, IA
Alvernia College, PA
Appalachian State University, NC
Arkansas State University, AR
Arkansas Tech University, AR
Atlantic Union College, MA
Auburn University, AL
Aurora University, IL
Averett University, VA
Bemidji State University, MN
Benedictine College, KS
Benedictine University, IL
Bethel University, MN
Bluffton University, OH
Brewton-Parker College, GA
Bridgewater College, VA
Buena Vista University, IA
California State University, Chico, CA
Cascade College, OR
Centenary College, NJ
Centenary College of Louisiana, LA
Central College, IA
Central Michigan University, MI
Central Missouri State University, MO
The Citadel, The Military College of South Carolina, SC
Coastal Carolina University, SC
College Misericordia, PA
College of St. Catherine, MN
Concordia University Wisconsin, WI
Cornerstone University, MI
Defiance College, OH
Dominican University of California, CA
Dordt College, IA
East Central University, OK
Eastern Michigan University, MI
Edinboro University of Pennsylvania, PA
Emory & Henry College, VA
Erskine College, SC
Eugene Bible College, OR
Fairmont State University, WV
Ferrum College, VA
Flagler College, FL
Florida Gulf Coast University, FL
Florida Southern College, FL
Fort Lewis College, CO
Francis Marion University, SC
Frostburg State University, MD
Georgia College & State University, GA
Georgia Institute of Technology, GA
Grambling State University, LA
Grand Valley State University, MI
Greenville College, IL
Hampden-Sydney College, VA
Hanover College, IN
Hardin-Simmons University, TX
Hawai'i Pacific University, HI
Heidelberg College, OH
Hollins University, VA
Idaho State University, ID
Illinois College, IL
Iowa Wesleyan College, IA
James Madison University, VA
Kent State University, OH
Kentucky Wesleyan College, KY
Lewis-Clark State College, ID
Limestone College, SC
Louisiana Tech University, LA
MacMurray College, IL
Mayville State University, ND
McKendree College, IL
Meredith College, NC
Mesa State College, CO
Miami University, OH
Michigan State University, MI
Michigan Technological University, MI
Midwestern State University, TX
Minnesota State University Mankato, MN
Mississippi State University, MS
Missouri State University, MO
Monmouth University, NJ
Montana State University–Billings, MT
Morehead State University, KY
Morningside College, IA
Murray State University, KY
New College of Florida, FL
Newman University, KS
New Mexico State University, NM
Northern Arizona University, AZ
Northern Michigan University, MI
Northwestern State University of Louisiana, LA
Northwest Nazarene University, ID
Nyack College, NY
The Ohio State University, OH
Ohio Wesleyan University, OH
Oklahoma Baptist University, OK
Oklahoma Panhandle State University, OK
Oklahoma State University, OK
Ouachita Baptist University, AR
Portland State University, OR
Ramapo College of New Jersey, NJ
Ripon College, WI
Robert Morris College, IL
Robert Morris University, PA
Roberts Wesleyan College, NY
St. Cloud State University, MN
Salem International University, WV
San Diego Christian College, CA
Shimer College, IL
Shorter College, GA
Simpson University, CA
Slippery Rock University of Pennsylvania, PA
Sonoma State University, CA
Southeastern Louisiana University, LA
Southeastern Oklahoma State University, OK
Southeast Missouri State University, MO
Southern Adventist University, TN
Southern Arkansas University–Magnolia, AR
Spring Arbor University, MI
State University of New York at Binghamton, NY

Non-Need Scholarships for Undergraduates
Special Characteristics

State University of New York at Plattsburgh, NY
State University of New York College at Brockport, NY
State University of New York, Fredonia, NY
Stephens College, MO
Tabor College, KS
Tennessee Technological University, TN
Texas Tech University, TX
Tiffin University, OH
Transylvania University, KY
The University of Akron, OH
The University of Alabama, AL
The University of Alabama at Birmingham, AL
University of Arkansas, AR
University of Arkansas at Monticello, AR
University of Cincinnati, OH
University of Colorado at Colorado Springs, CO
University of Florida, FL
University of Idaho, ID
University of Illinois at Springfield, IL
University of Illinois at Urbana–Champaign, IL
University of Kansas, KS
University of Maine, ME
University of Maine at Farmington, ME
University of Mary Hardin-Baylor, TX
University of Maryland, College Park, MD
University of Michigan, MI
University of Michigan–Dearborn, MI
University of Missouri–Columbia, MO
University of Missouri–Kansas City, MO
University of Nebraska at Kearney, NE
University of Nebraska at Omaha, NE
University of Nebraska–Lincoln, NE
University of Nevada, Las Vegas, NV
University of New Orleans, LA
University of North Alabama, AL
The University of North Carolina at Chapel Hill, NC
The University of North Carolina at Greensboro, NC
University of Northern Colorado, CO
University of North Florida, FL
University of Science and Arts of Oklahoma, OK
University of South Carolina, SC
University of Southern Indiana, IN
University of Southern Maine, ME
University of Southern Mississippi, MS
The University of Tennessee at Martin, TN
The University of Texas at Dallas, TX
The University of Texas at El Paso, TX
The University of Texas at San Antonio, TX
The University of Texas–Pan American, TX
University of Utah, UT
University of Wisconsin–La Crosse, WI
University of Wisconsin–Stevens Point, WI
University of Wisconsin–Stout, WI
University of Wisconsin–Whitewater, WI
University of Wyoming, WY
Virginia Military Institute, VA

Virginia Polytechnic Institute and State University, VA
Wartburg College, IA
Washington State University, WA
Wayne State College, NE
Wesleyan College, GA
Western Kentucky University, KY
Western New England College, MA
William Jewell College, MO
Winona State University, MN

Parents of Current Students
Alabama Agricultural and Mechanical University, AL
Aurora University, IL
Blue Mountain College, MS
Cascade College, OR
Cincinnati Christian University, OH
Franklin Pierce College, NH
Green Mountain College, VT
Huntington University, IN
Johnson Bible College, TN
Malone College, OH
Marymount University, VA
Maryville University of Saint Louis, MO
Mount Aloysius College, PA
Mount Marty College, SD
Mount Mary College, WI
New England College, NH
Northwest University, WA
Olivet Nazarene University, IL
Seton Hill University, PA
The University of Alabama at Birmingham, AL
University of Great Falls, MT
University of Hartford, CT
Wesleyan College, GA

Previous College Experience
Abilene Christian University, TX
Alma College, MI
Alvernia College, PA
American University, DC
Anna Maria College, MA
Benedictine University, IL
Bethel College, KS
Bloomfield College, NJ
Brevard College, NC
Carthage College, WI
Cedar Crest College, PA
Centenary College, NJ
Central College, IA
Central Missouri State University, MO
Central Washington University, WA
College Misericordia, PA
College of St. Joseph, VT
The College of St. Scholastica, MN
Defiance College, OH
East Central University, OK
Eastern Michigan University, MI
East Texas Baptist University, TX
Elmira College, NY
Emory & Henry College, VA
Florida Institute of Technology, FL
Hawai'i Pacific University, HI
Hendrix College, AR
Illinois College, IL

Illinois State University, IL
Lake Forest College, IL
Lancaster Bible College, PA
Lock Haven University of Pennsylvania, PA
MacMurray College, IL
Manchester College, IN
McDaniel College, MD
Memphis College of Art, TN
Meredith College, NC
Michigan Technological University, MI
Mississippi State University, MS
Monmouth University, NJ
Mount Mercy College, IA
New Mexico State University, NM
New York Institute of Technology, NY
The Ohio State University, OH
Oklahoma State University, OK
Pacific Lutheran University, WA
Palm Beach Atlantic University, FL
The Richard Stockton College of New Jersey, NJ
Ripon College, WI
Saint Louis University, MO
Slippery Rock University of Pennsylvania, PA
Sonoma State University, CA
Southeast Missouri State University, MO
Southern New Hampshire University, NH
Southwest Minnesota State University, MN
State University of New York College at Potsdam, NY
State University of New York, Fredonia, NY
State University of New York Institute of Technology, NY
Stephen F. Austin State University, TX
Sterling College, VT
The University of Alabama at Birmingham, AL
University of Arkansas, AR
University of Hartford, CT
University of Kansas, KS
University of Maine, ME
University of Michigan–Dearborn, MI
University of New Orleans, LA
University of Oklahoma, OK
University of Science and Arts of Oklahoma, OK
The University of Toledo, OH
University of West Georgia, GA
University of Wisconsin–Eau Claire, WI
University of Wisconsin–Stout, WI
Walsh College of Accountancy and Business Administration, MI
Warren Wilson College, NC
Western Washington University, WA

Public Servants
Arkansas Tech University, AR
College of Staten Island of the City University of New York, NY
Dowling College, NY
Grambling State University, LA
Hannibal-LaGrange College, MO
Hardin-Simmons University, TX
Louisiana Tech University, LA
Michigan State University, MI

Non-Need Scholarships for Undergraduates
Special Characteristics

New York Institute of Technology, NY
Nicholls State University, LA
Northwestern State University of Louisiana, LA
St. Francis College, NY
Southern Illinois University Carbondale, IL
Tennessee Technological University, TN
Tiffin University, OH
The University of Alabama at Birmingham, AL
University of Illinois at Springfield, IL
University of Maine, ME
University of Memphis, TN
University of New Orleans, LA
The University of Texas at Arlington, TX
The University of Texas at Dallas, TX
The University of Toledo, OH
Washington State University, WA

Relatives of Clergy

Abilene Christian University, TX
Albion College, MI
American University, DC
Ashland University, OH
Augsburg College, MN
Austin College, TX
Averett University, VA
Azusa Pacific University, CA
Barton College, NC
Belhaven College, MS
Bennett College For Women, NC
Bethany College, KS
Bethel College, KS
Bethel University, MN
Biola University, CA
Blue Mountain College, MS
Bluffton University, OH
Boston University, MA
Brevard College, NC
Brewton-Parker College, GA
Bryan College, TN
California Baptist University, CA
California Lutheran University, CA
Calvary Bible College and Theological Seminary, MO
Campbellsville University, KY
Carson-Newman College, TN
Carthage College, WI
Cedar Crest College, PA
Centenary College of Louisiana, LA
Chowan University, NC
Clarke College, IA
College Misericordia, PA
College of the Southwest, NM
Columbia College, SC
Concordia University, MI
Corban College, OR
Crown College, MN
Dallas Baptist University, TX
Davidson College, NC
Defiance College, OH
DePauw University, IN
Duquesne University, PA
Elon University, NC
Emory & Henry College, VA
Emory University, GA

Erskine College, SC
Eugene Bible College, OR
Faith Baptist Bible College and Theological Seminary, IA
Faulkner University, AL
Ferrum College, VA
Florida Christian College, FL
Florida Southern College, FL
Free Will Baptist Bible College, TN
Friends University, KS
Furman University, SC
Geneva College, PA
Georgetown College, KY
Gordon College, MA
Grace Bible College, MI
Grace College, IN
Green Mountain College, VT
Greenville College, IL
Hannibal-LaGrange College, MO
Hardin-Simmons University, TX
Hawai'i Pacific University, HI
Heidelberg College, OH
Hendrix College, AR
Houghton College, NY
Houston Baptist University, TX
Huntington University, IN
Iowa Wesleyan College, IA
Jamestown College, ND
John Brown University, AR
Johnson Bible College, TN
Judson College, AL
Kentucky Wesleyan College, KY
King College, TN
King's College, PA
LaGrange College, GA
Lancaster Bible College, PA
La Sierra University, CA
LeTourneau University, TX
Lipscomb University, TN
Lycoming College, PA
Malone College, OH
Maranatha Baptist Bible College, WI
The Master's College and Seminary, CA
Mercer University, GA
Merrimack College, MA
Messiah College, PA
Methodist College, NC
MidAmerica Nazarene University, KS
Midway College, KY
Millsaps College, MS
Montreat College, NC
Moravian College, PA
Mount Union College, OH
Mount Vernon Nazarene University, OH
Nebraska Wesleyan University, NE
Newberry College, SC
Niagara University, NY
North Greenville College, SC
Northwest Christian College, OR
Northwestern College, MN
Northwest Nazarene University, ID
Northwest University, WA
Nyack College, NY
Ohio Northern University, OH
Ohio Wesleyan University, OH
Oklahoma Baptist University, OK

Olivet Nazarene University, IL
Oral Roberts University, OK
Ouachita Baptist University, AR
Our Lady of Holy Cross College, LA
Pacific Lutheran University, WA
Pacific University, OR
Palm Beach Atlantic University, FL
Peace College, NC
Philadelphia Biblical University, PA
Randolph-Macon College, VA
Randolph-Macon Woman's College, VA
Regis College, MA
Roberts Wesleyan College, NY
Rosemont College, PA
St. Bonaventure University, NY
St. John's University, NY
Saint Mary's College of California, CA
Samford University, AL
San Diego Christian College, CA
Seattle Pacific University, WA
Sewanee: The University of the South, TN
Shasta Bible College, CA
Shenandoah University, VA
Simpson College, IA
Simpson University, CA
Southern Methodist College, SC
Southwest Baptist University, MO
Southwestern Christian University, OK
Southwestern University, TX
Spring Arbor University, MI
Stonehill College, MA
Taylor University Fort Wayne, IN
Texas Christian University, TX
Thiel College, PA
Toccoa Falls College, GA
Transylvania University, KY
Trevecca Nazarene University, TN
Union University, TN
The University of Alabama at Birmingham, AL
University of Mary Hardin-Baylor, TX
The University of North Carolina at Chapel Hill, NC
University of Portland, OR
University of St. Thomas, TX
University of South Carolina, SC
University of the Cumberlands, KY
University of the Ozarks, AR
University of Tulsa, OK
Valley Forge Christian College, PA
Valparaiso University, IN
Virginia Wesleyan College, VA
Wake Forest University, NC
Wayland Baptist University, TX
Wesleyan College, GA
Westminster College, MO
West Virginia Wesleyan College, WV
Whitworth College, WA
William Carey College, MS
William Jewell College, MO
Williams Baptist College, AR
William Woods University, MO
Wilson College, PA
Wingate University, NC
Wittenberg University, OH
Wofford College, SC

Non-Need Scholarships for Undergraduates
Special Characteristics

Religious Affiliation

Abilene Christian University, TX
Adrian College, MI
Agnes Scott College, GA
Alaska Bible College, AK
Alaska Pacific University, AK
Albertson College of Idaho, ID
Albertus Magnus College, CT
Alderson-Broaddus College, WV
Alvernia College, PA
American Baptist College of American Baptist Theological Seminary, TN
Armstrong Atlantic State University, GA
Ashland University, OH
Augustana College, SD
Averett University, VA
Avila University, MO
Azusa Pacific University, CA
Baldwin-Wallace College, OH
The Baptist College of Florida, FL
Barton College, NC
Belhaven College, MS
Benedictine College, KS
Bennett College For Women, NC
Bethel College, KS
Bethel University, MN
Beulah Heights Bible College, GA
Blue Mountain College, MS
Bluffton University, OH
Boston University, MA
Brevard College, NC
Brewton-Parker College, GA
Bridgewater College, VA
Brigham Young University–Hawaii, HI
Bryan College, TN
Buena Vista University, IA
California Lutheran University, CA
Calvin College, MI
Campbellsville University, KY
Carthage College, WI
The Catholic University of America, DC
Cedar Crest College, PA
Cedarville University, OH
Centenary College, NJ
Centenary College of Louisiana, LA
Central College, IA
Chestnut Hill College, PA
Chowan University, NC
Christian Brothers University, TN
Clarke College, IA
Clearwater Christian College, FL
College Misericordia, PA
College of St. Catherine, MN
College of St. Joseph, VT
The College of St. Scholastica, MN
Concordia University, CA
Concordia University, MI
Concordia University, St. Paul, MN
Concordia University Wisconsin, WI
Creighton University, NE
Culver-Stockton College, MO
Dallas Baptist University, TX
Dallas Christian College, TX
Davis & Elkins College, WV
Defiance College, OH
DePauw University, IN

Doane College, NE
Dordt College, IA
Duquesne University, PA
Eastern Michigan University, MI
East Texas Baptist University, TX
Eckerd College, FL
Edinboro University of Pennsylvania, PA
Elizabethtown College, PA
Elmhurst College, IL
Elms College, MA
Emmanuel College, MA
Emory & Henry College, VA
Emory University, GA
Emporia State University, KS
Endicott College, MA
Erskine College, SC
Eureka College, IL
Evangel University, MO
Fairfield University, CT
Ferrum College, VA
Finlandia University, MI
Florida Christian College, FL
Fresno Pacific University, CA
Friends University, KS
Furman University, SC
Gannon University, PA
Geneva College, PA
Georgetown College, KY
Georgia College & State University, GA
Graceland University, IA
Greenville College, IL
Hampden-Sydney College, VA
Hannibal-LaGrange College, MO
Hanover College, IN
Hardin-Simmons University, TX
Hawai'i Pacific University, HI
Heidelberg College, OH
Holy Names University, CA
Houghton College, NY
Huntington University, IN
Illinois College, IL
Iona College, NY
Iowa Wesleyan College, IA
Jamestown College, ND
Johnson Bible College, TN
Judson College, AL
Juniata College, PA
Kennesaw State University, GA
Kentucky Christian University, KY
Kentucky Wesleyan College, KY
LaGrange College, GA
Lakeland College, WI
Lancaster Bible College, PA
La Sierra University, CA
Loyola University Chicago, IL
Luther College, IA
Lyon College, AR
MacMurray College, IL
Malone College, OH
Manchester College, IN
Marian College, IN
Maryville College, TN
Maryville University of Saint Louis, MO
Marywood University, PA
McKendree College, IL
Medical College of Georgia, GA

Mercer University, GA
Meredith College, NC
Messenger College, MO
Messiah College, PA
Methodist College, NC
Michigan State University, MI
MidAmerica Nazarene University, KS
Midland Lutheran College, NE
Midway College, KY
Millsaps College, MS
Moravian College, PA
Mount Aloysius College, PA
Mount Marty College, SD
Mount Olive College, NC
Mount Vernon Nazarene University, OH
Newberry College, SC
Newman University, KS
Northwest Christian College, OR
Northwest Nazarene University, ID
Northwest University, WA
Nyack College, NY
Ohio Northern University, OH
Ohio Wesleyan University, OH
Oklahoma Baptist University, OK
Ouachita Baptist University, AR
Our Lady of Holy Cross College, LA
Randolph-Macon Woman's College, VA
Regis College, MA
Ripon College, WI
Roanoke College, VA
Roberts Wesleyan College, NY
Sacred Heart University, CT
St. Bonaventure University, NY
St. Edward's University, TX
St. John's University, NY
Saint Martin's University, WA
Salem International University, WV
San Diego Christian College, CA
Schreiner University, TX
Seattle Pacific University, WA
Shenandoah University, VA
Shorter College, GA
Simpson College, IA
Simpson University, CA
Southwestern Christian University, OK
Spring Arbor University, MI
State University of New York College at Brockport, NY
Stephen F. Austin State University, TX
Tabor College, KS
Taylor University, IN
Texas Christian University, TX
Texas Lutheran University, TX
Thiel College, PA
Thomas More College, KY
Toccoa Falls College, GA
Transylvania University, KY
Trevecca Nazarene University, TN
Trinity International University, IL
Trinity Lutheran College, WA
Union College, KY
Union University, TN
The University of Alabama at Birmingham, AL
University of Dayton, OH
University of Evansville, IN

Non-Need Scholarships for Undergraduates
Special Characteristics

University of Great Falls, MT
University of Hartford, CT
University of Mary Hardin-Baylor, TX
The University of North Carolina at Chapel Hill, NC
The University of North Carolina at Greensboro, NC
University of St. Francis, IL
University of St. Thomas, TX
University of South Carolina, SC
University of the Ozarks, AR
The University of Toledo, OH
University of Tulsa, OK
Urbana University, OH
Valparaiso University, IN
Villanova University, PA
Virginia Intermont College, VA
Virginia Wesleyan College, VA
Wake Forest University, NC
Waldorf College, IA
Warner Pacific College, OR
Warren Wilson College, NC
Wartburg College, IA
Washington State University, WA
Wesleyan College, GA
Western Kentucky University, KY
Westminster College, MO
Westminster College, PA
Wheeling Jesuit University, WV
William Carey College, MS
William Jewell College, MO
Williams Baptist College, AR
William Woods University, MO
Wilson College, PA
Wingate University, NC
Wittenberg University, OH

Siblings of Current Students

Albertson College of Idaho, ID
Albright College, PA
Alvernia College, PA
Anna Maria College, MA
Asbury College, KY
Atlantic Union College, MA
Augsburg College, MN
Augustana College, SD
Aurora University, IL
Avila University, MO
Azusa Pacific University, CA
Baldwin-Wallace College, OH
Barton College, NC
Becker College, MA
Beloit College, WI
Benedictine University, IL
Blue Mountain College, MS
Bridgewater College, VA
Bryant University, RI
Buena Vista University, IA
Cabrini College, PA
California Baptist University, CA
Calvary Bible College and Theological Seminary, MO
Carroll College, MT
Carroll College, WI
Carson-Newman College, TN
Carthage College, WI

Cascade College, OR
The Catholic University of America, DC
Cedar Crest College, PA
Centenary College, NJ
Central College, IA
Cincinnati Christian University, OH
Clarke College, IA
Clearwater Christian College, FL
Coe College, IA
College Misericordia, PA
College of Mount Saint Vincent, NY
College of St. Catherine, MN
The College of Saint Rose, NY
The College of St. Scholastica, MN
Concordia University, CA
Concordia University, MI
Corban College, OR
Creighton University, NE
Crown College, MN
Daemen College, NY
Doane College, NE
Dominican University, IL
Drexel University, PA
East Texas Baptist University, TX
Elizabethtown College, PA
Elmhurst College, IL
Elmira College, NY
Embry-Riddle Aeronautical University, FL
Emmanuel College, MA
Erskine College, SC
Faulkner University, AL
Ferrum College, VA
Finlandia University, MI
Florida Southern College, FL
Franklin Pierce College, NH
Gonzaga University, WA
Green Mountain College, VT
Greenville College, IL
Gwynedd-Mercy College, PA
Hanover College, IN
Harding University, AR
Hardin-Simmons University, TX
Hilbert College, NY
Houghton College, NY
Huntington University, IN
Iona College, NY
Ithaca College, NY
Jacksonville University, FL
James Madison University, VA
John Brown University, AR
Johnson Bible College, TN
Kentucky Wesleyan College, KY
Kettering University, MI
King's College, PA
Lakeland College, WI
Lancaster Bible College, PA
Lasell College, MA
La Sierra University, CA
Lee University, TN
Limestone College, SC
Loras College, IA
Lynn University, FL
MacMurray College, IL
Malone College, OH
Marian College, IN
Marian College of Fond du Lac, WI

Marymount University, VA
Maryville University of Saint Louis, MO
Marywood University, PA
McDaniel College, MD
Mercer University, GA
Merrimack College, MA
Messiah College, PA
Midland Lutheran College, NE
Montserrat College of Art, MA
Mount Aloysius College, PA
Mount Marty College, SD
Mount Mary College, WI
Mount St. Mary's University, MD
Mount Vernon Nazarene University, OH
Nazareth College of Rochester, NY
Nebraska Wesleyan University, NE
Newberry College, SC
New England College, NH
Newman University, KS
Nichols College, MA
North Greenville College, SC
Northwestern College, MN
Northwest Nazarene University, ID
Northwest University, WA
Northwood University, MI
Northwood University, Florida Campus, FL
Northwood University, Texas Campus, TX
Ohio Northern University, OH
Olivet Nazarene University, IL
Oral Roberts University, OK
Pacific Union College, CA
Palm Beach Atlantic University, FL
Philadelphia Biblical University, PA
Quinnipiac University, CT
Randolph-Macon College, VA
Regis College, MA
Ripon College, WI
Roberts Wesleyan College, NY
Rockhurst University, MO
Rosemont College, PA
Russell Sage College, NY
Sacred Heart University, CT
St. Bonaventure University, NY
Saint Francis University, PA
Saint Joseph's College, IN
Saint Joseph's College of Maine, ME
St. Lawrence University, NY
Saint Louis University, MO
Saint Martin's University, WA
Saint Mary's College, IN
San Diego Christian College, CA
Seton Hill University, PA
Shorter College, GA
Simpson College, IA
Simpson University, CA
Southeastern University, FL
Southern Adventist University, TN
Southern New Hampshire University, NH
Spring Hill College, AL
Stephens College, MO
Stonehill College, MA
Suffolk University, MA
Thiel College, PA
Toccoa Falls College, GA
Union University, TN

Non-Need Scholarships for Undergraduates
Special Characteristics

The University of Alabama at Birmingham, AL
University of Dallas, TX
University of Evansville, IN
University of Great Falls, MT
University of Hartford, CT
University of New England, ME
University of St. Francis, IL
University of Saint Francis, IN
University of the Cumberlands, KY
University of the Ozarks, AR
University of Tulsa, OK
Ursinus College, PA
Valley Forge Christian College, PA
Virginia Intermont College, VA
Wartburg College, IA
Webber International University, FL
Wesleyan College, GA
Western New England College, MA
Westminster College, MO
Whitworth College, WA
Widener University, PA
William Jewell College, MO
William Woods University, MO
Xavier University, OH

Spouses of Current Students
Alaska Bible College, AK
American University, DC
Arlington Baptist College, TX
Augustana College, SD
Aurora University, IL
Avila University, MO
The Baptist College of Florida, FL
Beulah Heights Bible College, GA
Blue Mountain College, MS
Bryan College, TN
Calvary Bible College and Theological Seminary, MO
Carroll College, MT
Carroll College, WI
Cascade College, OR
Cincinnati Christian University, OH
Elmhurst College, IL
Eugene Bible College, OR
Finlandia University, MI
Florida Christian College, FL
Franklin Pierce College, NH
Heritage Christian University, AL
Huntington University, IN
Jacksonville University, FL
Jamestown College, ND
Johnson Bible College, TN
Lancaster Bible College, PA
Lee University, TN
LeTourneau University, TX
Malone College, OH
Maranatha Baptist Bible College, WI
Marian College, IN
Maryville University of Saint Louis, MO
Marywood University, PA
Messiah College, PA
Mount Aloysius College, PA
Mount Marty College, SD
Mount Vernon Nazarene University, OH
New Mexico State University, NM

Northwest University, WA
Nyack College, NY
Olivet Nazarene University, IL
Palm Beach Atlantic University, FL
Pontifical Catholic University of Puerto Rico, PR
Russell Sage College, NY
Saint Joseph's College of Maine, ME
Saint Martin's University, WA
Simpson University, CA
Southern Adventist University, TN
Taylor University Fort Wayne, IN
The University of Alabama at Birmingham, AL
University of Great Falls, MT
University of Saint Francis, IN
University of Southern Indiana, IN
Urbana University, OH
Valley Forge Christian College, PA
Wesleyan College, GA

Spouses of Deceased or Disabled Public Servants
College of Staten Island of the City University of New York, NY
Francis Marion University, SC
Indiana University–Purdue University Fort Wayne, IN
Louisiana Tech University, LA
Michigan State University, MI
Mississippi State University, MS
Missouri State University, MO
New York Institute of Technology, NY
Northern Arizona University, AZ
Southern Illinois University Carbondale, IL
The University of Alabama, AL
The University of Alabama at Birmingham, AL
University of Kentucky, KY
University of South Carolina, SC
University of Utah, UT
Youngstown State University, OH

Twins
Becker College, MA
The Catholic University of America, DC
Cincinnati Christian University, OH
The College of Saint Rose, NY
Dominican University, IL
Drexel University, PA
East Texas Baptist University, TX
Finlandia University, MI
Lasell College, MA
Maryville University of Saint Louis, MO
Mount Aloysius College, PA
Ouachita Baptist University, AR
Randolph-Macon Woman's College, VA
Sacred Heart University, CT
Simpson College, IA
The University of Alabama at Birmingham, AL
University of Hartford, CT
Virginia Polytechnic Institute and State University, VA
Westminster College, MO

Veterans
Appalachian State University, NC
Arkansas State University, AR
Augustana College, SD
Austin Peay State University, TN
Barton College, NC
Brigham Young University–Hawaii, HI
Carroll College, MT
Cedarville University, OH
Central Michigan University, MI
The Culinary Institute of America, NY
Dickinson State University, ND
East Central University, OK
Edinboro University of Pennsylvania, PA
Emory University, GA
Emporia State University, KS
Eugene Bible College, OR
Excelsior College, NY
Fordham University, NY
Francis Marion University, SC
Free Will Baptist Bible College, TN
Frostburg State University, MD
Furman University, SC
Grambling State University, LA
Hollins University, VA
Maharishi University of Management, IA
Massachusetts College of Art, MA
Massachusetts Maritime Academy, MA
Michigan State University, MI
Midway College, KY
Midwestern State University, TX
Missouri State University, MO
Monmouth University, NJ
Montana State University–Billings, MT
Mount Vernon Nazarene University, OH
New Mexico State University, NM
New York Institute of Technology, NY
Northern Illinois University, IL
Northwestern State University of Louisiana, LA
Northwest Nazarene University, ID
Oklahoma Panhandle State University, OK
Pontifical Catholic University of Puerto Rico, PR
Robert Morris College, IL
Rochester Institute of Technology, NY
Shasta Bible College, CA
Sonoma State University, CA
South Dakota State University, SD
Southeastern Bible College, AL
Southern Connecticut State University, CT
Southern Illinois University Carbondale, IL
Southern New Hampshire University, NH
Southwest Minnesota State University, MN
State University of New York College at Brockport, NY
State University of New York, Fredonia, NY
Texas A&M University, TX
Texas Tech University, TX
Thomas Jefferson University, PA
The University of Alabama at Birmingham, AL
University of Connecticut, CT
University of Illinois at Springfield, IL

Non-Need Scholarships for Undergraduates
Special Characteristics

University of Illinois at Urbana–Champaign, IL
University of Kentucky, KY
University of Maine, ME
University of Massachusetts Amherst, MA
University of Massachusetts Dartmouth, MA
University of Minnesota, Morris, MN
University of Nebraska at Kearney, NE
The University of North Carolina at Asheville, NC
The University of North Carolina at Greensboro, NC
University of Northern Colorado, CO
University of Southern Mississippi, MS
The University of Texas at Dallas, TX
The University of Texas–Pan American, TX
University of the Virgin Islands, VI
The University of Toledo, OH
University of Wisconsin–Green Bay, WI
University of Wisconsin–Stevens Point, WI
University of Wisconsin–Stout, WI
University of Wyoming, WY
Washington State University, WA
Wayne State College, NE
Western Kentucky University, KY
Western Washington University, WA
Widener University, PA
William Carey College, MS
Wilson College, PA
Worcester State College, MA
Youngstown State University, OH

Veterans' Children
Appalachian State University, NC
Arkansas State University, AR
Benedictine College, KS
Brevard College, NC
Central Michigan University, MI
Coastal Carolina University, SC
College of Staten Island of the City University of New York, NY
Dickinson State University, ND
East Central University, OK
Edinboro University of Pennsylvania, PA
Emporia State University, KS
Eugene Bible College, OR
Excelsior College, NY
Fordham University, NY
Fort Lewis College, CO
Francis Marion University, SC
Free Will Baptist Bible College, TN
Frostburg State University, MD
Glenville State College, WV
Grambling State University, LA
Indiana State University, IN
Kennesaw State University, GA
Maharishi University of Management, IA
Michigan State University, MI
Mount Vernon Nazarene University, OH
New Mexico State University, NM
Northwestern State University of Louisiana, LA
Oklahoma Panhandle State University, OK
Pontifical Catholic University of Puerto Rico, PR
Shepherd University, WV
South Dakota State University, SD
Southeastern Louisiana University, LA
Southern New Hampshire University, NH
Southwest Minnesota State University, MN
State University of New York, Fredonia, NY
Texas A&M University, TX
Texas Tech University, TX
Tiffin University, OH
The University of Alabama at Birmingham, AL
University of California, San Diego, CA
University of Illinois at Springfield, IL
University of Illinois at Urbana–Champaign, IL
University of Kentucky, KY
University of Maine, ME
University of Maine at Farmington, ME
University of Maine at Presque Isle, ME
University of Minnesota, Morris, MN
University of Nebraska at Kearney, NE
University of Nebraska at Omaha, NE
University of Nebraska–Lincoln, NE
University of New Orleans, LA
The University of North Carolina at Asheville, NC
The University of North Carolina at Greensboro, NC
University of North Dakota, ND
University of Southern Indiana, IN
The University of Texas at Dallas, TX
The University of Toledo, OH
University of Wisconsin–Stout, WI
Virginia Commonwealth University, VA
Virginia Polytechnic Institute and State University, VA
Wayne State College, NE
Western Illinois University, IL
Western Kentucky University, KY
Youngstown State University, OH

Athletic Grants for Undergraduates

M = Men
W = Women

Archery
Texas A&M University, TX — W

Baseball
Abilene Christian University, TX — M
Adelphi University, NY — M
Alabama Agricultural and Mechanical University, AL — M
Albertson College of Idaho, ID — M
Alderson-Broaddus College, WV — M
Alice Lloyd College, KY — M
American International College, MA — M
Anderson University, SC — M
Appalachian State University, NC — M
Arizona State University, AZ — M
Arkansas State University, AR — M
Arkansas Tech University, AR — M
Armstrong Atlantic State University, GA — M
Ashford University, IA — M
Ashland University, OH — M
Auburn University, AL — M
Auburn University Montgomery, AL — M
Augustana College, SD — M
Austin Peay State University, TN — M
Avila University, MO — M
Azusa Pacific University, CA — M
Ball State University, IN — M
Barton College, NC — M
Baylor University, TX — M
Belhaven College, MS — M
Belmont Abbey College, NC — M
Belmont University, TN — M
Bemidji State University, MN — M
Benedictine College, KS — M
Bentley College, MA — M
Berry College, GA — M
Bethany College, KS — M
Biola University, CA — M
Blessing-Rieman College of Nursing, IL — M,W
Bloomfield College, NJ — M
Bloomsburg University of Pennsylvania, PA — M
Bluefield State College, WV — M
Bowling Green State University, OH — M
Bradley University, IL — M
Brevard College, NC — M
Brewton-Parker College, GA — M
Bryan College, TN — M
Butler University, IN — M
California Baptist University, CA — M
California Polytechnic State University, San Luis Obispo, CA — M
California State University, Chico, CA — M
California State University, Fresno, CA — M
California State University, Fullerton, CA — M
California State University, Sacramento, CA — M
Campbellsville University, KY — M
Campbell University, NC — M
Carson-Newman College, TN — M
Catawba College, NC — M
Cedarville University, OH — M
Centenary College of Louisiana, LA — M
Central Connecticut State University, CT — M
Central Michigan University, MI — M
Central Missouri State University, MO — M
Central Washington University, WA — M
Christian Brothers University, TN — M
The Citadel, The Military College of South Carolina, SC — M
Cleveland State University, OH — M
Coastal Carolina University, SC — M
College of Charleston, SC — M
The College of Saint Rose, NY — M
College of the Ozarks, MO — M
College of the Southwest, NM — M
The College of William and Mary, VA — M
Colorado School of Mines, CO — M
Columbus State University, GA — M
Concordia University, CA — M
Concordia University, MI — M
Concordia University, NE — M
Concordia University, St. Paul, MN — M
Coppin State University, MD — M
Corban College, OR — M
Creighton University, NE — M
Culver-Stockton College, MO — M
Dallas Baptist University, TX — M
Davidson College, NC — M
Davis & Elkins College, WV — M
Dickinson State University, ND — M
Doane College, NE — M
Dordt College, IA — M
Dowling College, NY — M
Drexel University, PA — M
Duke University, NC — M
Duquesne University, PA — M
East Carolina University, NC — M
East Central University, OK — M
Eastern Illinois University, IL — M
Eastern Michigan University, MI — M
East Stroudsburg University of Pennsylvania, PA — M
East Tennessee State University, TN — M
Eckerd College, FL — M
Elon University, NC — M
Embry-Riddle Aeronautical University, FL — M
Emporia State University, KS — M
Erskine College, SC — M
Evangel University, MO — M
Fairfield University, CT — M
Faulkner University, AL — M
Felician College, NJ — M
Flagler College, FL — M
Florida Atlantic University, FL — M
Florida College, FL — M
Florida Gulf Coast University, FL — M
Florida Institute of Technology, FL — M
Florida Southern College, FL — M
Florida State University, FL — M
Fordham University, NY — M
Fort Hays State University, KS — M
Francis Marion University, SC — M
Franklin Pierce College, NH — M
Freed-Hardeman University, TN — M
Friends University, KS — M
Furman University, SC — M
Gannon University, PA — M
Geneva College, PA — M
George Mason University, VA — M
Georgetown College, KY — M
Georgetown University, DC — M
Georgia College & State University, GA — M
Georgia Institute of Technology, GA — M
Georgia Southern University, GA — M
Georgia Southwestern State University, GA — M
Gonzaga University, WA — M
Goshen College, IN — M
Grace College, IN — M
Graceland University, IA — M
Grambling State University, LA — M
Grand Valley State University, MI — M
Grand View College, IA — M
Hannibal-LaGrange College, MO — M
Harding University, AR — M

Athletic Grants for Undergraduates
Baseball

School	
Harris-Stowe State University, MO	M
Hawai'i Pacific University, HI	M
Hofstra University, NY	M
Houston Baptist University, TX	M
Howard University, DC	M,W
Huntington University, IN	M
Illinois State University, IL	M
Indiana State University, IN	M
Indiana University Bloomington, IN	M
Indiana University of Pennsylvania, PA	M
Indiana University–Purdue University Fort Wayne, IN	M
Inter American University of Puerto Rico, Guayama Campus, PR	M
Iona College, NY	M
Iowa Wesleyan College, IA	M
Jacksonville State University, AL	M
Jacksonville University, FL	M
James Madison University, VA	M
Jamestown College, ND	M
Kansas State University, KS	M
Kennesaw State University, GA	M
Kent State University, OH	M
Kentucky Wesleyan College, KY	M
King College, TN	M
Lamar University, TX	M
Lehigh University, PA	M
Le Moyne College, NY	M
LeMoyne-Owen College, TN	M
Lewis-Clark State College, ID	M
Limestone College, SC	M
Lincoln University, MO	M
Lindenwood University, MO	M
Lindsey Wilson College, KY	M
Lipscomb University, TN	M
Lock Haven University of Pennsylvania, PA	M
Long Island University, Brooklyn Campus, NY	M
Louisiana State University and Agricultural and Mechanical College, LA	M
Louisiana Tech University, LA	M
Lubbock Christian University, TX	M
Lynn University, FL	M
Lyon College, AR	M
Malone College, OH	M
Manhattan College, NY	M
Mansfield University of Pennsylvania, PA	M
Marian College, IN	M
Marist College, NY	M
Marshall University, WV	M
The Master's College and Seminary, CA	M
Mayville State University, ND	M
McKendree College, IL	M
Mercer University, GA	M
Mercyhurst College, PA	M
Mesa State College, CO	M
Metropolitan State College of Denver, CO	M
Miami University, OH	M
MidAmerica Nazarene University, KS	M
Middle Tennessee State University, TN	M
Midland Lutheran College, NE	M
Millersville University of Pennsylvania, PA	M
Milligan College, TN	M
Minnesota State University Mankato, MN	M
Mississippi State University, MS	M
Missouri State University, MO	M
Molloy College, NY	M
Monmouth University, NJ	M
Montreat College, NC	M
Morehead State University, KY	M
Morningside College, IA	M
Mount Marty College, SD	M
Mount Olive College, NC	M
Mount St. Mary's University, MD	M
Mount Vernon Nazarene University, OH	M
Murray State University, KY	M
Newberry College, SC	M
Newman University, KS	M
New Mexico State University, NM	M
New York Institute of Technology, NY	M
Niagara University, NY	M
Nicholls State University, LA	M
North Carolina Agricultural and Technical State University, NC	M
North Carolina State University, NC	M
Northeastern University, MA	M
Northern Illinois University, IL	M
North Greenville College, SC	M
Northwestern Oklahoma State University, OK	M
Northwestern State University of Louisiana, LA	M
Northwestern University, IL	M
Northwest Nazarene University, ID	M
Northwood University, MI	M
Northwood University, Florida Campus, FL	M
Northwood University, Texas Campus, TX	M
Nova Southeastern University, FL	M
Nyack College, NY	M
The Ohio State University, OH	M
Ohio University, OH	M
Oklahoma Baptist University, OK	M
Oklahoma Panhandle State University, OK	M
Oklahoma State University, OK	M
Olivet Nazarene University, IL	M
Oral Roberts University, OK	M
Ouachita Baptist University, AR	M
The Pennsylvania State University University Park Campus, PA	M
Pepperdine University, CA	M
Philadelphia University, PA	M
Pikeville College, KY	M
Pittsburg State University, KS	M
Portland State University, OR	M
Purdue University, IN	M
Quincy University, IL	M
Quinnipiac University, CT	M
Radford University, VA	M
Rice University, TX	M
Rider University, NJ	M
Robert Morris College, IL	M
Rockhurst University, MO	M
Rollins College, FL	M
Sacred Heart University, CT	M
St. Andrews Presbyterian College, NC	M
St. Bonaventure University, NY	M
St. Cloud State University, MN	M
St. Edward's University, TX	M
St. Francis College, NY	M
St. John's University, NY	M
Saint Joseph's College, IN	M
Saint Joseph's University, PA	M
Saint Leo University, FL	M
Saint Louis University, MO	M
Saint Martin's University, WA	M
Saint Mary's College of California, CA	M
St. Thomas University, FL	M
Saint Vincent College, PA	M
Saint Xavier University, IL	M
Salem International University, WV	M
Samford University, AL	M
San Diego State University, CA	M
San Francisco State University, CA	M,W
San Jose State University, CA	M
Santa Clara University, CA	M
Seton Hill University, PA	M
Shepherd University, WV	M
Shippensburg University of Pennsylvania, PA	M
Shorter College, GA	M
Slippery Rock University of Pennsylvania, PA	M
Sonoma State University, CA	M
South Dakota State University, SD	M
Southeastern Louisiana University, LA	M
Southeastern Oklahoma State University, OK	M
Southeast Missouri State University, MO	M
Southern Arkansas University–Magnolia, AR	M
Southern Illinois University Carbondale, IL	M
Southern Illinois University Edwardsville, IL	M
Southern New Hampshire University, NH	M
Southern Polytechnic State University, GA	M
Southwest Baptist University, MO	M
Southwest Minnesota State University, MN	M
Spring Arbor University, MI	M
Spring Hill College, AL	M
Stanford University, CA	M
State University of New York at Binghamton, NY	M
State University of New York at Buffalo, NY	M
Stetson University, FL	M
Stonehill College, MA	M
Stony Brook University, State University of New York, NY	M

Athletic Grants for Undergraduates
Basketball

Tabor College, KS	M
Taylor University, IN	M
Temple University, PA	M
Tennessee Technological University, TN	M
Texas A&M University, TX	M
Texas Christian University, TX	M
Texas Southern University, TX	M
Texas State University-San Marcos, TX	M
Texas Tech University, TX	M
Tiffin University, OH	M
Towson University, MD	M
Trevecca Nazarene University, TN	M
Trinity International University, IL	M
Truman State University, MO	M
Tusculum College, TN	M
Tuskegee University, AL	M
Union College, KY	M
Union University, TN	M
University at Albany, State University of New York, NY	M
The University of Akron, OH	M
The University of Alabama, AL	M
The University of Alabama at Birmingham, AL	M
The University of Alabama in Huntsville, AL	M
University of Arkansas, AR	M
University of Arkansas at Monticello, AR	M
University of California, Berkeley, CA	M
University of California, Irvine, CA	M
University of California, Los Angeles, CA	M
University of California, Riverside, CA	M
University of California, Santa Barbara, CA	M
University of Central Oklahoma, OK	M
University of Connecticut, CT	M
University of Dayton, OH	M
University of Delaware, DE	M
University of Evansville, IN	M
The University of Findlay, OH	M
University of Florida, FL	M
University of Georgia, GA	M
University of Hartford, CT	M
University of Hawaii at Hilo, HI	M
University of Hawaii at Manoa, HI	M
University of Illinois at Urbana–Champaign, IL	M
The University of Iowa, IA	M
University of Kansas, KS	M
University of Kentucky, KY	M
University of Louisiana at Lafayette, LA	M
University of Louisville, KY	M
University of Maine, ME	M
University of Mary, ND	M
University of Maryland, Baltimore County, MD	M
University of Maryland, College Park, MD	M
University of Massachusetts Amherst, MA	M
University of Memphis, TN	M
University of Miami, FL	M
University of Michigan, MI	M
University of Minnesota, Duluth, MN	M
University of Minnesota, Twin Cities Campus, MN	M
University of Missouri–Columbia, MO	M
University of Missouri–St. Louis, MO	M
University of Nebraska at Kearney, NE	M
University of Nebraska at Omaha, NE	M
University of Nebraska–Lincoln, NE	M
University of Nevada, Las Vegas, NV	M
University of Nevada, Reno, NV	M
University of New Haven, CT	M
University of New Orleans, LA	M
University of North Alabama, AL	M
The University of North Carolina at Asheville, NC	M
The University of North Carolina at Chapel Hill, NC	M
The University of North Carolina at Greensboro, NC	M
The University of North Carolina at Pembroke, NC	M
The University of North Carolina Wilmington, NC	M
University of North Dakota, ND	M
University of Northern Colorado, CO	M
University of Northern Iowa, IA	M
University of North Florida, FL	M
University of Oklahoma, OK	M
University of Pittsburgh, PA	M
University of Portland, OR	M
University of Rhode Island, RI	M
University of Richmond, VA	M
University of St. Francis, IL	M
University of Saint Francis, IN	M
University of San Diego, CA	M
University of Science and Arts of Oklahoma, OK	M
University of South Carolina, SC	M
University of South Carolina Upstate, SC	M
The University of South Dakota, SD	M
University of Southern California, CA	M
University of Southern Indiana, IN	M
University of Southern Mississippi, MS	M
University of South Florida, FL	M
The University of Tampa, FL	M
The University of Tennessee at Martin, TN	M
The University of Texas at Arlington, TX	M
The University of Texas at Austin, TX	M
The University of Texas at San Antonio, TX	M
The University of Texas–Pan American, TX	M
University of the Cumberlands, KY	M
University of the Pacific, CA	M
The University of Toledo, OH	M
University of Utah, UT	M
University of Vermont, VT	M
University of Virginia, VA	M
The University of West Alabama, AL	M
University of West Georgia, GA	M
University of Wisconsin–Parkside, WI	M
Urbana University, OH	M
Valdosta State University, GA	M
Valley City State University, ND	M
Valparaiso University, IN	M
Vanderbilt University, TN	M
Vanguard University of Southern California, CA	M
Villanova University, PA	M
Virginia Commonwealth University, VA	M
Virginia Intermont College, VA	M
Virginia Military Institute, VA	M
Virginia Polytechnic Institute and State University, VA	M
Wake Forest University, NC	M
Waldorf College, IA	M
Washington State University, WA	M
Wayland Baptist University, TX	M
Wayne State College, NE	M
Wayne State University, MI	M
Webber International University, FL	M
Western Carolina University, NC	M
Western Illinois University, IL	M
Western Kentucky University, KY	M
Westmont College, CA	M
West Texas A&M University, TX	M
West Virginia University, WV	M
West Virginia Wesleyan College, WV	M
Wheeling Jesuit University, WV	M
Wichita State University, KS	M
William Carey College, MS	M
William Jewell College, MO	M
William Penn University, IA	M
Williams Baptist College, AR	M
William Woods University, MO	M
Wingate University, NC	M
Winona State University, MN	M
Winthrop University, SC	M
Wofford College, SC	M
Xavier University, OH	M
Youngstown State University, OH	M

Basketball

Abilene Christian University, TX	M,W
Adelphi University, NY	M,W
Alabama Agricultural and Mechanical University, AL	M,W
Albertson College of Idaho, ID	M,W
Alderson-Broaddus College, WV	M,W
Alice Lloyd College, KY	M,W
American International College, MA	M,W
American University, DC	M,W
Anderson University, SC	M,W
Appalachian State University, NC	M,W
Arizona State University, AZ	M,W
Arkansas State University, AR	M,W
Arkansas Tech University, AR	M,W
Armstrong Atlantic State University, GA	M,W
Asbury College, KY	M,W
Ashford University, IA	M,W
Ashland University, OH	M,W
Assumption College, MA	M,W

Athletic Grants for Undergraduates
Basketball

College	
Auburn University, AL	M,W
Auburn University Montgomery, AL	M,W
Augustana College, SD	M,W
Augusta State University, GA	M,W
Austin Peay State University, TN	M,W
Avila University, MO	M,W
Azusa Pacific University, CA	M,W
Ball State University, IN	M,W
Barton College, NC	M,W
Baylor University, TX	M,W
Belhaven College, MS	M,W
Belmont Abbey College, NC	M,W
Belmont University, TN	M,W
Bemidji State University, MN	M,W
Benedictine College, KS	M,W
Bentley College, MA	M,W
Berry College, GA	M,W
Bethany College, KS	M,W
Bethel College, KS	M,W
Biola University, CA	M,W
Black Hills State University, SD	M,W
Blessing-Rieman College of Nursing, IL	M,W
Bloomfield College, NJ	M,W
Bloomsburg University of Pennsylvania, PA	M,W
Bluefield State College, WV	M,W
Blue Mountain College, MS	W
Boston College, MA	M,W
Boston University, MA	M,W
Bowling Green State University, OH	M,W
Bradley University, IL	M,W
Brevard College, NC	M,W
Brewton-Parker College, GA	M,W
Brigham Young University–Hawaii, HI	M
Bryan College, TN	M,W
Bryant University, RI	M,W
Bucknell University, PA	M,W
Butler University, IN	M,W
California Baptist University, CA	M,W
California Polytechnic State University, San Luis Obispo, CA	M,W
California State University, Bakersfield, CA	M
California State University, Chico, CA	M,W
California State University, Dominguez Hills, CA	M,W
California State University, Fresno, CA	M,W
California State University, Fullerton, CA	M,W
California State University, Sacramento, CA	M,W
Campbellsville University, KY	M,W
Campbell University, NC	M,W
Carroll College, MT	M,W
Carson-Newman College, TN	M,W
Cascade College, OR	M,W
Catawba College, NC	M,W
Cedarville University, OH	M,W
Centenary College of Louisiana, LA	M,W
Central Connecticut State University, CT	M,W
Central Michigan University, MI	M,W
Central Missouri State University, MO	M,W
Central Washington University, WA	M,W
Chaminade University of Honolulu, HI	M
Christian Brothers University, TN	M,W
The Citadel, The Military College of South Carolina, SC	M
Clark Atlanta University, GA	M,W
Clemson University, SC	M,W
Cleveland State University, OH	M,W
Coastal Carolina University, SC	M,W
Colgate University, NY	M,W
College of Charleston, SC	M,W
College of Saint Mary, NE	W
The College of Saint Rose, NY	M,W
College of the Holy Cross, MA	M,W
College of the Ozarks, MO	M,W
The College of William and Mary, VA	M,W
Colorado School of Mines, CO	M,W
Colorado State University, CO	M,W
Columbia College, SC	W
Columbus State University, GA	M,W
Concordia University, CA	M,W
Concordia University, MI	M,W
Concordia University, NE	M,W
Concordia University, St. Paul, MN	M,W
Converse College, SC	W
Coppin State University, MD	M,W
Corban College, OR	M,W
Cornerstone University, MI	M,W
Creighton University, NE	M,W
Culver-Stockton College, MO	M,W
Daemen College, NY	M,W
Dakota State University, SD	M,W
Davidson College, NC	M,W
Davis & Elkins College, WV	M,W
DePaul University, IL	M,W
Dickinson State University, ND	M,W
Doane College, NE	M,W
Dominican University of California, CA	M,W
Dordt College, IA	M,W
Dowling College, NY	M,W
Drake University, IA	M,W
Drexel University, PA	M,W
Duke University, NC	M,W
Duquesne University, PA	M,W
East Carolina University, NC	M,W
East Central University, OK	M,W
Eastern Illinois University, IL	M,W
Eastern Michigan University, MI	M,W
Eastern Washington University, WA	M,W
East Stroudsburg University of Pennsylvania, PA	M,W
East Tennessee State University, TN	M,W
Eckerd College, FL	M,W
Edinboro University of Pennsylvania, PA	M,W
Elon University, NC	M,W
Embry-Riddle Aeronautical University, FL	M
Emporia State University, KS	M,W
Erskine College, SC	M,W
Evangel University, MO	M,W
The Evergreen State College, WA	M,W
Fairfield University, CT	M,W
Fairmont State University, WV	M,W
Faulkner University, AL	M
Felician College, NJ	M,W
Ferris State University, MI	M,W
Flagler College, FL	M,W
Florida Agricultural and Mechanical University, FL	M,W
Florida Atlantic University, FL	M,W
Florida College, FL	M
Florida Gulf Coast University, FL	M,W
Florida Institute of Technology, FL	M,W
Florida Southern College, FL	M,W
Florida State University, FL	M,W
Fordham University, NY	M,W
Fort Hays State University, KS	M,W
Fort Lewis College, CO	M,W
Francis Marion University, SC	M,W
Franklin Pierce College, NH	M,W
Freed-Hardeman University, TN	M,W
Fresno Pacific University, CA	M,W
Friends University, KS	M,W
Furman University, SC	M,W
Gannon University, PA	M,W
Geneva College, PA	M,W
George Mason University, VA	M,W
Georgetown College, KY	M,W
Georgetown University, DC	M,W
Georgia College & State University, GA	M,W
Georgia Institute of Technology, GA	M,W
Georgia Southern University, GA	M,W
Georgia Southwestern State University, GA	M,W
Glenville State College, WV	M,W
Gonzaga University, WA	M,W
Goshen College, IN	M,W
Grace College, IN	M,W
Graceland University, IA	M,W
Grambling State University, LA	M,W
Grand Valley State University, MI	M,W
Grand View College, IA	M,W
Hampton University, VA	M,W
Hannibal-LaGrange College, MO	M,W
Harding University, AR	M,W
Harris-Stowe State University, MO	M,W
Hawai'i Pacific University, HI	M
Hofstra University, NY	M,W
Holy Names University, CA	M,W
Houghton College, NY	M,W
Houston Baptist University, TX	M,W
Howard University, DC	M,W
Humboldt State University, CA	M,W
Huntington University, IN	M,W
Idaho State University, ID	M,W
Illinois State University, IL	M,W
Indiana State University, IN	M,W
Indiana University Bloomington, IN	M,W
Indiana University of Pennsylvania, PA	M,W
Indiana University–Purdue University Fort Wayne, IN	
Indiana University–Purdue University Indianapolis, IN	M,W
Indiana University South Bend, IN	M,W
Indiana University Southeast, IN	M,W
Inter American University of Puerto Rico, Guayama Campus, PR	M,W
Iona College, NY	M,W

Athletic Grants for Undergraduates
Basketball

College	
Iowa Wesleyan College, IA	M,W
Jacksonville State University, AL	M,W
Jacksonville University, FL	M,W
James Madison University, VA	M,W
Jamestown College, ND	M,W
John Brown University, AR	M,W
Judson College, AL	W
Kansas State University, KS	M,W
Kennesaw State University, GA	M,W
Kent State University, OH	M,W
Kentucky State University, KY	M,W
Kentucky Wesleyan College, KY	M,W
King College, TN	M,W
Lake Superior State University, MI	M,W
Lamar University, TX	M,W
Lee University, TN	M,W
Lehigh University, PA	M,W
Le Moyne College, NY	M,W
LeMoyne-Owen College, TN	M,W
Lesley University, MA	M,W
Lewis-Clark State College, ID	M,W
Limestone College, SC	M,W
Lincoln University, MO	M,W
Lindenwood University, MO	M,W
Lindsey Wilson College, KY	M,W
Lipscomb University, TN	M,W
Lock Haven University of Pennsylvania, PA	M,W
Long Island University, Brooklyn Campus, NY	M,W
Louisiana State University and Agricultural and Mechanical College, LA	M,W
Louisiana Tech University, LA	M,W
Loyola University Chicago, IL	M,W
Loyola University New Orleans, LA	M,W
Lubbock Christian University, TX	M,W
Lynn University, FL	M,W
Lyon College, AR	M,W
Malone College, OH	M,W
Manhattan College, NY	M,W
Mansfield University of Pennsylvania, PA	M,W
Marian College, IN	M,W
Marist College, NY	M,W
Marquette University, WI	M,W
Marshall University, WV	M,W
The Master's College and Seminary, CA	M,W
Mayville State University, ND	M,W
McKendree College, IL	M,W
Mercer University, GA	M,W
Mercyhurst College, PA	M,W
Merrimack College, MA	M,W
Mesa State College, CO	M,W
Metropolitan State College of Denver, CO	M,W
Miami University, OH	M,W
Michigan State University, MI	M,W
Michigan Technological University, MI	M,W
MidAmerica Nazarene University, KS	M,W
Middle Tennessee State University, TN	M,W
Midland Lutheran College, NE	M,W
Midway College, KY	W
Midwestern State University, TX	M,W
Millersville University of Pennsylvania, PA	M,W
Milligan College, TN	M,W
Minnesota State University Mankato, MN	M,W
Mississippi State University, MS	M,W
Missouri State University, MO	M,W
Molloy College, NY	M,W
Monmouth University, NJ	M,W
Montana State University, MT	M,W
Montana State University–Billings, MT	M,W
Montana Tech of The University of Montana, MT	M,W
Montreat College, NC	M,W
Morehead State University, KY	M,W
Morningside College, IA	M,W
Mountain State University, WV	M
Mount Marty College, SD	M,W
Mount Olive College, NC	M,W
Mount St. Mary's University, MD	M,W
Mount Vernon Nazarene University, OH	M,W
Murray State University, KY	M,W
Newberry College, SC	M,W
Newman University, KS	M,W
New Mexico State University, NM	M,W
New York Institute of Technology, NY	M,W
Niagara University, NY	M,W
Nicholls State University, LA	M,W
North Carolina Agricultural and Technical State University, NC	M,W
North Carolina State University, NC	M,W
Northeastern University, MA	M,W
Northern Arizona University, AZ	M,W
Northern Illinois University, IL	M,W
Northern State University, SD	M,W
North Georgia College & State University, GA	M,W
North Greenville College, SC	M,W
Northwest Christian College, OR	M,W
Northwestern Oklahoma State University, OK	M,W
Northwestern State University of Louisiana, LA	M,W
Northwestern University, IL	M,W
Northwest Nazarene University, ID	M,W
Northwest University, WA	M,W
Northwood University, MI	M,W
Nova Southeastern University, FL	M,W
Nyack College, NY	M,W
The Ohio State University, OH	M,W
Ohio University, OH	M,W
Oklahoma Baptist University, OK	M,W
Oklahoma Panhandle State University, OK	M,W
Oklahoma State University, OK	M,W
Olivet Nazarene University, IL	M,W
Oral Roberts University, OK	M,W
Ouachita Baptist University, AR	M,W
Paul Smith's College of Arts and Sciences, NY	M,W
The Pennsylvania State University University Park Campus, PA	M,W
Pepperdine University, CA	M,W
Philadelphia University, PA	M,W
Pikeville College, KY	M,W
Pittsburg State University, KS	M,W
Portland State University, OR	M,W
Purdue University, IN	M,W
Purdue University Calumet, IN	M,W
Quincy University, IL	M,W
Quinnipiac University, CT	M,W
Radford University, VA	M,W
Rice University, TX	M,W
Rider University, NJ	M,W
Robert Morris College, IL	M,W
Robert Morris University, PA	M,W
Roberts Wesleyan College, NY	M,W
Rockhurst University, MO	M,W
Rollins College, FL	M,W
Sacred Heart University, CT	M,W
St. Andrews Presbyterian College, NC	M,W
St. Bonaventure University, NY	M,W
St. Cloud State University, MN	M,W
St. Edward's University, TX	M,W
St. Francis College, NY	M,W
Saint Francis University, PA	M,W
St. John's University, NY	M,W
Saint Joseph's College, IN	M,W
Saint Joseph's University, PA	M,W
Saint Leo University, FL	M,W
Saint Louis University, MO	M,W
Saint Martin's University, WA	M,W
Saint Mary's College of California, CA	M,W
Saint Vincent College, PA	M,W
Saint Xavier University, IL	M
Salem International University, WV	M,W
Samford University, AL	M,W
San Diego Christian College, CA	M,W
San Diego State University, CA	M,W
San Francisco State University, CA	M,W
San Jose State University, CA	M,W
Santa Clara University, CA	M,W
Seattle Pacific University, WA	M,W
Seattle University, WA	M,W
Seton Hill University, PA	M,W
Shepherd University, WV	M,W
Shippensburg University of Pennsylvania, PA	M,W
Shorter College, GA	M,W
Slippery Rock University of Pennsylvania, PA	M,W
Sonoma State University, CA	M,W
South Carolina State University, SC	M,W
South Dakota School of Mines and Technology, SD	M,W
South Dakota State University, SD	M,W
Southeastern Louisiana University, LA	M,W
Southeastern Oklahoma State University, OK	M,W
Southeast Missouri State University, MO	M,W
Southern Arkansas University–Magnolia, AR	M,W
Southern Illinois University Carbondale, IL	M,W
Southern Illinois University Edwardsville, IL	M,W

Athletic Grants for Undergraduates
Basketball

School	
Southern New Hampshire University, NH	M,W
Southern Oregon University, OR	M,W
Southern Polytechnic State University, GA	M,W
Southern University and Agricultural and Mechanical College, LA	M,W
Southwest Baptist University, MO	M,W
Southwest Minnesota State University, MN	M,W
Spring Arbor University, MI	M,W
Spring Hill College, AL	M,W
Stanford University, CA	M,W
State University of New York at Binghamton, NY	M,W
State University of New York at Buffalo, NY	M,W
Stephen F. Austin State University, TX	M,W
Stetson University, FL	M,W
Stonehill College, MA	M,W
Stony Brook University, State University of New York, NY	M,W
Syracuse University, NY	M,W
Tabor College, KS	M,W
Taylor University, IN	M,W
Temple University, PA	M,W
Tennessee State University, TN	M,W
Tennessee Technological University, TN	M,W
Texas A&M University, TX	M,W
Texas A&M University–Commerce, TX	M,W
Texas Christian University, TX	M,W
Texas Southern University, TX	M,W
Texas State University-San Marcos, TX	M,W
Texas Tech University, TX	M,W
Texas Woman's University, TX	W
Tiffin University, OH	M,W
Towson University, MD	M,W
Trevecca Nazarene University, TN	M,W
Trinity International University, IL	M,W
Truman State University, MO	M,W
Tusculum College, TN	M,W
Tuskegee University, AL	M,W
Union College, KY	M,W
Union University, TN	M,W
Unity College, ME	M
University at Albany, State University of New York, NY	M,W
The University of Akron, OH	M,W
The University of Alabama, AL	M,W
The University of Alabama at Birmingham, AL	M,W
The University of Alabama in Huntsville, AL	M,W
University of Alaska Fairbanks, AK	M,W
University of Arkansas, AR	M,W
University of Arkansas at Monticello, AR	M,W
University of Arkansas at Pine Bluff, AR	M,W
University of California, Berkeley, CA	M,W
University of California, Irvine, CA	M,W
University of California, Los Angeles, CA	M,W
University of California, Riverside, CA	M,W
University of California, Santa Barbara, CA	M,W
University of Central Oklahoma, OK	M,W
University of Cincinnati, OH	M,W
University of Colorado at Boulder, CO	M,W
University of Colorado at Colorado Springs, CO	M,W
University of Connecticut, CT	M,W
University of Dayton, OH	M,W
University of Delaware, DE	M,W
University of Denver, CO	M,W
University of Evansville, IN	M,W
The University of Findlay, OH	M,W
University of Florida, FL	M,W
University of Georgia, GA	M,W
University of Great Falls, MT	M,W
University of Hartford, CT	M,W
University of Hawaii at Hilo, HI	M
University of Hawaii at Manoa, HI	M,W
University of Idaho, ID	M,W
University of Illinois at Springfield, IL	M,W
University of Illinois at Urbana–Champaign, IL	M,W
The University of Iowa, IA	M,W
University of Kansas, KS	M,W
University of Kentucky, KY	M,W
University of Louisiana at Lafayette, LA	M,W
University of Louisville, KY	M,W
University of Maine, ME	M,W
University of Mary, ND	M,W
University of Maryland, Baltimore County, MD	M,W
University of Maryland, College Park, MD	M,W
University of Massachusetts Amherst, MA	M,W
University of Massachusetts Lowell, MA	M,W
University of Memphis, TN	M,W
University of Miami, FL	M,W
University of Michigan, MI	M,W
University of Michigan–Dearborn, MI	M,W
University of Minnesota, Duluth, MN	M,W
University of Minnesota, Twin Cities Campus, MN	M,W
University of Missouri–Columbia, MO	M,W
University of Missouri–Kansas City, MO	M,W
University of Missouri–St. Louis, MO	M,W
University of Nebraska at Kearney, NE	M,W
University of Nebraska at Omaha, NE	M,W
University of Nebraska–Lincoln, NE	M,W
University of Nevada, Las Vegas, NV	M,W
University of Nevada, Reno, NV	M,W
University of New Hampshire, NH	M,W
University of New Haven, CT	M,W
University of New Orleans, LA	M,W
University of North Alabama, AL	M,W
The University of North Carolina at Asheville, NC	M,W
The University of North Carolina at Chapel Hill, NC	M,W
The University of North Carolina at Greensboro, NC	M,W
The University of North Carolina at Pembroke, NC	M,W
The University of North Carolina Wilmington, NC	M,W
University of North Dakota, ND	M,W
University of Northern Colorado, CO	M,W
University of Northern Iowa, IA	M,W
University of North Florida, FL	M,W
University of Oklahoma, OK	M,W
University of Oregon, OR	M,W
University of Pittsburgh, PA	M,W
University of Pittsburgh at Johnstown, PA	
University of Portland, OR	M,W
University of Puerto Rico, Mayagüez Campus, PR	M,W
University of Rhode Island, RI	M,W
University of Richmond, VA	M,W
University of St. Francis, IL	M,W
University of Saint Francis, IN	M,W
University of San Diego, CA	M,W
University of Science and Arts of Oklahoma, OK	M,W
University of South Carolina, SC	M,W
University of South Carolina Upstate, SC	M,W
The University of South Dakota, SD	M,W
University of Southern California, CA	M,W
University of Southern Indiana, IN	M,W
University of Southern Mississippi, MS	M,W
University of South Florida, FL	M,W
The University of Tampa, FL	M,W
The University of Tennessee at Martin, TN	M,W
The University of Texas at Arlington, TX	M,W
The University of Texas at Austin, TX	M,W
The University of Texas at El Paso, TX	M,W
The University of Texas at San Antonio, TX	M,W
The University of Texas–Pan American, TX	M,W
University of the Cumberlands, KY	M,W
University of the Pacific, CA	M,W
The University of Toledo, OH	M,W
University of Tulsa, OK	M,W
University of Utah, UT	M,W
University of Vermont, VT	M,W
University of Virginia, VA	M,W
The University of West Alabama, AL	M,W
University of West Georgia, GA	M,W
University of Wisconsin–Green Bay, WI	M,W
University of Wisconsin–Madison, WI	M,W
University of Wisconsin–Parkside, WI	M,W
University of Wyoming, WY	M,W
Urbana University, OH	M,W
Utah State University, UT	M,W
Valdosta State University, GA	M,W
Valley City State University, ND	M,W
Valparaiso University, IN	M,W
Vanderbilt University, TN	M,W

Athletic Grants for Undergraduates
Crew

College	
Vanguard University of Southern California, CA	M,W
Villanova University, PA	M,W
Virginia Commonwealth University, VA	M,W
Virginia Intermont College, VA	M,W
Virginia Military Institute, VA	M
Virginia Polytechnic Institute and State University, VA	M,W
Virginia Union University, VA	M,W
Wake Forest University, NC	M,W
Waldorf College, IA	M,W
Warner Pacific College, OR	M,W
Washington State University, WA	M,W
Wayland Baptist University, TX	M,W
Wayne State College, NE	M,W
Wayne State University, MI	M,W
Webber International University, FL	M,W
Western Carolina University, NC	M,W
Western Illinois University, IL	M,W
Western Kentucky University, KY	M,W
Western State College of Colorado, CO	M,W
Western Washington University, WA	M,W
Westmont College, CA	M,W
West Texas A&M University, TX	M,W
West Virginia University, WV	M,W
West Virginia Wesleyan College, WV	M,W
Wheeling Jesuit University, WV	M,W
Wichita State University, KS	M,W
William Carey College, MS	M,W
William Jewell College, MO	M,W
William Penn University, IA	M,W
Williams Baptist College, AR	M,W
William Woods University, MO	W
Wingate University, NC	M,W
Winona State University, MN	M,W
Winston-Salem State University, NC	M,W
Winthrop University, SC	M,W
Wofford College, SC	M,W
Xavier University, OH	M,W
Xavier University of Louisiana, LA	M,W
Youngstown State University, OH	M,W

Bowling

Arkansas State University, AR	W
Grambling State University, LA	W
Hampton University, VA	W
Lindenwood University, MO	M,W
Lindsey Wilson College, KY	M,W
McKendree College, IL	M,W
Newman University, KS	M,W
Pikeville College, KY	M,W
Robert Morris College, IL	M
Sacred Heart University, CT	W
Southern University and Agricultural and Mechanical College, LA	W
Texas Southern University, TX	W
West Texas A&M University, TX	M,W
Winston-Salem State University, NC	M,W

Cheerleading

Anderson University, SC	W
Austin Peay State University, TN	M,W
Avila University, MO	W
Benedictine College, KS	M,W
Bethany College, KS	M,W
Brevard College, NC	M,W
Brewton-Parker College, GA	M,W
California State University, Fresno, CA	M,W
Campbellsville University, KY	M,W
Campbell University, NC	W
Clark Atlanta University, GA	W
Culver-Stockton College, MO	M,W
Drake University, IA	M,W
East Texas Baptist University, TX	M,W
Emporia State University, KS	M,W
Freed-Hardeman University, TN	W
Georgetown College, KY	W
Grace College, IN	M,W
Hannibal-LaGrange College, MO	M,W
Harris-Stowe State University, MO	M,W
Hawai'i Pacific University, HI	M,W
Hofstra University, NY	M,W
Houston Baptist University, TX	M,W
Kent State University, OH	M,W
King College, TN	M,W
Limestone College, SC	M,W
Lindenwood University, MO	M,W
Lindsey Wilson College, KY	M,W
Manhattan College, NY	M,W
Marian College, IN	M,W
McKendree College, IL	M,W
Mercer University, GA	M,W
Methodist College, NC	M,W
Metropolitan State College of Denver, CO	M,W
MidAmerica Nazarene University, KS	M,W
Middle Tennessee State University, TN	M,W
Midwestern State University, TX	M,W
Montana State University, MT	M,W
Newberry College, SC	W
Newman University, KS	M,W
North Greenville College, SC	M,W
Northwestern Oklahoma State University, OK	M,W
Northwood University, MI	M,W
Nyack College, NY	M,W
Olivet Nazarene University, IL	M,W
Pittsburg State University, KS	M,W
Southeastern Louisiana University, LA	M,W
Southeast Missouri State University, MO	M,W
Southern Illinois University Carbondale, IL	M,W
Tabor College, KS	W
Tennessee Technological University, TN	M,W
Texas A&M University–Commerce, TX	M,W
Tiffin University, OH	M,W
Tusculum College, TN	W
Union College, KY	M,W
Union University, TN	W
The University of Alabama, AL	M,W
The University of Alabama in Huntsville, AL	M,W
University of Delaware, DE	M,W
University of Hawaii at Manoa, HI	W
University of Louisville, KY	M,W
University of Maryland, College Park, MD	W
University of Memphis, TN	M,W
University of Nevada, Las Vegas, NV	M,W
University of Oregon, OR	M,W
University of Saint Francis, IN	M,W
University of Science and Arts of Oklahoma, OK	M,W
University of the Cumberlands, KY	M,W
University of Utah, UT	M,W
University of West Georgia, GA	M,W
University of Wyoming, WY	M,W
Virginia Intermont College, VA	W
Wayland Baptist University, TX	M,W
Webber International University, FL	M,W
West Virginia University, WV	M,W
William Jewell College, MO	M,W
William Penn University, IA	M,W

Crew

Boston University, MA	M,W
California State University, Sacramento, CA	M,W
Clemson University, SC	W
Creighton University, NE	W
Drexel University, PA	M,W
Duke University, NC	W
Duquesne University, PA	W
Eastern Michigan University, MI	W
Florida Institute of Technology, FL	M,W
Fordham University, NY	W
Indiana University Bloomington, IN	W
Jacksonville University, FL	M,W
Kansas State University, KS	W
Lehigh University, PA	W
Lesley University, MA	M,W
Mercyhurst College, PA	M,W
Michigan State University, MI	W
Murray State University, KY	M,W
Northeastern University, MA	M,W
Nova Southeastern University, FL	W
Robert Morris University, PA	W
Sacred Heart University, CT	W
Saint Joseph's University, PA	M,W
Saint Leo University, FL	M,W
Stanford University, CA	W
State University of New York at Buffalo, NY	W
Syracuse University, NY	M,W
Temple University, PA	M,W
University of California, Berkeley, CA	M,W
University of California, Irvine, CA	M,W
University of Delaware, DE	W
The University of Iowa, IA	W
University of Kansas, KS	W
University of Louisville, KY	W
University of Massachusetts Amherst, MA	W
University of Miami, FL	W
The University of North Carolina at Chapel Hill, NC	W
University of Southern California, CA	W
The University of Tampa, FL	W
The University of Texas at Austin, TX	W
University of Tulsa, OK	W
University of Virginia, VA	W

Athletic Grants for Undergraduates
Crew

Villanova University, PA	W	
Washington State University, WA	W	
Western Washington University, WA	M,W	
West Virginia University, WV	W	

Cross-country running

Abilene Christian University, TX	M,W
Adelphi University, NY	M,W
Alabama Agricultural and Mechanical University, AL	M,W
Alderson-Broaddus College, WV	M,W
Alliant International University, CA	M,W
American University, DC	M,W
Anderson University, SC	M,W
Appalachian State University, NC	M,W
Arizona State University, AZ	M,W
Arkansas State University, AR	M,W
Arkansas Tech University, AR	W
Asbury College, KY	M,W
Ashford University, IA	M,W
Ashland University, OH	M,W
Auburn University, AL	M,W
Augustana College, SD	M,W
Augusta State University, GA	M,W
Austin Peay State University, TN	M,W
Azusa Pacific University, CA	M,W
Ball State University, IN	M,W
Barton College, NC	M,W
Baylor University, TX	M,W
Belhaven College, MS	M,W
Belmont Abbey College, NC	M,W
Belmont University, TN	M,W
Benedictine College, KS	M,W
Bentley College, MA	M,W
Berry College, GA	M,W
Bethany College, KS	M,W
Bethel College, KS	M,W
Biola University, CA	M,W
Black Hills State University, SD	M,W
Bloomfield College, NJ	M
Bloomsburg University of Pennsylvania, PA	M,W
Bluefield State College, WV	M,W
Boston College, MA	W
Boston University, MA	M,W
Bowling Green State University, OH	M,W
Bradley University, IL	M,W
Brenau University, GA	W
Brevard College, NC	M,W
Brigham Young University–Hawaii, HI	M,W
Bryan College, TN	M,W
Butler University, IN	M,W
California Polytechnic State University, San Luis Obispo, CA	M,W
California State University, Chico, CA	M,W
California State University, Fresno, CA	M,W
California State University, Fullerton, CA	M,W
California State University, Sacramento, CA	M,W
Campbellsville University, KY	M,W
Campbell University, NC	M,W
Carson-Newman College, TN	M,W
Cascade College, OR	M,W
Catawba College, NC	M,W
Cedarville University, OH	M,W
Centenary College of Louisiana, LA	M,W
Central Connecticut State University, CT	M,W
Central Michigan University, MI	M,W
Central Missouri State University, MO	M,W
Central Washington University, WA	M,W
Chaminade University of Honolulu, HI	M,W
The Citadel, The Military College of South Carolina, SC	M,W
Clark Atlanta University, GA	M,W
Clemson University, SC	M,W
Cleveland State University, OH	W
Coastal Carolina University, SC	M,W
College of Charleston, SC	M,W
College of Saint Mary, NE	W
The College of Saint Rose, NY	M,W
College of the Southwest, NM	M,W
The College of William and Mary, VA	M,W
Colorado School of Mines, CO	M,W
Colorado State University, CO	M,W
Columbus State University, GA	M,W
Concordia University, CA	M,W
Concordia University, MI	M,W
Concordia University, NE	M,W
Concordia University, St. Paul, MN	M,W
Converse College, SC	W
Coppin State University, MD	M,W
Corban College, OR	M,W
Cornerstone University, MI	M,W
Creighton University, NE	M,W
Daemen College, NY	M,W
Dakota State University, SD	M,W
Dallas Baptist University, TX	W
Davidson College, NC	M,W
Davis & Elkins College, WV	M,W
DePaul University, IL	M,W
Dickinson State University, ND	M,W
Doane College, NE	M,W
Dordt College, IA	M,W
Drake University, IA	M,W
Duquesne University, PA	M,W
East Carolina University, NC	M,W
East Central University, OK	M,W
Eastern Illinois University, IL	M,W
Eastern Michigan University, MI	M,W
Eastern Washington University, WA	M,W
East Stroudsburg University of Pennsylvania, PA	M,W
East Tennessee State University, TN	M,W
Eckerd College, FL	W
Edinboro University of Pennsylvania, PA	M,W
Elon University, NC	M,W
Emporia State University, KS	M,W
Erskine College, SC	M,W
Evangel University, MO	M,W
The Evergreen State College, WA	M,W
Felician College, NJ	M,W
Ferris State University, MI	M,W
Flagler College, FL	M,W
Florida Agricultural and Mechanical University, FL	M,W
Florida Atlantic University, FL	M,W
Florida Institute of Technology, FL	M,W
Florida Southern College, FL	M,W
Florida State University, FL	M,W
Fordham University, NY	M,W
Fort Hays State University, KS	M,W
Fort Lewis College, CO	M,W
Francis Marion University, SC	M,W
Fresno Pacific University, CA	M,W
Friends University, KS	M,W
Furman University, SC	M,W
Gannon University, PA	M,W
Geneva College, PA	M,W
George Mason University, VA	M,W
Georgetown College, KY	M,W
Georgetown University, DC	M,W
Georgia College & State University, GA	
Georgia Institute of Technology, GA	M,W
Georgia Southern University, GA	W
Glenville State College, WV	
Goshen College, IN	M,W
Grace College, IN	M,W
Graceland University, IA	M,W
Grand Valley State University, MI	M,W
Grand View College, IA	M,W
Hampton University, VA	M,W
Hannibal-LaGrange College, MO	M,W
Harding University, AR	M,W
Hawai'i Pacific University, HI	M,W
Hofstra University, NY	M,W
Holy Names University, CA	M,W
Houghton College, NY	M,W
Howard University, DC	M,W
Humboldt State University, CA	M,W
Huntington University, IN	M,W
Idaho State University, ID	M,W
Illinois State University, IL	M,W
Indiana State University, IN	M,W
Indiana University Bloomington, IN	M,W
Indiana University of Pennsylvania, PA	M,W
Indiana University–Purdue University Fort Wayne, IN	M,W
Indiana University–Purdue University Indianapolis, IN	M,W
Inter American University of Puerto Rico, Guayama Campus, PR	M,W
Iona College, NY	M,W
Jacksonville State University, AL	M,W
Jacksonville University, FL	W
James Madison University, VA	M,W
Jamestown College, ND	M,W
Kansas State University, KS	M,W
Kennesaw State University, GA	M,W
Kent State University, OH	M,W
Kentucky State University, KY	M,W
King College, TN	M,W
Lake Superior State University, MI	M,W
Lamar University, TX	M,W
Lee University, TN	M,W
Lehigh University, PA	M,W
Le Moyne College, NY	M,W
LeMoyne-Owen College, TN	M
Lewis-Clark State College, ID	M,W
Limestone College, SC	M,W
Lincoln University, MO	M,W
Lindenwood University, MO	M,W

Athletic Grants for Undergraduates
Cross-country running

College	
Lindsey Wilson College, KY	M,W
Lipscomb University, TN	M,W
Lock Haven University of Pennsylvania, PA	M,W
Long Island University, Brooklyn Campus, NY	M,W
Louisiana State University and Agricultural and Mechanical College, LA	M,W
Louisiana Tech University, LA	M,W
Loyola University Chicago, IL	M,W
Lyon College, AR	M,W
Malone College, OH	M,W
Manhattan College, NY	M,W
Mansfield University of Pennsylvania, PA	M,W
Marian College, IN	M,W
Marist College, NY	M,W
Marquette University, WI	M,W
Marshall University, WV	M,W
The Master's College and Seminary, CA	M,W
McKendree College, IL	M,W
Mercer University, GA	M,W
Mercyhurst College, PA	M,W
Merrimack College, MA	W
Mesa State College, CO	W
Miami University, OH	M,W
Michigan State University, MI	M,W
MidAmerica Nazarene University, KS	M,W
Middle Tennessee State University, TN	M,W
Midland Lutheran College, NE	M,W
Millersville University of Pennsylvania, PA	M,W
Milligan College, TN	M,W
Minnesota State University Mankato, MN	M,W
Mississippi State University, MS	M,W
Missouri State University, MO	M,W
Molloy College, NY	M,W
Monmouth University, NJ	M,W
Montana State University, MT	M,W
Montana State University–Billings, MT	M,W
Montreat College, NC	M,W
Morehead State University, KY	M,W
Morningside College, IA	M,W
Mount Marty College, SD	M,W
Mount Olive College, NC	M,W
Mount St. Mary's University, MD	M,W
Murray State University, KY	M,W
Newberry College, SC	M,W
Newman University, KS	M,W
New Mexico State University, NM	M,W
New York Institute of Technology, NY	M,W
Niagara University, NY	M,W
Nicholls State University, LA	M,W
North Carolina Agricultural and Technical State University, NC	M,W
North Carolina State University, NC	M,W
Northeastern University, MA	M,W
Northern Arizona University, AZ	M,W
Northern State University, SD	M,W
North Greenville College, SC	M,W
Northwestern Oklahoma State University, OK	M,W
Northwestern State University of Louisiana, LA	M,W
Northwestern University, IL	W
Northwest Nazarene University, ID	M,W
Northwest University, WA	M,W
Northwood University, MI	M,W
Northwood University, Texas Campus, TX	M,W
Nova Southeastern University, FL	M,W
Nyack College, NY	M,W
The Ohio State University, OH	M,W
Ohio University, OH	M,W
Oklahoma Baptist University, OK	M,W
Oklahoma Panhandle State University, OK	M,W
Oklahoma State University, OK	M,W
Olivet Nazarene University, IL	M,W
Oral Roberts University, OK	M,W
Ouachita Baptist University, AR	W
The Pennsylvania State University University Park Campus, PA	M,W
Pepperdine University, CA	M,W
Pikeville College, KY	M,W
Pittsburg State University, KS	M,W
Portland State University, OR	M,W
Purdue University, IN	M,W
Quinnipiac University, CT	M,W
Radford University, VA	M,W
Rice University, TX	M,W
Rider University, NJ	M,W
Robert Morris College, IL	M,W
Robert Morris University, PA	M,W
Roberts Wesleyan College, NY	M,W
Sacred Heart University, CT	M,W
St. Andrews Presbyterian College, NC	M,W
St. Bonaventure University, NY	M,W
St. Cloud State University, MN	M
St. Francis College, NY	M,W
Saint Francis University, PA	M,W
St. John's University, NY	W
Saint Joseph's College, IN	M,W
Saint Joseph's University, PA	M,W
Saint Leo University, FL	M,W
Saint Louis University, MO	M,W
Saint Martin's University, WA	M,W
Saint Mary's College of California, CA	M,W
St. Thomas University, FL	M,W
Saint Vincent College, PA	M,W
Saint Xavier University, IL	W
Salem International University, WV	M,W
Samford University, AL	M,W
San Diego Christian College, CA	M,W
San Diego State University, CA	W
San Francisco State University, CA	M,W
San Jose State University, CA	M,W
Santa Clara University, CA	M,W
Seattle Pacific University, WA	M,W
Seattle University, WA	M,W
Seton Hill University, PA	M,W
Shippensburg University of Pennsylvania, PA	M,W
Shorter College, GA	M,W
Slippery Rock University of Pennsylvania, PA	M,W
Sonoma State University, CA	W
South Carolina State University, SC	M,W
South Dakota School of Mines and Technology, SD	M,W
South Dakota State University, SD	M,W
Southeastern Louisiana University, LA	M,W
Southeastern Oklahoma State University, OK	W
Southeast Missouri State University, MO	M,W
Southern Arkansas University–Magnolia, AR	W
Southern Illinois University Carbondale, IL	M,W
Southern Illinois University Edwardsville, IL	M,W
Southern New Hampshire University, NH	M,W
Southern Oregon University, OR	M,W
Southern University and Agricultural and Mechanical College, LA	M
Southwest Baptist University, MO	M,W
Spring Arbor University, MI	M,W
Spring Hill College, AL	M,W
Stanford University, CA	M,W
State University of New York at Binghamton, NY	M,W
State University of New York at Buffalo, NY	M,W
Stephen F. Austin State University, TX	M,W
Stetson University, FL	M,W
Stonehill College, MA	M,W
Stony Brook University, State University of New York, NY	M,W
Syracuse University, NY	M,W
Tabor College, KS	M,W
Taylor University, IN	M,W
Tennessee State University, TN	M,W
Tennessee Technological University, TN	M,W
Texas A&M University, TX	M,W
Texas A&M University–Commerce, TX	M,W
Texas Christian University, TX	M,W
Texas Southern University, TX	M,W
Texas State University-San Marcos, TX	M,W
Texas Tech University, TX	M,W
Tiffin University, OH	M,W
Towson University, MD	M,W
Truman State University, MO	M,W
Tusculum College, TN	M,W
Union University, TN	W
Unity College, ME	M,W
University at Albany, State University of New York, NY	M,W
The University of Akron, OH	M,W
The University of Alabama, AL	M,W
The University of Alabama at Birmingham, AL	W
The University of Alabama in Huntsville, AL	M,W
University of Alaska Fairbanks, AK	M,W
University of Arkansas, AR	M,W

Athletic Grants for Undergraduates
Cross-country running

Institution	
University of California, Berkeley, CA	M,W
University of California, Irvine, CA	M,W
University of California, Los Angeles, CA	M,W
University of California, Riverside, CA	M,W
University of California, Santa Barbara, CA	M,W
University of Central Oklahoma, OK	M,W
University of Cincinnati, OH	M,W
University of Colorado at Boulder, CO	M,W
University of Colorado at Colorado Springs, CO	M,W
University of Connecticut, CT	M,W
University of Dayton, OH	M,W
University of Evansville, IN	M,W
The University of Findlay, OH	M,W
University of Florida, FL	M,W
University of Georgia, GA	M,W
University of Hartford, CT	M,W
University of Hawaii at Hilo, HI	M,W
University of Hawaii at Manoa, HI	W
University of Idaho, ID	M,W
University of Illinois at Urbana–Champaign, IL	M,W
The University of Iowa, IA	M,W
University of Kansas, KS	M,W
University of Kentucky, KY	M,W
University of Louisiana at Lafayette, LA	M,W
University of Louisville, KY	M,W
University of Maine, ME	M,W
University of Mary, ND	M,W
University of Maryland, Baltimore County, MD	M,W
University of Maryland, College Park, MD	M,W
University of Massachusetts Amherst, MA	M,W
University of Massachusetts Lowell, MA	M,W
University of Memphis, TN	M,W
University of Miami, FL	M,W
University of Michigan, MI	M,W
University of Minnesota, Duluth, MN	M,W
University of Minnesota, Twin Cities Campus, MN	M,W
University of Missouri–Columbia, MO	M,W
University of Missouri–Kansas City, MO	M,W
University of Nebraska at Kearney, NE	M,W
University of Nebraska at Omaha, NE	W
University of Nebraska–Lincoln, NE	M,W
University of Nevada, Las Vegas, NV	W
University of Nevada, Reno, NV	W
University of New Hampshire, NH	M,W
University of New Haven, CT	M,W
University of New Orleans, LA	M,W
University of North Alabama, AL	M,W
The University of North Carolina at Asheville, NC	M,W
The University of North Carolina at Chapel Hill, NC	M,W
The University of North Carolina at Greensboro, NC	M,W
The University of North Carolina at Pembroke, NC	M,W
The University of North Carolina Wilmington, NC	M,W
University of Northern Colorado, CO	W
University of Northern Iowa, IA	M,W
University of North Florida, FL	M,W
University of Oklahoma, OK	M,W
University of Oregon, OR	M,W
University of Pittsburgh, PA	M,W
University of Portland, OR	M,W
University of Puerto Rico, Mayagüez Campus, PR	M,W
University of Rhode Island, RI	M,W
University of Richmond, VA	W
University of St. Francis, IL	W
University of Saint Francis, IN	M,W
University of San Diego, CA	M,W
University of South Carolina, SC	W
University of South Carolina Upstate, SC	M,W
The University of South Dakota, SD	M,W
University of Southern California, CA	M,W
University of Southern Indiana, IN	M,W
University of Southern Mississippi, MS	M,W
University of South Florida, FL	M,W
The University of Tampa, FL	M,W
The University of Tennessee at Martin, TN	M,W
The University of Texas at Arlington, TX	M,W
The University of Texas at Austin, TX	M,W
The University of Texas at El Paso, TX	M,W
The University of Texas at San Antonio, TX	M,W
The University of Texas–Pan American, TX	M,W
University of the Cumberlands, KY	M,W
University of the Pacific, CA	W
The University of Toledo, OH	M,W
University of Tulsa, OK	M,W
University of Utah, UT	W
University of Vermont, VT	M,W
University of Virginia, VA	M,W
The University of West Alabama, AL	M,W
University of West Georgia, GA	M,W
University of Wisconsin–Green Bay, WI	M,W
University of Wisconsin–Madison, WI	M,W
University of Wisconsin–Parkside, WI	M,W
University of Wyoming, WY	M,W
Utah State University, UT	M,W
Valdosta State University, GA	M,W
Valparaiso University, IN	M,W
Vanderbilt University, TN	M,W
Vanguard University of Southern California, CA	M,W
Villanova University, PA	M,W
Virginia Commonwealth University, VA	M,W
Virginia Intermont College, VA	M,W
Virginia Military Institute, VA	M,W
Virginia Polytechnic Institute and State University, VA	M,W
Virginia Union University, VA	M,W
Wake Forest University, NC	M,W
Warner Pacific College, OR	M,W
Washington State University, WA	M,W
Wayland Baptist University, TX	M,W
Wayne State College, NE	M,W
Wayne State University, MI	M,W
Webber International University, FL	M,W
Western Carolina University, NC	M,W
Western Illinois University, IL	M,W
Western Kentucky University, KY	M,W
Western State College of Colorado, CO	M,W
Western Washington University, WA	M,W
Westmont College, CA	M,W
West Texas A&M University, TX	M,W
West Virginia University, WV	W
West Virginia Wesleyan College, WV	M,W
Wheeling Jesuit University, WV	M,W
Wichita State University, KS	M,W
William Jewell College, MO	M,W
William Penn University, IA	M,W
William Woods University, MO	M,W
Wingate University, NC	M
Winona State University, MN	W
Winston-Salem State University, NC	M,W
Winthrop University, SC	M,W
Wofford College, SC	M,W
Xavier University, OH	M,W
Youngstown State University, OH	M,W

Equestrian sports

Institution	
Auburn University, AL	W
Baylor University, TX	W
California State University, Fresno, CA	W
Midway College, KY	W
Molloy College, NY	M,W
Murray State University, KY	M,W
Oklahoma State University, OK	W
Sacred Heart University, CT	W
St. Andrews Presbyterian College, NC	M,W
Seton Hill University, PA	M,W
Texas A&M University, TX	W
University of Georgia, GA	M,W
University of South Carolina, SC	W
Virginia Intermont College, VA	M,W
West Texas A&M University, TX	W

Fencing

Institution	
California State University, Fullerton, CA	M,W
Cleveland State University, OH	M,W
Northwestern University, IL	W
The Ohio State University, OH	M,W
The Pennsylvania State University University Park Campus, PA	M,W
Sacred Heart University, CT	W
St. John's University, NY	M,W
Stanford University, CA	M,W
Temple University, PA	W
Wayne State University, MI	M,W

Field hockey

Institution	
American International College, MA	W
American University, DC	W
Appalachian State University, NC	W

Athletic Grants for Undergraduates
Football

College	
Ball State University, IN	W
Bentley College, MA	W
Bloomsburg University of Pennsylvania, PA	W
Boston College, MA	W
Boston University, MA	W
Catawba College, NC	W
Central Michigan University, MI	W
Colgate University, NY	W
The College of William and Mary, VA	W
Davidson College, NC	W
Drexel University, PA	W
Duke University, NC	W
East Stroudsburg University of Pennsylvania, PA	W
Fairfield University, CT	W
Franklin Pierce College, NH	W
Hofstra University, NY	W
Houghton College, NY	W
Indiana University of Pennsylvania, PA	W
James Madison University, VA	W
Kent State University, OH	W
Lehigh University, PA	W
Lindenwood University, MO	W
Lock Haven University of Pennsylvania, PA	W
Mansfield University of Pennsylvania, PA	W
Mercyhurst College, PA	W
Merrimack College, MA	W
Miami University, OH	W
Michigan State University, MI	W
Millersville University of Pennsylvania, PA	W
Missouri State University, MO	W
Monmouth University, NJ	W
Northeastern University, MA	W
Northwestern University, IL	W
The Ohio State University, OH	W
Ohio University, OH	W
The Pennsylvania State University University Park Campus, PA	W
Philadelphia University, PA	W
Quinnipiac University, CT	W
Radford University, VA	W
Rider University, NJ	W
Robert Morris University, PA	W
Sacred Heart University, CT	W
Saint Francis University, PA	W
Saint Joseph's University, PA	W
Saint Leo University, FL	W
Saint Louis University, MO	W
Saint Vincent College, PA	W
Seton Hill University, PA	W
Shippensburg University of Pennsylvania, PA	W
Slippery Rock University of Pennsylvania, PA	W
Stanford University, CA	W
Stonehill College, MA	W
Syracuse University, NY	W
Temple University, PA	W
Towson University, MD	W
University at Albany, State University of New York, NY	W
University of California, Berkeley, CA	W
University of Connecticut, CT	W
University of Delaware, DE	W
The University of Iowa, IA	W
University of Louisville, KY	W
University of Maine, ME	W
University of Maryland, Baltimore County, MD	W
University of Maryland, College Park, MD	W
University of Massachusetts Amherst, MA	W
University of Massachusetts Lowell, MA	W
University of Michigan, MI	W
University of New Hampshire, NH	W
The University of North Carolina at Chapel Hill, NC	W
University of Rhode Island, RI	W
University of Richmond, VA	W
University of the Pacific, CA	W
University of Vermont, VT	W
University of Virginia, VA	W
Villanova University, PA	W
Virginia Commonwealth University, VA	W
Wake Forest University, NC	W

Football

College	
Abilene Christian University, TX	M
Alabama Agricultural and Mechanical University, AL	M
American International College, MA	M
Appalachian State University, NC	M
Arizona State University, AZ	M
Arkansas State University, AR	M
Arkansas Tech University, AR	M
Ashland University, OH	M
Auburn University, AL	M
Augustana College, SD	M
Avila University, MO	M
Azusa Pacific University, CA	M
Ball State University, IN	M
Baylor University, TX	M
Belhaven College, MS	M
Bemidji State University, MN	M
Benedictine College, KS	M
Bethany College, KS	M
Bethel College, KS	M
Black Hills State University, SD	M
Blessing-Rieman College of Nursing, IL	M
Bloomsburg University of Pennsylvania, PA	M
Boston College, MA	M
Bowling Green State University, OH	M
California Polytechnic State University, San Luis Obispo, CA	M
California State University, Fresno, CA	M
California State University, Sacramento, CA	M
Campbellsville University, KY	M
Carroll College, MT	M
Carson-Newman College, TN	M
Catawba College, NC	M
Central Michigan University, MI	M
Central Missouri State University, MO	M
Central Washington University, WA	M
The Citadel, The Military College of South Carolina, SC	M
Clark Atlanta University, GA	M
Clemson University, SC	M
Coastal Carolina University, SC	M
The College of William and Mary, VA	M
Colorado School of Mines, CO	M
Colorado State University, CO	M
Concordia University, NE	M
Concordia University, St. Paul, MN	M
Culver-Stockton College, MO	M
Dakota State University, SD	M
Davidson College, NC	M
Dickinson State University, ND	M
Doane College, NE	M
Duke University, NC	M
East Carolina University, NC	M
East Central University, OK	M
Eastern Illinois University, IL	M
Eastern Michigan University, MI	M
Eastern Washington University, WA	M
East Stroudsburg University of Pennsylvania, PA	M
Edinboro University of Pennsylvania, PA	M
Elon University, NC	M
Emporia State University, KS	M
Evangel University, MO	M
Fairmont State University, WV	M
Ferris State University, MI	M
Florida Agricultural and Mechanical University, FL	M
Florida Atlantic University, FL	M
Florida State University, FL	M
Fort Hays State University, KS	M
Fort Lewis College, CO	M
Friends University, KS	M
Furman University, SC	M
Geneva College, PA	M
Georgetown College, KY	M
Georgetown University, DC	M
Georgia Institute of Technology, GA	M
Georgia Southern University, GA	M
Glenville State College, WV	M
Graceland University, IA	M
Grambling State University, LA	M
Grand Valley State University, MI	M
Hampton University, VA	M
Harding University, AR	M
Hillsdale College, MI	M
Hofstra University, NY	M
Howard University, DC	M
Humboldt State University, CA	M
Idaho State University, ID	M
Illinois State University, IL	M
Indiana State University, IN	M
Indiana University Bloomington, IN	M
Indiana University of Pennsylvania, PA	M
Iowa Wesleyan College, IA	M
Jacksonville State University, AL	M
James Madison University, VA	M
Jamestown College, ND	M

Athletic Grants for Undergraduates
Football

Kansas State University, KS	M
Kent State University, OH	M
Kentucky State University, KY	M
Kentucky Wesleyan College, KY	M
Lamar University, TX	M
Lehigh University, PA	M
Lincoln University, MO	M
Lindenwood University, MO	M
Lock Haven University of Pennsylvania, PA	M
Louisiana State University and Agricultural and Mechanical College, LA	M
Louisiana Tech University, LA	M
Malone College, OH	M
Mansfield University of Pennsylvania, PA	M
Marshall University, WV	M
Mayville State University, ND	M
McKendree College, IL	M
Mercyhurst College, PA	M
Mesa State College, CO	M
Miami University, OH	M
Michigan State University, MI	M
Michigan Technological University, MI	M
MidAmerica Nazarene University, KS	M
Middle Tennessee State University, TN	M
Midland Lutheran College, NE	M
Midwestern State University, TX	M
Millersville University of Pennsylvania, PA	M
Minnesota State University Mankato, MN	
Mississippi State University, MS	M
Missouri State University, MO	M
Montana State University, MT	M
Montana Tech of The University of Montana, MT	M
Morningside College, IA	M
Murray State University, KY	M
Newberry College, SC	M
New Mexico State University, NM	M
Nicholls State University, LA	M
North Carolina Agricultural and Technical State University, NC	M
North Carolina State University, NC	M
Northeastern University, MA	M
Northern Arizona University, AZ	M
Northern Illinois University, IL	M
Northern State University, SD	M
North Greenville College, SC	M
Northwestern Oklahoma State University, OK	M
Northwestern State University of Louisiana, LA	M
Northwestern University, IL	M
Northwood University, MI	M
The Ohio State University, OH	M
Ohio University, OH	M
Oklahoma Panhandle State University, OK	M
Oklahoma State University, OK	M
Olivet Nazarene University, IL	M
Ouachita Baptist University, AR	M
The Pennsylvania State University University Park Campus, PA	M
Pikeville College, KY	M
Pittsburg State University, KS	M
Portland State University, OR	M
Purdue University, IN	M
Quincy University, IL	M
Rice University, TX	M
Sacred Heart University, CT	M
St. Cloud State University, MN	M
Saint Joseph's College, IN	M
Saint Xavier University, IL	M
Samford University, AL	M
San Diego State University, CA	M
San Jose State University, CA	M
Seton Hill University, PA	M
Shepherd University, WV	M
Shippensburg University of Pennsylvania, PA	M
Slippery Rock University of Pennsylvania, PA	M
South Carolina State University, SC	M
South Dakota School of Mines and Technology, SD	M
South Dakota State University, SD	M
Southeastern Louisiana University, LA	M
Southeastern Oklahoma State University, OK	M
Southeast Missouri State University, MO	M
Southern Arkansas University–Magnolia, AR	M
Southern Illinois University Carbondale, IL	
Southern Oregon University, OR	M
Southern University and Agricultural and Mechanical College, LA	M
Southwest Baptist University, MO	M
Southwest Minnesota State University, MN	M
Stanford University, CA	M
State University of New York at Buffalo, NY	M
Stephen F. Austin State University, TX	M
Stonehill College, MA	M
Stony Brook University, State University of New York, NY	M
Syracuse University, NY	M
Tabor College, KS	M
Taylor University, IN	M
Temple University, PA	M
Tennessee State University, TN	M
Tennessee Technological University, TN	
Texas A&M University, TX	M
Texas A&M University–Commerce, TX	M
Texas Christian University, TX	M
Texas Southern University, TX	M
Texas State University-San Marcos, TX	M
Texas Tech University, TX	M
Tiffin University, OH	M
Towson University, MD	M
Trinity International University, IL	M
Truman State University, MO	M
Tusculum College, TN	M
Tuskegee University, AL	M
Union College, KY	M
University at Albany, State University of New York, NY	
The University of Akron, OH	M
The University of Alabama, AL	M
The University of Alabama at Birmingham, AL	M
University of Arkansas, AR	M
University of Arkansas at Monticello, AR	M
University of Arkansas at Pine Bluff, AR	M
University of California, Berkeley, CA	M
University of California, Los Angeles, CA	M
University of Central Oklahoma, OK	M
University of Cincinnati, OH	M
University of Colorado at Boulder, CO	M
University of Connecticut, CT	M
University of Delaware, DE	M
The University of Findlay, OH	M
University of Florida, FL	M
University of Georgia, GA	M
University of Hawaii at Manoa, HI	M
University of Idaho, ID	M
University of Illinois at Urbana–Champaign, IL	M
The University of Iowa, IA	M
University of Kansas, KS	M
University of Kentucky, KY	M
University of Louisiana at Lafayette, LA	M
University of Louisville, KY	M
University of Maine, ME	M
University of Mary, ND	
University of Maryland, College Park, MD	M
University of Massachusetts Amherst, MA	
University of Memphis, TN	M
University of Miami, FL	M
University of Michigan, MI	M
University of Minnesota, Duluth, MN	M
University of Minnesota, Twin Cities Campus, MN	M
University of Missouri–Columbia, MO	M
University of Nebraska at Kearney, NE	M
University of Nebraska at Omaha, NE	M
University of Nebraska–Lincoln, NE	M
University of Nevada, Las Vegas, NV	M
University of Nevada, Reno, NV	
University of New Hampshire, NH	
University of New Haven, CT	
University of North Alabama, AL	M
The University of North Carolina at Chapel Hill, NC	M
University of North Dakota, ND	M
University of Northern Colorado, CO	
University of Northern Iowa, IA	M
University of Oklahoma, OK	M
University of Oregon, OR	M
University of Pittsburgh, PA	
University of Rhode Island, RI	

Athletic Grants for Undergraduates
Golf

Institution	
University of Richmond, VA	M
University of St. Francis, IL	M
University of Saint Francis, IN	M
University of South Carolina, SC	M
The University of South Dakota, SD	M
University of Southern California, CA	M
University of Southern Mississippi, MS	M
University of South Florida, FL	M
The University of Tennessee at Martin, TN	M
The University of Texas at Austin, TX	M
The University of Texas at El Paso, TX	M
University of the Cumberlands, KY	M
The University of Toledo, OH	M
University of Tulsa, OK	M
University of Utah, UT	M
University of Virginia, VA	M
The University of West Alabama, AL	M
University of West Georgia, GA	M
University of Wisconsin–Madison, WI	M
University of Wyoming, WY	M
Urbana University, OH	M
Utah State University, UT	M
Valdosta State University, GA	M
Valley City State University, ND	M
Vanderbilt University, TN	M
Villanova University, PA	M
Virginia Military Institute, VA	M
Virginia Polytechnic Institute and State University, VA	M
Virginia Union University, VA	M
Wake Forest University, NC	M
Waldorf College, IA	M
Washington State University, WA	M
Wayne State College, NE	M
Wayne State University, MI	M
Webber International University, FL	M
Western Carolina University, NC	M
Western Illinois University, IL	M
Western Kentucky University, KY	M
Western State College of Colorado, CO	M
Western Washington University, WA	M
Westminster College, PA	M
West Texas A&M University, TX	M
West Virginia University, WV	M
West Virginia Wesleyan College, WV	M
William Jewell College, MO	M
William Penn University, IA	M
Wingate University, NC	M
Winona State University, MN	M
Winston-Salem State University, NC	M
Wofford College, SC	M
Youngstown State University, OH	M

Golf

Institution	
Abilene Christian University, TX	M
Adelphi University, NY	M
Alabama Agricultural and Mechanical University, AL	M
Albertson College of Idaho, ID	M,W
Alderson-Broaddus College, WV	M,W
American University, DC	M
Anderson University, SC	M,W
Appalachian State University, NC	M,W
Arizona State University, AZ	M,W
Arkansas State University, AR	M,W
Arkansas Tech University, AR	M
Armstrong Atlantic State University, GA	M
Ashford University, IA	M,W
Ashland University, OH	M,W
Auburn University, AL	M,W
Austin Peay State University, TN	M,W
Avila University, MO	W
Azusa Pacific University, CA	M
Ball State University, IN	M
Barton College, NC	M
Baylor University, TX	M,W
Belhaven College, MS	M,W
Belmont Abbey College, NC	M
Belmont University, TN	M,W
Benedictine College, KS	M,W
Berry College, GA	M,W
Bethany College, KS	M
Bethel College, KS	M,W
Bluefield State College, WV	M
Bowling Green State University, OH	M,W
Bradley University, IL	M,W
Brevard College, NC	M
Butler University, IN	M,W
California Polytechnic State University, San Luis Obispo, CA	M
California State University, Bakersfield, CA	M
California State University, Chico, CA	M,W
California State University, Fresno, CA	M
California State University, Sacramento, CA	M
California State University, San Marcos, CA	M
Campbellsville University, KY	M,W
Campbell University, NC	M,W
Carroll College, MT	W
Carson-Newman College, TN	M
Catawba College, NC	M
Cedarville University, OH	M
Centenary College of Louisiana, LA	M,W
Central Connecticut State University, CT	M,W
Central Missouri State University, MO	M
The Citadel, The Military College of South Carolina, SC	M,W
Clark Atlanta University, GA	M
Clemson University, SC	M
Cleveland State University, OH	M
Coastal Carolina University, SC	M,W
College of Charleston, SC	M,W
College of the Southwest, NM	M,W
Colorado School of Mines, CO	M
Colorado State University, CO	M,W
Columbus State University, GA	M
Concordia University, MI	M,W
Concordia University, NE	M,W
Concordia University, St. Paul, MN	W
Cornerstone University, MI	M
Creighton University, NE	M,W
Culver-Stockton College, MO	M,W
Daemen College, NY	M
Davidson College, NC	M
Davis & Elkins College, WV	M
DePaul University, IL	M
Dickinson State University, ND	M,W
Doane College, NE	M,W
Dordt College, IA	M
Drake University, IA	M
Drexel University, PA	M
Duke University, NC	M,W
Duquesne University, PA	M
East Carolina University, NC	M,W
East Central University, OK	M
Eastern Illinois University, IL	M,W
Eastern Michigan University, MI	M,W
Eastern Washington University, WA	W
East Tennessee State University, TN	M,W
Eckerd College, FL	M
Elon University, NC	M,W
Embry-Riddle Aeronautical University, FL	M
Evangel University, MO	M,W
Fairmont State University, WV	M
Ferris State University, MI	M,W
Flagler College, FL	M
Florida Agricultural and Mechanical University, FL	M,W
Florida Atlantic University, FL	M,W
Florida Gulf Coast University, FL	M,W
Florida Institute of Technology, FL	M,W
Florida Southern College, FL	M,W
Florida State University, FL	M,W
Fort Hays State University, KS	M
Fort Lewis College, CO	M
Francis Marion University, SC	M
Friends University, KS	M
Furman University, SC	M,W
Gannon University, PA	M,W
George Mason University, VA	M
Georgetown College, KY	M,W
Georgetown University, DC	M
Georgia College & State University, GA	M
Georgia Institute of Technology, GA	M
Georgia Southern University, GA	M
Glenville State College, WV	M,W
Goshen College, IN	M
Grace College, IN	M
Graceland University, IA	M,W
Grambling State University, LA	M,W
Grand Valley State University, MI	M,W
Grand View College, IA	M,W
Hampton University, VA	M,W
Hannibal-LaGrange College, MO	M
Hawai'i Pacific University, HI	M,W
Hofstra University, NY	M,W
Holy Names University, CA	M
Huntington University, IN	M
Idaho State University, ID	M,W
Illinois State University, IL	M,W
Indiana University Bloomington, IN	M,W
Indiana University of Pennsylvania, PA	M
Indiana University–Purdue University Indianapolis, IN	M
Iona College, NY	M
Iowa Wesleyan College, IA	M,W

Athletic Grants for Undergraduates
Golf

College		College		College	
Jacksonville State University, AL	M,W	New Mexico State University, NM	M,W	Santa Clara University, CA	M,W
Jacksonville University, FL	M,W	Niagara University, NY	M	Seton Hill University, PA	M,W
Jamestown College, ND	M,W	Nicholls State University, LA	M,W	Shorter College, GA	M,W
Kansas State University, KS	M,W	North Carolina State University, NC	M	Slippery Rock University of Pennsylvania, PA	M,W
Kennesaw State University, GA	M	Northern Arizona University, AZ	W	South Carolina State University, SC	M
Kent State University, OH	M,W	Northern Illinois University, IL	M,W	South Dakota State University, SD	M,W
Kentucky State University, KY	M	Northern State University, SD	W	Southeastern Louisiana University, LA	M
Kentucky Wesleyan College, KY	M,W	North Greenville College, SC	M	Southeast Missouri State University, MO	M
King College, TN	M,W	Northwestern Oklahoma State University, OK	M,W	Southern Illinois University Carbondale, IL	M,W
Lamar University, TX	M,W	Northwestern University, IL	M,W	Southern Illinois University Edwardsville, IL	M,W
Lee University, TN	M	Northwest Nazarene University, ID	M	Southern University and Agricultural and Mechanical College, LA	M,W
Lehigh University, PA	M	Northwood University, MI	M,W	Southwest Baptist University, MO	M
Le Moyne College, NY	M	Northwood University, Florida Campus, FL	M,W	Southwest Minnesota State University, MN	W
LeMoyne-Owen College, TN	M,W	Northwood University, Texas Campus, TX	M,W	Spring Arbor University, MI	M
Lewis-Clark State College, ID	M,W	Nova Southeastern University, FL	M,W	Spring Hill College, AL	M,W
Limestone College, SC	M,W	Nyack College, NY	M	Stanford University, CA	M,W
Lincoln University, MO	M	The Ohio State University, OH	M,W	State University of New York at Binghamton, NY	M
Lindenwood University, MO	M,W	Ohio University, OH	M,W	Stephen F. Austin State University, TX	M
Lindsey Wilson College, KY	M,W	Oklahoma Baptist University, OK	M,W	Stetson University, FL	M,W
Lipscomb University, TN	M,W	Oklahoma Panhandle State University, OK	M,W	Tabor College, KS	M,W
Long Island University, Brooklyn Campus, NY	M,W	Oklahoma State University, OK	M,W	Taylor University, IN	M
Louisiana State University and Agricultural and Mechanical College, LA	M,W	Olivet Nazarene University, IL	M	Temple University, PA	M
Louisiana Tech University, LA	M	Oral Roberts University, OK	M,W	Tennessee State University, TN	M
Loyola University Chicago, IL	M,W	Ouachita Baptist University, AR	M	Tennessee Technological University, TN	M,W
Lynn University, FL	M,W	The Pennsylvania State University University Park Campus, PA	M,W	Texas A&M University, TX	M,W
Lyon College, AR	M,W	Pepperdine University, CA	M,W	Texas A&M University–Commerce, TX	M,W
Malone College, OH	M,W	Philadelphia University, PA	M	Texas Christian University, TX	M,W
Manhattan College, NY	M	Pikeville College, KY	M,W	Texas Southern University, TX	M,W
Marian College, IN	M,W	Pittsburg State University, KS	M	Texas State University-San Marcos, TX	M,W
Marquette University, WI	M	Portland State University, OR	M,W	Texas Tech University, TX	M,W
Marshall University, WV	M,W	Purdue University, IN	M,W	Tiffin University, OH	M,W
The Master's College and Seminary, CA	M	Quincy University, IL	M,W	Towson University, MD	M
McKendree College, IL	M,W	Quinnipiac University, CT	M	Trevecca Nazarene University, TN	M,W
Mercer University, GA	M,W	Radford University, VA	M,W	Truman State University, MO	M,W
Mercyhurst College, PA	M,W	Rice University, TX	M	Tusculum College, TN	M
Mesa State College, CO	W	Rider University, NJ	M	Tuskegee University, AL	M
Miami University, OH	M	Robert Morris College, IL	M,W	Union College, KY	M,W
Michigan State University, MI	M,W	Robert Morris University, PA	M,W	Union University, TN	M
Middle Tennessee State University, TN	M,W	Roberts Wesleyan College, NY	M,W	University at Albany, State University of New York, NY	W
Midland Lutheran College, NE	M,W	Rockhurst University, MO	M,W	The University of Akron, OH	M
Millersville University of Pennsylvania, PA	M	Rollins College, FL	M,W	The University of Alabama, AL	M,W
Milligan College, TN	M	Sacred Heart University, CT	M,W	The University of Alabama at Birmingham, AL	M,W
Minnesota State University Mankato, MN	M,W	St. Andrews Presbyterian College, NC	M,W	University of Arkansas, AR	M,W
Mississippi State University, MS	M,W	St. Bonaventure University, NY	M	University of Arkansas at Monticello, AR	M
Missouri State University, MO	M,W	St. Cloud State University, MN	W	University of Arkansas at Pine Bluff, AR	M
Monmouth University, NJ	M,W	St. Edward's University, TX	M,W	University of California, Berkeley, CA	M,W
Montana State University, MT	W	Saint Francis University, PA	M,W	University of California, Irvine, CA	M,W
Montana Tech of The University of Montana, MT	M,W	St. John's University, NY	M,W	University of California, Los Angeles, CA	M,W
Montreat College, NC	M	Saint Joseph's College, IN	M,W	University of California, Santa Barbara, CA	M
Morehead State University, KY	M	Saint Joseph's University, PA	M	University of Central Oklahoma, OK	M,W
Morningside College, IA	M,W	Saint Leo University, FL	M,W		
Mount Olive College, NC	M,W	Saint Louis University, MO	M		
Mount St. Mary's University, MD	M,W	Saint Martin's University, WA	M,W		
Mount Vernon Nazarene University, OH	M	Saint Mary's College of California, CA			
Murray State University, KY	M,W	St. Thomas University, FL	M,W		
Newberry College, SC	M,W	Saint Vincent College, PA	M,W		
Newman University, KS	M,W	Saint Xavier University, IL	M		
		Samford University, AL	M,W		
		San Diego State University, CA	M,W		
		San Jose State University, CA	M,W		

Athletic Grants for Undergraduates
Ice hockey

Institution	
University of Cincinnati, OH	M
University of Colorado at Boulder, CO	M,W
University of Colorado at Colorado Springs, CO	M
University of Connecticut, CT	M
University of Dayton, OH	M,W
University of Denver, CO	M,W
University of Evansville, IN	M
The University of Findlay, OH	M,W
University of Florida, FL	M,W
University of Georgia, GA	M,W
University of Hartford, CT	M,W
University of Hawaii at Hilo, HI	M
University of Hawaii at Manoa, HI	M,W
University of Idaho, ID	M,W
University of Illinois at Urbana–Champaign, IL	M,W
The University of Iowa, IA	M,W
University of Kansas, KS	M,W
University of Kentucky, KY	M,W
University of Louisiana at Lafayette, LA	M
University of Louisville, KY	M,W
University of Mary, ND	M,W
University of Maryland, College Park, MD	M,W
University of Memphis, TN	M,W
University of Miami, FL	W
University of Michigan, MI	M,W
University of Minnesota, Twin Cities Campus, MN	M,W
University of Missouri–Columbia, MO	M,W
University of Missouri–Kansas City, MO	M,W
University of Missouri–St. Louis, MO	M,W
University of Nebraska at Kearney, NE	M,W
University of Nebraska–Lincoln, NE	M,W
University of Nevada, Las Vegas, NV	M
University of Nevada, Reno, NV	M,W
University of New Haven, CT	M
University of New Orleans, LA	M,W
University of North Alabama, AL	M
The University of North Carolina at Chapel Hill, NC	M,W
The University of North Carolina at Greensboro, NC	M,W
The University of North Carolina at Pembroke, NC	M
The University of North Carolina Wilmington, NC	M,W
University of Northern Colorado, CO	M,W
University of Northern Iowa, IA	M,W
University of North Florida, FL	M
University of Oklahoma, OK	M,W
University of Oregon, OR	M,W
University of Portland, OR	M,W
University of Rhode Island, RI	M
University of Richmond, VA	M,W
University of St. Francis, IL	M,W
University of Saint Francis, IN	M
University of San Diego, CA	M
University of South Carolina, SC	M,W
University of Southern California, CA	M,W
University of Southern Indiana, IN	M,W
University of Southern Mississippi, MS	M,W
University of South Florida, FL	M,W
The University of Tampa, FL	M
The University of Tennessee at Martin, TN	M
The University of Texas at Arlington, TX	M
The University of Texas at Austin, TX	M,W
The University of Texas at El Paso, TX	M
The University of Texas at San Antonio, TX	M
The University of Texas–Pan American, TX	M,W
University of the Cumberlands, KY	M,W
University of the District of Columbia, DC	M
University of the Pacific, CA	M
The University of Toledo, OH	M,W
University of Tulsa, OK	M,W
University of Utah, UT	M
University of Virginia, VA	M,W
University of Wisconsin–Madison, WI	M,W
University of Wisconsin–Parkside, WI	M
University of Wyoming, WY	M,W
Urbana University, OH	M,W
Utah State University, UT	M
Valdosta State University, GA	M
Vanderbilt University, TN	M,W
Virginia Commonwealth University, VA	M
Virginia Intermont College, VA	M
Virginia Military Institute, VA	M
Virginia Polytechnic Institute and State University, VA	M
Virginia Union University, VA	M
Wake Forest University, NC	M,W
Waldorf College, IA	M,W
Washington State University, WA	M,W
Wayland Baptist University, TX	M
Wayne State College, NE	M,W
Wayne State University, MI	M
Webber International University, FL	M,W
Western Carolina University, NC	M,W
Western Illinois University, IL	M
Western Kentucky University, KY	M,W
Western Washington University, WA	M,W
West Texas A&M University, TX	M,W
West Virginia Wesleyan College, WV	M
Wheeling Jesuit University, WV	M,W
Wichita State University, KS	M,W
William Jewell College, MO	M,W
William Penn University, IA	M
Williams Baptist College, AR	M
William Woods University, MO	M,W
Wingate University, NC	M,W
Winona State University, MN	M,W
Winthrop University, SC	M,W
Wofford College, SC	M,W
Xavier University, OH	M,W
Youngstown State University, OH	M

Gymnastics

Institution	
Arizona State University, AZ	W
Auburn University, AL	W
Ball State University, IN	W
Bowling Green State University, OH	W
California Polytechnic State University, San Luis Obispo, CA	W
California State University, Fullerton, CA	W
California State University, Sacramento, CA	W
Centenary College of Louisiana, LA	W
Central Michigan University, MI	W
The College of William and Mary, VA	M,W
Eastern Michigan University, MI	W
Illinois State University, IL	W
Kent State University, OH	W
Louisiana State University and Agricultural and Mechanical College, LA	W
Michigan State University, MI	W
North Carolina State University, NC	W
Northern Illinois University, IL	W
The Ohio State University, OH	M,W
The Pennsylvania State University University Park Campus, PA	M,W
San Jose State University, CA	W
Seattle Pacific University, WA	W
Southeast Missouri State University, MO	W
Stanford University, CA	M,W
Temple University, PA	M,W
Texas Woman's University, TX	W
Towson University, MD	W
The University of Alabama, AL	W
University of Arkansas, AR	W
University of California, Berkeley, CA	M,W
University of California, Los Angeles, CA	W
University of California, Santa Barbara, CA	W
University of Denver, CO	W
University of Florida, FL	W
University of Georgia, GA	W
University of Illinois at Urbana–Champaign, IL	M,W
The University of Iowa, IA	M,W
University of Kentucky, KY	W
University of Maryland, College Park, MD	W
University of Michigan, MI	M,W
University of Minnesota, Twin Cities Campus, MN	M,W
University of Missouri–Columbia, MO	W
University of Nebraska–Lincoln, NE	M,W
University of New Hampshire, NH	W
The University of North Carolina at Chapel Hill, NC	W
University of Oklahoma, OK	M,W
University of Pittsburgh, PA	W
University of Rhode Island, RI	W
University of Utah, UT	W
Utah State University, UT	W
West Virginia University, WV	W
Winona State University, MN	W

Ice hockey

Institution	
American International College, MA	M
Bemidji State University, MN	M,W

Athletic Grants for Undergraduates
Ice hockey

College	
Bentley College, MA	M
Boston College, MA	M
Boston University, MA	M,W
Bowling Green State University, OH	M
Clarkson University, NY	M,W
Colgate University, NY	M,W
The Colorado College, CO	M
Dordt College, IA	M
Ferris State University, MI	M
Lake Superior State University, MI	M
Lindenwood University, MO	M,W
Mercyhurst College, PA	M,W
Merrimack College, MA	M
Miami University, OH	M
Michigan State University, MI	M
Michigan Technological University, MI	M
Minnesota State University Mankato, MN	M,W
Niagara University, NY	M,W
Northeastern University, MA	M,W
The Ohio State University, OH	M,W
Quinnipiac University, CT	M,W
Rensselaer Polytechnic Institute, NY	M,W
Robert Morris University, PA	M
Sacred Heart University, CT	M
St. Cloud State University, MN	M,W
St. Lawrence University, NY	M,W
The University of Alabama in Huntsville, AL	M
University of Alaska Fairbanks, AK	M
University of Connecticut, CT	M,W
University of Denver, CO	M
University of Maine, ME	M,W
University of Massachusetts Amherst, MA	M
University of Massachusetts Lowell, MA	M
University of Michigan, MI	M
University of Minnesota, Duluth, MN	M
University of Minnesota, Twin Cities Campus, MN	M,W
University of Nebraska at Omaha, NE	M
University of New Hampshire, NH	M,W
University of North Dakota, ND	M,W
The University of Toledo, OH	M,W
University of Vermont, VT	M,W
University of Wisconsin–Madison, WI	M,W
Wayne State University, MI	M,W

Lacrosse

College	
Adelphi University, NY	M,W
American International College, MA	W
American University, DC	W
Belmont Abbey College, NC	M,W
Bentley College, MA	M,W
Boston College, MA	W
Boston University, MA	W
Butler University, IN	M
Central Connecticut State University, CT	W
Colgate University, NY	M,W
The College of William and Mary, VA	W
Davidson College, NC	W
Drexel University, PA	M,W
Duke University, NC	M,W
Duquesne University, PA	W
East Stroudsburg University of Pennsylvania, PA	W
Fairfield University, CT	M,W
Gannon University, PA	W
George Mason University, VA	W
Georgetown University, DC	M,W
Hofstra University, NY	M,W
Indiana University of Pennsylvania, PA	W
Iona College, NY	W
James Madison University, VA	W
The Johns Hopkins University, MD	M,W
Lehigh University, PA	M,W
Le Moyne College, NY	M,W
Limestone College, SC	M,W
Lindenwood University, MO	M,W
Lock Haven University of Pennsylvania, PA	W
Long Island University, Brooklyn Campus, NY	W
Manhattan College, NY	M,W
Marist College, NY	M,W
Mercyhurst College, PA	M,W
Merrimack College, MA	W
Millersville University of Pennsylvania, PA	W
Molloy College, NY	M,W
Monmouth University, NJ	W
Mount St. Mary's University, MD	M,W
New York Institute of Technology, NY	M
Niagara University, NY	W
Northwestern University, IL	W
The Ohio State University, OH	M,W
The Pennsylvania State University University Park Campus, PA	M,W
Philadelphia University, PA	W
Quinnipiac University, CT	M,W
Robert Morris University, PA	M,W
Sacred Heart University, CT	M,W
St. Andrews Presbyterian College, NC	M,W
Saint Francis University, PA	W
St. John's University, NY	M
Saint Joseph's University, PA	M,W
Saint Leo University, FL	M
Saint Vincent College, PA	M,W
Seton Hill University, PA	M,W
Shippensburg University of Pennsylvania, PA	W
Southern New Hampshire University, NH	M,W
State University of New York at Binghamton, NY	M,W
Stonehill College, MA	W
Stony Brook University, State University of New York, NY	M,W
Syracuse University, NY	M,W
Temple University, PA	W
Towson University, MD	M,W
University at Albany, State University of New York, NY	M,W
University of California, Berkeley, CA	W
University of Delaware, DE	M,W
University of Denver, CO	M,W
University of Hartford, CT	W
University of Maryland, Baltimore County, MD	M,W
University of Maryland, College Park, MD	M,W
University of Massachusetts Amherst, MA	M,W
University of New Hampshire, NH	W
University of New Haven, CT	W
The University of North Carolina at Chapel Hill, NC	M,W
University of Oregon, OR	W
University of Richmond, VA	W
The University of Toledo, OH	M,W
University of Vermont, VT	M,W
University of Virginia, VA	M,W
Vanderbilt University, TN	W
Virginia Military Institute, VA	M
Virginia Polytechnic Institute and State University, VA	W
Wheeling Jesuit University, WV	M
Wingate University, NC	M

Riflery

College	
Austin Peay State University, TN	W
Jacksonville State University, AL	M,W
Lindenwood University, MO	M,W
Mercer University, GA	M,W
Morehead State University, KY	M,W
Murray State University, KY	M,W
North Georgia College & State University, GA	M,W
Tennessee Technological University, TN	M,W
Texas Christian University, TX	W
University of Alaska Fairbanks, AK	M,W
University of Kentucky, KY	M,W
University of Memphis, TN	M,W
University of Missouri–Kansas City, MO	M,W
University of Nebraska–Lincoln, NE	W
University of Nevada, Reno, NV	M,W
The University of Tennessee at Martin, TN	M,W
Virginia Military Institute, VA	M,W
West Virginia University, WV	M,W
Xavier University, OH	M,W

Rugby

College	
Eastern Illinois University, IL	W
University of California, Berkeley, CA	M

Sailing

College	
Hampton University, VA	M,W

Skiing (cross-country)

College	
Montana State University, MT	M,W
St. Cloud State University, MN	W
University of Alaska Fairbanks, AK	M,W
University of Colorado at Boulder, CO	M,W
University of Denver, CO	M,W
University of Nevada, Reno, NV	M
University of New Hampshire, NH	M
University of Utah, UT	M,W
University of Vermont, VT	M,W
University of Wisconsin–Green Bay, WI	M,W
Western State College of Colorado, CO	M,W

Athletic Grants for Undergraduates
Soccer

Skiing (downhill)
Albertson College of Idaho, ID	M,W
Davis & Elkins College, WV	M,W
Montana State University, MT	M,W
Paul Smith's College of Arts and Sciences, NY	M,W
University of Colorado at Boulder, CO	M,W
University of Denver, CO	M,W
University of Massachusetts Amherst, MA	M,W
University of Nevada, Reno, NV	M,W
University of New Hampshire, NH	M,W
University of Utah, UT	M,W
University of Vermont, VT	M,W
Western State College of Colorado, CO	M,W

Soccer
Adelphi University, NY	M,W
Alabama Agricultural and Mechanical University, AL	M
Albertson College of Idaho, ID	M,W
Alderson-Broaddus College, WV	M
Alliant International University, CA	M,W
American International College, MA	M,W
American University, DC	M,W
Anderson University, SC	M,W
Appalachian State University, NC	M,W
Arizona State University, AZ	W
Arkansas State University, AR	W
Asbury College, KY	M,W
Ashford University, IA	M,W
Ashland University, OH	M,W
Auburn University, AL	W
Auburn University Montgomery, AL	M,W
Augustana College, SD	W
Austin Peay State University, TN	W
Avila University, MO	M,W
Azusa Pacific University, CA	M,W
Barton College, NC	M,W
Baylor University, TX	W
Belhaven College, MS	M,W
Belmont Abbey College, NC	M,W
Belmont University, TN	M,W
Bemidji State University, MN	W
Benedictine College, KS	M,W
Bentley College, MA	M,W
Berry College, GA	M,W
Bethany College, KS	M,W
Bethel College, KS	M,W
Biola University, CA	M,W
Blessing-Rieman College of Nursing, IL	M,W
Bloomfield College, NJ	M,W
Bloomsburg University of Pennsylvania, PA	M,W
Boston College, MA	M,W
Boston University, MA	M,W
Bowling Green State University, OH	M,W
Bradley University, IL	M
Brenau University, GA	W
Brevard College, NC	M,W
Brewton-Parker College, GA	M,W
Bryan College, TN	M,W
Butler University, IN	M,W
California Baptist University, CA	M,W
California State University, Bakersfield, CA	M
California State University, Chico, CA	M,W
California State University, Dominguez Hills, CA	M,W
California State University, Fresno, CA	M,W
California State University, Fullerton, CA	M,W
California State University, Sacramento, CA	M,W
Campbellsville University, KY	M,W
Campbell University, NC	M,W
Carroll College, MT	W
Carson-Newman College, TN	M,W
Cascade College, OR	M,W
Catawba College, NC	M,W
Cedarville University, OH	M,W
Centenary College of Louisiana, LA	M,W
Central Connecticut State University, CT	M,W
Central Michigan University, MI	W
Central Missouri State University, MO	W
Central Washington University, WA	W
Christian Brothers University, TN	M,W
The Citadel, The Military College of South Carolina, SC	M,W
Clemson University, SC	M,W
Cleveland State University, OH	M
Coastal Carolina University, SC	M,W
Colgate University, NY	M,W
College of Charleston, SC	M,W
College of Saint Mary, NE	W
The College of Saint Rose, NY	M,W
College of the Southwest, NM	M,W
The College of William and Mary, VA	M,W
The Colorado College, CO	W
Columbia College, SC	W
Columbus State University, GA	W
Concordia University, CA	M,W
Concordia University, MI	M,W
Concordia University, NE	M,W
Concordia University, St. Paul, MN	W
Converse College, SC	W
Corban College, OR	M,W
Cornerstone University, MI	M,W
Creighton University, NE	M,W
Culver-Stockton College, MO	M,W
Daemen College, NY	M,W
Dallas Baptist University, TX	W
Davidson College, NC	M,W
Davis & Elkins College, WV	M,W
DePaul University, IL	M,W
Doane College, NE	M,W
Dominican University of California, CA	M,W
Dordt College, IA	M,W
Dowling College, NY	M
Drake University, IA	M,W
Drexel University, PA	M,W
Duke University, NC	M,W
Duquesne University, PA	M,W
East Carolina University, NC	M,W
East Central University, OK	W
Eastern Illinois University, IL	M,W
Eastern Michigan University, MI	W
Eastern Washington University, WA	W
East Stroudsburg University of Pennsylvania, PA	M,W
East Tennessee State University, TN	W
Eckerd College, FL	M,W
Edinboro University of Pennsylvania, PA	W
Elon University, NC	M,W
Embry-Riddle Aeronautical University, FL	M,W
Emporia State University, KS	W
Erskine College, SC	M,W
The Evergreen State College, WA	M,W
Fairfield University, CT	M,W
Faulkner University, AL	M,W
Felician College, NJ	M,W
Flagler College, FL	M,W
Florida Atlantic University, FL	M,W
Florida Institute of Technology, FL	M,W
Florida Southern College, FL	M,W
Florida State University, FL	W
Fordham University, NY	M,W
Fort Lewis College, CO	M,W
Francis Marion University, SC	M,W
Franklin Pierce College, NH	M,W
Freed-Hardeman University, TN	M,W
Fresno Pacific University, CA	M,W
Friends University, KS	M,W
Furman University, SC	M,W
Gannon University, PA	M,W
Geneva College, PA	M,W
George Mason University, VA	M,W
Georgetown College, KY	M,W
Georgetown University, DC	M,W
Georgia College & State University, GA	W
Georgia Southern University, GA	M,W
Gonzaga University, WA	M,W
Goshen College, IN	M,W
Grace College, IN	M,W
Graceland University, IA	M,W
Grand Valley State University, MI	W
Grand View College, IA	M,W
Hannibal-LaGrange College, MO	M,W
Harding University, AR	M,W
Harris-Stowe State University, MO	M,W
Hawai'i Pacific University, HI	M,W
Hofstra University, NY	M,W
Holy Names University, CA	M,W
Houghton College, NY	M,W
Howard University, DC	M
Humboldt State University, CA	M,W
Huntington University, IN	M,W
Illinois State University, IL	W
Indiana State University, IN	W
Indiana University Bloomington, IN	M,W
Indiana University of Pennsylvania, PA	W
Indiana University–Purdue University Fort Wayne, IN	M,W
Indiana University–Purdue University Indianapolis, IN	M,W
Inter American University of Puerto Rico, Guayama Campus, PR	M
Iona College, NY	M,W
Iowa Wesleyan College, IA	M,W

Peterson's College Money Handbook 2007 — www.petersons.com

Athletic Grants for Undergraduates
Soccer

College	
Jacksonville State University, AL	W
Jacksonville University, FL	M,W
James Madison University, VA	M,W
Jamestown College, ND	W
John Brown University, AR	M,W
Kent State University, OH	W
Kentucky Wesleyan College, KY	M,W
King College, TN	M,W
Lee University, TN	M,W
Lehigh University, PA	M,W
Le Moyne College, NY	M,W
Limestone College, SC	M,W
Lindenwood University, MO	M,W
Lindsey Wilson College, KY	M,W
Lipscomb University, TN	M,W
Lock Haven University of Pennsylvania, PA	M,W
Long Island University, Brooklyn Campus, NY	M,W
Louisiana State University and Agricultural and Mechanical College, LA	W
Loyola University Chicago, IL	M,W
Lynn University, FL	M,W
Lyon College, AR	M,W
Malone College, OH	M,W
Manhattan College, NY	M,W
Mansfield University of Pennsylvania, PA	W
Marian College, IN	M,W
Marist College, NY	M,W
Marquette University, WI	M,W
Marshall University, WV	M,W
The Master's College and Seminary, CA	M,W
Mayville State University, ND	M,W
McKendree College, IL	M,W
Mercer University, GA	M,W
Mercyhurst College, PA	M,W
Merrimack College, MA	W
Mesa State College, CO	W
Metropolitan State College of Denver, CO	M,W
Miami University, OH	W
Michigan State University, MI	M
MidAmerica Nazarene University, KS	M,W
Middle Tennessee State University, TN	W
Midland Lutheran College, NE	M,W
Midway College, KY	W
Midwestern State University, TX	M,W
Millersville University of Pennsylvania, PA	M,W
Milligan College, TN	M,W
Minnesota State University Mankato, MN	W
Mississippi State University, MS	W
Missouri State University, MO	M,W
Molloy College, NY	M,W
Monmouth University, NJ	M,W
Montana State University–Billings, MT	M,W
Montreat College, NC	M,W
Morehead State University, KY	W
Morningside College, IA	M,W
Mount Marty College, SD	M,W
Mount Olive College, NC	M,W
Mount St. Mary's University, MD	M,W
Mount Vernon Nazarene University, OH	M,W
Murray State University, KY	W
Newberry College, SC	M,W
Newman University, KS	M,W
New York Institute of Technology, NY	M,W
Niagara University, NY	M,W
Nicholls State University, LA	W
North Carolina State University, NC	M,W
Northeastern University, MA	M,W
Northern Arizona University, AZ	W
Northern Illinois University, IL	M,W
Northern State University, SD	W
North Georgia College & State University, GA	M,W
North Greenville College, SC	M,W
Northwestern Oklahoma State University, OK	W
Northwestern State University of Louisiana, LA	W
Northwestern University, IL	M,W
Northwest Nazarene University, ID	W
Northwest University, WA	M
Northwood University, MI	M,W
Northwood University, Florida Campus, FL	M,W
Northwood University, Texas Campus, TX	M,W
Nova Southeastern University, FL	M,W
Nyack College, NY	M,W
The Ohio State University, OH	M,W
Ohio University, OH	W
Oklahoma State University, OK	W
Olivet Nazarene University, IL	M,W
Oral Roberts University, OK	M,W
Paul Smith's College of Arts and Sciences, NY	M,W
The Pennsylvania State University University Park Campus, PA	M,W
Pepperdine University, CA	W
Philadelphia University, PA	M,W
Portland State University, OR	W
Purdue University, IN	W
Quincy University, IL	M,W
Quinnipiac University, CT	M,W
Radford University, VA	M,W
Rice University, TX	W
Rider University, NJ	M,W
Robert Morris College, IL	M,W
Robert Morris University, PA	M,W
Roberts Wesleyan College, NY	M,W
Rockhurst University, MO	M,W
Rollins College, FL	M,W
Sacred Heart University, CT	M,W
St. Andrews Presbyterian College, NC	M,W
St. Bonaventure University, NY	M,W
St. Cloud State University, MN	W
St. Edward's University, TX	M,W
St. Francis College, NY	M
Saint Francis University, PA	M,W
St. John's University, NY	M,W
Saint Joseph's College, IN	M,W
Saint Joseph's University, PA	M,W
Saint Leo University, FL	M,W
Saint Louis University, MO	M,W
Saint Mary's College of California, CA	M,W
St. Thomas University, FL	M,W
Saint Vincent College, PA	M,W
Saint Xavier University, IL	M,W
Salem International University, WV	M
Samford University, AL	W
San Diego Christian College, CA	M,W
San Diego State University, CA	M,W
San Francisco State University, CA	M,W
San Jose State University, CA	M,W
Santa Clara University, CA	M,W
Seattle Pacific University, WA	M
Seattle University, WA	M,W
Seton Hill University, PA	M,W
Shepherd University, WV	M,W
Shippensburg University of Pennsylvania, PA	M,W
Shorter College, GA	M,W
Slippery Rock University of Pennsylvania, PA	M,W
Sonoma State University, CA	M,W
South Dakota State University, SD	W
Southeastern Louisiana University, LA	W
Southeast Missouri State University, MO	W
Southern Illinois University Edwardsville, IL	M,W
Southern New Hampshire University, NH	M,W
Southern Oregon University, OR	W
Southwest Baptist University, MO	W
Southwest Minnesota State University, MN	W
Spring Arbor University, MI	M,W
Spring Hill College, AL	M,W
Stanford University, CA	M,W
State University of New York at Binghamton, NY	M,W
State University of New York at Buffalo, NY	M,W
State University of New York College at Oneonta, NY	M
Stephen F. Austin State University, TX	W
Stetson University, FL	M,W
Stonehill College, MA	M,W
Stony Brook University, State University of New York, NY	M,W
Syracuse University, NY	M,W
Tabor College, KS	M,W
Taylor University, IN	M,W
Temple University, PA	M,W
Tennessee Technological University, TN	W
Texas A&M University, TX	W
Texas A&M University–Commerce, TX	W
Texas Christian University, TX	W
Texas Southern University, TX	W
Texas State University-San Marcos, TX	W
Texas Tech University, TX	W
Texas Woman's University, TX	W
Tiffin University, OH	M,W
Towson University, MD	M,W

Athletic Grants for Undergraduates
Softball

College	
Trevecca Nazarene University, TN	M,W
Trinity International University, IL	M,W
Truman State University, MO	M,W
Tusculum College, TN	M,W
Union College, KY	M,W
Union University, TN	M,W
Unity College, ME	M
University at Albany, State University of New York, NY	M,W
The University of Akron, OH	M
The University of Alabama, AL	W
The University of Alabama at Birmingham, AL	M,W
The University of Alabama in Huntsville, AL	M,W
University of Arkansas, AR	W
University of California, Berkeley, CA	M,W
University of California, Irvine, CA	M,W
University of California, Los Angeles, CA	M,W
University of California, Santa Barbara, CA	M,W
University of Central Oklahoma, OK	W
University of Cincinnati, OH	M,W
University of Colorado at Boulder, CO	W
University of Colorado at Colorado Springs, CO	M
University of Connecticut, CT	M,W
University of Dayton, OH	M,W
University of Delaware, DE	M,W
University of Denver, CO	M,W
University of Evansville, IN	M,W
The University of Findlay, OH	M,W
University of Florida, FL	W
University of Georgia, GA	W
University of Great Falls, MT	W
University of Hartford, CT	M,W
University of Hawaii at Manoa, HI	W
University of Idaho, ID	W
University of Illinois at Springfield, IL	M
University of Illinois at Urbana–Champaign, IL	W
The University of Iowa, IA	W
University of Kansas, KS	W
University of Kentucky, KY	M,W
University of Louisville, KY	M,W
University of Maine, ME	M,W
University of Mary, ND	M,W
University of Maryland, Baltimore County, MD	M,W
University of Maryland, College Park, MD	M,W
University of Massachusetts Amherst, MA	M,W
University of Memphis, TN	M,W
University of Miami, FL	W
University of Michigan, MI	W
University of Minnesota, Duluth, MN	W
University of Minnesota, Twin Cities Campus, MN	W
University of Missouri–Columbia, MO	W
University of Missouri–Kansas City, MO	M
University of Missouri–St. Louis, MO	M,W
University of Nebraska–Lincoln, NE	W
University of Nevada, Las Vegas, NV	M,W
University of Nevada, Reno, NV	W
University of New Hampshire, NH	M,W
University of New Haven, CT	M,W
University of North Alabama, AL	W
The University of North Carolina at Asheville, NC	M,W
The University of North Carolina at Chapel Hill, NC	M,W
The University of North Carolina at Greensboro, NC	M,W
The University of North Carolina at Pembroke, NC	M,W
The University of North Carolina Wilmington, NC	M,W
University of Northern Colorado, CO	W
University of Northern Iowa, IA	W
University of North Florida, FL	M,W
University of Oklahoma, OK	W
University of Oregon, OR	W
University of Pittsburgh, PA	M,W
University of Portland, OR	M,W
University of Rhode Island, RI	M,W
University of Richmond, VA	M,W
University of St. Francis, IL	M,W
University of Saint Francis, IN	M,W
University of San Diego, CA	M,W
University of Science and Arts of Oklahoma, OK	M,W
University of South Carolina, SC	M,W
University of South Carolina Upstate, SC	M,W
University of Southern California, CA	W
University of Southern Indiana, IN	M,W
University of South Florida, FL	M,W
The University of Tampa, FL	M,W
The University of Tennessee at Martin, TN	W
The University of Texas at Austin, TX	W
University of the Cumberlands, KY	M,W
University of the District of Columbia, DC	M
University of the Pacific, CA	W
The University of Toledo, OH	W
University of Tulsa, OK	M,W
University of Utah, UT	W
University of Vermont, VT	M,W
University of Virginia, VA	M,W
University of Wisconsin–Green Bay, WI	M,W
University of Wisconsin–Madison, WI	M,W
University of Wisconsin–Parkside, WI	M,W
University of Wyoming, WY	W
Urbana University, OH	M,W
Utah State University, UT	W
Valparaiso University, IN	M,W
Vanderbilt University, TN	M,W
Vanguard University of Southern California, CA	M,W
Villanova University, PA	M,W
Virginia Commonwealth University, VA	M,W
Virginia Intermont College, VA	M,W
Virginia Military Institute, VA	M
Virginia Polytechnic Institute and State University, VA	M,W
Wake Forest University, NC	M,W
Waldorf College, IA	M,W
Washington State University, WA	W
Wayne State College, NE	W
Webber International University, FL	M,W
Western Carolina University, NC	W
Western Illinois University, IL	M,W
Western Kentucky University, KY	M
Western Washington University, WA	M,W
Westmont College, CA	M,W
West Texas A&M University, TX	M,W
West Virginia University, WV	M,W
West Virginia Wesleyan College, WV	M,W
Wheeling Jesuit University, WV	M,W
Whitman College, WA	M,W
William Carey College, MS	M,W
William Jewell College, MO	M,W
William Penn University, IA	M,W
Williams Baptist College, AR	M,W
William Woods University, MO	M,W
Wingate University, NC	M
Winona State University, MN	W
Winthrop University, SC	M
Wofford College, SC	M,W
Xavier University, OH	M,W

Softball

College	
Abilene Christian University, TX	W
Adelphi University, NY	W
Albertson College of Idaho, ID	W
Alderson-Broaddus College, WV	W
American International College, MA	W
Anderson University, SC	W
Arizona State University, AZ	W
Armstrong Atlantic State University, GA	W
Ashford University, IA	W
Ashland University, OH	W
Auburn University, AL	W
Augustana College, SD	W
Austin Peay State University, TN	W
Avila University, MO	W
Azusa Pacific University, CA	W
Ball State University, IN	W
Barton College, NC	W
Baylor University, TX	W
Belhaven College, MS	W
Belmont Abbey College, NC	W
Belmont University, TN	W
Bemidji State University, MN	W
Benedictine College, KS	W
Bentley College, MA	W
Bethany College, KS	W
Biola University, CA	W
Bloomfield College, NJ	W
Bloomsburg University of Pennsylvania, PA	W
Bluefield State College, WV	W
Boston College, MA	W
Boston University, MA	W
Bowling Green State University, OH	W
Bradley University, IL	W
Brenau University, GA	W
Brevard College, NC	W
Brewton-Parker College, GA	W
Brigham Young University–Hawaii, HI	W
Butler University, IN	W

Peterson's College Money Handbook 2007

Athletic Grants for Undergraduates
Softball

College	
California Baptist University, CA	W
California Polytechnic State University, San Luis Obispo, CA	W
California State University, Bakersfield, CA	W
California State University, Chico, CA	W
California State University, Fresno, CA	W
California State University, Fullerton, CA	W
California State University, Sacramento, CA	W
Campbellsville University, KY	W
Campbell University, NC	W
Carson-Newman College, TN	W
Catawba College, NC	W
Cedarville University, OH	W
Centenary College of Louisiana, LA	W
Central Connecticut State University, CT	W
Central Michigan University, MI	W
Central Missouri State University, MO	W
Central Washington University, WA	W
Chaminade University of Honolulu, HI	W
Christian Brothers University, TN	W
Cleveland State University, OH	W
Coastal Carolina University, SC	W
Colgate University, NY	W
College of Charleston, SC	W
College of Saint Mary, NE	W
The College of Saint Rose, NY	W
College of the Southwest, NM	W
Colorado School of Mines, CO	W
Colorado State University, CO	W
Columbus State University, GA	W
Concordia University, CA	W
Concordia University, MI	W
Concordia University, NE	W
Concordia University, St. Paul, MN	W
Corban College, OR	W
Cornerstone University, MI	W
Creighton University, NE	W
Culver-Stockton College, MO	W
Davis & Elkins College, WV	W
DePaul University, IL	W
Dickinson State University, ND	W
Doane College, NE	W
Dominican University of California, CA	W
Dordt College, IA	W
Dowling College, NY	W
Drake University, IA	W
Drexel University, PA	W
East Carolina University, NC	W
East Central University, OK	W
Eastern Illinois University, IL	W
Eastern Michigan University, MI	W
East Stroudsburg University of Pennsylvania, PA	W
East Tennessee State University, TN	W
Eckerd College, FL	W
Edinboro University of Pennsylvania, PA	W
Elon University, NC	W
Emporia State University, KS	W
Erskine College, SC	W
Evangel University, MO	W
Fairfield University, CT	W
Faulkner University, AL	W
Felician College, NJ	W
Ferris State University, MI	W
Florida Atlantic University, FL	W
Florida Gulf Coast University, FL	W
Florida Institute of Technology, FL	W
Florida Southern College, FL	W
Florida State University, FL	W
Fordham University, NY	W
Fort Lewis College, CO	W
Francis Marion University, SC	W
Franklin Pierce College, NH	W
Freed-Hardeman University, TN	W
Friends University, KS	W
Furman University, SC	W
Gannon University, PA	W
Geneva College, PA	W
George Mason University, VA	W
Georgetown College, KY	W
Georgia College & State University, GA	W
Georgia Institute of Technology, GA	W
Georgia Southern University, GA	W
Georgia Southwestern State University, GA	W
Glenville State College, WV	W
Goshen College, IN	W
Grace College, IN	W
Graceland University, IA	W
Grand Valley State University, MI	W
Grand View College, IA	W
Hampton University, VA	W
Hannibal-LaGrange College, MO	W
Harris-Stowe State University, MO	W
Hawai'i Pacific University, HI	W
Hillsdale College, MI	W
Hofstra University, NY	W
Houston Baptist University, TX	W
Humboldt State University, CA	W
Huntington University, IN	W
Illinois State University, IL	W
Indiana State University, IN	W
Indiana University Bloomington, IN	W
Indiana University of Pennsylvania, PA	W
Indiana University–Purdue University Fort Wayne, IN	W
Indiana University–Purdue University Indianapolis, IN	W
Inter American University of Puerto Rico, Guayama Campus, PR	M,W
Iona College, NY	W
Iowa Wesleyan College, IA	W
Jacksonville State University, AL	W
Jacksonville University, FL	W
James Madison University, VA	W
Jamestown College, ND	W
Judson College, AL	W
Kennesaw State University, GA	W
Kent State University, OH	W
Kentucky Wesleyan College, KY	W
King College, TN	M,W
Lee University, TN	W
Lehigh University, PA	W
Le Moyne College, NY	W
LeMoyne-Owen College, TN	W
Limestone College, SC	W
Lincoln University, MO	W
Lindenwood University, MO	W
Lindsey Wilson College, KY	W
Lipscomb University, TN	W
Lock Haven University of Pennsylvania, PA	W
Long Island University, Brooklyn Campus, NY	W
Louisiana State University and Agricultural and Mechanical College, LA	W
Louisiana Tech University, LA	W
Loyola University Chicago, IL	W
Malone College, OH	W
Manhattan College, NY	W
Mansfield University of Pennsylvania, PA	W
Marian College, IN	W
Marist College, NY	W
Marshall University, WV	W
The Master's College and Seminary, CA	W
Mayville State University, ND	W
McKendree College, IL	W
Mercer University, GA	W
Mercyhurst College, PA	W
Merrimack College, MA	W
Mesa State College, CO	W
Miami University, OH	W
MidAmerica Nazarene University, KS	W
Middle Tennessee State University, TN	W
Midland Lutheran College, NE	W
Midway College, KY	W
Midwestern State University, TX	W
Millersville University of Pennsylvania, PA	W
Milligan College, TN	W
Minnesota State University Mankato, MN	W
Mississippi State University, MS	W
Missouri State University, MO	W
Molloy College, NY	W
Monmouth University, NJ	W
Montreat College, NC	W
Morehead State University, KY	W
Morningside College, IA	W
Mountain State University, WV	W
Mount Marty College, SD	W
Mount Olive College, NC	W
Mount St. Mary's University, MD	W
Mount Vernon Nazarene University, OH	W
Newberry College, SC	W
Newman University, KS	W
New Mexico State University, NM	W
New York Institute of Technology, NY	W
Niagara University, NY	W
Nicholls State University, LA	W
North Carolina State University, NC	W
Northern Illinois University, IL	W
Northern State University, SD	W

Athletic Grants for Undergraduates
Softball

College					
North Greenville College, SC	W	Sonoma State University, CA	W	University of California, Los Angeles, CA	W
Northwest Christian College, OR	W	South Carolina State University, SC	W	University of California, Riverside, CA	W
Northwestern Oklahoma State University, OK	W	South Dakota State University, SD	W	University of California, Santa Barbara, CA	W
Northwestern State University of Louisiana, LA	W	Southeastern Louisiana University, LA	W	University of Central Oklahoma, OK	W
Northwestern University, IL	W	Southeastern Oklahoma State University, OK	W	University of Colorado at Colorado Springs, CO	W
Northwest Nazarene University, ID	W	Southeast Missouri State University, MO	W	University of Connecticut, CT	W
Northwood University, MI	W	Southern Arkansas University–Magnolia, AR	W	University of Dayton, OH	W
Northwood University, Florida Campus, FL	W	Southern Illinois University Carbondale, IL	W	University of Delaware, DE	W
Northwood University, Texas Campus, TX	W	Southern Illinois University Edwardsville, IL	W	University of Evansville, IN	W
Nova Southeastern University, FL	W	Southern New Hampshire University, NH	W	The University of Findlay, OH	W
Nyack College, NY	W	Southern Oregon University, OR	W	University of Florida, FL	W
The Ohio State University, OH	W	Southern University and Agricultural and Mechanical College, LA	W	University of Hartford, CT	W
Ohio University, OH	W	Southwest Baptist University, MO	W	University of Hawaii at Hilo, HI	W
Oklahoma Baptist University, OK	W	Southwest Minnesota State University, MN	W	University of Hawaii at Manoa, HI	W
Oklahoma Panhandle State University, OK	W	Spring Arbor University, MI	W	University of Illinois at Springfield, IL	W
Oklahoma State University, OK	W	Spring Hill College, AL	W	University of Illinois at Urbana–Champaign, IL	W
Olivet Nazarene University, IL	W	Stanford University, CA	W	The University of Iowa, IA	W
Ouachita Baptist University, AR	W	State University of New York at Binghamton, NY	W	University of Kansas, KS	W
Philadelphia University, PA	W	State University of New York at Buffalo, NY	W	University of Kentucky, KY	W
Pikeville College, KY	W	Stephen F. Austin State University, TX	W	University of Louisiana at Lafayette, LA	W
Pittsburg State University, KS	W	Stetson University, FL	W	University of Louisville, KY	W
Portland State University, OR	W	Stonehill College, MA	W	University of Maine, ME	W
Purdue University, IN	W	Stony Brook University, State University of New York, NY	W	University of Mary, ND	W
Quincy University, IL	W	Syracuse University, NY	W	University of Maryland, Baltimore County, MD	W
Quinnipiac University, CT	W	Tabor College, KS	W	University of Maryland, College Park, MD	W
Radford University, VA	W	Taylor University, IN	W	University of Massachusetts Amherst, MA	W
Rider University, NJ	W	Temple University, PA	M,W	University of Michigan, MI	W
Robert Morris College, IL	W	Tennessee Technological University, TN	W	University of Minnesota, Duluth, MN	W
Robert Morris University, PA	W	Texas A&M University, TX	W	University of Minnesota, Twin Cities Campus, MN	W
Rockhurst University, MO	W	Texas Southern University, TX	W	University of Missouri–Columbia, MO	W
Rollins College, FL	W	Texas State University-San Marcos, TX	W	University of Missouri–Kansas City, MO	W
Sacred Heart University, CT	W	Texas Tech University, TX	W	University of Missouri–St. Louis, MO	W
St. Andrews Presbyterian College, NC	W	Texas Woman's University, TX	W	University of Nebraska at Kearney, NE	W
St. Bonaventure University, NY	W	Tiffin University, OH	W	University of Nebraska at Omaha, NE	W
St. Cloud State University, MN	W	Towson University, MD	W	University of Nebraska–Lincoln, NE	W
St. Edward's University, TX	W	Trevecca Nazarene University, TN	W	University of Nevada, Las Vegas, NV	W
St. Francis College, NY	W	Trinity International University, IL	W	University of Nevada, Reno, NV	W
Saint Francis University, PA	W	Truman State University, MO	W	University of New Haven, CT	W
St. John's University, NY	W	Tusculum College, TN	W	University of North Alabama, AL	W
Saint Joseph's College, IN	W	Union College, KY	W	The University of North Carolina at Chapel Hill, NC	W
Saint Joseph's University, PA	W	Union University, TN	W	The University of North Carolina at Greensboro, NC	W
Saint Leo University, FL	W	University at Albany, State University of New York, NY	W	The University of North Carolina at Pembroke, NC	W
Saint Louis University, MO	W	The University of Akron, OH	W	The University of North Carolina Wilmington, NC	W
Saint Martin's University, WA	W	The University of Alabama, AL	W	University of North Dakota, ND	W
Saint Mary's College of California, CA	W	The University of Alabama at Birmingham, AL		University of Northern Colorado, CO	W
St. Thomas University, FL	W	The University of Alabama in Huntsville, AL	W	University of Northern Iowa, IA	W
Saint Vincent College, PA	W	University of Arkansas, AR	W	University of North Florida, FL	W
Saint Xavier University, IL	W	University of Arkansas at Monticello, AR		University of Oklahoma, OK	W
Salem International University, WV	W	University of California, Berkeley, CA	W	University of Oregon, OR	W
Samford University, AL	W			University of Pittsburgh, PA	W
San Diego State University, CA	W				
San Francisco State University, CA	W				
Santa Clara University, CA	W				
Seattle University, WA	W				
Seton Hill University, PA	W				
Shepherd University, WV	W				
Shippensburg University of Pennsylvania, PA	W				
Slippery Rock University of Pennsylvania, PA	W				

Peterson's College Money Handbook 2007

Athletic Grants for Undergraduates
Softball

College	
University of Rhode Island, RI	W
University of St. Francis, IL	W
University of Saint Francis, IN	W
University of Science and Arts of Oklahoma, OK	W
University of South Carolina, SC	W
University of South Carolina Upstate, SC	W
The University of South Dakota, SD	W
University of Southern Indiana, IN	W
University of South Florida, FL	W
The University of Tampa, FL	W
The University of Tennessee at Martin, TN	W
The University of Texas at Arlington, TX	W
The University of Texas at Austin, TX	W
The University of Texas at San Antonio, TX	W
University of the Cumberlands, KY	W
University of the Pacific, CA	W
The University of Toledo, OH	W
University of Tulsa, OK	W
University of Vermont, VT	W
University of Virginia, VA	W
The University of West Alabama, AL	W
University of West Georgia, GA	W
University of Wisconsin–Green Bay, WI	W
University of Wisconsin–Madison, WI	W
University of Wisconsin–Parkside, WI	W
Urbana University, OH	W
Utah State University, UT	W
Valdosta State University, GA	W
Valley City State University, ND	W
Valparaiso University, IN	W
Vanguard University of Southern California, CA	W
Villanova University, PA	W
Virginia Intermont College, VA	W
Virginia Union University, VA	W
Waldorf College, IA	W
Wayne State College, NE	W
Wayne State University, MI	W
Webber International University, FL	W
Western Illinois University, IL	W
Western Kentucky University, KY	W
Western Washington University, WA	W
West Texas A&M University, TX	W
West Virginia Wesleyan College, WV	W
Wheeling Jesuit University, WV	W
Wichita State University, KS	W
William Carey College, MS	W
William Jewell College, MO	W
William Penn University, IA	W
Williams Baptist College, AR	W
William Woods University, MO	W
Wingate University, NC	W
Winona State University, MN	W
Winston-Salem State University, NC	W
Winthrop University, SC	W
Youngstown State University, OH	W

Swimming and diving

College	
Adelphi University, NY	M,W
American University, DC	M,W
Arizona State University, AZ	M,W
Asbury College, KY	M,W
Ashland University, OH	M,W
Auburn University, AL	M,W
Ball State University, IN	M,W
Bentley College, MA	M,W
Biola University, CA	M,W
Bloomsburg University of Pennsylvania, PA	M,W
Boston College, MA	W
Boston University, MA	M,W
Bowling Green State University, OH	M,W
California Baptist University, CA	M,W
California State University, Bakersfield, CA	M,W
California State University, Fresno, CA	W
Catawba College, NC	W
Centenary College of Louisiana, LA	M,W
Central Connecticut State University, CT	W
Clemson University, SC	M,W
Cleveland State University, OH	M,W
College of Charleston, SC	M,W
The College of Saint Rose, NY	M,W
The College of William and Mary, VA	M
Colorado School of Mines, CO	M,W
Colorado State University, CO	W
Davidson College, NC	M,W
Drexel University, PA	M,W
Duquesne University, PA	M,W
East Carolina University, NC	M,W
Eastern Illinois University, IL	M,W
Eastern Michigan University, MI	M,W
East Stroudsburg University of Pennsylvania, PA	W
Edinboro University of Pennsylvania, PA	M,W
Fairfield University, CT	M,W
Fairmont State University, WV	M,W
Florida Agricultural and Mechanical University, FL	M,W
Florida Atlantic University, FL	M,W
Florida State University, FL	M,W
Fordham University, NY	M,W
Gannon University, PA	M,W
George Mason University, VA	M,W
Georgia Institute of Technology, GA	M,W
Georgia Southern University, GA	W
Grand Valley State University, MI	M,W
Hillsdale College, MI	W
Howard University, DC	M,W
Illinois State University, IL	W
Indiana University Bloomington, IN	M,W
Indiana University of Pennsylvania, PA	W
Indiana University–Purdue University Indianapolis, IN	M,W
Iona College, NY	M,W
John Brown University, AR	M,W
Lehigh University, PA	M,W
Limestone College, SC	W
Lindenwood University, MO	M,W
Lock Haven University of Pennsylvania, PA	W
Louisiana State University and Agricultural and Mechanical College, LA	M,W
Manhattan College, NY	W
Marist College, NY	M,W
Marshall University, WV	W
Metropolitan State College of Denver, CO	M,W
Miami University, OH	M,W
Michigan State University, MI	M,W
Millersville University of Pennsylvania, PA	W
Minnesota State University Mankato, MN	M,W
Missouri State University, MO	M,W
Morningside College, IA	M,W
New Mexico State University, NM	W
Niagara University, NY	M,W
North Carolina Agricultural and Technical State University, NC	W
North Carolina State University, NC	M,W
Northeastern University, MA	W
Northern Arizona University, AZ	W
Northern Illinois University, IL	M,W
Northwestern University, IL	M,W
The Ohio State University, OH	M,W
Ohio University, OH	M,W
Ouachita Baptist University, AR	M,W
The Pennsylvania State University University Park Campus, PA	M,W
Pepperdine University, CA	W
Purdue University, IN	M,W
Radford University, VA	W
Rice University, TX	W
Rider University, NJ	M,W
Sacred Heart University, CT	W
St. Bonaventure University, NY	M,W
St. Cloud State University, MN	M,W
St. Francis College, NY	M,W
Saint Francis University, PA	M,W
Saint Leo University, FL	M,W
Saint Louis University, MO	M,W
Salem International University, WV	M,W
San Diego State University, CA	W
San Francisco State University, CA	M,W
San Jose State University, CA	W
Seattle University, WA	M,W
Shippensburg University of Pennsylvania, PA	M,W
Slippery Rock University of Pennsylvania, PA	M,W
South Dakota State University, SD	M,W
Southern Illinois University Carbondale, IL	M,W
Spring Hill College, AL	M,W
Stanford University, CA	M,W
State University of New York at Binghamton, NY	M,W
State University of New York at Buffalo, NY	M,W
Stony Brook University, State University of New York, NY	M,W
Syracuse University, NY	M,W
Texas A&M University, TX	M,W
Texas Christian University, TX	M,W
Towson University, MD	M,W

Athletic Grants for Undergraduates
Tennis

Truman State University, MO	M,W
The University of Alabama, AL	M,W
The University of Alabama at Birmingham, AL	W
University of Alaska Fairbanks, AK	W
University of Arkansas, AR	W
University of California, Berkeley, CA	M,W
University of California, Irvine, CA	M,W
University of California, Los Angeles, CA	W
University of California, Santa Barbara, CA	M,W
University of Cincinnati, OH	M,W
University of Connecticut, CT	M,W
University of Delaware, DE	W
University of Denver, CO	M,W
University of Evansville, IN	M,W
The University of Findlay, OH	M,W
University of Florida, FL	M,W
University of Georgia, GA	M,W
University of Hawaii at Manoa, HI	M,W
University of Illinois at Urbana–Champaign, IL	W
The University of Iowa, IA	M,W
University of Kansas, KS	W
University of Kentucky, KY	M,W
University of Louisville, KY	M,W
University of Maine, ME	W
University of Maryland, Baltimore County, MD	M,W
University of Maryland, College Park, MD	M,W
University of Massachusetts Amherst, MA	M,W
University of Massachusetts Lowell, MA	M
University of Miami, FL	W
University of Michigan, MI	M,W
University of Minnesota, Twin Cities Campus, MN	M,W
University of Missouri–Columbia, MO	M,W
University of Nebraska at Kearney, NE	W
University of Nebraska–Lincoln, NE	W
University of Nevada, Las Vegas, NV	M,W
University of Nevada, Reno, NV	W
University of New Hampshire, NH	W
The University of North Carolina at Chapel Hill, NC	M,W
The University of North Carolina Wilmington, NC	M,W
University of North Dakota, ND	W
University of Northern Colorado, CO	W
University of Northern Iowa, IA	W
University of North Florida, FL	W
University of Pittsburgh, PA	M,W
University of Puerto Rico, Mayagüez Campus, PR	M,W
University of Rhode Island, RI	M,W
University of Richmond, VA	W
University of San Diego, CA	W
University of South Carolina, SC	M,W
The University of South Dakota, SD	M
University of Southern California, CA	M,W
The University of Texas at Austin, TX	M,W
University of the Cumberlands, KY	M,W
University of the Pacific, CA	M,W
The University of Toledo, OH	M,W
University of Utah, UT	M,W
University of Vermont, VT	W
University of Virginia, VA	M,W
University of Wisconsin–Green Bay, WI	M,W
University of Wisconsin–Madison, WI	M,W
University of Wyoming, WY	M,W
Valparaiso University, IN	M,W
Villanova University, PA	W
Virginia Military Institute, VA	M
Virginia Polytechnic Institute and State University, VA	M,W
Washington State University, WA	W
Wayne State University, MI	M,W
Western Illinois University, IL	M,W
Western Kentucky University, KY	M,W
West Virginia University, WV	M,W
West Virginia Wesleyan College, WV	M,W
Wheeling Jesuit University, WV	M,W
Wingate University, NC	M,W
Xavier University, OH	M,W

Table tennis

Inter American University of Puerto Rico, Guayama Campus, PR	M,W
University of Puerto Rico, Mayagüez Campus, PR	M,W

Tennis

Abilene Christian University, TX	M,W
Adelphi University, NY	M,W
Albertson College of Idaho, ID	M,W
Alliant International University, CA	M,W
American University, DC	M,W
Anderson University, SC	M,W
Appalachian State University, NC	M,W
Arizona State University, AZ	M,W
Arkansas State University, AR	W
Arkansas Tech University, AR	W
Armstrong Atlantic State University, GA	M,W
Asbury College, KY	M,W
Auburn University, AL	M,W
Auburn University Montgomery, AL	M,W
Augusta State University, GA	M,W
Austin Peay State University, TN	M,W
Azusa Pacific University, CA	M
Ball State University, IN	M,W
Barton College, NC	M,W
Baylor University, TX	M,W
Belhaven College, MS	M,W
Belmont Abbey College, NC	M,W
Belmont University, TN	M,W
Bemidji State University, MN	W
Benedictine College, KS	M,W
Berry College, GA	M,W
Bethany College, KS	M,W
Bethel College, KS	M,W
Biola University, CA	W
Bloomsburg University of Pennsylvania, PA	M,W
Bluefield State College, WV	M,W
Blue Mountain College, MS	W
Boston College, MA	W
Boston University, MA	W
Bowling Green State University, OH	M,W
Bradley University, IL	M,W
Brenau University, GA	W
Brevard College, NC	M,W
Brigham Young University–Hawaii, HI	M,W
Bryan College, TN	M,W
Butler University, IN	M,W
California State University, Bakersfield, CA	W
California State University, Fresno, CA	M,W
California State University, Fullerton, CA	W
California State University, Sacramento, CA	M,W
Campbellsville University, KY	M,W
Campbell University, NC	M,W
Carson-Newman College, TN	M,W
Catawba College, NC	M,W
Cedarville University, OH	M,W
Centenary College of Louisiana, LA	M,W
Chaminade University of Honolulu, HI	M,W
The Citadel, The Military College of South Carolina, SC	M
Clark Atlanta University, GA	M,W
Clemson University, SC	M,W
Cleveland State University, OH	W
Coastal Carolina University, SC	M,W
College of Charleston, SC	M,W
College of Santa Fe, NM	M,W
The College of William and Mary, VA	M,W
Colorado School of Mines, CO	M,W
Colorado State University, CO	W
Columbia College, SC	W
Columbus State University, GA	M,W
Concordia University, NE	M,W
Converse College, SC	W
Coppin State University, MD	M,W
Creighton University, NE	M,W
Dallas Baptist University, TX	W
Davidson College, NC	M,W
DePaul University, IL	M,W
Dominican University of California, CA	M,W
Dordt College, IA	M,W
Dowling College, NY	M,W
Drake University, IA	M,W
Drexel University, PA	M,W
Duke University, NC	M,W
Duquesne University, PA	M,W
East Carolina University, NC	M,W
East Central University, OK	M,W
Eastern Illinois University, IL	M,W
Eastern Michigan University, MI	W
Eastern Washington University, WA	M,W
East Stroudsburg University of Pennsylvania, PA	M,W
East Tennessee State University, TN	M,W
Eckerd College, FL	M,W
Elon University, NC	M,W
Embry-Riddle Aeronautical University, FL	M
Emporia State University, KS	M,W
Erskine College, SC	M,W
Evangel University, MO	M,W

Peterson's College Money Handbook 2007

Athletic Grants for Undergraduates
Tennis

College	
Fairfield University, CT	M,W
Fairmont State University, WV	M,W
Ferris State University, MI	M,W
Flagler College, FL	M,W
Florida Agricultural and Mechanical University, FL	M,W
Florida Atlantic University, FL	M,W
Florida Gulf Coast University, FL	M,W
Florida Institute of Technology, FL	M,W
Florida Southern College, FL	M,W
Florida State University, FL	M,W
Fordham University, NY	M,W
Fort Hays State University, KS	W
Francis Marion University, SC	M,W
Franklin Pierce College, NH	M,W
Freed-Hardeman University, TN	M,W
Friends University, KS	M,W
Furman University, SC	M,W
Geneva College, PA	W
George Mason University, VA	M,W
Georgetown College, KY	M,W
Georgetown University, DC	W
Georgia College & State University, GA	M,W
Georgia Institute of Technology, GA	M,W
Georgia Southern University, GA	M,W
Georgia Southwestern State University, GA	M,W
Gonzaga University, WA	M,W
Goshen College, IN	M,W
Grace College, IN	M,W
Graceland University, IA	M,W
Grambling State University, LA	M,W
Grand Valley State University, MI	M,W
Hampton University, VA	M,W
Harding University, AR	M,W
Harris-Stowe State University, MO	M,W
Hawai'i Pacific University, HI	M,W
Hofstra University, NY	M,W
Howard University, DC	M,W
Huntington University, IN	M,W
Idaho State University, ID	M,W
Illinois State University, IL	M,W
Indiana State University, IN	M,W
Indiana University Bloomington, IN	M,W
Indiana University of Pennsylvania, PA	W
Indiana University–Purdue University Fort Wayne, IN	M,W
Indiana University–Purdue University Indianapolis, IN	M,W
Inter American University of Puerto Rico, Guayama Campus, PR	M,W
Jacksonville State University, AL	M,W
Jacksonville University, FL	M,W
John Brown University, AR	M,W
Judson College, AL	W
Kansas State University, KS	W
Kennesaw State University, GA	W
Kentucky State University, KY	M,W
King College, TN	M,W
Lake Superior State University, MI	M,W
Lamar University, TX	M,W
Lee University, TN	M,W
Lehigh University, PA	M,W
Le Moyne College, NY	M,W
LeMoyne-Owen College, TN	M,W
Lewis-Clark State College, ID	M,W
Limestone College, SC	M,W
Lincoln University, MO	W
Lindenwood University, MO	M,W
Lindsey Wilson College, KY	M,W
Lipscomb University, TN	M,W
Long Island University, Brooklyn Campus, NY	W
Louisiana State University and Agricultural and Mechanical College, LA	M,W
Louisiana Tech University, LA	W
Lynn University, FL	M,W
Lyon College, AR	M,W
Malone College, OH	M,W
Manhattan College, NY	M,W
Marian College, IN	M,W
Marist College, NY	M,W
Marquette University, WI	M,W
Marshall University, WV	W
McKendree College, IL	M,W
Mercer University, GA	M,W
Mercyhurst College, PA	M,W
Merrimack College, MA	W
Mesa State College, CO	M,W
Metropolitan State College of Denver, CO	M,W
Miami University, OH	W
Michigan State University, MI	M,W
Michigan Technological University, MI	W
Middle Tennessee State University, TN	M,W
Midland Lutheran College, NE	M,W
Midway College, KY	W
Midwestern State University, TX	M,W
Millersville University of Pennsylvania, PA	M,W
Milligan College, TN	M,W
Minnesota State University Mankato, MN	M,W
Mississippi State University, MS	M,W
Missouri State University, MO	M,W
Molloy College, NY	W
Monmouth University, NJ	M,W
Montana State University, MT	M,W
Montana State University–Billings, MT	M,W
Montreat College, NC	M,W
Morehead State University, KY	M,W
Morningside College, IA	M,W
Mount Olive College, NC	M,W
Mount St. Mary's University, MD	M,W
Murray State University, KY	M,W
Newberry College, SC	M,W
Newman University, KS	M,W
New Mexico State University, NM	M,W
Niagara University, NY	M,W
Nicholls State University, LA	W
North Carolina Agricultural and Technical State University, NC	M,W
North Carolina State University, NC	M,W
Northeastern University, MA	M
Northern Arizona University, AZ	M,W
Northern Illinois University, IL	M,W
Northern State University, SD	W
North Georgia College & State University, GA	M,W
North Greenville College, SC	M,W
Northwestern State University of Louisiana, LA	W
Northwestern University, IL	M,W
Northwood University, MI	M,W
Northwood University, Florida Campus, FL	M,W
Nova Southeastern University, FL	W
The Ohio State University, OH	M,W
Oklahoma Baptist University, OK	M,W
Oklahoma State University, OK	M,W
Olivet Nazarene University, IL	M,W
Oral Roberts University, OK	M,W
Ouachita Baptist University, AR	M,W
The Pennsylvania State University University Park Campus, PA	M,W
Pepperdine University, CA	M,W
Philadelphia University, PA	M,W
Pikeville College, KY	M,W
Portland State University, OR	M,W
Purdue University, IN	M,W
Quincy University, IL	M,W
Quinnipiac University, CT	M,W
Radford University, VA	M,W
Rice University, TX	M,W
Rider University, NJ	M,W
Robert Morris College, IL	W
Robert Morris University, PA	M,W
Roberts Wesleyan College, NY	M,W
Rockhurst University, MO	M,W
Rollins College, FL	M,W
Sacred Heart University, CT	M,W
St. Andrews Presbyterian College, NC	M,W
St. Bonaventure University, NY	M,W
St. Cloud State University, MN	M,W
St. Edward's University, TX	M,W
St. Francis College, NY	M,W
Saint Francis University, PA	M,W
St. John's University, NY	M,W
Saint Joseph's College, IN	M,W
Saint Joseph's University, PA	M,W
Saint Leo University, FL	M,W
Saint Louis University, MO	M,W
Saint Mary's College of California, CA	M,W
St. Thomas University, FL	M,W
Saint Vincent College, PA	M,W
Salem International University, WV	M,W
Samford University, AL	M,W
San Diego State University, CA	M,W
San Jose State University, CA	W
Santa Clara University, CA	M,W
Seton Hill University, PA	M,W
Shepherd University, WV	M,W
Shippensburg University of Pennsylvania, PA	W
Shorter College, GA	M,W
Slippery Rock University of Pennsylvania, PA	W
Sonoma State University, CA	M,W
South Carolina State University, SC	M,W
South Dakota State University, SD	M,W
Southeastern Louisiana University, LA	M,W

Athletic Grants for Undergraduates
Tennis

School	
Southeastern Oklahoma State University, OK	M,W
Southeast Missouri State University, MO	W
Southern Arkansas University–Magnolia, AR	W
Southern Illinois University Carbondale, IL	M,W
Southern Illinois University Edwardsville, IL	M,W
Southern New Hampshire University, NH	M,W
Southern Oregon University, OR	W
Southern University and Agricultural and Mechanical College, LA	M,W
Southwest Baptist University, MO	M,W
Southwest Minnesota State University, MN	W
Spring Arbor University, MI	M,W
Spring Hill College, AL	M,W
Stanford University, CA	M,W
State University of New York at Binghamton, NY	M,W
State University of New York at Buffalo, NY	M,W
Stephen F. Austin State University, TX	W
Stetson University, FL	M,W
Stonehill College, MA	M,W
Stony Brook University, State University of New York, NY	M,W
Syracuse University, NY	W
Tabor College, KS	M,W
Taylor University, IN	M,W
Temple University, PA	M
Tennessee State University, TN	M,W
Tennessee Technological University, TN	M,W
Texas A&M University, TX	M,W
Texas Christian University, TX	M,W
Texas Southern University, TX	M,W
Texas State University-San Marcos, TX	W
Texas Tech University, TX	M,W
Tiffin University, OH	M,W
Towson University, MD	M,W
Truman State University, MO	M,W
Tusculum College, TN	M,W
Tuskegee University, AL	M,W
Union College, KY	M,W
University at Albany, State University of New York, NY	W
The University of Akron, OH	M,W
The University of Alabama, AL	M,W
The University of Alabama at Birmingham, AL	M,W
The University of Alabama in Huntsville, AL	M,W
University of Arkansas, AR	M,W
University of California, Berkeley, CA	M,W
University of California, Irvine, CA	M,W
University of California, Los Angeles, CA	M,W
University of California, Riverside, CA	M,W
University of California, Santa Barbara, CA	M,W
University of Central Oklahoma, OK	M,W
University of Cincinnati, OH	M,W
University of Colorado at Boulder, CO	M,W
University of Colorado at Colorado Springs, CO	M,W
University of Connecticut, CT	M,W
University of Dayton, OH	M,W
University of Denver, CO	M,W
University of Evansville, IN	W
The University of Findlay, OH	M,W
University of Florida, FL	M,W
University of Georgia, GA	M,W
University of Hartford, CT	M,W
University of Hawaii at Hilo, HI	M,W
University of Hawaii at Manoa, HI	M,W
University of Idaho, ID	M,W
University of Illinois at Springfield, IL	M,W
University of Illinois at Urbana–Champaign, IL	M,W
The University of Iowa, IA	M,W
University of Kansas, KS	W
University of Kentucky, KY	M,W
University of Louisiana at Lafayette, LA	M,W
University of Louisville, KY	M,W
University of Mary, ND	M,W
University of Maryland, Baltimore County, MD	M,W
University of Maryland, College Park, MD	M,W
University of Massachusetts Amherst, MA	M,W
University of Massachusetts Lowell, MA	M,W
University of Memphis, TN	M,W
University of Miami, FL	M,W
University of Michigan, MI	M,W
University of Minnesota, Duluth, MN	M,W
University of Minnesota, Twin Cities Campus, MN	M,W
University of Missouri–Columbia, MO	W
University of Missouri–Kansas City, MO	M,W
University of Missouri–St. Louis, MO	M,W
University of Nebraska at Kearney, NE	M,W
University of Nebraska–Lincoln, NE	M,W
University of Nevada, Las Vegas, NV	M,W
University of Nevada, Reno, NV	M,W
University of New Hampshire, NH	W
University of New Haven, CT	M,W
University of New Orleans, LA	M,W
University of North Alabama, AL	M,W
The University of North Carolina at Asheville, NC	M,W
The University of North Carolina at Chapel Hill, NC	M,W
The University of North Carolina at Greensboro, NC	M,W
The University of North Carolina at Pembroke, NC	W
The University of North Carolina Wilmington, NC	M,W
University of Northern Colorado, CO	M,W
University of Northern Iowa, IA	W
University of North Florida, FL	M,W
University of Oklahoma, OK	M,W
University of Oregon, OR	M,W
University of Pittsburgh, PA	W
University of Portland, OR	M,W
University of Puerto Rico, Mayagüez Campus, PR	M,W
University of Rhode Island, RI	W
University of Richmond, VA	M,W
University of St. Francis, IL	M,W
University of Saint Francis, IN	M,W
University of San Diego, CA	M,W
University of South Carolina, SC	M,W
University of South Carolina Upstate, SC	M,W
The University of South Dakota, SD	M,W
University of Southern California, CA	M,W
University of Southern Indiana, IN	M,W
University of Southern Mississippi, MS	M,W
University of South Florida, FL	M,W
The University of Tampa, FL	W
The University of Tennessee at Martin, TN	M,W
The University of Texas at Arlington, TX	M,W
The University of Texas at Austin, TX	M,W
The University of Texas at El Paso, TX	W
The University of Texas at San Antonio, TX	M,W
The University of Texas–Pan American, TX	M,W
University of the Cumberlands, KY	M,W
University of the District of Columbia, DC	M,W
University of the Pacific, CA	M,W
The University of Toledo, OH	M,W
University of Tulsa, OK	M,W
University of Utah, UT	M,W
University of Virginia, VA	M,W
University of Wisconsin–Green Bay, WI	M,W
University of Wisconsin–Madison, WI	M,W
University of Wyoming, WY	W
Utah State University, UT	M,W
Valdosta State University, GA	M,W
Valparaiso University, IN	M,W
Vanderbilt University, TN	M,W
Vanguard University of Southern California, CA	M,W
Virginia Commonwealth University, VA	M,W
Virginia Intermont College, VA	M,W
Virginia Military Institute, VA	M
Virginia Polytechnic Institute and State University, VA	M,W
Virginia Union University, VA	M
Wake Forest University, NC	M,W
Washington State University, WA	W
Wayne State University, MI	M,W
Webber International University, FL	M,W
Western Carolina University, NC	W
Western Illinois University, IL	M,W
Western Kentucky University, KY	M,W
Westmont College, CA	M,W
West Virginia University, WV	W

Athletic Grants for Undergraduates
Tennis

West Virginia Wesleyan College, WV	M,W
Wichita State University, KS	M,W
William Jewell College, MO	M,W
Wingate University, NC	M,W
Winona State University, MN	M,W
Winston-Salem State University, NC	M,W
Winthrop University, SC	M,W
Wofford College, SC	M,W
Xavier University, OH	M,W
Xavier University of Louisiana, LA	M,W
Youngstown State University, OH	M,W

Track and field

Abilene Christian University, TX	M,W
Adelphi University, NY	M,W
Alabama Agricultural and Mechanical University, AL	M,W
Alliant International University, CA	M,W
American University, DC	M,W
Anderson University, SC	M,W
Appalachian State University, NC	M,W
Arizona State University, AZ	M,W
Arkansas State University, AR	M,W
Ashford University, IA	M,W
Ashland University, OH	M,W
Auburn University, AL	M,W
Augustana College, SD	M,W
Austin Peay State University, TN	W
Azusa Pacific University, CA	M,W
Ball State University, IN	M,W
Baylor University, TX	M,W
Belmont University, TN	M,W
Bemidji State University, MN	M,W
Benedictine College, KS	M,W
Bentley College, MA	M,W
Berry College, GA	M,W
Bethany College, KS	M,W
Bethel College, KS	M,W
Biola University, CA	M,W
Black Hills State University, SD	M,W
Bloomsburg University of Pennsylvania, PA	M,W
Boston College, MA	M,W
Boston University, MA	M,W
Bowling Green State University, OH	M,W
Bradley University, IL	W
Brevard College, NC	M,W
California Polytechnic State University, San Luis Obispo, CA	M,W
California State University, Bakersfield, CA	M,W
California State University, Chico, CA	M,W
California State University, Fresno, CA	M,W
California State University, Fullerton, CA	M,W
California State University, Sacramento, CA	M,W
Campbellsville University, KY	M,W
Campbell University, NC	M,W
Carson-Newman College, TN	M,W
Cascade College, OR	M,W
Cedarville University, OH	M,W
Central Connecticut State University, CT	M,W
Central Michigan University, MI	M,W
Central Missouri State University, MO	M,W
Central Washington University, WA	M,W
The Citadel, The Military College of South Carolina, SC	M,W
Clark Atlanta University, GA	M
Clemson University, SC	M,W
Cleveland State University, OH	W
Coastal Carolina University, SC	M,W
College of the Southwest, NM	M,W
The College of William and Mary, VA	M,W
Colorado School of Mines, CO	M,W
Colorado State University, CO	M,W
Concordia University, NE	M,W
Concordia University, St. Paul, MN	M,W
Coppin State University, MD	M,W
Cornerstone University, MI	M,W
Dakota State University, SD	M,W
Dallas Baptist University, TX	W
Davidson College, NC	M,W
DePaul University, IL	M,W
Dickinson State University, ND	M,W
Doane College, NE	M,W
Dordt College, IA	M,W
Drake University, IA	M,W
Duquesne University, PA	W
East Carolina University, NC	M,W
Eastern Illinois University, IL	M,W
Eastern Michigan University, MI	M,W
Eastern Washington University, WA	M,W
East Stroudsburg University of Pennsylvania, PA	M,W
East Tennessee State University, TN	M,W
Edinboro University of Pennsylvania, PA	M,W
Elon University, NC	W
Emporia State University, KS	M,W
Evangel University, MO	M,W
Felician College, NJ	M,W
Ferris State University, MI	M,W
Florida Agricultural and Mechanical University, FL	M,W
Florida Atlantic University, FL	W
Florida State University, FL	M,W
Fordham University, NY	M,W
Fort Hays State University, KS	M,W
Fresno Pacific University, CA	M,W
Friends University, KS	M,W
Furman University, SC	M,W
Geneva College, PA	M,W
George Mason University, VA	M,W
Georgetown College, KY	M,W
Georgetown University, DC	M,W
Georgia Institute of Technology, GA	M,W
Georgia Southern University, GA	W
Glenville State College, WV	M,W
Gordon College, MA	W
Goshen College, IN	M,W
Grace College, IN	M,W
Graceland University, IA	M,W
Grambling State University, LA	M,W
Grand Valley State University, MI	M,W
Grand View College, IA	M,W
Hampton University, VA	M,W
Harding University, AR	M,W
Harris-Stowe State University, MO	W
Hillsdale College, MI	M,W
Houghton College, NY	M,W
Howard University, DC	M,W
Humboldt State University, CA	M,W
Huntington University, IN	M,W
Idaho State University, ID	M,W
Illinois State University, IL	M,W
Indiana State University, IN	M,W
Indiana University Bloomington, IN	M,W
Indiana University of Pennsylvania, PA	M,W
Indiana University–Purdue University Fort Wayne, IN	W
Inter American University of Puerto Rico, Guayama Campus, PR	M,W
Iona College, NY	M,W
Iowa Wesleyan College, IA	M,W
Jacksonville University, FL	W
James Madison University, VA	M,W
Jamestown College, ND	M,W
Kansas State University, KS	M,W
Kent State University, OH	M,W
Kentucky State University, KY	M,W
King College, TN	M,W
Lake Superior State University, MI	M,W
Lamar University, TX	M,W
Lehigh University, PA	M,W
Lincoln University, MO	M,W
Lindenwood University, MO	M,W
Lindsey Wilson College, KY	M,W
Lock Haven University of Pennsylvania, PA	M,W
Long Island University, Brooklyn Campus, NY	M,W
Louisiana State University and Agricultural and Mechanical College, LA	M,W
Louisiana Tech University, LA	M,W
Loyola University Chicago, IL	M,W
Malone College, OH	M,W
Manhattan College, NY	M,W
Mansfield University of Pennsylvania, PA	M,W
Marian College, IN	M,W
Marist College, NY	M,W
Marquette University, WI	M,W
Marshall University, WV	M,W
McKendree College, IL	M,W
Miami University, OH	M,W
Michigan State University, MI	M,W
MidAmerica Nazarene University, KS	M,W
Middle Tennessee State University, TN	M,W
Midland Lutheran College, NE	M,W
Millersville University of Pennsylvania, PA	M,W
Minnesota State University Mankato, MN	M,W
Mississippi State University, MS	M,W
Missouri State University, MO	M,W
Monmouth University, NJ	M,W
Montana State University, MT	M,W
Morehead State University, KY	M,W
Morningside College, IA	M,W
Mount Marty College, SD	M,W
Mount St. Mary's University, MD	M,W
Murray State University, KY	M,W

Athletic Grants for Undergraduates
Track and field

Institution	
New Mexico State University, NM	W
New York Institute of Technology, NY	M,W
Nicholls State University, LA	M,W
North Carolina Agricultural and Technical State University, NC	M,W
North Carolina State University, NC	M,W
Northeastern University, MA	M,W
Northern Arizona University, AZ	M,W
Northern State University, SD	M,W
Northwestern State University of Louisiana, LA	M,W
Northwest Nazarene University, ID	M,W
Northwest University, WA	M,W
Northwood University, MI	M,W
Northwood University, Texas Campus, TX	M,W
The Ohio State University, OH	M,W
Ohio University, OH	M,W
Oklahoma Baptist University, OK	M,W
Oklahoma State University, OK	M,W
Olivet Nazarene University, IL	M,W
Oral Roberts University, OK	M,W
The Pennsylvania State University University Park Campus, PA	M,W
Pittsburg State University, KS	M,W
Pontifical Catholic University of Puerto Rico, PR	M,W
Portland State University, OR	M,W
Purdue University, IN	M,W
Quinnipiac University, CT	M,W
Radford University, VA	M,W
Rice University, TX	M,W
Rider University, NJ	M,W
Robert Morris University, PA	M,W
Roberts Wesleyan College, NY	M,W
Sacred Heart University, CT	M,W
St. Cloud State University, MN	M,W
St. Francis College, NY	M,W
Saint Francis University, PA	M,W
Saint Joseph's College, IN	M,W
Saint Joseph's University, PA	M,W
Saint Martin's University, WA	M,W
Samford University, AL	M,W
San Diego State University, CA	W
San Francisco State University, CA	M,W
Seattle Pacific University, WA	M,W
Seattle University, WA	M,W
Seton Hill University, PA	M,W
Shippensburg University of Pennsylvania, PA	M,W
Shorter College, GA	M,W
Slippery Rock University of Pennsylvania, PA	M,W
Sonoma State University, CA	W
South Carolina State University, SC	M,W
South Dakota School of Mines and Technology, SD	M,W
South Dakota State University, SD	M,W
Southeastern Louisiana University, LA	M,W
Southeast Missouri State University, MO	M,W
Southern Illinois University Carbondale, IL	M,W
Southern Illinois University Edwardsville, IL	M,W
Southern Oregon University, OR	M,W
Southern University and Agricultural and Mechanical College, LA	M,W
Spring Arbor University, MI	M,W
Stanford University, CA	M,W
State University of New York at Binghamton, NY	M,W
State University of New York at Buffalo, NY	M,W
Stephen F. Austin State University, TX	M,W
Stonehill College, MA	M,W
Stony Brook University, State University of New York, NY	M,W
Syracuse University, NY	M,W
Tabor College, KS	M,W
Taylor University, IN	M,W
Temple University, PA	M,W
Tennessee State University, TN	M,W
Tennessee Technological University, TN	W
Texas A&M University, TX	M,W
Texas A&M University–Commerce, TX	
Texas Christian University, TX	M,W
Texas Southern University, TX	M,W
Texas State University-San Marcos, TX	M,W
Texas Tech University, TX	M,W
Tiffin University, OH	M,W
Towson University, MD	M,W
Truman State University, MO	M,W
Tuskegee University, AL	M,W
University at Albany, State University of New York, NY	M,W
The University of Akron, OH	M,W
The University of Alabama, AL	M,W
The University of Alabama at Birmingham, AL	W
The University of Alabama in Huntsville, AL	M,W
University of Arkansas, AR	M,W
University of California, Berkeley, CA	M
University of California, Irvine, CA	M,W
University of California, Los Angeles, CA	M,W
University of California, Riverside, CA	M,W
University of California, Santa Barbara, CA	M,W
University of Cincinnati, OH	M
University of Colorado at Boulder, CO	M,W
University of Connecticut, CT	M,W
University of Dayton, OH	W
University of Delaware, DE	W
The University of Findlay, OH	M,W
University of Florida, FL	M,W
University of Georgia, GA	M,W
University of Hawaii at Manoa, HI	W
University of Idaho, ID	M,W
University of Illinois at Urbana–Champaign, IL	M,W
The University of Iowa, IA	M,W
University of Kansas, KS	M,W
University of Kentucky, KY	M,W
University of Louisiana at Lafayette, LA	M,W
University of Louisville, KY	M,W
University of Maine, ME	M,W
University of Mary, ND	M,W
University of Maryland, Baltimore County, MD	M,W
University of Maryland, College Park, MD	M,W
University of Massachusetts Amherst, MA	M,W
University of Massachusetts Lowell, MA	M,W
University of Memphis, TN	M,W
University of Miami, FL	M,W
University of Michigan, MI	M,W
University of Minnesota, Duluth, MN	M,W
University of Minnesota, Twin Cities Campus, MN	M,W
University of Missouri–Columbia, MO	M,W
University of Missouri–Kansas City, MO	M,W
University of Nebraska at Kearney, NE	M,W
University of Nebraska–Lincoln, NE	M,W
University of Nevada, Las Vegas, NV	W
University of Nevada, Reno, NV	W
University of New Hampshire, NH	M,W
University of New Haven, CT	M,W
University of New Orleans, LA	M,W
The University of North Carolina at Asheville, NC	M,W
The University of North Carolina at Chapel Hill, NC	M,W
The University of North Carolina at Pembroke, NC	M
The University of North Carolina Wilmington, NC	M,W
University of North Dakota, ND	M,W
University of Northern Colorado, CO	M,W
University of Northern Iowa, IA	M,W
University of North Florida, FL	M,W
University of Oklahoma, OK	M,W
University of Oregon, OR	M,W
University of Pittsburgh, PA	M,W
University of Portland, OR	M,W
University of Puerto Rico, Mayagüez Campus, PR	M,W
University of Rhode Island, RI	M,W
University of Richmond, VA	W
University of St. Francis, IL	W
University of Saint Francis, IN	M,W
University of South Carolina, SC	M,W
The University of South Dakota, SD	M,W
University of Southern California, CA	M,W
University of Southern Mississippi, MS	M,W
University of South Florida, FL	M,W
The University of Texas at Arlington, TX	M,W
The University of Texas at Austin, TX	M,W
The University of Texas at El Paso, TX	M,W
The University of Texas at San Antonio, TX	M,W
The University of Texas–Pan American, TX	M,W
University of the Cumberlands, KY	M,W

Peterson's College Money Handbook 2007

Athletic Grants for Undergraduates

Track and field

School	
University of the District of Columbia, DC	M,W
The University of Toledo, OH	M,W
University of Tulsa, OK	M,W
University of Utah, UT	W
University of Vermont, VT	M,W
University of Virginia, VA	M,W
University of Wisconsin–Madison, WI	M,W
University of Wisconsin–Parkside, WI	M,W
University of Wyoming, WY	M,W
Utah State University, UT	M,W
Vanderbilt University, TN	W
Vanguard University of Southern California, CA	
Villanova University, PA	M,W
Virginia Commonwealth University, VA	M,W
Virginia Intermont College, VA	M,W
Virginia Military Institute, VA	M,W
Virginia Polytechnic Institute and State University, VA	M,W
Virginia Union University, VA	M,W
Wake Forest University, NC	M,W
Washington State University, WA	M,W
Wayland Baptist University, TX	M,W
Wayne State College, NE	M,W
Webber International University, FL	M,W
Western Carolina University, NC	M,W
Western Illinois University, IL	M,W
Western Kentucky University, KY	M,W
Western State College of Colorado, CO	M,W
Western Washington University, WA	M,W
Westmont College, CA	M,W
West Virginia University, WV	W
West Virginia Wesleyan College, WV	M,W
Wheeling Jesuit University, WV	M,W
Wichita State University, KS	M,W
William Jewell College, MO	M,W
William Penn University, IA	M,W
Winona State University, MN	W
Winthrop University, SC	M,W
Wofford College, SC	M,W
Youngstown State University, OH	M,W

Volleyball

School	
Abilene Christian University, TX	W
Adelphi University, NY	W
Alabama Agricultural and Mechanical University, AL	W
Albertson College of Idaho, ID	W
Alderson-Broaddus College, WV	W
Alliant International University, CA	W
American International College, MA	W
American University, DC	W
Anderson University, SC	W
Appalachian State University, NC	W
Arizona State University, AZ	W
Arkansas State University, AR	W
Arkansas Tech University, AR	W
Armstrong Atlantic State University, GA	W
Asbury College, KY	W
Ashford University, IA	W
Ashland University, OH	W
Auburn University, AL	W
Augustana College, SD	W
Austin Peay State University, TN	W
Avila University, MO	W
Azusa Pacific University, CA	W
Ball State University, IN	M,W
Barton College, NC	W
Baylor University, TX	W
Belhaven College, MS	W
Belmont University, TN	W
Bemidji State University, MN	W
Benedictine College, KS	W
Bentley College, MA	W
Bethany College, KS	W
Bethel College, KS	W
Biola University, CA	W
Black Hills State University, SD	W
Blessing-Rieman College of Nursing, IL	M,W
Bloomfield College, NJ	W
Bluefield State College, WV	W
Boston College, MA	W
Bowling Green State University, OH	W
Bradley University, IL	W
Brenau University, GA	W
Brevard College, NC	W
Brewton-Parker College, GA	W
Brigham Young University–Hawaii, HI	W
Bryan College, TN	W
Butler University, IN	W
California Baptist University, CA	M,W
California Polytechnic State University, San Luis Obispo, CA	W
California State University, Bakersfield, CA	W
California State University, Dominguez Hills, CA	W
California State University, Fresno, CA	W
California State University, Fullerton, CA	W
California State University, Sacramento, CA	W
Campbellsville University, KY	W
Campbell University, NC	W
Carroll College, MT	W
Carson-Newman College, TN	W
Cascade College, OR	W
Catawba College, NC	W
Cedarville University, OH	W
Centenary College of Louisiana, LA	W
Central Connecticut State University, CT	W
Central Michigan University, MI	W
Central Missouri State University, MO	W
Central Washington University, WA	W
Chaminade University of Honolulu, HI	W
Christian Brothers University, TN	W
The Citadel, The Military College of South Carolina, SC	W
Clemson University, SC	W
Cleveland State University, OH	W
Coastal Carolina University, SC	W
Colgate University, NY	W
College of Charleston, SC	W
College of Saint Mary, NE	W
The College of Saint Rose, NY	W
College of the Ozarks, MO	W
College of the Southwest, NM	W
The College of William and Mary, VA	W
Colorado School of Mines, CO	W
Colorado State University, CO	W
Columbia College, SC	W
Concordia University, CA	W
Concordia University, MI	W
Concordia University, NE	W
Concordia University, St. Paul, MN	W
Converse College, SC	W
Coppin State University, MD	W
Corban College, OR	W
Cornerstone University, MI	W
Creighton University, NE	W
Culver-Stockton College, MO	W
Daemen College, NY	W
Dakota State University, SD	W
Dallas Baptist University, TX	W
Davidson College, NC	W
Davis & Elkins College, WV	W
DePaul University, IL	W
Dickinson State University, ND	W
Doane College, NE	W
Dominican University of California, CA	W
Dordt College, IA	W
Dowling College, NY	W
Drake University, IA	W
Drexel University, PA	W
Duke University, NC	W
Duquesne University, PA	W
East Carolina University, NC	W
Eastern Illinois University, IL	W
Eastern Michigan University, MI	W
Eastern Washington University, WA	W
East Stroudsburg University of Pennsylvania, PA	M,W
East Tennessee State University, TN	W
Eckerd College, FL	W
Edinboro University of Pennsylvania, PA	W
Elon University, NC	W
Embry-Riddle Aeronautical University, AZ	W
Embry-Riddle Aeronautical University, FL	W
Emporia State University, KS	W
Evangel University, MO	W
The Evergreen State College, WA	W
Fairfield University, CT	W
Faulkner University, AL	W
Ferris State University, MI	W
Flagler College, FL	W
Florida Agricultural and Mechanical University, FL	W
Florida Atlantic University, FL	W
Florida College, FL	W
Florida Gulf Coast University, FL	W
Florida Institute of Technology, FL	W
Florida Southern College, FL	W
Florida State University, FL	W
Fordham University, NY	W
Fort Hays State University, KS	W
Fort Lewis College, CO	W

Athletic Grants for Undergraduates
Volleyball

Francis Marion University, SC	W	Le Moyne College, NY	W	Newman University, KS	M,W
Franklin Pierce College, NH	W	LeMoyne-Owen College, TN	W	New Mexico State University, NM	W
Freed-Hardeman University, TN	W	Lesley University, MA	M,W	New York Institute of Technology, NY	W
Fresno Pacific University, CA	W	Lewis-Clark State College, ID	W	Niagara University, NY	W
Friends University, KS	W	Limestone College, SC	W	Nicholls State University, LA	W
Furman University, SC	W	Lindenwood University, MO	M,W	North Carolina Agricultural and Technical State University, NC	W
Gannon University, PA	W	Lindsey Wilson College, KY	W	North Carolina State University, NC	W
Geneva College, PA	W	Lipscomb University, TN	W	Northeastern University, MA	W
George Mason University, VA	M,W	Lock Haven University of Pennsylvania, PA	W	Northern Arizona University, AZ	W
Georgetown College, KY	W	Long Island University, Brooklyn Campus, NY	W	Northern Illinois University, IL	W
Georgetown University, DC	W			Northern State University, SD	W
Georgia Institute of Technology, GA	W	Louisiana State University and Agricultural and Mechanical College, LA	W	North Greenville College, SC	W
Georgia Southern University, GA	W			Northwestern State University of Louisiana, LA	W
Georgia Southwestern State University, GA		Louisiana Tech University, LA	W	Northwestern University, IL	W
Glenville State College, WV	W	Loyola University Chicago, IL	M,W	Northwest Nazarene University, ID	W
Gonzaga University, WA	W	Lubbock Christian University, TX	W	Northwest University, WA	W
Goshen College, IN	W	Lyon College, AR	W	Northwood University, MI	W
Grace College, IN	W	Malone College, OH	W	Northwood University, Florida Campus, FL	W
Graceland University, IA	M,W	Manhattan College, NY	W	Nova Southeastern University, FL	W
Grambling State University, LA	W	Marian College, IN	W	Nyack College, NY	W
Grand Valley State University, MI	W	Marist College, NY	W	The Ohio State University, OH	M,W
Grand View College, IA	W	Marquette University, WI	W	Ohio University, OH	W
Hampton University, VA	W	Marshall University, WV	W	Oklahoma Panhandle State University, OK	
Hannibal-LaGrange College, MO	W	The Master's College and Seminary, CA	W	Olivet Nazarene University, IL	W
Harding University, AR	W	Mayville State University, ND	W	Oral Roberts University, OK	W
Harris-Stowe State University, MO	W	McKendree College, IL	W	Ouachita Baptist University, AR	W
Hawai'i Pacific University, HI	W	Mercer University, GA	W	The Pennsylvania State University University Park Campus, PA	M,W
Hillsdale College, MI	W	Mercyhurst College, PA	M,W		
Hofstra University, NY	W	Merrimack College, MA	W	Pepperdine University, CA	M,W
Holy Names University, CA	M,W	Mesa State College, CO	W	Philadelphia University, PA	W
Houghton College, NY	W	Metropolitan State College of Denver, CO	W	Pikeville College, KY	W
Houston Baptist University, TX	W	Miami University, OH	W	Pittsburg State University, KS	W
Howard University, DC	W	Michigan State University, MI	W	Portland State University, OR	W
Humboldt State University, CA	W	Michigan Technological University, MI	W	Purdue University, IN	W
Huntington University, IN	W			Quincy University, IL	M,W
Idaho State University, ID	W	MidAmerica Nazarene University, KS	W	Quinnipiac University, CT	W
Illinois State University, IL	W	Middle Tennessee State University, TN	W	Radford University, VA	W
Indiana State University, IN	W			Rice University, TX	W
Indiana University Bloomington, IN	W	Midland Lutheran College, NE	W	Rider University, NJ	M,W
Indiana University of Pennsylvania, PA	W	Midwestern State University, TX	W	Robert Morris College, IL	W
Indiana University–Purdue University Fort Wayne, IN	M,W	Millersville University of Pennsylvania, PA	W	Robert Morris University, PA	W
		Milligan College, TN	W	Roberts Wesleyan College, NY	W
Indiana University–Purdue University Indianapolis, IN	W	Minnesota State University Mankato, MN	W	Rockhurst University, MO	W
				Rollins College, FL	W
Indiana University Southeast, IN	W	Mississippi State University, MS	W	Sacred Heart University, CT	M,W
Inter American University of Puerto Rico, Guayama Campus, PR	M,W	Missouri State University, MO	W	St. Andrews Presbyterian College, NC	W
		Molloy College, NY	W	St. Bonaventure University, NY	W
Iona College, NY	W	Montana State University, MT	W	St. Cloud State University, MN	W
Iowa Wesleyan College, IA	W	Montana State University–Billings, MT	W	St. Edward's University, TX	W
Jacksonville State University, AL	W			St. Francis College, NY	W
Jacksonville University, FL	W	Montana Tech of The University of Montana, MT	W	Saint Francis University, PA	M,W
James Madison University, VA	W			St. John's University, NY	W
Jamestown College, ND	W	Montreat College, NC	W	Saint Joseph's College, IN	W
John Brown University, AR	W	Morehead State University, KY	W	Saint Leo University, FL	W
Judson College, AL	W	Morningside College, IA	W	Saint Louis University, MO	W
Kansas State University, KS	W	Mount Marty College, SD	W	Saint Martin's University, WA	W
Kent State University, OH	W	Mount Olive College, NC	M,W	Saint Mary's College of California, CA	W
Kentucky State University, KY	W	Mount Vernon Nazarene University, OH	W		
Kentucky Wesleyan College, KY	W			St. Thomas University, FL	W
King College, TN	W	Murray State University, KY	W	Saint Vincent College, PA	W
Lake Superior State University, MI	W	Newberry College, SC	W	Saint Xavier University, IL	W
Lamar University, TX	W			Salem International University, WV	W
Lee University, TN	W				
Lehigh University, PA	W				

Athletic Grants for Undergraduates
Volleyball

School	Grants
Samford University, AL	W
San Diego Christian College, CA	W
San Diego State University, CA	W
San Francisco State University, CA	W
San Jose State University, CA	W
Santa Clara University, CA	W
Seattle Pacific University, WA	W
Seton Hill University, PA	W
Shepherd University, WV	W
Shippensburg University of Pennsylvania, PA	W
Shorter College, GA	W
Slippery Rock University of Pennsylvania, PA	W
Sonoma State University, CA	W
South Carolina State University, SC	W
South Dakota School of Mines and Technology, SD	W
South Dakota State University, SD	W
Southeastern Louisiana University, LA	W
Southeastern Oklahoma State University, OK	W
Southeast Missouri State University, MO	W
Southern Arkansas University–Magnolia, AR	
Southern Illinois University Carbondale, IL	W
Southern Illinois University Edwardsville, IL	W
Southern New Hampshire University, NH	W
Southern Oregon University, OR	W
Southern University and Agricultural and Mechanical College, LA	W
Southwest Baptist University, MO	W
Southwest Minnesota State University, MN	W
Spring Arbor University, MI	W
Spring Hill College, AL	W
Stanford University, CA	M,W
State University of New York at Binghamton, NY	W
State University of New York at Buffalo, NY	W
Stephen F. Austin State University, TX	W
Stetson University, FL	W
Stonehill College, MA	W
Stony Brook University, State University of New York, NY	W
Syracuse University, NY	W
Tabor College, KS	W
Taylor University, IN	W
Temple University, PA	W
Tennessee Technological University, TN	W
Texas A&M University, TX	W
Texas A&M University–Commerce, TX	W
Texas Christian University, TX	W
Texas Southern University, TX	W
Texas State University-San Marcos, TX	
Texas Tech University, TX	W
Texas Woman's University, TX	W
Tiffin University, OH	W
Towson University, MD	W
Trevecca Nazarene University, TN	W
Trinity International University, IL	W
Truman State University, MO	W
Tusculum College, TN	W
Tuskegee University, AL	W
Union College, KY	W
Union University, TN	W
Unity College, ME	W
University at Albany, State University of New York, NY	W
The University of Akron, OH	W
The University of Alabama, AL	W
The University of Alabama at Birmingham, AL	W
The University of Alabama in Huntsville, AL	W
University of Alaska Fairbanks, AK	W
University of Arkansas, AR	W
University of Arkansas at Pine Bluff, AR	W
University of California, Berkeley, CA	W
University of California, Irvine, CA	M,W
University of California, Los Angeles, CA	M,W
University of California, Riverside, CA	W
University of California, Santa Barbara, CA	M,W
University of Central Oklahoma, OK	W
University of Cincinnati, OH	W
University of Colorado at Boulder, CO	W
University of Colorado at Colorado Springs, CO	W
University of Connecticut, CT	W
University of Dayton, OH	W
University of Delaware, DE	W
University of Denver, CO	W
University of Evansville, IN	W
The University of Findlay, OH	W
University of Florida, FL	W
University of Georgia, GA	W
University of Great Falls, MT	W
University of Hartford, CT	W
University of Hawaii at Hilo, HI	W
University of Hawaii at Manoa, HI	M,W
University of Idaho, ID	W
University of Illinois at Springfield, IL	W
University of Illinois at Urbana–Champaign, IL	W
The University of Iowa, IA	W
University of Kansas, KS	W
University of Kentucky, KY	W
University of Louisiana at Lafayette, LA	W
University of Louisville, KY	W
University of Maine, ME	W
University of Mary, ND	W
University of Maryland, Baltimore County, MD	W
University of Maryland, College Park, MD	W
University of Massachusetts Amherst, MA	
University of Massachusetts Lowell, MA	
University of Memphis, TN	W
University of Miami, FL	W
University of Michigan, MI	W
University of Michigan–Dearborn, MI	W
University of Minnesota, Duluth, MN	W
University of Minnesota, Twin Cities Campus, MN	W
University of Missouri–Columbia, MO	W
University of Missouri–Kansas City, MO	W
University of Missouri–St. Louis, MO	W
University of Nebraska at Kearney, NE	W
University of Nebraska at Omaha, NE	W
University of Nebraska–Lincoln, NE	W
University of Nevada, Las Vegas, NV	W
University of Nevada, Reno, NV	W
University of New Hampshire, NH	W
University of New Haven, CT	M,W
University of New Orleans, LA	W
University of North Alabama, AL	W
The University of North Carolina at Asheville, NC	
The University of North Carolina at Chapel Hill, NC	
The University of North Carolina at Greensboro, NC	W
The University of North Carolina at Pembroke, NC	W
The University of North Carolina Wilmington, NC	W
University of North Dakota, ND	W
University of Northern Colorado, CO	W
University of Northern Iowa, IA	W
University of North Florida, FL	W
University of Oklahoma, OK	W
University of Oregon, OR	W
University of Pittsburgh, PA	W
University of Portland, OR	W
University of Puerto Rico, Mayagüez Campus, PR	M,W
University of Rhode Island, RI	W
University of St. Francis, IL	
University of Saint Francis, IN	
University of San Diego, CA	
University of South Carolina, SC	W
University of South Carolina Upstate, SC	W
The University of South Dakota, SD	W
University of Southern California, CA	M,W
University of Southern Indiana, IN	W
University of Southern Mississippi, MS	W
University of South Florida, FL	W
The University of Tampa, FL	W
The University of Tennessee at Martin, TN	W
The University of Texas at Arlington, TX	W
The University of Texas at Austin, TX	W
The University of Texas at El Paso, TX	
The University of Texas at San Antonio, TX	W
The University of Texas–Pan American, TX	W

Athletic Grants for Undergraduates
Wrestling

College	Type
University of the Cumberlands, KY	W
University of the District of Columbia, DC	W
University of the Pacific, CA	M,W
The University of Toledo, OH	W
University of Tulsa, OK	W
University of Utah, UT	W
University of Virginia, VA	W
The University of West Alabama, AL	W
University of West Georgia, GA	W
University of Wisconsin–Green Bay, WI	W
University of Wisconsin–Madison, WI	W
University of Wisconsin–Parkside, WI	W
University of Wyoming, WY	W
Urbana University, OH	W
Utah State University, UT	W
Valdosta State University, GA	W
Valley City State University, ND	W
Valparaiso University, IN	W
Vanguard University of Southern California, CA	W
Villanova University, PA	W
Virginia Intermont College, VA	W
Virginia Polytechnic Institute and State University, VA	W
Virginia Union University, VA	W
Wake Forest University, NC	W
Waldorf College, IA	W
Warner Pacific College, OR	W
Washington State University, WA	W
Wayland Baptist University, TX	W
Wayne State College, NE	W
Wayne State University, MI	W
Western Carolina University, NC	W
Western Illinois University, IL	W
Western Kentucky University, KY	W
Western State College of Colorado, CO	W
Western Washington University, WA	W
Westmont College, CA	W
West Texas A&M University, TX	W
West Virginia University, WV	W
West Virginia Wesleyan College, WV	W
Wheeling Jesuit University, WV	W
Whitman College, WA	M,W
Wichita State University, KS	W
William Jewell College, MO	W
William Penn University, IA	W
Williams Baptist College, AR	W
William Woods University, MO	M,W
Wingate University, NC	W
Winona State University, MN	W
Winston-Salem State University, NC	W
Winthrop University, SC	W
Wofford College, SC	W
Xavier University, OH	W
Youngstown State University, OH	W

Water polo

College	Type
Brigham Young University–Hawaii, HI	M
California Baptist University, CA	M,W
California State University, Bakersfield, CA	W
Chaminade University of Honolulu, HI	M
Colorado State University, CO	W
Fordham University, NY	M
Indiana University Bloomington, IN	W
Iona College, NY	W
Lindenwood University, MO	M,W
Marist College, NY	W
Mercyhurst College, PA	M,W
Pepperdine University, CA	M
St. Francis College, NY	M,W
Salem International University, WV	M,W
San Diego State University, CA	W
San Jose State University, CA	W
Santa Clara University, CA	M
Slippery Rock University of Pennsylvania, PA	M,W
Stanford University, CA	M,W
University of California, Berkeley, CA	M,W
University of California, Irvine, CA	M
University of California, Los Angeles, CA	M,W
University of California, Santa Barbara, CA	M,W
University of Hawaii at Manoa, HI	W
University of Maryland, College Park, MD	W
University of Puerto Rico, Mayagüez Campus, PR	M
University of Southern California, CA	M,W
University of the Pacific, CA	M,W

Weight lifting

College	Type
Coppin State University, MD	M,W
Inter American University of Puerto Rico, Guayama Campus, PR	M,W
University of Puerto Rico, Mayagüez Campus, PR	M

Wrestling

College	Type
American University, DC	M
Anderson University, SC	M
Appalachian State University, NC	M
Arizona State University, AZ	M
Ashland University, OH	M
Augustana College, SD	M
Bloomsburg University of Pennsylvania, PA	
Boston University, MA	M
California Polytechnic State University, San Luis Obispo, CA	M
California State University, Bakersfield, CA	
California State University, Fresno, CA	
California State University, Fullerton, CA	M
Campbellsville University, KY	M
Campbell University, NC	M
Carson-Newman College, TN	M
Central Michigan University, MI	M
Central Missouri State University, MO	M
The Citadel, The Military College of South Carolina, SC	M
Cleveland State University, OH	M
Colorado School of Mines, CO	M
Coppin State University, MD	M
Davidson College, NC	M
Dickinson State University, ND	M
Drexel University, PA	M
Duquesne University, PA	M
Eastern Illinois University, IL	M
Eastern Michigan University, MI	M
East Stroudsburg University of Pennsylvania, PA	M
Edinboro University of Pennsylvania, PA	M
Embry-Riddle Aeronautical University, AZ	M
Fort Hays State University, KS	M
Gannon University, PA	M
George Mason University, VA	M
Hofstra University, NY	M
Indiana University Bloomington, IN	M
Jamestown College, ND	M
Kent State University, OH	M
King College, TN	M
Lehigh University, PA	M
Limestone College, SC	M
Lindenwood University, MO	M
Lock Haven University of Pennsylvania, PA	M
McKendree College, IL	M
Mercyhurst College, PA	M
Michigan State University, MI	M
Millersville University of Pennsylvania, PA	M
Minnesota State University Mankato, MN	M
Morningside College, IA	M
Newberry College, SC	M
Newman University, KS	M
North Carolina State University, NC	M
Northern Illinois University, IL	M
Northern State University, SD	M
Northwestern University, IL	M
The Ohio State University, OH	M
Ohio University, OH	M
Oklahoma State University, OK	M
The Pennsylvania State University University Park Campus, PA	M
Portland State University, OR	M
Purdue University, IN	M
Rider University, NJ	M
Sacred Heart University, CT	M
St. Cloud State University, MN	M
San Francisco State University, CA	M
Shippensburg University of Pennsylvania, PA	M
Slippery Rock University of Pennsylvania, PA	M
South Dakota State University, SD	M
Southern Connecticut State University, CT	M
Southern Illinois University Edwardsville, IL	M
Southern Oregon University, OR	M
Southwest Minnesota State University, MN	M
Stanford University, CA	M
State University of New York at Binghamton, NY	M
State University of New York at Buffalo, NY	M
Truman State University, MO	M

Athletic Grants for Undergraduates
Wrestling

Institution	
University of Central Oklahoma, OK	M
The University of Findlay, OH	M
University of Great Falls, MT	M
University of Illinois at Urbana–Champaign, IL	M
The University of Iowa, IA	M
University of Mary, ND	M
University of Maryland, College Park, MD	M
University of Massachusetts Lowell, MA	M
University of Michigan, MI	M
University of Minnesota, Twin Cities Campus, MN	M
University of Missouri–Columbia, MO	M
University of Nebraska at Kearney, NE	M
University of Nebraska at Omaha, NE	M
University of Nebraska–Lincoln, NE	M
The University of North Carolina at Chapel Hill, NC	M
The University of North Carolina at Greensboro, NC	M
The University of North Carolina at Pembroke, NC	M
University of Northern Colorado, CO	M
University of Northern Iowa, IA	M
University of Oklahoma, OK	M
University of Oregon, OR	M
University of Pittsburgh, PA	M
University of Pittsburgh at Johnstown, PA	M
University of Puerto Rico, Mayagüez Campus, PR	M
University of the Cumberlands, KY	M,W
University of Virginia, VA	M
University of Wisconsin–Madison, WI	M
University of Wisconsin–Parkside, WI	M
University of Wyoming, WY	M
Virginia Military Institute, VA	M
Virginia Polytechnic Institute and State University, VA	M
Waldorf College, IA	M
Western State College of Colorado, CO	M
West Virginia University, WV	M
William Penn University, IA	M

Co-op Programs

Adrian College, MI
Alabama Agricultural and Mechanical University, AL
Albertson College of Idaho, ID
Alfred University, NY
American University, DC
Anderson University, SC
Andrews University, MI
Anna Maria College, MA
Antioch College, OH
Antioch University McGregor, OH
Arizona State University, AZ
Arkansas State University, AR
Armstrong Atlantic State University, GA
The Art Institute of Phoenix, AZ
Athens State University, AL
Atlantic Union College, MA
Auburn University, AL
Auburn University Montgomery, AL
Augsburg College, MN
Augustana College, SD
Augusta State University, GA
Avila University, MO
Azusa Pacific University, CA
Ball State University, IN
Barton College, NC
Bastyr University, WA
Bates College, ME
Becker College, MA
Belmont Abbey College, NC
Belmont University, TN
Bemidji State University, MN
Benedictine College, KS
Bennett College For Women, NC
Bennington College, VT
Berry College, GA
Beulah Heights Bible College, GA
Biola University, CA
Black Hills State University, SD
Bloomfield College, NJ
Bloomsburg University of Pennsylvania, PA
Boston University, MA
Bowling Green State University, OH
Bradley University, IL
Brenau University, GA
Brewton-Parker College, GA
Brigham Young University–Hawaii, HI
Burlington College, VT
Butler University, IN
Cabrini College, PA
California Institute of the Arts, CA
California Lutheran University, CA
California Polytechnic State University, San Luis Obispo, CA
California State University, Bakersfield, CA
California State University, Chico, CA
California State University, Dominguez Hills, CA
California State University, East Bay, CA
California State University, Fresno, CA
California State University, Fullerton, CA
California State University, Sacramento, CA
California State University, Stanislaus, CA
Calumet College of Saint Joseph, IN
Campbell University, NC
Capitol College, MD
Carnegie Mellon University, PA
Carroll College, MT
Carthage College, WI
Case Western Reserve University, OH
Cazenovia College, NY
Central Connecticut State University, CT
Central Missouri State University, MO
Central Washington University, WA
Champlain College, VT
Chapman University, CA
Chester College of New England, NH
Chestnut Hill College, PA
Christendom College, VA
Christopher Newport University, VA
The Citadel, The Military College of South Carolina, SC
City College of the City University of New York, NY
Clark Atlanta University, GA
Clarke College, IA
Clarkson University, NY
Clemson University, SC
Cleveland State University, OH
Coastal Carolina University, SC
College for Creative Studies, MI
College Misericordia, PA
College of Charleston, SC
College of Mount St. Joseph, OH
College of Santa Fe, NM
College of Staten Island of the City University of New York, NY
College of the Atlantic, ME
College of the Ozarks, MO
Colorado School of Mines, CO
Colorado State University, CO
Columbus State University, GA
Concordia University, NE
Coppin State University, MD
Cornell University, NY
The Culinary Institute of America, NY
Daemen College, NY
Dakota State University, SD
Davenport University, MI
David N. Myers University, OH
Davis & Elkins College, WV
Defiance College, OH
Delaware Valley College, PA
Denison University, OH
DePaul University, IL
Dickinson State University, ND
Doane College, NE
Dowling College, NY
Drake University, IA
Drexel University, PA
East Carolina University, NC
Eastern Michigan University, MI
Eastern Washington University, WA
East Tennessee State University, TN
Eckerd College, FL
Elmhurst College, IL
Embry-Riddle Aeronautical University, AZ
Embry-Riddle Aeronautical University, FL
Embry-Riddle Aeronautical University, Extended Campus, FL
Emory & Henry College, VA
Eugene Bible College, OR
Eureka College, IL
The Evergreen State College, WA
Fashion Institute of Technology, NY
Felician College, NJ
Ferris State University, MI
Ferrum College, VA
Five Towns College, NY
Florida Agricultural and Mechanical University, FL
Florida Atlantic University, FL
Florida Gulf Coast University, FL
Florida Institute of Technology, FL
Florida Metropolitan University–Pinellas Campus, FL
Florida Metropolitan University–Tampa Campus, FL
Florida State University, FL
Fort Lewis College, CO
Freed-Hardeman University, TN
Fresno Pacific University, CA
Friends University, KS
Gallaudet University, DC
Gannon University, PA
Geneva College, PA
George Mason University, VA
Georgetown College, KY
Georgia Institute of Technology, GA
Georgia Southern University, GA
Georgia Southwestern State University, GA
Glenville State College, WV
Gordon College, MA
Grace College, IN
Graceland University, IA
Grambling State University, LA
Grand Valley State University, MI
Grand View College, IA

783

Co-op Programs

Green Mountain College, VT
Greenville College, IL
Guilford College, NC
Gustavus Adolphus College, MN
Gwynedd-Mercy College, PA
Hampton University, VA
Hannibal-LaGrange College, MO
Harding University, AR
Harris-Stowe State University, MO
Hawai'i Pacific University, HI
Hendrix College, AR
Hilbert College, NY
Howard University, DC
Humboldt State University, CA
Husson College, ME
Illinois State University, IL
Indiana State University, IN
Indiana University Bloomington, IN
Indiana University East, IN
Indiana University Northwest, IN
Indiana University of Pennsylvania, PA
Indiana University–Purdue University Fort Wayne, IN
Indiana University–Purdue University Indianapolis, IN
International College, FL
Jacksonville State University, AL
Jacksonville University, FL
Jamestown College, ND
John Jay College of Criminal Justice of the City University of New York, NY
Johnson & Wales University, CO
Johnson & Wales University, FL
Johnson & Wales University, RI
Johnson Bible College, TN
Kansas City Art Institute, MO
Kansas State University, KS
Kean University, NJ
Keene State College, NH
Kennesaw State University, GA
Kent State University, OH
Kentucky Christian University, KY
Kentucky State University, KY
Kettering University, MI
Kuyper College, MI
Lake Superior State University, MI
Lamar University, TX
Lasell College, MA
Laura and Alvin Siegal College of Judaic Studies, OH
Lawrence Technological University, MI
Lehigh University, PA
Lehman College of the City University of New York, NY
LeMoyne-Owen College, TN
LeTourneau University, TX
Lewis-Clark State College, ID
Lexington College, IL
Life University, GA
Lincoln University, MO
Lincoln University, PA
Lindenwood University, MO
Lindsey Wilson College, KY
Lock Haven University of Pennsylvania, PA
Long Island University, Brooklyn Campus, NY

Loras College, IA
Louisiana State University and Agricultural and Mechanical College, LA
Louisiana Tech University, LA
Lynn University, FL
Macon State College, GA
Magdalen College, NH
Maharishi University of Management, IA
Malone College, OH
Manhattan College, NY
Marian College, IN
Marian College of Fond du Lac, WI
Marist College, NY
Marquette University, WI
Marshall University, WV
Maryville University of Saint Louis, MO
Massachusetts Institute of Technology, MA
Massachusetts Maritime Academy, MA
The Master's College and Seminary, CA
Mayville State University, ND
Medgar Evers College of the City University of New York, NY
Menlo College, CA
Mercer University, GA
Mercyhurst College, PA
Meredith College, NC
Merrimack College, MA
Mesa State College, CO
Messenger College, MO
Methodist College, NC
Metropolitan State College of Denver, CO
Miami University, OH
Michigan State University, MI
Michigan Technological University, MI
Middle Tennessee State University, TN
Midland Lutheran College, NE
Millersville University of Pennsylvania, PA
Milligan College, TN
Millsaps College, MS
Mississippi State University, MS
Missouri State University, MO
Molloy College, NY
Monmouth University, NJ
Monroe College, NY
Montana State University–Billings, MT
Montana Tech of The University of Montana, MT
Montclair State University, NJ
Montreat College, NC
Morehead State University, KY
Mountain State University, WV
Mount Holyoke College, MA
Mount Marty College, SD
Mount Olive College, NC
Mount Union College, OH
Mount Vernon Nazarene University, OH
Murray State University, KY
Nazareth College of Rochester, NY
Neumann College, PA
Newberry College, SC
New Jersey City University, NJ
Newman University, KS
New Mexico State University, NM
New York Institute of Technology, NY
New York University, NY
Niagara University, NY

Nicholls State University, LA
Nichols College, MA
North Carolina Agricultural and Technical State University, NC
North Carolina State University, NC
Northeastern Illinois University, IL
Northeastern University, MA
Northern Arizona University, AZ
Northern Illinois University, IL
Northern State University, SD
North Georgia College & State University, GA
Northland College, WI
Northwest Christian College, OR
Northwestern State University of Louisiana, LA
Northwestern University, IL
Northwest Nazarene University, ID
Northwest University, WA
Northwood University, MI
Nova Southeastern University, FL
Oglethorpe University, GA
Ohio Northern University, OH
The Ohio State University, OH
Ohio University, OH
Oklahoma Baptist University, OK
Oklahoma Panhandle State University, OK
Oklahoma State University, OK
Otis College of Art and Design, CA
Ouachita Baptist University, AR
Our Lady of Holy Cross College, LA
Pacific Lutheran University, WA
Pacific Union College, CA
Palm Beach Atlantic University, FL
Paul Smith's College of Arts and Sciences, NY
Pennsylvania College of Technology, PA
The Pennsylvania State University Abington College, PA
The Pennsylvania State University Altoona College, PA
The Pennsylvania State University at Erie, The Behrend College, PA
The Pennsylvania State University Berks Campus of the Berks–Lehigh Valley College, PA
The Pennsylvania State University Harrisburg Campus, PA
The Pennsylvania State University University Park Campus, PA
Philadelphia University, PA
Pittsburg State University, KS
Pitzer College, CA
Pontifical Catholic University of Puerto Rico, PR
Portland State University, OR
Presentation College, SD
Purdue University, IN
Purdue University Calumet, IN
Ramapo College of New Jersey, NJ
Reed College, OR
Rensselaer Polytechnic Institute, NY
Rider University, NJ
Robert Morris College, IL
Robert Morris University, PA
Roberts Wesleyan College, NY

Co-op Programs

Rochester Institute of Technology, NY
Rockhurst University, MO
Rocky Mountain College of Art & Design, CO
Roger Williams University, RI
Rose-Hulman Institute of Technology, IN
Russell Sage College, NY
Rutgers, The State University of New Jersey, Camden, NJ
Rutgers, The State University of New Jersey, Newark, NJ
Rutgers, The State University of New Jersey, New Brunswick/Piscataway, NJ
Sacred Heart University, CT
Sage College of Albany, NY
St. Francis College, NY
Saint Joseph's College of Maine, ME
St. Joseph's College, Suffolk Campus, NY
Saint Joseph's University, PA
Saint Louis University, MO
Saint Martin's University, WA
Saint Mary's College, IN
Saint Mary's University of Minnesota, MN
Saint Vincent College, PA
Saint Xavier University, IL
Samford University, AL
Samuel Merritt College, CA
San Francisco State University, CA
San Jose State University, CA
Santa Clara University, CA
Schreiner University, TX
Seattle Pacific University, WA
Shasta Bible College, CA
Shepherd University, WV
Shimer College, IL
Shippensburg University of Pennsylvania, PA
Silver Lake College, WI
Simpson College, IA
Sonoma State University, CA
South Carolina State University, SC
South Dakota School of Mines and Technology, SD
South Dakota State University, SD
Southeast Missouri State University, MO
Southern California Institute of Architecture, CA
Southern Connecticut State University, CT
Southern Illinois University Carbondale, IL
Southern Illinois University Edwardsville, IL
Southern Methodist College, SC
Southern New Hampshire University, NH
Southern Oregon University, OR
Southern Polytechnic State University, GA
Southern University and Agricultural and Mechanical College, LA
Southern Vermont College, VT
Southern Virginia University, VA
Southwest Baptist University, MO
State University of New York at Buffalo, NY
State University of New York at New Paltz, NY
State University of New York at Oswego, NY

State University of New York at Plattsburgh, NY
State University of New York College at Brockport, NY
State University of New York College at Cortland, NY
State University of New York College of Environmental Science and Forestry, NY
Stephens College, MO
Stevens Institute of Technology, NJ
Suffolk University, MA
Syracuse University, NY
Taylor University, IN
Taylor University Fort Wayne, IN
Temple University, PA
Tennessee State University, TN
Tennessee Technological University, TN
Texas A&M University, TX
Texas A&M University at Galveston, TX
Texas A&M University–Commerce, TX
Texas Southern University, TX
Texas Tech University, TX
Texas Woman's University, TX
Thiel College, PA
Thomas College, ME
Thomas Jefferson University, PA
Thomas More College, KY
Towson University, MD
Tri-State University, IN
Tuskegee University, AL
Union College, KY
Union College, NY
Union University, TN
Unity College, ME
The University of Akron, OH
The University of Alabama, AL
The University of Alabama at Birmingham, AL
The University of Alabama in Huntsville, AL
University of Alaska Fairbanks, AK
University of Alaska Southeast, AK
University of Arkansas, AR
University of Arkansas at Pine Bluff, AR
University of Baltimore, MD
University of California, Riverside, CA
University of California, San Diego, CA
University of California, Santa Barbara, CA
University of California, Santa Cruz, CA
University of Cincinnati, OH
University of Colorado at Boulder, CO
University of Colorado at Colorado Springs, CO
University of Colorado at Denver and Health Sciences Center—Downtown Denver Campus, CO
University of Connecticut, CT
University of Dayton, OH
University of Delaware, DE
University of Denver, CO
University of Evansville, IN
The University of Findlay, OH
University of Florida, FL
University of Georgia, GA
University of Great Falls, MT
University of Hartford, CT

University of Hawaii at Manoa, HI
University of Idaho, ID
University of Illinois at Springfield, IL
University of Illinois at Urbana–Champaign, IL
The University of Iowa, IA
University of Kansas, KS
University of Kentucky, KY
University of Louisiana at Lafayette, LA
University of Louisville, KY
University of Maine, ME
University of Maine at Presque Isle, ME
University of Mary, ND
University of Maryland, Baltimore County, MD
University of Maryland, College Park, MD
University of Mary Washington, VA
University of Massachusetts Amherst, MA
University of Massachusetts Dartmouth, MA
University of Massachusetts Lowell, MA
University of Memphis, TN
University of Michigan, MI
University of Michigan–Dearborn, MI
University of Michigan–Flint, MI
University of Minnesota, Twin Cities Campus, MN
University of Missouri–Columbia, MO
University of Missouri–Kansas City, MO
University of Missouri–St. Louis, MO
University of Nebraska at Kearney, NE
University of Nebraska at Omaha, NE
University of Nebraska–Lincoln, NE
University of Nevada, Las Vegas, NV
University of New England, ME
University of New Haven, CT
University of New Orleans, LA
University of North Alabama, AL
The University of North Carolina at Pembroke, NC
The University of North Carolina Wilmington, NC
University of North Dakota, ND
University of Northern Colorado, CO
University of Northern Iowa, IA
University of North Florida, FL
University of Oklahoma, OK
University of Pittsburgh, PA
University of Pittsburgh at Johnstown, PA
University of Puerto Rico, Mayagüez Campus, PR
University of Puget Sound, WA
University of Rhode Island, RI
University of Richmond, VA
University of Saint Francis, IN
University of South Carolina, SC
University of South Carolina Upstate, SC
University of Southern California, CA
University of Southern Indiana, IN
University of Southern Maine, ME
University of Southern Mississippi, MS
University of South Florida, FL
The University of Tampa, FL
The University of Tennessee at Martin, TN
The University of Texas at Arlington, TX
The University of Texas at Austin, TX

Co-op Programs

The University of Texas at Dallas, TX
The University of Texas at El Paso, TX
The University of Texas at San Antonio, TX
The University of Texas at Tyler, TX
The University of Texas–Pan American, TX
University of the Cumberlands, KY
University of the District of Columbia, DC
University of the Ozarks, AR
University of the Pacific, CA
The University of Toledo, OH
University of Utah, UT
University of Vermont, VT
University of Virginia, VA
University of West Georgia, GA
University of Wisconsin–Eau Claire, WI
University of Wisconsin–Green Bay, WI
University of Wisconsin–La Crosse, WI
University of Wisconsin–Madison, WI
University of Wisconsin–Stevens Point, WI
University of Wisconsin–Stout, WI
University of Wisconsin–Whitewater, WI
Urbana University, OH
Utah State University, UT
Utica College, NY
Valdosta State University, GA
Valley City State University, ND
Valparaiso University, IN
Vanderbilt University, TN
Vassar College, NY
Vaughn College of Aeronautics and Technology, NY
Vermont Technical College, VT
Villa Julie College, MD
Virginia Commonwealth University, VA
Virginia Polytechnic Institute and State University, VA
Virginia Union University, VA
Waldorf College, IA
Walla Walla College, WA
Warner Pacific College, OR
Warren Wilson College, NC
Washington State University, WA
Washington University in St. Louis, MO
Watkins College of Art and Design, TN
Wayne State College, NE
Wayne State University, MI
Webber International University, FL
Webb Institute, NY
Webster University, MO
Wentworth Institute of Technology, MA
Wesleyan College, GA
Western Carolina University, NC
Western Kentucky University, KY
Western State College of Colorado, CO
Western Washington University, WA
Westfield State College, MA
Westminster College, MO
Westmont College, CA
West Texas A&M University, TX
Whitman College, WA
Whitworth College, WA
Wichita State University, KS
Widener University, PA
Wilkes University, PA
Willamette University, OR
William Jewell College, MO
William Penn University, IA
Wilson College, PA
Winston-Salem State University, NC
Winthrop University, SC
Wittenberg University, OH
Worcester Polytechnic Institute, MA
Xavier University, OH
Xavier University of Louisiana, LA
York College of Pennsylvania, PA
York College of the City University of New York, NY
Youngstown State University, OH

ROTC Programs

Army

Adelphi University, NY*
Alabama Agricultural and Mechanical University, AL
Albertson College of Idaho, ID*
Alfred University, NY*
Allen College, IA*
Alliant International University, CA*
Alma College, MI*
Alvernia College, PA*
Alverno College, WI*
American International College, MA*
American University, DC*
Anderson University, SC*
Appalachian State University, NC
Arizona State University, AZ
Arizona State University at the Polytechnic Campus, AZ*
Arkansas State University, AR
Arkansas Tech University, AR*
Armstrong Atlantic State University, GA
Asbury College, KY*
Assumption College, MA*
Auburn University, AL
Auburn University Montgomery, AL
Augsburg College, MN*
Augusta State University, GA
Austin Peay State University, TN
Avila University, MO*
Azusa Pacific University, CA*
Babson College, MA*
Ball State University, IN
Becker College, MA*
Bellin College of Nursing, WI*
Belmont Abbey College, NC*
Belmont University, TN*
Benedictine College, KS
Benedictine University, IL*
Bennett College For Women, NC*
Bentley College, MA*
Bethany Lutheran College, MN*
Bethel University, MN*
Biola University, CA*
Black Hills State University, SD
Bloomfield College, NJ*
Bloomsburg University of Pennsylvania, PA
Boston College, MA*
Boston University, MA
Bowling Green State University, OH
Bradley University, IL
Brandeis University, MA*
Bridgewater State College, MA*
Brigham Young University–Hawaii, HI*
Bryant University, RI
Bucknell University, PA
Butler University, IN

Cabrini College, PA*
California Baptist University, CA*
California Institute of Technology, CA*
California Lutheran University, CA*
California Polytechnic State University, San Luis Obispo, CA
California State University, Dominguez Hills, CA*
California State University, Fresno, CA
California State University, Fullerton, CA
California State University, Sacramento, CA*
California State University, San Marcos, CA*
Calvin College, MI*
Campbell University, NC
Capitol College, MD*
Carnegie Mellon University, PA
Carroll College, MT
Carson-Newman College, TN
Carthage College, WI*
Cascade College, OR*
Case Western Reserve University, OH*
Catawba College, NC*
The Catholic University of America, DC*
Cazenovia College, NY*
Cedar Crest College, PA*
Cedarville University, OH*
Central Connecticut State University, CT*
Central Michigan University, MI
Central Missouri State University, MO
Central Washington University, WA
Centre College, KY*
Chaminade University of Honolulu, HI*
Champlain College, VT*
Chapman University, CA*
Christian Brothers University, TN*
Christopher Newport University, VA
The Citadel, The Military College of South Carolina, SC
City College of the City University of New York, NY*
Claremont McKenna College, CA
Clark Atlanta University, GA
Clarkson University, NY
Clark University, MA*
Clearwater Christian College, FL*
Clemson University, SC
Cleveland Institute of Music, OH*
Cleveland State University, OH*
Coe College, IA*
Colby College, ME*
Colgate University, NY*
College Misericordia, PA*
College of Mount St. Joseph, OH*
College of Mount Saint Vincent, NY*

The College of New Jersey, NJ*
College of Notre Dame of Maryland, MD*
College of Saint Benedict, MN*
College of Saint Mary, NE*
College of the Holy Cross, MA*
College of the Ozarks, MO
The College of William and Mary, VA
The Colorado College, CO*
Colorado School of Mines, CO
Colorado State University, CO
Columbia College, SC*
Columbus State University, GA
Concordia University, MI*
Concordia University, NE*
Concordia University at Austin, TX*
Concordia University, St. Paul, MN*
Converse College, SC*
Coppin State University, MD
Corban College, OR*
Cornell University, NY
Cornerstone University, MI*
Creighton University, NE
Curry College, MA*
Daemen College, NY*
Dallas Baptist University, TX*
Daniel Webster College, NH*
Dartmouth College, NH*
Davidson College, NC
Denison University, OH*
DePaul University, IL*
DePauw University, IN*
Dickinson College, PA
Doane College, NE*
Drake University, IA
Drew University, NJ*
Drexel University, PA
Duke University, NC
Duquesne University, PA
East Carolina University, NC
Eastern Illinois University, IL
Eastern Michigan University, MI
Eastern Washington University, WA
East Stroudsburg University of Pennsylvania, PA*
East Tennessee State University, TN
Eckerd College, FL*
Edinboro University of Pennsylvania, PA
Elmhurst College, IL*
Elmira College, NY
Elms College, MA*
Elon University, NC
Embry-Riddle Aeronautical University, AZ
Embry-Riddle Aeronautical University, FL
Emmanuel College, MA*
Endicott College, MA*
Evangel University, MO

program is offered at another college's campus

ROTC Programs
Army

Fairfield University, CT*
Fairmont State University, WV
Faulkner University, AL*
Ferris State University, MI*
Finlandia University, MI*
Florida Agricultural and Mechanical University, FL
Florida Atlantic University, FL*
Florida College, FL*
Florida Institute of Technology, FL
Florida Southern College, FL
Florida State University, FL
Fordham University, NY
Franklin Pierce College, NH*
Free Will Baptist Bible College, TN*
Furman University, SC
Gannon University, PA
Geneva College, PA*
George Mason University, VA
Georgetown College, KY*
Georgetown University, DC
Georgia College & State University, GA*
Georgia Institute of Technology, GA
Georgia Southern University, GA
Gettysburg College, PA*
Gonzaga University, WA
Gordon College, MA*
Goucher College, MD*
Grace Bible College, MI*
Grambling State University, LA
Grand View College, IA*
Grove City College, PA*
Gustavus Adolphus College, MN*
Hampden-Sydney College, VA*
Hampshire College, MA*
Hampton University, VA
Harding University, AR*
Harvard University, MA*
Harvey Mudd College, CA*
Hawai'i Pacific University, HI*
Heidelberg College, OH*
Hendrix College, AR*
Hofstra University, NY
Holy Names University, CA*
Hope College, MI*
Houghton College, NY*
Houston Baptist University, TX*
Howard University, DC
Husson College, ME*
Idaho State University, ID*
Illinois State University, IL
Illinois Wesleyan University, IL*
Indiana State University, IN
Indiana University Bloomington, IN
Indiana University Kokomo, IN*
Indiana University Northwest, IN
Indiana University of Pennsylvania, PA
Indiana University–Purdue University Indianapolis, IN
Indiana University South Bend, IN*
Indiana University Southeast, IN*
Inter American University of Puerto Rico, Guayama Campus, PR*
Iona College, NY*
Ithaca College, NY*
Jacksonville State University, AL

James Madison University, VA
John Brown University, AR*
The Johns Hopkins University, MD
Judson College, AL*
Kansas State University, KS
Kean University, NJ*
Kennesaw State University, GA
Kent State University, OH
King's College, PA
Lawrence Technological University, MI*
Lebanon Valley College, PA*
Lehigh University, PA
Lehman College of the City University of New York, NY*
Le Moyne College, NY*
LeMoyne-Owen College, TN*
Lewis-Clark State College, ID
Limestone College, SC*
Lincoln University, MO
Lincoln University, PA*
Lindenwood University, MO
Lindsey Wilson College, KY*
Lipscomb University, TN*
Lock Haven University of Pennsylvania, PA
Louisiana State University and Agricultural and Mechanical College, LA
Louisiana Tech University, LA*
Loyola College in Maryland, MD
Loyola University Chicago, IL*
Loyola University New Orleans, LA*
Lubbock Christian University, TX*
Lycoming College, PA*
Maine Maritime Academy, ME
Malone College, OH*
Manhattan Christian College, KS*
Manhattan College, NY*
Marian College, IN*
Marian College of Fond du Lac, WI
Marist College, NY
Marquette University, WI
Marshall University, WV
Mary Baldwin College, VA
Marymount University, VA*
Maryville University of Saint Louis, MO*
Marywood University, PA*
Massachusetts College of Pharmacy and Health Sciences, MA*
Massachusetts Institute of Technology, MA
Massachusetts Maritime Academy, MA*
Mayville State University, ND*
McDaniel College, MD
McKendree College, IL*
Menlo College, CA*
Mercer University, GA
Mercyhurst College, PA*
Meredith College, NC*
Methodist College, NC
Metropolitan State College of Denver, CO*
Miami University, OH*
Michigan State University, MI
Michigan Technological University, MI
MidAmerica Nazarene University, KS*
Middlebury College, VT*
Middle Tennessee State University, TN
Midway College, KY*
Millersville University of Pennsylvania, PA

Milligan College, TN*
Millsaps College, MS*
Milwaukee School of Engineering, WI*
Minnesota State University Mankato, MN
Mississippi State University, MS
Missouri State University, MO
Molloy College, NY*
Montana State University, MT
Moravian College, PA*
Morehead State University, KY
Morningside College, IA*
Mount Holyoke College, MA*
Mount Marty College, SD*
Mount Mary College, WI*
Mount St. Mary's University, MD*
Mount Union College, OH*
Murray State University, KY*
National University, CA*
Nazareth College of Rochester, NY*
Nebraska Wesleyan University, NE*
Neumann College, PA*
Newberry College, SC*
New England College, NH*
New Mexico State University, NM
New York Institute of Technology, NY
Niagara University, NY
Nichols College, MA*
North Carolina Agricultural and Technical State University, NC
North Carolina State University, NC
Northeastern Illinois University, IL*
Northeastern University, MA
Northern Arizona University, AZ
Northern Illinois University, IL
Northern Michigan University, MI
North Georgia College & State University, GA
North Greenville College, SC*
Northwest Christian College, OR*
Northwestern College, MN*
Northwestern State University of Louisiana, LA
Northwestern University, IL*
Northwest Nazarene University, ID
Northwest University, WA*
Occidental College, CA*
Ohio Northern University, OH*
The Ohio State University, OH
Ohio University, OH
Ohio University–Chillicothe, OH*
Ohio University–Lancaster, OH*
Ohio Wesleyan University, OH*
Oklahoma State University, OK
Olivet Nazarene University, IL
Oregon Health & Science University, OR*
Ouachita Baptist University, AR
Our Lady of Holy Cross College, LA*
Pacific Lutheran University, WA
Pacific University, OR*
Peace College, NC*
Pennsylvania College of Technology, PA*
The Pennsylvania State University Abington College, PA
The Pennsylvania State University Altoona College, PA

*program is offered at another college's campus

ROTC Programs
Army

The Pennsylvania State University at Erie, The Behrend College, PA*
The Pennsylvania State University Harrisburg Campus, PA*
The Pennsylvania State University University Park Campus, PA
Pepperdine University, CA*
Pittsburg State University, KS
Pitzer College, CA*
Plymouth State University, NH*
Pontifical Catholic University of Puerto Rico, PR*
Portland State University, OR
Princeton University, NJ
Purdue University, IN
Purdue University Calumet, IN*
Quinnipiac University, CT*
Radford University, VA
Randolph-Macon College, VA*
Regis College, MA*
Rensselaer Polytechnic Institute, NY
Rice University, TX*
Rider University, NJ*
Ripon College, WI
Robert Morris College, IL*
Robert Morris University, PA*
Roberts Wesleyan College, NY*
Rochester Institute of Technology, NY
Rockhurst University, MO*
Roger Williams University, RI
Rose-Hulman Institute of Technology, IN
Rosemont College, PA*
Rowan University, NJ*
Russell Sage College, NY*
Rutgers, The State University of New Jersey, Camden, NJ*
Rutgers, The State University of New Jersey, Newark, NJ
Rutgers, The State University of New Jersey, New Brunswick/Piscataway, NJ
Sacred Heart University, CT
St. Bonaventure University, NY
St. Cloud State University, MN
St. Edward's University, TX*
Saint Francis University, PA*
St. John Fisher College, NY*
St. John's University, NY
Saint Joseph's College of Maine, ME*
St. Joseph's College, Suffolk Campus, NY*
Saint Joseph's University, PA*
St. Lawrence University, NY*
Saint Leo University, FL
St. Louis College of Pharmacy, MO*
Saint Louis University, MO*
Saint Martin's University, WA*
Saint Mary's College, IN*
Saint Mary's College of California, CA*
Saint Mary's University of Minnesota, MN*
St. Norbert College, WI
St. Thomas University, FL*
Salisbury University, MD*
Salve Regina University, RI*
Samford University, AL*
Samuel Merritt College, CA*
San Diego Christian College, CA*

San Diego State University, CA
San Francisco State University, CA*
San Jose State University, CA
Santa Clara University, CA
Scripps College, CA*
Seattle Pacific University, WA*
Seattle University, WA
Seton Hill University, PA*
Shippensburg University of Pennsylvania, PA
Simmons College, MA*
Skidmore College, NY*
Slippery Rock University of Pennsylvania, PA
Smith College, MA*
Sonoma State University, CA*
South Carolina State University, SC
South Dakota School of Mines and Technology, SD
South Dakota State University, SD
Southeastern Louisiana University, LA*
Southeastern University, FL*
Southern Connecticut State University, CT*
Southern Illinois University Carbondale, IL
Southern Illinois University Edwardsville, IL
Southern New Hampshire University, NH*
Southern Polytechnic State University, GA*
Southern University and Agricultural and Mechanical College, LA
Southern Virginia University, VA*
Southwest Baptist University, MO*
Spring Arbor University, MI*
Spring Hill College, AL*
Stanford University, CA*
State University of New York at Buffalo, NY*
State University of New York at Oswego, NY*
State University of New York College at Brockport, NY
State University of New York College at Cortland, NY*
State University of New York College at Geneseo, NY*
State University of New York College at Old Westbury, NY*
State University of New York College at Potsdam, NY*
State University of New York College of Environmental Science and Forestry, NY*
State University of New York Institute of Technology, NY*
Stephen F. Austin State University, TX
Stephens College, MO*
Stetson University, FL*
Stevens Institute of Technology, NJ*
Stonehill College, MA
Stony Brook University, State University of New York, NY*
Suffolk University, MA*
Swarthmore College, PA*
Syracuse University, NY
Temple University, PA
Tennessee State University, TN*
Tennessee Technological University, TN

Texas A&M University, TX
Texas Christian University, TX
Texas Lutheran University, TX*
Texas Southern University, TX*
Texas State University-San Marcos, TX
Texas Tech University, TX
Texas Woman's University, TX*
Thomas More College, KY*
Tiffin University, OH*
Towson University, MD*
Transylvania University, KY*
Trevecca Nazarene University, TN*
Trinity College, CT*
Truman State University, MO
Tufts University, MA*
Tuskegee University, AL
Union College, KY*
Union College, NY*
Unity College, ME*
University at Albany, State University of New York, NY
The University of Akron, OH
The University of Alabama, AL
The University of Alabama at Birmingham, AL
The University of Alabama in Huntsville, AL*
University of Alaska Fairbanks, AK
University of Arkansas, AR
University of Arkansas at Pine Bluff, AR
University of Arkansas for Medical Sciences, AR*
University of Baltimore, MD*
University of California, Berkeley, CA
University of California, Davis, CA
University of California, Irvine, CA*
University of California, Los Angeles, CA
University of California, Riverside, CA*
University of California, San Diego, CA*
University of California, Santa Barbara, CA
University of California, Santa Cruz, CA*
University of Central Oklahoma, OK
University of Cincinnati, OH
University of Colorado at Boulder, CO
University of Colorado at Colorado Springs, CO
University of Colorado at Denver and Health Sciences Center—Downtown Denver Campus, CO
University of Connecticut, CT
University of Dallas, TX*
University of Dayton, OH
University of Delaware, DE
University of Denver, CO*
The University of Findlay, OH*
University of Florida, FL
University of Georgia, GA
University of Hartford, CT*
University of Hawaii at Manoa, HI
University of Idaho, ID
University of Illinois at Urbana–Champaign, IL
The University of Iowa, IA
University of Kansas, KS
University of Kentucky, KY
University of Louisiana at Lafayette, LA

program is offered at another college's campus

ROTC Programs

Army

University of Louisville, KY
University of Maine, ME
University of Maryland, Baltimore County, MD*
University of Maryland, College Park, MD
University of Massachusetts Amherst, MA
University of Massachusetts Dartmouth, MA*
University of Memphis, TN
University of Miami, FL
University of Michigan, MI
University of Michigan–Dearborn, MI*
University of Minnesota, Twin Cities Campus, MN
University of Missouri–Columbia, MO
University of Missouri–Kansas City, MO
University of Missouri–St. Louis, MO*
University of Nebraska at Omaha, NE*
University of Nebraska–Lincoln, NE
University of Nebraska Medical Center, NE*
University of Nevada, Reno, NV
University of New England, ME*
University of New Hampshire, NH
University of New Hampshire at Manchester, NH*
University of New Orleans, LA*
University of North Alabama, AL
The University of North Carolina at Chapel Hill, NC
The University of North Carolina at Greensboro, NC*
The University of North Carolina at Pembroke, NC
University of North Dakota, ND
University of Northern Colorado, CO
University of Northern Iowa, IA
University of Oklahoma, OK
University of Oregon, OR
University of Pennsylvania, PA*
University of Pittsburgh, PA
University of Pittsburgh at Bradford, PA*
University of Pittsburgh at Greensburg, PA*
University of Portland, OR
University of Puerto Rico, Mayagüez Campus, PR
University of Puget Sound, WA*
University of Rhode Island, RI
University of Richmond, VA
University of St. Thomas, MN*
University of St. Thomas, TX*
University of San Diego, CA*
University of South Carolina, SC
University of South Carolina Upstate, SC*
The University of South Dakota, SD
University of Southern California, CA
University of Southern Indiana, IN
University of Southern Maine, ME*
University of Southern Mississippi, MS
University of South Florida, FL
The University of Tampa, FL
The University of Tennessee at Martin, TN
The University of Texas at Arlington, TX
The University of Texas at Austin, TX
The University of Texas at Dallas, TX*
The University of Texas at El Paso, TX
The University of Texas at San Antonio, TX
The University of Texas Health Science Center at Houston, TX*
The University of Texas–Pan American, TX
University of the Cumberlands, KY
University of the District of Columbia, DC*
University of the Virgin Islands, VI
The University of Toledo, OH
University of Utah, UT
University of Vermont, VT
University of Virginia, VA
The University of West Alabama, AL*
University of West Georgia, GA
University of Wisconsin–Green Bay, WI
University of Wisconsin–La Crosse, WI
University of Wisconsin–Madison, WI
University of Wisconsin–Parkside, WI*
University of Wisconsin–Stevens Point, WI
University of Wisconsin–Whitewater, WI
University of Wyoming, WY
Utah State University, UT
Utica College, NY
Vanderbilt University, TN
Vaughn College of Aeronautics and Technology, NY*
Vermont Technical College, VT*
Villa Julie College, MD*
Villanova University, PA*
Virginia Commonwealth University, VA*
Virginia Military Institute, VA
Virginia Polytechnic Institute and State University, VA
Virginia Union University, VA*
Virginia Wesleyan College, VA*
Wabash College, IN*
Wake Forest University, NC
Warner Pacific College, OR*
Washington & Jefferson College, PA*
Washington and Lee University, VA*
Washington State University, WA
Washington University in St. Louis, MO
Wayland Baptist University, TX*
Waynesburg College, PA*
Wayne State College, NE*
Webster University, MO*
Wellesley College, MA*
Wentworth Institute of Technology, MA*
Western Illinois University, IL
Western Kentucky University, KY
Western New England College, MA
Western Oregon University, OR
Westfield State College, MA*
Westminster College, MO*
Westminster College, PA*
Westmont College, CA*
West Virginia University, WV
Wheaton College, IL
Wheaton College, MA*
Whittier College, CA*
Whitworth College, WA*
Widener University, PA
Wilkes University, PA*
William Carey College, MS*
Williams Baptist College, AR*
William Woods University, MO*
Wilson College, PA*
Wingate University, NC*
Winona State University, MN*
Winston-Salem State University, NC
Wittenberg University, OH*
Wofford College, SC
Worcester Polytechnic Institute, MA
Worcester State College, MA*
Xavier University, OH
Xavier University of Louisiana, LA*
Yale University, CT*
York College of Pennsylvania, PA*
York College of the City University of New York, NY*
Youngstown State University, OH

Naval

Armstrong Atlantic State University, GA*
Auburn University, AL
Augsburg College, MN*
Babson College, MA*
Becker College, MA*
Belmont University, TN*
Boston University, MA
Brigham Young University–Hawaii, HI*
California State University, San Marcos, CA*
Carnegie Mellon University, PA
The Catholic University of America, DC*
Christian Brothers University, TN*
The Citadel, The Military College of South Carolina, SC
Clark University, MA*
Cleveland State University, OH*
College of the Holy Cross, MA
Columbia College, SC*
Concordia University, St. Paul, MN*
Duquesne University, PA*
Eastern Michigan University, MI*
Embry-Riddle Aeronautical University, FL
Florida Agricultural and Mechanical University, FL
Florida State University, FL*
Fordham University, NY*
Georgetown University, DC*
Georgia Institute of Technology, GA
Hampton University, VA
Husson College, ME*
Indiana University–Purdue University Indianapolis, IN*
Indiana University South Bend, IN*
Jacksonville University, FL
Louisiana State University and Agricultural and Mechanical College, LA*
Louisiana Tech University, LA
Loyola University Chicago, IL*
Loyola University New Orleans, LA*
Macalester College, MN*
Maine Maritime Academy, ME
Marquette University, WI
Mary Baldwin College, VA*
Massachusetts Institute of Technology, MA
Massachusetts Maritime Academy, MA
Miami University, OH
Milwaukee School of Engineering, WI*
Molloy College, NY*

*program is offered at another college's campus

ROTC Programs
Air Force

North Carolina State University, NC
Northeastern University, MA*
Northwestern University, IL
Occidental College, CA*
The Ohio State University, OH
Peace College, NC*
The Pennsylvania State University University Park Campus, PA
Purdue University, IN
Radford University, VA*
Rensselaer Polytechnic Institute, NY
Rice University, TX
Rochester Institute of Technology, NY*
St. John Fisher College, NY*
Saint Joseph's University, PA*
Saint Mary's College, IN*
San Diego State University, CA
San Francisco State University, CA*
Seattle Pacific University, WA*
Simmons College, MA*
Southern Polytechnic State University, GA*
Southern University and Agricultural and Mechanical College, LA
Stanford University, CA*
State University of New York College at Brockport, NY*
Temple University, PA*
Tennessee State University, TN*
Texas A&M University, TX
Texas A&M University at Galveston, TX
Texas Southern University, TX*
Tufts University, MA*
University of California, Berkeley, CA
University of California, Davis, CA*
University of California, Los Angeles, CA
University of California, Santa Cruz, CA*
University of Colorado at Boulder, CO
University of Idaho, ID
University of Illinois at Urbana–Champaign, IL
University of Kansas, KS
University of Maine, ME
University of Maryland, College Park, MD*
University of Memphis, TN
University of Michigan–Dearborn, MI*
University of Missouri–Columbia, MO
University of Nebraska–Lincoln, NE
University of New Orleans, LA*
The University of North Carolina at Chapel Hill, NC
University of North Florida, FL*
University of Oklahoma, OK
University of Pennsylvania, PA
University of Pittsburgh, PA*
University of Rochester, NY
University of San Diego, CA
University of South Florida, FL
The University of Texas at Austin, TX
University of Utah, UT
University of Virginia, VA
University of Wisconsin–Madison, WI
Vanderbilt University, TN
Villanova University, PA
Virginia Military Institute, VA
Virginia Polytechnic Institute and State University, VA

Washington State University, WA
Widener University, PA*
William Woods University, MO*
Worcester Polytechnic Institute, MA*
Worcester State College, MA*
Xavier University of Louisiana, LA*

Air Force

Adelphi University, NY*
Agnes Scott College, GA*
Alverno College, WI*
American International College, MA*
American University, DC*
Anderson University, SC*
Anna Maria College, MA*
Arizona State University, AZ
Arizona State University at the Polytechnic Campus, AZ*
Asbury College, KY*
Assumption College, MA*
Auburn University, AL
Auburn University Montgomery, AL*
Augsburg College, MN*
Babson College, MA*
Baldwin-Wallace College, OH*
Baylor University, TX
Becker College, MA*
Belmont Abbey College, NC*
Bennett College For Women, NC*
Bethel University, MN*
Biola University, CA*
Bloomsburg University of Pennsylvania, PA*
Boston College, MA*
Boston University, MA
Bowling Green State University, OH
Brandeis University, MA*
Bridgewater State College, MA*
Brigham Young University–Hawaii, HI*
Bryn Mawr College, PA*
Butler University, IN*
California Baptist University, CA*
California Institute of Technology, CA*
California Lutheran University, CA*
California State University, Dominguez Hills, CA*
California State University, Fresno, CA
California State University, Sacramento, CA
California State University, San Marcos, CA*
Carnegie Mellon University, PA
Carroll College, WI*
Carson-Newman College, TN*
Carthage College, WI*
Cascade College, OR*
Case Western Reserve University, OH*
The Catholic University of America, DC*
Cazenovia College, NY*
Cedarville University, OH*
Central Connecticut State University, CT*
Central Missouri State University, MO*
Central Washington University, WA
Centre College, KY*
Chaminade University of Honolulu, HI*
Chapman University, CA*
Christian Brothers University, TN*

The Citadel, The Military College of South Carolina, SC
City College of the City University of New York, NY*
Claremont McKenna College, CA*
Clark Atlanta University, GA
Clarkson University, NY
Clark University, MA*
Clearwater Christian College, FL*
Clemson University, SC
Cleveland Institute of Music, OH*
Cleveland State University, OH*
Coe College, IA*
College Misericordia, PA*
College of Charleston, SC*
College of Mount St. Joseph, OH*
College of Mount Saint Vincent, NY*
The College of New Jersey, NJ*
College of St. Catherine, MN*
College of Saint Mary, NE*
The College of St. Scholastica, MN*
College of Santa Fe, NM*
College of the Holy Cross, MA*
Colorado State University, CO
Columbia College, SC*
Concordia University, MI*
Concordia University, NE*
Concordia University at Austin, TX*
Concordia University, St. Paul, MN*
Corban College, OR*
Cornell University, NY
Creighton University, NE*
Dakota State University, SD*
Dallas Baptist University, TX*
Daniel Webster College, NH*
Davidson College, NC*
DePauw University, IN*
Doane College, NE*
Dowling College, NY*
Drake University, IA*
Drew University, NJ*
Drexel University, PA*
Duke University, NC
Duquesne University, PA*
East Carolina University, NC
Eastern Michigan University, MI*
East Stroudsburg University of Pennsylvania, PA*
Eckerd College, FL*
Elmhurst College, IL*
Elmira College, NY*
Elms College, MA*
Elon University, NC*
Embry-Riddle Aeronautical University, AZ
Embry-Riddle Aeronautical University, FL
Emory University, GA*
Faulkner University, AL*
Finlandia University, MI*
Fitchburg State College, MA*
Florida Agricultural and Mechanical University, FL*
Florida Atlantic University, FL*
Florida College, FL*
Florida Southern College, FL*
Florida State University, FL
Fordham University, NY*

program is offered at another college's campus

ROTC Programs
Air Force

Franklin Pierce College, NH*
Free Will Baptist Bible College, TN*
George Mason University, VA*
Georgetown College, KY*
Georgetown University, DC*
Georgia Institute of Technology, GA
Gordon College, MA*
Grambling State University, LA
Grand View College, IA*
Hamline University, MN*
Harris-Stowe State University, MO*
Harvard University, MA*
Harvey Mudd College, CA
Hawai'i Pacific University, HI*
Heidelberg College, OH*
Holy Names University, CA*
Howard University, DC
Indiana State University, IN
Indiana University Bloomington, IN
Indiana University–Purdue University Indianapolis, IN*
Indiana University South Bend, IN*
Indiana University Southeast, IN*
Ithaca College, NY*
James Madison University, VA*
John Brown University, AR*
John Jay College of Criminal Justice of the City University of New York, NY*
The Johns Hopkins University, MD*
Kansas State University, KS
Kean University, NJ*
Keene State College, NH*
Kennesaw State University, GA
Kent State University, OH
Kentucky State University, KY*
King's College, PA
Lawrence Technological University, MI*
Le Moyne College, NY*
LeMoyne-Owen College, TN*
Lewis-Clark State College, ID*
Lincoln University, PA*
Lindenwood University, MO*
Linfield College, OR*
Lipscomb University, TN*
Louisiana State University and Agricultural and Mechanical College, LA
Loyola College in Maryland, MD*
Loyola University New Orleans, LA*
Lubbock Christian University, TX*
Lynn University, FL*
Macalester College, MN*
Malone College, OH*
Manhattan Christian College, KS*
Manhattan College, NY
Maranatha Baptist Bible College, WI
Marquette University, WI
Mary Baldwin College, VA*
Marywood University, PA*
Massachusetts College of Pharmacy and Health Sciences, MA*
Massachusetts Institute of Technology, MA
Mayville State University, ND
McKendree College, IL*
Mercyhurst College, PA*
Meredith College, NC*
Merrimack College, MA*

Methodist College, NC*
Metropolitan State College of Denver, CO*
Miami University, OH
Michigan State University, MI
Michigan Technological University, MI
MidAmerica Nazarene University, KS*
Middle Tennessee State University, TN*
Midwestern State University, TX*
Milwaukee School of Engineering, WI*
Mississippi State University, MS
Molloy College, NY*
Monmouth University, NJ*
Montana State University, MT
Montclair State University, NJ*
Montserrat College of Art, MA*
Mount Holyoke College, MA*
Mount Union College, OH*
National University, CA*
Nazareth College of Rochester, NY*
Nebraska Wesleyan University, NE*
New England College, NH*
New Mexico State University, NM
New York Institute of Technology, NY
North Carolina Agricultural and Technical State University, NC
North Carolina State University, NC
Northeastern Illinois University, IL*
Northeastern University, MA*
Northern Arizona University, AZ
Northern Illinois University, IL*
Northwestern College, MN*
Northwestern University, IL*
Occidental College, CA*
Ohio Northern University, OH*
The Ohio State University, OH
Ohio University, OH
Ohio University–Chillicothe, OH*
Ohio University–Lancaster, OH*
Oklahoma Baptist University, OK*
Oklahoma State University, OK
Oral Roberts University, OK*
Our Lady of Holy Cross College, LA*
Pacific University, OR*
Peace College, NC*
The Pennsylvania State University Abington College, PA*
The Pennsylvania State University Altoona College, PA
The Pennsylvania State University University Park Campus, PA
Pepperdine University, CA*
Philadelphia Biblical University, PA*
Pitzer College, CA*
Plymouth State University, NH*
Portland State University, OR*
Princeton University, NJ*
Purdue University, IN
Quinnipiac University, CT*
Ramapo College of New Jersey, NJ*
Rensselaer Polytechnic Institute, NY
Rice University, TX*
Robert Morris University, PA*
Roberts Wesleyan College, NY*
Rochester Institute of Technology, NY
Rose-Hulman Institute of Technology, IN
Russell Sage College, NY*

Rutgers, The State University of New Jersey, Camden, NJ*
Rutgers, The State University of New Jersey, Newark, NJ
Rutgers, The State University of New Jersey, New Brunswick/Piscataway, NJ
St. Edward's University, TX*
St. John Fisher College, NY*
St. Joseph's College, Suffolk Campus, NY*
Saint Joseph's University, PA
St. Lawrence University, NY*
Saint Leo University, FL*
St. Louis College of Pharmacy, MO*
Saint Louis University, MO
Saint Mary's College, IN*
Saint Mary's College of California, CA*
St. Thomas University, FL*
Saint Vincent College, PA*
Saint Xavier University, IL*
Samford University, AL
Samuel Merritt College, CA*
San Diego Christian College, CA*
San Diego State University, CA
San Francisco State University, CA*
San Jose State University, CA
Santa Clara University, CA*
Scripps College, CA*
Seattle Pacific University, WA*
Seattle University, WA*
Simmons College, MA*
Skidmore College, NY*
Sonoma State University, CA*
South Carolina State University, SC*
South Dakota State University, SD
Southeastern University, FL*
Southeast Missouri State University, MO
Southern Connecticut State University, CT*
Southern Illinois University Carbondale, IL
Southern Illinois University Edwardsville, IL
Southern New Hampshire University, NH*
Southern Polytechnic State University, GA*
Southern University and Agricultural and Mechanical College, LA*
Spring Hill College, AL*
Stanford University, CA*
State University of New York at Binghamton, NY*
State University of New York College at Brockport, NY*
State University of New York College at Cortland, NY*
State University of New York College at Geneseo, NY*
State University of New York College at Old Westbury, NY*
State University of New York College at Potsdam, NY*
State University of New York College of Environmental Science and Forestry, NY*
State University of New York Institute of Technology, NY*
Stephens College, MO*
Stevens Institute of Technology, NJ*
Stony Brook University, State University of New York, NY*

*program is offered at another college's campus

ROTC Programs
Air Force

Swarthmore College, PA*
Syracuse University, NY
Temple University, PA*
Tennessee State University, TN
Tennessee Technological University, TN*
Texas A&M University, TX
Texas Christian University, TX
Texas Lutheran University, TX*
Texas State University-San Marcos, TX
Texas Tech University, TX
Texas Woman's University, TX*
Thomas Jefferson University, PA*
Thomas More College, KY*
Tiffin University, OH*
Towson University, MD*
Transylvania University, KY*
Tufts University, MA*
Tuskegee University, AL
Union College, NY*
University at Albany, State University of New York, NY*
The University of Akron, OH
The University of Alabama, AL
The University of Alabama at Birmingham, AL*
University of Arkansas, AR
University of Baltimore, MD*
University of California, Berkeley, CA
University of California, Davis, CA*
University of California, Irvine, CA*
University of California, Los Angeles, CA
University of California, Riverside, CA*
University of California, Santa Cruz, CA*
University of Cincinnati, OH
University of Colorado at Boulder, CO
University of Colorado at Denver and Health Sciences Center—Downtown Denver Campus, CO*
University of Connecticut, CT
University of Dallas, TX*
University of Dayton, OH*
University of Delaware, DE
University of Denver, CO*
The University of Findlay, OH*
University of Florida, FL
University of Georgia, GA
University of Hartford, CT*
University of Hawaii at Manoa, HI
University of Idaho, ID*
University of Illinois at Urbana–Champaign, IL
The University of Iowa, IA
University of Kansas, KS
University of Kentucky, KY
University of Louisville, KY
University of Mary Hardin-Baylor, TX*

University of Maryland, College Park, MD
University of Massachusetts Amherst, MA
University of Massachusetts Lowell, MA
University of Memphis, TN
University of Miami, FL
University of Michigan, MI
University of Michigan–Dearborn, MI*
University of Minnesota, Duluth, MN
University of Minnesota, Twin Cities Campus, MN
University of Missouri–Columbia, MO
University of Missouri–Kansas City, MO*
University of Missouri–St. Louis, MO*
University of Nebraska at Omaha, NE
University of Nebraska–Lincoln, NE
University of Nebraska Medical Center, NE*
University of New Hampshire, NH
University of New Hampshire at Manchester, NH*
University of New Orleans, LA*
The University of North Carolina at Chapel Hill, NC
The University of North Carolina at Greensboro, NC*
The University of North Carolina at Pembroke, NC
University of North Dakota, ND
University of Northern Colorado, CO
University of Oklahoma, OK
University of Oregon, OR*
University of Pennsylvania, PA*
University of Pittsburgh, PA
University of Pittsburgh at Greensburg, PA*
University of Portland, OR
University of Puerto Rico, Mayagüez Campus, PR
University of Rochester, NY*
University of St. Thomas, MN
University of San Diego, CA*
University of South Carolina, SC
University of Southern California, CA
University of Southern Maine, ME*
University of Southern Mississippi, MS
University of South Florida, FL
The University of Tampa, FL*
The University of Texas at Arlington, TX*
The University of Texas at Austin, TX
The University of Texas at Dallas, TX*
The University of Texas at El Paso, TX
The University of Texas at San Antonio, TX
University of the District of Columbia, DC*
The University of Toledo, OH*
University of Tulsa, OK*
University of Utah, UT

University of Virginia, VA
The University of West Alabama, AL*
University of Wisconsin–Madison, WI
University of Wisconsin–Whitewater, WI
University of Wyoming, WY
Utah State University, UT
Utica College, NY*
Valdosta State University, GA
Valparaiso University, IN
Vanderbilt University, TN*
Vanguard University of Southern California, CA*
Vaughn College of Aeronautics and Technology, NY*
Villanova University, PA*
Virginia Military Institute, VA
Virginia Polytechnic Institute and State University, VA
Warner Pacific College, OR*
Washington & Jefferson College, PA*
Washington State University, WA
Washington University in St. Louis, MO*
Wayland Baptist University, TX*
Wayne State University, MI*
Webster University, MO*
Wellesley College, MA*
Wells College, NY*
Wentworth Institute of Technology, MA*
Wesleyan University, CT*
Western Kentucky University, KY*
Western New England College, MA*
Western Oregon University, OR*
Westfield State College, MA*
Westminster College, MO*
Westmont College, CA*
West Virginia University, WV
Wheaton College, IL*
Whittier College, CA*
Widener University, PA*
Wilkes University, PA
Willamette University, OR*
William Carey College, MS*
William Paterson University of New Jersey, NJ*
William Woods University, MO*
Wingate University, NC*
Winston-Salem State University, NC
Wittenberg University, OH*
Worcester Polytechnic Institute, MA
Worcester State College, MA*
Xavier University, OH*
Xavier University of Louisiana, LA*
Yale University, CT*
York College of the City University of New York, NY*
Youngstown State University, OH*

*program is offered at another college's campus

Tuition Waivers

Minority Students
Alice Lloyd College, KY
Assumption College, MA
Bloomsburg University of Pennsylvania, PA
Bridgewater College, VA
Dickinson State University, ND
Dowling College, NY
Edinboro University of Pennsylvania, PA
Fort Lewis College, CO
Geneva College, PA
Huntington University, IN
Illinois State University, IL
Indiana University of Pennsylvania, PA
John Brown University, AR
Lake Superior State University, MI
Lipscomb University, TN
Lock Haven University of Pennsylvania, PA
MacMurray College, IL
Mayville State University, ND
Messiah College, PA
Montana State University, MT
Montana State University–Billings, MT
Nazareth College of Rochester, NY
Northern Illinois University, IL
Portland State University, OR
Saint Joseph's College, IN
St. Thomas University, FL
Shepherd University, WV
Slippery Rock University of Pennsylvania, PA
Southeastern Oklahoma State University, OK
State University of New York at Buffalo, NY
State University of New York College at Potsdam, NY
Tennessee State University, TN
Texas Southern University, TX
University of Evansville, IN
University of Hawaii at Manoa, HI
University of Idaho, ID
University of Maine at Farmington, ME
University of Maine at Presque Isle, ME
University of North Dakota, ND
University of Rhode Island, RI
University of Southern Maine, ME
University of West Georgia, GA
University of Wisconsin–Eau Claire, WI
Utah State University, UT
Washington College, MD
Wayne State College, NE
William Jewell College, MO
Wittenberg University, OH

Children of Alumni
Adrian College, MI
Albertson College of Idaho, ID
Albion College, MI
Albright College, PA
Alliant International University, CA
Arkansas State University, AR
Ashland University, OH
Augsburg College, MN
Avila University, MO
Baldwin-Wallace College, OH
Barton College, NC
Bethany College, KS
Bethel College, KS
Bryan College, TN
Cabrini College, PA
Calumet College of Saint Joseph, IN
Carthage College, WI
Cedar Crest College, PA
Centenary College, NJ
Central Michigan University, MI
Central Missouri State University, MO
Centre College, KY
Christian Brothers University, TN
Clarke College, IA
Coe College, IA
The College of St. Scholastica, MN
Dominican University, IL
Dowling College, NY
Drake University, IA
Erskine College, SC
Eureka College, IL
Faulkner University, AL
Florida Southern College, FL
Grambling State University, LA
Hilbert College, NY
Hillsdale College, MI
Huntington University, IN
John Brown University, AR
Kentucky Wesleyan College, KY
Lake Superior State University, MI
Louisiana State University and Agricultural and Mechanical College, LA
Louisiana Tech University, LA
MacMurray College, IL
Marian College, IN
Marymount University, VA
Messiah College, PA
Michigan Technological University, MI
Midland Lutheran College, NE
Mississippi State University, MS
Missouri State University, MO
Moravian College, PA
Morehead State University, KY
Morningside College, IA
Mount Union College, OH
Murray State University, KY
Nazareth College of Rochester, NY
New England College, NH
Northwestern College, MN
Northwood University, MI
Northwood University, Florida Campus, FL
Northwood University, Texas Campus, TX
Ohio Wesleyan University, OH
Oklahoma State University, OK
Oral Roberts University, OK
Philadelphia Biblical University, PA
Ripon College, WI
Rockhurst University, MO
Saint Joseph's College, IN
Saint Martin's University, WA
St. Thomas University, FL
Silver Lake College, WI
South Dakota State University, SD
Southeastern Bible College, AL
Southeastern Oklahoma State University, OK
Southern Arkansas University–Magnolia, AR
Southern University and Agricultural and Mechanical College, LA
Taylor University Fort Wayne, IN
Texas Lutheran University, TX
Thomas More College, KY
University of Alaska Fairbanks, AK
University of Alaska Southeast, AK
University of Evansville, IN
The University of Findlay, OH
University of Idaho, ID
University of Louisiana at Lafayette, LA
University of Minnesota, Duluth, MN
University of Nebraska Medical Center, NE
University of Nevada, Las Vegas, NV
University of Nevada, Reno, NV
University of New England, ME
University of Rochester, NY
University of St. Francis, IL
University of Saint Francis, IN
University of Southern Mississippi, MS
University of Wisconsin–Whitewater, WI
University of Wyoming, WY
Urbana University, OH
Utah State University, UT
Valley City State University, ND
Washington State University, WA
Webber International University, FL
Wells College, NY
Westminster College, MO
William Jewell College, MO
William Woods University, MO
Wilson College, PA
Wittenberg University, OH

Tuition Waivers
Adult Students

Adult Students
Alaska Pacific University, AK
Albertson College of Idaho, ID
Anderson University, SC
Augustana College, SD
Barton College, NC
California State University, Stanislaus, CA
Clarke College, IA
Coe College, IA
College of the Atlantic, ME
Converse College, SC
Cornell College, IA
Creighton University, NE
Dowling College, NY
Goucher College, MD
Huntington University, IN
John Brown University, AR
Marquette University, WI
Mercyhurst College, PA
Messiah College, PA
Mount Union College, OH
Nebraska Wesleyan University, NE
New England College, NH
Randolph-Macon Woman's College, VA
St. Andrews Presbyterian College, NC
Simmons College, MA
Southern Adventist University, TN
Sweet Briar College, VA
Trinity College, CT
University of West Georgia, GA
Utah State University, UT
Webber International University, FL
Wittenberg University, OH

Senior Citizens
Alaska Pacific University, AK
Albertson College of Idaho, ID
Albertus Magnus College, CT
Albright College, PA
Alvernia College, PA
Anderson University, SC
Andrews University, MI
Arkansas State University, AR
Arkansas Tech University, AR
Armstrong Atlantic State University, GA
Asbury College, KY
Ashland University, OH
Athens State University, AL
Atlantic Union College, MA
Augsburg College, MN
Augustana College, SD
Augusta State University, GA
Aurora University, IL
Austin Peay State University, TN
Averett University, VA
Avila University, MO
Barton College, NC
Becker College, MA
Belmont Abbey College, NC
Belmont University, TN
Bemidji State University, MN
Benedictine College, KS
Bernard M. Baruch College of the City University of New York, NY
Berry College, GA
Bethel College, KS

Bethel University, MN
Black Hills State University, SD
Bloomfield College, NJ
Bloomsburg University of Pennsylvania, PA
Bluefield State College, WV
Boston University, MA
Bowling Green State University, OH
Bradley University, IL
Brevard College, NC
Brewton-Parker College, GA
Bridgewater College, VA
Bryn Mawr College, PA
Cabrini College, PA
California State University, Chico, CA
California State University, Fresno, CA
California State University, Fullerton, CA
California State University, Sacramento, CA
California State University, San Marcos, CA
California State University, Stanislaus, CA
Calumet College of Saint Joseph, IN
Campbellsville University, KY
Carroll College, MT
Carson-Newman College, TN
Cedarville University, OH
Centenary College, NJ
Central Connecticut State University, CT
Central Michigan University, MI
Central Missouri State University, MO
Central Washington University, WA
Champlain College, VT
Chestnut Hill College, PA
Chowan University, NC
Christopher Newport University, VA
The Citadel, The Military College of South Carolina, SC
City College of the City University of New York, NY
Clarke College, IA
Clemson University, SC
Cleveland State University, OH
Coastal Carolina University, SC
Coe College, IA
College of Charleston, SC
College of Mount St. Joseph, OH
College of Mount Saint Vincent, NY
The College of New Jersey, NJ
College of St. Catherine, MN
College of St. Joseph, VT
College of Saint Mary, NE
The College of St. Scholastica, MN
College of Santa Fe, NM
College of Staten Island of the City University of New York, NY
College of the Atlantic, ME
The College of William and Mary, VA
Columbus State University, GA
Connecticut College, CT
Converse College, SC
Cornell College, IA
Culver-Stockton College, MO
Daemen College, NY
Dakota State University, SD
Defiance College, OH
Dickinson State University, ND
Doane College, NE

Dominican University of California, CA
Dordt College, IA
Dowling College, NY
Drake University, IA
Drew University, NJ
Duquesne University, PA
East Carolina University, NC
East Central University, OK
East Stroudsburg University of Pennsylvania, PA
East Tennessee State University, TN
Elmhurst College, IL
Elms College, MA
Emporia State University, KS
Eureka College, IL
Ferrum College, VA
Fitchburg State College, MA
Florida Agricultural and Mechanical University, FL
Florida Atlantic University, FL
Florida Gulf Coast University, FL
Florida Institute of Technology, FL
Florida State University, FL
Fort Hays State University, KS
Francis Marion University, SC
Freed-Hardeman University, TN
Fresno Pacific University, CA
Frostburg State University, MD
Gannon University, PA
George Mason University, VA
Georgia College & State University, GA
Georgia Southern University, GA
Georgia Southwestern State University, GA
Glenville State College, WV
Goucher College, MD
Graceland University, IA
Grambling State University, LA
Grand View College, IA
Greenville College, IL
Hanover College, IN
Harding University, AR
Hilbert College, NY
Hofstra University, NY
Houghton College, NY
Houston Baptist University, TX
Huntington University, IN
Husson College, ME
Idaho State University, ID
Illinois State University, IL
Indiana University Northwest, IN
Indiana University–Purdue University Fort Wayne, IN
Iona College, NY
James Madison University, VA
John Brown University, AR
Kean University, NJ
Kennesaw State University, GA
Kentucky State University, KY
Kentucky Wesleyan College, KY
King's College, PA
Lake Superior State University, MI
Lebanon Valley College, PA
Lehigh University, PA
Lehman College of the City University of New York, NY
Lewis-Clark State College, ID

Tuition Waivers
Senior Citizens

Lincoln University, MO
Lindenwood University, MO
Linfield College, OR
Lock Haven University of Pennsylvania, PA
Loras College, IA
Louisiana Tech University, LA
Loyola University New Orleans, LA
Lynchburg College, VA
MacMurray College, IL
Macon State College, GA
Malone College, OH
Manhattan Christian College, KS
Mansfield University of Pennsylvania, PA
Marian College, IN
Marian College of Fond du Lac, WI
Marlboro College, VT
Marquette University, WI
Marshall University, WV
Marymount University, VA
Maryville University of Saint Louis, MO
Marywood University, PA
Mayville State University, ND
Merrimack College, MA
Messiah College, PA
Methodist College, NC
Metropolitan State College of Denver, CO
Michigan Technological University, MI
Middle Tennessee State University, TN
Midway College, KY
Midwestern State University, TX
Millersville University of Pennsylvania, PA
Minnesota State University Mankato, MN
Mississippi State University, MS
Missouri State University, MO
Monmouth University, NJ
Montana State University, MT
Montana State University–Billings, MT
Montclair State University, NJ
Morehead State University, KY
Morningside College, IA
Mountain State University, WV
Mount Mary College, WI
Mount Olive College, NC
Mount Vernon Nazarene University, OH
Murray State University, KY
Nebraska Wesleyan University, NE
New England College, NH
New Jersey City University, NJ
New Mexico State University, NM
New York Institute of Technology, NY
Niagara University, NY
North Carolina State University, NC
Northeastern University, MA
Northern Michigan University, MI
North Georgia College & State University, GA
Northwestern College, MN
Northwestern Oklahoma State University, OK
Northwestern State University of Louisiana, LA
Northwest University, WA
The Ohio State University, OH
Ohio University–Southern Campus, OH
Ohio University–Zanesville, OH
Oklahoma Baptist University, OK

Pacific Lutheran University, WA
Pacific Union College, CA
The Pennsylvania State University Abington College, PA
The Pennsylvania State University Altoona College, PA
The Pennsylvania State University at Erie, The Behrend College, PA
The Pennsylvania State University Berks Campus of the Berks–Lehigh Valley College, PA
The Pennsylvania State University Harrisburg Campus, PA
Pikeville College, KY
Plymouth State University, NH
Portland State University, OR
Presentation College, SD
Purdue University, IN
Purdue University Calumet, IN
Quincy University, IL
Radford University, VA
The Richard Stockton College of New Jersey, NJ
Roanoke College, VA
Rockhurst University, MO
Roosevelt University, IL
Rosemont College, PA
St. Andrews Presbyterian College, NC
St. Cloud State University, MN
St. John's University, NY
St. Joseph's College, Suffolk Campus, NY
Saint Mary's College, IN
Saint Vincent College, PA
Saint Xavier University, IL
Salisbury University, MD
San Francisco State University, CA
Seattle Pacific University, WA
Shasta Bible College, CA
Shepherd University, WV
Shippensburg University of Pennsylvania, PA
Shorter College, GA
Silver Lake College, WI
Simmons College, MA
Slippery Rock University of Pennsylvania, PA
South Carolina State University, SC
South Dakota School of Mines and Technology, SD
South Dakota State University, SD
Southeastern Louisiana University, LA
Southeastern Oklahoma State University, OK
Southeast Missouri State University, MO
Southern Adventist University, TN
Southern Arkansas University–Magnolia, AR
Southern Connecticut State University, CT
Southern Illinois University Carbondale, IL
Southern Illinois University Edwardsville, IL
Southern Methodist College, SC
Southern Oregon University, OR
Southern University and Agricultural and Mechanical College, LA
Spring Arbor University, MI

State University of New York College at Brockport, NY
State University of New York College at Old Westbury, NY
Suffolk University, MA
Sweet Briar College, VA
Taylor University, IN
Taylor University Fort Wayne, IN
Tennessee State University, TN
Texas A&M University–Commerce, TX
Texas Southern University, TX
Texas Tech University, TX
Thiel College, PA
Tiffin University, OH
Towson University, MD
Trevecca Nazarene University, TN
Truman State University, MO
Union College, KY
Union College, NY
University at Albany, State University of New York, NY
The University of Akron, OH
University of Alaska Fairbanks, AK
University of Alaska Southeast, AK
University of Arkansas, AR
University of Baltimore, MD
University of Colorado at Boulder, CO
University of Connecticut, CT
University of Dayton, OH
University of Delaware, DE
University of Evansville, IN
The University of Findlay, OH
University of Florida, FL
University of Georgia, GA
University of Great Falls, MT
University of Hartford, CT
University of Idaho, ID
University of Illinois at Springfield, IL
University of Illinois at Urbana–Champaign, IL
University of Kentucky, KY
University of Louisiana at Lafayette, LA
University of Louisville, KY
University of Maine at Farmington, ME
University of Maine at Presque Isle, ME
University of Mary, ND
University of Mary Washington, VA
University of Massachusetts Amherst, MA
University of Massachusetts Dartmouth, MA
University of Massachusetts Lowell, MA
University of Memphis, TN
University of Michigan, MI
University of Michigan–Dearborn, MI
University of Michigan–Flint, MI
University of Minnesota, Morris, MN
University of Minnesota, Twin Cities Campus, MN
University of Missouri–Columbia, MO
University of Missouri–St. Louis, MO
University of Nevada, Las Vegas, NV
University of Nevada, Reno, NV
University of New Hampshire, NH
University of New Hampshire at Manchester, NH
University of New Orleans, LA

Tuition Waivers
Senior Citizens

University of North Alabama, AL
The University of North Carolina at Asheville, NC
The University of North Carolina at Chapel Hill, NC
The University of North Carolina at Pembroke, NC
The University of North Carolina Wilmington, NC
University of North Dakota, ND
University of North Florida, FL
University of Oklahoma, OK
University of Rhode Island, RI
University of Saint Francis, IN
University of St. Thomas, MN
University of St. Thomas, TX
University of Science and Arts of Oklahoma, OK
University of South Carolina, SC
University of South Carolina Upstate, SC
The University of South Dakota, SD
University of Southern Indiana, IN
University of Southern Mississippi, MS
University of South Florida, FL
The University of Tennessee at Martin, TN
The University of Texas at Austin, TX
The University of Texas at Dallas, TX
The University of Texas at Tyler, TX
The University of Texas–Pan American, TX
University of the District of Columbia, DC
University of the Virgin Islands, VI
University of Utah, UT
University of Vermont, VT
University of Virginia, VA
University of West Georgia, GA
University of Wisconsin–Eau Claire, WI
University of Wisconsin–Green Bay, WI
University of Wisconsin–Parkside, WI
University of Wisconsin–Stevens Point, WI
University of Wisconsin–Whitewater, WI
University of Wyoming, WY
Urbana University, OH
Ursinus College, PA
Utah State University, UT
Utica College, NY
Valdosta State University, GA
Villanova University, PA
Virginia Commonwealth University, VA
Virginia Intermont College, VA
Virginia Wesleyan College, VA
Walla Walla College, WA
Wartburg College, IA
Wayne State University, MI
Webber International University, FL
Wells College, NY
Wesleyan College, GA
Western Carolina University, NC
Western Illinois University, IL
Western Kentucky University, KY
Western New England College, MA
Western State College of Colorado, CO
West Virginia University, WV
Wheeling Jesuit University, WV
Wichita State University, KS
Widener University, PA
William Jewell College, MO
William Paterson University of New Jersey, NJ
William Penn University, IA
William Woods University, MO
Winston-Salem State University, NC
Winthrop University, SC
Wittenberg University, OH
Worcester State College, MA
Xavier University, OH
York College of the City University of New York, NY
Youngstown State University, OH

Tuition Payment Alternatives

Abilene Christian University, TX	I,P	Barton College, NC	I	California Polytechnic State	
Academy of Art University, CA	I	Bates College, ME	I,P	University, San Luis Obispo, CA	I
Adelphi University, NY	D,I,P	Baylor University, TX	I	California State University, Chico, CA	D,I
Adrian College, MI	I	Becker College, MA	I	California State University,	
Agnes Scott College, GA	I	Belhaven College, MS	I	Dominguez Hills, CA	I
Alaska Bible College, AK	I	Bellin College of Nursing, WI	I	California State University,	
Alaska Pacific University, AK	D,G,I	Belmont Abbey College, NC	D,I	Fresno, CA	I
Albertson College of Idaho, ID	G	Belmont University, TN	D,I	California State University,	
Albertus Magnus College, CT	I	Beloit College, WI	I	Fullerton, CA	D,I
Albion College, MI	D,I,P	Bemidji State University, MN	I	California State University,	
Albright College, PA	I	Benedictine College, KS	I	Sacramento, CA	I
Alderson-Broaddus College, WV	I	Benedictine University, IL	I	California State University,	
Alfred University, NY	D,I,P	Bennett College For Women, NC	D	Stanislaus, CA	D,I
Alice Lloyd College, KY	D	Bennington College, VT	I	Calumet College of Saint Joseph, IN	I
Allegheny College, PA	I,P	Bentley College, MA	I	Calvin College, MI	I,P
Allen College, IA	I	Bernard M. Baruch College of the		Campbellsville University, KY	I
Alliant International University, CA	I	City University of New York, NY	D,I	Campbell University, NC	I
Alma College, MI	D,I	Berry College, GA	I	Capitol College, MD	D,I
Alvernia College, PA	I	Bethany College, KS	I	Carleton College, MN	I,P
Alverno College, WI	D,I	Bethany Lutheran College, MN	I	Carnegie Mellon University, PA	I
American Baptist College of American		Bethel College, KS	D,I	Carroll College, MT	I
Baptist Theological Seminary, TN	D	Bethel University, MN	I,P	Carroll College, WI	I
American University, DC	I,P	Biola University, CA	I	Carson-Newman College, TN	I
Amherst College, MA	D,I	Black Hills State University, SD	D,I	Carthage College, WI	I
Anderson University, SC	I	Blessing-Rieman College of		Cascade College, OR	I
Andrews University, MI	I	Nursing, IL	I	Case Western Reserve University, OH	I
Antioch College, OH	I	Bloomfield College, NJ	D,I	Catawba College, NC	I
Appalachian State University, NC	I	Bloomsburg University of		The Catholic University of	
Arizona State University, AZ	I	Pennsylvania, PA	I	America, DC	I,P
Arizona State University at the		Bluefield State College, WV	D,I	Cazenovia College, NY	I
Polytechnic Campus, AZ	I	Blue Mountain College, MS	I	Cedar Crest College, PA	I
Arizona State University West, AZ	I	Bluffton University, OH	I	Cedarville University, OH	I
Arkansas State University, AR	I	Boston College, MA	I,P	Centenary College, NJ	I
Arkansas Tech University, AR	D,I	Boston University, MA	I,P	Centenary College of Louisiana, LA	D,I
Arlington Baptist College, TX	I	Bowdoin College, ME	D,I	Central College, IA	I
Art Center College of Design, CA	I	Bowling Green State University, OH	I	Central Connecticut State	
The Art Institute of Phoenix, AZ	G,I	Bradley University, IL	D,I	University, CT	I
Asbury College, KY	D,I	Brandeis University, MA	I	Central Michigan University, MI	G,I
Ashland University, OH	I	Brenau University, GA	I	Central Missouri State University, MO	D,I
Assumption College, MA	I	Brevard College, NC	I	Centre College, KY	I
Atlantic Union College, MA	G	Brewton-Parker College, GA	I	Chaminade University of	
Auburn University, AL	I	Bridgewater College, VA	I	Honolulu, HI	I
Auburn University Montgomery, AL	D	Bridgewater State College, MA	I	Champlain College, VT	I
Augsburg College, MN	D,I	Brigham Young University–Hawaii, HI	I	Chapman University, CA	D,I,P
Augustana College, SD	I	Bryan College, TN	I	Chester College of New England, NH	I
Aurora University, IL	D,I	Bryant University, RI	I	Chestnut Hill College, PA	D,I
Austin College, TX	I	Bryn Mawr College, PA	I,P	Chowan University, NC	D,I
Austin Peay State University, TN	D,I	Bucknell University, PA	I	Christendom College, VA	I,P
Averett University, VA	I	Burlington College, VT	I	Christian Brothers University, TN	D,I
Avila University, MO	D,G,I	Butler University, IN	I	Christopher Newport University, VA	I
Azusa Pacific University, CA	I	Cabrini College, PA	I	City College of the City University of	
Babson College, MA	I	California Baptist University, CA	I	New York, NY	D
Baldwin-Wallace College, OH	D,I	California Institute of Technology, CA	D,I	Claremont McKenna College, CA	I,P
The Baptist College of Florida, FL	I	California Institute of the Arts, CA	D	Clark Atlanta University, GA	D
Bard College, NY	I,P	California Lutheran University, CA	I	Clarke College, IA	D,I
Barnard College, NY	D,I			Clarkson University, NY	I,P

D = deferred payment system; G = guaranteed tuition rate; I = installment payments; P = prepayment locks in tuition rate

Tuition Payment Alternatives

College	Code	College	Code	College	Code
Clark University, MA	I,P	DePaul University, IL	D,I	Gallaudet University, DC	I
Clearwater Christian College, FL	I	DePauw University, IN	D,I,P	Gannon University, PA	D,I
Clemson University, SC	I	Dickinson College, PA	I	Geneva College, PA	I
The Cleveland Institute of Art, OH	D	Doane College, NE	I	George Mason University, VA	D,I
Cleveland Institute of Music, OH	I	Dominican University, IL	I	Georgetown University, DC	D,I
Cleveland State University, OH	I	Dominican University of California, CA	I	Gettysburg College, PA	I,P
Coastal Carolina University, SC	D,I	Dordt College, IA	I	Glenville State College, WV	I
Coe College, IA	I	Dowling College, NY	D,I	Goddard College, VT	I
Colgate University, NY	D,I,P	Drake University, IA	I	Gonzaga University, WA	D,I
College Misericordia, PA	D,I	Drew University, NJ	D,I,P	Gordon College, MA	I
College of Charleston, SC	I	Drexel University, PA	I	Goshen College, IN	I
College of Mount St. Joseph, OH	D,I	Duquesne University, PA	D,I	Goucher College, MD	I,P
College of Mount Saint Vincent, NY	I	East Carolina University, NC	D,I	Grace Bible College, MI	I
The College of New Jersey, NJ	I	Eastern Illinois University, IL	I	Grace College, IN	I
College of Notre Dame of Maryland, MD	I	Eastern Washington University, WA	I	Graceland University, IA	I
College of Saint Benedict, MN	I,P	East Stroudsburg University of Pennsylvania, PA	I	Grambling State University, LA	D
College of St. Joseph, VT	I			Grand Valley State University, MI	D,I
College of Saint Mary, NE	D,I	East Tennessee State University, TN	D,I	Grand View College, IA	I
The College of Saint Rose, NY	D	East Texas Baptist University, TX	G,I	Green Mountain College, VT	I
The College of St. Scholastica, MN	I	Eckerd College, FL	I	Grove City College, PA	I
College of Santa Fe, NM	I	Edinboro University of Pennsylvania, PA	I	Guilford College, NC	I
College of Staten Island of the City University of New York, NY	I	Elizabethtown College, PA	I	Gustavus Adolphus College, MN	G,I,P
				Gwynedd-Mercy College, PA	I
College of the Atlantic, ME	I	Elmhurst College, IL	I	Hamline University, MN	I
College of the Holy Cross, MA	I	Elmira College, NY	I,P	Hampden-Sydney College, VA	I
College of the Ozarks, MO	I	Elon University, NC	I	Hampshire College, MA	I
College of the Southwest, NM	D	Emerson College, MA	I	Hampton University, VA	D
College of Visual Arts, MN	I	Emmanuel College, MA	I	Hannibal-LaGrange College, MO	I
The College of William and Mary, VA	I	Emmaus Bible College, IA	I	Hanover College, IN	I
The College of Wooster, OH	I	Emory & Henry College, VA	I	Harding University, AR	I
Collins College: A School of Design and Technology, AZ	G	Emory University, GA	I,P	Hardin-Simmons University, TX	D,G,I,P
		Emporia State University, KS	D,I	Harvard University, MA	I,P
The Colorado College, CO	I	Endicott College, MA	I	Harvey Mudd College, CA	I
Colorado School of Mines, CO	I	Erskine College, SC	I	Haverford College, PA	I
Colorado State University, CO	I	Eureka College, IL	I	Hawai'i Pacific University, HI	I
Columbia College, SC	I,P	Evangel University, MO	I	Heidelberg College, OH	D,I
Columbia University, School of General Studies, NY	D,P	The Evergreen State College, WA	I	Hendrix College, AR	I
		Excelsior College, NY	I	Heritage Christian University, AL	D,I
Columbus College of Art & Design, OH	D,I	Fairfield University, CT	I	Hilbert College, NY	D,I
		Fashion Institute of Technology, NY	I	Hillsdale College, MI	D,I,P
Concordia University, CA	D,I	Faulkner University, AL	D,I	Hobart and William Smith Colleges, NY	I,P
Concordia University, MI	I	Felician College, NJ	D,I	Hofstra University, NY	D,I
Concordia University, NE	I	Ferris State University, MI	D,I	Hollins University, VA	I
Concordia University, St. Paul, MN	I	Ferrum College, VA	I	Holy Names University, CA	I
Concordia University Wisconsin, WI	D,G,I	Finlandia University, MI	I	Hope College, MI	I
Connecticut College, CT	I	Fitchburg State College, MA	I	Houghton College, NY	I
Converse College, SC	I	Five Towns College, NY	I	Houston Baptist University, TX	I,P
Corban College, OR	I	Florida Agricultural and Mechanical University, FL	D,P	Howard University, DC	D
Corcoran College of Art and Design, DC	I			Huntington University, IN	G,I
		Florida Atlantic University, FL	D,I,P	Husson College, ME	I,P
Cornell College, IA	I	Florida Christian College, FL	G	Idaho State University, ID	D
Cornell University, NY	I	Florida College, FL	I	Illinois College, IL	D,I
Cornerstone University, MI	I	Florida Institute of Technology, FL	I	Illinois State University, IL	G,I
Creighton University, NE	I	Florida Metropolitan University–Tampa Campus, FL	I	Illinois Wesleyan University, IL	I
Crown College, MN	I			Indiana State University, IN	I
The Culinary Institute of America, NY	I	Florida Southern College, FL	I	Indiana University Bloomington, IN	D
Culver-Stockton College, MO	I	Florida State University, FL	I,P	Indiana University East, IN	D
Daemen College, NY	D,I	Fort Hays State University, KS	I	Indiana University Kokomo, IN	D
Dakota State University, SD	D,I	Francis Marion University, SC	I	Indiana University Northwest, IN	D,I
Dallas Baptist University, TX	I	Franklin and Marshall College, PA	D,I	Indiana University of Pennsylvania, PA	D,I
Daniel Webster College, NH	I	Freed-Hardeman University, TN	I,P		
Dartmouth College, NH	P	Free Will Baptist Bible College, TN	D,I	Indiana University–Purdue University Fort Wayne, IN	D,I
Davis & Elkins College, WV		Fresno Pacific University, CA	I		
Defiance College, OH	I	Frostburg State University, MD	D,I	Indiana University–Purdue University Indianapolis, IN	D,I
Denison University, OH	I	Furman University, SC	I		

D = deferred payment system; *G* = guaranteed tuition rate; *I* = installment payments; *P* = prepayment locks in tuition rate

Tuition Payment Alternatives

College	Code
Indiana University South Bend, IN	D
Indiana University Southeast, IN	D
International College, FL	I
Iona College, NY	I
Iowa Wesleyan College, IA	D,I
James Madison University, VA	I
Jamestown College, ND	I
John Brown University, AR	I
John Jay College of Criminal Justice of the City University of New York, NY	I
The Johns Hopkins University, MD	I
Johnson & Wales University, CO	D,G,I
Johnson & Wales University, FL	G,I
Johnson & Wales University, RI	D,I
Johnson Bible College, TN	I
Judson College, AL	I
Kansas State University, KS	D,I
Kean University, NJ	D,I
Keene State College, NH	I
Kennesaw State University, GA	D
Kent State University, OH	D,I,P
Kentucky State University, KY	D,I
Kentucky Wesleyan College, KY	D,I
Kenyon College, OH	I
Kettering University, MI	I
King College, TN	I,P
King's College, PA	D,I
Knox College, IL	I
Kuyper College, MI	I
LaGrange College, GA	I
Lake Forest College, IL	I
Lakeland College, WI	I
Lake Superior State University, MI	D,I
Lamar University, TX	I
Laura and Alvin Siegal College of Judaic Studies, OH	I
Lawrence Technological University, MI	I
Lawrence University, WI	I
Lebanon Valley College, PA	I
Lee University, TN	D
Lehigh University, PA	I,P
Lehman College of the City University of New York, NY	I
Le Moyne College, NY	D,I
LeMoyne-Owen College, TN	I
Lesley University, MA	I
LeTourneau University, TX	I
Lewis & Clark College, OR	I
Lewis-Clark State College, ID	D
Lexington College, IL	I
Limestone College, SC	I
Lincoln University, MO	I
Lincoln University, PA	D,I
Lindenwood University, MO	D,I
Lindsey Wilson College, KY	I
Linfield College, OR	I
Lipscomb University, TN	D,I
Lock Haven University of Pennsylvania, PA	D,I
Long Island University, Brooklyn Campus, NY	D
Loras College, IA	I
Louisiana State University and Agricultural and Mechanical College, LA	D
Louisiana Tech University, LA	D,I
Loyola University Chicago, IL	I
Loyola University New Orleans, LA	I
Lubbock Christian University, TX	I
Luther College, IA	I
Lycoming College, PA	I
Lynchburg College, VA	I
Lynn University, FL	D,I
Lyon College, AR	I
MacMurray College, IL	I
Maharishi University of Management, IA	I
Maine Maritime Academy, ME	I
Malone College, OH	I
Manchester College, IN	I
Manhattan Christian College, KS	D
Manhattan College, NY	I
Manhattan School of Music, NY	D,I
Mansfield University of Pennsylvania, PA	D,I
Marian College, IN	D,I
Marian College of Fond du Lac, WI	I
Marist College, NY	I
Marlboro College, VT	I
Marquette University, WI	I
Marshall University, WV	I
Mary Baldwin College, VA	I
Marymount University, VA	I
Maryville College, TN	I
Maryville University of Saint Louis, MO	D,I
Marywood University, PA	D,I
Massachusetts Institute of Technology, MA	I
Massachusetts Maritime Academy, MA	I
The Master's College and Seminary, CA	I
Mayville State University, ND	I
McDaniel College, MD	I
McKendree College, IL	D,I
Medgar Evers College of the City University of New York, NY	D,I
Menlo College, CA	I
Mercer University, GA	I
Mercyhurst College, PA	I
Meredith College, NC	I
Merrimack College, MA	I
Mesa State College, CO	I
Messenger College, MO	I
Messiah College, PA	I
Methodist College, NC	D,I
Metropolitan State College of Denver, CO	D,I
Miami University, OH	I
Michigan State University, MI	D
Michigan Technological University, MI	D,I
Middlebury College, VT	P
Middle Tennessee State University, TN	D
Midland Lutheran College, NE	I
Midway College, KY	D
Midwestern State University, TX	I
Millersville University of Pennsylvania, PA	I
Milligan College, TN	I
Millsaps College, MS	D,I
Milwaukee School of Engineering, WI	I
Minnesota State University Mankato, MN	I
Missouri State University, MO	D
Molloy College, NY	I
Monmouth University, NJ	I
Montana State University, MT	D,I
Montana State University–Billings, MT	I
Montclair State University, NJ	I
Montserrat College of Art, MA	I
Moore College of Art & Design, PA	I
Moravian College, PA	I
Morehead State University, KY	D,I
Morningside College, IA	I
Mountain State University, WV	I
Mount Aloysius College, PA	I
Mount Holyoke College, MA	P
Mount Marty College, SD	I
Mount Mary College, WI	I
Mount Mercy College, IA	I
Mount Olive College, NC	I
Mount St. Mary's University, MD	I
Mount Union College, OH	I,P
Mount Vernon Nazarene University, OH	I
Murray State University, KY	I
Nazareth College of Rochester, NY	I
Nebraska Wesleyan University, NE	D,I
New College of Florida, FL	D,I,P
New England College, NH	I
New England School of Communications, ME	I
New Jersey City University, NJ	D
Newman University, KS	I
New Mexico State University, NM	D,I
New York Institute of Technology, NY	I
New York School of Interior Design, NY	I
New York University, NY	D,I
Niagara University, NY	D,I
Nicholls State University, LA	D,I
North Carolina State University, NC	I
Northeastern University, MA	D,I
Northern Arizona University, AZ	I
Northern Illinois University, IL	I
Northern Michigan University, MI	D,I
Northern State University, SD	I
North Greenville College, SC	I
Northland College, WI	I
Northwest Christian College, OR	D,I
Northwestern College, MN	I
Northwestern Oklahoma State University, OK	I
Northwestern State University of Louisiana, LA	I
Northwestern University, IL	I
Northwest Nazarene University, ID	I,P
Northwest University, WA	I
Northwood University, MI	I

D = deferred payment system; G = guaranteed tuition rate; I = installment payments; P = prepayment locks in tuition rate

Tuition Payment Alternatives

College	Code
Northwood University, Florida Campus, FL	I
Northwood University, Texas Campus, TX	I
Nova Southeastern University, FL	D,I
Nyack College, NY	I
Occidental College, CA	I,P
Oglethorpe University, GA	I,P
Ohio Northern University, OH	I
The Ohio State University, OH	I
Ohio University, OH	I
Ohio University–Southern Campus, OH	I
Ohio Wesleyan University, OH	I
Oklahoma Baptist University, OK	I
Oklahoma Panhandle State University, OK	I
Oklahoma State University, OK	I
Olivet Nazarene University, IL	I
Oral Roberts University, OK	I
Otis College of Art and Design, CA	I
Pacific Lutheran University, WA	I
Pacific Oaks College, CA	I
Pacific Union College, CA	G,I
Pacific University, OR	D,I
Palm Beach Atlantic University, FL	I
Paul Smith's College of Arts and Sciences, NY	I
Peace College, NC	D,I
Pennsylvania College of Technology, PA	D
The Pennsylvania State University Abington College, PA	D
The Pennsylvania State University Altoona College, PA	D
The Pennsylvania State University at Erie, The Behrend College, PA	D
The Pennsylvania State University Berks Campus of the Berks–Lehigh Valley College, PA	D
The Pennsylvania State University Harrisburg Campus, PA	D
Pepperdine University, CA	D,I
Philadelphia Biblical University, PA	I
Philadelphia University, PA	D,I
Pikeville College, KY	I
Pittsburg State University, KS	I
Pitzer College, CA	D,I
Plymouth State University, NH	I
Pomona College, CA	I
Pontifical Catholic University of Puerto Rico, PR	D
Portland State University, OR	I
Prescott College, AZ	D,I
Presentation College, SD	I
Princeton University, NJ	D,I
Principia College, IL	I
Purdue University, IN	I
Purdue University Calumet, IN	D
Quincy University, IL	I
Quinnipiac University, CT	D,I
Radford University, VA	I
Randolph-Macon College, VA	I
Randolph-Macon Woman's College, VA	I
Reed College, OR	I
Regis College, MA	I
Rensselaer Polytechnic Institute, NY	I
Rice University, TX	I
The Richard Stockton College of New Jersey, NJ	D,I
Ringling School of Art and Design, FL	I
Ripon College, WI	G,I
Roanoke College, VA	I
Robert Morris College, IL	I
Robert Morris University, PA	D,I
Roberts Wesleyan College, NY	I
Rochester Institute of Technology, NY	D,I,P
Rockhurst University, MO	D,I
Roger Williams University, RI	D,I
Rollins College, FL	I
Roosevelt University, IL	D,I
Rose-Hulman Institute of Technology, IN	I,P
Rosemont College, PA	I
Rowan University, NJ	D
Russell Sage College, NY	D,I
Rutgers, The State University of New Jersey, Newark, NJ	I
Rutgers, The State University of New Jersey, New Brunswick/Piscataway, NJ	I
Sacred Heart University, CT	I
Sage College of Albany, NY	D,I
St. Andrews Presbyterian College, NC	I
St. Cloud State University, MN	I
St. Edward's University, TX	D,I
St. Francis College, NY	D,I
Saint Francis Medical Center College of Nursing, IL	I
Saint Francis University, PA	D,I
St. John Fisher College, NY	D,I
St. John's University, NY	D,G,I
Saint Joseph's College, IN	I
St. Joseph's College, New York, NY	I
Saint Joseph's College of Maine, ME	I
St. Joseph's College, Suffolk Campus, NY	I
Saint Joseph's University, PA	D,I
St. Lawrence University, NY	D,I
Saint Leo University, FL	I
St. Louis College of Pharmacy, MO	D
Saint Louis University, MO	I
Saint Martin's University, WA	I
Saint Mary's College, IN	I
Saint Mary's College of California, CA	I
Saint Mary's University of Minnesota, MN	I
St. Norbert College, WI	D,I
St. Thomas University, FL	I
Saint Vincent College, PA	I
Saint Xavier University, IL	I
Salisbury University, MD	I
Salve Regina University, RI	I
Samuel Merritt College, CA	I
San Diego Christian College, CA	I
San Diego State University, CA	I
San Francisco State University, CA	I
San Jose State University, CA	I
Santa Clara University, CA	D,I,P
Sarah Lawrence College, NY	I
School of the Museum of Fine Arts, Boston, MA	I
Schreiner University, TX	I
Scripps College, CA	I
Seattle Pacific University, WA	I
Seton Hill University, PA	D,I
Sewanee: The University of the South, TN	D,I
Shasta Bible College, CA	I
Shenandoah University, VA	I
Shepherd University, WV	I
Shippensburg University of Pennsylvania, PA	I
Shorter College, GA	I
Silver Lake College, WI	D,I
Simmons College, MA	I
Simpson College, IA	I
Simpson University, CA	D,I
Skidmore College, NY	I,P
Slippery Rock University of Pennsylvania, PA	I
Smith College, MA	I
Sojourner-Douglass College, MD	I
South Carolina State University, SC	D,I
South Dakota School of Mines and Technology, SD	I
South Dakota State University, SD	D,I
Southeastern Bible College, AL	I
Southeastern Louisiana University, LA	D,I
Southeastern University, FL	I
Southeast Missouri State University, MO	D,I
Southern Adventist University, TN	D,I,P
Southern Arkansas University–Magnolia, AR	I
Southern Connecticut State University, CT	I
Southern Illinois University Carbondale, IL	G,I
Southern Illinois University Edwardsville, IL	I
Southern New Hampshire University, NH	D,I
Southern Oregon University, OR	D
Southern Virginia University, VA	I
Southwest Baptist University, MO	I
Southwestern University, TX	D,I
Spring Arbor University, MI	D,I
Spring Hill College, AL	I
State University of New York at Binghamton, NY	I
State University of New York at Buffalo, NY	I
State University of New York at New Paltz, NY	I
State University of New York at Oswego, NY	I
State University of New York at Plattsburgh, NY	D,I
State University of New York College at Brockport, NY	D,I
State University of New York College at Geneseo, NY	D,I
State University of New York College at Old Westbury, NY	I

D = deferred payment system; G = guaranteed tuition rate; I = installment payments; P = prepayment locks in tuition rate

Tuition Payment Alternatives

Institution	Code
State University of New York College at Oneonta, NY	I
State University of New York College at Potsdam, NY	I
State University of New York College of Agriculture and Technology at Cobleskill, NY	I
State University of New York College of Environmental Science and Forestry, NY	D,I
State University of New York, Fredonia, NY	I
Stephen F. Austin State University, TX	I
Stephens College, MO	I
Sterling College, VT	I
Stetson University, FL	I
Stevens Institute of Technology, NJ	I
Stonehill College, MA	I,P
Stony Brook University, State University of New York, NY	I
Suffolk University, MA	D,I
Swarthmore College, PA	I
Sweet Briar College, VA	I
Syracuse University, NY	I
Tabor College, KS	I
Taylor University, IN	I
Taylor University Fort Wayne, IN	I
Temple University, PA	I
Tennessee Technological University, TN	I
Texas A&M University, TX	I
Texas A&M University at Galveston, TX	I
Texas A&M University–Commerce, TX	I
Texas Christian University, TX	I
Texas Lutheran University, TX	I
Texas Southern University, TX	I
Texas State University-San Marcos, TX	I
Texas Tech University, TX	I
Thiel College, PA	I
Thomas College, ME	D
Thomas More College, KY	D,I
Thomas More College of Liberal Arts, NH	I
Tiffin University, OH	I
Toccoa Falls College, GA	I
Towson University, MD	I
Transylvania University, KY	I
Trevecca Nazarene University, TN	I
Trinity College, CT	I
Trinity International University, IL	I
Trinity Lutheran College, WA	I
Tri-State University, IN	I
Truman State University, MO	I
Tufts University, MA	I,P
Tusculum College, TN	I
Tuskegee University, AL	I
Union College, KY	I
Union College, NY	I
Union University, TN	D,I
Unity College, ME	I
University at Albany, State University of New York, NY	I
The University of Akron, OH	I
The University of Alabama, AL	D,I
The University of Alabama in Huntsville, AL	D
University of Alaska Fairbanks, AK	I
University of Alaska Southeast, AK	D,I
University of Arkansas, AR	I
University of Baltimore, MD	D,I
University of California, Berkeley, CA	I
University of California, Davis, CA	D
University of California, Irvine, CA	I
University of California, Riverside, CA	D
University of California, San Diego, CA	D,I
University of California, Santa Cruz, CA	D,I
University of Central Oklahoma, OK	D,I
University of Cincinnati, OH	I
University of Colorado at Boulder, CO	D
University of Colorado at Denver and Health Sciences Center—Downtown Denver Campus, CO	D,I
University of Connecticut, CT	D,I
University of Dallas, TX	I
University of Dayton, OH	D
University of Delaware, DE	I
University of Denver, CO	D
University of Evansville, IN	I
The University of Findlay, OH	I
University of Florida, FL	P
University of Great Falls, MT	D,I
University of Hartford, CT	I,P
University of Idaho, ID	D,I
University of Illinois at Springfield, IL	G,I
University of Illinois at Urbana–Champaign, IL	G,I
The University of Iowa, IA	I
University of Judaism, CA	I
University of Kansas, KS	I
University of Kentucky, KY	I
University of Louisiana at Lafayette, LA	D
University of Louisville, KY	I
University of Maine, ME	I
University of Maine at Farmington, ME	I
University of Maine at Presque Isle, ME	D,I
University of Mary, ND	I
University of Mary Hardin-Baylor, TX	I
University of Maryland, College Park, MD	D,I
University of Mary Washington, VA	I
University of Massachusetts Amherst, MA	I
University of Massachusetts Dartmouth, MA	I
University of Massachusetts Lowell, MA	I
University of Memphis, TN	I
University of Miami, FL	D,G,I,P
University of Michigan, MI	I
University of Michigan–Dearborn, MI	I
University of Minnesota, Duluth, MN	I
University of Minnesota, Morris, MN	I
University of Minnesota, Twin Cities Campus, MN	G,I
University of Missouri–Columbia, MO	I
University of Missouri–Kansas City, MO	I
University of Missouri–St. Louis, MO	I
University of Nebraska at Kearney, NE	I
University of Nebraska at Omaha, NE	D,I
University of Nebraska–Lincoln, NE	I
University of Nevada, Las Vegas, NV	D
University of Nevada, Reno, NV	D
University of New England, ME	I
University of New Hampshire, NH	I
University of New Haven, CT	I
University of New Orleans, LA	D
University of North Alabama, AL	I
The University of North Carolina at Chapel Hill, NC	D,I
The University of North Carolina at Greensboro, NC	I
The University of North Carolina at Pembroke, NC	I
The University of North Carolina Wilmington, NC	I
University of North Dakota, ND	D
University of Northern Colorado, CO	D
University of Northern Iowa, IA	I
University of North Florida, FL	D
University of Oklahoma, OK	I
University of Oregon, OR	I
University of Pennsylvania, PA	I
University of Phoenix–Atlanta Campus, GA	D
University of Phoenix–Bay Area Campus, CA	D
University of Phoenix–Boston Campus, MA	D
University of Phoenix–Central Florida Campus, FL	D
University of Phoenix–Central Massachusetts Campus, MA	D
University of Phoenix–Central Valley Campus, CA	D
University of Phoenix–Charlotte Campus, NC	D
University of Phoenix–Chicago Campus, IL	D
University of Phoenix–Cincinnati Campus, OH	D
University of Phoenix–Cleveland Campus, OH	D
University of Phoenix–Columbus Georgia Campus, GA	D
University of Phoenix–Columbus Ohio Campus, OH	D
University of Phoenix–Dallas Campus, TX	D
University of Phoenix–Denver Campus, CO	D
University of Phoenix–Hawaii Campus, HI	D
University of Phoenix–Houston Campus, TX	D
University of Phoenix–Idaho Campus, ID	D

D = deferred payment system; *G* = guaranteed tuition rate; *I* = installment payments; *P* = prepayment locks in tuition rate

Tuition Payment Alternatives

Institution	Code
University of Phoenix–Indianapolis Campus, IN	D
University of Phoenix–Kansas City Campus, MO	D
University of Phoenix–Little Rock Campus, AR	D
University of Phoenix–Louisiana Campus, LA	D
University of Phoenix–Maryland Campus, MD	D
University of Phoenix–Metro Detroit Campus, MI	D
University of Phoenix–Nashville Campus, TN	D
University of Phoenix–New Mexico Campus, NM	D
University of Phoenix–Northern Virginia Campus, VA	D
University of Phoenix–North Florida Campus, FL	D
University of Phoenix–Oklahoma City Campus, OK	D
University of Phoenix Online Campus, AZ	D
University of Phoenix–Oregon Campus, OR	D
University of Phoenix–Philadelphia Campus, PA	D
University of Phoenix–Phoenix Campus, AZ	D
University of Phoenix–Pittsburgh Campus, PA	D
University of Phoenix–Puerto Rico Campus, PR	D
University of Phoenix–Raleigh Campus, NC	D
University of Phoenix–Richmond Campus, VA	D
University of Phoenix–Sacramento Valley Campus, CA	D
University of Phoenix–St. Louis Campus, MO	D
University of Phoenix–San Diego Campus, CA	D
University of Phoenix–Southern Arizona Campus, AZ	D
University of Phoenix–Southern California Campus, CA	D
University of Phoenix–Southern Colorado Campus, CO	D
University of Phoenix–South Florida Campus, FL	D
University of Phoenix–Spokane Campus, WA	D
University of Phoenix–Springfield Campus, MO	D
University of Phoenix–Tulsa Campus, OK	D
University of Phoenix–Utah Campus, UT	D
University of Phoenix–Washington Campus, WA	D
University of Phoenix–West Florida Campus, FL	D
University of Phoenix–West Michigan Campus, MI	D
University of Phoenix–Wichita Campus, KS	D
University of Phoenix–Wisconsin Campus, WI	D
University of Pittsburgh, PA	D,I
University of Pittsburgh at Bradford, PA	I
University of Pittsburgh at Johnstown, PA	I
University of Portland, OR	D,I
University of Puget Sound, WA	D,I
University of Redlands, CA	I
University of Rhode Island, RI	I
University of Richmond, VA	D,I
University of Rochester, NY	I,P
University of St. Francis, IL	I
University of Saint Francis, IN	D,I
University of St. Thomas, MN	D,I
University of St. Thomas, TX	D,I
University of San Diego, CA	I
University of Science and Arts of Oklahoma, OK	I
University of South Carolina, SC	D,I
University of South Carolina Upstate, SC	D
The University of South Dakota, SD	D
University of Southern California, CA	D,I,P
University of Southern Indiana, IN	I
University of Southern Maine, ME	I
University of Southern Mississippi, MS	I
University of South Florida, FL	I
The University of Tampa, FL	I
The University of Tennessee at Martin, TN	D
The University of Texas at Arlington, TX	I
The University of Texas at Austin, TX	I
The University of Texas at Dallas, TX	I
The University of Texas at El Paso, TX	I
The University of Texas at San Antonio, TX	D,I
The University of Texas at Tyler, TX	I
The University of Texas Health Science Center at Houston, TX	I
The University of Texas–Pan American, TX	I
University of the Cumberlands, KY	I
University of the District of Columbia, DC	D,I
University of the Ozarks, AR	I
University of the Pacific, CA	D
The University of Toledo, OH	I
University of Tulsa, OK	I,P
University of Utah, UT	I
University of Vermont, VT	D,I
University of Virginia, VA	I
The University of West Alabama, AL	D
University of Wisconsin–Eau Claire, WI	I
University of Wisconsin–Green Bay, WI	I
University of Wisconsin–La Crosse, WI	I
University of Wisconsin–Parkside, WI	I
University of Wisconsin–Stevens Point, WI	I
University of Wisconsin–Stout, WI	I
University of Wisconsin–Whitewater, WI	I
University of Wyoming, WY	D,I
Urbana University, OH	D,I
Ursinus College, PA	I
Utah State University, UT	D
Utica College, NY	D,I
Valley Forge Christian College, PA	I
Valparaiso University, IN	D,I
Vanguard University of Southern California, CA	I
Vassar College, NY	I
Vaughn College of Aeronautics and Technology, NY	I
Vermont Technical College, VT	D,I
Villa Julie College, MD	D,I
Villanova University, PA	I
Virginia Commonwealth University, VA	I
Virginia Intermont College, VA	I
Virginia Military Institute, VA	I
Virginia Polytechnic Institute and State University, VA	I
Virginia Union University, VA	D,I
Virginia Wesleyan College, VA	D,I
Wabash College, IN	I,P
Wake Forest University, NC	I
Waldorf College, IA	D,I
Walla Walla College, WA	I
Walsh College of Accountancy and Business Administration, MI	D
Warren Wilson College, NC	I
Wartburg College, IA	I
Washington & Jefferson College, PA	D,I
Washington College, MD	I,P
Washington State University, WA	I,P
Washington University in St. Louis, MO	I,P
Watkins College of Art and Design, TN	D,I
Wayland Baptist University, TX	I
Waynesburg College, PA	D,I
Wayne State College, NE	I
Wayne State University, MI	I
Webber International University, FL	I
Webster University, MO	I
Wellesley College, MA	I,P
Wells College, NY	I
Wentworth Institute of Technology, MA	I
Wesleyan University, CT	I
Wesley College, MS	I
Western Carolina University, NC	I
Western Illinois University, IL	G
Western Kentucky University, KY	I,P
Western New England College, MA	I,P
Western Oregon University, OR	D
Western State College of Colorado, CO	D,I
Western Washington University, WA	I
Westminster College, MO	I
Westminster College, PA	I
Westmont College, CA	I

D = deferred payment system; *G* = guaranteed tuition rate; *I* = installment payments; *P* = prepayment locks in tuition rate

Tuition Payment Alternatives

West Virginia University, WV	D	William Carey College, MS	D	Wittenberg University, OH	I
Wheaton College, IL	D,I	William Jewell College, MO	I,P	Wofford College, SC	I
Wheaton College, MA	I,P	William Paterson University of New Jersey, NJ	I	Woodbury University, CA	D,I
Wheeling Jesuit University, WV	I			Worcester Polytechnic Institute, MA	D,I
Whitman College, WA	D	William Penn University, IA	I	Worcester State College, MA	I
Whitworth College, WA	I	William Woods University, MO	I	Xavier University, OH	D,I
Wichita State University, KS	I	Wilson College, PA	I	Xavier University of Louisiana, LA	I
Widener University, PA	I	Wingate University, NC	I	York College of Pennsylvania, PA	I,P
Wilkes University, PA	D,I	Winston-Salem State University, NC	I	York College of the City University of New York, NY	D
Willamette University, OR	I	Winthrop University, SC	I	Youngstown State University, OH	I

D = deferred payment system; *G* = guaranteed tuition rate; *I* = installment payments; *P* = prepayment locks in tuition rate

THOMSON PETERSON'S

Get Matched With an Expert and Get In.

Put an expert in your corner.
Planning for college? Don't get overwhelmed—get in. Peterson's College Consulting matches you with your very own private advisor, trained by America's leading college consultants Howard and Matthew Greene.

- *Top-notch consultants, including former deans of admission*
- *Convenient, one-on-one telephone consultation*
- *Your own in-depth, personalized action plan*
- *Fast, 48-hour service*
- *Satisfaction guaranteed!*

 Visit www.petersons.com/pcc1

While you're there, be sure to check out our FREE Chat Series!

PCC2006

THOMSON PETERSON'S

FIND the right school.

PREPARE for your test.

UNCOVER great college deals.

EXPLORE career options.

SHAPE your future.

GET IN.

FIND   PREPARE   UNCOVER   EXPLORE   SHAPE   **GET IN.**

PETERSON'S
getting you there

 Visit **Petersons.com/gen1**
for everything you need. In print or online,
Thomson Peterson's can help.

www.petersons.com

TESTAD05